PENGUIN HANDBOOKS

The Penguin Guide to B

EDWARD GREENFIELD has been Record Critic of the *Guardian* since 1954 and, from 1964, its Music Critic too. At the end of 1960 he joined the reviewing panel of *Gramophone*, specializing in operatic and orchestral issues. He is a regular broadcaster on music and records for the BBC, not just on Radios 3 and 4 but also on the BBC World Service. In 1958 he published a monograph on the operas of Puccini. More recently he has written studies on the recorded work of Joan Sutherland and André Previn. He has been a regular juror on International Record awards and has appeared with such artists as Dame Elisabeth Schwarzkopf, Dame Joan Sutherland and Sir Georg Solti in public interviews.

ROBERT LAYTON studied at Oxford with Edmund Rubbra for composition and with Egon Wellesz for the history of music. He spent two years in Sweden at the universities of Uppsala and Stockholm. He joined the BBC Music Division in 1959 and has been responsible for such programmes as *Interpretations on Record*. He has contributed 'A Quarterly Retrospect' to *Gramophone* for a number of years and he has written books on Berwald and Sibelius and has specialized in Scandinavian music. His recent publications include a monograph on the Dvořák symphonies and concertos for the BBC Music Guides, of which he is General Editor, and the first two volumes of his translation of Erik Tawastsjerna's definitive study of Sibelius. In 1987 he was awarded the Sibelius Medal and in the following year was made a Knight of the Order of the White Rose of Finland for his services to Finnish music.

IVAN MARCH is a former professional musician. He studied at Trinity College of Music, London, and at the Royal Manchester College. After service in the RAF Central Band, he played the horn professionally for the BBC and travelled with the Carl Rosa and D'Oyly Carte opera companies. Now director of the Long Playing Record Library, the largest commercial lending library for classical music on compact discs in the British Isles, he is a well-known lecturer, journalist and personality in the world of recorded music. As a journalist he contributes to a number of record-reviewing magazines, including *Gramophone* and the new monthly, *Classics*, which concentrates on bargain repertoire.

The Penguin Guide to Bargain Compact Discs and Cassettes

Edward Greenfield, Robert Layton and Ivan March

Edited by Ivan March

Penguin Books

PENGUIN BOOKS

Published by the Penguin Group
Penguin Books Ltd, 27 Wrights Lane, London W8 5TZ, England
Penguin Books USA Inc., 375 Hudson Street, New York, New York 10014, USA
Penguin Books Australia Ltd, Ringwood, Victoria, Australia
Penguin Books Canada Ltd, 10 Alcorn Avenue, Toronto, Ontario, Canada M4V 3B2
Penguin Books (NZ) Ltd, 182–190 Wairau Road, Auckland 10, New Zealand

Penguin Books Ltd, Registered Offices: Harmondsworth, Middlesex, England

First published 1992
10 9 8 7 6 5 4 3 2 1

Made and printed in Great Britain by Clays Ltd, St Ives plc

Typeset in 8 on 9½ pt Times by Barbers Ltd, Wrotham, Kent

Contents

Preface

The enormous range of music available on compact disc at considerably less than premium price is breathtaking and, as our current survey demonstrates again and again, there is no longer any direct relation between the cost of a CD and its quality or desirability. Even those who insist on a modern digital recording, as distinct from digitally remastered analogue sound, will find a remarkably wide choice. This is partly because of the great competition brought about by the flood of new records over the past two years which has prompted the major record companies to reissue at mid-price (and sometimes in the bargain range) many of the first generation of digital records made in the early 1980s.

There has also been a stimulus from Eastern Europe, which has suddenly become a new source of recordings. Here basic costs are lower, and artists – eager to be heard in the West – are willing to work for reduced royalties or sometimes to waive royalties altogether. The digital CDs on the super-bargain Naxos label are already showing us what a wealth of talent is waiting to be tapped in the East.

The oldest and truest adage of the recording world is that newer is not necessarily better. Many of the greatest and most rewarding performances belong to the analogue stereo LP era, and these records can offer an illusion of realism to compare with almost anything achieved more recently. One thinks here not only of EMI/Angel and the Polygram labels – Decca/London, DG and Philips – but also of the early RCA recordings made in Chicago with Fritz Reiner, and of the steadily re-emerging Mercury records from the late 1950s and early 1960s, now lovingly being remastered by their original Recording Director, Wilma Cozart Fine. Leonard Bernstein's electrifying, early NYPO performances, plus Aaron Copland's and Igor Stravinsky's authoritative interpretations of their own music have also reappeared, usually sounding vividly refreshed on the Sony label.

Now the Vox, Saga and Vanguard catalogues are being steadily transferred to CD, almost always bringing considerable improvement in sound-quality, and we are especially delighted to rediscover the early piano records of Alfred Brendel and Walter Klien, which have a striking freshness and spontaneity. Artists of the calibre of Arthur Grumiaux, Stephen Kovacevich and Wilhelm Kempff, together with Peter Hurford's revelatory survey of Bach's organ music, all belong to the later vintage period of the 1960s and early 1970s, while the legacy of Sir Neville Marriner's Academy of St Martin-in-the-Fields' recordings on the Argo label is no less distinguished.

If we venture back further to the days of mono LPs and shellac 78-r.p.m. discs, the standard of music-making can be very special indeed and the sound often much better than we could possibly have expected. Names of conductors such as Barbirolli, Beecham, Furtwängler, Koussevitzky and Toscanini conjure up the image of a very special kind of music-making, while instrumental soloists such as Horowitz and Schnabel, Casals and Heifetz, bring memorably charismatic musical insights. First recordings, too, can offer a freshness of discovery that is unique; one thinks here of an unforgettable record by Heifetz of the Glazunov *Violin concerto*, made while the composer was still alive, that has never been surpassed since.

Preserving the sound of the human voice has been a role of the phonograph/gramophone from its very earliest days, and many famous singers and outstanding performances are available on CD within the lower price ranges. One of the joys of the Saga catalogue has been the reappearance of the earliest song recitals of Dame Janet Baker (as treasurable as the recorded presence of the late Kathleen Ferrier on Decca), while the vocal art of Victoria de los Angeles, Dame Elisabeth Schwarzkopf, Gérard Souzay and Dietrich Fischer-Dieskau is generously represented on the major labels. There are stars galore in the operatic firmament, with Caruso and Gigli alongside Pavarotti and Domingo, Rosa Ponselle and Leontyne Price alongside Callas, Tebaldi and Dame Joan Sutherland, to say nothing of the many famous names featured in the historical anthologies.

There remains the controversial issue of digital remastering and what it adds to or removes from an original recording. As the more perceptive of sound engineers have always realized, digital technology can bring extraordinary benefits in clarity; whether in a straight studio recording or in a digital transfer to CD, that very clarity has to be handled very carefully, however. A sense of presence, of tangible, well-focused sound retaining its body, ambience and illusion of hall decay is more important than extreme frequency range. With a good transfer, the benefits to be gained from

CD can be astonishing, the original quality transformed. But too often the major companies resurrecting their old recordings, whether historic or recent, have tended to put them through the same digital 'sausage machine', with extremely variable results. The big essential is that some sort of individual artistic monitoring should be undertaken to avoid the introduction of an edginess on top, which was not present on the original LP or 78-r.p.m. source.

Putting all these technical grumbles to one side, the acquisition of a CD player becomes the 'Open Sesame' to a vast treasure-house of records costing under £10 (sometimes half that much), usually giving an hour or more of music – although not always as well documented as they should be. The range of choice in the standard repertoire is remarkable, while, befitting his bicentennial, Mozart is represented by a magnificent tribute from Philips, whose distinguished Complete Mozart Edition offers virtually everything the composer ever wrote (and some music he failed to complete) in 45 mid-priced volumes of CDs which, on a single shelf, stretch half-way round the room!

Cassette alternatives are still available for a great many lower-priced recordings. They are very economical and remain a viable buy because of their extreme portability, especially for use in the car, where CDs – with their wider dynamic range – have little advantage. Moreover, just at the time when the tape medium is losing its prime hold on the marketplace, the manufacturing technology has been vastly improved so that the best cassettes can now give aural satisfaction, even on the most demanding domestic equipment. However, the sheer convenience of the compact disc, and its ease of access, has established it as the prime carrier for prerecorded music in the foreseeable future.

Edward Greenfield, Robert Layton, Ivan March

March 1992

Introduction

The object of *The Penguin Guide to Bargain Compact Discs and Cassettes* is to give the serious collector a comprehensive survey of the finest bargain recordings of permanent music, primarily on CD, but also on cassettes. As most records are issued almost simultaneously on both sides of the Atlantic and use identical international catalogue numbers, this *Guide* should be found to be equally useful in Great Britain and the USA. The internationalization of repertoire and numbers is increasingly applying to CDs issued by the major international companies and by many smaller ones too, while most of the smaller European labels are imported in their original formats into both Britain and the USA. Our coverage includes all CDs costing under £10 in the UK or under $12 in the USA.

The sheer number of records of artistic merit now available causes considerable problems in any assessment of overall and individual excellence. While in the case of a single popular repertoire work it might be ideal for the discussion to be conducted by a single reviewer, it has not always been possible for one person to have access to every version, and division of reviewing responsibility becomes inevitable. Also there are certain works and certain recorded performances for which one or another of our team has a special affinity. Such a personal identification can often carry with it a special perception too. We feel that it is a strength of our basic style to let such conveyed pleasure or admiration for the merits of an individual recording come over directly to the reader, even if this produces a certain ambivalence in the matter of choice between competing recordings. Where disagreement is more positive (and this has rarely happened), then readers will find an indication of this difference in the text.

We have considered and rejected the use of initials against individual reviews, since this is essentially a team project. The occasions for disagreement generally concern matters of aesthetics, for instance in the manner of recording balance, where a contrived effect may trouble some ears more than others, or in the matter of style, where the difference between robustness and refinement of approach appeals differently to listening sensibilities, rather than involving a question of artistic integrity. But over the years our views seem to grow closer together, rather than to diverge; perhaps we are getting mellower, but we are seldom ready to offer strong disagreement following the enthusiastic reception by one of the team of a controversial recording, if the results are creatively stimulating. Our perceptions of the advantages and disadvantages of performances of early music on original (as against modern) instruments seem fairly evenly balanced; again, any strong feelings are indicated in the text.

EVALUATION

Most recordings issued today by the major companies are of a high technical standard and offer performances of a quality at least as high as is experienced in the concert hall. In adopting a starring system for the evaluation of records, we have decided to make use of from one to three stars. Brackets round one or more of the stars indicate some reservations about its inclusion, and readers are advised to refer to the text. Brackets round all the stars usually indicate a basic qualification: for instance, a mono recording of a performance of artistic interest, where considerable allowances have to be made for the sound quality, even though the recording may have been digitally remastered.

Our evaluation system may be summarized as follows:

*** An outstanding performance and recording in every way.
** A good performance and recording of today's normal high standard.
* A fair performance, reasonably well or well recorded.

Our evaluation is normally applied to the record as a whole, unless there are two main works or groups of works, and by different composers. In this case, each is dealt with separately in its appropriate place. In the case of a collection of shorter works, we feel that there is little point in giving a separate starring to each item, even if their merits are uneven, since the record has to be purchased as a complete programme.

ROSETTES

To a very few records we have awarded a rosette: ❀.

Unlike our general evaluations, in which we have tried to be consistent, a rosette is a quite arbitrary compliment by a member of the reviewing team to a recorded performance which, he finds, shows special illumination, magic, or a spiritual quality, or even outstanding production values, that places it in a very special class. The choice is essentially a personal one (although often it represents a shared view), and in some cases it is applied to an issue where certain reservations must also be mentioned in the text of the review. The rosette symbol is placed before the usual evaluation and the record number. It is quite small – we do not mean to imply an 'Academy Award' but a personal token of appreciation for something uniquely valuable. We hope that, once the reader has discovered and perhaps acquired a 'rosetted' CD, its special qualities will soon become apparent.

DIGITAL RECORDINGS

The majority of bargain compact discs are digitally remastered analogue recordings, but an increasing number of digital recordings are now appearing, and we think it important to include a clear indication of the difference:

Dig. This indicates that the master recording was digitally encoded.

LISTINGS

Our listing of each recording first indicates its category, as follows:

(M) Medium-priced label

(B) Bargain-priced label

(BB) Super-bargain label

See below for price structures both for CDs and for cassettes in the UK and USA.

LAYOUT OF TEXT

We have aimed to make our style as simple as possible, even though the catalogue numbers of recordings are no longer as straightforward as they once were. So, immediately after the evaluation and before the catalogue number, the record make is given, usually in abbreviated form (a key to the abbreviations is provided on pages xvi–xvii). In the case of a set of two or more CDs, the number of units involved is given in brackets after the catalogue number.

AMERICAN CATALOGUE NUMBERS

The numbers which follow in square brackets are US catalogue numbers, while the abbreviation [id.] indicates that the American number is identical to the European, which is increasingly the case. If there is no [id.] indication, it could mean that the recording is available in the USA only as an import, which may imply a higher price. Alternatively, it could be that the recording has not yet arrived in the USA at our date of publication. Readers are advised to check the current *Schwann* catalogue and to consult their local record store.

There are certain small differences to be remembered by American readers. For instance, a CBS number could have a completely different catalogue number on either side of the Atlantic, or use the same digits with different alphabetical prefixes. Both will be clearly indicated. EMI/Angel use extra digits for their British compact discs; thus the US number CDM 47001 becomes CDM7 47001-2 in Britain (the -2 is the European indication that this is a compact disc). We have taken care to check catalogue information as far as is possible, but as all the editorial work has been done in England there is always the possibility of error; American readers are therefore invited, when ordering records locally, to take the precaution of giving their dealer the fullest information about the music and recordings they want.

The indication (M), (B) or (BB) immediately before the starring of a disc usually refers to both UK and US prices, although of course they are not identical. If the price range is different on either side of the Atlantic, this is clearly indicated.

ABBREVIATIONS

To save space we have adopted a number of standard abbreviations in listing orchestras and performing groups (a list is provided below), and the titles of works are often shortened, especially where they are listed several times. Artists' forenames are sometimes omitted if they are not absolutely necessary for identification purposes. Also we have not usually listed the contents of operatic highlights and collections; these can be found in *The Classical Catalogue*, published by *Gramophone* magazine (177–179, Kenton Road, Kenton, Harrow, Middlesex, England, HA3 0HA).

We have followed common practice in the use of the original language for titles where it seems sensible. In most cases, English is used for orchestral and instrumental music and the original language for vocal music and opera. There are exceptions, however; for instance, the Johann Strauss discography uses the German language in the interests of consistency.

ORDER OF MUSIC

The order of music under each composer's name broadly follows that adopted by *The Classical Catalogue*: orchestral music, including concertos and symphonies; chamber music; solo instrumental music (in some cases with keyboard and organ music separated); vocal and choral music; opera; vocal collections; miscellaneous collections.

The Classical Catalogue now usually includes stage works alongside opera; in the main we have not followed this practice, preferring to list, say, ballet music and incidental music (where no vocal items are involved) in the general orchestral group. Within each group our listing follows an alphabetical sequence, and couplings within a single composer's output are *usually* discussed together instead of separately with cross-references. Occasionally and inevitably because of this alphabetical approach, different recordings of a given work can become separated when a record is listed and discussed under the first work of its alphabetical sequence. The editor feels that alphabetical consistency is essential if the reader is to learn to find his or her way about.

CONCERTS AND RECITALS

Most collections of music intended to be regarded as concerts or recitals involve many composers, and it is quite impractical to deal with them within the alphabetical composer index. They are grouped separately, at the end of the book, in three sections. In each section, recordings are usually arranged in alphabetical order of the performers' names: concerts of orchestral and concertante music under the name of the orchestra, ensemble or, if more important, conductor or soloist; instrumental recitals under the name of the instrumentalist; operatic and vocal recitals under the principal singer or vocal group, as seems appropriate.

In certain cases where the compilation features many different performers, it is listed alphabetically under its collective title, or the key word in that title (thus *Favourite operatic duets* is listed under 'Operatic duets'). Sometimes, for complicated collections, and especially compilations of favourite operatic arias, only brief details of contents and performers are given; fuller information can usually be found in *The Classical Catalogue*.

CATALOGUE NUMBERS

Enormous care has gone into the checking of CD catalogue numbers and contents to ensure that all details are correct, but the editor and publishers cannot be held responsible for any mistakes that may have crept in despite all our zealous checking. When ordering CDs, readers are urged to provide their record-dealer with full details of the music and performers, as well as the catalogue number. If no UK catalogue number is indicated – i.e. only a number in square brackets is included – this means that the recording is available in the USA but still awaits issue in Britain.

DELETIONS

Compact discs are all the time succumbing to the deletions axe, and more are likely to disappear during the lifetime of this book. Sometimes copies may still be found in specialist shops, and there remains the compensatory fact that most really important and desirable recordings are eventually reissued.

COVERAGE

We believe our bargain coverage to be zealously comprehensive even if, for various reasons, it is impossible for us to mention *every* CD that is available on both sides of the Atlantic. On rare occasions a recording has been omitted simply because a review copy was not available; hopefully, anything which eludes us can always be included next time. We welcome suggestions from readers about such omissions if they seem to be of special interest and are inexpensive. But borderline music on specialist labels that are not readily and reliably obtainable on both sides of the Atlantic cannot be given any kind of priority.

BARGAIN PRICE RANGES – UK and USA

Compact discs and cassettes in all price-ranges are more expensive in Britain and Europe than they are in the USA but, fortunately, in nearly all cases the various mid-price, bargain and super-bargain categories are fairly consistent on both sides of the Atlantic. However, where records are imported in either direction, this can affect their domestic cost. For instance, (British) EMI's Classics for Pleasure and Eminence labels are both in the mid-price range in the USA, whereas CfP is a bargain series in the UK. Similarly Naxos, a super-bargain digital label in the UK, is a bargain label in the USA. LaserLight, however, is a super-bargain series in both markets.

Vox Boxes are exceptionally good value at super-budget price in America, while in Britain they are comparable with EMI's 'two for the price of one' series. Of course retail prices are not fixed in either country, and various stores may offer even better deals at times, so our price structure must be taken as a guideline only. One major difference in the USA is that almost all companies make a dollar surcharge (per disc) for opera sets (to cover the cost of librettos) and Angel applies this levy to all their boxed sets. The Pickwick RPO and MCD compact disc series is an upper-mid-price label in the UK (costing just under our upper limit of £10) and – like the ASV bargain label – appears to be available only as a special import in the USA. The Vanguard CD label (except for the 8000 Series, which retails at around $15) is upper-mid-price in the USA but lower-mid-price in the UK. In *listing* records we have not used the major record companies' additional label subdivisions (like Decca/London's Headline and Ovation, DG's Privilege, EMI's Studio, Philips's Concert Classics, and so on) in order to avoid further confusion, although these designations are sometimes referred to in the text of reviews.

(M) MID-PRICED SERIES (sets are multiples of these prices)
Includes: BMG/RCA; Chandos; Collins; Decca/London; DG; EMI/Angel (Studio and Références; Eminence); Erato/Warner (UK), Erato/WEA (USA); HM/BMG (UK), DHM/BMG (USA); Mercury; Philips; Saga; Sony (including Portrait and Essential Classics); Teldec/Warner (UK), Teldec/WEA (USA); Tuxedo (UK only); Unicorn (UK only).

UK

CDs: under £10; more usually £8–£9
Cassettes: under £5

USA

CDs: under $11
Cassettes: $5–$6.50

(B) BARGAIN-PRICED SERIES (sets are multiples of these prices)

Includes: BMG/RCA; Decca/London; CfP (UK only); DG; EMI Laser; Hungaroton White Label; MCA Double-decker (USA only); Philips; Pickwick; Sony.

UK

CDs: £5–6
Cassettes: under £4

USA

CDs: under $7
Cassettes: under $4

SPECIAL SETS: Vox Boxes cost only $5 per disc in the USA, but (alongside the Turnabout Doubles) are UK imports and are priced at around £5–£6 per disc in Britain where available. MCA Doubles are $6 per disc in the USA and, with one or two exceptions, have no British equivalent.

(BB) SUPER-BARGAIN SERIES – CDs

Includes: ASV (UK only); BMG/Victrola; LaserLight; Naxos; Pickwick (PWK); Virgin (Virgo).

UK

CDs: under £5

USA

CDs: under $7 (LaserLight under $4)

(In some cases equivalent cassettes are available, usually costing slightly less than bargain cassettes.)

An International Mail-Order Source for Recordings

Readers are urged to support a local dealer if he is prepared and able to give a proper service, and to remember that obtaining many CDs involves perseverence. If, however, difficulty is experienced locally, we suggest the following mail-order alternative, which operates world-wide:

PG Dept
Squires Gate Music Centre
Squires Gate Station Approach
Blackpool
Lancashire FY8 2SP
England
Tel: 0253 44360
Fax: 0253 406686

This organization (which is operated under the direction of the Editor of the *Penguin Guide to Bargain Compact Discs and Cassettes*) patiently extends compact disc orders which are temporarily unavailable from the manufacturers until they finally come to hand. A full guarantee of safe delivery is made on any order undertaken. Please write for further details, enclosing a stamped and self-addressed envelope if within the UK.

American readers seeking a domestic mail-order source may write to the following address where a comparable supply service is in operation (for both American and imported European labels). Please write for further details (enclosing a stamped, self-addressed envelope if within the USA) or send your order to:

PG Dept
Serenade Records
1713 G St, N.W.
Washington DC 20006
USA
Tel: (202) 638-6648
Fax: (202) 783-0372
Tel: (for US orders only) 1-800-237-2390

Acknowledgements

Our thanks, as ever, are due to Roger Wells, our Copy Editor, who has worked closely alongside us throughout the preparation of this book and, as a keen CD collector himself, also frequently made valuable creative suggestions. Kathleen March once again zealously checked the proofs for errors and reminded us when the text proved ambiguous, clumsily repetitive in its descriptive terminology, or just plain contradictory. Winifred Greenwood scrupulously checked our catalogue numbers and cassette references. Barbara Menard contributed to the titling – never an easy task, and especially complicated in the many boxed anthologies involving a bouquet of different performers. Our team of Penguin proof readers are also indispensable. Grateful thanks also go to all those readers who write to us to point out factual errors and remind us of important recordings which have escaped our notice.

Finally, we welcome back to our cover the whimsical portrait of Nipper, the most famous dog in the world. He is associated with a deservedly world-famous trademark and reminds us that fine records have been available from this source for almost exactly one hundred years!

Abbreviations

Ac.	Academy, Academic
AAM	Academy of Ancient Music
Amb. S.	Ambrosian Singers
Ang.	Angel
Ara.	Arabesque
arr.	arranged
ASMF	Academy of St Martin-in-the-Fields
ASV	Academy Sound and Vision
Bar.	Baroque
Bav.	Bavarian
BPO	Berlin Philharmonic Orchestra
Cal.	Calliope
Cap.	Caprice
CBSO	City of Birmingham Symphony Orchestra
CfP	Classics for Pleasure
Ch.	Choir; Chorale; Chorus
Chan.	Chandos
CO	Chamber Orchestra
COE	Chamber Orchestra of Europe
Col. Mus. Ant.	Musica Antiqua, Cologne
Coll.	Collegium
Coll. Aur.	Collegium Aureum
Coll. Mus.	Collegium Musicum
Concg. O	Royal Concertgebouw Orchestra of Amsterdam
cond.	conductor, conducted
Cons.	Consort
DG	Deutsche Grammophon
Dig.	digital recording
E.	England, English
ECO	English Chamber Orchestra
EMI	Electrical and Mechanical Industries
Ens.	Ensemble
Fr.	French
GO	Gewandhaus Orchestra
HM	Harmonia Mundi France
HM/RCA	Deutsche Harmonia Mundi
Hung	Hungaroton
L.	London
LAPO	Los Angeles Philharmonic Orchestra
LCO	London Chamber Orchestra
LMP	London Mozart Players
LOP	Lamoureux Orchestra of Paris
LPO	London Philharmonic Orchestra
LSO	London Symphony Orchestra
Mer.	Meridian
Met.	Metropolitan
movt	movement
N.	North

nar.	narrated
Nat.	National
NY	New York
O	Orchestra, Orchestre
O-L	Oiseau-Lyre
Op.	Opera (in performance listings); opus (in music titles)
orch.	orchestrated
ORTF	'Orchestre de la radio et télévision française
Ph.	Philips
Phd.	Philadelphia
Philh.	Philharmonia
PO	Philharmonic Orchestra
Qt	Quartet
R.	Radio
RCA	distributed in UK by BMG
ROHCG	Royal Opera House, Covent Garden
RPO	Royal Philharmonic Orchestra
RSO	Radio Symphony Orchestra
S.	South
SCO	Scottish Chamber Orchestra
Sinf.	Sinfonietta
SNO	Royal Scottish Orchestra
SO	Symphony Orchestra
Soc.	Society
Sol. Ven.	I Solisti Veneti
SRO	Suisse Romande Orchestra
Sup.	Supraphon
trans.	transcription, transcribed
V.	Vienna
Van.	Vanguard
VCM	Vienna Concentus Musicus
VPO	Vienna Philharmonic Orchestra
VSO	Vienna Symphony Orchestra
W.	West

Adam, Adolphe (1803–56)

Giselle (ballet): complete.
(M) *** Decca Dig. 433 007-2 (2) [id.]. ROHCG O, Richard Bonynge.

Giselle (1841) is the first of the great classical ballets. Bonynge's performance offers the complete original score, exactly as Adam scored it, with all repeats. Also included are the *Peasants' Pas de deux* in Act I with music by Frédéric Bürgmuller, and two other insertions, possibly by Minkus. The playing is polished and warmly sympathetic. Bonynge's tempi are very much of the ballet theatre, but the overall tension is maintained well and detail is affectionately vivid. Recorded in London's Henry Wood Hall, with its glowing acoustics, the sound is richly coloured and sumptuous, the bass resonance almost too expansive, and this is one of the most successful and satisfying of Bonynge's many ballet recordings made for Decca over the years. The recording, on two CDs, provides for well over two hours of musical pleasure and this makes a clear first choice, irrespective of price.

Giselle (ballet): original score (abridged).
(M) **(*) Decca 417 738-2; *417 738-4* [id.]. VPO, Karajan.

Karajan's performance offers sixty minutes of music: he effectively combines drama with an affectionate warmth, and the phrasing of the lyrical passages produces much lovely – if sometimes suave – playing from the Vienna strings. The more robust writing has plenty of vigour and colour. The recording was made in the Sofiensaal in 1961, and its original excellence is enhanced by the digital remastering, rather like the cleaning of a painting. Karajan is particularly good in the closing pages: when Giselle leaves her lover for ever, he creates a tellingly spacious romantic apotheosis. However, this now needs to be reissued at bargain price.

Giselle (ballet): *suite*.
(M) ** Sony SBK 46341 [id.]; *40-46341*. Phd. O, Ormandy – MEYERBEER: *Les Patineurs*; TCHAIKOVSKY: *Swan Lake*. **

Ormandy's eleven-minute suite concentrates mostly on the robust music of Adam's score and thus fails to give a complete picture of the ballet's charm. Characteristically polished playing, with Philadelphian vitality and sumptuously resonant mid-1970s sound.

Addinsell, Richard (1904–77)

Warsaw concerto.
(M) *** Decca Dig. 430 726-2; *430 726-4* [id.]. Ortiz, RPO, Atzmon – GERSHWIN: *Rhapsody* **(*); GOTTSCHALK: *Grand fantasia* ***; LITOLFF: *Scherzo* ***; LISZT: *Hungarian fantasia*. ***
(B) *** Decca Dig. 433 616-2; *433 616-4* [id.]. Ortiz, RPO, Atzmon – GERSHWIN: *American in Paris* etc. **

Richard Addinsell's pastiche niniature concerto, written for the film *Dangerous Moonlight* in 1942, is perfectly crafted and its atmosphere combines all the elements of the Romantic concerto to great effect; moreover it has a truly memorable main theme. Cristina Ortiz offers a warmly romantic account, spacious in conception, with the resonant ambience of Walthamstow Assembly Hall providing beguilingly rich string-timbres. This performance is offered with alternative couplings: the mid-priced digital programme, although (at 57 minutes) offering ten minutes' less music, is by far the more attractive of the two compilations.

Albéniz, Isaac (1860–1909)

Suite española (arr. Frühbeck de Burgos).
(M) *** Decca 417 786-2; *417 786-4*. New Philh. O, Frühbeck de Burgos – FALLA: *El amor brujo* *** (with GRANADOS: *Goyescas: Intermezzo* ***).

Here is a multi-coloured orchestral arrangement by the conductor, Raphael Frühbeck de Burgos, of Albéniz's early *Suite española* (originally written for piano). It offers light music of the best kind, colourful, tuneful, exotically scored and providing orchestra and recording engineers alike with a chance to show their paces, the sound bright and glittering. We are given seven pieces from the suite plus *Cordoba*, which is one of the *Cantos de españa* and has a very fetching melody to end the group graciously. The Granados *Intermezzo* from *Goyescas* makes a lusciously brilliant bonus item.

Iberia (complete).
(B) *(*) EMI CZS7 62889-2 (2). Aldo Ciccolini – GRANADOS: *Goyescas*. *(*)

Aldo Ciccolini's recording of *Iberia* comes in harness with the *Goyescas* of Granados and on the face of it offers good value in EMI's French 'two for the price of one' series. Book One, comprising the *Evocation*, *El Puerto* and *Fête-Dieu à Séville*, comes after the Granados on the first CD, the remaining three Books being accommodated on the second disc. The recordings were made in the Paris Salle Wagram and date from 1966. Unfortunately the sound is unappealing, a bit clattery and shallow in timbre.

Albinoni, Tommaso (1671–1750)

Adagio in G min. for organ and strings (arr. Giazotto).
(M) *** Decca 417 712-2; *417 712-4* [id.]. Stuttgart CO, Münchinger – PACHELBEL: *Canon* ***; VIVALDI: *4 Seasons*. **(*)
(B) *** Pickwick Dig. PCD 802; *CIMPC 802*. Scottish CO, Laredo (with *String masterpieces*. ***)

Münchinger's sumptuous yet stylish version is also available within a mid-priced concert of baroque lollipops (Decca 417 781-2).

No less telling is the bargain-priced, digitally recorded Pickwick account, strongly contoured and most responsively played by the Scottish Chamber Orchestra under Jaime Laredo. Other versions are listed in the Concerts section.

(i) *Adagio in G min.* (arr. Giazotto); (i; ii) *Oboe concerto in D min., Op. 9/2;* (iii; iv) *Double oboe concerto in F, Op. 9/3;* (iv) *Sinfonias for strings: in C; G; G min.*
(M) ** Erato/Warner 2292 45557-2 [id.]. (i) Saar R. CO, Ristenpart; (ii) with Jacques Chambon; (iii) Pierre Pierlot, Chambon; (iv) I Solisti Veneti, Scimone.

This, the first in the Erato/Warner Résidence series, is called 'Albinoni in Venice'; it brings better biographical and geographical documentation than information about the music. The Giazotto arrangement of the famous *Adagio* acts as bait, and those who succumb will be rewarded by some inventive and sometimes beautiful music in generally stylish performances. The splendid *Oboe concerto in D minor* is the highlight; the *Double concerto* is enjoyable too, though the balance of the soloists is rather close. The *Sinfonias* all have fine slow movements, but the outer movements, though lively, are more conventional. The recordings, made over a decade from 1964 to 1974, are fresh and cleanly transferred but have lost just a little of their original bloom.

12 Concerti a cinque, Op. 5.
(M) *** Ph. Dig. 422 251-2; *422 251-4* [id.]. Pina Carmirelli, I Musici.

Albinoni has been quite unjustly overshadowed by many of his contemporaries. His invention is unfailingly fresh and vital, and this fine body of concertos has variety and resource to commend it. I Musici, with Pina Carmirelli as the solo player, are every bit as fresh as the music, and they are accorded altogether first-rate sound. The digital recording is early (1982) but sounds excellent. Modern instruments are used to most convincing effect.

Concerti a cinque, Op. 7/2, 3, 5, 6, 8, 9, 11 & 12.
(M) *** DG 427 111-2; *427 111-4* [id.]. Holliger, Elhorst, Bern Camerata.

This splendid DG reissue contains eight of the twelve concertos comprising Albinoni's Op. 7, which were published in Amsterdam in 1715. Four of them are double oboe concertos (Nos. 2, 5, 8 and 11), four are for solo oboe, and the remainder are for strings. The ideas are memorable and there is a touching charm about many of the slow movements. The playing of Heinz Holliger, Hans Elhorst and the Bern Camerata is refined, persuasive and vital, and the CD could hardly be more truthful or better detailed.

Concerti a cinque, Op. 9/1, 4, 6, 7, 10 & 12.
(M) *** Ph. 426 080-2; *426 080-4*. Ayo, Holliger, Bourgue, Garatti, I Musici.

Albinoni's Op. 9 concertos in five parts feature one or two oboe soloists or a violin. This excellent mid-priced CD includes all the concertos with violin, plus two of the four double oboe concertos. The recording was first issued in 1968 and the concertos are played with characteristic finesse and style. There is much delightful music here and the recording, excellent for its period, sounds fresh and vivid, if a little dry.

Alfvén, Hugo (1872–1960)

Swedish rhapsody No. 1 (Midsummer watch), Op. 19; King Gustav II suite: Elegy.
(M) **(*) EMI CD-EMX 2176; *TC-EMX 2176*. Bournemouth SO, Berglund – GRIEG: *Peer Gynt* **(*); JÄRNEFELT: *Praeludium*. ***

Alfvén's *Rhapsody* has a justly famous principal theme – once made famous by Mantovani. But there is more to the piece than that, and it is all put together with imagination and skill. It is well played here with plenty of spirit although rather less charm. Nevertheless the remastered recording from 1974 sounds vivid, with plenty of colour; the engaging *Elegy* is affectionately done, and this makes an attractive compilation overall.

Alkan, Charles (1813–88)

Barcarolle; Gigue, Op. 24; Marche, Op. 37/1; Nocturne No. 2, Op. 57/1; Saltarelle, Op. 23; Scherzo diabolico, Op. 39/3; Sonatine, Op. 61.
(M) *** HM HMA 190 927 [id.]. Bernard Ringeissen.

Bernard Ringeissen could be more flamboyant but he is fully equal to the cruel technical demands of this music. The *Sonatine*, an extended, big-boned piece, is particularly successful, but all this music is of interest. The recording, from the beginning of the 1970s, is first class; it has splendid presence and body in its remastered format.

Allegri, Gregorio (1582–1652)

Miserere.
(M) *** Decca 421 147-2; *421 147-4* [id.]. King's College Ch., Willcocks – PALESTRINA: *Collection.* ***
(M) **(*) EMI Dig. CD-EMX 2180; *TC-EMX 2180.* St John's College, Cambridge, Ch., Guest – LASSUS: *Missa super bella* **(*); PALESTRINA: *Veni sponsa Christi.* ***

The famous King's performance of Allegri's *Miserere*, with its arresting treble solo so beautifully and securely sung by Roy Goodman, is now coupled with Palestrina at mid-price. The sound remains first class; the background quiet of the medium is a great blessing in this music, with the soaring treble line elysian in its purity.

The new digital recording from St John's is finely sung, and the three-dimensional balance is very realistic. Guest offers more verses (with subtly varied dynamics) and his performance runs to nearly 14 minutes. His unnamed treble soloist sings less ethereally than Roy Goodman, with a strong upward leap in his famous repeated phrase. The performance is otherwise impressive but has less magic than the King's version.

Anderson, Leroy (1908–75)

Arietta; Balladette; Belle of the ball; Blue tango; Bugler's holiday; The captains and the kings; China doll; Clarinet candy; Fiddle-faddle; The first day of spring; Forgotten dreams; The girl in satin; The golden years; Goldilocks (musical): (*Lady in waiting* (ballet music); *Pyramid dance (Heart of stone); Lazy moon; I never know when; The pussy foot; Shall I take my heart; Town House Maxixe; Pirate dance*). *Home stretch; Horse and buggy. Irish suite: (The Irish washerwoman; The minstrel boy; The Rakes of Mallow; The wearing of the green; The last rose of summer; The girl I left behind me). Jazz legato; Jazz pizzicato; The penny-whistle song; The phantom regiment; Plink, plank, plunk!; Promenade; Sandpaper ballet; Sarabande; Scottish suite: The bluebells of Scotland; Turn ye to me. Serenata; Sleigh ride; Song of the bells; Summer skies; The syncopated clock; Trumpeter's lullaby; The typewriter; The waltzing cat.*
(B) *** MCA Double-decker (2) [MCAD2-9815-A/B]. O cond. composer.

Belle of the ball; Bugler's holiday; Fiddle-faddle; Forgotten dreams; Jazz pizzicato; Plink, plank, plunk!; Sandpaper ballet; Sarabande; Serenata; Sleigh ride; Song of the bells; The syncopated clock; Trumpeter's lullaby; The typewriter.
(M) **(*) Van. 08.6008.71 [OVC 6008]. Utah SO, Maurice Abravanel.

Leroy Anderson, who studied under both Walter Piston and George Enesco, was in his varied musical career bandmaster, church organist, choirmaster, double-bass player and orchestral conductor. At the beginning of the 1950s he was asked by Arthur Fiedler to provide a series of specially written 'lollipops' for use as encores at the Boston Pops concerts. In response he produced a series of instantly memorable vignettes, wittily scored and usually melodically indelible. Over two decades he wrote two dozen such pieces in the best tradition of American popular music, and the finest of them sound as freshly attractive as the day they were written. Anderson might be regarded as the American equivalent of the British 'composer of tunes', Eric Coates – only his easy use of syncopation gives the music an unmistakable transatlantic flavour.

The composer was a naturally spontaneous exponent of his own music and he recorded a great deal of it for the American Decca label between 1950 and 1962. This MCA Double CD pack includes everything except the Christmas pot-pourris. It is extremely well documented, with first performance and recording dates for each item. A number of rather pleasant tunes are included from his musical, *Goldilocks*, plus mono recordings of his *Irish suite* (of which the arrangement of *The minstrel boy* as a haunting patrol is the highlight) and two numbers from a similar collection of Scottish airs. But it is for the orchestral encores that Anderson will be remembered and these are all played with great zest and affectionate lyrical feeling, and often the lightest possible touch, as in *Forgotten dreams*, where the composer plays the piano solo. The sound is bright and vivid, with a nicely judged hall ambience. The strings have less body here than on the shorter, Vanguard collection, but numbers like the the *Sandpaper ballet*, *The typewriter* and *The syncopated clock* have an extra rhythmic precision and sharpness of focus. This set is not currently available in the UK.

The collection by the Utah Symphony Orchestra under Maurice Abravanel is also very enjoyable, affectionate and polished, if not as racy as Anderson's own recordings. Numbers like *Bugler's holiday* and *Fiddle-faddle* are about half a minute longer than the composer's versions. Some might also feel that the Utah acoustic is a bit resonant for this lightly orchestrated writing, but it does not blunt the music's wit (the special effects in the *Sandpaper ballet* flit enthusiastically from speaker to speaker) and the glowing sound, richer in colour, gives an added warmth to the charming *Forgotten dreams* and the winsome *Trumpeter's lullaby*.

Arnold, Malcolm (born 1921)

(i) *Clarinet concerto No. 1;* (ii) *Flute concertos Nos. 1–2;* (iii) *Horn concerto No. 2;* (iv) *Oboe concerto;* (v) *Trumpet concerto.*
(M) *** EMI CDM7 63491-2. (i) Janet Hilton; (ii) Richard Adeney; (iii) Alan Civil; (iv) Gordon Hunt; (v) John Wallace; Bournemouth Sinf., (i; iii–v) Del Mar; (ii) Ronald Thomas.

Malcolm Arnold has more than eighteen concertos to his credit. Richard Adeney commissioned the flute concertos and premièred them in 1954 and 1973 respectively; he recorded both works in 1979. His playing of the cool cantilena which forms the *Andante* of the *First Concerto* is particularly beautiful, the ending quite ethereal; while the exhilarating finale, marked *con fuoco*, has superb dash. Even so, it is the engaging *Allegretto* finale of No. 2 which lingers in the memory, one of the composer's most engaging ideas: its gentle rhythmic inflexion is perfectly caught by the soloist. Janet Hilton in the *First Clarinet concerto* and Alan Civil in the *Second Horn concerto* are hardly less brilliant, while the *Oboe concerto*, written for Leon Goossens, is played with quite superb panache and virtuosity by Gordon Hunt. Having been a trumpeter, Arnold writes with uncommon skill for the instrument and John Wallace's articulation is dazzling. All this music is well crafted, enormously facile and easy to enjoy. The accompaniments, under Norman Del Mar and Neville Dilkes respectively, are excellent and the recordings are comparably vivid.

8 English dances.
(M) (***) Decca mono 425 661-2 [id.]. LPO, Boult – WALTON: *Façade* etc. *** ❀

Arnold's first essay in writing colourful regional pieces receives a vividly sympathetic performance under Boult, with the mono recording still sounding remarkably well, an unexpected but attractive coupling for a classic account of Walton's *Façade*.

The Sound Barrier (rhapsody) after film score, *Op. 38.*
(M) *** ASV Dig. CDWHL 2058; *ZCWHL 2058*. RPO, Kenneth Alwyn – BAX: *Malta G.C.* etc. ***

Malcolm Arnold's *Rhapsody*, adapted in 1952 from his film score, shows the composer at his most characteristically inventive. It has five tiny subdivisions but makes a satisfying whole, not a note too long, and is kaleidoscopically orchestrated. Kenneth Alwyn and the RPO clearly relish the virtuosity demanded of them, and the recording is equally brilliant.

(i) *Symphony No. 1;* (ii) *Concerto for 2 pianos* (3 hands), *Op. 104;* (iii) *English dances Nos. 3 & 5;* (i) *Solitaire: Sarabande; Polka;* (iii) *Tam O'Shanter: overture, Op. 51.*
(M) *** EMI CDM7 64044-2; *EG 764044-4*. (i) Bournemouth SO; (ii) Phyllis Sellick and Cyril Smith, CBSO; (iii) Philh. O; composer.

Malcolm Arnold in his late twenties made his first symphonic statement, one of total bitterness, a mood he was to find again much later in his life. But even here the idiom is direct and immediately recognizable. This is a strong performance under the composer. Arnold wrote his three-handed concerto especially for Phyllis Sellick and Cyril Smith (who had, sadly, lost the use of one hand but continued in a duo with his wife). The finale is an outrageous send-up of the pop music of the 1920s, banjo-strumming and all. A delightful, undemanding work, superbly played by the dedicatees, which makes a good foil for the *Symphony* alongside the rumbustious overture, *Tam O'Shanter*, a vividly compelling Burnsian evocation with its bacchanalian roistering, complete with bagpipes! Finally come the two pieces Arnold added to his *English dances* for the ballet *Solitaire*, and two of the most attractive of the *Dances*.

(i) *Symphony No. 2, Op. 40;* (ii) *Symphony No. 5, Op. 74.*(i) *Peterloo: overture.*
(M) *** EMI CDM7 63368-2 [id.]. (i) Bournemouth SO, Groves; (ii) CBSO, composer.

The recoupling of two of Arnold's most impressive symphonies can be warmly welcomed. Both recordings date from the 1970s. The *Second Symphony* is one of Malcolm Arnold's best pieces, far more complex in structure than it may initially seem. Arnold has developed the habit of hiding his deeper emotions behind a bright, extrovert manner and his *Fifth Symphony* brings out this dichotomy very clearly. It is a consciously elegiac work, written in memory of friends who died young; it contains some of his most intense and emotional music but remains easily approachable. The composer secures an excellent response from the Birmingham orchestra, as Groves, in Bournemouth, is equally dedicated. The CD transfer is outstandingly successful; indeed the sound approaches the demonstration class in its vivid detail, body and spaciousness. The *Overture* makes a highly effective encore. Splendid value at mid-price.

Auber, Daniel (1782–1871)

Crown Diamonds: Overture.
(M) *** Mercury 432 014-2 [id.]. Detroit SO,

Paray (with Concert: *'French opera highlights'* ***).

A splendidly polished account of one of Auber's very best overtures, given a genuine French accent in Detroit by Paul Paray. The 1960 Mercury recording is well up to standard. The rest of Paray's programme is equally enticing.

Bacarisse, Salvator (1898–1963)

Concertino in A min. for guitar and orchestra, Op. 72.
(B) **(*) DG Compact Classics 413 156-2 (2) [id.]. Yepes, Spanish R. & TV O, Alonso – CASTELNUOVO-TEDESCO: *Guitar concerto* ***; FALLA: *Nights in the gardens of Spain* ***; RODRIGO: *Concertos.* **

This is the least distinctive component in DG's two-CD bargain compilation of concertante works for guitar, harp and piano. Bacarisse was director of the Spanish Radio in Republican days. His *Concertino* is an unpretentious little work, brilliantly played by Yepes. It is monothematic and the somewhat ingenuous main idea is attractive in a straightforward way. In Yepes's hands the slow movement has plenty of atmosphere and the variations of the finale are pleasing enough. The 1973 recording is clear and fresh.

Bach, Carl Philipp Emanuel
(1714–88)

Cello concertos: in B flat, Wq.171; in A, Wq.172.
(B) **(*) Hung. White Label HRC 117 [id.]. Csába Onczay, Liszt CO, Rolla (with CHERUBINI: *13 Contredanses* **).

Onczay, who has a warm, well-focused tone, plays very sympathetically. The accompaniments for him are polished, elegant and alert, and the recording has a pleasing ambience. As an encore, we are given some attractive country dances by Cherubini, in which the recording is more confined but still agreeable. The disc has good documentation too. Excellent value.

Cello concerto in A, Wq.172.
(BB) *** Virgin/Virgo Dig. VJ7 91453-2; *VJ7 91453-4* [id.]. Caroline Dale, Scottish Ens., Jonathan Rees – J. S. BACH: *Violin concertos.* ***

Caroline Dale at a spacious Largo plays the slow movement of the splendid *A major Cello concerto* with full expressiveness, in principle using too romantic a style but bringing out a dark intensity that relates it to the greatest of the Passion music of the composer's father, J. S. Bach. With vigorous outer movements, this is a valuable work to have as makeweight for three of J. S. B.'s most popular violin concertos; and it makes an auspicious start for Virgo, the new bargain label from Virgin Classics. However, the musical notes, characteristic of the series, are sparse.

Flute concerto in D min., Wq. 22.
(BB) **(*) ASV CDQS 6012; *ZCQS 6012.* Dingfelder, ECO, Mackerras – HOFFMEISTER: *Concertos Nos. 6 & 9.* **(*)

Flute concertos: in A min.; in B flat, Wq. 166/7.
(M) **(*) DG 427 132-2 [id.]. Stephen Preston, E. Concert, Pinnock.

Stephen Preston plays a period instrument which is inevitably less strong in the bottom octave than the modern flute. He gives performances of considerable accomplishment and virtuosity; he makes much of the introspection of the slow movement of the *A minor* and tosses off the finales with enormous facility. He receives excellent support from Pinnock, and the recording quality has fine presence and detail; however, some ears may find this coupling, with its slightly abrasive upper string-sound, a little lacking in charm.

Those who are interested in the Hoffmeister coupling rather than a C. P. E. Bach collection will find Ingrid Dingfelder's playing both spirited and stylish, while Mackerras's accompaniments match polish with vigour. The sound-quality too is admirably vivid and this CD reissue is competitively priced.

Harpsichord concerto in D min., Wq.23.
(B) ** CfP CD-CFP 4571; *TC-CFP 4571.* Malcolm, Bath Festival O, Y. Menuhin – J. S. BACH: *Harpsichord concerto No. 6* etc. **

C. P. E. Bach composed about four dozen harpsichord concertos, this one being written in Potsdam in 1748. Its most striking movement is the finale, which gives off plenty of sparks and is here relished with zest. The other movements are thematically less memorable: the *Poco andante* is rather conventional from a melodic point of view. Malcolm plays a modern harpsichord, balanced within the orchestra, to counterbalance the strings which have greater tonal impact than would have been likely in the composer's day. The CD transfer is fresh and clean.

(i) *Harpsichord concerto in D min., Wq.23;* (i–ii) *Double harpsichord concerto in F, Wq.46;* (iii) *Oboe concerto in E flat, Wq.165.*
(M) **(*) HM/BMG GD77061 [77061-RG-2]. (i) Leonhardt, (ii) Curtis, (iii) Hucke; Coll. Aur., Maier.

The *F major concerto* for two harpsichords and strings with the addition of two horns and continuo, Wq.46, comes from Bach's Berlin years (its probable date is 1740) and it is thoroughly representative of this extraordinary composer. The better-known *D minor concerto*, Wq.23 (1748), could almost be said to look forward to the *Sturm und Drang*, and it receives a dashing and fiery performance from Gustav Leonhardt and the Collegium Aureum. The *Oboe concerto* is much later (1765) and is notable for its forward-looking and expressive slow movement. So far as baroque oboe playing is concerned, things have moved on since this record was made; however, the performances have a spirit and expressive vitality that are sometimes missing from more modern ensembles; the excellent recordings were made in the resonant acoustic of Schloss Kirchheim in 1965 (Wq.46) and 1968 (Wq.23 and 165), when the cellos, incidentally, were led by Anner Bylsma. By the side of modern-day period ensembles, the Collegium Aureum sound positively big-band, an impression no doubt reinforced by the acoustic; for those who are worried by such matters, they play at present-day pitch.

Oboe concertos: in B flat, Wq. 164; in E flat, Wq. 165; Sonata for oboe and continuo in G min., Wq. 135.
(M) *** Erato/Warner Dig. 2292 45430-2 [id.]. Ku Ebbinge, Amsterdam Bar. O, Koopman.

C. P. E. Bach's pair of *Oboe concertos* are very appealing in their wide range of mood, and the *Largo e mesto* of Wq. 164 is plaintively haunting in Ku Ebbinge's hands. His small, sweet authentic timbre is very appealing, his decoration is nicely judged, and he articulates nimbly in the the lively allegros. Koopman provides gracefully alert accompaniments and the recording balance is fresh and realistic, with textures transparent. The four-movement *Sonata* with its variation third movement makes an attractive bonus, played no less felicitously.

4 Hamburg sinfonias, Wq. 183/1–4; Sinfonias: in E min., Wq. 177; in C, Wq. 182/3.
(M) *** Ph. 426 081-2; *426 081-4* [id.]. ECO, Leppard.

Like their predecessors, the four *Sinfonias*, Wq. 183, are not merely interesting historically but are often characterized by an emotional insistence that is disturbing and by a capacity to surprise that is quite remarkable. Leppard's performances are full of drive and have an alert intensity appropriate to this astonishing composer. The recordings too are fresh and impeccably balanced; and this generous mid-priced Philips disc can be strongly recommended to those not insisting on original instruments.

CHAMBER AND INSTRUMENTAL MUSIC

Quartets (Trios) for fortepiano, flute and viola: in A min., D & G, Wq.93/95.
(M) *** HM/BMG GD 77052 [77052-2-RG]. Les Adieux.

Although these works were designated by Bach as *Quartets*, no bass part survives. Piano, flute and viola are musically handled so equally, and everything is so minutely written out, that an added cello would always remain 'the fifth wheel on the wagon'. Certainly the bright, transparent textures of the original instruments are as delightful as Bach's invention. The playing, too, matches the music in its finish, lightness of touch and spontaneity.

VOCAL MUSIC

Die letzten Leiden des Erlösers (The Last Sufferings of the Saviour), Wq. 233.
(M) *** HM/BMG GD 77042 [77042-2-RG]. Schlick, Reyghere, Patriasz, Prégardien, Egmond, Ghent Coll. Vocale, La Petite Bande, Kuijken.

Die letzten Leiden des Erlösers (1770) has moments of great inspiration; its invention has nobility and originality – though it must be admitted that there are some passages which are routine. However, the restless intelligence and sensibility which pervade so much of Bach's music are all in evidence. *Die letzten Leiden* has good claims to be considered one of Carl Philipp Emanuel's masterpieces, and it is given a first-class performance by the excellent team of soloists assembled here. The singing of the Collegium Vocale of Ghent is also eloquent, and the playing of La Petite Bande under Sigiswald Kuijken is predictably vivid and alive. Fine, well-balanced recording.

Magnificat, Wq. 215.
(M) *** Decca 421 148-2. Palmer, Watts, Tear, Roberts, King's College Ch., ASMF, Ledger – BACH, J. S.: *Magnificat*. ***

The magnificent opening chorus of C. P. E. Bach's *Magnificat* (repeated later in the setting of the *Gloria*) presents King's College Choir at its most exhilarating. This irresistible movement, here taken challengingly fast, leads to a whole series of sharply characterized numbers, including a sparkling tenor aria on *Quia fecit*. With vividly atmospheric recording, the performance under Philip Ledger comes electrically to life, with choir, soloists and orchestra all in splendid form. Aptly coupled with Johann Sebastian's earlier setting, this CD can be strongly recommended. It sounds extremely vivid.

Bach, Johann Christian (1735–82)

Bassoon concertos: in B flat; in E flat.
(B) ** Hung. White Label HRC 041 [id.]. Gábor Janota, Liszt CO, Rolla; or József Vajda, Budapest SO, Lehel – HUMMEL: *Bassoon concerto.* ***

These are smoothly straightforward works in the *galant* style. Good playing from both soloists (especially from Janota in the latter) and warm, polished accompaniments. The recording is full and pleasing, the overall effect a shade bland.

6 Sinfonias, Op. 3 (ed. Erik Smith).
(M) *** Ph. 422 498-2. ASMF, Marriner.

These Op. 3 symphonies are recorded here for the first time. Erik Smith, who has edited them, describes them as 'in essence Italian overtures, though with an unusual wealth of singing melody'. They are beguilingly played by the Academy of St Martin-in-the-Fields under Sir Neville Marriner, and beautifully recorded. The 1970 recording sounds wonderfully fresh and transparent.

Bach, Johann Sebastian
(1685–1750)

The Art of fugue, BWV 1080.
(M) ** DG Dig. 431 704-2; *431 704-4* [id.]. Col. Mus. Ant., Reinhard Goebel.

How to perform *The Art of fugue* has always presented problems, since Bach's own indications are so sparse. In the Cologne performance, the movements are divided between strings and solo harpsichord. The two harpsichord players are often imaginative and expressive, to contrast with the rhythmic vigour of the playing of the strings. It has genuine vitality, but the bite on the string-tone, and also the expressive bulges which are at times exaggerated, will pose a listening problem for some readers. The recording is remarkably clean and present. The digital sound is faithful.

Brandenburg concertos Nos. 1–6; (i) *Violin concertos Nos. 1–2;* (i; ii) *Double violin concerto.*
(B) ** VoxBox (3) [CD3X 3008]. (i) Susanne Lautenbacher; (ii) Dieter Vorholz; Mainz CO, Günter Kehr.

Many collectors will remember the Kehr/Mainz set of *Brandenburgs* with affection. They date from 1958 and had wide circulation on Turnabout LPs in the 1960s. On the whole the recording wears its years fairly lightly; it is resonant and, in its CD format, tuttis are robust rather than refined, but there is no lack of dynamic range, and there is good stereo separation. The playing is good-humouredly spontaneous and musically convincing. The wind solos are generally excellent, with the soloists (and even the trumpet in No. 2) balanced with the group. The harpsichord soloist distinguishes himself in No. 5, although the continuo playing is less imaginative elsewhere. The overall effect is of a fairly modest-sized chamber orchestra playing modern instruments with skill and conviction. In the *Violin concertos* the strings sound fuller and heavier than we would expect today and Suzanne Lautenbacher's degree of romantic warmth may raise some eyebrows. But her phrasing of slow movements is warmly musical (her interchanges with Dieter Vorholz in the *Largo* of the *Double concerto* are relaxed and expressively appealing) and allegros are buoyant and lively. This set still awaits reissue in the UK.

Brandenburg concertos Nos. 1–6, BWV 1046/51; Suites Nos. 1–4, BWV 1066/9.
(B) *** Ph. 426 145-2 (4) [id.]. ECO, Raymond Leppard.
(M) **(*) DG 423 492-2 (3). E. Concert, Pinnock.
(M) *(*) EMI CMS7 64150-2 (3). (i) Philh. O or (ii) New Philh. O, Klemperer (with RAMEAU: *Gavotte with 6 variations* **).

Leppard's early Philips recordings of the *Brandenburgs* and *Suites* are highly recommendable at bargain price and the sound is excellent. They are discussed below in greater detail; however, unless original instruments are mandatory, this set should give every satisfaction.

The merits of Pinnock's *Brandenburg concertos* are considerable – see below – but the *Suites* are somewhat more controversial, bringing a distinct loss of breadth and grandeur.

Klemperer's handling of the *Brandenburgs* is far more alert than one might have expected and, with such intensely felt performances, one misses the added ornaments very little. No. 3, however, provides the exception: beside the others it is comparatively dull, with strangely slack discipline, so that for once the slow speeds do tend to plod. The *Suites* are much more pedestrian. The set has its moments, of course, mainly in the music which gains most from majestic treatment. But the deadpan approach to repeats without added decoration, the absence of double-dotting and all the other features of the pre-war Bach performing tradition are difficult to accept alongside a set like Marriner's, where modern instruments are used but the more recent discoveries of scholarship are put at the service of the music. The Klemperer recordings were made at Abbey Road in 1960 (the *Brandenburgs*) and 1969 (the *Suites*) and are well transferred to CD.

Brandenburg concertos Nos. 1–6, BWV 1046/51.

(M) *** DG Dig. 435 081-2; *435 081-4* (*Nos. 1, 3 & 5*); 435 082-2; *435 082-4* (*Nos. 2, 4 & 6*) [id.]. E. Concert, Trevor Pinnock.

(B) *** Pickwick Dig. PCD 830; *CIMPC 830* (1–3); PCD 845; *CIMPC 845* (4–6) [id.]. ECO, Ledger.

(M) *** Ph. 420 345/6-2 [id.]; *420 345/6-4*. ECO Leppard.

(M) **(*) Decca 425 725-2; *425 725-4* (*Nos. 1–3*); 425 726-2; *425 726-4* (*Nos. 4–6*) [id.]. ECO, Britten.

(BB) ** Naxos Dig. 8.550047 (*Nos. 1–3*); 8.550048 (*Nos. 4–6*). Capella Istropolitana, Bohdan Warchal.

(B) * Ph. 426 970-2 (*Nos. 1–3*); 426 971-2 (*Nos.4–6*). I Musici.

Brandenburg concertos Nos. 1–6; Harpsichord concerto No. 2 in D, BWV 1054.

(BB) *(*) LaserLight 15 508 (*Nos. 1–3* & BWV 1054); ** 15 509 (*Nos. 4–6*). Berlin CO, Peter Wohlert.

Brandenburg concertos Nos. 3–5, BWV 1048/50.

(M) **(*) Ph. Dig. 432 037-2 [id.]. I Musici.

The reissue of Pinnock's set of *Brandenburgs* at mid-price could be a clear first recommendation for those favouring these works played on original instruments, were it not for the Linde EMI compilation – see below – which includes in addition the *Musical offering*. Undoubtedly Pinnock's DG versions represent the peak of his achievement as an advocate of authentic performance, with sounds that are clear and refreshing but not too abrasive. Interpretatively he tends to opt for faster speeds in outer movements, relatively slow ones in *Andantes*, with a warm but stylish degree of expressiveness, but from first to last there is no routine. Soloists are outstanding, and so is the 1982 recording, made in the Henry Wood Hall, London, with the CDs transferred at a very high level, giving the sound great immediacy, although the string focus is sharply delineated. This brings a degree more bite and abrasiveness than in the Linde performances, and some ears will find this stimulating.

On Pickwick, Ledger has the advantage of fresh and detailed digital recording. He directs resilient, well-paced readings of all six concertos, lively yet never over-forced. The slow movements in particular are most beautifully done, persuasively and without mannerism. Flutes rather than recorders are used in No. 4.

Leppard's Philips set, in the mid-priced range, is higher-powered than Ledger's, whose gentler manner will for many be easier to live with. But the exhilaration of the Leppard set is undeniable; there is much to enjoy here. The remastered analogue sound is full and ample.

Britten made his recordings in the Maltings concert-hall in 1968, not long before the serious fire there. The engineers had not quite accustomed themselves to the reverberant acoustic and, to compensate, they put the microphones rather close to the players. The result is a fairly ample sound that in its way goes well with Britten's interpretations. The disappointing element is the lack of delicacy, partly textural, in the slow movements of Nos. 1, 2, 4 and 6; but the bubbling high spirits of the outer movements are hard to resist, and the harspsichordist, Philip Ledger, follows the pattern he had set in live Britten performances, with Britten-inspired extra elaborations a continual delight. The CD transfer is very successful, the sound both full and bright, and the effect of these performances is joyfully life-enhancing.

Very well played and recorded, the Capella Istropolitana's set of the *Brandenburgs* offers comfortably old-fashioned performances, with speeds consistently on the slow side, both in Allegros and in slow movements. With rhythms generally well sprung, the results become sluggish only occasionally, as in No. 3 – but those who favour latter-day ideas on Bach interpretation should keep clear.

I Musici's 1984 digital set of *Brandenburgs* is already being issued at mid-price, although so far only Nos. 3–5 are available. These are sunny performances, very realistically recorded, lacking something in imagination in slow movements but not without energy in fast ones: witness the zestfully brisk finale of No. 3. The sound is first class, with a striking presence. Disgracefully for a major mid-priced series, there are no musical notes, only a list of the other records on the Laser Line label.

Philips have also reissued I Musici's earlier (1965) analogue set at bargain price (also without documentation). Although famous soloists are featured, including Maurice André, Heinz Holliger, and Frans Brüggen, the performances are much less attractive. The approach is rather solid, generally slow of tempo and unresilient of rhythm. The CD transfer is good, but the sound is less realistically focused than on the digital recording.

Peter Wohlert's performances are in the older German tradition associated with Münchinger and Richter. Tempi are very relaxed, though the finale of No. 3 has an attractive lightness of articulation; only in the first movement of No. 2 is tuning less than ideally defined. The second disc, including the last three concertos, is consistently enjoyable, with excellent solo playing.

The keyboard concerto with an unnamed soloist, included as a bonus on the first disc, is not an asset, rhythmically rigid and emphatic in its accents. The recording is pleasingly full and clear.

Brandenburg concertos Nos. 1–6; A Musical offering.
(M) *** EMI Dig./Analogue CMS7 63434-2 (2). Linde Cons.

The Linde Consort is one of the most stylish and responsive of authentic performing groups working in Europe, and their recording sounds very fresh and vivid on CD. It can be strongly recommended, with sprung rhythms and generally well-chosen tempi, and these CDs deserve to rank alongside Pinnock's set. But, quite apart from the considerable bonus of the *Musical offering*, many will prefer the Linde version of the *Brandenburgs*, for the 1981 EMI recording is rather fuller than the DG Archiv sound, with the strings very slightly less immediate. In *Brandenburg No. 3* there is a distinct gain in body and warmth, and No. 6 (also for strings alone) again brings a slightly more ample texture, without loss of inner definition. In the *Musical offering* (recorded a year earlier) Hans-Martin Linde draws on the thinking of the American scholar, Ursula Kirkendale, whose conclusion favours the same sequence of movements as that adopted by Spitta – not that this is necessarily a major consideration, since with a little effort the listener can exercise his or her own preferences in playing the disc. Generally speaking, Linde is as stylish and accomplished as any of his rivals, and he and his six colleagues offer the preferred version of this work using original instruments. They are again warmly as well as clearly recorded; indeed the analogue to digital transfer is particularly natural, and this set offers remarkable value.

Brandenburg concertos Nos. 1–3; Orchestral suite No. 1, BWV 1066.
(M) * DG Dig. 431 701-2; *431 701-4* [id.]. Col. Mus. Ant., Goebel.

Brandenburg concertos Nos. 4–6; Orchestral suite No. 4, BWV 1069.
(M) * DG Dig. 431 702-2; *431 702-4* [id.]. Col. Mus. Ant., Goebel.

Goebel's allegros are so fast and hectic in the *Brandenburg concertos* that they have you disbelieving your ears. It is hard not to laugh out loud at the speeds for both movements of No. 3 (the second more than the first), and even more at the sketchy strumming which purports to be the first movement of No. 6. At Goebel's headlong speed, the semiquaver arpeggios are hardly audible and even the repeated quavers sound rushed. It is a tribute to the virtuosity of the Cologne ensemble that otherwise they cope so well, usually playing with a good rhythmic spring. Slow movements, by contrast, are taken relatively conservatively, though Goebel's squeezy phrasing is often uncomfortable, with the ensemble characteristically edgy in its light, clear style. The speeds mean that there is room to fit one of the *Orchestral suites* on each of the two discs. With abrasive, choppy phrasing and again using squeeze techniques on sustained notes, they present a clear, lively view of what Goebel feels constitutes authentic performance, using a normal baroque-sized orchestral group with four first and four second violins. Fine recording, but this issue is mainly of curiosity interest.

Flute concertos: in D min., BWV 1052; in A min., BWV 1056; Italian concerto, BWV 971 (arr. for flute and strings by Mark Starr); *Suite No. 2 in B min., BWV 1067.*
(M) * Pickwick MCD 28; *MCC 28.* James Dower, L. Bach O, Malcolm Layfield.

The *Flute concertos* are nothing of the kind but, as their Schmieder numbers indicate, are transcriptions of the *D minor Clavier concerto* (itself transcribed from a lost violin concerto) and the *F minor Clavier concerto*. The *Italian concerto* is also an arrangement – by Mark Starr, who has also transposed it up a tone. Not that Bach himself would have thought this in any way unusual, nor would he have been displeased by the result. The *B minor Suite* is the only work here that has not been arranged. The disc is obviously a vehicle for the not inconsiderable musical skills of John Dower, but the results are all rather ordinary: the orchestral playing is inclined to be routine and pedestrian, and the recording, made in the bright acoustic of St John's, Smith Square, London, is a bit forward. The *B minor suite* is curiously wanting in sparkle; the dotted rhythms in the *Overture* are flabby.

Flute concertos: in C (from *BWV 1055*); *in E min.* (from movements of *Cantata No. 35*); *in G min.* (from *BWV 1056*); *Sinfonia* from *Cantata No. 209.*
(M) **(*) Sony Dig. MDK 46510 [id.]. Rampal, Ars Redivivia, Munclinger.

If you enjoy transcriptions of Bach for the flute – and they are easy to enjoy here – it is difficult to imagine them being played better than by Jean-Pierre Rampal. He is wonderfully nimble in the opening allegro of BWV 1055 and gives a radiantly beautiful account of the slow-movement cantilena of BWV 1056. Munclinger, who made the arrangements, provides sympathetic accompaniments, although rhythmically he does not quite display

Rampal's lightness of touch. Nevertheless, this is an attractive concert, made the more welcome by the inclusion of the *Sinfonia* from *Cantata No. 209*. The digital recording is very good indeed – and well balanced, too. However, those who count minutes will note that there are only 42½ of them here.

Harpsichord concertos Nos. 1 in D min., BWV 1052; 5 in F min., BWV 1056; Double harpsichord concerto No. 1 in C min., BWV 1060; Triple harpsichord concerto No. 2 in C, BWV 1064; Quadruple harpsichord concerto in A min., BWV 1065.
(M) *** Ph. 422 497-2; *422 497-4* [id.]. Leppard, Andrew Davis, Ledger, Verlet, ECO, Leppard.

Harpsichord concertos Nos. 2 in E, BWV 1053; 4 in A, BWV 1055; Double harpsichord concerto No. 2 in C, BWV 1061; Triple harpsichord concerto No. 1 in D min., BWV 1063.
(M) *** Ph. 426 084-2; *426 084-4* [id.]. Leppard, Andrew Davis, Ledger, ECO, Leppard.

Harpsichord concerto Nos. 3 in D, BWV 1054; 6 in F, BWV 1057; 7 in G min., BWV 1058; (i) *Double harpsichord concerto No. 3 in C min., BWV 1062.*
(M) *** Ph. 426 448-2; *426 448-4* [id.]. Leppard; (i) Ledger, ECO, Leppard.

These performances derive from a boxed set, recorded in 1973/4. Leppard and Davis play with skill and flair, as do their colleagues in the multiple concertos; the ECO shows plenty of life and the performances communicate such joy in the music that criticism is disarmed. The Philips sound is very realistic, the harpsichords life-size and not too forward; one does reflect that modern strings, however refined, create a body of tone which tends slightly to outweigh the more slender keyboard timbres. However, in the works for two or more harpsichords there is a pleasing absence of jangle.

Clavier concertos Nos. 1 in D min., BWV 1052; 2 in E, BWV 1053; 3 in D, BWV 1054.
(BB) *** Naxos Dig. 8.550422 [id.]. Hae-won Chang (piano), Camerata Cassovia, Robert Stankovsky.

Clavier concertos Nos. 4 in A, BWV 1055; 5 in F min., BWV 1056; 6 in F, BWV 10557; 7 in G min., BWV 1058.
(BB) *** Naxos Dig. 8. 550423 [id.]. Hae-won Chang (piano), Camerata Cassovia, Robert Stankovsky.

This splendid Naxos set marks the début both of the highly gifted young Korean pianist, Hae-won Chang, and of the excellent chamber ensemble drawn from members of the CSSR State Philharmonic Orchestra, based in Košice. Miss Chang is a highly sympathetic Bach exponent, playing flexibly yet with strong rhythmic feeling, decorating nimbly and not fussily. Robert Stankovsky directs freshly resilient accompaniments; and both artists understand the need for a subtle gradation of light and shade. Slow movements are highly imaginative and give much pleasure. The *Adagio* of the *D minor Concerto* (No. 1) and the *Siciliano* of the *E major* are appealingly thoughtful, while the famous *Largo* of the *F minor Concerto* is played with great delicacy of feeling. The *Larghetto* of the *A major* brings some memorably expressive dynamic contrasts from the Camerata strings. The imitative finale of the *F major* is attractively relaxed and brings some particularly felicitous ornamentation from the soloist. The digital recording, made in the House of Arts, Košice, is first class, with the piano balanced not too far forward.

Clavier concertos Nos. 1 in D min., BWV 1052; 2 in E, BWV 1053; 4 in A, BWV 1055; 5 in F min., BWV 1056.
(M) **(*) EMI Dig. CDD7 64055-2 [id.]; *ET 764055-4*. Andrei Gavrilov (piano), ASMF, Marriner.

In terms of dexterity and clarity of articulation Andrei Gavrilov cannot be faulted and he produces some beautiful sound when his playing is lyrical and relaxed. If at times one feels he is pushing on relentlessly and that his incisive touch can be a bit unremitting in some movements, there are a lot of memorable things, too. Indeed, in the slow movement of the *D minor* and *F minor Concertos*, there is playing of real poetry and delicacy – and, for that matter, in the finale of the *A major*. The 1986 Abbey Road recordings are excellently balanced, with the piano well integrated into the overall picture.

Clavier concertos Nos. 1 in D min., BWV 1052; 3 in D, BWV 1054; 5 in F min., BWV 1056; 6 in F, BWV 1057.
(M) *** Teldec/Warner Dig. 9031 74779-2 [id.]. Cyprien Katsaris (piano), Liszt CO, Rolla.

We thought well of these exhilarating performances when they first appeared at full price. Now that they are at mid-price their claims on the collector are even stronger. The *F major*, BWV 1057, is the transcription of the *Fourth Brandenburg Concerto*, and the others also derive from earlier works. Cyprien Katsaris possesses the most remarkable technique and feeling for colour, which are to be heard to excellent advantage in this vividly recorded and well-filled disc. He has an astonishingly vital musicality and keyboard resource. The playing of the Liszt Chamber Orchestra, surely one of the very finest chamber ensembles in the world, is splendidly supportive. Exhilarating and imaginative performances all round. This is one of the very best accounts of these concertos played on the piano currently available on CD, irrespective of cost.

Clavier concertos Nos. 1 in D min.; 4 in A; 5 in F min., BWV 1052 & 1055/6; (i) *Brandenburg concerto No. 5 in D, BWV 1050.*
(M) (***) EMI mono CDH7 63039-2. Edwin Fischer (piano) & CO; (i) Philh. O.

Edwin Fischer recorded the *Clavier concertos* with his own chamber orchestra in the 1930s and the *Fifth Brandenburg* in 1953 with the Philharmonia. Even the latter was also recorded for 78 r.p.m. discs, since there are long rallentandos as the side draws to a close. But these performances are riveting and have a compelling eloquence and sensitivity that banish all thoughts of sound-quality. It is good to hear Gareth Morris and Manoug Parikian again in the *Brandenburg*. Excellent transfers.

Harpsichord concerto No. 1 in D min., BWV 1052; Oboe d'amore concerto in A, BWV 1055; Violin concerto No. 1 in A min., BWV 1041; Double violin concerto in D min., BWV 1043.
(M) **(*) DG Dig. 435 084-2; *435 084-4* [id.]. Soloists, E. Concert, Pinnock.

Quadruple harpsichord concerto in A min., BWV 1065; Triple concerto in A min. for flute, violin and harpsichord, BWV 1044; Double concerto for oboe and violin in C min., BWV 1060; Violin concerto No. 2 in E, BWV 1042.
(M) **(*) DG Dig. 435 085-2; *435 085-4* [id.]. Soloists, E. Concert, Pinnock.

These are very persuasive performances, with excellent soloists. Rhythms are resilient and there is no lack of warmth; indeed the sound is admirably full and atmospheric. Those wanting these two programmes will be well pleased, but the selection is arbitrary and cuts across compilations offering complete sets of the keyboard concertos; one needs to buy both these records in order to obtain all three major violin concertos. Here the slight edge on Standage's solo timbre (and that of his partner in the *Double concerto*, Elizabeth Wilcock) will be no problem for those enjoying the authentic style.

Harpsichord concerto No. 6 in F, BWV 1057; (i) *Triple concerto in A min., for flute, violin and harpsichord, BWV 1044.*
(B) ** CfP CD-CFP 4571; *TC-CFP 4571.* Malcolm; (i) Bennett, Y. Menuhin; Bath Festival O, Menuhin – C. P. E. BACH: *Harpsichord concerto in D min.*

The *F major Concerto*, BWV 1057, is a transcription of the *Brandenburg concerto No. 4*, with recorder parts superbly played here by David Munrow and John Turner. George Malcolm is at his finest and Menuhin provides a sparkling accompaniment. There are good things, too, in the performance of the *Triple concerto*, especially the flute playing of William Bennett; but here the balance is slightly less well contrived and the performance has a shade less vitality. Bright and lively CD transfers.

Violin concertos Nos. 1 in A min.; 2 in E; Double concerto in D min., BWV 1041/3; Sonata in E min., BWV 1023 (arr. Respighi for violin and strings); *Suite 3, BWV 1068: Air.*
(BB) **(*) Naxos Dig. 8.550194 [id.]. Nishizaki, Jablokov, Capella Istropolitana, Oliver Dohnányi.

The first thing about the Naxos recording that strikes the ear is the attractively bright, gleaming sound of the orchestral string group, who play with fine resilience. Neither soloist is a strong personality and the espressivo in the *Adagio* of the *E major* solo *Concerto* and in the famous lyrical dialogue of the slow movement of the *Double concerto* brings rather deliberate phrasing. Yet these players are certainly musical and there is a sense of style here and plenty of vitality in allegros. The Respighi arrangement is effective enough and the concert ends with Bach's most famous string tune, played simply and eloquently.

Violin concertos Nos. (i) *1, BWV 1041;* (ii) *2, BWV 1042;* (iii) *Double violin concerto, BWV 1053;* (iv) *Double concerto for violin & oboe in D min., BWV 1060.*
❀ (M) *** Ph. 420 700-2; *420 700-4.* Grumiaux; (iii) Krebbers, (iv) Holliger; (i–iii) Les Solistes Romandes, Arpad Gerecz; (iv) New Philh. O, Edo de Waart.
(B) ** Ph. 426 075-2; *426 075-4.* (i; iii; iv) Michelucci; (ii; iii) Ayo; (iv) Leo Driehuys; I Musici.

Arthur Grumiaux recorded the violin concertos before in stereo (see below, in *Orchestral Suites*), but the present Swiss versions were made in 1978, when he was joined in the *Double concerto* by Hermann Krebbers. The result is an outstanding success. The way Grumiaux responds to the challenge of working with another great artist comes over equally clearly in the concerto with oboe, reconstructed from the *Double harpsichord concerto in C minor*. There the interplay of phrasing with Holliger is enchanting and, although the recording is earlier (1970), the sound is still good. Grumiaux's performances of the two solo concertos are equally satisfying, with a purity of line and an expressive response in slow movements that communicate very positively. Les Solistes Romandes under Gerecz provide crisply rhythmic allegros and are sensitively supportive in the expressive music. The digital remastering produces transparently fresh yet warm sound and gives the soloists great presence – indeed some may feel that the soloists are too forward, perhaps robbing the playing of some of its dynamic range.

On the Philips bargain label it is Felix Ayo who plays the *E major Violin concerto*, and with rather more flair than his colleague, Roberto Michelucci, shows in the *A minor Concerto*; but the two players join together for a spirited account of the *Double concerto*, and the work featuring the oboe is also a success. The clear, unaffected approach to all four concertos gives pleasure; the only snag is the reverberant acoustic, which rarely allows the harpsichord continuo to come through with any bite. But the sound itself is pleasing and this is acceptable value.

Violin concertos Nos. 1 in A min.; 2 in E; (i) *Double concerto, BWV 1041/3.*

(M) *** HM/BMG GD 77006; *GK 77006* [77006-2-RG; *77006-4-RG*]. Sigiswald Kuijken; (i) Lucy van Dael; La Petite Bande.

(M) *** DG 427 114-2 [id.]. Melkus, (i) Rantos; Vienna Capella Academica (with VIVALDI: *Concerto for viola d'amore and lute, RV 540* ***).

(M) (***) EMI mono CDH7 61018-2 (with *Partita No. 2, BWV 1004: Chaconne*) [MCA MCAD 25931]. Menuhin, Paris SO, Enescu or Monteux; (i) with Enescu (violin).

(B) **(*) Pickwick Dig. PCD 808 [id.]. Laredo, Scottish CO.

As we know from his admirable recordings of the Bach *Sonatas for violin and harpsichord* (see below) Kuijken is a fine Bach player, and these performances of the *Violin concertos* go to the top of the list for those wanting period performances on original instruments. The slight edge on the solo timbre is painless and La Petite Bande provide lively, resilient allegros, the playing both polished and alert. There are touches of individuality too, especially in slow movements, and the way Kuijken's solo melisma floats freely over the rather grave accompaniment in the *A minor concerto* is particularly appealing. In the *Largo* of the *Double concerto*, both soloists phrase their beautiful imitative line with gently separated notes, the expressive feeling enhanced without a hint of romantic overlay. Excellent, well-balanced, 1981 digital recording.

Melkus has the advantage of well-balanced DG recording from the early 1970s. He is not a soloist with a 'big' personality like Menuhin, but he is a musician of uncommon sensibility, and the way the recording balance allows him to form part of the overall ensemble, rather than enjoying a spotlight, gives special character to the music-making. Throughout, one has the impression of a happy balance between scholarship and musical freshness. His coupling is Vivaldi's *Concerto for viola d'amore and lute*, RV 540, in which he is ably partnered by Konrad Ragossnig. This is most memorably played and beautifully recorded.

Menuhin's 78 r.p.m. recording of the *Double concerto* with George Enescu his partner (and teacher) is legendary for its rapport and simple expressive beauty; the two solo *Concertos* are hardly less remarkable. All these records were made when Menuhin was between sixteen and nineteen years of age and show his unique instinctive musical vision, which came from within rather than from outside influences. The famous *Chaconne* is very impressive too, and all admirers of this great artist will not want to miss this reissue, even if the orchestral sound is dry and limited.

On the bargain-priced Pickwick CD, Laredo directs sympathetic traditional performances. The excellent Scottish Chamber Orchestra is well recorded with a realistic, well-judged balance except for the rather too prominent harpsichord continuo which in its relentlessness sometimes detracts from the generally well-sprung rhythms. Laredo's tone is a little thin at times, but that is a fault on the right side.

Violin concertos Nos. 2 in E, BWV 1042; in G min. (from *BWV 1056);* (i) *Double violin concerto in D min., BWV 1043.*

(BB) *** Virgin/Virgo Dig. VJ7 91453-2; *VJ7 91453-4* [id.]. Jonathan Rees, (i) with Jane Murdoch; Scottish Ens., Jonathan Rees – C. P. E. BACH: *Cello concerto.* ***

With forward and bright sound, well detailed, Jonathan Rees directs the Scottish Ensemble in warm, buoyant readings of three of Bach's violin concertos, the *G minor* being an arrangement of the *F minor Harpsichord concerto*, with its memorable central *Largo*. Allegros are infectiously sprung, while slow movements are allowed full expressiveness without sentimentality. In the clear digital recording the harpsichord continuo of Sally Heath is prominent without being distracting. The *Cello concerto* of C. P. E. Bach is a valuable makeweight.

The Musical offering, BWV 1079 (see also above, under *Brandenburg concertos*).

(M) ** Teldec/Warner 2292 42748-2 [id.]. VCM, Harnoncourt.

The Musical offering, BWV 1079; (i) *Suite No. 2 in B min, BWV 1067.*

(M) **(*) Decca 430 266-2; *430 266-4*. Stuttgart CO, Münchinger, (i) with Rampal.

Münchinger's 1976 version of the *Musical offer-*

ing is strikingly well recorded: it has fullness, presence and good detail. Moreover it offers playing of genuine breadth and eloquence, particularly in the *Trio sonata*. There is some fine dark colouring from Hans-Peter Weber's cor anglais, and the string textures often bring a sombre nobility which is very affecting. The canons are grouped together and come off well. Münchinger can be heavy-handed in Bach, but the performance here has many fine qualities and its cost is reasonable. For the reissue, the 1962 recording of the *B minor Suite* for flute and strings has been added, the best of the set, with some first-class playing from Jean-Pierre Rampal whose timbre and lightness of touch are most appealing.

Harnoncourt's recording dates from the early 1970s. It is musically sound, somewhat plainspun and a little lacking in imaginative vitality; but it is well recorded and offered at mid-price.

Orchestral Suites Nos. 1–4, BWV 1066/9.
(M) *** Decca 430 378-2; *430 378-4* [id.]. ASMF, Marriner.
(M) **(*) HM/BMG Dig. GD 77008 (2) [77008-2-RG]. La Petite Bande, Kuijken.
(M) **(*) Collins Dig. 3009-2 [id.]. L. Consort, Robert Haydon Clarke.

Orchestral Suites Nos. 1–4; Double Violin concerto, BWV 1043; Double concerto for violin & oboe, BWV 1060.
(M) ** Ph. 426 462-2 (2). Kremer, Szeryng, Hasson, Holliger, ASMF, Marriner.

Orchestral Suites Nos. 1–2, BWV 1066/7; Chorale variation; Prelude in B min.; Siciliano.
(BB) * Naxos Dig. 8.550244 [id.]. Capella Istropolitana, Jaroslav Dvořák.

Orchestral Suites Nos. 3–4, BWV 1068/9; Suite in G min. BWV 1070 (arr. David).
(BB) * Naxos Dig. 8.550245 [id.]. Capella Istropolitana, Jaroslav Dvořák.

Orchestral Suites Nos. 1 in C; 3 in D; 4 in D, BWV 1066, 1068 & 1069.
(M) *** Ph. 420 888-2. ECO, Leppard.

Orchestral Suite No. 2 in B min., BWV 1067; (i) *Violin concertos Nos. 1 in A min.; 2 in E, BWV 1041/2;* (ii) *Triple concerto for flute, violin and harpsichord in A min., BWV 1044.*
(M) *** Ph. 420 889-2. (i) Grumiaux; (ii) Garcia, Adeney, Leppard; ECO, Leppard.

We have always greatly enjoyed Marriner's 1970 recording of the Bach *Suites* with the ASMF. Now all four arrive on a single CD (77 minutes 48 seconds) and the remastering of the fine (originally Argo) recording is fresh and vivid, but without that over-lit quality and thinning of violin timbre which affected Decca's earlier reissue of the *Second* and *Third Suites* (see below). Thurston Dart, who plays the continuo, had a great deal to do with the preparation of these performances, and the exuberance of the music-making makes a fitting tribute to his scholarship which always sought to enhance the music's spirit, never to deaden it. The playing throughout is expressive without being romantic (the famous *Air* in the *Third Suite* is particularly successful) and always buoyant and vigorous. Perhaps the CD transfer loses a little of the weight of the originals but not their musical strength. William Bennett is the agile and sensitive flute soloist in the *Second Suite*; his decoration, never overdone, is particularly well judged in the closing *Badinerie*, played with nimble bravura. A fine bargain for those not insisting on original instruments; there is nothing remotely unstylish here.

For Philips's Silverline mid-price reissue of the four Bach *Orchestral Suites*, Grumiaux's 1964 performances of the two solo *Violin concertos* have been added (with their purity of line and matching vitality) plus an attractive version of the *Triple concerto*, its slow movement striking for the colourful interchanges of timbre. The *Suites* come from the pre-authentic era, but they are sparklingly played by excellent soloists; overall, Leppard's conception balances gravitas and elegance with baroque ebullience. The 1968 recording has been remastered successfully for CD, with the sound remaining full as well as being better defined.

Kuijken with La Petite Bande shows that authentic performance need not be acidly overabrasive. Set against a warm acoustic – more comfortable for the trumpet-sound, if not always helpful to clarity – these are brightly attractive performances with their just speeds and resilient rhythms. Solo work is most stylish, though ensemble is not always immaculate and intonation is somewhat variable. Nevertheless a good medium-price version if you are looking for performances on original instruments. The CDs are certainly impressive in their spaciousness, and definition is excellent. But they cost twice as much as the Marriner set.

Robert Haydon Clarke and the London Consort offer the first complete, mid-priced digital recording of all four *Suites* using modern instruments. The performances are fresh and pleasing, with tempi very close to those of Ledger on Virgo, though Haydon Clarke's lighter rhythmic pointing means that the playing has marginally less rhythmic character. This affects the overtures more than the dances, which are light in articulation and pleasingly elegant. One major difference is with the famous *Air* of the *Third Suite*, which the leader of the London Consort plays as a violin solo.

The spry flute soloist in the *Second Suite* decorates tastefully. The recording is very natural, although the warm acoustic means that inner detail is slightly less clearly observed than with Ledger or Marriner, who remains first choice, unless digital sound is essential.

Fine as it is – and despite the inclusion of two *Double concertos* – Marriner's second recording of the *Suites*, for Philips, is no match for his first, Argo/Decca set. The movements where he has changed his mind – for example in the famous *Air* from the *Suite No. 3*, which is here ponderously slow – are now almost always less convincing, and that reflects the very qualities of urgency and spontaneity which made the earlier Argo version so enjoyable.

Recorded on a larger scale, with weightier sound than on the same group's set of the *Brandenburgs*, the Capella Istropolitana's versions of the *Suites* bring extreme speeds in both directions. Though dance movements are done crisply enough, the *Allegro* for the *Suite No. 3*, for example, is hectically fast, challenging the players, while the great *Air* following it is heavy and sluggish. When competition is strong and the Naxos couplings are not generous, this gets a very qualified recommendation. The *Suite in G minor* (generally counted as spurious and, for all its charm, sounding un-Bach-like) is confusingly described as *Suite No. 5*.

Orchestral suites Nos. 1–3, BWV 1066/8.
(BB) **(*) Virgin/Virgo Dig. VJ7 91452-2; *VJ7 91452-4* [id.]. ECO, Ledger.
(M) ** DG Dig. 435 083-2; *435 083-4* [id.]. E. Concert, Trevor Pinnock.

Philip Ledger directs fresh and stylish performances of the first three *Suites*, very well recorded, with his own harpsichord continuo placed rather more prominently than in rival versions. The style is otherwise rather lighter than in the vintage Marriner performances on the Decca disc. Like the Pinnock reissue, this Virgo CD misses out the last *Suite*, an omission which many collectors will find unacceptable; but the price is markedly lower, and the excellent digital sound may be a further incentive. The accompanying notes, however, are very brief and barely adequate.

Pinnock's complete set of the *Suites* is available, harnessed to the *Brandenburgs* (see above). To be offered three out of the four is unsatisfactory, and the unprepared listener could well find the bright edge on the squeezed, vibrato-less string-timbre disconcerting, even though the recording has a full ambience. Playing is alert, with rhythms refreshingly sprung – not least in the slow introductions which, as one would expect, are anything but ponderous. In the *B minor Suite*, although there could be more contrast in feeling, there is no sense that reverence for supposed authenticity is stifling musical spontaneity. The recording is excellent; but any feeling of Baroque grandeur of the kind conveyed by Marriner in his Decca/Argo set is less apparent here.

Orchestral suites Nos. 2–3, BWV 1067/8; (i) *Flute concerto, BWV 1056;* (ii) *Concerto for violin and oboe, BWV 1060.*
(M) ** Decca 417 715-2 [id.]. ASMF, Marriner; (i) with Bennett; (ii) Kaine, Miller.

These spirited and polished performances come from Marriner's Argo recordings of the 1970s. The digital remastering has emphasized the bright lighting of the recording in the *Suites*, the violin timbre is thin (some might feel the effect to be more 'authentic') and the overall sound-balance rather dry in the bass. The two concertos (which date from 1975) are noticeably more expansive in quality.

CHAMBER MUSIC

(Unaccompanied) *Cello suites Nos. 1–6, BWV 1007/12.*
(M) *** DG 419 359-2 (2) [id.]. Pierre Fournier.
(M) (***) EMI mono CHS7 61027-2 (2) [Ang. CDH 61028/9]. Pablo Casals.
(M) *** Ph. 422 494-2; *422 494-4* (*Nos. 1, 4 & 6*); 422 495-2; *422 495-4* (*Nos. 2, 3 & 5*). Maurice Gendron.
(B) **(*) EMI CMS7 69431-2 (2). Paul Tortelier.

(Unaccompanied) Cello suites Nos. 1–6, BWV 1007/12; (i) *Viola da gamba sonatas Nos. 1–2, BWV 1027/8.*
(M) **(*) Mercury 432 756-2 (2) [id.]. Janos Starker, (i) with György Sebök.

Fournier's richly phrased and warm-toned performances were recorded in 1961 and dominated the catalogue during the 1960s. They carry an impressive musical conviction. This is not refined, introverted playing – the cellist dwelling within himself – but a bold and vigorous reading, obviously designed to project outwards to the listener. Fournier can be profound and he can lift rhythms infectiously in dance movements, but above all he conveys the feeling that this is music to be enjoyed. The recording, made in a resonant but not over-blown ambience, does not sound in the least dated.

It was Casals who restored these pieces to the repertory after long decades of neglect. Some of the playing is far from flawless; passage-work is rushed or articulation uneven, and he is often wayward. But he brought to the *Cello suites* insights that remain unrivalled. Casals brings one closer to this music than do most (one is tempted to say, any) of his rivals. Listen to the

Sarabandes from the *D minor* or *C minor Suites* and the humanity, nobility and wisdom of this playing will be immediately evident. The sound is inevitably dated but still comes over well in this transfer.

No one artist holds all the secrets in this repertoire, but few succeed in producing such consistent beauty of tone as Maurice Gendron, with the digital remastering firming up the focus of what was originally an excellent and truthful analogue recording. His phrasing is unfailingly musical and, although these readings have a certain sobriety (save perhaps for No. 6, which has distinct flair), their restraint and fine judgement command admiration. At mid-price (with the two discs available separately) they can certainly be given a warm welcome back to the catalogue.

The Mercury set is not to be confused with the incandescent set Janos Starker made in the early days of mono LP (issued in the UK on the old Nixa label). These later performances come from 1963 and 1965 and are of great integrity and dedication, without having quite the same electric communication of the earlier recording. The two *Viola da gamba sonatas* are not ideally balanced and favour György Sebök's piano; though there is no question of his artistry, the actual sound of his instrument is a bit shallow and wanting in colour. Recommended, but not in preference to Fournier.

With Tortelier's 1983 digital set at full price already holding an honoured place in the catalogue, EMI have now reissued his earlier analogue recording in their French 'two for the price of one' bargain series. Some might prefer it for its drier acoustic, and undoubtedly Tortelier's rhythmic grip is strong, his technique masterly and his intonation true. At the same time, however, there are touches of reticence: it is as if he is consciously resisting the temptation to give full rein to his musical and lyrical instinct. Nevertheless the faster movements are splendidly played, and the *Prelude* to the *E flat major Suite* finds him at his most imposing. The set is very good value and the recording, though made in the first half of the 1960s, sounds most realistic.

Flute sonatas Nos. 1–6, BWV 1030/35; in G min., BWV 1020; Partita in A min. (for solo flute), *BWV 1013.*
(M) **(*) Ph. 422 943-2 (2) [id.]. Maxence Larrieu, Rafael Puyana, Wieland Kuijken.
(B) ** Hung. White Label HRC 119 [id.] (*Nos. 2, 4–6 & BWV 1020*). Lóránt Kovács, János Sebestyén, Ede Banda.

The Philips set comes from 1967 and places the flute very much in the foreground, though it is otherwise well enough recorded. Maxence Larrieu plays a modern flute, Rafael Puyana an instrument modelled on a large German harpsichord of the eighteenth century, and Wieland Kuijken a seven-stringed viola da gamba from the Tyrol and probably dating from the second half of the eighteenth century. The performances are highly accomplished and often persuasive. Moreover the *G minor Sonata*, BWV 1020, is also included. There are doubts about its authenticity, but Carl Philipp Emanuel has claimed that his father wrote it; if so, it almost certainly pre-dates the other works included. Puyana has made a sensible, fairly straightforward reconstruction of the incomplete first movement of BWV 1032. The set, which is economically priced, makes very agreeable listening.

Lóránt Kovács makes an arbitrary selection of five *Sonatas*, and makes a good case for the unauthenticated works as well as for those confirmed as belonging to Bach. This is not for authenticists, as his timbre is rich; but he plays quite winningly and the continuo is more than adequate. Apart from the rather forward balance of the flute, the sound is very good and this inexpensive CD includes proper documentation.

(i) *Flute sonatas Nos. 1, 3, 5 & 6; Partita in A min., BWV 1013* (2 versions); (ii) *Concerto in D for strings* (arr. Brüggen from *BWV 1031*).
(M) ** HM/BMG GD 71964 (2). Brüggen, Leonhardt, Bylsma; Kuijken Ens.

Brüggen's RCA set is a curiosity. He plays those four *Sonatas* which he considers authentic very beautifully, and the flute timbre is nicely in scale with the continuo. Then come two versions of the *Partita*, one for solo flute, the second with the movements divided up between flute and various stringed instruments. Lastly we are offered Brüggen's own arrangement for strings of part of the *Sonata*, BWV 1031, which he admits is sketchy and 'still leaves much to be desired'. The 1975 sound is very good.

Viola da gamba sonatas Nos. 1–3, BWV 1027/9.
(M) *** HM/BMG GD 77044 [77044-2-RG]. Wieland Kuijken, Gustav Leonhardt.
(M) (**) Sony mono MPK 46445 [id.]. Pablo Casals, Paul Baumgartner (piano).
(M) *(*) Erato/Warner 2292 45659-2 [id.]. Paul Tortelier (cello), Robert Veyron-Lacroix (harpsichord).

Kuijken and Leonhardt are both sensitive and scholarly musicians, their tempi well judged and their artistry in good evidence. Their phrasing is finely shaped and natural, and there is no sense of the relentless flow that can so often impair the faster movements. The slow movement of the *G minor* is very slow, but the tempo obviously springs from musical conviction and as a result *feels* right. This is the most authentic account to have appeared on the market in recent years and is among the most rewarding. The recorded sound is faithful: it may be too immediate for some ears, but adjustment of the controls gives a satisfactory result.

Although there are some fine moments on this Sony mono recording, such as Casals' phrasing of the opening Adagio of the *D major Sonata*, BWV 1028, at times the playing seems curiously deliberate. The recording, made at the Prades Festival in 1950, is acceptable but somewhat lacklustre.

The 1963 Erato recording is not ideally balanced and finds Tortelier in the extreme foreground and his partner relegated to a secondary role. The playing is very expert, but Tortelier plays in an overtly expressive and romantic fashion which will not suite all tastes. Moreover the rather thick, opaque sound is not particularly appealing.

(i) *Viola da gamba sonatas Nos. 1–3, BWV 1027/9*; (ii) *Violin sonatas Nos. 1–6, BWV 1014/19*.
(M) ** Sony M2K 42414 (2) [id.]. (i) Leonard Rose or (ii) Jaime Laredo, Glenn Gould (piano).

Leonard Rose does not project a larger-than-life instrumental personality but his tone is subtly coloured and beautifully focused, his playing shows a fine sensibility, and his slightly introvert style is admirably suited to the *Viola da gamba sonatas* of Bach. Moreover he and Glenn Gould achieve a very close partnership indeed, although some of Gould's ornamentation is questionable. In allegros, the music-making has splendid vitality, and altogether these performances are rewarding, if highly idiosyncratic. In the *Violin sonatas* Jaime Laredo is also brought forward by the close balance, and this brings a degree of edge to his timbre, though the effect is not unpleasing; indeed it has an 'authentic' feel. But the close microphones do not spoil the dynamic range and there is some lovely quiet lyrical playing from Laredo. There is undoubtedly pleasure to be had from this pair of discs, for all the unconventionality of Gould's contribution.

(Unaccompanied) *Violin sonatas Nos. 1–3, BWV 1001, 1003 & 1005; Violin partitas Nos. 1–3, BWV 1002, 1004 & 1006*.
(M) *** DG 423 294-2 (2) [id.]. Milstein.
(M) *** Ph. 422 940-2; *422 940-4* (2). Felix Ayo.
(M) *** HM/BMG GD 77043 (2) [77043-2-RG]. Sigiswald Kuijken.
(M) (***) EMI mono CHS7 63035-2 (2) [Ang. CDHB 63035]. Yehudi Menuhin.
(M) (**(*)) BMG/RCA mono GD 87708 (2) [7708-2-RC]. Jascha Heifetz.
(M) (**) Sony mono MP2K 46721 (2) [id.]. Henryk Szeryng.

Milstein's set from the mid-1970s has been most realistically remastered and makes a first-class mid-price recommendation. Every phrase is beautifully shaped and there is a highly developed feeling for line. Intonation is not always absolutely impeccable, but there is no want of virtuosity and it is always put at the service of the music. The DG engineers served this artist well on the original LPs, and the CDs have not lost the lifelike sound-balance, while there is the usual gain in presence. These performances have an aristocratic poise and a classical finesse which are very refreshing.

Felix Ayo, closely associated with I Musici, is also renowned for his purity of intonation and fine musicianship, both of which are in evidence here. His beautiful tone brings a feeling of Italian sunshine to Bach; tempi are often more relaxed than with Milstein and his approach is mellower, although this is playing of much feeling. Ayo's readings are unmannered but have a distinct personality, and they are very easy to live with; they also have the advantage of very realistic sound, the violin image smoother and warmer than Milstein's.

Using a Grancino violin of 1700 restored to its original condition, Sigiswald Kuijken aims in his set to present an authentic period performance. Those who tire of the sweetness and beauty of even the finest modern performances will find the sharper sounds of Kuijken very refreshing. With wonderfully true intonation and G-string tone of gutty firmness, these accounts are as little painful or scratchy as you are ever likely to get in the authentic field. The recording is full and faithful, yet conveys chamber intimacy.

The Menuhin set brings together a masterly series he recorded between May 1934 and February 1936, mostly in Paris, rounding off his golden teenage. For anyone wanting to appreciate the impact his playing had at that period – strong, pure and disciplined, as well as warmly expressive in the way always associated with his name – this provides the most compelling evidence. Though the digital transfer reveals the occasional bump in the original recording, the vivid sense of presence quickly makes one forget any limitations.

The dry and limited mono sound of Heifetz's classic set, dating from the 1950s, does not prevent one being thrilled by the astonishing bravura of his playing. Speeds are often extremely fast – phenomenally so in the fugues – yet rhythms are superbly controlled. Though the power of the performances is overwhelming, the closeness and dryness of the acoustic give a kind of drawing-room intimacy. Heifetz's creative imagination in his phrasing has one consistently registering the music afresh.

Szeryng, recorded in 1953 (although the liner notes give the date as 1965!), plays with superb confidence and absolute technical security. There is no doubt that the famous *Chaconne* which concludes the *D minor Partita* is very commanding. Yet these readings, with their bold, purposeful manner, at times seem unrelenting, and Szeryng too seldom plays really quietly. The mono sound is very faithful and real, but he is placed very near the microphone and, although this gives a realistic presence, it reduces the dynamic range still further.

Transcriptions of works for unaccompanied violin: *Sonatas in G min.* (from *BWV 1001*); *in D* (from *BWV l005*); *Suite in D* (from *Suite for viola pomposa, BWV 1012*).
(M) *** HM/BMG GD 77014 [77014-2-RG]. Gustav Leonhardt (harpsichord).

One might have thought that the advent of the gramophone would render the art of transcription obsolete. What need is there of an arrangement when the original is so readily accessible? However, not only have recent years seen the extraordinary Liszt transcriptions of the Beethoven symphonies duplicated on records but they have also touched off a mini-explosion of others: Bach's *Italian concerto* and Vivaldi's *Four Seasons* on the flute, and now, from Gustav Leonhardt's expert fingers, two solo violin sonatas and the last of the six *Cello suites*. There are no lack of precedents both in the nineteenth century (Raff, Busoni, etc.) and in Bach's own time. The *Suite in D* (transposed up a tone from the C major original) fares particularly well from being fleshed out. Gustav Leonhardt plays a 1755 instrument of Nicholas Lefebvre of Rouen, restored by the Bremen maker, Martin Skowroneck, and the recording has excellent presence and bloom.

Violin sonatas (for violin and harpsichord) *Nos. 1–6, BWV 1014/9.*
(M) *** HM/BMG GD 77170 (2) [77170-2-RG]. Sigiswald Kuijken, Gustav Leonhardt.

Violin sonatas Nos. 1–6, BWV 1014/9; 1019a; Sonatas for violin and continuo, BWV 1020/4.
❀ (M) *** Ph. 426 452-2; *426 452-4* (2). Arthur Grumiaux, Christiane Jaccottet, Philippe Mermoud (in *BWV 1021 & 1023*).

The Bach *Sonatas for violin and harpsichord* and *violin and continuo* are much less well known than the works for unaccompanied violin or cello, but they contain music of great character and beauty. Who can forget the Siciliana which opens No. 4 or the charm of the brief *Largo* of BWV 1019; while the polyphony of the allegros is always engagingly fresh. Grumiaux's performances were recorded in 1978 and 1980 but are new to the UK catalogue. They are marvellously played, with all the beauty of tone and line for which he is renowned; they have great vitality too. His admirable partner is Christiane Jaccottet, and in BWV 1021 and 1023 Philippe Mermoud (cello) joins the continuo. Grumiaux's collection is all-embracing, even though the *Sonatas*, BWV 1020 and 1022, are not considered authentic. There is endless treasure to be discovered here, particularly when the music-making is so serenely communicative. The balance rather favours the violin, but the recording is very realistic and Grumiaux's tone is ravishingly pure.

Sigiswald Kuijken uses a baroque violin, and both he and Gustav Leonhardt give us playing of rare eloquence. This reissue is an admirable example of the claims of authenticity and musical feeling pulling together rather than apart. The violinist does not shrink from the intelligent use of vibrato, and both artists demonstrate in every bar that scholarship is at their service and is not an inhibiting taskmaster. As so often from this source, the harpsichord is very well recorded and the texture is lighter and cleaner than usual. This is a wholly delightful set and the transparency of the sound is especially appealing.

KEYBOARD MUSIC

The Art of fugue, BWV 1080; Italian concerto, BWV 971; Partita in B min., BWV 831; Prelude, fugue and allegro in E flat, BWV 998.
(M) *** HM/BMG GD 77013 (2) [77013-2-RG]. Gustav Leonhardt (harpsichord).

Gustav Leonhardt uses a copy by Martin Skowroneck of a Dulcken harpsichord of 1745, a responsive and beautiful instrument. Under the fingers of Leonhardt every strand in the texture emerges with clarity and every phrase is allowed to speak for itself. In the 12th and 18th fugues Leonhardt is joined by Bob van Asperen. Leonhardt does not include the unfinished fugue, but that will be the only reservation to cross the minds of most listeners. This is a very impressive and rewarding set, well recorded and produced.

(i) *Capriccio in B flat (on the departure of a beloved brother), BWV 992; Chromatic fantasia and fugue in D min., BWV 903; Fantasia in C min., BWV 906;* (ii) *French suite No. 6 in E, BWV 817;* (i) *Italian concerto in F, BWV 971; Toccata in C min, BWV 911.*

(BB) *(*) Naxos 8.550066 [id.]. (i) Joseph Banowetz; (ii) Monique Duphil (piano).

The reservation here concerns the recording, made in a rather dry acoustic which robs the instrument of timbre and bloom. Artistically it is worth more, for Joseph Banowetz is an intelligent player of the old school whose approach to Bach is imaginative and will engage the sympathies of those who have tired of the brisk metronomic canter so often encountered these days. Monique Duphil, who was a pupil of Marguerite Long and Jean Doyen, gives a lively enough account of the *E major French suite* and is better recorded. The playing of both these artists is accomplished and deserves less unglamorous sound.

Chromatic fantasia and fugue in D min., BWV 903; Italian concerto in F, BWV 971; Partita in B min., BWV 831; Toccata in D min., BWV 913.
(M) ** DG Dig. 435 086-2; *435 086-4* [id.]. Trevor Pinnock (harpsichord).

Trevor Pinnock's sense of style is matched by his technical expertise and there is no doubt that his explosive burst of bravura at the opening of the *Chromatic fantasia* is exciting. Sometimes his approach is rather literal, but at others he allows himself more expressive latitude, notably so in the *B minor Partita.* The playing is always rhythmically alive, but the close recording of the harpsichord and the high level combine to create a somewhat unrelenting dynamic level, without a great deal of light and shade, and the harpsichord timbre is metallic.

4 Duets, BWV 802–5; English suite No. 6 in D min., BWV 811; Italian concerto, BWV 971; Toccata in C minor, BWV 911.
(M) *** DG Dig. 429 975-2. Angela Hewitt (piano).

In both the *Italian concerto* and the *English suite* Angela Hewitt's playing is enormously alive and stimulating. Textures are clean, with every strand in perfect focus and every phrase clearly articulated. She plays with vital imaginative resource, totally free from idiosyncrasy and affectation. The piano is beautifully captured on this recording, which must be numbered as one of the most successful DG have given us, with fresh, life-like sound and vivid presence.

English suites Nos. 1–6, BWV 806/11.
(M) **(*) DG 427 146-2 (2) [id.]. Huguette Dreyfus (harpsichord).

Huguette Dreyfus recorded the *English suites* in 1972 but the recording does not sound dated. She plays very musically on an unnamed modern harpsichord and has plenty of rhythmic spirit; and this set, particularly given its competitive price, has a great deal to recommend it.

English suite No. 2 in A min., BWV 807; Partita No. 2 in C min., BWV 826; Toccata in C min., BWV 911.
(M) *** DG 423 880-2; *423 880-4* [id.]. Martha Argerich (piano).

Martha Argerich does not disappoint: her playing is alive and keenly rhythmic but also wonderfully flexible and rich in colour. Her finger control is consistently impressive. The textures are always varied and clean, and there is an intellectual and musical vitality here that is refreshing. Moreover Miss Argerich is very well recorded.

French suites Nos. 1–6, BWV 812/17.
(M) **(*) HM/BMG GD 71963 (2). Gustav Leonhardt (harpsichord).

French suites Nos. 1–6, BWV 812/17. Capriccio, BWV 992.
(M) *** DG 427 149-2 (2) [id.]. Huguette Dreyfus (harpsichord).

Huguette Dreyfus's analogue records come from 1972 and, as is so often the case with harpsichord, clavichord or lute recordings, need to be reproduced at a lower-level setting than usual. Her playing is admirably straightforward, authoritative and vital; she commands splendid articulation in handling ornaments and, though she shows a strong rhythmic grip, there is no sense of metronomic rigidity. There is clarity of texture and sound musicianship here. An enjoyable and recommendable set.

Leonhardt's recordings were made in 1975. He uses a Rubio, modelled on a Taskin, and it sounds well, the recording only a shade close. The playing is generally flexible; perhaps the rhythmic French style is over-assertive at times, but the livelier dance movements, like the famous *Gavotte* in BWV 816, have plenty of character.

Goldberg variations, BWV 988.
(M) *** HM/BMG GD 77149 [77149-2-RG]. Gustav Leonhardt (harpsichord).
(BB) *(*) Naxos Dig. 8.550078 [id.]. Chen Pi-hsien (piano).

Gustav Leonhardt's third (1978) version of the *Goldberg* is most beautifully recorded. His instrument is a Dowd copy of a Blanchet; the sound is altogether mellower and more appealing than in his 1967 record for Teldec. This is an introvert and searching performance, at times rhythmically very free and with the *Black Pearl* variation a case in point; but the reading is so thoughtful that no one can fail to draw illumination from it: this account is altogether fresher and more personal than his earlier one. The CD transfer is wholly convincing.

Chen Pi-hsien comes from Taiwan; she has made a considerable name for herself over the last few years, both in England and on the Continent, as an artist of refined musical intelligence and taste. Her account of the *Goldberg variations* is both clean in articulation and fluent; she takes a pretty brisk, no-nonsense view of the theme but, generally speaking, her tempi are not unduly fast. At the same time, hers is not as searching or as subtle a performance as one would expect from an artist of this repute or from one who has studied with Leygraf, Kempff and Nikolayeva. The piano sound as such is not in the first flight, and at times the piano seems in less than fresh condition. She plays the 'Black Pearl' variation with poetic feeling and good taste. Some repeats are made, but most are ignored. The recording, made in the Festeburgkirche in Frankfurt, is acceptable rather than good.

Goldberg variations, BWV 988; Chromatic fantasia and fugue, BWV 903; Italian concerto in F, BWV 971.
(M) (**) EMI mono CDH7 61008-2 [id.]. Wanda Landowska (harpsichord).

Wanda Landowska's version from the 1930s was the first ever complete recording of Bach's *Goldberg variations*; though on a clangy Pleyel – not helped by the close recording – the result is aggressive, the imagination of the soloist is endlessly illuminating on her own terms, as are her classic performances of the two other favourite Bach keyboard works.

Partitas Nos. 1–6, BWV 825/30.
(M) *** HM/BMG GD 77215 (2) [77215-2-RG]. Gustav Leonhardt (harpsichord).

Leonhardt's Deutsche Harmonia Mundi set was not conceived as an entity but was recorded over a longish period (1963–70) in the Cerdernsaal at Schloss Kirchheim. The *Second Partita* is heard at today's pitch, while the others are recorded a semitone lower. The sound of the CD transfer is admirable, with the instrument – a 1962 Martin Skowroneck copy of a 1745 Dulcken – set slightly back in an acoustic which provides ample space for the music to breathe, yet which is not too resonant. Variations of quality in the recordings of different partitas are minimal, and these are searching and often profound readings. There are occasional exaggerations (the *Allemande* of the *First Suite*, for example) and some of the dotted rhythms are overemphatic. Yet this still remains an impressive achievement, for the thoughts of this scholar-musician are always illuminating and his artistry compels admiration.

Partitas Nos. 3 in A min., 4 in D; 5 in G, BWV 827/9.
(BB) ** Naxos Dig. 8.550312 [id.]. Wolf Harden (piano).

These are crisply articulated, thoughtful performances, well recorded. Wolf Harden does not emerge as a very individual player, but he catches the character of the *Courantes*, *Sarabandes* and *Gigues* rather well, although the *Overture* of the *D major Partita* could do with more flair. Nevertheless many will enjoy its clean purity of style.

The Well-tempered Clavier (48 Preludes & fugues), BWV 846/893.
(M) (**(*)) EMI mono CHS7 63188-2 (3) [Ang. CDH 63188]. Edwin Fischer.
(M) (**(*)) DG mono 429 929-2 (3). Walter Gieseking (piano).
(M) ** BMG/RCA GD 60949 (4). Sviatoslav Richter (piano).

The Well-tempered Clavier, Book I, Preludes and fugues Nos. 1–24, BWV 846/69.
(M) *(**) HM/BMG GD 77011 (2) [RCA 77011-2-RG]. Gustav Leonhardt (harpsichord).
(M) (***) BMG/RCA mono GD 86217 (2) [6217-2-RC]. Wanda Landowska (harpsichord).

The Well-tempered Clavier, Book II, Preludes and fugues Nos. 25–48, BWV 870/93.
(M) *(**) HM/BMG GD 77012 (2) [RCA 77012-2-RG]. Gustav Leonhardt (harpsichord).
(M) (***) BMG/RCA mono GD 87825 (3) [7825-2-RC]. Wanda Landowska (harpsichord).

Gustav Leonhardt plays a copy of a Taskin by David Rubio for Book I and an instrument by Martin Skowroneck for Book II. It must be said straight away that the attractions of this reissue are diminished by their close balance. Even when the volume is reduced, the perspective seems unnatural, as if one were leaning into each instrument itself. Tastes in the matter of registration are bound to differ, but there is little with which to quarrel and much to admire, while Leonhardt's technique is effortless. His interpretative insights too are most impressive and, were the sound more sympathetic and appealing, this would be very highly recommendable, for Leonhardt combines scholarship, technique and sensibility in no small measure.

It is good that RCA have restored Landowska's celebrated records of the '48' to circulation, together with her original notes. They were recorded between 1949 and 1954 and are now accommodated on five well-filled

CDs. They still sound marvellous and have a colour, vitality, authority and grandeur that make it difficult to stop listening to them. Styles in Bach playing may have changed over the intervening forty years – it would be strange if they had not – but this playing still carries all before it. The CD transfer has the usual advantages of the medium. Strongly recommended.

Older collectors will recall Edwin Fischer's Bach with particular affection. His was the first ever 'Forty-Eight' to be put on shellac, being recorded in 1933–6. After more than half a century the sound is inevitably dated and the piano tone papery and shallow but – make no mistake – there is nothing shallow about these interpretations. Fischer has often been spoken of as an artist of intellect, but the approach here is never remote or cool. Moreover he produces a beauty of sound and a sense of line that is an unfailing source of musical wisdom and nourishment. The performance is economically laid out on three mid-price CDs, each accommodating close on 80 minutes. These discs are indispensable to the serious Bach collector.

Gieseking's vintage performance on the piano, recorded for Saar Radio in 1950, is strikingly different from the historic recording made even earlier for EMI by Fischer. Gieseking is straighter and heavier; where Fischer took three years over recording the cycle, Gieseking worked quickly, and that seems to have spurred him on. From his heavy start he rises masterfully to the full challenge of the great fugues of Book Two. Though transfers are good, one has to use a creative ear to cope with the boxy sound.

Sviatoslav Richter's recordings come from 1972–3, and the piano sound is very adequate, though at times it places the listener closer to the piano than is ideal. The quality seems to vary a little from piece to piece, but the image is very clean and pleasing in most of the Preludes and fugues – at least in Book I. Book II is lower in level and the sound a good deal less fresh and immediate than in its companion. Richter's playing is very often (though not always) thought-provoking and satisfying; there are moments when he seems to be on automatic pilot (the *D major Prelude* of Book II, for instance) but an artist of this distinction is rarely unrewarding. (Those wanting a modern recording of *The Well-tempered Clavier* played on the piano will find András Schiff on Decca well worth the premium price (Book 1: 414 388-2 (2); Book 2: 417 236-2 (2)).)

ORGAN MUSIC

Complete organ music

Volume 1: *Fantasias, BWV 562, 570, 572; Fantasias & fugues, BWV 537, 542, 561; Fugues, BWV 575/577, 579, 581, 946; Kleines harmonisches Labyrinth, BWV 591; Passacaglia & fugue, BWV 582; Pedal-Exercitium, BWV 598; Preludes & fugues, BWV 531/533, 535, 548/551; Toccata, adagio & fugue, BWV 564; Toccatas & fugues, BWV 538, 540, 565; Trios, BWV 583, 585.*

(M) *** Decca 421 337-2 (3) [id.]. Peter Hurford (organs of Ratzeburg Cathedral, Germany, Church of Our Lady of Sorrows, Toronto).

Volume 2: *Chorale preludes, BWV 672/675, 677, 681, 683, 685, 687, 689; 24 Kirnberger Chorale preludes, BWV 690/713; Clavier-Übung, Part 3: German organ Mass (Prelude & fugue in E flat, BWV 552 & Chorale preludes, BWV 669/671, 676, 678, 680, 682, 684, 686, 688); 6 Trio sonatas, BWV 525/530.*

(M) *** Decca 421 341-2 (3) [id.]. Peter Hurford (organs of Chapels at New College, Oxford, & Knox Grammar School, Sydney; Church of Our Lady of Sorrows, Toronto, Ratzeburg Cathedral).

Volume 3: *Canonic variations: Vom Himmel hoch, BWV 769; Chorale partitas: Christ, der du bist; O Gott, du frommer Gott; Sei gegrüsset, Jesu gütig, BWV 766/768; Chorale preludes, BWV 726/740; Schübler chorale preludes, BWV 645/650; Chorale variations: Ach, was soll ich sünder machen; Allein Gott in der Höh' sei Ehr, BWV 770/771. Concertos Nos. 1–6, BWV 592/597.*

❀ (M) *** Decca 421 617-2 (3) [id.]. Peter Hurford (organs as above, & Melk Abbey, Austria, and Eton College, Windsor).

Volume 4: *35 Arnstedt chorale preludes, BWV 714, 719, 742, 957 & 1090/1120* (from Yale manuscript, copied Neumeister); *18 Leipzig chorale preludes, BWV 651/58. Chorale preludes, BWV 663/668 & BWV 714/725.*

(M) *** Decca Dig./Analogue 421 621-2 (3) [id.]. Peter Hurford (Vienna Bach organ, Augustinerkirche, Vienna, & organs of All Souls' Unitarian Church, Washington, DC, St Catharine's College Chapel, Cambridge, Ratzeburg Cathedral, Knox Grammar School, Sydney, and Eton College, Windsor).

Volume 5: *Allabreve in D, BWV 589; Aria in F, BWV 587; Canzona in D min., BWV 588; Fantasias, BWV 563 & BWV 571; Fugues, BWV 574, BWV 578 & BWV 580; Musical offering, BWV 1079: Ricercar. Pastorale, BWV 590; Preludes, BWV 567/569; Preludes & fugues, BWV 534, 535a* (incomplete), *BWV 536, BWV 539, BWV 541, BWV 543/547; 8 Short Preludes & fugues, BWV 553/560; Prelude, trio & fugue,*

BWV 545b; Toccata & fugue in E, BWV 566; Trios, BWV 584, BWV 586 & BWV 1027a.
(M) *** Decca 425 631-2 (3). Peter Hurford (organs of the Church of Our Lady of Sorrows, Toronto; Ratzeburg Cathedral; Eton College, Windsor; St Catharine's College Chapel, Cambridge; New College, Oxford; Domkirche, St Pölten, Austria; Stiftskirche, Melk, Austria; Knox Grammar School, Sydney).

Volume 6: *Chorale preludes Nos. 1–46 (Orgelbüchlein), BWV 599/644. Chorale preludes, BWV 620a, BWV 741/748, BWV 751/2, BWV 754/5, BWV 757/763, BWV 765, BWV Anh. 55; Fugue in G min., BWV 131a.*
(M) *** Decca 425 635-2 (2) [id.]. Peter Hurford (organs of the Church of Our Lady of Sorrows, Toronto; St Catharine's College Chapel, Cambridge; Eton College, Windsor).

With the exception of the *Arnstedt chorale preludes*, which were added in 1986 (and are digital), Peter Hurford recorded his unique survey of Bach's organ music for Decca's Argo label over a period of eight years, 1974–1982. Performances are consistently fresh and engrossing in their spontaneity; there is no slackening of tension and the registration features a range of baroque colour that is almost orchestral in its diversity. Hurford plays a number of different organs, moving, say, from Sydney to Toronto, then on to Washington, DC, back to Ratzeburg Cathedral in Germany, and thence home again to Oxford and Windsor. The digital recording of the Vienna Bach organ, used for the recently discovered *Arnstedt chorale preludes*, is particularly beautiful. Hurford here omits the three pieces which were already familiar (BWV 601, 639 and 737) but includes BWV 714 (which in the Neumeister manuscript is 27 bars longer than previously known versions), BWV 719 and 742 (hitherto not thought to be authentic Bach), and BWV 957 (until now not regarded as an organ work). This brings about a duplication of BWV 714 and 719, which were also recorded in Sydney in 1977.

Anyone wishing to explore the huge range of this repertoire could hardly do better than begin with one of these boxes, and perhaps a good jumping-off point would be Volume 3, to which we award a token Rosette: this includes many of the *Chorale preludes* and *Chorale variations*, in particular the splendid half-dozen chorales which were published at the very end of Bach's life and which commemorate the name of an otherwise unknown music-engraver called Schübler. They are all especially beautifully recorded, demonstrating the character of the six organs which feature most importantly in this undertaking. Hurford understands the structural needs of all this music, yet he ceaselessly fascinates with his feeling for colour and care for detail. Both here and in the more ambitious works, Hurford's pacing always seems apt to the point of inevitability. There is never the faintest hint of routine nor of the fugues trundling on endlessly, as in some performances in the German pedagogic Bach tradition. Sometimes there is dash, at others a clear, unforced momentum, depending on the character of the writing, while the bigger set-pieces have no want of breadth. In the so-called *German organ Mass*, Hurford's approach is direct, with powerful contrasts made between weight and serenity. The recordings were originally in the demonstration class; the CD remastering marginally sharpens the focus and at times brightens the sound-picture at higher dynamic levels. In Volume 4, for instance, at the close of the Neumeister collection (recorded with digital smoothness) the analogue *Leipzig chorale preludes* immediately follow. The ear notices that in the first of these, BWV 651, there is an abrasive pungency on the reeds of the Washington organ, brought about by the slight treble emphasis; and elsewhere there is occasionally a slight element of harshness, with the upper partials not always quite clean. But this effect should not be overemphasized; the warm basic ambience is very appealing; the sound never clouds over and has great presence and depth.

Volume 5 concludes the set of *Preludes and fugues* begun in Volume 1. It opens with the eight short works, BWV 553/560, now considered to be inauthentic – indeed they are dated from around the time of Bach's death; but they are attractively individual pieces, here presented genially and spontaneously. In the mature *Preludes and fugues* Hurford's tempi tend to be rather steady. The various shorter pieces are used to diversify the programme. The *Trio in G major*, BWV 1027a, for instance, is based on a string sonata and the arrangement is not Bach's, but it makes an entertaining interlude. Like the more complex four-movement *Pastorale*, it is most engagingly registered. The *Toccata in E*, BWV 566, looks back to Buxtehude in style and has two following fugues.

The 46 *Chorales* from the *Orgelbüchlein* first appeared towards the end of the project (1981/2); they not only show Peter Hurford at his most imaginative in terms of registration and colour, but they also demonstrate the clarity with which the *cantus firmus* always emerges in his hands, however florid the texture. These are all played on the Toronto organ, which is beautifully recorded and seems ideal for this repertoire. Of the remaining twenty-three miscellaneous chorales, many are now known not to be authentic: BWV 749, 750 and 756 are omitted because they have no connection with Bach at all, and BWV 753 and 764 because they are not complete. Of the rest, some are now definitely attributed to other composers but are nevertheless included for their general musical interest. Hurford makes a good case for them.

The only real drawback to these otherwise admirable reissues is their sparse documentation. The organ specifications are included, but too little about the music itself. Volume 1, which includes many of the fantasias and fugues, preludes and fugues, and toccatas and fugues, is disgracefully inadequate in this respect, although Volumes 3 and 4 are much better. But with generous measure of music in each of the boxes, this remains overall the most rewarding assessment of Bach's organ music ever committed to record.

Adagio in C (from *BWV 565); Chorales: Herzlich tut mich verlangen, BWV 727; Liebster Jesu, BWV 730; Wachet auf, BWV 645; Fantasia and fugue in G min., BWV 542; Fugue in E flat (St Anne), BWV 552; Passacaglia and fugue in C min., BWV 582; Toccata and fugue in D min., BWV 565.*

(M) *** Decca 417 711-2 [id.]. Peter Hurford (various organs).

An admirable popular recital. Performances are consistently alive and the vivid recording projects them strongly. A self-recommending issue.

(i) *Allabreve, BWV 589; Canzona, BWV 588; Fantasia in G, BWV 572; Prelude in A min., BWV 569;* (ii) *Trio sonatas: Nos. 1 in E flat, BWV 525; 2 in C min., BWV 526; 5 in C, BWV 529.*

(M) *** DG Dig. 431 705-2; *431 705-4*. Ton Koopman (organs of (i) Grote Kerk, Massluis; (ii) Waalse Kerk, Amsterdam).

An excellent recital, with both organs beautifully recorded, with the single proviso that it was a pity to place the *Canzona* immediately after the *Allebreve*, as they are both slow pieces in rather similar style. But it is the *Trio sonatas* here which give the most pleasure; they are full of life and colour, and Koopman's buoyant playing of the allegros confirms the fact that their character is essentially that of music for chamber ensemble rather than the keyboard.

(i) *Chorale partita on Sei gegrüsset, Jesu gutig, BWV 768;* (ii) *Toccatas and fugues: in D min. (Dorian), BWV 538; D, BWV 565; E, BWV 566.*

(M) **(*) Ph. Dig. 432 610-2; *432 610-4* [id.]. Daniel Chorzempa (organ of (i) Domkirche, Arlesheim, Switzerland; (ii) Bovenkerk, Kampen, The Netherlands).

The *Chorale partita* on *Sei gegrüsset, Jesu gutig* is admirably designed to demonstrate the palette of a fine Swiss organ in the hands of an imaginative player; and here Daniel Chorzempa is on top form, in matters both of registration and of musical judgement. The *Toccatas and fugues*, however, are played in Kampen and, although the *Dorian Toccata* is buoyant enough, Chorzempa's performances are heftily conceived, with the massive sounds of the Bovenkerk organ contributing to this impression of weightiness. The fugues proceed in considered fashion and even the famous BWV 565, more often played flamboyantly, is here rather measured. The recording is spectacular.

Chorale preludes, BWV 614, 622, 683, 727; Chorale fughetta, BWV 703; Fantasia and fugue in A min., BWV 561; Fugue in G min., BWV 578; Preludes and fugues: in G min., BWV 542; in E flat, BWV 552; Toccata and fugue in D min., BWV 565.

(BB) * LaserLight 15 507 [id.]. Gabor Lehotka or Hannes Kästner.

The sound, though not from a digital master, is very good here, but the performances are in the deliberate German tradition of Bach playing. Even Bach's genial *G minor Fugue* (beloved of Stokowski) fails to take off, and the *Chorale preludes* are also slow. The documentation fails to identify the organs used.

Chorale preludes: Herzlich tut mich verlangen, BWV 727; Ich ruf' zu dir, BWV 639; In dulci jubilo, BWV 608; Nun freut euch, BWV 734, Valet will ich dir geben, BWV 736; Vom Himmel hoch, BWV 700; Passacaglia in C min., BWV 582; Pastorale in F, BWV 590; Preludes & fugues: in G min., BWV 535; in A, BWV 536; Toccata & fugue in D min., BWV 565.

(M) **(*) DG 435 090-2; *435 090-4* [id.]. Helmut Walcha (organs of St Laurenskerk, Alkmaar, and Saint Pierre-le-Jeune, Strasbourg).

An admirable reminder of Helmut Walcha's Bach style. The great organist, who died towards the end of last year, did much to establish Bach's organ music as a necessary part of any comprehensive record collection. His scholarly approach and slight reticence were offset by a keen feeling for registration; while his manner was seldom flamboyant, it was never pedagogic and dull. There are more dramatic performances of the famous *D minor Toccata and fugue* elsewhere, but the *C minor Passacaglia* is impressively structured. These are both played on the Alkmaar organ and were recorded in 1956 and 1962 respectively: the transfer to CD brings a rather dry sound from the pedals. The rest of the programme was recorded between 1969 and 1979 in Strasbourg; Walcha's skill with colour is readily shown in the chorale preludes and in his fine account of the *Pastorale*, although the registration of the *Preludes and fugues*, and particularly of the *A major Prelude*, readily demonstrates the attractive palette of the Saint Pierre-le-Jeune organ.

Concertos (for solo organ) *Nos. 1–6, BWV 592/7.*

(M) ** DG 431 119-2. Karl Richter (Silbermann organ, Arlesheim).

Bach's solo *Organ concertos*, based on the music of others, notably Nos. 2, 3 and 5, deriving from three string concertos by Vivaldi, require a more extrovert approach than is provided by Karl Richter, though his peal-like flourishes in the finale of No. 2 show him making a very firm response to this highly spontaneous music. But elsewhere at times his approach seems excessively scholarly. The Arlesheim organ is beautifully recorded, and his registration often finds some very attractive colouring, but in the last resort this playing is rather sober for music which is so often genial and outgiving. Nevertheless Richter includes all six *Concertos*, including the E flat major transcription, BWV 597, which is not now attributed to Bach. The source of its two movements is uncertain, but they are rather attractive, especially the second, a *Gigue*.

Fantasia in G, BWV 572; Preludes and fugues: in C, BWV 545; in C min.; in G, BWV 549/50; in G min., BWV 535; Pastorale, BWV 590; Toccata and fugue in D min., BWV 565.

(M) *** Ph. 420 860-2. Wolfgang Rübsam (organ of Frauenfeld, Switzerland).

A splendid collection of early works, nearly all dating from Bach's Arnstadt and Weimar periods and full of exuberance of spirit. The *Fugue in G*, BWV 550, is especially memorable, but undoubtedly the highlight of the recital is the superb performance of the *Fantasia in G*. It opens with an exhilarating *Très vitement* and after a massive *Grave* middle section comes a brilliantly lightweight bravura finale. Wolfgang Rübsam's articulation is deliciously pointed. The recording of the Metzler organ has a fairly long reverberation period, and Rübsam anticipates this in his playing most successfully. The quality of the recorded sound is splendid. Highly recommended.

Fantasia and fugue in G min., BWV 542; Prelude and fugue in F min., BWV 534; Toccata and fugue in D min., BWV 565; Toccata, adagio and fugue in C, BWV 564; Trio sonata No. 1 in E flat, BWV 525.

(M) ** DG 419 047-2 [id.]. Helmut Walcha (organ of St Laurenskerk, Alkmaar).

These recordings, made in 1963/4, sound extremely well in their CD format: the brightness is supported by an underlying depth and there is a sense of perspective too, particularly in the interplay of the famous *D minor Fugue* which shows Walcha at his more extrovert. The other performances are often very effectively registered, notably the *C major Fugue*, BWV 564, and the first movement of the *Trio sonata*, but Walcha's pulse seems determinedly steady in most of this music. Structures are well controlled and detail is lucid, but there is also a ponderous quality which will not appeal to everyone.

Passacaglia and fugue in C min., BWV 582; Preludes & fugues: in D, BWV 532; in A min., BWV 543; in E flat, BWV 552; Toccata and fugue in D min., BWV 565.

(B) ** Ph. 422 965-2; *422 965-4*. Daniel Chorzempa (organs of Our Lady's Church, Breda, or (in BWV 552) Bovenkerk, Kampen, Holland).

This is a beautifully recorded disc, with notable depth and resonance. All the items but one come from a successful 1970 recital, and here Chorzempa's playing is impressive throughout and often stimulating, even if his occasional dalliance with matters of colour can sometimes interfere with the music's forward impulse. In the great *Passacaglia and fugue in C minor* this certainly adds to the interest and individuality of the performance. Unfortunately this bargain reissue omits Chorzempa's own original sleeve-notes, which indicated the reasons for his elaborations of Bach's basic text; despite his apparently free approach, the playing has a pontificating character in places. The *E flat Prelude and fugue*, BWV 552, was recorded separately, in 1982, and is something of an artistic disaster. It is incredibly slow (23 minutes 19 seconds overall), and at its opening the fugue is leaden and sounds as though it will go on for ever. However, the rest of the recital is well worth its modest cost.

Pastorale in F, BWV 590; Preludes and fugues: in D, BWV 532; in E min., BWV 548; in E flat (St Anne), BWV 552; Toccata and fugue in D min., BWV 565.

(BB) * Naxos Dig. 8.550184 [id.]. Wolfgang Rübsam (organ of Oberlin College).

After Wolfgang Rübsam's earlier, excellent, analogue recital for Philips this is a great disappointment. The splendid Flenthrop organ at Oberlin College is spectacularly caught by the Naxos engineers, but the performances have little of the vitality which made Rübsam's earlier programme so rewarding. The massive opening *Prelude in E flat* is mannered and hangs fire, and the other works are little better. Even the *Pastorale* (which he included much more successfully before) seems laboured and lacks charm, while famous *Toccata in D minor* has eccentric phrasing.

6 Schübler chorales, BWV 645/650; Pastorale in F, BWV 590; Passacaglia in C min., BWV 582; Toccata, adagio & fugue in C, BWV 564; Toccata & fugue in D min., BWV 565.
(M) *** DG Dig. 427 801-2; *427 801-4*. Ton Koopman (organs of Grote Kerk, Maasluis, & Waalse Kerk, Amsterdam).

Ton Koopman uses two different organs here, principally the Grote Kerk, Maasluis; but the *Schübler chorales* are recorded on the Waalse Kerk, Amsterdam, whose reeds are livelier almost to the point of stridency, underscored by the emphatically rhythmic style of the playing. The effect is certainly full of character. The programme includes the famous *D minor Toccata and fugue*, BWV 565, and this performance has an engaging eccentricity in that Koopman introduces decoration into the opening flourishes. The performance has an excitingly paced fugue and is superbly recorded. Excellent contrast is provided by the *Pastorale* (an extended piece of some twelve minutes), where the registration features the organ's flute stops piquantly. The other performances are well structured and alive, if sometimes rather considered in feeling. The sound is generally first class, extremely vivid throughout.

Toccatas and fugues: in D min. (Dorian), BWV 538; in D, BWV 540; in D min., BWV 565; Toccata, adagio and fugue in C, BWV 564.
(B) ** DG 427 191-2; *427 191-4* [id.]. Helmut Walcha (organ of St Laurenskerk, Alkmaar).

Helmut Walcha is at his most buoyant in the *Fugue* of BWV 564, which is also most attractively registered. Elsewhere he is perhaps a shade didactic; but everything is laid out clearly and the performances, it hardly needs saying, are structurally impeccable. The famous Alkmaar organ sounds bright and reedy, but the remastering has dried out the bass a little, and one would have liked a degree more amplitude from the pedals. However, at bargain price this is well worth considering.

VOCAL MUSIC

Volume 1: *Cantatas Nos. 1: Wie schön leuchtet uns der Morgenstern; 2: Ach Gott, vom Himmel; 3: Ach Gott, wie manches Herzeleid; 4: Christ lag in Todesbanden.*
(M) *** Teldec/Warner 2292 42497-2 (2) [id.]. Treble soloists from V. Boys' Ch., Esswood, Equiluz, Van Egmond, V. Boys' Ch., Ch. Viennensis, VCM, Harnoncourt.

Volume 2: (i) *Cantatas Nos. 5: Wo soll ich fliehen; 6: Bleib bei uns;* (ii) *7: Christ unser Herr zum Jordan kam; 8: Liebster Gott.*
(M) *** Teldec/Warner 2292 42498-2 (2) [id.]. Esswood, Equiluz, Van Egmond, (i) Treble soloists from V. Boys' Ch., Ch. Viennensis, V. Boys' Ch., VCM, Harnoncourt; (ii) Regensburg treble soloists, King's College Ch., Leonhardt Cons., Leonhardt.

Volume 3: (i) *Cantatas Nos. 9: Es ist das Heil; 10: Meine Seele erhebt den Herrn;* (ii) *11: Lobet Gott in seinen Reichen.*
(M) *** Teldec/Warner 2292 42499-2 (2) [id.]. Esswood, Equiluz, Van Egmond; (i) Regensburg treble soloists, King's College Ch., Leonhardt Cons., Leonhardt; (ii) Treble soloists from V. Boys' Ch., Ch. Viennensis, V. Boys' Ch., VCM, Harnoncourt.

The remarkable Teldec project, a complete recording of all Bach's cantatas, began in the early 1970s and has now reached completion. The first CDs appeared during the tercentenary year and the digital remastering proved consistently successful. The original LP packaging included full scores. Inevitably, the CDs omit these but retain the English translations of the texts and excellent notes by Alfred Dürr. The authentic character of the performances means that boys replace women, not only in the choruses but also as soloists, and the size of the forces is confined to what we know Bach himself would have expected. The simplicity of the approach brings its own merits, for the imperfect yet other-worldly quality of some of the treble soloists refreshingly focuses the listener's attention on the music itself. Less appealing is the quality of the violins, which eschew vibrato – and, it would sometimes seem, any kind of timbre! Generally speaking, there is a certain want of rhythmic freedom and some expressive caution. Rhythmic accents are underlined with some regularity and the grandeur of Bach's inspiration is at times lost to view. Where there are no alternatives for outstanding cantatas, such as the marvellously rich and resourceful sonorities of the sinfonia to *Ach Gott, vom Himmel* (No. 2), with its heavenly aria, *Durchs Feuer wird das Silber rein*, choice is simple, and here the performance too is a fine one. There is so much fine music in Cantatas 2 and 3, not otherwise obtainable on record, that the first of these volumes is a must.

Cantatas Nos. 4: Christ lag in Todesbanden; 56: Ich will den Kreuzstab gerne tragen; 82: Ich habe genug.
(M) **(*) DG 427 128-2. Fischer-Dieskau, Munich Bach Ch. & O, Karl Richter.

In No. 4 the chorale melody is quoted in plain

or varied form in each movement and dominates proceedings. This is a cantata which, given the wrong approach, can all too readily sound dull and sombre, but Richter seems wholly in sympathy with the work and secures some splendid and dignified playing from the orchestra. The solo singing is distinguished. Perhaps in the two later cantatas Fischer-Dieskau is at times a little too expressive and over-sophisticated; yet these are certainly sensitive performances, even if here Richter is sometimes a trifle heavy-handed. The recording still sounds extremely well.

Cantata No. 10: Meine Seele erhebt den Herrn.
(M) *** Decca 425 650-2 [id.]. Ameling, Watts, Krenn, Rintzler, V. Ac. Ch., Stuttgart CO, Münchinger – *Easter oratorio.* ***

An excellent coupling for a first-rate account of the surprisingly little-recorded *Easter oratorio.* This fine cantata is very well sung and played, with all the performers at their best. The recording too is freshly vivid.

Volume 4: *Cantatas Nos. 12: Weinen, klagen, sorgen, zagen; 13: Meine Seufzer, meine Tränen; 14: Wär Gott nicht mit uns diese Zeit; 16: Herr Gott, dich loben wir.*
(M) *** Teldec/Warner 2292 42500-2 (2) [id.]. Gampert, Hinterreiter, Esswood, Equiluz, Van Altena, Van Egmond, Tölz Boys' Ch., King's Coll. Ch., Leonhardt Cons., Leonhardt.

There is much wonderful music in all four works here; performances and recordings are first class. In Cantata No. 12, *Weinen, klagen, sorgen, zagen* ('Weeping, lamenting, worrying, fearing') the alto aria is particularly fine (*Kreuz und Krone sind verbunden*) and the oboe obbligato is beautifully done. No. 14, *Wär Gott nicht mit uns diese Zeit*, has a splendid extended opening chorus, of considerable complexity and striking power.

Volume 5: *Cantatas Nos. 17: Wer Dank opfert, der preiset mich; 18: Gleichwie der Regen und Schnee vom Himmel; 19: Es erhub sich ein Streit; 20: O Ewigkeit, du Donnerwort.*
(M) *** Teldec/Warner 2292 42501-2 (2) [id.]. Treble soloists from V. Boys' Ch., Esswood, Equiluz, Van Egmond, V. Boys' Ch., Ch. Viennensis, VCM, Harnoncourt.

Cantata No. 17 has a long sinfonia and opening chorus combined; and in No. 19 the introductory fugal chorus is magnificent in its tumultuous polyphony. The closing chorus is simpler, but trumpets add a touch of ceremonial splendour. No. 20 also includes a memorable alto/tenor duet, *O Menschenkind, hör auf geschwind.* The sound is first class, fresh, vivid and clear.

Volume 6: *Cantatas Nos.* (i) *21: Ich hatte viel Bekümmernis;* (ii) *22: Jesus nahm zu sich die Zwölfe; 23: Du wahrer Gott und Davids Sohn.*
(M) **(*) Teldec/Warner 2292 42502-2 (2) [id.]. Esswood, Equiluz; (i) Walker, Wyatt, V. Boys' Ch., Ch. Viennensis, VCM, Harnoncourt; (ii) Gampert, Van Altena, Van Egmond, King's College Ch., Leonhardt Cons., Leonhardt.

The magnificent *Ich hatte viel Bekümmernis* lacks something in flair and Leonhardt is a little rigid in No. 22, *Jesus nahm zu sich die Zwölfe.* Harnoncourt tends in general to be freer; but a constant source of irritation through the series is the tendency to accentuate all main beats. This was the final appearance of the King's College Choir, which made a worthwhile contribution to many of the early performances in the series.

Volume 7: *Cantatas Nos. 24: Ein ungefärbt Gemüte; 25: Es ist nicht Gesundes an meinem Leibe; 26: Ach wie flüchtig, ach wie nichtig; 27: Wer weiss, wie nahe mir mein Ende!.*
(M) *** Teldec/Warner 2292 42503-2 (2). Esswood, Equiluz, Van Egmond, Nimsgern, V. Boys' Ch., Ch. Viennensis, VCM, Harnoncourt.

This volume is worth having in particular for the sake of the magnificent *Es ist nicht Gesundes*, a cantata of exceptional richness of expression and resource. No. 27, *Wer weiss, wie nahe mir mein Ende!*, is altogether magnificent too, and the performances are some of the finest to appear in this ambitious and often impressive survey. Certainly for those dipping into rather than collecting all this series, Volumes 1 and 7 would be good starting points, even though in the case of the latter all the cantatas are exceptionally short.

Cantatas Nos. 26: Ach wie flüchtig; 80: Ein feste Burg; 116: Du Friedefürst, Herr Jesu Christ.
(M) ** DG 427 130-2. Mathis, Schmidt, Schreier, Fischer-Dieskau, Munich Bach Ch. & O, Karl Richter.

It is pleasant to return to the vigorous, full-bodied Richter approach to Bach after an overdose of Leonhardt and Harnoncourt. The opening fugal chorus of *Ein feste Burg* and its later, more straightforward presentation are agreeably robust, and the music-making overall has plenty of vitality. The solo contributions are good too, particularly those of Schreier and Fischer-Dieskau. The sound is full and immediate, even if the choral focus is not absolutely clean; and these performances still have a place in the catalogue.

Volume 8: *Cantatas Nos. 28: Gottlob! nun geht das Jahr zu Ende; 29: Wir danken dir, Gott; 30: Freue dich, erlöste Schar.*
(M) *** Teldec/Warner 2292 42504-2 (2). Esswood, Equiluz, Van Egmond, Nimsgern, V. Boys' Ch., Ch. Viennensis, VCM, Harnoncourt.

Volume 9: *Cantatas Nos.* (i) *31: Der Himmel lacht! die Erde jubilieret;* (ii) *32: Liebster Jesu, mein Verlangen; 33: Allein zu dir, Herr Jesu Christ;* (i) *34: O ewiges Feuer, O Ursprung der Liebe.*
(M) *** Teldec/Warner 2292 42505-2 (2). (i) Esswood, Equiluz, Nimsgern, V. Boys' Ch., Ch. Viennensis, VCM, Harnoncourt; (ii) Gampert, Jacobs, Van Altena, Van Egmond, Hanover Boys' Ch., Leonhardt Cons., Leonhardt.

Volume 10: *Cantatas Nos. 35: Geist und Seele wird verwirret; 36: Schwingt freudig euch empor; 37: Wer da gläubet und getauft wird; 38: Aus tiefer Not schrei ich zu dir.*
(M) *** Teldec/Warner 2292 42506-2 (2). Esswood, Equiluz, Van der Meer, V. Boys' Ch., Ch. Viennensis, VCM, Harnoncourt.

These three boxes continue the high standard that has distinguished this enterprise. Of the new names in the roster of soloists one must mention the stylish singing of René Jacobs; Walter Gampert is the excellent treble soloist in *Liebster Jesu.* No. 34 is an especially attractive cantata; here, as throughout, one notes the liveliness as well as the authenticity of the performances, although the expressive writing is sensitively handled, too: the alto aria, *Wohl euch, ihr auser-wahlten, Seelen* ('Blessed ye hearts whom God has chosen'), with its atmospheric obbligato flutes is particularly memorable. No. 35 features an outstanding concertante organ solo; No. 36 uses a pair of oboi d'amore, and there are oboes in duet in No. 38. Most enjoyable, with excellent solo singing, and vividly clear, well-balanced sound.

Volume 11: *Cantatas Nos.* (i) *39: Brich dem Hungrigen dein Brot;* (i; ii) *40: Dazu ist erschienen der Sohn Gottes;* (iii) *41: Jesu, nun sei gepreiset; 42: Am Abend aber desselbigen Sabbats.*
(M) ** Teldec/Warner 2292 42556-2 (2). (i) Jacobs, Van Egmond, Hanover Boys' Ch., Leonhardt Cons., Leonhardt; (ii) Van Altena; (iii) Esswood, Equiluz, Van der Meer, V. Boys' Ch., Ch. Viennensis, VCM, Harnoncourt.

This is one of the less distinguished sets in this long and successful project. No. 41 probably fares best: one admires the light tone of the baroque brass instruments and the general sense of style that informs the proceedings, even if intonation, as inevitably seems to happen with authentic instruments, is not always true. The music is quite magnificent. So, too, is Cantata 42, but these artists do little to convey the feeling of the opening sinfonia, the oboe melody losing much of its expressive fervour. There is a loss of breadth also in No. 39, not altogether offset by the authenticity to which these performers are dedicated. No. 40 has some lively choruses, well sung, and there is also some excellent obbligato horn playing: here the music-making is undoubtedly spirited. But these performances sometimes radiate greater concern with historical rectitude (as these artists conceive it) than with communicating their pleasure in the music. The recordings are exemplary.

Volume 12: *Cantatas Nos.* (i) *43: Gott fähret auf mit Jauchzen; 44: Sie werden euch in die Bann tun;* (ii) *45: Es ist dir gesagt, Mensch, was gut ist; 46: Schauet doch und sehet.*
(M) *** Teldec/Warner 2292 42559-2 (2) [id.]. (i) Jelosits, Esswood, Equiluz, Van der Meer, V. Boys' Ch., Ch. Viennensis, VCM, Harnoncourt; (ii) Jacobs, Equiluz, Kunz, Hanover Boys' Ch., Leonhardt Cons., Leonhardt.

Cantata No. 46 is the one that includes the original *Qui tollis peccata* of the *B minor Mass.* This and No. 43 are not otherwise available; though the texture could be laid out more revealingly in No. 46, this is the only technical blemish in a very fine recording. All four performances are of the highest standard, and young Peter Jelosits, the boy treble, copes staunchly with the very considerable demands of Bach's writing. He really is astonishingly fine, and his companions in these records are no less accomplished. Leonhardt takes the chorale in No. 46 a little on the fast side; but enough of quibbles – this is a truly first-class box.

Volume 13: *Cantatas Nos. 47: Wer sich selbst erhöhet; 48: Ich elender Mensch, wer wird mich erlösen; 49: Ich geh' und suche mit Verlangen; 50: Nun ist das Heil und die Kraft.*
(M) *** Teldec/Warner 2292 42560-2 (2) [id.]. Jelosits, Esswood, Equiluz, Van der Meer, V. Boys' Ch., Ch. Viennensis, VCM, Harnoncourt.

The treble soloist in No. 49, *Ich geh' und suche mit Verlangen*, Peter Jelosits, really is remarkable. Perhaps the chorus in No. 50, *Nun ist das Heil und die Kraft*, is a shade overdriven; but by and large this is one of the best of the series, and the riches the music unfolds do not fail to surprise and reward the listener.

Volume 14: *Cantatas Nos. 51: Jauchzet Gott im allen Landen; 52: Falsche Welt, dir trau ihr nicht; 54: Widerstehe doch der Sünde; 55: Ich armer Mensch, ich Sündenknecht; 56: Ich will den Kreuzstab gerne tragen.*
(M) *** Teldec/Warner 2292 42422-2 (2) [id.]. Kweksilber, Kronwitter, Esswood, Equiluz, Schopper, Hanover Boys' Ch., Leonhardt Cons., Leonhardt.

A stunning set, arguably one of the most remarkable in the whole series. *Jauchzet Gott*, the most familiar, has an altogether superb soprano soloist in Marianne Kweksilber and Don Smithers' playing of the trumpet obbligato is no less impressive. There have been some splendid records of No. 51 in the past, but this eclipses them all; and the remaining cantatas in this box are all done with great distinction.

Volume 15: *Cantatas Nos. 57: Selig ist der Mann; 58: Ach Gott, wie manches Herzeleid; 59: Wer mich liebet, der wird mein Wort halten; 60: O Ewigkeit, du Donnerwort.*
(M) **(*) Teldec/Warner 2292 42423-2 [id.]. Jelosits, Kronwitter, Esswood, Equiluz, Van der Meer, Tölz Boys' Ch., VCM, Harnoncourt.

Volume 16: *Cantatas Nos. 61: Nun komm, der Heiden Heiland; 62: Nun komm, der Heiden Heiland; 63: Christen, ätzet diesen Tag; 64: Sehet, welch eine Liebe.*
(M) **(*) Teldec/Warner 2292 42565-2 (2) [id.]. Jelosits, Kronwitter, Esswood, Equiluz, Van der Meer, Tölz Boys' Ch., VCM, Harnoncourt.

These volumes maintain their high standards, even if their style is unlikely to appeal to all tastes. Nos. 57–60 are all short but the music is consistently fine, and they are now fitted on to a single CD. The boy soloist in No. 61 is not the equal of Peter Jelosits and he sounds short-breathed, while the vibratoless strings at the opening invite unfavourable comparisons with the Richter recording. Still, these slight inadequacies are a small price to pay for the general excellence and scholarship here.

Volume 17: *Cantatas Nos.* (i) *65: Sie werden aus Saba alle kommen*; (ii) *66: Erfreut euch, ihr Herzen; 67: Halt' im Gedächtnis Jesum Christ*; (i) *68: Also hat Gott die Welt geliebt.*
(M) ** Teldec/Warner 2292 42571-2 (2) [id.]. (i) Jelosits, Equiluz, Van der Meer, Tölz Boys' Ch., VCM, Harnoncourt; (ii) Esswood, Equiluz, Van Egmond, Hanover Boys' Ch., Ghent Coll. Vocale, Leonhardt Cons., Leonhardt.

The best thing in this volume is Leonhardt's broad and spacious account of No. 66, which also offers some stunning playing on the natural trumpet. Harnoncourt's versions of Nos. 65 and 68 are a little wanting in charm and poetry (the dialogue between the voice of Christ and the chorus in No. 67 is also prosaic). But there is fine solo singing, and that and the instrumental playing outweigh other considerations.

Cantatas Nos. 67: Halt'im Gedächtnis Jesum Christ; 130: Herr Gott, dich loben alle wir.
(M) **(*) Decca 433 175-2. Ameling, Watts, Krenn, Krause, Lausanne Pro Arte Ch., SRO, Ansermet – *Magnificat.* ***

A good and very enjoyable Bach cantata pairing. No. 130 is a particularly fine piece which, apart from the excellent choir and soloists, offers distinguished obbligato flute playing from André Pepin. The sound is good and the *Magnificat* coupling well worth while.

Volume 18: *Cantatas Nos. 69 & 69a: Lobe den Herrn, meine Seeele; 70: Wachet! betet! betet! wachet!; 71: Gott ist mein König; 72: Alles nur nach Gottes Willen.*
(M) *** Teldec/Warner 2292 42572-2 (2) [id.]. Esswood, Equiluz, Van der Meer, Visser, Tölz Boys' Ch., VCM, Harnoncourt.

No. 71 is an enchanting piece, full of invention and variety. This set also includes both versions of Cantata No. 69; only the numbers which differ, or are new in its adaptation in 1730, are re-recorded. No. 72 employs more modest forces than the others. Wilhelm Wiedl (from the Tölz Choir) is the excellent treble soloist throughout, and the other soloists and instrumentalists cannot be praised too highly. The choral singing is not above criticism but remains more than acceptable. Excellent sound.

Volume 19: *Cantatas Nos. 73: Herr, wie du willt, so schicks mit mir; 74: Wer mich liebet, der wird mein Wort halten; 75: Die Elenden sollen essen.*
(M) ** Teldec/Warner 2292 42573-2 [id.]. Erler, Klein, Esswood, Equiluz, Kraus, Van Egmond, Hanover Boys' Ch., Ghent Coll. Vocale, Leonhardt Cons., Leonhardt.

All three cantatas offered on this single CD come from 1723–5 and none is otherwise available. The music is certainly worth getting to know. However, some of the weaknesses of the Teldec series emerge here: some sedate and really rather weak choral work and a reluctance to permit 'expressive' singing deprive the music of some of its eloquence, and the boy trebles, though possessed of musical and pleasing voices, are not fully equal to Bach's taxing writing.

Volume 20: *Cantatas Nos.* (i) *76: Die Himmel erzählen die Ehre Gottes*; (ii) *77: Du sollt Gott, deinen Herren, lieben; 78: Jesu, der du meine Seele*; (ii) *79: Gott der Herr ist Sonn' und Schild.*
(M) **(*) Teldec/Warner 2292 42576-2 (2) [id.]. Esswood, (i) Wiedl, Equiluz, Van der Meer, Tölz Boys' Ch., VCM, Harnoncourt; (ii) Bratschke, Kraus, Van Egmond, Hanover Boys' Ch., Ghent Coll. Vocale, Leonhardt Cons., Leonhardt.

Two of the cantatas in this volume are not otherwise recorded at present, and all four are of outstanding interest. As almost always in these performances, one is aware of restraints and the ear longs for bolder colours and the greater power of modern instruments. However, there is too much good music here for such reservations to worry us for long.

Volume 21: *Cantatas Nos. 80: Ein' feste Burg; 81: Jesus schläft, was soll ich hoffen?; 82: Ich habe genug; 83: Erfreute Zeit im neuen Bunde.*
(M) *(*) Teldec/Warner 2292 42577-2 (2) [id.]. Esswood, Equiluz, Van der Meer, Huttenlocher, Van Egmond, Tölz Boys' Ch., V. Boys' Ch., Ch. Viennensis, VCM, Harnoncourt.

This is one of the less successful issues in the Teldec series. *Ich habe genug* has been performed more impressively on other recordings, and Philippe Huttenlocher, though intelligent and thoughtful, is not always secure. Some of the choral singing could also do with more polish and incisiveness.

Cantatas Nos. 80: Ein' feste Burg ist unser Gott; 140: Wachet auf, ruft uns die Stimme.
(M) ** Ph. 422 490-2 [id.]. Ameling, Finnie, Baldin, Ramey, L. Voices, ECO, Leppard.

In *Ein' feste Burg* Leppard uses the parts for three trumpets and drums. It is a well-prepared, straightforward account with some responsive singing from the chorus. *Wachet auf* is the less successful of the two and, even apart from the rather too measured tempo of the first of the duets, Elly Ameling's intonation is not completely true. There are good things, of course, and the actual sound is very good.

Cantata No. 82: Ich habe genug.
(M) (***) EMI CDH7 63198-2 [id.]. Hans Hotter, Philh. O, Bernard – BRAHMS: *Lieder.*(***)

One of the greatest cantata performances ever. Glorious singing from Hans Hotter and wonderfully stylish accompanying from Anthony Bernard and the Philharmonia. This 1950 mono recording was never reissued on LP, and it sounds eminently present in this fine transfer.

Cantatas Nos. (i; ii) *82: Ich habe genug;* (i; iii; iv) *159: Sehet, wir gehn hinauf gen Jerusalem;* (iii) *170: Vergnügte Ruh', beliebte Seelenlust.*
❀ (M) *** Decca 430 260-2; *430 260-4.* (i) Shirley-Quirk; (ii) Lord; (iii) J. Baker; (iv) Tear, St Anthony Singers; ASMF, Marriner.

John Shirley-Quirk's performance of *Ich habe genug* is much to be admired, not only for the sensitive solo singing but also for the lovely oboe obbligato of Roger Lord. The mid-1960s sound is also remarkably fresh and present. But this reissue is to be prized even more for the other two cantatas. *Sehet, wir gehn hinauf gen Jerusalem* is one of Bach's most inspired and surely ranks high on the shortlist of essential Bach. Particularly glorious is the penultimate meditation, *Es is vollbracht* ('It is finished'), again with a poignant oboe obbligato. Both Dame Janet Baker and Shirley-Quirk are in marvellous voice, and *Vergnügte Ruh'* makes a worthy companion. These are also from the mid-1960s and both are performed superbly and recorded very naturally; the CD transfer retains all the warmth and refinement of the original master. This is among the half-dozen or so cantata records that ought to be in every collection.

Volume 22: *Cantatas Nos.* (i) *84: Ich bin vergnügt mit meinem Glücke; 85: Ich bin ein guter Hirt; 86: Wahrlich, wahrlich, ich sage euch; 87: Bisher habt ihr nichts gebeten;* (ii) *88: Siehe, ich will viel Fischer aussenden; 89: Was soll ich aus dir machen, Ephraim?; 90: Es reisset euch ein schrecklich Ende.*
(M) ** Teldec/Warner 2292 42578-2 (2) [id.]. Esswood, Equiluz, (i) Wiedl, Van der Meer, Tölz Boys' Ch., VCM, Harnoncourt; (ii) Klein, Van Egmond, Hanover Boys' Ch., Ghent Coll. Vocale, Leonhardt Cons., Leonhardt.

If the performances here are of variable quality, the musical inspiration is not, and the set is worth acquiring for the sake of this neglected music, much of which is otherwise unobtainable.

Volume 23: *Cantatas Nos.* (i) *91: Gelobet seist du, Jesus Christ; 92: Ich hab' in Gottes Herz und Sinn*; (ii) *93: Wer nur den lieben Gott lässt walten; 94: Was frag' ich nach der Welt.*
(M) *** Teldec/Warner 2292 42582-2 (2) [id.]. Esswood, Equiluz, (i) Bratschke, Van Egmond, Hanover Boys' Ch., Ghent Coll. Vocale, Leonhardt Cons. Leonhardt; (ii) Wiedl, Van der Meer, Huttenlocher, Tölz Boys' Ch., VCM, Harnoncourt.

One of the most desirable of these Bach sets,

with assured and confident playing and singing from all concerned.

Volume 24: *Cantatas Nos.* (i) *95: Christus, der ist mein Leben; 96: Herr Christ, der ein'ge Gottesohn; 97: In allen meinen Taten*; (ii) *98: Was Gott tut, das ist wohlgetan.*
(M) **(*) Teldec/Warner 2292 42583-2 [id.]. Esswood, Equiluz, (i) Wiedl, Huttenlocher, Van der Meer, Tölz Boys' Ch., VCM, Harnoncourt; (ii) Lengert, Van Egmond, Hanover Boys' Ch., Ghent Coll. Vocale, Leonhardt Cons., Leonhardt.

There are occasional weaknesses here (Philippe Huttenlocher is not altogether happy in No. 96), but this CD is still well worth having.

Volume 25: *Cantatas Nos.* (i) *99: Was Gott tut, das ist wohlgetan*; (ii) *100: Was Gott tut, das ist wohlgetan;* (i) *101: Nimm von uns, Herr, du treuer Gott; 102: Herr, deine Augen sehen nach dem Glauben.*
(M) **(*) Teldec/Warner 2292 42584-2 (2) [id.]. Esswood, Equiluz, (i) Wiedl, Huttenlocher, Tölz Boys' Ch., VCM, Harnoncourt; (ii) Bratschke, Van Egmond, Hanover Boys' Ch., Ghent Coll. Vocale, Leonhardt Cons., Leonhardt.

With this box Teldec pass the century and, although there have been unevennesses in the series, it is no mean achievement. Cantata 99 fares less well than the others; but it would be curmudgeonly to dwell on the shortcomings of this box, given the interest of its contents.

Volume 26: *Cantatas Nos.* (i; ii) *103: Ihr werdet weinen und heulen*; (iii; iv) *104: Du Hirte Israel, höre*; (v; iv) *105: Herr, gehe nicht ins Gericht*; (vi; ii) *106: Gottes Zeit ist die allerbeste Zeit (Actus tragicus).*
(M) *** Teldec/Warner 2292 42602-2 [id.]. (i) Esswood, Equiluz, Van Egmond; (ii) Hanover Boys' Ch., Ghent Coll. Vocale, Leonhardt Cons., Leonhardt; (iii) Esswood, Huttenlocher; (iv) Tölz Boys' Ch., VCM, Harnoncourt; (v) Wiedl, Equiluz, Van der Meer; (vi) Klein, Harten, Van Altena, Van Egmond.

The best-known and most deeply moving cantata here is the *Actus tragicus*. No. 103, too, is a poignant and expressive piece that repays study. Both these performances are among the very finest to have reached us in this series. No. 105 is arguably one of the very deepest of all Bach cantatas; Harnoncourt is perhaps wanting in expressive weight here; but neither this fact nor the reservations one might feel about his account of No. 104 diminish the value of this excellent single-CD collection.

Volume 27: *Cantatas Nos.* (i) *107: Wass willst du dich betrüben*; (ii) *108: Es ist euch gut, dass ich hingehe; 109: Ich glaube, lieber Herr, hilf meinem Unglauben!; 110: Unser Mund sei voll Lachens.*
(M) *** Teldec/Warner 2292 42603-2 (2) [id.]. Equiluz, (i) Klein, Van Egmond, Hanover Boys' Ch., Ghent Coll. Vocale, Leonhardt Cons., Leonhardt; (ii) Wiedl, Frangoulis, Stumpf, Lorenz, Esswood, Van der Meer, Tölz Boys' Ch., VCM, Harnoncourt.

The highest standards of this series are maintained throughout this volume, and that applies to performance, recording, CD transfer and presentation.

Volume 28: *Cantatas Nos.* (i) *111: Was mein Gott will, das gescheh' allzeit; 112: Der Herr ist mein getreuer Hirt*; (ii) *113: Herr Jesu Christ, du höchstes Gut; 114: Ach, lieben Christen, seid getrost.*
(M) *** Teldec/Warner 2292 42606-2 (2) [id.]. Equiluz, (i) Huber, Esswood, Van der Meer, Tölz Boys' Ch., VCM, Harnoncourt; (ii) Hennig, Jacobs, Van Egmond, Hanover Boys' Ch., Ghent Coll. Vocale, Leonhardt Cons., Leonhardt.

The opening chorus of No. 112 is among the most beautiful of Bach's choral fantasias, and it must be said that Harnoncourt does it justice. Leonhardt's accounts of Cantatas Nos. 113 and 114 are free from pedantry, well shaped and unaffected. This is one of the sets that lovers of the Bach cantatas should acquire, even if they have ambivalent feelings about the series as a whole.

Volume 29: *Cantatas Nos.* (i; iii; iv) *115: Mache dich, mein Geist, bereit; 116: Du Friedefürst, Herr Jesu Christ*; (ii; v; vi) *117: Sei Lob und Erh dem höchsten Gut*; (i; iii; vii) *119: Preise, Jerusalem, den Herrn.*
(M) *** Teldec/Warner 2292 42608-2 (2) [id.]. (i) Tölz Boys' Ch., VCM, Harnoncourt; (ii) Equiluz, Hanover Boys' Ch., Ghent Coll. Vocale, Leonhardt Cons., Leonhardt; with (iii) Huber, Esswood; (iv) Huttenlocher; (v) Jacobs; (vi) Van Egmond; (vii) Holl.

No. 115 is rich in melodic invention. Its companion, No. 116, opens with a lively A major chorus, and that is given with plenty of vigour and spirit. There is a demanding trio for treble, tenor and bass, which taxes the soloists but rewards the listener with invention of great contrapuntal refinement. The imposing *Sei Lob und Ehr dem höchsten Gut* is the only cantata here conducted by Leonhardt; his tempi are excellently judged, although one grumble is the detached delivery of the chorale, which sounds unnecessarily jerky. In No. 119 Harnoncourt is in good form, and the recording is excellently balanced and splendidly truthful.

Volume 30: *Cantatas Nos. 120: Gott, mann lobet dich in der Stille; 121: Christum wir sollen loben; 122: Das neugebor'ne Kindelein; 123: Liebster Immanuel, Herzog der Frommen.*
(M) *** Teldec/Warner 2292 42609-2 (2) [id.]. Treble soloists from Tölz Ch., Esswood, Equiluz, Huttenlocher or Holl, Tölz Ch., VCM, Harnoncourt.

No serious grumbles about any of the performances here, even if one or two numbers fall short of perfection. The recordings are exemplary in every way.

Volume 31: *Cantatas Nos.* (i) *124: Meinen Jesum lass ich nicht; 125: Mit Fried und Freud ich fahr dahin; 126: Erhalt uns, Herr, bei deinem Wort*; (ii) *127: Herr Jesu Christ wahr' Mensch und Gott.*
(M) *** Teldec/Warner 2292 42615-2 [id.]. (i) Bergius, Rampf, Esswood, Equiluz, Thomaschke, Tölz Boys' Ch., VCM, Harnoncourt; (ii) Hennig, Van Egmond, Hanover Boys' Ch., Ghent Coll. Vocale, Leonhardt Cons., Leonhardt.

No. 124 is a piece of strong melodic vitality and is full of colour too. No. 125 is even finer, a grave, elevated work that is most affecting. The opening chorus is inspired and the alto solo which follows is wonderfully expressive and receives eloquent treatment from Paul Esswood. No. 126 is based on a Lutheran hymn and the bellicose spirit of the first verse inspires Bach to write real battle music, with a demanding trumpet part. No. 127 is another cantata of striking richness and inspiration and includes an extraordinarily beautiful soprano aria. It is an altogether marvellous piece and very well performed. This is another CD that collectors who are not automatically acquiring the whole series should not overlook.

Volume 32: *Cantatas Nos.* (i) *128: Auf Christi Himmelfahrt allein; 129: Gelobet sei der Herr, mein Gott;* (ii) *130: Herr Gott, dich loben alle wir; 131: Aus der Tiefen rufe ich, Herr, zu dir.*
(M) **(*) Teldec/Warner 2292 42617-2 (2) [id.]. Hennig, Bergius, Jacobs, Rampf, Equiluz, Van Egmond, Heldwein, Holl; (i) Hanover Boys' Ch., Ghent Coll. Vocale, Leonhardt Consort, Leonhardt; (ii) Tölz Boys' Ch., VCM, Harnoncourt.

Cantatas Nos. (i) *128: Auf Christi Himmelfahrt allein; 129: Gelobet sei der Herr, mein Gott*; (ii) *130: Herr Gott.*
(M) **(*) Teldec/Warner 2292 43055-2 [id.]. (recordings as above).

The singers here are excellent, but the strings have an edge that is razor-sharp and not pleasing. The brass playing in No. 129 is pretty rough; but the treble, Sebastian Hennig, acquits himself excellently in the glorious aria which forms the centrepiece of the cantata. No. 130 has a powerful opening chorus whose trumpets proclaim the Kingdom of God. All three cantatas are short and can be accommodated on a single CD. The two-CD set adds No. 131, the earliest of Bach's cantatas, not only more extended but a marvellous, inspired piece, whose grave beauty is eloquently conveyed by Harnoncourt, and it alone is almost worth the price of this volume. The recordings are of the high standard set by the series.

Volume 33: *Cantatas Nos. 132: Bereitet die Wege, bereitet die Bahn; 133: Ich freue mich in dir; 134: Ein Herz, das seinen Jesum lebend weiss; 135: Ach Herr, mich armen Sünder.*
(M) **(*) Teldec/Warner 2292 42618-2 (2) [id.]. Hennig, Jacobs, Van Altena, Van Egmond, Hanover Boys' Ch., Ghent Coll. Vocale, Leonhardt Cons., Leonhardt.

No. 132 is probably the best performance here: its young treble, Sebastian Hennig, is secure and in tune, and the cantata itself has grandeur. Since there is no final chorale, Leonhardt substitutes a chorale setting from Cantata No. 164. No. 133 comes off less well, thanks to an indifferent contribution from the Ghent Collegium Vocale, just as in its companion, No. 134, the tenor's intonation is not absolutely firm. But there is much to admire in his singing in the final cantata in the box (No. 135) and much in Leonhardt's performance that gives pleasure.

Volume 34: *Cantatas Nos. 136: Erforsche mich, Gott, und erfahre mein Herz; 137: Lobe den Herren, den mächtigen König der Ehren; 138: Warum betrübst du dich, mein Herz?; 139: Wohl dem, der sich auf seinen Gott.*
(M) ** Teldec/Warner 2292 42619-2 [id.]. Bergius, Rampf, Esswood, Equiluz, Holl, Heldwein, Hartinger, Tölz Boys' Ch., VCM, Harnoncourt.

Some relatively routine playing emerges straight away in the first of the four cantatas in this volume, all of them fitting on to a single CD. The solo singing is another matter: Paul Esswood's performance of the aria, *Es kömmt ein Tag*, is very distinguished indeed, as is Robert Holl's contribution. No. 137 is probably the best-known cantata here and it prompts some lovely singing from Alan Bergius. No. 138 is a particularly beautiful cantata; it opens with a strikingly poignant chorus which makes less effect than it might, thanks to some undistinguished singing and direction. Here the treble, Stefan Rampf, sounds distinctly insecure in the third section, *Er kann und will lasse nicht*. Nor can one say that the performance given to No. 139 is really worthy of it, with the two oboi d'amore sounding a little fragile at one point in the opening chorus. Still, the music is all very much worth having.

Volume 35: *Cantatas Nos.* (i) *140: Wachet auf, ruft uns die Stimme;* (ii) *143: Lobe den Herrn, meine Seele; 144: Nimm, was dein ist, und gehe hin;* (i) *145: Ich lebe, mein Herze, zu deinem Ergötzen; 146: Wir müssen durch viel Trübsal.*
(M) *** Teldec/Warner Dig. 2292 42630-2 (2) [id.]. Esswood, Equiluz, (i) Bergius, Hampson, Tölz Boys' Ch., VCM, Harnoncourt; (ii) Cericius, Pfeiffer, Van Egmond, Hanover Boys' Ch., Ghent Coll. Vocale, Leonhardt Cons., Leonhardt.

This two-CD set offers plenty of interest. The best known is No. 140, *Wachet auf, ruft uns die Stimme*, and, though the opening chorale is rather pedestrian, there is some felicitous singing elsewhere. Cantata No. 141 is by Telemann and No. 142 by an unknown hand; both are omitted. Leonhardt is in charge in No. 143, which is unusual in having three horns. There is a particularly fine treble contribution from Roger Cericius in the working of the chorale, *Du Friedefürst, Herr Jesu Christ*, and Leonhardt directs with vitality. No. 146 opens with the first movement of the *Harpsichord concerto in D minor* (BWV 1052) as its sinfonia with the organ as soloist, and the opening duet of No. 145 between Jesus and the Soul (Equiluz and Bergius) is beautifully done. As always in this venture, not everything is perfect, but this is one of the more satisfying of the series.

Volume 36: *Cantatas Nos.* (i) *147: Herz und Mund und Tat und Leben; 148: Bringet dem Herrn Ehre seines Namens;* (ii) *149: Man singet mit Freuden vom Sieg; 150: Nach dir, Herr, verlanget mich; 151: Süsser Trost, mein Jesus kömmt.*
(M) *** Teldec/Warner Dig. 2292 42631-2 (2) [id.]. Bergius, Hennig, Esswood, Equiluz, Hampson, Van Egmond; (i) Tölz Boys' Ch., VCM, Harnoncourt; (ii) Ghent Coll. Vocale, Leonhardt Cons., Leonhardt.

The best-known cantata here is the festive No. 147; No. 148, however, is relatively little heard and it proves an inventive and rewarding score. Paul Esswood's aria, *Mund und Herz steht dir offen*, is a delight. No. 149 is another festive cantata whose opening chorus draws on No. 208, *Was mir behagt*. Generally good playing here and some fine singing, particularly from the young treble, Sebastian Hennig. No. 150 is not assigned to any specific Sunday or feast-day; if doubt has been cast on its authenticity, surely there can be none as to its merit. There is a marvellous bassoon obbligato in the bass aria, *Kraft und Starke sei gesungen Gott*, which is expertly played. No. 151 is a Christmas cantata, and a delightful one, too.

Volume 37: *Cantatas Nos. 152: Tritt auf die Glaubensbahn; 153: Schau, lieber Gott, wie meine Feind; 154: Mein liebster Jesus ist verloren; 155: Mein Gott, wie lang, ach lange; 156: Ich steh' mit einem Fuss im Grabe.*
(M) **(*) Teldec/Warner Dig. 2292 42632-2 (2) [id.]. Wegmann, Bergius, Rampf, Esswood, Equiluz, Hampson, Tölz Boys' Ch., VCM, Harnoncourt.

No. 152 has some particularly felicitous instrumental invention: the *Sinfonia* is a delight. The playing of the Concentus Musicus is eloquent and the performance as a whole very enjoyable. Unfortunately, the young Christoph Wegmann is obviously beset by nerves, though the voice, if unsteady, is admirably pure. No. 153 is a rarity and is unusual in that it discards the usual opening chorus in favour of a simple chorale: indeed, the cantata has three chorales in all. No. 154 is a powerful and emotional piece. The oboi d'amore suffer from imperfect intonation in the fourth number, *Jesu, lass dich finden*. Generally speaking, however, this is an acceptable performance. The recording is very clean indeed, but perhaps a trifle dry, with relatively little ambience.

Volume 38: *Cantatas Nos.* (i) *157: Ich lasse dich nicht, du segnest mich denn; 158: Der Friede sei mit dir; 159: Sehet, wir geh'n hinauf gen Jerusalem;* (ii) *161: Komm, du süsse Todesstunde; 162: Ach! ich sehe, jetzt, da ich zur Hochzeit gehe; 163: Nur jedem das Seine.*
(M) ** Teldec/Warner Dig. 2292 42633-2 (2) [id.]. Eiwanger, Esswood, Equiluz, Van Egmond, Tölz Boys' Ch., (i) Wegmann, Ghent Coll. Vocale, Leonhardt; (ii) Iconomou, Holl, VCM, Harnoncourt.

Of the cantatas recorded here, the finest and most familiar is undoubtedly No. 159, with its moving combination of chorale and aria, *Ich folge dir nach*, and the highly expressive aria for bass and oboe. Hardly less impressive is No. 161, a much earlier work from Weimar. So, too, are its companions. No. 157 is a chamber cantata for tenor, bass, strings, flute and oboe d'amore. To be frank, it is less than inspired. Its companion, No. 158, though incomplete is far from routine Bach. Although the performances are touched by moments of inspiration and are beautifully recorded, they fall short of distinction. Wind intonation at times is less than ideal.

Cantatas Nos. 161: Komm, du süsse Todesstunde; 169: Gott soll allein mein Herze haben.

(B) ** Hung. White Label HRC 124 [id.]. Hamari, Réti, Liszt Ac. of Music Ch. & O, Sándor.

Julia Hamari's contribution here is sound rather than outstandingly eloquent, but her tenor partner in No. 161, József Réti, has a pleasing voice, and the choral singing is beautiful in both *Cantatas*. A pair of flutes add colour to the orchestra in No. 161, whereas No. 169 begins with an attractive sinfonia which is a bit like a Handel organ concerto; the excellent organist, Gábor Lehotka, also makes contributions elsewhere. This is all fine music, very well recorded; and these works are otherwise available only in the Harnoncourt/Leonhardt series, offering an entirely different sound-world.

Volume 39: *Cantatas Nos.* (i) *164: Ihr, die ihr euch von Christo nennet; 165: O heil'ges Geist und Wasserbad; 166: Wo gehest du hin?;* (ii) *167: Ihr Menschen, rühmet Gottes Liebe; 168: Tue, Rechnung! Donnerwort; 169: Gott soll allein mein Herze haben.*

(M) ** Teldec/Warner Dig. 2292 42634-2 (2) [id.]. Esswood, Equiluz, Tölz Boys' Ch.; (i) Wegmann, Eiwanger, Van Egmond, Ghent Coll. Vocale, Leonhardt Cons., Leonhardt; (ii) Iconomou, Immler, Holl, VCM, Harnoncourt.

In No. 164 at the beginning of the aria, *Nur durch Lieb und durch Erbarmen*, the intonation of the two flauto traverso and Paul Esswood is excruciating, and the direction here, under Leonhardt, laboured. Elsewhere things are much better. In No. 165 the treble copes well with the opening solo. Though one of the more rarely performed cantatas, this is both inventive and varied, as indeed is its successor on this disc, *Wo gehest du hin?* It has an inspired tenor aria – well sung, too. No. 169 draws on material from the *E major Concerto*, BWV 1053, and No. 167 is more pastoral in character. No. 168 opens with a spirited aria that evokes a superb response from the Vienna Concentus Musicus and finds the bass soloist in excellent form. Elsewhere there are moments when the performances sound as if they would have benefited from more rehearsal, though those under Harnoncourt are generally more lively. As usual, excellent recording and infinitely rewarding music.

Volume 40: *Cantatas Nos.* (i) *170: Vergnügte Ruh', beliebte Seelenlust;* (ii) *171: Gott, wie dein Name, so ist auch dein Ruhm;* (i) *172: Erschallet, ihr Lieder;* (ii) *173: Erhöhtes Fleisch und Blut; 174: Ich liebe den Höchsten von ganzem Gemüte.*

(M) **(*) Teldec/Warner Dig. 2292 42635-2 (2) [id.]. (i) Esswood, Van Altena, Van Egmond, Hanover Boys' Ch., Ghent Coll. Vocale, Leonhardt Cons., Leonhardt; (ii) Equiluz, Holl, Tölz Boys' Ch., VCM, Harnoncourt.

No. 170 is for alto and instruments and is without chorus or chorale. There is a moving alto aria, eloquently sung by Paul Esswood who copes with the demanding role very impressively. Leonhardt makes heavy weather of the aria, *Die Welt das Sundenhaus*. No. 171 falls to Harnoncourt. It is festive in character. The boy treble Helmut Wittek is quite remarkable in the aria, *Jesus soll mein erstes Wort*. No. 172 receives a rather laboured performance from Leonhardt; 173 is a reworking of an earlier secular cantata from Cöthen. No. 174 opens with the first movement of *Brandenburg No. 3*, scored for oboes, oboe di caccia, horns and strings, plus bassoon continuo. Excellent sound and eminently serviceable performances.

Volume 41: *Cantatas Nos.* (i) *175: Er rufet seinen Schafen mit Namen; 176: Es ist ein trotzig und verzagt Ding*; (ii) *177: Ich ruf zu dir, Herr Jesu Christ; 178: Wo Gott der Herr nicht bei uns hält; 179: Siehe zu, dass deine Gottesfurcht.*

(M) ** Teldec/Warner Dig. 2292 42428-2 (2) [id.]. (i) Echternach, Esswood, Van Altena, Van Egmond, Hanover Boys' Ch., Coll. Vocale, Leonhardt Cons., Leonhardt; (ii) Wittek, Iconomou, Equiluz, Holl, Tölz Boys' Ch., VCM, Harnoncourt.

No. 175 is pastoral in mood and has some lovely things in it. Some of the playing under Gustav Leonhardt sounds a little tentative, and the performance of No. 176, with its powerful opening fugal chorus, sounds a bit pedestrian. No. 177 falls to Harnoncourt and receives a solid rather than an inspired performance, with the heavily accented first beats in the opening chorus producing an earthbound effect, though the boy alto Panito Iconomou has a distinctive vocal personality. By far the most successful on all counts is No. 178, which has considerable vigour and power in Harnoncourt's hands. The chorus in 179 make heavy weather of their powerful opening number, but there is some eloquent singing later from Kurt Equiluz and Robert Holl. Excellent recorded sound, with excellent balance between the singers and instrumentalists.

Volume 42: *Cantatas Nos* (i) *180: Schmücke dich, o liebe Seele; 181: Leichtgesinnte Flattergeister;* (ii) *182: Himmelskönig, sei*

wilkommen; 183: Sie werden euch in den Bann tun; (i) *184: Erwunschtes Freudenlicht.*
(M) *** Teldec/Warner Dig. 2292 42738-2 (2) [id.]. (i) O'Farrell, Esswood, Equiluz, Van Egmond, Hanover Boys' Ch., Coll. Vocale, Leonhardt Cons., Leonhardt; (ii) Wittek, Holl, Hampson, Tölz Boys' Ch., VCM, Harnoncourt.

In No. 180 the orchestral playing under Leonhardt is a little pedestrian and the young soloist (Jan Patrick O'Farrell) at times is swamped. Paul Esswood is in splendid form. No. 181 receives a much livelier performance, with excellent singing, and has a more confident treble in Alexander Heymann. The Palm Sunday cantata, No. 182, is in every way a delight and the performance under Harnoncourt is expressive and unforced. Its companions, *Sie werden euch in den Bann tun* and *Erwunschtes Freudenlicht*, are no less interesting and the level of inspiration is high.

Volume 43: *Cantatas Nos.* (i) *185: Barmherziges Herze der ewigen Liebes; 186: Ärgre dich, o Seele, nicht;* (ii) *187: Es wartet alles auf dich;* (i) *188: Ich habe meine Zuversicht.*
(M) **(*) Teldec/Warner Dig. 2292 44179-2 (2). (i) Wittek, Equiluz, Hampson, Holl, Tölz Boys' Ch., VCM, Harnoncourt; (ii) Emmermann, Esswood, Van Egmond, Hanover Boys' Ch., Ghent Coll. Vocale, Leonhardt Cons., Leonhardt.

Barmherziges Herze der ewigen Liebes is a lovely piece and finds both Esswood and Hampson in excellent form. Four of the arias from No. 186 come originally from Weimar (1716) but form the basis of a much bigger cantata, also from Leipzig. The chromatic soprano aria is one of its highlights, but inspiration throughout is high and the singing good, even though the young boy soprano is under some strain. Kurt Equiluz is in impressive form both here and in No. 188. No. 187, probably performed most often of the four, finds Leonhardt at the helm. On the whole the set is rewarding, though the choral contribution is not always secure.

Volume 44: *Cantatas Nos.* (i) *192: Nun danket alle Gott;* (ii) *194: Höchsterwünschtes Freudenfest;* (iii) *195: Dem Gerechten muss das Licht immer wieder aufgehen.*
(M) **(*) Teldec/Warner Dig. 2292 44193-2 [id.]. (i) Wittek, (i; ii) Hampson, (ii) Stricker, Gienger, Equiluz, (iii) O'Farrell, Jacobs, Elwes, Van der Kamp; (i & ii) Tölz Boys' Ch., VCM, Harnoncourt; (iii) Hanover Boys' Ch., Ghent Coll. Vocale, Leonhardt Consort, Leonhardt.

Leonhardt and Harnoncourt omit cantatas Nos. 189–91 and 193. No. 190, *Singet dem Herrn ein neues Lied*, was partly lost, though a conjectural reconstruction of it (BWV 190a) has been recorded; No. 191, *Gloria in excelsis Deo*, is a Latin cantata, and contains music which Bach 'recycled' in the *B minor Mass*, while 193, *Ihr Tore zu Zion*, is incomplete. The biggest cantata here is *Höchsterwünschtes Freudenfest*, a twelve-movement two-part work with (as Alec Robertson put it in his book on the *Cantatas*) some charming music but not very interesting recitatives. The performance under Harnoncourt reveals some scrawny string-tone but there is some good singing. No. 195, under Leonhardt, is let down by some undistinguished choral singing in the fugal opening, but otherwise there is much to enjoy in this fine piece.

Volume 45: *Cantatas Nos.* (i) *196: Der Herr denket an uns;* (ii) *197: Gott ist unsrer Zuversicht;* (iii) *198: Lass, Fürstin, lass noch einen Strahl;* (iv) *199: Mein Herze schwimmt im Blut.*
(M) ** Teldec/Warner Dig. 2292 44194-2 (2) [id.]. (i) Wittek, Equiluz, Hampson, (ii; iii) O'Farrell, Jacobs, Van der Kamp, (iii) Elwes, (iv) Bonney; (i) Tölz Boys' Ch., (ii; iii) Hanover Boys' Ch., Ghent Coll. Vocale; (i; iv) VCM, Harnoncourt; (ii; iii) Leonhardt Consort, Leonhardt.

In the last volume in the series some measure of exhaustion must be noted. The choral singing both in No. 197, a wedding cantata from the late 1730s, and in No. 198, probably the best-known of the present set, is distinctly tired, and there is also some less than distinguished instrumental playing. However, there are good things too from the soloists, in particular from René Jacobs and young Jan Patrick O'Farrell.

Cantata No. 205: Der zufriedengestellte Äolus.
(M) *** Teldec/Warner Dig. 2292 42957-2 [id.]. Kenny, Lipovšek, Equiluz, Holl, Arnold-Schönberg Ch., VCM, Harnoncourt.

Bach describes this cantata as '*Dramma per musica*', and some of its invention comes as close to opera as anything he wrote. It is a long piece of fifteen numbers and is written for ambitious forces, all of whom serenade the learned scholar. The performance is very good indeed, though the heavy accents in the opening chorus of the winds and the wooden orchestral tutti in the second number must be noted. Alice Harnoncourt's obbligato in *Angenehmer Zephyrus* ('Delightful Zephyr') is a model of good style and is beautifully articulated. The singers, particularly Yvonne Kenny's Pallas and Kurt Equiluz's Zephyrus, are good; the recording has a decently spacious acoustic and no lack of detail. Recommended.

Christmas oratorio, BWV 248.

(M) **(*) Teldec/Warner 2292 42495-2 (3) [id.]. Treble soloists from V. Boys' Ch., Esswood, Equiluz, Nimsgern, V. Boys' Ch., Ch. Viennensis, VCM, Harnoncourt.

(M) ** BMG/RCA GD 77046; *GK 77046* (2) [77046-2-RG; *77046-4-RG*]. Bucchereil, Stein, Altmeyer, McDaniel, Tölz Boys' Ch., Coll. Aur., Schmidt-Gaden.

Christmas oratorio; Magnificat, BWV 243.

(M) *** Decca 425 441-2 (3) [id.]. Ameling, Watts, Pears, Krause, Ch., Stuttgart CO, Münchinger.

Münchinger directs an admirably fresh performance of the *Christmas oratorio*, sharp in tone and bright in recording (which dates from 1967). With an excellent team of soloists and with Lübeck trebles adding to the freshness, this is a good middle-of-the-road version, representative of modern scholarship as determined in the immediate pre-authentic era. Münchinger's recording of the *Magnificat* dates from 1969 and was another of his finest Bach performances. The soloists are uniformly good and so are the contributions of the Vienna Academy Choir and the Stuttgart Chamber Orchestra. Münchinger tends to stress the breadth and spaciousness of the *Magnificat* – though his reading has plenty of spirit – and the Decca engineers have captured the detail with admirable clarity and naturalness. The trumpets sound resplendent.

In his search for authenticity in Bach performance Harnoncourt has rarely been more successful than here. It will not be to everyone's taste to have a boy treble and male countertenor instead of women soloists, but the purity of sound of these singers is most affecting. Above all Harnoncourt in this instance never allows his pursuit of authentic sound to weigh the performance down; it has a lightness of touch which should please everyone. The sound, as usual from this source, is excellent and has transferred to CD with conspicuous success, but the use of three discs, even at mid-price, is disadvantageous.

The Collegium Aureum were pioneers in the period-performance movement, a less abrasive group than Nikolaus Harnoncourt's Concentus Musicus. Their recording of the *Christmas oratorio* was made in 1973 and, by latterday standards, it sounds too heavy and smooth for a period performance. Speeds are often surprisingly slow, not just for arias but also for recitatives. The all-male team of soloists includes not just a boy treble but a boy alto, who makes heavy weather of the cradle song in Cantata No. 2. Yet even with slow speeds, genuine joy is conveyed in the choruses, again with boys singing the upper parts.

Christmas oratorio: Arias and choruses.

(M) *** DG Dig. 435 088-2; *435 088-4* [id.]. Argenta, Von Otter, Bär, Blochwitz, Monteverdi Ch., E. Bar. Soloists, Gardiner.

This makes an excellent sampler of the finest recording available of Bach's joyous Christmas celebration, notable for the freshness of both singing and orchestral playing. The 70-minute selection offers choruses and arias from all six cantatas and includes the *Sinfonia* to introduce the four items from Part Two. The notes, however, concentrate on John Eliot Gardiner and say nothing about Bach and his music.

Easter oratorio.

(M) *** Decca 425 650-2 [id.]. Ameling, Watts, Krenn, Krause, Stuttgart CO, Münchinger – *Cantata No. 10.* ***

Münchinger is at his finest in the *Easter oratorio*, giving a spacious and impressive reading. He is well supported by his splendid team of soloists, and the Decca recording is well up to the lively standard of his Stuttgart series. With a generous and attractive coupling, this makes a reliable recommendation for this surprisingly little-recorded work.

Magnificat in D, BWV 243.

(M) *** Decca 421 148-2. Palmer, Watts, Tear, Roberts, King's College Ch., ASMF, Ledger – BACH, C.P.E.: *Magnificat.* ***

(M) *** Decca 433 175-2. Ameling, Van Borkh, Watts, Krenn, Krause, V. Ac. Ch., Stuttgart CO, Münchinger – *Cantatas Nos. 67 & 130.* **(*)

Philip Ledger's account, recorded by Argo in the late 1970s, is most attractive, highly recommendable if boys' voices are preferred in the chorus. The women soloists are outstanding, as is the St Martin's Academy; and the CD transfer brings added clarity and improves the overall balance.

Münchinger's performance and recording of the *Magnificat* is also as impressive as any in the catalogue. The soloists are uniformly good and so are the contributions of the Vienna Academy Choir and the Stuttgart orchestra. Münchinger tends to stress the breadth and spaciousness of the *Magnificat*, and the Decca engineers have captured the detail with admirable clarity and naturalness – and plenty of weight, too. However, most will prefer Ledger's coupling.

Mass in B min., BWV 232.

(M) (***) EMI mono CHS7 63505-2 (2) [Ang. CDHB 63505]. Schwarzkopf, Hoffgen,

Gedda, Rehfuss, Ch. & O of V. Gesellschaft der Musikfreunde, Karajan.
(M) ** Ph. 426 657-2 (2). Stich-Randall, Reynolds, Haefliger, Shirley-Quirk, Berlin RIAS Chamber Ch., Berlin RSO, Maazel.
(M) ** EMI CMS7 63364-2 (2) [Ang. CDMB 63364]. Giebel, J. Baker, Gedda, Prey, Crass, BBC Ch., New Philh. O, Klemperer.
(M) ** DG 415 622-2 (2) [id.]. Janowitz, Ludwig, Schreier, Kerns, Ridderbusch, V. Singverein, Karajan.

Recorded in 1952 with obbligato solos taken by the then principals of the Philharmonia in London, Karajan's historic recording combines the weight of a traditional performance with a freshness missing from most of the later and plushier Bach recordings he made in Berlin. This was one of Karajan's early collaborations with the producer, Walter Legge, and the casting of four clean-toned soloists reflects that, notably Legge's wife, Elisabeth Schwarzkopf. Though the opening *Kyrie* and the great *Sanctus* are slow and portentous in a traditional way, Karajan's intensity sustains them, with sweet rather than bright choral tone. Frequently Karajan's speeds are far faster and more resilient than was common in Bach performances at that time. This is a set full of delights to make you forget the limited mono sound, which is well transferred to CD. Dennis Brain's horn obbligato for *Qui sedes* is a wonder.

Maazel's is a thoughtful and sensitive interpretation, with the changing moods of music and text faithfully caught. Nothing sounds exaggerated and the recording is tonally beautiful and remarkably homogeneous. This suits the soloists, whose attitude to phrasing and melodic lines seems unusually consistent and admirable. The singing of the Berlin RIAS Chorus also flows smoothly and effortlessly, the upper voices soaring through Bach's expansive polyphony without strain. Indeed the contours are rounded a shade too self-consciously for the work's inherent drama to make its full effect, although there is no absence of majesty and breadth. Despite the fine solo contributions, there is an element of blandness here, even if the music's spiritual dimension is not lost.

Although the CD transfer of the 1967 Kingsway Hall recording is impressively full and clear, Klemperer's performance is disappointing. Leaving aside any questions of authenticity of scale, the sobriety of his reading, with plodding tempi and a dogged observance of the *Neue Bach-Ausgabe* (Bärenreiter), utterly unornamented, was no doubt predictable. Only when the drama of the Mass takes over in the *Crucifixus* and *Et resurrexit* does the majesty of Klemperer's conception become apparent. Dame Janet Baker stands out among the soloists with superb accounts of the *Qui sedes* and *Agnus Dei*. Whatever the initial shortcomings, Klemperer's *Sanctus* (faster than usual) has wonderful momentum, the *Osanna* is genuinely joyful and the concluding sections of this sublime work come vividly to life.

On DG, Karajan conveys intensity, even religious fervour, and the very opening brings an impressive first entry of the choir on *Kyrie*. But then, after the instrumental fugue, the contrapuntal entries are sung in a self-consciously softened tone. There is a strong sense of the work's architecture, and the highly polished surfaces do not obscure the depths of the music, but (despite a fine solo team) this is hardly a first choice.

Motets: *Singet dem Herrn ein Neues Lied, BWV 225; Der Geist hilft unser Schwachheit, BWV 226; Jesu meine Freude, BWV 227; Der Gerechte Kommt um Fürchte dich nicht, BWV 228; Komm, Jesu, Komm, BWV 229; Lobet den Herrn, BWV 230; Sei Lob und Preis mit Ehren, BWV 231.*
(M) *** DG 435 087-2; *435 087-4* [id.] (without *BWV 229*). Regensburger Domspätzen, Hamburg Bläserkreis, V. Capella Academica, Schneidt.
(M) **(*) EMI CDM7 63237-2 (without *BWV 231*). King's Coll. Ch., Willcocks.

As part of DG's Bach Edition, Hans-Martin Schneidt's set of six motets (*Komm, Jesu, komm* is omitted) brings highly enjoyable performances which have a lusty freshness, enhanced by the brightness of boy trebles. The accompaniments on period instruments at lower pitch add to the bluffness and, though speeds are often on the slow side, the resilience of the playing and singing makes them consistently convincing. Excellent, atmospheric recording.

Recorded in King's College Chapel in 1967 and 1970, the King's College versions represent an older order of Bach performance; however, with their fresh attack, warmly atmospheric sound and clean rhythms, and with no accompanying instruments, they are undistractingly satisfying for all but period-performance specialists. The characteristic timbre of the Cambridge trebles is caught well, with voices closely focused against the Chapel's lively acoustic and with the stereo spread underlining the antiphonal double-choir effects of *Singet dem Herrn*.

Motets: *Lobet den Herrn, alle Heiden, BWV 230; Sei Lob und Preis mit Ehren, BWV 231. Ich lasse dich nicht, du segnest mich denn, BWV*

Anh./App.159 (attrib. – probably by J. C. Bach).

(M) *** DG 427 142-2. Regensburg Domspätzen, V. Capella Academica, Schneidt – VIVALDI: *Gloria; Kyrie.* ***

These motets, including one probably written by Johann Christian, are admirably fresh and feature accompaniments with period instruments. They make a fine bonus for the two Vivaldi choral works.

St John Passion, BWV 245.

(M) **(*) Teldec/Warner 2292 42492-2 (2) [id.]. Equiluz, Van t'Hoff, Van Egmond, Villisech, Schneeweis, treble soloists from V. Boys' Ch., Ch. Viennensis, VCM, Harnoncourt.

(M) ** Ph. 426 645-2 (2). Giebel, Höffgen, Haefliger, Young, Berry, Crass, Netherlands R. Ch., Concg. O, Jochum.

Harnoncourt's version, using male voices only and period instruments, dates from 1971. This is a fresh, brisk tour through Bach's most dramatic choral work, helped by the light, distinctive narration of Kurt Equiluz and the bright singing of the Viennese choristers, men and boys. Soloists from the Vienna Boys' Choir sing the soprano and alto arias, and within its chosen approach this remains a positive and characterful reading, vigorous if not as resilient as some more recent performances using period instruments. The sound in the CD transfer is excellent.

The Concertgebouw under Jochum offer a relatively conventional interpretation of this work. The performance has some quite outstanding contributions from the soloists, particularly from Giebel and Haefliger, and some eloquent instrumental playing. As one would expect from Jochum, there is a splendid warmth and musical spontaneity about the set, which was recorded in a spacious acoustic and has considerable breadth of tone. It is not, however, particularly concerned with authenticity; the forces are of traditional size and the continuo role is divided between harpsichord and organ. Nevertherless there is much to enjoy and admire here, for the transfer to CD has improved both the immediacy of the sound and the projection of the performance.

St Matthew Passion, BWV 244.

(M) *** EMI CMS7 63058-2 (3). Pears, Fischer-Dieskau, Schwarzkopf, Ludwig, Gedda, Berry, Hampstead Parish Church Ch., Philh. Ch. & O, Klemperer.

(M) **(*) Decca 414 057-2 (3) [id.]. Pears, Prey, Ameling, Höffgen, Wunderlich, Krause, Stuttgart Hymnus Boys' Ch., Stuttgart CO, Münchinger.

(M) ** Teldec/Warner 2292 42509-2 (3) [id.]. Equiluz, Esswood, Sutcliffe, Bowman, Rogers, Ridderbusch, Van Egmond, Schopper, Regensburger Boys' Ch., King's College, Cambridge, Ch., VCM, Harnoncourt.

While it certainly will not appeal to the authentic lobby, Klemperer's 1962 Philharmonia recording of the *St Matthew Passion* represents one of his greatest achievements on record, an act of devotion of such intensity that points of style and interpretation seem insignificant. Klemperer's way is to take the chorales slowly, with pauses at the end of each line; he makes no concessions to recent scholarship on the question of introducing ornamentation. There is a matchless team of soloists, with Peter Pears at his peak in the role of Evangelist and Fischer-Dieskau deeply expressive as Jesus. The Philharmonia Choir sings with the finest focus. The whole cast clearly shared Klemperer's own intense feelings, and one can only sit back and share them too, whatever one's preconceptions.

Münchinger's direction does not attain the spiritual heights of an interpretation such as Klemperer's, but his version is consistently fresh and alert, and it has the degree of authenticity of its period (1965) – although much has happened to Bach performances since then. All the soloists are excellent, and Peter Pears shows that no tenor of his generation rivalled his insight as the Evangelist. Elly Ameling is sweet-toned and sensitive. The recording is first class, clear and brilliant and very well balanced, with the chorus sounding incisive and well defined, with just the right degree of weight. Some may object to the deliberate closeness with which the voice of Hermann Prey as Jesus has been recorded.

Harnoncourt's vocal sound remains unique in its total reliance on male voices (including boy trebles); the choral singing is incisive and lightweight. Among the soloists, Karl Ridderbusch and Paul Esswood are outstanding. Some of the other contributions are less reliable, and the use of boy trebles for the soprano arias produces a strangely detached effect, although the singing itself is usually technically good. Vivid recording.

St Matthew Passion: Arias and choruses.

(M) *** DG Dig. 435 089-2; *435 089-4* [id.]. Bonney, Monoyios, Von Otter, Chance, Crook, Hauptmann, Monteverdi Ch., L. Oratory Junior Ch., E. Bar. Soloists, Gardiner.

As with the *Christmas oratorio*, Gardiner's highly recommendable version of the *St Matthew Passion* is not just for period-performance enthusiasts, and this 66-minute sampler readily demonstrates the dramatic intensity of the music-making and the excellence of the recording, made in 1988 at The Maltings, Snape. A list of the contents is all the information we are offered about the music; the notes concentrate on the conductor.

Collections and vocal collections

'The world of Bach': (i) *Brandenburg concerto No. 2;* (ii) *Suite No. 2: Minuet & Badinerie. Suite No. 3: Air.* (iii) *Toccata & fugue in D min., BWV 565; Chorale: Wachet auf;* (iv) *Cantata No. 12: Sinfonia.* (v) *Cantata No. 147: Jesu, joy of man's desiring.* (i; vi) *Christmas oratorio: Opening chorus.* (vii) *Mass in B min. : Agnus Dei.* (i; viii) *St Matthew Passion: Final chorus.*
(B) *** Decca 430 499-2; *430 499-4* [id.]. (i) Stuttgart CO, Münchinger; (ii) ASMF, Marriner; (iii) Peter Hurford; (iv) SRO, Ansermet; (v) St John's College, Cambridge, Ch., Guest; (vi) Lubeck Ch.; (vii) Ferrier; (viii) Stuttgart Hymnus-Chorknaben.

An enjoyable concert of Bach favourites, well laid out for continuous listening, which could tempt the novice to explore further. The cast-list is strong, with Münchinger at his best in the *Second Brandenburg* and the splendid choruses. Kathleen Ferrier's contribution is particularly welcome. The tape would provide excellent in-car entertainment.

Arias and choruses from: *Christmas oratorio; Mass in B min.; St John Passion; St Matthew Passion.*
(M) **(*) DG 431 703-2; *431 703-4* [id.]. Argenta, Kwella, Nichols, Von Otter, Chance, Blochwitz, Bär, Hauptmann, Monteverdi Ch., E. Bar. Soloists, Gardiner.

Although it is hardly possible to sample Bach's four masterpieces properly in 62 minutes, the excerpts here are well laid out to provide a reasonable balance of contrast. Beginning, understandably, with the joyful opening chorus from the *Christmas oratorio*, the programme then moves to the *Agnus Dei* from the *Mass in B minor*, with Michael Chance movingly expressive, and back to the *Christmas oratorio* again, before Anne Sofie von Otter's *Buss und Reu* from the *St Matthew Passion*. Patrizia Kwella and Mary Nichols then join together for the duet, *Et in unum Dominum*, from the *Mass in B minor*, followed by the double chorus, *Osanna in excelsis*, and so on. Such distinguished music-making is undoubtedly rewarding when the sound is excellent too.

Arrangements: Bach–Stokowski

Adagio, BWV 564; Chorales: Christ lag in Todesbanden, BWV 4; Komm süsser Tod, BWV 478; Chorale prelude & fugue: Wir gläuben all' an einen Gott, BWV 680; Fugue in G min., BWV 578; Passacaglia & fugue in C min., BWV 582–3.
(M) ** Chan. CHAN 6532; *MBTD 6532* [id.]. Sydney SO, Robert Pikler.

The recording here is brighter and cleaner, if less sumptuous, than on Stokowski's own Czech disc (currently withdrawn by Decca). Robert Pikler's very free treatment of the famous *Toccata and fugue* will not convince everyone, and it is the chorales which come off best here, with the playing pleasingly expressive.

Baermann, Heinrich (1784–1847)

Adagio for clarinet and orchestra.
(M) **(*) Decca 417 643-2; *417 643-4* [id.]. Boskovsky, V. Octet (members) – BRAHMS: *Quintet* **(*); MOZART: *Quintet.* **

Heinrich Baermann's rather beautiful *Adagio* was once attributed to Wagner. Boskovsky is particularly languorous and well accompanied and recorded.

Balakirev, Mily (1837–1910)

Symphony No. 1 in C; Tamara (symphonic poem).
(M) *** EMI CDM7 63375-2 [id.]; *EG 763375-4*. RPO, Beecham.

This is a splendid symphony with a highly original first movement, a sparkling scherzo, an agreeably lyrical *Andante* and a breezy finale. It is an extended piece (40 minutes) but Balakirev's material and treatment can easily sustain the length, particularly when the performance is as persuasive as Beecham's. Admittedly Karajan was more dynamic and passionate in his old mono recording, but Beecham offers many felicities and he coaxes the sinuous oriental melodies of the slow movement with characteristically stylish languor. The early (1955) stereo has responded quite well to the CD face-lift: there is plenty of colour and atmosphere, although ideally one needs a great amplitude of string-tone. *Tamara* was recorded a year earlier and the mono sound-balance compares very favourably with the stereo in the *Symphony*. The performance has the characteristic Beecham panache; there is also flamboyance and subtlety, and he is especially fine in conveying the bitter-sweet atmosphere of the work's close.

Islamey (oriental fantasy).
(M) *** EMI CDM7 69125-2; *EG 769125-4*. Andrei Gavrilov – TCHAIKOVSKY: *Piano concerto No. 1* etc. **(*)
(M) (**(*)) Decca mono 425 961-2 [id.]. Julius Katchen – LISZT: *Funérailles* etc; MUSSORGSKY: *Pictures.*(**(*))

(BB) (*) Naxos Dig. 8.550044 [id.]. Jenö Jandó – MUSSORGSKY: *Pictures* etc. *

Gavrilov's dazzling account of Balakirev's fantasy is outstandingly charismatic. It is well recorded too; but unfortunately it comes in harness with a performance of the Tchaikovsky *B flat minor Concerto* which is rather less convincing.

Recorded in more than tolerable sound in 1954, Julius Katchen offers some pretty dazzling playing in Balakirev's remarkable display-piece. He was a notable musician and still only in his twenties when he made this recording.

Jenö Jandó is a gifted Hungarian pianist of the younger-to-middle generation, but he makes very heavy weather of this famous display piece. Not really recommendable, though the recording as such is acceptable enough.

Bantock, Granville (1868–1946)

Fifine at the fair (tone poem No. 3).

(M) (***) EMI mono CDM7 63405-2 [id.]. RPO, Sir Thomas Beecham – BAX: *Garden of Fand;* BERNERS: *Triumph of Neptune.* (***)

Bantock's *Fifine at the fair* (based on a Browning poem about man's inconstancy when tempted by feminine allure) is now almost the only piece by which the composer is remembered. Beecham always had a soft spot for it and his advocacy is so persuasive that one could wish for the piece to be restored to the repertoire. Certainly the famous clarinet solo, representing the nymphet heroine hovering over her intended lover in the shape of a butterly, is played most delectably by Jack Brymer. Later there is a lovely melody for veiled strings which is given wonderful luminosity, despite the early (1949) recording. Elsewhere, and notably in the fairground music, the sound is a bit confined and opaque, but it is full and not edgy, and one is readily seduced by the Beecham magic. The CD transfer makes the very most of the 78-r.p.m. master.

Barber, Samuel (1910–81)

Adagio for strings.

(M) *** DG Dig. 427 806-2; *427 806-4*. LAPO, Bernstein – BERNSTEIN: *Overture Candide; West Side Story; On the Town* ***; GERSHWIN: *Rhapsody in blue.* **(*)

(M) *** DG Dig. 431 048-2; *431 048-4* [id.]. LAPO, Bernstein – COPLAND: *Appalachian spring* ***; GERSHWIN: *Rhapsody in blue.* **(*)

Bernstein's powerfully expressive and deeply felt reading of Barber's *Adagio* was (appropriately) reissued just before his death. It has an expansively restrained, elegiac feeling, but his control of the climax – in what is substantially a live recording – is unerring. Bernstein's recording is available either coupled with Gershwin and some of his own music or with Copland's most famous ballet suite.

(i) *Adagio for strings, Op. 11;* (ii) *Essay No. 2 for orchestra; Music for a scene from Shelley; Serenade for strings, Op. 1;* (ii; iii) *A Stopwatch and an ordnance map, Op. 15;* (iv) Chorus: *Let down the bars, O Death!* (ii; v) *A Hand of Bridge* (chamber opera), *Op. 35.*

(M) *** Van. 08.4016.71 [OVC 4016]. (i) I Solisti di Zagreb, Antonio Janigro; (ii) Symphony of the Air, Golschmann; (iii) with Robert De Cormier Chorale; (v) with Neway, Alberts, Lewis, Maero; (iv) Washington Cathedral Ch., Callaway.

An admirable and highly rewarding anthology of works by a composer whose *Adagio for strings* has wrongly overshadowed his achievement elsewhere. The Hungarian performance of that famous piece is full of intensity: even if it moves away a little too quickly from the opening mood of serene melancholy, the playing is very compelling. It is the concise nature of Barber's writing that comes out in the other six works, yet the warmth of emotion is always clear, even in the early *Serenade* (1929) and especially in the haunting Shelley piece, inspired by *Prometheus Unbound* from which Barber quotes on the score ('Hearest thou not sounds i' the air which speak the love of all articulate beings?'). The *Essay* has a weight of expression beyond its time-length of fractionally over 10 minutes, and the brief but powerful chorale addressed to Death is no less musically succinct. *A Stopwatch and an ordnance map* proves to be a moving piece inspired by a Spender poem on the Spanish Civil War; and most strikingly concise of all is the so-called 'chamber opera', *A Hand of Bridge*, lasting exactly 9½ minutes. The libretto by Menotti brilliantly exploits the cross-currents of a bridge game, and Barber matches it with memorably effective music. Excellent singing and playing throughout, and a balance of warmth and vitality from Golschmann makes this collection stand out from other Barber records; the 1960 recording, vivid and with plenty of ambience, has been transferred very effectively to CD.

Medea (ballet): suite.

(M) *** Mercury 462 016-2 [id.]. Eastman-Rochester O, Howard Hanson – GOULD: *Fall River legend* etc. ***

Although the composer made a mono LP of the score, this was the first stereo recording of the *Medea suite*, which he said 'follows roughly the form of a Greek tragedy'. The influence of Stravinsky is clear and this pungent score contains some of Barber's most intensely serious music, as well as some of the most expressive. As with all good ballets, however, the rhythmic element is vital. Hanson's performance is both polished and dramatic, and the brilliant 1959 Mercury recording has astonishing clarity and vivid presence.

Summer music, Op. 31 (for woodwind quintet).
(M) **(*) Sony SMK 46250 [id.]. Members of the Marlboro Festival – NIELSEN: *Wood-wind quintet*; HINDEMITH: *Octet*. **

Barber's delightful *Summer music* is sensitively played by these artists who capture its air of tenderness and melancholy very well. Those who admire the sound produced by John de Lancie will enjoy the oboe playing here. The balance could perhaps have placed them a little more distantly and given a little more space round them, but the 1981 sound-quality is very acceptable and the coupling valuable.

Piano sonata, Op. 26.
(M) **(*) BMG/RCA GD 60415; *GK 60415* [60415-2-RG; *60415-4-RG*]. Van Cliburn – DEBUSSY: *Estampes* etc. **; MOZART: *Piano sonata No. 10*. **

Barber's *Sonata* was an almost mandatory repertoire piece for pianists in the 1960s and '70s. Van Cliburn's recording of it is pretty masterly and, although the sound could be more ingratiating and have a warmer ambience, it is still acceptable. It has greater sonority though not more virtuosity than the 1951 Horowitz account. Van Cliburn has refinement and intelligence to commend him, and readers with a special interest in the work should make a point of hearing him.

(i) *Andromache's farewell;* (ii) *Dover Beach;* (iii) *Hermit songs;* (iv) *Knoxville: summer of 1915.*
(M) (***) Sony mono/stereo MPK 46727 [id.]. (i) Arroyo, NYPO, Schippers; (ii) Fischer-Dieskau, Juilliard Qt; (iii) Leontyne Price, composer; (iv) Eleanor Steber, Dumbarton Oaks O, William Strickland.

This collection of vintage recordings makes a splendid mid-priced Barber compendium, representing four of his finest vocal works, all in superb performances. The two older recordings – of *Knoxville* and the *Hermit songs* – are in mono, dating from the early 1950s; but the sound, limited in range, vividly captures the voices, with the composer a most persuasive piano accompanist for the young Leontyne Price. Eleanor Steber in *Knoxville* may not quite match the wonderfully atmospheric sound that Price received for her RCA record, but it is still hauntingly evocative. Fischer-Dieskau's recording of the early *Dover Beach* is better known, a fine reading; but most vivid of all is the ripely romantic scena, *Adromache's farewell*, with text taken from Euripides' *The Trojan Women*, a superb vehicle for Martina Arroyo at her finest. Excellent CD transfers. No texts are provided but words are exceptionally clear.

Vanessa (opera): complete.
(M) *** BMG/RCA GD 87899 (2) [7899-2-RG]. Steber, Elias, Resnik, Gedda, Tossi, Met. Op. Ch. & O, Mitropoulos.

For long *Vanessa* was looked down on as plush and old-fashioned, but it is a work of much charm and warmth. It inhabits much the same civilized world as Strauss or Henry James. Although it has not held the stage, its melodic freshness and warmth will ensure a reversal of its fortunes some day. This, its only recording so far, was made at the time of its first performance in 1958, but no apologies are needed for its quality; it stands the test of time as well as does the opera itself. Eleanor Steber is in good voice in the title-role, as are Gedda as Anatol and Resnik as the old Baroness. In fact the first-production cast has no real weakness, and the orchestral playing under Mitropoulos is wholly committed; it is good to have this lovely opera back, sounding better than ever.

Barrios, Augustin (1885–1944)

Aconquija; Aire de Zamba; Le catedral; Cueca; Estudio; Una limosna por el amor de Dios; Madrigal (Gavota); Maxixa; Mazurka appasssionata; Minuet; Preludio; Un sueño en la floresta; Valse No. 3; Vallancico de Navidad.
(M) *** Sony SBK 47669 [id.]. John Williams – PONCE: *Folia de España*. ***

Agustin Barrios is a little-known Paraguayan guitarist and composer who had the distinction of making (in 1909) the first known recording of a guitar. His music essentially belongs to the previous century; its invention is fresh, if sometimes ingenuous, and the pieces here are well varied in style. In the expert hands of John Williams the collection provides a very entertaining recital, ideal for late-evening listening. Try the charming opening *Le catedral* (sweet but not sugary) or the irresistible *Sueño en la floresta*, where Williams creates a breathtaking haze of fluttering figurations that remind one of Tarrega's *Recuerdos de la Alhambra*. The recording is excellent. Although the guitar is closely balanced, there is plenty of ambience and the CD transfer is very realistic, with minimal analogue background noise. The remarkable extended set of Ponce *Variations* added for the CD reissue brings the total playing time up to 77 minutes.

Bartók, Béla (1881–1945)

Concerto for orchestra.
(M) *** Decca 417 754-2 [id.]. Chicago SO, Solti – MUSSORGSKY: *Pictures.* ***

Concerto for orchestra; Music for strings, percussion and celesta.
(M) **(*) BMG/RCA GD 60175 [60175-2-RG]. Chicago SO, Fritz Reiner.
(BB) *(*) Naxos Dig. 8.550261 [id.]. Belgian R. & TV PO (Brussels), Alexander Rahbari.

Solti gave Bartók's *Concerto for orchestra* its compact disc début. The upper range is very brightly lit indeed, which brings an aggressive feeling to the upper strings. This undoubtedly suits the reading, fierce and biting on the one hand, exuberant on the other. Superlative playing from Solti's own Chicago orchestra, and given vivid sound.

Reiner's version of the *Concerto for orchestra* was recorded in 1955, but the sound is unbelievably good, spacious and vivid. The performance is most satisfying, surprisingly straightforward from one brought up in Central Europe but with plenty of cutting edge. The *Music for strings, percussion and celesta*, recorded three years later, suffers from a forward balance which prevents any true pianissimo quality, even in the first movement. Moreover Reiner tends to iron out some of Bartók's complicated speed changes. However, the performance has plenty of atmosphere and grip and is by no means to be ignored.

Rahbari directs the Belgian orchestra in a warm and comfortable, rather than a brilliant, performance of the *Concerto for orchestra.* Though ensemble is not perfect, the impulse gives a feeling of live performance, with the night music of the slow movement beautifully atmospheric, helped by warmly reverberant sound. There is some first-rate solo playing from the woodwind, and the brass and percussion come over with satisfying weight. The *Music for strings, percussion and celesta* makes the ideal coupling; but, even more taxing in its technical demands, it brings a rougher performance, not always biting enough, but again warmly atmospheric in the slow third movement. At super-bargain price it deserves a qualified recommendation.

Concerto for orchestra; Dance suite; The Miraculous Mandarin: suite.
(M) *** Decca 425 039-2; *425 039-4* [id.]. LSO, Solti.

There will be many who prefer Solti's earlier (1965) LSO version of the *Concerto for orchestra*, for the 1960s' recording – outstanding in its day – shows its age only very marginally in the string-tone; in all other respects it is of high quality, and the Kingsway Hall affords a pleasing warmth of colouring. The performance has all the fire and passion one could wish for, but also a touch more of wit and idiosyncrasy than the later, digital, Chicago version (see above). There is more spontaneity, too, than in the later, digital account and one senses Solti's Hungarian upbringing more readily here, for he allows himself certain rubato effects not strictly marked in the score, absorbing the inflexions of Hungarian folksong, very much an influence of Bartók's last-period lyricism. The inclusion of two fill-ups is most welcome. The title, *Dance suite*, may suggest something rather trivial, but the beauty of Bartók's inspiration in this product of the early 1920s (generally his most dissonant period) lies in the way one can appreciate it on many different levels, especially when the performance is so strong and fiery. The streak of ruthlessness in Solti's make-up that sometimes mars performances of less barbaric music is then given full rein in *The Miraculous Mandarin suite*, recorded with comparable vividness and colour two years earlier, and again benefiting from the Kingsway Hall ambience.

(i) *Concerto for orchestra;* (ii) *Dance suite; 2 Portraits, Op. 5; Mikrokosmos* (orch. Serly): *Bourrée; From the diary of a fly.*
(M) *** Mercury 432 017-2 [id.]. (i) LSO; (ii) Philharmonia Hungarica, Dorati.

This generous, 71-minute Mercury compilation consists of two of Mercury's most highly regarded LPs. Dorati's electrifying version of the *Concerto for orchestra* dates from 1962 and many collectors still regard it as the account by which all later versions are to be judged. Dorati secures outstandingly brilliant and committed playing from the LSO, who open the work evocatively and combine bite with a fiery ardour in the outer movements. With the central sections strongly characterized – the *Elegia* touching and the *Giuoco della coppie* genial and bright-hued – and an exhilaratiing finale – the brass producing a spontaneous burst of excitement near the close – this can be strongly recommended. The recording, made in Wembley Town hall, shows characteristic expertise of balance. The rest of the programme was recorded in 1958 in the Grosse Saal of the Vienna Konzerthaus, which affords Dorati's fine orchestra of Hungarian émigrés plenty of body without blurring outlines. They play these highly attractive genre pieces with striking tonal vigour, and the luminous intensity of the strings and brass in particular is enhanced by the hall acoustics. Erwin Ramor is the soloist in the first of the *Two Portraits* and he plays his expressive movement with great beauty and purity of tone and with a sense of colour which suits the music's romantic feeling but without becoming voluptuous. Tibor Serly's orchestrations of two movements from *Mikrokosmos* are highly effective: the first shows Bartók in an almost elegant mood of neo-classicism, contrasting with the vignette of the buzzing fly which gets swatted at the end.

Piano concertos Nos. 1–3.
(M) *** Ph. 426 660-2. Stephen Kovacevich, LSO or BBC SO, C. Davis.

(i) *Piano concertos Nos. 1–3; Rhapsody for piano and orchestra; Concerto for orchestra.*
(M) *** DG 427 410-2 (2) [id.]. (i) Géza Anda, Berlin RSO, Fricsay.

(i) *Piano concertos Nos. 1–3*; (ii) *Sonata for 2 pianos and percussion.*
(M) *** Decca Dig./Analogue 425 573-2 (2) [id.]. Vladimir Ashkenazy; (i) LPO, Solti; (ii) Vovka Ashkenazy, D. Corkhill, Andrew Smith.

Kovacevich's direct, concentrated readings of the three *Piano concertos* come at mid-price in this generous coupling on a Philips Silver Line reissue. Though No. 2 was recorded (with the BBC SO) in 1968, and the other two in 1975, the sound is bright and clear, giving extra bite to the performances, although the effect of the original resonance remains. Sir Colin Davis accompanies sensitively and vigorously, with lifted folk-rhythms in No. 1 sharply pressed home and the violent finale exhilarating, with its many unexpected changes of tempo expertly controlled. After the fierceness of the first two, Kovacevich seems intent on countering the idea that No. 3 is a facile work, with the central *Adagio religioso* played with hushed dedication between spiky outer movements, giving concentrated intensity to compare with late Beethoven. The thrust of the scherzando passages in the first movement has a lively wit, and the finale, at a relatively fast and exuberant tempo, registers the 3/8 marking far more clearly than usual. At mid-price, this disc is hard to beat.

Ashkenazy's versions of both the *First Concerto* and the *Sonata* (with his son, Vovka) are tough, even aggressive performances, biting, never relaxing, spectacularly caught in (1984) digital sound with the widest range of dynamics. The *Second* and *Third Concertos*, recorded four years earlier, are analogue, but the recording, although reverberant, is comparably vivid and present. With the Slavonic bite of the soloist aptly matching the Hungarian fire of the conductor, the readings of both works are urgently involving and incisive, and these two concertos, from very different periods in Bartók's career, are made to seem far closer kin than usual. Tempi tend to be fast, while slow movements bring hushed inner concentration, beautifully captured in Decca's atmospheric recording. If anything, the *Third Concerto* is even more gripping than the *Second.*

Anda's recordings of the Bartók *Concertos* and the *Rhapsody*, which is attractively volatile, have acquired classic status. Anda seems ideally cast as soloist and Fricsay is a natural Bartókian. The performances are refined yet urgent, incisive but red-blooded too. The recording from 1960–61 has been vividly enhanced by the CD transfers. Fricsay's *Concerto for orchestra* was recorded in 1957 and is a first-class example of DG's expertise in the pre-stereo era. The Berlin Radio orchestra plays with considerable virtuosity, especially in the finale, and the pairs of instruments in the second movement combine wit with finesse. A most enjoyable performance and no apologies for the sound.

(i) *Piano concerto No. 1;* (ii) *The Miraculous Mandarin* (suite); *2 Portraits, Op. 5.*
(M) ** Sony MPK 46446 [id.]. (i) Serkin, Columbia SO, Szell; (ii) Phd. O, Ormandy.

Serkin is at his best here, finding the right combination of drama, aggressiveness and implied emotion, and he appreciates, as does Szell, that many of the effects, particularly in the fascinating slow movement, need subtlety as well as strength. The finale has great dash and bite. The recording is bold and forward but not without atmosphere. Anshel Brusilow, concertmaster of the Philadelphia, is the soloist in the first of the *Two Portraits* and he gives a gorgeously romantic reading of a piece which was written for a Swiss violinist, Stefi Geyer, with whom Bartók was then in love. Ormandy and his orchestra are equally at home in this work, and they then make the most of the grotesquerie of the second piece, a fast, almost bitter waltz. Predictably, Ormandy also draws a brilliant, polished performance of *The Miraculous Mandarin* from his players, though here the reverberation clouds the louder music, despite the close-up balance.

Viola concerto; Violin concerto No. 1; (i) *Rhapsodies Nos. 1–2.*
(M) *** EMI CDM7 63985-2 [id.]. Sir Yehudi Menuhin, New Philh. O, Dorati; (i) BBC SO, Boulez.

Menuhin was closely associated with Bartók in the last few years of the composer's life; he made the pioneering records of the 1938 *Second*

Concerto with Dorati and the Dallas Symphony Orchestra in 1946 and recorded it again in 1967. Here he plays the earlier concerto that Bartók wrote for Stefi Geyer. The work's two-movement form is not entirely satisfactory, for the romantic, post-Straussian first movement does not match the more spiky and sometimes disjointed finale, yet the commitment and creative artistry of Menuhin reconcile much of the unevenness. The *Viola concerto* is an even less finished example of Bartók's inspiration, although it comes from the very end of his career. The sketches merely were what existed at the time of the composer's death; however, Tibor Serly, who had worked closely with Bartók, fitted them together and constructed the outline of what Bartók undoubtedly intended. But clearly Bartók would have drawn the threads together more and filled out the rather sketchy ideas for orchestral accompaniment. The drawing-together process is helped enormously by an interpreter such as Menuhin with his strongly creative imagination: he plays the *Adagio religioso* central movement with characteristic nobility of feeling, and he and Dorati make much of the Hungarian dance rhythms of the finale. The mid-1960s Kingsway Hall recording has plenty of atmosphere, with the vivid remastering brightening the original sound. There is a comparably earthy, peasant manner in Menuhin's playing of the two *Rhapsodies*, and it is matched by Boulez's approach, warm and passionate rather than clinical. Menuhin's air of relaxation and authentic tang are well caught by the recording, made at Abbey Road in 1969, which has good ambience as well as vividness. The soloist is balanced rather close, and the remastering again is brightly lit in the treble; this affects mainly the orchestral violins, which have a degree of shrillness above the stave. However, the balance responds to the controls, and this remains one of Menuhin's most worthwhile reissues.

Violin concertos Nos. 1 and 2.
(M) *** Decca Dig./Analogue 425 015-2; *425 015-4* [id.]. Kyung Wha Chung, Chicago SO or LPO, Solti.

Decca's mid-price issue in the Ovation series brings a generous and apt coupling of two earlier recordings, No. 1 in digital sound done in Chicago in 1983, No. 2 done in London in 1976 with first-rate analogue sound, well transferred. Though the soloist is rather forwardly balanced, the hushed intensity of the writing, as well as bitingly Hungarian flavours, is caught superbly, thanks to the conductor as well as to the soloist. Though the expressive warmth behind Bartók's writing is fully brought out, there is no sentimental lingering. This leads the field in both works.

(i) *Violin concerto No. 2 in B min.;* (Solo) *Violin sonata.*
(M) (***) EMI mono CDH7 69804-2 [id.]. Yehudi Menuhin; (i) Philh. O, Furtwängler.

Menuhin's coupling of Bartók's two greatest violin works brings together historic recordings from the last days of 78 r.p.m. discs, here beautifully transferred, if with obvious limitations. One hardly associates Furtwängler with Bartók, but here in collaboration with Menuhin he is an inspired, warm interpreter, strongly coordinating a work that needs holding together tautly. Menuhin was also at his most inspired, both in the *Concerto* and in the solo *Violin sonata*, the work which he himself commissioned. This is among the very finest performances that Menuhin has ever put on record: strong, intense and deeply poetic.

Hungarian sketches; Roumanian folk dances.
(M) *** Mercury 432 005-2 [id.]. Minneapolis SO, Dorati – KODÁLY: *Dances; Háry János.* ***

Dorati, himself a Hungarian, provided the pioneer stereo recording of these works, yet the 1956 sound is vivid and full and wears its years very lightly indeed. The Minneapolis orchestra, on top form, provides plenty of ethnic feeling and colour. This is Bartók at his most winningly approachable, and the style of the music-making has an agreeable air of authenticity.

The Miraculous Mandarin (complete ballet).
(M) ** Decca 425 026-2; *425 026-4* [id.]. VPO, Dohnányi – STRAVINSKY: *Petrushka.* **

Dohnányi's direction of *The Miraculous Mandarin*, long regarded as an unusually barbaric score, is clean, precise and often beautiful. It is far less violent and weighty than usual, and not everyone will respond to what could almost be described as an unsuspected neo-classical element in the score. The playing of the VPO is very fine, helped by spacious recording, not very analytical in detail, and a faithful transfer.

4 Orchestral pieces, Op. 12; (i) *The Miraculous Mandarin* (complete ballet), *Op. 19;* (ii) *3 Village scenes.*
(M) *** Sony SMK 45837 [id.]. (i) Schola Cantorum; (ii) Camerata Singers; NYPO, Pierre Boulez.

The *Four Orchestral pieces* was the nearest Bartók came to writing a symphony. The layout is unconventional, with an expansive Prelude, followed by a Scherzo, then an *Intermezzo* and a closing *Marcia funèbre*; but in Boulez's hands there is no doubting the power of the music nor the quality of the invention, and it is surprising that this work (written in 1912 but not orchestrated until 1921) is not better known. The *Three Village scenes – Wedding*, *Lullaby* (with two soloists) and *Men's dance* – have a Stravinskian flavour as well as pungent folk influences: they are colourful and exciting. Boulez proves a strong and sympathetic advocate in all this music, and his approach is surprisingly warm. This is even more striking in *The Miraculous Mandarin*, which is a far more romantic-sounding version than Solti's and also is markedly less incisive. However, the New York orchestra responds with deeply expressive playing and, with spacious recording (originally made in quadrophony), many will prefer it on that account.

(i) *Contrasts. Mikrokosmos*: excerpts.
(M) (***) Sony mono MPK 47676 [id.]. Composer; (i) with Joseph Szigeti, Benny Goodman.

A disc of exceptional documentary interest. *Contrasts* was commissioned by Benny Goodman, at the suggestion of Szigeti; when it arrived in 1938, however, it was in two movements and lasted slightly longer than the eight minutes (or two sides of a 78-r.p.m. record) that the 'King of Swing' had suggested. In 1940 Bartók added a further movement, perhaps with a view to filling four 78 sides, and it was in this form that the three artists made their recording. That same year Bartók recorded 31 pieces from *Mikrokosmos*. Though his playing is handsomely represented on Hungarian discs (there were some thirteen LP sides taken from commercial and radio sources), these performances are among the best-recorded and are indicative of the wide range and delicacy of keyboard colour that Bartók commanded. The sound is surprisingly good, given that it is over half a century old! Bartók and Szigeti recorded some other works at this time (among them Beethoven's *Kreutzer*, the Debussy *Violin sonata* and Bartók's own *Second Sonata*) which we hope will appear shortly. An indispensable issue.

OPERA

Bluebeard's Castle (sung in Hungarian).
(M) **(*) DG 423 236-2 [id.]. Varady, Fischer-Dieskau, Bav. State O, Sawallisch.

This performance is warmly expressive rather than biting, as you might expect from Sawallisch and the Bavarian State Orchestra. Varady and Fischer-Dieskau give a Lieder-like intensity to the exchanges, full of refined detail. The voices are more forward than on some versions; but the separation from the orchestra is far cleaner than it was on LP and the sound of the Bavarian State Orchestra has satisfying weight. Libretto and notes are included.

Bax, Arnold (1883–1953)

The Garden of Fand (symphonic poem).
(M) (***) EMI mono CDM7 63405-2 [id.]. RPO, Sir Thomas Beecham – BANTOCK: *Fifine at the fair;* BERNERS: *Triumph of Neptune.* (***)

The Garden of Fand, with its magically evocative opening and ecstatic central episode, found a ready advocate in Sir Thomas Beecham, who related its atmospheric feeling to the music of Delius. It is played superbly here, although the 1947 recording is a bit confined and two-dimensional; it is very well transferred to CD, however. We look forward to the reappearance of Barbirolli's rapturously ardent, early stereo version; meanwhile this is an essential disc for Beecham fans, not least because of the couplings.

Malta G.C. (complete); *Oliver Twist: suite* (film-scores).
(M) *** ASV Dig. CDWHL 2058; *ZCWHL 2058*. RPO, Kenneth Alwyn – ARNOLD: *The Sound Barrier.* ***

Both these film-scores are in the form of a series of miniatures; on the whole, *Oliver Twist* stands up more effectively without the visual imagery. The use of concertante piano is effective in a brief nocturnal portrayal of Oliver and later in a sequence called *Oliver and Brownlow. Oliver and the Artful Dodger* and *Fagin's romp* both give rise to effective and inventive scherzando writing, and the finale brings a resplendent Waltonian jubilation. In *Malta G.C.* much of the score is concerned with wartime action: it is the gentler music, the *Intermezzo* and *Reconstruction* and again the final apotheosis, that brings the most memorable writing. Kenneth Alwyn conducts the RPO with fine flair and commitment, Eric Parkin is the brief soloist and the recording is brilliantly colourful and vivid, if at times a little lacking in the richest sonority. Originally issued by Cloud Nine, this is welcome back in the catalogue at mid-price, with Arnold's *Rhapsody* as a bonus.

Symphonies 1–7.
(M) *** Chan. Dig. CHAN 8906/10 [id.]. LPO or Ulster O, Bryden Thomson.

Chandos have repackaged the cycle of seven symphonies on five CDs. Nos. 3 and 7 have discs to themselves, while Nos. 1 and 6 share a disc. Only the *Fourth* is split between two discs: the first two movements are placed after the *Fifth Symphony* and the finale precedes the *Second Symphony*. Inevitably, the fill-ups that accompanied the symphonies first time around are sacrificed, notably *Tintagel*, originally coupled with the *Fourth Symphony*, and *Christmas Eve*. But, of course, it makes better sense for those primarily interested in these richly imaginative symphonies to pay for five rather than seven CDs, and the recordings continue to make a strong impression. Bax's *First Symphony* began life as a piano sonata in 1921. Bryden Thomson is completely inside the idiom and is boldly expressive, relaxing his pace when the natural flow of the music suggests it; and the results carry total conviction. Bax's splendid scoring is heard to excellent advantage in the Chandos recording.

The *Second Symphony* comes from 1924–6; it is a rich and engrossing work, closely related to nature. The strength of Bryden Thomson's account lies in its breadth and sweep: its evocation of and identification with the natural and spiritual world of this composer. He seems totally at one with Bax's sensibility and secures orchestral playing of total commitment. As with other issues in the series, the recording is of spectacular clarity and definition.

The *Third* is arguably the best, though the *Second* also has strong claims to be so regarded. The opening is one of the composer's finest inspirations and has a searching, visionary quality about it, while the slow movement is wholly unlike anything else in English music. Bryden Thomson is closely attuned to the Bax idiom, and it would be difficult to overpraise him and his fine players. The symphony is Bax's longest at nearly 50 minutes. The Chandos recording does full justice to Bax's sumptuous and opulent orchestral textures.

The *Fourth Symphony* was written in 1930–31; the seascapes that the score brings to mind are mainly those of the coast and islands of the Western Highlands where Bax spent each winter during the 1930s. The ideas may not be quite as memorable as those of the *Third* and *Fifth*, but the moods are still powerful and the colours vivid. The performance is altogether splendid. The CD is a demonstration disc even by the high standards Chandos have established in this field.

With the *Fifth* Bryden Thomson again proves himself completely inside the music's idiom, catching the breadth and sweep of Bax's inspiration and identifying himself consistently with the composer's natural and spiritual world. The playing of the LPO is totally committed and responsive and the Chandos recording well up to the high standards of the house.

The *Sixth Symphony* of 1934 is the last major work to find Bax in the fullness of his creative power. Bryden Thomson is scrupulously attentive to the dynamic and agogic markings of the score, and the LPO respond admirably. First-class recording, well up to the high standard of this series.

The *Seventh Symphony* comes from 1938, when Bax's creative fires were beginning to burn less brightly, but the slow movement, *In Legendary mood*, is particularly fine, and there is an epic breadth about the first which is impressive. The playing of the LPO for Bryden Thomson is exemplary in its passion and refinement in the *Symphony*. The recording has first-rate presence and body.

Beethoven, Ludwig van (1770–1827)

Piano concertos Nos. 1–5.

(M) *** Sony M3K 44575 (3) [id.]. Perahia, Concg. O, Haitink.

(i) *Piano concertos Nos. 1–5. 6 Bagatelles, Op. 126; Für Elise.*

(M) ** Decca 425 582-2 (3) [id.]. Ashkenazy (i) Chicago SO, Solti.

Piano concertos Nos. 1–5; (i) *Choral Fantasia, Op. 80.*

(M) *** EMI CMS7 63360-2 (3) [Ang. CDMC 63360]. Daniel Barenboim, New Philh. O, Klemperer, (i) with John Alldis Ch.

(B) **(*) Ph. 422 937-2 (3). Alfred Brendel, LPO, Haitink, (i) with LPO Ch.

(i) *Piano concertos Nos. 1–5; Piano sonata No. 32 in C min., Op. 111.*

(B) *** DG 427 237-2 (3) [id.]. Kempff; (i) BPO, Leitner.

This music always has greater depth than any single interpretation can fathom but, among recent versions, the Perahia brings us as close to the heart of this music as any. These are masterly performances, and it is good that their more competitive price will bring them within the reach of an even wider audience. The sound is full and well balanced.

Kempff's accounts offer an additional price advantage since, although the individual issues are all at mid-price, the set is offered at bargain price; the magisterial account of Op. 111 remains coupled with the *Emperor*. The performances all come from the early 1960s and still sound remarkably good for their age, and the wisdom Kempff dispensed is as fresh as ever. He opts for his own cadenzas in Nos. 2–4, which makes a refreshing change – and very authoritative they are. No collector should restrict him or herself to a single version of these masterpieces for no one pianist can uncover all their profundities, and the Kempff set is undoubtedly among the handful that occupy classic status in the catalogue.

The combination of Barenboim and

Klemperer, recording together in 1967/8, is nothing if not stimulating and, for every wilfulness of a measured Klemperer, there is a youthful spark from the spontaneously combusting Barenboim. The recordings were made much more quickly than usual, with long takes allowing a sense of continuity rare on record. The spontaneity easily compensates for any minor shortcomings (in the *Emperor*, for example, Barenboim has some slight fluffs of finger), but the concentration is formidable and especially compelling in the slow movements, whether in the earliest concerto, No. 2 – here given an interpretation that is anything but Mozartian, splendidly strong – or in the later concertos. No. 3 brings the most obviously wilful slow tempi but, with fine rhythmic points from soloist and orchestra, the result is still vivid and compelling. No. 4 is anything but a delicate, feminine work, with basic tempi measured enough to avoid the need for much slowing, when the lyrical counter-subjects emerge. The *Choral Fantasia* too is given an inspired performance, with the weaknesses of Beethoven's writing wonderfully concealed when the music-making is so intense. The remastered sound is vivid and clear and quite full, but orchestral tuttis are less refined than in the Kovacevich/Davis Philips recordings.

Given an artist of Brendel's distinction, it would be surprising if his analogue set with Haitink were not artistically rewarding, even if there are moments (for instance in the *Emperor*) when one's mind returns to his earlier Vox Turnabout recordings, which sounded less studied. Generally, however, there is no lack of spontaneity and the recordings are full and well balanced in the best Philips tradition. The perspective between soloist and orchestra is very well judged and the piano tone itself is lifelike, clean and well focused throughout its register.

The partnership of Ashkenazy and Solti is fascinating. Where Solti is fiery and intense, Ashkenazy provides an introspective balance. Ashkenazy brings a hushed, poetic quality to every slow movement, while Solti's urgency maintains a vivid forward impulse in outer movements. Sometimes, as in the *C minor Concerto*, one feels that the music-making is too intense. Here a more relaxed and lyrical approach can find in the first movement a warmth that Solti misses. But for the most part the listener is given an overriding impression of freshness, and the *Emperor* performance, while on the grandest scale, has a marvellous individual moment in the first movement when Ashkenazy lingers over the presentation of the second subject. The Chicago orchestral playing is characteristically brilliant, and the one real snag is the very bright recording, which on CD is made to sound uncomfortably fierce at times, while the piano timbre is not as full in sonority as Decca usually provides.

(i) *Piano concertos Nos. 1–5. Piano sonatas Nos. 14 in C sharp min. (Moonlight), Op. 27/2; 18 in E flat, Op. 31/3; 21 in C (Waldstein), Op. 53; 22 in F, Op. 54; 23 in F min., Op. 57; 26 in E flat (Les Adieux), Op. 81a; 31 in A flat, Op. 110; 32 in C min., Op. 111; 32 variations in C min., WoO 80.*

(M) *(**) EMI mono/stereo CZS7 67379-2 (5) [id.]. Claudio Arrau, (i) with Philh. O, Galliera.

The concertos were all recorded in the late 1950s and early 1960s and, with the exception of the *Fourth*, which was made in 1955, are in very well-focused stereo. There is some considerable magic, for example the coda of the first movement of the *C minor Concerto* or the introduction to the slow movement. Most of the sonatas are mono, with the *E flat*, Op. 31, No. 3, dating from as early as 1947; even the late sonatas, Opp. 101, 110 and 111, which were issued in 1958 having been recorded not long before, are mono. The exceptions are the stereo *Appassionata* and the little *F major*, Op. 54. In some ways these are fresher performances than the later, magisterial accounts with Haitink and the Concertgebouw Orchestra on Philips. Most of the sonatas were recorded in the dry acoustic of Abbey Road which – as transferred to CD – makes the sonority about the stave sound brittle and much of the middle range seem wanting in timbre. But the playing is unfailingly illuminating, and readers investing in the set will feel enriched by this or that insight. At times Arrau's rubato can seem idiosyncratic (in Chopin and Schubert), but there are few such instances here. Strongly recommended to admirers of this great artist – the performances are nearly all touched with distinction and the dry studio recording in the sonatas should not deter collectors, though it does inhibit a full three-star recommendation.

(i) *Piano concerto No. 1 in C;* (ii) *Triple concerto for piano, violin & cello, Op. 56.*

(M) **(*) DG 435 096-2; *435 096-4* [id.]. (i) Eschenbach; (ii) Zeltzer, Mutter, Ma; BPO, Karajan.

Eschenbach and Karajan choose a slow tempo for the first movement and, though the concentration holds the attention, the result here is closer to a chamber approach. A beautiful performance of the slow movement and a lightweight finale. The reading is attractive and interesting but, in its concentration on refinement, it misses any sort of greatness, although the recording does not lack weight in the orchestra. However, the *Triple concerto* coupling is generous and apt as, after Karajan's formidable opening crescendo – within his very positive opening tutti – the soloists seem rather small-scale. Yet there are benefits from the unity brought by the conductor when each of these young players has a positive contribution to make, no less effectively when the 1979 recording balance – for once in this work – does not favour the solo instruments unduly. The urgency, spontaneity and – in the slow movement – the depth of expressiveness make for an enjoyable version, well transferred to CD.

Piano concerto No. 1 in C, Op. 15; Rondo in B flat, WoO 6.
(BB) **(*) Naxos Dig. 8.550190 [id.]. Stefan Vladar, Capella Istropolitana, Wordsworth.

Stefan Vladar's performance of Beethoven's *C major Concerto* is among the finest in his Naxos super-bargain series. The first movement has striking freshness and spontaneity, and the spacious *Largo* makes an eloquent contrast with the sparkle of the joyful finale. Excellent accompaniments from Wordsworth and the Capella Istropolitana, alert and sympathetic and full of spirit. The coupling, however, is not generous, although here too the playing is strong in personality. Throughout, the digital recording is fresh, full and clean.

Piano concertos Nos. 1 in C, Op. 15; 2 in B flat, Op. 19.
(B) *** Ph. 422 968-2; *422 968-4* [id.]. Kovacevich, BBC SO, Sir Colin Davis.
(M) *** DG 419 856-2 [id.]. Kempff, BPO, Leitner.
(M) *** Ph. 420 882-2; *420 882-4*. Brendel, LPO, Haitink.
(M) *** Decca Dig. 425 012-2 [id.]. Radu Lupu, Israel PO, Mehta.

These first two works, ideally coupled, bring characteristically crisp and refreshing readings from Stephen Kovacevich with Sir Colin Davis, which convey their conviction with no intrusive idiosyncrasies. Kovacevich opts for the longest and weightiest of Beethoven's own cadenzas for the first movement of No. 1, and his account of the finale has rarely been matched in its sparkle and exhilaration, with wonderfully clear articulation. In No. 2, the pianist plays with a weight and intensity to heighten such visionary passages as the hushed quasi-recitative at the end of the slow movement, while keeping the whole reading in scale with early Beethoven. That these model performances and recordings come on the cheapest Philips label is something to marvel at.

Kempff's coupling is second to none, and the digitally remastered recording sounds remarkably fresh and vivid. The sense of repose is notable in the slow movements, the very profundity of Kempff's sense of calm creating an aura of great serenity. Leitner's contribution, too, is strong and sympathetic, and the orchestral response is memorable throughout. In the finales the playing sparkles joyously. The balance between piano and orchestra is particularly natural.

There is a spontaneity in Brendel's 1979 studio recordings with Haitink which eluded his later partnership with Levine in the concert hall. Nowhere is this more compelling than in the *First Concerto*, though both he and Haitink convey both the strength and charm of the *Second*, not least in the capriciousness of the finale, even if the slow movement could have been treated more gently. With very good recording, admirers of Brendel need not hesitate.

Lupu's readings with Mehta favour fast, resilient speeds. Slow movements are treated with lightness too, and throughout it is the pianist who dominates. Lupu's playing has sparkle and sensitivity and its poetry is ever apparent. These are marvellously articulated readings, and if the playing of the Israel Philharmonic is sometimes not very refined it is always sympathetic. Those looking for a mid-priced digital coupling of these works will find the balance is excellently judged and the sound both natural and clear.

Piano concertos Nos. 1 in C, Op. 15; 4 in G, Op. 58.
(M) **(*) EMI Dig. CD-EMX 2177; *TC-EMX 2177*. Kovacevich, Australian CO.

Unlike Kovacevich's superb EMI account of the *Emperor*, also with the Australian Chamber Orchestra, this coupling of the *First* and *Fourth Concertos* offers performances that do not quite match the masterly versions he recorded earlier with Sir Colin Davis for Philips. Controversially Kovacevich arpeggiates the first chord of No. 4, but that might be thought to enhance his thoughtful, characteristically searching manner. Later on, that movement loses some of the brightness and point that are typical of this pianist, though the slow movement is as poised and dedicated as before, and the finale is more relaxed. There are fewer reservations to be made about No. 1, though the fast speed for the finale runs the danger of becoming breathless. In both *Concertos* the solo instrument is not focused quite clearly enough over the orchestra.

Piano concertos Nos. 2; 5 (Emperor), Op. 73.
(M) **(*) Decca 417 703-2 [id.]. Ashkenazy, Chicago SO, Solti.

(BB) **(*) Naxos Dig. 8.550121 [id.]. Stefan Vladar, Capella Istropolitana, Barry Wordsworth.

In both concertos the partnership of Ashkenazy and Solti works well, with the vivid orchestral articulation matched by the responsive solo playing. The slow movement of No. 2 is strikingly beautiful and its hushed close creates a memorable feeling of serenity before the sparkling finale. The *Emperor* is an excitingly dramatic performance on the largest possible scale, yet one which is consistently imbued with poetry. The remastered recording is brilliantly vivid, the piano clear and believably focused, but the orchestral textures are leaner than the originals, and some will want a more ample sound in the *Emperor*.

Vladar's fine account of the *Emperor* (see below) is also available coupled with an infectiously vigorous performance of the *Second Concerto*, again very well accompanied by Wordsworth and his chamber group. The sound is full and open, though the 'twangy' Bösendorfer keyboard timbre may be a drawback for some listeners.

Piano concerto No. 3 in C min., Op. 37.
(M) ** EMI CDM7 69013-2 [id.]. Sviatoslav Richter, Philh. O, Muti – MOZART: *Piano Concerto No. 22.* **

Richter's 1978 version may be controversial – like its Mozart coupling – but clearly a master is at the keyboard and Muti draws a sympathetic accompaniment from the Philharmonia players. The performance is consciously wayward, essentially lyrical, but it has undoubted authority, and the remastered recording sounds well.

Piano concertos Nos. 3 in C min., Op. 37; 4 in G, Op. 58.
(B) *** Ph. 426 062-2 [id.]. Kovacevich, BBC SO, Sir Colin Davis.
(M) *** DG 419 467-2 [id.]. Kempff, BPO, Leitner.
(M) **(*) Ph. 420 861-2. Brendel, LPO, Haitink.
(BB) **(*) Naxos Dig. 8.550122 [id.]. Stefan Vladar, Capella Istropolitana, Barry Wordsworth.
(M) *(**) Tuxedo TUXCD 1016. Brendel, V. Pro Musica O or V. State Op. O, Wallberg.
(BB) ** Pickwick PWK 1153. Julius Katchen, LSO, Piero Gamba.
(M) ** Decca 417 740-2 [id.]. Ashkenazy, Chicago SO, Solti.

The Philips versions of Nos. 3 and 4 from Kovacevich and Sir Colin Davis would be top recommendations even if they cost far more. In both works the playing of the soloist has a depth and thoughtful intensity that have rarely been matched, and in his concentration he totally avoids the sort of wilfulness which becomes obtrusive on repeated hearing. The *Third Concerto* brings a first movement which erupts in a commanding account of the big cadenza and, after a central *Largo* taken very slowly and intensely, Kovacevich plays the finale with sparkling clarity. His account of the *Fourth Concerto* has a similar combination of strength, dedication and poetry. The refined Philips recording has transferred admirably to CD: the balance is altogether excellent.

The Kempff/Leitner performances on DG bring an outstanding mid-priced recommendation. The digital remastering has clarified the sound perceptibly without loss of bloom. In the *C minor Concerto* Kempff's approach is relatively measured, somewhat serious in mood; but in its unforced way, happily lyrical, brightly sparkling in articulation, it is refreshingly spontaneous. Again, in the *Fourth Concerto* Kempff's delicacy of fingerwork and his shading of tone-colour are as effervescent as ever, and the fine control of the conductor ensures the unity of the reading. In both concertos the recording of the orchestra is bright and resonant, the piano tone warm as well as clear.

On Philips, Brendel in No. 3 provides an easy, relaxed account of the first movement, spontaneous-sounding, with the timpani raps of the coda even more measured and mysterious than usual. If the other two movements are less tense, with the finale thrown off in a mercurial manner, this adds up to a strong, persuasive performance. No. 4 brings a contrastingly strong, even tough reading, not as immaculate as one might expect on detail, but producing an almost impressionistic thrust of urgency in the first movement. The slow movement is rapt in its simplicity, and the finale is treated almost flippantly, with some slips of ensemble which suggest the immediacy of live music-making, rather than the extra care of the studio. The remastered sound is impressively firm and realistic.

Vladar's cycle of Beethoven concertos for Naxos is recorded with a Bösendorfer piano, and the bright, rather dry sound in the instrument's higher tessitura stems from the character of this particular instrument. It adds classical bite to performances which are dramatic and fresh, with the slow movement of No. 3 strongly contrasted in its expressive feeling. The brightness in the piano's upper range seems less obvious in the *G major Concerto* – in all other respects the sound is very good in both works – and its essential lyricism is well understood by soloist and conductor alike. At super-bargain price, this is certainly recommendable.

Brendel's 1959 Vox performances (originally issued on Turnabout in the UK) are very welcome back to the catalogue. Both interpretations are deeply satisfying, with the most delicate tonal and rhythmic control married to intellectual strength. The slow movement of No. 3 combines depth with poetry, and the finale is engagingly jaunty. In No. 4 the orchestral accompaniment is unimaginative: the first-movement tutti, for example, is rhythmically stodgy; but Brendel's control of phrase and colour is such that his reading rides over this impediment and the contrasts of the slow movement are strongly and poetically made. It is noteworthy that he uses the second of the cadenzas written for the work, one not generally heard. In spite of the shrill, thin orchestral strings (cleanly remastered), many will count these among the finest Beethoven concerto recordings Brendel has committed to disc.

Julius Katchen's account of the *C minor Concerto* dates from 1959, the *G major* from five years later. Both were very well recorded (by Decca), though the remastering reveals their early dates by the sound of the fortissimo violins; the piano image, however, is most real, and there is a good balance and plenty of ambient warmth. The first movement of No. 3 takes a little while to warm up but, when Katchen enters, the performance springs splendidly to life. The slow movement is sustained with considerable tension, its beauty readily conveyed, and there is plenty of vigour and sparkle in the finale. Katchen is less penetrating in No. 4. His virtuosity is remarkable and the performance is by no means without feeling, but Kempff and Kovacevich find more expressive depth in this work than he does. Nevertheless, this is an enjoyable coupling and undoubtedly good value in the lowest price-range.

The Ashkenazy/Solti combination also brings playing full of character. The fierce intensity of the orchestral tuttis of the outer movements of the *C minor* may be counted controversial, emphasized by the coarsely lit recording. But the strength of the playing is in no doubt, and the slow movement is finely done, the contrasts stronger than usual. A more relaxed atmosphere pervades the *G major*; here the contrast between the personalities of soloist and conductor is most striking in the interplay of the *Andante*, where Solti's gruff boldness contrasts so tellingly with Ashkenazy's melting response. The 1973 recording produces an attractive piano image, but the orchestra is a bit fierce.

(i) *Piano concerto No. 3 in C min. Piano sonatas Nos. 8 in C min. (Pathétique), Op. 13; 17 in D min. (Tempest), Op. 31/2.*

(M) *** DG 435 097-2; *435 097-4* [id.]. Kempff, BPO, Leitner.

For most collectors, Kempff's coupling with the *G major Concerto* will seem the most desirable way of acquiring the C minor work; however, if the two named sonatas are preferred, the performances show Kempff's mastery of the solo repertoire. The recording of the solo piano in the *Sonatas* is clean and truthful but a little dry.

Piano concerto No. 4 in G, Op. 58.

(M) *** Sony MYK 44832 [MYK 37762]. Leon Fleisher, Cleveland O, Szell – MOZART: *Piano concerto No. 25.* ***

Fleisher's is a magical performance, memorable in every bar, to rival even Kempff's version. Starting with the genuine tension of a live performance and displaying throughout a commanding control of argument from soloist and conductor alike – the orchestral playing is superb – this is among the finest recordings of the work ever committed to disc. Fleisher's half-tones are most beautiful and his fingerwork is dazzling without ever giving the slightest impression of mere slickness. In some ways this scores over Kempff's more idiosyncratic approach, although the 1959 CBS recording is rather less agreeable than the DG balance. It has, however, been skilfully remastered for CD and can be made to sound well.

(i) *Piano concertos No. 4 in G, Op. 58;* (ii) *5 in E flat (Emperor), Op. 73.*

(B) *** EMI CDZ7 62607-2. Gieseking, Philh. O, Galliera.

(M) **(*) Decca Dig. 430 704-2; *430 704-4* [id.]. Vladimir Ashkenazy, VPO, Mehta.

(M) ** DG 435 098-2; *435 098-4* [id.]. Pollini, VPO, Boehm.

These are the recordings that Gieseking made in stereo in September 1955 and which were never issued at the time. Galliera's conducting is not always imaginative, but the Philharmonia gives strong and refined support for Gieseking's magnetic readings. Power was never his watchword, any more than it was with Kempff; yet the concentration and poetry in his playing, the ability to turn a phrase or passage-work in a totally individual way, make this record a fascinating document. He is at his finest in No. 4, where the delicacy of his playing is a constant delight. The slow movement of the *Emperor* tends to be over-inflected, beautiful though the playing is. The stereo sound is very good for its period, generally clear and with plenty of presence.

The relaxation and sense of spontaneity which mark Ashkenazy's Vienna cycle bring a performance of the *Fourth Piano concerto* which may lack something in heroic drive but which, in its relative lightness, never loses concentration and brings a captivating sparkle to the finale. Though this may not be as powerful as Ashkenazy's earlier, Chicago recording with Solti, and Mehta is a less individual accompanist, it is fresher and more natural, with fewer expressive hesitations. The spaciousness of the first movement of the *Emperor*, combined with clarity of texture, is most persuasive, and so is the unusually gentle account of the slow movement. Only in the finale does Ashkenazy's easy and relaxed approach bring a slackening of tension to reduce the impact of the reading. Excellent recording, full and brilliant; if this disc does not represent a first choice, the coupling remains enjoyable and rewarding.

There is an aristocratic feeling about Pollini's 1976 account of the *Fourth Concerto*, with classical poise and poetic sensibility delicately balanced. Boehm is a faithful accompanist, but the end result is a little chilly; and the same feeling is generated by the playing in the 1978 *Emperor concerto.* The clarity of Pollini's vision and his dedication are never in doubt, and the strong and wise accompaniment by Boehm and the Vienna Philharmonic provides considerable compensation. But the slow movement is elegant, lacking the depth which the finest versions give it, and the finale is urgent and energetic rather than joyful. The analogue orchestral recording is full and lively, the piano image brilliant and truthful but close. Both recordings were made in the Musikverein Grosser Saal.

Piano concerto No. 5 in E flat (Emperor), Op. 73.
(M) (***) BMG/RCA mono GD 87992 [7992-2-RG]. Horowitz, RCA Victor SO, Reiner – TCHAIKOVSKY: *Piano concerto No. 1.*(***) ❀
(M) **(*) EMI Dig. CDD7 63892-2 [id.]; *ET 763892-4*. Yuri Egorov, Philh. O, Sawallisch – MOZART: *Piano concerto No. 20.* **
(BB) **(*) Pickwick PWK 1146. Friedrich Gulda, VPO, Horst Stein.

(i) *Piano concerto No. 5 in E flat (Emperor). 2 Rondos, Op. 51/1–2; Piano sonatas Nos. 19 in G min.; 20 in G, Op. 49/1–2.*
(M) **(*) Decca Dig. 425 025-2; *425 025-4* [id.]. Radu Lupu, (i) Israel PO, Mehta.

(i) *Piano concerto No. 5 in E flat (Emperor);* (ii) *Piano sonata No. 15 in D (Pastoral), Op. 28.*
(BB) **(*) Naxos Dig. 8.550290 [id.]. (i) Stefan Vladar, Capella Istropolitana, Barry Wordsworth; (ii) Jenö Jandó.

(i) *Piano concerto No. 5 (Emperor); Piano sonata No. 28 in A, Op. 101.*
(M) **(*) Ph. 426 106-2. Casadesus; (i) Concg. O, Hans Rosbaud.

(i) *Piano concerto No. 5 in E flat (Emperor); Piano sonata No. 30 in E, Op. 109.*
(B) *** Ph. 422 482-2; *422 482-4*. Kovacevich; (i) LSO, C. Davis.

Piano concerto No. 5 (Emperor); Piano sonata No. 32 in C min., Op. 111.
(M) *** DG 419 468-2; *419 468-4* [id.]. Kempff, BPO, Leitner.

Piano concerto No. 5 in E flat (Emperor); Grosse Fuge in B flat, Op. 133.
❀ (M) *** EMI Dig. CD-EMX 2184; *TC-EMX 2184*. Stephen Kovacevich, Australian CO.

(i) *Piano concerto No. 5 (Emperor);* (ii) *Overtures: Coriolan; Leonora No. 2.*
(BB) ** LaserLight Dig. 15 523 [id.]. (i) Anton Dikov, Sofia PO, Emil Tabakov; (ii) Dresden PO, Herbert Kegel.

(i) *Piano concerto No. 5 in E flat (Emperor)*; (ii) *Choral Fantasia, Op. 80.*
(M) *(**) Tuxedo TUXCD 1038 [(d.) Turnabout PVC 7108]. (i) Brendel, V. Pro Musica O, Mehta; (ii) (mono) Wührer, Ac. Chamber Ch., VSO, Clemens Krauss.

Originally Stephen Bishop, later Bishop-Kovacevich, and now plain Kovacevich, this great pianist is unsurpassed today as an interpreter of this most magnificent of concertos. His superb account for Philips, now on Concert Classics, has set a model for everyone and, with its sonata coupling, remains highly recommendable. This new Eminence version, recorded at the Sydney Opera House in 1989 with the soloist directing from the keyboard, is recognizably from the same inspired artist, though speeds are consistently faster and the manner is sharper and tauter. So the first movement is now more thrillingly urgent, while presenting the same high contrast of bravura and poetry, along with absence of mannerism. The central *Adagio* is similarly rapt and pure, but the faster speed allows the soloist's melodic line to flow more easily, while the tension in the finale is even greater than before, with the faster speed still allowing the dotted rhythms to skip infectiously. The piano sound on the digital recording is aptly brighter and more faithful than on the Philips, making this a first choice for this much-recorded work, even with no allowance for price. For fill-up, Kovacevich conducts a comparably electrifying account of the *Grosse Fuge.*

On Philips, with alert, sharp-edged accompaniment from Sir Colin Davis, Kovacevich gives a clean, dynamic performance of the outer movements, then in the central slow movement finds a depth of intensity that completely explodes any idea of this as a lighter central resting-point. Even so he avoids weighing down the simple plan with unstylistic mannerisms: he relies only on natural, unforced concentration in the most delicate, hushed tones. After such raptness, the panache of the finale is all the more exhilarating. The 1969 sound begins to show its age, with the bass a little boomy and the piano rather clattery on fortissimos, though well defined. With volume set high, the recording is still very agreeable, and the magic of the performance is never impaired. For coupling there is one of the most deeply perceptive performances of a late Beethoven sonata on record. The recording, made in 1978, could be brighter but presents a natural piano tone over the full dynamic range.

Kempff's version remains very desirable. Although it is not on an epic scale, it has power in plenty and excitement, too. As ever, Kempff's range of tone-colour is extraordinarily wide, from the merest half-tone as though the fingers were barely brushing the keys to the crisp impact of a dry fortissimo. Leitner's orchestral contribution is of high quality and the Berlin orchestral playing has vigour and warmth. Some reservations need to be made about the sound of the digitally remastered CD. The bass is somewhat over-resonant and the orchestral tuttis are slightly woolly; the piano timbre is natural, but the slight lack of firmness in the orchestral focus is a drawback though it does not seriously detract from the music-making. Opus 111 is undoubtedly a great performance and makes a generous coupling.

Horowitz's fine record was made in Carnegie Hall in 1952 and few apologies need be made for the sound, which is full and resonant, although the piano timbre seems to harden a little at the opening of the finale. The *Emperor* was the work given in 1933 when the pianist was soloist for the first time with Toscanini. However, here Reiner is at the helm and the two great artists form a splendid partnership. Horowitz's virtuosity is always put at Beethoven's service and, for all the excitement of the outer movements, it is the *Adagio* that stays in the mind, classical in line, tender in poetic feeling.

Radu Lupu's *Emperor* was the first version to be issued on compact disc. Lupu gives a performance which, while not lacking strength, brings thoughtfulness and poetry even to the magnificence of the first movement, with classical proportions made clear. The slow movement has delicacy and fantasy, the finale easy exhilaration, though neither conductor nor orchestra quite matches the soloist's distinction. The upper range has the characteristically bright sound of Decca's early digital recordings, but there is plenty of weight and the orchestral layout is convincing; if the piano image seems a trifle near, it gives a commanding presence to the solo playing. The encores are generous and are played most beautifully: the two *Rondos* are immaculately done and are full of charm; the *Sonatas* are persuasive in their sense of scale, while still showing Lupu's characteristic sensibility. They are all very pleasingly recorded; though the *Sonatas* have an analogue source, their sound is truthful in both balance and colour.

This was Yuri Egorov's first concerto recording, made in 1982; it gives a refreshingly direct but still individual account of the opening allegro, helped by authoritative conducting from Sawallisch. The finale too has splendid drive and attack, with full digital sound. The slow movement, however, is the controversial point: it is taken at a very measured *Adagio* which might have flowed better had Egorov adopted a more affectionate style of phrasing. For its reissue it has been generously coupled with a good but less distinctive version of Mozart's *D minor Concerto.*

Casadesus and Rosbaud give a most beautiful interpretation, satisfyingly detailed and refined, and with a wonderfully serene Adagio. The Op. 101 *Sonata* is also impressively done, with the recording reasonably full and clear throughout. However, Kovacevich and Sir Colin Davis in a similar coupling are even more searching, and they cost less.

Stefan Vladar's super-bargain version on Naxos is both commanding and exciting. The bold opening flourish immediately indicates the very characteristic Bösendorfer timbre. The performance, while powerfully direct, still has many individual touches to indicate the degree of imagination at work both from the soloist and in Wordsworth's strong, sympathetic accompaniment. The *Adagio*, which is persuasively shaped, may lack something in idiosyncrasy, but there is a real sensitivity here and the finale is appropriately vigorous and joyful. The sound is splendidly full, with the solo instrument dominating, yet with the orchestra well in the picture. For an encore Jenö Jandó offers an appealing performance of the *Pastoral sonata*, also well recorded. The first two movements are a trifle subdued, but the scherzo is nicely buoyant and the finale catches the spirit of the work's sobriquet engagingly.

With its dramatically recorded opening (the tone of the Bösendorfer piano extremely vivid), Gulda's account of the first movement does not lack a robust quality, yet the passages in his reading that re-echo in the memory are the gentle and poetic ones, whether the half-tones of the second subject in the first movement or the serene phrases of the *Adagio*, given here with real *Innigkeit*. After this, the lively joy of the finale is the more telling. The Decca recording has been remastered brightly, and the orchestral sound may need just a little smoothing; although there are more individual performances available, this Pickwick bargain reissue will not disappoint the impulse-purchaser.

On Tuxedo, Brendel gives a splendidly bold and vigorous reading and he is well suppported (in 1959) by Zubin Mehta and the Vienna Pro Musica Orchestra. As for the (originally Vox/Turnabout) recording, the orchestral sound leaves much to be desired although (as in the coupling of Nos. 3 and 4) the piano image is convincing. But the performance generates a spontaneity which is less apparent in his later versions for Philips; it may be a reading without idiosyncrasy, but it is strong in style and personality. The beginning of the finale is prepared beautifully and the main rondo theme merges vividly and with great character. As a coupling, we are given the famous Vox pioneering mono recording of the *Choral Fantasia*, with enthusiastic if rough-and-ready vocal contributions from the Vienna Academy Chamber Choir, but with Friedrich Wührer undoubtedly powerful in the opening section. Fair recording.

Anton Dikov gives a strong, forthright performance of the *Emperor*. The music-making is energetically committed, even if it lacks the subtlety of Kovacevich's versions; nor does the playing of the Sofia orchestra, although very good, have the refinement of the LSO under Davis. Dikov's thundering octaves just before the recapitulation in the first movement are arresting indeed, while the score's gentler moments are also brought out well, and the slow movement has poise and a sense of line. The finale is appropriately joyful. Kegel's *Overtures* are exciting, and the Dresden orchestra displays greater polish and a full sonority – one wishes they could have accompanied the *Concerto*. But with vivid, modern digital sound, this whole record is invigoratingly enjoyable.

(i) *Piano concerto No. 5 (Emperor);* (ii) *Violin concerto, Op. 61;* (iii) *Fidelio: overture, Op. 72b* (CD only: (iv) *Leonora overture No. 2, Op. 72a;* (iii) *Leonora overture No. 3, Op. 72b*).

(B) *** DG Compact Classics 413 145-2 (2); *413 145-4* [id.]. (i) Eschenbach, Boston SO, Ozawa; (ii) Schneiderhan, BPO, Jochum; (iii) Dresden State O, Boehm. (CD only: (iv) BPO, Jochum).

Eschenbach gives a deeply satisfying interpretation of the *Emperor*, helped by the equally youthful urgency of his accompanist, Ozawa. With thoughtfulness, power and bravura nicely balanced, this interpretation is very impressive. Although detail is not as sharp as in some versions, the sound has fine weight and richness, with the piano timbre appropriately firm and bold. The recording dates from 1974, whereas the coupling (also available separately – see below) is from 1962. Schneiderhan's stereo version of the *Violin concerto* is among the greatest recordings of this work: the serene spiritual beauty of the slow movement, and the playing of the second subject in particular, have never been surpassed on record; the orchestra under Jochum provides a background tapestry of breadth and dignity. It is a noble reading with an innate sense of classicism, yet the first movement offers wonderful lyrical intensity. As an added point of interest, Schneiderhan uses cadenzas that were provided for the transcription of the work for piano and orchestra. The first-movement cadenza is impressive in scale and adds a solo part for the timpani. This makes a very real bargain for tape collectors. The pair of CDs offer the extra pair of overtures which are well worth having, particularly Jochum's *Leonora No. 2*. In either format this is an outstanding coupling.

(i) *Piano concerto No. 5 in E flat (Emperor)*; (ii) *Triple concerto for violin, cello and piano in C, Op. 56.*

(M) *** Sony SBK 46549 [id.]. (i) Leon Fleisher, Cleveland O, Szell; (ii) Stern, Rose, Istomin, Phd. O, Ormandy.

A unique coupling, for this is one of Sony's 'Essential Classics' that is justly named. Leon Fleisher is a pianist who worked with special understanding in the Szell regime at Cleveland, and by any count his reading of the *Emperor* is impressive for its youthful dramatic vigour, so the advantages of youth and experience are combined with exceptional intensity. Yet in one important detail this version relaxes more than its rivals. Szell has noted that at the very end of the slow movement Beethoven's autograph asks for pizzicato strings half a bar after the point where the indication appears in printed scores. With Szell, after a lyrical span of poised beauty, the first indication of the magical key-change comes gently on a sustained bowed note, instead of with the usual 'plonk', quite an important point. The 1961 recording is very bright, but the Severance Hall ambience ensures fullness too, and the bold presence given to the piano produces a riveting moment when Fleisher plays Beethoven's commanding octave passage in the first movement. For the coupling we move to Philadelphia and a recording made in the Town Hall there, three years later. Stern, Rose and Istomin – three friends who invariably reveal their personal joy in making music together – make a wonderful trio of soloists. Though Stern is undoubtedly the leader of the group, the dominance over his colleagues is benevolent and the individual expressiveness of each soloist keeps the attention riveted. Ormandy, too, proves to be a marvellous accompanist: his very opening pianissimo is full of tension and he begins the slow movement equally atmospherically, preparing the way for Leonard Rose's magical solo; indeed, the cello solos are so superbly expressive and the concentration of his colleagues so rapt that the movement acquires a depth beyond its spare proportions. The finale brings some wonderfully springy Polacca rhythms that take Beethoven very close to Eastern Europe. Unfortunately the CBS balance, as usual, favours the soloists so that the contrast of their soft playing is endangered; but the performance as a whole is so compelling that it would take a much more serious recording fault to undermine the concentration.

Violin concerto in D, Op. 61.

(M) *** EMI CD-EMX 2069; *TC-EMX 2069*. Yehudi Menuhin, VPO, Silvestri.

(M) (***) EMI mono CDH7 69799-2 [id.]. Yehudi Menuhin, Philh. O, Furtwängler – MENDELSSOHN: *Concerto*.(***)

(M) **(*) BMG/RCA Dig. GD 86536 [RCA 6536-2-RG]. Ughi, LSO, Sawallisch – MENDELSSOHN: *Concerto*. **(*)

(M) **(*) EMI CDM7 69261-2 [id.]. David Oistrakh, Fr. Nat. R. O, Cluytens – BRUCH: *Concerto No. 1*.(***)

(M) ** Sony SBK 47659 [id.]. Francescatti, Columbia SO, Bruno Walter – SIBELIUS: *Concerto*. **

(M) ** Decca Dig. 425 035-2; *425 035-4* [id.]. Kyung Wha Chung, VPO, Kondrashin – BRUCH: *Scottish fantasia*. ***

(i) *Violin concerto in D, Op. 61;* (ii) *Romances Nos. 1 in G, Op. 40; 2 in F, Op. 50.*

❀ (B) *** DG 427 197-2; *427 197-4* [id.]. (i) Schneiderhan, BPO, Jochum; (ii) D. Oistrakh, RPO, Goossens.

(B) *** Ph. 426 064-2; *426 064-4* [id.]. Grumiaux; (i) New Philh. O, Galliera; (ii) Concg. O, Haitink.

(M) *** Ph. 420 348-2; *420 348-4* [id.]. Grumiaux, (i) Concg. O, C. Davis; (ii) New Philh. O, De Waart.

(M) *** DG 435 099-2; *435 099-4* [id.]. Zukerman; (i) Chicago SO; (ii) LPO; Barenboim.

(BB) *** Naxos Dig. 8.550149 [id.]. Takako Nishizaki, Slovak PO (Bratislava), Kenneth Jean.

(i) *Violin concerto in D, Op. 61;* (ii) *Overtures: Coriolan; Creatures of Prometheus.*

(M) **(*) Chan. Analogue/Dig. CHAN 6521 [id.]. (i) Erich Gruenberg, New Philh. O, Horenstein; (ii) CBSO, Weller.

Violin concerto in D, Op. 61; Overture Egmont, Op. 84.

(B) *** Ph. 422 971-2; *422 971-4*. Hermann Krebbers, Concg. O, Haitink.

Schneiderhan's outstanding version of the Beethoven *Concerto* is here available without the Compact Classics coupling of the *Emperor* (see above). David Oistrakh's accounts of the *Romances* are of high quality too, and the remastering is well managed. It is fascinating to compare Oistrakh's strong, aristocratic way with Beethoven with Schneiderhan's pure inspirational lyricism.

Grumiaux recorded the Beethoven *Violin concerto* twice for Philips in stereo, the first occasion in the late 1960s with Galliera in London, and again in the mid-1970s with Sir Colin Davis in Amsterdam. The balance of advantage between the two versions – both among the finest ever committed to disc – is very difficult to resolve, although the earlier version has a price advantage. The Concertgebouw recording is fuller and richer, even if there is not absolute clarity, and there is less background noise. With sharper orchestral ensemble under Davis, the outer movements seem even more impressive than with the New Philharmonia under Galliera. Grumiaux imbues both performances with a spirit of classical serenity. But in the slow movement there is not quite the same sense of repose or of spontaneous magic in the later account. Both discs include the *Romances*, appealingly played, and in each instance the recording is of a slightly different vintage, brighter and clearer.

Another highly recommendable version comes from Zukerman and Barenboim, who take a spacious and persuasive view of the first movement, stretched to the limit but still held in complete concentration. If warmth and tonal richness are the qualities most wanted, then this is the ideal version, with the immaculate playing of the Chicago Symphony Orchestra ripely recorded in 1977. Like Schneiderhan and Grumiaux, Zukerman also offers fine accounts of the two *Romances*, recorded in London three years earlier.

It is good, too, to have Menuhin's first stereo recording with Silvestri back in the catalogue; it is far preferable to his more recent versions with Klemperer and Masur. This is a noble performance, very comparable with his mono record with Furtwängler, but of course the sound is greatly improved. Silvestri is surprisingly classical in his outlook and the VPO provide an accompaniment of great character. Menuhin's warmth and humanity show in his instinctive shaping of phrases, and his slightly slower tempi add breadth and boldness to a design that can easily be spoiled by ill-judged emphasis. His playing in the slow movement is particularly lovely, and the intonation here is rock-steady. The remastering is vividly successful, with the orchestra reasonably full-bodied.

Those looking for a super-bargain, digital version will find that Nishizaki's highly spontaneous performance can measure up to many accounts by more famous names. Helped by a strongly sympathetic backing from the excellent Slovak Philharmonic under Kenneth Jean, her playing is individual yet unselfconscious and has a fresh simplicity of approach which is consistently appealing, while in the first movement, at the close of the Kreisler cadenza, the reprise of the main theme is quite magical. The *Larghetto*, too, is poised and serene, with affectingly gentle embellishments in the variations, and the second subject is as melting as you could wish. The finale is nicely buoyant. The two *Romances* are also very well played, with the *F major* rather more rhapsodic and free than the *G major*. The digital recording, made in the Reduta Concert Hall in Bratislava, is first class, the violin well forward but with the resonantly full orchestral tapestry spaciously caught.

As a soloist Hermann Krebbers has not quite the commanding 'star' quality of David Oistrakh, Menuhin or even Grumiaux, but he plays with an appealing naturalness and a totally unforced spontaneity. In his hands the slow movement has a tender simplicity which is irresistible, and it is followed by a delightfully relaxed and playful reading of the finale. In the first movement Haitink and his soloist form a partnership which brings out the symphonic strength more than almost any other reading. If the balance of the soloist is a shade too close, the recording is otherwise excellent, and it has transferred with vivid fullness to CD.

Recorded only months before the conductor's death, Menuhin's version with Furtwängler is a classic which emerges with extraordinary freshness. The bond between the wrongly reviled conductor and his Jewish champion brought an extra intensity to a natural musical alliance between two inspirational artists, here both at their peak. Rarely if ever has the Beethoven *Violin concerto* been recorded with such sweetness and tenderness, yet with firm underlying strength. With its generous coupling, it is a compact disc which defies the years. One hardly registers that this is mono recording.

Ughi's version has first-class digital recording, realistic and very well balanced: this mid-priced CD is coupled with a strikingly fine performance of the Mendelssohn *Concerto* (also digitally recorded). The performance of the Beethoven is first rate, fresh and unaffected, marked by consistent purity of tone in every register. If the last degree of imagination, of the kind which creates special magic in the slow movement, is missing here, nevertheless this remains well worth considering for those with limited budgets.

David Oistrakh's strong, aristocratic reading dates from 1958, but the EMI recording still sounds well, with a spacious acoustic and resonant orchestral tone. The balance, however, places the soloist unnaturally forward, although he is recorded truthfully. The reading is characteristically assured, the soloist's phrasing and sense of line impeccable; but for some there is a suggestion of aloofness in the slow movement.

Horenstein provides a firm classical backing for Erich Gruenberg, who gives a refined and direct reading of the first movement. His timbre, already small, is thinned down a little by the recording, but the *Larghetto* brings beautiful pianissimo tone, especially at the ethereal reprise, and in the finale the lightness of the solo articulation adds to the spirit of the dance. The analogue orchestral recording has a slight tendency to harshness but the balance is good. Weller's accounts of the two overtures offer fine, modern, digital sound.

Francescatti's recording dates from 1961 and sounds well in its CD transfer; like the other Bruno Walter recordings of this period, the orchestral quality is full, and the vividness on top is supported by a firm, rich bass. Francescatti generally produces a beautiful tone, with a silvery upper register, although his intonation is occasionally slightly suspect. There is much to admire, however, and there are many passages of lyrical beauty in the first movement. The emotional tension is well held. Walter's orchestral contribution is spacious and strong, if with just a hint of heaviness, yet the slow movement is often most beautiful and the finale brings an attractive feeling of the dance. In the last resort this is not among the most memorable versions and the Oistrakh coupling of the Sibelius *Concerto* has less agreeable sound-quality.

Miss Chung gives a measured and thoughtful reading which lacks the compulsion one would have predicted. That is largely due to the often prosaic conducting of Kondrashin. There is poetry in individual moments – the minor-key episode of the finale, for example, which alone justifies the unusually slow tempo – but, with too little of the soloist's natural electricity conveyed and none of her volatile imagination, it must not be counted her final statement on a masterpiece. The early (1979) digital recording, made in the Sofiensaal, was outstanding in its day; the balance is natural, the effect impressively realistic. This has a very generous and desirable (analogue) coupling, but cannot rank high on the list of current recommendations.

(i) *Violin concerto in D;* (ii) *Violin sonata No. 9 (Kreutzer).*
(M) (***) EMI mono CDH7 63194-2 [id.]. Bronislaw Huberman; (i) VPO, Szell; (ii) Ignaz Friedman.

Huberman's is a legendary reading, recorded with George Szell and the Vienna Philharmonic in June 1934. What must strike the modern listener is that – whether or not influenced by the restrictions of short-playing 78-r.p.m. sides – the basic speed for the first movement is markedly faster than on most modern versions; yet there is no feeling of haste, and Huberman's immaculate intonation makes for ravishing sounds, particularly in the topmost register. Rarely has any later recording matched the rapt, sweet intensity of the coda in this version. The lovely third theme in the slow movement brings comparable intensity, though the close balance of the violin, typical of 78 recording, is not helpful, and Huberman, like other violinists of his generation, uses more portamento than is expected nowadays. The account of the *Kreutzer sonata*, which Huberman recorded with Ignaz Friedman in 1930, has similar bite and intensity, though with heavy surface hiss the sound shows its age more, and the piano is backwardly balanced. A generous coupling that gives a superb idea of the artistry of a master violinist long neglected.

(i) *Piano concerto in D* (arr. from *Violin concerto*), *Op. 61;* (ii) *Romances Nos. 1–2, Opp. 40 & 50.*
(M) **(*) DG 429 179-2; *429 179-4* [id.]. (i) Barenboim, ECO; (ii) Zukerman, LPO, Barenboim.

Beethoven's transcription of his *Violin concerto* into this piano version made little or no effort to rework the solo part in pianistic terms. The result is to alter the character of the music, bringing down the emotional scale and substituting charm where in the original there is great spiritual depth. The work could not receive a more dedicated or affectionate performance than it does here: Barenboim makes the most of the limited piano part, and he is delightful in the slow movement. (Incidentally, the special cadenzas featuring the timpani can also be heard in the outstanding Schneiderhan version of the original.) Zukerman's performances of the *Romances* are a welcome makeweight.

Konzertsatz (Concerto movement) in C, WoO 5; Romance No. 1 in G, Op.40.
(M) *** DG 431 168-2; *431 168-4* [id.]. Kremer, LSO, Tchakarov – SCHUBERT: *Konzertstück* etc. ***

The early *Concerto movement in C* reveals Beethoven at twenty writing on an ambitious scale but rarely, if ever, achieving the touches of individuality which mark his mature concertos. The piece is performed in a completion by Wilfried Fischer that is effective enough; and the mixed bag of Schubert which acts as coupling is certainly apt. All the music is beautifully played by Kremer; the 1978 recording, made in the London Sir Henry Wood Hall, has transferred splendidly to CD.

Triple concerto for violin, cello and piano in C, Op. 56.
(B) *** Pickwick Dig. PCD 917. Trio Zingara, ECO, Heath – BOCCHERINI: *Concerto No. 7.* ***
(B) **(*) EMI CDZ7 62854-2; *LZ 762854-4.* David Oistrakh, Knushevitzky, Oborin, Philh. O, Sargent – BRAHMS: *Double concerto.* ***
(B) ** DG 429 934-2 [id.]. Schneiderhan, Fournier, Anda, Berlin RSO, Fricsay – BRAHMS: *Double concerto.* **
(B) ** DG Compact Classics *415 332-4* [id.]. Schneiderhan, Starker, Anda, Berlin RSO, Fricsay – BRAHMS: *Double concerto*; MOZART: *Violin concerto No. 3.* **
(M) *(*) Ph. 426 631-2; *426 631-4.* Szeryng, Starker, Arrau, New Philh. O, Inbal – BRAHMS: *Double concerto.* *(*)

(i) *Triple concerto, Op. 56;* (ii) *Symphony No. 10: First movement* (realized & completed by Barry Cooper).
(M) *** Chan. Dig. CHAN 6501; *MBTD 6501* [id.]. (i) Kalichstein–Laredo–Robinson Trio, ECO, Gibson; (ii) CBSO, Weller.

(i) *Triple concerto, Op. 56; Piano sonata No. 17 in D min. (Tempest), Op. 31/2.*
(M) **(*) EMI CDM7 69032-2 [id.]; *EG 769032-4.* Sviatoslav Richter, (i) with D. Oistrakh, Rostropovich, BPO, Karajan.

The cellist in the Trio Zingara is Felix Schmidt, who is also the soloist in the Boccherini. In the Beethoven *Triple concerto* it is that instrument which continually takes the lead, and Schmidt plays with consistently beautiful, firm and clean tone, well matched by his two partners. It is not just a question of a regular trio working naturally together, but of them jointly – together with the conductor, Edward Heath – creating the illusion of live performance, full of bounce and vigour. At mid-price, in full and vivid digital sound and well coupled with the Boccherini, it makes an excellent recommendation.

The 1984 Chandos version of the *Triple concerto* with three young American soloists is exceptionally well recorded, with problems of balance resolved better than on any other version. The playing is immaculate, and Sharon Robinson, the cellist, takes the lead with pure tone and fine intonation, though both her partners are by nature more forceful artists. A clean-cut, often refreshing view of the work, it is now reissued coupled with Weller's strong version of Barry Cooper's completion of the first movement of Beethoven's projected *Tenth Symphony*, also very well recorded.

The star-studded cast on the EMI recording make a breathtaking line-up, and to have Karajan as well seems almost too good to be true. The results are predictably arresting, with Beethoven's priorities among the soloists well preserved in the extra dominance of Rostropovich over his colleagues. This is warm, expansive music-making that confirms even more clearly than before the strength of the piece. The resonant recording suffers from loss of focus in some climaxes, but this is not too serious. Richter's powerful reading of Beethoven's *D minor Sonata* makes a good coupling.

The EMI Laser recording, with its distinguished alternative Russian solo group, dates from the early days of stereo, but the balance (with Walter Legge producing) is very successful. Sargent does not direct the proceedings with Karajan's flair but he is authoritative and musical, and his soloists make a good team, as well as displaying plenty of individual personality. The slow movement is strikingly eloquent. In EMI's Laser series and with an outstanding version of the Brahms *Double concerto* as coupling, the bargain status is obvious.

The 1960 recording by Anda, Schneiderhan and Fournier was recorded in the Berlin Jesus-Christus Kirche, which means that there is plenty of atmosphere; but the balance is artificial, with the solo players (clearly separated) well forward and with their contribution dynamically nearly matching that of the orchestra, reducing the natural contrast. This gives the solo playing much more presence than that of the competing team on Philips, but Fricsay's vibrant orchestral tuttis have plenty of impact on the remastered CD. The performance has breadth and a genuine grasp of structure, with an eloquent contribution from each of the distinguished soloists. Only in the first movement does one sense a slight want of spontaneity, but the reading undoubtedly has more grip than the Philips/Inbal account. This version is also offered on a DG Compact Classics tape. Coupled with Brahms's *Double concerto* and Mozart's *Violin concerto No. 3*, this is generous value.

The Philips issue has spendidly full and spacious orchestral recording (dating from a decade later), but Arrau and his colleagues are less strongly projected and, by adopting very unhurried tempi, they run the risk of losing concentration. The central brief *Largo* is exquisitely done, and Starker's dedicated and spacious reading of the great cello solo has rarely been matched; but the outer movements, with the solo playing almost on a chamber scale, lack the bite and bravura of the finest rivals.

12 Contredanses, WoO 14; 12 German dances, WoO 8; 12 Minuets, WoO 17; 11 Mödlinger dances, WoO 17.
(BB) *** Naxos 8.550433 [id.]. Capella Istropolitana, Oliver Dohnányi.

It is always a delight to catch Beethoven relaxing and showing how warmly he felt towards the Viennese background in which he lived. These dances were intended for the ballroom; they are innocent in invention and are simply scored, with odd surprises now and then, like the 'Turkish' music (piccolo and percussion) introduced in WoO 8, No. 10, or the sudden entry of the posthorn to close the set; while orchestral horns are used strikingly in the Trio of the Minuet, WoO 17, No. 3. The theme of the *Eroica variations* pops up in the *Contredanse*, WoO 14, No. 7. The excellent Capella Istopolitana group used for the recording seems to be of exactly the right size, and they play the music with light rhythmic feeling, yet with plenty of spirit. Dipped into, this will give pleasure.

OVERTURES

Overtures: The Consecration of the house, Op. 124; Coriolan, Op. 62; The Creatures of Prometheus, Op. 43; Egmont, Op. 84; Fidelio, Op. 72c; King Stephen, Op. 117; Leonora Nos. 1–3, Opp. 138; 72a; 72b; The Ruins of Athens, Op. 113; Zur Namensfeier, Op. 115.
(M) *** DG 427 256-2 (2) [id.]. BPO, Karajan.

Karajan's set of overtures was recorded in the mid- and late 1960s. They are impressive performances that have stood the test of time. They show an imposing command of structure and detail as well as the customary virtuosity one expects from this conductor and the Berlin Philharmonic. The sound is fresh and bright in its remastered format; at Privilege price, this set is excellent value.

Overtures: The Consecration of the House, Op. 124; Coriolan, Op. 62; The Creatures of Prometheus, Op. 43; Egmont, Op. 84; Fidelio,

Op. 72c; King Stephen, Op. 117; Leonora No. 3, Op. 72b; The Ruins of Athens, Op. 113; Zur Namensfeier, Op. 115.
(B) *** Ph. 426 630-2; *426 630-4*. Leipzig GO, Kurt Masur.

This collection shows Kurt Masur and his Leipzig players at their very finest. These performances are more direct than those of Karajan and are wholly satisfying in their strong motivation and lack of mannerism. This is not to suggest they are without individuality: they have a combination of breadth and excitement that communicates readily – *Leonora No. 3* is every bit as gripping as Karajan's version. The Philips recording, from the early 1970s, is of high quality, and the remastering has enhanced its vividness and impact. This generous reissue (71 minutes) acts as a bargain sampler for the Silverline catalogue; but this means that its liner carries details of other records rather than notes about the music.

Overtures: The Consecration of the house, Op. 124; Coriolan, Op. 62; The Creatures of Prometheus, Op. 43; Egmont, Op. 84; Fidelio, Op. 72c; Leonora No. 3, Op. 72b; The Ruins of Athens, Op. 113.
(BB) ** Naxos Dig. 8.550072 [id.]. Slovak PO, Stephen Gunzenhauser.

This was one of Naxos's first recordings in Bratislava, and the Philharmonic Hall is made to sound too reverberant, notably at the very start of the first overture on the disc, *Fidelio*. The other items are affected in varying degrees, but the tension of the performances is never in doubt so that, even with this reservation, such a generous collection of seven overtures in vigorous interpretations, well played, makes an attractive bargain.

Overtures: Coriolan, Op. 62; The Creatures of Prometheus, Op. 43; Egmont, Op. 84; Leonora No. 1, Op. 138; Leonora No. 3, Op. 72b; The Ruins of Athens, Op. 113.
(M) *** Sony Dig. MDK 44790 [id.]. Bav. RSO, C. Davis.

This Sony/CBS CD is very well recorded – the sound is spacious and beautiful, full yet refined, and has a remarkably wide dynamic range. Sir Colin Davis secures playing of distinction from the Bavarian orchestra and, while it was a pity that *Leonora No. 2* was omitted, this remains a distinguished collection. Now reissued at mid-price, it too can be recommended with enthusiasm.

Overtures: Fidelio, Op. 72c; Leonora Nos. 1–3, Opp. 138; 72a; 72b.
(B) ** Pickwick IMPX 9034. Israel PO, Maazel.

Maazel goes for brilliance at all costs, and it is surprising how well the Israeli orchestra copes with the pressure. These performances are certainly exciting, but hard-driven too, and they hardly tell the whole story. The 1962 (originally Decca) recording sounds as if it was made in London rather than in Israel: the sound is full, the ambience resonant, though it does not mask detail. However, as usual with these Pickwick-licensed bargain reissues, the playing time is ungenerous at 42 minutes.

Romances for violin and orchestra Nos. 1 in G, Op. 40; 2 in F, Op. 50.
(B) *** DG Compact Classics 413 844-2 (2); *413 844-4* [id.]. D. Oistrakh, RPO, Goossens – BRAHMS: *Violin concerto* **(*); BRUCH: *Concerto No. 1* ** (CD only: DVOŘÁK: *Concerto* **(*)).

David Oistrakh's performances of the Beethoven *Romances* are of high quality and are very well recorded. If the other works on this DG Compact Classics tape are required, this is good value. The pair of digitally remastered CDs also includes an attractive account of the Dvořák *Concerto*.

SYMPHONIES

Symphonies Nos. 1–9.
(B) *** DG 429 036-2 (5) [id.]. Janowitz, Rössel-Majdan, Kmentt, Berry & V. Singverein (in No. 9), BPO, Karajan.
(BB) **(*) LaserLight Dig. 15 900 (5). Hungarian PO, Ferencsik (with Andor, Szirmay, Korondy, Solyom-Nagy & Budapest Philharmonic Ch. in No. 9).
(M) (**(*)) EMI mono CHS7 63606-2 (5). VPO or Stockholm PO, Furtwängler, (with soloists & Ch. in No. 9).
(M) ** Telarc Dig. CD 80200 (5) [id.]. Soloists, Ch., Cleveland O, Dohnányi.

Symphonies Nos. 1–9; Overtures: Coriolan; Creatures of Prometheus; Egmont; Fidelio; King Stephen; Leonora No. 3.
(M) ** DG 423 481-2 (6) [id.]. VPO, Bernstein (with soloists & V. State Op. Ch. in No. 9).

Symphonies Nos. 1–9; Overtures: Coriolan; The Creatures of Prometheus; Egmont; Fidelio; Leonora No. 3; The Ruins of Athens.
(M) *** DG 429 089-2 (6). Tomowa-Sintow, Baltsa, Schreier, Van Dam, V. Singverein, BPO, Karajan.

Symphonies Nos. 1–9; Overtures: Coriolan; Egmont; Fidelio; Leonora No. 3.
(M) ** Ph. 416 274-2 (6). Leipzig GO, Masur (with soloists and chorus in No. 9).

Symphonies Nos. 1–9; Overtures: Coriolan; Egmont; Leonora No. 3.

(B) *(**) Decca 430 792-2 (6). Lorengar, Minton, Burrows, Talvela, Chicago Ch. (in No. 9), Chicago SO, Solti.

Symphonies Nos. 1–9; Overture Leonora No. 3.
(M) (***) BMG/RCA mono GD 60324 (5) [60324-2-RG]. Farrell, Merriman, Peerce, Scott, Shaw Chorale (in No. 9), NBC SO, Toscanini.

When over the winter of 1961–2 Karajan and the Berlin Philharmonic recorded all nine *Symphonies*, it marked a breakthrough in the history of recording. The project was conceived from the start as a cycle in a way never attempted on record before. It then made its first appearance in boxed format, another important innovation which pointed to the future. Of Karajan's four recorded cycles this is the most consistent and in many ways the most compelling, combining high polish with a biting sense of urgency and spontaneity. There is one major disappointment, in the over-taut reading of the *Pastoral*, which in addition omits the vital repeat in the scherzo. Otherwise these are incandescent performances, superbly played. Designedly, Karajan left the *Eroica* and the *Ninth* till last in the intensive recording sessions, and that helped to give extra power of communication to those supreme masterpieces. On CD the sound is still excellent, the best-balanced in any of his Beethoven series and with a keener sense of presence, helped by the acoustic of the Jesus-Christus Kirche in Berlin. On five CDs at bargain price, this makes outstanding value for money.

Karajan's 1977 cycle is offered on six CDs at mid-price, including the major overtures. Interpretatively his view on Beethoven had changed relatively little, but some differences are significant. The *Eroica* presents the one major disappointment of this cycle, at least in the outer movements, which are faster and slightly rushed, though the *Funeral march* remains measured and direct. As against this, the first movement of the *Pastoral*, angular and tense in the 1962 cycle, has more elegance and joyfulness at tempi barely any slower. Otherwise the middle symphonies remain very much the same in both cycles, although in 1977 finales tend to be a little faster than before. Just as the cycle of 1962 established standards which were hard for any rival to match, so the 1977 cycle, different in emphasis on certain symphonies, is also very satisfying. The cycle is capped by a version of the *Choral Symphony* that is among the finest ever committed to disc. However, in terms of sound the later cycle does not necessarily show an improvement, and for most collectors the earlier set will prove the more rewarding purchase.

With Bernstein's electricity – partly achieved by recording at live performances – matched against the traditional warmth of Viennese playing, the results are consistently persuasive, culminating in a superb, triumphant account of the *Ninth* with a fast, tense first movement, a resilient scherzo, a hushed expansive reading of the *Adagio* and a dramatic account of the finale. Balances are not always perfect, with microphones placed in order to eliminate audience noise, but the results are generally undistracting. The CD transfers, as one would expect, clarify and freshen the sound, removing any gauziness; but they also make the occasional oddities of balance more obvious.

Ferencsik's excellent set of Beethoven *Symphonies* with the Hungarian Philharmonic Orchestra comes on five CDs at super-bargain price. Each has its own individual jewel-case, within a slip-case, and there is adequate documentation. These CDs are almost unbelievably inexpensive and well worth their modest price. The orchestral playing is of good quality, if without quite the finesse or rhythmic resilience of the very finest versions – as is noticeable immediately in the *First Symphony* – but ensemble is always impressive, and the players' undoubted commitment conveys a sense of enjoyment and usually a feeling of spontaneity. Often the playing is really exciting, as in the outer movements of the *Seventh* (a performance which grips from beginning to end) and in the rhythmically strong *Eroica* (given without the first-movement exposition repeat) and in the allegros of the earlier symphonies. Nos. 4 and 8 are particularly successful, and no one could fault the *Fifth* for lack of energy or impetus. The *Pastoral* is mellow and pleasingly paced. (Jochum is warmer, but more relaxed in his tempi.) The series is capped by a performance of the *Choral Symphony* which, while not lacking strength, begins a little soberly, offers a simple, rather withdrawn slow movement, and then explodes into a finale of great fervour, with soloists and chorus – most effectively balanced – joining in an exultant celebration of human joy, thrillingly caught by the engineers. Throughout, the recording is full and lively and without edge; the acoustics are resonant, but not excessively so.

As one of the first batch in the Toscanini Collection, BMG/RCA's big project to reissue all the recordings that the maestro himself approved, this uniquely intense cycle amply reinforces the claims of Toscanini as a supreme conductor in his time. These NBC versions are faster and more tense than the earlier Beethoven readings that he committed to records, but they are far from rigid or unloving, and they are crowned by performances of breathtaking power in the *Eroica* and the *Ninth*. Far more than memory has come to suggest, Toscanini drew out melodic lines with Italianate affection, even while he was presenting the whole at a high voltage, rarely matched. Listening to this Beethoven is never a relaxing experience, but it is a uniquely involving one. The new transfers have been lovingly remastered under the direction of John Pfeiffer, one of Toscanini's last recording producers. In the *Ninth*, treble emphasis needs taming, and the *Fourth* and *Fifth* are given in live (as opposed to studio) recordings, with more variable results. The recordings sound at their best at a high volume, but the intrusive hum which marred the first CD transfers has been virtually eliminated. Once one adjusts to the dry acoustic that Toscanini demanded – 'like seeing the score spread before you' was his comment – there is much pleasure to be had in these incandescent performances. *Leonora No. 3* was recorded much earlier, from a 1939 broadcast.

Kurt Masur's Beethoven cycle with the Leipzig Gewandhaus Orchestra has a very great deal to recommend it. In sheer naturalness of utterance, unforced expressiveness and the superlatively disciplined response of the orchestral playing, the Gewandhaus set has a good deal to offer. The *Eroica* is uncommonly fine, particularly its nobly paced slow movement which is totally free from excessive emphasis in expression. In the *Fourth Symphony* Masur is particularly successful, and the Gewandhaus Orchestra respond with marvellously alert playing. The digital remastering has produced sound which is considerably livelier than the originals; the violins above the stave are very brightly lit, though not edgy.

Superbly played and very well recorded, Dohnányi's Cleveland cycle brings straight, satisfying performances that can hardly be faulted on points of interpretation. No one will be seriously disappointed with this five-disc package, yet these are not readings which grip the attention as live performances do, but civilized run-throughs rather.

By unearthing a live recording of No. 2, made in the Royal Albert Hall in 1948, and borrowing a radio recording of No. 8 made in Stockholm, EMI managed to put together a complete Furtwängler cycle, and very impressive it is interpretatively. The sound of those two ad hoc recordings may be very rough indeed, with heavy background noise, but the performances – with one or two oddities – are electrifying. No. 9 comes in the dedicated performance given at Bayreuth in 1951, uniquely historic, but the others are EMI's studio versions, not always as inspired as Furtwängler's live performances but still magnetic and, with generally well-balanced mono sound, very well transferred.

Solti's epic cycle, recorded in the mid-1970s with his own Chicago orchestra, has a firm centrality to it, following the outstandingly successful version of the *Ninth* with which he started the cycle. The performance of the *Eroica* has comparable qualities, with expansive, steady tempi and a dedicated, hushed account of the slow movement. Here and elsewhere Solti shows a willingness to relax, as well as to press dramatically forward, and there is plenty of sunshine in the even-numbered symphonies, though Nos. 1 and 8 are arguably too weighty in their tone of voice. For the very first time on record, every repeat is observed throughout, but this means that the *Ninth* has the first movement on the fifth disc, with the rest on the sixth. That break is to be deplored; but, more seriously, the digital transfers underline the aggressive brightness of the Chicago sound, emphasizing the brilliance of the performances to the detriment of their more thoughtful qualities. However, at bargain price, Solti admirers will undoubtedly be tempted, particularly as these performances are generally more satisfying than his later, digital series.

Symphonies Nos. 1 in C, Op. 21; 2 in D, Op. 36.
(M) *** Ph. 432 274-2; *432 274-4* [id.]. ASMF, Sir Neville Marriner.

Marriner presents the first two symphonies on modern instruments but on an authentic scale with a Mozart-sized orchestra, and the result is fresh and lithe, with plenty of character but with few, if any, quirks and mannerisms. Nor are the dramatic contrasts underplayed, for the chamber scale is most realistically captured in the excellent 1970 recording, admirably remastered.

Symphonies Nos. 1 in C; 3 in E flat (Eroica), Op. 55.
(B) **(*) Decca 433 619-2; *433 619-4* [id.]. VPO, Hans Schmidt-Isserstedt.

Symphonies Nos. 2 in D, Op. 36; 7 in A, Op. 92.
(B) **(*) Decca 433 605-2; *433 605-4* [id.]. VPO, Hans Schmidt-Isserstedt.

For both the *First* and *Second Symphonies* Schmidt-Isserstedt adopts unusually slow tempi, giving each movement a hint of ponderousness, although the lively sound prevents the effect from seeming heavy. In the finales the measured approach is pure delight and, with nicely pointed playing from the Vienna Philharmonic and admirably clear recording, reveals detail normally submerged. These are not electrifying performances, but they give much pleasure.

The *Eroica*, too, is a very satisfying reading,

made to sound more dramatic by the vivid remastering. There is no first-movement exposition repeat, but the structuring is convincing; this is very much a performance to live with: its qualities (which include splendid horn playing in the scherzo) become more and more apparent with repetition.

Schmidt-Isserstedt gives a magnetic account of the *Seventh* that compels attention from the first bar to the last, with the vivid recording-quality given new life on CD. In general tempi are judged with perfect regard for the often conflicting requirements of symphony and dance – neither too ponderous nor too hectic – and with the Vienna Philharmonic in outstanding form.

Symphonies Nos. 1 in C, Op. 21; 3 in E flat (Eroica), Op. 55.

(M) (***) BMG/RCA mono GD 60252 [60252-2-RG]. NBC O, Toscanini.

It is welcome to have the individual issues in Toscanini's Beethoven cycle also available separately. The transfers are the same as in the Toscanini Edition boxed set, carefully remastered with the original hum almost eliminated but with the sound still inevitably dry and harsh. Nevertheless these are performances which convey breathtaking power, notably the magnificent account of the *Eroica*, never comfortable but far from rigid or unloving.

Symphonies Nos. 1 in C, Op. 21; 4 in B flat, Op. 60; Egmont overture.

(M) *** DG 419 048-2; *419 048-4* [id.]. BPO, Karajan.

Karajan's 1977 version of No. 1 is exciting, polished and elegant; in No. 4 the balance is closer, exposing every flicker of tremolando. Yet the body and ambience of the recording combine to give a realistic presence, and overall this is very impressive. Karajan conveys weight and strength and there is a wider range of dynamic than in the later, digital version. Only the extremely fast tempo for the finale marks a controversial development, but even there the brilliance and excitement are never in doubt.

Symphonies Nos. (i) *1 in C, Op. 21;* (ii) *6 in F (Pastoral), Op. 68.*

(M) *** BMG/RCA GD 60002 [60002-2-RG]. Chicago SO, Reiner.

(M) **(*) Sony SMK 45891 [id.]. Marlboro Festival O, Pablo Casals.

(BB) * Naxos Dig. 8.550179 [id.]. (i) Zagreb PO, Richard Edlinger; (ii) Slovak RSO (Bratislava), Halász.

Symphonies Nos. 1 in C, Op. 21; 6 in F (Pastoral), Op. 68; Overture Egmont, Op. 84.

(M) ** Sony SBK 46532 [id.]. Cleveland O, Szell.

In its newly remastered form, Reiner's 1961 *Pastoral* sounds wonderfully warm and full, once again demonstrating the beauty of the acoustics of the Chicago Orchestral Hall at that time. The performance too is among the finest ever recorded, outstandingly fresh and enjoyable. Throughout Reiner adopts a straightforward, unmannered approach, his shading is subtle, and there is atmosphere without any confusion of texture. The slow movement is particularly beautiful and all the tempi sound utterly unforced and natural. It is true that Reiner's speed in the finale is somewhat faster than usual, but with this degree of lyrical fervour it does not sound over-pressed, and his choice is justified in the firmness achieved. The exposition repeat is observed in the first movement, to add to the architectural strength. The *First Symphony*, recorded in the same year, is weighty and direct, less incandescent but still a considerable account.

Sony do not give the actual date of these Marlboro performances, which must come from the late 1960s or early 1970s, but they do publish a list of the orchestra's personnel, which includes some pretty distinguished names: Shmuel Ashkenazi, Jaime Laredo, Pina Carmirelli, Miklos Perényi, Richard Stoltzman and many others. The *Pastoral* radiates integrity and warmth. It is totally free from any expressive exaggeration and tempi are well judged. These are performances of a vital sensitivity and, paradoxically, although everything is kept on a pretty tight rein it all seems relaxed and unhurried. The recording quality is dryish but eminently acceptable.

In the *First Symphony*, the characteristic 1964 Cleveland sound with its absence of real pianissimo, very bright and rather fierce on CD, may prove disconcerting for some listeners; but the clarity, the polish, the dynamism, the unfailing alertness of Szell's performance make up for any absence of charm. In the *Pastoral* (recorded in 1962), where the quality is smoother and warmer, Szell is subtle in his control of phrasing, for all the firmness of his style. However, it is a pity that the close-up sound robs the slow movement of much of its gentleness and delicacy of atmosphere. The finale, by contrast, is attractively relaxed. The fill-up, a version of the *Egmont overture* recorded in 1966, is excellently performed in Szell's intense way.

The Naxos performance of No. 1, recorded in Zagreb, is crisper and more refined than that of the *Pastoral* from Bratislava, helped by warmer and fuller sound. Interpretations are unexceptionable, though Michael Halász's slow speed for the finale of the *Pastoral* means that rhythms tend to be stodgy. With Reiner's outstanding coupling available on RCA, this is a non-starter, even at super-bargain price.

Symphonies Nos. 1; 7 in A, Op. 92.
(BB) **(*) ASV CDQS 6066; *ZCQS 6066*. N. Sinfonia of England, Richard Hickox.
(M) **(*) EMI CDM7 63354-2 [id.]; *EG 763354-4*. Philh. O, Klemperer.

From Hickox comes a generous coupling in the super-bargain range for those wanting chamber-scale performances, though the warm acoustic of Trinity Hall, Newcastle, where the recordings were made, gives a result hardly smaller-sounding than from a full-scale symphony orchestra. Hickox's view of both works is unaffected and direct and so gets the best of both worlds: finely detailed yet substantial; and the very lack of idiosyncrasy makes for easy listening. No. 1 is a little wanting in dramatic tension, and in No. 7 the second-movement *Allegretto* is slow and at times over-expressive; but otherwise this is a sensible and invigorating account with a brightly genial first movement. The CD transfer is full and agreeable but provides a rather resonant bass.

With Klemperer the slow speeds and heavyweight manner in both works – in principle not apt for No. 1, while undermining the dance-like element in No. 7 – will for many get in the way of enjoyment. That said, the compulsion of Klemperer in Beethoven remains strong, with rhythmic pointing consistently preventing stagnation. The recordings (1958 and 1961 respectively) are full and vivid, if not quite among the best of the series.

Symphony No. 2 in D, Op. 36; Overture Egmont, Op. 84.
(M) ** Sony SMK 46247 [id.]. Marlboro Festival O, Casals – BRAHMS: *Variations on a theme by Haydn*. **

Casals' performance of the *Second Symphony* was recorded at Marlboro in 1969 and the *Egmont Overture* the following year. The *Second Symphony* is a performance of some stature and great integrity, with no whipped-up excitement or playing to the gallery. The recording is a bit dry and the balance not always perfect, but this is live music-making that is well worth hearing, despite the dated sound. Neither the symphony nor the overture has appeared before.

Symphonies Nos. 2 in D; 4 in B flat, Op. 60.
(M) *** EMI CDM7 63355-2 [id.]; *EG 763355-4*. Philh. O, Klemperer.
(M) (**) EMI mono CDH7 63192-2 [id.]. BPO, Furtwängler.

The coupling for CD emphasizes the consistency of Klemperer's approach to Beethoven, with both the *Second* and *Fourth* symphonies sounding the more powerful through weighty treatment. Only in the finale is the result rather too gruff. The *Fourth* brings one of the most compelling performances of all, with Klemperer's measured but consistently sprung pulse allowing for persuasive lyricism alongside power. Exposition repeats are observed in the first movements of both symphonies. The sound is fresh yet full.

This Furtwängler disc brings the most marked discrepancy in sound between the two symphonies, with the scrunching background for No. 2 very distracting, though the live performance, given in the Royal Albert Hall, is electrifying. No. 4 comes in one of Furtwängler's finest studio recordings; though it is heavier and not quite as freely expressive as his live performances, its individuality is most compelling.

Symphonies Nos. 2 in D; 5 in C min., Op. 67.
(M) **(*) Sony SBK 47651 [id.]. Cleveland O, George Szell.
(BB) ** Naxos Dig. 8.550177 [id.]. Zagreb PO, Richard Edlinger.

Szell, recording in 1963/4, takes what might be described as the American post-Toscanini approach. There is some marvellously clean articulation from the strings in the first movement of No. 2 and the adrenalin runs free; yet here, as in the similarly brilliant account of No. 5, Szell understands the need to give full scope to the lyrical elements. The recording is respectably transferred: because of the forward balance it cannot convey a real pianissimo and textures are not rich but, as usual, the Severance Hall ambience ensures an acceptable degree of amplitude.

Richard Edlinger directs the Zagreb orchestra in crisp, dramatic performances of both symphonies, generally adopting urgent speeds in reflection of modern ideas on Beethoven's metronome markings. Slow movements flow easily and rhythms in allegros are generally well sprung, though the scherzo of No. 2 brings a heavier style than in the rest. Well recorded, with horns ripely caught and lower strings warm and full, this disc is well worth its super-bargain price.

Symphonies Nos. 2 in D; 7 in A, Op. 92.
(M) *** DG 419 050-2; *419 050-4* [id.]. BPO, Karajan.
(M) (**) BMG/RCA mono GD 60253; [60253-2-RG]. NBC SO, Toscanini.

As with Karajan's coupling of Nos. 1 and 4, the digitally remastered versions of the 1977 recordings of the *D* and *A major Symphonies* are remarkably successful, the sound vivid and clear, yet with plenty of body. In No. 2 the firm lines give the necessary strength. The tempo for the slow movement is particularly well judged; the recording is now clearer in its newest format. The *Seventh* is tense and exciting, with the conductor emphasizing the work's dramatic rather than its dance-like qualities. The slow introduction, taken at a fastish tempo, is tough rather than monumental, and the main *Allegro* is fresh and bright, and not very lilting in its 6/8 rhythm.

Toscanini's fondness for fast speeds works well in No. 2, with results that are sometimes fierce but which never sound breathless. His feeling for lyrical line is the more persuasive at his flowing speed for the *Larghetto*, anticipating modern interpretative ideas. No. 7, fast and fierce, is less sympathetic and suffers seriously in comparison with his classic recording, made with the New York Philharmonic in 1936, which is marginally broader in the fast movements. The second movement by contrast is markedly slower, well shaped but less concerned with Beethoven's originality in conceiving an *Allegretto* slow movement. The transfers are bright and clear, like the others in the Toscanini series.

Symphony No. 3 in E flat (Eroica), Op. 55.
(M) (***) BMG/RCA mono GD 60271; *GK 60271* [60271-2-RG; *60271-4-RG*]. NBC SO, Toscanini – MOZART: *Symphony No. 40.* (**)
(M) ** DG 435 092-2; *435 092-4* [id.]. LAPO, Carlo Maria Giulini.

Symphony No. 3 (Eroica); Grosse Fuge, Op. 133.
(M) *** EMI CDM7 63356-2 [id.]; *EG 763356-4.* Philh. O, Klemperer.

(i) *Symphony No. 3 (Eroica);* (ii) *Overture, Coriolan.*
(B) *** Pickwick Dig. PCD 900; *CIMPC 900* [id.]. LSO, Wyn Morris.
(B) *** Sup. SUP 000004 [Urania US 5167-CD]. Czech PO, (i) Von Matačić; (ii) Kletzki.
(B) **(*) Sony MBK 42599 [id.]. Columbia SO, Walter.

Symphony No. 3 (Eroica); Overtures: Leonora Nos. 2 & 3.
(M) (***) EMI mono CDM7 63855-2 [id.]; *EG 763855-4.* Philh. O, Klemperer.

Symphony No. 3 (Eroica); Overture: Leonora No. 3.
(M) **(*) DG 419 049-2; *419 049-4* [id.]. BPO, Karajan.

The digital remastering of Klemperer's spacious 1961 version of the *Eroica* reinforces its magnificence, keenly concentrated to sustain speeds slower than in his earlier, mono account. The stoically intense reading of the *Funeral march* is among the most impressive on record, and only in the coda to the finale does the slow tempo bring some slackening. The reissue includes the stereo version of the *Grosse Fuge*, dating from 1957, now available for the first time, and the sound is first rate, vivid and well balanced.

The alternative, mono version by Klemperer was among the very first records he made with the Philharmonia for EMI, the start of a whole era of recording. Once Karajan took up his Berlin Philharmonic appointment, Walter Legge knew that he would be available for work with the Philharmonia less often, and the record producer shrewdly chose Klemperer as his replacement; in so doing, he created a new star among interpreters of the central classics. Till then Klemperer had made relatively few recordings, but the success of these first Beethoven works revealed his full strength. Even now they have an electricity that he did not quite match in his re-recordings in stereo, with the *Eroica* one of his supreme achievements. The overtures were originally done in 1954, the symphony in 1955, but the mono sound is astonishingly vivid and full in the excellent CD transfers.

Wyn Morris on the Pickwick label conducts a taut reading of the *Eroica*, dark and intense, with allegros consistently urgent. The *Funeral march* too is strong and positive, braving the tragedy. Morris observes the important exposition repeat in the first movement, and has the benefit of first-rate sound; and the LSO responds with both bite and refinement. At budget price and with a coupling, it makes an excellent bargain, matching and even outshining most full-price rivals.

Walter's interpretation has all the ripeness of the best of his work with the Vienna Philharmonic Orchestra between the wars. The digitally remastered recording retains the amplitude one needs for such a reading: its expansive qualities bring rich horns as well as full-bodied strings. The disc opens with a superb account of the *Coriolan overture*, spacious, warm and dramatic, and the sound-balance is especially telling.

Recorded live at Carnegie Hall, New York, in December 1953, Toscanini's version has a far keener emotional intensity than the studio recording which appeared earlier as part of his Beethoven cycle in the BMG Toscanini series. Speeds are fractionally broader in the first two movements, which allows a more flowingly expressive style, less fierce but without losing high voltage. The great *Funeral march* particularly gains, though the ensemble does not always have quite such pinpoint precision. Toscanini had a special insight into this of all

Beethoven's symphonies, making this disc a valuable addition to his discography, generously coupled with a strong and urgent account of Mozart's great *G minor Symphony* (although this is a studio recording).

A warm welcome to Lovro von Matačić's commanding 1959 performance of the *Eroica*, one of the classic accounts of the early analogue era. This has an impressive tension and grandeur, and was one of the few *Eroicas* to recall the famous pre-war Weingartner set. The playing has tremendous grip but is never overdriven. The sound remains remarkably fresh and realistic; this is still a most competitive release.

Not everyone will identify readily with the fiery intensity of fast tempi in the outer movements of Karajan's 1977 performance, even if this version includes a more intense account of the *Funeral march* than in earlier recordings. A point to consider is the absence of the exposition repeat in the first movement; but this is among the most polished as well as the most dramatic accounts available. An exciting performance of *Leonora No. 3* makes a very generous bonus. The sound, although it has ample fullness and weight, is better defined than in the newer, digital version.

Giulini's refined and individual reading, with its almost eccentrically measured view of the first movement, including the exposition repeat, was an early product of his love-affair with the Los Angeles orchestra. It remains an extraordinary example of a conductor transforming an orchestra's usual character, and at mid-price can be valued for its new revelations, with the CD successfully remastered from the 1978 analogue original: the sound is full and clear.

Symphonies Nos. 3 in E flat (Eroica); 8 in F, Op. 93.

(M) **(*) Sony SBK 46328 [id.]. Cleveland O, Szell.

(BB) * Naxos Dig. 8.550407 [id.]. Belgian R. & TV PO (Brussels), Alexander Rahbari.

Szell's is a fine performance in the Toscanini tradition, hard-driven and dramatic. The speed of the first movement is almost the same as Toscanini's, the reading more rugged than with Karajan, but with more changes of tempo. The slow movement is most impressive; the prominence of the trumpet in the great climax may strike some listeners as vulgar, but it cannot be denied that this is an exciting performance, and the final subdued disintegration of the theme is most deeply felt. The digital remastering of the recording (from the late 1950s) is very successful: the sound is firm, full and brilliant. The performance of the *Eighth* is also a compelling one. The first-movement repeat is taken and the performance is not over-driven; indeed, the finale is slower than usual, with plenty of consideration for the players' comfort. The 1962 recording is full and well detailed.

Rahbari's Naxos version of the *Eroica* is given a relaxed rather than a keenly dramatic reading. Both it and No. 8 are warmly and comfortably recorded, with reverberation obscuring detail only occasionally in tuttis. Apart from some slackness in the third-movement Minuet, No. 8 is given a fresh, well-pointed reading. But by paying a little more, one can get more satisfying versions than these.

Symphony No. 4 in B flat, Op. 60.

(M) ** Sony SMK 46246 [id.]. Marlboro Festival O, Casals – SCHUBERT: *Symphony No. 5.* **(*) ❀

Symphony No. 4 in B flat; Grosse Fuge in B flat, Op. 133.

(M) **(*) Ph. 432 509-2; *432 509-4* [id.]. ASMF, Marriner.

If Marriner and the Academy aim at a smaller scale than is usual with performances on modern instruments, the fullness and vividness of the 1974 recording prevent one from ever feeling any diminution of the music, and the stylishness and refinement of the playing make the result resiliently enjoyable. The *Grosse Fuge* is similarly vibrant, but it makes a singularly ungenerous coupling. Nevertheless, with such first-class sound this is an immensely stimulating account of the symphony.

Like his magisterial account of the *Seventh*, Casals's recording of the *Fourth Symphony* comes from the 1969 season at Marlboro when the orchestra comprised players of great renown. The present recording has not, however, appeared before and should be heard. There is a real sense of mystery at the opening and Casals keeps a firm grip on proceedings, with good choice of tempi and finely judged phrasing. For the latter, try the opening paragraph or so of the slow movement. As is the case with other Marlboro recordings, the acoustic is dryish and the balance far from perfect, but this is dedicated music-making which makes no concessions to the smooth surface perfection of the studio but which has a sense of musical purpose that puts you completely under its spell.

Symphonies Nos. 4 in B flat, Op. 60; 5 in C min., Op. 67.

(B) *** Pickwick Dig. PCD 869; *CIMPC 869* [id.]. LSO, Wyn Morris.

(M) **(*) Sony MK 42011. Columbia SO, Bruno Walter.

(BB) **(*) ASV Dig. CDQS 6054; *ZCQS 6054*. N. Sinfonia, Richard Hickox.

Wyn Morris's coupling of Nos. 4 and 5 makes a first-rate budget recommendation. He generally adopts speeds close to those of Karajan and, though he cannot match that master in sharpness of focus or pointed intensity, his urgency goes with fine, biting strength, helped by some first-rate playing from the LSO. These are readings which, more than most, convey the varying tensions of a live performance, and one suspects that the studio recordings were done in long takes. The sound is bright and slightly abrasive, but with enough body to sustain that. The weight of the readings is enhanced by the observance of all repeats. A bargain.

Walter's 1959 reading of the *Fourth* is splendid, the finest achievement of his whole cycle. There is intensity and a feeling of natural vigour which makes itself felt in every bar. The slow movement gives Walter the perfect opportunity to coax a genuinely singing tone from his violins as only he knows how; and the finale allows the wind department its measure of brilliance. All aspects of this symphony are welded together here and show what depths it really contains. The recording is full yet clear, sweet-toned with a firm bass. Here as in the *Fifth* the sound-balance is richer and more satisfying than in many modern recordings. In Walter's reading of the *Fifth*, the first movement is taken very fast, yet it lacks the kind of nervous tension that distinguishes Carlos Kleiber's famous (full-price) version. The middle two movements are contrastingly slow. In the *Andante* (more like *adagio*) there is a glowing, natural warmth, but the scherzo at this speed is too gentle. The finale, taken at a spacious, natural pace, is joyous and sympathetic, but again fails to convey the ultimate in tension. The digital remastering for CD has left behind a residue of pre-Dolby background hiss, but it is not too distracting. In the USA this coupling remains at full price.

At super-bargain price, Richard Hickox's versions of Nos. 4 and 5 make a generous and attractive coupling. Both works receive strong, direct readings, well scaled, with the reverberant recording giving a chamber-sized string-band plenty of body. No. 4 is the more successful, a buoyant performance which has the sharper impact through its full analogue recording. The *Fifth*, in which the digital recording distances the sound, lacks a degree of bite as well as of mystery, as at the start of the Scherzo, but the finale – at a brisk speed, with the exposition repeat observed – brings a powerful, flamboyant conclusion.

Symphonies Nos. 4 in B flat, Op. 60; 6 in F (Pastoral), Op. 68.

(M) (***) BMG/RCA mono GD 60254 [60254-2-RG]. NBC SO, Toscanini.

Toscanini's reading of the *Pastoral* contradicts one's preconceptions. This was one of his favourite Beethoven symphonies and he included it in his NBC concerts more frequently than any other; it largely escaped the tightening process which affected his other Beethoven interpretations. The first movement in this 1952 performance has a natural, unforced freshness which allows the most delicate shading and persuasive moulding between sections. The second movement flows beautifully, with elegant phrasing and, though the scherzo and *Storm* are fast and intense, the finale brings a fresh, simple manner, not as tender as it might be but still persuasive. No. 4 is more characteristic of the later Toscanini, though the fast, fierce manner in the first movement conveys joyful exuberance, and the slow movement brings fine moulding. The recording is coarser than in the *Pastoral*, with a heavier tape-hiss. Both are transferred with the bright clarity characteristic of the series.

Symphonies Nos. 4 in B flat; 7 in A, Op. 92.

(B) **(*) Ph. 422 967-2; *422 967-4*. Concg. O, Jochum.

(BB) ** Naxos Dig. 8.550180 [id.]. Zagreb PO, Richard Edlinger.

Jochum's Philips coupling comes from 1967/8 and offers a strong, compelling reading of No. 4, with a satisfying *Seventh*. The slow movement of the *B flat Symphony* is rather serious in mood (less radiant than in his earlier performance on Heliodor), and the outer movements of the *A major* find more extrovert excitement in some other performances; but overall this is rewarding, with the Concertgebouw playing as eloquent and polished as in the rest of this excellent series. The sound too is clear, with a full Concertgebouw sonority.

Each of these Beethoven symphonies begins with a grand ceremonial slow introduction, leading to a strongly rhythmic, dramatic first movement, and then involves a scherzo with a rondo-like middle section, which has a double return of the main section. Edlinger is rougher than many rivals, but there are few to match him for his immediacy of communication in works that always run the danger of being thought hackneyed.

Symphony No. 5 in C min., Op. 67.

(BB) ** Naxos Dig. 8.550289 [id.]. Zagreb PO, Edlinger – SCHUBERT: *Symphony No. 8*. **

Edlinger's urgent and dramatic reading of Beethoven's *Fifth*, discussed above coupled with *Symphony No. 2*, is also available with Schubert as coupling.

Symphonies Nos. 5; 7 in A, Op. 92.
(M) *** Decca Dig. 430 701-2; *430 701-4* [id.]. Philh. O, Ashkenazy.
(M) (***) EMI mono CDM7 63868-2 [id.]; *EG 763868-4*. Philh. O, Klemperer.
(M) (**(*)) EMI mono CDH7 69803-2 [id.]. VPO, Furtwängler.
(M) **(*) DG Dig. 435 093-2; *435 093-4* [id.]. VPO, Claudio Abbado.

Symphonies Nos. 5; 8 in F, Op. 93.
(B) *** Ph. 422 474-2. Concg. O, Jochum.
(B) **(*) Decca 421 166-2; *421 166-4* [id.]. VPO, Schmidt-Isserstedt.
(M) **(*) EMI CDM7 63357-2 [id.]; *EG 763357-4*. Philh. O, Klemperer.

Symphonies Nos. 5; 8; Fidelio: overture.
(M) *** DG 419 051-2; *419 051-4* [id.]. BPO, Karajan.

Symphonies Nos. 5; 8; Overture: Leonora No. 3.
(M) (**(*)) BMG/RCA mono GD 60255; [60255-2-RG]. NBC O, Toscanini.

Karajan's 1977 version of the *Fifth* is magnificent in every way, tough and urgently incisive, with fast tempi bringing weight as well as excitement but no unwanted blatancy, even in the finale. The recording has satisfying body and a wide dynamic range. The coupling is an electrically intense performance of the *Eighth* plus the *Fidelio overture.*

Ashkenazy's reading of the *Fifth* is urgent and vivid and is notable for its rich, Kingsway Hall recording. Well-adjusted speeds here (the *Andante* on the slow side, the finale somewhat quick), with joyful exuberance a fair substitute for grandeur. The reading of the *Seventh* is equally spontaneous, a generally direct performance taken steadily at unexaggerated speeds; the result is glowingly convincing, thanks to fine playing and recording that set new standards in this work, full and spacious yet warmly co-ordinated. After a grave and simple account of the slow introduction, the allegro at first sounds deceptively relaxed in pastoral mood, until the dramatic urgency of the movement takes over, its dance rhythms nicely lifted. The finale is a shade slower than usual, but effectively so. This mid-priced digital CD ranks high among records of these two symphonies, especially for those for whom outstanding recording quality is a priority.

Klemperer never surpassed these first EMI interpretations of either symphony. Though the recording is in mono only, both works have a clarity, immediacy and fidelity of balance that enhance electrifying readings, revealing Klemperer at his peak. The speeds are characteristically spacious, if not quite as expansive as in his later interpretations. These are among the finest versions of either symphony ever put on disc, and a generous coupling, too.

Jochum provides a highly satisfying bargain-price coupling of the *Fifth* and *Eighth Symphonies.* He launches into a vigorous reading of the *Fifth*, unmarred by any romantic exaggeration but gripping in a totally natural and unforced way. The finale is especially fine and beautifully prepared; the *Eighth*, too, is attractively unmannered, satisfyingly paced and superbly played. The sound is extremely good. An outstanding bargain.

Schmidt-Isserstedt offers strong readings of both the *Fifth* and *Eighth symphonies* and includes exposition repeats in both the first movements. The first movement of No. 8 is slower than usual in the interests of emphasizing that this is not simply Beethoven's 'little one' but a powerful, symphonic argument. In the *Fifth* the first movement has both bite and breathing-space, a nicely measured *Andante* and a triumphant finale. Only the scherzo invites controversy in its slow tempo. Excellent recording, vividly transferred to CD.

As with the others in his mid-priced series on EMI, Klemperer's renditions of Nos. 5 and 8 bring a clean and natural sound on top, notably in violin tone. The *Fifth* is plainly less electric than his earlier, mono version but, with exposition repeats observed in both outer movements, this retains its epic quality.

Furtwängler's coupling of the *Fifth* and the *Seventh Symphonies* on EMI brings together two of his finest Beethoven recordings, both made in the Musikvereinsaal in Vienna under studio conditions. Furtwängler's rhythmic control and his mastery of line exert a magnetic hold over the listener; the fateful power of No. 5 and the dance-apotheosis of No. 7 are celebrated with equal intensity. In both symphonies the recording is rather dry and limited, but in a good transfer this is undistracting enough to give much pleasure.

Abbado offers a weighty and spacious account of the *Fifth*, with powerful outer movements, but in which the speed for the *Andante* is dangerously slow. It is paired with an electrifying, incandescent performance of the *Seventh*, fresh and rhythmic. The *Seventh* has always been a favourite symphony with Abbado, and the main allegro of the first movement is beautifully judged at a fastish speed, which is nevertheless made resilient. The finale similarly blazes fearlessly but never becomes a gabble and, though the 1987 live recording is not ideally clear on inner detail, the sound is full and atmospheric, whereas in the *Fifth* it is thicker, with inner textures not sharply defined, yet the sense of weight and presence compensates for that.

(i) *Symphonies Nos. 5–6 (Pastoral); Overture: Egmont* (CD only: (ii) *Overtures: Consecration of the House; Namensfeier*; (iii) *The Ruins of Athens*).
(B) **(*) DG Compact Classics 413 144-2; *** *413 144-4* [id.]. (i) VPO, Boehm; (CD only: (ii) LOP, Markevitch; (iii) Bav. RSO, Jochum).

Boehm's Compact Classics account of the *Fifth* may not be the most powerful available, but the excellent playing and recording, rich and weighty in the bass as well as lively on top, make it a good version to live with. It pairs naturally with Boehm's warmly lyrical account of the *Pastoral* in its display of positive feeling and absence of neurosis. The reading of the *Pastoral* has a natural, unforced beauty, and is very well played (with strings, woodwind and horns beautifully integrated). In the first movement Boehm observes the exposition repeat (not many versions do); although the dynamic contrasts are never underplayed and the phrasing is affectionate, there is a feeling of inevitable rightness about Boehm's approach, no sense of an interpreter imposing his will. Only the slow movement with its even stressing raises any reservation, and that is very slight. The chrome-tape transfers of both works are very successful; in offering nearly 90 minutes of music, this is undoubtedly good value. The pair of CDs adds three more overtures, which many collectors will not consider an advantage. Jochum's *Ruins of Athens* is more distinguished than the other two, even if the Bavarian orchestral playing lacks the last ounce of polish. As it happens, the stylistic contrast is less distracting than one would expect, though naturally the Paris orchestra with its French vibrato on the horns does not always sound idiomatic. The recording is also more dated; indeed it sounds a bit fierce. Markevitch makes *The Consecration of the House* less weighty than usual, almost frivolous, but the interpretation of *Namensfeier* is clean and dramatic.

Symphony No. 5 in C min.; Wellington's Victory (Battle Symphony).
(M) ** Collins Dig. 3002-2 [id.]. LSO, Rafael Frühbeck de Burgos.

Frühbeck de Burgos's *Fifth* is eminently musical and quite strong, with an excellent response from the LSO. Detail is well observed in the slow movement, which is played most persuasively, but it is not until the finale that the adrenalin runs free and the performance becomes compulsive. *Wellington's Victory*, however, is a great success and the recording, hitherto very good, becomes spectacular, with impressive ordnance from the opposing troops and a joyous celebration at the close.

Symphony No. 6 in F (Pastoral), Op. 68.
(M) *** DG 413 721-2 (2) [id.]. VPO, Boehm – *Symphony No. 9.* ***

Symphonies No. 6 (Pastoral); Overtures: Coriolan; Creatures of Prometheus.
(BB) *** ASV CDQS 6053; *ZCQS 6053*. N. Sinfonia, Richard Hickox.

Symphony No. 6 (Pastoral); Overture: The Creatures of Prometheus; (i) *Egmont: Overture; Die Trommel geruhet; Freudvoll und leidvoll; Klarchens Tod, Op. 84.*
(M) *** EMI CDM7 63358-2 [id.]; *EG 763358-4*. Philh. O, Klemperer; (i) with Birgit Nilsson.

Symphony No. 6 (Pastoral); Overtures: The Creatures of Prometheus; Egmont; Fidelio.
(M) ** DG 435 094-2; *435 094-4* [id.]. VPO, Leonard Bernstein.

Symphony No. 6 (Pastoral); Overture Egmont, Op. 84.
(B) **(*) Pickwick Dig. PCD 912; *CIMPC 912* [id.]. LSO, Wyn Morris.

Symphony No. 6 (Pastoral); Overtures: Egmont; Leonora No. 3.
(M) *** Decca Dig. 430 721-2; *430 721-4* [id.]. Philh. O, Vladimir Ashkenazy.

Symphony No. 6 (Pastoral); Overture: Leonora No. 2, Op. 72a.
(B) *** Sony MYK 42536 [(d.) MYK 36720]. Columbia SO, Walter.
(B) *** Ph. 426 061-2; *426 061-4* [id.]. Concg. O, Jochum.

Among earlier versions of the *Pastoral*, Fritz Reiner's should also be considered, one of the finest ever recorded and sounding gloriously rich in its remastered format, coupled with No. 1 – see above. Tennstedt's fine digital account, paired with No. 8, should also not be forgotten – see below.

Ashkenazy's is essentially a genial reading, almost totally unmannered. But the performance has a beguiling warmth and it communicates readily. With generally spacious tempi, the feeling of lyrical ease and repose is most captivating, thanks to the response of the Philharmonia players and the richness of the recording, made in the Kingsway Hall. After a *Storm* that is civilized rather than frightening, the performance is crowned by a radiant account of the *Shepherds' thanksgiving*. The sound, with its fairly reverberant acoustic, is particularly impressive. The two overtures, though not electrifying, are enjoyably musical and spontaneous and make a thoroughly satisfactory makeweight.

Boehm's reading of the *Pastoral* (see above) is

here coupled with a fine digital version of the *Choral Symphony* on a pair of mid-priced discs.

Bruno Walter's recording dates from the beginning of the 1960s. The whole performance glows, and the gentle warmth of phrasing is comparable with Klemperer's famous version. The slow movement is taken slightly fast, but there is no sense of hurry, and the tempo of the *Peasants' merrymaking* is less controversial than Klemperer's. It is an affectionate and completely integrated performance from a master who thought and lived the work all his life. The sound is beautifully balanced, with sweet strings and clear, glowing woodwind, and the bass response is firm and full. The quality is very slightly shallower in the *Overture Leonora No. 2* which opens the disc, but this splendid performance shows Walter at his most dramatically spontaneous.

Hickox directs a persuasively paced reading, with a small orchestra used to give a performance of high contrasts, intimate in the lighter textures, as at the start, and elegant in the slow movement, but expanding dramatically in the tuttis, as in the *Storm*, while the finale, fresh and pure, brings a glowing climax. With warm, analogue recording giving a fine sense of presence, this is one of the best of the Hickox Beethoven series. The two *Overtures* come in vigorously dramatic readings; though the coupling is hardly generous, this is available in the lowest price-range.

Klemperer's account of the *Pastoral* is one of the very finest of all his records. The scherzo may be eccentrically slow but, with superbly dancing rhythms, it could not be more bucolic, and it falls naturally into place within the reading as a whole. The exquisitely phrased slow movement and the final *Shepherds' hymn* bring peaks of beauty, made the more intense by the fine digital transfer, reinforcing the clarity and balance of the original sound, with violin tone amazingly fresh and clean for 1958, although thinner than we would expect today. The *Egmont* music follows the *Symphony*, an unusual but valuable coupling with Nilsson in her prime, unexpectedly but effectively cast in the two simple songs, the first made to sound almost Mahlerian. The CD also offers the *Creatures of Prometheus overture*.

Jochum's Philips recording of the *Pastoral* dates from the end of the 1960s. It sounds extremely well in remastered form, resonantly full, vivid and clear. It is primarily a leisurely reading, the countryside relaxing in the sunshine. In the first movement Jochum is essentially undramatic until the radiant final climax in the coda, which he links with the similar burst of energy in the finale. The slow movement has an Elysian stillness and repose; the *Storm* is not over-romanticized. With beautiful playing from the Concertgebouw Orchestra, the reading is sustained without a hint of lethargy.

Morris takes a characteristically fresh and direct view of the *Pastoral*. The speed for the first movement is brisk, and he does not allow even a momentary easing for the entry of the second subject, let alone a slowing of tempo. Next to more relaxed readings, Morris sounds tense; on his own terms, however, it works well, as does his brisk treatment of the other movements. The piece becomes less atmospheric – with the entry into the *Storm* hardly suggesting raindrops – but one appreciates the structural originality the more. With a similarly taut account of the *Egmont overture* for fill-up, and with first-rate playing from the LSO, it makes a characterful bargain-price recommendation.

Bernstein's reading has plenty of character and, with its combination of joy and serenity, is persuasive, even if the performance fails to bite in the *Storm* sequence. But the inevitable inconsistencies of live recording – even with discreet editing between performances – come out more clearly on CD in the discrepancy between the symphony and the overtures, even though the venue, the Vienna Musikverein Grosser Saal, was the same throughout.

Symphonies Nos. 6 in F (Pastoral), Op. 68; 8 in F, Op. 93.

(M) *** EMI Dig. CDD7 63891-2 [id.]; *ET 763891-4*. LPO, Tennstedt.

(B) * DG 431 159-2; *431 159-4* [id.]. BPO, Karajan.

Tennstedt's fresh, alert and imaginative performance of the *Pastoral* comes in a generous coupling with the *Eighth*, given an equally enjoyable reading in which the second-movement *Allegretto* at a fast speed is made into a scherzo while the Minuet is spaciously lyrical. In the *Pastoral*, the slow movement brings a finely moulded performance from Tennstedt, a dramatic account of the *Storm* and a radiant reading of the finale. Well-balanced recording, bright and fresh. If the coupling is suitable, this is strongly recommendable.

Karajan's 1962 version of the *Pastoral* was by far the least appealing of his first Berlin Beethoven cycle, with hectically fast tempi. Ironically, his sharply dramatic reading of the *Eighth* offers an excellently performed fill-up. The playing throughout is very refined and the sound remarkably good for its period but, even at bargain price, this does not compete with the EMI/Tennstedt mid-price coupling of the same two symphonies.

Symphony No. 7 in A, Op. 92.

(BB) ** Pickwick PWK 1156. SRO, Ansermet.

Symphony No. 7; Overtures: Coriolan; Creatures of Prometheus; Egmont.
(B) *** DG 429 509-2; *429 509-4* [id.]. VPO, Boehm.

Symphony No. 7; Overture: The Creatures of Prometheus.
(M) *** EMI CDM7 69183-2 [id.]; *EG 769183-4*. Philh. O, Klemperer.

Symphony No. 7; (i) *The Ruins of Athens (Overture and incidental music), Op. 113.*
(M) *** EMI CDM7 69871-2. RPO, Beecham; (i) with Beecham Choral Soc.

(i) *Symphonies Nos. 7;* (ii) *8 in F, Op. 93.*
(B) **(*) Pickwick Dig. PCD 917; *CIMPC 917* [id.]. LSO, Wyn Morris.
(M) *(*) Sony SMK 45893 [id.]. Marlboro Festival O, Casals.

Klemperer's 1955 recording of the *Seventh* is among his very finest Beethoven interpretations on disc, and it sounds all the more vivid and full of presence in the stereo version, issued for the first time. Speeds are consistently faster, the tension more electric, with phrasing moulded more subtly, than in the later Philharmonia version. Though the later recording carries extra weight with its wider range, the 1955 sound is very acceptable, with good inner detail. The 1959 *Prometheus* is not a generous makeweight, but the disc comes at mid-price in the EMI Studio series.

Boehm's 1972 version with the VPO stands high among the lower-priced versions of this symphony. The recording is excellent, full and fresh, and the whole performance has lift and spontaneity. Boehm's direct style is most satisfying: in the first movement the well-articulated playing keeps the music very much alive, even though his basic speed isn't fast. The slow movement has a grave eloquence which is most moving, and the spirited scherzo makes way for a striking finale, full of impetus, yet with plenty of weight. The overtures go well too, especially *Egmont*.

Beecham's *Seventh* is one of the briskest accounts of the symphony ever; yet, such is his rhythmic control and his ability to clarify textures – well realized in the recording, which is astonishingly vivid for the late 1950s – the result is exhilarating. Only the slow movement reverts to old-fashioned slow manners in what is in effect an *Andante* rather than an *Allegretto*, but Beecham's rhythmic sense and care for phrasing still avoid heaviness. The fill-up of incidental music makes a valuable and enjoyable rarity, with Beecham roaring through the *Chorus of Dervishes* (finely sung by the Beecham Choral Society), whiskers obviously bristling. The 1958 sound has also been transferred well.

Wyn Morris directs strong, spontaneous-sounding readings of both *Symphonies*, not always as refined in execution as the finest, but superbly recorded. In a generous coupling on the bargain Pickwick label, they make an excellent recommendation. Though there are some distracting fluctuations of speed, Morris draws consistently resilient playing from the LSO, a vital quality in these two works written in parallel, with No. 8 becoming, like No. 7, an apotheosis of the dance.

Ansermet's Beethoven has always been underestimated. His Swiss players could not rival the finest international orchestras in discipline and polish; but this conductor never made a record that was not tinglingly alive, and so it is here. He starts well, with a poised introduction (taken rather fast) building up to a fine climax; both outer movements have plenty of adrenalin, and the final coda is thrilling. There is no lack of warmth either, and the 1960 recording, made in the Vicoria Hall, Geneva, is astonishingly vivid and full. This is by no means a general recommendation, but Ansermet admirers will not be disappointed.

The *Seventh Symphony* was recorded by Casals in 1969 and the *Eighth* six years earlier. The line-up is an impressive one: the violins include Shmuel Ashkenazi, Arnold Steinhardt, Pina Carmirelli, Zvi Zeitlin and others familiar as soloists and leaders of quartets, and the performances are of real stature and personality. There is a community of spirit about this playing and not the slightest trace of the recording studio. The first movement of the *Seventh* has impressive fire and momentum, and Casals keeps a firm grip on the architecture throughout. The *Eighth Symphony* is a more controversial performance and some may feel it too hard-driven; the rather dryish, coarse-grained sound certainly contributes to this impression. But its first movement has all the concentration of a white dwarf star and unleashes reserves of energy that seem inexhaustible. The 1969 sound is much cleaner than on the LP, but the 1963 recording still calls for tolerance and is constricted in range.

Symphony No. 8 in F, Op. 93.
(M) (***) EMI mono CDM7 63398-2 [id.]; *EG 763398-4*. RPO, Beecham – MENDELSSOHN: *Symphony No. 4*; SCHUBERT: *Symphony No. 8*. (***)

Though Beecham was never very sympathetic to the Beethoven of the great odd-numbered symphonies, he loved the *Eighth*, as this characteristic reading makes plain, rescued by EMI for the Beecham Edition from the CBS archive.

Speeds tend to be on the relaxed side, but Beecham's rhythmic spring never lets them drag. Such moments as the entry of the recapitulation in the first movement at the very culmination of the development have the thrill of first discovery, and the delicate pointing of that movement's gentle pay-off is very Beechamesque. The mono recording does not help the strings to sound very sweet, but this EMI transfer is far clearer than ever the original LPs were.

Symphony No. 9 in D min. (Choral), Op. 125.

(M) *** EMI Dig. CD-EMX 2186; *TC-EMX 2186*. Joan Rodgers, Della Jones, Peter Bronder, Bryn Terfel, Royal Liverpool PO Ch. & O, Sir Charles Mackerras.

(M) *** DG 415 832-2; *415 832-4* [id.]. Tomowa-Sintow, Baltsa, Schreier, Van Dam, V. Singverein, BPO, Karajan.

(M) *** Decca 430 438-2; *430 438-4* [id.]. Lorengar, Minton, Burrows, Talvela, Chicago Ch. & SO, Solti.

(B) *** Ph. 422 464-2; *422 464-4* [id.]. Rebmann, Reynolds, de Ridder, Feldhoff, Netherlands R. Ch., Concg. O, Jochum.

(M) *** DG 431 026-2; *431 026-4* [id.]. Gwyneth Jones, Schwarz, Kollo, Moll, V. State Op. Ch., VPO, Bernstein.

(M) *** DG 427 802-2; *427 802-4* [id.]. Norman, Fassbaender, Domingo, Berry, Concert Singers of V. State Op., VPO, Boehm.

(M) *** DG 413 721-2 (2) [id.]. Norman, Fassbaender, Domingo, Berry, Concert Singers of V. State Op., VPO, Boehm – *Symphony No. 6.* ***

(BB) *** Pickwick (Decca) PWK 1150. Sutherland, Procter, Dermota, Arnold van Mill, Brassus Ch., Ch. Vaudoise, SRO, Ansermet.

(B) *** Decca 433 617-2; *433 617-4* [id.]. Sutherland, Horne, King, Talvela, V. State Op. Ch., VPO, Schmidt-Isserstedt.

(M) **(*) Ph. 420 701-2 [id.]. Tomowa-Sintow, Burmeister, Schreier, Adam, Leipzig R. Ch. & GO, Masur.

(M) **(*) Sony Dig. MDK 44646 [id.]. Murphy, Watkinson, O'Neill, Howell, Tallis Chamber Ch., ECO, Tilson Thomas.

(M) (***) EMI mono CDH7 69801-2 [id.]. Schwarzkopf, Höngen, Hopf, Edelmann, Bayreuth Festival Ch. & O, Furtwängler.

(M) (**(*)) BMG/RCA mono GD 60256; [60256-2-RG]. Farrell, Merriman, Peerce, Scott, Shaw Ch., NBC O, Toscanini.

(M) *(**) EMI CDM7 69030-2 [id.]. Te Kanawa, Hamari, Burrows, Holl, LSO Ch., LSO, Jochum.

(M) ** EMI CDM7 63359-2 [id.]; *EG 763359-4*. Lövberg, Ludwig, Kmentt, Hotter, Philh. Ch. and O, Klemperer.

(M) ** EMI Dig. CDD7 63902-2 [id.]; *ET 763902-4*. Armstrong, Finnie, Tear, Tomlinson, Philh. Ch. & O, Sanderling.

(M) ** Ph. 432 039-2. J. Price, Finnilä, Laubenthal, Rintzler, Concg. Ch. & O, Haitink.

(M) *(*) Pickwick Dig. PCD 923; *CIMPC 923* [id.]. Hargan, Della Jones, Rendall, Howell, LSO Ch., LSO, Wyn Morris.

(BB) * Naxos Dig. 8.550181 [id.]. Lechner, Elias, Pabst, Holzer, Ch. & Zagreb PO, Edlinger.

Symphony No. 9 (Choral); Overture: Coriolan.

(M) *** DG 435 095-2; *435 095-2* [id.]. Janowitz, Rössel-Majdan, Kmentt, Berry, V. Singverein, BPO, Karajan.

Symphony No. 9 (Choral); Overture Fidelio, Op. 72b.

(M) **(*) Sony SBK 46533 [id.]; *40-46533*. Addison, Hobson, Lewis, Bell, Cleveland O Ch. & O, Szell.

Sir Charles Mackerras conducts the Royal Liverpool Philharmonic in an exceptional, inspired account of the *Ninth*, one which – more than any other with a traditional symphony orchestra – has learnt from the lessons of period performance. Articulation is light and clean, vibrato is used sparingly, making textures unusually clear; and, like Roger Norrington, Sir Charles has taken careful note of Beethoven's controversial metronome markings. However, he does not apply them quite so strictly, so that, though the great *Adagio* slow movement flows relatively quickly, the speed still allows tenderly expressive lyricism, while the drum-and-fife episode of the finale becomes a swinging march and does not sag, as Norrington's very slow (full-price) account does. The recording is among the very finest ever given to this symphony, warm yet transparent and with plenty of body; and the singing in the finale is splendid, even if the tenor, Peter Bronder, is on the strenuous side. The other soloists are outstanding, not least the bass, Bryn Terfel, who delivers a gloriously resonant account of his first entry, *O Freunde, nicht diese Töne*. Anyone wanting a refreshingly different version of the *Ninth*, which yet brings all the dramatic power and intensity of a more conventional reading, need not hesitate.

Of the three stereo recordings Karajan has made of the *Ninth*, his 1977 account is the most inspired in its insight, above all in the *Adagio*, where he conveys spiritual intensity at a slower tempo than in his earlier, 1962 version and more searchingly than in the later, digital recording, where the effect is more lyrical in its beauty. In the finale, the concluding eruption has an animal excitement rarely heard from this highly controlled conductor. The soloists make an excellent team, with contralto, tenor and bass all finer than their predecessors and the soprano markedly more secure than her successor in 1985. The sound has tingling projection and drama. Though Karajan's 1962 version is less hushed and serene in the slow movement, the finale blazes even more intensely, with Janowitz's contribution radiant in its purity. This reflected the Berlin sessions when it rounded off a cycle, recorded over two weeks. The disc opens with the fine 1965 recording of *Coriolan*, rather fuller in sound than the symphony.

Solti's 1972 recording of the *Ninth* is one of his outstanding gramophone achievements, long praised by us in its original LP and tape formats. If you regard the sublime slow movement as the key to this epic work, then Solti is clearly with you. With spacious, measured tempi he leads the ear on, not only with his phrasing but also with his subtle shading of dynamic down to whispered pianissimo. Here is *Innigkeit* of a concentration rarely heard on record, even in the *Ninth*. Solti in the first movement is searing in his dynamic contrasts – maybe too brutally so – while the precision of the finale, with superb choral work and solo singing, confirms this as one of the finest *Ninths* on CD. Recorded in Krannert Center at the University of Illinois, the analogue recording is full yet clean and bright, its various elements very well co-ordinated in the CD transfer.

On Philips's cheapest Concert Classics label, Jochum's 1969 version makes an excellent recommendation, powerfully conducted and intense, beautifully played with exceptionally crisp wind articulation and with the glory of the Concertgebouw string-tone well caught by the recording despite obvious signs of age. There is a demonic quality in Jochum's reading, be it in the rugged power of the first movement, the fierce dance of the scherzo or the sharp disruption at the start of the finale. That quality is strongly set against a rapt and spacious account of the slow movement and a reading of the finale which underlines the joy of the writing. Soloists are a clear and fresh team with no wobblers, and the chorus is powerful and responsive, not helped by being set behind the orchestra. The sound has good presence and clarity, though lacking a little in body and failing to expand as a more modern recording would.

Bernstein – recorded live, as in the rest of his Vienna cycle – directs a powerful and distinctive reading of the *Ninth*. The very start conveys immediate electricity, the scherzo is resilient, the *Adagio* deeply convincing in its distinctive contrasting of inner meditation with lighter, more carefree interludes. Though in the choral finale Gwyneth Jones has her raw moments, overall it is a superb account, sung and played with dedication. The recording is among the finest in the series, given extra space and presence in the CD transfer.

Just a few months before he died, Karl Boehm made his final statement on the work in this resplendent digital recording. With generally slow tempi, his reading is spacious and powerful – the first movement even has a certain stoic quality – and in its broad concept it has much in common with Klemperer's version. Yet overall there is a transcendent sense of a great occasion; the concentration is unfailing, reaching its peak in the glorious finale, where ruggedness and strength well over into inspiration. With a fine, characterful team of soloists and a freshly incisive chorus formed from singers of the Vienna State Opera, this is strongly recommendable. It is available separately at mid-price, and also coupled to another outstanding Boehm recording – of the *Pastoral Symphony*.

Ansermet's 1965 recording of the *Choral Symphony* was one of the first successful stereo versions to appear on a single LP. Now it makes its return to the catalogue as a super-bargain CD, still sounding vividly clear. Such clean detail (although there is atmosphere too) suits the direct style of the conductor; it seems that Ansermet was inspired beyond his usual achievement by the greatest challenge of all in Beethoven, helped by a fine group of soloists and incisive choral singing. In the first two movements he is clear-cut and rhythmically precise (though by no means inflexible), and the slow movement, if not wearing its heart on its sleeve, certainly does not lack expressive feeling. The finale is strong and exciting, with the quality of the recording telling, even if, like the first movement, it lacks some weight (as did the original LP). Ansermet demonstrates here that the Viennese tradition is not the only way with Beethoven.

Schmidt-Isserstedt, with no exaggeration and few if any high-flown purple patches, gives a most satisfying reading of the *Ninth* to act as a suitable culmination for his impressive cycle from the late 1960s. This (like his account of the *Eroica*) is in many ways easier to live with than more monumental, more obviously 'great' performances. The approach associates the work more readily than most with Beethoven's earlier symphonic achievements – the link with the *Pastoral* at the end of the slow movement, for example – but it is the fine singing of soloists and chorus in the finale that above all makes this one of the keenest recommendations in the bargain range. All four soloists are on peak form and few rival versions match the beauty and balance of ensemble. The recording quality is outstanding for its period (1965) and the CD transfer improves the focus without loss of weight and body: the choral sound is particularly natural.

Masur's Leipzig *Ninth* comes from his complete set of the mid-1970s. It is a spacious, well-proportioned and noble account, more conventional in its speeds than some, and less weighty, yet in the excellent digital remastering the choral sound is full and immediate and the extra clarity extends to the other movements.

Michael Tilson Thomas's version of the *Ninth* may – like the rest of his Beethoven cycle – involve limited forces approximating to the size of those originally used, but there is nothing miniature here. This is an unusually powerful reading, sharply rhythmic and with a fine sense of drama, well paced at traditional rather than 'authentic' tempi. The very opening has nothing of mystery in it, with the tremolos firmly placed in clear and immediate sound. That forwardness gives the first movement ample power, and the clarity of detail in the second adds to the joyful resilience of the dance rhythms. Paradoxically, one misses a full body of violins most of all in the lyrical expanses of the slow movement, which is done very sweetly. The whole of the last movement – often taken faster than usual – comes at white heat, with some first-rate solo work, notably from Gwynne Howell in a magnificent account of the opening solo, though the forward balance militates against any gentle singing. The Tallis Chamber Choir rather belies its name when, with more immediacy than choruses often get in the *Ninth*, the sound is so full as well as clear.

As bitingly dramatic as Toscanini in the first movement and electrically intense all through, Szell directs a magnetic, seemingly inevitable account of the *Ninth* which demonstrates the glories of the Cleveland Orchestra. With speeds never as extreme as Toscanini's, he yet captures a comparable fire. Though with close-up CBS recording, the slow movement never conveys anything like a pianissimo, the beauty of line in immaculate legato gives persuasive warmth and sweetness. The chorus sings with similarly knife-edged ensemble, set behind the orchestra but not too distantly. Soloists are well forward, so that words are exceptionally clear. The 1961 sound, bright and forward, has come up satisfyingly full-bodied, if with some analogue hiss. At mid-price a first-rate recommendation for those wanting a commanding reminder of a great conductor's work. The performance of the *Fidelio* overture is electrifying.

It is thrilling to have a CD transfer of the historic recording made at the re-opening of the Festspielhaus in Bayreuth in 1951. The chorus may sound washy in the distance, almost as though placed at the bottom of the Rhine, and the lack of perspective in the mono sound is brought out the more on CD (along with audience noises), but the extra clarity and freshness impressively enhance a reading without parallel. The spacious, lovingly moulded account of the slow movement is among Furtwängler's finest achievements on record and, with an excellent quartet of soloists, the finale crowns a great performance.

Toscanini's electrifying account of the *Ninth* is marred somewhat by the excessive treble emphasis, more noticeable than on the earlier, full-priced reissue.

Jochum's later EMI recording could have been even more recommendable than the earlier, Philips Concertgebouw version, but unfortunately the CD transfer has lost some of the bloom of the analogue master and is edgy and not ideally focused. The interpretation is similar, with the scherzo almost violent in its urgency and speeds generally on the fast side, the massive structures of the first and third movements held together seamlessly. With youthful-sounding voices among the soloists as well as in the chorus, the effect balances vitality with weight, and it is a pity that the sound is so disappointing.

Klemperer's 1958 sound is amazingly good for its period, with the finale fresher and better balanced than in many recent recordings. However, Klemperer's weighty vision is marred by a disappointing quartet of soloists; and the slow speeds for the first two movements – the scherzo seems to go on for ever – come to sound ponderous. Yet the flowing account of the slow movement shows Klemperer at his finest. The CD offers extra refinement, with the choral sound in the finale given astonishing presence and tangibility.

Sanderling's 1984 digital performance of the *Ninth* has a rugged directness – an unvarnished honesty, as one commentator put it – which has special links with the Philharmonia versions conducted by Klemperer. Like Klemperer, Sanderling prefers slowish tempi, steadily maintained. This *Ninth* may lack mystery at the start, and the finale is dangerously slow; but the power of the work is caught splendidly. The soloists make an excellent team, but the Philharmonia Chorus is just below its best form, the singing of the sopranos not always well supported. This record undoubtedly has its rewards to offer but, except for those insisting on digital recording, there are many more distinctive mid-priced alternatives.

Haitink's 1980 digital recording was made at

a live concert in the Concertgebouw, but one would not know that: there are few if any signs of an audience, and – disappointingly – the performance fails to convey the excitement of a live occasion. The reading is satisfyingly unidiosyncratic, direct and honest; but with this work one needs more. The sound is good, but this reissue includes no information about the music itself.

Wyn Morris's Beethoven cycle for Pickwick came to a disappointing conclusion with this account of the *Ninth* which displayed too many signs of haste in the recording; where most of the earlier issues in the series found the LSO in excellent form, the ensemble here is often slack. Even at mid-price, there are many versions finer than this; though it has the benefit of modern digital recording, the sound here is little more faithful than that on some of the vintage versions.

Edlinger's Naxos version from Zagreb fails to maintain full tension through this most dramatic of symphonies, nor is it helped by speeds on the expansive side. Yet, with a fresh-toned chorus and good soloists, notably the tenor, the choral finale makes an aptly exciting conclusion. Warm, digital recording.

Symphony No. 10 in E flat: 1st movement (realized and completed by Dr Barry Cooper – includes lecture by Dr Cooper).
(B) *** Pickwick Dig. PCD 911; *CIMPC 911* [id.]. LSO, Wyn Morris.

As re-created from Beethoven's sketches by Dr Barry Cooper, this movement from what was planned as the *Tenth Symphony* is, as Dr Cooper says, no more than an 'artist's impression'. What he has put together from those and other sketch sources makes a fascinating and satisfying symphonic concept: a noble slow movement in E flat with obvious echoes of the *Ninth Symphony*, in the centre of which is a compressed *Allegro* sonata-form movement in C minor, the whole lasting almost 20 minutes. The broad *Andante* sections with their *Ninth*-like descants to the *Pathétique*-like main theme are plausibly Beethovenian. What is far less convincing is the *Allegro*, based as it is on relatively feeble material, with conventional working-out but with one or two surprising strokes culled from the sketches which, for all their oddity, must be counted Beethovenian. The master would have moulded this into something far greater, but it is well worth hearing music that so dwells in the mind.

Wyn Morris in this first recording directs a broad, strong reading, very well played and recorded. Dr Cooper's half-hour lecture fascinatingly amplifies and illustrates his detailed notes, making clear his scholarly credentials as well as his devotion to what Beethoven planned.

CHAMBER MUSIC

Allegro and minuet in G for 2 flutes; Serenade (arr. for flute and piano), *Op. 41; Sonata in B flat* (for flute & piano); *6 Themes and variations for flute and piano, Op. 105; 10 Themes and variations for flute and piano, Op. 107; Trio in G for 3 flutes; Trio concertante in G, for flute, bassoon and piano.*
(B) *** VoxBox (2) [CDX 5000]. Rampal, Larde, Veyron-Lacroix.

The VoxBox sensibly gathers together all Beethoven's music featuring the solo flute, and, if the *Sonata in B flat* is almost certainly spurious, it is pleasing enough. The *Serenade* is offered in a transcription by other hands (perhaps those of Franz Xaver Kleinheinz), which Beethoven himself revised. With Rampal showing polish and finesse as well as vivacity, well partnered by Robert Veyron-Lacroix, it is more enjoyable here than in the original version, offered on the alternative, Turnabout set. The second set of 10 *Themes and variations*, Op. 107, were also part of the Thompson commission and engagingly feature Tyrolean, Irish (including *St Patrick's Day*), Welsh, Scottish and Russian airs. Good sound and a programme well worth dipping into. This is not yet available in the UK.

(i) *Allegro & minuet in G for 2 flutes; 6 Themes and variations for flute and piano, Op. 105; Trio for 3 flutes;* (ii) *Piano and wind quintet in E flat, Op. 16;* (iii) *Serenade in D for flute, violin & viola, Op. 25; Sonatinas for mandolin and harpsichord: in C min.; in C; Adagio in E flat; Variations in D, WoO 43/44;* (iv) *Violin sonata No. 5 in F (Spring), Op. 24.*
(B) ** Turnabout 0009 (2). (i) Rampal, Marion, Lardé, Veyron-Lacrox; (ii) Simon, Woodhams, Silfies, Pandolfi, Berry; (iii) Berg, Rabinovitsi; Barnes; (iv) Kunschak, Hinterleitner; Rosand, Flisser; (with SCHLICK: *Divertimento in D* *).

With these generously full Turnabout doubles one has to take a certain amount of music that is acceptable rather than memorable in order to secure the highlights. Of the pieces for two and three flutes, delightful in their ocarina-like piping but limited in colour range, the *Rondo* of the *Trio* is a winner, The *Themes and variations* are an offshoot of Beethoven's arrangements of British folksongs, inspired and commissioned by the Scottish publisher, Thomson. Five of the six are based on Scots or Irish airs. Surprisingly, *The last rose of summer* (with a melodic line lightly different from the familiar song) has a rather faded charm; the gems are *The cottage maid* (which opens the collection with engaging naïveté) and perhaps an even more ingenuous set on the Austrian tune, *A Schüssel und a Reindel*. Very good playing and clear, forward recording. The account of the *Serenade* (also flute-led) is lively but is less winning, partly because the violin is made to seem a little edgy by the recording, while the performance of the *Piano and wind quintet*, led by Abbey Simon, is bland and lacking in charisma. The balance is restored by Aaron Rosand's strong version of the *Spring sonata*, very well played, although the brisk first movement is vital rather than seeking to charm. But the miniatures for mandolin are delightful, especially when played so spontaneously and projected so crisply by the recording. The filler by Johann Schlick (1748–1825) is less interesting, a divertimento for two mandolins and continuo. Alas, the documentation included provides no information beyond listing the titles of the various works.

Cello sonatas Nos. 1–5; 7 Variations on Bei Männern (from Mozart's *Die Zauberflöte), WoO 45; 12 Variations on 'See the conqu'ring hero comes'* (from Handel's *Judas Maccabaeus), WoO 46; 12 Variations on Ein Mädchen, Op. 66*.
(M) *** EMI CMS7 63015-2 (2). Jacqueline Du Pré, Daniel Barenboim.
(M) *** DG 423 297-2 (2) [id.]. Pierre Fournier, Wilhelm Kempff.

The set of performances by Jacqueline Du Pré with Daniel Barenboim was recorded live for the BBC during the Edinburgh Festival of 1970. The playing may not have the final polish that studio performances would no doubt have achieved, but the concentration and intensity of the playing are wonderfully caught; and though the Scottish audience was often maddeningly bronchial, the performances remain totally compelling, with Barenboim bringing discipline, his wife drawing out lyrical intensity. The recording emerges with good presence on CD, not as full as it might be.

By a strange coincidence, Fournier and Kempff also recorded their cycle of the *Sonatas* at live festival performances. However, the Paris audience is considerably less intrusive than the Edinburgh ones on EMI and, like their younger colleagues, these artists were inspired by the occasion to produce intensely expressive playing, performances which are marked by light, clear textures and rippling scale-work, even in the slow introductions which are taken relatively fast. Some of the weight is missing; but such a stylish spontaneity is irresistible, and admirers of both artists can be warmly recommended to the set. The balances are not ideal, but there is no lack of CD presence.

Cello sonatas Nos. 1–2, Op. 5/1–2; 12 Variations in G on 'See the conqu'ring hero comes' (from Handel's *Judas Maccabaeus), WoO 46*.
(M) (**) Sony mono MPK 46725 [id.]. Pablo Casals, Rudolf Serkin.

These celebrated performances come from the early 1950s (the *F major Sonata* was recorded at Prades in 1953, the *G minor* in Perpignan two years earlier). If the playing is at an exalted level, younger collectors may be disappointed by the lacklustre recordings. In the *F major* the dryish acoustic robs Casals of some timbre and bloom, though the earlier recording is a good deal better in this respect. Indeed Serkin is at his most sensitive and, artistically, this is by far the more satisfying experience, though neither performance is free from the intrusive grunts and moans in which Casals indulged. Of the three recordings the *Judas Maccabaeus variations* calls for the greatest tolerance as it is thin and papery.

Cello sonatas Nos. 3 in A, Op. 69; 4 in C; 5 in D, Op. 102/1–2.
(BB) *(*) Naxos Dig. 8.550478 [id.]. Csaba Onczay, Jenö Jandó.

Cello sonatas Nos. 3 in A, Op. 69; 5 in D, Op. 102/2.
(M) *** EMI CDM7 69179-2; *EG 769179-4*. Jacqueline du Pré, Kovacevich.

The Du Pré/Bishop-Kovacevich recordings of Nos. 3 and 5 come from 1966, the year after Jacqueline had made her definitive record of the Elgar *Concerto*. The very opening of the *D major Sonata* underlines an unbuttoned quality in Beethoven's writing and when, after the hushed intensity of the slow introduction of Op. 69, the music launches into the allegro, both artists soar away fearlessly. More remarkable still is the range of expressiveness in the slow movement of Op. 102/2. Du Pré's tone ranges from full-blooded fortissimo to the mere whisper of a half-tone, and these artists allow the most free range of expressive rubato. With excellent recording, these performances are most welcome on CD, sounding crisp and present in their new format.

A rather unsatisfactory balance diminishes the attractions of the alternative Naxos coupling. The pianist is far too dominant and, though he is a responsive and at times sensitive partner, he can also be a little perfunctory. Indeed, some of his fortissimos are a shade brutal. Csaba Onczay is a musical player but his personality is swamped here. A pity, for the acoustic environment in which they are recorded is much more congenial than many others from this source. Not quite the bargain it first appears.

Clarinet trio in B flat, Op. 11.
(B) **(*) Pickwick PCD 959. David Campbell, Iwan Llewelyn-Jones, Lionel Handy – BRAHMS: *Clarinet trio.* **(*)

No quarrels with the Musicfest Trio (an umbrella group which can expand to an octet or even to a chamber orchestra and who have their origins in the Aberystwyth Festival), who play with evident spirit and vitality. They show sound musicianship and no mean sensitivity, and the only ground for reservation is the over-reverberant acoustic. A pity, as this is a very promising début.

Piano trios Nos. 1–9; 10 (Variations on an original theme in E flat), Op. 44; 11 (Variations on 'Ich bin der Schneider Kakadu'), Op. 121a.
(M) **(*) Sony SM4K 46738 (4) [id.]. Eugene Istomin, Isaac Stern, Leonard Rose.

Piano trios Nos. 1–11; Trio in E flat (from Septet), Op. 38; Trio in D (from *Symphony No. 2*); *Trio movement in E flat.*
(M) **(*) Ph. Analogue/Dig. 432 381-2 (5) [id.]. Beaux Arts Trio.

Piano trios Nos. 1–3; 5–7; 9–10 (Variations on an original theme in E flat); 11 (Variations on 'Ich bin der Schneider Kakadu'); Allegretto in E flat, Hess 48.
(M) **(*) EMI CMS7 63124-2 (3) [Ang. CDMC 63124]. Daniel Barenboim, Pinchas Zukerman, Jacqueline du Pré.

Piano trios Nos. 1–3; 5–7.
(M) **(*) DG 415 879-2 (3) [id.]. Kempff, Szeryng, Fournier.

Piano trio No. 5 in D (Ghost), Op. 70/1.
(M) *** Ph. 420 716-2 [id.]. Beaux Arts Trio – SCHUBERT: *Trout quintet.* **
(M) (**) Sony mono MPK 46447 [id.]. Rudolf Serkin, A. & H. Busch – BRAHMS: *Piano trio No. 2.* (**)

Piano trios Nos. 5 in D (Ghost), Op. 70/1; 7 in B flat (Archduke), Op. 97.
(M) **(*) DG 429 712-2; *429 712-4* [id.]. Kempff, Szeryng, Fournier.

Piano trios Nos. 7 (Archduke); 11 (Variations on 'Ich bin der Schneider Kakadu').
(B) *** Pickwick Dig. PCD 874; *CIMPC 874* [id.]. Kalichstein, Laredo, Robinson.

Unlike their earlier set, made in the late 1960s, the present Beaux Arts box offers absolutely everything Beethoven composed (or arranged) for this grouping. Four of the recordings are digital, and everything has been economically fitted on five CDs, four of which have playing times of over 70 minutes. The transfers are well up to the usual high Philips standard and the performances are as accomplished and musical as one would expect from this celebrated team. However, it has to be said that the earlier, analogue set had a freshness and sparkle that these new accounts do not wholly match. Also at mid-price they couple the *Ghost trio* with an enjoyable version of Schubert's *Trout quintet.* The *Ghost* comes off marvellously and sounds very fresh, and the 1979 recording has responded well to digital remastering; the sound is firm, clear and truthfully balanced. The *Trout*, however, is rather less successful; the violinist Isidore Cohen's timbre is made to sound thinner and edgier than it is.

The Barenboim/Zukerman/du Pré set (by omitting Nos. 4 and 8) is fitted economically on to three mid-priced CDs. Even more than usual, the individual takes involved long spans of music, often complete movements, sometimes even a complete work. The result is music-making of rare concentration, spontaneity and warmth. Any tendency to self-indulgence – and this aspect of the playing may seem intrusive to some ears – plus a certain leaning towards romantic expressiveness, is counterbalanced by the urgency and intensity. Speeds tend to be extreme in both directions, and the *Innigkeit* of some of the slow movements, especially in the *Ghost trio*, Op. 70, No. 1, has the depth of really mature artistry, extraordinary in the work of musicians so young at the time of the recordings. The excellent recording has been freshened on CD, and the players are given a natural presence; although at times the definition is not absolutely clean and there is a touch of dryness on fortissimo tuttis, overall the effect is pleasingly natural.

The Kempff–Szeryng–Fournier team recorded their survey of the Beethoven *Trios* in the early 1970s, and the DG engineers have been outstandingly successful in transferring them to the new medium. These are performances of distinction and well worth adding to any collection, given the excellence of the sound-quality. Wilhelm Kempff is an unfailingly interesting artist, and both Henryk Szeryng and that aristocrat of cellists, Pierre Fournier, are in impressive form throughout. On their separate coupling of the two most famous works, Kempff and his colleagues give a crystalline reading of the *Archduke*, and the performance of the *Ghost trio* is again relatively restrained. These are essentially lyrical readings and it is the clarity and imagination of Kempff's playing which grip the listener's attention with his many individual touches so that, by comparison, Szeryng and Fournier sound less inspired. The CD transfers are fresh and clear and the 1970 recording has plenty of fullness as well as a natural presence.

The Sony set includes everything but the

early *Allegretto in E flat*; it is therefore more complete than its two mid-priced competitors – but in doing so it runs to four discs and is thus considerably more expensive. Compared with the approach of Barenboim and his team, the playing of the Istomin/Stern/Rose group is more direct and straightforward. In New York the music-making is strong, polished and alive, and Istomin is always thoughtful and imaginative in slow movements, while Rose, although a less extovert artist than Stern, holds his own by the warmth and finesse of his lyrical phrasing. One of the highlights of the Sony set is the *Archduke*, bold and immediate, less controversial than the more wayward EMI account; the *Ghost trio* also shows these artists at their most communicative, while they do not miss the charm of the early Op. 1 works. The recording is characteristically forward in the CBS manner of the late 1960s: piano tone is comparatively shallow and Stern's upper range is given a degree of fierceness, and the effect is not entirely natural. Yet these are considerable performances, highly committed, unidiosyncratic and close to the spirit of Beethoven.

The Kalichstein–Laredo–Robinson Trio's interpretations of both the *Archduke* and the *Variations* are unaffected, supremely musicianly and thoughtful. Indeed their first movement of the *Archduke* is splendidly unhurried, and tempi throughout are excellently judged. There is formidable and distinguished opposition, but this team has nothing to fear from it. A marvellous performance and a very good, splendidly clean recording, even if it is bright and forward.

Adolf Busch was past his prime by the time this *Ghost trio* was recorded, but the fine musicianship and musical insight are still in evidence, despite the slightly wider vibrato and odd portamento. As far as the microphone is concerned, Serkin is rather dominant, but his playing is unfailingly responsive and articulate and without a trace of the mannerisms that affected him in the 1960s (banged pedals and ugly phrase-endings). Above all (and bearing in mind the sonic limitations) this is *real* chamber-music-making, far removed from the high-tech gloss of some modern ensembles. The players are wholly absorbed in the music and with what each has to say to the others, so it is well worth putting up with the balance and Busch's tonal frailties.

Piano and wind quintet in E flat, Op. 16.

(M) *** Decca 421 151-2; *421 151-4*. Ashkenazy, L. Wind Soloists – MOZART: *Quintet*. ***

(B) *** Hung. White Label HRC 169 [id.]. Sándor Fálvai, Hungarian Wind Qt – MOZART: *Quintet*. ***

(BB) *(*) Naxos Dig. 8.550511 [id.]. Jenö Jandó, Kiss, Kovács, Kevehazi, Vajda – MOZART: *Quintet*. *(*)

Ashkenazy's recording from 1966 is in every way recommendable. The *Andante cantabile* of the Beethoven is given a particularly appealing tranquillity, and the *Rondo* is both gracious and sprightly. The sound is first class in every way, the balance rather forward but very vivid and real.

The excellent, bargain-priced Hungaroton coupling stands up well to the distinguished competition. The three movements are admirably paced and spontaneously interrelated in mood, the woodwind playing is individually characterful yet well blended, and the pianist, Sándor Fálvai, dominates with fresh, rhythmic articulation and shapely phrasing. The Hungaroton recording is clear and natural, and the acoustic and balance are equally felicitous. Altogether most enjoyable.

The Naxos performance, though well recorded and naturally balanced, is a disappointment. It opens rather stoically, and the first movement then proceeds robustly, without ever really taking off. Jandó leads the *Andante* effectively enough, but the wind players, though blending well, proceed in a leisured but uninspired manner. The finale has plenty of spirit, again with Jandó dominating, but overall this will give but limited satisfaction.

Septet in E flat, Op. 20.

(M) *** Decca 421 093-2; *421 093-4* [id.]. V. Octet (members) – MENDELSSOHN: *Octet*. **(*)

Septet in E flat, Op. 20; (i) *Sextet in E flat, Op. 81b.*

(M) **(*) Ph. 426 091-2; *426 091-4*. BPO Octet (members); (i) with Manfred Klier.

This Decca recording was made by the older generation of the Vienna Octet – which consists of the first desks of the VPO. Their performance has elegance but also conveys a sparkle and a sense of enjoyment that are thoroughly exhilarating. The CD transfer is very successful.

An amiably refined performance from the excellent Berlin Philharmonic group on Philips, with plenty of life in the outer movements, but with rather a solemn view taken of the slow movement. The recording is first class; many will like its warmth and amplitude. The *Sextet*, for two horns and string quartet, is also very well played and recorded.

Serenade in D, Op. 8 (arr. Matiegka).

(M) ** BMG/RCA GD 87870; *GK 87870* [7870-

2-RG; *7870-4-RG*]. Heifetz, Primrose, Piatigorsky – SPOHR: *Violin concerto No. 8* etc.(***)

The Heifetz–Primrose–Piatigorsky record was made in 1960 at the same time as the *D major Trio*, Op. 9, No. 2. The sound is dry but not unacceptably so, and the playing is immaculate. It comes with an altogether remarkable account of Spohr's so-called *Gesangsszene concerto.*

Serenade in D for flute, violin and viola, Op. 25.
❀ (BB) *** Pickwick/CDI Dig. PWK 1139. Israel Flute Trio (with Recital: '*Flute Serenade*' ***).

The light and charming combination of flute, violin and viola inspired the youthful Beethoven to write in an unexpectedly carefree and undemanding way. The sequence of tuneful, unpretentious movements reminds one of Mozart's occasional music, and this delectable Israel performance brings out all its charm. Er'ella Talmi is a superb flautist and she receives admirable support from her colleagues. The recording is wonderfully natural in sound and balance: it is as if the players were making music in one's own room.

String quartets

String quartets Nos. 1–16; Grosse Fuge, Op. 133.
(M) (***) EMI mono CZS7 67236-2 (7). Hungarian Qt.
(M) **(*) DG 423 473-2 (7) [id.]. Amadeus Qt.

String quartets Nos. 1–16; Grosse Fuge; Quartet in F from Sonata, Op. 14/1 (transcription).
(B) ** DG Dig. 431 094-2 (9). Melos Qt.

Recorded in 1953 before the age of stereo, the Hungarian Quartet's first recorded cycle of the Beethoven *Quartets* has long been overshadowed by their later, stereo set of 1966. Yet this very welcome reissue, with the mono sound firm and full and with fine presence, brings out the palpable advantages of the earlier performances. Originally issued on the Columbia label, this was the first complete cycle made in the LP era, soon to be followed by cycles from the Budapest, Pascal and Végh quartets – their earlier mono versions. The Hungarians' matching is superb, with tonal beauty never an end in itself. The *senza vibrato* playing of the chorale in the great *Heilige Dankgesang* of Opus 132 has never been more perfectly achieved. Polished ensemble goes with a sense of spontaneity in readings fresher and more direct than those of 1966. The spacious, unhurried playing of the great slow movements here has rarely been matched. Those primarily concerned with the music as opposed to sound-quality will find little difficulty in adjusting to the recording; indeed, on first hearing, so vivid and full is the sound that it would be easy to believe one was listening to a very early stereo recording, while the layout on only seven discs (with each one offering well over 70 minutes of music) makes it a bargain too. Unlike the Amadeus's seven-disc cycle on DG, this one has exposition repeats observed.

The Amadeus are at their best in the Op. 18 quartets, where their mastery and polish are heard to good advantage. In the middle-period and late quartets, their sumptuous tone and refinement of balance are always in evidence, but they do not always penetrate very far beneath the surface, particularly in the late quartets. There is some superb quartet playing in this cycle, but there are more searching accounts to be found. The recording, from the beginning of the 1960s, is fresh and lifelike and the set is economically priced on seven CDs.

The performances by the Melos Quartet of the early and middle-period quartets offer a refined blend, impeccable intonation and superb ensemble. However, admiration rather than unalloyed pleasure is one's final reaction. Speeds are on the fast side, this group does not convey sufficient sense of pleasure in the courtly exchanges that take place between the instruments in the early quartets, and at times their playing has an aggressive edge. There are, of course, some very good things in the set, and there is no question as to the finesse and mastery of the playing or the vividness of the recording. But far too many of the finales are too fast - the first movement in Op. 59/1 is incredibly rushed. The Melos players seem most naturally attuned to the late quartets, where they are strong and positive in fast movements, deeply expressive in slow ones, although here the playing is not as hushed as it might be. As a novelty, they include Beethoven's own transcription of the *Sonata*, Op. 14, No. 1, which is not otherwise available. The complete set is now offered in a box, on nine bargain-priced CDs.

String quartets Nos. 1–6, Op. 18/1–6.
(M) **(*) Ph. 426 046-2 (3). Italian Qt.
(B) ** Hung. White Label HRC 156/7. Bartók Qt.
(M) *(*) BMG/RCA GD 60456; *GK 60456* (3) [60456-2-RG]. Guarneri Qt.

String quartets Nos. 5 in A; 6 in B flat, Op. 18/5–6.
(B) **(*) Ph. 426 049-2. Italian Qt.

The Italian performances are in superb style. The only reservations concern Nos. 2 and 4: the latter is perhaps a little wanting in forward movement, while the conventional exchanges at the opening of No. 2 seem a shade too deliberate. The recordings were made between 1972 (Nos. 1 and 3) and 1975 (Nos. 2 and 4) and, while the balance is truthful, the digital remastering does draw the ear to a certain thinness in the treble, slightly more noticeable in the earliest recordings. If all the recordings were to be issued on Philips's bargain label, they would remain highly competitive.

The Bartók Quartet plays with great elegance and aplomb, though they rarely penetrate far below the surface. The performances first appeared in the early 1970s and the recordings are satisfactory but no more. Tempi tend to be brisk: the first-movement exposition repeat in the *F major* is not observed, but all the others are. There are good things here, but they would not add up to more than a cautious recommendation, were they not economically priced. They are certainly good value on a pair of bargain discs, although the Italian Quartet bring greater musical rewards.

The Guarneri set dates from 1969 and is probably the best of their cycle. Three quartets are accommodated on the first CD, two on the second, and the *B flat* (No. 6) has a disc to itself. Room could surely have been found for, say, the *String quintet*, which the Guarneri recorded at about this time. The performances are very efficient, but the sound is inclined to be hard and wiry.

String quartets Nos. 7–9 (Rasumovsky Nos. 1–3), Op. 59/1–3; 10 in E flat (Harp), Op. 74; 11 in F min., Op. 95.
(M) *** Ph. 420 797-2 (3). Italian Qt.
(M) * BMG/RCA GD 60457; *GK 60457* (3) [60457-2-RG]. Guarneri Qt.

String quartets Nos. 7 in F; 9 in C (Rasumovsky Nos. 1 & 3), Op. 59/1 & 3.
(B) ** Hung. White Label HRC 153. Bartók Qt.

String quartets Nos. 8, Op. 59/2; 10 (Harp), Op. 74.
(B) *** Hung. White Label HRC 063. Bartók Qt.

The remastered Italian set still sounds well: the original recordings, made between 1971 and 1974, were strikingly natural in balance and there is now only a slight thinness on top to betray their age, with no lack of body and warmth in the middle range. Their superiority in terms of sheer quartet playing is still striking: purity of intonation, perfectly blended tone and superb ensemble and attack. Their tempi are perfectly judged and every phrase is sensitively shaped. Yet there is no attempt to 'beautify' Beethoven, and these performances remain very recommendable at mid-price.

The *F major*, Op. 59, No. 1, is the best thing in the Guarneri set, made in the late 1960s, and it is less overdriven than the others. In general the playing here is never less than brilliant and virtuosic, which is not enough in this repertoire. The finale of Op. 59, No. 3, is horribly scrambled and the *E minor* is brash and aggressive. The recording enhances this impression: it is rather dry, airless and hard.

Op. 59, Nos. 1 and 3, can easily be accommodated on one CD these days, even though the *F major* often takes longer than 40 minutes. The Bartók here get through both in 62 minutes flat by adopting pretty fast tempi and omitting exposition repeats. The performances are good, if less than searching, and the 1970s recordings are fully acceptable, if nothing out of the ordinary. But this CD is nevertheless economically priced. The Bartók Quartet give strong, well-paced readings of Op. 59/2 and the *Harp quartet*, with slow movements to match any rival versions at whatever price. With excellent Hungaroton recording, this is an outstanding bargain in the White Label series.

String quartets Nos. 7 in F; 8 in E min. (Rasumovsky), Op. 59/1–2.
(M) **(*) Sony SBK 46545 [id.]. Budapest Qt (Joseph Roisman; Alexander Schneider, Boris Kroyt, Mischa Schneider).

The Budapest Quartet on CBS were the first group to provide a complete stereo set of the Beethoven *Quartets*. The rugged masculinity of their approach (heard most strikingly here in the *Allegretto vivace* of Op. 59/1) is very suitable in such works, and it brings plenty of bite to both performances. They are closely balanced, which does not help in the provision of pianissimos, yet there is no real lack of light and shade. At times the leader's intonation is less than ideal; but this is powerfully felt playing of a kind we do not often encounter today – the *Adagio* of the *E minor*, Op. 59/2, shows this readily. Moreover the music-making is strongly communicative – the rough edges are caused by commitment to Beethoven, not by lack of rehearsal, and the ensemble playing generally has the most powerful unanimity. The sound on CD is balanced in favour of the leader, but otherwise is remarkably good, and the effect is very live.

String quartets Nos. 9 in C (Rasumovsky), Op. 59/3; 10 in E flat (Harp), Op. 59/3; Grosse Fuge in B flat, Op. 133.
(M) * Sony SBK 47665 [id.]. Budapest Qt.

The performance of Op. 59/3 suffers badly from the faults inherent in this series: too close a balance, scrawny violin-tone and suspect intonation in the first movement. The *Harp* fares rather better and the *Adagio* is eloquent, but the sound remains too forward and there is a reluctance to play softly. The *Grosse Fuge* is strong but shrill.

String quartet No. 10 in E flat (Harp), Op. 74.
(B) ** Pickwick Dig. PCD 831. Brodsky Qt – SCHUBERT: *String quartet No. 13.* **

The Brodsky recording comes from the mid-1980s. Their account of the *Harp quartet* is full of spirit and they are not lacking in imagination. But there are some rough edges here and there, and their vehemence in fortissimos is not helped by a rather forward recording balance.

String quartets Nos. 12 in E flat, Op. 127; 13 in B flat, Op. 130; 14 in C sharp min., Op. 131; 15 in A min., Op. 132; 16 in F, Op. 135; Grosse Fuge in B flat, Op. 133.
(M) **(*) Ph. 426 050-2 (4). Italian Qt.
(M) ** DG 431 141-2 (3). LaSalle Qt.
(M) * BMG/RCA GD 60458; *GK 60458* (3) [60458-2-RG]. Guarneri Qt.

The merits of the Italian Quartet's performances are considerable. The sonority that they produce is beautifully blended and splendidly focused and yet their prime concern is with truth, not beauty. The transfers to compact disc have been effected well, though the gain in clarity also entails a slight loss of warmth in the middle register. Now they do not sound as sumptuous as some modern quartet recordings, but their reissue on four medium-price CDs is less competitive than it might be, when their competitors are available on three. However, for many the Italians' searching and thoughtful interpretations will ultimately prove most satisfying.

Technically, the LaSalle Quartet are unfailingly impressive and they bring unanimity of ensemble and fine tonal blend to these awe inspiring scores. But there is no sense of mystery, little feeling of inwardness or depth. The recordings (made between 1973 and 1977) were of DG's best analogue quality, and they have been transferred cleanly and firmly to CD; but the Italians bring us much closer to this music.

The Guarneri are brash and hard, and rarely penetrate below the surface. Even if they did, it would be difficult in this day and age to recommend a set that manages to split Op. 127 over two CDs and also accommodates Op. 130 and the *Grosse Fuge* on separate discs.

String quartets Nos. 12 in E flat, Op. 127; 14 in C sharp min., Op. 131.
(B) *** Hung. White Label HRC 125. Bartók Qt.

The Bartók Quartet's very generous coupling of Opp. 127 and 131 comes in the inexpensive White Label series, making it another outstanding bargain, particularly when the performances – well recorded by Hungaroton in good analogue sound – have such concentration. The sweetness and purity of the string-playing matches that of any rival versions; but the sureness of control over the span of the sublime slow movements still makes this an outstanding version, even taking no account of price.

String quartets Nos. 12 in E flat, Op. 127; 16 in F, Op. 135.
(M) *** Ph. 422 840-2. Italian Quartet.

The Italians give a most searching account of the first movement of Op. 127, and their firmness of tone and accuracy of ensemble compel admiration; indeed, their account of the whole work goes far deeper than that of many full-priced rivals. Some may quarrel with their tempi in the inner movements of Op. 135; but on the whole this is a magnificent account which readers will find musically satisfying and sounding very fresh and immediate on this remastered CD.

(i) *String trio No. 1 in E flat, Op. 3;* (ii) *String quartet No. 11 in F min., Op. 95.*
(B) *(*) Hung. White Label HRC 158. (i) Kovács, Németh, Banda; (ii) Bartók Qt.

The *E flat String trio* is an underrated and masterly work, and it is given an eminently respectable performance by these distinguished players. The Bartóks' account of Op. 95 is of much the same vintage (the early 1970s) and is also workmanlike rather than inspired. The recording is fully acceptable.

String trio No. 2 in D, Op. 9/2.
(M) ** BMG/RCA GD 87873; *GK 87873* [7873-2-RG; *7873-4-RG*]. Heifetz, Primrose, Piatigorsky – BRAHMS: *Piano quartet in C min.*; SCHUBERT: *Fantaisie.* **

The performance of the *D major Trio* comes from 1960 and is the earliest of the recordings on this disc. The dryish sound remains a handicap but, as one would expect from these artists, the playing is magisterial.

Violin sonatas Nos. 1–10.
(M) *** Decca 421 453-2 (4). Itzhak Perlman, Vladimir Ashkenazy.
(M) *** DG 415 874-2 (3) [id.]. Yehudi Menuhin, Wilhelm Kempff.
(M) (***) Ph. mono 422 140-2 (3). Arthur Grumiaux, Clara Haskil.
(M) * HM/BMG GD 77163 (3) [77163-2-RG]. Jaap Schröder (violin), Jos Van Immerseel (fortepiano).

Perlman and Ashkenazy's set of the *Violin sonatas*, now reissued on four mid-priced CDs, is self-recommending. It was for the 1970s what Kreisler and Rupp were for the 1930s and

1940s, Grumiaux and Haskil for the 1950s and David Oistrakh and Oborin for the 1960s; and it will be difficult to surpass. These performances offer a blend of classical purity and spontaneous vitality that it is hard to resist; moreover the realism and presence of the recording in its CD format are very striking.

Inspirational artists of genius, Menuhin and Kempff met together in London in June 1970 to record this cycle of the Beethoven *Violin sonatas* in Conway Hall. Though these are not always the most immaculate performances on disc, they consistently reflect the joy and sense of wonder of pianist and violinist alike, often relaxed in tempo but magnetic from first to last. The brightness of the CD transfer at times gives too much edge to the violin tone, but these vintage recordings still sound well, with the rippling articulation of Kempff a constant delight.

Arthur Grumiaux and Clara Haskil made their celebrated recordings in 1956–7 and they sound remarkably well for their age. The performances are wonderfully civilized and aristocratic, and no one investing in them will regret it. They accommodate all ten *Sonatas* on three CDs at mid-price, as opposed to the four of Perlman and Ashkenazy.

Jaap Schröder plays an instrument by Joffredus Cappa of Saluzzo dating from 1684, while that most accomplished of fortepianists, Jos Van Immerseel, plays an 1824 fortepiano of the Viennese maker, Conrad Graf. Schröder's violin is often swamped by the fortepiano in the generously reverberant acoustic of the Vleeshuis Museum at Antwerp and sounds puny and scrawny by its side – admittedly not at the opening of the *Kreutzer* but certainly throughout the first movement of the *Spring*. The balance and the acoustic combine to diminish the success of this enterprise, though there are numerous artistic felicities from both artists.

Violin sonatas Nos. 5 in F (Spring), Op. 24; 7 in C min., Op. 30/2.

(M) (***) EMI CDH7 63494-2. Adolf Busch, Rudolf Serkin (with BACH: *Violin partita No. 2* (***)).

Music-making from another age, unhurried, humane and of supreme integrity. It seems as if the music plays itself, so selfless and musical are these great artists. The *Sonatas* were recorded in the early 1930s and the *Partita* in 1929, though the latter sounds more vivid, since the violin is placed more forwardly. Playing of such naturalness and artistry transcends the inevitable sonic limitations.

Violin sonatas Nos. 5 in F (Spring), Op. 24; 9 in A (Kreutzer), Op. 47.

(M) *** EMI CDM7 69021-2 [id.]; *EG 769021-4*. Pinchas Zukerman, Daniel Barenboim.

(M) *** DG 435 101-2; *435 101-4* [id.]. Sir Yehudi Menuhin, Wilhelm Kempff.

(B) *** DG Compact Classics *415 615-4* [id.]. Yehudi Menuhin, Wilhelm Kempff – BRAHMS: *Violin sonata No. 2.* ***

(BB) *** Naxos Dig. 8.550283 [id.]. Takako Nishizaki, Jenö Jandó.

(B) *(*) Hung. White Label HRC 105 [id.]. Dénes Kovács, Mihály Bächer.

Violin sonatas Nos. 5 in F (Spring); 9 in A (Kreutzer); 10 in G, Op. 96.

(M) **(*) Sony SBK 46342; *40-46342* [id.]. Zino Francescatti, Robert Casadesus.

Zukerman and Barenboim's coupling of the two favourites among Beethoven's *Violin sonatas*, taken from their 1973 cycle, brings disarmingly spontaneous-sounding performances. The CD transfer has warm, natural sound that scarcely betrays its age.

Menuhin has recorded three different versions of this coupling, two on EMI with partners from his own family, and the version on DG. There is no doubt that Menuhin and Kempff give inspirational accounts of both works, and the recording has striking presence and naturalness on CD. The Compact Classics tape offers an attractive coupling with Brahms.

Takako Nishizaki does not produce a large sound but the balance with Jandó is expertly managed, and the result is very natural and real. The performances are delightful in their fresh spontaneity. The opening of the *Spring sonata* is disarming in its simplicity, the variations in the *Kreutzer* are splendidly flowing and alive, and the finale, lightly pointed by both artists, has an irresistibly infectious sparkle. This is a bargain.

The Francescatti/Casadesus performances date from between 1959 and 1962. They are unfailingly musical and Casadesus's playing is always illuminating. Francescatti is warm-timbred, though not all ears will take to the slightly febrile quality of his vibrato. There is an occasional tendency to virtuosity at the expense of poise, although no one could fail to respond to the joyous vigour of the finale of the *Kreutzer*, following after a fine set of variations. Op. 96 is a more intimate performance and an appealing asset to the disc. Very good remastering: the piano tone is full and the overall effect is real, with good presence for both artists.

The Hungaroton White Label coupling is very acceptable, though Kovács' timbre as recorded is a little on the thin side. The balance, though, is good and these are fresh, straightforward performances.

Violin sonatas Nos. 6 in A; 7 in C min.; 8 in G, Op. 30/1–3.
(BB) **(*) Naxos Dig. 8.550286 [id.]. Takako Nishizaki, Jenö Jandó.

All three of the Op. 30 *Sonatas* on one CD represents very good value for money, particularly as these performances are of considerable quality. The Japanese violinist, Takako Nishizaki, produces a good sound and plays with fine musicianship and artistry, though she does not produce a big tone. Indeed hers is a reticent personality by the side of her Hungarian partner, though he shows keen musical responses. The recording, made in a Bratislava Radio studio, tends to favour the piano a little too much to warrant an unreserved three-star recommendation, and the instrument itself sounds just a bit bottom-heavy. However, these performances give much pleasure.

Violin sonata No. 8 in G, Op. 30/3.
(M) ** BMG/RCA GD 86264 [6264-2-RG]. Szeryng, Rubinstein – BRAHMS: *Sonatas Nos. 1 & 3.* **

A particularly successful account of the *G major Sonata* from Szeryng and Rubinstein, well recorded if rather drily, makes a good coupling for the two Brahms *Sonatas.*

Wind music

11 Dances, WoO 17; 3 Marches for military band in F and C, WoO 18/20; Octet in E flat, Op. 103; Rondino in E flat, WoO 25; Sextet in E flat, Op. 71; Variations on Mozart's 'Là ci darem la mano', WoO 28.
(M) *(**) EMI CDM7 64135-2; *EG 764135-4.* L. Bar. Ens., Karl Haas.

In the early LP era Karl Haas assembled the most distinguished players of the time for recordings by his London Baroque Ensemble. This sparkling collection brings together most of the recordings of Beethoven's wind music that he made between 1952 and 1959, with Dennis Brain, Alan Civil, Jack Brymer and Richard Adeney among the players listed; in the *Dances*, even Norbert Brainin and Siegmund Nissel from the Amadeus Quartet were brought in. The *Octet* and the *Sextet* are early works, despite their opus numbers; and the collections of marches and dances are, if anything, even more winning, the latter written for the local band in Mödling, where Beethoven spent his summer holidays. The *Marches* are great fun; the one in C major is especially bucolic (it is the second in order on the disc) and No. 2 in F has a virtuoso bassoon part which enlivens the texture agreeably. Clearly Beethoven is enjoying himself. The *Marches* are played with great spirit, but the wind chamber works are more relaxed, though the ear is coaxed by such expert musicianship and mellifluous blending, especially in the *Adagio* of the *Sextet.* The work's *Rondo* finale and the Minuet and Finale of the *Octet* are deliciously sprightly, and the gentle close of the *Rondino* is done most affectingly. Unfortunately, the recording has patches of distortion, notably in the first movement of the *Octet* and in the *Dances.* But the *Variations*, which are mono, recorded in 1952, are beautifully clean to match the delicately witty playing of Sidney Sutcliffe and Roger Lord (oboes) and Natalie James (cor anglais).

SOLO PIANO MUSIC

Piano sonatas Nos. 1–32 (complete).
❀ (M) (***) EMI mono CHS7 63765-2 (8) [Ang. CDHH 63765]. Artur Schnabel.
(B) *** DG 429 306-2 (9) [id.]. Wilhelm Kempff.
(M) *** EMI CZS7 62863-2 (10). Daniel Barenboim.
(M) **(*) Decca 425 590-2 (10). Vladimir Ashkenazy.

Piano sonatas Nos. 1–32; 6 Variations in F, Op. 43; Variations and fugue in E flat on a theme from Prometheus (Eroica), Op. 35; 32 Variations in C min., WoO 80.
(M) *** Ph. 432 301-2 (11) [id.]. Claudio Arrau.

Schnabel's survey originally appeared as part of a subscription venture (the Beethoven Sonata Society) in bulky albums of 78-r.p.m. shellac records. In the 1970s they were transferred to thirteen LPs and now, some twenty years on, can be accommodated on eight well-filled CDs – fewer than most of the competition. For many music-lovers and record collectors of an older generation, Schnabel was the voice of Beethoven; returning to this pioneering set again, one realizes that his insights were deeper than those of almost anyone who followed him, though his pianism has been surpassed. It was Schnabel who said that this music is better than it can ever be played, but his profound understanding of it shines through almost every bar. Of course his *Hammerklavier* has its moments of inelegance (to say the least) and his pianistic mannerisms are well in evidence in some of the earlier sonatas. Anyone can hear these moments of rough-and-ready playing, but no modern masters (Gilels the possible exception) have penetrated closer to the truth than he. No one has ever made the last movement of Op. 111 mean as much or found as much depth in Op. 110 as he did. This is one of the towering classics of the gramophone and, whatever other individual Beethoven sonatas you may have, this is an indispensable reference point.

Kempff's recordings, all dating from 1964/5, are to the 1960s what Schnabel's were to the pre-war years – performances that represent a yardstick by which all others are judged. The original LPs lacked the warmth of sonority and bloom of the very finest piano records of the analogue era, but the CD transfers bring a distinct improvement: the sound is fuller and firmer now, and the sense of presence is very striking. Some slight background hiss remains, but Kempff's shading of pianistic colour is so imaginative that the ear readily accommodates any slight dryness in the upper range. The interpretations have a commanding stature, yet Kempff brings his own individuality to every bar and a clarity and sparkle that make you want to go on listening. In his relatively measured speeds for fast movements Kempff is dramatic as well as fresh, while his flowing speeds in slow movements have a repose and concentration that belie the metronome. Where he is occasionally fast (in the slow movements of Opp. 26 and 110, for example) he is invariably illuminating. There is no doubting the inner compulsion and spiritual intensity which hold all these performances together. With his lucid and refreshing style, Kempff, more than any pianist of our time, has the power to make one appreciate and understand Beethoven in a new way, and that is so however many times one hears him. It makes a fascinating study to compare these interpretations not only with those of other pianists but with his own previous mono recordings. Above all, these magnificent records never fail to reveal his own spontaneity in the studio, his ability to rethink the reading on each occasion. The layout on nine CDs, presented in three separate jewel boxes within a slip-case, is admirably planned, and the records are offered at bargain price. Of the boxed sets of Beethoven's sonatas now before the public, this would be a first choice for many collectors, and rightly so.

Barenboim's earlier set of the Beethoven *Sonatas*, recorded for EMI when he was in his late twenties, remains one of his very finest achievements on record. Reissued on ten CDs at mid-price, it offers good value, with truthful recording and unique interpretations. The readings are sometimes idiosyncratic, with unexpected tempi both fast and slow, but the spontaneous style is unfailingly compelling. At times Barenboim's way is mercurial, with an element of fantasy. But overall this is a keenly thoughtful musician living through Beethoven's great piano cycle with an individuality that puts him in the line of master pianists. All three of the wonderful Op. 10 sonatas are given superb performances, and the last five show remarkable concentration, with the *Hammerklavier* providing a fitting culmination to the series.

Ashkenazy's comparable set occupied him over a decade or longer. These are eminently sound, well-recorded performances that deserve to rank among the best. Crisply articulated, intelligently shaped, not always inspired, they are never less than musically satisfying, although there is at times a hint of self-consciousness in the playing. The recording was generally of Decca's best quality in its LP format, but the CDs are not always as full and natural as the EMI transfers of the Barenboim cycle.

Whatever the merits of individual sonatas, Arrau's Beethoven cycle, recorded during the 1960s, is a survey of extreme distinction. The great Chilean pianist possessed a quite distinctive keyboard sonority, rich and aristocratic in its finesse. His tone was always perfectly focused and unusually rounded – and quite unlike that of anyone else. This sensitivity to tone-quality and awareness of beauty of tone shines through all these performances, though beauty is never given pride of place over truth. Even if one could part company with some of the expressive hesitations that occasionally disrupt the line, there is no doubt that they arise from deeply held musical conviction. The late sonatas show his artistry at its most consummate: one of the very finest of these performances (and one of the very finest records he ever made) is his *Hammerklavier*, which represents his art at its most fully realized. No apologies need be made for the recordings, which belie their age.

Piano sonatas Nos. 1 in F min.; 2 in A; 3 in C, Op. 2/1–3.

(BB) **(*) Naxos Dig. 8.550150 [id.]. Jenö Jandó.

Jenö Jandó's complete recording of the Beethoven *Piano sonatas* offers a consistently high standard of musicianship and excellent digital recording. The piano sound is real, full and bold, and well placed within the highly suitable acoustics of the Italian Institute of Budapest, which are neither dry nor too resonant. Apart from the ten separate issues discussed here, the records are also available in two flimsy slip-cases, each comprising five CDs (8.505002 and 8.505003). This first CD (actually Volume 3) establishes Jandó's credentials as a strong, unidiosyncratic Beethovenian. In the early sonatas, slow movements have a simple, unaffected eloquence, allegros are well paced, articulation is clean and often brilliant, and the classical structures are held together perceptively. If there is not the individuality of a Kempff or a Barenboim, the playing is always direct and satisfying, and if the *grazioso* finale of the *A major* seems a shade studied, the account here of *No. 3 in C major* is particularly fresh and enjoyable.

Piano sonatas Nos. 1 in F min., Op. 2/3; 5 in C min.; 6 in F, Op. 10/1–2; 9 in E; 10 in G, Op. 14/1–2; 13 in E flat; 14 in C sharp min. (Moonlight), Op. 27/1–2; 15 in D (Pastoral), Op. 28.
(B) **(*) VoxBox (2) [CDX 5056]. Alfred Brendel.

From the very start of the little F minor work which opens the greatest of all sonata cycles, Brendel makes clear the weight and seriousness of his approach. This is no mere Haydnesque reading, but a determined attempt to present the work as revolutionary, in the way it must have struck its first listeners. Yet the music flows spontaneously and the *Adagio* is poised and serene. Equally, in the two shorter sonatas from Op. 10, Brendel's clear, direct style suits the pithiness of the argument; although the *Adagio* of the *C minor Sonata* seems a little deliberate, the *Allegretto* of the F major work has plenty of colour. It is a pity, however, that the layout of the VoxBox prevents the usual arrangement of having all three Op. 10 sonatas together. The less ambitious but closely argued sonatas of Op. 14 are both fine works, despite their associations with piano lessons. Except perhaps in the great D minor slow movement, Brendel's strong, direct manner is consistently satisfying. For the first and less famous of the two Op. 27 *'Fantasy' Sonatas*, his concentration makes for satisfying results. Though fantasy in a strict sense is not one of his strongest suits, the work's opening is full of atmosphere. The *Moonlight* is hushed and gentle in its cool stillness, with veiled tone (a straight style helping, though there is no mystery). The finale, at a relaxed tempo, is beautifully pointed but does not seek extrovert excitement. The *Pastoral* is enjoyable in its relaxed simplicity. Brendel consistently holds the attention with his unforced and straightforward manner but by his very reticence misses some of the charm which a pianist like Barenboim in his more idiosyncratic way uses to heighten the music's effect. However, Brendel is at his finest in the elusive *G major Sonata*, Op. 79, which also offers good sound. The recordings, made between 1962 and 1964, have been excellently remastered: the piano image is bright bold and resonant with fine presence, the somewhat clattery quality of the original LPs now better controlled within the ambience, and no lack of sonority. Good notes. These first two Brendel Vox Boxes are not yet issued in the UK.

Piano sonatas Nos. 3 in C, Op. 2/3; 4 in E flat, Op. 7; 8 in C min. (Pathétique), Op. 13.
(BB) ** ASV CDQS 6056; *ZCQS 6056*. John Lill.

The *C major Sonata*, Op. 2/3, is one of John Lill's most successful performances and one of the best recorded. The slow movement makes a strong impression, though some will feel that the fortissimo outbursts are overcharacterized. In Op. 7 Lill's articulation from fingers of steel is thrilling, but the rhythms too rarely spring, and the rather formal *Largo, con gran espressione*, is given an uncompromising quality. The sound is believably present, though it seems shallower in the *Pathétique*, where the slow movement is thoughtful; but at times in the outer movements one has the impression that the drama is overdone.

Piano sonatas Nos. 4 in E flat, Op. 7; 13 in E flat, Op. 27/1; 19 in G min., 20 in G, Op. 49/1–2; 22 in F, Op. 54.
(BB) **(*) Naxos Dig. 8.550167 [id.]. Jenö Jandó.

Our copy of Jandó's Volume 8 is incorrectly documented: the notes (but not the listing) apply to another disc; however, we hope this will be corrected eventually. The performances of both the *E flat Sonata*, Op. 7, with its memorable slow movement, and the *Sonata quasi una fantasia*, Op. 27/1, in which Jandó is comparably responsive to Beethoven's wide expressive range, show the continuing excellence of this series, and the three shorter works are also freshly presented.

Piano sonatas Nos. 5 in C min.; 6 in F; 7 in D, Op. 10/1–3; 25 in G, Op. 79.
(BB) *** Naxos Dig. 8.550161 [id.]. Jenö Jandó.

The three splendid Op. 10 sonatas show Jandó at his most perceptive and unselfconscious. The performances are spontaneous and admirably paced, and the musical characterization is strong. Slow movements are thoughtful and have a natural expressive feeling. Op. 79 is also very appealing, and altogether Volume 5 may be regarded as one of the most successful in this excellent series.

Piano sonatas Nos. 8 in C min. (Pathétique), Op. 13; 9 in E; 10 in in G, Op. 14/1–2; 13 in E flat; 14 in C sharp min. (Moonlight), Op. 27/1–2.
(B) ** EMI CDZ7 62857-2; *LZ 762857-4*. Walter Gieseking.

These recordings were made in the early days of stereo, not long before Gieseking's death. He was undoubtedly a great pianist and there is distinguished playing here, of course; but there is something a little remote and cool about his approach to these *Sonatas*, and they cannot be said to compete in interpretative insight with the very finest versions now available. Even so, at bargain price they are by no means to be dismissed.

Piano sonatas Nos. 8 in C min. (Pathétique), Op. 13; 14 in C sharp min. (Moonlight), Op. 27/2; 15 in D (Pastoral), Op. 28; 23 in F min. (Appassionata), Op. 57; 26 in E flat (Les Adieux), Op. 81a (CD only: *17 in D min. (Tempest), Op. 31/2*).
(B) *** DG Compact Classics 413 435-2 (2); *413 435-4* [id.]. Wilhelm Kempff.

Piano sonatas Nos. 8 in C min. (Pathétique), Op. 13; 14 in C sharp min. (Moonlight), Op. 27/2; 15 in D (Pastoral), Op. 28; 24 in F sharp, Op. 78.
(M) *** DG 415 834-2; *415 834-4* [id.]. Wilhelm Kempff.

Kempff's masterly recordings show so well his ability to rethink Beethoven's music within the recording studio. Everything he does has his individual stamp, and above all he never fails to convey the deep intensity of a master in communion with Beethoven. The Compact Classics tape collection of five favourite named sonatas is an obvious bargain, while the digitally remastered two-CD set offers also the *Tempest*, and the piano quality has undoubtedly gained in firmness, although there is also a degree of hardness in both formats.

Piano sonatas Nos. 8 in C min. (Pathétique), Op. 13; 14 in C sharp min. (Moonlight), Op. 27/2; 23 in F min. (Appassionata), Op. 57.
(M) **(*) Sony MYK 42539 [id.]. Rudolf Serkin.
(BB) **(*) Naxos Dig. 8.550045 [id.]. Jenö Jandó.
(B) ** Pickwick Dig. PCD 828; *CIMPC 828* [id.]. John Ogdon.
(B) * Ph. 422 970-2; *422 970-4* [id.]. Claudio Arrau.

Serkin recorded remarkably few of the Beethoven sonatas, considering how eminent a pianist he was. Instead, he has concentrated on the popular named works, and these three in particular, each recorded by him several times before. His aristocratic approach is immediately apparent at the opening of the *Moonlight Sonata*, and in the allegros he is as incisive and dramatic as ever. As with all master pianists, one finds many points of insight emerging as well as one or two points of personal mannerism. The piano recording, from the early 1960s, is firmer and more real than in its previous LP incarnation.

Jandó's grouping of the three most famous named sonatas is in fact Volume 1 in his complete series and immediately establishes the lifelike nature of the Naxos recording. Jandó's clean, direct style and natural spontaneity are particularly admirable in the slow movements of the *Pathétique* and *Appassionata*, warmly lyrical in feeling, yet not a whit sentimental. Only in the coda of the finale of the *Appassionata* does one feel a loss of poise, when the closing *presto* becomes *prestissimo* and the exuberance of the music-making nearly gets out of control.

John Ogdon's mid-1980s record for Pickwick is far from negligible, even if it is not always completely satisfying. He is impressive in the outer movements of the *Moonlight* (the finale has admirable spirit and fire) but less so in the *Pathétique* and the *Appassionata* finale, which are wanting in concentration and at times are touched by routine. Yet Ogdon was a pianist of undoubted insights; the first movement of Op. 57 has great power. His admirers will want this, even if it does not represent him at his most consistently inspired.

This is one of Arrau's least successful Beethoven records. The *Grave* introduction of the *Pathétique*, the *Adagio* of the same sonata, the *Andante* of the *Appassionata* and the opening of the *Moonlight Sonata* are curiously studied and unspontaneous and, though there is impressive playing elsewhere and the recording is good if rather dry, this record can give but limited enjoyment.

Piano sonatas Nos. 8 in C min. (Pathétique), Op. 13; 14 in C sharp min. (Moonlight), Op. 27/2; 23 in F min. (Appassionata), Op. 57; 26 in E flat (Les Adieux), Op. 81a.
(M) * BMG/RCA GD 60356 [60356-2-RG]. Van Cliburn.

A disappointing collection. Van Cliburn takes the opening of the *Moonlight* quite fast and finds absolutely no atmosphere in the music; the slow movement of the *Pathétique* is similarly direct. The *Appassionata* comes off best here.

Piano sonatas Nos. 8 in C min. (Pathétique), Op. 13; 21 in C (Waldstein), Op. 53; 23 in F min. (Appassionata), Op. 57.
(M) **(*) Ph. 432 041-2; *432 041-4* [id.]. Claudio Arrau.

Arrau's performances are recorded magnificently. They were made at different times (1984–7) and in different places (Switzerland and New York), but the digital piano sonority is full and satisfying, the image bold and realistic. This helps to make Arrau's *Appassionata* very commanding indeed, with gloriously rich timbre in the central *Andante*. It is a distinguished performance, powerful and commanding in the same way as his *Emperor concerto*. The *Waldstein* is impressive too, though not as incandescent as Kempff's. The *Pathétique* (recorded in 1986 when Arrau was eighty-three) is just a little wanting in colour and vitality, and some listeners may feel that the *Adagio cantabile* is too measured. However, the playing throughout this record is impressive and, for all the individual mannerisms, the interpretations are authoritative and convincing. No musical notes are provided.

Piano sonatas Nos. 9 in E; 10 in G, Op. 14/1–2; 13 in E flat; 14 in C sharp min. (Moonlight), Op. 27/2.

(BB) ** ASV CDQS 6058; *ZCQS 6058*. John Lill.

For the two early sonatas Lill scales down the aggressiveness in his approach to Beethoven and the results are clear and refreshing, if lacking in charm. His account of No. 13 is thoughtful but not really imaginative enough, and memories of the marvellous range of colour that Schnabel produced in the first movement flood back. The opening of the *Moonlight* is simple and quite evocative, and Lill then attacks the finale with furious bravura. Bright, clear, late-1970s recording, not lacking sonority – the CD gives a good illusion of realism and presence.

Piano sonatas Nos. 9 in E; 10 in G, Op. 14/1–2; 24 in F sharp, Op. 78; 27 in E min., Op. 90; 28 in A, Op. 101.

(BB) *** Naxos Dig. 8.550162 [id.]. Jenö Jandó.

Volume 6 represents Jandó's finest achievement in the series so far. The readings are freshly immediate and communicative, very like being at a live recital. Opp. 90 and 101 show this artist at full stretch. These are demanding works and he does not fall short, particularly in the slow movements, which are very eloquent indeed. The piano sound is most believable.

Piano sonatas Nos. 11 in B flat, Op. 22; 29 in B flat (Hammerklavier), Op. 106.

(BB) **(*) Naxos Dig. 8.550234 [id.]. Jenö Jandó.

Volume 9 opens with another reading which demonstrates Jandó's direct and spontaneous style at its most impressive, although the articulation in the first movement of this *B flat Sonata*, Op. 22, (as in the *Waldstein*) is almost too clear and clean in its precision; the *Adagio*, however, is played most expressively. From its very opening bars the *Hammerklavier* is commanding; there is rapt concentration in the slow movement, and the closing fugue runs its course with a powerful inevitability. Again, most realistic recording.

Piano sonatas Nos. 12 in A flat, Op. 26; 16 in G; 18 in E flat, Op. 31/1 & 3.

(BB) **(*) Naxos Dig. 8.550166 [id.]. Jenö Jandó.

Volume 7 with its trio of middle-period sonatas can be recommended with few reservations. In No. 12 the *Andante con variazioni* is very engaging, but the *Marcia funebre* has moments when Jandó's articulation seems marginally overforceful; at the opening of the *Adagio* of No. 16, the accompaniment is very marked in its rhythmic emphasis and some ears may find this overdone. Yet No. 18 is a considerable success, and there is much to stimulate the listener's interest here. Excellent sound.

Piano sonatas Nos. 14 in C sharp min. (Moonlight), Op. 27/2; 17 in D min. (Tempest), Op. 31; 26 in E flat (Les Adieux), Op. 81a.

(M) **(*) DG Dig. 427 803-2; *427 803-4* [id.]. Daniel Barenboim.

A good example of Barenboim's spontaneous studio style in his second set of Beethoven sonatas, recorded digitally for DG in 1984. The slow movements of *Les Adieux* and the *Tempest* are memorable, and the finale of the latter work is infectiously communicative. Perhaps the opening of the *Moonlight* could be less withdrawn, but the rest of the work springs readily to life. Realistic recording, with a natural presence.

Piano sonatas Nos. 14 in C sharp min. (Moonlight), Op. 27/2; 21 in C (Waldstein), Op. 53; 23 in F min. (Appassionata), Op. 57.

(M) *** Decca 417 732-2. Vladimir Ashkenazy.

(M) **(*) BMG/RCA GD 60375 [60375-2-RG]. Vladimir Horowitz.

(M) **(*) DG Dig. 435 100-2; *435 100-4* [id.]. Daniel Barenboim.

(BB) **(*) Naxos Dig. 8.550294 [id.]. Jenö Jandó.

An excellent mid-priced grouping of three popular sonatas from Ashkenazy. All three recordings are given fine presence on CD. The *Waldstein* (1975) is splendidly structured and the *Appassionata* (1973) superb, although those who feel strongly about matters of tempo may well find Ashkenazy a little too free in the first movement.

Horowitz was not thought of primarily as a Beethoven pianist, but these recordings, made in 1956 (the *Moonlight* and *Waldstein*) and 1959, show how powerful he could be in the music of this composer. His delicacy, too, is equally impressive, as in the gentle *Adagio* which opens the *Moonlight Sonata* or in the way the lyrical theme steals in at the beginning of the finale of the *Waldstein*, where his reading has much in common with Kempff. There is prodigious bravura, too, as in the finale of the *Appassionata*, where he matches – and perhaps even surpasses – Richter in exuberance. The sound has been improved in the remastering process; there is some hardness on top but little shallowness, and the bass sonority is telling.

Barenboim plays the *Appassionata* with real panache, and his straightforwardly lyrical account of the *Waldstein* is more persuasive than was his earlier version for EMI, with its controversial tempi in the outer movements (and especially in the finale); this time all three movements are convincing in their lyricism. The lack of atmosphere in the first movement of the *Moonlight*, however, is a disappointment. No complaints about the recording, which is real and immediate.

This is a separate, alternative grouping of the named sonatas in Jandó's highly musical and well-recorded performances, not included in the boxed sets.

Piano sonatas: No. 15 in D (Pastoral), Op. 28; (Kurfürstensonaten) in E flat, F min., D, WoO 47/1–3; in C (incomplete), *WoO 51; Sonatinas: in G, F, Anh. 5/1–2.*
(BB) ** Naxos Dig. 8.550255 [id.]. Jenö Jandó.

This CD, Volume 10 in Jandó's integral set, acts mainly as an appendix to the major sonatas. The playing is fresh, clean and intelligent and, if the two *Sonatinas* are not authentic, they make agreeable listening here. The *Pastoral sonata* is admirably done.

Piano sonatas Nos. 15 in D (Pastoral), Op. 28; 21 in C (Waldstein), Op. 53; 26 in E flat (Les Adieux), Op. 81a.
(B) ** Ph. 426 068-2 [id.]. Claudio Arrau.

These are sound readings. Arrau is impressive in the *Andante* of the *Pastoral*, and he finds a similar lightness of touch in his introduction of the famous melody in the finale of the *Waldstein*. But the slow movement of the same sonata is overtly serious in mood, and elsewhere the impulsive and spontaneous character of these works is brought out less readily. The recordings were made between 1962 and 1966; the recording is truthful, if lacking something in colour in the middle range.

Piano sonatas Nos. 16 in G; 17 in D min. (Tempest); 18 in E flat, Op. 31/1–3; 19 in G min., Op. 49/1; 21 in C (Waldstein), Op. 53; 22 in F, Op. 54; 23 in F min. (Appassionata), Op. 57; 26 in E flat (Les Adieux), Op. 81a.
(B) **(*) VoxBox (2) [CDX 5052]. Alfred Brendel.

This box contains two of Brendel's very finest Beethoven performances. Op. 31/2 with its romantic echoes of Beethoven's improvisational style, produces electrically sharp playing and spontaneity; in the *Waldstein* too, Brendel's fresh and straightforward concentration produces a cleanly satisfying version, spontaneous-sounding but controlled. The finale, rippling and gentle, is very satisfying indeed, every bit the equal of Kempff's version. The *Appassionata*, however, is one of the less imaginative readings in Brendel's Vox cycle. The very opening is done simply and satisfyingly, in a way that would have been satisfactory enough in a lesser sonata but which here gives little expectation of the great statements to come. The coda is clean and sharp to round off the movement consistently, but the variations sound a little heavy, and the close of the finale hardly sweeps one away. The slow movement of *Les Adieux* lacks a hushed quality; the finale is strong and direct. The other sonatas here are well up to the standard of the series and there is more in this box to admire than to cavil at. Again the 1962–4 recordings have been remastered effectively and the piano recording has plenty of body and presence.

Piano sonatas Nos. 17 in D min. (Tempest), Op. 31/2; 21 in C (Waldstein), Op. 53; 26 in E flat (Les Adieux), Op. 81a.
(BB) **(*) Naxos Dig. 8.550054 [id.]. Jenö Jandó.

Volume 2 in Jandó's Naxos series contains the other three famous named sonatas, and very enjoyable they are in their direct manner, if lacking that little extra imaginative touch that Kempff, for one, can bring to the *Waldstein*, where Jandó's sharply articulated opening movement could ideally be more resilient. But *Les Adieux* has a simplicity that is disarming, and Op. 31/2 has strength and fine control of the work's emotional ebb and flow.

Piano sonatas Nos. 17 in D min. (Tempest), Op. 31/2; 29 in B flat (Hammerklavier), Op. 106.
(M) *** DG 419 857-2 [id.]. Wilhelm Kempff.

Kempff's *Hammerklavier* performance represents his interpretative approach to Beethoven at its most extreme and therefore controversial. Here his preference for measured allegros and fastish andantes gives a different weighting to movements from the usual, but there is a thoughtfulness of utterance which brings profundity, while in the finale Kempff's clarity of fingerwork brings a new freshness that lacks nothing in excitement. The coupling also has its own special insights, and the sound is clean and clear.

Piano sonatas Nos. 21 in C (Waldstein), Op. 53; 22 in F, Op. 54; 23 (Appassionata), Op. 57.
(BB) ** ASV CDQS 6061; *ZCQS 6061*. John Lill.

In the large-scale sonatas Lill's clean-cut, incisive style makes for performances that are generally refreshing but lacking in incandescence. The *Adagio* of the *Waldstein* is simple and restrained, and the entry of the main theme of the finale is prepared effectively, but later his powerful articulation, though strong, is somewhat inflexible. However, the lyrical directness of the two-movement *F major Sonata* is appealing and the *Appassionata* shows Lill's powerful fingers at their most arresting.

Piano sonatas Nos. 21 in C (Waldstein), Op. 53; 23 in F min. (Appassionata), Op. 57; 26 in E flat (Les Adieux), Op. 81a.
(M) *** DG 419 053-2 [id.]. Wilhelm Kempff.

Kempff's individuality in Beethoven is again established here. The *Appassionata* is characteristically clear, classically straight in the same way that the *Waldstein* is cooler and fresher than usual, with a wonderful classical purity in the rippling quavers. *Les Adieux*, like the *Appassionata*, may be less weightily dramatic than in other readings, but the concentration is irresistible. The digital remastering has brought clean sound to match.

Piano sonata No. 23 in F min. (Appassionata), Op. 57.
(M) *** BMG/RCA GD 86518 [RCA 6518-2-RG]. Sviatoslav Richter – BRAHMS: *Piano concerto No. 2.* ***

Richter's thrilling 1960 *Appassionata* is a superb example of a studio recording sounding like a live performance, with the wide dynamic range bringing out both the drama and passion of this boldly contrasted sonata. Some might feel that Richter goes over the top in the coda of the finale but the fervour is unmistakable, and this is an undeniably great interpretation. The recording brings out the percussive qualities of Richter's playing. But the remastering has made the most of the possibilities of the master-tape.

Piano sonatas Nos. 27 in E min., Op. 90; 28 in A, Op. 101; 29 in B flat (Hammerklavier), Op. 106; 30 in E, Op. 109; 31 in A flat, Op. 110; 32 in C min., Op. 111.
(B) **(*) VoxBox 1155952 (2) [CDX 5028]. Alfred Brendel.

The VoxBox devoted to Brendel's accounts of the late *Sonatas* is available in the UK and is far better value than the alternative pair of Tuxedo CDs – see below – offering first-rate transfers and much more music. There is no lack of *Innigkeit* in the wayward and elusive opening movement of Op. 90, to be followed by a smoothly flowing reading of the haunting second movement. However, there is less concentration in the last sonata of all, and the variations are somewhat disappointing.

Piano sonatas Nos. 27 in E min., Op. 90; 29 in B flat (Hammerklavier), Op. 106.
(BB) ** ASV CDQS 6063; *ZCQS 6063*. John Lill.

The *E minor Sonata* shows John Lill's thoughtful musical style at its most communicative, and he is most naturally recorded; but the *Hammerklavier* is more controversial. Lill's speed in the great *Adagio* is very slow indeed, and he does not sustain the movement with the necessary concentration; though the outer movements pack tremendous virtuosic punch, this does not match the finest versions.

Piano sonatas Nos. 28 in A, Op. 101; 29 in B flat (Hammerklavier), Op. 106.
(M) *** DG Dig. 429 485-2; *429 485-4* [id.]. Daniel Barenboim.

In his second digital cycle for DG, Barenboim was at his finest in the late *Sonatas*, and the sustained concentration of the slow movement of the *Hammerklavier* is like a live performance, with the finale hardly less eloquent. In No. 28, another fine performance with a melting opening, the brief Adagio before the *attaca* into the finale is another passage of Barenboim magic. Excellent recording, with real presence.

Piano sonatas Nos. 28 in A, Op. 101; 30 in E, Op. 109; 31 in A flat, Op. 109.
(M) ** Tuxedo TUXCD 1086. Alfred Brendel.

From the evidence of publication, it seems that when Brendel began his first Beethoven cycle in 1957 he recorded the late sonatas first, probably a mistake when here his playing lacks something of the depth and inner tension that distinguish the very best performances of the Vox cycle. None of these sonatas draws from him the *Innigkeit* one expects from such a master pianist, and the first movement of Op. 101 is disappointingly underplayed – yet, by most pianists' standards, these are still distinguished performances. The piano recording is remarkably good, full and clear, but the close microphones prevent a real pianissimo from registering.

Piano sonata No. 29 in B flat (Hammerklavier), Op. 106.
(M) **(*) Tuxedo TUXCD 1084. Alfred Brendel.

A fine, strong performance of Beethoven's most formidable sonata from Brendel on Tuxedo. The concentration and sense of drama of the first movement are most striking, and only the comparatively unhushed view of the *Adagio* – taken on the fast side – mars the interpretation. Brendel's later recordings for Philips sometimes have not quite the fire and sense of spontaneity that marked his invigorating Vox records – this one was made as early as 1957, yet the piano sound on CD is impressively full and present. (Only 43 minutes of music though, which reduces the disc's appeal.)

Piano sonatas Nos. 30 in E, Op. 109; 31 in A flat, Op. 110; 32 in C min., Op. 111.
(BB) *** Naxos Dig. 8.550151 [id.]. Jenö Jandó.

The last three sonatas of Beethoven, offered in Volume 4, are very imposing indeed in Jandó's hands. Moreover they are given very realistic recording, with great presence. There is serenity and gravitas in these readings and a powerful control of structure. The thoughtful concentration of the closing *Arietta* of No. 32 puts the seal on a cycle which can receive the strongest advocacy, even without taking into consideration the super-bargain status of the set.

Miscellaneous piano music

7 Bagatelles, Op. 33; 11 Bagatelles, Op. 119; 6 Bagatelles, Op. 126.
(B) *** Ph. 426 976-2; *426 976-4*. Stephen Kovacevich.

Beethoven's *Bagatelles*, particularly those from Opp. 119 and 126, have often been described as chips from the master's workbench; but rarely if ever has that description seemed so apt as in these searchingly simple and completely spontaneous readings by Kovacevich. The memorability and sparkle of each idea comes over with astonishing freshness and the crisp, clear recording projects the music-making admirably, with CD giving a real presence, yet bringing a natural warmth of colour to Beethoven's engaging *Andante* and *Allegretto* movements.

5 Variations on 'Rule Britannia', WoO 79; 7 Variations on 'God save the King' in C, WoO 78; 7 Variations on Winter's 'Kind, willst du ruhig schlafen' in F, WoO 75; 12 Variations on the Russian dance from Wranitzky's ballet 'Das Waldmädchen' in A, WoO 71; 24 Variations on Righini's arietta, 'Venni amore', WoO 65.
(M) *** Tuxedo TUXCD 1060 [id.]. Alfred Brendel.

The simplicity of Beethoven's variations on *God save the King* is disarming, and *Rule Britannia* is also without rhetoric. Brendel plays them eloquently and with the proper, unforced manner. His approach is stronger in some of the other divisions. Sometimes the toughness may seem too keen for these genre pieces, but Brendel's natural, spontaneous manner brings out many felicities and the playing is never merely matter-of-fact, even when, as in the longest set of variations here, on Righini's '*Venni amore*', he takes a fast tempo and fails to observe the repeats. The bright recordings have fine presence on CD.

6 Easy variations on a Swiss song in F, WoO 64; 6 Easy variations on an original theme in G, WoO 77; 8 Variations on Grétry's 'Une fièvre brûlante' in C, WoO 72; 9 Variations on Paisiello's 'Quant'è più bello l'Amor contadino' in A, WoO 69; 10 Variations on Salieri's 'La stessa, la stessissima' in B flat, WoO 73; 15 Variations and fugue on a theme from Prometheus in E flat (Eroica variations), Op. 35.
(M) **(*) Tuxedo TUXCD 1080. Alfred Brendel.

Brendel plays the well-known set of variations on the *Prometheus* theme with directness, brilliance and muscular fingerwork; the other sets are done with comparable integrity, in the manner of his first collection, above. However, here the recording, though still faithful and clear, is somewhat more brittle in timbre, especially in the *Eroica variations.*

32 Variations in C min., WoO 80.
(B) *** Decca 417 773-2. Radu Lupu – MOZART: *Piano concertos Nos. 12 and 21.* **(*)

Originally coupled with a less memorable version of Beethoven's *Third Piano concerto*, Lupu's fine account of the *32 Variations in C minor* makes a worthwhile addition to Decca's Weekend reissue of Mozart concertos.

33 Variations on a Waltz by Diabelli, Op. 120.
(B) *** Ph. 422 969-2; *422 969-4*. Stephen Kovacevich.

Kovacevich gives one of the most deeply satisfying performances ever recorded. Avoiding the idiosyncrasies of most other interpreters, he may at times seem austere, but his concentration is magnetic from first to last, and the variety of expression within his unmannered approach has one thinking direct to Beethoven, with fearless dynamic contrasts enhanced in the CD transfer. The reading culminates in the most dedicated account of the concluding variations, hushed in meditation and with no hint of self-indulgence. On the cheapest Philips label, it is a bargain that no Beethovenian should miss, and the remastering – with separate tracks for each variation – fully matches that of other, full-price versions.

15 Variations and fugue on a theme from Prometheus (Eroica variations), Op. 35.
(M) *(*) Teldec/Warner Dig. 9031 74782-2. Cyprien Katsaris – LISZT: *Variations* (*)*; RACHMANINOV: *Chopin variations.* **

As collectors who have heard his Liszt transcriptions of the Beethoven symphonies will know, Cyprien Katsaris possesses a formidable technique, and those who have heard him play any of them in the flesh will know that this is not the product of paste-and-scissors in the editing channel. However, his account of the *Eroica variations* disappoints. There are occasional agogic distortions that do not wear well on repetition and the thick, synthetic piano sonority is not particularly pleasing. Brendel is far to be preferred.

VOCAL MUSIC

Lieder: *Adelaide; Ich liebe Dich; Der Kuss; Resignation.*
(M) **(*) DG 429 933-2 [id.]. Fritz Wunderlich, Hubert Giesen – SCHUBERT: *Lieder*; SCHUMANN: *Dichterliebe.* ***

Wunderlich was thirty-five when he recorded these songs and the unique bloom of the lovely voice is beautifully caught. Though the accompanist is too metrical at times, the freshness of Wunderlich's singing makes one grieve again over his untimely death.

Ah! perfido (concert aria), *Op. 65.*
(M) ** EMI CMS7 63625-2 (2) [Ang. CDMB 63625]. Callas, Paris Conservatoire O, Rescigno – CHERUBINI: *Medea.* **

Recorded in 1964 at what proved to be the very end of her recording career, this Beethoven scena exposes the flaws that sadly emerged in the great Callas voice, but her fire-eating manner is irresistible. A welcome fill-up for the Cherubini opera.

Christus am Ölberge, Op. 85.
(M) **(*) Sony MPK 45878 [id.]. Raskin, Lewis, Herbert Beattie, Temple University Choirs, Phd. O, Ormandy.

This oratorio is a stronger and more interesting work than has often been thought. Though the Ormandy version dates from the mid-1960s, the CBS sound as transferred on the Sony disc is full and forward, with satisfyingly resonant strings. At mid-price a strong case can be made for it, when Ormandy is at his most purposeful and warmly understanding without self-indulgence, and the soloists are outstandingly fine, with the pure-toned Judith Raskin very aptly cast as the Seraph and with Richard Lewis at his freshest and most expressive as Jesus.

Egmont: Overture and incidental music: (2 Entr'actes, Die Trommel gerühret, Freudvoll und Leidvoll, Victory Symphony), Op. 84.
(M) *** Decca 425 972-2. Lorengar, VPO, Szell – TCHAIKOVSKY: *Symphony No. 4.* ***

Szell's splendid 1970 version of the *Egmont Overture and incidental music* comes as an odd but attractive fill-up to his searingly intense account of Tchaikovsky's *Fourth Symphony.* The Beethoven pieces are very well played and were recorded in the Sofiensaal in Vienna. For the reissue, the spoken dialogue included on the original LP has been excised, although the songs, movingly sung by Pilar Lorengar, remain, plus the two entr'actes, and the final brief *Victory Symphony.*

(i) *King Stephen* (incidental music), *Op. 117: Overture and excerpts. The Ruins of Athens* (incidental music), *Op. 113: Overture and excerpts.* (ii) *The Creatures of Prometheus overture.*
(B) *** Hung. White Label HRC 118 [id.]. (i) Hungarian R. & TV Ch., Budapest PO, Oberfrank; (ii) Hungarian State O, Kórodi.

This is a particularly useful issue in Hungaroton's enterprising bargain White Label series, as it will surely encourage collectors with limited budgets to explore repertoire that might otherwise be overlooked. Beethoven's incidental music, though not always characteristic, is full of imagination and vitality. The choruses (and five are included here from each score) bring a whiff of Weber, yet the finales of both scores have an epic, Beethovenian grandeur. *The Ruins of Athens* has an unexpectedly bizarre Turkish element, but it also includes a duet for baritone and soprano (the excellent Margit László and Sándor Sólyom-Nagy) that recalls *Fidelio.* The fervour of the singing of the Hungarian Radio Chorus adds much to the sparkle of the performances, admirably conducted by Géza Oberfrank; as an apt encore, András Kórodi directs a lively account of *The Creatures of Prometheus overture.*

Mass in C, Op. 86.
(M) *** Decca 430 361-2; *430 361-4* [id.]. Palmer, Watts, Tear, Keyte, St John's College, Cambridge, Ch., ASMF, Guest – BRUCKNER: *Motets.* ***
(B) ** DG 429 510-2; *429 510-4* [id.]. Janowitz, Hamari, Laubenthal, Schramm, Munich Bach Ch. & O, Richter – MOZART: *Mass No. 16.* **(*)

George Guest's reading of the *Mass in C* is designedly intimate, continually reminding one that this work was specifically designed as a successor to the late, great Haydn Masses, like them being commissioned for the Princess Esterhazy's name-day. Naturally, with boys' voices in the choir and a smaller band of singers, the results are less dramatic; but, with splendid recording, the scale works admirably and the result is refreshing.

Richter's account seems a little earthbound alongside Guest's, but it is soundly conceived and not without eloquence. The soloists are good and the 1970 recording has been given a highly effective facelift: the whole impression is fresher than on the original LPs; moreover it is coupled, at bargain price, with an excellent version of Mozart's *Coronation Mass*.

Mass in C, Op. 86; Missa solemnis in D, Op. 123.

(B) ** EMI CZS7 62693-2 [id.]. Ameling, J. Baker, Altmeyer, Rintzler, New Philh. Ch. & O, Giulini.

Giulini directs the *Mass in C* without apology – after all, it is only the dazzling splendour of the *Missa solemnis* that prevents this from being acclaimed as a Beethoven masterpiece; and in a performance as inspired, polished and intense as Giulini's, with a fine quartet of soloists and a superb choir, the effect is very compelling indeed. With so splendid a team, one expected even more from his version of the *Missa solemnis*. The recording is certainly vivid, but it rarely conveys any kind of hushed tension, an essential ingredient in this of all choral works, and the ensemble of the chorus is far from perfect; the excellent soloists are all balanced very close.

Missa solemnis in D, Op. 123.

(M) *** DG 423 913-2 (2) [id.]. Janowitz, Ludwig, Wunderlich, Berry, V. Singverein, BPO, Karajan – MOZART: *Mass No. 16*. **(*)

(M) *** Ph. 426 648-2 (2). Giebel, Höffgen, Haefliger, Ridderbusch, Netherlands R. Ch., Concg. O, Jochum.

(M) (**(*)) BMG/RCA mono GD 60272; *GK 60272* (2) [60272-RG-2; *60272-RG-4*]. Marshall, Merriman, Conley, Hines, Robert Shaw Ch., NBC SO, Toscanini – CHERUBINI: *Requiem*.(**(*))

(M) * Decca 425 844-2 (2). Popp, Minton, Walker, Howell, Chicago Ch. & SO, Solti – VERDI: *Sacred pieces*. **(*)

(i) *Missa solemnis in D;* (ii) *Choral Fantasia in C, Op. 80.*

(M) **(*) EMI CMS7 69538-2 (2) [Ang. CDMB 69538-2]. (i) Söderström, Höffgen, Kmentt, Talvela, New Philh. Ch.; (ii) Barenboim, Alldis Ch.; New Philh. O, Klemperer.

Karajan's earlier DG version of the *Missa solemnis* comes up marvellously well in the digital transfer to CD, far clearer and more faithful in sound than either of his later versions (for EMI and DG), to make it an outstanding recommendation on two mid-price discs, with a generous fill-up in Mozart's *Coronation Mass*. Both the chorus and, even more strikingly, the superbly matched quartet of soloists, never surpassed as a team in this work, convey the intensity and cohesion of Beethoven's deeply personal response to the liturgy, not so much a statement of conventional religious faith as of belief in humanity. Gundula Janowitz is even more meltingly beautiful here than in her later EMI recording for Karajan. Christa Ludwig, as there, is a firm and characterful mezzo, while Walter Berry is a warmly expressive bass. Best of all is the ill-fated Fritz Wunderlich, whose lovely, heroic but unstrained tenor adds supremely to the radiance of the performance, one of his great recordings. The balance between soloists, chorus and orchestra is far clearer and more precise than in most recent recordings, and the clarity of detail is exemplary.

Jochum's 1970 recording with the Netherlands Radio Chorus is also among the most inspired readings of the *Missa solemnis*, especially in the way it conveys the hushed inner intensity of the work. The soloists not only make a splendid team, they are individually finer than we had remembered. The CD transfer is excellent too, more vivid than the LPs were, heightening the incandescence of a performance which comes over with the sort of glow one experiences only rarely, even in the concert hall. To cap a superb reissue, the obbligato violin playing of Hermann Krebbers is movingly pure and beautiful. The performance, at 81 minutes, is just too long for a single CD and, maddeningly, Philips have reissued it on two mid-priced discs (instead of choosing a bargain format).

Klemperer's set has been transferred to CD very successfully. Its glory is the superb choral singing of the New Philharmonia Chorus; it is not just their purity of tone and their fine discipline but the real fervour with which they sing that makes the choral passages so moving. The soloists are less happily chosen: Waldemar Kmentt seems unpleasantly hard and Elisabeth Söderström does not sound as firm as she can be. It was, however, a happy idea to include the *Choral Fantasia* as a bonus.

Toscanini's tensely dramatic account of the *Missa solemnis* leaves you in no doubt as to the work's magisterial power, even if the absence of a true pianissimo makes it less meditative than usual. The supreme revelation comes at the end of the *Dona nobis pacem*, in which – after the menacing sounds of war – the final coda brings a sense of culmination such as few other conductors have achieved. Fine singing from choir and soloists alike, though the typical harshness of the recording is unappealing. It is a pity that RCA did not offer the whole performance on a single CD, instead of breaking before the final movement and putting the Cherubini on the second disc.

Solti's view of the work is essentially dramatic, hardly at all spiritual; moreover it is let down by less than crisp orchestral ensemble and poor co-ordination with the chorus. Thus the necessary bite is not always forthcoming. The solo team is balanced much too forwardly and is not well matched either: the women outweigh the men, and the contribution of the tenor, Mallory Walker, is indifferent. His colleagues all have splendid moments but overall, given the competition, this is a non-starter, not helped by a recording with a narrow range of dynamic.

OPERA

Fidelio (complete).

❀ (M) *** EMI CMS7 69324-2 (2) [Ang. CDMB 69324]. Ludwig, Vickers, Frick, Berry, Crass, Philh. Ch. & O, Klemperer.

(M) *** EMI CMS7 69290-2 (2) [Ang. CDMB 69290]. Dernesch, Vickers, Ridderbusch, Van Dam, Kelemen, German Op. Ch., BPO, Karajan.

(M) *(*) BMG/Eurodisc GD 69030; *GK 69030* (2). Altmeyer, Jerusalem, Adam, Nimsgern, Meven, Nossek, Wohlers, Leipzig R. Ch. & GO, Masur.

Klemperer's great set of *Fidelio* arrives on CD, sounding admirably fresh, to sweep the board in its new format. Its incandescence and spiritual strength are unique, with wonderful performances from all concerned and with a final scene in which, more than in any other recording, the parallel with the finale of the *Choral Symphony* is underlined.

Comparison between Klemperer's version and Karajan's strong and heroic reading is fascinating. Both have very similar merits, underlining the symphonic character of the work with their weight of utterance. Both may miss some of the sparkle of the opening scene, but it is better that seriousness should enter too early than too late. Since seriousness is the keynote, it is rather surprising to find Karajan using bass and baritone soloists lighter than usual. Both the Rocco (Ridderbusch) and the Don Fernando (Van Dam) lack something in resonance in their lower range. Yet they sing dramatically and intelligently, and there is the advantage that the Pizarro of Zoltan Kelemen sounds the more biting and powerful as a result – a fine performance. Jon Vickers as Florestan is if anything even finer than he was for Klemperer; and though Helga Dernesch as Leonore does not have quite the clear-focused mastery of Christa Ludwig in the Klemperer set, this is still a glorious, thrilling performance, outshining lesser rivals than Ludwig. The orchestral playing is superb.

Masur's version is offered in well-balanced, modern, analogue sound. It is played very well by the Leipzig orchestra, but this is a surprisingly small-scale view, lacking the full dramatic bite needed in this towering masterpiece. Neither Jeannine Altmeyer nor Siegfried Jerusalem had achieved their peak when they made the recording in 1982 and, though there is fine singing from the male members of the cast, the Marzelline of Carola Nossek is thin and unsteady. The whole performance has the feeling of a well-behaved run-through.

Fidelio: highlights.

(M) *** EMI CDM7 63077-2; *EG 763077-4* (from above set; cond. Karajan).

(B) **(*) Pickwick IMPX 9021. Rysanek, Haefliger, Fischer-Dieskau, Frick, Seefried, Engen, Bav. State Op. Ch. & O, Fricsay.

(B) *(*) DG Compact Classics *427 713-4* [id.] (from complete recording, with Gwyneth Jones, James King, Talvela, Crass, Leipzig R. Ch., Dresden State Op. O, Boehm) – MOZART: *Die Zauberflöte: highlights.* **(*)

Those who acquire Klemperer's classic set will welcome just under an hour of well-chosen highlights from the fine alternative Karajan recording, made in 1970. It opens with the *Overture* and includes key items like Pizarro's Act I aria, the *Abscheulicher!*, the *Prisoners' chorus* and the closing scene, all vividly presented in bright, clear sound. There is a brief synopsis but no libretto.

The Fricsay set dates from 1958, but the recording has responded well to the CD remastering and has both vividness and atmosphere. Fricsay's direction – from the *Overture* onwards – has the excitement and genuine tension of a Toscanini performance. Ernst Haefliger is a fine Florestan, and Frick and Fischer-Dieskau offer strong characterizations. Rysanek's Leonore is also impressive and her *Abscheulicher!* is very dramatic, helped by splendid Bavarian horn playing. By including snippets of dialogue the selection succeeds in linking the story from beginning to end in an hour of music (rather as happened during the mono LP era, with Fricsay's earlier highlights from Mozart's *Die Zauberflöte*, an ideal example of the genre). The snag with this CD is that here, unlike the original LP from which it is taken, there is no text with translation, only a brief synopsis.

Boehm's selection comes from his flawed 1969 Dresden recording, where none of the principals is shown in a flattering light. The sound is rather middle- and bass-orientated.

Bellini, Vincenzo (1801–35)

Norma (complete).

(M) *** Decca 425 488-2 (3) [id.]. Sutherland, Horne, Alexander, Cross, Minton, Ward, LSO Ch., LSO, Bonynge.

(M) **(*) EMI CMS7 63000-2 (3) [Ang. CDMC 63000]. Callas, Corelli, Ludwig, Zaccharia, Ch. & O of La Scala, Milan, Serafin.

Norma: highlights.
(M) **(*) EMI CDM7 63091-2 (from above complete set with Callas, Corelli; cond. Serafin).

In her first, mid-1960s recording of *Norma*, Sutherland was joined by an Adalgisa in Marilyn Horne whose control of florid singing is just as remarkable as Sutherland's own, and who sometimes even outshines the heroine in musical imagination. The other soloists are very good indeed, John Alexander and Richard Cross both young, clear-voiced singers. Sutherland's own contribution is dramatically very much after the school of Callas, while at the same time ensuring that something as near as possible to musical perfection is achieved, even if occasionally at the expense of masked diction. But overall this is a most compelling performance, helped by the conducting of Richard Bonynge, who keeps musical interest alive in the many conventional accompaniment figures with sprung rhythm and with the most subtle attention to the vocal line. The Walthamstow recording is vivid but also atmospheric in its CD format.

By the time Callas came to record her 1960 stereo version, the tendency to hardness and unsteadiness in the voice above the stave, always apparent, had grown more serious, but the interpretation was as sharply illuminating as ever, a unique assumption, helped – as her earlier mono performance was not – by a strong cast. Christa Ludwig as Adalgisa brings not just rich, firm tone but a real feeling for Italian style and, despite moments of coarseness, Corelli sings heroically. Serafin as ever is the most persuasive of Bellini conductors, and the recording is very good for its period – not surprisingly, as Walter Legge masterminded the original production. Those who already have the mono set will surely want the generous (63 minutes) highlights disc which includes, of course, *Casta diva* and the three principal Norma/Adalgisa duets.

Bennett, Robert Russell
(1894–1981)

Symphonic songs for band.
(M) *** Mercury 432 009-2 [id.]. Eastman Wind Ens., Fennell – HOLST: *Hammersmith* ***; JACOB: *William Byrd suite* ***; WALTON: *Crown Imperial.* *** ❀

Bennett's triptych, not surprisingly, relies more on colouristic manipulation and sonority than on content, although the opening *Serenade* is catchily rhythmic and the final *Celebration* is certainly rumbustious (if empty). Marvellous playing and Mercury's best recording. The disc also includes a *Fanfare and allegro* by Clifton Williams, which is self-descriptive and equally well presented.

Berg, Alban (1885–1935)

(i) *Chamber concerto;* (ii) *Violin concerto.*
(M) *** Decca Analogue/Dig. 430 349-2 [id.]. (i) Pauk, Crossley, L. Sinf., Atherton; (ii) Kyung Wha Chung, Chicago SO, Solti.

As a birthday tribute to Schoenberg, his friend and teacher, Berg wrote the *Chamber concerto*, his most concentratedly formalized work, a piece that can very easily seem cold and unexpressive. Atherton rightly takes the opposite view: that, for all its complexity, it is romantic at heart so that one hears it as a melodic work, full of humour, and the waltz rhythms are given a genuine Viennese flavour. György Pauk and Paul Crossley are outstanding soloists, the Sinfonietta plays with precision as well as commitment, and the 1980 analogue recording is excellent, cleanly detailed yet not too dry. The appropriate coupling is Kyung Wha Chung's fine 1983 version of the *Violin concerto*. Chung may not be as powerful as Perlman (at full price), but her tenderness and poetry bring an added dimension to the music. The violin is placed well in front of the orchestra, but not aggressively so, and the brilliant Chicago digital recording is more spacious than some from this source.

(i) *Chamber concerto;* (ii) *4 Pieces for clarinet and piano, Op. 5; Piano sonata, Op. 1.*
(M) *** DG 423 237-2 [id.]. Barenboim with (i) Zukerman & Ens. InterContemporain, Boulez; (ii) Antony Pay.

Boulez sets brisk tempi in the *Chamber concerto*, seeking to give the work classical incisiveness; but the strong and expressive personalities of the pianist and violinist tend towards a more romantic view. The result is characterful and convincing. The apt coupling combines the high-romantic *Piano sonata* in one movement with the *Clarinet pieces*; here Antony Pay is an outstanding soloist.

Violin concerto.
(M) *** EMI CDM7 63989-2 [id.]. Sir Yehudi Menuhin, BBC SO, Boulez – BLOCH: *Violin concerto.* ***
(M) *** DG 431 740-2. Szeryng, Bav. RSO, Kubelik – SCHOENBERG: *Concertos.* **(*)
(M) *** Ph. 422 136-2. Grumiaux, Concg. O, Markevitch – STRAVINSKY: *Violin concerto.* ***

Menuhin's is a warm and vibrant performance, one that shows him at his finest and that is manifestly on the largest scale and most expressive wavelength; one has no sense whatsoever of an intellectual serialist at work. Even more than usual, Menuhin puts this among the greatest Romantic violin concertos. The collaboration between the warm-hearted, inspirational soloist and the clear-headed micro-sensitive conductor works extraordinarily well, notably in the rapt final *Adagio*. Boulez's insistence on orchestral precision gives Menuhin extra confidence and, though technically this is not as dashing or immaculate a performance as several others on record, it is one that compels admiration on its own terms of greatness. The basically warm (1968) Abbey Road recording has been brightened in the remastering but retains its ambience and body.

An outstanding version of Berg's *Violin concerto* also comes from Henryk Szeryng, who gives a persuasive, perceptive and sympathetic account of this fine work, and is well accompanied by the Bavarian orchestra under Kubelik. Given such superb playing, and a recording that has transferred well to CD, this makes an attractive supplement to the two Schoenberg concertos with which it is coupled.

Grumiaux's splendid account is by no means an also-ran; as a performance it could hardly be bettered, and Markevitch gives him highly sympathetic support. There is a warmth and melancholy that make this as moving and convincing as any committed to disc, and the recording emerges freshly.

Lyric suite: 3 Pieces; 3 Pieces for orchestra, Op. 6.

(M) *** DG 427 424-2 (3) [id.]. BPO, Karajan – SCHOENBERG; WEBERN: *Orchestral pieces.* ***

Karajan's justly famous collection of music by the Second Viennese School is here available as a set of three mid-priced CDs. No more persuasive view could be taken – though, next to Schoenberg and Webern, Berg appears here as the figure who overloaded his music, rather than as the most approachable of the three composers. Beautiful, refined recording, admirably transferred to CD.

3 Pieces for orchestra, Op. 6; (i) *Lulu: symphonic suite.*

(M) *** Mercury 432 006-2 [id.]. (i) Helga Pilarczyk; LSO, Dorati – SCHOENBERG; WEBERN: *Orchestral pieces.* ***

In his pioneering 1962 Mercury coupling Dorati set the pattern for later recordings of this twentieth-century orchestral triptych, none recorded more clearly or vividly. Schoenberg's *Five Pieces*, Op. 16, are the parent work and Berg has taken and developed the emotional basis of his mentor's inspiration and treated it expansively – at least by the standard of the Schoenberg school – and to this Dorati readily responds. There is brilliance, even self-indulgence, which contrasts strongly with Webern's spare, introspective thought, revealed at its purest in his *Five Pieces*, Op. 10. The LSO plays fluently and warmly. For the CD reissue, the recording of the *Lulu suite*, recorded a year earlier, has generously been added. Its big emotions are underlined, at the expense of Berg's markings if necessary; but no one hearing this could possibly miss the fearsome power that erupted in the creation of this opera. Helen Pilarczyk, in her first recording, is most impressive: the murder produces the most bloodcurdling scream.

3 Pieces for orchestra, Op. 6; 5 Orchestral songs, Op. 4; (i) *Lulu: symphonic suite.*

(M) *** DG 423 238-2 [id.]. (i) M. Price; LSO, Abbado.

Abbado makes it clear above all how beautiful Berg's writing is, not just in the *Lulu* excerpts but in the early Opus 4 *Songs* and the Opus 6 *Orchestral pieces*, among which even the formidable march movement has sumptuousness as well as power. The recording from the early 1970s is still outstanding.

Lieder: *Nun ich der Riesen stärksten; Schlafen, schlafen; Schlafend trägt man mich; Warm die Lüfte.*

(M) *** DG 431 744-2 (2) [id.]. Fischer-Dieskau, Aribert Reimann – SCHOENBERG: *Gurrelieder* etc. **(*); WEBERN: *Lieder.* ***

These four early Berg songs form part of the generous fill-up for Schoenberg's *Gurrelieder* in Kubelik's refined and well-recorded reading. Fischer-Dieskau's performances, recorded in 1971, could not be more sensitive.

Berio, Luciano (born 1925)

Differences; 2 Pieces; (i) *Sequenza III;* (ii) *Sequenza VII;* (i) *Chamber music.*

(M) *** Ph. 426 662-2. (i) Cathy Berberian; (ii) Heinz Holliger; Juilliard Ens. (members), composer.

This is an excellent mid-price compilation of recordings made in the late 1960s with the composer himself in charge. The biggest work is *Differences* for five instruments and tape; but the two virtuoso solos – *Sequenza III* for voice (Cathy Berberian) and *Sequenza VII* for oboe (Heinz Holliger) – are if anything even more striking in their extensions of technique and expressive range. The *Two Pieces* and *Chamber music* are both collections of brief inspirations, the latter with voice as well as instrumental trio. First-rate sound, well transferred.

Coro (revised version).
(M) *** DG 423 902-2 [id.]. Cologne R. Ch. and SO, composer.

Coro is one of the most ambitious of Berio's works, with each of forty singers paired with an instrumentalist and with folk verse on basic themes contrasted with poems of Pablo Neruda. Of his generation of leading avant-gardists Berio remains the most approachable. The composer directs a committed performance here, helped by the impact of the forward sound.

A-Ronne; The Cries of London.
(M) *** Decca 425 620-2. Swingle II, composer.

A-Ronne, literally 'A–Z', is an extraordinary setting of a multilingual poem by Edoardo Sanguinetti. From time to time the eight voices briefly break into singing, but for the most part the characteristic musical collage consists of shouts, snarls and organized crowd-noises, with the fragmentary word-sequence run through some twenty times. *The Cries of London* is almost equally surrealistic, an updating of the cries used by Elizabethan madrigal composers but with musical references to medieval patterns. There is some jokiness, but much of the music in this cycle of seven vocal pieces is immediately beautiful. The performances by Swingle II are nothing less than brilliant and they are recorded with stunning immediacy. There are few more stimulating examples of the avant garde than this.

Berkeley, Michael (born 1948)

Or shall we die? (oratorio).
(M) *** EMI Dig. CDM7 69810-2. Harper, Wilson-Johnson, LSO Ch., LSO, Hickox.

Michael Berkeley's oratorio on the pain and problems of a nuclear world confidently uses an openly eclectic style that communicates immediately to any listener. The pity is that the biggest blemish comes at its very peak, where the Woman's agony as the mother of a nuclear bomb victim is most tenderly brought home, only to be resolved in banality, when doggerel verses are set in pop parody, intended bathos which defeats its own object. Despite the flaws, it is a strong, confident and colourful work which it is good to have on record. The recording is first rate.

Berlioz, Hector (1803–69)

Harold in Italy, Op. 16.
(BB) ** Pickwick PWK 1152. Daniel Benyamini, Israel PO, Mehta.

(i) *Harold in Italy, Op. 16. Overtures: Le carnaval romain, Op. 9; Le Roi Lear, Op. 4.*
(M) (*(**)) Sony mono MPK 47679 [id.]. (i) William Primrose; RPO, Beecham.

(i) *Harold in Italy, Op. 16;* (ii) Romance: *Rêverie et caprice, Op. 8.*
(M) ** EMI CDM7 63530-2; *EG 763530-4*. Y. Menuhin, Philh. O, (i) C. Davis; (ii) Pritchard.

When Beecham made his recording of *Harold in Italy* in 1951, William Primrose was incontestably the greatest viola-player in the world. His imagination here matches that of Beecham, though it is a sign of how viola-playing has progressed that he hardly measures up to the finest exponents today in sweetness of tone. He is not helped by the close balance of the solo instrument and, as though relieved to be rid of an artistic rival, Beecham finds an extra fire and intensity in the concluding movement, the *Brigands' orgy*, when the soloist's role is virtually eliminated. Beecham's genius there and throughout – as well as in the two overtures – is to give the sharpest focus to Berlioz's often fragmentary and jagged writing, while co-ordinating the pieces to form a tautly structured whole. The transfer of the mono recordings is clear but limited, with some harshness at the top. As in the EMI version of the *Symphonie fantastique*, you have both *Roman carnival* and *King Lear* for fill-up, but in 1954 recordings, the one slower than before, the other markedly faster, both in sound similar to that of the symphony.

Mehta draws sonorous playing from the Israel Philharmonic and the 1975 (Decca) recording has the sort of brilliance and separation that one used to associate with Mehta's Los Angeles analogue recordings, while there is also plenty of warmth and sense of spectacle. It is very effectively remastered; though the solo viola is balanced too close and some of Berlioz's subtlety is missing, this is certainly an enjoyable and often exciting account, worth its modest cost.

Menuhin asserts his personality strongly, even over that of Sir Colin Davis, and the 1963 recording of the Philharmonia openly treats the work as a concerto, with the soloist often dictating the rhythm, which the orchestra has to follow. Nevertheless this makes an enjoyable version, although the recording could ideally have greater warmth and bloom. It is now made slightly more competitive by including the *Rêverie et caprice*, made in 1965, but here Menuhin is placed rather too close to the microphone for comfort.

Overtures: Benvenuto Cellini; Le carnaval romain, Op. 9; Le Corsaire, Op. 21; Le Roi Lear, Op. 4; La damnation de Faust: Marche hongroise; Menuet des follets. Roméo et Juliette: Scène d'amour.
(BB) *(*) Naxos 8.550231 [id.]. Polish State PO (Katowice), Kenneth Jean.

The Polish orchestra generally plays very well and the recording has a spectacular concert-hall acoustic. There is plenty of enthusiasm here – especially from the brass – and there is excitement too, notably in the *Hungarian march*, which opens the programme vividly, and in the closing *Le Corsaire*, which goes swingingly. But one ideally needs more sophistication and Gallic flair. Kenneth Jean is rather heavy-handed in his lyrical phrasing, especially in the introduction to *Le Roi Lear*, and his *Scène d'amour* from *Roméo et Juliette* is no match for Ozawa's in subtlety of line and dynamic control. Incidentally, the listing and sleeve notes indicate that the *Danse des Sylphes* is included in the programme, but it turns out to be the *Minuet of the Will-o'-the-Wisps*.

Roméo et Juliette: Queen Mab scherzo.
(M) (**) BMG/RCA mono GD 60314 [60314-2-RG]. Phd. O, Toscanini – MENDELSSOHN: *Midsummer Night's Dream*. (***)

Toscanini's quicksilver reading of this fairy scherzo has much in common with his fine Philadelphia recording of Mendelssohn's fairy music. The 1941 recording is clear but lacking in dynamic subtlety.

Symphonie fantastique, Op. 14.
(M) **(*) EMI CMD7 64143-2 [id.]; *EG 764143-4*. Philh. O, Klemperer (with BEETHOVEN: *Leonora overture No. 1* ***; GLUCK: *Overture: Iphigénie en Aulide* *).
(BB) **(*) Pickwick PWK 1147. Paris Conservatoire O, Argenta.
(M) ** Sony SBK 46329; *40-46329* [id.]. Phd. O, Ormandy – DUKAS: *L'apprenti sorcier*; MUSSORGSKY: *Night*. ***
(M) *(*) Teldec/Warner Dig. 9031 74791-2 [id.]. VSO, Prêtre – SCHOENBERG: *Verklaerte Nacht*. **
(BB) * Naxos Dig. 8.550093 [id.]. CSR (Slovak) RSO, Bratislava, Pinchas Steinberg.

Symphonie fantastique; La damnation de Faust, Op. 21: Danse des sylphes; Marche hongroise; Menuet des follets; Overture: Le carnaval romain, Op. 9.
(M) **(*) EMI CDM7 63762-2 [id.]; *EG 763762-4*. Hallé O, Barbirolli.

(i) *Symphonie fantastique; Overture: Le carnaval romain, Op. 9.*
(B) **(*) Decca 433 611-2; *433 611-4* [id.]. (i) VPO, Haitink; (ii) Cleveland O, Maazel.

(i) *Symphonie fantastique;* (ii) *Overtures: Le carnaval romain, Op. 9; Le Corsaire, Op. 31.*
(BB) **(*) BMG/RCA VD 60478; *VK 60478* [60478-2-RV; *60478-4-RV*]. Boston SO, (i) Prêtre; (ii) Munch.

(i) *Symphonie fantastique; Overtures:* (ii) *Le Carnaval romain;* (iii) *Le Roi Lear.*
(M) (***) EMI mono CDM7 64032-2 [id.]; *EG 764032-4*. (i) O. Nat. de l'ORTF; (ii) LPO; (iii) RPO, Sir Thomas Beecham.

Symphonie fantastique; (i) *Roméo et Juliette, Op. 17: Scène d'amour.*
(M) **(*) DG 431 169-2; *431 169-4* [id.]. (i) New England Conservatory Ch.; Boston SO, Ozawa.

(i) *Symphonie fantastique; Les Troyens: Trojan march & Royal hunt and storm.*
(M) **(*) Erato/Warner Analogue/Dig. 2292 45566-2 [id.]. (i) O Nat. de France, James Conlon; (ii) French R. New PO, Gilbert Amy.

Barbirolli provides a reading of the *Symphonie fantastique* which is not only impulsively exciting but also possesses a breadth of imagination that is missing in many other performances. A lyrical spaciousness is felt in the slow movement, which is played most beautifully, yet the thunder at the end, on the timpani, bursts into the room and anticipates the mood of the *March to the scaffold*. This is full of energy and fire; and in the finale there is a demonic impulse, with the detailed realization of Berlioz's orchestration vividly projected, not least the plangent bell-toll. The overture is full of adrenalin too, but most striking of all are the three pieces from *La damnation de Faust*, vividly characterized and presented with great flair and spontaneity, with the *Danse des sylphes* given a gossamer delicacy. Unfortunately the (originally Pye) recording, dating from 1959, has been remastered fiercely and, although the original ambience remains to give fullness and atmosphere, the upper range needs a great deal of control to sound comfortable at fortissimo levels.

The Beecham Edition version of the *Symphonie fantastique* with the Orchestre National is not the one that has been generally available for the last 25 years, whether on LP or, latterly, on CD. That is in stereo, where the one now at last reissued is a mono recording, made only a short time before. What is surprising is to discover how different the two performances are. The mono version is faster in all five movements, with an astonishing difference in overall timing of six minutes in a three-quarter-hour work. The slow movement alone, the *Scène aux champs*, accounts for three minutes of that. More important is the difference of tension, with the final *March to the scaffold* and *Witches' sabbath* much more exciting in the faster, mono version. Beecham's incisive control of rhythm goes with the most persuasive feeling for overall line, not just in the symphony but in the two overtures that come as fill-up, *King Lear* and *Roman carnival*, both recorded much earlier, the one with the RPO in 1947, soon after that orchestra was founded, the other in 1936 with the LPO, one of Beecham's vintage pre-war recordings. Transfers are clean, but with some edge on top.

James Conlon is convincingly volatile in the first movement of the *Symphonie fantastique*, and his reading has a fine sense of spontaneity. The *Waltz* is engagingly *galant*, yet the element of neurosis is present and rises to the surface in a dazzlingly effective accelerando at its close. The slow movement brings beautifully serene playing from the strings, with textures radiant. The *March to the scaffold* has a jaunty air, and the exuberant finale is less overtly satanic than in some hands. The fairly close balance gives good detail and projection but the overall effect, although full, hasn't quite the ambient beauty of the Decca Haitink recording. Even so, this is a very enjoyable account, impetuously sensitive to the work's charismatic mood changes. It is reissued in Erato's Résidence series, which means that the notes are more concerned with linking Berlioz to Paris than with the music itself; but it does mean that a splendid performance, excitingly recorded, of Berlioz's *Royal hunt and storm* is added, as fine as any in the catalogue, plus other music from *Les Troyens*. It is not clear which of the recordings – made in 1982 and 1984 (the *Symphonie*) – are digital and which analogue, as there is very slight background noise throughout. Nevertheless this is a most enjoyable disc.

Weight is the keynote of Klemperer's reading, so individual that some will regard it as merely perverse in its avoidance of conventional, thrusting excitement. Yet the effect is always spontaneous and no one could be in any doubt that this was the work of a great conductor. From the first movement onwards – not without its impetuous feeling but far more clearly symphonic than usual – Klemperer conveys a rugged strength which, in the massiveness of the *Witches' sabbath* for example, brings you close to Satan himself. There is certainly no lack of adrenalin and the *March to the scaffold*, its rhythms clipped, is also given commanding power, while the close is made the more impressive by a recording that is outstanding for its period, sounding superbly expansive on CD with rich, resonant strings and full, sonorous brass. The Beethoven *Leonora No. 1* is an exciting and fresh performance from Klemperer's first Beethoven series in 1954, but an all-pervading heaviness of style quite ruins *Iphigénie en Aulide*.

It is good to welcome back to the catalogue Ataulfo Argenta's (originally Decca) recording from the earliest days of stereo. It was considered to be of demonstration standard in its day, and the overall balance is still very impressive, with the French brass full of character yet not sounding too blatant. The reading is individual and distinguished. The balance between reflection and neurosis in the first movement is admirable: the *Allegro agitato* is impetuous, yet never gets out of control. The *Waltz* is very poised and the *Adagio* is a thing of sheer beauty: the spirit of Beethoven is felt in the closing pages. Argenta observes the repeat in the *March to the scaffold* – for the first time on disc – and the finale is strong on atmosphere as well as drive.

Haitink with the Vienna Philharmonic may sound a little unidiomatic in French music, but the freshness and refinement of the reading, helped by atmospheric sound that is always full and warm, will suit those who prefer a degree of detachment in this boldly Romantic symphony. The *Marche au supplice* could be more sinister, but the second and third movements are beautifully played and the finale does not lack power. However, Maazel's contrastingly racy account of *Le carnaval romain*, which acts as a postlude, demonstrates the relative lack of high drama in the performance of the *Symphonie*.

Prêtre's excitingly chimerical Boston account has now reappeared on BMG/RCA's bargain Silver Seal label. It was recorded at about the same time as Argenta's, but the upper range is less full. However, the Boston ambience brings weight and the sound is otherwise resonantly spacious, with exciting projection for the brass. It is a highly volatile performance but Prêtre's sense of neurosis is convincing. The heart of the interpretation lies in the beautiful slow movement, but the *March to the scaffold* has a jaunty sense of melodrama, and the finale combines an element of the grotesque with high adrenalin flow. An individual and involving account. Munch's famous accounts of the two *Overtures* make a thrilling bonus, but here the sound tends to shrillness. With the treble cut back, however, this CD makes a very strong impression.

Ozawa's 1973 recording has come up splendidly in its CD transfer, with the recording full, atmospheric and vivid. The reading, characteristically flexible in expressiveness and rhythmically resilient (the *March to the scaffold*

– taken fast – has an almost balletic, jaunty rhythmic bite) does not lack excitement and is beautifully played; even if the last degree of demonic force is missing from the finale, this is enjoyable in its fresh, spontaneous feeling. The *Love scene* from *Roméo et Juliette*, which provides a considerable bonus, has all the warmth and glow required to sustain its span.

Ormandy's 1961 account, with the Philadelphia Orchestra playing brilliantly, is certainly gripping. There are one or two mannered touches in the first movement, and the very fast opening of the allegro rather overdoes the neurotic aspect of the music, but the *Waltz* has panache and the last two movements have plenty of pungency and spectacle; there is no doubting the Satanic feeling in the finale. The very brilliantly lit recording does not lack fullness, but tends to emphasize the hyperbole of the reading.

The Prêtre/Teldec CD offers a pretty weird coupling. It is hard to imagine anyone wanting the *Symphonie fantastique* being tempted by the prospect of so unrelated a work as *Verklaerte Nacht* or vice versa. Prêtre is generally underrated, though the Wiener Symfoniker is not. All the same, they play satisfactorily for him and are very well recorded. His reading begins promisingly enough but is prone to expressive exaggerations that would prove irksome on repetition. There is such stiff competition here that, in spite of decent digital sound and the generous playing time, this Teldec/Warner issue cannot really be considered a front runner.

Pinchas Steinberg's Naxos account is well played and recorded, but the reading is too comfortable to be really convincing: it is never really gripping, and the finale needs more Satanic feeling.

Solti's Chicago version – reissued on a mid-priced CD in the 'Solti Collection', coupled with *Les Francs-juges overture* – is no more successful, despite extremely vivid sound. Hardly a semiquaver is out of place, but the spirit of the music eludes the conductor (Decca 430 441-2; *430 441-4*).

Symphonie fantastique, Op. 14; (i) *Lélio (Le retour à la vie), Op. 14b.*

(B) *** EMI CZS7 62739-2 (2). (i) Gedda, Burles, Van Gorp, Sendrez, Topart, Ch. of R. France; ORTF Nat. O, Martinon.

Berlioz intended *Lélio* as a sequel to the *Symphonie fantastique*, and Martinon conveniently offers the works paired at bargain price. His account of the *Symphonie* shows a unique seductiveness. In its way it is as magically compelling as Beecham's version with the same orchestra. Martinon gives the first-movement exposition repeat and provides the often omitted extra brass parts; though the result is brilliant, he never presses on too frenetically. The *March to the scaffold* is aptly menacing. But most of all this reading is outstanding for its warm shaping of phrase, even if the finale, with its tolling bells of doom, has a flamboyance and power to match any available. The 1973 sound remains remarkably vivid.

Lélio is a strange work but, as so often with an oddity, the gramophone allows one to appreciate its genuine merits more clearly. Though the spoken narration and music for soloists (including a Goethe ballad setting for tenor with piano!) doesn't help the piece hold together, the six musical numbers make a fascinating suite. The work quotes the *idée fixe* from the *Symphonie*, which helps the listener to feel at home. It is difficult to imagine this performance being bettered, and the 1974 sound is suitably atmospheric. The coupling is offered as part of EMI's 'two for the price of one' 'Rouge et Noir' series.

VOCAL MUSIC

La damnation de Faust, Op. 24.

(M) **(*) DG 423 907-2 (2) [id.]. Mathis, Burrows, McIntyre, Paul, Tanglewood Festival Ch., Boston Boys' Ch. & Boston SO, Ozawa.

Ozawa's performance provides an admirable mid-priced version in a very moulded style. The relative softness of focus is underlined by the reverberant Boston acoustics; with superb playing and generally fine singing, however, the results are seductively enjoyable. The digital remastering has improved definition without losing the effect of the hall ambience.

Les nuits d'été (song-cycle), *Op. 7.*

(M) (***) Decca mono 425 988-2 [id.]. Suzanne Danco, Cincinnati SO, Thor Johnson – RAVEL: *2 Mélodies hébraïques* etc. (***)

(i) *Les nuits d'été* (song-cycle), *Op. 7;* (ii) *La mort de Cléopâtre* (lyric scena); (ii; iii) *Les Troyens, Act V, Scenes ii & iii.*

❀ (M) *** EMI CDM7 69544-2. Dame Janet Baker, (i) New Philh. O, Barbirolli; (ii) LSO, Gibson; (iii) with Greevy, Erwen, Howell & Amb. Op. Ch.

The collaboration of Dame Janet Baker at the peak of her powers and Sir John Barbirolli in what is probably the most beautiful of all orchestral song-cycles produces ravishing results. The half-tones in the middle songs are exquisitely controlled, and the elation of the final song, *L'île inconnue*, with its vision of an idyllic island, has never been captured more rapturously on record. Berlioz's early scena on the death of a famous classical heroine is also beautifully performed. But even more desirable is Dame Janet's deeply moving rendering of the concluding scenes of Berlioz's epic opera. This makes an essential supplement to the complete recording for any dedicated Berliozian. Baker, helped by a warm and sympathetic accompaniment under Gibson's direction, allows herself a range of tone-colour and a depth of expressiveness not matched elsewhere. Fine remastered sound.

Suzanne Danco's record, made in 1951, was the first complete version of Berlioz's magical song-cycle, when at 29 minutes it occupied the whole of one LP! The purity of her tone and diction, her poise and sense of style shine through. She evokes not only the heady atmosphere of these songs but also their essentially classical feeling. High expectations born of long-treasured memories are not disappointed and sonic limitations soon forgotten. Nor should Thor Johnson's contribution be forgotten either, for he draws playing of much sensitivity from the Cincinnati orchestra. Like the Mélisande she recorded in Geneva with Ansermet the following year, this is one of the classics of the gramophone and should not be missed. The ethereal sound Danco produces long resonates in the memory, and the Ravel coupling is no less magical.

(i) *Requiem Mass (Grande messe des morts), Op. 5;* (ii) *Te Deum, Op. 22.*

(M) **(*) Sony M2YK 46461 (2) [id.]. (i) Stuart Burrows, Ch. of R. France, O Nat. de France, O Philharmonique, Bernstein; (ii) Jean Dupory, Jean Guillov, Ch. d'Enfants de Paris, Maîtrise de la Resurrection, Paris Ch. & O, Barenboim.

In a characteristically powerful and vibrant reading, Bernstein adopts a moulded, consciously persuasive style, and the result is atmospheric and dramatic. In *Rex tremendae*, for example, his expansiveness is well in scale with the music. In the *Lacrymosa* he is faster and more urgent, with an irresistible, wave-like rhythm; and he is notable for warmth and expressiveness. The acoustic is reasonably ample, and this allows the chorus to sound larger than some. The remastering improves the effect enormously – indeed the impact of drums and brass in the *Dies irae* is almost overwhelming. At lower dynamic levels textures are fresh and appealing, the flutes especially radiant. Stuart Burrows's headily ardent solo in the *Sanctus* is tellingly projected, and altogether the performance communicates vividly. The coupling is hardly less exciting: recorded in 1977 during the quadraphonic era, Barenboim's Paris version of the *Te Deum* brings a strong and characterful performance, occasionally exaggerated, with fine choral singing and a stylish tenor soloist. The recording is not as sharply focused as it should be, although it is made much more immediate on CD; overall, this is hardly less compelling than the *Requiem*, to make this reissue a real bargain. Strongly recommended.

Berners, Lord (1883–1950)

The Triumph of Neptune (ballet suite): excerpts.

(M) (***) EMI mono CDM7 63405-2 [id.]. LPO, Sir Thomas Beecham – BANTOCK: *Fifine at the fair;* BAX: *Garden of Fand.* (***)

The Triumph of Neptune was a rare example of music by an English composer being commissioned and performed by Diaghilev's Ballets Russes (at the London Coliseum in 1926). The ballet was devised by Sacheverell Sitwell, the choreographer was Balanchine, and settings were based on Victorian scenic picture postcards. It was a promising mixture, and the result was a witty and elegant, if sometimes outrageous score (including a polka in which a baritone – here Robert Alva – interpolates an excerpt from *The last rose of summer*). Beecham recorded excerpts from it twice. This is the first set, taken from 78s (originally Columbia LX 697/8, which we remember with great affection); but alas, it omits *Cloudland* and *The frozen forest*, included on the later LP with the Philadelphia Orchestra. Nevertheless what is offered (the *Schottische*, *Hornpipe*, *Polka: the sailor's return*, *Harlequinade*, *Dance of the fairy princess*, *Intermezzo: Sunday morning* and *Apotheosis of Neptune*) is irresistible. The LPO playing has all the whimsical flair one would expect, and the CD transfer by Michael Dutton and John Holland admirably retains the fullness and atmosphere of those old shellac discs. The sound may be confined but it is never thinned out or made edgy.

Bernstein, Leonard (1918–90)

Candide: overture; Facsimile (choreographic essay); *Fancy free* (ballet); *On the town* (3 dance episodes).

(M) **(*) EMI Dig. CDD7 63905-2 [id.]; *ET 763905-4.* St Louis SO, Slatkin.

Though Slatkin cannot quite match Bernstein himself in the flair he brings to his jazzier inspirations, this is an attractive and generous collection. Next to Bernstein, Slatkin sounds a little metrical at times, but it is a marginal shortcoming, and he directs a beautiful, refined reading of the extended choreographic essay, *Facsimile.* As a gimmick, the song 'Big Stuff' before *Fancy Free* is recorded in simulation of a juke-box, complete with 78-r.p.m. surface-hiss and a blues singer with very heavy vibrato. The sound otherwise is full rather than brilliant, set in a helpful, believable acoustic.

(i) *Candide overture; Facsimile* (choreographic essay); *Fancy Free* (ballet); *On the Town* (3 dance episodes); (ii) *On the Town* (musical); (i) *On the Waterfront* (symphonic suite); (iii) *Trouble in Tahiti (opera in 7 scenes);* (i) *West Side story: Symphonic dances* (orch. Sid Ramin & Irwin Kostal).

(M) *** Sony SM3K 47154 (3) [id.]. (i) NYPO; (ii) Betty Comden, Adolph Green, Nancy Walker, John Reardon, Cris Alexander, George Gaynes, Ch. & O; (iii) Nancy Williams, Julian Patrick & Vocal Trio, Columbia Wind Ens.; all cond. composer.

Candide overture – placed at the beginning of Disc 2 – provides the perfect curtain-raiser for this indispensable box of Bernstein's vibrant, early recordings of his theatrical and film music. The New York Philharmonic, in cracking form, play the overture with exhilarating zest in just over four minutes. (Bernstein's later, London recording for the revised complete performance takes 21 seconds longer!) The New Yorkers display similar virtuosity and tremendous spirit in the ballet music and comparable gusto in the noisily pungent film score, plus a natural command of the jazz rhythms, while the tender moments in the *West Side story* dances have great poignancy. Of the ballets, *Fancy Free*, written in 1944 for the New York Ballet Theatre, is an attractive example of Bernstein's freely eclectic style, raiding Stravinsky, Copland and Gershwin and putting the result effectively together, thanks to his exuberant sense of colour and rhythm. *Facsimile* was also written for Jerome Robbins two years later and is another highly inventive and resourceful score, again eclectic but with no want of atmosphere and imagination. But Bernstein comes completely into his own in the music for the musical theatre. Both *On the Town* (1944), tinglingly presented here by most of the original Broadway cast, and *Trouble in Tahiti* (1952) were precursors to *West Side story*. *On the Town* is very much a traditional musical with Hollywood associations, but the style of *Trouble in Tahiti* (for which Bernstein wrote both words and music) lies somewhere between the musical and the opera house; it concerns a day in the life of a middle-class American couple who no longer communicate. In 1983 Bernstein incorporated his early score as a flashback sequence into a sequel, *A Quiet Place*, but there is no doubt that the earlier music has greater vitality, besides having a very strong lyrical element. There is no lack of good tunes and memorable rhythmic numbers in either piece, and the performances under the composer have great flair and theatrical adrenalin. The recordings were made in 1960 and 1973 respectively and are remarkably vivid. The NYPO orchestral sesssions date from between 1960 and 1963 and have been impressively remastered to sound more atmospheric than in their earlier, LP incarnations.

Candide: overture; On the town: 3 Dance episodes. On the Waterfront (symphonic suite); West Side story: Symphonic dances.

(M) **(*) Sony MYK 44773. NYPO, composer.

Bernstein's dazzling performance of the *Candide overture* with the NYPO was the most brilliant on record until his most recent version, recorded in London as part of the complete (full-price) recording of *Candide*. He did not quite match its zest himself in his later performance for DG. Both the *Symphonic dances* from *West Side story* and the film score, *On the Waterfront*, are comparably vibrant and are played superbly, but it is a pity that there is an element of harshness in the CBS sound (especially when compared with his later, DG versions).

(i) *Candide: overture;* (ii) *On the town: 3 Dance episodes;* (i) *West Side story: Symphonic dances;* (iii) *America.*

(M) *** DG Dig. 427 806-2; *427 806-4*. (i) LAPO; (ii) Israel PO; (iii) Troyanos with O; composer – BARBER: *Adagio* ***; GERSHWIN: *Rhapsody in blue*. **(*)

A mid-priced collection, duplicating others, to show the popular side of Bernstein's genius at its most electrifying. The *Overture* to *Candide* is one of the most dazzlingly brilliant of the century, and the composer directs it in this live recording with tremendous flair, his speed a fraction slower than in his New York studio recording for CBS. Early Bernstein is well represented in the colourful and vigorous dances from *On the town*, while the composer, recorded live, is at his most persuasive conducting a highly idiomatic account of the orchestral confection devised from his most successful musical, *West Side story*, with the players contributing the necessary shouts in the *Mambo* representing a street fight. Vivid if close-up sound.

(i) *3 Meditations* (for cello and orchestra) from *Mass; On the Waterfront* (symphonic suite); (ii) *Symphony No. 1 (Jeremiah).*

(M) *** DG Dig./Analogue 431 028-2; *431 028-4* [id.]. (i) Rostropovich; (ii) Christa Ludwig; Israel PO, composer.

This assembly of three works representing different sides of Bernstein's musical personality was put together for the mid-priced DG Bernstein Edition, and it works well. *Three Meditations*, a concertante piece for cello and orchestra, beautifully reflects the individual poetry of the artist for whom it was written and who performs masterfully here. The *Jeremiah Symphony* dates from Bernstein's early twenties and ends with a moving passage from Lamentations for the mezzo soloist. This performance with the Israel Philharmonic is not always quite as polished or as forceful as Bernstein's earlier recording in New York but it never fails to reflect the warmth of Bernstein's writing. The aggressive digital sound of the original recordings bites even more on CD, with a brilliant top and spectacular bass leaving the middle light. With Bernstein, such sound does little harm.

Symphonies Nos. (i) *1 (Jeremiah);* (ii) *2 (The age of anxiety) for piano and orchestra;* (i; iii) *3 (Kaddish): To the beloved memory of President Kennedy* (original version); (vi) *Prelude, fugue and riffs;* (iv) *Serenade after Plato's Symposium* (for solo violin, string orchestra, harp & percussion); (v) *Chichester Psalms.*

(M) *** Sony SM3K 47162 (3) [id.]. (i) Tourel; (ii) Entremont; (iii) F. Montealegre (speaker), Camerata Singers; Columbus Boychoir; (iv) Francescatti; (v) J. Bogart, Camerata Singers; (i–iv) NYPO; (vi) Benny Goodman, Columbia Jazz Combo; all cond. composer.

Bernstein's three symphonies span two decades of his creative life: the first dates from 1942, when he was 24, and the *Kaddish* (No. 3) was premièred in 1963. They have been undervalued because of his theatre music and his willingness to draw on popular influences, but their surface facility is deceptive: the writing has eloquence and depth and they will eventually find their way into the pantheon of memorable twentieth-century symphonies. The *Jeremiah* is a brilliant *tour de force*, the three movements – slow, fast, slow – cunningly integrated by the use of traditional Jewish material. The syncopations and jazz rhythms of the middle movement give it a recognizable flavour, but it is in fact the most closely argued movement of the three. The outer movements are essentially lyrical, and the finale is a moving setting of a passage from *Lamentations*: 'How she sits desolate, the city once full of people'. With Jennie Tourel as a warm-voiced soloist there is a strong reminder of the lament Prokofiev included in his *Alexander Nevsky* cantata, first recorded at about the time when Bernstein was writing his symphony.

W. H. Auden's poem, *The age of anxiety*, was taken as the dramatic basis of the *Second Symphony*, with the *Epilogue* resolving the conversation of its four characters depicted in ambitious philosophy. Rather oddly, Bernstein was content to write a purely instrumental work, reflecting moods, soliloquies and ideas in the most poetic way, rather than actually expressing them. But one can readily turn back to the poem itself (although unfortunately it is not included in the accompanying booklet). Philippe Entremont as solo pianist makes a distinguished contribution here, and the recording balances him convincingly.

The *Kaddish Symphony*, like No. 1, is a Jewish-based work, but one which was finally dedicated to the memory of John F. Kennedy. It features a series of apostrophes to God and includes some of the composer's most impressive music. This is the original version; Bernstein revised it later and chose in his DG recording to use a male speaker. One can see why, listening to the spoken dialogue recited here with melodramatic fervour by Felicia Montealegre (Mrs Bernstein at the time); this is a serious stumbling block to the present performance. The three movements are divided into separate sections to give something of the impression of a cantata rather than a symphony but, as usual in Bernstein, the immediate attractiveness of the writing conceals some ingenious argument. Bernstein's tinkering with twelve-note rows, for example, has nothing daunting about it. The performance is red-hot. All three recordings were made in the Manhattan Center, New York, in the early 1960s; the acoustic is agreeably spacious, the bass resonantly full and the strings have plenty of body, so that no apologies need be made for the sound-quality.

The *Chichester Psalms*, also impressively transferred to CD, was written in response to a commission from the Dean of Chichester, but Bernstein chose to use the original Hebrew for the actual setting of the Psalm texts. It is the central Psalm 100, with jazz rhythms reminiscent of *West Side story*, that is the most obviously appealing, but the *a cappella* setting of Psalm 133 has a distinctive beauty when the composer's direction is so vividly communicative. The *Serenade* is based on Plato's account of an Ancient Greek banquet in which those present take turns to soliloquize on the nature of love. Full of ideas, often thrilling and exciting, often moving, it must rank among Bernstein's most resourceful and inspired creations. Isaac Stern pioneered the work in its first, mono recording, but Francescatti responds naturally to the Hebrew flavour of the lyrical writing: his opening solo and his phrasing of the *Agathon Adagio* are very beautiful. But he is very closely balanced, as is the orchestra, and Bernstein's passionate climaxes are given an aggressive fierceness. Finally comes the *Prelude, fugue and riffs*, which Benny Goodman commissioned; so his performance is definitive, the rhythms stimulatingly cool, witty and strident by turns. With any reservations noted, this is a most stimulating box.

West Side story: Symphonic dances.
(B) **(*) DG Compact Classics 413 851-2 (2); *** *413 851-4* [id.]. San Francisco SO, Ozawa – GERSHWIN: *American in Paris* etc. **(*) (CD only: RUSSO: *3 Pieces for Blues band & orchestra, Op. 50* – with the Siegel-Schwall Band).

Ozawa's performance is highly seductive, with an approach that is both vivid and warm, yet concealing any sentimentality. The 1973 recording sounds equally brilliant in its tape and CD formats. However, the additional item on the pair of CDs by William Russo is no great asset, not very convincingly inhabiting that curiously indeterminate middle ground between popular and concert-hall music.

VOCAL MUSIC

Chichester Psalms.
(M) *** Pickwick/RPO Dig. CDRPO 7007; *ZCRPO 7007* [id.]. Aled Jones, LSO Ch., RPO, Hickox – FAURÉ: *Requiem.* ***

Bernstein's *Chichester Psalms* make an instant communication and respond to familiarity too, especially in Richard Hickox's fresh and colourful reading, with Aled Jones bringing an ethereal contribution to the setting of the 23rd Psalm. As a bonus for a fresh and sympathetic account of the Fauré *Requiem*, this can be recommended strongly. The recorded sound is firm and well focused.

(i) *Dybbuk* (ballet): complete; (ii) *Mass (for the death of President Kennedy).*
(M) *** Sony SM3K 47158 (3) [id.]. (i) David Johnson, John Ostendorf, NY City Ballet O; (ii) Alan Titus (celebrant), Scribner Ch., Berkshire Boys' Ch., Rock Band & O; composer.

Outrageously eclectic in its borrowings from pop and the avant garde, Bernstein's *Mass* presents an extraordinary example of the composer's irresistible creative energy. With a scenario that boldly defies all sense of good taste, the celebrant smashing the holy vessel before the altar, its impact is even more remarkable in the CD format, which loses nothing in atmosphere but increases the sense of spectacle. The recording was made partly at the J. F. Kennedy Center, Washington, DC, supplemented by New York studio sessions in 1971. It now assumes a historical as well as a musical significance, for Bernstein's all-embracing emotional theatricality sums up a decade in recent American history when all conventional beliefs were put in question by a new generation. Bernstein characteristically encapsulated both the doubt and the optimistic self-confidence in the future which is so much a part of the American experience.

Bernstein wrote his ghoulish ballet on lost spirits for Jerome Robbins and the New York City Ballet in 1974, when this splendidly atmospheric recording was made. Following up various lines in demonology and the mystical Jewish cabala, Bernstein developed his score with various crypto-serial techniques, based on numerology. But far from sounding serial, the score presents much the same happy and colourful amalgam of influences as you find in other Bernstein ballets, a touch of the *Rite of spring* here and a whiff of *West Side story* there – although, at 48 minutes, it is less concentrated than the shorter works. The vocal parts, although fairly substantial (and very well done here), are merely incidental.

Stage works

Candide (musical): *Overture and excerpts.*
(M) *** Sony SK 48017 [id.]. Adrian, Cook, Rounseville and original New York cast, Krachmalnick.

This exhilarating CBS record encapsulates the original 1956 Broadway production and has all the freshness of discovery inherent in a first recording, plus all the zing of the American musical theatre. Its highlight, the Rossini-style *Glitter and be gay*, is given a scintillating coloratura performance here by Barbara Cook. Max Adrian is hardly less memorable, and the Gilbert and Sullivan influences will surely endear the score to British listeners. The lyrics, by Richard Wilbur, give pleasure in themselves. Brilliantly lively sound.

West Side story: highlights.
(M) **(*) DG Dig. 431 027-2 (from complete recording, with Te Kanawa, Carreras, Troyanos, Horne, Ollman; cond. composer).

By cutting the dialogue, all the main numbers are included here, presented as vividly as on the complete (full-price) set; but with only just over 53 minutes of music included this is not especially good value, even though the highlights disc is now offered at mid-price. The moving *Tonight* sequence, for example, loses much without the spoken interchanges between the lovers, and clearly there was room for this on the disc. In the USA this selection is issued at full price.

Biber, Heinrich (1644–1704)

Rosenkranz sonatas Nos. 1–16.
(M) **(*) HM/BMG Dig. GD 77102 (2) [77102-

RG]. Franzjosef Maier, Franz Lehrndorfer, Max Engel, Konrad Junghänel.

Biber's *Sonatas* for violin and basso continuo, based on the Mysteries of the rosary, are unique in a number of respects. They represent the first attempt to introduce a programmatic content into the instrumental sonata and the first at a connected sequence of pieces (the Kuhlau *Biblical sonatas*, for keyboard instruments, are of later provenance). Each of the 15 *Sonatas* calls for a different tuning of the strings (*scordatura*) so that, instead of the strings being tuned in fifths, they can be at fourths, thirds or even seconds, thus producing an unusual timbre. The *Sonatas* include music of great poetic feeling and sensibility; each is prefaced by a small copperplate depicting one of the Mysteries, and these are reproduced in the accompanying booklet. Franzjosef Maier and his colleagues made their Harmonia Mundi set in 1981. The playing is of high quality and, although the recording could provide better internal definition, it is full and pleasing. When Archiv reissue their admirable set from 1967 by Eduard Melkus, Huguette Dreyfus, Lionel Rogg and Karl Scheit at mid-price, this will provide a useful alternative. Otherwise the Harmonia Mundi set should be considered, for it has considerable merits.

Bizet, Georges (1838–75)

L'Arlésienne (incidental music): *suite No. 1.*
(M) ** Sony Dig. MDK 46504 [id.]. Toronto SO, Andrew Davis – DVOŘÁK: *Slavonic dances, Op. 46.* **

L'Arlésienne (incidental music): *suite No. 2; Jeux d'enfants.*
(M) **(*) Sony MDK 46508 [id.]. Toronto SO, Andrew Davis – ROSSINI/RESPIGHI: *La boutique fantasque.* *** ❀

Andrew Davis gives an alert, quite stylish performance of the *First suite* from *L'Arlésienne* with the excellent Toronto Symphony Orchestra. The *Adagietto*, opening with a real pianissimo, is beautifully done and the digital recording is excellent. But it is a pity that the suites have been split up for reissue. Davis's *Second suite* is also well played and recorded (neither has the distinction or individuality of Stokowski), and the charming *Jeux d'enfants* has both sparkle and affection. This latter is more than acceptable as a bonus for the outstanding Rossini/Respighi coupling.

L'Arlésienne: suites Nos. 1–2; Carmen: suite No. 1.
(B) *** DG 431 160-2; *431 160-4* [id.]. BPO, Karajan (with OFFENBACH: *Contes d'Hoffmann: Barcarolle; Orpheus in the Underworld: overture* **(*)).
(M) *** DG 423 472-2; *423 472-4* [id.]. LSO, Abbado.

L'Arlésienne (incidental music): *suites Nos. 1 & 2; Carmen* (opera): *suites Nos. 1 & 2.*
(BB) **(*) Naxos Dig. 8.550061 [id.]. Slovak PO, Anthony Bramhall.
(B) *(*) LaserLight Dig. 15 614 [id.]. Budapest SO, Janos Sandor.

L'Arlésienne: suites Nos. 1–2; Carmen: suite No. 1; suite No. 2: excerpts.
(B) *** DG Compact Classics 413 422-2 (2); *413 422-4* [id.]. LSO, Abbado (with CHABRIER: *España*; DUKAS: *L'apprenti sorcier*; RIMSKY-KORSAKOV: *Capriccio espagnol* **(*) and on CD only: FALLA: *Three-cornered hat*: dances).
(B) **(*) Pickwick Dig. PCD 905 [MCA MCAD 6278]. LSO, Frühbeck de Burgos.

(i) *L'Arlésienne: suite No. 1; suite No. 2: Farandole. Carmen: suites 1 & 2;* (ii) *Fair maid of Perth suite.*
(B) ** Decca 421 632-2. (i) New Philh. O, Munch; (ii) SRO, Ansermet.

Among analogue couplings of *L'Arlésienne* and *Carmen suites*, Abbado's 1981 DG recording stands out, available either at medium price on CD only or, on Compact Classics at bargain price, on a pair of CDs or a double-length cassette. The orchestral playing is characteristically refined, the wind solos cultured and eloquent, especially in *L'Arlésienne*, where the pacing of the music is nicely judged. A vibrant accelerando at the end of the *Farandole* only serves to emphasize the obvious spontaneity of the music-making. There is warmth too, of course, and in the opening *Prélude* of the *Carmen suite* plenty of spirit. With vivid and truthful recording, the Compact Classics compilation is very attractive if the couplings are suitable, for both the CD and the tape transfers are splendidly managed. Abbado's selection from the *Carmen* suite is supplemented with two extra items, well played by the Hague Philharmonic Orchestra under Willem van Otterloo. The other highlight of this collection is Lorin Maazel's famous (1959) recording of Rimsky-Korsakov's *Capriccio espagnol*, lustrously played by the Berlin Philharmonic Orchestra in sparkling form. This remains the most electrifying account of Rimsky's famous orchestral showpiece in the current catalogue, and the remastering is extraordinarily vivid. There are also lively accounts of *L'apprenti sorcier* (Fiedler and the Boston Pops) and Chabrier's *España*, in a spirited performance by the Warsaw Philharmonic Orchestra under Jerzy Semkow. On the pair of

CDs, four dances from Falla's *Three-cornered hat*, brilliantly – if not distinctively – done by Maazel and the Berlin Radio Symphony Orchestra make a lively if none too generous bonus.

The metallic clash of the cymbals for the opening *Carmen Prélude* on Karajan's 1971 disc sets the seal on the brilliance of both the orchestral playing and the recording. Yet the acoustic is attractively resonant, allowing plenty of orchestral bloom. There is some marvellously crisp and stylish woodwind playing, and the characterization of the music is dramatic and vivid. This version is undoubtedly fresher than Karajan's later, digital recording with the same forces, in which the conductor sounds at times too languid. The two Offenbach encores, polished and vivacious, are welcome, although in the *Overture* the 1981 digital recording sounds rather dry.

Raphael Frühbeck de Burgos offers three more items than Abbado on his medium-price CD, and in an even cheaper price-range; he also has the advantage of full, modern digital recording, made in Watford Town Hall. The LSO playing is bright-eyed and polished, but Frühbeck's tempi are not always as naturally apt as those of Abbado, and the effect is rather less spontaneous. Nevertheless the Pickwick disc remains good value for those wanting an inexpensive modern recording of this colourful coupling.

Anthony Bramhall makes his Naxos début directing excellent performances with the Slovak Philharmonic Orchestra. The solo wind playing has an appealing delicacy of colour, the principal flute plays with finesse, and only the violin substituting for Michaela's aria is a little below the generally high standard. There is plenty of flair in the *Danse bohémienne* and the closing *Farandole* from *L'Arlésienne*; with vivid digital sound and a nicely atmospheric ambience, this inexpensive disc is most attractive.

Munch's disc was originally issued in 1967 as a Decca Phase 4 recording, and there is no doubt that the sound is both atmospheric and extraordinarily vivid. Generally the readings are stylish; if the last ounce of swagger is missing, the playing is still infectiously lively. Ansermet's *Fair maid of Perth* suite dates from 1960; it offers clean string-playing, and the overall effect has plenty of warmth and colour. A good bargain coupling, offering generous measure.

Sandor's selection is comprehensive, with over an hour of music; but the orchestral playing lacks the necessary zip and panache for these scores. The digital sound is good but not outstanding.

Jeux d'enfants (Children's games), Op. 22.

(B) *** CfP CD-CFP 4086; *TC-CFP 4086.* SNO, Gibson – RAVEL: *Ma Mère l'Oye;* SAINT-SAENS; *Carnival.* ***

(B) ** Pickwick Dig. PCD 932. LSO, Wordsworth – SAINT-SAENS: *Carnival* **; RAVEL: *Ma Mère l'Oye.* **(*)

From Classics for Pleasure a fresh approach, lively orchestral playing and excellent mid-1970s sound. The lyrical movements, shaped by Gibson with gentle affection, give much pleasure and, with excellent couplings, this is highly recommendable.

Barry Wordsworth draws crisp and sympathetic playing from the LSO, although there could be greater individuality. The recording is vivid at higher dynamic levels but seems to recede somewhat at pianissimos, and it is difficult to find a volume setting which suits both the gentle *Berceuse* and the brightly coloured opening *Marche.*

Symphony in C.

(M) *** Decca 417 734-2 [id.]. ASMF, Marriner – PROKOFIEV: *Symphony No. 1;* STRAVINSKY: *Pulcinella.* ***

(BB) **(*) Virgin/Virgo Dig. VJ7 91469-2; *VJ7 91469-4* [id.]. SCO, Saraste – RAVEL: *Ma Mère l'Oye* etc. ***

Marriner's performance is played with all the polish and elegance characteristic of the vintage ASMF records of the early 1970s; the slow movement has a delectable oboe solo and the finale is irrepressibly gay and high-spirited. The recording, originally rather reverberant, is now drier, the bass less expansive; but at mid-price and with highly desirable couplings, this remains excellent value.

With allegros brisk and well sprung, the first movement rhythmically bold and with the haunting slow movement taken spaciously, Saraste offers a refreshing, modern account of Bizet's youthful *Symphony.* The interpretation does not have the individuality of the Marriner Academy version, but this makes an unusual but apt coupling for Ravel's complete *Mother Goose.* Reverberant yet refined recording.

Symphony in C; Carmen: suites Nos. 1–2; Jeux d'enfants; Patrie: overture.

(M) ** EMI Dig. CDD7 63898-2 [id.]; *ET 763898-4.* O Nat. de France, Seiji Ozawa.

Eminently good performances from the Orchestre National de France and Ozawa, with the exception of the *Carmen* extended suite. Here, the music-making sounds too much like a rehearsal and refuses to spring fully to life; Ozawa's direction is lacking in flair. The EMI recording is vivid and clear, and this is certainly an attractive programme.

OPERA

Carmen (opera; complete).

(B) *** DG 427 440-2 (3) [id.]. Horne, McCracken, Krause, Maliponte, Manhattan Op. Ch., Met. Op. O, Bernstein.

(M) *** BMG/RCA GD 86199 (3) [6199-2-RG]. Leontyne Price, Corelli, Merrill, Freni, Linval, V. State Op. Ch., VPO, Karajan.

(M) ** EMI CMS7 63643-2 (2) [CDMB 63643]. Bumbry, Vickers, Freni, Paskalis, Les Petits Chanteurs à la Croix de Bois, Paris Op. Ch. & O, Frühbeck de Burgos.

(M) *(*) BMG/Eurodisc GD 69147 (2). Moffo, Corelli, Cappuccilli, Donath, Schönberg Boys' Ch., German Op. Ch. & O, Berlin, Maazel.

(M) * Decca 411 630-2 (2) [id.]. Resnik, Del Monaco, Sutherland, Krause, Geneva Grand Theatre Ch., SRO, Schippers.

(B) * Naxos Dig. 8.660005/7 [id.]. Alperyn, Lamberti, Titus, Palade, Schaechter, Liebeck, Slovak Philharmonic Ch., Bratislava Children's Ch., Slovak RSO (Bratislava), Alexander Rahbari.

Bernstein's 1973 *Carmen* was recorded at the New York Metropolitan Opera, the first recording undertaken there for many years. It was based on the Met.'s spectacular production with the same cast and conductor as on record, and the sessions plainly gained from being interleaved with live performances: Bernstein adopted the original version of 1875, with spoken dialogue but with variations designed to suit a stage production. Some of his slow tempi will be questioned, too; but what really matters is the authentic tingle of dramatic tension which permeates the whole entertainment. The full theatrical flavour of Bizet's score is strongly conveyed, and Marilyn Horne – occasionally coarse in expression – gives a most fully satisfying reading of the heroine's role, a great vivid characterization, warts and all. The rest of the cast similarly works to Bernstein's consistent overall plan. The singing is not all perfect, but it is always vigorous and colourful, and so (despite often questionable French accents) is the spoken dialogue. It is very well transferred and comes on three bargain CDs.

With Karajan's RCA version, made in Vienna in 1964, much depends on the listener's reaction to the conductor's tempi and to Leontyne Price's smoky-toned Carmen. Corelli has moments of coarseness, but his is still a heroic performance. Robert Merrill sings with gloriously firm tone, while Mirella Freni is, as ever, enchanting as Micaela. With often spectacular recording, this three-disc set, now offered at mid-price, remains a keen competitor.

Frühbeck uses the original 1875 version of Bizet's score without the cuts that were made after experience in the theatre, and with spoken dialogue instead of the recitatives which Guiraud composed after Bizet's early death. Quite apart from that, Grace Bumbry makes a disappointing, generally unimaginative Carmen, singing with good tone but with few of the individual touches that bring the words or musical phrases to life. Vickers makes a strong, heroic Don José, but he rarely sounds idiomatic; and, surprisingly, Frühbeck's conducting lacks sparkle. Paskalis makes a gloriously rich-toned Escamillo and Freni an exquisite Micaela.

Maazel's 1979 Eurodisc version of *Carmen*, using the expanded Fritz Oeser edition, makes a doubtful bargain. The casting is starry – with such celebrated singers as Arleen Augér and Jane Berbié in the small roles of Frasquita and Mercedes – but almost totally non-French and not always apt. Anna Moffo, lacking mezzo weight, is hardly an ideal Carmen, and she makes up for that by underlining her characterization too heavily. Franco Corelli too is heavy-handed as Don José, not as effective as he was for Karajan. Helen Donath makes a charming Micaela, light and sweet, while Piero Cappuccilli as Escamillo produces a stream of strong, firm tone, even if – like others in the cast – his French is not his strong point. Maazel as in his later, Erato version (the one used in Franco Rosi's film) directs a bright and forceful performance, dramatically tense, exaggerated by the fierceness of the recorded sound in tuttis. Otherwise the recording (not digital) is reasonably atmospheric.

One cannot imagine why Decca chose to reissue this early stereo *Carmen* conducted by Schippers (despite brilliant engineering). Resnik has a fruitier tone than her many rivals, but her aim is wild compared with many of her competitors. Del Monaco sings coarsely and, though Sutherland sings beautifully as Micaela, it sounds as though Lucia had strayed into the wrong opera. Schippers drives very hard indeed.

The Naxos version on three discs at budget price brings refined playing from the Czecho-Slovak Radio Symphony Orchestra but low tensions and little feeling of atmosphere. As Carmen, Graciela Alperyn sings with rich, firm tone and secure control but lacks all dramatic weight, making a colourless figure. Giorgio Lamberti is a coarse Don José and Doina Palade a fluttery Micaela, though Alan Titus is a good, virile Escamillo.

Carmen: highlights.

(M) *** Decca 421 300-2. Troyanos, Domingo, Van Dam, Te Kanawa, John Alldis Ch., LPO, Solti.

(B) **(*) Pickwick (Decca) IMPX 9016.

Marilyn Horne, Michael Molese, Soloists, RPO Ch., RPO, Henry Lewis.
(B) ** DG Compact Classics *427 719-4* [id.] (from above complete set with Horne, MacCracken, cond. Bernstein) – PUCCINI: *Tosca*: highlights. **(*)
(M) ** EMI CDM7 63075-2. Callas, Gedda, Massard, René Duclos Ch., Children's Ch., Paris Nat. Op. O, Prêtre.
(B) *(*) Decca 433 626-2; *433 626-4* [id.]. Resnik, Del Monaco, Kraus, Sutherland, Spanellys, Minton, Ch. & SRO, Schippers.

Solti's Decca performance is remarkable for its new illumination of characters whom everyone thinks they know inside out. Tatiana Troyanos is quite simply the subtlest Carmen on record. Escamillo too is more readily sympathetic, not just the flashy matador who steals the hero's girl, whereas Don José is revealed as weak rather than just a victim. Troyanos's singing is delicately seductive too, with no hint of vulgarity, while the others make up a most consistent singing cast. The reissued compilation of 'scenes and arias' from Solti's sharply characterful set is generous, and the remastered recording sounds better than the complete set.

The Pickwick (originally Decca Phase 4) selection of *Carmen* excerpts dates from 1970, some years before Marilyn Horne made her complete New York recording. She it was who provided the ghost voice behind Dorothy Dandridge in the film *Carmen Jones*; here, with a further decade of experience, she is even more searingly compelling as the fire-eating heroine. Not only is there dramatic presence but musical control too, and the voice is at its ripest. Henry Lewis's conducting has no lack of flair – although the 37-minute selection (after the *Prelude*) concentrates entirely on solos, duets and the quintet featuring the heroine, while Escamillo fails to appear at all! Yet the vivid projection of Horne's vocal personality on this excellently transferred bargain CD is well worth sampling.

Highlights from Bernstein's recording are offered on a bargain Compact Classics tape, coupled with a matching *Tosca* selection. The compilation is well made to demonstrate Marilyn Horne's seductively vibrant assumption of the title-role, although Bernstein's sometimes leisurely tempi are not helped by a preponderance of bass in the sound balance, noticeable immediately in the opening *Prelude*.

The selection from the Callas set, which is very generous with a playing time of 71 minutes 35 seconds, is not designed so much to highlight the heroine as to provide as many 'pops' as possible from the opera. In isolation, Callas's shortcomings – dramatic as well as vocal – are just as clear as in the complete (full-price) set, and Prêtre is hardly a sensitive or understanding Bizet conductor.

The most striking thing about the set of highlights from the Schippers recording is the brilliance and atmosphere of the vintage 1963 Decca recording. Resnik is by no means an unappealing Carmen, but her vibrato is brought out by the microphone. Sutherland's Micaela was one of the two memorable aspects of the complete set (the other was the sound of Carmen's hob-nailed boots in the *Habañera*) and it is disappointing that Decca included only her Act III aria in a 56-minute selection which matches the old LP without any additional material. Del Monaco's Don José is predictably coarse.

(i) *Les pêcheurs de perles* (complete). (ii) *Ivan IV: highlights.*
(M) ** EMI CMS7 69704-2 (2) [Ang. CDMB 69704]. (i) Micheau, Gedda, Blanc, Mars, Paris Opéra-Comique O, Dervaux; (ii) Roux, Micheau, Legay, Sénéchal, Noguera, Savignol, French R. Ch. & O, Tzipine.

Paul Dervaux is no more than an efficient conductor, and his lack of affection infects the principals, who are all stylish artists but here sing below their best, even the dependable Nicolai Gedda. On two mid-priced CDs the set might still be worth considering, however, when it also includes selections from the opera which Bizet wrote immediately after *Pearl-fishers*, *Ivan IV*. There is a fine scena for the heroine, beautifully sung by Janine Micheau; and the heady-toned tenor, Henri Legay, an outstanding artist, sings superbly in his vengeance aria. It is also good to hear the fine bass, Pierre Savignol. The package includes the libretto of *Pearl-fishers* but, as yet, no translation, and only garbled notes and synopsis for *Ivan IV*. The CD transfers hardly betray the age of the recordings.

Bliss, Arthur (1891–1975)

(i) *Piano concerto; March of homage.*
(M) **(*) Unicorn Dig. UKCD 2029. (i) Philip Fowke; Royal Liverpool PO, David Atherton.

Bliss wrote his *Piano concerto* for British Week at the New York World Fair in 1939 and he attempted a bravura work on a very large scale. From the dashing double octaves at the start the pianistic style throughout has much of Rachmaninov and Liszt in it, though the idiom is very much Bliss's own, with some of his most memorable material. It is a work which needs a passionately committed soloist, and that is what it finds in Philip Fowke, urgent and expressive, well matched by David Atherton and the Liverpool orchestra. The occasional piece is also given a lively performance. The digital recording is full and vivid, with the piano naturally balanced, less forward than is common. There is a tendency for the acoustic to be a shade over-resonant in the *Concerto* (noticeable at the opening) but the internal definition is somewhat improved on CD, which also brings a degree of fierceness to orchestral fortissimos.

Morning heroes.
(M) **(*) EMI CDM7 63906-2; *EG 763906-4.*
Westbrook (nar.), Royal Liverpool PO Ch. & O, Groves.

Morning heroes is an elegiac work, written as a tribute to the composer's brother and to all who fell in the First World War. The sincerity of the writing is never in doubt but there is less contrast here than in comparable war-inspired works by Vaughan Williams and Britten. One misses both the anger of those other composers and their passages of total simplicity; but it is good that one of Bliss's most ambitious works should be available in so strong a performance. Fine recording and an excellent transfer.

Bloch, Ernest (1880–1959)

Concerti grossi Nos. 1 & 2; (i) *Schelomo.*
(M) *** Mercury 432 718-2 [id.]. Eastman-Rochester O, Hanson, (i) with Miquelle.

Bloch's two *Concerti grossi* were written in 1925 and 1952 respectively. Although separated by more than a quarter of a uniquely fast-moving century, they are surprisingly similar in style. They may not be among Bloch's most deeply personal works but they are thoroughly enjoyable. The neo-classical style brings a piano continuo in the Baroque manner in No. 1; the second, for strings alone, is more intense in feeling. The performances here are admirable, lively and sympathetic, and the slightly spiky tinge to the otherwise full Mercury sound is like an attractive condiment although the violin timbre is distinctly astringent. *Schelomo*, with Georges Miquelle its soloist, makes a useful bonus for this mid-priced reissue. Hanson's orchestral backing is very dramatic and full-blooded and thus makes the strongest dynamic contrast with the less expansive solo image. Nevertheless Miquelle's playing is very sympathetic.

Violin concerto.
(M) *** EMI CDM7 63989-2 [id.]. Menuhin, Philh. O, Kletzki – BERG: *Violin concerto.* ***

Bloch's powerful and intensely atmospheric *Violin concerto* seems to have dropped out of the repertory, yet the colour and eloquence of this piece are undeniable. For long Szigeti's pioneering account with Charles Münch and the Paris Conservatoire had an intimidating effect on other performers, including (he said at the time) Menuhin himself, and his was only the second recording of this powerful work. This deeply felt and finely recorded 1963 account was a worthy successor to the Szigeti and (as far as the UK is concerned) remains the only current CD version of this evocative score at any price. Menuhin's playing is passionate and committed from the very first note, and any weaknesses in the score are quite lost when the playing is so compelling. Paul Kletzki accompanies with equal distinction and a real sense of atmosphere, and the Philharmonia playing is first rate. The 1964 Kingsway Hall recording sounds very well indeed, brighter than on LP but with plenty of ambient glow. At mid-price (and with a fine account of the Berg thrown in) this is a real bargain.

Schelomo: Hebrew rhapsody (for cello and orchestra).
(B) **(*) DG 429 155-2; *429 155-4* [id.].
Fournier, BPO, Wallenstein – DVOŘÁK: *Cello concerto* **(*); BRUCH: *Kol Nidrei.* **

Fournier's fervent advocacy of Bloch's *Hebrew rhapsody* is given sympathetic support by Alfred Wallenstein. Fournier is closely balanced, but the 1976 recording is warmly atmospheric and, if orchestral detail is not always fully revealed, the CD sound is otherwise impressive.

Blow, John (1649–1708)

(i) *Ode on the death of Mr Henry Purcell*; (ii) *Amphion Angelicus* (song collection): *Ah heaven! What is't I hear?; Cloe found Amintas lying all in tears; Loving above himself; Shepherds deck your crooks; Why weeps Asteria?; Epilogue: Sing, sing, ye muses.*
(M) **(*) HM/BMG GD 71962. (i) René Jacobs, James Bowman; (ii) Yamamoto, Van der Speek, Jacobs, Van Altena, Van Egmond, Ens., Leonhardt.

John Blow's *Ode on the death of Purcell*, a highly eloquent setting of an allegorical poem by John Dryden, makes a worthy memorial to the great English composer. It is an extended three-part structure some 25 minutes long, with René Jacobs and James Bowman ideally matched in the vocal centrepiece. The other items in the programme are taken from a collection of 50 songs, published in 1700, and admirably demonstrate the range and variety of Blow's art. Apart from the opening *Cloe found Amintas lying all in tears*, where the two soprano soloists, Nobuko Yamamoto and Nelly van der Speek, could blend more pleasingly, they are all effectively presented, especially the closing *Epilogue* for vocal quartet. Gustav Leonhardt and his chamber ensemble (two recorders are used in the main work) accompany authentically, and the 1973 recording has a good ambience and no lack of presence.

Venus and Adonis.
(M) *** HM/BMG GD 77117 (2). Kirkby, Tubb, King, Wistreich, Bonner, Holden, Cass, Nichols, Cornwell, Müller, Consort of Musicke, Rooley – GIBBONS: *Cupid and Death.* ***

Venus and Adonis, 'a masque for the entertainment of the king' dating from around 1682, was the first through-composed opera in English. *Dido and Aeneas* by Blow's pupil, Purcell, followed it before the end of the decade, and it is sad that so promising a start never led to the development of a school of English opera. In form, this is like a Lully opera in miniature. Its length makes it more likely to suit twentieth-century taste, with the Prologue and three brief Acts presenting a fast-moving sequence of choruses, dances and 'act-tunes' as well as arias, often with chorus. Rooley directs an elegant, lightly sprung performance, very well sung, recorded in good analogue sound (1984) in a warm acoustic. It takes up only part of the first disc of the two-disc set, now reissued by BMG at mid-price.

Boccherini, Luigi (1743–1805)

Cello concerto No. 2 in D, G.479.
(M) *** DG 429 098-2; *429 098-4.* Rostropovich, Zurich Coll. Mus., Sacher – TARTINI; VIVALDI: *Concertos.* ***
(B) *** DG Compact Classics *415 330-4* [id.]. Rostropovich, Zurich Coll. Mus., Sacher – HAYDN **; DVOŘÁK: *Cello concertos.* ***

Rostropovich in Boccherini offers a highly individual musical experience. Although essentially a performance in the grand manner (with Rostropovich providing his own cadenzas), the music-making has tremendous vitality, with extremely lively outer movements to balance the eloquence of the *Adagio.* The forceful nature of the performance is short on charm and so perhaps a little out of character for an essentially elegant composer like Boccherini; but Rostropovich is so compelling that reservations are swept aside. He is given an alert accompaniment by Sacher, and the recording has fine body and presence. This is among the most worthwhile of DG's series of bargain-price double-length Compact Classics tapes, for it includes a very fine account of the Dvořák *Cello concerto* partnering Fournier and Szell. The chrome-tape transfer has excellent range and detail.

Cello concerto No. 7 in G, G.480.
(B) *** Ph. 422 481-2. Gendron, LSO, Leppard – HAYDN: *Cello concerto in C.* ***
(B) *** Pickwick Dig. PCD 917. Felix Schmidt, ECO, Heath – BEETHOVEN: *Triple concerto.* ***

It was Maurice Gendron who originally unearthed this *G major Concerto* and made its first recording. It is admirably played and usefully coupled with Haydn's lesser-known *C major Concerto.*

The Boccherini *Concerto No. 7* makes an unusual but apt and attractive coupling for the Trio Zingara's excellent version of the Beethoven *Triple concerto.* This is the concerto from which Grützmacher extracted the slow movement in his phoney, cobbled-together 'Boccherini Concerto', the movement everyone remembers. The recording, as in the Beethoven, is full and vivid, an excellent recommendation on the bargain-price IMP label.

Cello concerto in B flat (arr Grützmacher).
(BB) *** Naxos Dig. 8.550059 [id.]. Ludovít Kanta, Capella Istropolitana, Peter Breiner – HAYDN: *Cello concertos Nos. 1 & 2.* ***

Ludovít Kanta distinguished himself at the Tchaikovsky Competition in 1982 and now leads the cellos of the Slovak Philharmonic, from whose members the Capella Istropolitana is drawn; he also plays in the Slovak Piano Trio. He is a very fine player and gives an eloquent account of the Boccherini *Cello concerto* in the Grützmacher version. Although he does not possess the commanding personality of Fournier or Rostropovich, there is nothing second-class about this performance. His playing is distinguished by imaginative and musicianly phrasing and a warm tone, and he commands considerable technical address. The Slovak players under Peter Breiner give a good account of themselves and the (perhaps slightly forward) recording is made in a bright, warm acoustic. This can hold its own against versions costing twice or three times as much.

Symphony in C min.
(M) ** Decca 433 169-2; *433 169-4* [id.]. Orchestra Rossini di Napoli, Franco Caracciolo – VIVALDI: *Concertos.* ***

This is a very conventional piece of writing with virtually none of the touches of *galant* colouring that make the best of Boccherini's chamber music attractive. The performance here is quite nicely turned, but the actual orchestral playing is better in the string departments than in the wind. The recording is clear and fresh, and this makes an agreeable enough bonus for a desirable collection of Vivaldi concertos.

CHAMBER MUSIC

Cello quintet, Op. 37/7 (Pleyel).

(B) **(*) Decca 421 637-2; *421 637-4*. ASMF – MENDELSSOHN: *Octet*. **(*)

This is an inspired piece: it would be worth getting for its own sake – and the coupled performance of the Mendelssohn *Octet* is a particularly fine one. Reissued on Decca's Weekend label, this is a bargain, even if the recording shows its age just a little in the upper range.

Guitar quintets Nos. 3 in B flat, G.447; 9 in C (La ritirata di Madrid), G.453.

(M) **(*) Ph. 426 092-2; *426 092-4*. Pepe Romero, ASMF Chamber Ens.

Both works here are arrangements. No. 3 comes from the *Piano quintet*, Op. 57/2; the first three movements of No. 9 originate in the *Piano quintet*, Op. 56/3, and the finale, which gives it its subtitle, *La ritirata di Madrid*, is familiar from the *String quintet*, Op. 30/6. The picturesque evocation of Spanish life is created with a set of twelve short variations set in a long, slow crescendo, followed by a similarly graduated decrescendo, a kind of Spanish patrol with the 'night watch' disappearing into the distance at the close. Both works are melodically engaging in Boccherini's elegant rococo style, and they are beautifully played. The guitar is well balanced within the string group, yet is able to dominate when required. On CD, detail is cleaner but the string timbre is slightly more astringent than it was on the original LP, not entirely to Boccherini's advantage. However, this remains an attractive coupling.

Guitar quintets: in D, G.449; in E min., G.451; String quintet in A, G.308.

(M) *(*) Sony SMK 47298 [id.]. Starobin, Carmirelli, Genualdi, Setzer, Paetsche, Naegele, Hoffman, Bolipata, Rosen, Wiley, Hoffman.

These engaging pieces were recorded at various times: the *D major Guitar quintet*, G.449, in 1979 and the beguiling *E minor Quintet* five years earlier. The fine playing of David Starobin and his eminent colleagues is spoilt by the uncomfortably close balance, though things are even worse in the *A major String quintet*. The performance of the latter is a little less finished than are the guitar quintets.

Guitar quintets Nos. (i) *4 in D (Fandango); 7 in E min., G.451; 9 in C (La ritirata di Madrid).*

(B) *** DG 429 512-2; *429 512-4* [id.]. Yepes, Melos Qt; (i) with Lucero Tena.

Guitar quintets Nos. 4 (Fandango); 9 (La ritirata di Madrid).

(B) ** Hung. White Label HRC 055 [id.]. Laszlo Szendrey-Karper, Tátrai Qt.

The DG bargain compilation (from 1971) offers a cleaner sound-picture than its Philips competitor: indeed the sound is very good, full yet lively and well projected. The playing is expert and, in the boisterous *Fandango* finale of No. 4, Lucero Tena makes a glittering contribution with his castanets.

The Hungaroton CD is not to be dismissed; the performances have vitality and the recording is vivid, if a trifle thin in string timbre. But the DG disc is first choice.

6 Oboe quintets, Op. 45.

(M) *** Decca 433 173-2 [id.]. Sarah Francis, Allegri Qt.

An attractive collection, very persuasively played and recorded. These *Quintets*, written in 1797, were published as Op. 45, though Boccherini's own catalogue lists them as 555. They have a sunny grace that is altogether beguiling, and a gentle, wistful lyricism that is unfailing in its appeal.

Piano quintets: in A min., Op. 56/2, G.412; in E flat, Op. 56/3, G.410; in E min., Op. 57/3, G.415; in C, Op. 57/6, G.418.

(M) *** BMG/RCA Dig. GD 77053 [77053-2-RG]. Les Adieux.

Two of the six Op. 56 *Quintets* (1797), the last work Boccherini composed in his capacity as court composer to Friedrich Wilhelm II of Prussia, are included, together with two from Op. 57 (1799) dedicated to the whole French nation, no less. The most haunting of them are the lovely *E minor* (Op. 57/3), which starts the disc, and the *A minor* (Op. 56/2); both have those hints of beguiling, almost sultry melancholy that makes this composer's musical language so distinctive. This accomplished period-instrument group turn in performances of great finesse and charm, though the recording balance places the listener very much in the front row of the salon. But this music has much more to it than it is given credit for.

Boieldieu, François (1775–1834)

Harp concerto in 3 tempi in C.

❀ (M) *** Decca 425 723-2; *425 723-4*. Marisa Robles, ASMF, Iona Brown – DITTERSDORF; HANDEL: *Harp concertos* etc. *** ❀

Boieldieu's *Harp concerto* has been recorded elsewhere but never more attractively. Iona Brown and the Academy set the scene with an alert, vigorous introduction and Miss Robles provides contrasting delicacy. Much play is made with the possibilities of light and shade, the harp bringing gentle echo effects in repeated phrases. The slow movement is delightful and the lilt of the finale irresistible. The (originally Argo) recording is still in the demonstration class and very sweet on the ear. To make the reissue even more attractive, three beguiling sets of *Variations* have been added, derived from a separate solo LP, including music by Handel, Beethoven's *Six Variations on a Swiss song* and a *Theme, variations and Rondo pastorale* attributed to Mozart.

Boito, Arrigo (1842–1918)

Mefistofele (opera): *Prologue.*

(M) (***) BMG/RCA mono GD 60276; *GK 60276* [60276-2-RG; *60276-4-RG*]. Moscona, Robert Shaw Ch., Columbus Boychoir, NBC SO, Toscanini – VERDI: *I Lombardi; Rigoletto*: excerpts. (**)

(M) **(*) DG 431 171-2 [id.]. Ghiaurov, V. State Op. Ch., VPO, Bernstein – R. STRAUSS: *Salome* etc. **(*)

Whatever the limitations of the sound, the hair-raising intensity of Toscanini's performance gives Boito's multi-layered *Prologue* a cogency never matched since on record. The dryness of sound even seems to help, when offstage choruses are accurately focused, and the singing of the Robert Shaw Chorale has thrillingly dramatic bite. This was taken from one of the very last broadcasts Toscanini ever made and with the Verdi items it makes a magnetically involving historic document.

The DG recording was made in Vienna in 1977 and finds Ghiaurov in excellent form. Bernstein, too, conducts this highly imaginative piece vividly and atmospherically. The CD transfer has greatly improved the focus and now the offstage choruses register impressively. This does not quite have the electricity of Toscanini but, for those wanting a modern version, it will serve admirably.

Borodin, Alexander (1833–87)

In the Steppes of Central Asia; Prince Igor: Polovtsian dances.

(BB) **(*) Naxos Dig. 8.550051 [id.]. Slovak PO, Nazareth – MUSSORGSKY: *Night* etc. **(*)

The sinuous oriental flavour of *In the Steppes of Central Asia* is well caught in the Naxos performance, although the first climax is rhythmically a little ponderous. The *Polovtsian dances*, if without the last degree of refinement, have plenty of zestful exuberance. Vivid digital sound makes this coupling with Mussorgsky excellent value.

(i) *Symphonies Nos. 1–3; Prince Igor:* (i; ii) *Overture and Polovtsian dances;* (iii) *In the steppes of Central Asia; Nocturne for string orchestra* (arr. Sargent).

(M) *(**) Sony M2YK 46459 (2). (i) Toronto SO, Andrew Davis, (ii) with Ch.; (iii) Phd. O, Eugene Ormandy.

Symphonies Nos. 1–2; 3 in A min. (completed & orch. Glazunov).

(BB) ** Naxos Dig. 8.550238 [id.]. Bratislava RSO, Stephen Gunzenhauser.

Though the *Second* is by far the best known of the Borodin symphonies, both its companions deserve greater popularity, especially the *First* which, in Andrew Davis's hands, sounds a fully mature work in its own right and not just a preparation for the well-known *Symphony in E flat.* It is colourful and ebullient, with a particularly appealing scherzo. The *Third* brings some most engaging playing from the Toronto woodwind. It is a pastoral two-movement torso, completed by Glazunov from sketches, and here it sounds delightfully spontaneous. In the *Second Symphony* Davis's tempi are admirably judged: the bold rhythmic figure of the first movement has both Russian power and bite, and the performance overall has striking colour and vitality, with a superb horn solo in the *Andante.* In short, these are easily the finest performances available and the Toronto orchestra find plenty of zest and romantic feeling for the *Prince Igor Overture*, provided as a bonus, while the *Polovtsian dances*, complete with unnamed chorus, bring a thrilling Beechamesque excitement and flair. Unfortunately the Toronto orchestra is not flattered by the 1977 CBS recording which, although fully acceptable, is lacking in natural ambience and bloom, its two-dimensional sound-picture all the more apparent on CD. The two encores from the Philadelphia Orchestra under Ormandy, recorded nearly two decades earlier, must be written off. The rich sounds which obviously emanate from the Philadelphia strings in their opulent account of the *Nocturne* are rendered sterile in the CD transfer by a piercingly thin sound for the violins above the stave, and *In the steppes of Central Asia* is even more disagreeable, with discoloration of the upper harmonics of the woodwind immediately noticeable at the opening.

The Naxos disc is an undoubted bargain in offering good recordings of all three symphonies (76 minutes) at a very modest price indeed. One ideally needs a more sumptuous body of sound for this music than the Bratislava Radio Symphony Orchestra can provide, but

Gunzenhauser brings plenty of buoyant vitality to the first movement of the *Second Symphony*. Altogether these are fresh, pleasing performances but not distinctive.

Symphony No. 2 in B min.; Prince Igor: Overture; Polovtsian dances.
(BB) ** ASV Dig. CDQS 6018; *ZCQS 6018*.
Mexico State SO, Bátiz.

Bátiz's bright, modern digital recording certainly makes a vivid impression and the performances are extremely spirited, although one is made to realize that the Mexican State Orchestra, though impressively rehearsed, cannot match the finest European orchestras in virtuosity and finesse. The *Polovtsian dances* are without a chorus, and the effect is slightly shrill; but the energy of the performance is arresting. This is issued in the super-bargain range and is very good value.

String quartet No. 2 in D.
(M) **(*) Decca 425 541-2; *425 541-4* [id.].
Borodin Qt – SHOSTAKOVICH; TCHAIKOVSKY: *Quartets*. **(*)

The Borodins' first version on Decca was recorded in 1962; this performance is hardly less fine than the later (full-price) versions and it is very generously coupled. However, the forward recording, though rich-textured, is given a boldly outlined treble, approaching fierceness in the CD transfer, and some will prefer a softer-grained effect.

Songs: *Arabian melody; Arrogance; The beauty no longer loves me; The false note; The fishermaiden; From my tears; From the shores of thy far native land; Listen to my song little friend; The magic garden; The queen of the sea; The sea; The sleeping princess; Song of the dark forest; There is poison in my songs; Those people; Why art thou so early, dawn?*
(M) *** EMI CMS7 63386-2 (3) [Ang. CDMC 63386]. Christoff, Tcherepnin, Reiss, Lamoureux O, Tzipine – *Prince Igor*. **(*)

Accompanied at the piano in all but three of the songs by the composer, Alexander Tcherepnin, Christoff gives glorious performances of these rare items. They were recorded in the 1960s, when the voice was at its richest and most expressive, providing an invaluable makeweight for Semkow's cut version of *Prince Igor*.

Prince Igor (opera) complete.
(M) **(*) EMI CMS7 63386-2 (3) [Ang. CDMC 63386]. Chekerliiski, Christoff, Todorov, Sofia Nat. Theatre Op. Ch. & O, Jerzy Semkow – *Songs*. ***

Recorded in Paris in 1966, the colourful EMI recording of *Prince Igor* was never given international circulation – except briefly in a highlights disc – until this mid-price CD transfer appeared in 1990. Its great flaw is that Act III is completely omitted, on the grounds that it was almost entirely the work of Rimsky-Korsakov and Glazunov. The great glory of the performance is the singing of Boris Christoff as both Galitszky and Konchak, easily outshining all rivals. Jerzy Semkow with his Sofia Opera forces is most sympathetic, but the other soloists are almost all disappointing, with the women sour-toned and the men often strained and unsteady. There is no libretto; but EMI is very generous with cueing points, and you can follow the story easily by checking them against the very detailed synopsis. The sound is limited but agreeably atmospheric.

Prince Igor: Overture and Polovtsian dances.
(B) *** Decca 417 689-2; *417 689-4*. LSO Ch., LSO, Solti – MUSSORGSKY: *Khovanshchina prelude; Night;* GLINKA: *Russlan overture*. ***

Prince Igor: Polovtsian dances.
(M) *** DG 419 063-2; *419 063-4* [id.]. BPO, Karajan – RIMSKY-KORSAKOV: *Scheherazade*. ***
(M) *** EMI CDM7 69041-2 [id.]. Philh. O, Karajan – GOUNOD: *Faust ballet* ***; OFFENBACH: *Gaîté parisienne* **(*); PONCHIELLI: *Dance of the hours*. ***
(M) **(*) Decca 417 753-2 [id.]. Welsh Nat. Op. Ch., RPO, Stokowski – RIMSKY-KORSAKOV: *Scheherazade* etc. *(**)

Karajan's Berlin Philharmonic version has great flair and excitement, though it lacks a chorus. The alternative Philharmonia account comes from 1960 but hardly shows its age – the recording sounds full as well as brilliant.

Solti's performance is also among the finest ever recorded, with good choral singing – even if the chorus takes a little while to warm up. The *Overture* too has fine dash, with the LSO players consistently on their toes.

Stokowski misses out the percussion-led opening *Dance of the Polovtsi maidens*. His performance is a mannered one, but there is no question of the sheer excitement he creates as the work reaches its final climax. The remastered 1969 recording is impressively vivid, with a sense of spectacle, even if the effect is not absolutely refined.

Boulez, Pierre (born 1926)

Rituel: In memoriam Bruno Maderna; Éclat-Multiples.
(M) *** Sony SK 45839 [id.]. BBC SO, Ens. InterContemporain, composer.

This CD reissue of two of Boulez's strongest and most immediately approachable works in his own authoritative performances could not be more welcome. *Éclat-Multiples* is a piece, begun in 1964, which may well never be completed to the composer's satisfaction. It started simply as *Éclat*, a brilliant showpiece, an exuberant mosaic of sounds; but then, in 1970, it started developing from there in the pendant work, *Multiples*. On this recording the two sections are played without a break. *Rituel* is even more remarkable, the most moving music that Boulez has ever written, inspired by the premature death of his friend and colleague, Bruno Maderna. Conceived more broadly than most of Boulez's music, this half-hour span, in fifteen clearly defined sections, brings what even an uninitiated listener will recognize as a great funeral procession, darkly intense, building up with an emotional intensity hardly less involving than a Mahler funeral march. Boulez himself does not resist the idea of the work being appreciated first on a direct emotional level, so long as the listener does not just wallow but looks below the surface. This record, very well played and recorded, provides both a challenge and a reward.

Le soleil des eaux.
(M) *** EMI CDM7 63948-2 [id.]. Nendick, McDaniel, Devos, BBC Ch. & SO, composer – KOECKLIN: *Les Bandar-Log*; MESSIAEN: *Chronochromie* etc. ***

Three of the perfomances on this CD were funded by the Gulbenkian Foundation. Boulez's cantata is best thought of initially in its atmospheric context, for it served originally as incidental music to a poetic radio drama about the poisoning of a river. As ever with Boulez, the concentration is formidable, but Josephine Nendick, the principal soloist, is breathtakingly precise and the result is far more enjoyable as a result. Both performance and recording reflect the high standard of the original series, and the CD transfer gives striking presence.

Boyce, William (1710–79)

Overtures Nos. 1–9.
(M) *** Chan. CHAN 6531; *MBTD 6531* [id.]. Cantilena, Adrian Shepherd.

The eight Boyce *Symphonies* have been recorded many times, but the composer's collection of a dozen *Overtures*, put together in 1770 – although including at least one work from as early as 1745 – has much of comparable vigour. As it happens, the first overture is not one of the best; but each has its attractions and those which bring out the brass are most exciting. In 1770 Boyce, already deaf, was regarded as old-fashioned and was never given a proper hearing with this music. This 73-minute disc includes nine of the set, and Cantilena's performances readily convey the freshness of Boyce's inspiration. The recording is oddly balanced but is both atmospheric and vivid and provides a refreshing musical experience.

(i) *Organ voluntaries Nos. 1, 2, 4 & 10.* Anthems: *By the waters of Babylon; I have surely built Thee a house; O where shall wisdom be found; Turn unto me, O Lord.*
(M) *** Saga SCD 9006. (i) Arthur Wills; (ii) Ely Cathedral Ch., Wills; Gerald Clifford.

Superbly recorded, this first of a series of Saga reissues from the 1970s is most welcome. Originally a bargain label, the CDs are now offered at medium price, but this one is well worth it. It is a salutary contrast to hear formal eighteenth-century settings of words which have been set dramatically in our own century by Sir William Walton; but the music of Boyce is most compelling, especially when sung with such warmth. The organ voluntaries are placed as interludes between the anthems and are very well played on an organ that gives them plenty of character. This makes a most stimulating introduction to valuable and rare repertoire, and the CD transfer catches the cathedral ambience to perfection.

Brade, William (1560–1630)

Hamburger Ratsmusik: Allemandes, Canzonas, Courantes, Galliards, Intradas (1609, 1614 & 1617 collections).
(M) *** HM/BMG Dig. GD 77168 (2) [77168-2-RG]. Hespèrion XX, Jordi Savall.

William Brade spent most of his life on the Continent, serving at the Court of Christian IV of Denmark in the 1590s, and subsequently at the Brandenburg Court in Berlin and in Bückenburg, Halle and in Hamburg, where he died in 1630. This collection of dances is based on the three main prints which appeared in 1609, 1614 and 1617 in Hamburg and Lübeck, and embraces all the contemporary forms, Allemand, Paduana, Galliard and a variety of descriptive pieces. Their realization is absolutely delightful, varied in both content and instrumental colour, and excellently played by Hespèrion XX under Jordi Savall, while the recording, from 1981, is very good indeed.

Brahms, Johannes (1833–97)

Piano concerto No. 1 in D min., Op. 15.
(M) **(*) Ph. 420 702-2; *420 702-4* [id.]. Arrau, Concg. O, Haitink.

(i) *Piano concerto No. 1;* (ii) *Variations on a theme of Haydn, Op. 56a.*
(M) *** EMI CDM7 63536-2; *EG 763536-4*

[id.]. (i) Barenboim, Philh. O; (ii) VPO; Barbirolli.

(i) *Piano concerto No. 1; 4 Ballades, Op. 10.*
(M) *** DG 431 595-2; *431 595-4* [id.]. Gilels, (i) BPO, Jochum.

(i) *Piano concerto No. 1; Variations and fugue on a theme of Handel, Op. 24.*
(M) **(*) BMG/RCA GD 60357 [60357-2-RG]. Van Cliburn; (i) Boston SO, Leinsdorf.

Gilels's reading of the *D minor Concerto* is to the 1970s what Curzon's was to the 1960s; it has a magisterial strength blended with a warmth, humanity and depth that are altogether inspiring. Jochum is a superb accompanist and the remastered 1972 recording has a better focus on CD, if slightly less glowing warmth than the original LP. The *Ballades*, recorded three years later, make a considerable bonus. They have never been played so marvellously on record, and the recording is very believable.

Barenboim recorded the two Brahms *Piano concertos* with Barbirolli in 1968, at almost exactly the same time as the conductor was doing his Vienna cycle of the *Symphonies*. It was by the choice of the pianist that tempi were so unusually slow, but it was a decision with which Barbirolli wholly sympathized, drawing even more loving playing from the Philharmonia than he had done from the Vienna Philharmonic in the orchestral works. Their performance of the *First Concerto* is among the most inspired ever committed to disc. If at first the opening tempo seems disconcertingly measured, it falls into place on a second hearing. The playing is heroic and marvellously spacious, and the performance is sustained by the intensity of concentration, especially in the pianissimo passages of the slow movement; the joyous finale uplifts the spirit and communicates a life-enhancing confidence. The *Variations*, laid out for the listener in affectionate detail, again show the conductor at his finest; the late-1960s recordings have transferred splendidly to CD, with plenty of body and the upper range brighter but without edginess.

With its rugged opening, Van Cliburn's account of the *D minor Concerto* soon develops a full head of steam. Leinsdorf is hardly less sympathetic than he is for Richter in No. 2, and this is a compelling reading, full of spontaneous vigour. The slow movement has eloquence and atmosphere, and the finale plenty of fire. What makes the disc especially attractive is the splendid account of the *Handel variations*, which acts as an exhilarating (26-minute) encore. Van Cliburn plays with splendid dash and often with great bravura, displaying a wide range of timbre and dynamic. He is never heavy-handed, yet the closing fugue is a *tour de force*. The 1964 sound in the *Concerto* is good if not always ideally expansive, in spite of the Boston acoustics, but the solo work, recorded a decade later, gives little if any cause for complaint. This is one of Van Cliburn's best records.

Arrau's reading has vision and power and, though there are some characteristic agogic distortions that will not convince all listeners, he is majestic and eloquent. There is never an ugly sonority even in the moments of the greatest vehemence. By the side of Gilels he seems idiosyncratic but, given the excellence of the digitally remastered recording and the warmth of Haitink's support, this is well worth considering in the medium-price range.

Piano concerto No. 2 in B flat, Op. 83.
(M) *** BMG/RCA GD 86518 [RCA 6518-2-RG]. Sviatoslav Richter, Chicago SO, Leinsdorf – BEETHOVEN: *Piano sonata No. 23.* ***
(M) *** DG 419 471-2 [id.]. Pollini, VPO, Abbado.
(M) **(*) Ph. 420 885-2 [id.]. Arrau, Concg. O, Haitink.
(M) ** Ph. 426 633-2; *426 633-4*. Brendel, Concg. O, Haitink.

(i) *Piano concerto No. 2 in B flat, Op. 83;* (ii) *Academic festival overture; Tragic overture.*
(M) *** EMI CDM7 63537-2; *EG 763537-4* [id.]. (i) Barenboim, Philh. O; (ii) VPO, Barbirolli.

(i) *Piano concerto No. 2. Intermezzi, Op. 117/1–2; Op. 119/1–3.*
(M) ** BMG/RCA GD 87942 [7942-2-RG]. Van Cliburn, (i) Chicago SO, Reiner.

(i) *Piano concerto No. 2. Intermezzo in B flat min., Op. 117/2.*
(M) (*) BMG/RCA mono GD 60523. Horowitz, (i) NBC SO, Toscanini (with SCHUBERT: *Impromptu, D.899/3*) – LISZT: *Années de pèlerinage* etc. (***)

(i) *Piano concerto No. 2 in B flat, Op. 83;* (ii) *6 Piano pieces, Op. 118.*
(B) **(*) DG 431 162-2; *431 162-4*. (i) Géza Anda, BPO, Karajan; (ii) Wilhelm Kempff.

Richter's 1960 RCA performance has all the intensity of a live occasion and finds him in splendid form. It is wayward, mannered in places, but the basic structure is always kept in sight; there is impressive weight and authority as well as a warm Brahmsian lyrical feeling, and it is far more spontaneous and dashing than his later recording with Maazel and the Orchestre de Paris for EMI. The Chicago acoustics ensure that the orchestral texture is full-bodied and atmospheric and the piano timbre sounds fuller than before. With an exciting account of Beethoven's *Appassionata Sonata* as coupling, this is highly recommendable.

Pollini's 1977 recording makes a good alternative choice, also at mid-price. His account is powerful, in many ways more classical in feeling than Richter's. He has the measure of the work's scale and breadth and is given first-rate support by the Vienna Philharmonic under Abbado. The remastered sound has a Brahmsian body and warmth and, although the upper range is not as open as a digital recording would be, it sounds more modern than the RCA CD.

While Barenboim's reading with Barbirolli remains an individual view, the tendency to slow tempi brings the advantage that the lyrical passages merge spontaneously into the whole. The first two movements remain grandly heroic and the slow movement has something of the awed intensity you find in the middle movement of the *First Concerto*, while the finale erupts gracefully into rib-tickling humour. Barenboim's touch here reminds one of Rubinstein's famous version. This is a performance to love in its glowing spontaneity; the first-rate 1968 recording has splendid Brahmsian body and breadth, and no lack of brilliance. Of the fill-ups, the *Tragic overture* is a performance of considerable subtlety in matters of mood and style, and has no lack of impulse; but many will feel that the measured account of the *Academic festival overture*, attractively affectionate as it is, could do with more sparkle.

Arrau's account of the concerto is competitive at medium price. There are one or two idiosyncratic touches, but the playing has a splendid combination of aristocratic finesse and warmth of feeling, and Haitink and the Concertgebouw Orchestra give excellent support. The engineers strike the right balance between the piano and orchestra, and the orchestral texture is better focused and cleaner than in the earlier Arrau recording.

The 1968 partnership of Anda with the BPO provides much fine playing from soloist and orchestra alike. The performance opens slowly and is rhapsodically free; it has plenty of impulse, but Anda is wayward at times, although he is always commanding. But there is poetry here, and undoubted power. The slow movement is often richly eloquent, and the finale has a persuasive, lyrical charm. There is much to enjoy, not least the glorious orchestral response. The recording is appropriately bold and full, and the balance is good; it sounds brighter now than originally, and internal detail is much clearer. As sound, this makes satisfying listening. In the six *Klavierstücke*, Op. 118, Kempff shines in exactly those pieces where many modern pianists fall short, emphasizing poetry rather than brilliance, subtle timbres rather than virtuosity, the gentle fancies of Brahms's last period, evocative and meaningful beyond the mere notes. The first piece, in A minor, sounds a little shallow as recorded here, but after that the piano timbre is full of colour.

Van Cliburn could not have a more committed or sympathetic accompanist than Reiner, and the Chicago orchestra create a richly spacious background tapestry for their soloist. Cliburn plays powerfully and shows a ready response to Brahmsian lyricism. There is much that is fine here, but the first movement lacks something in overall grip and the tension is not sustained consistently. The recording, from the early 1970s, is faithful and very well transferred. As a bonus, Cliburn offers five *Intermezzi*, but these are disappointingly lacking in spontaneity.

Brendel's is a finely recorded performance, but the performance falls a little below expectations. He seems too judicious and adopts a deliberately restrained approach, so keen is he to eschew the grand manner. The results, though always commanding respect, are not wholly convincing; but the engineers produce excellent sound.

The Horowitz/Toscanini version of the Brahms *B flat Concerto* dates from around the same time as their famous record of the Tchaikovsky *Concerto*. It was made in Carnegie Hall in May 1940, immediately following a benefit concert, and has the advantage of fairly full orchestral sound, although the piano is shallow. Toscanini generates little Brahmsian expansiveness (and Horowitz matches his lean textures with bare pedalling) and only in the finale does Horowitz's scintillating fingerwork restore the *grazioso* feeling. For all its energy and bravura, we are never drawn into this performance but remain detached and uninvolved. In the encores the piano timbre is much fuller and the Schubert (despite being played in an edited arrangement in the wrong key) has real magic, while the Liszt items show the pianist at his most commanding, with his own arrangement of the *Hungarian rhapsody* providing a glittering finale of astounding digital dexterity. This comes from a live recital and the audience's response at the end is understandable.

Violin concerto in D, Op. 77.

(M) *** Ph. 420 703-2; *420 703-4*. Grumiaux, New Philh. O, C. Davis – BRUCH: *Concerto No. 1*. **(*)

(B) *** Decca Dig. 433 604-2; *433 604-4* [id.].

Belkin, LSO, Fischer (with MASSENET: *Thaïs: Méditation*: Nigel Kennedy, National PO, Bonynge ***).
(M) (***) EMI mono CDH7 61011-2. Ginette Neveu, Philh. O, Issay Debrowen – SIBELIUS: *Concerto*. (***)
(BB) **(*) BMG/RCA VD 60479; *VK 60479* [60479-2-RV; *60479-4-RV*]. Ughi, Philh. O, Sawallisch – BRUCH: *Concerto No. 1*. **(*)
(M) **(*) EMI CDM7 69034-2 [id.]. David Oistrakh, French Nat. R. O, Klemperer.
(B) **(*) DG Compact Classics 413 844-2 (2); *413 844-4* [id.]. Ferras, BPO, Karajan – BEETHOVEN: *Romances* ***; BRUCH: *Violin concerto No. 1* **; (on CD only: DVOŘÁK: *Violin concerto*. **(*))
(BB) * Naxos Dig. 8.550195 [id.]. Nishizaki, Slovak PO, Gunzenhauser – BRUCH: *Concerto No. 1*. *(*)

(i) *Violin concerto;* (ii) *Hungarian dances Nos. 1, 3, 5, 6, 17–21.*
(B) *** EMI CDZ7 62608-2; *LZ 762608-4*. (i) Menuhin, BPO, Kempe; (ii) RPO, Kubelik.

(i) *Violin concerto in D; Tragic overture, Op. 81.*
(B) *** Ph. 422 972-2; *422 972-4*. (i) Hermann Krebbers; Concg. O, Haitink.

(i) *Violin concerto in D*; (ii) *Violin sonata No. 1 in G, Op. 78.*
(B) **(*) DG 429 513-2; *429 513-4* [id.]. Ferras, (i) BPO, Karajan; (ii) Pierre Barbizet.

(i) *Violin concerto in D;* (ii) *Violin sonata No. 2 in A, Op. 100.*
(M) **(*) DG 415 838-2; *415 838-4* [id.]. Zukerman; (i) O de Paris, Barenboim; (ii) Barenboim (piano).

Hermann Krebbers, concertmaster of the Concertgebouw Orchestra, but also a master violinist of the first order in his own right, here gives one of the most deeply satisfying readings of the Brahms *Violin concerto* ever recorded: strong and urgent yet tenderly poetic too, and always full of spontaneous imagination. The total commitment behind the performance is not just the achievement of the soloist but also that of his colleagues and their conductor, who perform as at a live concert. The vintage, 1973 recording has been successfully remastered: the effect, with the violin slightly forward but not too obtrusively so, is full and immediate. The *Tragic overture* makes a suitable encore after the *Concerto*.

Reissued in EMI's bargain Laser series, with Kubelik's group of *Hungarian dances* offered as an engaging additional incentive, Menuhin's recording from the end of the 1950s can be given the strongest recommendation. He was in superb form, producing tone of great beauty, while the reading is memorable for its warmth and nobility. He was splendidly accompanied by Kempe, and the Berlin Philharmonic was inspired to outstanding playing – the oboe solo in the slow movement is particularly fine. The sound remains satisfyingly well balanced, and now compares very favourably indeed with any of the top recommendations for this work.

Grumiaux's performance, it goes without saying, is full of insight and lyrical eloquence, and Sir Colin Davis lends his soloist the most sympathetic support; at mid-price, coupled with the Max Bruch *G minor Concerto* (a work with which Grumiaux, with his essentially classical style, has slightly less natural affinity), this excellent CD could well be first choice for many readers, particularly in view of the excellence of the remastered Philips sound, which is firm, detailed and refined, with believable presence and a warm ambience.

Those looking for a bargain digital recording should be well pleased with Boris Belkin's 1983 Decca issue. The performance is deeply felt, direct and spontaneous and makes a strong impression. The tempo of the first movement is measured and spacious, though not as slow as Nigel Kennedy's full-priced version; and it is Kennedy who plays very appealingly in the Massenet lollipop which acts as an encore. With excellent sound and as good balance, this reissue is very competitive.

Ginette Neveu's is a magnificent performance, urgently electric, remarkable not just for the sweetness of tone and her pinpoint intonation but for the precision and clarity of even the most formidable passages of double-stopping. This is a reading as remarkable for its toughness and power as for the warmth and poetry one would expect from an outstanding woman virtuoso. Though dynamic contrasts are limited, the transfer from the original 78s brings satisfyingly full-bodied sound, surprisingly good on detail. Coupled with the Sibelius on a mid-price Références disc, it makes an outstanding bargain.

Ughi's account has the advantage of a strong and passionate orchestral backing from Sawallisch and first-rate (1983) digital sound, with a good balance. As with the Bruch coupling, this is a fresh, direct reading, not as charismatic as some, but with moments of considerable lyrical intensity and by no means unimaginative in the control of light and shade. At bargain price, it is well worth considering.

The conjunction of two such positive artists as Oistrakh and Klemperer makes for a reading characterful to the point of idiosyncrasy, monumental and strong rather than sweetly lyrical. Oistrakh sounds superbly poised and confident and in the finale, if the tempo is a shade deliberate, the total effect is one of clear gain. The 1961 recording is quite full, but the bright CD transfer has brought an element of steeliness to the solo violin timbre.

Zukerman's is a well-conceived reading that has finish and facility and is sweet-toned, but his general approach can often seem a little bland by comparison with some other versions. He is exposed to a close balance, but this does not mask the Orchestre de Paris under Barenboim, who give excellent support and receive a well-detailed recording, in spite of the unrealistic perspective. For the reissue the *A major Violin sonata* has been added, but this is also available, more appropriately coupled, with the other two sonatas – see below.

Much depends on one's attitude to Ferras's tone-colour whether the Ferras/Karajan version is a good recommendation or not. DG have placed him close to the microphone so that the smallness of tone that in the concert hall is disappointing is certainly not evident here. Moreover, there is a jewelled accuracy about the playing that is most appealing, and Karajan conducts vividly. The recording is of good quality and the high-level transfer is of striking liveliness. The bargain-price Compact Classics CDs offer an enjoyable account by Edith Peinemann of the Dvořák *Violin concerto* as a bonus, while on the medium-price CD the *Violin sonata*, which is very pleasingly done by Barbizet, appropriately sounds more intimate and subdued.

Takako Nishizaki seems somehow not quite comfortable in this concerto, as if straining to make a bigger, more ardent reading than is natural to her. Some of the upper tessitura, so pressured, is not very sweet, and she makes Kreisler's first-movement cadenza sound laboured. The coupled Bruch suits her better, but this is not one of her recommendable records.

(i) *Violin concerto in D, Op. 77;* (ii) *Double concerto for violin, cello and orchestra, Op. 102.*

(M) (***) EMI mono CDH7 63496-2 [id.]. (i) Y. Menuhin, Lucerne O; (ii) Boskovsky, Emanuel Brabec, VPO; Furtwängler.

(M) **(*) Sony SBK 46335 [id.]; *40-46335*. Stern, (ii) with Rose; Phd. O, Ormandy.

Menuhin's 1949 recording of the Brahms *Violin concerto*, like his earliest version of the Beethoven which he made with the same forces, brings a towering performance. The unlikely and, at the time, controversial partnership brought a dedication that has rarely been matched, with each responding to the challenge of the other's highly individual artistry. As Menuhin himself said, it was 'an experience of almost religious intensity'. Even in the opening tutti, the playing of the orchestra is incandescent and, contrary to what one might expect, there is little self-indulgence in the reading, with the second movement pure and flowing and the finale given a persuasive Hungarian lilt at a relatively easy speed. The feeling of co-ordination is intensified by the natural, unspotlit balance of the violin. Even with the Cedar noise-reduction process, the 78 surfaces are heavier than usual; but with such magnetic playing one can easily listen through the interference. The *Double concerto* brings a live performance of comparable warmth, recorded in 1952. With the distinguished concertmaster and the principal cello of the Vienna Philharmonic, Furtwängler was prepared to allow his soloists the fullest freedom. The cellist in particular – for much of the time the senior partner – is ripely expansive. The result is again magnetic, not perfect in detail but a historic reading to cherish.

Stern's splendid 1959 account of the *Violin concerto* with Ormandy now returns to the catalogue satisfactorily remastered and, although the balance still spotlights the solo violin, the overall impression is of a better integration than in previous CD incarnations. For the first time we are also offered a coupling that is both generous and suitable, the mid-1960s' collaboration with Leonard Rose in the *Double concerto*. In the most naturally expressive way, relaxed yet commanding, the two soloists unfailingly match each other's playing. Each has a creative ear in pointing a comment so that the response is made to sound like an unfolding conversation, with Ormandy always an understanding accompanist. Both in the detailed pointing of phrasing (the opening of the finale has a most engagingly light touch), in the bite of bravura passages, and in the rich expansiveness of the slow movement, as a performance this compares very favourably with the Oistrakh/Fournier account. The forward balance of the soloists brings glorious tone, even if this means that there are no pianissimos (although one can tell when they are playing quietly from the tone-colour). The CD transfer is well managed; though light in bass, the sound overall is full and clear.

Double concerto for violin, cello and orchestra in A min., Op. 102.

(B) *** EMI CDZ7 62854-2; *LZ 762854-4*. D. Oistrakh, Fournier, Philh. O, Galliera – BEETHOVEN: *Triple concerto.* **(*)

(B) **(*) Sony MYK 44771 [id.]. Francescatti, Fournier, Columbia SO, Bruno Walter – SCHUMANN: *Piano concerto.* **(*)

(B) ** DG 429 934-2 [id.]. Schneiderhan,

Starker, Berlin RSO, Fricsay – BEETHOVEN: *Triple concerto.* **
(B) ** DG Compact Classics *415 332-4* [id.]. Schneiderhan, Starker, Berlin RSO, Fricsay – BEETHOVEN: *Triple concerto*; MOZART: *Violin concerto No. 3.* **
(M) *(*) Ph. 426 631-2; *426 631-4.* Szeryng, Starker, Concg. O, Haitink – BEETHOVEN: *Triple concerto.* *(*)

David Oistrakh's recording with Fournier dates from 1959, but it was balanced by Walter Legge and the sound remains remarkably satisfying. The performance is distinguished, strong and lyrical – the slow movement particularly fine – and, with Galliera and the Philharmonia providing excellent support, this version, coupled with Beethoven's *Triple concerto*, makes a good choice for bargain-hunters.

Bruno Walter's recording with Francescatti and Fournier dates from 1959, and the compact disc represents another example of successful digital remastering which enhances the original balance within an attractively warm ambience. Fournier is magnificent and, if one can adjust to Francescatti's rather intense vibrato, this can stand among the most satisfying of available versions. Walter draws playing of great warmth from the Columbia orchestra and oversees the reading as a whole with his customary humanity, yet tuttis are thrillingly expansive and vital.

We have always appreciated the Schneiderhan/Starker/Fricsay version of the *Double concerto* ever since it first came out on a ten-inch LP in 1961. The remastering for CD may have brightened the upper range, but the acoustic of the Berlin Jesus-Christus Kirche provides warmth, even though the two soloists are very forwardly balanced. Fricsay shapes the work splendidly and there is plenty of impetus. The same version of the *Double concerto*, coupled with Beethoven's *Triple concerto*, makes a fair bargain on a DG Compact Classics cassette which also includes Mozart.

The Szeryng/Starker version, recorded in 1970 in the Concertgebouw, has a richer orchestral tapestry; indeed the Philips sound is first class. Although the engineers also balance the soloists fairly closely, their account makes far less of an impact musically, however. This version remains obstinately unmemorable and is ultimately disappointing, though it is not easy to fault any individual detail and the *Andante* is songful.

Hungarian dances Nos. 1–21 (complete).
❀ (BB) *** Naxos Dig. 8.550110 (*Nos. 1–2; 4–21*) Budapest SO, István Bogár.
(BB) ** LaserLight Dig. 15501 [id.]. Hungarian PO, János Sándor.
(i) *Hungarian dances Nos. 1–21;* (ii) *Variations on a theme of Haydn, Op. 56a.*
(M) *** DG Dig./Analogue 431 594-2; *431 594-4* [id.]. (i) VPO; (ii) Dresden State O; Abbado.

The Budapest recording of the Brahms *Hungarian dances* is sheer delight from beginning to end. The playing has warmth and sparkle, and the natural way the music unfolds brings a refreshing feeling of rhythmic freedom. Yet there are also many delightful individual touches from the conductor, with the woodwind joyfully producing some most engaging colours. Bogár's rubato is wholly spontaneous; the strings bring plenty of temperament to their phrasing of the more sultry tunes, while their lighter articulation is infectious. The recording is warm and full, yet transparent, with just the right brilliance on top. This is an outright winner among the available versions, but there is a small snag with the layout and documentation. The *Third dance* (a charming *Allegretto in F major*, led by the woodwind) has inadvertently been added to track 2 and follows on immediately after the *Second dance.* The listing on the CD anticipates the presence of all 21 dances, separately banded and, from No. 3 (actually No. 4) onwards, gives the wrong timings, with each applying to the previous number. Even with this minor problem, which is primarily one of access, one would far rather have this set of dances (particularly on such an inexpensive disc) than any of the other alternative versions.

Abbado's fine complete digital set of the *Hungarian dances* now reappears at mid-price, coupled with his excellent 1972 Dresden account of the *Haydn variations*, a work he always did well.

Sándor's LaserLight CD offers what are essentially mellow performances, and the feeling of warmth is emphasized by the resonant acoustics of the auditorium. Even though this is a digital recording, it is comfortably subdued in the upper range. Some might feel, too, that these dances, although very well played and obviously idiomatic, could use a little more dash.

Hungarian dances Nos. 1, 3, 5, 6 18–19.
(M) **(*) Ph. 432 046-2; *432 046-4.* Leipzig GO, Masur – DVOŘÁK: *Slavonic dances.* **(*)

Those wanting just a selection from Masur's complete set of the *Hungarian dances* will find these performances are very sympathetic and well recorded. However, the coupling of Dvořák, with only twelve of the sixteen *Slavonic dances* included, does not seem very sensible planning, and no information about the music is included.

Serenade No. 1 in D, Op. 11.
(B) **(*) MCA Double-decker (2) [MCAD2-

9826-A/B]. Symphony of the Air, Stokowski – DAWSON: *Negro Folk Symphony.* **

Serenades Nos. 1 in D, Op. 11; 2 in A, Op. 16.
(B) **(*) Decca 421 628-2. LSO, Kertész.
(M) **(*) Ph. 432 510-2; *432 510-4* [id.]. Concg. O, Haitink.

The Kertész performances of the two *Serenades* are beautifully relaxed but at the same time alert, and the 1968 Decca recording emerges more clearly in detail, with a drier effect at the bass end, yet with the hall ambience retaining most of the bloom. But in some ways the original LPs sounded sweeter.

Haitink's account of the *D major Serenade* is finely proportioned, relaxed yet vital. The Concertgebouw wind-playing is particularly distinguished and, while the players obviously relish the many delights of this underrated score, the architecture is held together firmly and without the slightest trace of expressive indulgence. However, the resonant Concertgebouw acoustics, while giving agreeably full textures, do not afford the same degree of freshness and transparency to the sound-picture as on the competing Decca version: the effect is more symphonic, less light-hearted. The *A major Serenade* has lighter scoring (the string section does without violins altogether) and, while the recording is warm, it is yet more lucid in detail. Haitink's performance is similarly sound in conception and well shaped, and the conductor's warmth is obvious. Perhaps the Kertész performances have a slightly more vivid characterization and the Decca sound-quality is undoubtedly fresher and, if with less body to the strings, produces brighter wind colouring.

When playing 'straight', Stokowski was a great Brahmsian, and this account of the *D major Serenade* has exhilarating charisma. The *Adagio* has great warmth from the strings, the wind playing in the Minuet is delightful and the horns in the Scherzo are bucolic – they sound as if they are enjoying themelves hugely, and so do we. The 1961 recording is too forward, confined and studio-ish in acoustic – but no matter, it does not lack body, and the music-making is cherishable. Alas, the coupling is not – William Levi Dawson has very little indeed in common with Johannes Brahms. This set is not yet available in the UK.

Serenade No. 2 in A, Op. 16 – see also below, under *Symphony No. 3*.

Symphonies Nos. 1–4.
(M) **(*) HM/BMG Dig. GD 60085; *GK 60085* (3) [60085-2-RG; *60085-4-RG*]. N. German RSO, Wand.
(M) **(*) DG 429 644-2 (3) [id.]. BPO, Karajan.
(B) *(**) MCA Double-decker (2) [MCAD2-9817-A/B]. Pittsburgh SO, William Steinberg.

Symphonies Nos. 1–4; Academic festival overture, Op. 80; Tragic overture, Op. 81.
(B) ** Decca 430 799-2 (4) [id.]. Chicago SO, Solti.

Symphonies Nos. 1–4; Academic festival overture; Tragic overture; Variations on a theme of Haydn.
(B) **(*) Sony/CBS SM3K 45823 (3) [id.]. Cleveland O, George Szell.

Wand's complete cycle, originally on EMI and now reissued on three mid-priced Deutsche Harmonia Mundi discs, has the advantage of digital recording, although the sound brings a degree of fierceness on violin tone in all but No. 2. Wand's is a consistently direct view of Brahms, yet the reading of each symphony has its own individuality. In the opening movement of the *First*, he brings great intensity to the slow introduction by choosing an unusually fast speed, then leading naturally by modular pacing into the main allegro. The extra unity is clear. There is a comparable dramatic intensity in the finale, although his choice of a tempo for the main marching melody, far slower than the rest, brings uncomfortable changes of gear. Yet the performance is made convincing by its spontaneity. Even though he does not observe the exposition repeat, Wand's reading of the *Second* is the pick of his Brahms series, a characteristically glowing but steady reading, recorded with a fullness and bloom that are missing in his companion issues. In the *Third Symphony* Wand does observe the exposition repeat and his wise way with Brahms, strong and easy and steadily paced, works beautifully here, bringing out the autumnal moods, ending with a sober view of the finale. The bright sound underlines the reedy twang of the Hamburg woodwind – rather rough in the slow movement – while the horn could be more secure in his solo in the third movement. By contrast, the reading of No. 4 initially seems understated. At a fastish speed, the first movement is melancholy rather than tragic, while the slow movement, similarly steady and flowing, makes no great expansion for the big melody of the counter-subject. The third movement in jollity has plenty of light and shade, and the finale is rather brisk and tough, with the great flute passage in the *Passacaglia* tender but not drawn out. It is quite a strong reading, but marred by recording that is less than ideally clear, with edgy violins as in Nos. 1 and 3.

Broadly, Karajan's 1978 cycle shows that his readings of the Brahms *Symphonies*, with lyrical and dramatic elements finely balanced, changed little over the years. It is worth noting that his approach to No. 3 is stronger and more direct, with less mannered phrasing in the third movement, but that he continues to omit the first-movement exposition repeat. The playing of the Berlin Philharmonic remains uniquely cultivated: the ensemble is finely polished, yet can produce tremendous bravura at times, as in the finales to the *First* and *Second Symphonies*. The remastering has freshened the sound: textures are clear and clean, but the effect is slightly polarized, with a bright, clean treble and a strong, firmly focused bass. There is less emphasis in the middle frequencies so that the Brahmsian richness is conveyed less readily. On three mid-priced discs, this apppears to be good value, but there was plenty of room on the first and third discs to include the *Overtures* and the *Haydn variations*.

Szell's powerful view of Brahms is consistently revealed in this masterful series of performances, recorded in the 1960s when he had made the Cleveland Orchestra America's finest. His approach is generally plain and direct, crisp and detached rather than smooth and moulded. Speeds are broad, but only in the first movement of No. 4 does that undermine the electric tension of conductor and orchestra. In the manner of the time, no exposition repeats are observed, not even in No. 3. Though the sound, as transferred, is not as full as on the original LPs (when EMI had the CBS-Epic concession), it is clear and bright, with superb detail. Complete with all the shorter pieces on three discs, it makes an excellent bargain.

Steinberg's vintage recordings of all four symphonies, conveniently squeezed on to two discs (as first-movement exposition repeats are omitted), bring warm, powerful performances, superbly played. Steinberg's training of the Pittsburgh orchestra in the 1950s and '60s gave it the high-powered precision of the finest American groups, alongside the warmer and more expressive qualities of the Central European tradition. Steinberg's approach to Brahms is firm yet romantic, with some easing allowed of sensible speeds and broad treatment of slow movements. The CD transfers make high violins somewhat edgy; but only in No. 1 – where the bass is light, too – does this seem pronounced and the lack of body in the strings gets in the way of enjoyment. For American collectors this will seem quite a good bargain, but the set is not yet issued in the UK.

Sir Georg Solti's Chicago cycle was recorded in the less than ideal acoustics of the Medinah Temple in 1978/9. The remastered sound is not flattering: full-bodied, but with the upper strings rather grainy (especially in No. 1) and overlit. The bass is inclined to be rather weighty, and the whole effect is less than ideally refined. The layout on four discs is extravagant, even at bargain price. These are all spacious rather than impetuous readings, marked by poised playing from the Chicago orchestra. Solti's interpretations are soundly conceived; he is a true Brahmsian but, even at slow speeds, tension and electricity remain not always relaxed enough in lyricism.

Symphonies Nos. 1–4; Academic festival overture; (i) *Double concerto in A min., Op. 102. Hungarian dances Nos. 1, 17, 20 & 21; Tragic overture; Variations on a theme of Haydn;* (ii) *Liebeslieder-Walzer, Op. 52;* (iii) *Song of the Fates (Gesang der Parzen). Op. 89.*

(M) (***) BMG/RCA mono GD 60325 *GK 60325* (4) [60325-2-RG; *60325-4-RG*]. NBC SO, Toscanini, with (i) Mischakoff, Miller; (ii) Ch., Artur Balsam, Joseph Kahn; (iii) (without O) Robert Shaw Ch.

Though Toscanini's direction of the delightful *Liebeslieder waltzes* is impossibly regimented and lacking in lilt (he hardly needed to conduct with only two pianos), the rest of this set reveals the maestro as a much warmer and more spacious Brahmsian than has often been thought. The *First Symphony* starts very fast and intensely; but often speeds are surprisingly broad, and the *Fourth symphony*, Toscanini's favourite, brings a magnificent performance. The soloists in the *Double concerto* were principals in the NBC orchestra, Mischa Mischakoff and Frank Miller, both very fine artists, even though Toscanini allowed them less expressive freedom than they really needed. The CD transfers do everything possible for the dry and limited original sound. The extra items date mainly from 1948, recorded several years earlier than the symphonies.

Symphony No. 1 in C min., Op. 68.

(B) *** DG 431 161-2; *431 161-4* [id.]. BPO, Karajan – SCHUMANN: *Overture, Scherzo and Finale.* ***

(B) **(*) Sony MYK 44827 [id.]. Columbia SO, Bruno Walter.

(M) ** DG Dig. 427 804-2; *427 804-4* [id.] (with SCHUMANN: *Manfred overture*). LAPO, Giulini.

(M) ** DG Dig. 431 591-2; *431 591-4* [id.]. LAPO, Giulini.

Symphony No. 1; Academic festival overture, Op. 80.

(B) *** Pickwick Dig. PCD 882; *CIMPC 882* [id.]. Hallé O, Skrowaczewski.

Symphony No. 1; Academic festival overture; Tragic overture.

(M) *** EMI CDM7 69651-2 [id.]; *EG 769651-4*. Philh. O, Klemperer.
(M) *** Ph. 432 275-2; *432 275-4*. Concg. O, Haitink.

Symphony No. 1; Variations on a theme of Haydn, Op. 56a.
(M) *** DG 427 253-2 [id.]. BPO, Karajan.
(BB) **(*) Naxos Dig. 8.550278 [id.]. Belgian R. PO, Brussels, Alexander Rahbari.
(B) * Hung. White Label HRC 109 [id.]. (i) Budapest SO, Lehel; (ii) Hungarian State O, Németh.

(i) *Symphony No. 1 in C min.; Variations on a theme of Haydn;* (ii) *Hungarian dances Nos. 17–21.*
(M) **(*) Sony SBK 46534 [id.]. (i) Cleveland O, Szell; (ii) Phd. O, Ormandy.

Klemperer's monumental performance was recorded in the Kingsway Hall over a long time-span (between December 1955 and March 1957), yet the interpretation lost nothing in consistency. The spacious opening with its thundering, relentless timpani strokes is as compelling as ever and the close of the work has a comparable majesty. Elsewhere, other versions may find greater incandescence, but the reading remains unique for its feeling of authority and power, supported by consistently fine Philharmonia playing. The remastered recording has gained in clarity while retaining its fullness, but has lost a little in weight, although the bass is firmer and clearer than on LP. Even those who find Klemperer's approach too marmoreal must respond to its integrity. The *Tragic overture* suits Klemperer particularly well, but the *Academic festival overture* is made to sound grand rather than high-spirited.

Karajan's 1978 analogue recording – his fourth – is highly recommendable (especially at bargain price and now with its present Schumann coupling), and the sound is still remarkably good. The superbly committed response of the Berlin Philharmonic players, in repertoire to which they are completely attuned, is a joy in itself.

Haitink's 1972 recording of the *First Symphony* emerges splendidly in its remastered CD format. It is a strong, well-argued reading of considerable power, and superbly played. Haitink does not observe the first-movement exposition repeat but, that apart, it remains among the very finest versions, with recording that is full and spacious and well balanced. The *Tragic overture* is also a particularly arresting account, and the *Academic festival overture* has plenty of vitality.

Walter's first two movements have a white-hot intensity that shows this conductor at his very finest. He conveys the architecture of the first movement strongly. The second movement too is most impressive, warm and with natural, unforced phrasing. The third movement begins with a less than ravishing clarinet solo and, though the 6/8 section is lively enough, the playing is not as crisp as in the first two movements. In the finale the performance reasserts itself, although some might find the big string tune too slow. The remastered recording makes the strings sound richly beautiful here; and later the brass is comparably sonorous. The 1960 recording is full and well balanced; as sound, this is preferable to many more recent versions.

Szell's account of No. 1 is one of the most impressive of his set. His bold, direct thrust gives the outer movements plenty of power and impetus, and the inner movements bring relaxation and a fair degree of warmth. The *Variations* are strongly characterized, too, and have plenty of finesse in the matter of light and shade. But, as in the symphony, Szell does not seek to charm. The sound is remarkably good, bright and vivid, certainly, but not without the body so necessary in Brahms. For an encore Ormandy chooses the last five *Hungarian dances*, as orchestrated by Dvořák, and plays them with characteristic flair. They are enjoyable, but it is a pity that the recorded sound of the violins is not sweeter and more opulent above the stave.

Opening powerfully with thundering timpani in the manner of Klemperer, though with generally more relaxed tempi, Alexander Rahbari gives an account of Brahms's *First* that is certainly recommendable. It is a strong, direct reading, spacious yet with plenty of impetus. The inner movements are well contrasted, with soaring eloquence in the *Andante*, and though there are one or two minor idiosyncrasies in the finale the reading holds together convincingly, even the broadening at the end. The sound is full and rich, yet detail is clear. The *Variations* bring a lighter, more lyrical Brahms style but are no less spontaneously successful. A very good choice for those with limited budgets, although Jochum's Laser version is even finer.

Skrowaczewski conducts the Hallé in a powerful performance of No. 1, both warmly sympathetic and refined, with sound which is fresh, bright and clear and with a good, open atmosphere. The first movement is ideally paced, purposeful without undue rush – and also without the exposition repeat. Few other accounts of the slow movement are as delicate as Skrowaczewski's, with the hushed opening given simple gravity. His view of the finale is big and bold, but with a rather old-fashioned slowing for the final appearance of the chorale theme in the coda. With an account of the *Aca-*

demic festival overture textured with similar refinement, it makes an excellent bargain-price digital choice.

Giulini's spacious, 1982 digital recording with the Los Angeles Philharmonic Orchestra has been reissued at mid-price, coupled with Schumann's *Manfred overture*. His keen control of rhythm generally means that the slowness does not deteriorate into heaviness, but the speed for the big C major theme in the finale is so slow that it sounds self-conscious and the movement loses its concentration. This recording has also reappeared in DG's Brahms Edition. It is still at mid-price but is now without the coupling of Schumann's *Manfred overture*.

Although the Hungaroton disc is also in the bargain range, collectors would do better to look elsewhere. The sound is good, but the outer movements of the *Symphony* are lacking in thrust and momentum. The *Variations* (which shrewdly have been placed first) are more successful.

(i) *Symphonies Nos. 1;* (ii) *4 in E min., Op. 98;* (CD only: (iii) *Tragic overture;* (iv) *Variations on a theme of Haydn*).
(B) *** DG Compact Classics 413 424-2 (2); *413 424-4* [id.]. (i) BPO; (ii) VPO, Boehm (CD only: (iii) BPO, Maazel; (iv) LSO, Jochum).

Anyone learning their Brahms from Boehm's performances cannot go far wrong, and these very satisfying readings comprise one of the very finest issues in DG's Compact Classics series. His Berlin Philharmonic version of the *First* comes from the early 1960s (he recorded it again later, rather less successfully, with the VPO). It is a centrally recommendable version, with tempi that are steady rather than volatile; but, with polished playing from the Berliners, the performance is undoubtedly very compelling and the well-balanced recording emerges here to excellent effect. Boehm's account of the *Fourth* was the most successful performance in his Vienna cycle, with a spacious and noble reading of the first movement and a finely contrasted view of the final *Passacaglia*, lyrical and dramatic elements sharply defined. It remains among the very finest performances of this work ever committed to disc. The remastered sound is full-blooded and has plenty of life and warmth on CD and tape alike, with the bass rather more resonant on cassette. For the pair of digitally remastered CDs, Maazel's self-consciously brilliant account of the *Tragic overture* has been added, plus Jochum's LSO version of the *St Anthony Variations*. Jochum proves as naturally a Brahmsian as he is a Brucknerian, and this performance has a natural freshness which disguises the subtlety of detail.

Symphony No. 2 in D, Op. 73.
(M) *** DG 435 067-2; *435 067-4* [id.]. BPO, Karajan – SCHUMANN: *Symphony No. 2.* ***
(M) **(*) Unicorn UKCD 2036 [id.]. Danish RSO, Horenstein (with recorded interview between Jascha Horenstein and Alan Blyth).

Symphony No. 2; Academic festival overture, Op. 80.
(B) *** Sony MYK 44870. Columbia SO, Bruno Walter.

Symphony No. 2; Academic festival overture; Tragic overture.
(M) **(*) DG Dig. 431 592-2; *431 592-4* [id.]. VPO, Bernstein.

Symphony No. 2; Academic festival overture; (i) *Song of destiny.*
(M) **(*) EMI CDM7 63221-2; *EG 763221-4*. (i) Beecham Ch. Soc.; RPO, Beecham.

Symphony No. 2; Tragic overture, Op. 81.
(B) **(*) Pickwick Dig. PCD 857; *CIMPC 857* [id.]. Hallé O, Skrowaczewski.

Symphony No. 2; Serenade No. 2 in A, Op. 16.
(BB) * Naxos Dig. 8.550279 [id.]. Belgian R. & TV PO (Brussels), Alexander Rahbari.

Symphony No. 2; (i) *Alto rhapsody, Op. 53.*
(M) *** EMI CDM7 69650-2 [id.]; *EG 769650-4*. (i) Ludwig, Philh. Ch.; Philh. O, Klemperer.

Karajan's 1978 recording of the Brahms *Second* is strikingly fresh and direct, helped by superb playing from the Berlin Philharmonic on peak form. Overall the reading is more direct, less mellow than the earlier (1964) account – see below – and this is most striking in the third movement. The finale has even more impetus than before, its brilliant pacing challenging the Berliners to exciting virtuosity. Some will prefer the earlier version, but the sound here is obviously more modern; it is balanced relatively close, but with lively atmosphere.

Walter's performance of Brahms's *Second Symphony* is wonderfully sympathetic, with an inevitability, a rightness which makes it hard to concentrate on the interpretation as such, so cogent is the musical argument. As though to balance the romanticism of his approach on detail, Walter keeps his basic speeds surprisingly constant, yet little of the passion is lost in consequence. It is a masterly conception overall and one very easy to live with. The CD opens with a vigorous and yet expansive account of the *Academic festival overture*, sumptuously recorded; in the remastering of the *Symphony* there is some loss in the lower-middle and bass, which is less richly resonant than in the *First Symphony*. But the bloom remains and the middle string timbre is always fresh and warm. In the USA this appears to be still a full-priced issue [MK 42021].

Klemperer's is also a great performance, the product of a strong and vital intelligence. He may seem a trifle severe and uncompromising, but he was at his peak in his Brahms cycle and he underlines the power of the *Symphony* without diminishing its eloquence in any way. The *Alto rhapsody*, with Klemperer at his most masterful and Ludwig on fine form, is a beautifully expressive performance that brings out the work's strength as well as its lyricism. Ludwig sings gloriously in the opening section, and later her voice blends naturally with the male chorus. The remastered recording is outstanding here; the *Symphony* sounds full and clear, with telling viola and cello timbre; but there is a degree of shrillness on the *ff* massed violins.

Though the CD transfer of the *Symphony* brings some rough sound – less well focused than in the two fill-up items – the Beecham magic makes this volatile reading consistently compelling. The accompanying booklet reveals that it was recorded at no fewer than six separate recording sessions, spread between November 1958 and November 1959. The quirkiness of the performance rather reflects that. The horns at the opening may be disappointing, but the first movement is then urgently riveting at speeds faster than usual. Beecham is also on the fast side in the second-movement Adagio, but his fine detailing there and in the third movement is totally distinctive, and the finale, rough at times, predictably brings an exhilarating close. The fill-ups are equally desirable, particularly the rare *Song of destiny*, sung in Denis Vaughan's English translation.

With beautifully open and transparent sound, Skrowaczewski and the Hallé Orchestra give a measured and restrained reading, unsensational, fresh and thoughtful. The opening may seem sleepy, but Skrowaczewski's broad speeds and patient manner build up increasingly as the work progresses. With exposition repeat observed and a generous fill-up, plus excellent digital recording, luminous to match the performance, it is a good bargain-priced recommendation.

Bernstein's live 1982 recording is here reissued in DG's Brahms Edition, with the *Tragic overture* added to the original coupling. It is a warm, expansive account, notably less free and idiosyncratic than the others in Bernstein's Vienna cycle, yet comparably rhythmic and equally spontaneous-sounding. With good recording, considering the limitations of a live concert, this is worth considering at mid-price.

In course of rescuing as many Horenstein performances as possible from oblivion, Unicorn Kanchana lighted on this highly characterful account of the *Second Symphony*, recorded live in Copenhagen in March 1972. The reading – which includes the first-movement exposition repeat – is marked by spaciousness and lyricism, and only in the finale, which avoids any suspicion of whipping up excitement, will some listeners feel that the result is a shade reserved, though the performance does not lack spontaneous feeling. Well-balanced radio recording, which has transferred well to CD. The effect is not too studio-ish and has plenty of warmth; even if the Danish violins do not have the body of tone of, say, the Berlin Philharmonic, they play with fine ensemble and considerable ardour, and there is no shrillness. The recording includes a 20-minute BBC interview, with the conductor talking to Alan Blyth. This will be of interest to admirers of the conductor, although it has no connection with the present record; he talks about other composers, Mahler and Berg included.

Rahbari's reading of No. 2 is warm and persuasive, but the recording is almost impossibly cavernous, distantly placed with the reverberation totally obscuring detail in tuttis. The *Serenade No. 2 in A* for wind and lower strings fares better, though even there the focus should be sharper if the freshness of this early work is to be fully appreciated.

Symphonies Nos. 2–3.

(B) *** DG 429 153-2; *429 153-4* [id.]. BPO, Karajan.

(M) **(*) Ph. 426 632-2; *426 632-4*. Concg. O, Haitink.

(i) *Symphonies Nos. 2–3;* (ii) *Academic festival overture.*

(B) **(*) DG Compact Classics *415 334-4*. (i) VPO, Boehm; (ii) BPO, Abbado.

Karajan's 1964 reading of the *Second* is among the sunniest and most lyrical accounts, and its sound is fully competitive even now. The companion performance of the *Third* is marginally less compelling, but still very fine. He takes the opening expansively – which makes it surprising that he omits the exposition repeat. But clearly he sees the work as a whole: the third movement is also slow and perhaps slightly indulgent, but the closing pages of the finale have a memorable autumnal serenity. A bargain.

Haitink's account of No. 2 opens soberly. The tempo is slow, the manner bald and uncompromising. The sunshine quickly breaks through, however, so that the gentle high entry of the violins is magically sweet. This is a thoughtful reading, marked by beautifully refined string playing, but in a way it is too controlled. The *Third* is much more impressive. The playing of the Concertgebouw Orchestra here is distinguished by unanimity of attack and chording, wonderfully true intonation and homogeneity of tone; and Haitink's firmness of grip and lyrical eloquence make this a very satisfying account. The sound is fresh yet full in the Philips manner.

Boehm's readings of the two middle symphonies will seem to most Brahmsians more idiosyncratic than those of Nos. 1 and 4, though the conductor himself might have pointed out that he learned his Brahms interpretations from the composer's friend, Eusebius Mandyczewski. His approach to the *Second Symphony* is certainly volatile in the first movement, with the *Adagio* very expansive indeed. But here the conductor's moulded style rivets the attention and one quickly accepts the extra spaciousness. After a gracefully phrased *Allegretto*, the finale is strong. The *Third Symphony* is very broadly conceived, the reins held comparatively slackly throughout until the finale, where the increased momentum creates a sense of apotheosis. The recordings date from 1976 and sound well, with the Vienna strings given more body than in the original LP issue of No. 2. The excellent account of the *Academic festival overture* by Abbado makes a good bonus for a chrome cassette already offered at bargain price.

Symphony No. 3 in F, Op. 90.
(M) *** EMI CDH7 63085-2. Philh. O, Cantelli – SCHUMANN: *Symphony No. 4.*(***)

Symphony No. 3; Serenade No. 1 in D, Op. 11.
(BB) *(*) Naxos Dig. 8.550280 [id.]. Belgian R. & TV PO (Brussels), Alexander Rahbari.

(i) *Symphony No. 3;* (ii) *Serenade No. 2 in A, Op. 16; Academic festival overture.*
(M) **(*) EMI CDM7 69203-2 [id.]. (i) LSO; (ii) LPO, Sir Adrian Boult.

Symphony No. 3; Variations on a theme of Haydn, Op. 56a.
(B) *** Sony CD 42022 [id.]. Columbia SO, Bruno Walter.
(B) *** Pickwick Dig. PCD 906; *CIMPC 906* [id.]. Hallé O, Skrowaczewski.

Guido Cantelli's 1955 version with the Philharmonia offers one of the most glowing performances of the work ever put on record; and the early stereo CD transfer is astonishingly full and vivid. The *Andante* is taken broadly and expressively but without sentimentality; and the incandescence of the outer movements makes one regret all the more that such a genius of a conductor died so young. Coupled with his other great symphony recording with the Philharmonia, Schumann's *Fourth*, this is an outstanding issue in EMI's Références series.

Bruno Walter's *Third* is no less highly recommendable, both as a performance and as a recording. His pacing is admirable and the vigour and sense of joy which imbues the opening of the first movement (exposition repeat included) dominate throughout, with the second subject eased in with wonderful naturalness. The central movements provide contrast, though with an intense middle section in II. There is beautifully phrased string and horn playing in the *Poco Allegretto*. The finale goes splendidly, the secondary theme given characteristic breadth and dignity and the softening of mood for the coda sounding structurally inevitable. The CD transfer brings soaring upper strings, excellent detail with glowing woodwind, and a supporting weight. The account of the *Variations* is relaxed and smiling, with deft and affectionate detail, moving forward to a majestic restatement of the chorale. The recording is clear and spacious. In the USA this appears to be still in the premium-price range.

Skrowaczewski chooses consistently slow tempi for the central movements, yet with refined playing there is no hint of dragging. In the third movement he underlines the tender wistfulness, with a gorgeous horn solo in the reprise, full and spacious. The hush at the start of the finale then leads to a powerfully rhythmic performance, ending with a most refined account of the gentle coda. Only in the high violin lines at the very start of the work does the sound grow edgy, and that is more marked on some machines than on others. An excellent digital bargain-price version, well coupled with a fresh reading of the *Haydn variations*.

If there are slight reservations about the sound – which isn't ideally open, although there is no lack of Brahmsian warmth – Boult's mid-priced CD offers a happily unusual coupling. The 1971 performance of the *Third Symphony* has great dignity and spaciousness. Boult captures the autumnal feeling of the slow movement with great success, after including the exposition repeat in the first. It is essentially a mellow performance, keenly lyrical in feeling, but the LSO play with great enthusiasm and fire, so the music-making exudes vitality. After an expansive account of the *Academic festival overture*, the *Serenade in A major* is again glowingly lyrical.

Though the sound is not as reverberant in Rahbari's account of No. 3 as in the Naxos version of No. 2 from the same series, the recording is thinner, with less body. The first movement is strikingly slow, but well sustained, with exposition repeat omitted. The other movements are unexceptionably paced, and the pastoral quality of the *Serenade No. 1* is well brought out, offering some first-rate wind playing.

Symphonies Nos. 3–4.
(M) *** EMI CDM7 69649-2 [id.]; *EG 769649-4.* Philh. O, Klemperer.
(M) *** DG 431 593-2; *431 593-4* [id.]. BPO, Karajan.

With slow speeds and all repeats taken, Klemperer's timing in No. 3 is much more extended than usual. For all his expansiveness, however, Klemperer does not make the music sound opulent. There is a severity about his approach which may at first seem unappealing but which comes to underline the strength of the architecture. Similarly in No. 4, Klemperer's granite strength and his feeling for Brahmsian lyricism make his version one of the most satisfying ever recorded. The finale may lack something in sheer excitement, but the gravity of Klemperer's tone of voice, natural and unforced in this movement as in the others, makes for a compelling result. The remastering, like the others in the Klemperer/Brahms series, brings brightly lit violin timbre, with a hint of shrillness immediately noticeable at the surging opening of No. 3 but less so in No. 4. The orchestral focus is admirably clear, with woodwind fairly forward, and there is no lack of body in the middle, while the bass is firmer.

In his 1978 recording Karajan gives superb grandeur to the opening of the *Third Symphony* but then characteristically refuses to observe the exposition repeat which, in this of all Brahms's first movements, is necessary as a balance to the others. Comparing this reading with Karajan's earlier, 1964 version (coupled with No. 2), one finds him more direct, noticeably less mannered in his treatment of the third movement and strikingly more dynamic and compelling. Though one may criticize the recording balance, the result is powerful and immediate. In the *Fourth Symphony* Karajan refuses to overstate the first movement, starting with deceptive reticence. His easy, lyrical style, less moulded in this 1978 reading than in his 1964 account, is fresh and unaffected and highly persuasive. The scherzo, fierce and strong, leads to a clean, weighty account of the finale. The overall performance is very satisfying. The recording is vivid but, as with the *F major Symphony*, balances are not quite natural.

Symphony No. 4 in E min., Op. 98.
(M) **(*) EMI CDM7 69228-2 [id.]; *EG 769228-4.* Philh. O, Karajan – LISZT: *Les Préludes.* ***

Symphony No. 4; Academic festival overture; Tragic overture.
(M) ** Sony SBK 46330; *40-46330* [id.]. Cleveland O, Szell.
(B) * Hung. White Label HRC 108 [id.]. Budapest SO, Lehel.
(BB) (*) Naxos Dig. 8.550281 [id.]. Belgian R. PO, Brussels, Alexander Rahbari.

Symphony No. 4; Hungarian dances Nos. 1, 3 & 10.
(B) *** Pickwick Dig. PCD 897; *CIMPC 897* [id.]. Hallé O, Skrowaczewski.

Symphony No 4; Tragic overture, Op. 81.
(B) *** Sony MYK 44776 [id.]. Columbia SO, Bruno Walter.
(M) (***) EMI mono CDH7 69783-2 [id.]. BBC SO, Toscanini.

Symphony No. 4; Variations on a theme of Haydn (St Anthony chorale), Op. 56a.
(M) *** Decca 430 440-2; *430 440-4* [id.]. Chicago SO, Solti.

In considering recordings of the *Fourth Symphony*, Karl Boehm's outstanding VPO version should not be forgotten, coupled with No. 1 on DG's Compact Classics – see above.

Walter's opening is simple, even gentle, and the pervading lyricism is immediately apparent; yet power and authority are underlying. The conductor's refusal to linger by a wayside always painted in gently glowing colours adds strength and impetus, building a cumulative effect. The slow movement, essentially serene yet intense at its central climax, is balanced by a vivacious, exhilarating scherzo. The finale has an underlying impetus so that Walter creates a feeling of inevitability throughout. The *Tragic overture* opens the record powerfully, so that the mellow opening of the *Symphony* is the more striking. The CD brings full, well-balanced sound in an attractively spacious ambience, with glowing detail. Few versions are sonically balanced more appealingly.

Solti's *Fourth*, the finest of his cycle, returns to the catalogue at mid-price with a comparably fine account of the *Variations* as coupling. The reading shows him at his most vibrantly individual when, after a very direct, strongly motivated first movement, his view of the *Andante moderato* second movement is more an *Adagio*, unfailingly pure and eloquent. The scherzo has ebullience and the finale undoubted power. The playing of the Chicago orchestra is magnificent and the recording, full and precise, has been remastered for this latest CD appearance and the bass (previously boomily resonant) made firm.

The refinement of the very opening in Skrowaczewski's Pickwick version leads to an exceptionally satisfying reading, outstanding in the bargain-price range and finer than many full-price versions. The phrasing is affectionate without ever sounding self-conscious, and the alertness as well as the refinement of the Hallé playing confirms the excellence; if the coupling of only three *Hungarian dances* is hardly generous, they are certainly attractively presented.

Karajan's glowing EMI performance almost holds its own with his later, mid-1960s Berlin version. The keynote of the performance is its complete naturalness; the symphony unfolds at an unforced pace and possesses a glowing eloquence that is unfailingly impressive. The sound is remarkably good, given that it is over thirty years old. The Philharmonia play marvellously for Karajan and, with its Liszt bonus, this is a bargain.

Toscanini's version was recorded live in June 1935, and though the sound is inevitably limited and the playing is fallible, the interpretation brings out not only the tension of a Toscanini performance but also his warmth in freely expressive phrasing, very different from his much later NBC recording. The *Tragic overture* too has more colour and freedom than other versions he recorded.

György Lehel's leisurely approach to Brahms comes off better in the *Fourth Symphony* than in the *First*, but the overall effect is still somewhat enervating, especially in the finale; moreover the orchestral playing lacks polish and wind textures could ideally be more homogeneous. The two *Overtures* frame the main work.

After the success of his recording of Brahms's *First*, Rahbari's account of the *Fourth* is a great disappointment. His weighty approach to the outer movements brings a serious lack of momentum and the reading entirely fails to take off.

Variations on a theme by Haydn, Op. 56a.

(M) ** Sony SMK 46247 [id.]. Marlboro Festival O, Casals – BEETHOVEN: *Symphony No. 2* etc. **

The Casals account is a concert performance recorded at the Marlboro Festival, Vermont, in 1969 and is broad, spacious and eminently straightforward, an account that well deserves to be heard. The sound is of course somewhat dated, and the string-tone needs more bloom, but nothing Casals did was without stature or interest.

CHAMBER MUSIC

Cello sonatas Nos. 1 in E min., Op. 38; 2 in F, Op. 99.

(M) ** EMI CDM7 63298-2 [id.]; *EG 763298-4*. Jacqueline du Pré, Daniel Barenboim.

(M) (**) Decca mono 425 973-2. Fournier, Backhaus (with BACH: *Viola da gamba sonata in G, BWV 1027*, partnered by Ernest Lush).

This coupling shows the Du Pré/Barenboim partnership at its stylistically most self-indulgent. Many listeners will find the blatant change of tempo between the first and second subjects in the earlier work hard to accept. At least the players tackle the second and more taxing of the *Sonatas* with a sense of its heroic size. On the whole this is the more successful of the two performances, but neither is lacking in Brahmsian warmth and flair. The remastered recording is well balanced.

That aristocrat of cellists, Pierre Fournier, recorded the two Brahms *Sonatas* with Backhaus in 1955 in Victoria Hall, Geneva. The sound is surprisingly – though not unacceptably – dry and the frequency range is constricted. These fine performances are a welcome reminder of Fournier's art and it is worth making allowances for the sonic limitations.

Clarinet quintet in B min., Op. 115.

(M) *** EMI CDM7 63116-2 [id.]; *EG 763116-4*. Gervase de Peyer, Melos Ens. – MOZART: *Quintet.* ***

(B) *** Pickwick Dig. PCD 883; *CIMPC 883* [id.]. Keith Puddy, Delmé Qt – DVOŘÁK: *Quartet No. 12.* ***

(M) **(*) Decca 417 643-2; *417 643-4* [id.]. Boskovsky, V. Octet (members) – BAERMANN: *Adagio* **(*); MOZART: *Quintet.* **

(i) *Clarinet quintet in B min., Op. 115;* (ii) *Clarinet sonata No. 2 in E flat, Op. 120/2.*

(M) *** Chan. CHAN 6522 [id.]. Janet Hilton, (i) Lindsay Qt; (ii) Peter Frankl.

Gervase de Peyer's vintage performance of the *Clarinet quintet* with the Melos Ensemble, recorded in 1964, returns to the catalogue at mid-price in an apt and generous coupling with Mozart. It is a warmly lyrical reading, dominated by the clarinettist, who brings out wistfully autumnal overtones. The sound is full and immediate, set in a relatively dry acoustic.

Keith Puddy's warm tone is well suited to Brahms and, with spacious speeds in all four movements, this is a consistently sympathetic reading; the recording is equally fine, vivid and full. Excellent value.

Janet Hilton's essentially mellow performance of the *Clarinet quintet*, with the Lindsay

Quartet playing with pleasing warmth and refinement, has a distinct individuality. She creates quite a strong solo profile and is especially striking in the *Zigeuner* interlude at the centre of the *Adagio*, where she provides an exciting burst of bravura. Her lilting syncopations in the third movement are delightful and the theme and variations of the finale are full of character. The 1980 analogue recording has a natural presence without being obtrusively close. Hilton's partnership with Peter Frankl in the *E flat Clarinet sonata* is rather less idiosyncratic and individual; nevertheless this performance offers considerable artistic rewards, even if the resonance means that the aural focus is a little diffuse. The balance is otherwise natural and makes this a good mid-priced alternative.

Boskovsky's is a rich-toned, relaxed account; the first movement could be tauter and the slow movement is on the gentle side; with generous couplings and good sound, however, this is certainly attractive.

(i) *Clarinet quintet, Op. 115;* (ii) *Piano quintet, Op. 34; String quintets Nos. 1–2, Opp. 88 & 111; String sextets Nos. 1–2, Opp. 18 & 36.*

(M) **(*) DG 419 875-2 (3) [id.]. (i) Leister; (ii) Eschenbach; augmented Amadeus Qt.

These performances were first issued in 1969. The playing is consistently polished and tempi are well chosen. Karl Leister plays with considerable sensitivity in the *Clarinet quintet*, while in the *Piano quintet* Christoph Eschenbach gives a powerful account of the piano part. Perhaps it is at times over-projected, but the performance has no want of life. Elsewhere the element of suavity which at times enters the Amadeus contribution seems minimized by the immediacy of the sound, and there is much to enjoy here.

Clarinet sonatas Nos. 1 in F min.; 2 in E flat, Op. 120/1–2.

(M) **(*) BMG/RCA GD 60036 [60036-2-RG]. Richard Stoltzman, Richard Goode.

(M) ** Collins Dig. 3010-2 [id.]. David Campbell, Andrew Ball – MENDELSSOHN: *Clarinet sonata.* **(*)

Stoltzman's readings of both works have a relaxed, improvisatory style. Richard Goode makes a sensitive partner, but his piano timbre as recorded is a little dry, although the sound overall is balanced truthfully.

David Campbell and Andrew Ball provide strong rather than melting accounts of these two *Sonatas*, with the pianist's contribution very direct and often rhythmically forceful. Campbell phrases lyrically in slow movements, but overall a touch more idiosyncrasy and charm would have been welcome. The recording is realistic but rather forward.

Clarinet trio in A min., Op. 114.

(B) **(*) Pickwick PCD 959. David Campbell, Iwan Llewelyn-Jones, Lionel Handy – BEETHOVEN: *Clarinet trio.* **(*)

The Musicfest Trio, which began life at the Aberystwyth Music Festival, is a flexible ensemble which can vary in number and size and even reach chamber orchestra proportions. The three players recorded here give a good account of the Brahms *Clarinet trio* and they have no lack of spirit or sensitivity; as with the Beethoven coupling, however, the over-reverberant acoustic considerably diminishes its appeal.

Horn trio in E flat, Op. 40.

(M) EMI ** CDM7 63988-2 [id.]. Civil, Y. & H. Menuhin – MENDELSSOHN: *Violin sonata* *(*); SCHUBERT: *Fantasia.* **

(i) *Horn trio in E flat;* (ii) *String sextet No. 2 in G, Op. 36.*

❀ (M) **(*) Sony SMK 46249 [id.]. (i) Myron Bloom, Michael Tree, Rudolph Serkin; (ii) Pina Carmirelli, Toth, Naegele, Caroline Levine, Arico, Reichenberger.

(i) *Horn trio in E flat;* (ii) *Liebeslieder waltzes, Op. 52.*

(M) *(**) Sony stereo/mono MPK 46448 [id.]. Rudolph Serkin, with (i) Myron Bloom, Michael Tree; (ii) Fleisher, Valente, Kleinman, Conner, Singer.

The performance of the *Horn trio*, recorded at the Marlboro Festival in 1960, is quite splendid, the warmly romantic feeling of the first movement matched by subtlety of colour in the *Adagio* and the wonderful bite and rhythmic exhilaration of the scherzo and finale. Myron Bloom's horn playing is superb, and Michael Tree matches his lyrical feeling, while Serkin holds the performance together so that, when the fervour of the music-making brings a few slips in rhythmic precision, the listener is carried along by the exhilaration of the moment. The *Trio* comes paired with another Marlboro performance, of the *G major String sextet*, by a string group led by Pina Carmirelli. Recorded in 1967, this is at an altogether lower voltage. But even if the playing is not in any way memorable, its direct response to one of Brahms's most lyrical string works is not unappealing. The sound is quite well matched and balanced, if a little thin on top (though not edgy). But the *Horn trio* is unforgettable and earns our Rosette: one all too rarely experiences this kind of inspiration and fire in music-making on a record, and the sound is remarkably vivid.

The alternative coupling offering the

Liebeslieder waltzes is much less successful. The voice of the soprano, Benita Valente, does not seem tailor-made for this work and it is the gentler numbers that come off best; elsewhere, the presentation has more vigour than subtlety. The recording is fully acceptable.

The EMI account of the *Horn trio* was made in 1966; it brings an example of the flawless playing of the late lamented Alan Civil and also a relatively rare appearance on record by Yehudi Menuhin's sister, Hephzibah. Menuhin's own performance is less distinguished on this occasion and the recording is, if not subfusc, at least not in the front rank. All the same it is worth investigating for the sake of Alan Civil's masterly performance.

Piano quartets Nos. 1 in G min., Op. 25; 2 in A, Op. 26; 3 in A, Op. 60.
(B) *** VoxBox (2) [CDX 5052]. Eastman Qt.

The Eastman Quartet were recorded in 1968 but the sound, though more forward than ideal, is acceptably warm. (The quartet comprises professors at the Eastman School of Music at the University of Rochester.) The set is distinguished by some very fine playing, in particular from the pianist Frank Glazer, whose sensitivity and imagination are always in evidence. The musical insights that he brings and the fine musicianship and teamwork shown by his colleagues make this a particularly rewarding set. There is nothing sensational or jet-setting about this playing; it is relaxed, unforced and musical through and through. We missed these performances when they first appeared in the late 1960s and are sorry to have done so for, despite any minor reservations one might have, they are artistically superior to many, more celebrated, later recordings. It is a pity that three CDs were not used (perhaps for the price of two) as the *A major* is split between the two discs; so compelling are these readings that one regrets the distraction of having to change discs. This Vox Box still awaits issue in the UK.

Piano quartets Nos. 1 in G min.; 3 in C min., Op. 60.
(M) **(*) BMG/RCA GD 85677 [5677-2-RG]. Rubinstein, Guarneri Qt.

Rubinstein can be a persuasive Brahms advocate and here he is at his most commanding, clearly inspiring the Guarneri players to match his power and emotional warmth. The performances have tremendous spontaneity and conviction; however, the remastered recording, although well blended and properly balanced and clear, lacks something in warmth in the middle frequencies, although the upper range is not shrill.

Piano quartet No. 3 in C min., Op. 60.
(M) ** BMG/RCA GD 87873; *GK 87873* [7873-2-RG; *7873-4-RG*]. Lateiner, Heifetz, Schonbach, Piatigorsky – BEETHOVEN: *Trio*; SCHUBERT: *Fantaisie*. **

This is a powerful, big-boned performance of the *C minor Piano quartet* (at times perhaps a bit too high-powered, but let that pass). However, the dry, boxed-in acoustic diminishes the pleasure these players give.

Piano quintet in F min., Op. 34.
(BB) *** Naxos Dig. 8.550406 [id.]. Jenö Jandó, Kodály Qt – SCHUMANN: *Piano quintet*. ***

Although not quite as refined as some of its full-price competitors, this fine Naxos account has a great deal going for it, even though it does not include the first-movement exposition repeat. The playing is boldly spontaneous and has plenty of fire and expressive feeling. The opening of the finale has mystery too, and overall, with full-bodied recording and plenty of presence, this makes a strong impression. It is certainly a bargain.

(i) *Piano quintet in F min., Op. 34. String quartet No. 3 in B flat, Op. 67.*
(M) * Pickwick Dig. MCD 30. (i) Derek Han; New World Qt.

This is an attractive and generous coupling, and the performances are generally lively, but reservations are serious. The recording makes the piano sound wooden in the *Piano quintet*, with a limited upper range, and that makes the playing sound less inspired too, notably in the slow movement, which needs to be more persuasive. The last two movements are more successful, but neither there nor in the *Quartet* is the string-playing quite as finely disciplined or as consistent as one needs on disc. So the slow movement of the *String quartet* brings a warmly expressive opening violin solo, but the following movement misses the pointed delicacy needed in a Brahms *Allegretto*.

Piano trios Nos. 1 in B, Op. 8; 2 in C, Op. 87.
(M) *** Decca 421 152-2; *421 152-4*. Julius Katchen, Josef Suk, Janos Starker.

Piano trio No. 3 in C min., Op. 101; Cello sonata No. 2 in F, Op. 99; Scherzo for violin and piano in C min.
(M) *** Decca 425 423-2; *425 423-4*. Katchen, Suk, Starker.

The Katchen/Suk/Starker recordings were made in The Maltings in July 1968, representing Katchen's last sessions before his untimely death. The performances are warm, strong and characterful. The richness of the acoustics at The Maltings adds to the Brahmsian glow; and if the sound of the remastered disc is a little limited in the upper range, it provides a real Brahmsian amplitude which is very satisfying. The *Scherzo in C minor*, added for the reissue on CD, is an attractive bonus, not otherwise available.

Piano trio No. 2 in C, Op. 87.
(M) (**) Sony mono MPK 46447 [id.]. Rudolf Serkin, A. & H. Busch – BEETHOVEN: *Ghost trio.* (**)

Adolf Busch was well past his prime by the time this was recorded in Vermont in 1951 and his playing is technically far from immaculate: his tone has lost something of its bloom and focus; but the performance succeeds in communicating musical intentions, even though the dryish mono recording does not flatter them. The piano tends to dominate, though Serkin plays commandingly and responsively. Even if his sonority is no longer beautiful, Busch's phrasing is unfailingly musical and full of thought: this is chamber-music-playing of the old school, concentrating on a private discourse and less concerned with public projection or impressing an audience.

String quintets Nos. 1 in F, Op. 88; 2 in G, Op. 111.
(M) **(*) Ph. 426 094-2; *426 094-4*. BPO Octet (members).

These splendid works are quite well served by the 1970 Philips reissue. Although the remastering has brought a thinner, more astringent treble response than the original LP, the underlying sound is full and well balanced. The performances by the Berlin Philharmonic group are searching and artistically satisfying, combining freshness with polish, warmth with well-integrated detail.

String sextets Nos. 1 in B flat, Op. 18; 2 in G, Op. 36.
(M) **(*) EMI CDM7 63531-2 [id.]; *EG 763531-4*. Y. Menuhin, Masters, Aronowitz, E. Wallfisch, Gendron, Simpson.
(BB) *(*) Naxos Dig. 8.550436 [id.]. Stuttgart String Sextet.

Menuhin's group of star players integrate well together and transmit their enjoyment of these warmly lyrical works. The performances are relaxed and often agreeably affectionate, with the last two movements of the G major work particularly beguiling. Perhaps both opening movements could have more grip, but the spirit of the music is well projected; the mid-1960s recording has retained its original warmth and it now has greater freshness and is better defined, without edginess.

The Stuttgart Sextet are obviously an accomplished group but their accounts never attain a consistent level of distinction. They are recorded in the Tonstudio van Geest in Heidelberg, which is kinder to string players than it is to the piano; but the balance is still too close for comfort. Anyone buying this will soon find themselves wanting to move on to something better.

Violin sonatas Nos. 1 in G, Op. 78; 2 in A, Op. 100; 3 in D min., Op. 108.
(M) *** DG 431 599-2; *431 599-4* [id.]. Pinchas Zukerman, Daniel Barenboim.
(M) **(*) Decca 421 092-2; *421 092-4* [id.]. Josef Suk, Julius Katchen.
(M) ** Ph. 426 093-2; *426 093-4*. Arthur Grumiaux, György Sebok.

Zukerman and Barenboim are inspired to take an expansive view of Brahms to produce songful, spontaneous-sounding performances that catch the inspiration of the moment. The manner is warmer and less self-conscious – if at times less refined – than many of their full-price competitors. Recorded in 1975, the sound is ripe and warm to match.

Suk's personal blend of romanticism and the classical tradition is warmly attractive but small in scale. These are intimate performances and, in their way, very enjoyable, since the remastered 1967 recording remains smoothly realistic, with only a hint of rawness on top.

Mellifluous playing from Grumiaux, expertly partnered by György Sebok, but not helped by the remastered mid-1970s recording, which is very slightly thin on top. This is acceptable, but is no match for Zukerman and Barenboim in the same price range.

Violin sonatas Nos. 1 in G, Op. 78; 3 in D min., Op. 108.
(M) ** BMG/RCA GD 86264 [6264-2-RG]. Szeryng, Rubinstein – BEETHOVEN: *Sonata No. 8.* **

Szeryng and Rubinstein were recorded together in the early 1960s. Their performances are sophisticated yet committed, strongly felt yet careful in matters of detail and balance. The remastered recording is, however, rather dry in acoustic; ideally, Brahms's chamber music needs a warmer acoustic than this and a richer piano sound. But this remains very distinguished playing.

Violin sonata No. 2 in A, Op. 100.
(B) *** DG Compact Classics *415 615-4* [id.]. Christian Ferras, Pierre Barbizet – BEETHOVEN: *Violin sonatas Nos. 5 and 9.* ***

This intimately lyrical performance of the *A major Sonata* is most enjoyable. It is placed on side one of the Compact Classics cassette, immediately following the Menuhin/Kempff version of Beethoven's *Spring sonata*, and acts as an excellent foil to it. The recording is truthful and the transfers excellent.

PIANO MUSIC

4 Ballades, Op. 10; 7 Fantasias, Op. 116; Hungarian dances Nos. 1–10; (i) *Nos. 11–21. 3 Intermezzi, Op. 117; 8 Piano pieces, Op. 76; 6 Piano pieces, Op. 118; 4 Piano pieces, Op. 119; Piano sonata Nos. 1 in C, Op. 1; 2 in F sharp min., Op. 2; 3 in F min., Op. 5; 2 Rhapsodies, Op. 79; Variations on a Hungarian song, Op. 21/2; Variations on a theme by Paganini, Op. 35; Variations and fugue on a theme by Handel, Op. 24; Variations on a theme by Schumann, Op. 9; Variations on an original theme, Op. 21/1; Waltzes, Op. 39.*

(M) **(*) Decca mono/stereo 430 053-2 (6). Julius Katchen, (i) with Marty.

Brahms often brought out the best in Katchen, and he is particularly good in the impulsive early music. If at times one could make small criticisms, the spontaneity and understanding are always there, and of course the excitement that comes when bravura is controlled by a sensitive and musical mind. Katchen's style in Brahms is distinctive: there is a boldness about it that suits some works more than others. In general the bigger, tougher pieces come off better than the gentle *Intermezzi* of Opp. 116 and 117, which lack the sort of inner tension that Kovacevich can convey. Even so, there is much beautiful playing here, especially in Op. 117/1 and 2, while Katchen's free, musing rubato in Op. 119/1 is most appealing, and Op. 119/4 shows him at his most masterful. Such pieces as the two *Rhapsodies*, Op. 79, are splendidly done, and so are the *Ballades*. The *Waltzes*, brief trivial ideas but on the whole extrovert, come somewhere in between. Katchen's playing in the first two *Sonatas* hardly achieves the compelling intensity of some of his rivals, but the result is always exciting. The playing is extremely brilliant and assured, and a certain lack of resilience in the style scarcely mars the performances, rather giving them a tough individuality; and his account of Op. 5 is similarly commanding. The lesser-known *Variations on a Hungarian song* and *On an original theme*, plus those *On a theme by Schumann* are particularly successful. They are played with the utmost persuasiveness and artistry. On the other hand, the *Handel* and *Paganini* sets, Opp. 24 and 35, are very extrovert in style and, for all their pyrotechnical display, lack a degree of spontaneity, though not excitement. Katchen plays Book One of the *Hungarian dances*, usually given in their chamber version as piano duets, in Brahms's later arrangement for piano solo; the remaining dances are offered in the more traditional form with Jean-Pierre Marty as Katchen's partner. On CD the recordings, made between 1962 and 1966, are remarkably realistic, full in timbre and with good presence. The four *Ballades* are mono. A fine set which will give much satisfaction. But it is a pity that the cueing is so ungenerous in the *Variations* and (especially) the *Waltzes*.

3 Intermezzi, Op. 117; 6 Pieces, Op. 118; 4 Pieces, Op. 119; Scherzo, Op. 4.

(BB) * Naxos Dig. 8.550354 [id.]. Idil Biret.

In the Op. 117 *Intermezzi* Idil Biret plays with taste and an appropriate inwardness, and her playing is always the product of thought. But the close balance, together with the unventilated, claustrophobic acoustic of the Tonstudio van Geest, makes for aural fatigue. One longs for more space round the instrument.

Intermezzi: in E flat, Op. 117/1; in A, Op. 118/2; in B min., Op. 119/1; Rhapsody in G min., Op. 79/2; Waltzes: in E and A flat, Op. 39/2 & 15.

(B) *(*) Pickwick Dig. PCD 949. Annette Servadei – MENDELSSOHN; SCHUMANN: *Piano music.* *(*)

Annette Servadei's recital is intelligently chosen and offers some very musical but essentially small-scale playing. There is rather more to the *E flat Intermezzo* than she finds, and she makes somewhat heavy weather of the *Rhapsody in G minor*, where the piano sounds distinctly tired. Generally speaking, despite some felicitous touches at the beginning of the *A major Intermezzo*, there is a certain want of authority. The recording, made at St John's, Smith Square, in London, is very good.

8 Pieces, Op. 76; 2 Rhapsodies, Op. 79; 7 Fantasias, Op. 116.

(BB) * Naxos Dig. 8.550353 [id.]. Idil Biret.

The Naxos accounts of this repertoire are attractively priced but, as with other issues in this series, are let down by unsatisfactory recorded sound.

Piano sonatas Nos. 1 in C, Op. 1; 2 in F sharp min., Op. 2.

(BB) * Naxos Dig. 8.550351–2 [id.]. Idil Biret.

The Turkish-born Idil Biret gives a commanding and intelligent account of the *C major Sonata*, and her fine sense of architecture serves as a reminder that she was a pupil of Kempff. However, the studio environment in which these recordings were made is very unsympathetic: the close balance and brittle timbre of the instrument are unpleasing.

Variations and fugue on a theme by Handel, Op. 24.

(M) *** Decca 417 791-2. Jorge Bolet – REGER: *Variations.* ***

(BB) *(*) Naxos Dig. 8.550408 [id.]. Michael Ponti – LISZT: *Fantasia & fugue on B-A-C-H* etc. *(*)

This was Jorge Bolet's début record for Decca, and very impressive it is. His playing in Brahms's best-loved set of piano variations is incisive and brightly revealing, intensely refreshing and concentrated. With excellently remastered analogue sound, this makes a first-class coupling with music by Reger which is much less familiar.

Michael Ponti possesses a formidable technique and keen musical responses and, though his account of the *Variations and fugue on a theme by Handel* may not be the finest on disc, it is an eminently respectable one. The acoustic of the Tonstudio van Geest in Heidelberg is not quite big enough to cope with the fortissimo passages and – though there are worse – as sound this falls a long way short of the ideal.

Variations on a theme by Handel, Op. 24; Variations on a theme by Paganini, Op. 35; Variations on a theme by Schumann, Op. 9.

(BB) *(*) Naxos Dig. 8.550350 [id.]. Idil Biret.

On the face of it, this is outstanding value for money: good performances of the *Variations on a theme by Handel*, in which Idil Biret is occasionally a little heavy-handed, and with both sets of *Variations, on a theme by Paganini* and *on a theme by Schumann*, thrown in for good measure. The playing is often imaginative and sensitive and only rarely routine – but the acoustic of the Tonstudio van Geest in Heidelberg is really very unappealing and diminishes the pleasure this artist's playing gives.

VOCAL MUSIC

(i) *Alto rhapsody, Op. 53; Nänie, Op. 82; Schicksalslied (Song of destiny), Op. 54; Triumphlied, Op. 55.*

(M) *** DG Dig. 435 066-2; *435 066-4* [id.]. (i) Brigitte Fassbaender; Prague Philharmonic Ch., Czech PO, Sinopoli.

Alto rhapsody, Op. 53; Schicksalslied (Song of destiny), Op. 54.

(M) ** Sony MYK 45503 [id.]; *40-45503.* Mildred Miller, Occidental College Concert Ch., Columbia SO, Bruno Walter – MAHLER: *Lieder eines fahrenden Gesellen.* **

A splendidly generous (70 minutes) choral anthology. Brigitte Fassbaender makes a strong, noble soloist in the *Alto rhapsody*, but there is freshness and excitement in the other, rarer works, not least the one generally dismissesd as mere occasional music, the *Triumphlied* of 1870. Sinopoli, helped by incandescent singing from the Czech choir, gives it Handelian exhilaration. The recording is very convincingly balanced, with the orchestra vividly forward and the chorus set behind in a warm ambience.

Mildred Miller is a fresh rather than an inspirational soloist in the *Alto rhapsody* and, despite coaching from Walter (who had decided views on the interpretation of this fine work), she gives a somewhat strait-laced account of the opening pages. The *Song of destiny* is very satisfactory, however, and displays the capability of the chorus to good effect. The CD transfers are well managed, with the orchestral detail in the *Rhapsody*, and the fine choral singing in both works, showing that Walter's directing hand has a special contribution to make.

Lieder: *Dein blaues Auge hält; Dort in den Weiden; Immer leiser wird mein Schlummer; Klage I & II; Liebestreu; Des Liebsten Schwur; Das Mädchen; Das Mädchen spricht; Regenlied; Romanzen und Lieder, Op. 84; Salome; Sapphische Ode, Op. 94/4; Der Schmied;* (i) *2 Songs with viola, Op. 91; Therese; Vom Strande; Wie Melodien zieht es; Zigeunerlieder, Op. 103.*

(M) *** DG Dig. 431 600-2; *431 600-4* [id.]. Jessye Norman, Daniel Barenboim; (i) Wolfram Christ.

Jessye Norman's glorious Lieder recital with Barenboim, recorded in 1981/2, is one of the reissued mid-priced bargains in DG's Brahms Edition; the task of recording a complete set of women's songs seems in this instance to have added to the warmth and sense of spontaneity of both singer and pianist in the studio, while Wolfram Christ makes a distinguished contribution to Op. 91. The heroic scale of *Der Schmied* is superb, as is the open simplicity of the *Zigeunerlieder*, while the gentler songs find Norman's gloriously ample voice scaled down exquisitely. The recording is wonderfully vivid, giving the artists a tangible presence. This is one of the finest Lieder collections in the CD catalogue.

Vier ernste Gesänge, Op. 121; Lieder: *Auf dem Kirchhofe; Botschaft; Feldeinsamkeit; Im Waldeseinsamkeit; Minnelied III; Mondenschein; O wüsst ich doch den Weg züruck; Sapphische Ode; Sommerabend; Ständchen.*

(M) (***) EMI CDH7 63198-2 [id.]. Hotter, Moore – BACH: *Cantata No. 82: Ich habe genug.*(***)

Glorious singing from Hans Hotter, wonderfully accompanied by Gerald Moore. Those who have treasured the old LP will know how eloquent this is; others should not pass over singing and artistry of this eloquence. An excellent transfer.

German requiem, Op. 45.

(M) *** Teldec/Warner Dig. 9301 75862-2 [id.]. M. Price, Ramey, Amb. S., RPO, Previn.

(M) *** DG Dig. 429 486-2; *429 486-4*. Lucia Popp, Wolfgang Brendel, Prague Philharmonic Ch., Czech PO, Sinopoli.

(M) *** DG Dig. 431 598-2; *431 598-4* [id.] (as above, cond. Sinopoli).

(M) **(*) EMI CDM7 69229-2 [id.]; *EG 769229-4*. Tomowa-Sintow, Van Dam, V. Singverein, BPO, Karajan.

(M) (***) EMI mono CDH7 61010-2 [id.]. Schwarzkopf, Hotter, V. Singverein, VPO, Karajan.

(M) **(*) Sony SK 45853 [id.]. Cotrubas, Prey, New Philh. Ch. & O, Maazel.

(M) ** DG 427 252-2 [id.]. Janowitz, Waechter, V. Singverein, BPO, Karajan.

It is the seeming simplicity of Previn's dedicated approach, with radiant singing from the chorus and measured speeds held steadily, that so movingly conveys an innocence in the often square writing, both in the powerful opening choruses and in the simple, songful *Wie lieblich*. The great fugatos are then powerfully presented. Both soloists are outstanding, Margaret Price golden-toned, Samuel Ramey incisively dark. The recording is warmly set against a helpful church acoustic with the chorus slightly distanced.

Sinopoli's DG version of the *Deutsches Requiem* brings a performance of extremes: generally measured but consistently positive and often dramatically thrilling, helped by the wide-ranging recording, excellent soloists and an incisive contribution from the Prague Philharmonic Chorus. The hushed opening pianissimo soon expands powerfully, and the dynamic and emotional contrast is even more striking in the penultimate section (with baritone and chorus), which uses texts made famous in Handel's *Messiah*. The 1983 digital recording is full, clear and realistically balanced. This version is also to be had as part of DG's Brahms Edition.

The reissue of Karajan's 1977 EMI set on a mid-priced CD offers considerable competition to his later, digital version at full price. The chorus here is both full and clearly focused, and soloists and orchestral detail are vividly projected. Indeed the most striking difference between this and the (full-priced) digital DG set lies in the choral sound, here bigger and closer, with sharp dramatic contrasts. The soloists are both excellent: Tomowa-Sintow sings with a rich vocal colour, while José van Dam is equally expressive and with firm tone. The remastering is certainly a success, and this is generally also preferable to the alternative mid-priced Karajan reissue from DG. Though there is a good deal to praise and enjoy on the analogue DG disc, the EMI version brings better choral sound and solo contributions at least as fine.

Recorded in October 1947 and issued on ten short-playing 78-r.p.m. discs, Karajan's mono version of the *German requiem* was – surprisingly – the first ever complete recording of this work. It was also something of a breakthrough in Karajan's early career. It is in part a tribute to his unique collaboration with Walter Legge not only that this is a performance which has rarely been matched since on record, incandescent and intense, but that even now the sound has such vivid presence. There is inevitably some surface noise, but nothing too distracting, and the brightness and fullness of the sound is astonishing. The chorus is in superb, incisive form, and the two soloists are both at their peak, the young Schwarzkopf fresh-toned and Hotter far firmer than he later became.

Maazel on his mid-priced Sony disc gives a strong, unaffected performance, marked by superbly disciplined singing from the New Philharmonia Chorus, though the 1976 recording is not as clear on inner detail as it might be. Maazel sustains slow speeds most convincingly, and the two soloists, balanced rather close, are both warmly expressive, maybe too much so for some, with Cotrubas's vibrato giving a richer sound than is common in this work. Helpfully, Sony have put tracks on different sections within the seven movements.

(i) *Nänie, Op. 82;* (ii; iii) *Rinaldo, Op. 50;* (iii) *Schicksalslied, Op. 54.*

(M) ** Decca 425 030-2; *425 030-4* [id.]. (i) Suisse Romande & Lausanne Pro Arte Ch., SRO, Ansermet; (ii) King; (iii) Amb. Ch., New Philh. O, Abbado.

The cantata *Rinaldo* gives some idea of what a Brahms opera might have sounded like; but, unfortunately for dramatic impact, the text provides no music for the seducing Armida, and the score has only one soloist. Although Abbado directs strongly, James King is far from ideal in the role of Rinaldo. His Wagnerian Heldentenor is really too coarse for music that is much more easily lyrical than Wagner. However, there is a great deal for the chorus to do, and the Ambrosians clearly relish this music. The 1968 Kingsway Hall Decca recording, too, is first rate. The fine Ansermet performance of *Nänie* was recorded two years earlier in Geneva and makes an enjoyable bonus.

Brian, Havergal (1876–1972)

Symphonies Nos. 10 in C min.; 21 in E flat.
(M) **(*) Unicorn UKCD 2027. Leicestershire Schools SO, Loughran or Pinkett.

Both these *Symphonies* are works of old age; No. 10, a powerfully wrought and original one-movement piece, is the more appealing of the two; No. 21 dates from the composer's late eighties. There need be no serious reservations about the recordings, and the performances are astonishingly accomplished.

Bridge, Frank (1879–1941)

Cherry Ripe; Enter Spring (rhapsody); *Lament; The Sea* (suite); *Summer* (tone-poem).
(M) *** EMI CDM7 69870-2. Royal Liverpool PO, Groves.

Writing in the early years of the century, the composer confidently produced a magnificent seascape in the wake of Debussy, *The Sea*, but already by 1914 his responses were subtler, more original. *Summer*, written in that fateful year, was free of conventional pastoral moods, while in the last and greatest of Bridge's tone-poems, *Enter Spring*, he was responding to still wider musical horizons in experimentation which matches that of European contemporaries. Groves's warm advocacy adds to the impressiveness. First-rate recording, most successfully remastered.

Oration (Concerto elegiaco) for cello and orchestra.
(M) *** EMI Dig. CDM7 63909-2; *EG 763909-4*. Isserlis, City of L. Sinfonia, Hickox – BRITTEN: *Symphony for cello and orchestra.* ***

Completed in 1930, *Oration* is in effect a massive cello concerto in nine linked sections lasting a full half-hour. It is an elegiac work which, like Bridge's ambitious *Piano sonata* of 1924, reflects the composer's continuing desolation over the deaths of so many of his friends in the First World War. As in the *Sonata*, Bridge's idea of writing an elegiac work made for the opposite of comfortable consolation. In its often gritty textures and dark concentration it is fundamentally angry music, stylistically amazing – like other late Bridge – for a British composer to have been writing at the time. Though Isserlis is not always as passionate as Julian Lloyd Webber was on the earlier, Lyrita version, his focus is sharper, and with Hickox he brings out the originality of the writing all the more cleanly. It is fascinating to find some passages anticipating the more abrasive side of Britten, and specifically the *Cello symphony* with which this is coupled.

Britten, Benjamin (1913–76)

(i) *Piano concerto, Op. 13;* (ii) *Violin concerto, Op. 15.*
(M) *** Decca 417 308-2. (i) Sviatoslav Richter; (ii) Lubotsky; ECO, composer.

Richter is incomparable in interpreting the *Piano concerto*, not only the thoughtful, introspective moments but the Liszt-like bravura passages (many of them surprising from this composer). With its highly original sonorities the *Violin concerto* makes a splendid vehicle for another Soviet artist, Mark Lubotsky. Recorded in The Maltings, the playing of the ECO under the composer's direction matches the inspiration of the soloists. The 1971 recording sounds splendid on this reissued CD.

(i) *Matinées musicales; Soirées musicales;* (ii; iv) *Young person's guide to the orchestra;* (iii; iv) *Peter Grimes: 4 Sea interludes and Passacaglia.*
(M) *** Decca 425 659-2; *425 659-4* [id.]. (i) Nat. PO, Bonynge; (ii) LSO; (iii) ROHCG O; (iv) composer.
(M) (**) EMI mono CDM7 63777-2 [id.]; *EG 763777-4*. LPO, Boult, (ii) nar. Boult.

Britten wrote his *Soirées musicales* for a GPO film-score in the 1930s; the *Matinées* followed in 1941 and were intended as straight ballet music. Both are wittily if rather sparsely scored, deriving their musical content directly from Rossini. Bonynge's versions are brightly played and extremely vividly recorded in the best Decca manner. They are now reissued at mid-price, generously coupled with Britten's brilliant account of the *Young person's guide to the orchestra* and the *Sea interludes* and *Passacaglia* from *Peter Grimes.* The latter are taken from the complete recording, and this means that odd extracts from the vocal parts are included so that the general effect is not as tidy as the concert version. That proviso apart, these are wonderfully vital accounts of some superbly atmospheric music.

Although Boult gave many early performances of Britten's music, he never disguised the fact that he did not find an affinity with the composer's output to match the striking sympathy he so obviously had with the music of Elgar. Neverthless he conducts Britten's Rossini arrangements with evident relish, and the LPO plays them with gusto. The *Peter Grimes interludes*, however, are a disappointment. To get the full salty flavour of Britten's music you need crisper, more biting playing than this, and an overall control which, besides being sensitive to atmosphere, has a firm emotional grip. *The Young person's guide*, however, is admirably spirited and is made something of a collector's item in including here (for the first time)

Boult's own narration of Eric Crozier's script, which he does with characteristic disarming and gentlemanly simplicity. The early stereo is vividly unrefined, but quite acceptable.

(i) *Sinfonia da requiem, Op. 20;* (ii) *Symphony for cello and orchestra, Op. 68;* (iii) *Cantata misericordium, Op. 69.*

(M) *** Decca 425 100-2 [id.]. (i) New Philh. O; (ii) Rostropovich, ECO; (iii) Pears, Fischer-Dieskau, LSO Ch., LSO; composer.

Britten's own 1964 recordings of the *Sinfonia da requiem* and the *Cello symphony* appear on CD with the *Cantata misericordium* added for good measure. All the performances are definitive, and Rostropovich's account of the *Cello symphony* in particular is everything one could ask for. It is a marvellous piece, very much a new landscape in Britten's world. The CD transfers are admirably managed.

Symphony for cello and orchestra, Op. 68.

(M) *** EMI Dig. CDM7 63909-2; *EG 763909-4.* Stephen Isserlis, City of L. Sinfonia, Hickox – BRIDGE: *Oration.* ***

Stephen Isserlis provides a valuable mid-priced alternative to Rostropovich, inspirer of the *Cello symphony* and soloist in the first recording. With speeds generally a little slower, Isserlis is not quite as taut and electric as his rival, partly because the recording does not present the solo instrument so cleanly. It remains a powerful, dramatic performance and makes excellent value, if the Bridge coupling is suitable.

Variations on a theme of Frank Bridge, Op. 10.

(M) *** Decca 421 391-2; *421 391-4* [id.]. ASMF, Marriner – BUTTERWORTH: *Banks of green willow* etc.; WARLOCK: *Capriol suite.* ***

Although not even Marriner quite matches the natural warmth of expression of the composer himself in this music, his is a superb performance, if anything even more polished, and recorded with remarkable vividness, the CD giving the impression of great presence and immediacy. With beautiful Butterworth pieces plus the Warlock *Capriol suite* for coupling, this is a very attractive reissue.

The Young person's guide to the orchestra (Variations and fugue on a theme of Purcell), Op. 34.

(M) *** EMI Dig. CD-EMX 2165; *TC-EMX 2165* (without narration). LPO, Sian Edwards – PROKOFIEV: *Peter and the wolf* **(*); RAVEL: *Ma Mère l'Oye.* **

(B) **(*) Pickwick IMPX 9002. Sean Connery, RPO, Dorati – PROKOFIEV: *Peter and the wolf.* **(*)

(BB) ** Naxos Dig. 8.550499 [id.]. Slovak RSO (Bratislava), Lenárd – PROKOFIEV: *Peter* **; SAINT-SAENS: *Carnival.* **(*)

Sian Edwards, always impressive in the recording studio, provides an excellent mid-priced digital version of Britten's orchestral showpiece. She does not press the earlier variations too hard, revelling in the colour of her wind soloists, yet the violins enter zestfully and the violas make a touching contrast. The brass bring fine bite and sonority. The fugue has plenty of vitality and the climax is spectacularly expansive in the resonant acoustics of Watford Town Hall.

Sean Connery's voice is very familiar and his easy style is attractive. His narration should go down well with young people, even if some of the points are made rather heavily. The orchestral playing is first rate and the vivid, forwardly balanced recording – with a Decca Phase 4 source – is effective enough in this context. The performance has plenty of colour and vitality.

The Slovak Radio Orchestra play well enough; although they are not as naturally at home in the variations as British orchestras, they obviously enjoy the gusto of the fugue. Bright, digital sound, but this is not a distinctive version. Separate cues are provided for each of the orchestral sections – woodwind, strings, brass and percussion – but not for the individual instruments.

CHAMBER MUSIC

(i) *Cello sonata in C, Op. 65;* (Unaccompanied) *Cello suites Nos. 1, Op. 72; 2, Op. 80.*

(M) *** Decca 421 859-2 [id.]. Rostropovich; (i) with composer.

This strange five-movement *Cello sonata* was written specially for Rostropovich's appearance at the Aldeburgh Festival of 1961, and the recording was made soon after the first performance. Each of the five movements is poised and concentrated and it is an excellent work to wrestle with on a record, particularly when the performance is never likely to be outshone. Here it is coupled with two of the *Suites for unaccompanied cello.* This is rough, gritty music in Britten's latterday manner, but Rostropovich gives such inspired accounts that the music reveals more and more with repetition. The CD transfers serve to add presence to recordings which are already very impressive.

(i) *Sinfonietta, Op. 1;* (ii) *String quartets Nos. 2, Op. 36; 3, Op. 94.*

(M) *** Decca 425 715-2. (i) Vienna Octet; (ii) Amadeus Qt.

Britten's Opus 1 was written when he was in his teens. It has some characteristic fingerprints but points atypically towards Central Europe –

reflection no doubt of his desire at the time to study with Berg in Vienna. Its mixture of seriousness and assurance is not unappealing and its astringency is brought out well in this appropriately Viennese chamber performance. The *Third Quartet*, a late work, was written for the Amadeus, who play it convincingly. It is spare, seemingly wayward, but with an underlying depth of feeling which comes to the surface in its brooding *Passacaglia*. The *Second*, ending with a forceful *Chaconne*, was written in 1945 to commemorate the 250th anniversary of Purcell's death. The contrasts of style and mood are developed well here, in performances that could be regarded as definitive. On CD the recording is full, vivid and realistic.

VOCAL MUSIC

(i) *A Boy was born, Op. 3;* (ii) *The Little Sweep (Let's make an opera).*

(M) (***) Decca stereo/mono 430 367-2 [id.]. (i) Hartnett, Purcell Singers, English Op. Group Boys' Ch.; Choristers of All Saints', Margaret St; (ii) Vyvyan, Cantelo, Marilyn Baker, Soskin, Hemmings, Ingram, Fairhurst, Lyn Vaughan, Nancy Thomas, Pears, Anthony, Alleyn's School Ch., E. Op. Group O; composer.

Though Britten's own recording of *The Little Sweep* is in mono only, it sounds amazingly vivid still in the CD transfer, with voices in particular full and immediate. As a performance it has never been surpassed in its vigour and freshness, with the film-star-to-be, David Hemmings, here as impressive in the title-role for treble, as he also was in *The Turn of the Screw*. Others in the cast, like Jennifer Vyvyan and April Cantelo, represent the accomplished group of singers that Britten gathered for his Aldeburgh Festival performances. The choruses, usually sung by the audience, are here done by the school choir. The unaccompanied Christmas cantata, *A Boy was born*, the astonishing product of Britten's early maturity as a 19-year-old student, is a brilliant set of choral variations. Again, it has never been more convincingly recorded than here in the composer's own reading, which uses the revised text he prepared in 1955, in places simplifying the complex part-writing.

The Burning fiery furnace (2nd Parable), Op. 77.

(M) *** Decca 414 663-2. Pears, Tear, Drake, Shirley-Quirk, Ch. & O of E. Op. Group, composer and Viola Tunnard.

Britten's conception of the church parable, so highly individual with its ritual elements (the audience turned into a medieval congregation), yet allows the widest variety of construction and expression. The story of *Burning fiery furnace* is obviously dramatic in the operatic sense, with vivid scenes like the Entrance of Nebuchadnezzar, the Raising of the Idol, and the putting of the three Israelites into the furnace. Britten is as imaginative as ever in his settings, and one must mention also the marvellous central interlude where the instrumentalists process round the church, which is stunningly well conveyed by the recording. The performers, both singers and players, are the same hand-picked cast that participated in the first performance at Orford Parish Church, where this record was made. This is another example of the way Decca served Britten in providing definitive versions of his major scores for the guidance of all future performers, as well as for our enjoyment at home. The recording now emerges on CD with even greater vividness and presence.

Canticles Nos. 1, My beloved is mine, Op. 40; 2, Abraham and Isaac, Opp. 51; 3, Still falls the rain, Op. 55; 4, Journey of the Magi, Op. 86; 5, Death of St. Narcissus, Op. 89. A birthday hansel. (iii) Arr. of PURCELL: *Sweeter than roses.*

(M) *** Decca 425 716-2. Peter Pears, Hahessy, Bowman, Shirley-Quirk, Tuckwell, Ellis, composer.

This CD brings together on a single record all five of the miniature cantatas to which Britten gave the title 'Canticle', most of them performed by their original performers. To the new collection, the *Birthday hansel*, written in honour of the seventy-fifth birthday of Queen Elizabeth the Queen Mother, and a Purcell song-arrangement are added for good measure. The *Canticles* all share the spiritual intensity which stemmed from the composer's religious faith. A beautiful collection as well as a historical document, with recording that still sounds well.

A Ceremony of carols, Op. 28; Festival Te Deum; Hymn to St Colomba; Hymn to St Peter; Hymn to the Virgin; Jubilate Deo; Missa brevis; Rejoice in the Lamb, Op. 30.

(M) *** Decca 430 097-2; *430 097-4*. Tear, Forbes Robinson, St John's College Ch., Guest; Robles; Runnett.

An exceptionally attractive and generous compilation of St John's recordings, derived from the old Argo catalogue. Guest's account of the delightful *Ceremony of carols* has tingling vitality, spacious sound and a superb contribution from Marisa Robles who plays with masterly sensitivity, especially in her solo *Interlude.* The performance of *Rejoice in the Lamb* is very similar to Britten's own, but much better recorded, and the *Missa brevis* has the same striking excellence of style. Of the other items added for the CD reissue, the *Hymn to the Virgin* is an engaging early work written in 1930. All these shorter pieces show the choir in superb form and the Argo analogue engineering at its most impressive.

A Ceremony of carols; Hymn to St Cecilia, Op. 17; Hymn to St Peter; Hymn to the Virgin; Te Deum in C.
(BB) **(*) ASV Dig. CDQS 6030; *ZCQS 6030*. Christ Church Cathedral, Ch., Grier; Kelly.

There is an earthy quality in these performances which reflects the composer's own rejection of over-refined choirboy tone, but the *Hymn to St Cecilia* with its setting of a brilliant Auden poem (text not included) is a degree too rough, and it loses some impact when the choir is rather backwardly balanced. The coupling, however, is apt and most desirable; and for the rest the sound is excellent. For those wanting a budget digital collection including the *Ceremony of carols*, this is excellent value.

Curlew River (1st parable for church performance).
(M) *** Decca 421 858-2 [id.]. Pears, Shirley-Quirk, Blackburn, soloists, Instrumental Ens., composer and Viola Tunnard.

Few dramatic works have been based on a more unlikely idea than *Curlew River*, and the result is a dramatic entertainment that defies all convention. The work was initially inspired by Britten's recollection of a Noh-play which he saw in Japan. There are overtones too of Eastern music (Balinese rather than Japanese) in the highly original instrumentation and often free approach to rhythm, but mainly the work's ultimate success stems from the vividness of atmosphere within a monastery setting. Harold Blackburn plays the Abbot of the monastery who introduces the drama, while John Shirley-Quirk plays the ferryman who takes people over the Curlew River and Peter Pears sings the part of the madwoman who, distracted, searches fruitlessly for her abducted child. The recording is outstanding even by Decca standards, as the vivid CD transfer readily demonstrates.

Folk-song arrangements: *The ash grove; Avenging and bright; La belle est au jardin d'amour; The bonny Earl o' Moray; The brisk young widow; Ca' the yowes; Come you not from Newcastle; Early one morning; The foggy, foggy dew; How sweet the answer; The last rose of summer; The Lincolnshire poacher; The miller of Dee; The minstrel boy; Oft in the stilly night; O Waly, Waly; The plough boy; Le roi s'en va-t'en chasse; Sally in our alley; Sweet Polly Oliver; Tom Bowling.*
(M) *** Decca 430 063-2; *430 063-4* [id.]. Peter Pears, Benjamin Britten.

It is good to have the definitive Pears/Britten collaboration in the folksong arrangements back in the catalogue on CD. To the main LP recital, made in the Kingsway Hall in 1961, Decca have added four earlier recordings from 1959, including the most famous, *The foggy, foggy dew* and *The Lincolnshire poacher*, with its witty obbligato to match the whistle of *The plough boy*. Pears's voice was at its freshest, as can be heard in *Early one morning* and *The ash grove*, while the French song about the king going hunting is sheer delight. Excellent, faithful recording, well transferred to CD.

Folksong arrangements: *The ash grove; La belle est au jardin d'amour; The bonny Earl o' Moray; The brisk young widow; Ca' the yowes; Come you not from Newcastle?; The foggy, foggy dew; The Lincolnshire poacher; Little Sir William; The minstrel boy; O can ye sew cushions; Oliver Cromwell; O Waly, Waly; The plough boy; Quand j'étais chez mon père; Le roi s'en va-t'en chasse; The Sally Gardens; Sweet Polly Oliver; The trees they grow so high.*
(M) *** EMI CDM7 69423-2. Robert Tear, Philip Ledger.

Close as Robert Tear's interpretations are to those of Peter Pears, he does have a sparkle of his own, helped by resilient accompaniment from Philip Ledger. In any case, some of these songs are unavailable in the Pears versions, and the record is a delight on its own account. *Oliver Cromwell* is among the most delectable of pay-off songs ever written. Fine recording.

(i) *The Golden Vanity;* (ii) *Noye's Fludde.*
(M) *** Decca 425 161-2. (i) Wandsworth School Boys' Ch., Burgess, composer (piano); (ii) Brannigan, Rex, Anthony, East Suffolk Children's Ch. & O, E. Op. Group O, Del Mar.

The Golden Vanity is a 'vaudeville' written for the Vienna Boys' Choir. The tale of the cabin boy who sinks the threatening pirate ship and is then drowned by his wicked captain is simply and vividly told, with the help of the well-known folksong, and the recording does wonders in recapturing the fun of performance, with its play ritual round the stage. The Wandsworth Boys are completely at home in the music and sing with pleasing freshness. The coupling, Britten's infectious children's oratorio, setting words from the Chester Miracle Play, was recorded during the 1961 Aldeburgh Festival, and not only the professional choristers but the children too have the time of their lives to the greater glory of God. All the effects have been captured miraculously here, most strikingly the entry into the Ark, while a bugle band blares out fanfares which finally turn into a rollicking march. Altogether this coupling makes a wonderful record, with the stereo readily catching the sense of occasion and particularly the sound of *Eternal Father* rising above the storm at the climax of *Noye's Fludde.*

(i) *Les Illuminations* (song-cycle), *Op. 18;* (ii) *Serenade for tenor, horn and strings, Op. 31;* (iii) *Young person's guide to the orchestra.*
(M) **(*) DG 423 239-2. (i; ii) Robert Tear; (i) Philh. O; (ii) Clevenger, Chicago SO; (i; ii) Giulini; (iii) French Nat. R. O, Maazel.

The fact that these two excellent performances were recorded on opposite sides of the Atlantic adds to the attractiveness, for the Philharmonia produces playing of warmth and resonance to match that of the Chicago orchestra. Tear is at his finest in both cycles, more open than in his earlier recording of the *Serenade.* Dale Clevenger is a superb horn-player, and though some may find him unidiomatic in places it is good to have a fresh view in such music. Soloists are balanced rather close in an otherwise excellent, vivid recording. The Maazel version of the *Young person's guide to the orchestra* was recorded much earlier and, though well played, was hardly an imaginative way of offering a bonus.

(i) *St Nicholas, Op. 42;* (ii) *Rejoice in the Lamb, Op. 30.*
(M) (***) Decca mono 425 714-2. (i) Hemmings, Pears, St John Leman School, Beccles, Girls' Ch., Ipswich School Boys' Ch., Aldeburgh Festival Ch. & O; R. Downes; (ii) Hartnett, Steele, Todd, Francke, Purcell Singers, G. Malcolm; composer.

With rare exceptions, Britten's own first recordings of his own works have a freshness and vigour unsurpassed since. Here are two fine examples which vividly draw on the brightness of boys' voices – not least that of David Hemmings as the youthful St Nicholas. The expression may be direct but the emotions behind both these works are more complex than one might at first appreciate. Britten's performances capture the element of vulnerability, not least in the touching setting of words by the deranged poet, Christopher Smart, *Rejoice in the Lamb.*

The Prodigal Son (3rd parable), Op. 81.
(M) *** Decca 425 713-2. Pears, Tear, Shirley-Quirk, Drake, E. Op. Group Ch. & O, composer and Viola Tunnard.

The last of the parables is the sunniest and most heart-warming. Britten cleverly avoids the charge of oversweetness by introducing the Abbot, even before the play starts, in the role of Tempter, confessing he represents evil and aims to destroy contentment in the family he describes: 'See how I break it up' – a marvellous line for Peter Pears. An ideal performance is given here with a characteristically real and atmospheric Decca recording.

OPERA

Peter Grimes (complete).
(M) *** Ph. 432 578-2 (2) [id.]. Vickers, Harper, Summers, Bainbridge, Cahill, Robinson, Allen, ROHCG Ch. & O, C. Davis.

Sir Colin Davis takes a fundamentally darker, tougher view of *Peter Grimes* than the composer himself (whose Decca recording is at full price). In some ways the result on Davis's set is even more powerful, if less varied and atmospheric, with the Borough turned into a dark place, full of Strindbergian tensions, and Grimes himself, physically powerful (not a misplaced intellectual), turned into a Hardy-like figure. It was Jon Vickers's heroic interpretation in the Met. production in New York which first prompted Davis to press for this recording, and the result sheds keen new illumination on what arguably remains the greatest of Britten's operas, even if it cannot be said to supplant the composer's own version. Plainly close in frame and spirit to Crabbe's rough fisherman, Vickers, slow-spoken and weighty, is frighteningly intense. Heather Harper as Ellen Orford is very moving, and there are fine contributions from Jonathan Summers as Captain Balstrode and Thomas Allen as Ned Keene. The lack of atmospheric effects in this set reinforces Davis's contention that the actual notes need no outside aid. The recording is full and vivid, with fine balancing.

The Turn of the screw.
(M) (***) Decca mono 425 672-2 (2) [id.]. Pears, Vyvyan, Hemmings, Dyer, Cross, Mandikian, E. Op. Group O, composer.

Though the recording is in mono only, the very dryness and the sharpness of focus give an extra intensity to the composer's own incomparable reading of his most compressed opera. With such sound, the claustrophobic quality of this weird ghost story is intensified, along with the musical cogency of this sequence of fifteen closely knit scenes. Peter Pears as Peter Quint is superbly matched by Jennifer Vyvyan as the governess and by Joan Cross as the housekeeper, Mrs Grose. It is also fascinating to hear David Hemmings as a boy treble, already a confident actor. Excellent CD transfer.

Bruch, Max (1838–1920)

Violin concertos Nos. 1 in G min.; 2 in D min., Op. 44; 3 in D min., Op. 58; Adagio appas-

sionato, Op. 57; In Memoriam, Op. 65; Konzertstücke, Op. 84; Romanze, Op. 42; Serenade, Op. 75.

(M) *** Ph. 432 282-2 (3) [id.]. Salvatore Accardo, Leipzig GO, Kurt Masur.

This is an immensely valuable set of great distinction; it gathers together all Bruch's major works for violin and orchestra. Although no other piece quite matches the famous *G minor Concerto* in inventive concentration, the delightful *Scottish fantasia*, with its profusion of good tunes, comes near to doing so, and the first movement of the *Second Concerto* has two themes of soaring lyrical ardour. Even if the rest of the work has a lower level of inspiration, it is still richly enjoyable. The *Third Concerto* brings another striking lyrical idea in the first movement and has an endearing *Adagio* and a jolly finale. The engagingly insubstantial *Serenade*, a four-movement piece dating from the turn of the century, was originally intended to be a fourth violin concerto. Its nostalgic opening *Andante* is highly characteristic, then comes a balletic little march, a dreamy *Notturno* and a gay, Spanish-influenced finale, full of sparkling bravura. The two-movement *Konzertstück* dates from 1911 and is one of Bruch's last works. As in the case of the *Serenade*, Bruch had toyed with the idea of calling it a violin concerto, but he finally decided on *Konzertstück* since the piece has only two movements; the second, an *Adagio*, is really very touching. *In Memoriam* is finer still (Bruch himself thought highly of it); it has genuine depth and nobility. The *Adagio appassionato* and *Romanze* are strongly characterized pieces and their eloquence is striking in performances of this calibre. Throughout the set Accardo's playing is so persuasive in its restrained passion that even the less inspired moments bring pleasure, and there are many pages of music that show the composer nearing his finest form. When this set was first issued on LP in 1978, we thought it difficult to imagine it being surpassed for many years to come. This applies equally today – with the caveat that, because of the resonant Leipzig acoustics, the Philips engineers put their microphones rather too close to the soloist. With the sharpening of focus which comes with the CD remastering, his image is balanced very forwardly, almost out of the hall acoustic, and there is at times a degree of shrillness on his upper range. This is most noticeable on the first disc, containing the *G minor Concerto*, but the ear adjusts; throughout the rest of the collection one's pleasure is hardly diminished, for the orchestral recording is full and spacious.

Violin concerto No. 1 in G min., Op. 26.

(M) *** Sony/CBS Dig. MDK 44902; *40-44902* [id.]. Cho-Liang Lin, Chicago SO, Slatkin – MENDELSSOHN: *Concerto* *** (with Sandra Rivers (piano): SARASATE: *Introduction and Tarantella* ***; KREISLER: *Liebesfreud* ***).

(M) *** Decca 417 707-2 [id.]. Kyung Wha Chung, RPO, Kempe – SAINT-SAENS: *Havanaise*; TCHAIKOVSKY: *Concerto.* ***

(B) *** CfP Dig. CD-CFP 4566; *TC-CFP 4566* [Ang. CDB 62920]. Tasmin Little, Royal Liverpool PO, Handley – DVOŘÁK: *Concerto.* ***

(B) *** Pickwick Dig. PCD 829; *CIMPC 829* [id.]. Jaime Laredo, SCO – MENDELSSOHN: *Concerto.* ***

(M) *** EMI CDM7 69003-2 [id.]; *EG 769003-4.* Menuhin, Philh. O, Susskind – MENDELSSOHN: *Concerto.* ***

(M) **(*) Sony/CBS CD 45555 [MYK 37811]; *40-45555.* Stern, Phd. O, Ormandy – LALO: *Symphonie espagnole.* **(*)

(M) (***) EMI mono CDM7 69261-2 [id.]. David Oistrakh, LSO, Lovro von Matačić – BEETHOVEN: *Concerto.* **(*)

(B) **(*) EMI CDZ7 62519-2; *LZ 762519-4.* Menuhin, LSO, Boult – MENDELSSOHN: *Violin concerto.* **(*)

(M) **(*) Ph. 420 703-2. Grumiaux, New Philh. O, Wallberg – BRAHMS: *Concerto.* **(*)

(B) **(*) Sony MBK 44717 [id.]. Zukerman, LAPO, Mehta – LALO: *Symphonie espagnole.* **(*)

(BB) **(*) BMG/RCA VD 60479; *VK 60479* [60479-2-RV; *60479-4-RV*]. Ughi, LSO, Prêtre – BRAHMS: *Concerto.* **(*)

(M) (***) Ph. 426 639-2; *426 639-4.* Accardo, Leipzig GO, Masur – MENDELSSOHN: *Concerto.* ***

(B) ** DG Compact Classics 413 844-2 (2); *413 844-4* [id.]. Yong Uck Kim, Bamberg SO, Kamu – BEETHOVEN: *Romances* ***; BRAHMS: *Violin concerto* **((*) (CD only: DVOŘÁK: *Violin concerto* **(*)).

(BB) ** LaserLight Dig. 15 615 [id.]. Szenthelýi, Budapest PO, Sándor – MENDELSSOHN: *Concerto.* **

(BB) *(*) Naxos Dig. 8.550195 [id.]. Nishizaki, Slovak PO, Gunzenhauser – BRAHMS: *Concerto.* *

(BB) *(*) Pickwick PWK 1151. Ion Voicou, LSO, Frühbeck de Burgos – MENDELSSOHN: *Concerto.* *(*)

Sony, taking note of the competition, have now issued Cho-Liang Lin's radiantly beautiful 1986 account of the *G minor Concerto*, recoupled with the Mendelssohn, to make an outstanding mid-priced digital recommendation. There have been few accounts on record of Bruch's slow movement that begin to match the raptness of Lin. He is accompanied most sensitively by Slatkin and the Chicago orchestra, and this reading is totally compelling in its combination of passsion and purity, strength and dark, hushed intensity. The Kreisler and Sarasate bonuses, recorded three years earlier, are also presented with great flair. The recording is excellent.

The magic of Kyung Wha Chung, a spontaneously inspired violinist if ever there was one, comes over very beguilingly in her mid-priced Decca interpretation, while Kempe and the Royal Philharmonic give a sympathetic, if not always perfectly polished accompaniment, well caught in a glowing recording from the early 1970s which has responded well to its remastering. There may be more glossily perfect accounts of the *Concerto*, but Chung goes straight to the heart, finding mystery and fantasy as well as more extrovert qualities.

It was the Classics for Pleasure/Eminence label that promoted Nigel Kennedy's first concerto recording, and that enterprise is here followed up in the first recording by another highly talented young violinist, Tasmin Little, a generous and unique coupling of Bruch and Dvořák. The movement in the Bruch where Little's individuality comes out most clearly is the central *Adagio*, raptly done with a deceptive simplicity of phrasing, totally unselfconscious, that matches the purity of her sound. Her speeds in the outer movements are broader than those of such rivals as Lin. The finale may not have quite the thrusting excitement of Lin's in particular, but the clarity and precision of her playing are fair compensation, along with the fuller, more faithful sound. At full price this would be a first-rate recommendation: on CfP it is an outstanding bargain.

Jaime Laredo with consistently fresh and sweet tone gives a delightfully direct reading, warmly expressive but never for a moment self-indulgent. His is a beautiful, reflective account of the slow movement. The orchestral ensemble is particularly impressive, when no conductor is involved. With first-rate modern digital recording, this is a bargain, a highlight of the Pickwick budget-price catalogue.

Menuhin's performance has long held an honoured place in the catalogue. It was a work to which he made a particularly individual response, and he was in very good form when he made the disc. The performance has a fine spontaneity, the work's improvisatory quality very much part of the interpretation, and there is no doubting the poetry Menuhin finds in the slow movement or the sparkle in the finale. The bright, forward sound of the 1960 recording has transferred vividly to CD.

It is good to welcome back to the catalogue Stern's 1967-vintage recording with Ormandy. Although the balance is totally unrealistic, this is one of the great classic recordings of the work, gloriously warm-hearted and with a very involving account of the slow movement, which sustains the greatest possible intensity. The finale, too, has wonderful fire and spirit. Ormandy's accompaniment is first class and triumphs over the unrealistic balance and a less than refined orchestral image.

David Oistrakh's 1954 mono recording of this *Concerto* is rightly admired. His restraint brings a moving eloquence to the slow movement, especially its closing pages. The polished accompaniment matches the aristocratic feeling of the soloist, yet has plenty of impetus. Overall this makes a valuable corrective to more histrionic versions of this famous work and it shows the soloist at his finest. No apologies need be made for the excellently balanced recording.

Menuhin's second stereo recording of the Bruch *Concerto* was made in the early 1970s. While he is obviously on familiar ground, there is no sign of over-familiarity and the lovely slow movement is given a performance of great warmth and humanity. Boult accompanies admirably and the recording is obviously fuller and more modern than the earlier version with Susskind, even if the solo playing is technically less immaculate. On EMI's bargain Laser label, this coupling with Mendelssohn remains very competitive.

Grumiaux's version with Wallberg would not be counted a first choice; but as a coupling for an outstanding performance of the Brahms *Concerto* it offers a refreshingly different view, civilized, classical in its refinement, if slightly cool. Yet Grumiaux brings all his beauty of tone and expressive technique to this music-making, and he is well accompanied and recorded.

Zukerman's account of the *G minor Concerto* is splendidly eloquent, and the slow movement is played most beautifully. The late 1970s recording is also good and the balance convincing within a fairly resonant acoustic. On the whole the transfer is successful, and those seeking a coupling with Lalo might consider this at bargain price.

Those looking for a bargain coupling with the Brahms *Concerto* and very good (1982) digital recording might well choose Uto Ughi on RCA. His is a fresh, direct reading. It may not have the individuality of Lin or the extrovert ardour of Stern, but it is still a fine performance, and good value too.

Accardo's playing is very persuasive is its restrained eloquence. This is also outstanding in its way, and the slow movement generates considerable intensity; but the snag is the 1977 recording. The violin is forwardly balanced and, under pressure, the timbre catches the microphone and becomes edgy.

Miklós Szenthelýi's performance has an appealing lyrical ardour. His tone is full, and his account of the *Adagio* combines passionate feeling with tenderness, while the outer movements have plenty of eager momentum. There is certainly no lack of spontaneity here; although the forward balance, for both soloist and orchestra, brings an element of rawness to the string timbre, this is easily smoothed, and otherwise the digital sound is vivid, with plenty of ambience. Good value in the lowest price-range.

Yong Uck Kim's performance impresses by its purity of style and understated feeling. But such an approach is not entirely successful in this ripely romantic concerto which does not always respond to such delicacy of feeling. Unfortunately the orchestral response, though good, does not match the solo playing in finesse, but the recording is full and well balanced and the Compact Classics tape is well transferred. The digitally remastered pair of CDs also include a freshly enjoyable account of the Dvořák *Concerto*.

Takako Nishizaki plays the slow movement gently and sweetly, and the first movement goes quite well. But the finale lacks sparkle, and altogether this is not one of her recommendable couplings.

The Voicou/Frühbeck de Burgos performance (recorded by Decca in the mid-1960s) has some really fine moments. The opening sections of the first and second movements have expressive magic and the closing tutti of the latter brings great ardour, while the soloist often phrases with subtlety. The pity is that his timbre, as recorded, is somewhat febrile and (like the upper strings of the orchestra) made to sound wiry, and this spoils an otherwise impressive reading.

Kol Nidrei, Op. 47.

(M) *** Decca Dig. 425 020-2; *425 020-4* [id.]. Harrell, Philh. O, Ashkenazy – DVOŘÁK: *Cello concerto* **; TCHAIKOVSKY: *Rococo variations.* ***

(M) ** Mercury 432 001-2 [id.]. Starker, LSO, Dorati – DVOŘÁK: *Cello concerto*; TCHAIKOVSKY: *Rococo variations.* **

(B) ** DG 429 155-2; *429 155-4* [id.]. Fournier, LOP, Martinon – DVOŘÁK: *Cello concerto*; BLOCH: *Schelomo.* **(*)

Bruch's withdrawn, prayerful piece finds a natural response in Lynn Harrell, whose musical personality is often comparatively reticent; his account with Ashkenazy is both eloquent and atmospheric, and is certainly well recorded.

Although beginning rather solemnly, Starker's reading of Bruch's serene cantilena is very sensitive, without wearing its heart on its sleeve, and is accompanied most sympathetically. Indeed, Dorati opens and closes the piece with a striking feeling for the work's colour and atmosphere.

Fournier's performance, while not without feeling, is slightly lacking in romantic urgency. The recording is fully acceptable.

Scottish fantasia for violin and orchestra, Op. 46.

(M) *** Decca 425 035-2; *425 035-4* [id.]. Kyung Wha Chung, RPO, Kempe – BEETHOVEN: *Violin concerto.* **

(B) **(*) Pickwick IMPX 9031. Campoli, LPO, Boult – MENDELSSOHN: *Violin concerto.* **(*)

In the *Scottish fantasia*, Chung transcends the episodic nature of the writing to give the music a genuine depth and concentration, above all in the lovely slow movement. Kempe and the Royal Philharmonic, not always perfectly polished, provide a sympathetic accompaniment, well caught in a fine Decca analogue recording. The CD transfer is strikingly successful too, with the solo violin timbre sweet and perfectly focused.

Campoli made the recordings on this CD in 1958, when he was on peak form. His clean, sweet tone suits the ingenuous simplicity of Bruch's inspiration, and this is a delightful performance. Boult provides a characteristically accomplished account of the orchestral part and the (Decca) recording is vivid, though the CD transfer emphasizes the upper range and reveals some roughness in tuttis. Nevetheless this coupling affords much musical pleasure.

Bruckner, Anton (1824–96)

Symphonies Nos. 1–9 (original editions).

(M) ** Teldec/Warner Dig. 2292 46068-2 (10) [id.]. Frankfurt RSO, Inbal.

Eliahu Inbal's performances with the Frankfurt Radio Orchestra are obviously not a first choice since they commit to disc Bruckner's first thoughts rather than the finished works of art. The differences are most striking in the case of the 1874 version of No. 4, where the familiar scherzo is not to be found, and in the opening of the finale. There are, of course, major divergences in Nos. 3 and 8: Inbal gives us the 1873 edition of No. 3, the form in which it was first presented to Wagner. Inbal has a good feeling for Bruckner and there is no lack of atmosphere, but the set as a whole is variable. Nos. 5 and 6 do not come off well and, generally speaking, readers would be better advised to stick with rival versions, supplementing them for the sake of interest with Inbal's accounts of Nos. 1, 3, 4 and 8. The recordings are good though not top-drawer.

Symphonies Nos. 1–9.
(M) *** DG 429 648-2 (9) [id.]. BPO, Karajan.
(M) *** DG 429 079-2 (9) [id.]. BPO or Bav. RSO, Jochum.
(M) *** EMI CZS7 62935-2 (9) [Ang. CDZI 62935]. Dresden State O, Jochum.
(M) **(*) HM/BMG GD 60075 (10) [60075-2-RG]. Cologne RSO, Wand.
(M) ** BMG/RCA GD 69227 (10). Leipzig GO, Kurt Masur.

The reappearance of Karajan's magnificent cycle, long a yardstick by which others were measured – and at mid-price, too – must be warmly welcomed. No. 8, one of the peaks of the cycle, is his 1976 account, which is only marginally less magisterial than his recent Vienna performance. In No. 1, Karajan (like Günther Wand) opts for the 1891 edition, while Jochum gives us the Linz version of 1865–6. We have sung the praises of these recordings loud and long, and in their new format they are outstanding value.

Jochum's DG cycle was recorded between 1958 (No. 5) and 1967 (No. 2), all but four (Nos. 2, 3, 5 and 6) with the Berlin Philharmonic. It enjoys the advantage of accommodating one symphony per disc. No apology need be made for either the performances or the quality of the recorded sound, which wears its years lightly. Indeed one of the finest is the 1957 *Fifth.* Jochum brought a sense of mystery and atmosphere to Bruckner that was quite unique, and it more than compensates for the occasional freedom he permitted himself. His was the first overview of Bruckner on record – followed not long afterwards by Haitink on Philips – and he still has special claims as a guide in this terrain. He communicates a lofty inspiration to his players, and many of these readings can more than hold their own with later rivals.

Jochum's EMI set, made with the Staatskapelle Dresden between 1975 and 1980, has the advantage of more modern recorded sound (though readers will be surprised how well the 1957 stereo recording of the *Fifth Symphony* on DG actually sounds). Jochum's allegiance to the Novak editions remains unchanged and, apart from various odd details, so does his overall approach. His readings have a spirituality and nobility that remain rather special, notwithstanding the claims of his many distinguished rivals. Either the DG or the EMI set will give great satisfacton.

Günther Wand's more recent survey (1974–81) is with the Cologne Radio Symphony Orchestra. Wand is a dedicated Brucknerian who rarely falters in his majestic progress. His accounts of Nos. 5 and 6 do not match Jochum but elsewhere (in Nos. 2 and 8) he is perhaps to be preferred. The *Eighth* may be the least successful of the Jochum DG set, and the planners were wise to choose Wand's 1979 recording rather than his more recent and less convincing account. Except in No. 6, Wand is never less than perceptive and at times he and his fine orchestra achieve real inspiration.

Kurt Masur's survey comes from much the same period as Jochum's EMI series, and some – though by no means all – of the symphonies appeared on LP during the late 1970s. Generally speaking, it is what one might call a sound rather than an inspired cycle. Masur is a dedicated Brucknerian and the Leipzig Gewandhaus is a responsive body, but for those who (rightly) attach importance to continuity, it occupies ten as opposed to nine discs – like Wand's set with the Cologne Radio Orchestra.

Symphony No. 1 in C min.; (i) *Te Deum.*
(M) **(*) DG Dig. 435 068-2; *435 068-4* [id.]. Chicago SO, Barenboim; (i) with Jessye Norman, Minton, Rendall, Ramey, Chicago Symphony Ch.

It makes a generous coupling, having Barenboim's fine version of the *Te Deum* with its starry quartet of soloists and the magnificent Chicago Symphony Chorus as a fill-up for the *Symphony No. 1.* In both works he directs beautifully played, spontaneous-sounding performances that mould Brucknerian lines persuasively, but in the *Symphony* the dramatic tension is less keen, lacking something in concentration. The early digital recording is good but not ideally clear, with a brightness that needs a little taming.

Symphony No. 3 in D min.
(M) ** Sony MPK 45880. Cleveland O, George Szell.

Szell's way with Bruckner is reserved, almost severe. He opens atmospherically, but he does not indulge the listener in a gentle, moulded style. All the same, the reading has undoubted strength, and it is a pity that Szell uses the controversial 1890 edition, in which Bruckner was persuaded by Franz Schalk to cut large sections of the finale. This makes the piece much tauter, but many Brucknerians will resist the truncation. The orchestral playing is outstanding and the recording on CD is given a fairly wide dynamic range, in spite of the relatively close balance which does bring a degree of harshness.

Symphony No. 4 in E flat (Romantic).
(B) *** DG 427 200-2 [id.]. BPO, Jochum.

(B) *** Sony MYK 44871. Columbia SO, Walter.
(M) **(*) EMI Dig. CDD7 63895-2 [id.]; *ET 763895-4*. BPO, Tennstedt.
(M) **(*) EMI CDM7 69006-2 [id.]. BPO, Karajan.
(M) **(*) Sony SBK 47653 [id.]. Phd. O, Ormandy.
(M) **(*) EMI CDM7 69127-2 [id.]; *EG 769127-4*. Philh. O, Klemperer.
(BB) ** Naxos Dig. 8.550154 [id.]. Royal Flanders PO, Günther Neuhold.

Jochum's way with Bruckner is unique. So gentle is his hand that the opening of each movement or even the beginning of each theme emerges into the consciousness rather than starting normally. And when it is a matter of leading from one section to another over a difficult transition passage – as in the lead-in to the first-movement recapitulation – no one can match Jochum in his subtlety and persuasiveness. The purist may object that, in order to do this, Jochum reduces the speed far below what is marked, but Jochum is for the listener who wants above all to love Bruckner. The recording from the late 1960s still sounds vivid and firm.

Although not quite as impressive as his Bruckner *Ninth*, Bruno Walter's 1960 recording is transformed by its CD remastering, with textures clearer, strings full and brass sonorous. It is not quite as rich as some of the full-price competition, but it is still pretty impressive, and the superbly played 'hunting horn' scherzo is wonderfully vivid. Walter makes his recording orchestra sound remarkably European in style and timbre. The reading is characteristically spacious; the conductor's special feeling for Bruckner means that he can relax over long musical paragraphs and retain his control of the structure, while the playing has fine atmosphere and no want of mystery.

In Tennstedt's 1982 version the breadth of the recording is admirable, if with a degree of fierceness on fortissimos. This is a reading that combines concentration and a degree of ruggedness; plainness goes with pure beauty and natural strength in the first two movements. The scherzo is urgent, the finale resplendent. With one or two modifications, the Haas edition is used. Not a first choice, but nevertheless compelling.

Karajan's reading for EMI had undoubted electricity and combines simplicity and strength. The playing of the Berlin Philharmonic is very fine. The snag is the considerable resonance, which has led to a degree of harshness appearing in the tuttis with the added brilliance of the digital remastering, while pianissimos are relatively diffuse.

Eugene Ormandy has never been closely associated with Bruckner on record, yet this reading from 1967 has a warmth and power, a natural expressiveness, which are most persuasive. Made relatively soon after Bruno Walter's masterly reading, also for CBS, Ormandy's was inevitably overshadowed, yet at budget price this version makes a viable alternative recommendation, very well played with opulent Philadelphia string tone (very different from latterday recordings) and with glorious horns in the hunting motif of the Scherzo. There is some edge on high violins in the transfer, but the recording has plenty of body. The Nowak edition is used.

Klemperer's performance with the Philharmonia is for those primarily seeking architectural strength. The reading is magisterial and the finale has impressive weight and strength. Alongside Jochum's flexible account, Klemperer's view seems severe, even marmoreal. But there is no question concerning its power or the vividness of the remastered EMI recording, although there is a hint of fierceness on fortissimos.

Günther Neuhold uses the Nowak edition, and his is a wayward, if often powerful account. His basic tempi are slow – he begins very slowly – but his pacing is very volatile. The Royal Flanders orchestra produces a rich sonority with spectacular brass sounds, and they are obviously responsive. The digital recording has plenty of atmosphere, though the resonance means that the most expansive fortissimos are almost overwhelming. This could be regarded as an interesting and very free alternative reading; but Jochum, who is also inspirational in approach, brings more grip to the score.

Symphony No. 5 in B flat.

(M) **(*) Decca Dig. 425 008-2 (2) [id.]. Chicago SO, Solti – SCHOENBERG: *Variations.* **(*)
(M) **(*) EMI CDM7 63612-2; *EG 763612-4* [id.]. New Philh. O, Klemperer.
(M) *(**) Ph. 426 107-2. Concg. O, Jochum.

Solti's conducting undoubtedly gives off electric sparks and his precise control of this performance underlines dramatic contrasts, helped by the clarity and brilliance of the digital recording, with its extremely wide dynamic range, so striking on CD. The slow movement finds the necessary warmth with Solti in what, for him, may be called Elgarian mood; but it is the intensity and sharpness of profile that give the special character to this reading.

Klemperer's account is certainly expansive, though some may find it heavy-handed. Without doubt the conception is massive; this results in rich, powerful brass sonorities, with a cathedral-like breadth, but at times there is a suspicion of bombast, and this is heightened by the somewhat drier and sharper focus of the CD sound-picture. In the beautiful slow movement, where others are more lyrical, the second C major theme makes a stirring impact as presented by Klemperer; taking the reading overall, one has the impression that lyricism has been subordinated to architectural strength.

Jochum's Concertgebouw version was made at a concert in the Ottobeuren Abbey, West Germany, in 1964. The acoustic of the Philips recording is confined, with two-dimensional brass sonorities. The string timbre too is curiously dry and studio-ish for an ecclesiastical ambience. The performance undoubtedly has the electricity of live music-making, but most listeners will want a more expansive sound in this work.

Symphonies Nos. (i) *5 in B flat;* (ii) *7 in E.*
(B) *(*) Sony MY2K 45669 (2) [id.]. (i) Phd. O, Ormandy; (ii) Columbia SO, Walter.

An unfortunate and unnecessary coupling, as each symphony is complete on a single CD. Ormandy's *Fifth* with the Philadelphia Orchestra lacks atmosphere and mystery and the recording is two-dimensional, with little lustre to the strings. Walter is infinitely better recorded, but his reading of the *Seventh* suffers from the fault of concentrating on detail at the expense of structure. The outer movements bring many illuminating touches and the final climax of the first is imposingly built, but overall the tension is held loosely. In the *Adagio*, which is kept moving fairly convincingly, the climax is disappointing, made the more so by the absence of the famous cymbal clash, as Walter uses the original text. The 1963 recording has been opened up in its remastering for CD and sounds fuller and more spacious than the original LPs.

Symphony No. 6 in A.
(M) *** EMI CDM7 63351-2 [id.]; *EG 763351-4.* New Philh. O, Klemperer.

Klemperer's version of the *Sixth* was recorded in the Kingsway Hall in 1964. Starting with a spacious account of the first movement, grandly majestic, sharply architectural, he directs a characteristically strong and direct reading. It is disarmingly simple rather than expressive in the slow movement (faster than usual) but is always concentrated and strong, and the finale is particularly well held together. Splendid playing from the orchestra and clear, bright recording. Bruckner's massive climaxes are accommodated without strain and the brass is very telling. A little more warmth in the sound would have been ideal, but it is always clear and the brightness never harshens.

Symphony No. 7 in E.
(M) *** EMI CDM7 69923-2. BPO, Karajan.

Karajan's reading of No. 7 for EMI shows a superb feeling for the work's architecture, and the playing of the Berlin Philharmonic is gorgeous. The recording has striking resonance and amplitude, sounding well if not absolutely refined in its remastered format and making a good medium-price choice for this favourite Bruckner symphony.

Symphonies Nos. (i) *7 in E;* (ii) *8 in C min.*
(B) *(**) MCA Double-decker (2) [MCAD2-9825-A/B]. (i) Pittsburgh SO, Steinberg; (ii) Munich PO, Hans Knappertsbusch.

Both these vintage recordings offer strong, concentrated performances of late Bruckner in limited sound which irons out the big dynamic contrasts and leaves violin-tone rather thin and scrawny. Steinberg's plain, direct account of No. 7 gives a reminder of what a fine orchestra he had created in Pittsburgh and, though he misses subtler points of expression, this is a powerful reading that is well worth resurrecting in a bargain issue. Knappertsbusch's account of No. 8 with the Munich Philharmonic is unusually spacious, with a very slow Adagio for the third movement masterfully sustained but without the mystery of a great performance. The broad, bold reading of the finale makes it unusually rugged. The first movement of No. 8 is on the first disc with No. 7, leaving the second disc for the remaining three movements.

Symphony No. 8 in C min.
(M) *** EMI CMS7 63469-2 (2) [Ang. CDMB 63469]. BPO, Karajan – WAGNER: *Lohengrin; Parsifal: Preludes.* ***
(B) **(*) DG 431 163-2; *431 163-4.* BPO, Jochum.
(M) ** EMI CMS7 63835-2 (2) [Ang. CDMB 63835]. New Philh. O, Klemperer – HINDEMITH: *Nobilissima visione*: suite (**); WAGNER: *Die Walküre: Wotan's farewell.* **(*)

The transfer of Karajan's 1958 Berlin Philharmonic recording is amazingly successful. The EMI sound is wonderfully full and spacious, yet with excellent detail; the strings are gloriously rich and brass sonorities are thrilling. The performance has much in common with his later (full-price) versions for DG and has compelling power. The slow movement is very fine indeed, conveying dark and tragic feelings. This is very much worthwhile: as well as the advantage of economy, it offers outstanding performances of the *Preludes* to Acts I and III of both *Lohengrin* and *Parsifal*.

When Jochum's recording of Bruckner's *Eighth* was first issued on LP, we had some doubts concerning his somewhat wayward inspirational style. Jochum uses the Nowak Edition, which involves cuts in the slow movement and finale, and in addition he often presses the music on impulsively in both the outer movements and especially in his account of the *Adagio*, where the climax has great passion and thrust. One is undoubtedly caught up with this, and there is also some marvellously serene playing from the Berlin Philharmonic strings, with a noble contribution from the brass. The use of the Philharmonie instead of the Jesus-Christus Kirche for the 1964 recording brought a certain forceful and sometimes piercing brightness to the trumpets, and the recording needs to be reproduced at a high level for its breadth and fullness to be properly experienced; but there can be no doubting the skill of its remastering. The combination of the Nowak cuts and Jochum's accelerandos means that the overall playing time is just over 74 minutes, and the symphony fits on to a single bargain-priced CD – which is worth any Brucknerian's money.

Klemperer's version was impressively recorded in the Kingsway Hall in 1970, but the performance does little credit to his memory. It was one of his last records, and funereal tempi make it seem one of the longest. The performance also suffers from untidiness here and there and, although many details inspire respect and even moments of admiration, the set must regretfully be passed over.

Symphonies Nos. 8 in C min. (1890 version); *9 in D min.* (original version).
(B) **(*) EMI CZS7 67279-2 (2) [id.]. VPO, Carl Schuricht.

Carl Schuricht (1880–1967), a favourite in Vienna, made a number of fine recordings in the early days of LP, and it is welcome in this bargain box to have two compelling examples of his Bruckner conducting. His approach was freely romantic, rather in the manner of Furtwängler or of Eugen Jochum. Yet in both slow movements here, arguably the two greatest that Bruckner ever wrote, his flowing, less spacious manner binds the argument together in warmth of lyricism, rather than bringing out the spiritual depth, as Furtwängler and Jochum did. The rugged power of the allegros comes over splendidly and the early stereo recordings (1963 and 1961 respectively) are vividly atmospheric, if with some constriction in tuttis and an edge on high violins, brought in the CD transfer.

Symphony No. 9 in D min.
❀ (M) *** Sony MYK 44825 [id.]. Columbia SO, Bruno Walter.
(M) *** DG 429 904-2; *429 904-4* [id.]. BPO, Karajan.
(B) **(*) DG 429 514-2; *429 514-4* [id.]. BPO, Jochum.
(M) *(*) EMI CDM7 63916-2 [id.]; *EG 763916-4*. New Philh. O, Klemperer.

Bruno Walter's 1959 recording is a superb achievement. This was one of the most beautiful results of Walter's Indian summer in the CBS studio, and now the results are immeasurably enhanced, with a blend of rich, clear strings and splendidly sonorous brass. Walter's mellow, persuasive reading leads one on through the leisurely paragraphs so that the logic and coherence seem obvious where other performances can sound aimless. Perhaps the scherzo is not vigorous enough to provide the fullest contrast – though the sound here has ample bite – yet it exactly fits the overall conception. The final slow movement has a nobility which makes one glad that Bruckner never completed the intended finale. After this, anything would have been an anticlimax.

This DG Galleria reissue offers a glorious performance of Bruckner's last and uncompleted symphony, moulded in a way that is characteristic of Karajan and displaying a simple, direct nobility that is sometimes missing in this work. Here he seems to find it unnecessary to underline but, with glowing playing from the Berlin Philharmonic and spectacular recording, he gives the illusion of letting the music speak for itself. Yet no Bruckner interpreter has a clearer idea of the composer's architecture and, as one appreciates the subtle gradation towards the climax in the concluding slow movement, one knows how firmly Karajan's sights have been set on this goal all along. The differences between this superlative 1966 version and Karajan's later, full-price one, recorded with the same orchestra eight years later, are relatively small. The clue lies principally in the recording quality. Whereas the digital remastering of the mid-1960s version has brought a brighter, more boldly focused sound, the acoustics of the Jesus-Christus Kirche still provide a basically mellow ambience; the later (1977) recording balance is sharper and closer, to suggest that Karajan wanted to convey a tougher impression. Where the present, earlier version brings natural gravity and profound contemplation in greater measure, with manners a degree more affectionate, the later one concentrated on strength and impact. Even in a competitive field, this 1966 disc stands out at mid-price, to rank alongside Bruno Walter's noble 1959 version.

Jochum's reading has greater mystery than any other and the orchestral playing (at the individual level) reaches a degree of eloquence that disarms criticism. If at times Jochum tends to phrase too affectionately so that consequently the architecture does not emerge unscathed, he is still magnetic in everything he does. The 1966 recording sounds remarkably good and this issue is a genuine bargain, especially if treated as a supplement to Walter's version.

Klemperer's performance is slow and deliberate but far from unimpressive; it is more effectively held together than his *Eighth*, and the fine 1970 Kingsway Hall recording has transferred effectively to CD. Devotees of this conductor may feel this well worth pursuing, but for most collectors it will not seriously challenge the finest alternative versions.

CHAMBER MUSIC

String quintet in F.

(M) *** Decca 430 296-2; *430 296-4* [id.]. VPO Quintet with H. Weiss – SCHMIDT: *Piano quintet.* ***

Bruckner's beautiful *Quintet* dates from 1878, immediately after the revision of the *Third* and *Fourth Symphonies*. It is music of substance and depth and has not been better served on records since this account by the Vienna Philharmonic Quintet, recorded in the Sofiensaal in 1974. The Decca engineers were on top form and the quality is full and sweet.

VOCAL MUSIC

(i) *Masses Nos. 1 in D min.; 2 in E min.; 3 in F min.;* Motets: *Afferentur regi; Ave Maria; Christus factus est pro nobis; Ecce sacerdos magnus; Locus iste; Os justi medititur; Pange lingua; Tota pulchra es, Maria; Vexilla regis; Virga Jesse.* (ii) *Psalm 150; Te Deum.*

(M) **(*) DG 423 127-2 (4) [id.]. (i) Soloists, Bav. R. Ch. & SO; (ii) Soloists, Ch. of German Op., Berlin, BPO; Jochum.

Bruckner's choral music, like the symphonies, spans his musical career. Now Brucknerians have an excellent chance to get to know this unjustly neglected music, in highly sympathetic and dedicated performances from one of the composer's most understanding and eloquent advocates. With excellent soloists, including Maria Stader, Edith Mathis, Ernst Haefliger, Kim Borg and Karl Ridderbusch, the performances of the large-scale works have fine eloquence and admirable breadth and humanity and no lack of drama, although other accounts – of the *Te Deum*, for instance – have had more blazing intensity. But that is not Jochum's way, and the concentration of these performances is never in doubt, with much magic distilled, notably in the early *D minor Mass*, a noble and moving account. The original recordings tended to be distanced; in making the sound more present and clear, the CD remastering has lost some of the atmospheric fullness, although the effect is undoubtedly fresher and brighter, if not always absolutely clean on top. The beautiful motets are particularly successful.

Mass No. 2 in E min.

(M) *** Decca 430 365-2; *430 365-4* [id.]. Peter Hall, Schütz Ch. of London, Philip Jones Wind Ens., Norrington – R. STRAUSS: *Deutsche Motette* etc. ***

Roger Norrington's recording of Bruckner's fine *E minor Mass* was made for Argo in 1973, before the conductor turned his attention to original instruments. It was the finest of a number of distinguished analogue recordings of the work and now holds an equally strong position in the CD catalogue. It is sung with great feeling and perception and is recorded in a flattering acoustic which produces splendid depth and richness of sonority, the choir wonderfully underpinned by the brass. The rare Richard Strauss coupling increases the appeal of this Decca reissue.

Motets: *Afferentur regi virgines; Ecce sacerdos magnus; Inveni David; Os justi meditabitur sapientiam; Pange lingua gloriosa.*

(M) *** Decca 430 361-2; *430 361-4* [id.]. St John's College, Cambridge, Ch., ASMF, Guest – BEETHOVEN: *Mass in C.* ***

Although the motets are obviously not the main attraction here, they make a welcome coupling for the Beethoven *C major Mass*. The performances are of the highest quality and the recording is marvellously spacious. *Afferentur regi virgines*, *Inveni David* and the splendid *Ecce sacerdos magnus* all have trombones, the remaining two are unaccompanied.

Te Deum.

(M) * DG 429 980-2; *429 980-4* [id.]. Perry, Müller-Molinari, Winbergh, Malta, V. Singverein, VPO, Karajan – MOZART: *Coronation Mass.* **(*)

With Janet Perry a shrill soprano soloist, and with the big choral tuttis constricted in sound, the Bruckner *Te Deum* makes a disappointing fill-up for Karajan's latest version of the Brahms *Requiem*, though the majesty of his vision is never in doubt.

Burgon, Geoffrey (born 1941)

Requiem.
(M) *** Decca Dig. 430 064-2 [id.]. Jennifer Smith, Murray, Rolfe Johnson, LSO Ch., Woburn Singers, City of L. Sinfonia, Hickox.

Geoffrey Burgon is now in his early fifties and has a wide range of works to his credit. He is best known for his incidental music to John le Carré's *Tinker Tailor Soldier Spy* and Evelyn Waugh's *Brideshead Revisited* on television. In idiom his *Requiem* owes much to Benjamin Britten and perhaps early Messiaen. Much of the writing is static in feeling but highly atmospheric. The composer has shown considerable resource in his handling of texture and, though the melodic invention is unmemorable, the overall impression is quite powerful. The work enjoys committed advocacy from these artists and remarkably fine (1981) recorded quality. Although the aspirations of this music may not be matched by its substance, this score has the power to fascinate the listener and is well worth investigating. The 1981 Kingway Hall acoustic is used to frame sounds which are immensely vivid and atmospheric.

Busoni, Ferruccio (1866–1924)

Piano concerto, Op. 39.
(M) *** EMI CDM7 69850-2. John Ogdon, Alldis Ch., RPO, Revenaugh.

Busoni's marathon *Piano concerto* is unique, running to 70 minutes, roughly the same time as Beethoven's *Choral symphony*, with which it has another parallel in its choral finale. With such an ambitious design it must be expected that the music's inspiration will be uneven. Much of the most important material lies with the orchestra, the piano often tending to act more as a poetic obbligato to the work's main argument. John Ogdon's magisterial and powerful advocacy is matched by both his brilliance and his passionate commitment, making the music surge forward, and he is well supported by Daniel Revenaugh and the RPO, with an incandescent contribution from the John Alldis Choir. The EMI recording from the late 1960s sounds bold and immediate in its CD format. This issue makes an outstanding bargain at mid-price.

Doktor Faust (opera) complete.
(M) *** DG 427 413-2 (3) [id.]. Fischer-Dieskau, Kohn, Cochran, Hillebrecht, Bav. Op. Ch. & R. O, Leitner.

Busoni's epic *Doktor Faust* was left incomplete at the composer's death. Unfortunately, this recording is full of small but tiresome cuts; however, with a magnificent performance from Fischer-Dieskau in the name-part and superb, fierily intense conducting from Leitner, it fully conveys the work's wayward mastery, the magnetic quality which establishes it as Busoni's supreme masterpiece, even though it was finished by another hand. This performance, recorded in conjunction with a broadcast mounted by the European Broadcasting Union, fully substantiates the vision and originality of the opera. Being offbeat in its layout, the piece works more predictably on record than on stage. The cast is dominated by Fischer-Dieskau, here in 1969 at his very finest; and the only weak link among the others is Hildegard Hillebrecht as the Duchess of Parma. In the CD transfer the vividness of the sound is intensified. Though this is a mid-price set, the documentation is generous, with essays and synopsis and the complete libretto in English translation as well as the original German.

Butterworth, George (1885–1916)

The banks of green willow; 2 English idylls; A Shropshire lad (rhapsody).
(M) *** Decca 421 391-2; *421 391-4* [id.]. ASMF, Marriner – BRITTEN: *Variations on a theme of Frank Bridge*; WARLOCK: *Capriol suite.* ***

The banks of green willow; A Shropshire lad (rhapsody).
(M) **(*) EMI CDM7 69419-2; *EG 769419-4*. E. Sinfonia, Dilkes – MOERAN: *Symphony* etc. **(*)

Butterworth's *Shropshire lad* represents the English folksong school at its most captivatingly atmospheric, and the other works are in a similarly appealing pastoral vein. Marriner's performances with the Academy are stylishly beautiful, without the last degree of finesse but very fine indeed, with vivid, wide-ranging recording quality. The recording dates from 1976 and the CD remastering shows just how good it was.

The performances by Dilkes and the English Sinfonia are also sensitive if perhaps a shade too immediate for this atmospheric music; with fine, forward recording, this makes an attractive coupling for an excellent mid-priced version of the Moeran *Symphony*.

A Shropshire lad (song-cycle).
(M) *** Decca 430 368-2 [id.]. Benjamin Luxon, David Willison – VAUGHAN WILLIAMS: *Blake songs* etc. ***

Benjamin Luxon gives powerful, dramatic performances of songs which can take such treatment, not quite the miniatures they may sometimes seem. But while he can project his tone and the words with great power, his delicate half-tones are equally impressive, and he underlines the aptness of the music to words, often set by British composers but never more understandingly than here. Well-balanced recording and an admirable coupling.

Buxtehude, Diderik (*c.* 1637–1707)

Canzona in G, BuxWV 170. Chorales: *Ach Herr, mich armen Sünder, BuxWV 178; Erhalt uns, Herr, BuxWV 185; Es ist das Heil, BuxWV 186; Gott der Vater, BuxWV 190; Herr Jesu Christ, BuxWV 193; In dulci jubilo, BuxWV 197; Jesus Christus unser Heiland, BuxWV 198; Kommt her zu mir, BuxWV 201; Lobt Gott, ihr Christen allzugleich, BuxWV 202. Fugue in C (Gigue), BuxWV 174; Passacaglia in D min., BuxWV 161; Preludes & fugues: in D, BuxWV 139; in E, BuxWV 141; in F sharp, BuxWV 146.*
(M) *** Decca Dig. 430 262-2; *430 262-4.* Peter Hurford (organ of the Church of Our Lady of Sorrows, Toronto).

Turning to survey a wider Baroque field, Peter Hurford here alights on Buxtehude whom, the story goes, Bach walked 200 miles to visit. Hurford's recital subdivides into two sections, each opening with an impressively structured *Prelude and fugue* and the first ending with the *D minor Passacaglia*; the *E major Prelude and fugue* rounds off the second half. In between comes a series of agreeable and mellifluous chorales, obviously a model for Bach, but not imaginatively on a par with the latter's inspired embroidery. What catches the ear most strikingly here are the delightful *Canzona in G* and the captivating *'Gigue' Fugue in C*, uncannily like Bach's *Fugue à la gigue in G*, BWV 577. Hurford's registration here is agreeably apt, giving both pieces a piquant bite to offset the blander sounds he creates for the amiable chorale preludes. A distinguished recital, played with characteristic spontaneity on a splendid organ that is highly suitable for this repertoire.

Ciaconas: in C min.; E min., BuxWV 159/60; Passacaglia in D min., BuxWV 161; Preludes and fugues: in D; D min.; E; E min.; BuxWV 139/142; in F; F sharp min., BuxWV 145/146; in G min., BuxWV 149.
(M) *** DG 427 133-2. Helmut Walcha (organ of Church of SS Peter and Paul, Cappel, West Germany).

Buxtehude's organ music has a character of its own: his *Preludes and fugues* are more complex than Bach's straightforward two-part structures. Toccata-like passages and fugal sections alternate, and the writing here and in the *Ciaconas* is often exuberantly florid. Helmut Walcha has the full measure of this repertoire and these performances on the highly suitable Arp Schnitger organ in Cappel, Lower Saxony, are authoritative and spontaneous. The 1978 recording is excellent and the disc comprises generous measure: 73 minutes.

Byrd, William (1543–1623)

Ave verum corpus; Masses for 3, 4 & 5 voices.
(M) ** EMI Dig. CDM7 63441-2 [id.]. Hilliard Ens., Paul Hillier.

The Hilliard Ensemble, using one voice per part, present pure and detached readings. They were recorded in 1983 in St James's Church, Clerkenwell, London, but the effect is intimate rather than emphasizing the ecclesiastical acoustic. Arguably these were works which, when they were written in Elizabethen times, would have been sung in private recusant chapels rather than openly, but that situation itself argues a more involved response. The recording is full yet clear. The motet, *Ave verum corpus*, is presented in a rather similar style.

Mass for four voices; Mass for five voices.
(M) **(*) EMI Dig. CD-EMX 9505; *TC-EMX 2104* [Ang. CDM 62015]. St John's College, Cambridge, Ch., Guest.

There is no lack of enthusiasm in the performances of the Choir of St John's College, Cambridge, and they can at times be more persuasive than some professional groups. The *Five-part Mass* fares best and is given with genuine fervour. The balance of the recording is rather closer than is usual in this venue, though there is a reasonable glow round the singers. George Guest features rather more pronounced cadential ritardandi than are favoured in Early Music circles, but there is a sense of real music-making here.

Motets in paired settings: *Ave verum corpus* (with PHILIPS: *Ave verum corpus*); *Haec Dies* (with PALESTRINA: *Haec Dies*); *Iustorum animae* (with LASSUS: *Iustorum animae*); *Miserere mei* (with G. GABRIELI: *Miserere mei*); *O quam gloriosum* (with VICTORIA: *O quam gloriosum*); *Tu es Petrus* (with PALESTRINA: *Tu es Petrus*).
(B) *** CfP CD-CFP 4481; *TC-CFP 4481.* King's College, Cambridge, Ch., Sir David Willcocks.

This is an imaginatively devised programme of motets in which settings of Latin texts by Byrd are directly contrasted with settings of the same words by some of his greatest contemporaries. As was the intention, quite apart from adding variety to the programme, the juxtaposition makes one listen to the individual qualities of these polyphonic masters the more keenly, and to register their individuality. It is not just a question of contrasts between composers but of the greatness of each being underlined. The recording – one of the first made by EMI at King's College in the mid-1960s, emerges with remarkable freshness on CD, and the beauty of the singing is never in doubt.

Campra, André (1660–1744)

L'Europe galante (opera-ballet).

(M) *** HM/BMG GD 77059 (2) [77059-2-RG]. Yakar, Kweksilber, René Jacobs, La Petite Bande, Leonhardt – LULLY: *Bourgeois gentilhomme.* ***

The sheer tunefulness of *L'Europe galante* has ensured its appeal over the years. This record, the first with period instruments, dates from 1973 and gives us the complete entertainment – and very delightful it is. Like Couperin's *Les Nations*, though in a very different fashion, this enchanting divertissement attempts to portray various national characteristics: French, Spanish, Italian and Turkish. The three soloists all shine and the instrumentalists, directed by Leonhardt, are both expert and spirited. The recording too is well balanced and sounds very fresh on CD. The only snag is that this now comes in harness with Lully's *Le bourgeois gentilhomme*, which is musically much thinner. Full translations are provided.

Canteloube, Marie-Joseph (1879–1957)

(i) *Chants d'Auvergne:* Series 1 – 5 (complete); (ii) Appendix : Chants d'Auvergne et Quercy: *La Mère Antoine; Lorsque le meunier; Oh! Madelon, je dois partir; Reveillez-vous, belle endormie.* Chants paysans Bearn: *Rossignolet qui chants.* Chants du Languedoc: *La fille d'un paysan; Moi j'ai un homme; Mon père m'a plasée; O up!; Quand Marion va au moulin.* Chants des Pays Basques: *Allons, beau rossignole; Comment donc Savoir; Dans le tombeau; J'ai un douce amie; Le premier de tous les oiseaux.*

❀ (M) *** Van. 08.8002.72 [OVC 8001/2]. Netania Davrath, O, (i) Pierre de la Roche; (ii) Gershon Kingsley.

It was Netania Davrath who in 1963 and 1966 – a decade before the De los Angeles selection – pioneered a complete recording of Canteloube's delightful song-settings from the Auvergne region of France. Born in the Ukraine, she studied also in Dusseldorf and Israel and during this period folksong became second nature to her. For the Auvergne recordings she spent six months immersed in the dialect of the region, and her performances are more folksy in feeling than almost any others. While her voice has a lovely, sweet purity and freedom in the upper range, she also brings a special kind of colour and life to these infinitely varied settings. All 30 songs from the five series are included, plus an important appendix of 15 more, collected by Canteloube and admirably scored by Gershon Kingsley, very much in the seductive manner of the others. These include not only additional Auvergne items but songs from other areas too, including the Languedoc and the Basque country. They are quite as delightful as any of the more familiar *chants*, and some of them are unforgettable. One thinks of the nightingale singing in the gentle evening (from the Bearn region), the farmer's daughter getting married in the Languedoc, the delicious *O up!* ('Have you ever heard the cuckoo sing') from the same area, the Basque 'I have a sweetheart – she's neither short nor tall, but just in between' or, most memorable of all, *Reveillez vous, belle endormie*, a Quercy dialogue song of unattainable love (she's only fourteen years old!), which has a melody that could become as famous as *Baïlèro*, given proper exposure. This ends a programme of two hours of enchanting music which, when dipped into, will give endless pleasure. The accompaniments are freshly idiomatic, warm but not overupholstered, and the CD transfers retain all the sparkle and atmosphere of the original recordings, made in the agreeable ambience of Baumgartner Hall, Vienna.

Chants d'Auvergne: Series 1–5.

(M) *** EMI CDM7 63178-2 [id.]; *EG 763178-4.* Victoria de los Angeles, LOP, Jacquillat.

(M) **(*) Sony Dig. MDK 46509 [id.]. Frederica von Stade, RPO, Antonio de Almeida.

It is good to have Victoria de los Angeles' pioneering set of the *Chants d'Auvergne* (recorded in Paris in 1969 and 1974) now available at mid-price. There is some 70 minutes of music here, and the recording seems more vivid than ever.

Frederica von Stade is no less generous, offering 25 of the 30 songs. She has the advantage of 1982 digital sound, clean and immediate, if not as evocative as the EMI analogue recording for De los Angeles, or as vividly atmospheric as Jill Gomez's alternative (shorter) digital selection on EMI Eminence, also at offered mid-price. Fine as von Stade's singing is, she is stylistically and temperamentally not always as completely at home in Canteloube's lovely folksong settings as her colleagues. However, certain songs have more charm and obvious personal identification than others, and admirers of this artist will still find a good deal to enjoy here. Full texts and translations are provided.

Chants d'Auvergne: L'Aio dè rotso; L'Antouèno; Baïlèro; Brezairola; Malurous qu'o uno fenno; Passo pel prat; Pastourelle.
(M) *** BMG/RCA GD 87831 [7831-2-RG]. Anna Moffo, American SO, Stokowski – RACHMANINOV: *Vocalise*; VILLA-LOBOS: *Bachianas Brasileiras No. 5.* ***

Moffo gives radiant performances, helped by the sumptuous accompaniment which Stokowski provides. The result is sweet, seductively so. The recording, from the early 1960s, is opulent to match. With several favourites included, this makes an excellent shorter selection from Canteloube's famous settings, and the couplings are vintage Stokowski.

Chants d'Auvergne: L'Antouèno; Baïlèro; 3 Bourrées; Lou Boussu; Brezairola; Lou coucut; Chut, chut; La Delàssádo; Lo Fiolairé; Jou l'pount d'o Mirabel; Malurous qu'o uno fenno; Passo pel prat; Pastourelle; Postouro, sé tu m'aymo; Tè, l'co tè.
❀ (M) *** EMI Dig. CD-EMX 9500; *TC-EMX 2075* [Ang. CDM 62010]. Jill Gomez, Royal Liverpool PO, Handley.

Jill Gomez's selection of these increasingly popular songs, attractively presented on a mid-price label, makes for a memorably characterful record which, as well as bringing out the sensuous beauty of Canteloube's arrangements, keeps reminding us, in the echoes of rustic band music, of the genuine folk base. Jill Gomez's voice could not be more apt, for the natural radiance and the range of tone-colour go with a strong feeling for words and sentiment, helped by her intensive study of Provençal pronunciation. Vernon Handley's accompaniments have a directness as well as a warmth which supports the voice admirably, and the recording is outstandingly full and vivid. A splendid bargain and an ideal purchase for the collector who wants just a selection.

Casadesus, Robert (1899–1972)

Concerto for 3 pianos.
(M) ** Sony MPK 46730 [id.]. Robert, Gaby & Jean Casadesus, Colonne Concerts O, Dervaux – FRANCK: *Symphonic variations*; D'INDY: *Symphonie.* ***

Apart from his eminence as a pianist, Robert Casadesus was a prolific composer. His output includes no fewer than seven symphonies, a piano concerto dedicated to Mitropoulos, four string quartets, a sextet for piano and wind, four violin sonatas and, of course, a large amount of piano music: a set of 24 preludes, four sonatas and a set of eight studies. The *Concerto for three pianos*, Op. 65, was written in the mid-1960s for him, his wife and his son, Jean, who recorded it with the now defunct Orchestre des Concerts Colonne under Pierre Dervaux. There is a spiky first movement, an *Allegro marziale* which inhabits a no-man's land somewhere between Poulenc, Stravinsky and the Prokofiev of the piano concertos, and there is an atmospheric siciliano middle movement and a vigorous finale. It is an attractive piece whose ideals would harmonize with *Les Six*, but the thematic substance remains ultimately unmemorable. The recording is a bit on the dry side but not excessively so, and detail is very cleanly defined; the string-tone of the Colonne Orchestra is hardly sumptuous, though its placing (in the couplings) alongside the Philadelphia in its heyday under Ormandy is perhaps a little unfair.

Castelnuovo-Tedesco, Mario (1895–1968)

Guitar concerto in D, Op. 99.
(B) *** DG Compact Classics 413 156-2 (2). Yepes, LSO, Navarra – BACARISSE: *Concertino* **(*); FALLA: *Nights in the gardens of Spain* ***; RODRIGO: *Concertos.* **

Castelnuovo-Tedesco's *Guitar concerto* is a work of considerable charm, with its gently lyrical first movement and Andantino with a 'lollipop' tune that reminds one of something else. It is very well played by Yepes who is attentively accompanied by Navarro and the LSO, and the DG sound is fresh and vivid.

Violin concerto No. 2 (I Profeti).
(M) (**) BMG/RCA mono GD 87872; *GK 87872* [7872-2-RG; *7872-4-RG*]. Heifetz, LAPO, Wallenstein – FERGUSON: *Sonata No. 1* **; FRANÇAIX: *Trio* ***; K. KHACHATURIAN: *Sonata.* **

Castelnuovo-Tedesco is virtually a one-work composer, known almost exclusively for the *Guitar concerto*, first recorded by Segovia. His collaboration with Heifetz began in 1930 when the latter commissioned a work for violin and piano. The following year, Heifetz played the *First Violin concerto* of 1924 in New York, and in due course presented the *Second* (1931) at a concert conducted by Toscanini. It is subtitled *The Prophets* and, though free of programme associations, the composer sought to represent the fiery eloquence of the ancient prophets among the surrounding voices of the people and the voices of nature. It is a neo-romantic piece whose opening suggests Bloch or Vaughan Williams; but the idiom is predominantly sunny, though the thematic substance is thin. Heifetz plays with glorious, full-throated tone and the Los Angeles orchestra under Wallenstein give excellent support. The 1954 recording places the soloist far forward but is otherwise quite spacious and, despite some distortion in climaxes, is generally acceptable.

Castillon, Alexis de (1838–73)

(i) *Piano concerto in D, Op. 12; Esquisses symphoniques, Op. 15.*
(M) *** EMI CDM7 63943-2 [id.]. (i) Ciccolini; Monte Carlo PO, Prêtre.

Alexis de Castillon was intended by his parents for the army and he studied at the École Militaire de Saint-Cyr. He was recalled to service in the Franco-Prussian war of 1870, which undermined his health (he died when he was only 34). He found his way to music relatively late; in 1868 when he was thirty Duparc introduced him to César Franck and at the première of his *Piano concerto* in 1872 the soloist was Saint-Saëns. In his excellent book, *French Music from the Death of Berlioz*, Martin Cooper speaks of Castillon as 'still an amateur when he died, but an amateur of the most fertile and promising with ideals which might have won him a place beside the greatest of Franck's disciples had he lived'. The *Concerto* is much indebted to Schumann and Beethoven, influences which are by no means fully assimilated even in the *Esquisses symphoniques*, written not long before his death. The ideas have grace and facility, and there is an elegance and charm about some of the piano writing that offset the occasional infelicitous orchestral tutti. Aldo Ciccolini plays with virtuosity and much poetic feeling – though he is perhaps rather forwardly balanced – and Georges Prêtre gets good results from the Monte Carlo orchestra. Neither piece has the effortless inventive flow and polish of Saint-Saëns, but they are well worth investigating.

Catalani, Alfredo (1854–93)

La Wally (opera): complete.
(M) *** Decca 425 417-2 (2) [id.]. Tebaldi, Del Monaco, Diaz, Cappuccilli, Marimpietri, Turin Lyric Ch., Monte Carlo Op. O, Fausto Cleva.

This unashamed piece of hokum was much loved by Toscanini, who named his children after characters in it. The title-role prompts Renata Tebaldi to give one of her most tenderly affecting performances on record, a glorious example of her singing late in her career. Her poise and control of line in the celebrated aria, *Ebben? Ne andro lontana*, provide a model for any generation. The work's mixture of sweetness and melodrama has its attractions despite the absurdity of the story. The last Act leads to a concluding love-duet, set in the Swiss mountains, when the warbling of hero and heroine is curtailed by an avalanche. The hero is swept away, and the heroine distractedly throws herself after him. Tebaldi is well matched by a strong cast. Mario del Monaco begins coarsely, but the heroic power and intensity of his singing are formidable, and it is good to have the young Cappuccilli in the baritone role of Gellner. The sound in this late-1960s recording is superbly focused and vividly real, a fine example of Decca recording at a vintage period, with only a touch of over-brightness in the CD transfer. On two discs only (two Acts per disc) with libretto and translation, it will not easily be displaced.

Cererols, Joan (1618–76)

Missa de batalla; Missa de gloria.
(M) ** HM/BMG GD 77057 [77057-2-RG]. Escolania & Capella de Música Montserrat, Ars Musicae de Barcelona (Romà Escales), Ireneu Segarra.

Joan Cererols was one of the finest composers of the Catalan School during the Baroque era, but in more recent times his music came into its own only in the 1930s, when Pujol embarked on his complete edition, and began to attract the attention of record companies in the 1960s and 1970s. These recordings from the celebrated Escolania de Montserrat, where Cererols himself served, come from 1977; the *Missa de batalla* is the less successful, the sound being reverberant and opaque, despite the (too close) multi-mike techniques, and wanting in front-to-back perspective. There is little depth but greater transparency in the more interesting *Missa de gloria*. The collection of shawms, crumhorns and trombones make a colourful sound which deserves more skilful engineering. Even granted the interest of the repertoire and the modest price, this is short measure at 43 minutes.

Chabrier, Emmanuel (1841–94)

Bourrée fantasque; España (rhapsody); *Gwendoline: Overture. Marche joyeuse; Le Roi malgré lui: Danse slave; Fête polonaise. Suite pastorale.*
(M) *** Mercury 434 303-2 [id.]. Detroit SO, Paray – ROUSSEL: *Suite.* **(*)

The return of this finely played and idiomatically conducted collection of Chabrier's best orchestral pieces has been eagerly awaited by Mercury aficionados, and it does not disappoint. The CD transfer has refined the (basically) 1960 sound-picture and made it seem more natural, without loss of fullness. The bass resonance, which was a characteristic of the hall at Cass Technical High School, is better focused here than it was on LP. It brought a slightly more forward balance than would have been ideal but is most effective in the melodrama of the full-blooded Detroit performance of the *Gwendoline Overture*. Paray's whimsically relaxed and sparkling account of *España* gives great pleasure and his rubato in the *Fête polonaise* is equally winning. In both these pieces the remastering is fresh and clean, and there is only a hint of muddiness in the finale of the *Suite pastorale*. This is a wholly delightful account, given playing that is at once warm and polished, neat and perfectly in scale, with the orchestra beautifully balanced. The third movement, *Sous bois*, is rather fast, but the finish of the phrasing makes the effect convincing. The *Marche joyeuse* was recorded in Detroit's Old Orchestral Hall a year before the rest of the programme. The *Bourrée fantasque* and the Roussel *Suite* have been added as a bonus; they were made earlier, in the Ford Auditorium in 1957. The eagle ear will detect the acoustic differences.

España (rhapsody).
(M) **(*) EMI Dig. CDM7 63572-2 [id.]; *EG 763572-4*. Phd. O, Muti – FALLA: *Three-cornered hat*; RAVEL: *Rapsodie espagnole*. **(*)

Muti's manner is brisk but lilting in Chabrier's dance rhythms, an apt makeweight for two other works inspired by the Spanish sun. The brilliant (1980) digital recording has a touch of glare, but is one of the best from this source. However, with only 44 minutes of music, this is not remarkable value, even at mid-price.

Bourrée fantasque; Impromptu; 5 morceaux pour piano; 10 Pièces pittoresques; (i) *3 Valses romantiques.*
(M) (*) Sony MPK 46729 [id.]. Jean Casadesus; (i) Robert & Gaby Casadesus.

Chabrier's music for the piano, while not extensive, is of high quality. The *Bourrée fantasque* was his last work for the medium and, though he planned to orchestrate it, he never lived to do so; the familiar version we know is by Felix Mottl. Chabrier himself scored four of the *Pièces pittoresques* to form the charming *Suite pastorale*, though there is not a great deal of charm about Jean Casadesus's unaffectionate playing. He tosses off the *Bourrée fantasque* with more virtuosity than sparkle. But, to be fair, the recording is highly unflattering; it was made in a horribly dry New York studio in the mid-1960s, and the piano sounds brittle and two-dimensional. Casadesus *père et mère* are similarly ill-served in the *Trois Valses romantiques*. This is repertoire that would ideally suit artists like Rogé and Collard. This disc, however, is a real disappointment and conveys all too little of this music's charm.

Mélodies: *L'Ile heureuse; Villanelle des petites canards.*
(M) (**) Sony MPK 47684 [id.]. Piere Bernac, Poulenc – POULENC; SATIE: *Piano music.*

The two mélodies were recorded in 1950 and come off well. Bernac was a singer of enormous intelligence and imagination, but these songs cannot rescue the rest of this ungainly recital.

Charpentier, Gustave (1860–1956)

Louise (opera): complete.
(M) *** Sony S3K 46429 (3) [id.]. Cotrubas, Berbié, Domingo, Sénéchal, Bacquier, Amb. Op. Ch., New Philh. O, Prêtre.

Even more than Mascagni and Leoncavallo, Gustave Charpentier is a one-work composer, and one might be forgiven for thinking that that work, the opera *Louise*, is a one-aria opera. No other melody in the piece may quite match the soaring lyricism of the heroine's *Depuis le jour*, but this fine, atmospheric recording, the first in stereo, certainly explains why *Louise* has long been a favourite opera in Paris. It cocoons the listener in the atmosphere of Montmartre in the 1890s, with Bohemians more obviously proletarian than Puccini's, a whole factory of seamstresses and an assorted range of ragmen, junkmen, pea-sellers and the like making up a highly individual cast-list. Only four characters actually matter in a plot that remains essentially simple, even though the music (not counting intervals) lasts close on three hours. Louise is torn between loyalty to her parents and her love for the Bohemian, Julien. The opera starts with a love-duet and from there meanders along happily, enlivened mainly by the superb crowd scenes. One of them, normally omitted but included here, proves as fine as any, with Louise's fellow seamstresses in their workhouse (cue for sewing-machines in the percussion department) teasing her for being in love, much as Carmen is teased in Bizet's quintet. The love-duets too are enchanting and, although the confrontations with the boring parents are far less appealing, the atmosphere carries one over. Ileana Cotrubas makes a delightful heroine, not always flawless technically but charmingly girlish. Placido Domingo is a relatively heavyweight Julien and Jane Berbié and Gabriel Bacquier are excellent as the parents. Under Georges Prêtre, far warmer than usual on record, the ensemble is rich and clear, with refined recording every bit as atmospheric as one could want. A set which splendidly fills an obvious gap in the catalogue.

Charpentier, Marc-Antoine
(1634–1704)

Élévation; In obitum augustissimae nec non piissimae gallorum Reginae lamentum; Luctus de morte augustissimae Mariae Theresiae Reginae Galliae.
(M) *** Erato/Warner Dig. 2292 45339-2 [id.]. Degelin, Verdoodt, Smolders, Crook, Vandersteene, Widmer, Namur Chamber Ch., Musica Polyphonica, Devos.

The music here shows Charpentier at his most inspired, and this CD could well provide an introduction to the composer for many collectors. All three works lament the death in 1683 of Queen Maria Teresa, wife of Louis XIV of France since 1660. There is no evidence of their being performed in the composer's lifetime, but clearly the event moved Charpentier deeply, and each reflects the paradox of the Chrisian faith in contrasting grief with joy and hope in the life hereafter. *In obitum augustissimae* opens with Zeger Vandersteene as the Messenger bringing the news to the people; then Faith (Bernadette Degelin), Hope (Diana Verdoodt) and Charity (Marina Smolders) pay homage to the Queen's virtues; finally Kurt Widmer as the Angel extols the dramatic and joyous message of Salvation. *Élévation*, by no means as short as its title, is a motet in the form of a metaphorical duologue between Christ and Hunger, with obvious allusions to the Eucharist; while *Luctus de morte augustissimae* is another imaginatively expressive dialogue in which three male soloists, counter-tenor, tenor and bass, sing individually and together about the Queen's character and majesty in a mourning supplication of considerable intensity. The performance here could hardly be bettered, bringing out all the music's drama, joy and depth of feeling. The recording, made in a spacious acoustic, is also first class in every way. Very highly recommended.

(i) *Messe de minuit pour Noël (Midnight Mass for Christmas Eve);* (ii) *Te Deum.*
(M) ** EMI CDM7 63135-2. (i) Cantelo, Gelmar, Partridge, Bowman, Keyte, King's College Ch., ECO, Willcocks; (ii) Lott, Harrhy, Brett, Partridge, Roberts, King's College Ch., ASMF, Ledger.

There is a kinship between Charpentier's lovely *Christmas Mass* and Czech settings of the Mass that incorporate folk material; and the combination of verse anthems and carol-like pieces is attractive, even the *Kyrie* having a jolly quality about it. The King's performance is warm and musical, but there isn't much Gallic flavour. The organist, Andrew Davis, intelligently uses realizations of the organ interludes – which the composer directs shall be based on the carol themes – by Nicolas Le Bègue. The recording comes from the late 1960s and certainly now has more bite than it did; but reservations remain about the basic style of the singing. The coupling is the best-known of the *Te Deum* settings, and this time the King's performance has a vitality and boldness to match the music and catches also its *douceur* and freshness. The recording, made a decade later than the coupling, is also very successful and has been transferred well to CD.

Te Deum.
(M) *(*) Sony SBK 46344 [id.]. Beverley, K. Smith, Griffett, D. Thomas, Collegiate Church Ch., St Mary in Warwick, Malgoire – MOZART: *Requiem.* *(*)

The Sony version of the Charpentier *Te Deum* comes from the late 1970s and is, to be frank, a rather lacklustre affair. There is some vulnerable ensemble and some less-than-distinguished choral singing. The recording is acceptable rather than refined.

Chausson, Ernest (1855–99)

Poème (for violin and orchestra), *Op. 25.*
(M) *** Ph. Dig. 432 513-2. Kremer, LSO, Chailly (with *Concert* ***).

Kremer's poetic account of Chausson's *Poème* is part of a highly recommendable concert of French concertante works for violin and orchestra.

Chanson perpétuelle, Op. 37.
❀ (M) *** Decca 425 948-2 [id.]. Dame Janet Baket, Melos Ens. (with *French song recital* *** ❀).

Dame Janet Baker's magical performance of Chausson's setting of the Charles Cros poem – a declaration of passion to a departed lover, with the words inspiring continuous music – is part of a collection of French songs of the greatest distinction. It was originally issued on Oiseau-Lyre in 1967, recorded with the combination of atmosphere and presence for which that label was famous.

Poème de l'amour et de la mer.
(M) (***) EMI CMS7 63549-2 (3) [Ang. CDMC 63549]. Victoria de los Angeles, Lamoureux O, Jacquillat – MASSENET: *Manon* (*(**)).

Victoria de los Angeles, the most seductive Manon on record, is in just as glorious voice for Chausson's sensuous cantata, a generous fill-up on EMI's mid-price set of the opera.

Le roi Arthus (opera): complete.
(M) *** Erato/Warner Dig. 2292 45407 (3) [id.].

Zylis-Gara, Quilico, Winbergh, Massis, Fr. R. Ch. & New PO, Jordan.

This first ever recording of *Le roi Arthus* reveals it to be a powerful piece, full of overt Wagnerian echoes; it places Arthur, Guinevere and Lancelot in a sequence of situations closely akin to those of King Mark, Isolde and Tristan. The musical parallels are often bare-faced and the result could easily have emerged as just a big Wagnerian pastiche, but the energy and exuberant lyricism of the piece give it a positive life of its own. The vigour and panache of the opening suggest *Tannhäuser* and *Walküre* rather than *Tristan*, while the forthright side of *Parsifal* lies behind the noble music for Arthur himself, a more virile figure than King Mark. The love-duets in Tristan-style, of which there are several, have a way of growing ever more lusciously lyrical to bring them close to Massenet and Puccini. Armin Jordan directs a warmly committed performance which brings out the full stature of the work, far more than just a radio recording translated. Gino Quilico in the name-part sings magnificently, and the freshness and freedom of Gösta Winbergh's tone are very apt for Lancelot's music. Teresa Zylis-Gara, though not always ideally sweet-toned, is an appealing Guinevere; the recorded sound is generally full and well balanced. This makes a valuable addition to the catalogue and is guaranteed to delight many more than specialists in French opera.

Chávez, Carlos (1899–1978)

Symphonies Nos. 1 (Sinfonia de Antigona); 2 (Sinfonia India); 4 (Sinfonia romantica).

(M) **(*) Ph. 422 305-2 [id.]. NY Stadium O, composer.

The Philips performances carry the authority of the composer's own direction and include the best-known, *Sinfonia India*, which is based on true Indian melodies. It has a savage, primitive character that is very attractive. The recording is detailed and bright, if not absolutely sharp in focus and somewhat wanting in real depth and weight. It derives from the Everest catalogue and dates from the early days of stereo (1958).

Cherubini, Luigi (1760–1842)

String quartets Nos 1–6.

(M) *** DG 429 185-2 (3). Melos Qt.

Cherubini's *Quartets* are new to the CD catalogue and here have the advantage of authentic performing texts. No. 1 was composed when Cherubini was already in his fifties; the last four were written in the 1830s, when he was advanced in years. *No. 2 in C* is a reworking of the *Symphony in D*, though he composed a fresh slow movement. Cherubini's melodic inspiration is often both distinguished and distinctive, although there are times when it falls short of true memorability; but a fine musical intelligence and polished craftsmanship are always in evidence. The Melos Quartet play these works with real commitment and authority, while the remastered recorded sound is well balanced and clear.

(i) *Coronation Mass for King Charles X; Marche religieuse.* (ii) *Requiem in C min.;* (iii) *Requiem in D min. for male voices;* (iv) *Solemn mass in G for the Coronation of Louis XVIII.*

(M) *** EMI Dig./Analogue CMS7 63161-2 (4). (i) Philh. Ch. & O; (ii) Amb. S., Philh. O; (iii) Amb. S., New Philh. O; (iv) LPO Ch., LPO; Muti.

Three of these records are digital, the *D minor Requiem* (recorded in 1975) is analogue. They come in a handsome slip-case and, at mid-price, should bring this fine repertoire to a wider audience. Three of the four works are currently still available separately at full price, although they may disappear during the lifetime of this book. The *C minor Requiem*, the best known, was called by Berlioz 'the greatest of the greatest of his [Cherubini's] work', and he went on to claim that 'no other production of this great master can bear any comparison with it for abundance of ideas, fullness of form and sustained sublimity of style'. Muti directs a tough, incisive reading, underlining the drama, to remind one that this was a work also recorded by Toscanini some three decades earlier. Muti is well served both by his orchestra and by the relatively small professional choir; and the full, clear recording is most satisfying.

Requiem.

(M) (**(*)) BMG/RCA mono GD 60272; *GK 60272* (2) [60272-RG-2; *60272-RG-4*]. Marshall, Merriman, Conley, Hines, Robert Shaw Ch., NBC SO, Toscanini – BEETHOVEN: *Missa solemnis.* (**(*))

Toscanini, like his latterday disciple, Riccardo Muti, was an admirer of Cherubini's choral music, and though the start of this live performance of 1950 lacks the full Toscanini electricity, the Shaw Chorale, superbly disciplined, quickly responds to the maestro, to produce searingly incisive singing in such movements as the *Dies irae.* It makes a fair coupling for Toscanini's keenly dramatic account of Beethoven's *Missa solemnis*; but it would have been better to have had them separated, as could easily have been arranged. Characteristically dry recording.

OPERA

Medea (complete).

(M) ** EMI CMS7 63625-2 (2) [Ang. CDMB 63625]. Callas, Scotto, Pirazzini, Picchi, La Scala Ch. & O, Serafin – BEETHOVEN: *Ah! perfido*. **

Callas's 1957 studio recording of *Medea* may not bring out the full expressiveness of her historic reading of a long-neglected opera – live recordings reveal it better – but it is still a magnificent example of the fire-eating Callas. She completely outshines any rival. A cut text is used and Italian instead of the original French, with Serafin less imaginative than he usually was; but, with a cast more than competent – including the young Renata Scotto – it is an enjoyable set. Callas's recording of the Beethoven scena, *Ah! perfido*, makes a powerful fill-up, even though in this late recording (1963/4) vocal flaws emerge the more.

Chopin, Frédéric (1810–49)

CONCERTANTE AND ORCHESTRAL MUSIC

Chopiniana (ballet, arr. Glazunov).

(BB) ** Naxos Dig. 8.550324/5 [id.]. Slovak RSO (Bratislava), Lenárd – TCHAIKOVSKY: *Nutcracker*. **

The presentation and titling of the Naxos CDs (though not the documentation inside) suggest that *Chopiniana* is the same as *Les Sylphides*, which it is not. It opens robustly rather than evocatively, with the *Polonaise in A major*, and closes with the *Tarantella*, Op. 43. Glazunov's scoring for the most part has bright primary colours, effective in context, but the moonlit atmosphere of Roy Douglas's magical arrangement is only sporadic. This is not the fault of the excellent Slovak playing, which is bright and lively and vividly recorded. But this work fails to convince the listener that orchestral transcriptions of Chopin's piano music add anything new, whereas the Douglas *Les Sylphides* has quite the opposite effect.

Piano concertos Nos. 1 in E min., Op. 11; 2 in F min., Op. 21; Andante spianato & grand polonaise in E flat, Op. 22; Grand fantasy on Polish airs, Op. 14; Rondo à la Krakowiak, Op. 14; Variations on Mozart's 'Là ci darem la mano', Op. 2.

(B) VoxBox ** (2) [CDX 5002]. Abbey Simon, Hamburg SO, Beissel.

(i) *Piano concertos Nos. 1–2; Andante spianato & Grande polonaise brillante in E flat, Op. 22; Variations on Mozart's 'Là ci darem la mano', Op. 2. Berceuse in F sharp min., Op. 49; Fantaisie in F min., Op. 49; Impromptus Nos. 1–3; Fantaisie-impromptu, Op. 66.*

(B) ** Turnabout 0020 (2). Abbey Simon, (i) with Hamburg SO, Herbert Beissel.

Abbey Simon is a much-respected player who was better known to BBC audiences during the 1960s than he is now. He offers both concertos and Chopin's other music for piano and orchestra on two bargain discs. Vox are somewhat reticent about the date of the performances, but the analogue sound is perfectly decent; though the piano is a bit forwardly placed, the relationship between piano and orchestra is good and there is reasonable space round the aural image. The performances are enjoyable: Abbey Simon is often sensitive and poetic, though he does not project a very charismatic musical personality, and the orchestral playing is supportive. Not a first choice, but these performers are free from idiosyncratic mannerisms and prove sounder guides in this repertoire than some more celebrated artists.

The Turnabout Double offers an alternative selection. The *Berceuse* has an agreeable simplicity, but the *Fantaisie in F minor* and the *Impromptus*, although well played, have no special individuality. The transfers are very well managed and the recording of both piano and orchestra is realistic. Regrettably, no documentary information is provided except the titles of the works played.

Piano concertos Nos. (i) *1 in E min., Op. 11;* (ii) *2 in F min., Op. 21.*

(BB) *** Naxos Dig. 8.550123 [id.]. István Székely, Budapest SO, Gyula Németh.

(B) *** DG 429 515-2; *429 515-4* [id.]. Tamás Vásáry, BPO, Semkow or Kulka.

(M) ** Sony SBK 46336; *40-46336* [id.]. (i) Gilels, Phd. O, Ormandy; (ii) Watts, NYPO, Schippers.

(B) ** Hung. White Label HRC 084 [id.]. Sándor Falvai, Budapest PO, András Kórodi.

István Székely is particularly impressive in the *E minor Concerto*, but in both works he finds atmosphere and poetry in slow movements and an engaging dance spirit for the finales, with rhythms given plenty of character. Németh accompanies sympathetically, building the uncut opening ritornelli impressively, and the Budapest strings caress Chopin's lyrical melodies affectingly; the orchestral contribution here is quite refined. The recording is resonantly full in the Hungarian manner, not absolutely clear on detail; but the piano image is bold and realistic, and the brilliance of the pianist's articulation is crisply caught. A splendid bargain in every sense of the word.

Vásáry's approach is much more self-effacing: his gentle poetry is in clear contrast with the opulent orchestral sound (especially in No. 1, where the recording is more resonantly expansive than in No. 2). Yet soloist and orchestra match their styles perfectly in both slow movements, which are played most beautifully, and the finales have no lack of character and sparkle. In their way, these performances will give considerable pleasure and, with recording that retains its depth and bloom, this makes a fine bargain coupling.

Gilels's account of the *E minor Concerto* is one of the most thoughtful and dramatic currently available. He does not match the youthful fire of Pollini or Zimerman, but the lambent quality and the sensitivity of his playing, with every phrase breathing naturally, make the most poetic impression. Ormandy gives good support and the recording seems fuller and more pleasing in its CD format. However, André Watts's version of the *F minor Concerto*, although dreamily persuasive in the *Larghetto* and with plenty of life in the finale, is less distinctive overall, and this coupling cannot be recommended in preference to Székely or Vásáry, both of whom are even more competitively priced.

The Hungaroton performances are highly musical and pleasing, and the sound is smooth; but overall the impression is rather subdued and lacks a feeling of projection.

Piano concerto No. 1.
(BB) **(*) Naxos Dig. 8.550292 [id.]. Székely, Budapest SO, Németh – LISZT: *Concerto No. 1.* **(*)
(M) (**) EMI mono CDH7 63497-2 [id.]. Lipatti, Zurich Tonhalle O, Ackermann – GRIEG: *Piano concerto.*(***)

(i) *Piano concerto No. 1. Andante spianato et Grande polonaise brillante, Op. 22; Waltz No. 1 in E flat (Grande valse brillante), Op. 18.*
(M) *** DG 419 054-2; *419 054-4* [id.]. Krystian Zimerman, (i) Concg. O, Kondrashin.

(i; ii) *Piano concerto No. 1 in E min., Op. 11* (only first movement on cassette); (iii) *Ballade No. 1 in G min., Op. 23; Études: in E, Op. 10/3; in A min. (Winter wind), Op. 25/11;* (iv) *Fantaisie-impromptu, Op. 66;* (iii) *Mazurka in A min., Op. 68/2; Nocturnes: in E flat, Op. 9/2; in F sharp, Op. 15/2;* (v) *Polonaises: in A (Military), Op. 40/1;* (i) *in A flat, Op. 53;* (vi) *Preludes: in A; in D flat (Raindrop), Op. 28/7 & 15;* (i) *Sonata No. 2, Op. 35: Funeral march only;* (iii) *Waltzes: in E flat (Grande valse brillante), Op. 18; in D flat (Minute); in C sharp min., Op. 64/1–2.*
(B) **(*) DG Compact Classics 413 146-2 (2); ** *413 146-4* [id.]. (i) Argerich; (ii) LSO, Abbado; (iii) Vásáry; (iv) Szidon; (v) Cherkassky; (vi) Eschenbach.

(i) *Piano concerto No. 1. Ballade No. 1, Op. 23; Nocturnes Nos. 4 & 5, Op. 15/1–2.*
(M) *** EMI CDM7 69004-2 [id.]; *EG 769004-4.* Pollini, (i) Philh. O, Kletzki.

(i) *Piano concerto No. 1. Ballade No. 2 in F, Op. 38; Scherzo No. 4 in E, Op. 54.*
(M) *** DG Analogue/Dig. 431 580-2; *431 580-4.* Krystian Zimerman, (i) with Concg. O, Kondrashin.

(i) *Piano concerto No. 1 in E min.;* (ii) *Piano sonata No. 2 (Funeral march);* (iii) *Waltzes Nos. 1 in E flat (Grande valse brillante), Op. 18/1; 6 in D flat, Op. 64/1.*
(M) *(*) Erato/Warner 2292 45570-2. (i) Pires, Monte Carlo Op. O, Jordan; (ii) György Sebök; (iii) M. Boegner.

Pollini's classic recording still remains the best available of the *E minor Concerto.* This is playing of such total spontaneity, poetic feeling and refined judgement that criticism is silenced. The digital remastering has been generally successful. Orchestral texture is drier and clearer, with slight loss of bass, but there is better definition; the piano timbre is unimpaired. The additional items come from Pollini's first EMI solo recital, and the playing is equally distinguished, the recording truthful.

Zimerman's mid-priced version of the *E minor Concerto* comes from a live performance at the Concertgebouw in 1979. Zimerman gives a characteristically authoritative and poised performance and seems to have established a particularly good rapport with Kondrashin. He is balanced rather forwardly, and there is plenty of spontaneity (particularly in the slow movement and finale). The *Andante spianato* and the *Waltz* are drier and less open in acoustic; otherwise the sound is altogether excellent. This performance has also been reissued with his more recent, digital recording of the *F major Ballade* and the *Scherzo in E major* (which has some breathtaking passages), taken from his début recital, recorded rather dryly by Polskie Nagrania.

This Compact Classics issue is a new compilation centring on Martha Agerich's 1969 recording of the *First Piano concerto*, which helped to establish her international reputation. The distinction of this partnership is immediately apparent in the opening orchestral ritornello with Abbado's flexible approach. Argerich follows his lead and her affectionate phrasing provides some lovely playing, especially in the slow movement. Perhaps in the passage-work she is on occasion rather too intense, but this is far preferable to the rambling style we are sometimes offered. With excellent recording this is one of the most satisfactory versions available of this elusive concerto. The supporting programme is well chosen to include fine performances of many favourites: Vásáry makes a particularly distinguished contribution and the sound is excellent on CD and tape alike. The snag about the cassette is the omission of the second and third movements of the *Concerto*, and it is also a pity that CDs and tapes both offer only the *Funeral march* from the *B minor Sonata*, part of another charateristic Argerich performance.

Lipatti's is a lovely performance but, despite the expert ministrations of Keith Hardwick, its sonic limitations and limited frequency range will prove something of an obstacle to all but specialist collectors.

Maria João Pires recorded the Chopin *E minor Concerto* with the Monte Carlo orchestra in 1979 and, for all its merits (there are moments of some considerable poetry), it falls short of the distinction one expects from this artist. Nor is the orchestral support from Armin Jordan particularly special. Some pianistic touches are particularly felicitous (the phrasing at the opening of the finale, for instance) though they are spoiled by some ill-balanced and out-of-tune playing from the band. György Sebök's performance of the so-called *Funeral march sonata* is not lacking in fire or temperament, but the 1963 sound does not carry its years lightly and is a bit papery. Michèle Boegner's *Waltzes* were recorded in 1969 and sound a good deal better.

Piano concerto No. 2 in F min., Op. 21.

(M) *** Decca 417 750-2 [id.]. Ashkenazy, LSO, Zinman – TCHAIKOVSKY: *Piano concerto No. 1.* ***

(BB) ** ASV CDQS 6003; *ZCQS 6003.* Vásáry, N. Sinfonia – SCHUMANN: *Concerto.* **

(i) *Piano concerto No. 2 in F min.;* (ii) *Andante spianato et Grande polonaise brillante, Op. 22;* (i) *Fantasia on Polish airs, Op. 13.*

(M) * BMG/RCA GD 60404; *GK 60404* [60404-2-RG; *60404-4-RG*]. Artur Rubinstein, (i) Phd. O, Ormandy; (ii) Symphony of the Air, Wallenstein.

(i) *Piano concerto No. 2 in F min., Op. 21; Krakowiak (concert rondo), Op. 14. Fantaisie-impromptu, Op. 66.*

(M) ** Ph. 432 611-2; *432 611-4.* Bella Davidovich; (i) LSO, Marriner.

Ashkenazy's 1965 recording is a distinguished performance: his sophisticated use of light and shade in the opening movement, and the subtlety of phrasing and rubato, are a constant source of pleasure. The recitativo section in the *Larghetto*, which can often sound merely rhetorical, is here shaped with mastery and there is a delectable lightness of touch in the finale. David Zinman and the LSO are obviously in full rapport with their soloist, and the vintage recording has been remastered most satisfactorily.

Bella Davidovich's is a very musical reading, and there is undoubted poetry in the slow movement. She is beautifully recorded and the CD offers a particularly natural sound-picture, warmly ambient yet with excellent definition and detail. This is a pleasure to listen to, yet it must be admitted that the performance is somewhat undercharacterized. However, the attractions of this issue are increased by Davidovich's delightful account of the engaging *Krakowiak rondo*, sparkling and fresh, a very real bonus.

Vásáry's newest recording on ASV in which he not only plays but directs the Northern Sinfonia from the keyboard has the advantage of fresher and well-balanced sound, but the playing, while it has much delicacy and refinement, is not so boldly characterized nor so full of ardour and flair as was his earlier account on DG.

Rubinstein's 1968 recording of Chopin's *F minor Piano concerto* was one of his rare failures in the recording studio. He and Ormandy – normally such a sympathetic accompanist – failed to find an artistic rapport, and Rubinstein's playing is curiously unmelting. The recording isn't very special either. The *Fantasia on Polish airs* also fails to take off, and the closing *Kujawiak* is unspontaneous. The *Andante spianato*, recorded a decade earlier with Wallenstein, is a different matter, and Rubinstein gives an interpretation to the manner born, at once showy and emotional, yet sensitive. Incidentally, Chopin added the slow introduction to the more obvious showpiece when the work was published. The curious marking *spianato* underlines the steady pulse of the accompaniment, over which Rubinstein's right hand, in typical Chopin fashion, weaves florid decorations with the utmost magic.

Les Sylphides (ballet; orch. Douglas).

❀ (B) *** DG 429 163-2. BPO, Karajan – DELIBES: *Coppélia*; OFFENBACH: *Gaîté parisienne.* ***

(M) *** Sony SBK 46550 [id.]. Phd. O, Ormandy – DELIBES: *Coppélia; Sylvia:* suites ***; TCHAIKOVSKY: *Nutcracker suite.* **(*)

(M) **(*) Decca Dig. 430 723-2; *430 723-4* [id.]. National PO, Bonynge – ROSSINI/RESPIGHI: *Boutique fantasque.* **(*)

Karajan conjures consistently beautiful playing with the Berlin Philharmonic Orchestra, and he evokes a delicacy of texture which consistently delights the ear. The woodwind solos are played gently and lovingly, and one can feel the conductor's touch on the phrasing. The upper register of the strings is bright, fresh and clearly focused, the recording is full and atmospheric, and this is one of Karajan's very finest recordings. At bargain price it is unbeatable, coupled on CD with not only *Coppélia* (although the suite is not complete) but also Offenbach's *Gaîté parisienne.*

The Philadelphia strings are perfectly cast in this score and, although the CBS sound is less svelte than the DG quality for Karajan, it is still very good. Ormandy begins gently and persuasively but with the rhythmic moulding more positive in the opening *Prelude* and *Nocturne* than with Karajan, but not lacking in charm. Later the lively sections are played with irrepressible brilliance, and some might feel that this extrovert approach is almost overdone in the first *Waltz*, where Ormandy gives the upper strings their head. But later the playing has that rich, expansive excitement for which this orchestra is famous. Ormandy's couplings are more generous than the DG alternative, with nearly 76 minutes of ballet music, all equally charismatic.

Bonynge's performance shows a strong feeling for the dance rhythms of the ballet, and the orchestral playing is polished and lively. Bonynge also has the advantage of excellent 1982 digital recording, made in the Kingsway Hall. Even so, Karajan remains unsurpassed in this beautiful score and the Berlin Philharmonic playing has a warmth, elegance and grace which the London players do not quite match.

CHAMBER MUSIC

Cello sonata in G min., Op. 65.
(M) **(*) EMI CMS7 63184-2. Du Pré, Barenboim – FRANCK: *Cello sonata.* **(*)
(B) **(*) Hung. White Label HRC 171 [id.]. Miklós Perényi, Tibor Wehner – FAURÉ: *Cello sonatas.* ***

(i) *Cello sonata in G min., Op. 65; Introduction and polonaise brillante in C, Op. 3;* (ii) *Ballades Nos. 3 in A flat, Op. 47; 4 in F min., Op. 52.*
(M) *** DG 431 583-2; *431 583-4.* (i) Rostropovich, Argerich; (ii) Sviatoslav Richter.

With such characterful artists as Rostropovich and Argerich challenging each other, this is a memorably warm and convincing account of the *Cello sonata*, Chopin's last published work, a piece which clicks into focus in such a performance. The contrasts of character between expressive cello and brilliant piano are also richly caught in the *Introduction and polonaise*, and the recording is warm to match. The digital remastering for this reissue as part of DG's Chopin Edition is most successful; the sound always refined, with a good balance, is now firmer and clearer. Richter's 1961/62 accounts of the two *Ballades* have a commanding individuality, and the recording is remarkably good: No. 4 comes from a live recital.

The easy romanticism of the *Cello sonata* is beautifully caught by Jacqueline du Pré and Daniel Barenboim. Though the cellist phrases with all her usual spontaneous-sounding imagination, this is one of her more reticent records, while still bringing an autumnal quality to the writing which is very appealing. The recording is excellently balanced.

Though the Hungaroton performance has not the stature of the Rostropovich–Argerich account, it offers playing of quality. Miklós Perényi is not as well served by the engineers as he is in the coupled Fauré sonatas, where his tonal eloquence comes into its own, but he plays with real musical feeling and taste, and his pianist, Tibor Wehner, is excellent.

SOLO PIANO MUSIC

Ballades Nos. 1–4; Barcarolle, Op. 60; Fantaisie in F min; Impromptus Nos. 1–4; Nocturnes Nos. 1–21; Polonaise No. 7, Op. 61; Preludes Nos. 1–26; Scherzi Nos. 1–4; Waltzes Nos. 1–19.
(M) ** Ph. 432 303-2 (6) [id.]. Claudio Arrau.

Arrau was one of the greatest pianists of his day; his distinctive keyboard personality and tonal colour are incontrovertible. His Chopin, however, was more controversial than his Beethoven or Liszt for, while his aristocratic poise and commanding artistry are never in question, his rubato does not always convince – indeed, at times it is distinctly idiosyncratic. The excellent Philips recordings do justice to his particular sound-world and are admirably present, but the set as a whole can be recommended without reserve only to aficionados.

Ballades Nos. 1–4; Scherzi Nos. 1–4.
(M) *(**) Teldec/Warner Dig. 9031 74781-2 [id.]. Cyprien Katsaris.
(BB) * Naxos Dig. 8.550084 [id.]. István Székely.

Cyprien Katsaris is a player with an impressive technique and considerable power. He is a fiery interpreter of Chopin but displays no lack of poetic feeling. The *B minor Scherzo* is very brilliant indeed, though the virtuosity never distracts attention away from composer to interpreter. Unlike Gilels or Perahia, one is quite aware that the piano has hammers! The LP of these performances was awarded a prize at the 1985 Warsaw Chopin Competition as 'the finest recital of the last five years' (though one does not know what other Western recordings were available to the jury). As piano playing it is certainly very good, at times even distinguished, but the recording as such leaves much to be desired. The acoustic is not really big enough and the climaxes are overwhelming. At times one has the feeling that the attention of a tuner might not have come amiss and, while this is a subjective comment, the sound certainly does not compare with the best recordings of pianos by, say, Philips or Decca.

On Naxos we have the young Hungarian pianist, István Székely, a pupil of the composer Pál Kadosa and Zoltán Kocsis, in a generous coupling of the *Ballades* and *Scherzos*. His undoubted gifts are not shown to best advantage here; he gabbles the opening of the *B minor Scherzo*, though his treatment of the contrasting section is sensitive. His technical prowess and artistry are not in question, but they are not sufficient to make the pulse quicken or lift the spirits. The recording does not help matters, though it is marginally superior to that for the *Sonatas* and *Waltzes*. There is not quite enough air round the sound, and the overall effect is to induce aural fatigue.

Barcarolle in F sharp, Op. 60; Berceuse in D flat, Op. 57; Fantaisie in F. min., Op. 49; Nocturne No. 4 in F, Op. 15/1; Polonaise No. 4 in C min., Op. 40/2; Sonata No. 3 in B min., Op. 58.
(B) **(*) Pickwick Dig. PCD 834; *CIMPC 834* [id.]. John Ogdon.

John Ogdon's collection presents fresh and thoughtful performances, not as electrifying as some he recorded earlier in his career but often bold and full of individual insights. His speeds for the slower pieces are at times daringly extreme, but he sustains them well and the delicacy of much that he does is a delight, set in contrast to his natural strength in bravura. Bright, clear, realistic recording, giving the piano a powerful presence.

Études, Op. 10/1–12; Op. 25/1–12; Polonaises 1–7; 24 Preludes, Op. 28.
(B) *** DG 431 221-2 (3) [id.]. Maurizio Pollini.

The reissue of these works on three CDs at bargain price makes a most attractive package. Pollini offers playing of outstanding mastery as well as subtle poetry, and the DG engineers have accomplished the remastering with splendid freshness. Pollini has impeccable taste in handling rubato and the firmest sense of line and form. It is a pity, however, that the later *Preludes* are not included.

Études, Op. 10/1–12; Op. 25/1–12.
(M) *(**) Saga SCD 9002. Vladimir Ashkenazy.
(BB) * Naxos Dig. 8.550364 [id.]. Idil Biret.

Ashkenazy's set first appeared in the early 1960s on the Chant du Monde label. The playing has great brilliance and much poetic feeling: it is unfailingly rewarding. The sound is quite acceptable, though not distinguished; the piano timbre is rather lacking in bloom, although there is no lack of space round the instrument. A pity this Saga reissue is not in the bargain range, where it would have been very tempting indeed.

As has so often proved to be the case in the Naxos recordings made in the Tonstudio van Geest in Heidelberg, the artist is let down by a less than sympathetic studio environment. The instrument is rather closely balanced and, though it may not be the case, it sounds as if echo has been added, for the timbre of the piano is not completely natural. Idil Biret plays well enough, though she is not strong on poetry. This set is not really competitive, even at super-bargain price.

Mazurkas Nos. 1–51 (complete).
(BB) * Naxos Dig. 8.550358 (*Nos. 1–26*); 8.550359 (*Nos. 27–51*). Idil Biret.

Idil Biret plays very well and with good idiomatic feeling but, as has so often proved to be the case with recordings made in this venue (the Tonstudio van Geest in Heidelberg), the airless environment quickly induces aural fatigue. For all Idil Biret's artistry, this set is not very recommendable, even at super-bargain price.

Nocturnes Nos. 1–21.
(M) *** DG Dig. 423 916-2 (2) [id.]. Daniel Barenboim.

Barenboim's playing is of considerable eloquence, the phrasing beautifully moulded, and he is superbly recorded. His set will still give much pleasure with its relaxed, less than impetuous style, although occasionally there is just a hint of blandness.

Nocturnes Nos. 1–11.
(B) * Ph. 426 979-2; *426 979-4*. Nikita Magaloff.

Magaloff's *Nocturnes* do not command a strong recommendation, even at bargain price. The recording is good, though not quite as sonorous as on LP, but the playing is curiously measured and deliberate; one needs more incandescence and poetic feeling in this repertoire.

Nocturnes Nos. 1–11; 13–15; 19.
(BB) * Naxos Dig. 8.550257 [id.]. Sándor Falvay.

Like his colleagues in the Naxos Chopin series, Sándor Falvay is handicapped by a closely balanced recording and a distinctly unglamorous acoustic. Now in his early forties, he has studied at the Liszt Academy, where he now teaches, and in Moscow. He is a far from unsympathetic guide in the *Nocturnes* and he is much more imaginative than Székeley, to whom Naxos have entrusted the *Sonatas*. However, these performances fall short of real distinction and, even at bargain price, the dryish sound further limits their appeal.

Nocturnes Nos. 1–4; 7–10; 12–13; 15; 18–19.
(M) **(*) DG 431 586-2; *431 586-4*. Daniel Barenboim.

Barenboim's selection has been generously expanded for this reissue (72 minutes). The performances, taken from his complete set, are intense, thoughtful and poetic, following rather in the mid-European tradition. Compared with Rubinstein (at full price), they lack a mercurial dimension. The recording is first class.

Nocturnes Nos 1–7, 9–12, 13, 15, 19–20.
(B) ** DG 429 154-2; *429 154-4* [id.]. Tamás Vásáry.

This is playing of character and the selection is generous. Vásáry can mould a Chopin phrase with the best, but here he often seems too positive, although there are moments of poetry too. But the clean, rather dry piano timbre does not help provide a feeling of warm relaxation.

Polonaises Nos. 1–7.
(B) ** DG 429 516-2; *429 516-4*. [id.]. Shura Cherkassky.

Shura Cherkassky is sometimes an idiosyncratic artist and his playing has certain eccentricities of style and tempo. Compared with Pollini, he sometimes sounds wilful, and the famous *A major Polonaise* is rather deliberate. But for the most part his playing shows a redeeming spontaneity. The recording is good though not distinguished, bold but a little hard.

24 Preludes, Op. 28; Prelude No. 25 in C sharp min., Op. 26; Barcarolle, Op. 60; Berceuse, Op. 57; Impromptus Nos. 1–4; Fantaisie-impromptu.
(M) (**(*)) EMI mono CDH7 61050-2. Alfred Cortot.

Cortot's celebrated recording of the *Preludes* was made in 1933–4, as were the *Impromptus* and the *Barcarolle*. The *Prelude*, Op. 26, and the *Berceuse* come from a visit he made to England in 1949, when he had lost some of his technique but none of his poetry. (We remember hearing him in Oxford that year.) He was a stylist of the first order, a master of characterization and, as Jeremy Siepmann puts it in his notes, 'in his hands, phrases never really followed one another, they grew, in a continuous organic chain of cause and effect'. The sound of the 1930s' recordings is inevitably frail and papery, and the digital mastering does not seem a great improvement on the analogue LP that appeared in France some years ago.

24 Preludes, Op. 28; Preludes Nos. 25–26.
(M) ** EMI Dig. CD-EMX 2182; *TC-EMX 2182*. Dimitri Alexeev.

24 Preludes, Op. 28; Preludes Nos. 25–26; Barcarolle, Op. 60; Polonaise No. 6 in A flat, Op. 53; Scherzo No. 2 in B flat min., Op. 31.
(M) **(*) DG 415 836-2 [id.]. Martha Argerich.

24 Preludes, Op. 28; Preludes Nos. 25–26; 3 Mazurkas, Op. 59; Scherzo No. 3 in C sharp min., Op. 39.
(M) *** DG 431 584-2; *431 584-4* [id.]. Martha Argerich.

24 Preludes, Op. 28; Preludes Nos. 25–26; Impromptus Nos. 1–3; 4 (Fantaisie-impromptu).
(M) **(*) Ph. 426 634-2; *426 634-4*. Claudio Arrau.

24 Preludes, Op. 28; Preludes Nos. 25–26; Variations brillantes, Op. 12.
(BB) ** Naxos Dig. 8.550225 [id.]. Irina Zaritzkaya.

The *Preludes* show Martha Argerich at her finest, spontaneous and inspirational, though her moments of impetuosity may not appeal to all tastes. But her instinct is sure, with many poetic, individual touches. The other pieces are splendidly played. On her alternative CD, the *Mazurkas* are similarly volatile, and the *Scherzo* brings some glitteringly delicate articulation to make one catch one's breath. The recording of the *Preludes*, made in Watford Town Hall in 1977, was among the best she received from DG.

Arrau's *Preludes* date from the mid-1970s and are much admired. He certainly receives a full-bodied recording which does justice to his subtle nuances of tone; every *Prelude* bears the imprint of a strong personality. Arrau can sometimes sound a shade calculating (his rubato seeming arbitrary and contrived), but there is little evidence of this here. His *Preludes* appear to spring from an inner conviction, even if the outward results will not have universal appeal. The same thoughts might be applied to the *Impromptus*. Arrau's Chopin is seldom mercurial, but it is never inflexible and has its own special insights. The *Fantaisie-impromptu*, with its nobly contoured central melody, is a highlight here, with the richly coloured piano timbre contributing a good deal to the character of its presentation.

In some of the *Preludes* Alexeev is second to none and he is rarely unilluminating. However, although he carries all before him much of the time, elsewhere he leaves one impressed but unmoved. There is much fine artistry here, but this is not a first choice.

Irina Zaritzkaya is an artist of quality. She was placed second to Pollini in the 1960 Warsaw Competition and has not so far enjoyed the exposure on record to which her talents entitle her. She left the Soviet Union in 1972 to settle in Israel and has toured widely in the United States and South America. She has now settled in London, where she teaches. Artistically this is a three-star disc, for she plays with deep musical insight and a keen sense of poetry. Phrases breathe and she produces a wide range of keyboard colour; she even makes one momentarily unaware both of the acoustic deficiences of the Tonstudio van Geest in Heidelberg and of the tonal inadequacies of the instrument, which would benefit from the attentions of a technician. In the generally unsatisfactory Chopin series Naxos has produced this is an exception, and it is a pity that more repertoire was not entrusted to her.

Piano sonata No. 2 in B flat min. (Funeral march), Op. 35; Ballade No. 1 in G min., Op. 23; Barcarolle, Op. 60; Nocturnes: in F, F sharp, Op. 15/1–2; Scherzo No. 2 in B flat min., Op. 31.
(M) *** Decca 417 729-2 [id.]. Vladimir Ashkenazy.

Piano sonata No. 2; Barcarolle in F sharp, Op. 60; Polonaise No. 6 in A flat (Heroic), Op. 53; Polonaise-fantaisie in A flat, Op. 61.
(M) **(*) DG 431 582-2; *431 582-4* [id.]. Martha Argerich.

Ashkenazy's 1972 recording of the *Second Sonata* (plus the two *Nocturnes*) was made during a live recital at Essex University; the piano has splendid resonance and realism, and now the applause has been edited out. The performance of the *Sonata* is of the highest distinction; if the final *Presto* is not absolutely immaculate, who will cavil, with music-making of this quality? The two *Nocturnes*, recorded at the same time, have a comparable spontaneity; the rest of the programme, recorded earlier, is also distinguished.

Martha Argerich's *B flat minor Sonata* was recorded in 1975 and its combination of impetuosity and poetic feeling is distinctly individual. Her brilliance is admirably suited to the two *Polonaises*, and the *Barcarolle* (the earliest recording here) is also charismatic. The recording still sounds fresh and the CD transfer gives her plenty of presence.

Piano sonatas Nos. 2 in B flat min. (Funeral march), Op. 25; 3 in B min., Op. 58; Barcarolle in F sharp, Op. 60; Berceuse in D flat, Op. 57; Fantaisie-impromptu in C sharp min., Op. 66.
(BB) (*) Naxos Dig. 8.550071 [id.]. István Székely.

István Székely was a pupil of the composer Pál Kadosa and he also studied with Zoltán Kocsis. His undoubted keyboard talent is not matched by a strong enough musical personality or imagination to command the collector who has so rich a diversity of choice in this repertoire. These are in no way outstanding interpreptations and, even at so modest a price, collectors are unlikely to return to them very often. The recordings, made in the Italian Institute in Budapest, suffer from an unpleasing shallowness of tone.

Sonata No. 3 in B min., Op. 58; Fantaisie in F min., Op. 49; Tarantelle in A flat, Op. 43.
(M) (*) EMI mono CDH7 64025-2 [id.]. Arrau – SCHUMANN: *Carnaval.* (**)

Arrau's account of the Chopin *B minor Sonata* first appeared on Columbia blue-label in 1962, as did the *Fantaisie in F minor.* Neither shows the great pianist at his best; the recording is pretty monochrome and airless and does scant justice to the Arrau sound; his reading is very consciously thought out and his rubato may pose problems for some listeners. The *Tarantella* is a transfer of a Parlophone 78-r.p.m. disc from 1939 and has much greater sparkle.

(i) *Piano sonata No. 3 in B min., Op. 58;* (ii) *Polonaises Nos. 1 in C sharp min.; 2 in E flat min., Op. 26/1–2;* (i) *3 in A (Military); 4 in C min., Op. 40/1–2.*
(M) **(*) DG 431 587-2; *431 587-4* [id.]. (i) Emil Gilels; (ii) Lazar Berman.

Gilels's account of the *B minor Sonata* is thoughtful and ruminative, seen through a powerful mind and wholly individual fingers. There are some highly personal touches, for example the gentle undulating accompaniment, like quietly tolling bells, caressing the second group of the first movement, and a beautifully pensive and delicately coloured slow movement. The first movement is expansive and warmly lyrical, and there is not a bar that does not have one thinking anew about this music. An altogether haunting reading. The two *Polonaises* are also superb: they have majesty, grandeur and poetry, and the 1978 recording, made in the Berlin Jesus-Christus Kirche, is very satisfactory. For the reissue, DG have added the two Op. 26 *Polonaises*, recorded in Munich by Lazar Berman a year later. These readings possess a certain magisterial command and are also well recorded; but Berman does not invest each phrase with the intensity of Pollini or the sheer poetry of Gilels, and they have less character and colour than either of these artists provide.

Piano sonata No. 3 in B min., Op. 58; Waltzes Nos. 1–14.
(M) *(*) Sony SBK 46346 [id.]. Alexander Brailowsky.

Brailowsky's recordings date from the mid-1970s and, despite a certain character in the shaping of the *Waltzes*, do not show him at his best, either technically or artistically. There is a curious lack of flair, and the recording too is rather lacklustre.

Waltzes Nos. 1–19.
(BB) *(*) Naxos Dig. 8.550082 [id.]. István Székely.

Waltzes Nos. 1–14; Barcarolle, Op. 60; Mazurka in C sharp min., Op. 50/3; Nocturne in D flat, Op. 27/2.
❀ (M) (***) EMI CDH7 69802-2. Dinu Lipatti.

Waltzes Nos. 1–16.
(B) **(*) Decca 417 045-2; *417 045-4* [id.]. Peter Katin.

Lipatti's classic performances were recorded by Walter Legge in the rather dry acoustic of a Swiss Radio studio at Geneva in the last year of Lipatti's short life, and with each LP reincarnation they seem to have grown in wisdom and subtlety. Their appearance on a mid-priced CD, together with the *Barcarolle* and *Nocturne*, recorded in 1947, cannot be too warmly welcomed and the transfer has been accomplished most successfully. The reputation of these meticulous performances is fully deserved.

Peter Katin does not play the *Waltzes* in numerical order, as is customary, but in chronological order, which seems eminently sensible. The playing is thoughtful and affectionate, certainly assured and positive, especially in the more brilliant pieces, which are presented with flair. The bright yet quite full recording (from 1972) is very cleanly focused on CD and the piano is given striking presence. An excellent bargain recommendation.

Székely rather rattles off the first two waltzes, and as the recital proceeds one wonders whether he has a strongly enough developed musical personality to tempt one to return very often to his playing. Certainly alongside the innumerable major artists, from Ashkenazy to Zimerman, who have recorded this repertoire, he gives one less to think about. The recording, made in the Italian Institute in Budapest, is clean and well detailed but closely balanced, and one longs for more air round the aural image.

RECITAL COLLECTIONS

Andante spianato et Grande polonaise brillante, Op. 22; Ballade No. 1 in G min., Op. 23; Fantaisie in F min., Op. 49; Mazurkas: in G min.; in C; in B flat min., Op. 24/1, 2 & 4; Waltz in A flat, Op. 34/1.
(M) **(*) Analogue/Dig. DG 431 589-2; *431 589-4*. Krystian Zimerman.

Much of this programme derives from Zimerman's 1977 initial recital, recorded by Polskie Nagrania, when we commented: 'A remarkably promising début. This first recital leaves no doubts as to the astonishing security of Zimerman's technique (there are some breathtaking passages in the *Andante spianato*), nor the individual quality of his artistic personality. Here is an artist to watch.' And so it proved, as his later, mercurial, digital recordings of the *Fantaisie in F minor* and the *First Ballade* so readily demonstrate. The earlier recordings are dry and close, but the CD transfer makes them sound firmer than in their original LP format.

Andante spianato et Grande polonaise brillante, Op. 22; Ballades Nos. 1, Op. 23; 4, Op. 52; Barcarolle, Op. 60; Études: in G flat, Op. 10/5; in C sharp min., Op. 25/7; Polonaise-fantaisie, Op. 61; Waltz in A flat, Op. 69/1.
(M) *** BMG/RCA GD 87752 [7752-2-RG]. Vladimir Horowitz.

All these performances derive from live recitals. The *Andante spianato* (offering wonderful delicacy of articulation) was recorded in 1945 but still sounds well; the remaining performances date from between 1979 and 1982. The sound is modern: the *Polonaise-fantaisie*, the *Ballades* and the *Waltz* are digital, the rest analogue. The performances are fabulous; to the end of his career Horowitz's technique was transcendental and his insights remarkable. There is much excitement – but even more that is unforgettably poetic, and not a bar is predictable. With the sound so realistic, his presence is very tangible.

Andante spianato, Op. 22; Ballade No. 4 in F min., Op. 52; Études: in C min. (Revolutionary), Op. 10/12; in A min. (Winter wind), Op. 25/11; Impromptu in A flat, Op. 29/1; Fantaisie-impromptu, Op. 66; Mazurkas: in B flat min., Op. 24/4; in C, Op. 67/3; Nocturnes: in F, Op. 15/1; in C min., Op. 48/1; Scherzo No. 3 in C sharp min., Op. 39; Waltzes: in D flat (Minute); in C sharp min., Op. 64/1–2; in A flat, Op. 69/1.
(B) **(*) Pickwick Dig. PCD 872; *CIMPC 872*. Cristina Ortiz.

In the hands of Cristina Ortiz the *Andante spianato* sounds particularly engaging when it is presented with attractive simplicity. In the *Mazurkas* she does not show Rubinstein's subtle feeling for rubato; but in general her playing is agreeably flexible and highly musical, even if her structural approach is a shade impulsive at times. There are many favourites here, and the two *Impromptus* are particularly successful, while the bravura in the *Études* is impressive. Excellent recording.

Andante spianato et Grande polonaise brillante, Op. 22; Polonaises Nos. 4 in C min., Op. 40/2; 5 in F sharp min., Op. 44; 6 in A flat, Op. 53; 7 (Fantaisie-polonaise) in A flat, Op. 61.

(M) ** Van. 08.4023 71 [OVC 4023]. Alfred Brendel.

Although not possessing a natural affinity for the music of Chopin – the least effective piece here is the *Andante spianato* – nothing Brendel does is unstimulating, and these rather Schumannesque performances certainly have their interest. They were very well recorded (in 1968) and the natural piano timbre, with a full, resonant bass, has been expertly transferred to CD.

(i) *Ballade No. 1 in G min.; Barcarolle, Op. 60; Études: in F; in C min. (Revolutionary), Op. 10/8 & 12; in A flat; in G flat, Op. 25/1 & 9; Preludes: in A; in D flat (Raindrop), Op. 25/1 & 9;* (ii) *Études: in E; in G flat (Black keys), Op. 10/3 & 5; Mazurkas Nos. 10 in B flat, Op. 17/1; 41 in C sharp min., Op. 63/3; Nocturne No. 4 in F, Op. 15/1; Polonaise No. 6 in A flat (Heroic), Op. 53; Scherzo No. 1 in B min., Op. 20; Waltz No. 14 in E min., Op. posth.*

(M) *(*) EMI CDM7 64136-2; *EG 764136-4*. (i) Iso Elinson; (ii) Richard Farrell.

It is often a mistake to use two artists to make up a recital, especially if they are widely contrasted in age and experience. The recordings made in 1958 by Richard Farrell, the remarkably talented New Zealand pianist who died in a road accident later that same year, are (like his account of the Grieg *Concerto*) full of natural poetic feeling and technically brilliant. The piano timbre is full, if a little 'plummy'. Iso Elinson's contributions, however, do nothing to enhance his reputation. He was a distinguished teacher at the Royal Manchester College of Music and had many successful pupils, but his playing here is technically insecure and only sporadically springs to life.

Ballade No. 1 in G min., Op. 23; Barcarolle, Op. 60; Fantaisie-Impromptu, Op. 66; Mazurkas: in B flat, Op. 7/1; in D, Op. 33/2; Nocturnes: in E flat, Op. 9/2; in F sharp, Op. 15/2; in D flat, Op. 27/2; in G min., Op. 37/1; Polonaises: in A (Military), Op. 40/1; in A flat, Op. 53; Waltzes: in A flat, Op. 34/1; in D flat (Minute); in C sharp min., Op. 64/1–2.

(M) *** BMG/RCA GD 87725 [7725-2-RG]. Artur Rubinstein.

An outstanding mid-priced recital – there is no more distinguished miscellaneous Chopin collection in the catalogue – with fourteen contrasted pieces, well programmed. The recording is surprisingly consistent and Rubinstein's inimitable touch gives much pleasure. The programme ends admirably with the lovely *Nocturne in D flat*, followed by the *G minor Ballade*, coaxing and dazzling by turns.

'Favourites': Ballade No. 1 in G min., Op. 23; Fantaisie-impromptu, Op. 66; Mazurkas: in B flat, Op. 7/1; in D, Op. 33/2; Nocturnes: in E flat, Op. 9/2; in F sharp, Op. 15/2; in B, Op. 32/1; Polonaise in A flat, Op. 53; Scherzo in B flat min., Op. 31; Waltzes: in E flat (Grand valse brillante), Op. 18; in A min., Op. 34/2; in A flat; B min., Op. 69/1–2; in G flat, Op. 70/1.

(M) *** Decca Dig. 417 798-2; *417 798-4*. Vladimir Ashkenazy.

An exceptionally attractive recital, with many favourites, played with Ashkenazy's customary poetic flair and easy brilliance. The digital recordings were made at various times during the early 1980s but match surprisingly well: the sound has striking realism and presence.

Ballade No. 3 in A flat, Op. 47; Barcarolle in F sharp, Op. 60; Fantaisie in F min., Op. 49; Fantaisie-impromptu, Op. 66; Nocturnes Nos. 2 in E flat, Op. 9/2; 5 in F sharp, Op. 15/2; Prelude in D flat, Op. 28/15; Waltzes Nos. 7 in C sharp min., Op. 64/2; 9 in A flat, Op. 69/1.

(M) *** Ph. 420 655-2; *420 655-4* [id.]. Claudio Arrau.

A fine recital, showing both poetry and the thoughtful seriousness which distinguishes Arrau's Chopin, which is West rather than East European in spirit. The CD is admirably transferred, bringing the fullness of timbre and natural balance we expect of Philips.

Barcarolle, Op. 60; Berceuse, Op. 57; 24 Preludes, Op. 28; Sonata No. 2 (Funeral march), Op. 35.

(M) (**) BMG/RCA mono GD 60047; *GK 60047* [60047-2-RG; *60047-4-RG*]. Artur Rubinstein.

These recordings were made in 1946 and have been transferred very well from the original 78s; although the acoustic is dry and studio-ish, the piano image is truthful and reasonably full. The performance of the *Sonata* is authoritative, its slow movement especially fine; but in the *Preludes* Rubinstein sometimes seems to rush his fences, and the fast passage-work is not always clearly articulated.

Berceuse in D flat, Op. 57; Études, Op. 10/1–4, 6–7; Op. 25/1, 4, 6 & 7; Nocturnes: in G min., Op. 37/1; in B, Op. 62/1; Scherzo No. 1 in B

min., Op. 20; Waltzes: in E flat (Grand valse brillante), Op. 18; in A min., Op. 34/2; in C sharp min., Op. 64/2.
(M) **(*) DG 431 588-2; *431 588-4*. Tamás Vásáry.

An excellent recital compiled from Vásáry's mid-1960s recordings, showing this artist at his most impressive in this repertoire. The opening *Scherzo* is brilliantly and flexibly done and the *Études* are authoritative and commanding, the famous *E major*, Op. 10, No. 3, beautifully done. Perhaps the *Berceuse* is a shade deliberate; but both the *Nocturnes* and *Waltzes* have plenty of colour and their rubato is generally convincing. The layout is satisfyingly conceived, and the recital ends dashingly with the *Grand valse brillante*. The sound is generally very believable, with only a hint of brittleness in the opening *Scherzo*.

'The world of Chopin': (i) *Berceuse, Op. 57;* (ii) *Études: in E (Tristesse); in C min. (Revolutionary), Op. 10/3 & 12;* (iii) *in A min. (Winter wind), Op. 25/11;* (ii) *Fantaisie-impromptu, Op. 65; Mazurkas: in B flat, Op. 7/1; in D, Op. 33/2; Nocturnes:* (iii) *in E flat, Op. 9/2;* (ii) *in F min., Op. 55/1; Polonaises: in A, Op. 40/1;* (iv) *in A flat, Op. 53;* (v) *Prelude in D flat (Raindrop), Op. 28/15;* (i) *Sonata No. 2: Funeral march; Waltzes:* (ii) *in E flat (Grand valse brillante), Op. 18;* (iii) *in D flat (Minute), Op. 64/1;* (ii) *in C sharp min., Op. 64/2; in B min., Op. 69/2.*
(B) ** Decca Dig./Analogue 433 070-2; *433 070-4* [id.]. (i) Kempff; (ii) Ashkenazy; (iii) Bolet; (iv) Katchen; (v) De Larrocha.

Although Ashkenazy, who dominates this recital, is right inside this repertoire and the programme is attractive, the first three items on the disc are all played by Jorge Bolet, who is a less sympathetic Chopinian, impressive though his playing is technically. Kempff's gentle *Berceuse* and his characteristically thoughtful account of the famous *Funeral march* are the other highlights, alongside Katchen's stirring *A flat Polonaise*. The sound, often digital, is always crisp and clear in projection.

Études: in C min. (Revolutionary), Op. 10/12; in D flat, Op. 25/8; Impromptus Nos. 1 in A flat, Op. 29; 2 in F sharp, Op. 36; 3 in G flat, Op. 51; Fantaisie-impromptu, Op. 6; Mazurkas: in D; in C, Op. 33/2–3; in C sharp min., Op. 41/4; in C sharp min., Op. 63/3; in C, Op. 67/3; Nocturne in F sharp, Op. 15/2; Waltzes: in G, Op. 34/3; in E; in E flat; in A flat, Op. posth.
(M) ** DG Dig. 431 585-2; *431 585-4*. Stanislav Bunin.

Stanislav Bunin won the 1983 Marguerite Long Competition in Paris when he was only sixteen and the Warsaw Chopin Competition two years later. Still in his early twenties, he is a player of some fire and temperament, and these recordings (made during the course of the Warsaw Competition) show his remarkable technical address and musicianship – but also his idiosyncratic manner. His fingers are more than equal to this repertoire and he has a strong sense of style, but he is rather self-aware too. His rubato sometimes sounds studied, but his *Écossaises* have much rhythmic charm. The *Fantaisie-impromptu* and the *Revolutionary study* show him at his most brilliant, and the *A flat Impromptu* is impressively individual; but the *Grande valse brillante* is gabbled (though it evokes much applause at the close of the recital). The sound is realistic.

Fantasy in F min., Op. 49; Mazurkas: in C; in B flat min., Op. 24/2 & 4; in C sharp min., Op. 50/3; in C min., Op. 56/3; in C sharp min., Op. 63/3; Nocturnes: in F, Op. 15/1; in C sharp min., Op. 17/1; Scherzos Nos. 2 in B flat min., Op. 31; 3 in C sharp min., Op. 39.
(M) *(*) Polskie Nagrania PNCD 022. Witold Malcuzynski.

Malcuzynski made some famous recordings for EMI in the earliest days of stereo, notably a glittering set of *Waltzes* and some characterful *Mazurkas*. The present recital dates from the mid-1970s and is not helped by piano recording which is hard as well as bold and which, even in the *Nocturnes*, produces an unrelenting effect. The playing is at its most charismatic in the *Mazurkas* and the two *Scherzos*.

Cilea, Francesco (1866–1950)

Adriana Lecouvreur (complete).
(M) **(*) Sony CD 79310 (2) [M2K 34588]. Scotto, Domingo, Obraztsova, Milnes, Amb. Op. Ch., Philh. O, Levine.
(M) **(*) Decca 430 256-2 (2) [id.]. Tebaldi, Simionato, Del Monaco, Fioravanti, St Cecilia, Rome, Ac. Ch. & O, Capuana.

Renata Scotto gives a vibrant, volatile, dramatically strong account of the title-role, not as electrifying as Callas would have been (to judge by her recordings of the two big arias) but vividly convincing as a great actress. The tendency for her voice to spread on top is exaggerated by the closeness of the balance of the voices on CD, but her control of legato and a beautiful line amply compensate. Domingo, Milnes and Obraztsova make a strong supporting team, not always idiomatic but always relishing the melodrama, while Levine draws committed playing from the Philharmonia. This set still appears to be at full price in the USA.

Tebaldi's consistently rich singing misses some of the flamboyance of Adriana's personality and in her characterization both *Io son l'umile ancella* and *Poveri fiori* are lyrically very beautiful. But then, this is an opera that relies very largely on its vocal line for its effect. One wishes that Del Monaco had been as reliable as Tebaldi but, alas, there are some coarse moments among the fine, plangent top notes. Simionato is a little more variable than usual but a tower of strength nevertheless. The recording is outstanding for its time (early 1960s), brilliant and atmospheric.

Cimarosa, Domenico (1749–1801)

Double flute concerto in G.
(B) **(*) Decca 421 630-2; *421 630-4*. Aurèle and Christiane Nicolet, Stuttgart CO, Münchinger – MOZART: *Flute concertos.* ***

Although not momentous music, Cimarosa's *Concerto for two flutes* has undeniable charm, and its gay final rondo is quite memorable. The only drawback is the composer's emphasis on florid writing, with the two solo instruments playing consistently in thirds and sixths. The performance here is warmly gracious, with a good accompaniment and excellent sound.

Il maestro di cappella (complete).
(M) *** Decca 433 036-2 (2) [id.]. Fernando Corena, ROHCG O, Argeo Quadri – DONIZETTI: *Don Pasquale.* **(*)

Corena's classic assumption of the role of incompetent Kapellmeister has been out of the catalogue for too long. The Decca stereo allows his orchestral rehearsal to come over most vividly, with the poor man dashing first to the left then to the right, to one instrument after another, trying to keep each in order. Corena shows complete mastery of the *buffo* bass style, and he is so little troubled by the florid passages that he can relax in the good humour. The vintage 1960 recording is clear and atmospheric, with the directional effects naturally conveyed, and the CD transfer is quite admirable.

Clementi, Muzio (1752–1832)

Keyboard sonatas: in F min., Op. 14/3; in F sharp min., Op. 26/2; in C (quasi concerto), Op. 33/3; in G min., Op. 34/2; Rondo (from *Sonata, Op. 47/2*).
(M) *** BMG/RCA GD 87753 [7753-2-RC]. Vladimir Horowitz (piano).

These electrifying performances from the 1950s show a Clementi of greater substance and sterner mettle than the composer we thought we knew. In Horowitz's commanding hands these *Sonatas* sound almost worthy of Beethoven and, though the piano sound is shallow by the side of most up-to-date recordings, the quality is a great improvement upon either of the vinyl transfers with which we have compared it.

Piano sonatas: in E flat, Op. 24/3; in D, Op. 26/3; in C; in G, Op. 39/1–2.
(B) **(*) Hung. White Label HRC 092 [id.]. Donatella Failoni.

Donatella Failoni is a thoughtful and intelligent player, with a clean, direct style. She is particularly persuasive in the *D major Sonata* which in her hands almost has the calibre of Mozart; throughout, she makes a good case for these underrated works and she is given a bold, faithful recording. This is well worth exploring at its reasonable price.

Coates, Eric (1886–1958)

Ballad; By the sleepy lagoon; London suite; The Three Bears (phantasy); *The Three Elizabeths* (suite).
(M) *** ASV CDWHL 2053; *ZCWHL 2053*. East of England O, Malcolm Nabarro.

This is the first recording by the East of England Orchestra, formed in 1982 by Malcolm Nabarro, and it is appropriate that they should make their début with music by the East Midlander, Eric Coates – 'the man who writes tunes', as Dame Ethel Smyth described him. There are plenty of them here and one of the most memorable comes in the central movement of *The Three Elizabeths. Elizabeth of Glamis* celebrates the Queen Mother (who is charmingly pictured on the front of the disc) and draws a springtime evocation of Glamis Castle, not missing out the cuckoo. Its delightful main theme, complete with Scottish snap, is given to the oboe, and Gareth Hulse presents it simply but not too ripely, as is suitable for the Scottish climate. Nabarro has the full measure of Coates's leaping allegros: the first movement of the same suite – famous as the TV signature-tune of *The Forsyte Saga* – has admirable rhythmic spirit, and he plays the famous marches with crisp buoyancy. *The Three Bears* sparkles humorously, as it should; only in *By the sleepy lagoon* does one really miss a richer, more languorous string-texture. Excellent, bright recording, and the price is right.

(i) *By the sleepy lagoon;* (ii) *Calling all workers* (march); (iii) *Cinderella* (phantasy); *From meadow to Mayfair: suite; London suite; London again suite;* (i) *The Merrymakers overture;* (iii) *Music everywhere* (march); (iv) *Saxo-rhapsody;* (i) *The three bears* (phantasy); (ii) *The three Elizabeths* (suite); (i) *The three men* (suite): *Man from the Sea.* (iii) *Wood nymphs* (valsette).
(B) *** CfP CD-CFPD 4456; *TC-CFPD 4456* (2) [id.]. (i) LSO, Mackerras; (ii) CBSO,

Kilbey; (iii) Royal Liverpool PO, Groves; (iv) with Jack Brymer.

This collection of the music of Eric Coates with its breezy tunefulness is now issued on a pair of very inexpensive CDs, cleanly transferred. It includes, besides some very lively performances from Sir Charles Mackerras, several outstanding ones from the CBSO under Reginald Kilbey, who proves the ideal Coates conductor. The marches are splendidly alive and vigorous. Although the CDs bring out the brittleness in the upper range, notably in the Groves recordings, the ambient effect helps to prevent too great an imbalance towards the treble. This remains much the best Coates compilation currently available.

Copland, Aaron (1900–90)

Appalachian spring: ballet suite.
(M) *** DG 431 048-2; *431 048-4* [id.]. LAPO, Bernstein – BARBER: *Adagio* ***; GERSHWIN: *Rhapsody in blue.* **(*)

Bernstein's DG version of *Appalachian spring* was recorded at a live performance, and the conductor communicates his love of the score in a strong, yet richly lyrical reading, and the compulsion of the music-making is obvious. The recording is close but not lacking atmosphere, and it sounds extremely vivid. It is here recoupled with his rather less recommendable second recording of Gershwin's *Rhapsody in blue.*

(i) *Appalachian spring: ballet suite; Billy the Kid: ballet suite;* (ii) *Clarinet concerto;* (i) *Danzón Cubano; Fanfare for the common man; John Henry; Letter from home;* (i; iv) *Lincoln portrait;* (iii) *Music for movies;* (i) *Our Town; An Outdoor overture; Quiet city; Rodeo (4 Dance episodes);* (iii) *El Salón México;* (i) *Symphony No. 3; Las agachadas.*
(M) *** Sony SM3K 46559 (3) [id.]. (i) LSO; (ii) Benny Goodman, Columbia Symphony Strings; (iii) New Philh. O; (iv) with Henry Fonda; (v) New England Conservatory Ch., composer.

Sony here offer a comprehensive anthology of the major orchestral works, ballet suites and film scores dating from Copland's vintage period, 1936–48. The composer directs with unrivalled insight throughout. Alongside the many familiar scores there are three novelties: *John Henry*, the railroad ballad about the black folk hero who was regarded as the finest rail-layer and rock-crusher of his time; the engaging *Letter from home* ('It's very sentimental,' said Copland, 'but it *modulates*!'); and a vocal vignette which, as such, doesn't properly belong here but is very welcome neverthless, *Las agachadas* ('The shake-down song'), an unaccompanied choral piece, sung spiritedly in Spanish. Benny Goodman's instinctively idiomatic account of the *Clarinet concerto*, which he commissioned, is indispensable in such a collection, as is the *Third Symphony*. By the side of Bernstein's vibrant account, the composer's approach seems comparatively mellow – even gentle at times, as in the scherzo. But the natural authority is commanding, and the work's freshness of inspiration communicates anew. Any listener who responds to the famous *Fanfare for the common man* will be delighted to find it in use here as a launching-pad for the finale: in the composer's hands, the way it steals in is sheer magic. The remastering for CD is done most skilfully, retaining the ambience of the originals, while achieving more refined detail. With 226 minutes of consistently inspired music offered on three CDs, this is a bargain of the utmost distinction. But Bernstein's disc, below, makes an essential appendix.

(i) *Appalachian spring* (ballet) *suite; Billy the Kid* (ballet) complete; (ii) *Danzón cubano; El salón México.*
(M) *** Mercury 434 301-2 [id.]. (i) LSO; (ii) Minneapolis SO, Antal Dorati.

Dorati pioneered the first stereo recording of the complete *Billy the Kid* ballet, and the 1961 Mercury LP caused a sensation on its first appearance for its precision of detail and brilliance of colour, while the generous acoustics of Watford Town Hall added ambient warmth. The gunshots (track 13) were and remain electrifying, with their clean percussive transients, while the LSO playing combines tremendous vitality and rhythmic power with genuine atmospheric tension in the score's evocative sections. There is some delectable woodwind pointing in the *Celebration* after the gun-battle, and *Billy the Kid's waltz* which follows is appropriately doleful, although here the high violins are a bit shrill. The degree of fierceness on the violin timbre is more noticeable in *Appalachian spring* (striking at their first entry (track 2) and at the climax of the variations on the Shaker hymn (track 7)) but again the sound has plenty of colour and atmosphere and the clarity is remarkable. The orchestra's sprung rhythms are very engaging, especially in the sprightly *Dance of the bride* (track 5), and the closing section is very touching. Dorati has re-recorded the suite for Decca, see below, and the digital sound is even more spacious and beautiful, but the Mercury performance has all the freshness of new discovery. For the CD, earlier (1957) Minneapolis versions of the *Danzón cubano* and *El salón México* have been added.

Dorati, though always vital, is somewhat inflexible in his treatment of both pieces, which here lack a feeling of complete metrical freedom, even though the Mexican evocation piece has much sensuous charm. The recording is crisp and clean to suit his approach.

Appalachian spring (ballet): *suite; Billy the Kid* (ballet) *suite; Fanfare for the common man; Rodeo (four dance episodes).*
(BB) **(*) Naxos Dig. 8.550282 [id.]. Slovak RSO (Bratislava), Gunzenhauser.

One does not expect a Czech orchestra, excellent as the Bratislava players are, to achieve quite the exhilarating rhythmic precision that Bernstein and the NYPO bring to this music, but they play with such spontaneous enjoyment in *Rodeo* and *Billy the Kid* that one cannot help but respond. Gunzenhauser, a fine conductor of Czech music, is equally at home in Copland's folksy, cowboy idiom and all this music has plenty of colour and atmosphere. If some of the detail in *Appalachian spring* is less sharply etched than with Dorati, the closing pages are tenderly responsive. The recording is admirably colourful and vivid with a fine hall ambience, and the spectacle of the *Fanfare for the common man* is worth anybody's money. A bargain.

Appalachian spring (ballet suite); Dance Symphony; Fanfare for the common man; Rodeo: 4 dance episodes; El salón México.
(M) *** Decca Dig. 430 705-2; *430 705-4* [id.]. Detroit SO, Dorati.

Dorati has the full measure of Copland's masterly *Appalachian spring* score, creating a marvellous evocation at the opening and a feeling of serene acceptance at the close, while the affectionately witty portrayal of *The revivalist and his flock* is presented with sparklingly precise rhythms and splendid string and woodwind detail. The *Solo dance of the bride* is equally characterful; throughout, Dorati finds a balance between the nicely observed interplay of the human characters and the spacious and lonely grandeur of the Appalachian backcloth. The 1984 Decca digital recording is impressive in its range and beauty of texture, and again confirms the excellence of the acoustic of the Old Orchestral Hall, Detroit. The other works on this mid-priced CD were all digitally recorded in the United Artists Auditorium in 1981. They are notable for their bright, extrovert brilliance, having evidently been chosen for their immediate, cheerful, wide-open-spaces qualities. The playing demonstrates very clearly the degree of orchestral virtuosity available in Detroit, and the recording has a clarity and impact that suit the music. The only reservation is that, rather surprisingly, Dorati's treatment of jazzy syncopations – an essential element in Copland of this vintage – is very literal, lacking the lift we think of as idiomatic. Nevertheless, as sound this is very impressive and the performances have much vitality.

Appalachian spring (ballet suite); Fanfare for the common man.
(M) *** Decca 417 716-2; *417 716-4* [id.]. LAPO, Mehta – GERSHWIN: *American in Paris; Cuban overture; Rhapsody in blue.* **

Mehta's performance is one of the most distinguished of several fine recordings he made for Decca in the late 1970s which also included the spectacular *Fanfare for the common man.* Here the digital remastering gives riveting presence to the percussion at the opening, without quite going over the top like the full-price Telarc version. The sound is excellent in the ballet also, which is powerfully atmospheric: the work's climax is exhilarating and the closing pages movingly serene. The couplings are generous but less distinctive.

Billy the Kid (ballet): *suite; Fanfare for the common man; Rodeo (4 dance episodes).*
(B) ** VoxBox (2) [CDX 5035]. Dallas SO, Johanos – IVES: *Holidays Symphony;* RACHMANINOV: *Symphonic dances* etc. **

The Dallas orchestra play with idiomatic feeling and much warmth of atmosphere. Being Texans, they know what cowboy music is about and the barn-dance rhythms come naturally, while the gun-battle is done with the percussive effectiveness of familiarity. Good spacious recording.

Piano concerto.
(M) *** Van. 08.4029.71 [OVC 4029]. Earl Wild, Symphony of the Air, composer – MENOTTI: *Piano concerto.* **(*)

Copland has also recorded his *Piano concerto* for CBS, taking the solo role himself, with Leonard Bernstein conducting – see below. That performance, perhaps because of the influence of the conductor, is freer and more persuasive in the passages influenced by jazz. Yet this Vanguard record, with a supreme piano virtuoso providing a glittering account of the piano part, is very recommendable. The 1961 recording, with a vivid projection of the piano, is first rate, hardly showing its age in the crisp new CD transfer. The coupling is a fascinating curiosity.

(i; ii) *Piano concerto;* (iii) *Dance Symphony;* (ii) *Music for the theatre;* (iii) *2 Pieces for string orchestra; Short symphony (Symphony No. 2); Statements; Symphonic ode;* (iv; ii) *Symphony for organ and orchestra.*
(M) *** Sony SM2K 47232 (2) [id.]. (i) Com-

poser (piano); (ii) NYPO, Bernstein; (iii) LSO, composer; (iv) with E. Power Biggs.

This second Sony Copland collection covers early orchestral and concertante music written between 1922 and 1935 and is, if anything, more valuable than the first box. The material is rarer and it helps us to follow the composer's developing orchestral style; moreover the participation of both the composer and Leonard Bernstein is uniquely valuable. Bernstein's performances have all the freshness and sharpness of response that come with new discovery; indeed, much of Copland's earlier writing is more exuberantly dissonant, less accommodating than his later work. The *Rondino*, the second of his *Two Pieces for string orchestra*, is the earliest work here. Originally written in 1923 (during Copland's Paris years) for string quartet, it dances along engagingly in acerbic neo-classicism, with just a whiff of jazz, and an underlying bitter-sweet lyricism. It fits remarkably well with the *Lento molto* (which precedes it), written five years later, again conceived for string quartet. The *Lento* is a totally memorable piece which instantly establishes Copland's unique harmonic credentials and so has a familiar flavour. Hauntingly elegiac, it reaches a powerful climax and ought to be as familiar as Barber's *Adagio*, with which it has much in common. The *Symphony for organ and orchestra* is a powerful and strikingly innovative work, dating from 1924, when Copland was finishing his studies with Nadia Boulanger. The composer subsequently re-scored the piece as his *First Symphony*, but its character and personality stand out best in its original format. It opens gently, with the organ immersed in the orchestral patina, but produces excitingly explosive rhythmic climaxes in the last two movements, even though the finale begins by again taking up the opening mood of reverie. Textures are highly original and the brilliantly piquant scherzo allows the organist to imitate a harmonium. It is given an extremely idiomatic and responsive performance by Power Biggs, who is fully sensitive to its atmosphere, and Bernstein balances the overall sounds with great skill and a marvellous feeling for colour. The recording is spectacularly worthy of the playing. The *Piano concerto* (1927) is both abrasive and strongly jazz-influenced. With the composer playing his own piano part with obvious feeling and Bernstein directing brilliantly (one wonders if they ever thought of exchanging roles) the result is a most impressive example of 'symphonic jazz'. The pungently flamboyant *Symphonic ode*, commissioned by the Boston Symphony, helped the orchestra to celebrate its fiftieth anniversary: it was written between 1927 and 1929. The *Dance Symphony* was completed that same year, absorbing earlier fragments conceived between 1922 and 1925 and originally intended for a 'Vampire' ballet, after Copland had been fascinated by the German horror film, *Nosferatu*. The *Short Symphony* dates from 1931–3; both works are full of originality and energy and are tautly constructed. They are rewarding scores, though the collector approaching them for the first time may feel that, with their dissonance and complex rhythms, the influence of Stravinsky had then not been fully assimilated. *Statements* (1934–5), as the bald title suggests, is one of Copland's less expansive works, but its six vignettes, *Militant*, *Cryptic*, *Dogmatic*, *Subjective*, *Jingo* and *Prophetic*, reveal a compression of thought and sharpness of idea that are most refreshing. Appropriately, the final section looks forward to the atmosphere of both *Quiet city* and *Appalachian spring*. All these performances have a definitive authority combined with total spontaneity of response from the participants which makes them compelling listening, and the recordings – dating from between 1964 and 1967 – whether made in the New York Avery Fisher Hall or at Walthamstow, are very well engineered, the London sound rather mellower than the transatlantic balance, but both extremely vivid in the excellent CD transfers. *Music for the theatre*, however, was recorded in the St George Hotel, Brooklyn, in 1958; like Bernstein's ballet recordings, it shows early CBS stereo engineering at its best.

(i) *Connotations;* (ii) *Dance panels; Down a country lane;* (i) *Inscape;* (ii) *3 Latin-American sketches; Music for a great city; Orchestral variations; Preamble for a solemn occasion; The Red Pony* (film score).

(M) *(**) Sony SM2K 47236 (2) [id.]. (i) NYPO, Bernstein; (ii) LSO or New Philh. O, composer.

This third Copland box from Sony is something of a disappointment – not the music, which is even rarer than before and of great interest. *The Red Pony* is vintage Copland, a collection of vividly atmospheric genre pieces from a highly successful film-score, the most haunting being *Walk to the bunkhouse* and the equally superbly played *Orchestral variations* which, though strictly an orchestral version of the *Piano variations* of 1930, make a unique and impressive contribution to Copland's oeuvre. It was 27 years after their first composition that the composer decided to present them in this new form, but the instrumentation is so ingenious and imaginative that you would never suspect their history. The result is epigramatic and tough, yet unmistakably the work of Copland. *Connotations* is tougher still, and both this 1962 piece and to a lesser extent *Inscape*, the major work of the composer's final period, are serially orientated. *Dance panels* is an abstract ballet without a narrative line, and *Music for a great city*, with its jazz influences and nocturnal scene, derives from another film-score (*Something wild*) and was reworked into its present format in response to a 1964 commission from the LSO. The three *Latin-American sketches* are a late attempt by the composer to return to his earlier popular style; *Down a country lane* is an engaging piano piece (commissioned by *Life* magazine) and subsequently scored for small orchestra, while the *Preamble* is occasional music in the best sense. The performances are all extremely successful, but the CD transfers are over-bright and, for all their vividness of detail, tiring to the ear, particularly the thin violins and the more pungent climaxes of the later works. Moreover, while the documentation is basically admirable, nowhere – except minimally on the labels of the actual discs – is the track layout given; both the booklet and the insert leaflet at the back of the box list the music in order of performance, with no cues whatsoever!

Dance Symphony; Danzón cubano; Fanfare for the common man; Quiet city; Rodeo: 4 Dance episodes; El salón México.
(M) **(*) EMI Dig. CD-EMX 2147; *TC-EMX 2147*. Mexico City PO, Bátiz.

Bátiz is a lively interpreter of Copland and he is particularly good with *El salón México* and the *Danzón cubano*. The *Dance Symphony* is derived from an unperformed ballet composed with Diaghilev in mind. It was devised to fit a bizarre scenario involving dancing corpses, coffins and a vampire called Grohg, but as a ballet was stillborn; the music turned up in its present format in 1929. Bátiz has the full measure of its sparky rhythms and vivid scoring. Ensemble is not ideally polished overall, but the playing throughout has splendid vitality; the gentler moments of *Rodeo* are atmospherically caught, even if the orchestra could do with more body here and in the evocative *Quiet city*.

El Salón México.
(B) ** CfP CD-CFP 4583; *TC-CFP 4583*. Utah SO, Maurice Abravanel – GROFÉ: *Grand Canyon suite*. **

This is distinctly short measure; although there is plenty of local colour and lively rhythmic feeling projected by the Utah orchestra, this performance does not match Bernstein's for dynamism and precision. The CD transfer is vivid but sacrifices some of the opulence of the original analogue master.

(i) *Lincoln portrait. Our Town* (film music: suite); *An Outdoor overture; Quiet city.*
(M) **(*) Van. 08.4037.71 [OVC 4037]. (i) Charlton Heston; Utah SO, Abravanel – GOULD: *Latin American symphonette*. **

Maurice Abravanel has the full measure of this music and the playing of the Utah orchestra is most sympathetic. In the *Lincoln portrait*, Charlton Heston's warm, friendly voice is a pleasure to listen to. His delivery of Lincoln's words is slow and strong, more persuasive than Henry Fonda's relatively diffident manner, although there are moments of melodrama, and his repeated 'This is what he said' seems to come too many times. (Katharine Hepburn is far more vibrant than either, but she is at full price.) The sumptuous recorded sound is very beautiful throughout, much richer than the Sony balance, but the Utah reverberation inflates *Quiet city* almost into a trumpet concerto, with William Sullivan's fine solo contribution made to dominate the texture unduly.

Corelli, Arcangelo (1653–1713)

Concerti grossi, Op. 6/1–12.
(BB) *** Naxos Dig. 8.550402/3 [id.]. Capella Istropolitana, Jaroslav Kr(e)chek.
(M) *** HM/BMG GD 77007 (2) [77077-2-RG]. La Petite Bande, Kuijken.
(M) *** Decca 430 560-2 (2) [id.]. ASMF, Sir Neville Marriner.
(M) ** Ph. 426 453-2 (2). I Musici.
(B) ** VoxBox 1155942 (2) [CDX 5023]. SW German R. CO, Angerer.

Corelli's masterly Op. 6 are rich in melodic invention and harmonic resource. After long neglect they are at last coming into their own on record. At super-bargain price, the Naxos set by the Capella Istropolitana under Jaroslav Kr(e)chek represents very good value indeed. Each CD contains well over an hour's music and is available separately, and anyone collecting the one is unlikely to resist the temptation to go on to the other. The players are drawn from the Slovak Philharmonic and have great vitality and, when necessary, virtuosity to commend them. Readers wanting period instruments have La Petite Bande, but for those who prefer the warmer sonority of modern strings this version will offer much satisfaction. Although this ensemble may not be superior to the Franz Liszt Chamber Orchestra, they are at times its equal. The digital recording is clean and well lit, but not over-bright, and makes their version strongly competitive.

La Petite Bande offers a useful mid-price

alternative to the Naxos set. Authentic instruments are used to excellent effect, and the playing is always expressive and musical. The 1977 recordings were made in a highly sympathetic acoustic, that of Cedernsaal at Schloss Kirchheim; besides being splendidly lifelike, they are especially impressive in conveying the nobility and grandeur of Corelli.

The older Argo set, now reissued on Decca's Serenata label, was prepared with evident thought and care, and if one must cavil it is only at two small points: some fussy continuo playing here and there, and occasionally a certain want of breadth and nobility of feeling in some of the slow movements, a lack one does not expect from Marriner. But weighed against these are the vitality and intelligence of the performances, expertly played by the Academy and given vintage 1973/4 recording, made in the flattering acoustics of St John's, Smith Square. However, for those wanting this music played on modern instruments, the digital Naxos set, with its added economy, takes pride of place.

I Musici bring full sonority and expert musicianship to these *Concertos*. They are especially good in slow movements, where the playing has an agreeable lightness of touch and often creates delicately radiant textures. In allegros, rhythms are less bouncy than with Marriner, and the effect is less exhilarating. Yet there is an appealing warmth here, and certainly the Philips recording provides beautifully rich string-sound.

Paul Angerer's set of the Op. 6 *Concerti grossi* is also for collectors who prefer a straightforward, traditional approach. He is an excellent musician who proves a sound rather than an inspired guide in this repertoire. He gets good but not particularly subtle playing from the Sudwestfunk Kammerorchester and is decently recorded. Fair value and enjoyable, but the competition is strong.

Concerti grossi, Op. 6/1, 3, 7, 8 (Christmas), 11 & 12.

(M) *** DG Dig. 431 706-2; *431 706-4*. E. Concert, Trevor Pinnock.

We have given high praise to the (full-price) complete set from which these performances come. The English Concert are entirely inside the sensibility of this music and the playing of the continuo group is wonderfully fresh. At mid-price, with the *Christmas Concerto* included, this will admirably suit those collectors who want an original-instrument version and who are content with a single-disc selection.

Concerti grossi, Op. 6/5–8 (Christmas Concerto).

(M) ** Erato/Warner Dig. 2292 45215-2. Sol. Ven., Scimone.

I Solisti Veneti offer polished accounts of the set and are well enough recorded by the Erato engineers. They bring a robust vitality to some of the quicker movements – but are heavy-handed on occasion. On CD, the sound is fresh and full-bodied and the recorded image is very realistic; however, more transparency of texture and a lighter touch are needed in this repertoire, if modern stringed instruments are to be used.

Violin sonatas (for violin & continuo), *Op. 5/1–6.*

(B) ** Hung. White Label HRC 167 [id.]. Dénes Kovács, Ede Banda, János Sebestyén.

Those who do not find pleasure in period instruments might well consider these performances from Dénes Kovács, Ede Banda and János Sebestyén on Hungaroton White Label. Kovács uses an edition by Bernhard Paumgartner, and the violin part has been adapted by Günter Kehr. The analogue recordings were available here on LP during the 1970s, before the use of authentic instruments became so entrenched. Although it now sounds odd to hear a modern cello as a continuo instrument, there is a corresponding gain in warmth that is not unwelcome. Kovács is a player of some imaginative vitality and taste, and the recording is eminently satisfactory, with good separation.

Corigliano, John (born 1938)

(i) *Oboe concerto;* (ii; iii) *3 Irish folksong settings: The Sally Gardens; The foggy dew; She moved thro' the fair;* (ii; iv) *Poem in October.*

(M) *** BMG Analogue/Dig. GD 60395 [60395-2-RG]. (i) Humbert Lucarelli, American SO, Kazuyoshi Akiyama; (ii) Robert White; (iii) Ransom Wilson; (iv) Nyfenger, Lucarelli, Rabbai, American Qt, Peress (cond. from harpsichord).

John Corigliano's highly imaginative *Oboe concerto* (written in 1975 and given this superb première recording a year later) is an ambitious four-movement piece (26 minutes), requiring great flexibility and virtuosity from its soloist as well as the ability to provide beautiful tone and a sustained line in the haunting *Song*, the first of the two slow movements. The work opens ingeniously with the orchestra tuning up, and the music springs fairly naturally from this familiar aleatory pattern of sound. The composer calls his first movement *Tuning game*, and the soloist engages in a not entirely friendly interplay with each of the orchestra's instrumental groups as his 'A' is proffered seductively to each in turn. Later, the scherzo interrupts the end of the *Song* with what the composer describes as 'a polyrhythmic episode for oboe multiphonics and percussion, with harp and piano'. At a concert this crossover intervention might be fun, but on record a little of it goes a long way. The *Aria* has the style of a concerto grosso, with a string quartet concertino heard against orchestral tutti, the oboe providing a bravura cadenza, and the rondo finale is based on a ferocious Moroccan dance. Here the soloist is called on to imitate the rheita (or rhaita), an Arabic double-reed cousin of his own instrument, by playing 'without using his lips and tongue against the reeds'. Later the Moroccan timbre is contrasted with the Western oboe sound when the soloist plays a duet with the orchestra's principal oboe. The performance here is outstanding, expert and spontaneous and very well recorded.

The three *Folksong settings* are for tenor and flute; the latter's embroidery is effective, without adding anything very significant, but Robert White's headily distinctive light tenor gives much pleasure, as he does in the Dylan Thomas setting, *Poem in October*. Essentially lyrical, the music is in a rondo format with the instrumental interludes imaginatively separating the seven verses, and the composer's response, not just to the poem's imagery but to the richness of words and metaphor, is full of individuality and communicates readily. White's performance is most beautiful, especially in the poignant closing section. His diction is remarkably clear, but even so the omission of the texts in the accompanying leaflet is unforgivable.

Correa de Arauxo, Francisco
(*c.* 1576–1654)

Tientos for organ Nos. 10, 15, 16, 28, 34, 37, 47, 52 & 54.
(M) ** HM/BMG GD 77226. Gertrud Mersiovsky (organ of Granada Cathedral).

Francisco Correa de Arauxo was one of the leading Spanish organists and theorists of the first half of the seventeenth century. In 1646 he published his *Libro de Tientos y Discursos de Musica Practica y Theorica de organico*, which can be thought of as the Spanish equivalent of Frescobaldi's *Fiori Musicali* or Scheidt's *Tabulatura Nova*. It comprises some 62 *Tientos* and a handful of other pieces, preceded by a lengthy and important treatise on music. The *Tientos* is the Spanish equivalent of the Ricercare ('*tentar*' means to find), and there is much the same structural freedom. The sleeve-notes speak of Correa's 'austerity and measuredness, his mystical and fanatical exaltation, undisturbed serenity and apparent dynamism', though for the modern listener it will be difficult to discern many stylistic differences between this music and that of his contemporaries. It is not as consistent in interest as the writing of Frescobaldi.

These analogue recordings were made in Granada in 1977 and Gertrud Mersiovsky, successively professor of the organ at Lisbon Conservatory and in São Paulo, Brazil, gives committed accounts of all nine pieces. Decent sound.

Couperin, François (1668–1733)

Les Goûts-réunis: Nouveaux concerts Nos. 8; 9 (Ritratto dell'amore).
(M) **(*) HM/BMG GD 71968. Kuijken Ens.

The Kuijken Ensemble use original instruments, and one only has to sample the *Overture* of the *Eighth Concert* to find how attractive is their sound-world. The *Ninth Concert* has a linking programme and its eight dance movements contrast the many facets of love. The first, *Le charme*, marked *Gracieusement et gravement*, has all the delicacy of mood one would expect; and all these vignettes are engaging in their different ways. The playing here is idiomatic and pleasing; but the disc offers short measure: there is plenty of room for another *Concert*.

Les Nations (Ordres 1–4) complete.
(M) * DG Dig. 427 164-2 (2). Col. Mus. Ant.

This account by the Cologne Musica Antiqua has the benefit of recent scholarship which suggests that many of the dance movements were faster than had previously been believed. They certainly seem faster – yet, paradoxically, each of these suites feels longer; perhaps this is due to the want of tonal variety and generosity. This group is greatly respected in Early Music circles but, to be frank, their playing conveys little sense of the nobility and grandeur of this music, nor does it bring any sense of pleasure. The recording is satisfactory without being top-drawer. Recommended only to admirers of this ensemble.

Harpsichord suites, Book 1, Ordres 1–5.
(B) *** HM HMA 190351/3 [id.]. Kenneth Gilbert.

Harpsichord suites, Book 2, Ordres 6–12.
(B) *** HM HMA 190354/6 [id.]. Kenneth Gilbert.

Harpsichord suites, Book 3, Ordres 13–19.
(B) *** HM HMA 190357/8 [id.]. Kenneth Gilbert.

Harpsichord suites, Book 4, Ordres 20–27.
(B) *** HM HMA 190359/60 [id.]. Kenneth Gilbert.

The Canadian scholar Kenneth Gilbert has edited the complete keyboard works of Couperin, and his recording of them is made on an exact copy of an instrument by Henry Hemsch (1750) made by Hubbard in Boston. Professor Gilbert's performances are scrupulous in matters of registration, following what is known of eighteenth-century practice in France. There is no want of expressive range throughout the series and Gilbert plays with authority and taste – and, more to the point, artistry. He is also well served by the engineers. Readers should note that the sound throughout the series is of excellent quality and altogether on a par with the performances. It is impossible to dwell on the individual felicities of each *Ordre*. As with the *48*, there is little to be gained in making recommendations to start with any particular disc; the important thing is to start somewhere. Once started, the listener will want to explore this rewarding world more fully, and there is no doubt that Kenneth Gilbert is an eminently authoritative guide.

Harpsichord suites, Book 2, Ordres 6, 8 & 11.
(BB) ** Naxos Dig. 8.550460 [id.]. Alan Cuckson (harpsichord).

Harpsichord suites, Book 3, Ordres 13, 17 & 18; Book 4, Ordre 21.
(BB) **(*) Naxos Dig. 8.550461 [id.]. Alan Cuckson (harpsichord).

Harpsichord suites, Book 4, Ordres 22–23; 25–26.
(BB) **(*) Naxos Dig. 8.550462 [id.]. Alan Cuckson (harpsichord).

The three Naxos discs are generously filled; the first, accommodating the *Sixième*, *Huitième* and *Onzième Ordres*, runs to 77 minutes, which represents outstanding value for money. (All three offer over 70 minutes' playing time.) Alan Cuckson also enjoys a competitive advantage over Kenneth Gilbert, whose magisterial survey on Harmonia Mundi cannot be acquired either so conveniently (one disc at a time) or at quite so modest an outlay (even though it is not so very much more expensive). Moreover Cuckson provides more than adequate presentation notes, though they fail to give any indication of the instrument he uses. The recording will sound thunderous played at a normal volume setting, for the transfer has been effected at a very high level. However, when the volume is reduced sharply, the results are satisfactory, even though the balance is really a bit too close. Perhaps Kenneth Gilbert scores in his greater expressive range and variety of colour, though Cuckson has no want of expertise and artistry. At the same time the latter's playing does not have the imaginative flair or the persuasive eloquence which could justify the claim that Couperin was to the eighteenth century what Chopin was to the nineteenth.

Couperin, Louis (*c.* 1626–61)

Harpsichord suites: in A min.; in C; in F; Pavane in F sharp min.
(M) *** HM/BMG GD 77058 [77058-2-RG]. Gustav Leonhardt (harpsichord).

Gustav Leonhardt plays a copy by Skowroneck of a 1680 French harpsichord, and the sound is altogether vivid and appealing; the quality of the recording is completely natural and lifelike. Louis Couperin's invention is not always as rich in character as that of his nephew, and it needs playing of this order to show it to best advantage. Leonhardt has such subtlety and panache that he makes the most of the grandeur and refinement of this music to whose sensibility he seems wholly attuned. This is the best introduction to Louis Couperin's keyboard suites now before the public.

Czerny, Karl (1791–1857)

Variations on a theme by Rode: La Ricordanza, Op. 23.
(M) (**) BMG/RCA mono GD 60451 [60451-2-RG]. Vladimir Horowitz – MENDELSSOHN: *Variations sérieuses;* MOZART: *Sonata No. 12;* SCHUBERT: *Sonata No. 21.* (**)

Czerny's *Variations on a theme by Pierre Rode* is emphatically no masterpiece but, played with such elegance and virtuosity, one is almost persuaded that its neglect is undeserved. The recording was made in December 1944 and sounds remarkably good for its period, even if it is pretty two-dimensional.

Dawson, William Levi (born 1898)

Negro Folk Symphony.
(B) ** MCA Double-decker (2) [MCAD2-9826-A/B]. American SO, Stokowski – BRAHMS: *Serenade No. 1.* **(*)

William Dawson began life the son of a poor Alabama labourer. That he should have worked his way to become Director of Music at the Tuskegee Institute from such humble beginnings compels admiration and one does not want to seem patronizing about his *Negro Folk Symphony*, written in 1931 but revised in 1952. It purports to combine European influences (of which the principal ingredient is a distinct flavour of Dvořák's *New World Symphony*) and Negro folk-themes. But the sad fact is that the result is undistinguished, and the work fails to hold the listener's attention either by its architecture or by its musical ideas. The scoring, too, is thin, although it is not helped here by a two-dimensional recording. Stokowski's performance, however, is as persuasive as it could possibly be.

Debussy, Claude (1862–1918)

Berceuse héroïque; La Boîte à joujoux (complete ballet, orch. Caplet); *L'Enfant Prodique: Cortège et Air de danse.* (i) *Fantasy for piano and orchestra; Marche écossaise; Le Martyre de Saint-Sébastien: 2 Fanfares & symphonic fragments. Musiques pour le Roi Lear: Fanfare; Le sommeil de Lear. La plus que lente* (orch. composer); *Printemps* (orch. Büsser); (ii) *Première Rhapsodie for clarinet and orchestra;* (iii) *Rhapsodie for saxophone and orchestra. Le Triomphe de Bacchus* (Divertissment).
(B) ** VoxBox (2) [CDX 5053]. Psallette de Lorraine Vocal Ens., R. Luxembourg O, Louis de Froment; with (i) Marylene Dosse; (ii) Serge Dangain; (iii) Jean-Marie Londeix.

Berceuse héroïque; Marche écossaise; La Mer; Musiques pour le Roi Lear; Nocturnes; Prélude à l'après-midi d'un faune.
(M) **(*) EMI CDM7 69587-2. French R. & TV Ch. & O, Martinon.

Martinon's account of *La Mer* first appeared in the mid-1970s. It still has plenty of atmosphere and enjoys the idiomatic advantage of fine French orchestral playing. The *Musiques pour le Roi Lear* is a real rarity; the colourful *Fanfare* remains impressive, and *Le sommeil de Lear* is highly evocative. The *Nocturnes* are not quite the equal of the finest versions, but are still beautifully played. This is a fairly competitive recommendation, though in the digital remastering there is a slight edge at the upper end of the range, where the trumpets are shrill.

For readers who possess individual Debussy records in their collection, Martinon's records, made (like the present set) in the early 1970s, are an obvious first choice as they can be bought individually. They also offer more distinguished orchestral playing, but this Vox Box remains very good value. Not only are there such rarities as the *Musique pour Le roi Lear* and *Khamma*, which Martinon also includes, but also the four fragments from *Le Martyre de Saint-Sébastien* and *Le Triomphe de Bacchus*, which he does not. True, there are finer versions of the former, but the latter remains an only recording. It was written in 1882 after Debussy's return from Russia, where he had stayed with Madame von Meck (Tchaikovsky's patroness), but it bears the imprint of Rimsky-Korsakov rather than Tchaikovsky. Debussy never completed scoring the piece. Louis de Froment is a sensitive Debussian and there are some good performances here, though Marylene Dosse does not eclipse memories of Jean-Rudolph Kars's Decca account, also from the 1970s. Both this and the companion set have excellent notes by Richard Freed.

(i) *La Boîte à joujoux* (orch. Caplet): complete; (ii) *La Mer; Prélude à l'après-midi d'un faune;* (i) *Sarabande* (orch. Ravel).
(M) **(*) Erato/Warner 2292 45569-2 [id.]. (i) Basle SO, Jordan; (ii) Strasbourg PO, Lombard.

Debussy's delightful children's ballet score about adventures in a box of toys was orchestrated by André Caplet. Armin Jordan's 1982 analogue account is enjoyably alive and, though not distinguished by playing of the very highest order, it is helped by a vivid CD transfer. Jordan's sympathetic account of Ravel's arrangement of the *Sarabande* from *Pour le piano* is also most welcome. The addition of a passionately atmospheric Strasbourg *La Mer*, very well transferred to CD, and an acceptably sensuous *Prélude à l'après-midi d'un faune* (recorded earlier, in the mid-1970s) makes this CD excellent value, with a playing time of 71 minutes. Neither of the Strasbourg performances are as polished as, say, Karajan but they are played with strong idiomatic feeling. The sleeve-note writer seems to think that *Jeux* is included in the programme, as there is no mention of the children's ballet.

Danse (orch. Ravel); (i) *Fantaisie for piano and orchestra;* (ii) *La plus que lente;* (iii) *Khamma;* (iv) *Première Rhapsodie for clarinet and orchestra;* (v) *Rhapsodie for saxophone.*
(M) **(*) EMI CDM7 69668-2. (i) Aldo Ciccolini; (ii) John Leach; (iii) Fabienne Boury; (iv) Guy Dangain; (v) Londe; Fr. R. & TV O, Martinon.

The rarity here is *Khamma*, which Ansermet recorded in the 1960s, a ballet whose scoring Debussy entrusted to Charles Koechlin. The two *Rhapsodies* are underrated, and although there are alternative versions of all these pieces on CD, few are more generously coupled or more economically priced. Very acceptable performances and recordings.

(i) *Danses sacrée et profane;* (ii) *La Mer;* (iii) *Prélude à l'après-midi d'un faune.*
(B) *** DG Compact Classics 413 154-2 (2); *413 154-4* [id.]. (i) Zabaleta, Paul Kuentz CO, Kuentz; (ii) BPO, Karajan; (iii) Boston SO, Tilson Thomas – RAVEL: *Alborada; Boléro; Pavane; Rapsodie espagnole* (CD only: *Tombeau de Couperin; Valses nobles.* **(*))

Three fine performances. Zabaleta's *Danses sacrée et profane* come from the late 1960s and are beautifully played; Karajan's analogue *La Mer* is very much in a class of its own and Tilson Thomas's *Prélude* is refined and atmospheric, with excellent recording from the early 1970s. Ozawa's Ravel couplings have a less striking profile, though they again show the Boston orchestra on top form and offer very impressive sound in both formats. The pair of CDs includes two extra Ravel works.

Fantasy for piano and orchestra.
(M) *** Erato/Warner 2292 45086-2 [id.]. Anne Queffélec, Monte Carlo Op. O, Jordan – RAVEL: *Concertos.* ***

Debussy's *Fantasy*, an early work, does not find his musical language fully formed, but it is well worth investigating, for in Anne Queffélec's hands it makes a good impression. The warm recording too is persuasive.

Images (complete).
(M) *(*) DG Dig. 429 487-2; *429 487-4*. O de Paris, Barenboim – RAVEL: *Daphnis* etc. **

Barenboim secures a good response from the Orchestre de Paris and there are many felicitous touches. However, there is nothing very special here: the performance remains serviceable rather than distinguished and ultimately there is a lack of real profile which in the last resort is disappointing. The 1982 sound is well balanced, atmospheric and vivid.

Images; Jeux; Khamma; La Mer; Nocturnes; Prélude à l'après-midi d'un faune.
(B) ** VoxBox 1154922 (2) [CDX 5003]. Luxembourg R. O, de Froment.

Very decent performances from the Luxembourg Radio Orchestra under Louis de Froment, and acceptable recording too. The strings above the stave are wanting in bloom and a bit tizzy, but there is a good sense of space. Tuttis could be cleaner but, generally speaking, the sound is serviceable, if not the equal of Martinon on EMI. The female choir in *Sirènes* sing in tune and the *Fêtes* has admirable vitality. The second CD seems to be transferred at a slightly lower level and there is a curious misreading from the cor anglais at the opening of *Gigues* and some unbeautiful tone later on. Both *Jeux* and *Khamma* come off particularly well and the recordings have a decent sense of space round them. Although the set may not be a first choice, many pieces give pleasure and the recordings, though far from distinguished, are not unsatisfactory. Whatever its merits or shortcomings, this represents value for money.

Images: Ibéria.
❀ (M) *** BMG/RCA GD 60179 [60179-2-RG]. Chicago SO, Fritz Reiner – RAVEL: *Alborada* etc. *** ❀

Fritz Reiner and the Chicago orchestra give a reading that is immaculate in execution and magical in atmosphere. There have been superb modern accounts since this first appeared, over 30 years ago, but none that are more refined in terms of characterization. This marvellously evocative performance, and the Ravel with which it is coupled, has been underrated by the wider record-loving public over the years and has long been out of circulation. It should not be overlooked now, for the recorded sound with its natural concert-hall balance is greatly improved in terms of body and definition. It is amazingly realistic even without considering its vintage.

Images: Ibéria. La Mer; Nocturnes: Nuages; Fêtes. Prélude à l'après-midi d'un faune.
(M) (**(*)) BMG/RCA mono GD 60265 [60265-2-RG]. NBC SO, Toscanini.

There is nothing vague about Toscanini's view of Debussy. Anyone who is wanting mistily evocative readings of this generous group of Debussy's greatest orchestral works should look elsewhere; by emphasizing clarity, Toscanini with his electric intensity and sense of purpose consistently compels attention. One thinks of these supreme examples of musical impressionism, not as colour pieces, but as masterly structures of great originality in purely musical terms. Least effective is the account of the first of the *Nocturnes*, where Toscanini's metrical manner is unsympathetic, but *Fêtes* is exhilaratingly fast and brilliant, even if the procession is raced along mercilessly. Sadly, the third of the *Nocturnes* with its women's chorus is omitted. Clean, bright transfers.

Jeux; La Mer; Prélude à l'après-midi d'un faune.
❀ (M) *** EMI Dig. CD-EMX 9502; *TC-EMX 2090* [Ang. CDM 62012]. LPO, Baudo.

Serge Baudo's version of *La Mer* is first class and can be ranked alongside the finest accounts now on disc. The recording is beautifully natural and expertly balanced. The same may be said for his lovely account of *Prélude à l'après-midi d'un faune*, as atmospheric as any in the catalogue and more beautifully shaped than many. In the faster sections, *Jeux* is at times brisker than we are used to and well conveys the sense of the playfulness of the tennis match. Its competitive price makes it even more enticing.

La Mer.
(M) *** BMG/RCA GD 60875 [60875-2-RG]. Chicago SO, Reiner – RIMSKY-KORSAKOV: *Scheherazade.* ***
(M) **(*) EMI/Phoenixa CDM7 63763-2; *EG*

763763-4 [id.]. Hallé O, Barbirolli – RAVEL: *Daphnis et Chloé* etc. **(*)
(M) (**) EMI mono CDH7 69784-2. BBC SO, Toscanini – ELGAR: *Enigma variations*.(***)

La Mer; Images: Ibéria (only).
(M) (*) BMG/RCA mono GD 60311. Phd. O, Toscanini – RESPIGHI: *Feste romane*. (*)

La Mer; (i) *Nocturnes*.
(M) *** EMI CDM7 69184-2; *EG 769184-4*. Philh. O, Giulini, with Ch.
(M) *** EMI Dig. CDD7 64056-2 [id.]; *EG 764056-4*. LSO, Previn; (i) with Amb. S. – RAVEL: *Alborada* etc. ***
(B) **(*) EMI CZS7 62669-2 (2). O de Paris, Barbirolli; (i) with female Ch. (with Concert: *French music* ***).

(i) *La Mer;* (i; ii) *Nocturnes;* (iii) *Prélude à l'après-midi d'un faune*.
(B) *** Pickwick Dig. PCD 915; *CIMPC 915*. LSO, Frühbeck de Burgos, with Ch. in *Nocturnes*.
(BB) **(*) Naxos Dig. 8.550262 [id.]. Belgian Radio & TV O (Brussels), Alexander Rahbari.
(M) *(*) Ph. 426 635-2; *426 635-4*. Concg. O, (i) Inbal, (ii) with Netherlands R. Ch.; (iii) Fournet.
(M) * Decca Dig. 430 732-2; *430 732-4* [id.]. Cleveland O, Ashkenazy, with women's Ch. in *Nocturnes*.

La Mer; Prélude à l'après-midi d'un faune.
(M) *** DG 427 250-2. BPO, Karajan – RAVEL: *Boléro; Daphnis et Chloé*. ***
(M) ** Decca 430 444-2; *430 444-4* [id.]. Chicago SO, Solti – RAVEL: *Boléro* etc. *(*)

After more than two decades, Karajan's 1964 DG account of *La Mer* is still very much in a class of its own. So strong is its evocative power that one feels one can almost see and smell the ocean, and the superb playing of the Berlin orchestra, for all its virtuosity and beauty of sound, is totally at the service of the composer. The performance of the *Prélude à l'après-midi d'un faune* is no less outstanding, the cool perfection of the opening flute solo matched by ravishing string-playing in the central section.

Reiner's 1960 recording has not previously been available in the UK. It has all the warmth and atmosphere that make his version of *Ibéria*, recorded at about the same time – see above – so unforgettable. The pianissimo opening has enormous evocative feeling and the *Jeux des vagues* has the same haunting sense of colour. Of course the marvellous acoustics of the Chicago Hall contribute to the appeal of this superbly played account: the effect is richer and fuller than in Karajan's remastered DG version, and Reiner's record gives no less pleasure. With Karajan, one could picture the bracing air of the northern Atlantic, whereas with Reiner, although the dialogue of the wind and waves is no less powerful, one senses a more southern latitude.

Giulini's early EMI version of *La Mer* is also very distinguished. The Philharmonia are in splendid form, and the coupled *Nocturnes* are also played with great delicacy of feeling and refinement of detail; if *Nuages* is perhaps a little too dreamy, it is nevertheless full of atmosphere. *Sirènes*, however, is somewhat lacking in a sense of movement, slow to the point of sluggishness. Nevertheless, overall this is an impressive reissue.

Previn's *La Mer* is not quite as fine as Karajan's 1964 version, but it is a considerable achievement. His ocean is clearly in the southern hemisphere, with Debussy's orchestral colours made to sound more vividly sunlit. The playing of the LSO is extremely impressive, particularly the ardour of the strings. There is less subtlety than with Giulini, emphasized by the recording which has glittering detail and expands brilliantly at climaxes (though, even on CD, there is a slight loss of refinement at the very loudest peaks). The *Nocturnes* have even greater spontaneity. Some might feel that the *Sirènes* are too voluptuous but this matches Previn's extrovert approach. The spectacular qualities of the 1983 Abbey Road recording remain impressive for, although definition is very clear, there is no lack of ambient atmosphere. The reissue adds a pair of first-class Ravel performances and gives a total playing time of nearly 77 minutes.

Although strong in Mediterranean atmosphere, Frühbeck de Burgos's account of *La Mer* has an underlying grip, so he can concentrate on evocation at the opening and create a real pianissimo, helped by the wide dynamic range of the Walthamstow recording. Later he indulges in a moment of sultry rubato in the early part of the *Dialogue du vent et de la mer*, and yet he continues to lead the ear on spontaneously. Overall there is plenty of excitement, with the LSO's virtuosity in the finale matched by the rich-toned ardour of the strings when they rise to the emotional peak of *Jeux de vagues*. There is much subtlety of detail, both here and in the *Nocturnes*, where textures again have the sensuousness of southern climes, while the processional of *Fêtes* proceeds spectacularly, glittering with colour. The *Prélude à l'après-midi d'un faune* brings lovely delicate flute playing from Paul Edmund-Davies and a richly moulded string climax. If these are not conventional readings, they are full of impulse and superbly recorded.

Barbirolli's 1959 Hallé version of *La Mer*

readily demonstrates his special feeling for the atmosphere and rhapsodical freedom of Debussy's masterly score. The performance has remarkable grip and becomes increasingly exciting in its closing section. The remastering for CD of the (originally PRT) recording is a great success, cutting down background noise without losing vividness, and simultaneously improving the focus.

The later, French account, recorded in Paris in 1968, is also very sympathetic and certainly does not lack sensuous, evocative feeling. Barbirolli and the Orchestre de Paris are helped by the more modern sound; moreover the CD brings better-defined detail than the original LP, without losing the warmth of texture provided by the ambience of the Salle Wagram. There is some lack of inner tension about the playing, both here and in the *Nocturnes*, where the close balance of the female chorus in *Sirènes* reduces the ethereal effect, but, as in the earlier, Hallé recording, there is plenty of adrenalin flowing in the closing *Dialogue du vent et de la mer* of the former piece. This is now reissued in EMI's competitive French 'two for the price of one' series.

Judging from these Naxos performances, the Flemish section of the Belgian Radio Orchestra under its Iranian-born conductor, Alexander Rahbari, is in good shape. They give eminently respectable (and certainly very well-recorded) accounts of these familiar Debussy scores and, though they would not perhaps be a first choice among a discography that includes Reiner, Giulini and Karajan (whose Salzburg assistant Rahbari was), this certainly fits the bill for young (or even not so young) collectors with limited means just starting to explore classical music. Perhaps *Fêtes* could have slightly more pace and tension (though it is far from slack), but the strength of Rahbari's *Nocturnes* is the good female choir in *Sirènes*, which are well focused and in tune. The account of *La Mer* needs just a bit more excitement, though *Jeu de vagues* comes off very well. The atmospheric and very natural recording is a major plus. You can do worse than this with a full-price disc, and no one buying this is going to feel badly let down.

Whether or not influenced by the character of the Ravel coupling, Solti treats the evocative Debussy works as virtuoso showpieces. That works very well in the two fast movements of *La Mer* (helped by brightly analytical recording), but much of the poetry is lost in the opening movement, not to mention *L'après-midi*. The CD transfer brings vivid, clean sound without added edge.

Inbal's accounts do little to make the pulse beat faster. His tempi are brisk; however, though the orchestral playing is of a high standard, both *La Mer* and the *Nocturnes* sound prosaic and rarely rise above the routine.

Although Ashkenazy's Cleveland versions of these works have the advantage of superb 1987 digital sound, Ashkenazy seems unable to get inside the music, tempi are often unconvincing and the beautiful *Prélude à l'après-midi d'un faune* lacks shape without a really strong central climax.

Toscanini's 1935 recording of *La Mer* is extremely vivid and the sense of occasion is striking. However, it cannot quite compare with his much later NBC recording which, with far crisper ensemble, bites harder; the London recording, well handled by the engineers, is seriously marred by audience noises (there are some appalling coughs to disfigure the quiet opening section).

Toscanini's Debussy and Respighi are the least successful of his Philadelphia recordings made in the winter season of 1941–2. The sound is poorer than on the other Philadelphia discs, with the Debussy spoiled by heavy surface noise. The performances too are less sympathetic, more regimented, than those Toscanini recorded with the NBC and BBC Symphony Orchestras.

(i) *Nocturnes; Le Martyre de Saint Sébastien: 2 Fanfares & symphonic fragments; Printemps* (symphonic suite).

❀ (M) *** DG 435 069-2; *435 069-4* [id.]. (i) Ch.; O de Paris, Daniel Barenboim.

This is one of Barenboim's very finest records and in its reissued format (72 minutes) generously includes not only the early *Printemps* and the fragments from *Le Martyre de Saint Sébastien* but also his splendid set of *Nocturnes*. This performance, although highly individual in its control of tempo, has great fervour. *Sirènes* develops a feeling of soaring ecstasy, and the closing pages with the chorus are rapturously beautiful. Comparably in *Le Martyre* Barenboim succeeds in distilling an intense, rapt quality and brings to life its evocative atmosphere in a way that has not been matched since Cantelli's mono HMV recording. If Barenboim does not diffuse the score with quite the same delicacy of feeling that Cantelli secured, he still refrains from any expressive indulgence and allows the music to speak for itself. He is no less persuasive in *Printemps* (which had to be re-orchestrated by Henri Büsser – following the composer's instructions – when the original was lost in a fire). This receives a performance as good as any in the catalogue: Barenboim succeeds in balancing intensity with atmospheric feeling, and the result is very persuasive. The 1977/8 recordings, made in either Notre Dame du Liban or the Paris Mutualité, are spacious, rich in texture and well balanced, with good definition and range, and the CD transfer refines detail without reducing the sonic allure.

CHAMBER MUSIC

Beau soir (arr. Chesis/Cutler); *Children's corner* (arr. Salzedo); *Danse (Tarantelle styrienne); La fille aux cheveux de lin; L'isle joyeuse* (all arr. Noon); *Sonata for flute, viola & harp;* (i) *Chansons de Bilitis* (complete version).

(M) ** Pickwick MCD 23. Linda Chesis, Sara Cutler, New World Qt; (i) with Claire Bloom, Janet Paulus, Elizabeth Difelice.

This disc is largely a vehicle for the talents of the American flautist, Linda Chesis, and the harpist, Sara Cutler. It opens with the ethereal *Sonata for flute, viola and harp*, in which they are joined by the violist, Daniel Avshalomov; it is sensitively played but rather too forwardly recorded. The *Chansons de Bilitis* poems are offered in a good English translation, spoken with a slightly mid-Atlantic accent by Claire Bloom. However, the instruments are far more closely balanced than she, and the overall effect sounds a bit too creamy and overnourished. *Beau soir* is transcribed for flute and harp. The various piano pieces, *Children's corner*, *L'isle joyeuse*, *La fille aux cheveux de lin* and the *Danse*, are all heard in transcriptions of varying success for flute, harp and string quartet. Some listeners may find them enjoyable, though they would seem more suitable for the recital room than for repeated hearing at home. This is all undeniably accomplished music-making, though the sound is glamorized.

Cello sonata in D min.

(M) ** Erato/Warner 2292 45660-2 [id.]. Paul Tortelier, Jean Hubeau – FAURÉ: *Cello sonatas* etc. **

Tortelier's impassioned account of the *Sonata* comes with the two Fauré *Sonatas* and the *Élégie* and was recorded in 1962. The sound is very decent, if perhaps a little dryish, with the result that Jean Hubeau's piano is somewhat lacking in bloom.

(i) *Cello sonata in D min.;* (ii; iii) *Sonata for flute, viola and harp;* (iv) *Violin sonata in G min.;* (ii) *Syrinx.*

(M) *** Ph. 422 839-2; *422 839-4*. (i) Gendron, Françaix; (ii) Bourdin; (iii) Lequien, Challan; (iv) Grumiaux, Hajdu.

Though these excellent performances on Philips do not wholly dislodge others from one's affections, for example Rostropovich's account of the *Cello sonata* (at full price) or Chung's version of the *Violin sonata* on Decca, they are very nearly as fine. Gendron's version of the *Cello sonata* is most eloquent and is splendidly recorded.

String quartet in G min.

(M) *** Ph. 420 894-2 [id.]. Italian Qt – RAVEL: *Quartet*. ***

(BB) **(*) Naxos Dig. 8.550249 [id.]. Kodály Qt – RAVEL: *Quartet* etc. ***

(B) **(*) Hung. White Label HRC 122 [id.]. Bartók Qt – RAVEL: *Quartet* **(*); DVOŘÁK: *Quartet No. 12*. ***

It need hardly be said that the playing of the Italian Quartet is outstanding. Perfectly judged ensemble, weight and tone make this a most satisfying choice, and the recording engineers have produced a vivid and truthful sound-picture, with plenty of impact.

As we know from their Haydn recordings, the Kodály Quartet are an excellent ensemble and they give a thoroughly enjoyable account that can be recommended to those who do not want to spend that bit extra on the mid-priced Quartetto Italiano version. There are moments here (in the slow movement, for example) when the Kodály, too, are touched by distinction. This music-making has the feel of a live performance and is to be preferred to some of the glossier, mechanized accounts at full price: these players also have the benefit of a generous fill-up and very good recorded sound. Excellent value.

The account by the Bartók Quartet is full of character, and the *Andante* is certainly *doucement expressif*. The recording is good, too, and well balanced; with three quartets on offer, this record is a genuine bargain.

Violin sonata in G min.; Prélude (La fille aux cheveux de lin) arr. Arthur Hartmann.

(M) (**) BMG/RCA mono GD 87871; *GK 87871* [7871-2-RG; *7871-4-RG*]. Heifetz, Bay – MARTINŮ: *Duo* ***; RAVEL: *Trio* etc. (**); RESPIGHI: *Sonata*. (***)

(i) *Violin sonata in G min.;* (ii) *Sonata for flute, viola and harp.*

❀ (M) *** Decca 421 154-2; *421 154-4*. (i) Kyung Wha Chung, Radu Lupu; (ii) Melos Ens. (members) – FRANCK: *Violin sonata*; RAVEL: *Introduction and allegro*. *** ❀

(M) ** EMI CDM7 63986-2 [id.]. Sir Yehudi Menuhin, (i) Février; (ii) Debost, Laskine. – FAURÉ: *Andante* etc. **; RAVEL: *Piano trio*. *(*)

Kyung Wha Chung and Radu Lupu are superbly balanced and most truthfully recorded. Miss Chung plays with marvellous character and penetration, and her partnership with Radu Lupu could hardly be more fruitful. Nothing is pushed to extremes, and everything is in perfect perspective so far as both the playing and the recording are concerned. The *Sonata for flute, viola and harp* and the Ravel *Introduction and allegro* come from a famous Oiseau-Lyre record made in 1962. In both works the playing is wonderfully sensitive and the music's ethereal atmosphere well caught. The recording sounds admirably real.

While it is true that there are more polished and integrated accounts of the other-worldly *Sonata for flute, viola and harp*, as recorded by Menuhin with Michel Debost and the legendary Lili Laskine in 1974 in the Salle Wagram there is a wonderfully ethereal start to the first movement that more than counterbalances some inelegance from Menuhin's viola in the *Interlude* and the finale. Some will find it too loosely held together and too rhapsodic – these artists add three minutes to the Melos's timing – but all the same there are moments of beauty that almost redeem the occasional rough touches. Neither this nor the *Violin sonata* with Jacques Février, which was recorded at the same time, was issued in the UK, and it must be conceded that the recording itself is somewhat lacking in bloom.

Heifetz's immaculately played account of the *Violin sonata* was recorded in the 1950s and, although the golden tone is glorious, allowances have to be made for the dryish piano timbre – though not, of course, for Emanuel Bay's playing. Perhaps David Oistrakh and Frida Bauer achieved a more ethereal effect in the closing pages of the slow movement.

PIANO MUSIC

(i) *En blanc et noir* (for 2 pianos); *Petite suite* (for piano, 4 hands). (ii) *2 Arabesques; Berceuse héroïque; Children's corner; Danse bohémienne; Estampes; Hommage à Haydn; Masques; Mazurka; Le petit nègre; Pour le piano; Rêverie; Suite bergamasque; Valse romantique.*

(B) *** Turnabout 0004 (2). (i) Walter & Beatriz Klien; (ii) Peter Frankl – FAURÉ: *Dolly*. ***

En blanc et noir is a masterpiece and its comparative neglect is unaccountable, while the *Petite suite* is just as charming in its four-handed piano version as it is in full orchestral dress. The playing here from the Klien duo is sensitive and the recording good. The rest of the programme comes from Peter Frankl who is an eminently stylish Debussy player and is also well recorded. Readers need feel no hesitation in investing in this collection with its appealing Fauré bonus. However, it is a matter for regret that the documentation lists the works played and nothing more.

Solo piano music

2 Arabesques; Ballade; Danse bohémienne; Images I–II; Images (1894); Mazurka; Nocturne.

(M) *** Saga SCD 9020. Livia Rév.

For a long time Livia Rév was underrated as a pianist; it was these Debussy recordings which established her reputation, receiving wide and just acclaim when they first appeared on LP. This compilation (77 minutes 38 seconds) can hold its own with any in the catalogue. Livia Rév has sensibility, a finely developed sense of colour, a keen awareness of atmosphere and fleet fingers. What more could one ask for in this repertoire? She is moreover decently recorded in a spacious acoustic, and the CD transfers are extremely successful.

Arabesques 1–2; Ballade; Danse bohémienne; Danse (Tarantelle styrienne); Images (1894); *Nocturne; Pour le piano; Rêverie; Suite bergamasque; Valse romantique.*

(M) ** Pickwick MCD 24; *MCC 24* [id.]. Martino Tirimo.

Martino Tirimo's anthology shares two pieces, the *Arabesques* and the *Suite bergamasque*, with Klára Körmendi's programme on Naxos; and there is another similarity: a very close balance. If anything, Tirimo is more closely observed than she is, but he can withstand the closer scrutiny. His playing is the more distinguished and there is never any doubt as to his Debussian credentials. He plays only the two outer movements of the 1894 *Images*, arguing quite reasonably that the differences between the two versions of the *Sarabande* are very slight. But the balance is horribly close and the microphone even picks up the pedal mechanism (try the opening of the *Danse* (*Tarantelle styrienne*) on Track 8) to an unacceptable extent. The acoustic of Rosslyn Hill Chapel, Hampstead, does permit the sound to expand – but some slight background noise from the environs, which was probably what was posing problems for the engineer, would be better than putting the listener virtually on the piano stool.

2 Arabesques; Ballade; Images, Book 1: Reflets dans l'eau; Mouvement. Book 2: Poissons d'or. L'isle joyeuse; Préludes, Book 2: Feux d'artifice. Suite bergamasque.

(M) *** EMI CD-EMX 2055-2; *TC-EMX 2055*. Daniel Adni.

This collection dates from 1972 and was a follow-up to a similarly successful Chopin recital which had served as Daniel Adni's gramophone début the previous year and was equally well recorded. It is outstanding in every way: this young Israeli pianist proves himself a

Debussian of no mean order. His recital is well planned and offers playing that is as poetic in feeling as it is accomplished in technique.

2 Arabesques; Children's corner; Images I and II; Suite bergamasque.
(M) *** Decca 417 792-2; *417 792-4*. Pascal Rogé.

Pascal Rogé's playing is distinguished by a keen musical intelligence and sympathy, as well as by a subtle command of keyboard colour. Apart from the *Images* with their finesse and highly accomplished pianism, the *Suite bergamasque* is particularly successful, with genuine poetry in the famous *Clair de lune*. The well-defined Decca sound is most realistic. The quality is eminently secure and the bottom end of the piano reproduces in a most lifelike fashion.

Arabesques 1–2; Images I and II; Préludes, Book 1: *Des pas sur la neige; La fille aux cheveaux de lin; La danse de Puck;* Book 2: *Général Lavine: dans le style et le mouvement d'un cake-walk; Les terrasses des audiences du clair de lune; Feux d'artifice. Suite bergamasque.*
(BB) *(*) Naxos Dig. 8.550253 [id.]. Klára Körmendi.

The Hungarian pianist Klára Körmendi is a sympathetic advocate of Messiaen, Boulez, Berio and other contemporary composers and, judging from this recital, an idiomatic interpreter of Debussy, too. Moreover the recording, made at the Italian Institute in Budapest, at first seems more acceptable than some others Naxos have made at this venue. But when the level rises above *forte*, the sound dries out and hammers are all too evident: try *La plus que lente* (Track 5) and this will become clear. Martino Tirimo also is too closely observed in his very similar anthology (listed above), but there is room into which *fortes* can expand with comfort.

2 Arabesques; L'Isle joyeuse; Masques; La plus que lente; Pour le piano; Suite bergamasque; Tarantelle styrienne (Danse).
(B) *** DG 429 517-2; *429 517-4* [id.]. Tamás Vásáry.

Vásáry is at his very best in the *Suite bergamasque,* and *Clair de lune* is beautifully played, as are the *Arabesques*. *La plus que lente* receives the least convincing performance. Here Vásáry's rubato sounds slightly unspontaneous. But overall this is a satisfying recital and makes an excellent bargain, particularly as the piano is so realistic.

Berceuse héroïque; Études, Books 1–2; Morceau de concours; Suite bergamasque.
(M) *** Saga SCD 9027. Livia Rév.

The *Études* are not represented as generously in the catalogue as the *Préludes* or *Images*, so these fine performances are doubly welcome. Livia Rév is consistently imaginative and her playing has considerable poetic feeling, as well as great technical accomplishment. The *Suite bergamasque* is also highly sensitive. The 1980 recording is excellent and the disc offers 75 minutes of music.

Children's corner; Élégie; Hommage à Haydn; Page d'album; Préludes, Book 1; La plus que lente; Tarantelle styrienne (Danse).
(M) *** Saga SCD 9021. Livia Rév.

Livia Rév plays *Children's corner* very well, though without quite the elegance we find in Pascal Rogé's Decca recital. But her performance of the *Préludes* holds its own in terms of sensitivity and atmosphere. Her keyboard mastery is beyond question (just sample *La cathédrale engloutie*) and she is a fine colourist. The recording, too, is first class, full and natural, and admirably transferred to CD. Moreover the playing time of this programme is over 71 minutes.

Estampes; Images, Books 1–2; Préludes, Books 1–2.
(M) *** Ph. 432 304-2 (2) [id.]. Claudio Arrau.

Claudio Arrau's versions of these solo piano works by Debussy, praised by us in the past in their full-price format, have been re-released by Philips at mid-price as part of their Arrau Edition, commemorating the death of the great pianist. The piano timbre in these 1978/9 analogue recordings has a consistent body and realism typical of this company's finest work.

Estampes: La soirée dans Grenade; Jardins sous la pluie. Étude No. 5 pour les octaves. Images, Book 1: Reflets dans l'eau. Préludes, Book 2: La terrasse des audiences du clair de lune; Feux d'artifice.
(M) ** BMG/RCA GD 60415; *GK 60445* [60415-2-RG; *60415-4-RG*]. Van Cliburn – BARBER: *Sonata* **(*); MOZART: *Sonata No. 10.* **

Van Cliburn shows that he is no mean interpreter of Debussy in these sensitive performances, but he is handicapped a little by the lustreless recording. Nevertheless the disc is well worth having for the Barber *Sonata*.

Préludes, Books 1–2 (complete).
❀ (M) *** EMI mono CDH7 61004-2 [id.]. Walter Gieseking.
(M) (***) Sony mono MPK 45688 [id.]. Robert Casadesus.
(M) *** Pickwick Dig. MCD 16; *MCC 16*. Martino Tirimo.

In his day, Walter Gieseking was something of a legend as a Debussy interpreter, and this excellent CD transfer testifies to his magic. Background is almost vanquished; our copy produced some very slight noise near the opening, but for the most part this is simply not a problem. Gieseking penetrates the atmosphere of the *Préludes* more deeply than almost any other artist. This is playing of rare distinction and great evocative quality. However, the documentation is concerned solely with the artist and gives no information about the music save the titles and the cues.

Robert Casadesus's accounts of the *Préludes* are (like Gieseking's before him) legendary. His recordings were made in 1953/4 and the piano sound is faithful, though the second book has a warmer, fuller piano image. The performances of Book 2 show the pianist at his very finest: *Brouillards* and *Feuilles mortes*, for instance, are superbly atmospheric and *Feux d'artifice* glitters with fiery brilliance. At times in Book 1 he is a trifle cool. Nevertheless this is all distinguished playing and this CD is a must for Debussians.

No grumbles about value for money or about quality from Martino Tirimo on Pickwick; he accommodates both Books on the same disc. His playing is very fine indeed and can withstand comparison with most of his rivals – and, apart from the sensitivity of the playing, the recording is most realistic and natural. This is first choice for those wanting a modern digital record offering the complete set.

VOCAL MUSIC

Mélodies: (i) *Aimons-nous et dormons;* (ii) *Les Angelus;* (iii) *Ariettes oubliées;* (iv) *3 Ballades de François Villon; Beau soir;* (ii) *La Belle au Bois dormant;* (i) *Calmes dans le demi-jour;* (ii) *3 Chansons de Bilitis;* (iv) *Chanson de France;* (i) *4 Chansons de jeunesse;* (ii) *Les cloches;* (v) *Danse de jardin; L'échelonnement des haies; Fêtes galantes* (first group); (iv) *Fêtes galantes* (2nd group); (v) *Fleur de blés;* (i) *Jane;* (iv) *Mandoline; La mer est plus belle;* (v) *Noël des enfants qui n'ont plus de maison; Nuit d'étoiles;* (i) *Paysage sentimental;* (ii) *5 Poèmes de Charles Baudelaire;* (v) *3 Poèmes de Stéphane Mallarmé;* (iv) *Le promenoir des deux amants;* (v) *4 Proses lyriques;* (i) *Romance; Rondeau; Rondel chinois;* (iv) *Le son du cor s'afflige;* (i) *Voici que le printemps; Zéphyr.*

(M) *** EMI CMS7 64095-2 (3). (i) Mady Mesplé; (ii) Michèle Command; (iii) Frederica von Stade; (iv) Gérard Souzay; (v) Elly Ameling; all with Dalton Baldwin.

These three generously filled discs at mid-price offer no fewer than 55 of Debussy's songs out of a total of just over 80. Drawn from recordings made between 1971 and 1979, they were all done in the Salle Wagram in Paris with Dalton Baldwin accompanying. Arranged in the order of publication, they give an illuminating idea of the composer's development, from his earliest Fauré-like songs, through his vital discovery of the poet Verlaine as his most consistent source of inspiration, and on to the rarefied atmosphere of the late songs such as the Villon and Mallarmé settings. Charmingly, he followed those last two groups with a little simple song to words he had composed himself, *Noël des enfants qui n'ont plus de maison*, written in 1915 as a heartfelt response to the First World War. Though Mady Mesplé's bright soprano has a flutter in it as recorded, hers is the smallest contribution, and all the others are in splendid voice, with Michèle Command characterfully French and Gérard Souzay at his freshest. The most ravishing singing of all comes from Elly Ameling and Frederica von Stade. The latter sings ecstatically in Debussy's evocative setting of Verlaine's most famous poem, *Il pleure dans mon coeur* (from the *Ariettes oublieées*), with Baldwin bringing out the subtlety of the pattering accompaniment. Well-balanced, clear sound. The booklet provides an essay in English and French, with full texts in French only.

OPERA

Pelléas et Mélisande (complete).

(M) *** Erato/Warner 2292 45684-2 (3) [id.]. Tappy, Yakar, Huttenlocher, Loup, Taillon, Monte Carlo Op. Ch. & O, Jordan.

(M) **(*) Sony SM3K 47265 (3) [id.]. Shirley, Söderström, McIntyre, Ward, Minton, ROHCG Ch. & O, Boulez.

Armin Jordan's sensitive and idiomatic version of Debussy's masterpiece can be recommended on almost all counts. At its centre is the finely focused Golaud of Hottenlocher, fresh and expressive, well contrasted with the tenor of Eric Tappy, a brighter-toned singer than is usual for Pelléas, a role generally taken by a *bariton marin*. Rachel Yakar's vocal acting as Mélisande is first rate and, if neither the playing nor the recording quite matches that on the full-priced sets by Karajan and Dutoit, the whole performance is most convincing. The documentation includes a libretto translation, and this is excellent value.

Boulez's sharply dramatic view of Debussy's atmospheric score made a strong impact at Covent Garden at the end of the 1960s, and this admirable complete recording vividly recaptures the intense excitement of that experience. This is a performance which will probably not please the dedicated Francophile – for one thing there is not a single French-born singer in the cast – but it rescues Debussy from the languid half-tone approach which for too long has been accepted as authentic. Boulez's attitude may initially stem from a searching analysis of the musical structure – Debussy anticipating today's avant garde in so many ways – but the dramatic element has been focused more sharply too, for he sees the characters as flesh and blood, no mere wayward shadows. He is supported by a strong cast; the singing is not always very idiomatic but it has the musical and dramatic momentum which stems from sustained experience on the stage. In almost every way this has the tension of a live performance. The recording, made at EMI's Abbey Road Studios in December 1969 and January 1970, does not allow a true pianissimo, but it is still both vivid and atmospheric; indeed the balance is theatrically more convincing on CD than it was on LP. There is a well-produced booklet with full translation.

Delibes, Léo (1836–91)

Coppélia (ballet): complete.
(M) *** Decca 425 472-2 (2). SRO, Richard Bonynge – MASSENET: *Le Carillon.* ***

Bonynge secures a high degree of polish from the Swiss Romande Orchestra, with sparkling string and wind textures and sonority and bite from the brass. The Decca recording sounds freshly minted and, with its generous Massenet bonus, little-known music of great charm, this set is very competitive.

Coppélia (ballet): suite: excerpts.
(B) *** DG 429 163-2. BPO, Karajan – CHOPIN: *Les Sylphides* *** ❀; OFFENBACH: *Gaîté parisienne.* ***

(i) *Coppélia* (ballet): suite; (ii) *Sylvia* (ballet): suite.
(M) *** Sony SBK 46550 [id.]. Phd. O, Ormandy – CHOPIN: *Les Sylphides* ***; TCHAIKOVSKY: *Nutcracker suite.* **(*)
(BB) *** LaserLight Dig. 15 616. (i) Berlin RSO, Fricke; (ii) Budapest PO, Sandor – GOUNOD: *Faust ballet.* ***

Ormandy and the Philadelphia Orchestra are on top form here. The playing sparkles and has a fine sense of style. *Sylvia* is particularly successful: the gusto of the opening and closing sections is infectious, with its life-assertive geniality; the more delicate numbers, including the famous *Pizzicato*, are played with affection and polish. The selection of items from *Coppélia* is generous, each strongly characterized. Both suites are done in a continuous presentation but are, unfortunately, not banded. The recording is notably full and brilliant in the CBS manner.

Although the playing of the (East German) Berlin Radio orchestra is not quite as cultured as that of the Berlin Philharmonic under Karajan, it is still very fine, and Fricke displays a lighter touch in the *Csárdás.* He also includes more music, both at the opening and in the delectable *Music of the Automatons*, one of Delibes' most piquant and memorable inspirations. The digital recording is first class, with sparkle and warmth and an attractively warm ambient effect. The Budapest performance of *Sylvia* is also graceful and vividly coloured, and the recording again is first rate. A genuine superbargain.

Karajan secures some wonderfully elegant playing from the Berlin Philharmonic Orchestra, and generally his lightness of touch is sure. The *Csárdás*, however, is played very slowly and heavily, and its curiously studied tempo may spoil the performance for some. The recording is very impressive; but it is a pity that in assembling the CD the suite had to be truncated (with only 71 minutes' playing time, at least one more number could have been included). As it is, the *Scène et Valse de la Poupée*, *Ballade de l'Épi* and the *Thème slav varié*, all present on the original analogue LP, are omitted here.

Coppélia: suite; *Kassya: Trepak; Le roi s'amuse:* suite; *La Source:* suite; *Sylvia:* suite.
(BB) **(*) Naxos Dig. 8.550080 [id.]. Slovak RSO (Bratislava), Ondrej Lenárd.

An attractive hour of Delibes, with five key items from *Coppélia*, including the *Music for the Automatons* and *Waltz*, four from *Sylvia*, not forgetting the *Pizzicato*, and four from *La Source*. Perhaps most enjoyable of all are the six pastiche ancient *airs de danse*, provided for a ballroom scene in Victor Hugo's play, *Le roi s'amuse.* (The second of these, a haunting *Pavane*, is also used by Respighi in his collection of *Ancient airs and dances.*) They are played most gracefully here, and the excerpts from the major ballets are spirited and nicely turned. The overall effect is not as sumptuous or individual as Bonynge's Decca recordings, but the brightly lit digital sound has body too, and the acoustics of the Bratislava Concert Hall are not unflattering to Delibes's vivid palette. The tasteful solo horn-playing brings a vibrato (most strikingly in the melody which dominates the *Andante* of *La Source*), but this is to be expected in an East European orchestra; it would be unfortunate if such a feature was considered a deterrent. Excellent value, especially for those who have not already discovered Sir Thomas Beecham's recording of *Le roi s'amuse.*

Sylvia (ballet): complete.
(M) *** Decca 425 475-2 (2). New Philh. O, Richard Bonynge – MASSENET: *Le Cid.* ***

If the score for *Sylvia* does not quite brim over with hits in the way that *Coppélia* does, and some of the best tunes are presented more than once, it still contains much delightful music and characteristically felicitous scoring. It is played here with wonderful polish and affection, and the recording is full, brilliant and sparkling in Decca's best manner. The CDs offer a splendid Massenet bonus, another recording out of Decca's top drawer.

OPERA

Lakmé (complete).
(M) *** Decca 425 485-2 (2). Sutherland, Berbié, Vanzo, Bacquier, Monte Carlo Op. Ch. and O, Bonynge.

Lakmé is a strange work, not at all the piece one would expect knowing simply the famous *Bell song*. Predictably enough, at the beginning it has its measure of orientalism, but quickly comedy is introduced in the shape of Britons abroad, and Delibes presents it with wit and charm. This performance (with Monica Sinclair a gloriously outrageous Governess) seizes its opportunities with both hands, while the more serious passages are sung with a regard for beautiful vocal line that should convert anyone. Sutherland swallows her consonants, but the beauty of her singing, with its ravishing ease and purity up to the highest register, is what matters; and she has opposite her one of the most pleasing and intelligent of French tenors, Alain Vanzo. Excellent contributions from the others too, spirited conducting and brilliant, atmospheric recording. Highly recommended in this mid-price reissue which costs little more than the original LPs.

Lakmé: highlights.
(M) ** EMI CDM7 63447-2; *EG 763447-4*. Mesplé, Burles, Soyer, Millet, Paris Opéra-Comique Ch. & O, Lombard.

The *Flower duet*, made into a top classical pop by a British Airways TV commercial, is quite nicely sung here by Mady Mesplé and Danielle Millet, and those who seek it could choose this highlights disc. Otherwise the performance is marred by the thin and wobbly – if idiomatic – singing of Mesplé in the title-role. The rest of the cast give adequate support and Lombard conducts with understanding.

Delius, Frederick (1862–1934)

Air and dance; Fennimore and Gerda: Intermezzo; Hassan: Intermezzo and serenade; Koanga: La Calinda; On hearing the first cuckoo in spring; A Song before sunrise; Summer night on the river; A Village Romeo and Juliet: The Walk to the Paradise Garden.
(M) *** Decca 421 390-2; *421 390-4* [id.]. ASMF, Marriner.

No grumbles here: these are lovely performances, warm, tender and eloquent. They are played superbly and recorded in a flattering acoustic. The recording is beautifully balanced – the distant cuckoo is highly evocative – though, with a relatively small band of strings, the sound inevitably has less body than with a full orchestral group. Excellent value at mid-price.

2 Aquarelles (arr. Fenby); *Fennimore and Gerda: Intermezzo. Hassan: Intermezzo and serenade* (all arr. Beecham); *Irmelin: Prelude. Late swallows* (arr. Fenby); *On hearing the first cuckoo in spring; A Song before sunrise; Summer night on the river.*
(M) *** Chan. CHAN 6502 [id.]. Bournemouth Sinf., Norman Del Mar.

There are few finer interpreters of Delius today than Del Mar, once a protégé of Beecham; and this nicely balanced collection of miniatures, now reissued at mid-price, is among the most broadly recommendable of the Delius collections available. The 49-minute concert creates a mood of serene, atmospheric evocation – into which Eric Fenby's arrangement of *Late swallows* from the *String quartet* fits admirably – and the beauty of the 1977 analogue recording has been transferred very well to CD, with all its warmth and bloom retained to make a highlight in the Chandos budget Collect series, although the autumnal sleeve design seems hardly appropriate.

Brigg Fair; Eventyr; In a summer garden; A Song of summer.
(B) *** CfP CD-CFP 4568; *TC-CFP 4568*. Hallé O, Vernon Handley.

Although the tempi are sometimes controversial, Handley is an understanding and exciting Delian, and these pieces are beautifully played. The woodwind and horn solos in *Brigg Fair* are particularly delectable and the strings throughout make some lovely translucent sounds. The digital recording is of EMI's best quality, matching clarity of definition with ambient lustre and rich colouring. A bargain.

Brigg Fair; In a summer garden.
(BB) ** Naxos Dig. 8.550229 [id.]. CSR SO (Bratislava), Adrian Leaper – ELGAR: *Pomp and circumstance marches* etc. **

Entitled *'English Festival'*, this generous (70 minutes) Naxos collection, digitally recorded in the Concert Hall of Slovak Radio, is undoubtedly good value, for the acoustic is expansive and the playing (especially of the woodwind and the solo horn in *Brigg Fair*) is sensitive. Adrian Leaper's readings are sympathetic and well judged, although *In a summer garden* sounds rather episodic.

(i) *Cello concerto;* (ii) *Double concerto for violin and cello. Paris, the song of a great city.*
(M) *** EMI Dig. CD-EMX 2185; *TC-EMX 2185*. (i–ii) Rafael Wallfisch; (ii) Tasmin Little; Royal Liverpool PO, Mackerras.

Thanks largely to recordings, the *Double concerto*, for long neglected and regarded as a weakly rhapsodic work, has come to be appreciated as being among the most cogently argued of Delius's longer pieces. This superb new recording, with soloists who easily outshine their predecessors on record (however distinguished), confirms the strength of a piece which establishes its own logic, with each theme developing naturally out of the preceding one. Though the prevailing speed is leisurely, there is no sense of Delian meandering, with firm, square rhythms generally preferred to the composer's favourite triple or compound-time. Inspired by the playing of the sisters May and Beatrice Harrison, Delius completed the work in 1915, and then six years later went on to write the *Cello concerto*, also with Beatrice Harrison in mind. It was his own favourite among his concertos, another warmly persuasive piece, with a barcarolle-like theme at its heart. Wallfisch is just as persuasive here, and with the authority of Delius's helper and amanuensis, Eric Fenby, he and Mackerras have opted for an unusually fast tempo for the final *Allegramente* section based on a square folk-like melody. That may disconcert those who know earlier recordings, but the power and warmth of this latest performance are magnetic. Sir Charles proves just as understanding an interpreter of the composer in the big tone-poem, *Paris, the song of a great city*. Though his speeds are relatively fast, he moulds them with unerring persuasiveness, consistently drawing warmly committed playing from the Liverpool orchestra. The recording is comparably full and atmospheric.

(i) *Dance rhapsody No. 1; Eventyr;* (ii) *Life's dance; North country sketches; A Song of summer.*
(M) **(*) EMI CDM7 63171-2. (i) Royal Liverpool PO; (ii) RPO, Sir Charles Groves.

Recorded in 1971 in the Philharmonic Hall, Liverpool, and in EMI's Abbey Road No. 1 Studio in 1974, these Delius performances make an attractively generous (80 minutes) CD anthology. The collection contains a virtually unknown piece, *Lebenstanz*, or *Life's dance*, which was written in the 1890s immediately before the tone-poem *Paris*. It presents a fascinating contrast, beginning with an urgency not always associated with this composer. *Song of summer*, a typically evocative piece, comes from the other end of Delius's career; it was conceived just before he lost his sight and was subsequently dictated to his amanuensis, Eric Fenby. The *North country sketches*, depicting with Delian impressionism the seasons of the year, are equally welcome, as are the *Dance rhapsody* and *Eventyr*. Groves is a sensitive interpreter, even if he rarely matches the irresistible persuasiveness of a Beecham. The balance is vivid and warm, almost too close in sound to do justice to such delicately atmospheric music. The CD transfer is successful in retaining the fullness and bloom, although orchestral textures are not ideally transparent.

Fennimore and Gerda: Intermezzo. Irmelin: Prelude. Koanga: La Calinda (arr. Fenby). *On hearing the first cuckoo in spring; Sleigh ride; A Song before sunrise; Summer night on the river; A Village Romeo and Juliet: The Walk to the Paradise Garden.*
(B) *** CfP CD-CFP 4304; *TC-CFP 4304*. LPO, Vernon Handley.

This is a successful anthology, with expansive and imaginative phrasing; the woodwind playing of the LPO is particularly fine. Those looking for a bargain collection of Delius should find this very good value, although Handley's approach to *The Walk to the Paradise Garden* is strongly emotional, closer to Barbirolli than to Beecham. The CD brings enhanced clarity, if with slightly less sumptuous violin timbre.

(i) *Arabesk;* (ii) *Hassan* (incidental music); (iii) *Sea drift.*
(M) (*(**)) Sony mono MPK 47680 [id.]. (i) Nørby; (ii) Fry; (iii) Boyce; BBC Ch., RPO, Beecham.

It is sad that these three Delius recordings, though made between December 1954 and February 1958 after the advent of stereo, were done in mono only. These are all prime examples of music that cries out for the extra atmosphere of stereo. Even the magic of Beecham is not enough to compensate entirely. Once that is said, the results are persuasive in a way unsurpassed by any rival Delius interpreter, with the lyrical line of each passage, central to the argument, lovingly drawn out. Unlike the orchestra, which is placed well forward, the chorus – important in all three works – is more flatteringly caught in the distance, with the off-stage effects in the *Hassan* incidental music most evocative. *Arabesk*, the least well-known of the three pieces, is a setting of a Pan-worship poem by the Norwegian, Jens Peter Jacobsen, and makes a superb counterpart to the long-recognized masterpiece, *Sea drift*, setting the words of Walt Whitman. Both have a baritone soloist as well as chorus, and it is a pity that the two baritones chosen here sound unsteady, as caught by the microphone. Nevertheless this makes an indispensable disc for lovers of Delius's music and an apt selection of items for those who want to hear three of his finest works, one of them very rare, and one – the suite of pieces written as incidental music for James Elroy Flecker's play, *Hassan* – including his most approachable piece, the famous *Serenade*. The transfers are clear but have some roughness from the original recording.

Dittersdorf, Carl Ditters von (1739–99)

Harp concerto in A (arr. Pilley).
❀ (M) *** Decca 425 723-2; *425 723-4* [id.]. Marisa Robles, ASMF, Iona Brown – BOIELDIEU; HANDEL: *Harp concertos* etc. *** ❀

Dittersdorf's *Harp concerto* is a transcription of an unfinished keyboard concerto with additional wind parts. It is an elegant piece, thematically not quite as memorable as the Boieldieu coupling, but captivating when played with such style. The recording too is from the old Argo catalogue's top drawer. With its additional solo items (see under Boieldieu for details), this collection makes one of the most rewarding anthologies for harp ever issued.

Dohnányi, Ernst von (1877–1960)

(i) *Ruralia hungarica, Op. 32b;* (i; ii) *Variations on a nursery tune, Op. 25;* (iii) *Serenade in C (for string trio), Op. 10.*
(B) *** Hung. White Label HRC 121 [id.]. (i) Budapest SO, Lehel, (ii) with István Lantos; (iii) Kovács, Bársony, Botvay.

Ruralia hungarica, although a cultivated score, still has an element of peasant earthiness. There is also, in its five movements, wide variety of mood, and the music rises to considerable eloquence; it was admired by Bartók for its colourful scoring. György Lehel and the Budapest orchestra successfully convey its exuberance and poetry, and the pianist in the famous *Variations*, István Lantos, is characterful as well as brilliant. To make this record even more attractive, we are offered the *Serenade*, Op. 10, an expressive and inventive piece with a particularly beautiful slow movement. Again the playing here is accomplished and spontaneous. With excellent, well-balanced sound, this is one of the outstanding bargains on Hungaroton's White Label.

Donizetti, Gaetano (1797–1848)

Don Pasquale (complete).
(M) **(*) Decca 433 036-2 (2) [id.]. Corena, Sciutti, Oncina, Krause, V. State Op. Ch. & O, Kertész – CIMAROSA: *Il maestro di cappella*. ***

Kertész may have been Hungarian and the use of the Vienna State Opera Chorus and Orchestra may bring some moments suggestive rather of operetta than of Italian opera; but the important thing is that high spirits are conveyed all the time. This is done partly by allowing the characters to laugh and make jolly noises a great deal. Occasionally the effects may seem coarse if separated out of context but, heard as a whole, there is no doubt that this performance succeeds remarkably well; one can even forget that the standard of florid singing today is hardly what it was. Corena is an attractive *buffo*, even if his voice is not always focused well enough to sing semiquavers accurately. Juan Oncina, as often on record, sounds rather strained, but the tenor part is very small; and Krause makes an incisive Malatesta. Graziella Sciutti is charming from beginning to end, bright-toned and vivacious, and remarkably agile in the most difficult passages. The 1964 Decca recording is excellent, with plenty of atmosphere as well as sparkle.

L'Elisir d'amore (complete).
(M) *** Sony CD 79210 (2) [M2K 34585]. Cotrubas, Domingo, Evans, Wixell, ROHCG Ch. & O, Pritchard.
(M) **(*) Decca 411 699-2 (2). Gueden, Di Stefano, Corena, Capecchi, Mandelli, Maggio Musicale Fiorentino Ch. & O, Molinari-Pradelli.

Originating from a successful Covent Garden production, the CBS reissue presents a strong and enjoyable performance, well sung and well characterized. Delight centres very much on the delectable Adina of Ileana Cotrubas. Quite apart from the delicacy of her singing, she presents a sparkling, flirtatious character to underline the point of the whole story. Placido Domingo by contrast is a more conventional hero and less the world's fool that Nemorino should be. It is a large voice for the role and *Una furtiva lagrima* is not pure enough in its legato, but otherwise his singing is stylish and vigorous. Sir Geraint Evans gives a vivid characterization of Dr Dulcamara, though the microphone sometimes brings out roughness of tone and this is all the more noticeable with the added projection of CD. Ingvar Wixell is an upstanding Belcore. The stereo staging is effective and the remastered recording bright and immediate. This set remains at full price in the USA.

Decca's first stereo set of this opera dates from the mid-1950s but still sounds fresh. Giuseppe di Stefano was at his most headily sweet-toned and Hilde Gueden at her most seductive. Capecchi as Belcore and Corena as Dulcamara are both splendidly comic, and the performance overall conveys the sparkle and charm of Donizetti's inspiration admirably. Though without the sophistication of the later (full-price) Decca version with Sutherland and Pavarotti, this makes a fine alternative, mid-priced recommendation.

La Favorita (complete).

(M) **(*) Decca 430 038-2 (3). Cossotto, Pavarotti, Bacquier, Ghiaurov, Cotrubas, Teatro Comunale Bologna Ch. & O, Bonynge.

No opera of Donizetti shows more clearly than *La Favorita* just how deeply he influenced the development of Verdi. Almost every scene brings anticipations, not just of early Verdi but of the middle operas and even of such mature masterpieces as *Don Carlos* and *La forza del destino*. *La Favorita* may not have as many memorable tunes as the finest Donizetti operas, but red-blooded drama provides ample compensation. Set in Spain in the early fourteenth century, the story revolves around the predicament of Fernando – strongly and imaginatively sung here by Pavarotti – torn between religious devotion and love for the beautiful Leonora, who (unknown to him) is the mistress of the king. The recording, made in Bologna, is not ideal – showing signs that the sessions were not easy – but the colour and vigour of the writing are never in doubt. The mezzo role of the heroine is taken by Fiorenza Cossotto, formidably powerful if not quite at her finest, while Ileana Cotrubas is comparably imaginative as her confidante Ines, but not quite at her peak. Bacquier and Ghiaurov make up a team which should have been even better but which will still give much satisfaction. Bright recording, vividly transferred, but the effect is not quite out of Decca's top drawer.

Lucia di Lammermoor (complete).

(M) *** Decca 411 622-2 (2) [id.]. Sutherland, Cioni, Merrill, Siepi, St Cecilia Ac., Rome, Ch. & O, Pritchard.

(M) (***) EMI mono CMS7 63631-2 (2) [Ang. CDMB 63631]. Callas, Di Stefano, Panerai, Zaccaria, La Scala Ch. & O, Karajan.

(M) (***) EMI mono CMS7 69980-2 (2) [Ang. CDMB 69980]. Callas, Di Stefano, Gobbi, Arie, Ch. & O of Maggio Musicale Fiorentino, Serafin.

(M) **(*) Ph. 426 563-2 (2). Caballé, Carreras, Sardinero, Áhnsjö, Murray, Ramey, Amb. S., New Philh. O, Lopez-Cobos.

It was hardly surprising that Decca recorded Sutherland twice in the role with which she is inseparably associated. The 1961 Sutherland version of *Lucia* remains an attractive proposition in the mid-price range. Though consonants were being smoothed over, the voice is obviously that of a young singer and dramatically the performance was close to Sutherland's famous stage appearances of that time, full of fresh innocence. Though the text is not quite as full as the 1971 (full-price) version, a fascinating supplement is provided in an aria (from *Rosmonda d'Inghilterra*) which for many years was used as a replacement for the big Act I aria, *Regnava nel silenzio*). The recording remains very fresh and vivid, though not everyone will like the prominent crowd noises. Sutherland's coloratura virtuosity remains breathtaking, and the cast is a strong one, with Pritchard a most understanding conductor.

Recorded live in 1955, when Karajan took the company of La Scala to Berlin, for years this finest of Callas's recordings of *Lucia* was available only on pirate issues. Callas was an artist who responded vividly to an audience and an occasion, particularly with a great conductor in charge. Karajan's insight gives a new dimension to the work, even though the usual much-cut text is used. Despite the limited sound, Callas's voice is caught with fine immediacy. Her singing is less steely than in the 1953 studio recording, and far firmer than in the 1959 one.

Callas's earlier mono set, which dates from 1953, is given an effective remastering which brings out the solo voices well, although the acoustic is confined and the choral sound less well focused. Here, needless to say, is not the portrait of a sweet girl, wronged and wilting, but a formidably tragic characterization. The diva is vocally better controlled than in her later stereo set (indeed some of the coloratura is excitingly brilliant in its own right), and there are memorable if not always perfectly stylish contributions from Di Stefano and Gobbi. As in the later set, the text has the usual stage cuts, but Callas's irresistible musical imagination, her ability to turn a well-known phrase with unforgettable inflexions, supremely justifies the preservation of a historic recording.

The idea behind the set with Caballé is fascinating: a return to what the conductor, Jésus Lopez-Cobos, believes is Donizetti's original concept, an opera for a dramatic soprano, not a light coloratura. Compared with the text we know, transpositions paradoxically are for the most part upwards (made possible when no stratospheric coloratura additions are needed); but Cobos's direction hardly compensates for the lack of brilliance and, José Carreras apart, the singing, even that of Caballé, is not especially persuasive. Good, refined recording.

Lucia di Lammermoor: highlights.
(M) **(*) EMI CDM7 63934-2 [id.]; *EG 763934-4* (from complete set, with Callas, Tagliavini, Cappuccilli, Ladysz, Philh. Ch. & O, Serafin).

A satisfactory hour-long selection from Callas's 1959 Kingsway Hall recording, with Callas not as completely in vocal control as she was in her earlier, mono set, in which Di Stefano and Gobbi provide more memorable support. However, the present cast is adequate, and Callas's flashing-eyed interpretation remains unique. The stereo sound is very good for its period.

Lucrezia Borgia (complete).
(M) *** Decca 421 497-2 (2) [id.]. Sutherland, Aragall, Horne, Wixell, London Op. Voices, Nat. PO, Bonynge.
(M) *(*) BMG/RCA GD 86642 (2) [6642-2-RG2]. Caballé, Verrett, Kraus, Flagello, RCA Italiana Op. Ch. & O, Perlea.

Sutherland is in her element here. In one or two places she falls into the old swooning style but, as in the theatre, her singing is masterly, not only in its technical assurance but in its power and conviction, making the impossible story of poisoner-heroine moving and even sympathetic. Aragall sings stylishly too, and though Wixell's timbre is hardly Italianate he is a commanding Alfonso. Marilyn Horne in the breeches role of Orsini is impressive in the brilliant *Brindisi* of the last Act, but earlier she has moments of unsteadiness. Thanks to researches by Richard Bonynge, the set also includes extra material for the tenor, including an aria newly discovered, *T'amo qual dama un angelo*. The recording is characteristically full and brilliant.

Lucrezia Borgia was the opera which brought Montserrat Caballé overnight fame when she stepped in at the last minute at a stage performance in New York; so one approaches this 1966 recording with expectation. But in no way does she enter into the character of the wicked Lucrezia caught out by fate and, though there is much beautiful singing, the uninspired direction of Perlea does not help. Even when Caballé in the final Act enters the banquet where her enemies (and, unknown, her son) are being entertained to poisoned wine, she sounds like a hostess asking whether her guests would like more tea. Alfredo Kraus is the most successful soloist here, for even Shirley Verrett seems to have been affected by the prevailing lassitude. However, the remastered recording is excellent.

Maria Stuarda (complete).
(M) *** Decca 425 410-2 (2) [id.]. Sutherland, Tourangeau, Pavarotti, Ch. & O of Teatro Comunale, Bologna, Bonynge.

In Donizetti's tellingly dramatic opera on the conflict of Elizabeth I and Mary Queen of Scots the confrontation between the two Queens is so brilliantly effective that one regrets that history did not actually manage such a meeting between the royal cousins. Here the contrast between the full soprano Maria and the dark mezzo Elisabetta is underlined by some transpositions, with Tourangeau emerging as a powerful villainess in this slanted version of the story. Pavarotti turns Leicester into a passionate Italian lover, not at all an Elizabethan gentleman. As for Sutherland, she is at her most fully dramatic too, and the great moment when she flings the insult *Vil bastarda!* at her cousin brings a superb snarl. In the lovely prayer before the Queen's execution with its glorious melody, Sutherland is richly forthright but does not quite efface memories of Dame Janet Baker. Otherwise she remains the most commanding of Donizetti sopranos, and Richard Bonynge directs an urgent account of an unfailingly enjoyable opera. Unusually for Decca, the score is slightly cut. The recording is characteristically bright and full and the CD transfer first rate.

Mary Stuart (complete, in English).
(M) **(*) EMI Dig. CMS7 69372-2 (2). Dame Janet Baker, Plowright, Rendall, Opie, Tomlinson, E. Nat. Op. Ch. and O, Mackerras.

Mary Stuart was the opera chosen at the ENO just before Dame Janet decided to retire from the opera stage in 1982; happily, EMI took the opportunity to make live recordings of a series of performances at the Coliseum. Though far from ideal, the result is strong and memorable, with Dame Janet herself rising nobly to the demands of the role, snorting fire superbly in her condemnation of Elizabeth as a royal bastard, and above all making the closing scenes before Mary's execution deeply moving. Her performance is splendidly matched by that of Rosalind Plowright, though the closeness of the recording of the singers makes the voice rather hard. The singing of the rest of the cast is less distinguished, with chorus ensemble often disappointingly ragged, a point shown up by the recording balance. The acoustic has the listener almost on stage, with the orchestra relatively distant. It is a valuable and historic set, but the

Decca version (in Italian) with Sutherland gives a fuller idea of the work's power.

Mary Stuart: highlights (in English).
(M) **(*) EMI Dig. CDM7 63727-2 [id.]; *EG 763727-4* (from above complete recording; cond. Mackerras).

The highlight of Donizetti's dramatization of the conflict between Elizabeth I and Mary Queen of Scots reaches its climax at the confrontation between the two Queens, historically incorrect but dramatically irresistible. The meeting is the more communicative when the interchange occurs in English, with Dame Janet (as Mary Stuart) and Joan Plowright rising to the challenge superbly. This scene is at the centre of the 61 minutes of highlights from the memorable if uneven ENO performance. Many will enjoy this while not requiring the complete set. The balance is very close to the singers, with some hardness on the voices.

Dowland, John (1563–1626)

Lute songs: *Awake sweet love, thou art returned; Can she excuse my wrongs?; Come again! sweet love doth now invite; Fine knacks for ladies; Flow not so fast, ye fountains; Go, crystal tears; Lady, if you so spite me; Me, me and none but me; Shall I strive with words to move?; Shall I sue?; Sorrow stay; Tell me true love; What is I never speed?; When Phoebus first did Daphne love;* Lute lessons: *Captain Candish's galliard; Lady Laiton's almain; Preludium and Lachrimae pavan; Semper Dowland; Semper dolens.*
(M) *** Saga SCD 9004. James Bowman, Robert Spencer.

This admirable record contains songs from all three Bookes plus two from *A Pilgrim's Solace* (1612). The lute solos, played in exemplary fashion by Robert Spencer, provide two central interludes. This record makes a fine single-disc introduction to Dowland's art, since it includes such justly popular pieces as *Fine knacks for ladies*, *Come again! sweet love doth now invite*, and *Sorrow stay*. Moreover they are sung with wonderful artistry by James Bowman, who brings sensitivity and intelligence to each song and characterizes them tellingly. There is no lack of contrast, and each phrase is floated with imagination. The recording is very good too, real and present. Unless you have a disaffection for the special sound of a counter-tenor, this is highly recommended.

Dukas, Paul (1865–1935)

L'apprenti sorcier (The sorcerer's apprentice).
(M) *** Sony SBK 46329; *40-46329* [id.]. Phd. O, Ormandy – BERLIOZ: *Symphonie fantastique* **; MUSSORGSKY: *Night.* ***
(BB) **(*) BMG/RCA Dig. VD 87727 [7727-2-RV]. Dallas SO, Mata (with Concert ***).
(B) **(*) Pickwick Dig. PCD 921. Nat. Youth O of Great Britain, Christopher Seaman – STRAVINSKY: *Firebird ballet.* **(*)
(M) **(*) Chan. CHAN 6503 [id.]. SNO, Gibson – ROSSINI/RESPIGHI: *La boutique fantasque*; SAINT-SAENS: *Danse macabre.* **(*)

Ormandy's 1963 recording of Dukas's famous orchestral narrative, played with great orchestral bravura, is very exciting at the calamitous climax, yet it does not miss the underlying humour of the apprentice's predicament. The pacing is just right, and the imagery of Walt Disney's *Fantasia* springs readily to mind. Spectacular sound too.

Mata does not quite match Ormandy's zest but is genially enjoyable and is featured within a desirable collection, given demonstration-worthy recording – see our Concerts section. Previn, too, has made a lively recording with the LSO, included in a popular compilation of 'Classical Favourites': again, see our Concerts section, below.

Under Christopher Seaman, the National Youth Orchestra of Great Britain give a most attractive account of Dukas's orchestral scherzo, with ensemble and commitment that leave little to be desired. There is plenty of impulse here, and the modern digital recording is full and brilliant.

Gibson secures excellent playing from the SNO, if without the sheer panache of his Philadelphia competitors. His basic tempo is apt and there is fine momentum and zest. The recording (made in City Hall, Glasgow, in 1972) is less overtly brilliant than Ormandy's but has plenty of atmosphere. The Chandos disc, however, is ungenerous in playing time (37 minutes).

(i) *L'apprenti sorcier (The sorcerer's apprentice);* (ii) *Ariane et Barbe-bleue: Act III Prelude; La péri;* (iii) *Symphony in C.*
(M) **(*) EMI CDM7 63160-2. (i) (mono): Philh. O, Markevitch; (ii) (stereo): Paris Op. O, Dervaux; (iii) ORTF, Martinon.

The Dukas is one of the finest of the post-Franck symphonies, more vital in argument and more independent in outlook than the Chausson or either of the d'Indy symphonies. Martinon brings real vigour and feeling to it, and the (slightly but not excessively reverberant) 1974 recording comes up well. *La péri* was recorded in 1957 and wears its years well, though the orchestral playing is not first class (the wind intonation is not always true). Markevitch's 1953 Philharmonia account of

L'apprenti sorcier (mono, of course) is brilliantly played, but there is an ugly edit (cut-off reverberation) halfway through. Still, this is worth having.

Ariane et Barbe-bleue (opera): complete.
(M) *** Erato/Warner Dig. 2292 45663-2 (2) [id.]. Ciesinski, Bacquier, Paunova, Schauer, Blanzat, Chamonin, Command, Fr. R. Ch. & O, Jordan.

Ariane et Barbe-bleue is a rarity and this is its first appearance on CD. It is rich in invention and atmosphere, as one would expect from the composer of *La Péri* and *L'apprenti sorcier*, and its vivid colours should ensure its wide appeal. Dukas was enormously self-critical and consigned an earlier opera, *Horn and Rimenhild*, to oblivion, along with much other music. *Ariane* is, like Debussy's *Pelléas*, set to a Maeterlinck text but there is none of the half-lights and the dream-like atmosphere of the latter. The performance derives from a French Radio production and is, with one exception, well cast; its direction under the baton of Armin Jordan is sensitive and often powerful; the recording is eminently acceptable. The complete libretto is included, and this most enterprising and valuable reissue is strongly recommended.

Dutilleux, Henri (born 1916)

Le Loup (ballet): *symphonic fragments*.
(M) *** EMI CDM7 63945-2 [id.]. Paris Conservatoire O, Prêtre – MILHAUD: *Création du monde*; POULENC: *Les Biches*. ***

Dutilleux's score for *Le Loup*, with its 'Beauty and the Beast' storyline bringing a tragic ending, is dominated by a haunting, bitter-sweet waltz theme of the kind that, once heard, refuses to budge from the memory. But the invention throughout has plenty of colour and variety, and Dutilleux's orchestral palette is used individually to great effect. Prêtre makes a persuasive case for the suite, and this vivid recording is part of a highly attractive triptych of French ballet scores.

Métaboles.
(M) *** Erato/Warner 2292 45689-2 [id.]. French Nat. RO, Münch – HONEGGER: *Symphony No. 4*. ***

Métaboles comes from 1964 and was written for George Szell, who conducted it in Cleveland, Boston, Washington and Paris. It is a marvellously atmospheric piece, with the fastidious orchestral palette this composer commands: it has something of the hieratic quality and rhythmic energy of Stravinsky, the evocative atmosphere of Messiaen or of Szymanowski, but is wholly individual. It is played in splendid and exhilarating fashion by the Orchestre National de l'ORTF (as the French Radio Orchestra was cumbersomely known in the days of de Gaulle), and the recording could have been made yesterday. Strongly recommended.

Dvořák, Antonín (1841–1904)

Carnaval overture, Op. 92; The Golden spinning wheel, Op. 109; Hussite overture, Op. 67; In nature's realm, Op. 91; My home, Op. 62; The Noonday witch, Op. 108; Othello, Op. 93; Symphonic variations, Op. 78; The Water goblin, Op. 107; The Wild dove, Op. 110.
(M) *** DG 435 074-2 (2) [id.]. Bav. RSO, Rafael Kubelik.

Kubelik has a special feeling for Slavonic melodrama, as he showed in his imaginative recording of Smetana'a *Má Vlast*. There is plenty for him to cope with in Dvořák's symphonic poems, although the composer has a cheerfully extrovert way of approaching the morbid national legends his music seeks to illustrate. The heroine of *The Golden spinning wheel* (which Sir Thomas Beecham used to present with much flair and charm) is killed and mutilated by her stepmother; *The Wild dove* begins with a beautiful young widow burying the husband she has just poisoned; *The Noonday witch* is the traditional ogress threatened by distraught mothers upon their errant children, and here she gets her prey; *The Water goblin*, having ensnared his maiden, dashes their green-haired child, decapitated, at her feet when she escapes. The music is colourful, with attractive invention and characteristically imaginative orchestration. The watery scene of the *Goblin* provides the most evocative and imaginative writing, alongside the delightful horn-calls which open *The Golden spinning wheel*, while the elegy for the repenting widow in *The Wild dove* is most touching. Kubelik's performances are among his finest on record and they are superbly played. He is splendidly dashing in *Carnaval*; the two other pieces, Opp. 91 and 93 (all three linked by a recurring main theme) which Dvořák wrote immediately before his first visit to America in 1892, are comparably successful and full of colouristic subtlety. He is superbly passionate in the *Hussite overture*, without overdoing the rhetoric. The opening of *The Golden spinning wheel* is gentle and elfin-like, and there is some bewitching playing from the woodwind throughout this performance, at times delicately beautiful, at others scintillating; and this is matched by tender strings and the noble restraint of the trombones. The closing pages are spacious and exciting. In both *The Water goblin* and *The Noonday witch* Kubelik's dramatic urgency is most compulsive, with stabbing rhythms in the former and the lyrical sections of the score given with much poignancy. *The Wild dove* is more difficult to bring off, but here – as in the other two – there is magic and lustre in the orchestra, and the atmospheric tension is striking. The *Symphonic variations*, appropriately placed last in the collection, opens warmly and graciously, yet Kubelik is obviously determined to minimize the Brahmsian associations; his light touch and apt pacing lead on to the lively finale, which becomes a characteristic mixture of fugato and the spirit of the dance. The recordings, made in the Munich Hercules-Saal between 1973 and 1977, are freshly transferred to CD and generally sound excellent. At times one might have liked a warmer, fuller string patina, and the bass end (like other DG Kubelik recordings of this period) is a little dry; but the hall acoustic gives an attractive overall ambient effect and the balance is realistic. Each CD offers over 78 minutes of music, so the value is obvious; for the newcomer there is much to discover, and the pair of discs is well documented.

Cello concerto in B min., Op. 104.

(M) *** BMG/RCA GD 86531 (6531-2-RG]. Harrell, LSO, Levine – SCHUBERT: *Arpeggione sonata.* ***

(M) *** EMI CDM7 69169-2; *EG 769169-4.* Tortelier, LSO, Previn – TCHAIKOVSKY: *Rococo variations.* ***

(B) *** DG 429 155-2; *429 155-4* [id.]. Fournier, BPO, Szell – BLOCH: *Schelomo;* BRUCH: *Kol Nidrei.* **(*)

(B) *** DG Compact Classics *415 330-4* [id.]. Fournier, BPO, Szell – BOCCHERINI ***; HAYDN: *Cello concertos.* **

(B) **(*) Pickwick IMPX 9035. Christine Walevska, LPO, Gibson – TCHAIKOVSKY: *Rococo variations.* **(*)

(M) (***) EMI CDH7 63498-2 [id.]. Casals, Czech PO, Szell – ELGAR: *Concerto* (**(*)) (with BRUCH: *Kol Nidrei* (***)).

(M) ** Decca 425 020-2; *425 020-4* [id.]. Harrell, Philh. O, Ashkenazy – BRUCH: *Kol Nidrei*; TCHAIKOVSKY: *Rococo variations.* ***

(M) ** Mercury 432 001-2 [id.]. Starker, LSO, Dorati – BRUCH: *Kol Nidrei*; TCHAIKOVSKY: *Rococo variations.* **

Cello concerto; Rondo in G, Op. 94.

(B) **(*) Ph. 422 467-2; *422 467-4.* Gendron, LPO, Haitink – FAURÉ: *Élégie* *(*); SAINT-SAENS: *Concerto No. 1.* **

In Lynn Harrell's first RCA recording, made in the mid-1970s, his collaboration with James Levine in Dvořák's *Cello concerto* proved a powerful and sympathetic one. Richly satisfying accounts of the first and second movements culminate in a reading of the finale which proves the most distinctive of all. The main body of the movement is finely integrated, but it is the *andante* epilogue which brings the most memorable playing, very expansive but not at all sentimental, with a wonderful sense of repose. The recording is bright and full and has been remastered most successfully for CD.

The richness of Tortelier's reading of Dvořák's *Cello concerto* has long been appreciated on record; his 1978 recording with Previn has a satisfying centrality, not as passionately romantic as Rostropovich's (full-price) recording on DG, but with the tenderness as well as the power of the work held in perfect equilibrium. What is rather less perfect is the balance of the recording, favouring the cellist too much, although the digital remastering has improved overall clarity without loss of bloom.

Fournier's reading has a sweep of conception and richness of tone and phrasing which carry the melodic lines along with exactly the mixture of nobility and tension that the work demands. Fournier can relax and beguile the ear in the lyrical passages and yet catch the listener up in his exuberance in the exciting finale. The phrasing in the slow movement is ravishing, and the interpretation as a whole balances beautifully. DG's recording is forward and vivid, with a broad, warm tone for the soloist. Dating from 1962, it sounds newly minted on the Compact Classics chrome-tape transfer. With couplings of Haydn (Fournier stylish but less impressively accompanied) and Rostropovich's larger-than-life version of Boccherini, this is another fine DG tape bargain. Fournier's performance is also available on a single bargain-price CD and tape, coupled with Bloch and Bruch.

Christine Walevska's performance is attractively fresh and spontaneous, and Gibson provides an admirable accompaniment, full of character yet never overwhelming his soloist. The result is very enjoyable, with excellent 1971 (Philips) recording, notable for its good balance. Very good value in the lowest price-range.

Gendron's performance is unidiosyncratic, attractively fresh and lyrical, and it has the advantage of impeccable orchestral support under Haitink. There is a real spontaneity about this playing and its responsiveness is given good support by the Philips engineers. The *Rondo* makes an engaging bonus; alas, the other couplings, although generous, are less appealing.

Casals' celebrated account was recorded in Prague with George Szell, the year before the Nazi invasion. Casals plays with astonishing fire and the performance seems to spring to life in a way that eludes many modern artists; the rather dry acoustic of the Deutsches Haus, Prague, and the limitations of the 1937 recording are of little consequence. This disc is one of the classics of the gramophone – and when you recall that this CD accommodates nine old 78-r.p.m. discs which at the end of the war would have cost about £4.50 altogether, the present asking price is hardly inflationary!

Lynn Harrell's 1982 digital version of the Dvořák *Cello concerto* for Decca, while brilliantly recorded, is relatively disappointing compared with his fervent, earlier, analogue version with James Levine for RCA.

Starker and Dorati, Hungarians both, bring a partnership of contrasts to Dvořák's *Cello concerto.* The exciting orchestral introduction immediately establishes the electricity of Dorati's contribution, but Starker is a less extrovert artist. Although the latter plays with consistent eloquence and much beauty of phrase, he is not helped by a recording which produces a balance of cello timbre in which the upper partials predominate over the lower, without a balancing resonance in the bass. The orchestral recording is extremely vivid – some ears may find the upper focus a shade too brilliant – but the warm acoustics of Watford Town Hall add depth to the sound-image, and the solo cello is very naturally balanced. Not a first choice but, with generous couplings, worth considering by admirers of Starker.

(i) *Cello concerto in B min., Op. 104;* (ii) *Piano concerto in G min., Op. 33;* (iii) *Violin concerto in A min., Op. 53; Mazurek in E min.* (for violin & orchestra), *Op. 49;* (i) *Rondo in G min., Op. 94; Silent woods, Op. 68* (both for cello and orchestra).

(B) **(*) VoxBox 1154872 (2) [CDX 5015]. (i) Nelsova; (ii) Firkusný; (iii) Ricci; St Louis SO, Süsskind.

Zara Nelsova's version of the *Cello concerto* is, as one would expect, cultured and musicianly; it resists expressive exaggeration or any temptation to play to the gallery and it has the benefit of excellent support from Walter Süsskind. Rudolf Firkusný's aristocratic performance of the *Piano concerto* has a natural authority that is always persuasive; he has recorded it on no fewer than three occasions, and this one is as fine as the others. Ruggiero Ricci's reading of the *Violin concerto* is also far from negligible; no one wanting all three concertos at a modest cost need hesitate long. The shorter pieces are also enjoyably done, the early-1970s recordings are well balanced, and this box provides a worthwhile overall survey, even if individually there are finer performances available of each major work. Good value.

(i) *Cello concerto in B min., Op. 104;* (ii) *Violin concerto in A min., Op. 53.*

(M) ** Sony CD 46337; *40-46337* [id.]. (i) Leonard Rose; (ii) Isaac Stern; Phd. O, Ormandy.

Leonard Rose's reading of the *Cello concerto* is one of the utmost simplicity; its heart lies in the slow movement, which flows onward with an unruffled lyrical impulse. Other versions may have more extrovert feeling and greater imagination in matters of detail – but if you feel that this work is normally spoilt by too much ripe romanticism, this version provides a healthy antidote. Ormandy accompanies with his usual warmth and the recording is full and realistically balanced. Stern's performance of the *Violin concerto* has plenty of power and eloquence, although it is less natural in feeling than some more recent versions. The violin is forwardly balanced, though not as spotlit as on some of his records; and Ormandy's accompaniment is well in the picture.

Violin concerto in A min., Op. 53.

(B) *** CfP Dig. CD-CFP 4566; *TC-CFP 4566* [Ang. CDB 62920]. Tasmin Little, Royal Liverpool PO, Handley – BRUCH: *Concerto No. 1.* ***

(M) *** Ph. 420 895-2. Accardo, Concg. O, C. Davis – SIBELIUS: *Violin concerto.* ***

(B) *** Sup. 110601-2. Josef Suk, Czech PO, Ančerl – SUK: *Fantasy.* ***

(B) **(*) DG Compact Classics 413 844-2 (2) [id.]. Edith Peinemann, Czech PO, Peter Maag – BEETHOVEN: *Romances* ***; BRAHMS: *Violin concerto* **(*); BRUCH: *Violin concerto No. 1.* **

On the Classics for Pleasure label, Tasmin Little in her first concerto recording offers a bargain version that fully matches top-price rivals, and is generously coupled too. Little brings to this concerto an open freshness and sweetness, very apt for this composer, that are extremely winning. The firm richness of her sound, totally secure on intonation up to the topmost register, goes with an unflustered ease of manner, and the recording brings little or no spotlighting of the soloist; she establishes her place firmly with full-ranging, well-balanced sound that coordinates the soloist along with the orchestra. She is particularly successful in the finale, where she plays the syncopations of the dance-like main theme with a happy lilt that yet has no hint of rushing.

In his Philips recording, Accardo is beautifully natural and unforced, with eloquent playing from both soloist and orchestra. The engineering is altogether excellent, and in a competitive field this must rank high, especially at mid-price.

Suk's earlier performance is back in the catalogue at bargain price, effectively remastered, recoupled with the Suk *Fantasy*. Its lyrical eloquence is endearing, the work is played in the simplest possible way and Ančerl accompanies glowingly.

Edith Peinemann's poetic and pleasingly natural account of Dvořák's *Violin concerto* is the bonus item provided to fill out the pair of Compact Classics CDs, which otherwise match the equivalent DG cassette. She is well partnered by Peter Maag, and the Czech Philharmonic provide a vividly idiomatic accompaniment, especially in the very winning finale. The recording, although somewhat reverberant, can be made to yield excellent results.

Serenade for strings in E, Op. 22.
(BB) **(*) Naxos Dig. 8.550419 [id.]. Capella Istropolitana, Kr(e)chek – SUK: *Serenade.* ***
(M) *(*) DG Dig. 429 488-2. Orpheus CO – ELGAR: *Serenade* *(*); TCHAIKOVSKY: *Serenade.* **

Serenade for strings, Op. 22; Romance, Op. 11.
(B) *** Pickwick Dig. PCD 928; *CIMPC 928.* Laredo, SCO, Laredo – WAGNER: *Siegfried idyll.* ***

Serenade for strings, Op. 22; Slavonic dances Nos. 9–16, Op. 72/1–8.
(BB) **(*) LaserLight Dig. 15 605 [id.]. Berlin CO, Peter Wohlert.

Laredo's performance of Dvořák's lovely *Serenade* is volatile, full of spontaneous lyrical feeling. The SCO strings play beautifully, and their bright rich tone above the stave adds to the feeling of freshness. The recording, made in City Hall, Glasgow, is admirably balanced to give a true concert-hall effect and add ambient lustre to the string timbre. As an encore Laredo takes the solo role in the *F minor Romance*, which he plays with appealing simplicity.

Fine playing from the Capella Istropolitana on Naxos, and flexible direction from Jaroslav Kr(e)chek. His pacing is not quite as sure as in the delightful Suk coupling, and the *Adagio* could flow with a stronger current, but this is still an enjoyable and well-recorded performance.

Although the same artists are credited for both recordings on the LaserLight disc, the effect is entirely different. The *Serenade* is played simply and gracefully by a small body of strings. Wohlert's tempi are well chosen and the acoustic is both fresh and warm. For the *Slavonic dances* a larger group is used and the recording is more resonant, with the bass fairly weighty. But the playing itself is never heavy, and there are some felicitous woodwind solos. Peter Wohlert is again very sympathetic, his pacing and feeling for rubato find the music's Czech spirit. Some may want less reverberation, but otherwise the digital sound is well defined, with plenty of bloom on the wind and strings alike.

The Orpheus Chamber Orchestra starts with a disconcertingly limp and wayward account of the first movement at a very slow speed, and elsewhere, though the playing is refined, there is little feeling of the bright folk element. Good, clean recording.

Serenade for wind in D min., Op. 44.
(M) *** Ph. Dig. 434 219-2; *434 219-4.* ASMF, Marriner – TCHAIKOVSKY: *String serenade.* **

Marriner's 1981 recording of the *Wind serenade* is an outstanding success. Stylish and beautifully sprung, it is elegantly infectious, and the recording is strikingly vivid, with a gloriously rich and firm bass. A pity that the original coupling (the *String serenade*) has been exchanged for the comparable work by Tchaikovsky, which has a lower level of voltage.

Slavonic dances Nos. 1–8, Op. 46; 9–16, Op. 72.
(M) **(*) Decca Dig. 430 735-2; *430 735-4* [id.]. RPO, Dorati.
(M) **(*) Sup. Dig. SUP 000812 [id.]. Czech PO, Neumann.
(BB) ** Naxos Dig. 8.551043 [id.]. Slovak PO, Košler.
(M) ** Sony Dig. MDK 46504 [id.] (Nos. 1–8 only). Philh. O, Andrew Davis – BIZET: *L'Arlésienne suite No. 1.* **

Dorati's performances have characteristic brio, the RPO response is warmly lyrical when necessary, and the woodwind playing gives much pleasure. Sparkle is the keynote and there is no lack of spontaneity. The Kingsway Hall venue with its natural resonance seems to have offered more problems than usual, and on CD the louder tuttis are not as sweet in the upper range of the strings as one would expect. However, the digital sound is generally superior.

Neumann's Supraphon set was recorded in the House of Artists, Prague. The *Dances* are very well played, with much felicitous detail from the Czech orchestra, who clearly have not grown tired of this engaging music. The recording is clear and naturally balanced, with no artificial digital brightness; it is also a little dry at the lower end. But the alert vivacity of the music-making is winning.

Zdenék Košler's performances have the advantage of Slovak orchestral playing, which brings an obvious idiomatic flavour, and clean, bright, digital sound. But the performances are less exhilarating than Dorati's; in almost all cases the timings are longer. This brings a more laid-back effect, and although the vigorous dances are still lively they have less panache.

Andrew Davis's set of Op. 46, with the Philharmonia Orchestra, is lively and stylish, and very well played and recorded. But who wants Op. 46 without Op. 72 or, for that matter, Bizet's *L'Arlésienne suite No. 1* alone?

Slavonic dances, Op. 46/1–5.
(B) *** DG Compact Classics *413 159-4* [id.]. Bav. RSO, Kubelik – LISZT: *Hungarian rhapsodies* etc.; SMETANA: *Má Vlast* excerpts. ***

The performances on the Compact Classics cassette are part of an attractive compilation of popular Slavonic music (with Kubelik again conducting Smetana, and Karajan in Liszt). Kubelik's accounts of five of the *Slavonic dances* from Op. 46 offer polished, sparkling orchestral playing and very good sound.

Slavonic dances Nos. 1–8, Op. 46; 9–10, 12 & 15, Op. 72/1, 2, 4 & 7.
(M) **(*) Ph. Dig. 432 046-2; *432 046-4*. Leipzig GO, Masur – BRAHMS: *Hungarian dances.* **(*)

Masur's performances are highly sympathetic and very well played. Although the Leipzig auditorium brings some clouding of focus, the sound is otherwise ripe and pleasing. However, it seems perverse to omit just four dances from the complete set, in order to accommodate a Brahms coupling. There is no accompanying information about the music, apart from the titles.

Symphonies Nos. 1–9.
(M) *** Chan. Dig. CHAN 9008/13 [id.]. SNO, Neeme Järvi.

Symphonies Nos. 1–9; Overtures: Carnaval; Hussite; My home; Othello.
(M) **(*) Ph. 432 602-2 (6). LSO, Rowicki.

Symphonies Nos. 1–9; Overtures: Carnaval; In Nature's realm; My Home. Scherzo capriccioso.
❀ (B) *** Decca 430 046-2 (6). LSO, István Kertész.

Symphonies Nos. 1–9; Carnaval overture; Scherzo capriccioso; The Wild Dove, Op. 110.
(M) **(*) DG 423 120-2 (6). BPO, Kubelik.

Järvi has the advantage of outstanding, modern, digital recording, full and naturally balanced. The recordings were made between May 1986 and October 1987, in either the SNO Centre or the Henry Wood Hall, Glasgow. The sound is warmly atmospheric in typical Chandos style, not always sharply detailed but with a firm focus. Järvi's are strongly committed, red-blooded performances, often impetuous; sometimes, as in the *Adagio* of No. 3, he can sound unsettled but, by allowing himself a fair degree of expressive rubato, he is almost always most convincing. He is very persuasive indeed in Nos. 5 and 6; No. 7 is just a little plain-spun, but his affectionately rhapsodic view of No. 8 is very successful, and the exceptionally spacious reading of the *New World*, with a contrasting, swaggering finale, is both individual and satisfying. The set is offered at upper mid-price, six CDs for the price of four. Only the *Fourth Symphony* is split centrally between discs; all the others can be heard uninterrupted. But there are no fillers, as with Kertész on Decca.

For those not wanting to go to the expense of the digital Chandos Järvi set, Kertész's bargain box, recorded in the Kingsway Hall between 1963 and 1966, is an easy first choice among the remaining collections of Dvořák symphonies. The CD transfers are of Decca's best quality, full-bodied and vivid with a fine ambient effect. Only in the earliest recorded, No. 8, is there a noticeable touch of thinness in the violin timbre, most strikingly in the *Allegretto* third movement; No. 7, one of the more relaxed performances of the cycle, is given greater dramatic impact than on LP. It was Kertész who first revealed the full potential of the early symphonies, and his readings gave us fresh insights into these often inspired works. He pioneered the *First* in a version without cuts, and presented the others with a fresh directness of manner which disguised their structural weaknesses, revealed their lyrical melodiousness and rejoiced in their rhythmic felicity. Where influences from Brahms and Wagner were not to be ignored, he nevertheless underlined their Dvořákian individuality. His *New World* remains one of the finest versions ever, and the vibrant *Eighth* long held sway as a top recommendation during the analogue LP era. It was made the more attractive by its original coupling with a brilliant account of the *Scherzo capriccioso*, rightly also included in this box, together with the three overtures, linked by a recurring theme, of which *Carnaval* (highly vivacious here) is the most famous. To fit the symphonies and orchestral works on to six CDs some mid-work breaks have proved unavoidable, and these occur in Nos. 2 (after the first movement) and No. 5 (before the finale); but the set remains a magnificent memorial to a conductor who died sadly young.

Kubelik's set has much to recommend it: first and foremost the glorious playing of the Berlin Philharmonic and the natural warmth that Kubelik brings to his music-making. He seems less convinced by the earliest symphonies than Järvi and in No. 3 he sounds almost routine by the side of the Chandos recording. In spite of some idiosyncratic but not unidiomatic touches, however, he achieves glowing performances of Nos. 6–9. At mid-price this remains a desirable set; the bonus items are all well played and recorded and are equally idiomatic.

Rowicki's Dvořák cycle is overshadowed by the Kertész series with the same orchestra. Heard as a whole in this mid-price box, Rowicki's readings present a consistent and very satisfying view of Dvořák, slightly understating the expressiveness of slow movements and often in fast movements adding a touch of fierceness. The opening of No. 6, for example, with the syncopated accompaniment very clearly defined, sounds unusually fresh and individual, even if one would not always want to hear it interpreted in that way. The recordings, made between 1965 and 1972, are generally refined, warm and full-bodied in the Philips manner. The CD transfer has opened up the sound: although it is still resonantly weighty, the effect is more vivid than on LP. This is certainly enjoyable listening. However, this set would have been even more attractive at bargain price.

Symphony No. 1 in C min. (The Bells of Zlonice), Op. 3; Legends, Op. 59/1–5.
(BB) *** Naxos Dig. 8.550266 [id.]. Slovak PO, Czecho-Slovak RSO, Gunzenhauser.

Though on a super-bargain label, this Bratislava version rivals any in the catalogue both as a performance and in sound. The ensemble of the Slovak Philharmonic is rather crisper than that on the other modern rival, Järvi's Chandos disc, and the recording, full and atmospheric, has detail less obscured by reverberation. Though Gunzenhauser's speeds for the slow movement and the *Allegretto* third movement are relatively spacious, he moulds them beautifully, bringing out the folk flavour, and the outer movements are powerfully idiomatic though rhythmically rather plain. The first five of Dvořák's ten *Legends* make a generous coupling: colourful miniatures, colourfully played.

Symphony No. 2 in B flat, Op. 4; Legends, Op. 59/6–10.
(BB) *** Naxos Dig. 8.550267 [id.]. Slovak PO, Czecho-Slovak RSO, Gunzenhauser.

Dvořák's *Second* is by far his longest symphony, difficult to hold together. With speeds more expansive than those of his Chandos rival, Neeme Järvi, Gunzenhauser gives a taut, beautifully textured account, very well played and recorded, a formidable rival in every way, even making no allowance for price. The completion of the set of *Legends* makes a very generous coupling (73 minutes), so that this is the perfect counterpart of Gunzenhauser's disc of *Symphony No. 1*, both separately available.

Symphonies Nos. 3 in E flat, Op. 10; 6 in D, Op. 60.
(BB) *** Naxos Dig. 8.550268 [id.]. Slovak PO, Stephen Gunzenhauser.

These exhilarating performances of the *Third* and *Sixth Symphonies* are well up to the standard of earlier records in this splendid Naxos series. Gunzenhauser and his Bratislava orchestra sail off with fine lyrical impetus into the first movement of the E flat work, and in the slow movement the Dvořákian freshness triumphs readily over the Wagnerian influences, when Gunzenhauser keeps the music moving onwards. The vivace finale has great zest. Similarly in No. 6 the lyrical flow of the opening movement is matched by a serene *Adagio*, sustained by the eloquence of the orchestral response, with lovely wind and string playing. The scherzo/furiant has all the sparkle of a Slavonic dance and the lightest rhythmic touch, and the finale makes a joyous conclusion, again with the woodwind providing all the colour one could want. Gunzenhauser's pacing is admirably judged through both works, and rhythms are always lifted. Excellent, vivid recording in the warm acoustics of the Bratislava Concert Hall.

Symphonies Nos. 4 in D min., Op. 13; 8 in G, Op. 33.
(BB) **(*) Naxos Dig. 8.550269 [id.]. Slovak PO, Stephen Gunzenhauser.

Gunzenhauser's *Fourth* is very convincing. In his hands the fine lyrical theme of the first movement certainly blossoms and the relative lack of weight in the orchestral textures brings distinct benefit in the Scherzo, where the outer sections are rhythmically buoyant and the forceful centrepiece has an infectious vigour without crudeness. The slow movement, too, is lyrical without too much Wagnerian emphasis and the rhythmically repetitive finale avoids heaviness. The naturally sympathetic orchestral playing helps to make the *Eighth* a refreshing experience, even though the first two movements are rather relaxed and without the impetus of the finest versions. The digital sound is excellent, vivid and full, with a natural concert-hall ambience.

Symphonies Nos. 5 in F, Op. 76; 7 in D min., Op. 70.
(BB) *** Naxos Dig. 8.550270 [id.]. Slovak PO, Stephen Gunzenhauser.

Gunzenhauser's coupling, the finest so far of his super-bargain Naxos series, is recommendable even without the price advantage. Both symphonies are very well played and truthfully recorded within a convincing concert-hall acoustic. The beguiling opening of the *Fifth*, with its engaging Slovak wind solos, has plenty of atmosphere, and the reading generates a natural lyrical impulse. The *Seventh* has something in common with Païta's famous version, spontaneous throughout and with an eloquent *Poco adagio*, a lilting scherzo, and a finale that combines an expansive secondary theme with plenty of excitement and impetus.

Symphonies Nos. 7 in D min., Op. 70; 8 in G, Op. 88.
(M) *** Decca Dig. 430 728-2; *430 728-4* [id.]. Cleveland O, Christoph von Dohnányi.
(M) *** Ph. 420 890-2; *420 890-4* [id.]. Concg. O, C. Davis.
(M) ** DG Dig. 429 976-2; *429 976-4* [id.]. VPO, Maazel.

Dohnányi's coupling of Dvořák's *Seventh* and *Eighth Symphonies* with the Cleveland Orchestra is an unsurpassed bargain to rank alongside Kondrashin's splendid version of the *New World Symphony*. The reading of the *Seventh* can be spoken of in the same breath as Païta's famous, early digital record. Tempi are all aptly judged and, while the work's Brahmsian inheritance is acknowledged in the *Poco adagio*, the Dvořákian lyrical flavour is dominant and the lightly sprung scherzo is liltingly articulated and rhythmically infectious. Outer movements are strong, with exciting climaxes. The *Eighth*, although it includes a few self-conscious interpretative nudgings, is comparably spontaneous, with the playing of the Cleveland Orchestra so responsive that the overall impression is one of freshness, especially in the *Adagio*, warm and full of colour, and in the engagingly elegant *Allegretto grazioso*. The recording is in the demonstration class, using the acoustics of the Masonic Auditorium to give a convincingly natural balance, the internal definition achieved without any kind of digital edge.

The coupling of Sir Colin Davis's analogue recordings of the *D minor* and *G major Symphonies* is also highly recommendable. The recordings (from 1975 and 1978 respectively) have been remastered most successfully: there is very little loss to the body of the string timbre (indeed in the *Allegretto grazioso* third movement of No. 8 the violins sound engagingly fresh) and the Concertgebouw ambience casts a warm glow on woodwind and horns, while detail is cleaner, with the bass firm. Davis's performances, with their bracing rhythmic flow and natural feeling for Dvořákian lyricism, are appealingly direct, yet have plenty of life and urgency. In the famous scherzo of No. 7, with its striking cross-rhythms, he marks the sforzandos more sharply than usual, keeping rhythms very exact. The *Adagio* of No. 8 is hardly less eloquent, and there is an engagingly zestful exuberance in the outer movements.

Maazel's reluctance to relax in Dvořákian happiness and innocence produces a powerful, incisive performance of No. 7, with the slow movement spacious and refined, though the bright DG recording fails to place the orchestra against any defined acoustic, making fortissimos somewhat aggressive. The performance of the *Eighth* is a fierce one, lacking the glow or warmth one associates with this work. Despite excellent playing, the hardness of the reading is underlined by the recording balance, which favours a bright treble against a rather light bass. Though the trumpet fanfare heralding the start of the finale is wonderfully vivid, the sound lacks something in body.

(i) *Symphonies Nos. 7 in D min., Op. 70; 8 in G, Op. 88;* (ii) *Slavonic dances Nos. 9, 10 and 15, Op. 72/1, 2 and 7.*
(B) *** DG Compact Classics *419 088-4* [id.]. (i) BPO; (ii) Bav. RSO; Kubelik.

Kubelik gives a glowing performance of the *Seventh*, one of Dvořák's richest inspirations. His approach is essentially expressive, but his romanticism never obscures the overall structural plan and there is no lack of vitality and sparkle. The account of the *Eighth* is a shade straighter, without personal idiosyncrasy except for a minor indulgence for the phrasing of the lovely string theme in the trio of the scherzo. Throughout both works the playing of the Berlin Philharmonic Orchestra is most responsive, with the polish of the playing adding refinement. The orchestral balance in the *G major Symphony* is particularly well judged. The recordings come from 1971 and 1966 respectively and sound admirably fresh, full yet well detailed, the ambience attractive. They hardly sound dated; nor do the beguilingly shaped *Slavonic dances*, from 1975, with the Bavarian orchestra on top form. They are used as encores following the close of each symphony.

Symphonies Nos. 7 in D min., Op. 70; 9 (From the New World).
(M) **(*) EMI/Phoenixa CDM7 63774-2; *EG 763774-4* [id.]. Hallé O, Sir John Barbirolli.

Barbirolli's recordings derive from the Pye/Nixa label and date from 1957 and 1959. The remastering has successfully cleaned up the fizzy upper focus of the LP originals, and the sound, though a little limited on top, is now full and vivid. Indeed the *Seventh* emerges totally renewed. Its first movement has fine exhilaration and a superb burst of adrenalin in the closing pages; the *Poco adagio* has an engaging Dvořákian lyrical flow, and the scherzo is contagiously buoyant, after its gently seductive opening. The finale opens powerfully and gathers further momentum to reach a thrilling denouement. In the *New World* Barbirolli achieves memorability by the utmost simplicity of his approach. The first movement unfolds dramatically after a presentation of the second subject which achieves lyrical contrast with very little relaxation of tempo. There is an electrifying tightening of tension towards the end of the movement (an effect which is repeated with equal compulsion in the finale). The *Largo* is sustained with unaffected beauty, and the scherzo is notable for its woodwind colour and especially the delightful trills in the trio. The finale gathers the music's threads together before the exciting close, with a real sense of apotheosis. Altogether this is Barbirolli at his revelatory finest.

Symphony No. 8 in G, Op. 88.
(B) *** Sony MYK 44872 [id.]. Columbia SO, Bruno Walter – WAGNER: *Parsifal* excerpts. ***
(M) (***) EMI mono CDM7 63399-2 [id.]. RPO, Beecham – SIBELIUS: *Symphony No. 2.*(***)

(i) *Symphony No. 8 in G;* (ii) *Carnaval overture, Op. 92.*
(BB) **(*) ASV Dig. CDQS 6006; *ZCQS 6006.* (i) Royal Liverpool PO; (ii) LPO; Bátiz.

Symphony No. 8 in G; Carnaval overture; The wild dove, Op. 110.
(B) *** DG 429 518-2; *429 518-4* [id.]. BPO or Bav. RSO, Kubelik.

Symphony No. 8 in G; Legends Nos. 4, 6 & 7, Op. 59; Scherzo capriccioso.
❀ (M) *** EMI CDM7 64193-2; *EG 764193-4* [id.]. Hallé O, Sir John Barbirolli.

(i) *Symphony No. 8 in G, Op. 88;* (ii) *Serenade for strings in E, Op. 22.*
(M) **(*) Erato/Warner 2292 45673-2 [id.]. (i) Yomiuri Nippon SO, Guschlbauer; (ii) Paillard CO, Paillard.

Barbirolli's account of this symphony was one of his best Pye records: the reading has immense vitality and forward impetus, the kind of spontaneous excitement that is rare in the recording studio, and yet the whole performance is imbued with a delightful, unforced lyricism. There is, however, a slight lapse in the third movement when the strings take over the main tune of the Trio; here the combination of vibrato and a fruity portamento brings a characteristically indulgent underlining of the lovely melody. But this is a small blemish on an otherwise remarkably good performance. The *Scherzo capriccioso* is warm and very exciting too, and the *Legends* make a colourful bonus. This was always the finest of Barbirolli's late Dvořák symphonies technically, and the EMI documentation reveals why: it was made in 1957/8 in Manchester's recently rebuilt Free Trade Hall by the Mercury recording team, led by Wilma Cozart Fine. In remastered form it is tremendously real and vivid; more than any other of these reissued Barbirolli recordings, it gives the listener an electrifying illusion of sitting in a concert hall listening to a live performance.

Kubelik's *Eighth* is appealingly direct and without idiosyncrasy, except for a minor indulgence in the phrasing of the richly contoured string theme in the trio of the scherzo. The polished, responsive playing of the Berlin Philharmonic adds to the joy and refinement of the performance. The Bavarian Radio Orchestra provide the substantial encores, which are splendidly done. This is well worth considering in DG's bargain range: the 1966 sound is bright and clear, if a little dry; the overture and symphonic poem, which were recorded a decade later, are only slightly more atmospheric.

Walter's famous account of Dvořák's *Eighth* was recorded in 1962, just before he died. It is a strong yet superbly lyrical reading; but the overall lyricism never takes the place of virility and Walter's mellowness is most effective in the *Adagio*. His pacing is uncontroversial until the finale, which is steadier than usual, more symphonic, although never heavy. The sound was always warm and full but now is more naturally clear, the focus of all sections of the orchestra firmer, with upper strings sweet and the violas, cellos and basses expansively resonant. With its equally inspired coupling of the *Prelude and Good Friday music* from *Parsifal*, this bargain-priced issue ranks high in the CBS legacy.

Beecham always got rousing results, and this is an infectiously spirited and rumbustious performance, but full of glowing Dvořákian lyricism. The 'live' recording comes from 1959 and the Royal Festival Hall acoustics bring a somewhat dry ambience, with a bright sheen on the strings and a less-than-ideal balance for the brass – the trumpet fanfare in the finale is much too close and tuttis can be a bit fierce. Nevertheless the sound is fully acceptable and every bar of the music is alive.

An excellent digital bargain CD comes from Bátiz with consistently spirited playing from the Royal Liverpool Philharmonic Orchestra. The reading is direct, responsive and structurally sound and enjoyable in its easy spontaneity. The recording is vivid, yet does not lack warmth, although there is a touch of fierceness on climaxes. The overture is slightly less successful, but this is certainly good value.

The Japanese performance of the *G major*

Symphony is astonishingly idiomatic, with natural lyrical feeling. Guschlbauer's reading is direct and strong, exciting in outer movements and warmly flowing in the *Adagio*. With full, natural (1975) sound, remastered without loss of body or ambience, this is most enjoyable. The account of the *Serenade* is also refreshing, the *Larghetto* quite memorable in its gentle intensity, and the finale sparkling. The string timbre here is a little thinner, but the recording is again agreeably remastered.

Symphony No. 9 in E min. (From the New World), Op. 95.

(B) *** DG 429 676-2. BPO, Karajan – SCHUBERT: *Symphony No. 8.* ***

(M) **(*) EMI CDM7 69005-2 [id.]; *EG 769005-4*. BPO, Karajan – SMETANA: *Vltava.* ***

(M) **(*) EMI Dig. CDD7 63900-2 [id.]; *ET 763900-4*. BPO, Tennstedt – KODÁLY: *Háry János.* ***

(M) (***) BMG/RCA mono GD 60279; *GK 60279* [60279-2-RG; *60279-4-RG*]. NBC SO, Toscanini – KODÁLY: *Háry János*: suite (***); SMETANA: *Má Vlast: Vltava.* (**)

(M) ** EMI CDM7 63869-2 [id.]; *EG 763869-4*. Philh. O, Klemperer – SCHUBERT: *Symphony No. 5.* ***

(i) *Symphony No. 9 (New World);* (ii) *American suite, Op. 98b.*

(M) *** Decca Dig. 430 702-2; *430 702-4* [id.]. (i) VPO, Kondrashin; (ii) RPO, Dorati.

Symphony No. 9 (New World); Carnaval overture, Op. 92; Humoresque (arr. Foster).

(M) **(*) BMG/RCA GD 86530 [6530-2-RG]. Boston Pops O, Fiedler – ENESCU: *Rumanian rhapsody.* **(*)

Symphony No. 9 (New World); Carnaval overture; Scherzo capriccioso, Op. 66.

(M) **(*) Decca 417 724-2 [id.]. LSO, Kertész.

(i) *Symphony No. 9 (New World);* (ii) *Scherzo capriccioso.*

(B) *** DG 427 202-2; *427 202-4* [id.]. (i) BPO; (ii) Bav. RSO, Kubelik.

(i) *Symphony No. 9 (New World);* (ii) *Scherzo capriccioso;* (iii) *Serenade for strings in E, Op. 22.*

(B) *** DG Compact Classics *413 147-4*. (i) BPO; (ii) Bav. RSO; (iii) ECO; Kubelik.

(i) *Symphony No. 9 (New World);* (ii) *Serenade for strings.*

(M) **(*) Sony SBK 46331; *40-46331* [id.]. (i) LSO, Ormandy; (ii) Munich PO, Kempe.

(i) *Symphony No. 9 (New World);* (ii) *Symphonic variations, Op. 78.*

(B) *** CfP Dig. CD-CFP 9006; *TC-CFP 4382*. LPO, Macal.

(BB) **(*) Naxos Dig. 8.550271 [id.]. Slovak PO, Stephen Gunzenhauser.

(M) **(*) Ph. 420 349-2. (i) Concg. O; (ii) LSO; C. Davis.

Kondrashin's Vienna performance of the *New World Symphony* was one of Decca's first demonstration CDs, and its impact remains quite remarkable. Recorded in the Sofiensaal, the range of the sound is equalled by its depth. The ambience of the hall prevents a clinical effect, yet every detail of Dvořák's orchestration is revealed within a highly convincing perspective. Other performances may exhibit a higher level of tension, but there is a natural spontaneity here, with the first-movement exposition repeat fitting naturally into the scheme of things. The cor anglais solo in the *Largo* is easy and songful, and the finale is especially satisfying, with the wide dynamic range adding drama and the refinement and transparency of the texture noticeably effective as the composer recalls ideas from earlier movements. This splendid disc now returns to the top of the list of recommedations as a superb mid-priced bargain, enhanced by the inclusion of Dorati's RPO version of the engaging *American suite*, which also has clear influences from the New World. It was written first (in 1894) in a piano version, but was turned into an orchestral piece the following year. The Kingsway Hall recording balance seems to suit the scoring rather well; the music is slight but, given Dorati's characteristic brio, sounds very fresh. The orchestral response is warmly lyrical when appropriate, and the woodwind playing gives much pleasure.

Macal as a Czech takes a fresh and unsentimental view of the *New World Symphony*, with speeds far steadier than usual in the first movement. His inclusion of the repeat balances the structure convincingly. With idiomatic insights there is no feeling of rigidity, with the beauty of the slow movement purified, the scherzo crisp and energetic, set against pastoral freshness in the episodes, and the finale again strong and direct, bringing a ravishing clarinet solo. The *Symphonic variations*, which acts as coupling, is less distinctive but is well characterized. The digital recording is strikingly believable in its natural balance, with body as well as brilliance, and excellent definition. A fine bargain recommendation.

Karajan's 1964 DG recording held a strong place in the catalogue for two decades, and it is certainly far preferable to his digital version. It has a powerful lyrical feeling and an exciting build-up of power in the outer movements. The *Largo* is played most beautifully, and Karajan's element of detachment lets the orchestra speak for itself, which it does, gloriously. The rustic qualities of the scherzo are affectionately brought out, and altogether this is very rewarding. The recording is full, bright and open. This is now reissued at bargain price, generously coupled with Schubert's *Unfinished*, as a sampler for DG's Karajan Symphony Edition.

Kubelik's marvellously fresh account of the *New World*, recorded in the early 1970s, is certainly among the top versions. The hushed opening immediately creates a tension which is to be sustained throughout, and the *Largo* has a compelling lyrical beauty, with playing of great radiance from the Berlin Philharmonic. After a scherzo of striking character and a finale of comparable urgency, Kubelik then relaxes magically, when the composer recalls earlier themes as in a reverie. Kubelik's accounts of the *Scherzo capriccioso* and *String serenade* have a comparable freshness. The *Scherzo* is attractively spirited and colourful, while the account of the *Serenade* is beautifully lyrical yet strong in impulse. The playing of the ECO here is attractively polished as well as resilient. The recording is brightly lit and, like the *Symphony*, somewhat dry in the bass, but the chrome-tape transfers are of DG's finest quality. The *Symphony* is offered without a break. Kubelik's account has now also been reissued on DG's bargain Privilege label in digitally remastered form, which has brought a firmer bass and slightly clearer detail. The coupling is a reading of comparable freshness of the *Scherzo capriccioso*, with much felicitous detail from the Bavarian orchestra.

Among earlier analogue accounts Kertész's LSO version stands out, with a most exciting first movement (exposition repeat included), in which the introduction of the second subject group is eased in with considerable subtlety; the *Largo* brings playing of hushed intensity to make one hear the music with new ears. Kertész's exuberant *Carnaval overture* and his brilliant and lilting account of the *Scherzo capriccioso* are as attractive as any in the catalogue.

Karajan's 1977 *New World* for EMI is robust and spontaneous-sounding, but refined too, and the cor anglais solo of the *Largo* is fresh, at a nicely flowing tempo. The digital remastering has brightened the sound and given it excellent projection but, as usual with EMI's remastered analogue recordings of this period, the bass is drier and the overall effect slightly less atmospheric than the original. As in the earlier, DG version, the first-movement exposition repeat is omitted.

Gunzenhauser's is a vibrantly exciting reading, helped by sound that is more present and brilliant than in the earlier issues in his Dvořák cycle. Indeed the climaxes of the first movement (exposition repeat included) have just a hint of stridency. But the impact of the performance is undeniable, particularly the finale which moves forward with a consistently dramatic impetus. There is fine playing in the *Largo*, but this is not as melting as some versions. Where Gunzenhauser scores is in also offering a highly spontaneous account of Dvořák's engaging *Symphonic variations*, where the vivid orchestral response blows all the cobwebs off this underrated piece, full of the most attractive Dvořákian invention.

Tennstedt's is a warm, romantic reading, freely expressive at generally spacious speeds, very much in the German rather than the Czech tradition. Though he fails to observe the important exposition repeat in the first movement, the symphonic weight of the work is powerfully conveyed with full, forward recording and outstanding playing from the Berlin Philharmonic, not least the soloists. The natural, easy warmth of the famous cor anglais solo at the start of the slow movement has a pure felicity that it would be hard to match. The CD adds clarity to the rich, full recording; however, it also adds a degree of shrillness on the treble in fortissimos. The addition of the *Háry Jânos* suite to Tennstedt's *New World* adds greatly to the attractiveness of this budget-price CD.

Sir Colin Davis's very directness has its drawbacks. The cor anglais solo in the slow movement has an appealing simplicity, yet the effect is not very resilient and, later, when the horns echo the theme at the end of the opening section, the impression is positive rather than seductively nostalgic. The reading is completely free from egotistical eccentricity and, with beautiful orchestral playing throughout, this is satisfying in its way. The CD transfer is well managed, rich and full-bodied. The coupling, a first-class performance of the *Symphonic variations* – one of Dvořák's finest works, much underrated by the public – is very welcome and sounds fresh.

With speeds consistently fast and the manner clipped, Toscanini's reading of the *New World* is anything but idiomatic, but it still tells us something unique about Dvořák and his perennial masterpiece, presenting a fiery, thrilling experience. The sound is fuller than most from this source and the transfer brings that out, despite the usual dryness. With equally electric performances of Smetana and Kodály for coupling, it is a most valuable reissue in the Toscanini series.

Ormandy rarely made records outside the USA; his 1969 London recording of the *New World Symphony*, besides offering plenty of excitement, shows unusual care in preparation, even though the first-movement exposition is not repeated. The playing of the LSO has life and spontaneity, and the rhythmic freshness of the scherzo (achieved by unforced precision) is matched by the lyrical beauty of the *Largo* and the breadth and vigour of the finale. Perhaps the reading has not the individuality of the finest versions; but the sound is full and firm in the bass to support the upper range's brilliance: the opening of the finale has a striking lower sonority, which indicates immediately that the CBS engineers were working on the European side of the Atlantic. For coupling, we are offered an essentially mellow account of the *String serenade*, with sound to match. It is directed by Kempe with affectionate warmth, but has no lack of brilliance in the finale.

Arthur Fiedler's performance was recorded in 1959 and the sound is most naturally balanced and vivid, characteristic of RCA's early stereo techniques. The performance is satisfying in its direct simplicity, with responsive playing from every section of the orchestra, no interpretative eccentricities, and an attractively relaxed feeling, as if all the players were enjoying the music. Fiedler observes the first-movement exposition repeat, by no means an automatic procedure in the late 1950s, and his feeling for the work's structure is conveyed well. The dashing account of the *Carnaval overture* comes from 1964, and here the recording brightens and is slightly less natural in the matter of string timbre. After the very welcome Enesco *Rhapsody*, Fiedler provides an agreeable lollipop encore, Stephen Foster's outrageous arrangement of the *Humoresque*, intertwined with his own *Swanee River*.

Klemperer is given very good EMI recording, dating from 1963, and fine playing from the Philharmonia Orchestra. The *Largo* is very beautiful but, although the conductor's deliberation in the first movement brings a well-detailed account of the score, the scherzo and finale are too solid to be totally convincing. Admirers of this conductor's style will probably not be disappointed.

CHAMBER AND INSTRUMENTAL MUSIC

Piano quartets Nos. 1 in D, Op. 23; 2 in E flat, Op. 87; Piano quintet in A, Op. 81; Bagatelles, Op. 47.

(M) **(*) Sony M2YK 45672 (2) [id.]. Rudolph Firkusny, Juilliard Qt.

Firkusny is a fine Dvořákian, and the Juilliards play sympathetically throughout and with plenty of character too. Pacing is well judged, and undoubtedly these performances are tinged with distinction. One has only to sample the *Theme and variations* second movement of the *D major Piano quartet* or the engaging interplay between piano and cello (the unnamed cellist makes a memorable contribution throughout) at the beginning of the *Lento* of Op. 87, to find that this playing is warmly imaginative. It has brio and spirit too, and the *Piano quintet* has plenty of life. The snag is the forward balance, particularly in the latter work and in the *Bagatelles*, where the harmonium is presumably played by Firkusny, though no credit is given. Here the acoustic dryness is unsympathetic to this unusual but effective combination; more ambience would have produced a better blend with the strings. There is more space for the *Piano quartets*; here the sound is undistracting, and undoubtedly these performances make a very strong impression.

Piano quintet in A, Op. 81.

(M) *** Decca 421 153-2. Clifford Curzon, VPO Qt – FRANCK: *Quintet*. ***

(M) **(*) Van. 08.8003.71 [OVC 8003]. Peter Serkin, Schneider, Galimir, Tree, Soyer.

This wonderfully warm and lyrical (1962) performance of Dvořák's *Piano quintet* by Clifford Curzon is a classic record, one by which all later versions have come to be judged, and the CD transfer has not lost the richness and ambient glow of the original analogue master, yet has improved definition and presence. The piano timbre remains full and real.

A strongly expressive and at times ardent account from Peter Serkin and the accomplished Schneider group. They are very well recorded too (though the balance is forward) and, while the warmth of their approach leads to a hint of languishing in the lyrical writing, obviously this playing is felt and responsive and the performance has undoubted spontaneity. The 1965 sound is richer than the Decca Curzon version, and if this performance had a coupling it could be competitive.

Piano trios No. 3 in F min., Op. 65; 4 in E min. (Dumky), Op. 90.

(M) **(*) Ph. 426 095-2; *426 095-4*. Beaux Arts Trio.

The Beaux Arts' 1969 performances of Op. 65 and the *Dumky* still sound fresh and sparkling, though the recording on CD is a little dry in violin timbre; the *F minor*, arguably the finer and certainly the more concentrated of the two, is played with great eloquence and vitality.

String quartets Nos. 1–14; Cypresses, B.152; Fragment in F, B.120; 2 Waltzes, Op. 54, B.105.

(M) *** DG 429 193-2 (9). Prague Qt.

Dvořák's *Quartets* span the whole of his creative life: the *A major*, Op. 2, pre-dates the *First Symphony* and the *G major*, Op. 106, comes two years after the *New World*. This set was made in 1973–7 and first appeared on 12 LPs. In the new format, *No. 3 in D* (which, remarkably, takes 69 minutes 42 seconds) can be accommodated complete on one CD. The glories of the mature *Quartets* (Opp. 34, 51, 61, 80, 96 and 105–6) are well known, though it is only the so-called *American* which has achieved real popularity. The beauty of the present set is that it offers seven more *Quartets* (not otherwise available) plus two *Quartet movements*, in *A minor* (1873) and *F major* (1881), plus two *Waltzes* and *Cypresses* for good measure, all in eminently respectable performances and decent recordings.

String quartet No. 12 in F (American), Op. 96.
(B) *** Pickwick Dig. PCD 883; *CIMPC 883* [id.]. Delmé Qt – BRAHMS: *Clarinet quintet.* ***
(B) *** Hung. White Label HRC 122 [id.]. Bartók Qt – DEBUSSY; RAVEL: *Quartets.* **(*)

The Delmé Quartet on a superbly recorded Pickwick disc at bargain price give a winningly spontaneous-sounding performance, marked by unusually sweet matching of timbre between the players, which brings out the total joyfulness of Dvořák's American inspiration. The exuberant finale in particular has its rhythms sprung with delectable lightness, leading to an exhilarating close. The unusual coupling, a similarly warm reading of the Brahms *Clarinet quintet*, is both attractive and generous.

A splendidly alive and spontaneous account from the Bartók Quartet too, polished yet with plenty of warmth and lyrical feeling, and with a dance-like sparkle in the scherzo and finale. Good sound, generous couplings and the bargain status of this issue ensure its value.

String quartets Nos. 12 in F (American); 14 in E flat, Op. 105.
(BB) ** Naxos 8.550251 [id.]. Moyzes Qt.

The members of the Moyzes Quartet are drawn from the ranks of the Slovak Philharmonic Orchestra and they are obviously at home in this repertoire. The slow movement of the *American quartet* is played with much warmth, and their account of Op. 105 has comparable intensity. The bright recording projects them forwardly and, although the acoustic is quite sympathetic, the effect could ideally be more intimate. However, this coupling remains very good value.

(i) *String quartet No. 12 (American);* (ii) *String quintet in E flat, Op. 97.*
(M) *** Decca 425 537-2; *425 537-4* [id.]. (i) Janáček Qt; (ii) Vienna Octet (members).

The Janáček performance of the *American quartet* is strikingly fresh, the superb playing and ensemble ensuring that the fast tempi chosen for the outer movements are exciting without being rushed, while the *Lento* is warmly eloquent. This is virtuosity of a high order put completely at the service of the composer, and the fine 1964 recording has depth as well as realistic definition. The coupled *E flat Quintet*, another of the greatest works of Dvořák's American period, is given a comparably eloquent and characterful performance by members of the Vienna Octet. Again the recording is full, with an attractive ambience, and the focus is firmer than the orginal LP.

String quintet in G, Op. 77; String sextet in A, Op. 48.
(M) **(*) Decca 430 299-2; *430 299-4* [id.]. Vienna Octet (members).

The *Sextet*, Op. 48, was one of the pieces that served to establish Dvořák's name in England in the 1880s and it is undoubtedly one of the Czech master's most spontaneous and flowing works. The members of the Vienna Octet give it an eloquent performance. The *G major Quintet*, despite its late opus number, is an early work; it is sometimes documented as Op. 18. Its inspiration is more uneven, but there is plenty to be found in the beautiful slow movement and in the vital finale. The Viennese players are especially sympathetic to the lyrical elements in the music: the *Poco andante* is most beautiful, its drooping principal melodic phrase reminding one of Tchaikovsky. The scherzo lacks something in sparkle. It is not an easy movement to bring off since, although it has a dance-like quality, it is by no means a furiant. The Viennese group catches the gaiety of the finale more readily, although one misses the authentic Czech lilt. The recording, though not outstanding by Decca's high standards – there is a slight degree of edge in the CD focus of the violin timbre – is still fully acceptable.

VOCAL AND CHORAL MUSIC

Mass in D, Op. 86.
(M) *** Decca 430 364-2; *430 364-4* [id.]. Ritchie, Giles, Byers, Morton, Christ Church Cathedral Ch., Preston; Cleobury (organ) – LISZT: *Missa choralis.* ***

The *Mass in D* was originally scored for small forces, and this Christ Church version presents it in its original form. It was finished in 1887, a year or two before the *G major Symphony*, and though not a major work by any means it has many delights to offer. In such a beautifully shaped reading it is self-recommending, especially when coupled with a superb performance of Liszt's equally fresh *Missa choralis*. As so often, the CD remastering shows just how good was the original (Argo) recording, which is impeccably balanced.

Requiem, Op. 89.
(M) *** Decca 421 810-2 (2). Lorengar, Komlóssy, Isofalvy, Krause, Amb. S., LSO, Kertész – KODÁLY: *Hymn of Zrinyi; Psalmus Hungaricus.* ***

The *Requiem* reflects the impact on Dvořák of the English musical world of the day and has a good deal of relatively conventional writing in it. Kertész conducts with a total commitment to the score and secures from singers and orchestra an alert and sensitive response. Pilar Lorengar's vibrato is at times a trifle disturbing, but it is the only solo performance that is likely to occasion any reserve. The recording matches the performance: it has a lifelike balance and the CD remastering adds freshness and bite.

(i) *Stabat Mater, Op. 58;* (ii) *Legends, Op. 59.*
(M) *** DG 423 919-2 (2) [id.]. (i) Mathis, Reynolds, Ochman, Shirley-Quirk, Bav. R. Ch. & O; (ii) ECO, Kubelik.

Dvořák's devout Catholicism led him to treat this tragic religious theme with an open innocence that avoids sentimentality and, though a setting of a relatively short poem which stretches to 80 minutes entails much repetition of words, this idiomatic DG performance, with fine solo and choral singing and responsive playing, holds the attention from first to last. Kubelik is consistently persuasive and this is a work which benefits from his imaginative approach. The recording, made in the Munich Herkules-Saal, is of very good quality; the remastering adds presence (especially for the soloists) without too much loss of the attractive hall ambience. There are ten *Legends*, lyrical and romantic equivalents of the *Slavonic dances* but less robust in rhythmic style and more delicately coloured. They are presented here most persuasively and the 1976 recording, made in the London Henry Wood Hall, is pleasingly vivid and atmospheric.

OPERA

Rusalka: highlights.
(B) *** Sup. Dig. 110617-2. Beňačková-Čápová, Novak, Soukupová, Ochman, Drobkova, Prague Ch. & Czech PO, Neumann.

This is a first-class selection, available on a bargain-priced disc and offering an hour of music, although only a synopsis is provided. Dvořák's fairy-tale opera is given a magical performance by Neumann and his Czech forces, helped by full, brilliant and atmospheric recording which, while giving prominence to the voices, brings out the beauty and refinement of Dvořák's orchestration. Written right at the end of the composer's career in his ripest maturity but with Wagnerian influences at work, the piece has a unique flavour. The title-role is superbly taken by Gabriela Beňačková-Čápová. The voice is creamy in tone, characterfully Slavonic without disagreeable hooting or wobbling, and the famous *Invocation to the moon* is enchanting. Vera Soukupová as the Witch is just as characterfully Slavonic in a lower register, though not so even; while Wieslaw Ochman sings with fine, clean, heroic tone as the Prince, with timbre made distinctive by tight vibrato. Richard Novak brings out some of the Alberich-like overtones as the Watersprite, though the voice is not always steady.

Egk, Werner (1901–83)

The Temptation of St Anthony (cantata).
(M) *** DG 429 858-2 [id.]. J. Baker, Koekert Qt, Bav. RSO (strings), composer – MARTIN: *Everyman; The Tempest.* *** ❀

Werner Egk's song-cycle *The Temptation of St Anthony* comes from 1945 and is a setting for contralto, string quartet and string orchestra of some eighteenth-century verses. It has a certain folk-like simplicity; as a modest makeweight for the Martin *Everyman* songs it is not of comparable distinction. Dame Janet Baker was in particularly good voice at this period in her career and the recording, which dates from the mid-1960s, is very good.

Elgar, Edward (1857–1934)

(i) *Adieu; Beau Brummel: Minuet;* (ii) *3 Bavarian dances, Op. 27; Caractacus, Op. 35: Woodland interlude. Chanson de matin; Chanson de nuit, Op. 15/1–2; Contrasts, Op. 10/3; Dream children, Op. 43; Falstaff, Op. 68: 2 Interludes. Salut d'amour; Sérnade lyrique;* (ii; iii) *Soliloquy for oboe* (orch. Gordon Jacob); (i) *Sospiri, Op. 70; The Spanish Lady: Burlesco. The Starlight Express: Waltz. Sursum corda, Op. 11.*
(M) *** Chan. CHAN 6544; *MBTD 6544* [id.]. Bournemouth Sinf., (i) George Hurst; (ii) Norman Del Mar; (iii) with Goossens.

The real treasure in this splendid collection of Elgar miniatures is the *Soliloquy* which Elgar wrote right at the end of his life for Leon Goossens. It was the only movement completed of a projected suite, a wayward, improvisatory piece which yet has a character of its own. Here the dedicatee plays it with his long-recognizable tone-colour and feeling for phrase in an orchestration by Gordon Jacob. Most of the other pieces in Norman Del Mar's programme are well known but they come up with new warmth and commitment here, and the 1976 recording, made in the Guildhall, Southampton, has an appealing ambient warmth and naturalness; indeed it approaches demonstration standard. For the CD reissue Chandos have generously added some delightful Elgar rarities recorded by George Hurst a year earlier in Christchurch Priory. The most striking is the *Sursum corda* for organ, brass, strings and timpani (no woodwind), an occasional piece written for a royal visit to Worcester in 1894, which has real nobilmente depth. The *Burlesco*, a fragment from the unfinished Elgar opera, is engagingly done, and each of these items has its charms. Again the recording has plenty of fullness, but the CD transfer brings some thinness to the violins and the upper focus sounds somewhat more artificial than in the Del Mar recording. However, these items may be regarded as a substantial bonus for the main concert, giving the disc an overall playing time of nearly 76 minutes.

Caractacus, Op. 35: Woodland interlude. Crown of India (suite), Op. 66; Grania and Dermid, Op. 42: Funeral march. Light of Life, Op. 29: Meditation. Nursery suite; Severn suite, Op. 87.
(M) **(*) EMI CDM7 63280-2; *EG 763280-4*. Royal Liverpool PO, Groves.

It is good to have these performances by Sir Charles Groves – recorded while he was principal conductor of the Royal Liverpool Philharmonic Orchestra – restored to the catalogue. This is all music that he understands warmly, and the results give much pleasure. One does not have to be an imperialist to enjoy any of the occasional pieces, and it is interesting to find the patriotic music coming up fresher than the little interlude from *The Light of Life*, beautiful as that is. Both the *Nursery suite* (written for the Princesses Elizabeth and Margaret Rose) and the orchestral version of the *Severn suite* (written for a brass band contest) come from Elgar's very last period, when his inspiration came in flashes rather than as a sustained searchlight. The completely neglected *Funeral march* was written in 1901 for a play by W. B. Yeats and George Moore; it is a splendid piece. The CD transfer retains the bloom of the original recordings and adds to the vividness.

Cockaigne overture, Op. 40; Crown of India suite, Op. 66; Enigma variations (Variations on an original theme), Op. 36; Falstaff, Op. 68; Imperial march, Op. 32; Pomp and circumstance marches Nos. 1–5, Op. 39; Serenade for strings, Op. 20.
(M) **(*) Sony M2YK 46465 (2) [id.]. LPO or ECO, Barenboim.

Barenboim's habit of moulding the music of Elgar in flexible tempi, of underlining romantic expressiveness, has never been as convincing on record as here in *Falstaff*, where the big contrasts of texture, dynamic and mood are played for all they are worth. Rarely, even under the composer, has the story-telling element in Elgar's symphonic study been presented so captivatingly. The Gadshill episode with its ambush is so vivid, one can see the picture in one's mind's eye. *Cockaigne* is also given a colourful reading, though the recording is not ideally balanced. Barenboim's view of *Enigma* is full of fantasy. Its most distinctive point is its concern for the miniature element. Without belittling the delicate variations, Barenboim both makes them sparkle and gives them emotional point, while the big variations have full weight, and the finale brings extra fierceness at a fast tempo. Barenboim's readings of the ceremonial music are never less than interesting, but his judgement is not infallible. Tempi are surprisingly fast in the *Pomp and circumstance marches* (though Elgar's tended to be fast too), and not all Elgarians will approve of his updating of Edwardian majesty. The sound is clear and firm; ideally, one wants rather more opulence (especially in *Pomp and circumstance*), but the transfers are sophisticated and well balanced, with *Cockaigne*, the *Crown of India* and the *Serenade* notably fresh and clear.

(i) *Cockaigne overture, Op. 40;* (ii) *Froissart overture, Op. 19; Pomp and circumstance marches, Op. 39, Nos* (i) *1 in D;* (ii) *2 in A min.; 3 in C min.;* (i) *4 in G;* (ii) *5 in C.*
(M) *** EMI CDM7 69563-2; *EG 769563-4* (i) Philh. O; (ii) New Philh. O; Barbirolli.

(i) *Cockaigne overture, Op. 40;* (ii) *Enigma variations (Variations on an original theme), Op. 36;* (i) *Pomp and circumstance marches Nos. 1–5, Op. 39.*
(M) **(*) Decca 417 719-2. (i) LPO; (ii) Chicago SO; Solti.

It is good to have Barbirolli's ripe yet wonderfully vital portrait of Edwardian London at last on CD where the recording retains its atmosphere as well as its vividness. *Froissart* is very compelling too, and Barbirolli makes a fine suite of the five *Pomp and circumstance marches*, with plenty of contrast in Nos. 2 and 3 to offset the Edwardian flag-waving of Nos. 1 and 4.

Solti's *Cockaigne* is sharply dramatic and exciting; his view of the *Marches* is both vigorous and refined, with sharp pointing in the outer sections, spaciousness in the great melodies. In the *Marches* the CD remastering brings vivid sound with full-bodied strings; *Cockaigne* is somewhat brighter, especially in the brass, and there is a touch of glare. Although the opening of *Enigma* is affectionately Elgarian, with Solti the work becomes essentially a dazzling showpiece. *Nimrod* opens elegiacally but, with a basic tempo faster than usual, Solti allows himself to get faster and faster still, although there is a broadening at the end. This won't be to all tastes, but the brilliant recording suits the drama of the playing.

Cello concerto in E min., Op. 85.
(B) *** Pickwick Dig. PCD 930 [id.]. (i) Felix Schmidt; LSO, Frühbeck de Burgos – VAUGHAN WILLIAMS: *Tallis fantasia; Greensleeves.* **(*)
(M) *** Decca 421 385-2; *421 385-4* [id.]. Lynn Harrell, Cleveland O, Maazel – WALTON: *Violin concerto.* ***
(M) (**(*)) EMI mono CDH7 63498-2 [id.]. Casals, BBC SO, Boult – DVOŘÁK: *Concerto* (***) (with BRUCH: *Kol Nidrei* (***)).

(i) *Cello concerto. Elegy for strings, Op. 58; In the South (Alassio), Op. 50.*
(B) **(*) CfP CD-CFP 9003; *TC-CFP 40342.* (i) Robert Cohen; LPO, Del Mar.

(i) *Cello concerto. Introduction and allegro for strings, Op. 47; Overtures: Froissart, Op. 19; In the South (Alassio), Op. 50.*
(M) **(*) EMI CDM7 69200-2. (i) Tortelier; LPO, Boult.

Felix Schmidt, a young cellist with the widest expressive range, gives a bold, emotionally intense reading which finds a most satisfying middle ground between the romantic freedom typified by the unique Jacqueline du Pré (available only in a collection – see Concerts) and the steadier way of a Paul Tortelier. Schmidt's hushed, deeply meditative account of the slow movement is among the most moving of all. With his rich, full tone opulently recorded, his account can be recommended beside the very finest versions, depending on preference as to coupling, in this instance an unconventional linking with two of Vaughan Williams's most popular works.

Lynn Harrell's outstanding account with the Cleveland Orchestra on Decca offers a strong challenge. With eloquent support from Maazel and this fine orchestra (the woodwind play with appealing delicacy), this reading, deeply felt, balances a gentle nostalgia with extrovert brilliance. The slow movement is tenderly spacious, the scherzo bursts with exuberance and, after a passionate opening, the finale is memorable for the poignantly expressive reprise of the melody from the *Adagio*, one of Elgar's greatest inspirations. The recording of the orchestra is brightly lit; the solo cello is rich-timbred, a little larger than life, but convincingly focused.

On his earlier, EMI recording, Tortelier gives a noble and restrained performance; Boult accompanies with splendid tact and in addition gives fine accounts of the *Introduction and allegro*, the early *Froissart overture* – which combines orchestral links with Brahms with emergent fingerprints of the later Elgar – and *In the South*.

Robert Cohen's performance is firm and intense, with steady tempi, the colouring more positive, less autumnal than usual, relating the work more closely to the *Second Symphony*. Yet there is no lack of inner feeling. Del Mar's accompaniment is wholly sympathetic, underlining the soloist's approach. He also directs an exciting account of *In the South*, recorded in a single take and highly spontaneous in effect. The *Elegy* makes an eloquent bonus. The recording is wide-ranging and well balanced, but shows Cohen's tone as bright and well focused rather than as especially resonant in the bass.

Casals recorded the Elgar *Cello concerto* in London in 1946, and the fervour of his playing caused some raised eyebrows. In the first edition of *The Record Guide* (1951), Edward Sackville-West and Desmond Shawe-Taylor found that 'the great cellist's idiosyncrasies take us too far away from the composer's intentions'; the autumnal episode in the finale prompted their thoughts to turn to *Amfortas*! But if it is less than Elgarian in its reticence, the same also must be said of many later versions. A powerful account, not least for Sir Adrian's contribution, even though its eloquence would have been even more telling were the emotion recollected in greater tranquillity. A landmark of the gramophone all the same, and the strongly characterized Max Bruch *Kol Nidrei* makes a fine encore.

(i) *Cello concerto in E min., Op. 85*; (ii) *Violin concerto in B min., Op. 61.*
(M) (***) EMI mono CDH7 69786-2. (i) Beatrice Harrison, New SO; (ii) Menuhin, LSO, composer.

Even though the original master of the 1932 Menuhin/Elgar recording of the *Violin concerto* was wilfully destroyed many years ago, the tape transfer (originally made by A. C. Griffith) was of the highest quality and it emerges on CD with a superb sense of atmosphere and presence. As for the performance, its classic status is amply confirmed: in many ways no one has ever matched – let alone surpassed – the seventeen-year-old Menuhin in this work, even if the first part of the finale lacks something in fire. The response of conductor, soloist and orchestra has extraordinary magic, with great warmth but no self-indulgence. The performance of the *Cello concerto* has nothing like the same inspiration, when Beatrice Harrison's playing is at times fallible, and there are moments which seem almost perfunctory; but there is still much Elgarian feeling. Even with reservations about the *Cello concerto*, this record is indispensable for Menuhin's totally compulsive account of the *Violin concerto*, a very moving experience.

(i) *Cello concerto in E min., Op. 85. Elegy, Op. 58; Enigma variations (Variations on an original theme), Op. 36; Introduction and allegro, Op. 47.*
❀ (M) *** EMI stereo/mono CDM7 63955-2 [id.]; *EG 763955-4*. (i) Navarra, Hallé O, Barbirolli.

This is one of the most fascinating of all the Barbirolli reissues on the EMI Phoenixa label. The documentation reveals that, astonishingly, this Hallé version of the *Enigma variations* was recorded in the Manchester Free Trade Hall in 1956 by the Mercury team, Wilma Cozart and Harold Lawrence. In its new CD transfer the sound is extraordinarily good, and the performance is revealed as Barbirolli's finest account ever on record. There is a naturally spontaneous flow and marvellous detail, both affectionate and perceptive; *Nimrod* has never sounded as nobly resonant as here, and the finale is the most exciting of any performance in the catalogue. In the finale Barbirolli generates powerful fervour and an irresistible momentum: at the very end, the organ entry brings an unforgettable, tummy-wobbling effect which engulfs the listener thrillingly. The *Introduction and allegro* is mono and, though not quite so impressively recorded, has comparable passion – the recapitulation of the big striding tune in the middle strings has superb thrust and warmth. The concert closes with a moving account of the *Elegy*, simple and affectionate. In between comes Navarra's strong and firm view of the *Cello concerto*. With his control of phrasing and wide range of tone-colour this 1957 perfomance culminates in a most moving account of the Epilogue. Only the scherzo falls slightly short – slower than usual, but Navarra manages some beautifully light bowing, and the virtuoso passages of the finale are played with reliable intonation. Again, the recording is firmer and fuller on CD than it ever was on LP.

Violin concerto in B min., Op. 61.
❀ (M) *** EMI Dig. EMX 2058; *TC-EMX 2058*. Nigel Kennedy, LPO, Handley.
(M) (***) BMG/RCA mono GD 87966 [7966-2-RG]. Heifetz, LSO, Sargent – WALTON: *Concerto*. (***)

(i) *Violin concerto in B min., Op. 61; Overture Cockaigne, Op. 40.*
(BB) *** Naxos Dig. 8.550489 [id.]. Dong-Suk Kang, Polish Nat. RSO (Katowice), Adrian Leaper.

Violin concerto in B min.; Salut d'amour; La Capricieuse.
(M) *** Decca 421 388-2; *421 388-4* [id.]. Kyung Wha Chung, LPO, Solti.

Recorded before Nigel Kennedy had become a popular evangelist for the classics and changed his hair-style and manner of apparel to suit his new audience, this remains his finest achievement on record, arguably even finer than the long line of versions with star international soloists either from outside or within Britain. With Vernon Handley as guide it is a truly inspired and inspiring performance and the recording is outstandingly faithful and atmospheric. At mid-price it is a supreme Elgarian bargain.

Dong-Suk Kang, immaculate in his intonation, plays the Elgar with fire and urgency. This is very different from most latterday performances, with markedly faster speeds; yet those speeds relate more closely than usual to the metronome markings in the score, and they never get in the way of Kang's ability to feel Elgarian rubato naturally, guided by the warmly understanding conducting of Adrian Leaper. The flowing speed for the central *Andante* brings out a characteristically Elgarian elegance at the start which slower speeds tend to miss. The dashing, mercurial quality of the performance in the finale, very exciting, then leads on to a finely sustained account of the long accompanied cadenza. Irrespective of price – and this is a super-budget issue – this is a keenly competitive version, with excellent, wide-ranging digital sound, if with rather too forward a balance for the soloist. With the bonus of a finely detailed account of *Cockaigne*, it makes an outstanding bargain.

The extra clarity and sense of presence in the CD transfer intensify the impact of Kyung Wha Chung's heartfelt performance, with Solti responding with warmth to the wide-ranging expressiveness of the soloist. Chung's dreamily expansive playing in that middle movement is ravishing in its beauty, not least in the ethereal writing above the stave, and so too are the lyrical pages of the outer movements. The bravura passages draw from her a vein of mercurial fantasy, excitingly volatile, and no other recording brings a wider range of dynamic or tone in the soloist's playing. The two little violin pieces, accompanied by Philip Moll, act as encores. The 1977 analogue recording for the *Concerto* has been beautifully transferred.

Heifetz's view of Elgar, with speeds unusually fast, may not be idiomatic, but this recording brings a masterly example of his artistry, demonstrating very clearly that, for all the ease and technical perfection, he is in no way a cold interpreter of romantic music. The mono recording is limited, not helped by a low hum in the transfer, and the solo instrument is balanced very close; but such a historic document should not be missed, generously coupled with Heifetz's authoritative reading of the Walton, with the composer conducting.

Elegy for strings, Op. 58; Introduction and allegro for strings, Op. 47; Serenade for strings in E min., Op. 20; Sospiri, Op. 70; The Spanish Lady; suite (ed. Young).
(M) **(*) Decca 421 384-2; *421 384-4* [id.]. ASMF, Marriner – WARLOCK: *Serenade.* ***

Marriner's somewhat stiff manner in the *Introduction and allegro* will not appeal to everyone, but the subtlety and strength of his unique band of string players are never in doubt. The collection has the added interest of including the brief snippets arranged by Percy Young from Elgar's unfinished opera, *The Spanish Lady*. Marriner's version of the *Serenade*, warm and resilient, shows him at his finest. The (1968) sound on CD is fresh and full – but with just a touch of astringency in the violins, which adds to the bite of the *Introduction and allegro*. The Warlock *Serenade* has also been included for this reissue.

Enigma variations (Variations on an original theme), Op. 36.
(M) (***) EMI mono CDH7 69784-2. BBC SO, Toscanini – DEBUSSY: *La Mer.* (**)
(M) (***) BMG/RCA mono GD 60287 [60287-2-RG]. NBC SO, Toscanini – MUSSORGSKY: *Pictures.* (**)
(M) ** Ph. 432 276-2; *432 276-4*. Concg. O, Haitink – STRAUSS: *Ein Heldenleben.* ***

(i) *Enigma variations (Variations on an original theme), Op. 36;* (ii) *Viola concerto* (arr. Tertis from *Cello concerto*).
(BB) ** Virgin/Virgo Dig. VJ7 91455-2; *VJ7 91455-4* [id.]. (i) RPO, Litton; (ii) Braunstein, Ac. of London, Richard Stamp.

(i) *Enigma variations;* (ii) *Falstaff, Op. 68.*
(M) *** EMI CDM7 69185-2; *EG 769185-4* (i) Philh. O, (ii) Hallé O, Barbirolli.

Enigma variations; Introduction and allegro for strings.
(B) *(*) CfP CD-CFP 4022; *TC-CFP 4022.* LPO, Sir Adrian Boult.

Enigma variations; Introduction and allegro for strings, Op. 47; Serenade for strings, Op. 20.
(M) **(*) EMI Dig. CD-EMX 9503; *TC-EMX 2011.* LPO, Vernon Handley.

(i) *Enigma variations;* (ii) *Pomp and circumstance marches Nos. 1–5, Op. 39.*
(M) *** Chan. CHAN 6504 [id.]. SNO, Sir Alexander Gibson.
(M) *** DG 429 713-2; *429 713-4* [id.]. RPO, Norman Del Mar.
(M) *** EMI CDM7 64015-2 [id.]; *EG 764015-4.* (i) LSO or (ii) LPO, Sir Adrian Boult.
(B) **(*) Decca 417 878-2; *417 878-4* LSO, (i) Monteux; (ii) Bliss.

(i) *Enigma variations;* (ii) *Pomp and circumstance marches Nos. 1 and 3* (CD only: (iii) *Cello concerto in E min.*).
(B) *** DG Compact Classics 413 852-2 (2); *413 852-4* [id.]. (i) LSO, Jochum; (ii) RPO, Del Mar (CD only: (iii) Fournier, BPO, Wallenstein) – HOLST: *Planets.* **(*)

Enigma variations; Pomp and circumstance marches Nos. 1 & 4; Salut d'amour.
(BB) ** Naxos Dig. 8.550229 [id.]. CSR SO (Bratislava), Adrian Leaper – DELIUS: *Brigg Fair* etc. **

Ripe and expansive, Barbirolli's view of *Falstaff* is colourful and convincing; it has fine atmospheric feeling too, and the interludes are more magical here than in the Boult version. *Enigma*, too, was a work that Barbirolli, himself a cellist, made especially his own, with wonderfully expansive string-playing and much imaginative detail; the recording was made when he was at the very peak of his interpretative powers. The massed strings have lost some of their amplitude, but detail is clearer and the overall balance is convincing, with the Kingsway Hall ambience ensuring a pleasing bloom.

Sir Alexander Gibson's reading of *Enigma* has stood the test of time and remains very satisfying, warm and spontaneous in feeling, with a memorable climax in *Nimrod*. The 1978 recording, made in Glasgow's City Hall, remains outstanding, with the organ sonorously filling out the bass in the finale, which has real splendour. The *Pomp and circumstance marches*, too, have fine nobilmente and swagger. The CD transfers retain all the character and bloom of the original recordings, and this makes another highlight in Chandos's mid-priced Collect series, in spite of the unappealing picture of the composer on the cover.

In the *Enigma variations* Del Mar comes closer than any other conductor to the responsive rubato style of Elgar himself, using fluctuations to point the emotional message of the work with wonderful power and spontaneity. Recorded in Guildford Cathedral, with plentiful reverberation, this version has the advantage of a splendid contribution from the organ at the end. The RPO plays superbly, both here and in the *Pomp and circumstance marches*, given Proms-style flair and urgency – although some might feel that the fast speeds miss some of the nobilmente. The reverberant sound here adds something of an aggressive edge to the music-making; however, at mid-price this is a very competitive reissue.

Boult's *Enigma* comes from the beginning of the 1970s, but the recording has lost some of its amplitude in its transfer to CD: the effect is fresh, but the strings are less warm. The reading shows this conductor's long experience of the work, with each variation growing naturally and seamlessly out of the music that has gone before. *Nimrod* in particular glows, superbly sustained. Perhaps the finale lacks the fire that Barbirolli gives to it, but it has undoubted strength and forms a satisfying culmination. Boult's approach to the *Pomp and circumstance marches* is brisk and direct, with an almost no-nonsense manner in places. There is not a hint of vulgarity and the freshness is most attractive, though it is a pity he omits the repeats in the Dvořák-like No. 2. The brightened sound brings a degree of abrasiveness to the brass.

The Compact Classics issue combines Steinberg's exciting and brilliantly recorded complete set of the Holst *Planets* with Eugen Jochum's inspirational reading of *Enigma*, and bringing as a bonus two of Del Mar's extremely spirited *Pomp and circumstance marches*. The equivalent pair of CDs adds Fournier's moving and eloquent account of the *Cello concerto* which, by reason of the forward balance of the soloist, is made to sound more extrovert than usual. It has undoubted fervour and conviction, even if the close microphone placing, besides reducing the dynamic contrast of the solo playing, also obscures some of the orchestral detail. When Jochum recorded *Enigma* in 1975, he had not conducted it for several decades, but his thoughtful insight, in fresh study, produced an outstanding reading, consistently satisfying. The key to the whole work, as Jochum sees it, is *Nimrod*. Like others – including Elgar himself – Jochum sets a very slow *adagio* at the start, slower than the metronome marking in the score; unlike others, he maintains that measured tempo and, with the subtlest gradations, builds an even bigger, nobler climax than you find in *accelerando* readings. It is like a Bruckner slow movement in microcosm, around which revolve the other variations, all of them delicately detailed, with a natural feeling for Elgarian rubato. The playing of the LSO matches the strength and refinement of the performance. The remastered recording, however, sounds brighter and more vivid than before but has lost some of its richness. CD and tape are closely matched.

Vernon Handley's generously full Eminence collection is given brilliantly wide-ranging digital sound. In the string works, the CD makes the emphasis of the upper range at the expense of the middle the more striking; one needs more amplitude here. Handley's strong personal identification with the music brings a consciously moulded style that tends at times to rob the *Enigma variations* of its forward impulse. The performances of the string works are more direct.

Monteux's *Enigma* is famous for its individual account of *Nimrod*, where his electric pianissimo at the opening (the playing scarcely above a whisper) benefits from the background quiet of CD, enhancing the superb climax, built up in elegiac fashion. Bliss's *Pomp and circumstance marches* have a rumbustious vigour; here the recording sounds more dated; but in Decca's bargain range this makes an impressive coupling.

Toscanini's freely expressive BBC reading makes a fascinating contrast with his much later NBC orchestra recording, done live but in much more clinical conditions. Where the American orchestra plays the notes brilliantly but, as it seems, too literally, what is basically the same interpretation comes over with a far greater sense of fantasy, of idiomatic warmth and flair in the electric atmosphere of Queen's Hall, ending with a dazzling account of the finale, which promptly inspires an eruption of joy and excitement from the audience. Though elsewhere audience noises intrude, the sound – superbly mastered by Keith Hardwick, but given extra space on CD – is astonishingly vivid, especially for a transfer from 78 r.p.m., roughening at times as at the very end of the finale.

It is a pity that Toscanini's sharply focused but warmly expressive NBC reading of *Enigma* should come in an (admittedly generous) coupling with his severe account of the Mussorgsky. The Elgar, often expansive as well as affectionately phrased, as in the statement of the theme, gives a much more sympathetic view of the taskmaster conductor than most of his late recordings. Though traditionalist Elgarians may not always approve, it makes for an electrifying experience. The transfer is clean but not too aggressive.

The Naxos CD has excellent modern digital recording, made in the Concert Hall of Slovak Radio. Adrian Leaper's reading of *Enigma* is pleasingly fresh and idiomatic, and the orchestra responds with warmth to his understanding direction. The direct, naturally paced performance is not unlike Gibson's, with only marginally less character overall. The encores are vigorous, and *Salut d'amour* is not sentimentalized. Good value in the bargain basement.

On the comparably priced Virgo label, Litton's excellent version of *Enigma*, red-blooded and well paced, is recoupled with a welcome recording of an Elgar rarity, the arrangement of the *Cello concerto* which – with Elgar's approval – Lionel Tertis made for the viola. The American violist, Mark Braunstein, plays with fine, true intonation, but the reading totally lacks idiosyncrasy, sounding relatively characterless and lacking in warmth. Aptly, the recorded sound is more intimate than in the *Variations*.

Haitink's reading of the *Enigma variations*, while thoughtfully direct and beautifully played, nevertheless lacks the dynamism to weld the separate variations into a unity. The blood never tingles, as it does in the coupling of Strauss's *Ein Heldenleben*. Excellent, refined analogue recording.

Boult's LPO version on CfP was made a decade earlier than his set with the LSO; it is enjoyable enough, if rather less strongly characterized. The sound is well balanced and clear but has less substance than the later recording. The sound is even thinner in the *Introduction and allegro*, emphasizing the athletic thrust of the music-making rather than the warmth which undoubtedly underlies the playing.

Falstaff (symphonic study), *Op. 68; The Sanguine Fan* (ballet), *Op. 81;* BACH, arr. ELGAR: *Fantasia and fugue in C min. (BWV 537), Op. 86.*

(M) *** EMI CDM7 63133-2. LPO, Boult.

Falstaff, Op. 68; Introduction and allegro for strings, Op. 47; arr. of BACH: *Fantasia and fugue in C min., Op. 86.*

(B) *** Pickwick Dig. PCD 934; *CIMPC 934* [id.]. National Youth O of Great Britain, Christopher Seaman.

These works have rarely been given such heartfelt performances as those by Christopher Seaman and the National Youth Orchestra. The weight of string sound, combined with the fervour behind the playing, makes this an exceptionally satisfying reading of the *Introduction and allegro*, while *Falstaff* demonstrates even more strikingly how, working together intensively, these youngsters have learnt to keep a precise ensemble through the most complex variations of expressive rubato. There the weight of string-tone contrasts with the lightness of touch and wit that the players bring to the many scherzando passages, keeping keen concentration from first to last, not easy in this work. Some of the solo string passages betray that these are not adult professionals, but they are momentary and very rare, and most Elgarians will enjoy these performances – including the Bach arrangement, also done passionately – far more than cooler ones, however polished. Warm, full, digital recording adds to an outstanding bargain, though irritatingly there is no tracking of sections in *Falstaff*, over half an hour long.

Boult treats *Falstaff* essentially as a symphonic structure. It follows therefore that some of the mystery, some of the delicate sense of atmosphere that impregnates the interludes for example, is undercharacterized. But the crispness of the playing and Boult's unfailing alertness amply compensate for that. The little-known ballet score written during the First World War makes for an unexpected and enjoyable coupling, and Elgar's Bach arrangement is richly expansive. The remastering, as with Boult's other Elgar recordings, clarifies textures without too much loss of ambience and weight.

Serenade for strings in E min., Op. 20.

(B) *** Pickwick Dig. PCD 861; *CIMPC 861* [id.]. Serenata of London – GRIEG: *Holberg suite*; MOZART: *Eine kleine Nachtmusik* etc. ***

(M) *(*) DG Dig. 429 488-2. Orpheus CO – DVOŘÁK: *Serenade* *(*); TCHAIKOVSKY: *Serenade.* **

A particularly appealing account of Elgar's *Serenade*, with unforced tempi in the outer movements admirably catching its mood and atmosphere so that the elegiac *Larghetto*, beautifully and sensitively phrased, finds a natural place in the overall scheme. The Serenata of London is led rather than conducted by Barry Wilde; but this is a performance of undoubted personality, and it is recorded with remarkable realism and naturalness. With excellent couplings, this is an outstanding bargain.

The recording by the Orpheus Chamber Orchestra is disappointing. The sharply focused, vividly realistic recording of a string group that is plainly too few in number to be fully effective in this music also emphasizes the lack of ripeness in the reading.

Symphony No. 1 in A flat, Op. 55.

❀ (B) *** Pickwick Dig. PCD 956 [id.]. Hallé O, James Judd.

(B) *** CfP CD-CFP 9018; *TC-CFP 4541.* LPO, Vernon Handley.

Symphony No. 1 in A flat, Op. 55; Cockaigne overture.

(M) *** Decca 421 387-2; *421 387-4* [id.]. LPO, Solti.

Symphony No. 1 in A flat; Chanson de matin; Chanson de nuit; Serenade for strings, Op. 20.
(M) *** EMI CDM7 64013-2 [id.]; *EG 764013-4.* LPO, Sir Adrian Boult.

James Judd, more than any rival on disc, has learnt directly from Elgar's own recording of this magnificent symphony. He does not copy slavishly but uses his deep understanding of what Elgar achieves on record to enhance the Hallé's performance. So the reading has extra authenticity in the many complex speed-changes (sometimes indicated confusingly in the score), in the precise placing of climaxes and in the textural balances. Like Elgar, he draws out the horns and trombones thrillingly, and the Hallé brass, forwardly balanced, blazes out superbly, with the final coda thrust home magnificently. Above all, Judd outshines others in the pacing and phrasing of the lovely slow movement which in its natural flowing rubato has melting tenderness behind the passion, a throat-catching poignancy not fully conveyed elsewhere but very much a quality of Elgar's own reading. The refinement of the strings down to the most hushed pianissimo confirms this as the Hallé's most beautiful disc in years, recorded with warmth and opulence. Though there is no coupling, the bargain price is ample compensation.

Vernon Handley directs a beautifully paced reading which can be counted in every way outstanding, even making no allowance for price. The LPO has performed this symphony many times before but never with more poise and refinement than here. It is in the slow movement above all that Handley scores, spacious and movingly expressive. With very good sound, well transferred to CD, this is a highly recommendable alternative version.

Boult clearly presents the *First Symphony* as a counterpart to the *Second*, with hints of reflective nostalgia amid the triumph. Until this final version, made when Sir Adrian was eighty-seven, his recordings of the *First* had been among his less riveting Elgar interpretations. But the EMI disc contains a radiantly beautiful performance, with no extreme tempi, richly spaced in the first movement, invigorating in the syncopated march rhythms of the scherzo, and similarly bouncing in the Brahmsian rhythms of the finale. Most clearly distinctive is the lovely slow movement, presented as a seamless flow of melody, less 'inner' than with Handley, and above all glowing with untroubled sweetness. The CD remastering of the 1976 Abbey Road recording, as so often, has lost the exceptionally full-blooded quality of the original LP: the violin timbre is thinner and, although the brass is full, the sharpening of detail is not all gain. This applies also to the 1967 recording of the *Chansons* and the 1972 *Serenade* (recorded, like the finale of the *Symphony*, in Kingsway Hall). Here Boult's simplicity and tenderness are no less effective than a riper view.

Solti's version of the *First Symphony* is in Decca's mid-price British Collection series, aptly coupled with his sharply dramatic account of *Cockaigne*. The CD transfers bring out the fullness as well as the brilliance of the excellent 1970s sound, and though Solti's thrusting manner will give the traditional Elgarian the occasional jolt, his clearing away of the cobwebs stems from his study of the composer's own recording before he ever attempted to conduct the work at all.

Symphony No. 2 in E flat, Op. 63.
(B) *** CfP CD-CFP 4544; *TC-CFP 4544.* LPO, Vernon Handley.

Symphony No. 2 in E flat; Cockaigne overture, Op. 40.
(M) *** EMI CDM7 64014-2 [id.]; *EG 764014-4.* LPO, Sir Adrian Boult.

Symphony No. 2 in E flat; The Crown of India (suite), *Op. 66.*
(M) *** Chan. CHAN 6523; *MBTD 6523* [id.]. SNO, Gibson.

Symphony No. 2 in E flat; Imperial march, Op. 32; Sospiri, Op. 70. Dream of Gerontius: Prelude. CHOPIN, arr. Elgar: *Funeral march.*
(M) (***) EMI mono CDH7 63134-2. BBC SO, Boult.

Handley's is the most satisfying modern version of a work which has latterly been much recorded. What Handley conveys superbly is the sense of Elgarian ebb and flow, building climaxes like a master and drawing excellent, spontaneous-sounding playing from an orchestra which, more than any other, has specialized in performing this symphony. The sound is warmly atmospheric and vividly conveys the added organ part in the bass, just at the climax of the finale, which Elgar himself suggested 'if available': a tummy-wobbling effect. This would be a first choice at full price, but as a bargain CD there are few records to match it.

Gibson recorded the *Second Symphony* in 1977, the year before his outstanding account of *Enigma*. It shows his partnership with the SNO at its peak, and this performance captures all the opulent nostalgia of Elgar's masterly score. The reading of the first movement is more relaxed in its grip than Handley's, but its spaciousness is appealing and, both here and in the beautifully sustained *Larghetto*, the richly resonant acoustics of Glasgow City Hall bring out the full panoply of Elgarian sound. The finale has splendid nobilmente, with a thrilling reprise, and the relaxation of tension for the closing pages is most sensitively managed. In the *Crown of India* suite Gibson is consistently imaginative in his attention to detail, and the playing of the Scottish orchestra is again warmly responsive, especially in the score's more delicate moments.

For his fifth recording of the *Second Symphony* Sir Adrian Boult, incomparable Elgarian, drew from the LPO the most richly satisfying performance of all. Over the years Sir Adrian's view of the glorious nobility of the first movement had mellowed a degree. The tempo is a shade slower than before (and much slower than the composer's own in the great leaping 12/8 theme), but the pointing of climaxes is unrivalled. With Boult more than anyone else the architecture is clearly and strongly established, with tempo changes less exaggerated than usual. The peak comes in the great *Funeral march*, where the concentration of the performance is irresistible. The LPO strings play gloriously, with the great swooping violin phrases at the climaxes inspiring a frisson as in a live performance. The scherzo has lightness and delicacy, giving more room to breathe. In the finale, firm and strong, Boult cleverly conceals the repetitiveness of the main theme and gives a radiant account of the lovely epilogue. This is a version to convert new listeners to a love of Elgar, although, even more than in the *First Symphony* the ear notices a loss of opulence compared with the original LP. There is greater vividness, certainly, and this heightens the drama in the central section of the scherzo; throughout, however, the violins sound thinner and there is less warmth in the middle and lower strings. This is very striking in *Cockaigne*, which opens the disc, although it serves to emphasize the fresh directness of Boult's approach.

No more exhilarating account of Elgar's *Second* has ever been put on disc than the first of Boult's five recordings. The sessions in Bedford, where the orchestra was still evacuated, took place in the closing months of the Second World War and reflect the tense yet newly optimistic atmosphere of the time. It helped too that this was the first ever recording after the composer's own, a special event. Boult's noble reading of this work was at its very freshest here, with dramatic and emotional points thrust home unerringly. The transfer has some edge on it, not ideally rounded, but brings out the fine detail in what at the time marked a new development in hi-fi recording. The other items, all recorded in the 1930s, make welcome and generous fill-ups.

VOCAL AND CHORAL MUSIC

The Dream of Gerontius, Op. 38.

(M) **(*) Decca 421 381-2 (2) [id.]. Pears, Minton, Shirley-Quirk, King's College Ch., LSO Ch., LSO, Britten – HOLST: *Hymn of Jesus.* ***

(M) (**(*)) EMI mono CHS7 63376-2 [Ang. CDHB 63376]. Lewis, Thomas, Cameron, Huddersfield Ch. Soc., Royal Liverpool PO, Sargent – WALTON: *Belshazzar's Feast.* (**(*))

(i) *The Dream of Gerontius. Sea pictures.*

(M) **(*) EMI CMS7 63185-2 (2). Dame Janet Baker, Hallé O, Barbirolli; (i) with Richard Lewis, Kim Borg, Hallé & Sheffield Philharmonic Ch., Amb. S.

Barbirolli's red-blooded reading of *Gerontius* is the most heart-warmingly dramatic ever recorded; here it is offered, in a first-rate CD transfer, in coupling with one of the greatest Elgar recordings ever made: Dame Janet Baker's rapt and heartfelt account of *Sea pictures*, originally the coupling for Jacqueline du Pré's first version of the *Cello concerto*. No one on record can match Dame Janet in this version of *Gerontius* for the fervent intensity and glorious tonal range of her singing as the Angel, one of her supreme recorded performances; and the clarity of CD intensifies the experience. In pure dedication the emotional thrust of Barbirolli's reading conveys the deepest spiritual intensity, making most other versions seem cool by comparison. Barbirolli also scores even over the finest modern rivals in the forward immediacy of the chorus. The recording may have its hints of distortion, but the sound is overwhelming, not least in the great outburst of *Praise to the holiest*, and in the surge of emotion behind the radiant choruses ending each half. Richard Lewis gives one of his finest recorded performances, searching and intense, and, though Kim Borg is unidiomatic in the bass role, his bass tones are rich in timbre, even if his projection lacks the dramatic edge of Robert Lloyd on the full-price Boult set. The Barbirolli reissue has rather a high tape-hiss, but in such a performance one quickly forgets it after the Prelude; and the layout is preferable to the full-price Boult set, opening with the *Sea Pictures*, then offering Part One of the main work on the first CD, and Part Two complete on the second.

The Britten version brings searching and inspired conducting from a fellow-composer not generally associated with Elgar. Britten's approach is red-blooded, passionate and urgent and with speeds never languishing – as in this oratorio they can. The LSO Chorus – supplemented by the King's Choir – is balanced backwardly in the warmly atmospheric recording made at The Maltings, but the extra projection and precision of CD bring out how bitingly dramatic the singing is, even if the actual choral sound is not sharply focused. The soloists are a fine, responsive team, with Pears an involving if sometimes over-stressed Gerontius, and Yvonne Minton and John Shirley-Quirk both excellent. On CD the layout, with the Holst work placed first, allows the break between discs to come in the ideal place, between the oratorio's two parts.

Sargent directs a thoughtful and moving account of *Gerontius*, with the 1950s sound coming up remarkably well, but it is sad that his earlier (1945) recording, the first complete one ever issued, was not chosen instead, more intense, more dedicated, more spontaneous-sounding. But with three excellent soloists and the Huddersfield Choral Society at its traditional peak, this is an excellent example of Sargent's work in his most successful area, conducting an amateur chorus. The coupling is both generous and apt and, with Walton coming before Part 1 of the Elgar, it means that the break between discs is placed between the two Parts.

(i) *Sea pictures, Op. 37. Pomp and circumstance marches Nos. 1–5, Op. 39.*
(B) *** CfP CD-CFP 9004; *TC-CFP 40363.* (i) Bernadette Greevy; LPO, Handley.

Bernadette Greevy – in glorious voice – gives the performance of her recording career in an inspired partnership with Vernon Handley, whose accompaniments are no less memorable, and with the LPO players finding a wonderful rapport with the voice. The singer's imaginative illumination of the words is a constant source of delight. In the last song Handley uses a telling *ad lib.* organ part to underline the climaxes of each final stanza. The recording balance is excellent, although the CD suggests that the microphone was rather close to the voice, rich and clear against an orchestral background shimmering with atmospheric detail. The coupled *Marches* are exhilarating, and if Nos. 2 and (especially) 3 strike some ears as too vigorously paced, comparison with the composer's own tempi reveals an authentic precedent.

COLLECTION

'The world of Elgar': (i) *Introduction & allegro, Op. 47;* (ii) *Pomp and circumstance marches Nos. 1 & 4;* (iii) *Serenade for strings, Op. 20;* (iv) *Enigma variations: Nimrod.* (v) *Salut d'amour, Op. 12;* (vi) *Dream of Gerontius: But hark! a grand mysterious harmony . . . Praise to the holiest in the height.* (vii) *Give unto the Lord;* (viii) *There is sweet music.*
(B) ** Decca 430 094-2; *430 094-4.* (i) ECO, Britten; (ii) LSO, Bliss; (iii) ASMF, Marriner; (iv) LSO, Monteux; (v) Kyung Wha Chung, Moll; (vi) Soloists, LSO Ch., King's College Ch., LSO, Britten; (vii) Canterbury Cathedral Ch., Wicks; (viii) Louis Halsey Singers, Halsey.

This collection is worth its modest cost for Britten's individually creative account of the *Introduction and allegro*, full of ardour at the climax, and for Marriner's warmly elegant account of the *Serenade*, both sounding well on CD. Bliss's rumbustious *Pomp and circumstance marches* and Monteux's famous account of *Nimrod*, with its rapt opening pianissimo, are worth having, but the early recording brings a lack of amplitude in the violin timbre; and the rather brief excerpt from Britten's *Dream of Gerontius* lacks ideal clarity and bite in the choral focus. The welcome surprise is *There is sweet music*, a delightful performance by the Louis Halsey Singers.

Enescu, Georges (1881–1955)

Roumanian rhapsody No. 1.
(M) *** Mercury 432 015-2 [id.]. LSO, Dorati – LISZT: *Hungarian rhapsodies Nos. 1–6.* **(*)
(M) **(*) BMG/RCA GD 86530 [6530-2-RG]. Boston Pops, Fiedler – DVOŘÁK: *Symphony No. 9.* **(*)

Enescu's chimerical *First Roumanian rhapsody* combines a string of glowing folk-derived melodies with glittering scoring to make it the finest genre piece of its kind in laminating Eastern gypsy influences under a bourgeois orchestral veneer. Dorati finds both flair and exhilaration in the closing pages, and the Mercury sound, from the early 1960s, is well up to the standards of the house. The coupling with the Liszt *Hungarian rhapsodies* is entirely appropriate.

Fiedler's version has great dash; this was music the conductor of the Boston Pops did uncommonly well, and the orchestral playing is first rate. The recording, however, is not so rich as Dorati's.

Falla, Manuel de (1876–1946)

(i) *El amor brujo* (ballet; complete); (ii) *Nights in the gardens of Spain.*
❀ (M) *** Decca Dig. 430 703-2; *430 703-4* [id.]. (i) Tourangeau, Montreal SO, Dutoit; (ii) De Larrocha, LPO, Frühbeck de Burgos – RODRIGO: *Concierto.* *** ❀

(i; ii) *El amor brujo* (complete); (iii) *Nights in the gardens of Spain;* (ii) *The Three-cornered hat* (ballet): *suite.*

(M) ** EMI CDM7 69037-2; *EG 769037-4* [id.]. (i) De los Angeles; (ii) Philh. O, Giulini; (iii) Soriano, Paris Conservatoire O, Frühbeck de Burgos.

(i) *El amor brujo* (complete); (ii; iii) *Nights in the gardens of Spain;* (iii) *The Three-cornered hat: 3 dances.*

(M) **(*) Sony mono/stereo MPK 46449 [id.]. Phd. O, with (i) Shirley Verrett, cond. Stokowski; (ii) Philipe Entremont, (iii) Ormandy.

(i) *El amor brujo; The Three-cornered hat* (ballet): complete.

(M) *** Decca 417 786-2; *417 786-4.* (i) Nati Mistral, New Philh. O, Frühbeck de Burgos – ALBÉNIZ: *Suite española.* ***

Dutoit's brilliantly played *El amor brujo* has long been praised by us. With recording in the demonstration class, the performance has characteristic flexibility over phrasing and rhythm and is hauntingly atmospheric. The sound in the coupled *Nights in the gardens of Spain* is equally superb, rich and lustrous and with vivid detail. Miss de Larrocha's lambent feeling for the work's poetic evocation is matched by her brilliance in the nocturnal dance-rhythms. There is at times a thoughtful, improvisatory quality about the reading and the closing pages are particularly beautiful. Even if it were not offered at mid-price, with its generous and outstanding Rodrigo coupling this would still be one of the most attractive compilations of Spanish music in the catalogue.

Raphael Frühbeck de Burgos provides us with a completely recommendable mid-priced version of *El amore brujo*, attractively coupled with Albéniz. The score's evocative atmosphere is hauntingly captured and, to make the most striking contrast, the famous *Ritual fire dance* blazes brilliantly. Nati Mistral has the vibrant open-throated projection of the real flamenco artist, and the whole performance is idiomatically authentic and compelling. Brilliant Decca sound to match.

According to Oliver Daniel's discography in his biography of Stokowski, his recording of *El amor brujo* was made in 1960. (The Sony documentation would prefer the prospective purchaser to believe that it dates from 1979.) It is undoubtedly mono, yet the ear could almost be fooled for, though the treble is a bit spiky, the ambient effect is impressive. Stokowski's magnetism is undiluted: the dramatic effects are superbly strong, *El circulo magico* is drawn by a true magician of the orchestra, the seductive *Pantomime* is characteristically voluptuous, and there is a haunting, atmospheric delicacy for the ghostly *Escena* that precedes the *Canción del fuego fatuo.* This, like the other vocal interpolations, is unforgettably sung by Shirley Verrett with full-throated flamenco fire and darkly resonant timbre. The Philadelphia Orchestra, who play so vibrantly for Stokowski, are again at their most flamboyantly expressive in the spectacular 1964 recording of *Nights in the gardens of Spain.* Philip Entremont plays with coruscating brilliance: he is forwardly balanced but the orchestra is well in the picture (the climax of *En el Generalife* is almost overwhelming). Ormandy again demonstrates his skill in a concertante work; this is a true partnership, with pianistic and orchestral colours glowing, blending and glittering in an essentially extrovert performance which generates much electricity yet which has plenty of atmosphere plus a moulded, expressive diversity that is characteristic of Ormandy when he is not making routine responses. The sound is less opulent in the three dances from *The Three-cornered hat*: the violins are a bit glassy but there is Spanish sunshine too, and the playing is strong and fiery. *The Miller's dance* has an arrestingly bold horn solo, matched by a cor anglais response that is nearly as full-throated as Miss Verrett in her first solo of *El amor brujo.*

Giulini's performances come from the mid-1960s and include Soriano's excellent account of *Nights in the gardens of Spain.* The Philharmonia playing is polished and responsive, and Giulini produces civilized and colourful performances. But the recording, though brightly coloured, has lost some of its bloom in the digital remastering, and in any case *El amor brujo* is not as red-blooded here as it is in the hands of Dutoit.

Nights in the gardens of Spain.

(B) *** DG Compact Classics 413 156-2 (2); *413 156-4* [id.]. Margrit Weber, Bav. RSO, Kubelik – RODRIGO: *Concierto serenata* etc. ** (CD only: BACARISSE: *Concertino* **(*); CASTELNUOVO-TEDESCO: *Concerto.* ***)

(M) **(*) EMI Dig. CDD7 63886-2 [id.]; *ET 763886-4.* Ciccolini, RPO, Bátiz – RODRIGO: *Concierto de Aranjuez*; TURINA: *Danzas fantásticas.* **(*)

The DG recording is extremely vivid, with the performers going all out to bring the utmost grip and excitement to the score. With Margrit Weber giving a brilliant account of the solo part, particularly in the latter movements, the effect is both sparkling and exhilarating. A little of the fragrant atmosphere is lost, particularly in the opening section (where de Larrocha is gentler), but the performance, with its strong sense of drama, is certainly not without evocative qualities. This Compact Classics cassette is in the main devoted to the music of Rodrigo, and the three coupled recordings are of mixed appeal; but those wanting an inexpensive version of Rodrigo's delightful *Concierto serenata* for harp should not be disappointed with the Falla. The digitally remastered pair of CDs, which acts as an equivalent, also offers concertos by Castelnuovo-Tedesco and Bacarisse.

Bátiz is given digital recording that is brilliantly clear but not lacking in ambient warmth, and Aldo Ciccolini is a very good soloist. If some of the music's atmospheric mystery is lost when the sound-picture is so brilliantly lit and detail so sharply drawn, this very positive, 1984 version makes a striking and involving impression.

(i) *Nights in the gardens of Spain;* (ii) *The Three-cornered hat* (ballet): complete; *La vida breve: Interlude and dance.*
(M) *** Decca 417 771-2. (i) De Larrocha, SRO, Comissiona; (ii) SRO, Ansermet.

Alicia de Larrocha's earlier (1971) recording makes an excellent mid-priced recommendation, coupled with Ansermet's lively and vividly recorded complete *Three-cornered hat*; she receives admirable support from Comissiona. The Decca analogue recording was outstanding in its day and is very well balanced: it sounds first class in its remastered format, as does the Ansermet coupling, which entirely belies its age (1962). The *La vida breve* excerpts make an agreeable bonus.

The Three-cornered hat: Suites Nos. 1 & 2.
(M) **(*) EMI Dig. CDM7 63572-2; *EG 763572-4* [id.]. Phd. O, Muti – CHABRIER: *España*; RAVEL: *Rapsodie espagnole.* **(*)

Muti's reading of the colourful *Suites* is characteristically thrustful, lacking just a little in rhythmic subtlety but making up for that in bite. They incorporate the greater part of the ballet – although, with only 44 minutes' music on the disc, there would easily have been room for the complete score. The 1980 sound, typically reverberant and somewhat brash, is characteristic of early digital recordings from this source.

OPERA

La vida breve (complete).
(M) *** EMI CDM7 69590-2 [id.]. De los Angeles, Higueras, Rivadeneyra, Cossutta, Moreno, Orfeon Donostiarra Ch., Nat. O of Spain, Frühbeck de Burgos.

La vida breve is a kind of Spanish *Cavalleria Rusticana* without the melodrama. Unquestionably the opera's story is weak, the heroine expiring with a broken heart when her lover deserts her for another; but if the music for the final scene is weakened by a fundamental lack of drama in the plot, Frühbeck de Burgos makes the most of the poignancy of the closing moments. Victoria de los Angeles deepened her interpretation over the years, and her imaginative colouring of the words gives a unique authority and evocation to her performance. *Vivan les que ri'an* is most expressively done, with Frühbeck following the soloist with great skill. The flamenco singer in Act II (Gabriel Moreno) also matches the realism of the idiom with an authentic 'folk' style. The other members of the cast are good without being memorable; but when this is primarily a solo vehicle for De los Angeles, and the orchestral interludes are managed so colloquially, this is readily recommendable. The recording remains atmospheric, as well as having increased vividness and presence. It now fits conveniently on a single CD.

Fauré, Gabriel (1845–1924)

(i) *Ballade for piano and orchestra, Op. 19;* (ii) *Requiem, Op. 48; Cantique de Jean Racine, Op. 11.*
(M) **(*) EMI CDM7 69841-2; *EG 769841-4.* (i) John Ogdon; (ii) Burrowes, Rayner-Cook, CBSO Ch.; CBSO, Frémaux.

The elusive and delicate essence of Fauré's *Ballade* is not easy to capture, but Ogdon's warmly affectionate approach is enjoyable and is notably sensitive in the central and closing sections of the work. Frémaux has a moulded style in the *Requiem* which does not spill over into too much expressiveness, and there is a natural warmth about this performance that is persuasive. Norma Burrowes sings beautifully; her innocent style is most engaging. The originally reverberant recording has been refocused somewhat and does not lose too much of its warmth.

Dolly (suite, orch. Henri Rabaud), *Op. 56; Masques et bergamasques: suite; Pelléas et Mélisande: suite, Op. 80.*
(B) *** EMI CZS7 62669-2 (2). O de Paris, Serge Baudo (with Concert: *French music* ***).

Serge Baudo is at his most sympathetic and perceptive here. All three performances are well observed and are distinguished by eloquent string-playing that can be both passionate and tender. *Dolly* is Beechamesque in its gentle detail. The *Ouverture* of *Masques et bergamasques* has an engaging rhythmic spring and the closing *Pastorale* is quite lovely. The performance of *Pelléas et Mélisande* is dignified and the beautiful *Prélude* is given with much feeling. The Orchestre de Paris is a fine ensemble, and the warmth of the 1968/69 recording, made in the kindly acoustics of the Salle Wagram, has not been lost, while detail has been refined. This is part of a highly recommendable two-disc concert, now available in EMI's competitive French 'two for the price of one' series.

Élégie in C min. (for cello and orchestra), *Op. 24.*

(B) *** DG 431 166-2; *431 166-4.* Heinrich Schiff, New Philh. O, Mackerras – LALO: *Cello concerto*; SAINT-SAENS: *Cello concerto No. 1.* ***

(B) *(*) Ph. 422 467-2. Gendron, Monte Carlo Op. O, Benzi – DVOŘÁK: *Concerto* etc. **(*); SAINT-SAENS: *Concerto No. 1.* **

Heinrich Schiff gives an eloquent account of the *Élégie*, and he is finely accompanied and superbly recorded. This 1977 performance, coupled with equally enjoyable versions of the Saint-Saëns and Lalo *Cello concertos*, makes an outstanding bargain.

Gendron's performance is an excellent one, but it is disfigured by an undistinguished accompaniment, notably by some poor woodwind intonation.

CHAMBER MUSIC

(i) *Andante in B flat, Op. 75; Berceuse, Op. 16;* (ii) *Cello sonatas Nos. 1 in D min., Op. 109; 2 in G min., Op. 117; Élégie, Op. 24;* (iii) *Fantaisie, Op. 79; Morceau de concours;* (i) *Morceau de lecture;* (ii) *Papillon, Op. 77;* (i) *Romance, Op. 28;* (ii) *Serenade in B min., Op. 98; Sicilienne, Op. 78;* (i) *Violin sonatas Nos. 1 in A, Op. 15; 2 in E min., Op. 108;* (i; ii) *Trio in D min., Op. 120.*

(B) *** EMI CMS7 62545-2 (2). Jean-Philippe Collard, (i) Augustin Dumay; (ii) Frédéric Lodéon; (iii) Michel Debost.

Piano quartets Nos. (i; ii) *1 in C min., Op. 15;* (i; iii) *2 in G min., Op. 45; Piano quintets Nos. 1 in C min., Op. 89; 2 in D min., Op. 115;* (iii) *String quartet in E min., Op. 121.*

(B) *** EMI CMS7 62548-2 (2). (i) Jean-Philippe Collard; (ii) Augustin Dumay, Bruno Pasquier, Frédéric Lodéon; (iii) Parrenin Qt.

An essential acquisition. Dumay and Collard bring different and equally valuable insights, and the performances of the *Piano quartets* are masterly. In addition, there are authoritative and idiomatic readings of the two *Piano quintets*, the *Piano trio*, the two *Cello sonatas*, on the first set, above (what a fine player Lodéon is!), and the enigmatic and otherworldly *Quartet*, Fauré's last utterance, plus all the smaller pieces. This is enormously civilized music whose rewards grow with each hearing; however, one has to accept that, because the Paris Salle Wagram was employed for the recordings (made between 1975 and 1978), close microphones have been used to counteract the hall's resonance (the flute of Michel Debost in the *Fantaisie*, Op. 79, and the *Morceau de concours* is strikingly forward). The remastering has both increased the sense of presence and brought a certain dryness to the ambient effect, although the string timbres are fresh. Both sets have been reissued in EMI's French 'two for the price of one' series and are wonderful value for money.

Andante in B flat, Op. 75; Berceuse in D, Op. 16.

(M) ** EMI CDM7 63986-2 [id.]. Sir Yehudi & Jeremy Menuhin – DEBUSSY: *Sonata* etc. **; RAVEL: *Piano trio.* *(*)

These slight but lovely pieces form an attractive makeweight to an uneven concert of French music compiled recently to celebrate Menuhin's 75th birthday. These recordings, made with his son, Jeremy, in the Abbey Road Studios in 1970, sound fresher than the Debussy coupling.

Cello sonatas Nos. 1 in D min., Op. 109; 2 in G min., Op. 117.

(B) *** Hung. White Label HRC 171 [id.]. Miklós Perényi, Loránt Szücs – CHOPIN: *Cello sonata.* **(*)

Cello sonatas Nos. 1–2; Élégie, Op. 24.

(M) ** Erato/Warner 2292 45660-2 [id.]. Paul Tortelier, Jean Hubeau – DEBUSSY: *Sonata.* **

The distinguished Hungarian cellist Miklós Perényi seems completely attuned to the elusive world of late Fauré, and in both sonatas the engineers do justice to his tone. Loránt Szücs is an excellent partner, and those who want this repertoire will find little cause for complaint. The performances hold their own with most of the competition, though they are not to be preferred to Frédéric Lodéon and Jean-Philippe Collard in the generously filled, bargain two-CD Fauré compilation from EMI. But this disc is highly competitive.

Tortelier's performances with Jean Hubeau date from 1962 and find the celebrated cellist in good form. He is not quite as imaginatively supported or as well recorded as he was in his 1975 EMI recording with Eric Heidsieck – though this is not to suggest that Hubeau's playing is insensitive. The thirty-year-old recording is good, if on the dry side, and will still give pleasure.

Violin sonatas Nos. 1 in A, Op. 13; 2 in E min., Op. 108.

❀ (M) *** Ph. 426 384-2. Arthur Grumiaux, Paul Crossley – FRANCK: *Sonata*. **(*)

The two Fauré *Sonatas* are immensely refined and rewarding pieces, with strange stylistic affinities and disparities: the second movement of the *E minor* actually uses a theme intended for a symphony that Fauré had discarded more than thirty years earlier. Although they have been coupled before, they have never been so beautifully played or recorded as on the Philips issue. Indeed, this is a model of its kind: there is perfect rapport between Grumiaux and Crossley, and both seem totally dedicated to and captivated by Fauré's muse. Moreover the two artists sound as if they are in the living-room; the acoustic is warm, lively and well balanced. Reissued on Philips's 'Musica da camera' at mid-price and vividly transferred to CD, this coupling is more desirable than ever.

PIANO MUSIC

Dolly (suite for piano, 4 hands).
(B) *** Turnabout 0004. Walter & Beatriz Klien – DEBUSSY: *En blanc et noir* & Collection. ***

Dolly is highly effective in its four-handed piano version, especially when played as sympathetically and vivaciously as here by the admirable Klien duo. It is well recorded too, and it makes a fine bonus for a generous and valuable Debussy programme.

Solo piano music

Ballade in F sharp, Op. 19; Nocturnes Nos. 1–13 (complete); *9 Préludes, Op. 103; Theme and variations in C sharp min., Op. 73.*
(B) *** EMI CMS7 69149-2 (2). Jean-Philippe Collard.

This is glorious music which ranges from the gently reflective to the profoundly searching. The *Nocturnes* were composed over the best part of half a century: the first was sketched at the time of the *First Violin sonata* (1875–6) and the last dates from 1921. They offer a glimse of Fauré's art at its most inward and subtle; and they take a greater hold of the listener at each hearing, the quiet-spoken reticence proving more eloquent than one would ever suspect. Immensely civilized yet never aloof, this music offers balm to the soul. The *Préludes* are comparably intimate, and this is all music to which Jean-Philippe Collard is wholly attuned. Collard is indeed the foremost interpreter of this composer now before the public and there are no finer versions to be had. Collard's account of the *Theme and variations* is no less masterly, combining the utmost tonal refinement and sensitivity with striking keyboard authority. The recording is good, though it has not the bloom and body of the very finest piano records.

Barcarolles Nos. 1–13; (i) *Dolly. Impromptus Nos. 1–5; Mazurka, Op. 32; Pièces brèves Nos. 1–8, Op. 84; Romances sans paroles Nos. 1–3;* (i) *Souvenir de Bayreuth. Valses-caprices Nos. 1–4.*
(B) *** EMI CZS7 62687-2 (2) [id.]. Jean-Philippe Collard, (i) with Rigutto.

The *Barcarolles* span the best part of Fauré's life, the first (Op. 26) coming from 1883 and the last (Op. 116) from 1921; and they contain some of his most haunting inspiration. The first three of the *Impromptus* also come from 1883 and the last two from 1906 and 1910 respectively. Despite the long interruption, they sound well as a complete set. The rest of the music here, particularly the *Pièces brèves* and the charming *Dolly* suite, are equally welcome. Jean-Philippe Collard has the qualities of reticence yet ardour, subtlety and poetic feeling to penetrate Fauré's intimate world, and it is hard to think of any artist temperamentally better attuned to these pieces, which cast quite a spell on the listener. The recordings were made in the Salle Wagram but the acoustic sounds confined and, while Collard has exceptional beauty and refinement of tone at all dynamic levels, the only regret is that full justice is not done to it by the French engineers. While too much should not be made of this reservation, playing of this order deserves the very best, and the CD transfer brings a certain dryness of effect. This set, like its companion, above, comes in EMI's 'two for the price of one' series.

VOCAL MUSIC

Mélodies (complete): (i) *L'Absent;* (ii) *Accompagnement; Après un rêve; Arpège; Aubade;* (i) *Au bord de l'eau;* (ii) *Au cimetière; Aurore;* (i) *L'aurore; Automne;* (ii) *Barcarolle; Les berceaux; La bonne chanson* (song-cycle), *Op. 61;*(i) *2 Cantiques (En prière; Noël); C'est la paix!; Chanson;* (ii) *Chanson d'amour;* (i) *La chanson d'Ève* (song-cycle), *Op. 95;* (ii) *Chanson du pêcheur; Chanson de Shylock; Chant d'automne; Clair de lune; Dans la forêt de septembre;* (i) *Dans les ruines d'une abbaye;* (ii) *Le Don silencieux;* (i) *2 Duos for 2 sopranos (Puisqu'ici-bas; Tarentelle); La Fée aux chansons; Fleur jetée;* (ii) *La fleur qui va sur l'eau; L'horizon chimérique* (song-cycle), *Op. 118; Hymne; Ici-bas!;* (i) *Les jardins clos* (song-cycle), *Op. 106;* (ii) *Larmes; Lydia; Madrigal de Shylock; Mai; Les matelots;* (i) *Mélisande's song; 5 Mélodies de Venise;* (ii) *Mirages* (song-cycle), *Op. 113;* (i) *Nell;* (ii) *Nocturne;* (i) *Notre amour; Le papillon et la fleur; Le parfum impérissable;*

Le pays des rêves; (ii) *Pleurs d'or; Le plus doux chemin; 3 Poèmes de jour; Les présents; Prison; Le ramier; La rançon;* (i) *Rêve d'amour; La rose; Les roses d'Ispahan; Le secret;* (ii) *Sérénade du bourgeois gentilhomme; Sérénade toscane;* (i) *Seule; Soir;* (ii) *Spleen; Sylvie; Tristesse;* (i) *Vocalise-étude;* (ii) *Le voyageur.*
(M) *** EMI CMS7 64079-2 (4). (i) Elly Ameling, (ii) Gérard Souzay; Dalton Baldwin.

Recorded between 1971 and 1974, this complete collection of the solo songs of Fauré is all the more valuable for coming at mid-price. The songs were written over the fullest span of Fauré's life, during a period of no less than 60 years, starting with a jolly waltz-song written when the composer was sixteen. The most striking melodies tend to come in the earlier songs – with the second of the four CDs offering many favourite items like *Chanson d'amour* winningly done by Souzay and *Les roses d'Ispahan* bringing a ravishing example of Ameling at her most radiant. Even so, the style is astonishingly consistent throughout. In the late cycles, *La chanson d'Ève*, *Les jardins clos*, *Mirages* and *L'horizon chimérique*, there is an extra subtlety in the composer's restraint; but even in that last period Fauré allowed himself one extrovert return to an earlier style, a simple, jaunty song for soprano celebrating the Armistice of 1918, *C'est la paix!*. Souzay is not quite as even in his vocal production as at the beginning of his career, but no baritone of recent years has surpassed him in this repertory, and Ameling is at her very peak throughout, fresh and even in line with beautiful colourings. A helpful essay comes in English as well as in French, but the texts of the songs are given only in French.

La bonne chanson, Op. 61; Poème d'un jour, Op. 21; Les berceaux; La chanson d'Ève: Eau vivante; O mort, poussière d'étoiles. Le horizon chimérique; Le jardin clos: Exaucement; Je me poserai sur ton coeur. 5 Mélodies de Venise; Mirages.
(M) *** Ph. 420 775-2 [id.]. Gérard Souzay, Dalton Baldwin.

This is a self-recommending recital. Gérard Souzay had a unique sensibility in this repertoire, and his control of colour and feeling for the words is magical. The songs are drawn from two records, made in 1961 and 1965, and the sound is fresh, with good presence. Baldwin accompanies impeccably and is well in the picture.

Requiem, Op. 48.
(M) *** Pickwick/RPO Dig. CDRPO 7007; *ZCRPO 7007* [id.]. Aled Jones, Stephen Roberts, LSO Ch., RPO, Hickox.

(i) *Requiem, Op. 48; Cantique de Jean Racine, Op. 11;* (ii) *Messe basse.*
(M) *** Decca 430 360-2; *430 360-4* [id.]. (i) Jonathon Bond, Benjamin Luxon; (ii) Andrew Brunt; St John's College, Cambridge, Ch., ASMF, Guest – POULENC: *Mass* etc. ***

Requiem, Op. 48; Maria Mater gratiae, Op. 47/2; Tantum ergo, Op. 65/2.
(B) **(*) Pickwick Dig. PCD 896; *CIMPC 896.* Aidan Oliver, Harry Escott, David Wilson-Johnson, Westminster Cathedral Ch., City of L. Sinfonia, David Hill.

(i) *Requiem, Op. 48;* (ii) *Messe basse.*
(M) ** EMI Dig. CD-EMX 2166; *TC-EMX 2166.* (i) Augér, Luxon; (ii) Paul Smy; King's College Ch., ECO, Ledger.

Requiem; Pavane, Op. 50.
(M) *** EMI CDM7 69038-2 [id.]. Sheila Armstrong, Fischer-Dieskau, Edinburgh Fest. Ch., O de Paris, Barenboim.

(i) *Requiem. Pelléas et Mélisande; Masques et bergamasques.*
(B) *(*) Decca 421 026-2. (i) Danco, Souzay, Peilz Ch. Union; SRO, Ansermet.

George Guest's performance is on a smaller scale than the RPO version. The excellence of both is not in question, but in these matters tastes differ, although undoubtedly the St John's account has a magic that works from the opening bars onwards. Jonathon Bond and Benjamin Luxon are highly sympathetic soloists and the 1975 (originally Argo) recording is every bit as impressive as its digital competitor. It is wide-ranging, atmospheric and exceptionally truthful, and the smaller scale of the conception is probably nearer to Fauré's original conception. Moreover the Decca couplings are exceptionally generous and beautifully sung. This CD has a playing time of 74 minutes.

Richard Hickox opts for the regular full-scale text of the *Requiem*, yet, at speeds rather faster than usual – no faster than those marked – he presents a fresh, easily flowing view, rather akin to John Rutter's using the original chamber scoring on his full-price Conifer issue. Aled Jones sings very sweetly in *Pié Jesu*. This makes a strong alternative recommendation.

The Edinburgh Festival Chorus is freshly responsive in Barenboim's 1975 recording so that, although the sound is beefier than with Guest or Hickox, the effect is never heavy and the performance is given a strong dimension of drama. Yet there is splendidly pure singing from Sheila Armstrong and, although Fischer-Dieskau is not quite as mellifluous as he was earlier, he now brings a greater sense of drama.

Including a sensitive account of the *Pavane*, this is well worth considering in the budget range.

Using the usual full orchestral score, David Hill yet gives a performance which keeps a modest scale, set within a warm church acoustic – St Jude's, Hampstead, not Westminster Cathedral itself. Its special quality among current versions is that it uses boy trebles and male altos from the cathedral choir instead of women's voices. There is a very boyish, earnest quality to Aidan Oliver's singing of the *Pié Jesu* which is most winning, even if there are still more angelic accounts. The snag is that the choir is set at rather too great a distance in relation to the orchestra.

Ledger presents the *Requiem* on a small scale with more restraint than usual. The singing is refreshingly direct; but anyone who warms to the touch of sensuousness in the work, its Gallic quality, may be disappointed, in spite of the full, yet clear digital recording. It is not nearly as beautiful a performance as the earlier one from King's Choir under Sir David Willcocks. The *Messe basse*, also sweetly melodic, makes an apt coupling.

Ansermet's clear Decca recording serves only to emphasize the rather thin-toned contribution from the chorus. The solo singing is good but not memorable. This disc is most notable for the orchestral items, sympathetic and stylish performances, highly regarded in their day and still sounding well.

Ferguson, Howard (born 1908)

Violin sonata No. 1, Op. 2.

(M) ** BMG/RCA GD 87872; *GK 87872* [7872-2-RG; *7872-4-RG*]. Heifetz, Steuber – CASTELNUOVO-TEDESCO: *Concerto No. 2* (**); FRANÇAIX: *Trio* ***; K. KHACHATURIAN: *Sonata.* **

Howard Ferguson's *First Violin sonata* was written in 1931 when the composer was in his early twenties. It is beautifully crafted and, though not strongly individual (it springs from the tradition of Brahms and Elgar), is a satisfying musical experience, the product of a fastidious intelligence. The finale, which is the longest of the three movements, is particularly impressive. It was recorded in stereo in 1966, but in a dryish acoustic which does not flatter the bottom-heavy and closely balanced piano of Lillian Steuber. However, it comes in a particularly enterprising compilation and is not otherwise available.

Field, John (1782–1837)

Nocturnes Nos. 1–18.

(M) * Tuxedo TUXCD 1056 [id.]. Hans Kahn.

Field's *Nocturnes* – a form which he invented – at times uncannily anticipate those of Chopin, and it is curious how elusive they seem to be in the recording studio. This collection is generous (74 minutes) and Hans Kahn is quite realistically recorded. But his style is rhythmically too inflexible to capture the music's subtle inflexions and he misses its nostalgic atmosphere. Even in *Le Midi*, which is comparatively direct, he is rather matter of fact.

Finzi, Gerald (1901–56)

Dies natalis.

(M) *** EMI CDM7 63372-2; *EG 763372-4.* Wilfred Brown, ECO, Christopher Finzi – HOWELLS: *Hymnus paradisi.* ***

(i) *Dies natalis; For St Cecilia;* (ii) *In terra pax; Magnificat.*

(M) *** Decca 425 660-2; *425 660-4.* (i) Langridge, LSO Ch., LSO; (ii) Burrowes, Shirley-Quirk, Hickox Singers, City of L. Sinfonia; Hickox.

Dies natalis is one of Finzi's most sensitive and deeply felt works, using meditative texts by the seventeenth-century writer, Thomas Traherne, on the theme of Christ's nativity. Finzi's profound response to the words inspires five intensely beautiful songs; only the central *Rapture*, subtitled *Danza*, provides vigorous contrast to the mood of contemplation. *In terra pax* is another Christmas work, this time more direct, opening atmospherically with the baritone's musing evocation of the pastoral nativity scene. Then comes a burst of choral splendour at the appearance of the Angel of the Lord, and after her gentle declaration of the birth of Christ comes another even more resplendent depiction of the 'multitude of the heavenly host', and the music returns to the thoughtful, recessed mood of the opening. The cantata commissioned for the St Cecilia's Day celebration in 1947 has an opening full of pageantry in the Elgarian tradition; although the mood softens in the second section, this is an altogether more external work. Even so, Finzi was able to respond individually to the text which was specially written by his contemporary, Edmund Blunden. The concert ends with the fine *Magnificat* setting from 1951, an American commission. All the performances here are both strong and convincing in their contrasting moods; this generous Decca anthology, taken from vintage Argo recordings made in 1978/9, remains highly recommendable.

Finzi's setting is sung well here by Wilfred Brown. In a way, one may regard this as a preparation for Britten's later achievement in his orchestral song-cycles, and this record must be recommended to all interested in modern English song setting. The remastered recording sounds wonderfully fresh and is naturally balanced within a glowing acoustic. What a beautiful work this is!

Flotow, Friedrich (1812–83)

Martha (complete).
(M) *** Eurodisc 352 878 (2) [7789-2-RG]. Popp, Soffel, Jerusalem, Nimsgern, Ridderbusch, Bav. R. Ch. and O, Wallberg.

Martha is a charming opera that should be much better known in Britain than it is. The Eurodisc cast is as near perfect as could be imagined. Lucia Popp is a splendid Lady Harriet, the voice rich and full (her *Letzte Rose* is radiant) yet riding the ensembles with jewelled accuracy. Doris Soffel is no less characterful as Nancy, and Siegfried Jerusalem is in his element as the hero, Lionel, singing ardently throughout. Siegmund Nimsgern is an excellent Lord Tristan, and Karl Ridderbusch matches his genial gusto, singing Plunkett's *Porter-Lied* with weight as well as brio. Wallberg's direction is marvellously spirited and the opera gathers pace as it proceeds. The Bavarian Radio Chorus sings with joyous precision and the orchestral playing sparkles. With first-class recording, full and vivid, this is highly recommended, for the transfer to CD has been managed admirably.

Françaix, Jean (born 1912)

L'horloge de flore.
❀ (M) *** BMG/RCA GD 87989. John de Lancie, LSO, Previn (with SATIE: *Gymnopédies Nos. 1 & 3*) – IBERT: *Symphonie concertante;* R. STRAUSS: *Oboe concerto.* ***

Jean Françaix writes within an extremely limited range, but those who have discovered the exquisite *Piano concertino* will be equally delighted with *L'horloge de flore.* Inspired by the Linnaeus Flower Clock (which ingeniously conveys the time by its formation from various floral species, each of which blossoms at a different time between 3 a.m. and 6 p.m.), the music forms a suite of seven characteristically short and mainly gentle movements. The naïvely simple writing is deceptive: this is music of real memorability and much charm. John de Lancie, the sponsor of the piece, plays delightfully, the accompaniment is a model of felicity and good taste, and the recording is just about perfect. The only slight snag is that the movements are not cued separately. The Satie *Gymnopédies*, orchestrated by Debussy, which follows as an encore, are played slowly and gravely and not ineffectively.

String trio in C.
(M) *** Sony GD 87872; *GK 87872* [7872-2-RG; *7872-4-RG*]. Heifetz, De Pasquale, Piatigorsky – CASTELNUOVO-TEDESCO: *Concerto No. 2* (**); FERGUSON: *Sonata No. 1* **; K. KHACHATURIAN: *Sonata.* **

Jean Françaix's debonair *String trio* of 1933 is a delight, full of sophistication and tenderness. All four movements are far too short. Marvellously played by Heifetz, Joseph de Pasquale and Piatigorsky, recorded in 1964 – and, as if to remind us that they are human, there is even some tuning between the third and fourth movements that we don't recall from the LP!

Franck, César (1822–90)

Psyché (symphonic poem); *Symphony in D min.*
(M) *(*) DG 431 468-2; *431 468-4.* O de Paris, Daniel Barenboim.

In *Psyché* Barenboim limits himself to the purely orchestral passages of this extended work, leaving plenty of room for the *Symphony.* In the symphonic poem he draws rich, refined playing from the Paris orchestra, a little sleepy at times but suitably sensuous. But in the first movement of the *Symphony* he adopts a surprisingly plodding main tempo, the first subject lacking bite. There are places too where the reading is self-indulgent (Barenboim putting on his Furtwänglerian mantle) and, in an otherwise fine account of the slow movement, the cor anglais solo is disappointingly wooden. The 1976 sound, however, is firmer than the original and very acceptable.

Symphonic variations for piano and orchestra.
❀ (B) *** Decca 433 628-2; *433 628-4* [id.]. Curzon, LPO, Boult – GRIEG: *Concerto* ***; SCHUMANN: *Concerto.* **(*)
(M) *** Sony MPK 46730 [id.]. Robert Casadesus, Phd. O, Ormandy – CASADESUS: *Concerto for 3 pianos* **; D'INDY: *Symphonie.* ***
(B) * EMI CDZ7 62859-2; *LZ 762859-4.* John Ogdon, Philh. O, Barbirolli – GRIEG; SCHUMANN: *Piano concertos.* *

Clifford Curzon's 1959 recording of the Franck *Variations* has stood the test of time; even after three decades and more, there is no finer version. It is an engagingly fresh reading as notable for its impulse and rhythmic felicity as for its poetry. The vintage Decca recording is naturally balanced and has been transferred to CD without loss of bloom. The Grieg *Concerto* coupling is hardly less desirable.

Casadesus's classic recording of the *Symphonic variations* with the Philadelphia Orchestra comes from 1958 and has been much improved in this transfer. Everyone who heard the Philadelphia Orchestra in the flesh under Stokowski and Ormandy spoke of being overwhelmed by the sheer size and quality of their sonority; something of this feeling comes across at the very beginning of this performance. (All too often the CBS engineers of the 1960s drained their strings of timbre and, in a search for brilliance, made them sound strident above the stave.) The great French pianist is in masterly form throughout, and no one investing in this disc is likely to be disappointed.

John Ogdon opens in improvisatory style and the result is curiously unspontaneous; the best section is the finale, where a certain rhythmic spring catches the listener's previously flagging interest. Good 1963 recording.

Symphony in D min.

❀ (M) **(*) BMG/RCA GD 86805 [6805-2-RG]. Chicago SO, Monteux – D'INDY: *Symphonie sur un chant montagnard français* **(*) (with BERLIOZ: *Overture: Béatrice et Bénédict* ***).

(M) **(*) EMI CDM7 63396-2 [id.]. O Nat. de l'ORTF, Sir Thomas Beecham – LALO: *Symphony.* **(*)

(M) ** EMI CMD7 64145-2 [id.]; *EG 764145-4.* New Philh. O, Klemperer – SCHUMANN: *Piano concerto.* **

(B) * DG Compact Classics *413 423-4* [id.]. O de Paris, Barenboim – SAINT-SAENS: *Symphony No. 3; Danse macabre.* ***

Symphony in D min.; Prélude choral et fugue (orch. Pierné).

(BB) ** Naxos Dig. 8.550155 [id.]. Royal Flanders PO, Günter Neuhold.

Symphony in D min; (i) *Symphonic variations for piano and orchestra.*

(M) *** EMI Dig. CDD7 63889-2 [id.]; *ET 763889-4.* (i) Collard; Capitole Toulouse O, Plasson.

Monteux exerts a unique grip on this highly charged Romantic symphony, and his control of the continuous ebb and flow of tempo and tension is masterly, so that any weaknesses of structure in the outer movements are disguised. The splendid playing of the Chicago orchestra is ever responsive to the changes of mood: the fervour of the thrusting chromatic secondary tune of the first movement is matched by the dynamism of the transformation of the main theme of the *Andante* when it reappears in the finale, before the superbly prepared apotheosis of the coda. The sound on this new CD is greatly improved; the ingredient of harshness, caused by Franck's scoring of trumpets in his tuttis, now seems hardly a problem, merely adding a degree of pungency and providing a true French accent. The Chicago ambience ensures that the overall effect is properly spacious.

Plasson gives a straightforward and powerful account of the *Symphony* with his Orchestre du Capitole, Toulouse. His 1985 version has conviction and genuine lyrical fervour, equally strikingly in the chromatic secondary theme of the first movement and the impulsive gusto of the finale. At the same time Plasson handles the overall ebb and flow of tension convincingly. This may not seem as individual an account as that by Monteux, but it is certainly both exciting and satisfying, and the recording is much more impressive than RCA's recording for Monteux, even if it is not quite top-drawer EMI. Fortissimos are vividly projected but the score's quieter pages, though atmospheric, are less sharply detailed, notably in the slow movement. Jean-Philippe Collard's performance of the *Symphonic variations* is characteristically sensitive and full of imaginative colours and is touched by distinction. All in all, those looking for a mid-priced digital version of this coupling should be well satisfied.

Beecham's very last recordings were made in Paris on the first four days of December 1959, not with his own Royal Philharmonic Orchestra but with the Orchestre National of French Radio, ORTF. Aptly, this Beecham Edition CD couples both the French symphonies he then recorded, not only the *Symphony in D minor* of César Franck but also the *Symphony in G minor* by Franck's close contemporary, Lalo, which is rather less successful. The Franck, much duplicated, has never seemed richer or more powerful on disc. It is Beecham's ability to build tension, to control a melodic line so that the ear is magnetized, that gives symphonic tautness to a work which can seem diffuse. Beecham is also masterful in the rhythmic bite he gives to the great syncopated melodies that swagger their way through the outer movements – the second subject in the first movement and the opening theme of the finale. The recording has plenty of body, with a good sense of presence; but the transfer emphasizes an edge on top.

Almost everything Klemperer recorded is interesting, and this performance has its moments, particularly in the outer movements when, by illuminating a phrase or bringing the grand manner to a sonority, the conductor shows his individuality. But in essence this reading is too heavy in style, with little trace of a French accent; although such treatment often brings a stirring feeling of cathedral architecture to the first movement, especially as it draws to its close, the *Allegretto* is too grandiose and its charm is lost. The (1966) Abbey Road recording is good, full though not very transparent. (It is not in the same class as the Klemperer version of the Berlioz *Symphonie fantastique.*)

The Naxos version of the *Symphony in D minor* has more than economy in its favour in that it also brings a rarity in the form of Gabriel Pierné's orchestral transcription of the *Prélude choral et fugue.* The reading of the symphony under Günter Neuhold is well shaped, free from idiosyncrasy and sensitively phrased. The conductor is Austrian and was a pupil of Swarowski, before working in various German opera houses. The orchestral playing is more than just acceptable: it is very good indeed; the only snag is the recording quality. This is pleasingly resonant but is rather opaque and suffers from glare, becoming shrill and edgy above the stave in tuttis. The performance as such gives real pleasure, and the Pierné transcription makes an interesting fill-up.

Although he is well recorded, Barenboim's account is disappointing (see above). However, the coupling on the chrome Compact Classics tape brings two of his finest performances on record.

CHAMBER MUSIC

Piano quintet in F min.

(M) **(*) Decca 421 153-2. Clifford Curzon, VPO Qt – DVOŘÁK: *Quintet.* ***

Not as seductive a performance on Decca as the glorious Dvořák coupling, partly because the sound, though basically full, has a touch of astringency on top. But there is a case for not having too luscious textures and not letting the emotion spill over in this work, and Curzon and the VPO players are sensitive and firm at the same time. Curzon's playing is particularly fine. The CD transfer has undoubtedly enhanced the detail of the (1960) sound.

String quartet in D.

(M) **(*) Decca 425 424-2. Fitzwilliam Qt – RAVEL: *Quartet.* **

Franck's *Quartet*, highly ambitious in its scale, contains some of the composer's most profound and compelling thought; this magnificent performance by the Fitzwilliam Quartet, triumphing superbly over the technical challenge with totally dedicated, passionately convincing playing, completely silences any reservations. Very well recorded, with the thick textures nicely balanced, this was one of the finest chamber records of the 1980s. However, the CD transfer, in attempting to clarify the sound, has brought a degree of fierceness to the fortissimo violin timbre.

Violin sonata in A.

❀ (M) *** Decca 421 154-2; *421 154-4.* Kyung Wha Chung, Radu Lupu – DEBUSSY: *Sonatas*; RAVEL: *Introduction and allegro* etc. *** ❀

(M) *** DG 431 469-2; *431 469-4.* Kaja Danczowska, Krystian Zimerman – SZYMANOWSKI: *Mythes* etc. *** ❀

(M) **(*) Ph. 426 384-2; *426 384-4.* Arthur Grumiaux, György Sebok – FAURÉ: *Sonatas.* *** ❀

(BB) ** Naxos Dig. 8.550417 [id.]. Takako Nishizaki, Jenö Jandó – GRIEG: *Violin sonata* etc. **

Kyung Wha Chung and Radu Lupu give a glorious account, full of natural and not overprojected eloquence, and most beautifully recorded. The slow movement has marvellous repose and the other movements have a natural exuberance and sense of line that carry the listener with them. The 1977 recording is enhanced on CD and, with outstanding couplings, this record is in every sense a genuine bargain.

Kaja Danczowska was a pupil of Eugenia Uminska and the late David Oistrakh and, on the evidence of this 1980 début recording, she is an artist to reckon with. Her account of the Franck is distinguished by a fine sense of line and great sweetness of tone, and she is partnered superbly by Krystian Zimerman. Indeed, in terms of dramatic fire and strength of line, this version can hold its own alongside the finest, and it is perhaps marginally better-balanced than the Kyung Wha Chung and Radu Lupu recording. This DG issue has a particularly valuable and interesting coupling and would be worth acquiring for that alone. Certainly the sound is very immediate and present, and the acoustic is naturally resonant in a most attractive way.

Grumiaux's account, if less fresh than Miss Chung's, has nobility and warmth to commend it. He is slightly let down by his partner, who is not as imaginative as Lupu in the more poetic moments, including the hushed opening bars. The balance favours the violin, but remains lifelike. However, the coupling is indispensable.

Though she is an unfailingly sensitive player, Takako Nishizaki's vibrato is rather wider at the beginning of the sonata than in other of her records that we have heard, even if there is little cause for complaint elsewhere. She has both eloquence and artistry to commend her and Jenö Jandó proves an excellent partner. The recordings are made in a fairly resonant and pleasing acoustic, but the piano sounds less than freshly tuned at times.

Cello sonata in A (transcription of *Violin sonata*).

(M) **(*) EMI CDM7 63184-2. Du Pré, Barenboim – CHOPIN: *Sonata*. **(*)

Du Pré and Barenboim give a fine, mature, deeply expressive reading of a richly satisfying work. They are well balanced, but the effect of the music when transferred to the cello is inevitably mellower, less vibrant.

ORGAN MUSIC

(i) *Andantino in A flat; Final in B flat, Op. 21; Grand pièce symphonique, Op. 17; Pièce héroïque*; (ii) *Prélude, fugue et variation in B min., Op. 18.*

(B) **(*) Hung. White Label HRC 120 [id.]. (i) Gábor Lehotka (organ of Kodaly Music Centre, Kecskemét); (ii) Ferenc Gergely (organ of Péc Cathedral).

As recorded here, Czech organs seem to suit Franck's music rather well. The sound is fresh and bright, and detail emerges vividly. Both organists are sympathetic: the *Final* has plenty of impulse and the extended *Grand pièce symphonique* is very well structured, the listener's interest readily held throughout. Gergely's account of the last item is attractively registered and well contrasted. This makes an excellent survey in the lowest price range.

Cantabile; Fantaisie in A; Pièce héroïque; L'Organiste: 8 Pieces.

(M) **(*) Saga SCD 9019. Pierre Cochereau (organ of Notre Dame, Paris).

Cochereau's performances of the *Cantabile* and *Fantaisie* have far more life than usual and the *Pièce héroïque* is suitably massive. The eight miniatures from *L'Organiste* are charming – an adjective one did not expect to apply to Franck's organ music. The recording has the touch of harshness characteristic of a French organ. It is easy to reproduce and does not disappoint in the *Pièce héroïque*. But the playing time is ungenerous.

Frescobaldi, Girolamo (1583–1643)

Capricci, Book 1.

(M) ** HM/BMG GD 77071 [77071-2-RG]. Gustav Leonhardt, Harry Van Der Kamp.

Frescobaldi was one of the greatest keyboard masters of his day and, as organist of St Peter's, Rome, enjoyed a legendary reputation during his lifetime. The *Capricci* (the word means 'moods') were published in 1624 with a dedication to Prince Alfonso of Modena and were written for those interested in 'seriousness of style, a difficult and learned perfection', and were intended not only with didactic ends in mind but as intellectual relaxation for performers and audience. Gustav Leonhardt's analogue recording dates from 1979 and has splendid clarity and warmth. It first appeared briefly on EMI/Deutsche Harmonia Mundi, with almost 80 minutes' playing time, but did not stay in circulation long enough to be listed by us. It now reappears from RCA, albeit with one of the pieces, the *Capriccio cromatico con ligature*, omitted. Nevertheless, at 73 minutes and at mid-price, this is still good value for money, and the music is certainly rewarding. The recording is far too close and wanting in tonal variety; the effect can be improved somewhat by playing at a lower-than-usual level setting.

Gabrieli, Andrea (1520–86)

Laudate dominum.

(M) **(*) Decca 430 359-2; *430 359-4*. Magdalen College, Oxford, Ch., Wren O, Rose – G. GABRIELI: *Motets* **(*); PERGOLESI: *Miserere II* *** (with BASSANO: *Ave Regina* **(*)).

In modern times the name Gabrieli has usually suggested Giovanni, nephew of Andrea, but in their day they were both held in equal esteem; this fine setting of *Laudate dominum* for two five-part choirs helps to explain why. Also included is a splendid *Ave Regina* by Andrea's contemporary, Giovanni Bassano, which is laid out for three four-part choirs and brass in a similar polychoral style. Both are are well performed, if without strong individuality, and the recording is magnificently expansive.

Gabrieli, Giovanni (1557–1612)

Hodie Christus natus est; Plaudite; Virtute magna.

(M) **(*) Decca 430 359-2; *430 359-4* [id.]. Magdalen College, Oxford, Ch., Gowman (organ), Wren O, Rose – A. GABRIELI: *Laudate dominum* **(*); PERGOLESI: *Miserere II*. ***

This coupling of three comparatively rare pieces by Giovanni Gabrieli, as well as an item by his uncle Andrea, is welcome and apt. The Christmas motet, *Hodie Christus natus est*, is justly the most celebrated; but the other pieces too are most beautiful, notably *Plaudite* for three separate choirs. With the *Ave Regina* of the Gabrielis' contemporary, Giovanni Bassano, as makeweight, this makes a valuable bonus for the Pergolesi *Miserere*. The performances, though finely controlled, could be more positive and dramatic, but they are very well recorded.

Geminiani, Francesco (1687–1762)

Concerti grossi, Op. 2/5–6; Op. 3/3; Op. 7/2; in G min. (after Corelli, *Op. 5/5*); *in D min.* (after Corelli, *Op. 5/12*); *Theme & variations (La Follia).*
(M) *** BMG/RCA Dig. GD 77010 [77010-2-RG]. La Petite Bande, Sigiswald Kuijken.

A more considerable and innovative figure than is generally supposed, the quality of invention in the Geminiani concertos recorded here rises high above the routine. There is considerable expressive depth in some of the slow movements too. La Petite Bande is incomparably superior to many of the period-instrument ensembles; their string-tone is light and feathery, accents are never overemphatic, and there is a splendid sense of movement. Those who are normally allergic to the vinegary offerings of some rivals will find this record a joy. It is beautifully recorded too, and makes an admirable and economical introduction to this underrated and genial composer.

Gershwin, George (1898–1937)

An American in Paris; Catfish Row (suite from *Porgy and Bess*); (i) *Piano concerto in F. Cuban overture; 'I got rhythm' variations; Lullaby for string orchestra; Promenade;* (i) *Rhapsody in blue; Second Rhapsody for piano and orchestra.*
(B) *** VoxBox 1154832 (2) [CDX 5007]. (i) Jeffrey Siegel; St Louis SO, Leonard Slatkin.

These performances are greatly admired in the USA, and rightly so. The orchestral playing, projected by bold, vividly forward recording, has a tingling vitality throughout and the *Cuban overture* lifts off marvellously, helped by the exuberant percussive condiment, administered equally beguilingly in the sultry middle section. The same rhythmic effervescence is no less attractive in the *Piano concerto*, a splendid performance, full of verve and colour, with an authentic atmosphere in the *Andante*. The *Second Rhapsody* and the delightfully witty and affectionate account of the 'I got rhythm' variations are hardly less appealing, while there is a delicious clarinet solo from George Silfries to open the engaging *Promenade*; this is based on an Astaire dance-sequence in the film *Shall We Dance* and was reconstructed from the composer's sketches by Ira Gershwin. It is as persuasively stylish as the *Lullaby* (though here a silkier string-sound might have been advantageous). But above all it is the vibrancy of this music-making which is so telling, with Jeffrey Siegel not as subtle as Leonard Bernstein in the *Rhapsody in blue* but playing with genuine charisma, and Slatkin presents the central melody with an agreeable warmth. *Catfish Row*, Gershwin's own selection from *Porgy and Bess*, is strongly characterized, yet inevitably sounds more piecemeal than Robert Russell Bennett's famous *Symphonic picture*, while Slatkin's vigorous and characterful account of *An American in Paris*, if rhythmically a little mannered at times, is no less potent than the rest of this heady transatlantic mixture. Outstanding value.

(i) *An American in Paris;* (ii) *Piano concerto in F;* (iii) *Rhapsody in blue.*
(B) *** Pickwick Dig. PCD 909. (ii; iii) Gwenneth Pryor; LSO, Richard Williams.
(M) **(*) Ph. 420 492-2. (ii; iii) Werner Haas; Monte Carlo Op. O, De Waart.
(B) **(*) CfP CD-CFP 9012; *TC-CFP 4413*. (ii; iii) Blumenthal; ECO, Steuart Bedford.
(M) **(*) DG Dig. 427 806-2; *427 806-4*. Bernstein with LAPO – BARBER: *Adagio*; BERNSTEIN: *Candide overture* etc. ***
(B) **(*) DG Compact Classics 413 851-2 (2); *413 851-4* [id.]. (i) San Francisco SO, Ozawa; (ii) Szidon, LPO, Downes; (iii) Siegfried Stöckigt, Leipzig GO, Masur – BERNSTEIN: *West Side story: Symphonic dances.* *** (CD only: (i) RUSSO: *3 Pieces for Blues band and orchestra* – with Siegel-Schwall Band).
(BB) * Naxos Dig. 8.550295 [id.]. (ii; iii) Kathryn Selby; (i) CSR SO (Bratislava); (ii; iii) Slovak PO; Richard Hayman.

An American in Paris; (i) *Piano concerto in F; Rhapsody in blue; Variations on 'I got rhythm'.*
(M) **(*) BMG/RCA GD 86519 [RCA 6519-2-RG]. (i) Earl Wild; Boston Pops O, Fiedler.

(i) *An American in Paris;* (i; ii) *Piano concerto in F;* (iii) *Rhapsody in blue* (original version); *Who Cares?* (ballet from Gershwin Songbook, arr. Hershy Kay); arr. of songs for piano: *Clap your hands; Do, do, do it again; Nobody but you; Swanee.*
(M) **(*) Pickwick/RPO CDRPO 9002 (2) [id.]. (i) RPO, Henry Lewis; (ii) with Janis Vakarelis; (iii) Andrew Litton, with RPO.

From the opening glissando swirl on the clarinet, the performance of the *Rhapsody in blue* by Gwenneth Pryor and the LSO under Richard Williams tingles with adrenalin, and the other performances are comparable. The *Rhapsody* has splendid rhythmic energy, yet the performers can relax to allow the big expressive blossoming at the centre really to expand. Similarly in the *Concerto*, the combination of vitality and flair and an almost voluptuous response to the lyrical melodies is very involving. *An American in Paris*, briskly paced, moves forward in an exhilarating sweep, with the big blues tune vibrant and the closing section managed to perfection. The performances are helped by superb recording, made in the EMI No. 1 Studio; but it is the life and spontaneity of the music-making that enthral the listener throughout all three works.

Among British and European compilations, the Philips collection from Monte Carlo stands out. Digital remastering has brought noticeable improvement in the sound, which always had appealing body and warmth; now the treble is brighter but not edgier and, although the upper range is still not as wide as on more recent versions, there is no real feeling of restriction. The *Concerto* is particularly successful; its lyrical moments have a quality of nostalgia which is very attractive. Werner Haas is a volatile and sympathetic soloist, and his rhythmic verve is refreshing. Edo de Waart's *An American in Paris* is not only buoyant but glamorous too – the big blues melody is highly seductive and, as with all the best accounts of this piece, the episodic nature of the writing is hidden. There is a cultured, European flavour to this music-making that does not detract from its vitality, and the jazz inflexions are not missed, with plenty of verve in the *Rhapsody*.

Daniel Blumenthal gives performances of the two concertante pieces which convincingly combine Ravelian delicacy of articulation with genuine feeling for the jazz-based idiom. The syncopations are often naughtily pointed, to delightful effect, and Bedford and the ECO, unlikely accompanists as they may be, give warm and understanding support. *An American in Paris* is also done warmly but with less panache. For those seeking a cultured flavour in this music, however, this can be strongly recommended as an alternative to Haas.

The mid-priced reissue from RPO combines two CDs by different artists, originally (and more sensibly) issued separately. The performances of *An American in Paris* and the *Concerto in F* are strongly directed by Henry Lewis and have the advantage of a first-class digital recording, made in the Henry Wood Hall, London. The sound and balance are most realistic. The performance of the *Concerto* is spontaneously fresh, with the lyrical and rhythmic elements well contrasted and affectionately underlined: the blues theme in the slow movement produces an attractive, easy trumpet solo and an admirable response from the RPO woodwind. *An American in Paris* is vigorously done, though the fluent treatment of the blues tune lacks sentience; however, there is more first-class trumpet playing in the night-club sequence and the piece ends enthusiastically (though without motor horns), even if some of the accenting on the way lacks transatlantic rhythmic flair. But with only two works included, this disc is not very generous. Andrew Litton follows in Michael Tilson Thomas's footsteps by adopting the original Whiteman score of the *Rhapsody in blue*. The performance is lively enough, and thoughtful too, so it has some elements of the Bernstein approach, particularly in the improvisatory-like passage before the big tune arrives. When it does, its reedy textures emphasize the smaller, less inflated sound which Gershwin originally conceived, while earlier the brass tuttis have a jazzy exuberance, without the players sounding rushed off their feet. In its way, this is very enjoyable and very well recorded, but the rhythmic inflexions are clearly from this side of the Atlantic, and this applies even more strikingly to the (attractively) amiable performance of Hershy Kay's ballet-score adapted from Gershwin's own 'Song Book for Balanchine'. Litton then usefully plays as solo piano items the four remaining songs which Kay discarded, and plays them very well too. This companion CD plays for about an hour.

The mid-priced RCA CD is particularly generous (70 minutes) in including, besides the usual triptych, the *'I got rhythm' variations*, given plenty of rhythmic panache. Indeed these are essentially jazzy performances: Earl Wild's playing is full of energy and brio, and he inspires Arthur Fiedler to a similarly infectious response. The outer movements of the *Concerto* are comparably volatile and the blues feeling of the slow movement is strong. At the end of *An American in Paris* Fiedler adds to the exuberance by bringing in a bevy of motor horns. The brightly remastered recording suits the music-making, though the resonant Boston acoustics at times prevent absolute sharpness of focus: ideally, the spectacular percussion at the beginning of the *Concerto* should sound cleaner.

The DG Compact Classics tape provides a mid-European slant on Gershwin, although the performance of the *Rhapsody* comes from further east, with the Leipzig Gewandhaus Orchestra under Masur providing a cultured accompaniment to the extremely lively account of the piano part by Siegfried Stöckigt. The jazzy flavour is enhanced by the blend of saxophone and string timbre in the big tune, which has an air of pre-1939 Berlin. The performance of the *Concerto* is even finer, with Roberto Szidon treating the work as he would any other Romantic concerto; with rhythms superbly lithe and subtle tonal colouring, the result has both freshness and stature. The jazz idiom is seen here as an essential, but not overwhelmingly dominant, element. Downes and the LPO match the soloist in understanding and virtuosity. Ozawa's account of *An American in Paris* is both vivid and brilliant, with sound to match in both formats. The Bernstein coupling is no less attractive, but the Russo bonus item, which is included on the pair of CDs only, is far from indispensable.

The Naxos collection is totally unidiomatic. Everything is well played, even refined (especially the slow movement of the *Concerto*), but the rhythmic feeling of this music eludes these players: the *Rhapsody* is unmemorable and the blues tune in *An American in Paris* is square. Good modern recording, but the jazzy element is too diluted for this music-making to be fully convincing.

An American in Paris; Catfish Row (suite from Porgy & Bess); Cuban overture; Lullaby.
(M) *** EMI Dig. CDD7 64084-2 [id.]; *ET 764084-4* [id.]. St Louis SO, Leonard Slatkin.

An American in Paris; Cuban overture; (i) *Rhapsody in blue.*
(M) ** Decca 417 716-2; *417 716-4* [id.]. (i) Ivan Davis; Cleveland O, Maazel – COPLAND: *Appalachian spring* etc. ***

(i) *An American in Paris;* (ii) *Cuban overture;* (i; iii) *Rhapsody in blue;* (iv) *I got rhythm: Variations.*
(B) ** Decca 433 616-2; *433 616-4* [id.]. (i) L. Festival O, Stanley Black; (ii) Cleveland O, Maazel; (iii) Black (piano); (iv) David Parkhouse, L. Festival Ens., Herrmann – ADDINSELL: *Warsaw concerto.* ***

(i) *An American in Paris;* (ii) *Rhapsody in blue.*
(M) *** Sony [MYK 37242]. (i) NYPO, Bernstein; (ii) Bernstein with Columbia SO.

(i) *An American in Paris;* (i; ii) *Rhapsody in blue;* (ii) *3 Preludes;* (i) *Porgy and Bess: Symphonic picture* (arr. Robert Russell Bennett).
(M) ** EMI CDM7 63736-2. (i) Hollywood Bowl SO, Felix Slatkin; (ii) Leonard Pennario.

Bernstein's 1959 CBS (now Sony) coupling was recorded when (at the beginning of his forties) he was at the peak of his creativity, with *West Side Story* only two years behind him. This record set the standard by which all subsequent pairings of *An American in Paris* and *Rhapsody in blue* came to be judged. It still sounds astonishingly well as a recording; the *Rhapsody* in particular has better piano-tone than CBS often provided in the 1970s. Bernstein's approach is inspirational, exceptionally flexible but completely spontaneous. Although the jazzy element is not masked, it is essentially a concert performance, fully justifying the expanded orchestration, masterly in every way, with much broader tempi than in the composer's piano-roll version, but quixotic in mood, rhythmically subtle and creating a life-enhancing surge of human warmth at the entry of the big central tune. The performance of *An American in Paris* is vividly characterized, brash and episodic; an unashamedly American view, with the great blues tune marvellously timed and phrased as only a great American orchestra can do it. This coupling is newly remastered, the sound slightly brighter and brasher, which brings both gains and losses. Fortunately, the piano timbre remains unscathed in the *Rhapsody.* This uniquely desirable disc is apparently still available in the USA, although it has been withdrawn – we hope temporarily – in the UK.

Slatkin is clearly at home in *Catfish Row* and he relishes the sophistication of Gershwin's own suite from *Porgy and Bess*, while still bringing out the special effects (bell and wind-simulator in *Hurricane*). A similar sophistication in the brash *Cuban overture* does mean that some of the gutsy feeling of the piece (not one of Gershwin's best works) is lost; while for *An American in Paris*, although he often disguises the seams, he could at times be more extrovert. It is partly the gloriously ample acoustics of the Lowell Hall, St Louis, that makes everything seem opulent, and certainly on sonic grounds no one will be disappointed with this collection, especially by the *Lullaby* (which derives from *Blue Monday*), in which the St Louis strings sound particularly rich in timbre.

Stanley Black's performances of *An American in Paris* and the *Rhapsody in blue* were originally recorded in Decca's Phase 4 system, which brings an intentionally forward balance and sound which is brilliant to the point of brashness, an effect emphasized on CD. The perfomances show thoroughly idiomatic feeling and are spontaneously enjoyable. David Parkhouse is an excellent soloist in the *I got rhythm variations*, and both this and Maazel's racy *Cuban overture* are vividly recorded – although, coming after the demonstration digital quality of the Addinsell *Warsaw concerto* which opens the concert, the ear readily perceives the difference in sonic fullness.

Maazel's triptych dates from 1974. The performances of all three works are strikingly energetic (Ivan Davis both brilliant and sophisticated in the *Rhapsody*) and the boisterous account of the *Cuban overture* is immensely spirited, almost disguising its emptiness. But the big tune at the centre of the *Rhapsody* and the blues melody in *An American in Paris* (given an upbeat reading) are lacking in sensuous warmth, which means that a dimension is missing in both works.

Spirited, rumbustious performances on EMI, with the forward balance bringing a vividly brash sound-picture which serves to emphasize the episodic nature of Slatkin's readings of *An American in Paris* and the *Symphonic picture, Porgy and Bess*, in which the orchestral playing is superb. Pennario makes a distingushed contribution to an essentially jazzy version of the *Rhapsody* and is no less at home in the *Three Preludes*. A lively and enjoyable collection, but there are better versions of all three major works.

Piano concerto in F.
(M) ** Sony SBK 46338; *40-46338* [id.].
Entremont, Phd. O, Ormandy – RAVEL: *Concertos*. **

Entremont plays well enough in the *Concerto*, which has the appropriate transatlantic rhythmic verve, and Ormandy again directs the proceedings with flair. But the recording is not distinguished: piano-tone is rather shallow, the strings have a tendency to edginess and the drum resonance at the opening is not cleanly caught.

(i) *Cuban overture;* (i; ii) *'I got rhythm' variations; Second Rhapsody.* (i) *Porgy and Bess: symphonic picture* (arr. Bennett); (ii) *3 Piano preludes.*
(M) **(*) Ph. 432 511-2; *432 511-4*. (i) Monte Carlo Nat. Op. O, Edo de Waart; (ii) Werner Haas.

For those not seeking a strong transatlantic bias, these are most enjoyable recordings, given Philips's most refined, early-1970s sound. There is a cultured, European flavour about the music-making that does not detract from its vitality, and indeed the performance of the *Porgy and Bess symphonic picture* is first rate, with each melody given its own individuality and the warm acoustic adding evocative qualities and a certain elegance. Werner Haas is an excellent soloist in the *Second Rhapsody* and the *'I got rhythm' variations*, the rhythmic inflexions by no means clumsy, even if, as with the *Cuban overture*, the effect is less racy than in an American performance. This collection won't be to all tastes, but it is refreshing to have a new approach to this much-recorded repertoire.

Overtures: Funny Face; Let 'em Eat Cake; Oh Kay!. Girl Crazy: suite. Of Thee I Sing: Wintergreen for President (orch. Paul). *3 Preludes* (orch. Stone); (i) *Second Rhapsody* (for piano and orchestra).
(B) **(*) Pickwick (Decca) IMPX 9013. Boston Pops O, Fiedler; (i) with Ralph Votapek.

This (1979, Decca Phase 4) Gershwin concert has transferred splendidly to CD: the sound has warmth, sparkle and colour. There are plenty of good tunes hidden here (not least *'S Wonderful* from *Funny Face*) and the orchestrations sound authentic. *Wintergreen for President* quotes exuberantly from a number of sources (including a snippet from *The Pirates of Penzance*) and Fiedler, always lively, catches its roisterous ambience. The *Second Rhapsody*, one of Gershwin's near-misses, is given with considerable fervour, with Ralph Votapek sparking off a good orchestral response. The three piano *Preludes* do not readily transcribe for orchestra, but Fiedler makes the most of them.

Porgy and Bess: Symphonic picture (arr. Bennett).
(M) *** Decca 430 712-2; *430 712-4* [id.].
Detroit SO, Dorati – GROFÉ: *Grand Canyon suite*. ***

Robert Russell Bennett's famous arrangement of Gershwin melodies has been recorded many times, but never more beautifully than on this Decca digital version from Detroit. The performance is totally memorable, the opening evocatively nostalgic, and each one of these wonderful tunes is phrased with a warmly affectionate feeling for its character, yet is never vulgarized. The sound is quite superb: on CD the strings have a ravishing, lustrous radiance that stems from the refinement of the playing itself, captured with remarkable naturalness.

Rhapsody in blue (see also above, under *An American in Paris*).
(M) **(*) DG 431 048-2; *431 048-4* [id.].
Bernstein with LAPO – BARBER: *Adagio*; COPLAND: *Appalachian spring*. ***
(M) **(*) DG Dig. 427 806-2; *427 806-4*.
Bernstein with LAPO – BARBER: *Adagio*; BERNSTEIN: *Candide overture* etc. ***
(M) **(*) Decca Dig. 430 726-2; *430 726-4* [id.].
Katia & Marielle Labèque, Cleveland O, Chailly – ADDINSELL: *Warsaw concerto*; GOTTSCHALK: *Grand fantasia*; LISZT: *Hungarian fantasia*; LITOLFF: *Scherzo*. ***

In his most recent recording for DG, Bernstein rather goes over the top with his jazzing of the solos in Gershwin. Such rhythmic freedom was clearly the result of a live rather than a studio performance. The big melody in *Rhapsody in blue* is rather too heavily pointed for comfort. The immediacy of the occasion is most compellingly projected, but this does not match Bernstein's inspired 1959 analogue coupling for CBS. This version has been reissued at mid-price, coupled with Barber's *Adagio* and two extracts from Bernstein's own *West Side story*. Bernstein's later digital recording of the *Rhapsody in blue*, reissued again but differently coupled, has all the immediacy of live music-making, but it does not match his earlier, CBS version.

There seems no special reason for preferring the two-piano version of the *Rhapsody in blue*, and although the Labèque duo play charismatically their account is made somewhat controversial by the addition of an improvisatory element (more decorative than structural). However, the playing does not lack sparkle and the recording is first class.

Arrangements of songs: *Embraceable you; Fascinatin' rhythm; A foggy day; Funny face; He loves and she loves; I got rhythm; Lady be good; Liza; Love is here to stay; The man I love; Nice work if you can get it; Soon; Summertime; S'wonderful; They all laughed; They can't take that away from me.*
(M) *** EMI CDM7 69218-2 [id.]; *EG 769218-4*. Yehudi Menuhin, Stéphane Grappelli.

This is an attractive re-assembly of the Gershwin numbers taken from the famous Menuhin/Grappelli series of studio collaborations in which two distinguished musicians from different musical backgrounds struck sparks off each other to most entertaining effect. The songs are all famous and the treatments highly felicitous. The sound has excellent presence.

OPERA

Porgy and Bess: highlights.
(M) ** BMG/RCA GD 85234 [5234-2-RG]. Leontyne Price, William Warfield, John Bubbles, McHenry Boatwright, RCA Victor Ch. & O, Skitch Henderson.

The RCA studio compilation was recorded in 1963, a decade before the complete Decca and RCA versions appeared. Both Price and Warfield sing magnificently, and the supporting group is given lively direction by Skitch Henderson.

Gibbons, Christopher (1615–1676)

Cupid and Death (with Matthew Locke).
(M) *** HM/BMG GD 77117 (2). Kirkby, Tubb, King, Wistreich, Thomas, Holden, Cass, Nichols, Cornwell, King, Consort of Musicke, Rooley – BLOW: *Venus and Adonis*. ***

Cupid and Death, 'a masque in four entries', dates from 1653, or nearly 30 years before the better-known Blow work with which it is coupled. Gibbons, the son of Orlando Gibbons and the teacher of Blow, seems to have been the lesser partner in the project, with Matthew Locke providing the bulk of the music for this rustic fantasy on an ancient fable. Each of the five 'entries' or Acts is formally laid out in a set sequence of items – a suite of dances, a dialogue, a song and a chorus – and Rooley's team consistently brings out the fresh charm of the music. For repeated listening, the spoken sections, up to ten minutes long, can easily be programmed out on CD. A welcome reissue at mid-price.

Giordano, Umberto (1867–1948)

Andrea Chénier (complete).
(M) *** BMG/RCA GD 82046 (2) [RCD-2-2046]. Domingo, Scotto, Milnes, Alldis Ch., Nat. PO, Levine.
(M) **(*) Decca 425 407-2 (2) [id.]. Tebaldi, Del Monaco, Bastianini, Ch. & O of St Cecilia Ac., Rome, Gavazzeni.

Giordano always runs the risk – not least in this opera with its obvious parallels with *Tosca* – of being considered only in the shadow of Puccini, but this red-blooded score can, as here, be searingly effective with its defiant poet hero – a splendid role for Domingo at his most heroic – and the former servant, later revolutionary leader, Gérard, a character who genuinely develops from Act to Act, a point well appreciated by Milnes. Scotto gives one of her most eloquent and beautiful performances, and Levine has rarely displayed his powers as an urgent and dramatic opera conductor more potently on record, with the bright recording intensifying the dramatic thrust of playing and singing.

Apart perhaps from *La forza del destino*, the 1960 Decca set represents the most desirable of the Tebaldi/Del Monaco collaborations in Italian opera. The blood-and-thunder of the story suits both singers admirably and Gavazzeni is also at his best. Sample the final duet if you have any doubts concerning the power of this performance. Finer still than the soprano and tenor is Bastianini as Gérard. His finely focused voice is caught beautifully and he conveys vividly the conflicts in the man's character. Bold, vivid sound projects the drama splendidly.

Fedora (complete).
(M) **(*) Decca 433 033-2 (2) [id.]. Olivero, Del Monaco, Gobbi, Monte Carlo Nat. Op. Ch. & O, Gardelli – ZANDONAI: *Francesca da Rimini*. **(*)

Puccini was unique among his contemporaries in sustaining his operatic reputation over a long series of works. Giordano, like Leoncavallo, Mascagni and others, failed to live up to early success; with Giordano it is significant that this opera, like his most famous one, *Andrea Chénier*, dates from the earliest part of his career. He went on to marry the rich daughter of a hotelier, and prosperity was no doubt the bogey of invention. *Fedora* will always be remembered for one brief aria, the hero's *Amor ti vieta*; but, as this highly enjoyable recording confirms, there is much that is memorable in the score, even if nothing else quite approaches it. The piece is adapted from a Sardou melodrama designed for Sarah Bernhardt (parallel with *Tosca*), with an absurd plot involving a passionate *volte-face* when the heroine's hatred for the hero (her wicked brother's murderer) suddenly turns to love. Meaty stuff, which brings some splendid singing from Magda Olivero and (more intermittently) from Del Monaco, with Gobbi in a light comedy part. Fine, vintage (1969), atmospheric recording. Well worth trying by anyone with a hankering after *verismo*, especially given its rare Zandonai coupling, added for the CD reissue.

Glazunov, Alexander (1865–1936)

Chant du ménestrel (for cello and orchestra), *Op. 71.*
(M) *** DG 431 475-2; *431 475-4.*
Rostropovich, Boston SO, Ozawa – SHOSTAKOVICH: *Cello concerto No. 2*; TCHAIKOVSKY: *Andante cantabile.* ***

Glazunov's *Chant du ménestrel*, which dates from 1900, is an amiable four-minute piece which serves as an excellent encore for the Shostakovich and Tchaikovsky works which it follows on Rostropovich's CD. It is played with simple eloquence and is admirably recorded.

Violin concerto in A min., Op. 82.
❀ (M) (***) EMI mono CDH7 64030-2 [id.].
Heifetz, LPO, Barbirolli – SIBELIUS: *Violin concerto* (**); TCHAIKOVSKY: *Violin concerto.* (***)
(B) *** Pickwick Dig. PCD 966 [id.]. Udagawa, LPO, Klein – Concert ***.

Heifetz's recording of the Glazunov *Violin concerto* was made in 1934 when the composer was still alive. It has greater expressive breadth and spaciousness than his later record (still at full price on CD) with Walter Hendl and the Chicago orchestra which, though marvellously played, sounds relatively hard-driven by comparison. Here phrases breathe naturally and there is great warmth. The recording sounds somewhat opaque and the opening of the cadenza (track 9) finds the soloist suddenly a bit too close. Intonation is incredibly sure and the tone sweet. Surfaces are mostly silent in the CD transfer, though there are two passages where one is aware of background noise. Milstein recorded a superb account in the 1950s but, generally speaking, this first Heifetz version of the concerto has never been surpassed.

The Glazunov *Violin concerto*, the longest work in a fine collection of sweetmeat concertante pieces by Hideko Udagawa, receives a heartfelt performance which is just as compelling as the virtuoso stereo accounts from such master violinists as Heifetz and Perlman. In the finale she may not offer quite such bravura fireworks as they do but, with more open sound, the result is just as persuasive in its lilting way. The violin is balanced close but not so close as with Perlman or Heifetz, and there is far more space round the orchestral sound, which is full and warm to match the soloist.

Raymonda (ballet), *Op. 57* (complete).
(B) **(*) Pickwick Dig. DUET 36 CD (2).
Bolshoi Theatre O, Algis Zhuraitis.

Glazunov's *Raymonda* follows very much in the Tchaikovsky tradition, a Russian epic/romantic tale set in the Middle Ages. An attempted abduction of the heroine by her unwanted Saracen suitor is thwarted in the nick of time by the return of her true love from the Crusades. The ballet provides a whole stream of colourful and undemanding music, with the felicity of the orchestration giving constant pleasure. Zhuraitis has already given us a fine version of Prokofiev's *Romeo and Juliet* and here he shows himself as completely at home in Glazunov's more glamorous ballet. The Bolshoi Orchestra plays splendidly: there is much finesse in the wind solos and the strings are warm and sensitive – try the *Grande Valse* in Act I or the lovely veiled playing in the *Pas de deux* following the *Scène mimique* (track 5). The digital recording could be more sumptuous; it is a bit two-dimensional in relation to both violins and brass (the trumpeting is more blatant than we expect in Western Europe), but the backing ambience ensures a pleasing overall effect, even if tuttis bring a degree of brashness. The one snag is that, because this was recorded at a live performance, the music is punctuated by enthusiastic clapping which at times interrupts before the end of a number (particularly in the divertissements, with their individual variations). But this does have the effect of making one sense the presence of the dancers, and it certainly brings a spontaneous response from the orchestra. The documentation is barely adequate, failing to relate the plot synopsis to the detailed events of the narrative. However, the 33 separate cues are considerable compensation.

The Seasons (ballet) *Op. 67.*
(BB) **(*) Naxos Dig. 8.550079 [id.]. Czech RSO (Bratislava), Ondrej Lenárd – TCHAIKOVSKY: *Sleeping Beauty suite.* **

The Seasons (complete ballet), *Op. 67; Concert waltzes Nos. 1 in D, Op. 47; 2 in F, Op. 51; Stenka Razin, Op. 13.*
(M) ** Decca 430 348-2. SRO, Ernest Ansermet.

Ondrej Lenárd gives a pleasing account of Glazunov's delightful score, finding plenty of delicacy for the vignettes of *Winter*: *Frost*, *Ice* and *Snow*, and an appropriate warmth for the *Waltz of the cornflowers and poppies* of *Summer*. The entry of Glazunov's most famous tune at the opening of the *Autumn Bacchanale* is very virile indeed, helped by a slight rise in the recording level. The sound is first class, transparently atmospheric yet with plenty of fullness and weight at climaxes. The ear has an impression of a fairly modest string section, but the sounds they make are pleasing and graceful.

Ansermet, after his Diaghliev experience, had a very special way with ballet music. His meticulous feeling for detail and colour immediately catches the ear at the opening of Glazunov's *Seasons*, and every bar is tinglingly alive. One wishes that the remastered 1967 recording had a little more amplitude at these moments, but the Geneva acoustics have plenty of atmosphere and Ansermet's vivid woodwind colours gleam and glitter. The two slight *Concert waltzes* are played with affectionate delicacy and charm; the Suisse Romande is not one of the world's most opulent-sounding orchestras but, with Ansermet at the helm, their playing always has much character. *Stenka Razin* is a melodramatic, descriptive piece which uses the *Volga boat song* at the very opening and again at its Lisztian climax. The performance here is certainly dramatic enough, and Ansermet winningly catches the sinuous, oriental flavour of the secondary theme. The early (1954) stereo is somewhat primitive, but acceptable.

Glière, Reinhold (1875–1956)

(i) *Concerto for coloratura soprano, Op. 82;* (ii) *Harp concerto, Op. 74.*

(M) *** Decca 430 006-2. (i) Sutherland; (ii) Ellis, LSO, Bonynge – with Recital. **(*)

Glière's brilliant *Coloratura concerto* inspires Joan Sutherland to some dreamily beautiful singing. The first movement sounds like a Russian version of Villa-Lobos's famous *Bachianas brasileiras No. 5*, and the second movement has echoes of Johann Strauss, but with a Russian accent. The *Harp concerto* is as easy, unpretentious and tuneful as the vocal concerto, with Osian Ellis performing brilliantly. Excellent 1968 Kingsway Hall recording. For the rest of the collection, see under 'Sutherland' in the Vocal Recitals.

Symphony No. 3 in B min. (Ilya Murometz), Op. 42.

(M) **(*) Unicorn Dig. UKCD 2014/5. RPO, Farberman.

Glière's massive programme symphony manages to stretch thin material extraordinarily far. Farberman's conducting cannot be described as volatile, and he is never led into introducing urgent stringendos to add to the passion of a climax, but his very patience, helped by vivid recording, makes for very compelling results. The sound has natural balance and combines brilliance with warmth.

Glinka, Mikhail (1805–57)

Russlan and Ludmilla: Overture.

(B) *** Decca 417 689-2; *417 689-4*. LSO, Solti – MUSSORGSKY: *Khovanshchina prelude; Night;* BORODIN: *Prince Igor*: excerpts. ***

(M) *** BMG/RCA GD 60176 [60176-2-RG]. Chicago SO, Fritz Reiner – PROKOFIEV: *Alexander Nevsky* etc. ***

Solti's electrifying account of the *Russlan and Ludmilla overture* is perhaps the most exciting ever recorded, with the lyrical element providing a balancing warmth, though the sound is very brightly lit.

Reiner's performance is not quite as racy as Solti's, but it is still highly infectious, and the 1959 Chicago sound brings plenty of colour and warmth.

Gluck, Christophe (1714–87)

Le Cinesi (The Chinese women).

(M) *** HM/BMG Dig. GD 77174 [77174-2-RG]. Poulenard, Von Otter, Banditelli, De Mey, Schola Cantorum Basiliensis O, Jacobs.

Gluck's hour-long opera-serenade, written in 1754 for a palace entertainment given by Prince Joseph Friedrich of Saxe-Hildburghausen, provides a fascinating view of the composer's lighter side. In the comedy here one can even detect anticipations of Mozart, though with recitative taking up an undue proportion of the whole – including one solid span, near the beginning, of over ten minutes – Gluck's timing hardly compares. The chinoiserie of the story was reflected at that first performance in elaborate Chinese costumes, a novelty at the time; more importantly for us, Gluck, rather like Mozart in *Entführung*, uses jangling and tinkling percussion instruments in the overture to indicate an exotic setting. Otherwise the formal attitudes in Metastasio's libretto – written some twenty years before Gluck set it – are pure eighteenth century.

Orfeo ed Euridice (complete).

(M) **(*) BMG/RCA GD 87896 (2) [7896-2-RG]. Verrett, Moffo, Raskin, Rome Polyphonic Ch., Virtuosi di Roma, Fasano.

(M) ** EMI Dig. CMS7 63637-2 (2) [Ang. CDMB 63637]. Baltsa, Marshall, Gruberová, Amb. Op. Ch., Philh. O, Muti.

Clearly, if you have a mezzo as firm and sensitive as Shirley Verrett, then everything is in favour of your using the original Italian version rather than the later, Paris version with tenor. Quite apart from making a sensible decision over the text, Fasano uses the right-sized orchestra (of modern instruments) and adopts an appropriately classical style. Anna Moffo and Judith Raskin match Verrett in clean, strong singing, and the Rome Polyphonic Chorus is far more incisive than most Italian choirs. The recording is vivid and atmospheric, but on CD the close balance of the voices emphasizes the music's dramatic qualities rather than its tenderness. However, this makes a good mid-priced recommendation.

Muti chose to record the relatively severe 1762 version of *Orfeo ed Euridice* which eliminates some much-loved passages added later, but then opted for a most unstylish approach, sleek and smooth but full of romantic exaggerations. The pity is that the trio of principals was one of the strongest on record. Sadly, even Agnes Baltsa cannot make *Che farò* sound stylish when the speed is so leaden. The recording is warm and rounded and the sound generally first class.

Opera arias from *Alceste; Armide; Iphigénie en Aulide; Iphigénie en Tauride; Orfeo ed Euridice; Paride ed Elena; La rencontre imprévue.*
(M) *** Ph. 422 950-2; *422 950-4*. Dame Janet Baker, ECO, Raymond Leppard.

Helped by alert and sensitive accompaniments, Dame Janet Baker's singing of Gluck completely undermines any idea of something square or dull. The most famous arias bring unconventional readings – *Divinités du Styx* from *Alceste* deliberately less commanding, more thoughtful than usual – but the rarities are what inspire her most keenly: the four arias from *Paride ed Elena*, for example, are vividly contrasted in their sharply compact form. Outstanding recording, vividly remastered.

Goehr, Alexander (born 1932)

Metamorphosis/Dance, Op. 36; (i) *Romanza for cello and orchestra, Op. 24.*
(M) *** Unicorn Dig. UKCD 2039. (i) Moray Welsh; Royal Liverpool PO, Atherton.

Originally recorded in 1981 in first-rate digital sound, this invaluable issue, now on mid-price CD, offers two of the most representative works of a fine composer who has tended to be outshone by his younger colleagues from the New Manchester School, Peter Maxwell Davies and Harrison Birtwistle. Goehr wrote the *Romanza*, one of his most lyrical works, with Jacqueline du Pré in mind. Moray Welsh plays warmly and stylishly, but it is a pity that the dedicatee never recorded this piece which, in its serial argument, still requires persuasiveness, with its rhapsodic layout of *Aria* incorporating scherzo and cadenza. *Metamorphosis/Dance* was inspired by the Circe episode in the *Odyssey*, a sequence of elaborate variations, full of strong rhythmic interest. Not for nothing did the composer describe the piece as an 'imaginary ballet', though he would have done better to have chosen a less daunting title. The performance is excellent.

Gordon, Gavin (1901–70)

The Rake's Progress (ballet suite).
(M) (***) EMI mono CDH7 63911-2 [id.]. ROHCG O, Constant Lambert – LAMBERT: *Horoscope* etc.; RAWSTHORNE: *Street corner.* (***)

Gavin Gordon, a singer and actor as well as a composer, wrote his ballet based on Hogarth for the Sadler's Wells company in 1935. In its lively English idiom it had great success; as an attractive period piece the suite now makes a welcome fill-up to the colourful Lambert works. The 1946 mono recording is astonishingly vivid.

Gottschalk, Louis (1829–69)

(i; iii) *Grande fantaisie triomphale on the Brazilian national anthem* (arr. Adler); (i; iv) *Grande tarantelle for piano and orchestra;* (iii) *Marche solennelle (for orchestra and bands); Marcha triunfal y final de opera;* (iv) *Symphonies Nos. 1 (A Night in the Tropics)* (ed. Buketoff); *2 (A Montevideo);* (i; iv) *The Union: Concert paraphrase on national airs* (arr. Adler); *Variations on the Portuguese national anthem for piano and orchestra* (ed List). (ii) *5 Pieces* (for piano, 4 hands); (iv; v) *Escenas campestres (Cuban country scenes)*: opera in 1 Act.
(B) **(*) VoxBox 1154842 (2) [CDX 5009]. (i) Eugene List; (ii) Cary Lewis & Brady Millican; (iii) Berlin SO, Adler; (iv) V. State Op. O, Buketoff; (v) with Paniagua, Estevas, Garcia.

Louis Gottschalk was born in New Orleans of mixed German and French parentage. He studied music in Paris under Charles Hallé and then launched himself on a hugely successful career as composer/conductor/virtuoso pianist. He travelled widely, constantly moving throughout Europe and the USA, appealing to a society whose musical taste was without pretensions. As a touring star (perhaps comparable in many ways to the pop stars and groups of today) he was to some extent an isolated figure, cut off from serious musical influences. His subservience to public taste led to a continual infusion of national and patriotic airs into his scores and his music retained a refreshing naïveté to the last. This Vox Box offers a distinguished anthology, with obvious dedication from editors and executants alike. Eugene List (as we know from his Gershwin recordings) was just the man to choose as soloist. Whether tongue-in-cheek or not, he manages to sound stylish throughout and in *The Union concert paraphrase*, which is outrageous, he is superb. There is no space here to dwell on the felicities of Gottschalk's elegant vulgarity. If you want Lisztian bravura, try the concertante pieces; if you fancy romanticism mixed with popular national dance rhythms, sample the two symphonies. There is also an imitation of Tchaikovsky's *Marche slave* which does not quite come off. The solo piano pieces (very forwardly recorded) are more variable: *La Gallina* is particularly likeable. The programme ends with some attractive vocal music (the *Escenas campestres*), which is vividly sung. The recording is not of the very best quality; at the very opening of the *Grande tarantelle* one notices that the castanets are not quite clean and the upper range of the sound is inclined to be a bit shallow. Yet the effect, if sometimes two-dimensional, is always vivid and sparkling, and the bright, slightly hard piano timbre is not out of place here.

Grand fantasia triumfal for piano and orchestra.
(M) *** Decca Dig. 430 726-2; *430 726-4* [id.]. Ortiz, RPO, Atzmon – ADDINSELL: *Warsaw concerto* ***; GERSHWIN: *Rhapsody* **(*); LISZT: *Hungarian fantasia* ***; LITOLFF: *Scherzo.* ***

Gottschalk's *Grand fantasia* has naïvety, and a touch of vulgarity too, but the performers here give it an account which nicely combines flair and a certain elegance, and the result is a distinct success.

Gould, Morton (born 1913)

Fall River legend: suite; Spirituals for string choir and orchestra.
(M) *** Mercury 432 016-2 [id.]. Eastman-Rochester SO, Howard Hanson – BARBER: *Medea*: suite. ***

The grim narrative of *Fall River legend* concerns Lizzie Borden, a respectable American spinster of thirty-three who – according to the ballet, though not the decision of the court, which sympathetically pronounced her not guilty – murdered both her father and the malignant stepmother who had destroyed her hopes of happiness. It inspired an attractive sub-Copland score. On Mercury comes the composer's orchestral suite from the ballet, vividly played by the Eastman-Rochester Orchestra under the highly sympathetic Howard Hanson, who also gives an outstandingly vibrant account of the *Spirituals*, which resourcefully and wittily uses the massed string choir as an autonomous body in concertante with the rest of the orchestra. The 1959/60 recording has astonishing clarity, range and presence and makes one realize why Mercury engineering established such a high reputation early in the stereo era.

Latin American Symphonette.
(M) ** Van. 08.4037.71 [OVC 4071]. Utah SO, Abravanel – COPLAND: *Lincoln portrait* etc. **(*)

Abravanel's performance has plenty of colour and spirit, and is very well played, but the Utah acoustic with its wide reverberation brings problems, at times making the full-blooded scoring sound roisterously over the top. The result is infectious but noisy.

Gounod, Charles (1818–93)

Symphonies Nos. 1 in D; 2 in B flat.
(M) **(*) EMI CDM7 63949-2. Toulouse Capitole O, Plasson.

Gounod's two *Symphonies* sound astonishingly youthful, though they were composed in quick succession in his mid-thirties. When listening to No. 1, the Bizet *Symphony* springs to mind. The effortless flow of first-rate ideas and the mastery, both of the orchestra, which is handled with the greatest expertise, and of symphonic form, are very striking. The *Second Symphony* is very like the *First*, and both receive decent performance from Michel Plasson. He is thoroughly in sympathy with the composer's infectious style, as is the Orchestra of the Capitole, Toulouse, although the playing is not quite as finished or as accomplished as the music deserves. The EMI engineers have produced fresh, warm sound and the CD transfer is very successful.

Messe solennelle de Saint Cécile.
(M) *** DG 427 409-2 [id.]. Seefried, Stolze, Uhde, Czech Ch. & PO, Markevitch.

Markevitch's vintage version, recorded in the mid-1960s, still sounds remarkably well in DG's mid-price Dokumente series. In his straight-faced way Markevitch makes the incongruity of Gounod's jolly and vulgar tunes all the more delectable, and soloists, chorus and orchestra are all first rate.

Faust (complete).
(M) **(*) EMI CMS7 69983-2 (3) [Ang. CDMC 69983]. De los Angeles, Gedda, Blanc, Christoff, Paris Nat. Op. Ch. and O, Cluytens.
(M) ** Decca 421 240-2 (3) [id.]. Corelli, Suther-

land, Massard, Ghiaurov, Amb. S., Highgate School Ch., LSO, Bonynge.
(M) *(*) Erato/Warner 2292 45685-2 (3) [id.]. Caballé, Aragall, Plishka, Huttenlocher, Ch. of Op. du Rhin, Strasbourg PO, Lombard.

In the reissued Cluytens set the seductiveness of De los Angeles's singing is a dream and it is a pity that the recording hardens the natural timbre slightly. Christoff is magnificently Mephistophelian; the dark, rich, bass voice with all its many subtle facets of tone-colour is a superb vehicle for the part, at once musical and dramatic. Gedda, though showing some signs of strain, sings intelligently, and among the other soloists Ernest Blanc has a pleasing, firm voice, which he uses to make Valentin into a sympathetic character. Cluytens's approach is competent but somewhat workaday. He rarely offers that extra spring which adds so much to Gounod's score in sheer charm, and he shows a tendency to over-drive in the more dramatic passages. The recording is well balanced on the whole, although at times some of the soloists are oddly placed on the stereo stage. The layout of the five Acts over three CDs is just as it should be, and the libretto includes a full translation.

Decca provide a performance of *Faust* with only one Frenchman in the cast (Robert Massard as Valentin); in the event, it is not surprising if the flavour is only intermittently authentic. Richard Bonynge's conducting is fresh and stylish – the most consistently successful contribution – but much of the singing, including Sutherland's, falls short. It goes without saying that the heroine produces some exquisite sounds, but too often she indulges in her 'mooning' style, so that *Le Roi de Thule* provokes unclean attack all through, and ends with a really disagreeable last phrase on *Et doucement*. Corelli's faults are more than those of style, and his French is excruciating. Ghiaurov also hardly sounds at home in the music. But when Gounod's aim is clear, then all the singers' efforts click into place, and the final trio is wonderfully rousing. A memorable contribution from Monica Sinclair as Martha. The recording is more complete than that of any previous version and the quality of the sound is of Decca's best.

The Erato set is one of the disappointments in their normally excellent 'Affordable Opera' series, and it is not one of Alain Lombard's successes as an opera conductor. The unatmospheric recording and singing (either unstylish or dull) do not help. Caballé is the chief offender, plainly seeing herself as a prima donna whose vagaries and self-indulgences have to be wooed. Aragall produces some beautiful sounds, but he does not seem completely happy in French, and Paul Plishka lacks flair and devilry as Mephistopheles. The Cluytens set remains the most attractive available version.

Faust: ballet music (suite).
(M) *** EMI CDM7 69041-2 [id.]; *EG 769041-4*. Philh. O, Karajan – BORODIN: *Polovtsian dances* ***; OFFENBACH: *Gaîté parisienne* **(*); PONCHIELLI: *Dance of the Hours.* ***
(M) **(*) Decca Dig. 430 718-2; *430 718-4* [id.]. Montreal SO, Dutoit – OFFENBACH: *Gaîté parisienne.* **(*)

Karajan's 1960 recording offers elegant, sparkling playing from the Philharmonia at their peak. The sound is pleasingly full as well as bright.

Gounod's attractive suite is warmly and elegantly played by the Montreal orchestra under Dutoit, although the conductor's touch is not as light as one would have expected. The CD sounds first rate. However, there is also a splendidly 'French' performance conducted by Paul Paray on Mercury in a collection called 'French Opera Highlights' (Philips/Mercury 432 014-2) – see under Detroit Symphony Orchestra in our Concerts section, below.

Grainger, Percy (1882–1961)

(i) *Air from County Derry (Londonderry air); Country gardens;* (ii) *Danish folk music suite;* (i) *Handel in the Strand;* (ii) *The immovable 'Do'; In a nutshell suite;* (i) *Mock morris; Molly on the shore; Shepherd's hey;* (Piano) *Knight and shepherd's daughter; Walking tune.* Arrangements: FAURÉ: *Nell, Op. 18/1.* GERSHWIN: *Love walked in; The man I love.*
(M) *** EMI CDM7 63520-2; *EG 763520-4*. (i) Light Music Soc. O, Dunn; (ii) E. Sinfonia, Dilkes; (iii) Daniel Adni.

A useful and very generous Grainger anthology (79 minutes long). The performances under Sir Vivian Dunn are particularly spontaneous and the recording is bright and fresh, perhaps not as sumptuous in the *Londonderry air* as might be ideal. Of the Dilkes items, *In a nutshell* is an early work, a collection of original tunes colourfully set, with exotic percussion effects, while the *Danish folk music suite* is equally attractive and unpretentious, if less distinctive. *The immovable 'Do'* is a piece inspired by a time when Grainger had a 'cipher' on his harmonium and the note C went on sounding through everything. The inclusion of the piano pieces is particularly welcome. Daniel Adni plays them with a combination of sound musical instinct and good taste that gives unfailing pleasure, and he is very well recorded. The curiosities

here are the Fauré and Gershwin arrangements, models of their kind.

Blithe bells (Free ramble on a theme by Bach: Sheep may safely graze): Country gardens; Green bushes (Passacaglia); Handel in the Strand; Mock morris; Molly on the shore; My Robin is to the greenwood gone; Shepherd's hey; Spoon River; Walking tune; Youthful rapture.
(M) *** Chan. CHAN 6542 [id.]. Bournemouth Sinf., Montgomery.

Montgomery's anthology of Grainger's music stands out for the sparkling and sympathetic playing of the Bournemouth Sinfonietta and an engaging choice of programme. Among the expressive pieces, the arrangement of *My Robin is to the greenwood gone* is highly attractive, but the cello solo in *Youthful rapture* is perhaps less effective. Favourites such as *Country gardens*, *Shepherd's hey*, *Molly on the shore* and *Handel in the Strand* all sound as fresh as paint. The 1978 recording, made in Christchurch Priory, has retained all its ambient character in its CD transfer.

Duke of Marlborough fanfare; Green bushes (Passacaglia); Irish tune from County Derry; Lisbon; Molly on the shore; My Robin is to Greenwood gone; Shepherd's hey; Piano duet: *Let's dance gay in green meadow*; Vocal & choral: *Bold William Taylor; Brigg Fair; I'm seventeen come Sunday; Lord Maxwell's goodnight; The lost lady found; The pretty maid milkin' her cow; Scotch strathspey and reel; Shallow Brown; Shenandoah; The sprig of thyme; There was a pig went out to dig; Willow willow.*
(M) *** Decca 425 159-2. Pears, Shirley-Quirk, Amb. S. or Linden Singers, Wandsworth Boys' Ch., ECO, Britten or Steuart Bedford; Britten and V. Tunnard (pianos).

This is an altogether delightful anthology, beautifully played and sung by these distinguished artists. Grainger's talent was a smaller one than his more fervent advocates would have us believe, but his imagination in the art of arranging folksong was prodigious. The *Willow song* is a touching and indeed haunting piece and shows the quality of Grainger's harmonic resource. The opening fanfare too is strikingly original, and so is *Shallow Brown*. Vocal and instrumental items are felicitously interwoven, and the recording is extremely vivid, though the digital remastering has put a hint of edge on the voices.

Granados, Enrique (1867–1916)

Goyescas (complete).
(B) *(*) EMI CZS7 62889-2 (2). Aldo Ciccolini – ALBÉNIZ: *Iberia.* *(*)

Aldo Ciccolini's recording of the *Goyescas* looks like good value in EMI's 'two for the price of one' French series, particularly with *Iberia* thrown in for good measure. But the recordings, made in the Salle Wagram in Paris in 1966, are a bit subfusc. The piano-tone is clattery and shallow in timbre and does not show the admirable Ciccolini in the best light.

Graun, Johann Gottlieb (1703–71)

Oboe concerto in C min.
(M) *** DG 431 120-2. Holliger, Camerata Bern, Van Wijnkoop – KREBS: *Double concerto* **(*); TELEMANN: *Concerto.* ***

This Graun was the brother of the better-known composer of the opera *Montezuma*, and the *C minor Concerto* is delectable in its originality. All three movements are highly inventive, and the only pity is that this CD reissue omits the companion *G minor concerto*, included on the original LP. There would have been plenty of room for it, with a playing time here of only 55 minutes. Nevertheless this is a valuable reissue and, with Holliger at his most sparkling and with excellent sound, is well worth exploring.

Grieg, Edvard (1843–1907)

Piano concerto in A min., Op. 16.
(B) *** CfP Dig. CD-CFP 4574 [id.]; *TC-CFP 4574.* Pascal Devoyon, LPO, Maksymiuk – SCHUMANN: *Piano concerto.* ***
(B) *** Decca 433 628-2; *433 628-4* [id.]. Curzon, LSO, Fjeldstad – FRANCK: *Symphonic variations* *** ❀; SCHUMANN: *Concerto.* **(*)
(M) **(*) Decca 417 728-2 [id.]. Radu Lupu, LSO, Previn – SCHUMANN: *Concerto.* **(*)
(M) (***) EMI mono CDH7 63497-2. Lipatti, Philh. O, Galliera – CHOPIN: *Piano concerto No. 1.* (**)
(M) **(*) EMI Dig. CDD7 63903-2 [id.]; *ET 763903-4.* Cécile Ousset, LSO, Marriner – RACHMANINOV: *Piano concerto No. 2.* ***
(M) **(*) Sony SBK 46543 [id.]. Philippe Entremont, Phd. O, Ormandy – SCHUMANN: *Piano concerto* etc. *
(M) **(*) Sony/CBS CD 44849; *40-44849.* Fleisher, Cleveland O, Szell – SCHUMANN: *Concerto.* **(*)
(B) * EMI CDZ7 62859-2; *LZ 762859-4.* Ogdon, New Philh. O, Berglund – FRANCK: *Symphonic variations*; SCHUMANN: *Concerto.* *
(M) * Decca Dig. 430 719-2; *430 719-4.* George Bolet, Berlin RSO, Chailly – SCHUMANN: *Concerto.* *(*)
(B) (*) Hung. White Label HRC 181 [id.]. Jenö

Jandó. Budapest SO, Jansovics – RAVEL: *Concerto in G.* *

Piano concerto in A min.; Lyric pieces, Op. 12/1; Op. 43/1, 3 & 6; Op. 47/1 & 3; Op. 57/2; Op. 65/6; Op. 71/7.

(M) **(*) EMI/Phoenixa stereo/mono CDM7 63778-2; *EG 763778-4*. Richard Farrell, Hallé O, Weldon – LISZT: *Piano concerto No. 1.* ***

(i) *Piano concerto in A min.;* (ii) *Peer Gynt suites Nos. 1–2.*

(B) ** DG Compact Classics 413 158-2 (2); *413 158-4* [id.]. (i) Anda, BPO, Kubelik; (ii) Bamberg SO, Richard Kraus – SIBELIUS: *Finlandia; Karelia; Valse triste* *** (CD only: *En Saga; Legend: The Swan of Tuonela* ***).

The French pianist Pascal Devoyon is now in his thirties and has never enjoyed the recognition he so richly deserves on record. His account of the Grieg *Concerto* is characteristic of him: aristocratic without being aloof, pensive without being self-conscious, and brilliant without being flashy. He is a poetic artist whose natural musicianship shines through and this excellent account is very competitive. This is a very fine issue, with excellent playing from the LPO under Jerzy Maksymiuk.

The sensitivity of Clifford Curzon in the recording studio is never in doubt and, like the Franck coupling, his 1959 account of the Grieg *Concerto* sounds as fresh as the day it was made. The sound is bright and open and the recording hardly shows its age in this crisply focused CD transfer. Curzon's approach to Grieg is wonderfully poetic, and this is a performance with strength and power as well as lyrical tenderness. This ranks alongside Kovacevich and Perahia (both at full price), and the reading is second to none in distilling the music's special atmosphere.

Radu Lupu's recording dates from 1974 and is now even more brightly lit than it was originally, not entirely to advantage. But the performance is a fine one; there is both warmth and poetry in the slow movement; the hushed opening is particularly telling. There is a hint of calculation at the coda of the first movement; but the performance does not lack spontaneity, and the orchestral contribution under Previn is a strong one.

The famous 1947 Lipatti performance remains eternally fresh, and its return to the catalogue is a cause for rejoicing. Although the recording has greater clarity and definition, particularly at the top, put this CD alongside one of the LP transfers of the 1970s and the ear now notices a slightly drier quality and a marginal loss of bloom.

Ousset's is a strong, dramatic reading, not lacking in warmth and poetry but, paradoxically, bringing out what we would generally think of as the masculine qualities of power and drive. The result, with excellent accompaniment recorded in very full sound, is always fresh and convincing. A good choice for anyone wanting this unusual coupling with the Rachmaninov *Concerto No. 2.*

The outstanding New Zealand pianist, Richard Farrell, had his career tragically terminated at the age of thirty-two by a car accident in Sussex in 1958, not long after he had recorded this poetic account of an elusive romantic concerto of which he has the full measure. There is no lack of brilliance here, yet it is the gentle moments which one best remembers, with the most subtle tonal shading. George Weldon accompanies most sympathetically, and the recording is excellent: it does not in the least sound its age. The generous selection of *Lyric pieces* also shows Farrell's winning understanding of Grieg; if here the musical characterization is at times a shade less strong, this is still fine playing.

Entremont's, too, is a fresh, vital performance, with Ormandy as well as the soloist on top form. The orchestral opening of the slow movement is beautifully played and the piano entry is a moment of magic, while the finale is splendidly spirited. Characteristically lavish CBS/Philadelphia sound, brightly lit. Unfortunately, the Serkin Schumann coupling is very unenticing.

Fleisher is another outstanding artist, and his recordings are too little known in Europe. His performance of the Grieg ranks with the finest, combining strength with poetry in a satisfying balance. The Cleveland Orchestra gives a very positive accompaniment under Szell, with deeply expressive playing in the *Adagio*. There is plenty of sparkle in the outer movements. The recording is bold and clear – bordering on the fierce so far as the upfront orchestral presence is concerned – and tape-hiss seems more obtrusive than usual in the CD transfer.

Anda's account of the *Concerto*, offered on the DG Compact Classics issue, is more wayward than some, but it is strong in personality and has plenty of life. Kubelik's accompaniment is very good too and the early 1960s recording sounds well. A rather fuller selection from the *Peer Gynt suite No. 2* is offered on the pair of CDs. Grieg's perennially fresh incidental music is vividly played in Bamberg, but the early stereo recording here sounds a bit thin in the strings (in both formats). The Sibelius couplings, however, are first rate, with two of the performances conducted by Karajan, and excellent accounts under Okko Kamu of *En*

Saga and *The Swan of Tuonela* added to the CD programme.

John Ogdon's version is disappointing. Clearly the partnership with Berglund did not work well and the end result is dull, in spite of an often bold solo contribution and fine recording from the early 1970s, most effectively remastered.

Bolet shows little affinity with Grieg's delightful concerto. He seeks to give a spacious reading and the result is merely lethargic and heavy; even the first-movement cadenza drags. The recording is the best part of the affair – it is of Decca's finest quality.

Jenö Jandó would have been in his early twenties when he made this Hungaroton recording in 1975. Although it is not without merit, it is pretty unremarkable; the first movement is taken at a very slow tempo, the piano timbre is rather wooden and is a bit too closely balanced for comfort; and there is little freshness or sparkle. Nor does the orchestral playing rise much above the routine either.

(i; ii) *Piano concerto; Peer Gynt* (incidental music): *suites Nos.* (ii) *1, Op. 46;* (iii) *2, Op. 55.*
(BB) * LaserLight Dig. 15 617 [id.]. (i) Jenö Jandó; (ii) Budapest PO, János Sándor; (iii) VSO, Ahronovitch.

Jandó's account of the *Concerto* is bold and brilliant, missing much of its delicacy of romantic feeling, and Sándor's performance of the first *Peer Gynt suite* is rather square and unimaginative; *Anitra's dance* comes off best. Ahronovitch is much more convincing in the *Second Suite*, although he is melodramatic too, but *Solveig's song* is beautifully played. Full, brilliant, digital sound.

2 Elegiac melodies, Op. 34; Erotik; 2 Melodies, Op. 53; 2 Norwegian airs, Op. 63.
(BB) **(*) Naxos Dig. 8.550330 [id.]. Capella Istropolitana, Adrian Leaper – SIBELIUS: *Andante festivo* etc. **

The Capella Istropolitana is drawn from the Slovak Philharmonic and they prove themselves an excellent ensemble. Adrian Leaper secures responsive and sensitive playing from them in this Grieg collection and the recording is very good indeed, with the balance natural. There is the very slightest hint of glassiness from the upper strings, but not all systems would be troubled by this.

2 Elegiac melodies, Op. 34; Holberg suite, Op. 40; In Autumn (Concert overture) Op. 11; Lyric pieces: Evening in the mountains; At the cradle, Op. 68/4 & 5. Lyric suite, Op. 54; Norwegian dances, Op. 35; Peer Gynt suites Nos. 1, Op. 46; 2, Op. 55; Pictures from life in the country: Bridal procession (orch. Halvorsen), *Op. 19/3. Sigurd Jorsalfar (suite), Op. 56; Symphonic dances, Op. 64; Wedding day at Troldhaugen, Op. 65.*
(B) ** VoxBox (2) [CDX 5048]. Utah SO or CO, Maurice Abravanel.

This exceptionally generous collection (156 minutes) includes almost all Grieg's orchestral music. It is played with warmth, often with a vivid spontaneity, yet without idiosyncrasy. The *Lyric suite* is particularly memorable, as fine as any account on disc; the *Norwegian dances* too come off sparklingly, and the two evocative *Lyric pieces* are most beautifully played. The snag is that, to counter the Utah resonance, the recording engineers have put their microphones close to the violins which are thus robbed of tonal body. This is more detrimental on the first of the two discs, notably in the *Elegiac melodies* and the *Holberg suite*, both for strings alone, and in the *In Autumn concert overture* which is not very special anyway. However, the overall ambience lends colour to the wind and, although the cymbals clash very metallically, the sound otherwise is acceptable. Musically, there is much to enjoy here. This still awaits issue in the UK.

Holberg suite, Op. 40.
(B) *** Pickwick Dig. PCD 861; *CIMPC 861* [id.]. Serenata of London – ELGAR: *Serenade*; MOZART: *Eine kleine Nachtmusik.* ***

The performance by the Serenata of London is first class in every way, spontaneous, naturally paced and played with considerable eloquence. The ensemble is led by Barry Wilde, who asserts his personality much in the way Marriner did in the early days of the ASMF. The digital recording is most realistic and very naturally balanced. A bargain.

Holberg suite, Op. 40; Lyric suite, Op. 54; Sigurd Jorsalfar (suite), *Op. 56.*
(M) **(*) Ph. 432 277-2; *432 277-4.* ECO, Raymond Leppard.

Grieg's delightful *Lyric suite* is the finest of the performances here; very freshly played, it has warm, transparent string textures and the closing *March of the dwarfs* is earthily malignant. *Sigurd Jorsalfar* goes well, too: the remastering has made the recording sound more vivid and the opening *Prelude* is nicely paced. The relative disappointment here is the *Holberg suite*, in which the playing has an element of routine that is unexpected from this conductor. But the 1979 sound is very good indeed.

CHAMBER MUSIC

(i) *Violin sonata No. 3 in C min., Op. 45. Lyric*

pieces: Arietta, Op. 12/1; Berceuse, Op. 38/1; Cradle song, Op. 68/5; Little bird, Op. 43/4; Remembrances, Op. 71/7.
(BB) ** Naxos Dig. 8.550417 [id.]. (i) Takako Nishizaki; Jenö Jandó – FRANCK: *Violin sonata.* **

Takako Nishizaki and her Hungarian partner give a very spirited and vital account of the *Sonata* that is thoroughly enjoyable and very recommendable, given the modest outlay involved. Not that the resonant acoustic is ideal, for the piano tends to sound bottom-heavy and muddy in climaxes. But Jandó proves a most sensitive player in the middle movement. In the *Lyric pieces*, which are heard in transcriptions by Vladimir Godar, the balance is quite different, placing the soloist closer to the microphone.

Lyric pieces, Books 1–10 (complete).
(M) **(*) Unicorn Dig. UKCD 2033, *UKC 2033* (*1–4*); UKCD 2034, *UKC 2034* (*5–7*); UKCD 2035, *UKC 2035* (*8–10*) [id.]. Peter Katin.

Peter Katin is a persuasive and sensitive exponent of this repertoire, and he has the benefit of a recording of exceptional presence and clarity (though very occasionally it seems to harden in climaxes, when one notices that the microphone is perhaps a shade close). Katin has the measure of Grieg's sensibility and characterizes these pieces with real poetic feeling. His performances are by far the most sensitive and idiomatic survey of the complete set at present on offer.

Lyric pieces, Op. 12/1–2, 4–5, 7; Op. 38/2–7; Op. 43/2; Op. 47/1–4, 8; Op. 54/2; Op. 57/5; Op. 65/1; Op. 68/1, 3, 6; Op. 71/1–7.
(BB) ** Naxos Dig. 8.550450 [id.]. Baláza Szokolay.

Baláza Szokolay made a strong impression at the 1990 Leeds International Piano Competition where, like Louis Lortie before him, he was placed fourth. He is an imaginative and intelligent player, but the musical attractions of his recital are diminished by the close balance which he is given by the recording engineer. However, his playing has plenty of character and a good feeling for the idiom.

VOCAL MUSIC

Peer Gynt (incidental music), *Op. 23* (complete).
(M) *** Unicorn UKCD 2003/4 [id.]. Carlson, Hanssen, Björköy, Hansli, Oslo PO Ch., LSO, Dreier.

This excellent Unicorn analogue set comes from the end of the 1970s and sounds admirably fresh in its CD format, the quality not tampered with in the transfer. Per Dreier achieves very spirited results from his soloists, the Oslo Philharmonic Chorus and our own LSO, with some especially beautiful playing from the woodwind; the recording is generally first class, with a natural perspective between soloists, chorus and orchestra. The Unicorn set includes 32 numbers in all, including Robert Henrique's scoring of the *Three Norwegian dances*, following the revised version of the score Grieg prepared for the 1886 production in Copenhagen. This music, whether familiar or unfamiliar, continues to astonish by its freshness and inexhaustibility.

(i) *Peer Gynt:* extended excerpts; *Overture In Autumn, Op. 11; Symphonic dance No. 2.*
(M) *** EMI CDM7 69039-2 [id.]; *EG 769039-4.* (i) Ilse Hollweg, Beecham Ch. Soc.; RPO, Beecham.

All the single-disc compilations from *Peer Gynt* rest under the shadow of Beecham's, which is not ideal as a recording (the choral contribution lacks polish and is rather too forwardly balanced) but offers moments of magical delicacy in the orchestral playing. Beecham showed a very special feeling for this score, and to hear *Morning*, the gently textured *Anitra's dance*, or the eloquent portrayal of the *Death of Aase* under his baton is a uniquely rewarding experience. Ilse Hollweg makes an excellent soloist. The recording dates from 1957 and, like most earlier Beecham reissues, has been enhanced by the remastering process. The most delectable of the *Symphonic dances*, very beautifully played, makes an ideal encore after *Solveig's lullaby*, affectingly sung by Hollweg. The final item, the *Overture In Autumn*, not one of Grieg's finest works, is most enjoyable when Sir Thomas is so affectionately persuasive.

Peer Gynt: extended excerpts; *Sigurd Jorsalfar: suite;* (i) Songs: *Efterårsstormen; Jeg giver mit digt til våren; Og jeg vil ha mig en hjaertenskjaer; Til én Nos. 1–2.*
(B) *(**) Decca 425 512-2; *425 512-4.* LSO, Øivin Fjeldstad, (i) with Kirsten Flagstad.

Fjeldstad's wonderfully fresh *Peer Gynt* selection was one of the most beautiful records in Decca's early stereo catalogue. The digital remastering, while adding vividness, has not been beneficial to the string tone – originally radiant, now thin and edgy. Moreover, while Kirsten Flagstad's performances of the songs are very welcome, no translations or synopses are provided, and their reissue is almost pointless without them.

Peer Gynt (incidental music): *Overture; Suites 1–2. Lyric pieces: Evening in the mountain; Cra-*

dle song, Op. 68/5; Sigurd Jorsalfar: Suite, Op. 56; Wedding day at Troldhaugen, Op. 65/6.
(BB) **(*) Naxos Dig. 8.550140 [id.]. CSSR State PO, Košice, Stephen Gunzenhauser.

A generous Grieg anthology on Naxos (70 minutes, all but 3 seconds) and the performances by the Slovak State Philharmonic Orchestra in Košice (in Eastern Slovakia) are very fresh and lively and thoroughly enjoyable. There is wide dynamic range both in the playing and in the recording, and sensitivity in matters of phrasing. Their American conductor, Stephen Gunzenhauser, gets very good results and, though there may be more sumptuous recordings at full price, the sound is really very good indeed. No one investing in this need feel they are being short-changed. If it were at full price, it would still be competitive.

Peer Gynt: (i) *Suite No. 1, Op. 46;* (ii) *Suite No. 2, Op. 55.*
(M) **(*) EMI CD-EMX 2176; *TC-EMX 2176.* Bournemouth SO, Berglund – ALFVÉN: *Swedish rhapsody* **(*); JÄRNEFELT: *Praeludium.* ***
(B) ** Hung. White Label HRC 172 [id.]. (i) Debrecen PO, László Szabó; (ii) Budapest PO, Adám Medveczky – SIBELIUS: *Finlandia* etc. **

Peer Gynt: suite No. 1; suite No. 2: Ingrid's lament; Solveig's song.
(M) **(*) Decca 417 722-2 [id.]. VPO, Karajan – TCHAIKOVSKY: *Romeo and Juliet* **(*) (with R. STRAUSS: *Till Eulenspiegel* **(*)).

Peer Gynt: suites Nos. 1 & 2; Holberg suite; Sigurd Jorsalfar: suite.
(M) *** DG 419 474-2; *419 474-4* [id.]. BPO, Karajan.

Karajan's analogue set remains available on a mid-priced DG CD, where the highly expressive performances were played with superlative skill and polish. There is a touch of fierceness on the *Sigurd Jorsalfar* climaxes, but otherwise these performances are given good sound.

To offer a further choice, Decca have also reissued Karajan's Vienna recording of the *First Suite* plus two favourite items from the *Second*, which come from ten years earlier. The digital remastering is successful, the new sound-image, if not lustrously rich, is quite full and firm and with good ambient effect.

Berglund's performances are strongly characterized. *Morning* is undoubtedly fresh and *Ingrid's lament* is notably sombre. Although the orchestral playing is persuasive, there is some lack of charm here; the upper strings are made to sound unnaturally brilliant and fierce at the climax of the *Death of Aase* (something which derives from the balance of the original recording rather than the CD transfer).

While there is nothing extra special about the performance of the *First Suite* from *Peer Gynt* by the Debrecen orchestra under László Szabó, it is very decently played and well recorded too. No one buying it is likely to feel badly let down; and much the same goes for the *Second Suite*, played by the Budapest orchestra. The recording acoustic is ample without being excessively reverberant and the detail, particularly at either the top or the bass, is really very clean and present. It may not have quite the magic or character of a Beecham or a Karajan but it is more than just acceptable.

(i) *Peer Gynt: suites Nos. 1–2; Lyric suite, Op. 54; Sigurd Jorsalfar: suite.*
(M) *** DG Dig. 427 807-2; *427 807-4* [id.]. Soloists, Ch., Gothenburg SO, Järvi.

Järvi's excerpts from *Peer Gynt* and *Sigurd Jorsalfar* are extracted from his complete sets, so the editing inevitably produces a less tidy effect than normal recordings of the *Suites.* However, the performances are first class and so is the recording, and this comment applies also to the *Lyric suite*, taken from an earlier, digital orchestral collection.

Songs: *Den Saerde; En Drøm; Eros; En svane; Fra Monte Pincio; Guten; Med en primulaveris; Med en vandlilje; Millom Rosor; Modersorg; Og jeg vil ha mig en Hjertenskjaer; Prinsessen; Tak for dit Räd; Våren; Ved Rundarne. Peer Gynt: Solveigs song.*
(M) (***) EMI mono CDH7 63305-2 (with songs by Hurum; Lie; Alnaes; Bull; Grøndahl; Sinding). Kirsten Flagstad, Philh. O, Braithwaite; Susskind; Moore McArthur; Alnaes.

What an extraordinary and glorious sound Flagstad produced! These inimitable performances come from 1948, when her voice was in its prime, and remain unsurpassed. (Her later Grieg recitals, recorded for Decca in the 1950s, wonderful though they were, found the voice past its peak.) Her masterly pacing, sense of vocal colour and command of atmosphere in this repertoire are flawless. The recital includes 16 of Grieg's best-known songs and a handful of other Norwegian songs recorded in Oslo in 1929 (the earliest are songs by Sinding and Backer-Grøndahl, recorded in 1923). No collector of Grieg's music or of fine singing should overlook this compilation.

(i) *Sigurd Jorsalfar, Op. 22:* incidental music; *Funeral march in memory of Rikard Nordraak* (orch. Halvorsen); (i) *The Mountain spell, Op. 32.*

(M) *** Unicorn UKCD 2019. (i) Kåre Björköy; Oslo Philharmonic Ch., LSO, Per Dreier.

Grieg composed his incidental music for *Sigurd Jorsalfar* (*Sigurd the Crusader*) in 1872 for a production of Björnson's historical drama in Christiania (as Oslo was then known), though neither he nor the dramatist was particularly satisfied with it. The score comprised five movements in all, from which Grieg drew the familiar suite; but there were additional sections as well, most importantly the moving *Funeral march in memory of Nordraak* which is given here in Halvorsen's orchestral transcription. Even though it does not claim to be a first recording, *Den Bergtekne* (*The Mountain spell*) for baritone, strings and two horns is something of a rarity. *The Mountain spell* (or 'thrall', as it is sometimes translated) is somewhat later than *Sigurd Jorsalfar* and was one of Grieg's favourite pieces. It is a song of great beauty, and is alone worth the price of the CD. The Oslo Philharmonic Choir give a spirited account of themselves, as do the LSO, who play sensitively for Per Dreier. Kåre Björköy is an excellent soloist with well-focused tone. The recording is very good indeed and the perspective is agreeably natural.

Grofé, Ferde (1892–1972)

Grand Canyon suite.

(M) *** Decca 430 712-2; *430 712-4* [id.]. Detroit SO, Dorati – GERSHWIN: *Porgy and Bess.* ***

(B) ** CfP CD-CFP 4583; *TC-CFP 4583.* Utah SO, Maurice Abravanel – COPLAND: *El Salón México.* **

Antal Dorati has the advantage of superlative Decca recording, very much in the demonstration class, with stereoscopically vivid detail. Yet the performance combines subtlety with spectacle, and on CD the naturalness of the orchestral sound-picture adds to the sense of spaciousness and tangibility. With its outstanding coupling, and its price advantage, this version is very much in a class of its own.

The Utah orchestra under Abravanel also provide an attractive account of Grofé's picaresque score, making the most of its melodic content and finding plenty of colour and warmth in its pictorialism. *On the trail* is wittily and affectionately done and, in spite of rather primitive storm effects, *Cloudburst* is rather telling. The analogue recording has been effectively remastered. With only *El Salón México* offered as a coupling, however, it is ungenerous.

Halvorsen, Johan (1864–1935)

Air Norvégien, Op. 7; Danses Norvégiennes.

(BB) *** Naxos Dig. 8.550329 [id.]. Dong-Suk Kang, Slovak (Bratislava) RSO, Adrian Leaper – SIBELIUS: *Violin concerto*; SINDING: *Légende*; SVENDSEN: *Romance.* ***

Dong-Suk Kang plays the attractive *Danses Norvégiennes* with great panache, character and effortless virtuosity, and delivers an equally impeccable performance of the earlier *Air Norvégien.*

Handel, George Frideric (1685–1759)

Ballet music: *Alcina: overture; Acts I & III: suites. Il pastor fido: suite. Terpsichore: suite.*

(M) *** Erato/Warner Dig. 2292 45378-2 [id.]. E. Bar. Soloists, Gardiner.

As so often in the history of staged dance music, Handel wrote his ballet music for a specific dancer, in this case Marie Sallé, and her special skills demanded a high proportion of lyrical music. Handel rose to the challenge: the expressive writing here is very appealing; so is the scoring with its felicitous use of recorders. John Eliot Gardiner is just the man for such a programme. He is not afraid to charm the ear, yet allegros are vigorous and rhythmically infectious. The bright and clean recorded sound adds to the sparkle, and the quality is first class. A delightful collection, and very tuneful too.

Amaryllis (suite); *The Faithful shepherd* (suite); *The Gods go a'begging* (suite; all. arr. Beecham); *Handel at Bath* (suite, arr. Bennett); *Music for the Royal Fireworks; Water music:* suite (both arr. Baines); *Overture in D min.* (arr. Elgar); *Solomon: Arrival of the Queen of Sheba.*

(M) ** RPO/Pickwick CDRPO 9004 (2). RPO, Sir Yehudi Menuhin.

Menuhin's performances of the famous Beecham arrangements have neither the charisma nor the charm of Sir Thomas's own versions, although they are played warmly and vigorously (perhaps at times too assertively) by his old orchestra, helped by full and well-balanced digital recording. The *Fireworks* and *Water music* come in arrangements by Anthony Baines; the former, both grand and elegant, is the most sucessful performance here. Allan Bennett's *Handel at Bath* draws on the keyboard suites quite effectively and, like Beecham, he scores for a modern orchestra. Overall this is an agreeable but not a distinctive collection.

Amaryllis (suite): *Gavotte; Scherzo. The Gods go a-begging* (ballet): suite. *The Great elopement: Serenade.* (i) *Love in Bath* (complete).
(M) *** EMI CDM7 63374-2; *EG 763374-4*.
RPO, Sir Thomas Beecham, (i) with Ilse Hollweg.

This delightful CD collects together many of Beecham's most famous Handel arrangements and – unless you are an out-and-out purist – the result is irresistible. One must remember that in Beecham's time little of this music was often (if at all) heard in its original format. The new name, *Love in Bath*, in fact conceals the identity of Beecham's intended ballet, *The Great elopement*. It never received a stage performance, although Beecham recorded a suite under this title, from which the *Serenade*, an aria from *Il pastor fido* (*Un sospiretto d'un labro pallido*), is presented in its purely orchestral form as an appendix. In the (virtually complete) version of *Love in Bath* it is charmingly sung by Ilse Hollweg. The score also includes a *Rondeau* purloined from yet another Handel suite, while the introduction of the famous *Largo* in the finale, floating serenely over a rhythmically busy accompaniment, is an inspired highlight. The earlier ballet, *The Gods go a-begging*, was produced for the stage with choreography by Balanchine, and nine of its eleven numbers are included here; its delectable woodwind scoring is a special feature. Needless to say, the Royal Philharmonic play like angels – if occasionally not perfectly disciplined angels! – and the originally mellow sound has been freshly remastered with great skill: there is greater transparency and little loss of bloom.

Concerto grosso in C (Alexander's Feast); Oboe concertos Nos. 1–2; Organ concerto in D min.; Sonata a 5 in B flat.
(M) **(*) Teldec/Warner 2292 43032-2 [id.].
Schaeftlein, Tachezi, VCM, Harnoncourt.

There is nothing wrong with Harnoncourt's collection, dating from 1974, especially now it is available at mid-price. Jurg Schaeftlein is a fine oboist, but he omits the third concerto (HWV 287) in favour of Herbert Tachezi's spirited performance of a fairly attractive hybrid organ concerto, based on a sonata from the first set of Telemann's *Tafelmusik*. Alice Harnoncourt is the third soloist in the *Sonata a 5*. Good performances, all well recorded and cleanly transferred to CD.

Concerti grossi, Op. 3/1–6.
(M) *** Ph. 422 487-2; *422 487-4*. ECO, Leppard.
(BB) **(*) ASV CDQS 6024; *ZCQS 6024*. N. Sinfonia, Malcolm.

Concerti grossi, Op. 3/1–6; Overtures: Alcina; Ariodante.
(M) *** Decca 430 261-2; *430 261-4* [id.].
ASMF, Sir Neville Marriner.

Marriner's earlier (1964) Argo set, now reappearing on Decca's Serenata label, remains fully competitive (irrespective of price) for musical scholarship and, what is even more to the point, for musical expressiveness and spontaneity. Flutes and oboes are employed as Handel intended and the final concerto features the organ as a solo instrument, very much conjuring up the composer's spirit hovering in the background. The ASMF was in peak form when this recording was made and the sound is very well balanced and vivid. The two overtures, recorded a decade later, make an acceptable bonus.

Among budget versions of Handel's Op. 3, Leppard's set also stands high. The playing is lively and fresh, and the remastered recording sounds very good. Leppard includes oboes and bassoons and secures excellent playing all round. At times one wonders whether he isn't just a shade too elegant, but in general this CD offers one of the best versions of Op. 3 on modern instruments.

George Malcolm's performances are infectiously spirited and stylish, though rhythms are sometimes jogging rather than sprightly. The recording is strikingly vivid in its CD transfer, but the forward balance reduces the dynamic range, though the contrasts of light and shade within the strings are effective; and in the lowest price range this is excellent value.

12 Concerti grossi, Op. 6/1–12.
(M) **(*) Ph. 426 465-2; *426 465-4* (3). ECO, Leppard.
(M) ** DG 435 041-2 (2). BPO, Karajan.
(B) ** VoxBox (3) [CD3X 3005]. SW German CO, Pforzheim, Paul Angerer.

Leppard's 1967 set sounds splendid in its newly remastered format, not in the least dated. The main group is comparatively full-bodied, which means that his soloists stand out in greater relief. There is grace and elegance here, but rather less gravitas than with Iona Brown and the ASMF (at full price). These performances, too, have plenty of spirit and lively rhythmic feeling, while the richer orchestral texture brings added breadth in slow movements. With the sound newly minted, this is excellent value at mid-price, though Leslie Pearson's harpsichord continuo is dwarfed by the tuttis.

Karajan's set was recorded between between 1966 and 1968, and this is the first time all the performances have appeared together. Although there are minor differences between them – for instance the conductor himself plays the harpsichord continuo in Nos. 1, 5, 8 and 10–12 – the reverberant acoustic and the use of a fairly large string group ensure that these are of little moment. Karajan obviously cares about the music, but the sounds he creates are too sumptuous to suggest a truly Handelian texture. The playing is superb and the nobility and breadth of the writing are not missed but, despite considerable use of contrast, the true baroque spirit becomes submerged.

As the very opening suggests, the Vox performances are in the older German style and, although rhythms are often quite buoyant and the fugal movements bring contrapuntal detail that is graceful as well as clear, the conductor's tempi are at times rather easy-going; this effect is amplified by tuttis which are richly upholstered by the resonance. Though the playing does not match the BPO in finesse, it is polished and always warm. The recording balance brings a fuller sound than the remastered DG set, with both the solo group and the ripieno placed fairly forward, which also brings a reduction in dynamic range. But the players obviously enjoy the music and, if the effect is heavy at times, the expressive grandeur of Handel's Larghettos is certainly not lost, while in a movement like the *Air*, (*Lentemente*) from Op. 6/10, the hint of melancholy in the playing is touching. In short, though by no means a first choice, these inexpensive discs give pleasure, and the performance certainly makes plain that Handel's Op. 6 is a masterpiece of the highest order.

Concerti grossi, Op. 6/4–6; Concerto grosso, Op. 3/3.
(BB) * Naxos Dig. 8.550157 [id.]. Capella Istropolitana, Jozef Kopelman.

Concerti grossi, Op. 6/8, 10 & 12; in C (Alexander's Feast).
(BB) * Naxos Dig. 8.550158 [id.]. Capella Istropolitana, Jozef Kopelman.

As we know from their recordings of Bach, Haydn and Mozart, the Capella Istropolitana is an excellent group; their playing here is warm and polished, and the Naxos recording is flattering. But Jozef Kopelman's rhythmic manner is too easy-going – one needs more bite at the opening of Op. 6/5, and slow movements are often rather lazily expressive and almost bland.

Concerti grossi, Op. 6/4, 6, 9 & 11.
(B) ** Hung. White Label HRC 133 [id.]. Liszt CO, Rolla.

These performances use a double continuo but, while the organ increases the sonority of the ripieno, the harpsichord contribution is barely audible. Nevertheless the playing, both of soloists and of the main group, is attractively warm, alive and sympathetic and has plenty of personality. Those looking for a bargain sampler of Op. 6 will not be disappointed by the recording quality, which is resonantly full and firmly focused.

Harp concerto in B flat, Op. 4/5.
(B) *** DG 427 206-2. Zabaleta, Paul Kuentz CO – MOZART: *Flute and harp concerto*; WAGENSEIL: *Harp concerto*. ***

The DG recording sounds clear and immediate and the crystalline stream of sound is attractive. Zabaleta's approach is agreeably cool, with imaginative use of light and shade. The Privilege reissue also includes a set of variations by Spohr.

(i) *Harp concerto, Op. 4/6. Variations for harp.*
❀ (M) *** Decca 425 723-2; *425 723-4*. Marisa Robles, (i) ASMF, Iona Brown – BOIELDIEU; DITTERSDORF: *Harp concertos* etc. *** ❀

Handel's Op. 4/6 is well known in both organ and harp versions. Marisa Robles and Iona Brown make an unforgettable case for the latter by creating the most delightful textures, while never letting the work sound insubstantial. The ASMF accompaniment, so stylish and beautifully balanced, is a treat in itself, and the recording is well-nigh perfect. This collection (which also includes solo harp variations by Beethoven and a set attributed to Mozart) amounts to a good deal more than the sum of its parts.

Oboe concertos Nos 1–3, HWV 301, 302a & 287; Concerto grosso, Op. 3/3; Hornpipe in D, HWV 356; Overture in D, HWV 337/8; Sonata a 5 in B flat, HWV 288.
(M) **(*) Ph. 426 082-2; *426 082-4* [id.]. Heinz Holliger, ECO, Raymond Leppard.

Holliger, being a creative artist as well as a masterly interpreter, does not hesitate to embellish repeats; his ornamentation may overstep the boundaries some listeners are prepared to accept. His playing and that of the other artists in this collection is exquisite, and the recording is naturally balanced and fresh.

Organ concertos, Op. 4/1–6; in F (The cuckoo and the nightingale), HVW 295; in A, HWV 296; Sonata in D min. (Il trionfo del tempo a del disinganno), HWV 46a.
(M) *** Decca Dig. 430 569-2 (2). Peter Hurford, Concg. CO, Joshua Rifkin.

Peter Hurford's 1985 Decca set features the organ of Bethlehemkerk, Papendrecht, Holland, which has attractively fresh and bright registrations, particularly suited to the Op. 4 set. The highly engaging *Cuckoo and the nightingale concerto* is particularly successful – here Hurford interpolates a Telemann movement instead of improvising, as the composer would have done. The *Sonata* is also attractive and, with splendid recording, fresh and yet not lacking weight where needed, this is very enjoyable indeed. The sound is in the demonstration bracket, and this is highly recommendable.

Organ concertos, Op. 4/1 & 2; Op. 7/1 & 2.
(M) ** Teldec/Warner 2292 43434-2 [id.]. Karl Richter with CO.

Organ concertos, Op. 4/3 & 4; Op. 7/3 & 4.
(M) *** Teldec/Warner 2292 43540-2 [id.]. Karl Richter with CO.

Organ concertos, Op. 4/5 & 6; Op. 7/5 & 6.
(M) *** Teldec/Warner 2292 42412-2 [id.]. Karl Richter with CO.

These Teldec recordings come from a complete set which Karl Richter recorded in 1959. The sound is surprisingly undated and the performances have the merit of exactly the right kind of organ (St Mark's, Munich) and a small, flexible orchestral group which Richter directs from the keyboard. The element of extemporization is a limited feature, at first, especially in Op. 4; but later, in Op. 7, organ *ad libs* are effectively included. Throughout, the playing is attractively buoyant; the full sound of the strings, contrasted with imaginative registration, makes this series increasingly attractive. The second and third discs can be recommended strongly, and overall the set is excellent value.

Organ concertos, Op. 4/1 & 5; in F (Cuckoo and the nightingale); in A, HWV 296.
(M) ** EMI CD-EMX 2115; *TC-EMX 2115*. Simon Preston, Bath Festival O, Y. Menuhin.

In this EMI reissue from the late 1960s, Simon Preston uses the organ in Merchant Taylors Hall, London, and is partnered by Menuhin. They use the Neville Boyling edition and, though there are minor criticisms to be made of tempi and phrasing, on the whole these are enjoyably lively accounts. The CD transfer is very brightly lit.

Organ concertos, Op. 4/2; Op. 7/3–5; in F (Cuckoo and the nightingale).
(M) *** DG Dig. 431 708-2; *431 708-4* [id.]. Simon Preston, E. Concert, Pinnock.

This is more generous than the previous (full-price) sampler from Preston's series with Pinnock; all the Op. 7 works plus the *Cuckoo and the nightingale* are recorded on the organ at St John's, Armitage, in Staffordshire, which seems particularly well suited to this repertoire. Both performances and sound are admirably fresh.

Organ concertos, Op. 4/2, 4 & 5; Op. 7/1; in F (Cuckoo and the nightingale).
(BB) ** Naxos Dig. 8.550069 [id.]. Johann Aratore, Handel Festival CO, John Tingle.

Brisk tempi and a crisply robust (unidentified) organ image, placed forwardly, ensure that these performances project with plenty of life. The orchestral support is polished, rhythmically strong and sympathetic in slow movements. The digital recording is bright and faithful; but there is a hint of relentlessness at times.

Organ concertos, Op. 7/1–6; in D min., HWV 304; in F, HWV 305 & Appendix.
(M) *** Decca Dig. 433 176-2 (2). Peter Hurford, Concg. CO, Rifkin.

Peter Hurford's Op. 7 set has comparable sparkle, if not being quite as memorable as Op. 4. The effect (especially of the first four concertos) seems a little lightweight. But the digital recording is first class and the considerable bonuses are well worth having. Excellent value.

Overtures: Admeto; Alcina; Ariodante; Esther; Lotario; Orlando; Ottone; Partenope; (i) *Il pastor fido; Poro.*
(M) *** Ph. 422 486-2. ECO or (i) New Philh. O, Leppard.

Characteristically elegant performances from Leppard, richly recorded. The orchestral playing is gracious and polished, and the recording is bright and well balanced. The reissue includes two extra overtures, *Il pastor fido* and *Ariodante* (taken from the complete set), not included on the original LP. There is some fine music here: Handel's overtures are consistently tuneful and inventive and, at budget price, this disc is well worth exploring.

Music for the Royal Fireworks; Concerto grosso in C (Alexander's Feast); Concerti grossi, Op. 6/1 & 6.
(M) *** DG 431 707-2; *431 707-4*. E. Concert, Trevor Pinnock.

Pinnock's performance of the *Fireworks music* has tremendous zest; this is not only the safest but the best recommendation for those wanting a period-instrument version. The DG recording is outstanding in its combination of brightness and colour, and it certainly does not lack weight. The account of the *Alexander's Feast concerto* has both vitality and imagination and is no less recommendable; for those who already have a complete set of Op. 6, yet who want to experience Pinnock's way with this music, the disc proves a useful sampler. The performances have admirable lightness and an infectious spirit but have less of a sense of grandeur. Excellently balanced and truthful recording.

Music for the Royal Fireworks; Water music (complete).
(BB) *** Naxos Dig. 8.550109 [id.]. Capella Istropolitana, Bohdan Warchal.
(M) **(*) Decca Dig. 417-743-2 [id.]. Stuttgart CO, Münchinger.
(M) ** Decca 430 717-2; *430 717-4*. Concg. CO, Simon Preston.

Music for the Royal Fireworks; Water music: extended suite.
(M) **(*) Ph. 420 354-2; *420 354-4* [id.]. ECO, Leppard.

Music for the Royal Fireworks: suite; Water music; suite (arr. Harty and Szell); *The Faithful shepherd: Minuet* (ed. Beecham); *Xerxes: Largo* (arr. Reinhardt).
(B) *** Decca 417 694-2; *417 694-4*. LSO, Szell.

Bohdan Warchal directs the Capella Istropolitana in bright and lively performances of the complete *Water music* as well as the *Fireworks music*, well paced and well scaled, with woodwind and brass aptly abrasive, and with such points as double-dotting faithfully observed. Textures are clean, with an attractive bloom on the full and immediate sound. As always with Naxos – but not with all bargain labels – first-rate notes are provided; but the listing of movements fails to distinguish the three separate *Water music* suites, the more confusing in the later movements, when titling follows the old Chrysander score and not what has become common practice. However, this remains a strong bargain recommendation.

Münchinger's coupling of the complete *Water* and *Fireworks music* has first-class 1982 digital recording: the effect is vivid and well focused. His style is a compromise between authenticity and the German tradition. Some other versions of this music are more buoyant, but Münchinger is consistently sympathetic and never dull. With the additional advantage of economy, this is well worth considering.

Leppard's mid-priced Philips reissue also offers an excellent coupling. The remastering is very successful and the resonance of the sound in the *Fireworks music* matches the broad and spectacular reading, while the substantial extract from Leppard's complete *Water music* recording has comparable flair, combining rhythmic resilience with an apt feeling for ceremony. However, with other versions absolutely complete, this Philips disc now seems less competitive.

Although the very opening of the *Water music* could have a stronger rhythmic profile, on the whole both of Handel's great sets of occasional pieces are given alert performances by Simon Preston and the Concertgebouw Chamber Orchestra, while the boisterous horns and the bright, clean string textures readily show influences from the authentic school. So, too, does the performance of the famous *Air*, which lacks charm. In the last resort the effect here is too briskly stylish; there is no sense of glee in Handel's profusion of colourful melody. Excellent, modern, digital sound, and no doubt many will find the energy of the music-making stimulating.

Many readers will, like us, have a nostalgic feeling for the Handel–Harty suites from which earlier generations got to know these two marvellous scores. George Szell and the LSO offer a highly recommendable coupling of them on a Decca lower-mid-priced issue, with Handel's *Largo* and the *Minuet* from Beecham's *Faithful shepherd suite* thrown in for good measure. The orchestral playing throughout is quite outstanding, and the strings are wonderfully expressive in the slower pieces. The horns excel, and the crisp new Decca re-transfer makes for a good bargain.

(i) *Music for the Royal Fireworks; Water music* (both complete); (ii) *Harp concerto, Op. 4/6;* (iii) *Messiah: Sinfonia* (CD only: (iv) *Organ concerto in F, Op. 4/4*).
(B) **(*) DG Compact Classics 413 148-2 (2); *** *413 148-4*. (i) BPO, Kubelik; (ii) Zabaleta, Kuentz CO, Kuentz; (iii) LPO, Karl Richter (CD only: (iv) Michael Schneider, Bav. RSO, Jochum).

Kubelik's full-orchestral version of the complete *Water music* has been freshly remastered and combines a sense of grandeur and genuine Baroque feeling with liveliness. It is splendidly played, as is the *Fireworks music*, where the focus of the sound is slightly less clean. Zabaleta's approach to the *Harp concerto* is as cool as a spring stream and eminently musical, while the sound-balance is excellent. At bargain price this Compact Classics tape is good value. The pair of CDs includes also a lively account of the *Organ concerto in F*, Op. 4/4, not a particularly substantial bonus.

Water music: Suites Nos. 1–3 (complete).
(B) *(*) Hung. White Label HRC 178 [id.]. Liszt CO, Budapest, Frigyes Sándor.

Water music: Suites Nos. 1–3 (complete); *Solomon: Arrival of the Queen of Sheba. Ode for St Cecilia's Day: Minuet.*
(BB) ** LaserLight Dig.15 607 [id.]. Budapest Strings, Bela Banfalvi.

The Budapest Strings carry a wind contingent too, and – if the overture could be rhythmically more telling – on the whole the playing is quite fresh, though this is a case where the absence of a conductor has brought a somewhat anonymous impression. However, the recording is vivid and, with the attractive encores at the end also nicely done, this is fair value.

The Hungaroton White Label recording offers certain felicities. Some of the movements are played with grace and warmth but others are just a shade stolid. The recording, though perfectly acceptable and better than some, is not better than most. And the same applies to the performances, better than some but not special enough to be among the first recommendations.

CHAMBER MUSIC

Flute sonatas, Op. 1/1b, 5, 6, 8 & 9; & in D. Oboe sonatas Op. 1/8; in B flat (Fitzwilliam); & in F min.
(M) *** HM/BMG Dig. GD 77152 [77152-2-RG]. Camerata Köln.

Recorder sonatas, Op. 1/2, 4, 7 & 11; Recorder sonatas in B flat; in D; in G (Fitzwilliam); Trio sonata in F.
(M) *** HM/BMG Dig. GD 77104 [77104-2-RG]. Camerata Köln.

These two CDs by the Camerata Köln playing on period instruments give very satisfying accounts of this repertoire. What accomplished players they are! Michael Schneider in the recorder sonatas, Karl Keiser in those for transverse flute and Hans-Peter Westermann in the oboe sonatas: all play with artistry and sensitivity. The first disc is intelligently planned to give maximum variety of texture. The programme includes everything except Op. 1, No. 1a, an arrangement – not by Handel himself – of No. 1b. The accompanying notes give a lucid presentation of the state of scholarship concerning these sonatas, the various arrangements used, and the reasoning for adopting the chosen course in each work. Not only is the playing rewarding, but the quality of the 1985 sound has exemplary clarity, yet warmth too.

Harpsichord suites Nos. 1–8.
(M) *** DG 427 170-2 (2). Colin Tilney (harpsichord).

Colin Tilney plays two fine period instruments from Hamburg (both pictured in the accompanying booklet). The 1728 Zell (used for *Suites 1, 3, 6* and *7*) has two manuals and is gloriously decorated with nature paintings and subjects from ancient mythology. It must be one of the most beautiful restored harpsichords in existence. The 1710 Fleischer – the oldest surviving harpsichord known to have been made in Hamburg – is played in *Suites 2, 4, 5* (with its famous *Harmonious blacksmith* variations) and *8*; it has only one manual and its elegant design follows English models. Both suit this repertoire extremely well and there are subtle and occasionally striking differences in colour and resonance between the two instruments. One has to be a little careful with the volume control but both instruments are recorded within a proper ambience, and a most vivid and truthful image can be obtained. Tilney has a fine technique and a firm rhythmic grip and he shows awareness of stylistic problems (he plays the *Allemande* in the *A major Suite* in the French way), even if there are inconsistencies with double-dotting. His approach is direct and thoughtful, not inflexible, and at times has almost a rhapsodic element, as at the improvisatory flourish which forms the *Prelude* of the *Third Suite in D minor*. Altogether this playing has much to commend it in its vitality and consistency of style.

Harpsichord suites Nos. 1–5.
(BB) ** Naxos Dig. 8.550415 [id.]. Alan Cuckson (harpsichord).

Harpsichord suites Nos. 6–8; 2nd Collection: *Suite No. 4. Air and variations; Sonatina in D min.; Sonata in G min.; Toccata in G min.*
(BB) ** Naxos Dig. 8.550416 [id.]. Alan Cuckson (harpsichord).

Were Alan Cuckson less closely recorded, his Naxos set would deserve a higher star rating, but after a time the effect is just a little oppressive. The performances have undoubted qualities, but the playing is at times a little too judicious to be wholly persuasive. There are some minor fluffs and fingerslips here and there (in the *Capriccio in F major*, for example) which should have been corrected, and some inelegances elsewhere.

COLLECTIONS

(i) *Oboe concerto No. 1 in B flat;* (ii) *Organ concerto, Op. 7/1. Rodrigo: suite;* (iii) *Xerxes (Serse): suite.*
(M) ** EMI CDM7 63956-2 [id.]; *EG 763956-4.* (i) Rothwell; (ii) Chadwick; (iii) Lewis, Hallé O, Barbirolli (with PURCELL: *Suite for strings* **).

This collection is well recorded and Barbirolli's directing hand ensures that all the music is alive. The snag is the question of style, over which Barbirolli seems to have managed a not entirely happy compromise. He uses a fairly large modern orchestral group and includes a harpsichord to be on the safe side. *Ombra mai fù* therefore opens with a richly phrased orchestral ritornello, and, when Richard Lewis begins to sing, his purity of style is a little disconcerting. But Sir John plays both the orchestral suites with vigour, and some of this music is the kind that enjoys enthusiasm and warmth every bit as much as scholarship. Lady Barbirolli's playing is, as ever, delightful; if the effect of the *Organ concerto* is somewhat pontificatory, the grandeur of the piece comes over too. Sir John makes a good deal of the ground bass (a little like the last movement of the *Eroica Symphony*) which links and permeates the work's first two movements. With all one's reservations, this disc is full of personality. The sound is good, with an exciting dynamic range in the *Organ concerto*. The additional Purcell suite is also very welcome, arranged by Barbirolli from movements derived from various stage works. Incidentally, although described as being for strings, there is a demure flute solo in the Minuet from *The Virtuous Wife*.

VOCAL AND CHORAL MUSIC

(i) *Coronation anthems;* (ii) *Chandos anthem No. 9: O praise the Lord.*
(M) *** Decca 421 150-2. (i) King's College Ch., Willcocks; (ii) with E. Vaughan, A. Young, Forbes Robinson; ASMF, Willcocks.

(i) *Coronation anthems;* (ii) *Dixit Dominus.*
(M) ** EMI CDM7 69753-2. (i) King's College Ch., ECO, Ledger; (ii) Zylis-Gara, J. Baker, Lane, Tear, Shirley-Quirk, King's College Ch., Willcocks.

The reissued 1961 Argo recording of these four anthems, of which *Zadok the Priest* is the most famous, makes an admirable mid-priced recommendation, particularly as the extra clarity and presence given to the choir improve the balance in relation to the orchestra. The *Chandos anthem* makes a fine bonus.

On EMI Ledger directs a reading of the *Coronation anthems* which favours measured speeds. Though the choir is small, the recording balance in excellent digital sound has the voices standing out clearly to reinforce the weight of the reading. The use of a modern string sound also increases this effect. The inclusion of *Dixit Dominus* is generous, but this performance is rather less successful. The intonation of the soloists is not above reproach and the trio, *Dominus a dextris*, is not very comfortable. Vigour and enthusiasm are here, but not always the last degree of finesse.

Israel in Egypt (oratorio).
(M) **(*) DG 429 530-2 (2) [id.]. Harper, Clark, Esswood, Young, Rippon, Keyte, Leeds Festival Ch., ECO, Mackerras.

Mackerras's performance represents a dichotomy of styles, using the English Chamber Orchestra, sounding crisp, stylish and lightweight in the opening overture (borrowed from *Solomon*) and the full texture of the fairly large amateur choir, impressively weighty rather than incisive, but given strong projection on CD. Thus the work makes its effect by breadth and grandiloquence rather than athletic vigour. The recording balance also reflects the problems of the basic set-up, with the chorus sometimes virtually drowned by the orchestra in the epic pieces, and then suddenly coming to the fore for the lighter moments of the score. The solo singing is distinguished, but its style is refined rather than earthy – thus again contrasting with the choral manner (although this contrast is not unfamiliar in the English tradition of live performance) and it is the choruses which are the glory of this oratorio.

Lucrezia (cantata). Arias: *Ariodante: Oh, felice mio core . . . Con l'ali do constanza; E vivo ancore? . . . Scherza infida in grembo al drudo; Dopo notte. Atalanta: Care selve. Hercules: Where shall I fly? Joshua: O had I Jubal's lyre. Rodelinda: Pompe vane di morte! . . . Dove sei, amato bene? Serse: Frondi tenere e belle . . . Ombra mai fù (Largo).*
(M) *** Ph. 426 450-2; *426 450-4*. Dame Janet Baker, ECO, Leppard.

Even among Dame Janet's most impressive records this Handel recital marks a special contribution, ranging as it does from the pure gravity of *Ombra mai fù* to the passionate virtuosity in *Dopo notte* from *Ariodante*. Two extra items have been added to the original, 1972 selection. Leppard gives sparkling support and the whole is recorded with natural and refined balance. An outstanding disc, with admirable documentation.

Messiah (complete).
(M) *** Ph. 420 865-2; *420 865-4* (2) [id.]. Harper, Watts, Wakefield, Shirley-Quirk, LSO Ch., LSO, C. Davis.
(B) *** EMI CZS7 62748-2 (2) [Ang. CDMB 62748]. Harwood, J. Baker, Esswood, Tear, Herincx, Amb. S., ECO, Mackerras.
(M) *** Erato/Warner 2292 45447-2 (2) [id.]. Palmer, Watts, Davies, Shirley-Quirk, ECO Ch., ECO, Leppard.
(B) **(*) CfP CD-CFPD 4718; *TC-CFPD 4718* (2) [id.]. Morison, Thomas, Lewis, Milligan, Huddersfield Ch. Soc., Royal Liverpool PO, Sargent.
(M) **(*) Van. 08.4019.72 [OVC 4018/19]. M. Price, Minton, A. Young, Amor Artis Chorale, ECO, Somary.
(M) ** Decca 421 234-2 (2) [id.]. Ameling, Reynolds, Langridge, Howell, Ch. & ASMF, Marriner.
(M) *(*) EMI CMS7 63621-2 (3) [Ang. CDMC 63261]. Schwarzkopf, Hoffman, Gedda, Hines, Philh. Ch. & O, Klemperer.
(M) * Eurodisc/BMG GD 69088; *GK 69088* (2).

(Sung in German) Bjoner, Töpper, Traxel, Engen, St Hedwig's Cathedral Ch., Berlin SO, Karl Forster.

(i) Messiah (complete); Arias from: (ii) *Jephtha; Judas Maccabaeus;* (iii) *Samson.*
(M) ** Decca 433 003-2 (3) [id.]. (i) Sutherland, Bumbry, McKellar, Ward, LSO Ch., LSO, Boult; (ii) McKellar; (iii) Sutherland.

The Philips LSO recording conducted by Sir Colin Davis has not lost its impact and sounds brightly lit and fresh in its digitally remastered format. Textures are beautifully clear and, thanks to Davis, the rhythmic bounce of such choruses as *For unto us* is really infectious. Even *Hallelujah* loses little and gains much from being performed by a chorus of this size. Excellent singing from all four soloists, particularly Helen Watts who, following early precedent, is given *For He is like a refiner's fire* to sing, instead of the bass, and produces a glorious chest register. The performance is absolutely complete and is excellent value at mid-price.

The EMI/Mackerras set was first issued in 1967, just a few months after the Davis set. It provided a comparable new look, but also a clear alternative in its approach. The choruses on EMI have not quite the same zest as on Philips, but they have a compensating breadth and body. More than Davis, Mackerras adopted Handel's alternative versions, so the soprano aria *Rejoice greatly* is given in its optional 12/8 version, with compound time adding a skip to the rhythm. A male alto is also included – Paul Esswood, who was already making his mark in the Teldec series of Bach cantatas – and he is given some of the bass arias as well as some of the regular alto passages. Among the soloists, Dame Janet Baker is outstanding. Her intense, slow account of *He was despised* – with decorations on the reprise – is sung with profound feeling. Like Davis, Mackerras includes all the numbers traditionally omitted. The recording is warm and full in ambience and, with the added brightness of CD, sounds extremely vivid. It is offered as part of EMI's 'two for the price of one' 'Rouge et Noir' series.

Raymond Leppard presents a fine, enjoyable account of *Messiah*, which lies somewhere between Sir Colin Davis's earlier Philips set and the Mackerras EMI version. His tempi, unlike Davis's, are never exaggeratedly fast and his ornamentation is less fancy than Mackerras's on EMI. The closest Leppard comes to eccentricity is in his tempo for *The trumpet shall sound*, very fast indeed, like Davis's with the same baritone; *All we like sheep*, preceded by a delightful flourish from the organ, is even jauntier than Davis's account. Leppard has the same contralto, Helen Watts, as well as the same bass and, if anything, both are in finer form. Felicity Palmer is fresher-toned than she sometimes is on record, while Ryland Davies sings brightly and cleanly. The chorus is admirably resilient and luminous; although the acoustics of St Giles, Cripplegate, prevent an absolutely sharp focus, the fine 1976 Erato recording is obviously fuller and more modern than either the Davis/Philips or Mackerras/EMI sets.

It is good to have Sir Malcolm Sargent's 1959 recording now restored to the catalogue in full for, apart from the pleasure given by a performance that brings out the breadth of Handel's inspiration, it provides an important corrective to misconceptions about pre-authentic practice. Sargent writes a forthright note in which he is quite scathing about scholarly authenticity: he has no time for keyboard recitatives, and he is quite sure that Handel would have preferred to use large forces had he been able to get them. Sargent unashamedly fills out the orchestration (favouring Mozart's scoring where possible). By the side of Davis, his tempi are measured, but his pacing is sure and spontaneous and, with a hundred-strong Huddersfield group, no one will be disappointed with the weight or vigour of the choruses. There is some splendid singing from all four soloists, and Marjorie Thomas's *He was despised* is memorable in its moving simplicity. The success of the CD transfer is remarkable: the old analogue LPs never sounded as clear as this. At bargain price – though with traditional cuts – this is well worth sampling.

Johannes Somary directs a crisp, small-scale performance, yet one that does not lack expansive qualities and features sparkling orchestral playing plus first-rate singing from soloists and chorus alike. His direction is not always consistent and the overall reading does not have a strongly individual profile, but it is never dull. The 1970 recording, engineered by Robert Auger, is balanced most musically, and those who have a special fondness for any or all of the soloists will find that the CD transfer reflects the warm yet clean and bright 1970 analogue master faithfully.

Marriner's conception was to present *Messiah* as nearly as possible in the text followed at the first London performance of 1743. The losses are as great as the gains, but the result has unusual unity, thanks also to Marriner's direction. His tempi in fast choruses can scarcely be counted as authentic in any way: with a small professional chorus he has gone as far as possible towards lightening them and has thus made possible speeds that almost pass belief. Although Anna Reynolds' contralto is not ideally suited to recording, this is otherwise an excellent band of soloists – and in any case Miss Reynolds sings *He was despised* on a thread of sound. Vivid recording.

Boult's 1961 recording is nothing if not spacious, and his broad tempi produce a complete performance running for 198 minutes, too long for a pair of CDs. Decca's solution has been to add a half-hour selection of arias from Kenneth McKellar (in fine voice but not always naturally suited to the Handelian style) and Sutherland (sparkling but somewhat operatic). In *Messiah* it is she who gives due attention to the question of whether or not to use ornamentation in the repeats of the *da capo* arias. What she does is mostly in good taste, but none of the other singers does anything apart from giving us the notes as they stand in the score. Both Grace Bumbry and Kenneth MacKellar sing pleasingly, but neither they nor Joseph Ward produce a great deal of dramatic vitality. The distinction of the set lies in the choruses, splendidly recorded (the sound is of Decca's finest vintage analogue quality) and sung with great eloquence in the way they used to be presented before the dawn of the authentic era. *Messiah*, for all the importance of its choruses, ultimately stands or falls by its soloists. Yet so strong is Boult's warm directing personality that, with the full, vivid Decca recording, this remains very enjoyable.

The glory of the Klemperer set also lies in the singing of the chorus. There is a freshness, a clarity and an edge to it that shows up many of the rival performances on record. Nor is Klemperer's direction dull, despite his characteristic determination to underline the solidity of the music and, like Sargent, to pay no heed to scholarly ideas on the text. So far so good . . . but the soloists' contribution is far more questionable. Schwarzkopf sings beautifully in her way, and in the recitatives she is undoubtedly imaginative. But in the arias her line is not always impeccable: *I know that my Redeemer liveth*, for example, with its combined elements of Lieder and opera, sounds curiously unsympathetic. Even so, she is unfailingly stimulating – which is more than can be said for Grace Hoffman. *O thou that tellest* is sung badly, though *He was despised* is far better. Gedda is interesting but not always comfortable in the part; Jerome Hines, despite a big, dark voice, also seems out of his element and is scarcely imaginative. Both chorus and orchestra make some lovely sounds and, with the Kingsway Hall providing a fine ambient glow, the clarity of detail and natural balance of the CD transfer are most impressive. But EMI's use of three CDs for this set makes it highly uncompetitive.

The Eurodisc/BMG set, directed by Karl Forster, is sung straightforwardly in German. It is not absolutely complete. The soloists are good, particularly the soprano and bass. But the orchestral sound is as richly upholstered as the choral sound is solidly weighty and the St Hedwig's *Hallelujah* must be one of the longest on record. The documentation offers only a German text, without translation. Those wanting *Messiah* sung in German would do far better to consider Mackerras's Austrian DG performance of Mozart's version – see below.

Der Messias (sung in German, arr. Mozart): complete.

(M) **(*) DG 427 173-2 (2). Mathis, Finnilä, Schreier, Adam, Austrian R. Ch. & O, Vienna, Mackerras.

Mozart's arrangement of *Messiah* has a special fascination. It is not simply a question of trombones being added but of elaborate woodwind parts too – most engaging in a number such as *All we like sheep*, which even has a touch of humour. *Rejoice greatly* is given to the tenor (Peter Schreier sounding too heavy) and *The trumpet shall sound* is considerably modified and shortened. To avoid the use of a baroque instrument, Mozart shares the obbligato between trumpet and horn. Mackerras leads his fine team through a performance that is vital, not academic in the heavy sense. The remastered recording is excellent and a translation is provided.

Messiah (sung in English): highlights.

(M) *** EMI CDM7 69040-2 [id.]. Harwood, Janet Baker, Esswood, Tear, Herinx, Amb. S., ECO, Mackerras.

(B) **(*) CfP CD-CFP 9007. Morison, Marjorie Thomas, R. Lewis, Milligan, Huddersfield Ch. Soc., Royal Liverpool PO, Sargent.

(B) **(*) Pickwick Dig. PCD 803. Lott, Finnie, Winslade, Herford, Scottish Philharmonic Singers, Scottish SO, Malcolm.

(M) **(*) Decca 417 735-2 [id.]. Ameling, Reynolds, Langridge, Howell, Ch. & ASMF, Marriner.

(BB) **(*) ASV Dig. CDQS 6001; *ZCQS 6001*. Kwella, Cable, Kendal, Drew, Jackson, Winchester Cathedral Ch., L. Handel O, Neary.

(B) **(*) Decca 417 879-2; *417 879-4*. Sutherland, Bumbry, McKellar, Ward, LSO Ch. & O, Boult.

(M) ** Ph. Dig. 432 047-2; *432 047-4*. M. Price, Schwarz, Burrows, Estes, Bav. R. Ch. & SO, C. Davis.

Messiah: choruses.

(M) *** Decca Dig. 430 734-2; *430 734-4* [id.]. Chicago Ch. & SO, Solti.

As with the complete set, the great and pleasant surprise among the bargain selections is the Classics for Pleasure CD of highlights from Sir

Malcolm Sargent's 1959 recording. There is some splendid solo singing and the choruses emerge vigorously out of the fog of the old analogue master, with the words audible and the heaviness dissipated; no one will be disappointed with *Hallelujah*, while the closing *Amen* has a powerful sense of apotheosis.

Beautifully sung by excellent soloists (especially Felicity Lott) and choir, the Pickwick issue makes another good bargain-priced CD, very naturally and beautifully recorded in warmly atmospheric sound, though the performance could at times be livelier.

A highlights disc is probably the best way to sample the Marriner performance, and the same comment might apply to Boult's 1961 version, mainly notable for its choruses.

Brightly if reverberantly recorded in Winchester Cathedral, Martin Neary's collection of excerpts gives a pleasant reminder of the work of one of our finest cathedral choirs. In its authentic manner Neary's style is rather too clipped to convey deep involvement, but the freshness is attractive, with some very good solo singing.

Sir Colin Davis's 1984 digital set is disappointing, compared with his earlier, LSO version. Hanna Schwarz lets the side down among the otherwise excellent soloists; the chorus is lively, but the Bavarian Radio Orchestra is a degree too smooth. The selection plays for only a few seconds over an hour, so there would have been room for more, the notable omission being *The trumpet shall sound*. There are no notes about the music, just a list of the excerpts.

The choruses were a strong feature of Solti's fine complete set on Decca, and they are now available separately at mid-price.

OPERA

Alessandro (complete).
(M) **(*) HM/BMG GD 77110 (3) [77110-2-RG]. Jacobs, Boulin, Poulenard, Nirouët, Varcoe, Guy de Mey, La Petite Bande, Kuijken.

Sigiswald Kuijken directs his team of period-performance specialists in an urgently refreshing, at times sharply abrasive reading of one of Handel's key operas, the first in which he wrote roles for the rival prima donnas, Faustina and Cuzzoni, not to mention the celebrated castrato, Senesino. As a high counter-tenor, René Jacobs copes brilliantly with the taxing Senesino role of Alexander himself. His singing is astonishingly free and agile, if too heavily aspirated. Among the others, Isabelle Poulenard at her best sounds a little like a French Emma Kirkby, though the production is not quite so pure and at times comes over more edgily. The others make a fine, consistent team, the more effective when the recording so vividly conveys a sense of presence with sharply defined directional focus. Even though reissued at mid-price, the set is well documented and with full translation: the printing apparently uses period-style fonts. The three CDs have 70 separate points of access.

Giulio Cesare (Julius Caesar); abridged.
(M) ** BMG/RCA GD 86182 (2) [6182-2-RG]. Treigle, Sills, Forrester, Wolff, Malas, NY City Op. Ch. & O, Julius Rudel.

This RCA recording of *Julius Caesar* (first issued on LP in 1968) is fairly complete and based on a New York stage production. The conductor's approach is intelligent and tries to pay homage to scholarship, but one is not sure that the solution to the *da capo* arias – having a bare initial statement and reserving all the decoration to the reprise – is entirely successful. Nor does the singing of the name-part by a baritone (while effective on the stage) mean that the music lies exactly right for the voice. But with all reservations, the overall effect is accomplished, and the lively, atmospheric recording gives considerable enjoyment.

Julius Caesar (complete; in English).
(M) *** EMI Dig. CMS7 69760-2 (3). Dame Janet Baker, Masterson, Sarah Walker, Della Jones, Bowman, Tomlinson, E. Nat. Op. Ch. & O, Mackerras.

Dame Janet, in glorious voice and drawing on the widest range of expressive tone-colours, shatters the old idea that this alto-castrato role should be transposed down an octave and given to a baritone. Valerie Masterson makes a charming and seductive Cleopatra, fresh and girlish, though the voice is caught a little too brightly for caressing such radiant melodies as those for *V'adoro pupille* (*Lamenting, complaining*) and *Piangero* (*Flow my tears*). Sarah Walker sings with powerful intensity as Pompey's widow; James Bowman is a characterful counter-tenor Ptolemy and John Tomlinson a firm, resonant Achillas, the other nasty character. The ravishing accompaniments to the two big Cleopatra arias amply justify the use by the excellent ENO Orchestra of modern, not period, instruments. The full, vivid studio sound makes this one of the very finest of the invaluable series of ENO opera recordings in English.

Julius Caesar: highlights (in English).
(M) *** EMI Dig. CDM7 63724-2 [id.]; *EG 63724-4* (from above recording; cond. Mackerras).

A well-selected, generous compilation (68 minutes) for those not wanting the complete set.

Partenope (complete).
(M) *** HM/BMG GD 77109 (3) [77109-2-RG]. Laki, Jacobs, York, Skinner, Varcoe, Müller-Molinari, Hill, La Petite Bande, Kuijken.

By the time he wrote *Partenope* in 1730 Handel was having to cut his cloth rather more modestly than earlier in his career. In its limited scale this opera has few heroic overtones, yet a performance as fresh and alert as this amply demonstrates that the result can be even more invigorating. One problem for Handel was that at this time his company could call on only one each of soprano, tenor and bass; with an excellent team of counter-tenors and contralto, however, this performance makes light of that limitation. With the exception of René Jacobs, rather too mannered for Handel, the roster of soloists is outstanding, with Krisztina Laki and Helga Müller-Molinari welcome additions to the team. Though ornamentation is sparse, the direction of Sigiswald Kuijken is consistently invigorating, as is immediately apparent in the *Overture*. The 1979 recording sounds quite marvellous in its CD format, and the only irritation is that the English translation is printed separately – in an old-style font – from the Italian original. Each is cued, however – there are 74 points of access – so it is fairly easy to link the two.

Tamerlano (complete).
(M) *** Erato/Warner Dig. 2292 45408-2 (3) [id.]. Ragin, Robson, Argenta, Chance, Findlay, Schirrer, E. Bar. Soloists, Gardiner.

Recorded at a live concert performance for West German Radio immediately after a staging in Lyons and Göttingen, John Eliot Gardiner's set of *Tamerlano* presents a strikingly dramatic and immediate experience. One has no doubt whatever that this is one of Handel's most masterly operas. The pacing of numbers and of the recitative is beautifully thought out and, with a cast notable for clean, precise voices, the result is electrifying, the more so when, more than usual, in this opera Handel wrote ensemble numbers as well as solo arias, most of them crisp and compact. Leading the cast are two outstanding counter-tenors, whose encounters provide some of the most exciting moments: Michael Chance as Andronicus, firm and clear, Derek Ragin in the name-part equally agile and more distinctive of timbre, with a rich, warm tone that avoids womanliness. Nigel Robson in the tenor role of Bajazet conveys the necessary gravity, not least in the difficult, highly original G minor aria before the character's suicide; and Nancy Argenta sings with starry purity as Asteria. The only serious snag is the dryness of the sound, which makes voices and instruments sound more aggressive on CD than they usually do in Gardiner's recordings with the English Baroque Soloists. However, even that flaw might be thought to add to the dramatic impact.

COLLECTIONS

Opera arias: *Agrippina: Bel piacere. Orlando: Fammi combattere. Partenope: Funbondo spira il vento. Rinaldo: Or la tromba; Cara sposa; Venti turbini; Cor ingrato; Lascia ch'io pianga. Serse: Frondi tenere; Ombra mai fù.*
(M) **(*) Erato/Warner Dig. 2292 45186-2 [id.]. Marilyn Horne, Sol. Ven., Scimone.

Horne gives virtuoso performances of a wide-ranging collection of Handel arias. The flexibility of her voice in scales and trills and ornaments of every kind remains formidable, and the power is extraordinary down to the tangy chest register. The voice is spotlit against a reverberant acoustic. Purists may question some of the ornamentation, but voice-fanciers will not worry. The recording sounds well.

'The world of Handel': (i) *Berenice: Minuet.* (i; ii) *Organ concerto, Op. 4/2;* (i) *Solomon: Arrival of the Queen of Sheba.* (iii) *Water music:* excerpts. (iv) *Coronation anthem: Zadok the Priest.* (v) *Israel in Egypt: Hailstones chorus.* (vi; i) *Messiah: O thou that tellest;* (vii; i) *Halleluja.* (viii) *Rodelinda: Dove sei.* (ix) *Samson: Let the bright seraphim.* (x) *Semele: Where'er you walk.*
(B) **(*) Decca 430 500-2; *430 500-4* [id.]. (i) ASMF, Marriner; (ii) Malcolm; (iii) LSO, Szell; (iv) King's College Ch., Willcocks; (v) Handel Opera Society Ch. & O, Farncombe; (vi) Anna Reynolds; (vii) ASMF Ch.; (viii) M. Horne; (ix) J. Sutherland; (x) K. McKellar.

An enjoyable programme, not perhaps quite as successful as the companion Bach selection but, like that, probably best enjoyed in its tape format in the car. It is a pity that the full Handel/Harty suite from the *Water music* is not included instead of just three items; but it is good to have the reminder of Kenneth McKellar's lyric tenor in the famous excerpt from *Semele*.

'Great choruses': Coronation anthem: Zadok the Priest; Excerpts from: *Israel in Egypt; Jephtha; Judas Maccabaeus; Messiah; Saul; Solomon.*
(B) ** Pickwick IMPX 9011. Handel Opera Soc. Ch. & O, Charles Farncombe.

Enjoyably fresh and vigorous singing. The concert opens with a buoyant account of *Hallelujah* and an equally enthusiastic account of *See the conquering hero comes* from *Judas Maccabaeus* (with fine horn playing). Of the lesser-known choruses one highlight is *May no rash intruder* from *Solomon*, with its evocative pastoral scene. The small orchestral group is well balanced with the amateur choir, and the conveyed enjoyment and spontaneity here make up for any lack of polish. The recording is bright and forward. Not a generous concert (only 44 minutes long), but an invigorating one.

Hanson, Howard (1896–1981)

Symphonies Nos. 1 in E min. (Nordic), Op. 21; 2 (Romantic), Op. 30; (i) *Song of democracy.*
(M) *** Mercury 432 008-2 [id.]. Eastman-Rochester O, composer; (i) with Eastman School of Music Ch.

Hanson's own pioneering stereo recordings of his two best-known symphonies have a unique thrust and ardour, with the sense of the orchestral musicians being stimulated, both by the composer's direction and by the music's emotional force. The recordings date from 1958 and 1960 respectively and, while not having quite the fullness of records made three decades later, still sound astonishingly vivid. The *Song of democracy*, an effective occasional piece setting words by Walt Whitman, has plenty of dramatic impact and is also very well recorded.

Symphony No. 3; Elegy in memory of my friend Serge Koussevitzky, Op. 44; (i) *Lament for Beowulf.*
(M) *** Mercury 434 302-2 [id.]. Eastman-Rochester O, composer, (i) with Eastman School of Music Ch.

Serge Koussevitzky, for whom Hanson's fine *Elegy* was written, once suggested to the composer with a twinkle that the real beginning of American music dated from the early 1920s: '. . . that was when you came to Rochester and I came to Boston!' The great conductor championed all six Hanson symphonies but especially favoured the *Third*, which the composer recorded in 1963 in full, resonant sound. It is a powerful work, with strong Nordic feeling in the outer movements (Sibelius occasionally springs to mind), and has an eloquent slow movement, memorably melodic, with sonorous brass writing; the exultant finale recalls the main theme of the *Andante*. For those familiar with the earlier works, the musical terrain is familiar: the string threnodies surge purposefully forward, there are similar rhythmic patterns and confident rhetorical gestures. This is highly accessible music: Hanson's harmonic language is in no way difficult, there is a strong individuality of idiom and colour and the invention is always interesting. This applies also to the *Elegy*, which has considerable lyrical power and variety of colour. The cantata also makes an immediate impression and is very well sung, but is in fact a more conventional piece. However, here as in the orchestral works the 1958 Mercury sound is first rate.

Haydn, Josef (1732–1809)

Cello concerto in C, Hob VIIb/1.
(B) *** Ph. 422 481-2. Gendron, LSO, Leppard – BOCCHERINI: *Cello concerto.* ***

Cello concertos in C and D, Hob VIIb/1–2.
(BB) *** Naxos Dig. 8.550059 [id.]. Ludovít Kanta, Capella Istropolitana, Peter Breiner – BOCCHERINI: *Cello concerto.* ***
(M) **(*) EMI CDM7 69299-2 [id.]; *EG 769299-4*. Tortelier, Württemberg CO, Faerber.

Cello concerto in D, Hob VIIb/2.
(B) ** DG Compact Classics *415 330-4* [id.]. Fournier, Lucerne Festival O, Baumgartner – DVOŘÁK; BOCCHERINI: *Concertos.* ***

The Capella Istropolitana is drawn from the Slovak Philharmonic at Bratislava, of which Ludovít Kanta is principal cellist. The orchestra is a very fine one and the playing very alert and fresh (try the finale of the *C major*) and Kanta is a soloist of quality. The *Concerto in C major* was discovered only in the 1960s and first recorded by Miloš Sadló and then by Mstislav Rostropovich, who introduced cadenzas by Benjamin Britten – see below. Kanta also plays contemporary cadenzas. The excellent recording is made in a bright, resonant acoustic in which every detail is clearly registered, though the players are perhaps forwardly placed. The Boccherini coupling is recorded in the (rather endearing but outdated) Grützmacher arrangement, which may put some collectors off. However, in the cadenzas the acoustic changes as noticeably as does the style.

Tortelier gives warmly expressive performances of the two *Concertos*, more relaxed than some of his rivals, but not lacking spontaneity. He is sympathetically if not always immaculately accompanied by the Württemberg Chamber Orchestra. Clear yet warm digital sound to match, very pleasingly balanced.

Gendron's account of the *C major Concerto* is highly musical and is sensitively accompanied by Leppard. This coupling with Boccherini shows him at his finest, and the recording is of good Philips quality.

Fournier plays the *D major Concerto* with style and polish; if Baumgartner's accompaniment is relatively unimaginative, the 1968 recording sounds better here than it has in some previous incarnations. The Boccherini and Dvořák couplings are very attractive, and this

Compact Classics chrome tape certainly offers value for money.

(i) *Cello concerto in C, Hob VIIb/1;* (ii; iv) *Horn concertos Nos. 1–2;* (iii; iv) *Trumpet concerto in D.*
(M) *** Decca 430 633-2; 430 633-4 [id.]. (i) Rostropovich, ECO, Britten; (ii) Tuckwell; (iii) Alan Stringer; (iv) ASMF, Marriner.

(i) *Cello concerto in C, Hob VIIb/1;* (ii) *Horn concertos Nos. 1–2 in D, Hob VIId/3–4;* (iii) *Trumpet concerto in E flat.*
(M) *** Ph. Dig. 432 060-2; *432 060-4.* (i) Heinrich Schiff; (ii) Baumann; (iii) Hardenberger; ASMF, Marriner or I. Brown.

A self-recommending collection from Philips. All the solo playing is first class: Schiff is superbly stylish in the *C major Cello concerto*, Baumann's warm tone and fine sense of line in the works for horn are most appealing, and Hardenberger's famous account of the *Trumpet concerto* is unsurpassed. The accompaniments are admirable and the recording is of Philips's best, if rather resonant. There is no more enticing collection of Haydn concertos than this; the only snag is the total absence of information about the music.

Rostropovich's earlier (1964) stereo recording of the *C major Cello concerto* for Decca is undoubtedly romantic, and some may feel he takes too many liberties in the slow movement. But tempi are well judged and, with very sympathetic conducting from Britten, Rostropovich's expressiveness and beauty of tone-colour are bewitching. The coupling of first-class 1966 versions of both the *Horn concertos* by Tuckwell in peak form and Stringer's 1967 account of the *Trumpet concerto* (all deriving from Argo masters) is certainly tempting. Alan Stringer – who went on to become principal with the Royal Liverpool Philharmonic Orchestra – favours a forthright, open timbre, but he plays the famous slow movement graciously and the orchestral accompaniment, as in the *Horn concertos*, has striking elegance and finesse. All three CD transfers are first class, the Kingsway Hall ambience ensuring that the sound is full as well as bright. Another most desirable collection, offering 73 minutes of music.

(i) *Cello concerto in D, Hob VIIb/2;* (ii) *Piano concerto in D, Hob XVIII/2;* (iii) *Trumpet concerto in E flat.*
(M) ** Erato/Warner 2292 45675-2 [id.]. (i) Lodéon, Bournemouth Sinfonietta, Guschlbauer; (ii) Quéffelec, Lausanne CO, Jordan; (iii) André, Bamberg SO, Guschlbauer.

Three excellent performances here, let down a little by variable CD transfers. Frédéric Lodéon gives a warm and stylish account of the *D major Cello concerto*, and Anne Quéffelec displays even more personality in the best-known of Haydn's keyboard concertos, which she plays with much spirit. She is also given the best sound, although Lodéon is well balanced too. Needless to say, Maurice André is fully equal to all the demands of the *Trumpet concerto*: his crisp articulation is of the highest order. Moreover he uses a first-class cadenza of his own in the first movement to show his mettle and, after a warmly flexible *Andante*, the finale displays similar sparkling bravura. The snag is that, in trying to clarify the originally reverberant 1972 recording, the engineers have lost much of the bloom on the violins.

Harpsichord concerto in D, Hob XVIII/2; Double concerto for violin and harpsichord, Hob XVIII/6. Symphony No. 31 in D (Horn signal).
(B) ** Hung. White Label HRC 088 [id.].
Zsuzsa Pertis, János Rolla, Liszt CO, Rolla.

Engagingly vivacious accounts of Haydn's best-known keyboard concerto and the equally personable *Double concerto*, with a convincing balance for the harpsichord, especially considering the full-timbred orchestral sound. In the *Symphony*, which has some splendid horn playing, the recording becomes slightly more opaque with greater bass emphasis, but this inexpensive disc is worth having for the *Concertos* alone.

Horn concertos Nos. 1 in D, Hob VII/d3; 2 in D, Hob VII/d4.
(M) *** Teldec/Warner Dig. 9031 74790-2 [id.].
Dale Clevenger, Liszt CO, Rolla – M. HAYDN: *Concertino.* ***

Dale Clevenger, principal horn with the Chicago Symphony, gives superb accounts of the two *Horn concertos* attributed to Haydn (the second is of doubtful lineage). He is especially good in the slow movements, a little solemn in the *First*, but eloquently so, with the *Adagio* of its companion given an air of gentle melancholy. This is a movement that can seem too long, but not here. The dotted main theme of the first movement, nicely pointed, is most engaging, and the performance projects a *galant* charm of the kind we associate with Hummel. The accompaniments are supportive, polished and elegant. These performances have fine spirit and spontaneity and on CD the Telefunken recording, made in a nicely judged and warm acoustic, is in the demonstration class: when Clevenger plays his solo cadenzas, the tangibility of his presence is remarkable, yet the combination with the orchestra is hardly less convincing.

Horn concerto No. 1 in D, Hob VIId/3.
(M) *** Decca 417 767-2 [id.]. Barry Tuckwell, ASMF, Marriner – MOZART: *Concertos Nos 1–4.* ***

Haydn's *First Horn concerto* is a fine work, technically more demanding than any of the Mozart concertos – especially as played by Barry Tuckwell on Decca, with a profusion of ornaments and trills, witty or decorative. The finale is in the 'hunting' style of the period, but the highlight of the work is the *Adagio*, a beautifully shaped cantilena for the soloist. Tuckwell's playing throughout is of the highest order, and Marriner's vintage accompaniments are equally polished and full of elegance and vitality. The remastering is admirably fresh, though there is a hint of shrillness on the violins above the stave.

Trumpet concerto in E flat.
(B) *** CfP Dig CD-CFP 4589; *TC-CFP 4589.* Ian Balmain, Royal Liverpool PO, Kovacevich – MOZART: *Horn concertos.* ***

With Stephen Kovacevich as conductor, Ian Balmain, principal trumpet with the Royal Liverpool Philharmonic, favours extreme speeds for Haydn's delectable *Trumpet concerto*, playing brilliantly. If not quite as memorable as Hardenberger's version, it makes an apt and attractive coupling for Claire Briggs's fine recordings of all four Mozart *Horn concertos*, very well recorded.

Violin concerto in C, Hob VIIa/1.
(M) *** Teldec/Warner Dig. 9031 74784-2 [id.]. Zehetmair, Liszt CO – M. HAYDN: *Concerto* **(*); SIBELIUS: *Concerto.* **

Haydn's *C major Violin concerto* is given a superb performance by the young Hungarian violinist, Thomas Zehetmair, stylish, strong and resilient. He also directs the accompaniments which are alert and spirited in outer movements and responsive in the lovely *Adagio*. On his bow this central movement has a touching lyrical serenity, essentially classical in spirit yet expressively beautiful in timbre. The recording is first class, with the soloist given the most realistic presence on CD, yet with no sense that the microphones were placed too near. The orchestra is truthfully balanced within an attractively resonant acoustic.

Violin concertos: in C, Hob VIIa/1; in G, Hob VIIa/4.
(B) *** Ph. 426 977-2; *426 977-4.* Grumiaux, ECO or New Philh. O, Leppard – MOZART: *Adagio; Rondo*; SCHUBERT: *Rondo.* ***

Haydn's *Violin concertos* are early works; the *C major*, with its winding, serenade-like melody in the slow movement, is probably the finer, but the *G major* too has an eloquent *Adagio* and a bustling finale. They make perfect vehicles for Grumiaux's refined classicism; he shows a real feeling for the music's simple lines, and the central movement of No. 1 soars gently and engagingly. Grumiaux plays his own cadenzas. Good mid-1960s sound and alert, gracious support from Leppard. A pity there are no insert notes about the music.

SYMPHONIES

Symphonies Nos 1–104; A; B.
❀ (M) *** Decca 430 100-2 (32) [id.]. Philharmonia Hungarica, Antal Dorati.

Antal Dorati was ahead of his time as a Haydn interpreter when, in the early 1970s, he made his pioneering recording of the complete Haydn symphonies. Superbly transferred to CD in full, bright and immediate sound, the performances are a consistent delight, with brisk allegros and fast-flowing andantes, with textures remarkably clean. The slow rustic-sounding accounts of Minuets are more controversial, but the rhythmic bounce makes them very attractive too. The packaging is excellent, available either in eight separate boxes or as a complete set, with the sequence kept helpfully in numerical order. The time-length is generous, but it is a pity that no way was found of including the extra and alternative movements which Dorati originally recorded along with the complete cycle. That would make a valuable supplementary disc and could have been given free with the complete set.

Symphonies Nos. 1 in D; 2 in C; 3 in G; 4 in D; 5 in A; 6 in D (Le Matin); 7 in C (Le Midi); 8 in G (Le Soir); 9 in C; 10 in D; 11 in E flat; 12 in E; 13 in D; 14 in A; 15 in D; 16 in B flat.
(M) *** Decca 425 900-2 (4) [id.]. Philharmonia Hungarica, Antal Dorati.

By his own calculation Haydn did not start writing symphonies until he was twenty-five and, though his earliest symphonies make a long list, there is not an immature one among them. The urgent crescendo which opens *Symphony No. 1* at once establishes the high voltage of inspiration, and from then on there is no suspicion of a power failure. These works – antedated by one or two symphonies that are later in the Breitkopf numbering – come from the early Esterhazy period (1759–63) and show the young, formidably gifted composer working at full stretch, above all in the fairly well-known trilogy of symphonies, *Le Matin*, *Le Midi* and *Le Soir* (also available separately – see below) with their marvellous solos for members of the Esterhazy orchestra. Dorati left these symphonies until well on in his great pioneering recording project, and the combination of exhilaration and stylishness is irresistible.

Symphonies Nos. 6 in D (Le Matin); 7 in C (Le Midi); 8 in G (Le Soir).
(B) *** Decca 421 627-2 [id.]. Philh. Hungarica, Dorati.

Dorati is at his finest in these relatively well-known named symphonies, with their marvellous solos for members of the Esterhazy orchestra. The remastered recording sounds fresh and clear, but just a little of the body has been lost from the strings.

Symphonies Nos. 17 in F; 18 in G; 19 in D; 20 in C; 21 in A; 22 in E flat (Philosopher) (1st version); *23 in G; 24 in D; 25 in C; 26 in D min. (Lamentatione); 27 in G; 28 in A; 29 in E; 30 in C (Alleluja); 31 in D (Hornsignal); 32 in C; 33 in C.*
(M) *** Decca 425 905-2 (4) [id.]. Philharmonia Hungarica, Antal Dorati.

Because of the idiosyncrasies of the Breitkopf numbering, this sequence of symphonies includes one, *Lamentatione*, that is later than the rest, a transitional work leading into the dark, intense manner of Haydn's middle period. It gives marvellous perspective to the rest, all of them fascinating and many of them masterly. Even with familiarity, the sound Haydn creates, using two cors anglais in the opening chorale of the *Philosopher*, continues to tweak the ear, almost like an anticipation of *Zauberflöte*, and there are many other imaginative touches of colour in these works. The early festive symphonies, like Nos. 32 and 33, both in C major, with trumpets and timpani, have their individual marks of inspiration, for example in the C minor slow movement of No. 33. As in the rest of the cycle, Dorati's performances, helped by vivid recording, have you listening on from one symphony to the next, compulsively following the composer's career.

Symphonies Nos. 26 (Lamentatione), 35, 38–9, 41–2, 43 (Mercury), 44 (Trauer), 45 (Farewell), 46–7, 48 (Maria Theresia), 49 (La passione), 50–52, 58, 59 (Fire), 65.
(M) *** DG Dig. 435 001-2 (6). E. Concert, Trevor Pinnock.

This set lays out in chronological order (not in the normal Hoboken catalogue sequence) the so-called *Sturm und Drang Symphonies*, which Haydn composed during his early years at Eszterháza between 1766 and 1773, but including also Nos. 41, 48 and 65, which are outstanding examples, not of 'storm and stress', but of Haydn's ceremonial application of symphonic form. Pinnock's forces are modest (with 6.5.2.2.1 strings), but the panache of the playing conveys any necessary grandeur. The *Lamentatione*, written in 1768 or 1769, is mistakenly numbered No. 26; chronologically, the first two works here are Nos. 35 and 38 and they have little storm or stress; but the sharp incisiveness of the playing, coupled with the exhilarating rhythmic lift which Pinnock gives in his direction from the keyboard, makes the results very refreshing. It is a new experience to have Haydn symphonies of this period recorded in relatively dry and close sound, with inner detail crystal clear (harpsichord never obscured) and made the more dramatic by the intimate sense of presence, yet with a fine bloom on the instruments. Some may find a certain lack of charm at times, and others may quarrel with the very brisk one-in-a-bar minuets and – dare one say it! – even find finales a bit rushed. Converts to the authentic school will surely find such misgivings of little import, and certainly the recording is well balanced and extremely vivid.

Symphonies Nos. 26 in D min. (Lamentatione); 44 in E min. (Trauer); 45 in F sharp min. (Farewell).
(B) **(*) Hung. White Label HRC 102 [id.]. Hungarian CO, Vilmos Tátrai.

Symphonies Nos. 27 in G; 88 in G; 100 in G (Military).
(B) **(*) Hung. White Label HRC 090 [id.]. Hungarian CO, Tátrai or Adám Fischer.

Symphonies Nos. 43 in E flat (Mercury); 82 in C (The Bear); 94 in G (Surprise).
(B) **(*) Hung. White Label HRC 123 [id.]. Hungarian CO, Tátrai or János Ferencsik.

Symphonies Nos. 49 in F min. (La Passione); 59 in A (Fire); 73 in D (La Chasse).
(B) **(*) Hung. White Label HRC 103 [id.]. Hungarian CO, Tátrai.

This excellent series by the Hungarian Chamber Orchestra offers alert, well-characterized performances, played with zest and style. There is no lack of polish here and the expressive playing in slow movements is appealingly phrased and spontaneous. In short, this excellent chamber orchestra convey their enjoyment of the music. The recording is resonant and full but remains clear. Tempi are apt (in No. 88, for instance, they are somewhat measured, but this is still a fine performance) and this is an excellent way to explore this repertoire. However, the Wordsworth series on Naxos is even finer and costs less.

Symphonies Nos. 34 in D min.; 35 in B flat; 36 in E flat; 37 in C; 38 in C (Echo); 39 in G min.; 40 in F; 41 in C; 42 in D; 43 in E flat (Mercury);

44 in E min. (Trauer); 45 in F sharp min. (Farewell); 46 in B; 47 in G.
(M) *** Decca 425 910-2 (4) [id.]. Philharmonia Hungarica, Antal Dorati.

Despite the numbering, this set of symphonies arguably includes the very first symphony of all, *No. 37 in C*, revealing, as H. C. Robbins Landon points out in his absorbing commentary, 'impeccable craftsmanship and enormous energy'. The 3/8 finale is exhilarating – but then all of these works, as played by Dorati and the Philharmonia Hungarica, reflect the composer's unquenchable genius. This particular sequence brings us to the frontier in Dorati's interpretations between those using and not using harpsichord continuo. He switches over in the middle of *No. 40 in F* – not illogically, when the finale is a fugue in which continuo would only be muddling. The two named symphonies towards the end of the box (*Trauer* and *Farewell*) lead into the darker intensity of Haydn's so-called *Sturm und Drang* period. Unfailingly lively performances and abiding, brightly vivid sound.

Symphony No. 44 in E min. (Trauer).
(B) *** Pickwick Dig. PCD 820 [id.]. O of St John's, Smith Square, Lubbock – MOZART: *Symphony No. 40.* **(*)

Symphony No. 49 in F minor (La Passione).
(B) **(*) Pickwick Dig. PCD 819 [id.]. O of St John's, Smith Square, Lubbock – SCHUBERT: *Symphony No. 5.* **

The Orchestra of St John's are on their toes throughout their splendidly committed account of the *Trauersymphonie.* Outer movements are alert and vivacious – the finale has striking buoyancy and spring – and there is some lovely espressivo playing in the beautiful *Adagio* slow movement which brings out the forward-looking qualities of the writing. The recording too is in the demonstration class.

John Lubbock's version of Haydn's *La Passione* is not quite as convincing as his fine account of No. 44. With the opening *Adagio* overtly expressive and the allegros boldly assertive in their fast, crisp articulation, this is certainly responsive playing, but there is at times a sense of over-characterization of an already powerfully contrasted work. The recording is first class.

Symphonies Nos. 44 in E min. (Trauer); 88 in G; 104 in D (London).
(BB) *** Naxos Dig. 8.550287 [id.]. Capella Istropolitana, Barry Wordsworth.

Symphonies Nos. 45 in F sharp min. (Farewell); 48 in C (Maria Theresia); 102 in B flat.
(BB) *** Naxos Dig. 8.550382 [id.]. Capella Istropolitana, Barry Wordsworth.

Symphonies Nos. 82 in C (The Bear); 96 in D (Miracle); 100 in G (Military).
(BB) *** Naxos Dig. 8.550139 [id.]. Capella Istropolitana, Barry Wordsworth.

Symphonies Nos. 83 in G min. (The Hen); 94 in G (Surprise); 101 in D (The Clock).
(BB) *** Naxos Dig. 8.550114 [id.]. Capella Istropolitana, Barry Wordsworth.

Symphonies Nos. 85 in B flat (La Reine); 92 in G (Oxford); 103 in E flat (Drum Roll).
(BB) *** Naxos Dig. 8.550387 [id.]. Capella Istropolitana, Barry Wordsworth.

Like Barry Wordsworth's recordings of Mozart symphonies, also with the Capella Istropolitana on the Naxos label, this Haydn collection provides a series of outstanding bargains at the lowest budget price. The sound is not quite as clean and immediate as in the Mozart series, a little boomy at times in fact, and Wordsworth's preference for relatively relaxed speeds is a little more marked here than in Mozart, but the varied choice of works on each disc is most attractive. It is good that, in addition to named symphonies, Wordsworth includes two of the undoubted masterpieces among those unnamed, both with supremely beautiful slow movements, *No. 88 in G* and *No. 102 in B flat.* At their modest cost, these are well worth collecting alongside Dorati's Philharmonia Hungarica boxes.

Symphonies Nos. 45 in F sharp min. (Farewell); 48 in C (Maria Theresia).
(M) *** Sony Dig. MDK 46507 [id.]. L'Estro Armonico, Derek Solomons.

The musical marvel of No. 45 in the rare key (for Haydn's time) of F sharp minor brings one of Solomons' finest performances. The picturesque story of the departing players in the finale tends to obscure the work's status as one of the most powerful of this rare, dark series of symphonies, not to mention the sheer originality (practical motives apart) of that amazing close. Solomons keeps his ensemble of period instruments very small, with six violins but only one each of the other stringed instruments, a scale Haydn himself employed at Esterháza, and in the slow movement of the *Farewell* the effect is touchingly graceful, almost ethereal in texture. The robust Minuet which follows makes a striking contrast. Special mention must be made of the brilliant horn playing of Anthony Halstead (no concessions here to any technical problems) not only in this work but also in the slow movement of No. 48, again hauntingly beautiful. The invigorating opening movement of that same work, bursting with exuberance and with the first horn, crooked in C alto, shining out over the strings, brings thrilling sound, and the Minuet is no less impressive. Recorded in the pleasingly atmospheric acoustic of St Barnabas Church, Woodside Park, the sense of vibrant yet intimate music-making is most stimulating. Repeats are generously observed, which is why these two symphonies have a combined playing time of 66 minutes.

Symphonies Nos. 48 in C (Maria Theresia); 49 in F min. (La Passione); 50 in C; 51 in B flat; 52 in C min.; 53 in D (L'Impériale); 54 in G; 55 in E flat (Schoolmaster); 56 in C; 57 in D; 58 in F; 59 in A (Fire).
(M) *** Decca 425 915-2 (4) [id.]. Philharmonia Hungarica, Antal Dorati.

The nine symphonies which comprise the bulk of this box, from *Maria Theresia* onwards, show Haydn in the full flight of his *Sturm und Drang* period: tense, exhilarating music, full of anguished minor-key arguments that belie the idea of jolly 'Papa' Haydn working patiently for his princely master. Their emotional basis clearly points forward to the Romantic movement which, within decades, was to overtake music. Indeed the literary movement which gives the appellation *Sturm und Drang* itself marks the first stirrings of Romanticism. While individual performances of some of these symphonies have already appeared on CD, the special value of Dorati's box is that it enables the listener to hear the ongoing sequence of nine works and to experience their historical impact in the same way as Prince Esterhazy and his court must have done. The impact is the more powerful because of the splendid notes written by Profesor Robbins Landon, whose comments are fascinating at every level, whether for the specialist or the beginner. Such symphonies as *La Passione* and *Maria Theresia* are already quite well known, but the others without sobriquets are no less compelling; and it is impossible to become bored for a moment by the vigorous, committed performances given by Dorati and his orchestra of Hungarian exiles, especially as the last symphonies in this collection are already moving towards the stylistic changes which came in Haydn's middle period. The CD transfers continue to be outstandingly vivid.

Symphonies Nos. 59 in A (Fire); 100 in G (Military); 101 in D (Clock).
(M) *** Ph. 420 866-2 [id.]. ASMF, Marriner.

Marriner's recordings derive from the mid-1970s and the performances are very satisfactory, as is the remastering. The *Clock* is vital and intelligent, the playing of the Academy very spruce and elegant. There is perhaps not quite the depth of character that informs Sir Colin Davis's performances of this repertoire, but they do display finesse, and the readings are never superficial in expressive terms.

Symphonies Nos. 60 in C (Il Distratto); 61 in D; 62 in D; 63 in C (La Roxolane); 64 in A; 65 in A; 66 in B flat; 67 in F; 68 in B flat; 69 in C (Laudon); 70 in D; 71 in B flat.
(M) *** Decca 425 920-2 (4) [id.]. Philharmonia Hungarica, Antal Dorati.

Even Robbins Landon underestimates the mastery of these middle-period symphonies. All in major keys, they represent the comparatively extrovert period immediately after Haydn had worked through the bitterest tensions of his *Sturm und Drang* era but before he expanded into the international world of music-making with the *Paris* and *London Symphonies*. Even if they are not quite as fascinating as the surrounding works, these maintain an amazing standard of invention, with such movements as the Adagio and 6/8 finale of No. 61 endlessly interesting. With the exception of an occasional movement (No. 69/II or No. 70/III), this music is riveting, and even where the actual material is conventional, as in the theatrical first movement of No. 69 (nicknamed Laudon after a field marshal), the treatment is sparkling, with many surprising turns. The only serious flaw in Dorati's interpretations – and it is something to note in a few of the symphonies in other boxes too – is his tendency to take minuets rather slowly. In many of them Haydn had already moved half-way towards a scherzo. But the Philharmonia Hungarica maintains its alertness with amazing consistency, never giving the suspicion of merely running through the music. As in the other boxes, Professor Robbins Landon's notes provide an ideal preparation for listening with a historical ear, and even his tendency to understate the merits of the lesser-known works makes one tend to enjoy them the more in sheer defiance of his authority. Nos. 65 to 71 were included in the very first album of symphonies to be issued on LP in September 1970 in Decca's integral series, and the dynamic tone of the whole project was at once established with works that had previously been not just neglected but absurdly underrated. The continuing vividness of the playing is matched by the bright CD transfers.

Symphonies Nos. 72 in D; 73 in D (La chasse); 74 in E flat; 75 in D; 76 in E flat; 77 in B flat; 78 in C min.; 79 in F; 80 in D min.; 81 in G; 82 in C (L'Ours); 83 in G min. (La Poule).
(M) *** Decca 425 925-2 (2) [id.]. Philharmonia Hungarica, Antal Dorati.

This collection – apart from No. 72, which is an earlier work, and the two *Paris Symphonies* tacked on at the end – centres on nine symphonies written more or less consecutively over a compact period of just four years (1780–84). Robbins Landon emphasizes that these are much more courtly works than their *Sturm und Drang* predecessors and that at this time Haydn was regarding the symphony as a side concern, being mainly concerned with opera. Even so, what will strike the non-specialist listener is that, whatever the courtly manners of the expositions (and even there moods vary, particularly in the two minor-key symphonies), the development sections give a flashing reminder of Haydn's tensest manner, with kaleidoscopic sequences of minor keys whirling the argument in unexpected directions. On this showing, even when he was not really trying Haydn was incapable of being boring, and some of these works are in every way remarkable in their forward-looking reminders, often of Mozart's most visionary works. At that time Haydn had just made contact with Mozart and though, on chronological evidence, the direct similarities can only be accidental the influence is already clear. The performances achieve an amazing degree of intensity, with alertness maintained throughout.

Symphonies Nos. 84 in E flat; 85 in B flat (La Reine); 86 in D; 87 in A (Paris Symphonies); 88 in G; 89 in F; 90 in C; 91 in E flat; 92 in G (Oxford); 93 in D; 94 in G (Surprise); 95 in C min.
(M) *** Decca 425 930-2 (4) [id.]. Philharmonia Hungarica, Antal Dorati.

It is a pity that Decca's layout in four-CD groups, and employing a consistent numerical sequence, has meant that Dorati's sets of both the six *Paris* and the first six *London Symphonies* have each had to be split over two separate CD boxes. However, here we have not only the last four of the main *Paris* set (Nos. 84–7) but also the other Paris-based works, all given fresh and stylish performances. Even the least-known of the *Paris* set, No. 84, has a first movement of the most delicate fantasy, while No. 89 is rounded off with an extraordinarily witty movement that looks directly forward to the fun of Johann Strauss's polkas, with a delicious *portamento* in each reprise down to the main theme. Of the three *London Symphonies* included here, No. 93 brings one of the most delightful performances of Dorati's cycle, with a delectable, Ländler-like first movement; No. 94 is one of the more controversial, with a fast trotting slow movement (less of a 'surprise') and a fraction less delicacy in the playing. No. 95 is the only work in the set which lacks a slow opening section. Its compactness and the C minor tensions, however, recall the *Sturm und Drang* period.

Symphonies Nos. 88 in G; 89; 92 (Oxford).
(B) *** DG 429 523-2; *429 523-4* [id.]. VPO, Boehm.

Enjoyably cultured performances from Boehm and the Vienna Philharmonic, who play with great polish and tonal refinement. The finale of No. 88 and the Andante of No. 89 are most beautifully done and the slow movement of the former is gravely expansive. The remastering is very successful indeed in freshening the sound without losing its body and depth; some will want a less weighty effect, possible with a smaller group, but Boehm's touch can charm in allegros, as in the sprightly finale of the *Oxford Symphony*.

Symphonies Nos. 92 in G (Oxford); 94 in G (Surprise); 96 in D (Miracle).
(M) *** Sony SBK 46332 [id.]; *40-46332*. Cleveland O, Szell.

Symphonies Nos. 93 in D; 94 in G (Surprise); 95 in C min.; 96 in D (Miracle); 97 in C; 98 in B flat (London Symphonies).
(M) *** Sony MY2K 45673 (2) [id.]. Cleveland O, Szell.

With superb polish in the playing and precise phrasing it would be easy for such performances as these to sound superficial, but Haydn's music obviously struck a deep chord in Szell's sensibility and there is humanity underlying the technical perfection. Indeed there are many little musical touches from Szell to show that his perfectionist approach is a dedicated and affectionate one. There is also the most delectable pointing and a fine judgement of the inner balance. Szell's minuets have a greater rhythmic spring than Bernstein's, and his account of No. 96 compares favourably with Beecham's mono version, with Szell having the additional advantage of using modern editions of these scores. The finale is particularly felicitous, the orchestral articulation a delight. The recordings have been splendidly remastered and the sound is fuller and firmer than it ever was on LP, with the Cleveland ambience well caught. The underlying aggressiveness in the recording still produces a thinness in the violins in No. 95 and, to a far lesser extent, in No. 97. Both Nos. 97 and 98 are strong performances. Szell brings out the forceful maturity of first movements – the slow introduction of No. 98 is most arresting – and the beauty of the *Adagios*, both among Haydn's finest. These are most distinguished reissues, and all collectors should try the disc offering the three named symphonies.

Symphonies Nos. (i) *92 in G (Oxford);* (ii) *100 in G (Military); 101 in D (Clock).*
(B) **(*) DG Compact Classics *415 329-4* [id.]. (i) VPO, Boehm; (ii) LPO, Jochum.

On this Compact Classics tape Boehm conducts the *Oxford Symphony* and he secures finely disciplined playing from the VPO. The recording too is excellent, but the weightiness of the approach may not please all tastes, even if the phrasing has much finesse, and the finale is agreeably vivacious. Jochum's performances are another matter. He too is well recorded and inspires the LPO to fresh, polished performances that do not miss the genial side of Haydn. The performance of the finale of the *Military Symphony* is very good indeed and, throughout, the *Clock* is alert and sparkling. The sound, from the early 1970s, is naturally balanced and has transferred admirably in its tape format.

Symphonies Nos. 92 in G (Oxford); 101 in D (Clock).
(B) **(*) Hung. White Label HRC 089 [id.]. Hungarian State O, Ervin Lukács.

A useful supplement to the Hungarian Chamber Orchestra series, using a bigger band for late Haydn. The performances have plenty of life and are unidiosyncratic without losing character. The sound is full but not clouded.

Symphonies Nos. 92 in G (Oxford); 104 in D (London).
(B) *** Pickwick Dig. PCD 916; *CIMPC 916*. E. Sinfonia, Groves.

Sir Charles Groves makes an admirable case for a modern orchestra, especially when it is recorded so faithfully (in EMI's Abbey Road studio, but sounding like a concert hall), with agreeable ambient warmth, a bloom on strings and woodwind alike, yet with good definition. The performances are robust yet elegant as well; both slow movements are beautifully shaped, with Haydn's characteristic contrasts unfolding spontaneously. In the last movement of the *Oxford*, the dancing violins are a special delight in what is one of the composer's most infectious finales. The closing movement of the *London Symphony* is altogether stronger and has a satisfying feeling of apotheosis.

Symphonies Nos. 93–104 (London symphonies).
❀ (M) *** Ph. 432 286-2 (4) [id.]. Concg. O, Sir Colin Davis.
(M) **(*) DG Dig. 429 658-2 (4) [id.]. BPO, Karajan.

Symphonies Nos. 93 in D; 94 in G (Surprise); 100 in G (Military).
(M) **(*) DG Dig. 427 809-2; *427 809-4* [id.]. BPO, Karajan.

This Haydn series is one of the most distinguished recordings Sir Colin Davis has given us in recent years, and its blend of brilliance and sensitivity, wit and humanity, gives this box a special claim on the collector. There is no trace of routine in these performances and no failure of imagination. The excellence of the playing is matched by Philips's best recording quality and, with three symphonies to each CD, this is remarkable value too. The recordings were made between 1975 and 1981. Nos. 93, 94 and 96 are digital, the rest analogue, but all have been transferred to CD with fine body and range. For some, this could prove an antidote to the more abrasive Pinnock style in the earlier, *Sturm und Drang Symphonies*.

Karajan offers big-band Haydn – but what a band! At times the Berlin Philharmonic do not seem fully involved in this music, and many of the minuets are wanting in the sparkle and humour that distinguished Beecham's performances on a similar scale. But there is often tenderness in slow movements – witness the close of *No. 98 in B flat* – and there is no want of dignity and breadth. The sound of the Berlin Philharmonic is itself a joy. This set, we gather, enjoyed the imprimatur of no less an authority than H. C. Robbins Landon; but it inspires admiration rather than affection. As a fine sampler, the triptych of Nos. 93, 94 and 100 can be recommended. First-movement exposition repeats are observed and the playing undoubtedly has distinction. The sound is first class.

Symphonies Nos. 94 in G (Surprise); 96 in D (Miracle); 100 in G (Military).
(M) *** Decca 417 718-2 [id.]. Philh. Hungarica, Dorati.

These three symphonies, collected from Dorati's historic complete Haydn cycle, make a delightful group. Allegros are well sprung, with phrasing elegant and the wind playing an especial delight. The only controversial speed comes in the *Andante* of the *Surprise*, much faster than usual, but the freshness of the joke is the more sharply presented. Dorati's flair comes out in the bold reading of the military section of the slow movement of No. 100, and though the digital transfer exaggerates the brightness of upper frequencies, the warm acoustic of the hall in Marl, West Germany, where the recordings were done makes the result very acceptable.

Symphonies Nos. 94 in G (Surprise); 101 in D (Clock).
(M) *** DG 423 883-2 [id.]. LPO, Jochum.

Jochum's are marvellously fresh, crisp accounts of both symphonies, elegantly played and always judiciously paced. The sound remains first class, with added clarity but without loss of bloom, the bass cleaner and only slightly drier.

Symphonies Nos. 94 in G (Surprise); 103 in E flat (Drum Roll); 104 in D (London).
(B) *** DG Compact Classics *413 426-4* [id.]. LPO, Jochum.

Like Jochum's companion Compact Classics coupling (see above), these performances derive from the complete set of *London Symphonies* DG released in 1973, the *Surprise* having appeared the previous year as a trailer. The playing is elegant yet fresh, allegros marvellously crisp, slow movements warm and humane. This is among the musically most satisfying accounts of No. 104 in the catalogue; throughout, the recording is of DG's best analogue quality. A bargain.

Symphonies Nos. 96 in D (Miracle); 97 in C; 98 in B flat; 99 in E flat; 100 in G (Military); 101 in D (Clock); 102 in B flat; 103 in E flat (Drum Roll); 104 in D (London). Symphonies A in B flat; B in B flat; Sinfonia concertante in B flat (for oboe, bassoon, violin, cello & orchestra).
(M) *** Decca 425 935-2 (4) [id.]. Philharmonia Hungarica, Antal Dorati.

Dorati and the Philharmonia Hungarica, working in comparative isolation in Marl in (what was) West Germany, completed their monumental project of recording the entire Haydn symphonic *oeuvre* with not a suspicion of routine. These final masterpieces are performed with a glowing sense of commitment, and Dorati, no doubt taking his cue from the editor, H. C. Robbins Landon, generally chooses rather relaxed tempi for the first movements. In slow movements his tempi are on the fast side and, though an extra desk of strings has been added to each section, the results are authentically in scale, with individual solos emerging naturally against the glowing acoustic, and with intimacy comes extra dramatic force in sforzandos. The sound has immediacy and range, the bass is firmly defined and detail is clean. The playing is vital and sensitive and there is a splendid sense of style. Other versions of these late masterpieces may have a degree more refinement and polish, but the Philharmonia Hungarica provide a robust, spontaneous approach that is invigorating. As an appendix we are given the *Sinfonia concertante* and *Symphonies A* and *B*, which were not included in the numerical list simply because originally they were not thought to be symphonies at all. They are presented with characteristic vitality. Dorati's account of the *Sinfonia concertante* is a performance of few extremes, one which – not surprisingly, given the context – presents the work as a further symphony with unusual scoring, rather than as a concerto-styled work.

Symphony No. 104 in D (London).
(M) (**) DG mono 427 776-2 [id.]. BPO, Furtwängler – MOZART: *Symphony No. 39.* (**)

As one of Furtwängler's recently rediscovered wartime recordings, this account of No. 104 brings limited sound that tends to crumble in tuttis, but the performance consistently reveals what a fine classicist he could be, with an exuberant *allegro* in the first movement, a spaciously lyrical slow movement (but with appoggiatura interpreted oddly), a solidly weighty minuet and an exhilarating, sunny finale. This and the Mozart coupling are among the finest of the wartime Furtwängler series.

CHAMBER MUSIC

Duo sonatas for violin and viola Nos. 1–6.
(B) *** Hung. White Label HRC 071 [id.]. Dénes Kovács, Géza Németh.

Haydn composed these six duos some time in the late 1760s. They are all structured similarly: a central adagio is framed by a moderately fast opening movement and a closing Minuet; but Haydn's diversity of invention seems inexhaustible. The performances here are expert and spontaneous – the players are obviously enjoying the music, and so do we. The recording too is well balanced and has fine presence and realism. Ideal repertoire for a bargain label!

Piano trios (complete).
❀ (M) *** Ph. 432 061-2 (9). Beaux Arts Trio.

The original Beaux Arts set of the complete *Piano trios* was not only awarded a Rosette by us but was also named 1979 Record of the Year by *Gramophone* and went on in 1980 to win the 'Grand Prix International du Disque de l'Académie Charles Cros'. It is not often possible to hail one set of records as a 'classic' in quite the way that Schnabel's Beethoven sonatas can be so described; all too few performances attain that level of artistic insight, and such is the sheer proliferation of material today that records have to struggle increasingly for attention. Yet this set can be described in those terms, for the playing of the Beaux Arts Trio is of the very highest musical distinction. The contribution of the pianist, Menahem Pressler, is little short of inspired, and the recorded sound on CD is astonishingly lifelike. The performances follow the Critical Edition of H. C. Robbins Landon, whose indefatigable researches have increased the number of *Trios* we know in the standard edition from 31 to 43. This is the kind of inflation one welcomes! Most collectors will find something new in this box, and its riches will stand us in good stead for many decades. Here is music that is sane and intelligent, balm to the soul in a troubled world, and the recording is wonderfully natural. The CD transfer has enhanced detail without losing the warmth of ambience or sense of intimacy.

Piano trios, Hob XV, Nos. 24–27.
(M) *** Ph. 422 831-2. Beaux Arts Trio.

These are all splendid works. No. 25 with its *Gypsy rondos* is the most famous, but each has a character of its own, showing the mature Haydn working at full stretch (they are contemporary with the *London symphonies*). The playing here is peerless and the recording truthful and refined.

String quartets Nos. 17 in F (Serenade), Op. 3/5; 38 in E flat (Joke), Op. 33/2; 76 in D min. (Fifths), Op. 76/2.
(M) *** Decca 425 422-2; *425 422-4.* Janáček Qt.

These performances are strong and dedicated and careful to sense that the style of Haydn is not that of either Beethoven or Mozart. The music itself is highly civilized; whether Haydn or Hoffstetter wrote that delicious tune which forms the slow movement of the *Serenade quartet* seems irrelevant; it is an attractive little work and makes a good foil for the really splendid music of its companions. The recording (mid-1960s' vintage) always had good presence; the CD brings even more striking tangibility and plenty of body, within a well-judged ambience.

String quartets Nos. 17 in F (Serenade), Op. 3/5; 63 in D (Lark), Op. 64/5; 76 in D min. (Fifths), Op. 76/2.
(M) *** Ph. 426 097-2; *426 097-4.* Italian Qt.

First-class playing here, although the first movement of the *Lark* is a bit measured in feeling and could do with more sparkle. The *Serenade quartet* is made to sound inspired, its famous slow movement played with exquisite gentleness. The *D minor Quartet* is admirably poised and classical in feeling. This rivals the grouping by the Janáček Quartet on Decca, but the remastered Philips recording, although refined, is drier: the Decca has more bloom and warmth.

String quartets Nos. 50–56 (The Seven Last Words of Christ); 63–68, Op. 64 1–6 (Tost quartets).
(M) **(*) DG 431 145-2 (3). Amadeus Qt.

It is perhaps a pity that the Amadeus version of *The Seven Last Words of Christ* is linked on CD with Op. 64, for the immaculate Amadeus style, though not lacking in drama, does tend to smooth over the darker side of Haydn. The last six of the twelve *Tost quartets* are another matter. Dedicated to a rich, self-made patron, Johann Tost, they include a number of masterpieces, not least the *Lark*, Op. 64/5. Here the superb ensemble and cultivated playing are always easy on the ear when the recording is so well balanced and natural. There is no lack of life in allegros, for all their neat, spick-and-span precision; if other performances of some of the great slow movements have more intensity, the playing here is still certainly felt, as well as being assured and beautiful, with tempi aptly chosen and well sustained. Indeed, overall these performances give much pleasure.

String quartets Nos. 50–56 (The Seven Last Words of our Saviour on the Cross), Op. 51; 83 in B flat, Op. 103.
(BB) *** Naxos Dig. 8.550346 [id.]. Kodály Qt.

The Kodály Quartet give a memorable performance, strongly characterized and beautifully played, with subtle contrasts of expressive tension between the seven inner slow movements. They also offer an appropriate bonus in Haydn's last, unfinished, two-movement *Quartet.* He was working on this in 1803, at about the same time as he directed his last public concert, which was *The Seven Last Words.* The recording is first rate, vividly present yet naturally balanced, like the other isssues in this attractive Naxos series.

String quartets Nos. 57 in G; 58 in C; 59 in E, Op. 54/1-3.
(BB) *** Naxos Dig. 8.550395 [id.]. Kodály Qt.

The Op. 54 *Quartets* were the first of six dedicated to Johann Tost, a violinist who led the second violins of Haydn's Esterháza orchestra for five years from 1783; he then departed for Paris to become a musical entrepreneur and had chamber music dedicated to him by Mozart as well as by Haydn. The present works show Haydn at his most inventive; all have fine first movements, and Op. 54/1 has a particularly witty and zestful finale. Op. 54/2 contrasts a profound C minor *Adagio* with a catchy Minuet, leading to a highly original finale, beginning and ending *Adagio*, yet with a central *Presto* featuring unexpected pauses. The Kodály players enter animatedly into the spirit of the music and give a fine, direct account of Op. 54/1; the leader, Attila Falvay, shows himself fully equal to Haydn's bravura embellishments in the demanding first violin writing, both here and in Op. 54/3. The Naxos sound is fresh and truthful, well up to the standard of this excellent super-bargain series.

String quartets Nos. 60 in A; 61 in F min. (Razor); 62 in B flat, Op. 55/1–3 (Tost Quartets).

(BB) **(*) Naxos Dig. 8.550397. Kodály Qt.

Opus 55 brings playing which is undoubtedly spirited and generally polished, but the music-making at times seems plainer than usual in the Naxos series. The opening movement of the *A major Quartet* has some rather forceful accents, and its poised *Adagio cantabile* could have relaxed to find a degree more warmth. Even so, there is still much to enjoy, with the *B flat major Quartet*, Op. 55/3, the most spontaneous performance of the three, especially the sparkling finale. The recording is bright and clear, with a realistic presence. Incidentally, the origin of the title of the F minor work comes from an anecdote supplied by the English publisher, John Bland. Haydn was supposed to have offered 'his best quartet for a pair of decent razors', and that was how his music was paid for.

String quartets Nos. 63 in D, Op. 64/5; 82 in F, Op. 77/2.
(M) ** Tuxedo TUXCD 1026 [id.]. Hungarian Qt.

The Hungarians give a most sensitive account of the *Lark Quartet*, with the solo violin soaring with pleasing delicacy in the opening movement and the vivacious *moto perpetuo* finale played with sparkling precision. The late quartet is no less successful, with the *Adagio* finely sustained. The recordings come from 1957 and have been remastered most successfully for CD, the sound firm and with an appealing ambience. However, with only 38 minutes of music offered, recommendation must be qualified, when the Naxos series is far more generous – and less expensive too.

String quartets Nos. 69 in B flat; 70 in D; 71 in E flat, Op. 71/1–3; 72 in C; 73 in F; 74 in G min. (Reiter), Op. 74/1–3 (Apponyi quartets).
(BB) *** Naxos Dig. 8.550394 (*Nos. 69–71*); 8.550396 (*Nos. 72–74*) [id.]. Kódaly Qt.

The *Apponyi quartets* (so named because their 'onlie begetter' was Count Antal Apponyi) are among the composer's finest. The Naxos recordings by the Kodály Quartet are outstanding in every way and would be highly recommendable even without their considerable price advantage. The performances are superbly shaped, naturally paced and alive; the playing is cultivated, yet it has depth of feeling too, and the group readily communicate their pleasure in this wonderful music. The second disc, offering the three Op. 74 *Quartets*, is particularly fine, although the performance of Op. 71/3, a superb work, is hardly less memorable. The digital recording has vivid presence and just the right amount of ambience: the effect is entirely natural.

String quartets Nos. 69 in B flat; 70 in D; 71 in E flat, Op. 71/1–3; 72 in C; 73 in F; 74 in G min. (Reiter), Op. 74/1–3; Op. 77/1–2; in D min., Op. 103.
(M) *** DG 429 189-2 (3). Amadeus Qt.

This excellent set shows the Amadeus on their finest form; there is a sense of spontaneity as well as genuine breadth to these readings. Haydn's late quartets have much the same expansiveness and depth as the symphonies, and here the Amadeus succeed in conveying both their intimacy and their scale. The recordings have a warm acoustic and plenty of presence.

String quartets Nos. 75 in G; 76 in D min. (Fifths); 77 in C (Emperor); 78 in B flat (Sunrise); 79 in D; 80 in E flat, Op. 76/1–6.
❀ (BB) *** Naxos Dig. 8.550314 (*Nos. 75–77*); 8.550315 (*Nos. 78–80*). Kodály Qt.
(M) **(*) DG 415 867-2 (2) [id.]. Amadeus Qt.

String quartets Nos. 76 (Fifths); 77 (Emperor); 78 (Sunrise), Op. 76/2–4.
❀ (BB) *** Naxos Dig. 8.550129 [id.]. Kodály Qt.

Haydn's six *Erdödy quartets*, Op. 76, contain some of his very greatest music, and these performances by the Kodály Quartet are fully worthy of the composer's inexhaustible invention. We know that this Hungarian group do not enter the recording studio until they have spent much time together, immersing themselves in the composer, and feel ready to make a record. Their playing brings a joyful pleasure in Haydn's inspiration and a polished refinement than can only come from familiarity over a considerable period. Yet there is not the slightest suspicion of over-rehearsal or of routine: every bar of the music springs to life spontaneously, and these musicians' insights bring an ideal combination of authority and warmth, emotional balance and structural awareness. The group of three familiar named works (recorded in 1988 in the Italian Institute in Budapest) would make an ideal present for any novice coming to this repertoire for the first time. The opening movement of the *Emperor*, fresh and rhythmic, makes way for a sonorous blend of tone in the famous melody of the slow movement, and the finale has great character. The firm interplay on the interval of a fifth, which gives the first movement of Op. 76/2 its nickname, is most telling as the motif is passed among the players, and the charming *Andante* which follows then leads to a vibrant, so-called 'Witches' minuet', and on to the sparkling finale. The gently lyrical opening of the *Sunrise* suggests a more lightweight work, yet the *Adagio* is as intensely beautiful as any Haydn wrote, and the rapt response here is highlighted by glorious playing from the leader.

But the other works in the set, those without nicknames, are no less inspired. Opus 76/1 has a wonderfully serene *Adagio*, and the last of the series, in E flat, might be counted finest of all, with its *Allegretto* theme and variations to begin, another very beautiful slow movement, and a jolly Minuet with a wittily employed scalic Trio, first descending then ascending. As with others in this superb series, the recordings of the complete set, made in the Hungaroton Studios in Budapest in 1989, are absolutely natural in balance and combine a sense of intimacy with an admirably realistic projection: the players might well be at the end of one's room. Heard side by side, it is extraordinary how alike the two sets of performances of the three named works are, equally refreshing and spontaneous; and, with the producer (János Mátyás) the same in each instance, the balance and sound too are remarkably similar. Perhaps the acoustics of the Hungaroton Studios are slightly warmer, but there is little in it.

The Amadeus performances are certainly polished but, by the side of the Kodály Quartet, relatively mannered. Norbert Brainin's vibrato is a little tiresome on occasion; but, generally speaking, there is much to reward the listener here; the recordings are vivid and they have enhanced realism and presence in their new CD format. They are also offered at mid-price.

String quartet No. 77 in C (Emperor), Op. 76/3.
(M) *** Teldec/Warner 2292 42440-2 [id.]. Alban Berg Qt – MOZART: *Quartet No. 17.* ***

Back in the 1970s the Alban Berg displayed admirable polish, but the end-result was without that hint of glossy perfection which poses a problem with some of their more recent recordings. This performance of Haydn's *Emperor quartet*, dating from 1975, has playing of striking resilience and sparkle. The famous slow movement has seldom been put on record with such warmth and eloquence. The sound is bright, clear and well balanced, and the Mozart coupling is even finer.

String quartets Nos. 81 in G; 82 in F, Op. 77/1–2; 83 in D min., Op. 103.
(M) **(*) HM/BMG Dig. GD 77106 [77106-2-RG]. Smithson Qt.

The Smithson Quartet is led by Jaap Schröder and is one of the pre-eminent period-instrument ensembles in America. They are recorded in the generous acoustic of the Evangelical Church of Blumenstein near Berne, which helps to enrich the sonority. Readers who prefer their Haydn quartets with this purer timbre rather than with the traditional greater warmth of the modern string quartet will find much to admire here.

Piano sonatas Nos. 33 in C min., Hob XVI/20.
(M) (*(**) Saga mono SCD 9014. Sviatoslav Richter (with CHOPIN: *Ballade No.2 in F, Op. 38; Nocturne in B, Op. 9/3.* LISZT: *Mephisto Waltz No. 1* played by Vladimir Ashkenazy).

Haydn's *C minor Sonata* dates from 1771; written during the composer's *Sturm and Drang* period, it is one of his most individual and searching works for the keyboard. The first movement, with its interrupting ruminative passages, is spontaneously realized, an in the *Andante* the two-part counterpoint is made reminiscent of Bach. Indeed Richter has the work's full measure, yet his style has a disarming simplicity. The mid-1950s live recording appears to have been transfered direct from an LP pressing, since there are some minor clicks as well as tape background. The piano image is acceptable and the ear readily adjusts when the playing has such magnetism. The Ashkenazy recordings come from the same period, long before his Decca contract, and include a rare and charismatic Liszt performance alongside the more usual Chopin items, played with warmth and refinement. Here the piano sound, although limited and not perfactly focused, is fuller in timbre. Audience noises throughout, including the usual bronchial interpolations, are not too distracting.

VOCAL MUSIC

The Creation (*Die Schöpfung;* in German).
(M) *** DG 435 077-2 (2). Janowitz, Ludwig, Wunderlich, Krenn, Fischer-Dieskau, Berry, V. Singverein, BPO, Karajan.
(M) **(*) Decca Dig. 430 473-2 (2) [id.]. Burrowes, Wohlers, Morris, Greenberg, Nimsgern, Chicago Ch. & SO, Solti.

(i) *The Creation;* (ii) *Mass No. 7 in B flat (Little organ mass): Missa brevis Sancti Johannis de Deo.*
(M) *** Decca 425 968 (2). (i; ii) Ameling; (i) Krenn, Krause, Spoorenberg, Fairhurst; (ii) P. Planyavsky (organ); (i; ii) V. State Op. Ch., VPO, Münchinger.

Among versions of *The Creation* sung in German, Karajan's 1969 set remains unsurpassed and, at mid-price, is a clear first choice despite two small cuts (in Nos. 30 and 32). Here Karajan produces one of his most rapt choral performances; his concentration on refinement and polish might in principle seem out of place in a work which tells of religious faith in the most direct of terms, but in fact the result is outstanding. The combination of the Berlin Philharmonic at its most intense and the great Viennese choir makes for a performance that is not only polished but warm and dramatically strong too. The soloists are an extraordinarily fine team, more consistent in quality than those on almost any rival version. This was one of the last recordings made by the incomparable Fritz Wunderlich, and fortunately his magnificent contribution extended to all the arias, leaving Werner Krenn to fill in the gaps of recitative left unrecorded. The recording quality is both atmospheric and lively in its CD transfer.

Münchinger also provides an excellent mid-price *Creation*. It is a fine performance that stands up well, even in comparison with Karajan's set, and the Decca recording is much better balanced. Münchinger has rarely conducted with such electric tension on record and although his direct style is somewhat square, his soloists make a satisfying team. The set also includes Haydn's *Little organ mass*, so called because the solo organ is used to add colour to the soprano's *Benedictus*, a most delightful setting. Ameling here matches her appealing contribution to the main work and the choral singing is pleasingly crisp. The sound is first class, the remastering highly successful.

Solti is predictably fierce in some of the big choruses (*Die Himmel erzälen*, for example, taken at a spanking pace and producing a very exciting climax), but this generally presents a relatively genial view, helped by outstanding choral singing and vivid digital sound. Norma Burrowes is pleasingly fresh, charmingly bright in her girlish tone; but much of the other solo singing is variable, with James Morris's baritone not always taking kindly to the microphone. Nevertheless, for those seeking high-quality recording, the sound here is markedly superior to that of the remastered Karajan analogue set.

The Creation: Arias and choruses.
(M) **(*) DG Dig. 429 489-2. Mathis, Murray, Araiza, Van Dam, V. Singverein, VPO, Karajan).

This is a generous disc of excerpts, offering 72 minutes' playing time, but, without the continuity of the complete work, the ear is drawn to notice the contrived balance.

The Creation (complete; in English).
(M) **(*) EMI CMS7 69894-2 (2). Harper, Tear, Shirley-Quirk, King's College Ch., ASMF, Willcocks.

Quite apart from the fact that it is based on Milton, the idea of *The Creation* was first presented to Haydn in the form of an English libretto provided by the impresario Salomon. David Willcocks captures the work's genial, spirited vigour and it is good to have 'the flexible tiger' and 'the nimble stag' so vividly portrayed. Though Heather Harper is not always quite as steady or sweet-toned as usual, this is a first-rate team of soloists, and the choral singing and the playing of the Academy could hardly be more stylish.

Masses Nos. (i) *7 in B flat: Missa brevis Sancti Joannis de Deo (Little organ mass), Hob XXII/7;* (ii) *8 in C (Mariazellermesse): Missa Cellensis, Hob XXII/8;* (iii) *Organ concerto No. 1 in C, Hob XVIII/1.*
(M) *** Decca 430 160-2; *430 160-4* [id.]. (i) J. Smith; Scott; (ii) J. Smith, Watts, Tear, Luxon; (i; ii) St John's College, Cambridge, Ch., Guest; (i–iii) ASMF; (iii) Preston, Marriner.

The *Little organ mass* dates from 1775 and fares even better here than in the earlier Decca version under Münchinger, coupled with *The Creation*, good though that is. There is some fine invention in this piece, though it is not by any means the equal of the *Mariazellermesse* of 1782, which H. C. Robbins Landon called 'the most perfect large-scale work Haydn achieved' in this particular period. With excellent singing and fine orchestral playing, this is a very desirable issue in the splendid Guest series, and was originally recorded by Argo in 1977. The CD transfers are admirably fresh and well focused, and for a bonus we are given Simon Preston's persuasive account of an early organ concerto, written about 1756. Preston's vivid registration and Marriner's spirited accompaniment ensure the listener's pleasure, and the fine 1966 recording, sounding cleaner in the bass than in its original LP format, was also made at St John's.

Mass No. 9 in B flat (Heiligmesse): Missa Sancti Bernardi von Offida, Hob XXII/10.
(M) *** Decca 430 158-2; *430 158-4* [id.]. Cantelo, Minty, Partridge, Keyte, St John's College, Cambridge, Ch., ASMF, Guest – MOZART: *Litaniae de venerabili.* ***

Of all Haydn's Masses the *Heiligmesse* is one of the most human and direct in its appeal. Its combination of symphonic means and simple vocal style underlines its effectiveness. Haydn started writing this Mass in the first year after his return from London, at about the same time that he wrote the *Paukenmesse*; but it was not completed until later, and was finally dedicated to the memory of St Bernard of Offida, newly canonized by Pope Pius VI barely a century after his death. The name *Heiligmesse* derives from the church song on which Haydn based the *Sanctus*. Among the special points of interest in the work are the slow introduction to the *Kyrie*, very like the introductions to Haydn's late symphonies, and the subdued *Agnus Dei* in the (for the time) extraordinary key of B flat minor. Like the other records in this series, this is a splendid performance, and the vintage Argo sound has been transferred very successfully to CD. The solo singing is good, if not always equally distinguished, and the choral response is excellent. For its reissue, the Mass is generously joined with Mozart's *Litaniae de venerabili altaris sacramento*, recorded over a decade later.

Mass No. 10 in C: Missa in tempore belli (Paukenmesse), Hob XXII/9.

(M) *** Decca 430 157-2; *430 157-4* [id.]. Cantelo, Watts, Tear, McDaniel, St John's College, Cambridge, Ch., ASMF, Guest – MOZART: *Vesperae sollennes.* ***

This was the last of the six Haydn late Masses to be recorded by Guest and his St John's forces for Argo, in 1969, and it is well up to the standard previously set. Guest provides a clean, brightly recorded account with good soloists. The Argo performance sounds very fresh in its remastered format. It is now generously coupled with a fine Mozart recording, made a decade later.

Mass No. 11 in D min. (Nelson): Missa in angustiis.

(M) *** Decca 421 146-2. Stahlman, Watts, Wilfred Brown, Krause, King's College, Cambridge, Ch., LSO, Willcocks – VIVALDI: *Gloria.* ***

The CD of the famous Willcocks account, recorded by Argo in 1962, does not quite manage to control the focus of the resonant King's acoustic, but the effect is admirably full-bodied and vivid; those not wanting to stretch to Pinnock's full-priced digital CD will find this a satisfactory alternative with its very generous Vivaldi coupling.

Mass No. 12 in B flat (Theresienmesse), Hob XXII/12.

(M) *** Decca 430 159-2; *430 159-4* [id.]. Spoorenberg, Greevy, Mitchinson, Krause, St John's College, Cambridge, Ch., Guest – M. HAYDN: *Ave Regina*; MOZART: *Ave verum corpus.* ***

The *Theresa Mass* followed on a year after the *Nelson Mass*. It may be less famous but the inspiration is hardly less memorable, and Haydn's balancing of chorus against soloists, contrapuntal writing set against chordal passages, was never more masterly than here. Argo had started recording these late Masses with the other great Cambridge choir, at King's College; but after the *Nelson Mass* Argo moved down the road to St John's. George Guest injects tremendous vigour into the music (as in the *Harmoniemesse*, there is a 'military' conclusion in the *Donna nobis pacem*) and the St John's Choir, in splendid form, makes the very most of this fine work. Good solo singing and brilliant, vivid, 1965 recording.

Mass No. 13 in B flat (Schöpfungsmesse).

(M) *** Decca 430 161-2; *430 161-4* [id.]. Cantelo,, Watts, Tear, Forbes Robinson, St John's College, Cambridge, Ch., ASMF, Guest – MOZART: *Mass No. 12 (Spaur).* ***

The *Schöpfungsmesse* or 'Creation Mass' was the last but one of the magnificent series that Haydn wrote yearly in his retirement for his patron, Prince Esterházy. Guest again draws an outstanding performance from his own St John's College Choir and an excellent band of professionals, a fresh and direct reading to match the others of his highly successful Argo series. The very opening has superb weight and vigour, matched by the *Gloria*, rich with brass, and the exuberant *Credo*; while in the introduction to the *Benedictus* Haydn uses the horns to create a most forward-looking warmth of colour, before the richly textured vocal entry.

Mass No. 14 in B flat (Harmoniemesse), Hob XXII/14.

(M) *** Decca 430 162-2; *430 162-4* [id.]. Spoorenberg, Watts, Young, Rouleau, St John's College, Cambridge, Ch., Guest – MOZART: *Vesperae de Dominica.* ***

The *Harmoniemesse* was the last of the six Masses, all of them masterpieces, that Haydn wrote after his return from London. He had just completed *The Seasons* and, in 1802 when he wrote the Mass, the Esterházy orchestra was at its most expansive; typically, Haydn took advantage of the extra instruments available: his colourful scoring for a full range of wind and brass led to the German sobriquet. Haydn was over seventy when he started writing this Mass, but his freshness and originality are as striking as in any of the earlier works. In particular the last section of the Mass brings a wonderfully memorable passage when, after the genial, life-enhancing *Benedictus*, comes the contrast of a gentle setting of the *Agnus Dei*, with the spirit of Mozart hovering in the background. Then Haydn bursts out with fanfares into a vigorous, even aggressive *Donna nobis pacem*. The fine performance caps the others in this outstanding series. The quartet of soloists is strong, with Helen Watts in particular singing magnificently. The brilliant and well-balanced 1966 recording has been transferred splendidly to CD, which now offers a substantial bonus in the Mozart *Vespers*, recorded at St John's over a decade later.

The Seasons (Die Jahreszeiten: oratorio): complete (in German).
(M) *** DG 423 922-2 (2) [id.]. Janowitz, Schreier, Talvela, VSO, Boehm.
(M) **(*) Decca 425 708-2 (2). Cotrubas, Krenn, Sotin, Brighton Festival Ch., RPO, Dorati.
(B) *(*) VoxBox 1155972 (2) [CDX 5045]. Donath, Adalbert Kraus, Widmer, S. German Madrigal Ch., Ludwigsburger Schlossfestspiele O, Gönnenwein.

This work, essentially genial, is an expression of a simple faith and of a human being to whom life on the whole has been kind, and who was duly grateful to record the many earthly pleasures he had enjoyed. Boehm's performance enters totally into the spirit of the music. The soloists are excellent and characterize the music fully; the chorus sing enthusiastically and are well recorded. But it is Boehm's set. He secures fine orchestral playing throughout, an excellent overall musical balance and real spontaneity in music that needs this above all else. The CD transfer of the 1967 recording is admirably managed; the sound overall is a little drier, but the chorus have plenty of body and there is an excellent sense of presence.

Dorati brings to the work an innocent dedication, at times pointing to the folk-like inspiration, which is most compelling. This is not as polished an account as Boehm's in the same price-range but, with excellent solo singing and bright chorus work, it is enjoyable in its own right. The choruses of peasants in Part 3, for instance, are boisterously robust. Textually there is an important difference in that Dorati has returned to the original version and restored the cuts in the introductions to *Autumn* and *Winter*, the latter with some wonderfully adventurous harmonies. The performance as a whole is highly animated. With Dorati, this is above all a happy work, a point made all the more telling by the immediacy of the new transfer.

With the date of recording unidentified, this Vox Box offers forward and clean sound, with woodwind very prominent but with strings rather acid and the chorus set back too far. That is a pity when the choral singing is among the more enjoyable elements in the performance. Among the soloists Helen Donath is outstanding, fresh and girlish, but the tenor is too throaty and the baritone is clumsy and often unsteady. The rustic element in the work nevertheless comes over well; the great horn solos which mark the *Autumn* section in particular are ripely satisfying. Recitative tends to be recorded aggressively close.

The Seasons: highlights.
(M) **(*) Ph. Dig. 432 617-2; *432 617-4*. Mathis, Jerusalem, Fischer-Dieskau, Ch. & ASMF, Marriner.

Marriner's set of *The Seasons*, from which this selection is taken, is an easy first choice among modern (full-priced) digital versions, with three first-rate soloists and a chorus and orchestra of authentic size – though with modern instruments – providing the most refreshing results in the pleasing acoustics of St John's, Smith Square. The selection is generous (72 minutes) and well chosen, but this Laser Line series, disgracefully, provides no information whatsover about the work from which these excerpts are drawn, not even telling the purchaser from which section each comes.

Stabat Mater.
(M) *** Decca 433 172-2 [id.]. Augér, Hodgson, Rolfe Johnson, Howell, L. Chamber Ch., Argo CO, Laszlo Heltay.

Haydn's *Stabat Mater*, one of his first major masterpieces showing him at full stretch, was written in the early years at Esterháza. Scored for strings with oboes, the work is far bigger in aim than this scale might suggest, and some of the choruses include harmonic progressions which in their emotional overtones suggest music of a much later period. On record, as in the concert hall, the work is scandalously neglected and it is good that Heltay's reading conveys its essential greatness, helped by excellent soloists and vividly atmospheric recording.

Te Deum in C, Hob XXIIIc/2.
(M) **(*) BMG/RCA GD 86535 [6535-2-RG]. V. Boys' Ch., Ch. Viennensis, VCO, Gillesberger – MOZART: *Requiem mass; Ave verum.* **(*)

A fine, vigorous account of the *Te Deum* by these Viennese forces, very vividly recorded, coupled to a not inconsiderable account of Mozart's *Requiem.* At mid-price it is excellent value.

OPERA

Armida: excerpts; *La vera constanza*: excerpts.
(M) *** Ph. 426 641-2; *426 641-4*. Jessye Norman, Claes Ahnsjö, Lucerne CO, Dorati.

With both these operas currently out of the catalogue, this set of arias and duets is the more attractive, to whet the musical appetite for the complete works. Jessye Norman's voice is superbly captured in fine recording, with Claes Ahnsjö also impressive in two duets. Lively and sympathetic conducting from Dorati.

Haydn, Michael (1737–1806)

Concertino for horn and orchestra in D.
(M) *** Teldec/Warner Dig. 9031 74790-2 [id.]. Dale Clevenger, Liszt CO, Rolla – J. HAYDN: *Concertos.* ***

Michael Haydn's *Concertino* is in the form of a French overture, beginning with a slow movement, followed by a fast one, and closing with a minuet and Trio in which the soloist is featured in only the middle section. The music itself is attractive; the second-movement allegro is played with fine style by Dale Clevenger, whose articulation is a joy in itself. Rolla and his orchestra clearly enjoy themselves in the minuet, which they play with elegance and warmth and, in the absence of the soloist, the unnamed continuo player embroiders the texture gently and effectively. The recording, like the coupled concertos by Josef Haydn, is very realistic indeed, especially during the solo cadenzas which Dale Clevenger provides for the first two movements. An outstanding coupling.

Flute concerto in D.
(B) ** Hung. White Label HRC 107 [id.]. Lóránt Kovács, Györ PO, Sándor – MOZART: *Flute concertos Nos. 1–2.* **(*)

An agreeable if not distinctive work, well played and recorded.

Violin concerto in B flat.
(M) **(*) Teldec/Warner Dig. 9031 74784-2 [id.]. Zehetmair, Liszt CO – J. HAYDN: *Concerto* ***; SIBELIUS: *Concerto.* **

A *Violin concerto* from Michael Haydn (written in 1760) makes an enterprising coupling for the better-known work by his brother, Josef. It is not melodically as memorable as Josef's but is a fine piece, with a lively first movement, rather briskly paced here, and a central *Adagio* of some depth. The finale is the weakest part, though not lacking in spirit. The performance with Thomas Zehetmair combining roles of soloist and conductor is strongly characterized and very well recorded. One's only reservation concerns a tendency for the phrasing – notably in the slow movement – to have squeezed emphases, so that the melodic line swells out dynamically, though this is not an alternative to the use of vibrato, as in 'authentic' performances.

Serenade in D; Symphony in D, P.11.
(B) ** Hung. White Label HRC 100 [id.]. Budapest PO, János Sándor.

Michael Haydn's music represents a happy medium between the baroque and early classical styles. The *Serenade*, for small orchestra, is fairly ambitious, with six movements and an extended *Andante with variations* at its centre. It is undemanding but agreeably inventive, with anticipations of Mozart, notably in the lively first movement. Like the better-known *Symphony in D*, it receives an alert and stylish performance, and the sound is full and bright.

Symphonies Nos. 19 in C, P.10; 21 in C, P.12; 23 in D, P.43; 26 in G, P.16; 29 in C, P.19; 37 in B flat, P.28; 39 in F, P.30; 41 in F, P.32.
(B) **(*) VoxBox 1155012 (2) [CDX 5020]. Bournemouth Sinf., Harold Fabermann.

It is good that Harold Fabermann is exploring the symphonies of Michael Haydn, and even better that they are being recorded digitally – though at times one would not realize this, for the resonant recording often makes tuttis sound opaque and not too cleanly focused. The composer's inspiration is uneven but the slow movements are always pleasing. The scoring is agreeable too, with much use made of the oboe and bassoon. The first work to be offered in the programme, P.12 (No. 21), has a memorable *Andante* in A minor with a most engaging oboe melody, while the *Adagio* of P.32 (No. 41) offers a long, piquant bassoon solo, and the bassoon also makes a surprise entry in the second movement of P.16 (No. 26). This was the symphony which Mozart brought back from Vienna in 1793 and which has long been mistakenly attributed to him (as No. 37, K.444). However, Mozart's score omits the bassoon solo (perhaps he felt it sounded too comic!) so this is the first recording of what Michael Haydn actually wrote. No. 19 (P.10) is scored more ambitiously than usual, with three instead of two horns and the substitution of a pair of cors anglais for oboes in the *Andante*, though with no special sensitivity demonstrated by the composer to the change of colour. Many of the symphonies are notable for their helter-skelter finales (marked variously *Allegro molto*, *Vivace* or *Fugato-Vivace assai*) which have great energy, responsively generated by the Bournemouth players. The performances are well made and sympathetic, suitably athletic in the allegros; but they lack the final degree of flexibility and imagination in the expressive writing. Probably the finest work in the group included is the last on the second disc, No. 29 (P.19), resourcefully scored for a large classical band: highly inventive in the extended central *Rondeau* and generating real vitality in the outer movements. It is given one of the best performances too, and it ought to be in the repertoire. The documentation with the set is admirable; the Perger numbers, incidentally, realign the symphonies in order of composition. The individual movements are all indexed but are not given separate tracks as the backing slip suggests.

Symphony in C, P.12.
(M) *** Teldec/Warner Dig. 9031 74788-2 [id.]. Liszt CO, János Rolla – ROSSINI: *String sonatas.* ***

This *Symphony in C major*, if otherwise fairly conventional, contains a strikingly beautiful inspiration, the central elegiac *Andante in A minor* for strings with solo oboe. It is very well played throughout and is freshly recorded.

Ave Regina.
(M) *** Ph. 430 159-2; *430 159-4* [id.]. St John's College, Cambridge, Ch., Guest – J. HAYDN: *Theresienmesse*; MOZART: *Ave verum corpus.* ***

This lovely antiphon, scored for eight-part double choir, looks back to Palestrina and the Venetian school of the Gabrielis and the young Monteverdi. It is beautifully sung and recorded, and makes an unexpected yet welcome fill-up for the fine Guest version of the *Theresienmesse.*

Hely-Hutchinson, Victor (1901–47)

Carol Symphony.
(M) ** EMI CDM7 64131-2 [id.]; *EG 764131-4.* Guildford Cathedral Ch., Pro Arte O, Barry Rose – QUILTER: *Children's overture;* VAUGHAN WILLIAMS: *Fantasia on Christmas carols.* **

Hely-Hutchinson's *Carol Symphony* dates from the late 1920s. It was essentially a happy idea to construct a work of this kind, but the snag is that carols, if they are good ones, don't admit improvement by 'symphonic' treatment. All you can do with them is to alter their orchestral dress, their harmony (which is seldom an improvement) or – as Constant Lambert observed about the use of folksongs – play them again, louder. Hely-Hutchinson does all these things. His first movement could do with a little judicious pruning, the scherzo is quite effective and in the finale he gathers all the threads together and ends with a triumphal presentation of *O come, all ye faithful.* But it is the *Andante* which remains in the memory with its deliciously imaginative gossamer texture against which the solo harp embroiders *Nowell.* The performance here is lively and sensitive if not distinctive, but the close-miked recording is curiously dry and unexpansive, bearing in mind that the 1966 venue was Guildford Cathedral.

Henze, Hans Werner (born 1926)

(i) *Compases para preguntas ensimismadas* (music for viola & 22 players); (ii) *Violin concerto No. 2* (for solo violin, tape voices & 33 instrumentalists, using Hans Magnus Enzensberger's poem,'Homage à Gödel'); (iii) *Apollo et Hyazinthus.*
(M) *** Decca 430 347-2. (i) Hirofumi Fukai; (ii) Brenton Langbein; (iii) Anna Reynolds, John Constable; (i–iii) L. Sinf., composer.

Compases is a relatively gentle work, with the solo instrument supported by a shimmering orchestral texture, a piece than can easily seem flat and uneventful until you have a chance to hear it repeatedly on record. Of the *Violin concerto No. 2* Henze said that 'it is very nearly a stage piece but not quite' and, with a poem by Enzenberger sung and recited during its course, the drama of the music is strongly presented, with the violin as prime actor. *Apollo et Hyazinthus* is at one and the same time a miniature tone-poem and a harpsichord concerto. Its sonorities are admirably calculated and attractive. All these works are expertly performed and recorded under the composer's authoritative direction, and are of unfailing concern to all who are interested in his development. The music is all transferred brightly to CD, with the sharpest detail.

Symphonies Nos. (i) *1–5*; (ii) *6.*
(M) *** DG 429 854-2 (2) [id.]. (i) BPO, (ii) LSO, composer.

The Henze *Symphonies* are remarkable pieces which inhabit a strongly distinctive soundworld. The *First* with its cool, Stravinskyan slow movement is a remarkable achievement for a 21-year-old, though we hear it in a revision Henze made in early 1963. There is a dance-like feel to the *Third* (1950), written while Henze was attached to the Wiesbaden Ballet. It is rich in fantasy – the titles of its three movements, *Apollo*, *Dithyramb* and *Conjuring dance*, show its involvement in the dance. The *Fourth* was originally intended for the opera *König Hirsch* and was meant to connote 'an evocation of the living, breathing forest and the passing of the seasons'. It is among the most concentrated and atmospheric of his works; there is at times an overwhelming sense of melancholy and a strongly Mediterranean atmosphere to its invention. The *Fifth Symphony* comes from the period of the *Elegy for young lovers* and quotes from one of its arias; the language is strongly post-expressionist. One wonders, however, what its first audience, 'soldiers of the Cuban revolutionary army, sons of workers and students', must have made of the *Sixth Symphony*, composed while Henze was living in Havana! The performances, dating from 1966 and 1972, are excellent and the recorded sound amazingly vivid, even if a comparison between the CD transfer of No. 3 and the original LP reveals some compression – not in terms of dynamic or frequency range, quite the contrary – but in the sense of space occupied by the orchestra. An important and indispensable set, recommended with enthusiasm. Let us hope that DG will soon add the *Seventh Symphony* to their catalogue.

Hérold, Ferdinand (1791–1833)

La Fille mal gardée (ballet, arr. Lanchbery): complete.

(M) *** Decca Dig. *430 849-2* (2) [id.]. ROHCG O, Lanchbery – LECOCQ: *Mam'zelle Angot.* ***

Lanchbery himself concocted the score for this fizzingly comic and totally delightful ballet, drawing primarily on Hérold's music, but interpolating the famous comic *Clog dance* from Hertel's alternative score, which must be one of the most famous of all ballet numbers outside Tchaikovsky. There is much else of comparable delight. Here, with sound of spectacular Decca digital fidelity, Lanchbery conducts a highly seductive account of the complete ballet with an orchestra long familiar with playing it in the theatre, now reissued coupled with Gordon Jacob's equally delicious confection, based on the music of Lecocq.

Zampa: Overture.

(M) *** Mercury 432 014-2 [id.]. Detroit SO, Paray (with Concert: *'French opera highlights'* ***).

It is good to have this old warhorse of the bandstand, a favourite demonstration record of the era of 78s, back in the catalogue in a performance as exhilarating as it is colourful. Marvellous playing and top-class Mercury sound from 1960. The rest of the programme is pretty good too.

Herrmann, Bernard (1911–75)

Film scores: *Beneath the Twelve-mile Reef;* (i) *Citizen Kane: suite; Hangover Square:* (ii) *Concerto macabre. On Dangerous Ground: Death hunt. White Witch Doctor: suite.*

(M) *** BMG/RCA GD 80707; *GK 80707* [0707-2-RG; *0707-4-RG*]. Nat. PO, Gerhardt, (i) with Te Kanawa, (ii) Achucarro.

Bernard Herrmann's reputation as a film composer in the grand Hollywood tradition was immediately established with his remarkable 1940 score for *Citizen Kane.* It is well able to stand up on its own and includes a fascinating pastiche aria from a fictitious opera, *Salammbo*, eloquently sung here by Kiri Te Kanawa. The collection opens with an exhilarating example of the composer's ferocious chase music, the *Death hunt* from *On Dangerous Ground*, led by eight roistering horns with the orchestral brass augmented. *Beneath the Twelve-mile Reef* displays Herrmann's soaring melodic gift and his orchestral flair. The evocation of the undersea forest brings a tapestry backed by nine harps, with an imaginative amalgam of low woodwind, electric bass and organ pedals. The Busoni–Liszt-derived *Concerto macabre* is brilliantly played by Joaquin Achucarro, while *White Witch Doctor* offers opportunities for pseudo-exoticism and a wide range of drum effects, introduced with much colouristic skill. Charles Gerhardt and his splendid orchestra obviously relish the hyperbole and the recording is spectacular. Documentation is excellent and the illustrative stills include a hilarious bedroom encounter between Susan Hayward and a studio tarantula spider.

North by Northwest (film score).

(M) **(*) Unicorn Dig. UKCD 2040. London Studio SO, Laurie Johnson.

Although inventive and scored with Herrmann's usual feeling for atmosphere, this selection of incidental music runs for only 38 minutes. It has a distinctively attractive romantic theme, a simple phrase which becomes quite haunting, introduced first in a section called *Conversation piece* and reprised later in *Duo.* The rest of the score is a series of vignettes, representing various incidents in the screenplay; but one would have to know the film very well to link up much of the music with the narrative. Moreover, the most famous scene in the film – which is illustrated on the front of the CD – Cary Grant's eluding the menacing crop-dusting aircraft, is accompanied by silence! The playing is excellent and the digital recording of high quality.

Hildegard of Bingen (1098–1179)

Ordo virtutum (The Play of the Virtues).

(M) *** HM/BMG Dig. GD 77051 (2) [77051-2-RG; *77051-4-RG*]. Köper, Mockridge, Thornton, Laurens, Feldman, Monahan, Lister, Trevor, Sanford, Smith, Sequentia.

The more one learns about Abbess Hildegard of Bingen, the more astonishing her achievement appears. She was not just a leading poet and composer of the twelfth century, she was a major political figure who not only founded her own Abbey but corresponded with popes and emperors. *Ordo virtutum* is a mystery play, a genre which she may well have created. Where her motets and hymns are more reflective, this 90-minute piece includes strikingly dramatic passages, with the Devil himself intervening. This recording, made in collaboration with West German Radio of Cologne, is outstandingly fine, particularly recommendable for anyone to investigate who already knows the superb collection of shorter pieces recorded by Gothic Voices for Hyperion (at full price). The sound here is equally full, immediate and atmospheric, with the voices beautifully caught.

Hindemith, Paul (1895–1963)

Concert music for strings and brass, Op. 50; (i) *Horn concerto; Nobilissima visione (suite); Symphony in B flat for concert band.*

(M) *** EMI CDH7 63373-2 [id.]. (i) Dennis Brain; Philh. O, composer.

Recorded in 1956, Hindemith's own performances with the Philharmonia Orchestra of four of his most characteristic works come out with astonishing vividness in this digital transfer of well over three decades later; indeed the sheer bloom of the sound and the naturalness of the balance suggest that it could have been made in the 1970s. The *Horn concerto* – distinctly laid out in two fast movements followed by a longer, more formal slow movement as summary – is dazzlingly played by its original performer, Dennis Brain. That has been available in stereo before this latest issue, but it is a revelation to have the other three works, notably the fine ballet score, *Nobilissima visione*. Though there is much in Hindemith's output that is manufactured and arid, *Nobilissima visione*, the work he composed in the 1930s on the theme of St Francis, shows him at his most inspired. The slow movement has a grave beauty that is quite haunting, and its eloquence here should touch even those who regard him as normally outside their reach. There is also dignity and nobility in its splendid opening, and the composer proves a most persuasive interpreter of his own music, drawing refined and committed performances and finding wit in the *Symphony for concert band*. These 73 minutes of music make an ideal introduction to Hindemith's orchestral writing, and collectors can rest assured that the transfers are well managed throughout.

(i) *Concert music for brass and strings; Mathis der Maler* (symphony); (ii) *Viola concerto (Der Schwanendreher).*

(M) **(*) DG 423 241-2 [id.]. (i) Boston SO, Steinberg; (ii) Benyamini, O de Paris, Barenboim.

William Steinberg's accounts of *Mathis* and the *Concert music* were recorded in the early 1970s and are first class, even if the balance is a little recessed. The CD now carries a bonus in the shape of Daniel Benyamini's 1979 version of *Der Schwanendreher*. Hindemith was a fine violist and *Der Schwanendreher* is his third concerto for the instrument; it was completed only three months after he had finished work on *Mathis*. It is based on folksongs and the unusual title (*The Swan-Turner*) is of the tune he uses in the finale. Benyamini and the Orchestre de Paris under Barenboim give a very full-bodied account of it; Benyamini is rather forwardly balanced, but his rich (almost over-ripe) tone is glorious.

Nobilissima visione: suite.

(M) (**) EMI mono CMS7 63835-2 (2) [Ang. CDMB 63835]. Philh. O, Klemperer – BRUCKNER: *Symphony No. 8* **; WAGNER: *Die Walküre*: *Wotan's farewell.* **(*)

Klemperer recorded only the three-movement suite from *Nobilissima visione*, but the three movements incorporate music from all five numbers of the ballet. The Philharmonia play gravely and nobly (especially in the final *Passacaglia*) and Klemperer's rather austere style suits the music. The 1954 mono Kingsway Hall recording is remarkably good.

Octet (for wind and strings).

(M) ** Sony SMK 46250 [id.]. Members of the Marlboro Festival – BARBER: *Summer music* **(*); NIELSEN: *Woodwind quintet.* **

Those unsympathetic to the composer will find Hindemith at his ugliest and most manufactured in the *Octet* (1957–8). It is a divertimento-like piece of about 28 minutes, and even those who like his music may find it hard going at times. The artists recorded here play it more persuasively than most predecessors on disc, and the recording balance places slightly more air round the sound than in the Nielsen. The disc as a whole is well worth investigating.

When lilacs last in the dooryard bloom'd (Requiem).

(M) **(*) Sony/CBS MPK 45881. Louise Parker, George London, NY Schola Cantorum, NYPO, composer.

Hindemith's *When lilacs last in the dooryard bloom'd* was written at the end of the Second World War as the result of a commission from the Robert Shaw Chorale. Here Hindemith himself is at the helm, so the performance carries a special authority. The music has surpassing beauty and eloquence, and the work must be numbered among his most impressive achievements, from the dignified and noble prelude right through to the imposing finale. Why it is not performed more often is a mystery indeed. Louise Parker and George London are committed soloists and, though they are too forward in relation to the orchestra, the recording has a full and realistic acoustic and is perfectly acceptable in its CD format, given the interest of the composer's own interpretation.

(i) *Cardillac* (opera) complete; (ii) *Mathis der Maler*: excerpts.
(M) *** DG 431 741-2 (2) [id.]. Fischer-Dieskau, Grobe, (i) Kirschstein, Kohn, Cologne R. Ch. & SO, Keilberth; (ii) Lorengar, Berlin RSO, Ludwig.

Taken from a radio performance, this reissue of *Cardillac* shows Hindemith at his most vigorous. In the story of a Parisian goldsmith who resorts to murder in order to save his own creations, he uses academic forms such as fugue and passacaglia with Bachian overtones in the idiom but to striking dramatic effect. Fischer-Dieskau as the goldsmith has a part which tests even his artistry, and though the other soloists are variable in quality the conducting of Keilberth holds the music together strongly. This is the original, 1926 version of the score, fresher and more effective than Hindemith's later revision. As a generous and ideal coupling, the second disc contains an hour of excerpts from Hindemith's even more celebrated opera, *Mathis der Maler*, again with Fischer-Dieskau taking the lead, and with Donald Grobe in a supporting role. The selection concentrates on Mathis's solos and on his duets with his beloved, Regina, a role beautifully sung by Pilar Lorengar. The 1960s recordings of both operas are excellently transferred, with voices full and fresh. No texts are given, but instead there are detailed summaries of the plots, with copious quotations.

Hoffmeister, Franz (1754–1812)

Flute concertos: in D; in G.
(BB) **(*) ASV CDQS 6012; *ZCQS 6012*. Dingfelder, ECO, Mackerras; Leonard – C. P. E. BACH: *Concerto*. **(*)

Franz Hoffmeister's two *Flute concertos* are elegantly inventive, if not distinctive. They are well recorded and make pleasant late-evening listening. The performances are sprightly and polished, and the accompaniments have plenty of spirit. The sound is brightly lit, but not excessively so.

Holst, Gustav (1874–1934)

Hammersmith: Prelude and scherzo, Op. 52.
(M) *** Mercury 432 009-2 [id.]. Eastman Wind Ens., Fennell – BENNETT: *Symphonic songs* ***; JACOB: *William Byrd suite* ***; WALTON: *Crown Imperial*. *** ❀

Holst's highly original and characteristically individual piece was commissioned in 1930 by the BBC, but the planned first performance never took place, and Holst never heard the piece in its original form. It is scored for 25 individual wind instruments (there is no doubling of parts in this recording). Holst insisted that *Hammersmith* is not programme music, yet he admitted that the ever-flowing Thames nearby was part of his inspiration. The work has an indelible principal theme, its effects are colourful and imaginative, and its range of mood wide, from introspection to rather jolly folk-dance rhythms. Fennell's pioneering stereo recording is superbly played by these expert students from the Eastman School, and the effect is totally spontaneous. The recording remains demonstration-worthy, though it dates from 1958!

Military band suites Nos. 1–2. Hammersmith: Prelude and scherzo, Op. 52.
(BB) *** ASV CDQS 6021; *ZCQS 6021*. L. Wind O, Denis Wick – VAUGHAN WILLIAMS: *English folksong suite* etc. ***

The London performances have great spontaneity, even if they are essentially lightweight, especially when compared with the earlier, Fennell versions. In *Hammersmith*, however, the approach is freshly direct rather than seeking to evoke atmosphere. The sound is first class and the Vaughan Williams couplings are no less successful; this reissue is very competitively priced.

The Planets (suite), *Op. 32.*
(M) *** EMI CDM7 69045-2 [id.]; *EG 769045-4*. LPO, Boult (with G. Mitchell Ch.).
(M) *** Decca 417 709-2 [id.]. V. State Op. Ch., VPO, Karajan.
(B) **(*) DG Compact Classics 413 852-2 (2); *413 852-4* [id.]. Boston Ch. & SO, Steinberg – ELGAR: *Enigma variations; Pomp and circumstance* *** (CD only: *Cello concerto* ***).
(M) **(*) Decca 430 447-2; *430 447-4* [id.]. LPO & Ch., Solti (with ELGAR: *Pomp and circumstance marches Nos. 1, 4 & 5*. **(*))
(B) **(*) Pickwick Dig. PCD 890; *CIMPC 890* [id.]. LSO & Ch., Hickox.
(M) **(*) EMI Dig. CD-EMX 9513; *TC-EMX 2106*. Amb. S., Philh. O, Rattle.
(M) (***) EMI mono CDH7 63097-2. BBC SO & Ch., Boult (with ELGAR: *Introduction and allegro* (***)).

(i) *The Planets;* (ii) *Egdon Heath, Op. 47; The Perfect Fool* (suite); *Op. 39.*
(M) **(*) Decca 425 152-2; *425 152-4*. LPO, (i) Solti; (ii) Boult (with LPO Choir).

(i) *The Planets;* (ii) *The Perfect Fool* (suite).
(B) *** Decca 433 620-2; *433 620-4* [id.]. (i) LAPO, Mehta; (ii) LPO, Boult.
(BB) **(*) Virgin/Virgo Dig. VJ7 91457-2; *VJ7*

91457-4 [id.]. Royal Liverpool PO, Mackerras.

The Planets; Suite de ballet in E flat, Op. 10. (BB) ** Naxos Dig. 8.550193 [id.]. CRS SO, Bratislava, Adrian Leaper.

It was Sir Adrian Boult who, over sixty years ago, first 'made *The Planets* shine', as the composer put it, and if the opening of *Mars* – noticeably slower than in Boult's previous recordings – suggests a slackening, the opposite proves true: that movement gains greater weight at a slower tempo. *Mercury* has lift and clarity, not just rushing brilliance, and it is striking that in Holst's syncopations – as in the introduction to *Jupiter* – Boult allows himself a jaunty, even jazzy freedom which adds an infectious sparkle. The great melody of *Jupiter* is more flowing than previously but is more involving too, and *Uranus* as well as *Jupiter* has its measure of jollity, with the lolloping 6/8 rhythms delectably pointed. The recording has gained presence and definition with its digital remastering and yet not lost its body and atmosphere. At mid-price, this could well be a first choice for many.

Still very competitive indeed is Karajan's Decca version which still sounds remarkably vivid with its brilliantly remastered recording, now more precise in detail but retaining its atmospheric analogue sound-picture. There are many individual touches, from the whining Wagnerian tubas of *Mars*, *Venus* representing ardour rather than mysticism, the gossamer textures of *Mercury*, and the strongly characterized *Saturn* and *Venus*, with splendid playing from the Vienna brass, now given more bite. The upper range of the strings, however, has a touch of fierceness at higher dynamic levels.

Mehta's set of *Planets* set a new standard for sonic splendour when it was first issued in 1971; the previous (AAD) transfer, reissued on Decca's Weekend label, was quite stunning – particularly *Uranus* – with the brass (and the tuba especially) extraordinarily rich and tangible, the horns rollicking infectiously and the timpani quite riveting. The new ADD transfer still provides outstanding sound, but there is a touch more edge on the strings and the quality has lost just a little of its richness and amplitude; though definition is sharper, the background hiss is fractionally more noticeable. Even so, this is a superb disc and a clear first bargain choice. The power and impact of *Mars* are most impressive, *Saturn* is full of character, and *Jupiter* – with the horns again articulating joyously and the big central melody ample and resonant – is equally striking. This was the young Mehta at his inspirational best, before he went to the USA to take over the NYPO. As on the Solti *Planets*, Boult's splendid account of the ballet suite from *The Perfect Fool* has now been added. This was recorded a decade earlier, but the vintage Decca sound remains spectacular, with the LPO brass hardly less resplendent than their colleagues in Los Angeles.

Also recorded in 1971, Steinberg's Boston set of *Planets* was another outstanding version from a vintage analogue period. It remains one of the most exciting and involving versions and now sounds brighter and sharper in outline, though with some loss of opulence. Steinberg draws sumptuous playing from the Boston Symphony, and anyone who wants to wallow in the colour and power of this extrovert work will certainly be delighted. *Mars* in particular is intensely exciting. At his fast tempo, Steinberg may get to his fortissimos a little early, but rarely has the piece sounded so menacing on record. The testing point for most will no doubt be *Jupiter*, and here Steinberg the excellent Elgarian comes to the fore, giving a wonderful nobilmente swagger. In its Compact Classics reissue Steinberg's fine performance is coupled with Jochum's inspirational account of *Enigma* plus a dash of *Pomp and circumstance*. The pair of CDs also include Fournier's ardent reading of Elgar's *Cello concerto* as a substantial bonus.

The Decca recording for Solti's Chicago version is extremely brilliant, with *Mars* given a vivid cutting edge at the fastest possible tempo. Solti's directness in *Jupiter* (with the trumpets coming through splendidly) is certainly riveting, the big tune red-blooded and with plenty of character. In *Saturn* the spareness of texture is finely sustained and the tempo is slow, the detail precise; while in *Neptune* the coolness is even more striking when the pianissimos are achieved with such a high degree of tension. The analogue recording has remarkable clarity and detail, and Solti's clear-headed intensity undoubtedly brings refreshing new insights to this multi-faceted score, even if some will prefer a less tense, more atmospheric viewpoint. The CD gives the orchestra great presence, and the addition of Boult's classic versions of *Egdon Heath* and *The Perfect Fool* ballet music makes this reissue very competitive. Solti's *Planets* is also available in an alternative issue, less generously coupled. His accounts of the *Pomp and circumstance marches* are vigorous and polished and equally brilliantly recorded – but why only three from the set of five, when the disc has a playing time of only 67 minutes?

Richard Hickox's *Mars* is given an unremittingly fast pace and is angrily aggressive, the climax topped by ferocious percussion. The emphasized dissonance makes *Venus*, with its translucent serenity, the more striking, the playing cool and withdrawn. *Mercury* is attractively fleet, with a proper element of fantasy, and *Saturn* has an elegiac gravity of mood. The disappointments are *Jupiter* and *Uranus*: the former lacking in real jubilation, with the central melody rather square – though there is no lack of energy – and *Uranus* has a forcefulness of accentuation which precludes any geniality. The recording, with its wide dynamic range, is certainly spectacular; it has excellent transparency and detail but rather misses out on expansive warmth.

For Simon Rattle, EMI's digital recording provides wonderfully atmospheric sound, and the quality in *Venus* and *Mercury* is also beautiful, clear and translucent. Otherwise it is not as distinctive a version as one might have expected from this leading young conductor; it is sensibly paced but neither so polished nor so bitingly committed as Karajan or Boult.

Those looking for a modern digital version of the same coupling could well be happy with the Virgo super-bargain issue. Mackerras's usual zestful approach communicates readily and the Liverpool orchestra bring a lively response, but the over-reverberant recording tends to cloud the otherwise pungently vigorous *Mars*, and both *Venus* and *Saturn* seem a little straightforward and marginally undercharacterized, while again in the powerful climax of *Uranus* there is some blurring from the resonance. *The Perfect Fool*, with its vivid colouring and irregular rhythms, has much in common with *The Planets* and makes a fine coupling, especially when played with such flair.

Sir Adrian Boult's 1945 recording of *The Planets* is also most welcome on CD, if only to show nostalgic collectors how vividly the EMI engineers captured the music at the time, when Decca's first FFRR 78-r.p.m. discs were also extending the boundaries of recorded sound, prior to the arrival of LPs. The *Introduction and allegro* also sounds amazing for its period; of course Boult has since recorded both works in greatly improved sound.

On Naxos, the Slovak Radio Orchestra under an English conductor give a direct, straightforward reading, without much subtlety of detail but strong in effect, helped by excellent, full-bodied, digital recording. The big tune in *Jupiter*, taken spaciously, is sonorously eloquent. The novelty is the inclusion of Holst's early four-movement *Suite de ballet*, written in 1899 and revised in 1912. The invention is attractively robust, apart from the winningly fragile *Valse*, and the work is presented enthusiastially. Good orchestral playing throughout.

VOCAL MUSIC

Hymn of Jesus, Op. 37.

(M) *** Decca 421 381-2 (2) [id.]. BBC Ch., BBC SO, Boult – ELGAR: *Dream of Gerontius.* **(*)

Boult's superb performance of *The Hymn of Jesus*, a visionary masterpiece that brings some of Holst's most searching inspirations, comes as a generous and apt – if unusual – coupling for Elgar's great oratorio. The spatial beauty of Holst's choral writing is vividly caught with fine presence in the early-1960s recording.

OPERA

(i; ii) *Sávitri* (chamber opera; complete). (iii) *Choral hymns from the Rig Veda* (3rd group) *H.99. The Evening watch, H.159;* (ii) *7 Partsongs, H.162.*

(M) *** Decca 430 062-2; *430 062-4*. Purcell Singers with (i) J. Baker, Tear, Hemsley; (ii) ECO; (iii) Osian Ellis; Imogen Holst.

There are few chamber operas as beautifully scaled as *Sávitri*. With light texture and many slow tempi, it is a work which can fall apart in an uncommitted performance, but the interpreters on this reissued 1965 Decca (originally Argo) version could hardly be more imaginative. Dame Janet Baker produces some of her most intense and expressive singing. There is no mistaking that the piece is one of Holst's most perfectly conceived works. Aptly, the *Rig Veda hymns*, which follow the opera on this record, are also from a Sanskrit source, and the composer himself suggested that the last of them could, if necessary, be used as a postlude to *Sávitri* (something one can easily arrange with the facilities of CD). The opening *Hymn to the dawn* brings echoes of *Neptune* from *The Planets* and the fast, rhythmically fascinating *Hymn to the waters* is even more attractive. To fill up the disc, the no less imaginative *Partsongs* and the magical *Evening watch* have been added. Beautifully atmospheric Kingsway Hall recording, admirably remastered to match intense and sensitive performances.

Honegger, Arthur (1892–1955)

Pacific 231; Pastorale d'été; Rugby. (i) *Christmas cantata (Cantata de Noël).*

(M) **(*) EMI CDM7 63944-2 [id.]. O Nat. de l'ORTF, Martinon; (i) with Camille Maurane & Ch. d'Oratorio Maîtrise de l'ORTF.

These recordings all date from 1971; although in *Pacific 231* the quality is not quite as impressive as the very best modern sound, it is still very good indeed. The Orchestre National de l'ORTF (which after the reorganization of

French Radio in the 1970s became the Orchestre National de France) plays well for Jean Martinon, though we have heard more atmospheric accounts of *Pastorale d'été* (Martinon is not always responsive to pianissimo indications here). The *Cantata de Noël* is given a stronger performance than Ansermet's, though not even the expert French Radio choir manages the highly exacting demands of Honegger's difficult (and not always effective) choral writing. Generally these are good performances – although the programme offers rather short measure at 46 minutes.

Symphonies Nos. 2 & 3 (Symphonie liturgique).
❀ (M) *** DG 423 242-2 [id.]. BPO, Karajan.

This reissue includes arguably the finest versions of any Honegger works ever put on record. In No. 2 the Berlin strings have extraordinary sensitivity and expressive power, and Karajan conveys the sombre wartime atmosphere to perfection. At the same time, there is astonishing refinement of texture in the *Liturgique*, whose slow movement has never sounded more magical. The recording was always one of DG's best, and this transfer brings to life more detail and greater body and range. A great record, completely in a class of its own.

Symphonies Nos. 2; 4 (Deliciae Basiliensis); (i) *Christmas cantata.*
(M) ** Decca 430 350-2. SRO, Ansermet, (i) with Pierre Mollet, R. Lausanne Ch. & children's Ch.

Ansermet's performance of the *Second Symphony* is vigorous and spirited, and is well recorded for its time (1961). The *Fourth* is also presented characterfully, but the playing does not really do justice to its lightness and wit, although the 1968 sound remains impressive. The *Christmas cantata* is an effective and often moving work and Ansermet's performance is committed; though problems of intonation crop up from time to time, they do not detract too much from the impact of the music-making. However, there are preferable modern versions of all these works available now, so this disc will be mainly of interest to Ansermet devotees.

Symphonies Nos. 2 for strings; 5 (Di tre re).
(M) (***) BMG/RCA mono/stereo GD 60685 [60685-2-RG]. Boston SO, Charles Münch – MILHAUD: *La création du monde* etc. ***

Charles Münch made the first recordings of both *Symphonies*; in fact this transfer of the *Fifth* is one of them. The *Second*, made in 1953, is a bit harder-driven than his very first set on 78s – or, indeed, than his later version with the Orchestre de Paris. The *Fifth* originally appeared on LP coupled with Roussel's *Bacchus et Ariane Suite No. 2* and, though the sound is a bit dry, the performance is full of character. The witty and enigmatic middle movement has never been surpassed on record, though Baudo is more demonic in the finale. Some (but relatively little) allowance needs to be made for the actual sound-quality of the 1952 mono recording.

Symphony No. 4 (Deliciae Basilienses).
(M) *** Erato/Warner 2292 45689-2 [id.]. French Nat. RSO, Münch – DUTILLEUX: *Métaboles.* ***

Münch's 1967 account of the delightful *Fourth Symphony*, which was available on LP only fleetingly, remains by far the most characterful on disc – it is to be preferred to any of the full-price rivals, such as Dutoit (Erato) or Vásáry (Chandos), and has the right blend of energy and atmosphere. The recording is also eminently acceptable, with a decently balanced sound typical of a good broadcast. An additional attraction is the interesting coupling. What this lacks in playing time (it is only 43 minutes) it more than makes up for in quality and musical interest. Strongly recommended.

Le Roi David (complete).
(M) *** Van. 08.4038.71 [OVC 4038]. Davrath, Sorensen, Preston, Singher, Madeleine Milhaud, Utah University Ch., Utah SO, Abravanel.
(M) **(*) Decca 425 621-2 [id.]. Audel (nar.), Danco, De Montmollin, Martin, Hamel, Ch. & SRO, Ansermet.

Honegger's colourful oratorios never sat happily on LP as they spilled over on to a third side – but, at about 70 minutes, they are ideally suited to the CD medium. Listening to the present digital transfer of the Vanguard version, it is difficult to believe that the recording was made in 1961. It is remarkably vivid, well detailed and present, and the playing of the Utah Symphony under Maurice Abravanel is in many respects superior to that of the Suisse Romande for Ansermet. The recording also stands up well to the comparison, though one would welcome greater back-to-front perspective and slightly more air round the soloists. (Decca misleadingly list their set as dating from 1970, which was when the stereo version first appeared, but it was originally issued in mono in 1957.) The Ansermet has Danco, of course, a strong cast and amazingly good sound – but Netania Davrath is excellent too, and so is Madeleine Milhaud, the composer's wife, as the Witch of Endor. Ansermet fully reveals the vivid detail of Honegger's rich tapestry, but both are thoroughly recommendable. Faced with a choice between the two, the excellence of the sound in this transfer tips the scales in Vanguard's favour. This emerges in a much stronger light than it did in its original form.

Howells, Herbert (1892–1983)

Hymnus paradisi.

(M) *** EMI CDM7 63372-2; *EG 763372-4*. Harper, Tear, Bach Ch., King's College Ch., New Philh. O, Willcocks – FINZI: *Dies natalis*. ***

Hymnus paradisi is a dignified and beautifully wrought work but also and more importantly is both moving and powerful. Howells is not among the most original of English composers but, on the strength of this work, he is surely among the most civilized and disciplined. The performance is eloquently and warmly persuasive within the glowing Kingsway Hall acoustics, and the 1970 recording has been enhanced further in its CD transfer.

Hummel, Johann (1778–1837)

Bassoon concerto in F.

(B) ** Hung. White Label HRC 041 [id.]. Gábor Janota, Liszt CO, Frigyes Sándor – J. C. BACH: *Concertos*. **

Hummel's *Concerto* has much more florid and, generally, more interesting passage-work for the bassoon than its two J. C. Bach couplings, and its central *Romanza* has a distinctly *galant* charm. The work is very well played and nicely recorded within a characteristically reverberant Hungaroton acoustic. Not an indispensable disc, but a pleasant one.

(i) *Bassoon concerto in F;* (ii; iii) *Piano concertino in G, Op. 73* (arr. of *Mandolin concerto*); (ii; iv) *Piano concertos: in A min., Op. 85;* (ii; v) *in B min., Op. 89;* (ii; vi; iv) *Double concerto for piano and violin, Op. 17;* (ii) *La Galante Rondo* (for piano), *Op. 120.*

(B) ** Turnabout 0003 (2). (i) Zukerman, Württemberg CO, Faerber; (ii) Martin Galling; (iii) Berlin SO, Bünte; (iv) Stuttgart PO, Paulmüller; (v) Innsbruck SO, Robert Wagner; (v) with Lautenbacher.

Vox pioneered the Hummel concertos in stereo in the late 1960s and early 1970s, but the recordings were of uneven quality and the orchestral playing was seldom strong on finesse. The *Bassoon concerto*, however, is a winner, with much of the charm if not the depth of the famous work by Mozart. It is presented with a real appreciation of its genial humour by George Zukerman who shows himself an uncommonly good musician in matters of technique and phrasing. He is closely balanced and the clicks one hears are not pressing faults but the bassoonist's busy keys. Faerber accompanies warmly, though the orchestral sound is over-resonant in the bass. The arranged *Piano concertino* with its immediately catchy dotted melody in the first movement has a comparably *galant* quality and its amiable chatter is never empty. Again, full recording, though the piano timbre is 'plummy' and the violins are a bit thin on top. Still this is engaging music-making, for Martin Galling is a first-class pianist (as he proves in his solo *Rondo*, Op. 120). Of the two piano concertos the *A minor* is the better-known. Although it is structurally conventional, Hummel uses attractive melodic material, with the characteristically dotted little march theme in the first movement again catching the ear, and a lyrical idea in the finale worthy of Mendelssohn. It is well played and acceptably recorded, with the Stuttgart musicians entering into the spirit of the music alongside the soloist. The *B minor Concerto*, if less distinctive, also has some good tunes and is well made. There is some adventurous writing for the horns in the *Larghetto*, but the playing here (as of the orchestra generally) is not very refined. The soloist, however, is excellent and the sound acceptable. The *Double concerto* is a less interesting work, not helped by a highly modulated recording which places the soloists rather on top of the listener and makes Miss Lautenbacher's tone seem wiry. Still, the CD transfers retain the ambient fullness of the original masters, and there is 143 minutes of music here, so this set can certainly be counted good value.

(i) *Mandolin concerto in G;* (ii) *Partita in E flat for wind;* (iii) *Violin sonata in B flat, Op. 55/1.*

(M) ** Tuxedo TUXCD 1026. (i) Edith Bauer-Slais, V. Pro Musica O, Hladky; (ii) Prague Collegium Musicum; (iii) Zlato Topolski, Hans Kann.

The main attraction here is the *Mandolin concerto*, a charming, lightweight piece with an ingenuous set of variations for its central movement and a winsome finale. Hummel exploits the instrument's limited possibilities skilfully. It needs playing back at a low level to get the sound of the solo instrument in scale, then everything falls into place. It was originally coupled more appropriately with another similar concerto, but now we have more Hummel. The *Wind partita* has the good-natured jocularity that is the speciality of Czech players, but the recording lacks sonority; the *Violin sonata*, too, is rather a good piece, and it is well played and adequately recorded.

Piano quintet in E flat, Op. 87; Piano septet in D min., Op. 74.

(M) *** Decca 430 297-2; *430 297-4* [id.]. Melos Ens. – WEBER: *Clarinet quintet.* ***

These two highly engaging works show the composer at his most melodically fecund and his musical craftsmanship at its most apt. One can see how Hummel charmed nineteenth-century audiences into regarding him as being a greater composer than he was, for his facility and skill at shaping and balancing a movement can be impressive. It is the ideas themselves (as in all music) that can make or break the structure, and here they are entirely appropriate to music designed in the first instance to entertain. This these works certainly do in such spontaneous and polished performances – just try the opening movement of the *Septet* to sample the composer's felicity. Moreover the 1965 recording sounds absolutely first class in its CD format.

Humperdinck, Engelbert (1854–1921)

Hänsel und Gretel (complete).

(M) *** EMI CMS7 69293-2 (2) [Ang. CDMB 69293]. Schwarzkopf, Grümmer, Metternich, Ilsovay, Schürhoff, Felbermayer, Children's Ch., Philh. O, Karajan.

Karajan's classic 1950s set of Humperdinck's children's opera, with Schwarzkopf and Grümmer peerless in the name-parts, is enchanting; this was an instance where everything in the recording went right. The original mono LP set was already extremely atmospheric. In most respects the sound has as much clarity and warmth as rival recordings made in the 1970s. There is much to delight here; the smaller parts are beautifully done and Else Schürhoff's Witch is memorable. The snag is that the digital remastering has brought a curious orchestral bass emphasis, noticeable in the Overture and elsewhere, but notably in the *Witch's ride.*

Königskinder (complete).

(M) *** EMI CMS7 69936-2 (3). Donath, Prey, Dallapozza, Schwarz, Unger, Ridderbusch, Bav. R. Ch., Tolz Boys' Ch., Munich R. O, Wallberg.

The success of *Hänsel und Gretel* has completely overshadowed this second fairy-tale opera of Humperdinck, which contains much fine music. Humperdinck had expanded his incidental music for a play to make this opera, which was given its première in New York in 1910. In an entertainment for children, the sadness and cruelty of a typical German fairy-tale, not to mention the heavy vein of moralizing, are a serious disadvantage, but in a recording as fine as this it is a piece well worth investigation. Both the conducting and the singing of the principals are most persuasive.

Königskinder: highlights.

(M) *** EMI CDZ2 52379-2 (from above recording; cond. Wallberg).

Because of the English-language production at the London Coliseum, EMI have rushed out an attractive set of highlights (64 minutes), which many will find an ideal sampler of Humperdinck's little-known children's opera. The chosen excerpts have much lyrical appeal and even charm (track 6 includes an appropriate quotation from *Hansel and Gretel*). The singing is most persuasive and the recording is pleasingly atmospheric. Unfortunately, EMI have hurriedly issued the German edition of the disc with neither translation nor a synopsis.

Ibert, Jacques (1890–1962)

Escales (Ports of call).

(M) **(*) Mercury 432 003-2 [id.]. Detroit SO, Paray – RAVEL: *Alborada* etc. ***

Paray's recording catches the Mediterranean exoticism of *Escales* admirably, and the 1962 Mercury recording has plenty of atmosphere as well as glittering detail. The diaphanous strings in the opening *Palermo* are particularly impressive, and only in the loudest tuttis does the sound seem over-brilliant. The Ravel couplings are very impressive too.

Symphonie concertante (for oboe and string orchestra).

(M) *** BMG/RCA GD 87989. John de Lancie, LSO, Previn – FRANÇAIX: *L'horloge de flore* *** ❀; R. STRAUSS: *Oboe concerto.* ***

Ibert's *Symphonie concertante* was written for Paul Sacher and the Basle Chamber Orchestra in 1948/9, and its astringency of idiom is slightly at odds with Ibert's usually more light-hearted musical persona. The writing in the outer movements has enormous vitality and impulse and demands great virtuosity from the orchestra; here it produces an exhilarating response from the LSO strings, and the extended *Adagio* has a wan, expressive poignancy. John de Lancie is a first-class soloist. André Previn directs with much conviction and spirit; this came from his vintage recording period with RCA in 1966. The sound is very good – its slight lack of opulence suits the music.

d'Indy, Vincent (1851–1931)

Diptyque méditerranéan; Poème des rivages (symphonic suite).

(M) **(*) EMI Dig. CDM7 63954-2. Monte Carlo PO, Prêtre.

Neither work represents d'Indy at his most consistently inspired but there are still good things. As Martin Cooper put it in his study of French music, 'in the *Poème des rivages* [d'Indy] distilled the last drops of that honey he had gathered so assiduously in the garden of Franck'. The comparison often made between the *Diptyque* and the glorious *Jour d'été à la montagne* is not flattering. But the *Soleil matinal* of the *Diptyque* has a blend of the Wagner of *Parsifal* and that quality of conservative impressionism which d'Indy made so much his own after the turn of the century. There are considerable beauties in this piece and in the *Poème* and, though the recording is not top-drawer, string textures are transparent, even diaphanous at gentler moments, and the sound does not lack allure. This is well worth investigating for, despite some unevenness of inspiration, Prêtre holds the music together impressively.

La forêt enchantée, Op. 8; Istar (variations symphoniques), Op. 42; Wallenstein (trilogie), Op. 28.

(M) ** EMI CDM7 63953-2 [id.]. O Philharmonique des Pays de Loire, Pierre Dervaux.

Vincent d'Indy seems to be emerging from the shadows and his growing representation on CD is greatly to be welcomed. *La forêt enchantée* is an early work, written in his mid-twenties. Although reminders of Wagner and of *Le chasseur maudit* by his master, César Franck, are clearly in evidence, there is individuality and great exuberance. The *Wallenstein* trilogy occupied him between 1873 and 1878 but was not put into its final shape for another ten years. The outer movements, *Le camp de Wallenstein* and *La mort de Wallenstein*, are better known than the middle one, *Max et Técia*, and none is anywhere near as appealing in either the quality of its invention or orchestral presentation as *La forêt enchantée* or the much later *Istar* variations, though even these are thickly scored. These recordings date from 1978 except *Istar*, which was made three years earlier; they are serviceable rather than outstanding.

Symphonie sur un chant montagnard français (Symphonie cévenole).

(B) *** Hung. White Label HRC 106 [id.]. Gabriella Torma, Budapest PO, Tamás Pál – LALO: *Symphonie espagnole.* **(*)

(M) *** Sony MPK 46730 [id.]. Robert Casadesus, Phd. O, Ormandy – CASADESUS: *Concerto for 3 pianos* **; FRANCK: *Symphonic variations.* ***

(M) **(*) BMG/RCA GD 86805 [6805-2-RG]. Nicole Henriot-Schweitzer, Boston SO, Munch – FRANCK: *Symphony.* **(*) ❀

(i) *Symphonie sur un chant montagnard français (Symphonie cévenole);* (ii) *Symphony No. 2 in B flat, Op. 57.*

(M) *** EMI CDM7 63952-2. (i) Ciccolini, O de Paris, Baudo; (ii) Toulouse Capitole O, Plasson.

The *Symphonie sur un chant montagnard français* is the work by which Vincent d'Indy is best known in this country, though the *Second Symphony* is occasionally heard. So the present coupling in EMI's '*L'esprit français*' reissue series is propitious. Aldo Ciccolini gives a good account of himself in the demanding solo part of the former, and the Orchestre de Paris under Serge Baudo give sympathetic support. The music is charming and resourceful and the recording, if not outstanding, is pleasing and with a convincing piano image. The *Second Symphony* (1902–3) is as impressive as it is neglected. Although its cyclic organization betrays its francophilia, there is intellectual vigour, charm (as in the modal, folk-like *Modéré* of the third movement) and nobility in the arching lines of the fugue in the finale. Michel Plasson proves a sympathetic and committed advocate, and his orchestra, though not in the luxury bracket, responds with enthusiasm and sensitivity to his direction. The recording too is spacious, full and well focused. Those who complain about repeated duplications of the Franck *Symphony* should investigate this disc and discover one of the composer's most powerful works.

A sensitive and atmospheric account of the concertante piece from Gabriell Torma and the Budapest Philharmonic under Pál. The Hungaroton recording is warmly atmospheric and the piano is balanced well with the orchestra. There is no lack of vividness here, and these artists show great sympathy for this attractive music. The Lalo coupling is recommendable, too. A bargain.

Casadesus gives a commanding performance of d'Indy's once popular *Symphonie sur un chant montagnard français*, and the transfer does greater justice to the sonority of the fabulous Philadelphians than it did in its earlier, LP incarnations. The recording comes from the late 1950s but more than holds its own with later records from this illustrious orchestra. Indeed the transfer has recaptured some of the sumptuousness of the string tone, though the piano timbre is at times lacking in freshness.

Nicole Henriot-Schweitzer and Munch present a fresh and crisp performance which is certainly true to the atmosphere of the composer's inspiration, which he found in the mountains of the Cevennes. Munch's natural affinity and the bright-eyed response of the Boston players make for the happiest results, and Henriot-Schweitzer plays the piano part most sympathetically. The early (1958) stereo recording comes up well; there is not always absolute internal clarity, but the Boston acoustics are effective in this music, and the piano focus is bright and sharp.

Ives, Charles (1874–1954)

Holidays Symphony.

(B) ** VoxBox (2) [CDX 5035]. Dallas SO, Johanos – COPLAND: *Billy the Kid* etc.; RACHMANINOV: *Symphonic dances* etc. **

The so-called *Holidays Symphony* (also known as *New England holidays*) consists of four fine Ives pieces normally heard separately. The first three, *George Washington's birthday*, *Decoration Day* and *The Fourth of July*, with their still-startling clashes of impressionistic imagery, are well enough known. The fourth – full title: *Thanksgiving and/or Forefathers Day* – is a rarity, bringing in a full choir to sing a single verse of a hymn. The performances here are vividly enthusiastic if not absolutely refined. But the recording is impressive with its atmospheric effects, even if not perfectly balanced.

Symphony No. 3; Three places in New England.

(M) *** Mercury 432 755-2 [id.]. Eastman-Rochester O, Howard Hanson – SCHUMAN: *New England triptych* ***; MENNIN: *Symphony No. 5.* **(*)

Ives's quixotic genius is at its most individual in the *Three places in New England.* Written between 1903 and 1914, this music is still able to shock the ear, especially the second movement, *Putnam's Camp, Redding, Connecticut*, with its fantasy images inspired by a child's dream at a site connected with the American War of Independence. Although the work opens with a sense of magical evocation, the outer movements are also highly original and searingly atmospheric, especially the tumultuous climax of *From the Housatonic at Stockbridge* when all nature seems to erupt into the composer's consciousness. Both works are most understandingly presented here under Howard Hanson, who is equally at home in the folksy imagery of *The Camp meeting*, which is the subtitle of the *Third Symphony*, an immediately attractive triptych, full of colourful invention. The acoustics of the Eastman Theatre are less than ideally expansive, but the 1957 recording is remarkably full-bodied and vivid – though, particularly in the symphony, the forward balance brings a noticeable lack of dramatic dynamic contrast. Nevetheless, with the performances thoroughly sympathetic, this worthwhile reissue would make an excellent start for newcomers to Ives's extraordinary singularity.

(i) *Symphony No. 4; Robert Browning Overture;* (ii) Songs: *An Election, Lincoln the great commoner; Majority, They are There!*

(M) *** Sony MPK 46726 [id.]. (i) NY Schola Cantorum; (ii) Gregg Smith Singers; American SO, Stokowski

This reissue of three vintage Stokowski recordings of Ives makes a welcome addition to the Masterworks Portrait series, well transferred to CD. The (originally 1965) recording of the *Fourth Symphony*, made at the same period as the belated première of the work, brings a stunning performance, with sound that is still amazingly full and vivid. Stokowski also brings out the often aggressive vigour of the *Robert Browning Overture.* The choral songs with orchestra provide an attractive makeweight.

Jacob, Gordon (1895–1987)

William Byrd suite.

(M) *** Mercury 432 009-2 [id.]. Eastman Wind Ens., Fennell – BENNETT: *Symphonic songs* ***; HOLST: *Hammersmith* ***; WALTON: *Crown Imperial.* *** ❀

Gordon Jacob's arrangement of the music of Byrd is audaciously anachronistic, but it is very entertaining when played with such flair under that supreme maestro of the wind band, Frederick Fennell. The closing number, *The Bells* (*Variations on a ground*), is particularly successful. The recording is up to the usual high Mercury standard in this repertoire.

Janáček, Leoš (1854–1928)

Sinfonietta.

(M) *** Decca 425 624-2 [id.]. LSO, Abbado – *Glagolitic Mass.* ***

Sinfonietta; Lachian dances; Taras Bulba.

(BB) *** Naxos Dig. 8.550411 [id.]. Slovak RSO (Bratislava), Ondrej Lenárd.

Sinfonietta; Taras Bulba.

(M) *** Decca Dig. 430 727-2; *430 727-4* [id.]. VPO, Mackerras – SHOSTAKOVICH: *Age of gold.* ***

Mackerras's coupling comes as a superb supplement to his Janáček opera recordings with the Vienna Philharmonic. The massed brass of the *Sinfonietta* has tremendous bite and brilliance as well as characteristic Viennese ripeness, thanks to a spectacular digital recording. *Taras Bulba* too is given more weight and body than is usual, the often savage dance rhythms presented with great energy.

Abbado gives a splendid account of the *Sinfo-*

nietta and evokes a highly sympathetic response from the LSO. His acute sensitivity to dynamic nuances and his care for detail are felt in every bar, without any sense of excessive fastidiousness, and this is thoroughly alive and fresh playing. The recording balance, too, allows the subtlest of colours to register while still having plenty of impact. In its remastered CD format it sounds quite splendid.

On Naxos we have the normal LP coupling of the *Sinfonietta* and *Taras Bulba*, but with the *Lachian dances* thrown in for good measure, all played by musicians steeped in the Janáček tradition – and all at a very modest cost. The Slovak Radio Orchestra is very good indeed, though their strings are not equal in opulence to those of the Czech Philharmonic; nor does Ondrej Lenárd have quite the same grip on the proceedings as did Ančerl in the 1960s. All the same, these are excellent performances and well worth the money involved; the recording, made in a fairly resonant studio, is natural and free from any artificially spotlit balance.

Sinfonietta; Preludes: From the House of the Dead; Jealousy (original *Overture to Jenůfa*); *Katya Kabanova; The Makropulos affair.*
(M) *(**) EMI CDM7 63779-2; *EG 763779-4.*
Pro Arte O, Mackerras (with WEINBERGER: *Schwanda the Bagpiper: Polka & fugue;* SMETANA: *Bartered Bride: Overture* ***).

Sir Charles Mackerras (having studied in Prague with Václav Talich) became for the music of Janáček what Beecham before him had been for the promulgation of the works of Delius. The present (1959) performance has a fire and bite that are not quite matched even by Mackerras himself in his later, Decca record (see above). The playing of the Pro Arte Orchestra is immensely vivid; its lack of the last degree of refinement seems to increase its forceful projection. The brass sonorities (the work uses twelve trumpets) are pungent, and elsewhere the recording has striking detail and colour. The original coupling of the four operatic *Preludes* was an imaginative choice, and similar comments apply to the vibrant playing here. The only snag is that in this bright CD transfer the EMI engineers have rather gone over the top in the upper range, which is very brightly lit indeed to the point of shrillness. The two vivacious encores by Weinberger and Smetana have comparable colour and zest, plus excellent detail, and it is a pity that, even here, the upper range is a bit fierce.

String quartets Nos. 1 (Kreutzer); 2 (Intimate letters).
(M) *** Decca 430 295-2; *430 295-4* [id.].
Gabrieli Qt – SMETANA: *Quartet No. 1.* ***

Janáček's two *String quartets* come from his last years and are among his most deeply individual and profoundly impassioned utterances. The Gabrieli Quartet have the measure of this strikingly original music and give a highly idiomatic and strongly felt account of these masterpieces. They have the advantage of a well-focused and truthfully balanced recording, made in Rosslyn Hill Chapel in 1977, which has transferred well to CD and has maximum clarity and blend as well as considerable warmth. With its generous Smetana coupling, this CD plays for 73 minutes.

Piano sonata (1.X.1905); In the mist; On the overgrown path, Book 2; A recollection; Theme & variations.
(M) *** DG 429 857-2 [id.]. Rudolf Firkušný.

Rudolf Firkušný brings a special authority and sensitivity to this repertoire. As a small boy he played many of these pieces to the composer, but it is his selfless dedication to this music that tells. He recorded these pieces for DG in the early 1970s and he produces seamless legato lines, hammerless tone and rapt atmosphere. Given its competitive price, many collectors will opt for this anthology, which still sounds very good and also includes the *Zdenka Theme and variations.*

VOCAL MUSIC

Glagolitic Mass.
(M) *** Decca 425 624-2 [id.]. Kubiak, Collins, Tear, Schone, Brighton Festival Ch., RPO, Kempe – *Sinfonietta.* ***

(i) *Glagolitic Mass; Taras Bulba.*
(M) ** DG 429 182-2; *429 182-4* [id.]. (i) Lear, Rössl-Majdan, Haefliger, Crass, Bav. R. Ch.; Bav. RSO, Kubelik.

The Decca recording is an extremely good one. Kempe's reading is broad but has plenty of vitality, and the Brighton chorus sings vigorously. The playing of the Royal Philharmonic is wonderfully committed and vivid, and there is first-rate solo singing, with Teresa Kubiak particularly impressive. The sound on CD is splendidly lively and colourful, of vintage Decca quality.

The reissued DG coupling under Kubelik has considerable merits: there is some very fine playing in *Taras Bulba.* In a less competitive marketplace it would have been very welcome, but Kempe is preferable – the effect marginally less refined, perhaps, but with greater overall impact, even though the DG remastering gives a very lively effect.

Järnefelt, Armas (1869–1958)

Praeludium.
(M) *** EMI CD-EMX 2176; *TC-EMX 2176.* Bournemouth SO, Berglund – ALFVÉN: *Swedish rhapsody*; GRIEG: *Peer Gynt.* **(*)

Järnefelt's charming miniature has been absent from the catalogues for too long (it used to be very familiar because it fitted easily on to a 78-r.p.m. side). It is nicely played here and given bright, immediate recording. A pleasing lollipop, used as an encore for a well-planned concert of Scandinavian music.

Joachim, Joseph (1831–1907)

(i) *Violin concerto in the Hungarian manner, Op. 11. Overtures: Hamlet, Op. 4; Henry IV, Op. 7.*
(M) *** Pickwick Dig. MCD 27. (i) Elmer Oliveira; LPO, Leon Bottstein.

Joseph Joachim's fame rests as a legendary performer and the dedicatee of the Brahms *Violin concerto*, rather than as a composer – though his admirers included Tovey, who wrote a long analytical essay about the *Hungarian Concerto*. The conductor Leon Bottstein not only gives committed accounts of the splendid *Henry IV* and *Hamlet Overtures* but also provides a long and interesting note on the composer. Like Svendsen he gave up composition relatively early in his career – but for different reasons. Joachim abandoned composition not long after the *Hungarian Concerto* when he was twenty-three ('Why should one compose while there is a Brahms in the world?'). It is by no means a virtuoso concerto but, as Bottstein says, 'a major musical statement whose ambitions and musical ideas tower over those by Spohr, Vieuxtemps and Wieniawski'. It lasts over three-quarters of an hour (the first movement alone, at nearly 25 minutes, is longer than the Brahms) and is one of the most demanding works written for the instrument in the nineteenth century. Conservative in outlook and indebted to Mendelssohn and Beethoven, it is a very considerable achievement – as, for that matter, is the playing of Elmer Oliveira in this truthful, present and well-balanced recording. An enterprising and rewarding release.

Joplin, Scott (1868–1917)

Rags: *A Breeze from Alabama; The Cascades; The Chrysanthemum; Easy winners; Elite syncopations; The Entertainer; Maple leaf rag; Original rags; Palm leaf rag; Peacherine rag; Something doing; The Strenuous life; Sunflower slow drag; Swipesy; The Sycamore.*
(M) *** BMG/RCA GD 87993 [7993-2-RG]. Dick Hyman.

Dick Hyman's playing is first rate. His rhythmic spring (the crisp snap of the main phrase of *Original rags* is a splendid example), clean touch and sensibility in matters of light and shade – without ever trying to present this as concert music – mean that pieces which can easily appear stereotyped remain fresh and spontaneous-sounding throughout. The recording has fine presence; the piano image (not too rich, but not shallow either) seems just right. There is nearly an hour of playing time and this is essentially a recital to be dipped into rather than listened to at a single sitting.

Kabalevsky, Dmitri (1904–87)

The Comedians (suite), *Op. 26.*
(M) *** EMI Dig. CDD7 63893 [id.]; *ET 763893.* Bav. State O, Sawallisch (with Concert of Russian music ***).

Kabalevsky's suite has a certain brashness in its scoring at times, but the polished playing of the Bavarian State Orchestra adds a touch of elegance and these ten charming vignettes, full of colour and vitality, are made to sound very entertaining indeed. The most famous is the exuberant *Galop*, a knockabout circus piece, complete with xylophone; but the charming *Intermezzo* and the gentle *Little lyrical scene* are just as memorable in their contrasting restraint, while the Scherzo is worthy of Prokofiev. First-class sound, with plenty of ambience, so that the music can be boisterous without vulgarity.

Khachaturian, Aram (1903–78)

Gayaneh (ballet): *suite.*
(BB) *** BMG/RCA VD 87734 [7734-2-RV]. Boston Pops O, Fiedler – OFFENBACH: *Gaîté parisienne.* ***
(B) **(*) DG Compact Classics *413 155-4* [id.]. Leningrad PO, Rozhdestvensky – RIMSKY-KORSAKOV: *Scheherazade*; STRAVINSKY: *Firebird suite.* **(*)

Gayaneh: suite; Masquerade: suite; Spartacus: suite.
(B) **(*) Decca 417 062-2; *417 062-4.* LSO, Stanley Black.

Gayaneh: suite; Spartacus: suite.
(M) **(*) Decca 417 737-2 [id.]. VPO, composer – PROKOFIEV: *Romeo and Juliet.* ***

Fiedler's offering is a miniature suite; it includes the *Lesginka*, *Dance of the Rose Maidens* and *Dance of the Kurds*, plus an exhilarating *Sabre dance*, all played with zest and flair – but, alas, it omits the *Lullaby*. Fiedler and his

Bostonians are at their best, and the RCA sound is pretty good too. An excellent coupling for an outstanding bargain version of Offenbach's *Gaîté parisienne* ballet.

No one does the *Sabre dance* like the Russians, and with Rozhdestvensky it makes a sensational opening, exploding into the room at the end of Stravinsky's *Firebird suite.* The performance overall combines excitement with panache, and the original drawback of a rather fierce recording has been met here by the slight attenuation of the upper range of the chrome-tape transfer.

The composer's own first selection on Decca was recorded in 1962 and offers five items from *Gayaneh* and four from *Spartacus*, coupled to an intelligent selection from Maazel's complete Cleveland set of Prokofiev's *Romeo and Juliet*, dating from a decade later. Khachaturian achieves a brilliant response from the VPO and everything is most vivid, notably the famous *Adagio* from *Spartacus*, which is both expansive and passionate. It is a pity that the Decca remastering process has brought everything into such strong focus; the presence of the sound certainly makes an impact, but the massed violins now have an added edge and boldness of attack, at the expense of their richness of timbre.

Stanley Black understands the spirit of this music and the LSO make a colourful and vibrant response. The recording is forwardly balanced but extremely lively, and this is an inexpensive way of acquiring some of the composer's most memorable ideas.

Symphony No. 2; Gayaneh: suite.
(M) (***) Decca 425 619-2 [id.]. VPO, composer.

The *Symphony* was a propaganda piece, written during the war when the composer was evacuated from Moscow. Khachaturian lays the Armenian colour on very thickly but, unlike the splendid *Violin concerto* of two years earlier, this does not develop into a coherent argument. If the musical value is roughly in inverse proportion to the amount of noise made (and it is a long and very loud score indeed), one can still find the composer's earnest attempts to create a symphonic structure curiously endearing, and the lyrical moments are often quite attractive. The performance gives the music passionate advocacy and the recording is superbly spectacular (although the CD remastering doesn't help its garish qualities). When one turns to the *Gayaneh* coupling, splendidly done, one realizes where Khachaturian's talent really lies.

Khachaturian, Karen (born 1920)

Violin sonata in G min., Op. 1.
(M) ** BMG/RCA GD 87872; *GK 87872* [7872-2-RG; *7872-4-RG*]. Heifetz, Steuber – CASTELNUOVO-TEDESCO: *Concerto No. 2* (**); FERGUSON: *Sonata* **; FRANÇAIX: *Trio.* ***

Karen is the nephew of Aram Khachaturian and studied with Miaskovsky and Shostakovich in the late 1940s. Their tutelage shows in every bar of this eminently well-fashioned but not particularly individual piece. It is well laid out for the instruments and very accomplished for an Opus 1, and it has attracted the advocacy of David Oistrakh as well as of Heifetz. The work is beautifully played by Heifetz, though Lillian Steuber is not the most poetic of pianists. Goodish 1966 recording, but with not quite an ample enough acoustic.

Klemperer, Otto (1885–1973)

(i) *Symphony No. 2;* (ii) *String quartet No. 7.*
(M) ** EMI CMS7 64147-2 (2) [id.]. (i) New Philh. O, Klemperer; (ii) Philh. Qt – MAHLER: *Symphony No. 7.* **

Based on the evidence here, Klemperer was not a composer of great individuality, and he obviously found difficulty in resolving stylistic discrepancies between grittily chattering fast music (sometimes with a touch of Bartók in the *Quartet*) and slow, romantic music. The *Quartet* is the more vital work, though even here the concluding sweet slow movement does not quite belong, and the best movement is the charming and unpretentious Scherzo, which relaxes in a very Mahlerian way into a contrasting waltz theme. The *Symphony* has a passage – clarinet over pizzicato strings – that recalls Viennese operetta, but here the influence is unassimilated. For all the reservations, it is fascinating to find out what lies behind the interpretative façade of a great musician. The *Symphony* could have benefited from an extra rehearsal, but the *Quartet* is splendidly done.

Kodály, Zoltán (1882–1967)

(i) *Concerto for orchestra; Summer evening;* (ii) *Háry János: suite.*
(M) **(*) DG 427 408-2. (i) Budapest PO, composer; (ii) Berlin RSO, Fricsay.

Kodály's *Concerto for orchestra* does not set out to rival the Bartók *Concerto*, but in its own way it is attractive and easy to listen to. *Summer evening*, a pleasantly rhapsodic pastoral piece, dates from ten years earlier. Kodály's own recordings come from 1960 and originally sounded recessed, with little immediacy of impact. The improvement on CD is dramatic and the performances of both works sound much more vital, even if Kodály does not display the fervour and intensity which Fricsay brings to the *Háry János suite* (recorded a year later), with *The Battle and defeat of Napoleon* made very dramatic indeed. The Berlin Radio orchestra play splendidly and the sound is sparkling and clear.

(i) *Dances of Galánta; Marosszék dances;* (ii) *Háry János: suite.*
(M) *** Mercury 432 005-2 [id.]. (i) Philharmonia Hungarica; (ii) Minneapolis SO, Dorati – BARTÓK: *Hungarian sketches* etc. ***

Dances of Galánta; Dances of Marosszék; Háry János suite; Variations on a Hungarian folksong (The Peacock).
(M) *** Decca 425 034-2; *425 034-4* [id.]. Philharmonia Hungarica, Dorati.

From sneeze to finale, the Minneapolis orchestral playing in the *Háry János suite* is crisp and vigorous; the excellent 1956 Mercury stereo, while providing well-integrated tuttis, also gives simple separation for the solos and delicate highlighting of the more subtle percussion effects, especially the cimbalom. Dorati went on to record the other two sets of dances with the Philharmonia Hungarica in 1958. The playing of the woodwind soloists in the slow dances is intoxicatingly seductive, and the power and punch of the climaxes come over with real Mercury fidelity. An outstanding disc, since the Bartók couplings are equally successful.

When, in the early 1970s, Dorati and the Philharmonia Hungarica finished their monumental task of recording Haydn's symphonies complete, they returned to the music of their compatriot, Kodály. Though of course (by comparison with the Haydn set) the string section is augmented, there is the same sense of commitment. The performances of the *Galánta dances* and the familiar *Háry János suite* are first class, and the *Peacock variations* – luxuriantly extended, highly enjoyable and deserving of greater popularity – are equally fine. While the older, Mercury performances have a very special electricity of their own, the 1973 Decca recording is more modern and is of vintage quality; many collectors will also prefer to have the *Peacock variations* rather than the Mercury Bartók alternative couplings. The Decca disc plays for nearly 76 minutes.

Háry János suite.
(BB) *** Naxos Dig. 8.550142 [id.]. Hungarian State O, Mátyás Antal (with Concert: *'Hungarian festival'* ***).
(M) *** EMI Dig. CDD7 63900-2 [id.]; *ET 763900-4*. LPO, Tennstedt – DVOŘÁK: *Symphony No. 9.* **(*)
(M) (***) BMG/RCA mono GD 60279; *GK 60279* [60279-2-RG; *60279-4-RG*]. NBC SO, Toscanini – DVOŘÁK: *Symphony No. 9* (***); SMETANA: *Má Vlast: Vltava.*(**)

The Hungarian performance of the *Háry János suite* is wonderfully vivid, with the cimbalom – perfectly balanced within the orchestra – particularly telling. The grotesque elements of *The Battle and defeat of Napoleon* are pungently and wittily characterized and the *Entrance of the Emperor and his Court* also has an ironical sense of spectacle. The brilliant digital sound adds to the vitality and projection of the music-making, yet the lyrical music is played most tenderly.

Tennstedt might seem an unlikely conductor for Kodály's sharply characterized folk-based score, but his performance has sympathy as well as power and brilliance, drawing out the romantic warmth of the *Intermezzo*. Digital sound of the fullest, richest EMI vintage.

There is nothing relaxed about Toscanini's view of *Háry János*. He seems not to realize that a joke is involved; but the intensity of the performance gives the music a new and bigger scale, whether appropriate or not. A valuable and rare coupling for the fine examples of Toscanini conducting Czech music.

(i) *Hymn of Zrinyi*; (ii) *Psalmus Hungaricus.*
(M) *** Decca 421 810-2 (2). (i) Luxon, Brighton Festival Ch., Heltay; (ii) Kozma, Brighton Festival Ch., Wandsworth School Boys' Ch., LSO, Kertész – DVOŘÁK: *Requiem.* ***

Psalmus Hungaricus is Kodály's most vital choral work, and this Decca version comes as close to an ideal performance as one is likely to get. Here, with a chorus trained by a Hungarian musician, the results are electrifying, and the recording is outstandingly brilliant too. The light tenor tone of Lajos Kozma is not ideal for the solo part, but again the authentic Hungarian touch helps. The *Hymn of Zrinyi*, for unaccompanied chorus and baritone solo, celebrates a Magyar hero, and Heltay is persuasive. With first-class remastered sound, this generous coupling with Dvořák is strongly recommended.

Missa brevis: Agnus Dei. Psalms 114 and 121.
(M) ** Tuxedo TUXCD 1078 [id.]. Whikehart Ch., Lewis Whikehart – LISZT: *Missa choralis.* **

An acceptable if ungenerous coupling for Liszt's fine choral work (there would have been room for the whole *Missa brevis*). The performances are quite eloquent and the 1962 recording is very good. The Psalms are sung in German. But this CD plays for only 42 minutes.

Koechlin, Charles (1867–1961)

Les Bandar-log (symphonic poem), *Op. 176.*
(M) *** EMI CDM7 63948-2 [id.]. BBC SO, Dorati – BOULEZ: *Le soleil des eaux;* MESSIAEN: *Chronochromie* etc. ***

Les Bandar-log is the most immediately attractive of the works included in this Gulbenkian-sponsored collection. It is a symphonic poem based on the Kipling story, but used to satirize the vagaries of twentieth-century composers. Among his monkey tribe, Koechlin finds sham Debussians, sham Schoenbergians and sham neo-classicists; after illustrations from each, the spirit of the forest responds with inspired and beautiful working of the main themes. Koechlin – long neglected outside France – accomplishes his plan with fluent mastery and the score is aurally fascinating, especially in a performance as finely played and dedicated as this and with a 1964 recording which in its CD transfer approaches the demonstration class.

Korngold, Erich (1897–1957)

Film scores: *The Adventures of Robin Hood* (suite); *Captain Blood: Ship in the Night;* (i) *The Sea Hawk* (suite).
(M) *** BMG/RCA GD 80912; *GK 80912* [0912-2-RG; *0912-4-RG*]. Nat. PO, Charles Gerhardt; (i) with Amb. S. – STEINER: *Film scores.* ***

Korngold was the most distinguished of all the Hollywood film composers, and almost all his music makes agreeable entertainment separated from the screen images. His score for *Robin Hood* was justly celebrated and *The Sea Hawk* similarly combined animated battle-sequences with strong lyrical invention. Curiously, although this collection, centring on the swashbuckling movies of Erroll Flynn, is entitled *'Captain Blood'*, only a fragment – if a potent one – is included from Korngold's music for this film. Juxtaposed with the more flamboyant Steiner scores for other Flynn vehicles, this makes for one of the very best of these Hollywood anthologies, for the most part offering extended groups of excerpts and fairly generous measure overall. As in the rest of the series, the dedication of Charles Gerhardt and the superb playing of the National Philharmonic Orchestra, coupled with sumptuous RCA recording, means that these performances communicate strongly. The documentation is excellent, but only four illustrations are offered.

Film scores: excerpts from: *Another Dawn; Anthony Adverse; Deception:* (i) *Cello concerto in C, Op. 37. Of Human Bondage; The Prince and the Pauper; The Private Lives of Elizabeth and Essex; The Sea Wolf.*
(M) *** BMG/RCA GD 80185; *GK 80185* [0185-2-RG; *0185-4-RG*]. Nat. PO, Gerhardt, (i) with Gabarro.

This second disc, like the third, below, is entirely devoted to Korngold's music. The opening sequence of *The Private Lives of Elizabeth and Essex* (written for performance at the film's première) with its vivid thrust, admirably demonstrates the vigour of Korngold's inspiration. He drew on the attractive, lightweight score for *The Prince and the Pauper* as a basis for the variations in the last movement of the *Violin concerto*, while *Night scene* from *Another Dawn* – very effective in its own right – was to provide the principal theme of the first movement. For *Deception* he invented a miniature cello concerto, which is heard here in its expanded complete format. Nearly all this music is inventively rich and the performances by Gerhardt and the National Philharmonic are as persuasive as ever, with brilliant, spacious recording to match. Good documentation and six movie stills.

Film scores: excerpts from: *Anthony Adverse; Between Two Worlds;* (i) *The Constant Nymph; Deception; Devotion; Escape Me Never; King's Row; Of Human Bondage; The Sea Hawk* (suite); *The Sea Wolf* (suite).
(M) *** BMG/RCA GD 87890 [7890-2-RG]. Nat. PO, Gerhardt; (i) with Procter, Amb. S.

This was the first of the Korngold film collections to be reissued on CD and it makes a good summation of the scope of his achievement, particularly when, as throughout the series, the performances are so persuasively committed and the remastered recording, with its panoply of brass and strings, is attractively full and spacious. Hollywoodian hyperbole is heard at its most overwhelming in the *Between Two Worlds* sequence, while *The Constant Nymph* (about a composer) brings a characteristically flamboyant setting for contralto soloist (here Norma Procter) and chorus. *The Sea Wolf* contrasts a snarlingly pungent portrait of the main character (played by Edward G. Robinson) with a tenderly nostalgic romantic interlude. The *Elegy* for *Devotion* is equally touching, while the music for *The Sea Hawk* (an Errol Flynn vehicle) is vigorously exhilarating.

String quartets Nos. 1; 3.
(M) **(*) BMG/RCA GD 87889 [7889-2-RG]. Chilingirian Qt.

The *First* is the finer of the two quartets. It comes from 1923 and was written for Arnold Rosé, the brother-in-law of Mahler, whose string group gave its first performance. It comes from a period of some creative vitality and its inspiration is fresher than its later companion. The *Third Quartet*, dedicated to Bruno Walter, comes from 1945 and is a much feebler work, incorporating ideas used in some of Korngold's Hollywood scores. The Chilingirian give a good account of themselves and the 1977 recording still sounds very good.

OPERA

Die tote Stadt (complete).
(M) *** BMG/RCA GD 87767 (2) [7767-2-RG]. Neblett, Kollo, Luxon, Prey, Bav. R. Ch., Tölz Ch., Munich R. O, Leinsdorf.

At the age of twenty-three Korngold had his opera, *Die tote Stadt*, presented in simultaneous world premières in Hamburg and Cologne! It may not be a great work, but in a performance like this, splendidly recorded, it is one to revel in on the gramophone. The score includes many echoes of Puccini and Richard Strauss, but its youthful exuberance carries the day. Here René Kollo is powerful, if occasionally coarse of tone, Carol Neblett sings sweetly in the equivocal roles of the wife's apparition and the newcomer, and Hermann Prey, Benjamin Luxon and Rose Wagemann make up an impressive cast. Leinsdorf is at his finest.

Krebs, Johann Ludwig (1713–80)

Double concerto in B min. for harpsichord, oboe and strings.
(M) **(*) DG 431 120-2. Jaccottet, Holliger, Camerata Bern, Van Wijnkoop – GRAUN; TELEMANN: *Concertos.* ***

Krebs was a pupil of J. S. Bach; he left Leipzig with a glowing testimonial from the master and one can understand why from this delightful *Double concerto*, which makes a good coupling for the concertos of Graun and Telemann. Holliger as ever plays beautifully, but Christiane Jaccottet adopts too romantically expressive a style. However, this remains well worth hearing, and the recording is first rate.

Kreisler, Fritz (1875–1962)

Allegretto in the style of Boccherini; Allegretto in the style of Porpora; Caprice viennoise; Cavatina; La Chasse in the style of Cartier; La Gitana; Grave in the style of W. F. Bach; Gypsy caprice; Liebesfreud; Liebesleid; Praeludium and allegro in the style of Pugnani; Recitative and scherzo; Schön Rosmarin; Shepherd's madrigal; Sicilienne et rigaudon in the style of Francoeur; Toy soldiers' march; Viennese rhapsodic fantasia; arr. of *Austrian National Hymn.*
(BB) **(*) ASV CDQS 6039; *ZCQS 6039.* Oscar Shumsky, Milton Kaye.

A generous (67 minutes) and well-varied bargain recital of Kreislerian encores. To open with the famous *Austrian Hymn* played as a violin solo was not a very good choice, but most of the programme comes off splendidly. Oscar Shumsky's combination of technical mastery and musical flair is ideal for this music; and it is a pity that the rather dry recording and forward balance – well in front of the piano – makes the violin sound almost too close.

Caprice viennoise, Op. 2; La Gitana; Liebesfreud; Liebesleid; Polichinelle; La Précieuse; Recitativo and scherzo caprice, Op. 6; Rondo on a theme of Beethoven; Syncopation; Tambourin chinois; Zigeuner (Capriccio). Arrangements: ALBÉNIZ: *Tango, Op. 165/2.* WEBER: *Larghetto.* WIENIAWSKI: *Caprice in E flat.* DVOŘÁK: *Slavonic dance No. 10 in E min.* GLAZUNOV: *Sérénade espagnole.* GRANADOS: *Danse espagnole.*
(M) *** DG 423 876-2; *423 876-4* [id.]. Shlomo Mintz, Clifford Benson.

One can understand why DG chose to introduce Shlomo Mintz with this Kreisler programme in 1981 alongside his coupling of the Bruch and Mendelssohn concertos. He plays with a disarmingly easy style and absolute technical command, to bring out the music's warmth as well as its sparkle. Try *La Gitana* to sample the playing at its most genially glittering. A very attractive programme, given first-class recording and splendid presence without added edge on CD.

Kuhnau, Johann (1660–1722)

Biblische Historien Sonatas Nos. 1, 2, 3 & 6.
(B) ** Hung. White Label HRC 130 [id.]. Anikó Horváth (harpsichord).

This early example of keyboard programme music was written by Bach's predecessor at St Thomas's Church, Leipzig. Bible stories are used and the chosen examples here include descriptions of *The fight between David and Goliath*, *Saul cured by David through music*, *Jacob's wedding* (lasting nearly twenty minutes!) and *death and burial.* It is very doubtful whether anyone could begin to guess the narrative detail from the music itself, even knowing the subject-matter, although the music is strongly presented. The recording of the harpsichord is bold, a shade over-resonant. A curiosity.

Lalo, Eduard (1823–92)

Cello concerto No. 1 in D min., Op. 33.
(B) *** DG 431 166-2; *431 166-4.* Heinrich Schiff, New Philh. O, Mackerras – FAURÉ:

Élégie; SAINT-SAENS: *Cello concerto No. 1.* ***

(M) **(*) Mercury 432 010-2 [id.]. Janos Starker, LSO, Skrowaczewski – SAINT-SAENS; SCHUMANN: *Concertos.* ***

(M) *(*) Erato/Warner 2292 45688-2 [id.]. Navarra, LOP, Münch – SAINT-SAENS: *Concerto No. 1.* **

(i) *Cello concerto in D min.;* (ii) *Symphonie espagnole, Op. 21.*

(M) *(*) Erato/Warner 2292 45087-2 [id.]. (i) Lodéon, Philh. O, Dutoit; (ii) Pierre Amoyal, Monte Carlo Op. O, Paray.

This was Heinrich Schiff's début recording in 1977, made when he was still very young. His account of the Lalo *Concerto* is fresh and enthusiastic and very well recorded for its period. With its excellent coupling it makes a real bargain.

Janos Starker's 1962 recording with the LSO under Stanislaw Skrowaczewski sounds remarkably good for its age. Though the tutti chords are brutal and clipped, Starker plays splendidly, and the famous Mercury recording technique lays out the orchestral texture quite beautifully and with remarkable transparency.

André Navarra is very forwardly balanced and the recording is less detailed than the Mercury rival, which offers the additional inducement of the Schumann *Concerto.* Münch gets some good playing from the now defunct Lamoureux Orchestra, but this would not be a first choice.

Lodéon's performance of the *Cello concerto* is also recommendable in every way, with the Philharmonia under Dutoit providing excellent backing. For the coupling, Amoyal gives a warm and polished account of the *Symphonie espagnole*, rhythmically infectious and with many a seductive turn of phrase. Unfortunately here the Erato recording has a middle and bass emphasis which causes a muddy orchestral resonance, although the violin timbre remains sweet.

Symphonie espagnole (for violin and orchestra), *Op. 21.*

(M) *** DG Dig. 429 977-2 [id.]. Perlman, O de Paris, Barenboim – SAINT-SAENS: *Concerto No. 3.* ***

(M) **(*) Sony MPK 45555 [MYK 37811]; *40-45555.* Stern, Phd. O, Ormandy – BRUCH: *Concerto No. 1.* **(*)

(B) **(*) Ph. 422 976-2; *422 976-4* [id.]. Szeryng, Monte Carlo Op. O, Van Remoortel – PAGANINI: *Violin concerto No. 3.* ***

(B) **(*) Hung. White Label HRC 106 [id.]. Miklós Szenthelyi, Hungarian State O, Lukács – D'INDY: *Symphonie.* ***

(B) **(*) Sony MBK 44717 [id.]. Zukerman, LAPO, Mehta – BRUCH: *Concerto No. 1.* **(*)

Lalo's brilliant five-movement distillation of Spanish sunshine is well served by DG. The strongly articulated orchestral introduction from Barenboim combines rhythmic buoyancy with expressive flair and the lyrical material is handled with great sympathy. The richness and colour of Perlman's tone are never more telling than in the slow movement, which opens tenderly but develops a compelling expressive ripeness. The brilliance of the scherzo is matched by the dancing sparkle of the finale. The recording is extremely lively but fairly dry, and the forward balance of the soloist does not obscure orchestral detail.

Stern's version from the late 1960s has all the rich, red-blooded qualities which have made this artist world-famous; indeed this coupling with the Bruch *G minor Concerto* is one of his very finest records. Reservations concerning the close solo balance are inevitable (although Ormandy's fine accompaniment is not diminished); nevertheless the playing makes a huge impact on the listener and, although the actual sound-quality is far from refined, the charisma of the performance is unforgettable.

Szeryng's performance was recorded in 1970. He is in splendid form and brings out the work's Spanish sparkle, especially in the brilliant finale. The accompaniment is less distinctive, and the spotlighting of the soloist means that some of the orchestral detail, which is less strong in personality, is almost lost. Yet Szeryng's flair carries the day, and his Paganini coupling is outstanding too.

On Hungaroton, Miklós Szenthelyi brings an added Hungarian sparkle to this music without losing its seductive Spanish character. He is a fine, full-timbred player and this is an attractively spontaneous performance, well accompanied and with an effervescent finale. Although the resonant recording makes tuttis somewhat bass-heavy, detail is well observed and the slow movement is richly sonorous.

Zukerman's account of Lalo's five-movement *Symphonie espagnole* is first class in every way. The solo playing has real panache, Mehta accompanies vividly, and the recording is transferred well to CD, even if the balance is not ideal in its relationship of the soloist to the orchestra.

Symphony in G min.

(M) **(*) CDM7 63396-2 [id.]. O Nat. de l'ORTF, Sir Thomas Beecham – FRANCK: *Symphony.* **(*)

Symphony in G min.; Rapsodie norvégienne; Le roi d'Ys: overture.

(M) *** Ph. 432 278-2; *432 278-4.* Monte Carlo Opera O, Antonio de Almeida.

Lalo's *G minor Symphony* is not the strongest of nineteenth-century French symphonies but, as this Philips reissue demonstrates, it is worth an occasional airing. Beecham was a keen champion of out-of-the-way French music of this period, and his recording with the French Radio Orchestra has maintained public awareness of the work. The Monte Carlo orchestra is not as impressive an orchestra as the French group; but Almeida observes the repeat in the first movement and plays the work with evident affection. He is a most convincing advocate, particularly in the *Adagio* and finale. Moreover the 1974 Philips recording is superior to the early Beecham EMI alternative; both the *Rapsodie norvégienne* (especially the exciting *Presto* secondary section) and *Le roi d'Ys* are also very well played. Almeida, though not dull, refuses to go over the top in the latter piece, to good effect.

The *Symphony*'s second-movement scherzo with its delectable flute-writing has the sparkling memorability which has long made Lalo's concertante violin work, the *Symphonie espagnole*, an unfailing success, and that scherzo inspires Beecham to a delectably pointed performance; but he has to work harder with the rest, when the material is thinner, and the argument in the first movement lacks tautness. It is good to have Beecham's version of this colourful rarity in coupling with the other French symphony, also recorded at Beecham's very last sessions, in December 1959, but it has to be conceded that Almeida's account overall is more enjoyable. As in the Franck, the EMI recording has good body and presence, but the transfer adds an edge on top.

Lambert, Constant (1905–51)

Horoscope (ballet): *suite:* (i) *Dance for the Followers of Leo;* (ii) *Saraband for the followers of Virgo;* (i) *Valse for the Gemini;* (ii) *Bacchanale;* (i) *Invocation to the moon* and finale. (iii; ii) *The Rio Grande.* (ii) *Ballabile* (Chabrier, arr. Lambert); *Apparitions* (Liszt, arr. Lambert, orch. Jacob): *Galop; Cave scene.*

(M) (***) EMI mono CDH7 63911-2 [id.]. (i) Royal Liverpool PO; (ii) Philh. O; (iii) with Kyla Greenbaum, BBC Ch., Lambert – GORDON: *Rake's progress;* RAWSTHORNE: *Street corner.* (***)

Lambert made these recordings of some of his principal works between 1945 and 1951, and the sound is spectacularly good for its period, full and bright with a sense of presence that almost suggests stereo. The CD transfers are excellent too, giving plenty of body. More than any subsequent interpreter, Lambert himself captured the authentic jazz inflexions in his brilliant choral settings of Sacheverell Sitwell's 'Rio Grande', both in the vigorous sequences and in the languidly beautiful ones, often based on tango rhythm. Kyla Greenbaum is the similarly understanding piano soloist. Few British works so vividly capture the atmosphere of the 1920s, and the excerpts from the later ballets are comparably colourful and vigorous. From this one can see why for a long time Lambert was bracketed as a composer with his friend, William Walton. The highly engaging *Horoscope* suite, which is otherwise available only at full price (on Hyperion), is made up from recordings made at two different periods. The Rawsthorne and Gavin Gordon items make apt fill-ups.

Lassus, Orlandus (*c.* 1530–94)

Missa, Super bella Amfitrit' alterna.

(M) **(*) EMI Dig. CD-EMX 2180; *TC-EMX 2180.* St John's College, Cambridge, Ch., Guest – ALLEGRI: *Miserere* **(*); PALESTRINA: *Veni sponsa Christi.* ***

Amphitrite was not only the mythological goddess of the sea but also a nickname for Venice, and this Mass is almost certainly connected with the city rather than with Poseidon's wife. It is a complex and varied piece of remarkable textural diversity, and it is finely sung here, although perhaps a little more Latin fervour would have been in order. The digital recording is first class.

Musica Dei donum; Lauda Sion salvatorem; Missa Puisque j'ay perdu.

(M) *(*) HM/BMG GD 77083 [77083-2-RG]. Pro Cantione Antiqua, Bruno Turner.

The *Puisque j'ay perdu* Mass, as its title indicates, is a parody Mass based on the chanson of the same name by Johannes Lupi (its full title is *Missa ad imitationem moduli Puisque j'ay perdu cum quatuor vocum*). It was published in 1577 but was probably written in Munich around 1560. Its vast companion-piece on this disc, the motet *Lauda Sion salvatorem*, is in four sections and takes the best part of 23 minutes, and it represents Lassus at his most expansive and dignified. The performances by the Pro Cantione Antiqua and Bruno Turner date from 1975; for all their accomplishment and expressive ambition, they are less than wholly compelling: there is a certain uniformity of tone, and the vibrato of some of the singers is too wide for comfort and does not blend well. Just as the white, vibrato-less colour of some modern groups quickly induces monotony, so does the reverse. We like this group and admire much of Bruno Turner's work, but this is not one of their best records.

Lecocq, Alexandre (1832–1918)

Mam'zelle Angot (ballet, arr. Gordon Jacob).
(M) *** Decca 430 849-2 (2) [id.]. Nat. PO, Bonynge – HÉROLD: *La Fille mal gardée*. ***

La Fille de Madame Angot was a highly successful operetta of the 1870s. The ballet originated for Massine's post-Diaghilev company and was first danced in New York in 1943. It found its definitive form, however, in a later, Sadler's Wells, production, also choreographed by Massine. The narrative line follows the story of the operetta and much of the music is also drawn from that source; however, Gordon Jacob includes excerpts from other music by Lecocq. It is a gay, vivacious score with plenty of engaging tunes, prettily orchestrated in the modern French style. There are flavours from other composers too, from Adam to Sullivan, with Offenbach's influence strongly felt in the final carnival scene. Bonynge offers the first recording of the complete score, and its 39 minutes are consistently entertaining when the orchestral playing has such polish and wit. The Kingsway Hall recording is closely observed: the CD brings sharp detail and tangibility, especially at lower dynamic levels. The violin timbre is rather brightly lit, but the crisp focus of the recording suits the witty orchestration.

Lehár, Franz (1870–1948)

The Land of Smiles (Das Land des Lächelns; complete, in German).
(M) (***) EMI mono CHS7 69523-2 (2). Schwarzkopf, Gedda, Kunz, Loose, Kraus, Philh. Ch. & O, Ackermann.

Though Gedda does not have quite the passionate flair of Tauber in his famous *Dein ist mein ganzes Herz*, his thoughtful artistry matches a performance which effortlessly brings out the serious parallels without weighing the work down. Schwarzkopf and Kunz sing delectably and the transfer to CD of a well-balanced mono recording is very lively and full of presence.

The Merry Widow (Die lustige Witwe; complete, in German).
(M) (***) EMI mono CDH7 69520-2 [id.]. Schwarzkopf, Gedda, Kunz, Loose, Kraus, Philh. Ch. & O, Ackermann.

It was this set, of the early 1950s, which established a new pattern in recording operetta. Some were even scandalized when Schwarzkopf insisted on treating the *Viljalied* very seriously indeed at an unusually slow tempo; but the big step forward was that an operetta was treated with all the care for detail normally lavished on grand opera. Ten years later in stereo Schwarzkopf was to record the role again, if anything with even greater point and perception, but here she has extra youthful vivacity, and the *Viljalied* – ecstatically drawn out – is unique. Some may be troubled that Kunz as Danilo sounds older than the Baron, but it is still a superbly characterful cast, and the transfer to a single CD is bright and clear.

The Merry Widow (English version by Christopher Hassall): abridged.
(B) ** CfP CD-CFP 4485; *TC-CFP 4485*. Bronhill, Lowe, Glynne, McAlpine, Round, Dowling, Sadler's Wells Op. Ch. and O, William Reid.

The performance on Classics for Pleasure does not always have an *echt*-Viennese flavour; nevertheless it says much for the achievement of the Sadler's Wells production in the 1950s that their version is so successful. For many, the deciding factor will be the English words, sung in an admirable translation; but one is not sure that this is so important on a recording. The Sadler's Wells cast is strongly characterized; only in Howell Glynne's approach is there a suspicion of Gilbert and Sullivan. The chorus is outstandingly good (especially the men) in the big scenes. The 1959 recording sounds fresh, if slightly dated, but the voices and diction are clear and, though there is a touch of shrillness on top, there is an agreeable ambient feeling.

The Merry Widow (English version by Bonynge): highlights.
(M) **(*) Decca 421 884-2; *421 884-4* [id.]. Sutherland, Krenn, Resnik, Masterson, Ewer, Brecknock, Fryatt, Egerton, Amb. S., Nat. PO, Bonynge.

Although not everyone will take to Sutherland's Widow, this is generally an attractive English version. The exuberantly breezy overture (arranged by Douglas Gamley) introduces all the hits seductively, to set the mood of the proceedings; the slightly brash recording (the sheen on the strings sounding digitally bright, even though this a remastered 1977/8 analogue recording) is determinedly effervescent. The chorus sings with great zest and the ensembles are infectious. The whole of the closing part of the disc – the Finale of Act II, Njegus's aria (nicely done by Graham Ewer), the introduction of the girls from Maxim's and the famous *Waltz duet* – is certainly vivacious; the Parisian atmosphere may seem a trifle overdone, but enjoyably so. Earlier, Sutherland's *Vilja* loses out on charm because of her wide vibrato, but the *Waltz duet* with Krenn is engaging.

Leoncavallo, Ruggiero (1858–1919)

I Pagliacci (complete).

(M) *** EMI CMS7 63967-2 (2) [id.]. Amara, Corelli, Gobbi, La Scala, Milan, Ch. & O, Von Matačić – MASCAGNI: *Cavalleria Rusticana*. **(*)

(M) *** BMG/RCA GD 60865 (2) [60865-2]. Caballé, Domingo, Milnes, John Alldis Ch., LSO, Santi – PUCCINI: *Il Tabarro*. **(*)

(M) **(*) EMI CMS7 63650-2 (2). Scotto, Carreras, Nurmela, Amb. Op. Ch., Philh. O, Muti – MASCAGNI: *Cavalleria Rusticana*. **(*)

The EMI (originally Columbia) recording under Von Matačić dates from the early 1960s and is especially notable for the contribution of the tenor, Franco Corelli, as Canio, which calls for some superlatives. He is not not nearly as imaginative as some of the great tenors of the past, yet he shows a natural feeling for the phrases. It is not just a question of making a big, glorious noise – though of course he does that too – but of interpreting the music; and a performance like this puts several others, by more obviously starry names, in the shade. Gobbi is a predictably magnificent Tonio; true, there are some threadbare patches towards the top of the voice, but at that time it was still a most varied instrument and Gobbi used it to the greatest dramatic effect. Lucine Amara gives a thoroughly sound performance as Nedda, both vocally and dramatically, and the recording has a vivid sense of atmosphere and movement. The coupled *Cav.* is dramatically not quite so striking, but this still makes a clear first choice in the mid-priced range for those who want the pairing with Mascagni.

For those who do not want the obvious coupling with *Cavalleria Rusticana*, the RCA set is a first-rate recommendation, with fine singing from all three principals, vivid playing and recording, and one or two extra passages not normally included – as in the Nedda–Silvio duet. Milnes is superb in the Prologue, and though Caballé does not always suggest a young girl, this is technically the most beautiful account of Nedda available on record. The 1971 recording was made at Walthamstow Town Hall and the CD transfer has plenty of atmosphere and increased vividness. A full translation is provided.

Under Muti's urgent direction both *Cav.* and *Pag.* represent the music of violence. In both he has sought to use the original text, which in *Pag.* is often surprisingly different, with many top notes eliminated and Tonio instead of Canio delivering (singing, not speaking) the final *La commedia è finita*. Muti's approach represents the antithesis of smoothness, and the coarse rendering of the *Prologue* in *Pag.* by the rich-toned Kari Nurmela is disappointing. Scotto's Nedda goes raw above the stave, but the edge is in keeping with Muti's approach, with its generally brisk speeds. Carreras seems happier here than in *Cav.*, but it is the conductor and the fresh look he brings which will prompt a choice here. The sound is extremely vivid.

I Pagliacci: highlights.

(B) *** DG Compact Classics *427 717-4* [id.] (from complete recording with Joan Carlyle, Bergonzi, Benelli, Taddei, La Scala Milan Ch. & O, Karajan) – MASCAGNI: *Cavalleria Rusticana*: highlights. ***

(M) **(*) EMI CDM7 63933-2 [id.]; *EG 763933-2* (from above recording; cond. Muti) – MASCAGNI: *Cavalleria Rusticana*: highlights **(*).

(M) ** Decca 421 870-2; *421 870-4*. Freni, Pavarotti, Wixell, L. Op. Ch., Nat. PO, Patanè – MASCAGNI: *Cavalleria Rusticana*: highlights. **

Karajan's refined approach to Leoncavallo is matched by fine singing from all the principals and, with all the key items from the opera included, this is a very attractive Compact Classics tape coupling. The sound is excellent, although the choral focus is rather soft-grained.

On EMI, a good sampler of the vibrant Muti set with the key numbers vividly projected (27 minutes). The original text is used, which brings some surprises, and there are moments of coarseness too, particularly in the *Prologue*. But the red-blooded drama is very much to the fore.

On Decca, a reasonably generous coupling of excerpts from *Cav.* and *Pag.* with about half an hour from each opera. The sound is extremely lively and vivid, even if the performances are flawed. Pavarotti is obviously committed, though in both operas he seems reluctant to sing anything but loud. Voices are recorded rather close, and Freni is not helped by the balance, not as sweet-sounding as she usually is.

Liadov, Anatol (1855–1914)

(i) *Baba Yaga, Op. 56; The enchanted lake, Op. 62; Kikimora, Op. 63;* (ii) *8 Russian folksongs*.

(BB) **(*) Naxos Dig. 8.550328 [id.]. Slovak PO, (i) Gunzenhauser (ii) Kenneth Jean – Concert: *'Russian Fireworks'*.

It is good to have inexpensive recordings of these key Liadov works, particularly the *Russian folksongs*, eight orchestral vignettes of great charm, displaying a winning sense of orchestral colour. The performances are persuasive, and the digital recording is vivid and well balanced. They are part of an attractive concert of Russian music, much of it with a more extrovert appeal.

Ligeti, György (born 1923)

(i) *Chamber concerto for 13 instrumentalists;* (ii) *Double concerto for flute, oboe and orchestra; Melodien for orchestra;* (iii) *10 Pieces for wind quintet.*

(M) *** Decca 425 623-2. (i) L. Sinf., Atherton; (ii) with Nicolet, Holliger; (iii) Vienna Wind Soloists.

Over the last decade or so, Ligeti has developed a technique of micro-polyphony that produces strongly atmospheric and distinctive textures. The *Double concerto* makes great play with micro-intervals, not exactly quarter-tones but deviations. The resulting sonorities will not always please but should consistently interest or even exasperate the unprejudiced listener. The distinguished soloists and the London Sinfonietta give accomplished accounts of these complex scores and the Vienna performances of the wind pieces are hardly less stimulating.

Liszt, Franz (1811–86)

Piano concerto No. 1 in E flat.

(M) *** EMI/Phoenixa CDM7 63778-2; *EG 763778-4.* Richard Farrell, Hallé O, Weldon – GRIEG: *Concerto* etc. **(*)

(BB) **(*) Naxos Dig. 8.550292 [id.]. Joseph Banowetz, Czech RSO, Bratislava, Oliver Dohnányi – CHOPIN: *Concerto No. 1.* **(*)

(M) **(*) EMI CDM7 64144-2 [id.]; *EG 764144-4.* Annie Fischer, Philharmonia O, Klemperer (with Johann STRAUSS: *Overture: Die Fledermaus* **) – MENDELSSOHN: *A Midsummer Night's Dream.* ***

Even more than in the coupled Grieg, Liszt's *E flat Concerto* shows the flair and poetry of Richard Farrell's playing, and George Weldon is inspired to provide an equally charismatic accompaniment. The warm, poetic feeling of the *Poco adagio* is matched by the skittish wit of the scherzo and the dash and power of the finale. Fine recording, too. This record is a real bargain.

A splendid, energetic account of the *First Concerto* from Banowetz, well coupled with Chopin, has the full measure of the work's flamboyance and its poetry. The only snag is that the delicacy of texture in the engaging scherzo means that the triangle solo is only just audible. Otherwise the wide-ranging sound is excellent.

The Annie Fischer/Klemperer partnership works better here than in the Schumann *Concerto.* The Liszt performance is full-blooded but manages to play down the vulgarity at the same time. The famous triangle scherzando is particularly effective, less frothy but somehow more lyrical; instead of the usual flamboyance, the finale builds up a real feeling of power, with superb digital dexterity from the soloist. Excellent early-1960s Kingsway Hall recording. The concerto is prefaced by Strauss's *Die Fledermaus overture* played quite gracefully, but the conductor's serious approach lacks the appropriate lightness and unbuttoned zest.

Piano concertos Nos. 1 in E flat; 2 in A; Hungarian fantasia for piano and orchestra.

(M) **(*) Erato/Warner Dig. 2292 45206-2 [id.]. François-René Duchable, LPO, James Conlon.

(i) *Piano concertos Nos. 1–2;* (ii) *Les Préludes.*

(M) *** Tuxedo TUXCD 1013 [id.]. (i) Brendel, V. Prom Musica O, Michael Gielen; (ii) Hamburg SO, Hans-Jürgen Walther.

Piano concertos Nos. 1–2; Totentanz.

(M) *** Ph. 426 637-2; *426 637-4.* Alfred Brendel, LPO, Haitink.

(BB) ** Naxos Dig. 8.550187 [id.]. Joseph Banowetz, Slovak RSO (Bratislava), Oliver Dohnányi.

Piano concertos Nos. (i) *1 in E flat;* (ii) *2 in A. Années de pèlerinage: Sonetto 104 del Petrarca. Hungarian rhapsody No. 6; Valse oubliée.*

(M) *** Mercury 432 002-2 [id.]. Byron Janis, (i) Moscow PO, Kondrashin; (ii) Moscow RSO, Rozhdestvensky (also with SCHUMANN: *Romance in F sharp; Novellette in F.* FALLA: *Miller's dance.* GUION: *The harmonica player* ***).

(i) *Piano concertos Nos. 1–2. Années de pèlerinage: Vallée d'Obermann; Valses oubliées Nos. 1–2.*

(M) ** Ph. Dig. 432 612-2; *432 612-2.* Mischa Dichter, (i) Pittsburgh SO, André Previn.

Piano concertos Nos. 1–2; Étude transcendante d'après Paganini.

(B) **(*) DG Compact Classics 413 850-2 (2); *413 850-4* [id.]. Vásáry, Bamberg SO, Prohaska – RACHMANINOV: *Piano concerto No. 2* etc. ** (CD only: *Piano concerto No. 1* **).

Brendel's Philips recordings from the early 1970s hold their place at or near the top of the list. There is a valuable extra work offered here and the recording is of Philips's best. The performances are as poetic as they are brilliant, and those who doubt the musical substance of No. 2 will find their reservations melt away.

Brendel's earlier performances of the Liszt *Concertos*, made (for Vox) a decade before his Philips versions, are by no means superseded by the later accounts. Indeed, with spacious tempi from Gielen, they have a breadth (and in the case of the opening of the *First*) a majesty not approached by other performances. The orchestral support in No. 2 is not as polished as that provided by Haitink and the LPO, and the recording balance is more artificial, but the piano is richly resonant in the lower register. The playing is strikingly spontaneous, with a musing, improvisatory quality in the lyrical writing, especially in the A major work, and the bravura in both concertos is illuminating as well as exciting. The filler is a strong, slighty melodramatic account of *Les Préludes*, brightly played and somewhat brashly recorded. But the concertos are rather special.

Around the time they were recording Richter's (full-price) Liszt *Concertos* for Philips in London (1962), the Mercury engineers paid a visit to Moscow to record Byron Janis in the same repertoire, and his is a comparably distinguished coupling. The partnership between the soloist and both his Russian conductors is unusually close. Janis's glittering articulation is matched by his sense of poetry and drama, and there is plenty of dash in these very compelling performances, which are afforded characteristically brilliant Mercury sound, although the piano is too close. The encores which follow the two *Concertos* are also very enjoyable.

The generously coupled Compact Classics tape offers three concertos, plus solo items, and – while Vásáry's version of the Rachmaninov *C minor* is less impressive than his Liszt – this is still good value. His recording of Liszt's *E flat Concerto* still sounds very well indeed; the performance is distinguished by considerable subtlety and refinement, yet with no loss of impact, even if there is little barnstorming. His approach to the *A major*, too, is thoughtful and sensitive. The accompaniments under Prohaska are sympathetic, and the 1960 sound remains vivid and clear and is more brilliantly projected (in both formats) than in earlier issues. On the pair of CDs another concerto is added, and the Vásáry/Ahronovitch performance of Rachmaninov's *First* is agreeably impulsive and alive.

Those wanting a digital coupling of the Liszt *Concertos* could well find Duchable's Erato disc a worthwhile alternative. Duchable's performances are flamboyantly extrovert, and the bold, forwardly balanced piano helps to underline that effect. The orchestra makes a strong impression, however, and Conlon matches his soloist with firm and vigorous accompaniments. The *Second Concerto* comes first and is made to sound more melodramatic than usual. In both works, while the lyrical episodes do not lack expressive feeling, they are without the spontaneous feeling of Brendel's Tuxedo performances. The dash and brilliance of the playing best suit the *Hungarian fantasia*. Certainly on CD the sound has plenty of presence.

The Naxos recording does not have the same analytical clarity or atmosphere as the RPO recording for Janis Vakarelis, but Joseph Banowetz is the more thoughtful and poetic player. Nor is the orchestral playing as subtle as the RPO's for Rowicki or the LPO's for Haitink in Brendel's disc on Philips Silver Line. However, at super-bargain price it has its attractions.

It is odd that, instead of reissuing the Richter performances at mid-price, Philips should have cast another of their pianists in this repertoire. Mischa Dichter is an impressive player and the two *Valses oubliées* are beautifully done and very well recorded. So too are the concertos although, as so often, the piano looms too large. But the presence and projection of the music-making help performances about which there is nothing very special to say either in the solo contribution or in that of the orchestra, even though they are highly musical and enjoyable. There are no backing notes.

Piano concerto No. 2 in A.

(M) *** Pickwick/RPO Dig. CDRPO 5001 [id.]. Janis Vakarelis, RPO, Rowicki – PROKOFIEV: *Concerto No. 3.* **(*)

(BB) ** Pickwick PWK 1154. Katchen, LSO, Gamba – MENDELSSOHN: *Piano concerto No. 1.* **

Janis Vakarelis offers an unusual coupling: the Liszt *A major Concerto* and the Prokofiev No. 3; for those needing this repertoire, his 1985 account can be recommended. It has the benefit of a really first-class, modern, digital recording with excellent definition and range. The orchestral playing under the late Witold Rowicki is also of the highest quality. Vakarelis is an accomplished and thoughtful player and – although this would not necessarily be a first choice, given the existence of such fine accounts as Brendel's and Janis's – he is far from uncompetitive.

Katchen's is a commanding performance of the *A major Concerto*, and Gamba provides admirable support. This is exciting music-making, showing the pianist in his best light. But Katchen is even better in the *First Concerto*, which he recorded at the same time, and one can only lament its absence here. There would have been plenty of room for it, as the CD plays for only 41 minutes! The (originally Decca) recording, although dating from the very earliest days of stereo, is very good.

2 Episodes from Lenau's Faust: Der nächtliche Zug; Mephisto waltz No. 1 (Der Tanz in der Dorfschenke); 2 Legends; Les Préludes.
(M) **(*) Erato/Warner Dig. 2292 45256-2 [id.]. Rotterdam PO, James Conlon.

If this Liszt anthology falls short of the highest distinction, it is still impressive and enjoyable. James Conlon gives us the original orchestration of the *St Francis Legends* plus the rarely heard and highly imaginative *Der nächtliche Zug*. Conlon secures responsive playing from the Rotterdam orchestra, and the engineering is excellent without being in any way spectacular. There is a good, full-bodied and well-balanced sound-picture.

Fantasia on Hungarian folk tunes for piano and orchestra.
(M) *** Decca Dig. 430 726-2; *430 726-4* [id.]. Bolet, LSO, Ivan Fischer – ADDINSELL: *Warsaw concerto* ***; GERSHWIN: *Rhapsody* **(*); GOTTSCHALK: *Grand fantasia* ***; LITOLFF: *Scherzo.* ***

(i) *Fantasia on Hungarian folk tunes; Hungarian rhapsodies Nos. 2 & 5.*
(B) *** DG 429 156-2 [id.]. (i) Shura Cherkassky; BPO, Karajan (with BRAHMS: *Hungarian dances Nos. 17–20* ***).

(i) *Fantasia on Hungarian folk tunes; Hungarian rhapsodies Nos. 2 & 5; Mephisto waltz.*
(M) *** DG 419 862-2 [id.]. (i) Cherkassky; BPO, Karajan.

Shura Cherkassky's glittering 1961 recording of the *Hungarian fantasia* is an affectionate performance with some engaging touches from the orchestra, though the pianist is dominant and his playing is superbly assured. The rest of the programme is comparably charismatic, although the *Hungarian rhapsody* described as No. 2 is not the famous orchestral No. 2, but an orchestration of No. 12 for piano. The four Brahms *Hungarian dances* make a scintillating, lightweight encore. The Galleria mid-priced CD duplicates three of the items on the bargain disc. The *Mephisto waltz* is now added, brilliantly played and used to introduce the rest of the programme.

Bolet is a masterful soloist and he plays here with characteristic bravura. Like the pianist, the Hungarian conductor is an understanding Lisztian, and the accompaniment from the LSO is first rate, with a recording balance of demonstration quality.

A Faust symphony.
(M) *** DG 431 470-2; *431 470-4*. Kenneth Riegel, Tanglewood Festival Ch., Boston SO, Bernstein.
(M) *** EMI CDM7 63371-2 [id.]; *EG 763371-4*. Alexander Young, Beecham Ch. Soc., RPO, Beecham.

Bernstein recorded this symphony in the mid-1960s; but this 1976 version, made in Boston, is both more sensitive and more brilliant. Indeed, from the very opening its adrenalin surge is remarkable – it was the first modern recording to challenge Beecham's classic account, made in 1959. The DG sound is considerably superior and many will now consider it the best buy for this work, which can be as elusive in the concert hall as in the recording studio. Bernstein seems to possess the ideal temperament for holding together grippingly the melodrama of the first movement, while the lovely *Gretchen* centrepiece is played most beautifully (the Boston woodwind are an aural delight) with finely delineated detail and refined textures. Kenneth Riegel is an impressive tenor soloist in the finale, there is an excellent, well-balanced choral contribution, and the Boston Symphony Orchestra produce playing which is both exciting and atmospheric. The vividness of the recording overall is most compelling, and listening to the CD is undoubtedly a thrilling experience.

Sir Thomas Beecham's classic 1959 recording, well transferred to CD, shows this instinctive Lisztian at his most illuminatingly persuasive. His control of speed is masterly, spacious and eloquent in the first two movements without dragging, brilliant and urgent in the finale without any hint of breathlessness. Though in the transfer string-tone is limited in body, balances are very convincing, and the sound is unlikely to disappoint anyone wanting to enjoy a uniquely warm and understanding reading of an equivocal piece, hard to interpret.

Symphonic poems: *Hungaria; Mazeppa; Les Préludes; Tasso, lamento e trionfo.*
(M) ** Ph. 426 636-2; *426 636-4*. LPO, Haitink.

Haitink recorded all Liszt's symphonic poems with the LPO at the end of the 1960s, with variable degrees of success. The music of *Mazeppa*, *Les Préludes* and *Tasso* creates its scenic backgrounds with bold strokes of the brush. Haitink rather shirks the melodrama, but the LPO catches the music's idiom without self-consciousness, and *Hungaria* is effective with a limited degree of flamboyance. The added vividness of the CD transfer is certainly an advantage, and some listeners will enjoy *Les Préludes* with the rhetoric understated; but the dramatic denouement of *Mazeppa* is far more thrilling in Karajan's hands.

Hungarian rhapsodies Nos. 1–6.
(M) **(*) Mercury 432 015-2 [id.]. LSO, Dorati – ENESCU: *Roumanian rhapsody No. 1.* ***

Dorati's is undoubtedly the finest set of orchestral *Hungarian rhapsodies*. He brings out the gypsy flavour and, with lively playing from the LSO, there is both polish and sparkle, but the music does not become urbane. The use of the cimbalom within the orchestra brings an authentic extra colouring. The Mercury recording is characteristically vivid, if not quite as full in the upper range as we would expect today.

Hungarian rhapsodies Nos. 1–6; Symphonic poems: *Hunnenschlacht; Les Préludes; Mazeppa. Mephisto waltz.*
(B) **(*) MCA Double-decker (2) [MCAD2-9832-A/B]. V. State Op. O, Hermann Scherchen.

These performances have enormous flamboyance and excitement. The closing sections of the more volatile *Hungarian rhapsodies* have a thrilling impetus – there is a Beechamesque gusto in the way Scherchen drives his orchestra on. He is highly temperamental in his response to the ebb and flow of tempo elsewhere but he takes the orchestra with him. *Les Préludes* and *Mazeppa* are full of melodrama yet never quite go over the top. The early stereo (1957/8) is far from refined, but the charisma of these performances is unforgettable. A fine reminder of a conductor whose music-making was individual to the point of eccentricity but who was incapable of routine gestures. This set is not yet issued in the UK.

Hungarian rhapsody No. 2 in C sharp min.; Les Préludes.
(B) *** EMI CDZ7 62860-2; *LZ 762860-4* [id.]. Philh. O, Karajan – MUSSORGSKY: *Pictures.* ***

Les Préludes.
(M) *** EMI CDM7 69228-2 [id.]. Philh. O, Karajan – BRAHMS: *Symphony No. 4.* **(*)

Karajan's 1958 *Les Préludes* found much favour in its day, as well it should. It still sounds thrilling now, and demonstrates the fine musical judgement of the original balance engineers. Musically, this is the equal of any modern version. It is available either at mid-price, coupled with Brahms's *Fourth Symphony*, or on EMI's cheapest, Laser label, with the *Hungarian rhapsody No. 2* and a splendid version of Mussorgsky's *Pictures at an exhibition*.

Hungarian rhapsodies Nos. 2 and 4; Les Préludes.
(B) *** DG Compact Classics *413 159-4* [id.]. BPO, Karajan – DVOŘÁK: *Slavonic dances*; SMETANA: *Vltava* etc. ***

Karajan is completely at home in this repertoire. He goes over the top in *Les Préludes*, not helped by a very brightly lit recording which manages to make even the Berlin Philharmonic sound brash; but in the rest of the music here he secures marvellous playing and fine characterization. The approach to the *Hungarian rhapsodies* is somewhat urbane, yet there is plenty of sparkle. On this excellently engineered Compact Classics tape, these three popular works are featured as part of a well-organized anthology of Slavonic music.

Orpheus; (i) *Psalm 13.*
(M) *** EMI CDM7 63299-2. (i) Beecham Ch. Soc.; RPO, Beecham – R. STRAUSS: *Ein Heldenleben.* ***

Beecham's account of *Orpheus* originally appeared as the fill-up to his magisterial account of the *Faust symphony*. Inspired by an Etruscan vase in the Louvre depicting Orpheus singing to his lyre, it was partly designed to preface performances of Gluck's opera at Weimar. Beecham's recording remains the most poetic and unaffected yet to be committed to disc. Most listeners would place it as being recorded in the 1970s rather than in 1958! It sounds uncommonly fresh and spacious, and the performance is magical. The performance of *Psalm 13* is hardly less impressive. It is sung in English with the legendary Walter Midgely but is drier and more monochrome. All the same, an indispensable issue.

PIANO MUSIC

Années de pèlerinage: Après une lecture du Dante (Dante sonata); Sonetto 104 del Petrarca; Vallées d'Obermann; Les jeux d'eaux à la Villa d'Este. Ballade No. 2 in B min.; 6 Chants polonais de Chopin; Concert paraphrases on operas by Verdi; 2 Concert studies: Waldesrauschen; Gnomenreigen. 3 Études de concert; 12 Études d'exécution transcendante; Funérailles; Harmonies poétiques et religieuses: Bénédiction de Dieu dans la solitude; Sonata in B min.; Valse oubliée No. 1 in F sharp.
(M) *** Ph. Dig. 432 305-2 (5) [id.]. Claudio Arrau.

Claudio Arrau was one of the greatest pianists of our time and many of the volumes in the Philips commemorative collection are indispensable elements of any library. Of all modern players he possessed the most distinctive keyboard personality, with a rich, well-rounded sonority and a consummate technical address. His Liszt performances are, generally speaking, in a special class: they combine an aristocratic finesse with just the proper amount of virtuoso abandon. His rubato, which can seem idiosyncratic to some musicians in Chopin or Schubert, is never excessive and always idiomatic. The performances are always completely within the sensibility of the period, yet are completely of our time as well. The excellent Philips recordings do justice to his thoroughly individual sound-world and are admirably balanced, and the set can be recommended without any serious reservation.

Années de pèlerinage: Au bord d'une source; Au lac de Wallenstadt; Les jeux d'eau à la Villa d'Este. Bénédiction de Dieu dans le solitude; Liebestraum No. 3; Mephisto Waltz No. 1; Hungarian rhapsody No. 12; Variations on B-A-C-H.
❀ (BB) *** Virgo VC7 91458-2; *VC 791458-4* [id.]. Kun Woo Paik.

Kun Woo Paik is an outstanding Lisztian and this 78-minute recital, very realistically recorded and offered in the lowest price range, is in every way recommendable. Whether in the delicacy of Liszt's delightful watery evocations from the *Années de pèlerinage*, the devilish glitter of the upper tessitura of the *Mephisto Waltz*, or the comparable flamboyance of the *Hungarian rhapsody*, this is playing of a high order. The famous *Liebestraum* is presented more gently than usual and the wide range of mood of the *Bénédiction* is controlled very spontaneously; it is only in the climax of the *BACH variations* that perhaps a touch more restraint would have been effective. A most exciting issue and a very real bargain.

Années de pèlerinage: (lst Year: Switzerland) Au bord d'une source; (2nd Year: Italy) Sonetto 104 del Petrarca; Hungarian rhapsody No. 2 (arr. Horowitz).
(M) (***) BMG/RCA mono GD 60523. Vladimir Horowitz – BRAHMS: *Piano concerto No. 2.* (*)

Impressive playing from Horowitz but coupled with a rather cool and remote account of the Brahms *B flat Concerto.*

Années de pèlerinage, 1st Year: Au bord d'une source; 2nd Year: Sonnetto 104 del Petrarca; 3rd Year: Les jeux d'eau à la Villa d'Este; Supplement: Tarantella. Concert paraphrases of Schubert Lieder: *Auf dem Wasser zu singen; Die Forelle.* Concert studies: *Gnomenreigen; Un sospiro. Liebestraum No. 3.* (i)
SCHUBERT/LISZT: *Wanderer fantasia* (arr. for piano and orchestra).
(B) *** Decca Dig. 425 689-2 [id.]. Jorge Bolet; (i) with LPO, Solti.

Intended by Decca as a bargain sampler for Bolet's distinguished Liszt series, this makes a unique recital in its own right. Quite apart from including a splendid version of Liszt's transcription for piano and orchestra of Schubert's *Wanderer fantasia*, the recital demonstrates the composer's wide pianistic range, from the evocation of the *Années de pèlerinage* and the romanticism of *Un sospiro* and *Liebestraum* to the glittering brilliance of *Gnomenreigen*, in which Bolet's playing is breathtakingly assured. The recording is very real and present.

Concert paraphrases: Faust waltzes; Réminiscences de Don Juan (Mozart); Réminiscences de Robert le Diable: Valse infernale (Mayerbeer); Concert study: Gnomenreigen; Mephisto polka; Mephisto waltz No. 1.
(M) **(*) Van. 08.4035.71 [OVC 4035]. Earl Wild.

The title of this recital is *'The demonic Liszt'*, and as a display of brilliant piano playing it could hardly be bettered. Earl Wild's technique is prodigious. The articulation in *Gnomenreigen* has a fairy lightness and the *Mephisto polka* has a similar blithe delicacy of touch, while the more sinister waltz which follows is played with formidable energy and power. There is glittering upper tessitura in the *Don Juan fantasy*. But one ideally needs a programme designed to give more contrast, and the 1968 piano recording is on the dry side.

Études d'exécution transcendante (1838 version).
(M) **(*) Pickwick Dig. MCD 10. Janice Weber.

An interesting and impressive issue – and excellent value too. Janice Weber is an American pianist of formidable technique – and she needs it if she is to take on the 1838 version of the *Transcendental studies.* Liszt composed his *Étude en douze exercices* when he was fifteen, and in 1838 he reworked and expanded them into the present set. The form in which we know them now is the revision Liszt made in 1851. Ms Weber has not only excellent fingers but also refined musicianship and a good sense of keyboard colour. Lisztians will welcome the appearance of this excellently played and splendidly recorded account. But just as a great ballerina must make the most daunting difficulties seem easy, a virtuoso pianist must toss off the most hair-raising passage-work without apparent effort. This she does not quite manage, which is probably why Liszt made his revision.

Fantasia & fugue on 'B-A-C-H'; Variations on Bach's 'Weinen, Klagen, Sorgen, Zagen'.
(BB) *(*) Naxos Dig. 8.550408 [id.]. Michael Ponti – BRAHMS: *Handel variations.* *(*)

Michael Ponti is fully equal to the considerable artistic and physical demands these pieces pose and generates genuine atmosphere and excitement. The recording, made in a rather small studio, does not open out in climaxes and, though the artist and the engineer cope as well as they can with this handicap, there is no pretending that the piano sound equals that of, say, the best Philips or EMI recordings.

Harmonies poétiques et religieuses: Funérailles; Mephisto waltz No. 1; Hungarian rhapsody No. 12.

(M) (**(*)) Decca mono 425 961-2 [id.]. Julius Katchen – BALAKIREV: *Islamey*; MUSSORGSKY: *Pictures*.(**(*))

Julius Katchen's impressive pianistic fireworks are heard to excellent effect in this generous recital. He recorded the Liszt in 1953/4 and, though the sound is now no longer of the highest quality, Katchen's pianism and musicianship still sing loud and clear.

Hungarian rhapsodies Nos. 1–19.

(M) *** DG 423 925-2 (2) [id.]. Roberto Szidon.

At mid-price, Roberto Szidon's set of the *Hungarian rhapsodies* is highly recommendable. Szidon has been missing from the concert platform in recent years – at least so far as England is concerned – and has made few records. There is plenty of fire and flair here, and much that will dazzle the listener! The recording, too, sounds very good indeed.

Hungarian rhapsodies Nos. 2–3, 8, 13, 15 (Rákóczy march); 17; Csárdás obstinée.

(M) *** Van. 08.4024.71 [OVC 4024]. Alfred Brendel.

Although the Vanguard recording is not a recent one, it sounds very good in this excellent CD transfer, and the playing is very distinguished indeed. The Philips engineers provide Brendel elsewhere with more sonorous piano-tone and a wider dynamic range, but there are no more charismatic or spontaneous accounts of the *Hungarian rhapsodies* available, and there is no doubt about the brilliance of the playing nor the quality of musical thinking that informs it.

Piano sonata in B min.; Années de pèlerinage, 2nd Year (Italy): Après une lecture de Dante (Dante sonata); Harmonies poétiques et religieuses: Invocation; La lugubre gondola, Nos. 1–2.

(M) *** Ph Dig. 432 048-2; *432 048-4*. Alfred Brendel.

Brendel's latest account of the *Sonata* has received wide acclaim. It is certainly a more subtle and concentrated account than his earlier version, made in the mid-1960s – brilliant though that was – and must be numbered among the best now available. There is a wider range of colour and tonal nuance, yet the undoubted firmness of grip does not seem achieved at the expense of any spontaneity. It is most realistically recorded.

Variations on 'Weinen, Klagen, Sorgen, Zagen'.

(M) *(*) Teldec/Warner Dig. 9031 74782-2 [id.]. Cyprien Katsaris – BEETHOVEN: *Eroica variations* *(*); RACHMANINOV: *Chopin variations.* **

Cyprien Katsaris's account of Liszt's *Variations on 'Weinen, Klagen, Sorgen, Zagen'* come as part of an impressive collection, including Rachmaninov's imposing and inventive set based on the *C minor Prelude* of Chopin and the Beethoven *Eroica variations.* Masterful enough playing, but thick and synthetic sound-quality.

ORGAN MUSIC

Am Grabe Richard Wagners; Andante maestoso; Angelus; Ave maris stella; Gebet (Ave Maria); Missa pro organo; Ora pro nobis; Praeludium; Rosario; Salve Regina; Tu es Petrus; Weimars Volkslied.

(B) ** Hung. White Label HRC 095 [id.]. Sándor Marggittay, Endre Kovács, Gábor Lehotka (various organs).

Most of these are late works and many of the pieces were conceived in other, alternative versions. Of these the *Angelus* comes from the third year of the *Années de pèlerinage*, but sounds rather effective on the organ. The Wagner inspiration exists in three alternative versions but again suits the instrument well. Of the pieces conceived especially for the organ the *Salve Regina*, based on a Gregorian chant, has a striking, cool beauty. The most ambitious work is the *Missa pro organo*, an integral part of an organ-accompanied low Mass. All the music is presented well and the unnamed Hungarian organs sound bright and sonorous. Not an indispensable Liszt record but an interesting one.

VOCAL MUSIC

Missa choralis.

(M) *** Decca 430 364-2; *430 364-4* [id.]. Atkinson, Tinkler, Royall, Kendall, Suart, St John's College, Cambridge, Ch., Guest; Cleobury (organ) – DVOŘÁK: *Mass in D.* ***

(M) ** Tuxedo TUXCD 1078 [id.]. Thomann, Jahn, Wing, Kawwamura, Buchsbaum, V. Chamber Ch., Gillesberger; J. Nebois (organ) – KODÁLY: *Missa brevis: Agnus Dei* etc. **

Liszt's *Missa choralis* comes from the mid-1860s, after he received the tonsure. It is written for mixed choir and organ and is an impressive and moving work. Guest provides an inspired and beautifully sung version, with well-blended tone. It has the benefit of spacious and richly detailed (originally Argo) recording. It would be difficult to flaw this important reissue, which is more successful than any of the other versions recorded in the intervening years. The transfer to CD serves only to enhance the original excellent sound.

The alternative, 1961 Vox recording, reissued on Tuxedo, is also very realistically recorded, though with a more forward balance. The acoustic is not dry, but the effect here is rather of a concert performance, forthright but not unsubtle. The organ accompaniment is rather subdued at times, but in all other respects this is successful, although the Kodály couplings are far from generous.

Litolff, Henri (1818–91)

Concerto symphonique No. 4: Scherzo.
(M) *** Decca Dig. 430 726-2; *430 726-4* [id.]. Ortiz, RPO, Atzmon – ADDINSELL: *Warsaw concerto* ***; GERSHWIN: *Rhapsody* **(*); GOTTSCHALK: *Grand fantasia* ***; LISZT: *Hungarian fantasia.* ***

Cristina Ortiz's version may lack extrovert brilliance but it has an agreeable elegance. The intimacy of this version is emphasized by the balance, which places the piano within the orchestral group, making the gentle central section especially effective. The Decca couplings are all appealing and the CD is impressively natural.

Locatelli, Pietro (1695–1764)

The Art of the violin, Op.3/1–6.
(B) **(*) VoxBox 1154882 [CDX 5018]. Suzanne Lautenbacher, Mainz CO, Günter Kehr.

The Art of the violin, Op. 3/7–12.
(B) **(*) VoxBox 1155922 [CDX 5037]. Lautenbacher, Mainz CO, Kehr.

Pietro Locatelli was born in northern Italy in 1695. He was a pupil of Corelli and he travelled much as a virtuoso violinist until he finally settled in Amsterdam around 1729, where he spent the rest of his life. It was here in 1733 that he wrote the present remarkable work, in certain ways anticipating Paganini by more than half a century. The *Art of the violin* is a set of twelve violin concertos of undoubted individuality. The early baroque concerto style with alternations of solo and tutti is extended by including orchestral interjections within the solo passages, but orchestral textures are full and forward-looking, with Handelian linear richness. The most striking innovative feature is Locatelli's invention of the obvious ancestor of the modern cadenza. Each three-movement concerto is structured to include an extended *Capriccio* for the soloist in each of the outer movements, exploiting every facet of violin technique known to the composer. The writing does not anticipate the devilish upper tessitura using harmonics favoured by Paganini but still demands considerable resourcefulness from the soloist in the upper range. Indeed the last concerto of the set includes a *Capriccio* which the composer himself found so demanding that he called it '*Il laberinto armonico*' adding the humorous comment '*Facilis aditus, difficilis exitus*'. Needless to say, Suzanne Lautenbacher takes these problems in her stride, and she plays the gracious melodies in which the central *Largos* abound with much warmth. If the allegros are without the rhythmic vitality of Vivaldi, there is no lack of emotional breadth. Kehr directs the proceedings sympathetically. The Mainz Chamber Orchestra, of course, uses modern instruments with finesse, and the warmly resonant acoustic provides much beauty of texture; although at times there is also an element of blandness, the music-making makes highly agreeable listening, taken a concerto at a time.

Løvenskiold, Herman (1815–70)

La Sylphide (ballet) complete.
(M) *** Chan. Dig. CHAN 6546; *MBTD 6546* [id.]. Royal Danish O, David Garforth.

La Sylphide (1834) predates Adam's *Giselle* by seven years. It was commissioned by the great Danish dancing master, Bournonville who, like Petipa with Tchaikovsky, worked closely with the composer to ensure that the music matched his requirements, almost bar by bar. The result is less distinctive than Adam's score, but it is full of grace and the invention has genuine romantic vitality – indeed the horn writing in the finale anticipates Delibes. Although the Sylphide is given a very engaging melody (track 12), the work is not permeated with a memorably predominant *leitmotiv* as in Adam's ballet. The plot is almost *Giselle* in reverse, for here it is the Sylphide who lures the young Scottish hero away from his true love, even though she dies when he tries to draw her into the mortal world. The present performance (72 minutes) is based on the current performing edition used by the Royal Danish ballet but includes additional music, with the original Act II *Pas de deux*, hitherto unrecorded, added as an appendix. The wholly sympathetic playing is warm, elegant, lively and felicitous in its detailed delicacy, yet robust when necessary and always spontaneous. A most enjoyable disc, superbly recorded (in 1986) in the well-nigh perfect acoustics of the Old Fellows' Hall, Copenhagen.

Lully, Jean-Baptiste (1632–87)

Le bourgeois gentilhomme (comédie-ballet; complete).

(M) *** HM/BMG GD 77059 (2) [77059-2-RG]. Nimsgern, Jungmann, Schortemeier, René Jacobs, Tölz Ch., La Petite Bande, Leonhardt – CAMPRA: *L'Europe galante*. ***

Entertainment rather than musical value: in itself, Lully's score offers no great musical rewards. The melodic invention is unmemorable and harmonies are neither original nor interesting; but if the music taken on its own is thin stuff, the effect of the entertainment as a whole is quite a different matter. This performance puts Lully's music into the correct stage perspective and, with such sprightly and spirited performers as well as good 1973 recording, this can hardly fail to give pleasure. The orchestral contribution under the direction of Gustav Leonhardt is distinguished by a splendid sense of the French style.

Lutoslawski, Witold (born 1916)

Concerto for orchestra; Funeral music for string orchestra; Venetian games.

(M) ** Ph. 426 663-2. Warsaw Nat. PO, Rowicki.

The Lutoslawski *Concerto* is a brilliant, inventively scored work; its idiom is accessible and the ideas have character. It plumbs no great depths – but then nor do the composer's later and less accessible works. Rowicki gives it a thoroughly idiomatic performance and secures playing of real brilliance from the Warsaw orchestra. The *Funeral music* is an angular and rather empty piece whose feelings seem to reside very much on the surface. *Venetian games*, a work that contains randomly generated interpolations, is quite an attractive piece. Both are well played here. The recording is good but the strings are not ideally lustrous, and overall the sound could use a more vivid colouring.

MacDowell, Edward (1861–1908)

(i) *Piano concerto No. 2 in D min., Op. 23. Woodland sketches: To a wild rose, Op. 51/1.*

(M) **(*) BMG/RCA GD 60420; *GK 60420* [60420-2-RG; *60420-4-RG*]. Van Cliburn, (i) Chicago SO, Hendl – SCHUMANN: *Concerto*. **(*)

Edward MacDowell wrote his *Second Piano concerto* in Germany in 1884/5 and it is no accident that – especially in the first movement – Liszt's influence can be felt very strongly in the piano writing. MacDowell had previously studied in Paris, and the whiff of Saint-Saëns one gets in the orchestration here and there shows that the young composer was willing to follow in European traditions generally rather than attempt to create a new and individually American style. But the writing remains agreeably fresh and distinctly melodic. The work has a lyrical, rhapsodical first movement, a short but quite delightful Scherzo as a centrepiece, and a lively finale based on a strong and easily recognizable theme. A slow introduction to the third movement and a reflective middle section act in the place of a slow movement. The closing pages are a paean of virtuosity and emerge here in glittering fashion from Van Cliburn's nimble fingers. The pianist is not helped by a recording balance which consistently makes him sound rather too loud; but the performance otherwise has the advantage of warm Chicago acoustics, and Walter Hendl's vigorous and sympathetic support, with its fire and spontaneity, triumph over the technical problems. The Scherzo is superb. MacDowell's most famous solo piano piece makes a pleasing encore, though the performance is a trifle cool.

Machaut, Guillaume (*c.* 1300–77)

Messe de Notre Dame.

(M) *(*) HM/BMG GD 77064 [77064-2-RG]. Deller Consort, Coll. Aur., Alfred Deller (with ANON.: *Alleluja Christus ressurgens; Alleluja Nativitas; Clausula Mors; Pater noster cimmiserans* (conductus); MAGNUS: *Sederunt principes* (graduale); PHILLIPE LE CHANCELIER: *Dic Christi veritas* (conductus).

Specialist collectors will know the merits of the Deller account of the *Messe de Notre Dame* from the early 1960s. But the actual sound is pretty dated, very claustrophobic and unventilated. There are more satisfactory recordings at full price.

Mahler, Gustav (1860–1911)

Symphonies Nos. 1–9.

(B) *** Decca Dig./Analogue 430 804-2 (10). Buchanan, Zakai, Chicago Ch. (in No. 2); Dernesch, Ellyn Children's Ch., Chicago Ch. (in No. 3); Te Kanawa (in No. 4); Harper, Popp, Augér, Minton, Watts, Kollo, Shirley-Quirk, Talvela, V. Boys' Ch., V. State Op. Ch. & Singverein (in No. 8); Chicago SO, Solti.

Solti's achievement in Mahler has been consistent and impressive, and this bargain reissue on ten discs of a set that had previously been offered on fifteen (most at full price) is a formidable bargain that will be hard to beat. Nos. 1–4 and 9 are digital recordings, Nos. 5–8 are digitally remastered analogue. Solti draws stunning playing from the Chicago Symphony Orchestra, often pressed to great virtuosity, which adds to the electricity of the music-making; if his rather extrovert approach to Mahler means that deeper emotions are sometimes understated, there is no lack of involvement; and his fiery energy and commitment often carry shock-waves in their trail. In No. 1 the digital clarity takes away a little of the atmospheric magic, but the *Wunderhorn* charm is not missing; No. 2, always one of his most powerful readings, brings a culmination of breathtaking intensity. No. 4, the sunniest of the Mahler symphonies, is delightfully fresh, with Kiri Te Kanawa an ideal soloist in the finale. No. 5 brings very beautiful playing, but the performance lacks the 'inner' quality of the finest versions; and this also applies to No. 6, although this remains a persuasively strong reading. No. 7 is even more successful, the motivation full of dark implications. Tempi are challengingly fast, yet the *Nachtmusik* is very beguiling. The *Eighth* crowned the series superbly, and the Decca engineers, always providing sound of spectacular quality, here pulled out all the stops, so that Solti could provide an earth-shattering account of the closing hymn. If No. 9 lacks a sense of mystery and, like No. 3, is a little short on charm, no one could claim that it lacks power. All in all, an impressive achievement.

Symphony No. 1 in D (1893 version, including *Blumine*).

(M) **(*) EMI CDM7 64137-2 [id.]; *EG 764137-4*. New Philh. O, Wyn Morris.

In his 1970 recording, originally made for the short-lived Virtuoso label, Wyn Morris enterprisingly chose to follow the 1893 text of Mahler's *First*, which is the earliest that has survived. Like the original, 1888 score, it uses a normal romantic orchestra without the extra forces Mahler asked for in his definitive, 1899 edition. It makes the *Blumine* second movement much more consistent here than in rival versions that simply tack that extra movement on to the usual score. Detailed differences include muted horns instead of clarinets for the opening fanfares in the hushed introduction, timpani right at the start of the scherzo, solo cello with double-bass at the start of the slow movement, and quavers instead of crotchets for the falling octave which ends the work. Responding to the differences, Morris adopts a much slower speed than usual for *Blumine* and a faster one for the scherzo, which sounds more like a waltz than a Laendler. Morris's warmly expressive Mahlerian style works most persuasively, though ensemble is not quite as crisp as in most of his other Mahler recordings. The CD transfer has transformed the sound, which is bright with plenty of presence but with just a touch of harshness in tuttis.

(i) *Symphony No. 1 in D* (1896 version); (ii) *Blumine*.

(M) **(*) Collins Dig. 3005-2 [id.]. (i) LSO; (ii) Philh. O; Jacek Kaspszyk.

(B) **(*) Hung. White Label HRC 077 [id.]. Hungarian State O, Iván Fischer.

Kaspszyk has the advantage of excellent, modern, digital recording with a wide dynamic range and a spacious acoustic, another example of excellent concert-hall illusion that can be achieved at EMI's No. 1 Studio at Abbey Road. The LSO plays with commitment and drama and responds persuasively to the conductor's rather wayward reading, leading to a tense and exciting finale. The very opening is appealingly atmospheric and the slow movement conveys real warmth, as does the Philharmonia string-playing in *Blumine*, the discarded movement that came second in the composer's original scheme.

The bargain version on Hungaroton White Label also includes the original second movement, *Blumine*, placing it where the composer intended. Fischer's reading of the *Symphony* is spaciously conceived, with relaxed tempi throughout, but the Hungarian State Orchestra sustain his conception with very fine playing, especially from the strings in the last movement. With excellent analogue sound, full and well detailed, this is an inexpensive way to sample Mahler's initial layout.

Symphony No. 1 in D (Titan).

(M) *** DG Dig. 431 036-2; *431 036-4*. Concg. O, Bernstein.

(M) *** Decca 417 701-2 [id.]. LSO, Solti.

(M) *** Unicorn UKCD 2012. LSO, Horenstein.

(BB) **(*) LaserLight Dig. 15 529 [id.]. Prague Festival O, Pavel Urbanek.

(B) ** Ph. 426 067-2; *426 067-4* [id.]. Concg. O, Haitink.

(B) *(*) Pickwick IMPX 9005. Israel PO, Mehta.

(BB) * Naxos 8.550120 [id.]. Slovak PO, Zdenek Košler.

(B) * Pickwick Dig. PCD 941; *CIMPC 941* [id.]. LSO, Yondani Butt.

Symphony No. 1 in D min.; (i) *Lieder eines fahrenden Gesellen*.

(B) **(*) DG 429 157-2 [id.]. Bav. RSO, Kubelik; (i) with Fischer-Dieskau.

Bernstein and the Concertgebouw Orchestra, recorded live, give a wonderfully alert and imaginative performance of Mahler's *First*, with the opening movement conveying the youthful joys of spring in its *Wayfaring lad* associations, and the second at a relaxed Ländler tempo made more rustic than usual. In the slow movement the funeral march overtones are underlined, leading easily into what Bernstein calls the raucous 'Jewish wedding' episode. The finale has superb panache. This is among Bernstein's finest Mahler issues, very well recorded, even making no allowance for the extra problems encountered at live concerts.

The London Symphony Orchestra play Mahler's *First* like no other orchestra. They catch the magical opening with a singular evocative quality, at least partly related to the peculiarly characteristic blend of wind timbres, and throughout there is wonderfully warm stringtone. Solti's tendency to drive hard is felt only in the second movement, which is pressed a little too much, although he relaxes beautifully in the central section. Especially memorable are the poignancy of the introduction of the *Frère Jacques* theme in the slow movement and the exultant brilliance of the closing pages. The remastering for CD has improved definition without losing the recording's bloom. A fine mid-price recommendation.

Unicorn had the laudable aim of securing a relatively modern recording of Horenstein in Mahler's *First*, and the result has a freshness and concentration which put it in a special category among the many rival accounts. With measured tempi and a manner which conceals much art, Horenstein links the work more clearly with later Mahler symphonies. Fine recording from the end of the 1960s, though the timpani is balanced rather too close.

Kubelik gives an intensely poetic reading. He is here at his finest in Mahler, and though, as in later symphonies, he is sometimes tempted to choose a tempo on the fast side, the result could hardly be more glowing. The rubato in the slow funeral march is most subtly handled. In its bargain CD reissue the quality is a little dry in the bass and the violins have lost some of their warmth, but there is no lack of body. In the *Lieder eines fahrenden Gesellen* the sound is fuller, with more atmospheric bloom. No one quite rivals Fischer-Dieskau in these songs for his range and beauty of tone, conveying the heartache of the young traveller, and, with Kubelik equally persuasive, this is a very considerable bonus.

From the well-sustained opening pianissimo, the tension of the playing of the Prague Festival Orchestra under Pavel Urbanek holds the listener and, even though Urbanek's reading is unconventional in its control of Mahlerian structure, this is a highly spontaneous performance, not immaculate but full of character. The scherzo has exuberance, and the darkness of colour at the opening of the slow movement contrasts with the energetic excitement of the finale. The wide-ranging digital recording is extremely vivid, the upper strings bright but lacking just a little in body, but the ambient effect is well caught. At super-bargain price, this is distinctly competitive.

Haitink's 1962 version did not stay in the catalogue very long, and he re-recorded the work a decade later. That later version is generally preferable; the earlier performance had a lower level of tension. However, everything is beautifully laid out in front of the listener and, in its thoughtful way, with refined Concertgebouw playing, this could be quite appealing for those who enjoy Haitink's laid-back Mahler style.

Mehta's 1976 Decca recording has resurfaced on Pickwick's bargain label, and the sound is vividly full and brilliant; but the hard-driving, frenetic quality of the outer movements is unattractive and the warmth of the slow movement offers insufficient compensation. This is an approach to Mahler which is essentially outside the European tradition.

In sound so clear that the slow introduction lacks the necessary mystery, Košler directs the Slovak Philharmonic in a plain, unsubtle performance, lacking a degree of warmth. The Slovak Philharmonic here is not always as refined as on most Naxos issues, though the playing, like the recording, has plenty of weight.

Yondani Butt's version for IMP brings bold and brassy playing from the LSO but lacks rhythmic subtlety. Little spring is given to the *Wunderhorn* themes, and even the great melody in the finale is treated prosaically. The recording, made by EMI engineers at Walthamstow, is full and vivid, but the reverberation seriously obscures detail in rapid passages, notably in the first movement.

Symphonies Nos. (i) *1;* (ii) *2 (Resurrection).*

(B) *** Sony M2YK 45674. (i) Columbia SO; (ii) Cundari, Forrester, Westminster College Ch., NYPO; Bruno Walter.

(M) **(*) Decca 425 005-2 (2) [id.]. (ii) Harper, Watts, LSO Ch.; LSO, Solti.

(B) (**) MCA Double-decker (2) [MCAD2-9833-A/B]. (i) LPO; (ii) Coertse, West, V. Academy Ch., V. State Op. O, Scherchen.

Bruno Walter's recordings of Mahler's *Symphonies Nos. 1* and *2* are now economically coupled together on a pair of bargain-price discs with the sound further improved over the previous CD issues. The recording of No. 1 sounds splendid in this new format. The compellingly atmospheric opening is magnetic, heard against the almost silent background, and Walter is at his most charismatic here. While the recording's dynamic range is obviously more limited than more recent versions, the balance and ambient warmth are entirely satisfying, emphasizing the

Viennese character of the reading, with the final apotheosis drawn out spaciously and given added breadth and impact. The orchestral playing throughout is first class; other conductors have whipped up more animal excitement in the finale, but that is not Walter's way.

Even more than the *First Symphony*, the 1958 CBS set of the *Resurrection symphony* is among the gramophone's indispensable classics. In the first movement there is a restraint and in the second a gracefulness which provides a strong contrast with a conductor like Solti. The recording, one of the last Walter made in New York before his series with the Columbia Symphony Orchestra, was remarkably good for its period and the dynamic range is surprisingly wide. In remastering for CD, the CBS engineers have sought to remove as much as possible of the pre-Dolby background noise, and the treble response is noticeably limited, with the attractively warm ambience tending to smooth internal definition. But the glowing sound brings an evocative haze to the score's more atmospheric moments, and in the finale the balance with the voices gives the music-making an ethereal resonance, with the closing section thrillingly expansive.

Solti's 1964 LSO account of Mahler's *First Symphony* reappears in the Solti Edition, coupled with No. 2 which was also recorded in the Kingsway Hall two years later. This recording remains a demonstration of the outstanding results Decca were securing with analogue techniques at that time, although on CD the sharpness of focus (especially in No. 2) and the brilliance of the fortissimos, emphasized by the wide dynamic range, may not suit all ears. Yet in the slow Ländler of the second movement the clarity means that Solti can bring superb refinement of detail and a precise control of dynamic; while again in the third movement he concentrates with hushed intensity on precise control of dynamic and atmosphere; the natural ambience of the Kingsway Hall recording is particularly striking here. Helen Watts is wonderfully expressive in the chorale, conveying real inner feeling, while the chorus has a rapt intensity that is the more telling when the recording perspectives are so clearly delineated.

On MCA in both works the aged recording prevents the full range of colouring in Mahler's brilliant writing from being appreciated. The dynamic range is also very limited so that tuttis fail to expand as they should, with some fuzziness over detail. There are also odd balances, as in No. 1 when the triangle emerges as one of the loudest instruments. The lack of atmosphere is serious in both works, but Scherchen was a bold and sympathetic Mahlerian whose readings are well worth studying, able to sustain broad speeds with total concentration. Curiously, the Laendler movement in No. 2 is broad and lilting, while the Laendler in No. 1 is raced along. Despite the thin sound, the choral conclusion of the *Resurrection* is warmly convincing, with good solo work from the mezzo, Lucretia West, and the soprano, Mimi Coertse. The break between discs comes in the middle of the finale of the *Resurrection* and is placed, relatively conveniently, in the pause before the great unison horn call representing the Last Trump.

Symphony No. 2 in C min. (Resurrection).

(M) *** EMI CDM7 69662-2 [id.]; *EG 769662-4*. Schwarzkopf, Rössl-Majdan, Philh. Ch. & O, Klemperer.

(M) *** DG 427 262-2 (2) [id.]. Neblett, Horne, Chicago SO Ch. and O, Abbado.

(B) **(*) Pickwick Dig. DPCD 910 (2) [MCA MCAD 11011]. Valente, Forrester, LSO Ch., LSO, Kaplan.

(M) (**) Decca mono 425 970-2. Vincent, Ferrier, Amsterdam Toonkunstkoor, Concg. O, Klemperer.

The transfer of Klemperer's performance – one of his most compelling on record – on to a single CD (playing for over 79 minutes) is a considerable achievement, and the remastered sound is impressively full and clear, with the fullest sense of spectacle in the closing pages. The first movement, taken at a fairly fast tempo, is intense and earth-shaking, and that is surely as it should be in a work which culminates in a representation of Judgement Day itself. Though in the last movement some of Klemperer's speeds are designedly slow, he conveys supremely well the mood of transcendent heavenly happiness in the culminating passage, with chorus and soloists themselves singing like angels. The *Last Trump* brings a shudder of excitement, and the less grand central movements have their simple charm equally well conveyed.

The total conviction of Abbado's performance establishes itself in the very first bars, weighty yet marvellously precise on detail, with dotted rhythms sharply brought out. It proves a performance of extremes, with variations of tempo more confidently marked than is common but with concentration so intense there is no hint of self-indulgence. The delicacy of the Chicago orchestra in the second and third movements is as remarkable as its precision, while the great contrasts of the later movements prove a challenge not only to the performers but to the DG engineers, who produce sound of the finest analogue quality. Generally the singing is as splendid as the playing, but if there is even a minor disappointment, it lies in the closing pages which are just a little contained: Abbado keeps his sharpness of focus to the very end. However, while highly recommendable, this entails two CDs.

It would be easy but misguided to scoff at the achievement of the rich eccentric, Gilbert Kaplan, in his best-selling version of the *Resurrection Symphony*. It is the only music he ever conducts, or ever plans to; and whatever his musical training, by whatever means, the LSO plays with a biting precision and power to shame many an effort on record under a world-renowned conductor. Added to that, the sound is exceptionally brilliant and full, bringing home the impact of the big dramatic moments, which are what stand out in the performance. Though there are no *longueurs*, it becomes more a collection of salient sequences than a strongly co-ordinated whole, and in places the 'in-between bits' tend to plod a little or become less tense. The second-movement Ländler too is rhythmically heavy-handed, but even there the ensemble is splendid, with fine detail brought out. It is good to have the veteran Canadian mezzo, Maureen Forrester, as soloist, when her voice remains so rich and full. The soprano Benita Valente is less aptly fruity of tone; but she and Forrester as well as the fine chorus sing with a will, crowning a performance that is never less than enjoyable, thanks above all to the playing and to superb sound. The two discs come at bargain price, costing together the same as a single full-price disc. The documentation included is exceptionally generous, with a long essay and analysis by Kaplan in one booklet and a fascinating collection of Mahler's letters about the symphony in a second.

It is fascinating to eavesdrop on Klemperer's live performance, recorded from Dutch Radio on 12 July 1951, towards the end of Kathleen Ferrier's brief career. The mono sound is limited but reasonably clear. What is disappointing is the lack of that very quality one looks for in a live performance, the drive and thrust which are often difficult to recapture in the studio. Only in the final movement with its vision of heaven does the magic quality at last emerge at full intensity; but even there the later, Philharmonia studio performance gives a more complete idea of Klemperer's genius, and elsewhere there is no question of the superiority of the studio account, one of the conductor's strongest statements. The soloists are wonderfully characterful, Vincent as well as Ferrier. These are the two who appeared in the first performance of Britten's *Spring Symphony*, and they here provide the best justification for hearing the set.

Symphony No. 3 in D min.

(M) *** Unicorn UKCD 2006/7 [id.]. Procter, Wandsworth School Boys' Ch., Amb. S., LSO, Horenstein.

(M) *(*) Decca 414 254-2 (2) [id.]. Helen Watts, Amb. Ch., Boys from Wandsworth School, LSO, Solti.

More than the earlier issue of Mahler's *First Symphony*, this account of the Mahler *Third* shows Horenstein at his most intensely committed. The manner is still very consistent in its simple dedication to the authority of the score and its rejection of romantic indulgence; but with an extra intensity the result has the sort of frisson-creating quality one knew from live Horenstein performances. Above all the restraint of the finale is intensely compelling. Though the strings are rather backwardly balanced and the timpani are too prominent, the recording quality is both full and brilliant. Fine vocal contributions from Norma Procter, the Ambrosian Singers and the Wandsworth School Boys' Choir.

In Solti's earlier series of Mahler recordings for Decca with the LSO, the *Third Symphony* brought disappointment, notably in the brassy and extrovert account of the last movement, all the more apparent on CD. To compare these same players under Solti and under Horenstein is most illuminating, where on Decca in the finale there is no half-tone.

Symphony No. 4 in G.

(M) *** DG 419 863-2; *419 863-4* [id.]. Edith Mathis, BPO, Karajan.

(M) **(*) EMI CDM7 69667-2 [id.]; *EG 769667-4*. Schwarzkopf, Philh. O, Klemperer.

(M) **(*) Chan. Dig. CHAN 6505; *MBTD 6505* [id.]. Margaret Marshall, SNO, Gibson.

(B) ** DG 431 165-2; *431 165-4* [id.]. Elsie Morison, Bav. RSO, Rafael Kubelik.

Karajan's refined and poised, yet undoubtedly affectionate account remains among the finest versions of this lovely symphony, and Edith Mathis's sensitively composed contribution to the finale matches the conductor's meditative feeling. With glowing sound, this makes an outstanding mid-priced recommendation alongside Szell's renowned Cleveland CD with Judith Raskin – see below.

Klemperer is slow in the first movement and, strangely, fractionally too fast in the slow movement. Yet the Philharmonia make some ravishing sounds, and one can easily fall under Klemperer's spell. The two highlights of the reading are the marvellously beautiful Ländler, which forms the central section of the second movement, and the simplicity of Elisabeth Schwarzkopf's singing in the finale. This is a record to enjoy, but perhaps not the one to buy as a single representation of Mahler's *Fourth* in a collection.

Gibson has the advantage of modern digital recording and the warm acoustic of the Henry Wood Hall in the SNO Centre, Glasgow, which conveys the breadth and clarity of the sound impressively within an attractive ambient bloom. There is some delightfully fresh and stylish playing from the Scottish orchestra and this is a characteristically unmannered reading, slightly wanting in dramatic grip but not in tenderness. The finale, however, lacks some of the repose necessary in this child-song, with Margaret Marshall sounding a little tense.

The Bavarian orchestra phrase beautifully for Kubelik, and their playing has great vitality. With generally faster tempi than is common, the effect is light and luminous, with a charming, boyish account of the final song from Elsie Morison. This is fair value at bargain price, but the bright CD transfer means that the 1968 recording, though not lacking ambient warmth, shows its age a little in the violin timbre.

(i) *Symphony No. 4 in G;* (ii) *Lieder eines fahrenden Gesellen.*

❀ (M) *** Sony SBK 46535 [id.]; *40-46535.* (i) Judith Raskin, Cleveland O, Szell; (ii) Frederica von Stade, LPO, Andrew Davis.

(i) *Symphony No. 4 in G;* (ii) *Lieder (aus der Jugendzeit): Ablösung im Sommer; Erinnerung; Frühlingsmorgen; Hans und Grethe; Ich ging mit Lust durch einen grünen Wald; Nicht wiedersehen!; Scheiden und meiden; Starke Einbildungskraft.*

(M) (**) Sony mono MPK 46450 [id.]. (i) NYPO, Bruno Walter; (ii) Desi Halban, Bruno Walter.

George Szell's 1966 record of Mahler's *Fourth* represented his partnership with the Cleveland Orchestra at its highest peak. The digital remastering for CD brings out the very best of the original recording, making it sound translucently clear, yet without losing the ambient warmth. The performance remains uniquely satisfying: the interpretation has an element of coolness, but the music blossoms, partly because of the marvellous attention to detail (and the immaculate ensemble), but more positively because of the committed and radiantly luminous orchestral response to the music itself. In the finale Szell found the ideal soprano to match his conception: Judith Raskin sings without artifice, and her voice has an open colouring like a child's, yet the feminine quality subtly remains. An outstanding choice, generously coupled. In contrast with most other recorded performances, Frederica von Stade insinuates a hint of youthful ardour into her highly enjoyable account of the *Wayfaring Lad* cycle. If the playing of the LPO under Andrew Davis seems at times to lack refinement, this is partly the fault of close analogue recording.

Recorded in New York in 1945, the earlier was – astonishingly – the first ever complete recording of Mahler's most popular symphony to be issued commercially. Interpretatively, Walter CBS/Sony version still has much to show any rival, with delicately pointed rhythms and easily flexible speeds that consistently sound idiomatic. He brings out the pure joy behind the inspiration, culminating in the child-heaven finale, performed with delicious jauntiness. The aptly boyish-sounding soloist, Desi Halban, is not well focused in the recording, but she is even less flatteringly recorded in the fill-up, eight of Mahler's 'Youth' songs, *Aus der Jugendzeit*, with Walter accompanying at the piano. Recorded in an unattractively dry acoustic, Halban – daughter of the celebrated soprano, Selma Kurz – is made to sound edgy under pressure, and Walter's playing is often rhythmically lumpy, not nearly as persuasive as his conducting. Yet as a makeweight, the songs are well worth hearing. The closely balanced recording allows little dynamic range, with pianissimos eliminated, but, for its age, it has satisfying body and clarity.

Symphony No. 5 in C sharp min.

(M) *** EMI Dig. CD-EMX 2164; *TC-EMX 2164.* Royal Liverpool PO, Mackerras.

❀ (M) *** EMI CDM7 69186-2 [id.]; *EG 769186-4.* New Philh. O, Barbirolli.

(M) *** DG Dig. 431 037-2. VPO, Bernstein.

(M) **(*) Decca 430 443-2; *430 443-4* [id.]. Chicago SO, Solti.

(M) **(*) DG Dig. 427 254-2. Chicago SO, Abbado.

(M) (**) Sony mono MPK 47683 [id.]. NYPO, Bruno Walter.

(B) ** DG 429 519-2. Bav. RSO, Kubelik.

With brilliant, refined playing from the Liverpool orchestra, in warm, well-detailed sound, the Mackerras version at mid-price on Eminence is a match for any in the catalogue at whatever price, whether in performance or recording. Mackerras in his well-paced reading sees the work as a whole, building each movement with total concentration. There is a thrilling culmination on the great brass chorale at the end, with polish allied to purposefulness. Barbirolli in his classic reading may find more of a tear-laden quality in the great *Adagietto*; but Mackerras, with fewer controversial points of interpretation and superb modern sound, makes an excellent first choice.

Barbirolli's famous 1969 version has been digitally remastered on to one mid-priced CD. On any count it is one of the greatest, most warmly affecting performances ever committed to record, expansive yet concentrated in feeling. A classic version and a fine bargain.

Bernstein's is also an expansive version, characteristic of his latterday Mahler style. The lovely *Adagietto* was the music he conducted at the funeral of President John F. Kennedy, and the tempo this time is just as slow as before and just as elegiac, though the phrasing is less heavily underlined. The whole performance (recorded, in the Bernstein manner, at live concerts) has his personal stamp on it, at times idiosyncratic but luminous and magnetically compelling, one of the best in his new DG Mahler series and one of his finest recent records. The sound is more open and refined than in many of DG's Vienna recordings.

The opening *Funeral march* sets the tone of Solti's 1971 reading. At a tempo faster than usual, it is wistful rather than deeply tragic, even though the dynamic contrasts are superbly pointed and the string tone could hardly be more resonant. In the pivotal *Adagietto*, Solti secures intensely beautiful playing, but the result lacks the 'inner' quality one finds so abundantly in Barbirolli's interpretation. The recording is clear and brilliant.

Unlike Abbado's superb account of No. 2, his version of No. 5 lacks something in spontaneity. The *Adagietto*, for example, is hardly slow at all, but the phrasing sounds self-conscious. Nevertheless it is a polished reading, with first-rate digital sound, which can be recommended at mid-price to those collecting Abbado's Mahler series.

Bruno Walter followed up his 1945 recording of Mahler's *Fourth* with this account of No. 5, another persuasive reading marked by fine rhythmic pointing and natural expressiveness. It is transferred – evidently from the original 78s, not from tape – with a good body of sound but with a limited dynamic range. Even so, the celebrated *Adagietto* – taken much faster than has become the custom – has an easy warmth which makes one recognize it as idiomatic, naturally and unselfconsciously flexible in a song-like way. Mahler, one imagines, would have wanted it like this and might well have objected to the extra weight and depth which latterday slow readings bring. The ensemble is not always perfect – as at the end of the finale – and the recording gives an unwanted edge to high violins; but this is a classic reading that is very welcome indeed on a single mid-priced CD.

Although the opening brass fanfare is given dramatic projection on CD, in the first-movement funeral march Kubelik is gentle rather than tragic, and his relative lightness of manner, coupled with refined textures, underplays the epic qualities of this work. Nor does he succeed in disguising the patchwork structure of the last movement. The CD transfer gives the performance striking immediacy. The sound is slightly lacking in depth with a rather dry bass, but there is no lack of ambient glow in the *Adagietto*.

Symphony No. 6 in A min.

(M) *** Sony SBK 47654 [id.]. Cleveland O, Szell.

(M) *** Unicorn UKCD 2024/5. Stockholm PO, Jascha Horenstein.

This live recording, taken from a broadcast of October 1967, was not issued until after Szell's death; more than many of his studio recordings, it illustrates the subtlety and warmth as well as the power and concentration of his performances with the superb orchestra he had built up. The powerful outer movements are masterfully shaped and unerringly paced, with the second-movement scherzo a shade broader than the closely related first, beautifully sprung to bring out the grotesquerie. The *Andante moderato* then brings a uniquely delicate and moving account of an elusive movement. Unlike most others, Szell takes full account of the second word, *moderato*, as well as the first. At a whispered pianissimo, flowing easily, the result is hauntingly wistful, tender without a hint of sentimentality. The CD transfer gives a fuller, more atmospheric impression of what the orchestra sounded like in Severance Hall, Cleveland, than most of the studio recordings of the time. At budget price, squeezed on to a single disc (possible thanks to the omission of the first-movement exposition repeat) this is buried treasure, a historic issue for everyone, not just Mahlerians, and a fine counterpart to Szell's classic reading of Mahler's *Fourth*.

Horenstein's Unicorn-Kanchana set originates from live performances, recorded in Stockholm in April 1966; yet the sound is amazingly faithful and well balanced, with a firm bass, full strings, and a spacious concert-hall perspective. In the first movement Horenstein finds extra weight by taking a more measured tempo than most conductors. It is a sober reading that holds together with wonderful concentration. Not that this view of Mahler lacks flexibility, for the slow movement brings the most persuasive rubato. The finale brings another broad, noble reading, and the side-break which disfigured the LPs has disappeared. Yet some will feel that 33 minutes is short measure for the second CD, especially when Horenstein's recorded reminiscences with Alan Blyth, featured in the LP set, are not included here.

Symphony No. 7 in E min.
(M) ** EMI CMS7 64147-2 (2) [id.]. New Philh. O, Klemperer – KLEMPERER: *Symphony* etc. **

This is not one of Klemperer's most convincing Mahler performances. The 1968 recording sessions caught him and the orchestra below their peak, and one misses the concentrated sense of flow which normally runs through any of his performances, no matter how magisterially slow. There is, however, a magically sensitive account of the second *Nachtmusik* in which Klemperer's characteristic chunkinesss underlines a superbly refined contribution from the New Philharmonia wind players and beautiful string-tone. The rest, though, is comparatively disappointing, even if the Kingsway Hall sound is impressively bright and full-blooded in its CD transfer.

Symphony No. 9 in D min.
(M) *** EMI CDM7 63115-2 [id.]. BPO, Barbirolli.
(M) *** EMI CMS7 63277-2 (2) [Ang. CDMB 63277]. New Philh. O, Klemperer – WAGNER: *Siegfried idyll.* **(*)
(M) (**(*)) EMI mono CDH7 63029-2. VPO, Bruno Walter.
(M) ** Decca 430 247-2 (2) [id.]. LSO, Solti – WAGNER: *Siegfried idyll.* ***

Barbirolli greatly impressed the Berliners with his Mahler performances live, and this recording reflects the players' warmth of response. He opted to record the slow and intense finale before the rest, and the beauty of the playing makes it a fitting culmination. The other movements are strong and alert too, and the sound remains full and atmospheric, though now more clearly defined. An unquestionable bargain.

Klemperer's performance was recorded in 1967 after a serious illness, and his refusal to languish pays tribute to his physical and spiritual defiance. Characteristically, he insisted on a relatively close balance, with woodwind well forward, and the physical power is underlined when the sound is full-bodied and firmly focused. The sublimity of the finale comes out the more intensely, with overt expressiveness held in check and deep emotion implied rather than made explicit. In the second movement the rustic humour is beautifully pointed, and even the comparative heaviness of the third movement has its justification in bringing out Mahler's parody of academic forms. This is one of the very finest of Klemperer's later recordings and it is coupled with the much earlier Philharmonia chamber version of Wagner's *Siegfried idyll.*

Recorded live at a concert in the Musikvereinsaal on 16 January 1938, only a few weeks before Hitler invaded Austria, Bruno Walter's version with the Vienna Philharmonic was the first recording of this symphony ever issued. The opening is not promising, with coughing very obtrusive; but then, with the atmosphere of this hall caught more vividly than in most modern recordings, the magnetism of Walter becomes irresistible in music which he was the first ever to perform. Interestingly, his speeds in the great spans of the outer movements are faster than we have latterly grown used to, markedly so in the great *Adagio* finale. Ensemble is often scrappy in the first movement, but intensity is unaffected; and, even at its flowing speed, the finale brings warmth and repose with no feeling of haste.

Solti's 1967 version of Mahler's *Ninth* was an outstandingly successful example of Decca's vintage analogue techniques: there is a fantastic range of dynamic, combined with fine detail and a natural perspective. It is a brilliant, dramatic reading, but one which finally falls just a little short of being a great performance in its extrovert approach to the spiritual beauty of the finale. In the middle two movements it would be difficult to match Solti for the point and precision of the playing; the tempo for the second-movement Ländler may be slow but, with such pointing, the slowness is amply justified – quite apart from following Mahler's marking. The third movement is given the most brilliant account ever, but in the outer movements one feels that Solti is not penetrating deeply enough. He allows Mahler's passionate utterances to emerge too readily. He makes Mahler wear his heart on his sleeve and, although there may be justification for that, it misses something we have come to expect. The CD transfer, like the others in this series, achieves remarkable clarity of focus.

Symphony No. 10 in F sharp (unfinished): completed Deryk Cooke.
(M) ** Sony MPK 45882 [id.]. Phd O, Ormandy.

On a single CD, there is much to be said for the Ormandy version, when the performance has such emotional thrust and the playing such power and resonance, particularly in the strings. The mid-1960s recording still sounds well but, with a playing time of only 70 minutes, it means that the finale in particular does not have the spacious gravity and dark intensity of other versions, even though the opening hammerblows on the bass drum are thrillingly caught. A snag too is that this uses Cooke's original performing score (as distinct from the later, revised version) with rather balder, less Mahlerian scoring in the last two movements.

LIEDER AND SONG-CYCLES

Das klagende Lied: complete (Part 1, *Waldmärchen;* Part 2: *Der Spielmann;* Part 3, *Hochzeitsstücke*).
(M) *** Sony SK 45841 [id.]. Hoffman, Söderström, Haefliger, Nienstedt, Lear, Burrows, LSO, Boulez.

Das klagende Lied is the amazing inspiration of a teenage composer. Years after its completion, when Mahler came to revise the work he jettisoned the first of the three sections. It is arguable that he did not want it to be completely forgotten, for instead of destroying the score he gave it to a relative who was ultimately persuaded into allowing public performance. Boulez was given the rights to a first recording and in 1970 he promptly added his version of *Waldmärchen* to the other two parts, which he had already recorded using the same orchestra but with different soloists and a different venue, Walthamstow instead of Watford Town Hall. On record at least there is every argument for having the option of adding *Waldmärchen*, with Mahler's characteristic style and orchestration already identifiable, for it is almost as original as the other two parts, which stand as extraordinarily mature. Boulez is a distinctive Mahlerian. His clear ear concentrates on precision of texture, but the atmospheric ambience adds warmth despite the forward balance, which also ensures very little difference in sound between the two recordings. Certainly the chill at the heart of this gruesome story of the days of chivalry and knights in armour is the more sharply conveyed. *Waldmärchen* is less effective than the rest. Good singing from the chorus, less good from the soloists. But with any reservations noted, this excellently remastered CD is well worth exploring.

Des Knaben Wunderhorn; Lieder eines fahrenden Gesellen; 11 Lieder Aus der Jugendzeit; 4 Rückert Lieder.
(M) **(*) Sony SM2K 47170 (2) [id.]. Christa Ludwig, Walter Berry, Dietrich Fischer-Dieskau, Leonard Bernstein.

It is fascinating not only to compare Bernstein's playing for Fischer-Dieskau in the 'Youth' songs with that of Bruno Walter on the disc above but also to contrast Bernstein's style at the piano when accompanying the different singers. Where the *Wunderhorn* songs with Christa Ludwig and Walter Berry keep constantly in touch with the folk-inspiration behind them, the other groups with Fischer-Dieskau bring an even subtler and more sophisticated partnership between pianist and singer. It is true that, even in the *Wunderhorn* songs, Bernstein allows himself the most extreme rubato and tenuto on occasion. In the simple, tuneful *Rheinlegendchen*, for example, the piano introduction is pulled about astonishingly but then, with the entry of the voice, the folk-like quality is reflected in a simpler, more direct style. With the Fischer-Dieskau performances, both singer and pianist adopt a far more extreme expressive style all through, responding to each other in an almost impressionistic way, notably in the four Rückert Lieder, which inspire the singer to velvety legato. The eleven 'Youth' songs sound quite different here from the Halban/Walter recording, with '*Scheiden und Meiden*' given with exhilarating bounce and with a song such as '*Nicht wiedersehen*' treated expansively. Taken almost twice as slowly as on the rival version, it evokes a totally different, magical world. These 1968 recordings have not been released before, completing a collection which is a valuable supplement to Bernstein's Mahler recordings as a conductor.

Des Knaben Wunderhorn: Das irdische Leben; Wo die schönen Trompeten blasen; Urlicht. Rückert Lieder: Liebst du um Schönheit; Ich bin der Welt.
(M) **(*) Ph. 426 642-2; *426 642-4*. Jessye Norman, Irwin Gage – SCHUBERT: *Lieder.* **(*)

Jessye Norman recorded these Mahler songs in 1971, near the beginning of her career, and already the voice was developing magically. There is less detail here than in more recent performances, but the magisterial sustaining of long lines at very measured speeds is impressive. Irwin Gage accompanies sensitively, though he cannot efface memories of the orchestral versions. Good recording for its period, skilfully transferred to CD.

Lieder eines fahrenden Gesellen.
(M) ** Sony MYK 45503 [id.]. Mildred Miller, Columbia SO, Bruno Walter – BRAHMS: *Alto rhapsody* etc. **

Mildred Miller sings well enough, although her vocal production is at times a little restricted and, instead of long, resonant phrases, the listener sometimes receives an impression of short-term musical thought. Yet Walter keeps the performance dramatically alive and there is superb orchestral detail, brought out most vividly by the excellent CD transfer, which is atmospheric and refined. The tangibility of both voice and orchestra is striking and the balance is first class.

Das Lied von der Erde.
❀ (M) *** Ph. 432 279-2; *432 279-4* [id.]. Dame Janet Baker, James King, Concg. O, Haitink.
(M) *** DG 419 058-2; *419 058-4* [id.]. Ludwig, Kollo, BPO, Karajan.

(M) **(*) Sony MYK 45500 [id.]. Mildred Miller, Ernst Haefliger, NYPO, Bruno Walter.
(M) **(*) Decca 417 783-2 [id.]. James King, Fischer-Dieskau, VPO, Bernstein.

At last Dame Janet Baker's outstanding 1975 version arrives on CD, to dominate the field once again; indeed the combination of this most deeply committed of Mahler singers with Haitink, the most thoughtfully dedicated of Mahler conductors, produces radiantly beautiful and moving results, helped by refined and atmospheric recording. If these songs usually reflect a degree of oriental reticence, Dame Janet relates them more clearly to Mahler's other great orchestral songs, so complete is the sense of involvement, with the conductor matching his soloist's mood. The concentration over the long final *Abschied* has never been surpassed on record (almost all of it was recorded in a single take). Haitink opens the cycle impressively with an account of the first tenor song that subtly confirms its symphonic shape, less free in tempo than usual but presenting unusually strong contrasts between the main stanzas and the tender refrain, *Dunkel ist das Leben.* James King cannot match his solo partner, often failing to create fantasy, but his singing is intelligent and sympathetic. The balance is realistic; for this CD reissue the sound has been brightened and made more vivid, but not at the expense of the original bloom and warmth. The closing pages remain tellingly atmospheric.

Karajan presents *Das Lied* as the most seductive sequence of atmospheric songs, combining characteristic refinement and polish with a deep sense of melancholy. This way of presenting Mahler's orchestration in the subtlest tones rather than in full colours is arguably more apt. In any case what matters is that here Karajan conveys the ebb and flow of tension as in a live performance. He is helped enormously by the soloists, both of whom have recorded this work several times, but never more richly than here. The sound on CD is more sharply defined, and some of the ambient effect has gone, but the quality is admirably vivid and does not lack a basic warmth.

Though Bruno Walter's New York version does not have the tear-laden quality in the final *Abschied* that made his earlier Vienna account (in mono) with Kathleen Ferrier unique, that is its only serious shortcoming. Haefliger sparkles with imagination and Miller is a warm and appealing mezzo soloist, lacking only the last depth of feeling you find in a Ferrier; and the maestro himself has rarely sounded so happy on record, even in Mahler. The remastered recording has been considerably improved for CD and now sounds both warm and vivid.

Bernstein's tempi, although showing an individual hallmark, generally suit the music naturally. So the tenor songs sparkle as they should, and though the final *Abschied*, taken at a very slow tempo indeed, puts extra strain on everyone, Bernstein's intensity carries the performance through. Doubts do arise over the soloists. James King is a strong-voiced tenor, but at times his word-pointing and phrasing sound comparatively stiff. Fischer-Dieskau is as sensitive as ever, but it is doubtful whether even he can match the finest contralto in the role, for one needs a lightening of tone in the even-numbered songs rather than – as here – a darkening. However, the reissue on CD of Dame Janet Baker's version, also partnering James King, with the Concertgebouw Orchestra under Haitink, remains unsurpassed.

Marcello, Alessandro (1669–1747)

6 Oboe concertos (La Cetra).
(M) *** DG 427 137-2; *427 137-4* [id.]. Heinz Holliger, Louise Pellerin, Camerata Bern, Füri.

The six concertos of *La Cetra* are concertante exercises rather than concertos in the accepted sense of the word, and they reveal a pleasing mixture of originality and convention. As a composer Alessandro was perhaps not quite as accomplished as his brother, Benedetto, and occasionally there is a reliance on relatively routine gestures; but much of the time one is surprised by a genuinely alive and refreshing individuality. These performances are vital and keen, occasionally almost aggressively bright, but full of style and character, and the recording is faithful and well projected.

Martin, Frank (1890–1974)

(i) *Cello concerto; The Four elements.*
(M) *** Preludio PRL 2147 [id.]. (i) Jean Decroos, Concg. O, Haitink.

The Four elements was composed in 1963/4 for Ernest Ansermet's eightieth birthday and the *Cello concerto* in 1966 for Pierre Fournier. These two excellent performances come from Dutch Radio tapes, and the sound is unobtrusively natural and the balance beautifully judged, enabling Martin's subtle and expertly judged orchestral sonorities to register. Jean Decroos, from the first desk of the Concertgebouw, gives an impressive account of the *Cello concerto* and Haitink secures excellent playing from the Concertgebouw Orchestra. *The Four elements* is another Martin rarity, rich in invention and imaginative resource: its neglect is little short of scandalous. Both performances were recorded at public concerts in

1965 and 1970 respectively, but audience noise is minimal and the quality first rate.

Concerto for 7 wind instruments, timpani, percussion and strings; Études for strings; (i) *Petite symphonie concertante for harp, harpsichord, piano and double string orchestra.*
(M) (***) Decca mono 430 003-2. (i) Jamet, Vauchet-Clerc, Rossiaud, SRO, Ansermet.

This CD contains the pioneering record of Frank Martin's masterpiece, the *Petite symphonie concertante*, one of the very first Decca LPs. This authoritative performance has a concentration and an atmosphere that have not really been matched since. The three excellent soloists, Pierre Jamet (harp), Germaine Vauchet-Clerc (harpsichord) and Doris Rossiaud (piano) are at no point named in the documentation, but their contribution deserves recognition. The 1951 recording does not sound as spectacular as it seemed at the time, and the string-tone shows its age. No apologies need be made for the remarkably vivid recording of the *Études for strings* and the masterly *Concerto for 7 wind instruments*. An indispensable issue.

6 Monologues from Everyman; The Tempest: 3 excerpts.
❀ (M) *** DG 429 858-2 [id.]. Fischer-Dieskau, BPO, composer – EGK: *The temptation of St Anthony*. ***

The *Everyman Monologues* is a masterpiece – one of the great song-cycles of the twentieth century. Composed in the wake of *Der Cornet*, it is a setting of six monologues from Hofmannsthal's play on the theme of a rich man dying, and gives expression to both the fear of death and the doctrine of resurrection through love. The music is of extraordinary vision and imaginative power, and this classic performance from Fischer-Dieskau and the composer sounds as vivid and fresh as ever. The three excerpts from *The Tempest* make one long to hear the rest of the opera, which comes from the early 1950s, the same period as the *Violin concerto* and the *Harpsichord concerto*, to which it is related. The orchestral Prelude casts a strong and powerful spell and the two arias, from Act III (*My Ariel! Hast thou, which art but air*) and the Epilogue (*Now my charms are all o'erthrown*), are hardly less magical. This music impresses when one first encounters it, yet its beauties grow with each hearing.

Martinů, Bohuslav (1890–1959)

Symphonies Nos. 1–6 (Fantaisies symphoniques).
(M) *** Sup. 11 0382-2 (3) [id.]. Czech PO, Václav Neumann.

Neumann's complete set of the Martinů symphonies was recorded in the Dvořák Hall of the House of Artists, Prague, between January 1976 (No. 6) and 1978 (No. 5). The transfers to CD are excellently done: the sound is full, spacious and bright; it has greater presence and better definition than the original LPs, yet with no edginess in the strings. The orchestral playing, it hardly needs saying, is first class and Neumann's readings have a spacious intensity, a relaxed grip and a natural feeling for the colour and atmosphere of these works. The *First Symphony* dates from 1942, the year after Martinů arrived in the United States; like so much good music of the period, it was written in response to a commission from Koussevitzky. What Virgil Thomson described as the work's 'singing syncopation' lends the *Symphony* a forward thrust and subtlety which Neumann catches admirably. The *Second* (1943) is the most relaxed of the six; its ideas are unforced, its mood easy-going and bucolic. Much of it is exhilarating, particularly the delightful finale, and in Neumann's hands it has much charm in its pastoral slow movement. The coupling of the *Third* and *Fourth* on the second disc brings two of the finest performances in the cycle. The *Third* is in some ways the weightiest of the set; it is without doubt the most concentrated and powerful, with the possible exception of the *Sixth*. It has something of the dark purposefulness and vision of the *Double concerto*, and its splendid central slow movement brings great intensity of feeling and real depth from the Czech players, with the finale by no means an anticlimax. Neumann gives an authoritative reading, with well-shaped phrasing, and his conception is more spacious than was Sejna's in his post-war set. The *Fourth* is perhaps the most immediately attractive and appealing of all six, and Neumann's performance is eminently recommendable. The remastered recording, too, is strikingly vivid; its resonance does not blur the bright colours of the *Allegro vivo* second movement, and there is radiance in the violins at the sustained opening of the *Largo*. The *Fifth* (written for the Prague Spring Festival in 1946) is a marvellous piece. Its opening is invitingly confident (it is full of brightness and intensity with woodwind chirping and violins gleaming), while its closing pages radiate an almost incandescent quality and a life-enhancing power quite out of tune with the bleak post-war years that gave it birth. Neumann's account does not displace Ančerl's full-price version, but it is still powerfully communicative and has the spontaneity that distinguishes all the performances offered here. The *Sixth* is much later (1953) and was introduced to the gramophone by Charles Munch and the Boston Symphony, to whom the work is dedicated. The composer said that he wrote it to give pleasure to the conductor, and his comment that 'Munch's spontaneous approach to music, in which a composition freely acquires its form and flows out unrestrainedly', so that 'a hardly perceptible rippling or acceleration brings the melody to life', might be applied to the music itself. (It is also reassuring to find in the 1950s a great composer giving prime importance to melodic flow at a time when serious music was already entering a period when major figures were no longer able to find a central role for melody in their writing, to the consternation of the musical public, if not of the ivory-towered critical fraternity.) Yet Martinů's orchestration and imaginative design for the *Sixth* are by no means conservative or backward-looking. The exotic textures still intrigue the ear (the opening sounds for all the world like a cloud of Amazonian insects) and must initially, for the composer, have outweighed the musical cogency and sweep of his score, so that he was doubtful of its symphonic status. He subtitled it *Fantaisies symphoniques*, and even briefly asked for it not to be included in his numbered symphonies. Václav Neumann's performance has an impressive spaciousness and, though there could be more urgency and fire in places, the reading has life, colour and impetus, and is thoroughly compelling when the Czech orchestra play so vividly: witness the powerful trumpet solo in the finale.

CHAMBER MUSIC

Duo for violin and cello.

(M) *** BMG/RCA GD 87871; *GK 87871* [7871-2-RG; *7871-4-RG*]. Heifetz, Piatigorsky – DEBUSSY: *Sonata* etc.(**); RESPIGHI: *Sonata* (***); RAVEL: *Trio* etc.(**)

All the other works on the Heifetz disc are mono recordings from 1950 and, although the Respighi *Sonata* has never been surpassed, the Ravel *Trio* is wanting in atmosphere. The repertoire for violin and cello is not extensive (Kodály and Ravel wrote for this partnership) and Martinů composed two *Duos*, the first in 1927. A short but powerful piece, it was recorded in 1964 and, though the acoustic is a bit dryish, the playing is fabulous.

Mascagni, Pietro (1863–1945)

Cavalleria Rusticana (complete).

(M) **(*) EMI CMS7 63967-2 (2) [id.]. De los Angeles, Corelli, Sereni, Rome Op. Ch. & O, Santini – LEONCAVALLO: *Pagliacci* ***.

(M) **(*) Decca 425 985-2 [id.]. Tebaldi, Bjoerling, Bastianini, Maggio Musicale Fiorentino Ch. & O, Erede.

(M) **(*) EMI CMS7 63650-2 (2). Caballé, Carreras, Hamari, Manuguerra, Varnay, Amb. Op. Ch., Southend Boys' Ch., Philh. O, Muti – LEONCAVALLO: *I Pagliacci*. **(*)

(M) (***) BMG/RCA mono GD 86510 [RCA 6510-2-RG]. Milanov, Bjoerling, Merrill, Robert Shaw Chorale, RCA O, Cellini.

Though not as vibrant as Von Matačić's *Pagliacci* coupling, this beautifully sung, essentially lyrical EMI performance could give considerable satisfaction, provided the bitterness of Mascagni's drama is not a first consideration. Like the coupling, it shows Corelli in good form; both he and De los Angeles are given scope by Santini to produce soaring, Italianate singing of Mascagni's richly memorable melodies. The recording is suitably atmospheric.

The early (1957) Decca recording with Tebaldi offers a forthright, lusty account of Mascagni's piece of blood and thunder and has the distinction of three excellent soloists. Tebaldi is most moving in *Voi lo sapete*, and the firm richness of Bastianini's baritone is beautifully caught. As always, Bjoerling shows himself the most intelligent of tenors, and it is only the chorus that gives serious cause for disappointment. They are enthusiastic and accurate enough when accompanying Bjoerling's superb account of the drinking scene (in Italy no doubt the directions for wine were taken literally), but at other times they are very undisciplined. The CD sound is strikingly bright and lively.

There are fewer unexpected textual points in the EMI *Cav.* than in *Pag.*, but Muti's approach is comparably biting and violent, brushing away the idea that this is a sentimental score, though running the risk of making it vulgar. The result is certainly refreshing, with Caballé – pushed faster than usual, even in her big moments – collaborating warmly. So *Voi lo sapete* is geared from the start to the final cry of *Io son dannata*, and she manages a fine snarl on *A te la mala Pasqua*. Carreras does not sound quite so much at home, though the rest of the cast is memorable, including the resonant Manuguerra as Alfio and the veteran Astrid Varnay as Mamma Lucia, wobble as she does. The recording is forward and vivid.

Though Zinka Milanov starts disappointingly in the *Easter hymn*, the conjunction of three of the outstanding Met. principals of the early 1950s' period brings a warmly satisfying performance. Admirers of Milanov will not want to miss her beautiful singing of *Voi lo sapete*, and in the duet Merrill's dark, firm timbre is thrilling. Bjoerling brings a good measure of musical and tonal subtlety to the role of Turiddù, normally belted out, while Cellini's conducting minimizes the vulgarity of the piece.

Cavalleria Rusticana: highlights.
(B) *** DG Compact Classics *427 717-4* [id.] (from complete recording with Cossotto, Bergonzi, Guelfi, La Scala, Milan, Ch. & O, Karajan) – LEONCAVALLO: *Pagliacci*: highlights. ***
(M) **(*) EMI CDM7 63933-3 [id.]; *EG 763933-4* (from above complete recording; cond. Muti) – LEONCAVALLO: *Pagliacci*: highlights. **(*)
(M) ** Decca 421 870-2; *421 870-4*. Varady, Pavarotti, Cappuccilli, Gonzales, L. Op. Ch., Nat. PO, Gavazzeni – LEONCAVALLO: *I Pagliacci*: highlights. **

This Compact Classics highlights tape includes the key items from Karajan's set of *Cavalleria Rusticana*, with both Cossotto and Bergonzi in splendid form. There is some lack of bite in the choruses, but that is caused as much by the orginal recording balance as by the tape transfer, which is otherwise excellent.

With over a half an hour of music, the EMI CD provides an admirable sampler of Muti's pungent, earthy approach to *Cavalleria Rusticana*, with the recording ambience providing an atmospheric setting for the vivid projection of the drama.

The Decca excerpts from *Cavalleria Rusticana* include *Santuzza's Prayer* and *Voi lo sapete*, very welcome because Julia Varady is the most individual member of the cast. Pavarotti is loud and unsubtle as Turiddù, though the tone is often beautiful. The recording is brilliant, with striking presence and fine atmosphere.

Massenet, Jules (1842–1912)

Le Carillon (ballet): complete.
(M) *** Decca 425 472-2 (2). Nat. PO, Richard Bonynge – DELIBES: *Coppélia*. ***

Le Carillon was written in the same year as *Werther*. The villains of the story who try to destroy the bells of the title are punished by being miraculously transformed into bronze *jaquemarts*, fated to continue striking them for ever! The music of this one-act ballet makes a delightful offering – not always as lightweight as one would expect. With his keen rhythmic sense and feeling for colour, Bonynge is outstanding in this repertory, and the 1984 Decca recording is strikingly brilliant and colourful. A fine bonus (37 minutes) for a highly desirable version of Delibes' *Coppélia*.

Le Cid: ballet suite.
(M) *** Decca 425 475-2 (2). Nat. PO, Richard Bonynge – DELIBES: *Sylvia*. ***

Over the years, Decca have made a house speciality of recording the ballet music from *Le Cid* and coupling it with Constant Lambert's arrangement of Meyerbeer (*Les Patineurs*). Bonynge's version is the finest yet, with the most seductive orchestral playing, superbly recorded. Now it comes as an engaging encore for an equally recommendable complete set of Delibes' *Sylvia*, with the remastering for CD adding to the glitter and colour of Massenet's often witty scoring.

Cigale (ballet): complete.
(M) *** Decca 425 413-2 (3). Enid Hartle, Nat. PO, Bonynge – TCHAIKOVSKY: *Swan Lake*. **(*)

A late work, written with Massenet's characteristic finesse. *Cigale* was totally neglected after its première in 1904, until Richard Bonynge revived it in this admirable recording. The ballet recounts the La Fontaine fable about the grasshopper and the ant. The melodic invention does not match Massenet's finest, but the score is charming and colourful and is brightly and atmospherically played and sung and brilliantly recorded; and it makes a considerable coupling for Bonynge's complete set of Tchaikovsky's *Swan Lake*.

OPERA

Don Quichotte (complete).
(M) *** Decca 430 636-2 (2) [id.]. Ghiaurov, Bacquier, Crespin, SRO, Kord.

Massenet's operatic adaptation of Cervantes' classic novel gave him his last big success, written as it was with Chaliapin in mind for the title-role. It is a totally captivating piece with not a jaded bar in it, suggesting that Massenet might have developed further away from his regular romantic opera style. There is genuine nobility as well as comedy in the portrait of the knight, and that is well caught here by Ghiaurov, who refuses to exaggerate the characterization. Bacquier makes a delightful Sancho Panza, but it is Régine Crespin as a comically mature Dulcinée, who provides the most characterful singing, flawed vocally but commandingly positive. Kazimierz Kord directs the Suisse Romande Orchestra in a performance that is zestful and electrifying, and the recording is outstandingly clear and atmospheric.

Esclarmonde (complete).
(M) *** Decca 425 651-2 (3) [id.]. Sutherland, Aragall, Tourangeau, Davies, Grant, Alldis Ch., Nat. PO, Bonynge.

The central role of *Esclarmonde*, with its Wagnerian echoes and hints of both Verdi and Berlioz, calls for an almost impossible combination of qualities. In our generation Joan Sutherland is the obvious diva to encompass the demands of great range, great power and brilliant coloratura, and her performance is in its way as powerful as it is in Puccini's last opera. Aragall proves an excellent tenor, sweet of tone and intelligent, and the other parts, all of them relatively small, are well taken too. Richard Bonynge draws passionate singing and playing from chorus and orchestra, and the recording has both atmosphere and spectacle to match the story, based on a medieval romance involving song-contests and necromancy.

Manon (complete).

(M) (*(**)) EMI mono CMS7 63549-2 (3). De los Angeles, Legay, Dens, Boirthayre, Berton, Opéra-comique, Monteux – CHAUSSON: *Poème de l'amour et de la mer.* (***)

The combination of Victoria de los Angeles singing the role of the heroine with Pierre Monteux conducting is unbeatable in Massenet's most warmly approachable opera. There has never been a more winning Manon than De los Angeles, deliciously seductive from the start, making her first girlish solo, *Je suis encore tout étourdie*, sparkle irresistibly. The meeting with Des Grieux is then enchanting, with the hero's youthful wonderment breathtakingly caught by Henri Legay in his light, heady tenor. Though there are cuts – for example the end of Act I – this is a unique performance that defies the limitations of ancient mono recording. Unfortunately, the CD transfer emphasizes the top registers unduly while giving little body to lower registers. Voices can be made to sound vivid, but the orchestra remains thin and edgy. The original four LPs have been transferred to three CDs, with the bonus of De los Angeles' recording of the delightful Chausson cantata.

Werther (complete).

(M) *** DG 403 304-2 (2). Domingo, Obraztsova, Augér, Grundheber, Moll, Cologne Children's Ch. and RSO, Chailly.

(M) **(*) EMI CMS7 63973-2 (2) [id.]. Gedda, De los Angeles, Mesplé, Soyer, Voix d'Enfants de la Maîtrise de l'ORTF, O de Paris, Prêtre.

(M) ** EMI CMS7 69573-2 (2). Kraus, Troyanos, Manuguerra, Barbaux, Ch. & LPO, Plasson.

With a recording that gives fine body and range to the sound of the Cologne orchestra, down to the subtlest whisper from the pianissimo strings, the DG version stands at an advantage, particularly as Chailly proves a sharply masterful conductor, one who knows how to thrust home an important climax as well as how to create evocative textures, varying tensions positively. Placido Domingo in the name-part sings with sweetness and purity as well as strength, coping superbly with the legato line of the aria *Pourquoi me réveiller?*. Elena Obraztsova is richer and firmer than she usually is on record, but it is a generalized portrait, particularly beside the charming Sophie of Arlene Augér. The others make up a very convincing team.

Victoria de los Angeles, who has already given us a delectable portrayal of *Manon*, is equally attractive portraying Charlotte in *Werther*, and here she has the advantage of stereo. Her golden tones which convey pathos so beautifully are ideally suited to Massenet's gentle melodies and, though she is recorded too closely (closer than the other soloists), she makes an intensely appealing heroine. Though sweetness is the predominant quality, it would be a mistake to dismiss this score as sentimental, for Massenet's adaptation of Goethe is full of fine dramatic strokes. Gedda makes an intelligent romantic hero, though Prêtre's direction could be subtler.

It is sad that Alfredo Kraus, as a rule one of the most stylish of tenors, came to record *Werther* so late in his career. Listen to this account of *Pourquoi me réveiller?*, and the effortful underlining, with its chopping of the melodic line, is almost unrecognizable as his work. Troyanos makes a volatile Charlotte, but the voice as recorded is grainy. Manuguerra produces rich tone as the Bailiff, but the engineers have not been kind to the LPO strings, which sound rather thin.

Werther: highlights.

(M) ** EMI CDM7 63936-2 [id.]; *EG 763936-4* (from above complete recording; cond. Plasson).

With just under an hour of music included, this EMI highlights disc, pleasingly atmospheric – although the LPO strings could have more body – makes a good sampler of Plasson's set. Alfredo Kraus generally sings stylishly, though his tone is strained in *Pouquoi me réveiller?*, and Troyanos and Manuguerra both make quite impressive contributions.

Maxwell Davies, Peter (born 1934)

Ave maris stella; Image, reflection, shadow; (i) *Runes from a holy island.*

(M) *** Unicorn UKCD 2038; *UKC 2038*. Fires of London, (i) cond. composer.

This is a CD compilation of key Maxwell Davies works, more generously as well as more aptly coupled than on the original LPs. *Ave maris stella*, essentially elegiac, finds the composer at his most severe and demanding. The second piece, *Image, reflection, shadow*, is a kind of sequel; both of them are extended works for small chamber ensemble, which are played here without conductor. The one, using plainchant as its basis, suggested further exploration in the other, both ritualistic in their simple dedication yet not easy in their idiom. *Runes*, conducted by the composer, is much shorter yet just as intense in its rapt slowness. Ideal performances, well recorded, from the group for which all this music was written.

Sinfonia; Sinfonia concertante.
(M) *** Unicorn Dig. UKCD 2026 [id.]. SCO, composer.

In his *Sinfonia* of 1962 Peter Maxwell Davies took as his inspirational starting point Monteverdi's *Vespers* of 1610. Except perhaps in the simple, grave beauty of the second of the four movements, where the analogy is directly with *Pulchra es* from the *Vespers*, it is not a kinship which will readily strike the listener, but the dedication in this music, beautifully played by the Scottish Chamber Orchestra under the composer, is plain from first to last. The *Sinfonia concertante* of twenty years later, as the title implies, is a much more extrovert piece for strings plus solo wind quintet and timpani. The balance of movements broadly follows a conventional plan, but in idiom this is hardly at all neo-classical and, more than usual, the composer evokes romantic images, as in the lovely close of the first movement. Virtuoso playing from the Scottish principals, not least the horn. Well-balanced recording.

Sinfonia accademica; (i) *Into the labyrinth.*
(M) *** Unicorn UKCD 2022. (i) Neil Mackie; SCO, composer.

Into the Labyrinth, in five movements, might be regarded more as a song-symphony than as a cantata. The words by the Orcadian poet (and the composer's regular collaborator), George Mackay Brown, are a prose-poem inspired by the physical impact of Orkney, with the second movement a hymn of praise to fire, wind, earth and water, and the fourth – after a brief orchestral interlude in the third – bringing the centrepiece of the work, comprising almost half the total length, an intense meditation. The fine Scottish tenor, Neil Mackie, gives a superb performance, confirming this as one of Maxwell Davies's most beautiful and moving inspirations. The *Sinfonia accademica* provides a strong and attractive contrast, with its lively, extrovert outer movements and a central slow movement which again evokes the atmosphere of Orkney. Strong, intense performances under the composer, helped by first-rate recording.

Mendelssohn, Felix (1809–47)

Piano concerto No. 1 in G min., Op. 25.
(BB) ** Pickwick PWK 1154. Peter Katin, LSO, Anthony Collins – LISZT: *Concerto No. 2.* **

(i) *Piano concertos Nos. 1 in G min., Op. 25; 2 in D min., Op. 40;* (ii) *Capriccio brillant in B min., Op. 22.*
(B) ** Pickwick Dig. PCD 953; *CIMPC 953* [id.]. Anton Kuerti, LPO, Paul Freeman.
(M) (*) Sony MPK 45690 [id.]. Rudolf Serkin, (i) Columbia SO; (ii) Phd. O, Ormandy.

(i) *Piano concertos Nos. 1–2;* (ii) *Capriccio brillant, Op. 22; Rondo brillant, Op. 29.*
(B) **(*) Decca 425 504-2; *425 504-4.* Peter Katin; (i) LSO, Collins; (ii) LPO, Martinon.

(i) *Piano concertos Nos. 1–2;* (ii) *Violin concerto in E min., Op. 64.*
(M) * Sony SBK 46542 [id.]. (i) Rudolf Serkin, Phd. O or Columbia SO, Ormandy; (ii) Stern, Phd. O, Ormandy.

Katin's early (1955) coupling of the two *Piano concertos* has come up amazingly freshly on CD; the ambient warmth of the recording disguises its age and the piano recording is excellent. Katin has the full measure of these remarkably similar works. His crisp passagework prevents the outer movements from becoming either brittle or lifeless, and he offers a pleasingly light touch in the finales. In both slow movements his style is sensitive without sentimentality, a feature mirrored in the excellent accompaniments. The two occasional pieces were recorded much later (1971) and are equally accomplished and enjoyable. The Pickwick CD offers the *G minor Concerto* coupled only with Liszt. With only 41 minutes' playing time, however, there would have been plenty of room for another concerto here, whether by Mendelssohn or Liszt.

Anton Kuerti has a distinguished pedigree: he studied with Horszowski and Serkin and played with such conductors as Szell, Ormandy and Dutoit. These accounts of the two *Concertos* and the *Capriccio brillante* are perhaps stronger on speed than on charm, though there are some moments of poetry (the beginning of the slow movement of the *G minor Concerto*) and some sensitive playing elsewhere. The piano sound is very clean and truthful and the orchestra naturally balanced (the soloist is marginally forward), though this Pickwick CD would not hold up against either the competition now available at full price or Katin in the bargain range unless modern digital recording was essential. However, the playing gives pleasure and would give even more if it, were not quite so rushed. The finales of both *Concertos* are pretty breathless and the orchestral playing a trifle unenthusiastic.

Serkin's performances are brilliant in the extreme, but they lack the first essential in performances of Mendelssohn's piano music: a degree of charm, while the overall style in outer movements is much too bold and heavy. The aggressive 1960 sound makes things worse and, if anything, this is exaggerated by the CD transfer: the opening of the *G minor Concerto* is grotesquely clattery. The *Capriccio brillant*, recorded a decade later, brings much the same approach and even less refined sound. The two *Piano concertos* are also available, coupled with the *Violin concerto* on one of Sony's very inessential 'Essential classics' reissues. Those seeking Stern's superbly eloquent account of the latter work would be far better advised to turn to its pairing with the Tchaikovsky *Concerto*.

Violin concerto in E min., Op. 64.

(M) *** Sony Dig. MDK 44902; *40-44902* [id.]. Cho-Liang Lin, Philh. O, Tilson Thomas – BRUCH: *Concerto No. 1* *** (with encores by SARASATE and KREISLER ***).

(BB) *** Naxos Dig. 8.550153 [id.]. Nishizaki, Slovak PO, Jean – TCHAIKOVSKY: *Concerto*. ***

(B) *** Ph. 422 473-2; *422 473-4*. Grumiaux, New Philh. O, Krenz – TCHAIKOVSKY: *Concerto*. ***

(B) *** Pickwick Dig. PCD 829; *CIMPC 829* [id.]. Jaime Laredo, SCO – BRUCH: *Concerto No. 1*. ***

(M) *** EMI CDM7 69003-2 [id.]; *EG 769003-4*. Menuhin, Philh. O, Kurtz – BRUCH: *Concerto No. 1*. ***

(M) *** DG 419 067-2 [id.]. Milstein, VPO, Abbado – TCHAIKOVSKY: *Concerto*. ***

(M) *** Ph. 426 639-2; *426 639-4*. Accardo, LPO, Dutoit – BRUCH: *Concerto No. 1*.(***)

(B) **(*) Pickwick IMPX 9031. Campoli, LPO, Boult – BRUCH: *Scottish fantasia*. **(*)

(M) **(*) Sony CD 42537 [MYK 36724]. Stern, Phd. O, Ormandy – TCHAIKOVSKY: *Concerto*. **(*)

(M) (***) EMI mono CDH7 69799-2 [id.]. Yehudi Menuhin, BPO, Furtwängler – BEETHOVEN: *Concerto*.(***)

(B) **(*) EMI CDZ7 62519-2; *LZ 762519-4*. Menuhin, LSO, Frühbeck de Burgos – BRUCH: *Concerto No. 1*. **(*)

(B) **(*) Decca 417 687-2. Ricci, Netherlands R. PO, Fournet – TCHAIKOVSKY: *Concerto*. **(*)

(M) **(*) BMG/RCA Dig. GD 86536 [RCA 6536-2-RG]. Ughi, LSO, Prêtre – BEETHOVEN: *Concerto*. **(*)

(BB) ** LaserLight Dig. 15 615 [id.]. Verhey, Budapest SO, Joó – BRUCH: *Concerto No. l*. **

(BB) *(*) Pickwick PWK 1151. Ion Voicou, LSO, Frühbeck de Burgos – BRUCH: *Concerto No. 1*. *(*)

Cho-Liang Lin's vibrantly lyrical account now reappears with the Bruch *G minor* (plus some attractive encores) to make an unbeatable mid-priced coupling. These are both immensely rewarding and poetic performances, given excellent, modern, digital sound, and Michael Tilson Thomas proves a highly sympathetic partner in the Mendelssohn *Concerto*.

Takako Nishizaki gives an inspired reading of the *Concerto*, warm, spontaneous and full of temperament. The central *Andante* is on the slow side, but well shaped, not sentimental, while the outer movements are exhilarating, with excellent playing from the Slovak Philharmonic. Though the forwardly placed violin sounds over-bright, the recording is full and warm. A splendid coupling at super-bargain price.

Grumiaux's 1973 account of the Mendelssohn is characteristically polished and refined. He plays very beautifully throughout; the pure poetry of his playing is heard at its most magical in the key moment of the downward arpeggio which introduces the second subject of the first movement.

Laredo's version on a bargain-price CD brings an attractively direct reading, fresh and alert but avoiding mannerism, marked by consistently sweet and true tone from the soloist. The orchestral ensemble is amazingly good when you remember that the soloist himself is directing. The recording is vivid and clean.

The restrained nobility of Menuhin's phrasing of the famous principal melody of the slow movement has long been a hallmark of his reading with Efrem Kurtz, who provides polished and sympathetic support. The sound of the CD transfer is bright, with the soloist dominating but the orchestral texture well detailed.

Milstein's version comes from the early 1970s. His is a highly distinguished performance, very well accompanied. His account of the slow movement is more patrician than Menuhin's, and his slight reserve is projected by DG sound which is bright, clean and clear in its CD remastering.

Accardo's freshness of style is most appealing. Outer movements are lithe and sparkling; and the *Andante*, taken more slowly than usual, is expressive in a natural, unforced way. Some ears may find the refined phrasing a little understated here, but overall this reading is distinctive for its gentle, romantic feeling. Dutoit's accompaniment is in every way first class, and the sound here is very good, better balanced than in the Bruch coupling.

Campoli's sweet, perfectly formed tone and polished, secure playing are just right for the Mendelssohn *Concerto*, and this is a delightful performance, notable for its charm and disarming simplicity. The song-like eloquence of the *Andante* and the scintillating brilliance of the finale (with Boult and the LPO following closely) give much pleasure. The 1958 (originally Decca) recording is brightly lit in the CD transfer, and the vividness is marred by a degree of roughness in the orchestral focus; but no matter, this inexpensive record gives much pleasure and is a fine reminder of a superb violinist.

Ricci's later recording, with Fournet, in some ways is to be preferred to his (currently withdrawn) version with Gamba, also on Decca, although it is not so naturally balanced. Both versions are striking for their spontaneity and vivid sound.

Stern's performance has great bravura, culminating in a marvellously surging account of the finale. The slow movement too is played with great eloquence and feeling, but when pianissimos are non-existent – partly, but not entirely, the fault of the close recording balance – the poetic element is diminished.

Menuhin's unique gift for lyrical sweetness has never been presented on record more seductively than in his classic, earlier version of the Mendelssohn concerto with Furtwängler. The digital transfer is not ideally clear, yet one hardly registers that this is a mono recording from the early 1950s.

Menuhin's second stereo recording with Rafael Frühbeck de Burgos has its moments of roughness, but it has magic too: at the appearance of the first movement's second subject and in the slow movement. The recording sounds fuller than the earlier account with Kurtz, and this makes a good bargain on EMI's inexpensive Laser label.

Ughi's is a fresh, totally unsentimental reading; both the slow movement and the finale are very successful. Ughi lacks only the final individuality of artists like Lin or Menuhin; but he is highly musical and has the advantage of an excellent digital recording, clean and well balanced and set against a believable atmosphere.

Emmy Verhey's approach has simplicity and a lyrical ardour comparable to Accardo's. Her playing is gently honeyed and she displays a fine sense of line in the *Andante*. Hers is a less assertive account than some, and the balance is natural and slightly recessed to suit the style of the music-making. Arpád Joó provides a most sympathetic accompaniment, and this performance will suit those who like a degree of restraint in this work; the finale has both sparkle and a pleasing lightness of touch. Excellent value in the bargain basement.

The Voicou/de Burgos combination undoubtedly has its moments: the second subject of the first movement is genuinely touching, the *Andante* has a pleasing simplicity and the finale scintillates, when the soloist's articulation is light and feathery, and is nicely integrated with the accompaniment. But the 1965 Decca recording gives Voicou's timbre a febrile wiriness that is ill-suited to Mendelssohn's elegant lyricism.

(i) *Violin concerto in E min., Op. 64;* (ii) *Symphony No. 4 in A (Italian), Op. 90;* (iii) *A Midsummer Night's Dream: Overture and incidental music* (CD only: (iv) *Overture: A Calm sea and a prosperous voyage*).

(B) *** DG Compact Classics 413 150-2 (2); *413 150-4*. (i) Milstein, VPO, Abbado; (ii) BPO, Maazel; (iii) Mathis, Boese, Bav. RSO with Ch., Kubelik (CD only: (iv) LSO, Chmura).

This is one of the most attractive compilations in DG's Compact Classics series. Milstein's 1973 account of the *Violin concerto* (see above) is highly distinguished. With excellent recording and balance this is worthy to rank with the best, and it is greatly enhanced by the sensitivity of Abbado's accompaniment. Maazel's *Italian Symphony* offers a fast, hard-driven but joyous and beautifully articulated performance of the first movement and equal clarity and point in the vivacious finale. The Berlin Philharmonic playing is both infectious and superbly polished. The central movements are well sustained, and altogether this is highly enjoyable, the recording resonantly full-timbred. Kubelik's fairly complete version of the incidental music for *A Midsummer Night's Dream* is no less enjoyable and the sound is very good here, too. On the pair of CDs the *Midsummer Night's Dream* selection is extended, and a pleasing performance of the *Calm sea and prosperous voyage* overture is added. The collection from which this is derived is discussed below. The sound on both CDs and tape is fresh and bright but does not lack fullness.

Overtures: A Calm sea and prosperous voyage, Op. 27; Fair Melusina, Op. 32; The Hebrides (Fingal's Cave), Op. 26; A Midsummer Night's Dream, Op. 21; Ruy Blas, Op. 95.

(B) ** DG 423 025-2; *423 025-4*. LSO, Gabriel Chmura.

Gabriel Chmura errs on the side of expressive caution in *The Hebrides*, where his tempo is a bit too measured. This could have more romantic feeling, and *Ruy Blas*, too, needs more zest if it is to be really exciting. Yet he pays scrupulous attention to detail and is plainly both conscientious in his approach and deeply musical. The orchestral playing is obviously well prepared and has real finish, and the result is almost to bring a Mozartian classicism to these works. The 1977 recording is clean, well focused and bright, without being over-lit, and it has transferred very freshly to CD.

Symphonies Nos. 1–5.
(M) *** DG 429 664-2 (3). Mathis, Rebman, Hollweg, German Op. Ch., BPO, Karajan.
(B) ** Ph. 432 598-2 (3) [id.]. Donath, Hansmann, Kmentt, New Philh. Ch. (in *No. 2*), New Philh. O, Sawallisch.

Symphonies Nos. 1–5; Overtures: Calm sea and prosperous voyage; The Hebrides (Fingal's Cave).
(M) *** Decca 421 769-2 (3) [id.]. Soloists, V. State Op. Ch., VPO, Dohnányi.

Karajan's distinguished set of the Mendelssohn *Symphonies* was recorded in 1971/2 and, like other DG recordings made at that period in the Berlin Jesus-Christus Kirche, it has been successfully remastered for CD. The early C minor work sounds particularly fresh, and the *Hymn of praise* brings the fullest sound of all; the very fine choral singing is vividly caught. The soloists make a good team, rather than showing any memorable individuality; but overall Karajan's performance is most satisfying. The *Scottish Symphony* is a particularly remarkable account and the *Italian* shows the Berlin Philharmonic in sparkling form: the only drawback is Karajan's characteristic omission of both first-movement exposition repeats. The recording is brightly lit but not shrill. There are some reservations to be made about the *Reformation Symphony*, but the sound has been effectively clarified without too much loss of weight.

Dohnányi's Decca set (which includes also two key overtures) brings performances which are fresh and direct, often relying on faster and more flowing speeds than in Abbado's full-price set, more clearly rebutting any idea that this music might be sentimental. The most striking contrast comes in the *Hymn of praise*, where Dohnányi's speeds are often so much faster than Abbado's that the whole character of the music is changed, as in the second-movement scherzo, sharp in one, gently persuasive in the other. Many will prefer Dohnányi in that, particularly when the choral sound is brighter and more immediate too. The Decca engineers produced recording which was among the finest of its period and which still sounds well. The snag of the set is that Dohnányi, unlike Abbado, omits exposition repeats, which in the *Italian Symphony* means the loss of the substantial lead-back passage in the first movement.

The well-recorded and expertly transferred Sawallisch set is the least expensive way of acquiring the Mendelssohn symphonies complete, but Sawallisch is not really a committed enough Mendelssohnian to brazen his way through the less than inspired passages of the *Hymn of praise*, and the New Philharmonia Chorus for once sounds relatively uninvolved. The early *C minor Symphony*, however, is more successful and sounds anything but pretentious in Sawallisch's hands. The *Scottish Symphony* is a well-played but routine performance which lacks spontaneity and zest. Best of the set are the *Italian* and *Reformation Symphonies*, but these performances are already available separately (see below).

Symphony No. 2 in B flat (Hymn of praise), Op. 52.
(M) *** DG 431 471-2; *431 471-4*. Mathis, Rebmann, Hollweg, German Op. Ch., BPO, Karajan.
(M) *** Decca 425 023-2; *425 023-4* [id.]. Ghazarian, Gruberová, Krenn, V. State Ch., VPO, Christoph von Dohnányi.

We have already praised the 1972 Karajan recording of the *Hymn of Praise* within the context of his complete set of Mendelssohn symphonies above. In some ways Abbado's full-price digital version is even finer, if not more clearly recorded, but the Karajan CD has a price advantage and, although he has a less individual team of soloists, it is a very satisfying account, with the chorus vibrantly caught within the spacious acoustics of the Berlin Jesus-Christus Kirche.

Dohnányi's version relates the piece more to the choral than to the symphonic tradition. The chorus, not particularly large, yet sings incisively, and the wide-ranging 1976 Decca sound underpins the texture of the finale with resonant and superbly focused organ sound. In refinement and delicacy of shaping Dohnányi yields to a conductor like Karajan, and the 6/8 second movement lacks charm (the tempo is a fraction too fast); but overall this is a refreshing account and it is very well recorded indeed. The chorus makes a splendid impact and the acoustics of the Sofiensaal provides a most attractive overall bloom to the performance; those for whom fine sound is important will probably enjoy this more than the Karajan alternative.

Symphony No. 3 in A min. (Scottish), Op. 56; Overtures; Calm sea and a prosperous voyage; The Hebrides (Fingal's Cave); Ruy Blas.

(BB) **(*) Naxos Dig. 8.55022 [id.]. Slovak PO, Oliver Dohnányi.

Symphony No. 3 in A min. (Scottish); Overture: The Hebrides (Fingal's Cave).
(M) *** DG 419 477-2; *419 477-4* [id.]. BPO, Karajan.

Symphony No. 3 in A min. (Scottish); Overture: The Hebrides (Fingal's Cave); A Midsummer Night's Dream: Overture, Op. 21; Incidental music, Op. 61: Scherzo; Entry of the fairies; Intermezzo; Nocturne; Dance of the clowns; Wedding march.
(M) ** EMI CDM7 63957-2 [id.]; *EG 763957-4*. LPO, Sir Adrian Boult.

Symphonies Nos. 3 in A min. (Scottish); 4 in A (Italian), Op. 90.
(M) *** DG Dig. 427 810-2 [id.]. LSO, Abbado.
(M) *** EMI CDM7 69660-2. New Philh. O, Muti.
(BB) *** ASV CDQS 6004; *ZCQS 6004*. O of St John's, Lubbock.
(M) *** Decca 425 011-2; *425 011-4* [id.]. LSO, Abbado.
(M) **(*) EMI CDM7 63853-2 [id.]; *EG 763853-4*. Philh. O, Klemperer.
(BB) ** BMG/RCA VD 60483; *VK 60483* [60483-2-RV; *60483-4-RV*]. Boston SO, Munch.

Symphonies Nos. (i) *3 in A min. (Scottish), Op. 56;* (ii) *4 in A (Italian), Op. 90; Overture: The Hebrides, Op. 26.*
(M) **(*) Decca 417 731-2 [id.]. VPO, Dohnányi.
(M) **(*) Sony Dig./Analogue SBK 46536 [id.]. (i) Bav. RSO, A. Davis; (ii) Cleveland O, Szell.

Karajan's account of the *Scottish* is very fine indeed. The orchestral playing is superb – the pianissimo articulation of the strings is a pleasure in itself and the conductor's warmth and direct eloquence, with no fussiness, are irresistible. The scherzo is marvellously done and becomes a highlight, while there is no doubt that Karajan's final coda has splendid buoyancy and power. However, the coupling is ungenerous.

Abbado's fine digital recordings of the *Scottish* and *Italian Symphonies*, coupled together from his complete set, make a splendid mid-price bargain. The recording is admirably fresh and bright – atmospheric, too – and the ambience, if not absolutely sharply defined, is very attractive. Both first-movement exposition repeats are included. Allegros are exhilarating, but clean articulation means that the pace never seems forced and Abbado judges the espressivo with his usual combination of warmth and refinement.

Like Abbado, Muti observes the exposition repeats, and the remastered sound is fresh and clear, yet warm too. Muti's is a smiling performance of the *Scottish* but one which, with its wide dynamic range, also gives Mendelssohn his due weight, with whoopsing horns giving an exhilarating lift to the final coda. The account of the *Italian Symphony* is comparably glowing and fresh. He takes a strikingly uninhibited, even wild approach to the tarantella (*Saltarello*) finale which adds to the feeling of zest and excitement. The CD transfer is outstandingly successful, and this is every bit as attractive as Abbado's disc, and perhaps even more exhilarating.

Lubbock's coupling of the *Scottish* and *Italian Symphonies* makes an outstanding super-bargain issue, offering performances of delightful lightness and point, warmly and cleanly recorded. The string section may be of chamber size but, amplified by a warm acoustic, the result sparkles, with rhythms exhilaratingly lifted. The slow movements are both on the slow side but flow easily with no suspicion of sentimentality, while the *Saltarello* finale of No. 4, with the flute part delectably pointed, comes close to Mendelssohnian fairy music.

Abbado's outstanding 1968 Decca coupling with the LSO has now reappeared on Decca's Ovation label. His *Scottish* is beautifully played and the LSO responds to his direction with the greatest delicacy of feeling, while the *Italian Symphony* has a comparable lightness of touch, matched with lyrical warmth. The vintage 1968 Kingsway Hall recording is freshly detailed yet full, with glowing wind colour, and is in some ways preferable to the DG sound; however, the absence of the first-movement exposition repeat in the *Scottish Symphony* (though not in the *Italian*) is a drawback.

Dohnányi's mid-priced Decca reissue (part digital, part analogue) also includes a rather slow and romantic reading of *The Hebrides*. It is a refreshing account of the *Italian*, never pushed too hard, though the *Saltarello* is taken exhilaratingly fast; it is a pity that the first-movement exposition repeat is omitted. The *Scottish* too is fresh and alert, and the weighty recording helps to underline the stormy quality that Dohnányi aptly finds in the first movement, although in other movements this is a rather less characterful account.

The front of the Sony CD is misleading in implying that all three performances are by Szell, although on the back the performance details are given correctly. As it happens, the CBS digital recording of the *Scottish Symphony*, dating from 1980, is of high quality, and Andrew Davis's reading is freshly straightforward, supported by excellent playing from the Bavarian Radio Orchestra. But the score's pianissimo markings are much less strikingly contrasted here than in some other versions, and this is not just a matter of the forward balance. The scherzo is very successful (helped by the transparent detail of the sound) and the slow movement is memorable, nicely paced and beautifully shaped. The finale is alert and zestful. Szell and his Cleveland Orchestra then appear to present the rest of the programme, and are heard in bravura form in their recording of the *Italian Symphony* from 1962. This was the first stereo recording to include the first-movement exposition repeat, and Szell's approach is dramatic and often exhilarating but, as Klemperer has proved, the work's gaiety and sunlight can be readily captured with more relaxed tempi. Nevertheless the the precision of the playing is remarkable and there is never any hint of scurrying. The Cleveland sound is full as well as brilliant.

Klemperer's conception of the *Scottish Symphony* is broad and expansive, with an orchestral texture that is almost Brahmsian. There is no denying the weight and power of this reading, and the colourful Scherzo and richly played *Adagio* come off especially well. In the finale Klemperer's broad treatment of the maestoso section is quite convincing in context. In the *Italian Symphony*, Klemperer takes the first movement substantially more slowly than usual, but this is no heavily monumental and humourless reading: the playing has sparkling incandescence. The second movement is also taken at a moderate tempo, but the way Klemperer moulds and floats the main theme over the moving bass defeats all preconceptions in its sustained beauty. A fast pacing of the Minuet, but still with wonderful phrasing; and it is the beautiful shaping of a phrase that makes the finale so fresh and memorable. There is no lack of exhilaration yet none of that feeling of being rushed off one's feet. The 1960 recording is atmospheric, clearer than it was originally but still pleasingly full. This coupling is obviously not a first choice, but all admirers of the conductor will want it for his unique interpretation of the *Italian Symphony*.

Oliver Dohnányi conducts a joyful account of the *Scottish Symphony* on Naxos, given the more impact by forward recording. Mendelssohn's lilting rhythms in all the fast movements are delightfully bouncy, and though the slow movement brings few hushed pianissimos, its full warmth is brought out without sentimentality. The three overtures, also very well done, not least the underappreciated *Ruy Blas*, make an excellent coupling.

When Boult was forcibly retired from the directorship of the BBC Symphony Orchestra in 1950, he turned to the LPO and, later, to the Nixa/Westminster label to make his records. In 1954/5, when these recordings were made, the LPO (described as the 'Philharmonic Promenade Orchestra', for the orchestra still had a contractual agreement with EMI) was not able to match the Philharmonia in precision of ensemble, but Boult worked hard with them, and what they lacked in polish they made up for in vigour. The *Scottish Symphony* (although without its first-movement exposition repeat, standard recording practice at that time) is full of spontaneous combustion and has splendid freshness, especially in the exuberant scherzo and the *Adagio*, which Boult moves forward firmly. The coda is more contained, but the *Midsummer Night's Dream* selection has plenty of spirit and some felicitous solo wind-playing in the *Scherzo* and *Entry of the fairies*. The Walthamstow recording produces a good ambience but sounds a bit thin on top (especially the violins in the lively account of *Fingal's Cave*); it has supporting weight, however, and is greatly enhanced in this clear, bright CD transfer.

Munch secures some outstanding bravura from his Boston players: the scherzo of the *Scottish* is particularly nimble, while the clean articulation means that the allegros of the outer movements of the *Italian* can be hard-driven without stress. However, some may feel that Munch's style is emotionally too fierce in the first movement of the *A minor Symphony* and that a little more relaxation in the *Italian* would not come amiss. Nevertheless the excitement of these performances cannot be denied, and both slow movements are songful. The RCA engineers have done wonders with the 1958/9 recordings, which sound fuller and smoother than they did on LP. The omission of first-movement exposition repeats is a drawback here, however.

Symphony No. 4 in A (Italian), Op. 90.

(M) *** EMI Dig. CDD7 64085-2 [id.]; *ET 764085-4*. BPO, Tennstedt – SCHUBERT: *Symphony No. 9*. ***

(M) *** DG 415 848-2 [id.]. BPO, Karajan – SCHUBERT: *Symphony No. 8*. ***

(B) *** DG 429 158-2. BPO, Karajan – SCHUMANN: *Symphony No. 1*. ***

(M) (***) EMI mono CDM7 63398-2 [id.]; *EG 763398-4*. RPO, Beecham – BEETHOVEN: *Symphony No. 8*; SCHUBERT: *Symphony No. 8*.

(BB) *(*) Pickwick (Decca) PWK 1149. RPO, Vonk – SCHUBERT: *Symphony No. 8*. **

Tennstedt's account of the *Italian* is vividly articulated and obviously felt. The quality of the Berliners' playing is superb, with the *Saltarello* finale exhilarating in its witty, polished bravura and the woodwind achieving the lightest possible touch. The central movements are elegant and relaxed, with the *Andante* warmly flowing and gentle horns in the Trio of the Minuet. The digital sound has admirable body and clarity to recommend it and this is certainly a version to be considered if the splendid Schubert coupling is wanted.

Karajan's performance of the *Italian* is superbly polished and well paced. The reading is straighter than usual, notably in the third movement, though the effect of Karajan's slower pace is warm, never bland. The recording is very brightly lit in its remastered transfer and has lost some of its depth. The coupling with Schumann comes at bargain price, the coupling with Schubert at mid-price.

In all four movements of the *Italian* Beecham adopts speeds slower than usual, but only in the third-movement Minuet does that make for even a hint of sluggishness. In the rest – notably the outer movements, which at Beecham's speeds can be given the rhythmic lift and pointing they cry out for – he could not be more persuasive. Though the RPO strings were not at their sweetest in 1952, this makes a most cherishable issue in the Beecham Edition, generously coupled with the Beethoven and Schubert.

Hans Vonk, recorded by Decca in 1975, sets a very fast tempo in the first movement, with no exposition repeat and no really gentle playing. The originally Decca Phase 4 recording is on the coarse side for this composer, though the effect on CD is vivid enough.

Symphony No. 4 (Italian); Overtures: Fair Melusina, Op. 32; The Hebrides (Fingal's Cave), Op. 26; Son and stranger (Die Heimkehr aus der Fremde), Op. 89.

(B) *** Pickwick Dig. PCD 824; *CIMPC 824* [id.]. Berne SO, Peter Maag.

(i) *Symphony No. 4 in A (Italian); Overture: The Hebrides (Fingal's Cave);* (ii) *A Midsummer Night's Dream: Overture & incidental music: Scherzo; Intermezzo; Nocturne; Wedding march.*

(M) **(*) Decca Dig. 430 722-2; *430 722-4* [id.]. (i) VPO, Dohnányi; (ii) Montreal SO, Charles Dutoit.

Peter Maag, making a welcome return to the recording studio with his Berne orchestra, here offers a winningly relaxed performance of the *Italian Symphony* (including exposition repeat), plus an attractive group of overtures, which once more confirms him as a supreme Mendelssohnian. With fine ensemble from the Berne Symphony Orchestra – only marginally let down at times by the strings – the forward thrust is more compelling than with the taut, unyielding approach too often favoured today. *The Hebrides* receives a spacious reading and the two rarer overtures are a delight too, particularly *Son and stranger*, which in Maag's hands conveys radiant happiness. At bargain price, with full and brilliant recording, it is first rate.

Dohnányi's performances are also available, coupled with the *Scottish Symphony* – see above. Dutoit's contribution of the *Overture* and *suite* from *A Midsummer Night's Dream* offers even finer sound. The acoustics of St Eustache in Montreal are ideal for this transparently scored music, giving a pleasing bloom to the dancing strings of the *Overture* – which is, however, played rather coolly – and plenty of colour to the brisk but vivacious *Scherzo.* The *Wedding march* is grand without being pompous.

(i) *Symphony No. 4 (Italian);* (ii) *A Midsummer Night's Dream: Overture, Op. 21; Incidental music, Op. 61: Fairy march; Wedding march; Intermezzo; Nocturne; Dance of the Clowns; Scherzo.*

(BB) *** LaserLight Dig. 15 526 [id.]. (i) Philh. O, János Sándor; (ii) Budapest PO, Kovacs.

Symphony No. 4 in A (Italian); A Midsummer Night's Dream: Overture, Op. 21; Incidental music, Op. 61: Scherzo; Intermezzo; Nocturne; Wedding march.

(BB) ** Naxos Dig. 8.550055 [id.]. Slovak PO, Anthony Bramhall.

A first-class coupling in the super-bargain range from LaserLight. Sándor gives a fresh and exhilarating account of the *Italian Symphony*, with particularly elegant Philharmonia playing in his warm and nicely paced account of the *Andante.* Outer movements sparkle without being rushed, articulation is light and clean, and the digital sound is excellent. The performance of a generous selection from the *Midsummer Night's Dream* incidental music also shows the Budapest orchestra on top form: this is most beguiling and is recorded in a pleasingly warm acoustic which does not cloud detail.

Though the first movement of the *Italian Symphony* is less tense than the rest – clean and neat rather than exhilarating as it should be – this Naxos performance is an attractive, alert one, well recorded and aptly, if not very generously, coupled. A fair super-bargain alternative.

(i) *Symphony No. 4 (Italian) in A, Op. 90;* (ii) *Octet, Op. 20.*

(M) *(*) Sony SMK 46251 [id.]. (i) Marlboro Festival O, Casals; (ii) Laredo, Schneider, Steinhardt, Daley, Tree, Rhodes, Parnas, Soyer.

Casals's *Italian Symphony* was recorded in 1963 and the quality is rather rough-grained. The first movement has plenty of weight and is finely held together – though, surprisingly enough (considering his Schubert *Fifth*), the slow movement is a little sober and unsmiling. The finale, however, is among the most exhilarating on record. As always with Casals's music-making, there is no lack of personality and, though it is by no means a library recommendation, it is well worth hearing. The *Octet* (dating from 1965) is performed marvellously by the distinguished team of players, and there is a splendid sense of live music-making, with risks successfully ventured. There are plenty of sonic limitations here, though the sound is cleaner than in the *Symphony*; but it is the calibre of the music-making that counts.

Symphonies Nos. 4 (Italian); 5 (Reformation), Op. 107.

(B) ** Ph. 422 470-2. New Philh. O, Sawallisch.

Sawallisch's comparatively reticent Mendelssohnian style suits these two fine works. A fast tempo in the first movement of the *Italian* does not sound breathless, and Sawallisch's observance of the exposition repeat is to be welcomed. The *Reformation Symphony* is also a work that gains from not being over-inflated. Good, clear recording.

CHAMBER AND INSTRUMENTAL MUSIC

Clarinet sonata in C min.

(M) **(*) Collins Dig. 3010-2 [id.]. David Campbell, Andrew Ball – BRAHMS: *Sonatas.* **

The surface brilliance of the Mendelssohn *Clarinet sonata* finds a more natural response from David Campbell and Andrew Ball than the coupled Brahms works, and they play the outer movements with an appealing extrovert vitality and find charm in the *Andante*. The recording is truthful if rather too forward.

Octet in E flat, Op. 20.

(M) **(*) Decca 421 093-2; *421 093-4* [id.]. Vienna Octet (members) – BEETHOVEN: *Septet.* ***

(B) **(*) Decca 421 637-2; *421 637-4*. ASMF – BOCCHERINI: *Cello quintet.* **(*)

The 1973 Vienna version of the *Octet* is highly competitive at mid-price, coupled with an equally attractive account of Beethoven's *Septet*. The playing is polished and spontaneous and the recording has re-emerged freshly in its CD format, although the upper register of the strings is not quite as cleanly focused as the Beethoven coupling.

The 1968 (originally Argo) performance by the ASMF is fresh and buoyant, and the recording wears its years fairly lightly. It offered fine judgement in matters of clarity and sonority, and the digital remastering has not lost the original ambient bloom, although the violin timbre now has noticeable thinness. A good bargain version.

Octet in E flat, Op. 20; String quintet in B flat, Op. 87.

(B) Pickwick Dig. PCD 960 [id.]. Musicfest Quintet.

With muddy, ill-focused recording marred by distracting bumps, and with violins made to sound edgy, this is a disappointing disc of two of Mendelssohn's chamber-music masterpieces. The performances are energetic but a bit rough. Not recommended, even at bargain price.

String quartets: Nos. 1 in E flat, Op. 12; 2 in A min., Op. 13; 3–5, Op. 44/1–3; 6 in F min., Op. 80; 4 Movements, Op. 81.

(M) ** DG 415 883-2 (3) [id.]. Melos Qt.

The present set has both the merit of completeness and the advantage of good engineering. However, the performances succumb to the temptation to play far too quickly. There is more to these quartets than this brilliant ensemble finds; but, in the absence of any alternatives, this set is acceptable enough. It has been freshly remastered.

String quintets Nos. 1 in A, Op. 18; 2 in B flat, Op. 87.

(M) *** Sony/CBS CD 45883. Laredo, Kavafian, Ohyama, Kashkashian, Robinson.

A welcome addition to the catalogue. Laredo and his ensemble achieve good matching of timbre, and they give lively accounts of both these neglected works, lacking neither warmth nor finesse. The 1978 recording has responded well to remastering, and has body and presence.

Violin sonata in F.

(M) *(*) EMI CDM7 63988-2 [id.]. Y. Menuhin, Moore – BRAHMS: *Horn trio*; SCHUBERT: *Fantasia.* **

Menuhin recorded the *F major sonata* with Gerald Moore, and the 1953 mono recording now has a certain pallor and sounds its age. Neither of the distinguished performers brings the last ounce of finish to it, and the reading lacks the grace and elegance it needs.

PIANO MUSIC

Andante & rondo capriccioso, Op. 14; Duetto in A flat, Op. 38/6; Kinderstücke in E, Op. 72/2; Prelude in E min., Op. 35/1; Scherzo in E min., Op. 16/2; Songs without words: in E; in G min.

(Venetian gondola song), Op. 19/1 & 6; in E, Op. 30/2; in A (Spring song), Op. 62/6.
(B) *(*) Pickwick Dig. PCD 949. Annette Servadei – BRAHMS; SCHUMANN: *Piano music*. *(*)

Annette Servadei's programme is eminently well chosen and offers some very musical if unexceptional playing. The recital does not quite live up to the promise of its opening and, as it proceeds, the instrument needs the attentions of a technician, for one or two notes become tired. In terms of technical address she is not quite the equal of the greatest keyboard artists, but she plays with sensitivity. The recording, made at St John's, Smith Square, not the easiest venue for the piano, is very good.

Songs without words, Books 1–8 (complete); *Albumblatt, Op. 117; Gondellied; Kinderstücke, Op. 72; 2 Klavierstücke.*
(M) *** DG 423 931-2 (2) [id.]. Daniel Barenboim (piano).

This 1974 set of Mendelssohn's complete *Songs without words*, which Barenboim plays with such affectionate finesse, has dominated the catalogue for a decade and a half. For the mid-priced CD reissue, the six *Kinderstücke* (sometimes known as *Christmas pieces*) have been added, plus other music, so that the second of the two CDs plays for 73 minutes. The sound is first class.

Songs without words Nos. 5, Op. 19/5; 7–9, Op. 30/1–3; 15–16, Op. 38/3–4; 19–22, Op. 53/1–4; 25–6, Op. 62/1–2; 31–3; 35–6, Op. 67/1–3 & 5–6; 37–8, Op. 85/1–2; 40, Op. 85/4; 47–8, Op. 102/5–6.
(BB) *(*) Naxos Dig. 8.550316 [id.]. Péter Nagy.

Péter Nagy is a young Hungarian pianist who was in his late twenties when he made this recording. He is a gifted player who shows considerable artistry in his handling of these charming miniatures. Unfortunately he is handicapped, as so often in solo piano recordings on this label, by the quality of the recording, made in the Italian Institute at Budapest. It says much for his sensitivity to keyboard colour that, despite the unventilated acoustic, he succeeds in holding the listener for as long as he does.

Songs without words, Op. 19/1–2; Huntsman's song, Op. 19/3; Op. 19/4; Venetian gondola song, Op. 19/6; Op. 30/4–5; Venetian gondola song. Op. 30/6; Op. 38/1–2, 5 & 6; Op. 53/5–6; Op. 62/3–4; Venetian gondola song, Op. 62/5; Op. 62/6; Spinning song Op. 67/4; Op. 85/3, 5 & 6; Op. 102/1–2 & 4; 49 in D min. (Horseman's song).
(BB) *(*) Naxos Dig. 8.550453 [id.]. Péter Nagy.

Péter Nagy's second CD of Mendelssohn's *Songs without words* was made (a year after the first) with the same producer but, for part of the time, with a different engineer. There is, however, no significant difference; if anything, he is more closely balanced, at least in some of the pieces. As before, he plays with great poetic feeling and musical insight, and those who can adjust to the piano sound will find much to admire here.

Variations sérieuses, Op. 54.
(M) (**) BMG/RCA mono GD 60451 [60451-2-RG]. Vladimir Horowitz – CZERNY: *Variations;* MOZART: *Sonata No. 12;* SCHUBERT: *Sonata No. 21.* (**)

Impressively musical and highly sensitive playing from Horowitz which belies his image as a mere high-powered virtuoso – though he is all of that and more – and, although the 1946 sound leaves much to be desired, the sheer personality and colour of the playing carry the day.

VOCAL MUSIC

A Midsummer Night's Dream: Overture, Op. 21; Incidental music, Op. 61.
(M) *** DG 415 840-2 [id.]. Mathis, Boese, Bav. R. Ch. & SO, Kubelik – WEBER: *Overtures: Oberon; Der Freischütz.* ***
(M) *** EMI CMD7 64144-2 [id.]; *EG 764144-4*. Harper, J. Baker, Philh. Ch. & O, Klemperer – LISZT: *Piano concerto No. 1* etc. **(*)
(B) **(*) Hung. White Label Dig. HRC 049 [id.]. Kalmar, Bokor, Jeunesses Musicales Girls' Ch., Hungarian State O, Adám Fischer.
(M) (***) BMG/RCA mono GD 60314. Eustis, Kirk, University of Pennsylvania Women's Glee Club, Phd. O., Toscanini – BERLIOZ: *Romeo and Juliet: Queen Mab scherzo.* (**)

The version by the Bavarian Radio Orchestra takes pride of place; the playing and 1965 recording are strikingly fresh. Although Kubelik omits the melodramas, this makes room for an appropriate coupling of the two finest Weber overtures (both also associated with magic) and *Oberon* drawing an obvious parallel with Mendelssohn. They are marvellously played.

Klemperer's recording (which dates from 1960) was made when the Philharmonia was at its peak, and the orchestral playing is superb, the wind solos so nimble that even the *Scherzo*, taken more slowly than usual, has a light touch. The contribution of soloists (Heather Harper and Dame Janet Baker) and chorus is first class and the disc has the advantage of including the *Fairy march* and *Funeral march*. The quality is quite full and fresh, but the coupling with Liszt (plus the *Die Fledermaus overture*) although generous does not seem particularly appropriate.

The Hungaroton CD offers much lovely playing, and fine singing from the soloists too, although many will count it a disadvantage that the vocal numbers are sung in German. While the soft focus is attractively atmospheric, the resonant acoustic has to some extent subdued the sound, although the digital recording is full and natural. There is fine, delicate articulation from the woodwind and strings in the *Scherzo*; but the hint of vibrato on the horn solo of the *Nocturne* will not please all ears, although the playing is very responsive. Fischer includes the more important melodramas but omits Nos. 2, 4, 6 and 10. On Hungaroton's bargain White Label, this is competitive.

Toscanini's Philadelphia recording offers the seven most popular numbers from the *Midsummer Night's Dream* music, including the song with chorus, *You spotted snakes*, and the final melodrama. In sparkling performances it offers a fine example of his more relaxed manners in his one Philadelphia season.

A Midsummer Night's Dream: Overture, Op. 21; Scherzo; Nocturne; Wedding march, Op. 61.
(B) *** Ph. 426 071-2. Concg. O, Szell – SCHUBERT: *Rosamunde.* ***

Superlative playing from the Concertgebouw Orchestra under Szell. He seldom recorded in Europe, but when he did the results were always impressive. Here the lightness and clean articulation of the violins in the *Overture* are a delight; the wonderfully nimble wind-playing in the *Scherzo* is no less engaging, and there is a fine horn solo in the *Nocturne*. The recording, unbelievably, dates from 1957 and sounds admirably clear, without loss of bloom. Szell's coupled Schubert performances are equally rewarding. A similar selection at mid-price, recorded digitally by Levine in Chicago (DG 427 817-2) and including vivacious dances from Smetana's *Bartered Bride*, might be considered, but Szell's bargain disc is the more memorable.

Elijah (oratorio; sung in German), *Op. 70.*
(M) ** Sony M2YK 46455 (2). Augér, Schreckenbach, Tear, Nimsgern, Gächinger, Kantorei, Stuttgart RSO, Rilling.

There is room for a performance of *Elijah* in German, when Mendelssohn composed from a German text. However, this live recording from Stuttgart is hardly the answer, generally a rather dull performance with variable singing. Best among the soloists is the pure-toned Arlene Augér, and Robert Tear is as reliable as ever but hardly inspired. Nimsgern as Elijah himself sounds uninvolved, and Gabriele Schreckenbach is disappointingly monochrome. The CD transfer brings bright, vivid sound but (even at mid-price) this is only a stop-gap until the EMI/Frübeck de Burgos set returns to the catalogue.

St Paul, Op. 36.
(M) *** EMI CMS7 64005-2 (2) [Ang. CDMB 64005]. Donath, Schwarz, Hollweg, Fischer-Dieskau, Boys' Ch., Dusseldorf Musikverein & SO, Frühbeck de Burgos.

St Paul (or, in German, *Paulus*) was for long notorious as one of the most sanctimonious of Victorian oratorios. This sympathetic performance under the conductor who helped us review our ideas on *Elijah* – the return of his outstanding EMI/Philharmonia set, with gorgeous singing from Dame Janet Baker, cannot be too far away – gives the lie to that, a piece full of ideas well worthy of the composer of the *Italian Symphony*. Like *Elijah* ten years later, *Paulus* – completed in 1836 – was Mendelssohn's substitute for opera. In youthful zest it erupts in great Handelian choruses, and a Bachian style of story-telling is neatly updated in its choral interjections and chorales, with the soprano joining the traditional tenor in the narration. What reduces the dramatic effectiveness is that Mendelssohn, ever the optimist, comes to his happy resolution of the plot far too quickly and with too little stuggle involved. This performance glows with life. Fischer-Dieskau takes the name-part (as he did for *Elijah*), leading an excellent team of soloists and with admirable support from the Dusseldorf choir and orchestra. The recording is full and atmospheric, its vividness enhanced on CD.

Mennin, Peter (1923–83)

Symphony No. 5.
(M) **(*) Mercury 432 755-2 [id.]. Eastman-Rochester O, Howard Hanson – IVES: *Symphony No. 3* etc.; SCHUMAN: *New England triptych.* ***

Peter Mennin is not as individual a musical personality as William Schuman, let alone Charles Ives; but the *Canto* central movement of his *Fifth Symphony* has a piercing melancholy which is slightly reminiscent of the Barber *Adagio for strings*. The outer movements develop plenty of polyphonic energy, but the toccata-like linear writing lacks real memorability. Hanson's performance is persuasive and vital, and the 1962 Mercury sound makes the very most of the relatively unexpansive acoustics of the Eastman Theatre.

Menotti, Gian-Carlo (born 1911)

Piano concerto in F.
(M) **(*) Van. 08.4029.71 [OVC 4071]. Earl Wild, Symphony of the Air, Jorge Mester – COPLAND: *Concerto.* ***

Menotti's *Piano concerto*, like most of his music, is easy and fluent, never hard on the ear. Its eclectic style brings a pungent whiff of Shostakovich at the opening, and there are hints of Khachaturian elsewhere. As a coupling for the Copland it is very attractive, especially in a performance of such prodigious brilliance. Even if it is unlikely to bear repeated listening, the charisma and bravura of Earl Wild's playing make the music sound more substantial than it is. The accompaniment is vivacious, but the very present recording is marred by a balance favouring the piano unduly.

Messiaen, Olivier (born 1908)

(i) *Chronochromie;* (ii) *Et exspecto resurrectionem mortuorum.*
(M) *** EMI CDM7 63948-2 [id.]. (i) BBC SO, Dorati; (ii) O de Paris & Ens. de Percussion, Baudo – BOULEZ: *Le soleil des eaux*; KOECHLIN: *Les Bandar-log.* ***

Messiaen's *Chronochromie* characteristically has its inspiration in nature, the composer's long-established preoccupation with birdsong, and the culminating *Épode*, very difficult as a musical argument, is immediately and readily understandable as a climactic representation of the birds' dawn chorus. This fine performance and immensely vivid recording was sponsored by the Gulbenkian Foundation in 1964; for the reissue, however, EMI have added Serge Baudo's excellent 1968 recording of *Et exspecto resurrectionem mortuorum*, the wind-and-percussion work that Messiaen intended for performance in the wide open spaces. Baudo conducted its first performances in Paris and Chartres. It is not a work that will appeal to all tastes, but the greater openness of the EMI recording and its superior quality give this a lead over other versions by Boulez and Haitink.

Les offrandes oubliées.
(B) *** EMI CZS7 62669-2 (2). O de Paris, Serge Baudo (with Concert: *French music* ***).

Les offrandes oubliées (*The forgotten offerings*) is an early work, dating from 1930, when Messiaen was twenty-two, yet it is entirely characteristic. The outer sections of the triptych (*La Croix* and *L'Eucharistie*) have that magnetic mixture of sensuous mysticism and purity of spirit which makes this composer's music so haunting. In between comes the brief *Le Péché*, which is vehemently, self-evidently sinful. The work is played with great feeling for its atmosphere and power and is very well recorded. An excellent introduction to Messiaen's orchestral writing which even anticipates the *Turangalîla Symphony.*

Quatuor pour la fin du temps.
(M) *** Ph. 422 834-2; *422 834-4.* Beths, Pieterson, Bylsma, De Leeuw.
(M) **(*) BMG/RCA GD 87835 [7835-2-RG]. Tashi (Kavafian, Sherry, Stoltzman, Peter Serkin).
(M) **(*) DG 423 247-2 [id.]. Yordanoff, Tetard, Desurment, Barenboim.

(i) *Quatuor pour la fin du temps (Quartet for the end of time);* (ii) *Le merle noir.*
(M) *** EMI CDM7 63947-2 [id.]. (i) Gruenberg, De Peyer, Pleeth, Béroff; (ii) Zöller, Kontarsky.

Messiaen's visionary and often inspired piece was composed during his days in a Silesian prison camp. Among his fellow-prisoners were a violinist, a clarinettist and a cellist who, with the composer at the piano, made its creation possible. Messiaen tells us that lack of food gave him nightmares and multi-coloured visions. Certainly the instrumental colouring plays a large part in the *Quatuor* and, besides the visions of 'the Angel who announces the end of time', there are also the composer's beloved birdsongs. If a performance of this imaginative and eloquent score (very much a successor in spirit to Ravel's *Introduction and allegro*) is to be a success, the players must be capable of capturing the improvisatory style in ensemble (the sixth movement, *Dance of fury*, asks for unison playing of considerable virtuosity). The individual musicians (and the clarinet especially) are also given passages of gentle, ruminative poetry in which musical spontaneity is paramount. The 1968 EMI recording, led by Erich Gruenberg and with Gervase de Peyer the inspirational clarinettist, has been out of the catalogue for too long. The performance is in the very highest class, the players meeting every demand the composer makes upon them, and the fine, clear Abbey Road recording gives the group striking presence while affording proper background ambience. The bonus, too, is well worth having: *Le merle noir* exploits the composer's love of birdsong even more overtly. It is a delightful piece and is splendidly played and recorded here.

The Dutch team on Philips are also given the benefit of very good recording which has transferred well to CD; moreover their account has the merit of outstanding team-work and

Reinbert de Leeuw has a keen sense of atmosphere, though he does not dominate the proceedings. There is also some superbly eloquent playing from George Pieterson and Anner Bylsma.

With Peter Serkin at the piano it is not surprising that the RCA performance is a distinguished one. The clarinet solo, *Abyss of the birds*, is played with memorable eloquence by Richard Stoltzman, and the cellist, Fred Sherry, plays very beautifully in his *Praise to the eternity of Jesus*, while Ida Kavafian's long violin melisma has a striking, improvisatory quality. Considerable tension is movingly created in the work's closing section; and if there are minor reservations about the forward balance, the players certainly project as real and tangible.

Barenboim and his colleagues recorded the *Quatuor pour la fin du temps* in the presence of the composer. Barenboim is a strong personality who carries much of this performance in his hands and inspires his colleagues with his own commitment to the music. The recording was originally a good one; while increasing its presence, the digital remastering has added a degree of edginess to the sound on CD, making it less attractive than the original analogue LP from which the recording derives.

Préludes (complete); *Vingt regards sur l'enfant Jésus.*

(B) **(*) EMI CMS7 69161-2 (2) [id.]. Michel Béroff (piano).

The *Préludes* are early works, dating from 1929, and their recording in 1978 marked the occasion of Messiaen's seventieth birthday. *Vingt regards* were recorded earlier, in 1969, and show Béroff at his most inspired, generating the illusion of spontaneous creation. Time has not dimmed the appeal of this performance and, even if the catalogue were full of rival accounts, this would be difficult to beat. Even for listeners not wholly attuned to Messiaen's sensibility and language, this can be strongly recommended – and it may even make converts to this original master. Clean, well-focused sound – but, even though the venue was the Salle Wagram, the close balance brings a lack of rich sonority.

Vingt regards sur l'Enfant-Jésus.

(M) ** Decca 430 343-2 (2). John Ogdon.

John Ogdon is unfailingly thoughtful and conscientious, but one needs more spontaneity and a greater feeling for atmosphere than he finds in this extended work. The 1969 recording, made by Argo engineers in Decca's West Hampstead studio, is bold and clear.

ORGAN MUSIC

La Nativité du Seigneur (9 meditations).

(M) *** Decca 425 616-2 (2) [id.]. Simon Preston (organ of Westminster Abbey) – *La Transfiguration.* ***

Simon Preston is a convinced advocate of this score and conveys its hypnotic power most successfully. The recording reproduces with great fidelity, and in Preston's hands the Westminster Abbey organ produces the right kind of veiled colours to evoke the work's mysticism. This performance is by no means second best and makes a very generous bonus for *La Transfiguration.*

La Transfiguration de Notre Seigneur Jésus-Christ.

(M) *** Decca 425 616-2 (2) [id.]. Sylvester, Aquino, Westminster Symphonic Ch., Loriod, Instrumental Soloists, Washington Nat. SO, Dorati – *La Nativité du Seigneur.* ***

This massive work of fourteen movements, divided into two parallel septenaries, seems to sum up the whole achievement of Messiaen. Though the unconverted may feel it has its longueurs, no one can doubt the dedication of the composer and his ability, beyond that of almost any other contemporary, to convey his personal religious exaltation through his music. Dorati magnificently holds the unwieldy structures together, and, though such an evocative work might suggest a more reverberant acoustic, the brilliance and immediacy of the recording are most impressive. The opening percussion effects are very tangible, while the internal balance between singers and instrumentalists is managed ideally – the blend between chorus and orchestra rich yet transparent in detail – indeed everything is clearly interrelated within a sympathetic ambience.

Chants de terre et de ciel; Harawi (Chants d'amour et de mort). 3 Mélodies (Pourquoi; Le sourire; La fiancée); Poèmes pour Mi.

(M) *** EMI CMS7 64092-2 (2). Michèle Command, Marie-Madeleine Petit.

This collection of Messiaen's solo songs, offered at mid-price on only two discs, presents this key composer at his most approachable, a winning set for anyone wanting an easy introduction to his music. Michèle Command, impressive enough in her contributions to the EMI Debussy box, is here even more characterful and firmly focused, with her accompanist just as warmly idiomatic. The three early songs of 1930 lead naturally to the two cycles from the late 1930s, more complex in their melodic lines. It is then that the ambitious *Harawi* cycle of

1945, subtitled *Chant d'amour et de mort* ('Song of love and death'), in another logical development reveals the full scope of the mature Messiaen's style, with its echoes of birdsong. Harawi is the ancient Peruvian word for that concept of love and death. This hour-long cycle belongs to what the composer regarded as his 'Tristan and Isolde' trilogy, along with the *Turangalîla Symphony* and the choral cycle, *Cinq Rechants*. Clear, undistracting sound.

Meyerbeer, Giacomo (1791–1864)

Les Patineurs (ballet suite, arr. & orch. Lambert).

(M) *** Decca 425 468-2 (3). Nat. PO, Richard Bonynge – TCHAIKOVSKY: *Sleeping Beauty.* **(*)

(M) ** Sony SBK 46341 [id.]; *40-46341.* Phd. O, Ormandy – ADAM: *Giselle*; TCHAIKOVSKY: *Swan Lake.* **

Les Patineurs was arranged by Constant Lambert using excerpts from two of Meyerbeer's operas, *Le Prophète* and *L'Étoile du Nord.* Bonynge's approach is warm and comparatively easy-going but, with such polished orchestral playing, this version is extremely beguiling. The sound too is first rate.

Ormandy takes the *pesante* marking in the opening number rather literally, but otherwise this playing is invigoratingly polished, and is recorded in the usual resonant Philadalphia manner. There is plenty of flair and rhythmic energy here, but less in the way of subtlety.

Les Huguenots (complete).

(M) *** Decca 430 549-2 (4) [id.]. Sutherland, Vrenios, Bacquier, Arroyo, Tourangeau, Ghiuselev, New Philh. O, Bonynge.

Meyerbeer's once-popular opera of epic length has recently returned to the stage in London, so it is opportune that Bonynge's 1970 set should reappear in the catalogue on CD. At the time, he prepared for the recording with a concert performance in the Royal Albert Hall, and both then and in the recording itself his own passionate belief in the music was amply evident. It is good too to have Sutherland augmenting the enticing sample of the role of the Queen which she gave in one of her earlier recorded recitals ('*The art of the Prima Donna*' – see below). The result is predictably impressive, though once or twice there are signs of a 'beat' in the voice, previously unheard on Sutherland records. The rest of the cast is uneven, and in an unusually episodic opera, with passages that are musically less than inspired (Meyerbeer's melodic invention was often very square), that brings disappointments. Gabriel Bacquier and Nicola Ghiuselev are fine in their roles and, though Martina Arroyo is below her best as Valentine, the star quality is unmistakable. The tenor, Anastasios Vrenios, can easily be criticized in the role of Raoul in that this is too small a voice for a heroic part; but very few other tenors – and certainly not those who have been applauded in stage performances – can cope with the extraordinarily high tessitura and florid diversions. Vrenios sings the notes, which is more than almost any rival could. Fine recording to match this ambitious project, well worth investigating by lovers of French opera. The work sounds newly minted on CD.

Milhaud, Darius (1892–1974)

La création du monde.

(M) *** EMI CDM7 63945-2 [id.]. Paris Conservatoire O, Prêtre – DUTILLEUX: *Le Loup*; POULENC: *Les Biches.* ***

La création du monde; Suite provençale.

(M) *** BMG/RCA GD 60685 [60685-2-RG]. Boston SO, Charles Münch – HONEGGER: *Symphonies Nos. 2 & 5.* (***)

Prêtre's recording of *La création du monde* is unsurpassed in catching both the bitter-sweet sensuousness of the creation scene and the jazzy pastiche of the mating dance – the rhythmic touch is very much in the authentic spirit of 1920s' French jazz. The 1961 sound has been transformed in the CD remastering: it is fresh and vivid, yet admirably atmospheric. The couplings are no less attractive.

Both Münch performances come from the early 1960s and are full of all the style and spirit you would expect from this combination. We enjoyed these performances when they were coupled together on one LP in the early 1960s. Münch's account of *La création du monde* has greater virtuosity and panache, if not more jazz feeling, than the rival mid-priced account from Georges Prêtre and the Paris Conservatoire Orchestra, made at about the same time, though the latter has much greater clarity and detail. The Boston recording always sounded a bit too reverberant, and still does. Milhaud always spoke of himself as a Mediterranean composer (he was born in Aix-en-Provence 100 years ago this year) and the *Suite provençale*, based on tunes by another Provençal composer, André Campra, is one of his most captivating pieces. A thoroughly enjoyable disc and, with two symphonies by his friend and exact contemporary, Honegger, thrown in, even at mid-price it is an outstanding bargain.

Music for wind: *La Cheminée du Roi René, Op. 105; Divertissement en trois parties, Op. 399b; Pastorale, Op. 47; 2 Sketches, Op. 227b; Suite d'après Corrette, Op. 161b.*

(M) **(*) Chan. CHAN 6536; *MBTD 6536* [id.]. Athena Ens., McNichol.

Two of these pieces were derived from film music: *La Cheminée du Roi René* is based on a score Milhaud wote to *Cavalcade d'Amour*, set in the fifteenth century; and the *Divertissement* draws on material composed for a film on the life of Gauguin. The *Suite d'après Corrette* features music written for a Paris production of *Romeo and Juliet*, using themes by the eighteenth-century French master, Michel Corrette. Though none of this is first-class Milhaud, it is still full of pleasing and attractive ideas, and the general air of easy-going, life-loving enjoyment is well conveyed by the alert playing of the Athena Ensemble. One's only quarrel with this issue is the somewhat close balance, which picks up the mechanism of the various keys and which does less than justice to the artists' pianissimo tone. However, this can be remedied a little by a lower-level setting, and there is far too much to enjoy here to inhibit a recommendation. The CD transfer increases the sense of presence: the effect is very real and, even if the overall playing time is not very generous, this is an excellent entertainment.

Moeran, Ernest J. (1894–1950)

Symphony in G min.; Lonely waters; Whythorne's shadow.
(M) **(*) EMI CDM7 69419-2; *EG 769419-4*. E. Sinfonia, Dilkes – BUTTERWORTH: *Banks of green willow* etc. **(*)

Dilkes's fine, lusty performance is perhaps not as powerful as Handley's (full-price) superb version on Chandos, nor has it quite the subtlety of rubato that Handley draws from the Ulster Orchestra. With a smaller string band, recorded relatively close, the sound is vivid and immediate; the reading remains a satisfying one and it certainly does not lack urgency. The two lovely orchestral miniatures are most beautifully played and recorded and make a very worthwhile bonus alongside the two better-known Butterworth pieces which have been added to make this mid-priced disc even more attractive, although here especially the recording ideally could be more distanced.

Monteverdi, Claudio (1567–1643)

Madrigals: *Altri canti di Marte; Ardo avvampo; Hor che'l ciel e la terra; Ballo: Movete al mio bel suon; O ciecchi, ciecchi; Questi vaghi concenti.* (i) *Sestina: Lagrime d'amante al sepolcro dell'amata.*
(M) *** Decca *433 174-2* [id.]. Palmer, Holt, Bowen, Evans, Elwes, Thomas, Heinrich Schütz Ch., Norrington; (i) Schütz Cons.

These fine madrigals are given crisp, well-drilled performances by Norrington, not as relaxedly expressive as Leppard's outstanding Philips set (which we hope will soon reappear on CD), but most refreshing. The ample acoustic of St John's, Smith Square, adds agreeable atmosphere. The eloquent and moving *Sestina* is added for the CD reissue.

OPERA AND OPERA-BALLET

Il ballo delle ingrate; Il combattimento di Tancredi e Clorinda (opera-ballets).
(M) *** Ph. 426 451-2; *426 451-4*. Harpur, Watson, Howells, Alva, Wakefield, Dean, Amb. S., ECO, Leppard.

Monteverdi's mastery in these earliest examples of opera is brought out readily in these finely sung performances under Leppard. The famous dramatic narrative of *Tancredi and Clorinda*, brother and sister tragically and unknowingly matched in mortal combat, is perfectly coupled with *Il ballo delle ingrate*, which tells of the 'ungrateful' ladies who were condemned to the domain of Pluto, not for profligacy but for refusing to yield to their lovers' caresses. (Clearly the 'moral' of the story was aimed directly at the bride of the Duke of Mantua, at whose nuptial celebrations the work received its première.) The poignant climax to this remarkably expressive piece comes with the beautiful aria sung by a 'lost spirit', who stays behind to plead the cause of her companions. The recorded sound is very beautiful, the balance excellent and the vocal projection very present and natural against an attractively warm ambience.

Mozart, Wolfgang Amadeus (1756–91)

Adagio in E, K.261; Rondo in C, K.373 (both for violin & orchestra).
(B) *** Ph. 426 977-2; *426 977-4*. Grumiaux, New Philh. O, Leppard – HAYDN: *Violin concertos*; SCHUBERT: *Rondo.* ***

These two Mozart movements are far from slight: the *Adagio* is really lovely on Arthur Grumiaux's bow and the *Rondo* sparkles. Excellent, stylish accompaniments and very good sound. This makes a strong contribution to a splendid bargain anthology.

Adagio and fugue in C minor: see also below, in VOCAL MUSIC, under Complete Mozart Edition, Volume 22

(i) *Adagio and fugue in C min., K.456;* (ii) *Piano concerto No. 25 in C, K.503;* (iii) *Serenade No. 12 in C, K.388.*
(M) **(*) EMI CDM7 63620-2 [id.]; *EG 763620-*

4. (i) Philh. O; (ii) Barenboim, New Philh. O; (iii) New Philh. Wind Ens., Klemperer.

Barenboim recorded K.503 earlier for EMI in his series with the ECO, directing from the keyboard; but here, with Klemperer conducting, the manner is different, predictably weightier. It is one of the few Mozart concertos that could benefit from such a collaboration, and the other two items bring similar Klemperer revelations, rugged performances defying Mozartian convention, beautifully played.

Cassations Nos. 1 in G, K.63; 2 in B flat, K.99; 3 Divertimenti for strings, K.136/8. Divertimenti Nos. 1 in E flat, K.113; 2 in D, K.131; 7 in D, K.205; 10 in F, K.247; 11 in D, K.251; 15 in B flat, K.287; 17 in D, K.334. Serenades Nos. 1 in D, K.100; 2 in D, K.131; 3 in D, K.185; 4 in D (Colloredo), K.203; 5 in D, K.204; 6 in D (Serenata notturna), K.239; 7 in D (Haffner), K.250; 8 in D (Notturno for 4 orchestras), K.286; 9 in D (Posthorn), K.320; 13 in G (Eine kleine Nachtmusik), K.525. A Musical joke, K.522.
(M) *** Decca 430 311-2 (8) [id.]. V. Mozart Ens., Willi Boskovsky.

There are many delights in these justly famous Boskovsky performances, recorded in the 1960s and '70s. Unlike the Marriner survey, which involves two separate boxes, this single collection includes nearly all the major *Divertimenti* and *Serenades* which are not intended solely for wind instruments. The delightful *First Cassation* has two enchanting slow movements. The first is an atmospheric *Andante*, reminiscent of *Così fan tutte* in mood; the second introduces a cantilena for solo violin. The invention in the other works, too, usually finds Mozart at his most gracious and smiling. Beecham's account of the *Divertimento in D*, K.131, remains firmly in the memory but, even by Beecham's standards, these are all fine performances. Indeed the playing is so totally idiomatic and masterly that one scarcely thinks of the artists at all, only of the music. K.334, for instance, with its famous Minuet, offers sparkling, unaffected music-making of great spontaneity. The *Serenades* are hardly less distinguished. K.203, for instance, written – when Mozart was eighteen – for the name-day of Archbishop Colloredo, embraces a violin concerto, and the solo part is played here by Aldred Staar with great distinction; the *Night music* for muted strings is altogether delightful. The *Haffner* and *Posthorn Serenades* are marvellously alive, with admirable phrasing and feeling for detail. *Eine kleine Nachtmusik* and *A Musical joke* (which, like the *Posthorn Serenade*, are also available separately – see below) are as fine as any in the catalogue. The recordings were made over a decade between 1967 and 1978 in the Sofiensaal, and the remastering throughout is strikingly fresh and vivid, with the warm Viennese ambience bringing bloom to the overall sound. The violins are brightly lit and in K.203 (the earliest, made in 1967) there is a degree of fierceness in tuttis, and this appears again in the *Haffner Serenade* and, to a lesser extent, in the *Posthorn*. But generally the transfers are most impressively managed.

Complete Mozart Edition, Volume 3: *Cassations Nos. 1 in G, K.63; 2 in B flat, K.99; Divertimento No. 2 in D, K.131; Galimathias musicum, K.32; Serenades Nos. 1 in D, K.100* (with *March in D, K.62); 3 in D, K.185* (with *March in D, K.189); 4 in D (Colloredo), K.203* (with *March in D, K.237); 5 in D, K.204* (with *March in D, K.215); 6 in D (Serenata notturna), K.239; 7 in D (Haffner), K.250* (with *March in D, K.249); 8 in D (Notturno for 4 orchestras), K.286; 9 in D (Posthorn), K.320* (with *Marches in D, K.335/1–2); 13 in G (Eine kleine Nachtmusik), K.525.*
(M) *** Ph. Dig. 422 503-2 (7) [id.]. ASMF, Sir Neville Marriner.

Marriner and his Academy are at their very finest here and make a very persuasive case for giving these works on modern instruments. The playing has much finesse, yet its cultivated polish never brings a hint of blandness or lethargy; it is smiling, yet full of energy and sparkle. These performances of the major *Serenades* include the 'entry' marches, and their spirit carries forward into the allegros. In the concertante violin roles Iona Brown is surely an ideal soloist, her playing full of grace. The novelty is the inclusion of the amazingly mature-sounding *Galimathias musicum*, written in 1766 when the composer was ten years old. Leopold Mozart described it as 'A Quodlibet . . . for two violins, two oboes, two horns, obbligato harpsichord, two bassoons, viola and bass. All the instruments have their solos and at the end there is a fugue with all the instruments on a Dutch song called "Prince William".' The scoring and invention are delightfully fresh and the seventeen movements are engagingly varied, even interpolating a brief chorus in No. 8, presumably meant to be sung by the orchestra, but here performed with considerable refinement. Throughout this set the digital recording brings an almost ideal combination of bloom and vividness, achieving a natural balance without loss of inner definition, even though the acoustic is fairly reverberant.

CONCERTOS

Complete Mozart Edition, Volume 9: (i) *Bassoon concerto;* (ii) *Clarinet concerto;* (iii) *Flute concertos Nos. 1–2; Andante in C for flute & orchestra;* (iii; iv) *Flute and harp concerto;* (v) *Horn concertos Nos. 1–4; Concert rondo in E flat for horn and orchestra;* (vi) *Oboe concerto. Sinfonia concertante in E flat, K.297b; Sinfonia concertante in E flat, K.297b* (reconstructed R. Levin).

(M) **(*) Ph. Dig. 422 509-2 (5) [id.]. (i) Thunemann; (ii) Leister; (iii) Grafenauer; (iv) Graf; (v) Damm; (vi) Holliger; ASMF, Marriner (except (vi) Holliger).

The principal wind concertos here are recent digital versions. They are all well played and recorded, notably the works for flute, while Holliger does not disappoint in the *Oboe concerto* (this is his third recording). However, there is a slightly impersonal air about the accounts of the *Bassoon* and *Clarinet concertos*, well played though they are; and there are more individual sets of the works for horn. The *Sinfonia concertante* is offered both in the version we usually hear (recorded in 1972, with the performance attractively songful and elegant) and in a more modern recording of a conjectural reconstruction by Robert Levin, based on the material in the four wind parts.

(i; vii) *Bassoon concerto, K.191;* (ii; vii) *Clarinet concerto, K.622;* (iii; vii) *Flute concertos Nos. 1–2, K.313/4;* (iv; viii) *Flute & harp concerto, K.299;* (iii; vii) *Andante for flute & orchestra, K.315;* (v; vii) *Horn concertos Nos. 1–4;* (vi; vii) *Oboe concerto, K.314.*

(B) *(*) Erato/Warner 9031 73743-2 (3) [id.]. (i) Turković; (ii) Klöcker; (iii) Schultz; (iv) Glass, Stein; (v) Baumann; (vi) Schaeftlein; (vii) Salzburg Mozarteum O, Leopold Hager; (viii) S. German CO, Rolf Reinhardt.

The bulk of these performances derive from 1977 and 1979; the sole exception is the *Concerto for flute and harp*, K.299, which hails from 1953. The latter is well enough played by Willy Glass and Rose Stein but is handicapped by quite execrable sound. Otherwise the recording is fairly clean, though the closer-than-ideal balance in the *Flute concertos* produces some coarse string-quality in tuttis. The chaste, rather plain sound that Jürg Schaeftlein gives us in the *Oboe concerto* has a certain appeal, and he plays the work with great taste. There is more space round the participants in the *Horn concertos*, in which Hermann Baumann is the impressive and imaginative soloist. He plays marvellously throughout, though the orchestral response under Leopold Hager falls short of distinction and the accompaniments lack grace and affection. In the *Clarinet concerto* Dieter Klöcker is sensitive, but the upper strings produce a hard, uningratiating sound reminiscent of some mono records. Milan Turković dispatches the *Bassoon concerto* effortlessly and elegantly, but again the Salzburg Mozarteum strings lack bloom. Given the excellent alternatives now before the public, this is not particularly competitive. There are no notes.

(i) *Bassoon concerto in B flat, K.191;* (ii) *Clarinet concerto in A, K.622;* (iii) *Flute concerto No.1 in G, K.313; Andante in C, K.315;* (iii; iv) *Flute and harp concerto in C, K.299;* (v) *Horn concertos Nos. 1–4;* (vi) *Oboe concerto in C, K.314; Sinfonia concertante in E flat, K.197b.*

(M) *** DG Dig. 431 665-2 (3). (i) Morelli; (ii) Neidlich; (iii) Palma; (iv) Allen; (v) Jolley or Purvis; (vi) Wolfgang; Orpheus CO.

(M) ** Sony SM3K 47215 (3) (without *Andante & Flute & harp concerto*). (i) Garfield; (ii) Gigliotti; (iii) Kincaid; (v) Mason Jones; (vi) John de Lancie; Phd. O, Ormandy.

Most of these Orpheus performances are available separately at mid-price – see below – and have been highly praised by us. Randall Wolfgang's plaintive, slightly reedy timbre is especially telling in the *Adagio* of the *Oboe concerto* and he plays the finale with the lightest possible touch, as does Susan Palma the charming Minuet which closes the *Flute concerto*. The *Sinfonia concertante* for wind has three new soloists (Stephen Taylor, David Singer and Steven Dibner) plus William Purvis, and is pleasingly fresh; the players match their timbres beautifully in the *Adagio*, and again the last movement is delightful with its buoyant rhythmic spirit. All the works are given excellent modern recordings and this is a very persuasive collection, probably a 'best buy' for those wanting all the music in a digital format.

American readers will be attracted to the Philadelphia collection featuring famous soloists from the orchestra. Ormandy accompanies with his usual skill, though the ensemble is on the large side and the effect is occasionally a bit heavy (as in the finale of the *Flute concerto*). The remastered recordings, mostly from 1960/61, are generally satisfactory. The *Sinfonia concertante* is earlier (1957) but comes off especially well: the slow movement is most beautiful and the closing *Andantino con variazioni* is deliciously debonair. This is a highlight, as is Bernard Garfield's unforgettable account of the *Bassoon concerto*, wonderfully full of character – his timbre is uniquely appealing and he catches the work's changing moods to perfection. William Kincaid is suitably poised in the *Flute concerto*, and both John de Lancie and Anthony Gigliotti are expert too; although neither is particularly individual: the *Clarinet concerto* projects the more strongly, partly because of Ormandy's warmth. Mason Jones is unfailingly musical in the *Horn concer-*

tos. His tone is broad rather than glowing, but the phrasing is appealing. Ormandy obviously enjoys himself providing the beautifully polished accompaniments to these four works, and it is a pity that here the violins are made to sound a bit thin in tuttis. An enjoyable set but, with the *Flute and harp concerto* not included, this hardly competes with the Orpheus box from DG.

(i) *Bassoon concerto;* (ii) *Clarinet concerto;* (iii) *Oboe concerto, K.314.*
(M) *** DG 429 816-2; *429 816-4* [id.]. (i) Zeman; (ii) Prinz; (iii) Turetschek, VPO, Boehm.
(BB) **(*) Naxos Dig. 8.550345 [id.]. (i) Turnovský; (ii) Ottensamer; (iii) Gabriel, V. Mozart Academy, Wildner.

On DG, Dietmar Zeman gives a highly accomplished account of the *Bassoon concerto*, a distinguished performance by any standards. Prinz's account of the *Clarinet concerto* is also beautifully turned; both deserve a position of honour in the field. Turetschek is eminently civilized in the *Oboe concerto*, though his bright timbre is an individual one. The 1974/5 recordings are truthful and well balanced, with the upper range freshened on CD without being edgy.

Very acceptable recordings of all three works on Naxos, though the strings could have been set further back throughout. In the *Oboe concerto* the soloist, Martin Gabriel, is excellent. The clarinettist, Ernst Ottensamer, is also a sensitive player, his slow movement is full of feeling; and there is an accomplished performance of the *Bassoon concerto* from Stepan Turnovský (the son of the Czech conductor, Martin Turnovský), who has the measure of the work's character and wit. Recommendable, particularly at the price.

(i) *Bassoon concerto in B flat, K.191;* (ii) *Clarinet concerto in A, K. 622;* (iii) *Violin concerto No. 3 in G, K.216.*
(M) **(*) EMI stereo/mono CDM7 63408-2 [id.]; *EG 763408-4*. (i) Brooke; (ii) Brymer; (iii) De Vito; RPO, Beecham.

The Beecham Edition disc offers a vintage group of Mozart concerto recordings. His romantically expansive reading of the Mozart *Clarinet concerto* with Jack Brymer the glowing soloist is a classic recording, totally individual in every phrase, with conductor and soloist inspiring each other. The account of the *Bassoon concerto* has equal magic, thanks to the comparable partnership between Beecham and Gwydion Brooke, another of the 'royal family' of wind soloists which the great conductor gathered for his Royal Philharmonic Orchestra. But the surprise here is the equally inspired and highly personal account of the *G major Violin concerto*, with Gioconda de Vito as soloist. She too conveys magic comparable to Beecham's own, with the slow movement again luxuriantly expansive. It may be significant that soon afterwards she married one of Beecham's favourite collaborators in the recording world, the producer David Bicknell who was responsible for this very recording, made in 1958. The sound in the *Clarinet* and *Bassoon concertos* has fine body and presence, but with some emphasis on the top in the transfer (which has developed since its earlier appearance). The 1949 mono recording of the *Violin concerto* is similar, but with a more limited range.

(i) *Bassoon concerto;* (ii) *Horn concertos Nos. 1–4.*
(M) **(*) DG Dig. 431 284-2; *431 284-4*. (i) Frank Morelli; (ii) David Jolley (*1* & *4*), William Purvis (*2–3*); Orpheus CO.

Frank Morelli has an engagingly woody tone and plays a very nimble bassoon in the opening allegro of K.191, while his lively decoration of the gracious Minuet finale is full of imaginative use of light and shade. The *Andante*, too, is phrased most pleasingly. The appropriately named David Jolley is very personable in the *First* and *Fourth* of the *Horn concertos*; he brings a winning flair and crisp articulation to his solo role, and the slow movement of K.495 (No. 4) is particularly imaginative. In the remaining two concertos William Purvis plays fluently and agreeably, if without quite the same strength of personality as his colleague. Accompaniments throughout are well up to Orpheus standard in matters of finesse, warmth and polish, and the recorded sound is most believable. At medium price this is worth considering by those who require modern, digital versions of these works.

Clarinet concerto in A, K.622; Bassoon concerto in B flat (arr. for clarinet).
(M) ** BMG/RCA GD 60379 [60379-2-RG]. Richard Stolzman, ECO, Schneider.

Richard Stolzman's performance of the *Clarinet concerto* is distinctive, particularly in matters of light and shade, and he plays the slow movement beautifully. The recording too has been vastly improved in its present transfer, the solo instrument both clear and full-timbred, and very present against a warmly expansive orchestral backcloth. The *Bassoon concerto*, however, loses much of its character in this transcription, and the clarinet image here is rather more reedy.

Clarinet concerto; Flute concerto No. 1, K.313; Andante for flute & orchestra, K.315; Flute &

harp concerto; Oboe concerto; Horn concertos Nos. 1–4; Rondo for horn & orchestra, K.371.

(B) *** Ph. 426 148-2 (3). Brymer, Claude Monteux, Ellis, Black, Civil, ASMF, Marriner.

The Philips performances are among the finest available and, although the forward balance tends to make the soloists sound larger than life, the sound is otherwise realistic and eminently truthful in timbre. Jack Brymer's recording of the *Clarinet concerto* is the third he has made; in some ways it is his best, for he plays with deepened insight and feeling. The *Flute* and *Oboe concertos* are hardly less recommendable and the *Flute and harp concerto* is delightful, even if the instruments are made to seem jumbo-sized! Alan Civil's third recording of the *Horn concertos* is included, and this is discussed below.

(i) *Clarinet concerto;* (ii) *Flute concerto No. 1 in G, K.313;* (iii) *Flute and harp concerto* (CD only: (iv) *Oboe concerto in C, K.314*).

(B) **(*) DG Compact Classics 413 428-2 (2); *413 428-4* [id.]. (i) Prinz, VPO, Boehm; (ii) Linde, Munich CO, Stadlmair; (iii) Schulz, Zabeleta, VPO, Boehm (CD only: (iv) Holliger, Munich CO, Stadlmair).

Prinz's 1974 recording of the *Clarinet concerto* is here available on an excellent Compact Classics tape alongside Linde's impeccably played account of the *G major Flute concerto.* This has a touch of rigidity in the outer movements, but in the slow movement the playing is beautifully poised and the melody breathes in exactly the right way. Boehm's *Flute and harp concerto* comes from 1976 and the performance could hardly be bettered. The balance, as far as the relationship between soloists and orchestra is concerned, is expertly managed, and this is altogether refreshing. The sound throughout these recordings is excellent, except that Linde's 1966 *Flute concerto* shows its earlier date in the quality of the string timbre. On the CDs, Holliger's first recording of the *Oboe concerto* is added. His playing, needless to say, is first class, his tone appealing and his style and technique serving the music's grace and elegance. But Stadlmair's accompaniment is crisply straightforward rather than especially imaginative.

(i) *Clarinet concerto in A, K.622;* (ii; iii) *Flute and harp concerto in C, K.299.* (ii) *Andante for flute and orchestra in C, K.315.*

(M) *** DG Dig. 431 283-2; *431 283-4.* (i) Charles Neidlich; (ii) Susan Palma; (iii) Nancy Allen; Orpheus CO.

Susan Palma is an essentially gentle flautist and her playing in the *C major Andante* has a disarming innocence; the *Flute and harp concerto* too, in which Nancy Allen makes a sympathetic partner, is striking for its delicacy of feeling and texture. Some might feel that the orchestra leans a little strongly in formulating the opening phrase of the *Andantino*, but the flute entry dispels any doubts and the finale has the lightest possible touch. Charles Neidlich's account of the *Clarinet concerto* has an altogether stronger profile. He rightly chooses the basset clarinet and clearly relishes not only its range but also its colour. In the very spirited finale he produces some captivating lower tessitura, while in the *Adagio* he plays radiantly, after a bright, briskly paced first movement, essentially fresh and spring-like. At the reprise of the main theme in the second movement he drops to pianissimo and then decorates the lovely melody simply and affectionately; this leads to a glorious blossoming as the orchestra takes up the melody. The recording is very realistic and well balanced throughout.

(i) *Clarinet concerto;* (ii) *Flute and harp concerto in C, K.299.*

(B) *** Pickwick Dig. PCD 852; *CIMPC 852* [id.]. (i) Campbell; (ii) Davies, Masters; City of L. Sinfonia, Hickox.

(B) *** Decca 421 023-2. (i) Prinz; (ii) Tripp, Jellinek; VPO, Münchinger.

David Campbell's agile and pointed performance of the clarinet work brings fastish speeds and a fresh, unmannered style in all three movements. Though some will prefer a weightier or more individual approach, and the reverberant recording tends not to differentiate the soloist sharply enough, his tonal shading is very beautiful. The earlier flute and harp work is just as freshly and sympathetically done, with a direct, unmannered style sounding entirely spontaneous.

The Decca bargain coupling dates from 1963 and the recording is smooth, rich and well judged in reverberation. The balance between soloists and orchestra is finely calculated and the performances are admirable, sounding as fresh as the day they were made. Refinement and beauty of tone and phrase are a hallmark throughout, and Münchinger provides most sensitive accompaniments.

(i) *Clarinet concerto in A, K.622;* (ii) *Oboe concerto in C, K.314.*

(BB) **(*) HM/BMG Dig. VD 77509 [Victrola 77509-2-RV]. (i) Heinz Deinzer; (ii) Helmut Hucke; Coll. Aur., Franzjosef Maier.

Anyone looking for a bargain coupling of these concertos played on authentic instruments (Heinz Deinzer is pictured using a basset clarinet to good effect) will find these performances characterful and spontaneous, with both soloists fluently mastering technical difficulties. Helmut Hucke's woody oboe timbre is distinctly appealing; if Deinzer gives a rather straight account of the central *Adagio* of the work for clarinet, this is otherwise an enjoyably fresh performance. The acoustics of the Cedernsaal in the Schloss Kirchheim bring a resonant mellowness to the violins: there is no acidity of timbre here, yet the digital sound has good definition. However, these Deutsche Harmonia Mundi Mozart Edition reissues have no back-up documentation.

(i) *Clarinet concerto;* (ii) *Clarinet quintet in A, K.581.*

(M) **(*) Ph. 420 710-2; *420 710-4.* Brymer, (i) LSO, C. Davis; (ii) Allegri Qt.

Jack Brymer's second recording of the *Clarinet concerto* has a warm, autumnal feeling, and its soft lyricism is appealing in the slow movement, but there is not quite the magic of the earlier version with Beecham, until a fast speed for the finale brings extra exhilaration. The *Quintet* is comparably warm and smiling; the sound is bright and fresh.

Flute concerto No. 1 in G, K.313; Andante in C, K.315; (i) *Flute and harp concerto in C, K.299.*

(M) *** BMG/RCA GD 86723; *GK 86723.* James Galway; (i) Lucerne Festival O, Baumgartner; (ii) with Marisa Robles, LSO, Mata.

(M) *** Ph. 420 880-2. Claude Monteux; (i) Ellis; ASMF, Marriner.

Flute concertos Nos. (i) *1 in G, K.313;* (ii) *2 in D, K.314.*

(B) *** Pickwick Dig. PCD 871; *CIMPC 871.* Judith Hall, Philh. O, Peter Thomas.

(B) *** Decca 421 630-2; *421 630-4.* William Bennett, ECO, Malcolm – CIMAROSA: *Double flute concerto.* **(*)

(B) *** Pickwick PCD 807; *CIMPC 807.* Galway, New Irish Chamber Ens., Prieur.

(B) **(*) Hung. White Label HRC 107 [id.]. Lóránt Kovács, Hungarian State O, Ervin Lukács – M. HAYDN: *Concerto.* **

(B) ** DG 427 211-2 [id.]. (i) Linde, Munich CO, Stadlmair; (ii) Nicolet, Lucerne Festival O, Baumgartner – SALIERI: *Concerto for flute and oboe.* ***

Flute concertos Nos. 1 in G, K.313; 2 in D, K.314; Andante in C, K.315.

(BB) **(*) Naxos Dig. 8.550074 [id.]. Herbert Weissberg, Capella Istropolitana, Sieghart.

(B) **(*) Ph. 426 074-2. Aurèle Nicolet, Concg. O, Zinman.

(M) ** HM/BMG GD 77054; *GK 77054.* Barthold Kuijken, La Petite Bande, Sigiswald Kuijken.

Judith Hall produces a radiantly full timbre. Moreover she is a first-class Mozartian, as she demonstrates in her cadenzas as well as in the line of the slow movements, phrased with a simple eloquence that is disarming. There is plenty of vitality in the allegros, and Peter Thomas provides polished, infectious accompaniments to match the solo playing. The balance is most realistic and the sound overall is in the demonstration bracket.

William Bennett also gives a beautiful account of the *Flute concertos*, among the finest to have appeared in recent years. Every phrase is shaped with both taste and affection, and the playing of the ECO under George Malcolm is fresh and vital. The recording is clean, well detailed and with enough resonance to lend bloom to the sound.

James Galway's silvery timbre is instantly recognizable and his RCA performance of the solo concerto from the mid-1970s has virtuosity, charm and refinement. He seems as unlike an original instrument as could possibly be imagined. Galway is well supported by the Lucerne orchestra, rather reverberantly recorded, with the solo flute placed well forward. The coupled *Flute and harp concerto* has seldom sounded more lively than it does here, with an engaging element of fantasy in the music-making, a radiant slow movement and a very spirited finale. Marisa Robles makes a characterful match for Galway and they are well accompanied. The balance of the soloists is again forward, but not unrealistically so.

Galway's Pickwick alternative is a bargain. The accompaniments, ably directed by André Prieur, are reasonably polished and stylish, and the recording (although it gives a rather small sound to the violins) is excellent, clear and with good balance and perspective. It might be argued that Galway's vibrato is not entirely suited to these eighteenth-century works and that his cadenzas, too, are slightly anachronistic. But the star quality of his playing disarms criticism.

Exquisite playing on the Philips record (with Claude Monteux) from all concerned. The only reservation is that the solo instruments sound larger than life as balanced. In every other respect this splendidly remastered disc is highly recommendable.

The Naxos record by Herbert Weissberg and the Capella Istropolitana under Martin Sieghart can hold its head quite high alongside the competition. Weissberg does not have the outsize personality of some of his rivals but he is a cultured player, and the quality of the recording is excellent. In short, good value for money and very pleasant sound.

The Nicolet/Zinman performances are very positive, with the flute balanced well forward and dominating the proceedings, though David Zinman's accompaniments are alert and strong. Both finales are particularly attractive, briskly paced, and the solo playing throughout is expert and elegantly phrased. However, Galway displays a lighter touch generally and is to be preferred.

The performances by Lóránt Kovács have winning simplicity of line, and these are thoroughly musical accounts. The accompaniments are stylish too; the minuet finale of No. 1 has striking character. The recording is full, the flute forwardly balanced.

Two different soloists on the DG Privilege reissue, with Linde rather less flexible in allegros than Nicolet, but both playing impeccably and offering poised slow movements. The sound is lively and fresh, and the coupling is attractive.

Those who seek authentic performances of Mozart's three major concertante works for flute will find that playing and recording under Kuijken are eminently satisfactory, if a little reserved. Other versions yield more individuality and colour.

Flute concertos Nos. 1–2; (i) *Flute and harp concerto, K.299.*
(M) *** DG 429 815-2; *429 815-4* [id.]. Zöller, (i) Zabaleta; VPO, Boehm.

Karlheinz Zöller is a superb flautist. K.313 is a little cool but is played most elegantly, with pure tone and unmannered phrasing; the charming minuet finale is poised and graceful. The performance of K.314 is more relaxed and smiling. Zöller favours the use of comparatively extended cadenzas, and one wonders whether they will not seem too much of a good thing on repetition. However, the 1974 recording gives him a radiant timbre and he is very persuasive. The admirably played *Flute and harp concerto* is discussed above in its alternative bargain coupling.

(i) *Flute concerto No. 1 in G, K.313; Andante in C, K.315;* (ii) *Oboe concerto in C, K.314;* (iii) *Sinfonia concertante in E flat, K.279b; Serenade No. 10 in B flat for 13 wind instruments; K.361.*
(B) ** EMI CZS7 67306-2 (2). (i) Debost, (ii) Bourgue, O de Paris; (iii) ECO (members); all cond. Barenboim.

The *Flute* and *Oboe concertos* are well played here but are not especially distinctive and the digital remastering has lost some of the bloom in trying to clarify the resonance of the 1977 recording, made in the Salle Wagram. The *Sinfonia concertante*, made at Abbey Road in 1967, fares rather better, and this performance with four fine wind soloists (Peter Graeme, Thea King, Ifor James and Martinn Gatt) and full-blooded direction from Barenboim has plenty of life and personality. It is the *Wind Serenade*, however, that is the highlight of the collection, and we hope this may reappear separately; it is most distinguished. Here we have expertly blended wind-tone, free from the traces of self-indulgence that occasionally mars Barenboim's music-making. Tempi are a little on the brisk side (particularly in the first movement), but none the worse for that when the playing itself is so resilient. The quality of the original recording was warm yet beautifully focused, with no want of body and definition. The remastering has lost a little of the warmth, and the attempt to sharpen the focus still further has not been entirely successful.

(i) *Flute concerto No. 1 in G, K.313;* (ii) *Sinfonia concertante in E flat, K.297b.*
(M) **(*) EMI CD-EMX 2181; *TC-EMX 2181.* (i) Snowden; (ii) Theodore, Hill, Price, Busch; LPO, Mackerras.

Mackerras is characteristically brisk in the first movement of the *Sinfonia concertante* for wind, and his performance has plenty of life throughout, and charm too, in the closing variations. The solo playing is of high quality; the *Adagio* is persuasive, if with no striking individuality. Jonathan Snowden's account of the *Flute concerto* is also attractive, sprightly, stylish and polished (though some might not take to his comparatively elaborate cadenzas). With excellent, digital recording, an enjoyable if not a memorable coupling.

Flute and harp concerto in C, K.299.
(B) *** DG 427 206-2. Zöller, Zabaleta, BPO, Märzendorfer – HANDEL; WAGENSEIL: *Harp concertos.* ***

The outer movements of this DG performance have an attractive rhythmic buoyancy. The flautist is a most sensitive player and his phrasing is a constant pleasure, while Zabaleta's poise and sense of line knit the overall texture of the solo-duet together most convincingly. Märzendorfer conducts with warmth yet with a firm overall control. In short, with fresh, clear recorded sound, this is highly successful.

(i) *Flute and harp concerto in C, K.299;* (ii) *Oboe concerto in C, K.314.*
(M) ** EMI Dig. CD-EMX 9510; *TC-EMX 2116.* (i) Snowden, Thomas; (ii) Hunt, LPO, Litton.

The performance of the *Flute and harp concerto* is the more winning here. Where Gordon Hunt in the *Oboe concerto* seems a less natural concerto soloist, the flautist Jonathan Snowden, in collaboration with Caryl Thomas on the harp, is both sparkling and sensitive, a natural soloist, regularly imaginative in his individual phrasing.

(i) *Flute and harp concerto, K.299;* (ii) *Piano concerto No. 12 in A, K.414;* (iii) *Violin concerto No. 4 in D, K.218.*
(M) (***) EMI mono CDH7 63820-2 [id.]. (i) Le Roy, Laskine; (ii) Kentner; (iii) Heifetz; (i; iii) RPO; (ii) LPO; Beecham.

This CD assembles three classic performances from the 1940s conducted by Beecham. The *Concerto for flute and harp* has a cool elegance in this 1947 performance with René Le Roy and Lili Laskine; and listening to Louis Kentner's much earlier (1940) record of the *Piano concerto in A major*, K.414, which is very enjoyable indeed, makes one wish that this much-underrated musician had recorded the lot. The Heifetz is a bit high-powered – but is marvellously played, of course. If the performance does not have that sense of carefree joy that made Beecham's Mozart so peerless, it still sparkles; at mid-price, this triptych makes a splendid bargain. The transfers are much smoother than the Beecham/Mozart symphonies, and in the *Piano concerto* Louis Kentner's tone has fine naturalness and colour.

(i) *Flute and harp concerto in C, K.299; Sinfonia concertante in E flat, K. 297b.*
(BB) *** Naxos Dig. 8.550159 [id.]. (i) Jiri Válek, Hana Müllerová; Capella Istropolitana, Richard Edlinger.

Richard Edlinger may not be Beecham nor the Capella Istropolitana the pre-war LPO, but this account of the *Flute and harp concerto* is thoroughly fresh and stylish, and the two soloists are excellent. Although the *Sinfonia concertante in E flat*, K.297b, is not quite so successful, it is still very impressive, and it should (and indeed does) give pleasure. Perhaps the first movement is just a little too measured and the wind-playing, though very good, falls short of the last ounce of distinction. Both performances are very decently recorded in a warm, lively acoustic; in the lowest price-range they are a real bargain.

Horn concertos Nos. 1 in D, K.412; 2–4 in E flat, K.417, 447 & 495.
(M) (***) EMI mono CDH7 61013-2 [id.]. Dennis Brain, Philh. O, Karajan.
(M) *** Decca 417 767-2. Barry Tuckwell, LSO, Maag – HAYDN: *Concerto No. 1.* ***
(B) *** CfP Dig. CD-CFP 4589; *TC-CFP 4589.* Claire Briggs, Royal Liverpool PO, Stephen Kovacevich - HAYDN: *Trumpet concerto.* ***
(M) *** Teldec/Warner 2292 42757-2 [id.]. Hermann Baumann (hand-horn), VCM, Harnoncourt.
(M) *** DG 429 817-2; *429 817-4* [id.]. Gerd Seifert, BPO, Karajan.

Horn concertos Nos. 1–4; Concert rondo in E flat, K.371 (ed. Civil or E. Smith).
(M) *** EMI CD-EMX 2004; *TC-EMX 2004.* Alan Civil, RPO, Kempe.
(M) *** Ph. 420 709-2; *420 709-4.* Alan Civil, ASMF, Marriner.

Horn concertos Nos. 1–4; Concert rondo, K.371 (ed. Tuckwell); *Fragment, K.494a.*
(M) *** EMI CDM7 69569-2; *EG 769569-4.* Barry Tuckwell, ASMF, Marriner.

We are pleased to report that the EMI Références reissue of Dennis Brain's famous 1954 record with Karajan has been remastered; the violins now sound sweeter and much fuller than when these performances first appeared on CD. The horn timbre is wonderfully full and rich. Brain's glorious tone and phrasing – every note is alive – is life-enhancing in its warmth; the *espressivo* of the slow movements is matched by the joy of the Rondos, spirited, buoyant, infectious and smiling. Karajan's accompaniments, too, are a model of Mozartian good manners and the Philharmonia at their peak play wittily and elegantly.

Tuckwell's first (1960) stereo recording of the *Horn concertos* (perhaps even more spontaneous than his later, digital, full-priced version) re-emerges freshly on Decca's mid-price label, now shorn of the *Fragment*, K.494a, but offering instead Haydn's best concerto to make it more competitive. Peter Maag's accompaniments are admirably crisp and nicely scaled, giving his soloist buoyant support, and the vintage recording still sounds astonishingly well.

However, EMI have also effectively remastered Tuckwell's second set with Marriner, and the 1972 recording sounds fuller, with slightly more body to the violins. Marriner's direction of the accompaniments is agreeably warm and elegant. This CD has the advantage of including not only the *Concert rondo* but also the *Fragment in E* which ends where Mozart left it at bar 91. Altogether the vigour and grace of this music-making commend this record highly.

Alan Civil, like Tuckwell, recorded the concertos three times, but the earliest set, with Kempe, is the freshest and most rewarding. He plays with a simple eloquence, a full tone and a flawless technique. His sensitivity is present in every bar and Kempe accompanies benignly and with great affection. The warm 1967 recording has been cleanly remastered, although the RPO violins sound somewhat thinner above the stave than on the Tuckwell/Marriner recordings.

For those seeking a bargain digital set, Claire Briggs, formerly principal horn of the Royal Liverpool Philharmonic and latterly transferring to the City of Birmingham orchestra, here gives brilliant performances of all four *Concertos*, with the celebrated finale of No. 4 taken exceptionally fast. Even that is superbly articulated without any feeling of breathlessness, though it lacks some of the fun that others have brought. The Haydn *Trumpet concerto* in another fine performance makes an attractive fill-up.

Hermann Baumann successfully uses the original hand-horn, without valves, for which the concertos were written, and the result is a *tour de force* of technical skill, not achieved at the expense of musical literacy or expressive content. Inevitably this implies at least some alterations in timbre, as certain notes have to be 'stopped', with the hand in the bell of the instrument, if they are to be in tune. Baumann is not in the least intimidated by this problem; he lets the listener hear the stopped effect only when he decides that the tonal change can be put to good artistic effect. In his cadenzas he also uses horn chords (where several notes are produced simultaneously by resonating the instrument's harmonics), but as a complement to the music rather than as a gimmick. While the horn is given added presence and tangibility in the digital remastering, the brightness of the strings has brought some roughness of focus, since the original recording was mellow and reverberant.

Alan Civil's most recent set was made in 1973. The recording is obviously more modern and the performances are highly enjoyable, with Sir Neville Marriner's polished and lively accompaniments giving pleasure in themselves. The balance has the effect of making the horn sound slightly larger than life.

Gerd Seifert has been principal horn of the Berlin Philharmonic since 1964, and his velvety, warm tone is familiar on many records. His articulation is light and neat here and his nimbleness brings an effective lightness to the gay Rondos. Karajan almost matches his earlier accompaniments for Dennis Brain, and the orchestral playing is strong in character, although he never overwhelms his soloist. The 1969 recording now brings just a hint of overbrightness on the *forte* violins, but this adds to the sense of vitality without spoiling the elegance.

Piano concertos

Complete Mozart Edition, Volume 7: (i) *Piano concertos, K.107/1–3;* (ii) *Nos. 1–4;* (iii) *5, 6, 8, 9, 11–27; Concert rondos 1–2;* (iii; iv) *Double piano concertos, K.242 & K.365*; (v) *Triple concerto in F, K.242.*

(M) **(*) Ph. Analogue/Dig. 422 507-2 (12) [id.]. (i) Ton Koopman, Amsterdam Bar. O; (ii) Haebler, Vienna Capella Academica, Melkus; (iii) Brendel, ASMF, Marriner; (iv) Imogen Cooper; (v) Katia and Marielle Labèque, Bychkov, BPO, Bychkov.

Piano concertos Nos. 1–6; 8–9; 11–27; Rondo in D, K.382.

(M) *** EMI CZS7 62825-2 (10). Daniel Barenboim, ECO.

(M) ** DG 429 001-2 (10) (without *Rondo*). Géza Anda, Salzburg Mozarteum.

Piano concertos Nos. 1–6; 8–9; 11–27; Rondos Nos. 1–2, K.382 & 386.

(M) *** Sony Analogue/Dig. SK12K 46441 (12). Murray Perahia, ECO.

By omitting the four early concertos after J. C. Bach, Sony have been able to reissue the Perahia set on twelve mid-priced CDs, costing more than the Barenboim EMI set but in most respects offering the best buy in this much-recorded repertoire. The cycle is a remarkable achievement; in terms of poetic insight and musical spontaneity, the performances are in a class of their own. There is a wonderful singing line and at the same time a sensuousness that is always tempered by spirituality. There is one slight snag: about half the recordings are digital and of excellent quality, but the remastering of the earlier, analogue recordings, especially those made in 1976/7, has not enhanced the violin timbre. Nos. 5, 12, 21, 22, 24 and 27 are acceptable, although there is a loss of bloom; but Nos. 8, 11 and especially 20 have varying amounts of edginess or shrillness, while Nos. 9, 13 and 14 have a lesser degree of thinness – which admirers of the authentic school may welcome. Others will prefer the rounder, more natural sound of the digital recordings.

The sense of spontaneity in Barenboim's performances of the Mozart concertos, his message that this is music hot off the inspiration line, is hard to resist, even though it occasionally leads to over-exuberance and idiosyncrasies. On balance, fast movements are faster than usual and slow movements slower, but that view has powerful backing and any inconsistencies or romantic touches seem merely incidental to the forward drive. These are as nearly live performances as one could hope for on record, and the playing of the English Chamber Orchestra is splendidly geared to the approach of an artist with whom the players have worked regularly. They are recorded with fullness, and the sound is generally freshened very successfully in the remastering, with the piano tone remaining natural. Certainly this is the most invigorating cycle available at what amounts to bargain price, taking the number of discs into consideration.

The Philips Mozart Edition *Piano concertos* box is based on Brendel's set with the ASMF under Marriner. Throughout, his thoughts are never less than penetrating. The transfers are consistently of the very highest quality, as is the playing of the Academy of St Martin-in-the-Fields under Sir Neville Marriner. To make the set complete, Ingrid Haebler gives eminently stylish accounts of the first four *Concertos* on the fortepiano, accompanied by Melkus and his excellent Vienna Capella Academica; the sound is admirably fresh. However, on disc two the ear gets rather a shock when Ton Koopman presents the three works after J. C. Bach. The abrasive opening tutti of K.107/1 takes the listener by surprise into an entirely different sound-world. Convincing though these performances are, it seems a strange idea to offer an authentic approach to these three concertos alone, particularly as at the end of the disc we return to a delightfully cultured performance on modern instruments of the alternative version for three pianos of the so-called *Lodron Concerto*, K.242, provided by the Labèque duo plus Semyon Bychkov, with the Berlin Philharmonic Orchestra accompanying in the most sophisticated modern fashion.

Were the competition not so fierce, Anda's performances could carry a stronger recommendation. They are beautifully poised and have excellent feeling for style; some are quite memorable for their unidiosyncratic freshness. The recordings do not quite match those of Barenboim, and Anda is a less individual artist, but the sound is clean and well balanced and gives consistent enjoyment. But this set would have been better reissued on DG's bargain label.

Piano concertos Nos. 5, 6, 8, 9, 11–27; (i) *Double piano concerto, K.365;* (i; ii) *Triple piano concerto, K.242. Concert Rondos 1–2.*

(M) *** DG Dig. 431 211-2 (9) [id.]. Malcolm Bilson (fortepiano), E. Bar. Soloists, Gardiner, (i) with Robert Levin; (ii) Melvin Tan.

Malcolm Bilson's complete set of the Mozart *Piano concertos* appears on nine mid-price CDs. Bilson is an artist of excellent musical judgement and good taste, and his survey is the only one at present available on the fortepiano, though we gather that one is underway from Melvyn Tan, who features here in the *Triple concerto*. We have discussed most of the issues separately and see no cause to modify our general welcome. Going back to the set, there are some occasions when one feels that Bilson could have been a little more unbuttoned and others where he is too judicious. For the most part, however, there is little to quarrel with and much to enjoy.

Piano concertos Nos. 5 in D, K.175; 16 in D (Coronation), K.537; Rondo in D, K.382.

(BB) ** Naxos Dig. 8.550209 [id.]. Jenö Jandó, Concentus Hungaricus, Mátyás Antal.

Volume 9 of Jandó's Mozart series offers music-making which is fresh and direct yet somewhat lacking in individuality. There are stronger versions of K.537 available, although there are no complaints here about the digital sound, which is vivid and well balanced.

Piano concertos Nos. 6 in B flat, K.238; 8 in C, K.246; 19 in F, K.459.

(BB) *** Naxos Dig. 8.550208 [id.]. Jenö Jandó, Concentus Hungaricus, Mátyás Antal.

Volume 8 in Jandó's series is one of the finest. *No. 19 in F* is a delightful concerto and it receives a most attractive performance, aptly paced, the slow movement gently poised and with fine woodwind playing, the finale crisply sparkling. No. 6 is hardly less successful, the engaging melody of its *Andante un poco adagio* beautifully shaped and the finale most sprightly. If No. 8 seems plainer, it is still admirably fresh. With excellently balanced recording this is a genuine bargain.

Piano concertos Nos. 6 in B flat, K.238; 21 in C, K.467.

(BB) ** Pickwick Dig. PWK 1144. Arie Vardi, Israel CO.

The warm acoustic lends this Pickwick coupling what some would call a slightly 'plummy' quality, though it is not unpleasing and the recording is agreeably spacious. Arie Vardi is an Israeli pianist, a composition pupil of Boulez and Stockhausen who has played with such conductors as Paul Paray, Carlo Zecchi and Zubin Mehta, yet who has enjoyed little exposure on record. He is a sensitive player who obviously enjoys a close rapport with his colleagues in the Israel Chamber Orchestra, from whom he draws some ravishing sounds. He does not really put a foot (or, rather, a hand) wrong in either concerto – but at the same time neither reading has the strong, commanding profile of a Casadesus or Perahia. The playing is very musical indeed and very enjoyable, but perhaps lacking in that ultimate quality of distinction that would prompt one to return to it very often.

Piano concertos Nos. 8 in C (Lützow), K.246; 9 in E flat (Jeunehomme), K.271; Concert rondo in A, K.386.

(B) * Pickwick Dig. PCD 931 [id.]. Diana Ambache, Ambache CO.

Though Diana Ambache is a sympathetic Mozartian, these performances are without a strong profile, particularly in the orchestra. The opening of K.271 (which comes first) could be more alert, and the following *Andantino* ideally needs a more positive onward flow. The first movement of K.246 has more rhythmic character, but neither of the finales sparkle as they might.

Piano concertos Nos. 8 in C, K.246; 23 in A, K.488; 26 in D (Coronation), K.537.
(BB) ** HM/BMG VD 77560; *VK 77560* [77560-2-RV; *77560-4-RV]*. Jörg Demus (fortepiano), Coll. Aur.

The Collegeum Aureum are recorded in the generous acoustic of the Cedernsaal in Schloss Kirchheim, which lends a pleasing warmth to the string-tone: indeed the sound is quite big by the side of Demus's fortepiano. They also play at modern pitch. The so-called *'Lützow' Concerto*, K.246, and the *Coronation*, K.537, were recorded in 1970 and the *A major*, K.488, five years later. Demus plays well enough, though he has neither the poetic flair of the finest modern pianists nor the effortless mastery of Bilson, whose box of concertos is available at mid-price. Bilson has the more vital musical intelligence and sensibility, and on balance he is to be preferred in all three concertos. However, the present disc is very inexpensive.

(i) *Piano concertos Nos. 9 in E flat, K.271; 14 in E flat, K.449. Fantasia in C min., K.396.*
(M) *** Van. 8.4015.71 [OVC 4015]. Alfred Brendel; (i) I Solisti di Zagreb, Janigro.

Brendel's 1968 performance of No. 9 is quite outstanding, elegant and beautifully precise. The classical-sized orchestra is just right and the neat, stylish string-playing matches the soloist. Both pianist and conductor are sensitive to the gentle melancholy of the slow movement, and in the contrasting middle section of the finale Brendel's tonal nuance is beautifully shaded. The performance of K.449 is also first rate, with a memorably vivacious finale. Altogether this is an outstanding reissue with natural sound which hardly shows its age in the clean remastering. The rather serious account of the *Fantasy*, which comes first on the record, has a much drier acoustic and the forward balance brings a less natural effect.

Piano concertos Nos. 9 in E flat, K.271; 23 in A, K.488.
(M) * Sony MYK 45506 [id.]. Rudolf Serkin, Marlboro Festival O or Columbia SO, Schneider.

Of course, both soloist and conductor have things to say about this music, though there is at times a strange lack of pianistic finesse. Moreover the recordings show their age badly: they come from 1957–8, not the best period for CBS, and the digital remastering has produced (or not tempered) some scrawny, tizzy string-tone, which greatly diminishes pleasure. The *Concerto in E flat*, K.271, the so-called *Jeunehomme*, is the less satisfactory, though it would be idle to pretend that the *A major Concerto*, K.488, is ideal either. Serkin does not always bring to either concerto those poetic insights which he undoubtedly commanded; indeed his playing here can at times be pretty routine.

Piano concertos Nos. 9 in E flat (Jeunehomme), K.271; 27 in B flat, K.595.
(BB) **(*) Naxos Dig. 8.550203 [id.]. Jenö Jandó, Concentus Hungaricus, András Ligeti.

In Volume 3 of Jandó's ongoing series, the earlier concerto is the more consistently successful, refreshing in its alert vigour in outer movements, with the simple *Andantino* contrasting nicely with the exhilarating finale. K.595 does not lack strength, but this performance does not have the individuality of the finest versions. Excellent sound, the piano forward but with a realistic overall balance.

Piano concertos Nos. 11 in F, K.413; 22 in E flat, K.482.
(BB) **(*) Naxos Dig. 8.550206 [id.]. Jenö Jandó, Concentus Hungaricus, Mátyás Antal.

Jenö Jandó is a highly musical Mozartian and his accounts of both concertos have a good deal to offer, even if in K.482 he plays the Hummel cadenza rather heavily. In this work there are moments of poetry as well as some of prose; however, there is a liveliness and enthusiasm about the whole performance that is likeable. This is well worth considering if you are on a tight budget. The recording uses the Italian Institute in Vienna (the piano is a bit too close) and produces very acceptable results.

Piano concertos Nos. 12 in A, K.414; 14 in E flat, K.449; 21 in C, K.467.
(BB) *** Naxos Dig. 8.550202 [id.]. Jenö Jandó, Concentus Hungaricus, András Ligeti.

Volume 2 in the Naxos series makes an impressive bargain triptych. In Jandó's hands the first movement of K.449 sounds properly forward-looking; the brightly vivacious K.414 also sounds very fresh here, and its *Andante* is beautifully shaped. Similarly the famous slow movement ever associated with the film, *Elvira Madigan*, is most sensitive, with a gently poignant cantilena from the strings. The resonance of the Italian Institute in Budapest, where this series of recordings is made, adds warmth and generally provides fullness and bloom without clouding detail. The excellent orchestral response distinguishes the first movement of K.467: both grace and weight are here, and some fine wind playing. An added interest in this work is provided by Jandó's use of cadenzas provided by Robert Casadesus. Jandó is at his most spontaneous throughout these performances and this is altogether an excellent disc.

Piano concertos Nos. 12 in A, K.414; 21 in C, K.467.
(B) **(*) Decca 417 773-2. Lupu, ECO, Segal – BEETHOVEN: *32 Variations in C min.* ***

There is much that is beautiful here, including hushed playing from Radu Lupu in the slow movements of both concertos. The music-making has life and sensibility, and both performances are very enjoyable. The recording is rather brightly lit, but this is excellent value.

(i) *Piano concerto No. 12 in A, K.414;* (i; ii) *Double piano concerto in E flat, K.365;* (iii) *Piano trio in E flat, K.502.*
(M) * Sony SMK 46255 [id.]. Rudolf Serkin; (i) Marlboro Festival O, Schneider; (ii) with Peter Serkin; (iii) with Jaime Laredo, Madeline Foley.

Serkin's performance of the *A major concerto*, K.414, has felicitous touches, but there is some insensitivity and inelegance at the ends of phrases and some matter-of-fact passage-work. The *Double concerto in E flat*, K.365, has well-chosen tempi – except for the finale, which is a bit overdriven – but there are others (Gilels and his daughter; Brendel and Klien) who radiate more joy. The 1973 recordings are acceptable rather than distinguished. But neither in the concertos nor in the *E flat trio*, K.502, which is badly balanced, would this in any way be a first choice or anywhere near it.

Piano concertos Nos. (i) *13 in C, K.415;* (ii) *15 in B flat, K.450;* (i) *23 in A, K.488.*
(M) (*) EMI mono CDH7 63819-2 [id.]. Michelangeli, (i) O Alessandro Scarlatti, Caracciolo; (ii) Milan CO, Gracis.

The *B flat concerto*, K.450, with Ettore Gracis, recorded with the Milan Chamber Orchestra in 1951, strains the bounds of tolerance; the tape seems to have suffered much deterioration. The *C major*, K.415, and *A major*, K.488, are better, though the sound is barely passable and the strings sound pretty scrawny. Michelangeli's playing is a vast improvement over his recent DG recordings and has something of the cool distinction we associate with him. But despite some felicitous touches in the *C major concerto*, this is no match for other recordings of the period by Solomon or Gieseking.

Piano concertos Nos. 13 in A, K.415; 20 in D min., K.466.
(BB) **(*) Naxos Dig. 8.550201 [id.]. Jenö Jandó, Concentus Hungaricus, András Ligeti.

This is Volume 1 in the planned complete recording of the Mozart piano concertos by Naxos with Jenö Jandó and the excellent Concentus Hungaricus, a polished chamber group using modern instruments, here directed to stylish effect by András Ligeti. These performances set a high standard in their communicative immediacy, and if they have not quite the individuality of Perahia or Ashkenazy, they are worth a place in any collection and are very modestly priced. Here the early *A major Concerto* comes up with enticing freshness, allegros are crisp and alert and the slow movement has a disarming simplicity. Ligeti creates a sense of anticipatory tension at the opening of the coupled *D minor Concerto* and this performance has plenty of drama, with the *Romance* very appealingly shaped. Jandó uses Beethoven's cadenzas with impressive authority. The balance and recording are most believable and there is good documentation throughout this series.

Piano concertos Nos. 14 in E flat, K.449; 15 in E flat, K.450; 16 in D, K.451.
(M) *** EMI CDM7 69124-2 [id.]; *EG 769124-4.* Barenboim, ECO.

Barenboim's playing is spontaneous and smiling, while the orchestra respond with genuine vitality and sparkle. K.451 is particularly enjoyable, with a brisk, jaunty account of the first movement, a flowing, expressive slow movement and an exuberant finale. Good recording throughout, and a sensible price.

(i) *Piano concertos Nos. 15 in B flat, K.450;* (ii) *23 in A, K.488; 24 in C min., K.491.*
(M) (***) EMI mono CDH7 63707-2 [id.]. Solomon, Philh. O, (i) Ackermann; (ii) Menges.

At last EMI have restored Solomon's classic Mozart concerto accounts to circulation. It is astonishing that this company has been so tardy in paying due recognition to one of the greatest pianists of the present century. These records all come from 1953–5 and have that classical purity and tonal finesse for which Solomon was so famous. They are a model of style and have an extraordinary poise and authority. The recordings come up very well, and no apologies need be made for the sound quality or the recorded balance. Essential listening for all Mozartians.

Piano concerto No. 15 in B flat, K.450; (i) *Double piano concertos: in F (Lodron), K.242; in E flat, K.365.*

(M) **(*) Naxos Dig. 8.550210 [id.]. Jenö Jandó, (i) with Dénes Várjon; Concentus Hungaricus, Antal.

Jandó is at his most spontaneous in K.450, embellishing the theme of the *Andante* most stylishly, and he is as bright and witty as one could wish in the brilliantly good-humoured finale. In the pair of *Double concertos* he is joined by Dénes Várjon in an effective partnership, and these performances are agreeably fresh and alive; compared with Brendel and Klien, however, the interchanges between the two soloists are much more plainspun. The modern Naxos sound is a considerable advance on the earlier record, with the violins sounding much better-nourished, and this is certainly good value. But Brendel and Klien bring a magic to their performance which makes one forget any inadequacies in the orchestral backing.

(i) *Piano concerto No. 15 in B flat, K.450; Symphony No. 36 (Linz), K.425.*

(M) **(*) Decca 417 790-2. (i) Bernstein (piano); VPO, Bernstein.

An enjoyably light-hearted Mozartian coupling. In the performance of the *Linz Symphony*, one relishes the carefree quality in the playing. The *Concerto*, even more than the *Symphony*, conveys the feeling of a conductor enjoying himself on holiday. Bernstein's piano playing may not be poised in every detail, but every note communicates vividly – so much so that in the slow movement he even manages to make his dual tempo convincing – faster for the tuttis than for the more romantic solos. The finale is taken surprisingly slowly, but Bernstein brings it off. The sound projects vividly in its new format.

Piano concertos Nos. 16 in D, K.451; 25 in C, K.503; Rondo in A, K.386.

(BB) *** Naxos Dig. 8.550207 [id.]. Jenö Jandó, Concentus Hungaricus, Mátyás Antal.

Jenö Jandó is far from unimaginative here, and he gives a very spirited and intelligent account of the relatively neglected *D major Concerto*, K.451, in which he receives sensitive and attentive support from the excellent Concentus Hungaricus under Mátyás Antal. The performance has warmth and conveys a genuine sense of delight. The players sound as if they are enjoying themselves and, although there are greater performances of the *C major Concerto*, K.503, on record, they are not at this extraordinarily competitive price. The recording engineers place the soloist rather too forward but the recording is very agreeable; the acoustic is warm and there is plenty of space round the instruments.

Piano concertos Nos. 17 in G, K.453; 18 in B flat, K.456.

(BB) *** Naxos Dig. 8.550205 [id.]. Jenö Jandó, Concentus Hungaricus, Mátyás Antal.

Volume 5 is one of the finest so far in Jandó's excellent super-bargain series. The orchestral response under Mátyás Antal is very persuasive, with the finesse of the string playing immediately apparent at the very opening of K.453, and the final *Allegretto* similarly stylish. Tempi are admirably judged and both slow movements are most sensitively played. The variations which form the *Andante* of K.456 are particularly appealing in their perceptive use of light and shade, while the very lively *Allegro vivace* finale of the same work is infectiously spirited. Jandó uses Mozart's original cadenzas for the first two movements of K.453 and the composer's alternative cadenzas for K.546. Excellent sound. This may not quite match Perahia's full-priced analogue coupling of the same two concertos, but it is thoroughly worthwhile in its own right and remarkably inexpensive.

Piano concertos Nos. 17; 20; 22; 24; 25; Rondo in D, K.382. Piano sonatas Nos. 10, K.330; 11, K.331; Fantasias, K.396 & K.475; Romanze, K.Anh.205; Minuet, K.1.

(M) (***) EMI mono CHS7 63719-2 (3). Edwin Fischer, various orchestras & conductors.

Edwin Fischer's record of the *G major Concerto*, K.453, directed from the keyboard, is among the classics of the gramophone; it could still serve as a model of style in 1991, for it has radiant vitality, freshness and spirit and its 1937 sound is very good indeed. The first CD couples it with an almost equally magisterial account of the *D minor*, K.466, with the *C major Sonata* as a fill-up. Fischer's pre-war recording of K.482, with Barbirolli and the LPO, on the second CD is hardly less powerful, wonderfully paced, concentrated and alive, as is his *C minor*, K.491, with Lawrance Collingwood and the Barbirolli Chamber Orchestra. The last CD brings us a post-war account of the *C major*, K.503, with the Philharmonia under Josef Krips, not quite of the same stature as K.453 and K.482 but full of illuminating touches and fine musicianship. There is much for any Mozartian to learn throughout this set: Fischer plays his own cadenzas, an object lesson in themselves. Listening to these performances, one understands why this artist is so admired by later generations of Mozartians – pianists like Denis Matthews, Alfred Brendel and Murray Perahia. By comparison with the French LP transfer of K.453 some years back, the sound is a little dried-out but is still generally very good.

Piano concertos Nos. 17 in G, K.453; 21 in C, K.467.
(B) **(*) DG 429 522-2; *429 522-4* [id.]. Géza Anda, Camerata Academica of Salzburg Mozarteum.

In the *G major*, K.453, Anda, who is soloist and conductor, errs a little on the side of heaviness in style. But these Salzburg performances have both strength and poetry. Anda continues with a successful performance of K.467, notable for a beautifully poised orchestral introduction to the slow movement. One notices a certain rhythmic rigidity, and a lighter touch in the finale would have been acceptable; but on the whole this is a satisfying reading and the recording is excellent. There is plenty of life in the strings and a balancing orchestral richness; indeed this 1961 coupling wears its years lightly.

Piano concertos Nos. 17 in G, K.453; 27 in B flat, K.595.
(M) *** Tuxedo TUXCD 1027 [id.]. Alfred Brendel, V. State Op. O, Paul Angerer.

Brendel was an inspired Mozartian when he made his earlier Mozart recordings for the Vox Turnabout label at the end of the 1950s and beginning of the 1960s; these performances have a radiant freshness and spontaneity which he did not quite match in his later, Philips versions. The recording is on the thin side in the matter of violin timbre, although it has a good ambience, and at Brendel's entry one forgets this fault, for the piano is realistically recorded and very convincingly balanced in relation to the orchestra. Brendel is helped by a vivacious orchestral contribution in both works, with the strings neat, graceful and polished; the orchestra is given a very slightly more resonant image in K.595 than in K.453. Brendel's phrasing of the second subject of the first movement of the *G major* is a delight, and the *Andante*, too, is a constant source of pleasure, while both soloist and orchestra share in the high spirits of the finale. No. 27 is also very distinguished and can be spoken of in the same breath as Gilels's version. It is beautifully proportioned, the lyrical phrasing is most winning, with Brendel's sure feeling for nuance and tempo lighting up the *Andante* and the final Allegretto engagingly nimble.

Piano concertos Nos. 18 in B flat, K.456; 19 in F, K.459.
(M) *** EMI CDM7 69123-2 [id.]; *EG 769123-4*. Barenboim, ECO.

Barenboim's account of K.456 is among the most sparkling of his cycle, full of imaginative touches which have one chuckling with delight. K.459, with its *Figaro* overtones, prompts another remarkable performance, brisk in its march rhythms in the first movement, tender in the Susanna-like sweetness of the *Andante* and strong and resilient in the finale, with its great fugal tutti. Excellent sound.

Piano concertos Nos. 19–21; 24; 27; (i) *Double piano concerto in E flat, K.365. Piano sonatas Nos. 12 in F, K.332; 16 in B flat, K.570; Rondo in A min., K.511.*
(M) (***) EMI mono CHS7 63703-2 (3) [Ang. CDHC 63703]. Artur Schnabel; (i) with Karl Ulrich Schnabel; various orchestras & conductors.

Schnabel's Mozart is every bit as personal and impulsive as one would expect, more fiery and impetuous than Gieseking and less polished and poised. He occasionally thrusts ahead and makes much of the pre-echoes of Beethoven in the *C minor*, K.491, recorded with the Philharmonia under Walter Süsskind in 1948. His own cadenza, which serves to remind us that he was himself a composer, plunges us into an entirely different world which approaches Busoni in its wild harmonies and sudden modulations. His K.595 was much earlier (1934) and sounds extraordinarily good for the period, though allowances must be made for the very different style of string-playing of the LSO, with Barbirolli producing some period *portamenti*. The *Double concerto*, made with the LSO and Sir Adrian Boult at about the same time as the Bach *C major*, has plenty of sparkle and spontaneity. His K.467 (recorded with Sargent in 1937) also has a Schnabel cadenza which, though less celebrated than the one for the *C minor*, is engagingly out of period. There are great musical insights, particularly in the slow movement of K.595 and the *A minor Rondo*, K.511 (like the *F major Sonata*, a post-war recording). However, among the pianists of the time, if you find Gieseking too cool and well-bred and Schnabel too full of temperament, and you set greater store by sheer keyboard finesse and elegance, Edwin Fischer is a far better choice, for he brings to Mozart both the dedication and thoughtfulness of Schnabel and the perfect sense of style and mastery of colour of Gieseking.

Piano concertos Nos. 19 in F, K.459; 23 in A, K.488.
(M) *** DG 429 812-2; 429 812-4 [id.]. Pollini, VPO, Boehm.

Pollini is sparkling in the *F major*, and in the *A major* has a superbly poised, vibrant sense of line. Every phrase here seems to speak, and he is given excellent support from Boehm and the Vienna orchestra. Good, well-detailed and finely balanced analogue recording, which has transferred very freshly to CD, make this one of the finest Mozart concerto records DG have given us. Excellent value, and it is now offered at mid-price.

Piano concertos Nos. (i) *19 in F, K.459;* (ii) *27 in B flat, K.595.*
(M) (**) DG mono 431 872-2 [id.]. Clara Haskil, (i) BPO; (ii) Bav. State O; Fricsay.

Clara Haskil's recording of the *F major Concerto*, K.459, with Fricsay was made in Berlin in 1955 and the *B flat*, K.595, in the excellent acoustic of the Herkules-Saal, Munich, in 1957. Not much time was to pass before both artists died and this is a valuable record of their collaboration. Technically the recordings are very respectable, though the balance places the solo instrument rather more forward than is ideal. They are humane, unhurried and civilized performances, and the only criticism of note concerns the slow movement of K.595 where, in their determination to avoid too valedictory a feeling, they adopt a rather faster tempo than usual and the resulting effect is curiously bland. (They are, for example, twice as fast in this movement as Serkin and Ormandy.) However, admirers of Haskil's beautifully singing, lyrical playing need not hesitate. She was a stylist, as was Fricsay, and the inevitable limitations of the mono sound are soon forgotten.

Piano concerto No. 20 in D min., K.466.
(M) ** EMI CDD7 63892-2 [id.]; *ET 763892-4.* Yuri Egorov, Philh. O, Sawallisch – BEETHOVEN: *Piano concerto No. 5.* **(*)

A generous coupling for an imaginative if slightly controversial account of the *Emperor concerto*. The Mozart performance, though well played, is less distinctive, even though Egorov is stylish and Sawallisch finds plenty of drama in the outer movements and begins the finale, the most striking of the three, with great energy and bustle. Good, bright, 1985 EMI digital recording, made at Abbey Road.

(i; iii) *Piano concerto No. 20 in D min., K.466;* (iii) *3 German dances, K.605; Overtures: La clemenza di Tito; La finta giardiniera; Le nozze di Figaro; Serenade No. 13 (Eine kleine Nachtmusik), K.525; Symphonies Nos. 38 in D (Prague);* (iv) *39 in E flat, K.453;* (iii) *41 in C, K.551 (Jupiter);* (ii; iii) *Requiem Mass, K.626.*
(M) (**) EMI mono CHS7 63912-2 (3) [id.]. (i) Bruno Walter (piano); (ii) Schumann, Thorborg, Dermota, Kipnis, V. State Op. Ch.; (iii) VPO; (iv) BBC SO; all cond. Walter.

Bruno Walter had originally planned to become a pianist but a visit to Bayreuth in 1891 prompted him to change course. He remained a good accompanist and continued to direct Mozart concertos from the keyboard. To judge from his 1938 recording (it sounds earlier) of the *D minor Concerto*, K.466, he was no match for Edwin Fischer: his rhythmic control is far from flawless and his playing lacks the very last ounce of finish. All the same, there is the familiar humanity and warmth, which are much in evidence in the other performances. He and Koussevitzky were among the first guests whom Boult invited to conduct his newly formed BBC Symphony Orchestra, and the 1934 account of the *E flat Symphony* has great sparkle and freshness. The *Requiem* was recorded in 1937 at the Théâtre des Champs Elysées, Paris, with a distinguished team of soloists, but Walter never approved its release (there were minor blemishes of the kind one encounters in a concert) and it did not appear until a 1986 LP. For all their sonic frailty, these performances are rewarding and well worth having.

Piano concertos Nos. 20 in D min., K.466; 21 in C, K.467.
(M) *** BMG/RCA GD 87967 [7967-2-RG]. Rubinstein, RCA Victor SO, Wallenstein (with HAYDN: *Andante & variations in F min.* ***).
(BB) **(*) Naxos Dig. 8.550434 [id.]. Jenö Jandó, Concentus Hungaricus, András Ligeti.
(M) **(*) DG 429 811-2; *429 811-4* [id.]. Friedrich Gulda, VPO, Abbado.
(M) *(*) DG 431 278-2; *431 278-4* [id.]. Rudolf Serkin, LSO, Abbado.

(i) *Piano concertos Nos. 20 in D min., K.466; 21 in C, K.467;* (ii) *Don Giovanni: overture.*
(BB) ** BMG/RCA VD 60484; *VK 60484.* (i) Géza Anda, VSO; (ii) Chicago SO, Reiner.

Rubinstein has seldom been caught so sympathetically by the microphones, and the remastered 1961 recording has the orchestral sound admirably freshened. In each concerto the slow movement is the kernel of the interpretation. Rubinstein's playing is melting, and in the famous *Andante* of K.467 the silky smoothness of the string theme catches the intensity of the pianist's inspiration. The opening of the first movement of K.466, taken fairly briskly, is full of implied drama. Altogether Wallenstein is an excellent accompanist, for finales have plenty of sparkle. The Haydn *Andante and variations*, a substantial bonus recorded a year earlier, again demonstrates Rubinstein's aristocratic feeling for a classical melodic line: it is played most beautifully.

At super-bargain price Jenö Jandó's disc with the Concentus Hungaricus and András Ligeti can be recommended, if with certain reservations. The depth in the slow movement of the *D minor*, K.466, eludes him and he rushes the finale – but then, so did Barenboim. In the *C major Concerto*, K.467, he is eminently vital and spirited. This is a straightforward and unfussy performance, though it would be a mistake to stake too strong a claim for it (he is not as searching or poetic a player as, say, Casadesus). This will certainly reward the modest outlay involved and provide a good deal of pleasure. The recording is excellent, well detailed, warm and fresh, and the orchestral playing first class. Not an unqualified three-star recommendation but an enjoyable disc.

With Gulda the piano tone is crisp and clear, with just a hint of the character of a fortepiano about it, and admirably suited to these readings, which have an element of classical restraint yet at the same time are committed and do not lack warmth. Abbado's accompaniment shows him to be a first-class Mozartian, and the orchestral wind-playing is delightful. The recording (from 1975) now has added clarity and the bass is firmer; there is little loss of ambient bloom, but the upper string timbre has been slightly thinned out. This is good value at mid-price, but Rubinstein is even more distinctive.

The RCA recordings were made in 1973 after Géza Anda's complete cycle for DG. The two performances offered here do not add greatly to what has been said before, although K.466 is strikingly dramatic, rather more individual than K.467. Excellent recording. Reiner's fizzing 1959 account of the *Don Giovanni overture* makes an enjoyable encore, with splendid Chicago sound.

It is sad that Serkin had to leave it until his eighties to attempt a full series of the Mozart concertos. Though his thoughtfulness as an artist is often clear, his passage-work in these performances is scrappy and, though there are flashes of authority, the ends of phrases are not beautifully turned. Refined accompaniments from Abbado and the LSO, but even there the styles clash. There are stronger and more sensitive accounts of both concertos, though few that are better recorded, even to the point of including the soloist's vocal additions.

Piano concertos Nos. 20–21; 26 in D (Coronation), K. 537 (CD only: *27 in B flat, K.595*).
(B) ** DG Compact Classics 413 427-2 (2); *(*) *413 427-4* [id.]. Géza Anda, Salzburg Mozarteum O.

Anda's versions from the early 1960s are reasonably competitive in Compact Classics format. The recording sometimes sounds a little dated now in the matter of string timbre, but the piano is clearly focused and truthful. *No. 20 in D minor* is one of Anda's stronger performances, with solo playing that is both stylish and spontaneous; No. 21 is notable for its poised introduction to the famous slow movement. One notices a certain rhythmic rigidity, and a lighter touch in the finale would have been acceptable, but on the whole this is satisfying. The *Coronation concerto*, however, is disappointing. Anda's reading lacks the magisterial quality of the finest accounts and there is a slightly routine feeling about the accompaniment. The balance is restored, however, on the pair of CDs, by the addition of Mozart's last concerto. Anda's performance of K.595 is one of the finest available. His playing is authoritative, deft and lively, and the recording is clear and fresh to match the music-making.

Piano concertos Nos. 20 in D min., K.466; 23 in A, K.488.
(B) **(*) Ph. 422 466-2; *422 466-4*. Kovacevich, LSO, C. Davis.
(M) **(*) Ph. Dig. 432 049-2; *432 049-4*. Mitsuko Uchida, ECO, Jeffrey Tate.

If the coupling of the *D minor* and the *A major* from Kovacevich and Davis lacks some of the magic of their earlier pairing of the two *C major Concertos*, it is largely that the playing of the LSO is less polished. Nevertheless the minor-key seriousness of the outer movements of K.466 and the F sharp minor *Adagio* of K.488 come out superbly. It is a token of the pianist's command that, without any expressive exaggeration, the K.488 slow movement conveys such depth and intensity. The recording is full and clear in its new format.

Although Uchida's superbly recorded disc represents excellent value at mid-price and both performances are beautifully played, there is a sense of reserve about the reading of K.466 which loses some of its dramatic cohesion. About the *A major Concerto*, K.488, there can be no reservations: Uchida's gentle manner never becomes self-effacing and her restrained, lyrical feeling is very affecting when the the contribution of the ECO under Tate has a matching sensibility. The only snag is the lack of any information about the music itself.

(i) *Piano concertos Nos. 20; 23–25*; (ii) *Piano and wind quintet, K.452.*
(M) (***) EMI mono CHS7 63709-2 (2). Walter Gieseking, with (i) Philh. O, Karajan or Rosbaud; (ii) Philh. Wind Qt.

There is some very distinguished playing here, far more memorable and characterful than the set of complete solo keyboard music on which Gieseking embarked immediately after these recordings. The *D minor* and *C major Concertos* (K.466 and K.503) were recorded in 1953 under Hans Rosbaud, and their appearance serves as a timely reminder of what a fine conductor he was. In the *D minor* Gieseking plays the Beethoven cadenzas and in the *C major* his own. The *A major*, K.488, and *C minor*, K.491 (in which he plays the Hummel cadenza), were made with Karajan at much the same time. The *A major* unfolds in a wonderfully serene and spacious fashion, and the Philharmonia wind are in superb form. Gieseking's celebrated record of the *Piano and wind quintet* with the Philharmonia Wind Quartet, all glorious players (Sidney Sutcliffe, Bernard Walton, the legendary Dennis Brain and Cecil James), was made in 1955 and has enjoyed classic status ever since, despite the rather unexpansive acoustic. The electrical hum in K.448 and K.503, for which the sleeve apologizes, is not a real problem and should not deter Gieseking aficionados or even the non-specialist collector, for the transfers are very well managed indeed.

Piano concertos Nos. (i) *20 in D min., K.466;* (ii) *24 in C min., K.491.*
(M) **(*) Decca 417 726-2 [id.]. Vladimir Ashkenazy, (i) LSO, Schmidt-Isserstedt; (ii) Philh. O.

Piano concertos Nos. 20 in D min., K.466; 24 in C min., K.491; Concert rondo No. 1 in D, K.382.
(M) *** Ph. 420 867-2; *420 867-4.* Alfred Brendel, ASMF, Marriner.

The two minor-key *Concertos* are superbly played and the analogue recording is of Philips's best. Perhaps the last ounce of tragic intensity is missing but, at mid-price and with the *D major Rondo* now included, there is nothing to inhibit a three-star recommendation.

The mid-priced Decca reissue recouples recordings from 1968 and 1979. They sound quite different: the *D minor* very immediate and fresh; the *C minor*, more distantly balanced, with sound natural but more diffuse. The former is conducted by Hans Schmidt-Isserstedt; it is a performance of some personality although perhaps a little too regulated in emotional temperature (the *Romance* is rather precise), yet it has no want of vividness and life. Ashkenazy directs the orchestra himself in the *C minor*; his is a balanced view of the first movement: he avoids investing it with excessive intensity yet never loses impact. He is equally impressive in the slow movement and finale.

Piano concertos Nos. (i) *20 in D min., K.466;* (ii) *27 in B flat, K.595.*
(M) **(*) Sony MYK 42533 [id.]. Rudolf Serkin, (i) Columbia SO, Szell; (ii) Phd. O, Ormandy.

Both of Serkin's performances come from the early 1960s and, although the piano tone sounds a bit shallow, there is nothing shallow about the playing in either concerto. Szell was much (and rightly) admired as a Mozartian, but it is Ormandy, much underrated in this repertoire, who proves an even more sensitive and attentive partner. In the slow movement of the *D minor Concerto*, K.466, Serkin in his anxiety to avoid sentimentality adopts a very flowing tempo, which some may find a shade too fast. Elsewhere, pace is expertly judged, and in the *B flat Concerto* both artists have the measure of the depths of the slow movement and the sparkle of the finale. This is obviously big-band Mozart but sensitively and intelligently handled. Though the quality of the recording leaves something to be desired, it is far from unacceptable.

Piano concerto No. 21 in C, K.467.
(M) (*(**)) EMI mono CDH7 69792-2. Dinu Lipatti, Lucerne Festival O, Karajan – SCHUMANN: *Concerto.* (***)

Lipatti's performance derives from a broadcast from the 1950 Lucerne Festival and there is some discoloration and, at climaxes, distortion. However, nothing can detract from the distinction of Lipatti's playing or its immaculate control. This obviously occupies a rather special place in the catalogue and will be wanted by all admirers of this great artist.

(i) *Piano concerto No. 21 in C, K.467;* (ii) *Violin concerto No. 5 in A (Turkish), K.219.*
(BB) * Naxos Dig. 8.550293 [id.]. Capella Istropolitana, with (i) Peter Lang; (ii) Nishizaki; (i) Erberlee; (ii) Gunzenhauser.

There is nothing at all special about this performance of the *C major Piano concerto.* The first movement is somewhat square and the finale very fast, and even the famous *Romanza* is not particularly enticing. Takako Nishizaki's performance of the *Fifth Violin concerto* is a different matter, but this is also available coupled with No. 3, a splendid disc – see below.

Piano concertos Nos. (i) *21 in C, K.467;* (ii) *22 in E flat, K.482; 23 in A, K.488;* (i) *24 in C min., K.491;* (ii) *26 in D (Coronation), K.537; 27 in B, K.595;* (iii) *Double piano concerto in E flat, K.365.*
❀ (M) **(*) Sony SM3K 46519 (3) [id.]. Robert Casadesus, with (i) Cleveland O, Szell; (ii) Columbia SO, Szell; (iii) Gaby Casadesus, Phd. O, Ormandy.

A very distinguished set, effectively transferred to CD. Casadesus's Mozart may at first seem understated, but the imagination behind his readings is apparent in every phrase and the accompaniment could hardly be more stylish. Casadesus takes the finale of No. 21 at a tremendous speed, but for the most part this is exquisite Mozart playing, beautifully paced and articulated. While not scaling the heights of Casadesus's earlier accounts with Bigot and Münch, the present versions with the Cleveland Orchestra still sound pretty marvellous, for all the shortcomings of the recording balance and the sometimes over-tense precision of Szell. In fact the balance is better than we had remembered it. Although the orchestra tends to dwarf the soloist in tuttis, the placing of the piano is very pleasing, and the subtleties of the solo playing are naturally caught. In No. 22, Casadesus is second to none: he has space and proportion on the one hand and a marvellously alive sense of detail and phrasing on the other. He is first rate in the *A major* too, accompanied in this and No. 22 by Szell again but this time with the Columbia Symphony Orchestra. Mozart's last piano concertos inspire two extremely memorable performances, each of them underlining the dramatic contrast of soloist and orchestra, almost as a meeting of heroine and hero. The *Double concerto* is essentially a genial work, and this is the one quality completely missing from Casadesus's performance, which has a matching dry recording. All the solo concertos, however, were recorded in Severance Hall, Cleveland, between 1959 and 1962 (except for No. 23, which dates from 1969) and the hall ambience provides an attractive fullness to the overall sound.

Piano concertos Nos. 21 in C, K.467; 24 in C min., K.491.
(B) *** Sony MYK 42594 [MYK 38523]. Robert Casadesus, Cleveland O, Szell.
(B) *** Pickwick Dig. PCD 832; *CIMPC 832* [id.]. Howard Shelley, City of L. Sinfonia.

Casadesus is on top form: he plays most delectably in the first movement of K.467 and its ravishing central *Andante* has seldom sounded so magical. He takes the finale at a tremendous speed but brings it off; and both here and in the coupled K.491 (where, unusually, he chooses a cadenza by Saint-Saëns) this is exquisite Mozart playing, beautifully paced and articulated. Szell's precision gives a special character to the accompaniments. He is not as flexible as Davis is for Kovacevich, but the orchestral playing is superbly crisp. The 1965 recording sounds remarkably fresh and full, and this disc should belong in any Mozartian's library.

Howard Shelley gives delightfully fresh and characterful readings of both the popular *C major* and the great *C minor* concertos, bringing out their strength and purposefulness as well as their poetry, never overblown or sentimental. His Pickwick disc makes an outstanding digital bargain, with accompaniment very well played and recorded.

Piano concertos Nos. 21 in C, K.467; 25 in C, K.503.
❀ (B) *** Ph. 426 077-2; *426 077-4*. Kovacevich, LSO, C. Davis.

Piano concertos Nos. 21 in C, K.467; 25 in C, K.503; Adagio in B min., K.540.
(BB) ** Virgin/Virgo Dig. VJ7 91459-2; *VJ7 91459-4* [id.]. Diana Ambache, Ambache CO.

This is among the most searching and satisfying records of Mozart piano concertos available. The partnership of Kovacevich and Davis almost invariably produces inspired music-making, and here their equal dedication to Mozart, their balancing of strength and charm, drama and tenderness, make for performances which retain their sense of spontaneity but which plainly result from deep thought. Never has the famous slow movement of K.467 sounded more ethereally beautiful on record than here, with superb LSO string-tone, and the weight of both these great C major works is formidably conveyed. The 1972 recording is well balanced and refined; though the CD transfer has brightened the violins, there is plenty of supporting body and depth to the sound-picture, and the piano image is particularly appealing and cleanly focused.

As an added attraction on the Virgo issue there is a supplement in the lovely *B minor Adagio* for solo piano. Diana Ambache is a stylish Mozartian, imaginative and spontaneous-sounding, consistently playing with clean attack and crisp, light articulation. Tuttis do not always sound quite immediate enough, with thin violin tone, and ensemble is not always flawless, but such a movement as the finale of K.503 comes over with wit and point. However, while the outstanding Kovacevich/Philips CD coupling of these same two concertos remains available, this Virgo disc must be very much a second choice.

Piano concertos Nos. 21 in C, K.467; 27 in B flat, K.595.
(BB) ** HM/BMG VD 77564; *VK 77564* [77564-2-RV; *77564-4-RV*]. Jörg Demus (fortepiano), Coll. Aur.

Jörg Demus recorded the *C major Concerto* in 1975 and the *B flat*, K.595, six years earlier. The latter offers the warmer recorded sound and, though the Collegeum Aureum play on period instruments, they do so at modern pitch. In the *C major* Demus plays a Grober, an instrument-maker from Innsbruck, of about 1800, though this is not stated on the sleeve – which comes, as do others in this series, without presentation. In the past the Collegeum

Aureum have suffered from the suggestion emanating from the original instruments lobby that, if their sonority was euphonious and musical, it could not really be 'authentic', and there is nothing here to displease ears brought up on modern instruments. On the other hand, there are no special insights either. Demus is an excellent player, but neither in technical finesse nor in musical imagination is he the equal of a Malcolm Bilson. This is far from routine but less than distinguished.

Piano concerto No. 22 in E flat, K.482.
(M) ** EMI CDM7 69013-2 [id.]. Sviatoslav Richter, Philh. O, Muti – BEETHOVEN: *Concerto No. 3.* **

Richter's 1983 recording is clearly looking forward towards Beethoven, particularly in the slow movement. He plays with all the poise and authority one would expect, and there are numerous felicities. He uses cadenzas by Benjamin Britten. Muti draws lively and sympathetic support from the Philharmonia – though, following Richter's example, the finale is weighty, if not without rhythmic bounce. Good remastered sound.

Piano concertos Nos. 22 in E flat, K.482; 23 in A, K.488.
(M) **(*) EMI CDM7 69122-2 [id.]; *EG 769122-4.* Barenboim, ECO.

Barenboim gives a persuasive, at times even wilful account of K.482, relishing its expansiveness with dozens of spontaneous-sounding inflexions. The account of K.488 is enchanting. There are moments when his delicacy of fingerwork comes close to preciosity, but it never quite goes over the edge. Indeed his playing has all the sparkle and sensitivity one could ask for, and the orchestral accompaniment is admirably alive. One's only reservation concerns the somewhat fast tempo he adopts in the finale. Good remastered sound, firm, full and clear.

Piano concertos Nos. 22 in E flat, K.482; 25 in C, K.503.
(M) *** Tuxedo TUXCD 1046. Alfred Brendel, VCO or V. State Op. O, Paul Angerer.
(M) *(*) DG Dig. 429 978-2; *429 978-4* [id.]. Rudolf Serkin, LSO, Abbado.

Another unforgettable early Brendel coupling, recorded in 1958 but with the sound very respectable in its CD transfer. The string-tone remains thin, but the *E flat Concerto* is better focused than on LP and the excellent wind playing is well caught. Brendel plays the first movement of K.482 with authority, the *Andante* variations very beautifully and the finale enchantingly. Paul Angerer brings plenty of character and imagination to the accompaniments and is especially good in shaping the more serious *Andantino cantabile* episode which is Mozart's surprise in the otherwise sprightly finale. No. 25 shows Brendel at his most commanding, and Angerer sets the scene admirably with an imposing opening, even if the recording focus is less clean in this work. Again the solo phrasing is eminently stylish, with the secondary lyrical theme of the first movement giving much pleasure, the *Andante* classically serene and the finale given the lightest touch.

Serkin made some distinguished Mozart concerto records way back in the days of shellac; some of his later recordings for CBS with Szell and Ormandy are also now reappearing on Sony. At the beginning of the 1980s he embarked on a new cycle as the eightieth year of his own life was fast approaching. Unfortunately he is now no match for the current competition, and no one listening to these versions would imagine that this was the same Serkin whose playing so captivated listeners to the old Busch Chamber Players' account of the *Brandenburg No. 5.* That sparkled with delight; this is hard work, with only the occasional glimmer of past glories.

Piano concertos Nos. 23 in A, K.488; 24 in C min., K.491.
❀ (M) *** DG 423 885-2 [id.]. Kempff, Bamberg SO, Leitner.
(B) *** Decca 430 497-2; *430 497-4.* Clifford Curzon, LSO, Kertész (with SCHUBERT: *Impromptus: in G flat & A flat, D.899/3 & 4* ***).
(B) **(*) CfP CD-CFP 4511; *TC-CFP 4511.* Ian Hobson, ECO, Sir Alexander Gibson.
(BB) **(*) Naxos Dig. 8.550204 [id.]. Jenö Jandó, Concentus Hungaricus, Mátyás Antal.
(M) *(*) DG Dig. 431 279-2; *431 279-4* [id.]. Rudolf Serkin, LSO, Abbado.

(i) *Piano concertos Nos. 23 in A, K.488;* (ii) *24 in C min., K.491; Rondo in A, K.511.*
(M) *** BMG/RCA GD 87968 [7968-2-RG]. Rubinstein, RCA Victor SO, (i) Alfred Wallenstein; (ii) Josef Krips.

Kempff's outstanding performances of these concertos are uniquely poetic and inspired, and Leitner's accompaniments are comparably distinguished. The 1960 recording still sounds well, and this is strongly recommended at mid-price.

Rubinstein brings characteristic finesse and beauty of phrasing to his coupling of two of Mozart's finest concertos. K.488 is especially beautiful, with Wallenstein providing a most sympathetic accompaniment. In K.491 the crystal-clear articulation is allied to the aristocratic feeling characteristic of vintage Rubinstein: the slow movement is memorable in its poise. Krips's accompaniment, like the solo part, is smoothly cultured and acts as a foil to the tragic tone of this great and wonderfully balanced work. The recordings, from 1958 and 1961 respectively, sound fresh and full, although in K.488 the violin timbre is rather bright. The *Rondo*, recorded in 1959, is equally distinguished – much more than just an encore.

Curzon's account of these two concertos is immaculate; no connoisseur of the piano will fail to derive pleasure and refreshment from them. Curzon has the advantage of sensitive support both from Kertész and from the Decca engineers and the remastering has added life and vividness to the music-making. The sound is fuller than on the Kempff disc, and the slow movement of K.488 is full of colour. Two of the Schubert Op. 90 *Impromptus*, added as an attractive fill-up, are undoubtedly distinguished and add to the attractiveness of this reissue.

Ian Hobson, winner of the fourth prize in the 1978 Leeds Piano Competition who then came back to win that international event three years later, is generally associated with virtuoso piano music, but here shows himself a stylish Mozartian, if a somewhat reticent one. These are clean, generally refreshing performances, remarkably free of mannerism and lacking only the last degree of individuality. Speeds are unexceptionable, the accompaniment admirable and the sound first rate, making this an excellent bargain, clear and vivid. Hobson contributes his own tasteful cadenza for the first movement of K.491.

Antal's tempo in the first movement of the well-loved *A major Concerto* is bracingly brisk. The effect is undoubtedly fresh, but some ears may find the music could do with a touch more relaxation. This certainly comes in the *Adagio*, which has a simple melancholic nostalgia, and the energy returns appropriately in the vivacious closing *Allegro assai*. The operatic drama inherent in the first movement in the *C minor Concerto* is brought out well, and Jandó imaginatively and effectively chooses a cadenza by Hummel for this movement. Then, after the refined sensibility of the *Larghetto*, the finale is quite admirably paced. Recording is well up to the standard of the series.

Serkin's performances are for aficionados only. His playing is short on finish and elegance, nor is this offset on the balance sheet by the interpretative insights that distinguished his pre-war Mozart records. Well recorded as it is, the playing is just too unmelting to convey pleasure in K.588, and is insufficiently searching in the great *C minor*.

Piano concertos Nos. 23 in A, K.488; 26 in D (Coronation), K.537.
(M) *** Sony MPK 45884 [id.]. Casadesus, Cleveland O, Szell.

Here is a coupling to match that by these artists of Nos. 21 and 24. K.537 inspires Casadesus and Szell to a really outstanding performance. Casadesus is marvellous in No. 23, too; though neither Kempff nor Pollini is displaced, this disc is the pick of the three records included in the box discussed above. Szell's accompaniments could hardly be more stylish. The transfers to CD are excellently managed; the sound has good ambience and fullness. This is a splendid disc.

Piano concertos Nos. 23 in A, K.488; 27 in B flat, K.595.
(M) *** Ph. 420 487-2; *420 487-4* [id.]. Alfred Brendel, ASMF, Marriner.

On Philips, two of the best of Brendel's Mozart concertos. Both performances come from the early 1970s and sound wonderfully fresh in these digitally refurbished transfers. But allegiance to Gilels in K.595 remains strong.

Piano concerto No. 25 in C, K.503.
(M) *** Sony MYK 44832 [MYK 37762]. Leon Fleisher, Cleveland O, Szell – BEETHOVEN: *Piano concerto No. 4.* ***

Fleisher and Szell achieve a memorable partnership in this 1959 recording. The kernel of the performance is the beautiful slow movement, classically serene; Szell's accompaniment matches the soloist in poise, and the music is given a Beethovenian depth. The commanding outer movements have great vitality: Fleisher shapes the first movement's second subject most engagingly and is wonderfully nimble in the finale, while Szell's orchestral detail is a constant source of pleasure. The coupling is equally outstanding, and the recording emerges freshly on CD.

Piano concertos Nos. 25 in C, K.503; 27 in B flat, K.595.
(M) *(*) DG Dig. 431 280-2; *431 280-4* [id.]. Rudolf Serkin, LSO, Abbado.

If Rudolf Serkin's present Mozart was as good as the pre-war vintage – or, for that matter, as some of the recordings he made at Marlboro in the 1960s – this would be a most valuable recoupling. There is much to admire, including a clear, well-focused recording and refined accompaniments from Abbado – the opening of K.595 is measured and spacious – with an excellent response from the LSO. But even there Serkin is wanting in the grace he once commanded: the insights this distinguished Mozartian brings to these concertos do not compensate for the ungainly passage-work and other infelicities. His vocal melisma is also slightly distracting.

Piano concertos Nos. (i) *26 in D (Coronation), K.537;* (ii) *27 in B flat, K.595.*
(M) *** DG 429 810-2; *429 810-4* [id.]. (i) Vásáry, BPO; (ii) Gilels, VPO, Boehm.

Tamás Vásáry is a fine Mozartian with exemplary taste and judgement, and his account of the *Coronation concerto* has grandeur as well as vitality. The quality of the 1974 sound is very good in this transfer. Gilels's account of K.595 is in a class of its own, and those who do not require his coupling with the *Double piano concerto*, K.365 – see below – will find this a worthwhile alternative, although Vásáry's K.543 does not sparkle quite as brightly as the performances of his finest rivals.

Piano concerto No. 27 in B flat, K.595; (i) *Double piano concerto in E flat, K.365.*
❀ (M) *** DG 419 059-2; *419 059-4* [id.]. Emil Gilels, VPO, Boehm, (i) with Elena Gilels.

Gilels's is supremely lyrical playing that evinces all the classical virtues. No detail is allowed to detract from the picture as a whole; the pace is totally unhurried and superbly controlled. All the points are made by means of articulation and tone, and each phrase is marvellously alive. This is playing of the highest order of artistic integrity and poetic insight, while Boehm and the Vienna Philharmonic provide excellent support. The performance of the marvellous *Double concerto* is no less enjoyable. Its mood is comparatively serious, but this is not to suggest that the music's sunny qualities are not brought out; the interplay of phrasing between the two soloists is beautifully conveyed by the recording without exaggerated separation. The quality on CD is first class, refining detail yet not losing ambient warmth.

Double piano concerto in E flat, K.365; (i) *Triple piano concerto in F (Lodron), K.242.*
(M) **(*) EMI Dig. CD-EMX 2124; *TC-EMX 2124*. Eschenbach, Frantz; (i) Helmut Schmidt; LPO, Eschenbach.

Eschenbach's 1981 version of the *Double concerto* which he directs from the keyboard is the only one to include the clarinets, trumpets and timpani published in the orchestral material by Breitkopf & Härtel in 1881. These instruments were added for the Vienna performance of 1781, but there is some doubt as to their authenticity. Both Eschenbach and Frantz are lively and persuasive in the concerto, though comparison with the Gilels version on DG, coupled with K.595, is not to their advantage: that is a glorious record. In the *Triple concerto* the third pianist is Helmut Schmidt, at the time of the recording Chancellor of West Germany, who makes a creditable showing. The digital recording is very good indeed in both formats, but the coupling does not displace Gilels in K.365.

(i) *Double piano concerto in E flat, K.365. Double piano sonata in D, K.448; Fugue for 2 pianos in C min., K.426.*
❀ (M) *** Tuxedo TUXCD 1028 [id.]. Alfred Brendel, Walter Klien; (i) Vienna State Op. O, Paul Angerer.

Like Brendel, Walter Klien is a very distinguished Mozartian, having also made a splendid complete set of the *Piano sonatas* for Vox (see below). Their version of the *Double concerto* is second to none, not even that by the Gilels duo; if they do not have the advantage of the VPO, Angerer still provides admirable support, and the mood here is sunnier, and no less authoritative, than the DG version. The stereo places the pianos very positively to the left and the right, and the separation, while not exaggerated, is more positive than it would be in the concert hall. But the interplay between the two artists is a continuous delight, with Klien responding to Brendel in the most engaging way and the rapport between them one of equals. The lightness of bass in the recording of the orchestra (though the piano timbre has plenty of sonority) means that the left-hand side of the spectrum is slightly stronger than the right, but the effect remains very convincing. The couplings are an equal success, again displaying these artists' joy in Mozart's genial and skilful antiphonal writing.

Violin concertos

Violin concertos Nos. 1–7; Adagio, K.261; Rondos Nos. 1–2, K.269 & K.373 (all for violin and orchestra).
(BB) *** BMG/Eurodisc VD 69255 (3) [69255-2-RG]. Josef Suk, Prague Chamber O, Libor Hlaváček.
(B) ** Pickwick Dig. PCD 946, *CIMPC 946* (*Concertos Nos. 1, 3 & 7*); PCD 947, *CIMPC 947* (*Concertos Nos. 4 & 6; Rondos*); PCD 948, *CIMPC 948* (*Concertos Nos. 2 & 5; Adagio*). Ernst Kovacic, SCO.

Josef Suk's recordings date from 1972. He includes Nos. 6 and 7 which are almost certainly spurious (although some authorities suggest that No. 7 is largely the work of Mozart). Yet if these works are accepted by the listener simply as late-eighteenth-century concertos of better-than-average quality, they can be enjoyed for their own sake. Suk makes a good case for them and throughout the set his performances are highly distinguished. The solo playing has character, warmth and humanity, and its unaffected manner is especially suited to the first two concertos: No. 1 is as fine as any in the catalogue. That is not to say that the other works are any less appealing, though he plays Henri Marteau's cadenza in No. 3, which will not be to all tastes. The Prague Chamber Orchestra has less personality and impact, and at times the players are not ideally relaxed and unforced in their response to their soloist; Hlaváček does not always make enough of the dynamic contrasts and, throughout, this music-making is dominated by Suk. This is partly a matter of the recording balance, with the orchestra set back in a warm acoustic. The digital remastering increases the feeling of the soloist's presence and adds a brighter lighting to his timbre, particularly noticeable at the opening of No. 4. But with any reservations noted, these are delightful performances; and admirers of Suk, among whom we are numbered, should in no way be disappointed by this box, which is extremely competitively priced (even if it includes no notes about the music).

In full and vivid sound Kovacic's fresh and alert performances (available separately) provide a fair recommendation for Mozart's violin concertante music. Generally urgent and direct, they lack something in individuality and Mozartian sparkle. That they remain rather straight-faced, with rhythms at times a little square, probably reflects the absence of conductor.

Complete Mozart Edition, Volume 8: (i) *Violin concertos Nos 1–5; 7 in D, K.271; Adagio in E, K.361; Rondo in B flat, K.269; Rondo in C, K.373.* (i; ii) *Concertone, K.190;* (iii; iv) *Double Concerto in D for violin, piano and orchestra, K.315f;* (iii; v; vi) *Sinfonia concertante in A, for violin, viola, cello and orchestra, K.320e.* (iii; v) *Sinfonia concertante in E flat, K.364.*

(M) **(*) Ph. Analogue/Dig. 422 508-2 (4). (i) Szeryng, (ii) with Poulet, Morgan, Jones; New Philh. O, Gibson; (iii) Iona Brown, with (iv) Shelley; (v) Imai; (vi) Orton; ASMF, Marriner.

Volume 8 in the Philips Complete Mozart Edition is even more interesting than most, when it contains very convincing reconstructions of works that Mozart left as fragments. Philip Wilby has not only completed the first movement of an early *Sinfonia concertante for violin, viola and cello* (Mozart's only music with concertante cello) but also, through shrewd detective work, has reconstructed a full three-movement *Double concerto* from what Mozart left as 'a magnificent torso', to use Alfred Einstein's description; it is for violin, piano and orchestra, and Wilby's premiss is that – for reasons which he gives in fair detail – the *Violin sonata in D*, K.306, was in fact a reworking of the *Double concerto* which Mozart said he was writing in 1778 and which he could well have completed. The result here is a delight, a full-scale 25-minute work which ends with an effervescent double-variation finale, alternately in duple and compound time. That is superbly done with Iona Brown and Howard Shelley as soloists; and the other ASMF items are very good too, with Iona Brown joined by Nobuko Imai most characterfully on the viola in the great *Sinfonia concertante*, K.364. What is a shade disappointing – even in a well-filled set at mid-price – is to have Henryk Szeryng's readings of the main violin concertos from the 1960s, instead of the Grumiaux set. Szeryng is sympathetic but a trifle reserved and not as refreshing as Grumiaux.

(i) *Violin concertos Nos. 1 in B flat, K.207;* (ii) *2 in D, K. 211;* (iii) *3 in C, K.216;* (ii) *4 in D, K.218;* (i) *5 in A (Turkish), K.219;* (ii) *Adagio in C, K.261; Rondo No. 2 in C, K.373; Haffner Serenade, K.250: Rondo* (all for violin & orchestra); (iv) *Sinfonia concertante in E flat, K.364;* (v) *Divertimento in E flat for string trio (violin, viola & cello), K.563.*

(M) **(*) Sony SM3K 46523 [id.]. Isaac Stern, with (i) Columbia SO, Szell; (ii) ECO, Schneider; (iii) Cleveland O, Szell; (iv) Zukerman, ECO, Barenboim; (v) Pinchas Zukerman, Leonard Rose.

Unlike most sets of the Mozart *Violin concertos*, Stern's recordings were made at different times and with different conductors, with somewhat variable results. It goes without saying that the solo playing is always splendid; it is simply that he is not always as sensitive on detail as his rivals, and this especially applies to No. 1 and rather less so to No. 5 where the accompaniment is provided by the Columbia Symphony Orchestra under Szell. The interpretation of No. 3, however, displays Stern's qualities of sparkling stylishness at their most intense in a very satisfying reading, with a beautifully poised and pointed accompaniment from the same conductor but now with the splendid Cleveland Orchestra. Here the beauty of Stern's contribution easily triumphs over the comparatively undistinguished sound. In Nos. 2 and 4, Stern has the benefit of rather fuller recording and his playing, as always, is full of personality. Stern recorded the great *Sinfonia concertante* for CBS at least twice before this version, which stands among the finest available and is certainly the jewel in this set, presenting as it does two soloists of equally strong musical personality. The central slow movement is taken at a very expansive *Andante* but the concentration intensifies the beauty, and the finale is sparkling and resilient – more so than on Stern's previous version which he conducted himself. Fair, if somewhat aggressive recording, with the two soloists too closely balanced. The trio of famous virtuosi, Stern, Zuckerman and Rose, brings an individually characterized performance of the *Divertimento for string trio* with hushed playing accurately conveyed and the players clearly separated within an atmospheric acoustic, even though the recording is rather close and bright. Besides the *Adagio*, K.261, beautifully played, and the *Rondo*, K.373, Stern also offers the fourth-movement *Rondo* of the *Haffner Serenade*, which has a fizzing concertante violin part.

Violin concertos Nos. 1–5.
(B) *** Ph. 422 938-2 (2). Arthur Grumiaux, LSO, C. Davis.
(M) ** Pickwick/RPO Dig. CDRPD 9003 (2). Young Uck Kim, LPO, Eschenbach.

Violin concertos Nos. 1–5; Adagio in E, K.261; Rondos for violin and orchestra Nos. 1 in B flat, K.269; 2 in C, K.373.
(M) **(*) Ph. 422 256-2 (2). Henryk Szeryng, New Philh. O, Gibson.

Violin concertos Nos. 1 in B flat, K. 207; 3 in G, K. 216; 5 in A (Turkish), K. 219.
(M) *** Decca Dig./Analogue 433 170-2 [id.]. Iona Brown, ASMF.

Violin concertos Nos. 2 in D, K. 211; 4 in D, K. 218; (i) *Sinfonia concertante in E flat, K. 364.*
(M) *** Decca Dig./Analogue 433 171-2 [id.]. Iona Brown, (i) Josef Suk; ASMF.

Grumiaux's accounts of the Mozart *Violin concertos* come from the early 1960s and are among the most beautifully played in the catalogue at any price. The orchestral accompaniments have sparkle and vitality and Grumiaux's contribution has splendid poise and purity of tone. There are many delights here and the music-making has warmth as well as refinement; the recording sounds remarkably good, with clean, fresh string-tone and well-defined bass.

Iona Brown's (originally Argo) set of the Mozart *Violin concertos*, on a pair of mid-priced Decca Serenata discs, has the advantage of including a fine account of the great *Sinfonia concertante*, in which she is joined by Josef Suk. The performances of the solo concertos, too, are first rate. The playing has a freshness and vigour that are winning and the participants convey a sense of pleasure in what they are doing. There is a spring-like feeling about the outer movements of the *G major* (No. 3) and a sultry, Mediterranean warmth in the middle movement. Yet Iona Brown's playing does not suffer from excessive vibrato and is admirably coloured. Not everyone responds equally to her tone, which does not cultivate mellifluousness or beauty for its own sake; but all these performances have an engaging liveliness and are very well integrated. The recordings are part digital, part analogue (K.216 and K.218), but all produce bright, realistic quality on CD.

Szeryng plays with great purity of style and musicianly insight, though at times some might find his approach a trifle cool. But Sir Alexander Gibson's orchestral support is always alive, well shaped and responsive; and the 1971 Philips recording, musically balanced and truthful in timbre, is transferred immaculately to CD. Szeryng offers worthwhile bonuses and the Philips sound has an attractive Mozartian scale.

The Korean-born American violinist Young Uck Kim is an artist of real quality and his playing has great purity of tone and stylistic finesse to commend it; it is a pity that in the *G major* and *A major Concertos* the orchestral playing under Christoph Eschenbach is at times touched by routine. In Nos. 1, 2 and 4, the sound is slightly brighter and the playing fresher. Like Grumiaux and Sir Colin Davis, all five *Concertos* are accommodated on two discs, but the latter – albeit at bargain price – are not available separately. Good performances and recordings, but not a first choice at upper mid-price when the Iona Brown set includes also the *Sinfonia concertante.*

Violin concertos Nos. 1 in B flat, K.207; 2 in D, K.211; Rondo in B flat, K.269; Andante in F (arr. Saint-Saëns from *Piano concerto No. 21, K.467*).
(BB) **(*) Naxos Dig. 8.550414 [id.]. Takako Nishizaki, Capella Istropolitana, Johannes Wildner.

Violin concertos Nos. 1 in B flat, K.207; 2 in D, K.211; 3 in G, K.216.
(M) **(*) Sony Dig. SBK 46539 [id.]. Zukerman, St Paul CO.

Violin concertos Nos. 1 in B flat, K.207; 2 in D, K.211; 3 in G, K.216; Rondo in C, K.373.
(M) **(*) EMI CDM7 69176-2; *EG 769176-4*. David Oistrakh, BPO.

Violin concertos Nos. 1 in B flat, K.207; 2 in D, K.211; 5 in A (Turkish), K.219.
(M) ** DG Dig. 431 281-2; *431 281-4* [id.]. Gidon Kremer, VPO, Harnoncourt.

Violin concertos Nos. 1 in B flat, K.207; 5 in A (Turkish), K.219; Adagio in E, K.261.
(M) **(*) DG Dig. 427 813-2; *427 813-4* [id.]. Itzhak Perlman, VPO, Levine.

David Oistrakh is predictably strong and positive as a Mozartian, and he is well accompanied by the Berlin Philharmonic Orchestra. The slow movement of the *G major*, K.216, is memorably expressive, and the *Rondo*, K.373, is also very pleasing. The original resonance means that orchestral tuttis are not always absolutely clean, but in general the quality on CD is very good.

Perlman's version of K.207 is first class in every way and, like the particularly graceful account of the *Adagio*, K.261, receives accompaniments which are beautifully played and perfectly integrated in a recording which is ideally balanced and very truthful. K.219 is also drawn from the 1986 complete set but is treated rather more like a virtuoso showpiece than is common. For some the tone will be too sweet for Mozart, though Levine and the VPO are again in good form. This is certainly enjoyable, though the soloist is balanced very forwardly.

Zukerman's set has the advantage of excellent digital recording and a good balance, the violin forward but not distractingly so. The playing of outer movements is agreeably simple and fresh, and in the slow movements of both the *D major* and *G major Concertos* Zukerman's sweetness of tone will appeal to many, although his tendency to languish a little in his expressiveness, particularly in the *G major*, may be counted a less attractive feature. The St Paul Chamber Orchestra is clearly in rapport with its soloist/director and accompanies with stylish warmth.

This was the last disc to be recorded (in 1990) of Takako Nishizaki's fine survey of the violin concertos. The opening movement of K.207 is brisk and fresh, with the bright, digital sound emphasizing the immediacy; although the *Adagio* is played with an agreeable, simple eloquence, this is the least individual of Nishizaki's readings. The *Second Concerto*, K.211, although still admirably direct, has rather more flair, the *Andante* touchingly phrased, and the finale has a winning lightness of touch. The *Rondo* is also an attractively spontaneous performance, and as an encore we are offered Saint-Saëns's arrangement of the famous *'Elvira Madigan'* theme from the *C major Concerto*, K.467. Obviously the French composer recognized a 'lollipop' when he heard one.

Neither Kremer nor Harnoncourt is entirely consistent in their approach to these three concertos. Kremer's playing is expert throughout but, for all his finesse, the *B flat Concerto* is curiously uninvolving and the digital recording is inclined to be fierce in the treble. Harnoncourt's opening movement of K.211 is brisk and clean, then the slow movement is purposefully moulded. With Kremer playing sweetly throughout, this is undoubtedly enjoyable, and the finale is attractively spirited. The recording, too, made in the Musikverein, is fuller, if still brightly lit. In No. 5, the last to be recorded (in 1987), Kremer's elegant vitality is again apparent, although there are individual touches in both phrasing and dynamic contrast which may not appeal to all. Harnoncourt's tuttis are strong and direct and the partnership is generally successful, with the fine VPO playing always providing an anchor for the soloist, while remaining resilient at all times. The recording is full and clear, but remains very bright.

Violin concertos Nos. 2 in D, K.211; 4 in D, K.218.

(B) **(*) Ph. 422 468-2. Krebbers, Netherlands CO, Zinman.

With his immaculate intonation and subtle rhythmic sense, Krebbers gives splendid performances, very brightly recorded and with crisply alert accompaniments from the excellent Netherlands Chamber Orchestra. The earlier *D major Concerto* brings the most beautiful high-floated solo entries in the central slow movement, and relaxed tempi, nicely sprung, in the outer movements. The only snag is that the remastering emphasizes the forward balance of the soloist.

(i) *Violin concertos Nos. 2; 5 (Turkish), K.219;*
(ii) *Divertimento for string trio in E flat, K.563.*

(B) ** DG Compact Classics *423 289-4* [id.]. (i) Wolfgang Schneiderhan, BPO; (ii) Italian String Trio.

Violin concerto No. 3 in G, K.216.

(B) ** DG Compact Classics *415 332-4* [id.]. Wolfgang Schneiderhan, BPO – BEETHOVEN: *Triple concerto*; BRAHMS: *Double concerto.* **

Violin concertos Nos. 3 in G, K.216; 4 in D, K.218; Rondos (for violin & orchestra) Nos. 1 in B flat, K.269; 2 in B flat, K.373.

(M) *** DG Dig. 431 282-2; *431 282-2.* Itzhak Perlman, VPO, Levine.

Violin concertos Nos. 3 in G, K.216; 4 in D, K.218; 5 in A (Turkish), K.219.

(BB) **(*) LaserLight Dig. 15 525 [id.]. Christian Altenburger, German Bach Soloists, Winschermann.

(B) ** DG 429 159-2; *429 159-4* [id.]. Wolfgang Schneiderhan, BPO.

Violin concertos Nos. 3 in G, K.216; 5 in A (Turkish), K.219.

(M) *** DG 429 814-2; *429 814-4* [id.]. Anne-Sophie Mutter, BPO, Karajan.

(BB) *** Naxos Dig. 8.550063 [id.]. Takako

Nishizaki, Capella Istropolitana, Stephen Gunzenhauser.

Extraordinarily mature and accomplished playing from Anne-Sophie Mutter, who was a mere fourteen years old when her recording was made. The instinctive mastery means that there is no hint of immaturity: the playing has polish, but fine artistry too and remarkable freshness. Karajan is at his most sympathetic and scales down the accompaniment to act as a perfect setting for his young soloist. The recording has been brilliantly transferred to CD; some might feel that the orchestral strings are a shade too brightly lit.

Perlman likes to be closely balanced, and in K.216 one is very conscious of his virtuosity. But this element of self-consciousness does not seriously detract from the Mozartian spirit, thanks to the calibre of the playing and the finesse and warmth of his phrasing. In No. 4 the artistic rapport between soloist and orchestra is particularly striking. Once again Perlman's bravura is effortless and even more charismatic, and the orchestral playing is glorious. The perspective of the recording seems rather more natural here. The two engaging *Rondos* are played with fine style.

This is the finest of Nishizaki's three discs of the Mozart violin concertos on Naxos. The readings are individual and possess the most engaging lyrical feeling, stemming directly from the lovely solo timbre and the natural response of the soloist to Mozartian line and phrase. In the opening movement of K.219 (which comes first on the disc), Gunzenhauser's introduction is full of life and, at the expressive violin entry, Nishizaki holds the tempo back just a little and then sails off into the allegro with great zest. The *Adagio* is tender and serene, and the contrasting episodes of the finale are sparklingly handled, with the 'Turkish' interlude full of character. A sprightly vigour also informs the outer movements of K.216 and the *Adagio* has a gentle beauty, with the light-hearted finale providing a perfect contrast. A good balance, the soloist forward, but convincingly so, and the orchestral backcloth, always polished and supportive, in natural perspective. A real bargain.

Christian Altenburger is an appealing soloist, playing with full timbre and classical feeling, even if he is without a strong individual personality. Winschermann and the German Bach Soloists give polished and sympathetic support. Allegros are alive and the Turkish Minuet/Rondo finale of K.219 admirably contrasts elegance with sparkle. Slow movements, too, are appealingly poised, and the scale of these performances is well judged, with modern instruments used to convincing effect. Excellent digital sound, bright and open. A genuine bargain.

Schneiderhan's performances come from a complete set, made with the Berlin Philharmonic Orchestra at the end of the 1960s. He plays with effortless mastery and a strong sense of classical proportion. The Berlin orchestra accompany well for him, though there is a slightly unsmiling quality at times. The tape transfers are very successful, smooth and vivid. The recording of the masterly *Divertimento for string trio* also sounds well in its tape format. The performance is remarkable for its accuracy of intonation. The Italian String Trio is a wonderfully polished group – in a sense too polished, for their trim, fast speeds reveal rather too little temperament. Even so, this is very acceptable when it is so generously coupled.

Violin concerto No. 4 in D, K.218; (i) *Sinfonia concertante in E flat, for violin, viola and orchestra, K.364.*

(BB) **(*) Naxos Dig. 8.550332 [id.]. Takako Nishizaki, (i) Ladislav Kyselak; Capella Istropolitana, Stephen Gunzenhauser.

A fine account of No. 4, with Takako Nishizaki's solo playing well up to the high standard of this series and with Stephen Gunzenhauser's perceptive pacing, especially of the tranquil *Andante cantabile* and the engaging finale with its contrasting duo-tempi, adding to our pleasure. The *Sinfonia concertante* is very enjoyable too, if perhaps slightly less distinctive. It does not lack intensity of feeling from the well-matched soloists; indeed, at their expressive entry at the end of the exposition – which has a strong orchestral tutti with some fine horn playing – there is a brief passage of affectionate indulgence. The finale is infectious in its liveliness, its rhythms buoyantly pointed. Again, a good balance and excellent sound.

Violin concertos Nos. 4 in D, K.218; 5 in A (Turkish), K.219; Adagio in E, K.261; Rondo in C, K.373.

(M) **(*) Sony SBK 46540 [id.]. Zukerman, St Paul CO.

Zukerman's account of K.218 is unmannered and stylish, admirably direct in approach, though the *Andante* is taken rather slowly. The pacing of the last movement is somewhat idiosyncratic. His admirers will not be disappointed with K.219, although his sweet tone and effortless facility do not always engage one's sympathies. He languishes lovingly in the slow movement (though rather less so than in the *G major*, K.219) and is not always subtle in his expression of feeling. The shorter pieces are played with some flair, the *Adagio* most appealingly. The St Paul Chamber Orchestra obviously contains some fine players and the accompaniments, which Zukerman also directs, are polished, the recording vivid and rather brightly lit.

Violin concerto No. 5 in A (Turkish), K.219.
(M) *** BMG/RCA GD 87869 [7869-2-RG]. Heifetz with CO – *String quintet, K.516* etc. ***

Marvellously exhilarating Mozart from Heifetz, though his actual entry in the first movement is quite ethereal. He directs the accompanying group himself, the only time he did so on record. The early (1954) stereo is fully acceptable and the performance memorable, with the crystalline clarity of articulation matched by warmth of timbre and aristocratic phrasing. The 'Turkish' interludes of the finale are brought off with great élan and the slow movement has a superb line and much grace and subtlety of detail.

Concertone in C, K.190; Sinfonia concertante in E flat, for violin, viola and orchestra, K.364.
(BB) **(*) HM/BMG Dig. VD 77501; *VK 77501* [77501-2-RV; *77501-4RV*]. Schröder, McDonald, Smithsonian CO, Schröder.

Versions of Mozart's great *Sinfonia concertante in E flat* on period instruments are not thick on the ground, and the BMG account with Jaap Schröder, Marilyn McDonald and the Smithsonian orchestra is a welcome addition to the catalogue. There is an unforced quality about the outer movements that is very likeable, though the solo playing in the slow movement is a little cool (Schröder is at times not untouched by routine). There is also some particularly felicitous oboe-playing in the *Concertone* from Stephen Hammer (as well as the two soloists, of course) and in both works the Smithsonian orchestra play admirably. The recording is very good, but there is no presentation material.

Dances and Marches

Complete Mozart Edition, Volume 6: *La Chasse, KA.103/K.299d; Contredanses, K.101; K.123; K.267; K.269b; K.462; (Das Donnerwetter) K.534; (La Bataille) K.535; 535a; (Der Sieg vom Helden Koburg) K.587; K.603; (Il trionfo delle donne) K.607; (Non più andrai) K.609; K.610; Gavotte, K.300; German dances, K.509; K.536; K.567; K.571; K.586; K.600; K.602; K.605; Ländler, K.606; Marches, K.214; K.363; K.408; K.461; Minuets, K.61b; K.61g/2; K.61h; K.94, 103, 104, 105; K.122; K.164; K.176; K.315g; K.568; K.585; K.599; K.601; K.604; Minuets with Contredanses, K.463; Overture & 3 Contredanses, K.106.*
❀ (M) *** Ph. 422 506-2 (6). Vienna Mozart Ens., Willi Boskovsky.

Philips have chosen to use Willi Boskovsky's famous series of recordings of the dance music, made for Decca in the mid-1960s, for Volume 6 of their Complete Mozart Edition. Much of the credit for this remarkable undertaking should go to its expert producer, Erik Smith, who, besides providing highly stylish orchestrations for numbers without Mozart's own scoring, illuminates the music with some of the most informative and economically written notes that ever graced a record. On the completion of the orginal project, H. C. Robbins Landon cabled his praises and hailed 'the most beautiful Mozart playing and most sophisticated sound I know'. The CD transfers preserve the excellence of the sound: it is a shade crisper in definition and outline but has not lost its bloom. The layout is historical, with the music grouped into five sections: Salzburg and Italy (1769–77); Paris (1778); Vienna and Salzburg (1782–4); Prague (1787); and Dances for the Redoutensaal (1788–91). The collector might feel that he or she is faced here with an *embarras de richesses* with more than 120 *Minuets*, nearly 50 *German dances* and some three dozen *Contredanses*, but Mozart's invention is seemingly inexhaustible, and the instrumentation is full of imaginative touches. As Erik Smith comments, 'In the late dances Mozart seems to have used the medium of dance music to experiment in. Here is instrumentation as rich as Brahms, yet utterly lucid. There is nothing quite like it in the late symphonies and only a little in *Così fan tutte* and *Die Zauberflöte*.' Of course these are records to be dipped into rather than played a whole disc at a time; but there are surprises everywhere, and much that is inspired.

2 Contredanses, K.603; Contredanse, K.610; 19 German Dances, K.571/1–6; K.600/1–6; K.602/1–4; K.605/1–3; Marches: in D, K.335/1; in C & D, K.408/1–3; 10 Minuets, K.599/1–6; K.601/1–4.
(M) *** Decca 430 634-2; *430 634-4* [id.]. V. Mozart Ens., Willi Boskovsky.

A self-recommending single-disc selection from Boskovsky's admirable survey of Mozart's dance music, recorded between 1964 and 1966. The selection, of course, includes the famous *Sleigh ride* (within K.605) which has some superb post-horn playing, and there are other special effects, notably the charming hurdy-gurdy of K.602. One must remember that Mozart wrote this music to be *danced* to and its style is relatively formal. The disc plays for over 76 minutes – but, delightful as the music is, it is not to be taken all at once! The transfers are impeccable and Erik Smith's introductory notes are succinctly informative. A pity, though, that the individual dances were not cued or indexed.

12 German dances, K.586; 6 German dances, K.600; 4 German dances, K.602; 3 German dances, K.605.
(BB) *** Naxos Dig. 8.550412 [id.]. Capella Istropolitana, Johannes Wildner.

Fresh, bright, unmannered performances of some of the dance music Mozart wrote right at the end of his life. The very last item here, the third of the K.605 *Dances*, is the most famous with its sleigh-bells and two posthorns and nick-named *The Sleigh-ride.* The note with the disc suggests that the three shorter groups of dances were designed to fit together – but, whether that is so or not, they make a charming collection. The playing is excellent and the recording is bright and full. An excellent super-bargain alternative to the Boskovsky Decca CD.

3 German dances, K.605; Overtures: *Così fan tutte; Don Giovanni; Die Entführung aus dem Serail; La finta giardinera; Idomeneo; Le nozze di Figaro; Der Schauspieldirektor; Die Zauberflöte. Serenades Nos. 6 (Serenata Notturna), K.239; 13 (Eine kleine Nachtmusik), K.525.*
(B) ** EMI CDZ7 62858-2; *LZ 762858-4.* RPO or Philh. O, Sir Colin Davis.

Sir Colin Davis and the Philharmonia are most successful in Mozart's two nocturnal serenades. The *Nachtmusik* is relaxed yet entirely convincing and spontaneous, and the orchestral soloists in the *Serenata notturna* are of a high order. It is a pity that the CD transfer over-brightens the violin timbre, so that one needs to soften the upper range in playback. The overtures are stylishly conceived performances with polished RPO playing, especially from the first violins and woodwind. There is no lack of drama here, though a lighter touch is given to the charming *La finta giardiniera*, and *Così fan tutte* bubbles vivaciously. Slight reservations remain about the over-brilliant recording.

Complete Mozart Edition, Volume 45: *'Rarities and curiosities': Contredanses in B flat & D* (completed Smith); *The London Sketchbook:* (i) *3 Contredanses in F; 2 Contredanses in G; 6 Divertimenti.* (ii) *Wind divertimenti* arr. from operas: *Don Giovanni* (arr. Triebensee); *Die Enführung aus dem Serail* (arr. Wendt) & (i) *March, K 384.* (i; iii) *Rondo in E flat for horn and orchestra, K 371* (completed Smith); (iv) *Larghetto for piano and wind quintet, K 452a;* (v) *Modulating prelude in F/E min.* (vi) *Tantum ergo in B flat, K 142; in D, K 197;* (vii) *Idomeneo: Scene & rondo.* (viii) *Musical dice game, K.516.*
(M) *** Ph. 422 545-2 (3) [id.]. (i) ASMF, Marriner; (ii) Netherlands Wind Ens.; (iii) Timothy Brown; cond. Sillito; (iv) Uchida, Black, King, Farrell, O'Neil; (v) Erik Smith (harpsichord); (vi) Frimmer, Leipzig R. Ch. & SO, Schreier; (vii) Mentzler, Hendricks, Bav. RSO, C. Davis; (viii) Marriner & Smith.

The last box in the Philips Complete Mozart Edition contains three CDs, and most of the real curiosities are to be found on the third. The first includes the innocent little piano pieces from the child Mozart's 'London Notebook' (written while his father was ill). Erik Smith has orchestrated them and, if the results may not be important, they charm the ear at least as much as Mozart's early symphonies, with many unexpected touches. Marriner and the Academy are ideal performers and the 1971 recording is warm and refined. Then come the arrangements for wind of selections from two key operas (though why not *Nozze di Figaro* which Johann Wendt also scored and which exists in a Decca recording by the London Wind Soloists?). However, what we are offered, elegantly played by the Netherlands Wind Ensemble, is so gracious and satisfying – especially used as background music for a dinner party – that one almost forgets about the missing voices. Finally come the rarities and curiosities, the *Rondo for horn and orchestra* with the missing 60 bars (discovered only in 1989) now added, and the other music made good by Erik Smith: a not very important fragment for piano and wind quintet; two extra *Contredanses* and a pair of *Tantum ergo* settings that may or may not be authentic. There is an extra aria for *Idomeneo*, a March first intended for *Die Entführung* then abandoned, and a curious finale in which Erik Smith and Sir Neville Marriner participate (with spoken comments) in a *Musical dice game* to decide the order of interchangeable phrases in a very simple musical composition. The result, alas, is something of a damp squib.

Divertimenti and Serenades

Complete Mozart Edition, Volume 4: *Divertimenti for strings Nos. 1–3, K.136/8; Divertimenti for small orchestra Nos. 1 in E flat, K.113; 7 in D, K.205* (with *March in D, K.290); 10 in F, K.247* (with *March in F, K.248); 11 in D, K.251; 15 in B flat, K.287; 17 in D, K.334* (with *March in D, K.445); A Musical joke, K.622; Serenade (Eine kleine Nachtmusik), K.525.*
(M) *** Ph. Dig. 422 504-2 (5) [id.]. ASMF CO.

This is one of the most attractive of all the boxes in the Philips Mozart Edition. The music itself is a delight, the performances are stylish, elegant and polished, while the digital recording has admirable warmth and realistic presence and definition.

Divertimenti for strings Nos. 1–3, K.136–8; Divertimento No. 7 in D, K.205.
(BB) ** Naxos Dig. 8.550108 [id.]. Capella Istropolitana, Richard Edlinger.

Pleasing performances in a welcoming and warm acoustic. The Capella Istropolitana, which is drawn from the Slovak Philharmonic, play well for Richard Edlinger. They are not quite as characterful or spirited as the (somewhat more expensive) Franz Liszt Chamber Orchestra on Hungaroton, but they are better recorded.

Divertimenti for strings Nos. 1–3, K.136–8; Divertimento No. 10 in F, K.247.
(B) ** Hung. White Label HRC 187 [id.]. Liszt CO, Budapest, Sándor.

The Franz Liszt Chamber Orchestra is one of the finest ensembles of its kind, and this 1972 recording was made before János Rolla assumed its direction. The playing has plenty of vitality and, although the sound does not have the freshness and bloom of their Slovak rival on Naxos, the performances have greater personality. With the ASMF under Marriner around, neither would be a first choice; however, despite the minor deficiencies of the analogue remastering, this remains quite good value for money.

Divertimenti for strings Nos. 1–3, K.136–8; Serenades Nos. 6 (Serenata notturna); 13 in G (Eine kleine Nachtmusik), K.525.
(M) *** Ph. Dig. 432 055-2; *432 055-4*. I Musici.
(M) **(*) Decca 417 741-2 [id.]. ASMF, Marriner.
(M) **(*) Ph. 420 712-2 [id.]. I Musici.
(M) ** DG 429 805-2; *429 805-4*. BPO, Karajan.

(i) *Divertimenti for strings Nos. 1, K.136, & 3, K.138; Serenade No. 6 (Serenata Notturna);* (ii) *Serenade No. 13 (Eine kleine Nachtmusik);* (iii) *Sinfonia concertante in E flat, K.297b* (CD only: (iv) *Serenade No. 12 in C min., K.388*).
(B) **(*) DG Compact Classics 413 152-2 (2); *413 152-4* [id.]. (i) BPO, Karajan; (ii) VPO, Boehm; (iii) BPO, Boehm (CD only: (iv) VPO Wind Ens.).

The newest digital recording of the Salzburg *Divertimenti* by I Musici is particularly successful, extremely vivid and clean, bringing the players before one's very eyes. Their outstanding recording of the three *String divertimenti* is now joined with their remarkably fresh account of *Eine kleine Nachtmusik*, as fine as any in the catalogue and better than most. The vivid digital sound has excellent balance and striking presence throughout. A self-recommending mid-priced reissue, except for the lack of any information about the music being included. Their earlier, analogue recording from 1974, however, still sounds well in its mid-priced reissue. The playing is spirited and beautifully stylish. With the *Night music* added to the *Serenata notturna* as couplings, this is fair value.

The playing of the Academy is marvellous, with Marriner's choice of tempi equally apt. The same stylishness distinguishes the *Serenata notturna*, while *Eine kleine Nachtmusik* is presented delightfully. However, the remastered recordings from the late 1960s and early 1970s are very brightly lit, with the violins noticeably thin above the stave in *Eine kleine Nachtmusik*; the touch of shrillness is less striking in the three *Divertimenti*.

Karajan's (late 1960s) performances of the *String divertimenti* and the *Serenata notturna* are beautifully played, and as such they prompt the liveliest admiration. At the same time there is a predictably glossy elegance that seems to militate against spontaneity. The recording is well balanced, though the violins as remastered sound a little undernourished. Boehm's contribution is another matter. His 1976 VPO version of Mozart's *Night music* is among the finest of those played by a full complement of strings, polished and spacious, with a neat, lightly pointed finale. The account of the *Sinfonia concertante* is of first-class quality, sounding idiomatic and well blended, with the balance between soloists and orchestra nicely managed. This is altogether refreshing and the sound is very good in both formats. The pair of CDs also include the *Wind Serenade*, K.388, and here there are some reservations about the overall matching of timbres. The Viennese oboe is thinner and reedier than one would like, though the clarinet is particularly smooth in tone. This well-recorded performance will undoubtedly give pleasure, but ideally one needs a rather more homogeneous blend in Mozart.

Complete Mozart Edition, Volume 5: *Divertimentos for wind Nos. 3 in E flat, K.166; 4 in B flat, K.186; 6 in C, K.188; 8 in F, K.213; 9 in B flat K.240; 12 in E flat, K.252; 13 in F, K.253; 14 in B flat, K.270; 16 in E flat, K.289; in E flat, K.Anh. 226; in B flat, K.Anh. 227; Divertimentos for 3 basset horns, K.439b/1–5; Duos for 2 horns, K.487/1–12; Serenades for wind No. 10 in B flat, K.361; 11 in E flat, K.375; 12 in C min., K.388; Adagios: in F; B flat, K.410–11.*
(M) *** Ph. Analogue/Dig. 422 505-2 [id.]. Holliger Wind Ens. (or members of); Netherlands Wind Ens., De Waart (or members of); ASMF, Marriner or Laird.

Mozart's wind music, whether in the ambitious

Serenades or the simpler *Divertimenti*, brings a naturally felicitous blending of timbre and colour unmatched by any other composer. There is a considerable variety of instrumentation here and an unending diversity of invention. It seems that even when writing for the simplest combination of wind instruments, Mozart is incapable of being dull. The works for two horns are conjecturally allocated. The principal role involves some hair-raising bravura; thus it is suggested by some authorities that they were intended for basset horns. But given the kind of easy virtuosity they receive here, from Iman Soeteman and Jan Peeters, they get our vote in favour of horns every time. To afford maximum variety, they are presented in groups of three movements, interspersed with the other divertimenti. The playing of the more ambitious works is admirably polished and fresh, and it is interesting to note that Holliger's group provides a stylishly light touch and texture with the principal oboe dominating, while the blending of the Netherlanders is somewhat more homogeneous, though the effect is still very pleasing. It is very easy to enjoy both, when the recording is so well balanced and realistic.

Divertimento No. 7 in D, K.205.
(M) **(*) Decca 421 155-2; *421 155-4.* Vienna Octet (members) – SCHUBERT: *Octet.* **

Mozart's *Divertimento in D* is given a peerless performance by the Vienna Octet, and its quality of invention shows the composer at his most gracious and smiling. The recording, however, dates from 1964 and betrays a certain thinness in the string timbre, although there is plenty of ambient warmth.

Divertimenti Nos. 7 in D, K.205; 10 in F, K.247; Serenade No. 13 in G (Eine kleine Nachtmusik), K.525.
(BB) *(*) HM/BMG VD 77521 [Victrola 77521-2-RV]. Coll. Aur., Fanzjosef Maier.

Polished performances of both these fine *Divertimenti*, effectively using original instruments; but the playing has a definite absence of charm, and the violin timbre is rather grainy, especially in K.247, recorded in 1964. *Eine kleine Nachtmusik* is later (1975, like K.205) and comes off much better, the playing agreeably fresh and spontaneous; here the string texture is distinctly more pleasing.

Divertimenti Nos. 7 in D, K.205; 17 in D, K.334; March in D, K.290.
(B) *** Hung. White Label HRC 080 [id.]. Liszt CO, Rolla or Sándor.

An outstanding bargain coupling of two of Mozart's finest *Divertimenti*, in stylish chamber orchestra versions, elegantly played and truthfully recorded in a most pleasing acoustic. K.205 is scored for string trio, plus horns and bassoon, but Mozart's part-writing skilfully ensures that the basic texture is rich; and in the *Adagio* the interplay between violins and violas is especially felicitous. The work is introduced by the march used for its première at Dr Mesmer's garden party in August 1773. K.334 is perhaps the most familiar of all Mozart's large-scale works in this form, and its famous Minuet has more natural rhythmic pulse here than in the Decca version by members of the Vienna Octet.

Divertimenti Nos 10 in F, K.247; 17 in D, K.334.
(M) **(*) Decca 425 540-2; *425 540-4* [id.]. Vienna Octet.

This is a generous recoupling for CD of two major *Divertimenti*, recorded at the beginning of the 1960s. The performance of No. 10 is lively but not especially imaginative and the playing is rather unsmiling until towards the end, when it enlivens itself for a very spirited finale. The more familiar D major piece is given with fine verve, and here the style of the leader (Anton Fietz) in his many solo passages is exactly right for this kind of music-making. This is in fact just how to play Mozart, with no stiffness anywhere, although the rhythmic emphasis of the famous 'Boccherinian' Minuet may strike some ears as overdone. The Viennese acoustic is warm and the sound is extremely vivid, although some of the original smoothness in the treble has been lost in the CD mastering.

Divertimento No. 15 in B flat, K.287; Serenades Nos. 6 in D (Serenata notturna), K.239; 13 in G (Eine kleine Nachtmusik).
(M) **(*) DG Dig. 431 272-2; *431 272-4* [id.]. BPO, Karajan.

Karajan uses a full body of strings; the Berlin Philharmonic play with marvellous unanimity and their phrasing is the soul of elegance. This is an unfashionable approach to Mozart but it is easy to enjoy. The *Divertimento* is a 1987 recording; the *Night music* (1982) has appeared before and been praised by us for its cultured playing and well-sprung rhythms; the elegant if slightly bland account of the *Serenata notturna* is now added for good measure. The Philharmonie sound is especially full and real in K.287, rather more brightly lit in the *Serenade*, but still very believable in its presence.

Divertimento No. 17 in D, K.334; Notturno (Serenade) in D, K.286; Serenade No. 13 in G (Eine kleine Nachtmusik), K.525.

(B) *** Decca 430 496-2; *430 496-4*. ASMF, Marriner.

Mozart's innocently tricky *Notturno for four orchestras*, with its spatial interplay, is here played with superb style and is very well recorded. The *Divertimento*, equally, finds the Academy of St Martin's at its peak, relishing the technical problems of co-ordinating music which is often performed by solo strings and playing with great finesse. Versions of *Eine kleine Nachtmusik* which have such fresh, unaffected refinement are rare, but this analogue recording from the old Argo catalogue of the most popular of Mozart's serenades is delightfully played and wears its years lightly, like the others on this disc. A fine and generous bargain triptych.

Complete Mozart Edition, Volume 25: (i) *Idomeneo* (ballet music), *K.367;* (ii) *Les petits riens* (ballet), *K.299b; Music for a pantomime (Pantalon und Colombine), K.446* (completed and orch. Beyer); *Sketches for a ballet intermezzo, K.299c* (completed and orch. Erik Smith); (iii) *Thamos, King of Egypt* (incidental music), *K.345.*

(M) *** Ph. 422 525-2 (2) [id.]. (i) Netherlands CO, David Zinman; (ii) ASMF, Marriner; (iii) Eickstädt, Pohl, Büchner, Polster, Adam, Berlin R. Ch. & State O, Klee.

This volume collects together Mozart's theatre music and makes a particularly enticing package. Zinman and his Netherlanders give a neatly turned account of the ballet from *Idomeneo*, musical and spirited, and the 1974 recording sounds well. Marriner takes over with modern digital sound for *Les petits riens* and the two novelties, and the ASMF playing has characteristic elegance and finesse. Mozart wrote *Les petits riens* for a performance in 1778, sharing the composition with others and contributing about two-thirds of the total score. The music then disappeared for a century, and of the 20 pieces it is not certain which are authentically Mozart's. The selection here of 11 items plus the *Overture* is arbitrary but the music is certainly attractive. The two novelties are almost more enticing. The *Sketches for a ballet intermezzo* survive only in a single-line autograph, but Erik Smith's completion and scoring provide a series of eight charming vignettes, most with descriptive titles, ending with a piquant *Tambourin*. The music for *Pantalon and Columbine* (more mime than ballet) survives in the form of a first violin part, and Franz Beyer has skilfully orchestrated it for wind and strings, using the first movement of the *Symphony*, K.84, as the overture and the last movement of *Symphony*, K.120, as the finale. In the original (1783) performance, Mozart himself – after taking dancing lessons – had played Harlequin and his sister-in-law was Columbine. The writing is characteristically inventive and tuneful and the scoring most felicitous, the individual numbers more substantial and with greater internal contrast than in the *Ballet intermezzo*. Beautifully played as it is here, full of grace and colour, this is a real find and the digital recording is first rate. *Thamos, King of Egypt* comes from 1779 when Mozart was commissioned to provide incidental music for Gebler's play; it was eventually used for another play. Some of the choruses look forward to *Zauberflöte*, though in general one is reminded most of *Idomeneo*. In any event, it is marvellous music which it is good to have on record, particularly in such persuasive hands as these. The choral singing is impressive and the orchestral playing is excellent. The 1973 recording was made in the Jesus Christus-Kirche, Berlin, and is well balanced and faithful.

Masonic funeral music: see also below, in VOCAL MUSIC, under Complete Mozart Edition, Volume 22

Masonic funeral music, K.477; Overtures: Così fan tutte; The Impresario; Le nozze di Figaro; Die Zauberflöte; Serenade No. 13 (Eine kleine Nachtmusik), K.525.

(B) **(*) Sony MYK 42593 [MYK 37774]. Columbia SO, Bruno Walter.

Walter conducts all this music with evident affection; even if some may feel that he is almost too loving at times, particularly in *Eine kleine Nachtmusik*, there is still something very special about this music-making. His tempi in the overtures are unerringly apt. The account of the *Masonic funeral music* is particularly fine. The recording is characteristic of this highly successful CBS series, warm and full, with an ample bass, but a remarkably fresh upper range, with sweet violins.

A Musical joke, K.522; Notturno for 4 orchestras, K.286; Serenades Nos. 6 (Serenata notturna), K.239; 13 (Eine kleine Nachtmusik), K.525.

(M) *** Decca 430 259-2; *430 259-4*. V. Mozart Ens., Boskovsky.

This delightful collection shows just how good Boskovsky and his Vienna Mozart Ensemble were in their prime. The recordings were made in the Sofiensaal in 1968–9 and 1978 (K.239 and K.286); in remastered form they all sound wonderfully fresh and realistic. One wonders who would want to listen to Mozart on acerbic 'authentic' violins after experiencing the transparency and elegance of the string playing here. We have often praised this version of *Eine kleine Nachtmusik* for its grace and spontaneity

– one has the impression that one is hearing the piece for the first time – and the same comment could be applied to the string playing in the *Musical joke* (especially the delectable Minuet and the neat, zestful finale which ends with spectacular dissonance). The horns are superbly po-faced in their wrong notes in the former and Boskovsky's 'misjudged' scale at the end of the *Adagio* has comparable aplomb. The *Notturno for four orchestras* is a less inspired piece, but its spatial echoes are ingeniously contrived and their perspective admirably conveyed by the recording.

Overtures: *Apollo et Hyacinthus; Bastien und Bastienne; La clemenza di Tito; Così fan tutte; Don Giovanni; Die Entführung aus dem Serail; La finta giardiniera; Idomeneo; Lucio Silla; Mitridate, rè di Ponto; Le nozze di Figaro; Il rè pastore; Der Schauspieldirektor; Die Zauberflöte.*
(BB) *** Naxos Dig. 8.550185 [id.]. Capella Istropolitana, Barry Wordsworth.

Wordsworth follows up his excellent series of Mozart symphonies for Naxos with this generous collection of overtures, no fewer than 14 of them, arranged in chronological order and given vigorous, stylish performances. In Italian overture form, *Mitridate* and *Lucio Silla*, like miniature symphonies, have separate tracks for each of their three contrasted sections. Very well recorded, the disc is highly recommendable at super-bargain price.

Overtures: *La clemenza di Tito; Così fan tutte; Don Giovanni; Die Entführung aus dem Serail; Idomeneo; Lucio Silla; Le nozze di Figaro; Der Schauspieldirektor; Die Zauberflöte.*
(M) **(*) Ph. 432 512-2; *432 512-4*. LPO, Haitink.

Haitink's are essentially concert performances, with a warm, resonant acoustic giving suitable gravitas to the introductions for *Don Giovanni* and *Die Zauberflöte*, yet the brightness added by the remastering ensures that *Le nozze di Figaro* sounds fresh. There is sparkling playing from the LPO strings in the less well-known pieces, which they clearly enjoy, while the woodwind shine in *Così fan tutte*. This is certainly worthwhile, but only nine overtures are offered against Barry Wordworth's fourteen on Naxos at super-bargain price.

Serenades Nos. 3 in D, K.185; 4 in D (Colloredo), K.203.
(BB) *** Naxos Dig. 8.550413 [id.]. Salzburg CO, Harald Nerat.

Well-played, nicely phrased and musical accounts on Naxos, recorded in a warm, reverberant acoustic, but one in which detail clearly registers. The Salzburg Chamber Orchestra has real vitality, and most readers will find these accounts musically satisfying and very enjoyable. This offers particularly good value in terms of playing time.

Serenade No. 4 in D (Colloredo), K.203; March in D, K.237.
(BB) **(*) HM/BMG Dig. VD 77536; *VK 77536* [77536-2-RV; *77536-4-RV*]. Coll. Aur., Franzjosef Maier.

Serenade No. 5 in D, K.204; March in D, K.215.
(BB) **(*) HM/BMG Dig. VD 77568; *VK 77568* [77568-2-RV; *77568-4-RV*]. Coll. Aur., Franzjosef Maier.

Serenade No. 7 in D (Haffner), K.250; 5 Contredanses, K.609.
(BB) **(*) HM/BMG VD 77548; *VK 77548* [77548-2-RV; *77548-4-RV*]. Coll. Aur., Franzjosef Maier.

These recordings of K.203 and K.204 date from 1982/3. They were made in the kindly acoustics of the Schloss Kirchheim: the sound is resonantly warm and full, disguising astringencies, if there are any, brought about by the use of original string instruments. The phrasing, too, comes before the days of mercilessly squeezing the melodic line, so that the main aural difference is in the woodwind timbres. Both the *Serenades*, K.203 and K.204, encompass a three-movement violin concerto in their midst, played very well indeed by Franzjosef Maier. Tempi are occasionally a bit problematic. In the *Haffner Serenade* – recorded earlier, in 1970 – the effect is a shade bland, despite the neat, polished playing, and the last Minuet of K.204 is positively funereal. But there are enough good things here to make the performances enjoyable, and these reissues are inexpensive. The five *Contredanses* (recorded in 1979 and sounding very fresh) make a most attractive encore for the *Haffner Serenade*. They are played with much spirit by a chamber group (2 violins, double-bass, flute and drum) and have real Viennese flair: the first quotes directly from *Le nozze di Figaro* and the last is a hurdy-gurdy simulation. It is a great pity that this Collegium Aureum series is not provided with adequate musical documentation.

Serenades Nos. 6 in D (Serenata notturna), K.239; 13 in G (Eine kleine Nachtmusik), K.525.
(B) *** Pickwick Dig. PCD 861; *CIMPC 861* [id.]. Serenata of London – ELGAR: *Serenade*; GRIEG: *Holberg suite*. ***

The performance of the *Night music* by the Serenata of London is as fine as any available. There is not a suspicion of routine here; indeed the players, for all the excellence of their ensemble, give the impression of coming to the piece for the first time. The *Serenata notturna* is perhaps not quite so inspired a work, but these excellent players make a good case for it and are agreeably sprightly whenever given the opportunity. The recording has striking naturalness and realism; this is an outstanding CD bargain.

Serenades Nos. 6 in D (Serenata notturna), K.239; 13 (Eine kleine Nachtmusik), K.525; (i) *Sinfonia concertante in E flat, K.364.*
(B) **(*) DG 427 208-2; *427 208-4.* BPO, Boehm; (i) with Brandis, Cappone.

Boehm's performance of *Eine kleine Nachtmusik* is very enjoyable; it is gracious and stylishly phrased, with a gentle finale. If the *Sinfonia concertante* really requires more individual solo playing (especially in the slow movement) than Messrs Brandis and Cappone provide, the strong directing personality of the conductor keeps the music alive throughout and the sound has been clarified, yet remains well balanced.

Serenade No. 7 in D (Haffner); March, K.249.
(BB) **(*) Naxos Dig. 8.550333 [id.]. Takako Nishizaki, Capella Istropolitana, Johannes Wildner.

The K.249 *March* is given twice, as both prelude and postlude to the main *Serenade* in the authentic manner. Wildner brings out the vigour rather than the charm of the fast movements, with the Minuets on the heavy side, but with the big final allegro superbly articulated and erupting in rustic jollity. The important violin solos in earlier movements are played superbly by Takako Nishizaki. Bright, full recording. Even with the above reservations, this is an excellent bargain.

(i) *Serenade No. 7 in D (Haffner);* (ii) *Wind divertimento in B flat, K.186.*
(M) ** DG 429 806-2; *429 806-4* [id.]. (i) BPO, Boehm; (ii) VPO Wind Ens.

The Berlin Philharmonic play with such polish and vivacity, and articulation is so beautifully crisp, that one is inclined to accept Boehm's uncharacteristic lack of mellowness and his willingness to drive the allegros rather hard. Thomas Brandis is the excellent violin soloist, but at times there is more exhilaration here than charm. The freshened recording sounds just a little fierce at times in its remastered format and is not absolutely refined in focus. The performance of the *Wind divertimento* is sympathetic, polished and well integrated, but the bright recording tends to make the wind balance slightly top-heavy.

Serenade No. 9 in D (Posthorn), K.320; A Musical joke, K.522.
(BB) *** HM/BMG VD 77544; *VK 77544* [77544-2-RV; *77544-4-RV*]. Coll. Aur., Franzjosef Maier.

Serenade No. 9 in D (Posthorn); Notturno for 4 orchestras in D, K.286.
(BB) ** Naxos Dig. 8.550092 [id.]. Capella Istropolitana, Martin Turnovsky.

(i) *Serenade No. 9 in D (Posthorn);* (ii) *Wind divertimenti: in E flat, K.166; in B flat, K.227.*
(M) **(*) DG 429 807-2; *429 807-4* [id.]. (i) BPO, Boehm; (ii) VPO Wind Ens.

Serenades Nos. 9 in D (Posthorn); 13 (Eine kleine Nachtmusik), K.525.
(B) *** Decca 417 874-2; *417 874-4.* V. Mozart Ens., Boskovsky.

Bargain hunters should be well pleased with Decca's Weekend reissue of Boskovsky's performance with its natural musicality and sense of sparkle. The newest transfer is a little dry in the matter of string timbre, but there is plenty of bloom on the wind, detail is clean and the posthorn is tangible in its presence. The coupled *Night music* is one of the freshest and most attractive performances of this much-played work in any format, and the small string group is most realistically balanced and vividly projected.

Aficionados should certainly not overlook the Collegium Aureum version of the *Posthorn Serenade*, particularly as it is now offered at superbargain price. The playing is sensitive and vital and never sounds pedantic. About twenty-five instrumentalists take part, playing period instruments or copies, and the problems of intonation are altogether minimal. Indeed the woodwind sounds in the first-movement *Allegro con spirito* are full of character and quite delightful in the concertante, *Andante grazioso.* If, in the latter and the other concertante movement, the tempos are a little leisurely, the effect is so musical that this seems of little account. The remastered recording (from 1976), made in the spacious acoustics of Schloss Kirchheim, brings a brighter sound than in the earlier *Serenades* and gives the players a striking presence. The *Musical joke* (recorded in 1979) is effectively presented on a chamber sextet. The jokes are boldly made, and if this hasn't quite the charm of Boskovsky's version (see above), the use of one instrument to each part is especially telling in the vivacious finale. This is the most successful of the Collegium Aureum *Serenades* series.

Boehm's 1971 Berlin Philharmonic recording of the *Posthorn Serenade* sounds particularly fresh in its digitally remastered format. The playing is characteristically polished, warm and civilized. Incidentally, as well as naming the excellent posthorn soloist, the documentation reveals the principal flautist as James Galway and the fine oboist as Lothar Koch. Two attractive *Wind divertimenti* are now offered as couplings. Like their companion included with Boehm's *Haffner serenade*, they are sensitively played and well blended, but the digital mastering sounds a bit top-heavy.

Very well played, Turnovsky's account of the *Posthorn Serenade* is lively if not quite as elegant as the finest versions. At a slow speed the lovely minor-key *Andantino*, which is the fifth of the seven movements, is a degree too heavy-handed, for example; but at bargain price, with a generous fill-up and well recorded, it is a fair recommendation. The *Notturno* for four orchestras, with its antiphonal effects, also has its charms.

Serenade No. 9 in D (Posthorn); Symphony No. 31 in D (Paris), K.297.

(M) ** DG 431 271-2; *431 271-4* [id.]. VPO, James Levine.

Levine's account of the *Posthorn Serenade* is made more competitive at mid-price. Levine's tempi are well judged and the VPO contribution is distinguished. The early digital recording (1983) is a shade clinical, though well balanced. The inclusion of the *Paris Symphony*, a lithe, alert account if a little lacking in individuality, may attract some collectors. The (inadequate) documentation refers mainly to the symphony.

Serenade No. 10 in B flat for 13 wind instruments, K.361.

(B) **(*) CfP CD-CFP 4579; *TC-CFP 4579*. LPO Wind. Ens.

(B) **(*) Hung. White Label HRC 076 [id.]. Hungarian State Op. Wind Ens., Ervin Lukacs.

(M) **(*) DG Dig. 431 273-2; *431 273-4*. Orpheus CO.

(BB) ** HM/BMG Dig. VD 77540; *VK 77540* [77540-2-RV; *77540-4-RV*]. Coll. Aur., Franzjosef Maier.

(BB) ** Naxos Dig. 8.550060 [id.]. German Wind Soloists.

(M) ** DG Dig. 429 979-2; *429 979-4* [id.]. BPO (members).

(BB) ** Naxos Dig. 8.55060 [id.]. Amadeus Wind Ens.

Outstanding playing from the wind ensemble of the London Philharmonic, richly blended, warmly phrased and full of character. The articulation and rhythmic feeling of the outer movements and the *Theme and variations* are particularly spontaneous; however, in the slower sections, notably the third-movement *Adagio*, one feels the need of a conductor's directing hand: there is some loss of character both here and, occasionally, elsewhere. Even so, with modern digital recording, attractively coloured by the ambience and refined in detail, this is good value at bargain price.

Of the bargain versions of Mozart's large-scale wind serenade the Hungaroton is the other one to go for. The blending of the wind players from the Hungarian State Opera is impressive and their performance has an attractively robust character with buoyant allegros, and plenty of flexibility in slow movements. The sound is excellent, naturally vivid within an attractive ambience.

The Orpheus Chamber Orchestra give a refined, finely detailed reading, which yet rather lacks the individual character of the finest versions, though ensemble is splendid, and the slow movements are very smoothly done, with finely controlled dynamics. Good, full-toned recording.

The Collegium Aureum version, without being an obvious first choice, is an eminently satisfactory reading and gains considerable character by the unabrasive use of original instruments, although the blend is less homogeneous than in some more modern versions. The very plain rhythmic style will not suit all ears, though the relaxed manner of the variation movement is most attractive. The recording is warm and truthful, yet vivid.

Very well drilled but not always blending as well as some rival groups, the German Wind Soloists give a fresh and attractive account of the great *Serenade for 13 instruments*, often dubbed the '*Gran partita*'. The finest versions are rather more elegant than this, and the lovely third-movement *Adagio* – the most famous, thanks to its use in the film *Amadeus* – is rather too heavy at a slow speed, though beautifully pointed with warmly expressive solos. Clean, full-bodied recording.

The DG digital recording by the Berlin Philharmonic Orchestra's wind players is somewhat controversial. Some ears find the balance too analytical – although it is only fair to say that the sound is robust as well as clearly detailed. The playing of the BPO wind, while in its way impeccable, is curiously bland: there is none of the feeling of fresh discovery here and many moments when the dead hand of routine seems to touch their music-making. This is not the case in the glorious variation movement, but otherwise the performance is wanting in real personality.

The source of the group on the Naxos CD, the so-called Amadeus Wind Ensemble, is not made clear. They have a less characterful blend than the Hungaroton group and, although their performance is enjoyable, it has marginally less rhythmic character.

Serenades Nos. 10 in B flat; 11 in E flat, K.375.
(M) *** Ph. 420 711-2. Netherlands Wind Ens., Edo de Waart.
(M) *** Decca 425 421-2; *425 421-4*. L. Wind Soloists, Jack Brymer.
(M) **(*) EMI CDM7 63349-2; *EG 763349-4*. (i) L. Wind Quintet & Ens.; (ii) New Philh. Wind Ens., Klemperer.

The Netherlanders offer not only the *B flat Serenade* but also the *E flat*, K.375, a very substantial bonus. Their performances are fresh and alive, admirably sensitive both in feeling for line and in phrasing, but never lingering too lovingly over detail. Both works are enhanced by the presence and sonority of the recording.

Brymer's group gives a strong, stylish performance of the large-scale *B flat major Serenade* with plenty of imagination in matters of phrasing. The Decca balance is rather close, which gives excellent inner clarity but sometimes means that the overall blend is not perfectly balanced. But this has always been one of the best versions and now, with an equally fine account of K.375 added for the reissue, it is again very competitive; the digital remastering has great presence.

Admirers of Klemperer will find this reissued EMI CD worthwhile in combining two characteristic performances from 1961 and 1973 respectively. Though tempi tend to be on the slow side, the rhythmic control and fine ensemble make for performances which, despite their seriousness, remain bright and refreshing, not heavy. They are far from being conventional readings but, as the expression of a unique Mozart interpreter, they are undoubtedly illuminating. The sound is clean and clear.

Serenades Nos. 11 in E flat, K.375; 12 in C min., K.388; (i) *6 Notturni for voices & woodwind, K.346, K.436–9, K.549.*
(M) *** EMI mono/stereo CDM7 63958-2; *EG 763958-4*. (i) Emerentia Scheepers, Monica Sinclair, Sir Geraint Evans; L. Bar. Ens., Karl Haas.

Mozart's *C minor Serenade* is dark in mood and colouring and is obviously intended to be taken seriously rather than simply to divert, and this is emphasized by the lean if by no means inexpressive style of the performance here, which is distinguished by its strength of character. Mozart's genius for part-writing and for the perfect blending of wind voices ensures that a wide range of colour and expression is possible with such a combination, and this is especially apparent in the fine set of variations which closes the piece. Both this work and its companion in E flat receive wonderfully smooth yet alive playing from the London Baroque Ensemble (including such charismatic names as Jack Brymer, Bernard Walton, Dennis Brain and Alan Civil in its roster of distinguished wind virtuosi) under Karl Haas, and very well-balanced recording. The charming *Notturni*, mostly love-songs, thought to have been performed first by Mozart's wife Constanze at social gatherings, are accompanied by either two clarinets and a basset horn or three basset horns. This was their first (1953) recording, mono, but smooth and faithful.

Serenades Nos. (i) *11 in E flat, K.375;* (ii) *12 in C min., K.388;* (i) *13 (Eine kleine Nachtmusik), K.525.*
(M) ** Sony SMK 47295 [id.]. Marlboro Festival O (members), (i) Casals; (ii) Schneider.

Very good playing from all concerned in the 1968 account of the *C minor Serenade*, K.388, conducted by Alexander Schneider and decent, if dry, recorded sound; much the same must be said of the 1972 account of the *E flat Serenade*, K.375. The *Eine kleine Nachtmusik* is splendidly played, but the 1967 sound is a little grainy.

Serenade No. 12 in C min., K.388; Wind divertimenti Nos. 12 in E flat, K.252; 13 in F, K.253; 14 in B flat, K.270; 16 in E flat, K.289.
(M) *** Decca 430 298-2; *430 298-4* [id.]. London Wind Soloists, Jack Brymer.

These admirable performances are part of a complete survey of Mozart's wind divertimenti and serenades undertaken by Jack Brymer and his group of virtuosi, which caused quite a stir when they appeared on LP in the early 1960s. They were produced by Erik Smith within the ideal acoustics of Decca's No. 3 Studio, West Hampstead, and the recording sounds wonderfully fresh on CD. The playing is of the very highest order. These artists do not miss the sombre quality of the *C minor Serenade* but they are not intimdated by it, and the *Andante* has a winningly gentle poignancy. The other *Divertimenti* are all minor masterpieces. Throughout, the ear delights in the captivating oboe-playing of Terence MacDonagh (his colleague is James Brown; Brymer and Walter Lear are the clarinettists, Roger Birnstingle and Ronald Waller the bassoonists; and the horn players are Alan Civil and Ian Beers). There are countless felicities: all the finales have a wonderfully light touch, but one remembers especially the engaging three-movement *Divertimento in F*, K.253, with its charming first-movement theme and variations and its slow Minuet with its playful Trio.

Sinfonia concertante in E flat for oboe, clarinet, horn, bassoon and orchestra, K.297b; (i) *Horn concerto No. 3 in E flat, K.447.*
(BB) ** HM/BMG VD 77505 [Victrola 77505-2-

RV]. (i) Hubert Crüts; Coll. Aur., Franzjosef Maier.

A good, robust account of the *Sinfonia concertante* on original instruments, with the warm resonance of the Cedernsaal of Schloss Kirchheim as usual disguising any acerbity in the upper string range. In the concerto Hubert Crüts plays his hand-horn fluently, demonstrating that this work can be presented effectively with only minor slips in intonation, using a minimum of stopped notes. However, few collectors will crave a disc, playing for only 45 minutes, which offers only one of the four *Horn concertos.*

(i) *Sinfonia concertante in E flat for violin, viola and orchestra, K.364;* (ii) *Sinfonia concertante in E flat for oboe, clarinet, horn, bassoon and orchestra, K.297b.*

(M) ** DG 429 813-2; *429 813-4* [id.]. (i) Brandis, Cappone, BPO; (ii) Lehmayer, Schmidl, Högner, Faltl, VPO; Boehm.

These are uneven performances on DG, recorded a decade apart. Boehm's direction of K.364 is stylish and sure, but this work really requires more positive and individual solo playing than Messrs Brandis and Cappone provide, although the performance is not without spontaneity. Moreover the 1966 recording of the orchestra is not ideally focused in its CD transfer. The 1976 Vienna account of the companion work for wind is a different matter: it sounds remarkably idiomatic and well blended. The soloists exert plenty of personality and the recording too is better. This is altogether refreshing.

(i) *Sinfonia concertante in E flat for violin, viola and orchestra, K.364;* (ii) *Symphony No. 39 in E flat, K.543.*

(M) ** Chan. Dig. CHAN 6506; *MBTD 6506* [id.]. (i) Brainin, Schidlof, ECO, Gibson; (ii) LPO, Handley.

Brainin and Schidlof bring plenty of warmth and character to K.364. However, their responsive playing does bring a degree of romanticism to the slow movement, and their phrasing employs tenutos, at times rather indulgently. Yet there is no lack of vitality in outer movements, and Sir Alexander Gibson's accompaniments are stylish and strong. The symphony is more of a routine affair, although the *Andante* is beautifully played. The digital sound is first class in both works.

Complete Mozart Edition, Volume 21: (i) *Sonatas for organ and orchestra (Epistle sonatas) Nos. 1–17* (complete). *Adagio & allegro in F min., K.594; Andante in F, K.616; Fantasia in F min., K.608.*

(M) **(*) Ph. 422 521-2 (2). Daniel Barenboim (organs at Stift Wilhering, Linz, Austria; Schlosspfarrkirche, Obermarchtal, Germany – K.594; K.608); (i) German Bach Soloists, Helmut Winschermann.

Brightly recorded accounts of these pleasing and lively works, with plenty of ambience. The *Epistle sonatas* are so called because they were intended to be heard between the Epistle and the Gospel during the Mass. The balance folds the organ within the strings, perhaps rather too much so, especially in the later works where the obbligato solo part is more important. The final *Sonata*, K. 263, becomes a fully fledged concerto. The set is completed with the other works by Mozart which are usually heard on the organ, and here Barenboim's registration is particularly appealing. Indeed the performances are expert and can be recommended.

SYMPHONIES

Symphonies Nos. 1–47 (including alternative versions); in C, K.35; in D, K.38; in F, K.42a; in B flat, K.45b; in D, K.46a (K.51); in D, K.62a (K.100); in B flat, K.74g (K.216); in F, K.75; in G, K.75b (K.110); in D, K.111a; in D, K.203, 204 & 196 (121); in G, K.425a (K.444); in A min. (Odense); in G (New Lambacher).

(M) *** O-L Analogue/Dig. 430 639-2 (19) [id.]. AAM, Schröder, Hogwood.

The monumental complete recording of the Mozart *Symphonies*, using authentic manners and original instruments, now arrives as a complete set on 19 mid-priced CDs. With Jaap Schröder leading the admirably proportioned string group (9.8.4.3.2) and Christopher Hogwood at the keyboard, this was a remarkably successful joint enterprise. The playing has great style, warmth and polish and, if intonation is not always absolutely refined, that is only to be expected with old instruments. The survey is complete enough to include No. 37 – in fact the work of Michael Haydn but with a slow introduction by Mozart. The *Lambacher* and *Odense Symphonies* are also here, plus alternative versions, with different scoring, of No. 40; while the *Paris Symphony* is given two complete performances with alternative slow movements. Not all ears respond favourably to the non-vibrato tang of the Academy of Ancient Music's exploratory string-sound, and in certain of the earlier symphonies textures are sometimes thinned even further by the use of solo strings in sections of the music, which seems a questionable practice. However, the vitality and resilience of allegros is consistently refreshing and, although some listeners will prefer a more relaxed and less metrical style in slow movements, this remains a remarkable achievement.

Complete Mozart Edition, Volume 1: *Symphonies Nos. 1 in E in E flat, K.16; 4 in D, K.19; in F, K.19a; 5 in B flat, K.22; 6 in F, K.43; 7 in D, K.45; in G (Neue Lambacher), G.16; in G (Alte Lambacher), K.45a; in B flat, K.45b; 8 in D, K.48; 9 in C, K.73; 10 in G, K.74; in F, K.75; in F, K.76; in D, K.81; 11 in D, K.84; in D, K.95; in C, K.96; in D, K.97; 12 in G, K.110; 13 in F, K. 112; 14 in A, K.114; 15 in G, K.124; 16 in C, K.128; 17 in G, K.129; 18 in F, K.130; 19 in E flat, K.132* (with alternative slow movement); *20 in D, K.133; in D, K.161 & 163; in D, K.111 & 120; in D, K.196 & 121; in C, K.208 & 102. Minuet in A, K.61g/1.*
(M) *** Ph. 422 501-2 (6) [id.]. ASMF, Marriner.

The reissue, in the Philips Complete Mozart Edition, of Marriner's recordings of the early symphonies confirms the Mozartian vitality of the performances and their sense of style and spontaneity. There are some important additions, recorded digitally in 1989, notably the *Symphony in F*, K.19a, written when the composer was nine. This reappeared as recently as 1981, when a set of parts was discovered in Munich. Also now included is an alternative Minuet for the Salzburg *Symphony No. 14 in A*, K.114, and another charmingly brief (56 seconds) *Minuet in A*, K.61g/1, previously associated with this work. Modern research suggests that it was written a year earlier (1770), in Italy. The layout remains on six compact discs and the ear is again struck by the naturalness and warm vividness of the transfers. Except perhaps for those who insist on original instruments, the finesse and warmth of the playing here is a constant joy.

Complete Mozart Edition, Volume 2: *Symphonies Nos. 21–36; 37: Adagio maestoso in G, K.44* (Introduction to a symphony by M. Haydn); *38–41; Minuet for a Symphony in C, K.409.*
(M) **(*) Ph. 422 502-2 (6) [id.]. ASMF, Marriner.

As with the early works, the later symphonies in the Marriner performances, as reissued in the Philips Mozart Edition, are conveniently laid out on six mid-priced CDs, offered in numerical sequence, without a single symphony having to be divided between discs. No. 40 is now restored to its expected position, where in the earlier CD box it was out of order. However, the over-resonant bass remains in the recording of this work and also in the *Haffner* (both of which date from 1970, nearly a decade before the rest of the cycle was recorded). Otherwise the transfers are of Philips's best quality, and the performances generally give every satisfaction, even if their style does not show an awareness of the discoveries made – in terms of texture and balance – by the authentic school.

Symphonies Nos. 1 in E flat, K.16; in A min. (Odense), K.16a; 4 in D, K.19; in F, K.19a.
(M) **(*) Unicorn Dig. UKCD 2018. Odense SO, Vetö.

It was in Odense that the lost symphony, K.16a, was discovered by the archivist, Gunnar Thygesen. Alas for everyone's hopes, it seems very unlikely, from stylistic evidence and even the key, A minor, that it is genuine Mozart. It remains a charming work in the *Sturm und Drang* manner, and is well coupled here with an apt group of other early Mozart symphonies, done with warmer tone than those in the Hogwood complete set. First-rate recording.

Symphonies Nos. 18 in F, K.130; 19 in E flat, K.132; 20 in D, K.133; 21 in A, K.134; 22 in C, K.162; 23 in D, K.181; 25 in G min., K.183; 50 in D, K.141a (K.161 & 163: Overture: Il sogno di Scipione).
(B) ** VoxBox 1156012 (2) [CDX 5030]. Mainz CO, Günter Kehr.

An eminently serviceable pair of discs for those interested in exploring the early Mozart symphonies up to and including the G minor masterpiece, K.183. Günter Kehr certainly matches Boehm in Mozartian spirit. The playing is crisp and clean and certainly not without warmth. The acoustic is agreeable, but the resonance produces well-upholstered tuttis, with plenty of bass, perhaps a shade too much.

Symphonies Nos. 21 in A, K.134; 22 in C, K.162; 23 in D, K.181; 24 in B flat, K.182; 25 in G min., K.183.
(B) *** Ph. 426 973-2; *426 973-4*. Concg. O, Josef Krips.

Krips's bargain Concertgebouw sequence of Mozart symphonies leading up to the early masterpiece in G minor (which is done most persuasively) is worth any collector's money. The Dutch players bring the necessary warmth, as well as proving characteristically stylish in phrasing and execution. The *Allegro con spiritoso* movements of Nos. 23 and 24 are certainly spirited and, in the former work, Krips makes the most of the charm of the *Andantino grazioso*, if at a slower tempo than Mackerras (at full price). The 1973/4 sound is full, yet the remastering has brought improved detail and freshness. This is one of the best of the Krips series.

Symphonies Nos. 24–36; 38–41 (Jupiter); Masonic funeral music; Minuet & Trio, K.409.
(M) **(*) EMI Dig. CMS7 63856-2 (6). ASMF, Marriner.

Marriner's third set of Mozart symphony

recordings is the most beautifully recorded of all. The playing, too, is graceful and elegant. With bracing rhythms and brisker pacing than in his earlier, Philips set, these readings are positive yet unidiosyncratic. Phrasing is supple and the Mozartian spirit is always alive here. There is not quite the incandescent freshness of his earliest, Argo/Decca series (see below), and there is a degree of disappointment in the *Haffner* and *Jupiter Symphonies*, which are slightly undercharacterized. For the most part, however, this music-making will give a great deal of pleasure. The six individual CDs are offered here at mid-price, in their original jewel-boxes, within a slip-case.

Symphonies Nos. 25 in G min., K.183; 26 in E flat, K.184; 27 in G, K.199; 29 in A, K.201; 32 in G, K.318.
(M) *** Decca 430 268-2; *430 268-4*. ASMF, Marriner.

A splendidly generous reissue (70 minutes) which makes a fascinating comparison with Marriner's most recent digital recordings for EMI. Although the remastered Argo sound – which is brighter and with rather more edge to the violins – has something to do with it, there is no doubt that in 1969 and 1971 the Academy playing had greater rhythmic bite than it displays in the late 1980s. With an aptly sized group, very well balanced by the engineers, Marriner secures effervescent performances of the earlier symphonies, especially the little *G minor*, the first of the sequence of really great works. The pointing of phrases is done with great vitality and a superb sense of style. The scale of No. 29 is broad and forward-looking, yet the continuing alertness is matched by lightness of touch, while the imaginative detail of any interpretative freedoms adds positively to the enjoyment. The spacious acoustic is well controlled on CD and, though textures are less glowingly rich than in the EMI series, that doesn't seem aurally disadvantageous.

Symphonies Nos. 25 in G min., K.183; 32 in G, K.318; 41 in C (Jupiter), K.551.
(BB) *** Naxos Dig. 8.550113 [id.]. Capella Istropolitana, Barry Wordsworth.

Symphonies Nos. 27 in G, K.199/161b; 33 in B flat, K.319; 36 in C (Linz), K.425.
(BB) *** Naxos Dig. 8.550264 [id.]. Capella Istropolitana, Barry Wordsworth.

Symphonies Nos. 28 in C, K.200; 31 in D (Paris), K.297; 40 in G min., K.550.
(BB) *** Naxos Dig. 8.550164 [id.]. Capella Istropolitana, Barry Wordsworth.

Symphonies Nos. 29 in A, K.201; 30 in D, K.202; 38 in D (Prague). K.504.
(BB) *** Naxos Dig. 8.550119 [id.]. Capella Istropolitana, Barry Wordsworth.

Symphonies Nos. 34 in C, K.338; 35 in D (Haffner), K.385; 39 in E flat, K.543.
(BB) *** Naxos Dig. 8.550186 [id.]. Capella Istropolitana, Barry Wordsworth.

Symphonies Nos. 40 in G min., K. 550; 41 in C (Jupiter), K.551.
(BB) *** Naxos Dig. 8.550299 [id.]. Capella Istropolitana, Barry Wordsworth.

Barry Wordsworth's series of 15 symphonies on the Naxos super-bargain-priced label brings consistently refreshing and enjoyable performances. The Capella Istropolitana consists of leading members of the Slovak Philharmonic Orchestra of Bratislava; though their string-tone is thinnish, it is very much in scale with the clarity of a period performance but tonally far sweeter. The recording is outstandingly good, with a far keener sense of presence than in most rival versions and with less reverberation to obscure detail in tuttis. Very strikingly indeed, the sound here allows a genuine terracing, with the wind instruments, and the horns in particular, rising clear of the string band. Wordsworth observes exposition repeats in first movements, but in the finales only in such symphonies as Nos. 38 and 41, where the movement particularly needs extra scale. In slow movements, as is usual, he omits repeats. Consistently a principal concern with him is clarity of texture. That means he often adopts speeds that are marginally slower than we expect nowadays in chamber-scale performances; but, with exceptionally clean articulation and infectiously sprung rhythms, the results never drag, even if No. 29 is made to sound more sober than usual. In every way these are worthy rivals to the best full-priced versions, and they can be recommended with few if any reservations. Anyone wanting to sample might try the coupling of Nos. 34, 35 and 39 – with the hard-stick timpani sound at the start of No. 39 very dramatic, preferable even to the near-rival, full-price coupling from Tate (of Nos. 32, 35 and 39). The *Linz* too is outstanding. For some, the option of having the last two symphonies coupled together will be useful.

Symphonies Nos. 25 in G min., K.183; 29 in A, K.201; Serenade No. 6 in D (Serenata notturna), K.239.
(B) *** Decca 430 495-2; *430 495-4*. ECO, Britten.

Several years before his untimely death Benjamin Britten recorded these exhilarating performances of the two greatest of Mozart's early symphonies. Inexplicably, the record remained unissued, finally providing a superb codicil to

Britten's recording career. Now it reappears on CD at bargain price. It is striking that in many movements his tempi and even his approach are very close to those of Marriner on his early, Argo recordings; but it is Britten's genius, along with his crisp articulation and sprung rhythms, to provide the occasional touch of pure individual magic. Britten's slow movements provide a clear contrast, rather weightier than Marriner's, particularly in the little *G minor*, where Britten, with a slower speed and more expressive phrasing, underlines the elegiac quality of the music. Full, well-balanced recording. The addition of the *Serenata notturna*, played most engagingly, serves only to make this analogue collection more desirable.

Symphonies Nos. 25 in G min., K.183; 29 in A, K.201; 31 (Paris); 33 in B flat, K.319; 34 in C, K.338; 35 (Haffner); 36 (Linz); 38 (Prague); 39 in E flat, K.543; 40 in G min., K.550; 41 (Jupiter).
(M) ** EMI CMS7 63344-2 (3) [Ang. CDMD 63272]. Philh. O or New Philh. O, Klemperer.

Klemperer's Mozart performances with the Philharmonia were made over a decade between 1957 (*No. 25 in G minor* – sounding a little rough in the remastered transfer) and 1966. His achievement was uneven. The spirit of Beethoven often makes its presence felt, beneficially in the large-scale symphonies, notably in Nos. 38 and 39, but sometimes merely bringing heaviness, as in the *Haffner* and the *Linz*, where the weightiness and portentous feeling step outside the boundaries of Mozartian sensibility. Yet with wonderfully refined playing from the Philharmonia, usually in peak form, there are rare insights. The finale of No. 34 with its scampering triplets is the movement to try first: the rhythmic urgency makes it a delicious experience, while the beautiful *Andante* of the *G minor* (No. 25) has genuine incandescence. In the *Paris Symphony* there is a gain in strength, while the slow movement has a memorable classical poise. The 1963 performance of *No. 40 in G minor* was chosen rather than the earlier (late-1950s) version, because of better recording, but the reading is altogether heavier. The finest performances are undoubtedly the *Prague* and *No. 39 in E flat*, which combine virility and power in the outer movements with grace and elegance in slow movements: the orchestra respond throughout with a spontaneous sense of joy. Surprisingly, however, the *Jupiter* lacks a sense of occasion: while alert and structurally impressive, it never really catches fire. The remastered recording is fresh, bright and usually clean, with no lack of weight.

Symphonies Nos. 25 in G min., K.183; 38 in D (Prague), K. 504.
(M) ** DG Dig. 431 270-2; *431 270-4* [id.]. VPO, James Levine.

There have been more characterful and distinctive readings of No. 25 than this; but the Levine formula of fast allegros, brilliantly played, and a crisp slow movement, all marked by refined Viennese playing, works well enough. The *Prague* has rather more individuality; it certainly shows the VPO on top form in all departments. The sound is good.

Symphonies Nos. 26 in E flat, K.184; 27 in G, K.199; 28 in C, K.200; 29 in A, K.201.
(B) *** Ph. 426 974-2; *426 974-4*. Concg. O, Josef Krips.

Mozart wrote these four key works – which show his symphonic writing moving into maturity – in Salzburg during 1773 and early 1774. Krips recorded them exactly 200 years later; he secures superbly characterful playing from the Concertgebouw Orchestra: the *Molto presto* of No. 26 is bracingly vigorous, yet the work's lyrical counterpart is eminently graceful. Both the previously underrated No. 28 in C and the first great masterpiece in A major are very persuasively done, with apt pacing and almost ethereal delicacy from the strings in the beautiful *Andante* of No. 29, and the horns thrusting exuberantly in the coda of the finale. The CD transfers are exemplary, greatly improving the original LPs' sound, with extra firmness and better-focused detail, yet with no added edge in the treble. The appealing Concertgebouw acoustic adds bloom but does not blur textures. Unfortunately there is no documentation with this Philips series.

Symphonies Nos. 27 in G, K.199; 28 in C, K.200; 34 in C, K.338.
(B) **(*) Pickwick Dig. PCD 933; *CIMPC 933* [id.]. E. Sinfonia, Sir Charles Groves.

Crisp, clean, alert performances of these early symphonies from Sir Charles Groves and no lack of finesse in the playing of the English Sinfonia. Perhaps at times accents seem a shade strong, but rhythms are not unresilient and the *Andante* of No. 34 is shaped elegantly and affectionately, while remaining thoroughly stylish. Compared with Marriner and Mackerras there is perhaps a lack of idiosyncrasy in the readings but, at bargain price and with fine, modern, digital sound, well balanced and with the resonance nicely judged, this is excellent value.

Symphonies Nos. 29–36; 38–41; Divertimento No. 7 in D, K.205; 2 Marches, K.335.
(M) **(*) EMI CZS7 67301-2 (4). ECO, Barenboim.

Barenboim's recordings were made at Abbey Road over a five-year span, between 1966 and 1971, and represented EMI's first serious survey of the major symphonies attempting a proper chamber scale, thus offering an alternative to Marriner and his ASMF working for Argo. This use of an authentic-sized orchestra of modern instruments ensures that the balance between sections is accurate, although the sound caught by the EMI engineers is forward and full-bodied, with a resonant bass. With fine rhythmic pointing and consistently imaginative phrasing, these performances certainly have a place in the catalogue. Nos. 29 and 34, which are among the most exhilarating of the Mozart symphonies with their heaven-scaling finales, are particularly successful, and the *Paris* (No. 31) is also given an outstanding performance, the contrasts of mood in the first movement underlined and the finale taken at a hectic tempo that would have sounded breathless with players any less brilliant than the ECO. The later symphonies are also available separately and are discussed below, although they have been remastered again for the present box and the sound is now fuller, especially for the strings, bringing added weight. The box also includes the *D major Serenade*, K.205, which responds well to Barenboim's affectionate treatment, while the two *Marches* are attractively jaunty and colourful. Of its kind, this is a first-class compilation, though some ears may want a more transparent texture in Mozart.

Symphonies Nos. 29; 31 (Paris); 34; 35 (Haffner); 36 (Linz); 38 (Prague); 39–41 (Jupiter).
(M) (**(*)) EMI mono CHS7 63698-2 (3) [Ang. CDHC 63698]. LPO, Sir Thomas Beecham.

Beecham's pre-war accounts of the Mozart symphonies with the LPO on the old Columbia blue label hold a special place in the affections of older collectors – and rightly so, for, good though his post-war versions with the RPO were, these had a purity of style and a vitality of spirit that he never completely recaptured. The playing as such is marvellous and the lightness of rhythmic accent and plasticity of phrasing have few equals. The *Prague* and the *G minor Symphonies* enjoy special status, even among these classic readings. It goes without saying that these performances are three star and more, but the sound does not compare favourably with the last LP reissue on World Records; it suffers just a little from what can best be described as dehydration (a too common affliction with CD transfers, which means that collectors who have stayed loyal to analogue LPs can claim with justification that they are able to achieve more realistic reproduction). The basically warm studio ambience remains, but the real problem is the sound of the violins above the stave, which are piercing and shrill at peaks. Such a technical drawback is, however, not serious enough to discourage the Beecham enthusiast who has an efficient treble roll-off on his or her reproducer. But this was not how these records sounded on a normal domestic reproducer of the 1940s (especially using 'fibre' needles), which could then compare with the quality of a BBC live broadcast; it ought to have been possible to make CD transfers without this degree of shrillness in the upper range. Even so, this remains a mandatory acquisition for all Mozartians with a CD player.

Symphonies Nos. 29 in A, K.201; 32 in G, K.318; 33 in B flat, K.319; 35 (Haffner), 36 (Linz); 38 (Prague); 39 in E flat, K.543; 40 in G min., K.550; 41 (Jupiter).
(M) *** DG 429 668-2 (3) [id.]. BPO, Karajan.

With Nos. 29, 32 and 33 added to the original LP box, these are beautifully played and vitally alert readings; and the recordings, made between 1966 and 1979, are well balanced and given full, lively transfers to CD. There are details about which some may have reservations, and the opening of the *G minor*, which is a shade faster than in Karajan's earlier, Vienna performance for Decca, many not be quite dark enough for some tastes. But the *Jupiter*, although short on repeats, has weight and power as well as surface elegance.

Symphonies Nos. 29 in A, K.201; 32 in G, K.318; 33 in B flat, K.319.
(M) **(*) Pickwick Dig. PCD 922; *CIMPC 922* [id.]. E. Sinfonia, Sir Charles Groves.

Again Sir Charles Groves shows himself at home in this repertoire, with well-paced readings, cleanly and brightly articulated, especially the rhythmically buoyant minuets and the spirited finales which produce an attractively neat response from the strings and a light touch overall. The slow movements of all three works are gently graceful and beautifully played; the *Andante* of the *A major Symphony* has rather more warmth in Boehm's hands, but many will like Sir Charles's delicacy, helped by an appealing, transparent recording. Indeed the sound is very good indeed, with EMI's No. 1 Studio once more producing a concert-hall impression, with just the right amount of resonance.

Symphonies Nos. 29 in A, K.201; 35 in D (Haffner), K.385; Masonic funeral music, K.477.
(M) **(*) DG 429 803-2; *429 803-4* [id.]. VPO, Karl Boehm.

These performances, which first appeared not long before Boehm's death, are distinguished by finely groomed playing from the Vienna Philharmonic. The first movement of the *A major* is on the slow side, but Boehm's warmth sustains it and there is some lovely expressive playing in the second. Although these performances are weightier than his earlier, complete set with the Berlin Philharmonic, they have a relaxed quality and a glowing resonance which make them endearing, the mature products of octogenarian wisdom. They may sometimes lack drive but they remain compelling. The *Masonic funeral music*, darkly characterful, makes a worthwhile bonus. The 1981 recordings have responded to CD remastering; some of the heaviness has been mitigated, while the orchestral quality is full and naturally balanced within its attractive ambience.

Symphonies Nos. 29 in A, K.201; 35 in D (Haffner), K.385; 40 in G min., K.550.
(M) **(*) Ph. 420 486-2 [id.]. ASMF, Marriner.

Marriner uses original scorings of both the later works – minus flutes and clarinets in the *Haffner*, minus clarinets in No. 40. The readings are finely detailed but dynamic too, nicely scaled against warm recording, with a degree of excess bass resonance. No. 29 was recorded in 1979, but the sound matches up quite well.

Symphonies Nos. 29 in A, K.201; 39 in E flat, K.543.
(M) **(*) DG Dig. 431 268-2; *431 268-4* [id.]. BPO, Karajan.

Karajan's 1968 coupling is now reissued at mid-price in DG's 3D Mozart Collection. Although this is very much big-band Mozart with full, weighty sound, it is easy to respond to the warmth of Karajan's approach to the *A major Symphony*. There is some radiant string playing from the Berlin orchestra – the sounds produced utterly different from the textures of Hogwood's Academy – and if the *E flat Symphony* has a degree of heaviness (like the Minuet of K.201), the strength of the reading is in no doubt and the woodwind detail of the finale is perceptively illuminated.

Symphonies Nos. 29 in A, K.201; 41 in C (Jupiter), K.551; Overture: Die Zauberflöte.
(M) ** EMI CDM7 63959-2 [id.]; *EG 763959-4*. Hallé O, Barbirolli.

As with certain others of the old Pye/Barbirolli records reissued on EMI's Phoenixa label, the sound here has been immeasurably improved in the CD remastering and is strikingly firmer and better focused. The *Jupiter Symphony* is given a much stronger profile. There is still the Italianate warmth in the slow movement and the Minuet's main theme floats gracefully over its accompanying chords, but the finale now sounds more purposeful and dramatic. Some may feel that Barbirolli's warmth in No. 29 brings a degree of slackness, but this is still a charismatic reading, which the conductor's admirers will not want to be without.

Symphonies Nos. 30 in D, K.202; 33 in B flat, K.319; 34 in C, K.338.
(B) **(*) Ph. 422 978-2. Concg. O, Josef Krips.

Krips's performances on this bargain CD and its companions listed below were recorded in 1972/3. The ample Concertgebouw sound, with its resonant bass, emphasizes the breadth of scale of the music-making, yet the digital remastering gives an attractive freshness to the violins, although the Minuets sound rather well upholstered. Krips's tempi are aptly judged and the orchestral playing is a pleasure in itself, especially nimble in finales, which are never raced. Slow movements are graciously phrased, and altogether the music-making here shows Krips as a highly sympathetic if not a specially individual Mozartian.

Symphonies Nos. 30 in D, K.202; 35 in D (Haffner), K.385; Serenade No. 13 in G (Eine kleine Nachtmusik), K.525.
(M) ** DG Dig. 427 811-2; *427 811-4* [id.]. VPO, James Levine.

These performances are characteristic of Levine's Mozart series with the VPO. Strong and stylish, with brisk, well-polished allegros, they lack a little in distinctiveness, although in the *Night music* Levine's direct, elegant manner is in some ways more telling. The digital sound is clean and lively, less well balanced than later issues in the series (No. 30 was one of the first to be recorded).

Symphonies Nos. 31 in D (Paris), K.297; 35 in D (Haffner), K.385; 36 in C (Linz), K.425.
(B) **(*) Ph. 426 063-2. Concg. O, Josef Krips.

These are generally excellent performances, polished, alert and attractively recorded, if the warm Concertgebouw acoustics are not felt to be too weighty. Krips's pacing is relatively steady, but his readings again show a genuine Mozartian sensibility, and have vitality too.

(i) *Symphonies Nos. 31 in D (Paris); 35 in D (Haffner); 40 in G min., K.550; 41 in C (Jupiter)* (CD only: *Symphony No. 32 in G, K.318;* (ii) *Masonic funeral music, K.477*).
(B) **(*) DG Compact Classics 413 151-2 (2); *413 151-4* [id.]. (i) BPO; (ii) VPO, Karl Boehm.

These symphony recordings date from between 1960 and 1966 and come from Boehm's complete Berlin cycle. The playing is first class and the recordings sound well in their remastered format. In the *G minor Symphony* Boehm's featuring of oboes in place of clarinets (he uses Mozart's earlier version of the score) is hardly noticed, so mellifluous is the playing. This is excellent value at Compact Classics price, even if the later Vienna recordings (notably of Nos. 40 and 41) have rather more character. *No. 32 in G* (the recording rather brighter than in the others) plus Boehm's VPO strong and dignified account of the *Masonic funeral music* are added to fill out the pair of CDs attractively.

(i) *Symphonies Nos. 31 in D (Paris), K.297; 36 in C (Linz), K.425;* (ii) *Overture: Le nozze di Figaro.*
(BB) *** ASV CDQS 6033; *ZCQS 6033.* (i) LSO; (ii) RPO, Bátiz.

After a sprightly account of the *Figaro overture* from the RPO, the LSO under Bátiz provide two spirited and polished accounts of favourite named symphonies. Tempi in outer movements are brisk, but the *Presto* finale of the *Linz* (for instance) produces some sparkling playing from the strings; and in both slow movements the phrasing is warm and gracious. With excellent digital recording, this makes an enjoyable super-bargain-priced pairing.

Symphonies Nos. 31 (Paris); 40 in G min.; 41 in C (Jupiter).
(B) *** DG 427 210-2; *427 210-4* [id.]. BPO, Boehm.

Boehm's way with Mozart is broader and heavier in texture than we are used to nowadays, and exposition repeats are the exception rather than the rule; but these are warm and magnetic performances with refined and strongly rhythmic playing, sounding remarkably vivid in their digital transfer.

Symphonies Nos. 32 in G, K.318; 33 in B flat, K.319; 35 in D (Haffner), K.385; 36 in C (Linz), K.425.
(M) *** DG 435 070-2; *435 070-4* [id.]. BPO, Karajan.

With four symphonies now offered instead of the original three, this is excellent value. Here is Karajan's big-band Mozart at its finest. Although there may be slight reservations about the Minuet and Trio of the *Linz*, which is rather slow (and one might quibble at the broadening of tempo at bar 71 of the first movement) and the other minuets are also somewhat stately, overall there is plenty of life here and slow movements show the BPO at their most graciously expressive. The remastered sound is clear and lively, full but not over-weighted.

Symphonies Nos. 33 in B flat, K.319; 35 in D (Haffner), K.385; 36 in C (Linz), K.425.
(BB) ** HM/BMG VD 77525 [77525-2-RV]. Coll. Aur., Franzjosef Maier.

The Collegium Aureum, led rather than conducted by Franzjosef Maier, was one of the earlier groups to play Mozart on original instruments; these excellent analogue recordings, made in the warm acoustics of the Cedernsaal of Schloss Kirchheim, have none of the acerbic, squeezed string timbres which characterized a later generation. Indeed the effect is very like that of a normal chamber orchestra, often quite weighty, as in the first movement of the *Haffner Symphony*. The playing is polished and well paced but the readings are in no way distinctive, although the finale of the *B flat Symphony* is very felicitous.

Symphonies Nos. 35 in D (Haffner), K.385; 36 in C (Linz), K. 425.
(M) ** DG Dig. 431 269-2; *431 269-4*. VPO, James Levine.

Levine's coupling brings characteristically brisk and athletic performances marked by superb playing from all sections of the VPO. There is more life in these readings of the better-known works than in his versions of the earlier symphonies. Repeats are observed and the sound is clean and fresh. But this is not really distinctive.

Symphonies Nos. 35 (Haffner); 36 (Linz); 38 (Prague); 39 in E flat; 40 in G min.; 41 (Jupiter).
(B) *** Sony M2YK 45676 (2). Columbia SO, Bruno Walter.

Walter's set of Mozart's last and greatest symphonies comes from the beginning of the 1960s, his final recording period. The sound remains wonderfully fresh and full; some may feel that the bass resonance is occasionally too ample, but the upper range is sweet and clear and there is no imbalance. The performances are crisp and classical, while still possessing humanity and warmth. Slow movements are outstanding for their breadth and the natural flow of the phrasing. Melodic lines are moulded nobly and pacing always seems inevitable. Walter achieves just the right balance of tempi in the two sections of the first movement of the *Prague*, for instance, and draws from the *Andante* all the sweetness and lyrical power he is capable of. Finales are sparkling and brilliant, but never forced. The *G minor Symphony* is given a treasurable performance; in the *Jupiter*, if neither the first-movement exposition nor the finale carries repeats, Walter structures his interpretation accordingly, and the reading wears an Olympian quality.

'The birth of a performance': (recorded rehearsals of *Symphony No. 36*). *Symphonies Nos. 35 (Haffner); 36 (Linz); 38 (Prague); 39 in E flat; 40 in G min.; 41 (Jupiter).*

(M) *** Sony stereo/mono SM3K 46511 (3) [id.]. Columbia SO, Bruno Walter.

This set includes Walter's earlier version of the *Linz*, recorded in mono in New York City in 1955. Also included are the famous rehearsals of the *Linz Symphony*, called 'The birth of a performance', occupying the first disc. The second disc comprises Walter's mono performance of the *Linz* together with the *Prague* and No. 40, while the third disc contains performances of the *Haffner*, No. 39 and the *Jupiter* symphonies. These stereo recordings are all discussed in detail above.

(i) *Symphonies Nos. 35 in D (Haffner), K. 385; 36 in C (Linz);* (ii) *Rondo for violin and orchestra in B flat, K. 269.*
(M) *** Sony Dig. MDK 44647 [id.]. (i) Bav. RSO, Kubelik; (ii) Zukerman, St Paul CO.

First-class performances from Kubelik and the Bavarian Radio orchestra, well paced and alive in every bar. The *Haffner* is particularly strong, and Kubelik's spacious presentation of the *Linz* is also satisfying. Both slow movements are beautifully played. At the end, Zukerman provides a sparkling encore. The CBS recording is admirable, full, yet clear and well balanced.

Symphonies Nos. 35 (Haffner); 36 (Linz); 38 (Prague).
(B) *** DG 429 521-2; *429 521-4* [id.]. BPO, Boehm.

A splendid bargain triptych showing Boehm on his best form. His Berlin account of the *Linz* is one of his finest Mozart performances, balancing vitality with warmth. It was recorded in 1966 and the sound is first class; its companions were made six years earlier, yet the difference in quality is only marginal and the remastering brings plenty of warmth as well as adding freshness to the violins. The *Haffner* and the *Prague* are also alert and sensitive, and the playing is again of the highest order.

Symphonies Nos. 35 in D (Haffner), K.385; 40 in G min., K.550; 41 in C (Jupiter), K.551.
(M) *** Sony SBK 46333 [id.]; *40-46333*. Cleveland O, Szell.

As in his companion triptych of late Haydn symphonies, Szell and his Clevelanders are shown at their finest here. The sparkling account of the *Haffner* – the first movement incisively brisk but with the daintily rhythmic secondary theme deliciously pointed – is exhilarating, and the performances of the last two symphonies are equally polished and strong. Yet there is a tranquil feeling to both *Andantes* that shows Szell as a Mozartian of striking sensibility and finesse. He is at his finest in the *Jupiter*, which has great vigour in the outer movements and a proper weight to balance the rhythmic incisiveness; in spite of the lack of repeats, the work's scale is not diminished. Here the sound is remarkable considering the early date (late 1950s), and the remastering throughout is impressively full-bodied and clean.

Symphonies Nos. 35 in F (Haffner), K.385; 41 in C (Jupiter), K. 551.
(B) **(*) Pickwick Dig. PCD 914. O of St John's, Smith Square, Oliver Gilmour.

Oliver Gilmour's coupling of the *Haffner* and the *Jupiter* has the benefit of excellent sound, setting genuine chamber-orchestra performances in a believable acoustic. The playing is consistently neat, crisp and transparent; if the finale of the *Jupiter* brings some falling away in weightiness, there is compensation in added zest and spontaneity. Next to the finest versions these are rather plain readings, lacking something in individuality, though the fast movements of the *Haffner* are winningly bold and energetic.

Symphonies Nos. 38 in D (Prague), K.504; 39 in E flat, K.543.
(M) *** Sony Dig. MDK 44648 [id.]. Bav. RSO, Rafael Kubelik.
(M) *** DG 429 802-2; *429 802-4* [id.]. BPO, Karajan.

Symphonies Nos. 38 in D (Prague), K.504; 39 in E flat, K.543; (i) *Rondo in C* (for violin & orchestra), *K.373.*
(BB) **(*) HM/BMG VD 77529 [77529-2-RV]. Coll. Aur., Franzjosef Maier, (i) with Maier (violin).

Kubelik has the advantage of first-class modern digital recording, and this coupling is well up to the standard of the other two discs in his series of late Mozart symphonies. The playing has verve and is highly responsive. No. 39 is especially invigorating in its racy finale but has plenty of strength too.

Karajan's record, too, is strongly recommended. Generally speaking, the playing is so superlative and the sense of pace so well judged that one surrenders to the sheer quality of this music-making: the impression is one of resilience as well as of strength. The remastered recording is of high quality, appropriately weightier in the bass than in the disc offering the earlier symphonies.

This is among the most impressive of the Collegium Aureum recordings made in the Schloss Kirchheim, now reissued in the German Harmonia Mundi Mozart Edition. The weighty, rather grand effect, not at all what one expects from original instruments, suits these two symphonies and especially *No. 39 in E flat*, which is given an expansive reading, very well played. The violins are sweet but lithe, and the orchestral sound is as full as that of a modern chamber orchestra. Franzjosef Maier is the soloist in an attractive account of the *Rondo*, K.373, and here the leonine solo timbre does sound rather more 'authentic'. There is no back-up documentation with this series.

Symphonies Nos. 38 in D (Prague), K.504; 40 in G min., K.550.

(B) *** Decca 430 494-2; *430 494-4.* ECO, Britten.

In his perfomance of No. 40, Britten takes all repeats – the slow movement here is longer than that of *Eroica* – but is nevertheless almost totally convincing, with the rich Maltings sound to give added weight and resonance. In the *Prague* as in No. 40, Britten conveys a real sense of occasion, from the weighty introduction through a glowing and resilient account of the *Allegro* to a full, flowing reading of the *Andante*.

Symphony No. 39 in E flat, K.543.

(M) (**) DG mono 427 776-2 [id.]. BPO, Furtwängler – HAYDN: *Symphony No. 104.* (**)

Though recorded in 1944 in the Berlin State Opera, after the Philharmonie had been bombed, conductor and orchestra were undeterred by any such problems, giving a strong, vigorous performance typical of Furtwängler, a far more stylish classicist than his reputation has generally allowed. The manner is often weighty – notably in the biting, un-Ländler-like account of the Minuet – but the elegance of Mozart is never far away. The sound tends to crumble in loud tuttis, but the performance remains compelling.

Symphonies Nos. 39 in E flat, K.543; 41 in C (Jupiter), K.551.

(BB) *** Virgin/Virgo Dig. VJ7 91461-2; *VJ7 91461-4* [id.]. SCO, Saraste.

(B) ** Ph. 422 974-2. Concg. O, Josef Krips.

Jukka-Pekka Saraste's bargain issue on the Virgo label offers two of the finest performances of these late symphonies available on any disc: fresh, light and resilient in allegros, elegant in the slow movements and with clean, transparent recording. Wordsworth with the Capella Istropolitana may have more weight in these works, but Saraste has extra polish and refinement, with generally brisker speeds, notably in slow movements and minuets. The accompanying notes, however, are almost unbelievably sparse.

This is the least appealing of Krips's three reissued couplings. No. 39 goes well enough, but in the *Jupiter* Krips holds the tension much more slackly and there is something unmemorable and wanting in character that does not do full honour to the fine Mozartian Krips was.

Symphony No. 40 in G min., K.550.

(B) **(*) Pickwick Dig. PCD 820 [id.]. O of St John's, Smith Square, Lubbock – HAYDN: *Symphony No. 44.* ***

(M) (**) BMG/RCA mono GD 60271; *GK 60271* [60271-2-RG; *60271-4-RG*]. NBC SO, Toscanini – BEETHOVEN: *Symphony No. 3.* (***)

Lubbock's is a pleasingly relaxed account of Mozart's *G minor Symphony*, well played – the Minuet particularly deft – and nicely proportioned. The last ounce of character is missing from the slow movement, but the orchestra is responsive throughout, and the recording is in the demonstration class.

Dating from March 1950, Toscanini's version was recorded in the notoriously dry Studio 8-H in Radio City, New York; though the sound is uncomfortable, the high voltage of the interpretation makes considerable amends, with expressive warmth tempering the conductor's characteristic urgency. The slow movement is elegantly done, and even though the finale brings a measure of fierceness, Toscanini eases lovingly into the second subject. A valuable coupling for the maestro's outstanding 1953 account of Beethoven's *Eroica*.

Symphonies Nos. 40 in G min., K.550; 41 in C (Jupiter), K.551.

❀ (M) *** DG Dig. 431 267-2; *431 267-4* [431 040-2; *431 040-4*]. VPO, Leonard Bernstein.

(M) *** Sony Dig. MDK 44649 [id.]. Bav. RSO, Kubelik.

(B) *** CfP CD-CFP 4253; *TC-CFP 40243.* LPO, Mackerras.

(M) **(*) Decca Dig. 430 713-2; *430 713-4* [id.]. AAM, Hogwood.

(M) **(*) EMI Dig. CDD7 63897-2 [id.]; *ET 763897-4.* ASMF, Marriner.

(M) ** Decca Dig. 430 437-2; *430 437-4* [id.]. COE, Solti.

Symphonies Nos. (i) *40 in G min.;* (ii) *41 (Jupiter); Die Zauberflöte: Overture.*

(BB) **(*) LaserLight 15 511 [id.]. (i) Hungarian CO, Tátrai; (ii) LPO, Sándor.

(M) (*) DG mono 431 874-2 [id.]. Berlin State O, Richard Strauss.

This re-coupling represents the finest single issue from the 25 discs which make up DG's mid-priced 3D Mozart Collection, and is perhaps the most distinguished of Bernstein's Mozart records. Both recordings were made in the Musikverein Grosser Saal in January 1984 and were edited together from live performances. Bernstein's electrifying account of No. 40 is keenly dramatic, individual and stylish, with the finale delightfully airy and fresh. If anything, the *Jupiter* is even finer: it is exhilarating in its tensions and observes the repeats in both halves of the finale, making it almost as long as the massive first movement. Bernstein's electricity sustains that length, and one welcomes it for establishing the supreme power of the argument, the true crown in the whole of Mozart's symphonic output. Pacing cannot be faulted in any of the four movements and, considering the problems of making live recordings, the sound is first rate, lacking only the last degree of transparency in tuttis.

Like his excellent coupling of the *Haffner* and *Linz Symphonies*, these performances by Kubelik are strong and beautifully played, with well-integrated tempi and highly responsive phrasing – both slow movements are very appealingly shaped. Kubelik favours first-movement exposition repeats, but here he misses the chance of extending the finale of the *Jupiter*, although the performance certainly does not lack weight. The CBS recording is first class, and Kubelik's disc is fully competitive.

On Classics for Pleasure, Mackerras directs excellent, clean-cut performances which can stand comparison with any at whatever price. He observes exposition repeats in the outer movements of the *G minor* but not the *Jupiter*, which is a pity for so majestic a work. Some may prefer a more affectionate style in slow movements but, with clean (though not especially rich) modern recording, this is well worth considering in the bargain range.

Now reissued at medium price, this separate issue of Nos. 40 and 41 from Hogwood's collected edition makes a first-rate recommendation for those wanting period performances: brisk and light, but still conveying the drama of No. 40 and the majesty of the *Jupiter*; though the lack of expressive feeling typical of slow movements will be disappointing for some. Excellent 1983 digital recording.

On EMI, Marriner is at his best in No. 40, a work he always did very sympathetically. In the last two movements he is strikingly dramatic, with crisper articulation and faster speeds than in his earlier recording for Philips, and this time in the slow movement he observes the first-half repeat. The *Jupiter* is also very well done, but the effect is less charismatic – though, as in No. 40, the recording is first rate.

In the super-bargain range, the LaserLight issue is highly competitive and it offers an excellent version of *The Magic flute overture* as an encore. Sándor's account of the *Jupiter* brings fine playing from the LPO and has plenty of vitality, while the overall length of the performance, with necessary repeats, is 35 minutes, fully conveying the breadth of Mozart's architectural span. Again, in the *G minor Symphony* Tátrai includes the repeats in the outer movements; the playing is polished and there is a nice sense of scale. Both works have agreeable expressive warmth in slow movements, helped by the full, resonant recording, which is obviously modern. There is not quite the individuality of Bernstein here, but both performances communicate strongly.

The talented young players of the Chamber Orchestra of Europe respond acutely to Solti's direction with finely disciplined ensemble, paradoxically producing an interpretation which in many places is uncharacteristic of the conductor, unforced and intimate rather than fiery. The middle movements of No. 40 are disappointing for opposite reasons, the *Andante* too self-consciously pointed and the Minuet too heavy. The *Jupiter* is plainer and much more successful, brightly detailed and crisply articulated. The recording, made in Frankfurt, has plenty of bloom on the sound as well as good detail.

In his day Richard Strauss was a legendary interpreter of Mozart and enjoyed the reputation of conducting with the minimum of fuss and without the slightest expressive exaggeration. These performances come from the 1920s: the *Jupiter* from 1926, the *G minor Symphony* from the following year. Although the ear adjusts, the sound is not particularly good for its period (the acoustic is on the dry side) and the orchestral playing, it must be said, is not particularly distinguished either. Something of a disappointment.

CHAMBER MUSIC

Complete Mozart Edition, Volume 14: (i) *Adagio in C for glass harmonica, K.356;* (i; ii) *Adagio in C min. & Rondo in C for glass harmonica, flute, oboe, viola & cello;* (iii) *Clarinet trio in E flat (Kegelstatt), K.498;* (iv; v) *Piano quartets Nos. 1–2;* (iv) *Piano trios Nos. 1–6; Piano trio in D min., K.442;* (vi) *Piano and wind quintet in E flat, K.452.*

(M) *** Ph. Dig./Analogue 422 514-2 (5) [id.]. (i) Bruno Hoffmann; (ii) with Nicolet, Holliger, Schouten & Decroos; (iii) Brymer, Kovacevich, Ireland; (iv) Beaux Arts Trio; (v) with Giuranna; (vi) Brendel, Holliger, Brunner, Baumann, Thunemann.

It is a comment on the strength of the Philips back catalogue that this compilation of Mozart's chamber music with piano has no weak link. The last three discs contain the complete set of the Mozart *Piano trios* recorded by the Beaux Arts Trio in 1987, a first-rate cycle which includes not only the six completed trios but also the composite work, put together by Mozart's friend, the priest Maximilian Stadler, and listed by Köchel as K.442. It is made up of three unrelated movements that Mozart left unfinished, with an allegro (evidently later than the rest) which is far more inspired. The Beaux Arts' teamwork – with the pianist Menahem Pressler leading the way – brings consistently fresh and winning performances, as it also does in the two great *Piano quartets* where, in recordings made in 1983, they are joined by the viola-player, Bruno Giuranna. The *Piano and wind quintet*, K.452, recorded in 1986, subtly contrasts the artistry of Alfred Brendel at the piano with that of the oboist, Heinz Holliger, leading a distinguished team of wind-players. The only non-digital recordings are those of the *Kegelstatt trio*, characterfully done by Stephen Bishop-Kovacevich with the clarinettist Jack Brymer and the viola-player Patrick Ireland, and of the two shorter works involving glass harmonica. Those last are conveniently included here as an extra, both with Bruno Hoffmann playing that rare instrument, so titillating to the ear if heard in fairly brief spans.

Canons for strings; Canons for woodwind: see below, under VOCAL MUSIC: Complete Mozart Edition, Volume 23.

Complete Mozart Edition, Volume 10: (i; vi) *Clarinet quintet;* (ii) *Flute quartets Nos. 1–4;* (iii; vi) *Horn quintet;* (iv; vi) *Oboe quartet;* (v) *Sonata for bassoon and cello, K.292.* (vi) Fragments: *Allegro in F, K.App. 90/580b for clarinet, basset horn, & string trio; Allegro in B flat. K.App. 91/K.516c for a clarinet quintet; Allegro in F, K.288 for a divertimento for 2 horns & strings; String quartet movements: Allegro in B flat, K.App. 72/464a; Allegro in B flat, K.App. 80/514a; Minuet in B flat, K.68/589a; Minuet in F, K.168a; Movement in A, K.App. 72/464a. String quintet No. 1 in B flat, K.174: 2 Original movements: Trio & Finale. Allegro in A min., K.App. 79 for a string quintet. Allegro in G, K.App. 66/562e for a string trio* (completed, where necessary, by Erik Smith).

(M) *** Ph. Analogue/Dig. 422 510-2 (3) [id.]. (i) Pay; (ii) Bennett, Grumiaux Trio; (iii) Brown; (iv) Black; (v) Thunemann; Orton; (vi) ASMF Chamber Ens.

These highly praised performances of the major chamber works featuring modern wind instruments (Antony Pay uses a normal clarinet) are also available on two separate mid-priced CDs: those with solo clarinet, horn and oboe on 422 833-2, *422 833-4*; and William Bennett's superb set of *Flute quartets* on 422 835-2, *422 835-4*. The *Duo for bassoon and cello* is also very engaging, although the balance somewhat favours the bassoonist, Klaus Thunemann, at the expense of his partner, Stephen Orton. But it is the fragments which make this box particularly enticing. Erik Smith tells us in the notes that, with a single exception, he confined himself to 'filling in the missing instrumental parts without adding any more bars'. The exception is the *Movement in A*, K.464a, planned at the finale for the *String quartet No. 18*, K.464: 'The temptation to complete this extensive fragment and make its lovely music playable proved too strong for me,' says E. S., and he goes on to tell how he ingeniously incorporated a 12-bar sketch of a fugue in G minor, changing the key and building it into the unfinished movement with linking material from elsewhere in the movement. The result is a great success. The rest of the items are by no means inconsequential offcuts but provide music of high quality, notably the *String quartet movement*, K.514a. The *Minuet in B flat*, K.589a, in the rhythm of a polonaise and possibly the first draft for the finale of the *Hunt quartet*, is a real charmer which, had it received more exposure, might well have become a Mozartian lollipop like the famous and not dissimilar Minuet in the *D major Divertimento*, K.334. The two pieces with solo clarinet are also very winning (we have had them before, from Alan Hacker on Amon Ra at full price). The performances here are all polished and spontaneous and beautifully recorded.

Clarinet quintet in A, K.581.

(M) *** EMI CDM7 63116-2 [id.]; *EG 763116-4*. Gervase de Peyer, Melos Ens. – BRAHMS: *Quintet*. ***

(M) ** Decca 417 643-2; *417 643-4* [id.]. Boskovsky, Vienna Octet (members) – BAERMANN: *Adagio*; BRAHMS: *Clarinet quintet*. **(*)

(B) ** Decca 433 647-2; *433 647-4* [id.]. Peter Schmidl, New Vienna Octet (members) – SCHUBERT: *Trout quintet*. **(*)

(i) *Clarinet quintet;* (ii) *Oboe quartet in F, K.370.*

(B) *** CfP CD-CFP 4377; *TC-CFP 4377*. (i) Andrew Marriner; (ii) Gordon Hunt, Chilingirian Qt.

(B) *** Pickwick Dig. PCD 810 [id.]. (i) Puddy; (ii) Boyd, Gabrieli Qt.

Having de Peyer's vintage account of the Mozart *Clarinet quintet* in coupling with his equally inspired reading of the Brahms *Quintet* makes an outstanding bargain on a mid-price disc. This clean, fresh, well-pointed performance with the Melos Ensemble is consistently satisfying, recorded in immediate sound in a relatively dry acoustic.

On the bargain-priced CfP version, recorded in 1981, the young Andrew Marriner's persuasive account occupies the front rank, quite irrespective of price. It is coupled with an equally fine performance of the delightful *Oboe quartet* by Gordon Hunt, another young musician and principal oboe with the Philharmonia at the time of the recording. Marriner's playing in the *Quintet* is wonderfully flexible; it reaches its apex in the radiantly beautiful reading of the slow movement, although the finale is also engagingly characterized. The *Oboe quartet* is delectable too, with Hunt a highly musical and technically accomplished soloist. The Chilingirian players contribute most sympathetically to both works, and the performances are generous in repeats. The CfP issue was recorded in the Wigmore Hall and the sound-balance is most believable.

The bargain-priced Pickwick CD brings a reading of the *Clarinet quintet* which is clean and well paced and, if lacking the last degree of delicacy in the slow movement, is never less than stylish. The young oboist, Douglas Boyd, then gives an outstanding performance in the shorter, less demanding work, with the lilting finale delectably full of fun. The digital recording is vividly immediate and full of presence, with even the keys of the wind instruments often audible.

Boskovsky's account from the mid-1960s is gracious and intimate, a little lacking in individuality, but enjoyable in its unforced way. The sound is excellent, well defined and sweet, to match the mellow approach.

It is difficult to fault the playing in the warm and simple account by Peter Schmidl and members of the New Vienna Octet, and the 1978 recording is far richer than the Schubert coupling. But the overall effect is rather bland.

(i) *Clarinet quintet, K.581;* (ii) *Flute quartet No. 1 in D, K.285;* (iii) *Oboe quartet, K.370.*
(M) *** DG 429 819-2; *429 819-4* [id.]. (i) Gervase de Peyer; (ii) Andreas Blau; (iii) Lothar Koch; Amadeus Qt.

Gervase de Peyer gives a warm, smiling account of the *Clarinet quintet*, with a sunny opening movement, a gently expressive *Larghetto* and a delightfully genial finale. The performance is matched by the refinement of Koch in the *Oboe quartet*. With creamy tone and wonderfully stylish phrasing he is superb. The inclusion of just one of the four *Flute quartets* seems less than ideal, as most Mozartians will want all four. However, it must be admitted that Andreas Blau's playing is delightful, sprightly and full of grace. The Amadeus accompany with sensibility, and the recordings, which date from 1976 and 1978, are flawless, sounding fresh and immediate in their CD format.

(i) *Clarinet quintet in A, K.581;* (ii) *Horn quintet in E flat, K.407*; (iii) *Oboe quartet in F, K.370.*
(M) *** Ph. 422 833-2; *422 833-4*. (i) Antony Pay; (ii) Timothy Brown; (iii) Neil Black; ASMF Chamber Ens.

It is a delightful idea to have the *Clarinet quintet*, *Oboe quartet* and *Horn quintet* on a single CD. Here, Antony Pay's earlier account of the *Clarinet quintet*, played on a modern instrument, with the Academy of St Martin-in-the-Fields players must be numbered among the strongest now on the market for those not insisting on an authentic basset clarinet. Neil Black's playing in the *Oboe quartet* is distinguished, and again the whole performance radiates pleasure, while the *Horn quintet* comes in a well-projected and lively account with Timothy Brown. The recording, originally issued in 1981, is of Philips's best.

(i) *Clarinet quintet, K.581;* (ii) *Piano quartet No. 1, K.478;* (iii) *Serenade (Eine kleine Nachtmusik), K.525;* (iv) *String quintets Nos. 1–6.*
(M) (**(*)) Sony mono/stereo SM3K 46527 (3) [id.]. Budapest Qt, with (i) Oppenheim; (ii) Horzowski; (iii) Julius Levine; (iv) Walter Trampler or Milton Katims.

The accompanying notes mention that the Budapest Quartet was blessed by the tremendous vitality of its inner voices, notably Boris Kroyt's Deconnet viola and Alexander Schneider's Strad. In its prime there wasn't much wrong with the outer voices either! The performances assembled here are of various provenance and the earlier ones are mono. The *C minor String quintet*, K.406, comes from 1946 and the actual sound-quality calls for tolerance, as does the great *C major quintet*, K.515, recorded the previous year. In both cases (but particularly in the latter) tolerance is well worth extending, as the performance is beautifully proportioned and has considerable tonal finesse. The tempi are just right, unhurried yet with an underlying sense of movement and musical tension. The *G minor Quintet*, K.516, is even earlier (1941) and is artistically the highlight of the set. If it is not quite as profoundly searching as the classic Pro Arte version, made a few years earlier and recently reissued on EMI, there is precious little to choose between them. Sonic limitations are soon forgotten, for the quartet's beauty of blend and sonority shine through. A thoughtful and moving performance. The later performances are less impressive, though the *B flat String quintet*, K.174, recorded in 1956, is very fine. The *Clarinet quintet* comes from 1959 and is marred by some vulnerable intonation in the first trio section of the minuet and, though David Oppenheim is obviously a sensitive player, he does not produce as rich a sound as some rivals. The *G minor Piano Quartet*, K.478, is worth hearing for the sake of Horszowski, though the account of the quartet itself leaves something to be desired in terms not only of intonation but also of sonority. All the same, there is some very distinguished playing in this set, which must be recommended, warts and all.

(i) *Clarinet quintet in A, K.581*; (ii) *String quintet No. 4 in G min., K.516.*
(M) **(*) DG Dig. 431 286-2; *431 286-4.* (i) Eduard Brunner, Hagen Qt; (ii) Melos Qt with Franz Beyer.

It was a happy idea to couple what are perhaps Mozart's two greatest quintets, even if the performances are uneven. In the *Clarinet quintet* Eduard Brunner provides a mellifluous tone-quality and blends ideally with the fine Hagens. Everything is musically turned out and tempi are unfailingly sensible, relaxed and unforced. Brunner uses a modern instrument, and those not requiring the use of the more authentic basset clarinet will find this highly musical and the DG recording excellent. The Melos Quartet with their second violist, Franz Beyer, give a finely prepared and thoughtfully conceived account of the *G minor String quintet*, with the overall structure well held together.The famous Adagio is played simply and quite eloquently; but here, as elsewhere, their dynamic range does not vary greatly, and one feels the need for more expressive intensity. Again the sound is natural and well balanced.

Complete Mozart Edition, Volume 13: (i) *Divertimento in E flat for string trio, K.563;* (ii) *Duos for violin and viola Nos. 1–2, K.423/4;* (i) *6 Preludes and fugues for string trio, K.404a;* (iii) *Sonata (String trio) in B flat, K. 266.*
(M) *** Ph. 422 513-2 (2) [id.]. (i) Grumiaux, Janzer, Szabo; (ii) Grumiaux, Pelliccia; (iii) ASMF Chamber Ens.

The *Divertimento in E flat* is one of the richest of Mozart's last-period chamber works, far too rarely heard in the concert hall. Grumiaux's 1967 recorded performance remains unsurpassed; he is here joined by two players with a similarly refined and classical style. They may be an ad hoc group, but their unanimity is most striking, and Grumiaux's individual artistry gives the interpretation extra point. The hushed opening of the first-movement development – a visionary passage – is played with a magically intense half-tone, and the lilt of the finale is infectious from the very first bar. The recording has been remastered again and the excess brightness tamed for its reissue in Philips's Complete Mozart Edition: the balance still favours Grumiaux but he also dominates the performance artistically (as he does also in the *Duos*) and the result is now fully acceptable. In the *Duos*, which are ravishingly played, the balance is excellent, and Arrigo Pelliccia proves a natural partner in these inspired and rewarding works. The *Sonata for string trio* dates from 1777 and has a somewhat bland *Adagio/Andante*, followed by a jaunty Minuet. It is no missing masterpiece but is well played by the ASMF Chamber Ensemble and it has a modern, digital recording. Of the six *Preludes and fugues*, the first three derive from Bach's *Well-tempered clavier*, the fourth combines an *Adagio* from the *Organ sonata*, BWV 527, with *Contrapunctus 8* from the *Art of fugue*, the fifth is a transcription of two movements from the *Organ sonata*, BWV 526, and the sixth uses music of W. F. Bach. Mozart made these arrangements in the early 1780s for Baron Gottfried van Swieten in Vienna, composing *Adagio* introductions for Nos. 1–3 and 6. The performances here are sympathetic and direct, the recorded sound bold, clear and bright.

Divertimento in E flat for string trio, K.563; Duos for violin and viola, Nos 1–2, K.423/4.
(B) **(*) Hung. White Label HRC 072 [id.]. Dénes Kovács, Géza Németh, Ede Banda.

If not quite a match in subtlety for the Grumiaux version, the account of this masterly *Divertimento* by the three Hungarian players is freshly enjoyable, the playing vital, spontaneous and agreeably without mannered idiosyncrasy. Dénes Kovács, the leader, dominates the music-making, both in the *Trio* and in the highly rewarding pair of *Duos* which make the substantial coupling. His athletic style and strong personality add to the life of the performances; if his viola colleague in K.423/4 is less forceful, this remains a proper partnership. The Hungaroton recording is forward but better balanced than the Philips disc; it has a pleasing ambience, and this inexpensive CD is well worth its modest cost.

(i) *6 Divertimenti for 2 clarinets and bassoon, K.439b; 12 Duos (Kegelduette), K.487.*
(M) **(*) DG 431 472-2 (2). Alfred Prinz, Peter Schmidl, (i) with Dietmar Zeman.

Neither of these sets of works is in Mozart's own catalogue, nor can the *Divertimenti* be dated accurately; furthermore their intended instrumentation is uncertain, although scholars suggest that they were intended for three basset-horns. On the other hand, it seems almost certain that the *Duos*, K.487, were written for a pair of horns; even though the writing demands considerable virtuosity from the players, the layout of notes is in the range of the hand-horn, and the very first piece immediately sounds like horn-writing. Moreover, the twelve individual movements are nearly all quite brief. All the *Divertimenti* consist of five movements each: they were originally published as 25 separate items but fit naturally together in groups, especially *Divertimenti Nos. 5* and *6*, which contain some of the most attractive ideas. Mozart's part-writing for wind instruments was incomparable and, whatever the intended instrumentation, the blend of two clarinets and bassoon sounds most felicitous, especially in the delightful *Adagios* of Nos. 5 and 6. Alfred Prinz, Peter Schmidl and Dietmar Zeman match their timbres elegantly and play this music in excellent style, even if at times one feels that their approach is just a little sober. Prinz and Schmidl then use basset-horns characterfully enough in the *Duos*, even if one feels that the music would sound more exciting on hand-horns. The recording (made in Vienna in 1978/9) is immaculate and the CD transfers bring a natural presence to each group. But this is music to dip into rather than to be taken a whole disc at a time.

Flute quartets Nos. 1 in D, K.285; 2 in G, K.285a; 3 in C, K.285b; 4 in A, K.298.

(M) *** Van. 08.4001.71 [OVC 4001]. Paula Robinson, Tokyo Qt (members).

(M) *** Ph. 422 835-2; *422 835-4*. Bennett, Grumiaux Trio.

(BB) ** HM/BMG VD 77517 [77517-2-RV]. Barthold Kuijken, Coll. Aur. (members), Maier.

(BB) ** Naxos Dig. 8.550438 [id.]. Jean Claude Gérard, Villa Musica Ens.

This Vanguard recording of the *Flute quartets* (presumably from the 1960s – no date is given) is most winning. Paula Robinson displays a captivating lightness of touch and her silvery timbre seems eminently suited to Mozart. Needless to say, the Tokyo Quartet provide polished accompaniments which combine warmth with much finesse. Textures are transparent and the recording is most naturally balanced. Just sample the delightful *Adagio* of K.285 in which the flute cantilena floats gently over its pizzicato accompaniment, or the charm and diversity of the two alternative sets of Themes and variations which act as the closing section of K.285b, or the opening movement of K.298, to experience Mozartian spontaneity at its most refreshing.

There also seems to be general agreement about the merits of the William Bennett/Arthur Grumiaux Trio accounts of the *Flute quartets*. They are, to put it in a nutshell, exquisitely played and very well recorded, in every way finer than most other versions which have appeared and disappeared over the years. The freshness of both the playing and the remastered 1971 recording gives very great pleasure.

Those wanting the *Flute quartets* played on a period flute will find the performances by Barthold Kuijken elegantly agreeable. His support from the forwardly balanced members of the Collegium Aureum, recorded within the ample acoustics of the Jagdsaal of the Schloss Schwetzingen, is warm and somewhat larger than life. As usual with this group, the string sound is much mellower than the timbre one normally expects from original instruments.

On Naxos, rather upfront recording with insufficient room round the cello. Good playing from all concerned and, if the level is reduced, the results are acceptable, though lengthy exposure to the sound induces a certain acoustic claustrophobia. There is nothing wrong with the performances, which all give pleasure. Excellent value in the lowest price-range.

(i) *Horn quintet in E flat, K.407;* (ii) *String quartets Nos. 21 in D, K.575; 22 in B flat, K. 589 (Prussian Quartets Nos. 1–2).*

(B) **(*) Hung. White Label HRC 174 [id.]. (i) Ferenc Tarjáni, Kodály Qt; (ii) Eder Qt.

Ferenc Tarjáni is a characterful and sensitive horn player, managing a judicious degree of vibrato with finesse, yet phrasing eloquently and articulating the closing rondo with spirit. He is well partnered by the Kodály players. The Eder Quartet are only slightly less striking in the two *Prussian Quartets*; their playing is polished and sympathetic and they are smoothly recorded. Indeed the sound throughout is vivid and without edginess. Good value.

Piano quartets Nos. 1 in G min., K.478; 2 in E flat, K.493 (see also above, under Complete Mozart Edition, Volume 14).

(B) *** Hung. White Label HRC 170 [id.]. Gyula Kiss, Tátrai Trio.

(M) **(*) Van. 08.8007.71 [id.]. Peter Serkin, Schneider, Tree, Soyer.

Another fine record in Hungaroton's bargain-priced chamber music series brings a very enjoyable pairing of the two *Piano quartets.* Gyula Kiss, the pianist, is a fine and characterful Mozartian, and he dominates performances which are convincingly paced and alive, with the Tátrai string group making an excellent partnership. Both slow movements show the pianist at his most sensitive and the finales have a contrasting lightness of touch that is most appealing. Natural sound with good presence yet no edginess on the strings.

Now that they are paired together, the Vanguard performances are much more competitive. They were recorded in 1965 and the sound, though forward, is very good indeed. Because of the forwardness, the opening of both works is made to sound rather robust; but the music-making is individual, fresh in its Mozartian manners and easy to enjoy. There is a particularly sensitive response to the *Larghetto* of No. 2 and a light-hearted finale. If this were in the bargain range, it would be a very viable alternative to the Hungaroton version.

(i) *Piano quartets Nos 1–2;* (i) *Horn quintet in E flat, K.407.*

❀ (M) *** Decca mono 425 960-2 [id.]. (i) Clifford Curzon, Amadeus Qt; (ii) Dennis Brain, Griller Qt.

All versions of the Mozart *Piano quartets* rest in the shadow of the recordings by Clifford Curzon and members of the Amadeus Quartet (Norbert Brainin, Peter Schidlof and Martin Lovett). No apologies need be made for the 1952 mono recorded sound. An early example of the work of John Culshaw, it may be somewhat two-dimensional but is better balanced than many stereo recordings of chamber music. The warm integration of the strings, with the piano dominating but never dwarfing the ensemble, is ideal. The performances have a unique sparkle, slow movements are elysian, especially the beautiful account of the *Larghetto* of K.493, and the finale of the same work is the epitome of grace. One's only criticism is that the *Andante* of K.478 opens at a much lower dynamic level than the first movement, and some adjustment of the controls needs to be made. The *Horn quintet* coupling was recorded in 1944 and the transfer to CD is even more miraculous. The slight surface rustle of the 78-r.p.m. source is in no way distracting and the sound is unbelievably smooth and beautiful. Dennis Brain's horn contribution is superbly graduated to balance with the textures created by his colleagues, but again the ear registers the remarkable overall blend, with the string players (Sydney Griller, Philip Burton, Max Gilbert and Christopher Hampton) matching timbres in the true spirit of chamber music. There is not a suspicion of wiriness from the leader. The performance itself combines warmth and elegance with a spirited spontaneity, and the subtleties of the horn contribution are a continuous delight. A wonderful disc that should be in every Mozartian's library.

(i) *Piano quartets Nos 1–2. String quartet No. 17 in B flat (Hunt), K.458.*

(M) **(*) Decca 425 538-2; *425 538-4* [id.]. (i) André Previn; V. Musikverein Qt.

Previn's sparkling playing gives these parallel masterpieces – especially the *G minor* – a refreshing spontaneity. Though the tuning of the Musikverein Quartet is not as sweet as that of the Beaux Arts on Philips, the vitality of the Decca coupling – recorded in the warm acoustics of the Kingsway Hall in 1981 – commands attention. For those looking for a modern mid-priced CD, this could well be the answer, particularly as the bonus is a fine version of the *Hunt Quartet*. There is a relaxed, unforced quality about the playing here, though there is no want of brilliance either. This recording dates from 1979 and the CD transfer is more brightly lit, so that the upper string timbre is less smooth.

(i) *Piano quartets Nos. 1 in G min., K.478; 2 in E flat, K.493;* (ii) *Violin sonatas Nos. 17 in C, K.296; 18 in G, K.301.*

(M) (**) Sony mono/stereo MPK 47685 [id.]. George Szell (piano); (i) Budapest Qt (members); (ii) Raphael Druian.

The documentation gives the date of the Szell–Budapest Mozart *Piano quartets* as 1946 though it is difficult to believe it. Indeed they could easily be twenty years later, were it not for the mono sound. The playing is vital yet unforced, and slow movements are relaxed yet held together well. The 1967 stereo sound in the two *Violin sonatas* is drier and altogether less pleasant, and the performances give far less pleasure. But the disc is worth investigating for the *Piano quartets* alone.

(i) *Piano quartet No. 1 in G min., K.478. String quartet No. 16 in E flat, K.428;* (ii) *String quintets Nos. 3 in C, K.515; 4 in G min., K.516; 5 in D, K.593.*

(M) (***) EMI mono CHS7 63870-2 (2) [Ang. CDHB 63870]. (i) Schnabel; Pro Arte Qt, (ii) with A. Hobday.

These classic accounts from the 1930s are in some ways unsurpassed and withstand the passage of time. Schnabel was sometimes wanting in the pianistic grace we associate with later Mozartians, but these are among his best chamber music records; and the playing of the Pro Arte has a very special wisdom and humanity. The slow movement of the *E flat Quartet* will be a revelation to readers who have not encountered this ensemble before and who are used to the hard-boiled Mozart we are offered so often nowadays. The Pro Arte Quartet and Alfred Hobday find more depth and pathos in the *Adagio* fourth movement of the *G minor Quintet* than any ensemble since, and they bring us very close to the spirit of Mozart. A special issue –

even in a year that has been rich in historic Mozartiana.

Piano trios – see above, under Complete Mozart Edition, Volume 14.

Piano and wind quintet in E flat, K.452.
(M) *** Decca 421 151-2; *421 151-4.*
Ashkenazy, L. Wind Soloists – BEETHOVEN: *Quintet.* ***
(B) *** Hung. White Label HRC 169 [id.]. Sándor Fálvai, Hungarian Wind Quintet – BEETHOVEN: *Quintet.* ***

Piano and wind quintet in E flat, K.452; Adagio & rondo for glass harmonica, flute, oboe, violin & viola, K.617.
(BB) *(*) Naxos Dig. 8.550511 [id.]. Jenö Jandó, Kiss, Kovács, Keveházi, Vajda, Kovács, Konrád, Koó – BEETHOVEN: *Quintet.* *(*)

Ashkenazy's performance in Mozart's engaging *Quintet* is outstandingly successful, polished and urbane, yet marvellously spirited. His wind soloists are a distinguished team and their playing comes fully up to expectations. The balance and sound-quality are of the highest order and the CD sounds very natural, although the balance is forward. A first-class mid-priced alternative to the full-price versions led by Perahia and Lupu.

An enjoyably fresh performance from Sándor Fálvai and the excellent Hungarian wind players, given a most natural and realistic sound-balance in a pleasing acoustic. The playing has vitality and finesse, and an attractive degree of robustness too. Yet the *Andante* is appealingly serene and gentle, to act as a foil to the infectious finale.

Like its Beethoven coupling the Naxos performance, although excellently recorded, finds little magic in Mozart's delightful *Quintet.* The first movement is brisk and alive but has no added imaginative touches, and the *Larghetto* proceeds on its leisurely course uneventfully. The finale, however, is quite sprightly. The coupling, in which Jandó changes over to the celeste, is charming in its delicate textures but hardly affects one's response to the main work.

Complete Mozart Edition, Volume 12: *String quartets Nos. 1–23.*
(M) *** Ph. 422 512-2 (8) [id.]. Italian Qt.

String quartets Nos. 1–23; Divertimenti, K.136/8.
(M) ** DG 423 300-2 (6) [id.]. Amadeus Qt.

Those who do not already own the survey of Mozart's *String quartets* by the Quartetto Italiano should lose no time in obtaining Volume 12 of the Philips Complete Mozart Edition. Admittedly the earliest recordings now begin to show their age (notably the six *Haydn Quartets*, which date from 1966): the violin timbre is thinner than we would expect in more modern versions. But the ambience of La Chaux-de-Fonds, Switzerland, is ideal for chamber music and this project continued into the early 1970s. The quality is generally very satisfactory, for the Philips sound-balance is admirably judged. As a set, the performances have seen off all challengers for two decades or more; one is unlikely to assemble a more consistently satisfying overview of these works, or one so beautifully played. They hold a very special place in the Mozartian discography.

DG amazingly accommodate the complete *Quartets* on six mid-priced CDs, so this certainly represents value for money. The performances span more than a decade, and it goes without saying that there are good things among them. However, they do not compete in naturalness of expression or tonal beauty with the Quartetto Italiano on Philips. Although the latter involves a slightly greater outlay, it is well worth the extra cost.

String quartets Nos. 14 in G, K.387; 15 in D min., K.421; 16 in E flat, K.428; 17 in B flat (Hunt), K458; 18 in A, K.464; 19 in C (Dissonance), K.465 (Haydn quartets).
(M) (**(*)) Sony mono SM2K 47219 (2) [id.]. Budapest Qt.
(M) * O-L 433 048-2 (3). Esterhazy Qt.
(B) (**) VoxBox [CD3X 3009] (3). New Hungarian Qt.

These performances are very different from the *Quintets* that the Budapest players recorded only a few years later with Walter Trampler. Mozart's *Haydn Quartets* were made in 1953 with the exception of the *E flat*, K.428, which dates from three years earlier and sounds very good indeed. Although that performance does not have the classic stature of the pre-war Pro Arte set, it is still very fine; though the recording is dry, everything is very clear and well defined. The others offer various felicitous touches and, even if the sound throughout is dryish, it is tonally agreeable. In the early 1950s the Budapest were still in very good form and produced a well-blended sonority. There have been more subtle accounts since, but these performances still give a good deal of pleasure.

The Salomon Quartet have shown that authentic performances of this repertoire can be very successful. The Esterhazy also use period instruments and impose the restraint of no vibrato. However, the gain in textural clarity here is offset by a loss of warmth and of richness of feeling. This is particularly evident in slow movements. The severity of the approach is at first striking but soon appears inhibited and self-conscious and, though the playing itself is of the highest order of accomplishment, it does not bring us close to Mozart. The group are recorded well, but the effect is clinical.

There is nothing wrong and much that is right with the playing of the New Hungarian Quartet; but they are let down by the recording, the sound of which, apart from the (not unacceptably) dryish acoustic, discolours on all forte or sforzato chords. It does not exactly distort, but one instinctively goes to clean the dust from the stylus (or, as 78 collectors will recall, sharpen the fibre needles). The quality at full-room volume is very rough.

String quartets Nos. 14–17 (Hunt); 18–19 (Dissonance); 20–23.
(M) *(*) EMI Dig. CMS7 63858-2 (5). Alban Berg Qt (original CDs packaged in a slip case).

Immensely polished performances, but without quite the grace and elegance the ensemble brought to this repertoire earlier in their career. Their earlier, Teldec discs (or those of the Quartetto Italiano) are much to be preferred.

String quartets Nos. 14 in G, K.387; 15 in D min., K.421.
(B) *(*) Pickwick Dig. PCD 958; *CIMPC 958* [id.]. Alberni Qt.

Straightforward and unaffected performances that would prompt applause in the concert hall, but not quite polished or characterful enough to entice one to return to them. The Alberni play both repeats in the first-movement exposition, which is to be applauded, and they are well if closely recorded.

String quartets Nos. 16 in E flat, K.428; 17 in B flat (Hunt), K.458.
(M) **(*) Ph. 422 832-2. Italian Qt.

String quartets Nos. 18 in A, K.464; 19 in C (Dissonance), K.465.
(M) **(*) Ph. 426 099-2; *426 099-4*. Italian Qt.

The Italian players give a fine, unaffected account of the *Hunt quartet*, although some may feel that it is a shade undercharacterized in places. The other quartets are beautifully done, however; the *Dissonance* is especially successful, and the playing throughout is unfailingly perceptive and most musical. The remastered recording sounds fresh and transparent, if slightly dry in the treble. The ambient effect remains pleasing, but the upper range is less smooth than the (full-price) CRD recording for the Chilingirians.

String quartet No. 17 in B flat (Hunt), K.458.
(M) *** Teldec/Warner 2292 42440-2 [id.]. Alban Berg Qt – HAYDN: *Quartet No. 77.* ***
(M) ** DG Dig. 429 491-2; *429 491-4*. Amadeus Qt – SCHUBERT: *Quartet No. 14.* **(*)

The warmest possible welcome must be given to the return of this early Teldec coupling by the Alban Berg Quartet. At that period in their history these players had not yet acquired the glossy surface veneer that sometimes detracts from their more recent digital recordings. Their version of the *Hunt quartet* dates from 1979 and is still possibly the finest account on the market. It has much greater polish and freshness even than the Quartetto Italiano, the Melos or the Amadeus, and well withstands all the competition that has come since. Although dynamic gradations are steep, there is no sense of exaggeration – on the contrary, there is only a sense of total dedication about this wholly excellent performance, which is recommended with enthusiasm. No reservations about the transfer.

The Amadeus Quartet previously recorded Mozart's *Hunt quartet* in the mid-1960s and it was one of their popular successes. The digital repetition does not quite match the success of the older, analogue version: there is a distinct absence of charm. Moreover, although the CD sound has striking presence, it is a little edgy in the treble. However, at mid-price and coupled with a quite recommendable version of Schubert's *Death and the Maiden quartet*, this seems fair value.

String quartets Nos. 17 in B flat (Hunt), K.458; 19 in C (Dissonance), K.465.
(BB) **(*) Naxos Dig. 8.550105 [id.]. Moyzes Qt.
(M) ** DG 429 818-2; *429 818-4* [id.]. Melos Qt.

The Moyzes Quartet come from Bratislava and are an accomplished ensemble, distinguished by a generally sweet and light tone and decently recorded in the clean acoustic of the Concert Hall of Slovak Radio. The performances are very well prepared and neatly played, phrasing is musical and often sensitive. Greater diversity of colour would be welcome, and the players do not command quite a wide enough range of dynamics, so that the overall effect is just a little bland. But the performances still have a lot going for them and can be recommended.

The Melos performances are soundly conceived and finely executed. The playing is unmannered and thoughtful, and the remastered 1977/8 recording is well balanced and lifelike. The *Dissonance* is certainly enjoyable and the *Hunt* has no lack of vitality. Yet the phrasing seems rather predictable, as if familiarity with these masterpieces has taken its toll of freshness of response.

String quartets Nos. 18 in A, K.464; 19 in C (Dissonance), K.465.

(M) *** EMI CDM7 69102-2 [id.]. Smetana Qt.

The vintage analogue coupling from the Smetana Quartet is excellent in every way. The playing has impetus and feeling, finesse and vitality, and the sound is well balanced, full and clear. Excellent value at mid-price.

String quartets Nos. 20 in D (Hoffmeister), K.499; 21 in D, K.575; 22 in B flat, K.589; 23 in F, K.590 (Prussian Quartets Nos. 1–3).

(M) **(*) DG Dig./Analogue 431 153-2 (2). Melos Qt.

The Melos coupling of the *Second* and *Third Prussian Quartets*, K.589/590, is the most attractive of their Mozart recordings. These works were written for the Prussian king, Friedrich Wilhelm II, who was a keen cellist, and the Melos group possesses a particularly fine cellist in Peter Buck. He has a strong personality and a positive sense of characterization. These artists bring plenty of warmth to the slow movements of both quartets, and the transfer of the 1979/80 analogue recordings is fresh and clear. The other two quartets of the set were recorded digitally in 1981 and 1983. Here there is very accomplished playing, with all the musical intelligence and expertise one expects from this ensemble. In the first movement of the *Hoffmeister* they move things along with the right feeling of musical continuity and rhythmic momentum, but do so at the cost of a certain grace – and this strikes the listener more forcibly in the wonderful Minuet. Nevertheless these performances have many virtues: fine internal balance between the players, a keen responsiveness, superb ensemble and beauty of sound. The recording is excellent.

Complete Mozart Edition, Volume 11: *String quintets Nos. 1–6.*

(M) *** Ph. 422 511-2 (3). Grumiaux Trio, with Gerecz, Lesueur.

String quintets Nos. 1–6.

(M) **(*) DG 431 149-2 (3). Amadeus Qt, with Cecil Aronowitz.

(B) *(*) Hung. White Label HRC 085 (*Nos. 1 & 3*); HRC 086 (*Nos. 2 & 4*); HRC 096 (*Nos. 5–6*). Tátrai Qt with Anna Mauthner.

The Grumiaux recordings of the *String quintets* reappear (now at upper mid-price) as Volume 11 in the Philips Mozart Edition, while DG have now reissued their Amadeus set, recorded between 1968 (K.406, K.515) and 1970 (K.516). While the Grumiaux set is still to be preferred in terms both of interpretation and of recorded sound, the Amadeus is also distinguished by fine playing and the recordings are remarkably successful in their CD transfers, with only a slight degree of thinness on top to date the earlier sessions. The Amadeus accounts of the *C minor* (K.406) and *C major* (K.515) works are particularly searching and spontaneous, and obviously much thought and skill have gone into the matter of internal balance as well as the interpretations. Their account of the *G minor* (K.516) with its elysian slow movement has also been admired, and there is no question about the refinement and polish of the playing, both here and in the *D major* (K.593). Yet overall the Grumiaux performances are fresher and purer in utterance.

Great disappointment has to be expressed concerning the reissues on Hungaroton White Label of the Tátrai performances. The *Adagio* of K.515 is beautifully done and the reading of the great *G minor Quintet* is highly satisfactory. The first movement of the *C minor* (K.406) is rhythmically strong and the Andante refreshingly poised. The last two *Quintets* are splendidly alive, with slow movements thoughtful and finales sparkling. The snag is the sound-balance, with the violins in general impossibly shrill at higher dynamic levels. This seems likely to have come about with the digital remastering, since the recording is basically truthful, with firm cello tone.

String quintets Nos. 3 in C, K.515; 4 in G min., K.516.

(M) (*) Sony mono MPK 45692. Budapest Qt with Walter Trampler.

The two performances recorded here should not be confused with those issued as part of the three-CD set of the Budapest Quartet's Mozart *String quintets*, reviewed above. They come from 1956–7 and are in mono, when the Budapest Quartet was past its prime. No first-movement exposition repeats are observed (nor are they in the earlier versions) and the dry, rather uningratiating sound diminishes the appeal of the set. There are some rough edges here and there: listen to the leader at the beginning of the development of the first movement of the *C major Quintet*, K.515 (Track 1, about 3 minutes 50 seconds in), or the rather off-hand opening of the *G minor*. Lacklustre recording and some pretty rough-and-ready playing (though not from Walter Trampler).

(i) *String quintet No. 4 in G min., K.516;* (i) *Violin sonata No. 26 in B flat, K.378.*

(M) *** BMG/RCA GD 87869 [7869-2-RG]. Heifetz, with (i) Baker, Primrose, Majewski, Piatigorsky; (ii) Brooks Smith – *Violin concerto No. 5.* ***

This recording of the *G minor Quintet* was made at the time of the Pilgrimage Theatre Concerts, given in Hollywood in the autumn of 1961. The illustrious ensemble adopts a very fast pace for the first movement, and some might feel that its urgency is over-pressed; yet so fine is the playing that, after a minute or two, one adjusts as at a live performance. There are wonderful moments in the rest of the work, not least the viola playing of William Primrose. The great slow movement is rapt in its intensity and the opening of the finale is similarly compelling, until the allegro brings the sun out from behind the Mozartian clouds. The acoustic is a little dry, but the sound itself is full and warmly blended, with good detail. The *Violin sonata* was recorded two years later and shows splendid rapport between the great violinist and his partner, Brooks Smith.

Complete Mozart Edition, Volume 15: *Violin sonatas Nos. 1–34; Sonatinas in C & F, K.46d & 46e; Sonatina in F (for beginners), K.547; Sonata in C, K.403* (completed Stadler); *Adagio in C min., K.396; Allegro in B flat, K.372; Andante & allegretto in C, K.404; Andante in A & Fugue in A min., K.402* (completed Stadler); *12 Variations on 'La bergère Célimène', K.359; 6 Variations on 'Hélas, j'ai perdu mon amant', K.360.*
(M) **(*) Ph. Analogue/Dig. 422 515-2 (7). Gérard Poulet, Blandine Verlet; Arthur Grumiaux, Walter Klien; Isabelle van Keulen, Ronald Brautigan.

Two of the seven CDs in Volume 15 of Philips's Complete Mozart Edition are analogue and are from the mid-1970s. The early sonatas, from K.6 through to K.31, were recorded by Gérard Poulet with Blandine Verlet on harpsichord. The various fragments, sonatinas, sonatas (K.46d, K.46e, K.403 and K.547) and variations were recorded in 1990 by Isabelle van Keulen and Ronald Brautigan. For the remaining four CDs, Philips have turned to the set by Arthur Grumiaux and Walter Klien, recorded digitally in the early 1980s. There is a great deal of sparkle and some refined musicianship in these performances, and pleasure remains undisturbed by the balance which, in the 1981 recordings, favours the violin. The later recordings, from 1982 and 1983, are much better in this respect. It goes without saying that there is some distinguished playing here, even if the two artists are not quite so completely attuned as were Grumiaux and Haskil in their earlier, mono set (still at full price).

Violin sonatas Nos. 17–28; 32–4; Sonatina in F, K.547.
(M) *** DG Dig. 431 784-2 (4) [id.]. Itzhak Perlman, Daniel Barenboim.
(M) *** Decca 430 306-2 (4). Szymon Goldberg, Radu Lupu.

Perlman and Barenboim made their recordings in groups, beginning in 1983, returning to the studio in 1984, then again in 1986, and completing the set with the late works four years later. The interpretations (and the recordings) have a remarkable consistency and reflect a genuinely creative musical symbiosis and a spontaneous joy in the music. The digital recordings are beautifully balanced, and this will probably be a first choice for most collectors, although Goldberg and Lupu are by no means outclassed.

Both Goldberg and Lupu bring humanity and imagination to their performances of the mature sonatas, and the playing has freshness and sensitivity. There is no doubt that in these works Goldberg shows a wisdom, born of long experience, that is almost unfailingly revealing. Lupu gives instinctive musical support to his partner; and the recordings, made in the Kingsway Hall in 1975, are expertly balanced and have transferred vividly and realistically to CD. The sense of natural presence is remarkable. An outstanding set in every way.

Violin sonatas Nos. 17 in C, K.296; 18 in G, K.301; 25 in F, K.377.
(M) *** DG Dig. 431 276-2; *431 276-4*. Itzhak Perlman, Daniel Barenboim.

Violin sonatas Nos. 21 in E min., K.304; 23 in D, K.306; 24 in F, K.376.
(M) *** DG Dig. 431 277-2; *431 277-4*. Itzhak Perlman, Daniel Barenboim.

The *Sonata in C*, K.296, is the first of what Alfred Einstein described as Mozart's concertante sonatas; even here, however, the piano is dominant, a point reflected in the fact that, for all Perlman's individuality, it is Barenboim who leads. This is playing of a genial spontaneity that conveys the joy of the moment with countless felicitous details. Excellent, vivid recording, with lots of presence, but neither disc offers particularly generous measure (around 50 minutes).

Violin sonatas Nos. 17 in C, K.296; 24 in F, K.376; 25 in F, K.377.
(BB) * HM/BMG VD 77552. Jaap Schröder, Jos van Immerseel.

For all the renown of these artists, these performances fall short of distinction. There is not much sparkle about Jaap Schröder's playing of the *C major*, and ensemble is not always impeccable. Jos van Immerseel is a much admired and often impressive fortepianist, but the rather resonant acoustic lends his instrument an unwelcome clattery sound which, combined with the rather thin violin sonority, gives less pleasure.

Violin sonatas Nos. 17 in C, K.296; 24 in F, K.376; 26 in B flat, K.378.
(BB) ** Naxos Dig. 8.550065 [id.]. Takako Nishizaki, Wolf Harden.

Takako Nishizaki does not produce a big (or always a particularly beautiful) tone and at times she is covered by Wolf Harden's crisp accompaniment, which the engineer favours. All the same, she is a far from insensitive artist and her playing is always tasteful. However, this is not as good as some of her other records on this label. Wolf Harden is an excellent pianist and always supportive.

Violin sonatas Nos. 26 in B flat, K.378; 27 in G, K.379; 28 in E flat, K.380.
(BB) * HM/BMG VD 77556. Jaap Schröder, Jos van Immerseel.

In the *B flat Sonata*, K.378, which opens the disc, Jos van Immerseel's fortepiano sounds very clangorous, so resonant is the studio. Matters improve somewhat when the level setting is substantially reduced, though Jaap Schröder produces some uningratiating tone at times. The recordings derive from the early 1980s and are presented without notes.

Violin sonatas Nos. 33 in E flat, K.481; 34 in A, K.526; Violin sonatina in F, K.547.
(M) *** Decca 425 420-2. Szymon Goldberg, Radu Lupu.

Goldberg's playing has great depth, though at times his age perhaps begins to show (a slight lack of bloom on his tone); but this does not inhibit the strength of the recommendation, for Lupu is marvellously sensitive. The CD transfer is first class, and this is one of the most rewarding single discs of these *Sonatas*.

PIANO MUSIC

Complete Mozart Edition, Volume 16: (i) *Andante with 5 variations, K.501; Fugue in C min., K.426; Sonatas for piano duet in C, K.19d; D, K.381; G, K.357; B flat, K.358; F, K.497; C, K.521; Sonata in D for two pianos, K.448;* (ii) *Larghetto and Allegro in E flat* (reconstructed Badura-Skoda).
(M) ** Ph. 422 516-2 (2) [id.]. (i) Ingrid Haebler, Ludwig Hoffman; (ii) Jörg Demus, Paul Badura-Skoda.

This two-CD set includes all the music Mozart composed for piano duet or two pianos, in elegant (if at times a little too dainty) performances by Ingrid Haebler and Ludwig Hoffman in recordings dating from the mid-1970s. Also included is a Mozart fragment, the *Larghetto and Allegro in E flat*, probably written in 1782–3 and completed by Paul Badura-Skoda, who recorded it in 1971 for the Amadeo label with Jörg Demus. Despite the occasional distant clink of Dresden china, all these performances give pleasure and are very decently recorded.

Piano duet

Adagio & allegro in F min. (for mechanical organ), *K.594; Andante with 5 variations in G, K.501; Fantasia in F min.* (for mechanical organ), *K.608; Sonatas for piano duet in C, K.19d; B flat, K.358; D, K.381; F, K.497; C, K.521; Sonata in D for 2 pianos, K.448.*
(M) *** DG 435 042-2 (2) [id.]. Christoph Eschenbach, Justus Frantz.

Adagio & allegro in F min., K.594; Andante with variations, K.501; Fantasia in F min., K.608; Sonatas for piano duet in C, K.19b; in B flat, K.358; Sonata for 2 pianos in D, K.381.
(M) *** DG 429 809-2; *429 809-4*. Christoph Eschenbach, Justus Frantz.

We thought well of these performances when they first appeared, and they stand up to the test of time. (They were made between 1972 and 1975.) The major *Sonatas* are magnificent works. Eschenbach and Frantz play with exemplary ensemble and fine sensitivity. The pieces for mechanical clock show (alongside the *Sonatas*) these artists' care for detail, and here as elsewhere they readily convey their own pleasure in the music. The recordings are clean and well balanced, if occasionally a shade dry. They are certainly given good presence on CD.

Solo piano music

Complete solo piano music.
(M) (**) EMI mono CHS7 63688-2 (8). Walter Gieseking.

Gieseking recorded his complete Mozart cycle between 1953 and 1955 for the Columbia label, possibly the first time that any company had embarked on a complete survey of this particular repertoire by a single artist. Such an ambitious survey, comprising some nine hours of music, enjoys intermittent successes and it must be conceded that the playing (like the music) is of variable quality. The 1955 edition of the *Record Guide* spent over two pages discussing the first two LPs and, writing of the earliest pieces, was 'a little surprised that Gieseking does not accord them more charm . . . and we have heard him turn more pearly ornaments than he does here [in K.3 and 4]', but admired 'his eggshell delicacy of tone' elsewhere. Dipping into this set reaffirms the reputation enjoyed in their day by the original LPs; however, while they never fell below a certain level of artistry, they rarely rose to the greatest heights. At times, particularly in the variations, Gieseking is perfunctory; even in such masterpieces as the *C minor Fantasy*, K.475, and *Sonata No. 14 in C minor*, K.457, he is less illuminating than one might expect. Despite the occasional felicities, there are many records that do greater justice to Gieseking's memory than these. The recordings were always a trace dry, and the remastering by Paul Baily enhances the originals considerably.

Piano sonatas Nos. 1–18 (complete).
(M) *** EMI CZS7 67294-2 (5). Daniel Barenboim.

Piano sonatas Nos. 1–10.
❀ (B) *** VoxBox (2) [CDX 5026]. Walter Klien.

Piano sonatas Nos. 11–18; Fantasy in C min., K.475.
❀ (B) *** VoxBox (2) [CDX 5046]. Walter Klien.

Complete Mozart Edition, Volume 17: *Piano sonatas Nos. 1–18; Fantasia in C min., K.475.*
❀ (M) *** Ph. Dig. 422 517-2 (5) [id.]. Mitsuko Uchida.
(M) *** Decca 430 333-2 (5). András Schiff.

Piano sonatas Nos. 1–18; Adagio in B flat, K.540; Fantasias: in D min., K.397; in C min., K.475; Rondos: in D, K.485; in A min., K.511.
(M) ** Ph. 432 306-2 (7) [id.]. Claudio Arrau.

Walter Klien's set was first issued on Turnabout LPs at the beginning of the 1970s as part of his integral recording of all Mozart's piano music; it now reappears, beautifully transferred to CD, with greater naturalness than before. Moreover all 18 *Sonatas* (including the *F major*, which is an amalgam of the *Allegro and Andante*, K.533, with the *Rondo*, K.494), plus the *Fantasia in C minor*, K.475, have been successfully accommodated on four bargain-priced discs. Klien is an outstanding Mozartian; his playing has consistent freshness and is in exemplary taste. It gives enormous pleasure and is at times slightly more robust in its vitality than the playing of Mitsuko Uchida. There is nothing remotely self-conscious about it; the phrasing is unfailingly musical and every detail is beautifully placed without there being the slightest suggestion of preciosity. One has only to sample the opening allegro of the initial sonata included in the first box (*No. 5 in G*, K.283) or the delightful *Andante* which follows, to discover the disarming simplicity of Klien's style and the magic which invests his phrasing, or the spirited articulation of the outer movements of the *C major*, K.309, to find out how special is this music-making. The second box begins with the glorious *A major*, K.311, with its lovely opening *Andante with variations*. Klien captures the grazioso mood of the theme to perfection and later, in the famous closing *Rondo alla Turca*, his buoyant accenting is hardly less captivating. The balance is rather forward (the piano seems just behind the speakers and the sound-image is widely spread), but the tone is rounded and full, and the brightness in the treble never becomes brittle. There is a minimum of background, which never becomes obtrusive. These Vox Boxes still await issue in the UK.

On Philips, Mitsuko Uchida's self-recommending collection, with beautiful and naturally balanced digital recording made in the Henry Wood Hall, London, has now been reissued on 5 mid-priced CDs by omitting the shorter pieces, except for the *C minor Fantasia*. Miss Uchida's set of the Mozart *Sonatas* brings playing of consistently fine sense and sound musicianship. There is every indication that this will come to be regarded as a classic series to set alongside those of Gieseking and Walter Klien. Every phrase is beautifully placed, every detail registers, and the early *Sonatas* are as revealing as the late ones. Throughout, allegros are unerringly paced and impeccably stylish; each movement and each work is seen as a whole, yet detail is consistently illuminated. The slow movements generally bring the kind of sensibility we associate with Perahia in the concertos. The piano recording is completely realistic, slightly distanced in a believable ambience.

András Schiff's earlier, Decca recordings now also reappear, in a box in the same price-range, and they remain in groups, rather than being presented in Köchel-number order like the Philips set. Schiff, without exceeding the essential Mozartian sensibility, takes a somewhat more romantic and forward-looking view of the music. His fingerwork is precise, yet mellow, and his sense of colour consistently excites admiration. He is slightly prone to self-indulgence in the handling of some phrases but such is the inherent freshness and spontaneity of his playing that one accepts the idiosyncrasies as a natural product of live performance. The piano is set just a little further back than in the Philips/Uchida recordings, and the acoustic is marginally more open, which suits his slightly more expansive manner. The realism of the piano image is very striking, and there is only a faint remnant of analogue background noise remaining. This is a fine achievement and these records are very satisfying.

Barenboim's distinguished set of the Mozart *Piano sonatas* is reissued not only at mid-price but now on five CDs instead of the original six. Barenboim, while keeping his playing well within scale in its crisp articulation, refuses to adopt the Dresden china approach to Mozart's *Sonatas.* Even the little *C major*, K.545, designed for a young player, has its element of toughness, minimizing its 'eighteenth-century drawing-room' associations. Though – with the exception of the two minor-key sonatas – these are relatively unambitious works, Barenboim's voyage of discovery brings out their consistent freshness, with the orchestral implications of some of the allegros strongly established. The recording, with a pleasant ambience round the piano sound, confirms the apt scale.

Arrau's Mozart has all the distinctive hallmarks of his pianism: great aristocratic finesse and the cultured, well-rounded sonority that distinguished all his playing. All the same there is a slightly studied and self-conscious quality about some of it. Of course the pianism is immaculate and the slight agogic hesitations may not disturb all listeners. However, these sonatas benefit from a greater directness and immediacy of feeling – and, it must be said, greater sparkle. Although admirers will undoubtedly want this handsomely packaged commemorative edition of his Philips records, this set is not for the uninitiated. As always, the Philips recordings do him proud and are generally very well balanced.

Piano sonatas Nos. 1 in C, K.279; 2 in F, K.280; 3 in B flat, K.281; 4 in E flat, K.282; 5 in G, K.283.
(M) **(*) Denon Dig. DC-8071 [id.]. Maria João Pires.

Piano sonatas Nos. 6 in D, K.284; 7 in C, K.309; 8 in A min., K.310; Rondo in D, K.485.
(M) **(*) Denon Dig. DC-8072 [id.]. Maria João Pires.

Piano sonatas Nos. 9 in D, K.311; 10 in C, K.330; 11 in A, K.331; Rondo in A min., K.511.
(M) **(*) Denon Dig. DC-8073 [id.]. Maria João Pires.

Piano sonatas Nos. 12 in F, K.332; 13 in B flat, K.333; 14 in C min., K.457.
(M) **(*) Denon Dig. DC-8074 [id.]. Maria João Pires.

Piano sonatas Nos. 15 in F, K.533/494; 16 in C, K.545; 17 in B flat, K.570; 18 in D, K.576; Fantasia in D min., K.397.
(M) **(*) Denon Dig. DC-8075 [id.]. Maria João Pires.

Maria João Pires is a good Mozartian: a refreshingly unmannered stylist with clean articulation and admirable technical address. These performances on Denon were recorded in the mid-1970s in Tokyo and show consistent intelligence and refinement. Her complete cycle, available on five separate CDs at mid-price, makes a possible alternative to the Uchida, though the recording is not as rich-toned or full-bodied as the Philips.

Piano sonatas Nos. 1 in C, K.279; 4 in E flat, K.282; 5 in G, K.283; 6 in D, K.284.
(BB) ** Naxos Dig. 8.550447 [id.]. Jenö Jandó.

Piano sonatas Nos. 3 in B flat, K.281; 7 in C, K.309; 11 in A, K.331; 17 in D, K.576.
(BB) ** Naxos Dig. 8.550448 [id.]. Jenö Jandó.

Piano sonatas Nos. 8 in A min., K.310; 10 in C, K.330; Allegro & Andante, K.533; Rondo, K.494.
(BB) ** Naxos Dig. 8.550445 [id.]. Jenö Jandó.

Piano sonatas Nos. 9 in D, K.311; 12 in F, K.332; 15 in C, K.545; 16 in B flat, K.570.
(BB) ** Naxos Dig. 8.550446 [id.]. Jenö Jandó.

Piano sonatas Nos. 11 in A, K.331; 14 in C min., K.457; Fantasia in C min., K.475; Variations on 'Ah, vous dirai-je, maman', K.265.
(BB) ** Naxos Dig. 8.550258 [id.]. Jenö Jandó.

Jenö Jandó again here proves himself a thoughtful and intelligent Mozartian and seeks a crisp, classical profile for the Mozart *Sonatas.* They are presented very directly, with brisk, strong allegros and slow movements played simply rather than invested with any deeper feelings. The recordings, made in Budapest Unitarian church, use close microphones to create a clean, bright piano image against the background resonance; however, this results in some ugliness in loud passages. Compared with artists like Ashkenazy and Brendel, these readings offer no added illumination, even if they are often delicate and always alert and sensitive.

Piano sonatas Nos. 3 in B flat, K.281; 10 in C, K.330; 13 in B flat, K.333.
(M) **(*) DG 431 274-2; *431 274-4* [id.]. Vladimir Horowitz.

It is sensible to have Horowitz's Mozart sonata recordings gathered together. There have to be slight reservations about the sound: the quality in K.333 is rather dry, while K.281 is the most satisfactory. But this was still just about the best recording he received, apart from his live recitals for RCA, and the playing is remarkable, quite unlike any other. It is not always free from affectation but is never less than elegant. A distinguished contribution to DG's 3D Mozart Edition.

Piano sonata No. 8 in A min., K.310; Fantasia in C min., K.396; Rondo in A min., K.511; 9 Variations on a Minuet by Duport, K.573.
(M) **(*) Van. 08.4025.71 [OVC 4025]. Alfred Brendel.

Fine, strong performances from Brendel with a

particularly good set of Variations, where the care with shaping and detail raises the interest of the listener and the stature of the music. The 1968 recording is firm and full. But the measure (51 minutes) could be more generous.

Piano sonatas Nos. 8 in A min., K.310; 14 in C min., K.457; Fantasia in C min., K.475; Rondo: Alla turca (from *Sonata No. 11, K.331*).

(M) *** DG Dig. 431 275-2; *431 275-4*. Maria João Pires.

Maria João Pires is a stylist and a fine Mozartian, as those who have heard any of her cycle on Denon will know. Pires is always refined but is never wanting in classical feeling, and she has a vital imagination. The performance of the *C minor* is particularly fine and her *Rondo Alla turca* engagingly varied in dynamic range: it begins quite gently. Good, clear piano recording, bright but realistic.

Piano sonatas Nos. 8 in A min., K.310; 17 in D, K.576; (i) *Double piano sonata in D, K.448. Rondo in A min., K.511.*

(M) **(*) Decca 425 031-2; *425 031-4* [id.]. Vladimir Ashkenazy; (i) with Malcolm Frager.

Ashkenazy shows impeccable judgement and taste in the solo sonatas. His playing is immaculate and fresh, and this collection can be counted among his finest analogue records. The transfers of 1967/8 Kingsway Hall recordings are very well managed. The *Sonata for two pianos*, however, is on a lower level of tension; although the playing is bold and fluent and the recording excellent, the end result is less individual. Brendel and Klien are much to be preferred (see above). But this is still well worth having for the solo works.

Piano sonata No. 10 in C, K.330.

(M) ** BMG/RCA GD 60415; *GK 60415* [60415-2-RG; *60415-4* RG]. Van Cliburn – DEBUSSY: *Estampes* etc. **; BARBER: *Sonata*. *(*)

Van Cliburn's record, made in the mid-1960s, offers intelligent playing but sound that is wanting in timbre and sonority. The Debussy and Barber are better in this respect but still dryish.

Piano sonatas Nos. 11 in A, K.331; 14 in C min., K.457; 15 in C, K.545; Fantasy in C min., K.475; Variations on 'Ah, vous dirai-je Maman', K.265.

(M) ** DG 429 808-2; *429 808-4* [id.]. Christoph Eschenbach.

Eschenbach's recital calls for little detailed comment. He gives cool, elegant performances, without affectation or mannerism. The playing is not without strength of personality; if it is rather short on charm, it is very tasteful: the first movement of the *C major Sonata* is strikingly crisp and clean. The piano recording is realistic and has good presence but in its remastered format is a trifle over-bold in focus.

Piano sonata No. 12 in F, K.332.

(M) (**) BMG/RCA mono GD 60451 [60451-2-RG]. Vladimir Horowitz: CZERNY: *Variations;* MENDELSSOHN: *Variations sérieuses;* SCHUBERT: *Sonata No. 21*. (**)

Horowitz was recorded in 1947 and the sound is very papery and shallow. There is nothing shallow about the playing though: his Mozart was underrated in this period of his career, just as it was a bit overrated towards the end of his career. No exposition repeat in the first movement, and a moment of unsteady pitch just before the development.

Complete Mozart Edition, Volume 18: *8 Variations in G, K.24; 7 Variations in D, K.25; 12 Variations in C, K.179; 6 Variations in G, K.180; 9 Variations in C, K.264; 12 Variations in C, K.265; 8 Variations in F, K.352; 12 Variations in E flat, K.353; 12 Variations in E flat, K.354; 6 Variations in F, K.398; 10 Variations in G, K.455; 12 Variations in B flat, K.500; 9 Variations in D, K.573; 8 Variations in F, K.613; Adagio in B min., K.540; Eine kleine Gigue in G, K.574; Fantasia in D min., K.397; Minuet in D, K.355; Rondos: in D, K.485; in A min., K.511; 21 Pieces for keyboard, K.1, K.1a–1d;1f; K.2–5; K.5a; K.33b; K.94; K.312; K.394–5; K.399–401; K.408/1; K.453a; K.460.*

(M) ** Ph. Analogue/Dig. 422 518-2 (5) [id.]. Ingrid Haebler or Mitsuko Uchida (both piano), Ton Koopman (harpsichord).

The first three of the five CDs in this collection are taken from Ingrid Haebler's survey of the complete piano music, recorded in the mid-1970s. Although the gentle clink of Dresden china can occasionally be heard, she is an intelligent and perceptive artist who characterizes these variations with some subtlety. The quality of the sound is very good indeed: there is both warmth and presence. Mitsuko Uchida gives us various short pieces, such as the *A minor Rondo*, K.511, and the *B minor Adagio*, K.540, which she plays beautifully – though at less than 40 minutes her disc offers rather short measure. However, Haebler and Koopman make up for that, the latter offering 21 short pieces, including some juvenilia, which he dispatches with some degree of brusqueness. He is very brightly recorded. Recommended, though there is less musical nourishment on the Koopman disc than on its companions.

VOCAL MUSIC

Complete Mozart Edition, Volume 22: (i) *Adagio and fugue in C min., K.546; Maurerische*

Trauermusik, K.477. (ii) *La Betulia liberata* (oratorio), *K.118.* (iii) *Davidde penitente* (cantata), *K.469.* (iv) *Grabmusik (Funeral music), K.42.* (v; i) Masonic music: *Dir, Seele des Weltalls, K.429; Ihr unsre neuen Leiter, K.484; Die ihr unermesslichen Weltalls Schöpfer, ehrt, K.619; Lasst uns mit geschlung'gnen Händen, K.623; Laut verkünde unsre Freude, K.623; Lied zur Gesellenreise, K.468; Lobgesang auf die feierliche Johannisloge, K.148; Die Maurerfreude, K.471; Zerfliesset heut, geliebte Brüder, K.483.* (vi) *Passionslied: Kommet her, ihr frechen Sünder, K.146.* (vii) *Die Schuldigkeit des ersten Gebots* (Singspiel), K.35.

(M) **(*) Ph. Analogue/Dig. 422 522-2 (6) [id.]. (i) Dresden State O, Schreier; (ii) Schreier, Cotrubas, Berry, Fuchs, Zimmermann, Salzburg Chamber Ch. & Mozarteum O, Hagen; (iii) M. Marshall, Vermillion, Blochwitz; (iv) Murray, Varcoe; (v) Schreier, Blochwitz, Schmidt, Leipzig R. Ch.; (vi) Murray; (vii) M. Marshall, Murray, Nielsen, Blochwitz, Baldin; (iii; iv; vi; vii) Stuttgart RSO, Marriner.

The six discs in this volume of the Philips Complete Edition cover choral music from the full range of Mozart's career. The two big oratorios are both early works, *La Betulia liberata* and (even earlier, dating from his twelfth year) *Die Schuldigkeit des ersten Gebots* ('The Duty of the First Commandment'). *Davide penitente* is the cantata largely derived from the torso of the *C minor Mass*, while the sixth disc, in many ways the most inspired of all, contains the Masonic music, vividly done in Dresden under the direction of Peter Schreier. For convenience that disc also includes the purely instrumental Masonic music, the *Mauerische Trauermusik* and the *Adagio and fugue in C minor.* Directed by Leopold Hager, the recording of *La Betulia liberata*, originally recorded by DG in 1978, belongs to the Salzburg Mozarteum series, mainly devoted to the early operas, a plain, well-sung performance that does not quite disguise the piece's excessive length. The orchestral sound is thinner than on the other discs, though voices are well caught. Sir Neville Marriner is the conductor both of *Die Schuldigkeit* and of *Davide penitente*, giving sparkle to the early oratorio and vigour to the cantata, a fine piece. Full texts are given, and informative notes on individual works.

Complete Mozart Edition, Volume 20: (i) *Alma Dei creatoris, K.277;* (ii) *Ave verum corpus, K.618;* (i) *Benedictus sit Deus Pater, K.117; Cibavit eos ex adipe frumenti, K.44;* (iii) *Dixit et Magnificat, K.193;* (i) *Ergo interest, an quis, K.143;* (ii) *Exsultate jubilate, K.165;* (i) *God is our refuge* (motet), *K.20; Inter natos Mulierum, K.72;* (iii) *Litaniae de BMV (Lauretanae), K.109 & K.195;* (i) *Kyries, K.33; K.90–91; K.322–3;* (ii) *Kyrie, K.341;* (iii) *Litaniae de venerabili altaris sacramento, K.125 & K.243;* (i) *Miserere mei, Deus, K.85; Misercordias Domini, K.222; Quaerite primum regnum Dei, K.86; Regina coeli, laetare, K.108; K.127; K.276; Sancta Maria, mater Dei, K.273; Scande coeli limina, K.34; Sub tuum praesidium, K.198; Te Deum laudamus, K.141; Veni, Sancte Spiritus, K.47; Venite, populi, venite, K.260;* (ii) *Vesperae solennes de confessore, K.339;* (iii) *Vesperae solennes de Domenica, K.321.*

(M) *** Ph. 422 520-2 (5) [id.]. (i) Nawe, Reinhardt-Kiss, Schellenberger-Ernst, Selbig, Burmeister, Lang, Büchner, Eschrig, Ribbe, Pape, Polster; (ii) Te Kanawa, Bainbridge, Ryland Davies, Gowell, LSO Ch. & O, Sir Colin Davis; (iii) Frank-Reinecke, Shirai, Burmeister, Riess, Büchner, Polster, (i; iii) Leipzig R. Ch. & SO, Kegel.

The five discs in this volume of the Philips Edition cover the Litanies and Vespers, as well as some shorter pieces. It is fascinating to find that the boy Mozart's very first religious piece is an unaccompanied motet, written in London to an English text, *God is our refuge* – which here the Leipzig singers very forgivably pronounce 'reefuge'. Herbert Kegel with the Dresden Staatskapelle and his Leipzig Radio Choir are responsible for the great majority of the pieces here, fresh and alert if on occasion rhythmically too rigid. The big exception is the great setting of the *Solemn vespers*, K.339, for which Sir Colin Davis's 1971 version has understandably been preferred, when the young Kiri Te Kanawa sings the heavenly soprano setting of *Laudate Dominum* so ravishingly. She is also the soloist in the early cantata *Exsultate jubilate* with its brilliant *Alleluia.* Those 1971 recordings, made in London, are bass-heavy but the voices are still brightly caught. The rest – much of it recorded recently with some excellent soloists – brings very fresh and clean recording, with the choir generally more forwardly placed than in the recordings of Mozart's Masses, made by the same forces.

Complete Mozart Edition, Volume 23: (i) *2 Canons for strings; 14 Canons for woodwind; 10 Interval canons for woodwind*; (ii) *6 Canons for female voices; 3 Canons for mixed voices; 13 Canons for male voices; 4 puzzle canons for mixed voices.* (iii) *53 Concert arias. Aria* (with ornamentation by Mozart) for: J. C. BACH: *Adriano in Siria.* (iv) *8 Vocal Duets, Trios and Quartets.* (v) Alternative arias and duets for: *Così fan tutte; Don Giovanni; Die Entführung aus dem Serail; La finta semplice; Idomeneo; Lucio Silla; Mitridate; Le nozze di Figaro.*

(M) *** Ph. 422 523-2 (8) [id.]. (i) Bav. RSO (members); (ii) Ch. Viennensis, Mancusi or Harrer; (iii) Moser, Schwarz, Popp, Mathis, Gruberová, Sukis, Araiza, Ahnsjö, Lloyd, Berry, Kaufmann, Blochwitz, Lind, Burrows, Eda-Pierre; (iv) Blochwitz, Schariner, Pape, Kaufman, Lind, Jansen, Schreier; (v) Blochwitz, Szmytka, Wiens, Gudbjörnson, Vermillion, Schreier, Mathis, Burrows, Tear, Terfel, Kaufmann, Lind, Scharinger.

Taking three more records than the Decca collection of concert arias (see below), the Philips set offers substantial extras, not just a collection of a dozen or so ensembles and a whole disc of 35 canons (some of them instrumental) but some fascinating alternative versions and substitute arias for different Mozart operas, from *La finta semplice* and *Mitridate* through to the three Da Ponte masterpieces. It is fascinating to have Bryn Terfel, for example, as Figaro in a varied recitative and slightly extended version of the Act I aria, *Non piu' andrai*. Eva Lind is vocally a less happy choice for the items involving Susanna and Zerlina, and generally the sopranos chosen for this collection, stylish Mozartians as they are, have less sumptuous voices than those on the Decca set. Broadly, the arias are presented in chronological order, with full texts, as given in the Decca set, though general essays are provided rather than individual commentaries on each of the many dozens of items. The arias on the first four discs are taken from a series recorded for DG between 1979 and 1982, with most of the rest done recently in digital sound.

Complete Mozart Edition, Volume 24: (i) Lieder: *Abendempfindung; Als Luise die Briefe ihres ungetreuen Liebhabers; Die Alte; An Chloe; An die Freude; An die Freundschaft; Die betrogene Welt; Dans un bois solitaire; Geheime Liebe; Der Frühling; Gessellenreise; Die grossmütige Gelassenheit; Ich würd' auf meinem Pfad; Das Kinderspiel; 2 Kirchenlieder (O Gottes Lamm; Als aus Ägypten); Des kleinen Friedrichs Geburtstag; Die kleine Spinnerin; Komm, liebe Zither, komm; Lied der Freiheit; Das Lied der Trennung; Un moto di gioia; Oiseaux, si tous les ans; Ridente la calma; Sehnsucht nach dem Frühling; Sei du mein Trost; Das Traumbild; Das Veilchen; Verdankt sei es dem Glanz der Grossen; Die Verschweigung; Warnung; Wie unglücklich bin ich nit; Der Zauberer; Die Zufriedenheit (2): (Was frag' ich viel nach Geld und Gut; Wie sanft, wie ruhig fühl' ich hier); Die Zufriedenheit im niedrigen Stande.* (ii) 6 *Notturni for voices and woodwind, K.346; K.436/9 & K.549.*

(M) *** Ph. 422 524-2 (2) [id.]. Elly Ameling, (i) with Dalton Baldwin (piano or organ) or Benny Ludemann (mandolin); (ii) with Elisabeth Cooymans, Peter van der Bilt, Netherlands Wind Ens. (members).

These two discs, containing not just Mozart's solo songs but the six *Nocturnes* for solo voices and wind, make up one of the most delightful volumes in the Philips Complete Mozart Edition. Elly Ameling is the ideal soprano for such fresh and generally innocent inspirations, with her voice at its purest and sweetest when she made the recordings in 1977. In the 1973 recordings of the *Notturni* (setting Italian texts by Metastasio) she is well matched by her soprano and baritone partners, though these are mostly plainer, less distinctive miniatures. The songs may have regularly been dismissed as mere chips from the master's workbench, but it is astonishing what intensity of feeling Ameling conveys, even in the boyhood works. Included are two hymns with organ and two tiny songs with mandolin, while aptly the very last of the series, K.598, is one of the lightest of all, *Children's games*, sparklingly done. The recordings come up with fine freshness and presence.

51 Concert arias (complete).

(M) *** Decca Dig./Analogue 430 300-2 (5) [id.]. Te Kanawa, Berganza, Gruberová, Hobarth, Laki, Winbergh, Fischer-Dieskau, Corena; various orchestras & conductors.

The Decca collection of the Mozart concert arias is based on the set issued in the early 1980s of all the arias for soprano. As in that, the approach has been to give each of the singers a varied group, an attractive arrangement for sequential listening, when each has been shrewdly chosen for Mozartian qualities as well as for characterful and beautiful voice. With most of the recordings made in the Sophiensaal in Vienna – in full-bodied sound, analogue except for the items sung by the tenor, Gösta Winbergh – and with Gyorgy Fischer a warmly sympathetic accompanist in the soprano items, these five well-filled discs make a most attractive set.

Concert arias: (i) *Ah se in ciel, benigne stelle, K.538;* (ii) *Alcandro, lo confesso, K.294;* (i) *Mia speranza adorata, K.416; Nehmt meinen Dank, K.383; No, che non sei capace, K.419; Popoli di Tessaglia, K.316; Vado ma dove?, K.583; Vorrei spiegarvi, K.418.* (iii) Arias from: *Die Entführung aus dem Serail; Il rè pastore; Die Zauberflöte.*

(M) **(*) DG stereo/mono 431 875-2 [id.]. Rita Streich, (i) Bav. RSO, Mackerras; (ii) Salzburg Mozart Academica, Paumgartner; (iii) Berlin RIAS SO, Fricsay.

The collectors' items in this compilation are the recordings of the Queen of the Night's two arias, made in 1955 for Ferenc Fricsay's complete recording of *Zauberflöte*. They have rarely been matched for their fluency and natural brilliance, even though the close balance in the mono recording gives an impression of a bigger voice than Streich actually possessed. The recordings of Blonde's two arias from *Entführung* also come from a complete Fricsay recording in mono, equally assured; and it is a shade disappointing that the voice is not so well focused in the stereo recordings which make up the rest of the disc. Those with Sir Charles Mackerras, originally occupying a complete LP, make the voice sound a little fluttery, exaggerating a rapid vibrato, but the singing is most stylish. Like Schwarzkopf, Streich was a pupil of Maria Ivogun and she always represented the German tradition at its finest.

Concert arias: *A questo seno . . . Or che il cielo, K.374; Basta, vincesti . . . An non lasciarmi, K.486a; Voi avete un cor fedele, K.217. Exsultate, jubilate* (motet), *K.165. Litaniae de venerabili altaris sacramento, K.243: Dulcissimum convivium. Vesperae de Dominica, K.321: Laudate dominum.*
(B) *** Ph. 426 072-2; *426 072-4*. Elly Ameling, ECO, Leppard.

Elly Ameling's natural reserve can sometimes bring a coolness to her presentation, but here the singing, besides being technically very secure, has a simple radiance in the phrasing which is very beautiful. She is equally happy in the concert arias, sung with delightful flexibility of phrase, and in the ecclesiastical music, where the style has a serene simplicity, while *Exsultate, jubilate* has an infectious sense of joy. With well-balanced, sympathetic accompaniments and full, vivid 1969 recording, this is well worth exploring on Philips's bargain Concert Classics label.

Concert arias: *Ah! lo previdi . . . Ah t'invola, K.272; Bella mia fiamma . . . Resta oh cara, K.528; Chi sa, K.582; Nehmt meinen Dank, ihr holden Gönner, K.383; Non più, tutto ascolta . . . Non temer, amato bene, K.490; Oh temerario Arbace! . . . Per quel paterno amplesso, K.79/K.73d; Vado, ma dove?, K.583.*
(M) *** Decca 417 756-2 [id.]. Kiri Te Kanawa, V. CO, György Fischer.

Kiri Te Kanawa's Decca set of Mozart's concert arias for soprano, recorded in 1982, makes a beautiful and often brilliant recital. Items range from one of the very earliest arias, *Oh temerario Arbace*, already memorably lyrical, to the late *Vado, ma dove*, here sung for its beauty rather than for its drama. Atmospheric, wide-ranging recording, which has transferred well to CD.

Concert arias: *Alma grande e nobil core, K.578; Ch'io mi scordi di te?, K.505; Nehmt meinen Dank, K.383; Vado, ma dove?, K.583.* Lieder: *Abendemfindung; Als Luise die Briefe; Die Alte; An Chloë; Dans un bois solitaire; Im Frühlingsanfang; Das Kinderspiel; Die kleine Spinnerin; Das Lied der Trennung; Oiseaux, si tous les ans; Ridente la calma; Sehnsucht nach dem Frühling; Das Trumbild; Das Veilchen; Der Zauberer; Die Zuhfriedenheit.*
(M) *** EMI CDH7 63702-2 [id.]. Schwarzkopf, Gieseking; Brendel; LSO, Szell.

On an earlier full-price CD (EMI CDC7 47326-2) Schwarzkopf's classic series of the Mozart songs with Gieseking was used incomplete as a fill-up for her recordings of Schubert with Edwin Fischer. In this Schwarzkopf Edition issue at mid-price the missing songs are restored – including the most famous one, *Das Veilchen*. With such inspired performances, it comes as an added pleasure that they can now be heard in stereo in this issue. As a generous coupling, the disc also includes Schwarzkopf's much later recordings, with Szell conducting four concert arias – including the most taxing of all, *Ch'io mi scordi di te*. Though the voice is not quite so fresh in the concert arias, the artistry and imagination are supreme, and stereo recording helps to add bloom.

Ave verum corpus, K.618.
(M) *** Decca 430 159-2; *430 159-4* [id.]. St John's College, Cambridge, Ch., Guest – J. HAYDN: *Theresienmesse*; M. HAYDN: *Ave regina.* ***

This simple and eloquent account of Mozart's choral lollipop is beautifully recorded and, it is to be hoped, may introduce some collectors to the inspired late Haydn Mass with which it is coupled.

(i; ii) *Ave verum corpus, K.618;* (iii; iv) *Exsultate, jubilate, K.165; Masses Nos.* (i; ii; iii; v) *10 in C (Missa brevis): Spatzenmesse, K.220;* (ii; iii; vi) *16 in C (Coronation), K.317.*
(M) *** DG 419 060-2. (i) Regensburg Cathedral Ch.; (ii) Bav. RSO, Kubelik; (iii) Edith Mathis; (iv) Dresden State O, Klee; (v) Troyanos, Laubenthal, Engen; (vi) Procter, Grobe, Shirley-Quirk, Bav. R. Ch.

Kubelik draws a fine, vivid performance of the *Coronation Mass* from his Bavarian forces and is no less impressive in the earlier *Missa brevis*, with excellent soloists in both works. Then Edith Mathis gives a first-class account of the *Exsultate, jubilate* as an encore. The concert ends with Bernard Klee directing a serenely gentle account of the *Ave verum corpus* (recorded in 1979). The digital remastering is entirely beneficial.

(i) *Exsultate, jubilate, K.165;* (ii) *Litaniae lauretanae, K.195; Mass No. 16 in C (Coronation), K.137.*

(M) *** Decca 417 472-2. (i) Erna Spoorenberg, Ledger; (ii) Cotrubas, Watts, Tear, Shirley-Quirk, Schola Cantorum of Oxford, ASMF, Marriner.

Marriner's fine 1971 coupling of two of Mozart's most appealing early choral works has been linked with Erna Spoorenberg's radiant and sparkling account of the *Exsultate, jubilate.* In the two more extended works, the solo singing is again outstandingly good, notably the contribution of Ileana Cotrubas; and the Oxford Schola Cantorum are impressively vibrant. The Academy provides the most sensitive and stylish accompaniments and, with the sound full of presence, this reissue must receive the warmest welcome.

Litaniae de venerabili altaris sacramento, K.243.

(M) *** Decca 430 158-2; *430 158-4* [id.]. Marshall, Cable, Evans, Roberts, St John's College, Cambridge, Ch., Wren O, Guest – HAYDN: *Heiligmesse.* ***

Mozart made four settings of the Litany, of which this is the last, written in 1776. It is ambitiously scored for an orchestra of double wind, two horns and three trombones – used to add sonorous gravity to many of the choral passages and to bring point and drama to the choral fugue, *Pignus futurae gloriae.* The opening *Kyrie* and the later *Hostia sancta* integrate the vocal quartet with the chorus almost operatically; among the solo items is a lively, florid tenor contribution to the *Panis vivus*, while in the beautiful *Dulcissimum convivium* the solo soprano is accompanied with flutes added to the orchestra in place of the oboes. Then the trombones return to introduce the *Viaticum in Domino morientium*, sung by the choral sopranos in unison against a pizzicato accompaniment; and later, in the soprano's lovely *Agnus Dei*, both obbligato flute and oboe are used in the scoring. It is Mozart at his most imaginative and vital; the artists here rise to the occasion and give a highly responsive performance, with Margaret Marshall outstanding among the soloists. Excellent 1980 sound.

Masonic music

Music for Masonic occasions: *Adagio in B flat* (for 2 clarinets & 3 basset horns); *Adagio and fugue in C min.* (for string quartet), *K.546; Adagio and rondo in C* (for flute, oboe, viola, cello & celesta), *K.617; Canonic adagio in F* (for 2 basset horns and bassoon), *K.410; Masonic funeral music (Maurerische Trauermusik), K.477;* (Vocal): *Ave verum corpus, K.618; De profundis clamavi (Psalm 129), K.92; Dir, Seele des Weltalls, K.429; Die ihr des unermesslichen Weltalls Schöpfer ehrt, K.619; Die ihr einen neuen Grade, K.468; Ihr unsre neuen Leiter, K.484; Lasst uns mit geschlungnen Händen, K.623a; Laut verkünde unsere Freude, K.623; Die Maurerfreude, K.471; O heiliges Band, K.148; Santa Maria, Mater Dei, K.272; Zerfliesset Heut', geliebte Brüder, K.483.*

(B) **(*) Turnabout 0015 (2). Equiluz, Resch, Hoppe, V. Volksoper Ch. & O, Maag; K. Rapf; Wind Ens. (with *Mass No. 6 in F (Missa brevis), K.192* – Soloists, V. Ac. Chamber Ch., V. Volsoper O, Grossman).

(B) **(*) VoxBox [CDX 5055] (2) (as above, but without *Mass*).

This may be thought an ingenious way of collecting some of Mozart's shorter works together; but in fact, whether or not all this music was intended for Masonic purposes by its composer (*De profundis*, for instance, was written when Mozart was only fifteen), it is now used by the Viennese Lodge, of which the conductor (an excellent Mozartian) is himself a member. If perhaps the best-known music comes off least well, much of the rest is attractive, especially the miniature cantatas. The instrumental music creates pleasing interludes, although Mozart would have been surprised to hear the *Adagio and rondo in C* in this format (charming as it is) since the celesta was a discovery of Tchaikovsky's for the *Nutcracker* ballet! Nevertheless the recording is excellent – the acoustic has the right degree of spaciousness – and the performers catch the moods of the music, sombre or joyful, and make up in vitality and commitment what they lack in polish. A fresh, if not especially refined account of the early *Missa brevis* makes a good bonus on the Turnabout Double. However, this series does not offer musical notes, whereas the VoxBox documentation attempts to relate the music to its Masonic purpose.

Masonic music: *Masonic funeral music (Maurerische Trauermusik), K.477; Die ihr des unermesslichen Weltals Schöpfer ehrt* (cantata), *K.619; Die ihr einen neuen Grade, K.468; Dir, Seele des Weltalls* (cantata), *K.429; Ihr unsre neuen Leiter* (song), *K.484; Lasst uns mit geschlungnen Händen, K.623a; Laut verkünde unsre Freude, K.623; O heiliges Band* (song), *K.148; Sehen, wie dem starren Forscherange, K.471; Zerfliesset heut', geliebte Brüder, K.483.*

(M) *** Decca 425 722-2; *425 722-4*. Werner Krenn, Tom Krause, Edinburgh Festival Ch., LSO, Kertész.

This Decca reissue is among the most worthwhile of those stimulated by the Bicentenary. It contains the more important of Mozart's masonic music in first-class performances, admirably recorded. Most striking of all is Kertész's strongly dramatic account of the *Masonic funeral music*; the two lively songs for chorus, *Zerfliesset heut'* and *Ihr unsre neuen Leiter*, are sung with warm humanity and are also memorable. Indeed the choral contribution is most distinguished throughout, and Werner Krenn's light tenor is most appealing in the other items which he usually dominates.

Complete Mozart Edition, Volume 19: *Masses Nos. 1 in G (Missa brevis), K.49; 2 in D min. (Missa brevis), K.65; 3 in C ('Dominicus'), K.66; 4 in C min. (Waisenhaus), K.139; 5 in G (Pastoral), K.140; 6 in F (Missa brevis), K.192; 7 in C (Missa in honorem Ssmae Trinitatis), K.167; 9 in D (Missa brevis), K.194; 10 in C (Spatzenmesse; 'Sparrow Mass'), K.220; 11 in C ('Credo'), K.257; 12 in C (Spaur-Messe), K.258; 13 in C ('Organ solo'), K.259; 14 in C (Missa longa), K.262; 15 in B flat (Missa brevis), K.275; 16 in C ('Coronation'), K.317; 17 in C (Missa solemnis), K.337; 18 in C min. (Great), K.427; 19 in D min. (Requiem), K.626.*

(M) **(*) Ph. Analogue/Dig. 422 519-2 (9) [id.]. Mathis, Donath, M. Price, McNair, Montague, Shirai, Casapietra, Trudeliese Schmidt, Lang, Schiml, Markert, Burmeister, Knight, Schreier, Araiza, Heilmann, Baldin, Ryland Davies, Rolfe Johnson, Ude, Jelosits, Adam, Polster, Andreas Schmidt, Hauptmann, Rootering, Grant, Eder; Leipzig R. Ch.; Monteverdi Ch.; V. Boys' Ch.; John Alldis Ch.; Ch. Viennensis; Leipzig RSO; E. Bar. Soloists; Dresden State O; LSO; VSO; Dresden PO; Kegel; C. Davis; Gardiner; Schreier; Harrer.

One hardly thinks of Mozart as a profoundly religious composer, but these 18 Masses bear witness to the vigour of his inspiration when setting liturgical words, even in his boyhood and even when repeating the same exercise many times over. It adds to the attractions of this collection, one of the most massive of the volumes in the Philips Complete Mozart Edition, that one has variety of performers. Only one Mass, but that the great *C minor*, has period performers. John Eliot Gardiner's inspired reading, with superb soloists as well as his Monteverdi Choir and English Baroque Soloists, has rightly been chosen in preference to others from the Philips catalogue, and the *Requiem* comes in another outstanding modern version, with the Dresden Staatskapelle and Leipzig Radio Choir conducted by Peter Schreier, as imaginative a conductor as he is a tenor. That same choir and orchestra under the choir's regular conductor, Herbert Kegel, is responsible for the great bulk of the rest of the Masses, three of the early works recorded in 1973, but mostly done in the 1980s. With the chorus tending to be placed a little backwardly, it does not always sound its freshest, but performances – with consistently clean-toned soloists, including latterly Mitsuko Shirai – are bright and well sprung. Sir Colin Davis and the LSO in the earliest recording here, dating from 1971, take a weightier view than any in the *Credo Mass*, K.257, with sound bass-heavy, but again his vigour and freshness are very compelling. Two favourite Masses, the *Coronation Mass* and the *Spatzenmesse* (Sparrow Mass), come in performances conducted by Uwe Christian Harrer with the Vienna Symphony Orchestra and the Vienna Boys' Choir; boys also distinctively take the soprano and alto solos. Though Harrer's speeds tend to be slow, the rhythmic buoyancy is most compelling, with choral sound full and forward. As in all the boxes of the Philips Edition, the notes are first rate, including comments on each Mass individually.

Mass No. 4 in C min. (Weisenhausmesse), K.139.

(M) *** DG 427 255-2. Janowitz, Von Stade, Moll, Ochman, V. State Op. Ch., VPO, Abbado.

By any standards this is a remarkably sustained example of the thirteen-year-old composer's powers, with bustling allegros in the *Kyrie*, *Gloria* and *Credo*, as well as at the end of the *Agnus Dei*, while the *Gloria* and *Credo* end with full-scale fugues. This far from negligible piece sounds at its very best in Abbado's persuasive hands. His is a most characterful account, and the remastered DG recording sounds admirably lively, with the soloists in good perspective.

Mass No. 12 in C (Spaur), K.258.

(M) *** Decca 430 161-2; *430 161-4* [id.]. Palmer, Cable, Langridge, Roberts, St John's College, Cambridge, Ch., Wren O, Guest – HAYDN: *Schöpfungsmesse.* ***

The *Spaur Mass* is not among Mozart's most inspired, but its directness is appealing and the *Benedictus*, which offers a fine Mozartian interplay of chorus and soloists, is very appealing. In a vigorous performance like this, with trombones justifiably doubling some of the choral lines, it is most enjoyable. Excellent Argo sound, 1979 vintage.

Mass No. 16 in C (Coronation), K.317.

(M) **(*) DG 423 913-2 (2) [id.]. Tomowa-Sintow, Baltsa, Krenn, Van Dam, V. Singverein, BPO, Karajan – BEETHOVEN: *Missa solemnis.* ***

(M) **(*) DG Dig. 429 980-2; *429 980-4* [id.]. Battle, Schmidt, Winbergh, Furlanetto, V.

Singverein, VPO, Karajan – BRUCKNER: *Te Deum*. *

(B) **(*) DG 429 510-2; *429 510-4* [id.]. Stader, Dominguez, Haefliger, Roux, Brasseur Ch., LOP, Markevitch – BEETHOVEN: *Mass in C*. **

(i) *Mass No. 16 in C (Coronation), K.317;* (ii; iii) *Missa brevis in C (Spatzenmesse), K.220*; (iii) *Ave verum corpus;* (iv) *Exsultate, jubilate, K.165; Vesperae solennes de Confessore, K.339: Laudate Dominum.*

(M) **(*) DG 429 820-2; *429 820-4* [id.]. (i) Tomowa-Sintow, Baltsa, Krenn, Van Dam, V. Singverein, BPO, Karajan; (ii) Mathis, Troyanos, Laubenthal, Engen; (iii) Regensberger Cathedral Ch., Bav. RSO, Kubelik; (iv) Mathis, Dresden Ch. & State O, Klee.

Karajan's 1976 recording of the *Coronation Mass* is a dramatic reading, lacking something in rhythmic resilience perhaps; but, with excellent solo singing as well as an incisive contribution from the chorus, there is no lack of strength and the score's lyrical elements are sensitively managed. Kubelik draws a fine, lively account of the earlier *Missa brevis*, and again the solo singing is of high quality. Bernard Klee contributes a serene performance of the lovely *Ave verum corpus*, and Edith Mathis offers a first-class account of the *Exsultate, jubilate* and a slightly less appealing *Laudate Dominum* (recorded in 1979, six years after the motet). The remastering is vivid: although the choral focus in the two main works is not absolutely sharp, the sound is otherwise impressive, the ambience agreeably expansive.

Karajan's 1985 recording of Mozart's *Coronation Mass* is certainly vibrant, with fine choral singing and good soloists. Kathleen Battle sings beautifully in the *Agnus Dei*, and the recording is bright, if not ideally expansive. But the Bruckner coupling is much less recommendable.

Markevitch's performance, though not always completely refined, is incisively brilliant and its sheer vigour is infectious. That is not to say that its lyrical moments are not equally successful. He has an impressive team of soloists and they are well matched in ensemble as well as providing very good individual contributions; the *Agnus Dei* is especially fine. The brightly remastered recording has plenty of life and detail.

(i) *Mass No. 16 in C (Coronation), K.317;* (ii) *Requiem Mass in D min., K.626.*

(B) **(*) DG Compact Classics *419 084-4* [id.]. (i) Mathis, Procter, Grobe, Shirley-Quirk, Bav. R. Ch. and SO, Kubelik; (ii) Mathis, Hamari, Ochman, Ridderbusch, V. State Op. Ch., VPO, Boehm.

A characteristically generous Compact Classics coupling, with good sound throughout. Both recordings were made in the early 1970s. Kubelik draws a fine, mellow-toned performance of the *Coronation Mass* from his Bavarian forces, lacking something in exuberance but still alive and well sung. Boehm's account of the *Requiem* is also spacious but has more power, and the majesty of the closing *Agnus Dei* is very involving. The recording loses little in its chrome-tape transfer and is strikingly well balanced.

Mass No. 18 in C min. (Great), K.427.

(M) *** DG Dig. 431 287-2; *431 287-4*. Hendricks, Perry, Schreier, Luxon, V. Singverein, BPO, Karajan.

(i) *Mass No 18 in C min. (Great), K.427. Masonic funeral music, K.477.*

(B) **(*) DG 429 161-2; *429 161-4* [id.]. (i) Stader, Töpper, Haefliger, Sardi, St Hedwig's Cathedral Ch.; Berlin RSO, Fricsay.

In his 1982 digital recording of the *C minor Mass* Karajan gives Handelian splendour to this greatest of Mozart's choral works and, though the scale is large, the beauty and intensity are hard to resist. Solo singing is first rate, particularly that of Barbara Hendricks, the dreamy beauty of her voice ravishingly caught. Woodwind is rather backward, yet the sound is both rich and vivid – though, as the opening shows, the internal balance is not always completely consistent.

Fricsay's powerful 1960 recording of the *C minor Mass* brings often bitingly dramatic choral singing. The performance is not without its eccentricities – the accelerando at the close of the *Osanna*, for instance – but the conductor's volatile approach adds to the feeling of freshness. Maria Stader distinguishes herself in the *Laudamus te* and concludes the *Credo* most beautifully. Hertha Töpper, however, is less satisfactory and in the *Domine Deus* she tends to mar the duet she shares with Stader by conveying a lack of comfort in certain high passages where a similar phrase passes from one singer to the other. But even with such blemishes this music-making communicates very directly, and the focus on CD is remarkably clear, with plenty of depth to back up the bright upper range. The performance of the *Masonic funeral music* is also distinctive, bringing out the special colour which gives this remarkable miniature its character.

Requiem Mass (No. 19) in D min., K.626.

(BB) *** Virgin/Virgo Dig. VJ7 91460-2; *VJ7 91460-4* [id.]. Yvonne Kenny, Alfreda

Hodgson, Arthur Davies, Gwynne Howell, N. Sinfonia Ch., LSO Ch., N. Sinfonia, Richard Hickox.

(M) *** DG Dig. 431 288-2; *431 288-4*. Tomowa-Sintow, Müller Molinari, Cole, Burchuladze, V. Singverein, VPO, Karajan.

(M) *** DG 429 821-2; *429 821-4* [id.]. Tomowa-Sintow, Baltsa, Krenn, Van Dam, V. Singverein, BPO, Karajan.

(B) **(*) EMI CZS7 62892-2 (2) [Ang. CDZB 62892]. Armstrong, J. Baker, Gedda, Fischer-Dieskau, Alldis Ch., ECO, Barenboim – VERDI: *Requiem*. **

(M) **(*) Ph. 420 353-2; *420 353-4* [id.]. Donath, Minton, Ryland Davies, Nienstedt, Alldis Ch., BBC SO, C. Davis.

(B) **(*) EMI CDZ7 62518-2; *LZ 762518-4*. Donath, Ludwig, Tear, Lloyd, Philh. Ch. & O, Giulini.

(B) **(*) CfP CD-CFP 4399; *TC-CFP 4399*. Mathis, Bumbry, Shirley, Rintzler, New Philh. Ch., New Philh. O, Frühbeck de Burgos.

(M) ** DG Dig. 431 041-2; *431 041-4*. McLaughlin, Ewing, Hadley, Hauptmann, Ch. & Bayreuth RSO, Bernstein.

(B) ** DG 429 160-2; *429 160-4* [id.]. Lipp, Rössl-Majdan, Dermota, Berry, V. Singverein, BPO, Karajan.

(BB) *(*) Naxos Dig. 8.550235 [id.]. Hajóssyova, Horská, Kundlák, Mikuláš, Slovak PO & Ch., Košler.

(B) *(*) Decca 417 681-2; *417 681-4*. Ameling, Horne, Benelli, Franc, V. State Op. Ch., VPO, Kertész.

(M) *(*) Sony SBK 46344 [id.]. Alliot-Lugaz, Visse, Hill, Reinhardt, Regional Ch. Nord-pas-de-Calais, Grande Écurie et La Chambre du Roy, Malgoire – CHARPENTIER: *Te Deum*. *(*)

Requiem Mass, K.626; Ave verum corpus, K.618.

(M) **(*) BMG/RCA GD 86535 [RCA 6535-2-RG]. Equiluz, Eder, Vienna Boys' Ch., V. State Op. Ch. & O, Gillesberger; or VSO, Froschauer – HAYDN: *Te Deum*. **(*)

At superbargain price, Richard Hickox's excellent version of the *Requiem Mass* on the Virgo label matches any in the catalogue. With generally brisk speeds and light, resilient rhythms, it combines gravity with authentically clean, transparent textures in which the dark colourings of the orchestration, as with the basset horns, come out vividly. All four soloists are outstandingly fine, and the choral singing is fresh and incisive, with crisp attack. The voices, solo and choral, are placed rather backwardly; otherwise the recording is excellent, full and clean to match the performance.

Karajan's 1987 digital version of the *Requiem* is a large-scale reading, but one that is white-hot with intensity and energy. The power and bite of the rhythm are consistently exciting. The solo quartet is first rate, though Helga Müller Molinari is on the fruity side for Mozart. Vinson Cole, stretched at times, yet sings very beautifully, and so does Paata Burchuladze with his tangily distinctive Slavonic bass tone. The close balance adds to the excitement, though the sound, both choral and orchestral, lacks transparency.

Unlike his earlier analogue recording (see below), Karajan's 1976 version is outstandingly fine, deeply committed. The toughness of his approach is established from the start with incisive playing and clean-focused singing from the chorus, not too large and set a little backwardly. The fine quartet of soloists is also blended beautifully. The remastered recording sounds first class.

The surprise version is Gillesberger's. Using treble and alto soloists from the Vienna Boys' Choir, who sing with confidence and no little eloquence, this performance also has the advantage of a dedicated contribution from Kurt Equiluz. Gillesberger's pacing is well judged and the effect is as fresh as it is strong and direct. The 1982 recording is excellent, vivid yet full, and the result is powerful but not too heavy. Mozart's *Ave verum* is also very well sung.

Barenboim's earlier EMI account is greatly to be preferred to his later, French recording for the same label. However, at bargain price on Laser it now comes in harness with Barbirolli's less than outstanding set of Verdi's *Requiem*. In the Mozart, Barenboim's exuberance may raise a few eyebrows. The *Dies irae*, for instance, has such zest that one senses the chorus galloping towards the Day of Judgement with enthusiasm. Yet the underlying drama and musicality of the performance as a whole disarm criticism. The lyricism is beautifully calculated and, with a good solo team, excellent choral singing and fine orchestral playing (the opening of the *Lacrimosa* very well managed), this is a splendidly alive performance, and the remastered sound is very good.

Davis with a smaller choir gives a more intimate performance than is common, and with his natural sense of style he finds much beauty of detail. In principle the performance should have given the sort of 'new look' to the Mozart *Requiem* that was such a striking success in Handel's *Messiah*, but Davis does not provide the same sort of 'bite' that in performances on this scale should compensate for sheer massiveness of tone. The BBC Symphony Orchestra is in good form and the soloists – although varying in quality – keep up a laudably high standard. Anyone wanting a version on this scale need not hesitate, but this is plainly not the definitive version. The recording is good but not ideally sharp in focus, although it is fully acceptable on CD.

Giulini, in his bargain version also on EMI Laser, directs a large-scale performance which brings out rather more Mozartian lyricism than Mozartian drama. The choir is in excellent, incisive form and the soloists are a first-rate quartet. The 1979 recording now sounds fresher and clearer, without too much loss of weight.

The glory of Frühbeck's Classics for Pleasure reissue is the singing of the New Philharmonia Chorus. Frühbeck does not have a very subtle Mozart style, but as an interpretation it stands well in the middle of the road, not too romantic, not too frigidly classic; quite apart from the choral singing – recorded with good balance – the soloists are all first rate. The remastering has brought added clarity, and this is quite competitive in the bargain price-range.

Bernstein, in preparation for this recording of a work he had long neglected, made a special study not only of textual problems but also of most of the existing recordings, not least those which use period instruments. He also opted to make the recording in a church of modest size. Yet Bernstein's romantic personality engulfs such gestures towards authenticity and the result is a rich, warm-hearted reading, marked by a broad, expressive style in the slower sections. With weighty choral singing to match and with good, if flawed, solo singing, it is a strongly characterized reading, which yet hardly makes a first choice.

Karajan's earlier (1962) recording, now reissued on DG's bargain label, took a suave view of the work. The chief objection to this version is that detail tends to be sacrificed in favour of an almost bland richness of choral texture, massive in its weight. With measured tempi, in its way the effect cannot fail to be impressive, particularly as the remastered CD has firmed up the choral focus. The solo quartet are wonderfully blended, a rare occurrence in this work, and the spirited playing of the Berlin Philharmonic is another plus point. While both Karajan's later versions, digital and analogue, are greatly preferable, this is by no means without appeal.

Though the chorus and soloists are first rate on the Naxos issue, recorded in Bratislava, the style of the performance is on the heavy side, with generally slow speeds and rhythms that are often square and plodding. The four soloists are all firm and fresh-toned, though their tuning together is not always impeccable.

Kertész offers yet another large-scale view of Mozart's last work, but unfortunately he cannot rely on a really first-rate chorus. Much of the choral singing here is rather wild and smudgy, enthusiastic but not stylish enough for Mozart; and the impression is worsened by the forward balance of the singers against the orchestra.

There are good things, of course, in the Malgoire version, though the recording is distinctly subfusc and the choir does not always produce firmly focused tone, particularly the sopranos. Not a serious contender, even though it offers generous playing time.

Vesperae de dominica, K.321.

(M) *** Decca 430 162-2; *430 162-4* [id.]. Marshall, Cable, Evans, Roberts, St John's College, Cambridge, Ch., Wren O, Guest – HAYDN: *Harmoniemesse.* ***

Aptly coupled with Haydn's *Harmoniemesse*, Mozart's vibrant *Vesperae de dominica* opens with a series of brilliant choral settings (with contrasting solo quartet), accompanied by trumpets and strings, without violas – *Dixit Dominus . . . Confitebor . . . Beatus vir* – followed by a *Laudate pueri* 'in the learned style'. Margaret Marshall is appropriately agile in the lively soprano solo of the *Laudate Dominum*, and the work closes with an ambitious *Magnificat* in which all the participants are joined satisfyingly together. The St John's performance is full of vigour and Guest creates a proper sense of apotheosis in the work's closing section. The 1980 recording is full and vivid, and the CD transfer demonstrates the excellence of the original Argo sound-balance.

Vesperae solennes de confessore, K.339.

(M) *** Decca 430 157-2; *430 157-4* [id.]. Palmer, Cable, Langridge, Roberts, St John's College, Cambridge, Ch., Wren O, Guest – HAYDN: *Paukenmesse.* ***

Although Guest's version of Mozart's masterpiece does not always match the full-price recording by Sir Colin Davis for Philips – Felicity Palmer is a less poised soloist than Kiri Te Kanawa – the Decca account has the advantage of authenticity in the use of boys in the chorus. Moreover the CD transfer of the 1979 Argo recording is preferable to the less well-defined Philips sound: the Decca remastering is cleanly focused, yet has plenty of warmth and atmosphere.

OPERA

Complete Mozart Edition, Volume 26: *Apollo et Hyacinthus* (complete).

(M) *** Ph. 422 526-2 (2) [id.]. Augér, Mathis, Wulkopf, Schwarz, Rolfe Johnson, Salzburg Chamber Ch. & Mozarteum O, Hager.

This recording was made in Salzburg in 1981

for DG and has been passed over to Philips for their integral series. The opera was written when Mozart was eleven, with all but two of the parts taken by schoolchildren. The style of the writing and vocalization is rather simpler than in other dramatic works of the boy Mozart, but the inspiration is still remarkable, astonishingly mature. The orchestration is assured and full of imaginative touches. Specially delightful is the eighth of the nine numbers, a duet between the heroine, Melia, and her father after her brother, Hyacinthus, has died. The accompaniment of muted violins with pizzicato second violins and bass with divided violas is magical. The performance here is stylish and very well sung. If, as so often in early Mozart, recitatives seem too long, the CD banding allows one to make one's own selection if not requiring the whole opera. Excellent, clear and well-balanced recording, admirably transferred to CD. The voices are forward but not excessively so.

Complete Mozart Edition, Volume 30: *Ascanio in Alba* (complete).
(M) **(*) Ph. 422 530-2 (3) [id.]. Sukis, Baltsa, Mathis, Augér, Schreier, Salzburg Chamber Ch., Salzburg Mozarteum O, Hager.

Mozart provided this '*Festa teatrale*' as a festive entertainment for the coronation of the Archduke Ferdinand to an Italian princess in Milan in 1771. Written when he was fifteen, it came between the boy composer's two other Milan commissions, *Mitridate* and *Lucio Silla*. At 2¾ hours it is comparably expansive, though as a classical celebration of marriage – with Ascanio representing the young Archduke and the nymph Silvia representing the bride he had never previously seen, Maria Beatrix d'Este – it lacks the dramatic qualities of those other imaginative examples of *opera seria*. At its first performance it scored an immediate success with its unquenchable inventiveness, completely eclipsing the other newly commissioned work for the coronation, an opera by Hasse. Though it hardly compares with what Mozart was to do later, it brings one delightful number after another. Interspersed between the arias are choruses of comment, far more so than is usual in an *opera seria*. The final trio leads on, very imaginatively for the time, to a recitative and separate cabaletta, before the final brief chorus. Hager makes an excellent start with an exceptionally lively account of the delightful overture, but then the choruses seem relatively square, thanks to the pedestrian, if generally efficient singing of the Salzburg choir. Hager's speeds are sometimes on the slow side, but the singing is excellent, with no weak link in the characterful cast, though not everyone will like the distinctive vibrato of Lilian Sukis as Venus. The analogue recording, made in collaboration with Austrian Radio in 1976, is full and vivid.

Complete Mozart Edition, Volume 27: *Bastien und Bastienne* (complete); Lieder: *Komm, liebe Zither, komm; Die Zufriedenheit.*
(M) *** Ph. Dig. 422 527-2 [id.]. Dominik Orieschnig, Georg Nigl, David Busch, V. Boys' Ch., VSO, Harrer.

Mozart's second opera, written at the age of twelve, is a German Singspiel so simple in style that often, as here, it is performed by boy trebles instead of the soprano, tenor and bass originally intended. Members of the Vienna Boys' Choir give a refreshingly direct performance under Uwe Christian Harrer, missing little of the piece's charm,, though a modern recording with adult singers would still be welcome. The two songs with mandolin accopmpaniment, also sung by one of the trebles, make an attractive fill-up. First-rate 1986 digital sound.

Complete Mozart Edition, Volume 44: *La clemenza di Tito* (complete).
(M) *** Ph. 422 544-2 (2) [id.]. Dame Janet Baker, Minton, Burrows, Von Stade, Popp, Lloyd, ROHCG Ch. & O, Sir Colin Davis.

La clemenza di Tito (complete).
(M) *** DG 429 878-2 (2) [id.]. Berganza, Varady, Mathis, Schreier, Schiml, Adam, Leipzig R. Ch., Dresden State O, Boehm.
(M) ** Decca 430 105-2 (2) [id.]. Krenn, Berganza, Casula, Popp, Fassbaender, Franc, VPO Ch. & O, Kertész.

Sir Colin Davis's superb set is among the finest of his many Mozart recordings. Not only is the singing of Dame Janet Baker in the key role of Vitellia formidably brilliant, with every roulade and exposed leap flawlessly attacked; she actually makes one believe in the emotional development of an impossible character, one who progresses from villainy to virtue with the scantiest preparation. The two other mezzo-sopranos, Minton as Sesto and Von Stade in the small role of Annio, are superb too, while Stuart Burrows has rarely if ever sung so stylishly on a recording as here; he makes the forgiving Emperor a rounded and sympathetic character, not just a bore. The recitatives add to the compulsion of the drama, while Davis's swaggering manner in the pageant music heightens the genuine feeling conveyed in much of the rest, transforming what used to be dismissed as a dry *opera seria*. Excellent recording, which gains in brightness and immediacy in its CD format.

In his mid-eighties Karl Boehm at last managed to record *La clemenza di Tito*, and he gave the work warmth and charm, presenting the piece more genially than we have grown used to. The atmospheric recording helps in that, and the cast is first rate, with no weak link, matching at every point that of Sir Colin Davis on his full-price Philips set. Yet, ultimately, even Julia Varady for Boehm can hardly rival Dame Janet Baker for Davis, crisper and lighter in her coloratura. Davis's incisiveness, too, has points of advantage; but, to summarize, any Mozartian can safely leave the preference to his feelings about the two conductors, the one more genial and glowing, the other more urgently dramatic.

Kertész attacks Mozart's last opera with fine dramatic directness, but over the span of this formal *opera seria* one cannot help missing a more individual interpretative hand. He seems to have no idea about the grammar of the *apoggiatura*, for the endings of phrases requiring them are regularly left blunt. The recitative too is taken ponderously and one longs to have more pace and contrast in the story-telling. But with very vivid recording and production, generally excellent singing – particularly from Teresa Berganza as Sesto – and strong playing, this might be considered, although Boehm's mellower DG set (which also includes Teresa Berganza) is far more persuasive.

Complete Mozart Edition, Volume 42: *Così fan tutte* (complete).
(M) *** Ph. 422 542-2 (3) [id.]. Caballé, Dame Janet Baker, Cotrubas, Gedda, Ganzarolli, Van Allan, ROHCG Ch. & O, Sir Colin Davis.

Così fan tutte (complete).
❀ (M) *** EMI CMS7 69330-2 (3) [Ang. CDMC 69330]. Schwarzkopf, Ludwig, Steffek, Kraus, Taddei, Berry, Philh. Ch. & O, Boehm.
❀ (M) (***) EMI mono CHS7 69635-2 (3) [Ang. CDHC 69635]. Schwarzkopf, Otto, Merriman, Simoneau, Panerai, Bruscantini, Philh. Ch. & O, Karajan.
(M) **(*) EMI Dig. CMS7 69580-2 (3). Margaret Marshall, Battle, Baltsa, Araiza, Morris, Van Dam, V. State Op. Ch., VPO, Muti.
(M) **(*) DG 429 824-2 (2) [id.]. Janowitz, Fassbaender, Grist, Schreier, Prey, Panerai, V. State Op. Ch., VPO, Boehm.
(M) (***) EMI mono CHS7 63864-2 (2) [Ang. CDHB 63864]. Souez, Helletsgruber, Nash, Domgraf-Fassbaender, Brownlee, Eisinger, Glyndebourne Festival Ch. & O, Fritz Busch.
(M) **(*) BMG/RCA GD 86677 [6677-2-RG] (3). L. Price, Troyanos, Raskin, Shirley, Milnes, Flagello, Amb. Op. Ch., New Philh. O, Leinsdorf.
(M) **(*) EMI CMS7 63845-2 (3) [Ang. CDMC 63845]. M. Price, Minton, Popp, Alva, Evans, Sotin, Alldis Ch., New Philh. O, Klemperer.
(M) ** Decca 430 101-2 (3). Lorengar, Berganza, R. Davies, Krause, Bacquier, Berbié, ROHCG Ch., LPO, Solti.
(B) ** Naxos Dig. 8.660008/10 [id.]. Borowska, Yachmi, John Dickie, Martin, Coles, Mikulas, Slovak Philharmonic Ch., Capella Istropolitana, Johannes Wildner.

First choice remains with Boehm's classic set, reissued on three mid-priced CDs, with its glorious solo singing, headed by the incomparable Fiordiligi of Schwarzkopf and the equally moving Dorabella of Christa Ludwig, a superb memento of Walter Legge's recording genius. It still bears comparison with any other recordings, made before or since.

Commanding as Schwarzkopf is as Fiordiligi in the 1962 Boehm set, also with the Philharmonia, the extra ease and freshness of her singing in the earlier (1954) version makes it even more compelling. Nan Merriman is a distinctive and characterful Dorabella, and the role of Ferrando has never been sung more mellifluously on record than by Leopold Simoneau, ravishing in *Un aura amorosa*. The young Rolando Panerai is an ideal Guglielmo, and Lisa Otto a pert Despina; while Sesto Bruscantini in his prime brings to the role of Don Alfonso the wisdom and artistry which made him so compelling at Glyndebourne. Karajan has never sparkled more naturally in Mozart than here, for the high polish has nothing self-conscious about it. Though the mono recording is not as clear as some others of this period, the subtleties of the music-making are very well caught. In such a performance, one hardly worries that some recitative and one or two numbers are cut. An essential purchase for Mozartians as a supplement to the Boehm set.

The energy and sparkle of Sir Colin Davis are here set against inspired and characterful singing from the three women soloists, with Montserrat Caballé and Janet Baker proving a winning partnership, each challenging and abetting the other all the time. Cotrubas equally is a vivid Despina, never merely arch. Though Gedda has moments of rough tone and Ganzarolli falls short in one of his prominent arias, they are both spirited, while Richard van Allan sings with flair and imagination. Sparkling recitative, and recording which has you riveted by the play of the action.

Muti's recording of *Così fan tutte* is vivid, vigorous and often very beautiful. Ensemble is not always flawless, but this is far more polished than Boehm's eightieth-birthday performance, also recorded live (for DG) at the Kleines Festspielhaus. Muti's vigour is infectiously captured, as is his ability to relax into necessary tenderness. Though purists will prefer the extra precision of a studio performance – Boehm's Philharmonia set or Karajan's stand out – this newer EMI version gives an irresistible flavour of the theatre and the sparkle of Mozartian comedy, even if the sound is rough and lacks body, compared with the best versions.

Boehm's third recording makes a delightful memento and, offered on a pair of mid-priced CDs, it is worth considering, despite its obvious flaws. It was recorded live during the Salzburg Festival performance on the conductor's eightieth birthday, and though the zest and sparkle of the occasion come over delightfully, with as splendid a cast as you could gather, the ensemble is not ideally crisp for repeated listening. The balance favours the voices, with stage noises made the more prominent on CD.

Available during the LP era for only a very brief period as an import from France, the legendary Glyndebourne performance, the first ever recording of *Così fan tutte*, is the finest of the three pioneering sets recorded on 78s in the mid-1930s with the newly founded Glyndebourne company. The sound in the CD transfer, though limited, is amazingly vivid, with voices very well focused and with a keener sense of presence than on many recordings of the 1990s. Busch at the time was a progressive Mozartian, preferring athletic treatment – occasionally to excess, as in the concluding ensemble of Act I – but this is as efferverscent as any more recent recording, and nowadays even the use of a piano for the recitatives instead of a harpsichord seems less outlandish with the emergence of the fortepiano. John Brownlee as Don Alfonso is very much the English aristocrat, with 'fruffly-fruffly' English vowels instead of Italianate ones, but he is a fine, stylish singer. Ina Souez and Luise Helletsgruber as the two sisters outshine all but the very finest of their successors on record, technically superb; and Heddle Nash and Willi Domgraf-Fassbaender as their lovers are at once stylish and characterful, with Irene Eisinger as a delightfully soubrettish Despina. Cuts are made in the recitatives according to the custom of the time and, more seriously, four numbers disappear – including, amazingly, Ferrando's *Tradito, schernito* and Dorabella's *E amore un ladroncello.* The bonus is that, with those cuts, the opera fits on to only two mid-price CDs.

On the RCA set Leinsdorf is not an elegant Mozartian, but he was at his most relaxed in his 1967 recording of *Così fan tutte*, using a sextet of some of the finest American singers of the time. With Leontyne Price scaling her voice down well as Fiordiligi, with fine playing from the Philharmonia and with recording full of presence, it is a viable mid-price version, even though it can hardly match – except in its more complete text – its direct EMI rivals from Karajan and Boehm.

Klemperer's last opera set was predictably idiosyncratic. When the record company jibbed at his suggestion of recording this sparkling comedy, he is alleged to have protested (aged eighty-six at the time), 'What do you want? A posthumous interpretation?' The result proved by no means as funereal as had been predicted, with fine rhythmic pointing to lighten the slow tempi. There is fine singing too from the whole cast (Alva alone at times disappointing) to make the whole a satisfying entertainment, a different view of Mozart to be heard at least once. It is a pity the recitatives are not more imaginatively done. An excellent transfer to CD.

Solti's set will please those who want high voltage at all costs even in this most genial of all Mozart comedies. There is little relaxation and little charm, which underlines the shortcomings of the singing cast, notably of Pilar Lorengar, whose grainy voice is not treated kindly by the microphone and who here in places conveys uncertainty. It is a pity that the crackling wit of Solti's Covent Garden performances was not more magically captured on record. Brilliant recording.

On three budget-price CDs (each costing slightly more than this super-bargain label's orchestral and instrumental repertory) the Naxos version comes out at a price comparable to the Glyndebourne two-disc set, yet provides a text without the omissions of the latter, and the modern digital recording is fresh and bright. But with the exception of Joanna Borowska as a strong, stylish Fiordiligi, the Czech cast is in a different league. After Borowska, Peter Mikulas is the most successful of the soloists, a forthright, clean-toned Don Alfonso. John Dickie, as recorded, sounds rather too throaty as Ferrando and Rohangiz Yachmi as Dorabella has too fruity a vibrato for Mozart. After a gabbled overture, Wildner directs a well-played, generally well-paced performance. It is worth remembering that for the price of these discs one would be well pleased to come across such a performance in the opera house, be it in Bratislava or elsewhere.

Così fan tutte: highlights.

(M) **(*) DG Dig. 431 290-2; *431 290-4* [id.] (from recording with Te Kanawa, Murray, McLaughlin, Blochwitz, Hampson, Furlanetto, VPO, cond. Levine).

(M) ** DG 429 824-2 [id.] (from above recording, with Janowitz, Fassbaender, Grist, Schreier, Prey, Panerai; cond. Boehm).

A generous selection (75 minutes) from Levine's brisk, rather unsmiling *Così*, especially useful for sampling Dame Kiri's Fiordiligi, one of her finest Mozartian performances on record, and Thomas Hampson's characterfully rich portrayal of Guglielmo. Marie McLaughlin is a splendid Despina, so there is much to enjoy here, although Ann Murray's Dorabella is a disappointment.

Although an hour's playing time is indicated on the back liner-leaflet, this selection from Boehm's live 1974 Salzburg Festival recording (his third) runs to over 72 minutes, and the sparkle of the occasion is well conveyed. This is a good way of approaching a set where ensemble is at times less than perfect but which offers a splendid cast and some fine individual contributions. Unusually for DG, however, the documentation is wholly inadequate.

(i) *Così fan tutte*: highlights; (ii) *Le nozze di Figaro*: highlights.
(B) **(*) DG Compact Classics *427 712-4* [id.]. From complete sets with (i; ii) Janowitz; (i) Ludwig, Loose, Dermota, Kunz, Schoeffler, Vienna State Op. Ch., VPO; (ii) Mathis, Troyanos, Fischer-Dieskau, Prey, German Op. Ch. & O; Boehm.

This Compact Classics tape combines highlights from the 1977 Salzburg Festival recording of *Così* with an earlier, 1968 studio recording of *Figaro*. Boehm conducts both with his customary stylish warmth, and if in *Così*, understandably, the live performance is less than ideally polished, the sparkle of the singing projects splendidly, especially as the tape transfer is so lively, with the balance favouring the voices. The *Figaro* cast is very strong with Janowitz, common to both operas, in ravishing voice. An excellent tape for the car.

Complete Mozart Edition, Volume 41: *Don Giovanni* (complete).
(M) *** Ph. 422 541-2 (3) [id.]. Wixell, Arroyo, Te Kanawa, Freni, Burrows, Ganzarolli, ROHCG Ch. & O, Sir Colin Davis.

Don Giovanni (complete).
(M) *** Decca 411 626-2 (3). Siepi, Danco, Della Casa, Corena, Dermota, V. State Op. Ch., VPO, Krips.
(M) (***) EMI mono CHS7 63860-2 (3) [Ang. CDHB 63860]. Siepi, Schwarzkopf, Berger, Grümmer, Dermota, Edelmann, Berry, Ernster, V. State Op. Ch., VPO, Furtwängler.
(M) **(*) EMI CMS7 63841-2 (3) [Ang. CDMC 63841] Ghiaurov, Watson, Gedda, Ludwig, Berry, Freni, Montarsolo, Crass, New Philh. O & Ch., Klemperer.
(M) (***) EMI mono CHS7 61030-2 (3) [Ang. CDHB 61030]. Brownlee, Souez, Von Pataky, Helletsgruber, Baccaloni, Henderson, Mildmay, Glyndebourne Fest. Ch. & O, Fritz Busch.
(M) ** DG 429 870-2 (3) [id.]. Fischer-Dieskau, Arroyo, Nilsson, Grist, Schreier, Flagello, Prague Nat. Theatre Ch. & O, Boehm.
(M) ** Decca 425 169-2 (3). Weikl, M. Price, Burrows, Sass, Bacquier, Popp, Sramek, Moll, London Op. Ch., LPO, Solti.
(M) *(*) EMI CMS7 63976-2 (3) [id.]. Soyer, Sgourda, Harper, Donath, Evans, Alva, Scottish Op. Ch., ECO, Barenboim.

Sir Colin Davis has the advantage of a singing cast that has fewer shortcomings than almost any other on disc and much positive strength. For once one can listen, untroubled by vocal blemishes. Martina Arroyo controls her massive dramatic voice more completely than one would think possible, and she is strongly and imaginatively contrasted with the sweetly expressive Elvira of Kiri Te Kanawa and the sparkling Zerlina of Mirella Freni. As in the Davis *Figaro*, Ingvar Wixell and Wladimiro Ganzarolli make a formidable master/servant team with excellent vocal acting, while Stuart Burrows sings gloriously as Don Ottavio, and Richard Van Allan is a characterful Masetto. Davis draws a fresh and immediate performance from his team, riveting from beginning to end, and the recording, now better defined and more vivid than before, is still refined in the recognizable Philips manner.

Krips's recording of this most challenging opera has kept its place as a mid-priced version that is consistently satisfying, with a cast of all-round quality headed by the dark-toned Don of Cesare Siepi. The women are not ideal, but they form an excellent team, never overfaced by the music, generally characterful, and with timbres well contrasted. To balance Siepi's darkness, the Leporello of Corena is even more saturnine, and their dramatic teamwork is brought to a superb climax in the final scene – quite the finest and most spine-tingling performance of that scene ever recorded. The 1955 recording – genuine stereo – still sounds remarkably well.

The historic Furtwängler performance was recorded live by Austrian Radio at the 1954 Salzburg Festival, barely three months before the conductor's death. Far from taking a weightily Germanic view, he consistently brings out the sparkle in this '*Dramma giocoso*', to use Mozart's term on the title-page. Though speeds are often slow by today's standards, his springing of rhythm never lets them sag. Even the very slow speed for Leporello's catalogue aria is made to seem charmingly individual. With the exception of a wobbly Commendatore, this is a classic Salzburg cast, with Cesare Siepi a fine, incisive Don, dark in tone, Elisabeth Schwarzkopf a dominant Elvira, Elisabeth Grümmer a vulnerable Anna, Anton Dermota a heady-toned Ottavio and Otto Edelmann a clear and direct Leporello. Stage noises often suggest herds of stampeding animals, but both voices and orchestra are satisfyingly full-bodied in the CD transfer, and the sense of presence is astonishing.

The lumbering tempo of Leporello's opening music will alert the listener to the predictable Klemperer approach and at that point some may dismiss his performance as 'too heavy' – but the issue is far more complex than that. Most of the slow tempi which Klemperer regularly adopts, far from flagging, add a welcome breadth to the music, for they must be set against the unusually brisk and dramatic interpretation of the recitatives between numbers. Added to that, Ghiaurov as the Don and Berry as Leporello make a marvellously characterful pair. In this version, the male members of the cast are dominant and, with Klemperer's help, they make the dramatic experience a strongly masculine one. Nor is the ironic humour forgotten with Berry and Ghiaurov about, and the Klemperer spaciousness allows them extra time for pointing. Among the women, Ludwig is a strong and convincing Elvira, Freni a sweet-toned but rather unsmiling Zerlina; only Claire Watson seriously disappoints, with obvious nervousness marring the big climax of *Non mi dir*. It is a serious blemish but, with the usual reservations, for those not allergic to the Klemperer approach, this stands as a good recommendation – at the very least a commanding experience.

There are those who still count the early Glyndebourne set the finest of all, with Fritz Busch an inspired Mozartian, pointing the music with a freshness and absence of nineteenth-century heaviness rare at the time. A piano is used for the *secco* recitatives and the chords are played very baldly and without elaboration; but the interplay of characters in those exchanges has never been caught more infectiously on disc. John Brownlee as Giovanni may have a rather British-stiff-upper-lip Italian accent (noticeable for the most part in the recitatives) but his is a noble performance, beautifully sung, and he is brilliantly set against the lively, idiomatically Italian Leporello of Salvatore Baccaloni. The three ladies are both contrasted and well matched, with Audrey Mildmay as Zerlina a delightful foil for the excellent, if otherwise little-known Ina Souez and Luise Helletsgruber. Koloman von Pataky uses his light, heady tenor well as Ottavio, and the British stalwarts, David Franklin and Roy Henderson, are first rate as the Commendatore and Masetto respectively. Altogether this version is a delight, and Keith Hardwick's digital transfers are astonishingly vivid, with very little background noise.

The Boehm set chosen for reissue is the earlier of his two versions for DG, recorded in Prague, with Dietrich Fischer-Dieskau singing powerfully if sometimes roughly in the title-role. Birgit Nilsson does wonders in scaling down her Wagnerian soprano for the needs of Mozart, making a characterful if hardly a flawless Donna Anna. Similarly, the Verdian Martina Arroyo is characterful as Elvira, even if she has ungainly moments. The partnership between Fischer-Dieskau and Ezio Flagello as Leporello is most appealing, and Reri Grist makes a charming Zerlina. A flawed set, enjoyable but scarcely matching the others in the Boehm cycle.

Solti directs a crisp, incisive performance, with generally fast tempi and very well-directed recitatives. If it shows no special signs of affection, it contains one glorious performance in Margaret Price's Anna, pure in tone and line but powerfully dramatic too, always beautiful. Next to her, Sylvia Sass as a somewhat gusty Elvira sounds rather miscast, characterful though her singing is. The two baritones, Bernd Weikl and Gabriel Bacquier, are clearly contrasted as Giovanni and Leporello respectively, though the microphone is not kind to either. The recording is brilliant in its realistic clarity.

Barenboim's recording is directly based on the stage production at the 1974 Edinburgh Festival, but the often slack and unsparkling performance recorded here can scarcely reflect the live account. Surprisingly, Barenboim seems to be echoing Klemperer in his steady approach and exaggeratedly slow tempi. However, with Klemperer himself there was a granite-like solidity; with Barenboim, uncharacteristically, the rhythms sag. Roger Soyer's performance as the Don is refreshingly youthful in feeling, and it is good to have Sir Geraint Evans's Leporello on disc, but Luigi Alva's Ottavio is disressingly unsure. Heather Harper as Elvira and Helen Donath as Zerlina battle well against the tempi, but Antigone Sgourda as Anna uses her big, floppy voice in hit-or-miss fashion.

Don Giovanni: highlights.

(M) *** DG Dig. 431 289-2; *431 289-4* (from recording with Ramey, Tomowa-Sintow, Baltsa, Battle, Winbergh, Furlanetto, Malta, Burchuladze, BPO, cond. Karajan).

(M) *** EMI CDM7 63078-2. Waechter, Schwarzkopf, Sutherland, Alva, Frick, Sciutti, Taddei, Philh. Ch. & O, Giulini.

(M) **(*) EMI CDM7 69055-2 [id.] (from above

recording, with Ghiaurov, Watson, Freni, Ludwig, Gedda, Berry; cond. Klemperer).
(M) **(*) DG 429 823-2; *429 823-4* [id.]. Milnes, Tomowa-Sintow, Zylis-Gara, Mathis, Schreier, Berry, V. State Op. Ch., VPO, Boehm.
(B) ** Pickwick (DG) IMPX 9023 (from above recording, with Fischer-Dieskau, Arroyo, Nilsson, Grist, Schreier, Flagello; cond. Boehm).
(M) *(*) Decca 421 875-2; *421 875-4*. Siepi, Nilsson, L. Price, Ratti, Valletti, Corena, V. State Op. Ch., VPO, Leinsdorf.

A generous selection (66 minutes) from Karajan's digital set, most of the favourite items included and all the principals given a chance to sparkle, in solos, duets and ensembles. The selection opens with the *Overture* and closes with the powerful final scene.

Not surprisingly, the Giulini EMI selection concentrates on Sutherland as Donna Anna and Schwarzkopf as Donna Elvira, so that the Don and Leporello get rather short measure; but Sciutti's charming Zerlina is also given fair due.

Klemperer's set of highlights is well chosen to show his version's many merits and one hardly notices the spacious tempi. Ghiaurov as the Don and Berry as Leporello are first rate and, among the women, Ludwig is well up to form as Elvira and Freni makes a characterful Zerlina. Klemperer's measured pacing is controversial but by no means ponderous; this is a sampler of a very distinctive performance.

Like its companion collection of highlights from *Così fan tutte*, Boehm's DG selection is very generous (76 minutes) and is taken from live performances at Salzburg (recorded in 1977). It makes a welcome representation of a set centring round Sherrill Milnes's unusually heroic assumption of the role of the Don, and he sings with a richness and commitment to match his swaggering stage presence. The rest of the cast give stylish performances without being deeply memorable but, unlike *Così* where ensembles were less than ideally crisp, this live *Giovanni* presents strong and consistently enjoyable teamwork. The balance again favours the voices but is especially vivid in the culminating scene. However, the documentation, as with *Così*, offers only period pictures and a list of contents.

On Pickwick, a good sampler for Boehm's first Prague set, which is uneven but which has some fine, characterful performances and is worth hearing for Birgit Nilsson's unexpected casting as Donna Anna, represented here by *Or sai chi l'onore*. The selection is a little short on quantity (56 minutes), but the major participants are all given a chance to shine.

Although the selection is generous (70 minutes), there is little else to recommend in Leinsdorf's 1960 recording. It begins with a fierce, fast version of the *Overture* and elsewhere has drama without charm, for Leinsdorf's direction is largely uninspired. Nilsson again makes a gusty Donna Anna and Leontyne Price is equally poorly cast. Siepi and Corena are reliable but are better served in the Krips version. The sound is vivid but lacks bloom.

(i) *Don Giovanni:* highlights; (ii) *Die Entführung aus dem Serail:* highlights.
(B) *** DG Compact Classics *431 181-4* [id.]. (i) Milnes, Tomowa-Sintow, Zylis-Gara, Mathis, Schreier, Berry, V. State Op. Ch., VPO; (ii) Augér, Grist, Schreier, Neukirch, Moll, Leipzig R. Ch., Dresden State O, Boehm.

With sparkling sound, this is one of the finest operatic tape bargains in the DG Compact Classics catalogue. The *Don Giovanni* highlights were recorded live at the 1977 Salzburg Festival. The strong cast is dominated by a swaggering Don in Sherrill Milnes, and Anna Tomowa-Sintow proves a generally creamy-toned Donna Anna. Teresa Zylis-Gara and Edith Mathis are good too, and Walter Berry is a genial Leporello. The selection is well chosen and it is joined by an equally attractive set of excerpts from Boehm's superb *Entführung*, with Arleen Augér at her very finest in the role of Constanze, Kurl Moll relishing the characterization of Osmin, and the rest of the cast almost equally impressive. Again the transfer is vivid, and both overtures are included.

Complete Mozart Edition, Volume 38: *Die Entführung aus dem Serail* (complete).
(M) ** Ph. 422 538-2 (2) [id.]. Eda-Pierre, Stuart Burrows, Norma Burrowes, Tear, Lloyd, Jürgens, Alldis Ch., ASMF, Sir Colin Davis.

Die Entführung aus dem Serail (complete).
(M) *** DG 429 868-2 (2) [id.]. Augér, Grist, Schreier, Neukirch, Moll, Leipzig R. Ch., Dresden State O, Boehm.

(i) *Die Entführung aus dem Serail* (complete). (ii) Arias from: *La clemenza di Tito; Die Entführung; Idomeneo.*
(M) **(*) EMI stereo/mono CHS7 63715-2 (2). (i) Lois Marshall, Hollweg, Simoneau, Unger, Frick, Beecham Ch. Soc., RPO, Beecham; (ii) Léopold Simoneau.

Boehm's is a delectable performance, superbly cast and warmly recorded. Arleen Augér proves the most accomplished singer on record in the role of Constanze, girlish and fresh, yet rich, tender and dramatic by turns, with brilliant, almost flawless coloratura. The others are also outstandingly good, notably Kurt Moll whose powerful, finely focused bass makes him a superb Osmin, one who relishes the comedy too. Using East German forces, Boehm uncovers a natural, unforced Mozartian expression which carries the listener along in glowing ease. The warm recording is beautifully transferred, to make this easily the most sympathetic version of the opera on CD, with the added attraction of being at mid-price.

There is much to treasure in Beecham's vivid but idiosyncratic reading, not least the incomparable portrayal of Osmin by the great German bass, Gottlob Frick, thrillingly dark and firm, characterizing superbly. His aria, *O wie will ich triumphieren*, like the *Overture* and the *Chorus of Janissaries* in Act I, finds Beecham fizzing with energy, spine-tingling in intensity. Léopold Simoneau as Belmonte has rarely been matched on record for mellifluous beauty and flawless line, and Gerhard Unger is a charming Pedrillo, not least in the spoken dialogue. The two women soloists are more variable; Lois Marshall is technically fine as Constanze, but the voice has a hint of rawness, while Ilse Hollweg, bright and clear, could also be more characterful. The oddity of the set lies in the text. Beecham, dissatisfied with the heroine's two big arias following each other so closely, moved the second, heroic one, *Martern aller Arten*, to Act III and he also made an unwarranted cut in *Traurigkeit*. He also moved Belmonte's *Wenn der Freude* to the beginning of Act III, where it replaces *Ich baue ganz*, a curious decision. The transfer of early stereo sound is first rate. The four mono recordings of Mozart arias sung by Simoneau – including the missing *Ich baue ganz* – make an excellent bonus.

Sir Colin Davis, using a smaller orchestra, the St Martin's Academy, than he usually has in his Mozart opera recordings, produces a fresh and direct account, well but not outstandingly sung. There are no performances here which have one remembering individuality of phrase, and even so characterful a singer as Robert Tear does not sound quite mellifluous enough in the role of Pedrillo; while Robert Lloyd as Osmin is outshone by both his rivals, especially by the incomparable Gottlob Frick in the Beecham set. Crisp as the ensembles are, Davis's reading rather lacks the lightness and sparkle, the feeling of comedy before our eyes, which makes the Boehm version on DG such a delight from beginning to end. The Philips set, however, does include five alternative arias and duets. The recording is clear and refined in the Philips manner, and the CD transfer adds immediacy without losing the ambient atmosphere.

Complete Mozart Edition, Volume 33: *La finta giardiniera* (complete).
(M) *** Ph. 422 533-2 (3) [id.]. Conwell, Sukis, Di Cesare, Thomas Moser, Fassbaender, Ihloff, McDaniel, Salzburg Mozarteum O, Hager.

Complete Mozart Edition, Volume 34: *Die Gärtnerin aus Liebe* (*La finta giardiniera* sung in German) (complete).
(M) **(*) Ph. 422 534-2 (3) [id.]. Unger, Hollweg, Donath, J. Norman, Cotrubas, N. German R. Ch. & SO, Schmidt-Isserstedt.

This is the only *opera buffa* written by Mozart in his youth that can be regarded as a preparation for *Figaro*, particularly as you find Mozart at nineteen confidently using techniques in the extended finales which he was to perfect in the Da Ponte masterpiece. The story is unconvincing. In the manner of the time, every possible excuse (including bouts of madness for both hero and heroine) is used to prevent true love from being fulfilled until the end of Act III; yet, with Mozart, the more improbable the story the more inspired the music.

By the time Leopold Hager came to record the opera in 1980 with Salzburg Mozarteum forces, the text of the recitatives in Italian had been rediscovered and he was able to use the original language. He has a strong vocal team, with three impressive newcomers taking the women's roles – Jutta-Renate Ihloff, Julia Conwell (in the central role of Sandrina, the marquise who disguises herself as a garden-girl) and Lilian Sukis (the arrogant niece). Brigitte Fassbaender sings the castrato role of Ramiro, and the others are comparably stylish. It is a charming – if lengthy – comedy, which here, with crisply performed recitatives, is presented with vigour, charm and persuasiveness. The recording, made with the help of Austrian Radio, is excellent and has been brightly and freshly transferred to CD.

Hans Schmidt-Isserstedt's set was made in Hamburg a decade earlier, and he was forced to record the version that used the clumsy German Singspiel translation, in use until the discovery of the Italian recitatives. However, though this performance is slow in getting off the ground, it readily makes up for this later, with particularly delightful performances from Eleana Cotrubas and Hermann Prey in the roles of the two servants. The sound too is very pleasing, although the violin tone is a little on the thin side; but the CD transfer does not exaggerate this and retains an attractive ambience.

Complete Mozart Edition, Volume 28: *La finta semplice* (complete).

(M) *** Ph. Dig. 422 528-2 (2) [id.]. Hendricks, Lorenz, Johnson, Murray, Lind, Blochwitz, Schmidt, C. P. E. Bach CO, Schreier.

Peter Schreier draws sparkling playing from the C. P. E. Bach Orchestra of East Berlin, so that, with an excellent cast, this completely new recording in the Philips Complete Mozart Edition is one of the most delectable of all the sets of early Mozart operas. The plot, adapted from a Goldoni comedy, is a conventional one of love and intrigue, involving two rich, unmarried brothers (both described as 'foolish gentlemen'), and the trickery of the women in each getting the man of her choice. What is astonishing is that the invention of the 12-year-old Mozart was no less winning than that of anything he wrote in his early teens, starting with an overture guaranteed to raise the spirits. In every way Schreier's version replaces the earlier, Orfeo full-priced set from Leopold Hager, particularly when it comes at mid-price on two discs instead of three. The digital recording is wonderfully clear, with a fine sense of presence, capturing the fun of the comedy. Ann Murray has never sung more seductively in Mozart than here as Giacinta, and the characterful Barbara Hendricks is a delight in the central role of Rosina.

Complete Mozart Edition, Volume 37: *Idomeneo* (complete with ballet music).

(M) ** Ph. 422 537-2 (3) [id.]. Araiza, Mentzer, Hendricks, Allen, Lewis, Alexander, Heilmann, Hollweg, Peeters, Bav. R. Ch. & RSO, Sir Colin Davis.

Idomeneo (complete).

(M) *** DG 429 864-2 (3) [id.]. Ochman, Mathis, Schreier, Varady, Winkler, Leipzig R. Ch., Dresden State O, Boehm.

(M) **(*) Teldec/Warner 2292 42600-2 (3) [id.]. Hollweg, Schmidt, Yakar, Palmer, Zürich Op. O, Harnoncourt.

(M) **(*) EMI CMS7 63990-2 (3) [id.]. Rothenberger, Edda Moser, Gedda, Dallapozza, Schreier, Adam, Leipzig R. Ch., Dresden State O, Schmidt-Isserstedt.

(M) (***) EMI mono CHS7 63685-2 (2) [Ang. CDHB 63685]. Richard Lewis, Simoneau, Jurinac, Glyndebourne Fest. Ch. & O, Pritchard.

Textually Boehm's version of *Idomeneo* gives grounds for regrets. The score is snipped about and, like previous recordings, it opts for a tenor in the role of Idamante. That said, however, it is an enormously successful and richly enjoyable set. Boehm's conducting is a delight, often spacious but never heavy in the wrong way, with lightened textures and sprung rhythms which have one relishing Mozartian felicities as never before. As Idomeneo, Wieslaw Ochman, with tenor tone often too tight, is a comparatively dull dog, but the other principals are generally excellent. Peter Schreier as Idamante also might have sounded more consistently sweet, but the imagination is irresistible. Edith Mathis is at her most beguiling as Ilia, but it is Julia Varady as Elettra who gives the most compelling performance of all, sharply incisive in her dramatic outbursts, but at the same time precise and pure-toned, a Mozartian stylist through and through. Hermann Winkler as Arbace is squarely Germanic, and it is a pity that the secco recitatives are done heavily; whatever incidental reservations have to be made, however, this is a superbly compelling set which leaves one in no doubt as to the work's status as a masterpiece. The first-class recording has transferred vividly to CD.

Using a text very close to that of the Munich première of Mozart's great *opera seria*, and with the role of Idamante given to a soprano instead of being transposed down to tenor register, Harnoncourt presents a distinctive and refreshing view, one which in principle is preferable to general modern practice. The vocal cast is good, with Hollweg a clear-toned, strong Idomeneo, and with no weak link. Felicity Palmer finds the necessary contrasts of expression as Elettra. With remastering for CD, the sound is transformed and the edginess, present in the original LP format, smoothed without loss of presence. It is surprising that, in an account which aims at authenticity, appoggiature are so rarely used. This is hardly a performance to warm to, but it is refreshing and alive.

Schmidt-Isserstedt's version of Mozart's great essay in *opera seria* dates from 1971 and was first isssued as a timely memorial soon after the conductor's death. Though not perfect, it is most stylishly performed and at the time was the most complete version available. The only cuts are of recitative – and those relatively minor. It was a pity that the role of Idamante was given to a tenor, and the decision is the more irritating when Adolf Dallapozza is by far the least accomplished soloist. Otherwise the cast is strong, with Gedda heroic as Idomeneo, Rothenberger an appealing Ilia and Edda Moser a richly characterful Elektra. Altogether this is a very commanding version with fine concern for detail and very good recording, full and warm as well as vivid in its CD transfer.

The very first 'complete' recording of the opera, recorded in 1955 with Glyndebourne forces under John Pritchard, makes a timely reappearance on CD. Though it uses a severely cut text and the orchestral sound is rather dry, it wears its years well. The voices still sound splendid, notably Sena Jurinac as a ravishing Ilia, Richard Lewis in the title-role, and Léopold Simoneau so delicate he almost reconciles one to the casting of Idamante as a tenor (from Mozart's compromised Vienna revision). The cuts mean that the whole opera is fitted on to two discs.

To have a major new opera-set like this, issued from the start on a mid-priced label, is generous, but Sir Colin Davis's second version of Mozart's great *opera seria* was designed as part of the Philips Complete Mozart Edition and is priced accordingly. It comes with the fine qualities of presentation associated with the series; the text aims at completeness, with an appendix on the third disc containing major numbers like Arbace's two arias, omitted in the main text, as well as the ballet music designed to be performed after the drama is over. It also has the advantage over Davis's previous recording that the role of Idamante is given to a mezzo instead of a tenor, following Mozart's original Munich text. Such a number as the great Quartet of Act III benefits much by that – but unfortunately, as in Davis's previous version, there are flaws in the casting; his reading has also grown smoother and less incisive, less fresh than before, if now at times grander. Francisco Araiza's efforts to produce the heroic tone needed often sound strained, and he is not clean enough in his attack; while Barbara Hendricks as Ilia adopts an even less apt Mozartian style, with too much sliding and under-the-note attack, missing the purity needed for this character. Uwe Heilmann as Arbace is also disappointing, and it is as well his arias are left to the appendix. Others in the cast are far finer, but the total result is less than completely satisfactory, particularly arriving so soon after John Eliot Gardiner's brilliant and dramatic full-priced version for DG Archiv using period instruments. The Philips recording is full and warm, but the Gardiner set is well worth its extra cost.

Complete Mozart Edition, Volume 32: *Lucio Silla* (complete).
(M) *** Ph. 422 532-2 (3) [id.]. Schreier, Augér, Varady, Mathis, Donath, Krenn, Salzburg R. Ch. & Mozarteum Ch. & O, Hager.

The sixteen-year-old Mozart wrote his fifth opera, on the subject of the Roman dictator Sulla (Silla), in double quick time; and although the formal story has its longueurs (the total timing is three and a half hours) the speed of the composition is electrically communicated, with most of the arias urgently fast and strong symphonic ideas developed at surprising length. There are many pre-echoes of later Mozart operas, not just of the great *opera seria*, *Idomeneo*, but of *Entführung* and even of *Don Giovanni*. Though the formal limitations inhibit ensembles, there is a superb one at the end of Act I, anticipating the Da Ponte masterpieces. A rousing chorus is interrupted by an agonized G minor lament for the heroine and leads finally to an ecstatic reunion duet. The castrato roles are here splendidly taken by Julia Varady and Edith Mathis, and the whole team could hardly be bettered. The direction of Hager is fresh and lively, and the only snag is the length of the *secco* recitatives. However, with CD one can use these judiciously. The 1975 analogue recording, originally DG, has been taken over for the Philips Mozart Edition and the remastering is vivid and natural, although it is a pity that, in fitting the work on to CD, the first break had to come nine minutes before the end of Act I, in the middle of the scena described above, just before the duet.

Lucio Silla: overture.
(M) ** Teldec/Warner Dig. 9031 74785-2 [id.]. Concg. O, Harnoncourt – SCHUBERT: *Symphony No. 8 (Unfinished)* etc. *

In three brief movements (tracked separately here) the overture to Mozart's early *opera seria* is like a miniature symphony. With the Royal Concertgebouw instead of the Vienna SO, this fill-up brings a performance that is altogether sharper than the Schubert items with which it is coupled.

Complete Mozart Edition, Volume 29: *Mitridate, rè di Ponto* (complete).
(M) **(*) Ph. 422 529-2 (3) [id.]. Augér, Hollweg, Gruberová, Baltsa, Cotrubas, Salzburg Mozarteum O, Hager.

Mozart at fourteen attempted his first full-scale *opera seria* and showed that he could fully encompass the most ambitious of forms. Not all the 22 arias are of the finest quality; some are too long for their material, and the Metastasio libretto is hardly involving dramatically. But a fresh and generally lively performance (the rather heavy recitatives excepted) brings splendid illumination to the long-hidden area of the boy Mozart's achievement. Two of the most striking arias (including an urgent G minor piece for the heroine, Aspasia, with Arleen Augér the ravishing soprano) exploit minor keys most effectively. Ileana Cotrubas is outstanding as Ismene, and the soloists of the Salzburg orchestra cope well with the often important obbligato parts. This is a specially useful volume in Philips's Complete Mozart Edition and, like the others in Hager's series, has a DG source. The recording is bright and fresh, the CD transfer vivid and forward and a little lacking in atmosphere.

Complete Mozart Edition, Volume 40: *Le nozze di Figaro* (complete).
(M) *** Ph. 422 540-2 (3) [id.]. Freni, Norman, Minton, Ganzarolli, Wixell, Grant, Tear, BBC Ch. & SO, Sir Colin Davis.

Le nozze di Figaro (complete).
❀ (B) *** CfP CD-CFPD 4724; *TC-CFPD 4724* (2). Sciutti, Jurinac, Stevens, Bruscantini, Calabrese, Cuenod, Wallace, Sinclair, Glyndebourne Ch. & Festival O, Gui.
(M) *** EMI CMS7 63266-2 (2) [Ang. CDMB 63266]. Schwarzkopf, Moffo, Cossotto, Taddei, Waechter, Vinco, Philh. Ch. & O, Giulini.
(M) **(*) Decca 417 315-2 (3) [id.]. Gueden, Danco, Della Casa, Dickie, Poell, Corena, Siepi, V. State Op. Ch., VPO, Erich Kleiber.
(M) *** DG 429 869-2 (3) [id.]. Janowitz, Mathis, Troyanos, Fischer-Dieskau, Prey, Lagger, German Op. Ch. & O, Boehm.
(M) (**(*)) EMI mono CMS7 69639-2 (2) [Ang. CDMB 69639]. Schwarzkopf, Seefried, Jurinac, Kunz, Majkut, London, V. State Op. Ch., VPO, Karajan.
(M) **(*) EMI CMS7 63849-2 (3) [Ang. CDMC 63849]. Grist, Söderström, Berganza, Evans, Bacquier, Hollweg, Alldis Ch., New Philh. O, Klemperer.
(M) ** EMI CMS7 63646-2 (3) [Ang. CDMC 63646]. Harper, Blegen, Berganza, Fischer-Dieskau, G. Evans, Alldis Ch., ECO, Barenboim.

The most effervescent performance of *Figaro* on disc, brilliantly produced in early but well-separated stereo, the 1955 Glyndebourne recording makes a bargain without equal on only two CDs from CfP. The transfer on CD brings sound warmer, more naturally vivid and with more body than on many modern recordings. There is no added edginess, as occurs on so many CD transfers involving voices (in that respect it is far superior to the disappointing Decca CD transfer of the vintage Decca Kleiber set from the same period). The realistic projection instantly makes one forget any minimal tape-hiss, and the performance, recorded in the studio immediately after a vintage Glyndebourne season, offers not only unsurpassed teamwork, witty in its timing, but also a consistently stylish and characterful cast. Just as Sesto Bruscantini is the archetypal Glyndebourne Figaro, Sena Jurinac is the perfect Countess, with Graziella Sciutti a delectable Susanna and Risë Stevens a well-contrasted Cherubino, vivacious in their scenes together. Franco Calabrese as the Count is firm and virile, if occasionally stressed on top; and the three character roles have never been cast more vividly, with Ian Wallace as Bartolo, Monica Sinclair as Marcellina and the incomparable Hugues Cuenod as Basilio. The only regret is that Cuenod's brilliant performance of Basilio's aria in Act IV has had to be omitted (as it so often is on stage) to keep the two discs each within the 80-minute limit. There is no libretto, but a detailed synopsis is provided with cueing points conveniently indicated.

Like his set of *Don Giovanni* – also recorded in 1959 – the Giulini version is a classic, with a cast assembled by Walter Legge that has rarely been matched, let alone surpassed. If the fun of the opera is more gently presented by Giulini than by some others, he provides the perfect frame for such a characterful line-up of soloists. Taddei with his dark bass-baritone makes a provocative Figaro; opposite him, Anna Moffo is at her freshest and sweetest as Susanna. Schwarzkopf as ever is the noblest of Countesses, and it is good to hear the young Fiorenza Cossotto as a full-toned Cherubino. Eberhard Waechter is a strong and stylish Count. On only two mid-priced discs instead of the original four LPs, it makes a superb bargain, though – as in the other EMI two-disc version, the Gui on CfP – Marcellina's and Basilio's arias are omitted from Act IV. The break between discs is neatly managed towards the end of the Act II finale. The transfer is excellent, giving a focus and sense of presence often not achieved in modern digital recordings. Unlike many mid-priced opera sets from EMI, this one comes in a slip-case, complete with full libretto and translation, bringing an advantage over the CfP set.

The pacing of Sir Colin Davis has a sparkle in recitative that directly reflects experience in the opera house, and his tempi generally are beautifully chosen to make their dramatic points. Vocally the cast is exceptionally consistent. Mirella Freni (Susanna) is perhaps the least satisfying, yet there is no lack of character and charm. It is good to have so ravishingly beautiful a voice as Jessye Norman's for the Countess. The Figaro of Wladimiro Ganzarolli and the Count of Ingvar Wixell project with exceptional clarity and vigour, and there is fine singing too from Yvonne Minton as Cherubino, Clifford Grant as Bartolo and Robert Tear as Basilio. The 1971 recording has more reverberation than usual, but the effect is commendably atmospheric and on CD the voices have plenty of presence. The CD transfer is altogether smoother than Decca have managed for the Kleiber set, with the break in the middle of Act II coming earlier and much better placed. This is undoubtedly one of the most enjoyable versions of this opera from the analogue era.

Kleiber's famous set was one of Decca's Mozart bicentenary recordings of the mid-1950s. It remains an outstanding bargain at mid-price, an attractively strong performance with much fine singing. Few if any sets since have matched its constant stylishness. Gueden's Susanna might be criticized but her golden tones are certainly characterful and her voice blends with Della Casa's enchantingly. Danco and Della Casa are both at their finest. A dark-toned Figaro in Siepi brings added contrast and, if the pace of the recitatives is rather slow, this is not inconsistent within the context of Kleiber's overall approach. It is a pity that the Decca remastering, in brightening the sound, has brought a hint of edginess to the voices, though the basic atmosphere remains. Also, the layout brings a less than felicitous break in Act II, which Kleiber shapes with authoritative inevitability. In this respect the cassettes were superior – and they had smoother sound, too.

Boehm's version of *Figaro* is also among the most consistently assured performances available. The women all sing most beautifully, with Janowitz's Countess, Mathis's Susanna and Troyanos's Cherubino all ravishing the ear in contrasted ways. Prey is an intelligent if not very jolly-sounding Figaro, and Fischer-Dieskau gives his dark, sharply defined reading of the Count's role. All told, a great success, with fine playing and recording, enhanced on CD, and now offered at mid-price.

Recorded in 1950, Karajan's first recording of *Figaro* offers one of the most distinguished casts ever assembled; but, curiously at that period, they decided to record the opera without the secco recitatives. That is a most regrettable omission when all these singers are not just vocally immaculate but vividly characterful – as for example Sena Jurinac, later the greatest of Glyndebourne Countesses, here a vivacious Cherubino. The firmness of focus in Erich Kunz's singing of Figaro goes with a delightful twinkle in the word-pointing, and Irmgard Seefried makes a bewitching Susanna. Schwarzkopf's noble portrait of the Countess – not always helped by a slight backward balance in the placing of the microphone for her – culminates in the most poignant account of her second aria, *Dove sono*. Erich Majkut is a delightfully bright-eyed Basilio. Karajan at this early period was fresher as a Mozartian than later, sometimes hurrying his singers but keeping a necessary lightness. The sound, though obviously limited, presents the voices very vividly. Conveniently, each of the CDs contains two Acts.

Klemperer may seem to have been the most solemn of conductors but he had a great sense of humour. Here he shows very clearly how his humour fits in with the sterling characteristics we all recognize. Though the tempi are often slow, the pointing and shading are most delicate and the result, though hardly sparkling, is full of high spirits. A clue to the Klemperer approach comes near the beginning with Figaro's aria *Se vuol ballare*, which is not merely a servant's complaint about an individual master but a revolutionary call, with horns and pizzicato strings strongly defined, to apply to the whole world: 'I'll play the tune, sir!' Geraint Evans is masterly in matching Klemperer; though his normal interpretation of the role of Figaro is more effervescent than this, he is superb here, singing and acting with great power. Reri Grist makes a charming Susanna and Teresa Berganza is a rich-toned Cherubino. Gabriel Bacquier's Count is darker-toned and more formidable than usual, while Elisabeth Söderström's Countess, though it has its moments of strain, gives ample evidence of this artist's thoughtful intensity. Though this is not a version one would regularly laugh over, it represents a unique experience. The recording has transferred very well to CD.

For so lively a Mozartian, Barenboim takes a strangely staid view of *Figaro* in both his recordings. His EMI one, now reissued at mid-price, was recorded soon after live performances at the Edinburgh Festival and with substantially the same cast. Though recitatives are sharp enough, the result lacks sparkle, despite the characterful – if at times unsteady – Figaro of Sir Geraint Evans, in a classic characterization. The others too, on paper a fine, starry team, fail to project at full intensity, often thanks to slow speeds and unlifted rhythms. Those interested in individual singers might consider the set, but there are far finer versions than this.

Le nozze di Figaro: highlights.

(M) *** DG 429 822-3 (from above set, cond. Karl Boehm).

(M) **(*) Decca 421 317-2. Tomowa-Sintow, Cotrubas, Von Stade, Van Dam, Bastin, Krause, VPO, Karajan.

Boehm's selection includes many of the key numbers, but with a little over an hour of music it is less generous than its companion highlights discs. Like them, it is inadequately documented, but the singing is first class and the sound vivid.

Though overall Karajan's Decca Vienna recording of *Figaro* with its wilful speeds is too slick for so fizzing a comedy, such polish and refinement deserve to be sampled – notably Frederica von Stade's Cherubino.

Complete Mozart Edition, Volume 39: *L'Oca del Cairo* (complete).

(M) *** Ph. Dig. 422 539-2 [id.]. Nielsen, Wiens, Coburn, Schreier, Johnson, Fischer-Dieskau, Scharinger, Berlin R. Ch. (members), C. P. E. Bach CO, Schreier – *Lo sposo deluso.* ***

We owe it to the Mozart scholar and Philips recording producer, Erik Smith, that these two sets of Mozartian fragments, *L'Oca del Cairo* and *Lo sposo deluso*, have been prepared for performance and recorded. Dating from 1783–4, they anticipate the great leap forward in the history of comic opera represented by *Le nozze di Figaro* in 1786. Though it is doubtful whether even Mozart could have developed the ideas they contain into comparable masterpieces, the incidental delights are many. *L'Oca del Cairo* ('The Cairo goose'), containing roughly twice as much music as *Lo sposo deluso*, involves six substantial numbers, most of them ensembles, including an amazing finale to the projected Act I. It is as extended as the comparable finales of *Figaro* and *Così fan tutte*, with contrasted sections following briskly one after the other. The score left by Mozart has the vocal parts virtually complete, as well as the bass line and the occasional instrumental indications. Smith has sensitively filled in the gaps to make a satisfying whole, very well conducted by Peter Schreier, who also takes part as one of the soloists. Dietrich Fischer-Dieskau takes the *buffo* old-man role of Don Pippo, and Anton Scharinger is brilliant in the patter aria in tarantella rhythm for the major-domo, Chichibio, bringing a foretaste of Donizetti.

Lo sposo deluso, for which Smith did his completion much earlier, involves only four numbers, preceded by a splendid overture, but their invention is sharper and even more clearly anticipates the style of Mozart's Da Ponte operas. Sir Colin Davis directs an excellent (mainly British) cast, with the 1975 analogue recording as fresh and bright as the 1990 digital recording for *L'Oca del Cairo*. This is an ideal disc for anyone wanting a sampler of the Philips Mozart Edition.

Complete Mozart Edition, Volume 35: *Il rè pastore* (complete).

(M) **(*) Ph. Dig. 422 535-2 (2) [id.]. Blasi, McNair, Vermilion, Hadley, Ahnsjö, ASMF, Marriner.

Il rè pastore, the last of Mozart's early operas, is best known for the glorious aria, *L'amero*, one of the loveliest he ever wrote for soprano. The whole entertainment, described as a 'Serenata, on the subject of the shepherd-king nominated by Alexander the Great as his successor', is among the most charming of his early music, a gentle piece which works well on record. This version by Marriner and the Academy is completely new, specially recorded for the Complete Mozart Edition with a first-rate cast. Brisk and bright, with plenty of light and shade, and superbly played, it yet does not efface memories of the 1979 DG version conducted by Leopold Hager, which offered even purer singing. Here Angela Maria Blasi, despite a beautiful voice, attacks notes from below, even in *L'amero*. Excellent sound.

Complete Mozart Edition, Volume 36: *Der Schauspieldirektor* (complete).

(M) **(*) Ph. 422 536-2 (2) [id.]. Welting, Cotrubas, Grant, Rolfe Johnson, LSO, Sir Colin Davis – *Zaïde.* ***

Der Schauspieldirektor (*The Impresario*): complete.

(M) *** DG 429 877-2 (3) [id.]. Grist, Augér, Schreier, Moll, Dresden State O, Boehm – *Die Zauberflöte.* **(*)

The DG performance of *Der Schauspieldirektor* is without dialogue, so that it is short enough to make a fill-up for Boehm's *Zauberflöte.* Reri Grist's bravura as Madame Herz is impressive, and Arleen Augér is pleasingly fresh and stylish here. The tenor and bass make only minor contributions, but Boehm's guiding hand keeps the music alive from the first bar to the last.

There is no contest whatsoever between the two rival prima donnas presented in the Philips recording. *Ich bin die erste Sängerin* ('I am the leading prima donna'), they yell at each other; but here Ileana Cotrubas is in a world apart from the thin-sounding and shallow Ruth Welting. Davis directs with fire and electricity a performance which is otherwise (despite the lack of spoken dialogue) most refreshing and beautifully recorded (in 1975) in a sympathetic acoustic.

Complete Mozart Edition, Volume 31: *Il sogno di Scipione* (complete).

(M) *** Ph. 422 531-2 (2) [id.]. Popp, Gruberová, Mathis, Schreier, Ahnsjö, Thomas Moser, Salzburg Chamber Ch. & Mozarteum O, Hager.

Mozart described this early piece as a *serenata* or *azione teatrale* rather than an opera: it was written for the enthronement of Colloredo, the Archbishop with whom Mozart had his celebrated dispute. It presents an allegorical plot with Scipio set to choose between Fortune and Constancy; and in effect it consists of a sequence of 11 extended arias using three tenors and two sopranos. As a modern entertainment it outstays its welcome, but a recording as stylish and well sung as this certainly has its place in the Complete Mozart Edition. Given the choice of present-day singers, this cast could hardly be finer, with Edita Gruberová, Lucia Popp and Edith Mathis superbly contrasted in the women's roles (the latter taking part in the epilogue merely), and Peter Schreier is joined by two of his most accomplished younger colleagues. Hager sometimes does not press the music on as he might, but his direction is always alive, and the Salzburg Mozarteum Orchestra plays with fine point and elegance – witness the winningly sprightly violins in the *Overture*. With fine recording, vividly and atmospherically transferred to CD, the set is not likely to be surpassed in the immediate future.

Complete Mozart Edition, Volume 39: *Lo sposo deluso*.

(M) *** Ph. 422 539-2 [id.]. Palmer, Cotrubas, Rolfe Johnson, Tear, Grant, LSO, Sir Colin Davis – *L'Oca del Cairo* ***.

The music presented here from *Lo sposo deluso* is the surviving music from an unfinished opera written in the years before *Figaro*, and it contains much that is memorable. The *Overture*, with its trumpet calls, its lovely slow middle section and recaptitulation with voices, is a charmer, while the two arias, reconstructed by the recording producer and scholar, Erik Smith, are also delightful: the one a trial run for Fiordiligi's *Come scoglio* in *Così*, the other (sung by Robert Tear) giving a foretaste of Papageno's music in *The Magic Flute*.

Complete Mozart Edition, Volume 36: *Zaïde*.

(M) *** Ph. 422 536-2 (2) [id.]. Mathis, Schreier, Wixell, Hollweg, Süss, Berlin State O, Klee – *Der Schauspieldirektor*. **(*)

Zaïde, written between 1779 and 1780 and never quite completed, was a trial run for *Entführung*, based on a comparable story of love, duty, escape and forgiveness in the seraglio. It has nothing like the same sharpness of focus dramatically, which may perhaps account for Mozart's failure to complete the piece when within sight of the end. For whatever reason, he left it minus an overture and a finale, but it is simple enough for both to be supplied from other sources, as is done here: the *Symphony No. 32* makes an apt enough overture, and a *March* (K.335/1) rounds things off quickly and neatly. Much of the music is superb, and melodramas at the beginning of each Act are strikingly effective and original, with the speaking voice of the tenor in the first heard over darkly dramatic writing in D minor. Zaïde's arias in both Acts are magnificent: the radiantly lyrical *Ruhe sanft* is hauntingly memorable, and the dramatic *Tiger aria* is like Constanze's *Martern aller Arten* but briefer and more passionate. Bernhard Klee directs a crisp and lively performance, with excellent contributions from singers and orchestra alike – a first-rate team, as consistently stylish as one could want. The 1973 recording is most refined, and the CD transfer retains the appealingly warm ambient atmosphere, making this an attractively compact Mozartian entertainment.

Complete Mozart Edition, Volume 43: *Die Zauberflöte* (complete).

(M) *(*) Ph. Dig. 422 543-2 (3) [id.]. M. Price, Serra, Schreier, Moll, Melbye, Venuti, Tear, Dresden Kreuzchor, Leipzig R. Ch., Dresden State O, Sir Colin Davis.

Die Zauberflöte (complete).

(M) *** EMI CMS7 69971-2 (2) [Ang. CDMB 69971]. Janowitz, Putz, Popp, Gedda, Berry, Frick; Schwarzkopf, Ludwig, Hoffgen (3 Ladies), Philh. Ch. & O, Klemperer.

❀ (M) *** EMI mono CHS7 69631-2 (2) [Ang. CDHB 69631]. Seefried, Lipp, Loose, Dermota, Kunz, Weber, V. State Op. Ch., VPO, Karajan.

(M) **(*) DG 429 877-2 (3) [id.]. Lear, Peters, Otto, Wunderlich, Fischer-Dieskau, Hotter, Crass, Berlin RIAS Chamber Ch., BPO, Boehm – *Der Schauspieldirektor*. ***

(M) ** Decca 414 362-2; *414 362-4* (2) [id.]. Lipp, Gueden, Loose, Simoneau, Berry, Böhme, V. State Op. Ch., VPO, Boehm.

(M) (**) EMI mono CHS7 61034-2 (2) [Ang. CDHB 61034]. Lemnitz, Roswaenge, Berger, Hüsch, Strienz, Ch. & BPO, Beecham.

Klemperer's conducting of *The Magic Flute* is one of his finest achievements on record; indeed he is inspired, making the dramatic music sound more like Beethoven in its breadth and strength. But he does not miss the humour and point of the Papageno passages, and he gets the best of both worlds to a surprising degree. The cast is outstanding – look at the distinction of the Three Ladies alone – but curiously it is that generally most reliable of all the singers, Gottlob Frick as Sarastro, who comes nearest to letting the side down. Lucia Popp is in excellent form, and Gundula Janowitz sings Pamina's part with a creamy beauty that is just breathtaking. Nicolai Gedda too is a firm-voiced Papageno. The transfer to a pair of CDs, made possible by the absence of dialogue, is managed expertly – the whole effect is wonderfully fresh, the balance strikingly good.

As with the companion mono version of *Così fan tutte*, there has never been a more seductive recording of *Zauberflöte* than Karajan's mono version of 1950. The Vienna State Opera cast here has not since been matched on record: Irmgard Seefried and Anton Dermota both sing with radiant beauty and great character, Wilma

Lipp is a dazzling Queen of the Night, Erich Kunz as Papageno sings with an infectious smile in the voice, and Ludwig Weber is a commanding Sarastro. There is no spoken dialogue; but on two mid-priced CDs instead of three LPs, it is a Mozart treat not to be missed, with mono sound still amazingly vivid and full of presence.

One of the glories of Boehm's DG set is the singing of Fritz Wunderlich as Tamino, a wonderful memorial to a singer much missed. Fischer-Dieskau, with characteristic word-pointing, makes a sparkling Papageno on record (he is too big of frame, he says, to do the role on stage) and Franz Crass is a satisfyingly straightforward Sarastro. The team of women is well below this standard – Lear taxed cruelly in *Ach, ich fühl's*, Peters shrill in the upper register (although the effect is exciting), and the Three Ladies do not blend well – but Boehm's direction is superb, light and lyrical, but weighty where necessary to make a glowing, compelling experience. Fine recording, enhanced in the CD set, which has also found room for Boehm's admirable account of *Der Schauspieldirektor*, a very considerable bonus to this mid-priced reissue.

The principal attraction of the Decca reissue is the conducting of Karl Boehm. With surprisingly good recording quality (vintage 1955), vivid, warm and full in the bass, that might well be counted enough recommendation, in spite of the absence of dialogue, particularly when the Tamino of Léopold Simoneau and the Papageno of Walter Berry are strongly and sensitively sung. But the rest of the singing is rather variable, with Hilde Gueden a pert, characterful Pamina unhappy in the florid divisions, Wilma Lipp an impressive Queen of the Night, but Kurt Böhme a gritty and ungracious Sarastro. Although, with such remarkably atmospheric sound, this is certainly enjoyable, there are far stronger recommendations available in the mid-price range, not least Karajan's outstanding 1950 mono set, while Klemperer's inspired version is one of his outstanding achievements on record. Both these sets are also without dialogue.

Recorded in Berlin between November 1937 and March 1939, Beecham's recording of *Zauberflöte* was also the first opera set produced by Walter Legge. It brings a classic performance, and though Helge Roswaenge was too ungainly a tenor to be an ideal Tamino, the casting has otherwise been matched in only a few instances on record. Beecham too was at his peak, pacing each number superbly. Like other early recordings of this opera, this one omits the spoken dialogue; but the vocal delights are many, not least from Tiana Lemnitz as a radiant Pamina, Erna Berger as a dazzling Queen of the Night and Gerhard Hüsch as a delicately comic Papageno, bringing the detailed art of the Lieder-singer to the role. The disappointment of the EMI set is the dryness of the transfer to CD, with a limited top, little sense of presence and no bloom on the voices. As this was one of the first major issues transferred by the new CEDAR process, it provided a warning that technology should always be questioned.

The last of Sir Colin Davis's recordings of Mozart's major operas, and the only one made outside Britain, is also the least successful. With speeds often slower than usual and the manner heavier, it is a performance of little sparkle or charm, one which seems intent on bringing out serious, symbolic meanings. Thus, although Margaret Price produces a glorious flow of rich, creamy tone, she conveys little of the necessary vulnerability of Pamina in her plight. Luciana Serra sings capably but at times with shrill tone and not always with complete security; while Peter Schreier is in uncharacteristically gritty voice as Tamino, and Mikael Melbye as Papageno is ill-suited to recording, when the microphone exaggerates the throatiness and unevenness of his production. The greatest vocal glory of the set is the magnificent, firm and rich singing of Kurt Moll as Sarastro. The recording is excellent.

Die Zauberflöte: highlights.

(M) *** EMI CDM7 63451-2; *EG 763451-4* (from above recording, cond. Klemperer).

(M) *** DG Dig. 431 291-2; *431 291-4* (from complete recording, with Mathis, Ott, Perry, Araiza, Hornik, Van Dam, BPO, cond. Karajan).

(M) **(*) DG 429 825-2; *429 825-4* [id.] (from above recording, with Lear, Peters, Otto, Wunderlich, Fischer-Dieskau, Hotter, Crass; cond. Karl Boehm).

(B) **(*) DG Compact Classics *427 713-4* [id.]. From above set, with Lear, Peters, Otto, Wunderlich, Fischer-Dieskau, Hotter, Crass; cond. Boehm – BEETHOVEN: *Fidelio* highlights. *(*)

(M) ** Ph. Dig. 431 618-2; *431 618-4* (from above recording; cond. Sir Colin Davis).

(M) ** Decca 421 302-2; *421 302-4* (from complete set, with Lorengar, Deutekom, Burrows, Fischer-Dieskau, Prey, Talvela, V. State Op. Ch., VPO; cond. Solti).

Those looking for a first-rate set of highlights from *Die Zauberflöte* will find the mid-priced Klemperer disc hard to beat. It makes a good sampler of a performance which, while ambitious in scale, manages to find sparkle and humour too. A synopsis details each individual excerpt, and in this case the inclusion of the

Overture is especially welcome. The remastered sound has plenty of presence, but atmosphere and warmth too.

The Karajan set of highlights is reasonably generous (61 minutes); it includes the *Overture* and most of the key numbers, including the Papageno/Papagena items, and it demonstrates the overall strength of a generally first-rate cast. At mid-price this is probably a best buy for a highlights disc from this opera, alongside the Klemperer selection.

The hour of (very inadequately documented) excerpts from Boehm's recording is not obviously directed towards bringing out its special qualities. One would have liked more of Wunderlich's Tamino, one of the great glories of the set. However, the key arias are all included and the sound is fresh and full. The Compact Classics *Magic flute* highlights are much more successful than the Beethoven coupling. The male soloists shine especially brightly, and it is a pity that the selection does not include very much of Fischer-Dieskau's engaging Papageno. The *Overture* is included. The sound is pleasing but somewhat bass-orientated.

A highlights disc is probably the best way to approach Sir Colin Davis's 1984 digital *Zauberflöte*, and it includes Sarastro's two principal arias, the most memorable items in a 65-minute selection. However, only a list of titles is included by way of documentation.

The Solti highlights disc displays the characteristics of the complete set from which it is taken; the reading is tough, strong and brilliant, and it is arguable that in this opera these above all are the required qualities, but the almost total absence of charm is disconcerting. The drama may be consistently vital, but ultimately the full variety of Mozart's inspiration is not achieved.

'Famous arias': from *La clemenza di Tito; Così fan tutte; Don Giovanni; Le nozze di Figaro; Il re pastore; Zaïde; Die Zauberflöte.*

(M) **(*) Decca 421 311-2. Berganza, Lorengar, Ghiaurov, Tom Krause, S. Burrows, Bacquier, Fassbaender, Tomowa-Sintow, Popp, Krenn, Deutekom.

It is the men who provide the most memorable singing here: Stuart Burrows melting in *Il mio tesoro* from *Don Giovanni*, Gabriel Bacquier hardly less engaging in the *Serenade* (*Deh! vieni alla finestra*) from the same opera, and Ghiaurov bringing a sparkle to the *Catalogue song*. Among the ladies, Brigitte Fassbaender does not let us forget that Cherubino is a breeches role when she sings *Voi che sapete* stylishly but very directly; and Anna Tomowa-Sintow's account of the Countess's *Dove sono*, also from *Figaro*, is a trifle cool too. Yet Pilar Lorengar is very moving in *Per pietà* from *Così fan tutte*, an outstanding performance; and Lucia Popp's contributions from *Il re pastore* and *Zaïde* leaven an otherwise popular collection; the recording adds a suspicion of hardness to her voice but is mostly vividly atmospheric.

Arias: *Don Giovanni; Die Entführung aus dem Serail; Idomeneo; Le nozze di Figaro; Die Zauberflöte.*

(M) (***) EMI mono CDH7 63708-2. Elisabeth Schwarzkopf (with various orchestras & conductors, including John Pritchard).

Just how fine a Mozartian Schwarzkopf already was early in her career comes out in these 12 items, recorded between 1946 and 1952. The earliest are Konstanze's two arias from *Entführung*, and one of the curiosities is a lovely account of Pamina's *Ach ich fühl's*, recorded in English in 1948. The majority, including those from *Figaro* – Susanna's and Cherubino's arias well as the Countess's – are taken from a long-unavailable recital disc conducted by John Pritchard. Excellent transfers.

ANNIVERSARY ANTHOLOGIES

The Mozart Almanac: The Early Years (Volumes 1–2); 1775–91 (Volumes 3–20) (recordings selected by H. C. Robbins Landon).

(M) *** Decca Dig./Analogue 430 111-2 (20). Various artists.

Devised by H. C. Robbins Landon, a musicologist who wears his scholarship more lightly than almost any rival, Decca's 'Mozart Almanac' is the most imaginative of the Mozart compilations issued to celebrate bicentenary year. Landon's shrewd eye and ear are evident on every one of the twenty discs. The first two cover the period from when the boy started composing in 1761, to 1774. Then the year of his death, 1791, has two whole discs devoted to it, with *Zauberflöte* and *Clemenza* represented alongside the *Clarinet concerto* and *Requiem*; each of the years in between is covered by a single disc. In his choice of works, as well as of specific recordings, Landon repeatedly gives magic to the idea, with essays in each volume to illustrate particular themes related to the period; Mozart is vividly brought to life against his background. So Landon inserts unexpected musical gems among the popular masterpieces, for example the interludes from *Thamos, King of Egypt* on the 1779 disc (offering the *Coronation Mass*, *Symphony No. 32* and wind *Sinfonia concertante*). Complete works are the rule, though operas are represented by individual items merely – not by popular arias as a rule, but often by the long, musically revolutionary finales to Acts. A high proportion of recordings are digital, and many period performances are included – generally overlooked in the other bicentenary series. With generous measure on each disc, all twenty make excellent and illuminating bargains at mid-price.

'The Complete Mozart Edition': highlights. Excerpts from: *Horn concerto No. 4, K.495; Piano concerto No. 5 in D, K. 175; Serenade No. 12 in C min., K.388; Symphony No. 29, K. 201; Flute quartet No. 1 in D, K.285; Piano trio No. 4 in E, K.542; Allegretto in B flat for string quartet, K.App.68* (completed by Erik Smith); *String quartet No. 22 in B flat, K.589; Violin sonata No. 25 in F, K.377; Piano sonata No. 8 in A min., K.310; Exsultate Jubilate, K.165. Die kleine Spinnerin.* Excerpts from: *Requiem Mass, K.626; La clemenza di Tito; Così fan tutte; Don Giovanni; Die Entführung aus dem Serail; Le nozze di Figaro; Die Zauberflöte.*
(B) *** Ph. Dig./Analogue 426 735-2 [id.]. Various artists.

Issued as a sampler for Philips's Complete Mozart Edition and designed to tempt purchasers to explore further, this is a thoroughly worthwhile anthology in its own right. Rather modestly, Erik Smith suggests in the introduction that his selection cannot claim to represent the Edition very seriously, as twenty other items might be 'just as valid'. But he goes on to explain that 'In general the pieces have been chosen for the delight they can give out of context with their charm and melodiousness', and he notes two exceptions to this: Don Giovanni's dramatic final scene with the Commendatore, and an excerpt from the *Requiem* which includes the opening of the *Lacrymosa*, the last music Mozart wrote. The major novelty, previously unrecorded, is the *Allegretto for string quartet* in polonaise rhythm, of which Mozart completed only the first eight bars but then continued with 68 bars for the first violin alone. Smith reconstructed this himself, and very worthwhile it proves. The rest of the programme fits together uncannily well and includes artists of the calibre of the Beaux Arts Trio, Brendel, Grumiaux, Marriner and Uchida, plus many famous vocal soloists, making a fine and certainly a tempting entertainment. The recording is consistently real and refined in the best Philips manner, and the CD offers some 76 minutes of marvellous music. To make this issue even more of a bargain, the accompanying 204-page booklet offers an excellent potted biography, directly related to Mozart's output, with much about the social background against which his works were composed. Of course it also includes details of the 180 CDs which comprise the 45 volumes of the Edition, and it provides pictures and information about the principal performing artists. Finally, the Index gives a complete Köchel listing of Mozart's works, together with the volume number in which each appears.

'Fifty Years of Mozart singing on record': (i) *Concert arias;* Excerpts from: (ii) *Mass in C min., K.427;* (iii) *La clemenza di Tito;* (iv) *Così fan tutte;* (v) *Don Giovanni;* (vi) *Die Entführung aus dem Serail;* (vii) *La finta giardiniera;* (viii) *Idomeneo;* (ix) *Le nozze di Figaro;* (x) *Il re pastore;* (xi) *Zaïde;* (xii) *Die Zauberflöte.*
(M) (***) EMI mono CMS7 63350-2 (4) [id.]. (i) Rethberg, Ginster, Francillo-Kaufmann; (ii) Berger; (iii) Kirkby-Lunn; (iv) V. Schwarz, Noni, Grümmer, Hahn, Kiurina, Hüsch, Souez, H. Nash; (v) Vanni-Marcoux, Scotti, Farrar, Battistini, Corsi, Leider, Roswaenge, D'Andrade, Pinza, Patti, Maurel, Renaud, Pernet, McCormack, Gadski, Kemp, Callas; (vi) Slezak, L. Weber, Tauber, Lehmann, Nemeth, Perras, Ivogün, Von Pataky, Hesch; (vii) Dux; (viii) Jurinac, Jadlowker; (ix) Stabile, Helletsgruber, Santley, Gobbi, Lemnitz, Feraldy, Schumann, Seinemeyer, Vallin, Rautawaara, Mildmay, Jokl, Ritter-Ciampi; (x) Gerhart; (xi) Seefried; (xi) Fugère; Wittrisch; Schiøtz, Gedda, Kurz, Erb, Kipnis, Galvany, Hempel, Sibiriakov, Frick, Destinn, Norena, Schöne, Kunz.

This is an astonishing treasury of singing, recorded over the first half of the twentieth century. It begins with Mariano Stabile's resonant 1928 account of Figaro's *Se vuol ballare*, snail-like by today's standards, while Sir Charles Santley in *Non piu andrai* a few tracks later is both old-sounding and slow. The stylistic balance is then corrected in Tito Gobbi's magnificently characterful 1950 recording of that same aria. Astonishment lies less in early stylistic enormities than in the wonderful and consistent purity of vocal production, with wobbles – so prevalent today – virtually non-existent. That is partly the result of the shrewd and obviously loving choice of items, which includes not only celebrated marvels like John McCormack's 1916 account of Don Ottavio's *Il mio tesoro* (breaking all records for breath control, and stylistically surprising for including an appoggiatura), but many rarities. The short-lived Meta Seinemeyer, glorious in the Countess's first aria, Germaine Feraldy, virtually unknown, a charming Cherubino, Johanna Gadski formidably incisive in Donna Anna's *Mi tradi*, Frieda Hempel incomparable in the Queen of the Night's second aria – all these and many dozens of others make for compulsive listening, with transfers generally excellent. There are far more women singers represented than men, and a high proportion of early recordings are done in languages other than the original; but no lover of fine singing should miss this feast. The arias are gathered together under each opera, with items from non-operatic sources grouped at the end of each disc. Helpfully, duplicate versions of the same aria are put together irrespective of date of recording, and highly informative notes are provided on all the singers.

'The magic of Mozart': (i) *Horn concerto No. 4, K.495;* (ii) *Piano concerto No. 21 in C, K.467;* (iii) *Serenade: Eine kleine Nachtmusik. Così fan tutte:* (i) *Overture;* (iv) *Soave sia il vento; Come scoglio. Don Giovanni:* (v) *Là ci darem la mano; Batti, batti. Le nozze di Figaro:* (vi) *Non più andrai.*
(B) *** EMI Miles of Music *TC2-MOM 137* [id.]. (i) Tuckwell, ASMF, Marriner; (ii) Annie Fischer, Philh. O, Sawallisch; (iii) Philh. O or RPO, Sir Colin Davis; (iv) Schwarzkopf, Ludwig, Berry; (v) Waechter, Sciutti; (vi) Taddei.

For once the sobriquet here is correct: there is over 92 minutes of magic on this tape, admirably designed for motorway listening. The upper range is rather restricted, but the balance is good and the voices reproduce pleasingly. All three major works are complete, and Annie Fischer's 1959 account of the *C major Piano concerto* (with cadenzas by Busoni) is distinctive. The excerpts from the Giulini sets of *Don Giovanni* and *Nozze di Figaro* are delightful, but most ravishing of all is the glorious Trio from Boehm's 1963 *Così fan tutte*, followed by Schwarzkopf's superb *Come scoglio.*

'The world of Mozart': Excerpts from: *Clarinet concerto; Piano concerto No. 21, K.467. Masonic funeral music, K.477.* Excerpts from: *A Musical joke; Serenade: Eine kleine Nachtmusik; Symphonies Nos. 25 in G min., K.183; 40 in G min., K.550; Piano sonata No. 11, K.331 (Rondo alla turca). Ave verum corpus.* Excerpts from: *Requiem Mass; Così fan tutte; Le nozze di Figaro.*
(B) **(*) Decca 430 498-2; *430 498-4*. Various artists.

There are some fine performances here, notably Ashkenazy's lovely *Andante* from the *Piano concerto No. 21*, Solti's vivacious *Nozze di Figaro Overture*, followed by Kiri Te Kanawa's *Dove sono.* Kertész's very characterful *Masonic funeral music* is given complete, and another highlight is András Schiff's *Alla turca*, which most effectively alternates delicate articulation with strong rhythmic feeling. But overall the collection is inclined to feel piecemeal and thus does not quite amount to the sum of its parts. Characteristically bright Decca transfers. However, with 75 minutes of music, the tape should prove useful in the car.

Muffat, Georg (1653–1704)

Sonatas in G; in G min.; Suites in D (Nobilis juventus); in G (Laeta poesis).
(M) ** HM/BMG GD 77074 [77074-2-RG] [id.]. La Petite Bande, Kuijken.

Muffat, with his cosmopolitan mixtures of style, is more than a figure of historical interest; he is a diverting and inventive (if sometimes uneven) composer. Some of the pieces, including the *G major Sonata* (or Concerto) which opens the disc, will strike some listeners as dull, nor does it seem wholly to engage the enthusiasm of the normally excellent La Petite Bande. Their playing is often somewhat inhibited. The disc is worth investigating, however, for the sake of the *G major Suite*, *Laeta poesis*, with its rather delightful gastronomic programme, and the eloquent and expressive *G minor Sonata* which is worth the money alone. These recordings come from 1974 and are very serviceable.

Mussorgsky, Modest (1839–81)

Night on the bare mountain (original version).
(M) *** Ph. 420 898-2 [id.]. LPO, Lloyd-Jones – RIMSKY-KORSAKOV: *Scheherazade.* ***

Although it uses some of Mussorgsky's basic material, the piece we know as *Night on the bare mountain* is much more the work of Rimsky-Korsakov, who added much music of his own. The original has undoubted power and fascination, but its construction is considerably less polished. David Lloyd-Jones's performance makes a good case for it, bringing out all the crude force of its Satanic vision. The new digital transfer is also first class, and this makes an exciting bonus for an outstanding version of Rimsky-Korsakov's *Scheherazade.*

Night on the bare mountain (orch. Rimsky-Korsakov).
(M) *** Sony SBK 46329; *40-46329* [id.]. Phd. O, Ormandy – BERLIOZ: *Symphonie fantastique* **; DUKAS: *L'apprenti sorcier.* ***
(M) *** Mercury 432 004-2 [id.]. LSO, Dorati – PROKOFIEV: *Romeo and Juliet suites.* ***
(M) **(*) Decca Dig. 430 700-2; *430 700-4* [id.]. Montreal SO, Dutoit – RIMSKY-KORSAKOV: *Capriccio espagnol*; TCHAIKOVSKY: *1812* etc. **(*)

Night on the bare mountain; Khovanshchina: Prelude (both arr. Rimsky-Korsakov).
(B) *** Decca 417 689-2; *417 689-4*. LSO, Solti – BORODIN: *Prince Igor: Overture and*

Polovtsian dances; GLINKA: *Russlan overture.* ***

Solti's *Night on the bare mountain* can stand up to all competition in its vintage 1967 recording with its fine amplitude and great brilliance. This remains one of Solti's finest analogue collections, offering also the highly atmospheric *Khovanshchina Prelude*, which is beautifully played.

With virtuoso playing from the Philadelphia Orchestra, Ormandy's 1967 recording has plenty of thrills, with its shrieking banshees and darkly sonorous brass. As in the coupled *Sorcerer's apprentice* of Dukas, the potent imagery of Walt Disney's *Fantasia* springs readily to mind.

Dorati's fine 1960 account of *Night on the bare mountain* comes as an encore for Skrowaczewski's outstanding Prokofiev, and it is interesting at the end of *Romeo and Juliet* to note the subtle shift of acoustic from the Minneapolis auditorium to Wembley Town Hall.

Dutoit's *Night on the bare mountain* is strong and biting, but the adrenalin does not flow as grippingly as in, say, Ormandy's version. The brilliant, atmospheric recording is naturally balanced, with the bloom characteristic of the Montreal sound.

(i) *Night on the bare mountain* (arr. Rimsky-Korsakov); (ii) *Pictures at an exhibition* (orch. Ravel).

(B) *** DG Compact Classics 413 153-2 (2); *413 153-4* [id.]. (i) Boston Pops O, Fiedler; (ii) Chicago SO, Giulini – TCHAIKOVSKY: *1812* etc. **(*) (CD only: BORODIN: *In the Steppes of central Asia* **).

(BB) **(*) Naxos 8.550051 [id.]. Slovak PO, Nazareth – BORODIN: *In the Steppes of Central Asia* etc. **(*)

It is interesting that Giulini's memorably successful account of the *Pictures* should use the Chicago orchestra, thus repeating Reiner's success of the early days of stereo. The modern recording, however, is noticeably more refined and detailed, with brilliant percussive effects (a superb bass drum in *The Hut on fowl's legs*). With superlative orchestral playing and strong characterization, this is highly recommendable; the new transfer is outstandingly vivid and full-bodied in both CD and tape formats. It is here paired with an excitingly volatile account of *Night on the bare mountain*, directed by Fiedler. Both sound well on this bargain-price Compact Classics issue, generously coupled with Tchaikovsky. The pair of CDs also includes a romantically atmospheric performance of Borodin's *In the Steppes of Central Asia*, very well played by the Dresden State Orchestra under Kurt Sanderling, if with the violins sounding a little undernourished in the CD transfer. Mussorgsky's *Pictures* are also available on a single CD, coupled with Ravel, which makes an attractive alternative pairing.

The super-baragain Naxos coupling is vividly played and recorded and is well worth its modest price. *A night on the bare mountain* is played flexibly, yet does not lack excitement. The *Pictures*, too, have plenty of character. The climax of *Bydlo* is dramatically enhanced by a fortissimo contribution from the timpanist, and the detail throughout is well observed, from the bleating Schmuyle to the chirping chicks. *Tuileries* and *Limoges* bring lightly etched orchestral bravura, while the closing picture of the Kiev Gate has architectural grandeur and a sense of majesty. Enjoyable, if lacking the last touch of individuality.

Pictures at an exhibition (orch. Ravel).

(B) *** DG 429 162-2; *429 162-4* [id.]. BPO, Karajan – STRAVINSKY: *Rite of spring.* ***

(BB) *** BMG/RCA Dig. VD 87729 [7729-2-RV]. Dallas SO, Mata – RAVEL: *La valse* etc. ***

(M) *** DG 415 844-2 [id.]. Chicago SO, Giulini – RAVEL: *Ma mère l'Oye; Rapsodie espagnole.* ***

(B) *** EMI CDZ7 62860-2; *LZ7 62860-4* [id.]. Philh. O, Karajan – LISZT: *Hungarian rhapsody No. 2* etc. ***

(M) *** Decca Dig. 417 754-2 [id.]. Chicago SO, Solti – BARTÓK: *Concerto for orchestra.* ***

(M) *** Decca Dig. 430 446-2; *430 446-4* [id.]. Chicago SO, Solti – PROKOFIEV: *Symphony No. 1* *(*); TCHAIKOVSKY: *1812.* **(*)

(M) ** Decca Dig. 430 709-2; *430 709-4*. Concg. O, Chailly – STRAVINSKY: *Rite of spring.* **(*)

(M) (**) BMG/RCA mono GD 60287 [60287-2-RG]. NBC SO, Toscanini – ELGAR: *Enigma variations.* (***)

Karajan's 1966 record stands out. It is undoubtedly a great performance, tingling with electricity from the opening Promenade to the spaciously conceived finale, *The Great Gate of Kiev*, which has real splendour. Other high points are the ominously powerful climax of *Bydlo* as the Polish ox-wagon lumbers into view very weightily, and the venomously pungent bite of the brass – expansively recorded – in the sinister *Catacombs* sequence, which is given a bizarre majesty. Detail is consistently pointed with the greatest imagination, not only in the lighter moments, but for instance in *The hut on fowl's legs*, where the tuba articulation is sharp and rhythmically buoyant. Throughout, the glorious orchestral playing, and especially the brass sonorities, ensnare the ear; even when Karajan is relatively restrained, as in the nostalgic melancholy of *The old castle*, the underlying tension remains. The remastered analogue recording still sounds pretty marvellous; it is little short of demonstration standard and is very well balanced, apart from an odd spot of bass resonance.

The sumptuousness of the Dallas sound, its amplitude and richness of colouring are ideal for Mussorgsky's *Pictures*. Mata's performance has one or two idiosyncrasies – he treats *Tuileries* rather freely, with a little *tenuto* on the opening phrase – but the obvious affection justifies his indulgence. The orchestral playing is consistently responsive and the brass come into their own (after opening the work resonantly) in the *Catacombs* and the brilliant *Hut on fowl's legs*. The closing *Great Gate of Kiev* is splendidly paced, and Mata's eloquent preparation of the closing pages, measured yet purposeful, is underpinned by the gloriously full digital recording, as fine as any in the catalogue. A remarkable bargain in the lowest price-range.

Giulini's 1976 Chicago recording had always been among the front runners. He is generally more relaxed and often more wayward than Karajan, but this is still a splendid performance and the finale generates more tension than Karajan's most recent, digital version, though it is not as overpowering as the earlier, analogue recording. What makes the Giulini very attractive is the generous Ravel couplings which show him at his finest.

Karajan's Philharmonia recording of Mussorgsky's *Pictures* was made in the Kingsway Hall in 1955–6. The quality is astonishing, yet another tribute to the skill of Walter Legge as producer. There is extraordinary clarity and projection, yet no lack of body and ambience, and it is matched by the brilliantly polished detail of the orchestral playing – the Philharmonia offering breathtaking standards of ensemble and bite. The presentation of each picture is outstandingly strong, even if some other versions, including Karajan's own analogue Berlin Philharmonic recording, are at times pictorially more vivid. But *The Great Gate of Kiev* brings a frisson-creating climax of great breadth and splendour, achieved as much by Karajan's dignified pacing as by the spread of the sound.

Solti's performance is fiercely brilliant rather than atmospheric or evocative. He treats Ravel's orchestration as a virtuoso challenge, and with larger-than-life digital recording it undoubtedly has demonstration qualities, and the transparency of texture, given the forward balance, provides quite startling clarity. Now very generously recoupled at mid-price with Solti's outstanding version of Bartók's *Concerto for orchestra*, it makes a formidable bargain. Solti's account is also available with Prokofiev and Tchaikovsky, but these later couplings are less recommendable.

Chailly's brilliant Concertgebouw recording – one of the first discs he made with them after being appointed their music director – takes an oddly metrical view of the score. This means that the *Promenade* links sound square and plodding while the final *Great Gate of Kiev*, at a very slow and steady speed, is shattering in the wrong way as well as in the right one. But the light, brilliant numbers are done delightfully; and the Decca recording has spectacular range.

Toscanini was no colourist, and his regimented view of the exotic Mussorgsky–Ravel score is at its least sympathetic in the opening statement of the opening *Promenade*, not just rigidly metrical but made the coarser by the cornet-like trumpet tone. Many of the individual movements are done with greater understanding – for example, the *Ballet of the unhatched chicks* – but too often Toscanini's lack of sympathy undermines the character of this rich score. Clean, bright transfer. This version is still worth considering for the sake of Toscanini's unique account of the Elgar.

(i) *Pictures at an exhibition* (orch. Ravel); (ii) *Pictures at an exhibition* (original piano version).

(M) *** Ph. 420 708-2; *420 708-4*. (i) Rotterdam PO, Edo de Waart; (ii) Misha Dichter.

(M) ** Ph. Dig. 432 051-2; *432 051-4*. (i) VPO, Previn; (ii) Alfred Brendel.

Those seeking the natural pairing of the original piano version of Mussorgsky's *Pictures* with Ravel's orchestration will hardly better this analogue Philips CD. The Rotterdam orchestra play splendidly throughout, and Edo de Waart's performance has a natural, spontaneous momentum, with each picture aptly characterized and the final climax admirably paced and excitingly powerful. The 1975 recording is rather resonant, but detail comes through well enough. The weight in the bass emphasizes the strong contribution from the drums in *Baba-Yaga* and the closing section. The surprise here, however, is Misha Dichter's outstanding performance of the original piano score, among the finest on record. Each separate picture is telling and he perceptively varies the mood of each Promenade to provide an appropriate link. After a riveting account of *Baba-Yaga*, demonstrating great keyboard flair, the closing *Great Gate of Kiev* is overwhelmingly powerful. Dichter often seems a reticent pianist in the recording studio, but not here – Mussorgsky's spectacular finale has seldom sounded more gripping; and the piano's sonority is splendidly caught by the Philips recording.

What looks to be a fascinating juxtaposition

of the orchestral version under Previn and Brendel playing the piano original proves a little disappointing in the event, although it is easy for the listener to move backwards and forwards between piano and orchestra by using the cues provided on the liner leaflet at the back of the disc. Previn's performance was recorded during live performances in Vienna, and obviously the Philips engineers had problems with the acoustics of the Musikvereinsaal: the bass is noticeably resonant and inner definition could be sharper. The performance, though not lacking spontaneity, is not distinctive, and there is a lack of the grip which makes Karajan's readings so unforgettable. Brendel's account of the original piano version has its own imaginative touches and some fine moments: *The Ballet of the unhatched chicks* is delightfully articulated, and both *Bydlo* and *Baba-Yaga* are powerful, the latter coming after a darkly evocative *Catacombs/Cum mortuis* sequence. The closing pages, however, need to sound more unbuttoned. Brendel is weighty but fails to enthral the listener. The recording is admirably faithful.

Pictures at an exhibition (original piano version).
(M) *** DG 431 170-2; *431 170-4*. Lazar Berman – PROKOFIEV: *Romeo and Juliet*. ***
(M) (***) Ph. mono 420 774-2. Sviatoslav Richter (with *Recital* (***))
(M) (**(*)) Decca mono 425 961-2 [id.]. Julius Katchen – BALAKIREV: *Islamey*; LISZT: *Funérailles* etc. (**(*))

Pictures at an exhibition; Une larme; On the southern shore of the Crimea: Gurzuf; Capriccio; Sorochintsy Fair: Hopak.
(BB) * Naxos Dig. 8.550044 [id.]. Jenö Jandó – BALAKIREV: *Islamey*. (*)

Pictures at an exhibition (piano version, ed. Horowitz); *Sunless: By the water*.
(M) *** BMG/RCA GD 60449; *GK 60449* [60449-2-RG]. Vladimir Horowitz – TCHAIKOVSKY: *Piano concerto No. 1*. (***)

Horowitz's famous 1951 recording, made at a live performance at Carnegie Hall, is as thrilling as it is perceptive. Mussorgsky's darker colours are admirably caught (and this applies also in the pianist's own arrangement of the final song from the *Sunless* cycle, which is played as a sombre encore). The rhythmic angularity, forcefully accented, projects *Bydlo* potently and the lighter scherzando evocations are dazzlingly articulated. But it is the closing pictures which are especially powerful, the pungent *Baba-Yaga*, and the spectacular *Great Gate of Kiev*, where Horowitz has embroidered the final climax to add to its pianistic resplendency. The piano image is bold and clear, somewhat hard but not lacking fullness.

Like Horowitz, Lazar Berman brings an uncompromisingly fast pacing to the opening *Promenade*. One can picture him striding brusquely round the exhibition, hands behind his back. But when he stops, he is strongly involved in each picture, and his playing makes a very direct communication with its arresting power and atmosphere, notably so in *Bydlo*, *Catacombs* and *Cum mortuis*, although the *Ballet of the unhatched chicks* finds him more concerned with articulation (the playing is superb) than with humorous evocation. The *Great Gate of Kiev* makes a riveting climax. It is rather less flamboyant than with Horowitz, but effective in its sparer way, using just the notes Mussorgsky wrote. Recorded in 1977, this is undoubtedly among the most compelling versions to have appeared in recent years, and the CD transfer brings an impressively realistic piano image.

The Philips reissue offers Sviatoslav Richter's 1958 Sofia recital. The mono recording has been remastered using this company's NoNoise digital background reduction system, but alas this cannot suppress the audience's bronchial afflictions, and a troublesome tape roar also remains. Nevertheless, the magnetism of Richter's playing comes over and his enormously wide dynamic range brings a riveting final climax, even if, with the piano backwardly positioned, some of the pianissimo playing is not too cleanly focused. Besides the Mussorgsky, the recital offers a generous programme, including Schubert *Impromptus* and a *Moment musical*, the Chopin *Étude in E*, Op. 10, No. 3, two Liszt *Valses oubliées* and excerpts from the *Transcendental studies*, all readily demonstrating the Richter magic in spite of indifferent sound.

Decca have reissued their 1950 account of *Pictures* as part of a tribute to Julius Katchen, whose masterly performance has not been available for many years. It is undeniably impressive, though it does not have quite the mystery and incandescence of Horowitz or Richter. The sound is good but not outstanding for its period; older collectors with fond memories of Katchen's artistry will want it.

Jandó's *Pictures* are not strong on colour or imagination, nor are the other rarities played with the distinction he has brought to other repertoire. Despite the modest outlay required, this is not money well spent, given the quality of the competition. Apart from Béroff's now deleted recordings, the shorter Mussorgsky pieces are not well served on disc; they are well worth the attention of pianists, and it is a pity that these accounts are relatively pedestrian.

Pictures at an exhibition (arr. for brass by Elgar Howarth).
(M) *** Decca 425 022-2; *425 022-4* [id.]. Philip Jones Brass Ens., Howarth – SAINT-SAENS: *Carnival of the animals.* **

There is no reason why Mussorgsky's famous piano work should not be transcribed for brass as effectively as for a full symphony orchestra, and Elgar Howarth's imaginatively inspired arrangement fully justifies the experiment. There is never any suggestion of limited colour; indeed, in the pioneering 1977 Philip Jones recording (originally Argo), the pictures of the marketplace at Limoges and of the unhatched chicks have great pictorial vividness, and the evocation of the dead (in *Catacombs*) has an almost cinematic element of fantasy. The *Great Gate of Kiev* is as thrilling here as in many orchestral recordings, and the splendidly rich and sonorous Kingsway Hall recording remains in the demonstration bracket in its Decca CD format. If the Saint-Saëns coupling is rather less successful in transcription, that is no fault either of players or of engineers.

The Complete Songs.
❀ (M) (***) EMI mono CHS7 63025-2 (3) [Ang. CHS 63025]. Boris Christoff, Alexandre Labinsky, Gerald Moore, French R. & TV O, Georges Tzipine.

Boris Christoff originally recorded these songs in 1958; they then appeared in a four-LP mono set with a handsome book, generously illustrated with plates and music examples, giving the texts in Russian, French, Italian and English, and with copious notes on each of the 63 songs. Naturally the documentation cannot be so extensive in the CD format – but, on the other hand, one has the infinitely greater ease of access that the new technology offers. The Mussorgsky songs constitute a complete world in themselves, and they cast a strong spell: their range is enormous and their insight into the human condition deep. Christoff was at the height of his vocal powers when he made the set with Alexandre Labinsky, his accompanist in most of the songs; and its return to circulation cannot be too warmly welcomed. This was the first complete survey, and it still remains the only one.

Newman, Alfred (1901–70)

Film music: *20th Century-Fox Fanfare.* Excerpts from: *Airport; Anastasia; Best of Everything; The Bravados; Captain from Castile;* (i) *Conquest. Down to the Sea in Ships; How to Marry a Millionaire (Street scene).* (i; ii) *The Robe.* (ii) *The Song of Bernadette. Wuthering Heights.*
(M) *** BMG/RCA GD 80184; *GK 80184* [0184-2-RG; *0184-4-RG*]. Nat. PO, (i) with Band of the Grenadier Guards; (ii) Amb. S.; Charles Gerhardt.

Alfred Newman was Hollywood's own man. Unlike his émigré colleagues, Korngold, Rózsa and Waxman, he was born in Connecticut, and Hollywoodian hyperbole was an intrinsic part of his musical nature. He was good at rumbustious, rather empty marches (as in *Captain from Castile*) and tended to overscore. The very first piece here (after the famous *Twentieth Century-Fox Fanfare*, which will ensure his immortality) is genuinely memorable. *Street scene*, a Gershwinesque evocation originally written in 1931 for a film of the same name but more recently made familiar by its re-use as an introduction for *How to Marry a Millionaire*, combines strong thematic interest with a real feeling for atmosphere. For the rest, there is sentimentality (*Cathy's theme* from *Wuthering Heights*), orchestral inflation, the occasional vivid evocation (the vision sequence in *The Song of Bernadette* very effective, even if essentially tasteless) and luscious religiosity (*The Robe*). Charles Gerhardt's committed advocacy and the splendid orchestral playing ensure maximum impact throughout and, if one accepts the noise, there is something almost endearing about such ingenuous vulgarity, when the end result was exactly what the directors and producers wanted to match the spectacular cinematography of the period. As usual in this series, there are good notes but not enough movie stills.

Nicolai, Carl Otto (1810–49)

The merry wives of Windsor (Die lustigen Weiber von Windsor): complete.
(M) **(*) EMI CMS7 69348-2 (2) [Ang. CDMB 69348]. Frick, Gutstein, Engel, Wunderlich, Lenz, Hoppe, Putz, Litz, Mathis, Ch. & O of Bav. State Op., Heger.

The great glory of this fine EMI set is the darkly menacing Falstaff of Gottlob Frick in magnificent voice, even if he sounds baleful rather than comic. It is good too to have the young Fritz Wunderlich as Fenton opposite the Anna Reich of Edith Mathis. Though the others hardly match this standard – Ruth-Margret Putz is rather shrill as Frau Fluth – they all give enjoyable performances, helped by the production, which conveys the feeling of artists who have experienced performing the piece on stage. The effectiveness of the comic timing is owed in great measure to the conducting of the veteran, Robert Heger. From the CD transfer one could hardly tell the age of the recording, with the voices particularly well caught.

Nielsen, Carl (1865–1931)

Violin concerto, Op. 33.

(M) *(*) EMI mono CDM7 63987-2 [id.]. Y. Menuhin, Danish State RSO, Wöldike – SIBELIUS: *Violin concerto.* *(*)

Despite some felicities, neither Menuhin's Nielsen *Violin concerto*, recorded with Mogens Wöldike and the Danish State Radio Orchestra in 1952, nor its coupling with Sir Adrian Boult and the LPO from 1956 shows Menuhin at his very best. Intonation is not always secure and he does not always make a beautiful sound either. The Nielsen is well represented on CD now at premium price, and either Cho-Liang Lin on Sony or Kim Sjögren on Chandos are worth the extra money.

Symphonies Nos. 1–6.

(M) **(*) Unicorn UK CD 2000/2 [id.]. Gomez, Rayner-Cook (in No. 3), LSO, Schmidt.

Symphonies Nos. (i) *1, Op. 7;* (ii) *2 (Four Temperaments);* (iii) *3 (Espansiva);* (ii) *4 (Inextinguishable); 5, Op. 50;* (i) *6 (Sinfonia Semplice);* (iv; ii) *Clarinet concerto;* (v; ii) *Flute concerto;* (i) *Helios overture; Maskarade: Overture; Prelude, Act II; Pan and Syrinx; Rhapsodic overture.*

(M) ** Sony SM4K 45989 (4) [id.]. (i) Phd. O, Ormandy; (ii) NYPO, Bernstein; (iii) Guldbaek, Møller, Royal Danish O, Bernstein; (iv) Drucker; (v) Baker.

The performances on Unicorn Kanchana are ablaze with life, warmth and a sense of discovery. The recordings were always a bit rough, but the digital remastering represents an undoubted (though not spectacular) improvement, for the texture still remains coarse in tuttis. However, the brass is less garish and better integrated into the overall aural picture. In No. 2 and the last three symphonies Ole Schmidt is a sure and penetrating guide. Whatever quibbles one might have (Schmidt may be a little too fervent in the slow movement of the *First Symphony* for some tastes), his readings have an authentic ring to them, for he has real feeling for this glorious music. They obviously represent good value.

The complete symphonies and much else besides on four mid-price Sony CDs seems quite a bargain, though these performances are all from the period 1962–73 when CBS was going through a rough patch so far as recorded sound was concerned. The strings still retain their unpleasant edge (try the slow movement of the *Inextinguishable* or the opening of the *Second*). Ormandy's recordings of Nos. 1 and 6, made in 1966–7, are on the first CD and are marginally improved; even so, they still do not do justice to the sound this great partnership made – nor, to be fair, were the performances particularly outstanding. Bernstein's accounts of Nos. 2 and 4 come on the second CD, and again the improvement is marginal, though, for all their fire and intensity, neither performance really holds up against Ole Schmidt's later version. Oddly enough, the *Espansiva*, which Bernstein recorded in Copenhagen in 1965 with the Royal Danish Orchestra, sounds best, even if its finale is rather too deliberate in pace and self-conscious in phrasing. The slow movement is also just a shade too intense. All the same, it has a lot going for it: vitality, enthusiasm and a certain freshness. In the 1970s many of these performances were competitive, and there are still some powerful insights in Bernstein's account of the *Fifth*, which he recorded first of all. This has many admirers and rightly so, as it is both a perceptive and a deeply felt performance, even if allowances have to be made for the sound. The last disc contains the two concertos with Bernstein conducting (the *Clarinet concerto* is particularly fine), and the *Helios overture*, *Pan and Syrinx* and the *Rhapsodic overture* (*An imaginary journey to the Faeroes*) under Ormandy. All in all, there are good things here, even if there are better modern alternatives.

Symphony No. 4 (Inextinguishable), Op. 29.

(M) ** EMI Phoenixa CDM7 63775-2; *EG 763775-4.* Hallé O, Barbirolli – SIBELIUS: *Pohjola's Daughter; Scènes historiques.* **

Symphony No. 4 (Inextinguishable), Op. 29; An Imaginary journey to the Faroe Islands (Rhapsodic overture); Pan and Syrinx, Op. 49.

(M) **(*) Chan. CHAN 6524; *MBTD 6524* [id.]. SNO, Gibson – SIBELIUS: *The Dryad* etc. ***

Sir Alexander Gibson has well-judged tempi and an obvious sympathy for the *Inextinguishable*, and there is no want of commitment from the Scottish players. Perhaps the strings do not have quite the weight that is required, and one misses the last ounce of fire. Yet there is much to admire, including a well-balanced (1979) analogue sound-picture, truthfully transferred to CD. Both *Pan and Syrinx* and the much later *Rhapsodic overture* are given perceptive readings that realize much of the mystery these scores evoke, and the Sibelius couplings bring a similar sensitivity to atmosphere and colour. At mid-price this is worth considering.

Sir John Barbirolli's account of the symphony was the first to be made in stereo: it dates from 1958 and was well regarded in its day. The performance has plenty of fire and warmth; but the sound is far from ideal, even though it is now considerably cleaned up. The timpani in the finale are a bit clattery and some coarseness remains in climaxes. There is some fine playing, particularly from the woodwind in the second movement, and Sir John obviously had a strong feeling for the work.

Symphony No. 5; En Sagadrøm, Op. 39.
(M) **(*) Unicorn UKCD 2023. New Philh. O, Horenstein.

Symphony No. 5, Op. 50; Helios overture, Op. 17.
(M) **(*) Chan. CHAN 6533; *MBTD 6533* [id.]. SNO, Gibson – SIBELIUS: *Night ride and sunrise* etc. **(*)

Horenstein gives a dignified but slightly detached account of the *Fifth Symphony*. His feeling for the overall structure of the work is strong, but poetic detail is not savoured to the same extent as in Tuxen's old set. The string-playing of the New Philharmonia is extremely fine, though they do not have quite the lyrical fervour of the new Blomstedt/San Francisco full-price version. Horenstein's record has the advantage of an interesting fill-up, the tone-poem *En Sagadrøm*, which is poetically done and beautifully recorded. In the *Symphony* the balance gives far too great a prominence to the percussion and not quite enough weight to the strings. In that respect the new Decca digital recording is infinitely better judged and, although at full price, this offers also the *Fourth Symphony*.

Gibson's is a likeable performance of the *Fifth Symphony*, bringing some idiomatic playing from the Scottish orchestra. The approach is fresh and enthusiastic, and the music unfolds organically and naturally. One bar before fig. 3 in the first movement there is a B flat instead of a natural, which will worry some collectors on repetition; but this is a small blemish to put in the balance-sheet against some imaginative and committed playing. A poetic and eloquent account of the *Helios overture* serves as an encore, and for the reissue Chandos have added two of Gibson's atmospheric Sibelius performances. As usual with this label, the 1978 recording, made in Glasgow City Hall, has been transferred admirably to CD. The recording is full, with excellent ambience, though just a little lacking in transparency.

(i) *String quartets Nos. 1 in G min., Op. 13; 2 in F min., Op. 5; 3 in E flat, Op. 14; 4 in F, Op. 44;* (ii) *String quintet in G;* (iii) *Wind quintet, Op. 43.*
(M) *(*) DG 431 156-2 (2). (i) Carl Nielsen Qt, (ii) with Børge Mortensen; (iii) Vestjysk Chamber Ens.

All four works here are worth representing in any comprehensive collection, particularly Nos. 3 and 4; but they really need to be played much better than they are in these DG recordings from the 1970s. The playing of the eponymous Carl Nielsen Quartet is all very unpolished and their tone distinctly wanting in lustre. Nor do these players sound very much better in the early *G major Quintet* of 1888, which is much indebted to Svendsen. In the *Wind quintet* of 1922 the West Jutland ensemble are a good deal better, but all the same there are much better versions on the market. This set can only serve as a stop-gap until something better comes along.

Wind quintet, Op. 43.
(M) ** Sony SMK 46250 [id.]. Members of the Marlboro Festival – BARBER: *Summer Music* **(*); HINDEMITH: *Octet.* **

The Marlboro performance of the *Wind quintet* dates from 1971 and is a good one. If it is not an automatic recommendation, this is not because of any artistic reservations but rather because of the recording balance, which places the listener just a little too close to the players. There are some perceptive things here, and these players penetrate the spirit of the poignant preamble that opens the *Theme and variations.*

Offenbach, Jacques (1819–80)

Gaîté parisienne (ballet, arr. Rosenthal): complete.
(BB) *** BMG/RCA VD 87734 [7734-2-RV]. Boston Pops O, Fiedler – KHACHATURIAN: *Gayaneh suite.* ***
(M) **(*) Decca Dig. 430 718-2; *430 718-4.* Montreal SO, Dutoit – GOUNOD: *Faust: ballet music.* **(*)
(M) ** EMI CDM7 63136-2. Monte Carlo Op. O, Rosenthal – WALDTEUFEL: *Waltzes.* ***

A sparkling, racy – and indeed irresistible – account from Fiedler of the Rosenthal ballet, concocted from some of Offenbach's most memorable ideas. The orchestra are kept exhilaratingly on their toes throughout and are obviously enjoying themselves, not least in the elegantly tuneful waltzes and in the closing *Barcarolle*, which Fiedler prepares beautifully. The percussion, including bass drum in the *Can can*, adds an appropriate condiment, and the warm resonance of the Boston hall adds bloom yet doesn't blunt or coarsen the brilliance.

Dutoit has the advantage of digital sound that is bright and has good projection, though the acoustic is resonant and detail is not especially clear; but the recording undoubtedly emerges from Decca's top drawer. He opens the music racily and there are many admirable touches, yet as the ballet proceeds there is a hint of blandness in the lyrical moments, and the *Barcarolle* is somewhat disappointing; however, some may like the extra feeling of breadth Dutoit generates. The disc has the advantage of including also the *Faust* ballet music, warmly and elegantly played, but here also Dutoit's touch is a shade heavy. The feeling in both works is redolent of the concert hall rather than of the ballet theatre, and this effect is enhanced on the excellent CD.

Maurice Rosenthal's absolutely complete version from the mid-1970s has now been restored to the catologue, together with the documentation giving the sources for all the music in the score, the snag being that the identification is not always accurate. The performance, though often idiomatically persuasive, has not the verve and glamour of that by Fiedler and Karajan. The sound, however, has been greatly improved, with the original excess resonance considerably tempered.

Gaîté parisienne (ballet, arr. Rosenthal): extended excerpts.

(B) *** DG 429 163-2. BPO, Karajan – CHOPIN: *Les Sylphides* *** ❀; DELIBES: *Coppélia*: Suite excerpts. ***

(M) **(*) EMI CDM7 69041-2 [id.]. Philh. O, Karajan – BORODIN: *Polovtsian dances*; GOUNOD: *Faust ballet*; PONCHIELLI: *Dance of the hours.* ***

Karajan's selection is generous. On the DG disc, only Nos. 3–5, 7 and 19–21 are omitted. The remastering of the 1972 recording is highly successful. Textures have been lightened to advantage and the effect is to increase the raciness of the music-making, while its polish and sparkle are even more striking. On the whole this is preferable to the 1958 Philharmonia version. The London orchestra also plays with great brilliance, the players obviously revelling in the bravura, but the remastered sound is a little dry. However, the couplings are highly attractive.

Le Papillon (ballet): complete.

(M) *** Decca 425 450-2. LSO, Richard Bonynge – TCHAIKOVSKY: Nutcracker. **(*)

Le Papillon is Offenbach's only full-length ballet and it dates from 1860. If the tunes do not come quite as thick and fast as in Rosenthal's confected *Gaîté parisienne*, the quality of invention is high and the music sparkles from beginning to end. In such a sympathetic performance, vividly recorded (in 1974) it cannot fail to give pleasure. Highly recommended to all lovers of ballet and Offenbach.

OPERA

Les Contes d'Hoffmann: highlights.

(M) *** Decca 421 866-2; *421 866-4*. Sutherland, Domingo, Tourangeau, Bacquier, R. Suisse Romande & Pro Arte Ch., SRO, Bonynge.

(M) ** EMI CDM7 63448-2 [id.]; *EG 763448-4*. Schwarzkopf, De los Angeles, D'Angelo, Gedda, Ghuiselev, London, Blanc, Duclos Ch., Paris Conservatoire O, Cluytens.

The Decca highlights disc is one of the finest compilations of its kind from any opera. With over an hour of music, it offers a superbly managed distillation of nearly all the finest items and is edited most skilfully.

With such a starry cast-list it is disappointing that the EMI set was not more successful. In particular André Cluytens proved quite the wrong conductor for this sparkling music. Fortunately, most of the best moments are included in the highlights disc, including the Schwarzkopf/Gedda duet from the Venetian scene, not to mention the famous *Barcarolle* and the brilliant *Septet.* De los Angeles (sadly out of voice) and George London (unpleasantly gruff-toned) provide the vocal disappointments.

La Périchole (complete).

(M) *** Erato/Warner 2292 45686-2 (2) [id.]. Crespin, Vanzo, Bastin, Lombard, Friedmann, Trigeau, Rhine Op. Ch., Strasbourg PO, Lombard.

Dating from 1976, this recording of one of Offenbach's most delectable operettas features in the principal roles two of the singers who represent the French tradition at its very finest. Though both Régine Crespin in the title-role and Alain Vanzo as her partner, Piquillo, were past their peak at that time, their vocal control is a model in this music, with character strongly portrayed but without any hint of vulgar underlining. That is strikingly true of Crespin's account of the most famous number, the heroine's tipsy song, *Ah! quel diner*, which makes its point with delectable slyness. Crespin is fresh and pointed too in the letter song in waltz-time, which precedes it, an equally celebrated number. Vanzo, firm and clear and betraying few signs of age, produces heady tone in his varied arias, some of them brilliant. Jules Bastin is charactereful too in the subsidiary role of Don Andres, Viceroy of Peru. Lombard secures excellent precision of ensemble from his Strasbourg forces, only occasionally pressing too hard. The recorded sound is vivid and immediate, and the only disappointment is that spoken dialogue is omitted even in numbers described as *Melodrame.* Instead, the libretto provides a detailed synopsis of the action between the texts and translations of numbers.

Orff, Carl (1895–1982)

Carmina Burana.

❀ (M) *** Sony SBK 47668 [id.]. Harsanyi, Petrak, Presnell, Rutgers University Ch., Phd. O, Ormandy.

(M) *** DG 423 886-2; *423 886-4* [id.]. Janowitz, Stolze, Fischer-Dieskau, Schöneberger Boys' Ch., Berlin German Op. Ch. & O, Jochum.

(M) *** Decca 417 714-2; *417 714-4* [id.]. Burrows, Devos, Shirley-Quirk, Brighton Festival Ch., Southend Boys' Ch., RPO, Dorati.

(B) *** Pickwick Dig. PCD 855 [id.]. Walmsley-Clark, Graham-Hall, Maxwell, Southend Boys' Ch., LSO Ch., LSO, Hickox.

(M) *** BMG/RCA GD 86533 [RCA 6533-2-RG]. Mandac, Kolk, Milnes, New England Conservatory Ch. & Children's Ch., Boston SO, Ozawa.

(B) **(*) DG Compact Classics *413 160-4* [id.]. Janowitz, Stolze, Fischer-Dieskau, Schöneberger Boys' Ch., German Op. Ch. & O, Jochum – STRAVINSKY: *Rite of spring.* **(*)

(BB) ** Naxos Dig. 8.550196 [id.]. Jenisová, Dolezal, Kusnjer, Slovak Philharmonic Ch., Czech RSO (Bratislava), Gunzenhauser.

Ormandy and his Philadelphians have just the right panache to bring off this wildly exuberant picture of the Middle Ages by the anonymous poets of former days, and there is no more enjoyable version. It has tremendous vigour, warmth and colour and a genial, spontaneous enthusiasm from the Rutgers University choristers, men and boys alike, that is irresistible. *Veni, veni venias* (in *Cours d'amour*) is a *tour de force* that makes the nape of the neck tingle, while the boys obviously enjoy themselves hugely in *Tempus est iocundum*, and the closing *Ave formosissima* and reprise of *O Fortunata* are quite glorious. The soloists are excellent, especially the baritone, Harvey Presnell, who is outstanding – though the tenor, Rudolf Petrak, is pretty good too, and the lament of the poor roasting swan sounds less strained than usual. The soprano sings her lovely *In trutina* seductively enough, aided by Ormandy, even if her voice sounds a little uncovered in her passionate upward leap of submission later. But it is the chorus and orchestra that steal the show; the richness and eloquence of the choral tone is a joy in itself. The recording was made in 1960 in the Broadwood Hotel, Philadelphia. Presumably a ballroom was used, but it sounds like a concert hall, for the resonant acoustic gives the work a wonderful breadth and spaciousness, and the Philadelphia Orchestra have seldom emerged on record with such a fullness and variety of colour, with the strings and woodwind glowing. The reverberation prevents the last degree of sharpness of detail and bite in the choral sound, but the effect is wholly natural and the remastering engineer is to be congratulated that he did not try to provide an artificial brightening. This is quite splendid, one of Ormandy's most inspired recordings; it is certainly an 'Essential Classic' and, even if you already have the work in your collection, this exhilarating version will bring additional delights.

The CD reissue of Jochum's 1968 recording of *Carmina Burana* is outstandingly successful. Originally the choral pianissimos lacked immediacy, but now this effect is all but banished and the underlying tension of the quiet singing is very apparent. The recording has a wide dynamic range and when the music blazes it has real splendour and excitement. Fischer-Dieskau's singing is refined but not too much so, and his first solo, *Omnia sol temperat*, and later *Dies, nox et omnia* are both very beautiful, with the kind of tonal shading that a great Lieder singer can bring; he is suitably gruff in the Abbot's song – so much so that for the moment the voice is unrecognizable. Gerhard Stolze too is very stylish in his falsetto *Song of the roasted swan.* The soprano, Gundula Janowitz, finds a quiet dignity for her contribution and this is finely done. The closing scene is moulded by Jochum with wonderful control, most compelling in its restrained power. On the Compact Classics cassette the recording is well transferred on chrome stock. The Stravinsky coupling is rather less successful because of a resonant acoustic, but this remains good value, even if there is no supporting translation or detailed analysis.

Dorati's 1976 version was originally recorded in Decca's hi-fi-conscious Phase 4 system, and the balance is rather close; but the Kingsway Hall ambience helps to spread the sound and the dynamic range is surprisingly wide. It is a characteristically vibrant account; Dorati's speeds are generally brisk and the effect is exhilaratingly good-humoured, with the conductor showing a fine rhythmic sense. The characterization of the soloists is less sensuous than in some versions, but John Shirley-Quirk's account of the *Abbot's song* is very dramatic, with the chorus joining in enthusiastically. Because of Dorati's thrust, this is more consistently gripping than Hickox's otherwise first-rate Pickwick account and, if there are moments when the overall ensemble is less than perfectly polished, the feeling of a live performance is engendered throughout, even though this is a studio recording. No translation is provided and the synopsis is cursory, which earns Decca a black mark.

Richard Hickox, on his brilliantly recorded Pickwick CD, like Previn uses the combined LSO forces, but adds the Southend Boys' Choir who make sure we know they understand all about sexual abandon – their *'Oh, oh, oh, I am bursting out all over'* is a joy. Penelope Walmsley-Clark, too, makes a rapturous contribution: her account of the girl in the red dress is equally delectable. The other soloists are good but less individual. The performance takes a little while to warm up (Hickox's tempi tend to be more relaxed than Dorati's), but the chorus rises marvellously to climaxes and is resplendent in the *Ave formosissima*, while the sharp articulation of consonants when the singers hiss out the words of *O Fortuna* in the closing section is also a highlight. The vivid orchestral detail revealed by the bright digital sound adds an extra dimension. The documentation provides a vernacular narrative for each band but no translation.

On RCA Ozawa's strong, incisive performance brings out the bold simplicity of the score with tingling immediacy, rather than dwelling on its subtlety of colour. The soloists, too, are all characterful, especially Sherrill Milnes. The tenor, Stanley Kolk, sounds a little constrained with his *Roast swan*, but otherwise the solo singing is always responsive. Overall this is a highly effective account and the blaze of inspiration of Orff's masterpiece comes over to the listener in the most direct way, when the sound is so well projected, yet without any unnatural edge. The snag is the absence of a translation or of any kind of documentation beyond a listing of the 25 cued sections.

The Slovak Chorus sing Orff's hedonistic cantata with lusty, Slavonic enthusiasm, and it is a pity that some of the score's quieter passages are somewhat lacking in bite because of the resonance. But the Tavern scene comes across especially vividly and the culminating *Ave formosissima* and *O Fortuna* are splendidly expansive. The soprano, Eva Jenisová, is the most impressive of the three soloists, who generally do not match their Western rivals. This is an enjoyable performance, with exciting moments, but the Ormandy and Jochum versions are worth the extra outlay.

De temporum fine comoedia.

(M) (***) DG 429 859-2 [id.]. Ludwig, Schreier, Greindl, Boysen, Cologne R. Ch., RIAS Chamber Ch., Tölz Boys' Ch., Cologne RSO, Karajan.

There must be some merit in this tiresome, meretricious stuff. Musical invention is not its strong suit; the simplicity and melodic spontaneity that one encounters in *Carmina burana* are not to be found here. The performance offers the very highest standards and the recording is extremely lively and vivid, but musically this is a very thin brew, whatever impact it may have had as theatre.

(i) *Die Kluge;* (ii) *Der Mond.*

(M) *** EMI CMS7 63712-2 (2) [Ang. CDMB 63712]. (i) Cordes, Frick, Schwarzkopf, Wieter, Christ, Kusche; (ii) Christ, Schmitt-Walker, Graml, Kuen, Lagger, Hotter; Philh. Ch. & O, Sawallisch.

(M) **(*) BMG/Eurodisc GD 69069 (2) [69069-2-RG]. (i) Stewart, Frick, Popp, Kogel, Schmidt, Nicolai, Gruber; (ii) Van Kesteren, Friedrich, Kogel, Gruber, Kusche, Grumbach, Buchta, Kiermeyer Kinderchor; Bavarian R. Ch., Munich R. O, Kurt Eichhorn.

Sawallisch's pioneering Orff recordings of the mid-1950s were regularly used as demonstration recordings in the early days of stereo; the sound, well balanced, is still vivid and immediate on CD, with such effects as the thunderbolt in *Der Mond* impressive still. The recording producer was Walter Legge, using all his art of presentation, and the casts he assembled would be hard to match. His wife, Elisabeth Schwarzkopf, is here just as inspired in repertory unusual for her as in Mozart, characterful and dominant as the clever young woman of the title in *Die Kluge*. It is good too to hear such vintage singers as Gottlob Frick and Hans Hotter in unexpected roles. Musically, these may not be at all searching works, but both short operas provide easy, colourful entertainment, with Sawallisch drawing superb playing from the Philharmonia. No texts are provided, but the discs are very generously banded.

Eichhorn's Eurodisc version of the early 1970s provides an excellent alternative, with casts equally consistent. *Der Mond* is given in Orff's revised, 1970 version, and the composer himself is credited with having supervised the production of the recordings. Certainly their great merit is the fun and jollity they convey, beautifully timed if not always quite as crisp of ensemble as the EMI versions. The sound as transferred is shriller and brighter than the 1950s EMI, rather wearingly so, with voices not quite so cleanly focused. German texts are given but no translation.

Pachelbel, Johann (1653–1706)

Canon in D.

(M) *** Decca 417 712-2; *417 712-4* [id.]. Stuttgart CO, Münchinger – ALBINONI: *Adagio* ***; VIVALDI: *Four Seasons.* **(*)

Among budget-price recordings, Münchinger's

is as good as any; but many other enjoyable performances are listed in the Concerts section.

Padilla, Juan Gutierrez de (*c.* 1590–1664)

Missa: Ego flos campi. Stabat Mater.
(B) *** Pickwick Dig. PCD 970; *CIMPC 970* [id.]. Mixolydian, Piers Schmidt – VICTORIA: *Missa surge propera* etc. ***

Juan Gutierrez de Padilla was born in Málaga around 1590 and held musical appointments at the cathedrals of Jérez and Cádiz, before moving to Puebla in Mexico, where he remained 'maestro de capilla' at the cathedral, spending over four decades there. He wrote Masses, motets, psalms, two sets of *Lamentations* and works for double choir. His Mass *Ego flos campi* is for double choir, and throughout its *Credo* one choir interrupts the other, constantly punctuating the flow of the words with repetitions of the word '*credo*'. His Mass setting is more homophonic than much of his other music, certainly than his motets for five or six voices, which Bruno Turner describes as in a 'thoroughly conservative polyphonic style of great assurance'. The Mass is nevertheless full of interest, though of course the comparison which the sleeve-writer makes between the two composers on the disc is not to Victoria's disadvantage. Padilla's setting of the *Stabat Mater* lacks the expressive depth of that Renaissance master. Dedicated performances and excellent recording.

Paganini, Niccolò (1782–1840)

Violin concertos Nos. 1 in D, Op. 6; 2 in B min. (La Campanella), Op. 7.
(B) *** DG 429 524-2; *429 524-4* [id.]. Shmuel Ashkenasi, VSO, Esser.

Violin concertos Nos. 1–2; Le Streghe (Witches' dance); 4 Caprices, Op. 1.
(B) *** DG Compact Classics *413 848-4* [id.]. Accardo, LPO, Dutoit.

Accardo has a formidable technique, marvellously true intonation and impeccably good taste and style; it is a blend of all these which makes these performances so satisfying and enjoyable. These recordings are taken from the complete set he made in the mid-to-late 1960s. He is beautifully accompanied by the LPO under Dutoit and the sound is very good. The recording's resonance has meant that DG's tape transfer is rather lower than usual, but the image has not lost its immediacy. Apart from the witchery of *Le Streghe*, Accardo includes also four *Caprices*, including the most famous, on which the multitude of variations are based.

At bargain price on CD, Ashkenasi's coupling of the two favourite Paganini *Concertos* is also very good value. He surmounts all the many technical difficulties in an easy, confident style and, especially in the infectious *La Campanella* finale of No. 2, shows how completely he is in control. The microphone is close and he clearly has a smaller sound than Accardo, but his timbre is sweet and the high tessitura and harmonics are always cleanly focused. The orchestra is set back in a warm but not too resonant acoustic and the accompaniments are nicely made. The digital remastering is smooth and does not make the upper range edgy. There is less conscious flamboyance than with his main rivals, but this playing is easy to enjoy.

Violin concerto No. 3 in F.
(B) *** Ph. 422 976-2; *422 976-4* [id.]. Szeryng, LSO, Gibson – LALO: *Symphonie espagnole.* **(*)

Henryk Szeryng gave the first posthumous performance of the *F major Concerto* and made the present record. The performance is dazzling technically, with assured bravura in the spectacular pyrotechnics which the composer kept in reserve for the extended finale. The first movement is even longer – the opening ritornello lasts for four minutes – but, apart from an engaging *Allegro marziale* theme, is not of great musical interest. The best movement is undoubtedly the central *Cantabile spianato*, a brief aria-like piece, its theme engagingly introduced over pizzicatos in the orchestra. Not a lost masterpiece, then, but uncommonly well played here, and given a vivid CD transfer.

24 Caprices, Op. 1.
(M) *** DG 429 714-2; *429 714-4* [id.]. Salvatore Accardo.

Accardo succeeds in making Paganini's most routine phrases sound like the noblest of utterances and he invests these *Caprices* with an eloquence far beyond the sheer display they offer. There are no technical obstacles and, both in breadth of tone and in grandeur of conception, he is peerless. He observes all the repeats and has an excellent CD transfer.

Palestrina, Giovanni Pierluigi di (1525–94)

Hodie Beata Virgo; Litaniae de Beata Virgine Maria in 8 parts; Magnificat in 8 parts (Primi Toni); Senex puerum portabat; Stabat Mater.
(M) *** Decca 421 147-2; *421 147-4* [id.]. King's College Ch., Willcocks – ALLEGRI: *Miserere.* ***

This is an exceptionally fine collection dating from the mid-1960s. The flowing melodic lines and serene beauty which are the unique features of Palestrina's music are apparent throughout this programme, and there is no question about the dedication and accomplishment of the performance. Argo's recording is no less successful, sounding radiantly fresh and clear.

Missa Assumpta est Maria; Missa L'homme armé.
(B) **(*) Pickwick Dig. PCD 952; *CIMPC 952* [id.]. Pro Cantione Antiqua, Mark Brown.

Palestrina is not generously represented in this price range, and this bargain account of these two beautiful Masses by the Pro Cantione Antiqua under Mark Brown could hardly be bettered in terms of ensemble and accomplishment. Unlike most commercial records of the *Assumpta est Maria* Mass, the Pro Cantione Antiqua is an all-male ensemble (there are twelve singers in all, counter-tenors, tenors and basses), and the forces are modest – one to a part for much of the time – with resultant textural clarity, though the vocal colour is inevitably dark. The balance could with advantage have been more distant, as it is in the chants with which the Mass movements are interspersed; more air round the voices would have given greater aural variety and relief, though a somewhat lower than usual level setting helps matters. The singing itself is superb.

Missa Papae Marcelli; Stabat Mater.
(B) *** Pickwick PCD 863 [MCA MCAD 25191]. Pro Cantione Antiqua, Mark Brown.

Pro Cantione Antiqua on the budget-priced Pickwick label bring not only an outstandingly fresh and alert account of Palestrina's most celebrated Mass but one which involves keen scholarship. With an all-male choir and no boy trebles, and with one voice per part, this chamber choir yet sings with power and resonance against a warm and helpful church acoustic. The authentic atmosphere is enhanced by the inclusion of relevant plainchants between the sections of the Mass. The magnificent eight-part *Stabat Mater* also receives a powerful performance, warm and resonant.

Veni sponsa Christi.
(M) *** EMI Dig. CD-EMX 2180; *TC-EMX 2180*. St John's College, Cambridge, Ch., Guest – ALLEGRI: *Miserere*; LASSUS: *Missa super bella*. **(*)

Veni sponsa Christi is a parody Mass – which implies no suggestion of satirical mimicry, but simply means that it uses pre-existing music, here an earlier Palestrina motet based on Gregorian chant. Every section of the Mass is introduced by the same idea with much subtle variation, and this impressive work ends with two *Agnus Dei* settings, the second with an additional tenor part. It receives an eloqent, imaginatively detailed and finely shaped performance here, and the relative restraint of the Anglican choral tradition suits Palestrina's flowing counterpoint better than it does the Lassus Venetian coupling.

Panufnik, Andrzej (1914–91)

(i) *Autumn music; Heroic overture;* (i, ii) *Nocturne;* (iii) *Sinfonia rustica;* (i) *Tragic overture.*
(M) *** Unicorn UKCD 2016. (i) LSO, Horenstein; (ii) with Anthony Peebles; (iii) Monte Carlo Op. O, composer.

The two overtures are early pieces and of relatively little musical interest, but the *Autumn music* and *Nocturne* are worth hearing. They may strike some listeners as musically uneventful, but the opening of the *Nocturne* is really very beautiful indeed and there is a refined feeling for texture and a sensitive imagination at work here. The *Sinfonia rustica* is the most individual of the works recorded here and has plenty of character, though its invention is less symphonic, more in the style of a sinfonietta. The performance under the composer is thoroughly committed. The LSO under Horenstein play with conviction and they are very well recorded.

(i) *Concerto festivo;* (ii) *Concerto for timpani, percussion and strings; Katyń epitaph; Landscape;* (iii) *Sinfonia sacra (Symphony No. 3).*
(M) *** Unicorn UKCD 2020. (i) LSO, (ii) with Goedicke & Frye; (ii) Monte Carlo Op. O, composer.

Andrzej Panufnik's music is invariably approachable, finely crafted and fastidiously scored. His feeling for atmosphere and colour obviously comes from a refined sensibility. This splendidly recorded collection might be a good place for collectors to begin exploring his output. The *Concertos* are both readily communicative and the *Katyń epitaph* is powerfully eloquent. Oddly enough, at one point it is reminiscent of the atmosphere of the last pages of Britten's *A Time there was*, though the Panufnik was written some years earlier. The best of this music is deeply felt. The *Sinfonia sacra* serves to demonstrate the spectacular quality of the vividly remastered recording, with its compelling introductory 'colloquy' for four trumpets, followed by a withdrawn section for strings alone. In the finale of the second part of the work, *Hymn* (which is not separately cued as suggested by the contents details) the trumpets close the piece resplendently.

Paray, Paul (1886–1979)

Mass for the 500th anniversary of the death of Joan of Arc.

(M) **(*) Mercury 432 719-2 [id.]. Yeend, Bible, Lloyd, Yi-Kwei-Sze, Rackham Ch., Detroit SO, Paul Paray – SAINT-SAENS: *Symphony No. 3.* ***

An unexpected coupling for the Saint-Saëns *Organ Symphony*, but Paray's harmonic language is comfortable enough for admirers of that work to enjoy his *Mass*, much admired by the composer Florent Schmitt. It could hardly have a more eloquent performance, with the *Gloria* (the most extended section) particularly heady, and the thrustful, energetic *Sanctus*, erupting on the brass, and the chorus following on with spontaneous élan. The soloists are good and the choir are inspired to real fervour by their conductor, who at the close (in a brief recorded speech) expresses his special satisfaction with the singing of the closing, very romantic *Agnus Dei*. Excellent (1957) Mercury stereo, using the Ford Auditorium in Detroit. A collectors' item as a work for which one could find affection, even if the writing is without a strong individuality.

Pergolesi, Giovanni (1710–36)

Magnificat.

(M) **(*) Decca 425 724-2; *425 724-4*. Vaughan, J. Baker, Partridge, Keyte, King's College Ch., ASMF, Willcocks – VIVALDI: *Gloria; Magnificat.* **(*)

This Pergolesi *Magnificat* – doubtfully attributed, like so much that goes under this composer's name – is a comparatively pale piece to go with the Vivaldi *Magnificat* and *Gloria*. But the King's Choir gives a beautiful performance, and the recording matches it in intensity of atmosphere. The CD transfer is expertly managed.

Miserere II in C min.

(M) *** Decca 430 359-2; *430 359-4*. Wolf, James, Covey-Crump, Stuart, Magdalen College, Oxford, Ch., Wren O, Bernard Rose – A. and G. GABRIELI: *Motets.* **(*)

Pergolesi's *Miserere* was long listed under doubtful or spurious works, but modern opinion seems to favour its probable authenticity. In the liner-note which accompanies this CD, Dr Rose argues its similarity to the *Stabat Mater*, where there are striking parallels in melodic lines, motifs and harmonic progressions. Whatever the case, this work is both ambitious and moving. It consists of fifteen numbers: seven solo arias, two trios and six choruses. The singers are all of quality, particularly Richard Stuart, and Bernard Rose secures expressive and persuasive results from the Magdalen College Choir and the Wren Orchestra. The (originally Argo) recording, made in Magdalen College Chapel in 1979, is warm and atmospheric and sounds magnificently real and vivid in its CD format.

Pfitzner, Hans (1869–1949)

Palestrina (opera) complete.

(M) *** DG 427 417-2 (3) [id.]. Gedda, Fischer-Dieskau, Weikl, Ridderbusch, Donath, Fassbaender, Prey, Tölz Boys' Ch., Bav. R. Ch. & SO, Kubelik.

This rich and glowing performance goes a long way to explaining why in Germany the mastery of this unique opera is trumpeted so loudly. Though Pfitzner's melodic invention hardly matches that of his contemporary, Richard Strauss, his control of structure and drawing of character through music make an unforgettable impact. It is the central Act, a massive and colourful tableau representing the Council of Trent, which lets one witness the crucial discussion on the role of music in the church. The outer Acts – more personal and more immediately compelling – show the dilemma of Palestrina himself and the inspiration which led him to write the *Missa Papae Marcelli*, so resolving the crisis, both personal and public. At every point Pfitzner's response to this situation is illuminating, and this glorious performance with a near-ideal cast, consistent all through, could hardly be bettered in conveying the intensity of an admittedly offbeat inspiration. This CD reissue captures the glow of the Munich recording superbly and, though this is a mid-price set, DG has not skimped on the accompanying booklet, in the way some other companies have tended to do with sets of rare operas.

Pierné, Gabriel (1863–1937)

Les Cathédrales: Prelude (No. 1); Images, Op. 49; Paysages franciscains, Op. 43; Viennoise (suites de valses et cortège blues), Op. 49 bis.

(M) *** EMI CDM7 63950-2. Loire PO, Pierre Dervaux.

Gabriel Pierné was a leading figure in French musical life during the years of Debussy and Ravel. The music recorded here is urbane, civilized and charming and should make him many new friends, particularly in view of the persuasive account of these scores given by Pierre Dervaux and the Orchestre Philharmonique des Pays de Loire. The opening *Prélude* to *Les Cathédrales* (1915) is an evocation of the desolation caused by war; while *Images* is a late work, composed in 1935, only two years before Pierné's death. It derives from a divertissement of a pastoral character which shows not only the composer's virtuosity as an orchestrator but his subtlety as a composer. The score is full of touches of pastiche – a reference to Dukas's *La Péri* in the opening, an allusion to Debussy's *Gigues*, and so on – and there follows a set of pieces, *Viennoise*, in which Pierné developed two of the numbers in the divertissement as '*valses et cortège blues*'. The three picturesque *Paysages franciscains* (1920) betray the composer's love of Italy. All of this is rewarding music in the best French tradition, extremely well played. The 1978 recording has plenty of warmth and atmosphere, and the CD brings a greater sense of transparency without drying out the ambience.

Piston, Walter (1894–1976)

Symphony No. 2.

(M) *** DG 429 860-2 [id.]. Boston SO, Tilson Thomas – RUGGLES: *Sun-treader*; SCHUMAN: *Violin concerto.* ***

Walter Piston has greater reticence and refinement than Aaron Copland and is less a prisoner of his own mannerisms than Roy Harris. His wartime *Second Symphony* (1943) makes a good entry point if you are starting to collect his music. It is more than finely crafted: it has a generosity of melodic invention and in the slow movement possesses a nobility that makes a strong impression. Michael Tilson Thomas and the Boston Symphony are very persuasive in its advocacy and the recording from the early 1970s is very good.

Ponce, Manuel (1882–1948)

Folia de España (Theme and variations with fugue).

(M) *** Sony SBK 47669 [id.]. John Williams (guitar) – BARRIOS: *Collection.* ***

Ponce's *Variations* on *'Folia de España'* are subtle and haunting, and their surface charm often conceals a vein of richer, darker feeling. This piece, with its fugue, extends for 24 minutes and the writing is resourceful and imaginative. Perhaps it is least successful when Ponce attempts imitative textures, but there is a refined harmonic awareness in some of the more reflective variations. The performance is first rate and the sound admirably clean and finely detailed, yet at the same time warm. The CD transfer adds presence without any adverse effect on the ambience.

Ponchielli, Amilcare (1834–86)

La Gioconda: Dance of the hours.

(M) *** EMI CDM7 69041-2 [id.]. Philh. O, Karajan – BORODIN: *Polovtsian dances* ***; OFFENBACH: *Gaîté parisienne* **(*); GOUNOD: *Faust ballet.* ***

Ponchielli's miniature romantic ballet is much more familiar than the opera from which it derives. The imaginative charm of the music is most engaging when presented with such elegance and spirit and the Philharmonia players obviously relish this attractive succession of tunes, glowingly scored. The 1960 recording, with its pleasingly full ambience, hardly sounds dated at all. Besides the listed couplings, this generous anthology also includes four minutes of Verdi's ballet from Act II of *Aida*, equally vividly played and recorded.

Poulenc, Francis (1899–1963)

(i) *Les animaux modèles;* (ii; iii) *Les Biches* (complete ballet); (ii) *Bucolique;* (i; iv) *Concerto champêtre* (for harpsichord & orchestra); (i; v) *Double piano concerto in D min.* (vi) *2 Marches et un intermède* (for chamber orchestra); *Les mariés de la Tour Eiffel (La baigneuse de Trouville; Discourse du Général).* (ii) *Matelote provençale; Pastourelle;* (vi) *Sinfonietta; Suite française.*

(B) *** EMI Analogue/Dig. CZS7 62690-2 (2). (i) Paris Conservatoire O; or (ii) Philh. O; (iii) with Amb. S.; (iv) with Van der Wiele, or (v) composer and Février; (vi) O de Paris; all cond. Prêtre.

A fascinating and valuable orchestral collection, including a great deal of music not otherwise available, made all the more attractive by being offered on two discs for the price of one. *Les Biches* comes in its complete form, with the choral additions that Poulenc made optional when he came to rework the score. The title is untranslatable: it means 'The Does' and is also a term of endearment. But the atmosphere surrounding the young girls of the ballet is a uniquely French combination of surface innocence and a subtle underlying concupiscence. The music is a delight, and so too is the group of captivating short pieces, digitally recorded at the same time (1980): *Bucolique*, *Pastourelle* and *Matelote provençale.* High-spirited, fresh, elegant playing and sumptuous recorded sound enhance the claims of all this music. The strings have freshness and bloom and there is no lack of presence. The set is worth having for this music alone – we gave it a Rosette when it was first issued on a single LP and cassette.

The *Suite française* is another highlight. It is based on themes by the sixteenth-century composer, Claude Gervaise; they are dance pieces which Poulenc has freely transcribed, and the wind and brass writing is very colourful. It is well played and recorded in a pleasing, open acoustic. The two *Concertos* are also enjoyable, although the sound is rather resonant. Poulenc himself was a pianist of limited accomplishment, but his interpretation (with partner) of his own skittish *Double concerto* is infectiously jolly. One could never mistake the tone of voice intended. In the imitation pastoral concerto for harpsichord, Aimée van de Wiele is a nimble soloist, but here Prêtre's inflexibility as a conductor comes out the more, even though the finale has plenty of high spirits. The *Sinfonietta*, too, could have a lighter touch, but it does not lack personality. *Les animaux modèles* is based on the fables of La Fontaine, with a prelude and a postlude. *Les deux coqs* brings a witty reminder of Saint-Saëns, but here the recording is rather lacking in bloom, and the *Deux Marches* are also a trifle overbright. But for the most part the resonance gives colour and ambience to the transfers from the late 1960s. With nearly 156 minutes' playing time, these CDs are well worth exploring.

Les Biches (ballet suite).
(M) *** EMI CDM7 63945-2 [id.]. Paris Conservatoire O, Prêtre – DUTILLEUX: *Le Loup;* MILHAUD: *Création du Monde.* ***

Prêtre has re-recorded *Les Biches* digitally in its complete format (see above). This 1961 recording of the suite, omitting the chorus, is well worth having in its own right: the racy style of the orchestral playing is instantly infectious in the opening *Rondeau* with its catchy trumpet solo. The remastered sound-picture is much better focused than in its old LP format; and this is one example where the bright vividness of CD is entirely advantageous, for there is just the right degree of ambient atmosphere. With excellent couplings this is a most desirable triptych.

Les Biches (ballet): suite; (i) *Piano concerto;* (ii) *Gloria.*
(M) *** EMI CDM7 69644-2. (i) Ortiz; (ii) N. Burrowes, CBSO Ch.; CBSO, Frémaux.

Cristina Ortiz advances an alert and stylish account of Poulenc's disarming *Piano concerto* and is given splendid support from Louis Frémaux and the Birmingham orchestra. The latter's performance of *Les Biches*, too, is good-humoured, even if the opening trumpet tune is almost too fast in its racy vigour. The Birmingham account of the *Gloria* competes with Prêtre's fine version, but that is at full price; Frémaux also secures excellent results and he has a sympathetic soloist in Norma Burrowes. The recording, originally designed for quadraphony, is brightly remastered but retains much of its sense of spectacle.

(i) *Concert champêtre for harpsichord and orchestra;* (ii) *Concerto in G min. for organ, strings and timpani.*
(M) *** Erato/Warner Dig. 2292 45233-2 [id.]. (i) Koopman; (ii) Alain; Rotterdam PO, Conlon.

The *Organ concerto* has never come off better in the recording studio than on this Erato recording, made in Rotterdam's concert hall, the Doelen, with its excellent Flentrop organ. Marie-Claire Alain is fully equal to the many changes of mood, and her treatment of the *Allegro giocoso* racily catches the music's rhythmic humour. The balance is very well managed and the CD is in the demonstration bracket in this work. The *Concert champêtre* always offers problems of balance, as it is scored for a full orchestra, but the exaggerated contrast was clearly intended by the composer. Here the orchestral tapestry sounds very imposing indeed, against which the harpsichord seems almost insignificant. Those who like such a strong contrast will not be disappointed, for the performance is most perceptive, with a particularly elegant and sparkling finale. James Conlon provides admirable accompaniments.

(i) *Concert champêtre; Organ concerto in G min.;* (ii) *Gloria.*
(M) *** Decca 425 627-2. (i) Malcolm (hapsichord/organ), ASMF, Iona Brown; (ii) Greenbert, SRO Ch., SRO, Lopez-Cobos.

George Malcolm's excellent version of the *Organ concerto* is also available coupled with Saint-Saëns – see below – but pairing it with the *Concert champêtre* is even more attractive. In the latter work the engineers did not succumb to the temptation to make the harpsichord sound larger than life, and on CD the beautifully focused keyboard image contrasts wittily with the designedly ample orchestral tuttis. Some might feel that in the finale Malcolm rushes things a bit but the music effervesces, and in every other respect this is an exemplary account. Lopez-Cobos gives a fine account of the *Gloria*, expansive yet underlining the Stravinskian elements in the score. The pioneering version by Prêtre has a certain authenticity of feeling that Lopez-Cobos does not wholly capture, but his performance is enjoyable and is undoubtedly much better recorded. Indeed, the sound throughout this CD is in the demonstration bracket.

Organ concerto in G min. (for organ, strings and timpani).
(M) *** Decca 417 725-2 [id.]. George Malcolm, ASMF, Iona Brown – SAINT-SAENS: *Symphony No. 3.* **(*)

Poulenc's endearing and inventive *Organ con-*

certo is in one continuous movement, divided into seven contrasting sections, the last of which has a devotional quality very apt for its time. The remastered 1979 Argo recording, reissued on Decca Ovation, is a triumphant success, and George Malcolm gives an exemplary account, his pacing consistently apt and with the changing moods nicely caught. The playing of the Academy is splendidly crisp and vital.

CHAMBER MUSIC

Cello sonata; Clarinet sonata; Duo sonata for 2 clarinets; Sonata for clarinet and bassooon; Élégie for horn & piano; Flute sonata; Oboe sonata; Sextet for piano, flute, oboe, clarinet, bassoon and horn; Sonata for horn, trombone and trumpet; Trio for piano, oboe and bassoon; Violin sonata.
(B) ** EMI CZS7 62736-2 (2). Fournier, Février, Portal, Gabai, Wallez, Civil, Bourgue, Debost, Casier, Boutard, Faisandier, Bergès, Wilbraham, Iveson, Y. Menuhin.

This is a another generous EMI Poulenc collection of some 145 minutes of music on two CDs (offered for the price of one) and much of it (the chattering *Duo for two clarinets*, for instance) has an appeal and charm that deserve to reach a wider audience. Not all the performances are equally distinguished, and Jacques Février's pianism does not always have the finish such repertoire ideally demands. It is good to have Fournier's elegant account of the *Cello sonata* restored to the catalogue, though in the *Violin sonata* Menuhin gives less pleasure. Bourgue's account of the *Oboe sonata* is enjoyable, though he has since recorded it again (at full price) for Decca with Pascal Rogé, to even greater effect. Both the *Trio for piano, oboe and bassoon* and the *Sextet* are rather dryly recorded (and the CD transfer doesn't improve matters); however, although the playing could be more elegant, there is a high-spirited, knockabout quality that is eminently likeable. The brass trio is one of the disc's highlights, most entertainingly played and given better sound, too. The recordings were made betwen 1964 and 1974 and are acceptable, if often forwardly balanced and without a great deal of bloom. But with the reservations noted, this is a serviceable and modestly priced introduction to some delightful music.

PIANO MUSIC

Bourrée au pavillon d'Auvergne; Française d'après Claude Gervaise; Humoresque; 15 Improvisations; 3 Intermezzi; Mélancolie; Mouvements perpétuels; Napoli; 3 Novelettes; 8 Nocturnes; Pastourelle; 3 Pièces; Pièce brève sur le nom d'Albert Roussel; Presto in B flat; Les soirées de Nazelles; Suite française d'après Claude Gervaise; Suite in C. Thème varié; Valse-improvisation sur le nom de Bach. Villageoises.
(B) ** EMI CMS7 62551-2 (2). Gabriel Tacchino.

Gabriel Tacchino's two-CD compilation now reappears in EMI's 'two for the price of one' series, which makes it more competitive; it derives from various recordings he had made between 1966 and 1983. The quality of the recordings, all made at the Salle Wagram, is closely balanced and often shallow, although it is always acceptable; and the CD remastering has made the effect more consistent and improved the focus. The playing is characterful but does not have anywhere near the charm or the *gamin* quality which are ideally required, nor is the recording really distinguished. All the same, one cannot complain about the playing time.

Mouvements perpétuels; Nocturne No. 1 in C; Suite français.
(M) Sony MPK 47684 [id.]. Composer – CHABRIER: *Mélodies* (**); SATIE: *Piano music.*

It is always of interest to hear a composer's thoughts on his own music; but Poulenc is a rather ungainly player and sounds as if he has not bothered to practise for quite some time. There is little range of colour or subtlety in his playing and none in the very monochrome, dry (1950) recording. Even at his best, in his partnership with Pierre Bernac, he lacked the last ounce of elegance.

4 Motets pour un temps de pénitence.
(M) *** Decca 430 346-2. Christ Church Cathedral, Oxford, Ch., L. Sinf., Simon Preston – STRAVINSKY: *Canticum sacrum* etc. ***

These motets are of great beauty and they are vibrantly performed here; indeed Simon Preston's account of them with the Christ Church Catherdral Choir could hardly be improved on, and the 1973 (originally Argo) recording produces rich timbre and a clean focus within an ideal ambience.

VOCAL MUSIC

(i) *Mass in G. Salve regina.*
(M) *** Decca 430 360-2; *430 360-4* [id.]. (i) Bond; St John's College, Cambridge, Ch., Guest – FAURÉ: *Requiem* etc. ***

As a generous coupling for the Fauré *Requiem*, the choir of St John's College, Cambridge, offers the pre-war *Mass in G major* together with the motet, *Salve regina*, a finely wrought piece, in performances of great finish. The St John's forces cope admirably with the delicacy and sweetness of Poulenc's chromatic harmony, and the recorded sound is eminently realistic and truthful in its CD format.

Praetorius, Michael (1571–1621)

Dances from Terpsichore (Suite de ballets; Suite de voltes). (i) Motets: *Eulogodia Sionia: Resonet in laudibus; Musae Sionae: Allein Gott in der Höh sei Ehr; Aus tiefer Not schrei ich zu dir; Christus der uns selig macht; Gott der Vater wohn uns bei; Polyhymnia Caduceatrix: Erhalt uns, Herr, bei deinem Wort.*

(M) *** EMI CDM7 69024-2 [Ang. CDM 69024]. Early Music Cons. of L., Munrow, (i) with boys of the Cathedral and Abbey Church of St Alban.

Terpsichore is a huge collection of some 300 dance tunes used by the French-court dance bands of Henri IV. They were enthusiastically assembled by the German composer, Michael Praetorius, who also harmonized them and arranged them in four to six parts; however, any selection is conjectural in the matter of orchestration. One of the great pioneers of the 'authentic' re-creation of early music, David Munrow's main purpose was to bring the music fully to life and, at the same time, imaginatively to stimulate the ear of the listener. This record, made in 1973, is one of his most successful achievements. The sound is excellent in all respects. Munrow's instrumentation is imaginatively done: the third item, a *Bourrée* played by four racketts (a cross between a shawm and comb-and-paper in sound) is fascinating. The collection is a delightful one, the motets reminding one very much of Giovanni Gabrieli.

Prokofiev, Serge (1891–1953)

Chout (*The Buffoon;* ballet), *Op. 21: suite; Romeo and Juliet* (ballet), *Op. 64:* excerpts.

(M) *** Decca 425 027-2; *425 027-4* [id.]. LSO, Claudio Abbado.

It is difficult to see why a well-selected suite from *Chout* should not be as popular as any of Prokofiev's other ballet scores. It is marvellously inventive music which shows Prokofiev's harmonic resourcefulness at its most engaging. Abbado's version with the LSO offers a generous part of the score, including some of the loosely written connecting material, and he reveals a sensitive ear for balance of texture. The excerpts from *Romeo and Juliet* are also well chosen: they include some of the most delightful numbers, which are often omitted from selections, such as the *Dance with mandolins*, the *Aubade* and so on. The *Dance of the girls* is very sensuous and rather slow, far slower than Prokofiev's own 78s. But Abbado brings it off, and elsewhere there is admirable delicacy and a lightness of touch that are most engaging, while the wit of the humorous narrative is readily caught. The analogue recording, made in the Kingsway Hall in 1966, was a model of its kind, with a beautifully balanced perspective; the remastering has brought an added intensity of impact without losing the ambient warmth and colour. This was one of the prophetic records which helped to establish Abbado's international reputation, a quarter of a century before he acceded to the throne at the Berlin Philharmonie on the death of Karajan.

Cinderella: suite No. 1, Op. 107; Lieutenant Kijé (suite); *The Love for 3 Oranges: March; Scherzo; The Prince and Princess. Romeo and Juliet: Madrigal; Dance of the girls with lilies.*

(BB) *** Naxos Dig. 8.550381 [id.]. Slovak State PO, (Košice), Andrew Mogrelia.

An excellent Prokofievian ballet sampler, well chosen, vividly played and excellently recorded in a sympathetic acoustic. The calibre of this excellent Slovak orchestra is well demonstrated, and its perceptive conductor, Andrew Mogrelia (who studied at the Royal College of Music, London, with Norman Del Mar), is at his finest in his gently humorous portrait of *Lieutenant Kijé*, full of fantasy and gentle irony. The admirable selection of the three 'best bits' from *The Love for Three Oranges* brings out Prokofiev's Rimskian inheritance of Russian colour, rather than emphasizing the music's abrasive edge. The charming items from *Romeo and Juliet* are not duplicated in the fuller selection below.

Piano concertos Nos 1–5.

(M) **(*) Decca 425 570-2 (2) [id.]. Ashkenazy, LSO, Previn.

(i) *Piano concertos Nos. 1–5;* (ii) *Overture on Hebrew themes. Visions fugitives, Op. 22.*

(B) *** EMI CMS7 62542-2 (2). Michel Béroff; (i) with Leipzig GO, Masur; (ii) with Portal, Parrenin Qt.

Honours are more evenly divided between Ashkenazy and Béroff than one might expect. Ashkenazy's staggering virtuosity is often challenged by the young Frenchman, and he too plays masterfully; indeed, both sets of performances prove remarkably distinguished on closer acquaintance. However, for some the remastered Decca recording, which now has a top-heavy balance (the original analogue LPs were bottom-heavy!), will be a drawback. There is a fair amount of edginess and the upper strings tend to sound shrill at higher dynamic levels. The balance in the EMI version is slightly better, although the overall sound-picture is not wholly natural. The EMI CD transfer brings a fairly spiky sound to the violins – one would not guess that this was the Leipzig Gewandhaus Orchestra in the opening tutti of the *First Concerto*, which is bright rather than rich-textured. Nevertheless there is plenty of ambience and the somewhat acerbic sounds are not inappropriate for Prokofiev. Slow movements have plenty of atmosphere. Béroff is a pianist of genuine insight where Prokofiev is concerned, and Masur gives him excellent support. He is free of some of the agogic mannerisms that distinguish Ashkenazy (in the first movement of No. 2 and the slow movement of No. 3) and he has great poetry. Ashkenazy has marvellous panache, of course; Previn is a sensitive accompanist and, for all its too-brilliant lighting, the Decca recording is extremely vivid, although the piano is made stereoscopically prominent. What may clinch the matter for many collectors is the generous bonuses offered by the EMI set, which is reissued in their French 'two for the price of one' series. Béroff's account of the *Visions fugitives* is particularly distinguished, and the piano recording gives little cause for complaint.

(i) *Piano concertos Nos. 1 in D flat, Op. 10; 2 in G min., Op. 16; 3 in C, Op. 26; 4 in B flat for the left hand, Op. 53; 5 in G, Op. 55;* (ii) *Violin concertos Nos. 1 in D, Op. 19; 2 in G min., Op. 63;* (iii) *Sinfonia concertante in E min., Op. 125.*
(B) *(*) VoxBox (3) [CD3X 3000]. (i) Tacchino; (ii) Ricci; (iii) Varga; R. Luxembourg O, de Froment.

On the face of it the VoxBox Prokofiev concertos look to be good value – but, alas, they prove a very mixed bag. The first disc, coupling the *Sinfonia concertante* and the *Second Violin concerto*, is transferred at a surprisingly low level and sounds pale and rough; Laszló Varga's account of the former was a very acceptable one. The *Piano concertos* fare better, though by present-day standards they do not prove competitive either as sound or as performances. Tacchino's records are not without merit artistically and there is sensitive playing from him and the orchestra under Louis de Froment. The Ricci accounts of the *Violin concertos* are acceptable, but do not wear their years well either.

(i) *Piano concertos Nos. 1 in D flat, Op. 10; 3 in C, Op. 26. Piano sonata No. 3 in A min., Op. 28.*
(M) **(*) Sony MYK 44876 [id.]; *40-44876.* Gary Graffman; (i) Cleveland O, George Szell.

These are performances of great virtuosity and stunning brilliance. They have wit and humour too, and the orchestral playing is superb. (Try the ethereal opening, by the strings, of the *Andante* of No. 1, which comes second on the CD, or the perky woodwind at the beginning of the central movement of No. 3.) Just occasionally these artists emphasize the motoric, mechanistic side of Prokofiev, but the lyrical geniality comes over too. The playing has considerable thrust but is never unrelenting. The early-1960s recording has the advantage of the attractive Cleveland ambience and the piano balance is more realistic than in many CBS recordings from this period; moreover its upper range is smoother than Decca's remastered Ashkenazy recordings, which now sound rather too brightly lit.

Piano concerto No. 3 in C, Op. 26.
(M) **(*) Pickwick/RPO CDRPO 5001 [id.]. Janis Vakarelis, RPO, Rowicki – LISZT: *Concerto No. 2.* ***
(M) **(*) Chan. CHAN 6509; *MBTD 6509* [id.]. Terence Judd, Moscow PO, Lazarev – TCHAIKOVSKY: *Concerto No. 1.* **(*)

The Greek pianist Janis Vakarelis gives a very good account of the Prokofiev *C major Concerto*, though the excellence of the recording and sympathetic orchestral support from the RPO under the late Witold Rowicki would not tip the scales in its favour when put alongside the Béroff version with Masur. Vakarelis is decidedly on the slow side in the variations movement, where he does not show quite enough tenderness. However, the performance has no lack of brilliance and zest.

Recorded live when the late Terence Judd was competing in the 1978 Moscow Tchaikovsky Competition, his urgent and dynamic account of the Prokofiev makes up in impulse and conviction what it lacks in refinement. The recording favours the piano but has come up very vividly on CD. Like the unbridled Tchaikovsky performance with which it is coupled, this music-making is full of electricity, and its reissue gives a valuable and compelling reminder of a talent tragically cut off.

(i) *Piano concerto No. 3 in C, Op. 26;* (ii; iii) *Violin concertos Nos. 1–2;* (iii) *Lieutenant Kijé suite;* (iv) *March in B flat, Op. 99; Overture on Hebrew themes;* (iii) *Scythian suite;* (iv) *Symphony No. 1 (Classical);* (v) *Alexander Nevsky.*
(M) *** DG Analogue/Dig. 435 151-2 (3) [id.]. (i) Argerich, BPO; (ii) Mintz; (iii) Chicago SO; (iv) COE; (v) Obraztsova, LSO Ch., LSO; all cond. Abbado.

Not all of this collection is essential Prokofiev, but the *Hebrew overture* and the ebullient *March* are superbly played, and the *Classical*

Symphony is one of the very finest available recorded performances. So is *Alexander Nevsky*, which has great intensity and tragic power as well as refinement of detail. The digital remastering of the 1979 recording is very impressive in its combination of body and bite; and the same could be said of *Lieutenant Kijé* and the *Scythian suite* (both 1977), which have plenty of atmosphere. The earliest recording (1967) is of the *Piano concerto*, and the sound here does show its age a little, but Martha Argerich's performance is outstandingly rewarding and individual, and there is certainly no lack of vividness. Mintz's 1983 versions of the *Violin concertos* hold up well against the full-priced competition and, like all the other performances here, show that Abbado has a special feeling for the composer's sound-world, finding much subtlety of colour and dynamic nuance, with the music's vitality undiminished. As with the COE recordings, the sound here is of DG's best digital quality.

(i) *Piano concerto No. 3 in C, Op. 26. Contes de la vieille grand-mère, Op. 31/2 & 3; Étude, Op. 52; Gavotte No. 2, Op. 25; Gavotte No. 3, Op. 32; Paysage, Op. 59; Sonatine pastorale, Op. 59; Sonata No. 4, Op. 29: Andante. Suggestions diaboliques, Op. 4/4; Visions fugitives, Op. 22/3, 5, 6, 9–11, 16–18.*
(M) (***) Pearl mono GEMMCD 9470. Composer, (i) LSO, Piero Coppola.

An invaluable disc that gives us the only recordings Prokofiev ever made of his own music as a pianist. He recorded the *Third Piano concerto* with Piero Coppola and the LSO on three shellac discs in 1932; three years later, he made three more records of his own piano music, all of which are assembled on this disc. The critic, Boris de Schloezer, described Prokofiev's playing as 'brilliant, rather dry, but extremely polished, pure and finished', and in a memorable image Poulenc described how his 'long spatulate fingers held the keyboard as a racing car holds the track!'. Prokofiev's playing has the same wit and character as the music itself and, although interpretatively he is straightforward, there is a really strong musical personality in evidence. The recordings, though a bit monochrome and dry, are good for the period. Not to be missed.

Piano concerto No. 4 in B flat for the left hand, Op. 53.
(M) (***) Sony MPK 46452 [id.]. Rudolph Serkin, Phd. O, Ormandy – REGER: *Piano concerto.* **

Prokofiev's *Fourth Piano concerto* is still the least often played of the five (recordings of it usually come within complete sets). It was commissioned by the one-armed pianist and philosopher, Paul Wittgenstein, but was never played by him; he rejected it on the grounds that it was too aggressively modern (a curious reason, when the argument is as clear as crystal to us today) and it remained unperformed until 1956, well after the composer's death. Serkin's recording was made only two years later and the performance is not likely to be bettered. His mastery helps to disguise some of the work's defects, though even he cannot quite conceal the fact that the *vivace* finale is far too short to balance the rest properly. The mono recording is excellent, better balanced and with more agreeable sound than its Reger coupling, which nevertheless also has considerable documentary value.

Violin concertos Nos. 1 in D, Op. 19; 2 in G min., Op. 63.
(M) *** Decca 425 003-2; *425 003-4*. Kyung Wha Chung, LSO, Previn – STRAVINSKY: *Concerto.* ***

Kyung Wha Chung gives performances to emphasize the lyrical quality of these *Concertos*, with playing that is both warm and strong, tender and full of fantasy. The melody which opens the slow movement of No. 2 finds her playing with an inner, hushed quality and the ravishing modulation from E flat to B, a page or so later, brings an ecstatic frisson. Previn's acompaniments are deeply understanding. The Decca sound has lost only a little of its fullness in the digital remastering, and the soloist is now made very present.

(i) *Violin concerto No. 1 in D, Op. 19;* (ii) *Sinfonia concertante for cello and orchestra, Op. 125.*
(M) **(*) Erato/Warner Dig. 2292 45708-2 [id.]. (i) Mutter, Nat. SO, Washington, Rostropovich; (ii) Rostropovich, LSO, Ozawa.

Anne-Sophie Mutter's must be the most inorganic account of the first movement of Prokofiev's Op. 19 on record: its exposition is highly self-conscious; but she plays with stunning virtuosity and tonal refinement, particularly in the scherzo. In its way this is an exciting performance, and the playing of the Washington orchestra for Rostropovich is very vital and sensitive. However, both artists indulge in some idiosyncratic point-making and some of the fairy-tale innocence of the opening is lost. The recording of the *Sinfonia concertante* (which arose, phoenix-like, from the ashes of Prokofiev's pre-war *Cello concerto in E minor*) is another matter. Rostropovich is in glorious form throughout and Ozawa shows great sensitivity to dynamic nuance. There is a small mannerism a little way into the first movement where he pulls back to make an expressive effect (no doubt at the soloist's instigation) which some will find disruptive, but this is a relatively trivial point. The orchestral balance is excellent, with a truthful overall perspective.

Lieutenant Kijé (incidental music): *suite, Op. 60.*
(M) *** EMI Dig. CDD7 64105-2 [id.]; *ET 764105-4.* LPO, Tennstedt – SHOSTAKOVICH: *Symphony No. 10.* ***

Prokofiev's colourful suite drawn from film music makes an unusual coupling for the *Tenth Symphony* of Shostakovich. Tennstedt's reading, in repertory with which he is not usually associated, is aptly brilliant and colourful, with rhythms strongly marked. Excellent recording, especially vivid and present in its CD format.

Lieutenant Kijé (suite), *Op. 90; The Love for 3 Oranges* (suite); *Symphony No. 1 in D (Classical).*
(M) **(*) Sony Dig. MDK 46502 [id.]. O Nat. de France, Lorin Maazel.
(M) **(*) Ph. 426 640-2; *426 640-4.* LSO, Marriner.

After a brilliant account of the *Classical Symphony*, very well played and brightly lit, Maazel gives exceptionally dramatic and strongly characterized accounts of Prokofiev's two colourful suites. Though he does not miss the romantic allure in the portrait of *The Prince and Princess* from *The Love for three Oranges* or the nostalgia of *Kijé*, it is the Prokofievian sharpness of the rhythms and the crisp pointing of detail that register most strongly, helped by the resonant acoustic, which adds an effective pungency of colour to Prokofiev's bolder scoring. Inner detail registers vividly at all dynamic levels; while Maazel is clearly seeking a strongly presented projection rather than refinement and gentle irony, the committed orchestral response is certainly exhilarating.

On Philips, with good playing and recording, there is nothing to disappoint. Individually these pieces are available in other versions that are as good as (or better than) this compilation, but these are lively performances, and the remastered sound is fresh and open.

(i) *Love for 3 oranges* (suite); (ii) *La pas d'acier:* suite, *Op. 41 bis;* (i) *Scythian suite, Op. 20.*
(B) (**) EMI mono CZS7 62647-2 (2) [Ang. CDMB 62647]. (i) French Nat. R. O; (ii) Philh. O, Markevitch – STRAVINSKY: *Le baiser de la fee* etc. (***)

Sharply characterized performances from Markevitch, brilliantly played. No apologies need be made for the mono sound, which is both brilliant and atmospheric and is transferred to CD without added edge or thinness. However, it is the Stravinsky coupling which makes this reissue distinctive. The pair of CDs are now offered in EMI's French 'two for the price of one' series.

(i) *Love for three oranges* (suite), *Op. 33a; Scythian suite, Op. 20;* (ii) *Symphony No. 5, Op. 100.*
(M) **(*) Mercury 432 753-2 [id.]. (i) LSO; (ii) Minneapolis SO, Antal Dorati.

Dorati's account of Prokofiev's powerful and atmospheric *Scythian suite* was among the first in stereo; it was recorded at Watford Town Hall in 1957. The remastering confirms the excellence of the original engineering, with the stark brutality of the *Invocation to Veles and Ala* and the nightmarish forcefulness of the evocation of *The Evil God* and *Dance of the Pagan Monsters* set in bold relief against the winningly atmospheric nocturnal sequence. The suite from the *Love for three oranges* is similarly striking in its characterization and vivid primary colours, with the resonance not blunting the rhythms. The CD is worth considering for these two performances; but the *Fifth Symphony*, recorded in Minneapolis two years later, is less successful. Dorati's reading is similarly forceful but the effect is hard and often unsympathetic, while the Minneapolis recording produces an undernourished violin patina. The scherzo and *Allegro giocoso* finale come off best.

Peter and the wolf, Op. 67.
(BB) *** ASV CDQS 6017; *ZCQS 6017.* Angela Rippon, RPO, Hughes – SAINT-SAENS: *Carnival.* ***
(B) **(*) Pickwick IMPX 9002. Sean Connery, RPO, Dorati – BRITTEN: *Young person's guide.* **(*)
(M) **(*) EMI Dig. CD-EMX 2165; *TC-EMX 2165.* William Rushton, LPO, Sian Edwards – BRITTEN: *Young person's guide* ***; RAVEL: *Ma Mère l'Oye.* **
(BB) ** Naxos Dig. 8.550499 [id.]. Jeremy Nicholas, Slovak RSO (Bratislava), Lenárd – BRITTEN: *Young person's guide* **; SAINT-SAENS: *Carnival.* **(*)

(i; ii) *Peter and the wolf;* (iii) *Lieutenant Kijé: suite;* (iv) *Love for 3 oranges: suite;* (ii) *Symphony No. 1 in D (Classical).*
❀ (B) *** Decca 433 612-2; *433 612-4* [id.]. (i) Sir Ralph Richardson, (ii) LSO, Sargent; (iii) Paris Conservatoire O, Boult; (iv) LPO, Weller.

Sir Ralph Richardson brings a great actor's feeling for words to the narrative; he dwells lovingly on their sound as well as their meaning, and this genial preoccupation with the manner in which the story is told matches Sargent's feeling exactly. There are some delicious moments when that sonorous voice has exactly the right coloration, none more taking than Grandfather's very reasonable moral: '. . . and if Peter had not caught the wolf . . . what then?' But of course he did, and in this account it was surely inevitable. Sir Malcolm Sargent's direction of the accompaniment shows his professionalism at its very best, with finely prepared orchestral playing and many imaginative little touches of detail brought out, yet with the forward momentum of the action well sustained. The original coupling, Sargent's amiable, polished account of the *Classical Symphony* has now been restored. All the tempi, except the finale, are slow but Sir Malcolm's assured elegance carries its own spontaneity. The sound is vivid – Sir Ralph Richardson is afforded striking presence – but the remastering has taken some of the bloom from the violins, although the warm ambience remains. Boult's Paris recording of *Lieutenant Kijé* offers more gusto than finesse, but the result is exhilaratingly robust and the very early (1955) stereo comes up remarkably well. Weller's *Love for three oranges* is a different matter, a first-class performance with a rich palette of colour, generating exciting orchestral bravura and given top-drawer 1977 recording. But our Rosette is for *Peter and the wolf.*

Angela Rippon narrates with charm yet is never in the least coy; indeed she is thoroughly involved in the tale and thus also involves the listener. The accompaniment is equally spirited, with excellent orchestral playing, and the recording is splendidly clear, yet not lacking atmosphere. This makes an excellent superbargain recommendation.

Sean Connery uses a modern script by Gabrielle Hilton which brings a certain colloquial friendliness to the narrative and invites a relaxed style, to which the actor readily responds. If you can accept such extensions as 'dumb duck' and a pussy cat who is 'smooth, but greedy and vain', you will not be disappointed with Connery's participation in the climax of the tale, where Dorati supports him admirably. Both pieces on this record start with the orchestra tuning up, to create an anticipatory atmosphere, and the introductory matter is entirely fresh and informal. The recording – from a vivid Decca source – has plenty of colour and projection.

Although narrative and orchestral commentary were recorded separately on the Eminence recording, it is remarkable how well the two fit together. But the flair and professionalism of Sian Edwards meant that William Rushton was able to add his story-telling to a vividly colourful orchestral tapestry which had its momentum already established. He is a personable narrator, adding touches of his own like a 'vast' grey wolf and 'nothing to report' from the bird; but his delivery does not have the relish for the words that makes the version by Sir Ralph Richardson so memorable. However, this remains a direct, sparkling presentation, brightly and realistically recorded, which cannot fail to entertain children of all ages.

On Naxos, Jeremy Nicholas is recorded in a separate acoustic from the orchestra and his contribution was obviously laminated on afterwards, since the players do not always take over the narrative flow very spontaneously. The narration is gentle, mellow, even cosy, and young children will almost certainly respond to it. The orchestral sound is colourful, the drum shots especially dramatic. This is fair value, but there are far more distinctive versions available. However, with some 20 (descriptive) cues provided, young listeners can re-enter the story at any point.

Romeo and Juliet (ballet), *Op. 64* (complete).
(B) **(*) CfP CD-CFPD 4452; *TC-CFPD 4452* (2). Bolshoi Theatre O, Zuraitis.

Zuraitis's bargain version of *Romeo and Juliet* includes an important supplement in addition to the usual complete ballet score. Having studied the original manuscript material, he adds three movements finally omitted in the ballet, the *Nurse and Mercutio* (using familiar material), a sharply grotesque *Moorish dance* and a so-called *Letter scene* which provides a sketch for what eight years later became the scherzo of the *Fifth Symphony.* Zuraitis has scored this last with reference to the symphony. The performance generally may lack something in orchestral refinement, compared with the full-price versions of Previn and Maazel, but not Russian feeling. With strikingly bright digital sound of colour and power, not always perfectly balanced, it is excellent value. The 1982 Melodiya recording has a touch of blatancy at climaxes, mainly caused by the Russian brass style, but is otherwise vivid and full. Moreover the documentation is remarkable for a bargain issue in providing plenty of information about the music, plus a synopsis directly related to the 55 separate cues.

Romeo and Juliet (ballet), *Op. 64:* extended excerpts.
(BB) **(*) Naxos Dig. 8.550380 [id.]. Slovak State PO (Košice), Andrew Mogrelia.

The Naxos selection draws on the three suites, offering 55 minutes of music, and is very vividly recorded. The Slovak orchestral playing has plenty of character and there is no lack of emotional bite, even if the strings do not have the weight of their colleagues in Minneapolis or

Cleveland. Prokofiev's colours are given a strikingly individual tang by these excellent East European musicians, and this is both rewarding and excellent value for money.

Romeo and Juliet (ballet): *suites Nos. 1 & 2, Op. 64.*
(M) *** Mercury 432 004-2 [id.]. Minneapolis SO, Skrowaczewski – MUSSORGSKY: *Night on the bare mountain.* ***

Skrowaczewski's recording of the two ballet suites was made in 1962. The playing of the Minneapolis orchestra is on a virtuoso level: the string ensemble is superbly assured, the horn playing spectacular, and the wind solos are at one with the special character of Prokofiev's orchestral palette. The crystal-clear acoustic of the hall in Edison High School, with its backing ambience, seems ideally suited to the angular melodic lines and pungent lyricism of this powerful score, to underline the sense of tragedy without losing the music's romantic sweep. There are many marvellous moments here, and the fidelity and spectacle of the Mercury engineering reach a zenith in the powerful closing sequence of *Romeo at Juliet's tomb.*

Romeo and Juliet (ballet): *suite.*
(M) *** Decca 417 737-2 [id.]. Cleveland O, Maazel – KHACHATURIAN: *Gayaneh; Spartacus.* **(*)

An intelligently chosen selection of six pieces (including *Juliet as a young girl*, the *Balcony scene* and *The last farewell*) makes a generous coupling for Decca's Khachaturian ballet scores.

Romeo and Juliet: suites Nos. 1 and 2: excerpts.
(B) *** DG Compact Classics *413 430-4* [id.]. San Francisco SO, Ozawa – TCHAIKOVSKY: *Sleeping Beauty; Swan Lake.* **(*)

This is one of Ozawa's finest recordings. He draws warmly committed playing from the San Francisco orchestra, helped by vividly rich recording, and this shorter selection from Prokofiev's ballet is well chosen. In his coupled excerpts from *Swan Lake* the music-making is at a lower voltage, but Rostropovich's companion suite from the *Sleeping Beauty* is marvellous. At bargain price, with excellent transfers, this is good value.

Romeo and Juliet: suite.
(M) *** DG 431 170-2; *431 170-4*. Lazar Berman – MUSSORGSKY: *Pictures.* ***

Prokofiev made these piano transcriptions of the *Romeo and Juliet* music and played them in public in 1937 before the ballet itself was staged at the Bolshoi. Berman characterizes each piece to excellent effect and is well served by the engineers, who produce bold and well-focused tone. The music's inspiration comes over remarkably well in pianistic colouring.

Symphonies Nos. 1 – 7 (including both original and revised versions of *No. 4*).
(M) *(*) Erato/Warner Dig. 2292 45737-2 (4) [id.]. O Nat. de France, Rostropovich.

Symphonies Nos. 1 – 7; Overture russe, Op. 72; Scythian suite, Op. 20.
(M) **(*) Decca 430 782-2 (4). LSO or LPO, Walter Weller.

Weller's set of the Prokofiev symphonies was recorded in the Kingsway Hall over a period of three and a half years, between the spring of 1974 and the autumn of 1977. Weller began with the LSO (Nos. 1, 5 and 7) then turned to the LPO. The performances are polished and very well played, though at times they are emotionally a little earthbound and there is a tendency to beautify textures. The *Classical Symphony* is cultured and elegant but slightly bland, and for some reason the transfer has brought a degree of shrillness to the strings. Elsewhere, any added bite seems advantageous and the violins are full and expansive. The recordings were regarded as being of demonstration quality in their day, and transfers are very well managed, though there is some loss of naturalness in the upper range. The finest of the set is No. 2, which is an altogether impressive account of a problematic score; the playing of the LPO has great finesse as well as power. No. 3 is less gripping and could do with more thrust, but the playing and sound are both impressive. Weller chooses the revised, 1947 score of No. 4, and this account is distinctly enjoyable, with the work's balletic origins colourfully caught. The playing could do with more edge and attack, but there is no question about the polish and accomplishment of the orchestral response. No. 5 also has undoubted merits, even if the reading is let down by the slow movement, which lacks tautness and forward impetus (it is much slower than the metronome marking), while in the scherzo Weller makes too much of the *l'istesso tempo*. In the *Sixth*, too, the bitter tang of Prokofiev's language is again toned down and the hard-etched lines smoothed over. The *Seventh* suits Weller's approach more readily and he catches the atmosphere of its somewhat balletic second movement particularly well. The *Russian overture* has plenty of energy but the *Scythian suite*, too, needs more abrasiveness, and Night (the third movement) could be more atmospheric. However, those who normally find Prokofiev's orchestral writing too pungent could well be won over by these performances.

There are few grumbles about the playing of

the Orchestre National or the quality of their responses. The Erato recording, too, is generally impressive, both in body and range. However, throughout the set Rostropovich is overemphatic and laboured; one longs for a lighter touch throughout. He certainly makes a meal of the *Classical Symphony* and No. 6. Although the 1930 version of the *Fourth Symphony* is much tauter than the 1947 revision, it certainly does not seem so here: the opening is very relaxed and the slow movement interminable. The most successful is probably the *Second*, which he plays for all the decibels it is worth and to some effect.

Symphony No. 1 in D (Classical), Op. 25.
(M) *** Decca 417 734-2 [id.]. ASMF, Marriner – BIZET: *Symphony*; STRAVINSKY: *Pulcinella*. ***
(M) *(*) Decca Dig. 430 446-2; *430 446-4* [id.]. Chicago SO, Solti – MUSSORGSKY: *Pictures* ***; TCHAIKOVSKY: *1812*. **(*)

Symphony No. 1 in D (Classical); Romeo and Juliet: excerpts.
(M) *(*) Decca Dig. 430 731-2; *430 731-4*. Chicago SO, Solti.

Marriner's famous recording has been remastered effectively and sounds very fresh; although there has been some loss of bass response, the ambient warmth ensures that the sound retains its body and bloom. Marriner's tempi are comparatively relaxed, but the ASMF are in sparkling form and play beautifully in the slow movement. Detail is stylishly pointed and the finale is vivacious, yet elegant too.

The outer movements of Solti's performance of the *Classical Symphony* could do with more spontaneity and sparkle; the slow movement, however, has an occasional moment of charm. As far as the sound is concerned, there is spectacular presence and impact, a wide dynamic range and maximum detail. Alas, there is little distance to lend enchantment, and many collectors will find everything fiercely overlit. There are many other accounts of this work that are preferable. Alongside the new couplings, Decca have also restored the original pairing with *Romeo and Juliet*, also at mid-price. Here Solti compiles a suite of his own from the ballet. He is wholly unmannered and secures a brilliant response from the Chicago orchestra, but the sound is again very much up-front.

Symphonies Nos. 1 in D (Classical); 4 in C, Op. 47 (original, 1930 version); *5 in B flat, Op. 100; 7 in C sharp min., Op. 131; Overture on Hebrew themes, Op. 34b; Russian overture, Op. 72.*
(B) (**) VoxBox [CDX 5001] (2). O Nat. de l'ORTF, Martinon.

Jean Martinon's records originally appeared singly on Turnabout LPs in the early 1970s. The distinguished French conductor was a sympathetic interpreter of Prokofiev and will be remembered for an early RCA account of the *Seventh Symphony*. All the four symphonies recorded here are well enough played, though one suspects that the conductor might have welcomed additional rehearsal time. Tempi in the *Fifth Symphony* are eminently well judged, but he takes the *Fourth* (recorded in this set in its original, 1930 version) at a very leisurely pace. Unfortunately, the quality of the recordings which was distinctly subfusc on LP is, if anything, worse now, with climaxes sounding as if they were coming close to distortion. The quality of the strings in both the *Fifth* and *Seventh* is not clean, and tutti come close to discoloration.

Symphonies Nos. 1 in D (Classical), Op. 25; 5 in B flat, Op. 100.
(BB) **(*) Naxos Dig. 8.550237 [id.]. Slovak PO, Stephen Gunzenhauser.

The Naxos recording coupling the most popular of the Prokofiev symphonies, Nos. 1 and 5, on the face of it is very good value indeed. The recording is altogether first class: there is splendid detail and definition, and the balance is extremely well judged. Moreover the American conductor, Stephen Gunzenhauser, gets very good playing from the excellent Slovak Philharmonic and the performances have the merit of being straightforward and unaffected. Gunzenhauser is not a high-voltage conductor, and artistically neither symphony is as well served as it is by Karajan's mid-1960s recording, currently out of circulation but due back before long. All the same, tempi are generally well judged in No. 5. The first movement of the *'Classical' Symphony* is a bit sedate and wanting in sparkle; the finale comes off best.

Symphonies Nos. 1 (Classical); 7, Op. 131; Love for 3 oranges (opera): *suite.*
(B) *** CfP CD-CFP 4523; *TC-CFP 4523*. Philh. O, Malko.

Malko's performances were recorded in 1955, and the accounts of the two symphonies were the first stereo EMI ever made. All the performances are quite excellent, and the *Seventh Symphony*, of which Malko conducted the UK première, is freshly conceived and finely shaped. What is so striking is the range and refinement of the recording: the excellence of the balance and the body of the sound are remarkable. No less satisfying is the suite from *Love for three oranges*, an additional bonus making this outstanding value.

Symphonies Nos. 2 in D min., Op. 40; 3 in C min., Op. 44; 6 in E flat min., Op. 111; Chout (suite), *Op. 21.*

(B) ** VoxBox (2) [CDX 5054]. Nat. O of ORTF, Jean Martinon.

These are thoroughly idiomatic performances and, though the quality of the sound is variable, it is generally better than in the companion volume (see above). The first movement of the *Second Symphony* sounds as if it had enough rehearsal time for a broadcast rather than for a commercial record, but the slow variation movement is phrased with great poetic feeling. A good account of the *Third Symphony* too, though some of the orchestral detail is not clearly in focus (compare the opening of the slow movement in the Martinon with Weller's less searching Decca account). Anyway, the recording of the *Chout* suite, played with real panache by Martinon and the ORTF Orchestra, is a good deal brighter, and the *Sixth* is very well played indeed. This is far from ideal but, at the price, quite serviceable.

VOCAL MUSIC

Alexander Nevsky (cantata), *Op. 78*.
(M) *** EMI CDM7 63114-2. Anna Reynolds, LSO Ch., LSO, Previn – RACHMANINOV: *The Bells*. ***

Alexander Nevsky (cantata), *Op. 78; Ivan the Terrible, Op. 116* (film music, arr. in oratorio form by Stasevich); *Lieutenant Kijé:* (suite), *Op. 60*.
(B) **(*) VoxBox 1155022 (2) [CDX 5021]. St Louis SO & Ch., Slatkin.

(i) *Alexander Nevsky, Op. 78; Lieutenant Kijé* (suite), *Op. 60*.
(M) *** BMG/RCA GD 60176 [60176-2-RG]. (i) Rosalind Elias, Chicago SO Ch.; Chicago SO, Reiner – GLINKA: *Russlan Overture*. ***

(i) *Alexander Nevsky, Op. 78;* (ii) *Romeo and Juliet, Op. 64:* excerpts.
(M) ** Sony/CBS CD 45557. (i) Lilli Chookasian, Westminster Ch., NYPO, Schippers; (ii) NYPO, Mitropoulos.

All the weight, bite and colour of the score are captured by Previn, and though the timbre of the singers' voices may not suggest Russians, they cope very confidently with the Russian text; Previn's direct and dynamic manner ensures that the great *Battle on the ice* scene is powerfully effective. Anna Reynolds sings the lovely *Lament* for the dead most affectingly. The sound is sharply defined, with plenty of bite; just a little of the old analogue ambient fullness has gone. The coupling with Rachmaninov's *Bells* is an obvious (and generous) one, as Previn's performance of this other great Russian choral work is similarly successful.

Reiner's version, recorded in 1959, was another of the astonishingly vivid early achievements of the RCA stereo catalogue. The performance is gripping from the first bar to the last. The sinister evocation of the Teutonic invaders is matched by the power of the *Battle on the ice*. With choral singing of great fervour and a movingly eloquent contribution from Rosalind Elias in the great *Lament*, one hardly notices that the English-language performance inevitably sounds less idiomatic with an American accent. The *Lieutenant Kijé suite*, recorded two years earlier, is another colourful example of the Chicago orchestra at their peak, the sound again full and atmospheric.

The two-disc bargain VoxBox offers excellent performances of all three of the concert works derived from Prokofiev's film-scores, with Stasevich's arrangement of the *Ivan the Terrible* music taking up the first disc and the other two works the second. No date is given for the analogue recordings, but the sound is fuller and more forward than on the companion recordings of Rachmaninov from St Louis, made in the mid-1970s. The chorus too sings more incisively than in Rachmaninov and, except in the first two choruses of *Alexander Nevsky*, the balance is not too distant. Vocally, the greatest glory is the darkly expressive singing of Claudine Carlson in the *Lament for the dead* in *Nevsky*, with the chest register revealing a glorious contralto quality. She is the soloist in items from *Ivan the Terrible* too. Very good value.

Schippers' mid-priced reissue dates from 1961, but the remastering is vividly managed and there is some brilliant brass playing from the NYPO. With slow tempi in the first and third movements, Schippers does not always avoid portentousness, and the singing of Lilli Chookasian in the lament for the dead does not have the weight of emotion of Anna Reynolds' account for Previn. The CBS disc brings a generous selection from Mitropoulos's vibrant and distinguished set of excerpts from *Romeo and Juliet*, recorded in 1957 and still sounding very impressive.

Ivan the Terrible, Op. 116 (film music, arr. in oratorio form by Stasevich).
(M) *** EMI CDM7 69584-2; *EG 769584-4*. Arkhipova, Mokrenko, Morgunov (narrator), Ambrosian Ch., Philh. O, Muti.

This oratorio was put together long after Prokofiev's death by the scholar Abram Stasevich, and the result is diffuse; the device of adding a spoken narration (in Russian) could well prove irritating on repetition. Nevertheless, with fine playing and choral singing, there are many imaginative ideas here to relish, not least those using broad, folk-like melodies. The Kingsway Hall recording is admirably spacious, and though the histrionic style of the narrator, Boris Morgunov, is unappealing, the two other soloists are excellent in their limited roles. The remastering has been highly successful and the effect is often thrillingly vivid, with the chorus especially telling.

OPERA

War and peace (complete).

❀ (M) *** Erato/Warner 2292 45331-2 (4) [id.]. Vishnevskaya, Miller, Ciesinski, Tumagian, Ochman, Ghiuselev, Smith, Paunova, Petkov, Toczyska, Zakai, Gedda, Fr. R. Ch. & Nat. O, Rostropovich.

Here in the first really complete recording of *War and peace* Rostropovich magnificently fulfils the promise he made to the composer, not long before the latter's death, to do all he could to get this masterpiece fully appreciated. Though the components may suggest too facile a representation of Tolstoi's vast novel, a performance like this shows triumphantly how tautly they cohere to make a comparably epic work of art. Flawed as some of the casting is in this Paris recording, the performance confirms the piece as one of the greatest operas of the century, in which Prokofiev produces one haunting melody after another. The recording is vividly atmospheric, both in the evocative love-scenes and ball-scenes of the first half (Peace) or in the battle-scenes of the second half (War). The emotional thrust is overwhelming, with the energy and warmth of Rostropovich's conducting building to a climax, when the whole work culminates in a great patriotic chorus using the most memorable melody of all, heard first in General Kutuzov's solo after the Council of Fili. The French Radio Chorus sings with fervour both there and elsewhere, notably in the Choral epigraph – telling of the invasion of Russia – which Rostropovich logically places, not at the beginning of the opera, but immediately before the scenes of war. Instead, at the start he includes an optional overture which rehearses some of the main melodies. Though Galina Vishnevskaya was already in her early sixties when she made the recording, she characterizes the young Natasha with wonderful vividness, only occasionally raw in tone. Lajos Miller, not flawless either, is a clear-voiced Andrei, and Wieslaw Ochman is a first-rate Pierre, with the veteran Nicolai Gedda brought in as Kuragin. Katherine Ciesinski is a warm-toned Sonya, but Dimiter Petkov is disappointingly unsteady as Natasha's father, Count Rostov. The small role of Napoleon is strongly taken by Eduard Tumagian, while Nicola Ghiuselev is a noble Kutuzov, in some ways the most impressive of all. Even with a total playing time of over four hours, the opera yet seems compact. It fits neatly on the four CDs, with the first two devoted to the scenes of peace, and the last two to the scenes of war, without a single scene being broken in the middle. The booklet contains English, French and German translations, but no transliteration of the original Russian.

Puccini, Giacomo (1858–1924)

La Bohème (complete).

(M) *** Decca 425 534-2 (2). Tebaldi, Bergonzi, Bastianini, Siepi, Corena, D'Angelo, St Cecilia Ac. Ch. & O, Serafin.

(M) **(*) EMI CMS7 63657-2 (2) [id.]. Freni, Gedda, Basiola, Badioli, La Scala, Milan, Ch. & O, Schippers.

(B) ** CfP CD-CFP 4708; *CD-CFP 4708* (2). Scotto, Kraus, Milnes, Neblett, Plishka, Manuguerra, Trinity Boys' Ch., Amb. Op. Ch., Nat. PO, Levine.

(M) (**) EMI mono CHS7 63335-2 (2) [Ang. CDHB 63335]. Albanese, Gigli, Poli, Baracchi, Baronti, La Scala, Milan, Ch. & O, Berrettoni.

(M) (**) BMG/RCA GD 60288; *GK 60288* (2) [60288-2-RG; *60288-4-RG*]. Albanese, Peerce, Valentino, McKnight, Moscona, Cehanovsky, NBC Ch., NBC SO, Toscanini.

(B) ** Naxos Dig. 8.660003/4 [id.]. Orgonasova, Welch, Gonzales, Previati, Senator, Slovak Philharmonic Ch., Slovak RSO (Bratislava), Will Humburg.

Joan Sutherland has said that she regards Renata Tebaldi's vocal assumption of the role of Mimi as the finest of all modern performances, and certainly Tebaldi's Decca set with Bergonzi dominated the catalogue in the early days of stereo; technically it was an outstanding recording in its day. Vocally the performance achieves a consistently high standard, with Tebaldi as Mimi the most affecting: she offers some superbly controlled singing, but the individuality of the heroine is not as indelibly conveyed as with Freni. Carlo Bergonzi is a fine Rodolfo; Bastianini and Siepi are both superb as Marcello and Colline, and even the small parts of Benoit and Alcindoro (as usual taken by a single artist) have the benefit of Corena's magnificent voice. The veteran Serafin was more vital here than on some of his records. The recording, now thirty years old, has its vividness and sense of stage perspective enhanced on CD, with minimal residual tape hiss, though the age of the master shows in the string timbre above the stave.

Freni's characterization of Mimi is so enchanting that it is worth ignoring some of the less perfect elements. The engineers placed Freni rather close to the microphone, which makes it hard for her to sound tentative in her first scene, but the beauty of the voice is what one remembers, and from there to the end her performance is conceived as a whole, leading to a supremely moving account of the Death scene. Nicolai Gedda's Rodolfo is not rounded in the traditional Italian way but there is never any doubt about his ability to project a really grand manner of his own. Thomas Schippers' conducting starts as though this is going to be a hard-driven, unrelenting performance, but quickly after the horse-play he shows his genuinely Italianate sense of pause, giving the singers plenty of time to breathe and allowing the music to expand. The resonant, 1964 recording has transferred vividly to CD.

In the bargain range, on CfP comes the 1980 HMV set, conducted by James Levine. Alfredo Kraus's relatively light tenor sets the pattern at the very start for a performance that is strong on comedy. One registers the exchanges more sharply than usual on record, and though Kraus (no longer as sweet of timbre as he was) tends to over-point in the big arias, it is a stylish performance. Scotto – who first recorded the role of Mimi for DG in 1962 – is not flatteringly recorded here, for the rawness and unevenness which affect her voice at the top of the stave are distracting, marring an affectionate portrait. Milnes makes a powerful Marcello and Neblett a strong Musetta, a natural Minnie in *Fanciulla* transformed into a soubrette. Levine, brilliant in the comic writing of Acts I and IV, sounds less at home in the big melodies. The recording has plenty of warmth and atmosphere and the CD transfer is first class so that the voices ride naturally over the rich, vibrant orchestral texture. This is undoubtedly excellent value and it includes an excellent extended synopsis of the stage action, closely linked to 42 separate cues, well placed over the four Acts.

The pre-war EMI set conducted by Berrettoni is dominated – as was planned at the time of recording – by the great tenor, Beniamino Gigli, a superstar of his day. The way he spices the role of Rodolfo with little Gigli chuckles is consistently charming. From first to last his facial expression comes over vividly in his strongly characterized singing, and the pity is that he is not well served by the conducting (unimaginative) or the recording, which is markedly less vivid than in the parallel recording of *Tosca* with Gigli as Cavaradossi. Licia Albanese, later to sing the same role for Toscanini in his 1946 concert performance and recording, is tenderly affecting but, thanks to the recording, the voice is recessed. Afro Poli sings firmly, but proves a colourless Marcello, and Tatiana Menotti is an edgy, fluttery Musetta.

Toscanini's 1946 set is taken from the first of his concert performances of opera in New York, recorded in 1946. The sound is even drier than most from this source, but the voices are vivid in their forward placing, and fortunately the singers had been chosen for their clean focus. Albanese, though held in an expressive straitjacket by the conductor, sounds fuller and sweeter as Mimi than in her earlier recording with Gigli; indeed she is delightfully fresh, even though no pianissimos are possible in the NBC acoustic. Jan Peerce as Rodolfo and Francesco Valentino as Marcello are reliable rather than imaginative – not surprising with the conductor such a disciplinarian – and Anne McKnight makes a bright, clear Musetta. Toscanini is heavy-handed and often rigid in his direction, but his love of this score, which he knew from its earliest performances, shines out all through, not least in his loud and endearing vocal obbligatos during the big tunes.

Well played and atmospherically recorded, the Naxos version of *La Bohème* offers an outstanding performance by Luba Orgonosova as Mimi. The creamy quality of the voice, coupled with her warm expressiveness and her vocal poise, brings out the tenderness of the character to the full; and it is a pity that none of the others match her. Jonathan Welch as Rodolfo and Fabio Previati as Marcello are both strained and unsteady at times, while Carmen Gonzales tries too hard as Musetta. Yet with Will Humburg pacing the opera effectively, and with the well-disciplined Slovak Philharmonic Chorus adding to the atmospheric beauty, this is a fair bargain.

La Bohème: highlights.

(M) **(*) Decca 421 301-2. Tebaldi, Bergonzi, Bastianini, Siepi, Corena, D'Angelo, St Cecilia Ac. Ch. & O, Rome, Serafin.

(M) **(*) EMI CDM7 63932-2; *EG 763932-4*. Freni, Gedda, Basioli, Serei, Ch. & O of Rome Opera, Schippers.

(B) Pickwick (DG) IMPX 9024. Scotto, Poggi, Gobbi, Maneguzzer, Maggio Musicale Fiorentino Ch. & O, Votto.

Most collectors will surely want a reminder of the vintage set with Tebaldi and Bergonzi at the height of their powers. The selection is well made, and the disc is competitively priced.

The selection from the Schippers set is reasonably generous (60 minutes) and contains most of the key items; it is certainly well transferred.

This Pickwick highlights disc comes from a singularly unsuccessful DG *Bohème*, recorded at the beginning of the 1960s; it might be considered a collector's item that Gianni Poggi's

Che gelida manina easily wins the prize for the crudest performance on record! Even Tito Gobbi is less than a success as Marcello, and Scotto's voice is caught not at all well.

La Fanciulla del West (*The Girl of the Golden West;* complete).

❀ (M) *** Decca 421 595-2 (2) [id.]. Tebaldi, Del Monaco, MacNeil, Tozzi, St Cecilia Ac., Rome, Ch. & O, Capuana.

(M) ** EMI CMS7 63970-2 (2) [id.]. Nilsson, Mongelli, Gibin, La Scala, Milan, Ch. & O, Von Matačić.

Like Karajan's classic 1961 *Tosca* (see below), the Decca set of *La Fanciulla del West* has been remastered for CD with spectacular success. The achievement is the more remarkable when one considers that the original recording was made in 1958; but this is vintage Decca sound, both atmospheric and vivid. Tebaldi gives one of her most warm-hearted and understanding performances on record, and Mario del Monaco displays the wonderfully heroic quality of his voice to great – if sometimes tiring – effect. Cornell MacNeil as the villain, Sheriff Rance, sings with great precision and attack, but unfortunately has not a villainous-sounding voice to convey the character fully. Jake Wallace's entry and the song *Che faranno i viecchi miei* is one of the high spots of the recording, with Tozzi singing beautifully. Capuana's expansive reading is matched by the imagination of the production, with the closing scene wonderfully effective.

The difference between the Rome and Milan performances is obvious from the very first bar: Capuana on Decca is the more refined, Matačić the more passionate. The EMI sound is closer and not so atmospheric, though it has excellent directional separation too. Nilsson makes a formidable Minnie, not as warm-toned as Tebaldi, nor as gloriously expansive as Carol Neblett on DG, but thrilling as a budding Brünhilde was bound to be (she recorded this in 1959). Joao Gibin is a degree more imaginative than Del Monaco and has a good, distinctive timbre, and Mongelli's Rance is a splendid characterization. One or two brief passages are omitted, whereas the Decca (and full-price DG) versions are complete, so this must be very much a third choice, though it offers much that is stimulating, and the CD transfer gives it a new lease of life.

Madama Butterfly (complete).

(M) *** BMG/RCA GD 84145 (2) [4145-2-RG]. Moffo, Elias, Valletti, Cesari, Catalani, Rome Op. Ch. & O, Leinsdorf.

(M) *** EMI CMS7 69654-2 (2) [Ang. CDMB 69654]. Scotto, Bergonzi, Di Stasio, Panerai, De Palma, Rome Op. Ch. & O, Barbirolli.

(M) **(*) Decca 425 531-2 (2) [id.]. Tebaldi, Bergonzi, Cossotto, Sordello, St Cecilia Ac. Ch. & O, Serafin.

(M) **(*) EMI CMS7 63634-2 (2) [Ang. CDMB 63634]; *TC-CFPD 4446*. De los Angeles, Bjoerling, Pirazzini, Sereni, Rome Op. Ch. & O, Santini.

(M) (***) EMI mono CHS7 69990-2 (2) [Ang. CDHB 69990]. Toti dal Monte, Gigli, Palombini, Basiola, Rome Opera Ch. & O, Serafin.

(B) ** Naxos Dig. 8.660015/6 (2). Gauci, Ramiro, Tichy, Ch. & Slovak RSO (Bratislava), Rahbari.

Anna Moffo's Butterfly proves delightful, fresh and young-sounding. *Un bel dì* has some sliding at the beginning, but the end is glorious, and the *Flower duet* with Rosalind Elias is enchanting. Valletti's Pinkerton has a clear-voiced, almost Gigli-like charm – preferable to most rivals – and with Corena as the Bonze the only blot on the set vocally is the unimaginative Sharpless of Renato Cesari. Leinsdorf is efficient and undistracting and, with vivid recording (balanced in favour of the voices), this makes a first-class mid-priced recommendation, costing less than half the price of the Decca Karajan set with Freni, Ludwig and Pavarotti.

Under Sir John Barbirolli, players and singers perform consistently with a dedication and intensity rare in opera recordings made in Italy, and the whole score glows more freshly than ever. There is hardly a weak link in the cast. Bergonzi's Pinkerton and Panerai's Sharpless are both sensitively and beautifully sung; Anna di Stasio's Suzuki is more than adequate, and Renata Scotto's Butterfly has a subtlety and perceptiveness in its characterization that more than make up for any shortcoming in the basic beauty of tone-colour. It is on any count a highly individual voice, used here with great intelligence to point up the drama to its tragic climax. On CD the violins have lost a little of their original opulence, but in all other respects the recording combines vividness with atmosphere.

Serafin's reading is sensitive and beautifully paced. Tebaldi is at her most radiant; though she was never the most deft of Butterflies dramatically, her singing is consistently rich and beautiful, sometimes breathtakingly so. The excellence of Decca engineering in 1958 is amply proved in the CD transfer, with one serious exception: the absence of bass at the very opening brings a disagreeably shrill and thin sound, improved once the orchestration grows fuller, with voices very precisely and realistically placed.

In the late 1950s and early 1960s, Victoria de los Angeles was memorable in the role of Butterfly, and her 1960 recording displays her art at its most endearing, her range of golden tone-colour lovingly exploited, with the voice well recorded for the period, though rather close. Opposite her, Jussi Bjoerling was making one of his last recordings, and, though he shows few special insights, he produces a flow of rich tone to compare with that of the heroine. Mario Sereni is a full-voiced Sharpless, but Miriam Pirazzini is a disappointingly wobbly Suzuki; Santini is a reliable, generally rather square and unimaginative conductor who rarely gets in the way. With recording quality freshened, this fine set is most welcome either on a pair of mid-priced CDs or, still sounding bright and clear, in its CfP cassette format (offered in a chunky box with a synopsis rather than a libretto).

There has never been as endearing a portrait of Pinkerton on record as Gigli's. The perennial smile in his voice makes one immediately forget how totally caddish the American lieutenant's behaviour is. One simply revels in the beauty of the sound and the imagination of the phrasing, only occasionally self-indulgent. The Butterfly of Toti dal Monte is something of an acquired taste. The 'little-girl' sound is often exaggerated, but it is a classic performance nevertheless. Serafin as ever is a master of timing; but this mono recording of 1939, sounding very well for its age, is a set to get above all for the great tenor and his unique performance.

Rahbari conducts a warm, well-paced reading of *Butterfly* with an excellent young Maltese soprano in the name-part, Miriam Gauci. She sings with a warm vibrato which yet does not disturb her attractively girlish portrait. The light-toned Yordy Ramiro is here more successful in Puccini as Pinkerton than he is in his Verdi recordings for Naxos. Though Gabriel Tichy makes a colourless Sharpless and the final Suicide scene is lacking in orchestral bite, this makes an enjoyable, atmospherically recorded version. As with other Naxos operas, there is a full text but no translation. The tracking is exceptionally generous, neatly linked with a detailed synopsis.

Madama Butterfly: highlights.

(M) *** EMI CDM7 63411-2; *EG 763411-4*. Scotto, Bergonzi, Di Stasio, Panerei, Rome Op. Ch. & O, Barbirolli.

(M) ** Decca 421 873-2; *421 873-4* [417 733-2] (from complete recording, with Tebaldi, Bergonzi, Cossotto; cond. Serafin).

The EMI selection (54 minutes) offers only slightly more music than the Tebaldi selection, but it does include the essential *Humming chorus*. For those owning another complete set, it offers a fine sampler of Barbirolli's deeply felt performance with its admirably consistent cast. Scotto's Butterfly was one of her finest recorded performances. The transfer does reveal the age of the 1966 recording in the orchestral sound, but the voices are full and vividly projected.

The Tebaldi/Bergonzi Decca set dates from 1958 but the sound is rich in ambience, and the dated upper string sound is seldom distracting, for the voices are vividly projected. The magnetism of the singing is very compelling, but the 51 minutes' selection is ungenerous and still omits the *Humming chorus*. Readers would be much better advised to invest in the complete set which is one of Tebaldi's major recording achievements.

(i) *Madama Butterfly:* highlights; (ii) *Manon Lescaut:* highlights.

(B) *** DG Dig. Compact Classics *431 182-4* [id.]. (i; ii) Freni, (i) Carreras, Berganza, Pons, Amb. Op. Ch.; (ii) Domingo, Bruson, ROHCG Ch., Philh. O, Sinopoli.

This outstanding set of combined highlights from two of Sinopoli's finest opera sets marks a new level of sophistication in tape transfer for DG's bargain Compact Cassettes. Both these recordings are digital, and the sound here is remarkably clean, fresh and vivid. Mirella Freni sings ravishingly, whether as Mimi or Manon, and the supporting casts are admirable, with Domingo both stirring and providing subtle detail in his portrait of Manon's lover, Des Grieux. The finesse of the transfer ensures that the *Humming chorus* from *Butterfly*, sung at a haunting pianissimo, registers magically.

Manon Lescaut (complete).

(M) **(*) Decca 430 253-2 (2) [id.]. Tebaldi, Del Monaco, Corena, St Cecilia Ac., Rome, Ch. & O, Molinari-Pradelli.

(M) (***) BMG/RCA mono GD 60573 (2) [60573-2-RG]. Albanese, Bjorling, Merrill, Rome Op. Ch. & O, Perlea.

At mid-price, the Decca set with Tebaldi, dating from the mid-1950s, is still well worth considering. The Decca recording still sounds well, with good detail, and the direction of Molinari-Pradelli is warm and intense. While Tebaldi is not quite the little woman of Puccini's dreams, she still produces a flow of gorgeous, rich tone. Only the coarseness of Mario del Monaco as Des Grieux mars the set, but this is exciting, red-blooded singing and he does not overwhelm Tebaldi in the duet sequences.

Perlea's 1954 recording, well paced, fresh and vigorous, makes a valuable addition to the excellent Victor Opera series. The mono sound may be limited (with the orchestra in this transfer not given the body it originally had on LP), but no Puccinian should miss it, when Jussi Bjoerling gives the finest ever interpretation on record of the role of Des Grieux. This is one of Bjoerling's best recordings, passionately committed and gloriously sung; and Robert Merrill too is superb as Manon's brother, giving delightful irony to the closing scene of Act I which has rarely sounded so effervescent. The Manon of Licia Albanese is sensitively sung, but the voice is not at all girlish, even less so than in her two classic recordings as Mimi in *Bohème* – with Gigli in 1939 and in Toscanini's concert performance in 1946.

La Rondine (complete).
(M) ** BMG/RCA GD 60489 (2) [4801-2-RG]. Moffo, Sciutti, Barioni, De Palma, Sereni, RCA Italiana Op. Ch. & O, Molinari-Pradelli.

Anna Moffo leads a good cast and the performance, though not ideal, is still highly enjoyable, with understanding direction from Molinari-Pradelli. The recording too has come up well.

Il Tabarro (complete).
(M) **(*) BMG/RCA GD 60865 (2) [60865-2]. Leontyne Price, Domingo, Milnes, John Alldis Ch., New Philh. O, Leinsdorf – LEONCAVALLO: *I Pagliacci*. ***

The unforgettably atmospheric colouring in Puccini's essay in Grand Guignol is beautifully caught by the atmospheric RCA recording, made in Walthamstow Town Hall in 1971, and the refinement of the New Philharmonia playing is an added attraction. Leontyne Price may not be ideally cast as the bargemaster's wife, but she is fully in character, even though she does not point word-meanings in enough detail. Sherrill Milnes is rather young-sounding for the bargemaster, but he sings memorably in the climactic aria, *Nulla silenzio*, sustaining an unusually slow termpo. Placido Domingo makes a fresh-voiced and well-characterized young bargee, while Leinsdorf is at his most sympathetic. The CD transfer increases the sense of presence, yet retains the ambient evocation. A full translation is provided.

Tosca (complete).
(M) *** Decca 421 670-2 (2) [id.]. Leontyne Price, Di Stefano, Taddei, V. State Op. Ch., VPO, Karajan.
(M) (***) EMI mono CHS7 63338-2 (2) [Ang. CDHB 63338]. Caniglia, Gigli, Borgioli, Dominici, Rome Op. Ch. & O, Fabritiis.
(M) ** Decca 411 871-2 (2) [id.]. Tebaldi, Del Monaco, London, St Cecilia Ac., Rome, Ch. & O, Molinari-Pradelli.
(M) ** EMI CMS7 69974-2 (2) [Ang. CDMB 69974]. Callas, Bergonzi, Gobbi, Paris Op. Ch. & Conservatoire O, Prêtre.
(B) *(*) Naxos Dig. 8. 660001/2 [id.]. Miricioiu, Lamberti, Carroli, Slovak Philharmonic Ch., Slovak R. SO (Bratislava), Alexander Rahbari.

On Decca, Karajan deserves equal credit with the principal singers for the vital, imaginative performance recorded in Vienna. Some idea of its quality may be gained from the passage at the end of Act I, just before Scarpia's *Te Deum*. Karajan takes a speed far slower than usual, but there is an intensity which takes one vividly to the Church of San Andrea while at the same time building the necessary tension for the depiction of Scarpia's villainy. Taddei himself has a marvellously wide range of tone-colour, and though he cannot quite match the Gobbi snarl, he has almost every other weapon in his armoury. Leontyne Price is at the peak of her form and Di Stefano sings most sensitively. The sound of the Vienna orchestra is enthralling – both more refined and richer than usual in a Puccini opera, and it sounds quite marvellous in its digitally remastered format, combining presence with atmosphere and making a superb bargain at mid-price.

Collectors with long memories will be nostalgic about what inevitably, if illogically, must be described as 'the Gigli Tosca'; in the days of 78s, it was one of the glories of Puccini representation in the catalogue. The transfer brings astonishingly vivid sound, as in the rasping trombones on the opening Scarpia chords, along with a fine sense of presence. The great tenor dominates the whole performance, his facial expressiveness consistently beaming out through his voice, while Maria Caniglia, not characterful enough to be a memorable Tosca, sings with warmth and total commitment. Armando Borgioli is a young-sounding, virile Scarpia, forceful and upstanding rather than sinister. The conducting of Fabritiis brings far more natural and convincing timing than you find on many a more recent recording.

Tebaldi's early stereo *Tosca* is outclassed by most later versions. Yet Tebaldi is splendidly dramatic and often sings very affectingly. The set is well worth hearing for her classic assumption of the role, but unfortunately the other two principals do not match her.

The Callas stereo *Tosca* is exciting and disappointing in roughly predictable proportions. There are few points of improvement over the old (full-price) mono set, with Callas in the title-role and De Sabata conducting far more imaginatively than takes place here. When it comes to vocal reliability, the comparison of the new with the old is just as damaging, as an impartial observer might have predicted. Gobbi is magnificent still, but no more effective than he was in the mono recording, and Bergonzi's Cavaradossi, intelligent and attractive, is not helped by a recording balance not in his favour.

The Naxos version at budget price is worth hearing for the vibrant and strong performance of Nelly Miricioiu as Tosca, a soprano who deserves to be recorded far more. She is not helped by the principals around her and least of all by the conductor, Alexander Rahbari, whose preference for slow speeds undermines any tension the soprano builds up. Yet she both brings echoes of Maria Callas in her dramatic moments and gives a beautifully thoughtful and inward account of *Vissi d'arte*, finely controlled at a spacious speed. Giorgio Lamberti is a coarse-grained Cavaradossi, hammy in his underlining, and Silvano Carroli, despite a fine, weighty voice, is a rough-edged Scarpia, too often shouting rather than vocalizing. Good digital sound and refined playing.

Tosca: highlights.

(B) **(*) DG Compact Classics *427 719-4* [id.] (from complete set, with Vishnevskaya, Bonelli, Manuguerra, French R. Ch., O Nat. de France, Rostropovitch) – BIZET: *Carmen*: highlights. **

There is plenty of drama in Rostropovich's set of *Tosca* highlights, with all three principals at their best and Manuguerra a particularly compelling Scarpia. Vishnevskaya has her rough moments but is otherwise very compelling, and Bonelli sings with comparable ardour as Cavaradossi. The selection includes the complete final scene of the opera from *E lucevan le stelle* onwards. Good, vivid sound.

Il Trittico: (i) *Il Tabarro;* (ii) *Suor Angelica;* (iii) *Gianni Schicchi.*

(M) **(*) RCA/Eurodisc Dig. GD 69043 (3) [7775-2-RC: *Il Tabarro*; 7806-2-RC: *Suor Angelica*; 7751-2-RC: *Gianni Schicchi*]. (i) Nimsgern, Lamberti, Auer, Tokody; (i; iii) Pane; (ii) Popp, Lipovšek, Schimi, Jennings; (iii) Panerai, Donath, Baniewicz, Seifert; Bav. R. Ch., Munich R. O, Patanè.

(M) ** Decca 411 665-2 (3). Tebaldi, Del Monaco, Simionato, Merrill, Corena, Maggio Musicale Fiorentino Ch. & O, Gardelli.

Puccini's three one-act operas show him musically and dramatically at the peak of his achievement. They are balanced like the movements of a concerto: *Il Tabarro*, sombre in its portrait of the cuckolded bargemaster, but made attractive by the vividness of the atmosphere and the sweetness of the love music; *Suor Angelica*, a lyrical slow movement with its picture of a nunnery, verging on the syrupy but never quite falling; and *Gianni Schicchi*, easily the most brilliant and witty one-act comedy in the whole field of opera.

Patanè's Munich recordings of the three *Trittico* one-acters first appeared separately, but here come, attractively packaged, on three mid-price CDs. Patanè directs consistently well-paced, idiomatic performances of all three operas, well played and atmospherically recorded. Neither Lucia Popp as Angelica nor Maria Lipovšek as the vindictive Zia Principessa is ideally cast in the central opera of the triptych – the one overstressed, the other sounding too young – but these are both fine artists who sing with consistent imagination. Nimsgern as Michele in *Tabarro* gives a memorable, well-projected performance, and so does the characterful Rolando Panerai as Schicchi in the comic final opera, both central to the success of the performances. In the USA the three operas are available separately but at premium price.

On grounds of recording the early Decca set remains very impressive, but the performances are variable. Fernando Corena's Schicchi is too coarse-grained, both vocally and dramatically. This is buffo-bass style with too much parlando 'acting'. Nor is Tebaldi entirely at home in the open-eyed part of the young Lauretta, though she sings *O mio babbino caro* very sweetly. She is more at home in the role of Sister Angelica and gives a rich-voiced and affecting portrayal, only slightly troubled by the top notes at the end. Simionato makes a fine, firm Zia Principessa: one can really believe in her relentlessness, while Gardelli keeps the performance moving forward gently but firmly, and in a somewhat static piece this is most important. The scene of *Il Tabarro* is set on a barge on the banks of the Seine, in Paris, and though the Decca production team capture all of Puccini's background effects, the result has not so much a Parisian flavour as the acoustic of an empty opera-house. Merrill sings very strongly as the cuckolded bargemaster, and Tebaldi and del Monaco are good in a conventional, whole-hogging Italian way. The recording has been effectively remastered and sounds a shade drier than when first issued, but the voices are vividly projected on CD, and the sense of atmosphere remains.

Turandot (complete).

(M) *** EMI CMS7 69327-2 (2) [Ang. CDMB 69327]. Nilsson, Corelli, Scotto, Mercuriali, Giaiotti, Rome Op. Ch. & O, Molinari-Pradelli.

The EMI set brings Nilsson's second assumption on record of the role of Puccini's formidable princess. As an interpretation it is very similar to the earlier, RCA performance, but its impact is far more immediate, thanks to the conducting of Molinari-Pradelli. Corelli may not be the most sensitive prince in the world, but the voice is in glorious condition. Scotto's Liù is very beautiful and characterful too. With vividly remastered sound, this makes an excellent mid-priced recommendation, though the documentation, as yet, does not include an English translation.

Turandot: excerpts.
(M) (***) EMI mono CDH7 61074-2 [id.].
Dame Eva Turner, Martinelli, Albanese, Favero, Tomei, Dua, ROHCG Ch., LPO, Barbirolli.

The Références issue of Dame Eva Turner in extracts from *Turandot* has live recordings made at Covent Garden during the Coronation season of 1937, with Sir John Barbirolli conducting and with Giovanni Martinelli as a unique Calaf. The excerpts were recorded at two separate performances and fascinatingly duplicate most of the items, with the second performance in each pair marginally more spacious and helpful in sound, and generally warmer and more relaxed as a performance. Martinelli's heroic timbre may be an acquired taste, but he is stirringly convincing, and Dame Eva Turner gloriously confirms all the legends, even more commanding than in her earlier studio accounts of the big aria, *In questa reggia*. Keith Hardwick's excellent transfers, for all the obvious limitations of recording on stage at Covent Garden, give a superb sense of presence.

Turandot: highlights.
(M) **(*) EMI CDM7 63410-2; *EG 763410-4*.
Caballé, Carreras, Freni, Plishka, Sénéchal, Rhine Op. Ch., Strasbourg PO, Lombard.

Caballé's Turandot is well worth having on disc, even if, like the others in EMI's Puccini highlights series, the selection (52 minutes) is far from generous. All the singers are recorded very close, which is not always flattering, and Lombard is not a very idiomatic Puccinian. But the combination of Caballé and Freni (as Liù) is a fascinating one: it works well dramatically, and not in the most predictable way.

COLLECTIONS

Arias from: *La Bohème; Fanciulla del West; Gianni Schicchi; Madama Butterfly; Manon Lescaut; Suor Angelica; Tosca; Turandot.*
(B) ** CfP CD-CFP 4569; *TC-CFP 4569*.
Gedda; Scotto; Campora; Stella; Freni; ROHCG Ch. & O, Gardelli; Caballé and Marti; Charles Craig, Cavalli, Corelli, Amy Shuard.

Nicolai Gedda opens this Classics for Pleasure recital with a characteristically sensitive *Che gelida manina*, although he is not quite heroic enough in *Nessun dorma*. Charles Craig, one of the few British tenors to make a name in Italian opera, sings strongly in excerpts from *Manon Lescaut* and *Tosca*, but the remastering of these 1959 recordings does not flatter the voice. On the other hand, Amy Shuard's 1962 *In questa reggia* is thrillingly projected, and Mirella Freni is on fine form both in Liù's farewell from the same opera and in the most famous *Butterfly* aria. The rest is less distinctive, though the women are more refined than the men. As so often, a collection of histrionics like this needs singing of the highest quality to make an enjoyable continuous entertainment.

Arias and duets from: *La Bohème; Gianni Schicchi; Madama Butterfly; Manon Lescaut; Tosca; Turandot.*
(B) *** EMI CDZ7 62520-2; *LZ 762520-4*.
Caballé, Domingo, Di Stefano, Gedda, Freni, Dimitrova, Bruson, De los Angeles, Bjoerling, Scotto, Corelli.

This is a particularly well-ordered collection, containing many of Puccini's deservedly popular highlights in performances of sterling quality arranged to provide a satisfying concert. Placido Domingo opens with *Donna non vidi mai* from *Manon Lescaut* and is equally stirring in *Recondita armonia* from *Tosca*; Caballé is often ravishing in arias from *Manon Lescaut*, *Bohème*, a splendid *Vissi d'arte* from *Tosca*, *Un bel dì* from *Butterfly* and *Tu che di gel sei cinta*. Gedda and Freni combine passionately for *O soave fanciulla*, and Victoria de los Angeles and Jussi Bjoerling offer the Love scene from *Butterfly*. Room is also found for a fine 1957 mono version by Giuseppe di Stefano of *Che gelida manina*. The voices are given strong presence; the orchestral sound is vivid but not sumptuous. Excellent value at bargain price.

'Great arias' from: *La Bohème; La Fanciulla del West; Gianni Schicchi; Madama Butterfly; Manon Lescaut; La Rondine; Suor Angelica; Tosca; Turandot.*
(M) *** Decca 421 315-2. Freni, Pavarotti, Harwood, Tebaldi, Milnes, Caballé, Corelli, Nilsson, Sutherland, Chiara.

Opening with Freni's *One fine day* and following with Pavarotti's *Che gelida manina* and Freni returning for *Sì, mi chiamano Mimì*, this recital begins splendidly and offers many highlights, including Caballé's *Signora ascolta* and Sutherland's *In questa reggia* (both from *Turandot*). Maria Chiara is melting in arias from *Manon Lescaut* and *Suor Angelica*; and Tebaldi reminds us how ravishingly she could turn a phrase in *O mio babbino caro* from

Gianni Schicchi. Vivid sound throughout and few real disappointments.

Purcell, Henry (1659–95)

The Gordian Knot unty'd: suite. The Old Bachelor: suite. Sonata in D for trumpet and strings.
(M) **(*) Sony MDK 44644 [id.]. ECO, Leppard – VIVALDI: *4 Seasons*. **(*)

Those who like a rich orchestral tapestry in baroque music will be well satisfied with Leppard's collection of Purcell's theatre music, with its keenly resilient rhythms and nicely judged, expressive playing. The writing itself is consistently inventive. The forward balance and resonant acoustic produce attractively warm sound-quality – but it may be too well upholstered for those accustomed to the Academy of Ancient Music.

Harpsichord music (complete): *Suites Nos. 1–8* (with alternative *Prelude* for *Suite No. 4*). *Abdelazar: Jig. 4 Airs; Canary; Celebrate the festival: Gavotte. Dioclesian: Trumpet tune. The Double Dealer: Air. Hornpipe; The Indian Queen: Trumpet tune. 2 Marches; The Married Beau: March. The Old Bachelor: Hornpipe. Minuet; A New ground; New Irish tune; New minuet; New Scotch tune; Prelude in G min.; Round O; The Queen's dolour; Raise the voice: Minuet. Rigadoon; Saraband with division; Sefauchi's farewell; 2 Song tunes; Suite of 5 Lessons; Timon of Athens: Chaconne. Trumpet tune called The Cibell.*
(M) *** Saga SCD 9009/10. Robert Woolley (harpsichord).

Robert Woolley is a fine player. He was still in his mid-twenties when he made these recordings at the beginning of the 1980s. He plays copies of two eighteenth-century instruments by Benjamin Slade and his pupil, Thomas Hitchcock, and how well they sound! As usual, it is important not to set the volume level too high; then the harpsichord image is very natural and most attractive to the ear, crisply focused, full-bodied and presented within a nicely judged acoustic. The playing itself is vital and imaginative: Woolley can hold his own against senior and better-known rivals. The selection offers much that is not otherwise available, and Purcell's arrangements include many cherishable miniatures. A good deal of the music, including the *Suites*, derives from *A Choice Collection of Lessons* (published posthumously in 1696); other items are from *A Banquet of Musick* (1688) and many of the transcriptions come from the *Second Part of Musick's-Handmaid*, published by Playford in 1689, and were 'carefully revised and corrected by the same Mr Henry Purcell'. An indispensable set for those interested in English keyboard music.

VOCAL MUSIC

(i) *Come ye sons of art (Ode on the birthday of Queen Mary, 1694); Anthems:* (ii) *My beloved spake;* (iii) *Rejoice in the Lord alway (Bell anthem);* (iv) *Welcome to all the pleasures (Ode on Cecilia's Day, 1683).*
(M) **(*) Van. 08.8027.71 [OVC 8027]. Alfred Deller, Deller Consort; (i) Mark Deller, Mary Thomas, Bevan, Oriana Concert Ch. & O; (ii) Cantelo, English, Bevan; (iii; iv) Kalmar O; (iii) Thomas, Sheppard, Tear, Worthley; Oriana Concert O. (iv) Cantelo, McLoughlin, English, Grundy, Bevan.

An enjoyable anthology showing Deller at his finest in *Strike the viol*, with its engaging obbligato for two flutes (from *Come ye sons of art*) and *Here the Deities approve* in *Welcome to all pleasures*. The other soloists are good too, especially the tenor, Gerald English, in *Beauty thou scene of love* from the latter ode. The two anthems make a fine centrepiece, responding to the demand of Charles II for composers 'not to be too solemn' and to 'add symphonies, etc., with instruments' to their sacred vocal music. The *Bell anthem* is so called because of the repeated descending scales in the introduction. The warm, expressively played accompaniments are rather different from the effect one would achieve today with original instruments. The recording is closely balanced; although made at either Walthamstow or Cricklewood Church, the effect is not quite as spacious as one would expect, though pleasingly full. In the USA, this disc is very much in the upper-mid-price category.

(i) *Funeral music for Queen Mary;* (ii) Anthems and verse anthems: *Blessed are they that fear the Lord; Hear my prayer, O Lord; My beloved spake; Rejoice in the Lord alway; Remember not, Lord, our offences.*
(M) **(*) EMI CD-EMX 2172; *TC-EMX 2172*. Soloists, King's College Ch., Ledger; with (i) Philip Jones Brass Ens.; (ii) ASMF.

(i) *Funeral music for Queen Mary* (complete); *Jubilate Deo in D; Te Deum laudamus in D.* (ii) Verse anthems: *I was glad; O give thanks O Lord God of hosts.*
(M) **(*) Decca 430 263-2; *430 263-4*. (i) Bowman, Brett, Partridge, Forbes Robinson, Consort of Sackbuts, ECO; (ii) Esswood, Partridge, Anthony Dawson; (i; ii) St John's College, Cambridge, Ch., George Guest.

The *Funeral music for Queen Mary* consists of far more than the unforgettable *March* for lugrubious sackbuts with punctuating timpani (later repeated without timpani), which still sounds so modern to our ears. In the event, this brings the least effective performance on the 1972 Decca (originally Argo) collection, not as bitingly tragic as it might have been. The rest of the work is beautifully done, and so are the grand ceremonial settings of the *Te Deum* and *Jubilate*, although the solo contributions are a little uneven. The verse anthems – intended for Charles II's Chapel Royal – were recorded three years later. Though their direction could be more flamboyant, the singing is superb, with Paul Esswood and Ian Partridge especially fine among the soloists. The recording is vivid and atmospheric, though the focus on CD is not absolutely sharp.

Philip Ledger has the benefit of superbly expansive 1975 sound for his darkly memorable performance of the *March* with the Philip Jones Brass Ensemble, but the funeral anthems are given less alert performances than on the rival St John's reissue. However, the verse anthems are very impressively sung, and the remastered recording has much splendour on CD. The soloists are from the choir.

O sing unto the Lord; Praise the Lord, O Jerusalem; They that go down to the sea in ships (Anthems); *Ode: My heart is inditing; Te Deum and Jubilate Deo in D.*

(M) *** DG 427 124-2. Ch. of Christ Church Cathedral, Oxford, E. Concert, Preston.

This mid-priced collection includes, alongside favourite anthems, the big setting of the morning service canticles and the coronation ode, *My heart is inditing*. The performances are full of character, vigorous yet with the widest range of colour and feeling. The recording, made in London's Henry Wood Hall, is both spacious and well detailed.

Ode on St Cecilia's Day (Hail! bright Cecilia).

(M) *** DG 427 159-2 [id.]. Woolf, Esswood, Tatnell, Young, Rippon, Shirley-Quirk, Tiffin Ch., Amb. S., ECO, Mackerras.

A splendid all-male performance of Purcell's joyous *Ode* on DG, with an exceptionally incisive and vigorous choral contribution matched by fine solo singing. Simon Woolf is ideally cast here and the recording is excellent, although the balance between soloists and tutti does not make much distinction in volume between the smaller and the larger groups.

STAGE WORKS AND THEATRE MUSIC

Dido and Aeneas (complete).

❀ (M) *** Decca 425 720-2; *425 720-4*. Dame Janet Baker, Herincx, Clark, Sinclair, St Anthony Singers, ECO, Anthony Lewis.

(M) (***) EMI mono CDH7 61006-2 [id.]. Flagstad, Schwarzkopf, Hemsley, Mermaid Theatre Singers & O, Geraint Jones.

It was Janet Baker's 1962 recording of *Dido* for the Oiseau-Lyre label that established her as a recording star of the front rank: it is a truly great performance. The radiant beauty of the voice is obvious enough, but here she goes beyond that to show what stylishness and insight she can command. The emotion is implied, as it should be in this music, not injected in great uncontrolled gusts. Listen to the contrast between the angry, majestic words to Aeneas, *Away, away!*, and the dark grief of the following *But death alas I cannot shun*, and note how Baker contrasts dramatic soprano tone-colour with darkened contralto tone. Even subtler is the contrast between the opening phrase of *When I am laid in earth* and its repeat a few bars later: it is a model of graduated *mezza voce*. Then with the words *Remember me!*, delivered in a monotone, she subdues the natural vibrato to produce a white tone of hushed, aching intensity. When this record was first issued, we suggested that it would be surprising if a more deeply satisfying interpretation were recorded within the foreseeable future, and so it has proved: three decades later, this reissue still occupies the top of the recommended list. Anthony Lewis chooses fast speeds, but they challenge the ECO (Thurston Dart a model continuo player) to produce the crispest and lightest of playing which never sounds rushed. The other soloists and chorus give very good support. Herincx is a rather gruff Aeneas, but the only serious blemish is Monica Sinclair's Sorceress. She overcharacterizes in a way that is quite out of keeping with the rest of the production. Generally, by concentrating on musical values, Lewis and his singers and instrumentalists make the clear, simple dramatic point of the opera all the more telling, and it proves a most moving experience. Like most vintage Oiseau-Lyre recordings, this was beautifully engineered: the remastering thins out the upper range a little, but the effect is to increase the feeling of authenticity, for the ambient bloom remains.

Though Flagstad's magnificent voice may in principle be too weighty for this music – one might point to the latter-day equivalent of Jessye Norman – she scales it down superbly in her noble reading, which brings beautiful shading and masterly control of breath and tone. Schwarzkopf is brightly characterful as Belinda, and though Thomas Hemsley is not ideally sweet-toned as Aeneas, he sings very intelligently; even in this age of period performance, this traditional account under Geraint Jones sounds fresh and lively still, not at all heavy.

The mono sound, obviously limited, yet captures the voices vividly, and this above all is Flagstad's set.

The Fairy Queen (complete).

(M) *** Decca 433 163-2 (2) [id.]. Vyvyan, Bowman, Pears, Wells, Partridge, Shirley-Quirk, Brannigan, Norma Burrowes, Amb. Op. Ch., ECO, Britten.

The Fairy Queen, a classic example of a masterpiece rendered moribund by changed theatrical conditions, possesses a score which is crammed with the finest Purcellian inspiration which, happily, CD can help to keep alive. Britten's version from the early 1970s used a newly reshaped arrangement of the music made by Britten himself in collaboration with Imogen Holst and Peter Pears. The original collection of individual pieces is here grouped into four satisfying sections: *Oberon's birthday*, *Night and silence*, the *Sweet passion* and the *Epithalamium.* This version was first heard at the Aldeburgh Festival in 1967, and here the authentic glow of a Maltings performance (1971 vintage) is beautifully conveyed in the playing, the singing and the recording. Philip Ledger's imaginative harpsichord continuo is placed too far to one side, but otherwise the sound can scarcely be faulted. The cast is consistently satisfying, with Peter Pears and Jennifer Vyvyan surviving from the much earlier mono version of Anthony Lewis on Oiseau-Lyre.

(i) *The Indian Queen* (incidental music); (ii) *King Arthur* (complete).

❀ (M) *** Decca 433 166-2 (2) [id.]. (i) Cantelo, Wilfred Brown, Tear, Partridge, Keyte, St Anthony Singers, ECO, Mackerras; (ii) Morison, Harper, Mary Thomas, Whitworth, Wilfred Brown, Galliver, Cameron, Anthony, Alan, St Anthony Singers, Philomusica of L., Lewis.

The Indian Queen is another of the Purcellian entertainments that fit into no modern category, a semi-opera. The impossible plot matters little, for Purcell's music contains many delights; indeed the score seems to get better as it proceeds. This Decca Serenata (originally Oiseau-Lyre) version dates from 1966 and the recording, from a vintage era, remains first rate. With stylish singing and superb direction and accompaniment (Raymond Leppard's harpsichord continuo playing must be singled out), this is an invaluable reissue. Charles Mackerras shows himself a strong and vivid as well as scholarly Purcellian.

The Rosette, however, is for the pioneering 1959 set (also Oiseau-Lyre) of *King Arthur*, fully worthy to stand alongside the companion recording of *Dido and Aeneas*, made three years later – see above. Here the success of the interpretation does not centre on the contribution of one inspired artist, but rather on teamwork among a number of excellent singers and on the stylish and sensitive overall direction of Anthony Lewis. Oiseau-Lyre's excellent stereo also plays a bit part. This was an early set, but one would never guess it from the pleasing ambience and the sophistication of the antiphonal effects. A very happy example is the chorus *This way, that way*, when the opposing spirits (good and evil) make a joint attempt to entice the King, while the famous freezing aria will surely send a shiver through the most warm-blooded listener. Indeed *King Arthur* contains some of Purcell's most memorable inspiration, not just the items mentioned above and the famous song, *Fairest isle*, but a whole range of lively and atmospheric numbers which are admirably realized here by a very strong cast.

Theatre music (collection).

Disc 1: *Abdelazar: Overture & suite. Distressed Innocence: Overture & suite. The Gordian Knot Untied: Overture & suite; The Married Beau: Overture & suite. Sir Anthony Love: Overture & suite.*

Disc 2: *Bonduca: Overture and suite. Circe: suite. The Old Bachelor: Overture and suite. The Virtuous Wife: Overture and suite.*

Disc 3: *Amphitrion: Overture and suite; Overture in G min.; Don Quixote: suite.*

Disc 4: *Overture in G min. The Double Dealer: Overture and suite. Henry II, King of England: In vain, 'gainst love, in vain I strove. The Richmond Heiress: Behold the man. The Rival Sisters: Overture; 3 songs. Tyranic Love: Hark my Damilcar!* (duet); *Ah! how sweet it is to love. Theodosius*: excerpts. *The Wives' Excuse:* excerpts.

Disc 5: *Overture in D min.; Cleomenes, the Spartan Hero: No, no, poor suff'ring heart. A Dialogue between Thirsis and Daphne: Why, my Daphne, why complaining?. The English Lawyer: My wife has a tongue:* excerpts. *A Fool's Preferment:* excerpts. *The History of King Richard II: Retir'd from any mortal's sight. The Indian Emperor: I look'd and saw within. The Knight of Malta: At the close of the ev'ning. The Libertine:* excerpts. *The Marriage-hater Match'd: As soon as the chaos . . . How vile are the sordid intregues. The Massacre of Paris: The genius lo* (2 settings). *Oedipus:* excerpts. *Regulus: Ah me! to many deaths. Sir Barnaby Whigg: Blow, blow, Boreas, blow. Sophonisba: Beneath the poplar's shadow. The Wives' excuse:* excerpts.

Disc 6: *Chacony; Pavans Nos. 1–5; Trio sonata for violin, viola de gamba & organ. Aureng-Zebe: I see, she flies me. The Canterbury Guests: Good neighbours why?. Epsom Wells: Leave these useless arts. The Fatal Marriage: 2 songs. The Female Virtuosos: Love, thou art best. Love Triumphant: How happy's the husband. The Maid's Last Prayer:* excerpts. *The Mock Marriage: Oh! how you protest; Man is for the woman made. Oroonoko: Celemene, pray tell me. Pausanius: Song (Sweeter than roses) and duet. Rule a Wife and Have a Wife: There's not a swain. The Spanish Friar: Whilst I with grief.*

(M) *** O-L 425 893-2 (6). Kirkby, Nelson, Lane, Roberts, Lloyd, Bowman, Hill, Covey-Crump, Elliott, Byers, Bamber, Pike, David Thomas, Keyte, Shaw, George, Taverner Ch., AAM, Hogwood.

This set of six CDs creates an anthology from the contents of a selective but wide-ranging series of LPs recorded between 1974 and 1983. Most of the music Purcell wrote for the theatre is relatively little heard, and one must remember that the 'suites' assembled here were not originally intended for continuous performance. If in the earlier discs they do not provide the variety and range one would expect from works conceived as a whole, much of the music comes up with striking freshness in these performances using authentic instruments. As well as the charming dances and more ambitious overtures, as the series proceeds we are offered more extended scenas with soloists and chorus, of which the nine excerpts from *Theodosius*, an early score (1680), are a particularly entertaining example. Before that, on Disc 3 we have already had the highly inventive Overture and incidental music for *Don Quixote.* Purcell was one of three contributors on this occasion (there were three plays to service, all by Thomas D'Urfey and based on Cervantes' famous novel). Though the music was written at high speed, much of it was attractively lively and it deserves to be resurrected in such stylish performances, with much enchanting singing from both the soprano soloists, Emma Kirkby and Judith Nelson. Disc 4 also includes a delightful duet from *The Richmond Heiress*, representing a flirtation in music. There are other attractive duets elsewhere, for instance the nautical *Blow, blow, Boreas, blow* from *Sir Barnaby Whigg*, which could fit admirably into *HMS Pinafore* (Rogers Covey-Crump and David Thomas) and the jovial *As soon as the chaos* from *The Marriage-hater Match'd.* In *Ah me! to many deaths* from *Regulus*, Judith Nelson is at her most eloquent while, earlier on Disc 5, she sings charmingly the familiar *Nymphs and shepherds*, which comes from *The Libertine*, a particularly fine score with imaginative use of the brass. The equally famous *Music for a while*, beautifully sung by James Bowman, derives from *Oedipus.* The last disc again shows Judith Nelson at her finest in a series of arias, but it also includes a splendidly boisterous Quartet from *The Canterbury Guests.* The collection is appropriately rounded off by members of the Academy giving first-class performances of some of Purcell's instrumental music, ending with the famous *Chacony.* The sharpness of inspiration comes over very compellingly on original instruments, though Hogwood tends to prefer tempi faster than one might expect. The sound is admirably fresh throughout, with clean transfers retaining the warmth and bite of the original analogue recordings, yet without adding any abrasive edge. The discs are comprehensively documented and with full texts included.

Quilter, Roger (1877–1953)

A Children's overture.

(M) ** EMI CDM7 64131-2; *EG 764131-4.* Light Music Society O, Sir Vivian Dunn (with TOMLINSON: *Suite of English folk dances*) – HELY-HUTCHINSON: *Carol Symphony;* VAUGHAN WILLIAMS: *Fantasia on Christmas carols.* **

This charming overture, skilfully constructed from familiar nursery rhymes, hitherto has not been available on CD except in an old mono recording. Its neglect is inexplicable. Sir Vivian Dunn gives a good if not remarkable performance and the recording too is pleasing rather than outstanding. But the music itself is a delight. Ernest Tomlinson's suite of six folk-tunes, simply presented and tastefully scored, makes an attractive bonus. Again the sound is acceptable but could be richer.

Rabaud, Henri (1873–1949)

Divertissement sur les chansons russes, Op. 2; Églogue (Poème virgilien), Op. 7; Marouf, Savetier du Caire (Danses); La Procession nocturne.

(M) **(*) EMI CDM7 63951-2 [id.]. O Philharmonique des pays de Loire, Pierre Dervaux.

Henri Rabaud is best known to music-lovers for his orchestration of the *Dolly Suite* by Fauré, whom he succeeded as Director of the Paris Conservatoire. His music is generally neglected, though both *La Procession nocturne* and the opera *Maroûf, Savetier du Caire* were recorded in the LP era. The *Dances* from the opera are an appealing exercise in exoticism; but by far the best pieces are the sensitively scored *La Proces-*

sion nocturne and the *Églogue*. Rabaud was a pupil of Massenet, and his musical language belongs far more to the world of Franck and d'Indy than to that of Debussy. Good performances from the Loire orchestra under Pierre Dervaux; they play with evident sympathy and acceptable, if reverberant, recording. An interesting disc for anyone who likes exploring the byways of French music.

Rachmaninov, Sergei (1873–1943)

Caprice bohémien, Op. 12; The Isle of the dead (symphonic poem), *Op. 29; Prince Rostislav* (symphonic poem after Alexei Tolstoy); *The Rock* (fantasy for orchestra), *Op. 7; Scherzo in F; Symphonic dances, Op. 45; Vocalise, Op. 34/14; Youth Symphony;* (i) *The Bells, Op. 35; 3 Russian folksongs, Op. 41; Spring* (cantata), *Op. 20.*

(B) **(*) VoxBox (3) [CD3X 3002]. St Louis SO, Slatkin; (i) with Voketaitis, Christos, Planté & Ch.

This three-disc bargain box brings an invaluable collection of all Rachmaninov's orchestral works other than the symphonies. Recorded in 1979–80, it covers not only the well-established works like *The Isle of the dead* and the magnificent choral symphony, *The Bells*, but also such rarities as the *Caprice bohémien* (one of the less inspired pieces) and youthful works such as the *Scherzo in F major* (like Mendelssohn with a Russian accent) and the first-movement structure labelled *Youth Symphony*. At the other end of Rachmaninov's career come the *3 Russian folksongs* (sung rather slackly by the St Louis chorus) and his last work of all, the *Symphonic dances*. The playing of the St Louis Symphony is first rate, with all sections, notably the violins, able to respond to Slatkin's subtle use of rubato and with some excellent individual playing, as in the cor anglais solo in the last movement of *The Bells*. The recording is refined and well detailed but fails to make its full impact when not only is the chorus too distantly balanced – underlining an absence of bite in much of the singing – but the orchestral sound lacks immediacy. Nevertheless this box adds up to more than the sum of its component parts. It still awaits issue in the UK.

Piano concertos Nos. 1–4.

(M) *(**) Decca 425 576-2 (2) [id.]. Ashkenazy, LSO, Previn.

Piano concertos Nos. 1–4; Rhapsody on a theme of Paganini, Op. 43.

(M) ** VoxBox 1154942 (2) [CDX 5008]. Simon, St Louis O, Slatkin.

Decca's digital remastering of Ashkenazy's 1972 set with Previn sounds disappointingly brash. The original analogue sound cast a warm glow over the proceedings and any lack of clarity was more than compensated for by the rich atmospheric ambience. Now the sound-picture, including the piano image, is starkly clear and brilliant, and the strings have lost much of their bloom. The *Third Concerto* was originally bathed in a pleasing haze; now it is much clearer, but the fortissimo massed violins are strident. The performances are one of Ashkenazy's major achievements. The *Second Concerto*'s slow movement is particularly beautiful; and the individuality and imagination of the solo playing throughout, combined with the poetic feeling of Previn's accompaniments, provide special rewards. But the recording demands the aural equivalent of dark glasses.

On a two-CD VoxBox, Abbey Simon gives well-turned-out performances of the concertos and the *Rhapsody on a theme of Paganini* with the Saint Louis Orchestra under Leonard Slatkin, recorded in very decent analogue sound and offered at bargain price. There is some musicianly and often brilliant playing from all concerned, for example in the first movement of No. 3, where he plays the cadenza that Rachmaninov himself recorded – but, not to put too fine a point upon it, there are other accounts on the market that are higher-voltage and more commanding. It is all highly accomplished, but less than riveting.

Piano concertos Nos. 1 in F sharp min., Op. 1; 3 in D min., Op. 30.

(M) ** DG 429 715-2; *429 715-4* [id.]. Tamás Vásáry, LSO, Ahronovich.

Ahronovich's direction is nothing if not impetuous, and this DG performance of the *First Concerto* is full of vigour, with its bursts of vivid romanticism. Vásáry's more introvert manner seems to fit well within this dashing framework and there is no doubt about the freshness of the music-making. In the *Third Concerto*, Vásáry uses the longer version of the first-movement cadenza but not always with complete spontaneity. The slow movement is indulgent, too, and lacks momentum. Vásáry's playing itself is clean, often gentle in style, but the conductor's extremes of tempi are less appropriate here than in the *First Concerto*. Taken as a whole, the performance is not without its poetry and excitement (especially in the finale) but, in the last analysis, its impetuosity of mood remains unsatisfying.

Piano concerto Nos. 1 in F sharp min., Op. 1; 4 in G min., Op. 40.

(M) **(*) Decca 425 004-2; *425 004-4*. Ashkenazy, LSO, Previn.

Piano concertos Nos. 1 in F sharp min., Op. 1; 4 in G min., Op. 40; Rhapsody on a theme of Paganini, Op. 43.
(M) **(*) Sony SBK 46541 [id.]. Philippe Entremont, Phd. O, Ormandy.

Entremont gives a marvellously dashing account of both early and late concertos, rivalling the composer himself in the sheer effrontery of his bravura. By rights, no ten fingers could possibly play like this and, as with Rachmaninov himself, the speeds have one on the edge of one's seat. Where Entremont falls short – and he is not helped by the American recordings (dating from 1963 and 1961 respectively) which boosts pianissimos – is in the gentler music, where he could be more affectionate. The recording quality could be sweeter too, and the piano tone is rather clattery. In the *Rhapsody on a theme of Paganini*, recorded in in 1958, Ormandy oversees a strongly directed performance, with Entremont rising excitingly to the challenge. The balance here is rather more natural, and if overall there have to be some reservations about the brightly lit and larger-than-life sound-quality, this remains vividly compelling playing, and the coupling is very generous.

On Decca, the transfers of Nos. 1 and 4 are the most satisfactory of Ashkenazy's set; the brilliance is less plangent than in Nos. 2 and 3, and the performances are certainly exciting.

Piano concerto No. 2 in C min., Op. 18.
(M) *** EMI Dig. CDD7 63903-2 [id.]; *ET 763903-4*. Cécile Ousset, CBSO, Rattle – GRIEG: *Concerto*. **(*)

Cécile Ousset gives a powerful, red-blooded performance in the grand manner, warmly supported by Simon Rattle and the CBSO. Her rubato may often be extreme but it never sounds studied, always convincingly spontaneous; and the EMI recording copes well with the range of the playing. Those wanting a coupling with the Grieg *Concerto* will find Ousset's account similarly strong.

Piano concertos Nos. 2 in C min., Op. 18; 3 in D min., Op. 30.
(M) *** Chan. CHAN 6507; *MBTD 6507* [id.]. Earl Wild, RPO, Horenstein.

Piano concertos Nos. (i) *2 in C min, Op. 18;* (ii) *3 in D min., Op. 30. Preludes: in C sharp min., Op. 3/2; in E flat, Op. 23/6.*
❀ (M) *** Mercury 432 759-2 [id.]. Byron Janis; (i) Minneapolis SO; (ii) LSO, Antal Dorati.

We have long admired these Mercury performances; coupled together, they make an unbeatable bargain, representing Byron Janis's very finest record. Janis has just as much technical command as Earl Wild and he is equally compulsive, but his ability to relax without loss of concentration is especially telling in the music of Rachmaninov. He has the full measure of this music: his shapely lyrical phasing and natural response to the ebb and flow of the melodic lines is a constant source of pleasure. The climax of the first movement of the *C minor Concerto* is very exciting, but the closing section is no less memorable, and he is equally tender in the coda of the *Adagio*, beautifully played with Dorati providing admirable support. Then in the finale there is all the sparkling bravura one could ask for, but the great lyrical tune is made beguilingly poetic, so that the bold final statement is the more telling. Although the 1960 recording has plenty of ambience, the Minneapolis violins lack the richness of the LSO strings, recorded at Watford in 1961. The simple opening of the *Third Concerto* benefits from the extra warmth, and Janis lets the theme unwind with appealing spontaneity. The romantic glow which Dorati infuses into the blossoming second subject is matched by the atmosphere of the *Adagio*, and in the great closing climax of the finale the passion is built up – not too hurriedly – to the greatest possible tension. Janis makes two cuts (following the composer's own practice), one of about ten bars in the second movement and a rather longer one in the finale. Two favourite *Preludes*, with the *E flat* coming first, most persuasively played, make an excellent encore.

Earl Wild's performances derive from a complete set produced by Charles Gerhardt for RCA and recorded at the Kingsway Hall in 1965, to be issued subsequently in a subscription series through *Reader's Digest* magazine, and this mid-priced reissue must be counted a great success. The first movement of the *C minor Concerto* is faster than usual, but the expressive fervour is in no doubt; the *Adagio*, too, blossoms readily. The *Third Concerto* is among the very finest versions of this work on record and, in terms of bravura, is in the Horowitz class. The digital remastering is a great success, the overall balance is truthful and the hall ambience brings a rich orchestral image and plenty of brilliance. However, unfortunately there are three cuts, one in the second movement and two in the third, a total of 55 bars.

Piano concerto No. 2 in C min.; Rhapsody on a theme of Paganini, Op. 43.
(M) *** Decca 417 702-2 [id.]. Ashkenazy, LSO, Previn.
(BB) *** Naxos Dig. 8.550117. Jandó, Budapest SO, Lehel.

(B) *** CfP Dig. CD-CFP 9017; *TC-CFP 4383*. Tirimo, Philh. O, Levi.

(B) **(*) Decca 417 880-2; *417 880-4*. Katchen, LSO, Solti; or LPO, Boult.

Piano concerto No. 2; Rhapsody on a theme of Paganini; Vocalise, Op. 34/14 (arr. Kocsis).

(M) ** Ph. Dig. 432 044-2; *432 044-4*. Kocsis, San Francisco SO, Edo de Waart.

Decca's recoupling of Ashkenazy's earlier recordings with Previn is a very desirable CD indeed. At mid-price it makes a clear first choice. In the *Concerto*, Ashkenazy's opening tempo, like Richter's, is slow, but the tension is finely graduated towards the great climax; and the gentle, introspective mood of the *Adagio* is very beautiful indeed. The finale is broad and spacious rather than electrically exciting, but the scintillating, unforced bravura provides all the sparkle necessary. The *Rhapsody* too is outstandingly successful, the opening variations exhilaratingly paced and the whole performance moving forward in a single sweep, with the eighteenth variation making a great romantic blossoming at the centre. The Kingsway Hall sound is rich and full-bodied in the best analogue sense; unlike the complete set from which this is taken, the digital remastering has here retained all the bloom, especially in the slow movement of the *Concerto*, among the most beautiful on record. Detail is somewhat sharper in the *Rhapsody*; in the *Concerto*, however, atmosphere rather than clarity is the predominating factor, unlike the remastered complete set above, where the focus is much sharper and the quality less sweet.

Outstanding in the Naxos super-bargain series, Jenö Jandó's performances of both works are strongly recommendable. Although the *Concerto* opens modestly, the tempo relatively measured, it moves to a splendid climax, the piano astride the orchestra in a most exciting way. Jandó has the full measure of the ebb and flow of the Rachmaninovian phraseology, and the slow movement is romantically expansive, the reprise particularly beautiful, while the finale has plenty of dash and ripe, lyrical feeling. The *Rhapsody* is played brilliantly, as fine as any performance in the catalogue. The digital recording is satisfyingly balanced, with a bold piano image and a full, resonant orchestral tapestry, although it is a pity that the variations in the *Rhapsody* are not separately cued.

Concentrated and thoughtful, deeply expressive yet never self-indulgent, Tirimo is outstanding in both the *Concerto* and the *Rhapsody*, making this one of the most desirable versions of this favourite coupling, irrespective of price. Speeds for the outer movements of the *Concerto* are on the fast side, yet Tirimo's feeling for natural rubato makes them sound natural, never breathless, while the sweetness and repose of the middle movement are exemplary. The digital recording is full, clear and well balanced.

Katchen's coupling comes from 1958/60 and, while the Decca recording remains clear and vivid, the sound is slightly dated in the upper range of the *Concerto*, though the violins sound admirably full in the *Rhapsody*. The piano timbre is excellent. Katchen's accounts of both works offer drama and excitement in plenty – the outer movements of the *Concerto* reach the highest pitch of excitement, with bravura very much to the fore. Solti makes an excellent partner here; and Boult sees that the *Rhapsody* is superbly shaped and has diversity and wit, as well as romantic flair.

Zoltán Kocsis has fleet fingers and here combines dash with panache. But in No. 2 he gives the listener all too little time to savour incidental beauties or to surrender to the melancholy of the slow movement. He is just too carried away with his own virtuosity and, although this playing is thrilling enough, it is not the whole story.

(i) *Piano concerto No. 2 in C min.; Rhapsody on a theme of Paganini. Lilacs, Op. 21/5; Moment musical in E min., Op. 16/4; Preludes Nos. 16 in G, Op. 32/5; 21 in B min., Op. 32/10.* arr. of MENDELSSOHN: *Scherzo from A Midsummer Night's Dream.*

(M) **(*) EMI stereo/mono CDH7 63788-2. Benno Moiseiwitsch; (i) Philh. O, Rignold.

Older readers will remember Moiseiwitsch's 'plum-label' 78-r.p.m. discs of Rachmaninov's *Second Piano concerto*, with Walter Goehr, which some collectors prized more highly than the composer's own recording on the more prestigious 'red label'. Moiseiwitsch plays pretty impressively, too, on this 1955 coupling of the *Concerto* and *Rhapsody* and, although Hugo Rignold does not exert an ideal grip over the readings and there is less dramatic intensity than before, there is no lack of brilliance or concentration in the solo contribution; with superb Philharmonia playing, the first-movement climax is expansive and exciting. The early stereo sound, made at the Abbey Road Studio, is astonishly full and vivid, with a very lifelike piano quality. The solo items, recorded much earlier in mono, include a brilliant account of Rachmaninov's Mendelssohn arrangement, which Moiseiwitsch regarded as the best recording he ever made.

(i) *Piano concerto No. 2 in C min.;* (ii) *Preludes Nos. 3 in B flat; 8 in C min., Op. 23/2 & 7; 13 in*

B flat min., Op. 32/2 (CD only: (i) *Piano concerto No. 1 in F sharp min., Op. 1*).
(B) ** DG Compact Classics 413 850-2 (2); *413 850-4*. (i) Vásáry, LSO, Ahronovitch; (ii) Sviatoslav Richter – LISZT: *Concertos Nos. 1–2* etc. **(*)

Vásáry and Ahronovitch make quite an effective partnership in the *C minor Concerto* and the performance of the first movement has a fine climax. But after that the voltage is lower, and the *Adagio* does not distil the degree of poetry which makes the finest versions so memorable. The DG recording is bold and colourful, but the piano timbre is drier for Richter's masterly performances of the three *Preludes*, used as a makeweight on this Compact Classics chrome cassette. On the equivalent pair of CDs, the *First Concerto* is added as a substantial bonus, which is also available coupled with No. 3 – see above.

(i) *Piano concerto No. 2 in C min., Op. 18. Preludes Nos. 6 in G min., Op. 23/5; 16 in G, Op. 32/5; 23 in G sharp min., Op. 32/12.*
(M) ** EMI CDM7 63525-2; *EG 763525-4*. John Ogdon, (i) Philh. O, Pritchard – TCHAIKOVSKY: *Piano concerto No. 1*. **

John Ogdon's 1962 performance of the *C minor Concerto* is sensitive and introspective, and it is easy to enjoy the relaxed, lyrical beauty of the first two movements. But the partnership with Pritchard did not strike any sparks, and there is a lack of impulse and romantic virility, especially in the finale. The recording still sounds excellent, both in the *Concerto* and in the *Preludes*, which are splendidly played: the *G major* is especially delectable.

Piano concerto No. 3 in D min., Op. 30.
(M) *(*) EMI Dig. CD-EMX 2171; *TC-EMX 2171*. Dimitris Sgouros, BPO, Simonov.

Dimitris Sgouros made this record in 1984 when he was fifteen. It was his first concerto recording and much of the playing is pretty dazzling as such. But, however remarkable it may be, the standards of the gramophone differ from those of the concert hall; much of the musical meaning of this concerto seems to escape him and the bravura passages are thus rendered relatively ineffective. Compare the main theme in the hands of a Rachmaninov or a Horowitz, and it is evident that Sgouros is an artist of enormous facility and promise, rather than one of fulfilment. He plays the second cadenza, rather than the shorter one chosen by Rachmaninov. The digital recording itself is serviceable rather than distinguished: the Berlin Philharmonic does not produce its characteristic rich sonority for Yuri Simonov.

(i) *Piano concerto No. 3;* (ii) *Rhapsody on a theme of Paganini, Op. 43.*
(M) **(*) BMG/RCA GD 86524 (RCA 6524-2-RG]. (i) Ashkenazy, Phd. O, Ormandy; (ii) Pennario, Boston Pops O, Fiedler.

(i) *Piano concerto No. 3 in D min.; Preludes: in C sharp min., Op. 3/2; in B flat; in G min., Op. 23/2 & 5; in B min.; in D flat, Op. 32/10 & 13.*
(M) **(*) Decca 417 764-2 [id.]. Ashkenazy; (i) LSO, Previn.

(i) *Piano concerto No. 3. Sonata No. 2 in B flat min., Op. 36; Moment musical in E flat min., Op. 16/2; Polka; Prelude in C, Op. 32/5.*
(M) (***) BMG/RCA GD 87754 [7754-2-RC-]. Vladimir Horowitz; (i) with RCA SO, Reiner.

Horowitz's RCA account with Reiner dates from 1951. As a performance it is full of poetry, yet electrifying in its excitement. In spite of its dated sound and a less than ideal balance, its magic comes over and it is to be preferred to his later performance with Ormandy. The *Sonata* comes from live concerts in 1980 and is also pretty electrifying. He plays the conflation he made (and which Rachmaninov approved) of the 1913 original and the 1931 revision plus a few further retouchings he subsequently added. An indispensable part of any Rachmaninov collection which, in its digitally remastered form, sounds better than it has before.

Ashkenazy has recorded this concerto four times; as a work, it seems to prove elusive for him. His very first recording with Fistoulari had ardour and spontaneity. So too had his 1976 RCA version, recorded in Philadelphia with Eugene Ormandy. If one can adjust to its unflattering piano-sound, then the mid-1970s performance has much to offer: it has great charisma, and Ormandy, too, is at his finest. The coupling is a prodigiously brilliant account of the *Rhapsody* from Leonard Pennario and Fiedler which is certainly compulsive; the snag here is that the forward balance, coupled to the bright digital remastering, makes orchestral fortissimos sound shrill.

Ashkenazy's account with Previn has more in common with his most recent, digital version conducted by Haitink. It has moments of undoubted insight and touches of sheer magic, but in the last analysis it remains not quite satisfying as a whole. The remastering for CD is very successful, with the sound-picture clearer and firmer yet still warmly atmospheric. The well-chosen selection of *Preludes* is taken from his complete full-price set.

(i) *Piano concerto No. 3; Rhapsody on a theme of Paganini;* (ii) *The Isle of the dead, Op. 29.*
(B) **(*) DG Compact Classics *419 392-4* [id.].

(i) Vásáry, LSO, Ahronovitch; (ii) BPO, Maazel.

Vásáry's Compact Classics tape is excellent value, as it also includes Maazel's fine version of *The Isle of the dead.* In the *Concerto* Vásáry uses the longer version of the first-movement cadenza; his playing is highly musical, clean and often gentle in style. The impetuous Ahronovitch offers some extremes of tempi; taken as a whole, however, this performance has both poetry and excitement (especially in the finale). The conductor's chimerical style is more obviously suited to the *Rhapsody*, with its opening faster than usual and with strong contrasts of tempo and mood between brilliant and lyrical variations. The sound is very good.

The Isle of the dead, Op. 29; Symphonic dances, Op. 45.
(M) *** Decca Dig. 430 733-2; *430 733-4.* Concg. O, Ashkenazy.

The Isle of the dead, Op. 29; Symphonic dances, Op. 45; Aleko: Intermezzo & Women's dance. Vocalise, Op. 34/14.
(M) *** EMI CDM7 69025-2 [id.]. LSO, Previn.

Ashkenazy's is a superb coupling, rich and powerful in playing and interpretation. One here recognizes *The Isle of the dead* as among the very finest of Rachmaninov's orchestral works, relentless in its ominous build-up, while at generally fast speeds the *Symphonic dances* have extra darkness and intensity too, suggesting no relaxation whatever at the end of Rachmaninov's career. The splendid digital recording highlights both the passion and the fine precision of the playing. Previn's alternative, analogue EMI CD offers extra music, but the Decca remains a marginal first choice.

Previn's original full-priced issue (from 1976) offered the same coupling as Ashkenazy, but now it has been digitally remastered with great success and the vividly wide-ranging sound is highly spectacular, among EMI's most successful analogue reissues. The added clarity and sparkle have a balancing weight in the bass and the effect is very exciting. The addition of the *Aleko* excerpts, plus a fine lyrical account of the *Vocalise*, makes a generous mid-priced CD, which competes in every respect with Ashkenazy's digital alternative.

Rhapsody on a theme of Paganini, Op. 43.
(M) *** BMG/RCA GD 87945 [7945-2-RG]. Van Cliburn, Phd. O, Ormandy – CHOPIN: *Piano concerto No. 1.* *

Van Cliburn, in repertoire for which he seems ideally suited, gives an excitingly committed account of Rachmaninov's *Rhapsody*, with much attractive detail: the scherzando playing in Variation 15 is a delight. The romantic blossoming at Variation 18 brings a wonderful expansion from Ormandy and the Philadelphia strings, a moment beautifully prepared in the previous section. With excellent 1970 recording, this stands alongside Van Cliburn's outstanding earlier coupling at full price of Rachmaninov's *Second Concerto* and Tchaikovsky's *First* with Reiner. All the variations are cued separately.

Symphonic dances, Op. 45; Vocalise, Op. 34/14.
(B) ** VoxBox (2) [CDX 5035]. Dallas SO, Johanos – COPLAND: *Billy the Kid* etc.; IVES: *Holidays Symphony.* **

It seems a curious idea to couple Rachmaninov with Copland and Ives, although Donald Johanos seems equally at home with all three composers. His Rachmaninov, however, is not distinctive. These are pleasant, mellow performances, recorded in a reverberant acoustic without too much bite. Either Ashkenazy or Previn is preferable.

Symphonies Nos. 1–3.
(B) **(*) VoxBox (2) [CDX 5034]. St Louis SO, Slatkin.

Symphonies Nos. 1–3; Youth Symphony (1891).
(M) *** Decca Dig. 421 065-2 (3). Concg. O, Ashkenazy.

Ashkenazy's set – offered at mid-price – can be given an unqualified recommendation. The performances, passionate and volatile, are intensely Russian; the only possible reservation concerns the slow movement of the *Second*, where the clarinet solo is less ripe than in some versions. Elsewhere there is drama, energy and drive, balanced by much delicacy of feeling, while the Concertgebouw strings produce great ardour for Rachmaninov's long-breathed melodies. The vivid Decca sound within the glowing Concertgebouw ambience is ideal for the music.

Having all three of Rachmaninov's *Symphonies* in ripely idiomatic performances on two budget-priced VoxBox discs makes an excellent bargain, even if the recording lacks something in immediacy. Recorded between 1976 and 1979, they reveal that already, early in his career as the St Louis music director, Slatkin had welded this second-oldest American orchestra into a most responsive ensemble, able in Rachmaninov's ripest melodies to play with both polish and a warmly flexible expressiveness. The sound in No. 1, presumably recorded last, is rather fuller and more forward than in the other two symphonies, but there is plenty of detail in each. This does not match the digital Decca/Ashkenazy box, but it is excellent value.

Symphony No. 2 in E min., Op. 27.
(B) *** Pickwick Dig. PCD 904; *CIMPC 904* [id.]. LSO, Rozhdestvensky.
(BB) **(*) BMG/RCA VD 60132 [60132-RV]. Phd. O, Ormandy.

Symphony No. 2; The Isle of the dead, Op. 29.
(M) **(*) DG Dig. 429 490-2; *429 490-4*. BPO, Maazel.

Symphony No. 2; The Rock, Op. 7.
(BB) **(*) Naxos Dig. 8.550272 [id.]. Slovak RSO (Bratislava), Stephen Gunzenhauser.

Rozhdestvensky gives a very Tchaikovskian reading of Rachmaninov's *E minor Symphony*. There is plenty of vitality, but it is the conductor's affectionate warmth in the secondary material of the first two movements, with the big string melodies blossoming voluptuously, that is especially memorable. The slow movement, after a beguiling opening clarinet solo, has a climax of spacious intensity, and its power is almost overwhelming; the finale is flamboyantly broadened at the end, and the feeling of apotheosis is very much in the Tchaikovsky mould. With the LSO responding superbly, this is a most satisfying account, and the richness, brilliance and weight of the recording, made in All Saints', Tooting, adds to the compulsion of the music-making.

Gunzenhauser directs the Slovak Radio Symphony Orchestra – on this showing not quite so refined a band as the Slovak Philharmonic, also from Bratislava – in a warmly expressive reading of the Rachmaninov *Second*, with rubato consistently persuasive and idiomatic-sounding. The playing at times lacks bite, and the great clarinet solo in the slow movement is balanced too far back, but the red-bloodedness of Rachmaninov's inspiration is never in doubt. The slow movement brings sumptuous climaxes, and the finale is given attractively bouncy treatment at a more measured speed than usual. Highly recommendable at super-bargain price, with very good sound.

From the brooding opening, Maazel moves the allegro away very swiftly (ignoring the composer's marking of *moderato*) and the powerful forward impulse creates considerable electricity. The scherzo is crisp and brilliant, while the *Adagio*, with long-breathed phrasing, reaches a powerful climax, only to be capped in the exhilaratingly brilliant finale with an apotheosis of even greater fervour. The brightly lit digital recording enhances the excitement; but in this work one ideally needs a warmer, more sumptuous sound. *The Isle of the dead* makes a generous fill-up. Again choosing a fast speed, Maazel's view is less sombre than usual, but the climaxes are most powerful and the result is intensely compelling.

In 1973 Ormandy made his fourth recorded performance of the *E minor Symphony*. No doubt prodded by rivals on record, he opened out all the old disfiguring cuts and, with refined string-playing and expansive recording, produced a characteristically exciting, full-blown performance. The Philadelphia strings certainly make it involving and their body of tone is well conveyed on CD. Next to the finest versions, however, it lacks subtlety in expressiveness, for Ormandy in this music tends to pull out all the emotional stops too soon.

Symphony No. 3 in A min., Op. 44.
(M) *** EMI CDM7 69564-2; *EG 769564-4*. LSO, Previn – SHOSTAKOVICH: *Symphony No. 6*. ***

Previn's EMI CD brings an outstanding performance; the digital remastering brings plenty of body alongside the sharpened detail, even if some of the amplitude has been exchanged for clarity. There is much that is elusive in this highly original structure, and Previn conveys the purposefulness of the writing at every point, revelling in the richness, but clarifying textures. The LSO has rarely displayed its virtuosity more brilliantly in the recording studio, and, with its generous Shostakovich coupling, this is first choice for this symphony.

Symphony No. 3 in A min., Op. 44; Symphonic dances, Op. 45.
(M) **(*) DG Dig. 429 981-2 [id.]. BPO, Maazel.

Maazel takes a highly personal view of both these Rachmaninov masterpieces. The symphony is unusually fierce and intense, with refined, incisive playing spotlit by the overtly clear digital recording. The result is sharper and tougher than one expects, less obviously romantic, with the great second-subject melody sounding detached and rather chilly. The finale is made to sound like a Walton comedy overture at the start, brilliant and exciting, but at the end it lacks joyful exuberance. The reading of the *Symphonic dances* is crisp and light-textured. Brilliance there is in plenty, but full warmth of lyricism is lacking. Bright, spacious recording, made in the Philharmonie in 1983 and characteristic of the digital sound the DG engineers were achieving at the time.

PIANO MUSIC

Barcarolle in G min., Op. 10/3; Études-tableaux, Op. 39/4 & 6; Humoresque in G, Op. 10/5; Lilacs, Op. 21/5; 5 Morceaux de fantaisie, Op. 3: (Élégie in E flat min.; Prelude in C sharp min.; Mélodie in E; Polichinelle in F sharp min.; Sérénade in B flat min.); Polka de V. R.; Prelude

in G min., Op. 23/5. Transcriptions: MUSSORGSKY: *Hopak.* SCHUBERT: *Wohin?.* RIMSKY-KORSAKOV: *Flight of the bumble-bee.* KREISLER: *Liebeslied; Liebesfreud. The Star spangled banner.*
(M) *** Decca 425 964-2 [id.]. Sergei Rachmaninov (Ampico Roll recordings, 1919–29).

Daisies, Op. 38/5; Études-tableaux, Op. 33/2 & 7; Op. 39/6; Humoresque, Op. 10/5; Lilacs, Op. 21/5; Mélodie, Op. 3/5; Moment musical, Op. 16/2; Oriental sketch; Polka de V. R.; Preludes: in C sharp min., Op. 3/2; in G flat, Op. 23/10; in E, F min. & F, Op. 32/3, 6 & 7; Serenade, Op. 3/5. Transcriptions: BACH: *Violin Partita No. 2: Prelude; Gavotte; Rondo; Gigue.* MENDELSSOHN: *Midsummer Night's Dream: Scherzo.* KREISLER: *Liebesfreud.* SCHUBERT: *Wohin?.* MUSSORGSKY: *Hopak.* TCHAIKOVSKY: *Lullaby, Op. 16/11.* RIMSKY-KORSAKOV: *The Flight of the bumble-bee.*
(M) (***) BMG/RCA mono GD 87766 [7766-2-RG]. Sergei Rachmaninov.

These two records make a fascinating comparison. The RCA collection includes virtually all Rachmaninov's electric 78-r.p.m. recordings, made between 1925 and 1942, with most dating from 1940. The second offers the composer's Ampico piano-roll recordings, made during a shorter time-span, between 1919 and 1929, when Rachmaninov was at his technical peak. The Ampico recordings were reproduced on a specially adapted Estonia concert grand in the Kingsway Hall and recorded in stereo in 1978/9. On CD the sound is outstandingly real and the impression on the listener is quite uncanny when the recital opens with the *Élégie in E flat minor*, which was put on roll in October 1928 yet has all the spontaneity and presence of live music-making. A number of items are common to both discs, so it is possible to make direct comparisons. The Ampico system at that time could accurately reflect what was played, including note duration and pedalling, but the *strength* at which the notes were struck had to be edited on to the roll afterwards by a skilled musician/technician, who annotated his score while the artist performed. Wrong notes could also be edited out, and the recording had finally to be approved by the performer after hearing a playback. It can only be said that listening to these Ampico recordings never brings a feeling of any mechanical tone graduation, and in pieces like the *Humoresque in G major* or the *Polka de V. R.* not only does Rachmaninov's scintillating bravura sound absolutely natural, but also his chimerical use of rubato is more convincing on the earlier recordings. On the RCA CD, the opening *Preludes* bring a curiously hollow piano timbre, and the effect throughout is shallow, partly the effect of the dry studio acoustic. Rachmaninov's performances were usually remarkably consistent – witness his sombre account of the famous *Prelude in C sharp minor*, while *The Flight of the bumble-bee*, a *tour de force* of exuberant articulation, brings only one second's difference in playing time between the two versions. However, in the closing *Liebesfreud* on the Decca disc, with its coruscating decorative cascades, his virtuosity is dazzling and the performance takes about a minute less than on the RCA version. It sounds good on both discs, but on the Decca version one has the impression of Rachmaninov sitting at the end of one's room. A remarkable achievement.

Élégie, Op. 13/1; Études-tableaux, Op. 39/3 & 5; Moments musicaux, Op. 16/3–6; Preludes, Op. 23/1, 2, 5 & 6; Op. 32/12.
(M) *** EMI Dig. CDD7 64086-2 [id.]; *ET 764086-4.* Andrei Gavrilov – SCRIABIN: *Preludes.* ***

There is some pretty remarkable playing here, especially in the stormy *B flat major Prelude*, while the *G sharp minor* from Op. 32 has a proper sense of fantasy. More prodigious bravura provides real excitement in the *F sharp minor Étude-tableau*, Op. 39/3, and in the *E minor Moment musical*, while Gavrilov relaxes winningly in the *Andante cantabile* of Op. 16/3 and the *Élégie.* Sometimes his impetuosity almost carries him away, and the piano is placed rather near the listener so that we are nearly taken with him, but there is no doubt about the quality of this recital.

Études tableaux, Opp. 33 & 39 (complete).
(BB) (*) Naxos Dig. 8.550347 [id.]. Idil Biret.

On the face of it, Idil Biret's disc of both the Opp. 33 and 39 sets of the *Études tableaux* represents good value for money; after all, it costs less than half as much as Vladimir Ovchinnikov's full-price EMI set. However, it would represent a false economy: the Naxos piano recordings, made in this venue, do not constitute a real challenge to existing recommendations.

Études-tableaux, Op. 33; (i) *Suites for 2 pianos, Nos. 1 (Fantasy), Op. 5; 2, Op. 17.*
(M) *** Decca 425 029-2; *425 029-4* [id.].
Vladimir Ashkenazy; (i) with André Previn.

Ashkenazy's 1981 account of the Op. 33 *Études-tableaux* is very impressive indeed, but it is for the *Suites* that this reissue is especially valuable. The colour and flair of Rachmaninov's writing are captured with wonderful imagination, reflecting a live performance by Ashkenazy and Previn in London in the summer of 1974. The recordings were made in All Saints' Church, Petersham, and the pianos are fairly closely observed against the resonant acoustic; the sound is bold and has striking presence.

10 Preludes, Op. 23; 5 Morceaux de fantaisie, Op. 3.
(BB) (**) Naxos Dig. 8.550348 [id.]. Idil Biret.

No major quarrels with Idil Biret here. She sounds at home in this repertoire – but, as with so many of the piano records she has made for Naxos in the Heidelberg studios, the quality of the sound is in every respect unsatisfactory.

13 Preludes, Op. 32; arr. of KREISLER: *Liebesleid; Liebesfreud.*
(BB) (**) Naxos Dig. 8.550466 [id.]. Idil Biret.

It is impossible to recommend Idil Biret's account of the Op. 32 set of *Preludes*. Her playing sounds thoroughly idiomatic, but the claustrophobic, clatttery sound is distinctly unpleasant.

Piano sonata No. 2 in B flat min., Op. 36; Moments musicaux, Op. 16; Variations on a theme of Corelli, Op. 42.
(BB) (*) Naxos Dig. 8.550349 [id.]. Idil Biret.

Idil Biret plays with a good deal of authority, but the small acoustic is quite unsuited to this kind of repertoire and cannot accommodate powerful fortissimo passages with any degree of comfort.

Variations on a theme of Chopin, Op. 22.
(M) ** Teldec/Warner Dig. 9031 74782-2 [id.]. Cyprien Katsaris – BEETHOVEN: *Eroica variations*; LISZT: *Variations* *(*).

Rachmaninov's impressive set of *Variations*, Op. 22, on the *C minor Prelude* of Chopin is not otherwise available except at full price. In this range the Bolet and Ashkenazy accounts, both on Decca, bring better sound and have a more naturally aristocratic feel than Cyprien Katsaris's strongly extrovert approach. The Teldec recording is very close, thick and synthetic, though the ear quickly adjusts to it; this is the most rewarding of the three performances comprising Katsaris's recital.

VOCAL MUSIC

The Bells, Op. 35.
(M) *** EMI CDM7 63114-2. Sheila Armstrong, Robert Tear, John Shirley-Quirk, LSO Ch., LSO, Previn – PROKOFIEV: *Alexander Nevsky.* ***

In *The Bells*, as in Previn's equally fresh and direct account of the other Russian choral work included on this CD, Prokofiev's *Alexander Nevsky*, the LSO Chorus sings convincingly in the original language. The timbre may not be entirely Russian-sounding (cleaner and fresher in fact), but in what amounts to a choral symphony Previn's concentration on purely musical values as much as on evocation of atmosphere produces powerful results, even when the recording as transferred to CD has lost just a little of its ambient warmth in favour of added presence and choral brilliance.

Vocalise, Op. 34/14 (arr. Dubensky).
(M) *** BMG/RCA GD 87831 [7831-2-RG]. Anna Moffo, American SO, Stokowski – CANTELOUBE: *Songs of the Auvergne;* VILLA-LOBOS: *Bachianas Brasileiras No. 5.* ***

Rachmaninov's *Vocalise* was a favourite showpiece of Stokowski, usually in a purely orchestral arrangement; but here with Moffo at her warmest it is good to have the vocal version so persuasively matching the accompaniment.

Raff, Joachim (1822–82)

Symphony No. 5 (Lenore).
(M) *** Unicorn UKCD 2031. LPO, Bernard Herrmann.

Raff left eleven symphonies; No. 5, with its colourful programmatic writing, is generally counted the finest of his cycle. In some ways it is a very naïve work, based as it is on a high romantic ballad by the poet Bürger. A dead soldier-lover calls upon the girl he has left behind, and on a devil's ride he disconcertingly turns into a skeleton. The first two movements merely provide preparation for that dramatic development, while the third depicts the lovers' parting, with the main march heard first in crescendo then diminuendo to represent the arrival and departure of a troop of the lover's regiment – a piece much beloved by the Victorians. A thoroughly enjoyable Mendelssohnian symphony, colourfully performed with clean and vivid recording, given extra projection on CD, especially the percussion.

Rameau, Jean Philippe (1683–1764)

Hippolyte et Aricie: orchestral suite.
(M) *** HM/BMG GD 77009 [77009-2-RG]. La Petite Bande, Kuijken.

During Rameau's lifetime there were three productions of *Hippolyte et Aricie*, for which various instrumental additions were made. This record collects virtually all the orchestral music from the three in performances so lively and winning that the disc is irresistible. Sigiswald Kuijken gets delightful results from his ensemble; the melodic invention is fresh and its orchestral presentation ingenious. In every way an outstanding release – and not least in the quality of the sound.

Music for harpsichord: *Book 1* (1706); *Pièces de clavecin* (1724); *Nouvelles suites de pièces de clavecin* (*c.* 1728); *5 Pièces* (1741); *La Dauphine* (1747).
(M) *** DG 427 176-2 (2). Kenneth Gilbert (harpischord).

Pièces de clavecin, Book 1 (1706); *Nouvelles suites* (*c.* 1728).
(BB) ** Naxos Dig. 8.550463 [id.]. Alan Cuckson (harpsichord).

Pièces de clavecin (1724, revised 1731); *5 Pièces* (1741); *La Dauphine* (1747).
(BB) ** Naxos Dig. 8.550465 [id.]. Alan Cuckson (harpsichord).

Rameau's keyboard music is among the finest of the whole Baroque era, and Kenneth Gilbert is not just a scholar but an artist of genuine insight and stature. He uses three harpsichords here, all from the Paris Conservatoire and all from the period: a Goujon (1749), a Hemsch (1761), and a third by Dumont (1679) restored by Pascal Taskin in 1789. They are superb instruments and are excellently recorded too (in 1977); although the CD brings added presence, the instruments remain in a good perspective. There is no need to dwell on details here, for this is an indispensable set.

Alan Cuxton's survey of Rameau's keyboard music is doubly welcome in the lowest price-range. Each disc is generously filled and the first, comprising the *Premier Livre* of 1706 and the *Nouvelles suites*, runs to 75 minutes. But first a word of warning: both discs sound thunderous if played at a normal playback level. Even when the volume is drastically cut, the balance remains too close to be ideal. At a time when presentation material is minimal or non-existent on many budget CDs, it is a pleasure to record that Alan Cuckson's notes are informative and, relatively speaking, extensive. All the same, this set does not offer a serious challenge to Kenneth Gilbert's survey on two Archiv CDs; the latter has far greater elegance and finish.

Pièces de clavecin en concerts: 1st Concert: *La coulican; La livri; La vézinet;* 2nd Concert: *La laborde; La boucon; L'agaçante; Menuets 1–2;* 3rd Concert: *La poplinière; La timide, Rondeaux 1–2; Tambourines 1–2 en rondeau;* 4th Concert: *La pantomime; L'indiscrète; La Rameau;* 5th Concert: *La Forqueray; La Cupis; La Marais.*
(BB) *(*) Naxos Dig. 8.550464 [id.]. Alan Cuckson, Elisabeth Parry, Kenneth Mitchell, Alison Crum.

As with Alan Cuckson's companion records of Rameau on Naxos, the close balance does the artists a disservice. Not that these performances are strong on elegance (there are some tentative moments and the intonation of the flautist is momentarily vulnerable) and, though Alan Cuckson himself plays with spirit, the performances overall communicate more rectitude than pleasure.

OPERA-BALLET AND OPERA

Pygmalion (complete).
(M) **(*) HM/BMG GD 77143 [77143-2-RG]. Elwes, Van der Sluis, Vanhecke, Yakar, Paris Chapelle Royal Ch., La Petite Bande, Leonhardt.

Leonhardt's 1980 account with John Elwes as Pygmalion and Mieke van der Sluis as Céphise is welcome back to the catalogue. Leonhardt's direction is rather leisurely, but his soloists make a good team. The use of period instruments brings attractive transparency of texture and, thanks to the excellence of the original recording, this is enhanced on CD. The documentation (including full translation) is first class.

Zoroastre (complete).
(M) **(*) HM/BMG GD 77144 (3) [77144-2-RG]. Elwes, De Reyghere, Van der Sluis, Nellon, Reinhart, Bona, Ghent Coll. Vocale, La Petite Bande, Kuijken.

Zoroastre may not have quite the inspiration of *Les Boréades* in modifying once rigid conventions; but frequently, as in the monologue of the villain, Abramane, in Act III, Rameau was clearly taking a leaf out of Gluck's book in the dark originality of the instrumentation, here made transparent in finely detailed recording. Though Kuijken's characteristically gentle style with his excellent authentic group, La Petite Bande, fails to give the piece the bite and urgency that John Eliot Gardiner brings to *Les Boréades* in his full-price Erato recording, it is a fine presentation of a long-neglected masterpiece, with crisp and stylish singing from the soloists, notably John Elwes in the name-part and Gregory Reinhart as Abramane. The Ghent Collegium Vocale, placed rather close, sing with vigour in the choruses, but the individual voices fail to blend. The five Acts (with Rameau here abandoning the old convention of an allegorical Prologue) are now offered on three mid-priced CDs against the original set on four LPs. The excellent documentation (144 pages, including translations) puts the mid-priced issues of many of the large international companies to shame.

Ravel, Maurice (1875–1937)

Alborada del gracioso; Une barque sur l'océan; Boléro; (i) *Piano concerto in G; Piano concerto for the left hand. Daphnis et Chloé* (complete ballet); *L'Éventail de Jeanne: Fanfare. Menuet antique; Ma Mère l'Oye* (complete); *Pavane pour une infante défunte; Rapsodie espagnole; Le tombeau de Couperin; La valse; Valses nobles et sentimentales.*

❀ (M) *** Decca 421 458-2 (4). Montreal SO with Ch. and (i) Pascal Rogé; Dutoit.

(i) *Alborada del gracioso;* (ii) *Une barque sur l'océan; Boléro;* (i; iii) *Piano concerto for the left hand;* (ii; iv) *Daphnis et Chloé* (complete ballet); (ii) *Fanfare pour L'Éventail de Jeanne; Menuet antique; Ma Mère l'Oye* (complete ballet); (i) *Pavane pour une infante défunte; Rapsodie espagnole;* (ii) *Shéhérazade: Ouverture de feerie. Le tombeau de Couperin; La valse; Valses nobles et sentimentales.*

(M) **(*) Sony SM3K 45842 (3) [id.]. (i) Cleveland O; (ii) NYPO; Boulez; (iii) with Entremont; (iv) Camerata Singers.

Anyone coming new to this repertoire will find Dutoit's four-disc mid-price box unbeatable value: the orchestral playing is wonderfully sympathetic and the recording ideally combines atmospheric evocation with vividness of detail. In the concertos, Pascal Rogé finds gracefulness and vitality for the *G major* work and, if there is less dynamism in the *Left-hand concerto*, there is no lack of finesse. The balance is very realistic and the recording throughout is in the demonstration class.

Boulez's distinguished Sony set unfortunately comes into direct competition with Dutoit's outstanding Montreal box of four CDs, also at mid-price. However, Sony do offer very good value. Three CDs are used, yet only the *G major Piano concerto* is missing and instead we are offered a glitteringly iridescent account of the *Ouverture de feerie*, which is omitted by Dutoit. Entrement's account of the *Left-hand concerto* is strong and characterful and not lacking in poetic colour; but the rather forward CBS sound is a little fierce at the orchestral climax and does not altogether flatter the piano timbre. On the whole, however, the remastering makes the most of recordings which were originally among the best of their period (1972–5) from this source, even if they were at times balanced artificially in the interests of internal clarity and strong projection. Both orchestras respond with splendid virtuosity to Boulez's direction. The *Alborada* is quite brilliant and, throughout, Boulez allows all the music ample time to breathe; gentler textures have the transluscence for which this conductor is admired. *Une barque sur l'océan* has a genuine magic, while the complete *Daphnis et Chloé* has a sense of ecstasy and an ability to transport the listener into the enchanted landscape that this work inhabits, with its wonder, its vivid colours and innocence. The playing of the New York Philharmonic here is beyond praise: every detail is affectionately phrased, there is effortless virtuosity and brilliance and, despite some highlighting, the recording produces a warmly atmospheric quality, although again there is a touch of aggressiveness at climaxes. Boulez is also at his very best in *Ma Mère l'Oye*: the luminous textures of the gentle music are matched by the glitter and impact of the score's more dramatic moments. The *Menuet antique* has a pleasing directness of manner; the effect is most refreshing. Boulez's *Rapsodie espagnole* is equally distinctive: it is beautifully shaped and atmospheric in an entirely different way from Karajan's; the latter is heavy with exotic scents and sultry half-lights, whereas Boulez's Spain is brilliant, dry and well lit. The recording is more discreetly balanced and here, as in the *Valses nobles et sentimentales*, after a spectacular opening the delectably refined woodwind colours are kept in reasonable perspective. Both *Boléro* and *La valse* generate considerable tension and have powerful climaxes. There is no doubt that this music-making with its cleanly etched sound is immensely strong in character, and many listeners will respond to it very positively. There is excellent internal cueing, with even *Boléro* subdivided and the *Valses nobles et sentimentales* individually accessible.

Alborada del gracioso; Une barque sur l'océan; Boléro; Menuet antique; Ma Mère l'Oye (complete); *Pavane pour une infante défunte; Rapsodie espagnole; Le tombeau de Couperin; La valse; Valses nobles et sentimentales.*

(B) *** EMI CMS7 69165-2 (2). Paris Conservatoire O, André Cluytens.

This two-disc set (offered for the cost of a single premium-priced CD) includes all Cluytens's distinguished Ravel recordings made in the Paris Salle Wagram in 1962. As usual in this hall, the resonance ensures plenty of bloom and the effect is seldom noticeably dated. Cluytens gives a brilliant account of the *Alborada*, and *Une barque sur l'océan* sounds totally magical in his hands; his complete *Ma Mère l'Oye* is also most beautifully played, with textures gently glowing and, although some will find the wide horn vibrato in the *Pavane* a little off-putting, the performance has a noble serenity. *Boléro* maintains a consistent tempo: this is a vivid and unaffected account, if in the last analysis not as exciting as some. His account of the *Rapsodie espagnole* is excellent too: the recording here has warmth and glitter; and *Le tombeau de Couperin* is eminently stylish. *La valse* has both languor and tension, and the *Valses nobles et sentimentales* is second to none: there is fine atmosphere and a genuine feeling for movement and rubato as well as elegance. Here as elsewhere, one is struck by the excellence of the original recordings, well defined, full, yet with plenty of presence. Good value.

Alborada del gracioso; Une barque sur l'océan; Ma Mère l'Oye (ballet); *Pavane pour une infante défunte; Le tombeau de Couperin.*
(M) *** EMI CDM7 69567-2 [id.]; *EG 769567-4.* O de Paris, Martinon.

Like his version of *Daphnis et Chloé*, Martinon's *Ma Mère l'Oye* is exquisite, among the finest ever put on record (and one does not forget Dutoit or Previn). The other works are also played beautifully, with the Orchestre de Paris on its finest form. The analogue recording was of EMI's vintage quality, and it has been effectively remastered.

Alborada del gracioso; Une barque sur l'océan; Boléro; Menuet antique; Pavane pour une infante défunte; La valse.
(M) **(*) DG 415 845-2; *415 845-4* [id.]. Boston SO, Ozawa.

Ozawa is at his finest in catching the atmosphere of *Une barque sur l'océan*, and throughout this collection he secures admirable orchestral playing. If the last degree of character is missing, the 1975 recording is first class, beautifully balanced, with the hall ambience colouring the textures most naturally.

(i) *Alborado del gracioso; Boléro;* (ii) *Piano concerto in G;* (i) *Menuet antique; Pavane pour une infante défunte; Rapsodie espagnole; Valses nobles et sentimentales;* (iii) *String quartet in F.*
(B) ** VoxBox 1155992 (2) [CDX 5031]. (i) Minnesota O, Skrowaczewski; (ii) Simon, R. Luxembourg O, de Froment; (iii) New Hungarian Qt.

Abbey Simon's account of the *Piano Concerto in G* with the Luxembourg Radio Orchestra conducted by Louis de Froment is not really in the front rank nowadays (the piano is dryish and too forward). The New Hungarian Quartet maintains its link with its famed predecessor through the violist Dénes Koromzay and their account of the *Quartet* is very well played, though one could do with more space round the aural image and the group is too forwardly balanced. By far the best things here are the *Rapsodie espagnole* and the *Valses nobles et sentimentales*, both played with a seductive sensuousness by Skrowaczewksi and recorded in a much more spacious acoustic than the synthetic mixing of the Luxembourg studio. These performances linger in the memory; so good are they that the box is worth considering on their account. They deserve three stars for performance and, though the recording is not quite so outstanding by present-day standards, it is still very good indeed.

(i) *Alborada del gracioso; Boléro;* (ii) *Pavane pour une infante défunte;* (i) *Rapsodie espagnole* (CD only: (i) *Le tombeau de Couperin; Valses nobles et sentimentales*).
(B) **(*) DG Compact Classics 413 154-2 (2); *413 154-4* [id.]. Boston SO, (i) Ozawa; (ii) Abbado – DEBUSSY: *Danses sacrée; La Mer* etc. ***

Even though Ozawa's Ravel performances are somewhat faceless, *Boléro* moves to its climax steadily and powerfully. The Boston orchestral playing is superb and the recording first class. *Rapsodie espagnole* has plenty of glitter and the sound has warmth and much beauty of texture. *Le tombeau de Couperin*, cool and poised, showing Ozawa at his best, and the *Valses nobles et sentimentales* are added to fill out the pair of CDs, but this music-making makes its strongest impression heard on tape in the car. Abbado's performance of the *Pavane* is characteristically refined, and the Debussy couplings are similarly distinguished.

Alborada del gracioso; Boléro; Rapsodie espagnole; Le tombeau de Couperin; La valse.
(BB) *** BMG/RCA VD 60485; *VK 60485* [id.]. Dallas SO, Mata.

Mata and his excellent Dallas orchestra give impressive performances of the virtuoso showpieces and find both delicacy and grace for *Le tombeau de Couperin*. There are more individual accounts of several of these works in the lower price-range (one thinks of Reiner, Karajan and Paray) but, now that RCA have made this bargain reissue generous in playing time (68 minutes), it is very competitive, helped by digital recording of great range and the glowing, yet not over-resonant ambience of the Dallas Hall. This gives an advantage in the *Alborada*, compared with the Karajan/EMI version, while *Boléro* develops from a whisper of a pianissimo at the start to a formidably powerful climax, though the detailed balancing is not always consistent.

Alborada del gracioso; Boléro; Rapsodie espagnole; La valse.
(M) ** Sony Dig. MDK 46501. O Nat. de France, Lorin Maazel.

Maazel's 1981 collection is brilliantly played and his extrovert sentience in the *Rapsodie* is certainly involving. *La valse* is high-powered, with an indulgent treatment of the climax. The sound is resonant and brightly lit. Frankly, this is not in the same league as Dutoit, and it costs more than Mata's excellent Dallas collection, which is more enticingly recorded and includes also *Le tombeau de Couperin*.

Alborada del gracioso; Pavane pour une infante défunte; Rapsodie espagnole; Le tombeau de Couperin; La valse.
(M) *** Mercury 432 003-2 [id.]. Detroit SO, Paray – IBERT: *Escales.* **(*)

Paray's Ravel performances enjoyed a high reputation in the 1960s. His *Rapsodie espagnole* can be spoken of in the same breath as the Reiner/RCA and Karajan/EMI versions, with its languorous, shimmering textures and sparkling *Feria*. His *Alborada* glitters and the *Pavane* is glowingly elegiac. *La valse*, too, is impressively shaped and subtly controlled. *Le tombeau de Couperin* has great refinement and elegance: the solo oboist plays beautifully. This last item was recorded in the old Detroit Orchestral Hall, with its mellow acoustic; the rest of the programme was done at Cass Technical High School, and the sound is that bit brighter and more vivid. All have been excellently remastered.

Alborada del gracioso; Pavane pour une infante défunte; Rapsodie espagnole; Valses nobles et sentimentales.
❀ (M) *** BMG/RCA GD 60179 [60179-2-RG]. Chicago SO, Reiner – DEBUSSY: *Ibéria.* *** ❀

These performances are in an altogether special class. In the *Rapsodie espagnole*, the *Prélude à la nuit* is heavy with fragrance and atmosphere; never have the colours in the *Feria* glowed more luminously, while the *Malagueña* glitters with iridescence. In the thirty years since it first appeared, this is the recording we have turned to whenever we wanted to hear this work for pleasure. No one captures its sensuous atmosphere as completely as did Reiner. Its appearance on CD together with its companions is a cause for celebration, and the recorded sound with its natural concert-hall balance is greatly improved in terms of clarity and definition.

Alborada del gracioso; Rapsodie espagnole; Le tombeau de Couperin; La valse.
(M) *** EMI CDM7 63526-2; *EG 763526-4* [id.]. O de Paris, Karajan.

These superb performances were recorded just a decade after Karajan's DG analogue *Daphnis et Chloé suite*, one of the best things he ever did for the gramophone. The Orchestre de Paris, while not the Berlin Philharmonic – the horn vibrato, though unobtrusive, may not be appreciated by all ears – responds splendidly to Karajan's sensuous approach to these scores. The dynamic range is very wide and the acoustic somewhat too resonant. The *Alborada* is on the slow side, and doubtless the reverberation prompted this. But, even if the atmospheric quality of these performances is not wholly free from a trace of self-consciousness, there is no doubt about the mastery of *La valse*, which is extremely fine, or of the *Rapsodie espagnole*, the best performance since Reiner's. The remastering for CD is extremely successful.

Alborada del gracioso; Valses nobles et sentimentales.
(M) *** EMI Dig. CDD7 64056-2 [id.]; *EG 764056-4*. RPO, Previn – DEBUSSY: *La Mer* etc. ***

Previn's is a provocatively languorous account of the *Valses nobles et sentimentales*, lazy of tempo and affectionately indulgent, and afforded glowing 1985 Abbey Road recording; then the *Alborada* provides a brilliant close to a concert which has already given the listener two outstanding Debussy performances.

(i) *Une barque sur l'océan;* (ii) *Piano concerto for the left hand in D;* (i) *Daphnis et Chloé: suites Nos. 1–2; Fanfare; Ma Mère l'Oye* (ballet; complete); *Le tombeau de Couperin; La valse.*
(B) **(*) VoxBox (2) [CDX 5032]. (i) Minnesota O, Skrowaczewski; (ii) Simon, R. Luxembourg O, de Froment.

The second Voxbox Ravel compilation is even more worthwhile. Again the weakness is the *Concerto for the left hand*, well enough played but not good enough to excite superlatives. The complete *Ma Mère l'Oye* from the Minnesota Orchestra under Stanislaw Skrowaczewski is a totally different matter, as are the two suites from *Daphnis et Chloé*. These date from 1974 and are glorious; indeed the former is one of the best versions of the score on disc and can hold its own with Dutoit, Abbado or any newcomer.

Boléro.
(M) **(*) EMI CDM7 69007-2 [id.]; *EG 769007-4*. BPO, Karajan – DEBUSSY: *La mer* etc. **(*)

Karajan's digitally remastered 1978 version of *Boléro* has fine presence and a splendid forward impetus.

Boléro; (i) *Daphnis et Chloë: suite No. 2; Ma Mère l'Oye (suite); Valses nobles et sentimentales.*
(BB) *** Naxos Dig. 8.550173 [id.]. (i) Slovak

Philharmonic Ch.; Slovak RSO (Bratislava), Kenneth Jean.

The American conductor Kenneth Jean draws some sensitive readings of the suite from *Ma Mère l'Oye* and, for that matter, of the *Valses nobles et sentimentales.* The Slovak Radio Orchestra, which is a fine body and is superbly recorded, respond to him more warmly than they do on their (very good) companion disc reviewed below. At the price, this is very good value indeed; the *Ma Mère l'Oye* can hold its own alongside all but the most distinguished competition: indeed *Les entretiens de la belle et de la bête* is as keenly characterized as either Giulini or Dutoit, both long at mid-price, and *Le jardin feerique* is enchanting. For those wanting these pieces this is a real bargain.

Boléro; Daphnis et Chloé: suite No. 2.
(M) *** DG 427 250-2. BPO, Karajan – DEBUSSY: *La mer; Prélude.* ***

Karajan's 1964 *Boléro* is a very characteristic performance, marvellously controlled, hypnotic and gripping, with the Berlin Philharmonic at the top of its form. The 1965 *Daphnis et Chloé* suite is outstanding, even among all the competition. He has the advantage of the Berlin Philharmonic at their finest and it would be difficult to imagine better or more atmospheric playing. The CD has opened up the sound spectacularly although now there is a touch of glare.

Boléro; (i) *Daphnis et Chloé: suite No. 2; Pavane pour une infante défunte; La valse.*
(M) *** Decca Dig. 430 714-2; *430 714-4* [id.]. Montreal SO, Dutoit; (i) with chorus.

A further permutation of Dutoit's beautifully made Montreal recordings, warmly and translucently recorded at St Eustache, now reissued at mid-price. The *Daphnis et Chloé* suite is drawn from the highly praised complete set. If this programme is suitable, the performances and recordings cannot be bettered.

Boléro; Ma Mère l'Oye (suite); Pavane pour une infante défunte; Rapsodie espagnole.
(B) ** Hung. White Label HRC 176 [id.]. Budapest PO, András Kórodi.

The Hungaroton White Label anthology from the Budapest Philharmonic under András Kórodi has much to commend it – but not enough, given the present range of choice, to make it strongly competitive. The playing, though not the last word in elegance and sumptuousness, is still pretty good, and Kórodi is far from insensitive in handling phrasing and balancing textures. At the same time, this is not special and there are so many versions of this repertoire that are. The recording is from 1972 and is natural and spacious without being spectacular; given the relatively short playing time by 1992 standards (54 minutes), this collection is not much of a bargain.

Boléro; Menuet antique; Rapsodie espagnole; Shéhérazade: Overture de feerie; La valse.
(M) **(*) EMI CDM7 69565-2 [id.]; *EG 769565-4.* O de Paris, Martinon.

Martinon's performances are distinguished and very well played, even if *La valse* – not helped here by rather harsh fortissimo sound – is not among the finest versions available. The transfers are clearer than the originals and do not lack ambient warmth, but the upper range has a degree of shrillness under pressure.

Boléro; Le tombeau de Couperin.
(M) *(*) Decca 430 444-2; *430 444-4* [id.]. Chicago SO, Solti – DEBUSSY: *La Mer* etc. **

Solti's metrically vigorous (analogue) *Boléro* builds to its climax relentlessly and the recording makes a most powerful effect. *Le tombeau de Couperin* is well played but sounds hard and brilliant rather than classically elegant. The recording is partly to blame, with close-up sound reducing the sense of ambience.

Piano concerto in G (see also above, under *Alborado del gracioso*).
(B) * Hung. White Label HRC 181 [id.]. Jenö Jandó, Budapest SO, Jansovics – GRIEG: *Concerto.* (*)

Jenö Jandó's 1975 recording of the *G major Concerto* is an improvement on the lacklustre Grieg with which it is coupled. However, while it is not insensitive, it is neither magical nor memorable.

(i) *Piano concerto in G. Gaspard de la nuit; Sonatine.*
(M) *** DG 419 062-2 [id.]. Argerich, (i) BPO, Abbado.

Argerich's half-tones and clear fingerwork give the *G major Concerto* unusual delicacy, but its urgent virility – with jazz an important element – comes over the more forcefully by contrast. The compromise between coolness and expressiveness in the slow minuet of the middle movement is tantalizingly sensual. Her *Gaspard de la nuit* abounds in character and colour, and the *Sonatine* is a similarly telling performance. The *Concerto* balance is very successful and there is crisp detail, while the solo piano has fine presence and no want of colour.

(i) *Piano concerto in G;* (ii) *Piano concerto in D for the left hand.*
(M) *** Erato/Warner 2292 45086-2 [id.]. Anne Queffélec, Strasbourg PO, Lombard – DEBUSSY: *Fantasy.* ***
(M) ** Sony SBK 46338; *40-46338* [id.].

Entremont, (i) Phd. O, Ormandy; (ii) Cleveland O, Boulez – GERSHWIN: *Concerto in F.* **

Anne Queffélec's accounts of both *Concertos* are thoughtful and imaginative. She is a thorough musician with no mean sense of poetry. The excellent Strasbourg orchestra under Alain Lombard give her admirable support, and the well-balanced recording sounds fresher in its CD format. The rare Debussy coupling is also well worth having.

Entremont's account of the *G major Concerto* is not especially sensitive, nor is it helped by the crude recording. The *Left-hand concerto* fares much better, although the sound is still rather resonant. This is among the most highly characterized readings available; the partnership with Boulez produced the most vivid results.

(i) *Piano concerto for the left hand; Gaspard de la nuit; Pavane pour une infante défunte.*
(M) *** EMI CDM7 69026-2. Gavrilov; (i) LSO, Rattle.

Gavrilov's recording of the *Left-hand concerto* is altogether dazzling. He plays with effortless virtuosity, brilliance and, when required, great sensitivity. The *Pavane* is also very distinguished; apart from the strangely impulsive closing bars, this too is beautiful playing. *Gaspard de la nuit* is not quite so distinctive: both *Ondine* and *Le gibet* have an element of reserve. But *Scarbo* has superb dash, and the whole performance has impeccable style. The digital remastering is spectacular in its vividness.

Daphnis et Chloé (ballet; complete).
(M) *** BMG/RCA GD 60469 [60469-2-RG]. New England Conservatory Ch., Boston SO, Münch – ROUSSEL: *Bacchus et Ariane.* (***)
(M) ** DG Dig. 429 982-2. VPO, Levine.

Daphnis et Chloé (complete); *Pavane pour une infante défunte; Rapsodie espagnole.*
(M) *** Decca 425 956-2 [id.]. ROHCG Ch., LSO, Pierre Monteux.

(i) *Daphnis et Chloé* (complete); (ii) *Rapsodie espagnole.*
(M) *** EMI Dig. CDD7 63887-2 [id.]; *ET 763887-4.* (i) LSO Ch. & LSO; (ii) RPO, André Previn.

Daphnis et Chloé (complete); *Valses nobles et sentimentales.*
(M) *** EMI CDM7 69566-2; *EG 769566-4.* Paris Op. Ch., O de Paris, Martinon.

Charles Münch's Boston account is one of the great glories of the 1950s, superior in every way to his later version from the 1960s. The playing in all departments of the Boston orchestra is simply electrifying. Although Monteux's slightly later (1959) account has the advantage of a more vividly coloured and spacious recording (one of Decca's best from that vintage), it is not as compelling as the present issue. The sound here may not be as sumptuous as the Decca, but the richness of colour lies in the playing, and there is a heady sense of intoxication that at times sweeps you off your feet. A wonderful, glowing account, recorded before the virtuosity which Münch and his Bostonians commanded had become hard-driven. A performance to set beside the finest newcomers. Spot-on intonation from the choir – the LSO's chorus did not hold their pitch so securely for Monteux. The strings do not have ideal bloom and transparency (this was one of the first stereo recordings) and the sound does not open out. But try the *Danse de supplication de Chloé* (track 15) and the ensuing scene in which the pirates are put to flight, and you will get a good idea of just how dazzling this is and how little the sonic limitations matter.

With rhythm more important than atmosphere, Previn directs a very dramatic performance of *Daphnis et Chloé*, clear-headed and fresh. It is certainly made vivid, full-bodied too, yet with textures sharply defined. The original full-priced issue had very few internal cues, and it is good to see that, for the reissue, EMI have now provided a total of 18. Previn's unashamedly sultry 1985 *Rapsodie espagnole* with the RPO has also been added for good measure. Both recordings were made at Abbey Road, but the balance gives a concert-hall effect, and the glowing ambience in the *Rapsodie* nicely offsets the glitter. (Excellent value: 73 minutes.)

Monteux conducted the first performance of *Daphnis et Chloé* in 1912; Decca's 1959 recording, a demonstration disc in its day, captured his poetic and subtly shaded reading in the most vivid colours within an agreeably warm ambience. The performance was one of the finest things Monteux did for the gramophone. The CD transfer has opened up the sound, with generally impressive results. Perhaps just a little of the atmospheric allure has been lost (though *Daybreak* still sounds ravishing), but the sound generally is more transparent, without loss of body. Decca have added his 1962 recording of the *Pavane*, wonderfully poised and played most beautifully, and the *Rapsodie espagnole*, in which Monteux inspirationally achieves a balance and a contrast between the mood of quiet introspection for the opening and flashing brilliance for the *Feria*.

Martinon's *Daphnis et Chloé* has an intoxicating atmosphere: its sense of ecstasy and Dionysian abandon are altogether captivating. The delicacy of colouring in the *Nocturne*, the naturalness with which every phrase unfolds, and the virtuosity of the Orchestre de Paris are a constant source of delight. The *Valses nobles and sentimentales* are not quite so outstanding – there are preferable versions – but are still enjoyable. The sound, originally luminously opulent, is now clearer with only slight loss of richness.

With ripe Viennese horns adding opulence to Ravel's rich textures, Levine's reading could hardly be more high-powered, with superb playing from the Vienna Philharmonic. He has a natural feeling for Ravelian rubato, but what the reading consistently lacks is poetry, for in even the gentlest moments there is a want of evocative warmth. Despite the excessive contrasts between loud and soft and some hardness on violin tone, the recording is one of the most brilliant the DG engineers have made recently in Vienna.

Daphnis et Chloé: suite No. 2.
(M) **(*) Sony SBK 47664 [id.]. Cleveland O, Szell – STRAVINSKY: *Firebird* etc. **(*)
(M) (***) DG mono 427 783-2 [id.]. BPO, Wilhelm Furtwängler – SIBELIUS: *En Saga*; R. STRAUSS: *Till Eulenspiegel.* (***)

In spite of the essential brilliance of the 1963 Cleveland performance, Szell does not miss Ravel's sense of languor. *Daybreak* expands luxuriously, with the orchestra superbly responsive; later, the famous flute solo is electrifying in its rhapsodically free, glittering bravura, while the finale is a blaze of virtuosity. The recording, though forward, has plenty of backing ambience.

A *Daphnis suite* from a most unlikely source – Furtwängler, with whom we hardly associate the French master, and the Berlin Philharmonic Orchestra, recorded in 1944. Sonic limitations are soon forgotten, for this has a sense of colour and an ecstasy that elude most modern interpreters. Everything seems just right and the texture glows in a way that quite transcends the physical sound.

Daphnis et Chloé: suite No. 2; Ma Mère l'Oye (ballet): *suite; La valse.*
(M) **(*) EMI/Phoenixa stereo/mono CDM7 63763-2; *EG 763763-4* [id.]. Hallé O, Barbirolli – DEBUSSY: *La Mer.* **(*)

Barbirolli's languorous shaping of Ravel's great yearning string phrase in *Daybreak* really tugs at the heartstrings, its sense of ecstasy is profound and unforgettable. He has the advantage of using a chorus, very well balanced into the texture; indeed the 1959 recording is astonishingly full and luminous, more immediate in focus than the Debussy coupling. The flute playing in the *Pantomime* is wonderfully brilliant and sensitive; the *Danse générale* sparkles, with the chorus (not credited in the performance details) contributing very vividly to the climax. *La valse* also has plenty of temperament and excitement, and *Ma Mère l'Oye* great delicacy and innocence; the Hallé textures are ravishing, and the ear could hardly guess that this later recording derives from a 1957 mono master, so transluscent is the sound.

Daphnis et Chloé: suite No. 2; Pavane pour une infante défunte; Rapsodie espagnole; La valse.
(BB) **(*) Naxos Dig. 8.550424 [id.]. Slovak RSO (Bratislava), Kenneth Jean.

The Naxos version of the *Daphnis et Chloé suite* serves to remind us why the Hungarian White Label anthology, listed above, is not really competitive. Kenneth Jean has the advantage of altogether excellent recording, with splendid detail, definition and body and a natural recording acoustic. Moreover the Slovak Radio Orchestra is every bit the equal of the Hungarian body – if not its superior – and the performances are not only eminently well prepared but also well thought out. Kenneth Jean is an unfamiliar name in the UK, though he has been an associate conductor with the Chicago Symphony and served with the Detroit orchestra too. A three-star recording and not far off three-star performances, missing just the very last ounce of distinction and character, but often coming very close. Not quite as magical as the *Ma Mère l'Oye* and *Valses nobles* on the companion disc, listed above, but thoroughly enjoyable all the same, and well worth the money.

Daphnis et Chloé: suite No. 2; La valse.
(M) ** DG Dig. 429 487-2; *429 487-4.* O de Paris, Barenboim – DEBUSSY: *Iberia.* *(*)

Barenboim's *La valse* is on the slow side, but the seductive phrasing makes it sound lusciously idiomatic. The suite from *Daphnis et Chloé* is even more persuasive. The recorded sound is sumptuous to match, but it could have more air round it; moreover the Debussy coupling is much less appealing.

Ma Mère l'Oye (complete ballet).
(B) **(*) Pickwick Dig. PCD 932. LSO, Barry Wordsworth – BIZET: *Jeux d'enfants*; SAINT-SAENS: *Carnival.* **

Ma Mère l'Oye (complete); *Pavane pour une infante défunte.*
(BB) *** Virgin/Virgo Dig. VJ7 91469-2; *VJ7 91469-4* [id.]. SCO, Saraste – BIZET: *Symphony.* **(*)

Ma Mère l'Oye (complete); *Rapsodie espagnole.*
(M) *** DG 415 844-2 [id.]. LAPO, Giulini – MUSSORGSKY: *Pictures.* ***

Saraste directs a most sensitive, beautifully scaled and well-paced reading of the complete *Mother Goose* ballet. He catches its fantasy and tenderness as well as its glitter; and the Scottish players produce lovely sounds in the gentler music, yet can flare up vividly when the composer calls for virtuosity. The *Pavane* is serenely spacious and with a very fine horn solo. Generously coupled with the youthful Bizet *Symphony* and given warmly atmospheric recording, this makes an excellent bargain issue. The accompanying notes, however, are totally inadequate.

The Giulini Los Angeles performance conveys much of the sultry atmosphere of the *Rapsodie espagnole.* Indeed some details, such as the sensuous string responses to the cor anglais tune in the *Feria*, have not been so tenderly caressed since the intoxicating Reiner version. The *Ma Mère l'Oye* suite is also sensitively done; though it is cooler, it is still beautiful.

Barry Wordsworth finds the balletic grace in Ravel's beautiful score and creates some lovely diaphanous textures. There is plenty of vitality too, and the LSO response is consistently sympathetic. This hasn't the distinction of Dutoit but it is very well recorded, and the wide dynamic range suits this music rather better than the couplings.

Ma Mère l'Oye (ballet): *suite.*

(B) *** CfP CD-CFP 4086; *TC-CFP 4086.* SNO, Gibson – BIZET: *Jeux d'enfants;* SAINT-SAENS; *Carnival.* ***

(M) ** EMI Dig. CD-EMX 2165; *TC-EMX 2165.* LPO, Sian Edwards – BRITTEN: *Young person's guide* ***; PROKOFIEV: *Peter and the wolf.* **(*)

Gibson is highly persuasive, shaping the music with obvious affection and a feeling for both the innocent spirit and the radiant textures of Ravel's beautiful score. The orchestral playing is excellent and the recording very good, if perhaps wanting a little in atmosphere. But the CD transfer is well managed and, with excellent couplings, this is very recommendable.

Warm and beautiful orchestral playing from the LPO under Sian Edwards, but Ravel's magical score does not yield all its secrets here; its sense of gentle, innocent ecstasy is missing. Sian Edwards will present this music more perceptively when she has lived with it a little longer. Excellent recording.

Rapsodie espagnole.

(M) **(*) EMI CDM7 63572-2; *EG 763572-4* [id.]. Phd. O, Muti – CHABRIER: *España*; FALLA: *Three-cornered hat.* **(*)

Muti directs a performance which is aptly refined in its orchestral detail and also strikingly vigorous in the sharp definition of the dance rhythms. With a brightly lit recording, drenching everything in mid-day sunlight, the work here sounds more Spanish music than French. The vividness of the sound is matched by the virtuosity – often suitably restrained – of the players. But the concert overall (at 44 minutes) is short measure.

Tzigane (for violin and orchestra).

(M) **(*) Ph. 420 887-2. Szeryng, Monte Carlo Op. O, Remoortel – SAINT-SAENS: *Violin concerto No. 3* etc. **

Szeryng was at the height of his powers when he recorded this splendidly strong and committed account of Ravel's *Tzigane*, flexible and responsive as well as brilliant in execution. The recording spotlights him so that the rather less distinguished orchestral contribution, well enough held together by Eduard van Remoortel, emerges less strongly.

La valse; Valses nobles et sentimentales.

(BB) *** BMG/RCA Dig. VD 87729 [7729-2-RV]. Dallas SO, Mata – MUSSORGSKY: *Pictures.* ***

These are distinguished performances, very well played and superbly recorded – the very opening of the *Valses nobles* immediately impresses by its dynamic range, and the climax of *La valse* is engulfing.

CHAMBER MUSIC

Introduction and allegro for harp, flute, clarinet and string quartet.

❀ (M) *** Decca 421 154-2; *421 154-4.* Osian Ellis, Melos Ens. – DEBUSSY; FRANCK: *Sonatas.* *** ❀

The beauty and subtlety of Ravel's sublime septet are marvellously realized by this 1962 Melos account. The interpretation has great delicacy of feeling, and the recording hardly shows its age at all.

Piano trio in A min.

(M) *(*) EMI CDM7 63986-2 [id.]. Sir Yehudi Menuhin, Cassadó, Kentner – DEBUSSY: *Violin sonata* etc.; FAURÉ: *Andante* etc. **

The Menuhin–Cassadó–Kentner recording of the *Piano trio* comes from 1960 but enjoyed limited currency at the time. Possibly the best thing about it is the sensitive playing of Louis Kentner, though the balance allows Menuhin to dominate rather more than perhaps he should or would want to. There is some beautiful playing, but there are finer versions to be had.

(i) *Piano trio in A min.;* (ii) *Sonatine: Menuet.*

(M) (**) BMG/RCA mono GD 87871; *GK*

87871 [7871-2-RG; *7871-4-RG*]. Heifetz; (i) Rubinstein, Piatigorsky; (ii) Bay – DEBUSSY: *Sonata* etc.(**); RESPIGHI: *Sonata* (***); MARTINŮ: *Duo*. ***

It goes without saying that the million-dollar trio (Heifetz, Rubinstein and Piatigorsky), recorded in 1950, play the Ravel like a million dollars, yet its inspired opening is curiously lacking in magic and atmosphere. Peerless though the playing is, this is not a version to which one would often be tempted to return when the Beaux Arts is to hand.

String quartet in F.
(M) *** Ph. 420 894-2. Italian Qt – DEBUSSY: *Quartet*. ***
(B) **(*) Hung. White Label HRC 122 [id.]. Bartók Qt – DEBUSSY: *Quartet* **(*); DVOŘÁK: *Quartet No. 12*. ***
(M) ** Decca 425 424-2; *425 424-4*. Carmirelli Qt – FRANCK: *Quartet*. **(*)

String quartet in F; (i) *Introduction & allegro for harp, flute, clarinet and string quartet.*
(BB) *** Naxos Dig. 8.550249 [id.]. Kodály Qt; (i) with Maros, Gyöngyössy, Kovács – DEBUSSY: *Quartet*. **(*)

For many years the Italian Quartet held pride of place in this coupling. Their playing is perfect in ensemble, attack and beauty of tone, and their performance remains highly recommendable, one of the most satisfying chamber-music records in the catalogue.

At super-bargain price, the Naxos account of the *Quartet* represents splendid value for money. Indeed their Naxos version can more than hold its own against a number of discs offered at premium price, and those coming fresh to this repertoire are unlikely to be disappointed. While they do not surpass the Quartetto Italiano, they are still very good indeed and play with a sensitivity and accomplishment that give great pleasure. Artistically and technically this is a satisfying performance which has the feel of real live music-making. The *Introduction and allegro* is not as magical or as atmospheric as that of the Melos Ensemble from the 1960s, nor is it as well balanced (the players, save for the harp, are a bit forward), but it is still thoroughly enjoyable.

The Bartók Quartet on Hungaroton's cheapest label also give a sympathetic and well-characterized reading, only marginally less perceptive than the Italian version; and they too are well recorded. Moreover they offer an additional work. Those collectors looking for a bargain will not be disappointed here.

It is tempting to pass over the Carmirelli, which is offered as a bonus to the Franck *Quartet*. But this would be unjust, for their playing, if not as distinguished as that of their finest competitors, is still very good, and the recording is perfectly acceptable, even though it dates from the mid-1950s. In its CD transfer it is smoother than the Franck coupling.

SOLO PIANO MUSIC

(i) *À la manière de Borodine; À la manière de Chabrier. Gaspard de la nuit;* (i) *Habanera. Jeux d'eau; Menuet antique; Menuet sur le nom de Haydn;* (i) *Ma Mère l'Oye; Miroirs. Prelude in A min.;* (i) *Sonatine. Le tombeau de Couperin; Valses nobles et sentimentales.*
(M) (*(*)) Sony mono MP2K 46733 (2). Robert Casadesus; (i) with Gaby Casadesus.

In his day Robert Casadesus was a great exponent of this repertoire and these mono recordings were eagerly sought by collectors, despite their rather two-dimensional sound. Returning to the set, now forty years old, proved something of a disappointment. The performances are authoritative and sure-fingered, of course, and one admires the crystalline clarity of the *Noctuelles* and *Une barque sur l'océan*, but the special qualities with which memory invested them are curiously elusive. Unlike Casadesus's Mozart concertos, which hold up very well indeed in their CD incarnation, these strike one as less remarkable than they had once seemed; indeed the *Sonatine* is quite offhand. The pianism is sometimes less than subtle and the unexpansive, colourless studio and relatively compressed range of dynamics do not do Casadesus full justice.

À la manière de Borodine; À la manière de Chabrier; Gaspard de la nuit; Jeux d'eau; Menuet antique; Menuet sur le nom d'Haydn; Miroirs; Pavane pour une infante défunte; Prélude; Sonatine; Le tombeau de Couperin; La valse; Valses nobles et sentimentales.
(B) ** VoxBox (2) [CDX 5012]. Abbey Simon.

Good, reliable performances from Abbey Simon, albeit sometimes wanting the last ounce of magic and poetry, as for example in *Ondine* from *Gaspard de la nuit*. Yet he gives a highly effective account of *Le gibet* and again of *Oiseaux tristes* from *Miroirs*, though the rather forward microphones capture some gentle moaning.

Gaspard de la nuit; Jeux d'eaux; Miroirs; Valses nobles et sentimentales.
(M) *(*) Decca 425 002-2. Pascal Rogé.

These were among Pascal Rogé's first recordings of French repertoire for Decca, made in 1974/5, and they proved to be disappointing. He does not match Argerich in *Gaspard de la nuit* in terms of authority and panache. In the *Miroirs* he is a shade pallid and undercharacterized, though he produces some finely coloured tone; his *Jeux d'eaux*, though nicely played, is curiously faceless. He is well recorded, but he was to be much more successful in his later recordings of Debussy, Poulenc and Satie.

Gaspard de la nuit; Menuet antique; Pavane pour une infante défunte; Sonatine; Le tombeau de Couperin.

(BB) *(*) Naxos Dig. 8.550254 [id.]. Klára Körmendi.

Klára Körmendi belongs to the middle generation of Hungarian pianists and has specialized in contemporary music. She is a very capable player but, as so often in recordings from this source, is handicapped by a less than flattering recording acoustic. Although not as dry as in some of the Naxos recordings made in Heidelberg, the rather close balance robs this music of much of its magic and atmosphere. The sound is more three-dimensional than for Casadesus, recorded in the early 1950s; but we are well served in this repertoire and this disc does not pose a strong challenge.

VOCAL MUSIC

Chansons madécasses; 3 Poèmes de Stéphane Mallarmé.

❀ (M) *** Decca 425 948-2 [id.]. Dame Janet Baker, Melos Ens. (with *Recital of French songs* *** ❀).

Superb singing from Dame Janet, her voice at its most radiant in 1966, and a wonderfully sympathetic accompaniment from members of the Melos group, matched by a recording which spins a lovely web of atmospheric sound.

2 Mélodies hébraïques; 3 Poèmes de Stéphane Mallarmé; Shéhérazade.

(M) (***) Decca mono 425 988-2 [id.]. Suzanne Danco, SRO, Ansermet – BERLIOZ: *Les nuits d'été.* (***)

The great Belgian-born soprano recorded Ravel's *Shéhérazade* with Ansermet and the Suisse Romande Orchestra in the days of 78s, but her second and hardly less magical recording, made towards the end of 1954, is rightly chosen, for Decca engineering had made remarkable advances in the intervening years. Danco evokes a sense of enchantment in the opening song, *Asie*, and the other-worldly quality of sound she produces is ideal for *La flûte enchantée.* Her performance of the three Mallarmé *Songs* has probably never been surpassed in sheer purity of sound. Ansermet's orchestra was in good shape at this time, and the mono sound is impressively detailed and atmospheric.

Rawsthorne, Alan (1905–71)

Overture: Street corner.

(M) (***) EMI mono CDH7 63911-2 [id.]. Philh. O, Lambert – LAMBERT: *Horoscope* etc.; GORDON: *Rake's progress.* (***)

Street corner, following very much the mood of Walton's comedy overtures, is among Rawsthorne's most colourful and appealing works. It makes a welcome fill-up to the Lambert pieces in this première recording, made in 1946 and sounding astonishingly vivid.

Reger, Max (1873–1916)

Piano concerto in F min., Op. 114.

(M) ** Sony MPK 46452 [id.]. Rudolf Serkin, Phd. O, Ormandy - PROKOFIEV: *Piano concerto No. 4.* (***)

Reger's *Piano concerto* is a remarkable and powerful composition. Its dark opening momentarily suggests Shostakovich! No one but Reger, however, could have conceived the rugged, Brahmsian piano writing. The slow movement is a contemplative, rapt piece that touches genuine depths. Less successful, perhaps, is the rhetorical finale. Serkin gives a magisterial performance and is well supported by the Philadelphia Orchestra under Ormandy; this record has considerable documentary value, even though the early-1960s sound is not very inviting and is even rather harsh in its CD transfer (the outstanding mono coupling is much more agreeable!).

Variations and fugue on a theme of Bach, Op. 81.

(BB) **(*) Naxos Dig. 8.550469 [id.]. Wolf Harden – SCHUMANN: *Humoreske.* **(*)

Wolf Harden is a highly talented German pianist in his late twenties. He proves a sensitive and imaginative interpreter of the Schumann *Humoreske*, and his account of the Reger *Variations and fugue on a theme of Bach*, Op. 81, is every bit as fine. Unfortunately there is far less air or sense of space round the piano here and the instrument sounds much drier than in the Schumann. Yet such is the compelling quality of his playing (and the rarity of this remarkable piece on record) that it would be curmudgeonly to withhold a recommendation on this count.

Variations and fugue on a theme by Telemann, Op. 134.

(M) *** Decca 417 791-2. Jorge Bolet – BRAHMS: *Handel variations.* ***

Reger's *Telemann variations*, his last major work for solo piano, makes a challenging and compelling coupling for Bolet's superb account of Brahms's *Handel* set. The virtuosity is phenomenal, not least in the fugue at the end, which was once considered unplayable. Bolet breasts all difficulties with commanding strength. A thrilling experience with first-rate remastered recording.

Reich, Steve (born 1936)

Drumming; Music for mallet instruments, voices and organ; 6 Pianos.
(M) **(*) DG 427 428-2 (2) [id.]. Instrumental & Vocal Ens., composer.

At almost 90 minutes, *Drumming* is Steve Reich's longest work, with different groups of percussion instruments exploited in each of the four long parts or movements. *Six Pianos* uses that combination in the same way; and the most attractive piece on this pair of discs is the shortest, *Music for mallet instruments, voices and organ*, where at least textures are more varied and often charm the ear. Excellent performances and recording.

Respighi, Ottorino (1879–1936)

Ancient airs and dances: suites Nos. 1–3.
(M) **(*) DG 419 868-2 [id.]. Boston SO, Ozawa.

Ozawa is at his best in the *Second suite*, where the luminous Boston wind playing combines with strong contrasts of dynamic and tempo to dramatic effect. Rhythmically very positive throughout, as so often his music-making brings a feeling of ballet to the score. He is less memorable in the *Third suite*; but with brightly vivid sound this makes an enjoyable mid-price version.

(i) *The Birds* (suite); *Brazilian impressions;* (ii) *The Fountains of Rome; The Pines of Rome.*
(M) **(*) Mercury 432 007-2 [id.]. (i) LSO; (ii) Minneapolis SO, Antal Dorati.

This Mercury reissue combines the contents of two analogue LPs, one of which had not previously been issued in the UK, probably because of the established and justly famous RCA/Reiner/Chicago coupling of the same music. This has reappeared on CD in the USA at full price [RCA RCD1-5407] but is still awaited in the UK. The Minneapolis Northrop Auditorium – for all the skill of the Mercury engineers – never produced a web of sound with quite the magical glow which Orchestral Hall, Chicago, could provide in the late 1950s. Nevertheless, in Dorati's hands the opening and closing evocations of the *Fountains of Rome*, cleanly focused as they are by the use of Telefunken 201 microphones, have a unique, shimmering brightness which certainly suggests a sun-drenched landscape, although the turning of the Triton fountain brings a shrill burst of sound that almost assaults the ears. The tingling detail in the companion *Pines of Rome* is again matched by Dorati's powerful sense of atmosphere, so that the sepulchral Catacombs sequence, with its haunting nightingale's song, has a disturbing melancholy, while the finale has an overwhelming juggernaut forcefulness. The coupling of *The Birds* and *Brazilian impressions* was made in the smoother, warmer acoustics of Watford Town Hall in 1957, and here the vividness of detail particularly suits Dorati's spirited account of *The Birds*, bringing pictorial piquancy of great charm and strongly projected dance-rhythms. The liveliness of the LSO playing is most appealing. Respighi wrote *Brazilian impressions* while spending the summer of 1927 in Rio de Janeiro. The triptych recalls Debussy's *Ibéria*, though it is much less subtle. The second impression invokes the *Dies irae* in sinister fashion; it is named after Butantan, famous for its reptile institute, where poisonous snakes are bred in large numbers for the production of serum. The finale, *Canzone e danza*, certainly glitters in Dorati's hands even if overall this work does not represent Respighi at his finest.

The Birds (suite); The Fountains of Rome; The Pines of Rome.
(B) *** Decca 425 507-2; *425 507-4*. LSO, Istvan Kertész.

This was one of Kertész's most impressive records and (made in 1969) it has the advantage of vintage Decca recording. It still sounds pretty spectacular. *The Birds* is very engaging in its spirited elegance; seldom before has the entry of the nightingale's song been so beautifully prepared in the central section of *The Pines of Rome*, where Kertész creates a magical, atmospheric frisson. The iridescent brilliance of the turning on of the Triton fountain in the companion-piece is matched by the grandeur of the Trevi processional, when Neptune's chariot is imagined to be seen crossing the heavens. In sharpening detail the remastering loses only a little of the original ambient warmth and depth.

Feste romane.
(M) (*) BMG/RCA mono GD 60311. Phd. O, Toscanini – DEBUSSY: *La Mer.* (*)

Feste romane; The Fountains of Rome; The Pines of Rome (symphonic poems).
(M) *** DG 415 846-2 [id.]; *415 846-4*. Boston SO, Ozawa.
(BB) **(*) BMG/RCA VD 60486; *VK 60486*. Phd. O, Ormandy.
(M) (**(*)) BMG/RCA mono GD 60262; *GK*

60262 [60262-2-RG; *60262-4-RG*]. NBC SO, Toscanini.

Ozawa's CD offering some of his finest performances on record has been digitally remastered for its Galleria reissue and remains very competitive at mid-price; however, while sharpening the focus and refining detail, the brighter treble has brought a hint of harshness to the loudest fortissimos.

Ormandy plays all three works with enormous gusto and panache, and the orchestral virtuosity is thrilling, with the robust vulgarity of *Feste romane* breathtaking in its unbuttoned zest. The cascade at the turning on of the Triton fountain is like a dam bursting, and all the pictorial effects spring vividly to life. The 1973/4 recording is immensely spectacular. It is atmospheric too, but brightly lit to the point of garishness, and not all ears will respond to the tingling brilliance. But the performances make an unforgettable impact.

Toscanini's recordings of the Roman trilogy are in a class of their own; they (and Reiner in the *Pines* and the *Fountains*, still awaited on CD in the UK) are the yardstick by which all others are measured. This is electrifying playing, which comes over well in this transfer – though, to be fair, the old LPs (particularly the German RCA pressings of the *Feste romane*) had a rounder, fuller (less acidulated) tone on the strings above the stave.

Violin sonata in B min.

(M) (***) BMG/RCA mono GD 87871; *GK 87871* [7871-2-RG; *7871-4-RG*]. Heifetz, Bay – DEBUSSY: *Sonata* (**); RAVEL: *Trio* etc.(**); MARTINŮ: *Duo.* ***

Heifetz and Emanuel Bay recorded this sonata in 1950 (on the day after the Debussy with which this is coupled) and their performance has never been surpassed, not even by the superbly played and sumptuously recorded version by Kyung Wha Chung and Krystian Zimerman at full price. The latter remain the obvious recommendation, for it is difficult to summon up great enthusiasm for the Heifetz–Rubinstein–Piatigorsky Ravel *Trio.* All these performances, save the Martinů, are in mono.

Rimsky-Korsakov, Nikolay

(1844–1908)

Capriccio espagnol, Op. 34.

(B) *** DG Compact Classics 413 422-2 (2); *413 422-4* [id.]. BPO, Maazel – BIZET: *L'Arlésienne; Carmen*; DUKAS: *L'apprenti sorcier*; CHABRIER: *España.* **(*) (CD only: FALLA: *Three-cornered hat:* dances **).

(M) **(*) Decca Dig. 430 700-2; *430 700-4.* Montreal SO, Dutoit – MUSSORGSKY: *Night*; TCHAIKOVSKY: *1812* etc. **(*)

Maazel's 1960 recording of the *Capriccio espagnol* remains one of the very finest of recorded performances. With gorgeous string and horn playing, and a debonair, relaxed virtuosity in the *Scene e canto gitano* leading to breathtaking bravura in the closing section, every note in place, this is unforgettable. With Claudio Abbado's splendid account of Bizet's *L'Arlésienne* and *Carmen* suites, this is worth acquiring for the car, even if some duplication may be involved with the other items. The pair of CDs also includes excerpts from Falla's *Three-cornered hat* ballet. On both discs and tape the remastered sound is exceptionally vivid.

Dutoit's *Capriccio espagnol* is given a genial rather than an electrifying performance, though one not lacking in brilliance in terms of the orchestral playing. The recording is characteristic of the Montreal acoustic: full and warm, with luminous detail.

Le coq d'or: suite. Mlada: suite. The Snow Maiden: suite.

(BB) ** Naxos Dig. 8.550486 [id.]. Slovak RSO (Bratislava), Donald Johanos.

Donald Johanos finds a light touch for Rimsky's more piquant orchestral effects, and the *Dance of the birds* in the *Snow Maiden suite* sparkles engagingly. If the famous *Dance of the Tumblers* lacks the last degree of unbuttoned zest, the Suite from *Le coq d'or* has attractively picaresque detail, although here the music for Queen Shemakha is lacking in sensuous allure. However, the famous *Cortège* from *Mlada* ends the programme with boisterous exuberance. The recording is vividly detailed and atmospheric, but not sumptuous.

Scheherazade (symphonic suite), *Op. 35.*

(M) *** BMG/RCA GD 60875 [60875-2-RG]. Chicago SO, Fritz Reiner – DEBUSSY: *La Mer.* ***

(M) *** Ph. 420 898-2 [id.]. LPO, Haitink – MUSSORGSKY: *Night on the bare mountain.* ***

(M) *** DG 419 063-2; *419 063-4* [id.]. BPO, Karajan – BORODIN: *Polovtsian dances.* ***

(B) **(*) Pickwick Dig. PCD 880; *CIMPC 880* [id.]. LSO, John Mauceri.

(B) **(*) DG Compact Classics *413 155-4* [id.]. Boston SO, Ozawa – STRAVINSKY: *Firebird suite*; KHACHATURIAN: *Gayaneh.* **(*)

(BB) *(**) BMG/RCA VD 87743 [7743-2-RV]. RPO, Stokowski.

(i) *Scheherazade;* (ii) *Capriccio espagnol.*

(M) *(**) Decca 417 753-2 [id.]. (i) LSO; (ii)

New Philh. O, Stokowski – BORODIN: *Polovtsian dances.* **(*)
(BB) ** LaserLight Dig. 15 608 [id.]. Hungarian State O, János Sándor.

Scheherazade; Le coq d'or: Introduction & Cortège. Sadko, Op. 5.
(BB) ** Naxos Dig. 8.550098 [id.]. Czech RSO (Bratislava), Ondrej Lenárd.

(i) *Scheherazade;* (ii) *May night overture; Sadko, Op. 5.*
(B) *** Decca 421 400-2. (i) LSO, Monteux; (ii) SRO, Ansermet.

Scheherazade; Russian Easter festival overture.
(B) ** Decca 433 615-2; *433 615-4* [id.]. Cleveland O, Maazel.

(i) *Scheherazade, Op. 35;* (ii) *Russian Easter festival overture, Op. 36;* (i) *Tsar Saltan, Op. 57: March; Flight of the bumble-bee.*
(BB) **(*) BMG/RCA VD 60487; *VK 60487.* (i) LSO, Previn; (ii) Chicago SO, Stokowski.

Reiner's classic (1960) recording at last reappears on CD, coupled with an equally outstanding version of Debussy's *La Mer* which is new to the British catalogue. The CD transfer retains all the warmth and opulence of the analogue master. The first movement opens richly and dramatically and has a strong forward impulse. The unnamed orchestral leader, naturally balanced, plays most seductively, and the two central movements have beguiling colour, helped by the glowing ambience. Reiner's affectionate individual touches have much in common with Beecham's (full-price) version and sound comparably spontaneous. The third movement is wonderfully languorous and the finale, brilliant and very exciting, has a climax of resounding power and amplitude. The Chicago Hall ambience makes up in body and spaciousness for any lack of internal clarity, and the sound is richer if less refined in detail than the Philips recording for Haitink.

Haitink's LPO record dates from 1974. The recording shows its age just a little in the string timbre, but in all other respects it is exceptionally truthful in both sound and perspective. It is a relief to hear a solo violin sounding its natural size in relation to the orchestra as a whole. Yet Rodney Friend, who plays the solos subtly, dominates the performance with his richly sinuous picture of Scheherazade herself as narrator of each episode. The playing of the LPO is both sensitive and alert, Haitink's interpretation wholly unaffected and totally fresh in impact.

Karajan's 1967 recording is greatly enhanced in its CD format. The extra vividness brings more life and sparkle to the central movements, which are superbly played, and the brass fanfares in the second have a tingling immediacy. The added presence also increases the feeling of ardour from the glorious Berlin strings in the *Andante*. The outer movements have great vitality and thrust, and the bright percussion transients add to the feeling of zest. Yet Michel Schwalbé's sinuously luxuriant violin solos are still allowed to participate in the narrative. The fill-up is a sizzling account of the Borodin *Polovtsian dances*, with no chorus, but managing perfectly well without.

The recordings from Monteux and Ansermet on the Decca Weekend CD come from the earliest days of stereo. Monteux's version of *Scheherazade* is, if anything, even more vivid than Haitink's and the recording remains brilliant and sparkling, the performance sensuous and exciting, full of charisma. Ansermet finds all the colour in the *May night overture* and *Sadko*, an exotic Rimskian fairy-tale with a colourful storm for a climax; while the Decca engineers, working in Geneva, provided both atmosphere and the fullest orchestral palette. In the finale of *Scheherazade* Monteux holds back the climax – another storm – until the last minute and then unleashes his forces with devastating effect. The orchestral playing is not as polished as the LPO under Haitink, but it has tremendous zest and spontaneity, and this makes a fine bargain recommendation, even though the upper range lacks something in opulence.

On the bargain-price IMP label, John Mauceri conducts a powerful, dramatic reading marked by incisive, crisply disciplined playing from the LSO, just as impressive in the warmly expressive rubato of the great lyrical passages. To match this, the recording is brilliant rather than sensuously beautiful, clear, well balanced and with fine presence. Michael Davis is a persuasive violin soloist, and in Mauceri's hands the melodic line of the third movement is appealingly supple, while there is no lack of excitement in the finale.

Previn's tempi are expansive, but the first movement is commandingly spacious. The inner movements are unexpectedly cool, the very opposite of vulgar, but, with rhythmic pointing which is characteristically crisp, the result grows attractive on repetition, while the finale brings one of the most dramatic and brilliant performances of that showpiece ever recorded. Previn's fill-ups provide a charming bonus, particularly the *Tsar Saltan march.* The recording is outstanding for its late-1960s vintage and it has been richly and vividly transferred to CD. With Stokowski's brilliant and colourful (1968) account of the *Russian*

Easter festival overture added for good measure, this remains competitive in the bargain range.

Ozawa's version, available on a Compact Classics cassette, makes a fair bargain alternative if the couplings, Maazel's early stereo recording of the *Firebird suite* and Rozhdestvensky's *Gayaneh*, are suitable. It is an attractive performance, richly recorded. The first movement is strikingly spacious, building to a fine climax; if the last degree of vitality is missing from the central movements, the orchestral playing is warmly vivid. The finale is lively enough, if not earth-shaking in its excitement; the reading as a whole has plenty of colour and atmosphere, however, and it is certainly enjoyable. The chrome-tape transfer is sophisticated.

Stokowski's Decca performance is eccentric and wilful – with changes to the score – yet the LSO play brilliantly and there is no lack of excitement. But the 1964 sound is coarse-grained as remastered and lacks the necessary sumptuousness. The *Capriccio espagnol* coupling features the New Philharmonia and the recording, made a decade later, is much more acceptable. The performance brings surprisingly relaxed tempi, with jaunty gypsy rhythms deliciously underlined. In many ways this is memorable, but the score is slightly cut and rearranged by the conductor.

For the 1975 RCA recording, Stokowski turned to the RPO and, originally on LP, achieved some sensuously beautiful orchestral sound. With Erich Gruenberg providing a sweet-toned commentary, this is certainly compelling, with Stokowski at his most characteristic in the slow movement. But here his nudgings of rubato are not entirely spontaneous and, although there is no lack of drama, the reading overall does not show him at his very best. Moreover the RCA remastering brings an excess of brilliance, producing thin violin timbres and moments of shrillness.

Maazel generates a fine thrust in the opening movement of *Scheherazade* and plenty of adrenalin in the finale, but in the central movements his straightness, his reluctance to indulge in conventional expressiveness, sharpens the attention on purely musical matters in what should have a sinuous, romantic flexibility and affectionate colouring. Haitink, as one among rivals, gets the best of both worlds, where Maazel can sound stiff and relatively unsympathetic. The performance of the *Russian Easter festival overture* is another matter, full of imaginative touches, so that one has the sense of hearing the score for the first time. The recordings, dating from the late 1970s, are both spectacular, approaching demonstration standard in the ripely coloured overture.

There is not a great deal to choose between the two super-bargain versions. They both offer vivid digital sound and are well played. The Hungarian recording has slightly more glamour because of a marginally warmer recording acoustic. Neither has quite the finesse or the body of string tone of the finest Western versions but both offer excellent wind solos and plenty of excitement in the finale. Couplings could dictate choice. On the whole, those on Naxos are preferable; although it is a pity that the whole *Coq d'or* suite was not chosen, the performance of *Sadko* has plenty of atmosphere and a really spectacular climax. The *Capriccio espagnol* is also quite attractive but could be more exciting in the closing *Fandango asturiano.*

Rodrigo, Joaquín (born 1902)

(i) *Concierto Andaluz* (for 4 guitars); (ii) *Concierto de Aranjuez;* (ii; iii) *Concierto madrigal* (for 2 guitars); (ii) *Concierto para una fiesta; Fantasia para un gentilhombre.* Solo guitar pieces: *Bajando de la Meseta; En los Trigales; Fandango; Junto al Generalife; 3 Little Pieces; Romance de Durandarte; Sonata a la española; Tiento antiquo.*

(M) *** Ph. 432 581-2 (3) [id.]. (i) Los Romeros; (ii) Pepe Romero; (iii) Angel Romero; ASMF, Marriner.

This distinguished set gathers together all Rodrigo's major concertante guitar works in first-class performances and adds a rewarding recital of solo works as a postlude, all played with natural spontaneity and complete authority by an artist who feels this music from his innermost being. The *Sonata* is no less strongly Spanish in character and the genre pieces are comparably picturesque in evoking Mediterranean atmosphere and local dance-rhythms. Los Romeros make the very most of the *Concierto Andaluz* with its infectious tunefulness in the outer sections and plenty of romantic atmosphere. The highly engaging *Concierto madrigal*, in which Pepe and Angel Romero duet persuasively, is based on an anonymous Spanish Renaissance melody, treated in variation style. The work is divided into ten titled episodes, of which the first seven are brief and the last three, *Arieta*, *Zapateado* and *Caccia a la española*, are more extended. If the *Concierto para una fiesta* does not quite repeat the success of the *Concierto de Aranjuez*, it still has plenty of Andalusian colour, and Pepe Romero's performance has all the freshness of new discovery. He is equally magnetic in the solo items. Throughout, Marriner and the Academy provide accompaniments which are thoroughly polished and have much warmth, and the

Philips sound is most natural and beautifully balanced.

Concierto de Aranjuez (for guitar and orchestra).
❀ (M) *** Decca Dig. 430 703-2; *430 703-4* [id.]. Carlos Bonell, Montreal SO, Dutoit – FALLA: *El amor brujo* etc. *** ❀
(M) *** BMG/RCA GD 86525 [6525-2-RG]. Bream, Monteverdi O, Gardiner – VILLA-LOBOS: *Concerto* etc. ***
(M) **(*) EMI Dig. CDD7 63886-2 [id.]; *ET 763886-4*. Alfonso Moreno, LSO, Bátiz – FALLA: *Nights*; TURINA: *Danzas fantásticas*. **(*)
(BB) ** LaserLight Dig. 15 602 [id.]. Zoltán Tokos, Budapest Strings, Bela Banfalvi (with SOR: *Sonata*; GRANADOS: *Spanish dance No. 2*; ALBÉNIZ: *Castilla*; FALLA: *Homage à Debussy; Spanish dance*. Monika & Jürgen Rost).

Concierto de Aranjuez; (i) *Concierto madrigal* (for 2 guitars); *Fantasia para un gentilhombre*.
(M) *** Ph. 432 828-2; *432 828-4* [id.]. Pepe Romero; (ii) Angel Romero; ASMF, Marriner.

Concierto de Aranjuez; Fantasia para un gentilhombre.
(M) *** Decca Dig. 417 748-2 [id.]. Carlos Bonell, Montreal SO, Dutoit (with FALLA: *Three-cornered hat* ***).

(i) *Concierto de Aranjuez; Fantasia para un gentilhombre;* (ii) *Concierto serenata for harp and orchestra*.
(M) ** Ph. 420 714-2 [id.]. (i) Lagoya, (ii) Michel; Monte Carlo Op. O, Almeida.

Decca have reissued the much-praised Bonell/Dutoit recording of the *Concierto* a second time, now re-coupled with Alicia de Larrocha's splendid digital recording of Falla's *Nights in the gardens of Spain* plus Dutoit's outstanding complete *El amor brujo*. This is a very attractive pairing and the reasons for the success of the Rodrigo performance remain unaltered: an exceptionally clear, atmospheric and well-balanced digital recording plus Bonell's imaginative account of the solo part, and the strong characterization of the orchestral accompaniments by Charles Dutoit and his excellent Montreal orchestra. A feeling of freshness pervades every bar of the orchestral texture. De Larrocha's luminous account of *Nights in the gardens of Spain* is equally distinguished, and this makes one of the most desirable compilations of Spanish music in the catalogue.

The Bonell/Dutoit *Concierto* was originally paired with the *Fantasia para un gentilhombre*. Decca then made this issue even more attractive by adding a bonus of three dances from Falla's *Three-cornered hat* (taken from Dutoit's complete set) and by placing the recording on their mid-priced Ovation label. In the *Fantasia*, the balance between warmly gracious lyricism and sprightly rhythmic resilience is no less engaging; here again, the orchestral solo playing makes a strong impression.

Pepe Romero's performance of the *Concierto de Aranjuez* has plenty of Spanish colour, the musing poetry of the slow movement beautifully caught. The account of the *Fantasia* is warm and gracious, with the Academy contributing quite as much as the soloist to the appeal of the performance. Although inner detail is less sharply focused than on the Bonell digital version, it hardly matters, as the warm beauty of the analogue atmosphere emphasizes the Mediterranean feeling. Angel joins Pepe for the Renaissance-inspired duet, *Concierto madrigal*, which is very attractive indeed, making this a very viable alternative to the Decca coupling.

Bream recorded the *Concierto de Aranjuez* twice in the analogue era; this is the first of his analogue recordings and it has a little more dash than the later one with Sir Colin Davis, yet the differences are too subtle for easy analysis. Sufficient to say that this is excellent value at mid-price and that the couplings are also valuable.

The Moreno/Bátiz partnership works well enough in this famous concerto, with the digital recording lending a bright-as-a-button effect to a performance which is thoroughly sympathetic without being really distinctive. However, the equally vivid couplings are well played, and altogether this makes quite an attractive Spanish triptych.

A super-bargain digital recording of Rodrigo's famous *Concierto* obviously has its attractions and Zoltán Tokos is a sympathetic soloist. He is accompanied by a chamber-sized group with good ensemble and a bright violin line: the balance is excellent. The first two movements bring an attractive intimacy, and the famous *Adagio* has an atmospheric, ruminative, improvisatory feel. The finale, however, could do with a lighter rhythmic touch and its *moto perpetuo* is interrupted when Banfalvi lets both the tension and the momentum slip at the point where the soloist is given a pizzicato accompaniment. The coupling is a recital of guitar music by an excellent duo who bring the colourful genre pieces by Granados, Albéniz and Manuel de Falla vividly to life. But the opening Op. 22 *Sonata* of Sor is curiously wan, and not only because the recording level drops after the finale of the *Concierto*.

Lagoya is a good player, but he does not always project strongly, except perhaps in the slow movement of the *Concierto*, which he plays with considerable feeling. The outer movements are agreeable, if not as sprightly as some versions. However, we are now also offered an attractive account of the delectable *Concierto serenata* for harp, with Catherine Michel a splendid soloist and very good 1973 sound, well balanced, full and immediate.

(i) *Concierto de Aranjuez; Fantasia para un gentilhombre;* (ii) *Concierto serenata for harp and orchestra.*

(B) ** DG Compact Classics 413 156-2 (2); *413 156-4* [id.]. (i) Yepes, Spanish R. & TV O, Alonso; (ii) Zabaleta, Berlin RSO, Marzendorfer – FALLA: *Nights in the gardens of Spain* *** (CD only: BACARISSE: *Guitar concertino* **(*); CASTELNUOVO-TEDESCO: *Guitar concerto* ***).

The DG Compact Classics reissue offers Yepes' 1970 coupling of the two most famous Rodrigo concertante works, with Odon Alonso not the most imaginative conductor (he is rhythmically rather stiff in the finale of the *Concierto*). Yepes is at his finest in the *Adagio* and plays nobly in the *Fantasia*, which is generally more successful. The *Concierto serenata* is played with much piquancy and charm by Zabaleta. The remastered recording has gained in vividness, especially in the *Concierto de Aranjuez*. The pair of CDs includes two extra concertos.

Rosetti, Antoni (1750–92)

Horn concertos: in E flat, K.3:39; in E, K.3:42; in E, K3:44.

(B) *** CfP Dig. CD-CFP 4578; *TC-CFP 4578.* Barry Tuckwell, ECO.

The Bohemian composer, born Franz Anton Rössler, who adopted an Italian version of his name, wrote prolifically for the horn; the present concertos are characteristic of the taxing melodic line he provides for the soloist, with high-ranging lyrical tessitura contrasting with very florid arpeggios. He was especially good at rondo finales and the *E major Concerto*, K.3:42, shows him at his melodically most exuberant. Tuckwell's style is agreeably robust and he is very well recorded. He directs his own accompaniments with polish and spirit. This EMI collection is well worth having for anyone who enjoys horn concertos, although the invention here is far more conventional than those of Mozart. The EMI CD has exceptional realism and presence.

Rossini, Gioacchino (1792–1868)

La boutique fantasque (ballet, arr. Respighi) complete.

❀ (M) *** Sony Dig. MDK 46508 [id.]. Toronto SO, Andrew Davis – BIZET: *L'Arlésienne: suite No. 2* etc. **(*)

(M) **(*) Decca Dig. 430 723-2; *430 723-4* [id.]. National PO, Bonynge – CHOPIN: *Les Sylphides.* **(*)

At last comes a really outstanding complete CD of *La boutique fantasque*, one of the great popular triumphs of Diaghilev's Ballets Russes. Respighi created a fully integrated and wonderfully colourful score from tuneful Rossinian miniatures, enhancing the originals with sumptuously brilliant orchestration imbued with an Italianate feeling for atmosphere. In the sympathetic hands of Andrew Davis there is never a dull bar, for Respighi's linking passages (usually omitted) are ingeniously crafted and he leads the ear on affectionately. The Toronto orchestra is on peak form, playing with glittering bravura and warmth; the gentler second half of the ballet is particularly enticing. The digital recording has a spectacularly wide dynamic range; the magical opening (here taken faster than usual) with gentle pizzicato strings evoking gleaming horn chords, at first a mere whisper, then expands gloriously. The vividness of the CBS sound is balanced by a glowing underlying warmth, and this becomes a demonstration disc for the digital era which recalls Ansermet's famous Decca mono LP of the early 1950s, made with the LSO in the Kingsway Hall, London.

Bonynge goes for sparkle and momentum above all in Respighi's brilliant arrangement of Rossini. The Decca recording has great brilliance and the orchestral colours glitter within the Kingsway Hall ambience. But compare the very opening with Andrew Davis, and here there is much less magic and – more surprisingly – less atmosphere, while the dynamic range of the Toronto recording is much more dramatic.

La boutique fantasque (ballet, arr. Respighi): *suite.*

(M) **(*) Chan. CHAN 6503; *MBTD 6503* [id.]. SNO, Gibson – DUKAS: *L'apprenti sorcier*; SAINT-SAENS: *Danse macabre.* **(*)

(M) **(*) Sony SBK 46340 [id.]; *40-46340.* Phd. O, Ormandy – TCHAIKOVSKY: *Sleeping Beauty:* highlights. **

Gibson's version of the suite is strikingly atmospheric. Helped by the glowing acoustics of Glasgow's City Hall, his performance sounds for all the world as if the Scottish conductor had first listened to Ansermet's famous Decca mono LP. Tempi are similar and the opening has much of the evocation that the Swiss maestro created. The orchestra is on its toes and plays with warmth and zest, and the 1973 recording has transferred vividly to CD. The only snag is the short playing time (37 minutes).

Ormandy presents Respighi's glittering orchestration with much brilliance and dash, and the Philadelphia Orchestra has all the sumptuousness one could ask for. This is more extrovert music-making than Gibson's and it is undoubtedly exhilarating, even if the effect of the recording is less refined. The playing time of the Sony CD is much more generous too, but not everyone will want the rather inflated coupling.

Overtures: (i) *Il Barbiere di Siviglia;* (ii) *La cambiale di matrimonio;* (iii) *La Cenerentola;* (ii) *La gazza ladra;* (iv) *L'inganno felice;* (v) *L'Italiana in Algeri; La scala di seta;* (vi) *Il Signor Bruschino;* (i) *Il viaggio a Reims;* (v) *William Tell.*

(B) **(*) EMI CDZ7 67255-2; *LZ 767255-4.* (i) VPO, Sargent; (ii) RPO, Beecham; (iii) Philh. O, Serafin; (iv) Polish CO, Maksymiuk; (v) Philh. O, Galliera; (vi) RPO, C. Davis.

An exceptionally generous helping (76 minutes) of Rossinian high spirits, with Sir Thomas Beecham ensuring plenty of style and verve in two of the ten included overtures. Although the Polish Chamber Orchestra does not create a very wide dynamic range, Jerzy Maksymiuk produces exciting virtuosity in *L'inganno felice*, which is quite as arresting as Sir Thomas's side-drums at the opening of *La gazza ladra*. There is some delightfuly delicate Philharmonia oboe and string playing in *L'Italiana in Algeri* and *La scala de seta*; although Galliera's opening flourish could be more poised in the latter, in *William Tell* his robust vigour is exhilarating. With *Il Signor Bruschino*, it sounds as if the bow-tapping is done by the first desk alone, but otherwise this shows Sir Colin Davis as a natural Rossinian; and Sir Malcolm Sargent's elegantly witty performance of *Il viaggio a Reims* is one of the highlights of the programme. Nearly all the recordings come from the beginning of the 1960s and are brightly transferred, with good ambience, even if at times one could wish for rather more bloom on the violins.

Overtures: *Il Barbiere di Siviglia; La Cenerentola; La gazza ladra; L'Italiana in Algeri; Le siège de Corinthe; Il Signor Bruschino.*

(M) *** DG 419 869-2; *419 869-4* [id.]. LSO, Abbado.

Brilliant, sparkling playing, with splendid discipline, vibrant rhythms and finely articulated phrasing – altogether invigorating and bracing. There is perhaps an absence of outright geniality here, but these are superb performances and this remains one of the very finest collections of Rossini overtures ever, for the wit is spiced with a touch of acerbity, and the flavour is of a vintage dry champagne which retains its bloom, yet has a subtlety all its own.

Overtures: *Il Barbiere di Siviglia; La Cenerentola; La gazza ladra; La scala di seta; Il Signor Bruschino; William Tell.*

❀ (M) *** BMG/RCA GD 60387 [60387-2-RG]. Chicago SO, Fritz Reiner.

As with the others in RCA's remastered Reiner/Chicago series, the sound-quality has been improved phenomenally; no one could possibly guess that these recordings were made over thirty years ago (in 1958) for, as sound, they are preferable to most digital collections. The blaze of brass tone, supported by a rich orchestral backcloth and resonant bass drum, at the gallop in the *William Tell overture*, is all-engulfing, a thrilling moment indeed. The Chicago Symphony was always famous for its brass department, and this is an excellent reminder of how resplendent the playing could be; at the same time the scurrying violins display the utmost virtuosity. Reiner is equally impressive at the grandiloquent opening of *La gazza ladra*, where the hall acoustics again add a magnificent amplitude to the full orchestral tutti. But it is the sparkle and vivacity of these performances that one remembers above all – and, in *La Cenerentola*, the wit, as well as fizzing orchestral bravura. One would have liked the opening flourish of *La scala di seta* to be neater – it is presented too lavishly here – but this is the solitary reservation over a magnificent achievement.

Overtures: *Il Barbiere di Siviglia; La gazza ladra; L'Italiana in Algeri; La scala di seta; Semiramide; Le Siège de Corinthe; Tancredi.*

(BB) *(*) LaserLight Dig. 15 506 [id.]. Plovdiv PO, Rouslan Raychev.

These performances are quite well played by a good provincial orchestra but are not presented with much flair. The recording is bright and clear but not sumptuous. With collections by Reiner, Abbado and Karajan available inexpensively, it is false economy to invest in a record of this kind. This is music that above all needs wit and high polish.

Overtures: *Il Barbiere di Siviglia; La gazza ladra; L'Italiana in Algeri; La scala di seta; William Tell.*

(B) *** DG Compact Classics *431 185-4* [id.]. BPO, Karajan – VERDI: *Overtures.* ***

Karajan's virtuoso Rossini performances are superbly polished and vivid. *La scala di seta* abandons almost all decorum when played as brilliantly as here, but this music-making is nothing if not exhilarating. The 1971 recordings are crisply transferred with plenty of supporting weight and good ambience. With equally distinguished Verdi for coupling, this is one of the finest of the later Compact Classics tapes.

Overtures: *Il Barbiere di Siviglia; La gazza ladra; L'Italiana in Algeri; Semiramide; Il Signor Bruschino; William Tell.*
(B) ** Hung. White Label HRC 062 [id.]. Budapest SO, Adám Fischer.

These are lively performances – *William Tell* has splendid gusto – and the recording is both brilliant and open, while not lacking fullness. The orchestral playing is always good and generally characterful. Fair value in the lower price-range.

Overtures: *Il Barbiere di Siviglia; La gazza ladra; La scala di seta; Semiramide; William Tell.*
(B) **(*) Decca 417 692-2; *417 692-4*. LSO, Pierino Gamba.

Gamba's performances are taut and involving, the orchestral playing alive and polished. A strong disciplining force is felt in every piece, and care in phrasing is noticeable at every turn. The only quality missing is a touch of geniality – but, even so, *La scala di seta* is not overdriven. The very good recording re-emerges vividly and with plenty of ambient atmosphere, but the brightly lit violins, although not edgy, have a slightly artificial timbre.

Overtures: *Il Barbiere di Siviglia; La gazza ladra; L'Italiana in Algeri; La scala di seta.*
(B) *** DG 429 164-2. BPO, Karajan – VERDI: *Overtures and Preludes.* ***

These performances are all taken from Karajan's 1971 collection and offer orchestral playing of supreme polish and bravura. The recording is extremely realistic at *piano* and *mezzo forte* levels, with inner detail refined, and the digital remastering is fresh and vivid, if perhaps a little overbright in the treble.

Overtures: *La cambiale di matrimonio; La Cenerentola; Matilde di Shabran; Il viaggio à Reims; William Tell. La boutique fantasque* (ballet, arr. Respighi): *suite.*
(BB) *(*) LaserLight Dig. 15 520 [id.]. Plovdiv PO, Rouslan Raychev.

The second LaserLight collection has some rare repertoire and quite a good horn solo in *La cambiale di matrimonio*, beloved of Sir Thomas Beecham. It also includes a really fine account of *Il viaggio à Reims*, relaxed, stylish and with an element of wit. But *William Tell* is no match for Reiner's spectacular account. The short suite from *La boutique fantasque* appears to use a reduced orchestration; it lacks the sumptuousness of Respighi's fuller version, but in any case the performance has not a great deal of balletic feeling.

Overtures: Elisabetta, Regina d'Inghilterra; La scala di seta; Semiramide; Tancredi; Il Turco in Italia; William Tell.
(BB) **(*) BMG/RCA VD 87814 [7814-2-RV]. LSO, Abbado.

Zestful performances from Abbado, with exhilaratingly fast tempi, the LSO players kept consistently on their toes and obviously revelling in their own virtuosity. The exuberance comes to the fore especially in *Tancredi* – there is even a brief clarinet glissando – in a revised version by Philip Gosset. But some might feel that *La scala di seta* would be more effective if a fraction more relaxed. *William Tell* opens with elegant cellos, then offers an unashamedly vulgar storm sequence and a final *Galop* taken at breakneck pace. *Elisabetta, Regina* is our old friend *The Barber of Seville* but with a subtle change (a triplet consistently repeated in the first theme of the allegro): again stylish but fast. The remastered recording is more brightly lit than the original and may need a little taming on some machines.

String sonatas Nos. 1–6.
(M) **(*) Decca 430 563-2 (2). ASMF, Marriner (with DONIZETTI: *String quartet in D* (arr. for string orchestra); CHERUBINI: *Étude No. 2 for French horn and strings;* BELLINI: *Oboe concerto in E flat* **(*))

The Academy versions of Rossini's *String sonatas*, the astonishingly assured work of a precocious twelve-year-old, have always been admired for their freshness, polish and youthful high spirits. The playing time, at fractionally over 80 minutes, means that two CDs have been used (although we are reliably informed that it is now possible to get up to 82 minutes on one!). The 1966 recording was considered demonstration-worthy in its day: the violins now sound a bit sparer in texture, but they are still very pleasing because of the attractive ambience. The string-orchestral version of the Donizetti *Quartet* is particularly appropriate as it has a Rossinian flavour, especially in the delectable finale. Although a 'prentice work, it is beautifully crafted, with a pervading sunny lyricism. The Cherubini *Étude for French horn and strings* is rather less memorable but the unnamed horn player is persuasive, and Bellini's winningly operatic *Oboe concerto*, with another splendid soloist, fits the bill no less aptly. However, the overall playing time of 112 minutes means that there would have been room for even more music.

String sonatas Nos. 1 in G; 2 in A; 3 in C; 6 in D.
(B) ** DG 429 525-2 [id.]. BPO, Karajan.

Alongside Marriner, Karajan's Berlin Philharmonic performances sound a little suave, and the 1969 recording shows its age in the slight thinning-down of the violin timbre by the digital remastering. But there is plenty of bloom and the music cannot help but be effective when the playing is so polished and elegant; this disc also has a price advantage.

String sonatas Nos. 1 in G; 4 in B flat; 5 in E flat; 6 in D.
(M) *** Teldec/Warner 9031 74788-2 [id.]. Liszt CO, János Rolla – M. HAYDN: *Symphony, P.12.* ***

The merits of the Liszt Chamber Orchestra and János Rolla, who directs from the first desk, are by now well known. They are hardly less less virtuosic or less polished than Marriner's ASMF, and they have the advantage of very natural digital sound. Moreover the attractive Michael Haydn coupling is considerable compensation for the two missing sonatas.

Stabat Mater.
(M) **(*) Decca 417 766-2. Lorengar, Minton, Pavarotti, Sotin, LSO Ch., LSO, Kertész.

Kertész's approach brings out an unexpected degree of beauty, notably in the fine choral singing, and even *Cujus anima* is given extra delicacy, with Pavarotti singing most beautifully and linking back to the main theme with a subtle half-tone. Some may feel that Kertész underplays the work in removing the open-hearted vulgarity, but he certainly makes one enjoy the music afresh. Soprano, mezzo and bass may not have all the idiomatic Italian qualities, but their singing matches Kertész's interpretation.

OPERA

Il Barbiere di Siviglia (complete).
(M) *** EMI CMS7 64162-2 (2) [id.]; (B) CfP *TC-CFPD 4704*. De los Angeles, Alva, Cava, Wallace, Bruscantini, Glyndebourne Festival Ch., RPO, Gui.
(M) *** BMG/RCA GD 86505 (3) [RCA 6505-2-RG]. Roberta Peters, Valletti, Merrill, Corena, Tozzi, Met. Op. Ch. & O, Leinsdorf.
(M) **(*) Decca 417 164-2 (2) [id.]. Berganza, Ausensi, Benelli, Corena, Ghiaurov, Rossini Ch. & O of Naples, Varviso.

Victoria de los Angeles is as charming a Rosina as you will ever find: no viper this one, as she claims in *Una voce poco fa*. Musically it is an unforceful performance – Rossini's brilliant *fioriture* done lovingly, with no sense of fear or danger – and that matches the gently rib-nudging humour of what is otherwise a 1962 recording of the Glyndebourne production. It does not fizz as much as other Glyndebourne Rossini on record but, with elaborate stage direction in the stereo production and with a characterful line-up of soloists, it is an endearing performance which in its line is unmatched. The recording still sounds well. Tape collectors should be very well satisfied with the CfP equivalent, issued at bargain price on two cassettes in a chunky box, with synopsis instead of libretto. The transfer is kind to the voices and generally vivid, and this costs about half as much as the CDs.

Roberta Peters is a sparkling Rosina, a singer too little known in Europe, who here lives up to her high reputation at the Met., dazzling in coloratura elaborations *in alt.* Robert Merrill may not be a specially comic Figaro, but the vocal characterization is strong, with the glorious voice consistently firm and well focused. Valletti, Corena and Tozzi make up a formidable team, and Leinsdorf conducts with a lightness and relaxation rare for him on record. Good, clear sound of the period, set against a reverberant, helpful acoustic.

Vocally the Decca set, with Teresa Berganza an agile Rosina, is very reliable, and Silvio Varviso secures electrifying effects in many of Rossini's high-spirited ensembles. There remain important reservations, however. Manuel Ausensi as Figaro himself is rather gruff, both vocally and dramatically, though he was chosen specifically because of the authenticity of having a darker-toned voice than usual in the part. Ugo Benelli is charming as the Count, a free-voiced 'tenorino', though he sounds nervous in his first aria. Corena's fine Dr Bartolo is well known, and Ghiaurov sings with characteristic richness as Basilio. This version, while textually not quite complete, does contain much more than usual, including the often omitted Act II tenor aria which uses the *Non più mesta* theme from *Cenerentola.* It is very well recorded – the 1964 sound is noticeably fuller than the earlier, RCA version.

Il Barbiere di Siviglia: highlights.
(M) *** EMI CDM7 63076-2; *EG 763076-4* (from complete set with Callas, Alva, Gobbi, Ollendorff, Philh. Ch. & O, Galliera).
(M) *** BMG/RCA GD 60188; *GK 60188* [60188-2-RG; *60188-4-RG*] (from above recording with Peters, Valletti, Merrill cond. Leinsdorf).
(B) * Pickwick (DG) IMPX 9022. Gianna d'Angelo, Capecchi, Monti, Tadeo, Bav. RSO, Bartoletti.

Gobbi and Callas were here at their most inspired and, with the recording quality nicely refurbished, the EMI is an outstanding set of highlights. Callas remains supreme as a minx-like Rosina, summing up the character superbly in *Una voce poco fa*. In the final ensemble, despite the usual reading of the score, Rosina's verse is rightly given premier place at the very end. The disc offers most of the key solo numbers from Act I, while in Act II it concentrates on Rossini's witty ensembles, including the extended Second Act *Quintet*. The *Overture* is included and, while it is stylishly played, it would have been better to have offered more of the vocal music.

The selection from the Leinsdorf *Barber* is generous (71 minutes) and well chosen, and the documentation relates the excerpts to an excellent synopsis. The 1958 recording sounds a little shrill in the treble (the violins in the *Overture* are thin), but it responds to the controls.

The Pickwick/DG selection is reasonably generous (58 minutes) and includes most of the key numbers. Gianna d'Angelo sings very sweetly as Rosina, her coloratura is impressively clean, but there is little of the minx in her characterization. Capecchi's *Largo al factotum* is breezy, but elsewhere he gives a somewhat over-respectable account of the Barber. The recording emerges vividly enough on CD but, curiously, opens with a truncated account of the *Overture*, lasting 2 minutes 47 seconds!

Il Barbiere di Siviglia: highlights; *La Cenerentola:* highlights.
(B) **(*) DG Compact Classics *427 714-4* [id.] (from complete recordings, with Berganza, Alva, Prey, Capecchi, Amb. Op. Ch. or Scottish Op. Ch., LSO, Abbado).

Abbado's 1972 recordings of two favourite Rossini operas have a pleasing freshness. Both overtures are included, and the lack of theatrical feeling matters less in highlights; certainly Teresa Berganza, with her agile coloratura, and the stylish Luigia Alva together lead a reliable cast, with Herman Prey as Figaro in *The Barber* and Renato Capecchi as Dandini in *Cenerentola* bringing plenty of sparkle to their performances. The tape transfer reproduces the voices most naturally.

La Cenerentola (complete).
(M) *(*) Decca 433 030-2 (2) [id.]. Simionato, Benelli, Montarsolo, Bruscantini, Ch. & O of Maggio Musicale Fiorentino, Fabritiis.

Until Marriner's highly recommendable, full-price, Philips set arrived (420 468-2) *La Cenerentola* had not been lucky on records. This Decca version is a good example of earlier failures. With never very refined singing from any of his soloists, Fabritiis makes the piece sound longer and less interesting than it is. Simionato is well below her best vocally, wobbling far more than she ought to, and it is small consolation that the Decca recording is so brilliant.

Guillaume Tell (William Tell) (sung in French).
(M) **(*) EMI CMS7 69951-2 (4). Bacquier, Caballé, Gedda, Mesplé, Hendrikx, Amb. Op. Ch., RPO, Gardelli.

The interest of the 1973 EMI set is that it is sung in the original French. Gardelli proves an imaginative Rossini interpreter, allying his formidable team to vigorous and sensitive performances. Bacquier makes an impressive Tell, developing the character as the story progresses; Gedda is a model of taste, and Montserrat Caballé copes ravishingly with the coloratura problems of Mathilde's role. While Chailly's full-price Decca set puts forward a strong case for using Italian with its open vowels, this remains a fully worthwhile alternative, with excellent CD sound. The one considerable snag is that no English translation is provided.

L'Italiana in Algeri (complete).
(M) *** Erato/Warner 2292 45404-2 (2) [id.]. Horne, Palacio, Ramey, Trimarchi, Battle, Zaccaria, Prague Ch., Sol. Ven., Scimone.
(M) *** Decca 417 828-2 (2). Berganza, Alva, Corena, Panerai, Maggio Musicale Fiorentino Ch. & O, Varviso.
(M) (**) EMI mono CHS7 64041-2 (2). Petri, Sciutti, Valletti, Simionato, Cortis, La Scala O & Ch., Giulini.

Scholarship as well as Rossinian zest have gone into Scimone's highly enjoyable version, beautifully played and recorded with as stylish a team of soloists as one can expect nowadays. The text is complete, the original orchestration has been restored (as in the comic duetting of piccolo and bassoon in the reprise in the overture) and alternative versions of certain arias are given as an appendix. Marilyn Horne makes a dazzling, positive Isabella, and Samuel Ramey is splendidly firm as Mustafa. Domenico Trimarchi is a delightful Taddeo and Ernesto Palacio an agile Lindoro, not coarse, though the recording does not always catch his tenor timbre well. Nevertheless the sound is generally very good indeed, and the fullness and atmosphere come out the more vividly on CD.

Under Varviso the opera has Rossinian sparkle in abundance and the music blossoms readily. Teresa Berganza makes an enchanting Italian girl, and the three principal men are all characterful. The recording is vintage Decca, vividly remastered, and adds greatly to the sparkle of the whole proceedings. With excellent documentation this is a fine bargain, even if many may still opt for the later and more complete Scimone version.

Set in a dry, intimate acoustic, Giulini's mono version wears quite well in this CD reissue, with the rhythmic point of his conducting bringing plenty of sparkle, even if the singing is flawed. The characterful Simionato, in one of her most cherished roles as Isabella, is relatively disappointing, lacking charm. Her powerful mezzo is made to sound a little fluttery, less flatteringly caught than in her Decca recordings and with coloratura plentifully aspirated. Mario Petri produces woolly tone as the Bey, Mustafa, but the tenor, Cesare Valletti, a pupil of Tito Schipa, is excellent, and the Taddeo of Marcello Cortis is fresh and clear, while Graziella Sciutti is a delight in the role of Mustafa's wife, Elvira. The text is seriously cut, and the booklet gives only the Italian text without translation.

Semiramide (complete).
(M) *** Decca 425 481-2 (3) [id.]. Sutherland, Horne, Rouleau, Malas, Serge, Amb. Op. Ch., LSO, Bonynge.

The story of *Semiramide* is certainly improbable, involving the love which almost all the male characters bear for the Princess Azema, a lady who rather curiously appears very infrequently in the opera. Instead, Rossini concentrates on the love of Queen Semiramide for the Prince Arsace (a mezzo-soprano), and musically the result is a series of fine duets, superbly performed here by Sutherland and Horne (in the mid-1960s when they were both at the top of their form). What a complete recording brings out, however, is the consistency of Rossini's drama, the music involving the listener even when the story falls short. In Sutherland's interpretation, Semiramide is not so much a Lady Macbeth as a passionate, sympathetic woman and, with dramatic music predominating over languorous cantilena, one has her best, bright manner. Horne is well contrasted, direct and masculine in style, and Spiro Malas makes a firm, clear contribution in a minor role. Rouleau and Serge are variable but more than adequate, and Bonynge keeps the whole opera together with his alert, rhythmic control of tension and pacing. The vintage Decca recording has transferred brilliantly to CD.

COLLECTION

L'assedio de Corinto: Avanziam' . . . Non temer d'un basso affetto! . . . I destini tradir ogni speme . . . Signormche tutto puio . . . Sei tu, che stendi; L'ora fatal s'appressa . . . Giusto ciel. La Donna del lago: Mura Felici; Tanti affetti. Otello: Assisa a pie d'un salice. Tancredi: Di tanti palpiti.
❀ (M) *** Decca 421 306-2 [id.]. Marilyn Horne, Amb. Op. Ch., RPO, Henry Lewis.

Marilyn Horne's generously filled recital disc in Decca's mid-price Opera Gala series brings one of the most cherishable among all Rossini aria records ever issued. The voice is in glorious condition, rich and firm throughout its spectacular range, and is consistently used with artistry and imagination, as well as brilliant virtuosity in coloratura. By any reckoning this is thrilling singing, the more valuable for covering mostly rarities – which, with Horne, makes you wonder at their neglect. The sound is full and brilliant, showing its age hardly at all.

Roussel, Albert (1869–1937)

Bacchus et Ariane (ballet): *suite No. 2.*
(B) *** EMI CZS7 62669-2 (2) [Ang. CDMB 62647]. O de Paris, Serge Baudo (with Concert: *French music* ***).
(M) (***) BMG/RCA mono GD 60469 [60469-2-RG]. Boston SO, Münch – RAVEL: *Daphnis et Chloé.* ***

Many collectors will rest content with a suite from Roussel's vivid ballet. Serge Baudo achieves a performance of striking colour and intensity. The music's passion is projected as vehemently as its rhythmic feeling, and the Salle Wagram in Paris again provides an acoustic which brings out the rich colours as well as the evocation of the haunting introduction. The CD transfer of the 1969 recording is first class.

The Boston orchestra was still under Koussevitzky's spell in 1952 when the memorable RCA account of the second suite of Roussel's ballet was made. Münch re-recorded it twice during the 1960s but never with greater virtuosity than here. The recording is mono and the playing quite electrifying. A few bars are missing, perhaps due to the original tapes being damaged, or Münch himself may have made a cut in performance.

Suite in F, Op. 33.
(M) **(*) Mercury 434 303-2 [id.]. Detroit SO, Paul Paray – CHABRIER: *Bourrée fantasque* etc. ***

The outer movements of Roussel's *Suite in F* have a compulsive drive which also infects the harmonically complex, bittersweet central *Sarabande*. The scoring is rich (some might say thick), and the resonance of the Detroit Ford Auditorium makes it congeal a little. It is well played and alive, with Paray at his best in the closing *Gigue*.

Ruggles, Carl (1876–1971)

Sun-treader.

(M) *** DG 429 860-2 [id.]. Boston SO, Tilson Thomas – PISTON: *Symphony No. 2*; SCHUMAN: *Violin concerto.* ***

Carl Ruggles belongs to the same generation as Ives, whose exploratory outlook he shared, though not his carefree folksiness. Ruggles's music is expressionist and powerful, and he always structures finished works of art. *Sun-treader* takes its inspiration from Browning and, like so much of Ruggles's music, is uncompromising and it makes tough but rewarding listening. Tilson Thomas and the Boston orchestra make out a very good case for it.

Saint-Saëns, Camille (1835-1921)

Allegro appassionato for cello and orchestra, Op. 43; Caprice in D for violin and orchestra (arr. Ysaÿe); *Carnival of the animals: Le cygne. Cello concerto No. 1 in A min., Op. 33; Wedding-cake (caprice-valse) for piano and orchestra, Op. 76; Le Déluge: Prelude, Op. 45.*

(M) **(*) EMI CDM7 69386-2. Yan Pascal and Paul Tortelier, Maria de la Pau, CBSO, Frémaux.

Paul Tortelier gives an assured account of the *A minor Cello concerto*, but fails to make much of the busy but uninspired *Allegro appassionato.* Yan Pascal Tortelier plays with charm in the *Caprice* and with pleasing simplicity in the *Prelude* to the oratorio *Le Déluge*, which has a concertante part for the solo violin. The *Wedding-cake caprice* is also nicely done, even though Maria de la Pau does not reveal a strong personality. This is quite an attractive anthology, well recorded.

Carnival of the animals.

(B) *** CfP CD-CFP 4086; *TC-CFP 4086.* Katin, Fowke, SNO, Gibson – BIZET: *Jeux d'enfants;* RAVEL: *Ma Mère l'Oye.* ***

(BB) *** ASV CDQS 6017; *ZCQS 6017.* Goldstone, Brown, RPO, Hughes – PROKOFIEV: *Peter.* ***

(BB) **(*) Naxos Dig. 8.550499 [id.]. Lapšansky, Toperczer, Slovak RSO, Lenárd – BRITTEN: *Young person's guide;* PROKOFIEV: *Peter.* **

Carnival of the animals (chamber version).

(B) ** Pickwick Dig. PCD 932 [id.]. Julian Jacobson, Nigel Hutchinson, LSO (members), Barry Wordsworth – BIZET: *Jeux d'enfants* **; RAVEL: *Ma Mère l'Oye.* **(*)

On CfP the solo pianists, Peter Katin and Philip Fowke, enter fully into the spirit of the occasion, with Gibson directing his Scottish players with affectionate, unforced geniality. The couplings are attractive and the CD transfer confirms the vivid colourfulness and presence of the mid-1970s recording.

The two pianists on ASV also play with point and style, and the accompaniment has both spirit and spontaneity. *The Swan* is perhaps a trifle self-effacing, but otherwise this is very enjoyable, the humour appreciated without being underlined. The recording is excellent, and this makes a good super-bargain CD recommendation.

The Slovak Radio performance is given very attractive sound by the ambience of the Bratislava Hall, with pianos well balanced and the individual orchestral soloists naturally projected. Although Ondrej Lenárd begins rather seriously, the performance develops plenty of life and character. The pianists are particularly good at being *Kangaroos.* This is the most enjoyable of the three performances on this Naxos disc.

Barry Wordsworth opts for the original chamber version for flute, clarinet, string quintet and percussion. The two pianists make a lively contribution and the wide dynamic range of the recording means that the opening and closing sections of the work have their high spirits projected strongly. When the percussive condiment is added, the group makes a considerable impact, but in the more gentle zoological portraits the effect is a bit wan, and the imagery tends to recede. It is difficult here to achieve a volume setting which does not offer problems of changing levels within the domestic circumstances which Saint-Saëns envisaged.

(i) *Carnival of the animals;* (ii) *Danse macabre, Op. 40; Suite algérienne, Op. 60: Marche militaire française. Samson et Dalila: Bacchanale.* (ii; iii) *Symphony No. 3 in C min., Op. 78.*

(M) *** Sony SBY 47655 [id.]. (i) Entremont, Gaby Casadesus, Régis Pasquier, Yan-Pascal Tortelier, Caussé, Yo-Yo Ma, Lauridon, Marion, Arrignon, Cals, Cerutti; (ii) Phd. O, Ormandy; (iii) with E. Power Biggs.

It would be churlish to bracket the third star for this very generous collection (75 minutes 35 seconds) of what are certainly 'essential classics' because the *Carnival of the animals* – performed in its original chamber version – strikes the listener as somewhat lacking in lustre at the opening. The ear adjusts to the rather dry effect (L'Église du Liban, Paris, was used for the 1978 recording, and no doubt the microphones were placed very closely to counteract the ecclesiastical resonance). The evocations of the *Hens and Cocks* and *Wild asses* seem a bit clinical. But then things pick up. The tortoises are gently lugubrious, the elephantine double-bass solo is agreeably gruff, the aquarium delectably watery, and no one could complain that *Les oiseaux* fail to chirp merrily in their *Volière*, even if later the *Pianists* are bit stoical. It is a starry cast: Yo-Yo Ma personifies *The Swan* gently and gracefully, and the finale is extremely spirited. Ormandy and his splendid orchestra play the other orchestral lollipops with fine panache – the exuberance at the end of the *Samson et Dalila Bacchanale* is overwhelming, with thundering drums. The catchy *French military march* also goes with a swing, though the CD transfer makes the brass sound a bit coarse at the climax. (These short pieces were recorded in Philadelphia Town Hall in the mid-1960s, except for the enjoyable *Danse macabre*, which was made in 1959 in the Broadwood Hotel, another excellent recording venue.) No complaint about the 1962 sound in the *Symphony* – recorded at the Philadelphia Academy of Music, the source of many of Stokowski's 78-r.p.m. records, and offering far better acoustics than many of the halls used in recent years. The performance is fresh and vigorous, with the conductor's affection fully conveyed. The alert, polished Philadelphia playing brings incisive articulation to the first movement and scherzo, while the *Poco Adagio* is warmly expressive without being sentimentalized. E. Power Biggs has the full measure of the hall's Aeolian-Skinner organ, and he makes a spectacular contribution to the finale, which Ormandy structures most excitingly.

(i) *Carnival of the animals;* (ii) *Symphony No. 3 in C min.*

(M) **(*) Decca Dig. 430 720-2; *430 720-4* [id.]. (i) Rogé, Ortiz, L. Sinf.; (ii) Peter Hurford, Montreal SO; Dutoit.

Dutoit's *Carnival of the animals*, given a crisp and clean digital recording, is a sad disappointment. At almost every point the Gibson CfP version is superior in detailed characterization and lightness of touch, and *The Swan* is here played in a very matter-of-fact way. However, this may be regarded as merely a bonus for a fine performance of the *Organ Symphony*. Here Dutoit brings his usual gifts of freshness and a natural sympathy to Saint-Saëns's attractive score. The recording is very bright, with luminous detail, the strings given a thrilling brilliance above the stave. One notices a touch of digital edge, but there is a balancing weight. The reading effectively combines lyricism with passion. In the finale, Hurford's entry in the famous chorale melody is more pointed, less massive than usual, although Dutoit generates a genial feeling of gusto to compensate. With its wide range and bright lighting, this is a performance to leave one tingling, after Dutoit's final burst of adrenalin.

Carnival of the animals (arr. for brass by Peter Reeve).

(M) ** Decca 425 022-2; *425 022-4* [id.]. Philip Jones Brass Ens., Jones – MUSSORGSKY: *Pictures*. ***

A promising idea which proves disappointing in the execution, despite superb sound and plenty of colour – if very different from the original. But the pianists are sorely missed and a horn solo is no substitute for the cello in capturing the grace of Saint-Saëns's portrayal of *The Swan*. The wit, too, is coarsened, even if the geniality of the playing is evident.

Cello concerto No. 1 in A min., Op. 33.

(M) *** Mercury 432 010-2 [id.]. Janos Starker, LSO, Dorati – LALO: *Concerto* **(*); SCHUMANN: *Concerto*. ***

(B) *** DG 431 166-2; *431 166-4*. Heinrich Schiff, New Philh. O, Mackerras – FAURÉ: *Élégie*; LALO: *Cello concerto*. ***

(M) ** Erato/Warner 2292 45688-2 [id.]. André Navarra, LOP, Münch – LALO: *Concerto*. *(*)

(B) ** Ph. 422 467-2; *422 467-4*. Gendron, Monte Carlo Op. O, Benzi – DVOŘÁK: *Concerto* etc. **(*); FAURÉ: *Élégie*. *(*)

The Mercury CD brings three concertos in performances of striking quality. Starker plays the Saint-Saëns *A minor* with charm and grace, and Dorati provides first-class support. The 1964 recording comes up amazingly well and is excellently (and naturally) balanced, while the orchestral texture is beautifully clean without being in the least overlit or analytical.

Schiff was very young at the time of this recording (1977), but there are no signs of immaturity here. He gives as eloquent an account of this concerto as any on record. He sparks off an enthusiastic response from Mackerras, and the recorded sound and balance are excellent. At bargain price, this deserves the strongest recommendation.

André Navarra's recording was made a year later than the Starker. The balance places him unnaturally forward, at times masking orchestral detail. The performance is a very good one and Münch gets responsive playing from the now defunct Orchestre Lamoureux; but the Starker account is undoubtedly better value.

A good performance from Gendron with an adequate accompaniment. But the recording is not especially distinguished: the soloist is balanced too far forward.

(i) *Cello concerto No. 1 in A min., Op. 33;* (ii) *Piano concerto No. 2 in G min., Op. 22;* (iii) *Violin concerto No. 3, Op. 61.*

❀ (M) *** Sony/CBS Dig. MDK 46506 [id.]. (i)

Yo-Yo Ma, O Nat. de France, Maazel; (ii) Cécile Licad, LPO, Previn; (iii) Cho-Liang Lin, Philh. O, Tilson Thomas.

Three outstanding performances from the early 1980s are admirably linked together in this highly desirable CBS mid-price reissue. Yo-Yo Ma's performance of the *Cello Concerto* is distinguished by fine sensitivity and beautiful tone. One is tempted to speak of him as being 'hypersensitive', so fine is his attention to light and shade, yet there is not a trace of posturing or affectation. The Orchestre National de France respond with playing of the highest quality throughout. Superb recorded sound which reflects great credit on the engineers, with added refinement and transparency of texture on CD.

Cécile Licad and the LPO under Previn turn in an eminently satisfactory reading of the *G minor Piano concerto* that has the requisite delicacy in the Scherzo and seriousness elsewhere. It is a satisfying and persuasive performance of strong contrasts, with both power and thoughtfulness in the opening movement and a toccata-like brilliance of articulation in the finale. The recording is very realistic, with the acoustic of the London Henry Wood Hall pleasingly atmospheric, the orchestral focus a little diffuse, but attractively so, with the centrally placed piano dominating the proceedings, as much by the strength of Miss Licad's musical personality as by the actual balance.

Cho-Liang Lin's account of the *B minor Violin concerto* with the Philharmonia Orchestra and Michael Tilson Thomas is exhilarating and thrilling; indeed, this is the kind of performance that prompts one to burst into applause. Bernard Shaw's famous remark about the Saint-Saëns *Concerto* as consisting of 'trivially pretty scraps of serenade music sandwiched between pages from the great masters' has always seemed almost on target, but Cho-Liang Lin manages to persuade one otherwise. He is given excellent recording from the CBS engineers and, in terms of both virtuosity and musicianship, his version is certainly second to none and is arguably the finest yet to have appeared. The CD format is admirably 'present'.

Piano concertos Nos. 1–5.

(B) *** EMI CMS7 69443-2 (2). Aldo Ciccolini, O de Paris, Serge Baudo.

(B) (*) Sony M2YK 45624 (2). Philippe Entremont, O du Capitole, Toulouse, Plasson.

This makes an immensely enjoyable collection on EMI. There may be little development of style between the *First Concerto*, written when the composer was twenty-three, and the *Fifth* (*The Egyptian*), written at Luxor when he was in his fifties; but this is first-rate gramophone material. Beethoven, Bach and Mendelssohn all receive their due in the *First Concerto*; the *Second* and *Fourth* are already well known; but No. 5 is here unexpectedly attractive, with oriental atmosphere tingeing the music rather than overwhelming it. The finale, in which Egyptian ideas are punctuated in turn by early honky-tonk and a big Tchaikovsky-style melody, is delightful. Only No. 3 falls short in its comparatively banal ideas – and even in that there is a hilarious finale which sounds like a Viennese operetta turned into a concerto. The performances from Ciccolini and his colleagues are admirably spirited and emerge freshly on CD. The vibrant, at times slightly brash, 1970 sound gives the music-making strong character and projection, with a bold and often glittering piano image, and the warm acoustics of the Salle Wagram providing plenty of ambience. This is another very welcome reissue in EMI's French 'two for the price of one' series.

Entremont is a vigorously persuasive interpreter of French music, but the (originally late-1970s) CBS recording did less than justice to his gentler qualities, with the forward balance reducing the dynamic range. The CD remastering has made matters worse, with orchestral tuttis sounding crude and fierce and no bloom given to the piano, which becomes clattery and aggressive under pressure.

Piano concertos Nos. 2 in G min., Op. 22; 4 in C min., Op. 44.

(BB) **(*) Naxos Dig. 8.550334 [id.]. Idil Biret, Philh. O, James Loughran.

At least on this occasion Idil Biret has the benefit of decent sound, for the recording was made at St Barnabas, London. She makes rather heavy weather of the opening of the *G minor Concerto* and her performance sounds just a little portentous and wanting in charm, though the scherzo is played with delicacy and character. The accompaniment by the Philharmonia Orchestra under James Loughran is very good and the recording is very good indeed. There are performances of greater subtlety to be had – albeit not at this price – and, generally speaking, those wanting these two engaging concertos will not be disappointed – certainly not by the very natural but vivid recording, even if the piano is a bit too closely balanced. There is much to enjoy here.

Violin concerto No. 3 in B min., Op. 61.

(M) *** DG Dig. 429 977-2 [id.]. Perlman, O de Paris, Barenboim – LALO: *Symphonie espagnole.* ***

Violin concerto No. 3 in B min., Op. 61; Havanaise, Op. 83; Introduction and rondo capriccioso, Op. 28.

(M) ** Ph. 420 887-2. Szeryng, Monte Carlo Op. O, Remoortel – RAVEL: *Tzigane*. **(*)

On DG, Perlman achieves a fine partnership with his friend Barenboim, who provides a highly sympathetic accompaniment in a performance that is both tender and strong, while Perlman's verve and dash in the finale are dazzling. The forward balance is understandable in this work, but orchestral detail could at times be sharper.

Clean and immaculate performances from Szeryng, whose approach is aristocratic rather than indulgent. The orchestral contribution, adequate rather than distinguished, is not helped by the balance of the recording, which spotlights the violin and does not add a great deal of lustre to the accompaniment.

Danse macabre, Op. 40.

(M) **(*) Chan. CHAN 6503; *MBTD 6503* [id.]. SNO, Gibson – DUKAS: *L'apprenti sorcier*; ROSSINI/RESPIGHI: *La boutique fantasque*. **(*)

Gibson's performance is well played and vividly recorded, but this CD offers rather short measure (37 minutes), even at mid-price.

Danse macabre, Op. 40; (i) *Havanaise, Op. 83; Introduction and rondo capriccioso, Op. 28. Le jeunesse d'Hercule, Op. 50; Marche héroïque, Op. 34; Phaéton, Op. 39; Le rouet d'Omphale, Op. 31.*

(M) *** Decca 425 021-2; *425 021-4* [id.]. (i) Kyung Wha Chung, RPO; Philh. O; Charles Dutoit.

A splendidly conceived anthology. The symphonic poems are beautifully played, and the 1979 Kingsway Hall recording lends the appropriate atmosphere. Charles Dutoit shows himself an admirably sensitive exponent, revelling in the composer's craftsmanship and revealing much delightful orchestral detail in the manner of a Beecham. *La jeunesse d'Hercule* is the most ambitious piece, twice as long as its companions; its lyrical invention is both sensuous and elegant. The *Marche héroïque* is flamboyant but jolly, and *Phaéton*, a favourite in Victorian times, is engagingly dated but not faded. It is the delightful *Omphale's spinning wheel* and the familiar *Danse macabre* that show Saint-Saëns at his most creatively imaginative. To make the collection more generously attractive, Decca have now added Kyung Wha Chung's equally charismatic and individual 1977 accounts of what are perhaps the two most inspired short display-pieces for violin and orchestra in the repertoire. Here, as Chung makes very clear, the brilliance of the upper tessitura doesn't exist for its own sake but is part of the music's essentially lyrical fabric.

Havanaise, Op. 83.

(M) *** Decca 417 707-2 [id.]. Kyung Wha Chung, RPO, Dutoit – BRUCH: *Concerto No. 1*; TCHAIKOVSKY: *Concerto*. ***

Kyung Wha Chung shows rhythmic flair and a touch of the musical naughtiness that gives the *Havanaise* its full charm. Dutoit accompanies most sympathetically, and the recording is excellent.

Symphonies in A; in F (Urbs Roma); Symphonies Nos. 1–3.

(B) *** EMI CZS7 62643-2 (2) [Ang. CDMB 62643]. French Nat. R. O, Martinon (with Bernard Gavoty, organ de l'église Saint-Louis des Invalides in *No. 3*).

Martinon was the most persuasive advocate of Saint-Saëns, and this complete set of the five *Symphonies*, recorded in Paris between 1972 and 1975, is very welcome to the CD catalogue. The A and F major works were totally unknown and unpublished at the time of their recording and have never been dignified with numbers. Yet the A major, written when the composer was only fifteen, is a delight and may reasonably be compared with Bizet's youthful work in the same genre. Not surprisingly, it betrays the influence of Mozart as well as Mendelssohn (who is very 'present' in the first movement) and, consciously or not, Saint-Saëns uses a theme from the *Jupiter Symphony*. Scored for strings with flute and oboe, the charming scherzo survived the early ban as a separate piece and, with its delectable *moto perpetuo* finale, the whole work makes delightful gramophone listening. More obviously mature, the *Urbs Roma Symphony* came six years later, postdating the official No. 1. The writing is perhaps a shade more self-conscious, but more ambitious too, showing striking imagination in such movements as the darkly vigorous scherzo and the variation movement at the end.

The first of the numbered symphonies was written when Saint-Saëns was eighteen. It is a well-fashioned and genial piece, again much indebted to Mendelssohn, and to Schumann too, but with much delightfully fresh invention. The *Second*, written much later, in 1878, is full of excellent ideas and makes a welcome change from the familiar *Third*. Martinon directs splendid performances of the whole set, well prepared and lively; one can sense the pleasure of the French orchestral players in their discovery of the early works. The account of the *Third* ranks with the best: freshly spontaneous in the opening movement, then comes a spacious *Poco adagio*, a rumbustious scherzo and the threads are knitted powerfully together at the end of the finale. Here the recording could do with rather more sumptuousness, for the remastering has lost some of the original amplitude. Elsewhere the quality is bright and fresh, with no lack of body, and it suits the Saint-Saëns textures very well. This is now very competitively priced in EMI's French 'two for the price of one' series.

Symphony No. 3 in C min., Op. 78 (see also under *Carnival of the animals*).
(B) *** Pickwick Dig. PCD 847; *CIMPC 847* [id.]. Chorzempa, Berne SO, Maag.
(M) *** Mercury 432 719-2 [id.]. Marcel Dupré, Detroit SO, Paray – PARAY: *Mass.* **(*)
(M) **(*) Decca 417 725-2 [id.]. Priest, LAPO, Mehta – POULENC: *Organ concerto.* ***
(B) ** CfP Dig. CD-CFP 4572; *TC-CFP 4572.* Parker-Smith, LPO, Baudo (with WIDOR: *Organ symphony No. 5: Toccata. Organ symphony No. 6: Finale* **).

(i) *Symphony No. 3;* (ii) *Danse macabre, Op. 40.*
(B) *** DG Compact Classics *413 423-4* [id.]. (i) Litaize, Chicago SO; (ii) O de Paris, Barenboim – FRANCK: *Symphony.* *

(i) *Symphony No. 3;* (ii) *Danse macabre; Le Déluge: Prélude, Op. 45; Samson et Dalila: Bacchanale.*
(M) *** DG 415 847-2 [id.]. (i) Litaize, Chicago SO, Barenboim; (ii) O de Paris, Barenboim.

Symphony No. 3; Le rouet d'Omphale; Samson et Dalila: Bacchanale.
(BB) ** Naxos Dig. 8.550138 [id.]. Slovak RSO (Bratislava), Stephen Gunzenhauser.

From the many versions of César Franck's most popular symphony one could hardly better Barenboim's inspirational 1976 version which has dominated the catalogue for so long. Among the reissue's three attractive bonuses is an exciting account of the *Bacchanale* from *Samson et Dalila*. The performance of the *Symphony* glows with warmth from beginning to end. In the opening 6/8 section the galloping rhythms are pointed irresistibly, while the linked slow section has a poised stillness in its soaring lyricism which completely avoids any suspicion of sweetness or sentimentality. A brilliant account of the Scherzo leads into a magnificently energetic conclusion, with the Chicago orchestra excelling itself with radiant playing in every section. The digital remastering, as so often, is not wholly advantageous: while detail is sharper, the massed violins sound thinner and the bass is drier. In the finale, some of the bloom has gone, and the organ entry has a touch of hardness. The Compact Classics tape offers the *Symphony* uninterrupted in a transfer made from the original analogue master, and includes a fine account of *Danse macabre*; even if the coupled Franck *Symphony* is a much less attractive proposition, this is well worth considering for the car.

Maag's extremely well-recorded Berne performance has a Mendelssohnian freshness and the sprightly playing in the Scherzo draws an obvious affinity with that composer. The first movement has plenty of rhythmic lift and the *Poco Adagio* is eloquently elegiac, yet no one could be disappointed with the organ entry in the finale, which is certainly arresting, while the rippling delicacy of the piano figurations which follow is most engaging. The closing pages have a convincing feeling of apotheosis and, although this is not the weightiest reading available, it is an uncommonly enjoyable one in which the sound is bright, full and suitably resonant.

The fine Paray/Mercury recording dates, astonishingly, from 1957. The early date brings just a hint of shrillness to the violins in the first movement, which Paray presents engagingly with a skittishly light touch; otherwise the sound remains bold, full and remarkably well detailed; it is very successfully remastered for CD. The organ is well balanced in the slow movement, which Paray treats very affectionately (if perhaps a shade indulgently), before a light, brilliantly energetic performance of the scherzo. Then comes Marcel Dupré's weighty organ entry and a finale which is powerfully co-ordinated, building to an impressive climax. However, not everyone may want the coupling, enjoyable as it is.

Mehta draws a well-disciplined and exuberant response from all departments. The slow movement cantilena sings out vividly on the strings, helped by the brightened recording. The digital remastering produces a less sumptuous effect than on the original 1979 LP, and in the finale the focus of the more spectacular sounds is not absolutely clean; even so, this is very enjoyable.

Baudo on Classics for Pleasure has the advantage of modern digital recording, made at Watford Town Hall. There is a hint of shrillness in the upper strings, but otherwise the quality is full and refined in detail. The recording has a wide dynamic range and uses the organ of Paisley Abbey, which is laminated on to the orchestra effectively. The performance is at its most vivacious in the opening movement. In the finale, the organ entry is very spacious and grandiloquent, but Baudo steadily increases his grip and pulls everything together in the coda. The Widor encores are analogue and were recorded a decade earlier in Westminster Cathedral. The effect is certainly spectacular – Jane Parker-Smith is at her most exciting in the famous *Toc-*

cata – and the pedals resonate expansively, if without the sharpest focus.

Gunzenhauser directs a fearless performance of the Saint-Saëns *Organ Symphony*, not always ideally refined and scorning the dangers of vulgarity. With big, weighty organ sound, the boldness is most convincing, even if the slow movement becomes too sugary. This super-bargain issue is made the more attractive by its apt coupling of shorter pieces, all vividly played.

Samson et Dalila (opera): complete.
(M) **(*) DG 413 297-2 (2). Obraztsova, Domingo, Bruson, Lloyd, Thau, Ch. & O de Paris, Barenboim.

Barenboim proves as passionately dedicated an interpreter of Saint-Saëns here as he did in the *Third Symphony*, sweeping away any Victorian cobwebs. It is important, too, that the choral passages, so vital in this work, be sung with this sort of freshness, and Domingo has rarely sounded happier in French music, the bite as well as the heroic richness of the voice well caught. Renato Bruson and Robert Lloyd are both admirable too; sadly, however, the key role of Dalila is given an unpersuasive, unsensuous performance by Obraztsova, with her vibrato often verging on a wobble. The recording is as ripe as the music deserves.

Samson et Dalila: highlights.
(M) ** EMI CDM7 63935-2; *EG 763935-4*. Gorr, Vickers, Blanc, Diakov, Ch. René Duclos, O of Paris Nat. Op., Prêtre.

Many will rest content with a set of highlights from *Samson et Dalila*, and this 53-minute EMI selection just about passes muster. Jon Vickers and Rita Gorr sing vibrantly and make an appealing duo, and the 1962 recording has plenty of atmosphere. The only drawback is the direction of Georges Prêtre. Rather than any lack of tension in his conducting, there is rather too much tautness in the score's more relaxed moments.

Salieri, Antonio (1750-1825)

Concerto for oboe, flute and orchestra in C.
(B) *** DG 427 211-2 [id.]. Holliger, Nicolet, Bamberg SO, Maag – MOZART: *Flute concertos.* **

Heinz Holliger and Aurèle Nicolet form an expert and sensitive partnership in their earlier version of Salieri's *Double concerto*. The recording too is fresh.

(i) *Double concerto for flute, oboe and orchestra;* (ii) *Piano concerto in B flat.*
(M) *** Erato/Warner 2292 45245-2 [id.]. (i) Hoogendoorn, Borgonovo; (ii) Badura-Skoda; Sol. Ven., Scimone (with Franceso SALIERI: *La Tempesta di Mare (Sinfonia in B flat* ***).

Antonio Salieri has been given a certain notoriety by his role as arch-villain in the film, *Amadeus*, but at least it has reawakened interest in his music. He is no Mozart, but in the outer movements of the *Double concerto* the flute and oboe chatter together quite winningly and the central *Largo* is gracious. The performance here is persuasive. The *Piano concerto*'s first movement lasts for 11 minutes, but it seems longer; the *Adagio*, however, is fairly memorable with the soloist in dialogue with muted strings – there are no woodwind. The finale is a pleasing Minuet with variations. This is a typical *galant* piece, and Paul Badura-Skoda, playing on a period fortepiano, has its full measure. The accompaniments are first class, animated and polished, and I Solisti Veneti are at their finest in *La Tempesta di Mare*. This work is closest to Mozart in spirit and craftsmanship, an attractive three-movement Italian Overture. But the manuscript suggests it was written by Antonio's elder brother, Francesco, about which nothing is known, not even his dates. With excellent recording, this collection is worth exploring.

Sarasate, Pablo (1844–1908)

(i) *Carmen fantasy;* (ii) *Zigeunerweisen, Op. 20.*
(M) *** EMI CDM7 63533-2; *EG 763533-4*. Perlman, (i) RPO, Foster; (ii) Pittsburgh SO, Previn – *Concert.* ***

Perlman's superb 1972 account of the *Carmen fantasy* is one of his most dazzling recordings. On the mid-priced EMI record, *Zigeunerweisen* (recorded with Previn five years later) is added for good measure, and again the playing is both virtuosic and idiomatic. Here the microphone balance is rather too close, but Perlman can survive any amount of scrutiny.

Satie, Erik (1866-1925)

Les aventures de Mercure (ballet); *La belle excentrique: Grand ritournelle. 5 Grimaces pour 'Un songe d'une nuit d'été'; Gymnopédies Nos. 1 & 3; Jack-in-the-box* (orch. Milhaud); *3 Morceaux en forme de poire; Parade* (ballet); *Relâche* (ballet).
(M) **(*) Van. 8.4030.71 [OVC 4030]. Utah SO, Maurice Abravanel.

A generous budget collection of Satie's orchestral music, well played and given full, vivid recording from the beginning of the 1970s. The Utah Symphony Orchestra made a number of adventurous excursions into European repertoire at that time and, if Abravanel fails to throw off some of the more pointed music with a fully idiomatic lightness of touch, these are still enjoyable performances; the ballet scores have plenty of colour and rhythmic life.

(i) *Les aventures de Mercure;* (ii) *Gymnopédies 1 & 3* (orch. Debussy); (iii) *Les pantins dansent;* (iv) *Choses vues à droite et à gauche (sans lunettes);* (v; i) *Geneviève de Brabant* (orch. Desormière); (vi) *Messe des pauvres;* (v; vii; iii) *Le piège de Méduse* (comédie lyrique); (viii; i) *Socrate* (drame symphonique).
(B) *(**) EMI CZS7 62877-2 (2). (i) O de Paris, Dervaux; (ii) Paris Conservatoire O, Auriacombe; (iii) LOP, Ciccolini; (iv) Yan-Pascal Tortelier, Ciccolini (piano); (v) Mesplé, Benoit, Paris Op. Ch.; (v) Pierre Bertin (nar.); (vi) René Duclos Ch. (members); Gaston Litaize (organ de l'Église Saint François-Xavier); (vii) Deschamps, Falcucci, Laurence; (viii) Millet, Guiot, Esposito, Mesplé.

A fascinating collection, offering much music that is not otherwise available, but, alas, given inadequate documentation. In Auriacombe's account of the familiar *Gymnopédies* the burden of expressiveness is carried by the fine Paris woodwind soloists rather than the conductor, but Dervaux (although hampered a little by the resonant acoustic) brings reasonable spirit and no lack of warmth to the engagingly scored *Les aventures de Mercure.* He finds the necessary elegance for the *Danses des grâces* in the Second Tableau and real *tendresse* for the charming *Nouvelle danse* in the Third. Later Ciccolini, taking over the conductor's baton, is suitably sprightly in the quirkily rhythmic *Les patins dansent.* There is some fine singing in *Socrate*; the performance catches well the calm, expressive serenity of the melodic lines. But no libretto or translation is provided either here or in the two works with narrator, *Le piège de Méduse* and *Geneviève de Brabant.* This latter cantata, commemorating the saint yet conceived as a puppet play, tells of a medieval heroine banished for infidelity but who returns to clear her name. It opens with a narration lasting nearly 12 minutes before the music begins and, although Pierre Bertin is eloquent as only a Frenchman can be, the non-French-speaker will be dismayed to find that the entry of the the music is not even cued! Yet there is much that is attractive in Satie's piquant word-settings, both here and in the cabaret-styled *Le piège de Méduse* (with its reminders of Offenbach); however, without the written words or separating tracks, the listener's patience will be sorely tried. The *Messe des pauvres* is a lively Rosicrucian organ Mass, often forcefully played on a bold, grainy-sounding organ, with soprano and bass voices *ad lib.* interrupting the opening *Kyrie* and *Dixit Dominus.* The three brief *Choses vues à droite et à gauche* are scored for violin and piano. Here Yan-Pascal Tortelier joins Ciccolini (who moves over to the piano) to present them with engaging finesse and wit. The recordings were all made in the Salle Wagram between 1967 and 1974, and the transfers are of excellent quality. This pair of discs (for the price of one) is temptingly inexpensive and would have been highly recommendable had Noel Goodwin's succinct notes been backed up with the words of the vocal works.

PIANO MUSIC

Aperçus désagréables; La belle excentrique (fantaisie sérieuse) (both for 4 hands); *Croquis et agaceries d'un gros bonhomme en bois; Descriptions automatiques; Embryons desséchés; En habit de cheval* (for 4 hands); *Le fils des étoiles, wagnerie kaldéenne du Sar Peladan; 6 Gnossiennes; 3 Gymnopédies; Jack-in-the-box; 3 Mouvements en forme de poire* (for 4 hands); *3 Nocturnes; Peccadilles importunes; 3 Petites pièces montées* (for 4 hands); *Pièces froides; Prèludes flasques (pour un chien); Première pensée et sonneries de la Rose Croix; 3 Sarabandes; Sonatine bureaucratique; Sports et divertissements; 3 Valses distinguées du précieux dégoûté.*
(B) **(*) EMI CZS7 67282-2 (2). Aldo Ciccolini.

This is one of the most comprehensive collections of Satie's piano music available (158 minutes on the two CDs – offered for the price of one) and as such it is self-recommending. Although Satie's achievement is sometimes overrated by his admirers, about much of this music there is a desperate melancholy and a rich poetic feeling which are altogether unique. The *Gymnopédies*, *Gnossiennes*, *Sarabandes* and *Pièces froides* show such flashes of innocence and purity of inspiration that criticism is disarmed, while the wit of the sharper vignettes is most engaging. (In the *Sonatine bureaucratique*, a busy burst of bravura, one can visualize the French officials rushing about with their papers.) Aldo Ciccolini is widely praised as a Satie interpreter, and he plays here with unaffacted sympathy. He certainly understands the *douloureux* feeling of the famous *Gymnopédies*, with which his recital opens, and he also finds the '*conviction et tristesse rigoureuse*' of the *Gnossiennes.* There is a noble, aristocratic dignity expressed in the *Première pensée et sonneries de la Rose Croix*, yet *La belle excentrique* is thrown off with great dash and élan. In the works where (by electronic means) Ciccolini provides all four hands, the percussive edge of the pianism seems somewhat accentuated by the recording (and this occasionally happens with the bolder articulation in some of the solo pieces too), but generally the piano recording is most realistic, and the CD transfer has plenty of colour and sonority. Altogether this forms an excellent introduction to Satie's world.

Avant-dernières pensées; Chapitres tournés en tous sens; Croquis et agaceries d'un gros bonhomme en bois; Danses gothiques; Descriptions automatiques; Embryons desséchés; Enfantillages pittoresques; 3 Gnossiennes; 3 Gymnopédies; Heures séculaires et instantanées; Menus propos enfantins; 5 Nocturnes; Ogives; Les pantins dansent; Passacaille; Peccadilles importunes; Pièces froides; 4 Préludes; Prélude en tapisserie; Préludes de la porte héroïque du ciel; Premier menuet; Rêverie de l'enfance de Pantagruel; 3 Sarabandes; Sonatine bureaucratique; Sports et divertissements; 3 Valses distinguées du précieux dégoûté; Veritables préludes flasques; Vieux séquins et vieilles cuirasses.

(B) **(*) VoxBox 1154862 [CDX 5011]. Frank Glazer.

Vox offers a great deal of Satie's solo piano music on two CDs in excellent performances by Frank Glazer, and this VoxBox scores over the EMI competition by offering slightly more music (though, curiously, not the last three *Gnossiennes*). Glazer seems to penetrate the character of each of these aphoristic and haunting miniatures with genuine flair and insight. In some ways his are more searching and sympathetic performances than those of Aldo Ciccolini, and the recording, although rather reverberant and a little veiled in the treble, is full-bodied and faithful. The Vox CD transfer slightly enhances the original piano-sound and there is no drying-out of timbre or ambience. However, in the numbers requiring very pointed articulation, Ciccolini's more percussive style brings a degree more sparkle, even if the actual piano-tone is harder, less easy on the ear. Some of these pieces are insubstantial, but those attracted to the idiom of the music will find this a safe investment.

Avant-dernières pensées; Croquis et agaceries d'un gros bonhomme en bois; Descriptions automatiques; 3 Gnossiennes; 3 Gymnopédies; Nocturne No. 1; Valses chantées: Je te veux; Poudre d'or. 3 Valses distinguées du précieux dégoûté.

(B) **(*) Sony MYK 45505 [id.]. Philippe Entremont.

Entremont's tempi tend to be on the slow side, and the gentler pieces have a grave melancholy and a dark colour which is very affecting. He finds plenty of wit in the picaresque items and, although the *Valses chantées* could perhaps have a lighter rhythmic touch, this is still distinctive playing. The CBS recording is modern and attractively full in timbre.

Avant-dernières pensées; Croquis et agaceries d'un gros bonhomme en bois; Descriptions automatiques; Gnossienne No. 3; Gymnopédies Nos. 1 & 3; Sarabande No. 2.

(M) Sony mono MPK 47684 [id.]. Francis Poulenc – CHABRIER: *Mélodies* (**); POULENC: *Piano music.*

Satie was a kind of mascot for *Les Six* for he sympathized with the young. However, Poulenc's playing is too unpolished and lacking in elegance to serve these pieces properly – he sounds as if he hasn't practised for months! The 1950 sound is pretty primitive and monochrome. Not recommendable.

Avant-dernières pensées; Embryons desséchés; Fantaisie-Valse; 3 Gnossiennes; 3 Gymnopédies; Jack-in-the-Box; Je te veux; Le Picadilly; Poudre d'or; Prélude en tapisserie; Sports et divertissements; Les trois valses distinguées du précieux dégoûté; Valse-ballet.

(M) ** EMI CD-EMX 9507; *TC-EMX 2071* [Ang. CDM 62017]. Angela Brownridge.

The fun of Satie is well represented in Angela Brownridge's collection. It is sensitively arranged as a programme to have *Gymnopédies* and *Gnossiennes* alternating with the lighter pieces echoing popular music. The playing is bright and stylish, sensitively reflecting the sharply changing moods and lacking only the last touches of poetry.

Chapitres tournés en tous sens; Croquis et agaceries d'un gros bonhomme en bois; Descriptions automatiques; Embryons desséchés; Enfantillages pittoresques; 6 Gnossiennes; 3 Gymnopédies; Menus propos enfantins; Passacaille; Pas trop vif; 6 Pièces de la période; Ragtime Parade; Véritables préludes flasques.

(B) (*) Naxos Dig. 8.550305 [id.]. Klára Körmendi.

Klára Körmendi's recital on Naxos is not really recommendable. The playing is less at fault than the recording. The sound itself is very hard and unappealing, and it is very difficult to derive much pleasure from it.

Chapitres tournés en tous sens; Croquis et agaceries d'un gros bonhomme en bois; Gnossiennes Nos. 2 and 4; 3 Gymnopédies; Heures séculaires et instantanées; Nocturnes Nos. 2 and 4; Nouvelles pièces froides; Passacaille; Le Piège de Méduse; Prélude No. 2 (Le Fils des étoiles); Sonatine bureaucratique.

(B) ** CfP CD-CFP 4329; *TC-CFP 40329* [id.]. Peter Lawson.

Satie's deceptively simple piano writing has to

be played with great sensitivity and subtlety if justice is to be done to its special qualities of melancholy and irony. Peter Lawson's recital opens with the famous *Gymnopédies*, played coolly but not ineffectively. The highlight is a perceptive and articulate characterization of *Le Piège de Méduse*, seven epigrammatic *morceaux de concert*. Elsewhere his way is quietly tasteful, and though he catches something of Satie's gentle and wayward poetry he is less successful in revealing the underlying sense of fantasy. Good recording.

Scarlatti, Alessandro (1660–1725)

Il giardino di amore (*The garden of love*: cantata).
(M) *** DG 431 122-2. Gayer, Fassbaender, Munich CO, Stadlmair.

Scarlatti called this delightful work a '*serenata*', for there are only two characters and the orchestra is basically a string group with colourful obbligatos for recorder, violin and trumpet. The names of the two principal characters, Venus and Adonis, will recall the somewhat earlier work by Blow. Here the (originally castrato) role of Adonis is attractively sung by a soprano, Catherine Gayer, with Brigitte Fassbaender providing a foil in her portrayal of Venus. The two voices are well matched and the singing has both charm and character. Repeats are skilfully ornamented and the whole production has an engaging spontaneity to match its stylishness. There are some delightful pictorial touches in Scarlatti's word-settings and they are imaginatively realized. The nightingale song (with recorder obbligato) is especially memorable, as is the aria *Con battaglia die fiero tormento*, which has a trumpet obbligato worthy of Handel. The excellent 1964 recording has transferred vividly to CD, and the documentation includes a full translation.

(i) *St Cecilia Mass;* (ii) *Motets: Domine, refugium factus et nobis; O magnum mysterium.*
(M) *** Decca 430 631-2; *430 631-4* [id.]. (i) Harwood, Eathorne, Cable, Eans, Keyte, St John's College Ch., Wren O, Guest; (ii) Schütz Ch. of L., Norrington.

In this celebratory setting of the Mass, the most elaborate and expansive that Scarlatti wrote, he applied to church music the techniques he had already used in opera. This is far more florid in style than Scarlatti's other Masses and it receives from Guest a vigorous and fresh performance. The soloists cope with their difficult fioriture very confidently and they match one another well. The 1978 recording is atmospheric, yet sets choir and orchestra firmly in place. The two motets are fine pieces that show how enduring the Palestrina tradition was in seventeenth-century Italy. They are noble in conception and are beautifully performed under Roger Norrington.

Scarlatti, Domenico (1685-1757)

Keyboard sonatas, Kk. 1, 9, 11, 87, 96, 132, 135, 141, 146, 159, 198, 208, 247, 322, 380, 435, 466, 474 & 481.
(BB) ** Naxos Dig. 8.550252 [id.]. Balázs Szokolay (piano).

Balázs Szokolay is the son of the composer of the opera, *Blood Wedding*, and he made a strong impression at the last Leeds International Competition. His Scarlatti recital suffers from the airless acoustic of the Italian Institute in Budapest, though there is no doubt that he is a good stylist. The colourless sound greatly diminishes pleasure, but the playing is often so alert and intelligent (as in the *G major*, Kk. 146 (Longo 349) or the *C major*, Kk. 159 (Longo 194)) as to make one forget the sonic limitations! The two stars are a compromise: the playing is worth three, the recording barely rates one.

Keyboard sonatas, Kk. 28, 52, 132–3, 208–9, 490–92, 544–5.
(B) *** CfP CD-CFP 4538; *TC-CFP 4538.* Valda Aveling (harpsichord).

Valda Aveling plays a Goff harpsichord, not an authentic period instrument or copy. Indeed there is little period flavour here, for this artist favours frequent changes of registration. However, she plays with superb panache and is splendidly vital; and the full and vivid recording is an additional attraction. The robust effect will not suit purists; but this recital may well win over listeners new to this repertoire. The 1975 recording has added life on CD.

Keyboard sonatas, Kk. 32, 95, 99, 107, 158, 162–4, 193, 208, 210, 213, 215, 246–7, 262, 304, 318, 378–80, 394, 443, 461, 474, 481, 484, 500, 513, 531, 540, 550.
(M) **(*) Collins Dig. 3016-2 [id.]. Fou Ts'ong (piano).

This is the most generous Scarlatti recital in the catalogue, with 32 sonatas included and 73 minutes of music. Fou Ts'ong is not the first name to spring to mind in connection with this repertoire and, not unexpectedly, his approach is at times rather wayward, though stopping short of being overtly romantic. The very first sonata on the disc, the *D minor Sonata* (Kk. 31), has a rather appealing, ruminative quality, and the following *D major Sonata* (Kk. 164) is measured and thoughtful. But in those numbers in which keen articulation is called for (Kk. 484 in

D and Kk. 378 in F, for instance) the playing is agreeably fresh, the ornamentation crisp and not fussy. Sometimes he overdoes the flamboyance a bit, or is a shade too brittle in staccato (Kk. 540 in F), but there is much to enjoy here; dipped into, this recital will give pleasure: it certainly reveals Scarlatti's inexhaustible invention. The recording was produced by Fou Ts'ong himself and recorded at St John's Polish Roman Catholic Church, London, in 1984. The ambience is attractive, but the microphones are perhaps a shade too close to the piano (especially noticeable at the very opening). Nevertheless the image is convincing and without an artificial presence.

Keyboard sonatas: Kk. 39, 54, 96, 146, 162, 198, 209, 332, 335, 380, 424, 455, 466, 474, 525, 531.
(M) (***) Sony MK 42410 [id.]. Vladimir Horowitz (piano).

Recorded at various times between 1962 and 1968, the playing is of extraordinary elegance and refinement, and Horowitz's virtuosity is altogether remarkable. Unfortunately the improvement in sound-quality is minimal: the timbre is still dry and papery – so the three stars are exclusively for the playing.

Schillings, Max von (1868–1933)

Mona Lisa (opera): suite.
(B) *(*) VoxBox (2) [CDX 5043]. Westphalian SO (Rechlinghausen), Landau – SCHREKER: *The Birthday of the Infanta;* WEILL: *Violin concerto* etc. *(*)

Max von Schillings, a celebrated conductor as well as composer, was a contemporary of Richard Strauss. He wrote in a satisfyingly warm, late-Romantic style, which yet lacked the individuality of his more celebrated colleague. The *Mona Lisa suite* is a sequence of linked episodes, exotic and atmospheric, taken from his opera based on the supposed story behind Leonardo da Vinci's masterpiece of portraiture. It makes an attractive fill-up for the Weill Vox Box, but sound and performance are relatively coarse.

Schmidt, Franz (1874-1939)

Symphony No. 4 in C.
(M) **(*) Decca 430 007-2. VPO, Mehta – SCHOENBERG: *Chamber symphony No. 1.* **(*)

Schmidt's noble *Fourth Symphony* is much loved in Vienna, as the playing of the VPO on this Decca recording readily testifies. The work is given the intensity of Mahler, without the hint of hysteria, and the breadth and spaciousness of Bruckner – though it is very different from either: Mehta finds also a dignity that reminds one a little of Elgar. The brightened recording gains in vividness in its CD transfer but loses a little of its fullness, though the Vienna ambience remains very telling.

Piano quintet in G (arr. Wührer).
(M) Decca 430 296-2; *430 296-4* [id.]. Eduard Mrasek, VPO Qt – BRUCKNER: *String quintet.* ***

Franz Schmidt's *Piano quintet in G* is the first of three that he wrote for Paul Wittgenstein, the one-armed pianist for whom Ravel and Prokofiev both composed concertos. The quintets were subsequently arranged for two hands by Friedrich Wührer. This is rewarding music, full of unexpected touches; it also possesses a vein of genuine nobility, as one would expect from the composer of the *Fourth Symphony.* The performance is elegant and was beautifully recorded in the Sofiensaal in 1974. The CD retains the fullness and the natural, well-judged balance.

Schoenberg, Arnold (1874-1951)

Chamber symphony No. 1, Op. 9.
(M) **(*) Decca 430 007-2. LAPO (members), Mehta – SCHMIDT: *Symphony No. 4.* **(*)

It was to Los Angeles that Schoenberg moved to live out his last years, and it would have gladdened him that his local philharmonic orchestra had achieved a degree of brilliance to match that of any other orchestra in America. The *First Chamber symphony* is given a rich performance under Mehta, arguably too fast at times but full of understanding for the romantic emotions which underlie much of the writing. The 1969 recording is appropriately brilliant, but the CD transfer is very brightly lit.

(i) *Piano concerto in C, Op. 42;* (ii) *Violin concerto, Op. 36.*
(M) **(*) DG 431 740-2. (i) Brendel; (ii) Zeitlin; Bav. RSO, Kubelik – BERG: *Violin concerto.* ***

Schoenberg devotees tend to suggest that both these works, consciously echoing the world of the romantic concerto in twelve-note serial terms, present the most approachable road to appreciating the master. For some that may be so, particularly in performances as sympathetic as these; but, more than usual in these relatively late works, the thick textures favoured by Schoenberg obscure the focus of the argument rather than making it sweeter on the ear. Brendel – who made a recording for Vox very early in his career – remains a committed Schoenbergian, and Zeitlin is impressive too.

Though even the CD transfer does not manage to clarify the thorny textures completely, the sound, as transferred, is very good. With the Berg *Violin concerto* offered as coupling, this is excellent value in DG's 20th Century Classics series.

Pelleas und Melisande, Op. 5; Variations for orchestra, Op. 31; Verklaerte Nacht (orchestral version), *Op. 4.*
(M) *** DG 427 424-2 (3) [id.]. BPO, Karajan – BERG: *Lyric suite; 3 Pieces;* WEBERN: *Collection.* ***

These are superb performances which present the emotional element at full power but give unequalled precision and refinement. *Pelleas und Melisande*, written at the same time as the Debussy opera but in ignorance of the rival project, is in its way a Strauss-like masterpiece, while the Op. 31 *Variations*, the most challenging of Schoenberg's orchestral works, here receives a reading which vividly conveys the ebb and flow of tension within the phrase and over the whole plan. Superb recording, excellently remastered.

5 Pieces for orchestra, Op. 16.
(M) *** Mercury 432 006-2 [id.]. LSO, Dorati – BERG: *3 Pieces; Lulu suite*; WEBERN: *5 Pieces.* ***

Schoenberg put evocative titles on his *Five Pieces*, but it would be misleading to think of them as programmatic items. His titles were prompted by his publisher, and the arguments – colourful as they may be – had been established without them. Here for the first time he was writing 'abstract' instrumental music in his new role as atonalist, and even today it is amazing that such forward-looking music could have been written in 1909. Nowadays it is the combination of clarity and colour, with a big orchestra used in chamber style, that still seems intensely original and new. Dorati, in his pioneering coupling with other works written at the same period by Schoenberg's emergent pupils, used the version the composer made in 1949, with a slightly reduced orchestra. The performance is strong and vivid; the 1962 sound is admirably vivid and clear.

Variations, Op. 31.
(M) **(*) Decca 425 008-2 (2) [id.]. Chicago SO, Solti – BRUCKNER: *Symphony No. 5.* **(*)

Solti's reading of the challenging Schoenberg *Variations* is characteristically strong and forceful, with the Chicago orchestra playing with virtuoso brilliance; but Karajan's recording has shown what extra depths this initially difficult music contains. The Decca sound is bright and clear, rather firmer than it was on LP.

Verklaerte Nacht.
(M) **(*) Decca 430 002-2. ASMF, Marriner – R. STRAUSS: *Metamorphosen* **(*); WEBERN: *5 Movements.* ***
(M) ** Teldec/Warner Dig. 9031 74791-2 [id.]. Israel CO, Talmi – BERLIOZ: *Symphonie fantastique.* *(*)

Marriner's interpretation of Schoenberg's sensuous string work is relatively reticent until the culminating climaxes, when the final thrust is more powerful than that of almost any rival. The 1974 recording, still atmospheric, has lost some of its allure in the remastering, and the fortissimo violins become fierce.

The Israel Chamber Orchestra under Yoav Talmi give a perfectly acceptable if at times rather overheated account of *Verklaerte Nacht.* They are quite well recorded; but neither this nor Prêtre's account of the *Symphonie fantastique* would be a first choice.

(i) *Verklaerte Nacht, Op. 4* (string sextet version); *String trio, Op. 45.*
(M) ** DG 423 250-2 [id.]. LaSalle Qt; (i) with D. McInnes, J. Pegis.

For those who feel that Schoenberg's *Verklaerte Nacht* is best served by the version for solo strings, the LaSalle Quartet give a superbly efficient, virtuosic account with no lack of expressive feeling. At times they are inclined to rush things, but they are well – if rather too brightly – recorded; and the *String trio*, played with effortless mastery, makes a welcome coupling.

Die eiserne Brigade (march for string quartet and piano); (i) *Pierrot lunaire, Op. 21;* (ii) *Serenade, Op. 24* (for clarinet, bass clarinet, mandolin, guitar, violin, viola, cello and bass voice).
(M) *** Decca 425 626-2. (i) Mary Thomas; (ii) Shirley-Quirk; L. Sinf., Atherton.

These performances derive from David Atherton's distinguished 1973 survey of Schoenberg's chamber music, including vocal works. *Pierrot lunaire* is among the most incisive and dramatic yet recorded and, although not even these performers can make the humour of the *Serenade* anything but Teutonic, the performance remains compelling.

Piano music: *3 Pieces, Op. 11; 6 Small Pieces, Op. 19; 5 Pieces, Op. 23; 3 Pieces, Op. 33a & b; Suite, Op. 25.*
(M) *** DG 423 249-2 [id.]. Maurizio Pollini.

This CD encompasses Schoenberg's complete piano music. Pollini plays with enormous authority and refinement of dynamic nuance and colour, making one perceive this music in a totally different light from other performers. He is accorded excellent sound (very slightly on the dry side), extremely clear and well defined.

VOCAL MUSIC

(i) *Gurrelieder;* (ii) Lieder: *Die Aufgeregten; Erwartung; Geübtes Herz; Ich darf nich dankend; Sommermüd; Tot; Verlassen; Der verlorne Haufen.*
(M) **(*) DG 431 744-2 (2) [id.]. (i) Schachtschneider, Borkh, Töpper, Engen, Fehenberger, Bavarian R. Ch. & O, Kubelik; (ii) Fischer-Dieskau, Aribert Reimann – BERG; WEBERN: *Lieder.* ***

The mid-1960s DG set under Kubelik won golden opinions (and rightly so) for the eloquence of the performance and the excellence of the analogue recording. The balance is most musically done and Kubelik's approach shows both sympathy and insight, while his team of soloists works well together. But in the last analysis, there is a slight coolness of manner which dilutes the music's red-blooded dramatic qualities, and this performance will suit best those for whom refinement is more important than dynamism. Yet at mid-price and with Fischer-Dieskau in a generous, 45-minute collection of Lieder (mainly early works) by all three of the Second Viennese School, this makes a welcome bargain. Full texts and translations are given of both the main work and the songs.

Music for chorus: *2 Canons; 3 Canons, Op. 28; Dreimal Tausend Jähre, Op. 50a; Friede auf Erden, Op. 13; 3 Folksongs, Op. 49; 3 German folksongs; Kol Nidre, Op. 39; 4 Pieces, Op. 27; 6 Pieces, Op. 35; Psalm 130, Op. 50b; Modern Psalm No. 1, Op. 50 C; A Survivor from Warsaw, Op. 46.*
(M) *** Sony S2K 44571 (2) [id.]. John Shirley-Quirk, Günther Reich, BBC Singers, BBC SO, Pierre Boulez.

This superb collection of choral music, recorded by CBS between 1976 and 1986, is issued here in a handsome two-disc package by Sony. Though *A Survivor from Warsaw*, vividly dramatic and atmospheric, was issued earlier in one of CBS's Schoenberg boxes, it is shocking that the rest has had to wait so long to reappear. With passionately committed performances from the BBC Singers, the result explodes any idea that Schoenberg was a cold composer. In his choral pieces, particularly when inspired by a Jewish theme, as in the magnificent *Kol Nidre* of 1938 for narrator, mixed chorus and orchestra, his full romanticism broke out. His adoption of an idiom far removed from abrasive atonality in most of these pieces makes this one of the most approachable of Schoenberg sets, with the use of a narrator in three of the works adding spice to the mixture. The early motet, *Friede auf Erden*, very taxing for the chorus, is here made to sound mellifluous, and only the little middle-period *Pieces*, Opp. 27 and 28, show anything like the full rigour of Schoenbergian argument. The later works, written in America, use twelve-note technique with astonishingly warm, rich results. First-rate recording over the series, all done in the BBC's Maida Vale Studio. There is an extended essay in German in the booklet, but regrettably only summaries of it in English, French and Italian, though translations are given of the full texts.

Pierrot Lunaire, Op. 21.
(M) *** Chan. CHAN 6534; *MBTD 6534* [id.]. Jane Manning, Nash Ens., Rattle – WEBERN: *Concerto.* ***

Jane Manning is outstanding among singers who have tackled this most taxing of works, steering a masterful course between the twin perils of, on the one hand, actually singing and, on the other, simply speaking. As well as being beautifully controlled and far more accurate than is common, her sing-speech brings out the element of irony and darkly pointed wit that is an essential too often missed in this piece. In a 1977 recording originally made for the Open University, Rattle draws strong, committed performances from the members of the Nash Ensemble and, apart from some intermittently odd balances, the sound is excellent. The recording contains an important fill-up in the late Webern piece, and the transfer offers a clear, atmospheric sound-picture.

Schreker, Franz (1878–1934)

The Birthday of the Infanta (ballet-pantomime).
(B) *(*) VoxBox (2) [CDX 5043]. Hamburg SO, Grüber – SCHILLINGS: *Mona Lisa;* WEILL: *Violin concerto* etc. *(*)

Like Max von Schillings, Franz Schreker represented an older generation of composer than Kurt Weill, the main contributor to this Vox Box, the 'Berlin Project'. His brand of updated romanticism made his operas very popular in pre-Hitler Germany, but he has been seriously neglected since. He wrote this brief ballet, based on Oscar Wilde's short story, in 1908, an attractive, exotic piece in a style which led directly towards Hollywood film music. The string sound in the rather coarse recording is thin, and the performance is lively but lacks finesse.

Schubert, Franz (1797–1828)

(i) *Konzertstück, D.345; Polonaise in B flat, D.580; Rondo in A, D.438;* (ii) *Impromptus Nos. 1–4, D.899; 5–8, D.935; 3 Klavierstücke, D.946; Moments musicaux Nos. 1–6, D.780.*
(B) ** Turnabout Double 0006 (2). (i)

Lautenbacher, Württemberg CO, Faerber; (ii) Alfred Brendel.

Schubert was twenty when he wrote these three concertante pieces, the nearest he came to a violin concerto. They are not especially individual but are all attractive. Susanne Lautenbacher plays them simply and is well accompanied, although the recording does not have a great deal of bloom and her timbre is made to sound slightly wiry. Brendel's performances of the *Impromptus* are another matter. They have an unaffected eloquence which is most appealing, and the *Moments musicaux* are comparable, disarming in their simplicity of manner. The sound is good, too.

Rondo in A for violin and strings, D.438.
(B) *** Ph. 426 977-2; *426 977-4*. Grumiaux, New Philh. O, Leppard – HAYDN: *Violin concertos*; MOZART: *Adagio; Rondo*. ***

Schubert's *Rondo* has never danced more engagingly than on Grumiaux's bow, and Leppard captures the music's rhythmic lilt equally pleasingly. Excellent 1967 sound. A bargain.

Rosamunde: Overture (Die Zauberharfe), D.644; Ballet music No. 2; Entr'actes Nos. 1 & 3, D.797.
(B) *** Ph. 426 071-2; *426 071-4*. Concg. O, George Szell – MENDELSSOHN: *Midsummer Night's Dream*. ***

Those looking for a bargain coupling of Schubert and Mendelssohn could hardly do better than Szell's 1957 reissue, which sounds amazingly fresh. The orchestral playing is first class, the *Overture* has an engaging rhythmic spring, and the *Ballet* and *Entr'acte* match polish with charm. Recommended. A similar digital selection from the Chicago Symphony Orchestra under Levine at mid-price (DG Dig. 427 817-2) misses out the first *entr'acte* but offers instead Smetana's dances from *The Bartered Bride*. Despite the latter's more modern recording, the Szell collection is the more memorable.

Symphonies Nos. 1–7; 8 (Unfinished); 9 (Great).
(M) **(*) DG 419 318-2 (4). BPO, Karl Boehm.

Symphonies Nos. 1–7; 8 (Unfinished); 9 (Great); Overtures: Fierabras; In the Italian style in C; Des Teufels Lustschloss.
(B) **(*) Decca 430 773-2 (4). VPO, István Kertész.

Symphonies Nos 1–6; 8–9; Rosamunde: Overture and incidental music.
(M) **(*) BMG/RCA GD 60096 (5); [60096-2-RG]. Cologne RSO, Wand.

Performing honours between the Boehm and Kertész sets are fairly evenly divided. Boehm's recordings were made over a decade between 1963 and 1973. Although he does not always smile as often as Schubert's music demands, he is always sympathetic, and the Berlin Philharmonic plays with striking warmth and finesse throughout. Certainly the Berlin wind are a joy to listen to in most of these symphonies, and in Nos. 6, 8 and 9 Boehm is the best of Schubertians. It is only in the early symphonies that he does not quite capture the youthful sparkle of these delightful scores, although in its way No. 1 is brightly and classically done. The remastered sound is remarkably fine, fresh and clear and without loss of bloom. But with no fillers this set is overpriced.

Kertész, too, recorded these works over a fairly long period (between 1963 and 1971). He began with Nos. 8 and 9 and the overtures (which are well worth having), and these two symphonies are the finest performances in the cycle. The *Ninth* is fresh, dramatic and often very exciting, the *Unfinished* highly imaginative and comparably dramatic in its wide dynamic contrasts. Nos. 4 and 5 came next (in 1970) and, apart from a few extreme tempi – a fast minuet in No. 4, a fast opening movement and a slow start to the *Andante* in No. 5 – this is attractive, stylish Schubert playing. Nos. 1, 2, 3 and 6 completed the cycle in 1971. In the two early symphonies Kertész scores with the spirited VPO playing and a light touch, and this also applies to Nos. 3 and 6, even if they are without the last ounce of character and distinction. The playing of the VPO is beyond reproach throughout, and if Kertész's Schubert manner is less coaxing than Beecham's, less affectionate than Boehm's, it has a pervading freshness, helped by the transparent yet full Decca sound, recorded in the very suitable ambience of the Sofiensaal and admirably remastered. Given the bargain price, this is worth considering.

The freshness and bluff honesty of Gunter Wand in Schubert shine through all his performances. Now collected on five mid-price CDs, his cycle offers first-rate sound, engineered by West German Radio. Nos. 3, 5 and 6 as well as the *Rosamunde* music are the only digital recordings. Note that the Boehm set takes only four mid-price CDs, but has no makeweight, and is less generous over repeats.

Symphonies Nos. 3 in D, D.200; 5 in B flat, D.485; 6 in C, D.589.
❀ (M) *** EMI CDM7 69750-2; *EG 769750-4*. RPO, Beecham.

Beecham's are magical performances in which every phrase breathes. There is no substitute for imaginative phrasing and each line is shaped with affection and spirit. The *Allegretto* of the *Third Symphony* is an absolute delight. The delicacy of the opening of the *Fifth* is matched by the simple lyrical beauty of the *Andante*, while few conductors have been as persuasive as Beecham in the *Sixth* 'little' *C major Symphony*. The rhythmic point and high spirits of the first movement and scherzo are irresistible, and the finale, taken rather more gently than usual, is wonderfully graceful and delectably sprung. The sound is now just a shade drier in Nos. 3 and 6 than in their last LP incarnation but is generally faithful and spacious. This is an indispensable record or tape for all collections and a supreme bargain in the Schubert discography.

Symphonies Nos. 3 in D, D.200; 8 in B min. (Unfinished), D.759.
(B) *** Pickwick Dig. PCD 848; *CIMPC 848* [id.]. City of L. Sinfonia, Hickox.

Hickox's coupling makes a first-rate bargain recommendation on the Pickwick label. These are fresh and direct readings, never putting a foot wrong, very well recorded, with a chamber orchestra sounding full and substantial. Others may find more individuality and charm, but the crisp resilience of the playing is consistently winning.

Symphony No. 5 in B flat, D.485.
(M) *** EMI CDM7 63869-2 [id.]; *EG 763869-4*. Philh. O, Klemperer – DVOŘÁK: *Symphony No. 9.* **
❀ (M) **(*) Sony SMK 46246 [id.]. Marlboro Festival O, Casals – BEETHOVEN: *Symphony No. 4.* **
(B) ** Pickwick Dig. PCD 819 [id.]. O of St John's, Smith Square, Lubbock – HAYDN: *Symphony No. 49.* **(*)

More charm here than one might have expected from Klemperer, but basically his conception is stronger than most, so that something like an ideal balance is kept between Schubert's natural lyricism and the firmness of sonata form. The Philharmonia Orchestra is on top form, and rarely has Klemperer recorded a more exhilarating performance than this 1963 version. Recording excellent.

The Casals account is a concert performance, recorded at the Marlboro Festival in Vermont in 1970, and it is very special indeed. The orchestra is a roll-call of celebrities (the strings include Shmuel Ashkenazi, Miriam Fried, Pina Carmirelli, Edith Peinemann, Nuboko Imai and Miklós Perényi) which responds with warmth to Casals' direction. The reading is spacious and unhurried, eminently straightforward and unaffected, yet unfailingly illuminating. There are some extraneous noises at the beginning of the slow movement (and elsewhere), though they do not deflect attention from either the musical imagination that illumines the playing or the tenderness of the phrasing. The recording inhibits an unreserved recommendation; the string-tone needs more bloom and tutti are a bit rough-grained – but never mind, the performance is full of insight.

With tempi fractionally on the brisk side, Lubbock's pacing is nevertheless convincing; there is no want of character here, and the recording is first class; but ultimately this is not a performance to resonate in the memory, though the slow movement has grace. Very good sound, and the price is very competitive.

Symphonies Nos. 5 in B flat, D.485; 8 in B min. (Unfinished), D.759.
(M) *** Decca Dig. 430 439-2; *430 439-4* [id.]. VPO, Solti.
(M) *** Sony MK 42048 [id.]. Columbia SO or NYPO, Bruno Walter.
(M) **(*) EMI CDM7 69016 [id.]; *EG 769016-4*. BPO, Karajan.
(B) ** Decca 417 680-2; *417 680-4*. VPO, Istvan Kertész.
(B) ** Hung. White Label HRC 152; *WLMC 152* [id.]. Hungarian State O, Ferencsik.

As with Solti's fresh, resilient and persuasive (full-price) reading of the *Great C major* with the Vienna Philharmonic, his coupling of Nos. 5 and 8 brings one of his most felicitous recordings. There have been more charming versions of No. 5 but few that so beautifully combine freshness with refined polish. The *Unfinished* has Solti adopting measured speeds but with his refined manner keeping total concentration. Excellent recording.

Bruno Walter's famous coupling, recorded in 1960 and 1958, has now been reissued by Sony at mid-price, still with its earlier, premium-price catalogue number. Walter brings special qualities of warmth and lyricism to the *Unfinished*. Affection, gentleness and humanity are the keynotes of this performance; while the first movement of the *Fifth* is rather measured, there is much loving attention to detail in the *Andante*. The recording emerges fresh and glowing in its CD format and, like the rest of the Walter series, completely belies its age. The sound is still richly expansive as well as clear, and the CD is in every way satisfying.

Karajan's EMI coupling is taken from the complete cycle of Schubert symphonies which he recorded in the late 1970s. The performance of the *Unfinished* may lack the mystery and dark intensity of his DG recording of the work (see below), but both No. 5 and No. 8 here find Karajan at his freshest and least complicated.

In the *B flat Symphony* Kertész does not always find the smile in Schubert's writing, but the playing of the VPO is stylishly beyond reproach. The *Unfinished* was one of the finest of his cycle, spacious and unaffected. The recording, of good quality throughout, has a wider dynamic range here, so that the woodwind solos in the second movement tend to sound a little distant, yet the pianissimo at the opening immediately creates a degree of tension that is to be sustained throughout the performance.

Ferencsik's *Fifth* is graceful and strong, with the *Andante* flowing and the scherzo genial, yet with an attractive rhythmic feeling. The *Unfinished* is less individual, but has no lack of drama or momentum. The orchestral playing has character and polish in both works, and the Hungaroton recording is full and vivid.

Symphonies No. 5 in B flat, D.485; 8 in B min. (Unfinished) (completed and orch. Newbould).
(M) *** Ph. Dig. 432 045-2; *432 045-4*. ASMF, Marriner.

The balance in the *Fifth Symphony* is not quite ideal in the relationship between wind and strings, and the recording is not as clearly defined internally as one might expect. Nevertheless this remains a highly desirable performance, among the finest in Marriner's series. The *Unfinished* is here completed, with Schubert's Scherzo filled out and the *Rosamunde B minor Entr'acte* used as finale. Given a fresh, direct performance, the work becomes fully convincing in its own right.

Symphonies Nos. 5 in B flat, D.485; 9 in C (Great). Rosamunde: Ballet music No. 1, D.797.
(B) *** DG Compact Classics *419 389-4* [id.]. BPO, Boehm.

On the DG Compact Classics tape, Boehm's version of No. 5 makes a perfect coupling for his *Great C major*: the first movement is wonderfully light and relaxed; the slow movement, though also relaxed, never seems to outstay its welcome; and in the last two movements the Berlin playing makes for power as well as lightness. Boehm's Berlin *Ninth* stands in the lyrical Furtwängler tradition. His modification of tempo in the various sections of the first movement is masterly in its finesse, often so subtle that it requires close attention to be spotted. In the slow movement the rhythmic spring to the repeated quavers is delectable. Nor is there any lack of drama in the performance, although in the finale, taken rather fast, the playing is slightly less gripping; even so, there is excitement in plenty. The recording is full and resonant.

Symphony No. 8 in B min. (Unfinished), D.759.
❀ (M) *** DG Dig. 427 818-2; *427 818-4* [id.]. Philh. O, Sinopoli – SCHUMANN: *Symphony No. 3*. ***
(B) *** DG 429 676-2. BPO, Karajan – DVOŘÁK: *Symphony No. 9 (New World)*. ***
(M) *** DG 415 848-2; *415 848-4* [id.]. BPO, Karajan – MENDELSSOHN: *Symphony No. 4*. ***
(M) (***) EMI mono CDM7 63398-2 [id.]; *EG 763398-4*. RPO, Beecham – BEETHOVEN: *Symphony No. 8*; MENDELSSOHN: *Symphony No. 4*.(***)
(M) (**) Sony SMK 47297 [id.]. Marlboro Festival O, Casals – SCHUMANN: *Symphony No. 2*. **
(BB) ** Pickwick (Decca) PWK 1149. VPO, Münchinger – MENDELSSOHN: *Symphony No. 4*. *(*)
(BB) ** Naxos Dig. 8.550289 [id.]. Slovak PO, Michael Halász – BEETHOVEN: *Symphony No. 5*. **

Symphony No. 8 (Unfinished); Rosamunde: Overture (Die Zauberharfe), D.644; Incidental music, D.797; Intermezzi in D, B flat & B min.; Ballets in G & B min.
(B) ** Hung. White Label Dig. 15 527 [id.]. Budapest PO, János Kovacs.

Symphony No. 8 in B min. (Unfinished); Rosamunde: Overture (Die Zauberharfe); Ballet music Nos. 1–3.
(M) * Teldec/Warner Dig. 9031 74785-2 [id.]. VSO, Harnoncourt – MOZART: *Lucio Silla overture*.

Sinopoli secures the most ravishingly refined and beautiful playing; the orchestral blend, particularly of the woodwind and horns, is magical. It is a deeply concentrated reading of the *Unfinished*, bringing out much unexpected detail, with every phrase freshly turned in seamless spontaneity. The contrast, as Sinopoli sees it, is between the dark – yet never histrionic – tragedy of the first movement, relieved only partially by the lovely second subject, and the sunlight of the closing movement, giving an unforgettable, gentle radiance. The exposition repeat is observed, adding weight and substance. This takes its place among the recorded classics. The warmly atmospheric recording, made in Kingsway Hall, is very impressive.

Karajan's 1965 DG recording of the *Unfinished* sounds fresher still in remastered form, yet has not lost its fullness and warmth of bass response. Its merits of simplicity and directness are enhanced by the extraordinary polish of the orchestral playing, lighting up much that is often obscured. The first movement is extremely compelling in its atmosphere; the slow movement too brings tinglingly precise attack and a wonderful sense of drama. A superb bargain in its coupling with Dvořák's *New World Symphony*.

Beecham's 1951 mono recording, borrowed from the CBS archives for one of the first issues in the Beecham Edition, brings a magical example of his work. Though the first movement is taken relatively fast, a genuine allegro, Beecham's moulding of phrase and line could hardly be more persuasive. The build-up during the development section is thrilling, with the rasp of trombones vividly caught; and the slow movement is sweet and spacious, even though the RPO strings are not at their purest. Coupled with the Beethoven and the Mendelssohn, it makes a generous issue at mid-price.

The dry and rather constricted acoustic of the Music Shed and the occasional grunt are the drawbacks in Casals's 1968 account of the most sublime of Schubert's symphonies. These problems are more than offset by the deep musicianship and humanity that distinguish Casals's reading. Each phrase is beautifully but unselfconsciously moulded, and the distinguished musicians playing under his baton respond to his direction wonderfully. This is very special music-making.

At the beginning of his reading of the *Unfinished*, Münchinger achieves a degree of pianissimo rare even on CD – cellos and basses barely audible – and the exposition is slow, steady and rather withdrawn. Then in the development Münchinger suddenly comes out into the open. The orchestral sound is brighter and freer: it is as though the climax is the real argument of the work, with the sun suddenly appearing from behind the clouds. The moment of high drama is short-lived, for at the recapitulation we return to the withdrawn mood of the opening. The second movement is less idiosyncratic, thoughtful and again withdrawn. The reading is altogether refreshingly different, almost Byronic is its romanticism. The recording is early, 1959, but its wide dynamic range does not mean that the sound is not robust, and the CD medium with its background quiet adds to the sense of dramatic contrast.

Kovacs's account on Hungaroton is not especially dramatic, with the tempi of the two movements very similar. But the orchestral playing is warm and quite spontaneous, and the *Rosamunde overture* has a strikingly graceful touch. This selection of incidental music is more generous than is usual with this coupling and it is well characterized. The digital sound is full and natural.

Michael Halász's very plain reading of the *Unfinished* comes as an alternative coupling for Richard Edlinger's account of the Beethoven *Fifth*. It may lack mystery at the start, and the second subject is presented simply and with little expressive pointing, but the first movement still builds inexorably to the big crescendo at the start of the development, and the second movement has a folk-like freshness. Well recorded and aptly coupled, it has its clear place among versions in the least expensive category.

Harnoncourt, often electrifying in Mozart or Beethoven, is rhythmically too stodgy in these Schubert items with the Vienna Symphony Orchestra. The reading of the *Unfinished* sounds undercharacterized, even though it brings sharp dynamic contrasts. What is traditionally known as the *Rosamunde Overture* is described pedantically on the packaging as *Die Zauberharfe*. Even at mid-price in first-rate sound, this is not very competitive, though the Mozart fill-up is far finer.

Symphonies Nos. 8 in B min. (Unfinished), D.759; 9 in C (Great), D.944.

(M) **(*) EMI CDM7 63854-2 [id.]; *EG 763854-4*. Philh. O, Klemperer.

Klemperer's approach to the *Unfinished* is utterly individual. Gone is any attempt to charm; instead the work is seen as a massive symphonic structure. And massive it is if one regards the two movements in relation to the first halves of other symphonies. But Klemperer's approach is anything but stodgy, for his determination to play the score straight has inspired his players to keen, alert playing that never lets the attention wander. The opening is deliberately grim but, when the second subject finally arrives, there is no attempt to beautify the melody: it simply fends for itself and acquires an unusual purity thereby. So throughout the whole performance, recorded in 1963. This will hardly please everyone, but it remains an outstanding example of Klemperer's interpretative genius. In the *Great C Major*, recorded in 1960, Klemperer's view is certainly individual, with a measured performance, deliberately literal and rather heavy, particularly in the first movement. But once the speeds and the severe approach are accepted, the fascination of the reading becomes clear; there is some glorious playing from the Philharmonia: the oboe solo at the beginning of the slow movement is deliciously pointed. Like others in the Klemperer Edition, this coupling will appeal primarily to those interested in tracing the career of a great but individual conductor.

Symphony No. 9 in C (Great), D.944.

(M) *** EMI Dig. CDD7 64085-2 [id.]; *ET 764085-4*. BPO, Tennstedt – MENDELSSOHN: *Symphony No. 4.* ***

(M) *** DG 419 484-2 [id.]. Dresden State O, Boehm.

(M) **(*) Decca 425 957-2 [id.]. LSO, Josef Krips – SCHUMANN: *Symphony No. 4.* **

(B) **(*) Sony MYK 44828 [id.]. Columbia SO, Bruno Walter.
(M) **(*) DG Dig. 429 983-2 [id.]. Chicago SO, Levine.
(M) (**) BMG/RCA mono GD 60313. Phd. O, Toscanini.

Symphony No. 9 in C (Great); Symphonic fragments in D, D.615.
(M) *** Ph. Dig. 434 218-2; *434 218-4* [id.]. ASMF, Sir Neville Marriner.

Tennstedt's is an incandescent reading that brings home afresh how Schubert, even in this last and grandest of his symphonies, was still youthfully energetic. With superb playing from the Berlin Philharmonic Orchestra this is certainly among the very finest versions available, irrespective of price, and, coupled with an equally exhilarating account of Mendelssohn's *Italian Symphony*, makes a clear digital first choice in the lower price ranges. The 1983 sound is not quite as cleanly focused as the Mendelssohn, but it has fine body, a natural warmth and plenty of presence.

Boehm's Dresden performance is more volatile than the glowing one included in his cycle of the Schubert symphonies, with a notable relaxation for the second subject in the first movement and extreme slowing before the end. The slow movement is fastish, with dotted rhythms crisply pointed and a marked slowing for the cello theme after the great dissonant climax. The Scherzo is sunny and lilting, the finale fierce and fast. It may not be quite as immaculate as the studio-recorded version, but it is an equally superb document of Boehm's mastery as a Schubertian, and the recording, though a little edgy on brass, has fine range.

Taken from his collected edition of Schubert symphonies, Sir Neville Marriner's account of the *Great C major* makes up for any lack of weight with the fresh resilience of the playing, consistently well sprung. Though all repeats are observed, bringing the timing of the *Symphony* to over an hour, an attractive fill-up is provided in the little two-movement fragment, D.615, orchestrated by Brian Newbould. Written just after the *Sixth Symphony*, it consists of a slow introduction and first-movement exposition, plus a fragment of a sonata-rondo finale, which similarly breaks off. First-rate recording.

Josef Krips never made a finer record than his 1956 account of Schubert's *Great C major*. The performance has a direct, unforced spontaneity which shows Krips's natural feeling for Schubertian lyricism at its most engaging. The playing is polished yet flexible, strong without ever sounding aggressive. In the final two movements Krips finds an airy exhilaration which makes one wonder how other conductors can ever keep the music earthbound as they do. The pointing of the Trio in the scherzo is delectable, and the feathery lightness of the triplets in the finale makes one positively welcome every one of its many repetitions. As a whole, this reading represents the Viennese tradition at its finest. The recording, outstanding in its day, retains the glowing bloom over the orchestra; but the remastering has, alas, brought a degree of stridency to fortissimos.

Bruno Walter's 1959 CBS recording has been impressively enhanced on CD; the warm ambience of the sound – yet with no lack of rasp on the trombones – seems ideal for his very relaxed reading. The performance has less grip than Furtwängler's, but in the gentler passages there are many indications of Walter's mastery, not least in the lovely playing at the introduction of the second subject of the *Andante*. There is much to admire, even if this never quite achieves the distinction of the conductor's earlier recordings of this symphony.

Levine conducts a refined performance, beautifully played and excellently recorded, which is commendably free from mannerism, yet which may on that account seem undercharacterized. He omits the exposition repeats in the outer movements (just as was universally done until recently). Conversely, all the repeats in the Scherzo are observed, which unbalances the structure.

Those who know Toscanini's NBC recording of the *Great C major* will be surprised how much more sympathetic – more lyrical and less rigid – his Philadelphia performance is. Speeds tend to be brisk, as in the second-movement *Andante*, but rhythms are well sprung. The 1941 recording has been refurbished well to give it fair body, though there is still some harshness.

CHAMBER AND INSTRUMENTAL MUSIC

Arpeggione sonata, D.821 (arr. for cello).
(M) *** BMG/RCA GD 86531 [RCA 6531-2-RG]. Lynn Harrell, James Levine – DVOŘÁK: *Cello concerto.* ***

Lynn Harrell's account of the *Arpeggione* with James Levine makes an excellent medium-price choice. He is refreshingly unmannered and yet full of personality. Vital, sensitive playing excellently recorded, though the digitally remastered sound is rather light in bass.

Fantaisie in C, D.934.
(M) ** EMI CDM7 63988-2 [id.]. Y. Menuhin, Kentner – BRAHMS: *Horn trio* **; MENDELSSOHN: *Violin sonata.* *(*)
(M) ** BMG/RCA GD 87873; *GK 87873* [7873-2-RG; *7873-4-RG*]. Heifetz, Brooks Smith –

BEETHOVEN: *String trio No. 3*; BRAHMS: *Piano quartet No. 3*. **

Menuhin recorded the Schubert *C major Fantasia* in 1958 but the sound is, if anything, fresher than in the Brahms coupling. There are moments when his vibrato may pose problems for some listeners – though there are, of course, many felicities here. High among the latter is the beautiful playing of Louis Kentner, which is impeccable and makes one regret that he did not record any of the Schubert sonatas.

Heifetz's account of the *C major Fantasy* was recorded in 1968, though the dry studio acoustic almost suggests an earlier provenance. Brooks Smith is a fine player but not quite as imaginative as Kentner who had recorded this with Menuhin a few years earlier. Heifetz is his incomparable self.

Octet in F, D.803.

(M) ** Decca 421 155-2; *421 155-4*. Vienna Octet – MOZART: *Divertimento No. 7*. **(*)

The Decca record dates from as early as 1956 and, while the stereo with its clean separation was always impressive, there is a thinness to the violin timbre that betrays the age of the recording. The performance has the glow of the Vienna Octet at its peak under the leadership of Willi Boskovsky, and the horn has a Viennese fruitiness to make the sound that much more authentic. The digital remastering adds clarity of focus but tends to draw the ear to the thinness of the violin timbre.

Piano quintet in A (Trout), D.667.

(B) **(*) Decca 433 647-2; *433 647-4* [id.]. Clifford Curzon, Vienna Octet (members) – MOZART: *Clarinet quintet*. **

(M) ** Ph. 420 716-2 [id.]. Beaux Arts Trio (augmented) – BEETHOVEN: *Piano trio No. 5 (Ghost)*. ***

Piano quintet in A (Trout) Notturno in E flat, D.897.

(BB) ** Naxos Dig. 8.550057 [id.]. Leonard Hokanson, Villa Musica Ens.

(i) *Piano quintet in A (Trout)*; (ii) *Rondo in A, D.438*; (iii) *Impromptu in B flat, D.935/3.*

(BB) * LaserLight Dig. 15 522 [id.]. (i) Emmy Verhey, Colorado Qt; (ii) Dechenne; (iii) Jenö Jandó.

(i) *Piano quintet in A (Trout);* (ii) *String quartet No. 14 (Death and the Maiden).*

(M) **(*) Decca 417 459-2; *417 459-4* [id.]. (i) Curzon, Vienna Octet (members); (ii) VPO Qt.

(M) **(*) Sony SBK 46343 [id.]; *40-46343*. (i) Horszowski, Budapest Qt (members), Julius Levine; (ii) Juilliard Qt.

(M) **(*) Teldec/Warner Dig. 9031 74783-2 [id.]. (i) Medjimorec, V. Haydn Trio, Arad, Streicher; (ii) Vermeer Qt.

(i) *Piano quintet in A (Trout);* (ii) *String trios, D.471 & D.581.*

(M) *** Ph. 422 838-2; *422 838-4*. (i) Haebler, Grumiaux, Janzer, Czako, Cazauran; (ii) Grumiaux String Trio.

Piano quintet in A (Trout), D.667; Violin sonata in A, D.574.

(M) ** Van. 8.8005.71 [OVC 8005]. Peter Serkin, Schneider Ens.

(i) *Piano quintet in A (Trout);* (ii) *Der Hirt auf dem Felsen.*

(B) **(*) Pickwick PCD 868; *CIMPC 868* [id.]. (i) Nash Ens.; (ii) Lott, Collins, Brown.

Clifford Curzon's 1958 recording of the *Trout* sounds its age in the thin violin timbre, although the piano tone has plenty of colour and it has a warm ambience. It remains a classic performance, with a distinguished account of the piano part and splendidly stylish support from the Vienna players. Schubert's warm lyricism is caught with remarkable freshness. Some might find the brilliant Scherzo a little too fierce to match the rest of the performance, but such vigorous playing introduces an element of contrast at the centre of the interpretation and makes possible a relaxed account of the last movement. There are alternative couplings.

There is some admirably unassertive and deeply musical playing from Miss Haebler and from the incomparable Grumiaux; it is the freshness and pleasure in music-making that render this account memorable. These artists do not try to make 'interpretative points' but are content to let the music speak for itself. The balance is not altogether perfect, but the quality of the recorded sound is good. As an extra enticement, Philips have added a pair of *String trios*, given characteristically refined performances by Grumiaux and his companions, delightful music superbly played.

Horszowski's contribution to the *Trout* is undoubtedly distinguished and his clean, clear playing dominates the performance which, although full of imaginative detail, is a little on the cool side – though refreshingly so, for all that. The Juilliard Quartet are far from cool in the *Death and the Maiden quartet*. They begin the famous slow movement with a rapt pianissimo, and the variations are played with great feeling and the widest range of expression and dynamic. The scherzo has a comparable *agitato* character, but the bite and crispness of ensemble bring a firm sense of control, and the middle section is beautifully contrasted. The finale is infectiously alert and vigorous, the unanimity of ensemble consistently impressive. A fine performance overall, among the best in the catalogue. In both works the sound is a little dry, but not confined.

A generally unaffected performance of the ubiquitous *Trout* comes from the Vienna Haydn Trio playing with Atar Arad and Ludwig Streicher, though they choose a rather brisk tempo for the *Andante* movement. Be that as it may, there is much to enjoy in this performance, which has the merit of a lively, warm acoustic and well-balanced 1982 recording (some may think the piano a shade dominant) with excellent, sensitive playing by the pianist, Heinz Medjimorec. The 1983 Vermeer account of the *Death and the Maiden quartet* is recorded in a much drier acoustic and, as one would expect from this eminent group, it is impeccable in terms of ensemble and tonal refinement. Everything is finely shaped, but the performance has a little less warmth than some rival accounts. Good value and recommendable, though not perhaps a first choice.

The Nash Ensemble on Pickwick brings a fill-up in the shape of *The Shepherd on the rock*. They are recorded rather forwardly here and their account is just a little wanting in the spontaneity that distinguishes the finest of the current versions. Ian Brown is, as always, a sensitive artist.

The Naxos budget recording by Leonard Hokanson and the Villa Musica Ensemble was made in the normally cramped acoustic of the Tonstudio Van Geest in Heildelberg, but this is one of the most satisfactory recordings to have emerged from that venue. Of course one would welcome a greater back-to-front perspective and more air round the piano, but fortunately the formidable sensitivity and artistry of Leonard Hokanson dominate an account which is both highly musical and spontaneous.

Peter Serkin and Schneider's group give a bold, vigorous account of the *Trout* with a well-shaped set of variations. The wistful side of Schubert is missing here, but this music-making is easy to enjoy for its spontaneity. The recording is full and forward, the double-bass nicely resonant; but the violin timbre discloses the mid-1960s recording date.

The Beaux Arts *Trout* is a delightfully fresh performance. Every phrase is splendidly alive, there is no want of vitality or sensitivity, and the recording is basically well balanced. The snag is the digital remastering, which gives undue prominence to Isidore Cohen's violin, lighting it up brightly and thinning down the timbre.

The LaserLight super-bargain version is a brisk, no-nonsense account, completely lacking in charm. The bright, forward recording doesn't help, with its absence of warm resonance for the double-bass, which makes a meagre impression. The *Rondo* is altogether more successful, both as a performance and as a recording, and Jandó's account of the famous *Impromptu* has an appealing simplicity.

(i) *Piano trios Nos. 1 in E flat, D.890; 2 in B flat, D.929; Nocturne in E flat, D.897; Sonata in B flat, D.28; in E flat, D.929;* (ii) *Piano quintet in A (Trout), D.667; Adagio & Rondo concertante in F, D.487.*

(B) *(*) VoxBox 1156002 (2) [CDX 5033]. (i) Trio Concertante; (ii) Rochester Chamber Players.

The Trio Concertante are musical and vital performers and in Benedikt Kehlen have a sensitive and imaginative pianist, while the violist and cellist are also artists of some quality. The *B flat Trio*, which is placed on the second CD, is the drier recording of the two. Both trios are shorn of their first-movement exposition repeats. The Rochester Chamber Players, drawn presumably from the staff of the Eastman School of Music, include the pianist Eugene List, and they give a very acceptable account of the *Trout quintet* (again, no first-movement exposition repeat). Good though the playing is, the slightly constricted frequency range and the absence of any information on the box, make one suspect that these recordings are of earlier rather than later provenance. The first three movements of the *Trout* are accommodated on the first disc, along with the *E flat Trio* and the *Sonata in B flat*, D.28. The *B flat Trio* and the *Quintet* could easily have shared the same disc without any loss of continuity at just under 70 minutes. There is a rarity in the shape of the *Adagio and Rondo concertante in F*, D.487, but most collectors can do better elsewhere.

Piano trio No. 1 in B flat, D.898.

(M) ** BMG/RCA GD 86262 [6262-2-RG]. Szeryng, Fournier, Rubinstein – SCHUMANN: *Piano trio No. 1.* **

(M) ** Sony MPK 45697 [id.]. Eugene Istomin, Isaac Stern, Leonard Rose.

Piano trio No. 1 in B flat; Notturno in E flat, D.897.

(M) **(*) Ph. 422 836-2; *422 836-4.* Beaux Arts Trio.

(B) ** Hung. White Label HRC 173 [id.]. Ferenc Rados, Dénes Kovács, Ede Banda.

Piano trio No. 1 in B flat; Sonata movement in B flat, D.28.

(BB) **(*) Naxos Dig. 8.550131 [id.]. Stuttgart Piano Trio.

The Beaux Arts performance has impeccable ensemble, with the pianist, Menahem Pressler, always sharply imaginative and the string playing sensitive in both line and phrase. The performance is perhaps on the lightweight side, although the slow movement has a disarming simplicity. The *Notturno*, eloquently played, makes an attractive bonus. The recording, from the late 1960s, sounds fresh, although its age shows a little in the timbre of the violin.

The Stuttgart Piano Trio are a well-respected ensemble who have now been in existence almost a quarter of a century. Their Schubert may be at budget price but it is not a bargain-basement performance; the playing is musicianly and intelligent. First-movement exposition repeats are observed and there are many sensitive touches. The recording was made in the Tonstudio Van Geest in Heildelberg – not a venue which inspires confidence, given the quality of some of the Naxos piano recordings made there. But the engineer on this occasion has succeeded in getting rather more acceptable results. Although the sound is still less than ideal, there is slightly more air round the three instruments.

Szeryng, Fournier and Rubinstein were recorded in 1974 in a rather dryish studio so that this impeccably played version sounds just a little wanting in freshness and bloom. Apart from the rather measured finale, tempi are ideally judged and there is a good sense of momentum. A fine performance.

The artists on Sony convey their enjoyment with a fairly relaxed approach to Schubert, especially the slow movement. It is a good but not distinctive account, well recorded (in 1965), if closely balanced. However, the overall playing time of 38 minutes is short measure these days.

Like the Stuttgart Piano Trio on Naxos, Ferenc Rados, Dénes Kovács and Ede Banda on Hungaroton White Label are balanced rather too forwardly, though their 1981 recording has slightly more natural warmth. Expressive playing throughout, but one wishes one was placed further back from the artists.

Piano trio No. 2 in E flat, D.929.

(M) * Sony MPK 45560 [id.]. Eugene Istomin, Isaac Stern, Leonard Rose.

Piano trio No. 2 in E flat; Notturno in E flat, D.897.

(BB) (**) Naxos Dig. 8.550132 [id.]. Stuttgart Piano Trio.

Piano trio No. 2 in E flat; Sonata in B flat (for piano trio), *D.28.*

(M) **(*) Ph. 426 096-2; *426 096-4* [id.]. Beaux Arts Trio.

The Beaux Arts Trio's ensemble is superbly polished here, and the pianist's contribution is consistently imaginative, with the cellist, Bernard Greenhouse, bringing simple dedication to such key passages as the great slow-movement melody of the *E flat Trio*. The extra item gives this disc an added appeal. Written during Schubert's student days, the attractive early *Sonata in B flat* has the same kind of fluency as Beethoven's *First Piano trio*, though the lyrical flow has the unmistakable ring of Schubert. The 1967 recording has fine freshness and immediacy, but the CD remastering brings a degree of dryness to the upper range.

Coming to the Stuttgart Piano Trio's disc of the *E flat Trio* after its predecessor is something of a disappointment. The recording venue and team may be the same, but there is greater airlessness and tutti passages come close to discoloration. The playing is very good and deserves a high rating; it is even stronger in character and finesse than the *B flat Trio*, but the oppressive and unpleasant sound militates against it and it comes close to 'breaking up' at the very beginning.

The Stern–Istomin–Rose recording comes from 1970 and is recorded in a horribly dry studio acoustic. The performance has an intensity and drive absent from many rivals, but the brittle, monochrome sound diminishes pleasure.

String quartets Nos. 1–15.

(M) ** DG 419 879-2 (6) [id.]. Melos Qt of Stuttgart.

The early quartets have an altogether disarming grace and innocence, and some of their ideas are most touching. The Melos are an impressive body whose accounts of this repertoire are unmannered and on the whole sympathetic. They are let down by recording quality that is less than distinguished, but the remastering has brought added presence.

String quartets Nos. 12 (Quartettsatz); 13 in A min., D.804; 14 (Death and the Maiden); 15 in G.

(M) *(**) Sony M2YK 45617 (2) [id.]. Juilliard Qt.

(B) (*) VoxBox (2) [CDX 5022]. New Hungarian Qt.

String quartets Nos. 12 in C min. (Quartettsatz), D.703; 14 in D min. (Death and the Maiden), D.810.

(BB) **(*) Naxos Dig. 8.550221 [id.]. Mandelring Qt.

(M) ** Sony MYK 42602 [id.]. Juilliard Qt.

String quartet No. 14 in D min. (Death and the Maiden), D.810.

(M) *** Ph. 420 876-2. Italian Qt – DVOŘÁK: *Quartet No. 12* *** (with BORODIN: *Nocturne* *).

(M) **(*) DG Dig. 429 491-2; *429 491-4*.

Amadeus Qt – MOZART: *String quartet No. 17 (Hunt).* **

The Italian Quartet offer a fine coupling with Dvořák, and the Borodin *Nocturne* is thrown in for good measure. They bring great concentration and poetic feeling to this wonderful score, and they are free of the excessive point-making to be found in some rival versions. The sound of the reissue is vivid and clear.

The Mandelring Quartet, from Germany, are a young family group (two brothers and one sister, plus a violist) like the rather older and more celebrated Hagens. They are not quite in the Hagens' class, but they are very good indeed. The performances are sensitively and sensibly played and very decently recorded and, though the playing is not as polished as, say, the Quartetto Italiano's *Death and the Maiden*, anyone tempted by this Naxos disc will not be disappointed for so modest an outlay.

The 1983 Amadeus version of *Death and the Maiden* offers much to admire. The performance has a powerful momentum and, though there is some rough playing from Brainin, there is relatively little sentimentality. The actual sound is not as pure as in their very first mono recording, when their blend was superb and the leader's vibrato unobtrusive. Now the balance seems a trifle close.

On Sony, unaffected but largely unaffecting performances of these Schubert masterpieces. The playing is of the highest standard of accomplishment and everything is highly professional; the architecture of the music is well held together and there are of course many moments of real poetic feeling, but the dry sound diminishes the appeal of the set. Here the *Quartettsatz*, usually heard as a single movement, also includes the *Andante*, which ends at the moment Schubert left it as an incomplete fragment. The recordings date from the early 1980s, but one might be tempted to guess they were earlier. The *A minor Quartet* is split over the two discs.

On a two-disc VoxBox set, the New Hungarian Quartet give very well-thought-out and musical performances. However, they are let down by the very rough-and-ready recorded sound. Anything above forte comes close to discoloration and the unventilated acoustic and close balance are unpleasing.

String quartet No. 13 in A min., D.804.
(B) ** Pickwick PCD 831. Brodsky Qt – BEETHOVEN: *String quartet No. 10.* **

A promising CD début by this young British group who play with commendable vitality and spirit. There is some roughness of tone, exacerbated no doubt by the balance, but this is offset by a strong sense of line and much warmth of feeling. All the same, the greater refinement of the Hagen and Lindsays – at full price – tells.

String quartets Nos. 13 in A min., D.804; 14 in D min. (Death and the Maiden), D.810.
(M) *** Ph. 426 383-2; *426 383-4* [id.]. Italian Qt.
(M) (**) Sony mono MPK 45676 [id.]. Budapest Qt.

The Italians omit the exposition repeat in the first movement of the *A minor Quartet*; the slow movement is spacious – some may feel it is a bit too slow – and has an impressive command of feeling. Their account of *Death and the Maiden* is also very fine. Here the slow movement is particularly telling, showing a notable grip in the closing pages. Technically the playing throughout is quite remarkable. The recordings are well balanced and truthful, sounding a little dryer now in their CD remastering.

The Budapest versions are mono and were first published in 1954. The constricted frequency-range and dry studio acoustic are hurdles to overcome. The performances as such have greater warmth and breadth than the Juilliard listed above, but they do not have the stature of some of the Budapest accounts of the Mozart *Haydn Quartets*, where sonic limitations are largely banished by the concentration of the music-making. These Schubert recordings are no longer really competitive.

String quartets Nos. 14 in D min. (Death and the Maiden); 15 in G.
(M) (***) EMI (mono) CDH7 69795-2 [id.]. Busch Qt.

The Busch Quartet's account is more than fifty years old, but it brings us closer to the heart of this music than any other. The slow movement of the *Death and the Maiden quartet* is a revelation, and the same must be said of the *G major*, which has enormous depth and humanity and a marvellous eloquence. For its age, the sound is still amazing, and the musical wisdom is timeless.

String quintet in C, D.956.
(M) *** Saga SCD 9011. Aeolian Qt with Bruno Schreker.
(M) ** DG 435 071-2; *435 071-4*. LaSalle Qt with Lynn Harrell – SCHUMANN: *Piano quintet.* *(*)
(B) (*) Hung. White Label HRC 056 [id.]. Tátrai Qt with László Szilvásy.

String quintet in C, D.956; String quartet No. 12 in C min. (Quartettsatz), D.703.
(M) ** Decca 421 094-2; *421 094-4*. Weller Qt (augmented in *Quintet*).

String quintet in C, D.956; String trio in B flat, D. 581.

(BB) *** Naxos Dig. 8.550388 [id.]. Villa Musica Ens.

The augmented Aeolian Quartet give a strong, virile performance of what is arguably Schubert's greatest chamber work. Their style is direct with no mannerisms whatsoever. It might seem bald, were it not for the depth of concentration that the players convey in every bar. The finale, for example, is fresh and rustic-sounding, not because of its pointing of the rhythm but because of the very simplicity of utterance. In the slow movement the Aeolians daringly adopt the slowest possible *Adagio*, and the result might have seemed static but for the inner tension which holds one breathless through hushed pianissimos of the most intense beauty. Never before on record, not even in Casals's old Prades (mono) version had the profundity of this music been so compellingly conveyed. The analogue recording, though not of the clearest in terms of individual definition of instruments, has been transferred to CD with remarkable presence and the engineers have resisted the temptation to sharpen the imagery so that the body of tone has not been lost. This is a clear first bargain choice, and there are few premium-priced issues which approach, let alone match, its intensity.

The Ensemble Villa Musica is a group, based on Mainz, which on this showing is of the highest quality. Not only do these performances offer polish and refinement, with immaculate matching and intonation, but also a satisfying thrust of attack. The great *C major Quintet*, completed in the last months of Schubert's life, is among the most taxing of chamber works, and the Villa Musica players tackle it with a freshness and concentration that are consistently compelling, even if the finale is neat and clean rather than urgently dramatic. The little *String trio*, written when the composer was twenty, makes an attractive and generous fill-up, another assured and stylish performance. With clear, well-balanced recording this super-budget issue makes an outstanding bargain and offers an excellent alternative to the Saga version for those wanting digital sound.

The LaSalle version presents a refined but somewhat cool reading. Lynn Harrell makes an outstandingly positive second cellist, but there are more compelling readings than this, and the remastered recording is clear rather than glowing.

Fine playing from the Weller Quartet, though a trifle sweet and suave. The *Quartettsatz* makes an attractive fill-up. The sound too is good and does not seem too dated.

The Tátrai performance is acceptable but not distinctive, with no real magic in the great *Adagio*. The players are not helped by the digital remastering, which – like the Mozart *Quintets* on the same label – makes the violins sound impossibly shrill.

Duo in A, D.574; Violin sonatina, D.385; Fantaisie in C, D.934.

(M) **(*) Decca 425 539-2; *425 539-4*. Szymon Goldberg, Radu Lupu.

Violin sonatinas: in D, D.384; in A min., D.385; in G min., D.408; Duo in A, D.574.

(M) **(*) Ph. 426 385-2; *426 385-4* [id.]. Arthur Grumiaux, Robert Veyron-Lacroix.

Violin sonatinas in D, D.384; in A min., D.385; in G min., D.408; Fantasy in C, D.934.

(BB) *(**) Naxos Dig. 8.550420 [id.]. Dong-Suk Kang, Pascal Devoyon.

There is an unaffected, Schubertian feeling in the Goldberg/Lupu performances that is most appealing. Indeed Goldberg is vulnerable in that he almost undercharacterizes the line, and at times one could do with a greater variety of dynamic nuance and tonal colour. Yet the presence of Radu Lupu ensures that these performances give much pleasure: his playing has a vitality and inner life that are consistently rewarding. The remastered recording also sounds full and natural, and is very realistically balanced.

Instead of reissuing Grumiaux's set with Paul Crossley, the earlier, 1972 performances with Robert Veyron-Lacroix have been chosen, and the latter does not emerge as quite so strong a personality as his partner. However, his response is admirably musical and the Philips sound is fresh and clear, even though the acoustic is resonant.

Korean-born Dong-Suk Kang plays with style and panache and is given excellent support by Pascal Devoyon. Neither is well served by the recording, however, made in a cramped studio that robs the piano-tone of some of its timbre, while the close balance does less than complete justice to the sound this fine violinist makes in the flesh. Nevertheless it still gives pleasure. Performances three star; the recording one.

PIANO MUSIC

Allegretto in C min., D.915; Impromptus, D.899/1–4; Piano sonatas Nos. 13 in A, D.664; 19 in C min., D.958; 20 in A, D.959; 21 in B flat, D.960.

(M) ** Ph. Dig. 432 307-2 (3) [id.]. Claudio Arrau.

Undoubtedly Claudio Arrau was one of the keyboard giants of the twentieth century, and the handsomely packaged commemorative collection of his Philips recordings serves as an impressive representation of his art. Arrau's Schubert shows all the distinctive hallmarks of his pianism: great, aristocratic finesse and the familiar, cultured, well-rounded sonority. For all his tonal sophistication and undoubted depth, there remains an innocence about so much of this music that eludes him somewhat. The rubati in the great *B flat Sonata*, D.960, sound very studied; and whether in the late *Sonatas* or in the *Impromptus* the great pianist seldom seems to let the music speak for itself. As always, the pianism is immaculate and the Philips recording exemplary.

Allegretto in C min., D.915; Moments musicaux Nos. 1–6, D.780; 2 Scherzi, D.953; 12 Valse nobles, D.969.
(M) **(*) DG 435 072-2; *435 072-4*. Daniel Barenboim.

Some of the finest playing here comes in the two *Scherzi*. In the first, Barenboim's pointing is a delight, and he is equally persuasive in the Trio of the second. The *Allegretto in C minor* is given an effective, improvisatory quality, but the twelve *Valses nobles* are played too forcefully for their full charm to be revealed. In the *Moments musicaux* there is much to admire: Barenboim's mood is often thoughtful and intimate; at other times we are made a shade too aware of the interpreter's art and there is an element of calculation that robs the impact of freshness. There are good things, of course, but this does not challenge Lupu's set. The piano-tone on DG has impressive presence and weight and seems firmer than on LP, though it lacks something in ultimate richness.

Fantasia in C (Wanderer), D.760.
(M) *** Ph. 420 644-2. Alfred Brendel – *Sonata No. 21.* ***

Brendel's playing is of a high order, and he is truthfully recorded and coupled with what is perhaps Schubert's greatest *Sonata*, so this is excellent value at mid-price.

Impromptus Nos. 1–4, D. 899; 5–8, D.935.
(M) **(*) DG 415 849-2; *415 849-4* [id.]. Daniel Barenboim.
(BB) **(*) Naxos Dig. 8.550260 [id.]. Jenö Jandó.

Daniel Barenboim plays the *Impromptus* with characteristic sensitivity and refinement. His tempi are rather slow and there are occasional moments of self-consciousness. Barenboim's touch is quite ethereal at times and, whatever one's response may be, the playing is enormously positive and full of character. The recording is realistic, with presence and clarity to recommend it, though the CD transfer has brought a degree of hardness. A fair mid-price choice.

Though his set of the *Impromptus* is not ideally recorded (the microphones are a bit too close, with unpleasing results in fortissimo passages), Jandó has been worse served by the engineers. He is a very musical player and his unaffected (and often perceptive) readings are more than acceptable. The Perahia and (earlier) Brendel versions (at full price) are unchallenged, but no one investing in the present set is likely to be greatly disappointed.

4 Impromptus, D.899; Impromptu in B flat, D.935/3; Moments musicaux, D.780/1, 2 & 6.
(B) *** LaserLight Dig. 15609 [id.]. Jenö Jandó.

At last Jenö Jandó is heard, recorded in an acoustic that does justice to his talent. The sound, at least in the opening *B flat major Impromptu* of D.935, is fresh and truthful, the ambience is warm, and the playing is very good. The balance is not as good in the three *Moments musicaux* or in the D.899 *Impromptus*: it is closer and marginally drier. There is probably a very good reason why Jandó didn't record all four of D.935 or all six of the *Moments musicaux*, but the incompleteness diminishes the attractiveness of a good recital.

Moments musicaux Nos. 1–6, D.780; 3 Klavierstücke, D.946; Allegretto in C min., D.915.
(BB) **(*) Naxos Dig. 8.550259 [id.]. Jenö Jandó.

Though the venue is the Italian Institute in Budapest, Jandó is much better recorded here than he is in some other contexts. He proves a thoroughly sympathetic and sensitive Schubertian, but he is still too upfront (try the opening of the fifth *Moment musical*, where the hammers and the piano mechanism are distinctly audible). The opening of the *Drei Klavierstücke* is a shade too fast (Jandó does not completely convey its dark, disturbing overtones) but the middle section is beautifully judged. The little *Allegretto in C minor*, D.915, is also very nicely played. Thoughtful and intelligent music-making, acceptably recorded, and very good value for money.

Piano sonatas Nos. 1 in E, D.157; 14 in A min., D.784; 20 in A, D.959.
(M) *** Decca 425 033-2; *425 033-4* [id.]. Radu Lupu.

The early *E major Sonata* was written in 1815. Its finale was never composed and only three movements survive. Lupu is sensitive and poetic throughout and he effectively turns the lively Minuet into a brilliant closing movement. He is no less searching in the later *A minor Sonata.* In the *A major* work he strikes the perfect balance between Schubert's classicism and the spontaneity of his musical thought, and at the same time he leaves one with the impression that the achievement is perfectly effortless. The scherzo has great sparkle and delicacy, and the slow movement has an inner repose and depth of feeling that remain memorable long after the record has ended. Yet the strength of the interpretation lies in its sensitivity to detail and appreciation of the structure as a whole. Excellent vintage Decca recording, made in the Kingsway Hall in the late 1970s.

Piano sonatas Nos. 4 in A min., D.537; 20 in A, D.959; Andante in C min. (from D.840).
(M) * Pickwick Dig. MCD 33; *MCC 33.* Anton Kuerti.

The opening of the *A minor Sonata*, D.537, is pulled about in an intolerable fashion by Anton Kuerti, as is that of the slow movement. It is not always easy to follow the musical reasoning behind his agogic mannerisms. Nor is the powerful opening of the great *A major Sonata*, D.959, free from disruptive surges. Anton Kuerti's name is listed before Schubert's on the spine and features again on the front of the jewel case – and rightly so, for he figures more prominently in this musical experience than the composer! The Pickwick recording is very truthful.

Piano sonatas Nos. 13 in A, D.664; 18 in G, D.894.
(M) * Pickwick Dig. MCD 29; *MCC 29.* Anton Kuerti.

With Anton Kuerti the opening movement of the *G major Sonata* is insufferably affected. Those who recall the eloquent simplicity of Solomon in the *A major*, D. 664, or the Schubert sonatas of such artists as Gilels and Lupu will wonder what to make of all this self-conscious posturing. The star is for a good recording and for the nearly always beautiful sound this artist produces.

Piano sonatas Nos. 14 in A min., D.784; 18 in G, D.894; 12 Waltzes, D.145.
(M) *** Decca 425 017-2; *425 017-4* [id.]. Vladimir Ashkenazy.

This is a recoupling for CD. Ashkenazy's account of the *A minor Sonata* surpasses the pianist's own high standards. There is an astonishing directness about this performance, a virility tempered by tenderness that is very compelling indeed. On the other hand, the *G major Sonata* (which comes first on the disc) is altogether more controversial. The first movement should certainly be leisurely if it is to convey the self-communing as well as the sense of peace that lies at its heart. But Ashkenazy is very slow indeed: he robs it of its normal sense of momentum. If further hearings prove more convincing, this is largely because Ashkenazy's reading is so totally felt and, equally, perceptive. He succeeds in making the piano sound exceptionally expressive. This is a most searching and poetic account, and both sonatas are given highly realistic recording, the *G major* slightly fuller in the bass. The *Waltzes* make an attractive and generous encore.

Piano sonatas Nos. 15 in C (Unfinished), D.840; 19 in C min., D.958; 16 German Dances, D.783.
(M) *** Van. 08.4026.71 [OVC 4026]. Alfred Brendel.

Brendel was at his finest and most spontaneous in the 1960s, after his Vox contract was terminated. There is a freshness in his approach to Schubert here that is not absolutely consistent in his analogue Schubert recordings for Philips. The *C minor Sonata* is particularly fine, with no sense of agogic distortion of the flow, rather a thoughtful, improvisatory feeling in the slow movement which is consistently illuminating. The two-movement *C major Sonata* also has a memorable *Andante*, and the *German Dances* are an endless delight, lilting in their rhythms and full of imaginative touches. The recording is full and bold and gives every satisfaction, even if it does not bring such a naturally wide range of dynamic as his later, Philips records.

Piano sonata No. 19 in C min., D.958; Moments musicaux Nos. 1–6, D.780.
(M) *** Decca Dig. 417 785-2; *417 785-4* [id.]. Radu Lupu.

Lupu's performance has a simple eloquence that is most moving. His *Moments musicaux* are very fine indeed. The Decca recording is very natural and, at mid-price, this is extremely competitive.

Piano sonata No. 21 in B flat, D.960.
(M) *** Ph. 420 644-2. Alfred Brendel – *Wanderer fantasia.* ***
(M) (**) BMG/RCA mono GD 60451 [60451-2-RG]. Vladimir Horowitz – CZERNY: *Variations;* MENDELSSOHN: *Variations sérieuses;* MOZART: *Sonata No. 12.* (**)

Brendel's performance is as impressive and full of insight as one would expect. He is not unduly wayward, for his recording has room for the *Wanderer fantasy* as well, and he is supported by excellent Philips sound.

There is some wonderful pianism in Horowitz's performance of the *B flat Sonata*, recorded live at his 1953 Carnegie Hall recital and, as one would expect, some searching musical insights. His tempo in the first movement is a good deal faster than that adopted by artists like Kempff and Richter – though, even so, he omits the exposition repeat – and his slow movement, though full of magical things, will also be a little too fast-moving for those brought up on Schnabel and Richter. All the same, there is playing of some stature here. The two-dimensional (and, in the middle and lower register, boxy) recorded sound calls for some tolerance.

VOCAL MUSIC

Lieder: *Alinde; Am Tage aller Seelen; An die Entfernte; An die Laute; Auf dem Wasser zu singen; Auf der Riesenkoppe; Die Bürgschaft; Du bist die Ruh; Der Fischer; Der Fischers Liebesglück; Fischerweise; Die Forelle; Die Götter Griechenlands; Greisengesang; Heidenröslein; Das Heimweh; Im Walde; Der Jüngling an der Quelle; Der Jüngling und der Tod; Lachen und Weinen; Lied des gefangenen Jägers; Das Lied im Grünen; Nachtgesang; Nachtstück; Nähe des Geliebten; Normans Gesang; Der Schiffer; Sei mir gegrüsst; Seligkeit; Das sie hier gewesen; Ständchen; Strophe aus Die Götter; Der Strom; Der Tod und das Mädchen; Der Wanderer; Der Winterabend; Das Zügenglöcklein; Der zürnende Barde.*
(M) *** EMI CMS7 63566-2 (2) [Ang. CDMB 63566]. Dietrich Fischer-Dieskau, Gerald Moore; Karl Engel.

Dating from 1965, most of the items in this collection of Schubert songs superbly represent the second generation of Fischer-Dieskau recordings with Gerald Moore, deeper and more perceptive than his mono recordings, yet with voice and manner still youthfully fresh. Like this, there is no male Lieder-singer to match him. The contrast is fascinating, if subtle, between that main collection and the last nine songs on the second disc: they were recorded six years earlier, with three of them accompanied by Karl Engel, and with the voice still younger but presented in drier sound. With favourite songs comprising a substantial proportion of the programme, this delightful selection makes a valuable basic Lieder collection.

Lieder: *Am Bach in Frühling; An den Mond II; An die Nachtigall; Auf der Donau; Ave Maria; Berthas Lied in der Nacht; Dass sie hier gewesen; Frühlingsglaube; Gretchen am Spinnrade; Im Abendrot; Die junge Nonne; Kennst du das Land; Klärchens Lied; Der König in Thule; Lachen und Weinen; Lied der Anna Lyle; Lilla an die Morgenröte; Das Mädchen; Des Mädchens Klage; Mignon Lied I–III; Mignon Romanze; Sehnsucht;* (i) *Ständchen; Der Tod und das Mädchen; Wehmut; Der Zwerg.*
(M) *(*) DG 431 476-2 (2). Christa Ludwig, Irwin Gage, (i) with women's voices of Fr. R. Ch.

This reissue combines two collections by Christa Ludwig, made in 1974 and 1975 (each CD contains a complete recital). Neither shows her at her finest. She is most effective in the dramatic songs on the first disc; *Auf der Donau* and *Der Tod und das Mädchen* are both strikingly done, and the *Mignon Romanze* is beautiful. But *Ave Maria* is not relaxed enough and the simpler songs are lacking in charm. This applies even more to the second group, a challenging sequence of songs which fails to live up to the detailed imagination of her earlier Schubert performances on record. The results are often disappointingly lacking in charisma. Moreover, the microphones were evidently placed very near the singer, and the digital remastering, while giving striking projection of the dramatic songs, at times adds a hint of edge to the vocal timbre. However, Irwin Gage's sympathetic accompaniments are well in the picture.

Lieder: *An die Entfernte; Auf dem Wasser zu singen; Du bist die Ruh'; Der Erlkönig; Die Forelle; Heidenröslein; Das Heimweh; Der Jüngling an der Quelle; Der Jüngling und der Tod; Das Lied im Grünen; Litanei auf das Fest Aller Seelen; Nachtgesang; Der Schiffer; Sei mir gegrüsst!; Ständchen; Der Strom; Der Tod und das Mädchen; Der Wanderer; Der Winterabend; Das Zügenglöcklein; Der zürnende Barde.*
(M) *** EMI CDM7 69503-2 [id.]; *EG 769503-4*. Dietrich Fischer-Dieskau, Gerald Moore.

EMI's mid-price collection of vintage Fischer-Dieskau recordings makes an ideal sampler of favourite Schubert songs. Early in his career the voice was at its freshest and most beautiful and, though the comparably early stereo recording is less atmospheric than on more recent issues, there is a face-to-face immediacy which with such an artist could not be more revealing. A bargain.

Lieder: *An die Musik; An Sylvia; Auf dem Wasser zu singen; Ave Maria; Du bist die Ruh'; Die Forelle; Ganymed; Gretchen am Spinnrade; Heidenröslein; Im Frühling; Die junge Nonne; Litanei; Mignon und der Harfner; Der Musensohn; Nacht und Träume; Sei mir gegrüsst; Seligkeit.*
(B) *** Pickwick Dig. PCD 898; *CIMPC 898* [id.]. Felicity Lott, Graham Johnson.

At bargain price, Felicity Lott's collection brings an ideal choice of songs for the general collector. With Graham Johnson the most imaginative accompanist, even the best-known songs emerge fresh and new. Though Lott's voice loses some of its sweetness under pressure, the slight distancing of the recording gives a pleasant atmosphere, and gentle songs like *Litanei* are raptly beautiful.

Lieder: *An die Musik; An Sylvia; Auf dem Wasser zu singen; Ganymed; Gretchen am Spinnrade; Im Frühling; Die junge Nonne; Das Lied im Grünen; Der Musensohn; Nachtviolen; Nähe des Geliebten; Wehmut.*
(M) (***) EMI mono CDH7 640262 [id.]. Elisabeth Schwarzkopf, Edwin Fischer.

Schwarzkopf at the beginning of her recording career and Fischer at the end of his make a magical partnership, with even the simplest of songs inspiring intensely subtle expression from singer and pianist alike. Though Fischer's playing is not immaculate, he left few records more endearing than this, and Schwarzkopf's colouring of word and tone is masterly. The mono sound has been freshened, with the voice given a touch more aural mascara than on the original CD version which sounded even more natural – if more limited – than this. That earlier (full-price) disc, unlike this one in the Références series, offered a coupling – eleven of Schwarzkopf's Mozart song recordings with Gieseking.

Lieder: *An die Laute; An Silvia; An die Musik; Der Einsame; Im Abendrot; Liebhaber in allen Gestalten; Lied eines Schiffers an die Dioskuren; Der Musensohn; Ständchen.*
(M) *** DG 429 933-2 [id.]. Fritz Wunderlich, Hubert Giesen – BEETHOVEN: *Lieder* **(*); SCHUMANN: *Dichterliebe.* ***

Few tenors have matched the young Wunderlich in the freshness and golden bloom of the voice. The open manner could not be more appealing here in glowing performances well coupled with other fine examples of this sadly short-lived artist's work.

Lieder: *Ave Maria; Jäger, ruhe von der Jagd; Raste Krieger!; Schwestergruss; Der Zwerg.*
(M) **(*) Ph. 426 642-2; *426 642-4.* Jessye Norman, Irwin Gage – MAHLER: *Des Knaben Wunderhorn* etc. **(*)

These five Schubert songs come as fill-ups to Jessye Norman's early (1971) recordings of songs from Mahler's *Des Knaben Wunderhorn*, plus two *Rückert Lieder*, all sensitively done, if with less detail than she would later have provided. Good recording for its period, well transferred.

Lieder: *Die schöne Mullerin: Wohin?; Des Baches Wiegenlied. Schwanengesang: Liebesbotschaft. Winterreise: Die Post; Frühlingstraum. An die Geliebte; An die Musik; An die Nachtigall; An mein Klavier; Auf dem Wasser zu singen; Ave Maria; Das sie hier gewesen; Du bist die Ruh'; Der Einsame; Des Fischers Liebesglück; Fischerweise; Die Forelle* (2 versions); *Frühlingsglaube; Geheimes; Gretchen am Spinnrade; Heidenröslein; Das Heimweh;* (i) *Der Hirt auf dem Felsen; Im Abendrot; Die junge Nonne; Der Jüngling an der Quelle; Der Jüngling und der Tod; Lachen und Weinen; Liebhabner in allen Gestalten; Das Lied im Grünen; Litanei; Das Mädchen; Der Musensohn; Nacht und Träume; Nachtviolen; Nahe des Geliebten; Nur wer die Sehnsucht kennt; Der Schmetterling; Seligkeit; So lasst mich scheinen; Ständchen; Schweizerlied; Die Vögel; Wiegenlied. Claudine von Villa Bella, D.239: Hin und wieder fliegen Pfeile* (2 versions); *Liebe schwärmt. Rosamunde, D.797: Der Vollmond strahlt.*
(M) (***) EMI mono CHS7 63040-2 (2) [Ang. CDHB 63040]. Elisabeth Schumann (various pianists); (i) Reginald Kell.

The irresistible charm and pure, silvery tones of Elisabeth Schumann make this collection of Schubert songs a delight from first to last. On the two CDs are collected 49 songs, with *Der Hirt auf dem Felsen* (*The Shepherd on the rock*) given separate billing on the cover. The recordings were made between 1927 and 1949, but mostly come from Schumann's vintage period in the 1930s. Transfers capture the voice well but, with a brighter top than on LP, the piano sound has less body. What matters is the vivid personality of the singer, never more sparkling than in such favourite songs as *Wohin?* (one of the earliest, made in 1927), *Heidenröslein* (from 1932) or *Die Forelle*, with a fascinating contrast between the brisk 1936 account and the more cautious but more delicate version of ten years later.

Masses Nos. 4 in C, D.452; 5 in A flat, D.678.
(M) *** EMI CDM7 69222-2 [id.]; *EG 769222-4.* Popp, Donath, Fassbaender, Araiza, Dallapozza, Fischer-Dieskau, Bav. R. Ch. & SO, Sawallisch.

This medium-priced reissue from Sawallisch's excellent choral series combines two settings of the Mass, including the finest (in A flat). The singing is outstanding from chorus and soloists alike, and the remastered recording has retained most of its fullness and gained in clarity and presence.

Masses Nos. (i) *5 in A flat, D.678;* (ii) *7 in C, D.961.*
(M) **(*) Decca 430 363-2; *430 363-4.* (i) Eathorne, Greevy, Evans, Keyte, St John's College, Cambridge, Ch., ASMF, Guest; (ii)

Bryn-Johnson, De Gaetani, Rolfe Johnson, King, L. Sinf. Ch., L. Sinf., Atherton.

The *A flat Mass* dates from 1822, although it was probably begun a few years earlier and was certainly revised later. It has many beauties and in a fervently inspired reading can sound most impressive. Guest's performance is faithful but just lacks the distinction that marked his earlier recordings of the Haydn *Masses*; neither the singing nor the playing is in the least routine but they lack the personality that these musicians brought to the Haydn and the late *E flat* Schubert *Mass* (see below). The 1976 (originally Argo) recording sounds splendid in its CD transfer, finer than the Sawallisch HMV version; but that performance is more vibrantly distinctive. Schubert's *C major Mass* setting is less deeply inspired but, in a lively performance like Atherton's, this last of the four early *Masses* has refreshment to offer. The recording is again very impressive, not absolutely clear but full and atmospheric, and admirably transferred to CD.

(i) *Mass No. 6 in E flat, D.950;* (ii; iii) *Gesang der Geister über den Wassern, D.714;* (ii) *Eine kleine Trauermusik: Minuet and finale in D for wind, D.79.*
(M) *** Decca 430 362-2; *430 362-4.* (i) Palmer, Watts, Bowen, Evans, Keyte, St John's College, Cambridge, Ch., ASMF, Guest; (ii) L. Sinf. Ch.; (iii) L. Sinf. (members), Atherton.

Mass No. 6 in E flat, D.950; Offertorium, D.963; Tantum ergo, D.962.
(M) *** EMI CDM7 69223-2 [id.]; *EG 769223-4.* Donath, Popp, Fassbaender, Schreier, Araiza, Dallapozza, Fischer-Dieskau, Bav. R. Ch. & SO, Sawallisch.

Having made vibrantly dramatic records of all of Haydn's late *Masses*, George Guest and the St John's Choir went on, first to the Beethoven *C major Mass* (a direct successor), then to this previously neglected work of Schubert. It may not have quite the electric originality of those other masterpieces, but in every way it is a richly rewarding work, product of the last year of Schubert's short life. The freshness of the singing here (the chorus far more important than the soloists) and the resilient playing of the Academy make this a delightful performance, given superb 1974 (Argo) sound. As a coupling, secular music brings equally memorable inspiration, above all in Schubert's last setting of Goethe's *Song of the spirits over the water*, a magical piece. The mourning music is very early indeed, remarkable for its solemn brass writing. The 1979 recording is pleasingly atmospheric and the CD transfer has improved the focus.

The EMI record is centred on the *E flat Mass*, Schubert's masterpiece in this form; while the *Tantum ergo* (in C) also undoubtedly has its charm. Though the chorus is not flawless in the *Mass*, Sawallisch's performances here are warmly understanding and the recording is both vivid and atmospheric.

Die schöne Müllerin (song cycle), *D.795.*
(B) (*) Pickwick Dig. PCD 925; *CIMPC 925* [id.]. Adrian Thompson, Roger Vignoles.

It is sad that Adrian Thompson's tenor is caught so badly. As balanced, with breathing made very audible, the microphone brings out a serious unsteadiness in all sustained notes, with results so gritty that at times the vocal line almost becomes sing-speech.

Song-cycles: *Die schöne Müllerin, D.795; Schwanengesang, D.957; Winterreise, D.911.* Lieder: *Du bist die Ruh'. Erlkönig; Nacht und Träume.*
(M) (***) EMI mono CMS7 63559-2 (3) [Ang. CDMC 63559]. Dietrich Fischer-Dieskau, Gerald Moore.

Fischer-Dieskau's early mono versions may not match his later recordings in depth of insight, but already the young singer was a searching interpreter of these supreme cycles, and the voice was at its freshest and most beautiful, so that one misses stereo remarkably little. Gerald Moore was, as ever, the most sympathetic partner.

Winterreise (song cycle), *D.911.*
❀ (M) *** Decca 417 473-2 [id.]. Peter Pears, Benjamin Britten.

Winterreise (song-cycle), *D.911;* Lieder: *Erlkönig; Ganymed; Im Abendrot; Nachtgesang; Wanderers Nachtlied.*
(B) *** DG Compact Classics *427 724-4.* Dietrich Fischer-Dieskau, Gerald Moore.

Schubert's darkest song-cycle was in fact originally written for high voice, not low; quite apart from the intensity and subtlety of the Pears/Britten version, it gains enormously from being at the right pitch throughout. When the message of the poems is so gloomy, a dark voice tends to underline the sombre aspect too oppressively, whereas the lightness of a tenor is even more affecting. That is particularly so in those songs where the wandering poet in his despair observes triviality – as in the picture of the hurdy-gurdy man in the last song of all. What is so striking about the Pears performance is its intensity. One continually has the sense of a live occasion and, next to it, even Fischer-Dieskau's beautifully wrought singing sounds too easy. As for Britten, he re-creates the music, sometimes with a fair freedom from Schubert's markings, but always with scrupulous concern for the overall musical shaping and sense of atmosphere. The sprung rhythm of *Gefror'ne Tränen* is magical in creating the impression of frozen teardrops falling, and almost every song brings similar magic. The recording, produced by John Culshaw, was made in the Kingsway Hall in 1963, and the CD transfer is exceptionally successful in bringing a sense of presence and realism.

In the early 1970s Fischer-Dieskau's voice was still at its freshest, yet the singer had deepened and intensified his understanding of the greatest of song-cycles to a degree where his finely detailed and thoughtful interpretation sounded totally spontaneous. Moore exactly matches the hushed concentration of the singer, consistently imaginative. It might be argued that this 1972 account is the finest of all Fischer-Dieskau's recorded performances of the cycle. This Compact Classics tape is very smoothly transferred and adds five other favourite Lieder for good measure, to make a genuine bargain.

Schuman, William (born 1910)

Violin concerto.
(M) *** DG 429 860-2 [id.]. Zukofsky, Boston SO, Tilson Thomas – PISTON: *Symphony No. 2*; RUGGLES: *Sun-treader.* ***

William Schuman's *Violin concerto* was commissioned by Samuel Dushkin, who had partnered Stravinsky in the 1930s. It was revised twice and was championed by Isaac Stern, who played both versions in 1950 and 1956 respectively; but this later reworking dates from 1959. It is a tough but thoughtful piece with moments of characteristic dramatic intensity and poignant lyricism. Paul Zukofsky rises to its considerable technical demands with imposing virtuosity.

New England triptych.
(M) *** Mercury 432 755-2 [id.]. Eastman-Rochester O, Howard Hanson – IVES: *Symphony No. 3* etc. ***; MENNIN: *Symphony No. 5.* **(*)

A powerful and appropriate coupling for Ives's masterly *Three places in New England* and *Third Symphony*. William Schuman is not as outrageously original as Ives, but his sound-world is individual and wholly American. This work is drawn from what Schuman describes as the 'spirit of sinewy ruggedness, deep religiosity and patriotic fervour' which characterizes the music of an earlier American composer, William Billings (1746–1800). He tells us further: 'These pieces do not constitute a fantasy or variations on [Billings's] themes, but rather a fusion of styles and musical language.' Each of the three pieces is an orchestral anthem, the first a thrustingly vibrant *Hallelujah*; the second is in the form of a round, and the finale features a marching song. Splendidly alive playing and excellent (1963) Mercury recording, admirably transferred to CD.

Schumann, Robert (1810–56)

Cello concerto in A min., Op. 129.
(M) *** Mercury 432 010-2 [id.]. Janos Starker, LSO, Skrowaczewski – LALO: *Concerto* **(*); SAINT-SAENS: *Concerto.* ***

The Schumann *Cello concerto* is not generously represented at the mid-price or bargain end of the catalogue; Janos Starker gives a persuasive account of it that is thoroughly sensitive to the letter and spirit of the score. Skrowaczewski accompanies with spirit and without the rather explosive, clipped tutti chords that rather disfigure the Lalo with which it is coupled. The 1962 recording is amazing for its age: people make great claims for these early Mercury recordings and, judging from this expertly engineered disc, rightly so!

(i) *Cello concerto in A min., Op. 129;* (ii) *Piano concerto in A min., Op. 54.*
(M) *(*) DG Dig. 427 819-2; *427 819-4* [id.]. (i) Maisky; (ii) Frantz; VPO, Bernstein.

Both these recordings are taken from live performances. In the *Cello concerto* Bernstein seems reluctant to let the music speak for itself, and this affects the eloquent, generous-toned soloist, who similarly has moments of self-indulgence. There are reservations too about the *Piano concerto*. Justus Frantz's account seems a little wanting in spontaneity and does not have quite the delicacy of feeling or subtlety of nuance that the music requires.

(i) *Cello concerto in A min., Op. 129;* (ii) *Piano concerto in A min., Op. 54;* (iii) *Violin concerto in D min., Op. posth.;* (iv) *Fantasy in C, Op. 131;* (ii) *Introduction and allegro appassionato in G, Op. 92; Introduction and allegro in D min., Op. 134;* (v) *Konzertstück in F, Op. 86.*
(B) ** VoxBox 1155912 (2) [CDX 5027]. (i) Varga, Westphalian SO (Rechlinghausen), Landau; (ii) Frankl, Bamberg SO, Fürst; (iii) Lautenbacher, R. Luxembourg O, Cao; (iv) Ricci, Leipzig GO, Masur; (v) Frankl, Orval, Tommasini, Desprez, Janssens, R. Luxembourg O, Cao.

It is a good idea to assemble all three Schumann *Concertos* together and, though inevitably this is a variable compilation, it is inexpensive. The *Piano concerto* is one of the most recorded of all works; though Peter Frankl's version with the Bamberg orchestra has many merits, it does not rank among the most memorable versions. Still it is good to have his accounts of the other pieces (Opp. 86, 92 and 134) which are unjustly neglected. The *Violin concerto*, which came to light only in the 1930s, is one of the least recorded of the species and Suzanne Lautenbacher and the Radio Luxembourg Orchestra give a serviceable enough account of it, as for that matter does Laszlo Varga of the *Cello concerto*. The *C major Fantasy*, the two *Introductions and allegros* and the *Konzertstücke*, Op. 86, are rarities, of course, though there are some alternatives; but there is nothing outstanding here to make the pulse quicken.

Piano concerto in A min., Op. 54.

(M) (***) EMI mono CDH7 69792-2. Lipatti, Philh. O, Karajan – MOZART: *Piano concerto No. 21.* (*(**))

(M) **(*) BMG/RCA GD 60420; *GK 60420* [60420-2-RG; *60420-4-RG*]. Van Cliburn, Chicago SO, Reiner – MACDOWELL: *Concerto No. 2.* **(*)

(BB) **(*) Pickwick PWK 1148. Friedrich Gulda, VPO, Andrae – TCHAIKOVSKY: *Piano concerto No. 1.* ***

(B) **(*) Decca 433 628-2; *433 628-4* [id.]. Gulda, VPO, Andrae – FRANCK: *Symphonic variations* *** ⊛; GRIEG: *Concerto.* ***

(M) **(*) Sony/CBS CD 44849; *40-44849* [id.]. Fleisher, Cleveland O, Szell – GRIEG: *Concerto.* **(*)

(B) **(*) Sony MYK 44771 [id.]. Istomin, Columbia SO, Bruno Walter – BRAHMS: *Double concerto.* **(*)

(M) **(*) Decca 417 728-2 [id.]. Radu Lupu, LSO, Previn – GRIEG: *Concerto.* **(*)

(BB) ** ASV CDQS 6003; *ZCQS 6003.* Vásáry, N. Sinf. – CHOPIN: *Concerto No. 2.* **

(M) ** EMI CDM7 64145-2 [id.]; *EG 764145-4.* Annie Fischer, Philh. O, Klemperer – FRANCK: *Symphony.* **

(M) *(*) Decca Dig. 430 719-2; *430 719-4.* Jorge Bolet, Berlin RSO, Chailly – GRIEG: *Concerto.* *

(B) * EMI CDZ7 62859-2; *LZ 762859-4* [id.]. John Ogdon, New Philh. O, Berglund – FRANCK: *Symphonic variations*; GRIEG: *Concerto.* *

Piano concerto in A min.; Konzertstück for piano and orchestra in G, Op. 92.

(M) * Sony SBK 46543 [id.]. Rudolf Serkin, Phd. O, Ormandy – GRIEG: *Concerto.* **(*)

(i) *Piano concerto in A min. Arabeske in C, Op. 18.*

(M) *** Mercury 432 011-2 [id.]. Byron Janis, Minneapolis SO, Skrowaczewski – TCHAIKOVSKY: *Piano concerto No. 1.* **(*)

Byron Janis's Schumann *Concerto* is a lovely performance, and the 1962 recording sounds amazingly improved over its previous incarnations, especially in regard to the orchestra. The piano is full and firm, if forward, and the orchestral sound has body as well as range. Janis's reading finds an almost perfect balance between the need for romantic ardour and intimacy in the *Concerto* – the exchanges between the piano and the woodwind soloists in the first movement are most engagingly done. Skrowaczewski provides admirable support throughout, and this is highly recommendable.

Dinu Lipatti's celebrated EMI recording has acquired classic status and will more than repay study. The transfer is excellent. A splendidly aristocratic account in very acceptable sound.

Van Cliburn made his record in 1960 and the Chicago acoustics give plenty of warmth to Reiner's sympathetic accompaniment; the piano-tone is bright but not shallow and the balance is remarkably good: in short, this is a considerable improvement on the original LP. Van Cliburn's performance is very persuasive, the first movement rhapsodical in feeling, certainly poetic but exciting too. The *Intermezzo* is pleasingly fresh and the finale admirably buoyant and spirited. Altogether this is most attractive, and so is the unusual MacDowell coupling.

Gulda's account is refreshingly direct, with a brisk basic tempo for the first movement (the tempo of the coda is really nippy); yet, with light, crisp playing, the movement never sounds rushed. Similarly the *Intermezzo* is moved along but remains delicate in feeling, with nicely pointed pianism. The finale is just right, with an enjoyable rhythmic lift. This performance has not the distinction of its Franck and Grieg couplings, but it is enjoyably spontaneous and the early stereo (1956), though a little dated, is fully acceptable. It is also available on Pickwick, paired with Tchaikovsky.

Fleischer's 1960 account with Szell is also distinguished, the reading combining strength and poetry in a most satisfying way, yet with a finale that sparkles. In the first movement Szell relaxes the tempo for the famous piano and woodwind dialogues, and the effect is beguilingly intimate, in spite of a very bold, upfront orchestral recording, which tends to sound a little fierce. If the piano timbre is shallower than we would expect in a European recording, the effect remains warm and this makes a vivid listening experience.

Istomin's performance attractively combines strength and poetry, with bold contrasts in the first movement, a nicely lyrical *Intermezzo* and a fluent, well-paced finale. Bruno Walter's directing personality is strong and the recording sounds remarkably fine in its digital remastering, the warm ambience preventing any feeling of aggressiveness being generated by the dramatic tuttis.

Lupu's clean boldness of approach to the first movement is appealingly fresh, but the fusing together of the work's disparate masculine and feminine Romantic elements has not been solved entirely. The digital CD transfer is especially telling in the quieter moments, but tuttis are less transparent than with a digital recording.

Tamás Vásáry directing from the keyboard gives a characteristically refined yet strong account of the concerto, free from eccentricity and thoroughly straightforward. Poetic, likeable and decently recorded, this is recommendable for those wanting a bargain coupling. The recording is excellent.

The Annie Fischer/Klemperer partnership does not work especially productively. It has some fine moments and a certain noble romanticism, but the slow movement lacks a really delicate touch and the reading as a whole does not fulfil the promise of the opening bars. Good, full (1962) recording.

Jorge Bolet's Schumann is rather more successful than the Grieg with which it is coupled, but he does not show any true feeling for this repertoire. The performance is agreeably relaxed – the short central movement comes off best – but the interplay between wind soloists and pianist in the first movement seems disappointingly matter-of-fact and the finale tends towards heaviness. The recording is admirable.

John Ogdon, as in the other works on this well-transferred CD, is unexpectedly below form in what should be one of the most poetic of piano concertos. Clearly the partnership with Berglund did not work well. The interchanges with the orchestral wind soloists in the first movement are lucklustre and the performance overall refuses to catch fire.

Serkin's harshly overdriven reading of Schumann's ever-fresh *Concerto* misses the spirit of the music altogether. Surprisingly, the performance of the *Konzertstück*, which follows on afterwards, is much more sympathetic, in spite of garish recorded quality.

Piano concerto in A min.; Introduction and allegro appassionato, Op. 92; Introduction and allegro, Op.134.
(BB) ** Naxos Dig. 8.550277 [id.]. Sequeira Costa, Gulbenkian O, Gunzenhauser.

Despite his considerable reputation and distinction, the Portuguese pianist Sequeira Costa has made relatively few commercial records. This 1984 recording of the *A minor concerto* is unidiosyncratic and very well played, but perhaps not sufficiently special or insightful to offer much of a challenge to Byron Janis or Lipatti. This collection deserves some consideration for bringing the *Introduction and allegro appassionato*, Op. 92, to wider notice and for offering the *Introduction and allegro*, Op. 134. Good and musicianly though these performances are, they fall short of real distinction and suffer from the dryish recording in which orchestral tutti do not sufficiently expand.

Violin concerto in D min., Op. posth.
(M) **(*) EMI Dig. CDD7 63894-2 [id.]; *ET 763894*. Gidon Kremer, Philh. O, Muti – SIBELIUS: *Violin concerto*. **(*)

The Schumann *Violin concerto*, with its vein of introspection, seems to suit Gidon Kremer, who gives a generally sympathetic account of it and has very good support from the Philharmonia Orchestra under Riccardo Muti. It is not Schumann at his most consistently inspired, but there are good things in it, including a memorable second subject and a characteristic slow movement. The recording is full-bodied and vivid, balanced in favour of the soloist. It is good to have this recording reissued at mid-price, as it may tempt collectors to try the work.

Overture, Scherzo and Finale in E, Op. 52.
(B) *** DG 431 161-2; *431 161-4*. BPO, Karajan – BRAHMS: *Symphony No. 1*. ***

This serves merely as a bonus for Karajan's fine 1964 recording of the Brahms *First Symphony*. He and his great orchestra are equally at home in the music of Schumann, and this performance is second to none. One could make the criticism that the CD transfer has lost some of the original weight and resonance in the bass, but the result is undoubtedly fresh and there is no suggestion here of the supposed thickness of Schumann's orchestration.

Symphonies Nos. 1–4.
(M) *** DG 429 672-2 (2) [id.]. BPO, Karajan.

Symphonies Nos. 1–4; Symphony in G min. (Zwickau); Overture, Scherzo and Finale, Op. 52.
(B) ** Ph. 426 186-2 (3). New Philh. O, Inbal.

Symphonies Nos. 1–4; Overtures: Die Braut von Messina; Hermann und Dorothea, Op. 136; Die Braut von Messina, Op. 100.
(B) **(*) EMI CZS7 67319-2 (2). Philh. or New Philh. O, Muti.

Symphonies Nos. 1–4; Manfred overture, Op. 115.
(M) **(*) Sony/CBS M2YK 45680 (2) [id.]. Bav. RSO, Kubelik.

Symphonies Nos. 1 in B flat (Spring), Op. 38; 4 in D min., Op. 120; Overture, scherzo and finale, Op. 52.

(M) *** EMI CDM7 69471-2 [id.]; *EG 769471-4*. Dresden State O, Sawallisch.

Symphonies Nos. 2 in C, Op. 61; 3 in E flat (Rhenish), Op. 97.
(M) *** EMI CDM7 69472-2 [id.]; *EG 769472-4*. Dresden State O, Sawallisch.

The Dresden CDs of the Schumann *Symphonies* under Sawallisch are as deeply musical as they are carefully considered; the orchestral playing combines superb discipline with refreshing naturalness and spontaneity. Sawallisch catches all Schumann's varying moods, and his direction has splendid vigour. These recordings have dominated the catalogue, alongside Karajan's, for some years and they are most welcome on CD. Although the reverberant acoustic brought a degree of edge to the upper strings, the sound-picture has the essential fullness which the Karajan transfers lack, and the remastering has cleaned up the upper range to a considerable extent.

Karajan's interpretations of the Schumann *Symphonies* stand above all other modern recordings. No. 1 is a beautifully shaped performance, with orchestral playing of the highest distinction; Karajan has a natural feeling for the ebb and flow of the music and his control of tempo is subtly varied to follow the musical line. His No. 2 is among the most powerful ever recorded, combining poetic intensity and intellectual strength in equal proportions; and No. 3 is also among the most impressive versions ever commited to disc: its famous fourth-movement evocation of Cologne Cathedral is superbly spacious and eloquent, with quite magnificent brass playing. No. 4 can be classed alongside Furtwängler's famous record, with Karajan similarly inspirational, yet a shade more self-disciplined than his illustrious predecessor. However, the reissued complete set brings digital remastering which – as with the Brahms symphonies – has leaner textures than before, while in tuttis the violins above the stave may approach shrillness. Everything is clean and clear but, although the basic ambience remains, the brass have lost sonority and, above *mezzo forte*, textures are noticeably less warmly expansive than they were on LP. Nos. 1 and 3 are also available separately – see below.

Reissued to celebrate Muti's fiftieth birthday, this Schumann cycle, recorded in the late 1970s, is not quite as successful as his Philharmonia set of the Tchaikovsky symphonies. But Muti is a spirited and warm-hearted interpreter of Schumann, and all four symphonies are most enjoyable. The very opening of No. 1 brings what is probably the most controversial speed in the whole set, so hectic that the spring-like lightness is rather missed. But it is is a purposeful reading, and Muti brings out the reserve of the *Second Symphony*; the dark inward quality of No. 3 is given a noble reading, and No. 4 (recorded first) an exhilarating, glowing one. Though the Philharmonia strings are not always as polished as they have since become, both playing and recording are warm and ripe. *The Bride of Messina*, an overture to Schiller's play, was composed in the last few years of Schumann's life, as was its companion, *Hermann und Dorothea*, which includes an engagingly lightweight quotation from the *Marseillaise*. Muti gives fresh, invigorating accounts of both works. The CD transfer has brightened the sound and, although the focus is not completely clear, there is plenty of fullness; the effect is obviously more modern than with the Karajan and Sawallisch sets.

In his CBS/Sony set from the end of the 1970s Kubelik was recording the complete Schumann symphonies for the second time. The readings display the same bright and alert sensitivity to Schumann's style as did his set for DG, but the playing is less polished than that of the Berlin Philharmonic. Even so, it has plenty of life and vitality and the brass is impressive in the *Rhenish Symphony*. The recording is wide-ranging and emerges vividly on CD. It has rather more body and depth than the remastered DG sound but also has an element of coarseness in music which ideally needs refined textures. However, the performances have undoubted spontaneity and conviction and are enjoyable despite the above reservations.

Eliahu Inbal's set of the Schumann *Symphonies* comes from the early 1970s and has one special claim to attention in that it offers the early *G minor Zwickau Symphony*. The doyenne of Schumann scholars, Joan Chissell, speaks of it as 'an exercise, saluting Mozart, Schubert and Beethoven as well as including some bold individual strokes, a student flash-in-the-pan with only the first two movements complete enough for Marc Andrae to publish in 1972'. This recording was presumably made before Andrae's edition appeared, for Inbal omits the *Andantino* movement. The performances have been in and out of the catalogue over the years but have never stayed very long – not surprisingly, considering that the Karajan and Sawallisch versions were in circulation. The *Overture, Scherzo and Finale* is well played, and the other performances are what one might call eminently serviceable but ultimately wanting in the last ounce of distinction. Good recording but, despite the presence of the first movement of the *Zwickau Symphony*, not a real bargain. One can do better elsewhere.

Symphony No. 1 in B flat (Spring), Op. 38.
(B) *** DG 429 158-2 [id.]. BPO, Karajan – MENDELSSOHN: *Symphony No. 4.* ***

Symphonies Nos. 1 (Spring); 4 in D min., Op. 120.
(M) **(*) Ph. Dig. 432 059-2; *432 059-4.* Concg. O, Haitink.

Haitink conducts thoughtful and unexaggerated readings of the *First* and *Fourth Symphonies*, beautifully paced and with refined playing from the Concertgebouw Orchestra. His chosen speeds are never controversial, and the playing is both polished and committed, to make these consistently satisfying performances. The only snag is the recording quality which, with works that from the start are thick in their orchestration, is too reverberant. It is an ample, pleasing sound, but something sharper would have helped more to rebut criticism of Schumann's orchestration.

Symphony No. 2 in C, Op. 61.
(M) *** DG 435 067-2; *435 067-4* [id.]. BPO, Karajan – BRAHMS: *Symphony No. 2.* ***

Symphony No. 2 in C, Op. 61.
(M) ** Sony SMK 47297 [id.]. Marlboro Festival O, Casals – SCHUBERT: *Symphony No. 8 (Unfinished).* (**)

Karajan's powerful account of Schumann's *C major Symphony* has great eloquence and is marvellously played. The recording here sounds rather more expansive than in the boxed set.

Casals directs a wonderfully humane account of the *Second*, arguably the greatest of Schumann's symphonies. The recording comes from 1970 and has not appeared before, perhaps because of minor imperfections that are likely to occur in live performances. The orchestra has some distinguished players; the strings include Pina Carmirelli, Michel Schwalbé (onetime leader of the Berlin Philharmonic), Nobuko Imai, Henri Honegger and Miklós Perényi1, and their response is vital, joyous and marvellously natural. There have been fine accounts of this work from Karajan, Kubelik and Sawallisch, but this is still specially inspiriting despite the essentially dry, cramped acoustic of the Music Shed, which in this transfer has been treated to produce very acceptable results.

Symphony Nos. 2; 3 in E flat (Rhenish), Op. 97.
(B) *** DG 429 520-2 [id.]. BPO, Kubelik.

An excellent bargain coupling from Kubelik. No. 2 is beautifully played and eloquently shaped, and in the *Rhenish* Kubelik's straightforward, unmannered approach, coupled to a natural warmth, provides a musical and thoroughly enjoyable account. The remastering of the 1964/5 recordings is most successful: they have more body and warmth than the Karajan complete set.

Symphony No. 3 in E flat (Rhenish), Op. 87.
(M) *** DG Dig. 427 818-2; *427 818-4* [id.]. LAPO, Giulini – SCHUBERT: *Symphony No. 8 (Unfinished).* *** ❀

Giulini's *Rhenish* is completely free of interpretative exaggeration and its sheer musical vitality and nobility of spirit are beautifully conveyed. The Los Angeles players produce a very well-blended, warm and cultured sound that is a joy to listen to in itself. The recording is extremely fine, too. Now recoupled with Sinopoli's inspired version of Schubert's *Unfinished*, this makes an excellent recommendation.

Symphony No. 4 in D min., Op. 120.
(M) (***) EMI mono CDH7 63085-2. Philh. O, Cantelli – BRAHMS: *Symphony No. 3.* ***
(M) **(*) Decca 425 957-2 [id.]. LSO, Josef Krips – SCHUBERT: *Symphony No. 9.* ***

Cantelli's version of Schumann's *Fourth* brings an inspired performance, with incandescent playing from the Philharmonia. Having Cantelli's two finest symphony recordings with the Philharmonia on a single CD makes the perfect memorial for a conductor who promised supreme greatness before his tragic death.

The *Fourth Symphony* with its taut cyclic form demands dramatic treatment, and Krips's lyrical manner suits the inner movements better than the outer ones. However, the work is well played and the brightly remastered 1956 Kingsway Hall recording makes more impact than the original LP.

CHAMBER MUSIC

Abendlied, Op. 85/2; Adagio and allegro in A flat, Op. 70; Fantasiestücke, Op. 73; 3 Romances, Op. 94; 3 Pieces in Folk style, Op. 102/2–4.
(M) *** Ph. 426 386-2; *426 386-4.* Heinz Holliger, Alfred Brendel.

On this delightful record Heinz Holliger gathers together pieces written in 1849, the most fruitful of composing years for Schumann. The three *Romances* are specifically for oboe, but Holliger – pointing out that Schumann never heard any of the pieces except on the violin – suggests that the others too are suitable for oboe, since the composer himself gave different options. One misses something by not having a horn in the *Adagio and allegro*, a cello in the folk-style pieces, or a clarinet in the *Fantasiestücke* (the oboe d'amore is used here); but Holliger has never sounded more magical on record and, with superbly real recording and deeply imaginative accompaniment, the result is an unexpected revelation.

(i) *Andante and variations for 2 pianos, 2 cellos and horn in B flat;* (ii) *Ballszenen, Op. 109; 6 Impromptus (Bilder aus dem Osten), Op. 66; Kinderball, Op. 130; 12 Pieces for little and big children, Op. 85;* (iii) *Studies for the pedal piano, Op. 56; 8 Polonaises, Op. 111; Sketches for the pedal piano, Op. 58.*
(B) **(*) VoxBox (3) [CD3X 3001]. Peter Frankl; (i; ii) András Schiff; with (i) Halstead, Varga, Hegedüs; (iii) A. Frankl.

Not all the music is inspired, but enough of it is to make this a thoroughly enjoyable set. Moreover these artists make out the best possible case for it: the *Andante and variations for two pianos, cellos and horn in B flat*, which is a transcription of the Op. 46 two-piano piece, has rarely sounded more eloquent. The other pieces on this three-disc set are no less persuasive. Despite the close balance, the recordings yield pleasing results, for the studio has a warm, natural acoustic. The bulk were made in London in 1978; the pieces for pedal piano, Opp. 56 and 58, recorded in a small Paris studio by Peter and Annie Frankl, sound far less pleasing, thanks to the cramped acoustic. However, the whole set is well worth having. It is not yet available in the UK.

Piano quintet in E flat, Op. 44.
(BB) *** Naxos Dig. 8.550406 [id.]. Jenö Jandó, Kodály Qt – BRAHMS: *Piano quintet.* ***
(M) *(*) DG 435 071-2; *435 071-4.* Levine, LaSalle Qt – SCHUBERT: *String quintet.* **

A strongly characterized performance of Schumann's fine *Quintet* from Jenö Jandó and the Kodály Quartet, bringing out the sombre character of the March of the second movement without being too doleful and finding plenty of energy for the scherzo and finale. Jandó has the right kind of personality for this work and he forms a genuine partnership with his colleagues. One notices the warm tone of the cellist in the first movement's secondary theme. This is robust music-making, romantic in spirit, and its spontaneity is well projected by a vivid recording, made in an attractively resonant acoustic. With its comparable Brahms coupling, this makes an excellent bargain.

A rather hard-driven opening does not endear one to the DG version of the *Piano quintet*, although there is some sensitive playing from James Levine. The sound, too, is clear, with good presence, but in no way outstanding in terms of body and warmth.

Piano trio No. 1 in D min., Op. 63.
(M) ** BMG/RCA GD 86262 [6262-2-RG]. Szeryng, Fournier, Rubinstein – SCHUBERT: *Piano trio No. 1.* **

Szeryng, Fournier and Rubinstein are very persuasive. Their performance is taut and vital, yet gives full rein to Schumann's lyricism. The recording dates from 1972 but sounds earlier, with the piano tone a bit dry; and there is a certain want of bloom.

Piano trios Nos. 1 in D min., Op. 63; 3 in G min., Op. 110.
(M) Erato/Warner 2292 45726-2 [id.]. Jean Hubeau, Henri Merckel, Paul Tortelier.

On Erato the sound is opaque and boomy. The three players are all very upfront so that there is little back-to-front perspective. The recording dates from 1960 but is not good for the period; Henri Merckel sounds past his prime: his instrument sounds dry and wanting in timbre. Neither performance gave pleasure and it is difficult to get through them. Not recommended.

Funf Stücke (5 Pieces) im Volkston (for cello and piano).
(M) *** Decca 417 833-2 [id.]. Rostropovich, Britten – SCHUBERT: *Sonata* **(*); DEBUSSY: *Sonata.* ***

Though simpler than the Debussy *Sonata* with which it is coupled, this is just as elusive a work; but in the hands of masters these *Five Pieces in folk style* have a rare charm, particularly the last, with its irregular rhythm. Excellent recording.

PIANO MUSIC

Albumblätter, Op. 99; Arabeske, Op. 18; Études symphoniques, Op. 13.
(BB) *** Naxos Dig. 8.550144 [id.]. Stefan Vladar.

The young Austrian pianist, Stefan Vladar, is recorded in the cramped acoustic of the Tonstudio van Geest in Heidelberg; it says much for his artistry that, except at climaxes, he almost (but not completely) makes one forget this unsuitable venue. He intersperses the additional studies that Schumann published as an appendix into the *Études symphoniques.* His account is quite simply superb in every respect and deserves recording of comparable excellence. There are some tired notes on the instrument itself during the course of the music-making. His account of the *Albumblätter* is hardly less masterly. Artistically this rates three stars, with the compelling quality of the playing transcending the sonic limitations of the recording.

Arabeske in C, Op. 18; Aufschwung (from *Fantasiestücke*), *Op. 12/2; Fantasie Tanz* (from *Albumblätter*), *Op. 124/5; Intermezzo in E flat*

min. (from *Faschingschwank aus Wien*), *Op. 26/4; Romance in F sharp, Op. 28/2; Thema in E flat; Vogel als Prophet* (from *Waldscenen*), *Op. 82/7.*
(B) *(*) Pickwick Dig. PCD 949. Annette Servadei – BRAHMS; MENDELSSOHN: *Piano music.* *(*)

Annette Servadei is a musical but essentially small-scale player. She comes with impressive credentials, including the endorsement of no less an authority than Kempff. She makes rather heavy weather of the *Aufschwung* from the *Fantasiestücke*, Op. 12, and the *E flat minor Intermezzo* from *Faschingschwank aus Wien* finds her dangerously near to going through her tone. There are some out-of-tune notes which diminish pleasure too.

Arabesque in C, Op. 18; Blumenstück, Op. 19; Carnaval, Op. 9; Davidsbündlertänze, Op. 6; Fantasia in C, Op. 17; 8 Fantasiestücke, Op. 12; 3 Fantasiestücke, Op. 111; Faschingsschwank aus Wien, Op. 26; Humoresque in B flat, Op. 20; Kinderszenen, Op. 15; 4 Nachtstücke, Op. 23; Novelettes, Op. 21; Papillons, Op. 2; 3 Romances, Op. 28; Piano sonatas Nos. 1 in F sharp min., Op. 11; 2 in G min., Op. 22; Waldszenen, Op. 82.
(M) **(*) Ph. 402 308-2 (7) [id.]. Claudio Arrau.

Philips's handsomely packaged commemorative collection of Claudio Arrau's recordings of Schumann has a great deal to commend it. The playing has warmth, poise and the distinctive, aristocratic finesse that graced everything this artist touched. Arrau has the measure of Schumann's impulsive temperament and is almost always perfectly attuned to his sensibility. There is the cultured, full-bodied depth and beauty of sonority one expects from this great artist as well as the impeccable control of colour. Not all the rubati ring true and there are moments that seem a little self-conscious. But there is a very great deal to admire in this compilation, and few collectors will be greatly disappointed. The Philips recordings were made over several years in the 1970s and are mostly of the high standard we expect from this source. Kempff's four-CD collection is undoubtedly the safer choice for those embarking on this repertory, but there are some good things here too.

Carnaval, Op. 9.
(M) (**) EMI mono CDH7 64025-2 [id.]. Arrau – CHOPIN: *Piano sonata No. 3* etc. (*)

EMI's Arrau *Carnaval* is in monochrome but acceptable sound, coming from Parlophone 78s. The playing has great character and flair and is more compelling than the Chopin. All the same, this disc is not 'essential' Arrau.

Carnaval; Faschingsschwank aus Wien, Op. 26; Kinderszenen, Op. 15.
(B) *** DG 431 167-2; *431 167-4*. Daniel Barenboim.

Barenboim's 1979 reading of *Carnaval* is one of his finest recording achievements in his role as pianist rather than as conductor. His lively imagination lights on the fantasy in this quirkily spontaneous sequence of pieces and makes them sparkle anew. It is as if he were in the process of improvising the music, yet his liberties of expression are never too great. He may allow himself free rubato in such a piece as *Valse noble*, but the result remains noble, not sentimental. The 'Masked ball' piece (*Carnival jest from Vienna*) is more problematic, but the challenge inspires Barenboim, and here too he is at his most imaginative and persuasive, bringing out the warmth and tenderness as well as the brilliance. The recital opens with a tender and charismatic reading of *Kinderszenen*, sensitive yet unmannered, and with the gentle opening bringing the lightest touch and the closing *Der Dichter sprich* wonderfully serene. The 1979 recording is bold and truthful, but the CD transfer has lost a little of the fullness in the bass that made the *Marche des Davidsbündler contre les Philistins* at the end of *Carnaval* so resonantly expansive on LP. Even so, this reissue offers a genuine bargain.

Carnaval, Op. 9; Kinderszenen, Op. 15; Papillons, Op. 2.
(BB) (*) Naxos Dig. 8.550076 [id.]. Jenö Jandó.

Unlike Jandó's Schubert *Impromptus*, recorded in the same venue with the same producer but with a different engineer, this is unsuccessful: the sound is dry and brittle and the fortissimos a little way into the sixth of the *Kinderszenen*, *An important event*, are quite intolerably ugly. Almost certainly this is no fault of Jandó's, for so close a balance in so uncongenial an acoustic inevitably starves the sound of timbre.

Fantasia in C, Op. 17; Fantasiestücke, Op. 12.
(M) **(*) EMI CDM7 63576-2 [id.]. Martha Argerich.

A rather exaggerated beginning to the *Fantasia* from Martha Argerich, with wide dynamic range and slightly mannered rubato, but with fabulous tone-production. She is always a fascinating artist; here, however, there are too many agogic distortions and touches of impetuosity to make one feel entirely happy with it as the only version for one's collection. There are many beautiful moments throughout this record, but her view of the *Fantasiestücke* is also too personal to be recommended without reservation. The recording is good but rather close.

Humoreske in B flat, Op. 20.
(BB) **(*) Naxos Dig. 8.550469 [id.]. Wolf Harden – REGER: *Variations.* **(*)

Wolf Harden is a gifted German pianist who was still in his mid-twenties when this record was made. His performance of the Schumann *Humoreske* is highly imaginative, idiomatic and full of sensitive touches. The actual sound is also vastly superior to many of the other piano recordings emanating from this source. There is plenty of air round the aural image. However, in a work of this scale the piano is bound to need retouching, and the absence of a technician at the sessions must be presumed, since some notes become tired and twangy towards the end of the work.

VOCAL MUSIC

Dichterliebe, Op. 48.
(M) *** DG 429 933-2 [id.]. Fritz Wunderlich, Hubert Giesen – BEETHOVEN: *Lieder* **(*); SCHUBERT: *Lieder.* ***

Wunderlich, had he lived, would no doubt have surpassed this early recording of a favourite Schumann song-cycle but, even with an often unimaginative accompanist, his freshness here is most endearing, irresistible with so golden a voice.

Frauenliebe und Leben (song-cycle), *Op. 42.*
❀ (M) *** Saga SCD 9001 [id.]. Dame Janet Baker, Martin Isepp (with Lieder recital ***).

Janet Baker's range of expression in her earlier, Saga recording of the Schumann cycle runs the whole gamut from a joyful golden tone-colour in the exhilaration of *Ich kann's nicht fassen* through an ecstatic half-tone in *Süsser Freund* (the fulfilment of the line *Du geliebter Mann* wonderfully conveyed) to the dead, vibrato-less tone of agony at the bereavement in the final song. Martin Isepp proves a highly sensitive and supportive partner, and the recording balance – originally curiously artificial – has been immeasurably improved by the CD transfer.

Frauenliebe und Leben (song-cycle), *Op. 42; Liederkreis* (song-cycle), *Op. 39.* Lieder: *Aus den östlichen Rosen; Meine Rose; Mignon (Kennst du das Land?); Der Nussbaum; Requiem; Die Soldenbraut; Widmung.*
(M) ** Pickwick Dig. MCD 22 [id.]. Felicity Lott, Graham Johnson.

Felicity Lott's soprano is caught at its freshest and most girlish in this fine Schumann collection, based on the two principal song-cycles suitable for a woman's voice, both *Frauenliebe und Leben* and the Opus 39 *Liederkreis* setting poems by Eichendorff. The seven extra songs make a generous and attractive coupling, including as they do the most popular of all, *Der Nussbaum*, and Schumann's *Kennst du das Land?*, very different from Wolf's more celebrated version. The singer reserves for *Frauenliebe* her most intense and intimate expression, developing the sequence compellingly through its wide range of moods, but finding it hard to darken the voice sufficiently for the tragic final song. Speeds are relatively relaxed both there and in the Opus 39 cycle, and Lott concentrates on producing beautiful tone and persuasive phrasing even at the expense of word-meaning – as in the sinister reference to the Lorelei in the third of the Opus 39 songs, *Waldesgespricht*, which fails to make its full impact. Graham Johnson matches the sweetness in lightly pointed playing.

Scenes from Goethe's Faust.
❀ (M) *** Decca 425 705-2 (2). Harwood, Pears, Shirley-Quirk, Fischer-Dieskau, Vyvyan, Palmer, Aldeburgh Fest. Singers, ECO, Britten.

Britten made this superb recording of a major Schumann work, long neglected, in 1973, soon after a live performance at the Aldeburgh Festival. Though the reasons for neglect remain apparent – this episodic sequence of scenes is neither opera or cantata – the power and imagination of much of the music, not least the delightful garden scene and the energetic setting of the final part, are immensely satisfying. Britten inspired his orchestra and his fine cast of singers to vivid performances, which are outstandingly recorded against the warm Maltings acoustic. The CD mastering has effectively retained the ambience yet added to the projection of both solo voices and chorus. This is magnificent music, and readers are urged to explore it – the rewards are considerable.

Schütz, Heinrich (1585–1672)

(i) *Christmas oratorio (Historia der Geburt Jesu Christi);* (ii) *Deutsche Magnificat;* Motets for double choir: *Ach, Herr, straf mich nicht* (Psalm 6); *Cantate Domino* (Psalm 96); *Herr unser Herrscher* (Psalm 8); *Ich freu mich des* (Psalm 122); *Unser Herr Jesus; Wie lieblich* (Psalm 84).
(M) **(*) Decca 430 632-2; *430 632-4* [id.]. (i) Partridge, soloists, Schütz Ch., Instrumental Ens., Philip Jones Brass Ens.; (ii) Schütz Ch., Symphoniae Sacrae Chamber Ens.; Norrington.

Norrington's Argo recording of the *Christmas oratorio* was made before he espoused the cause of original instruments. It offers some extremely fine singing from Ian Partridge as the Evangelist, while the Heinrich Schütz Choir phrases with great feeling and subtlety; indeed, some may feel that their singing is a little too self-consciously beautiful for music that is so pure in style. The instrumental accompaniment on modern instruments may also strike some listeners as too much of a good thing: the brass has more than a suspicion of heaviness at times and textures are ample. For all that, however, this version offers much to admire, and the 1970 recording has great detail and sonority. A similar comment might be made about the Motets; yet again, the choral singing is impressively firm and undoubtedly moving, and here the brass though sonorous has more edge, while the recording does full justice to the antiphonal effects. The *Cantata Domino*, by the way, may well be by Giovanni Gabrieli, with whom Schütz studied in Venice in the early years of the seventeenth century. The *Deutsche Magnificat* is given with admirable authority, and this splendid example of Schütz's last years (he was eighty-five when he wrote it) is one of the best things in a very generous (75 minutes) and rewarding collection.

Madrigals (Book 1).
(M) *** HM/BMG Dig. GD 77118 [77118-2-RG]. Cons. of Musicke, Rooley.

Schütz's *Primo Libro de Madrigali* was published in Venice in 1611, towards the end of his period of study with Giovanni Gabrieli. Apart from Gabrieli, whom Schütz venerated as his only master and whose polychoral technique is to be heard in the nineteenth and final madrigal, *Vasco mar, nel ciu seno* (*O vast ocean*), the influence by Monteverdi on the 1603 and 1605 madrigal books is also in evidence. Schütz was still in his mid-twenties when he composed the set and, while they have great beauty and are highly accomplished, these madrigals do not differ markedly from those of his Italian contemporaries. The Consort of Musicke sing with exemplary intonation (there is a momentary lapse in the first part of *Alma affitta, che fai?*) and style and are given a very well-balanced and clean, digital recording.

Scriabin, Alexander (1872–1915)

Études, Op. 8/7 & 12; Op. 42/5. Preludes, Op. 11/1, 3, 9, 10, 13, 14, 16; Op. 13/6; Op. 15/2; Op. 16/1 & 4; Op. 27/1; Op. 48/3; Op. 51/2; Op. 59/2; Op. 67/1. Sonatas Nos. 3, Op. 23; 5, Op. 53.
(M) (***) BMG/RCA mono/stereo GD 86215 [6215-2-RC]. Vladimir Horowitz.

The RCA engineers have done wonders to these recordings from the 1950s though there is naturally a limit to what they can accomplish, and some of the original shallowness and clatter remains. The *Preludes* and the legendary account of the *Third Sonata* come from 1956 and give the impression of greater range and firmer focus than in their last vinyl incarnation. The *Fifth* is much later, coming from the mid-1970s, and has more bloom. The performances are obviously three star and form an essential part of any good Horowitz collection.

Preludes, Op. 11, Nos. 2, 4–6, 8–14, 16, 18, 20, 22 & 24.
(M) *** EMI Dig. CDD7 64086-2 [id.]; *ET 764086-4*. Andrei Gavrilov – RACHMANINOV: *Élégie* etc. ***

Gavrilov's selection from Opus 11 is arbitrary. At times his approach is impetuous, and dynamics can be exaggerated, but playing of this order is still pretty remarkable. The balance is not too close, yet the CD brings a tangible presence and the piano timbre is well caught.

Piano sonatas Nos. 1–10.
(M) *** Decca 425 579-2 (2) [id.]. Vladimir Ashkenazy.

Piano sonatas Nos. 1–10; Piano sonata in E flat min. (1887–9); Sonata fantaisie in G sharp min.
(M) **(*) DG 431 747-2 (3). Roberto Szidon.

The Scriabin *Piano sonatas* encompass two decades, the first dating from 1892 when he was twenty, while the last five were composed in quick succession from 1911 to 1913. It is good to have all ten in Vladimir Ashkenazy's commanding and authoritative performances, recorded between 1972 and 1984, all on two medium-priced discs. Ashkenazy is clearly attuned to this repertoire, though he is at his finest in the earlier sonatas. The last three are given with brilliance and vision, and there is no lack of awareness of the demonic side of Scriabin's musical personality. In Nos. 9 and 10 Horowitz had more abandon and intensity without losing any of his imperious control. However, these are fine performances and are well recorded.

Roberto Szidon recorded all ten sonatas as well as the two early sonatas and the Op. 28 *Fantasy* in 1971, and this DG reissue offers the whole set. Szidon seems especially at home in the later works. His version of the *Black Mass sonata* (No. 9) fares best and conveys real excitement. At medium price this is an attractive reissue and can be considered alongside Ashkenazy's series. The DG recording is good but not ideal and the tone tends to harden at climaxes.

Shostakovich, Dmitri (1906–75)

The Age of gold: suite, *Op. 22.*
(M) *** Decca Dig. 430 727-2; *430 727-4* [id.].

LPO, Haitink – JANÁČEK: *Sinfonietta* etc. ***

The joky *Age of gold* suite makes an unexpected if attractive makeweight for the vibrant Mackerras Janáček performances. When it was first heard in 1930, the celebrated *Polka* established Shostakovich's reputation as the *enfant terrible* of Russian music, but the seductive *Adagio* and *Dance*, the latter with its piquant simulation of accordions, are no less sharply characterful. The performances combine wit and feeling and are brilliantly recorded.

Cello concerto No. 1 in E flat, Op. 107.
(M) *** EMI CDM7 63020-2. Tortelier, Bournemouth SO, Berglund – WALTON: *Concerto.* ***

Tortelier's reading of the first of Shostakovich's two *Cello concertos* does not always quite match the example of the dedicatee and first performer, Rostropovich, in sheer precision of bravura passages, but Tortelier does match the Russian master in urgency and attack. Berglund and the Bournemouth orchestra provide colourful and committed accompaniment, and the recording has retained its fullness and is even more vivid on CD.

(i) *Cello concerto No. 1 in E flat, Op. 107; Piano concertos Nos.* (ii) *1 in C min., Op. 35*; (iii) *2 in F, Op. 101.*
(M) *** Sony MPK 44850 [id.]. (i) Rostropovich, Phd. O, Ormandy; (ii) Previn; (iii) Bernstein; NYPO, Bernstein.

Rostropovich made this recording of the *Cello concerto No. 1* within a few months of the first performance in Russia. Shostakovich himself attended the recording session in Philadelphia and gave his approval to what is a uniquely authoritative reading. Ormandy and the Philadelphia Orchestra accompany superbly, with a precision and warmth rare with new scores. The recording is clear and spacious but the balance places the soloist too prominently, and certain other features of the score are highlighted, notably the glockenspiel at the end of the first movement. Sony have now shrewdly made an attractive triptych for CD by including Bernstein's radiant account of the *Second Piano concerto*, along with Previn's equally striking account of No. 1. Though these New York performances bring somewhat dated recording, both pianists have a way of turning a phrase to catch the imagination, and a fine balance is struck between Shostakovich's warmth and his rhythmic alertness.

Cello concerto No. 2, Op. 126.
(M) *** DG 431 475-2; *431 475-4* [id.]. Rostropovich, Boston SO, Ozawa – GLAZUNOV: *Chant du ménestrel*; TCHAIKOVSKY: *Andante cantabile.* ***

Shostakovich's *Second Cello concerto* first appeared in the mid-1960s; whereas Rostropovich recorded the *First* almost immediately, this concerto languished, unrepresented in the catalogue for a decade. The *Second* is completely different from its predecessor: its first movement is closer to the ruminative *Nocturne* of the *First Violin concerto* than to the taut, concentrated *Allegro* of the *First Cello concerto.* At first it appears to lack density of musical incident and seems deceptively rhapsodic, but closer acquaintance reveals its strength. Indeed it is an evocative and haunting work and the rhapsodic opening *Largo* seems curiously dreamlike until one realizes how purposeful is the soloist's course through its shadowy landscape. There is a short but succinct scherzo (in some ways, musically the least substantial of the three movements) and a haunting, lyrical finale, gently discursive, at times sadly whimsical and tinged with a smiling melancholy that suggests deeper sorrows. At first this finale, too, seems insubstantial, but it possesses concentration of mood rather than of musical content and lingers in the listener's mind long after the performance is over. Rostropovich plays with beautifully controlled feeling, and Seiji Ozawa brings sympathy and fine discipline to the accompaniment, securing admirably expressive playing from the Boston orchestra. The analogue recording is first class; if Rostropovich is forward in the aural spectrum, the balance is otherwise impeccably judged and the most is made of the spacious and warm acoustic, although in the CD transfer the snares of the side drum in the closing *Allegretto* are not absolutely sharply in focus.

Piano concertos Nos. (i; ii) *1 in C min., Op. 35;* (i; iii) *2 in F, Op. 102;* (iv) *The age of gold (ballet suite), Op. 22; Symphonies Nos. 1 in F min., Op. 10;* (v) *5 in D min., Op. 47.*
(B) (**) MCA stereo/mono Double-decker (2) [MCAD2-9823-A/B]. (i) Eugene List; (ii) Wesenigk, Berlin Op. O, Georg Jochum; (iii) V. State Op. O, Desarzens; (iv) Nat. SO of Washington, Howard Mitchell; (v) L. O, Artur Rodzinski.

Each of the two discs begins with one of the *Piano concertos*, played by Eugene List, the two most successful performances here and the only two in stereo (recorded in 1960). Though the orchestral sound in both is thin and muddy, the forward balance of the piano allows you to appreciate Eugene List's splendidly muscular yet warmly expressive playing. His articulation is phenomenal and his readings of the slow movements are intense and persuasive. None of the other performances match those, with even older mono sound hardly flattering to undistinguished performances. Howard Mitchell's Washington account of the *Symphony No. 1* lacks tension and his reading of the *Age of gold*, though brighter, is also coarse. Rodzinski's account of No. 5 with the pseudonymous London Orchestra is interesting for adopting unusually fast speeds in all four movements. With limited dynamic range there is none of the hushed intensity needed, though the fast and furious account of the finale has its excitement.

Piano concertos Nos. 1–2; The Unforgettable year 1919, Op. 89; The Assault on beautiful Gorky (for piano and orchestra).
(B) *** CfP Dig. CD-CFP 4547; *TC-CFP 4547.*
Alexeev, Philip Jones, ECO, Maksymiuk.

Alexeev is a clear first choice in both *Concertos*, and his record would sweep the board even at full price. The digital recording is excellent in every way and scores over its rivals in clarity and presence. Artistically he has more personality than his rivals and has the advantage of sensitive and idiomatic support from the ECO and Jerzy Maksymiuk. There is a fill-up in the form of a miniature one-movement *Concerto* from a film-score called *The Unforgettable year 1919*. Given the quality of both the performance and the sound, this record should make new friends for the two *Concertos*, particularly at such an attractive price.

The Gadfly (film music): *Suite, Op. 97a.*
(B) **(*) CfP CD-CFP 4463; *TC-CFP 4463.*
USSR Cinema SO, Emin Khachaturian.

The score for *The Gadfly* was turned into a twelve-movement suite, published in 1960 and recorded two years later. At times the music is quite pleasing but at others is wholly uncharacteristic. On CfP, a musically committed and well-recorded issue, although the brightening of the sound in the digital remastering has lost some of the smoothness of the original LP.

Symphony No. 5 in D min., Op. 47.
(M) *** BMG/RCA GD 86801 [6801-2-RG].
LSO, Previn (with RACHMANINOV: *The Rock* ***).
(B) ** Pickwick Dig. PCD 940; *CIMPC 940* [id.]. Hallé O, Skrowaczewski.

Previn's RCA version, dating from early in his recording career (1965), remains at the top of the list of bargain recommendations. This is one of the most concentrated and intense readings ever, superbly played by the LSO at its peak. What has always marked out Previn's reading is the spaciousness of the first and third movements, held together masterfully. In the third movement he sustains a slower speed than anyone else, making it deeply meditative in its dark intensity; and the purity and beauty of the Previn version have never been surpassed, notably in the long-legged second subject, while his build-up in the central development section brings playing of white heat. The bite and urgency of the second and fourth movements are also irresistible. Only in the hint of analogue tape-hiss does the sound fall short of the finest modern digital recordings – and it is more vividly immediate than most.

Well played and vividly recorded, Skrowaczewski's version brings a refined, clean-cut reading worth considering at bargain price, but lacking some of the demonic bite which should mark the second-movement scherzo and the finale. Echoing Stravinsky's criticism of Karajan conducting the *Rite of spring*, one might describe this as a domestic animal rather than a wild one, a degree too civilized. Though Rahbari's Naxos version is less perfectly under control, its extra bite as well as its extra expressiveness makes it more enjoyable and, at a lower price, it comes with No. 9 as coupling.

Symphonies Nos. 5 in D min., Op. 47; 9 in E flat, Op. 70.
(BB) *** Naxos Dig. 8.550247 [id.]. Belgian R. & TV O, Alexander Rahbari.

It is a fair sign of the quality of the Belgian Radio Orchestra that the great exposed violin melody of the second subject of No. 5 comes over with such poise and sweetness. Both in the hushed intensity of the lyrical passages and in the vigour and bite of Shostakovich's violent allegros Rahbari's reading is most convincing, with dramatic tensions finely controlled in a spontaneous-sounding way. In No. 9 Rahbari opts for a controversially slow *Moderato* second movement but sustains it well, and the outer movements are deliciously witty in their pointing. The playing of all sections is first rate, and the sound is full and brilliant. An outstandingly generous coupling makes this a most attractive issue, even with no allowance made for the very low price.

Symphony No. 6 in B min., Op. 54.
(M) *** EMI CDM7 69564-2; *EG 769564-4.*
LSO, Previn – RACHMANINOV: *Symphony No. 3.* ***

Here Previn shows his deep understanding of Shostakovich in a powerfully drawn, unrelenting account of the opening movement, his slow tempo adding to the overall impact. After that the offhand wit of the central Scherzo comes over the more delicately at a slower tempo than usual, leaving the hectic finale to hammer home the deceptively joyful conclusion to the argument. Excellent recording, impressively remastered.

Symphonies Nos. (i) *9 in E flat;* (ii) *10 in E min.*
(M) (***) Sony mono MPK 45698 [id.]. NYPO, (i) Efrem Kurtz; (ii) Dmitri Mitropoulos.

Dmitri Mitropoulos's pioneering account of the *Tenth Symphony* with the New York Philharmonic was for many years the yardstick by which later versions were judged. It still is. In spite of the inevitable sonic limitations, it penetrates more deeply into the heart of this score than any of the recent newcomers; only Karajan's mid-1960s version can be put alongside it. It comes with Efrem Kurtz's 1949 version of the *Ninth* (not quite pioneering, since Koussevitzky had beaten him to it) with the same orchestra, playing with great virtuosity. The sound is remarkably good for its period (an edit has removed one note from the opening phrase of the scherzo), but apart from that hiccup this is a stunning performance. Two great performances on one disc must represent one of the bargains of the year.

Symphony No. 10 in E min., Op. 93.
(M) *** EMI CDD7 64105-2 [id.]; *ET 764105-4*. LSO, André Previn – PROKOFIEV: *Lieutenant Kijé*. ***
(B) *** Pickwick Dig. PCD 955 [id.]. Hallé O, Skrowaczewski.
(M) (***) Saga mono SCD 9017 [id.]. Leningrad PO, Mravinsky.
(M) **(*) DG 429 716-2; *429 716-4* [id.]. BPO, Karajan.
(M) ** EMI CDM7 63096-2. Bournemouth SO, Berglund.
(BB) ** Naxos Dig. 8.550326 [id.]. Belgian R. & TV O, Alexander Rahbari.

Previn's is a strong and dramatic reading marked by a specially compelling account of the long first movement, which steers an ideal course between expressive warmth and architectural strength. At marginally slower speeds than usual, Previn's rhythmic lift both in the scherzo and in the finale brings exhilarating results, sparkling and swaggering. The digital recording is early (1982) but strikingly full and firm, less aggressive-sounding than Karajan's analogue version.

Recorded in full, brilliant and weighty sound, Skrowaczewski's version of the *Tenth* prompts none of the reservations which precluded his earlier account of the *Fifth* from being a top recommendation. Here the second-movement scherzo has a sharply dramatic intensity that fully brings out its barbaric thrust and, after the hushed introduction to the fourth movement, the final allegro has point and bite in plenty. Above all, the spacious *moderato* of the long first movement has a natural power and concentration which put it among the finest versions, with the Hallé brass superbly focused at the great climaxes. This is one of Skrowaczewski's most memorable recordings with the Hallé.

Shostakovich's finest symphony has been well served on record. Mitropoulos, Ančerl and Efrem Kurz all gave first-class accounts of it on mono LP, but the finest of all was by Mravinsky, who conducted its première but whose mono LP was originally let down by dim recording. The sound has been improved on CD: the violins still sound thin but detail is cleaner and there is a firmer outline and more body overall. In the long first movement Mravinsky captures the doleful melancholy of the opening and he moves to the bitter desperation of the climax with great eloquence. The Leningrad Philharmonic plays the scherzo with staggering virtuosity and the work is satisfyingly resolved in the finale.

Karajan's 1967 reading is superbly moulded, with genuine tragic feeling and authenticity. The Berlin Philharmonic play magnificently and the 1967 recording combines ambient atmosphere with a fierce brilliance to project the score's climaxes pungently – indeed, some may feel that the CD is too brightly lit in the violins.

Berglund has a strong grip on the architecture of the work and is refreshingly straight. He draws playing of high quality from the Bournemouth orchestra and has a genuine sense of the music's scale; but ultimately he is let down by a want of inner tension. Nevertheless this performance is not without strength or atmosphere, although there is an element of literalness and sobriety.

Unlike Skrowaczewski, Rahbari is less successful in No. 10 than he was in No. 5, with the playing a degree less polished and the recording more distanced and less involving. Even so, his natural expressiveness is most persuasive, and the ironic flavour in the third-movement *Allegretto* is beautifully caught.

CHAMBER AND INSTRUMENTAL MUSIC

String quartet No. 8, Op. 110.
(M) **(*) Decca 425 541-2; *425 541-4* [id.]. Borodin Qt – BORODIN; TCHAIKOVSKY: *Quartets*. **(*)

As the central motif of this fine *Quartet* Shostakovich used a group of four notes derived, cipher-like, from his own name. It proves at least as fruitful as the famous one in the name 'Bach', and the argument throughout this impressive work is most intense. The Borodins' performance is outstanding and the recording real and vivid, although the balance means that in the CD transfer the effect is very forward, almost too boldly immediate.

Sibelius, Jean (1865–1957)

Andante festivo; Canzonetta, Op. 62a; Rakastava, Op. 14; Romance in C, Op. 43.
(BB) **(*) Naxos Dig. 8.550330 [id.]. Capella Istropolitana, Adrian Leaper – GRIEG: *Elegiac melodies* etc. **(*)

Adrian Leaper has proved himself a reliable Sibelian, though at times he adopts rather brisker tempi than are ideal. Anyone sampling the composer's own version of the *Andante festivo* will discover that his broader tempo enables him to communicate greater intensity and dignity. Likewise the *Canzonetta*, which derives from the music to *Kuolema*, loses something of its allure. No such reservations apply in either the *Romance in C* or *Rakastava* – the latter is particularly eloquent and the closing paragraphs of the last movement are movingly done. Generally speaking this is a sensitively played anthology, and only a certain fierceness from the upper string-tone inhibits a three-star recommendation.

Violin concerto in D min., Op. 47.
(M) *** Ph. 420 895-2. Accardo, LSO, C. Davis – DVOŘÁK: *Violin concerto.* ***
(M) (***) EMI mono CDH7 61011-2. Ginette Neveu, Philh. O, Susskind – BRAHMS: *Concerto.*(***)
(BB) *** Naxos Dig. 8.550329 [id.]. Dong-Suk Kang, Slovak (Bratislava) RSO, Adrian Leaper – HALVORSEN: *Air Norvégien* etc.; SINDING: *Légende*; SVENDSEN: *Romance.* ***
(M) **(*) EMI Dig. CDD7 63894-2 [id.]; *ET 763894-4* [id.]. Gidon Kremer, Philh. O, Muti – SCHUMANN: *Concerto.* **(*)
(M) ** Sony SBK 47659 [id.]. David Oistrakh, Phd. O, Ormandy – BEETHOVEN: *Violin concerto.* **
(M) (**) EMI mono CDH7 64030-2 [id.]. Heifetz, LPO, Beecham – GLAZUNOV *Violin concerto* (***) ❀; TCHAIKOVSKY: *Violin concerto.* (***)
(M) ** Teldec/Warner Dig. 9031 74784-2 [id.]. Zehetmair, Leipzig GO, Masur – J. HAYDN: *Concerto* ***; M. HAYDN: *Concerto.* **(*)
(M) *(*) EMI mono CDM7 63987-2 [id.]. Y. Menuhin, LPO, Boult – NIELSEN: *Concerto.* *(*)

Of the mid-price versions, Salvatore Accardo and Sir Colin Davis would be a first choice. There is no playing to the gallery, and no schmaltz – and in the slow movement there is a sense of repose and nobility. The finale is exhilarating, and there is an aristocratic feeling to the whole which is just right.

Ginette Neveu's reading of the Sibelius is a classic recording, a precious reminder of a great artist who died tragically young. The magnetism of Neveu in this, her first concerto recording, is inescapable from her opening phrase onwards, warmly expressive and dedicated, yet with no hint of mannerism. The finale is taken at a speed which is comfortable rather than exciting, but the extra spring of the thrumming dance-rhythms, superbly lifted, is ample compensation, providing a splendid culmination.

Dong-Suk Kang gave a commanding performance of the Sibelius *Violin concerto* at a 1990 (televised) BBC Prom. and is familiar to both concert and radio audiences on both sides of the Atlantic. He chooses some popular Scandinavian repertoire pieces, such as the charming Svendsen *Romance in G*, as makeweights. Although this newcomer is very fine, he is perhaps a little wanting – albeit only a little – in tenderness as opposed to passion in the slow movement, but there is splendid virtuosity in the outer movements. The orchestral playing is decent rather than distinguished. In the bargain basement, this enjoys a strong competitive advantage, but even if it were at full price it would feature quite high in the current lists.

Kremer presents the *Concerto* essentially as a bravura showpiece and his is a vibrantly extrovert reading. While the recording balance places the soloist well forward, the orchestral texture has plenty of impact and good detail, and the fortissimo brass blaze out excitingly. There is undoubted poetry in the slow movement, and throughout Muti gives his soloist splendid support. This is hardly a first choice, but it is now much more competitive at mid-price, and it has an interesting and unique coupling.

David Oistrakh's first stereo recording of the *Concerto* was made for CBS in 1959. It is a predictably powerful performance, assured and full of ardour, and Ormandy accompanies with his usual warmth and sympathy. However, although the orchestral sound does not lack sonority, the upper range becomes fierce and unrefined under pressure.

Sibelius and Glazunov were born in the same year and each composed only one violin concerto – and at about the same time (1905). Heifetz's EMI CD contains their première recordings. The Sibelius comes from 1935 and was first issued in an HMV Sibelius Society edition of seven 78-r.p.m. discs, so that it never gained the same currency as the post-war account by Ginette Neveu and Dobrowen. Although many first recordings have something special that stands out (such as Koussevitzky's *Harold in Italy* or Prokofiev *Fifth Symphony*, Beecham's account of Sibelius's *Fourth* and Kajanus's *Tapiola*), the Heifetz/Beecham Sibelius *Violin concerto*, marvellous though it is, excites admiration rather than affection. And despite Sir Thomas's direction, Heifetz gave the more powerful account of it in his later, Chicago recording with Walter Hendl in the early days of stereo. (The reverse was the case with the Glazunov.) A good transfer nevertheless, and well worth having – the Glazunov is particularly fine. (Heifetz's stereo recording of the Sibelius remains at full price and is well worth its extra cost.)

Neither as a performance nor as a recording is Thomas Zehetmair's account of the *Concerto* a front-runner, though it has many merits. The recording gets full marks for the natural balance between soloist and orchestra, but the listener is placed half-way back in a resonant hall, and the orchestral tutti are woolly and detail is wanting in real transparency. Zehetmair is obviously a fine player, though there are one or two zigeuner-like slides that are controversial. Given the richness and distinction of the competition, this is not a strong contender, although it is certainly enjoyable if the couplings by Josef and Michael Haydn are of interest.

Menuhin recorded the Sibelius *Concerto* with Sir Adrian in 1956, and even his most fervent admirers would hesitate to claim that it was one of his finest recordings. His playing falls well short of his distinguished best and can be recommended only to those who must have everything that this great artist has done.

(i) *Violin concerto; Symphony No. 5 in E flat, Op. 82; Tapiola.*
(B) **(*) DG Compact Classics *415 619-4* [id.]. (i) Ferras; BPO, Karajan.

Christian Ferras's account of the *Violin concerto* is a very good one and is well recorded. Although he begins the work with a winningly golden tone, when he is under stress, at the end of the first movement and in the finale, his intonation and general security are less than impeccable. However, there is still much to enjoy, and Ferras again develops a richly romantic tone for the main tune of the slow movement. Karajan's 1964 recording of the *Fifth Symphony* is undoubtedly a great performance. The orchestral playing throughout is glorious and the effect is spacious and atmospheric. Karajan finds an engrossing sense of mystery in the development section of the first movement, and there is jubilation in the finale. The only snag is that the Compact Classics tape is transferred at the highest level and there is a degree of harshness in the climaxes of the symphony, but this tape remains a formidable bargain.

The Dryad, Op. 45/1; En Saga, Op. 9.
(M) *** Chan. CHAN 6524; *MBTD 6524* [id.]. SNO, Gibson – NIELSEN: *Symphony No. 4* etc. **(*)

Sir Alexander Gibson's analogue recordings of the Sibelius tone-poems date from the late 1970s and were originally issued by RCA. The recordings have been digitally remastered with great success; the slightly distant sound-balance is admirably suited to the music, with the spacious acoustic of Glasgow City Hall generally flattering the orchestra and creating a suitable ambient atmosphere. Gibson's affinity with the Sibelius idiom is at its most convincing here, particularly in an elusive piece like *The Dryad*, although *En Saga*, which opens the collection, is also evocative and shows an impressive overall grasp. The fine playing and natural perspectives of the recording contribute a great deal to the music-making. Although both ends of the sound spectrum are less sharply focused than in a digital recording (most noticeably in *En Saga*), climaxes are made excitingly expansive, with the brass superbly sonorous. At mid-price and offered coupled with the Nielsen *Fourth*, these versions make rewarding listening.

En Saga.
(M) (***) DG mono 427 783-2 [id.]. BPO, Wilhelm Furtwängler – RAVEL: *Daphnis et Chloé*; R. STRAUSS: *Till Eulenspiegel.* (***)

Furtwängler's account of *En Saga* has the right air of narrative and magic, and its sense of atmosphere and space completely transcends the sonic limitations inevitable in a 1944 recording.

En Saga; Finlandia; Karelia suite, Op. 11; Legend: The Swan of Tuonela; (i) *Pohjola's daughter.*
(M) *** EMI CDM7 63367-2 [id.]; *EG 763367-4*. VPO or (i) BBC SO, Sir Malcolm Sargent.

Sargent's collection is highly successful and a fine reminder of his affinity with this repertoire. Each performance has conviction and character, and the five pieces complement one another, making a thoroughly enjoyable CD programme. The Vienna Philharmonic bring a distinctive freshness to their playing of music which must have been unfamiliar to them and Sir Malcolm Sargent imparts his usual confidence. The brass is especially full-blooded in *En Saga*, a performance full of adrenalin (as is *Pohjola's daughter*, the one item featuring the BBC Symphony Orchestra). *Finlandia* sounds unhackneyed and, with brisk tempi, *Karelia* has fine impetus and flair. The recordings, made in the Musikverein in 1961 and Kingsway Hall in 1958, are remarkably full and vivid; one would never suspect their age from these vibrant CD transfers, of EMI's best vintage.

En Saga, Op. 9; Finlandia, Op. 26; Karelia suite, Op. 11; Tapiola, Op. 112.
(M) *** Decca Dig. 417 762-2 [id.]. Philh. O, Ashkenazy.

These are all digital recordings of the first order – Decca sound at its very best. The performances are among the finest available, especially *En Saga* which is thrillingly atmospheric, while the *Karelia suite* is freshly appealing in its directness. The climax of *Tapiola* is almost frenzied in its impetus – some may feel that Ashkenazy goes over the top here; but this is the only real criticism of a distinguished collection and a very real bargain.

(i) *Finlandia, Op. 26;* (ii) *Karelia suite, Op. 11;* (i) *Kuolema: Valse triste, Op. 44* (CD only: (ii) *En Saga, Op. 9; Legend: The Swan of Tuonela, Op. 22/2*).
(B) *** DG Compact Classics 413 158-2 (2); *413 158-4* [id.]. (i) BPO, Karajan; (ii) Helsinki R. O, Kamu – GRIEG: *Piano concerto; Peer Gynt.* **

The bargain Compact Classics tape includes, alongside the fine Karajan performances of *Finlandia* and *Valse triste*, Kamu's splendid *Karelia suite*, as fine as almost any available, the outer movements atmospheric and exciting and the *Ballade* eloquently played, without idiosyncrasy. The pair of CDs further adds Kamu's admirable versions of *En Saga* and *The Swan of Tuonela*. The sound is very good throughout. If the couplings are suitable (and Géza Anda's account of the Grieg *Piano concerto*, if not among the finest available, is certainly enjoyable), this is excellent value.

Finlandia; Karelia suite, Op. 11. Kuolema: Valse triste. Legends: Lemminkäinen's return, Op. 22/4; Pohjola's daughter, Op. 49.
(M) **(*) EMI CDM7 69205-2 [id.]. Hallé O, Barbirolli.

Although the orchestral playing is not as polished as that of a virtuoso orchestra, it is enthusiastic and has the advantage of excellent recording from the mid-1960s. *Pohjola's daughter* is extremely impressive, spacious but no less exciting for all the slower tempi. *Lemminkäinen's return* is also a thrilling performance. Overall, a desirable introduction to Sibelius's smaller orchestral pieces, with admirable stereo definition.

Finlandia, Op. 26; Karelia suite, Op. 11; Legend: The Swan of Tuonela, Op. 22/2.
(B) ** Hung. White Label HRC 172 [id.]. Debrecen PO, László Szabó – GRIEG: *Peer Gynt suites.* **

On Hungaroton White Label come three Sibelius pieces from the 1890s in very decently played and well-recorded accounts by the Debrecen Philharmonic under László Szabó. *Finlandia* is a bit rushed perhaps, and there are finer versions of both *The Swan of Tuonela* and the *Karelia* suite on the market; but these are perfectly acceptable in every way, and the recording is really very warm and atmospheric.

Finlandia, Op. 26; Karelia suite, Op. 11; Scènes historiques: Festivo, Op. 25/3; The Chase; Love song; At the drawbridge, Op. 66/1–3; The Tempest (incidental music): *suites Nos. 1–2, Op. 109.*
❀ (M) (***) EMI mono CDM7 63397-2 [id.]; *EG 763397-4*. RPO, Beecham.

Beecham's mono performance of the incidental music for *The Tempest* is magical – no one has captured its spirit with such insight. A pity that he omits the *Prelude*, which he had done so evocatively on 78s, though the last number of the second suite covers much of the same ground. The four *Scènes historiques* are beautifully done, with the most vivid orchestral colouring: *The Chase* is particularly delectable. No apologies whatsoever need be made about the sound here, though in the *Intermezzo* from *Karelia* (which has a 78-r.p.m. source) the quality is curiously crumbly at the opening and close: surely a better original could have been found. The *Alla marcia* is better, although no one would buy this record for *Finlandia*.

Finlandia, Op. 26; Legend: The Swan of Tuonela, Op. 22/2; The Oceanides, Op. 73; Pohjola's daughter, Op. 49; Tapiola, Op. 112.
(M) **(*) Chan. CHAN 6508; *MBTD 6508* [id.]. SNO, Gibson.

Gibson has a real feeling for Sibelius, and these very well-played performances are given an atmospheric and convincingly balanced analogue recording which makes a very realistic impression. *The Oceanides* is particularly successful and, if Karajan finds even greater intensity in *Tapiola*, Gibson's account certainly captures the icy desolation of the northern forests. He is at his most persuasive in an elusive piece like *The Dryad*, although *En Saga* is also evocative, showing an impressive overall grasp. The SNO are at the peak of their form throughout these performances.

4 Legends, Op. 22 (Lemminkäinen and the maidens of Saari; The Swan of Tuonela; Lemminkäinen in Tuonela; Lemminkäinen's return). Finlandia, Op. 26.

(M) ** Collins Dig. 3013-2 [id.]. RPO, Sir Alexander Gibson.

Sir Alexander Gibson made an outstanding set of the *Legends* with the Scottish National Orchestra for Chandos in 1979 and this is surely due to appear at mid-price before too long. Alas, this Collins CD is no match for it. It is finely played and the mistily impressionistic recording aids Gibson's feeling for Sibelian colour and atmosphere, although the climaxes are made to sound spacious rather than electrifying, notably so in the otherwise impressive *Lemminkäinen in Tuonela.* But that is partly the fault of the performances which, though affectionately refined in detail, lack the underlying tension and grip of the earlier readings.

Night ride and sunrise, Op. 55; Spring song, Op. 16.
(M) **(*) Chan. CHAN 6533; *MBTD 6533* [id.]. SNO, Gibson – NIELSEN: *Symphony No. 5* etc. **(*)

Gibson's performances show a natural feeling for Sibelian colour: *Night ride and sunrise* has plenty of atmosphere, the playing not too tense in the opening sequence, with the music blossoming naturally but not headily at the first light of what is essentially a dawn in the northern hemisphere. *Spring song* is rarer, an early work (1894), and Gibson presents it with a nice balance between warmth and lyrical reticence. Excellent 1977 sound, the music enhanced by the ambience of Glasgow's City Hall.

The Oceanides, Op. 73; Pelléas et Mélisande: suite, Op. 46; Symphony No. 7 in C, Op. 105; Tapiola, Op. 112.
(M) *** EMI CDM7 63400-2 [id.]; *EG 763400-4*. RPO, Beecham.

The Oceanides, recorded at the composer's behest, is one of Beecham's greatest performances on record and is a must. It is Sibelius's most poetic evocation of the sea, and this marvellous playing captures every nuance of the score. The *Pelléas et Mélisande suite* was a yardstick by which all others have been measured ever since. Only Karajan matches it, and even the Berlin Philharmonic textures do not sound more luminous and magical than here, for the CD transfer is wonderfully refined. However, Beecham omits the *By the sea* movement. *Tapiola* is also very impressive: it has all the requisite brooding power and must be numbered among the very finest accounts committed to disc. Only the *Seventh Symphony* disappoints – and that only relatively speaking.

Symphonies Nos. 1–7.
(M) *** Decca Dig. 421 069-2 (4). Philh. O, Ashkenazy.
(M) **(*) Decca 430 778-2 (3). VPO, Maazel.
(M) **(*) Chan. Dig. CHAN 6559 (3). SNO, Sir Alexander Gibson.

(i) *Symphonies Nos. 1–7;* (ii) *Night ride and sunrise;* (i) *The Oceanides; Scene with cranes.*
(M) **(*) EMI CMS7 64118-2; *EX 764118-4* (4). (i) CBSO, (ii) Philh. O, Simon Rattle.

Ashkenazy's Sibelius series makes a rich and strong, consistently enjoyable cycle. Ashkenazy by temperament brings out the expressive warmth, colour and drama of the composer rather than his Scandinavian chill, reflecting perhaps his Slavonic background. The recordings are full and rich as well as brilliant, most of them of demonstration quality, even though they date from the early digital period. On four CDs at mid-price, the set makes a most attractive recommendation.

Simon Rattle's performances with the City of Birmingham Symphony Orchestra are available both as a four-CD boxed set and as individual discs. The best advice is probably to opt for the individual disc for the *Fourth* and *Sixth*, coupled together. They are both impressive, as is his *Seventh*, coupled with the *Fifth* and the highly atmospheric *Scene with cranes.* Also on the same disc is his Philharmonia recording of *Night ride and sunrise* – grievously neglected in the concert hall but powerful in his hands. He swoons a little towards the end of the slow movement of the *First Symphony* and the scherzo is a bit too measured, but this comes with an absolutely superb *Oceanides* – the best since Beecham's. Similarly the *Second*, which is a bit overblown and has a self-indulgent slow movement, comes with a generally excellent *Third.* As a set the box is worth considering, but it would not be first choice.

Maazel's set was recorded in the Sofiensaal between 1963 and 1968, with the project initiated by John Culshaw (No. 1) and Erik Smith producing the rest of the series. It still remains pretty impressive. By far the best performances are the *First* and *Fourth Symphonies* which are, of course, available on a separate disc. The latter is a reading of great power, one of the most intense and uncompromising since the celebrated 1937 Beecham version. The *Seventh Symphony*, too, is another landmark in the Sibelius discography and, apart from the occasional sweetness of the string vibrato, which may worry some more than it does us, has great majesty and breadth. The *Second* is also successful, but the *Fifth* and, more particularly, the *Sixth* do not come off as well. Many conductors, among them Barbirolli, claimed not to understand No. 6. To judge by his performance – not on CD, alas – even so authoritative a Sibelian as Koussevitzky made only intermittent contact with it, so Maazel is in good company. He sounds uninvolved in both works: the *Third* has a very good first movement but a faster-than-ideal second. The Decca analogue sound is excellent and is vividly transferred, and readers need not hesitate on that score.

Sir Alexander Gibson has been a doughty champion of Sibelius over the years and has recorded Nos. 1, 2 and 5 no fewer than three times, and Nos. 3 and 7 twice. His Sibelius cycle with what was the Scottish National and is now the Royal Scottish Orchestra was made over the period 1982–4. It is impressive, both musically and from an engineering point of view; there are no weak spots anywhere. (Indeed, one respected critic chose Gibson's version of No. 1 as his first choice on a BBC 'Record Review' some years ago.) At the same time it must be conceded that the peaks do not dwarf, say, the Maazel *Fourth* or *Seventh*. The performances are eminently sane, sound and reliable, and no one investing in the set is likely to be at all disappointed. Taken individually, none would be an absolute first choice.

Symphony No. 1 in E min., Op. 39.
(BB) *(*) ASV CDQS 6040; *ZCQS 6040*. Melbourne SO, Serebrier – TCHAIKOVSKY: *Romeo and Juliet*. *(*)

Symphony No. 1; The Oceanides.
(M) **(*) EMI Dig. CDM7 64119-2 [id.]; *EG 764119-4*. CBSO, Simon Rattle.

If the whole symphony was as fine as the first movement in Rattle's hands, this would be a clear first recommendation. He has a powerful grasp of both its structure and character and elicits an enthusiastic response from his players. The slow movement is for the most part superb, with excellent playing from the wind and brass of the Birmingham orchestra; but he makes too much of the commas at the end of the movement, which are so exaggerated as to be disruptive. The Scherzo has splendid character but is a good deal slower than the marking. The Oceanides were the nymphs who inhabited the waters of Homeric mythology, and the opening of the piece has an atmosphere that is altogether ethereal. Simon Rattle has its measure and conveys all its mystery and poetry. This is a subtle and masterly performance.

With José Serebrier's Melbourne account, both the playing and recording are good (or, at any rate, decent) and Serebrier sounds as if he is enjoying the work; but the performance, it must be admitted, is not really special.

Symphonies Nos. 1; 3 in C, Op. 52.
(B) **(*) DG 429 526-2; *429 526-4*. Helsinki R. O, Kamu.

Kamu's Helsinki version of the *First Symphony* does not lack excitement, but it is not distinctive. The *Third*, however, is among the finest ever put on disc and this bargain reissue is well worth exploring on its account alone. Tempi are invariably well judged and the atmosphere is thoroughly authentic, particularly in the slow movement, whose character seems to have eluded so many distinguished conductors. The recording is excellent, but the digital remastering, in seeking to clarify further a full-bodied sound, rich in ambience, gives an occasional hint of minor congestion. The effect is marginal and does not inhibit enjoyment of a magnificent performance overall.

Symphonies Nos. 1; 4 in A min., Op. 63.
(M) *** Decca 417 789-2; *417 789-4*. VPO, Maazel.
(M) **(*) Chan. Dig. CHAN 6555; *MBTD 6555* [id.]. SNO, Sir Alexander Gibson.

Maazel's VPO performance of the *First Symphony* dominated the LP catalogue during the 1970s: it has freshness of vision to commend it, along with careful attention to both the letter and the spirit of the score. The Vienna Philharmonic responds with enthusiasm and brilliance and the Decca engineers produce splendid detail (except for the important timpani part in the first movement echoing the main theme, which might have been more sharply defined). The climaxes of the outer movements are very exciting. The *Fourth* is equally impressive. The orchestral tone is less richly upholstered than in some more modern versions; but the players make the closest contact with the music, and Maazel's reading brings great concentration and power: the first movement is as cold and unremitting as one could wish. Apart from the slow movement, which could be a little more poetic, there are no real reservations to be made, and the remastered sound is brightly lit. A fine bargain.

Gibson's set, like Maazel's on Decca, fits on to three mid-priced CDs – only, in the case of the Chandos series, each CD is also available separately. The Scottish orchestra is excellently recorded in the warm acoustics of the Glasgow SNO Centre and one of the hallmarks of the set is Gibson's instinctive northern feeling for Sibelian colour and texture. The fine (1982/3) digital sound brings a natural concert-hall balance. All the performances are enjoyable; although No. 1 does not have the tension and power of, say, Ashkenazy or Maazel, in the closing pages Gibson draws the music together expansively. The playing of the Scottish orchestra is always committed and, if it lacks something in refinement both here and in the *Fourth*, the impact and authenticity of the latter reading is never in doubt.

Symphonies Nos. 1; 5 in E flat, Op. 82.
(M) **(*) EMI Phoenixa CDM7 64139-2 [id.]; *EG 764139-4*. Hallé O, Barbirolli.

Not to be confused with Barbirolli's later Sibelius recordings for EMI, these Hallé versions, made for Pye-Nixa, date from 1957. Though the sound is less refined, with some roughness in tuttis and with the dynamic range limited, the performances have an extra passion and spontaneity, excellent examples of Barbirolli's work with the orchestra he built up from its wartime trough. Speeds are consistently slow, at times extraordinarily so, but Barbirolli's concentration and his ability to mould the music with persuasive rubato prevent them from ever sounding sluggish, and for many Sibelians they will be more sympathetic than tauter, more urgent readings. The horns in the great ostinato of the finale in No. 5 come out magnificently. A most enjoyable coupling.

Symphonies Nos. 1; 6 in D min., Op. 104.
(M) *** EMI Dig. CDD7 63896-2 [id.]; *ET 763896*. BPO, Karajan.

In the *First Symphony* Karajan, a great Tchaikovsky interpreter, identifies with the work's inheritance. But there is a sense of grandeur and vision here, and the opulence and virtuosity of the Berliners helps to project the heroic dimensions of Karajan's performance. The early digital recording (1981) is not top-drawer: the bass is overweighted, but the full upper strings sing out gloriously with the richest amplitude in the finale, which has an electrifying climax; the brass is comparably rich and resonant. Karajan's version of the *Sixth* was made in 1981 and it brings to life the other-worldly quality of this score: the long white nights of the northern summer and their 'fragile melancholy', that the slow movement (or, for that matter, the opening polyphony) conjures up. Even though this is a spacious account, we are never unaware of the sense of forward movement. Although this performance seems more spacious and more unhurried than the DG account recorded in 1967, each movement is in fact marginally quicker. In short, this is Karajan at his finest: not even Beecham made the closing pages sound more magical. This recording is better than its predecessor, and the EMI team have achieved a more spacious acoustic ambience. The French critic, Marc Vignal, spoke of Sibelius as 'the aristocrat of symphonists', and this, surely, is the aristocrat of performances.

Symphonies Nos. 1 in E min., Op. 39; 7 in C, Op. 105.
(M) *** Decca Dig. 425 028-2; *425 028-4* [id.]. Philh. O, Ashkenazy.

Ashkenazy's digital coupling of the *First* and *Seventh Symphonies*, recorded in 1982 and 1984 respectively, is outstandingly successful; at mid-price, it will become a ready first choice for most collectors. The performance of the *First* is held together well and is finely shaped. Ashkenazy is exactly on target in the Scherzo. The resultant sense of momentum is exhilarating and here, as when echoing the main theme of the first movement, the timpani make a riveting effect. Throughout, the sheer physical excitement that this score engenders is tempered by admirable control. Only at the end of the slow movement does one feel that Ashkenazy could perhaps have afforded greater emotional restraint, but the big tune of the finale is superbly handled. The recording has splendid detail and clarity of texture, and there is all the presence and body one could ask for, with the bass-drum rolls particularly realistic. The *Seventh Symphony* is also very fine. Ashkenazy does not build up this work quite as powerfully as some others do, but he has the measure of its nobility and there is much to admire – indeed, much that is thrilling in his interpretation. As in the *First Symphony*, the playing of the Philharmonia Orchestra, like the recording, is of the very first order.

Symphony No. 2 in D, Op. 43.
(M) (***) EMI mono CDM7 63399-2 [id.]; *EG 763399-4*. BBC SO, Beecham – DVOŘÁK: *Symphony No. 8*. (***)
(M) (*(*)) EMI mono CDH7 63307-2 [id.]. BBC SO, Toscanini.

Symphony No. 2; Kuolema: Valse triste; Legend: The Swan of Tuonela; Pohjola's daughter.
(BB) **(*) BMG/RCA VD 60489; *VK 60489*. Phd. O, Ormandy.

Symphony No. 2; Legend: The Swan of Tuonela, Op. 22/2.
(B) **(*) Pickwick Dig. PCD 927; *CIMPC 927* [id.]. LSO, Mackerras.

Sir Charles Mackerras gives an eminently well-judged account of the *Second Symphony*. The tempo of the first movement is apt, a real allegretto, fast but without going to quite the same extreme as Järvi on BIS (at full price). There is no lack of tenderness and he shapes phrases with sensitivity. The fill-up, too, has no lack of atmosphere. The recording, made in the EMI Abbey Road studios, is bright and clean. Barbirolli perhaps brings greater warmth, and the playing of the Berlin Philharmonic for Karajan has greater electricity, but this Pickwick version has a lot going for it.

The overall impression of Ormandy's mid-1970s account is of a superbly disciplined response from the Philadelphians, well recorded, but wanting that extra degree of freshness and character to justify the exposure that repeated hearing will give it. Yet there is no doubt that the rich sweep of the Philadelphia strings in the big tune of the finale is very compulsive in its intensity. *Pohjola's daughter*, too, generates an exciting climax, while *The Swan of Tuonela* is darkly atmospheric. The digital remastering is vivid but not always absolutely refined, and the brass at the close of the *Symphony* has an element of coarseness.

Beecham's performance comes from a BBC tape of serviceable quality made at London's Royal Festival Hall in 1954. It is a pretty incandescent performance and the BBC orchestra, spurred on by various vocal exhortations from the conductor, play with great enthusiasm. Beecham admirers will not want to be without it.

Toscanini's BBC recording was made during his 1938 visit to London, but it is not quite as electrifying as his Wagner and Debussy of 1935. He tends to press ahead, as indeed he does in his two subsequent performances. The BBC Symphony Orchestra was a splendidly responsive instrument at this time but, high-voltage though it is, there is not the sense of atmosphere or conviction as in the Koussevitzky and Beecham issues. The ends of each movement are barbarously cut off without any atmosphere.

Symphonies Nos. 2 in D; 3 in C, Op. 52.
(M) *** EMI CDM7 64120-2 [id.]; *EG 7644120-4*. CBSO, Simon Rattle.

Rattle's EMI record offers a new coupling with the *Third Symphony*. In No. 2 the CBSO play with fervour and enthusiasm except, perhaps, in the first movement where the voltage is lower – particularly in the development, which is not easy to bring off. The slow movement is full-bodied and gutsy, convincing even when Rattle arrests the flow of the argument by underlining certain points. The Scherzo is bracing enough, though in the Trio the oboe tune is caressed a little too much; however, the transition to the finale is magnificent and Rattle finds the *tempo giusto* in this movement. The Birmingham strings produce a splendidly fervent unison both here and elsewhere in the *Symphony*. The recording is very alive, though the perspective needs greater depth. Rattle's account of the *Third* is vastly superior to his *First* and *Second*. He is convincing not only in his pacing but also in his capacity to relate the parts to the whole. The slow movement is particularly fine; few have penetrated its landscape more completely, and the movement throughout is magical. The way in which he gradually builds up the finale is masterly and sure of instinct. The recording, made in the Warwick Arts Centre, sounds very well balanced, natural in perspective and finely detailed.

Symphonies Nos. 2 in D; 5 in E flat, Op. 82.
(M) **(*) Chan. Dig. CHAN 6556; *MBTD 6556* [id.]. SNO, Sir Alexander Gibson.

The *Second* is among the best of Gibson's cycle and scores highly, thanks to the impressive clarity, fullness and impact of the 1982 digital recording. Gibson's reading is honest and straightforward, free of bombast in the finale. Tempos are well judged: the first movement is neither too taut nor too relaxed: it is well shaped and feels right. Overall this is most satisfying, as is the *Fifth*, which has similar virtues: at no time is there any attempt to interpose the personality of the interpreter, and the finale has genuine weight and power. The interpretation has the authenticity which comes from the conductor being constantly immersed in these scores since the early 1960s.

Symphonies Nos. 2 in D; 7 in C, Op. 105.
(BB) **(*) Naxos Dig. 8.550198 [id.]. Slovak PO, Adrian Leaper.

Adrian Leaper is a genuine Sibelian, but in No. 2 his first movement is a little low-key and wanting in tension. The horns, too, have a rather wider vibrato than is desirable, though this proves less obtrusive later on. There are some odd quirks of balance: the timpani sticks out at about one minute into the finale; but on the whole this is enjoyable. The *Seventh Symphony*, on the other hand, is really very impressive. This gifted conductor certainly knows how this music should move and what it is all about; he shapes phrases sensitively and with an instinctive feel for the idiom. Good recording, and excellent value at super-bargain price.

Symphonies Nos. 3 in C, Op. 52; 4 in A min., Op. 63.
(BB) ** Naxos Dig. 8.550199 [id.]. Slovak PO, Adrian Leaper.

Adrian Leaper has a good feel for this composer, but the tempo for the slow movement of the *Third Symphony* is far too fast for comfort. The first movement is pretty brisk too, but he has the measure of its power and momentum. The *Fourth Symphony* is far more impressive and the Slovak orchestra, for whom this must be rare material, play with great feeling and insight. Tubular bells rather than glockenspiel are employed in the finale. Superb recording – were the *Third* as successful as the *Fourth*, this issue would rate three stars.

Symphonies Nos. 3 in C; 6 in D min., Op. 104; 7 in C, Op. 105.

(M) *** Chan. CHAN 6557; *MBTD 6557* [id.]. SNO, Sir Alexander Gibson.

With three symphonies offered, some 74 minutes overall, this is a fine bargain and an excellent way to experience Gibson's special feeling for this composer. The SNO is in very good form. The first movement of the *Third* has real momentum and the Scottish orchestra play with genuine fire and enthusiasm. The *Andantino* is fast, faster than the composer's marking. One feels that Gibson has learned this symphony from Anthony Collins's famous mono Decca version. Such a tempo, while it gives the music-making fine thrust, means that Gibson, like Collins before him, loses some of the fantasy of this enigmatic movement. But there is more here to admire than to cavil at. The *Sixth* is impressive too, with plenty of atmosphere and some radiant playing from the Scottish violin section; as in the *Third*, the Chandos recording is vivid, full and well detailed. The *Seventh* has a rather relaxed feeling throughout, but it does not lack warmth and, as in No. 1, Gibson draws the threads together at the close with satisfying breadth.

(i) *Symphony No. 4 in A min., Op. 63;* (ii) *Symphony No. 5 in E flat, Op. 82.*
(M) *(*) Finlandia FACD 022 [id.]. Finnish RSO, Berglund; (ii) Helsinki PO, Jorma Panula.

Berglund's recording of the *Fourth Symphony* comes from the late 1960s and is in most respects impressive. In the 1970s it would have figured high in the lists, and it still counts as a reading of power and integrity. Not so its companion under Jorma Panula, which does not rise much above the routine. Both recordings sound quite good for their age, but there are better accounts to be had at all price levels.

Symphonies Nos. 4 in A min.; 6 in D min.
(M) *** EMI CDM7 64121-2 [id.]; *EG 764121-4*. CBSO, Simon Rattle.

Symphonies Nos. (i) *4 in A min, Op. 63;* (ii) *6 in D min., Op. 104;* (i) *The Bard, Op. 64; Lemminkäinen's return, Op. 22/4; The Tempest: Prelude.*
❀ (M) (***) EMI mono CDM7 64027-2 [id.]. (i) LPO, (ii) RPO, Sir Thomas Beecham.

In its colour Beecham's account of the *Fourth Symphony* reflects his feeling that, far from being an austere work, as is often claimed, it is ripely romantic. In his concert-programmes, he used unashamedly to replace standard symphonies at the last minute with this allegedly 'difficult' work, disconcerting some in the audience but proving his point. (This had the additional advantage of affording the orchestra familiarity with the music and providing extra rehearsal time to make a recording possible on a limited budget.) No performance brings one closer to the music, while the recording, made over fifty years ago, sounds astonishingly fresh and bleak in this excellent transfer. The sound is well rounded, with plenty of body and presence. To judge from the composer's correspondence, this performance comes very close to his wishes, and there is a concentration, darkness and poetry that few rivalled. Beecham's 1947 account of the *Sixth Symphony* was said to be Sibelius's favourite recording of all his symphonies; it has been out of general circulation for the best part of forty years. Its eloquence is no less impressive. In the three shorter works on the disc – also taken from the old Beecham Society volumes on 78-r.p.m. discs – Beecham's rhythmic sharpness and feeling for colour vividly convey the high voltage of Sibelius's strikingly original writing. *Lemminkäinen's homeward journey* is positively electrifying, with the horse galloping at frenzied speed and excitement, while the *Prelude* to *The Tempest* is every bit as awesome an evocation of a storm as we had remembered. No subsequent performance is as chilling. All these performances except the *Sixth Symphony* come from the late 1930s, but few allowances need be made, for they spring vividly to life in these remarkable transfers. Indispensable for all Sibelians.

Simon Rattle's account of the *Fourth* with the Birmingham orchestra is also one of the best to have appeared in recent years. He invokes a powerful atmosphere in its opening pages: one is completely transported to its dark landscape with its seemingly limitless horizons. The stringtone is splendidly lean without being undernourished and achieves a sinisterly whispering pianissimo in the development. The slow movement is magical. The finale is hardly less masterly: Rattle builds up most convincingly to the final climax and the enigmatic, almost resigned coda. His account of the *Sixth* is almost equally fine. In the slow movement Rattle does not have the tremendous grip that Karajan's DG version commands or quite the concentration that he achieves elsewhere; but that is still awaiting reissue, and – make no mistake – Rattle's is still a *Sixth* to reckon with and its closing bars are memorably eloquent.

Symphony No. 5 in E flat, Op. 82; Belshazzar's feast (suite), *Op. 51; En Saga, Op. 9.*
(BB) *(*) Naxos Dig. 8.550200 [id.]. Slovak PO, Adrian Leaper.

Adrian Leaper favours rather faster tempi than are ideal in the *Fifth Symphony* though he begins impressively. The transition to the scherzo section of the first movement is a bit precipitate and the rest of the movement goes far too fast. The exquisite music to Hjalmar Procopé's *Belshazzar's feast* has great atmosphere – but, again, would be heard to better effect if Leaper had let it take its time. We need a really poetic account of *Belshazzar's feast* and had hoped that Leaper, who has shown himself a sympathetic interpreter of Sibelius, would have brought it off. The Slovak orchestra play splendidly throughout and the recording is first class.

Symphony No. 5 in E flat; Pohjola's daughter, Op. 49.
(M) **(*) Sony CD 44720 [MYK 38474]; *40-44720.* NYPO, Bernstein.

Bernstein's earlier NYPO *Fifth* is splendidly played and totally unmannered. It is a reading of genuine stature, among the very finest on record. Although the recording is not ideal – it could have more richness of texture and less brilliance – the quality of this performance earns it the strongest recommendation. The coupling is a finely proportioned reading of *Pohjola's daughter*, again lacking amplitude in the sound, but certainly a thrilling performance.

Symphonies Nos. 5 in E flat; 7 in C; Kuolema: Scene with Cranes. Night ride and sunrise.
(M) *** EMI CDM7 64122-2 [id.]; *EG 764122-4.* CBSO, Simon Rattle.

Simon Rattle's record of the *Fifth Symphony* has collected numerous prizes in Europe – and deserves them all. From the very outset one feels that he has found the right tempo. Rattle is scrupulous in observing every dynamic nuance to the letter and, one might add, spirit. What is particularly impressive is the control of the transition between the first section and the scherzo element of the first movement. This relationship is ideally balanced and enables Rattle to convey detail in just the right perspective. There is a splendid sense of atmosphere in the development and a power unmatched in recent versions, save for the Karajan. The playing is superb, with recording to match. The *Seventh* is hardly less powerful and impressive: its opening is slow to unfold and has real vision. This is one of the finest *Sevenths* of recent years. With the addition of an imaginative and poetic account of the *Scene with cranes* from the incidental music to *Kuolema* and a good, if less distinctive, *Night ride and sunrise*, this is a record not to be missed, the finest single disc in Rattle's Birmingham cycle.

Simpson, Robert (born 1921)

(i) *Symphony No. 3;* (ii) *Clarinet quintet.*
(M) *** Unicorn UKCD 2028. (i) LSO, Jascha Horenstein; (ii) Bernard Walton (clarinet), Aeolian Qt.

The *Third Symphony* is in two long movements: the first hammering home in a developed sonata structure the contrast of adjacent tonal centres, B flat against C; the second combining the functions of slow movement, scherzo and finale in a gradually accelerating tempo. There is something Sibelian about the way that, in the first movement, Simpson gradually brings together fragments of musical ideas; but generally this is a work which (within its frankly tonal idiom) asks to be considered in Simpson's own individual terms. The *Clarinet quintet* is a thoughtful, searching piece, dating from 1968 and among Simpson's profoundest utterances. It is played with total commitment here. Both works are given extremely vivid sound.

Sinding, Christian (1856–1941)

Légende, Op. 46.
(BB) *** Naxos Dig. 8.550329 [id.]. Dong-Suk Kang, Slovak (Bratislava) RSO, Adrian Leaper – HALVORSEN: *Air Norvégien* etc.; SIBELIUS: *Violin concerto*; SVENDSEN: *Romance.* ***

Dong-Suk Kang plays Sinding's *Légende* with great conviction and an effortless, songful virtuosity. It is by no means as appealing as the Halvorsen and Svendsen pieces but makes a good makeweight for an excellent collection in the lowest price range.

Smetana, Bedřich (1824–84)

Má Vlast (complete).
(M) **(*) Teldec/Warner Dig. 9031 74778-2 [id.]. Frankfurt RSO, Eliahu Inbal.
(M) **(*) DG 429 183-2; *429 183-4* [id.]. Boston SO, Rafael Kubelik.
(B) **(*) Decca 433 635-2; *433 635-4* [id.]. Israel PO, Walter Weller.
(B) **(*) EMI CDZ7 62606-2; *LZ 762606-4.* RPO, Sargent.
(M) ** Eurodisc/BMG GD 69074 [69074-2-RG]. Bamberg SO, Gustav Kuhn.

The Teldec digital recording of *Má Vlast* is outstandingly fine, very much in the demonstration class. Technically it sweeps the board, and this is music where colourful, richly spacious yet naturally balanced sound can be especially telling. The orchestral playing is first class, too, and Inbal's reading is very dramatic. The progress of the *Vltava* river is vividly detailed with expansive orchestral climaxes and *From Bohemia's woods and fields* has plenty of strong contrasts. Šárka is certainly exciting and if, here and in the last two pieces, the patiotic fervour brings powerful accenting and bold brass, the balancing pastoral folk idiom in *Blaník* is atmospherically caught. This is not as subtle a performance as Kubelik's, but it is certainly compelling.

Among other bargain and mid-priced single-disc versions, Kubelik's 1971 recording with the Boston Symphony Orchestra has much in its favour. Kubelik is careful to temper the bombast which too readily comes to the surface in the later sections of the work, and his skill with the inner balance of the orchestra brings much felicitous detail. The two unquestioned masterpieces of the cycle, *Vltava* and *From Bohemia's woods and fields*, are very successful. The DG recording, however, has been brightly remastered – cymbal clashes sound very metallic – and one could have wished for more ample orchestral textures, although the sound is fully acceptable.

Weller's set is given top-quality 1978 Decca analogue sound which is strikingly full and lively, basically richer than Kubelik's DG recording. But the characteristically dry Tel Aviv acoustic means that the opening of *Vyšehrad* is not as evocative as it might be, and at times climaxes are not ideally expansive (This is the effect of the hall, not the fault of the engineers.) But these are fine, strongly characterized performances. *Vltava* has attractive detail and plenty of drama and a flowing current worthy of a great river. *From Bohemia's woods and fields* brings some fine string playing, and Weller is at his best in the later, more patriotically melodramatic pieces which he presents strongly, yet without going over the top. The orchestral response is persuasive, and at bargain price this is certainly excellent value.

Sargent's version of *Má Vlast* was recorded in 1965 and emerges with striking presence on this remastered CD. The performance has all the zest and spontaneity for which he was famous in the concert hall. Though the readings are not quite as individual and imaginative as some others, they are characteristically well shaped and alive. The opening *Vyšehrad* sets the mood, with the harp balanced closely and the orchestral layout fresh and clear, the romanticism not over-indulged. *Vltava* and *From Bohemia's woods and fields* are very successful and here, as in *Tábor* and *Blaník*, Sargent's directness of manner is appealing, tempering the bombast in the last two pieces. The recording helps too, by its clarity and the bright – yet not overwhelming – brass sonorities. The strings have excellent body yet add to the feeling of freshness; in every way the remastering has given the original sound – always warm and pleasing – more life and projection, while retaining the ambient atmosphere. Good value at bargain price.

The opening, larger-than-life harp solo of Kuhn's version immediately demonstrates the orchestral balance, with bold, forward projection against a very resonant acoustic. The effect certainly gives a richly romantic aura to an essentially spacious performance (which at 79 minutes only just fits on to a single CD). But detail is muddied and the bolder tuttis – the St John's rapids in *Vltava* and the patriotic spectacle of the work's closing sections – are spectacularly ample rather than refined. Nor is the reading subtle in its rhythmic feeling; it misses the vivid Czech folk-dance influence that refreshes Pešek's full-price version. There is no lack of impact here and the playing has plenty of impetus and weight, but there is no feeling of an imaginative freshness of approach.

Má Vlast: Vltava.

(M) *** EMI CDM7 69005-2 [id.]; *EG 768005-4*. BPO, Karajan – DVOŘÁK: *Symphony No. 9*. ***

(M) (**) BMG/RCA GD 60279; *GK 60279* [60279-2-RG; *60279-4-RG*]. NBC SO, Toscanini – DVOŘÁK: *Symphony No. 9*; KODÁLY: *Háry János suite*. (***)

As a fill-up for an excellent version of Dvořák's *New World symphony* Karajan's EMI account of Smetana's most popular piece is comparably vivid, sounding more robust in its digital remastering, but still expressively refined in detail and spontaneous-sounding.

Recorded several years earlier than the other two items on Toscanini's disc, *Vltava* has painfully dry and close sound; but the intensity of Toscanini's performance still makes it a valuable document, along with the searing accounts of Dvořák and Kodály.

Má Vlast: Vltava; Vyšehrad.

(B) *** DG Compact Classics *413 159-4* [id.]. Bav. RSO, Kubelik – DVOŘÁK: *Slavonic dances*; LISZT: *Hungarian rhapsodies; Les Préludes*. ***

Part of a generally attractive collection of Slavonic music. Kubelik's excellent performances come from his complete set and are splendidly played and very well recorded, although the acoustic is slightly dry.

String quartet No. 1 (From my life).

(M) *** Decca 430 295-2; *430 295-4* [id.]. Gabrieli Qt – JANÁČEK: *String quartets Nos. 1–2*. ***

Artistically, the Gabrieli performance of Smetana's autobiographical *First Quartet* is first class; technically, it offers vivid and well-balanced 1977 recorded sound, although the upper range of the violin timbre is marginally less smooth than in the Janáček coupling, even though it was recorded at the same time in the warm acoustics of Rosslyn Hill Chapel.

Spohr, Ludwig (1784–1859)

(i) *Violin concerto No. 8 in A min. (In modo d'una scena cantate), Op. 47;* (ii) *Double quartet in D min., Op. 65.*

(M) (***) BMG/RCA mono GD 87870; *GK 87870* [7870-2-RG; *7870-4-RG*]. Heifetz, with (i) RCA Victor O, Izler Solomon; (ii) Baker, Thomas, Piatigorsky, Amoyal, Rosenthal, Harshman, Lesser – BEETHOVEN: *Serenade.* **

Spohr's *Gesangszenekonsert* is in mono and dates from 1954. A dazzling performance which, in sheer beauty and refinement of tone, remains unsurpassed. Although the recording acoustic could with advantage have been more ample, this is still very good sound for its period and in some ways is more appealing than the dryish, 1968 stereo recording of the *D minor Double quartet*, Op. 65, made with various artists including the young Pierre Amoyal, then his pupil, who leads the second (and more subservient) quartet. The first violin dominates the texture, a reminder both of Spohr's prowess as a violinist and – certainly – of Heifetz's. His distinctive timbre and glorious tone shine through. Incomparable playing, without doubt, though they do not exactly produce a homogeneous quartet-blend. But, given Heifetz's sound, who cares!

Stainer, John (1840–1901)

The Crucifixion.

(B) *** CD-CFP 4519; *TC-CFP 4519.* David Hughes, John Lawrenson, Guildford Cathedral Ch., Barry Rose; Gavin Williams.

The Classics for Pleasure version (from the late 1960s) is of high quality and, although one of the congregational hymns is omitted, in every other respect this can be recommended. John Lawrenson makes a movingly eloquent solo contribution and the choral singing is excellent. When the remastered recording sounds as good as this, there seems little reason to pay more.

Steiner, Max (1888–1971)

Film scores: *The Adventures of Don Juan; Dodge City; They Died With Their Boots On* (suites).

(M) *** BMG/RCA GD 80912; *GK 80912* [0912-2-RG; *0912-4-RG*]. Nat. SO, Charles Gerhardt (with WAXMAN: *Objective Burma!: Parachute Drop.* FRIEDHOFER: *The Sun Also Rises: Prologue; The Lights of Paris* ***) – KORNGOLD: Film scores. ***

Max Steiner, Viennese born, emigrated to the USA in 1914 and, after working as a conductor/arranger/pianist on the East Coast, was lured out West with the coming of the talkies in 1929. He worked first for RKO (providing music for some 135 pictures), then moved to the Selznick studio and on to Warner Brothers, where he wrote scores for 155 more films. Selznick borrowed him back for *Gone with the Wind.* Steiner would wait until a film was completed and edited before producing his ideas; he would then develop the finished work quickly and spontaneously, but would leave the orchestration to others. He understood that music could slow up as well as enhance a scene, and his professionalism was justly admired. His style is unashamedly eclectic, but his writing never sounds thin in ideas. The first disc, which Steiner shares with Korngold and others, concentrates on swashbuckling Errol Flynn movies. *The Adventures of Don Juan* combines sumptuous and exuberant orchestration and attractive lyrical ideas. Here as in *Dodge City* the use of orchestral colour is in the most spectacular Hollywood tradition. The main-title sequence of the latter film immediately establishes the atmosphere of a Western and the music combines grandiloquence with some attractive swing-along cowboy tunes, while *They Died With Their Boots On* (which whitewashes General Custer) is generous with trumpet calls but also develops the most luscious romanticism, again bringing gloriously full textures from the National Philharmonic violins; then Steiner jauntily interpolates *Garry Owen*, the actual march of the US 7th Cavalry, before the battle sequence. The brief Waxman item is as dramatic as its title suggests, and Friedhofer's bitter-sweet waltz theme for *The Sun Also Rises* makes a gentle interlude after the strongly motivated action-sequences of the other contributors.

Film scores: *All This and Heaven too; Beyond the Forest; Dark Victory; In This Our Life; Jezebel; The Letter; Now Voyager; A Stolen Life.*

(M) **(*) BMG/RCA GD 80183; *GK 80183* [0183-2-RG; *0183-4-RG*]. Nat. PO, Charles Gerhardt (with KORNGOLD: *The Private Lives of Elizabeth and Essex: Elizabeth. Juarez: Carlotta.* WAXMAN: *Mr Skeffington: Forsaken.* NEWMAN: *All About Eve: Main title.* ***)

As can be guessed from the titles above, this collection concentrates on the highly charged Bette Davis dramas for which Steiner appropriately wrote emotionally drenched string themes. The disc opens with the big tune from *Now, Voyager* (included again below) and, while the *Waltz* from *Jezebel* brings a lighter and more frivolous mood, the prevailing mood is mostly melodramatic. Steiner was expert in creating a high level of tension and then suddenly relaxing into simplicity and charm, as in the attractive group of excepts from *All This and Heaven too.* The two vignettes from Korngold have more subtlety (his portrait of Queen Elizabeth I is most winning), while Alfred Newman's introduction to *All About Eve* has characteristic vitality. Many of the excerpts here are brief title-sequences, and the overall selection at around 40 minutes could have been more generous.

Film scores: *The Big Sleep* (suite); *The Charge of the Light Brigade: The charge; The Fountainhead* (suite). (i) *Four Wives: Symphonie moderne.* (ii) *The Informer* (excerpts). *Johnny Belinda* (suite); *King Kong* (excerpts); *Now Voyager* (excerpts); *Saratoga Trunk: As long as I live. Since you went away:* Title sequence.
(M) *** BMG/RCA GD 80136; *GK 80136* [0136-2-RG; *0136-4-RG*]. National PO, Charles Gerhardt, with (i) Earl Wild; (ii) Amb. S.

Steiner could always produce a good tune on demand, with the luscious themes for *Now Voyager* and *As long as I live* from *Saratoga Trunk* almost approaching the famous *Gone with the Wind* melody in memorability; and a dulcet touch was available for the wistful portrayal of *Johnny Belinda. King Kong* and *The Big Sleep* introduce appropriate elements of menace, and in *The Informer* the Ambrosian Singers provide a characteristic outpouring of Hollywood religiosity at the final climax (the death of the principal character). Charles Gerhardt is a master of the grand orchestral gesture and presents all this music with enormous conviction and with care for atmospheric detail. The orchestra (92 strong) are obviously enjoying themselves hugely, and the recording offers a fine blend of spaciousness and spectacle. There are excellent notes, but one would have welcomed more movie stills – only *Now Voyager*, *King Kong* and Erroll Flynn leading *The Charge of the Light Brigade* are represented pictorially.

Film scores: *The Big Sleep: Love theme; The Caine Mutiny: March; Casablanca* (suite); *Key Largo* (suite); *Passage to Marseilles: Rescue at sea; The Treasure of the Sierra Madre* (suite); *Virginia City* (excerpts). (Also includes music by WAXMAN: *To Have and Have Not; The Two Mrs Carrolls.* HOLLANDER: *Sabrina.* YOUNG: *The Left Hand of God.* ROZSA: *Sahara.*)
(M) ** BMG/RCA GD 80422; *GK 80422* [0422-2-RG; *0422-4-RG*]. National PO, Gerhardt.

This collection concentrates on the key Humphrey Bogart movies and certainly shows Steiner's versatility. The changes of mood in the five brief sequences from *The Treasure of the Sierra Madre* are mirrored most imaginatively. However, the evocative piano solo, so famous in *Casablanca*, is not very successful here, although there is some touchingly romantic lyrical writing in *Key Largo.* Among the items by other composers, the Waxman excerpts and the eloquent Victor Young melody for *The Left Hand of God* stand out. This is one of the least repeatable of the Gerhardt compilations, although performances, recording and CD transfers are all well up to standard. Again good notes, but only three movies are represented pictorially.

Gone with the Wind (film score).
(M) *** BMG/RCA GD 80452; *GK 80452* [0452-2-RG; *0452-4-RG*]. National PO, Charles Gerhardt.

It was sensible of Steiner not to associate his most potent musical idea in *Gone with the Wind* with one or more of the principal characters, but instead to centre it on Tara, the home of the heroine. Thus he could work it as a leitmotif and have it return again and again through a complex score of some two and a half hours to remind the audience nostalgically that Tara represented permanence and continuity against a foreground of changing human destinies. It says something for the quality of Steiner's tune that its ability to haunt the memory is not diminished by its many reappearances. The rest of the music is professionally tailored to the narrative and makes agreeable listening, although the quality of the lyrical invention inevitably becomes more sentimental as the film nears its close. As ever, Charles Gerhardt is a splendid advocate and he secures fine playing and obvious involvement from his orchestra. The recording, too, is both full and brilliant.

Sterndale Bennett, William
(1816–75)

(i) *Piano concerto No. 4 in F min.; Symphony in G. min.;* (i) *Fantasia in A, Op. 16.*
(M) *** Unicorn Dig. UKCD 2032. (i) Binns; Milton Keynes CO, Hilary Wetton.

Mendelssohn conducted the first performance (in 1839) of William Sterndale Bennett's *Fourth Piano concerto* in Leipzig. The work reflects Chopin rather more than Mendelssohn himself and is agreeable and well structured. Its lollipop slow movement is a winner, an engaging *Barcarolle*, and Sterndale Bennett's device of putting a cluster of piano filigree over a gentle pizzicato accompaniment was justly admired by the critics of the day. The *Symphony* is amiable, not unlike the Mendelssohn string symphonies, and the slow movement brings another ingenious device of repeated overlapping woodwind notes. Overall it is very slight, but enjoyable enough. Both performances are uncommonly good ones. There is nothing whatsoever second rate about the Milton Keynes Chamber Orchestra; the string ensemble is spirited and clean and the wind playing is first class. Malcolm Binns is a persuasive advocate of the *Concerto*, and he has the full measure of the appealing slow movement, while Hilary Wetton paces both works admirably and clearly has much sympathy for them. The solo *Fantasia* (with echoes of Mendelssohn and Schumann – to whom it is dedicated) has been added for the CD issue, which offers excellent sound and a good balance.

Stradella, Alessandro (1644–82)

La Susanna (oratorio).
(M) ** EMI CMS7 63438-2 (2) [id.]. Kweksilber, Nelson, Jacobs, Hill, Cold, Bar. Instrumental Ens., Curtis.

Recorded in Amsterdam in 1978, this period performance of Stradella's biblical oratorio, based on the story of Susanna and the Elders, begins disconcertingly. That was the time when baroque strings (the group here is violin, cello and violone, with theorbo, chittarone and harpsichord) used an abrasive squeeze technique on sustained notes. The slow Prelude, recorded close, is unpleasantly abrasive, but then the fine qualities of this lively performance emerge more and more, with an excellent cast of soloists, including the aptly named Marjanne Kweksilber silver-toned in the title-role. The oratorio is in two sections, lasting just over an hour and a half in all, and including no fewer than 25, mainly brief, numbers, linked by fluid recitative. Outstanding are the three substantial arias for Susanna near the beginning of Part Two, including a lament lasting nearly seven minutes. With its simple descending ground bass and languishing melodic lines, it directly echoes Monteverdi's celebrated *Lamento della Ninfa*. That is not the only likeness to the earlier composer, with many brief duets and trios also recalling Monteverdi's madrigals. Though the booklet provides a helpful essay about Stradella himself, there is too little information specifically about *La Susanna*, no text and not even a synopsis, though with bright, close-up sound the Italian words are exceptionally clear.

Strauss, Johann Jnr (1825–99)

(All music listed is by Johann Strauss Jnr unless otherwise stated)

Le Beau Danube (ballet, arr. Désormière); *Cinderella* (*Äschenbrodel;* ballet, rev. and ed. Gamley); *Ritter Pásmán* (ballet music).
(M) **(*) Decca Dig./Analogue 430 852-2 (2) [id.]. Nat. PO, Richard Bonynge.

Johann Strauss did not live to finish his only full-length ballet, *Äschenbrodel*. Most of Act I was completed, but the rest was pieced together and scored by Joseph Bayer; this version has been further revised and edited by Douglas Gamley. It would be nice to have discovered a hidden masterpiece, but this is not it. (Mahler was so unimpressed that he even doubted the work's authenticity, though he revised that view later.) The music is felicitously scored, but the most memorable moment is when the *Blue Danube* is quoted as a barrel-organ effect but sounding piquantly like an ocarina. Decca provide digital sound of spectacular excellence and Bonynge does his utmost to engage the listener, securing warm, elegant and sparkling playing. But as the *Ritter Pásmán* ballet suite, which is rather more memorable, shows, Strauss's setting of the Cinderella story is inconsequential, though pleasing enough as wallpaper music. *Le beau Danube* is another matter. Désormière draws on vintage Strauss material for *Le beau Danube* and, although his score is not chosen as adroitly as Dorati's *Graduation Ball* (which we urgently need on CD), it opens racily and is very entertaining. Bonynge presents it all with effervescent sparkle and the Decca analogue recording is first class.

(i) *Overtures: Die Fledermaus;* (ii) *Waldmeister*. (iii) *Perpetuum mobile*. Polkas: (iv) *Annen;* (v) *Auf der Jagd;* (vi) *Leichtes Blut;* (iv) *Pizzicato* (with Josef); (vii) *Tritsch-Tratsch;* (iv) *Vergnügungszug*. (viii) *Quadrille on themes from Verdi's 'Un ballo in maschera'*. Waltzes: (ix) *Accelerationen;* (x) *An der schönen blauen Donau;* (xi) *Du und Du;* (iv) *Frühlingsstimmen;* (vi) *Geschichten aus dem Wienerwald;* (xii) & (xiii) & (v) *Kaiser;* (iii) *Rosen aus dem Süden;* (ii) *Wein, Weib und Gesang*. Josef STRAUSS: (iv) *Dorfschwalben aus Österreich;* (v) *Sphärenklänge*. (iv) Johann STRAUSS, Snr: *Radetzky march*.
(M) *** DG mono/stereo 435 335-2 (2). VPO, (i) Maazel; (ii) Boskovsky; (iii) Boehm; (iv) Clemens Krauss; (v) Karajan; (vi) Knappertsbusch; (vii) Mehta; (viii) Abbado; (ix) Josef Krips; (x) Szell; (xi) Erich Kleiber; (xii) Bruno Walter; (xiii) Furtwängler.

This delectable compilation for the 150th anniversary of the Vienna Philharmonic brings recordings of Strauss made between 1929 and 1990. Surprisingly, only four of the 23 items are from DG sources, with the rest borrowed from rival companies, notably from EMI, whose recordings of Erich Kleiber, Clemens Krauss and George Szell (made in the late 1920s and early 1930s) are particularly atmospheric, very well transferred. Other Clemens Krauss performances, plus more by Boskovsky and Knappertsbusch, come from the Decca label, justly famous in this repertoire. It is fascinating to compare Bruno Walter (1937), Wilhelm Furtwängler (1950) and Karajan (1987), all in the *Emperor waltz*. Karajan's other major contribution dates from 1949 (*Sphärenkläange*), and the many well-known favourites are well spiced with a few charming rarities.

Banditen-Galopp; Kaiser Franz Joseph I: Rettungs-Jubel-Marsch; Russischer Marsch. Polkas: *Champagner; Eljen a Magyar!; Neue Pizzicato; Unter Donner und Blitz.* Waltzes: *Künstlerleben; Liebeslieder; Morgenblätter; Wiener Blut; Wiener Bonbons.* Josef STRAUSS: *Auf Ferienreisen polka; Dorfschwalben aus Österreich (Village swallows) waltz.*
(M) *** Decca 425 428-2; *425 428-4*. VPO, Boskovsky.

Egyptischer Marsch. Polkas: *Annen; Auf der Jagd; Pizzicato* (with Josef); *Tritsch-Tratsch.* Waltzes: *An der schönen blauen Donau; Carnevals-Botschafter; Frühlingsstimmen.* Josef STRAUSS: Polkas: *Feuerfest; Jokey; Polka-mazurka: Die Schwätzerin.* Waltzes: *Dynamiden; Sphärenklänge.* Eduard STRAUSS: *Fesche Geister waltz.* Johann STRAUSS Snr: *Wettrennen-Galopp.*
(M) *** Decca 425 425-2; *425 425-4*. VPO, Boskovsky.

Persischer Marsch. Polkas: *Bitte schön; Leichtes Blut; 'S gibt nur a Kaiserstadt; Tik-Tak; Vergnügungszug.* Waltzes: *Acccelerationen; Kaiser; Rosen aus dem Süden; Schneeglöckchen.* Johann STRAUSS Snr: *Loreley-Rhein-Klänge waltz.* Josef STRAUSS: *Die Emancipirte polka-mazurka; Delirien waltz.* Eduard STRAUSS: *Mit Extrapost polka.*
(M) *** Decca 425 429-2. VPO, Boskovsky.

Perpetuum mobile; Spanischer Marsch. Polkas: *Demolirer; Stürmisch in Lieb' und Tanz.* Waltzes: *Du und Du; Freuet euch des Lebens; Geschichten aus dem Wienerwald; Lagunen.* Josef STRAUSS: *Brennende Liebe polka mazurka; Eingesendet polka; Aquarellem waltz.* Eduard STRAUSS: *Bahn frei! polka; Frauenherz polka mazurka.* Johann STRAUSS Snr: *Radetzky march. Piefke und Pufke polka.*
(M) *** Decca 425 426-2; *425 426-4*. VPO, Boskovsky.

Decca have reassembled and carefully remastered the famous vintage Boskovsky/VPO recordings on to five CDs (of which they have have subsequently withdrawn one), each containing between 73 and 75 minutes of music. The cream of the Strauss family repertoire is here, and that includes some memorable items from Josef: the (so-called) *Village swallows waltz* and *Delirien*, some engaging polkas such as *Eingesendet*, *Brennende Liebe* and the spectacular *Feuerfest*. Eduard too offers some memorable pieces, of which the most famous is the infectious *Bahn frei!* with its opening whistle. Each CD is introduced by a famous waltz from Johann and is attractively programmed to alternate other waltzes with polkas, while the charming polka-mazurkas and marches offer further variety. The recordings date from between 1958 and 1976 but their age is partly disguised, since the warm acoustics of the Vienna Sophienbad-Saal (where many of the recordings were made) are agreeably flattering, although the upper string sound is less sumptuous than one would expect today. But the performances remain unsurpassed; one has only to sample the zither solo at the opening of *Tales from the Vienna Woods* to relish the special Viennese flavour.

'The world of Johann Strauss': Egyptischer Marsch; Perpetuum mobile; Polkas: *Auf de Jagd; Pizzicato* (with Josef); Waltzes: *An der schönen blauen Donau; Frühlingsstimmen; Geschichten aus dem Wienerwald; Rosen aus dem Süden; 1001 Nacht; Wiener Blut.*
(B) *** Decca 430 501-2; *430 501-4*. VPO, Boskovsky.

A further generous and inexpensive Decca permutation of the justly famous Boskovsky/VPO recordings, which still dominate the Strauss family listings. If the programme suits, this is excellent value.

Waltzes: *An der schönen blauen Donau; Carnevals-Botschafter; Donauweibchen; Du und du; Feuilleton; Flugschriften; Die Leitartikel; Morgenblätter; Wein, Weib und Gesang; Wiener Frauen.*
(M) **(*) EMI Dig. CDD7 64108-2; *ET 764108-4*. Johann Strauss O of Vienna, Boskovsky.

These recordings date from 1982 and 1984. The fuller digital sound is obviously more modern than that on Boskovsky's remastered VPO records made for Decca; but the effect is for the music-making to sound more robust, though the playing is warm and stylish and there is a genuine Viennese lilt. The *Blue Danube* is a splendid performance, Boskovsky at his finest; *Morning papers* is very enjoyable too, and the novelties sound admirably fresh, especially the two concerning the ladies, *Donauweibchen* and *Wiener Frauen*. This collection is generous (78 minutes) and is thoroughly worthwhile; if the playing does not have quite the magic of Boskovsky's finest VPO performances, it is still very easy to enjoy.

New Year's Day concert (1979): Polkas: *Auf der Jagd* (with encore); *Bitte schön! Leichtes Blut; Pizzicato* (with Josef); *Tik-Tak.* Waltzes: *An der schönen blauen Donau; Bei uns zu Haus; Wein, Weib und Gesang.* Josef STRAUSS: *Moulinet polka; Sphärenklänge waltz.* Johann STRAUSS, Snr: *Radetzky march.*
(M) **(*) Decca Dig. 430 715-2; *430 715-4.* VPO, Boskovsky.

Decca chose to record Boskovsky's 1979 New Year's Day concert in Vienna for one of their very first digital issues on LP. The clarity, immediacy and natural separation of detail are very striking throughout, although the upper strings of the Vienna Philharmonic are very brightly lit indeed and there is some lack of bloom at the top. The CD does not include the whole concert, and one notices that there is not the degree of ambient glow that Decca were to achieve in digital recordings made only a year or so after this. The music-making itself is another matter. It gains much from the spontaneity of the occasion, and the electricity is very apparent; it reaches its peak when the side-drum thunders out the introduction to the closing *Radetzky March*, a frisson-creating moment which, with the audience participation, is quite electrifying.

'Best of the New Year Concerts' (1980–83): Overtures: *Die Fledermaus; Waldmeister; Perpetuum mobile.* Polkas: *Eljen a Magyar!; Pizzicato* (with Josef); *Tritsch-Tratsch; Unter Donner und Blitz; Vergnügungszug.* Waltzes: *Accelerationen; An der schönen blauen Donau; Geschichten aus dem Wienerwald; Kaiser; Morgenblätter; Rosen aus dem Süden.* Josef STRAUSS: Polkas: *Frauenherz; Die Libelle; Ohne Sorgen; Die tanzende Muse.* Waltzes: *Aquarellen; Delirien; Sphärenklänge; Transactionen.* Johann STRAUSS Snr: *Radetzky march.*
(M) ** DG Dig. 429 562-2 (2). VPO, Lorin Maazel.

Waltzes: *An der schönen blauen Donau; Geschichten aus dem Wienerwald; Kaiser; Rosen aus dem Süden; Wiener Blut; Wiener Bonbons.* Josef STRAUSS: *Delirien.*
(M) ** DG Dig. 427 820-2 (from above). VPO, Lorin Maazel.

Maazel did not take on Boskovsky's mantle very readily; for all the brilliance of the playing, the impression is one of energy rather than of charm. Maazel can certainly shape the beginnings and ends of the waltzes elegantly, and the performances of the *Blue Danube* and *Tales from the Vienna Woods* are not without lilt; but elsewhere the feeling of the music-making can seem too high-powered. The *Radetzky march*, for instance, for all the enthusiasm of the audience response, is tightly disciplined. The digital recording gives good presence – especially in the *Pizzicato polka* – but less atmosphere, and when the applause comes one almost registers surprise. As well as the two-disc mixed compilation, there is a collection of favourite waltzes, all at mid-price. But Boskovsky and Karajan convey greater enjoyment in this repertoire.

'1989 New Year Concert in Vienna': Overture: *Die Fledermaus.* Csárdás: *Ritter Pásmán.* Polkas: *Bauern; Eljen a Magyar!; Im Krapfenwald'l; Pizzicato* (with Josef). Waltzes: *Accelerationen; An der schönen blauen Donau; Bei uns zu Haus; Frühlingsstimmen; Künstlerleben.* Josef STRAUSS: Polkas: *Jockey; Die Libelle; Moulinet; Plappermäulchen.* Johann STRAUSS Snr: *Radetzky march.*
(M) **(*) Sony M2K 45564 (2) [id.]. VPO, Carlos Kleiber.

In style this is very similar to Kleiber's controversial complete recording of *Fledermaus*, for though he allows all the rhythmic flexibility a traditionalist could want – and sometimes more – his pursuit of knife-edged precision prevents the results from sounding quite relaxed enough, with the Viennese lilt in the waltzes analysed to the last micro-second instead of just being played as a dance. In the delicious polka, *Im Krapfenwald'l*, the cheeky cuckoo-calls which comically punctuate the main theme are made to sound beautiful rather than rustic, and fun is muted elsewhere too. But in one or two numbers Kleiber really lets rip, as in the Hungarian polka, *Eljen a Magyar!* (*Hail to Hungary!*) and the *Ritter Pásmán Csárdás.* Warm, full recording, with the presence of the audience nicely implied without getting in the way. With 87 minutes of music on two discs, this is not generous measure, even at mid-price.

Overture: *Die Fledermaus.* Polkas: *Annen; Auf der Jagd; Explosionen.* Waltzes: *Frühlingsstimmen; Rosen aus dem Süden; Wein, Weib und Gesang; Windsor echoes.* Josef STRAUSS: *Feuerfest polka* (with ZIEHRER: *Kissing polka*).
(B) *** Pickwick PCD 902; *CIMPC 902* [id.]. LSO, Georgiadis.

Entitled '*An Evening in Vienna*', the performances have nevertheless a British flavour – which is not to say that there is any lack of lilt or beguiling warmth in the waltzes; they are beautifully done, while the polkas all go with an infectious swing. There are no superimposed sound-effects in the *Explosions polka*; one waits until the very end, when there is a spectacular 'collapse' of the whole percussion department. The sound is very good indeed, well balanced with a pleasing ambient bloom. This is very enjoyable and is John Georgiadis's best record to date.

Egyptischer Marsch. Overtures: *Die Fledermaus. Der Zigeunerbaron; Perpetuum mobile.* Polkas: *Annen; Auf der Jagd; Pizzicato; Tritsch-Tratsch* (CD only: *Eljen a Magyar!; Unter Donner und Blitz*). Waltzes: *An der schönen blauen Donau; Geschichten aus dem Wienerwald; Kaiser; Rosen aus dem Süden; Wiener Blut* (CD only: *Morgenblätter*).
(B) **(*) DG Compact Classics 413 432-2 (2); *413 432-4* [id.]. Berlin R. O, Fricsay; BPO, Karajan; VPO, Boehm.

This Compact Classics compilation juxtaposes the contrasting personalities of Ferenc Fricsay, Boehm and Karajan – all effective Johann Strauss exponents – in a fairly generous collection of favourites. Fricsay's volatile temperament brings individuality to the *Blue Danube* and *Emperor* waltzes, and he is at his most charismatic in *Tales from the Vienna Woods* and in registering the changing moods of the *Fledermaus overture.* Boehm and Karajan are at their most exuberant in *Roses from the South* and *Vienna blood* respectively, while the *Egyptian march* has striking panache in Karajan's hands. The recordings come from the 1960s, the earliest 1961; while the sound is variable, it does not seem obviously dated. For the pair of CDs, two extra polkas and one waltz have been added, as indicated in the listing.

Egyptischer Marsch; Kaiser Franz Josef Marsch; Banditen-Galopp. Polkas: *Eljen a Magyar!; Furioso; Tritsch-Tratsch; Unter Donner und Blitz.* Waltzes: *An der schönen blauen Donau; Rosen aus dem Süden; 1001 Nacht; Wiener Blut; Wiener Bonbons.* Josef STRAUSS: *Die Libelle polka; Perlen der Liebe waltz.*
(M) ** Chan. Dig. CHAN 6528; *MBTD 6528* [id.]. Johann Strauss O, leader Jack Rothstein (violin).

This reshuffling for Chandos's mid-priced Collect series brings fairly generous measure (69 minutes) and many will be attracted by the bright digital recording, which has plenty of bloom. The polkas go with an infectious swing and there is no lack of lilt in the waltzes, although Josef's *Perlen der Liebe* is a shade disappointing. Otherwise there is no lack of spontaneity here; good though Rothstein is, however, he does not equal Georgiadis in this repertoire.

Perpetuum mobile; Polkas: *Champagne; Pizzicato* (with Josef); *Tritsch-Tratsch; Unter Donner und Blitz;* Waltzes: *An der schönen blauen Donau; Kaiser; Wiener Blut; Wo die Zitronen bluh'n.* J. STRAUSS Snr: *Radetzky march.*
(B) ** Pickwick Dig. PCD 856; *CIMPC 856* [id.]. LSO, Georgiadis.

This is very spirited music-making, given brilliant, modern digital recording (the violins lacking something in sumptuousness above the stave). There is no lack of either polish or affection, but the extra magic of the best Viennese performances is missing.

Polkas: *Czech; Pizzicato* (with Josef). Waltzes: *Kaiser; Rosen aus dem Süden; Sängerlust; Wiener Blut; Wiener Bonbons.* J. STRAUSS, Snr: *Radetzky march.* Josef STRAUSS: Polkas: *Feuerfest; Ohne Sorgen.*
(BB) **(*) ASV CDQS 6020; *ZCQS 6020.* LSO, leader Georgiadis (violin).

The LSO is on top form and the rhythmic feel of the playing combines lilt with polished liveliness. There is delicacy (the *Czech polka* is enchanting) and boisterousness, as in the irresistible anvil effects in the *Feuerfest polka.* The closing *Radetzky march* is as rousing as anyone could wish, while the waltzes combine vitality and charm. With good recording in a suitably resonant acoustic, which tends to emphasize the bass, this is recommendable, especially at budget price.

Polka: *Unter Donner und Blitz.* Waltzes: *An der schönen blauen Donau; Kaiser; Künsterleben; Morgenblätter; Rosen aus dem Süden; Schatz; Wiener Blut.* Josef STRAUSS: Waltzes: *Dorfschwalben aus Österreich; Mein Lebenslauf ist Lieb' und Lust.*
(M) *** BMG/RCA GD 60177 [60177-2-RG]. Chicago SO, Reiner.

Reiner's collection was recorded in 1957 and 1960, and the sound is voluptuous with the warmth of the Chicago Hall ambience. The performances are memorable for their lilting zest and the sumptuous richness of the Chicago strings, although the *Thunder and lightning polka* has an unforgettably explosive exuberance. Reiner – Budapest born – fully understands how this music should be played and conveys his affection in every bar. A fine appendix for the Boskovsky series – it will give equal pleasure.

Waltzes: (ii) *Accelerationen;* (i) *An der schönen blauen Donau; Frühlingsstimmen;* (ii) *Geschichten aus dem Wienerwald;* (i) *Kaiser;* (i) *Künsterleben;* (ii) *Morgenblätter;* (i) *Rosen aus dem Suden; Wein, Weib und Gesang;* (ii) *Wiener Blut.*
(M) ** Ph. 422 277-2; *422 277-4.* VSO, (i) Sawallisch; (ii) Paul Walter.

There are 72 minutes of music here and so virtually all the favourite Johann Strauss waltzes are offered on a single disc. Sawallisch conducts with élan and no lack of rhythmic nuance: his *Blue Danube*, *Emperor* and *Roses from the South* are very enjoyable. The VSO is not the VPO and their string patina is less sumptuous, but the warmly resonant hall ambience is flattering. The snag is that some of the waltzes, including all four conducted, very ably, by Paul Walter, are truncated and this applies too, alas, to *Tales from the Vienna Woods*. But if you just want all the famous Strauss melodies and are not worried about the composer's artistically tailored introductions and postludes, then the present selection should meet the bill.

Waltzes: *An der schönen blauen Donau; Geschichtem aus dem Wienerwald; Kaiser; Künsterleben; Morgenblätter; Schatz; Wiener Blut; Wo die Zitronen blüh'n.*
(BB) ** BMG/RCA VD 60490; *VK 60490*. Phd. O, Ormandy.

Vividly recorded in the late 1960s, these performances have plenty of zest and panache, with the Philadelphia string section making the very most of the sumptuous melodies. Ormandy is clearly enjoying himself and, although there are a few eccentricities of pulse and phrasing and these are obviously not Viennese performances, they are enjoyable for their ready vitality.

Die Fledermaus (complete).
(M) (***) EMI mono CHS7 69531-2 (2) [Ang. CDHB 69531]. Schwarzkopf, Streich, Gedda, Krebs, Kunz, Christ, Philh. Ch. & O, Karajan.
(M) *** EMI CMS7 69354-2 (2) [Ang. CDMB 69354]. Rothenberger, Holm, Gedda, Fischer-Dieskau, Fassbaender, Berry, V. State Op. Ch., VSO, Boskovsky.
(B) **(*) CfP CD-CFPD 4702; *TC-CFPD 4702* (2) [Ang. CDMB 62566]. Lipp, Scheyrer, Ludwig, Dermota, Terkal, Waechter, Berry, Philh. Ch. & O, Ackermann.

The mono recording of Karajan's 1955 version has great freshness and clarity, along with the polish which for many will make it a first favourite. Tempi at times are unconventional, both slow and fast, but the precision and point of the playing are magical and the singing is endlessly delightful. Schwarzkopf makes an enchanting Rosalinde, not just in the imagination and sparkle of her singing but also in the snatches of spoken dialogue (never too long) which leaven the entertainment. As Adèle, Rita Streich produces her most dazzling coloratura; Gedda and Krebs are beautifully contrasted in their tenor tone, and Erich Kunz gives a vintage performance as Falke. The original recording, crisply focused, has been given a brighter edge but otherwise left unmolested.

The Boskovsky version, recorded with the Vienna Symphoniker instead of the Philharmonic, now heads the CD list of stereo *Fledermice*. Rothenberger is a sweet, domestic-sounding Rosalinde, relaxed and sparkling, while among an excellent supporting cast the Orlofsky of Brigitte Fassbaender must be singled out as quite the finest on record, tough and firm. The entertainment has been excellently produced for records, with German dialogue inserted, though the ripe recording sometimes makes the voices jump between singing and speaking. The remastering is admirably vivid.

On a pair of CfP CDs, with a synopsis rather than a libretto, comes a vintage *Fledermaus* from 1960. It makes a superb bargain, for the singing is consistently vivacious. Gerda Scheyrer's Rosalinde brings the only relative disappointment, for the voice is not ideally steady; but Wilma Lipp is a delicious Adèle and Christa Ludwig's Orlofsky is a real surprise, second only to Brigitte Fassbaender's assumption of a breeches role that is too often disappointing. Karl Terkal's Eisenstein and Anton Dermota's Alfred give much pleasure, and Erich Kunz's inebriated Frosch in the finale comes off even without a translation. Ackermann's direction has not the sparkle and subtlety of Karajan, but the final result is polished and with a real Viennese flavour. The sound has come up remarkably vividly – there is a nice combination of atmosphere and clarity.

A Night in Venice (Eine Nacht in Venedig): complete.
(M) (***) EMI mono CDH7 69530-2 [id.]. Schwarzkopf, Gedda, Kunz, Klein, Loose, Dönch, Philh. Ch. & O, Ackermann.

A Night in Venice, in Erich Korngold's revision, is a superb example of Walter Legge's Philharmonia productions, honeyed and atmospheric. As a sampler, try the jaunty little waltz duet in Act I between Schwarzkopf as the heroine, Annina, and the baritone Erich Kunz as Caramello, normally a tenor role. Nicolai Gedda as the Duke then appropriates the most famous waltz song of all, the *Gondola song*; but with such a frothy production purism would be out of place. The digital remastering preserves the balance of the mono original admirably.

Wiener Blut (complete).
(M) (***) EMI mono CDH7 69529-2 [id.]. Schwarzkopf, Gedda, Köth, Kunz, Loose, Dönch, Philh. Ch. & O, Ackermann.

To have Schwarzkopf at her most ravishing, singing a waltz song based on the tune of *Morning Papers*, is enough enticement for this Philharmonia version of the mid-1950s, showing Walter Legge's flair as a producer at its most compelling. Schwarzkopf was matched by the regular team of Gedda and Kunz and with Emmy Loose and Erika Köth in the secondary soprano roles. The original mono recording was beautifully balanced, and the facelift given here is most tactfully achieved.

Der Zigeunerbaron (The Gypsy Baron): complete.
(M) (***) EMI mono CHS7 69526-2 (2) [id.]. Schwarzkopf, Gedda, Prey, Kunz, Köth, Sinclair, Philh. Ch. & O, Ackermann.

This superb Philharmonia version of *The Gypsy Baron* from the mid-1950s has never been matched in its rich stylishness and polish. Schwarzkopf as the gypsy princess sings radiantly, not least in the heavenly Bullfinch duet (to the melody made famous by MGM as *One day when we were young*). Gedda, still youthful, produces heady tone, and Erich Kunz as the rough pig-breeder gives a vintage *echt*-Viennese performance of the irresistible *Ja, das schreiben und das lesen.* The CD transcription from excellent mono originals gives fresh and truthful sound, particularly in the voices.

Strauss, Richard (1864–1949)

An Alpine Symphony, Op. 64.
(M) *** Decca 417 717-2 [id.]. LAPO, Mehta.

Those wanting a medium-priced version of the *Alpine Symphony* could hardly do better than turn to Mehta, whose performance is among the best Strauss he has given us, and the vintage 1976 recording is successful in combining range and atmosphere with remarkable detail. It is more brightly lit in its digital transfer, but the Decca engineers let every strand of the texture tell without losing sight of the overall perspective. The effect remains spectacular.

Also sprach Zarathustra; Death and transfiguration, Op. 24; Don Juan, Op. 20.
(M) **(*) Decca 417 720-2. VPO, Karajan.

Karajan's earlier Vienna performances of *Also sprach*, *Don Juan* and *Death and transfiguration*, dating from 1959/60, are available on Decca, impressively remastered. The sound of the Vienna orchestra is more leonine than that of the Berlin Philharmonic – see below – but does not lack either body or attack. Indeed the performances of both *Don Juan* and *Death and transfiguration* are among the very finest – the *Don* has great zest and passion. *Also sprach Zarathustra* had an enormously wide dynamic range; only now, some three decades after it was made, does the technology of CD permit its degree of contrast to register without difficulty. Even so, the slightly backward balance means that the *Joys and passions* section does not sound as sumptuous as on the DG recording.

Also sprach Zarathustra; Don Juan; Macbeth, Op. 23.
(M) **(*) Decca Dig. 430 708-2; *430 708-4* [id.]. Detroit SO, Dorati.

Dorati's *Zarathustra* is well played but not so firmly held together as with Karajan. *Macbeth* is a good rather than a distinctive account. It is an early work whose first version appeared in 1887 when Strauss was barely twenty-three; but the composer revised it at the instigation of von Bülow and it was completed in its definitive form after *Don Juan* – hence the later opus number. Dorati's view of *Don Juan* is heroic, the sensuality played down by the sound-balance, brilliant rather than sumptuous. After a central love scene which is tenderly delicate, there is satiety and disillusion at the end. The recording has remarkable clarity of inner detail throughout.

(i) Also sprach Zarathustra; (ii) *Don Juan; Till Eulenspiegel.*
(M) *** Collins Dig. 3002-2 [id.]. LSO, Jacek Kaspszyk.
(M) *** EMI Dig. CDD7 64106-2 [id.]; *ET 764106-4.* (i) Phd. O, Ormandy; (ii) VPO, André Previn.
(M) **(*) Decca 430 445-2; *430 445-4* [id.]. Chicago SO, Solti.

Choice between the new Collins CD and the EMI alternative of this favourite Richard Strauss triptych is not easy. The Collins disc has the advantage of the very finest modern digital recording, with the orchestra set back naturally in a concert-hall acoustic. Perhaps Ormandy's reading of *Zarathustra* is detailed slightly more individually, but Kaspszyk's LSO account has fine breadth and momentum, with the LSO consistently on their toes, and with a memorable contribution from the leader, John Georgiadis, in the violin solos. The strings play with affecting sensuality – radiantly sumptuous when they soar above the stave – and this applies to *Don Juan* too, a performance which combines tenderness and passion with the excitement of the chase. *Till* is portrayed with an enjoyably genial vitality. Detail is wittily observed, the trial and execution scene very dramatic, making the epilogue the more touching. The recording throughout is very much in the demonstration bracket: all Strauss's spectacular effects are extravagantly realized, and the climax of *Also sprach Zarathustra* makes just as powerful an impression as the famous opening. An additional advantage is the nine cues which help the listener to find his or her way around the complex and almost bizarre programmatic content of this work.

Ormandy's 1979 *Also sprach Zarathustra* is one of his very finest records. The performance unleashes enormous ardour and the superb playing of the Philadelphia Orchestra, especially the strings, is consistently gripping in its extrovert passion. Ormandy's reading moves forward in a single sweep from the first bar to the last, yet with the contrasting episodes admirably characterized. This can be spoken of in the same breath as the Karajan versions, although its emotional feeling is more unbridled. The early recording was made in the Old Met., Philadelphia, by EMI engineers, but with JVC equipment; on the original LP it was excessively brightly lit, but the balance has been improved vastly and, although one might cavil over points of detail, there is now no want of opulence. The climax at the very opening is superbly graduated, the sound immensely spectacular, while the closing section, too, is memorably sustained. It is a pity that the internal episodes are unbanded. Previn's *Don Juan* and *Till Eulenspiegel* were made a year later in the Musikverein, and their style is quite different. This was the conductor's first recording with the VPO and plainly their response is wholehearted. But these are not at all Viennese-type performances: they are relatively direct, strong and urgent, rather than affectionate, refreshing rather than idiomatic. The characterization brings memorable moments; the great central love-scene in *Don Juan* has an affecting, languorous sentience and the picaresque detail of *Till*, lightly delineated, has an engaging scherzando quality, with the dramatic closing sequence and its postlude bringing a telling culmination. The sound is full and bright but not as open and brilliant as the Philadelphia recording.

Solti's performances come from analogue originals of the mid-1970s, and the coupling is apt and generous. Solti is ripely expansive in *Also sprach Zarathustra* and throughout there is glorious playing from the Chicago orchestra in peak form. This is Solti at his strongest, with this most Germanic of American orchestras responding as to the manner born. The transfer to CD is impressive, even if the finest digital versions aerate the textures more.

Also sprach Zarathustra; Macbeth.
(M) ** DG Dig. 427 821-2; *427 821-4* [id.]. VPO, Maazel.

The main attraction of Maazel's *Zarathustra* resides in the coupling, *Macbeth*, which is something of a rarity. It is powerful and does not deserve the neglect it suffers in the concert hall. It is played brilliantly here, as is the more famous work. This was one of the earliest of DG's digital recordings (1983), however, and the sound, though well balanced, is very brightly lit. It does not lack spectacle but misses the richness of texture of the finest analogue recordings, nor is it as finely detailed as the best of its current digital rivals.

Also sprach Zarathustra; Till Eulenspiegel; Salome: Salome's dance.
(M) *** DG 415 853-2; *415 853-4* [id.]. BPO, Karajan.

Karajan's 1974 DG version of *Also sprach Zarathustra* is coupled with his vividly characterized performance of *Till Eulenspiegel* plus his powerfully voluptuous account of *Salome's dance*. This account of *Also sprach* has long held sway and generally makes a strong recommendation. The Berlin Philharmonic plays with great fervour (the timpani strokes at the very opening are quite riveting) and creates characteristic body of tone in the strings, although the digital remastering has thrown a much brighter light on the violins, only just short of glare.

Also sprach Zarathustra; (i) *Salome:* final scene.
(M) **(*) EMI Dig. CD-EMX 2153; *TC-EMX 2153.* (i) Ruth Falcon; LPO, Mark Elder.

Mark Elder gives an agreeably unspectacular *Also sprach Zarathustra* – which is not to say unexciting. However, he does not strive after effect or succumb to exaggeration and he secures very opulent sound from the London Philharmonic. An altogether excellent balance too from the recording engineer. However, Ruth Falcon has far too excessive a vibrato to be wholly convincing in the final scene from *Salome*.

Also sprach Zarathustra, Op. 30; (i) *Don Quixote, Op. 35.*
(M) **(*) Sony SBK 47656 [id.]. Phd. O, Ormandy; (i) with Lorne Munroe.
(M) (**) Decca mono 425 974-2 [id.]. (i) Fournier; VPO, Clemens Krauss.

Ormandy's 1963 Sony *Also sprach Zarathustra*, if not so overwhelming as the later, EMI version, has much virtuoso orchestral playing to commend it and many felicities of characterization. There is no trace of vulgarity – apart from what is in the score – but complete fidelity to the composer's intentions. His (1961) *Don Quixote* will also give considerable pleasure. There is little of the strident edge that used to disfigure the Philadelphia strings on CBS LPs of the 1960s and, although there are more sumptuous recordings on the market, the Sony remastering is more than acceptable. There is some marvellous orchestral playing and the two soloists play splendidly with plenty of character but without the 'star soloist' approach favoured by so many record companies. A very competitive coupling – perhaps not a first choice, but very good value for money and thoroughly enjoyable.

The Fournier/Clemens Krauss *Don Quixote* was recorded in 1953 and, along with the somewhat earlier Tortelier/Beecham version on HMV, long reigned supreme in the catalogue. Deryck Cooke was particularly vocal in its praises in an *'Interpretations on Record'* broadcast in the mid-1960s – and rightly so. It has great humanity and psychological insight. The sound is a vast improvement on a dreadfully tizzy cassette transfer that appeared in the 1970s, though the strings are still wanting in bloom. Memories of the original yellow-label LXT may be deceptive, but one wonders whether it was as fierce and forward as this seems to be. Clemens Krauss's account of *Also sprach Zarathustra* comes from the days when this piece was a rarity both on record and in the concert hall. The work cries out for the opulent sound of modern stereo and, excellent though this 1950 performance was, it is unlikely to satisfy the younger collector on this count. All the same, the *Don Quixote* is something special.

Aus Italien, Op. 16; Die Liebe der Danae (symphonic fragment); *Der Rosenkavalier: waltz sequence No. 2.*
(BB) *** Naxos Dig. 8.550342 [id.]. Slovak PO, Zdenék Košler.

A very well-recorded and vividly detailed account of *Aus Italien* with an excellent sense of presence. The orchestra plays very well for Zdenék Košler both here and in the ten-minute symphonic fragment Clemens Krauss made from *Die Liebe der Danae* and in the *Rosenkavalier* waltz sequence. The Slovak Philharmonic is a highly responsive body, with cultured strings and wind departments and, given the quality of the recorded sound, this represents a real bargain.

Le bourgeois gentilhomme (suite), *Op. 60:* excerpts; (i) *Don Quixote, Op. 35.*
(M) (***) EMI mono CDH7 63106-2. (i) Tortelier; RPO, Beecham.

Tortelier and Beecham recorded their *Don Quixote* in 1947 during Strauss's visit to London. The playing is pretty electrifying, with the newly formed RPO on their best form. Tortelier had performed the work under Strauss himself and here plays for all the world as if his life depended on it. There is great delicacy in *Le bourgeois gentilhomme* and some delicious playing from the RPO's then leader, Oscar Lampe.

(i) *Horn concertos Nos. 1 in E flat, Op. 11; 2 in E flat;* (ii) *Oboe concerto in D;* (iii) *Duet concertino for clarinet, bassoon, strings and harp.*
(M) *** EMI CDM7 69661-2. (i) Peter Damm; (ii) Manfred Clement; (iii) Manfred Weise, Wolfgang Liebscher; Dresden State O, Kempe.

Peter Damm's performances of the *Horn concertos* are second to none and although his use of a (judicious) degree of vibrato may be a drawback for some ears, his tone is gloriously rich. The big striding theme at the centre of the *Andante* of No. 1 is superbly expansive, and the articulation in the finales of both *Concertos* is joyously deft and nimble. Similarly, while Manfred Clement's *Oboe concerto* is a sensitive reading, his creamily full timbre may not appeal to those brought up on Goossens. There can be no reservations whatsoever about the *Duet concertino*, where the sounds from bassoon and clarinet are beguilingly succulent, while the intertwining of both wind soloists with the dancing orchestral violins of the finale has an irresistible, genial finesse. Throughout, the superb playing of the Dresden orchestra adds an extra dimension to the music-making. Kempe's benign control of the music's ebb and flow shows him always a warmly understanding Straussian. The remastered recording, made in the Dresden Lukaskirche, retains an agreeable ambient glow which greatly pleases the ear.

Oboe concerto.
(M) *** BMG/RCA Dig. GD 87989. John de Lancie, CO, Max Wilcox – FRANÇAIX: *L'horloge de flore* *** ❀; IBERT: *Symphonie concertante.* ***

In the summer of 1945 a young American musician/GI (who before the war had been an oboist with the Pittsburgh Symphony Orchestra) was stationed in the Bavarian Alps; on several occasions he visited the ageing Richard Strauss at his home in Garmisch-Partenkirchen (a photo within the notes of this CD records the meeting). He suggested that Strauss write an oboe concerto, and only months later the eighty-one-year-old composer produced his famous work and, mixing up the cities, inscribed the score as 'inspired by an American soldier (oboist from Chicago)'. That same oboist, John de Lancie, recorded it in 1987, playing persuasively and with much finesse. The chamber accompaniment could ideally sound riper, but the balance is realistic and the sound real.

(i) *Oboe concerto; Metamorphosen for 23 solo strings;* (ii) *4 Last songs (Vier letzte Lieder).*
(M) **(*) DG 423 888-2 [id.]. (i) Koch; (ii) Janowitz; BPO, Karajan.

Karajan's 1971 account of the *Metamorphosen*

is self-recommending, and it sounds excellent in its remastered format, full yet better defined. In the *Four last songs* Gundula Janowitz produces a beautiful flow of creamy soprano tone, at the same time leaving the music's deeper and more subtle emotions underexposed. Lothar Koch's oboe timbre is creamy, too: he is forwardly balanced, but Karajan's accompaniment is relatively athletic, emphasizing the neoclassical style rather than the pastoral implications.

Death and transfiguration, Op. 24.
(M) (***) BMG/RCA mono GD 60312. Phd. O, Toscanini – TCHAIKOVSKY: *Symphony No. 6.* (***)

Toscanini's characteristically taut control of tension goes with what was for him a more warmly expressive style than usual, thanks to the influence of the Philadelphia Orchestra. With the transfer giving good body to the limited sound, it is comparable with his equally intense reading of Tchaikovsky's *Pathétique* from the same period.

Death and Transfiguration; Don Juan; Till Eulenspiegel.
(M) *** DG Dig. 429 492-2; *429 492-4*. LSO, Abbado.
(BB) ** Naxos Dig. 8.550250 [id.]. Slovak PO, Zdeněk Košler.

The performances under Claudio Abbado have plenty of dash and their brilliance is tempered with sensitivity. Some may feel that *Don Juan* veers too much towards the exuberant showpiece and vehicle for display, but both this and *Till Eulenspiegel* must be numbered among the best available. *Death and Transfiguration* has a marvellously spacious opening. The strings produce some splendidly silky tone and there is much sensitive wind playing too. Compared with the Philips Concertgebouw sound for Haitink, the DG upper range is less smoothly natural, but Abbado's CD now has a price advantage.

Anyone impulsively picking up Košler's record of Strauss's three favourite symphonic poems may be surprised at how enjoyable it is. The Slovak Philharmonic Orchestra cannot match Abbado and the LSO in dash and brilliance, but their voluptuously relaxed, sentient feeling in *Don Juan* and the powerful atmosphere at the close of *Death and transfiguration* give the readings plenty of character, even if Košler's structural grip is rather loose. Similarly, the Bratislava solo horn opens *Till* most personably, and the work's picaresque detail is observed with pleasing geniality, but the powerful execution scene at the close is prepared rather too broadly. The digital recording makes a fine impact here, and the warm acoustic ambience of the Reduta Hall, Bratislava, gives a pleasing opulence to the Straussian textures. Haitink's outstanding Philips record of these three masterpieces should be returning to the catalogue at mid-price soon; when it does, it will constitute a clear first recommendation.

Death and transfiguration; Don Juan; Metamorphosen for 23 solo strings; Salome: Dance of the 7 veils.
(M) *** EMI CDM7 63350-2 [id.]. Philh. O, Klemperer.

This generous CD admirably assembles Klemperer's Richard Strauss recordings in convenient form. In his hands it is the *Metamorphosen* and *Death and transfiguration* that excite the greatest admiration. With Klemperer the work for strings has a ripeness that exactly fits Strauss's last essay for orchestra, while *Death and transfiguration* is invested with a nobility too rarely heard in this work. Not everyone will respond to Klemperer's spacious treatment of the other works. His account of *Salome's dance* is splendidly sensuous and *Don Juan* is clearly seen as 'the idealist in search of perfect womanhood'. But with marvellous Philharmonia playing and a recording (made in the Kingsway Hall in 1960/61) which still sounds full-bodied and in the case of *Metamorphosen* has added refinement of detail, this collection is certainly not lacking in strength of characterization.

Death and transfiguration; Don Juan; Salome: Dance of the 7 veils.
(BB) *** BMG/RCA Dig. VD 60135 [60135-2-RV]. Dallas SO, Mata.

The sound of this bargain CD approaches the demonstration class and it is undoubtedly excellent value. These three works are all brilliantly played and, if Mata's reading of *Death and transfiguration* does not quite match Karajan's or Klemperer's, this inexpensive CD still gives considerable satisfaction.

(i) *Don Juan, Op. 20; Till Eulenspiegel;* (ii) *Duet concertino for clarinet and bassoon.*
(B) **(*) Hung. White Label HRC 082 [id.]. (i) Budapest SO, Kobayashi; (ii) Berkes, Fülemile, Budapest PO, Kórodi.

On Hungaroton White Label a spirited *Don Juan* from Kobayashi, while András Kórodi conducts a very sensitive and sympathetic account of the late *Duet concertino* with Kálmán Berkes and Tibor Fülemile as soloists. There are some occasional moments of self-consciousness in *Till Eulenspiegel* but they are few and do not detract from the rather strong impression this performance makes. Of course, as playing this offers no challenge to the Karajan DG mid-price CDs but, taken on its own merits, the disc will give pleasure, especially as the analogue sound is very good indeed, with a very natural balance and back-to-front perspective.

(i) *Don Quixote, Op. 35; Death and transfiguration.*
(M) *** DG 429 184-2 [id.]. (i) Fournier; BPO, Karajan.

Karajan's 1966 recording of *Don Quixote* sounds new-minted in its remastered CD format. Detail is clarified, while there is plenty of body to the sound, and the analogue ambience remains highy effective. Fournier's partnership with Karajan is outstanding. His portrayal of the Don has no less nobility than previous rivals and compares well with more recent versions. He brings great subtlety and (when required) repose to the part. The finale and Don Quixote's death are very moving in Fournier's hands, while Karajan's handling of orchestral detail is quite splendid. Although Fournier is forwardly balanced, in every other respect the recording is of DG's very finest quality and (given its price) this can be strongly recommended, more particularly since the disc includes Karajan's superlative 1973 analogue version of *Death and transfiguration*, which still remains a showpiece among his earlier Strauss recordings with the Berlin Philharmonic. Textures sound leaner than originally, but the quality is both vivid and refined in detail.

Don Quixote, Op. 35; Salome (opera): *Salome's dance.*
(B) *** Hung. White Label HRC 081 [id.]. Perényi, Hungarian State O, János Ferencsik.

János Ferencsik was a much underrated conductor and his account of *Don Quixote*, with Miklós Perényi and László Bársony as the excellent soloists and the Hungarian State Orchestra, can be recommended with confidence. It is in the old, humane tradition of conductors like Clemens Krauss and Rudolf Kempe, full of human insights and with orchestral virtuosity worn lightly. The sound is very good indeed and, though both the sleeve and label give a 1988 recording date (Ferencsik died in 1984!) and nowhere declares its exact provenance – perhaps late 1970s – there need be no worries on sonic grounds. It does not displace the Fournier and Karajan partnership but can be recommended alongside that fine version.

Ein Heldenleben, Op. 40.
(M) *** Ph. 432 276-2; *432 276-4*. Concg. O, Haitink – ELGAR: *Enigma variations.* **
(M) *** EMI CDM7 63299-2. RPO, Beecham – LISZT: *Orpheus* etc. ***

Ein Heldenleben; Don Juan, Op. 20.
(M) *** DG 429 717-2 [id.]. BPO, Karajan.

Ein Heldenleben; Macbeth.
(M) *** EMI CDM7 69171-2. Dresden State O, Kempe.

Haitink's 1970 version of *Ein Heldenleben* is one of his finest records. He gives just the sort of performance, brilliant and swaggering but utterly without bombast, which will delight those who normally resist this rich and expansive work. With a direct and fresh manner that yet conveys consistent urgency, he gives a performance that makes even such fine rival versions as Karajan's 1959 recording sound just a little lightweight. In the culminating fulfilment theme, a gentle, lyrical 6/8, Haitink finds a raptness in restraint, a hint of agony within joy, that links the passage directly with the great Trio from *Der Rosenkavalier*. The Philips sound is admirably faithful and skilfully remastered. By any standards, the Haitink reissue is a splendid record, even if its Elgar coupling has less concentration and dynamism.

Karajan's 1959 *Heldenleben* on DG still sounds amazingly fresh. It is a superb performance, and at mid-price it can certainly be recommended, in harness with *Don Juan*. Playing of great power and distinction emanates from the Berlin Philharmonic and, in the closing section, an altogether becoming sensuousness and warmth. The remastering has plenty of ambient atmosphere, combined with excellent detail; *Don Juan*, made over a decade later, brings only a marginal difference in body and none in breadth.

Beecham's valedictory *Heldenleben* sounds fabulous. He liked to work on a large scale and his 1961 performance is immensely vigorous but tender and sensuous when the music calls for it. There is also a marvellously unforced sense of naturalness in the phrasing, together with refined playing from strings and wind and an excellent solo contribution from the leader, Steven Staryk. The recording is quite full and has a transparency of texture inherent in the original balance. Beecham's magic exercises its own special pull and this reissue is a classic of the gramophone, splendidly remastered and not to be missed, particularly at its competitive price.

Rudolf Kempe's classic account of *Ein Heldenleben* is a noble performance in the grand manner, and the recording strikes the proper balance between richness of tone and analysis of detail. Its claims on the collector are strengthened by the fill-up, a strongly characterized account of *Macbeth*, a reading that has never been bettered on record.

Metamorphosen for 23 solo strings.
(M) **(*) Decca 430 002-2. ASMF, Marriner – SCHOENBERG: *Verklaerte Nacht* **(*); WEBERN: *5 Movements.* ***

Marriner's version is not as strongly characterized as Karajan's full-priced digital account, but it is finely played, although the CD transfer brings a touch of shrillness to the upper range of the otherwise excellent and certainly clear 1968 recording.

Sinfonia domestica, Op. 53.
(M) *** EMI CDM7 69571-2. BPO, Karajan.

Sinfonia domestica; (i) *Death and transfiguration.*
(M) *** BMG/RCA stereo/mono GD 60388 [60388-2-RG]. Chicago SO; (i) (mono) RCA Victor O; Fritz Reiner.

Strauss's much-maligned *Sinfonia domestica* is quite admirably served by this mid-priced CD of Karajan's 1973 recording. The playing is stunningly good and the Berlin strings produce tone of great magnificence. The remastered recording demonstrates the wide range of the original; detail is better focused and the ambient atmosphere remains.

Reiner's account of the *Sinfonia domestica* comes from 1956, the earliest days of stereo, and is a wonderful performance, a reading of stature, worthy to rank alongside the Karajan alternative. The Chicago orchestra play with warmth and virtuosity; the recording is inevitably lacking a little in upper range, but it still sounds remarkably good for its age. *Death and transfiguration* is a 1950 mono recording, and it was perverse of RCA not to include his marvellous 1957 Vienna Philharmonic version (in surprisingly good stereo even now).

Till Eulenspiegel.
(M) (***) DG mono 427 783-2 [id.]. BPO, Wilhelm Furtwängler – RAVEL: *Daphnis et Chloé*; SIBELIUS: *En Saga.* (***)

Furtwängler's excellence as a Strauss conductor is well known, and this wartime performance is well worth hearing. It comes with quite magical accounts of Ravel's *Daphnis et Chloé suite* and Sibelius's *En Saga.*

VOCAL MUSIC

Lieder: *Des Dichters Abendgang; Freundliche Vision; Heimliche Aufforderung; Ich trage meine Minne; Liebeshymnus; Morgen!; Das Rosenband; Ständchen; Traum durch die Dämmerung; Verführung; Waldseligkeit; Zueignung.*
(M) (***) Ph. Dig. 432 614-2; *432 614-4.* Siegfried Jerusalem, Leipzig GO, Masur.

Starting with an account of *Heimliche Aufforderung* that is both heroic and glowingly beautiful, Siegfried Jerusalem's collection of Strauss Lieder in orchestral arrangements provides a male counterpart to Jessye Norman's magnificent (full-price) disc, also recorded with Masur and the Leipzig Gewandhaus Orchestra. The shading of tone which Jerusalem commands is most sensitive, as in *Morgen* or a delicate rendering of *Ständchen.* Naturally balanced recording, warmly reverberant to bring out the ravishing beauty of Strauss's orchestrations. However, the reissue has no documentation whatsoever apart from a list of titles, and it is quite unforgivable that Philips should issue an important recital of this kind without translations.

Deutsche Motette, Op. 62; Hymne, Op. 34/1.
(M) *** Decca 430 365-2; *430 365-4* [id.]. Cash, Temperley, Evans, Varcoe, Schütz Ch. of L., Norrington – BRUCKNER: *Mass No. 2.* ***

Strauss, usually the most business-like and practical of composers, made these unaccompanied choral pieces so difficult for any choir to sing that they have been almost totally neglected. The *German motet*, with sixteen chorus lines, has the sopranos soaring to top D flat and staying there, while at one point the basses go down to bottom B, and the shifting harmonies make one's head reel. The *Hymn*, too, is written in sixteen parts and has a remarkably expressive range. But what matters is that, in superb performances like these, the music is richly poetic, quite distinctive within the whole choral repertory, with glowing reminders of some of Strauss's loveliest music. The CD transfer confirms the gloriously rich quality of the (originally Argo) recording.

8 Lieder, Op. 10; 5 Lieder, Op. 15; 6 Lieder, Op. 17; 6 Lieder, Op. 19; Schlichte Weisen, Op. 21; Mädchenblumen, Op. 22; 2 Lieder, Op. 26; 4 Lieder, Op. 27; Lieder, Op. 29/1 & 3; 3 Lieder, Op. 31; Stiller Gang, Op. 31/4; 5 Lieder, Op. 32; Lieder, Op. 36/1–4; Lieder, Op. 37/1–3 & 5–6; 5 Lieder, Op. 39; Lieder, Op. 41/2–5; Gesänge älterer deutscher Dichter, Op. 43/1 & 3; 5 Gedichte, Op. 46; 5 Lieder, Op. 47; 5 Lieder, Op. 48; Lieder, Op. 49/1 & 2; 4–6; 6 Lieder, Op. 56; Krämerspiegel, Op. 66; Lieder, Op. 67/4–6; Lieder, Op. 68/1 & 4; 5 kleine Lieder, Op. 69; Gesänge des Orients, Op. 77; Lieder, Op. 88/1–2; Lieder ohne Opuszahl.
(M) *** EMI CMS7 63995-2 (6). Dietrich Fischer-Dieskau, Gerald Moore.

Fischer-Dieskau and Moore made these recordings of the 134 Strauss songs suitable for a man's voice between 1967 and 1970, tackling them in roughly chronological order. With both artists at their very peak, the results are endlessly imaginative, and the transfers are full and immediate, giving fine presence to the voice. Compared with the later recordings of many of these songs which Fischer-Dieskau recorded for DG with Wolfgang Sawallisch accompanying, these readings are less volatile and more intimate, with the voice a degree fresher and sweeter. As in the original LP set, the booklet contains full texts and translations, as well as a perceptive essay by the singer on Strauss and his songs; yet it would have been helpful to have had a more detailed chronology of the songs.

Four Last songs (Vier letzte Lieder); Arabella: excerpts; *Ariadne auf Naxos: Ariadne's lament; Capriccio:* Closing scene.
(M) (**) Decca mono 425 959-2 [id.]. Lisa della Casa, VPO, Boehm, Moralt, Hollreiser.

Lisa della Casa with her creamily beautiful soprano was a radiant Straussian, as these precious excerpts demonstrate. Her account of the *Four Last songs* (given in the original order, not that usually adopted) has a commanding nobility. *Ariadne's lament* also receives a heartfelt performance, soaring to a thrilling climax, and the *Arabella* duets with Gueden, Schoeffler and Poell are hauntingly tender. When these recordings appeared in the early and mid-1950s they were always contrasted with those of Elisabeth Schwarzkopf, and so they must be now, when EMI's Schwarzkopf issue in the Références series not only has the *Four Last songs* but the same three duets from *Arabella* and the Closing scene from *Capriccio*. Consistently Schwarzkopf is the more animated, della Casa the more restrained. Sadly, in the transfer the Decca historic issue falls far short of the EMI, with the voice not as forward and vivid, and with the orchestra shrill and papery, lacking the body of the original LPs.

(i) *Four Last songs*. (ii) *Arabella* (opera): excerpts. (i) *Capriccio* (opera): Closing scene.
(M) (***) EMI mono CDH7 61001-2 [id.]. Elisabeth Schwarzkopf, (i) Philh. O, Ackermann; (ii) Metternich, Gedda, Philh. O, Von Matačić.

Schwarzkopf's 1953 version of the *Four Last songs* comes on the mid-price Références label with both its original coupling, the closing scene from *Capriccio*, also recorded in 1953, and the four major excerpts from *Arabella* which she recorded two years later. The *Four Last songs* are here less reflective, less sensuous, than in Schwarzkopf's later version with Szell, but the more flowing speeds and the extra tautness and freshness of voice bring equally illuminating performances. Fascinatingly, this separate account of the *Capriccio* scene is even more ravishing than the one in the complete set, and the sound is even fuller, astonishing for its period.

OPERA

Die Ägyptische Helena (complete).
(M) **(*) Decca 430 381-2 (2) [id.]. Dame Gwyneth Jones, Hendricks, Kastu, Detroit SO, Dorati.

Last of the six operas in which Strauss collaborated with Hugo von Hofmannsthal, this grand classical extravaganza was initially designed as a vehicle for the glamorous soprano Maria Jeritza (famous above all for her provocative Tosca) and the tenor, Richard Tauber. Hofmannsthal's device of mingling two Helen legends has an element of jokiness in it, but Ancient Greece, as so often with Strauss, prompted some heavyweight orchestral writing (echoes of *Elektra*), and Dorati, using the original Dresden version of the score, draws magnificent sounds from the Detroit orchestra, richly and forwardly recorded. The vocal sounds are less consistently pleasing. Gwyneth Jones has her squally moments as Helen, though it is a commanding performance. Matti Kastu manages as well as any Heldentenor today in the role of Menelaus, strained at times but with a pleasing and distinctive timbre. The others too are not always helped by the closeness, but this remains a richly enjoyable as well as a valuable set.

Ariadne auf Naxos (complete).
❀ (M) (***) EMI mono CMS7 69296-2 (2) [Ang. CDMB 69296]. Schwarzkopf, Schock, Rita Streich, Dönch, Seefried, Cuenod, Philh. O, Karajan.

Elisabeth Schwarzkopf makes a radiant, deeply moving Ariadne, giving as bonus a delicious little portrait of the Prima Donna in the Prologue. Rita Streich was at her most dazzling in the coloratura of Zerbinetta's aria and, in partnership with the harlequinade characters, sparkles engagingly. But it is Irmgard Seefried who gives perhaps the supreme performance of all as the Composer, exceptionally beautiful of tone, conveying a depth and intensity rarely if ever matched. Rudolf Schock is a fine Bacchus, strained less than most, and the team of theatrical characters includes such stars as Hugues Cuenod as the Dancing Master. The fine pacing and delectably pointed ensemble add to the impact of a uniquely perceptive Karajan interpretation. Though in mono and with the orchestral sound a little dry, the voices come out superbly. Though the absence of a translation in the libretto is to be regretted, the many index-points on CD, cued to the synopsis, can be used almost as easily as a translation alongside the original German words.

Elektra (complete).
(M) ** DG 431 737-2 (2) [id.]. Madeira, Borkh, Schech, Uhl, Fischer-Dieskau, Dresden State Op. Ch. & State O, Boehm.

The voices in this 1960 recording, made in the helpful acoustic of the Lukaskirche in Dresden, have warmth and immediacy, underlining the power of Inge Borkh, tough in the title-role with an apt touch of rawness, of Jean Madeira as Klytemnestra, firm and positive, and of Dietrich Fischer-Dieskau, incomparable as Orestes. Their contributions are very vivid; but the distancing of the orchestra, and with it the relative thinness of the strings, means that a vital element in this violent opera is underplayed. Such great moments as the recognition scene between Elektra and Orestes and the orchestral comment at the end of Elektra's great solo on the word '*Seliger*' ('Happier') fail to have the impact they should. The clarity of CD with its full body of sound brings an improvement on the original LPs, but Karl Boehm's masterly timing in this opera deserves to have a more substantial showing. The only weakness to note in the cast is the Chrysothemis of Marianne Schech, thin and unsteady and with touches of shrillness.

(i) *Elektra* (complete); (ii; iii) *Salome* (final scene – 2 versions).
(M) (***) Standing Room Only mono SRO 833-2 (2). (i) Nilsson, Rysanek, Resnik, Windgassen, VPO, Boehm; (ii) Rysanek, Varnay, Hopf, O, Leitner; (iii) Nilsson, Bergstrom, Henriksen, O, Ehrling – WAGNER: *Walküre:* excerpts. (**)

The main work on this Standing Room Only set is a live recording of *Elektra* made at the Vienna State Opera in December 1965. It is a superb performance with an almost incomparable cast and with Boehm even more intense and electrifying than in his studio recording, now reissued by DG. The broadcast sound is limited but very forward and vivid, with voices sounding immediate. The oddity is that Nilsson's vibrato makes her tone warmer than usual, with none of her characteristic 'hoot', suggesting in places that this role may be misatttributed. Yet no possible rival is likely to have sung the part with such precision and brilliance. The climactic moment of her solo, following the Recognition scene, brings an ecstatic moment on the word '*Seliger*', with a perfectly controlled crescendo. The first two of the three fill-ups are devoted to live recordings of the closing scene from *Salome*, with Rysanek at her finest with Leitner in 1974, and the young Nilsson already powerful but less detailed in Stockholm with Ehrling in 1953. The briefer Wagner items make up an exceptionally generous coupling.

(i) *Elektra: Soliloquy; Recognition scene; Finale. Salome: Dance of the seven veils; Finale.*
(M) *** BMG/RCA GD 60874 [60874-2-RG]. Inge Borkh, Chicago SO, Fritz Reiner; (i) with Schoeffler, Yeend, Chicago Lyric Theatre Ch.

Inge Borkh never sang *Elektra* at the Met., but this 40-minute group of excerpts, made in 1956, gives a tantalizing indication of what such a performance might have been like. With Borkh singing superbly in the title-role alongside Paul Schoeffler and Francis Yeend, this is a real collectors' piece. Reiner provides a superbly telling accompaniment; the performance of the Recognition scene and final duet are as ripely passionate as Beecham's old 78-r.p.m. excerpts and outstrip the complete versions. By no means does the balance project the singers at the expense of orchestral detail, and the orchestral sound is thrillingly rich, the brass superbly expansive. The CD transfer again confirms the glory of the Chicago acoustics during the Reiner era. For the reissue, Reiner's full-blooded account of *Salome's dance* has been added, and Borkh is comparably memorable in the finale scene. Here the 1955 recording is slightly less sumptuous, the voice less flattered on top, but the sound is still characteristically full and vivid. No Straussian should miss this disc.

Die Frau ohne Schatten (complete).
(M) ** Decca 425 981-2 (3) [id.]. Rysanek, Loose, Hopf, Terkal, Höngen, Böhme, V. State Op. Ch., VPO, Boehm.

This 1955 recording is reissued in Decca's Historical series, but it is an example of very early stereo, thanks to a rescue attempt from the original master-tape made by the recording manager, Christopher Raeburn. With the exception of Leonie Rysanek as the Empress, the singing on the Decca set is variable, with a high proportion of wobblers among the soloists, and Hans Hopf often producing coarse tone as the Emperor. However, once one accepts the strange symbolism of Hofmannsthal's libretto, one can go on to appreciate the richness of Strauss's inspiration, a score utterly different from anything else he ever did, in many ways more ambitious. It is a work that deserves the closest attention of Straussians and many may feel tempted to try this version, in spite of its vocal limitations, for it is above all Boehm's set, and his direction is masterly. The recording is remarkably good for its period.

Der Rosenkavalier (complete).
(M) (**(*)) Decca mono 425 950-2 (3) [id.].

Reining, Weber, Jurinac, Gueden, V. State Op. Ch., VPO, Erich Kleiber.

Decca's set with Erich Kleiber was the first ever complete recording of *Rosenkavalier*, and it has long enjoyed cult status. It has many glories, quite apart from the inspired conducting of Kleiber senior. Sena Jurinac is a charming Octavian, strong and sympathetic, and Hilde Gueden a sweetly characterful Sophie, not just a wilting innocent. Ludwig Weber characterizes deliciously in a very Viennese way as Ochs; but the disappointment is the Marschallin of Maria Reining, very plain and lacking intensity, even in the great scene with Octavian at the end of Act I. She is not helped by Kleiber's refusal to linger; with the singers recorded close, the effect of age on what was once a fine voice is very clear, even in the opening solo of the culminating trio. And though the Vienna Philharmonic responds in the most idiomatic way to the waltz rhythms, ensemble is not good, with even the prelude to Act I a muddle. One recalls the notorious castigation of the VPO in rehearsal, when George Szell returned to conduct this opera after the war: 'Gentlemen, you do not seem to know this score!' On that prelude more than anywhere, the CD transfer brings out a shrillness and lack of body in the orchestral sound, though voices are well caught. On three mid-price CDs, one per Act, this remains a classic set.

Der Rosenkavalier: highlights.
(M) *** EMI CDM7 63452-2; *EG 763452-4*. Schwarzkopf, Ludwig, Stich-Randall, Edelmann, Waechter, Philh. Ch. & O, Karajan.

On EMI we are offered the Marschallin's monologue to the end of Act I (25 minutes); the Presentation of the silver rose and finale from Act II; and the Duet and Closing scene, with the Trio from Act III, flawlessly and gloriously sung and transferred most beautifully to CD.

Salome (complete).
(M) *** BMG/RCA GD 86644 (2) [6644-2-RG]. Caballé, Richard Lewis, Resnik, Milnes, LSO, Leinsdorf.

Montserrat Caballé's formidable account of the role of Salome was recorded in 1968, utterly different from that of Birgit Nilsson on Decca and much closer to the personification of Behrens on the Karajan set on EMI (both at full price). For some listeners Caballé might seem too gentle, but in fact the range of her emotions is even wider than that of Nilsson. There are even one or two moments of fantasy, where for an instant one has the girlish skittishness of Salome revealed like an evil inverted picture of Sophie. As for the vocalization, it is superb, with glorious golden tone up to the highest register and never the slightest hesitation in attack. Lewis, Resnik and Milnes make a supporting team that matches the achievement of the Decca rivals, while Leinsdorf is inspired to some of his warmest and most sympathetic conducting on record. The sound has not the pin-point atmosphere of the Decca, but is nearer to the EMI set in its fullness and vivid projection. The price advantage, too, makes this well worth considering.

Salome: Dance of the 7 veils; Closing scene. Lieder: *Cäcilie; Ich liebe dich; Morgen; Wiegenlied; Zueignung.*
(M) **(*) DG 431 171-2 [id.]. Caballé, Fr. Nat. O, Bernstein – BOITO: *Mefistofele.* **(*)

One of Caballé's earliest and most refreshingly imaginative opera sets was Strauss's *Salome* with Leinsdorf conducting. This version of the final scene, recorded over a decade later with a very different conductor, has much of the same imagination, the sweet and innocent girl still observable next to the bloodthirsty fiend. The remainder of the recital is less recommendable, partly because Caballé underlines the expressiveness of works that remain Lieder even with the orchestral accompaniment. Bernstein too directs an over-weighted account of the *Dance of the seven veils.* The recording is warm and full.

Arias from: *Die Ägyptische Helena; Ariadne auf Naxos; Die Frau ohne Schatten; Guntram; Der Rosenkavalier; Salome.*
(M) *** RCA GD 60398; *GK 60398* [60398-2-RG; *60398-4-RG*]. Leontyne Price, Boston SO or New Philh. O, Leinsdorf; LSO, Cleva.

Leontyne Price gives generous performances of an unusually rich collection of Strauss scenes and solos, strongly accompanied by Leinsdorf (or Cleva in *Ariadne*), always at his finest in Strauss. Recorded between 1965 and 1973, Price was still at her peak, even if occasionally the voice grows raw under stress in Strauss's heavier passages. It is particularly good to have rarities as well as such regular favourites as the Marschallin's monologue from *Rosenkavalier*, the closing scene from *Salome* and Ariadne's lament. Among the luscious items are the solos from *Guntram* and *Die Ägyptische Helena* and the Empress's awakening from *Die Frau ohne Schatten*, one of the finest of all the performances here.

Stravinsky, Igor (1882–1971)

The Stravinsky edition: Volume 1, Ballets, etc.: (i) *The Firebird;* (i) *Fireworks;* (iii) *Histoire du soldat;* (i) *Pétrushka;* (iv, iii) *Renard the fox;* (i) *The Rite of spring;* (i) *Scherzo à la russe;* (ii)

Scherzo fantastique; (v) *The Wedding* (*Les Noces).*

Volume 2, Ballets etc.: (vi) *Agon;* (i) *Apollo;* (i) *Le baiser de la fee;* (i) *Bluebird (pas de deux);* (vii) *Jeux de cartes;* (viii) *Orphée;* (ix, i) *Pulchinella;* (ii) *Scènes de ballet.*

Volume 3, Ballet suites: (i) *Firebird; Pétrouchka; Pulchinella.*

Volume 4, Symphonies: (i) *Symphony in E;* (ii) *Symphony in C;* (i) *Symphony in 3 movements;* (x, ii) *Symphony of Psalms;* (i) Stravinsky in rehearsal: *Apollo; Piano concerto; Pulchinella; Sleeping beauty; Symphony in C; 3 Souvenirs.*

Volume 5, Concertos: (xi, i) *Capriccio for piano and orchestra* (with Robert Craft); *Concerto for piano and wind;* (xii, i) *Movements for piano and orchestra;* (xiii, i) *Violin concerto in D.*

Volume 6, Miniatures: (i) *Circus polka; Concerto in D for string orchestra; Concerto in E flat for chamber orchestra;* (ii) *4 Études for orchestra;* (i) *Greeting prelude;* (ii) *8 Instrumental miniatures; 4 Norwegian moods; Suites Nos. 1–2 for small orchestra.*

Volume 7, Chamber music and historical recordings: (iii) *Concertino for 12 instruments;* (xiv, xv) *Concerto for 2 solo pianos;* (xv, xvi) *Duo concertant for violin and piano;* (xvii, xviii) *Ebony Concerto (for clarinet and big band);* (iii) *Octet for wind;* (xix, iii) *Pastorale for violin and wind quartet;* (xv) *Piano rag music;* (xviii) *Preludium;* (xx, iii) *Ragtime* (for 11 instruments); (xv) *Serenade in A;* (iii) *Septet;* (xii) *Sonata for piano;* (xxi) *Sonata for 2 pianos;* (xviii) *Tango;* (xxii) *Wind symphonies.*

Volume 8, Operas and songs: (xxiii, iii) *Cat's cradle songs;* (xxiii, xxiv) *Elegy for J. F. K.;* (xxv, ii) *Faun and shepherdess;* (xxvi,iii) *In memoriam Dylan Thomas;* (xxvii, iii) *3 Japanese Lyrics* (with Robert Craft); (xxvii, xxix) *The owl and the pussycat;* (xxvii, iii) *2 poems by K. Bal'mont;* (xxx, i) *2 poems of Paul Verlaine;* (xxiii,i) *Pribaoutki (peasant songs);* (xxiii, i) *Recollections of my childhood;* (xxviii, xxxi) *4 Russian songs;* (xxxvii) *4 Russian peasant songs;* (xxiii, iii) *3 songs from William Shakespeare;* (xxvii, i) *Tilim-Bom (3 stories for children);* (xxxii) *Mavra;* (xxxiii) *The Nightingale.*

Volume 9: (xxxiv) *The Rake's progress.*

Volume 10, Oratorio and melodrama: (xxxv, i) *The Flood* (with Robert Craft); (i) *Monumentum pro Gesualdo di Venosa (3 madrigals recomposed for instruments);* (vii) *Ode;* (xxxvi) *Oedipus Rex;* (xxxvii, xxxviii, i) *Perséphone.*

Volume 11, Sacred works: (x) *Anthem (the dove descending breaks the air);* (x) *Ave Maria;* (xxxix, x, i) *Babel;* (xxviii, xxvi, x, iii) *Cantata;* (xl) *Canticum sacrum;* (x, ii) *Credo;* (x, iii) *Introitus (T. S. Eliot in Memoriam);* (xli) *Mass;* (x, i) *Pater noster;* (xlii, i) *A Sermon, a narrative & a prayer;* (xliii, i) *Threni;* (x, i) *Chorale: Variations on: Vom Himmel hoch, da komm ich her* (arr.); *Zvezdoliki.*

Volume 12, Robert Craft conducts: (xliv, i) *Abraham and Isaac;* (iii) *Danses concertantes;* (xlv) *Double canon: Raoul Dufy in memoriam;* (xlvi) *Epitaphium;* (i) *Le chant du rossignol* (symphonic poem); (i) *Orchestral variations: Aldous Huxley in memoriam;* (xlvii) *Requiem canticles;* (i) *Song of the nightingale (symphonic poem).*

(M) *** Sony SX 22K 46290 (22) [id.]. (i) Columbia SO; (ii) CBC SO; (iii) Columbia CO; (iv) Shirley, Driscoll, Gramm, Koves; (v) Allen, Sarfaty, Driscoll, Samuel Barber, Aaron Copland, Lukas Foss, Roger Sessions, American Chamber Ch., Hills, Columbia Percussion Ens.; (vi) Los Angeles Festival SO; (vii) Cleveland O; (viii) Chicago SO; (ix) Jordan, Shirley, Gramm; (x) Festival Singers of Toronto, Iseler; (xi) Philippe Entremont; (xii) Charles Rosen; (xiii) Isaac Stern; (xiv) Soulima Stravinsky; (xv) Igor Stravinsky; (xvi) Szigeti; (xvii) Benny Goodman; (xviii) Columbia Jazz Ens.; (xix) Israel Baker; (xx) Tony Koves; (xxi) Arthur Gold, Robert Fizdale; (xxii) N. W. German RSO; (xxiii) Cathy Berberian; (xxiv) Howland, Kreiselman, Russo; (xxv) Mary Simmons; (xxvi) Alexander Young; (xxvii) Evelyn Lear; (xxviii) Adrienne Albert; (xxix) Robert Craft; (xxx) Donald Gramm; (xxxi) Di Tullio, Remsen, Almeida; (xxxii) Belinck, Simmons, Rideout, Kolk; (xxxiii) Driscoll, Grist, Picassi, Smith, Beattie, Gramm, Kolk, Murphy, Kaiser, Bonazzi, Washington, D. C., Op. Society Ch. & O; (xxxiv) Young, Raskin, Reardon, Sarfaty, Miller, Manning, Garrard, Tracey, Colin Tilney, Sadler's Wells Op. Ch., John Baker, RPO; (xxxv) Laurence Harvey, Sebastian Cabot, Elsa Lanchester, John Reardon, Robert Oliver, Paul Tripp, Richard Robinson, Columbia SO Ch., Gregg Smith; (xxxvi) Westbrook (nar.), Shirley, Verrett, Gramm, Reardon, Driscoll, Chester Watson Ch., Washington, D. C., Op. Society O; (xxxvii) Gregg Smith Singers, Gregg Smith; (xxxviii) Zorina, Molese, Ithaca College Concert Ch., Fort Worth Texas Boys' Ch.; (xxxix) John Calicos (nar.); (xl) Robinson, Chitjian, Los Angeles Festival Ch. & SO; (xli) Baxter, Albert, Gregg Smith Singers, Columbia Symphony Winds & Brass; (xlii) Verrett, Driscoll, Hornton (nar.); (xliii) Beardslee, Krebs, Lewis, Wainner, Morgan, Oliver, Schola

Cantorum, Ross; all cond. composer. (xliv) Richard Frisch; (xlv) Baker, Igleman, Schonbach, Neikrug; (xlvi) Anderson, Bonazzi, Bressler, Gramm, Ithaca College Concert Ch., Gregg Smith; cond. Robert Craft.

On these 22 discs, a revised and remastered version of the 1982 CBS set originally issued on LP, you have the unique archive of recordings which Stravinsky left of his own music. Presented in a sturdy plastic display box that enhances the desirability of the set, almost all the performances are conducted by the composer, with a few at the very end of his career – like the magnificent *Requiem canticles* – left to Robert Craft to conduct, with the composer supervising. In addition there is a handful of recordings of works otherwise not covered, mainly chamber pieces. With some recordings of Stravinsky talking and in rehearsal (included in the box devoted to the symphonies) it makes a vivid portrait.

Stravinsky may not have been a brilliant conductor, but in the recording studio he knew how to draw out alert, vigorous performances of his own music, and every one of these items illuminates facets of his inspiration which other interpreters often fail to notice. There are few if any rival versions of the *Rite of spring* – nowadays, astonishingly, his most frequently recorded work – to match his own recording of 1960 in its compelling intensity and inexorable sense of line.

Nevertheless, there are some disappointments in the set. It is a pity that Stravinsky's earlier, mono version of *Oedipus Rex* (with Jean Cocteau as narrator and Peter Pears in the title-role) was not preferred to his much less taut, stereo remake, and sadly the spoken items fail to include his intensely memorable talk, *Apropos le sacre*, originally issued with his 1960 recording of *The Rite*. It ends unforgettably with the thought: 'I was the vessel through which *Le sacre* passed.' But transfers have been done very well, clarifying and refining the original analogue sound.

Of the major ballets, *Petrushka* and *The Firebird* are valuable, but *The Rite* is required listening: it has real savagery and astonishing electricity. The link between *Jeu de cartes* from the mid-1930s and Stravinsky's post-war opera, *The Rake's progress*, is striking and Stravinsky's sharp-edged conducting style underlines it, while the curiously anonymous-sounding *Scènes de ballet* certainly have their attractive moments. *Orpheus* is a post-war score, written for Balanchine, and has a powerful atmosphere, although one of Stravinsky's most classically restrained works. A good performance, with the composer's own authority lending it special interest. However, its invention is less memorable and distinguished than *Apollo*, one of Stravinsky's most gravely beautiful scores. *Agon* is one of the most stimulating of Stravinsky's later works. Again composed for Balanchine, all the pieces are modelled on a French dance manual of the mid-seventeenth century. The sonorities are as individual and astringent as one expects, and the performance and recording are both of a high order. The orchestra respond with tremendous alertness and enthusiasm to Stravinsky's direction. The recording of *Le baiser de la fee* is a typical CBS balance with forward woodwind. However, if the recorded quality does not inspire too much enthusiasm, the performance of this enchanting score, based on themes by Tchaikovsky, certainly does. There is a ruthlessness in the composer's own reading of *Les Noces* which exactly matches the primitive robustness in this last flowering of Russian nationalism in Stravinsky. It must be a long time since four distinguished composers paid such a tribute as this in playing the work of a fifth. The earlier parts are perhaps too rigid, but as the performance goes on so one senses the added alertness and enthusiasm of the performers. The recording is good, but the balance favours the voices. *Renard* is a curious work, a sophisticated fable which here receives too unrelenting a performance. The voices are very forward and tend to drown the instrumentalists. Stravinsky began *Le chant du rossignol* in 1909, but when Diaghilev commissioned *The Firebird* he put it aside and did not take it up again until after *Petrushka* and *The Rite of spring*. Much has been made of the stylistic discrepancy which resulted, but one doubts if many listeners would object if they did not already know the history of the work's composition. It is unashamedly exotic in a way that sets it aside from almost every other work Stravinsky has ever written, even *The Firebird*. It is perhaps surprising that Stravinsky wanted to record it, but his handling shows that what can seem over-exotic acquires an almost barbaric strength in his hands.

In the early *Symphony in E flat*, Op. 1, the young Stravinsky's material may be comparatively conventional and the treatment much too bound to the academic procedures taught him by his master, Rimsky-Korsakov, but at least in this performance the music springs to life. Each movement has its special delights to outweigh any shortcomings. The performance is obviously as near definitive as it could be. The composer's account of the *Symphony in three movements* is an object lesson for every conductor who has tried to perform this work. Stravinsky shows how, by vigorous, forthright treatment of the notes, the emotion implicit is made all the more compelling. The Columbia Symphony plays superbly and the recording is full and brilliant. Stravinsky never quite equalled the intensity of the pre-war 78-r.p.m. performance of the *Symphony of Psalms*. That had many more technical faults than his later, stereo version, and it is only fair to say that this new account is still impressive. It is just that, with so vivid a work, it is a shade disappointing to find Stravinsky as interpreter at less than maximum voltage.

The iron-fingered touch of Philippe Entremont has something to be said for it in the *Capriccio for piano and wind*, with the bright echoes of cake-walk and early jazz, and even in the Bach-like florid writing in the slow movement, but this performance conveys too little of the music's charm. The *Movements for piano and orchestra* are far more formidable. Here serial technique is applied strictly, and even Stravinsky admitted that the work's harmony is more complex than anything he had previously attempted. Despite the fearsome idiom, however, one really *wants* to understand the argument, and the composer's conducting could hardly be more compelling. Stravinsky wrote the *Concerto for piano and wind* to play himself on his concert tours. A strange work which at first seems brittle and arid, this performance reveals a steely strength. Sometimes conductor and soloist are over-dramatic – but then Stravinsky himself is – and firmness and vitality are the main essentials. The recording is excellent. Stern's account of the *Violin concerto in D* adds a romantic perspective to the framework, and at one time, no doubt, Stravinsky would have objected. But an expressive approach to Stravinsky is permissible in a soloist, when the composer is there to provide the bedrock under the expressive cantilena. Plainly this has the forthright spontaneity of a live performance.

The collection of Stravinsky's shorter pieces begins with the very brief prelude on 'Happy birthday to you' which Stravinsky wrote for Pierre Monteux. Most of the suites were adapted from piano-duet works written for children. The *Circus polka* was written for a Barnum & Bailey elephant and erupts magnificently into a distortion of Schubert's *Marche militaire*. The *Dumbarton Oaks concerto* with its obvious echoes of Bach's *Brandenburgs* is one of the most warmly attractive of Stravinsky's neo-classical works, all beautifully played and acceptably recorded. The *Octet for wind* of 1924 comes out with surprising freshness and, throughout, the unexpected combination of neo-Bach and neo-Pop is most refreshing. The *Ragtime* dates from the end of Stravinsky's Russian period, when he was beginning to dabble in the exotic sounds of Western music. The performance could be more lighthearted, but Stravinsky gives the impression of knowing what he wants. The *Ebony concerto*, in this version conducted by the composer, may have little of 'swung' rhythm, but it is completely faithful to Stravinsky's deadpan approach to jazz.

Of the piano music, the *Concerto for two pianos* was written for the composer and his son to play, yet it presents formidable technical difficulties. It is a taut, four-movement work that deserves to be better known. The *Sonata* is much easier, musically and technically, and the *Eight easy pieces* are better known in their later transformation into the two *Suites for orchestra*.

The songs represent a fascinating collection of trifles, chips from the master's workbench dating from the earliest years. There are many incidental delights, not least those in which the magnetic Cathy Berberian is featured.

In Stravinsky's opera, *The Rake's progress*, the Rake of Alexander Young is a marvellous achievement, sweet-toned and accurate and well characterized. In the choice of other principals, too, it is noticeable what store Stravinsky set by vocal precision. Judith Raskin makes an appealing Anne Trulove, sweetly sung if not particularly well projected dramatically. John Reardon too is remarkable more for vocal accuracy than for striking characterization, but Regina Sarfaty's Baba is marvellous on both counts. The Sadler's Wells Chorus sings with even greater drive under the composer than in the theatre, and the Royal Philharmonic play with a warmth and a fittingly Mozartian sense of style to match Stravinsky's surprisingly lyrical approach to his score.

The *Mass* is a work of the greatest concentration, a quality that comes out strongly if one plays this performance immediately after *The Flood*, with its inevitably slack passages. In 1951 when it first appeared, the *Mass* was criticized by some for its perfunctory treatment of the words of the service. What this performance under the composer shows conclusively is that there is a difference between unseemly haste and genuine concentration. As with other Stravinsky works – the *Wind symphonies* and *Movements for piano and orchestra* – the argument is so concentrated that it is almost a musical shorthand. This is a microcosm of a *Mass*. As directed in the score, trebles are used here, and it is a pity that the engineers have not brought them further forward: their sweet, clear tone is sometimes lost among the lower strands. Otherwise the quality is up to the standard of CBS's other Stravinsky recordings. In *The Flood*, originally written for television, it is difficult to take the bald narrations seriously, particularly when Laurence Harvey sanctimoniously keeps talking of the will of 'Gud'. The Disneyland hill-billy style of narration quite destroys enjoyment and it is difficult to know what its dramatic aim was, fascinating though the work is. *Perséphone* is full of that cool lyricism that marks much of Stravinsky's music inspired by classical myths. As with many of these vocal recordings, the balance is too close, and various orchestral solos are highlighted.

The *Cantata* of 1952 is a transitional piece between Stravinsky's tonal and serial periods. However, of the two soloists, Alexander Young is much more impressive than Adrienne Albert, for her voice is entirely unsuitable, with an unformed choirboy sound somehow married to wide vibrato. For the sake of Stravinsky one endures her. The *Canticum sacrum* dates from the mid-1950s and includes music that some listeners might find tough (the strictly serial choral section). But the performance is a fine one and the tenor solo from Richard Robinson is very moving. The Bach *Chorale variations* has a synthetic modernity that recalls the espresso bar, though one which still reveals underlying mastery. The *Epitaphium* and the *Double canon* are miniatures, dating from the composer's serial period. but the *Canon* is deliberately euphonious.

Of the items recorded by Robert Craft, the *Requiem canticles* stands out, the one incontrovertible masterpiece among the composer's very last serial works and one of the most deeply moving works ever written in the serial idiom. Even more strikingly than in the *Mass* of 1948, Stravinsky conveys his religious feelings with a searing intensity. The *Aldous Huxley variations* are more difficult to comprehend but have similar intensity. Valuable, too, are the ballad *Abraham and Isaac* and the brief *Introitus for T. S. Eliot*.

(i) *Le baiser de la fee (Divertimento);* (ii) *Petrushka:* excerpts: *(Danse russe; Chez Petrushka; La fête populaire);* (i) *Pulcinella: suite;* (ii) *The Rite of spring* (complete ballet).
(B) (***) EMI mono CZS7 62647-2 (2) [Ang. CDMB 62647]. (i) French Nat. R. O; (ii) Philh. O, Markevitch – PROKOFIEV: *Love for three oranges* etc. (**)

Markevitch's electrifying 1959 stereo recording of *The Rite of spring* has long been famous, even though the documentation suggests that it is mono. The Philharmonia playing is superbly exciting, and the conductor's rhythmic vitality and ruthless thrust are matched by an amazingly spectacular recording which hardly sounds dated even now. One of the highlights of the performance is the dramatic use of the tam-tam, and in Part 2 the drums are thrillingly crisp and make a powerful impact. The elegant *Divertimento*, which Stravinsky culled from his Tchaikovskian ballet *Le baiser de la fee*, was made famous by Ansermet's mono recording, but the French orchestral playing here has rather more finesse: the horns in their attractive ostinato (taken from a Tchaikovsky piano piece) articulate buoyantly, and the whole performance has flair. The three excerpts from *Petrushka* are similarly lively and colourful, and only *Pulcinella* is slightly disappointing: the trombones blow rasberries in their famous *Vivo* duet with the double basses, and elsewhere Markevitch dilutes the music's charm by his forcefulness. However, in EMI's 'two for the price of one' French series this is certainly value for money.

(i) *Capriccio for piano and orchestra* (1929, rev. 1949); *Concerto for piano and wind* (1924, rev. 1950); *Movements for piano and orchestra.* (Piano): *8 Easy pieces on 5 notes; 4 Études; 3 Movements from Petrushka; Piano rag music; Scherzo; Serenade in A; Sonata in F sharp min.* (1903/4); *Sonata* (1924); *Souvenir d'une marche bouche; Tango; Valse pour les enfants; Waltz for children.*
(B) *** EMI CZS7 67276-2 (2) [id.]. Michel Béroff; (i) O de Paris, Seiji Ozawa.

Only the *Capriccio*, the *Concerto for piano and wind* and the *Movements* have been available before in the UK, but specialist dealers did import the solo works and no one who acquired them could have been disappointed. Michel Béroff was still in his early twenties when he made the concerto recordings in the somewhat reverberant acoustic of the Salle Wagram. They are still better than those of most rivals and certainly better than those in the Sony *Stravinsky Edition*. The *Petrushka* excerpts are wonderfully alert and vital, and splendidly characterized. There is occasionally a very slight glare about the piano sound, recorded in the 1970s, but, among bargain, mid- and full-price discs, this is a first choice for this repertoire.

Concerto in D for strings; Danses concertantes; Dumbarton Oaks concerto in E flat; (i) *Cantata on old English texts.*
(M) *** Decca 425 622-2. ECO, Sir Colin Davis; (i) with Kern, Young, St Anthony Singers.

The *Danses concertantes* is one of Stravinsky's most light-hearted pieces and the highly original scoring is a constant delight. Together with the other two instrumental works included in this outstanding collection, it has a neo-classicism to which anyone who has enjoyed Bach's *Brandenburgs* must surely respond. Indeed Stravinsky himself admitted that the *Brandenburgs* were his starting point for the *Dumbarton Oaks concerto*. Sir Colin Davis brings enormous vitality as well as the right degree of dry humour to these works, and the 1962 recording sounds as fresh as the day it was made in this very successful CD transfer. Detail is crisp and the ambience is exactly right for the music. The *Cantata* (recorded a year later) has a much cooler atmosphere, its chilling setting of the *Lye-Wake Dirge* more relentless than Britten's; but the sharp originality of the concept makes its inspiration readily felt in a performance that so strikingly captures its harsh mood and strange beauty. Both soloists are excellent and the chorus is vividly caught.

Concerto in D for strings; Symphony in C; (i) *Symphony of Psalms* (1948 version).
(M) ** DG 423 252-2. BPO, Karajan, (i) with German Op. Ch.

These are extreme examples of Karajan's refined Stravinsky style. Though undeniably he brings elegance to the *Concerto* and to the *Symphony in C*, both these examples of Stravinsky's late neo-classicism lose their characteristic acerbity, with lines smoothed over and rhythms weakened. The *Symphony of Psalms* is equally unidiomatic, but the greatness of this masterpiece can stand deviation, and the final *Alleluias* are most beautifully done. The originally smooth, refined recording has gained in vividness on CD and so projection is improved.

Violin concerto in D.
(M) *** Decca 425 003-2; *425 003-4*. Kyung Wha Chung, LSO, Previn – PROKOFIEV: *Concertos 1–2.* ***
(M) *** Ph. 422 136-2. Grumiaux, Concg. O, Bour – BERG: *Concerto.* ***

Kyung Wha Chung is at her most incisive in the spikily swaggering outer movements, which with Previn's help are presented here in all their distinctiveness, tough and witty at the same time. In the two movements labelled *Aria*, Chung brings fantasy as well as lyricism, less overtly expressive than Perlman (at full price) but conveying instead an inner, brooding quality. Brilliant Decca recording, the soloist diamond-bright in presence, but with plenty of orchestral atmosphere.

A lithe and beautifully refined account of the *Concerto* from Grumiaux. In some respects this is the most thoroughly enjoyable account on record and compares favourably with the Perlman. It is enormously vital but its energy is controlled and the tone never becomes unduly aggressive or spiky. The remastered recording is faithful and preserves an excellent balance between violin and orchestra.

The Firebird (ballet; complete).
(B) **(*) Pickwick Dig. PCD 921. Nat. Youth O of Great Britain, Christopher Seaman – DUKAS: *L'apprenti sorcier.* **(*)

On Pickwick, *Firebird* is a work which inspires the young players of the current National Youth Orchestra to phenomenal feats of virtuosity. This is played at least as brilliantly as most versions by fully professional orchestras, with ensemble just as precise. Only in *Kaschei's dance*, taken a little cautiously, does the weight of the challenge show itself. The popular Dukas piece makes an attractive fill-up, and the modern digital recording is full and brilliant.

The Firebird (complete); *Le chant du rossignol; Fireworks; Scherzo à la russe.*
❀ (M) *** Mercury 432 012-2 [id.]. LSO, Dorati.

Many collectors have been eagerly awaiting the return of Dorati's electrifying, 1960 Mercury version of *The Firebird* with the LSO. The CD transfer makes the recording sound as fresh and vivid as the day it was made; the brilliantly transparent detail and enormous impact suggest a modern digital source rather than an analogue master made over 30 years ago. The stereo has remarkable atmosphere too, and the balance is very natural. The performance sounds completely spontaneous and the LSO wind playing is especially sensitive. Only the sound of the massed upper strings reveals the age of the original master, although this does not spoil the ravishing final climax; the bite of the brass and the transient edge of the percussion are thrilling. The recording of Stravinsky's glittering symphonic poem, *The song of the nightingale*, is hardly less compelling, with sparkle in the upper range and an impressive bass drum. Dorati's reading is urgent and finely pointed, yet is strong, too, on atmosphere. The other, shorter pieces also come up vividly. On CD one can order the programme to taste, and this remains one of the most stimulating Stravinsky compilations in the catalogue.

The Firebird: suite (1919 version); *Petrushka* (1947 version). *Orchestral Suites Nos. 1–2.*
(BB) * Naxos Dig. 8. 550263 [id.]. Belgian R. & TV O (Brussels), Alexander Rahbari.

Though the Belgian Radio Orchestra is a lively band, playing here with colour and expressiveness, the washy recording in the 1919 *Firebird suite* obscures far too much detail, and even *Kaschei's dance* lacks bite. The recording for *Petrushka*, though still reverberant, is better focused but, irritatingly, what would have been a complete performance is shorn off before the final section, when the ghost of Petrushka returns. Stravinsky did suggest that concert performances might end with a loud cadence in this way after the Masqueraders section, but it now seems unfortunate to record it this way. That is particularly so when there would have been plenty of room to include the hauntingly atmospheric coda for the full ballet version. As it is, the two relatively trivial *Suites* for chamber orchestra come as makeweight.

(i) *The Firebird* (complete); (ii) *The Rite of spring* (complete).
(BB) *** ASV CDQS 6031; *ZCQS 6031.* (i) RPO, Dorati; (ii) Nat. Youth O of Great Britain, Simon Rattle.

The ASV CD coupling of the two complete ballets is made possible because Dorati's tempi in the *Firebird* are comparatively fast. But this matches his dramatic approach, as does a recording balance which is rather close, although there is no serious lack of atmosphere in the score's gentler pages of evocation. Not surprisingly with Simon Rattle at the helm, the performance of the National Youth Orchestra in the once-feared showpiece coupling is not just 'good considering', but 'good absolute'; the youngsters under their young conductor (the recordings here date from 1976/7) produce warm and spontaneous playing, and the penalty of having a few imprecisions and errors is minimal. The sound here is slightly more atmospheric than in the coupling, but again there is plenty of bite and the timpani make a fine effect.

The Firebird: suite (1919 version).
(B) **(*) DG Compact Classics *413 155-4* [id.]. Berlin RSO, Maazel – KHACHATURIAN: *Gayaneh*; RIMSKY-KORSAKOV: *Scheherazade.* **(*)

(i) *The Firebird: suite* (1919 version); (ii) *Petrushka: suite* (1911 version).
(M) **(*) Sony SBK 47664 [id.]. (i) Cleveland O, Szell; (ii) Phd. O, Ormandy – RAVEL: *Daphnis: suite No. 2.* **(*)

The Firebird suite (1919 version); *The Rite of spring.*
(M) *** DG 415 854-2; *415 854-4* [id.]. LSO, Abbado.

Abbado's *Firebird suite* is a performance of great vitality and sensitivity; the conductor's feeling for colour and atmosphere is everywhere and the CD transfer loses nothing of the evocation of the analogue original. There is a degree of detachment in *The Rite of spring*; but on points of detail it is meticulous. There is a hypnotically atmospheric feeling at the opening of Part Two, emphasizing the contrast with the brutal music which follows. The drama is heightened by the wide dynamic range of the recording, and the effect is forceful without ever becoming ugly.

Szell's 1961 recording of the *Firebird suite* is extremely vivid and strong in character – *Katchei's dance infernale* is electrifying – and the Cleveland playing in the iridescent *Dance of the Firebird* has almost unbelievably crisply articulated detail. The Philadelphia Orchestra aren't exactly reticent in the matter of virtuosity either. Ormandy's 1964 *Petrushka* offers the bulk of the score with the concert ending; his approach is very rhythmic but never stiff. The *Dance of the ballerina*, with its crisp side-drum snares, is arresting and the closing tableau has great excitement and colour. It is a pity that the recording, though spacious, is a bit forward and harsh. But the orchestral bravura is always compelling.

Maazel's reading of the *Firebird suite* has an enjoyable éclat and he has the advantage of the most beautiful woodwind playing; indeed the Berlin Radio Orchestra is consistently on top form. The recording dates from 1960 and tended to betray its age by the sound of the massed upper strings. However, in the present transfer the DG engineers have smoothed off the upper partials and in consequence the recording, although still impressive, has lost some of its bite.

Jeux de cartes (ballet) complete; (i) *Pulcinella* (ballet after Pergolesi) complete.
(M) *** DG 423 889-2 [id.]. (i) Berganza, Davies, Shirley-Quirk; LSO, Abbado.

Abbado gives a vividly high-powered reading of the neo-classical score of *Pulcinella.* If he is in danger of over-colouring, the bite and flair are entirely and convincingly Stravinskian, with rhythms sharply incisive. Not just the playing but the singers too are outstandingly fine. The 1979 recording in its digital remastering has become slightly drier and more acerbic in timbre, adding point to the playing. *Jeux de cartes*, recorded five years earlier, also sounds somewhat drier than it did originally, but the detail, presence and impact remain very telling. The LSO plays with superb virtuosity and Abbado's feeling for atmosphere and colour is everywhere in evidence, heard against an excellently judged perspective.

Petrushka (1947 score; complete).
(M) ** Decca 425 026-2; *425 026-4* [id.]. VPO, Dohnányi – BARTÓK: *Miraculous Mandarin.* **

Petrushka (1911 version); *The Rite of spring.*
(M) *** Ph. 420 491-2 [id.]. LPO, Haitink.

Petrushka (1947 version); *The Rite of spring.*
(M) ** DG Dig. 429 493-2. Israel PO, Bernstein.

Haitink's 1974 *Petrushka* has been remastered with great success. There is a sense of expansion of the dynamic range and the performance is given added projection by the vivid sense of presence. It is a very involving account, with detail imaginatively delineated. The rhythmic feeling is strong, especially in the Second Tableau and the finale, where the fairground bustle is vivid. The LPO wind playing is especially fine; the recording's firm definition and the well-proportioned and truthful aural perspective make it a joy to listen to. The natural, unforced quality of Haitink's *Rite* also brings real compulsion. Other versions may hammer the listener more powerfully, thrust him or her along more forcefully; but the bite and precision of the playing here is most impressive.

Dohnányi directs a genial and well-paced reading, slightly lacking in sparkle and imagination but revealing the Vienna Philharmonic as a band surprisingly sympathetic to repertory not normally associated with it. Though the piano and trumpet might have been placed closer with advantage, the CD transfer of refined analogue sound is impressive, though detail is not sharply etched.

Sonic limitations qualified the enthusiasm with which Bernstein's digital version of *Le Sacre* could be greeted; his *Petrushka* was recorded in the same unglamorous acoustic of the Mann Auditorium, Tel Aviv. However, the results are by no means as uncongenial, though still too dry and unventilated. Bernstein coaxes some highly responsive playing from the Israel Philharmonic and secures much pleasing string-tone – not always to be found from this body. Perhaps this *Petrushka* is not as touching as his earlier, New York account made in the 1960s, surely one of the most vital and sensitively characterized versions of the work, but it is still vividly projected and keenly felt.

(i) *Petrushka* (1911 version); (ii) *The Rite of spring;* (ii; iii) *Le Roi des étoiles* (cantata).
(M) **(*) DG 435 073-2; *435 073-4* [id.]. (i) LSO, Dutoit; (ii) Boston SO, Tilson Thomas, (iii) with New England Conservatory Ch.

Charles Dutoit's brilliantly realized *Petrushka* was made almost impromptu and, in the event, did much to establish the conductor's recording reputation. In October 1975 a planned DG opera recording fell through and sessions were hastily reallotted with little advance planning. The result is triumphantly spontaneous in its own right, with rhythms that are incisive yet beautifully buoyant, and a degree of expressiveness in the orchestral playing that subtly underlines the dramatic atmosphere and is especially magical in the Third Tableau. The final section too is strongly coloured so that the gentle closing pages make a touching contrast to the gaiety of the early part of the scene. The recording is vivid, the only fault of balance being the prominence of the concertante piano soloist, Tamás Vásáry. The pairing is Tilson Thomas's equally lively account of the *Rite of spring* (also available on a Compact Classics tape, differently coupled – see below), reverberantly recorded but now given all the needed bite by the digital remastering (the cymbals in the *Dance of the earth* are positively explosive). Indeed the sound of these new transfers of both ballets has a spikiness in the treble not apparent on the original LPs. The brief makeweight is the rare motet of the same period as *The Rite*, unperformed for several decades, but here shown as an intensely imaginative and evocative choral work. The overall playing time of this issue is nearly 76 minutes.

Pulcinella (ballet): *suite.*
(M) *** Decca 417 734-2 [id.]. ASMF, Marriner – BIZET: PROKOFIEV: *Symphonies.* ***

Those wanting merely the orchestral suite can rest content with Marriner's vintage version, one of the first recordings by which the Academy spread its wings in the music of the twentieth century. The results are superb and the sound of the digitally remastered CD has all the bite one could ask for. It remains a demonstration disc with its sharp separation of instruments, particularly the trombones against double basses in the *Vivo.*

Pulcinella (ballet): suite; *Symphony in 3 movements.*
(M) * EMI CDM7 64142-2 [id.]; *EG 764142-4.* Philh. O, Klemperer – WEILL: *Kleine Dreigroschenmusik.* ***

In the 1930s Klemperer was a dedicated advocate of new music and his later canonization as an apostle of Beethoven, Brahms and Mahler makes one overlook his earlier reputation. But this account of the 1945 Stravinsky *Symphony* is far too often leaden and heavy-handed to be acceptable in this repertoire. Coolly received when it made its first appearance, there is no reason, on renewing acquaintance, to modify the general feeling of disappointment this disc aroused. The humour and high spirits of *Pulcinella* also elude Klemperer and, despite the excellence of the orchestral playing and the very good quality of the early-1960s recording – strikingly fresh on CD – this performance is characteristic neither of Stravinsky nor of Klemperer at his best.

The Rite of spring (complete ballet) (see also above, under *Petrushka*).
(B) *** DG 429 162-2; *429 162-4* [id.]. BPO, Karajan – MUSSORGSKY: *Pictures.* ***
(M) **(*) Decca Dig. 430 709-2; *430 709-4.*

Cleveland O, Chailly – MUSSORGSKY: *Pictures*. **
(B) **(*) DG Compact Classics *413 160-4* [id.]. Boston SO, Tilson Thomas – ORFF: *Carmina Burana*. **(*)

The Rite of spring (orchestral & pianola versions).
(M) *** Pickwick Dig. MCD 25; *MCC 25*. Boston PO, Zander.

(i) *The Rite of spring;* (ii) *Pulcinella* (ballet): *suite*.
(M) *(**) Sony MK 44709 [id.]. (i) LSO; (ii) NYPO; Bernstein.

The most fascinating of the new recordings of Stravinsky's *Rite of spring* is Benjamin Zander's live recording with the Boston Philharmonic, full and vivid if slightly confined in sound. It brings a hard-hitting, colourful performance, directly related to the pianola version with which it is coupled. Stravinsky himself in the 1920s supervised the original Pleyela piano roll recording, which Rex Lawson 'plays' very effectively on a resonant Bösendorfer Imperial. With this pianola system (unlike the reproducing rolls which captured the actual playing of a concert pianist) the piano roll represented a form of transcription of the printed score, accurate in note lengths and time values. The pianolist playing the score back uses pedals to create dynamic levels and accents, and levers to phrase and sustain and bring the music back to life. The speeds at which everything is presented remain predetermined and unalterable; and here the most striking point on speed is the very fast tempo for the opening of the final *Sacrificial dance*, markedly faster even than Stravinsky's own on the last – and finest – of his three recordings. With tracks correlated between the two performances, it is very easy to make illuminating comparisons. Zander suggests (and he offers additional documentary evidence from Marie Rambert, the Russian ballerina, quoting comments made by the composer at the original dance rehearsals of the ballet) that Stravinsky intended a faster pacing for the ballet's finale and that he modified the tempo only when he discovered that orchestras could not cope with the music at his intended speed (even his own 1960 recording contains inaccuracies). There is no doubt that, played up to this faster tempo, the *Danse sacrale* is electrifying and, once experienced, the slower speed to which we are all accustomed seems comparatively restrained. It is a final irony that the first recording of the suggested intended 'original' tempo made since Pierre Monteux's somewhat chaotic attempt with a Paris orchestra in 1929 is presented on CD by a semi-professional group (of considerable excellence) which now projects rhythms with biting confidence that defeated professionals 70 years earlier! This CD is offered at upper medium price.

Karajan's earlier, 1966 version of the *Rite of spring* (now coupled with Mussorgsky's *Pictures*) came in for criticism from the composer, who doubted whether Berlin Philharmonic traditions could encompass music from so different a discipline. Yet listening to the vibrant sounds coming from the remastered CD, one cannot fully accept the composer's response. Certainly the playing of the Berlin Philharmonic is marvellously polished and civilized, yet it is not without bite or excitement, and the lack of malignancy serves to increase the feeling of symphonic strength, while the beauty of the sound created in the lyrical sections brings a potent nostalgia.

With speeds faster than usual – markedly so in Part Two – Chailly's taut and urgent reading brings one of Decca's sound spectaculars. The bass-drum, so important in this work, leaps out with a power, precision and resonance to startle the listener. It may not be the easiest version to live with, and the fast speeds in Part Two provide less contrast than usual before the onslaught of the final *Sacrificial dance*; but anyone wanting the Mussorgsky coupling – or, for that matter, to startle friends with the *Rite* – will be well pleased.

Michael Tilson Thomas's reading is dramatic enough but warmly expressive too, missing some of the music's bite. The amply reverberant acoustic emphasizes his approach but, with fine playing from the Boston orchestra and the advantage of continuity, this Compact Classics tape is well worth considering, as it also contains Jochum's outstanding account of Orff's *Carmina Burana*, which has the composer's imprimatur.

Bernstein's LSO version dates from 1972 at the time of quadraphonic experiments. The problems of conducting in the round led Bernstein finally to suggest at the sessions that he should simply conduct a straight performance. That is substantially what appears on the record, a larger-than-life, colourfully romantic view with tremendous impact. As transferred to CD, the sound is full and spacious, less aggressive than it originally was on LP. Bernstein's New York account of the *Pulcinella suite*, recorded in 1960, brings rather edgy sound, making the performance seem overheavy for Stravinsky's wittily neo-classical inspirations.

The Soldier's tale (suite).
(M) *** Van. 08.8013.71 [OVC 8013]. Instru-

mental Ens., Leopold Stokowski – THOMSON: *Film scores.* ***

Stokowski works his magic upon this surprisingly neglected score, making the most of its lyrical warmth as well as the more abrasive Devil's music which has plenty of rhythmic bite. The septet of expert instrumentalists is naturally recorded in a studio acoustic, but one which has plenty of ambience. The solo violinist (Charles Tarack) and the trumpeter (Theodore Weis) are fully up to the considerable demands placed on them. This disc comes at upper-mid-price in the USA.

(i) *Symphonies of wind instruments;* (ii) *3 Pieces for string quartet;* (iii) *3 Easy pieces: March. Rite of spring:* excerpts. (iv) *Les cinq doigts, Nos. 1, 2 & 6; Ragtime; Studies, Op. 7/1 & 4.* (v; i) *3 Japanese lyrics;* (v; vi) *2 Poems of Bal'mont; 3 Little songs: The Jackdaw. 4 Russian songs: The Drake. Mavra* (opera): *Parasha's aria.*
(M) **(*) Chan. CHAN 6535; *MBTD 6535* [id.]. (i) Nash Ens., Rattle; (ii) Chilingirian Qt; (iii) Shasby & McMahon; (iv) Lumsden; (v) Manning; (vi) Rodney Bennett.

The performances here are lively enough; but the purpose of the original LP, designed to accompany a course on the rise of modernism (1890–1920) and including five brief excerpts from *The Rite of spring* in piano-duet form, renders its appeal limited. Nothing lasts for more than two minutes except *Ragtime* and, of course, the *Symphonies of wind instruments.* However, both performances and recordings are very good – the *Symphonies of wind* is done superbly – and the CD transfer is immaculate.

VOCAL MUSIC

(i) *Canticum sacrum;* (ii) *Mass;* (iii) *Symphony of Psalms.*
(M) *** Decca 430 346-2. Christ Church Cathedral, Oxford, Ch., Simon Preston; with (i) Morton, Creed; (i; iii) Philip Jones Ens.; (iii) N. Jones, Giles, Cave, Lindley, Herron, L. Sinf. – POULENC: *Motets.* ***

It is fascinating to hear Stravinsky's rapt and masterly *Symphony of Psalms* in a performance with boys' voices, as the composer said he had in mind. The freshness of the choral sound and its ethereal clarity make this a most moving performance, as though sung by an angel choir. The *Canticum sacrum*, more taxing still in its serial austerity, brings another superb example of the artistry of these youngsters. Here again Stravinsky's markings suggest that he may have had such a tone-colour in mind, though in normal circumstances it would seem all but impossible to achieve. The *Symphony* lacks some of the weight and bite of larger-scale performances but, with atmospheric, resonant yet well focused sound, the effect is most moving. The comparably spare but very beautiful *Mass* for voices and instruments, given a direct, classical reading, is hardly less impressive and is equally well transferred to CD. The recordings (originally Argo) date from 1973/4.

4 Cat's cradle songs; 4 Chants; Elegy for JFK; In memoriam Dylan Thomas; 3 Japanese lyrics; Pastorale; 2 Poems by Konstantin Bal'mont; 2 Poems by Paul Verlaine; Pribaoutki (4 songs); *Recollections of childhood* (3 songs); *2 Sacred songs* (from WOLF: *Spanish Lieder Book*); *3 Shakespeare songs; 4 Songs; Tilim-bom. Mavra: Parasha's aria.*
(M) *** DG 431 751-2 [id.]. Bryn-Julson, Murray, Tear, Shirley-Quirk, Ens. InterContemporain, Boulez.

Anyone who thinks a Stravinsky song could not be utterly charming should try the first item of this recital, the *Pastorale*, a song without words for voice and four wind instruments: Phyllis Bryn-Julson's performance is captivating. Practically all of Stravinsky's songs are accommodated on this useful CD, reissued in DG's 20th Century Classics series. The early songs occupy more than half of the collection: he wrote the bulk of his vocal output before or during the First World War, after which there is a long gap (1919–53) during which he abandoned the medium. (The *Chanson de Parasha* from *Mavra* was published as a separate song, but that is the sole exception.) All the singing here is very persuasive and well characterized. The Verlaine songs are, oddly enough, given in Russian (Stravinsky originally set them in French), but Shirley-Quirk makes them sound very appealing nevertheless. The record also includes a 1968 transcription of two of Wolf's Spanish songs, his very last opus. The CD transfer is immaculate, with natural, well-focused sound, and translations are provided where necessary.

Oedipus Rex (opera-oratorio).
(M) **(*) Decca 430 001-2. McCowen (narrator), Pears, Meyer, McIntyre, Dean, Ryland Davies, Luxon, John Alldis Ch., LPO, Solti.

Solti's view of this highly stylized work is less sharp-edged than one would expect, and the dominant factor in the performance is not so much the conductor's direction as the heartfelt singing of Peter Pears in the title-role. It was he who sang the part in the composer's first LP recording, twenty years earlier, and here the crispness and clarity of his delivery go with an ability to point the key moments of deep emotion with extraordinary intensity. The rest of the vocal team is good, if not outstanding, and the narration (in English) of Alec McCowen is apt and undistracting. The transfer to CD is outstandingly vivid and brilliant.

(i) *Renard. The Soldier's tale;* (ii) *3 Pieces for clarinet solo; Ragtime;* (iii) *3 Japanese lyrics.*
(B) *** Hung. White Label HRC 078. Budapest Chamber Ens., András Mihály, (i) Gulyás, Keonch, Polgar, Bordas; (ii) Berkes; (iii) Adrienne Csengery.

Mihály's well-planned Stravinsky collection, colourfully performed and recorded, makes an outstanding bargain in Hungaroton's White Label series. The oddity is that *The Soldier's tale* has the full text of the entertainment, over half an hour long, but without any dramatic dialogue. Both in the dramatic scena, *Renard* – with four excellent soloists – and in *Ragtime*, the cimbalom plays a prominent part and, aptly in Budapest performances, Marta Fabian's brilliant, idiomatic playing of that Hungarian instrument is put well to the fore. The clear, silvery soprano, Adrienne Csengery, gives delightful performances of the *Japanese lyrics* and Kálmán Berkes is an agile clarinettist in the unaccompanied pieces.

Suk, Josef (1874–1935)

Fantasy in G min. (for violin and orchestra), *Op. 24.*
(B) *** Sup. 110601-2. Josef Suk, Czech PO, Ančerl – DVOŘÁK: *Violin concerto.* ***

Suk's *Fantasy* is a brilliant piece which relates to the traditional essays in violin wizardry as well as to the Czech nationalist tradition. The work has music of characteristic fantasy, though the rhetorical brilliance is equally strong. Suk's playing is refreshing and the orchestral accompaniment under Ančerl is no less impressive. Good remastered 1960s sound.

Serenade for strings in E flat, Op. 6.
(BB) *** Naxos 8.550419 [id.]. Capella Istropolitana, Kr(e)chek – DVOŘÁK: *String serenade.* **(*)

An entirely delightful account of Suk's *Serenade*, which ought to be far better known. The innocent delicacy of the opening is perfectly caught and the charm of the dance movement which follows is just as winning. The *Adagio* is played most beautifully and then, with a burst of high spirits (and excellent ensemble), the finale bustles to its conclusion with exhilarating zest. The recording is first class, fresh yet full-textured, naturally balanced and transparent.

Sullivan, Arthur (1842–1900)

(i) *Pineapple Poll: ballet music* (arr. Mackerras); (ii) *Savoy dances* (arr. Robinson); (i) *Overtures: Iolanthe; Mikado.*
(M) **(*) EMI CDM7 63961-2; *EG 763961-4.* Pro Arte O, (i) John Hollingsworth; (ii) Stanford Robinson.

Hollingsworth offers a lively reading of *Pineapple Poll*, supported by good orchestral playing, and the slightly brash recorded quality quite suits the ebullience of the score. The upper register is over-bright but can be smoothed out. With its tuneful bonuses more smoothly done, this is enjoyable and quite good value for money.

Overtures: *Cox and Box; The Gondoliers; HMS Pinafore; Iolanthe; The Mikado; Patience; The Pirates of Penzance; Princess Ida; Ruddigore; The Sorcerer; The Yeomen of the Guard.*
(B) ** CfP CD-CFP 4529; *TC-CFP 4529* [id.]. Pro Arte O, Sir Malcolm Sargent.

Overtures: (i; ii) *Di Ballo;* (i; iii) *The Gondoliers;* (iv; v) *HMS Pinafore;* (i; iii) *Iolanthe; The Mikado;* (iv; iii) *The Pirates of Penzance;* (iv; vi) *The Yeomen of the Guard.*
(B) ** Pickwick IMPX 9014 [id.]. (i) New SO of L; (ii) Collins; (iii) Godfrey; (iv) RPO; (v) Walker; (vi) Sargent.

Among bargain collections, Sargent's must be the best buy. It includes eleven overtures, and the performances are characteristically bright and polished, although they do not always have quite the flair Godfrey brought to this music. The recordings date from between 1957 and 1961 (which brings less than ample strings) and have been brightly transferred to CD.

The Decca performances (on Pickwick) reflect the unfailing sparkle and lyrical feeling (witness the quotation of *Leave me not to pine alone* in *The Pirates of Penzance*) which Godfrey brought to his performances. *HMS Pinafore* is directed by James Walker, a Decca recording producer, who conducted the D'Oyly Carte Company briefly when Godfrey died, while *The Yeomen of the Guard* shows Sargent at his very best. The recordings have more colour and ambience than the EMI versions. As a bonus we are offered a vivacious account of *Di Ballo*, admirably presented by Anthony Collins (better known for his Sibelius!). This must date from the mid-1950s yet still provides stereo of excellent quality. The transfers to CD are very well managed but, with only seven items included, one wonders why a more complete anthology was not assembled from the Decca/D'Oyly Carte archives for this reissue.

OPERAS

(i) *Cox and Box* (libretto by F. C. Burnand) complete; (ii) *Ruddigore* (complete, without dialogue).

(M) *** Decca *417 355-4* (2). (i) Styler, Riordan, Adams; New SO of L.; (ii) J. Reed, Round, Sandford, Riley, Adams, Hindmarsh, Knight, Sansom, Allister, D'Oyly Carte Op. Ch., ROHCG O, Godfrey.

Cox and Box is a superb performance in every way. It is given a recording which, without sacrificing clarity, conveys with perfect balance the stage atmosphere. It was written in 1867 and thus pre-dates the first G & S success, *Trial by Jury*, by eight years. One must notice the lively military song *Rataplan* – splendidly sung by Donald Adams, an ideal Bouncer – which was to set the style for many similar later pieces with words by Gilbert, and also the captivating *Bacon 'Lullaby'*, so ravishingly sung by Joseph Riordan. Later on, in Box's recitative telling how he 'committed suicide', Sullivan makes one of his first and most impressive parodies of grand opera, which succeeds also in being effective in its own right.

Ruddigore, too, comes up surprisingly freshly, though it was a pity the dialogue was omitted. The performance includes *The battle's roar is over*, which is (for whatever reason) traditionally omitted. There is much to enjoy here (especially Gillian Knight and Donald Adams, whose *Ghosts' high noon* song is a marvellous highlight). Godfrey is his inimitable sprightly self and the chorus and orchestra are excellent. A fine traditional D'Oyly Carte set, then, brightly recorded.

N.B.: This set is currently available only on cassette.

The Gondoliers (complete, with dialogue).

(M) *(**) Decca 417 177-2; *425 254-4* (2). Reed, Skitch, Sandford, Round, Styler, Knight, Toye, Sansom, Wright, D'Oyly Carte Op. Ch., New SO of L., Godfrey.

One welcomes back *The Gondoliers* to the catalogue. Isidore Godfrey's conducting is vividly alive and Decca provided a large and excellent orchestra. The solo singing throughout is consistently good. Jeffrey Skitch and Jennifer Toye are a well-matched pair of lovers, and the two Gondoliers and their wives are no less effective. Thomas Round sings *Take a pair of sparkling eyes* very well indeed. The ensemble singing is very well balanced and always both lively and musical. The *Cachucha* is captivating and goes at a sparkling pace. Kenneth Sandford, who is a rather light-voiced Don Alhambra, makes much of his spoken part, as well as singing his songs with fine style. John Reed is a suitably dry Duke of Plaza-Toro: he makes the part his own and is well partnered by Gillian Knight. The drawback lies in the digitally remastered recording, which has been miscalculated – the treble is fierce, making the strings edgy and the female voices peaky.

HMS Pinafore (complete, with dialogue).

❀ (M) *** Decca 414 283-2; *414 283-4*. Reed, Skitch, Round, Adams, Hindmarsh, Wright, Knight, D'Oyly Carte Op. Ch., New SO of L., Godfrey.

It would be difficult to imagine a better-recorded performance than the 1960 Decca D'Oyly Carte set, complete with dialogue. Donald Adams is a totally memorable Deadeye and his larger-than-life personality underpins the whole piece. Among the others, Jeffrey Skitch is a first-class Captain; Jean Hindmarsh is absolutely convincing as Josephine, and she sings with great charm. Thomas Round is equally good as Ralph Rackstraw. Little Buttercup could be slightly more colourful, but this is a small blemish; among the minor parts, George Cook is a most personable Bill Bobstay. The choral singing is excellent, the orchestral playing good, and Isidore Godfrey conducts with marvellous spirit and lift. The recording has splendid atmosphere and its vintage qualities are very apparent in this remastered form.

Iolanthe (complete, with dialogue).

(M) *** Decca 414 145-2; *414 145-4* (2). Sansom, Reed, Adams, Round, Sandford, Styler, Knight, Newman, D'Oyly Carte Op. Ch., Grenadier Guards Band, New SO, Godfrey.

This was the first (1960) stereo *Iolanthe*, not the later and generally inferior remake under Nash. Even though Decca's budget had not yet stretched to the Royal Philharmonic Orchestra, the production was given added panache by introducing the Grenadier Guards Band into the *March of the Peers*, with spectacular effect. John Reed's characterization is wittily immediate, and the famous *Nightmare song* undoubtedly has greater freshness. Mary Sansom is a convincing Phyllis, and if her singing has not the sense of style Elsie Morison brings to the (currently withdrawn) Sargent EMI set, she is marvellous with the dialogue. Her Act II discourse with the two Earls – portrayed to perfection by Donald Adams and Thomas Round – is sheer delight. Alan Styler makes a vivid personal identification with the role of Strephon. Iolanthe's final aria (sung by Yvonne Newman) is a shade disappointing: here the voice does not sound quite secure. But this is a minor lapse in a first-rate achievement. The chorus is excellent, and the orchestral detail has the usual light

Godfrey touch. The remastering is very successful, the sound bright but with an admirable acoustic ambience which allows every word to project clearly.

The Mikado (complete, without dialogue).
(M) *** Decca 425 190-2 (2). Ayldon, Wright, J. Reed, Sandford, Masterson, Holland, D'Oyly Carte Op. Ch., RPO, Nash.

The 1973 stereo re-recording of *The Mikado* by the D'Oyly Carte company directed by Royston Nash is a complete success in every way and shows the Savoy tradition at its most attractive. The digital remastering for CD adds to the brightness: its effect is like a coat of new paint, so that the G & S masterpiece emerges with a pristine sparkle. Musically this is the finest version the D'Oyly Carte company have ever put on disc. The choral singing is first rate, with much refinement of detail. The glees, *Brightly dawns* and *See how the fates*, are robust in the D'Oyly Carte manner but more polished than usual. The words are exceptionally clear throughout. Of the principals, John Reed is a splendid Ko-Ko, a refined and individual characterization. Kenneth Sandford gives his customary vintage projection of Pooh-Bah and Valerie Masterson is a charming Yum-Yum. Colin Wright's vocal production has a slightly nasal quality; but one soon adjusts to it, and his voice has the proper bright freshness of timbre for Nanki-Poo. John Ayldon's Mikado has not quite the satanic glitter of Donald Adams's classic version, but he provides a laugh of terrifying bravura. Katisha (Lyndsie Holland) is commanding, and her attempts to interrupt the chorus in the finale of Act I are superbly believable and dramatic. On CD the singers are given striking presence, though the bright lighting of the sound has brought more sibilance.

The Mikado: highlights.
(B) *** Decca 433 618-2; *433 618-4* [id.]. Soloists, D'Oyly Carte Op. Ch., RPO, Royston Nash.

An hour of highlights taken from the above 1973 set and including almost all the key numbers. This bargain issue includes an excellent synopsis of the plot but, strangely, no cast list.

Patience (complete, with dialogue).
(M) *** Decca 425 193-2 (2). Sansom, Adams, Cartier, Potter, J. Reed, Sandford, Newman, Lloyd-Jones, Toye, Knight, D'Oyly Carte Op. Ch. & O, Godfrey.

Patience comes up superbly in its digitally remastered format. The military numbers are splendidly projected and vividly coloured – *When I first put this uniform on* and *The soldiers of our Queen* have an unforgettable vigour and presence, with Donald Adams in glorious voice. Everything seems to be freshened, and the D'Oyly Carte soloists, chorus and orchestra have never sounded better. Mary Sansom takes the lead charmingly and she is especially good in the dialogue. Both Bunthorne and Grosvenor are very well played. The dialogue is at a slightly lower dynamic level than the music, but that only reflects the reality of the theatre. Overall, this is irresistible.

The Pirates of Penzance (complete, with dialogue).
(M) *** Decca 425 196-2. J. Reed, Adams, Potter, Masterson, Palmer, Brannigan, D'Oyly Carte Op. Ch., RPO, Godfrey.

For compact disc issue, Decca have chosen the second (1968) D'Oyly Carte recording, and Isidore Godfrey is helped by a more uniformly excellent cast than was present on the earlier set. The dialogue is included, theatrical spontaneity is well maintained, and the spoken scenes with the Pirate King are particularly effective. Christene Palmer's Ruth is not quite so poised, but her singing is first rate – her opening aria has never been done better. John Reed's characterization of the part of the Major-General is strong, while Valerie Masterson is an excellent Mabel; if her voice is not creamy throughout its range, she controls it with great skill. Her duet with Frederic, *Leave me not to pine alone*, is enchanting, sung very gently. Godfrey's conducting is as affectionate as ever; but perhaps the greatest joy of the set is Owen Brannigan's Sergeant of Police, a part this artist was surely born to play. It is a marvellously humorous performance, yet the humour is never clumsy; the famous *Policeman's song* is so fresh that it is almost like hearing it for the first time. The recording is superbly spacious and clear throughout, with a fine sense of atmosphere. While a slight degree of edge appears on the voices at times, the sense of theatrical feeling is greatly enhanced and the dialogue interchanges have an uncanny realism.

(i) *The Yeomen of the Guard* (complete, without dialogue); (ii) *Trial by Jury*.
(M) *** Decca 417 358-2; *417 358-4*. Hood, J. Reed, Sandford, Adams, Raffell; (i) Harwood, Knight; (ii) Round; D'Oyly Carte Op. Ch.; (i) RPO, Sargent; (ii) ROHCG O, Godfrey.

Sir Malcolm Sargent recorded *The Yeomen of the Guard* in stereo twice very successfully. The later, Decca set has marginally the finer recording and Sir Malcolm's breadth of approach is at once apparent in the overture, and when the chorus enters (*Tower warders*) the feeling of opera rather than operetta is striking. Indeed one has seldom heard the choruses expand with such power, nor indeed has the orchestra (especially the brass) produced such a regal sound. As the work proceeds the essential lyricism of Sargent's reading begins to emerge more and more, and the ensemble singing is especially lovely. There is no lack of drama either, and indeed the only aspect of the work to be played down somewhat is the humorous side. The pathos of the famous Jester's song in Act II is played up, and the only moment to raise a real smile is the duet which follows, *Tell a tale of cock and bull.* But with consistently fine singing throughout from all the principals (and especially Elizabeth Harwood as Elsie), this *Yeomen* is unreservedly successful with its brilliant and atmospheric Decca recording. The CD transfer has splendid presence and immediacy.

'The best of Gilbert & Sullivan': excerpts from: *The Gondoliers; HMS Pinafore; Iolanthe; The Mikado; The Pirates of Penzance.*
(B) *** EMI CDZ7 62531-2; *LZ 762531-4*. Morison, Graham, Sinclair, Marjorie Thomas, Lewis, Young, George Baker, Cameron, Brannigan, Sir Geraint Evans, Milligan, Wallace, Glyndebourne Festival Ch., Pro Arte O, Sargent.

With a maximum amount of music included, this makes a fine bargain sampler for Sargent's (currently withdrawn) G & S series on EMI. The longest selection comes from *The Mikado* (with nine items included), not the strongest of the performances but with many felicities. The slow tempo for the *Cachucha* remains a curious drawback in the excerpts from *The Gondoliers*; but the items from *Iolanthe*, *The Pirates* and *Pinafore* have plenty of zest, and the lyrical singing is a pleasure throughout when the cast is so strong. The transfers are fresh and clear, with an abundance of ambience.

Highlights from: *The Gondoliers; HMS Pinafore; Iolanthe; The Mikado; The Pirates of Penzance; The Yeomen of the Guard.*
(B) **(*) CfP CD-CFP 4238; *TC-CFP 4238* [id.]. Soloists, Glyndebourne Festival Ch., Pro Arte O, Sargent.

Another attractive selection of highlights offering samples of six of Sargent's vintage EMI recordings. There is some distinguished solo singing and, if the atmosphere is sometimes a little cosy (once again one notices that the *Cachucha* from *The Gondoliers* sounds slower than ever heard out of context of the complete performance), there is a great deal to enjoy. The recordings have transferred well.

'The Best of Gilbert and Sullivan': excerpts from: *The Gondoliers; HMS Pinafore; The Mikado; The Pirates of Penzance.*
(B) *** EMI Miles of Music *TC2-MOM 106*. Morison, Sinclair, Graham, Thomas, Lewis, Young, Baker, Cameron, Brannigan, Evans, Milligan, Wallace, Glyndebourne Festival Ch., Pro Arte O, Sargent.

'Gilbert and Sullivan favourites': excerpts from: *The Gondoliers; HMS Pinafore; Iolanthe; The Mikado; Patience; The Pirates of Penzance; Ruddigore; The Yeomen of the Guard.*
(B) *** EMI Miles of Music *TC2-MOM 114*. (artists as above, plus) Anthony, Harwood, Bowden, Rouleau; Glyndebourne Festival Ch., Pro Arte O, Sargent.

Sargent's vintage studio recordings of the Savoy Operas were recorded between 1957 and 1963, with a wholly admirable cast. They blew a fresh breeze through the D'Oyly Carte performing tradition (of which Sargent himself had theatrical experience) and set very high musical standards. These two admirable cassette compilations, each offering over 80 minutes of music, should prove stimulating motorway entertainment; the first offers extensive selections from four favourite operas, while the second ranges more widely; however, as nothing is duplicated, they are complementary. The lollipops are fairly evenly divided: Owen Brannigan's immortal account of the *Policeman's song* from *Pirates* is on *TC2-MOM 114* (which is a marginal first choice), while the longer groups of numbers from that same opera, *Iolanthe* and *Pinafore* on *TC2-MOM 106* contain much that is very engaging indeed. Excellent, fresh transfers, with the words coming through clearly.

'The world of Gilbert and Sullivan': excerpts from: (i) *The Gondoliers; HMS Pinafore; Iolanthe;* (ii) *The Mikado;* (i) *The Pirates of Penzance;* (iii) *The Yeomen of the Guard.*
(B) *** Decca 430 095-2; *430 095-4*. Soloists, D'Oyly Carte Op. Co., New SO or RPO, (i) Godfrey; (ii) Nash; (iii) Sargent.

A quite admirable selection from the vintage series of Decca D'Oyly Carte recordings made between 1959 (*HMS Pinafore* – still the finest of the whole series) and 1973 (Royston Nash's *Mikado*). This was the right choice, as it is much more strongly cast than the earlier, Godfrey set, with John Reed shining brightly as Koko. His 'Little list' song is wonderfully relaxed, and *Tit willow* is charming. He is equally good as Sir Joseph Porter, KCB, in *Pinafore*, where his splendid *I am the monarch of the sea* is preceded by some highly atmospheric stage business. Owen Brannigan's unforgettable portrayal of the Sergeant of Police is demonstrated in the excerpts from *The Pirates of Penzance* (as is Valerie Masterson's charming

Mabel), and two of the most delectable items are the Second Act trios from *Pinafore* and *Iolanthe*, both liltingly infectious. Sargent's fine *Yeomen of the Guard* is only briefly represented, so we must hope that further selections are to follow. The recording has fine atmosphere and presence throughout; *The Gondoliers*, however, betrays the same slightly degraded treble response of the complete recording. But overall, with 62 minutes of music offered, this is a real bargain which will give much delight.

Suppé, Franz von (1819–95)

Overtures: *Beautiful Galathea; Fatinitza; Flotte Bursche; Jolly robbers; Light Cavalry; Morning, noon and night in Vienna; Pique dame; Poet and peasant. March: O du mein Österreich.*
(BB) **(*) LaserLight Dig. 15 611 [id.]. Hungarian State Op. O, János Sándor.

Sándor's LaserLight collection is very generous and the Hungarian State Opera Orchestra know just how to play this repertoire: the zigeuner section in the middle of *Light Cavalry* is most winning, while the cello solo in *Morning, noon and night* has an attractive, romantic simplicity. There is plenty of sparkle and the small group of first violins ensures that the ensemble is clean and agile in the music's racier moments. Sándor duplicates Dutoit's full-price programme and offers two extra novelties in *Flott Bursche* (which brings an amiable quotation of *Gaudeamus igitur*) and a vivid Viennese-style march. The digital recording is basically full-bodied but has brilliance too, and this is a real bargain.

Svendsen, Johan Severin (1840–1911)

Romance in G, Op. 26.
(BB) *** Naxos Dig. 8.550329 [id.]. Dong-Suk Kang, Slovak (Bratislava) RSO, Adrian Leaper – HALVORSEN: *Air Norvégien* etc.; SIBELIUS: *Violin concerto*; SINDING: *Légende.* ***

Svendsen's once-popular *Romance in G* is otherwise available only in Grumiaux's version from the 1960s. Dong-Suk Kang plays it without sentimentality but with full-hearted lyricism. The balance places him a little too forward, but the recording is very satisfactory.

Sweelinck, Jan (1562–1621)

Chorale variations: Da pacem, Domine, in diebus nostris; Puer nobis nascitur; Echo fantasia No. 12 in A min.; Fantasia No. 4 in D min; Hexachord fantasia; Toccata No. 17 in A.
(M) ** HM/BMG GD 77148 [77148-2-RG]. Gustav Leonhardt (organ of Grote of St Jakobswerk, The Hague).

It is good to have an authoritative introduction to Sweelinck's organ music played on a splendid Dutch organ, but the recording, though faithful, is less than ideal in its close balance which – together with Gustav Leonhardt's playing – seems too often to project the music on an unvarying dynamic level. Leonhardt's registrations are often attractive, and he clearly has the measure of the composer's often complex contrupuntal devices (as in the *Hexachord fantasia*), but one feels more could have been made of the imitation in the *Echo fantasia*, achieved by the repetition of a phrase on a different manual, or played an octave lower. We hope Peter Hurford may turn his attention to this repertoire.

Szymanowski, Karol (1882–1937)

Symphonies Nos. 2, Op. 19; (i) *3 (Song of the night), Op. 27.*
(M) *** Decca Dig. 425 625-2 [id.]. (i) Ryszard Karczykowski, Jewell Ch.; Detroit SO, Dorati (with BARTÓK: *2 Pictures* ***).

This 1980 Decca coupling was the first Western commercial recording of either of these symphonies. The *Second* is not as rewarding a score as the *Third*, but it is unusual formally: there are only two movements, the second being a set of variations culminating in a fugue. The influences of Strauss and Scriabin are clearly audible and not altogether assimilated. *The Song of the night* is one of the composer's most beautiful scores, and much of its heady, intoxicated – and intoxicating – atmosphere is captured here, together with its extraordinarily vivid colouring and sense of rapture; the detail and opulence of the orchestral textures are fully revealed and the chorus is clear and well balanced. A most valuable reissue, and the Bartók coupling is apt, though here the recording has an analogue master.

Mythes, Op. 30; Kurpian folk song; King Roger: Roxana's aria (both arr. Kochanski).
❀ (M) *** DG 431 469-2; *431 469-4.* Kaja Danczowska, Krystian Zimerman – FRANCK: *Violin sonata.* ***

The violinist Kaja Danczowska, a pupil of Eugenia Uminska and David Oistrakh, brings vision and poetry to the ecstatic, soaring lines of the opening movement of *Mythes*, *The Fountains of Arethusa*. Her intonation is impeccable, and she has the measure of these other-worldly, intoxicating scores. There is a sense of rapture here that is totally persuasive, and Krystian Zimerman plays with a virtuosity and imagination that silence criticsm. An indispensable issue, the more so as the CD transfer of this 1980 analogue recording is so vividly realistic.

Tallis, Thomas (*c.* 1505–85)

The Lamentations of Jeremiah the Prophet; Spem in alium (40-part motet).
(B) ** Pickwick Dig. PCD 806 [id.]. Pro Cantione Antiqua, Mark Brown – ALLEGRI: *Miserere.* **

On Pickwick, a strong, generally well-sung performance (although there are moments in the motet when intonation is not absolutely secure). The microphone balance brings a thickening of tone to the expansive climax of *Spem in alium* and less than ideal transparency of texture. But this CD may be counted good value.

Tartini, Giuseppe (1692–1770)

Cello concerto in A.
(M) *** DG 429 098-2; *429 098-4.* Rostropovich, Zurich Coll. Mus., Sacher – BOCCHERINI; VIVALDI: *Concertos.* ***

As with the other works in this fine 1978 collection, Rostropovich's view of Tartini's *A major Concerto* is larger than life; but the eloquence of the playing disarms criticism, even when the cellist plays cadenzas of his own that are not exactly in period. The lively accompaniment is matched by bright, vivid recording that sounds splendid on CD.

Violin concertos: in E min., D.56; in A, D.96; in A min., D.113.
(M) *** Erato/Warner Dig. 2292 45380-2 [id.]. Uto Ughi, Sol. Ven., Scimone.

Tartini is a composer of unfailing originality, and the three violin concertos on this record are all very rewarding. The *Concerto in A major*, which comes last on the disc, has an additional (probably) alternative slow movement, a *Largo Andante* which is particularly beautiful. Uto Ughi's performances are distinguished by excellent taste and refinement of tone, and I Solisti Veneti are hardly less polished. The harpsichord continuo is somewhat reticent but otherwise the recording is exemplary. Highly recommended.

Tchaikovsky, Peter (1840–93)

Andante cantabile for cello and orchestra, Op. posth.
(M) *** DG 431 475-2; *431 475-4* [id.]. Rostropovich, BPO – GLAZUNOV: *Chant du ménestrel*; SHOSTAKOVICH: *Cello concerto No. 2.* ***

The composer himself arranged the *Andante cantabile* for cello and orchestra from his *D major String quartet*, transposing it from B flat to B major, but it was not published until after his death. Rostropovich indulges himself affectionately in the work, and the balance – all cello with a discreet orchestral backing – reflects his approach. The sound is warm and pleasing.

Capriccio italien, Op. 45.
(BB) *** BMG/RCA Dig. VD 87727 [7727-2-RV]. Dallas SO, Mata (with *Concert* ***).

Capriccio italien, Op. 45; 1812 overture, Op. 49; Francesca da Rimini, Op. 32; Marche slave, Op. 31.
(B) **(*) Ph. 422 469-2. Concg. O, Haitink.

Capriccio italien, Op. 45; 1812 Overture; Marche slave, Op. 31; Romeo and Juliet (fantasy overture).
(BB) *** Naxos Dig. 8.550500 [id.]. RPO, Adrian Leaper.

Capriccio italien, Op. 45; Nutcracker suite, Op. 71a; Sleeping Beauty (ballet) *suite, Op. 66a.*
(M) *** DG 431 610-2; *431 610-4* [id.]. BPO, Rostropovich.

We have given the highest praise (and a Rosette) to the Rostropovich triptych combining the three Tchaikovsky ballet suites, which added *Swan Lake* to the two listed here (see below) and that still seems the most appropriate coupling; but anyone whose collection has room for *Capriccio italien* rather than *Swan Lake* will find the present reissue hardly less rewarding. Here the vulgarity inherent in the principal theme (which Tchaikovsky thought was a folksong but which proved to be a local Italian 'pop' tune of the time) evaporates, so decoratively elegant is the playing of the Berlin Philharmonic, especially the violins. The finale, too, has an attractive burst of exuberance, and the bright CD transfer lightens any hint of rhythmic heaviness in the fully scored reprise of the main tune. These were among the finest recordings the DG engineers made in the Philharmonie in the late 1970s.

Like Sian Edwards, Adrian Leaper is a natural Tchaikovskian; whether in the colourful extravagance of the composer's memento of his Italian holiday, the romantic ardour and passionate conflict of *Romeo and Juliet*, the sombre expansiveness of *Marche slave* with its surge of adrenalin at the close, or in the extrovert celebration of *1812*, he produces playing from the RPO that is spontaneously committed and exciting. The brilliantly spectacular recording, with plenty of weight for the brass, was made in Watford Town Hall, with realistic cannon and an impressively resonant imported carillon to add to the very exciting climax of *1812*. A splendid disc that would still be recommendable if it cost far more.

Tchaikovsky's *Capriccio italien* was given an extraordinarily successful compact disc début on Mata's Dallas disc. The concert-hall effect of the recording is very impressive indeed, with the opening fanfares sonically as riveting as the silences when the reverberation dies away naturally. The performance is colourful and exciting, and the piece is issued within an attractive compilation of favourite orchestral showpieces (see Concerts section, below).

Haitink's *Capriccio italien* is warm-blooded, with the string-playing elegantly turned. The restatement of the main theme at the end is given striking weight and thereafter the coda is rather slow in getting under way; but otherwise this is distinctly successful, as is *1812*, which has brilliance and momentum and a touch of dignity at the end, with the bangs well integrated into the orchestral texture. *Francesca da Rimini* is finely played – the central clarinet solo beautifully done – but lacks a sense of high nervous tension in its closing section. The sound is vividly remastered.

Piano concertos Nos. 1–3; Concert fantasia (for piano and orchestra), *Op. 56.*

(M) **(*) EMI Dig. CMS7 63658-2 (2); *EX 763658-4*. Peter Donohoe, Bournemouth SO, Rudolf Barshai.

If only Peter Donohoe could have repeated the success of his recording of the *Second Piano concerto* (which won the *Gramophone* magazine's Concerto Award in 1988 and a Rosette from us) when he returned to the Poole Arts Centre to record these other Tchaikovsky works, this mid-priced box would have been a very attractive proposition. But the account of the *B flat minor Concerto*, although thoroughly sympathetic and spaciously conceived, lacks the thrust and indeed the electricity of the finest versions. The *Third Piano concerto* is altogether more successful, dramatic and lyrically persuasive, and well held together by Barshai; this is now available at full price, sensibly coupled with the *Second*, and is a better buy than the present box. The *Concert fantasia* is even more in need of interpretative cohesion. It is laid out in two balancing movements, lasting about half an hour. The first opens with charming *Nutcracker* overtones yet develops a powerful central cadenza, which Donohoe plays grandly and rumbustiously. The second movement brings a series of chimerical changes of mood and tempo, which both pianist and conductor negotiate with zestful, spontaneous abandon. The lyrical interludes have a pleasing Russian folksiness, and the rhetoric of the allegros brings an exhilarating dash which almost carries the performers away with it. A little more poise would have been welcome, but there is no denying the spontaneous combustion of the music-making, and the recording – but for a little too much resonance for the solo cadenza in the opening movement – is effectively spectacular.

Piano concerto No. 1 in B flat min., Op. 23.

❀ (M) (***) BMG/RCA mono GD 87992 [7792-2-RG]. Horowitz, NBC SO, Toscanini – BEETHOVEN: *Piano concerto No. 5.* (***)

(M) (***) BMG/RCA mono GD 60449; *GK 60449*. Horowitz, NBC SO, Toscanini – MUSSORGSKY: *Pictures.* ***

(M) *** Decca 417 750-2 [id.]. Ashkenazy, LSO, Maazel – CHOPIN: *Concerto No. 2.* ***

(BB) *** Pickwick PWK 1148. Peter Katin, LSO, Eric Kundell – SCHUMANN: *Concerto.* **(*)

(M) **(*) Mercury 432 011-2 [id.]. Byron Janis, LSO Menges – SCHUMANN: *Concerto.* ***

(M) **(*) Chan. CHAN 6509; *MBTD 6509* [id.]. Terence Judd, Moscow PO, Lazarev – PROKOFIEV: *Concerto No. 3.* **(*)

(M) ** EMI CDM7 63525-2; *EG 763525-4*. John Ogdon, Philh. O, Barbirolli – RACHMANINOV: *Concerto No. 2* etc. **

(i) *Piano concerto No. 1 in B flat min., Op. 23. Theme and variations, Op. 19/6.*

(M) **(*) EMI CDM7 69125-2 [id.]; *EG 769125-4*. Gavrilov, (i) Philh. O, Muti (with LISZT: *La Campanella*) – BALAKIREV: *Islamey.* ***

Horowitz's famous account of the *B flat minor Concerto*, recorded at a concert in Carnegie Hall in 1943 with his father-in-law conducting, has dwarfed almost every record of the work made since. Somehow the alchemy of the occasion – which raised eleven million dollars in War Bonds! – was unique, and the result is unforgettable. The recording of the orchestra is confined and lacks body, some surface rustle remains from the 78-r.p.m. pressings, while the violins need a judicious degree of filtering, and even then don't sound very rich. But the piano itself is gloriously full and bold. Such is the magnetism of the playing, however, that the ear forgets the sonic limitations within moments. Toscanini's accompaniment is remarkable not only for matching the adrenalin of his soloist but for the tenderness he finds for the lyrical passages of the first movement. The powerful cadenza becomes its climax, wonderfully varied in colour, and with one passage in which there almost seem to be two pianists in duet, rather than just one pair of human hands. Toscanini's moments of delicacy extend to the *Andantino*, which is truly *simplice* (as the composer indicated), even when accompanying the coruscating pianistic fireworks of the central section.

The finale carries all before it, with Horowitz's riveting octave passage-work leading on to a tremendously exciting restatement of the big tune and then storming off furiously to the coda. The applause at the end is welcome for once, if only as a release of tension.

Horowitz's earlier version, coupled with the Mussorgsky, was made in Carnegie Hall, in 1941, under studio conditions. The recording is altogether better balanced than the famous live performance by the same artists two years later, and the orchestral sound is much fuller; indeed the quality brooks no real criticism. The performance has all the thrills and electricity of the 1943 version and the playing is prodigious in its bravura. But throughout one feels that Toscanini – with his soloist responding readily – is forcing the pace, creating enormous urgency in the first movement, which here is nearly a minute and a half shorter. The finale, too, has even more dazzling *fuoco*. This is an exhilarating listening experience; but the sense of occasion of the live performance created a really great performance which is undoubtedly more satisfying despite its sonic limitations.

Ashkenazy's performance is offered in alternative couplings: the Chopin is the more attractive, being at mid-price. This is not high-powered but it is lyrically satisfying. The soloist refuses to be stampeded by Tchaikovsky's rhetoric, and the biggest climaxes of the first movement are made to grow naturally out of the music. In the *Andantino* too, Ashkenazy refuses to play flashily and he uses the middle section rather as a contrasting episode to set in the boldest relief the delicate return of the opening tune. The finale is very fast and brilliant, yet the big tune is broadened at the end in the most convincing way. The remastering is highly successful: the piano sounds splendidly bold and clear while the orchestral balance is realistic.

Peter Katin's performance from the beginning of the 1970s is alive and direct, the opening big tune taken fast but with a fine sweep which continues through the first movement. The *Andantino* is played very stylishly, and the finale has plenty of bravura. With vintage Decca sound this is an enjoyable bargain, and the coupled Schumann *Concerto* is equally characterful.

Byron Janis's account is in many ways as dazzling as his Rachmaninov recordings (newly issued on CD). Menges is not as strong an accompanist as Dorati, most noticeably so in the finale. But this remains a memorable performance, with much dash and power from the soloist in the outer movements and the *Andantino* agreeably delicate. There are plenty of thrills, not least Janis's final stormy octaves before the bold restatement of the great tune in the finale. The Mercury sound is excellent, full and resonant, with a big piano image up front. There will be many who will enjoy this reading for its warmth of response in the lyrical material of the first movement, taking it nearer the (coupled) Schumann *Concerto* in romantic feeling.

The unbridled opening of the Terence Judd performance must be just about the fastest on record. He contributed this urgent and powerful reading at the 1978 Tchaikovsky Piano Competition in Moscow, and, though it has its moments of roughness and the recording is badly balanced and not exactly refined (yet not thin), the compulsion and urgency of the playing are hard to resist. This is hardly a version for general listening but, with the Prokofiev equally magnetic, it is a splendid reminder of a fine young pianist who died tragically young. The CD transfer makes the very most of the original sound.

Gavrilov is stunning in the finale of the *Concerto*; however, the final statement of the big tune is broadened so positively that one is not entirely convinced. Similarly in the first movement, contrasts of dynamic and tempo are extreme, and the element of self-consciousness is apparent. The *Andante* is full of tenderness and the *prestissimo* middle section goes like quicksilver, displaying the vein of spontaneous imagination that we recognize in Gavrilov's other records. The recording is full and sumptuous with a big, bold forward piano-image, so that the work's famous opening makes an immediate impact. In the *Variations*, Op. 19, Tchaikovsky's invention has great felicity. Gavrilov's playing is stylishly sympathetic here, and the Liszt *Paganini study*, *La Campanella*, which is his final encore, is dazzling.

The Ogdon/Barbirolli performance brings many highly musical touches, especially in its lyrical moments – the *Andantino*, with its natural simplicity, is most successful. But the barnstorming element is missing, and the finale seems underpowered. The 1962 recording still sounds very good.

Piano concertos Nos. 1 in B flat min.; 3 in E flat, Op. 75.

(M) **(*) EMI CD-EMX 2001. Gilels, New Philh. O, Maazel.

At medium price the Gilels/Maazel coupling from 1973 leads the field for those wanting these two concertos together. The recording is first class; though the piano is placed well forward, the sound is much better than in Gilels's CBS version. The *Third Concerto* is not lacking in memorable ideas and Gilels plays it with authority and freshness. The account of No. 1 is in many ways distinguished too, and it is certainly exciting, but it has a very fast opening that is exhilarating in its way. Many Tchaikovskians will feel, however, that this – one of his broadest melodies – needs a more expansive treatment.

(i) *Piano concerto No. 1 in B flat min., Op. 23;* (ii) *Violin concerto in D, Op. 35.*

(BB) *** BMG/RCA VD 60491; *VK 60491* [60491-2-RV; *60491-4-RV*]. (i) John Browning; (ii) Erick Friedman, LSO, Ozawa.

(M) *** Erato/Warner 2292 45674-2 [id.]. (i) Devoyon; (ii) Amoyal; Philh. O, Dutoit.

(B) **(*) DG 429 166-2; *429 166-4* [id.]. (i) Lazar Berman; (ii) Christian Ferras, BPO, Karajan.

(M) **(*) Sony Dig. MDK 44643 [id.]. (i) Gilels, NYPO; (ii) Zukerman, Israel PO; Mehta.

(M) **(*) Sony Dig./Analogue SBK 46339 [id.]; *40-46339.* (i) Gilels, NYPO, Mehta; (ii) D. Oistrakh, Phd. O, Ormandy.

(M) **(*) DG Analogue/Dig. 431 609-2; *431 609-4* [id.]. (i) Argerich, RPO, Dutoit; (ii) Kremer, BPO, Maazel.

(BB) **(*) LaserLight 15 516 [id.]. (i) Jenö Jandó, Budapest PO, Andras Ligeti; (ii) Emmy Verhey, Budapest SO, Arpad Joo.

(M) (*) Decca 430 725-2; *430 725-4* [id.]. (i) Postnikova, VSO, Rozhdestvensky; (ii) Kyung Wha Chung, Montreal SO, Dutoit.

The BMG/RCA coupling is an outstanding reissue, combining performances recorded in the mid-1960s. Browning's interpretation of the solo role in the *Piano concerto* is remarkable, not only for power and bravura but for wit and point in the many *scherzando* passages. His slow movement has an attractively cool simplicity, and in the finale he adopts a fast and furious tempo to compare with Horowitz. Erick Friedman, Heifetz's pupil, is a thoughtful violinist who gives a keenly intelligent performance of the companion work, imbued with a glowing lyricism and with a particularly poetic and beautiful account of the slow movement. There is plenty of dash and fire in the finale, and Ozawa gives first-rate support to both soloists. The recording was always excellent but now seems even firmer with the digital remastering, which gives the soloists excellent presence and the orchestra a more arresting impact at the opening of the *Piano concerto.* Two performances to match those of almost any rival; moreover this disc is in the lowest price-range.

Two most enjoyable performances on Erato, given excellent, modern, analogue recording, well transferred to CD. The performance of the *Piano concerto* is the very opposite of barnstorming. It opens and closes spaciously and, even in the big final statement of the finale, the participants hold back from unleashing a torrent of rhetoric. The result is refreshing. There is no lack of spontaneity and the first movement unfolds grandly, its lyrical impulse fully realized. With Dutoit in charge, the Philharmonia playing is predictably polished and committed and the soloist, Pascal Devoyon, is persuasive too, refusing to be stampeded at any point. While there are fewer switchback thrills here than usual, there is much that is satisfying. About Amoyal's account of the *Violin concerto* there can be no reservations. He plays with passionate commitment, his slow movement is particularly beautiful, and he is extremely sensitively accompanied. Dutoit gets exciting results from the Philharmonia and the analogue recording from the early 1980s is first class (the solo violin sounds particularly sweet and full-toned, without a suspicion of edginess). The disc is issued in Erato's Résidence series, so the notes link both works to Tchaikovsky's association with St Petersburg.

Berman's 1976 recording with Karajan makes a formidable bargain issue, well coupled with Christian Ferras's much earlier version of the *Violin concerto.* Berman's character is firmly established in the massive chords of the introduction; from there his revelling in dramatic contrast – whether of texture, tone-colour, dynamic or tempo – makes this one of the most exciting readings ever put on record. It is not just a question of massive bravura but of extreme delicacy too, so that in the central scherzando of the slow movement it almost sounds as though Berman is merely breathing on the keyboard, hardly depressing the notes at all. The ripe playing of the Berlin Philharmonic backs up the individuality of Berman's reading, and the recording is massively brilliant to match. Ferras's characteristic tone, with its rather close vibrato in lyrical passages, will not be to all tastes. But his is a well-conceived reading, with Karajan shaping the work as a whole very convincingly. The recording is excellent, rather warmer and more atmospheric than that provided for the *Piano concerto.*

CBS's digital coupling costs slightly more than the DG disc. There are more reservations about the Gilels performance than the Zukerman. The former offers less than first-class orchestral playing and not very distinguished sound, but Gilels's own playing is masterly. In Israel, the sound is much better, and Mehta secures generally good results from the Israel orchestra. The soloist is balanced closely and is made very tangible; Zukerman's warmth is most attractive, and the performance overall has both excitement and spontaneity.

Having already offered Gilels's 1980 digital

recording of the *Piano concerto* together with Zukerman's version of the *Violin concerto*, Sony now try again, choosing an alternative pairing with David Oistrakh's performance, recorded with Ormandy a decade earlier. It is, not surprisingly, an excellent performance but, perhaps because of the close microphones, Oistrakh's tone sounds thinner than usual. Such moments as the recapitulation of the second subject high among the ledger lines are beautifully done, but elsewhere the effect is not always as ravishing as one might expect. As usual, Ormandy provides a sympathetic accompaniment, although the imagery of the recording is slightly overblown, with the solo image made larger than life-size.

Argerich's 1971 version of the *Piano concerto* with Dutoit remains among the finest ever made, and the recording still sounds marvellous, bold and full and with striking presence. Kremer's was the first digital recording of the *Violin concerto*. This artist blends keen nervous energy with controlled lyrical feeling; it goes without saying that his virtuosity is impressive. Self-regarding agogic distortions are few (bars 50–58 and the first-movement cadenza are instances) and there is no lack of warmth – yet there is something missing. An outstanding performance of this work refreshes the spirit and resonates in the mind (Campoli's version – see below – does just this). With Kremer, although the playing of the Berlin Philharmonic under Maazel and the 1979 recording are both excellent, there is not the humanity and perception of a special kind which are needed if a newcomer is to take pride of place in a collection. The Compact Classics issue of Argerich's performance (see below) is a much better investment.

Although the name of the violinist is unknown in the West, both soloists on the LaserLight coupling are excellent players and the performances give real satisfaction. The overall balance in the *Piano concerto* is forward, which means some reduction in dynamic range, but the recording is admirably full and the performance has a direct spontaneity and power, with a strong forward momentum and plenty of excitement in the outer movements, while Jandó's controlled virtuosity in the *prestissimo* section of the *Andantino* is matched by his exciting bravura in the finale. The work's lyrical side is well realized too, more delicately in the *Andantino*, but the orchestral reprise of the big tune in the last movement is powerfully spontaneous. The *Violin concerto* is equally impressive. Emmy Verhey plays with a full tone, sparkling virtuosity and a sense of fantasy, while the slow movement has a tender simplicity and warmth. The recorded balance is natural and the orchestral texture is given plenty of body and ambient warmth yet is rather more open than the *Piano concerto*.

It was extraordinarily bad planning to recouple Kyung Wha Chung's engagingly volatile digital account of the *Violin concerto* with Postnikova's dull and mannered version of the *First Piano concerto*. Chung's tenderly affecting central *Canzonetta* contrasts only too obviously with Postnikova's studied reading of the *Andante* of the work for piano. Clearly, on this occasion the husband-and-wife partnership was not artistically stimulating. The famous opening of the *Piano concerto* is disconcertingly slow and later, in the first movement and other places, Postnikova's expressive fluctuations sound unspontaneous. This is most unenticing, though the digital recording of both works is excellent.

(i) *Piano concerto No. 1;* (ii) *Violin concerto in D, Op. 35;* (iii) *Serenade for strings: Waltz* (CD only: *Serenade for strings:* complete). (iv or v) *Variations on a rococo theme, Op. 33.*

❀ (B) *** DG Compact Classics 413 161-2 (2); *413 161-4*. (i) Argerich, RPO, Dutoit; (ii) Milstein, VPO, Abbado; (iii) BPO, Karajan (cassette only: (iv) Rostropovich, Leningrad PO, Rozhdestvensky; CD only: (v) Rostropovich, BPO, Karajan).

This extended-length chrome tape was the jewel in the crown of DG's Walkman series (now renamed Compact Classics), always generous but here exceptionally so, both in quality of performances and recording, as well as in the amount of music offered. We awarded it a Rosette as the outstanding Tchaikovsky bargain compilation. Now for their 2-CD equivalent, DG have gone one better by replacing Karajan's elegant and polished *Waltz* from the *String serenade* (which remains on the tape) with the remastered analogue performance of the work from which it was drawn. Moreover, on CD Rostropovich's later recording of the *Rococo variations*, with Karajan, is substituted for his earlier version with Rozhdestvensky. Rostropovich and Karajan find a splendid symbiosis, and this performance is superb in every way, and very well recorded. Yet tape collectors need not feel deprived, for Rostropovich's earlier (1961) version also offers playing with just the right amount of jaunty elegance as regards the theme and the first few variations; and when the virtuoso fireworks are let off, they are brilliant, effortless and breathtaking in their éclat. Indeed Rostropovich needs no superlatives, and Rozhdestvensky shows a mastery all his own. Argerich's account of the *B flat minor Piano concerto* is second to none; Milstein's (1973) performance of the *Violin concerto* is equally impressive, undoubtedly one of the finest available, while Abbado secures playing of genuine sensitivity and scale from the Vienna Philharmonic. The only slight drawback on the cassette is that the turnover comes between the first and second movements of the *Piano concerto*. But it is difficult to see how this could have been avoided within the chosen format. The sound is excellent in both formats.

(i) *Piano concerto No. 1;* (ii) *Violin concerto;* (iii) *Variations on a rococo theme for cello and orchestra.*
(B) ** Pickwick DUET 12 CD (2). (i) Graffman, Cleveland O, Szell; (ii) Isaac Stern; (iii) Leonard Rose, Phd. O, Ormandy.

This bargain-price Pickwick set is not especially generous, with the *Piano concerto* (at 34 minutes) alone on the first disc. However, Graffman's partnership with Szell produces a performance in which the electricity crackles, with the spirit of Horowitz and Toscanini evoked at the finale. Its atmosphere may be tense but the impact is undeniable, and lyrical contrast is not forgotten; an engaging delicacy pervades the outer sections of the *Andante*. The snag is the over-brilliant recording. Similarly in Stern's powerfully romantic reading of the *Violin concerto* the balance is too forward: his tone is rich but pianissimos consistently become *mezzo fortes*. Rose gives a warm, slightly reticent but admirably eloquent account of the *Rococo variations* and the sound here is quite good, though throughout this disc orchestral tuttis are without a desirable Tchaikovskian opulence.

Violin concerto in D, Op. 35.
(M) *** Decca 417 707-2 [id.]. Kyung Wha Chung, LSO, Previn – BRUCH: *Concerto No. 1*; SAINT-SAENS: *Havanaise.* ***
(BB) *** Naxos Dig. 8.550153 [id.]. Takako Nishizaki, Slovak PO, Kenneth Jean – MENDELSSOHN: *Concerto.* ***
(B) *** Ph. 422 473-2; *422 473-4*. Grumiaux, New Philh. O, Krenz – MENDELSSOHN: *Concerto.* ***
(M) *** DG 419 067-2 [id.]. Milstein, VPO, Abbado – MENDELSSOHN: *Concerto.* ***
(M) (***) EMI mono CDH7 64030-2 [id.]. Heifetz, LPO, Barbirolli – GLAZUNOV: *Violin concerto* (***) ❀; SIBELIUS: *Violin concerto.* (**)
(BB) **(*) Pickwick PWK 1145 [id.]. Campoli, LSO, Argenta.
(B) **(*) Decca 417 687-2 [id.]. Ricci, Netherlands R. PO, Fournet – MENDELSSOHN: *Concerto.* **(*)
(B) **(*) Sony CD 42537 [MYK 36724]. Stern, Phd. O, Ormandy – MENDELSSOHN: *Concerto.* **(*)

(i; ii) *Violin concerto in D;* (ii) *Capriccio italien*; (iii) *Francesca da Rimini.*
(M) **(*) EMI Dig. CDD7 63890-2 [id.]; *ET 763890-4*. (i) Vladimir Spivakov; (ii) Philh. O; (iii) BPO; Ozawa.

Those happy with the coupling with Bruch and Saint-Saëns should be well satisfied with Chung's 1970 version, which is still among the finest in the catalogue and in which Previn's accompanying is highly sympathetic and responsive. This has warmth, spontaneity and discipline; every detail is beautifully shaped and turned without a trace of sentimentality. Chung refuses to sentimentalize the central *Canzonetta*, choosing a flowing, easily songful speed. The result is the more tenderly affecting. The recording is well balanced and detail is clean, though the acoustic is warm.

Takako Nishizaki gives a warm and colourful reading, tender but purposeful and full of temperament. As in the Mendelssohn with which this is coupled, the central slow movement is on the measured side but flows sweetly, while the finale has all the necessary bravura, even at a speed that avoids breathlessness. Unlike many, Nishizaki opens out the little cuts which had become traditional. With excellent playing and recording, this makes a first-rate recommendation in the super-bargain bracket.

Grumiaux's playing has the usual aristocratic refinement and purity of tone to recommend it. His reading, too, is beautifully paced and has a particularly fine slow movement, less overtly emotional than some; both here and in the brilliant finale he shows superb aplomb and taste. With an excellent accompaniment from Krenz, this ranks among the finest budget versions, for the 1970s recording has a wide range and is firmly focused in its CD format.

Milstein's fine 1973 version with Abbado is here coupled with the Mendelssohn *Concerto* and remains one of the best mid-price reissues.

Heifetz's first recording of the Tchaikovsky *Violin concerto*, made in 1937, has tremendous virtuosity and warmth. The sound is opaque by modern standards but the ear quickly adjusts, and the performance is special even by Heifetz's own standards. The playing has even greater freshness and poetic feeling than his later recording with Reiner – though that, too, has a humanity that one does not always associate with this great violinist. The transfer, too, is very good and, coming as it does with a classic account of the Glazunov and a fascinating Sibelius, is a real bargain.

Campoli's performance has a lyrical simplicity and a natural warmth and spontaneity that are very appealing. Ataulfo Argenta accompanies with much sensitivity and shows his feeling for Tchaikovsky's orchestral colouring – especially in the *Canzonetta*, which has much wistful charm – as well as creating plenty of excitement and contrast in the tuttis: the polacca treatment of the main theme in the first movement is infectiously joyous. The finale brings fireworks from all concerned. The 1958 Decca recording, outstanding in its day, hardly shows its age, although a little judicious smoothing at the top is useful, for the sound has plenty of bloom. In today's marketplace a CD of this work, playing for 34 minutes and offering no coupling, can hardly be considered competitive, but anyone buying this super-bargain disc on impulse could well be surprised at the pleasure which it offers.

Ricci's characteristic, intense vibrato may not be to all tastes, but the ear readily submits to the compulsion and colour of the playing, which shows a rock-steady technique and a splendid lyrical feeling, so that the rich stream of tone is always securely based and the larger-than-life image is attractive, when the orchestral impact and detail are so vividly conveyed. The CD transfer is full and clear.

Spivakov takes a relatively heavyweight view of the *Concerto*, rich and warm, helped by strikingly full (even if early – 1981) digital recording, made at EMI's Abbey Road Studio. With Ozawa directing the Philharmonia in a most persuasive accompaniment, this is simultaneously a reading which brings out the almost Mozartian elegance of much of the writing, emphasizing the happiness of the inspiration. A joyful performance, too, of the *Capriccio italien*, the original fill-up; only the additional Berlin Philharmonic *Francesca da Rimini* (made in the Philharmonie in 1984) brings disappointment. Its essential neurosis means that at the end of the middle section Ozawa begins his accelerando much too early (at the cor anglais scalic figure) and, while what follows is undoubtedly thrilling, it turns Tchaikovsky's construction into melodrama.

Stern was on peak form when he made his first stereo recording with Ormandy, and it is a powerfully lyrical reading, rich in timbre and technically immaculate. The playing has undoubted poetry but is not helped by the very close balance of the soloist, so that pianissimos consistently become mezzo fortes. The orchestral sound is vivid but lacks amplitude.

Violin concerto; Sérénade mélancolique, Op. 35; Souvenir d'un lieu cher, Op. 42: (Méditation; Scherzo; Mélodie; orch. Glazunov).
(BB) *(**) Naxos Dig. 8.550124. Mariko Honda, Slovak PO or CSR SO, Keith Clark.

It was an excellent idea for Naxos to put all Tchaikovsky's music for violin and orchestra on a single super-bargain CD. In fact the *Souvenir d'un lieu cher* includes the *D minor Méditation*, originally intended as the slow movement for the *Concerto*, plus two other pieces, a *Scherzo* and a *Mélodie*, here orchestrated by Glazunov. Together they almost form another miniature concerto (though with the fast movement at the centre). Mariko Honda is wholly in sympathy with the specifically Tchaikovskian melancholy which permeates these shorter, lyrical pieces, and even in the *Concerto* her account of the slow movement and the lyrical episodes of the finale bring a darker colouring than with many soloists. Yet her playing can sparkle too, though overall her chosen tempi are comparatively relaxed. These are all performances of considerable intensity, well accompanied, and it is a pity that the brilliant digital recording balances her so closely, so the microphones do not always flatter her tone in the more histrionic upper tessitura. The orchestral sound is also brightly vivid.

1812 Overture, Op. 49.
(M) **(*) Decca Dig. 430 446-2; *430 446-4*. Chicago SO, Solti – MUSSORGSKY: *Pictures* ***; PROKOFIEV: *Symphony No. 1*. *(*)

1812 Overture; Francesca da Rimini, Op. 32.
(M) **(*) Decca Dig. 430 700-2; *430 700-4* [id.]. Montreal SO, Dutoit – MUSSORGSKY: *Night*; RIMSKY-KORSAKOV: *Capriccio espagnol*. **(*)

1812 Overture; Francesca da Rimini, Op. 32; Marche slave, Op. 31.
(M) ** DG 431 608-2; *431 608-4* [id.]. Chicago SO, Barenboim.

1812 Overture; Francesca da Rimini; Marche slave; Romeo and Juliet (fantasy overture).
(M) *** EMI Dig. CD-EMX 2152; *TC-EMX 2152*. Royal Liverpool PO, Sian Edwards.

(i) *1812 Overture;* (ii) *Marche slave;* (iii) *Romeo and Juliet* (CD only: (iv) *Capriccio italien*).
(B) **(*) DG Compact Classics 413 153-2 (2); *413 153-4*. (i) Boston Pops O, Fiedler; (ii) BPO, Karajan; (iii) San Francisco SO, Ozawa; (iv) BPO, Rostropovich – MUSSORGSKY: *Pictures* etc. ***

(i) *1812 Overture; Serenade for strings, Op. 48; Eugene Onegin: Polonaise and waltz.*
(M) **(*) DG 415 855-2; *415 855-4* [id.]. (i) Don Cossack Ch.; BPO, Karajan.

Sian Edwards's reading of *Francesca da Rimini* can be spoken of in the same breath as Stokowski's famous version. The control of the music's emotional ebb and flow shows her as an instinctive Tchaikovskian, moving through the work surely and compulsively, after the doom-laden opening stroke of the tam-tam has created an impending sense of nemesis. Francesca's clarinet entry is melting and the work's middle section has a Beechamesque sense of colour. The passionate climax, representing the discovery of the lovers, falls only just short of the vehement force of the Stokowski version, while the spectacular recording gives great impact to the closing whirlwind sequence and the despair-laden final chords, where the tam-tam makes its presence felt very pungently. *1812* is also very enjoyable indeed, full of vigour and flair, with the lyrical Russian folk melodies on strings and woodwind relished colourfully, and a majestic final sequence with superbly resounding cannon. In *Romeo and Juliet*, the love-theme is ushered in very naturally and blossoms with the fullest ardour, while the feud music combined with the Friar Lawrence theme reaches a very dramatic climax; again the final chords carry a real sense of tragedy. *Marche slave*, resplendently high-spirited and exhilarating, makes a perfect foil. The full-bodied recording is well balanced and thrilling in the proper Tchaikovskian way, with plenty of sonority and weight from the brass and a full string patina. Anything these performances lack in final polish they make up for in commitment and vitality.

Fiedler's account of *1812* has plenty of adrenalin and is brilliantly recorded, with the effective display of pyrotechnics at the end adding spectacle without drowning the music. The direct manner of the performance does all Tchaikovsky asks, if with no special individuality. Nevertheless, with Karajan's *Marche slave* plus Ozawa's excellent *Romeo and Juliet*, and first-class sound throughout, this Compact Classics chrome tape, coupled with Mussorgsky, is certainly good value. The pair of CDs add Kurt Sanderling's idiomatic and romantic version of Borodin's *In the Steppes of Central Asia*, which suffers a little from thin violin tone, plus Rostropovich's splendid BPO version of the *Capriccio italien* (see above) which is in every way recommendable.

Dutoit's performances are individually characterized and by no means conventional in approach. *1812*, complete with cannon provided by the 22nd Regiment of Quebec, is exciting without making one sit on the edge of one's seat. The sound is refined and luminous but lacks the sumptuous weight which is needed to give Tchaikovsky's climaxes a physical thrill. *Francesca da Rimini* has both weight and strength, backed up by a recording of spectacular range, but with less variation of tension than in the very finest versions.

Solti's *1812*, like the coupled Mussorgsky, is exciting and spectacular, and the engineering is impressively brilliant, apart from a rather inexact focus for the carillon that accompanies the very precise cannonade at the end.

Karajan's *1812* (with chorus) is very professional and quite exciting, but the chorus used to open the piece is not very sonorously recorded and the work, complete with cannon, doesn't show much engineering flair. His earlier reading of the *Serenade* is also brilliantly played. The two central movements are superb, the *Waltz* bringing masterly control of rubato and colour (the strings make a lovely sound) while the *Élégie* is freely passionate. The brightness of the sound brings a slight feeling of aggressiveness to the outer movements and especially to the finale. The *Polonaise* and *Waltz* from *Eugene Onegin* have fine panache.

Barenboim's are enjoyable performances, but he is too ready to let the tension relax to be entirely convincing throughout this programme, although his affection for the music is never in doubt. In *1812*, the lyrical string-melody is appealingly expansive; but by the finest Chicago standards the playing, although not without excitement, has less than the usual grip. *Marche slave* is slow and solemn, while the middle section of *Francesca da Rimini* yields some beguilingly languorous wind playing and its passionate string climax has ardour. Yet in the outer sections the frenzied nervous tension of the whirlwinds is partly subdued by the conductor's partiality for breadth, although the coda is exciting enough. The digital recording is vivid but could expand more.

Francesca da Rimini, Op. 32; Romeo and Juliet (fantasy overture).

(M) * Ph. Dig. 434 220-2; *434 220-4*. Concg. O, Edo de Waart.

The early (1980) Philips recording for Edo de Waart has none of the sparkle and clarity one associates with digital techniques; indeed the sound is muddy and bass-heavy, with poor transients. The performances are played well but are in no any way memorable; indeed *Romeo and Juliet* is distinctly pedestrian.

Manfred Symphony, Op. 58.

(M) *** Collins Dig. 3001-2 [id.]. LSO, Yuri Simonov.

Although Simonov's tempi overall are spacious rather than thrusting (the very opening could have more rhythmic point) and the recording balance is a little recessed, this is still a highly involving and romantically powerful account of what is perhaps the most difficult of all Tchaikovsky's major works to bring off successfully. But Simonov has its measure and his reading reaches its climax with the massive organ entry in the finale, a moment of great drama.

The pastoral *Andante* also has a fine lyrical warmth, and the scherzo is lilting and colourful. Perhaps the big moment of the horns at the end of the first movement (with bells raised) is a little submerged in the rich ambience of the hall, but the strings are sumptuous and the sound overall has a natural concert-hall balance and plenty of impact. However, the best versions of *Manfred* are available only within sets: Ashkenazy's splendid version comes in harness with *Symphonies Nos. 4–6* and the finest account of all, by Jansons and the Oslo Philharmonic, is offered by Chandos along with all six numbered symphonies.

The Nutcracker (ballet), *Op. 71* (complete).
(M) **(*) Decca 425 450-2 (2) [id.]. Nat. PO, Richard Bonynge – OFFENBACH: *Le Papillon.* ***
(BB) ** Naxos Dig. 8.550324/5 [id.]. Slovak RSO (Bratislava), Lenárd – CHOPIN/GLAZUNOV: *Chopinina.* **

(i) *The Nutcracker* (ballet) complete; (ii) *Serenade for strings in C, Op. 48.*
(M) *** Mercury 432 750-2 (2). (i) LSO; (ii) Philharmonia Hungarica, Antal Dorati.

Undoubtedly Dorati's LSO version is the finest of the mid- and bargain-priced analogue *Nutcrackers.* Mercury had pioneered the very first complete mono recording in 1953, and the charming original cover-design for that set is reinstated for this stereo version, made in 1962 in Watford Town Hall. The engineering is sophisticated, with a natural balance; the hall ambience provides wamth and bloom, yet detail is characteristically refined (the harp comes over resplendently). The performance retains all the freshness of an enchanting score which – at the time the earlier, mono records were made – was still little-known, apart from the famous suite. The party sequence of Act I can often sound flat, but not here: Dorati relishes every detail, his characterization is strong, and the playing is full of life and elegance. When the magic begins to work, there is an immediate atmospheric frisson, the clock strikes midnight, and the toy battle has splendid mock ferocity. The *Journey through the pine forest* expands magnificently while the choral delicacy of the *Waltz of the snowflakes* is full of charm. In Act II the characteristic dances have much colour and vitality. Dorati's accelerando at the end of the *Trepak* reminds one of Beecham, and the *Waltz of the flowers* has an agreeably stylish élan in the crisply articulated string phrases. Altogether a great success. The *Serenade for strings* is less compelling. It was recorded four years earlier, in the Grosse Saal of the Vienna Konzerthaus, with the microphones hung just outside the proscenium arch. The slightly dry effect does not capture quite enough of the hall ambience and turns a close scrutiny on ensemble from the Philharmonia Hungarica, who could at times be more polished. It is an affectionate performance, but not an especially vital one, and Dorati overdoes the pause after the first movement's introduction. On the other hand, the relaxed close of the *Élégie* leading on to the gentle opening of the bustling finale is rather effective. In any case, however, this set is worth having for the ballet performance alone. Excellent documentation, although the plot synopsis (related to the cueing) is closely aligned with Balanchine's choreography for the New York City Ballet.

Bonynge's set is made the more attractive by its rare and substantial Offenbach coupling. His approach is sympathetic and the orchestral playing is polished, even if in the opening scene he misses some of the atmosphere. With the beginning of the magic, as the Christmas tree expands, the performance becomes more dramatically involving, and in the latter part of the ballet Bonynge is at his best, with fine passion in the Act II *Pas de deux* and plenty of colour in the characteristic dances. The Decca recording is brilliant and vivid, but not as expansive as the full-price Mackerras Telarc set. However, it is good value at mid-price.

The Naxos super-bargain *Nutcracker* is played with great zest in Bratislava, and there is no lack of polish either. There is never a dull moment here, and the famous 'characteristic dances' of the Act II *Divertissement* emerge vividly. The digital recording has the brightest colouring and the effect overall could never be described as dull. But there are snags: there is a relative absence of charm and the *Waltz of the snowflakes* is minus its children's chorus. The Bolshoi Ballet did it that way at a London performance, but the omission of a highly engaging and appealingly innocent effect from a record is not easy to forgive. The *Waltz of the flowers*, too, lilts much more persuasively in Ormandy's hands – see below – even though he takes liberties with it. The break between the two Naxos CDs is at an awkward spot, just before the arrival of the Spanish dancers in the *Divertissement*, and the listener is left 'in mid-air' until the second disc continues the music.

(i) *The Nutcracker* (ballet) complete. (ii) *Sleeping Beauty* (ballet): *suite*; *Swan Lake* (ballet): *suite.*
(B) ** Sony M2YK 45619 (2). (i) Toronto SO, Andrew Davis; (ii) Phd. O, Ormandy.

Taken individually, the CBS performances are impressive, but the coupling is ill-matched. Andrew Davis's complete *Nutcracker* comes from the late 1970s and is given good, modern recording. The performance very much evokes the ballet theatre; the playing has a neat sense of stylish elegance, yet readily matches Tchaikovsky's more expansive moments. Ormandy's pair of suites, sumptuously recorded more than a decade earlier, conversely are ripely spectacular, full of life but not refined or subtle, although the orchestral playing – with plenty of rhythmic life – is polished as well as enthusiastic. The music is enjoyable in an opulently colourful way.

(i) *The Nutcracker* (ballet) complete; (ii) *Swan Lake* (ballet): highlights.
(B) **(*) Pickwick DUET 20 CD [MCAD2 9801]. (i) LPO, Artur Rodzinski; (ii) Utah SO, Abravanel.

Rodzinski's *Nutcracker* derives from the old Westminster label and dates from the earliest days of stereo. It must be one of the most involvingly dramatic and exciting accounts of the complete score ever recorded. The tingling vitality of the playing brings infectious zest to the party scene of Act I – and a smile to the face of the listener, when the clock striking midnight to herald the beginning of the magic is recognized, incongruously, as none other than Big Ben! Later the gorgeous *Journey through the pine forest* brings a frisson of pleasure in its breadth and intensity, while the great Act II *Pas de deux* has even greater passion. The studio recording – immensely improved in the CD transfer – is not always completely refined (the percussion and brass sometimes too forward) nor is there a great deal of transparency in the characteristic dances. Yet it has a glowing richness of string texture, so effective in the lilting *Waltz of the flowers*. The rather robust contribution of the chorus robs the *Waltz of the snowflakes* of some of its essential delicacy; yet the whole performance is so grippingly involving that reservations are of less moment, with the set in the bargain range. Fortunately the coupling has comparable vividness and excitement; the recording here is less opulent, brighter and with better internal definition. In a generous selection from *Swan Lake* Abravanel produces often electrifying playing from his splendid Utah orchestra – the *Scène final* is thrilling, yet there is much that is elegant and stylish too, not least the charming *Dance of the little swans* and the eloquently played violin/cello duet in the *Danse des cygnes*.

The Nutcracker (ballet): excerpts, *Op. 71*.
(M) *** Sony Dig. MDK 44656 [id.]. Amb. S., Philh. O, Tilson Thomas.

The Tilson Thomas CD can be given a strong recommendation: the bright-eyed Philharmonia playing is always alive and zestful and the CBS recording is brilliant and well balanced.

The Nutcracker (ballet): highlights; *Swan Lake* (ballet): highlights.
(B) * Pickwick DUET 6 CD (2). Phd. O, Ormandy.

These recordings come from the same CBS source as the selections joined with the (much more attractive) complete *Nutcracker* – see above. The sound is glossily over-brilliant and, although the playing is polished and often exciting, it hasn't much allure, as presented here. Moreover there is little point in joining these two discs together when the overall playing time of 102 minutes still leaves ample room for more music.

Nutcracker suite, Op. 71a.
(M) **(*) Sony SBK 46550 [id.]. Phd. O, Ormandy – CHOPIN: *Les Sylphides*; DELIBES: *Coppélia; Sylvia: Suites*. ***

Ormandy's 1963 recording of the suite is obviously derived from a more complete version, for the *Sugar Plum Fairy* is given her extended exit music as in the ballet, rather than the coda which Tchaikovsky provided for the concert suite. The Philadelphia Orchestra made this wonderful music universally famous in Walt Disney's *Fantasia* and they know how to play it just as well under Ormandy as they did under Stokowski. Perhaps there is less individuality in the characteristic dances, but the music-making has suitable moments of reticence (as in the neat *Ouverture miniature*) as well as plenty of flair. In the *Waltz of the flowers* Ormandy blots his copybook by taking the soaring violin tune an octave up on its second appearance, both at the beginning and in the reprise, but the Philadelphia violins make such a brilliant effect that one can almost forgive the excess.

Nutcracker suite, Op. 71a; Romeo and Juliet (fantasy overture); Swan Lake suite, Op. 20.
(M) *** Decca Dig. 430 707-2; *430 707-4*. Chicago SO, Solti.

Solti's digital recording of the *Swan Lake suite* was originally coupled with the *Fifth Symphony*. Now it comes in what is an attractive triptych, given Decca's best standard Chicago recording. *Romeo and Juliet* has an unexpected element of restraint and the love-theme, very tender and gentle when it first appears on the cor anglais, finds a yearning passion without histrionics; the battle sequences have plenty of bite in the strings, and at the climax the trumpets ring out resplendently. The *Nutcracker suite* produces marvellously characterful solo playing and much subtle detail.

Nutcracker suite; Sleeping Beauty: suite; Swan Lake: suite.

❀ (M) *** DG 429 097-2; *429 097-4* [id.]. BPO, Rostropovich.

(M) *** EMI CDM7 69044-2; *EG 769044-4*. LSO, Previn.

(M) **(*) Decca 417 700-2. VPO, Karajan.

Rostropovich's triptych of Tchaikovsky ballet suites is very special. His account of the *Nutcracker suite* is enchanting: the *Sugar plum fairy* is introduced with ethereal gentleness, the *Russian dance* has marvellous zest and the *Waltz of the flowers* combines warmth and elegance with an exhilarating vigour. The *Sleeping Beauty* and *Swan Lake* selections are hardly less distinguished. There is plenty of Slavonic intensity in the sweeping climaxes, and in the former the glorious *Panorama* melody is floated over its gently syncopated rocking bass with magical delicacy. Equally, the whimsical portrait of the cats is matched by the sprightly fledgling swans. The 1979 recording, with full strings and a lustrous ambience, expands spectacularly at climaxes, the CD remastering entirely beneficial, combining bloom with enhanced detail. 69 minutes of sheer joy, and at mid-price too.

The digital remastering has been very successful on the EMI disc, freshening the sound of the excellent recordings, taken from Previn's analogue complete sets (which means that the *Dance of the sugar plum fairy* in *The Nutcracker* has the longer coda rather than the ending Tchaikovsky devised for the *Suite*). The performances are at once vivid and elegant, warm and exciting.

The VPO triptych was made during Karajan's Decca period in the 1960s. As sound, this is very satisfactory; tuttis are well focused by the digital transfer, and overall this record offers fine playing, even if the VPO textures seem more leonine, less sumptuous than those of the Berlin Philharmonic under Rostropovich.

(i) *Nutcracker suite;* (ii) *Sleeping Beauty: suite;* (iii) *Swan Lake:* excerpts.

(B) ** Ph. 426 975-2; *426 975-4*. LSO, (i) Dorati; (ii) Fistoulari; (iii) Monteux.

There is some fine music-making here, especially under Fistoulari and Monteux. Dorati is lively but his *Waltz of the flowers*, though rhythmically neat, lacks something in glamour. However, apart from the *Nutcracker*, the selections are arbitrary and not particularly generous. To have a *Swan Lake* 'suite' without *the* oboe tune seems extraordinarily bad planning. On DG, costing only a little more, Rostropovich offers nine more minutes of music and secures superlative playing from the Berlin Philharmonic, while the DG engineers enhance his very special music-making with recording that is both lustrous and spectacular.

(i) *The Nutcracker; Sleeping Beauty; Swan Lake:* excerpts.

(B) **(*) EMI CZS7 62816-2 (2) [id.]. LSO, André Previn, (i) with Amb. S.

By the use of two CDs, offering some 148 minutes of music, this EMI box (issued in the 'two for the price of one' series) covers a substantial proportion of the key numbers from all three ballets. *The Nutcracker* selection is particularly generous in including, besides virtually all the most famous characteristic dances, the 13-minute episode in Act I starting with the Battle sequence, continuing with the magical Pine forest journey and finishing with the delightful choral *Waltz of the snowflakes*. Previn and the LSO provide vivacious, charismatic playing and the recording is full, bright and vivid. The remastering, however, loses some of the smoothness and refinement of focus of the original, analogue recordings in the interest of a lively upper range. But this remains very enjoyable and excellent value.

The Nutcracker; Sleeping Beauty; Swan Lake: highlights.

(M) *** EMI Dig. CDD7 641109-2 [id.]; *ET 764109-4*. Philh. O, Lanchbery.

(B) *** EMI CDZ7 62861-2; *LZ 762861-4*. Philh. O, Efrem Kurtz.

Those wanting a single disc of highlights from Tchaikovsky's three major ballets will surely find Lanchbery's selection fits the bill readily enough. Although it is perhaps a pity that the whole *Nutcracker suite* was not included, the favourite items are here, and there are eight popular excerpts from *Swan Lake* and seven from the *Sleeping Beauty* score. There are 79 minutes of music in all, played with great flair, warmth and polish, and given EMI's top-drawer digital sound.

At bargain price, the alternative collection from Kurtz, with the Philharmonia at its absolute peak, is also very recommendable. The early (late 1950s) stereo sounds astonishingly full, and the performances combine elegance and finesse with sparkle and colour. Here all of the *Nutcracker suite* is included except the *Chinese dance*, an inexplicable omission that would have nicely fitted on, as the programme plays for 77 minutes 39 seconds.

Nutcracker suite, Op. 71a; Symphony No. 4 in F min., Op. 36.

(M) (***) EMI mono CDM7 63380-2 [id.]; *EG 763380-4*. RPO, Sir Thomas Beecham.

Beecham himself praised the balance in the *Nutcracker suite*, one of his own favourite records.

It was recorded for American Columbia in Walthamstow Assemby Hall in 1953; when it was later reissued on LP, however, a wrong take was used for the *Dance of the flutes*. This has now been rectified by the skilful dubbing of the correct take from a commercial 78-r.p.m. pressing. It was a missing percussion condiment that caused the retake and, endearingly, the tambourine player in the characteristically zestful account of the *Trépak* almost gets left behind at the end. The performance overall has a Mozartian elegance; the *Dance of the flutes*, seductively slow, is ravishing and so is the closing *Waltz of the flowers*. It is a great pity that Sir Thomas was unenthusiastic about stereo in its early days and so allowed his performance of the *Fourth Symphony* to be recorded in mono, though it was made as late as 1957/8. Even so, the sound is outstandingly vivid, and the ear could easily be fooled into thinking it was stereo, so full are the strings and so rich the brass, with their glorious depth of sonority. The performance is unforgettably full of charisma. In the famous rocking crescendo in the first movement, Beecham manages to be urbane while at the same time building up the tension spontaneously; it is his cultivated approach to Tchaikovsky's marvellous orchestration that makes the reading so individual, while the account is second to none in generating excitement, with the thrilling coda of the last movement creating all the adrenalin of a live occasion.

Romeo and Juliet (fantasy overture).
(M) **(*) Decca 417 722-2 [id.]. VPO, Karajan – GRIEG: *Peer Gynt* **(*) (with R. STRAUSS: *Till Eulenspiegel* **(*)).
(BB) *(*) ASV CDQS 6040; *ZCQS 6040*. Sydney SO, Serebrier – SIBELIUS: *Symphony No. 1*. *(*)

Karajan's Decca recording of *Romeo and Juliet* comes from the early 1960s. The performance is marvellously shaped and has superb ardour and excitement: his later DG accounts never quite recaptured the spontaneous freshness of this version. The remastered sound is full, firm and clear.

José Serebrier's account of *Romeo and Juliet* with the Sydney Symphony Orchestra is respectable and comes with an acceptable account of the *First Symphony* of Sibelius. An odd coupling, given the competition in both works, even at the bargain end of the catalogue, and not a strong contender in either. Looking at it in cold, commercial terms, there is better value to be had elsewhere, even if the Sydney account is not lacking in merit.

Serenade for strings in C, Op. 48.
(M) ** DG Dig. 429 488-2. Orpheus CO – DVOŘÁK; ELGAR: *Serenades*. *(*)
(M) ** Ph. Dig. 434 219-2; *434 219-4* [id.]. ASMF, Marriner – DVOŘÁK: *Wind serenade*. ***

Serenade for strings; Souvenir de Florence, Op. 70.
(BB) **(*) Naxos Dig. 8.550404 [id.]. Vienna CO, Philippe Entremont.

Entremont's performances of Tchaikovsky's two major string works communicate above all a feeling of passionate thrust and energy. The first movement of the *Serenade* opens strongly, the pointedly rhythmic secondary theme is crisply accented, and the running passages which follow are imaginatively detailed. The *Waltz*, with its neatly managed tenutos, has a nice touch of romantic feeling and, after the ardour of the *Élégie*, the finale steals in persuasively, again producing an unflagging impetus, with dance-rhythms bracing and strong. The unaccountably neglected *Souvenir de Florence* has comparable momentum and eagerness. The dashing main theme of the first movement swings along infectiously, while the wistful secondary idea also takes wing. The finale has yet another indelible tune which responds to the impulsive energy generated by these Viennese players. The two central movements are hardly less memorable in their melodic inspiration, the *Adagio* opening delicately, then, after a quickening of tempo, producing a characteristically Tchaikovskian solo violin and cello duet. Entremont brings out the charm and responds easily to the variety of mood, both here and in the *Allegretto*, permeated with a flavour of Russian folksong. Throughout, the commitment and ensemble of the VCO bring the most persuasive advocacy and make one wonder why the *Souvenir* does not have a more central place in the string repertoire.

No one could accuse the Orpheus Chamber Orchestra of lack of energy in the outer movements; indeed the finale has tremendous vigour, the sheer nervous energy communicating in exhilarating fashion. Overall it is an impressive performance, even if the problems of rubato without a conductor are not always easily solved. Yet there is much that is fresh here, and one cannot but admire the precision of ensemble. The sound is first class, with the acoustics of the Performing Arts Center at New York State University providing plenty of warmth as well as clarity and a full, firm bass-line, very important in this work.

Marriner's 1982 recording of the *Serenade* for Philips is nicely played and well recorded. But it is no match for the earlier Decca/Argo analogue account, recorded when the Academy was at its early peak. By the side of this, the new performance seems a routine affair.

The Sleeping Beauty (ballet), *Op. 66* (complete).
(M) **(*) Decca 425 468-2 (3). Nat. PO, Richard Bonynge – MEYERBEER: *Les Patineurs.* ***

Bonynge secures brilliant and often elegant playing from the National Philharmonic Orchestra and his rhythmic pointing is always characterful. As recorded, however, the upper strings lack sumptuousness; otherwise, the sound is excellent and there is much to give pleasure, notably the drama of the awakening scene and the Act III *Divertissement.* The Decca sound has a fine sparkle here, and the solo violin (Mincho Minchev) and cello (Francisco Gabarro) provide most appealing solo contributions.

Sleeping Beauty (ballet): highlights.
(M) ** Sony SBK 46340 [id.]; *40-46340.* Phd. O, Ormandy – ROSSINI: *Boutique fantasque.* **(*)

Ormandy provides a sumptuously glossy selection, with nearly an hour's music (the CD plays for 76 minutes overall). Superbly polished and often exciting playing but, with a forward balance, the effect is somewhat overwhelming. The sound is opulently brilliant rather than refined.

Sleeping Beauty (ballet): *Suite.*
(BB) ** Naxos Dig. 8.550079 [id.]. Czech RSO (Bratislava), Ondrej Lenárd – GLAZUNOV: *The Seasons.* **(*)

The Czech Radio Orchestra under Ondrej Lenárd play Tchaikovsky's ballet suite with spirit and colour, and the recording has plenty of weight and ambience and no lack of brilliance. The *Waltz* goes especially well, but before that the *Panorama* is disappointing, taken fast and with a lack of subtlety in the rocking bass rhythm.

Sleeping Beauty: suite; Swan Lake: suite.
(M) *** EMI CD-EMX 2067; *TC-EMX 2067.* Philh. O, Karajan (with MUSSORGSKY: *Khovanshchina: Dance of the Persian slaves* ***).

Karajan has recorded this Tchaikovsky coupling three times in stereo and this, the first, with the Philharmonia Orchestra on peak form, shows Walter Legge's balancing skills at their most striking, for the recording is still impressive three decades after it was made. There is a rich ambient bloom and a resonant bass; the very slight lack of upper range means that the violin tone remains quite full-bodied while still retaining a brilliant sheen in the remastering, although the sound in *Sleeping Beauty* is a little less ample than in *Swan Lake.* Even so, the effect is amazingly vivid and full for a recording from the late 1950s. The orchestral playing in such items as the violin/cello duet and the dapper *Dance of the little swans* in *Swan Lake* or the lustrous *Rose Adagio* and seductive *Panorama* of *Sleeping Beauty* makes this issue especially desirable. The sinuous *Dance of the Persian slaves* from Mussorgsky's *Khovanshchina* proves a welcome bonus.

(i) *Sleeping Beauty: suite;* (ii) *Swan Lake, Op. 20:* excerpts.
(B) **(*) DG Compact Classics *413 430-4* [id.]. (i) BPO, Rostropovich; (ii) Boston SO, Ozawa – PROKOFIEV: *Romeo and Juliet.* ***

Rostropovich's *Sleeping Beauty suite* is highly distinguished, as fine as any in the catalogue, and the collection of *Swan Lake* excerpts from Ozawa is generous. Here the sophistication of playing and recording, within the warm Boston acoustic, is impressive; while the individual items have less individuality of approach than with Rostropovich, the orchestral response is first class and the final climax expands magnificently. Combined with an excellent selection from Prokofiev's *Romeo and Juliet*, this Compact Classics tape is very good value.

(i) *Suites Nos. 2 in C, Op. 53; 4 in G (Mozartiana), Op. 61;* (ii) *Sérénade mélancolique, Op. 26; Mélodie, Op. 42/3.*
(M) **(*) Sony/CBS Dig. MDK 46503 [id.]. (i) Philh. O, Tilson Thomas; (ii) Zukerman, Israel PO, Mehta.

Michael Tilson Thomas makes a very good case for Tchaikovsky's *Mozartiana suite*, finding both sparkle and elegance in the music and effectively balancing the personalities of both the composers represented. The Philharmonia's response is first class, and the *Second Suite* is also played with great vitality. The bright, slightly dry, early digital recording (made in EMI's No. 1 Studio at Abbey Road), which suits *Mozartiana* rather well, makes the more extrovert, fully scored first movement of the *Second*, *Jeu de sons*, seem a little aggressive in its brilliance, although the sharp focus is just right for the *Scherzo burlesque*, bustling with its accordions. Tilson Thomas finds elegance in the *Valse* and a wistful charm in the *Rêves d'enfant*; he directs the closing *Danse baroque* most stylishly. The fill-ups, if brief, are scarcely apt but are tenderly played and very appealing. Zukerman is closely balanced and his G string tone in the *Sérénade mélancolique* is ravishing without being too schmaltzy. This is a very good disc, and reservations about the recording are not serious; there is no lack of basic ambience.

Swan Lake (ballet), *Op. 20* (complete).
(B) *** CfP Dig. CD-CFPD 4727; *TC-CFPD 4727* (2). Philh. O, John Lanchbery.
(M) **(*) Decca 425 413-2 (3) [id.]. Nat. PO, Richard Bonynge – MASSENET: *Cigale.* ***
(BB) ** Naxos Dig. 8.550246/7 [id.]. Slovak RSO (Bratislava), Ondrej Lenárd.

Lanchbery's 1982 *Swan Lake* makes a superb bargain and, at this price, must now be a clear first choice among available versions. The CfP reissue on a pair of CDs, which play for 79 minutes and 75 minutes respectively, accommodates Acts I and II on the first disc and Acts III and IV on the second. The EMI set includes the extra music (a *Pas de deux*) which Tchaikovsky wrote to follow the *Pas de six* in Act III, when Siegfried dances with Odile, mistakenly believing her to be Odette. However, the Naxos set omits this sequence, even though the documentation suggests it is included – and, with Ondrej Lenárd's brisk tempi, there would have been ample room for it. Undoubtedly Lanchbery's pacing is preferable. The EMI recording, made at Abbey Road, is very fine indeed: spacious, vividly coloured and full, with natural perspective and a wide (but not uncomfortably wide) dynamic range. The orchestral playing is first class, with polished, elegant string phrasing matched by felicitous wind solos. Lanchbery's rhythmic spring is a constant pleasure; everything is alert, and there is plenty of excitement at climaxes. Other conductors – notably Fistoulari – have made this score sound more romantically passionate, but there is no lack of emotional commitment here, even if Lanchbery seldom overwhelms the listener. The score's marvellous detail is revealed with long theatrical experience. The documentation is good, with an adequate synopsis of the narrative, but without linking track cues; in this respect the Naxos set is superior: the banding is directly linked to the stage action. On the other hand, the Naxos cueing is much less generous (separate dances and variations within a group are not individually accessible).

Bonynge's approach is essentially strong and vigorous, bringing out all the drama of the score, if less of its charm. The forward impulse of the music-making is immediately striking. As in the other sets of his Decca Tchaikovsky series, the string timbre is somewhat leonine; overall there is fullness without sumptuousness. The brass sounds are open and vibrant and the upper range is brightly lit. The balance is managed well although the (very well-played) violin solos sound rather larger than life. While this lack of ripeness may not appeal to all ears, there is a consistent freshness here, and the moments of spectacle often make a thrilling impact.

Recorded in the Concert Hall of the Slovak Radio (Bratislava) in 1989, Lenárd's complete *Swan Lake* is both exhilarating and full-blooded and does not lack refinement or colour either. The sound is wide-ranging and full, and the very quality of racy excitement which makes his complete *Nutcracker* seem too hard-driven, here, more appropriately adds zest, although at times tempi are very fast indeed. This emphasizes the lyrical contrasts (as does the very wide dynamic range of the recording) and the famous oboe tune is always presented gracefully. Wind and brass playing is vivid, and altogether this makes a lively entertainment and, with the whole ballet offered on two discs, very economic too.

Swan Lake (ballet), *Op. 20:* highlights.
(B) *** CfP CD-CFP 4296; *TC-CFP 40296* [Ang. CDB 62713]. Sir Yehudi Menuhin, Philh. O, Efrem Kurtz.
(M) **(*) DG 431 607-2; *431 607-4* [id.]. Boston SO, Ozawa.
(M) ** Sony SBK 46341 [id.]; *40-46341*. Phd. O, Ormandy – ADAM: *Giselle*; MEYERBEER: *Les Patineurs.* **

A fine bargain selection on CfP with Menuhin present for the violin solos. He finds a surprising amount to play here; besides the famous duet with cello in the *Danse des cygnes*, which is beautifully done, he includes a ravishing account of the *Danse russe* as a postlude to the main selection. The 1960 recording matches the exuberance which Kurtz brings to the music's climaxes with an expansive dynamic range, and it has atmosphere as well as brilliance. The Philharmonia are on top form and the woodwind acquit themselves with plenty of style, while the string playing is characteristically elegant.

The DG disc offers some 59 minutes from the complete 1978 Boston/Ozawa set. The sophistication of the playing here, especially of the strings, is impressive, and Ozawa has a genuine rhythmic feeling for the world of ballet. Yet there is at times a lack of individuality in the score's lyrical moments. The CD transfer has made the analogue sound brighter and more vivid, if somewhat less refined, but the final climax expands spectacularly.

Ormandy's *Swan Lake* has much the same characteristics as his *Sleeping Beauty* selection, highly polished playing and sumptuously resonant sound which tends to detract from a sense of musical refinement. Yet the ebullient spirit of the music-making and the superb orchestral response cannot fail to make an effect in such a vividly coloured selection, with impeccable contributions from all the orchestral soloists.

SYMPHONIES

Symphonies Nos. 1–6.
(M) *** DG 429 675-2 (4) [id.]. BPO, Karajan.
(B) *** Ph. 426 848-2 (4) [id.]. LSO, Markevitch.

Symphonies Nos. 1–6; Capriccio italien; Manfred Symphony.
❀ (M) *** Chan. Dig. CHAN 8672/8 (7) [id.]. Oslo PO, Jansons.

Symphonies Nos. 1–6; Romeo and Juliet (fantasy overture).
(M) *** EMI CZS7 67314-2 (4) [Ang. CDMB 67314]. Philh. O, Muti.
(B) *** Decca 430 787-2 (4) [id.]. VPO, Lorin Maazel.

Jansons' outstanding Tchaikovsky series, which includes *Manfred*, is self-recommending. The full romantic power of the music is consistently conveyed and, above all, the music-making is urgently spontaneous throughout, with the Oslo Philharmonic Orchestra always committed and fresh, helped by the richly atmospheric Chandos sound. The seven separate CDs offered here are packaged in a box priced as for five premium discs.

Muti recorded his Tchaikovsky cycle over a period of six years in the late 1970s, during which time the New Philharmonia, thanks to its principal conductor, was restored both to its original name and to its earlier quality. The set of *Symphonies* is now appropriately reissued to celebrate the conductor's fiftieth birthday. It represented not only the high point of his recording partnership with that orchestra but also the peak of his interpretative career. The performances are as fine as any ever made, full of a kind of thrustful spontaneity he now finds less easy to achieve. It is a measure of Muti's success that even the first of the series to be recorded, No. 1, brings a performance as refined and persuasive as it is exciting, and the three early symphonies all bring orchestral playing which is both sophisticated and colourful. Throughout the cycle, and especially in the strong, urgent No. 4, Muti's view is brisk and dramatically direct, yet never lacking in feeling or imagination. In No. 5 he underlines the symphonic strength of the first movement rather than the immediate excitement. The Waltz may lack a little in charm but the slow movement is beautifully shaped, at first noble in feeling, with the passion held back for the climax. The finale then presents a sharp contrast, with its fast tempo and controlled excitement. In the *Pathétique* tempi are again characteristically fast, yet the result is fresh and youthful, with the flowing first-movement second subject given an easy expressiveness, The March, for all its urgency, never sounds brutal and the finale has satisfying depth and power. The sound generally is well up to EMI's best analogue standard of this period, and it has been transferred to CD very impressively, with the focus firm and no lack of body and weight. The layout involves just one break between discs in the middle of a symphony. Nos. 1 and 2 are on the first disc; The *Polish* and the first three movements of No. 4 are on the second; the finale of No. 4 and all of No. 5 are together on the third disc; and the final CD offers the *Pathétique* plus Muti's superb analogue *Romeo and Juliet*, one of the finest available, and full of imaginative touches.

Karajan's set, however, offers a quite outstanding bargain. Without *Manfred* (a work he never recorded), the six symphonies are fitted on to four mid-priced CDs, the only drawback being that Nos. 2 and 5 are split between discs. From both a performance and a technical point of view, the accounts of the last three symphonies are in every way preferable to his later, VPO digital versions. They date from 1975–6, whereas the first three symphonies were recorded in 1979; all offer peerless playing from the Berlin Philharmonic which the Oslo Philharmonic cannot always quite match, for all their excellence.

Maazel's performances from the mid-1960s have been remastered and reissued on four CDs, necessitating a break only at the centre of No. 4. The recordings come from a vintage Decca period and are remarkably full and vivid. In the early symphonies the hint of edge in the digital remastering (and it is very minimal) increases the bite and sense of urgency at the expense of charm (this is not a strong feature of Nos. 2 and 3 anyway). But in Nos. 4–6 (and especially in No. 4) the performances, always grippingly spontaneous, sound newly minted, helped by the freshness of the VPO, playing in their first complete cycle in the recording studio and obviously relishing the experience. Maazel's readings are well judged and clearly thought out. Perhaps No. 5 lacks the fullest expansive qualities, but there are few more effective accounts of the March/Scherzo from the *Pathétique*. *Romeo and Juliet* is exciting too, with plenty of romantic flair.

The admirable Philips set represents the least expensive way to acquire first-class versions of the six Tchaikovsky *Symphonies*. They were recorded between 1962 and 1966 and, then as now, had to compete with distinguished sets from Karajan, Haitink and Muti. Now they come into their own as a genuine bargain alternative. The recording is resonant and full-bodied; the CDs retain the ambient bloom on the strings and provide a fine weight and sonority for the brass. The layout on four CDs means that *Symphonies Nos. 2* and *5* are centrally divided between movements, but the other four works are uninterrupted. Markevitch is a genuine Tchaikovskian and his readings have fine momentum and plenty of ardour. In the *First Symphony* he finds the Mendelssohnian lightness in his fast pacing of the opening movement, while there is real evocation in the *Adagio*, and a sense of desolation at the reprise of the *Andante lugubre*, before the final rousing peroration. In the *Little Russian Symphony* the opening horn solo is full of character and the allegro tautly rhythmic. The *marziale* marking of the *Andantino* is taken literally, but its precise rhythmic beat is well lifted. The finale is striking for its bustling energy rather than its charm. The *Polish Symphony* has a comparably dynamic first movement, but the central movements are expansively warm, the ballet-music associations not missed. The finale is strongly full-blooded. No. 4 is as exciting as almost any available. It has a superb, thrusting first movement and, although Markevitch allows himself a lilting degree of rubato in the rocking crescendo passage, he then produces an exhilarating stringendo and relaxes naturally for the second subject. The close of the movement, like the coda of the finale, brings the highest degree of tension and a real sense of triumph over adversity. The central movements are no less striking, with a vigorous dotted climax to the *Andante* contrasting with the repose of the outer sections, and a swift scherzo, where the duple rhythms of the woodwind in the Trio are emphasized, to bring out the peasant imagery. No. 5 has a less flexible first movement, and some might feel that here the forward momentum is too hard pressed to let the secondary material really blossom. The slow movement has plenty of passion, but the other controversial point is that the final statement of the big tune in the finale is slow and rather stolid. But Markevitch is fully back on form in the *Pathétique*. He takes the first-movement allegro at a brisk pace, then produces a stringendo which further tautens the climax at the reprise of the second subject. The second movement has both warmth and elegance and the scherzo/march is treated broadly, providing suitable contrast before a deeply felt performance of the finale, where the second subject is introduced with great tenderness. The close of the symphony has an elegiac quality to complete a reading which has a wide emotional range and is gripping from first to last.

Symphonies Nos. 1–3.
(M) *** Ph. 420 751-2 (2). Concg. O, Haitink.

Haitink's readings are satisfyingly consistent and they have genuine symphonic strength. His special advantage, in addition to the superb Concertgebouw playing, is the Philips recording, which sounds splendid in its remastered form: rich yet fresh, refined in detail and not lacking weight. Haitink's choice of speeds, though not always conventional, always seems apt and natural, and in the *First Symphony* it is typical of his flair for balance that the big horn solo which comes at the end of the slow movement has nothing vulgar in it. Similarly in the *Little Russian*, the solemn nobility of the opening introduction has nothing of pomposity about it and, in the finale, the long and loud coda is given genuine joyfulness, with no blatancy. The *Polish Symphony* has a disarmingly direct freshness of approach. The slow movement is not as passionate as in some readings, but the delicacy of the scherzo is capped by a finale in which the rhetoric is minimized.

Symphony No. 1 in G min. (Winter daydreams), Op. 13; (i) *Variations on a rococo theme for cello and orchestra, Op. 33.*
(M) *** DG 431 606-2; *431 606-4* [id.]. BPO, Karajan; (i) with Rostropovich.

Karajan's performance of the *Winter daydreams symphony* is second to none and the playing of the Berlin Philharmonic is quite marvellous. Although he takes the opening *Allegro tranquillo* of the first movement quite fast, there is no feeling of breathlessness: it is genuinely *tranquillo*, though the rhythmic bite of the syncopated passages, so important in these early symphonies, could hardly be sharper. If the folk element is underplayed, the beautiful *Andante cantabile* has genuine Russian melancholy, while the fugato in the last movement is given classical strength and the final peroration has regality and splendour. Rostropovich's account of the published score of the *Rococo variations* is hardly less distinguished, and Karajan accompanies him warmly. Both analogue recordings are among DG's best, the *Symphony* dating from 1979 and the *Variations* from a decade earlier. Neither is lacking in brilliance or fullness, and both have a realistic ambience.

Symphonies Nos. (i) *2 (Little Russian), Op. 17;* (ii) *4 in F min.*
❀ (B) *** DG 429 527-2; *429 527-4.* (i) New Philh. O; (ii) VPO, Claudio Abbado.
❀ (M) *** DG 431 604-2; *431 604-4.* (i) New Philh. O; (ii) VPO, Abbado.

Abbado's coupling of Tchaikovsky's *Second* and *Fourth Symphonies* is one of the supreme bargains of the current catalogue. His account of the *Little Russian Symphony* is very enjoyable, although the first movement concentrates on refinement of detail and is a shade too deadpan. The *Andantino* is very nicely done and the scherzo is admirably crisp and sparkling. The finale is superb, with fine colour and thrust and a memorably spectacular stroke on the tam-tam before the exhilarating coda. The 1967 recording still sounds excellent. But this is merely a bonus for an unforgettable account of the *Fourth Symphony*, unsurpassed on record and sounding marvellous in its remastered CD format, brilliant yet atmospheric, with a balancing resonance and depth. Abbado's control of the structure of the first movement is masterly. The superbly graduated exposition climax is built from a fragile pianissimo of gently rocking violins and erupts into a blazing culmination from the horns. The secondary material is refined and colourful, the counter-melody graceful in the strings, yet Abbado maintains the intensity to the end of the movement. The *Andantino*, with its gentle oboe solo, really takes wing in its central section. Its delectable reprise is followed by a wittily crisp scherzo, while the finale has sparkle as well as power, epitomizing the Russian dance spirit which was Tchaikovsky's inspiration. It was recorded in 1975 in the Musikverein and still sounds very good indeed.

At the time of going to press, the bargain Privilege issue is still available. Should it disappear, however, the second listing above is more than worth its slightly higher price, although the insert leaflet still includes nothing about the music!

Symphony No. 3 in D (Polish), Op. 29; Serenade for strings in C, Op. 48.
❀ (M) *** DG Analogue/Dig. 431 605-2; *431 605-4* [id.]. BPO, Karajan.

Karajan's version of the *Polish Symphony* ranks with the finest, and no other version offers more polished orchestral playing. The first movement is full of flair, and in the central movements Karajan is ever conscious of the variety of Tchaikovsky's colouring. He even finds an affinity with Brahms in the second movement, and yet the climax of the *Andante* is full of Tchaikovskian fervour. In the finale the articulation of the *Polacca* is both vigorous and joyful and it brings a sense of symphonic strength often lacking in other versions. The 1979 analogue recording is bold, brilliant and clear, with the ambience of the Philharmonie well conveyed. The *String Serenade* is equally compelling, with taut, alert and superbly articulated playing in the first movement, a passionately intense *Élégie* and a bustling, immensely spirited finale. And no group plays the Waltz with more panache and elegance than the Berlin Philharmonic. The digital recording is early (1980), but satisfyingly well balanced, with a firm, resonant bass-line to balance the bright upper range.

Symphonies Nos. 4–6 (Pathétique).
(M) ** EMI CMS7 63838-2 (2) [Ang. CDMB 63838]. Philh. O, Klemperer.

Symphonies Nos. 4–6; Manfred symphony.
(M) *** Decca 425 586-2 (3) [id.]. Philh. O, Ashkenazy.

Ashkenazy's set is highly competitive on three mid-priced discs, although the CD layout splits No. 5 between the second and third movements. Apart from the emotional power and strong Russian feeling of the readings, the special quality which Ashkenazy conveys is spontaneity. The freshness of his approach, his natural feeling for lyricism on the one hand and for drama on the other, is consistently compelling, even if at times the orchestral ensemble is not as immaculate as with Karajan. The inclusion of the superb, inspirational account of *Manfred* sets the seal on his achievement. The remastering has brought just a degree of digital brightening to the fortissimo violins but adds to the transparency and tangibility of the sound picture overall. The recording quality remains outstandingly full and atmospheric, with the brass gloriously sonorous and a satisfying weight in the bass.

Klemperer was not a conductor who took naturally to Tchaikovsky, but nothing he recorded was without certain insights, and these recordings are no exception. Klemperer's view of the first movement in the *Fourth* is weighty yet relaxed. The basic dotted rhythm sometimes recalls Beethoven's *Seventh*, and many listeners will feel that coasting along in the first movement – even with the feeling of real power inherent underneath – does not really catch the almost barbaric Russian spirit that other interpreters find in the movement. There are no complaints elsewhere and, throughout, the Philharmonia solo playing is highly pleasing, especially in the very attractive Scherzo. The bright, vivid yet full-bodied 1963 recording ensures that the finale makes a suitable impact. The reading of the *Fifth*, however, is surprisingly successful in a way one would not perhaps expect. There is an expanding emotional warmth in the treatment of the opening movement, with the second subject blossoming in a ripely romantic way. The slow movement too, if not completely uninhibited, is played richly, with a fine horn solo from Alan Civil. The Waltz is perhaps marginally disappointing, but the finale has splendid dignity and the recording (again from 1963) has transferred impressively to CD. Klemperer's *Pathétique*, however, is surely a record to be heard rather than lived with. The outer movements are best, although the finale is not entirely convincing. The opening of the first movement goes well; it has great poise and dignity, and the beginning of the allegro is well managed. Later the climaxes are restrained without losing too much intensity and the coda is nicely moulded. The *Allegro con grazia* is heavy and without grace, and the March forgets that it is a Scherzo too; it has little cumulative excitement. The recording is spacious and full, with a good brass (and a notable bass-drum).

Symphonies Nos. 4–6; The Nutcracker; Sleeping Beauty; Swan Lake: ballet suites.
(M) (***) EMI mono/stereo CMS7 63460-2 (3) [Ang. CDMC 63460]. Philh. O, Karajan.

The Philharmonia in the early 1950s was an extraordinary body, and these early records are worth having even if you already possess Karajan's later accounts with the Berlin Philharmonic. Nos. 4 and 5 are mono, but the 1959 *Pathétique* is stereo. Exhilarating performances that still sound amazing for their period.

Symphony No. 4 in F min., Op. 36.
(M) *** Decca 425 972-2. LSO, Szell – BEETHOVEN: *Egmont.* ***
(M) (*(**)) Van. 08.8012.71 [OVC 8012]. American SO, Leopold Stokowski (with SCRIABIN: *Étude in C sharp min., Op. 2/1*, arr. Stokowski ***).

Symphony No. 4; Andante cantabile; Marche slave, Op. 31.
(M) *** EMI CDM7 63960-2 [id.]. Hallé O, Barbirolli (with rehearsal sequence).

Symphony No. 4; Capriccio italien.
(M) *** DG 419 872-2 [id.]. BPO, Karajan.
(M) **(*) Pickwick/RPO Dig. CDRPO 7008 [id.]. RPO, Kazuhiro Koizumi.

Symphony No. 4; (i) *Overture 1812. Marche slave.*
(M) ** Sony SBK 46334 [id.]; *40-46334.* Phd. O, Ormandy; (i) with Mormon Tabernacle Ch.; Valley Forge Military Ac. Band.

Symphony No. 4; Marche slave.
(B) **(*) Pickwick Dig. PCD 867; *CIMPC 867* [id.]. LSO, Rozhdestvensky.

Szell's white-hot performance is one of the very finest ever put on disc. At the sessions in 1962 the irascible conductor was in an angry mood, and John Culshaw deliberately prodded him still further by having the first playback in dull sound. Szell then unleashed a force in the subsequent takes that has to be heard to be believed. It was a recording that was not released until after his death – he would not allow it – but it was one of his very finest. It now sounds superb on CD, clean, forward and full, with thrillingly immediate brass. Tape-hiss is audible but undistracting, and the interpretation at ideally chosen speeds has a freshness rarely matched. The *Egmont* fill-up is odd but attractive, and is very well recorded in the Sofiensaal.

As with others in EMI's Phoenixa series of Barbirolli's recordings from the end of the 1950s and early 1960s, the sound has been immeasurably improved, and one can appreciate the sheer power and drive of the performance which, as with the *Fifth*, has much in common with Szell's version in its highly charged romanticism. The outer movements are electrifying in their excitement, and the elegantly structured *Andantino* has many characteristic touches of individuality, so that the performance overall can be spoken of in the same breath as Abbado's reading in its feeling for Tchaikovskian ebb and flow. After the *Symphony* comes a complete contrast in a refined and delicate account of the *Andante cantabile*; then comes a thrilling *Marche slave*, although here the recording is somewhat shrill. The disc ends with a rehearsal sequence, made during the preparation of the *Symphony*, not especially illuminating but valuable in letting us hear the way Barbirolli communcated with his orchestra who so often approached greatness under his baton.

Karajan's 1977 version is undoubtedly more compelling than his previous recordings and is in most respects preferable to the newer Vienna version too. After a dramatically robust fanfare at the start of the first movement, the theme of the *Allegro* steals in and its atmosphere has a tinge of melancholy. Yet it is the vitality and drive of the performance as a whole that one remembers, although the beauty of the wind playing at the opening and close of the slow movement can give nothing but pleasure. The finale has tremendous force to sweep the listener along, and the wide dynamic range of the recording makes the most dramatic effect. The CD transfer is extremely vivid. The ubiquitous *Capriccio italien* is offered as a filler.

After the fanfare, Rozhdestvensky's performance takes a little while to warm up, but when the first climax arrives it is very impressive. The lyrical secondary material is presented very beguilingly and the rocking string theme at the *Ben sostenuto* is positively sensuous. The slow movement is basically simple, although Rozhdestvensky allows himself a mannered emphasis at its climax. The Scherzo, light and gentle, has the feeling of an arabesque, and the finale is strongly articulated and expansive. With first-class digital recording and a powerful response from the LSO in both the *Symphony* and the coupled *Marche slave*, this is certainly worth considering in the bargain-price range.

Koizumi on the RPO label gives a robust, colourful reading, not always subtle in its pointing but with excellent solo work and clean ensemble, all helped by full and forward recording, transferred to CD at a high level. In the second-movement *Andantino*, with a finely moulded oboe solo, Koizumi keeps the music flowing, even at a slow speed, and in the finale he finds plenty of excitement, though the reverberant recording obscures a fair amount of detail. In his fill-up, he starts *Capriccio italien* rather stodgily but secures brilliant playing from all sections of the RPO in the sequence of dance-sections, defying any thought of vulgarity. The disc provides a first-rate recommendation for anyone who wants a completely new digital version of the symphony at upper mid-price, complete with a worthwhile coupling. However, Rozhdestvensky's bargain version (also on Pickwick), although without a coupling, offers strong competition.

Ormandy's account of the *Fourth* comes from the early 1960s and is a flamboyant reading, with moments of physical excitement but with specific mannerisms too, as in the broadened coda of the first movement or the rather heavy phrasing of the string theme which answers the oboe solo in the *Andantino*. The 'balalaika' scherzo shows the orchestra at its finest, but the resonant recording brings a degree of crudeness to the fortissimos of the outer movements. Ormandy's famous recording of *1812* comes from a decade later and in it the Mormon Tabernacle choir make a spectacular contribution to the work's opening section. Heard in quadraphony, their crescendo near the opening was thrilling, and the closing pages, with cannon shots all around, were equally impressive. Now the upper strings sound fierce and the climax has brilliance without a matching depth of sonority. *Marche slave* is exciting too, but again the sound has an element of harshness.

Stokowski's is a fascinating but exasperatingly eccentric performance. The pity is that the magnetism and basic understanding are in no doubt. Without the numerous minor interferences with the composer's score and the music's rhythmic flow, this could have been a great performance. Even as it is, it has splendid moments: the *Andantino* with its thrilling central climax and wonderfully touching coda is really memorable. But immediately at the opening of the first movement Stokowski makes his intentions clear. At the end of the third bar the trombones are added to the horns, anticipating the brass tutti Tchaikovsky has so carefully prepared for the seventh bar. Then, when the *Moderato con anima* begins, there is a flagrant tenuto on the opening phrase which is repeated at the end of the third bar; and this type of rhythmic distortion is employed in both the principal themes of the first movement. Only the scherzo (brilliantly done) is comparatively free from interference, while the end of the finale is grotesque. The amazing thing is that, through all these excesses, Stokowski carries the orchestra with him and at the same time maintains the tension at a higher pitch than almost any other performance. The recording is spectacularly spacious, with only a touch of harshness. As a fill-up Stokowski offers a richly indulgent orchestration of a Scriabin *Étude*. A collector's item – but for Stokowskians rather than Tchaikovskians! This reissue comes at upper-mid-price in the USA.

Symphony No. 5 in E min., Op. 64.
(M) ** DG Dig. 427 822-2; *427 822-4* [id.]. LSO, Karl Boehm.

Symphony No. 5; Capriccio italien.
(B) **(*) Pickwick Dig. PCD 875; *CIMPC 875* [id.]. LSO, Rozhdestvensky.

(i) *Symphony No. 5;* (ii) *Marche slave.*
(M) *** DG 419 066-2; *419 066-4* [id.]. BPO, Karajan.
(BB) **(*) LaserLight 15 620 [id.]. (i) Prague Fest. O, Pavel Urbanek; (ii) Hungarian State O, Adám Fischer.
(BB) * Naxos Dig. 8.550191 [id.]. Slovak PO, Stephen Gunzenhauser.

Symphony No. 5; Nutcracker suite.
(M) (*) Decca mono 425 958-2 [id.]. LPO, Sergiu Celibidache.

Symphony No. 5; Romeo and Juliet (fantasy overture).
(M) ** DG 431 603-2; *431 603-4* [id.]. (i) Boston SO, (ii) San Francisco SO, Ozawa.

(i) *Symphony No. 5;* (ii) *Serenade for strings in C, Op. 48.*
(M) *** EMI CDM7 63962-2 [id.]; *EG 763962-4*. (i) Hallé O; (ii) LSO, Barbirolli.

Symphony No. 5; (i) *Eugene Onegin: Tatiana's letter scene.*
❀ (M) *** EMI Dig. CD-EMX 2187; *TC-EMX 2187*. LPO, Sian Edwards; (i) with Eilene Hannan.

Sian Edwards has already given us a truly memorable account of *Francesca da Rimini*; now she conducts an equally electrifying and warm-hearted reading of Tchaikovsky's *Fifth*. With refined playing from the LPO and brilliant recording, it matches any version in the catalogue, particularly when it comes with an unusual and exceptionally attractive fill-up, Tchaikovsky's greatest inspiration for soprano, *Tatiana's letter scene*. That is freshly and dramatically sung, in a convincingly girlish impersonation, by the Australian, Eilene Hannan, too long neglected by the record companies. Sian

Edwards's control of rubato is exceptionally persuasive, notably so in moulding the different sections of the first movement of the symphony, while the great horn solo of the slow movement is played with exquisite delicacy by Richard Bissell. With fine concentration Edwards sustains an exceptionally slow tempo for that movement, building to a passionate climax. The Waltz third movement is most tenderly done, as though for a ballet, while the finale brings a very fast and exciting allegro, challenging the orchestra to brilliant, incisive playing. The booklet includes a transliteration of the Russian text of the vocal item, together with an English translation.

Karajan's 1976 recording stands out from his other recordings of the *Fifth*. The first movement is unerringly paced and has great romantic flair; in Karajan's hands the climax of the slow movement is grippingly intense, though with a touchingly elegiac preparation for the horn solo at the opening. The Waltz has character and charm too – the Berlin Philharmonic string playing is peerless – and in the finale Karajan drives hard, creating a riveting forward thrust. The remastered recording brings a remarkable improvement; the bass is more expansive and, although the overall sound-picture is brilliantly lit, it has depth and weight too, besides strong projection and impact. The CD at mid-price makes a fine bargain.

As with the *Fourth*, Barbirolli's urgent, thrustfully romantic reading of the *Fifth* has much in common with Szell, particularly in the way its irresistible forward momentum springs from the very essence of the music. Tempi are unerrringly apt, not only in themselves but also in the way they interrelate. The reading has passion and drama (the entries of the motto theme in the *Andante* are almost cataclysmic), and the energy of the finale is matched by the nobility with which Barbirolli invests the great main tune when it is introduced in the strings; yet, at its final appearance in the coda, the blazing trumpets have no inhibition whatsoever. The orchestra are galvanized into playing of remarkable emotional tension and, as the final hammered chords die away at the end, the listener is left to take a deep breath and recover from the adrenalin flow. EMI have recoupled this Pye reissue with one of their own recordings of the *Serenade for strings* (made in 1964), characteristically ripe and romantic, especially in the *Élégie*. In the first movement Barbirolli is surprisingly metrical when the second subject arrives, but the effect is not in the least heavy. He is naturally expressive in the Waltz and prepares the bustling finale with subtle, loving anticipation. A suberb disc: any lack of refinement in the recording is forgotten when the playing is so consistently involving.

Though less brightly recorded than its companions in Rozhdestvensky's LSO series for Pickwick, with strings a little cloudy, this version of the *Fifth* brings a strong, passionate performance, with the middle movements in particular beautifully done. The *Capriccio italien* is also given a sunny and relaxed reading at relatively spacious speeds.

Although the orchestral ensemble is not immaculate, the Prague Festival Orchestra's super-bargain version is very exciting. The tension slowly builds through the first movement and is then maintained to the end. Moreover, the slow movement has a quite glorious horn solo, spacious and warm-timbred. The *Marche slave*, which serves for an encore, not unexpectedly has plenty of sombre Slavonic feeling. The digital recording is well balanced to give a ripe brass sound and plenty of weight to the strings.

Boehm's 1981 account of the *Fifth*, given really excellent digital sound, has a splendid first movement, full of character and warm, romantic colour. But Boehm refuses to press the music ahead from his very steady basic start in the slow movement and the result is disappointingly heavy, and the finale too is wanting in thrust and ardour.

Ozawa has the advantage of excellent DG sound. In the finale the brass is superb: this is undoubtedly the finest movement; the music-making springs vividly to life and the listener is swept along by the impact and projection of the Boston orchestra. But the first three movements are disappointing, and until the finale the performance is a routine one. In the *Romeo and Juliet* overture, however, Ozawa is at his best, drawing warmly committed playing from the San Francisco orchestra.

Stephen Gunzenhauser's account with the Slovak Philharmonic is less refined and detailed as an interpretation than the best of its competitors. Rhythms sometimes grow heavy and not all Western ears will adjust to the fruity horn solo, while the finale lacks a little in tension. It has good, warm, digital sound, but in the super-bargain range the LaserLight Prague version is far preferable.

Celibidache's records of the *Fifth Symphony* and the *Nutcracker suite* come from the late 1940s and are wilful and eccentric in the extreme. He pulls the symphony completely out of shape, and the *Nutcracker* is pretty idiosyncratic too.

Symphonies Nos. 5 – 6 (Pathétique).
(B) **(*) DG Compact Classics *413 429-4* [id.].
LSO, VPO, Abbado.

The Compact Classics chrome cassette couples Abbado's lightweight but refreshingly individual DG accounts of Tchaikovsky's two most popular symphonies. The performance of the *Fifth* is both sophisticated and sparkling: there is lyrical intensity and the outer movements have plenty of vigour; the finale is genuinely exciting, yet with no sense of rhetoric. There are more powerful accounts available but none more spontaneously volatile. The *Pathétique* is also slightly underpowered but may have many attractions for those who prefer a reading that is not too intense. There is a strong impulse throughout, with the third movement essentially a Scherzo, the march-rhythms never becoming weighty and pontifical. The recordings have transferred well to tape, that of the *Fifth* richer than the *Sixth*, which is slightly dry.

Symphony No. 6 in B min. (Pathétique), Op. 74.
(M) (***) DG 419 486-2 [id.]. BPO, Karajan.
(M) (***) BMG/RCA mono GD 60312. NBC SO, Toscanini – R. STRAUSS: *Death and transfiguration.* (***)
(M) **(*) DG Dig. 431 046-2; *431 046-4.* NYPO, Bernstein.
(M) ** DG Dig. 431 602-2; *431 602-4* [id.]. LAPO, Giulini.

Symphony No. 6 (Pathétique); Capriccio italien; Eugene Onegin: Waltz & Polonaise.
(M) **(*) Sony SBK 47657 [id.]. Phd O, Ormandy.

(i) *Symphony No. 6 (Pathétique);* (ii) *Overture 1812.*
(BB) *(*) LaserLight Dig. 15 524 [id.]. (i) Prague Fest. O, Pavel Urbanek; (ii) Hungarian State O, Adám Fischer.

Symphony No. 6 (Pathétique); (i) *Francesca da Rimini, Op. 32.*
(B) *** EMI CDZ7 62603-2; *LZ 762603-4.* Philh. O, Giulini; (i) New Philh. O, Barbirolli.
(BB) ** Naxos Dig. 8.550097 [id.]. Slovak RSO (Bratislava), Ondrej Lenárd.

(i) *Symphony No. 6 (Pathétique);* (ii) *Hamlet* (fantasy overture), *Op. 67a.*
(B) *** Ph. 422 478-2. (i) LSO, (ii) New Philh. O, Markevitch.

Symphony No. 6 (Pathétique); Romeo and Juliet (fantasy overture).
(M) ** EMI stereo/mono CDM7 63776-2 [id.]; *EG 763776-4.* Hallé O, Barbirolli.
(M) *(*) Decca Analogue/Dig. 430 442-2; *430 442-4* [id.]. Chicago SO, Solti.

Symphony No. 6 (Pathétique); The Storm, Op. 76.
(B) **(*) Pickwick Dig. PCD 878; *CIMPC 878* [id.]. LSO, Rozhdestvensky.

Karajan has a very special affinity with Tchaikovsky's *Pathétique Symphony*; he has recorded it five times in stereo. For many, the 1976 version is the finest – but the current issue on CD of this performance must be treated with extreme caution. The bright recording has been remastered fiercely and the upper range is so sharp-edged as to make the ear cringe in the louder passages. Undoubtedly the impact of Tchaikovsky's climaxes – notably those of the first and third movements – is tremendously powerful, the articulation of the Berlin players precise and strong. In the 5/4 movement Karajan allows the middle section to increase the elegiac feeling, against a background of remorseless but distanced drumbeats, like a tolling bell. The finale has great passion and eloquence, with two gentle sforzandos at the very end to emphasize the finality of the closing phrase. We must hope that DG will consider a further remastering of this recording.

Giulini's EMI performance was recorded with the Philharmonia at its peak in 1959, and this bargain reissue still sounds excellent in the CD transfer. It comes most generously coupled with Barbirolli's colourful and intense 1969 version of *Francesca da Rimini* with the New Philharmonia, one of his very finest recordings from his last years. Giulini takes a spacious view of the *Pathétique*. There is a degree of restraint in the way he interprets the big melodies of the first and last movements, which are given an almost Elgarian nobility. Yet passionate intensity is conveyed by the purity and concentration of the playing, which equally builds up electric tension and excitement without hysteria.

Ormandy's fine 1960 performance was recorded (like his *Carmina Burana*) in the Broadwood Hotel, Philadelphia, which proved far more flattering for the orchestra than the usual Pennsylvania venues. It is a reading of impressive breadth, dignity and power, with no suggestion of routine in a single bar. The orchestra makes much of the first-movement climax and plays with considerable passion and impressive body of tone in both outer movements; yet there is an element of restraint in the finale which prevents any feeling of hysteria. The 5/4 movement has an attractive, melancholy warmth, the repeats effectively taken; the scherzo combines weight with sparkle (the march theme emerges as a real march). In short, this is most satisfying, a performance to live with; the CD transfer, while brightly lit, avoids glare in the upper range. The *Capriccio italien* and the *Eugene Onegin* excerpts were recorded in Philadelphia Town Hall in 1965/6, and the acoustic effect is less subtle. But Ormandy's panache and gusto give the Italian piece plenty of life without driving too hard, and the dances are rhythmically infectious.

Toscanini's Philadelphia version of the *Pathétique* glows with the special magic that developed between him and the orchestra over the winter season of 1941–2. Though far more disciplined than most readings, it is altogether warmer than his NBC recording, with the great second-subject melody of the first movement tender in its emotions, not rigid in its easy rubato. He even eases the tempo sympathetically for the fortissimo entries of the march in the third movement. Alongside a magnificent account of the Strauss – an apt link, with death the theme – it makes a superb historic document.

Markevitch brings great intensity to his account of the first movement. He takes the *Allegro* at a fast pace and drives hard throughout, producing a stringendo that further tautens the climax at the reprise of the second subject. The effect is undoubtedly powerful but, with a touch of harshness to the recording, some might feel that Markevitch is too aggressive, even though the performance is always under emotional control. The second movement has both warmth and elegance, and the march is treated broadly, providing suitable contrast before a deeply felt performance of the finale, where the second subject is introduced with great tenderness. The close of the *Symphony* has an elegiac quality to complete a reading which has a wide emotional range and is gripping from first to last. The performance of *Hamlet* is exciting, with a particularly telling closing section. The portrayal of Ophelia is rather striking, but the remastered recording produces less than ideal fullness for the massed violins.

The timings in Bernstein's version make you suspect that someone has made a mistake with the stopwatch. At 59 minutes overall, it is the slowest *Pathétique* ever, over a quarter of an hour longer than Jansons' (by no means rushed) version. To an amazing degree the conductor's magnetism and his ability to sustain electric tension, not least in hushed pianissimos of fine delicacy, justify his view, but this is an eccentric version by any count, a live recording that is fascinating to hear once but which is not for repeated listening. The wide-ranging DG recording is one of the best made in Avery Fisher Hall.

Rozhdestvensky's performance with the LSO on the bargain-price Pickwick label, generously coupled and very well recorded in modern digital sound, makes an obvious bargain. His passionate reading fails to match the finest in precision of ensemble – the slow finale is warm rather than tense or tragic – but the sense of spontaneity is most compelling.

The 1958 Barbirolli version brings a characteristically gutsy performance, at once firm in purpose and passionate. Inevitably the recording has a high tape-hiss and is limited in range, with violins often rough-sounding, but the EMI transfer has transformed it, so that the sense of presence is vivid, and the sound is full and satisfying enough to let one enjoy the central strength of the interpretation, although there is a degree of fierceness at climaxes. Barbirolli's reading begins rather coolly, but the secondary theme is beautifully phrased and the slight restraint adds to the contrast of the development, which opens with a dramatic fortissimo; the Hallé strings, however, ideally need to be able to produce a greater body of tone at the climax, though it does not lack fervour. The second movement is light and gracious and the third is a genuine scherzo, with Sir John holding back the big guns until the final peroration. The most powerful playing comes in the finale, which is passionately impulsive though not lacking dignity. The (mono) *Romeo and Juliet*, recorded in 1957, is notable for Barbirolli's delicacy of feeling at the introduction of the great love-theme, yet the performance is exciting enough.

On Naxos, Ondrej Lenárd conducts a relatively low-key account of the *Pathétique* which yet, with generally neat playing from the Slovak Radio Symphony Orchestra, is sympathetically refreshing. Even if the fortissimo entries of the march in the third movement lack a sense of drama, the crispness of the approach at a relatively relaxed speed is attractive, and Lenárd moulds the great melodies of the outer movements with natural sympathy. *Francesca da Rimini* brings a more keenly dramatic performance, a generous fill-up for a disc at superbargain price, warmly and atmospherically recorded.

Giulini's digital *Pathétique* is curiously lightweight, the mood set with the almost *scherzando* quality of the opening Allegro. The 5/4 movement is relatively unlilting and, though the march is impressive, it is no match for the Ashkenazy version. The finale does not lack eloquence, but Giulini's Philharmonia version of two decades earlier had more individuality than this. The digital recording is impressive, if slightly dry. The CD tends to emphasize rather than disguise the recording's faults, especially the close balance.

Solti's *Pathétique* – reissued in the 'Solti Collection' – brings dangerously fast tempi throughout the first and third movements, and the feeling of hysteria is never far away. The element of nobility, so necessary to provide emotional balance, is missing. The March/scherzo loses all charm at this hectic pace; indeed the march element almost disappears altogether. The finale is more under control but does not resolve the performance in any satisfactory way. Brilliantly clear recording to match the playing. *Romeo and Juliet* – digitally recorded – has greater restraint and is altogether more successful as a performance.

The LaserLight *Pathétique* is disappointingly lightweight after the Prague orchestra's successful *Fifth*. This is a symphony that needs maximum intensity and one wishes that it had as much as the coupled *1812*, which is enjoyably exciting and has a spectacular close, with Adám Fischer broadening the final peroration to achieve maximum grandiloquence.

Symphony No. 7 in E flat (reconstructed Bogatyryev); (i) *Variations on a rococo theme for cello and orchestra, Op. 33.*
(M) ** Sony MPK 46453 [id.]. Phd. O, Ormandy; (i) with Leonard Rose.

In 1892 Tchaikovsky began a new symphony, but he was not satisfied with the way his ideas were working out and decided that the material was more suitable for a piano concerto – and, if one listens to the one-movement *Third Concerto*, one might well feel that the composer was right, even though the work has never gained a place in the repertoire. Tchaikovsky discarded the rest of his material, but the sketches for the symphony as originally planned were not destroyed and it was to these that the Soviet musicologist, Bogatyryev, turned. As there was no scherzo, one was provided from a set of piano pieces written in 1893. Skilfully scored, it recalls the scherzo from *Manfred*, with its middle section introduced by oboe and harp and then taken up by the strings. The finale, however, is bizarre and here sounds rumbustious, blatant, even vulgar, with the reprise of the main theme against a side-drum in no way characteristic of Tchaikovsky's symphonic writing. Ormandy's performance has great fervour and is superbly played; but the recording, although spectacular, also has the harshness one associates with this source. Leonard Rose's warm and elegant account of the *Rococo variations* comes like balm to the ears after the noisy finale of the symphony. However, this CD does have distinct curiosity value.

Variations on a rococo theme for cello and orchestra, Op. 33.
(M) *** EMI CDM7 69169-2 [id.]; *EG 769169-4*. Paul Tortelier, N. Sinfonia, Yan Pascal Tortelier – DVOŘÁK: *Concerto.* ***
(M) *** Decca 425 020-2; *425 020-4* [id.]. Harrell, Cleveland O, Maazel – BRUCH: *Kol Nidrei* ***; DVOŘÁK: *Cello concerto.* ***
(B) **(*) Pickwick IMPX 9035. Christine Walevska, LPO, Gibson – DVOŘÁK: *Cello concerto.* **(*)
(M) ** Mercury 432 001-2 [id.]. Starker, LSO, Dorati – BRUCH: *Kol Nidrei*; DVOŘÁK: *Cello concerto.* **

A finely wrought account from Tortelier *père*, accompanied by the Northern Sinfonia under Tortelier *fils*. This is very enjoyable, if perhaps not quite so distinguished as Rostropovich on DG. Well worth considering at mid-price.

An assured, vividly characterized set of *Variations* from Lynn Harrell, with plenty of matching colour from the Cleveland woodwind. Harrell begins a little briskly, but there is no lack of poise here. Expressive feeling and sparkle are nicely matched, as is shown by the elegant account of the *Andante* (Variation 6) which acts as an interlude before the exhilarating finale. The analogue recording is bright and colourful, with the Cleveland ambience adding warmth and the cellist given a spotlight.

Christine Walevska has not the strength of profile of a Rostropovich, but she gives a spontaneous and musically enjoyable account of Tchaikovsky's elegant *Variations*, with plenty of bravura and sparkle in the closing section. She is accompanied sensitively by Gibson, and the 1971 (originally Philips) recording is well balanced and has realistic presence. Not a first choice, but very good value in the super-bargain range.

Starker's performance is elegant, and his precise, clean playing brings out the music's elegance, if not always its full charm. Dorati accompanies sympathetically and the 1964 recording is very believable.

CHAMBER AND INSTRUMENTAL MUSIC

String quartet No. 1 in D, Op. 11.
(M) **(*) Decca 425 541-2; *425 541-4* [id.]. Gabrieli Qt – BORODIN; SHOSTAKOVICH: *Quartets.* **(*)

The coupling of Tchaikovsky's *D major Quartet* (including the famous *Andante cantabile*) with the Borodin work containing the comparable *Nocturne* is good planning, especially with Shostakovich added to provide a touch of twentieth-century acerbity. The Gabrielis give a finely conceived performance of the Tchaikovsky, producing well-blended tone-quality, and the 1977 recording is clean and alive; but ideally the upper range could be less forcefully projected.

Capriccioso in B flat, Op. 19; Danse russe in A min., Op. 40; Dialogue in B, Op. 72; Dumka in C min., Op. 59; L'espiègle in E, Op. 72; Humoresque in E min., Op. 10; Mazurka in D, Op. 40; Nocturne in F, Op. 10; Polacca de concert in E

flat, Op. 72; Polka in B min., Op. 52; Rêverie in D, Op. 9; Rêverie du soir in G min., Op. 19; Romances in F min., Op. 5; in F, Op. 51; Scherzo in F, Op. 2; Tendre reproches in C sharp min., Op. 72.
(BB) *(*) Naxos Dig. 8.550504 [id.]. Ilona Prunyi.

Ilona Prunyi is recorded in the same acoustic, but with a different team and three years later than, her *Seasons*. The sound is not quite so oppressively close, though it is still forward and shallow. She plays this much-underrated repertoire with great vitality and musical intelligence; but anyone who has heard some of these miniatures played by a great pianist will know how much more there is to this music.

The Seasons, Op. 37b; Chanson triste in G min.; Nocturne in C sharp min.; Songs without words in A min.; in F.
(BB) (*) Naxos Dig. 8.550233 [id.]. Ilona Prunyi.

No quarrels here with Ilona Prunyi's musical response in *The Seasons* and other Tchaikovsky pieces, which she plays with evident sympathy. Every quarrel with the dreadfully close balance, which makes it difficult to get very far into the year. This upfront, two-dimensional sound gives no pleasure.

OPERA

Eugene Onegin: highlights.
(M) **(*) DG 431 611-2; *431 611-4* [id.] (from recording with Freni, Thomas Allen, Schicoff, Von Otter, Burchuladze, cond. Levine).

This 68-minute selection from the Levine DG set makes an admirable entertainment. It includes the *Letter scene* (with Freni a freshly charming Tatiana), the *Waltz* and *Polonaise* scenes (with the excellent Leipzig Radio Chorus), other key arias, all strongly characterized, and the entire closing scene (11 minutes). The recording, made in the Dresden Lukaskirche, is too closely balanced and surprisingly unexpansive; but this still makes an impressive sampler.

Telemann, Georg Philipp
(1681–1767)

Double concerto in F for 2 horns; Concerto in B flat for 3 oboes & 3 violins; Double concerto in F for recorder, bassoon & strings; Concerto in G for 4 violins.
(M) *** Teldec/Warner 2292 43543-2 [id.]. Soloists, VCM, Harnoncourt.

One of the best Telemann discs currently available. The *Concerto for two horns* shows the composer at his most characteristic (natural horns are used), and the performances are most persuasive. The oboes also sound splendidly in tune – not always the case with the baroque instrument – and phrasing is alive and sensitive. Indeed these 1966 performances are extremely fine, and only the *Concerto for recorder and bassoon* lets the disc down a little; it is not as well played as the others. The quality is good and the digital remastering has not tried to clarify artificially what is basically a resonant recording with inner detail mellowed by the ambience.

(i) *Oboe concertos: in C min.; D min.; E min.; F min.;* (ii) *Sonatas: in G; E min.* (from *Essercizii Musici*); *G min.* (from *Tafelmusik*, Part 3).
(M) **(*) EMI Dig. CDM7 63068-2. Hans de Vries; (i) Amsterdam Alma Music; (ii) Van Asperen, Moller.

Hans de Vries is a fine player and he produces an attractively full timbre on his baroque oboe; the accompaniments for him in the four *Concertos* are alert and stylish. The snag is the very forward balance of the solo instrument, which makes everything sound on one dynamic level. All four *Concertos* are characteristically inventive – but the three *Sonatas* are a delight; in the work taken from the *Tafelmusik* Telemann offers no fewer than seven movements, all full of character. Apart from the balance, the sound is very vivid and the harpsichord image in the *Sonatas* is particularly pleasing.

Oboe d'amore concerto No. 2 in A.
(M) *** DG 431 120-2. Holliger, Camerata Bern, Füri – GRAUN: *Concerto* ***; KREBS: *Double concerto.* **(*)

Telemann's *Oboe d'amore concerto* is in four engaging movements, opening with a lovely Siciliana which Holliger plays beautifully. It is a highly inventive work throughout, and this excellent performance and recording make the very most of it.

(i) *Double concerto for recorder, bassoon and strings. Suite in A min. for recorder and strings.*
(B) ** Hung. White Label HRC 042 [id.]. László Czidra; (i) Jószsef Vajda; Liszt CO, Sándor.

László Czidra proves a beguiling soloist with Jószsef Vajda a lively partner in the *Double concerto*, and he plays with considerably virtuosity in the more familiar *A minor Suite*. More air round the Franz Liszt Chamber Orchestra would have helped produce more pleasing string-tone, though there is nothing seriously wrong with this serviceable (and presumably 1970s) recording. The music, as so often with Telemann, is full of inventive resource. However, room could have been found for a third work.

(i) *Viola concerto in G. Don Quichotte: suite; Overture in C (Hamburger Ebb und Flut); Overture in D.*
(M) **(*) Decca 430 265-2; *430 265-4*. (i) Stephen Shingles; ASMF, Marriner.

This ASMF collection from the late 1970s presents a nicely varied group of works, not just the relatively well-known *Viola concerto* (with Stephen Shingles a stylish soloist) but also the colourful and endearing *Don Quichotte suite*, a vivid example of early programme music. The *Hamburg Ebb and Flow* also has programmatic implications in the manner of Vivaldi; but the musical descriptions are never too literal and the titular associations with the figures of classical mythology serve only to fire the composer's imagination. Finally we are given the *Overture* (Suite) *in D*, written in 1765 when Telemann was well into his eighties but still retained all his creative flair. Each movement is intensely individual and the work climaxes with a graceful *Carillon* for oboes and pizzicato strings and a rumbustious *Tintamare*. The only reason for our reservation bracket is that the digital remastering has brought a brighter, tighter sound to the upper range and a drier bass response. On the original Argo LPs the strings were gloriously resonant, as rich and refined as any on record; but now some of this amplitude has been lost, although the transparency of detail and most of the ambient bloom remain.

(i) *Viola concerto in G;* (ii) *Suite in A min. for recorder and strings; Tafelmusik,* Part 2: (iii) *Triple violin concerto in F;* Part 3: (iv) *Double horn concerto in E flat.*
❀ (BB) *** Naxos Dig. 8.550156 [id.]. (i) Kyselak; (ii) Stivín; (iii) Hoelblingova, Hoelbling, Jablokov; (iv) Z. & B. Tylšar, Capella Istropolitana, Richard Edlinger.

Our Rosette is awarded for enterprise and good planning – to say nothing of good music-making. It is difficult to conceive of a better Telemann programme for anyone encountering this versatile composer for the first time and coming fresh to this repertoire, having bought the inexpensive Naxos CD on impulse. There must be a vibrant musical life in Bratislava, for the excellent Capella Istropolitana consists of members of the Slovak Philharmonic, which is based there, and the soloists here are drawn from its ranks. Ladislav Kyselak is a fine violist and is thoroughly at home in Telemann's splendid four-movement concerto; Jiři Stivín is an equally personable recorder soloist in the masterly *Suite in A minor*; his decoration is a special joy. The *Triple violin concerto* with its memorable *Vivace* finale and the *Double horn concerto* also show the finesse which these musicians readily display. Richard Edlinger provides polished and alert accompaniments throughout: he is especially good at pacing the eight diverse movements of the *Suite*, which has so much in common with Bach's similarly scored *Suite in B minor*. The digital sound is first class.

Darmstadt overtures (suites): in C, TWV 55: C 6; in D, TWV 55: D 15; in D min., TWV 55: D 3; in G min., TWV 55: G 4; Tafelmusik, Part 1: *Overture (suite) in E min.; Concerto in A for flute and violin;* Part 2: *Overture (suite) in D; Concerto for three violins in F;* Part 3: *Overture (suite) in B flat. Concerto for 2 horns in E flat.*
(M) *** Teldec/Warner 2292 42723-2 (3) [id.]. Concerto Amsterdam, Brüggen; VCM, Harnoncourt.

What strikes one with renewed force while listening to these once again is the sheer fertility and quality of invention that these works exhibit. This is music of unfailing intelligence and wit and, although Telemann rarely touches the depths of Bach, there is no lack of expressive eloquence either. Renewing acquaintance with this music has been a pleasure, for it is easy to forget how rewarding these pieces are. The performances are light in touch and can be recommended with real enthusiasm. This would make an excellent start to any Telemann collection.

Tafelmusik: Overtures (suites): in E min. (from Part 1); *in D* (from Part 2); *in B flat* (from Part 3).
(M) *** Teldec/Warner 2292 43546-2 [id.]. Concerto Amsterdam, Brüggen.

Essentially, these works are made up of French dance-movements of considerable diversity, and the *E minor Suite* is engagingly scored for a pair of recorders with strings; although it has no *Badinerie*, its sound is not unlike Bach's B minor work; while Telemann's *D major*, with its forthright use of a trumpet, similarly reminds one of the Bach *Third Suite*, even though its invention has nothing in it as memorable as Bach's famous *Air*. The third suite here is perhaps the most agreeable of all, using two oboes with considerable flair. All this music is expertly played by the Concerto Amsterdam under Frans Brüggen, and the remastered 1970 recording is fresh and full, so that the disc sounds hardly dated at all. Offered at mid-price, it represents first-rate value.

CHAMBER MUSIC

Essercizii musici: Recorder sonatas in C & D min.; Der Getreue Music-Meister: Recorder sonatas in A; C; D; F. Sonata in F min.
(M) ** HM/BMG Dig. GD 77153 [77153-2-RG]. Schneider, Camerata Köln.

There is some highly accomplished and stylish playing here from Michael Schneider and his two colleagues of the Camerata Köln, but the 1984 recording could with advantage have subjected the recorder to less close scrutiny. Still, this is enjoyable music-making of rare repertoire.

Paris quartets, First Series, *Nos. 1: Concerto in G; 3: Sonata in A; 4: Sonata in G min.; 5: Suite in E min.*
(B) ** Hung. White Label HRC 087 [id.].
Kovács, Hungarian Baroque Trio, Nagy.

These are most inventive works, and the level of inspiration is extraordinarily even. No doubt Brüggen's complete set with the Amsterdam Quartet will return soon on Teldec; meanwhile these Hungarian performances are fresh and enjoyable. They are well recorded, too, though the close balance means that the range of dynamic is limited.

VOCAL MUSIC

(i) *Der Tag des Gerichts (The Day of Judgement;* oratorio): complete; (ii) *Pimpinone* (opera): complete; (iii) *Paris quartets Nos. 1 & 6.*
(M) **(*) Teldec/Warner 2292 42722-2 (3) [id.].
(i) Landwehr-Herrmann, Canne-Meijer, Equiluz, Van Egmond, soloists from Vienna Boys' Ch., Hamburg Monteverdi Ch., VCM, Harnoncourt; (ii) Spreckelsen, Nimsgern, Tachezi, Florilegium Musicum Ens., Hirsch; (iii) Amsterdam Qt.

Although these discs are offered at mid-price, the layout seems extravagant, since *Pimpinone* fits on to a single CD and could have been offered separately. This charming chamber opera anticipates *La Serva padrona* and offers music of great tunefulness and vivacity. The opera, here given uncut at 70 minutes, has only two characters, no chorus whatever, and a small orchestra. Yet its music is as witty as its libretto, and from the very opening one can sense that Telemann is enjoying every moment of this absurd comedy about a serving maid (Vespetta) who battens on a wealthy but stupid gentleman (Pimpinone), eventually persuading him not only to marry her but to give her the freedom of his purse and at the same time to do her bidding. Uta Spreckelsen and Sigmund Nimsgern are perfectly cast, and there is both charm and sparkle, while Hirsch accompanies in suitably spirited fashion. Excellent (1975) recording, with the voices given good presence. *The Day of Judgement* – the last of Telemann's great oratorios, coming from 1761–2 – is less convincing. Although there are moments of considerable inspiration in a work subtitled 'a poem for singing in four contemplations', one feels that Telemann was far too urbane a master to measure himself fully against so cosmic a theme. But the work is well worth sampling, particularly as the performers give it so persuasive and musical an advocacy and are, moreover, given the advantage of well-balanced recording. Nevertheless this is not a work that would figure high on the list of priorities for most Telemann admirers. The 1966 sound has been effectively remastered and, although the choral focus is not always completely clean, the overall effect is vivid. Since it runs to some 84 minutes' length, the last contemplation is placed on a separate CD, and two of the highly inventive *Paris quartets* are used as the fill-up; with the personnel of the Amsterdam group consisting of Frans Brüggen, Jaap Schröder, Anner Bylsma and Gustav Leonhardt, one can expect a high order of virtuosity put at the service of the composer. The main snag is the close recording, vivid enough but with dynamic contrast relatively limited. The other drawback is the absence of translations – only the German words are given.

Thomson, Virgil (1896–1989)

Film scores: *The Plow that broke the Plains; The River* (suites).
(M) *** Van. 08.8013.71 [OVC 8013].
Symphony of the Air, Leopold Stokowski – STRAVINSKY: *Soldier's Tale.* ***

Virgil Thomson's orchestral music may be sub-Copland (he too uses cowboy tunes like *Old paint*), but in Stokowski's charismatic hands these two film scores emerge with colours glowing and their rhythmic, folksy geniality readily communicating. The recording is resonantly atmospheric, but vivid too. Most enjoyable, and with a worthwhile coupling. This is at upper mid-price in the USA.

Tiomkin, Dimitri (1894–1979)

Film scores: *The Big Sky: suite. The Fourposter: Overture. Friendly Persuasion: Love scene in the barn. The Guns of Navarone: Prelude.* (i) *Lost Horizon* (extended excerpts); *Search for Paradise:* choral finale.
(M) ** BMG/RCA GD 81669; *GK 81669* [1669-2-RG; *1669-4-RG*]. Nat. PO, Charles Gerhardt; (i) with John Alldis Ch.

Tiomkin's score for *Lost Horizon* may have been just what Frank Capra wanted, but it is unadulterated oriental kitsch and stands up poorly away from the visual images. The composer is heard to better effect in the brief *Prelude* for *The Guns of Navarone* (with a pithy theme a little like Walton's fugal idea for *The First of the Few*). There is plenty of atmosphere in the score for *The Big Sky*, but Tiomkin is at his most attractively lyrical in the love scene for *Friendly Persuasion*, light-hearted rather than intense like the choral finale of *Search for Paradise.* As ever, performances are persuasive and the recorded sound is full and atmospheric, although it has less sharpness of definition than some reissues in this series. There are three very striking stills as illustrations.

Tippett, Michael (born 1905)

(i) *Concerto for double string orchestra;* (ii) *Fantasia concertante on a theme of Corelli;* (iii; iv) *Piano concerto;* (v) *String quartet No. 1;* (iii) *Piano sonatas Nos. 1–2.*

(M) *(**) EMI CMS7 63522-2 (2). (i) Moscow CO & Bath Festival O, Barshai; (ii) Y. Menuhin, Masters, Simpson, Bath Festival O, composer; (iii) John Ogdon; (iv) Philh. O, Sir Colin Davis; (v) Edinburgh Qt.

This is a useful and interesting compilation (provided with the composer's own notes on the music), and it is a pity that reservations have to be expressed concerning the sound of the CD transfers. Tippett's eloquent *Concerto for double string orchestra* is well served by Barshai's performance, which has both warmth and vitality. The recording is lively but a shade dry in the upper range. The string textures are clear but not ideally expansive. The *Fantasia concertante*, written for the 1953 Edinburgh Festival, is not as immediately striking as its predecessor but, with the composer in charge and Menuhin as principal soloist, its inventiveness and expressive feeling are never in doubt. The only snag is that the music by Corelli, with which it opens, is more obviously memorable than anything which follows. Again, the sound is clear and vivid but could be more sumptuous. The *Piano concerto* dates from around the same period – it was first performed in 1956 – and again represents Tippett's complex-textured and starkly conceived earlier style. None of the themes is specially memorable, and one gets the impression of too many notes chasing too few ideas. Ogdon gives it a fine performance, although he does not rescue it from waywardness, while the recording, if not ideal, now sounds clearer than originally. The *First String quartet* is an early work (1934–5) which the composer rewrote, changing it from a four-movement structure to a unitary piece in three sections (banded here, but played without a break). The piece is not difficult to come to grips with, although it is the outer movements which are most characteristic, and the *Molto lento e tranquillo* seems less striking. It is played rather slackly here and is more effective in a tauter performance; the sound is on the thin side. The difference between the style of the two *Piano sonatas* is the more striking for having them juxtaposed, particularly as Ogdon plays them both well and is especially convincing in the *First.* This is undeniably a work of power and originality, even though its relentless diatonicism may strike some listeners as limiting. The first movement is a set of variations and the *Andante* is a brief rondo using the Scottish folksong, *Ca' the yowes*, as its main idea. The finale is also a rondo with a hint of jazz in its principal theme. The work has a vitality of invention that it is easy to admire, even if as piano writing it is not as effective in the traditional sense as Tippett's later essay in this form. This is much more compressed in its argument, by way of kaleidoscopic reshuffling of tiny motifs rather than by conventional development, and though a more uninhibited approach can bring out the point of Tippett's scheme better, Ogdon displays his usual integrity, as well as virtuosity. The recording is faithful but a shade hard.

Symphonies Nos. (i) *1–2;* (ii; iii) *3; 4; Suite for the birthday of Prince Charles.*

(M) *** Decca 425 646-2 (3) [id.]. (i) LSO, C. Davis; (ii) Chicago SO, Solti; (iii) Heather Harper.

All the symphonies have previously been available separately, the *First* and *Third* on Philips, the *Second* on Argo and the *Fourth* on Decca. The Polygram merger permits all four to be accommodated in a box of three CDs (since possessing the *First* and *Fourth* originally involved duplication, as they were both coupled with the *Suite for the birthday of Prince Charles*, this new format is obviously attractive). The transfers are splendidly vivid.

Tosti, Francesco (1846–1916)

Songs: *L'alba sepàra della luce l'ombra; Aprile; 'A vucchella; Chanson de L'adieu; Goodbye; Ideale; Malia; Marechiare; Non t'amo; Segreto; La serenata; Sogno; L'ultima canzone; Vorrei morire.*

(M) *** Ph. 426 372-2. José Carreras, ECO, Muller.

Tosti (knighted by Queen Victoria for his services to music) had a gently charming lyric gift in songs like these, and it is good to have a tenor with such musical intelligence – not to mention such a fine, pure voice – tackling once-popular trifles like *Marechiare* and *Goodbye.* The arrangements are sweetly done, and the recording is excellent.

Turina, Joaquín (1882–1949)

Danzas fantásticas.

(M) **(*) EMI Dig. CDD7 63886-2 [id.]; *ET*

763886-4. LPO, Bátiz – FALLA: *Nights*; RODRIGO: *Concierto de Aranjuez*. **(*)

Bátiz certainly evokes a Mediterranean feeling in these three famous *Danzas* and he persuades the LPO to bring out the Latin colours and atmosphere. He is particularly beguiling in the gentle yet sultry charms of the central *Ensueño* ('Dream fantasy'), with a sensuous response from the LPO strings. The *Orgia* has plenty of energy and fire. The 1982 recording, made in – of all unlikely places – St Peter's Church, Morden, in Surrey – has an agreeably warm ambience, but fortissimos are very bright, in the way of early digital recordings; at times the ear craves rather more voluptuousness, although the effect is partly the result of Turina's brilliantly sunlit scoring.

Varèse, Edgar (1883–1965)

Ameriques; Arcana; Density 21.5; Intégrales; Ionisation; Octandre; Offrandes.
(M) *** Sony Analogue/Dig. SK 45844 [id.]. Yakar, NYPO, Ens. InterContemporain, Boulez.

This welcome mid-priced reissue combines two previous LPs, bringing together all of Varèse's most important works. In the inter-war period he was regarded as a wild man of the avant-garde in writing a work like *Ionisation* for percussion alone and abandoning conventional argument in favour of presenting blocks of sound. Yet performances like these show what a genius he had – not for assaulting but for tickling the ear with novelty. Boulez brings out the purposefulness of his writing, not least in the two big works for full orchestra, the early *Ameriques* and *Arcana*, written for an enormous orchestra in the late 1920s. Those two works are here played by the New York Philharmonic and are not digitally recorded. The selection recorded more recently in digital sound covers his smaller but just as striking works for chamber ensembles of various kinds, with Rachel Yakar the excellent soprano soloist in *Offrandes*.

Vaughan Williams, Ralph (1872–1958)

Concerto grosso; (i) *Oboe concerto; English folksongs suite; Fantasia on Greensleeves;* (ii) *Romance* (for harmonica and strings).
(M) **(*) Decca 421 392-2; *421 392-4*. (i) Nicklin; (ii) Reilly; ASMF, Marriner.

A somewhat mixed bag of lightweight Vaughan Williams. Celia Nicklin gives a most persuasive account of the elusive *Oboe concerto*, while the *Concerto grosso* is lively and polished. The atmospheric *Romance* is not one of the composer's most inspired works, but it is still worth having on disc. The recordings generally sound well, if with a touch of astringency in the string timbre.

(i) *Oboe concerto; English folksongs suite; Fantasia on Greensleeves; Fantasia on a theme by Thomas Tallis; Partita for double string orchestra*.
(M) **(*) EMI Dig. CD-EMX 2179; *TC-EMX 2179*. (i) Small; Royal Liverpool PO, Handley.

The charmingly lyrical *Oboe concerto* is given a delectable performance here by Jonathan Small, the flowing pastoralism of its first movement perfectly caught and the more demanding finale impressively handled by conductor and soloist alike. The rarer *Partita for string orchestra* (one without double-basses) is more ambitious even than the *Tallis fantasia*, and is some five minutes longer. This is also very well played and sonorously recorded. It is chiefly remembered for the *Intermezzo* headed 'Homage to Henry Hall' a unique tribute to the 1940s' leader of a dance-band, whose signature-tune, 'Here's to the next time', is hinted at in the first string group, while the second provides a jazzy pizzicato bass. The work is attractive, but elsewhere is not as catchy as one always hopes. Handley gives an essentially rhapsodic account of the *Tallis fantasia*, relaxing in its central section and then creating an accelerando to the climax. The inner string group creates radiantly ethereal textures, but ideally the recording needs just a little more resonance – the work was written to be first performed in Gloucester Cathedral – although it is rich-textured and truthful.

(i) *Violin concerto in D min.;* (ii) *Flos campi*.
(M) (***) EMI mono CDH7 63828-2. (i) Yehudi Menuhin, LPO; (ii) William Primrose (viola), Philh. O; Boult – WALTON: *Viola concerto* etc.(***)

Though the 1946 mono sound inevitably limits the atmospheric beauty of *Flos campi*, this première recording of a masterpiece brings revelatory playing from Primrose, as well as deeply understanding conducting from Boult. The soloist's degree of classical detachment adds to the intensity of emotion conveyed. It is almost the opposite with Menuhin's reading of what in its neo-classical figuration can seem a chilly work. Though there have been more immaculate performances on record since, none matches this in its heartfelt intensity, whether in the thrust and vigour of the outer movements or, most of all, in the yearning lyricism of the central *Adagio*, here revealed as among the composer's most tenderly beautiful slow movements. The recording, made in 1952 but never issued at the time, is also limited; but with excellent CD transfers and equally valuable Walton works as a generous coupling, this is a historic CD to cherish.

English folksongs suite; Fantasia on Greensleeves; In the Fen Country; (i) *The Lark ascending; Norfolk rhapsody No. 1;* (ii) *Serenade to music.*

(M) *** EMI CDM7 64022-2 [id.]; *EG 764022-4*. LPO, LSO or New Philh. O, Sir Adrian Boult; (i) with Hugh Bean; (ii) 16 soloists.

An attractive coupling of four works that originally appeared as fill-ups to Boult versions of the symphonies, all beautifully performed and recorded. Hugh Bean understands the spirit of *The Lark ascending* perfectly and his performance is wonderfully serene. For the CD reissue two others works have been added, the colourful *English folksongs suite* and Vaughan Williams's fine arrangement of one of the loveliest of all traditional melodies, *Greensleeves.* The transfers are fresh and pleasing, with only a marginal loss of body and the ambient atmosphere still providing bloom; in the lovely *Serenade* (which Boult does in the original version for 16 soloists) the voices are given greater presence, yet the overall balance remains convincing.

English folksongs suite; Toccata marziale.

(BB) *** ASV CDQS 6021; *ZCQS 6021*. London Wind O, Denis Wick – HOLST: *Military band suites* etc. ***

As in the Holst suites, the pace of these performances is attractively zestful, and if the slow movement of the *English folksongs suite* could have been played more reflectively, the bounce of *Seventeen come Sunday* is irresistible. The first-class analogue recording has been transferred vividly to CD.

(i) *Fantasia on Greensleeves;* (ii) *Fantasia on a theme of Thomas Tallis;* (i) *Overture: The Wasps;* (i; iii; iv) *Serenade to music;* (iv) *Towards the unknown region.*

(M) *** EMI CDM7 63382-2 [id.]. (i) LSO; (ii) Philh. O; (iii) Elsie Morison, Marjorie Thomas, Duncan Robertson, Trevor Anthony; (iv) Chorus; Sargent.

Here is a splendid reminder of the art of Sir Malcolm Sargent, or 'Flash Harry' as he was none too affectionately known by orchestral players, to whom he could be inordinately rude. He was not a modest man, but he knew how to woo the amateur choristers who sang at his many annual *Messiahs*, and he was a great favourite with the wider musical public, becoming the first celebrity musician on radio through his broadcasts on the wartime 'Brains Trust'. His orchestral command was considerable and he did much to proselytize British music overseas, especially the works of Vaughan Williams. *The Wasps overture* was one of his favourite showpieces, and his reading is delightfully spick and span. When he played it once at a concert in Carnegie Hall, a local review described it engagingly as 'a pleasant trifle that sounds like Rimsky-Korsakov with bowler, mackintosh and umbrella'. But he could find an unexpected depth and sense of infinity as well as strength in the *Tallis fantasia* (which is why he performed Elgar's *Dream of Gerontius* so intuitively). Vaughan Williams's great string work is superbly played here by the 1959 Philharmonia strings. The recording producer was Walter Legge, and the sound is wonderfully full, yet clear, with a lovely ethereal effect from the solo group. In the *Serenade to music* Sargent chose the first of the composer's performing alternatives. Rather than using sixteen solo singers, he divided their music up between four, and expanded to a chorus where the sixteen voices unite. Moreover he chose two of his favourite soloists, Elsie Morison and Majorie Thomas, for the recording, and the work's closing section sounds particularly beautiful. *Towards the unknown region* further demonstrates Sargent's choral skills in a reading of considerable eloquence. All the LSO recordings here were made in the Abbey Road No. 1 Studio in 1957, with Peter Andry in charge, and they sound remarkably good.

Fantasia on Greensleeves; Fantasia on a theme of Thomas Tallis.

(B) **(*) Pickwick Dig. PCD 930 [id.]. LSO, Frühbeck de Burgos – ELGAR: *Cello concerto.* ***

Though Frühbeck is rather heavy-handed in his treatment of these Vaughan Williams favourites, the playing of the LSO is refined and the recording first rate. On the bargain-price Pickwick label, it makes an unconventional coupling for Felix Schmidt's outstanding reading of the Elgar *Cello concerto.*

Five variants of Dives and Lazarus; (i) *The Lark ascending; The Wasps: Overture and suite.*

(M) *** EMI Dig. CD-EMX 9508; *TC-EMX 2082*. (i) David Nolan; LPO, Handley.

The immediacy of the recording allows no mistiness in *The Lark ascending*, but it is still a warm, understanding performance. The overture is spaciously conceived and it leads to charming, colourful accounts of the other, less well-known pieces in the suite, tuneful and lively. The *Five Variants of Dives and Lazarus* finds Vaughan Williams using his folksong idiom at its most poetic, here superbly played and recorded. The sound is fresh and clear, if rather brightly lit.

Symphonies Nos. 1–9; English folksongs suite; Fantasia on Greensleeves; Fantasia on a theme by Thomas Tallis; In the Fen Country; The Lark ascending; Norfolk rhapsody No. 1; Serenade to music; The Wasps: Overture and suite.
(M) *** EMI CMS7 63098-2 (7). LPO, New Philh. O or LSO, Boult.

Boult's approach to Vaughan Williams was firmly symphonic rather than evocative, and his cycle of the symphonies for EMI, here supplemented by many of the shorter orchestral pieces, brings warm and mature readings, which benefit from full-bodied, well-focused sound. EMI's mid-price offer gathers in a box the seven full-price CDs as originally issued, without any modification of format. Between them they present a comprehensive portrait of the composer, unmatched by any other single issue.

A Sea Symphony (No. 1).
(M) *** EMI CDM7 64016-2 [id.]; *EG 764016-4*. Armstrong, Carol Case, LPO Ch., LPO, Boult.
(M) **(*) EMI Dig. CD-EMX 2142. Rodgers, Shimell, Liverpool PO Ch., Royal Liverpool PO, Handley.
(M) *** BMG/RCA GD 90500 [60580-2-RG]. Harper, Shirley-Quirk, LSO Ch., LSO, Previn.
(M) (***) Decca mono 425 658-2. Baillie, Cameron, LPO Ch., LPO, Boult.

Boult's stereo version is a warm, relaxed reading of Vaughan Williams's expansive symphony. If the ensemble is sometimes less perfect than one would like, the flow of the music consistently holds the listener, and this is matched by warmly atmospheric recorded sound. Boult, often thought of as a 'straight' interpreter, here demonstrates his affectionate style, drawing consistently expressive but never sentimental phrasing from his singers and players. John Carol Case's baritone does not sound well on disc with his rather plaintive tone-colour, but his style is right, and Sheila Armstrong sings most beautifully. The set has been remastered with outstanding success. The balance is wholly natural, with the soloists seemingly just beyond the loudspeakers and the chorus spaciously laid out behind. Yet there is a vivid impact and the words are remarkably clear. There is no finer version.

Vernon Handley conducts a warmly idiomatic performance, which sustains relatively slow speeds masterfully. The emotional thrust of the work is caught powerfully from the very start, both in the big dramatic moments and in the tenderness of the quieter passages. The reading is crowned by Handley's rapt account of the slow movement, *On the beach at night alone*, as well as by the long duet in the finale, leading on through the exciting final ensemble, *Sail forth*, to a deeply satisfying culmination in *O my brave Soul!*. Joan Rodgers makes an outstandingly beautiful soprano soloist, with William Shimell drier-toned but expressive. There are two reservations: the first section of that long finale is less tense than the rest of the performance, and the recording, full and warm, presents problems in its extreme dynamic range, while placing the two soloists rather distantly. EMI has promised a remastering. That could well help to eliminate the problems, which in any case will not worry everyone – the organ, for example, is better defined here than in any other version. To have such a performance in modern digital sound on a mid-price issue is self-recommending.

Previn's is a fresh, youthful reading of a young composer's symphony. The conductor's nervous energy is obvious from the very start. He does not always relax even where, as in the slow movement, he takes a rather measured tempo. In the Scherzo, Previn is lighter and cleaner, holding more in reserve. The finale similarly is built up over a longer span, with less deliberate expressiveness. The culminating climax with Previn is not allowed to be swamped with choral tone, but has the brass and timpani still prominent. The *Epilogue* may not be so deliberately expressive, but it is purer in its tenderness and exact control of dynamics. Previn has clear advantages in his baritone soloist and his choir. The recording has been digitally remastered and detail clarified, yet the rich ambience remains, with the performers set slightly back.

It is good also to have Boult's 1954 Decca mono recording of the *Sea Symphony* back again on CD. In its original LP form it was one of the first really spectacular demonstration records (once used in the Royal Albert Hall) and it has not lost its power to surprise in the famous opening sequence. As for the performance, Boult was at his most inspired. However diffuse the argument may be, conveyed here is the kind of urgency one normally gets only at a live performance. What comes out above all in a rehearing is the way the work forecasts later Vaughan Williams and what a striking achievement it was for a composer who has been far too readily dubbed a 'late developer'. He was present at the recording sessions.

A London Symphony (No. 2); (i) *Concerto accademico; The Wasps: Overture.*

(M) *** BMG/RCA GD 90501 [60581-2-RG]. LSO, Previn; (i) with James Buswell.

A London Symphony (No. 2): Fantasia on a theme of Thomas Tallis.
(M) *** EMI CDM7 64017-2; *EG 764017-4.* LPO, Boult.

A London Symphony (No. 2); Partita for double string orchestra.
(M) (**(*)) Decca mono/stereo 430 366-2. LPO, Sir Adrian Boult.

On RCA, though the actual sonorities are subtly and beautifully realized by Previn, the architecture is presented equally convincingly, with the great climaxes of the first and last movements powerful and incisive. Most remarkable of all are the pianissimos which here have great intensity, a quality of frisson as in a live performance. The LSO play superbly and the digitally remastered recording, made in Kingsway Hall, still sounds well with its wide range of dynamic. The fill-ups are welcome, especially James Buswell's fine account of the *Concerto.*

The sound remains spacious on Boult's splendid 1970 version and the orchestral playing is outstandingly fine. The outer movements are expansive, less taut than in his much earlier mono version for Decca. The central *tranquillo* episode of the first movement, for instance, is very relaxed; but here, as in the slow movement, the orchestra produces lovely sounds, the playing deeply committed; and criticism is disarmed. The Scherzo is as light as thistledown and the gentle melancholy which underlies the solemn pageantry of the finale is coloured with great subtlety. With Boult's noble, gravely intense account of the *Tallis fantasia* offered as a coupling, this remains an attractive alternative to Previn. The new CD transfer is remarkably successful. Detail is refined, yet the massed strings are full and rich both in *Tallis* and in the slow movement of the symphony.

Boult's 1952 recording of the *London Symphony* has great atmosphere and intensity. His later, EMI performance is warmer, but the voltage of this first LP version is very compelling, bringing the feeling of a live performance. The mono sound is spacious and basically full, but the violins sound thin and edgy above the stave, and the remastering has not improved matters, especially in the glorious slow movement. But such is the magnetism of the music-making that the ear readily adjusts. The *Partita* was recorded in the earliest days of stereo in 1956. It is not one of the composer's most remarkable works (it was originally a double string trio) and it does not inspire Boult as does the symphony; but it is well played and the string sound here is more agreeable, if not outstanding.

A London Symphony (No. 2); Symphony No. 8 in G min.
(M) *** EMI CDM7 64197-2; *EG 764197-4* [id.]. Hallé O, Sir John Barbirolli.

There is a very special place in the catalogue for this coupling. Barbirolli's 1957 recording of the *London Symphony* was an inspirational performance, entirely throwing off the fetters of the studio. The reading gathers power as it proceeds and the slow movement has great intensity and eloquence, with the Hallé strings surpassing themselves; its climax sounds surprisingly full. Indeed the recording, besides having a wide dynamic range, has plenty of atmosphere and warmth. The digital remastering is wholly successful, with the background subdued. The new coupling of the *Eighth Symphony* makes the CD doubly attractive. 'Glorious John' (the composer's appreciative description of the work's dedicatee) gave its première, and this record was made (by Mercury engineers) just a month afterwards. It is a robust performance rather than a subtle one, but full of character and feeling, matched by most vivid sound.

(i) *A Pastoral Symphony (No. 3); Symphony No. 4 in F min.*
(M) *** BMG/RCA GD 90503 [60583-2-RG]. (i) Heather Harper; LSO, Previn.

One tends to think of Vaughan Williams's pastoral music as essentially synonymous with the English countryside, and it is something of a shock to discover that in fact the *Pastoral Symphony* was sketched in Northern France while the composer was on active service in 1916, and the initial inspiration was a Corot-like landscape in the sunset. But the music remains English in essence, and its gentle rapture is not easily evoked. Previn draws an outstandingly beautiful and refined performance from the LSO, the bare textures sounding austere but never thin, the few climaxes emerging at full force with purity undiminished. In the third movement the final coda – the only really fast music in the whole work – brings a magic tracery of pianissimo in this performance, light, fast and clear. In the *F minor Symphony* only the somewhat ponderous tempo Previn adopts for the first movement lets it down. But on the whole this is a powerful reading, and it is vividly recorded.

(i) *A Pastoral Symphony (No. 3);* (ii) *Symphony No. 5 in D.*
(M) *** EMI CDM7 64018-2; *EG 764018-4.* (i) Margaret Price, New Philh. O; (ii) LPO, Boult.
(M) (***) Decca mono 430 060-2; *430 060-4* [id.]. (i) Margaret Ritchie; LPO, Boult.

On EMI, in the *Pastoral Symphony* Boult is not entirely successful in controlling the tension of the short but elusive first movement, although it is beautifully played. The opening of the *Lento moderato*, however, is very fine, and its close is sustained with a perfect blend of restraint and intensity. After the jovial third movement, the orchestra is joined by Margaret Price, whose wordless contribution is blended into the texture most skilfully. Boult gives a loving performance of the *Fifth Symphony*, one which links it directly with the great opera *The Pilgrim's Progress*, from which (in its unfinished state) the composer drew much of the material. It is a gentle performance, easier and more flowing than some rivals', and some may prefer it for that reason, but the emotional involvement is a degree less intense, particularly in the slow movement. Both recordings have been very successfully remastered, retaining the fullness and atmosphere (while refining detail) to help the tranquil mood which is striking in both works. The effect is glowing and radiant.

It is good to have the earlier Kingsway Hall recordings back in the catalogue. They were made in 1952/3 with the composer present; although allowances have to be made for the pinched sound of the upper string climaxes, the recording is basically full and luminous. The transluscent textures Boult creates in the *Pastoral Symphony* (the opening is hauntingly ethereal) and his essential delicacy of approach are balanced by his intensity in the *Fifth*, where the climax of the first movement has wonderful breadth and passion. The LPO play with great sympathy and warmth in music that was still new, the *Fifth* only a decade old, at the time this record was made.

Symphonies Nos. 4 in F min.; 6 in E min.
(M) **(*) EMI CDM7 64019-2 [id.]; *EG 764019-4*. New Philh. O, Sir Adrian Boult.

Boult's was the first stereo recording of the *Fourth*; although it would be possible to imagine a performance of greater fire and tenacity, few will find much to disappoint them in this persuasive account. Sir Adrian procures orchestral playing of the highest quality from the New Philharmonia, and the slow movement, one of the composer's finest inspirations, is particularly successful. The recording, too, is first class; in this remastered form it sounds admirably fresh and combines body and clarity with spaciousness. There is plenty of bite in the sound, and this increases the sense of attack in the first movement of the powerful *Sixth Symphony*. Here Boult's performance is without the high voltage of his first mono recording for Decca with the composer present, and the reading is not as searching as that earlier account. The strange finale is played beautifully, with its finely sustained pianissimo enhanced on CD, and the atmosphere is not without a sense of mystery, but a greater degree of underlying tension is needed.

Symphony No. 5 in D; The England of Elizabeth: 3 Portraits (arr. Mathieson).
(M) *** BMG/RCA GD 90506 [60586-2-RG]. LSO, Previn.

Symphony No. 5 in D; (i) *Flos campi* (suite).
❀ (M) *** EMI Dig. CD-EMX 9512; TC-EMX 2112 [Ang. CDM 62029]. Royal Liverpool PO, Handley; (i) with Christopher Balmer & Liverpool Philharmonic Ch.

Vernon Handley's disc is outstanding in every way, a spacious yet concentrated reading, superbly played and recorded, which masterfully holds the broad structure of this symphony together, building to massive climaxes. The warmth and poetry of the work are also beautifully caught. The rare and evocative *Flos campi*, inspired by the Song of Solomon, makes a generous and attractive coupling, equally well played, though the viola solo is rather closely balanced. The sound is outstandingly full, giving fine clarity of texture.

If anyone ever doubted the dedication of Previn as an interpreter of Vaughan Williams, his glowing RCA disc will provide the clearest rebuttal. In this most characteristic – and, many would say, greatest – of the Vaughan Williams symphonies, Previn refuses to be lured into pastoral byways. His tempi may be consistently on the slow side, but the purity of tone he draws from the LSO, the precise shading of dynamic and phrasing, and the sustaining of tension through the longest, most hushed passages produce results that will persuade many not normally convinced of the greatness of this music. It is some tribute to Previn's intensity that he can draw out the *diminuendi* at the ends of movements with such refinement and no sense of exaggeration. This is an outstanding performance, very well transferred to CD. The *England of Elizabeth suite* is a film score of no great musical interest but undoubtedly pleasant to listen to.

(i) *Symphony No. 6* (includes original and revised Scherzo); (ii) *The Lark ascending;* (iii) *Song of thanksgiving*.
(M) (***) EMI mono CDH7 63308-2 [id.]. (i) LSO; (ii) Pougnet, LPO; (iii) Dolemore, Speight (nar.), Luton Ch. Soc. & Girls' Ch., LPO, Boult.

This is a valuable compilation of Sir Adrian Boult's early post-war recordings of Vaughan Williams's music, sounding surprisingly well in excellent transfers. One adjusts almost immediately to the flatter mono effect in the recording of the *Sixth Symphony*, made very soon after the first performance in 1948, so soon in fact that it was originally done with the unrevised version of the scherzo. As soon as the revision was written, Sir Adrian re-recorded that movement alone, and this disc includes both. On CD one can programme the player to include whichever of the two one chooses. Jean Pougnet, leader of the LPO at the time, is a natural soloist for *The Lark ascending* with his exceptionally pure tone, while the *Song of thanksgiving*, originally entitled 'Thanksgiving for victory', is an attractive period piece designed for victory celebrations after the Second World War. It proved rather more than an occasional piece but has never been recorded since. One has to make no apology for either of these recordings, and in the latter work the chorus sounds strikingly firm and clear.

Symphonies Nos. 6 in E min.; 9 in E min.
(M) *** BMG/RCA GD 90508 [60588-2-RG]. LSO, Previn.

The *Sixth Symphony*, with its moments of darkness and brutality contrasted against the warmth of the second subject or the hushed intensity of the final other-worldly slow movement, is a work for which Previn has a natural affinity. In the first three movements his performance is superbly dramatic, clear-headed and direct, with natural understanding. His account of the mystical final movement with its endless pianissimo is not, however, on the same level, for the playing is not quite hushed enough, and the tempo is a little too fast. The *Ninth*, Vaughan Williams's last symphony, stimulates Previn to show a freshness and sense of poetry which prove particularly thought-provoking and rewarding. The RCA recording is highly successful, and the string-tone is expansive and well balanced in relation to the rest of the orchestra.

(i) *Sinfonia Antartica (No. 7); Serenade to music.*
(M) *** EMI Dig. CD-EMX 2173; *TC-EMX 2173*. (i) Alison Hargan; Royal Liverpool PO and Ch., Vernon Handley.

Vernon Handley in his Vaughan Williams series for EMI Eminence directs a warmly atmospheric reading of the *Antartica*. This is a most satisfyingly symphonic view of a work that can seem merely illustrative. As in his other Vaughan Williams recordings, Handley shows a natural feeling for expressive rubato and draws refined playing from the Liverpool orchestra. At the end of the epilogue Alison Hargan makes a notable first appearance on disc, a soprano with an exceptionally sweet and pure voice. In well-balanced digital sound it makes an outstanding bargain, particularly when it offers an excellent fill-up. Handley directs a warmly understanding reading of the *Serenade to music*, though in this lovely score a chorus never sounds as characterful as a group of well-chosen soloists.

Sinfonia Antartica (No. 7); The Wasps (incidental music): *Overture and suite.*
(M) **(*) EMI CDM7 64020-2 [id.]; *EG 764020-4*. LPO, Sir Adrian Boult.

Sir Adrian gives a stirring account and is well served by the EMI engineers. There is not really a great deal to choose between this and Previn's version as performances: both are convincing. Perhaps the EMI recording has slightly greater range and a more natural balance; certainly the CD transfer brings an attractively firm focus. However, the inclusion of Vaughan Williams's Aristophanic suite, *The Wasps*, with its endearing participation of the kitchen utensils plus its indelibly tuneful *Overture*, is a bonus for the Boult issue, although in the *Overture* the upper strings sound a bit thin.

(i) *Sinfonia Antartica (No. 7); Symphony No. 8 in D min.*
(M) *** BMG/RCA GD 90510 [60590-2-RG]. (i) Heather Harper, Ralph Richardson, LSO Ch.; LSO, Previn.

The coupling of the *Sinfonia Antartica* with the *Eighth* is the most generous in Previn's cycle. In the former, the RCA recording in its relatively distant balance, as well as Previn's interpretation, concentrates on atmosphere rather than drama in a performance that is sensitive and literal. Because of the recessed effect of the sound, the portrayal of the ice-fall (represented by the sudden entry of the organ) has a good deal less impact than on Vernon Handley's version. Before each movement Sir Ralph Richardson speaks the superscription written by the composer on his score. Previn's account of the *Eighth* brings no reservations, with finely pointed playing, the most precise control of dynamic shading, and a delightfully Stravinskian account of the bouncing Scherzo for woodwind alone. Excellent recording, which has been opened up by the digital remastering and made to sound more expansive.

Symphonies Nos. 8 in D min.; 9 in E min.
(M) *** EMI CDM7 64021-2 [id.]; *EG 764021-4*. LPO, Sir Adrian Boult.

The coupling of Vaughan Williams's *Eighth* and *Ninth Symphonies* is generous and apt, both having been seriously underestimated. Boult's account of the *Eighth* is an essentially genial one. It may not be as sharply pointed as

Previn's version, but some will prefer the extra warmth of the Boult interpretation with its rather more lyrical approach. The *Ninth* contains much noble and arresting invention, and Boult's performance is fully worthy of it. He draws most committed playing from the LPO, and the recording is splendidly firm in tone. The digital remastering is well up to the high standard EMI have set with these reissues of Boult's recordings. There is a slight loss of amplitude but the clean focus has added to the bite of the performance of the *D minor Symphony*, especially in the witty *Scherzo alla marcia*.

VOCAL MUSIC

(i) *10 Blake songs* (for voice and oboe); (ii) *Songs of travel*. Songs: *Linden Lea; Orpheus with his lute; The water mill; Silent noon*.

(M) *** Decca 430 368-2. Robert Tear; (i) Neil Black; (ii) Philip Ledger – BUTTERWORTH: *Shropshire lad*. ***

Robert Tear, recorded in 1972, cannot match Ian Partridge in his wonderfully sensitive account (currently withdrawn) of the *Blake songs*, but his rougher-grained voice brings out a different kind of expressiveness, helped by Neil Black's fine oboe playing. The *Songs of travel*, here presented complete with the five extra songs published later, are also most welcome, as are the other four songs, notably *Silent noon*, added for this reissue. Ledger is a most perceptive accompanist and, with the bonus of the Butterworth coupling, this excellently recorded recital is well worth seeking out.

(i) *Fantasia on Christmas carols*. arr. of carols: *And all in the morning; Wassail song* (also includes: TRAD., arr. Warlock: *Adam lay ybounden; Bethlehem down*).

(M) ** EMI CDM7 64131-2 [id.]; *EG 764131-4*. Guildford Cathedral Ch., Pro Arte O, Barry Rose; (i) with Barrow – HELY-HUTCHINSON: *Carol Symphony;* QUILTER: *Children's overture*. **

Vaughan Williams's joyful *Fantasia on Christmas carols* is comparatively short. It was written for performance in 1912 in Hereford Cathedral, so the acoustic at Guildford Cathedral is well chosen. The performance here is suitably exuberant, and John Barrow is a good soloist, but not everyone will respond to his timbre and style, and the King's performance with Hervey Alan is marginally preferable (see below, under '*The world of Vaughan Williams*'). But the Christmas carol arrangements are delightful, beautifully sung and recorded, and this reissue is worthwhile for its interesting couplings.

'The world of Vaughan Williams': (i) *English folksongs suite;* (ii) *Fantasia on Greensleeves;* (ii; iii) *The Lark ascending;* (iv; v) *Fantasia on Christmas carols;* (vi) *Linden Lea;* (vii; viii) *O clap your hands;* (vii) *O taste and see;* (v) *3 Shakespeare songs;* (vi) *Silent noon; The vagabond*.

(B) **(*) Decca 430 093-2; *430 093-4*. (i) Boston Pops O, Fiedler; (ii) ASMF, Marriner; (iii) with Iona Brown; (iv) Hervey Alan & LSO; (v) King's College Ch., Willcocks; (vi) Tear, Ledger; (vii) Canterbury Cathedral Ch., Allan Wicks; (viii) Philip Jones Brass Ens; David Flood.

Many collectors will feel that any single-disc summation of Vaughan Williams's art without the symphonies must include the great *Tallis fantasia*. It would certainly have been a welcome substitute for the *Folksongs suite*, breezily done though that is. Otherwise the selection is quite well made, as long as there is no objection to having songs with piano sandwiched between *Greensleeves* and Iona Brown's Elysian performance of *The Lark ascending*. *O clap your hands* is most welcome, a splendid, spectacular miniature, and so is the fine *Fantasia on Christmas carols*, a surprisingly rare work, presented here with much spirit.

Verdi, Giuseppe (1813–1901)

Overtures and Preludes: *Aida* (prelude); *Un ballo in maschera* (prelude); *La forza del destino* (overture); *Nabucco* (overture); *La Traviata* (prelude to Act I); *I vespri siciliani* (sinfonia).

(B) *** DG 429 164-2. BPO, Karajan – ROSSINI: *Overtures*. ***

Overtures and Preludes: *Un ballo in maschera* (prelude); *La Battaglia di Legnano; Il Corsaro* (sinfonias); *Ernani* (prelude); *La Forza del destino; Luisa Miller* (overtures); *Macbeth; I Masnadieri* (preludes); *Nabucco* (overture); *Rigoletto; La Traviata* (preludes); *I vespri siciliani* (sinfonia).

(M) *** DG 419 622-2 [id.]. BPO, Karajan.

Make no mistake, this playing is in a class of its own and has an electricity, refinement and authority that sweep all before it. Some of the overtures are little known (*Il Corsaro* and *La Battaglia di Legnano*) and are given with tremendous panache and virtuosity. These are performances of real spirit and are vividly recorded, even if the climaxes could expand more.

Overtures and Preludes: *Aida; Il Corsaro; Luisa Miller; Macbeth; Rigoletto; La Traviata (Act I); I vespri siciliani*.

(B) *** DG Compact Classics *431 185-4* [id.]. BPO, Karajan – ROSSINI: *Overtures*. ***

Not a predictable collection on this excellently transferred Compact Classics cassette. Karajan is in his element, with the polished BPO players producing both elegance (in the *Traviata Prelude*) and plenty of high drama. Most enjoyable!

Overtures and Preludes: *Aida; La forza del destino; Giovanna d'Arco; Luisa Miller; La Traviata (Acts I & III); I vespri siciliani. Macbeth:* Ballet music.
(B) ** Ph. 426 078-2; *426 078-4*. New Philh. O, Markevitch.

A good bargain collection with strongly dramatic performances and excellent CD transfers. *Giovanna d'Arco* and *I vespri siciliani* are especially vivid, and the *Traviata Preludes* are well done too. At times the sonorous brass tends almost to overwhelm the strings, but generally the sound is impressive.

Requiem Mass.
(M) (**(*)) EMI mono CDH7 63341-2 [id.]. Caniglia, Stignani, Gigli, Pinza, Rome Op. Ch. & O, Serafin.
(M) **(*) DG 413 215-2; *413 215-4* (2) [id.]. Freni, Ludwig, Cossutta, Ghiaurov, V. Singverein, VPO, Karajan.
(B) ** EMI CZS7 62892-2 (2) [Ang. CDZB 62892]. Caballé, Cossotto, Vickers, Raimondi, New Philh. Ch. & O, Barbirolli – MOZART: *Requiem*. **(*)

(i) *Requiem Mass;* (ii) *4 Sacred pieces.*
(M) (***) DG mono 429 076-2 (2) [id.]. Stader, Dominguez, Carelli, Sardi, St Hedwig's Cathedral Ch., Berlin RIAS Chamber Ch. & RSO, Fricsay.
(M) **(*) Decca 421 608-2 (2) [id.]. (i) L. Price, Elias, Bjoerling, Tozzi, V. Musikverein, VPO, Reiner; (ii) Minton, Los Angeles Master Ch., LAPO, Mehta.

Fricsay's version (not to be confused with his studio recording of 1950) is of a live performance given in 1960, the very last he conducted before his untimely death. It is a commanding account, often at measured speeds but with a biting sense of drama and a gravity that plainly reflect the conductor's own emotions during his last illness. Like him, the two male soloists are Hungarian, and both are first rate, with the tenor, Gabor Carelli, pleasingly Italianate of tone. Maria Stader, also Hungarian-born, sings with a pure, clear tone, very occasionally suffering intonation problems. Oralia Dominguez is the fruity mezzo, and the chorus is superbly disciplined, with the mono recording remarkably full and spacious. The *Four Sacred pieces* were also recorded live, but ten years earlier. Fricsay gives another dedicated performance. This duplicates the coupling EMI provides for Giulini's classic 1964 account of the *Requiem* (at full price), and it comes remarkably close to matching that peerless set.

Reiner's opening of the *Requiem* is very slow and atmospheric. He takes the music at something like half the speed of Toscanini and shapes everything very carefully. Yet as the work proceeds the performance quickly sparks into life, and there is some superb and memorable singing from a distinguished team of soloists. The recording has a spectacularly wide dynamic range, enhanced by the CD format, and, with the chorus singing fervently, the *Dies irae* is almost overwhelming. Mehta's performance of the *Sacred pieces* has much more brilliant, sharply focused recording than Giulini's, but in every other way Giulini's performance of Verdi's last work (or group of works) provides a deeper, more searching experience. However, that is at full price.

Serafin's classic 1939 recording brings a glowing performance, beautifully shaped, warm and dramatic without drawing attention to itself. Maria Caniglia was not the most sensitive of Italian sopranos, but she ends here with a powerful *Libera me*, while the others could not be more characterful. Ebe Stignani and Ezio Pinza have never been surpassed in this music and Gigli, for all his stylistic peccadillos – with the vocal line often punctuated by aspirates and little sobs – is unique in his persuasiveness and honeyed tone. The choral singing is strong and dramatic, but the CD transfer requires some knob-twiddling if it is not to sound dull.

Karajan's earlier recording of the *Requiem* has been greatly enhanced in its CD transfer, with the whole effect given greater presence and immediacy. He has a fine team of soloists, too. However, Karajan's reading still smooths over the lines of Verdi's masterpiece. The result is often beautiful, but, apart from the obvious climaxes, such as the *Dies irae*, there is a lack of dramatic bite.

Barbirolli favours slow tempi, but his concentration is not enough to sustain the necessary drama. It is an enjoyably lyrical approach, but more is needed; though the solo quartet is strong, Montserrat Caballé is well below her finest form.

(i; ii) *Requiem Mass;* (iii; iv) *Inno delle nazione;* (ii) *Te Deum;* (iii) *Luisa Miller: Quando le sere al placido.* (iv) *Nabucco: Va pensiero.*
(M) (***) BMG/RCA mono GD 60299; *GK 60299* (2) [60299-RG-2; *60299-RG-4*]. (i) Nelli, Barbieri, Di Stefano, Siepi; (ii) Robert Shaw Ch.; (iii) Jan Peerce; (iv) Westminster Ch.; NBC SO, Toscanini.

Toscanini's account of the *Requiem* brings a

supreme performance, searingly intense. The opening of the *Dies irae* has never sounded more hair-raising, with the bass-drum thrillingly caught, despite the limitation of dry mono recording. And rarely has the chorus shone so brightly in this work on record, with the Robert Shaw Chorale balanced well forward in sharp focus. Nelli sings well with clear, Italianate purity, while the others are near-ideal, a vintage team – Fedora Barbieri, the young Giuseppe di Stefano and Cesare Siepi. The other works make fascinating listening, too. The *Te Deum* was one of Toscanini's very last recordings, a performance more intense than usual with this work, and it is good to have the extraordinary wartime recording of the potboiling *Hymn of the Nations*. The *Internationale* is added to Verdi's original catalogue of national anthems, to represent the ally, Soviet Russia.

4 Sacred pieces.

(M) **(*) Decca 425 844-2 (2). Chicago Ch. & SO, Solti – BEETHOVEN: *Missa solemnis*. *

Solti's brand of dedication is one of brightness and tension: he draws finely shaded performances from his forces and the electricity is never in doubt. The climaxes in the *Stabat Mater* and *Te Deum* are thrilling, and their effect is enhanced by the bold, brilliant recording. However, many will demand a more spiritual and more devotional manner in this music.

OPERA

Aida (complete).

(M) *** EMI CMS7 69300-2 (3) [Ang. CDMC 69300]. Freni, Carreras, Baltsa, Cappuccilli, Raimondi, Van Dam, V. State Op. Ch., VPO, Karajan.

(M) *** Decca 414 087-2 (3) [id.]. Tebaldi, Simionato, Bergonzi, MacNeil, Van Mill, Corena, V. Singverein, VPO, Karajan.

(M) (***) BMG/RCA mono GD 86652 (3) [6652-2-RG]. Milanov, Bjoerling, Barbieri, Warren, Christoff, Rome Op. Ch. & O, Perlea.

(M) (**) BMG/RCA mono GD 60300; *GK 60300* (3/2) [60300-RG-2; *60300-RG-4*]. Nelli, Gustavson, Tucker, Valdengo, Robert Shaw Ch., NBC SO, Toscanini.

On EMI, Karajan's is a performance of *Aida* that carries splendour and pageantry to the point of exaltation. At the very end of the Triumphal scene, when the march resumes with brass bands, there is a lift, a surge of emotion, such as is captured only rarely on record. For all the power of the pageantry, Karajan's fundamental approach is lyrical. Arias are often taken at a slow speed, taxing the singers more, yet Karajan's controversial choice of soloists is amply justified. On record at least, there can be little question of Freni lacking power in a role normally given to a larger voice, and there is ample gain in the tender beauty of her singing. Carreras makes a fresh, sensitive Radames, Raimondi a darkly intense Ramphis and Van Dam a cleanly focused King, his relative lightness no drawback. Cappuccilli here gives a more detailed performance than he did for Muti on EMI, while Baltsa as Amneris crowns the whole performance with her fine, incisive singing. Despite some overbrightness on cymbals and trumpet, the Berlin sound for Karajan, as transferred to CD, is richly and involvingly atmospheric, both in the intimate scenes and, most strikingly, in the scenes of pageant, which have rarely been presented on record in greater splendour.

There is also a place in the catalogue for Karajan's early stereo version from Decca, which stood unrivalled for many years for its spectacle in this most stereophonic of operas. On Decca, as on EMI, Karajan was helped by having a Viennese orchestra and chorus; but most important of all is the musicianship and musical teamwork of his soloists. Bergonzi in particular emerges here as a model among tenors, with a rare feeling for the shaping of phrases and attention to detail. Cornell MacNeil too is splendid. Tebaldi's creamy tone-colour rides beautifully over the phrases and she too acquires a new depth of imagination. Vocally there are also flaws: notably at the end of *O patria mia*, where Tebaldi finds the cruelly exposed top notes too taxing. Among the other soloists Arnold van Mill and Fernando Corena are both superb, and Simionato provides one of the very finest portrayals of Amneris we have ever had in a complete *Aida*. The recording has long been famous for its technical bravura and flair. CD enhances the overall projection and helps the pianissimos register in a recording with a very wide dynamic range for its period (late 1950s), but the brightness on top at times strikes the ear rather too forcibly. Nevertheless this remains a remarkable technical achievement.

All four principals on the historic RCA set are at their very finest, notably Milanov, whose poise and control in *O patria mia* are a marvel. Barbieri as Amneris is even finer here than in the Callas set, and it is good to hear the young Christoff resonant as Ramfis. Perlea conducts with great panache.

Toscanini's 1949 performance of *Aida* is the least satisfying of his New York opera recordings. Richard Tucker sings well but makes a relatively colourless Radames, and Herva Nelli lacks weight as Aida, neatly though she sings and with some touching moments. Nancy

Gustavson's Amneris lacks all menace, and Valdengo as Amonasro is the only fully satisfying principal. Yet Toscanini is so electrifying from first to last that his admirers will accept the limited, painfully dry recording.

Aida: highlights (scenes & arias).
(M) *** Decca 417 763-2 [id.] (from above set, with Tebaldi, Bergonzi, cond. Karajan).

Aida: highlights.
(M) (***) BMG/RCA mono GD 60201 [60201-2-RG] (from above recording with Milanov, Bjoerling; cond. Perlea).
(M) *** Decca 421 860-2; *421 860-4* [id.] (from complete recording, with Leontyne Price, Gorr, Vickers, Merrill, Tozzi; cond. Solti).

By far the most interesting compilation is the Decca 'Scenes and arias' from John Culshaw's Karajan recording from the early stereo era. The RCA highlights disc is valuable above all for providing a sample of one of Milanov's most compelling performances on record, poised and commanding.

A fairly generous mid-priced reminder of Solti's excellent set, with Price an outstandingly assured Aida.

(i) *Aida:* highlights; (ii) *Don Carlos:* highlights.
(B) **(*) DG Compact Classics *427 715-4* [id.]. From complete sets with (i; ii) Ricciarelli, Domingo, Nucci, Raimondi, Ghiaurov; (i) Obraztsova; (ii) Valentini Terrani; La Scala, Milan, Ch. & O, Abbado.

Five of the principals are common to both these fine Abbado sets, neither of which is a first choice in its complete format but both of which offer some superb singing, although in *Aida* Ricciarelli's contribution is flawed. Abbado's *Don Carlos* was the first recording to use French, the language of the original. Well-balanced if not brilliant tape transfers.

Attila (complete).
(M) *** Ph. 426 115-2 (2). Raimondi, Deutekom, Bergonzi, Milnes, Amb. S., Finchley Children's Music Group, RPO, Gardelli.

With its dramatic anticipations of *Macbeth*, the musical anticipations of *Rigoletto* and the compression which (on record if not on the stage) becomes a positive merit – all these qualities, helped by a fine performance under Gardelli, make this Philips version of *Attila* an intensely enjoyable set. Deutekom, not the most sweet-toned of sopranos, has never sung better on record, and the rest of the cast is outstandingly good. The 1973 recording is well balanced and atmospheric, but the remastering for CD has been able to make only a marginal improvement in definition, with the chorus less sharply focused than one would expect on a modern digital set.

Un ballo in maschera (complete).
(M) *** BMG/RCA GD 86645 (2) [6645-2-RG]. L. Price, Bergonzi, Merrill, Grist, Verrett, Flagello, RCA Italiana Op. Ch. & O, Leinsdorf.
(M) *** EMI CMS7 69576-2 (2) [Ang. CDMB 69576]. Arroyo, Domingo, Cappuccilli, Grist, Cossotto, Howell, ROHCG Ch., New Philh. O, Muti.
(M) **(*) Ph. 426 560-2 (2) [id.]. Caballé, Carreras, Wixell, Payne, Ghazarian, ROHCG Ch. & O, C. Davis.
(M) * Decca 425 655-2 (2). Bergonzi, Nilsson, MacNeil, Simionato, St Cecilia Ac., Rome, Ch. & O, Solti.

The reissued RCA set makes a fine bargain. All the principals are in splendid voice, and Leinsdorf's direction – too often inflexible in Italian opera – here has resilience as well as brilliance and urgency. Leontyne Price is a natural for the part of Amelia and, with one notable reservation, hers comes near to being a model interpretation, spontaneous-sounding and full of dramatic temperament. Only in the two big arias does Price for a moment grow self-conscious, and there are one or two mannered phrases, overloaded with the wrong sort of expressiveness. Robert Merrill, sometimes thought of as an inexpressive singer, here seems to have acquired all sorts of dramatic, Gobbi-like overtones to add to the flow of firm, satisfying tone. Bergonzi is a model of sensitivity, while Reri Grist makes a light, bright Oscar, and the Ulrica of Shirley Verrett has a range of power, richness and delicacy coupled with unparalleled firmness that makes this one of her most memorable recorded performances. Excellent recording, hardly showing its age, with the voices rather forward.

On EMI the quintet of principals is also unusually strong, but it is the conductor who takes first honours in a warmly dramatic reading. Muti's rhythmic resilience and consideration for the singers go with keen concentration, holding each Act together in a way he did not quite achieve in his earlier recording for EMI of *Aida*. Arroyo, rich of voice, is not always imaginative in her big solos, and Domingo rarely produces a half-tone, though the recording balance may be partly to blame. The sound is vivid, but no translation is provided for this mid-price reissue.

Davis's version, based on a Covent Garden production, is particularly good in the way it brings out the ironic humour in Verdi's score. Caballé and Carreras match Davis's lightness, but the dramatic power is diminished. Despite fine recording this is less satisfying than the above alternative versions.

In spite of an impressive cast, Solti's earlier version is very disappointing, with its opera-house atmosphere only adding to the impression of uninterested singing and playing.

Un ballo in maschera: highlights.
(M) ** Decca 421 874-2; *421 874-4* [id.] (from complete set with Tebaldi, Pavarotti, Milnes, Donath, Resnik, St Cecilia Academy, Rome, Ch. & O, Bartoletti).

The complete Decca set from which the quite generous (64 minutes) and well-chosen excerpts are taken is seriously flawed, but the selection can be recommended to those who want to sample the singing of Tebaldi, obviously past her prime but still strong and distinctive. With Pavarotti as Riccardo and Milnes as Renato also well featured, there is much to enjoy here. The 1970 Decca sound is certainly vivid, but the remastering brings a drier, brighter effect than the original LPs.

(i) *Un ballo in maschera:* highlights; (ii) *Macbeth:* highlights.
(B) *** DG Compact Classics *431 184-4* [id.]. (i) Ricciarelli, Domingo, Bruson, Obraztsova, Gruberová, Raimondi; (ii) Cappuccilli, Verrett, Ghiaurov, Domingo, La Scala, Milan, Ch. & O, Abbado.

Another fine Abbado pairing in DG's bargain Compact Classics tape series, offering 90 minutes of music drawn from two outstanding sets, *Un ballo in maschera*, dating from 1976, and *Macbeth*, made five years earlier. Both are highly compelling performances and strongly cast, *Macbeth* notable for fine teamwork from all the principals, and *Un ballo* for memorable individual characterizations. Ricciarelli is at her finest and most individual, Domingo in freshest voice, and Bruson superb as the wronged husband, Renato. The La Scala Chorus makes a strong contribution in *Macbeth* and the sound is vividly focused in both operas.

La Battaglia di Legnano (complete).
(M) *** Ph. 422 435-2 (2). Ricciarelli, Carreras, Manuguerra, Ghiuselev, Austrian R. Ch. & O, Gardelli.

La Battaglia di Legnano is a compact, sharply conceived piece, made the more intense by the subject's obvious relationship with the situation in Verdi's own time. One weakness is that the villainy is not effectively personalized, but the juxtaposition of the individual drama of supposed infidelity against a patriotic theme brings most effective musical contrasts. Gardelli directs a fine performance, helped by a strong cast of principals, with Carreras, Ricciarelli and Manuguerra all at their finest. Excellent recording, with the depth of perspective enhanced on CD.

Il Corsaro (complete).
(M) *** Ph. 426 118-2 (2). Norman, Caballé, Carreras, Grant, Mastromei, Noble, Amb. S., New Philh. O, Gardelli.

By the time he had completed the score, Verdi had fallen out of love with his subject, an adaptation of Byron. Only latterly has the composer's own poor view of *Il Corsaro* been revised in the light of closer study, and Piave's treatment of Byron turns out to be not nearly so clumsy as had been thought. Though the characterization is rudimentary, the contrast between the two heroines is effective, with Gulnara, the Pasha's slave, carrying conviction in the *coup de foudre* which has her promptly worshipping the Corsair, an early example of the Rudolph Valentino figure. The rival heroines are taken splendidly here, with Jessye Norman as the faithful wife, Medora, actually upstaging Montserrat Caballé as Gulnara. Gardelli, as in his previous Philips recordings of early Verdi, directs a vivid performance, with fine singing from the hero, portrayed by José Carreras. Gian-Piero Mastromei, not rich in tone, still rises to the challenge of the Pasha's music. Excellent, firmly focused and well-balanced Philips sound.

Don Carlos (complete).
(M) *** EMI CMS7 69304-2 (3) [Ang. CDMC 69304]. Carreras, Freni, Ghiaurov, Baltsa, Cappuccilli, Raimondi, German Op. Ch., Berlin, BPO, Karajan.

Karajan opts firmly for the later, four-Act version of the opera, merely opening out the cuts he adopted on stage. The results could hardly be more powerfully dramatic, one of his most involving opera performances, comparable with his vivid EMI *Aida*. The *Auto da fé* scene is here superb, while Karajan's characteristic choice of singers for refinement of voice rather than sheer size consistently pays off. Both Carreras and Freni are most moving, even if *Tu che le vanità* has its raw moments. Baltsa is a superlative Eboli and Cappuccilli an affecting Rodrigo, though neither Carreras nor Cappuccilli is at his finest in the famous oath duet. Raimondi and Ghiaurov as the Grand Inquisitor and Philip II provide the most powerful confrontation. Though the sound is not as analytically detailed as the earlier, EMI version with Giulini, it is both rich and atmospheric, giving great power to Karajan's uniquely taut account of the four-Act version.

Don Carlos: highlights.
(M) *** EMI CDM7 63089-2; *EG 763089-4*

(from complete set with Domingo, Caballé, Verrett, Milnes; cond. Giulini).

Giulini's disc of highlights can be highly recommended. In selecting from such a long opera, serious omissions are inevitable; nothing is included here from Act III, to make room for the *Auto da fé* scene from Act IV – some 37 minutes of the disc is given to this Act. With vivid sound this is most stimulating; the only reservation concerns Caballé's *Tu che le vanità*, which ends the selection disappointingly.

I due Foscari (complete).
(M) *** Ph. 422 426-2 (2). Ricciarelli, Carreras, Cappuccilli, Ramey, Austrian R. Ch. & SO, Gardelli.

I due Foscari brings Verdian high spirits in plenty, erupting in swinging cabalettas and much writing that anticipates operas as late as *Simon Boccanegra* (obvious enough in the Doge's music) and *La forza del destino* (particularly in the orchestral motifs which act as labels for the principal characters). The cast here is first rate, with Ricciarelli giving one of her finest performances in the recording studio to date and with Carreras singing tastefully as well as powerfully. The crispness of discipline among the Austrian Radio forces is admirable, but there is less sense of atmosphere here than in the earlier, London-made recordings in the series; otherwise the Philips sound is impressively present and clear.

Ernani (complete).
(M) **(*) BMG/RCA GD 86503 (2) [6503-2-RG]. Leontyne Price, Bergonzi, Sereni, Flagello, RCA Italiana Op. Ch. & O, Schippers.

At mid-price in RCA's Victor Opera series on two CDs instead of three LPs, Schippers' set, recorded in Rome in 1967, is an outstanding bargain. Leontyne Price may take the most celebrated aria, *Ernani involami*, rather cautiously, but the voice is gloriously firm and rich, and Bergonzi is comparably strong and vivid, though Mario Sereni, vocally reliable, is dull, and Ezio Flagello gritty-toned. Nevertheless, with Schippers drawing the team powerfully together, it is a highly enjoyable set, with the digital transfer making voices and orchestra sound full and vivid.

Falstaff (complete).
(M) (***) BMG/RCA mono GD 60251; *GK 60251* (2) [60251-RG-2; *60251-RG-4*]. Valdengo, Nelli, Merriman, Elmo, Guarrera, Stich-Randall, Robert Shaw Ch., NBC SO, Toscanini.

Toscanini's fizzing account of Verdi's last masterpiece has never been matched on record, the most high-spirited performance ever, beautifully paced for comedy. Even without stereo, and recorded with typical dryness, the clarity and sense of presence in this live concert performance set the story in relief. The cast is excellent, led by the ripe, firm baritone, Giuseppe Valdengo. Such singers as Nan Merriman as Mistress Page, Cloe Elmo as a wonderfully fruity Mistress Quickly and Frank Guarrera as Ford match or outshine any more recent interpreters. Toscanini's favourite soprano in his last years, Herva Nelli, is less characterful as Mistress Ford, rather over-parted but still fresh and reliable.

La Forza del destino (complete).
(M) *** BMG/RCA GD 87971 (3) [4515-2-RG]. Leontyne Price, Tucker, Merrill, Tozzi, Verrett, Flagello, Foiani, RCA Italiana Op. Ch. & O, Schippers.
(M) ** Decca 421 598-2 (3) [id.]. Tebaldi, Del Monaco, Bastianini, Siepi, St Cecilia Academy, Rome, Ch. & O, Molinari-Pradelli.

No soprano of her generation had natural gifts more suited to the role of Leonora in *Forza* than Leontyne Price. Her admirers will cherish this early recording quite as much as her later, full-price one with James Levine, also from RCA. The voice in 1964 was fresher and more open; though the clearer, less ambient recording from the Rome studio exposes it in greater detail, on balance this is a more tender and delicate performance than the weightier one she recorded with Levine. Richard Tucker as Alvaro is here far less lachrymose and more stylish than he was earlier in the Callas set, producing ample, heroic tone, if not with the finesse of a Domingo. Robert Merrill as Carlo also sings with heroic strength, consistently firm and dark of tone; while Shirley Verrett, Giorgio Tozzi and Ezio Flagello stand up well against any rivalry. The sound is remarkably full and vivid for its age, with a fine illusion of presence which quickly makes one forget any analogue hiss.

Tebaldi, as always, makes some lovely sounds, and the *mezza voce* in the soaring theme (first heard in the overture) in *Madre, madre, pietosa Vergine* is exquisite. Mario del Monaco never really matches this. He sings straight through his part – often with the most heroic-sounding noises – with little attention to the finer points of shading that Verdi expects. That the whole performance fails to add up to the sum of its parts is largely the fault of the conductor, Molinari-Pradelli. He is exciting enough in the proper places but his control of ensemble is a marked weakness. Fortunately this deficiency in the conducting is not nearly enough to mar enjoyment of the performance. The brilliance and atmosphere of the recording add much to the listener's pleasure.

(i) *La forza del destino:* highlights; (ii) *Nabucco:* highlights.
(B) *** DG Compact Classics *431 183-4* [id.].(i) Plowright, Carreras, Bruson, Burchuladze, Baltsa, Amb. Op. Ch., Philh. O; (ii) Cappuccilli, Dimitrova, Nesterenko, Domingo, German Op. Ch. & O; Sinopoli.

Sinopoli's Compact Classics cassette, pairing selections from *Forza del destino* and *Nabucco*, generously offers 92 minutes of music and in *Nabucco* includes the three most famous choruses, including a memorable *Va, pensiero*, with its hushed opening pianissimo. *La forza del destino* is very much a spacious reading, but Rosalind Plowright's *Pace, pace, mio Dio* is gloriously sustained, while Agnes Baltsa's *Rataplan* makes a lively contrast. *Nabucco* brings strong performances all round and this tape can be recommended also for the vividness of the transfer. Dimitrova is superb, noble in her evil, as is Cappucilli as Nabucco, and, with Domingo in a relatively small role and Nestorenko very impressive as the High Priest, Zaccaria, this is a brightly recorded set.

Un giorno di regno (complete).
(M) *** Ph. 422 429-2 (2). Cossotto, Norman, Carreras, Wixell, Sardinero, Ganzarolli, Amb. S., RPO, Gardelli.

Un giorno di regno may not be the greatest comic opera of the period, but this scintillating performance under Gardelli clearly reveals the young Verdi as a potent rival even in this field to his immediate predecessors, Rossini and Donizetti. The Rossinian echoes are particularly infectious, though every number reveals that the young Verdi is more than an imitator, and there are striking passages which clearly give a foretaste of such numbers as the duet *Si vendetta* from *Rigoletto*. Despite the absurd plot, this is as light and frothy an entertainment as anyone could want. Excellent singing from a fine team, with Jessye Norman and José Carreras outstanding. The recorded sound is even more vivid on CD.

I Lombardi (complete).
(M) *** Ph. 422 420-2 (2). Deutekom, Domingo, Raimondi, Amb. S., RPO, Gardelli.

If you are looking for sophisticated perfection, *I Lombardi* is not the opera to sample, but the directness of Verdi's inspiration is in no doubt. *Otello* is anticipated in the arias, with Pagano's evil *Credo* and the heroine Giselda's *Salve Maria*. The work reaches its apotheosis in the famous *Trio*, well known from the days of 78-r.p.m. recordings. By those standards, Cristina Deutekom is not an ideal Verdi singer: her tone is sometimes hard and her voice is not always perfectly under control, yet there are also some glorious moments and the phrasing is often impressive. Domingo as Oronte is in superb voice, and the villain Pagano is well characterized by Raimondi. Among the supporting cast Stafford Dean and Clifford Grant must be mentioned, and Gardelli conducts dramatically. The recording's atmosphere is well transferred and the action projects vividly.

(i) *I Lombardi, Act III: Trio.* (ii) *Rigoletto, Act IV* (complete).
(M) (**) BMG/RCA mono GD 60276; *GK 60276* (2); [60276-2-RG; *60276-4-RG*]. (i) Della Chiesa, Peerce, Moscona; (ii) Warren, Milanov, Peerce, Moscona, Merriman, All City Highschool Ch. & Glee Clubs, NBC SO, Toscanini – BOITO: *Mefistofele: Prologue.* (***)

These two fascinating Verdi items are wartime recordings, even more limited in sound than most of Toscanini's in his last years. The *Lombardi Trio* finds the acoustic of the notorious Studio 8H in Radio City at its driest, but the conductor's love for the music still dominates. It is interesting to find a little-known singer, Vivian della Chiesa, emerging strongly alongside Jan Peerce and Nicola Moscona. Equally impressive is the dazzling performance of the NBC Orchestra's concert-master, Mischa Mischakoff, in the virtuoso violin solo of the introduction. The last Act of *Rigoletto* was given in a wartime fund-raising concert in Madison Square Garden and, though the brittleness of sound is at times almost comic and the tautness of Toscanini's control was unrelenting, the performances of the principals are formidable, with Zinka Milanov at her most radiant. With Toscanini's searing account of the *Mefistofele Prologue*, this makes a generous compilation.

Luisa Miller (complete).
(M) *** BMG/RCA GD 86646 (2) [6646-2-RG]. Moffo, Bergonzi, Verrett, MacNeil, Tozzi, Flagello, RCA Italiana Op. Ch. & O, Cleva.

In many ways the RCA set provides a performance to compete with the full-price versions and is just as stylish, with Moffo at her very peak, singing superbly, Carlo Bergonzi unfailingly intelligent and stylish, and Verrett nothing less than magnificent in her role as a quasi-Amneris. MacNeil and Tozzi are also satisfyingly resonant, and Fausto Cleva tellingly reveals his experience directing the opera at the Met. Good recording.

Macbeth (complete).

(M) **(*) BMG/RCA GD 84516 (2) [4516-2-RG]. Warren, Rysanek, Bergonzi, Hines, Met. Op. Ch. & O, Leinsdorf.

(M) **(*) Decca 433 039-2 (2) [id.]. Taddei, Nilsson, Prevedi, Doiani, St Cecilia Ac., Rome, Ch. & O, Schippers.

On two mid-price discs in the Victor Opera series, the Leinsdorf version makes a good bargain, bringing a large-scale performance featuring three favourite principals from the Met. Leonie Rysanek here gives one of her finest performances on record, producing her firmest, creamiest sound for the Sleepwalking scene, even though the coloratura taxes her severely. Leonard Warren, much admired in this part before his untimely death (on stage, singing Don Carlo in *La forza del destino*), gives a strong, thoughtful reading, marred by the way the microphone exaggerates his vibrato. Carlo Bergonzi is a stylish, clear-toned Macduff. Good sound for its period.

On Decca Birgit Nilsson makes a fearsomely impressive Lady Macbeth, sounding like the devil of Verdi's imaginings, but with glorious tone and spot on the note. It is her success and that of Taddei as Macbeth himself that makes it all the more irritating that Schippers was allowed to cut the score (about a quarter of an hour of music is missing). With the variations between the editions, this is always a difficult opera to get right textually, but the solution of whittling down the roles of the witches and the murderers reduces the appeal of this Decca set considerably. Their rum-ti-tum choruses may not be the greatest Verdi, but without that music the opera loses its balance and the central tragedy is weakened by not being set in relief. Schippers' direction is on the whole less effective than that of Leinsdorf on the competing RCA Metropolitan set, but the 1964 Decca recording has transferred vividly to CD and the singing of the two principals is memorable.

I Masnadieri (complete).

(M) *** Ph. 422 423-2 (2). Caballé, Bergonzi, Raimondi, Cappuccilli, Amb. S., New Philh. O, Gardelli.

As this excellent Philips recording makes plain, the long neglect of *I Masnadieri* is totally undeserved, despite a libretto which is a bungled adaptation of a Schiller play. Few will seriously identify with the hero-turned-brigand who stabs his beloved rather than lead her into a life of shame; but, on record, flaws of motivation are of far less moment than on stage. The melodies may only fitfully be out of Verdi's top drawer, but the musical structure and argument often look forward to a much later period with hints of *Forza*, *Don Carlo* and even *Otello*. With Gardelli as ever an urgently sympathetic Verdian, and a team of four excellent principals, splendidly recorded, the set can be warmly welcomed.

Nabucco: highlights.

(M) *** Decca 421 867-2; *421 867-4* (from complete recording, with Gobbi, Suliotis, Cava, Previdi, V. State Op. Ch. & O, Gardelli).

(M) ** EMI CDM7 63092-2; *EG 763092-4*. Manuguerra, Scotto, Ghiaurov, Luchetti, Obraztsova, Amb. Op. Ch., Philh. O, Muti.

Suliotis's impressive contribution is well represented on the Decca highlights disc, and there are fine contributions too from Gobbi. Needless to say, the chorus *Va, pensiero* is given its place of honour (the performance rhythmically a little mannered but eloquent enough), and *Gli arredi festivi* opens the selection, which runs for 58 minutes. The 1965 recording sounds splendid.

Though the EMI disc offers generous measure (nearly 65 minutes) and has an impressive cast-list, it is much less involving, although the famous chorus, *Va, pensiero*, sounds well enough.

Otello (complete).

(M) *** BMG/RCA GD 81969 (2) [1969-2-RG]. Vickers, Rysanek, Gobbi, Rome Op. Ch. & O, Serafin.

(M) *** EMI CMS7 69308-2 (2) [Ang. CDMB 69308]. Vickers, Freni, Glossop, Ch. of German Op., Berlin, BPO, Karajan.

The Serafin version in RCA's Victor Opera series makes an outstanding bargain on two mid-priced discs. No conductor is more understanding of Verdian pacing than Serafin and, with sound that hardly begins to show its age (1960), it presents two of the finest solo performances on any *Otello* recording of whatever period: the Iago of Tito Gobbi has never been surpassed for vividness of characterization and tonal subtlety; while the young Jon Vickers, with a voice naturally suited to this role, was in his prime as the Moor. Leonie Rysanek is a warm and sympathetic Desdemona, not always ideally pure-toned but tender and touching in one of her very finest recorded performances. The sense of presence in the open, well-balanced recording is the more vivid on CD, thanks to a first-rate transfer.

Karajan directs a big, bold and brilliant account, for the most part splendidly sung and with all the dramatic contrasts strongly underlined. There are several tiny, but irritating, statutory cuts, but otherwise on two mid-price CDs this is well worth considering. Freni's Desdemona is delightful, delicate and beautiful, while Vickers and Glossop are both positive and characterful, only occasionally forcing their tone and losing focus. The recording is clarified on CD, with better focus and more bloom than on the much more recent EMI set under Maazel.

Otello: highlights.
(M) *** EMI CDM7 63454-2; *EG 763454-4* [id.] (from above recording, cond. Karajan.).
(M) **(*) EMI Dig. CDM7 69059-2; *EG 769059-4*. Domingo, Ricciarelli, Diaz, La Scala, Milan, Ch. & O, Maazel.

The Karajan highlights disc offers a generally well-managed selection (though of less than an hour), including excerpts from all four Acts, with a substantial excerpt from Act IV including Freni's touching *Willow song* and *Ave Maria*, then moving on to the tragic finale. The sound is full, appropriately weighty in the score's more spectacular moments.

Maazel's version, used as soundtrack for the Zeffirelli film but with the text uncut (unlike that of the film), brings a fine performance from Domingo and taut, subtle control from Maazel, particularly good in the spacious, tenderly emotional treatment of the final scene. In many ways Domingo shows how he has developed since he made his earlier recording with Levine; but with a disappointingly negative, unsinister Iago in Justino Diaz, the result often loses in dramatic bite, and Maazel's direction occasionally sags, as in the closing pages of Act II at the end of the oath duet. Ricciarelli, though not the ideal Desdemona, sings most affectingly, with pianissimos beautifully caught in the *Willow song* and *Ave Maria*. One snag is the sound, which is curiously recessed, with the voices often not quite in focus and with little sense of presence.

Otello (complete; in English).
(M) **(*) EMI CMS7 63012-2 (2). Charles Craig, Plowright, Howlett, Bottone, E. Nat. Op. Ch. & O, Mark Elder.

Recorded live at the Coliseum in London, the ENO version of *Otello* is flawed both vocally and in the sound; but those who seek records of opera in English need not hesitate, for almost every word of Andrew Porter's translation is audible, despite the very variable balances inevitable in recording a live stage production. Less acceptable is the level of stage noise, with the thud and rumble of wandering feet all the more noticeable on CD. The performance itself is most enjoyable, with dramatic tension building up compellingly. Charles Craig's Otello is most moving, the character's inner pain brought out vividly, though top notes are fallible. Neil Howlett as Iago may not have the most distinctive baritone, but finely controlled vocal colouring adds to a deeply perceptive performance. Rosalind Plowright makes a superb Desdemona, singing with rich, dramatic weight but also with poise and purity. The Death scene reveals her at her finest, radiant of tone, with flawless attack.

Otello (highlights; in English).
(M) **(*) EMI Dig. CDM7 63723-2; *EG 763723-4* (from above recording; cond. Mark Elder).

A good hour-long sampler of the ENO's *Otello*, recorded live in 1983, will suit those who want the complete opera sung in the original language. The recording makes the words vividly clear – and also the stage noises. There are other flaws, but the spontaneous drama of the occasion is well conveyed and the power of Charles Craig's memorable portrayal of Otello is well balanced by Rosalind Plowright's moving Desdemona, beautifully sung. A translation is included.

Rigoletto (complete).
(M) **(*) BMG/RCA GD 86506 (2) [6506-2-RG]. Merrill, Moffo, Kraus, Elias, Flagello, RCA Italiana Op. Ch. & O, Solti.
(M) ** BMG/RCA GD 60172 (2) [60172-2-RG]. Merrill, Peters, Bjoerling, Tozzi, Rome Op. Ch. & O, Perlea.
(BB) ** Naxos Dig. 8.660013/4 (2) [id.]. Tumagian, Ferrarini, Ramiro, Ch. & Slovak RSO (Bratislava), Rahbari.

Anna Moffo makes a charming Gilda in the Solti set of 1963, well transferred on two mid-price CDs in the Victor Opera series. Solti at times presses too hard, but this is a strong and dramatic reading, with Robert Merrill producing a glorious flow of dark, firm tone in the name-part. Alfredo Kraus is as stylish as ever as the Duke, and this rare example of his voice at its freshest should not be missed. A good bargain, though there are statutory cuts in the text.

The second RCA set is mainly of interest for Jussi Bjoerling's contribution. It opens well and generally the conductor, Jonel Perlea, controls the music effectively. But he is hampered by Robert Merrill's rather hammy Rigoletto and the fact that Roberta Peters, although singing nicely, does not project the character of Gilda at all. Indeed the whole atmosphere of the set is of a concert performance, and the close of the opera degenerates into melodrama. The 1956 recording has no lack of vividness.

Rahbari conducts a neat but rather underpowered account of *Rigoletto*, well played and recorded but lacking full Verdian bite. Though Eduard Tumagian is young-sounding baritone for the title-role of the hunchback jester, lacking dramatic weight, he sings cleanly and with feeling. The Gilda of Alida Ferrarini is bright and fresh, agile in *Caro nome* with a tight trill at the end. There and elsewhere her singing is slightly marred by an overfondness for under-the-note coloration which, with so precise a voice, often sounds flat. Yordy Ramiro is over-parted as the Count, with much of his singing crisp and clean, though often strained on top. The quartet in the final Act is made the more attractive by having four fresh young voices.

Rigoletto: highlights.
(M) **(*) Ph. Dig. 432 619-2; *432 619-4* [id.]. Bruson, Gruberová, Shicoff, Fassbaender, Lloyd, St Cecilia Ac., Rome, Ch. & O, Sinopoli.

Sinopoli's *Rigoletto* has the most consistent cast on record and, although his tempi are unconventional, this generous (71 minutes) and vividly recorded set of highlights is highly recommendable, with Gruberová's brilliantly sung yet tender portrayal of Gilda matched by Neil Schicoff's Duke, and Renato Bruson memorably powerful in the name-part. Unfortunately and disgracefully, the CD offers no notes or translation, instead wasting a dozen or so pages on listing other reissues in the digital Laser Line series! Such misguided hype is likely to put a disgruntled buyer off rather than encourage further purchases!

Rigoletto (highlights; in English).
(M) **(*) EMI Dig. CDM7 63726-2; *EG 736726-4*. Rawnsley, Field, Davies, Tomlinson, Rigby, E. Nat. Op. Ch. & O, Mark Elder).

Unlike the ENO *Otello*, *Rigoletto* was recorded in the studio (also in 1983), but there is no lack of intensity and, even if you normally resist opera in English, this 63 minutes of excerpts is well worth trying. The standard of singing is high, especially the appealing portrayal of the Duke by Arthur Davies, though Helen Field's *Caro nome* would not disgrace any operatic stage in the world. Excellent, vivid sound and a libretto provided, although the words are admirably clear.

Simon Boccanegra (complete).
(M) (***) EMI mono CMS7 63513-2 (2) [Ang. CDMB 63513]. Gobbi, Christoff, De los Angeles, Campora, Monachesi, Dari, Rome Op. Chor & O, Santini.

Tito Gobbi's portrait of the tragic Doge of Genoa is one of his greatest on record, and it emerges all the more impressively when it is set against equally memorable performances by Boris Christoff as Fiesco and Victoria de los Angeles as Amelia. The Recognition scene between father and daughter has never been done more movingly on record; nor has the great ensemble, which crowns the Council Chamber scene, been so powerfully and movingly presented, and that without the help of stereo recording. The transfer is full and immediate, giving a vivid sense of presence to the voices, though tape-hiss is on the high side.

Stiffelio (complete).
(M) *** Ph. 422 432-2 (2). Carreras, Sass, Manuguerra, Ganzarolli, V. ORF Ch. & SO, Gardelli.

Coming just before the great trio of masterpieces, *Rigoletto*, *Il Trovatore* and *La Traviata*, *Stiffelio* was a total failure at its first performance in 1850. To make *Aroldo* six years later, the score was in effect destroyed, and only through the discovery of two copyists' scores in the 1960s was a revival made possible. Though it lacks some of the beauties of *Aroldo*, *Stiffelio* is still a sharper, more telling work, largely because of the originality of the relationships and the superb final scene in which Stiffelio reads from the pulpit the parable of the woman taken in adultery. Gardelli directs a fresh performance, at times less lively than Queler's of *Aroldo* but with more consistent singing, notably from Carreras and Manuguerra. First-rate recording from Philips, typical of this fine series.

La Traviata (complete).
(M) **(*) Decca 411 877-2 (2) [id.]. Sutherland, Bergonzi, Merrill, Ch. & O of Maggio Musicale Fiorentino, Pritchard.
(M) (*(**)) EMI mono CMS7 63628-2 (2) [Ang. CDMB 63628]. Callas, Di Stefano, Bastianini, La Scala Ch. & O, Giulini.
(BB) *(*) Naxos 8.660011/2 (2) [id.]. Krause, Ramiro, Tichy, Ch. & Slovak RSO (Bratislava), Rahbari.
(M) * Decca 430 250-2 (2) [id.]. Tebaldi, Poggi, Protti, St Celia Ac., Rome, Ch. & O, Molinari-Pradelli.

In Sutherland's 1963 recording of *La Traviata*, it is true that her diction is poor, but it is also true that she has rarely sung on record with such deep feeling as in the final scene. The *Addio del passato* (both stanzas included and sung with an unexpected lilt) merely provides a beginning, for the duet with Bergonzi is most winning, and the final death scene, *Se una pudica vergine*, is overwhelmingly beautiful. This is not a sparkling Violetta, true, but it is vocally closer to perfection than almost any other in a complete set. Bergonzi is an attractive Alfredo and Merrill an efficient Germont. Pritchard sometimes tends to hustle things along with too little regard for shaping Verdian phrases, but the recording quality is outstandingly good in its CD format.

Callas's version with Giulini comes into rivalry with another live recording of her in this role, also from EMI but recorded in Lisbon and conducted by Ghione – but that is still a full-price set. This La Scala performance was recorded in 1955, three years before the other, when the voice was fresher. In the presence of a great conductor, one who often challenged her with unusually slow speeds, Callas responded with even greater depth of expression. There is no more vividly dramatic a performance on record than this, unmatchable in conveying Violetta's agony; sadly, the sound, always limited, grows crumbly towards the end. It is sad too that Bastianini sings so lumpishly as Germont père, even in the great duet of Act II, while di Stefano also fails to match his partner in the supreme test of the final scene. The transfer is fair, though in places it sounds as though an echo-chamber has been used.

Like the parallel recording of *Rigoletto*, the Naxos version of *La Traviata* is often under-powered and lacks bite but offers an attractive performance from Monika Krause as Violetta. The big test of *Ah dita alla giovine* in her duet with Germont in Act II brings an exquisitely shaded pianissimo, and her *Addio del passato* in Act III is no less touching for being taken at a genuine andante, with less rhythmic freedom than usual. As in *Rigoletto*, Yordy Ramiro sounds over-parted as Alfredo, with a flutter in the voice occasionally becoming intrusive, but he generally sings cleanly. The Germont of Georg Tichy is among the most prosaic on disc, wooden and unresponsive even to Krause's most exquisite singing. The sound, as in other Bratislava recordings, is clean and atmospheric. As in other Naxos operas, copious tracking is linked to a detailed synopsis and full Italian text.

Recorded in 1954, the Tebaldi version of *La Traviata* emerges on CD with the benefit of stereo, a very early example and one which certainly helps to give body to the voices. Though Violetta was not Tebaldi's ideal role – the coloratura of Act I is negotiated accurately rather than with joy – there is much superb singing from her here. The delicacy of her phrasing is a delight, bringing a most tender portrait, though the *Addio del passato* brings a suspicion of intrusive aitches. Her refinement contrasts with the coarseness of Gianni Poggi as Alfredo and the lack of imagination of Aldo Protti as Germont. Yet this is well worth hearing for Tebaldi in her early prime.

La Traviata: highlights.
(M) *** EMI CDM7 63088-2; *EG 763088-4*. Scotto, Kraus, Bruson, Amb. Op. Ch., Philh. O, Muti.

Muti's complete set is at full price and it isn't a first choice, so many will be glad to have this fairly generous (61 minutes) mid-price disc of highlights, including both the Act I and Act III *Preludes* and a well-balanced selection from each of the three Acts, with most of the key numbers included.

La Traviata (complete, in English).
(M) **(*) EMI CMS7 63072-2 (2). Masterson, Brecknock, Du Plessis, E. Nat. Op. Ch. & O, Mackerras.

Mackerras directs a vigorous, colourful reading which brings out the drama, and Valerie Masterson is at last given the chance on record she has so long deserved. The voice is caught beautifully, if not always very characterfully, and John Brecknock makes a fine Alfredo, most effective in the final scene. Christian Du Plessis' baritone is less suitable for recording. The conviction of the whole enterprise is infectious – but be warned, Verdi in English has a way of sounding on record rather like Gilbert and Sullivan.

La Traviata (sung in English): highlights.
(M) **(*) EMI CDM7 63725-2 [id.]; *EG 763725-4* (from above complete recording; cond. Mackerras).

Those wanting to sample this excellent performance in English will find that the 63-minute selection is fairly evenly divided over the three Acts and it is vividly transferred.

Il Trovatore (complete).
(M) (***) BMG/RCA mono GD 86643 (2) [6643-2-RG]. Milanov, Bjoerling, Warren, Barbieri, Robert Shaw Ch., RCA Victor O, Cellini.
(M) **(*) EMI CMS7 69311-2 (2) [Ang. CDMB 69311]. Leontyne Price, Bonisolli, Obraztsova, Cappuccilli, Raimondi, German Op. Ch., Berlin, BPO, Karajan.
(M) ** EMI CMS7 63640-2 (2) [Ang. CDMB 63640]. Corelli, Tucci, Simionato, Merrill, Rome Op. Ch. & O, Schippers.
(M) ** Ph. Dig. 426 557-2 (2). Ricciarelli, Carreras, Mazurok, Toczyska, ROHCG Ch. & O, C. Davis.

Though dating from 1952, using a cut text as in the Met. production, the Cellini version brings a vivid reminder of that great opera house at a key period. Milanov, though at times a little raw in Leonora's coloratura, gives a glorious, commanding performance, never surpassed on record, with the voice at its fullest. Bjoerling and Warren too are in ringing voice, and Barbieri is a superb Azucena, with Cellini – rarely heard on record – proving an outstanding Verdian.

The Karajan set with Leontyne Price promised much but proved disappointing, largely because of the thickness and strange balances of the recording, the product of multi-channel techniques exploited over-enthusiastically. So the introduction to Manrico's aria *Di quella pira* provides full-bodied orchestral sound, but then the orchestra fades down for the entry of the tenor, who in any case is in coarse voice, although in other places he sings more sensitively. CD clarifies the sound, but makes the flaws in the original recording all the more evident.

The Schippers set of *Il Trovatore* is a long way short of the ideal, but Merrill's Conte di Luna is characterful and firmly sung, if sometimes ungainly. Simionato is an excellent Azucena; Tucci, though less assured than her colleagues, sings very beautifully. Corelli is at his powerful best as Manrico, a really heroic, if not always subtle, tenor. His *Di quella pira* displays rather crude histrionics, but its gutsiness is welcome when Schippers' conducting is inclined to be rigid, somewhat preventing the temperature from rising; otherwise Schippers' incisiveness is compelling in an atmospheric recording that is characteristic of the Rome Opera House.

Sir Colin Davis offers a fresh and direct reading which in many ways is the antithesis of Karajan's Berlin version with its overblown sound. The refinement of the digital recording makes for a wide, clean separation but, with the backward placing of the orchestra, the result does not have the dramatic impact of the finest versions. The *Anvil chorus* sounds rather clinical and other important numbers lack the necessary swagger. Ricciarelli's Leonora is most moving, conveying an element of vulnerability in the character, but Carreras lacks the full confidence of a natural Manrico. He is less effective in the big, extrovert moments, best in such inward-looking numbers as *Ah si ben mio*. Toczyska's voice is presented rather grittily in the role of Azucena. Mazurok similarly is not flattered by the microphones but, with clean, refined ensemble, this emerges as the opposite of a hackneyed opera.

Il Trovatore: highlights.
(M) (***) RCA mono GD 60191 [60191-2-RG] (from above recording; cond. Cellini).
(M) **(*) Decca 421 310-2; *421 310-4*. Sutherland, Pavarotti, Horne, Wixell, Ghiaurov, L. Op. Ch. & Nat. PO, Bonynge.

For many, a highlights CD will be the ideal way to approach this outstanding 1952 recording, much admired in its day. Two dozen excerpts (68 minutes) span the opera very effectively.

The selection from Bonynge's Decca set is especially valuable as a reminder of Sutherland's Leonora. The size of the voice and its flexibility are splendidly caught, though a latter-day beat afflicts the more sustained passages, and Bonynge does not conduct with his usual urgency. Pavarotti may be stretched by the role of Manrico, but he is nearly always magnificent. Horne is represented by her powerful *Stride la vampa*, Wixell by an undernourished *Il Balen*.

COLLECTIONS

Arias: *Aida: Celeste Aida. Un ballo in maschera: La rivedrà; Di, tu se fedele; Ma se m'è forza perderti. I due Foscari: Dal più remote esilio. Luisa Miller: Quando le sere. Macbeth: Ah, la paterna mano. Rigoletto: Questa o quella; Parmi veder; La donna è mobile. La Traviata: De' miei bollenti. Il Trovatore: Di quella pira.*
(M) *** Decca 417 570-2. Luciano Pavarotti (with various orchestras & conductors).

Taken mainly from a recital which Pavarotti recorded early in his career with Edward Downes and the Vienna State Opera Orchestra, this Verdi collection on the mid-price Opera Gala label can be warmly recommended, a generous collection of favourite items, plus one or two rarer arias.

Arias & duets: *Un ballo in maschera: Teco io sto. Il Corsaro: Egli non riede ancora! Don Carlos: Non pianger, mia compagna. Giovanna d'Arco: Qui! Qui! Dove più s'apre libero il ciela; O fatidica foresta. Jérusalem: Ave Maria. I Masnadieri: Dall'infame banchetto io m'involai; Tu del mio; Carlo vive. Otello: Già nella notte densa; Ave Maria. Il Trovatore: Timor di me; D'amor sull'ali rosee; Tu vedrai che amor in terr. I vespri siciliani: Arrigo! Ah, parli a un cor.*
(M) *** BMG/RCA GD 86534 (6534-2-RG]. Katia Ricciarelli, Placido Domingo, Rome PO or St Cecilia Ac. O, Gavazzeni.

At mid-price this collection of Verdi arias and duets from two star singers, both in fresh voice, makes a good bargain. The inclusion of rarities adds to the attractions, and though the sound is not the most modern, it is more than acceptable in the digital transfer. The quality is very bright; although the orchestral timbre is a bit thin, both voices are given a good presence.

Choruses: *Aida: Triumphal march and ballet music. Attila: Urli rapine. La Battaglia di Legnano: Giuriam d'Italia. I Lombardi: O Signore dal tetto natio. Nabucco: Gli arredi festivi; Va pensiero. Otello: Fuoco di gloria. Il Trovatore: Vedi! le fosche; Squilli, echeggi.*
(M) ** Decca 417 721-2; *417 721-4* [id.]. Ch. & O of St Cecilia Ac., Rome, Carlo Franci.

Although the basic recording seems too brightly lit, in all other respects the quality is very good, inner detail is sharp and the big climaxes open up well. The performances are vivid, with a willingness to sing softly and, indeed, sometimes a degree of refinement in the approach surprising in an Italian chorus. The *I Lombardi* excerpts are especially appealing, but all the little-known items come up freshly. The trumpets in the *Aida* Triumphal scene get the full stereo treatment.

Choruses from: *Aida; La Battaglia di Legnano; Don Carlo; Ernani; La forza del destino; Macbeth; Nabucco; Otello; La Traviata; Il Trovatore.*
(BB) *** Naxos Dig. 8.550241 [id.]. Slovak Philharmonic Ch. & RSO, Oliver Dohnányi.

The super-bargain Naxos collection by the excellent Slovak Philharmonic Choir, trained by Marian Vach, brings very realistic sound and the slightly recessed choral balance in the Bratislava Radio Concert Hall is very natural: it certainly does not lack impact and, in the *Fire chorus* from Otello, detail registers admirably. Under Oliver Dohnányi's lively direction the chorus sings with admirable fervour. *Patria oppressa* from *Macbeth* is particularly stirring, and *Va, pensiero*, with a well-shaped line, is movingly projected. The *Soldiers' chorus* from *Il Trovatore* has a jaunty rhythmic feeling, the two novelties from *La Battaglia di Legnano* were well worth including: the second, *Giuramento*, includes four impressive male soloists. The collection ends resplendently with the Triumphal scene from *Aida*, omitting the ballet but with the fanfare trumpets blazing out on either side most tellingly. With a playing time of 56 minutes this is excellent value in every respect.

Victoria, Tomás Luis de (*c* 1548–1611)

Missa Surge propera; Stabat Mater.
(B) *** Pickwick Dig. PCD 970; *CIMPC 970* [id.]. Mixolydian, Piers Schmidt – PADILLA: *Missa Ego flos campi* etc. ***

Like the old examination questions, this record 'contrasts and compares' two Spanish composers of the sixteenth and seventeenth centuries. Tomás Luis de Victoria was undoubtedly Spain's greatest Renaissance master, while Juan Gutierrez de Padilla is relatively little known or performed. Whatever Padilla's merits (and he is a musician of both substance and interest), this disc serves to underline Victoria's stature as a composer of rich, expressive feeling and a powerful musical mind. Listen to the *Agnus Dei* from the Mass *Surge propera* and you will have few doubts as to his stature or the quality of his invention. The *Missa Surge propera* is a five-voiced parody Mass, published in 1583, the only one of his works to be based on Palestrina. It is a beautiful work and is very well sung by Mixolydian under Piers Schmidt and recorded with exemplary skill.

Villa-Lobos, Heitor (1887–1959)

Guitar concerto; 5 Preludes.
(M) *** BMG/RCA GD 86525 [6525-2-RG]. Bream, LSO, Previn – RODRIGO: *Concierto.* ***

Bream's highly distinguished account of the *Guitar concerto* with Previn has now been reissued at mid-price, coupled with Rodrigo, an excellent idea.

Bachianas Brasileiras Nos. 1; 2 (includes *The little train of the Caipira*); (i) *5* (for soprano & 8 cellos); (ii) *6* (for flute & bassoon); *9.*
(M) (**) EMI mono CDH7 61015-2 [id.]. French Nat. R. O, composer, with (i) De los Angeles; (ii) Fernand Dufrêne, René Plessier.

It is good to have on EMI's historic Références label this generous collection of the composer's own recordings, not immaculate in performance and with depressingly dry and boxy recording, but full of colour and life. Though even Victoria de los Angeles' golden voice loses some of its bloom, her account of the famous No. 5 is ravishing, and no one has been more persuasive than the composer himself in the other favourite, the *Little train of the Caipira.*

Bachianas Brasileiras No. 5 for soprano and cellos.
(M) *** BMG/RCA GD 87831 [7831-2-RG]. Anna Moffo, American SO, Stokowski – CANTELOUBE: *Chants d'Auvergne*; RACHMANINOV: *Vocalise.* ***

Anna Moffo gives a seductive performance of the most famous of the *Bachianas Brasileiras*, adopting a highly romantic style (matching the conductor) and warm tone-colour.

Vivaldi, Antonio (1675–1741)

L'Estro armonico, Op. 3 (complete).
(M) *** Decca 430 557-2 (2) [id.]. ASMF, Sir Neville Marriner.

As so often, Marriner directs the Academy in radiant and imaginative performances of Baroque music and yet observes scholarly good manners. The delightful use of continuo – lute and organ as well as harpsichord – the sharing of solo honours and the consistently resilient string-playing of the ensemble make for compelling listening. The early 1970s' (originally Argo) recording is superb, rich in timbre, yet with excellent detail and presence. The twelve concertos fit conveniently on the two discs, six on each.

L'Estro armonico (12 Concertos), Op. 3.
(M) *** Ph. 426 932-2 (2) [id.]. Michelucci, Gallozzi, Cotogni, Vicari, Colandrea, Altobelli, Garatti, I Musici.

La Stravaganza (12 Concertos), Op. 4.
(M) *** Ph. 426 935-2 (2) [id.]. Ayo, Gallozzi, Altobelli, Garatti, I Musici.

Besides offering an almost overwhelming commemoration of the bicentennial of Mozart's death, Philips now remind us that 1991 also marked 250 years since the death of Vivaldi. Drawing on a distinguished series of analogue recordings, originally published in 1978 to commemorate the 300th anniversary of the Italian composer's birth, this company now offers a mid-priced Vivaldi Edition, containing everything published from Op. 1 to Op. 12. These 19 CDs are available complete in a cardboard slipcase (426 925-2) or in a dozen separate issues. Volumes 3 and 4 draw on recordings made (mostly in the highly suitable acoustics of La Chaux-de-Fonds, Switzerland) in 1962/3. The transfers to CD are admirable. These are refreshing and lively performances; melodies are finely drawn and there is little hint of the routine which occasionally surfaces in I Musici – and, for that matter, in Vivaldi himself. As when originally issued, these two sets come into direct competition with Argo versions by the Academy of St Martin-in-the-Fields under Marriner or Iona Brown; the latter sets have crisper textures and greater imaginative enthusiasm, but I Musici remain a good choice and are certainly thoroughly recommendable to collectors of this Edition. Maria Teresa Garatti's continuo features a chamber organ as well as harpsichord in Op. 4, to excellent effect.

La Stravaganza, Op. 4 (complete).
❀ (M) *** Decca 430 566-2 (2) [id.]. ASMF, Sir Neville Marriner.

It has been held that, like *La Cetra*, *La Stravaganza* does not match the invention of *L'Estro armonico*; but if the quality of the earlier concertos of the set does not always show Vivaldi at his very best, from about halfway (from No. 6 onwards) one is constantly astonished at the music's vitality. Even earlier, in the finale of No. 3 or in the poetic slow movement of No. 4, Vivaldi provides some marvellously imaginative music; but the later works have consistency and show the composer at his most enticing. Marriner's performances make the music irresistible. The solo playing of Carmel Kaine and Alan Loveday is superb and, when the Academy's rhythms have such splendid buoyancy and lift, it is easy enough to accept Marriner's preference for a relatively sweet style in the often heavenly slow movements. As usual, the contribution of an imaginatively varied continuo (which includes cello and bassoon, in addition to harpsichord, theorbo and organ) adds much to the colour of Vivaldi's score. The recording, made in St John's, Smith Square, in 1973/4, is of the very highest quality and, as with Op. 3, the CD transfers are in the demonstration class. We awarded this set a Rosette on its original LP issue and we see no reason to withhold it now.

6 Violin concertos, Op. 6.
(M) **(*) Ph. 426 939-2 [id.]. Pina Carmirelli, I Musici.

These concertos are not otherwise available and, while their invention is more uneven than in the named sets, their rarity will undoubtedly tempt keen Vivaldians. The 1977 performances, with Pina Carmirelli a stylish and responsive soloist, are polished and with well-judged tempi, if with no special imaginative flair. Excellent sound.

12 Concertos (for violin or oboe), Op. 7.
(M) *** Ph. 426 940-2 (2) [id.]. Accardo or Holliger (Opp. 7/1 & 7), I Musici.

The Op. 7 set is relatively unfamiliar and is certainly rewarding – indeed, much of the invention is vital and appealing. The playing of Accardo and Holliger is altogether masterly, and they have fine rapport with their fellow musicians in I Musici. The 1975 sound-balance is first class (the acoustically sympathetic venue is La Chaux-de-Fonds, Switzerland) and the two CDs are economically priced. This is among the most desirable of the boxes in the Philips Vivaldi Edition.

The Trial between harmony and invention (12 Concertos), Op. 8.
(M) **(*) Ph. 426 943-2 (2) [id.]. Felix Ayo, Garatti, I Musici.
(M) **(*) Sony M2YK 46465 (2) [id.]. Pinchas Zuckerman, Neil Black, ECO, Philip Ledger.

Op. 8 is available in comparative abundance, and Ayo's *Four Seasons* (which are the first four concertos of the set) date from as early as 1959. The recording still sounds well, though, with the warm, resonant sound disguising its age. Ayo produces lovely tone throughout and he plays as stylishly as ever, but the accompaniment is short on imaginative detail. At times the ensemble is a shade heavy-handed in the remaining concertos; but Ayo's contribution has both polish and vitality, and there is still a great deal to enjoy in these performances. The later concertos were recorded in 1961/2 and are transferred vividly.

Zuckerman's solo playing is distinguished throughout, and the ECO provide unfailingly alert and resilient accompaniments. In *Concerto No. 9 in D min.* oboist Neil Black takes the solo position and provides a welcome contrast of timbre – Vivaldi designed this concerto as optionally for violin or oboe, but it probably sounds more effective on the wind instrument. The recording throughout is lively, with a close balance for the soloists. The sound is attractive on CD and does not lack fullness.

The Four Seasons, Op. 8/1–4.
(M) *** DG 431 479-2; *431 479-4*. Schneiderhan, Lucerne Festival Strings, Baumgartner (with ALBINONI: *Adagio*; PACHELBEL: *Canon & Gigue*; PURCELL: *Chacony*; BACH: *Suite No. 3, BWV 1068: Air* ***).
(M) *** DG 431 172-2; *431 172-4*. Gidon Kremer, LSO, Abbado.
(M) *** EMI CDM7 69046-2 [id.]; *EG 769046-4*. Itzhak Perlman, LPO.
(B) *** Pickwick Dig. PCD 800; *CIMPC 800* [id.]. Jaime Laredo, SCO.
(M) **(*) Sony Dig. MDK 44644 [id.]. Zukerman, St Paul CO – PURCELL: *Theatre music*. **(*)
(M) **(*) EMI Dig. CD-EMX 2183; *TC-EMX 2183*. Stanley Ritchie, Baroque O of London.
(B) **(*) CfP CD-CFP 9001; *TC-CFP 40016*. Kenneth Sillito, Virtuosi of England, Davison.
(BB) ** BMG/RCA VD 87732 [7732-2-RV]. Accardo, O de Camera Italiana.
(M) **(*) EMI CD-EMX 2009; *TC-EMX 2009*. Krzysztof Jakowicz, Polish CO, Jerzy Maksymiuk.
(M) **(*) Decca 417 712-2; *417 712-4* [id.]. Konstanty Kulka, Stuttgart CO, Münchinger – ALBINONI: *Adagio* ***; PACHELBEL: *Canon*. ***
(M) ** Chan. CHAN 6510; *MBTD 6510* [id.]. Ronald Thomas, Bournemouth Sinf.
(M) *(*) Ph. Dig. 432 615-2; *432 616-4* [id.]. Christopher Warren-Green, Philh. O, Wilbrandt.

The Four Seasons, Op. 8/1–4; L'Estro armonico: Concertos in A min., RV 356; D, RV 230, Op. 3/6 & 9.
(B) *** Ph. 422 479-2; *422 479-4*. Henryk Szeryng, ECO.

(i) *The Four Seasons, Op. 8/1–4;* (ii) *L'Estro armonico: Double violin concerto in A min., Op. 3/8;* (iii) *Double trumpet concerto in C, RV 537.*
(BB) *** Virgin/Virgo Dig. VJ7 91463-2; *VJ7 91463-4* [id.]. (i) Andrew Watkinson, (ii) with Nicholas Ward; (iii) Crispian Steele-Perkins, Michael Meeks; City of L. Sinfonia, Watkinson.

The Four Seasons; Violin concertos: in B flat (La Caccia), Op. 8/10; in A (per eco in lontana), RV 552.
(M) **(*) Ph. 420 356-2 [id.]. Roberto Michelucci, I Musici.

The Four Seasons; Concerto for strings (Alla rustica) in G, RV 151.
(BB) ** Naxos Dig. 8.550056 [id.]. Takako Nishizaki, Capella Istropolitana, Gunzenhauser.

(i) *The Four Seasons, Op. 8/1–4*; (ii) *Concertos: in C, per la solennità di San Lorenzo, RV 556; in G min., per l'orchestra di Dresda, RV 577.*
(M) *** Ph. 422 484-2. (i) Felix Ayo, Berlin CO; (ii) Dresden State O (members); Negri.

(i) *The Four Seasons, Op. 8/1–4;* (ii) *Double violin concerto in C min., RV 510; Triple concerto for 2 violins & cello in D min., Op. 3/11; Quadruple violin concerto in D, Op. 3/1.*
(M) ** EMI Dig. CDD7 63888-2 [id.]; *ET 763888-4*. Y. Menuhin, (i) with Hu Kun, Mi-Kyung Lee, Eduardo Vassallo; Camerata Lysy Gstaad, Alberto Lysy.

(i) *The Four Seasons;* (ii) *Flute concertos, Op. 10/1–3.*
(M) *** BMG/RCA GD 86553. (i) La Petite Bande, Kuijken; (ii) Brüggen, O of 18th Century.

(i; ii) *The Four Seasons;* (iii) *Recorder concerto in C, RV 443;* (ii) *Double violin concerto in A (Echo), RV 552* (CD only: (ii) *L'Estro armonico: Concerto No. 1 in D min., Op. 3/1, RV 549;* (iii) *Cello concerto in C min., RV 401*).
(B) **(*) DG Compact Classics 413 142-2 (2); *413 142-4* [id.]. (i) Schneiderhan; (ii) Lucerne Festival Strings, Baumgartner; (iii) Linde, Emil Seiler CO, Hofmann (with: ALBINONI: *Adagio* (arr. Giazotto). CORELLI: *Concerto grosso in G min. (Christmas), Op. 6/8.* PACHELBEL: *Canon and Gigue in D* ***).

On the bargain Virgo label Andrew Watkinson directs the City of London Sinfonia from the solo violin in one of the very finest versions available of Vivaldi's *Four Seasons*, superbly played and beautifully recorded with clean, forward sound. Anyone wanting a version on modern instruments cannot do better than this, with fresh, resilient playing in allegros, reflecting lessons learnt from period performance, and with sweet, unsentimental expressiveness in slow movements. The two double concertos provide a valuable makeweight, though the orchestra is more backwardly balanced in the *Concerto for two trumpets*. The accompanying notes, however, are extremely inadequate, and the documentation is also poor.

Schneiderhan's 1959 version of *The Four Sea-*

sons re-emerges, as fresh as paint, on DG's Archiv Galleria label, now well buttressed by an excellent supporting list of Baroque ephemera. Pachelbel's *Canon*, Purcell's *Chacony* and the famous Bach *Air* all sound serenely spacious, while the Albinoni/Giazotto *Adagio* also has a certain refined dignity. These recordings are later (1966/7) and are pleasingly warm and full yet not too opulent. The *Four Seasons*, too, have a firmer focus than before, and Schneiderhan's timbre, pure and sweetly classical, suits Vivaldi very well indeed. The aptly chamber-scaled performance, with brisk tempi and alert orchestral playing, is full of life, with the pictorial detail emerging naturally (*Winter* as cold as you like, and the springtime shepherd's dog very much in the picture, but not too gruff) but without being overcharacterized.

On the Compact Classics tape the couplings are even more generous and include Vivaldi's ingenious *Echo concerto*, where the echo effects are not just confined to the soloists but feature the ripieno too; plus the engaging *Concerto for sopranino recorder*, RV 443, and Corelli's *Christmas concerto*. The pair of CDs also offer two other Vivaldi string concertos. Performances are of high quality throughout and the transfer is consistently vivid.

For his 1975 recording, Felix Ayo chose a talented accompanying group from East Berlin (with Jeffrey Tate at the harpsichord). The playing has microscopic precision and plenty of atmosphere; slow movements are often delicately ethereal in their lightness of texture. Ayo's playing is as sweetly lyrical as ever and, although the result is not as sensuously beautiful as his earlier, I Musici set, the reading is rather more strongly characterized, notably the opening movement of *Winter* which is quite fast and sharply articulated. What makes this issue doubly attractive is the inclusion of the two orchestral concertos. The complicated orchestrations suggested by the composer are not followed to the letter, with clarinos (trumpets) introduced very effectively to celebrate the 'solemnity of San Lorenzo'. The *G minor Concerto*, dedicated to its original Dresden performers, also produces some aurally fascinating textures. Negri ensures throughout that all the playing is alert and polished and chooses apt tempi. The sound is bright, yet not lacking fullness.

Kremer's version of *The Four Seasons* with Abbado is an enormously vital one, full of pictorial drama. The summer storms have never raged with more fury than here, yet the delicacy of the gentle zephyrs is matched by the sensuous somnolence of the slow movement of *Autumn*. The brilliant recording suits the music-making, and this version now becomes fairly competitive again at mid-price, even though it has no fill-up.

Perlman's finesse as a great violinist is evident from first to last. Though some will demand more reticence in baroque concertos, Perlman's imagination holds the sequence together superbly, and there are many passages of pure magic, as in the central *Adagio* of *Summer*. The digital remastering of the 1976 recording is managed admirably, the sound firm, clear and well balanced, with plenty of detail.

On RCA, La Petite Band (soloist unnamed, but presumably Kuijken) offer an authentic version of considerable appeal. Although the accompanying group can generate plenty of energy when Vivaldi's winds are blowing, this is essentially a small-scale reading, notable for its delicacy. The small, pure violin line is particularly appealing in slow movements and one notes how closely the soloist follows Vivaldi's instructions in the second movement of *Spring*: *Largo e pianissimo sempre*. But this issue offers not just the four concertos of Op. 8 but also three favourite *Flute concertos* from Op. 10: *Tempesta di mare*, *La notte* and *Il gardinello*. With the master-instrumentalist, Frans Brüggen, playing a period instrument and directing the Orchestra of the 18th Century, the excellence of these performances, vividly recorded, can be taken for granted.

A first-rate bargain version comes from Szeryng, and the only reservation is that the very soft-grained tone of the harpsichord in the continuo does not come through readily because of the reverberation; the chamber proportions of the recording are retained however, and the digital remastering has improved definition. Szeryng's performances are eloquent and beautifully played, and the alert, resilient accompaniments are stylish. The balance places the violin well forward, but the resonance gives the orchestra plenty of body. As a considerable bonus, Szeryng offers two concertos from Op. 3, also played immaculately.

Jaime Laredo's Pickwick CD is another fine bargain. The performance has great spontaneity and vitality, emphasized by the forward balance which is nevertheless admirably truthful. The bright upper range is balanced by a firm, resonant bass. Laredo plays with bravura and directs polished, strongly characterized accompaniments. Pacing tends to be on the fast side; although the reading is extrovert and the lyrical music – played responsively – is made to offer a series of interludes to the vigour of the allegros, the effect is exhilarating rather than aggressive.

Generously coupled with suites of Purcell's theatre music directed by Raymond Leppard, Zukerman's digitally recorded set is among the best of the modern versions, finding a nice balance between the work's musical and programmatic features; the full recording, however, may be a shade too ample in the bass for some tastes.

Stanley Ritchie's version appears to use original instruments, although nowhere on the disc or documentation are claims made to this effect. The orchestra is of modest size (4,4,2,2,1 with theorbo and harpsichord continuo). The solo playing is both sensitive and lively, and textures are light and pleasing, with good use of dramatic contrast. Many will like the gentle haze of *Summer*, less overtly sensuous than usual, while the slow movement of *Autumn* is mysteriously veiled and delicate. Yet the summer storms have plenty of energy, generated by the sheer vitality of the playing. In the last resort, one's allegiance to this version depends on one's response to the slightly austere yet often coolly beautiful violin line.

The performance by Kenneth Sillito with the Virtuosi of England under Arthur Davison stands out for its bold, clear sound, beautifully focused and full of presence. Indeed the soloist is a shade too present, and this detracts a little from gentler expressiveness. Yet Sillito's playing is both poetic and assured and, with such vivid projection, this music-making is full of personality in its CD format.

Philips have also reissued Michelucci's 1970 version, sounding extremely well. I Musici must have played this work countless times and probably find it more difficult than most groups to bring freshness to each new recording. Roberto Michelucci is a first-class soloist, displaying bursts of bravura in the outer movements but often musingly thoughtful in the slower ones. His expressiveness is finely judged, and the group are naturally balanced, with the harpsichord coming through in the right way, without exaggeration. The last degree of spontaneity is sometimes missing, but this is certainly enjoyable. This version is made the more tempting by the inclusion of two extra named *Violin concertos*, both very well played and recorded.

Not unexpectedly, Accardo on his earlier, RCA Victrola record makes an accomplished and appealing soloist and the Orchestra de Camera Italiana offer full, bright supporting textures. The programmatic drama is conveyed well, but musical values are paramount and this is enjoyable in its fresh, direct manner, if not especially memorable. The sound is vivid, and this might be considered at super-bargain price, even though it has no couplings; but there are many other, more striking, versions.

The performance by Krzysztof Jakowicz and the Polish Chamber Orchestra, although on a slightly smaller scale, is not unlike the Kremer/Abbado version. It bustles with vigour, with strong dynamic contrasts and a similar balance between the fast, energetic allegros – rhythms crisp and incisive – and the gentle sostenuto of the lyrical music. However, the fast tempi at times bring the feeling that the music is driven very hard. The solo playing offers arresting bravura but is also sensitive, so that the gentle breezes and summer languor are as readily communicated as the violent storms and the icy briskness of what is plainly seen as a harsh Polish winter. The 1980 recording is bright, not edgy, but somewhat dry in timbre.

On Decca, Kulka gives a first-class solo performance, while Münchinger and the Stuttgart Chamber Orchestra, whose early LPs did so much to reawaken interest in Vivaldi, bring a stylish and lively manner to the accompaniments. This was always a strong recommendation in the mid-price range but, with digital remastering, the brightly lit recording has become vivid to the point of astringency in its CD format, and the ear is drawn to this when the bonus items sound much mellower.

The super-bargain Naxos version is given first-class digital sound, warm, fresh and well balanced (though the continuo does not come through very impressively). Takako Nishizaki plays beautifully, displaying an appropriate degree of bravura, and the accompaniment under Stephen Gunzenhauser is modest in scale and pleasingly finished. These are amiably musical performances, but Vivaldi's pictorial imagery is understated: the shepherd's dog has obviously just returned from an exhausting spring walk and *Winter* has seemingly been mellowed by the depletion of the ozone layer.

Menuhin's early (1979) digital recording of *The Four Seasons* was designed as much to provide a framework for the youthful Camerata Lysy as for its illustrious soloist, whose timbre is without much bloom above the stave and whose rhythmic control is not always stable (notably in the opening movement of *Autumn*). It is a characteristically extrovert account, robust and exuberant rather than refined. The continuo is insignificant and, while Menuhin's directness communicates readily, this hardly rates a strong recommendation in such a competitive marketplace; even if the sound has brilliant clarity, detail is not registered very subtly. Three multiple string concertos, recorded six years later, make an attractive bonus. Menuhin is a persuasive leader here, and the performances are all fresh and understanding, lively if not immaculate. The recording is rather dry and studio-ish, but not disagreeably so.

Ronald Thomas's approach on Chandos emphasizes the music's breadth and lyricism rather than its colourful scene-painting, so that the shepherd's dog yaps gently and the winds blow amiably, certainly never reaching gale force. In its way this is pleasing, but there is distinct undercharacterization here, in spite of vivid recording.

Christopher Warren-Green's full-priced Virgin Classics version of *The Four Seasons* with the LCO is one of the very finest of all recordings of this much-recorded work. But his new Philips account is not in same class. Again tempi are very brisk, but here the effect is hard-driven and perfunctory. It is as if the summer winds have arrived too early and blown all the leaves off the trees, while the raindrops of *Winter* have obviously frozen into swift-falling sleet. The accompaniments are efficient, and this effect is emphasized by the bright recording. There is no coupling: the overall playing time is 36 minutes.

The Four Seasons, Op. 8/1–4 (arr. for flute and strings).

(M) *** BMG/RCA GD 60748; *GK 60748* [60748-2-RG; *60748-4-RG*]. James Galway, Zagreb Soloists.

James Galway's transcription is thoroughly musical and so convincing that at times one is tempted to believe that the work was conceived in this form. The playing itself is marvellous, full of detail and imagination, and the recording is excellent, even if the flute is given a forward balance, the more striking on CD.

Violin concertos, Op. 8/5 (La tempesta di mare); 6 (Il piacere); 7–8; 10 (La caccia); 11–12.

(BB) **(*) Naxos Dig. 8.550189 [id.]. Béla Bánfalvi, Budapest Strings.

Very good (though not outstanding) performances of the violin concertos from the Op. 8 set come from Béla Bánfalvi and the Budapest Strings. Decent orchestral playing and well-balanced, fresh, recorded sound. Good value for money.

La Cetra (12 Violin concertos), Op. 9.

(M) **(*) Ph. 426 946-2 (2) [id.]. Ayo, Cotogni (in Op. 9/9), Altobelli, Garatti, I Musici.

I Musici's *La Cetra* dates from 1964 and is again recorded at La Chaux-de-Fonds, which ensures a realistic and pleasing sound-balance. With Felix Ayo the principal soloist, the playing is spirited, characterful and expressively rich, though the overall effect is less individual than in the finest versions from the past. One drawback is that solo passages are given no continuo support, though Maria Teresa Garatti provides an organ continuo for the ripieno. Overall this is good value at mid-price.

6 Flute concertos, Op. 10.

(M) *** Ph. 422 260-2; *422 260-4*. Gazzelloni, I Musici.

(M) *** Ph. 426 949-2 [id.]. Gazzelloni, I Musici.

(B) *** Pickwick Dig. PCD 961; *CIMPC 961* [id.]. Judith Hall, Divertimenti of L., Paul Barritt.

(M) **(*) EMI Dig. CD-EMX 9504; *TC-EMX 2105* [Ang. CDM 62014]. William Bennett, ECO, Malcolm.

Severino Gazzelloni's version of the six *Concertos*, Op. 10, has been in circulation throughout the 1970s and its merits are well established; it is a safer recommendation for the general collector than the authentic rivals, good though the best of these is. With fresh, remastered sound this is an excellent mid-price recommendation with two alternative catalogue numbers.

Judith Hall's record of the Op. 10 *Flute concertos* is fresh and brightly recorded. She plays with considerable virtuosity and a great deal of taste. The Divertimento of London is a modern-instrument group and the players are both sensitive and alert. The recording is so clean and forward that one would at times welcome greater atmosphere. But there's plenty of sensitivity and atmosphere about the performances.

Though beefier in approach than some rival versions, William Bennett's issue on the mid-price Eminence label brings highly enjoyable performances, marked by fine solo playing and sparkling and imaginative continuo from George Malcolm. Good, warm, modern recording.

6 Violin concertos, Op. 11.

(M) *** Ph. 426 950-2 [id.]. Salvatore Accardo, I Musici.

6 Violin concertos, Op. 12.

(M) *** Ph. 426 951-2 [id.]. Salvatore Accardo, I Musici.

More rare repertoire here. The Opp. 11 and 12 concertos are perhaps of uneven quality, but the best of them are very rewarding indeed and, played so superlatively by Salvatore Accardo, they are likely to beguile the most unwilling listener. Recorded in 1974/5, these two individual CDs are among the most desirable of the Philips Vivaldi Edition, and their CD transfers are among the best in the series.

Bassoon concertos: in C, RV 473; in F, RV 490; in G, RV 493; in G min., RV 496; in A min., RV 497; in B flat (La notte), RV 501.

(B) **(*) Hung. White Label HRC 043 [id.]. Gábor Janota, Liszt CO, Budapest, Frigyes Sándor.

Very good playing from Gábor Janota and lively and sensitive support from the Liszt Chamber Orchestra under Frigyes Sándor.

These concertos are unfailingly inventive and, unlike Perényi's recording of *Cello concertos* (listed below), the (presumably 1970s) recording is well balanced, with both soloist and orchestra present or pleasingly forward and with no lack of bloom and freshness to the sound. At about an hour's music, good value.

Cello concertos: in C, RV 398; in G, RV 413.
(M) *** DG 429 098-2; *429 098-4.*
Rostropovich, Zurich Coll. Mus., Sacher – BOCCHERINI; TARTINI: *Concertos.* ***

Performances of great vigour and projection from Rostropovich. The playing is superbly brilliant and immensely strong in character; it may be somewhat large-scale for Vivaldi's two quite short concertos, but undoubtedly every bar comes fully to life. Spendidly lively accompaniments and excellent CD transfers, bright and clean with no lack of depth. Like Tortelier's collection – see below – with which there is no conflict of repertoire, this is for those who primarily care about the communication of joy in great music.

Cello concertos: in C, RV 400; C min., RV 401; B min., RV 424; for (i) *2 cellos in G min., RV 531;* (i; ii) *violin & 2 cellos in C, RV 561.*
(M) *** EMI CDM7 69835-2; *EG 769835-4.*
Paul Tortelier, with (i) Maude Tortelier, (ii) Jacques Manzone; L. Mozart Players, Ledger.

This is one of Tortelier's finest records. The performances here are strong and alive, the slow movements expressive without being overromanticized. Philip Ledger directs the full-bodied accompanying group and provides a continuo with some flair. The playing is undoubtedly stylish, though the overall effect is not aimed at the 'authentic' lobby, rather at those who seek primarily a warmly understanding response to the composer's inspiration and readily communicated musical enjoyment. The sound is excellent, with the CD remasterings highly successful.

Cello concertos: in E flat, RV 408; in G, RV 413; in B min., RV 424; (i) *Double cello concerto in G min., RV 531.*
(B) * Hung. White Label HRC 044 [id.]. Miklós Perényi; (i) László Mezö; Liszt Academy of Music O, Albert Simon.

Miklós Perényi is Hungary's most distinguished cellist, an eloquent player who phrases with finesse and elegance. Note that the band is not the celebrated Franz (or Ferenc) Liszt Chamber Orchestra but that of the Liszt Academy; the playing, though mostly good, is not always distinguished: Albert Simon can at times produce sluggish results. The 1978 recording is very upfront, with little depth or perspective, and the result of the close balance is some coarseness of texture. Perényi's contribution makes it almost worth while but, at not much more than 46 minutes, it is not generous measure by present-day standards.

Flute concertos: in A min., RV 108; in F, RV 434; Double flute concerto in C, RV 533; Sopranino recorder concertos: in C, RV 443 & RV 444; in A min., RV 445.
(BB) *** Naxos Dig. 8.550385 [id.]. Jálek, Novotny, Stivin, Capella Istropolitana, Oliver Dohnányi.

The Capella Istropolitana, who are drawn from the excellent Slovak Philharmonic, play with vitality and sensitivity for Oliver Dohnányi and the soloists show appropriate virtuosity and flair. As always, there are rewards and surprises in this music, but readers are not recommended to listen to the last nine tracks without a break (or an aspirin), since three consecutive sopranino recorder concertos are too much of a good thing, despite Jíři Stivin's undoubted artistry. The sound is very good indeed, and so is the balance.

Guitar concertos: in C, RV 425; for 2 guitars in G, RV 532; for 4 guitars in D, RV 93; in B min., RV 580 (from L'Estro armonico, Op. 3/10); for guitar, violin, viola & cello in A, RV 82.
(B) ** Ph. 426 076-2; *426 076-4.* Los Romeros, San Antonio SO, Alessandro.

Though their composer did not conceive these works with guitars in mind, they sound quite effective in their present formats. Vivaldi's concertos of this kind are often more enjoyable when grouped in a miscellaneous collection with varying solo timbres. However, guitar and mandolin enthusiasts should find this satisfactory, for the recording is truthful, if a little studio-ish in feeling.

L'Estro armonico: Double violin concerto in A min.; Quadruple violin concerto in B min.; Triple concerto in D min., for 2 violins and cello, Op. 3/8, 10–11. Triple violin concerto in F.
(B) **(*) Pickwick Dig. PCD 809 [id.]. Soloists, SCO, Laredo.

The three concertos from *L'Estro armonico* are among Vivaldi's finest; they receive vigorous performances from members of the Scottish Chamber Orchestra, with their director, Jaime Laredo, again creating the lively spontaneity that informs his successful version of *The Four Seasons.* While the solo playing occasionally lacks the last touch of polish, there is excellent team spirit, and the phrasing has more light and shade than in Laredo's companion collection of wind concertos, below. The recording is a shade overbright, but there is a firm supporting bass line and the acoustic is attractive, adding ambience and warmth without blurring detail. On Pickwick's bargain-price CD label, this seems excellent value.

Violin concertos: in D min. for 2 violins and cello, Op. 3/11; in E flat (La tempesta di mare); in C (Il piacere), Op. 8/5 – 6; in E (L'amoroso), RV 271; in A min. for 2 violins, RV 523; in F for 3 violins, RV 551.

(BB) *** BMG/RCA Dig. VD 87741; *VK 87741* [7741-2-RV]. Fontanarosa, Agostini, Vernikov, Filippini, I Nuovi Virtuosi di Roma.

I Nuovi Virtuosi di Roma use modern instruments but are recorded in a drier acoustic than that usually afforded to their illustrious colleagues, I Musici, on Philips; the rather more athletic style of their playing brings brighter and quite sharply defined textures, which will appeal to ears already weaned on authenticity. There is certainly no lack of expressive feeling in the *Cantabile* slow movement of *L'amoroso* or indeed in the memorable *Largo e spiccato* of Op. 3, No. 11; while the clean articulation of the accompanying group is striking in the spirited finale of the former work, and indeed in the fugato which closes the first movement of the latter. All the soloists are drawn from the group itself, and the overall standard of playing is high. At bargain price and with modern digital sound, this is excellent value, with a playing time of just over an hour.

Violin concertos, Op. 8, Nos. 5 in E flat (La Tempesta di mare), RV 253; 6 in C (Il Piacere), RV 180; 10 in B flat (La Caccia), RV 362; 11 in D, RV 210; in C min. (Il Sospetto), RV 199.

(B) *** CfP Dig. CD-CFP 4522; *TC-CFP 4522.* Sir Yehudi Menuhin, Polish CO, Jerzy Maksymiuk.

Menuhin's collection of five concertos – four of them with nicknames and particularly delightful – brings some of his freshest, most intense playing in recent years. Particularly in slow movements – notably that of *Il Piacere* ('Pleasure') – he shows afresh his unique insight in shaping a phrase. Fresh, alert accompaniment and full digital recording.

(i) *Violin concertos: in A min., Op. 9/5; in E min. (Il favorito), Op. 11/2; in G min., Op. 12/1; in E min. (L'amoroso), RV 271. Orchestral concertos (con molti stromenti) in C, RV 558; in G min., RV 576.*

(M) *** Ph. 432 281-2; *431 281-4.* (i) Arthur Grumiaux; Dresden State O (members), Vittorio Negri.

Arthur Grumiaux never disappoints, and this is one of the most attractive collections of Vivaldi's *Violin concertos* in the catalogue. The *G minor*, Op. 12/1, is a particularly fine work and brings a highly imaginative response; and his playing is hardly less engaging in *L'amoroso*, full of lightness and grace. Negri accompanies sympathetically and the 1973 sound is excellent though fuller in texture than we would expect today. But the solo playing offers endless pleasure. What makes this reissue doubly attractive is the inclusion of the orchestral concertos *con molti stromenti*. The *G minor* work was dedicated to its Dresden performers, though not the present group! Its piquant textures bring oboe and violin soloists, with a ripieno including 2 flutes, 2 oboes, bassoon and strings. RV 558 is aurally even more fascinating, with its delicacy of scoring for flutes, theorbos, mandolins, salmò, 2 violins *in tromba marina*, cello and strings. The performances are full of life and colour, and the 1970 recording is excellent.

Concerto for strings in D min., RV 129; Double violin concerto in A (Echo), RV 522; Double concerto in B flat for violin and cello, RV 547; Concerto for 2 violins and 2 cellos in D, RV 564; Sonata a quattro in E flat, RV 130.

(B) ** Ph. 432 678-2 [id.]. Soloists, I Musici.

This not particularly generous bargain collection (49 minutes) is intended as a sampler for the Philips Vivaldi Edition. In the event, it is not a very tempting collection. By far the most attractive item is the *Concerto in A major con violino principale con altro violino per eco in lontana*, where Vivaldi's ingeniously devised echo effects are pleasingly brought off. Elsewhere, however, although all the performances are polished, there is at times an element of routine.

Violin concertos: in D min. (Senza cantin), RV 243; in E (Il riposo), RV 270; in E min. (Il favorito), RV 277; in F (Per la solennità di San Lorenzo), RV 286.

(B) **(*) CfP Dig. CD-CFP 4536; *TC-CFP 4536.* Accardo, I Solisti delle Settimane Musicali Internazionali di Napoli.

Salvatore Accardo plays each of the four concertos on this record on a different instrument from the collection of the Palazzo Communale, Cremona. He plays the *E major*, *Il riposo*, on the Niccolo Amati, *Il favorito* on the Cremonose of 1715, the darker-hued *Concerto senza cantin* ('without using the E string') on the Guarnieri del Gesù, and the *Concerto per la solennità di San Lorenzo* on the Andrea Amati of Charles IX of France. But this is more than a record for violin specialists: it offers playing of the highest order by one of the finest violinists of our time. Accardo himself directs the excellent ensemble, and the EMI recording is very vivid and clear but also rather dry in the manner of some early digital recordings. We would expect a warmer, more ample string-sound today. These are distinguished performances, but not all ears will respond to the relative lack of bloom.

MISCELLANEOUS CONCERTO COLLECTIONS

L'Estro armonico: Quadruple violin concerto in D; Double violin concerto in D min., Op. 3/1 & 11; Bassoon concerto in E min., RV 484; Flute concerto in G min. (La notte), Op. 10/2; Double mandolin concerto in G, RV 532; Oboe concerto in B flat, RV 548; Orchestral concerto (con molti stromenti) in C, RV 558; Concerto for strings in G (Alla rustica), RV 151.

(M) *** DG Dig. 431 710-2; *431 710-4* [id.]. Soloists, E. Concert, Trevor Pinnock.

This DG Archiv digital reissue is impressive for quantity as well as quality: eight concertos and 70 minutes must be some kind of record for a single Vivaldi disc! The collection of very varied works shows Pinnock and the English Concert at their liveliest and most refreshing, although not always so strong on charm. (The account of the *Bassoon concerto* is perhaps an unintentional exception, for the solo timbre has a certain bovine character.) The *Concerto for four violins* is very lithe, and throughout the concert the solo playing is predictably expert. The *Orchestral concerto* involves an astonishing array of instruments; it is also available as listed above, played on modern instruments by the Dresden orchestra, but authenticists will prefer the spicier timbres displayed here. Excellent recording, giving a most realistic impression on CD.

L'Estro armonico: Quadruple violin concerto in D, Op. 3/1; Flute concerto in D (Il gardellino), Op. 10/3; Oboe concerto in C, RV 446; Double concerto in G for oboe & bassooon, RV 545; Concerto for strings in B flat, RV 166; Viola d'amore concerto in D, RV 392; Double concerto in F for violin, organ and strings, RV 542.

(M) *** Ph. Dig. 432 059-2; *432 059-4*. Carmirelli, Nicolet, Holliger, Thunemann, Paris, Perez, Garatti, I Musici.

A generous and well-planned collection, drawn from different sources but given a convincing overall relationship by all being digitally recorded in the excellent acoustics of La Chaux-de-Fonds, Switzerland. With distinguished names among the soloists the performances are predictably fresh, and they all show Vivaldi's amazing fecundity of invention appealingly, not least the miniature *Concerto for strings and continuo*. The work for four violins is also very successful, and Holliger and Thunemann are as expressively appealing as they are nimble. The only slight reservation concerns Aurèle Nicolet's bird imitations in *Il gardellino*, engaging enough, but stylistically somewhat over the top.

L'Estro armonico: Quadruple violin concerto in B min., Op. 3/10; La Stravaganza: Violin concerto in B flat, Op. 4/1; Cello concerto in C min., RV 401; Double horn concerto in F, RV 539; Concerto in F for 2 oboes, bassoon, 2 horns and violin, RV 569; Double trumpet concerto in C, RV 537.

(M) *** Decca 425 721-2; *425 721-4*. ASMF, Marriner.

Another excellent collection from the considerable array of Vivaldi concertos recorded by Marriner and his ASMF (on modern instruments) between 1965 and 1977. The soloists are all distinguished, offering playing that is constantly alert, finely articulated and full of life and imagination. The special interest here is that Neville Marriner himself is the first of four equals in the concerto from *L'Estro armonico*. Accompaniments are predictably stylish, and the recordings still sound admirably fresh in their CD transfers, with only a touch of shrillness on the *Double trumpet concerto*.

(i) *The Trial between harmony and invention: Violin concertos Nos. 5 in E flat (La tempesta di mare); 6 in C (Il piacere), Op. 8/5–6;* (ii) *Bassoon concertos: in C, RV 472; in C min., RV 480; in A min., RV 498; in B flat, RV 504.*

(M) *** Chan. CHAN 6529; *MBTD 6529* [id.]. (i) Ronald Thomas, Bournemouth Sinf.; (ii) Robert Thompson, L. Mozart Players, Ledger.

The two concertos included here from *The Trial between harmony and invention* were among the best of the complete set recorded by Ronald Thomas in 1980. The use of modern instruments does not preclude a keen sense of style, and the balance is convincing. The bassoonist Robert Thompson turns a genial eye on his four concertos. He is rather forwardly projected but the performances are direct and personable and, like the sound, agreeably fresh, among the most attractive accounts of Vivaldi's bassoon concertos available on CD. An enjoyable collection.

Bassoon concerto in A min., RV 498; Flute concerto in C min., RV 441; Oboe concerto in F, RV 456; Concerto for 2 oboes in D min., RV 535; Concerto for 2 oboes, bassoon, 2 horns and violin in F, RV 574; Piccolo concerto in C, RV 444.

(M) *** Decca 417 777-2; *417 777-4*. ASMF, Marriner.

The playing here is splendidly alive and characterful, with crisp, clean articulation and well-pointed phrasing, free from overemphasis. The *A minor Bassoon concerto* has a delightful sense of humour. Altogether the musical substance may not be very weighty, but Vivaldi was rarely more engaging than when, as here, he was writing for wind instruments, particularly if he had more than one in his team of soloists. Well-balanced and vivid recording; this is highly recommendable for all those who do not insist on original instruments in this repertoire. The recordings were made in 1976/7 and have been transferred to CD with pleasing freshness.

Double cello concerto in G min., RV 531; Lute (Guitar) concerto in D, RV 93; Oboe concerto in F, F.VII, No.2 (R.455); Double concerto for oboe and violin; Trumpet concerto in D (trans. Jean Thilde); *Violin concerto in G min., Op. 12/1; RV 317.*

(BB) *** Naxos Dig. 8 550384 [id.]. Capella Istropolitana, Jaroslav Kr(e)chek.

This is a recommendable disc from which to set out to explore the Vivaldi concertos, especially if you are beginning a collection. Gabriela Krcková makes a sensitive contribution to the delightful *Oboe concerto in F major*, F.VII, No. 2 (R.455), and the other soloists are pretty good too. Should this programme meet your particular needs, there is no need for hesitation. The fresh, well-balanced recorded sound makes this attractive CD well worth its modest cost.

Cello concerto in B min., RV 424; Oboe concerto in A min., RV 461; Double concerto in C min. for oboe and violin, RV Anh.17; Violin concerto in D, RV 208; Sinfonia in B min., RV 169; Sonata à 4 in E flat for 2 violins, viola and continuo, RV 130.

(M) ** Teldec/Warner 2292 43436-2 [id.]. Soloists, Concerto Amsterdam, Schröder.

There is an element of too much rectitude here, and the forward balance seems to emphasize the somewhat stiff approach, although allegros are alert and lively. The recording readily captures the robust and somewhat plangent timbres, and those who favour Vivaldi played on baroque instruments will certainly find the sound faithful; the digital remastering is clean without loss of ambience, and the 1978 analogue recording sounds quite modern.

Double concertos: for 2 cellos in G min., RV 531; 2 flutes in C, RV 533; 2 oboes in D min., RV 535; 2 mandolins in G, RV 532; 2 trumpets in C, RV 537; 2 violins, RV 523.

(M) *** Ph. 426 086-2; *426 086-4*. I Musici.

This makes an attractively diverse collection. Most of these concertos are admirably inventive and the performances show I Musici at their very best, on sparkling form. The sound is good too.

Concertos: for 2 cellos in G min., RV 531; 2 mandolins in G, RV 532; recorder in C min., RV 441; in C, RV 443; Trio for violin, lute & continuo in G min., RV 85.

(M) *** DG Dig. 427 824-2; *427 824-4*. Demenga, Häusler, Söllscher, Copley, Camerata Bern, Füri.

An excellent mid-priced digital collection, assembled from various records made by the Camerata Bern, which will especially suit those who like their Vivaldi on original instruments. Söllscher's account of the *Duet concerto* for mandolins (in which he takes both solo roles) is quite outstanding, and there is some breathtaking virtuosity from Michael Copley in the *Recorder concertos*. Further variety is provided by the *Trio* which is also an attractive work. The well-balanced recording has splendid presence and realism.

Double cello concerto in G min., RV 531; Concertos for strings: in G (Alla rustica), RV 151; in A, RV 158; in B min. (Al santo sepolcro), RV 177; Double violin concerto in B flat, RV 524; Triple violin concerto in F, RV 551.

(M) *** Decca 433 169-2; *433 169-4* [id.]. Soloists, Lucerne Festival Strings, Baumgartner – BOCCHERINI: *Symphony in C.* **

It is unusual to see the Lucerne Festival Strings on the Decca label; but this disc, made in the Vienna Sofiensaal in 1973, was a successful venture of Christopher Raeburn. Although all these works are well represented in the current catalogue, readers coming new to Vivaldi may well choose this brightly recorded collection. The playing is splendidly alert and vigorous, and the overall impression is enormously fresh. The solemn *Concerto, Al santo sepolcro* is particularly characterful. Baumgartner is not always the most resilient of conductors, but on this occasion the Lucerne orchestra were clearly on their toes throughout. The soloists are excellent too, and it is good to hear the more robust sound of modern instruments in the concerto for a pair of cellos. The *Triple violin concerto*, incidentally, is the only violin work (out of some 280 which Vivaldi composed for one or more violins) which actually features three; it has a fine, melancholy central *Largo* which is reminiscent of *The Four Seasons*. Excellent notes, though curiously the documentation still uses the old Pincherle numbers.

Flute concerto in G min. (La Notte), Op. 10/2; Concertos for strings: in D min. (Madrigalesco), RV 129; in G (Alla rustica), RV 151; Violin concertos: in D (L'inquietudine), RV 234; in E

(L'amoroso), RV 271; Double violin concerto in A, RV 523; Sinfonia in B min. (Al Santo Sepolcro), RV 169.
(B) **(*) DG 429 167-2; *429 167-4*. Soloists, BPO, Karajan.

This collection dates from 1971 (except for the *Flute concerto*, which was recorded a decade later) and shows Karajan indulging himself in repertoire which he clearly loves but for which he does not have the stylistic credentials. Yet the sheer charisma of the playing and the glorious body of tone the orchestra creates within a resonant acoustic, notably in the extraordinary *Sinfonia al Santo Sepolcro*, is difficult to resist. The orchestra dominates even the solo concertos and the soloists seem to float, concertante style, within the resonantly glowing ambience.

Double flute concerto in C, RV 533; Double oboe concerto in D min., RV 535; Double horn concerto in F, RV 539; Double trumpet concerto in C, RV 537; Concerto for 2 oboes, 2 clarinets and strings, RV 560.
(B) **(*) Pickwick Dig. PCD 811 [id.]. Soloists, Scottish CO, Laredo.

An attractive bargain-priced compilation, with soloists and orchestra set back in good perspective in a believable acoustic. The resonance tends to make the trumpet timbre spread, but otherwise the sound is very good. The solo playing is accomplished, although rather more light and shade between phrases would have made the performances even more enticing, while Jaime Laredo's direction of the slow movements is not especially imaginative.

Concerto in C for 2 flutes, 2 salmò, 2 violins 'in tromba marina', 2 mandolins, 2 theorbos, cello & strings, RV 558; Guitar concerto in D, RV 93; Mandolin concerto in C, RV 425; Double mandolin concerto in G, RV 532; Concerto for viola d'amore and guitar, RV 540.
(B) ** DG 429 528-2; *429 528-4* [id.]. Yepes, Takashi, Ochi, Fransca-Colombier, Paul Kuentz CO, Kuentz.

An intimate programme, suitable for the late evening, given mellow recording which is retained in the CD transfer. The *Mandolin concertos* are beautifully recorded, the miniature imagery of the solo instruments truthfully captured in relation to the orchestra. The *Duet concerto* has a gentle charm. RV 93 and RV 540 were intended for lute rather than guitar, but Yepes is persuasive here, particularly in the memorable *Largo* of the latter piece. The concertante work rounds off the programme with a burst of colour. A pleasant rather than a distinctive concert.

CHAMBER MUSIC

Cello sonatas: in E min., RV 40; in F, RV 41; in A min., RV 43; in B flat, RV 45–7.
(M) ** Erato/Warner 2292 45658-2 [id.]. Paul Tortelier, Robert Veyron-Lacroix.

These performances of the Op. 14 *Cello sonatas* come from 1964 and, unlike some other Erato reissues in the '*Hommage à Paul Tortelier*' series, have the benefit of altogether fresh and well-ventilated sound. Tortelier's playing has predictable warmth and a strong sense of line; the balance very much favours the cellist (in the *A minor Sonata*, RV 43, unacceptably so), but this is nevertheless far more recommendable than the Bach *Viola da gamba sonatas* or the Schumann *Trios* he has also recorded.

12 Sonatas for 2 violins & continuo, Op. 1.
(M) *** Ph. 426 926-2 (2) [id.]. Accardo, Gulli, Canino, De Saram.

12 Violin sonatas, Op. 2.
(M) *** Ph. 426 929-2 (2) [id.]. Accardo, Canino, De Saram.

For the collector satiated by too many recordings of *The Four Seasons*, the two boxes offering the *Violin sonatas* should provide an admirable place to start. It is unlikely that Salvatore Accardo's performances, so ably supported by Bruno Canino and Rohan de Saram (and in Op. 1 by Franco Gulli), could be surpassed in terms of sympathetic fluency, musicianship and sheer beauty of tone. Textures are fuller and warmer than would be the case with original instruments, yet the recording balance brings admirable transparency, with the harpsichord coming through naturally. The shadow of Corelli still hangs over the earlier set, yet slow movements often have those specially memorable Vivaldian harmonic inflexions (sample the *Adagio* third movement of Op. 1/1, the *Grave* introduction of Op. 1/2 or the Adagio of the last of the set, Op. 1/6. The dance movements are genially vigorous and the invention is remarkably pleasing and fresh. Most of the sonatas in Op. 1 have four or five quite short movements, whereas in Op. 2 there are three or four, usually treating the material more ambitiously, over a longer span. Collectors will find unexpected rewards in both sets, and the CD transfer of recordings made in 1977 are completely natural yet vivid in Philips's best manner.

Violin sonatas (for violin and continuo), *Op. 2/1, 2, 4, 6, 8, 9, 11–12 (RV 1, 9, 16, 20, 23, 27, 31 & 32).*
(B) *** Hung. White Label HRC 062 [id.].
Dénes Kovács, János Sebestyén, Mária Frank.

Readers who are looking for a group of these

sonatas, very well played on modern instruments and decently recorded, will find these accounts by the Hungarian violinist, Dénes Kovács, give much pleasure. He is a player of aristocratic quality and good musical judgement; his continuo support is excellent and the analogue recordings, which presumably date from the 1970s, (the label would have us believe 1987) have warmth and freshness. This disc is not quite as distinctive as Accardo's complete set on Philips, but it is still thoroughly worthwhile in its own right and is reasonably priced.

6 Violin sonatas, Op. 5.
(M) **(*) Ph. 426 938-2 [id.]. Accardo, Gazeau (in Op. 5/5–6), Canino, De Saram.

Warm, mellifluous playing from Salvatore Accardo in the Op. 5 *Sonatas* of 1716–17, four being solo works with continuo and the remainder *Trio sonatas*. The music is not quite as interesting or inventive as Opp. 1 and 2, but those collecting this Edition will still find much that is rewarding. The 1977 sound is well up to the excellent standard of this series.

VOCAL MUSIC

Beatus vir, RV 597; Credo, RV 592; Magnificat, RV 610.
(M) *** Ph. 420 651-2. Soloists, Alldis Ch., ECO, Negri.

Beatus vir, RV 598; Dixit Dominus in D, RV 594; Introduzione al Dixit: Canta in prato in G, RV 636 (ed. Geigling); *Magnificat in G min., RV 611* (ed. Negri).
(M) *** Ph. 420 649-2. Lott, Burgess, Murray, Daniels, Finnie, Collins, Rolfe-Johnson, Holl, Alldis Ch., ECO, Negri.

Crediti propter quod, RV 105; Credo, RV 591; Introduction to Gloria, RV 639; Gloria, RV 588; Kyrie, RV 587; Laetatus sum, RV 607.
(M) *** Ph. 420 650-2. M. Marshall, Lott, Finnie, Rolfe-Johnson, Alldis Ch., ECO, Negri.

Dixit dominus, RV 595; In exitu Israel, RV 604; Sacrum, RV 586.
(M) *** Ph. 420 652-2. Alldis Ch., ECO, Negri.

Introduction to Gloria, RV 642; Gloria in D, RV 589; Lauda Jerusalem in E min., RV 609; Laudate Dominum in D min., RV 606; Laudati pueri Dominum in A, RV 602.
(M) *** Ph. 420 648-2. Marshall, Lott, Collins, Finnilä, Alldis Ch., ECO, Negri.

Beatus vir, RV 597; Canta in prato, RV 636; Credo, RV 591; Dixit dominus (2 settings), *RV 594 & RV 595; Gloria* (2 settings), *RV 588 & RV 589; In furore, RV 626; Kyrie, RV 587; Lauda Jerusalem, RV 609; Magnificat, RV 610; Nisi dominus, RV 608; Nulla in mundo pax sincera; O qui caeli, RV 631; Stabat mater, RV 621.*
(M) **(*) Erato/Warner 2292 45716-2 (4) [id.]. Soloists; Lausanne Vocal Ens. & CO; Lisbon Gulbenkian Foundation Ch. & O; E. Bach Festival Ch. & Baroque O; Corboz.

These Philips recordings come from the late 1970s. Vittorio Negri does not make use of period instruments, but he penetrates as deeply into the spirit of this music as many who do. When they first appeared, we found them lively, stylish performances, beautifully recorded – and they come up splendidly in their new format, digitally refurbished. Any lover of Vivaldi is likely to be astonished that not only the well-known works but the rarities show him writing with the keenest originality and intensity. There is nothing routine about any of this music, or any of the performances either.

Whereas Negri's recordings are conveniently offered on a series of individual CDs, the Corboz collection is grouped in a box, even though the recordings come from three different sources. Those from the English Bach Festival, which include the *Gloria*, RV 588 (shorn of the three-movement *Introduction* on a non-liturgical text), and *Nisi Dominus* (beautifully sung by Helen Watts), offer baroque orchestral playing on authentic instruments. The *Gloria*, RV 589, *Kyrie*, *Credo*, *Beatus vir*, *Magnificat* and the motets *Lauda Jerusalem* and *Nulla in mundo pax sincera* come from Lausanne and modern instruments are used to produce a warm, well-focused sound; the acoustic is spacious and the performances vital and musical. The professional singers of the Lausanne Choir are generally admirable and the soloists are sweet-toned. The *Magnificat* is given in its simpler, first version, on a relatively small scale with the chorus singing the alto solo, *Fecit potentiam*. The *Kyrie*, with its double chorus, double string orchestra plus four soloists, makes a fine contrast in its magnificence. The *Dixit dominus*, RV 594, and *Stabat Mater* (a most affecting piece, thought to have been composed at great speed) were recorded in Lisbon, and here the performances are pleasingly old-fashioned, with robust tone and modern instruments. The acoustic is cavernous (that of São Vicente da Fora Church) and, though warmth and space are desirable, some listeners may find this too much of a good thing. In spite of the woolly acoustic here, the solo singers and instrumentalists are fairly well focused. There is much to enjoy within these four CDs and the transfers are well managed, but the stylistic contrasts suggest that in the long term Negri on

Philips will prove the more satisfying investment.

Gloria in D, RV 589.
(M) *** Decca 421 146-2. Vaughan, J. Baker, King's College, Cambridge, Ch., ASMF, Willcocks – HAYDN: *Nelson Mass.* ***

(i) *Gloria in D, RV 589;* (ii) *Magnificat, RV 610.*
(M) **(*) Decca 425 724-2; *425 724-4.* (i) Vaughan, J. Baker; (ii) Castle, Cockerham, King; King's College Ch., ASMF; (i) Willcocks; (ii) Ledger – PERGOLESI: *Magnificat.* **(*)

The CD remastering of the stylish 1962 Willcocks recording of Vivaldi's *Gloria* is strikingly vivid and, with excellent choral and solo singing, this makes a fine and generous bonus for the Haydn *Nelson Mass.*

The Willcocks version of the *Gloria* uses comparatively small forces and, save for the occasional trace of preciosity, it is very stylish. It has excellent soloists and is very well recorded, though some might feel that the exaggerated consonants are tiresome. Ledger also offers the small-scale setting of the *Magnificat* and opts for boys' voices in the solos such as the beautiful duet, *Esurientes*; though the singers are taxed by ornamentation, the result has all the accustomed beauty of this choir's recordings. Excellent transfers.

Gloria in D, RV 589; Kyrie in G min., RV 587.
(M) *** DG 427 142-2. Regensburg Cathedral Ch., V. Capella Academica, Schneidt – BACH: *Motets.* ***

In the superb setting of the *Kyrie*, and the well-known *Gloria*, Schneidt with his fresh-toned Regensburg Choir (the celebrated Domspatzen, 'cathedral sparrows') brings out what may seem a surprising weight for an 'authentic' performance. Alongside the brilliant numbers in both these works, one can find music of Bach-like intensity. The use of semi-chorus for solo numbers is more questionable, but no one hearing these performances is likely to dismiss the music as trivial. The excellent 1977 recordings have been transferred to CD most effectively, with three favourite Bach motets now added as a bonus.

Juditha triumphans (oratorio) complete.
(M) *** Ph. 426 955-2 (2). Finnilä, Springer, Hamari, Ameling, Burmeister, Berlin R. Soloists Ch. & CO, Negri.

Issued as an adjunct to the Philips Vivaldi Edition, this excellent 1974 recording re-emerges vividly in its CD format. Described as a 'military' oratorio, *Juditha triumphans* demonstrates its martial bravado at the very start, as exhilarating a passage as you will find in the whole of Vivaldi. The vigorous choruses stand as cornerstones of commentary in a structure which, following convention, comes close to operatic form, with recitatives providing the narrative between formal *da capo* arias. Though Vivaldi fell into routine invention at times, the wonder is that so much of this music is so vividly alive, telling the story from the Apocrypha of Judith cutting off the head of the enemy general, Holofernes. As the cast-list will suggest, this Philips version rightly gives the castrato roles to women, with a generally stylish line-up of singers. It is a pity that the role of Judith is taken by one of the less interesting singers, Birgit Finnilä, and that Elly Ameling takes only a servant's role, though that is one which demands more brilliant technique than any. Overall, however, this is a considerable success.

OPERA

L'Olimpiade: highlights.
(B) **(*) Hung. White Label HRC 078 [id.]. Kováts, Takács, Zempleni, Miller, Horvath, Kaplan, Gati, Budapest Madrigal Ch., Hungarian State O, Szekeres.

In the inexpensive White Label series of Hungaroton recordings, a generous collection of highlights from Vivaldi's opera, *L'Olimpiade*, is well worth investigating. An early delight in this selection is the work's most attention-grabbing number, a choral version of what we know as *Spring* from *The Four Seasons.* Ferenc Szekeres' conducting of the Hungarian State Orchestra is too heavy by today's standards, now that we are attuned to period performance, but the singing of soloists and choir is good, and the recording is brightly focused, with clean directional effects.

Wagenseil, George (1715–77)

Harp concerto in G.
(B) *** DG 427 206-2. Zabaleta, Paul Kuentz CO – HANDEL: *Harp concerto*; MOZART: *Flute and harp concerto.* ***

Wagenseil's *Harp concerto* is a pleasant example of the *galant* style; the felicity of the writing in the first two movements is capped by a very jolly finale. Both performance and recording here can be commended and the remastering is fresh and clear.

Wagner, Richard (1813–83)

Siegfried idyll.
(B) *** Pickwick Dig. PCD 928. SCO, Jaime Laredo – DVOŘÁK: *String serenade* etc. ***
(M) *** Decca 430 247-2 (2) [id.]. VPO, Solti – MAHLER: *Symphony No. 9.* **
(M) **(*) EMI CMS7 63277-2 (2) [Ang. CDMB

63277]. Philh. O, Klemperer – MAHLER: *Symphony No. 9.* ***

A beautiful performance from Jaime Laredo and the Scottish Chamber Orchestra, warm and poised and ending serenely, yet moving to a strong central climax. The recording, made in Glasgow City Hall, has a pleasingly expansive ambience, yet textures are clear.

So full is the sound, recorded by John Culshaw in the Sofiensaal in 1965, that in Solti's performance of the *Siegfried idyll* in its original chamber scoring one is never conscious of any asceticism. The playing is similarly warm and committed; only in the central climax does one sense the need for a larger body of strings, yet the reading as a whole is so compelling as to confound criticism.

Klemperer also favours the original chamber-orchestra scoring and the Philharmonia players are very persuasive, especially in the score's gentler moments. However, the balance is forward and, although the sound is warm, the ear craves a greater breadth of string tone at the climax.

Siegfried idyll. Der fliegende Holländer: Overture. Lohengrin: Prelude to Act I. Die Meistersinger: Overture. (i) *Tannhäuser: Overture and Venusberg music.*

(M) *** Sony MPK 45701 [id.]. Columbia SO, Bruno Walter, (i) with Occidental College Ch.

Bruno Walter draws a lovingly warm account of the *Siegfried idyll* from his players, and the poise of the opening of the *Pilgrims' chorus* is equally full of quiet tension, while the reprise of this famous melody, before the introduction of the Venusberg section, is wonderfully gentle. With the central section thrillingly sensuous, the closing pages – the Occidental College Choir distantly balanced – bring a radiant hush. In digitally remastered form, the recording is most impressive. The detail in the fugato middle section of *Die Meistersinger* is characteristically affectionate, and all the threads are satisfyingly drawn together in the expansive closing pages. The *Lohengrin Prelude* is rather relaxed but beautifully controlled. With fine orchestral playing throughout, this stands among the most rewarding of all available compilations of Wagnerian orchestral excerpts.

(i) *Siegfried idyll;* (ii) *Der fliegende Holländer: Overture; Lohengrin:* (i) *Prelude to Act I;* (iii) *Bridal Chorus;* (i) *Die Meistersinger: Prelude;* (iv) *Tannhäuser: Overture;* (i) *Tristan und Isolde: Prelude and Liebestod;* (v) *Die Walküre: Ride of the Valkyries* (CD only: (vi) *Parsifal: Prelude and Good Friday music*).

(B) **(*) DG Compact Classics 413 849-2 (2); *413 849-4* [id.]. (i) BPO, Kubelik; (ii) Bayreuth Festival O, Boehm; (iii) Bayreuth Festival Ch., Pitz; (iv) cond. Gerdes; (v) cond. Karajan.

This Wagner Compact Classics concert centres on some fine performances made in 1963 by Kubelik and the Berlin Philharmonic, including the *Siegfried idyll.* Karajan contributes a lively *Ride of the Valkyries*; Gerdes's *Tannhäuser overture* comes from his (deleted) complete set; while the *Bridal chorus* from *Lohengrin* has a Bayreuth hallmark although in fact recorded in the studio. The sound is generally very good; only the opening *Flying Dutchman overture*, actually made at Bayreuth under Boehm, sounds slightly less refined than the rest of the concert. To fill out the pair of CDs, DG have added Jochum's inspirational account of the *Parsifal Good Friday* music, which was a famous early highlight of the stereo LP catalogue. The recording dates from 1958 but still sounds spacious and full in the present transfer, although the trumpets now sound penetratingly bright.

Siegfried idyll. Lohengrin: Preludes to Acts I & III. Die Meistersinger: Prelude to Act I. Parsifal: Prelude to Act I. Tristan und Isolde: Prelude and Liebestod.

(M) *** Ph. 420 886-2. Concg. O, Haitink.

The addition of Haitink's simple, unaffected reading of the *Siegfried idyll* to his 1975 collection of *Preludes* enhances the appeal of a particularly attractive concert. The rich acoustics of the Concertgebouw are surely ideal for *Die Meistersinger*, given a memorably spacious performance, and Haitink's restraint adds to the noble dignity of *Parsifal.* The *Lohengrin* excerpts are splendidly played. The digital remastering is almost entirely beneficial.

ORCHESTRAL EXCERPTS FROM THE OPERAS

Der fliegende Holländer: Overture. Lohengrin: Prelude to Act I. Die Meistersinger: Overture; Prelude to Act III; Dance of the Apprentices; Entry of the Masters. Tannhäuser: Overture. Tristan und Isolde: Prelude & Liebestod.

(M) EMI CDM7 64141-2 [id.]; *EG 764141-4.* Hallé O, Sir John Barbirolli.

Barbirolli's Hallé performances of the *Meistersinger* and *Tannhäuser Overtures* – recorded, like the rest of this programme, in the Free Trade Hall in 1959 – have a certain significance in the history of disc stereo. They were used by Pye-Nixa at their early public demonstrations, when this small label jumped the gun and, with American technical assistance, presented the first British stereo LPs to a record trade caught off-guard and unprepared to market them. The pressings were technically inadequate (legend has it that the channels were out of phase), but one remembers that the distorted stereo still carried a certain something that mono records could not supply. The present remastering demonstrates the excellence of the original recordings, produced by John Snashall and balanced by Robert Auger: the sound is certainly brilliant and, if it lacks something in opulence, is spacious and impressively balanced. The playing is full of characteristic electricity, and the Hallé strings produced some astonishingly good playing in the demanding high tessitura of the *Lohengrin Prelude* and the passionate fervour of the *Liebestod* from *Tristan*. Barbirolli's *Meistersinger overture* has a thrilling quickening of tension at its close, and the Apprentices dance with much vitality. Although recorded without an audience, all the performances give the impression of a live concert in their free-flowing adrenalin, and listening to the whole programme (74 minutes) is emotionally exhausting.

Der fliegende Holländer: Overture. Lohengrin: Prelude to Act III. Die Meistersinger: Preludes to Acts I & III. Tannhäuser: Overture and Venusberg music. Die Walküre: Ride of the Valkyries.
(M) ** EMI Dig. CD-EMX 2167; *TC-EMX 2167*. LPO, Mark Elder.

Direct, well-played but unmemorable performances, brightly but not particularly richly recorded. The *Ride of the Valkyries* comes off best, but it seems curious to include the *Venusberg music* from *Tannhäuser* without the chorus.

Overtures: Der fliegende Holländer; Die Meistersinger; Tannhäuser (original version). *Tristan und Isolde: Prelude and Liebestod.*
(M) **(*) Decca 430 448-2; *430 448-4* [id.]. Chicago SO, Solti.

A quite attractive collection of Wagner overtures, very well played. Except for the *Flying Dutchman overture*, these are newly made recordings, not taken from Solti's complete opera sets. So this is the self-contained *Tannhäuser overture* from the Dresden version, and the *Liebestod* comes in the purely orchestral version. Perhaps surprisingly, comparison between Solti in Chicago and Solti in Vienna shows him warmer in America. The CD has been digitally remastered and emphasizes the different recording balances: *Der fliegende Holländer* very brightly lit, *Die Meistersinger* (recorded in Illinois) richer and mellower. The Medinah Temple, Chicago, where the other items were recorded, seems here to produce somewhat variable results.

Der fliegende Holländer: Overture. Die Meistersinger: Overture. (i) *Tannhäuser: Overture and Venusberg music. Tristan: Prelude and Liebestod.*
(M) *** EMI CDM7 69019-2 [id.]; *EG 769019-4*. BPO, Karajan; (i) with German Op. Ch.

All the music here is played excellently, but the *Overture and Venusberg music* from *Tannhäuser* (Paris version, using chorus) and the *Prelude and Liebestod* from *Tristan* are superb. In the *Liebestod* the climactic culmination is overwhelming in its sentient power, while *Tannhäuser* has comparable spaciousness and grip. There is an urgency and edge to the *Flying Dutchman overture*, and *Die Meistersinger* has weight and dignity, but the last degree of tension is missing. Moreover the digitally remastered sound produces a touch of fierceness in the upper range of these pieces; the *Tannhäuser* and *Tristan* excerpts are fuller, though some of the original bloom has gone.

Der fliegende Holländer: Overture. Die Meistersinger: Overture. Tristan und Isolde: Preludes to Acts I & III; Liebestod. Die Walküre: Ride of the Valkyries.
(M) * DG Dig. 427 825-2; *427 825-4*. O de Paris, Daniel Barenboim.

Barenboim's collection does not lack intensity, but the snag is that the Orchestre de Paris – particularly the brass section, with its excessive vibrato – does not sound authentic and the recording acoustic is not helpful, failing to give the necessary resonance to the deeper brass sounds.

Götterdämmerung: Dawn and Siegfried's Rhine journey; Funeral march. Lohengrin: Preludes to Acts I & III. Die Meistersinger: Overture; Dance of the apprentices. Die Walküre: Ride of the Valkyries.
(B) *** CfP Dig. CD-CFP 9008; *TC-CFP 4412*. LPO, Rickenbacher.

Karl Anton Rickenbacher, formerly principal conductor with the BBC Scottish Symphony Orchestra, here makes an impressive recording début. He secures first-class playing from the LPO with the strings at their peak in the radiant opening of the *Lohengrin Prelude*. Rickenbacher's tempi are far from stoically Teutonic and he presses the music on convincingly, yet retains a sense of breadth. Some might feel his pacing of the *Die Meistersinger overture* is fractionally fast. The CD improves remarkably on the sound of the original LP: the sound is firmer and fuller, with a more expansive bass response; indeed the *Prelude to Act III* of *Lohengrin* makes a splendid demonstration recording; an exciting performance, particularly vividly projected.

Götterdämmerung: Dawn and Siegfried's Rhine journey; Siegfried's death and funeral march. Das Rheingold: Entry of the gods into Valhalla. Siegfried: Forest murmurs. Die Walküre: Ride of the Valkyries; Wotan's farewell and Magic fire music.
(M) **(*) Decca 417 775-2; *417 775-4*. Nat. SO of Washington, Dorati.
(M) **(*) Sony CD 44769 [MYK 36715]. Cleveland O, Szell.

Dorati's selection from *The Ring* is essentially dramatic. The *Ride of the Valkyries* comes off especially well, as do the three excerpts from *Götterdämmerung* (with a superbly played horn solo in *Siegfried's Rhine journey*). But in the final scene from *Die Walküre* the lack of richness and body of the string-tone that this orchestra can produce limits the effect of Dorati's eloquence.

Breathtaking orchestral playing and very exciting performances from Szell, with some really spectacular moments. The recording could ideally be more opulent, but it has body as well as brilliance, and there is no doubt about the adrenalin running here.

Lohengrin: Preludes to Acts I & III. Parsifal: Preludes to Acts I & III.
(M) *** EMI CMS7 63469-2 (2) [Ang. CDMB 63469]. BPO, Karajan – BRUCKNER: *Symphony No. 8*. ***

Karajan's Act I *Lohengrin Prelude* is graduated superbly; the *Parsifal* excerpts, too, are nobly shaped, yet here the tension is held at a slightly lower level. Nevertheless this is magnificent playing, and the 1975 recording has an attractively wide amplitude.

Parsifal: Prelude and Good Friday music.
(B) *** Sony MYK 44872 [id.]. Columbia SO, Bruno Walter – DVOŘÁK: *Symphony No. 8*. ***

A glorious account of the *Prelude* and *Good Friday music* from Walter, recorded in 1959, but with the glowingly rich recording never hinting at its age. The digital remastering is a superb achievement.

VOCAL MUSIC

Wesendonk Lieder: Der Engel; Stehe still; Im Treibhaus; Schmerzen; Träume. Götterdämmerung: Starke Scheite schichet mir dort. Siegfried: Ewig war ich. Tristan: Doch nun von Tristan?; Mild und leise.
(M) (***) EMI mono CDH7 63030-2 [id.]. Kirsten Flagstad, Philh. O, Furtwängler, Dobrowen.

Recorded in the late 1940s and early '50s, a year or so before Flagstad did *Tristan* complete with Furtwängler, these performances show her at her very peak, with the voice magnificent in power as well as beautiful and distinctive in every register. Not that there is as much bloom on the voice here as in the complete *Tristan* recording. The *Liebestod* (with rather heavy surface noise) may be less rapt and intense in this version with Dobrowen than with Furtwängler but is just as expansive. For the *Wesendonk Lieder* she shades the voice down very beautifully, but this is still monumental and noble rather than intimate Lieder-singing. Like other Références issues, this single CD gives no texts or even notes on the music.

OPERA

Der fliegende Holländer (complete).
(M) ** Decca 417 319-2 (2) [id.]. London, Rysanek, Tozzi, ROHCG Ch. & O, Dorati.
(M) ** EMI CMS7 63344-2 (3) [Ang. CDMC 63344]. Adam, Silja, Talvela, Kozub, Unger, Burmeister, BBC Ch., New Philh. O, Klemperer.

The outstanding quality of Dorati's set is the conducting and the general sense of teamwork. Both orchestra and chorus are on top form, the recording is splendidly clear and vivid and the reissue is offered on two mid-price CDs. George London's Dutchman is the drawback; the voice is comparatively ill-defined, the phrasing sometimes clumsy. Rysanek is not always the steadiest of Sentas but she sings with character, and the rest of the cast is vocally reliable.

Predictably Klemperer's reading is spacious in its tempi – involving a third disc in its CD reissue – and the drama hardly grips you by the throat. But the underlying intensity is irresistible. This could hardly be recommended as a first choice, but any committed admirer of the conductor should try to hear it. It is a pity that Anja Silja was chosen as Senta, even though she is not as squally in tone here as she can be. Otherwise a strong vocal cast, much beautiful playing (particularly from the wind soloists) and a lively if not particularly atmospheric recording, made to sound drier still in its CD format.

Der fliegende Holländer: highlights.
(M) *** EMI CDM7 63449-2 [id.]; *EG 763449-4* (from complete set, with Van Dam, Vejzovic, Moll, Hoffmann, Moser, Borris, V. State Op. Ch., BPO, cond. Karajan).
(M) **(*) Ph. Dig. 434 216-2; *434 216-4*. Estes, Balslev, Salminen, Schunk, Bayreuth Festival (1985) Ch. & O, Nelsson.

The selection here (67 minutes) offers the key numbers and includes the Dutchman's Act I monologue and the powerful closing scene. The remastered transfer is vivid but has plenty of atmosphere.

Here is another digital set of highlights on the Philips Laser Line label which has been issued without proper documentation, synopsis or translation. The 76-minute selection gives an admirable survey of the opera, which has here a more consistent cast than any other on record. The live recording at the 1985 Bayreuth Festival brings stage noises but alongside them comes marvellous music-making, with the chorus particularly fine.

Götterdämmerung (complete).

(M) **(*) RCA/Eurodisc Dig. GD 69007 (4) [69007-2-RG]. Altmeyer, Kollo, Salminen, Wenkel, Nocker, Nimsgern, Sharp, Popp, Leipzig R. Ch., Berlin R. Ch., Dresden State Op. Ch., Dresden State O, Janowski.

With sharply focused digital sound, Janowski's studio recording hits refreshingly hard, at least as much so as in the earlier *Ring* operas. Speeds rarely linger but, with some excellent casting – consistent with the earlier operas – the result is rarely lightweight. Jeannine Altmeyer as Brünnhilde rises to the challenges not so much in strength as in feeling and intensity, ecstatic in Act I, bitter in Act II, dedicated in the Immolation scene. Kollo is a fine heroic Siegfried, only occasionally raw-toned, and Salminen is a magnificent Hagen, with Nimsgern again an incisive Alberich on his brief appearances. Despite an indifferent Gunther and Gutrune and a wobbly if characterful Waltraute, the impression is of clean vocalization matched by finely disciplined and dedicated playing, all recorded in faithful studio sound with no sonic tricks. On the four CDs the background silence adds to the dramatic presence and overall clarity, which is strikingly enhanced, and this mid-priced reissue is well worth considering.

Lohengrin (complete).

(M) **(*) EMI CMS7 69314-2 (4) [Ang. CDMD 69314]. Kollo, Tomowa-Sintow, Nimsgern, Vejzovic, Ridderbusch, German Op. Ch., Berlin, BPO, Karajan.

Karajan, whose full-price DG recording of *Parsifal* was so naturally intense, failed in this earlier but related opera to capture comparable spiritual depth. So some of the big melodies sound a degree over-inflected and the result, though warm, expressive, dramatically powerful and with wide-ranging recording, misses an important dimension. Nor is much of the singing as pure-toned as it might be, with René Kollo too often straining and Tomowa-Sintow not always able to scale down in the necessary purity her big dramatic voice. The booklet offers the libretto without an English translation but with a synopsis instead.

Lohengrin: highlights.

(M) **(*) EMI CDM7 63453-2 [id.] *EG 763453-4* (from above set; cond. Karajan).

Another fairly generous EMI sampler (69 minutes) of a set which cannot be counted among Karajan's most successful Wagner recordings. The sound is vivid, with strong forward projection.

Die Meistersinger von Nürnberg (complete).

(M) **(*) Ph. 432 573-2 (4) [id.]. Ridderbusch, Bode, Sotin, Hirte, Cox, Stricker, (1974) Bayreuth Festival Ch. & O, Varviso.

(M) (***) EMI mono CHS7 63500-2 (4) [Ang. CDHD 63500]. Schwarzkopf, Edelmann, Kunz, Hopf, Unger, Bayreuth Festival Ch. & O, Karajan.

(M) ** BMG/RCA GD 69008 (4) [Eurodisc 69008-2-RG]. Wiener, Hotter, Watson, Thomas, Thaw, Hoppe, Kusche, Metternich, Bav. State Op. Ch., Bav. State O, Keilberth.

Die Meistersinger is an opera which presents serious problems for an engineer intent on recording it at a live performance. Not only do the big crowd scenes, with their plentiful movement, bring obtrusive stage noises; the sheer length of the work means that, by Act III, even the most stalwart singer is flagging. It follows that the Bayreuth performance, recorded during the Festival of 1974, is flawed; but the Swiss conductor Silvio Varviso still proves the most persuasive Wagnerian, one who inspires the authentic ebb and flow of tension, who builds up Wagner's scenes concentratedly over the longest span and who revels in the lyricism and textural beauty of the score. It is not a lightweight reading and, with one exception, the singing is very enjoyable indeed, with Karl Ridderbusch a firmly resonant Sachs and the other Masters, headed by Klaus Hirte as Beckmesser and Hans Sotin as Pogner, really singing their parts. Jean Cox is a strenuous Walther, understandably falling short towards the end; Hannelore Bode as Eva brings the one serious disappointment but she is firmer here than on Solti's later (and full-price) set. For all the variability, the recording, retaining its atmosphere in the CD transfer, gives enjoyment, even if the stage noises are the more noticeable.

Recorded live at the 1951 Bayreuth Festival, Karajan's EMI version has never quite been matched since for its involving intensity. The mono sound may be thin and the stage noises often distracting, but, with clean CD transfers, the sense of being present at a great event is irresistible, with the great emotional moments –

both between Eva and Walther and, even more strikingly, between Eva and Sachs – bringing a gulp in the throat. The young Elisabeth Schwarzkopf makes the most radiant Eva, singing her Act III solo *O Sachs, mein Freund!* with touching ardour before beginning the Quintet with flawless legato. Hans Hopf is here less gritty than in his other recordings, an attractive hero; while Otto Edelmann makes a superb Sachs, firm and virile, the more moving for not sounding old. There are inconsistencies among the others but, in a performance of such electricity generated by the conductor in his early prime, they are of minimal importance. The four mid-price CDs are generously indexed and come with a libretto but no translation. EMI should have indicated the index points not just in the libretto, but in the English synopsis as well.

The Keilberth set was recorded at the very first performance given in the rebuilt Opera House in Munich in November 1963. That brings inevitable flaws, but the voices are generally bright and forward, and the atmosphere is of a great occasion. The team of masters includes such distinguished singers as Hans Hotter as Pogner and Josef Metternich as Kottner; but Otto Wiener in the central role of Hans Sachs is too unsteady to be acceptable on record. Jess Thomas makes a ringing and accurate if hardly subtle Walther and Claire Watson a fresh-toned but uncharacterful Eva. Keilberth paces well but tends to bring out the rhythmic squareness. Like Karajan's inspired Bayreuth recording of 1951, this comes on four mid-price CDs, but has the advantage of stereo sound.

Die Meistersinger: highlights.
(M) **(*) EMI CDM7 63455-2; *EG 763455-4* (from complete set, with Adam, Evans, Kelemen, Ridderbusch, Kollo, Schreier, Donath, Hess, Leipzig R. Ch., Dresden State Op. Ch. & State O, Karajan).

Many will prefer to have a sampler rather than investing in the complete Karajan stereo set, which is let down by the casting of Theo Adam as Sachs. The selection runs to nearly 68 minutes.

Das Rheingold (complete).
(M) **(*) RCA/Eurodisc Dig. GD 69004 (2) [69004-2-RG]. Adam, Nimsgern, Stryczek, Schreier, Bracht, Salminen, Vogel, Buchner, Minton, Popp, Priew, Schwarz, Dresden State O, Janowski.

In Marek Janowski's digital recording, the studio sound has the voices close and vivid, with the orchestra rather in the background. Donner's hammer-blow in the Eurodisc set comes up with only a very ordinary 'ping' on an anvil, and the grandeur of the moment is missing. Theo Adam as Wotan has his grittiness of tone exaggerated here, but otherwise it is a fine set, consistently well cast, including Peter Schreier, Matti Salminen, Yvonne Minton and Lucia Popp, as well as East German singers of high calibre. Complete on two mid-priced CDs, it is certainly good value.

The Rheingold (complete, in English).
(M) **(*) EMI CMS7 64110-2 (3). Bailey, Hammond-Stroud, Pring, Belcourt, Attfield, Collins, McDonnall, Lloyd, Grant, English Nat. Op. O, Goodall.

Goodall's slow tempi in *Rheingold* bring an opening section where the temperature is low, reflecting hardly at all the tensions of a live performance, even though this was taken from a series of Coliseum presentations. The recording too, admirably clean and refined, is less atmospheric than *Siegfried*, the first of the series to be recorded. Nevertheless the momentum of Wagner gradually builds up so that, by the final scenes, both the overall teamwork and the individual contributions of such singers as Norman Bailey, Derek Hammond-Stroud and Clifford Grant come together impressively. Hammond-Stroud's powerful representation of Alberich culminates in a superb account of the curse. The spectacular orchestral effects (with the horns sounding glorious) are vividly caught by the engineers and impressively transferred to CD, even if balances (inevitably) are sometimes less than ideal.

Rienzi (complete).
(M) ** EMI CMS7 63980-2 (3) [id.]. Kollo, Wennberg, Martin, Adam, Hillebrand, Vogel, Schreier, Leipzig R. Ch., Dresden State Op. Ch., Dresden State O, Hollreiser.

It is sad that the flaws in this ambitious opera prevent the unwieldy piece from having its full dramatic impact. This recording is not quite complete, but the cuts are unimportant and most of the set numbers make plain the youthful, uncritical exuberance of the ambitious composer. The accompanied recitatives are less inspired, and no one could count the Paris-stye ballet music consistent with the rest, delightful and sparkling though it is. Except in the recitative, Heinrich Hollreiser's direction is strong and purposeful, but much of the singing is disappointing. René Kollo at least sounds heroic, but the two women principals are poor. Janis Martin in the breeches role of Adriano produces tone that does not record very sweetly, while Siv Wennberg as the heroine, Rienzi's sister, slides most unpleasantly between notes in the florid passages. Despite good recording, this can only be regarded as a stop-gap.

Der Ring des Nibelungen (complete).

❀ (M) *** Decca 414 100-2 (15) [id.]. Nilsson, Windgassen, Flagstad, Fischer-Dieskau, Hotter, London, Ludwig, Neidlinger, Frick, Svanholm, Stoltze, Böhme, Hoffgen, Sutherland, Crespin, King, Watson, Ch. & VPO, Solti.

(M) *** DG 435 211-2 (15) [id.]. Veasey, Fischer-Dieskau, Stolze, Kelemen, Dernesch, Dominguez, Jess Thomas, Stewart, Crespin, Janowitz, Vickers, Talvela, Brilioth, Ludwig, Ridderbusch, BPO, Karajan.

(M) *** Ph. 420 325-2 (14) [id.]. Nilsson, Windgassen, Neidlinger, Adam, Rysanek, King, Nienstedt, Esser, Talvela, Böhme, Silja, Dernesch, Stewart, Hoeffgen, Bayreuth Festival (1967) Ch. & O, Boehm.

(M) *** BMG/RCA Dig. GD 69003 (14) [69003-2-RG]. Altmeyer, Kollo, Adam, Schreier, Nimsgern, Vogel, Minton, Wenkel, Salminen, Popp, Jerusalem, J. Norman, Moll, Studer, Leipzig R. Ch., Dresden State Op. Ch. & O, Janowski.

(M) (***) EMI mono CZS7 67123-2 (13) [Ang. CDZM 67123]. Suthaus, Mödl, Frantz, Patzak, Neidlinger, Windgassen, Konetzni, Streich, Jurinac, Frick, RAI Ch. & Rome SO, Furtwängler.

The Decca set – one of the great achievements of the gramophone – has at last been reissued on CD in a special edition of 15 discs at medium price, a bargain of bargains for those who have not already invested in the separate issues. Solti's was the first recorded *Ring* cycle to be issued, and it has never been surpassed. Whether in performance or in vividness of sound, it continues to set standards three decades after Decca's great project was completed. That project was the brainchild of the Decca recording producer of the time, John Culshaw, whose concept was to portray in sound as vividly as possible the full impact of Wagner's stage directions, whether they related to what was possible in the theatre or not. To that degree, sound recording was made to transcend the opera house. First recorded was *Rheingold*, which caused a sensation when it was issued, not least because of the closing scenes with Donner's great hammer-blow and the rainbow-bridge, which remain demonstration passages even now, superbly transferred to CD. As for the casting, that too has never been surpassed, certainly not by latter-day studio recordings. Even the role of the Woodbird in *Siegfried* is uniquely cast, with the young Joan Sutherland outshining all rivals. Nilsson and Windgassen as Brünnhilde and Siegfried may not be as spontaneous-sounding in this studio performance as in their live, Bayreuth recording for Boehm, but the freshness and power are even greater. Solti's remains the most electrifying account of the tetralogy on disc, sharply focused if not always as warmly expressive as some. Solti himself developed in the process of making the recording, and *Götterdämmerung* represents a peak of achievement for him, commanding and magnificent. Though CD occasionally reveals bumps and bangs inaudible on the original LPs, this is a historic set that remains as central today as when it first appeared.

Karajan's recording of *The Ring* followed close on the heels of Solti's for Decca, providing a good alternative studio version which equally stands the test of time. The manner is smoother, the speeds generally broader, yet the tension and concentration of the performances are maintained more consistently than in most modern studio recordings. Though the recordings were linked with stage productions in Salzburg and at the Met. in New York, they preceded the stagings and bring a broadly contemplative rather than a searingly dramatic view of Wagner. Casting is generally good, with few failures, again generally better than in modern studio recordings. Casting is not quite consistent between the operas, with Régine Crespin as Brünnhilde in *Walküre*, but Helga Dernesch at her very peak in the last two operas. The casting of Siegfried is changed between *Siegfried* and *Götterdäammerung*, from Jess Thomas, clear and reliable, to Helge Brilioth, just as strong but sweeter of tone. The original CD transfers are used without change for this mid-price compilation. The recording, pleasantly reverberant, is not as immediate or involving as Solti's Decca, with fewer dramatic sound effects.

Anyone who prefers the idea of a live recording of the *Ring* cycle can be warmly recommended to Boehm's fine set, more immediately involving than any. Recorded at the 1967 Bayreuth Festival, it captures the unique atmosphere and acoustic of the Festspielhaus very vividly. Birgit Nilsson as Brünnhilde and Wolfgang Windgassen as Siegfried are both a degree more volatile and passionate than they were in the Solti cycle, recorded earlier for Decca, with Nilsson at her most incandescent in the final Immolation scene, triumphant at the end of her long performance. Gustav Neidlinger as Alberich is also superb, as he was too in the Solti set; and the only major reservation concerns the Wotan of Theo Adam, in a performance searchingly intense and finely detailed but often unsteady of tone even at that period. Boehm's preference for urgent speeds, never letting the music sag, makes this an exciting experience, and in *Rheingold* it brings the practical advantage that the Vorabend comes on only two CDs instead of three, bringing the total for the set to 14 instead of 15 discs. The sound, only occasionally constricted, has been vividly transferred.

Dedication and consistency are the mark of the Eurodisc *Ring*, a studio recording made with German thoroughness by the East German record company, VEB. Originally packaged cumbersomely by Eurodisc on 18 CDs, RCA here reissue it on 14 mid-price discs, to make it much more attractive. Voices tend to be balanced well forward of the orchestra, but the digital sound is full and clear to have one concentrating on the words, helped by Janowski's direct approach to the score. Overall this is a good deal more rewarding than many of the individual sets that have been issued at full price over the last five years.

When in 1972 EMI first transferred the Italian Radio tapes of Furtwängler's studio performances of 1953, the sound was disagreeably harsh, making sustained listening unpleasant. In this digital transfer, the boxiness of the studio sound and the closeness of the voices still take away some of the unique Furtwängler glow in Wagner, but the sound is acceptable and actually benefits in some ways from extra clarity. Each Act was performed on a separate day, giving the advantage of continuous performance but with closer preparation than would otherwise have been possible. Furtwängler gives each opera a commanding sense of unity, musically and dramatically, with hand-picked casts including Martha Mödl as a formidable Brünnhilde, Ferdinand Frantz a firm-voiced Wotan and Ludwig Suthaus (Tristan in Furtwängler's recording) a reliable Siegfried. In smaller roles you have stars like Wolfgang Windgassen, Julius Patzak, Rita Streich, Sena Jurinac and Gottlob Frick.

The Ring 'Great scenes': Das Rheingold: Entry of the Gods into Valhalla. Die Walküre: Ride of the Valkyries; Magic fire music. Siegfried: Forging scene; Forest murmurs. Götterdämmerung: Siegfried's funeral march; Brünnhilde's immolation scene.
(M) *** Decca 421 313-2. Nilsson, Windgassen, Hotter, Stolzel, VPO, Solti.

These excerpts are often quite extended – the *Entry of the Gods into Valhalla* offers some 10 minutes of music, and the *Forest murmurs* from *Siegfried* starts well before the orchestral interlude. Only *Siegfried's funeral march* is in any sense a 'bleeding chunk' which has to be faded at the end; and the disc closes with 20 minutes of Brünnhilde's Immolation scene.

Der Ring: excerpts: *Das Rheingold: Zur Burg führt die Brucke* (scene iv). *Die Walküre: Ein Schwert verhiess mir der Vater; Ride of the Valkyries; Wotan's farewell and Magic fire music. Siegfried: Notung!; Brünnhilde's awakening. Götterdämmerung: Brünnhilde, heilige Braut! Siegfried's death and Funeral music.*
(B) *** DG 429 168-2; *429 168-4* (from complete recording; cond. Karajan).

The task of selecting highlights to fit on a single disc, taken from the whole of the *Ring* cycle, is an impossible one. But the DG producer of this record has managed to assemble 70 minutes of key items, mostly nicely tailored, with quick fades. The one miscalculation was to end with *Siegfried's funeral march* from *Götterdämmerung*, which leaves the listener suspended; it would have been a simple matter to add the brief orchestral postlude which ends the opera. Nevertheless there is much to enjoy, and this makes a genuine sampler of Karajan's approach to the *Ring* – even the *Ride of the Valkyries* is comparatively refined. The late-1960s sound is excellent.

Siegfried (complete).
(M) **(*) RCA/Eurodisc Dig. GD 69006 (4) [69006-2-RG]. Kollo, Altmeyer, Adam, Schreier, Nimsgern, Wenkel, Salminen, Sharp, Dresden State O, Janowski.

With Janowski, direct and straight in his approach and securing superb playing from the Dresdeners, the RCA/Eurodisc set lacks a degree of dramatic tension, for he does not always build the climaxes cumulatively. Thus the final scene of Act II just scurries to a close, with Siegfried in pursuit of a rather shrill woodbird in Norma Sharp. The singing is generally first rate, with Kollo a fine Siegfried, less strained than he has sometimes been, and Peter Schreier a superb Mime, using Lieder-like qualities in detailed characterization. Siegmund Nimsgern is a less characterful Alberich, but the voice is excellent; and Theo Adam concludes his portrayal of Wotan/Wanderer with his finest performance of the series. The relative lightness of Jeannine Altmeyer's Brünnhilde comes out in the final love-duet more strikingly than in *Walküre.* Nevertheless the tenderness and femininity are most affecting as at the entry of the idyll motif, where Janowski in his dedicated simplicity is also at his most compelling. Clear, beautifully balanced digital sound, with voices and instruments firmly placed.

Siegfried (complete, in English).
(M) *** EMI CMS7 63595-2 (4). Remedios, Hunter, Bailey, Dempsey, Hammond-Stroud, Grant, Collins, London, Sadler's Wells Op. O, Goodall.

Compounded from three live performances at the Coliseum, this magnificent set gives a superb sense of dramatic realism. More tellingly than in almost any other Wagner opera recording, Goodall's spacious direction here conveys the genuine dramatic crunch that gives the experience of hearing Wagner in the opera house its unique power, its overwhelming force. In the *Prelude* there are intrusive audience noises, and towards the end the Sadler's Wells violins have one or two shaky moments; but this is unmistakably a great interpretation caught on the wing. Remedios, more than any rival on record, conveys not only heroic strength but clear-ringing youthfulness, caressing the ear as well as exciting it. Norman Bailey makes a magnificently noble Wanderer, steady of tone, and Gregory Dempsey is a characterful Mime, even if his deliberate whining tone is not well caught on record. The sound is superbly realistic, even making no allowances for the conditions. Lovers of opera in English should grasp the opportunity of hearing this unique set. The transfer is remarkably vivid and detailed, kind to the voices and with a natural presence so that the words are clear, yet there is no edge or exaggeration of consonants. This was the first of Goodall's *Ring* cycle to be transferred to CD and the orchestral recording is drier than in the others of the series: the brass sound brassier, less rounded than in *The Twilight of the Gods* for instance, but not less effective. The strings, however, have plenty of body and bloom.

Tristan und Isolde (complete).
(M) *** EMI CMS7 69319-2 (4) [Ang. CDMD 69319]. Vickers, Dernesch, Ludwig, Berry, Ridderbusch, German Op. Ch., Berlin, BPO, Karajan.

Karajan's is a sensual performance of Wagner's masterpiece, caressingly beautiful and with superbly refined playing from the Berlin Philharmonic. He is helped by a recording (not ideally balanced, but warmly atmospheric) which copes with an enormous dynamic range. Dernesch as Isolde is seductively feminine, not as noble as Flagstad, not as tough and unflinching as Nilsson; but the human quality makes this account if anything more moving still, helped by glorious tone-colour through every range. Jon Vickers matches her, in what is arguably his finest performance on record, allowing himself true pianissimo shading. The rest of the cast is excellent too. Though CD brings out more clearly the occasional oddities of balance, the 1972 sound has plenty of body, making this an excellent first choice, with inspired conducting and the most satisfactory cast of all.

Tristan und Isolde (slightly abridged).
(M) (***) EMI mono CHS7 64037-2 (3).
Melchior, Flagstad, Herbert Janssen, Margarete Klose/Sabine Kalter, Sven Nilsson/Emanuel List, ROHCG Ch., LPO, Beecham/Reiner.

What was originally promised as a complete recording of Beecham conducting *Tristan* at Covent Garden in the Coronation season of 1937 proved to be a mixture of recordings made, not only then, but in the previous year as well. In both recordings Melchior and Flagstad take the title-roles, with Herbert Janssen as Kurwenal, three legendary singers in those roles, but the parts of King Mark and Brangane were sung by different singers in each year – and, above all, Fritz Reiner was the conductor in the 1936 recordings. It says much that the end result, a jig-saw of pieces lovingly put together by Keith Hardwick, is so consistent. It is astonishing to find that the warmly expansive account of Act I is the work of Reiner, while it is Beecham who is responsible for the urgent view of Act II with its great love duet – part of it cut following the manner of the day. Act III is divided between Beecham in the first part, Reiner in the second. Whatever the inconsistencies, the result is a thrilling experience, with Flagstad fresher and even more incisive than in her studio recording with Furtwängler of 15 years later, and with Melchior a passionate vocal actor, not just the possessor of the most freely ringing of all Heldentenor voices. Though the orchestral sound is mostly dim and distant, the voices come over vividly and it is easy to forget the limitations. Each Act – with cuts in Act III as well as in Act II – is fitted conveniently and economically on a single disc.

Die Walküre (complete).
(M) (***) EMI mono CHS7 63045-2 (3) [Ang. CHS 63045]. Mödl, Rysanek, Frantz, Suthaus, Klose, Frick, VPO, Furtwängler.
(M) *** RCA/Eurodisc Dig. GD 69005 (4) [69005-2-RG]. Altmeyer, Norman, Minton, Jerusalem, Adam, Moll, Dresden State O, Janowski.
(M) ** Decca 430 391-2 (3) [id.]. Vickers, Brouwenstijn, Ward, Gorr, Nilsson, London, LSO, Leinsdorf.

In this superb reissue on three mid-price CDs Furtwängler's 1954 recording of *Die Walküre*, made in Vienna only months before the conductor's death, stands as the keenest possible competitor to the latest digitally recorded versions – in most ways outshining them. Except for those totally allergic to mono sound even as well balanced as this, the EMI Références set could well be the answer as a first choice, when not only Furtwängler but an excellent cast and the Vienna Philharmonic in radiant form match any of their successors. Even more than in *Tristan*, Ludwig Suthaus proves a satisfyingly clear-toned Heldentenor, never strained, with the lyricism of *Wintersturme* superbly sustained. Neither Léonie Rysanek as Sieglinde nor Martha Mödl as Brünnhilde is ideally steady, but the intensity and involvement of each is irresistible, classic performances both, with detail finely touched in and well contrasted with each other. Similarly, the mezzo of Margarete Klose may not be very beautiful, but the projection of words and the fire-eating character match the conductor's intensity. Rather in contrast with the women soloists, both bass and baritone are satisfyingly firm and beautiful. Gottlob Frick is as near an ideal Hunding as one will find, sinister but with the right streak of arrogant sexuality; while the Wotan of Ferdinand Frantz may not be as deeply perceptive as some, but to hear the sweep of Wagner's melodic lines so gloriously sung is a rare joy. The 1954 sound is amazingly full and vivid, with voices cleanly balanced against the inspired orchestra. Far more than Furtwängler's live recording of *The Ring* from Rome, this *Walküre* (the first of a *Ring* project which sadly went no further) is a superb memorial to his Wagnerian mastery. The only snag of the set is that, to fit the whole piece on to only three CDs, breaks between discs come in mid-Act.

Janowski's direct approach matches the relative dryness of the acoustic, with voices fixed well forward of the orchestra – but not aggressively so. That balance allows full presence for the singing from a satisfyingly consistent cast. Jessye Norman might not seem an obvious choice for Sieglinde, but the sound is glorious, the expression intense and detailed, making her a superb match for the fine, if rather less imaginative Siegmund of Siegfried Jerusalem. The one snag with so commanding a Sieglinde is that she overtops the Brünnhilde of Jeannine Altmeyer who, more than usual, conveys a measure of feminine vulnerability in the leading Valkyrie even in her godhead days. Miss Altmeyer may be slightly overparted, but the beauty and frequent sensuousness of her singing are the more telling, next to the gritty Wotan of Theo Adam. With its slow vibrato under pressure, his is rarely a pleasing voice, but the clarity of the recording makes it a specific, never a woolly sound, so that the illumination of the narrative is consistent and intense. Kurt Moll is a gloriously firm Hunding, and Yvonne Minton a searingly effective Fricka. On CD, the drama and urgency of the recording have even greater bite; and, as with the others in this series, the mid-priced reissue (on four CDs instead of the original five) makes this set far more competitive.

The early Decca set of *Die Walküre* hardly matches what Solti was later to achieve. The LSO playing is first class, Leinsdorf is vigorous and efficient, and the result is always exciting; but there is a monotony about his continual hard driving, and this affects the singers. Vickers misses the point of the spring greeting in a strangely ham-fisted piece of singing. Fortunately this is very much an exception with him: most of the performance is superbly rich and heroic. Gré Brouwenstijn is even finer as Sieglinde; her voice is pure-sounding and radiant. David Ward is a resonant Hunding, Rita Gorr a strong Fricka. Nilsson is predictably excellent as Brünnhilde but not impeccable. It is the Wotan of George London that is the most serious blot on the set: the voice sounds coarse-grained and, since the recording is otherwise of Decca's best vintage quality, one can hardly blame the technicians.

The Valkyrie (complete; in English).
(M) *** EMI CMS7 63918-2 (4). Hunter, Remedios, Curphey, Bailey, Grant, Howard, E. Nat. Op. Ch. & O, Goodall.

Like *Siegfried*, this was recorded live at the Coliseum and, with minor reservations, it fills the bill splendidly for those who want to enjoy the *Ring* cycle in English. With the voices balanced a little more closely than in *Siegfried*, the words of Andrew Porter's translation are a degree clearer but the atmosphere is less vivid. The glory of the performance lies not just in Goodall's spacious direction but in the magnificent Wotan of Norman Bailey, noble in the broadest span but very human in his illumination of detail. Rita Hunter sings nobly too, and though she is not as commanding as Nilsson in the Solti cycle she is often more lyrically tender. Alberto Remedios as Siegmund is more taxed than he was as Siegfried in the later opera (lower tessituras are not quite so comfortable for him) but his sweetly ringing top register is superb. If others, such as Ann Howard as Fricka, are not always treated kindly by the microphone, the total dramatic compulsion is irresistible. The CD transfer increases the sense of presence and at the same time confirms the relative lack of sumptuousness.

Die Walküre, Act I (complete).
(M) (***) EMI mono CDH7 61020-2 [id.]. Lehmann, Melchior, List, VPO, Bruno Walter.
(M) **(*) Decca 425 963-2 [id.]. Flagstad, Svanholm, Van Mill, VPO, Knappertsbusch.

Though in the days of 78-r.p.m. discs the music had to be recorded in short takes of under five minutes, one is consistently gripped by the continuity and sustained lines of Walter's reading, and by the intensity and beauty of the playing of the Vienna Philharmonic. Lotte Lehmann's portrait of Sieglinde, arguably her finest role, has a depth and beauty never surpassed since, and Lauritz Melchior's heroic Siegmund brings singing of a scale and variety – not to mention beauty – that no Heldentenor today begins to match. Emanuel List as Hunding is satisfactory enough, but his achievement at least has latterly been surpassed.

Flagstad may not have been ideally cast as Sieglinde, but the command of her singing with its unfailing richness, even after her official retirement, crowns a strong and dramatic performance, with Svanholm and Van Mill singing cleanly. The early stereo still sounds vivid.

Die Walküre: excerpts: Act II: *Kehrte der Vater nur Heim!;* Act III: *Schützt mich helft in höchster Not.*
(M) (**) Standing Room Only SRO 833-2. Nilsson, Rysanek, King, Bayreuth Festival O, Boehm – R. STRAUSS: *Elektra* etc. (***)

These *Walküre* excerpts were recorded live at the 1965 Bayreuth Festival, not as refined in sound or as performances as on the complete Boehm Philips recording. With such a cast they make a valuable fill-up for the exceptionally generous Strauss coupling from Standing Room Only.

Die Walküre: Act III (complete).
(M) *** Decca 425 986-2 [id.]. Flagstad, Edelmann, Schech, VPO, Solti.

This recording was made in 1957. Flagstad came out of retirement to make it, and Decca put us eternally in their debt for urging her to do so. She sings radiantly. This great artist seemed to have acquired an extra wisdom and an extra maturity in interpretation in her period away from the stage. The meticulousness needed in the recording studio obviously brought out all her finest qualities, and there is no more than a touch of hardness on some of the top notes to show that the voice was no longer as young as it had been. Edelmann is not the ideal Wotan but he has a particularly well-focused voice, and when he sings straight, without sliding up or sitting under the note, the result is superb and he is never wobbly. But it is Solti's conducting that prevents any slight blemishes from mattering. His rethinking of the score means that time and time again, at particularly dramatic points, one finds that the increased excitement engendered is merely the result of a literal following of all Wagner's markings. Not surprisingly, the recording too is remarkably vivid, anticipating the excellence of the great *Ring* project which was to follow.

Die Walküre: Act III: *Wotan's farewell.*
(M) **(*) EMI CMS7 63835-2 (2) [Ang. CDMB 63835]. Norman Bailey, New Philh. O, Klemperer – BRUCKNER: *Symphony No. 8* **; HINDEMITH: *Nobilissima visione*: suite. (**)

In places in *Wotan's farewell* there is almost a hint of self-parody in Klemperer's reading with its measured tempi and gruff manner, despite superb singing from Norman Bailey. Nevertheless, with thrilling orchestral playing and splendid 1970 recording, this remains very dramatic indeed.

VOCAL COLLECTIONS

'Wagner singing on record': Excerpts from: (i) *Der fliegende Holländer;* (ii) *Götterdämmerung;* (iii) *Lohengrin;* (iv) *Die Meistersinger von Nürnberg;* (v) *Parsifal;* (vi) *Das Rheingold;* (vii) *Siegfried;* (viii) *Tannhäuser;* (ix) *Tristan und Isolde;* (x) *Die Walküre.*
(M) EMI mono/stereo CMS7 640082 (4) [id.]. (i) Hermann, Nissen, Endrèze, Fuchs, Beckmann, Rethberg, Nilsson, Hotter; (ii) Austral, Widdop, List, Weber, Janssen, Lawrence; (iii) Rethberg, Pertil, Singher, Lawrence, Spani, Lehmann, Lemnitz, Klose, Wittrisch, Rosavaenge; (iv) Schorr, Thill, Martinelli, Bockelmann, Parr, Williams, Ralf, Lemnitz; (v) Leider, Kipnitz, Wolff; (vi) Schorr; (vii) Nissen, Olszewska, Schipper, Leider, Laubenthal, Lubin; (viii) Müller, Lorenz, Janssen, Hüsch, Flagstad; (ix) Leider, Marherr, Larsen-Todsen, Helm, Melchior, Seinemeyer, Lorenz; (x) Lawrence, Journet, Bockelmann.

This collection, compiled in Paris as '*Les Introuvables du Chant Wagnerien*', contains an amazing array of recordings made in the later years of 78-r.p.m. recording, mostly between 1927 and 1940. In 49 items, many of them substantial, the collection consistently demonstrates the reliability of the Wagner singing at that period, the ability of singers in every register to produce firm, well-focused tone of a kind too rare today. Some of the most interesting items are those in translation from French sources, with Germaine Lubin as Isolde and Brünnhilde and with Marcel Journet as Wotan, both lyrical and clean-cut. The ill-starred Marjorie Lawrence, a great favourite in France, is also represented by recordings in French, including Brünnhilde's Immolation scene from *Götterdämmerung.* Not only are such celebrated Wagnerians as Lauritz Melchior, Friedrich Schorr, Frida Leider, Lotte Lehmann and Max Lorenz very well represented, but also singers one might not expect, including the Lieder specialist, Gerhard Husch, as Wolfram in *Tannhäuser* and Aureliano Pertile singing in Italian as *Lohengrin*. Significantly, Meta Seinemeyer, an enchanting soprano who died tragically young, here gives lyric sweetness to the dramatic roles of Brünnhilde and Isolde; and among the baritones and basses there is none of the roughness or ill-focus that marks so much latter-day Wagner singing. It is a pity that British-based singers are poorly represented, but the Prologue duet from *Götterdämmerung* brings one of the most impressive items, sung by Florence Austral and Walter Widdop. First-rate transfers and good documentation.

Arias: *Götterdämmerung:* (i) *Zu neuen Taten; Starke Scheite schichter mire dort. Lohengrin: Euch Lüften mein Klagen. Parsifal:* (i) *Ich sah' das King. Tristan: Mild und leise. Die Walküre: Du bist der Lenz; Ho-jo-ho!.*

(M) (***) RCA mono GD 87915 [87915-2-RG]. Flagstad, (i) with Melchior, San Francisco Op. O, or Victor SO (both cond. Edwin McArthur); Phd. O, Ormandy

Recorded for RCA in America between 1935 and 1940, this first generation of Wagner recordings by Flagstad reveals the voice at its noblest and freshest, the more exposed in consistently close balance on the 78s of the period. It is a pity that only two of the shortest items – from *Lohengrin* and *Walküre* – have Ormandy conducting. Most of the rest are conducted by Flagstad's protégé, Edwin McArthur, including the two longest, the big duet for Parsifal and Kundry and Brünnhilde's Immolation scene. Yet the grandeur of Flagstad's singing is never in doubt, the commanding sureness, and, though the orchestral sound is unflatteringly dry, the voice is gloriously caught in clean transfers.

'Wagner gala': Lohengrin: Prelude to Act III. Rienzi: Overture. Excerpts from: *Der fliegende Holländer; Lohengrin; Die Meistersinger; Rienzi; Tannhäuser; Tristan und Isolde; Die Walküre.*

(M) **(*) Decca 421 877-2; *421 877-4*. London; G. Jones; J. King; Flagstad; Krause; Nilsson; VPO, Solti or Stein.

A generous and vivid concert (74 minutes) but hardly a gala occasion. It was a happy idea to open the programme with James King's appealing account of Rienzi's *Prayer*, based on the gorgeous lyrical tune which makes us all remember the *Overture*. He also sings Walther's *Prize song* from *Die Meistersinger* nobly. Other highlights include Kirsten Flagstad in *Die Männer Sippe* from *Die Walküre* and *Elsa's dream* from *Lohengrin* and Birgit Nilsson's comparatively restrained, early 1960s account of the *Tristan Liebestod*, spaciously recorded with Knappertsbusch, before she undertook the complete set.

Choruses from: *Der fliegende Holländer; Götterdämmerung; Lohengrin; Die Meistersinger; Parsifal; Tannhäuser.*

(B) **(*) DG 429 169-2 [id.]. Elisabeth Schärtel, Josef Greindl, Bayreuth Festival Ch. & O, Wilhelm Pitz.

This 1958 collection was recommended in our very first hardback *Stereo Record Guide* and it still sounds remarkably fresh. The female voices are not quite as impressive as the men's, but the tenors sing lustily and usually with fine, crisp discipline under their famous Bayreuth chorus master. Even though this was very early stereo, the spread and depth of the sound is remarkably realistic and in the *Parsifal* excerpt the distanced perspective for the female voices is expertly managed. The singing has ample conviction throughout and it is good to have such a vivid *Grand march* scene from *Tannhäuser*, with brilliant trumpets and an exhilarating sense of joy. The soloists (who have not very much to sing) are not overwhelmingly good. Josef Greindl has a somewhat heavy vibrato in his *Hoi-ho!* piece, but he has the right sort of voice. The remastering has added to the projection and sharpness of choral focus and has lost very little of the original atmosphere.

Choruses from: *Der fliegende Holländer; Lohengrin; Die Meistersinger; Parsifal; Tannhäuser.*

(M) *** Decca 421 865-2 (from complete sets, cond. Solti).

Solti's choral collection is superb, with an added sophistication in both performance and recording – especially in the subtle use of ambience and perspectives – to set it apart from the DG Bayreuth disc, good though that is. The collection opens with a blazing account of the *Lohengrin* Act III *Prelude*, since of course the *Bridal chorus* grows naturally out of it. But the *Pilgrims' chorus*, which comes next, creates an electrifying pianissimo and expands gloriously, while the excerpts from *Die Meistersinger* and *Parsifal* show Solti's characteristic intensity at its most potent.

Arias from: *Götterdämmerung; Lohengrin; Die Meistersinger; Rienzi; Siegfried; Tannhäuser; Tristan; Die Walküre.*

(M) (***) EMI mono CDH7 69789-2. Lauritz Melchior, LSO, Barbirolli; or Berlin State Op. O, Leo Blech.

No Heldentenor on record has outshone

Lauritz Melchior in this Wagner repertory. This collection in the Références series brings together 15 items recorded in his first full maturity between 1928 and 1931, when the magnificent voice was at its freshest. Not that the *Walküre* excerpts here improve on his incomparable performance as Siegfried in Bruno Walter's complete Act I of 1936 (also on Références CD – see above); but, fascinatingly, Barbirolli in the second of the three excerpts, *Wintersturme*, relaxes him more than Leo Blech did on the other two. The selection ends with Melchior's glorious singing of Walther's two arias from *Meistersinger*, noble and shining. Excellent transfers, with the voice given astonishing presence.

Waldteufel, Emil (1837–1915)

Waltzes: *Acclamations; España; Estudiantina; Les Patineurs.*

(M) *** EMI CDM7 63136-2. Monte Carlo Nat. Op. O, Boskovsky – OFFENBACH: *Gaîté parisienne.* **

Boskovsky's collection has the advantage of including, besides the three favourites, *Acclamations*, which he opens very invitingly. His manner is *echt*-Viennese, but *The Skaters* responds well to his warmth and there is no lack of sparkle here. The remastering of the mid-1970s recording is admirably fresh.

Walton, William (1902–83)

Capriccio burlesco; Coronation marches: Crown imperial; Orb and sceptre. Funeral march from Hamlet; Johannesburg festival overture; Richard III: Prelude & suite; Scapino overture; Spitfire prelude & fugue.

(M) **(*) EMI CDM7 63369-2; *EG 763369-4*. Royal Liverpool PO, Sir Charles Groves.

The 1969 collection of Walton's shorter orchestral pieces was made in Studio 2 (EMI's hi-fi-conscious equivalent of Decca's Phase 4) and now seems slightly over-bright with its digital remastering. The sound tends to polarize, with a lack of opulence in the middle range, so necessary in the *nobilmente* of the big tunes of the stirring *Spitfire Prelude and fugue* and *Crown imperial.* The Shakespearean film music was recorded much later (1984) and the quality is fuller, more warmly atmospheric. Although the two *Coronation marches* could do with a little more exuberance, Groves is otherwise a highly sympathetic interpreter of this repertoire, and the playing of the Liverpool orchestra is excellent.

Cello concerto.

(M) *** EMI CDM7 63020-2. Tortelier, Bournemouth SO, Berglund – SHOSTAKOVICH: *Cello concerto No. 1.* ***

Tortelier's version of Walton's *Cello concerto* is openly extrovert in its emotional response, offering a highly involving approach. After the haunting melancholy of the first movement, the central scherzo emerges as a far weightier piece than with Ma and Previn (both at full price), while the final variations are developed with a strong sense of compulsion. With full, vivid recording, Tortelier's reading remains very competitive.

(i) *Viola concerto;* (ii) *Sinfonia concertante.*

(M) (***) EMI mono CDH7 63828-2. (i) William Primrose, Philh. O; (ii) Phyllis Sellick, CBSO; composer – VAUGHAN WILLIAMS: *Violin concerto* etc. (***)

In the inter-war period William Primrose set new standards of virtuosity on the viola and here gives a formidable account of the greatest of viola concertos, with the composer conducting. Recorded in 1946, within weeks of the other viola work on the disc, Vaughan Williams's *Flos campi*, the mono sound fails to capture a genuine pianissimo, but otherwise the combination of romantic warmth tempered by classical restraint provides a lesson to some more recent interpreters. Unlike them, Primrose adopts an aptly flowing speed for the opening *Andante comodo*, refusing to sentimentalize it. The scherzo is phenomenally fast, sometimes sounding breathless, but the virtuosity is astonishing; and the spiky humour of the finale is delightfully pointed, leading to a yearning account of the epilogue. The *Sinfonia concertante* is another historic recording well deserving study, made in 1945, the first ever of this work. It is also a superb memento of a great pianist too little heard on record. Phyllis Sellick, in piano writing that is often ungrateful to the player, readily matches the composer-conductor in the thrusting urgency and romantic power of the performance. More than any more recent account it reveals the piece, Walton's first big symphonic work (completed in 1927), as a clear, warm-hearted precursor of the much better-known *Viola concerto* of two years later. The brilliant young *enfant terrible* who had written *Façade* was already a romantic. Excellent transfers of both concertos, generously coupled with the two Vaughan Williams works.

Violin concerto.

(M) *** Decca 421 385-2; *421 385-4* [id.]. Kyung Wha Chung, LSO, Previn – ELGAR: *Cello concerto.* ***

(M) (***) BMG/RCA mono GD 87966 [7966-2-

RG]. Heifetz, Philh. O, composer – ELGAR: *Concerto.* (***)

In the brooding intensity of the opening evocation, Kyung Wha Chung presents the first melody with a depth of expression, tender and hushed, that has never been matched on record, not even by Heifetz. With Previn as guide and with the composer himself a sympathetic observer at the recording sessions, Chung then builds up a performance which must remain a classic, showing the *Concerto* as one of the greatest of the century in this genre. Outstandingly fine recording, sounding the more vivid in its CD format.

It was Heifetz who commissioned the Walton *Concerto* and who gave the first performances, as well as making a wartime recording in America. This is the later version, first issued in 1951, which Heifetz made with Walton conducting, using the revised score. Speeds are often hair-raisingly fast, but few Heifetz records convey as much passion as this. The mono recording is dry, with a distracting hum in the transfer, but the high-voltage electricity has never been matched in this radiant music.

Crown Imperial (concert band version).
❀ (M) *** Mercury 432 009-2 [id.]. Eastman Wind Ens., Fennell – BENNETT: *Symphonic songs*; HOLST: *Hammersmith*; JACOB: *William Byrd suite.* ***

Paced with dignity, yet with joyously crisp articulation, Fennell's splendidly paced performance is part of a highly recommendable collection of music for concert band; the entry of the organ at the climax brings a frisson-creating dynamic expansion which is unforgettably exciting. The coda, too, is quite superb. The Mercury sound, from the late 1950s, remains in the demonstration bracket.

(i) *Façade* (complete); (ii) *Siesta; Overtures: Portsmouth Point; Scapino.*
❀ (M) *** Decca mono 425 661-2; *425 661-4* [id.]. (i) Sitwell, Pears, E. Op. Group Ens., Collins; (ii) LPO, Boult – ARNOLD: *English dances.* (***)

Anthony Collins's 1954 recording of *Façade* is a gramophone classic, sounding miraculously vivid and atmospheric in a CD transfer that seems almost like modern stereo. Dame Edith Sitwell had one of the richest and most characterful of speaking voices, and here she recites her early poems to the masterly, witty music of the youthful Walton with glorious relish. Peter Pears is splendid too in the fast poems, rattling off the lines like the *grande dame* herself, to demonstrate how near-nonsense can be pure poetry. Of course there are flaws in Dame Edith's contribution over rhythm. She has no idea whatever of offbeat accentuation or jazz syncopation in *Old Sir Faulk*, but even so the voice itself is incomparable. The Boult mono versions of *Scapino* and *Siesta* make a valuable coupling, although *Portsmouth Point* misses some of the rhythmic bite of his first 78-r.p.m. disc. Malcolm Arnold's own première recording of his masterly *English dances*, full of exuberance and colour, completes a fascinating programme that no lover of English music should miss.

Symphonies Nos. (i) *1;* (ii) *2.*
(M) ** EMI CDM7 63269-2 [id.]. (i) New Philh. O, Sargent; (ii) LSO, Previn.

Previn's outstanding version of No. 2 sounds very vivid and immediate in its CD transfer, with the 1974 sound providing a keen sense of presence. Sadly, Sargent's 1966 recording of No. 1 seems tepid beside it, generally a well-behaved reading, but one which lacks Waltonian bite, an essential ingredient in this work.

Symphony No. 1 in B flat min..
(M) *** BMG/RCA GD 87830 [7830-2-RG]. LSO, Previn (with VAUGHAN WILLIAMS: *Wasps overture* ***).

On RCA Previn gives a marvellously biting account of the magnificent *First Symphony.* His fast tempi may initially make one feel that he is pressing too hard, but his ability to screw the dramatic tension tighter and tighter until the final resolution is most assured, and certainly reflects the tense mood of the mid-1930s, as well as the youthful Walton's own personal tensions at that time. '*Presto con malizia*' says the score for the scherzo, and malice is exactly what Previn conveys, with the hints of vulgarity and humour securely placed. In the slow movement Previn finds real warmth, giving some of the melodies an Elgarian richness; and the finale's electricity here helps to overcome any feeling that it is too facile, too easily happy a conclusion. The bright recording – made by Decca engineers in the vintage 1960s – has splendid focus in its CD remastering, yet does not lack body. Previn has rarely made a record as powerfully intense as this, and as a performance it is unsurpassed.

Symphony No. 2; Partita for orchestra; Variations on a theme by Hindemith.
❀ (M) *** Sony MPK 46732 [id.]. Cleveland O, Szell.

In a letter to the conductor, Walton expressed himself greatly pleased with this performance of the *Second Symphony*: 'It is a quite fantastic and stupendous performance from every point of view. Firstly it is absolutely right musically speaking, and the virtuosity is quite staggering, especially the Fugato; but everything is phrased and balanced in an unbelievable way.' Listening to the splendidly remastered CD of this 1961 recording, one cannot but join the composer in responding to the wonderfully luminous detail in the orchestra, while the *Lento assai* is very moving, with richly sombre brass playing. In the first-movement allegro, the violins above the stave are miraculously firm and radiant, and the orchestral playing has an exhilarating flair and impulse. Szell's performance of the *Hindemith variations* is no less praiseworthy. Again the music-making is technically immaculate, and under Szell there is not only a pervading warmth, but each fragment is perfectly set in place. Finally comes the *Partita*, which was commissioned by the Cleveland Orchestra and given its première a year before the recording was made. The infectious writing is typical of the composer's earlier style. The recordings are bright, in the CBS manner, but the ambience of Severance Hall brings a backing warmth and depth, and these are technically among the finest of Szell's recordings in this venue. This Cleveland disc occupies a very special place in the Walton discography.

CHORAL MUSIC

Belshazzar's Feast; Coronation Te Deum; Gloria.

(M) (**(*)) EMI CHS7 63376-2 [Ang. CDHB 63376]. Milligan, Huddersfield Ch. Soc., Royal Liverpool PO, Sargent – ELGAR: *Dream of Gerontius.* (**(*))

The Sargent version, dating from the late 1950s, brings a good example of his 'Hudderspool' work in other than the traditional repertory. This is no match in electric tension for the very first ever recording of *Belshazzar*, made with the same choir and orchestra in 1943 under the composer; but, with generally brisk speeds, it is still fresh and dramatic. James Milligan, a singer cut off in his early prime, is an excellent soloist. The coupling is a generous and apt one, though it would have been far better to have had the earlier versions, Walton's own of *Belshazzar* and Sargent's earlier one of *Gerontius.*

Warlock, Peter (1894–1930)

Capriol suite for strings.

(M) *** Decca 421 391-2; *421 391-4* [id.]. ASMF, Marriner – BRITTEN: *Variations on a theme of Frank Bridge*; BUTTERWORTH: *Banks of green willow* etc. ***

The playing of the St Martin's Academy under Marriner is lively, polished and stylish here and readily reveals the freshness of Warlock's invention, based on Elizabethan dances. The recording is first rate: it dates from 1970 and has added realism and presence without loss of body. The Britten and Butterworth couplings are equally attractive.

Serenade for strings (for the sixtieth birthday of Delius).

(M) *** Decca 421 384-2; *421 384-4* [id.]. ASMF, Marriner – ELGAR: *Elegy for strings* etc. **(*)

Warlock's gentle *Serenade*, written for Delius, is beautifully played and recorded here, an unjustly neglected work receiving its due.

Waxman, Franz (1906–67)

Film scores: *Bride of Frankenstein: Creation of the female monster; Old Aquaintance: Elegy for strings. Philadelphia Story: Fanfare; Main title; True love. A Place in the Sun: suite. Prince Valiant: suite. Rebecca: suite. Sunset Boulevard: suite. Taras Bulba: suite.*

❀ (M) *** BMG/RCA GD 80708; *GK 80708* [0708-2-RG; *0708-4-RG*]. Nat. PO, Charles Gerhardt.

Of the many European musicians who crossed the Atlantic to make careers in Hollywood, Franz Waxman was among the most distinguished. Born in Upper Silesia, he had his early musical training in Germany. He was immensely gifted, and much of his music can stand on its own without the screen images it originally served to accompany. His first important score was for James Whale's *Bride of Frankenstein*, a horror movie to which many film buffs give classic status. His marvellously evocative music (a haunting, almost Wagnerian crescendo built over a throbbing timpani beat) for *The creation of the female monster* (visually most compelling in the film sequence) was restored by the conductor, mainly from listening to the film soundtrack, as the orchestral parts are lost. It builds on a memorable three-chord motif which seems instantly familiar. Readers will soon discover its associations for themselves: suffice to say that the more familiar use of this melodic fragment comes from a score written by another composer some fourteen years later. The *Bride of Frankenstein* music dates from 1935. Waxman stayed on to write for 188 films over 32 years. The opening of the first item on this CD and tape, the *Suite* from *Prince Valiant*, immediately shows the vigour of Waxman's invention and the brilliance of his Richard Straussian orchestration, and this score includes one of those sweeping string tunes which are the very epitome of Hollywood film music. Perhaps the finest of these comes in *A*

Place in the Sun, and in the *Suite* it is used to preface an imaginative rhapsodical movement for solo alto sax (brilliantly played here by Ronnie Chamberlain). The reprise of the main tune, also on the alto sax but decorated by a characteristic counter-theme in the upper strings, is a moment of the utmost magic. In this work, incidentally, there is another curious anticipation of music written by another composer: a fugal section of Waxman's score is remarkably like the end of the second movement of Shostakovich's *Eleventh Symphony* (written seven years after the film, which was not shown in the Soviet Union). To make the coincidence complete, it was Waxman who conducted the West Coast première of the symphony in 1958. The collection ends with *The ride to Dubno* from *Taras Bulba* (Waxman's last film-score), which has thrilling impetus and energy and is scored with great flair. All the music here is of high quality, and for any movie buff this is desert-island material. It nostalgically includes the famous MGM introductory title fanfare, which Waxman wrote as a backcloth for Leo the Lion. The orchestral playing throughout is marvellously eloquent, and the conductor's dedication is obvious. The recording is rich and full, with no lack of brilliance in this very successful transfer to compact disc. Four film-stills are included, notably the quintessential *Bride of Frankenstein* (Elsa Lanchester) plus a picture of the composer conducting in Hollywood.

Weber, Carl Maria von (1786–1826)

Clarinet concerto No. 1 in F min., J.114.
(M) **(*) BMG/RCA GD 60035 [60035-2-RG]. Stolzman, Mostly Mozart Festival O, Schneider (with ROSSINI: *Theme and variations in C* ***; MOZART: *Andante in C, K.315* **).

Stolzman's account of the *F minor Clarinet concerto* displays plenty of character, an easy bravura and a succulent tone in the *Adagio*. Here too the orchestra accompanies warmly, with some fine horn playing; but some might feel that in the outer movements the tuttis are too overwhelming in their expansiveness. Although the *Introduction* is a shade bland, the coupled Rossini *Variations* sparkle operatically once they get fully underway; but the Mozart *Andante*, conceived for the flute, needs a lighter touch if it is to be heard on the clarinet.

Clarinet concertos Nos. 1 in F min., Op. 73; 2 in E flat, Op. 74; Clarinet concertino in E flat, Op. 26.
(BB) *** Naxos Dig. 8.550378 [id.]. Ernst Ottensamer, Slovak State PO (Košice), Johannes Wildner.

Neither the soloist nor the conductor is a household name. Ernst Ottensamer is a highly sensitive clarinettist, who has played with the major Viennese orchestras and is a member of the Vienna Wind Ensemble. His account of the two *Clarinet concertos* can hold its own against the competition in the current catalogue in any price category. The Košice orchestra also responds well to Johannes Wildner's direction, and the recorded sound is very natural and well balanced. A real bargain.

Overtures: *Abu Hassan; Der Beherrscher der Geister; Euryanthe; Der Freischütz; Oberon; Peter Schmoll; Invitation to the dance* (orch. Berlioz), *Op. 65.*
(M) *** DG 419 070-2 [id.]. BPO, Karajan.

Karajan's performances have great style and refinement. Weber's overtures are superbly crafted and there are no better examples of the genre than *Oberon* and *Der Freischütz*, both epitomizing the spirit of the operas which they serve to introduce. Needless to say, the Berlin horn playing is peerless in these two pieces. Karajan's stylish performance of another Weberian innovation, the *Invitation to the dance* (in Berlioz's orchestration), makes a valuable bonus. On CD the sound is drier and brighter than originally, with a loss of weight in the bass.

Overtures: *Der Freischütz; Oberon.*
(M) *** DG 415 840-2 [id.]. Bav. RSO, Kubelik – MENDELSSOHN: *Midsummer Night's Dream.* ***

Kubelik offers Weber's two greatest overtures as a fine bonus for his extended selection from Mendelssohn's *Midsummer Night's Dream* incidental music. The playing is first class and compares favourably with the Karajan versions.

Clarinet quintet in B flat, Op. 34.
(M) *** Decca 430 297-2; *430 297-4* [id.]. Gervase de Peyer, Melos Ens. – HUMMEL: *Piano quintet* etc. ***

Weber's *Quintet* was written at a time when the clarinet was still fighting for acceptance as a solo instrument; even though Mozart, Beethoven and Schubert had used its novel colours with the utmost felicity, there remained plenty of scope for more virtuosic treatment. This Weber undertook in his concertos and in this *Quintet*, which is delightful music as well as being a willing vehicle for the soloist's immaculate display of pyrotechnics. Gervase de Peyer is in his element here and the strings give him admirable support. The 1959 (originally Oiseau-Lyre) recording is first class; it is vivid, with plenty of atmosphere, and does not sound at all dated.

OPERA

Euryanthe (complete).
(M) *** EMI CMS7 63509-2 (3) [Ang. CDMC 63509]. Jessye Norman, Hunter, Gedda, Krause, Leipzig R. Ch., Dresden State O, Janowski.

Much has been written about the absurdity of the plot of *Euryanthe*, as unlikely a tale of chivalry and troubadours as you will find; as this fine recording bears out, however, the opera is far more than just a historic curiosity. The juxtaposition of two sopranos, representing good and evil, is formidably effective, particularly when the challenge is taken by singers of the stature of Jessye Norman and Rita Hunter. Hunter may not be the most convincing villainess, but the cutting edge of the voice is marvellous; and as for Jessye Norman, she sings radiantly, whether in her first delicate cavatina or in the big aria of Act III. Tom Krause as the villain, Lysiart, has rarely sung better and Nicolai Gedda, as ever, is the most intelligent of tenors. Good atmospheric recording (as important in this opera as in *Freischütz*) and vivid remastering, while the direction from Marek Janowski makes light of any longueurs.

Der Freischütz (complete).
(M) *** EMI CMS7 69342-2 (2). Grümmer, Otto, Schock, Prey, Wiemann, Kohn, Frick, German Op. Ch., Berlin, BPO, Keilberth.

Keilberth's is a warm, exciting account of Weber's masterpiece which makes all the dated conventions of the work seem fresh and new. In particular the *Wolf's glen* scene on CD acquires something of the genuine terror that must have struck the earliest audiences and which is far more impressive than any mere scene-setting with wood and cardboard in the opera house. The casting of the magic bullets with each one numbered in turn, at first in eerie quiet and then in crescendo amid the howling of demons, is superbly conveyed. The bite of the orchestra and the proper balance of the voices in relation to it, with the effect of space and distance, helps also to create the illusion. Elisabeth Grümmer sings more sweetly and sensitively than one ever remembers before, with Agathe's prayer exquisitely done. Lisa Otto is really in character, with genuine coquettishness. Schock is not an ideal tenor, but he sings ably enough. The Kaspar of Karl Kohn is generally well focused, and the playing of the Berlin Philharmonic has plenty of polish. The overall effect is immensely atmospheric and enjoyable.

Oberon (complete).
(M) *** DG 419 038-2 (2) [id.]. Grobe, Nilsson, Domingo, Prey, Hamari, Schiml, Bav. R. Ch. & SO, Kubelik.

Rarely has operatic inspiration been squandered so cruelly on impossible material as in Weber's *Oberon.* We owe it to Covent Garden's strange ideas in the mid-1820s as to what English opera should be that Weber's delicately conceived score is a sequence of illogical arias, scenas and ensembles strung together by an absurd pantomime plot. Although, even on record, the result is slacker because of that loose construction, one can appreciate the contribution of Weber, in a performance as stylish and refined as this. The original issue included dialogue and a narrative spoken by one of Oberon's fairy characters. In the reissue this is omitted, cutting the number of discs from three to two, yet leaving the music untouched. With Birgit Nilsson commanding in *Ocean, thou mighty monster*, and excellent singing from the other principals, helped by Kubelik's ethereally light handling of the orchestra, the set can be be recommended without reservation, for the recording remains of excellent quality.

Webern, Anton (1883–1945)

Concerto for 9 instruments, Op. 24.
(M) *** Chan. CHAN 6534; *MBTD 6534* [id.]. Nash Ens., Simon Rattle – SCHOENBERG: *Pierrot Lunaire.* ***

This late Webern piece, tough, spare and uncompromising, makes a valuable fill-up for Jane Manning's outstanding version of Schoenberg's *Pierrot Lunaire*, a 1977 recording originally made for the Open University. First-rate sound and a beautifully clean CD transfer.

(i) *Concerto for nine instruments, Op. 24; 5 Movements for string quartet* (orchestral version), *Op. 5; Passacaglia, Op. 1; 6 Pieces for large orchestra, Op. 6; 5 Pieces for orchestra, Op. 10; Symphony, Op. 21; Variations for orchestra, Op. 30.* Arrangements of: BACH: *Musical offering: Fugue* (1935). (ii) SCHUBERT: *German dances* (for small orchestra), *Op. posth.* Chamber music: (iii) *6 Bagatelles for string quartet, Op. 9; 5 Movements for string quartet, Op. 5*; (iv; v) *4 Pieces for violin and piano, Op. 7;* (v; vi) *3 Small pieces for cello and piano, Op. 11;* (v; vii) *Quartet, Op. 22* (for piano, violin, clarinet & saxophone); (iii) *String quartet, Op. 28; String trio, Op. 20;* (v) *Variations for piano, Op. 27.* (Vocal) (viii; i) *Das Augenlicht, Op. 26;* (ix; x) *5 Canons on Latin texts, Op. 16;* (viii; ix; i) *Cantata No. 1, Op. 29;* (viii; ix; xi; i) *Cantata No. 2, Op. 31;* (viii) *Entflieht auf leichten Kähnen, Op. 2;* (ix; x) *5 Sacred songs, Op. 15;* (xii; v) *5 Songs,*

Op. 3; 5 Songs, Op. 4; (xii; x) *2 Songs, Op. 8;* (xii; v) *4 Songs, Op. 12;* (xii; x) *4 Songs, Op. 13; 6 Songs, Op. 14;* (ix; x; xiii) *3 Songs, Op. 18;* (viii; i) *2 Songs, Op. 19;* (xii; v) *3 Songs, Op. 23;* (ix; v) *3 Songs, Op. 25;* (ix; x) *3 Traditional rhymes, Op. 17.*

(M) *** Sony SM3K 45845 (3) [id.]. (i) LSO (or members), Pierre Boulez; (ii) Frankfurt R. O, composer (recorded December 1932); (iii) Juilliard Qt (or members); (iv) Stern; (v) Rosen; (vi) Piatigorsky; (vii) Majeske, Marcellus, Weinstein; (viii) John Alldis Ch.; (ix) Lukomska; (x) with Ens., Boulez; (xi) McDaniel; (xii) Harper; (xiii) with John Williams. Overall musical direction: Boulez.

These three CDs contain all Webern's works with opus numbers, as well as the string orchestra arrangements of Op. 5 and the orchestration of the *Fugue* from Bach's *Musical offering*. A rare recording of Webern himself conducting his arrangement of Schubert dances is also included. Though the recording quality varies somewhat, the CD transfers are remarkably consistent, considering that the items included were made over a period of eleven years. The orchestral music was done in the sympathetic acoustics of Barking Town Hall in 1969 and has atmosphere as well as vivid clarity, while the chamber music, recorded mostly in New York over the following three years, brings both immediacy and clean, realistic textures, even if the balance is close. The quality of the music-making is very high and, more importantly, all these performances convey the commitment without which such spare writing can sound merely chill. What Pierre Boulez above all demonstrates in the orchestral works (including those with chorus) is that, for all his seeming asceticism, Webern was working on human emotions. The spareness of the writing lets us appreciate how atonality can communicate tenderly, evocatively, movingly, not by any imitation of romantic models (as Schoenberg's and Berg's music often does) but by reducing the notes to the minimum. The Juilliard Quartet and the John Alldis Choir convey comparable commitment; though neither Heather Harper nor Halina Lukomska is ideally cast in the solo vocal music, Boulez brings out the best in both of them in the works with orchestra. Rarely can a major composer's whole *oeuvre* be appreciated in so compact a span. There are excellent notes, every item is cued, and perhaps it is carping to regret that the *Passacaglia* and *Variations for orchestra* were not indexed. With such consistently successful transfers and a realistic price, this set can be recommended to anyone who wants to come to grips with one of the key figures of the twentieth century.

5 Movements, Op. 5.

(M) *** Decca 430 002-2. ASMF, Marriner – SCHOENBERG: *Verklaerte Nacht*; R. STRAUSS: *Metamorphosen.* **(*)

The CD remastering of Marriner's 1974 recording brings a more sharply etched sound, almost to match the original string quartet medium in clarity and bite. With dedicated playing, the result is very satisfying, even if the music is inevitably made more romantic.

5 Movements, Op. 5; Passacaglia, Op. 1; 6 Pieces for orchestra, Op. 6; Symphony, Op. 21.

(M) *** DG 427 424-2 (3) [id.]. BPO, Karajan – BERG: *Lyric suite; 3 Pieces;* SCHOENBERG: *Pelleas und Melisande; Variations; Verklaerte Nacht.* ***

(M) *** DG 423 254-2 [id.]. BPO, Karajan.

Available either separately or within Karajan's three-CD compilation of music of the Second Viennese School, made in the early 1970s, this collection, devoted to four compact and chiselled Webern works, is in many ways the most remarkable of all. Karajan's expressive refinement reveals the emotional undertones behind this seemingly austere music, and the results are riveting – as for example in the dramatic and intense *Funeral march* of Op. 6. Opus 21 is altogether more difficult to grasp, but Karajan still conveys the intensity of argument even to the unskilled ear. Indeed, if Webern always sounded like this, he might even enjoy real popularity. Karajan secures a highly sensitive response from the Berlin Philharmonic, who produce sonorities as seductive as Debussy. Incidentally, he plays the 1928 version of Op. 6. A strong recommendation, with excellent sound.

5 Pieces for orchestra, Op. 10.

(M) *** Mercury 432 006-2 [id.]. LSO, Dorati – BERG: *3 Pieces; Lulu suite*; SCHOENBERG: *5 Pieces.* ***

Webern's *Five pieces*, Op. 10, written between 1911 and 1913, mark a radical point in his early development. Their compression is extreme, and their play with almost inaudible fragments may make the unsympathetic listener lose patience too quickly. What we have now gradually come to appreciate, thanks to such performances as this, is that, like so much of Berg and Schoenberg, they have their emotional point to make. The couplings could hardly be more fitting, and the whole record can be strongly recommended to anyone wanting to explore the early work of Schoenberg and his followers before they formalized their ideas in twelve-note technique. Bright, clear, 1962 recording to match the precision of the writing.

6 Bagatelles for string quartet, Op. 9; 5 Movements for string quartet, Op. 5; Slow movement for string quartet (1905); *String quartet* (1905); *String quartet, Op. 28.*
(M) *** Ph. 420 796-2 [id.]. Italian Qt.

Readers who quail at the name of Webern need not tremble at the prospect of hearing this record. The early music in particular is most accessible, and all of it is played with such conviction and beauty of tone that its difficulties melt away or at least become manageable. The recording is of outstanding vividness and presence, and it is difficult to imagine a more eloquent or persuasive introduction to Webern's chamber music than this.

Lieder: *Am Ufer; An Bachesranft; Bild der Liebe; Dies ist ein Lied; Gefunden; Ihr tratet zu dem Herde; Noch zwingt mich treue; So ich traurig bin; Vorfrühling.*
(M) *** DG 431 744-2 (2) [id.]. Fischer-Dieskau, Aribert Reimann – BERG: *Lieder* ***; SCHOENBERG: *Gurrelieder* etc. **(*)

These early Webern songs, most sensitively sung by Fischer-Dieskau, come as part of the generous fill-up for Kubelik's refined account of Schoenberg's *Gurrelieder.*

Weill, Kurt (1900–1950)

(i) *Violin concerto; Kleine Dreigroschenmusik* (suite for wind orchestra from *The Threepenny Opera*).
(M) *** DG 423 255-2 [id.]. (i) Lidell; L. Sinf., Atherton.

Weill's *Concerto* for violin and wind instruments is an early work, resourceful and inventive, the product of a fine intelligence and a good craftsman. The style is somewhat angular (as was that of the young Hindemith) but the textures are always clear and the invention holds the listener's attention throughout. It is splendidly played by Nona Lidell and the wind of the London Sinfonietta, and well recorded too. The *Suite* from *The Threepenny Opera* is given with good spirit and élan.

(i) *Violin concerto, Op. 12;* (ii) *Kleine Dreigroschenmusik* (suite for wind orchestra from *The Threepenny Opera*); (iii) *Quodlibet, Op. 9; Rise and fall of the city of Mahagonny (Songspiel).*
(B) *(*) VoxBox (2) [CDX 5043]. (i) Lautenbacher, Detmold Wind Ens., Michaels; (ii) Music for Westchester SO, Landau; (iii) Westphalian SO (Rechlinghausen), Landau; (iv) Jerusalem SO, Foss – SCHILLINGS: *Mona Lisa;* SCHREKER: *The Birthday of the Infanta.* *(*)

This Vox Box, described as 'The Berlin Project', rightly concentrates on the four very characteristic Weill works, offering rarities by Schreker and von Schillings as previously unpublished extras. Recordings from different sources made in the early 1970s are very forwardly balanced and rather coarse, which suits the *Threepenny opera* and *Mahagonny Songspiel* well enough but takes necessary subtlety away from the *Violin concerto*, where the solo instrument tends to be swallowed up in the wind ensemble, despite its acid tone. The crisply constructed *Quodlibet* in four substantial movements makes a welcome appearance, using material drawn from the 1922 'pantomime', *Zaubernacht* ('Magic night'). Performances are generally lively, but the vocal ensemble in the Jerusalem recording of *Mahagonny* is rough.

Happy End (play by Brecht with songs); *Die sieben Todsünden (The Seven deadly sins).*
(M) *** Sony mono/stereo MPK 45886 [id.]. Lotte Lenya, male quartet & O, Ch. & O, Brückner-Rüggeberg.

An outstandingly valuable and generous coupling offering some 73 minutes of music. Originally recorded in mono in the mid-1950s, the CBS performance of *The Seven deadly sins*, with the composer's widow as principal singer, underlines the status of this distinctive mixture of ballet and song-cycle as one of Weill's most concentrated inspirations. The rhythmic verve is irresistible and, though Lenya had to have the music transposed down, her understanding of the idiom is unique. The recording is forward and slightly harsh, though Lenya's voice is not hardened, and the effect is undoubtedly vivid. *Happy end*, intended as the work's successor and still more savagely cynical, took far longer to be appreciated. The present recording was made in Hamburg-Harburg in 1960. Lenya turned the songs into a kind of cycle (following a hint from her husband), again transposing where necessary, and her renderings in her individual brand of vocalizing are so compelling they make the scalp tingle. Many of these numbers are among the finest that Weill ever wrote. The excellent notes by David Drew are preserved with the CD, but the texts are printed out in German without any translations. The sound is again forwardly balanced, but the CD transfer still provides a backing ambience.

Die Dreigroschenoper (The Threepenny Opera): complete.
(M) ** Ph. 426 668-2; *426 668-4.* Teichmann, Korta, Huebner, Mey, Kutschera, Brammer, Frankfurt Op. Ch. & O, Wolfgang Rennert.

A mid-priced version of *The Threepenny Opera* is welcome, and the 1966 performance here has plenty of bite, even if some of the women's voices have little of the snarling character that one really wants in this 'black' music. However, for anyone except the most fluent German-speaker, a full text is essential; instead, here one has only an essay on how the Weill work relates to the *Beggar's Opera*, plus a very compressed synopsis of the story. The numbers are all separately cued, with the titles translated; but one sometimes needs to do a detective job to discover which characters are singing what. Without the right information, a work which relies far more than most operas on its words (by Brecht) can only be partially appreciated, even though the recording is lively, with the voices given a vivid presence.

Kleine Dreigroschenmusik (suite).
(M) *** EMI CDM7 64142-2 [id.]; *EG 764142-4*. Philh. O, Klemperer (with J. STRAUSS, Jr: *Wiener Blut* (waltz) ***) – STRAVINSKY: *Pulcinella* etc. *

Klemperer is thoroughly at home in the Kurt Weill *Suite*, readily evoking the mood and style of the first performance in 1929 by the Prussian State Military Band (the arrangement – by the composer – is for wind and brass only). His stately and ironically Prussian version of *Mack the Knife* is particularly striking. The Strauss waltz, too, is surprisingly successful, liltingly affectionate yet zestful, with some marvellous playing from the Philharmonia violins. Clearly, Klemperer is enjoying himself and this is hardly less memorable. The 1961 Kingsway Hall recording is excellent and given a first-rate CD transfer. These items need recoupling.

Weiss, Silvius (1686–1750)

Overture in B flat; Suite in D min.; Suite No. 17 in F min.
(M) *** BMG/RCA GD 77217 [77217-2-RG]. Konrad Junghänel (lute).

The Silesian composer Silvius Leopold Weiss was an almost exact contemporary of J. S. Bach and was regarded in his day as the greatest lutenist of the Baroque. He composed about 100 works, none of which was published in his lifetime: his preferred form was the cyclic suite. Konrad Junghänel's excellently focused recording comes from 1984. He plays a Baroque 13-string lute by Nico van der Waals with splendid authority and musicianship, though, as so often with recordings of soft-spoken instruments like the lute or the clavichord, the level is too high and best results are obtained by playing this at a lower volume setting. There are long and interesting presentation notes.

Suonate per il Liuto (Partita grande) Dresden No. 11; in D (Dresden No. 17). Partitia in D min. (Mosocow MS).
(BB) *(*) Naxos Dig. 8.550470 [id.]. Frenklin Lei (lute).

Frenklin Lei's playing conveys greater sensitivity and intelligence than authority. The colouring is often subtle and tasteful, and there is a rhapsodic, improvisatory feeling which is appealing, though certain moments sound curiously tentative. The recording needs to be played at a lower level setting than usual.

Wolf, Hugo (1860–1903)

Italienisches Liederbuch (Italian Song-book, Parts 1 and 2): complete.
(M) *** EMI CDM7 63732-2 [id.]; *EG 763732-4*. Elisabeth Schwarzkopf, Dietrich Fischer-Dieskau, Gerald Moore.

The 46 songs of Wolf's *Italienisches Liederbuch* were published in two parts, in 1892 and 1896. All of them are here, on a CD playing for two seconds over 79 minutes, generous measure indeed at mid-price. These songs show the composer at his most captivatingly individual. Many of them are very brief fragments of fantasy, which call for the most intense artistry if their point is to be fully made. No one today can match the searching perception of these two great singers in this music, with Fischer-Dieskau using his sweetest tones and Schwarzkopf ranging through all the many emotions inspired by love. Note particularly the little vignette, *Wer rief dich denn?*, the song Schwarzkopf was rehearsing when she first met her husband-to-be, Walter Legge, and which she interprets more vividly than anyone else: scorn mingling with hidden heartbreak. Gerald Moore is at his finest, and Walter Legge's translations will help bring the magic of these unique songs even to the newcomer. The well-balanced 1969 recording has been admirably transferred, giving the artists a fine presence.

6 Lieder für eine Frauenstimme. Goethe-Lieder: Die Bekehrte; Ganymed; Kennst du das Land; Mignon I, II & III; Philine; Die Spröde. Lieder: *An eine Aeolsharfe; Auf einer Wanderung; Begegnung; Denk es, o Seele; Elfenlied; Im Frühling; Sonne der Schlummerlosen; Wenn du zu den Blumen gehst; Wie glänzt der helle Mond; Die Zigeunerin.*
(M) **(*) EMI CDM7 63653-2; *EG 763653-4*. Elisabeth Schwarzkopf, Gerald Moore or Geoffrey Parsons.

This is a superb collection, issued as part of Schwarzkopf's 75th birthday edition, representing the peak of her achievement as a Lieder singer. It is disgraceful that no texts or translations are provided as this will seriously reduce its appeal for some collectors; but the selection of items could hardly be better, including many songs inseparably associated with Schwarzkopf's voice, like *Mausfallen spruchlein* and, above all, *Kennst du das Land.* That supreme Lied may not be quite as intensely moving in this studio recording as in Schwarzkopf's two live recordings, also issued by EMI, but it is commanding in its perfection.

Spanisches Liederbuch (complete).
(M) *** DG 423 934-2 (2) [id.]. Schwarzkopf, Fischer-Dieskau, Moore.

In this superb CD reissue the sacred songs provide a dark, intense prelude, with Fischer-Dieskau at his very finest, sustaining slow tempi impeccably. Schwarzkopf's dedication comes out in the three songs suitable for a woman's voice; but it is in the secular songs, particularly those which contain laughter in the music, where she is at her most memorable. Gerald Moore is balanced rather too backwardly – something the transfer cannot correct – but gives superb support. In all other respects the 1968 recording sounds first rate, the voices beautifully caught. A classic set.

Wood, Hugh (born 1932)

(i) *Cello concerto;* (ii) *Violin concerto.*
(M) *** Unicorn UKCD 2043. (i) Parikian; (ii) Welsh; Royal Liverpool PO, Atherton.

Hugh Wood has so far been represented on record only by his chamber music. For his CD début Unicorn have reissued this excellent 1978 coupling of two of his most important bigger pieces: the *Cello concerto* of 1969 and the *Violin concerto*, first heard two years later. Wood is a composer of integrity who has steeped himself in the music of Schoenberg and Webern, yet emerged richer for the experience – in contrast to many post-serial composers. His music is beautifully crafted and far from inaccessible. Here he is given the benefit of good recording, and the performances are thoroughly committed. Those who like and respond to the Bartók concertos or even to the Walton should try this. Excellently balanced recording, well transferred to CD.

Zandonai, Riccardo (1883–1944)

Francesca da Rimini: excerpts from Acts II, III & IV.
(M) **(*) Decca 433 033-2 (2) [id.]. Olivero, Del Monaco, Monte Carlo Op. O, Rescigno - GIORDANO: *Fedora.* **(*)

Magda Olivero is a fine artist who has not been represented nearly enough on record, and this rare Zandonai selection, like the coupled set of Giordano's *Fedora*, does her some belated justice. It would have been preferable to have a complete version of this ambitious opera – the publisher Tito Ricordi tended to think more highly of it than of the contemporary operas of his other, more famous, client, Puccini – but these selections give a fair flavour. Decca opted to have three substantial scenes recorded rather than snippets and, though Mario del Monaco as Paolo is predictably coarse in style, his tone is rich and strong and he does not detract from the achievement, unfailingly perceptive and musicianly, of Olivero as Francesca herself. Excellent, vintage 1969, Decca sound.

Zelenka, Jan (1679–1745)

Capriccios Nos. 1–5; Concerto in G; Hipocondrie in A; Overture in F; Sinfonia in A min..
❀ (M) *** DG 423 703-2 (3) [id.]. Camerata Bern, Van Wijnkoop.

In this superb orchestral collection, as in the companion Archiv issue of Zelenka *Sonatas* (see below), this long-neglected composer begins to get his due, some 250 years late. On this showing he stands as one of the most distinctive voices among Bach's contemporaries, and Bach himself nominated him in that role, though at the time Zelenka was serving in a relatively humble capacity. As in the sonata collection, it is the artistry of Heinz Holliger that sets the seal on the performances, but the virtuosity of Barry Tuckwell on the horn is also a delight, and the music itself regularly astonishes. One of the movements in the *Capriccio No. 5* has the title *Il furibondo (The angry man)* and, more strikingly still, another piece has the significant title *Hipocondrie* and sounds amazingly like a baroque tango. What comes out from this is that, in this period of high classicism, music for Zelenka was about emotion, something one recognizes clearly enough in Bach and Handel but too rarely in lesser composers. And in his bald expressiveness Zelenka often comes to sound amazingly modern, and often very beautiful, as in the slow *Aria No. 2* of the *Fourth Capriccio.* Superb recording, to match Van Wijnkoop's lively and colourful performances, makes these CDs very welcome indeed.

6 Sonatas for 2 oboes and bassoon with continuo.
❀ (M) *** DG 423 937-2 (2) [id.]. Holliger, Bourgue, Gawriloff, Thunemann, Buccarella, Jaccottet.

This second outstanding DG Archiv collection offers yet more music by the remarkable contemporary of Bach, Jan Dismas Zelenka, born in Bohemia but who spent most of his musical working life in Dresden. In these *Trio sonatas* it is almost as though Zelenka had a touch of Ives in him, so unexpected are some of the developments and turns of argument. The tone of voice is often dark and intense, directly comparable to Bach at his finest; and all through these superb performances the electricity of the original inspiration comes over with exhilarating immediacy. Fine recording, admirably remastered. Another set to recommend urgently to any lover of Baroque music.

Lamentationes Jeremiae Prophetae (Lamentations for Holy Week).

(M) *** HM/BMG GD 77112 [77112-2-RG]. Jacobs, De Mey, Widmer, Instrumentalists of the Schola Cantorum Basiliensis, Jacobs.

These solo settings of the six *Lamentations* for the days leading up to Easter reinforce Zelenka's claims as one of the most original composers of his time, one warmly commended by Bach himself. The spacious melodic lines and chromatic twists in the harmonic progressions are often very Bachian, but the free-flowing alternation of arioso and recitative is totally distinctive. This mid-price issue of René Jacobs's 1983 recording for Deutsche Harmonia Mundi follows close on a very recommendable full-price version on the Hyperion label with the Chandos Baroque Players. Here, too, all three soloists are excellent, with the least-known, the baritone Kurt Widmer, easily matching the other two in his exceptionally sweet and fresh singing. But, quite apart from price, this BMG disc has the advantage of focusing the voices more cleanly and offering a rather less abrasive instrumental accompaniment, with speeds generally more flowing. Unlike the Hyperion issue, however, this one has separate tracks only for the six different *Lamentations*, not for each section.

Zeller, Carl (1842–98)

Der Vogelhändler (complete).

(M) *** EMI CMS7 69357-2 (2). Rothenberger, Holm, Litz, Dallapozza, Berry, Unger, Forster, Dönch, V. Volksoper Ch., VSO, Boskovsky.

Boskovsky's vivacious and lilting performance of Zeller's delightfully tuneful operetta is in every way recommendable. The cast is strong; Anneliese Rothenberger may be below her best form as Princess Marie, but Renate Holm is a charmer as Christel, and Adolf Dallapozza sings the title-role with heady virility. There are many endearing moments, and the combination of infectious sparkle and style tempts one to revalue the score and place it, alongside *The Merry Widow* and *Die Fledermaus*, among the finest and most captivating of all operettas. For English-speaking listeners some of the dialogue might have been cut, but this is an international set and it is provided with an excellent libretto translation (not always the case in this kind of repertoire). The recording is excellent, combining atmosphere with vividness and giving lively projection of the principal characters.

Zemlinsky, Alexander von

(1871–1942)

String quartets Nos. 1, Op. 4; 2, Op. 15; 3, Op. 19; 4, Op. 25.

(M) *** DG Dig. 427 421-2 (2). LaSalle Qt.

The *First Quartet* gained the imprimatur of Brahms, to whom Zemlinsky had shown some of his other early compositions, and the last, which was written at exactly the same time as Schoenberg's *Fourth*, pays his erstwhile pupil the double compliment of a dedication and an allusion to *Verklaerte Nacht*. None of the four is in the least atonal: the textures are full of contrapuntal interest and the musical argument always proceeds with lucidity. There is diversity of mood and a fastidious craftsmanship, and the listener is always held. The musical language is steeped in Mahler and, to a lesser extent, Reger, but the music is undoubtedly the product of a very fine musical mind and one of considerable individuality. Collectors will find this a rewarding set: the LaSalle play with polish and unanimity, and the recording is first class, as is the admirable documentation.

Collections
Concerts of Orchestral and Concertante Music

Academy of St Martin-in-the-Fields, Sir Neville Marriner

VAUGHAN WILLIAMS: *Fantasia on Greensleeves; English folksongs suite.* ELGAR: *Serenade for strings in E min., Op. 20.* BUTTERWORTH: *The Banks of green willow.* WARLOCK: *Capriol suite.* DELIUS: *On hearing the first cuckoo in spring. A Village Romeo and Juliet: The walk to the Paradise Garden.*
(M) *** Decca 417 778-2; *417 778-4.*

All these vintage performances are available in other formats and couplings, many discussed within these pages. If the present assembly is attractive, there are no grounds for withholding a strong recommendation, for the recordings are first class and the digital remastering most successful.

Trumpet concertos (with (i) Alan Stringer; (ii) John Wilbraham): (i) HAYDN: *Concerto in E flat.* (ii) HUMMEL: *Concerto in E flat.* ALBINONI: *Concerto in C.* L. MOZART: *Concerto in D.* TELEMANN: *Concerto in D.*
(M) *** Decca 417 761-2.

Alan Stringer favours a forthright, open timbre for the Haydn *Concerto*, but he plays the famous slow movement graciously. John Wilbraham is superbly articulate and stylish in the rest of the programme, and his partnership with Marriner in the captivating Hummel *Concerto* makes for superb results. Albinoni's *Concerto* divides the spotlight between trumpet and three supporting oboes to add textural variety, and both the Leopold Mozart and Telemann works are among the finest of their genre. Throughout, the orchestral accompaniments have striking elegance and finesse, and plenty of vitality too; and the recording is bright, with plenty of presence for the soloists.

'English music for strings': HOLST: *St Paul's suite.* DELIUS (arr. Fenby): *2 Aquarelles.* PURCELL: *Chacony.* VAUGHAN WILLIAMS: *Rhosymedre: Prelude.* WALTON: *Henry V* (film music): *Death of Falstaff; Touch her soft lips and part.* BRITTEN: *Simple Symphony, Op. 4.*
(M) *** EMI CD-EMX 2170; *TC-EMX 2170.*

This attractively varied concert brings playing at once refined and resilient, delicately strong and warmly expressive by turns. Britten's *Simple Symphony* seems to be on a more impressive scale than usual in the fast movements, more openly romantic in the *Sentimental sarabande.* Holst's *St Paul's suite* brings wonderfully pointed rhythms in all four movements, while the Vaughan Williams (an arrangement of a haunting organ solo) and the Walton are finely atmospheric, against the sympathetic acoustic of EMI's Abbey Road Studio. The Delius too, atmospheric music *par excellence*, prepares the way for the bold and comparative astringency of the magnificent Purcell *Chacony*, which has never sounded more convincing on modern instruments. The remastered (1972) recording, while bringing string textures which are a little sparer than on the original analogue LP (most noticeably so in the Britten slow movement, which sounds less opulent), has refined detail and provides a somewhat firmer focus.

Concert: WAGNER: *Siegfried idyll.* SUPPÉ: *Overture Light Cavalry.* GRIEG: *2 Elegiac melodies, Op. 34.* TCHAIKOVSKY: *Andante cantabile.* DVOŘÁK: *Nocturne, Op. 40.* PONCHIELLI: *La Gioconda: Dance of the hours.* NICOLAI: *Overture The Merry Wives of Windsor.* FAURÉ: *Pavane, Op. 50.* BOCCHERINI: *Minuet (from Op. 13/5).*
(M) *** EMI Dig. CDD7 64107-2 [id.]; *ET 764107-4.*

This is a demonstration concert for those who have to think of their neighbours. Many of the pieces here are relatively gentle and they are given radiant performances, recorded in digital sound with ravishingly vivid results. As in his previous Decca/Argo version of the *Siegfried idyll*, Marriner uses solo strings for the gentle passages, a fuller ensemble for the climaxes, here passionately convincing. Other items which are especially beautiful are the Grieg, Dvořák and Tchaikovsky string pieces, while the *Dance of the hours* sparkles with colour and élan. The programme plays for 75 minutes, and both sound and performances are quite exceptional.

'Baroque masterpieces': HANDEL: *Solomon: Arrival of the Queen of Sheba. Concerto grosso in A min., Op. 6/4; Overture Berenice.* CORELLI: *Concerto grosso, Op. 6/1.* GABRIELI: *Canzona noni toni.* TELEMANN: *Viola concerto in G* (with Simon Streatfield). VIVALDI: *L'Estro armonico: Concerto for 4 violins, Op. 3/10* (with Marriner, Nelson, Howard, Connah).
(BB) **(*) Pickwick IMPX 9020.

This is a baroque feast. The programme is certainly made up of masterpieces, given glorious performances from the Academy's vintage Argo years during the mid-1960s. Marriner himself is a soloist in the highly stimulating account of

Vivaldi's *Quadruple violin concerto* and, alongside the joys of Corelli's Op. 6, we are given a reminder of the splendour of the Academy's first recording of Handel's comparable opus. It is a pity that the CD transfers are a bit edgy – the Queen of Sheba's entry is very brightly lit indeed – but there is no lack of ambience or fullness, and a treble cut works wonders.

Adler, Larry (harmonica)

'Larry Adler in Concert' (with (i) Pro Arte O, Francis Chagrin or Eric Robinson; (ii) Gerald Moore; (iii) LSO, Basil Cameron; (iv) Gritton, BBC SO, Sargent): (i) ENESCU: *Rumanian rhapsody No. 1.* GERSHWIN: *Rhapsody in blue.* (ii) *Porgy and Bess: It ain't necessarily so.* (i) BIZET arr. Adler: *Carmen fantasy.* RAVEL: *Boléro.* GRANADOS: *Spanish dance No. 5.* BENJAMIN: *Jamaican rumba;* (iii) *Harmonica concerto.* (i) CHAGRIN: *Roumanian fantasy.* (iv) VAUGHAN WILLIAMS: *Romance for harmonica with strings and piano.*
(M) *** EMI stereo/mono CDM7 64134-2 [id.]; *EG 764134-4* [id.].

It was Larry Adler who, more than anyone else, established the harmonica – or mouth-organ, as he always prefers to call it – as a respectable instrument. When in 1952 Vaughan Williams wrote his *Romance* for Adler, he expanded the expressive range of the instrument, using its chordal potential more imaginatively than any previous composer; and the Arthur Benjamin *Concerto* of the following year similarly brings a surprising range of expression. Both those works were recorded almost at once in the early 1950s in these outstanding performances, and they and the shorter items (for the most part recorded in stereo in 1957) consistently bring out Adler's artistry, his ability to transcend the limitations of the instrument and his creative feeling for phrasing. Indeed this whole programme reflects what Jascha Heifetz said of the mouth-organ: that it comes closer than other instruments to the human voice. It is only sad that Adler's unforgettable music for the film *Genevieve* was not also included on the disc, and room should also have been found for his uniquely haunting version of Debussy's *Maid with the flaxen hair.*

André, Maurice (trumpet)

Trumpet concertos (with LPO, López-Cobos): HAYDN: *Concerto in E flat.* TELEMANN: *Concerto in F.* ALBINONI: *Concerto in D min.* MARCELLO: *Concerto in C min.*
(M) *** EMI CDM7 69189-2 [id.]; *EG 769189-4.*

Maurice André's cultured playing gives much pleasure throughout this collection. Slow movements are elegantly phrased and communicate an appealing, expressive warmth. The stylishness and easy execution ensure a welcome for the Albinoni and Marcello works, which are transcriptions but are made thoroughly convincing in this format. Excellent, lively accompaniments from the LPO under López-Cobos, and good sound, the more vivid on CD.

Trumpet concertos (with (i) ECO, Mackerras; (ii) Munich Bach O, Karl Richter; (iii) Munich CO, Stadlmair): (i) VIVIANI: *Sonata for trumpet & organ in C* (with Hedwig Bilgram). VIVALDI: *Double trumpet concerto in C, RV 537.* TELEMANN: *Concerto-Sonata in D.* (ii) HANDEL: *Concerto in G min.* (arr. from *Oboe concerto No. 3*). (iii) M. HAYDN: *Trumpet concerto in D.* J. HAYDN: *Trumpet concerto in E flat.*
(M) *** DG 419 874-2; *419 874-4.*

This DG collection (well recorded in the late 1960s and late 1970s) represents Maurice André's art most impressively. The only transcription included is from a Handel *Oboe concerto*, and that is reasonably effective. Michael Haydn's *Concerto*, a concertante section of a seven-movement *Serenade*, has incredibly high tessitura, with the D trumpet taken up to high A (the fourth ledger-line above the treble stave), the highest note in any classical trumpet concerto. It is just a peep but, characteristically, Maurice André reaches up for it with consummate ease. He is completely at home in all this repertoire: his version of the Joseph Haydn *Concerto* is stylish and elegant, with a memorably eloquent account of the slow movement, the line gracious and warmly serene. The *Sonata for trumpet and organ* by Giovanni Buonaventura Viviani (1638–*c.* 1692) is also an attractive piece, comprising five brief but striking miniatures, each only a minute or so in length. In the Vivaldi *Double concerto* André plays both solo parts.

Ballet

'Nights at the ballet' (with (i) RPO, Weldon; (ii) Philh. O; (iii) Kurtz; (iv) Irving; (v) RPO, Fistoulari; (vi) CBSO, Frémaux; (vii) New Philh. O, Mackerras): excerpts from: (i) TCHAIKOVSKY: *Nutcracker; Swan Lake.* (ii; iii) PROKOFIEV: *Romeo and Juliet.* (ii; iv) ADAM: *Giselle.* (v) LUIGINI: *Ballet Égyptien* (suite). (vi) SATIE: *Gymnopédies Nos 1 and 3.* (vii) DELIBES: *Coppélia.* GOUNOD: *Faust* (suite).
(B) *** EMI *TC2-MOM 111.*

Here (on tape only) is nearly an hour and a half of the most tuneful and colourful ballet music ever written. Kurtz's three excerpts from

Romeo and Juliet are distinguished, if a little sombre, the inclusion of the Fistoulari recording of *Ballet Égyptien* is most welcome, and Mackerras is at his sparkling best in the *Coppélia* and *Faust* selections. Weldon's Tchaikovsky performances lack the last degree of flair, but they are alert and well played. The sound is admirable both for home listening and in the car.

Baroque Classics

'Baroque classics: Vivace!' (with (i) Cantilena, Shepherd; (ii) SCO, Gibson; (iii) Soloists of Australia, Thomas): (i) HANDEL: *Solomon: Arrival of the Queen of Sheba.* (ii) *Water music: Overture; Alla hornpipe.* (iii) BACH: *Violin concerto No. 2 in E, BWV 1042.* (i) *Suite No. 3: Air.* PACHELBEL: *Canon.* VIVALDI: *Concerto for strings in A, RV 159.* (iii) *L'Estro armonico: Quadruple violin concerto in B min., Op. 3/10.* (i) CORELLI: *Concerto grosso in G min. (Christmas), Op. 6/8.*
(M) **(*) Chan. Dig. CHAN 6527; *MBTD 6527* [id.].

Overall an agreeable late-evening concert. Pachelbel's *Canon* is serene but rather bland; otherwise the selection does not lack vitality, and the contributions from Ronald Thomas (especially the Bach *Violin concerto*) and Sir Alexander Gibson make one wish they had a greater share of the programme. However, the Corelli *Concerto grosso* is very pleasing, and the sound is excellent throughout.

Baroque music

'The sound of baroque' (with (i) Royal Liverpool PO, Groves; (ii) Scottish CO, Tortelier; (iii) LPO, Boult; (iv) Menuhin, Ferras, Bath Fest. O; (v) Bournemouth Sinf., Montgomery; (vi) Reginald Kilbey and Strings; (vii) RPO, Weldon, (viii) ASMF, Marriner): (i) ALBINONI: *Adagio for strings and organ* (arr. Giazotto). (ii) BACH: *Suite No. 3 in D, BWV 1068: Air.* (iii) *Brandenburg concerto No. 3 in G, BWV 1048.* (iv) *Double violin concerto in D, BWV 1043.* (i) GLUCK: *Orfeo: Dance of the Blessed Spirits.* (v) HANDEL: *Messiah: Pastoral symphony. Berenice: overture.* (v) *Solomon: Arrival of the Queen of Sheba.* (vi) *Serse: Largo.* (vii) *Water music: suite* (arr. Harty). (viii) PACHELBEL: *Canon.*
(B) *** EMI *TC2-MOM 103.*

One of the first of EMI's 'Miles of Music' tapes, planned for motorway listening as well as at home, and offering about 80 minutes of favourite baroquerie, this is recommendable in every way. The sound is full and lively, the performances are first class, with Bach's *Double violin concerto* and *Brandenburg No. 3* (Boult) bringing substance among the lollipops.

Bavarian State Orchestra, Wolfgang Sawallisch

Russian orchestral music: KABALEVSKY: *The Comedians* (suite), *Op. 26.* RIMSKY-KORSAKOV: *Capriccio espagnole, Op. 34.* GLINKA: *Overture: Russlan and Ludmilla.* BORODIN: *In the steppes of Central Asia.* MUSSORGSKY (arr. Rimsky-Korsakov): *Night on the bare mountain.* PROKOFIEV: *The Love for 3 Oranges, Op. 33: March & Scherzo.*
(M) *** EMI Dig. CDD7 63893-2 [id.]; *ET 763893-4.*

This splendid concert of Russian music was included in EMI's first reissued release of mid-priced digital repertoire, although it had not appeared before in the UK. It was made in the Herkulessaal, Munich, in 1987. The sound is splendid, resonantly full, coloured by the attractive ambient bloom characteristic of this famous hall, yet vivid and lively too. Apart from offering the best-ever version of the winning Kabalevsky suite, the Rimsky-Korsakov performance is comparably memorable for its sophisticated and brilliant orchestral playing and for sustaining warmth and excitement throughout without ever going over the top. The Glinka and Mussorgsky pieces are similarly distinctive and *In the steppes of Central Asia* is particularly appealing, not overtly romantic but refreshingly direct. The programme ends with Prokofiev, sparkling and witty, but not too abrasive, like the Kabalevsky at the opening.

BBC Symphony Orchestra, Sir Colin Davis

'The Last Night of the Proms' (with BBC Chorus & Choral Society, Jessye Norman): ELGAR: *Cockaigne overture, Op. 40; Pomp and circumstance march No. 1, Op. 39.* BERLIOZ: *Les Troyens: Hail, all hail to the Queen.* WAGNER: *Wesendonk Lieder: Schmerzen; Träume.* MENDELSSOHN: *Octet: Scherzo.* WOOD: *Fantasia on British sea-songs.* HANDEL: *Judas Maccabaeus: See, the conqu'ring hero comes.* ARNE: *Rule Britannia.* PARRY: *Jerusalem* (arr. Elgar).
(M) *** Ph. 420 085-2; *420 085-4.*

Although the vociferous clapping is sometimes almost overwhelming, this CD (recorded on two 'last nights', in 1969 and 1972) fully captures the exuberant atmosphere of the occasion. Only the *Cockaigne overture* is slightly below par. The full humour of the *Sea songs* extravaganza is well caught, with the clapping coming totally to grief in the *Sailor's hornpipe*. But the fervour of the singing in *Land of hope and glory* and *Rule Britannia* is caught superbly, and the entry of the organ crowns a frisson-making version of Parry's *Jerusalem*.

Bergen Philharmonic Orchestra, Dimitri Kitayenko

'The Sorcerer's apprentice': DUKAS: *The sorcerer's apprentice*. RAVEL: *Ma Mère l'Oye: suite*. DEBUSSY: *Prélude à l'après-midi d'un faune*. RAVEL: *Boléro*. MUSSORGSKY: *A Night on the bare mountain* (original version).
(BB) *** Virgo Dig. VJ7 91471-2; *VJ 791471-4*.

This is an enjoyable concert, vividly played and given first-class digital recording. It is an inexpensive way to get to know Mussorgsky's original scheme for *Night on the bare mountain* before Rimsky-Korsakov laminated his own ideas (including an interpolated brass fanfare) on to the score. Even without the melancholy closing section, the piece plays for half as long again as Rimsky's refurbishment. It is crude, rambling and repetitive, but it sounds strikingly primitive and bizarrely individual. The opening Dukas showpiece is glowingly animated, and the other works come off well too. The performances are direct and atmospheric, while *Boléro* mores steadily forward to produce a strong climax. Excellent value, but inadequate documentation.

Berlin Philharmonic Orchestra, Herbert von Karajan

'Karajan à Paris': RAVEL: *Boléro*. BIZET: *L'Arlésienne: suite No. 2*. CHABRIER: *España*. GOUNOD: *Faust: ballet suite*. BERLIOZ: *La Damnation de Faust: Hungarian march*.
(M) **(*) EMI CDM7 63527-2; *EG 763527-4*.

The original LP was short measure, so EMI have added *Boléro*, which is exciting enough but does not match Karajan's DG analogue version. The climax, too, is fierce. The rest of the programme finds the conductor in Beecham territory, but his approach is less incandescent, and his phrasing sometimes seems heavy for a volatile French concert. His view is broad (some might say rhythmically sluggish) in the Bizet, taut in the Chabrier, while nevertheless presenting this colourful music with brilliance and flair; indeed *España* has an infectious, tingling zest. The *Faust* ballet music is very attractive too, the playing full of warmth and elegance; but the Berlioz march, although exciting, does not sound very French. This is partly the fault of the recording which is very well upholstered although brightened by the CD transfer. The result is extremely vivid but lacks something in refinement at climaxes.

Christmas concertos: CORELLI: *Concerto grosso in G min., Op. 6/8*. MAREDINI: *Concerto grosso in C, Op. 3/12*. TORELLI: *Concerto a 4 in forma di pastorale per il santissimo natale*. LOCATELLI: *Concerto grosso in F min., Op. 1/8*. G. GABRIELI: *Canzona a 8*. SCHEIDT: *In dulci jubilo*. ECCARD: *Vom Himmel hoch; Es ist ein Ros' entsprungen*. GRUBER: *Stille Nacht*.
(M) **(*) DG 419 413-2 [id.].

Karajan's collection of baroque Christmas concertos brings first-class playing from the Berlin Philharmonic; but concentration on sensuous beauty of texture (the string sonorities are often ravishing) does tend to be self-defeating when four pieces with a similar pastoral inspiration are heard together. So DG had the bright idea of interspersing the concertos with carol-like chorales, played by the Berlin Philharmonic brass, ending the concert with Gruber's *Silent Night*. While purists and authenticists are warned to stay clear, others may find a good deal to enjoy here. The remastered 1970s recording is still very good.

GRIEG: *Holberg suite, Op. 40*. SIBELIUS: *Finlandia, Op. 26*. SMETANA: *Má Vlast: Vltava*. LISZT: *Les Préludes*.
(M) *** DG Dig. 427 808-2; *427 808-4*.

Four characterful performances, digitally recorded, superbly played and showing the Karajan charisma at its most impressive. At mid-price this is self-recommending, although Karajan's earlier, EMI recording of the Liszt symphonic poem is even more telling.

'Karajan Festival': BRAHMS: *Hungarian dances Nos. 1, 3, 5, 6, 17–20*. BORODIN: *Prince Igor: Polvtsian dances*. TCHAIKOVSKY: *Eugene Onegin: Polonaise & Waltz*. SMETANA: *The Bartered Bride: Polka; Furiant; Dance of the Comedians*. GRIEG: *Peer Gynt suites 1 & 2*. SIBELIUS: *Finlandia, Op. 26. Kuolema: Valse triste. Tapiola, Op.112*. RAVEL: *Boléro; Daphnis et Chloé: suite No. 2*. DEBUSSY: *La Mer; Prélude à l'après-midi d'un faune*. ROSSINI: *Overtures: Il barbiere di Siviglia; L'Italiana in Algeri; La gazza ladra; La scala di seta*. VERDI: *Overtures & Preludes: Nabucco; La Traviata; I vespri siciliani; Un ballo in maschera; La forza del destino; Aida*. SMETANA: *Má Vlast: Vltava; Vyšehrad*. DVOŘÁK: *Scherzo capriccioso*. LISZT: *Les Préludes; Hungarian rhapsody No. 4*.
(B) **(*) DG 429 436-2 (5) [id.].

There are many favourite Karajan warhorses here, played with finesse and brilliance. Everything sounds alive, but the CD transfers are often very brightly lit, notably the Brahms and

Tchaikovsky items and the Rossini overtures. However, this is fair value at bargain price, and the Smetana, Grieg and Sibelius performances show Karajan at his finest, while the Ravel and Debussy coupling represents one of the conductor's indispensable recording achievements.

Boskovsky Ensemble, Willi Boskovsky

'Viennese bonbons': J. STRAUSS, Snr: *Chinese galop; Kettenbrücke Waltz; Eisele und Beisele Sprünge. Cachucha galop.* J. STRAUSS, Jnr: *Weine Gemüths waltz; Champagne galop; Salon polka.* LANNER: *Styrian dances; Die Werber & Marien waltzes; Bruder halt galop.* MOZART: *3 Contredanses, K.462; 4 German dances, K.600/1 & 3; K.605/1; K.611.* SCHUBERT: *8 Waltzes & Ländler.*
(M) *** Van. 8.8015.71 [OVC 8015].

This is a captivating selection of the most delightful musical confectionery imaginable. Just over an hour of music is transferred here from a much-praised Boskovsky LP from the early 1970s. The ensemble is a small chamber group, similar to that led by the Strausses, and the playing has an appropriately intimate Viennese atmosphere. Not surprisingly, Boskovsky shows a strong personality as leader and soloist, and this colourful writing bubbles with good spirits and attractive melodies. The programme is made up almost entirely of rare repertoire and it makes one realize what an inexhaustible wealth of rare vintage there is in the Viennese musical cellars. The transfer is impeccable and the recording, made in the Baumgarten Hall, Vienna, is fresh, smooth and clear, with a nice bloom on sound which is never too inflated.

Boston Symphony Orchestra, Serge Koussevitzky

COPLAND: *El Salón México.* FOOTE: *Suite in E min., Op. 63.* HARRIS: *Symphony (1933); Symphony No. 3.* MCDONALD: *San Juan Capistrano – Two Evening Pictures.*
(M) (***) Pearl mono GEMMCD 9492.

This valuable CD brings some classic American music in classic performances. For many collectors, the Boston Symphony has never produced as fine a sonority or as consummate a virtuosity as it did for Koussevitzky. His performance of the Roy Harris *Third Symphony* has never been equalled in intensity and fire – even by Toscanini or Bernstein – and Copland himself never produced as exhilarating an *El Salón México.* Older collectors who cherish special memories of these electrifying performances will find that they are better even than they remembered. The 1933 Harris *Symphony* was the first American symphony ever to be put down on wax; the recording was made at its first New York performance, when the engineers missed the opening timpani note! Minor patching took place later. The Arthur Foote *Suite* is unpretentious and has great charm. Sonic limitations are soon forgotten, for these performances have exceptional power and should not be missed.

Brüggen, Frans (recorder)

Recorder concertos (with VCM, Harnoncourt): VIVALDI: *Concerto in C min., RV 441.* SAMMARTINI: *Concerto in F.* TELEMANN: *Concerto in C.* NAUDOT: *Concerto in G.*
(M) *** Teldec/Warner 2292 43547-2 [id.].

Frans Brüggen is an unsurpassed master of his instrument, and he gives the four assorted concertos his keen advocacy on this excellent record, reissued from 1968. (In the Vivaldi he even takes part in the tutti.) In his hands, phrases are turned with the utmost sophistication, intonation is unbelievably accurate and matters of style exact. There is spontaneity too and, with superb musicianship, good recording and a well-balanced orchestral contribution, this mid-priced CD can earn nothing but praise.

Capella Istropolitana, Adrian Leaper

'English string festival': DOWLAND: *Galliard a 5.* ELGAR: *Elegy, Op. 58; Introduction and allegro, Op. 47; Serenade, Op. 20.* BRIDGE: *Lament.* PARRY: *An English suite; Lady Radnor's suite.*
(BB) **(*) Naxos Dig. 8.550331 [id.].

It is fascinating and rewarding to hear these excellent Slovak players turn their attention to essentially English repertoire, and with a considerable degree of success. The brief Dowland *Galliard* makes a strong introduction, and the attractive pair of neo-Baroque Parry suites of dance movements, played with warmth, finesse and spirit, are given bright and lively sound. In the Elgar *Introduction and allegro* the violins above the stave have their upper partials overbrilliantly lit by the digital recording, the focus not quite sharp; but otherwise the sound is full, with plenty of resonant ambience. The playing is strongly felt, but the fugue is a bit too measured, and the great striding theme, played in unison on the G string, could also do with more pace, especially when it returns. Otherwise this is persuasive, and the *Serenade* is presented simply, combining warmth and finish. At superbargain price, this is worth exploring.

Chamber Orchestra of Europe, Judd

'Music of the Masters': BEETHOVEN: *Creatures of Prometheus overture, Op. 43.* MOZART: *Divertimento No. 1 in D for strings, K.136.* ROSSINI: *Il Barbiere di Siviglia: Overture.* FAURÉ: *Pavane, Op. 50.* WAGNER: *Siegfried idyll.*
(B) **(*) Pickwick Dig. PCD 805.

An enjoyable and well-balanced programme with first-class ensemble from these young players and excellently balanced digital recording. The presence and naturalness of the sound are especially striking in the Fauré *Pavane* (with a beautiful flute solo) and the *Siegfried idyll*, using only a small string group. James Judd brings stylish, thoroughly musical direction, although the overall presentation is a shade anonymous.

Chicago Symphony Orchestra, Barenboim

SMETANA: *Má Vlast: Vltava.* DVOŘÁK: *Slavonic dances, Op. 46/1 and 8.* BRAHMS: *Hungarian dances Nos. 1, 3 & 10.* BORODIN: *Prince Igor: Polovtsian dances.* LISZT: *Les Préludes.*
(M) *** DG 415 851-2.

The *Polovtsian dances* have splendid life and impetus. Indeed one hardly misses the chorus, so lively is the orchestral playing. Both *Vltava* and *Les Préludes* show Barenboim and the Chicago orchestra at their finest. *Vltava* is highly evocative – especially the moonlight sequence – and beautifully played; *Les Préludes* has dignity and poetry as well as excitement. The Brahms and Dvořák *Dances* make attractive encores. The only slight snag is that, in the digital remastering, the recording has lost some of its original glow and the strings sound thinner above the stave. But this is striking only in the violin timbre of the big tune of *Vltava*.

City of Birmingham Symphony Orchestra, Louis Frémaux

French music: RAVEL: *Boléro.* DEBUSSY: *Prélude à l'après-midi d'un faune.* DUKAS: *L'apprenti sorcier.* SAINT-SAËNS: *Danse macabre.* CHABRIER: *España.* OFFENBACH: *Overture: La vie parisienne.* HONEGGER: *Pacific 231.* SATIE: *Gymnopédies 1 & 3.* LITOLFF: *Concerto symphonique: Scherzo* (with John Ogdon).
(M) **(*) EMI CDM7 63023-2; *EG 763023-4.*

A generous programme from a successful earlier CBSO era when Frémaux gave the orchestra something of a French accent. The Offenbach *Overture* is as racy as anyone could desire; *The Sorcerer's apprentice* also has plenty of sparkle and Chabrier's *España* is hardly less vivid, while *Danse macabre* is both lively and exciting. Contrasts come with the Debussy *Prélude* and the fresh melancholy of the Satie. Ogdon is a brilliant if not a subtle soloist in the famous Litolff *Scherzo*. The recordings were originally very reverberant and the remastering has generally improved definition, most effectively in the powerful evocation of Honegger's *Pacific 231*, now sounding massive yet not oppressive at its spectacular climax.

Cleveland Orchestra, Lorin Maazel

Overtures: VERDI: *La forza del destino.* BEETHOVEN: *Creatures of Prometheus.* BERLIOZ: *Le carnaval romain.* GLINKA: *Russlan and Ludmilla.* BRAHMS: *Academic festival overture.* ROSSINI: *La gazza ladra.*
(B) *** Pickwick IMPX 9027.

A most enjoyable collection of overtures, very well recorded by Decca in 1976 and enjoying the splendid acoustics of the Cleveland Hall. Maazel's charisma is especially well demonstrated by the opening *Forza del destino* and there is no more effective modern recording of *Le carnaval romain*, in which the hall ambience makes an impressive effect with the brass. The orchestral response is as spontaneous as it is polished throughout a vivid programme. The timing is only 47 minutes 40 seconds, but this is fair value in the bargain range.

Cleveland, Royal Philharmonic or Philharmonia Orchestras, Vladimir Ashkenazy

'Capriccio italien': TCHAIKOVSKY: *Capriccio italien.* DEBUSSY: *Prélude à l'après-midi d'un faune; Nocturnes: Fêtes.* SIBELIUS: *Finlandia.* R. STRAUSS: *Salome's dance.* BRUCH: *Kol Nidrei.* RIMSKY-KORSAKOV: *Flight of the bumble-bee.* BORODIN: *Prince Igor: Polovtsian dances* (with London Opera Ch.).
(M) *** Decca 430 730-2; *430 730-4* [id.].

This highly succesful compilation offers Decca's top-quality digital sound throughout; the recordings were made in different venues between 1980 and 1988, yet every piece is in the demonstration bracket. The opening *Capriccio italien* is superb, spectacular, elegant and possessed of exhilarating impetus. *Finlandia* is hardly less exciting, and the performance of the *Polovtsian dances* carries all before it, yet also produces some richly lyrical singing from the chorus. *Salome's dance* has great sensuous feeling and a powerful dénouement, while Lynn Harrell provides a contrasting, mellower interlude with Bruch's *Kol Nidrei.* Ashkenazy's Debussy is unconventional, the *Prélude à l'après-midi d'un faune* freely rhapsodical and given a will-o'-the-wisp delicacy by the transparency of the Cleveland recording, while the climax of *Fêtes* is grippingly extrovert.

Consort of London, Robert Haydon Clark

Baroque concert: HANDEL: *Solomon: Arrival of the Queen of Sheba.* BACH: *Concerto for violin and oboe, BWV 1060.* ALBINONI: *Adagio* (arr. Giazotto). ZIPOLI: *Elevazione for cello & oboe.* GLUCK: *Orpheus: Dance of the Furies; Dance of the Blessed Spirits & Interlude.* BOYCE: *Symphony No. 4 in F.* PACHELBEL: *Canon.* PURCELL: *The Indian Queen: Trumpet tune.*
(M) ** Collins Dig. 3011-2.

The Queen of Sheba here arrives rather demurely and the playing overall, though warm and polished, is just a trifle bland. The Bach *Concerto* is very well played and the Boyce is enjoyable too, but the music-making really springs fully to life in the closing Purcell trumpet piece. Good sound, but this is in no way distinctive.

'Country gardens'

English music (various artists, including Bournemouth SO, Silvestri; Hallé O, Barbirolli; Royal Liverpool PO, Groves; E. Sinfonia, Dilkes): VAUGHAN WILLIAMS: *The Wasps: Overture. Rhosymedre.* WARLOCK: *Capriol suite.* DELIUS: *Summer night on the river. A Song before sunset.* GRAINGER: *Country gardens. Mock Morris; Shepherd's Hey.* arr. BRIDGE: *Cherry Ripe.* COLERIDGE TAYLOR: *Petite suite de concert* (excerpts). GERMAN: *Nell Gwyn: 3 Dances.* COATES: *Meadow to Mayfair: In the country. Summer Days: At the dance. Wood Nymphs.* ELGAR: *Chanson de matin. Salut d'amour.*
(B) **(*) EMI *TC2-MOM 123.*

A recommendable tape-only collection, essentially lightweight but never trivial. Barbirolli's Delius and Neville Dilkes's *Capriol suite* are among the highlights, and certainly it makes a most entertaining concert for use on a long journey, with the lively Grainger, Coates and German pastoral dances providing an excellent foil for the lyrical music. On domestic equipment the quality is slightly variable, with side two noticeably brighter than side one. Thus the opening *Wasps overture* is a little bass-heavy and the attractive *Capriol suite* has a more restricted upper range here than when it appears on EMI's companion tape collection '*Serenade*' (see below). But the rest of the programme sounds well.

Dallas Symphony Orchestra, Eduardo Mata

TCHAIKOVSKY: *Capriccio italien, Op. 45.* MUSSORGSKY: *Night on the bare mountain.* DUKAS: *L'apprenti sorcier.* ENESCU: *Rumanian rhapsody No. 1.*
(BB) *** BMG/RCA Dig. VD 87727 [7727-2-RV].

One of the outstanding early digital orchestral demonstration CDs. The acoustic of the Dallas Hall produces a thrilling resonance without too much clouding of detail. The Mussorgsky piece is rather lacking in menace when textures are so ample. *The Sorcerer's apprentice* is spirited and affectionately characterized, yet there is no sense of real calamity at the climax. But the Tchaikovsky and Enescu are richly enjoyable, even if the latter lacks the last degree of unbuttoned exuberance in its closing pages. A very real bargain in the lowest price-range.

Detroit Symphony Orchestra, Paul Paray

'French opera highlights': HÉROLD: *Overture: Zampa.* AUBER: *Overture: The Crown diamonds.* GOUNOD: *Faust: ballet suite; Waltz* (from Act II). SAINT-SAENS: *Samson et Dalila: Bacchanale.* BIZET: *Carmen: Danse bohème.* BERLIOZ: *Les Troyens: Royal hunt and storm.* MASSENET: *Phèdre overture.* THOMAS: *Mignon: Gavotte.*
(M) *** Mercury 432 014-2 [id.].

Paul Paray's reign at Detroit tempted the Mercury producers to record a good deal of French music under his baton, and here is a good example of the Gallic verve and sparkle that were achieved. The two overtures combine colour and flair with high spirits, while the highly animated *Faust ballet music* has much elegance, with the famous *Waltz* joyfully following at the end, with superb rhythmic lift. The *Danse bohème* from *Carmen* has comparable dash. The only disappointment is the unslurred horn phrasing at the magical opening and close of the *Royal hunt and storm.* This may be authentic but, under Beecham and Munch, the gently moulded effect is much more evocative. However, this piece does not lack excitement, and one's only other complaint is that the deliciously polished account of the very Parisian *Gavotte* from *Mignon*, which acts as a bonne-bouche at the end, makes one wish for the whole overture instead.

Du Pré, Jacqueline (cello)

'Impressions': ELGAR: *Cello concerto in E min., Op. 85* (with LSO, Barbirolli). HAYDN: *Cello concerto in C* (with ECO, Barenboim). BEETHOVEN: *Cello sonata No. 3 in A, Op. 69* (with Barenboim): *Piano trio No. 5 in D (Ghost), Op. 70/1* (with Barenboim and Zukerman).
(M) *** EMI CMS7 69707-2 (2).

A medium-priced anthology that is self-recommending if the mixed programme is of appeal. The chamber-music performances have the same qualities of spontaneity and inspiration that have made Du Pré's account of Elgar's *Cello concerto* come to be treasured above all others; if some find her approach to Haydn too romantic, it is nevertheless difficult to resist in its ready warmth. The sound-quality is fairly consistent, for all the remastered transfers are successful.

Eastman Wind Ensemble, Frederick Fennell

'Screamers' (Circus marches): HEED: *In storm and sunshine.* ALLEN: *Whip and spur.* KING: *Invictus; The big cage; Robinson's grand entree; Circus days.* FILLMORE: *Bones trombone; Circus bee; Rolling thunder.* HUFFINE: *Them basses.* JEWELL: *The screamer.* FUČIC: *Thunder and lightning.* FARRAR: *Bombasto.* HUFF: *The squealer.* RIBBLE: *Bennett's triumphal.* DUPLE: *Bravura. 'March time'*: GOLDMAN: *Bugles and drum; Illinois march; Children's march; The Interlochen Bowl; Onward-upward; Boy Scouts of America.* FILLMORE: *Americans we.* BROWNE HALL: *Officer of the day.* SEITZ: *Grandioso.* REEVES: *Second Regiment, Connecticut National Guard march.* ALFORD: *The mad major.* RODGERS: *Victory at sea: Guadalcanal march.*
(M) *** Mercury 432 019-2 [id.].

This 66-minute CD combines the contents of two analogue LPs recorded five years apart, although the earlier (1957) collection is just as demonstration-worthy of Mercury engineering brilliance. It offers an exhilarating collection of circus marches, notable for their fast pacing and for playing of much bravura and remarkably nimble articulation. Karl King was official bandmaster to Barnum & Bailey, but Henry Fillmore was his equal in good-natured razzmatazz. He was a trombone player and gleefully takes the mickey out of his instrument in *Bones trombone* which is gloriously vulgar. All the music has great exuberance, but the most familiar piece to British ears will be Fučik's *Thunder and lightning*, played with enjoyable verve and brashness. When the second (1962) collection opens with *Bugles and drums*, the pacing seems almost too slow by contrast, though in fact the style is admirably peppy. The six Goldman marches are impressively inventive, especially the *Children's march*, audaciously quoting from nursery rhymes. Kenneth Alford's *The Mad major* is appropriately played in a more relaxed, British style and becomes almost flaccid; the freshest march here is the one by Richard Rodgers.

'The (American) Civil War – its music and its sounds' (with Martin Gabel, narrator, and the reactivated Battery B, 2nd New Jersey Light Artillery): *Band and field music including camp, garrison and field calls for fifes and drums, cavalry bugle calls and signals; songs of the Union and Confederate troops. Firearms of the Civil War. The Appomattox bugle. The sounds of conflict: Gettysburg to Appomattox.*
(M) *** Mercury 432 591-2 (2) [id.].

This extraordinarily diverse collection – the music ranges from *Hail Columbia* and *Dixie* to a tune from Weber's *Der Freischütz*, arranged as a quickstep – has been lovingly and indefatigably assembled by Frederick Fennell. He used the original band-parts (one was unreadable, having been holed by a bullet and rendered illegible by water) and original instruments. Many of the latter were uniquely designed with their bells facing backwards, over the shoulder, so that the troops following the band could hear the music more easily. For the recording, the clarinets and piccolos had their backs to the conductor and watched him through mirrors; thus the projection of sound from forward- and backward-facing instruments could be co-ordinated for the microphones. Similarly, the recordings of ordnance were made with authentic guns, using the actual battlefield of Gettysburg. A British military diarist, Colonel Arthur Freemantle, who was an observer (up in a tree) with Robert E. Lee's army at that famous battle, wrote: 'When the cannonade was at its height, a Confederate band of music, between the cemetery and ourselves, began to play polkas and waltzes, which sounded very curious, accompanied by the hissing and bursting of shells.' This bizarre experience is re-created here, alongside many of the other sounds which were part of this terrible four-year conflict which left 714,245 Americans dead or wounded. The documentation accompanying the CD could hardly be better, and the contribution of the narrator, Martin Gabel, is admirable. Needless to say, the recordings are spectacularly realistic.

GRAINGER: *Lincolnshire posy. Hill song No. 2.* PERSICHETTI: *Symphony No. 6 for band.*

KHACHATURIAN: *Armenian dances.* W. HARTLEY: *Concerto for 23 winds.* B. ROGERS: *3 Japanese dances.*
(M) **(*) Mercury 432 754-2 [id.].

Marvellous playing and fine recording (incredibly, dating from as early as 1958/9) but the music is of varying interest. Grainger's folksy six-movement *Lincolnshire posy*, wittily and strongly characterized, and the *Hill song* are the highlights. Persichetti's *Symphony* also seems to have a folk element and is brilliantly conceived for the idiom. Its first movement offers some original effects, while the central *Adagio* and *Allegretto* are fairly attractive. But the work falls off at the end. Walter Hartley's *Concerto* is also striking in its blending of colours and it has a cool *Lento* which is rather agreeable. The *Japanese dances* of Bernard Rogers (1893–1968) are ingenuously pentatonic, yet the scoring titillates the ear, especially when so well caught by the recording; but Khachaturian's pair of *Armenian dances* are run-of-the-mill and thin in invention.

English Chamber Orchestra, Raymond Leppard

ALBINONI: *Sonata a 5 in A, Op. 2/3; Sonata a 5 in G min., Op. 2/6.* VIVALDI: *Concertos: in D, P.175; in G min., P.392; Sonata in E flat (Al Santo sepolcro), P.441.* CORELLI: *Concerto grosso in F, Op. 6/9.*
(B) *** CfP CD-CFP 4371; *TC-CFP 4371.*

An outstanding collection of Italian string concertos, recorded in 1970 and sounding first class in digitally remastered form: there is fullness, yet everything sounds fresh. The two Albinoni *Sonatas* are particularly attractive: the four contrasted movements of Op. 2, No. 3, are individually characterized, with the richness of the five-part ensemble obvious in the two slow movements and the fugal allegros sprightly and resilient, and with Leppard adding some witty harpsichord comments in the finale. The Corelli *Concerto grosso* has six equally diverse movements and, while Vivaldi's *Al Santo sepolcro* has only two, they are strongly contrasted. The standard of invention throughout the concert is high and the playing is polished and committed. Except for those who can accept only original instruments, this is a fine concert for the late evening.

'Baroque favourites': M.-A. CHARPENTIER: *Te Deum in D: Introduction.* PACHELBEL: *Canon in D.* BACH: *Chorale preludes: Ich ruf' zu dir; Wir Eilen mit Schwachen; Erbarm' dich. Cantata No. 156: Sinfonia. Suite No. 3 in D: Air. Suite No. 2 in B min.: Badinerie.* HANDEL: *Solomon: Arrival of the Queen of Sheba. Harpsichord suite in D min.: Sarabande. Berenice: Minuet.* GLUCK: *Orfeo: Dance of the Blessed Spirits.* MARCELLO: *Oboe concerto in D min.: 2nd movement.* VIVALDI: *Violin concerto in D, Op. 3/9:* Slow movement. PURCELL: *Abdelazer: suite.*
(M) **(*) Sony Dig. MDK 44650 [id.].

Opening regally with trumpets, Leppard's concert includes many of the usual baroque lollipops, including an engagingly elegant version of the famous Pachelbel *Canon*, and some fine solo oboe contributions from Neil Black, notably in the cantilena from the Bach *Sinfonia* and the slow movement from Alessandro Marcello's *D minor Oboe concerto*. The original programme has been filled out by a substantial suite of Purcellian theatre music from *Abdelazer*, which includes a brisk presentation of the famous tune Britten used as the basis for his *Young person's guide to the orchestra.* Excellent, vivid digital recording.

English Sinfonia, Sir Charles Groves

'Entente cordiale': FAURÉ: *Masques et bergamasques, Op. 112; Pavane, Op. 50.* ELGAR: *Chanson de nuit; Chanson de matin, Op. 15/1–2.* DELIUS: *On hearing the first cuckoo in spring.* RAVEL: *Pavane pour une infante défunte.* WARLOCK: *Capriol suite.* BUTTERWORTH: *The Banks of green willow.* SATIE: *Gymnopédies Nos. 1 & 3* (orch. Debussy).
(B) *** Pickwick Dig. PCD 926.

Having given us some attractive Haydn recordings with the English Sinfonia, Sir Charles Groves now offers a happy juxtaposition of French and British music. He opens with a performance of Fauré's *Masques et bergamasques* which is sheer delight in its airy grace, and later he finds passion as well as delicacy in the Butterworth rhapsody, very effectively followed by Debussy's languorous orchestrations of the Satie *Gymnopédies.* Groves's approach to Warlock's *Capriol* dances is essentially genial (Marriner's version has more zest); but all this music-making is easy to enjoy. The playing is polished and spontaneous and the recording, made at Abbey Road, quite splendid.

English String Orchestra or English Symphony Orchestra, William Boughton

'The spirit of England': ELGAR: *Overture Cockaigne; Introduction and allegro, Op. 47; Sospiri, Op. 70.* DELIUS: *Summer evening.* BUTTERWORTH: *The banks of green willow; A Shropshire lad.* FINZI: *Suite from Love's*

Labour's Lost; *Clarinet concerto* (with Alan Hacker). VAUGHAN WILLIAMS: *The lark ascending* (with Michael Bochmann); *Oboe concerto* (with Maurice Bourgue); *Fantasia on a theme of Thomas Tallis; Fantasia on Greensleeves.* PARRY: *Lady Radnor's suite.* BRIDGE: *Suite for string orchestra.* HOLST: *St Paul's suite.* WARLOCK: *Capriol suite.* BRITTEN: *Variations on a theme of Frank Bridge, Op. 10.*
❀ (B) *** Nimbus Dig. NI 5210/3 [id.].

From 1984 onwards Nimbus have been carefully building a catalogue of English orchestral works, much of it drawn from our great legacy of string music, played by the Birmingham-based English String and Symphony Orchestras under William Boughton. He is completely at home in this repertoire and also has the gift of making a studio recording sound like live music-making. One has only to sample his excitingly animated account of Holst's *St Paul's suite* (which also has much delicacy of feeling), the ideally paced Warlock *Capriol suite*, or the vibrant account of Britten's *Frank Bridge variations*, to discover the calibre of this music-making. The recordings were made in the Great Hall of Birmingham University which, with its warm reverberation, gives the strings a gloriously rich body of tone, supported by sumptuous cello and bass sonorities. At the very opening of the Britten *Variations* one might feel a certain excess of resonance at the bottom end but, when the great *Funeral march* arrives, one revels in its amplitude and physical impact. The Elgar *Introduction and allegro* expands wonderfully at its climax (yet the fugue is not blurred) and in Vaughan Williams's *Lark ascending*, where the violin solo is exquisitely played with wonderful purity of tone by Michael Bochmann, the closing pianissimo seems to float in the still air. The work most suited to such an expansive acoustic is Vaughan Williams's *Tallis fantasia*, a deeply expressive performance which gives the listener the impression of sitting in a cathedral, with the solo string group, perfectly matched and blended in timbre, evoking a distant, ethereal organ. The lovely Butterworth pieces are tenderly sympathetic, and Alan Hacker's rhapsodically improvisatory account of Finzi's *Clarinet concerto* is full of colour and warmth. Perhaps Maurice Bourgue's oboe is balanced a little too closely in Vaughan Williams's *Oboe concerto* but the ear adjusts. On the other hand, the flutes melt magically into the strings in the famous *Greensleeves fantasia*. Delius's *Summer evening*, an early work, is quite memorable, and the suites of Parry and Finzi are full of colourful invention. The Bridge *Suite for strings* brings a lively response, with sumptuous textures. Because of the consistency of the acoustic illusion given to the listener, it is easy to sit back and be enveloped by this very involving music-making, which is made more rather than less communicative by its distancing. Only the opening *Cockaigne overture* of Elgar is a little lacking in profile and drama – and even here Boughton's relaxed, lyrical approach is enjoyable, for he broadens the final climax very satisfyingly. Very reasonably priced, this box makes an outstanding bargain.

Gothenburg Symphony Orchestra, Neeme Järvi

'Intermezzo': Intermezzi from: MASCAGNI: *Cavalleria Rusticana; L'amico Fritz.* CILEA: *Adriana Lecouvreur.* PUCCINI: *Manon Lescaut; Suor Angelica.* LEONCAVALLO: *Pagliacci.* WOLF-FERRARI: *Jewels of the Madonna.* SCHMIDT: *Notre Dame.* MUSSORGSKY: *Khovanshchina.* MASSENET: *Thaïs: Méditation.* VERDI: *La Traviata: Preludes to Acts I & III.* OFFENBACH: *Contes d'Hoffmann: Barcarolle.* PONCHIELLI: *La Gioconda: Dance of the hours.*
(M) *** DG Dig. 429 494-2; *429 494-4* [id.].

At mid-price this has obvious attractions, though the modern digital sound could ideally be more sumptuous. But these are distinctive performances: there is plenty of temperament in the more passionate interludes and a balancing restraint in the splendidly shaped *Traviata Preludes*. The vivacious excerpt from *The Jewels of the Madonna* sparkles, and only the *Dance of the hours* gives cause for raised eyebrows with some curiously mannered, hesitant rhythmic distortions.

'Greensleeves'

English music (with (i) Sinfonia of L. or Hallé O, Barbirolli; (ii) New Philh. O, LPO or LSO, Boult; (iii) Williams, Bournemouth SO, Berglund; (iv) E. Sinfonia, Dilkes): (i) VAUGHAN WILLIAMS: *Fantasia on Greensleeves.* (ii) *The Lark ascending* (with Hugh Bean). (iii) *Oboe concerto in A min.* (ii) *English folksongs suite.* (i) DELIUS: *A Village Romeo and Juliet: Walk to the Paradise Garden. On hearing the first cuckoo in spring.* (iv) BUTTERWORTH: *The Banks of green willow.* (ii) ELGAR: *Serenade for strings, Op. 20.* (iii) MOERAN: *Lonely waters.*
(B) *** EMI *TC2-MOM 104.*

Looking at the programme and artists' roster, the reader will hardly need the confirmation that this is a very attractive tape anthology. Performances never disappoint, the layout is excellent, and for the car this is ideal. On domestic equipment the sound is a little variable, although the tape has been remastered since its first issue and now sounds pleasantly smooth on top. Often the quality is both vivid and rich, as in the title-piece and the Elgar *Serenade*. Vaughan Williams's *Oboe concerto*, stylishly played by John Williams, is admirably fresh. This is excellent value.

Hallé Orchestra, Sir John Barbirolli

'Romantic overtures': VERDI: *La forza del destino*. NICOLAI: *The Merry Wives of Windsor*. WEBER: *Oberon*. HUMPERDINCK: *Hansel and Gretel*. MENDELSSOHN: *The Hebrides (Fingal's Cave)*. ROSSINI: *Semiramide; William Tell*. DONIZETTI: *Don Pasquale*.
(M) **(*) EMI CDM7 64138-2 [id.]; *EG 764138-4*.

The programme opens with a superb account of *La forza del destino*, given ripe (1967) Abbey Road recording. Sir John shapes Verdi's great string-tune indulgently with such affectionate magnetism that the result is unforgettable. The other performances were recorded at various times between 1957 and 1959, with the exception of the vivacious *Don Pasquale*, which is mono (1951) but sounds colourful and vivid. Elsewhere, if the sound is sometimes a little dated, the remastering has been highly successful and the performances are full of life, with the two Rossini overtures (like the Verdi) showing the conductor at full stretch.

Hallé Orchestra, Maurice Handford

'Hallé encores': COPLAND: *Fanfare for the Common Man*. KHACHATURIAN: *Spartacus: Adagio of Spartacus and Phrygia*. GOUNOD: *Mors et Vita: Judex*. MACCUNN: *Overture: Land of the Mountain and the Flood*. SATIE: *Gymnopédies Nos. 1 and 3* (orch. Debussy). MASSENET: *Thaïs: Méditation*. TRAD.: *Suo Gan*. BARBER: *Adagio for strings*.
(B) *** CfP CD-CFP 4543; *TC-CFP 4543*.

Maurice Handford and the Hallé offer an exceptionally attractive collection of miscellaneous pieces, beautifully recorded. Many of the items have achieved popularity almost by accident through television and the other media (how else would the MacCunn overture have come – so rightly – to notice?), but the sharpness of the contrasts adds to the charm. The Hallé violins sound a little thin in Barber's beautiful *Adagio*, but otherwise the playing is first rate. What is particularly attractive about this concert is the way the programme is laid out so that each piece follows on naturally after its predecessor. The CD transfer is vivid.

Haskil, Clara (piano)

Concertos (with various orchestras & conductors): MOZART: *Piano concertos Nos. 9 in E flat, K.271; 20 in D min., K.466; 23 in A, K.488; 24 in C min., K.491*. CHOPIN: *Piano concerto No. 2 in F min., Op. 21*. FALLA: *Nights in the gardens of Spain*. SCHUMANN: *Piano concerto in A min., Op. 54*. (Solo piano) *Kinderszenen, Op. 15; Waldszenen, Op. 82*.
(B) *** Ph. 426 964-2 (4) [id.].

These celebrated performances have come up well: they made their first reappearance in a five-LP box and the recording quality largely belies their years – even the Mozart *A major*, K.488, made in Vienna with Sacher in 1954, sounds more than acceptable. The *D minor* (K.466) and *C minor* (K.491) *Concertos*, with Markevich and the Lamoureux Orchestra, are remarkably fresh for 1960 and offer beautifully rounded quality. Haskil rarely puts a foot – or, rather, a hand – wrong here, and though she does no more than hint at the darker dramatic fires of the *D minor*, K.466, she never beautifies the piano writing or reaches for the Dresden china. The Chopin and Falla, again both with Markevich, come from 1960, the last year of her life, and they serve as a reminder that she had a stronger temperament and a wider command of keyboard than her reputation as a Mozartian showed. Her Schumann *Concerto*, recorded in The Hague in 1951 under Willem van Otterloo, is particularly sympathetic, though the piano sound is not quite so fresh on this last disc. The solo Schumann pieces, recorded in the early 1950s, are entirely inside the composer's sensibility and, though again allowances must be made for the engineering, they are fewer than one might have expected. Not only is this set a welcome tribute to an artist of vision and gentleness that her admirers will want to collect, it is one that will give much quiet musical satisfaction.

Heifetz, Jascha (violin)

'The Acoustic recordings 1917–1924' (with André Benoist; Samuel Chotzinoff; O, Pasternak): SCHUBERT: *Ave Maria*. DRIGO: *Valse bluette*. ELGAR: *La Capricieuse, Op. 17*. SARASATE: *Malagueña, Habanera, Op. 21/1 & 2; Introduction and tarantelle, Op. 43; Zapateado, Op. 23/2; Zigeunerweisen, Op. 20/1; Carmen fantasy, Op. 25*. BAZZINI: *La ronde des lutins*. BEETHOVEN: *Ruins of Athens: Chorus of Dervishes; Turkish march*. WIENIAWSKI: *Scherzo-Tarantelle, Op. 16; Concerto No. 2, Op.*

22: Romance. ACHRON: *Hebrew melody, Op. 33; Hebrew lullaby, Hebrew dance, Op. 35; Stimmung, Op. 32.* PAGANINI: *Moto perpetuo; Caprices, Nos. 13 & 20.* KREISLER: *Minuet; Sicilienne et Rigaudon.* GLAZUNOV: *Meditation; Valse.* MOSZKOWSKI: *Guitarre, Op. 45/2.* CHOPIN: *Nocturnes, Op. 9/2; Op. 27/2.* TCHAIKOVSKY: *Souvenir d'un lieu cher: Scherzo, Op. 42/2. Serenade: Valse, Op. 48/2. Concerto, Op. 35: Canzonetta. Sérénade mélancolique, Op. 26.* MENDELSSOHN: *On wings of song, Op. 34/2; Concerto in E min.: finale.* DVOŘÁK: *Slavonic dances, Op. 46/2; Op. 72/2 & 8.* SCHUMANN: *Myrthen: Widmung, Op. 25/1.* LALO: *Symphonie espagnole, Op. 21: Andante.* MOZART: *Divertimento No. 17, K.334: Minuet. Haffner Serenade, K.250: Rondo.* D'AMBROSIO: *Serenade, Op. 4.* JUON: *Berceuse, Op. 28/3.* GOLDMARK: *Concerto in A min., Op. 28: Andante.* GODOWSKY: *Waltz in D.* BRAHMS: *Hungarian dance No. 1 in G min.* HAYDN: *Quartet (Lark), Op. 64/5: Vivace.* GRANADOS: *Danzas españolas, Op. 37/5; Andaluza.* BOULANGER: *Nocturne in F; Cortège.* SCOTT: *The gentle maiden.* SAINT-SAENS: *Havanaise, Op. 83.*
(M) (***) BMG/RCA mono GD 80942 [0942-2-RG] (3).

These recordings first appeared on LP during the mid-1970s and their reissue on CD serves as a salutary reminder of Heifetz's extraordinary powers. The earliest records come from the year of the Russian Revolution, when Heifetz was still sixteen and only five years after he had made his début in St Petersburg. As always with Heifetz, even the highest expectations are surpassed: his effortless technical mastery is dazzling, the golden tone strong and pure, the accuracy of his intonation almost beyond belief and his taste impeccable. The collector will also be agreeably surprised by the quality of sound; the earliest was made only two weeks after his Carnegie Hall début, when the art of recording was still relatively primitive, and the original 78-r.p.m. disc was single-sided. One critic, writing in 1918, said of the then seventeen-year-old boy, 'Kreisler is king, Heifetz the prophet, and all the rest violinists.' Seventy or more years later, his brilliance remains undimmed. The recordings are arranged in chronological order, though the differences during the period are relatively small. This set is a mandatory purchase for all who care about the art of violin playing.

American concertos (with (i) LAPO, Wallenstein; (ii) Dallas SO, Hendl; (iii) Piatigorsky and CO; (iv) RCA Victor SO, Voorhees): (i) KORNGOLD: *Violin concerto, Op. 35.* (ii) RÓZSA: *Violin concerto, Op. 24;* (iii) *Theme and variations, Op. 29a.* (iv) WAXMAN: *Fantasy on Bizet's 'Carmen'.*
(M) *** BMG/RCA mono/stereo GD 87963 [7963-3-RD].

Heifetz's playing in this 1953 mono recording of the Korngold *Violin concerto* is dazzling, the lyrical music sounds gorgeous and the material, drawn from film scores, is always appealing – and especially when presented like this. The Rózsa *Concerto* is slightly less memorable but still worth hearing in such a performance. In the *Theme and variations* he is joined by Piatigorsky, also in very good form. Waxman's *'Carmen' fantasy* is simply a string of Bizet's hit tunes, and they are presented with a panache that is little short of astonishing. Few reservations have to be made about the recording; the Rózsa pieces are in stereo, but the Korngold mono sounds just as good. Anyone who cares about fabulous violin-playing should not miss this disc.

Heifetz, Jascha (violin), RCA Victor SO, William Steinberg or Izler Solomon

LALO: *Symphonie espagnole, Op. 21.* SAINT-SAENS: *Havanaise, Op. 83; Introduction and Rondo capriccioso, Op. 28.* SARASATE: *Zigeunerweisen, Op. 20.* CHAUSSON: *Poème.*
(M) (***) BMG/RCA mono GD 87709 [7709-2-RG].

These recordings come from 1951–2 and are inevitably limited in range and body. Heifetz plays the Lalo *Symphonie espagnole* without the central *Intermezzo* movement, as was the custom before the war – and how he plays it! The virtuosity is dazzling and quite transcends the period sound. The Chausson *Poème*, in which the conductor is Izler Solomon, is quite unlike other versions: stripped of sentimentality, it is curiously affecting.

Holliger, Heinz (oboe)

Concertos (with (i) Frankfurt RSO, Inbal; (ii) ECO, Leppard): (i) BELLINI: *Oboe concerto in E flat.* MOLIQUE: *Oboe concertino in G min.* MOSCHELLES: *Concertante in F for flute and oboe* (with Aurèle Nicolet). RIETZ: *Konzertstück in F min., Op. 33.* (ii) FIALA: *Cor anglais concerto in E flat.* HUMMEL: *Adagio, theme and variations in F.*
(B) **(*) Ph. 426 972-2; *426 972-4.*

The playing here is of high quality and the measure generous: six concertante works with a playing time of 76 minutes. The recording is very good too, if rather resonantly inflated orchestrally, and the cost is modest. So perhaps this collection (mostly recorded in the mid-1970s) may be acquired for the two-movement Bellini concerto which is delightful, and the Moschelles double concerto is attractively inventive too, with a very fetching tune in the Rondo finale. The other works are more conventional and rather anonymous; although the Fiala is agreeable enough, the main theme of the Hummel sounds a trifle faded in its intended charm. But Holliger makes the most of all his many opportunities for stylish bravura throughout this disc, and he is well accompanied too.

Hollywood Bowl Symphony Orchestra, Carmen Dragon

'Fiesta': MASSENET: *Le Cid: Aragonaise.* BIZET: *Carmen: Chanson bohème.* arr. DRAGON: *La Paloma.* GLINKA: *Jota aragonesa.* MONTERDE: *La Virgen de la Macarena.* DE CAMPO: *La Chiapanecas.* DELIBES: *Maids of Cadiz.* GRANADOS: *Andaluza; Goyescas: Intermezzo.* BENJAMIN: *Jamaican rumba.* SERRADELL: *La Golandrina.* LARA: *Granada.* CHABRIER: *España.* LECUONA: *Andalucia.* PONCE: *Estrelita.* LECUONA: *Malagueña.*
(M) **(*) EMI stereo/mono CDM7 63734-2 [id.].

This was the best of a series of recordings, originally issued on LP on the Capitol label at the very beginning of the 1960s. Carmen Dragon proved to be a master of this popular Latin repertoire and produced orchestral playing that was both brilliant and seductive, and always polished. The recording acoustic is rather dry and the CD transfer tends to emphasize this effect. But the performances of pieces like *La Golandrina*, Dragon's own enticing arrangement of *La Paloma*, and Arthur Benjamin's catchy *Jamaican rumba* are very appealing when the presentation is so sympathetic and sparkling. Chabrier's *España* is also highly successful; though this, like the last three pieces listed and the Granados *Goyescas Intermezzo*, is a mono recording, the sound remains full and immediate.

Hollywood Bowl Symphony Orchestra, Felix Slatkin

'Symphonic dances': TCHAIKOVSKY: *Sleeping Beauty: Waltz.* KABALEVSKY: *The Comedians: Galop.* GRIEG: *Norwegian dance No. 2.* WEINBERGER: *Schwanda the Bagpiper: Polka.* GLIÈRE: *The Red Poppy: Russian sailors' dance.* BIZET: *L'Arlésienne: Farandole.* DELIBES: *Sylvia: Pizzicato.* KHACHATURIAN: *Gayaneh: Sabre dance.* SAINT-SAENS: *Samson et Dalila: Bacchanale.* MENDELSSOHN: *Midsummer Night's Dream: Scherzo.* OFFENBACH, arr. ROSENTHAL: *Gaîté parisienne* (ballet; complete).
(B) ** CD-CFP 4588; *TC-CFP 4588.*

The original collection issued under this title on analogue LP was a great success, offering a stream of good tunes, brilliantly played and recorded, and producing a fair degree of variety. For the reissue EMI have added the complete score of Offenbach's *Gaîté parisienne* (38 minutes), racily played but with sound that is very bright and somewhat two-dimensional, and with the studio acoustic the more noticeable.

'Boléro': RAVEL: *Boléro; Pavane pour une infante défunte.* ALBÉNIZ: *Iberia: Triana.* RIMSKY-KORSAKOV: *Capriccio espagnol.* MASSENET: *Le Cid: Navarraise.* WALDTEUFEL: *España waltz.* GOULD: *Latin-American symphonette.*
(M) ** EMI CDM7 63738-2.

The star item here is Gould's engaging *Latin-American Symphonette*, written in 1940; all the movements are based on dance themes, with the *Scherzo-Guaracha* particularly witty. The performance is as fine as any available and the vividly forward balance suits the music, although in Ravel's *Boléro* it reduces the overall dynamic range somewhat. The other short pieces are all brightly done, with the gentle melancholy of Ravel's *Pavane* caught well; but the account of Rimsky's *Capriccio espagnol* is not distinctive, and the climax of *Triana* is rather brittle and overlit.

Hungarian State Orchestra, Mátyás Antal

'Hungarian festival': KODÁLY: *Háry János: suite.* LISZT: *Hungarian rhapsodies for orchestra Nos. 1, 2 & 6* (arr. Doeppler). HUBAY: *Hejre Kati* (with Ferenc Balogh). BERLIOZ: *Damnation de Faust: Rákóczy march.*
(BB) *** Naxos Dig. 8.550142 [id.].

The Hungarian State Orchestra are in their element in this programme of colourful music for which they have a natural affinity. There is no more characterful version of the *Háry János suite* (we have already mentioned it in the Composer index) and Hubay's concertante violin piece, with its gypsy flair, is similarly successful, even if the violin soloist is not a particularly strong personality. The special interest of the Liszt *Hungarian rhapsodies* lies in the use of the Doeppler orchestrations, which are comparatively earthy, with greater use of brass solos than the more sophisticated scoring most often used in the West. The performances are suitably robust and certainly have plenty of charisma. The brilliant digital recording is strong on primary colours but has atmosphere too, and produces plenty of spectacle in the Berlioz *Rákóczy march*.

(Philip) Jones Brass Ensemble

'Baroque brass': BIBER: *Sonata a 7*. ANON.: *Sonata from Die Bankelsangerlieder*. M. FRANCK: *Intrata*. HASSLER: *Intrada V*. SPEER: *Sonata for trumpet & 3 trombones; Sonata for 3 trombones; Sonata for 4 trombones; Sonata for 2 trumpets and 3 trombones*. SCHEIDT: *Canzona a 10*. BACH: *Chorale: Nun danket alle Gott. Capriccio on the departure of a beloved brother, BWV 992: Aria & fugue in imitation of the postillion's horn (arr. Breuer). Cello suite No. 1: Menuetto & Courante* (arr. Fletcher for solo tuba). D. SCARLATTI: *Keyboard sonatas, Kk.380; Kk.430; Kk.443* (arr. Dodgson). C. P. E. BACH: *March*.
(M) *** Decca 425 727-2; *425 727-4*.

An imaginative and highly rewarding programme, among the best of the Philip Jones anthologies. The music of Daniel Speer is strikingly inventive and the Bach and Scarlatti arrangements are highly engaging – the latter with no attempt at miniaturization. The C. P. E. Bach *March* makes a superbly vigorous coda. If the Baroque idiom and the sound of modern brass instruments combine easily in your aural consciousness, this can be recommended, though not to be taken all at once. The recording is first class.

British music for brass (directed by Elgar Howarth, John Iveson & Howard Snell): BLISS: *Antiphonal fanfare for 3 brass choirs; Greetings to a city (Flourish for 2 brass orchestras); Fanfare for the Lord Mayor of London*. BRITTEN: *Fanfare: The Eagle has two heads. Russian funeral; Fanfare for St Edmondsbury*. ARNOLD: *Symphony, Op. 123; Quintet*. TIPPETT: *Fanfare*. BAX: *Fanfare for the wedding of Princess Elizabeth (1947)*. BRIAN: *The Cenci: Fanfare*. WALTON, arr. Howarth: *Spitfire prelude & fugue*.
(M) *** Decca 430 369-2 [id.].

Not everything here is as original and arresting as the three Britten pieces, especially the (1936) *Russian funeral*, based on a theme also used by Shostakovich in his *Eleventh Symphony*. But the Arnold *Quintet* has real wit and the *Symphony* is a considerable piece, essentially serious. There is plenty of traditional brass splendour from Bliss and Bax, and Elgar Howarth's transcription of Walton's film music for *The First of the Few* is spectacularly vivid. Expert playing throughout and brilliant, sonorous sound of Decca's best analogue quality.

'Virtuoso brass': CLARKE: *Trumpet voluntary*. PURCELL: *Trumpet tune and air*. G. GABRIELI: *Canzona: Sol, sol, la sol; Sonata pian' e forte* (both ed. Gardiner). SUSATO: *Suite* (arr. Iveson). BYRD: *Earl of Oxford's march*. LOCKE: *Music for His Majesty's sackbuts and cornetts*. TRAD.: *Greensleeves*. HANDEL: *La Rejouissance*. SCHEIDT: *Battle suite*. C. P. E. BACH: *March*.
(B) *** Decca 433 640-2; *433 640-4*.

For those who like superbly alive and polished brass-playing and spectacular sonorities, this collection of Baroque and Renaissance music on Decca's Headline bargain label should prove excellent value. The recordings are taken from various anthologies made for Argo/Decca, and the remastering is bright and clean. There are some striking antiphonal effects, as in the *Galliard battaglia* of Scheidt and C. P. E. Bach's *March*, and the melodic invention of the programme is consistently striking. The notes, too, are excellent.

Kremer, Gidon (violin)

Concert (with (i) LSO, Chailly; (ii) Elena Bashkirova): CHAUSSON: (i) *Poème, Op. 25*. MILHAUD: *Le Boeuf sur le toit*; (ii) *Le printemps*. SATIE: (i) *Choses vues à droite et à gauche (sans lunettes)*. VIEUXTEMPS: (i) *Fantasia appassionata*.
(M) *** Ph. Dig. 432 513-2.

One of Kremer's best records, this has stood up well to repetition. The repertoire is enticing. He plays the Milhaud and Satie pieces with charm, and the Chausson has poetic feeling. Kremer can often seem a self-conscious and narcissistic player but here he is heard at his very best. The 1980–81 recording is altogether excellent.

Laskine, Lily (harp)

Concertos for harp (with Paillard CO; or (i) Lamoureux O, Mari): HANDEL: *Concerto in B flat, Op. 4/8*. BOIELDIEU: *Concerto in C*. KRUMPHOLZ: *Concerto No. 6*. (i) BOCHSA: *Concerto No. 1*.
(M) ** Erato/Warner 2292 45084-2 [id.].

Although not quite as distinctive as Zabaleta's bargain DG disc (which duplicates the Handel), this is still an enjoyable collection for those who enjoy the concertante harp. Lily Laskine produces much delicate embroidery to entice the ear, and her accompaniments are well managed and atmospherically recorded, even if the orchestral sound is not especially transparent. All three of the lesser-known works are agreeably inventive in an undemanding way.

Lipatti, Dinu (piano)

(with Nadia Boulanger; Philh. O, Zürich Tonhalle O, Lucerne Festival O; Galliera, Ackermann, Karajan): BACH: *Chorale, Jesu, joy of man's desiring* (arr. Hess, from BWV 147); *Chorale preludes, BWV 599 & 639* (both arr. Busoni); *Partita No. 1, BWV 825; Siciliana* (arr. Kempff, from BWV 1031). D. SCARLATTI: *Sonatas, Kk. 9 & 380.* MOZART: *Piano concerto No. 21 in C, K.467; Piano sonata No. 8 in A min., K.310.* SCHUBERT: *Impromptus Nos. 2–3, D.899/2 & 3.* SCHUMANN: *Piano concerto in A min., Op. 54.* GRIEG: *Piano concerto in A min., Op. 16.* CHOPIN: *Piano concerto No. 1 in E min., Op. 11; Barcarolle, Op. 60; Études, Op. 10/5 & 25/5; Mazurka No. 32, Op. 50/3; Nocturne No. 8, Op. 27/2; Piano sonata No. 3 in B min., Op. 58; Waltzes Nos. 1–14.* LISZT: *Années de pèlerinage, 2nd Year: Sonnetto 104 del Petrarca.* RAVEL: *Alborada del gracioso.* BRAHMS: *Waltzes* (4 hands), *Op. 39/1–2, 5–6, 10, 14–15.* ENESCU: *Piano sonata No. 3 in D, Op. 25.*

❀ (M) (***) EMI CZS7 67163-2 (5).

This set represents Lipatti's major recording achievements. Whether in Bach (*Jesu, joy of man's desiring* is unforgettable) or Chopin – his *Waltzes* seem to have grown in wisdom and subtlety over the years – Scarlatti or Mozart, these performances are very special indeed. The remastering is done well, and this is a must for anyone with an interest in the piano.

London Gabrieli Brass Ensemble

'The splendour of baroque brass': SUSATO: *La Danserye: suite.* G. GABRIELI: *Canzona per sonare a 4: La Spiritata.* SCHEIDT: *Suite.* PEZEL: *Ceremonial brass music.* BACH: *The Art of fugue: Contrapunctus IX.* CHARPENTIER: *Te Deum: Prelude in D.* arr. James: *An Elizabethan suite.* CLARKE: *The Prince of Denmark's march.* HOLBORNE: *5 Dances.* STANLEY: *Trumpet tune.* LOCKE: *Music for His Majesty's sackbutts and cornetts.* PURCELL: *Trumpet tune and ayre. Music for the funeral of Queen Mary* (with Chorus).

❀ (BB) *** ASV CDQS 6013; *ZCQS 6013.*

This is one of the really outstanding brass anthologies, and the digitally remastered analogue recording is very realistic. The brass group is comparatively small: two trumpets, two trombones, horn and tuba; and that brings internal clarity, while the ambience adds fine sonority. The opening Susato *Danserye* is splendid music, and the Scheidt *Suite* is similarly inventive. Pezel's *Ceremonial brass music* is also in effect a suite – it includes a particularly memorable *Sarabande*; while Matthew Locke's *Music for His Majesty's sackbutts and cornetts* opens with a very striking *Air* and offers six diverse movements overall. With the Gabrieli *Canzona*, Purcell's *Trumpet tune and ayre* and the Jeremiah Clarke *Prince of Denmark's march* (better known as the *Trumpet voluntary*) all familiar, this makes a superb entertainment to be dipped into at will. The closing *Music for the funeral of Queen Mary* brings an eloquent choral contribution. Introduced by solemn drum-beats, it is one of Purcell's finest short works and the performance here is very moving. The arrangements throughout the concert (usually made by Crispian Steele-Perkins, who leads the group both sensitively and resplendently) are felicitous and the documentation is excellent. This is a very real bargain.

London Symphony Orchestra, Ahronovich

'Russian spectacular': KHACHATURIAN: *Gayaneh: Sabre dance. Spartacus: Adagio of Spartacus and Phyrigia. Masquerade: Waltz.* PROKOFIEV: *Lieutenant Kijé: Troika. Love of 3 Oranges: March.* BORODIN: *Prince Igor: Polovtsian dances.* GLINKA: *Overture: Russlan and Ludmilla.* MUSSORGSKY: *Night on the bare mountain.* SHOSTAKOVICH: *The Gadfly: Folk festival.*

(B) **(*) Pickwick Dig. PCD 804.

An excellent collection of characteristically vivid Russian orchestral genre pieces, played with plenty of spirit and polish by the LSO, who are in excellent form. Yuri Ahronovich may not be a subtle conductor, but his pacing here is notably convincing in Mussorgsky's *Night on the bare mountain*, while the piquant Prokofiev *March* is crisply rhythmic and nicely pointed. The *Sabre dance* and *Polovtsian dances* have no lack of energy and fire. The recording combines brilliance with weight; this CD is excellent value in Pickwick's bargain-priced series, even though the ambience is a little dry.

London Symphony Orchestra, Rafael Frühbeck de Burgos

'Spanish spectacular': RIMSKY-KORSAKOV: *Capriccio espagnol.* ALBÉNIZ: *Suite española: Granada* (arr. Frühbeck de Burgos). FALLA: *El amor brujo: Pantomime; Ritual fire dance. Three-cornered hat: 3 dances.* RAVEL: *Alborada del gracioso.* GRANADOS: *Goyescas: Intermezzo.*

(B) **(*) Pickwick Dig. PCD 924.

Rafael Frühbeck de Burgos is obviously completely at home in this repertoire and there is much here that is vividly coloured and exciting. He finds an extra degree of languor in the central section of Ravel's *Alborada* and a Mediterranean eloquence for the Granados *Intermezzo.* Rimsky-Korsakov's *Capriccio* has plenty of glitter and does not lack vitality; however, one does wish the performance could have generated the same degree of unbuttoned exuberance in its final section that Frühbeck finds for the three dances from *The Three-cornered hat*, which make a really exciting end to the concert. Vivid and certainly spectacular sound throughout.

London Symphony Orchestra, André Previn

'Classical favourites': BERNSTEIN: *Overture: Candide.* BARBER: *Adagio for strings.* WALTON: *Orb and sceptre (Coronation march).* DUKAS: *The Sorcerer's apprentice.* HUMPERDINCK: *Overture: Hansel and Gretel.* ALBINONI: *Adagio* (arr. Giazotto). DVOŘÁK: *Slavonic dance No. 9, Op. 72/1.* ENESCU: *Rumanian rhapsody No. 1.*
(M) *** EMI CD-EMX 2127; *TC-EMX 2127.*

A most enjoyable and generous collection of favourites, recorded between 1972 and 1977, demonstrating Previn's charisma at the peak of his success with the LSO. The playing sparkles and the musical characterization is strong. This is one of the most attractive accounts of *The Sorcerer's apprentice* available, while the *Candide overture* rivals the composer's own version. The delectable Enescu *Rumanian rhapsody* and the Dvořák *Slavonic dance* have splendid life and colour, while the account of Barber's *Adagio* is movingly intense. The sound-quality varies a little between items but is always vivid and often first rate.

London Symphony Orchestra, Leopold Stokowski

'Stokowski conducts' (also with: Czech PO; RPO & Welsh Nat. Op. Ch.): CLARKE: *Trumpet voluntary.* MUSSORGSKY: *Night on the bare mountain* (arr. Stokowski). ELGAR: *Enigma variations: Nimrod.* BORODIN: *Prince Igor: Polovtsian dances.* WAGNER: *Die Walküre: Ride of the Valkyries.* BACH: *Toccata & fugue in D min., BWV 565* (arr. Stokowski). SCHUBERT: *Moment musical No. 3 in F min.* TCHAIKOVSKY: *Chant sans paroles, Op. 40/6; Marche slave.* DVOŘÁK: *Slavonic dance, Op. 72/2.*
(B) *(*) Pickwick IMPX 9033.

A perfectly acceptable bargain collection, but the Mussorgsky and Borodin items and the Tchaikovsky *Marche slave* are available in superior transfers on the Decca disc, below. Here the focus is less clean (this also affects the famous *Toccata and fugue* transcription) and in the Tchaikovsky the violins are fierce and thin. However, the *Trumpet voluntary* is a Stokowski collectors' item, with its sweetly anachronistic violins in the middle section.

Russian orchestral music (also with RPO & RPO Ch.; Welsh Nat. Op. Ch.; New Philh. O): TCHAIKOVSKY: *Marche slave; Overture 1812.* BORODIN: *Prince Igor: Polovtsian dances.* MUSSORGSKY: *Night on the bare mountain* (arr. Stokowski). RIMSKY-KORSAKOV: *Capriccio espagnol.*
(B) **(*) Decca 433 625-2; *433 625-4* [id.].

Marche slave (taken from Stokowski's sixtieth-anniversary concert with the LSO) has a characteristic force and vigour, but elsewhere there are plenty of eccentricities. In *1812* he treats the big lyrical string-tune slowly and indulgently; at the final climax the RPO Chorus suddenly appears out of nowhere, makes a strong but remarkably brief contribution and then disappears again, and the cannon and bells take over, the latter continuing their resonance after the music has finished. The contribution of the Welsh National Opera Chorus in a colourful and sometimes wayward set of *Polovtsian dances* is also telling. In *Night on the bare mountain* Stokowski's arrangement returns to Mussorgsky's original, missing out the brass motive familiar in the Rimsky version, but adding some sinister high string harmonics. The gentle close is done in an atmosphere of characteristic, romantically drenched ecstasy. *Capriccio espagnol* brings surprisingly relaxed tempi, especially in the *Alborada*, but the jaunty gypsy rhythms are deliciously underlined and there is plenty of energy at the close. The work is slightly cut and rearranged by the conductor, but there is no doubt that Stokowski's magnetism communicates throughout this programme. The CD transfers are brilliant but do not lack warmth and allure, but the Phase 4 source means that the balance is artificial.

Ma, Yo-Yo (cello)

'Great cello concertos': HAYDN: *Concerto in D, Hob VIIb/2* (with ECO, Garcia). SAINT-SAËNS: *Concerto No. 1, Op. 33* (with O Nat. de France, Maazel). SCHUMANN: *Concerto in A min., Op. 129* (with Bav. RSO, C. Davis). DVOŘÁK: *Concerto in B min., Op. 104* (with BPO, Maazel). ELGAR: *Concerto in E min., Op. 85* (with LSO, Previn).
(M) *** Sony Dig./Analogue M2K 44562 (2) [id.].

An enticing mid-priced package, offering at least two of the greatest of all cello concertos, in Yo-Yo Ma's characteristic and imaginatively refined manner. Only the performance of the Haydn gives cause for reservations and these are slight; many will enjoy Ma's elegance here. He is also lucky in his accompanists, and the CBS sound gives no reasons for complaint. The account of the Saint-Saëns has wonderful finesse, and his Schumann is warmly affectionate, even if at times his range of dynamic seems almost hypersensitive. In the Elgar his rapt concentration brings a performance as intense as it is poised, while the Dvořák concerto combines ardour with much subtlety of colour. Here the partnership with the more extrovert Maazel works strikingly well.

Menuhin, Yehudi (violin)

'75th Birthday Edition' (with various artists): BARTÓK: *Violin concerto No. 1; Viola concerto; Rhapsodies 1–2.* RAVEL: *Piano trio in A min.* DEBUSSY: *Violin sonata; Sonata for flute, viola & harp.* FAURÉ: *Andante in B flat, Op. 75; Berceuse in D, Op. 16.* SIBELIUS: *Violin concerto, Op. 47.* NIELSEN: *Violin concerto, Op. 33.* SCHUBERT: *Fantasia in C, D.934.* MENDELSSOHN: *Sonata in F.* BRAHMS: *Horn trio in E flat, Op. 40.* BERG: *Violin concerto.* BLOCH: *Violin concerto.*
(M) *(**) EMI mono/stereo CMS7 63984-2 (5) [Ang. CDME 63984].

This mid-price CD compilation restores a number of valuable Menuhin performances to the catalogue, most of them from the mid-1960s and now also available separately. Not all of them show this great artist on top form, but nothing he touches is without musical insights, and it is good to have this fascinating retrospective, warts and all. However, all these performances are currently available separately. Despite some felicities, neither the Nielsen *Concerto*, recorded with Mogens Wöldike and the Danish State Radio Orchestra in 1952, nor the Sibelius with Sir Adrian Boult and the LPO (1956) shows Menuhin at his very best, but his classic 1964 account of the Bloch *Concerto*, made with Paul Kletzki and the Philharmonia, is an altogether different matter. For a considerable period Szigeti's pioneering account with Charles Münch and the Paris Conservatoire had an intimidating effect upon other performers, including (as he told us at the time) Menuhin himself. His was only the second recording of this powerful work, and this deeply felt and finely balanced account is a worthy successor to the Szigeti, which so far has not been transferred to CD in the UK. Menuhin's thus remains the only current CD version of this intense and evocative score. His account of the Berg, with Boulez conducting the BBC Orchestra, also comes up well.

Murphy, Maurice (trumpet), Consort of London, Robert Haydon Clark

'Favourite trumpet concertos': ARUTIUNIAN: *Concerto.* CLARKE: *Prince of Denmark's march.* HAYDN: *Concerto in E flat.* HUMMEL: *Concerto in E flat.* PURCELL: *Trumpet tune and air.*
(M) **(*) Collins Dig. 3008-2 [id.].

Maurice Murphy is a first-class soloist; anyone wanting the Haydn and Hummel concertos, plus the piece we used to know as the '*Trumpet voluntary*', on a single disc should be well satisfied. The solo timbre is gleamingly bright and there is bravura and sparkle and warm phrasing in slow movements. There is not quite the stylistic distinction of Hardenberger here, but the music-making is enjoyable and well recorded. However, few collectors will want to return to the Arutiunian work very often: it is colourful and fluent but not much else.

I Musici

BARTÓK: *Rumanian folk dances* (with R. Michelucci). BRITTEN: *Simple Symphony, Op. 4.* HINDEMITH: *Trauermusik for viola and strings* (with Cino Ghedin). MARTIN: *Études.* NIELSEN: *Little Suite, Op. 1.* ROUSSEL: *Sinfonietta, Op. 52.*
(M) **(*) Ph. 426 669-2; *426 669-4* [id.].

A valuable anthology. The Britten *Simple Symphony*, recorded in 1962, is perhaps the least convincing and needs more tonal bloom, but otherwise few qualifications need be made. The Frank Martin *Studies* are played marvellously: tone is always in focus and everyone is in the middle of the note, so that the timbre is particularly rich and full. I Musici play these and most of the other pieces with tremendous virtuosity; the Hindemith *Funeral music*, written in a few hours on the death of King George V, is given with real feeling. The first movement of the Nielsen is a bit on the fast side, but otherwise this record gives much pleasure; at the time of writing, no other CD version of the Roussel *Sinfonietta* is available. The recordings are mostly from 1968 and come up very well indeed.

National Philharmonic Orchestra, Leopold Stokowski

'Stokowski showcase': *Overtures:* BEETHOVEN: *Leonora No. 3.* MOZART: *Don Giovanni* (arr. Stokowski). SCHUBERT: *Rosamunde (Die*

Zauberharfe). BERLIOZ: *Le carnaval romain.* ROSSINI: *William Tell.* TCHAIKOVSKY: *Solitude, Op. 73/6.* SOUSA: *The Stars and Stripes forever* (both arr. Stokowski). CHABRIER: *España.* SAINT-SAENS: *Danse macabre.* IPPOLITOV-IVANOV: *Caucasian sketches: Procession of the Sardar.*
(M) *** EMI CDM7 64140-2; *EG 764140.*

Stokowski's collection of overtures dates from just before his ninety-fourth birthday – yet, as with so many of the recordings made during his 'Indian summer', the electricity crackles throughout and his charisma is apparent in every bar. The Beethoven is immensely dramatic – the distanced trumpet especially effective – while *Rosamunde* combines high romanticism with affectionate warmth. Dissatisfied with Mozart's ending to *Don Giovanni*, Stokowski extends this piece to include music from the opera's finale. The pacing in *William Tell* is fast, but here as elsewhere the players obviously relish the experience and, if ensemble slips a little, the music-making is enjoyably infectious. Here the reverberant acoustics of West Ham Central Mission (as unlikely a venue as one could imagine!) blur some of the detail, but the resonance also adds ambient bloom to sound which is also extremely vivid. The extra items, added for the 76-minute CD programme, were recorded at about the same time and are just as charismatic, especially *Danse macabre* (with Sidney Sax the seductive violin soloist) and the exhilarating *Stars and Stripes forever*, re-scored by the conductor to include an *ad lib.* xylophone.

NBC Symphony Orchestra, Arturo Toscanini

'The Toscanini collection': BEETHOVEN: *Leonora overture No. 3.* VERDI: *Nabucco: Va pensiero* (with Westminster Ch.). SMETANA: *Má Vlast: Vltava.* BERLIOZ: *Roméo et Juliette: Queen Mab scherzo.* BRAHMS: *Academic festival overture.* WAGNER: *Die Walküre: Ride of the Valkyries.* PUCCINI: *La Bohème: Ehi! Rodolfo!; O soave fanciulla* (with Albanese, Peerce, Cehanovsky, Moscona, Valentino). ROSSINI: *William Tell: Overture.*
(BB) (**(*)) BMG/RCA VD 60340; *VK 60340* [60340-2-RV; *60340-4-RV*].

This generous limited-edition super-bargain sampler for the BMG/RCA Toscanini Edition offers 68 minutes of Toscanini recordings. It is one of the tragedies of recording history that the great Italian maestro did not have a producer with the strength of personality of a Walter Legge to supervise his recordings. (Indeed, Elisabeth Schwarzkopf has recounted the occasion when her husband and Toscanini eventually met and – to her dismay – Legge fearlessly criticized the Toscanini recorded legacy. Toscanini's response was surprisingly positive, and he agreed, almost ruefully, that perhaps he had needed someone of Legge's calibre as his producer.) However, we have to accept what there is and that includes the excrably dry sounds afforded by the notorious Studio 8-H, which is used for the Beethoven and Brahms *Overtures* and the *La Bohème* excerpt, totally without atmosphere. Verdi's *Va pensiero*, with its clear chorus, and Smetana's *Vltava* sound rather better, although the latter has some distortion. The Carnegie Hall recordings are more attractive, notably the marvellously played *Queen Mab scherzo* and the brilliantly charismatic *William Tell overture.*

(i) New Philharmonia or (ii) ROHCG O, Sir Charles Mackerras

French ballet music: (i) DELIBES: *Coppélia:* excerpts; *Sylvia:* suite. (ii) MESSAGER: *Les deux pigeons:* suite. (i) GOUNOD: *Faust* (ballet): suite.
(B) **(*) EMI CDZ7 62515-2; *LZ 762515-4.*

Mackerras is at his sprightly and exhilarating best in this programme of French ballet music, securing polished and often elegant playing from both orchestras. *Les deux pigeons* dates from as early as 1958, yet the recording has been remastered most successfully. The rest of the programme is much later (1970) and only in the massed violins is the quality noticeably dated. There is a good balance and an attractive ambient effect. Excellent value.

Northern Sinfonia, Jean-Bernard Pommier

'French impressions': DEBUSSY: *Petite suite* (orch. Büsser). FAURÉ: *Ballade for piano and orchestra; Masques et bergamasques: suite.* RAVEL: *Pavane pour une infante défunte; Ma Mère l'Oye (suite).*
(BB) **(*) Virgo Dig. VJ7 914667-2; *VJ 791467-4* [id.].

Although wanting in the last degree of intensity, these warm, rather laid-back performances are easy to enjoy. They were recorded at EMI's No. 1 Abbey Road Studio, yet the slightly hazy sound-picture gives a feeling of French impressionist colours. Debussy's *Petite suite* perhaps needs a slightly stronger profile, and the central dance movements of *Masques et bergamasques*, like the *Ballade for piano and orchestra* (in which Pommier moves over to the keyboard), are very relaxed. But *Ma Mère l'Oye* glows beguilingly – *The Fairy garden* is quite lovely – and the refined orchestral playing gives pleasure throughout. As with the rest of this series, the documentation is very sparse.

Orchestra of St John's, Smith Square, John Lubbock

'On hearing the first cuckoo in spring': VAUGHAN WILLIAMS: *Fantasia on Greensleeves. Rhosymedre.* GRIEG: *Peer Gynt: Morning.* RAVEL: *Pavane.* DELIUS: *On hearing the first cuckoo in spring.* FAURÉ: *Masques et bergamasques: Overture. Berceuse, Op. 56.* SCHUBERT: *Rosamunde: Entr'acte No. 2; Ballet music No. 2.* MOZART: *Divertimento in D, K.136: Presto.*

(BB) **(*) ASV Dig. CDQS 6007; *ZCQS 6007.*

An enjoyable bargain collection of essentially atmospheric music for late evening. Fine playing throughout: tempi are very relaxed, notably in the Grieg, Fauré and Schubert items, but the evocation is persuasive. The digital recording is first class, full and clear, yet not too clinical in its detail. Some might feel that the music-making here verges on the somnolent in its consistently easy-going manner – the Delius piece is indicative of the conductor's style – but the closing Mozart *Presto* ends the concert with a sparkle.

Orchestre de Paris, (i) Sir John Barbirolli or (ii) Serge Baudo

'French music': (i) DEBUSSY: *La Mer; Nocturnes* (with female chorus). (ii) RAVEL: *Ma Mère l'Oye: suite.* FAURÉ: *Dolly, Op. 56. Masques et bergamasques; Pelléas et Mélisande: suite.* ROUSSEL: *Bacchus et Ariane: suite.* MESSIAEN: *Les offrandes oubliées.*

(B) *** EMI CZS7 62669-2 (2) [Ang. CDMB 62669].

As can be seen, Serge Baudo has the lion's share of this highly recommendable collection, admirably recorded in the Paris Salle Wagram in 1968–9 and now available in EMI's very competitive French 'two for the price of one' series. His performances are perceptive and sensitive and the Orchestre de Paris plays beautifully. Barbirolli's music-making has plenty of sensuous warmth too, but his earlier, Hallé version of *La Mer* has more grip. Nevetheless the Fauré, Messiaen and Roussel items (all discussed separately under their individual composers) make this concert well worth having. Incidentally, the French documentation by Jean Roy is worth taking the trouble to translate: it is more colourful and often has more of interest to say about the music than the English notes by Barry Millington.

Osipov State Russian Folk Orchestra, Vitaly Gnutov

'Balalaika favourites': BUDASHIN: *Fantasy on two folk songs.* arr. GORODOVSKAYA: *At sunrise.* KULIKOV: *The Linden tree.* OSIPOV: *Kamarinskaya.* MIKHAILOV/SHALAYEV: *Fantasy on Volga melodies.* ANDREYEV: *In the moonlight; Under the apple tree; Waltz of the faun.* SOLOVIEV/SEDOY: *Midnight in Moscow.* TCHAIKOVSKY: *Dance of the comedians.* SHISHAKOV: *The living room.* arr. MOSSOLOV: *Evening bells.* arr. POPONOV: *My dear friend, please visit me.* RIMSKY-KORSAKOV: *Flight of the bumble-bee.*

❀ (M) *** Mercury 432 000-2 [id.].

The Mercury recording team visited Moscow in 1962 in order to make the first recordings produced in the Soviet Union by Western engineers since the Revolution. Wilma Cozart Fine, the recording director, recalls that every morning, more in hope than expectation, they would set up their equipment (although they lacked official permission from the bureaucracy, because of arguments over royalty rights), and every morning the musicians would appear, arriving in all kinds of conveyances and carrying balalaikas plus other instruments; and, full of enthusiasm, the sessions would begin. The spirit of that unique occasion is captured wonderfully here – analogue atmosphere at its best. The rippling waves of balalaika sound, the accordion solos, the exhilarating accelerandos and crescendos that mark the style of this music-making: all are recorded with wonderful immediacy. Whether in the shimmering web of sound of *The Linden tree* or *Evening bells*, the sparkle of the folksongs or the sheer bravura of items like *In the moonlight*, which gets steadily faster and louder, or in Rimsky's famous piece (sounding like a hive full of bumble-bees), this is irresistible, and the recording is superbly real in its CD format.

Perahia, Murray (piano)

'The art of Murray Perahia': BARTÓK: *Sonata for 2 pianos & percussion.* BRAHMS: *Variations on a theme by Haydn* (for 2 pianos), *Op. 60* (with Solti, Corkhill & Glennie). BEETHOVEN: *Piano concerto No. 5 (Emperor)* (with Concg. O, Haitink); *Piano sonatas Nos. 7 in D, Op. 10/3; 23 (Appassionata).* BRAHMS: *Piano quartet No. 1 in G min., Op. 15* (with members of Amadeus Qt); *Rhapsody in B min., Op. 79/1.* CHOPIN: *Piano sonatas Nos. 2 in B flat min. (Funeral march); 3 in B min., Op. 48.* GRIEG: *Piano concerto in A min.* SCHUMANN: *Piano concerto in A min.* (both with Bavarian RSO, C. Davis). MENDELSSOHN: *Piano concertos Nos. 1–2*

(with ASMF, Marriner); *Prelude & fugue, Op. 35/1; Rondo capriccioso, Op. 14; Variations sérieuses, Op. 54; Piano sonata, Op. 61.* SCHUBERT: *Wanderer fantasia, Op. 15; Impromptu in E flat, D.899/2.* SCHUMANN: *Fantasia in C, Op. 17; Études symphoniques, Op. 13,* with posthumous *Études*; *Papillons, Op. 2; 3 Fantasiestücke, Op. 12.* LISZT: *Consolation No. 3; Rapsodie espagnole.*
(M) *** Sony Dig./Analogue SX11K 48153 (11).

This box offers many of Perahia's most distinguished recordings, nearly all of them digital (the Chopin *Sonatas*, Mendelssohn *Concertos* and the major Schumann pieces are analogue but here the sound is always fully acceptable, with the CD transfers adding presence without degrading the quality). Of the eleven CDs, ten are simple reissues in their original packaging (which means that we get three Mendelssohn piano works twice!), and there is a bonus recital disc which, apart from including only a single movement from Beethoven's *Tempest Piano sonata*, Op. 31/2, is an attractive mixture, obviously intended to tempt the listener into exploring further among Perahia's recordings. The set is offered at upper mid-price but this is a limited edition; we are assured that it should remain available during the lifetime of this book, but prospective purchasers should not delay too long.

Perlman, Itzhak (violin)

Spanish music: SARASATE: *Carmen fantasy* (with RPO, Foster); *Zigeunerweisen* (with Pittsburgh SO, Previn). *Danzas españolas: Malagueña; Habanera, Op. 21/1–2; Playera and Zapateado, Op. 23; Spanish dance, Op. 26/8. Caprice basque, Op. 24; Romanza andaluza, Op. 22.* FALLA, arr. KOCHANSKI: *Suite populaire espagnole.* GRANADOS: *Spanish dance.* HALFFTER: *Danza de la gitana.* ALBÉNIZ: *Malagueña, Op. 165/5* (all with Samuel Sanders, piano).
(M) *** EMI CDM7 63533-2; *EG 763533-4*.

Perlman's dazzling account of Sarasate's *Carmen fantasy* is offered here with a collection of popular Spanish pieces. Perlman demonstrates a delight in virtuosity in the most joyful way, but some may feel that the balance is a shade too close, and this effect is emphasized somewhat on CD.

Philadelphia Orchestra, Leopold Stokowski

'Fantasia': BACH, orch. Stokowski: *Toccata and Fugue in D min.* DUKAS: *L'apprenti sorcier.* MUSSORGSKY, arr. Stokowski: *A Night on the Bare Mountain.* STRAVINSKY: *The Rite of spring.* TCHAIKOVSKY: *Nutcracker Suite.*
(M) (***) Pearl mono GEMMCD 4988.

A self-recommending disc for the older generation – and, given the excellently refurbished VHS video of the Disney film, the younger generations too. (Incidentally, the early stereo CDs of the soundtrack are disappointingly shrill.) These recordings were made much earlier than you might think; *The Rite of spring* comes from 1929–30 (oddly enough, Stokowski never remade it) and the *Nutcracker* as early as 1926, though one would never believe it. Everything Stokowski did at this period was full of character, and the engineers obviously performed miracles. The latest recording is Stokowski's amazing arrangement of *A Night on the Bare Mountain*, which dates from 1940. Such is the colour and richness of sonority Stokowski evokes from the fabulous Philadelphians that surface noise and other limitations are completely forgotten. The performances are too familiar to need detailed comment, though it is worth recalling that his *Rite* was infinitely more masterly and even more exciting than Stravinsky's own account, made at much the same time. Collectors with wide-ranging equipment (and even those without) will be surprised how much sense of presence the HMV (or, rather, Victor) engineers managed to get on to wax in those days. Those who have the old 78s of *The sorcerer's apprentice* will remember the impossible side-breaks, which the CD now joins up. The transfers are very good.

Philadelphia Orchestra, Arturo Toscanini

'The Philadelphia recordings, 1941–2': DEBUSSY: *La Mer; Images: Ibéria.* RESPIGHI: *Feste romane.* TCHAIKOVSKY: *Symphony No. 6 in B min. (Pathétique), Op. 74.* R. STRAUSS: *Death and transfiguration, Op. 24.* MENDELSSOHN: *A Midsummer Night's Dream: Overture, Op. 21, & incidental music, Op. 61.* BERLIOZ: *Romeo et Juliette: Queen Mab scherzo.* SCHUBERT: *Symphony No. 9 in C (Great), D.644.*
(M) (**(*)) BMG/RCA GD 60328; *GK 60328* (4) [60328-2-RG; *60328-4-RG*]. Phd. O, Toscanini.

During the winter season of 1941/2 Toscanini was resident maestro in Philadelphia, and he made a series of recordings with the orchestra, at the peak of its form, many of which – though not all – bring a more relaxed style of performance than he often achieved in New York at that time. Most successful are the performances of Schubert's *Great C major Symphony* and

Tchaikovsky's *Pathétique*, although the *Midsummer Night's Dream* selection brings a pleasing lightness of touch to match his Berlioz *Queen Mab scherzo*. The Strauss tone-poem, too, has the right kind of tension. The disappointments are the Debussy and Respighi, which he recorded more successfully elsewhere; the recording too is much less satisfactory in these works. These records are now all available separately.

Philharmonia Orchestra, Herbert von Karajan

BARTÓK: *Concerto for Orchestra; Music for strings, percussion and celesta.* BRITTEN: *Variations on a theme of Frank Bridge.* DEBUSSY: *La Mer.* HANDEL arr. HARTY: *Water music.* KODÁLY: *Háry János suite.* RAVEL: *Rapsodie espagnol.* SIBELIUS: *Finlandia; Symphonies Nos. 4, 6 & 7; Tapiola.* VAUGHAN WILLIAMS: *Fantasia on a theme of Thomas Tallis.*
❀ (M) (***) EMI mono CMS7 63464-2 (4).

Of the many Karajan/Philharmonia recordings published by EMI this is the one you should on no account miss. The Vaughan Williams and the Britten have hardly ever been played more beautifully, and they are recorded marvellously. Karajan's mid-1950s Sibelius is leaner and more austere than his later versions with the Berlin orchestra (and earned the composer's plaudits). Only No. 7 disappoints, and it is a pity that his earlier No. 5 did not replace it. Also there is something special about the Bartók, which was almost (but not quite) a first recording: Harold Byrns just beat him to it; but, like the Bartók *Concerto*, it has the excitement of discovery.

Philharmonia or New Philharmonia Orchestra, Otto Klemperer

'Romantic overtures': WEBER: *Der Freischütz; Euryanthe; Oberon.* SCHUMANN: *Manfred, Op. 115; Genoveva, Op. 81.* HUMPERDINCK: *Hansel and Gretel,* with *Dream pantomime.* KLEMPERER: *Merry waltz.*
(M) *(*) EMI CDM7 63917-2; *EG 763917-4.*

This is strictly in the list of reissues 'for Klemperer fans only'. *Der Freischütz* is impressive in a Teutonic kind of way, and *Hansel and Gretel* is is on the whole successful, while Klemperer's Schumann has a certain massive strength. But elsewhere a lighter touch is needed. The sound, from the 1960s, is generally full and clear. Klemperer's own piece is undistinguished.

Primavera

Music for strings: ROUSSEL: *Sinfonietta, Op. 52.* VAUGHAN WILLIAMS: *Fantasia on Greensleeves; Fantasia on a theme by Thomas Tallis.* ELGAR: *Serenade for strings, Op. 20; Sospiri, Op. 70.* DEBUSSY: *Danses sacrée et profane for harp and strings.*
(M) **(*) Collins Dig. 3006-2 [id.].

This is a very enjoyable concert, most realistically recorded. It opens bracingly with Roussel's astringently lyrical *Sinfonietta* and includes a warmly atmospheric account of the beautiful Debussy work for harp and strings. The English music is also very well played, although in the *Tallis fantasia* there is not quite enough contrast between the main string body and the secondary group of players, who are not made to sound ethereal enough. Ideally a more resonant acoustic was needed for this piece, written to be first performed in a cathedral at the Three Choirs Festival. But the programme as a whole offers polished, vital performances to which one readily responds.

Richter, Sviatoslav (piano)

'Sviatoslav Richter plays': GRIEG: *Concerto in A min., Op. 16.* SCHUMANN: *Concerto in A min., Op. 54* (with Monte Carlo Opera O, Matačić). MOZART: *Concerto No. 22 in E flat, K.482.* BEETHOVEN: *Piano concerto No. 3 in C min., Op. 37* (with Philh. O, Muti). *Sonatas Nos. 1 in F min., Op. 2/1; 7 in D, Op. 10/3; 17 in D min. (Tempest), Op. 31/2.* SCHUBERT: *Wanderer fantasy, D.760; Sonata No. 13 in A, D.664.* SCHUMANN: *Faschingsschwank aus Wien, Op. 26.*
(B) **(*) EMI CZS7 67197-2 (4).

Some reservations have to be expressed here, of course: the performances of the Grieg and Schumann *Concertos* are very wilful, but the commanding mastery of this playing is truly remarkable. The standard of the recorded sound, too, is often very realistic, particularly the solo recordings Peter André made of Schubert and Schumann from recitals in Paris and Italy. They need to be reproduced at a high volume level; then the artist's presence is uncanny, while the playing here shows Richter at his most poetically charismatic: the slow movement of the Schubert *A major* is unforgettable. The Beethoven *Sonatas* are pretty impressive too, and can be ranked alongside the versions of Gilels. In the concertos Richter is never less than illuminating; and overall this box has many insights to offer and much musical stimulation.

Piano concertos (with var. orchestras & conductors): MOZART: *Concerto No. 20 in D min., K.466.* BEETHOVEN: *Concerto No. 3 in C min., Op. 37; Rondo for piano & orchestra in B flat, G.151.* RACHMANINOV: *Concerto No. 2 in C min., Op. 18.* TCHAIKOVSKY: *Concerto No. 1 in B flat min., Op. 54.* SCHUMANN: *Piano concerto in A min., Op. 54.* PROKOFIEV: *Concerto No. 5 in G min., Op. 55.*
(B) **(*) DG 429 918-2 (3).

Although there are severe reservations about the Tchaikovsky *Concerto*, where Richter and Karajan fail to see eye to eye over choice of tempi, and though the Beethoven does not show the great pianist at his very best, there are some outstanding performances here, not least the Prokofiev, which is a classic of the gramophone. At bargain price this is quite tempting.

Rimon, Meir (horn), Israel Philharmonic Orchestra

Horn concertos: HANDEL: *Double horn concerto in F* (arr. Rimon). BARSANTI: *Concerto grosso in D for 2 horns, timpani and strings, Op. 3/4.* HAENSEL: *Double horn concerto in F, Op. 80.* FRANZ: *Concert piece in F, for 2 horns and orchestra, Op. 4.* HÜBLER: *Concerto in F for 4 horns and orchestra.* SCHUMANN: *Konzertstück in F for four horns and orchestra, Op. 86.*
(M) *** Pickwick MCD 31.

There is much that is new and fascinating to discover in this almost entirely winning collection of horn music, in which Meir Rimon – with digital, electronic assistance – not only plays all the solo horn lines with remarkable virtuosity but also conducts the orchestra with aplomb. The result is the finest existing recording of the Schumann *Konzertstück*, full of exhilarating bravura, climaxing a programme which is rewarding throughout. The Handel *Double concerto* includes outer movements familiar from the *Water music*, but Rimon has interpolated an effective slow movement with a stately melody to make a satisfying whole. The Barsanti *Concerto grosso* combines a winning interplay between the horns and the ripieno with a quite beautiful central *Adagio* for strings alone. The subtitle for Oscar Franz's *Concert piece*, 'In a happy mood', is an apt description for an infectious piece with its melodic line taken from the operetta theatre, yet post-Weberian in manner; however, the musical fabric of Haensel's *Double concerto* is altogether less distinguished. This is something of a musical turkey, and its solo writing (mostly in thirds) is very conventional. However, Hübler's *Concerto for 4 horns* is another matter. Obviously inspired by the Schumann *Konzertstück*, which was written only five years earlier, it is ripely romantic, splendidly written for the four solo instruments and with an unforgettably exuberant finale. The recording is fully worthy of this highly spontaneous music-making: the engineers have discovered a – hitherto unsuspected – resonant warmth in the Tel-Aviv Mann Auditorium which gives a pleasing glow to the proceedings, produces rich horn timbres and flatters the orchestra. A most appealing disc in every respect.

'Romantic Overtures'

'Romantic Overtures' (played by: (i) LPO, Inbal; (ii) Spanish R. & TV O, Markevitch; (iii) BBC SO, C. Davis; (iv) LPO, Leppard): (i) WEBER: *Overtures: Oberon; Euryanthe;* (ii) *Preciosa.* (iii) BEETHOVEN: *Overture Leonora No. 1.* WAGNER: *Prelude: Die Meistersinger.* MENDELSSOHN: *The Hebrides (Fingal's Cave).* (iv) SCHUBERT: *Overtures: in E min., D.648; in B flat, D.470.*
(B) **(*) Ph. 426 978-2; *426 978-4.*

A useful bargain collection and well recorded throughout (mostly during the early 1970s). The LPO play beautifully at the opening of *Oberon*, to get the concert off to an atmospheric start and, if otherwise the two Inbal performances have no special charisma, they are enjoyably polished and fluent. There is plenty of vitality and sparkle in Markevitch's *Preciosa*, and Sir Colin Davis brings breadth to Beethoven and Wagner and evokes Mendelssohn's seascapes with dramatic effect. The two Schubert novelties are not otherwise available: not great music, but agreeable when Leppard's touch is affectionate.

Royal Liverpool Philharmonic Orchestra, Sir Charles Groves

'Meditation': CHOPIN, arr. JACOB: *Les Sylphides: Nocturne in A flat, Op. 32/2.* MASSENET: *Thaïs: Méditation.* ALBINONI/GIAZOTTO. *Adagio in G min.* (both with Clifford Knowles). BORODIN/SARGENT: *Nocturne for strings.* MENDELSSOHN: *A Midsummer Night's Dream: Nocturne.* GLUCK: *Orfeo: Dance of the Blessed Spirits.* FAURÉ: *Pavane, Op. 50.*
(B) ** CfP CD-CFP 4515; *TC-CFP 4515.*

Recorded in Liverpool's Philharmonic Hall in the late 1960s, the remastering has been beneficial in removing any soupiness from the sound, and nearly all these pieces come up fresh, particularly Sir Malcolm Sargent's famous string arrangement of the *Nocturne* from Borodin's *D major Quartet.* Gordon Jacob's scoring of Chopin, too, makes a welcome change from the usual Roy Douglas version. All the performances are alive and well played, and Clifford

Knowles is an excellent soloist in the two items needing a concertante violin. The principal flautist of the orchestra at that time was Atarah Ben-Tovin, who went on to become famous in the North-west, arranging special concerts to introduce children to the world of music. She plays beautifully in the Gluck and Fauré pieces, though, in the former, Groves's tempo is slow and the style on the heavy side.

'Rule Britannia': ELGAR: *Pomp and circumstance marches Nos. 1 & 4.* HOLST: *Marching song.* VAUGHAN WILLIAMS: *Coastal Command: Dawn patrol.* WALFORD DAVIES: *RAF March past.* WALTON: *Henry V: Touch her soft lips and part; Agincourt song.* WOOD: *Fantasia on British sea songs: Hornpipe.* COATES: *Dambusters march.* BLISS: *Processional.* ALFORD: *On the quarterdeck.* ARNE: *The British Grenadiers; Rule Britannia* (with Anne Collins & RLPO Ch.).
(B) ** CfP CD-CFP 4567; *TC-CFP 4567.*

A genial patriotic collection, nicely varied in content, with Holst, Vaughan Williams and Walton items to contrast with the breezy vitality of the Coates *Dambusters* and the Walford Davies *RAF March past* – a truly splendid march. Anne Collins's consonants seem to be somewhat overemphasized by the microphone in the closing spectacular, a favourite, like Sir Henry's Wood's *Hornpipe*, at the Proms. Sir Charles Groves directs throughout with spirit and affection, if with no striking individuality. Clean, bright, vividly remastered sound (from 1977).

Royal Philharmonic Orchestra, Sir Thomas Beecham

French music: BIZET: *Carmen suite No. 1.* FAURÉ: *Pavane, Op. 60; Dolly suite, Op. 56.* DEBUSSY: *Prélude à l'après-midi d'un faune.* SAINT-SAËNS: *Le rouet d'Omphale.* DELIBES: *Le Roi s'amuse* (ballet suite).
❀ (M) *** EMI CDM7 63379-2 [id.]; *EG 763379-4.*

No one conducts the *Carmen Prelude* with quite the flair of Sir Thomas, while the last movement of the *Dolly suite*, *Le pas espagnole*, (in Rabaud's orchestration) has the kind of dash we associate with Beecham's Chabrier. But for the most part the ear is beguiled by the consistently imaginative and poetic phrasing that distinguished his very best performances. The delicacy of string textures and wind playing (notably the flute) in *Le rouet d'Omphale* and the other *Dolly* numbers – the *Berceuse*, *Le jardin de Dolly* and *Tendresse* – is exquisite, and Debussy's *Prélude à l'après-midi d'un faune* brings a ravishingly diaphanous web of sound. Delibes' pastiche ballet-score, *Le Roi s'amuse*, is given the special elegance that Sir Thomas reserved for music from the past unashamedly rescored to please the ear of later generations. The remastering is marvellously managed and all the recordings (from between 1957 and 1961) sound wonderfully vivid and fresh.

'Lollipops': TCHAIKOVSKY: *Eugene Onegin: Waltz.* SIBELIUS: *Kuolema: Valse triste.* BERLIOZ: *Damnation of Faust: Menuet des follets; Danses des sylphes. Les Troyens: Marche.* DVOŘÁK: *Legend in G min., Op. 59/3.* DEBUSSY: *L'enfant prodigue: Cortège et Air de danse.* CHABRIER: *Marche joyeuse.* GOUNOD: *Roméo et Juliette: Le sommeil de Juliette.* VIDAL: *Zino-Zina: Gavotte.* GRIEG: *Symphonic dance No. 2 in A, Op. 64/2.* DELIUS: *Summer evening.* SAINT-SAËNS: *Samson et Dalila: Danse des prêtresses de Dagon; Bacchanale.* MOZART: *Thamos, King of Egypt: Entr'acte. Divertimento in D, K.131: Minuet. March in D (Haffner), K.249.*
(M) **(*) EMI CDM7 63412-2 [id.]; *EG 763412-4.*

It was Beecham who first used the word 'lollipop' to describe his brand of succulent encore pieces. In this selection of 17 examples, Beecham's devotion to French music shines out, with over half of the items by French composers. They include not just three pieces by Berlioz and two by Saint-Saëns but also a delectable rarity by the little-known Paul Vidal (1863–1931), a *Gavotte* from the ballet *Zino-Zina.* Items by Mozart, Dvořák, Sibelius and his special favourite, Delius, also conform to the Beecham definition of a lollipop as a musical sweetmeat; but the account of the *Waltz* from Tchaikovsky's *Eugene Onegin* chosen to start the disc is totally untypical of Beecham, with its metrical, unlilting rhythms. The transfers generally convey a good sense of presence but tend to emphasize an edge on top, which is an unfortunate addition to previous incarnations of this music on disc.

Royal Philharmonic Orchestra, Rudolf Kempe

'Bohemian festival': SMETANA: *The Bartered Bride: Overture & suite.* DVOŘÁK: *Scherzo capriccioso.* WEINBERGER: *Schwanda the Bagpiper: Polka & Fugue.*
(B) ** CfP CD-CFP 4587; *TC-CFP 4587.*

This is certainly an enjoyable concert. The programme, although not generous (40 minutes), is sensibly compiled and very well played, with brilliance and warmth nicely balanced. The performance of the Dvořák *Scherzo capriccioso* has an attractive Slavonic lilt and the Smetana

Dances are full of energy. However, the CD transfer of what were originally rather mellow (1962) recordings is shrill, with an edge given to the violins. The upper range needs a deal of damping down to become acceptable.

Royal Philharmonic Orchestra, Adrian Leaper

'Orchestral spectacular': CHABRIER: *España*. RIMSKY-KORSAKOV: *Capriccio espagnol*. MUSSORGSKY: *Night on the bare mountain* (arr. Rimsky-Korsakov). BORODIN: *Prince Igor: Polovtsian dances*. RAVEL: *Boléro*.
(BB) *** Naxos Dig. 8.550501 [id.].

Recorded in Watford Town Hall by Brian Culverhouse, this concert would be highly recommendable even if it cost far more. All these performances spring to life, and the brilliant, full-bodied sound certainly earns the record its title. The brass in the Mussorgsky/Rimsky-Korsakov *Night on the bare mountain* has splendid sonority and bite, and in the *Polovtsian dances* the orchestra 'sings' the lyrical melodies with such warmth of colour that the chorus is hardly missed. Leaper allows the *Capriccio espagnol* to relax in the colourful central variations, but the performance gathers pace towards the close. Chabrier's *España* has an attractive rhythmic lilt, and in Ravel's ubiquitous *Boléro* there is a strong impetus towards the climax, with much impressive playing on the way (the trombone solo, with a French-style vibrato, is particularly strong).

Scottish Chamber Orchestra, Laredo

'String masterpieces': ALBINONI: *Adagio in G min.* (arr. Giazotto). HANDEL: *Berenice: Overture. Solomon: Arrival of the Queen of Sheba*. BACH: *Suite No. 3, BWV 1068: Air. Violin concerto No. 1 in A min., BWV 1041: Finale*. PACHELBEL: *Canon*. PURCELL: *Abdelazer: Rondo. Chacony in G min.*
(B) *** Pickwick Dig. PCD 802.

An excellent issue. The playing is alive, alert, stylish and committed without being overly expressive, yet the Bach *Air* has warmth and Pachelbel's *Canon* is fresh and unconventional in approach. The sound is first class, especially spacious and convincing on CD, well detailed without any clinical feeling. The Purcell *Rondo* is the tune made familiar by Britten's orchestral guide; the *Chaconne* is played with telling simplicity.

Scottish Ensemble, Jonathan Rees

Baroque music: ALBINONI: *Adagio for strings and organ* (arr. Giazotto). PACHELBEL: *Canon and gigue for 3 violins and continuo*. VIVALDI: *The Trial between harmony and invention: Violin concerto in B flat (La Caccia), Op. 8/10; L'Estro armonico: Concerto for 2 violins and cello in D min., Op. 3/11*. PURCELL: *Chacony* (arr. Britten). CORELLI: *Concerto grosso in D, Op. 6/4*. BACH: *Suite No. 3 in D: Air*. LOCATELLI: *Concerto grosso, Op. 1/11*.
(BB) *** Virgo Dig. VJ7 91464-2; *VJ 791464-4* [id.].

A most refreshing concert. The Scottish strings play their allegros with bracingly resilient vigour and slow movements with an appealingly refined espressivo. Thus Albinoni's ubiquitous *Adagio* is serene but not too lush, and Pachelbel's *Canon* has vitality, with textures more refined than usual. The soloists, Jonathan Rees, Jane Murdoch and Caroline Dale, are first class in the two highly individual Vivaldi concertos. The Britten arrangement of Purcell is given the strongest possible profile, while the famous Bach *Air* makes a gentle interlude. Excellent sound, generous measure (65 minutes), but totally inadequate back-up documentation.

'Serenade for strings'

Serenades (with (i) Philh. O, C. Davis; (ii) LSO, Barbirolli; (iii) N. Sinfonia, Tortelier; (iv) RPO, Sargent; (v) E. Sinfonia, Dilkes; (vi) Bournemouth Sinf., Montgomery; (vii) LPO, Boult): (i) MOZART: *Serenade No. 13 in G (Eine kleine Nachtmusik), K.525*. (ii) TCHAIKOVSKY: *String serenade, Op. 48: Waltz*. (iii) GRIEG: *Holberg suite, Op. 40. Elegiac melody: Heart's wounds, Op. 34/1*. (iv) DVOŘÁK: *String serenade, Op. 11: 1st & 2nd movts*. (v) WARLOCK: *Capriol suite*. (vi) WIRÉN: *String serenade, Op. 11: March*. (vii) ELGAR: *Introduction and allegro for strings, Op. 47*.
(B) *** EMI *TC2-MOM 108*.

This was the finest of EMI's first release of 'Miles of Music' tapes with an attractive programme, good (and sometimes distinguished) performances and consistent sound-quality, slightly restricted in the upper range, but warm, full and clear. Tortelier's Grieg and Boult's complete version of Elgar's *Introduction and allegro* are obvious highlights, and this certainly makes an attractive background for a car journey, yet can be enjoyed at home too.

Serenata of London

BRITTEN: *Simple Symphony*. R. STRAUSS: *Till Eulenspiegel*. DVOŘÁK: *String quintet in G, Op. 77*.
(M) **(*) Collins Dig. 3007-2 [id.].

The Serenata of London is essentially a chamber music group, and Britten's *Simple Symphony* is given by a string quintet – and very effectively too. The acoustic is pleasingly resonant, so the *Sentimental sarabande*, played with touching simplicity, does not lack breadth of timbre, while the *Playful pizzicato* has plenty of bounce. The Dvořák *Quintet* is also a warmly felt, polished account with plenty of vitality and a genuine feeling for its Czech colour and rhythmic idiom. Again the players are afforded exceptional fullness by the ambience, creating an almost orchestral body of tone. The novelty is a concise version (8 minutes 35 seconds) of *Till Eulenspiegel* in which the string group is joined by clarinet, bassoon and horn. The performance sparkles wittily and the result is very entertaining, if not quite what the composer had in mind.

Serkin, Rudolf (piano)

'The Legendary concerto recordings': MOZART: *Piano concertos Nos. 21 in C, K.467* (with Columbia SO, Scheider); *25 in C, K.503* (with Columbia SO, Szell). SCHUMANN: *Concerto in A min., Op. 54*. BEETHOVEN: *Concerto No. 5 (Emperor), Op. 73*. BRAHMS: *Concerto No. 2 in B flat, Op. 83*. R. STRAUSS: *Burleske in D min.*
(M) (**) Sony mono SM3K 47269 (3) [id.].

These recordings were made in the early years of LP (1950–56), and the Sony transfer engineers have achieved excellent results. The 1956 Schumann *A minor Concerto* still sounds quite fresh, though it is an unlikeable performance, with some often brutal touches from the distinguished soloist. But there is a commanding (if dryly recorded) account from the same year of the Brahms *B flat Concerto* and a splendid version of the Strauss *Burleske*, arguably finer than the later recording he made in stereo. There is also a masterful and stylish 1953 record of the Mozart *C major Concerto*, K.503, though the recording is dry and monochrome. There are other good things in this set which will encourage devotees of Serkin to investigate it.

Slovak Philharmonic Orchestra

'Russian Fireworks' (cond. (i) Richard Hayman; (ii) Kenneth Jean; (iii) Stephen Gunzenhauser; (iv) Michael Halász): (i) IPPOLITOV-IVANOV: *Caucasian sketches: Procession of the Sardar*. (ii) LIADOV: *8 Russian folksongs*. KABALEVSKY: *Comedian's galop*. MUSSORGSKY: *Sorochinski Fair: Gopak. Khovanshchina: Dance of the Persian slaves*. (iii) LIADOV: *Baba Yaga; The enchanted lake; Kikimora*. (iv) RUBINSTEIN: *Feramor: Dance of the Bayaderes; Bridal procession. The Demon: Lesginka*. (ii) HALVORSEN: *Entry of the Boyars*.
(BB) *** Naxos Dig. 8.550328 [id.].

A vividly sparkling concert with spectacular digital sound, more than making up in vigour and spontaneity for any lack of finesse. The Liadov tone-poems are especially attractive and, besides the very familiar pieces by Ippolitov-Ivanov, Halvorsen and Mussorgsky, it is good to have the Rubinstein items, especially the *Lesginka* which has a rather attractive tune.

I Solisti Veneti, Claudio Scimone

Baroque mandolin concertos (with Ugo Orlandi): PAISIELLO: *Concertos: in E flat; in C*. LECCE: *Concerto in G*. ANTONIO MARIA GIULIANI: *Concerto in E for 2 mandolins and viola* (with D. Frati and J. Levitz).
(M) **(*) Erato/Warner Dig. 2292 45239-2 [id.].

The Giuliani on this record is not Mauro but Antonio Maria; neither he nor Francesco Lecce are exactly household names and they are not liberally documented in the accompanying liner-notes. However, whatever their stature, the music is appealing and its invention far from pale. Pleasant out-of-the-way repertoire, nicely played and recorded.

Solomon (piano)

'Great recordings of the century' (with (i) Liverpool PO, Boult; (ii; iii) Philh. O; (ii) Dobrowen; (iii) Susskind): (i) BLISS: *Piano concerto*. (ii) SCRIABIN: *Piano concerto in F sharp min., Op. 20*. (iii) LISZT: *Hungarian fantasia*.
(M) (***) EMI mono CDH7 63821-2.

Solomon's pioneering account of the Bliss *Piano concerto* was made during the war. Neither the music nor the recorded sound wear their years lightly, though the slow movement has more to recommend it than its more flamboyant neighbours. (It must be said, however, that some listeners find the ambitiously grand overstatement of the first movement rather endearing.) Solomon, of course, plays marvellously and the disc is important in offering us what would have been the first recording to be issued of the Scriabin *Piano concerto in F sharp minor* had Solomon and Dobrowen passed it for release. It is a lovely reading, every bit as poetic and polished as one would expect, and the sound is not bad for its period. It was made in 1949, at the same time as Solomon recorded the Tchaikovsky, which EMI must surely reissue soon. The Liszt *Hungarian fantasia* accompanied the Bliss when it came out on LP, and it is a pretty dazzling performance. The sonic limitations cannot diminish the sheer aristocratic finesse of this great pianist.

Steele-Perkins, Crispian (trumpet)

Six Trumpet concertos (with ECO, Anthony Halstead): HAYDN: *Concerto in E flat.* TORELLI: *Concerto in D.* M. HAYDN: *Concerto No. 2 in C.* TELEMANN: *Concerto for trumpet, two oboes and strings.* NERUDA: *Concerto in E flat.* HUMPHRIES: *Concerto in D, Op. 10/12.*
(B) *** Pickwick PCD 821.

Collectors who have relished Håkan Hardenberger's famous full-price collection of trumpet concertos might well go on to this equally admirable concert, which duplicates only the Haydn – and that in a performance hardly less distinguished. Crispian Steele-Perkins has a bright, gleaming, beautifully focused timbre and crisp articulation, with easy command of the high tessitura of the Michael Haydn work and all the bravura necessary for the sprightly finales of all these concertos. His phrasing in the slow movement of Joseph Haydn's shapely *Andante* is matched by his playing of the *Largo* of the Neruda and the *Adagio–Presto–Adagio* of the Torelli, another fine work. Anthony Halstead with the ECO gives him warmly sympathetic support. The recording balance gives the soloist plenty of presence, but the orchestra is recorded rather reverberantly, an effect similar to that on the Hardenberger record.

'Mr Purcell's trumpeter': (with City of L. Baroque Sinfonia, Hickox): PURCELL: *The Indian Queen: incidental music. Trumpet sonata in D. King Arthur: Act V tunes. Suite in C.* CLARKE: *Ayres for the theatre: Cebel; Trumpet song; 3 Minuets; Round-O (Prince of Denmark's march); Serenade: Gigue.* ANON.: *(Mr Shore's tunes): Shore's trumpet; Trumpett; Prince Eugene's march; Song (Prince Eugene's march into Italy); Shore's tune.* FINGER: *Trumpet and oboe sonata in C* (with A. Robson, oboe). BIBER: *Sonata in G min. for trumpet, violin and 2 violas* (with D. Woodcock, R. Nalden & M. Kelly).
(M) *** EMI Dig. CDM7 63931-2; *EG 763931-2.*

The title of this collection celebrates Purcell's trumpeter, John Shore, and some of the repertoire comes from Shore's personal collection. Both the *Sonatas* of Biber and Gottfried Finger are excellent works; and the programme is agreeably diverse, including an engaging account of *Shore's Tune*, allotted to the treble recorder. The famous *Trumpet voluntary* by Jeremiah Clarke is stirringly done and, with excellent accompaniments from Hickox and fine recording, this record is highly recommendable for trumpet fanciers.

Stuttgart Chamber Orchestra, Karl Münchinger

PACHELBEL: *Canon and gigue.* ALBINONI: *Adagio* (arr. Giazotto). BACH: *Jesu, joy of man's desiring; Sheep may safely graze; Suite No. 3: Air. Fugue in G min., BWV 542.* BOCCHERINI: *Minuet* from *Op. 13/5.* HOFSTETTER: *Serenade.* HANDEL: *Concerto grosso, Op. 6/6: Musette. Solomon: Arrival of the Queen of Sheba. Organ concerto, Op. 4/4. Overture: Berenice.*
(M) **(*) Decca 417 781-2; *417 781-4* [id.].

The recording quality of Münchinger's analogue concert is first class and the programme generous; the performances will suit those who prefer their Baroque lollipops played expansively on modern instruments. The balance is close, which does not permit much dynamic contrast in the Pachelbel *Canon*, although the *Gigue* certainly sounds gracious. The Boccherini *Minuet* and the famous *Serenade* once attributed to Haydn are pleasingly done, and among the Handel items the *Organ concerto* (with Ulrich Bremsteller) is nicely registered. The other Handel excerpts produce rich textures from the strings, and the Albinoni *Adagio* is sumptuous. Those who prefer something more authentic can turn to the Taverner Players on EMI – see below.

Baroque concert: PACHELBEL: *Canon.* ALBINONI: *Adagio in G min.* (arr. Giazotto). BACH: *Orchestral suites Nos. 2–3, BWV 1067/8.* HANDEL: *Organ concerto in F (Cuckoo and the nightingale* (with M. Haselböck).
(M) *(*) Decca Dig. 430 706-2; *430 706-4* [id.].

Münchinger is a little heavy-handed in the famous *Canon*, but the strongly expressive account of Albinoni's *Adagio* is convincing. The *Cuckoo and the nightingale organ concerto* (with Martin Haselböck an excellent soloist) also comes off well, but the Bach *Suites* are not an asset, unattractively heavy, with rhythms unlifted. Very good sound.

Taverner Players, Andrew Parrott

PACHELBEL: *Canon and gigue.* HANDEL: *Solomon: Arrival of the Queen of Sheba. Harp con-*

certo in B flat, Op. 4/6 (with A. Lawrence-King, harp). PURCELL: *3 Parts upon a ground; Suite of Theatre music.* BACH: *Sinfonias from Cantatas 29, 31, 106, 156, 174* and *Christmas oratorio. Cantata 147: Jesu, joy of man's desiring.*
(M) *** EMI Dig. CDM7 69853-2.

This really outstanding collection of Baroque favourites shows that authentic performance can produce both charm and charisma: there is not a whiff of sterile, scholarly rectitude here. Indeed Pachelbel's famous *Canon* sounds delightfully fresh, heard in its original chamber scoring, while Handel's *Queen of Sheba* arrives in exhilarating fashion. The *Harp concerto*, too, sounds delectable when the effect is so neat and stylish. The Bach *Sinfonias* are varied in content (that from No. 29 includes a bravura organ obbligato, played with considerable flair by John Toll), with No. 174 bringing a real novelty in being a different version of Bach's *Brandenburg concerto No. 3*, attractively expanded in scoring to include horns and oboes. First-class digital recording makes this a highly desirable compilation at a very reasonable price.

Udagawa, Hideko (violin)

Concertante works (with LPO, Klein):
GLAZUNOV: *Violin concerto in A min., Op. 82.*
TCHAIKOVSKY: *Souvenir d'un lieu cher, Op. 42.*
CHAUSSON: *Poème, Op. 25.* SARASATE: *Romanze andaluza, Op. 22/1.* SAINT-SAENS: *Caprice, Op. 52.*
(B) *** Pickwick Dig. PCD 966; *IMPC 966* [id.].

This is a generous collection (64 minutes) of mostly sugar-plum works for violin and orchestra, played with uninhibited romanticism by the rich-toned Udagawa. In a rather old-fashioned way she allows herself the occasional portamento and her passionate commitment to each work is clear in every note. With the violin balanced forward, the Glazunov receives a heartfelt performance which rivals almost any, even if the finale does not offer quite such bravura fireworks as Itzhak Perlman (at full price). It is valuable to have all three of the haunting pieces which Tchaikovsky called *Souvenirs d'un lieu cher* – the *Méditation* and *Mélodie*, much better known than the central *Scherzo.* They are here done in Glazunov's orchestral arrangements. The Chausson *Poème* is warmly convincing if a little heavy-handed, the Sarasate Andalusian *Romanze* dances delightfully, and only in the final Saint-Saëns *Caprice* does Udagawa's playing sound a little effortful in its virtuosity. Warm, full recording to match.

Ulster Orchestra, Vernon Handley or Bryden Thomson

'An Irish rhapsody': HARTY: *The Londonderry air. Irish Symphony: The fair day (scherzo). In the Antrim Hills.* STANFORD: *Irish rhapsody No. 4 (The Fisherman of Loch Neagh and what he saw), Op. 141; Symphony No. 3 (Irish): Scherzo.* MOERAN: *In the mountain country (symphonic impressions).* BAX: *In the faery hills; Roscatha.*
(M) *** Chan. Dig. CHAN 6525; *MBTD 6525* [id.].

It was a happy idea for Chandos to create this Irish anthology from a catalogue rich in music influenced by that country. It is especially good to have the *Scherzo* from Harty's *Irish Symphony* (a real lollipop), together with the skippity jig from the similar work by Stanford. His *Irish rhapsody No. 4* is also very colourful, and the two Bax pieces offer a strong contrast: one atmospheric, the other more dramatic and lively. Excellent performances throughout; all the recordings except the obligatory (and analogue) *Londonderry air* are of Chandos's best digital quality.

Vienna Philharmonic Orchestra

150th anniversary: R. STRAUSS: *Till Eulenspiegel* (cond. Clemens Krauss; mono). BEETHOVEN: *Symphony No. 3 (Eroica)* (cond. Erich Kleiber; mono). MAHLER: *Das Lied von der Erde* (with Kathleen Ferrier, Julius Patzak; cond. Bruno Walter; mono). BEETHOVEN: *Egmont: Overture & incidental music* (with Pilar Lorengar; cond. George Szell). R. STRAUSS: *Death and transfiguration* (cond. Fritz Reiner). WAGNER: *Tristan und Isolde: Prelude, Act I; Isolde's Liebestod* (with Birgit Nilsson; cond. Hans Knappertsbusch). HAYDN: *Symphonies Nos. 94 in G (Surprise); 101 in D (Clock)* (cond. Pierre Monteux). SCHUBERT: *Symphony No. 8 (Unfinished)* (cond. Josef Krips). SCHUMANN: *Symphony No. 1 (Spring)* (cond. Zubin Mehta). R. STRAUSS: *Don Quixote* (cond. Lorin Maazel). MOZART: *Piano concerto No. 15 in B flat, K.450* (with Leonard Bernstein, piano); *Symphony No. 36 in C (Linz), K.425* (cond. Bernstein). BEETHOVEN: *Symphony No. 8 in F;* BRAHMS: *Symphony No. 1 in C min.* (cond. Claudio Abbado). J. STRAUSS, Jnr: *Waltzes: An der schönen blauen Donau; Geschichten aus dem Wienerwald; Ägyptischer Marsch; Waltz: Wein, Weib und Gesang; Tritsch-Tratsch polka. Waltz: 1001 Nacht; Auf der Jagd polka; Perpetuum mobile; Kaiser waltz; Champagner polka; Frühlingsstimmen waltz;* J. STRAUSS, Snr: *Radetzky march* (cond. Willi Boskovsky). R.

STRAUSS: *Also sprach Zarathustra;* BRAHMS: *Symphony No. 3 in F* (cond. Herbert von Karajan). BRUCKNER: *Symphony No. 4 (Romantic)* (cond. Karl Boehm). MENDELSSOHN: *Symphonies Nos. 3 (Scottish); 4 (Italian); Overture The Hebrides (Fingal's Cave)* (cond. Christoph von Dohnányi). WAGNER: *Siegfried: Forest murmurs. Götterdämmerung: Siegfried's funeral march;* SCHUBERT: *Symphony No. 9 in C (Great)* (cond. Sir Georg Solti).
(M) **(*) Decca 433 330-2 (12) [id.].

Decca's collection of recordings celebrating the 150th anniversary of the Vienna Philharmonic Orchestra covers no fewer than 17 conductors, a wider range than that on the DG set but not such a historic choice. These are Decca's own recordings, newly compiled, and, unlike the DG discs, these are available only as a package in the 12-disc box. The big disappointment is that no opportunity was taken to remaster the disagreeably scrawny transfer of Bruno Walter's 1952 recording of Mahler's *Das Lied von der Erde* with Kathleen Ferrier, with far less body in the sound than on the original LPs. The even earlier recordings of Strauss's *Till Eulenspiegel* under Clemens Krauss and of Beethoven's *Eroica* under Erich Kleiber are much more successfully transferred. Otherwise the quality of Decca studio recordings brings excellent sound in the age of stereo, though some of the specific choices are odd – as for example the coupling of Mehta doing Schumann's *Spring Symphony* and Maazel conducting Strauss's *Don Quixote*. The separate discs, unlike those in the DG set, provide no individual documentation, and the booklet with the set is devoted mainly to a brief history of the orchestra, an account of Decca's association with it and a list of the company's Vienna recordings.

150th Anniversary Edition: HAYDN: *Symphony No. 102 in B flat;* RAVEL: *Piano concerto in G* (Leonard Bernstein piano/cond.: 435 322-2). SCHOENBERG: *Pelleas und Melisande, Op. 5;* R. STRAUSS: *Death and transfiguration* (cond. Karl Boehm: 435 323-2). BEETHOVEN: *Overture: Leonora No. 3; Grosse Fuge, Op. 133;* BRAHMS: *Symphony No. 2 in D* (cond. Wilhelm Furtwängler (mono): 435 324-2). BEETHOVEN: *Symphony No. 9 in D min. (Choral)* (with Irmgard Seefried, Rosette Anday, Anton Dermota, Paul Schoeffler, Vienna Singakademie; cond. Furtwängler (mono): 435 325-2). BRUCKNER: *Symphony No. 9 in D min.* (cond. Herbert von Karajan: 435 326-2). SCHUBERT: *Symphony No. 8 (Unfinished);* BEETHOVEN: *Symphony No. 5 in C min.* (cond. Otto Klemperer: 435 327-2). SCHMIDT: *Variations on a Hussar's song;* SCHUBERT: *Symphony No. 9 in C (Great)* (cond. Hans Knappertsbusch (mono): 435 328-2). BEETHOVEN: *Missa solemnis* (with Trude Eipperle, Luise Willer, Julius Patzak, Georg Hann, Konzertvereinigung of V. State Opera); STRAVINSKY: *Pulcinella: suite;* DUKAS: *L'apprenti sorcier* (cond. Clemens Krauss (mono): 435 329-2 – 2 CDs). BRUCKNER: *Symphony No. 5 in B flat* (cond. Carl Schuricht: 435 332-2). WAGNER: *Die Meistersinger: Overture;* R. STRAUSS: *Sinfonia domestica; Till Eulenspiegel* (cond. Richard Strauss (mono): 435 333-2). MOZART: *Symphony No. 38 in D (Prague);* MAHLER: *Symphony No. 4* (cond. Bruno Walter (mono): 435 334-2).
(M) (***) DG 435 321-2 (12) [id.].

This collection of live recordings made between 1940 and 1976 provides a handsome celebration of the 150th anniversary of the Vienna Philharmonic, with most of the greatest conductors associated with the orchestra over that period represented. With excellent documentation, not least on the individual conductors and their special associations and with each disc available separately, there is much treasure here, even for those who are not primarily concerned with the orchestra. Austrian Radio and its predecessor, Rot-Weiss-Rot, have provided most of the recordings, with radio going over to stereo long after it was normal in studio recording. So even the Boehm disc has only one of its two items in stereo. His account of Strauss's *Death and transfiguration* is in mono only but, with firm, vividly atmospheric sound, it makes an outstanding coupling for the early Schoenberg tone-poem when this was a Strauss piece for which the conductor had special affinity. The Bernstein and Karajan discs are also in stereo, with both CDs giving an extra slant on the conductors compared with their studio recordings of the same works. So Bernstein conveys extra joy in the Haydn and plays with extra expressive freedom in the Ravel, while Karajan's account of Bruckner's *Ninth*, recorded in Salzburg in 1976, is among the most passionate performances ever heard from him on disc. From this, one could never accuse him, for all his characteristic polish, of being cold or over-calculating. The earliest recordings are those of Clemens Krauss in Beethoven's *Missa solemnis*, an exceptionally spacious reading of 1940 lasting almost 90 minutes, with Julius Patzak the thrilling tenor soloist. The heavy surface on what presumably were 78-r.p.m. discs is initially distracting, but the concentrated intensity of the performance makes one ignore it. Stravinsky's *Pulcinella* – done raggedly but very amiably – and Dukas's *Sorcerer's apprentice* make curious bed-fellows, but they indicate the range of Krauss's sympathies. The Strauss discs, containing recordings made in 1944, again bring playing that is less disciplined than one expects of the Vienna Philharmonic, but with a lyrical flow that makes the *Sinfonia domestica* magically persuasive.

The two disappointments are of Klemperer in 1968 conducting Beethoven and Schubert – lacking tension, compared with his Philharmonia recordings – and Beethoven's *Ninth*, as recorded by Furtwängler in 1953, not just ragged but much slacker than his historic, Bayreuth recording of 1951. The other Furtwängler disc, again often with ragged ensemble, is yet far preferable, each time – whether in Beethoven (*Leonore 3* and *Grosse Fuge*) or Brahms's *Second Symphony* – building up to a thrilling culmination.

Schuricht's account of Bruckner's *Fifth* confirms the power and persuasiveness he also displays in the EMI recordings of Nos. 8 and 9, but this is thinner mono sound. The Knappertsbusch disc offers not just a glowing account of Schubert's *Great C major*, comfortably romantic and not self-indulgent, but also a rarity in Franz Schmidt's *Variations on a Hussar song*, full-blooded recordings of 1957. Lastly there is Bruno Walter conducting Mozart and Mahler in 1955. His account of Mozart's *Prague Symphony*, impulsively brisk in the outer allegros, may have its roughness, but the carefree joy conveyed in the Mahler could not be more winning. It makes this a very valuable supplement to Walter's only commercial recording of the piece, the earliest of his CBS series, much less relaxed than this. Clean transfers of radio recordings.

Vienna Philharmonic Orchestra, (i) Sir Georg Solti or (ii) Willi Boskovsky

'Light Cavalry': Overtures: (i) SUPPÉ: *Light Cavalry; Poet and peasant; Morning, noon and night; Pique dame;* (ii) *Beautiful Galatea.* NICOLAI: *The merry wives of Windsor.* REZNIČEK: *Donna Diana.* STRAUSS, Johann Jnr: *Die Fledermaus.*
(B) **(*) Decca 421 170-2; *421 170-4.*

Suppé overtures represented some of the first repertoire recorded by Solti for Decca in the days of mono LP (when he wanted to record Wagner!). These are his later, stereo versions, first issued in 1960. They generate characteristic intensity and excitement, and the recording has a spectacularly wide dynamic range – too wide for the cello solos in *Morning, noon and night* and *Poet and peasant*, where the instrument is backwardly balanced and sounds more like a viola. Boskovsky's performances are altogether more mellow, yet in *Donna Diana* the exhilarating but relaxed forward impulse is nicely judged. The sound is appropriately bright and vivid, especially brilliant in the four favourite Suppé overtures conducted by Solti.

Vienna Volksoper Orchestra, Franz Bauer-Theussl

'Popular Waltzes': IVANOVICI: *Donauwellen (Danube waves).* WALDTEUFEL: *Estudiantina; Les Patineurs (The skaters); Très jolie.* ZIEHRER: *Wiener Bürger.* LEHÁR: *Gold and silver; Ballsiren.* ROSAS: *Sobre las olas (Over the waves).*
(M) ** Ph. Dig. 434 222-2; *434 222-4.*

These performances have an agreeable warmth and a full, resonant recording to match. The result is easy on the ear but a bit bland. Franz Bauer-Theussl's rubato is not subtle but is often effective in its way. He shapes the main theme of Ivanovici's *Donauwellen* very persuasively; on the other hand Lehár's *Gold and silver* could do with more sparkle, as could the Waldteufel waltzes. The opening of *Les Patineurs* with its horn solo is cut. Pleasingly undemanding music-making, made effective by the rich recording.

'Weekend at the Zoo'

'Weekend at the Zoo': SAINT-SAËNS: *Carnival of the animals* (Katchen, Graffman, LSO, Skitch Henderson). RAMEAU: *La Poule.* DAQUIN: *Le coucou.* F. COUPERIN: *Le moucheron.* D. SCARLATTI: *Cat fugue.* SCHUMANN: *Waldszenen: The prophet bird.* MUSSORGSKY: *Pictures: Ballet of the unhatched chicks.* LISZT/SCHUBERT: *Die Forelle.* DEBUSSY: *Images: Poissons d'or.* DUTILLEUX: *The Blackbird.* IBERT: *Le petit âne blanc.* BARTÓK: *Mikrokosmos: From the diary of a fly.* COPLAND: *The cat and the mouse* (Varda Nishry). RIMSKY-KORSAKOV: *Flight of the bumble-bee* (SRO, Ansermet). ROSSINI: *The thieving magpie: overture* (LSO, Gamba).
(B) **(*) Decca 425 505-2; *425 505-4.*

The performance of Saint-Saëns's zoological fantasy is somewhat larger than life yet has great vitality and a starry solo contribution. Then comes an agreeable pianistic menagerie, played with some flair by Varda Nishry; and the two familiar orchestral items round off a concert/recital to be dipped into rather than played all at one go. Decca's sound is characteristically brilliant.

Williams, John (guitar)

Guitar concertos (with ECO, (i) Sir Charles Groves; (ii) Daniel Barenboim): (i) GIULIANI: *Concerto No. 1 in A, Op. 30.* VIVALDI: *Concertos in A and D.* RODRIGO: *Fantasia para un gentilhombre;* (ii) *Concierto de Aranjuez.* VILLA-LOBOS: *Concerto.* (i) CASTELNUOVO-TEDESCO: *Concerto No. 1 in D, Op. 99.*
(M) *** Sony M2YK 45610 (2) [id.].

This bouquet of seven concertante works for guitar from John Williams could hardly be better chosen, and the performances are most appealing. Moreover the transfers are very well managed. Only the Vivaldi concertos (unidentified but attractive, especially the *D major* with its striking central *Largo*) bring quality which sounds in the least dated. Elsewhere the orchestral texture is full and pleasing and, if the guitar is very forward and larger than life, the playing is so expert and spontaneous that one hardly objects. All these performances are among the finest ever recorded, and Groves and Barenboim provide admirably polished accompaniments, matching the eager spontaneity of their soloist. The Rodrigo works seem as fresh as the day when they were written, the Castelnuovo-Tedesco has no want of charm (although John Williams's earlier account with Ormandy and the Philadelphia Orchestra had rather more pace), and the account of the Villa-Lobos makes it seem a stronger work than usual. (This is also available separately, coupled with the Rodrigo *Concierto* – see above under the relevant composers.)

Instrumental Recitals

Bate, Jennifer (organ)

'Virtuoso French organ music' (organ of Beauvais Cathedral): BOËLLMANN: *Suite gothique.* GUILMANT: *Cantilène pastorale; March on 'Lift up your heads'.* SAINT-SAËNS: *Improvisation No. 7.* GIGOUT: *Toccata in B min.; Scherzo; Grand choeur dialogué.*
(M) **(*) Unicorn Dig. UKCD 2045.

The playing here has enormous flair and thrilling bravura. Jennifer Bate's imaginative touch makes Boëllmann's *Suite gothique* sound far better music than it is. In the closing *Toccata*, as in the spectacular Guilmant march based on Handel's famous chorus, the panache and excitement of the playing grip the listener firmly, and the clouding of the St Beauvais acoustic is forgotten. But in the swirling Saint-Saëns *Improvisation* and the Gigout *Scherzo* detail is masked. In the massive *Grand choeur dialogué*, the clever timing makes the firm articulation register, but, although the Unicorn engineers achieve a splendidly sumptuous sound-image, elsewhere there is blurring caused by the wide reverberation of the empty cathedral.

Britton, Harold (organ)

Organ of Royal Albert Hall: *'Organ spectacular':* SUPPÉ: *Light Cavalry overture.* LEMARE: *Andantino in D flat.* VERDI: *Aida: Grand march.* ALBINONI: *Adagio* (arr. Giazotto). WAGNER: *Ride of the Valkyries.* BACH: *Toccata and fugue in D min., BWV 565.* TCHAIKOVSKY: *None but the lonely heart.* ELGAR: *Pomp and circumstance march No. 1.* SOUSA: *Liberty Bell.* WIDOR: *Symphony No. 5: Toccata.*
(BB) *** ASV CDQS 6028; *ZCQS 6028.*

If one is to have a collection mainly of arrangements of orchestral lollipops on an organ, the instrument at the Royal Albert Hall is surely an ideal choice: it offers the widest dynamic range, including an effective recession of quieter passages readily at the player's command – used to good purpose in *Light Cavalry* – but can also produce truly spectacular fortissimos, with a wide amplitude and a blaze of colour from its multitude of stops. Harold Britton is obviously fully at home on the instrument and plays in an aptly extrovert style for such a recital, obviously enjoying himself. The CD is in the demonstration class – there are few problems of muddying from reverberation.

Cambridge Buskers

'Classic Busking'.
(B) *** DG Compact Classics *415 337-4.*

This highly diverting collection is ideal entertainment for a long car journey – though, for all its effervescence and wit, it is best taken a side at a time. The Cambridge Buskers are a duo, Michael Copley (who plays the flute, piccolo and various recorders, with often astonishing bravura) and Dag Ingram, the hardly less fluent accordionist. They met at Cambridge, and these recordings date from the end of the 1970s. There are 34 items here, including a remarkably wide range of classical lollipops. The recital immediately establishes the stylistic credentials of the players by opening with an engaging account of the *Rondo* from Mozart's *Eine kleine Nachtmusik.* The programme ranges from Chopin and Praetorius to Bach and Vivaldi, with ear-tickling operatic excerpts by Bizet, Gluck, Rossini, Mozart and Verdi. With tongue-in-cheek irreverence, they manage to include not only the *Quartet* from *Rigoletto*, but even the *Ride of the Valkyries* – which sounds a good deal more enticing than some over-enthusiastic orchestral versions. The players clearly delight in their more outrageous transcriptions, and they are such natural musicians that good taste comes easily. With crisp, clean recording and 83 minutes of music, this is certainly value for money.

Davies, Philippa (flute), Thelma Owen (harp)

'The Romance of the flute and harp': HASSELMANS: *La Source, Op. 44; Feuilles d'automne.* GODARD: *Suite, Op. 16: Allegretto.* GODEFROID: *Étude de concert.* FAURÉ: *Berceuse, Op. 16; Impromptu, Op. 86.* DOPPLER: *Mazurka.* MENDELSSOHN: *Spring song, Op. 62/3.* THOMAS: *Watching the wheat.* SAINT-SAENS: *Le Cygne.* BIZET: *Fair maid of Perth: Intermezzo.* PARISH-ALVARS: *Serenade.* DEBUSSY: *Syrinx; Suite bergamasque: Clair de lune.*
(B) *** Pickwick Dig. PCD 835.

An unexpectedly successful recital which effectively intersperses harp solos with music in which the flute takes the leading role. The playing is most sensitive and the recording is very realistic indeed. The programme, too, is well chosen and attractively laid out. Highly recommended for playing on a pleasant summer evening.

Du Pré, Jacqueline (cello)

Early BBC recordings, Vol. 1 (with Stephen Kovacevich, Ernest Lush): BACH: (Unaccompanied) *Cello suites Nos. 1 in G; 2 in D min., BWV 1007/8.* BRITTEN: *Cello sonata in C, Op. 65; Scherzo; Marcia.* FALLA: *Suite populaire espagnole* (arr. Maréchal).
(M) (***) EMI mono CDM7 63165-2.

Early BBC recordings, Vol. 2 (with Ernest Lush, (i) William Pleeth): BRAHMS: *Cello sonata No. 2 in F, Op. 99.* F. COUPERIN: (i) *13th Concert a 2 instrumens* (*Les Goûts-réunis*). HANDEL: *Cello sonata in G min.* (arr. Slatter).
(M) (***) EMI mono CDM7 63166-2.

These two discs on the mid-priced Studio label gather together some of the radio performances which Jacqueline du Pré gave in her inspired teens. Her 1962 recordings of the first two Bach *Cello suites* may not be immaculate, but her impulsive vitality makes phrase after phrase at once totally individual and seemingly inevitable. In two movements from Britten's *Cello sonata in C*, with Stephen Kovacevich as her partner, the sheer wit is deliciously infectious, fruit of youthful exuberance in both players. The first of the two discs is completed by Falla's *Suite populaire espagnole*, with the cello matching any singer in expressive range and rhythmic flair. The second has fascinating Couperin duets played with her teacher, William Pleeth; the Handel *Sonata* is equally warm and giving. Best of all is the Brahms *Cello sonata No. 2*, recorded at the 1962 Edinburgh Festival. Though there are incidental flaws, the broad sweep of this magnificent work is conveyed masterfully. Few of Du Pré's later records give a more vivid portrait of her than these. The quality of the mono sound varies but, with clean transfers, the vitality of the performances is unimpaired.

Eden, Bracha and Alexander Tamir (piano duet)

'Dances around the world': RACHMANINOV: *Polka italienne.* MOSZKOWSKI: *Spanish dances, Op. 65/1–2.* GRIEG: *Norwegian dances Nos. 2–3.* BRAHMS: *Hungarian dances and Waltzes.* DVOŘÁK: *Slavonic dances, Op. 46/6–7; Op. 72/8.* SCHUBERT: *Waltzes.* BARBER: *Souvenirs: Pas de deux.* DEBUSSY: *Petite suite: Menuet and ballet.*
(BB) *** Pickwick Dig. PWK 1134.

Eden and Tamir travel the world as a piano duo, and this record is exactly like going to one of their concerts: it is both exhilarating and beguiling, full of variety and spontaneity. They sound as if they are enjoying everything they play, and so do we. Very good sound too.

Fábián, Márta (cimbalom)

Baroque music for cimbalom (with Ágnes Szakály, cimbalom, Imre Kovács, flute, Béla Sztankovits, guitar): BACH: *French suites Nos. 2 in C min., BWV 813; 3 in B min., BWV 814; 5 in G, BWV 816.* PACHELBEL: *Partita in C min.* TELEMANN: *Trio sonata.*
(B) *** Hung. White Label HRC 097.

In order to play Bach's *French suites* on the cimbalom, two instruments and four hands are needed, and here Hungary's most famous virtuoso on the national instrument is joined by her colleague to do just that. The effect is piquantly effective. To make the recital even more rewarding, the solo cimbalom is also joined by flute and guitar to play a winningly tuneful six-movement *Partita* by Pachelbel and a no less engaging *Trio sonata* by Telemann. With excellent recording this is a disc that is as rewarding as it is unusual.

'French Impressions'

'French impressions' (played by: Er'ella Talmi, flute; Avigail Amheim, clarinet; Gad Levertov, viola; Alice Giles, harpsichord; Kaminkovsky Quartet): RAVEL: *Introduction and allegro.* DEBUSSY: *Sonata for flute, viola & harp.* ROUSSEL: *Trio, Op. 58.* CAPLET: *Conte fantastique.*
(BB) *** Pickwick/CDI Dig. PWK 1141.

Excellent, highly sensitive playing throughout an interesting and rewarding programme. This is one of the finest modern versions of Ravel's magically atmospheric *Introduction and allegro*, and the improvisatory nature of the lovely Debussy *Sonata* is captured equally well. The Roussel is of a drier vintage, but the programme ends in high drama with André Caplet's imaginative story in music based on Edgar Allan Poe's *Masque of the Red Death.* As always in this fine series, the recording has a remarkable illusion of presence and realism, and the ambience is perfectly judged.

Gilbert, Kenneth (harpsichord)

Pièces de clavecin: CLÉRAMBAULT: *Suites Nos. 1 in C; 2 in C min.* D'ANGELBERT: *Gailliarde et Double; Chaconne du vieux gautier.* L. COUPERIN: *Pavane in F sharp min.* GASPARD LE ROUX: *Suite No. 5 in F.* MARAIS: *Polonaise in D min.* LEBÈGUE: *Les cloches in F.*
(M) *** DG Dig. 431 709-2; *431 709-4* [id.].

The two Clérambault suites recorded here represent only a fraction of this composer's output for the harpsichord, but they are all that survive. Both suites were published during the composer's lifetime, in 1702 or 1704. They have splendid improvisatory preludes, rather in the style of Louis Couperin, and are notated without bar-lines; they also have a genuine vein of lyricism, not inappropriate in a composer of so much vocal music. Gaspard Le Roux's *Suite* also dates from the same period (1705) and is attractively inventive, especially its impressive fifth movement, *Chaconne*. There is also much of appeal in the rest of the progamme here, not least the engaging piece by Lebègue, *Les cloches*, which is something of a find. Kenneth Gilbert plays persuasively and authoritatively; most appropriately he uses a modern copy, by David Rubio, of the 1680 Vaudry harpsichord from the Victoria and Albert Museum. The 1981 recording, made in the Henry Wood Hall in London, is vividly real.

Horowitz, Vladimir (piano)

Recital: SCHUMANN: *Kinderszenen, Op. 15; Toccata in C, Op. 7.* D. SCARLATTI: *Sonatas: in G, Kk. 455; in E, Kk. 531; in A, Kk. 322.* SCHUBERT: *Impromptu No. 3 in G flat, D. 889.* SCRIABIN: *Poème, Op. 32/1; Études: in C sharp min., Op. 2/1; in D sharp min, Op. 8/12.*
(B) **(*) Sony MYK 42534.

Horowitz's 1968 recital offers marvellous playing of repertoire he knew and loved, recorded when he was still at his technical peak. The recording is dry (there is a hint of wow, but it appears only once or twice); even so, this is magical playing: the Schumann and Scarlatti are superb – but then so is the Scriabin, and Schubert's *G flat Impromptu* is infinitely subtle in its gradations of dynamic and colour.

'Encores': BIZET/HOROWITZ: *Variations on a theme from Carmen.* SAINT-SAËNS/LISZT/HOROWITZ: *Danse macabre.* MOZART: *Sonata No. 11, K.331: Rondo alla turca.* MENDELSSOHN/LISZT/HOROWITZ: *Wedding march and variations.* MENDELSSOHN: *Élégie, Op. 85/4; Spring song, Op. 62/6; The shepherd's complaint, Op. 67/5; Scherzo a capriccio: Presto.* DEBUSSY: *Children's corner: Serenade of a doll.* MOSZKOWSKI: *Études, Op. 72/6 & 11; Étincelles, Op. 36/6.* CHOPIN: *Polonaise in A flat, Op. 53.* SCHUMANN: *Kinderszenen: Träumerei.* LISZT: *Hungarian rhapsody No. 15; Valse oubliée No. 1.* RACHMANINOV: *Prelude in G min., Op. 23/5.* SOUSA/HOROWITZ: *The Stars and stripes forever.*
(M) (***) BMG/RCA mono GD 87755; *GK 87755* [7755-2-RG; *7755-4-RG*].

These encore pieces have been around for some time and, apart from the Rachmaninov *Prelude* and the Mendelssohn, derive from the days of the 78-r.p.m. record and the mono LP. Allowances have to be made for the quality which, as one would expect in this kind of compilation, is variable. So in its different way is the playing, which varies from dazzling to stunning!

Hurford, Peter (organ)

Sydney Opera House organ: *'Great organ works':* BACH: *Toccata and fugue in D min., BWV 565; Jesu, joy of man's desiring.* ALBINONI: *Adagio* (arr. Giazotto). PURCELL: *Trumpet tune in D.* MENDELSSOHN: *A Midsummer Night's Dream: Wedding march.* FRANCK: *Chorale No. 2 in B min.* MURRILL: *Carillon.* WALFORD DAVIES: *Solemn melody.* WIDOR: *Organ symphony No. 5: Toccata.*
(M) **(*) Decca Dig. 425 013-2; *425 013-4* [id.].

Superb sound here, wonderfully free and never oppressive, even in the most spectacular moments. The Widor is spiritedly genial when played within the mellow registration of the magnificent Sydney instrument, and the pedals have great sonority and power. The Murrill *Carillon* is equally engaging alongside the Purcell *Trumpet tune*, while Mendelssohn's wedding music has never sounded more resplendent. The Bach is less memorable, and the Albinoni *Adagio*, without the strings, is not an asset to the collection either.

'Organ spectacular': WIDOR: *Symphony No. 5: Toccata. Symphony No. 6: Allegro.* KARG-ELERT: *Marche triomphale: Nun danket alle Gott.* FRANCK: *Choral No. 3.* BACH: *Toccata and fugue in D min., BWV 565.* MENDELSSOHN: *Midsummer Night's Dream: Wedding march.* BOELLMAN: *Suite gothique, Op. 25.* LISZT: *Fantasia and fugue on B-A-C-H.*
(M) *** Decca Dig. 430 710-2; *430 710-4* [id.].

This Ovation collection centres on the Ratzeburg Cathedral organ, but Hurford uses the instrument in St Sermin, Toulouse, for the Franck *Choral*, while the Bach and Mendelssohn items feature the magnificent Sydney organ, which has striking sonority and power. The ever-popular Widor *Toccata* leads to other pieces that are just as efficient at bringing out the variety of organ sound possible at Ratzeburg, such as the Karg-Elert or the spectacle of Liszt's venture into Bach polyphony. The digital recording is in the demonstration class and the recital offers 69 minutes of music.

Hurford, Peter; Simon Preston (organ)

'The King of instruments (Organ favourites)': BACH: *Toccata and fugue in D min., BWV 565;*

Chorale prelude: Wachet auf. FRANCK: *Pièce héroïque; Choral No. 2 in B min.* MENDELSSOHN: *A Midsummer Night's Dream: Wedding march.* BOELLMANN: *Toccata.* ELGAR: *Imperial march.* PURCELL: *Trumpet tune.* GUILMANT: *March on a theme of Handel.* WIDOR: *Organ symphony No. 5: Toccata.*
(B) **(*) Decca Dig./Analogue 433 610-2; *433 610-4.*

Peter Hurford duplicates two items (the Mendelssohn and Boëllman) included on the Ovation collection above, and adds the Franck *Pièce héroïque* (also digital), using the organ of the Royal Festival Hall. The only relative disappointment is the Bach *Chorale* (recorded in Toronto), which shows Hurford not as spontaneous as usual. The rest of the 64-minute concert is analogue and is shared with Simon Preston, who plays most of his programme on the organ of Westminster Abbey, which has much tonal opulence and a wide reverberation period. But there is no lack of spectacle, even if the effect is less immediate at times. Good value at bargain price.

Israeli Flute Ensemble

'Flute Serenade': BEETHOVEN: *Serenade in D, Op. 25*❀. MOZART: *Flute quartet No. 1 in D, K.285.* SCHUBERT: *String trio in B flat, D.471.* HOFFMEISTER: *Flute quartet in A.*
(BB) *** Pickwick/CDI Dig. PWK 1139.

We have already praised this delightful account of Beethoven's *D major Serenade* in our composer index. The rest of the concert is hardly less winning, including not only one of the more memorable of Mozart's *Flute quartets* but also Hoffmeister's ingenious transcription of a favourite Mozart piano sonata, with its *Rondo Alla turca* finale sounding very sprightly in the arrangement for flute, violin and piano. The Schubert *String trio* makes a graceful interlude and an attractive change of texture; and the recording adds to the listener's pleasure by its complete naturalness of timbre and balance: one can readily imagine the players sitting at the end of one's room.

Kang, Dong-Suk (violin), Pascal Devoyon (piano)

French violin sonatas: DEBUSSY: *Sonata in G min.* RAVEL: *Sonata in G.* POULENC: *Violin sonata.* SAINT-SAËNS: *Sonata No. 1 in D min.*
(BB) *** Naxos Dig. 8.550276 [id.].

One of the jewels of the Naxos catalogue, this collection of four of the finest violin sonatas in the French repertoire is self-recommending. The stylistic range of this partnership is evident throughout: they seem equally attuned to all four composers. This is warm, freshly spontaneous playing, given vivid and realistic digital recording in a spacious acoustic. A very real bargain.

Kayath, Marcelo (guitar)

'Guitar classics from Latin America': PONCE: *Valse.* PIAZZOLA: *La muerte del angel.* BARRIOS: *Vals, Op. 8/3; Choro de saudade; Julia florida.* LAURO: *Vals venezolanos No. 2; El negrito; El marabino.* BROUWER: *Canción de cuna; Ojos brujos.* PERNAMBUCO: *Sons de carrilhões; Interrogando; Sono de maghia.* REIS: *Si ela perguntar.* VILLA-LOBOS: *5 Preludes.*
(B) *** Pickwick Dig. PCD 853; *CIMPC 853* [id.].

Marcelo Kayath studied in Rio de Janeiro and is a master of this repertoire – indeed his flexibly inspirational accounts of the Villa-Lobos *Preludes* can stand comparison with the finest performances on record. He has the rare gift of playing in the studio as at a live recital; obviously he soon becomes unaware of his surroundings, for he plays everything here with consummate technical ease and the most appealing spontaneity. His rubato in the Barrios *Vals* is particularly effective, and he is a fine advocate too of the engaging Lauro pieces and the picaresque writing of João Pernambuco, a friend of Villa-Lobos. The recording, made in a warm but not too resonant acoustic, is first class, and there is a fine illusion of presence. Even though this is a budget-priced issue, it carries excellent notes.

'Guitar classics from Spain': TARREGA: *Prelude in A min.; Capricho arabe; Recuerdos de la Alhambra.* GRANADOS: *La Maja de Goya.* ALBÉNIZ: *Granada; Zambra; Grandina; Sevilla; Mallorca.* TORROBA: *Prelude in E; Sonatina; Nocturno.* RODRIGO: *Zapateado.* TRAD.: *El Noy de la mare.*
(B) *** Pickwick Dig. PCD 876; *CIMPC 876* [id.].

Following the success of his first, Latin-American recital, Marcelo Kayath gives us an equally enjoyable Spanish collection, full of colour and spontaneity. By grouping music by several major composers, he provides a particularly revealing mix. The two opening Tarrega pieces are predominantly lyrical, to bring an effective contrast with the famous fluttering *Recuerdos de la Alhambra*, played strongly. Then after the Granados come five of Albéniz's most colourful and tuneful geographical evocations, while the Torroba group includes the *Sonatina*, a splendid piece. After Rodrigo he closes with the hauntingly memorable *El Noy de la mare*. There is over an hour of music and the recording has a most realistic presence; but take care not to set the volume level too high.

Kremer, Gidon (violin), Elena Bashkirova (piano)

SCHUBERT: *Fantasia in C, D.934.* STRAVINSKY: *Duo concertante.* PROKOFIEV: (Solo) *Violin sonata, Op. 115.* RAVEL: *Sonate posthume.* SATIE: *Choses vues droite et à gauche (sans lunettes).*
(M) *** Ph. 426 387-2; *426 387-4.*

This is perhaps the finest of all Gidon Kremer's records: he is superbly partnered by Elena Bashkirova and given a (1980) Philips recording of great realism and presence. The disc is worth having just for Ravel's posthumously published *Sonata*, a youthful work in a single movement that is surprisingly mature and with many magical anticipations of the future. It is a delightful piece, played marvellously. So too are the Prokofiev and Stravinsky works, full of bravura, yet with the latter displaying an agreeably cool lyrical element; while the Satie miniatures combine wit and sparkle with an attractive finesse. The Schubert *Fantasia* is full of spontaneous romantic flair, and the recital ends with another surprise, Milhaud's delicious *Printemps*, a real lollipop, yet not in the least trivial.

Larrocha, Alicia de (piano)

'Spanish fireworks': FALLA: *3 Dances.* M. ALBÉNIZ: *Sonata.* I. ALBÉNIZ: *Iberia: Trianna. Navarra; Sevilla; Asturias.* MOMPOU: *Secreto.* GRANADOS: *Zapateado; Allegro de concierto; Danzas españolas No. 5 (Andaluza); Quejas o la majas el Ruisenor; El Pele.* TURINA: *Sacro-monte; Zapateado.*
(M) *** Decca Dig./Analogue 417 795-2; *417 795-4.*

Although the title is slightly misleading, for this is essentially cultivated playing, Alicia de Larrocha can certainly provide bravura when called for, as in the glittering Granados *Allegro de concierto.* But this is a recital that relies for its appeal on evocation and colour – as in the same composer's haunting *Quejas o la majas el Ruisenor*, the excerpts from the Isaac Albéniz *Suite española*, or the atmospheric Mompou *Secreto* – and the sheer distinction and character of its pianism, coolly shown in the delectable *Sonata* of Mateo Albéniz. At 71 minutes the programme is very generous, and the recording, partly digital and partly analogue, is consistently realistic.

LaSalle Quartet

Chamber music of the Second Viennese School: BERG: *Lyric suite; String quartet, Op. 3.* SCHOENBERG: *String quartets: in D; No. 1 in D min., Op. 7; No. 2 in F sharp min., Op. 10/3* (with Margaret Price); *No. 3, Op. 30; No. 4, Op. 37.* WEBERN: *5 Movements, Op. 5; String quartet* (1905); *6 Bagatelles, Op. 9; String quartet, Op. 28.*
(M) *** DG 419 994-2 (4) [id.].

DG have compressed their 1971 five-LP set on to four CDs, offering them at a reduced and competitive price. They have also retained the invaluable and excellent documentary study edited by Ursula Rauchhaupt – which runs to 340 pages! It is almost worth having this set for the documentation alone. Now that the Juilliard version on CBS is out of circulation, this is the only complete survey of the Schoenberg *Four Quartets* plus the early *D major* before the public. The LaSalle Quartet give splendidly expert performances, even if at times their playing seems a little cool; and they are very well recorded. An invaluable issue for all who care about twentieth-century music.

Lipatti, Dinu (piano)

CHOPIN: *Sonata No. 3 in B min., Op. 58.* LISZT: *Années de pèlerinage: Sonetto del Petrarca, No. 104.* RAVEL: *Miroirs: Alborada del gracioso.* BRAHMS: *Waltzes, Op. 39/1, 2, 5, 6, 10, 14 & 15* (with Nadia Boulanger). ENESCU: *Sonata No. 3 in D, Op. 25.*
(M) (***) EMI mono CDH7 63038-2.

The Chopin *Sonata*, the Liszt and the Ravel were recorded in 1947–8, the Brahms *Waltzes*, with Nadia Boulanger, as long ago as 1937; while the Enescu *Sonata* comes from a 1943 wartime broadcast from Swiss Radio. The Chopin is one of the classics of the gramophone, and it is good to have it on CD in this excellent-sounding transfer. The Brahms *Waltzes* are played deliciously with tremendous sparkle and tenderness; they sound every bit as realistic as the post-war records. The Enescu *Sonata* is an accessible piece, with an exuberant first movement and a rather atmospheric *Andantino*, but the sound is not as fresh as the rest of the music on this valuable CD. A must for all with an interest in the piano.

Lloyd Webber, Julian (cello)

'The romantic cello' (with Yitkin Seow, piano): POPPER: *Elfentanz, Op. 39.* SAINT-SAENS: *Carnival of the animals: The Swan. Allegro appassionato, Op. 43.* FAURÉ: *Après un rêve.* MENDELSSOHN: *Song without words, Op. 109.*

RACHMANINOV: *Cello sonata, Op. 19:* slow movt. DELIUS: *Romance.* CHOPIN: *Introduction and polonaise brillante, Op. 3.* ELGAR: *Salut d'amour, Op. 12.*
(BB) **(*) ASV CDQS 6014; *ZCQS 6014.*

Julian Lloyd Webber has gathered together a most attractive collection of showpieces for the cello, romantic as well as brilliant. Such dazzling pieces as the Popper – always a favourite with virtuoso cellists – is on record a welcome rarity. The recording, a little edgy, if with undoubted presence, favours the cello and is vivid, with good body and range.

Lympany, Moura (piano)

'Best-loved piano classics', Volume 1: CHOPIN: *Fantaisie-impromptu, Op. 66; Études, Op. 10/4 & 5.* BRAHMS: *Waltz, Op. 39/15.* MOZART: *Sonata No. 11, 'Alla Turca', K.331.* BEETHOVEN: *Minuet in G; Für Elise.* SCHUMANN: *Kinderszenen: Träumerei.* LISZT: *Concert study: Un sospiro.* DVOŘÁK: *Humoresque. Op. 101/7.* MACDOWELL: *To a wild rose.* CHAMINADE: *Autumn.* DEBUSSY: *Suite bergamasque: Clair de lune. Children's corner: Golliwog's cakewalk.* RACHMANINOV: *Prelude in C sharp min., Op. 3/2.* RUBINSTEIN: *Melody in F, Op. 3/1.* GRANADOS: *Goyescas: The Maiden and the nightingale.* FALLA: *El amor brujo: Ritual fire dance.* ALBÉNIZ: *Tango, Op. 165/2.*
(M) *** EMI Dig. CDZ7 62523-2; *LZ 762523-4.*

The popularity and generosity of the programme here speak for themselves. Moreover these are not old recordings rehashed but a brand-new recital, digitally recorded at Abbey Road in 1988. Miss Lympany has lost none of the flair and technical skill which earned her her reputation: the whole programme has the spontaneity of a live recital. At times the playing has a masculine strength, and pieces like *Träumerei* and *Clair de lune* emerge the more freshly through a total absence of sentimentality. Liszt's *Concert study: Un sospiro* is played with commanding passion, and even the more trivial items sound newly minted. At medium price this is very good value, with the Spanish pieces ending the collection memorably, the bold Falla *Fire dance* contrasting with the more lyrical Granados and Albéniz items. The piano timbre is faithful and realistic, if a little dry.

'Best-loved piano classics, Volume 2': BACH, arr. Hess: *Jesu, joy of man's desiring.* DAQUIN: *Le Coucou.* HANDEL: *Suite No. 5: Air and variations (The harmonious blacksmith).* BEETHOVEN: *Rondo a capriccio, Op. 129; Piano sonata No. 14 (Moonlight)*: lst movt. DEBUSSY: *Images: Reflets dans l'eau. Préludes*, Book 1: *La fille aux cheveux de lin; La cathédrale engloutie.* CHOPIN: *Waltzes: in C sharp min., Op. 64/2; in G flat, Op. 70/1; Mazurka in A min., Op. 17/4.* ALBÉNIZ: *Malagueña, Op. 165/3.* RAVEL: *Jeux d'eau.* PADEREWSKI: *Minuet in G, Op. 14/1.* SCHUMANN: *Waldszenen: Der Vogel als Prophet.* SATIE: *Gymnopédie No. 1.* SCRIABIN: *Étude in D sharp min., Op. 8/12.*
(M) *** EMI Dig. CDZ7 67204-2; *LZ 767204-4.*

Moura Lympany begins here with Myra Hess's famous arrangement of Bach's *Jesu, joy of man's desiring*, presented with an innocent simplicity of line which is immediately appealing. She is equally good in Handel's famous set of variations and in the French impressionism. There is sparkle in the Chopin and Albéniz, and she is equally captivating in Daquin and Satie. As in her first recital, the piano image is clear and vivid with plenty of presence, and at 71 minutes the programme is certainly generous.

Menuhin, Sir Yehudi and Stéphane Grappelli (violins)

'Menuhin & Grappelli play Gershwin, Kern, Porter, Rodgers and Hart, "Jealousy" and other great standards'.
(M) **(*) EMI Analogue/Dig. CMS7 63939-2; *EX 763939-4* (3).

'Menuhin and Grappelli play Berlin, Kern, Porter and Rodgers & Hart': BERLIN: *Cheek to cheek; Isn't this a lovely day; The Piccolino; Change partners; Top Hat; I've got my love to keep me warm; Heat wave.* KERN: *The way you look tonight; Pick yourself up; A fine romance; All the things you are; Why do I love you?* C. PORTER: *I get a kick out of you; Night and day; Looking at you; Just one of those things.* RODGERS: *My funny valentine; Thou swell; The lady is a tramp; Blue moon.*
(M) **(*) EMI CDM7 69219-2; *EG 769219-4.*

'Jealousy and other great standards': Jealousy; Tea for two; Limehouse blues; These foolish things; The Continental; A Nightingale sang in Berkeley Square; Sweet Sue; Skylark; Laura; Sweet Georgia Brown; I'll remember April; April in Paris; The things we did last summer; September in the rain; Autumn leaves; Autumn in New York; Button up your overcoat.
(M) **(*) CfP CD-CFP 4576; *TC-CFP 4576.*

The partnership of Menuhin and Grappelli started in the television studio; their brief duets (tagged on to interviews) were so successful that the idea came of recording a whole recital, which between 1973 and 1985 became a series of five. These two CDs offer some of the best numbers extracted from all five. One of the secrets of the partnership's success lies in the choice of material. All these items started out as first-class songs with striking melodies which live in whatever guise; and here with ingenious arrangements they spark off the individual genius of each violinist, both as a challenge and towards the players' obvious enjoyment. The high spirits of each occasion are caught beautifully with no intimidation from the recording studio ambience; while the playing styles of each artist are different, they are also complementary and remarkably close in such matters as tone and balance. The result is delightful. The snag is that the digital remastering, in an attempt to add presence, has made the overall sound drier and, more noticeably in the second collection (entitled '*Jealousy*'), there is a degree of edge on the violin timbre. Menuhin and Grappelli fans will want the three-disc collection. The general collector will perhaps be satisfied with one of the individual issues while they remain available. Perhaps the Gershwin recital is most attractive of all.

'Strictly for the birds' (with Instrumental Ens., Max Harris): *A Nightingale sang in Berkeley Square. Lullaby of Birdland. When the red, red robin. Skylark. Bye, bye, blackbird. Coucou. Flamingo. Dinah. Rosetta. Sweet Sue. Once in love with Amy. Laura. La Route du Roi. Sweet Georgia Brown.*
(B) *** CfP Dig. CD-CFP 4549; *TC-CFP 4549.*

This digitally recorded collection dates from 1980. It is the lyrical tunes like the famous opening song, the atmospheric *Laura* and Grappelli's own engaging *Coucou* that are the most memorable, although in pieces like *Bye, bye, blackbird* and *Sweet Georgia Brown* the high spirits of the collaboration are caught well.

Organ Toccatas

'Grand Toccatas for organ' (played on various organs): BACH: *Toccata and fugue in D min., BWV 565.* CORETTE: *Carillon en F.* ALAIN: *Litanies* (Jean-Louis Gill). BUXTEHUDE: *Toccata and fugue in F, BuxWV 157.* KERLL: *Capriccio sopra 'Coucou'.* MOZART: *Fantasia in F min., K.608.* LISZT: *Prelude & fugue on the name, B-A-C-H* (Lionel Rogg). PACHELBEL: *Toccata in C.* MUFFAT: *Toccata No. 11 & Fugues Nos. 2, 4 & 6.* DANDRIEU: *Magnificat* (Werner Jacob). CLÉRAMBAULT: *Caprice sur les grands jeux* (Marie-Madeleine Duruflé). COUPERIN: *Offertoire sur les grands jeux* (Maurice Duruflé). BOELY: *Toccata in B min.* SAINT-SAENS: *Fantaisie in E flat* (Daniel Roth). MENDELSSOHN: *Prelude & fugue in C min., Op. 37/1.* BRAHMS: *Prelude and fugue in G min.* (Viktor Lukas). REGER: *Toccata in D min., Op. 59/5.* MULET: *Carillon-sortie.* DURUFLÉ: *Suite No. 5: Toccata* (Noel Rawsthorne). MURRILL: *Carillon* (Simon Preston). FRANCK: *Pièce héroïque.* GIGOUT: *Toccata in B min.* BOELLMANN: *Suite gothique, Op. 25: Toccata.* WIDOR: *Symphony No. 5: Toccata* (Guy Morançon). VIERNE: *Toccata in B flat, Op. 53* (Gaston Littaize). TOURNEMIRE: *Fantaisie de l'Épiphanie* (André Marchal). GRISON: *Toccata in F* (Jane Parker-Smith). DUPRÉ: *Le tombeau de Titelouze: Toccata (Placare Christe servulis)* (Philip Ledger). JONGEN: *Toccata* (Jan Valach). MESSIAEN: *L'Ascension: Transports de joie d'une âme devant la gloire du Christ qui est la sienne* (Olivier Messiaen).
(B) *** EMI CZS7 67291-2 (2) [id.].

An extraordinarily diverse anthology – using a wide geographical range of organs – assembled with dedication and perception. Many of the players use more than one instrument and, after the famous Bach introduction, the music is arranged in approximate chronological order. Not surprisingly, as the source is French EMI, there is a strong bias towards French repertoire and organs but, when so much of the programme has a strong appeal, there is no reason to grumble. The choice includes several engaging examples of *Carillons*, notably those by Corette (which has a throaty exuberance) and our own Herbert Murrill. Overall, the variety of mood is remarkable: Pachelbel is sombre, Johann Kaspar Kerll spring-like with his cuckoo imitations, and Dandrieu grandiloquent. Towards the end of the first disc, the German repertoire brings a more massive style, capped at the beginning of the second disc by Noel Rawsthorne's powerful Liszt *Prelude and fugue*, recorded in Liverpool. Then after Saint-Saëns has charmed the ear, the second half produces a whole series of first-class French pieces, ending with ear-catching items like Mulet's *Carillon-sortie*, Jongen's *Toccata* and Alain's rhythmically quirky *Litanies.* Messiaen then provides an appropriately mystical end-piece. Vibrant transfers throughout; sometimes, as in the four pieces played by Guy Morançon on the Rouen Cavaillé-Coll instrument, the sound is a shade harsh, but almost never muddy – except, perhaps, in the 1956 Messiaen excerpt.

Ortiz, Cristina (piano)

'French impressionist piano music': DEBUSSY: *2 Arabesques; Prélude: La cathédrale engloutie. Images: Reflets dans l'eau. Children's corner: Golliwog's cakewalk. Suite bergamasque: Clair de lune; L'isle joyeuse.* CHABRIER: *Pièce pittoresque No. 7: Danse villageoise.* SATIE: *Gymnopédie No. 1.* FAURÉ: *Impromptu No. 3, Op. 34.* IBERT: *10 Histoires: Le petit âne blanc.*

POULENC: *Mélancolie.* MILHAUD: *Saudades de Brasil: Copacabana, Op. 67/4.* RAVEL: *Jeux d'eau; Alborada del gracioso.*
(B) **(*) Pickwick Dig. PCD 846; *CIMPC 846* [id.].

As usual with Pickwick, this is a very generous recital and it is most realistically recorded. Cristina Ortiz shows her versatility in this wide-ranging French repertoire and projects plenty of charm – Ibert's *Little white donkey* is a notable highlight, while Ravel's *Jeux d'eau* is full of evocative feeling. Sometimes in the bravura her playing goes a little over the top, and one would have liked more poise, but there is no lack of commitment and spontaneity, and there is much to reward here. The Debussy pieces come off especially well, and *Reflets dans l'eau* and *La cathédrale engloutie* are as atmospheric as the Ravel pieces.

Paik, Kun Woo (piano)

POULENC: *Nocturnes Nos. 1, 5 & 6; Presto; Improvisations Nos. 10, 12 & 15. Intermezzo; Mouvements perpétuelles Nos. 1–3.* DEBUSSY: *Pour le piano; Suite bergamasque: Clair de lune.* SATIE: *Gnossiennes Nos. 4 & 5; Ogives Nos. 1–2: Vaisseaux; Casque. Celui qui parle trop; Españaña; Embryons desséchés; Gymnopédies Nos. 1–3.*
(BB) *** Virgo Dig. VJ7 91465-2; *VJ 791465-4* [id.].

The distinguished Korean pianist Kun Woo Paik has already given us a splendid Liszt recital on Virgo; if his collection of French music is slightly more idiosyncratic, there is still much to relish, notably Poulenc's *Mouvements perpétuelles* – and indeed the other pieces by this composer. His withdrawn performance of *Clair de lune* is a little indulgent and the *Gnossiennes* also find him a shade mannered, while the *Gymnopédies* are very languorous. But the outer movements of Debussy's *Pour le piano* bring some electrifying bravura, and his imagination is given full rein in the quirkier Satie miniatures. There is 75 minutes of music here and, even though the back-up documentation is disappointingly sparse, this is undoubtedly a bargain.

Petri, Michala (recorder or flute)

'Greensleeves' (with Hanne Petri, harpsichord, David Petri, cello): ANON.: *Greensleeves to a grounde; Divisions on an Italian ground.* EYCK, Jacob van: *Prins Robberts Masco; Philis Schoon Herderinne; Wat Zal Men op den Avond Doen; Engels Nachtegaeltje.* CORELLI: *Sonata, Op. 15/5: La Folia.* HANDEL: *Andante.* LECLAIR: *Tambourin.* F. COUPERIN: *Le rossignol vainqueur; Le rossignol en amour.* J. S. BACH: *Siciliano.* TELEMANN: *Rondino.* GOSSEC: *Tambourin.* PAGANINI: *Moto perpetuo, Op. 11.* BRUGGEN: *2 Studies.* CHRISTIANSEN: *Satie auf hoher See.* HENRIQUES: *Dance of the midges.* SCHUBERT: *The Bee.* MONTI: *Czárdás.* HERBERLE: *Rondo presto.* RIMSKY-KORSAKOV: *Flight of the bumble-bee.*
(M) *** Ph. Dig. 420 897-2.

Marvellously nimble playing from Michala Petri, and 71 minutes, digitally recorded at mid-price, so one can afford to pick and choose. Some of the music opening the recital is less than distinctive, but the Couperin transcriptions are a delight and Paganini's *Moto perpetuo* vies with Henriques' *Dance of the midges* for sparkling bravura. There are some attractively familiar melodies by Bach and Handel, among others, to provide contrast, and Henning Christiansen's *Satie auf hoher See* is an unexpected treat. Monti's *Czárdás* ends the programme infectiously.

'Piano pops'

'Piano Pops' (played by: (i) Garrick Ohlsson; (ii) Ronald Smith; (iii) Moura Lympany; (iv) Cyril Smith and Phyllis Sellick; (v) Daniel Adni; (vi) John Ogdon): (i) CHOPIN: *Polonaise No. 5 in F sharp min., Op. 55;* (ii) *Mazurkas Nos. 1 in F sharp min.; 2 in C sharp min.; 4 in E flat min., Op. 6/1, 2 & 4; 34 in C, Op. 56/2; 47 in A min., Op. 67/4;* (iii) *Nocturnes Nos. 2 in E flat, Op. 9/2; 5 in F sharp, Op. 15/2.* (iv) DEBUSSY: *Petite suite:* 4th movement. RACHMANINOV: *Lilacs.* BENJAMIN: *Mattie rag; Jamaican rumba.* SCOTT: *Water wagtail.* BIZET: *Jeux d'enfants: La bal.* FAURÉ: *Dolly: Berceuse.* WALTON: *Façade: Popular song.* MILHAUD: *Scaramouche: Brazileira.* (v) MENDELSSOHN: *Songs without words: Venetian gondola song, Op. 19/6;* (i) *Midsummer night's dream: Scherzo* (trans. Rachmaninov). (vi) BEETHOVEN: *5 Variations on Rule Brittania.* (i) TCHAIKOVSKY: *Lullaby.* RIMSKY-KORSAKOV: *Flight of the bumble-bee* (both trans. Rachmaninov). (v) GRIEG: *Lyric pieces: Melody; Norwegian dance (Halling), Op. 47/3–4; Nocturne; Scherzo, Op. 54/4–5.* GRAINGER: *Irish tune from County Derry; Molly on the shore; Shepherd's hey.*
(B) *** EMI *TC2-MOM 130.*

It is difficult to imagine a more attractively varied collection of piano genre pieces than this. Moreover, with a fine roster of artists to draw on, the performances are consistently distinguished. Highlights include Moura Lympany's Chopin *Nocturnes*, meltingly played; Daniel Adni sympathetic in Grieg and sprightly in Percy Grainger; Garrick Ohlsson bringing prodigious bravura to the Rachmaninov transcriptions, and John Ogdon showing Beethoven in a spontaneously light-hearted mood. But the undoubted pearl of the collection is the set of nine pieces played with consistent charm and sparkle by Cyril Smith and Phyllis Sellick (piano duo, three hands). Excellent, fresh transfers: this sounds splendid in the car.

Preston, Simon (organ)

'The world of the organ' (organ of Westminster Abbey): WIDOR: *Symphony No. 5: Toccata.* BACH: *Chorale prelude, Wachet auf, BWV 645.* MOZART: *Fantasia in F min., K.608.* WALTON: *Crown imperial* (arr. Murrill). CLARKE: *Prince of Denmark's march* (arr. Preston). HANDEL: *Saul: Dead march.* PURCELL: *Trumpet tune* (arr. Trevor). ELGAR: *Imperial march* (arr. Martin). VIERNE: *Symphony No. 1: Finale.* WAGNER: *Tannhäuser: Pilgrims' chorus.* GUILMANT: *March on a theme of Handel.* SCHUMANN: *Study No. 5* (arr. West). KARG-ELERT: *Marche triomphale (Now thank we all our God).*

(B) *** Decca 430 091-2; *430 091-4.*

A splendid bargain compilation from the Argo catalogue of the early to mid-1960s, spectacularly recorded, which offers 69 minutes of music and is in every sense a resounding success. Simon Preston's account of the Widor *Toccata* is second to none, and both the Vierne *Finale* and the Karg-Elert *March triomphale* lend themselves admirably to Preston's unashamed flamboyance and the tonal splendour afforded by the Westminster acoustics. Walton's *Crown imperial*, too, brings a panoply of sound which compares very favourably with an orchestral recording. The organ has a splendid trumpet stop which makes both the Purcell piece and Clarke's *Prince of Denmark's march*, better known as the '*Trumpet voluntary*', sound crisply regal.

Richter, Sviatoslav (piano)

DEBUSSY: *Estampes; Préludes, Book I: Voiles; Le vent dans la plaine; Les collines d'Anacapri.* PROKOFIEV: *Visions fugitives, Op. 22, Nos. 3, 6 & 9; Sonata No. 8 in B flat, Op. 84.* SCRIABIN: *Sonata No. 5 in F sharp, Op. 53.*

❀ (M) *** DG 423 573-2.

The Debussy *Préludes* and the Prokofiev *Sonata* were recorded at concerts during an Italian tour in 1962, while the remainder were made the previous year in Wembley Town Hall. The former sound more open than the rather confined studio acoustic – but what playing! The Scriabin is demonic and the Debussy could not be more atmospheric. The performance of the Prokofiev *Sonata* is, like the legendary Gilels account, a classic of the gramophone.

Schiller, Allan (piano)

'Für Elise': Popular piano pieces: BEETHOVEN: *Für Elise.* FIELD: *Nocturne in E (Noontide).* CHOPIN: *Mazurka in B flat, Op. 7/1; Waltz in A, Op. 34/2. 3 Écossaises, Op. 72/3; Fantaisie-impromptu, Op. 66.* MENDELSSOHN: *Songs without words: Venetian gondola song, Op. 19; Bees' wedding, Op. 67.* LISZT: *Consolation No. 3 in D flat.* DE SEVERAC: *The music box.* DEBUSSY: *Suite bergamasque: Clair de lune. Arabesques Nos. 1 and 2. Prélude: The girl with the flaxen hair.* GRIEG: *Wedding day at Trodhaugen; March of the dwarfs.* ALBÉNIZ: *Granada; Tango; Asturias.*

(BB) *** ASV CDQS 6032; *ZCQS 6032.*

A particularly attractive recital, diverse in mood, spontaneous in feeling and very well recorded. The acoustic is resonant, but the effect is highly realistic. There are many favourites here, with Allan Schiller at his most personable in the engaging Field *Nocturne*, De Severac's piquant *Music box* and the closing *Asturias* of Albéniz, played with fine bravura. The Chopin group, too, is particularly successful, with the Scottish rhythmic snap of the *Écossaises* neatly articulated and the famous *B flat Mazurka* presented most persuasively.

Thibaud, Jacques (violin), Pablo Casals (cello), Alfred Cortot (piano)

BEETHOVEN: *Piano trios Nos. 7 in B flat (Archduke), Op. 97; 11 (Variations on 'Ich bin der Schneider Kakadu'); 7 Variations in E flat on 'Bei Männern'* (from Mozart's *Die Zauberflöte*) *for cello and piano; Violin sonata No. 9 in A (Kreutzer), Op. 47.* SCHUBERT: *Piano trio No. 1 in B flat, D.898.* MENDELSSOHN: *Piano trio No. 1 in D min., Op. 63.* HAYDN: *Piano trio in G, Op. 73/2.* BRAHMS: *Double concerto in A min. for violin, cello and orchestra, Op. 102* (with Barcelona Orchestra).

(M) (**(*)) EMI mono CHS7 640572 (3) [id.].

Older collectors will have treasured these records in their original form or in such LP transfers as have appeared. The Brahms *Double concerto*, recorded in 1929 and the first recording of the work, has tremendous intensity which shines through the less than sumptuous sound. Cortot appears as conductor (he conducted the *Ring* in France before the turn of the century) and draws playing of a radiant vitality from the Barcelona Orchestra. Those who grew up with this performance will, of course, find this a nostalgic experience, but newcomers will surely find its fervour and directness of utterance inspiring. The Mendelssohn *D minor Trio* was also long a classic and shows what real chamber-music playing is about. Nothing is done to impress the public; this performance conveys the sense of music-making among friends. The 1927 sound calls for tolerance, though one suspects that the originals, reproduced on appropriate equipment, would yield more natural results. There have been better performances than the 1929 Thibaud–Cortot *Kreutzer* (Cortot was always more intent on the spirit than the letter) but few finer of the Schubert *B flat Trio*, made in 1926, among the best-sounding of the lot. A valuable document, for the most part adequately transferred.

Vaidman, Vera (violin), Emanuel Krasovsky (piano)

'Romantic strings': TCHAIKOVSKY: *Méditation; Mélodie, Op. 42/1 & 2; Valse-Scherzo, Op. 34.* DVOŘÁK: *Violin sonatina in G.* SCHUBERT: *Violin sonatina in A min., D.835.* KREISLER: *Schön Rosmarin; Liebeslied; Liebesfreud.*
(BB) *** Pickwick/CDI Dig. PWK 1137.

Misguidedly mistitled, this collection is a recital of the highest calibre. Though the three memorable Tchaikovsky pieces are played superbly, the highlight is the wonderfully spontaneous account of the Dvořák *Sonatina*, written during the composer's American period and with a melodic inspiration to match the *New World Symphony*. It is played here with all the freshness of new discovery. The charm of the Schubert work is equally well caught, and the three Kreisler lollipops make splendid bonnes-bouches at the end. This is an outstanding partnership in every way, and the recording is absolutely real and natural.

Wild, Earl (piano)

'The virtuoso piano': HERZ: *Variations on 'Non più mesta' from Rossini's La Cenerentola.* THALBERG: *Don Pasquale fantasy, Op. 67.* GODOWSKY: *Symphonic metamorphosis on themes from Johann Strauss's Kunsterleben (Artist's life).* RUBINSTEIN: *Étude (Staccato), Op. 23/2.* HUMMEL: *Rondo in E flat, Op. 11.* PADEREWSKI: *Theme and variations, Op. 16/3.*
(M) *** Van. 08.4033.71 [OVC 4033].

Earl Wild's famous performances from the late 1960s re-emerge on CD with their scintillating brilliance given even greater projection by the digital remastering. The piano sound is slightly dry but not lacking in depth of sonority, especially in the two Liszt operatic paraphrases, which are splendidly authoritative here. Wild's technique is prodigious and his glittering bravura in the engaging Herz *Rossini variations* and Thalberg's equally entertaining *Don Pasquale fantasy* is among the finest modern examples of the grand tradition of virtuoso pianism. Godowsky's piece may have a heavy title, but in Earl Wild's hands, for all the decorative complexities, the lilting waltz-rhythms are still paramount.

Williams, John (guitar)

'Spanish guitar favourites': ALBÉNIZ: *La torre bermeja.* PONCE: *3 Mexican songs* (arr. Segovia). VILLA-LOBOS: *Prelude No. 1 in E min.* GOMEZ-CRESPO: *Nortena.* DUARTE: *Variations on a Catalan folksong.* SOR: *Introduction & variations on a theme by Mozart.* SEGOVIA: *Oracion; Estudio.* MADRIGUERA: *Humorada.* TANSMAN: *Barcarolle.* GRANADOS: *Goyescas: La maja de Goya.* LAURO: *Valse criollo.*
(B) (**) Decca mono 433 632-2; *433 632-4.*

John Williams made this first recorded recital in 1958 when he was seventeen years old. The talent is obvious and prodigious; but his style, though already tangibly rhythmic, is still only in chrysalis, the musical personality a little pale. Yet he can charm the ear, as in the Sor *Mozart variations* or in the two gentle Segovia pieces; and his rubato in the Tansman *Barcarolle* is nicely flowing. The mono recording is absolutely faithful and in scale, the studio acoustic a little dry, but not unacceptably so. There are excellent notes.

'Spanish guitar music': I. ALBÉNIZ: *Asturias; Tango; Cordoba; Sevilla.* SANZ: *Canarios.* TORROBA: *Nocturno; Madroños.* SAGRERAS: *El Colibri.* M. ALBÉNIZ: *Sonata in D.* FALLA: *Homenaje; Three-cornered hat: Corregidor's dance; Miller's dance. El amor brujo: Fisherman's song.* CATALAN FOLKSONGS: *La Nit de Nadal; El noy de la mare; El testamen de Amelia.* GRANADOS: *La maja de Goya. Spanish dance No. 5.* TARREGA: *Recuerdos de la Alhambra.* VILLA-LOBOS: *Prelude No. 4 in E min.* MUDARRA: *Fantasia.* TURINA: *Fandanguillo, Op. 36.*
(M) *** Sony SBK 46347 [id.].

This generous (74 minutes) recital is drawn from two LPs, recorded in the mid-1970s and highly praised by us at the time. John Williams has the full measure of this repertoire. He can show strong Latin feeling, as in the vibrant *Farruca* of the *Miller's dance* from Falla's *Three-cornered hat*, or create a magically atmospheric mood, as in the hauntingly registered transcription of the *Fisherman's song* from *El amor brujo*. He can play with thoughtful improvisatory freedom, as in the Villa-Lobos *Prelude*, with its pianissimo evocation, or be dramatically spontaneous, as in the memorable performance of Turina's *Fandanguillo*, which ends the recital magnetically. He does not create quite the degree of tension that Julian Bream achieves in the central section of the Granados *Spanish dance No. 5* or in the Albéniz *Cordoba*, but these pieces bring imaginative rubato and are full of colour. The instinctive control of atmosphere and dynamic is constantly rewarding throughout a varied programme, and the technique is phenomenal, yet never flashy, always at the service of the music. The remastering brings a clean and truthful, if very immediate, image. Background is minimal and never intrusive.

Yamash'ta, Stomu (percusssion)

20th-Century music: HENZE: *Prison song.* TAKEMITSU: *Seasons.* MAXWELL DAVIES: *Turis campanarum sonantium.*
(M) *** Decca 430 005-2 [id.].

Henze's remarkable *Prison song* was written especially for Yamash'ta; whether or not it is a masterpiece, the performance here is totally compelling. The words of the poem (from the *Prison Diary of Ho Chi Minh*) are mixed in with a prerecorded *musique concrète* tape, and to this the percussionist adds his own rhythmic commentary. Yamash'ta both recites (if that is the word – the vocal delivery is quite different from anything one might expect) and plays, and the result is an artistic *tour de force.* Toru Takemitsu's *Seasons* is strong in atmosphere but does not quite match the imaginative quality of Peter Maxwell Davies's *Turis campanarum sonantium.* In this work, perhaps the most ambitious of the three here recorded, Yamash'ta creates and holds the strongest possible tension and builds a climax of tremendous power. The Decca recording is truly spectacular, and this is a reissue not to be missed by those interested in twentieth-century avant-garde writing.

Yepes, Narciso (guitar)

Spanish guitar music: TÁRREGA: *Recuerdos de la Alhambra; Capricho arabe; Serenata; Tango; Alborada; Marieta mazurka.* SOR: *Theme and variations, Op. 9; Minuet in G, Op. 11/1. Variations on Marlborough, Op. 28.* SANZ: *Spanish suite.* RODRIGO: *En los trigales.* GRANADOS: *Spanish Dance No. 4.* ALBÉNIZ: *Rumores de la Caleta; Malagueña, Op. 165. Suite española: Asturias (Leyenda).* Arr. LLOBET: *La canço del lladre; La filla del marxant* (Catalan folksongs). SEGOVIA: *El noi de la mare.* YEPES: *Forbidden games* (film score): *Romance.* VILLA-LOBOS: *Prelude No. 1.* RUIZ PIPÓ: *Canción and Danza No. 1* (CD only: ALBÉNIZ: *Piezas caracteristicas No. 12.* MOMPOU: *Canco i danca.* ASENCIO: *Collectici itim*).
⊛ (B) *** DG Compact Classics 413 434-2 (2); *413 434-4.*

This cassette can be recommended with the utmost enthusiasm to anyone wanting an inexpensive, generous (88 minutes) and representative programme of Spanish guitar music. Narciso Yepes is not only an outstanding exponent of this repertoire, he also has the rare gift of consistently creating electricity in the recording studio, and all this music springs vividly to life. In popular favourites like the famous opening *Recuerdos de la Alhambra* of Tárrega, the exciting transcription of Falla's *Miller's dance*, the earlier Baroque repertoire (the *Suite* of Sanz is particularly appealing), and in the communicative twentieth-century items by Rodrigo and Ruiz Pipó, Yepes' assured and always stylish advocacy brings consistent pleasure. The tape transfer level is quite high and the attendant hiss is not a problem. There are three extra items, all valuable, on the pair of CDs, which sound first class – but this is surely a case where the tape is the best buy: it costs much less and can be used both domestically and in the car.

Vocal Recitals and Choral Collections

Albanese, Licia (soprano)

Arias from: PUCCINI: *Madama Butterfly; La Bohème; Manon Lescaut; Tosca; Turandot; La Rondine; Suor Angelica.* VERDI: *La Traviata.* MOZART: *Le nozze di Figaro.* CILEA: *Adriana Lecouvreur.* CHARPENTIER: *Louise.* TCHAIKOVSKY: *Eugene Onegin.*
(M) (***) BMG/RCA mono GD 60384 [60394-2-RG].

With the distinction of having sung the role of Mimi in two historic recordings, opposite Gigli in 1938 and with Toscanini conducting in New York in 1946, Licia Albanese was a favourite singer at the Met. in the immediate post-war period. As the range of these recordings indicates, she was not limited to the Puccini repertory, though that was always at the centre, above all *Butterfly*. Her bright, clear voice might have seemed ideal for recording, but sadly a trick of vibrato often marred the sweetness and purity and made it sound older than it was, particularly under pressure. These recordings, mostly made between 1945 and 1950, present her at her peak, and consistently the charm and power of characterization make each item compelling. Fascinatingly, the last and longest of the items, of Tatiana's letter scene from Tchaikovsky's *Eugene Onegin*, was from a role she never sang on stage. Here Stokowski conducting his own orchestra adds to the natural warmth and expressiveness. Good bright transfers.

Angeles, Victoria de los (soprano)

Opera arias from: VERDI: *Ernani; Otello.* PUCCINI: *La Bohème.* BOITO: *Mefistofele.* ROSSINI: *La Cenerentola.* MASCAGNI: *Cavalleria Rusticana.* CATALANI: *La Wally.* MOZART: *Le nozze di Figaro.* WAGNER: *Tannhäuser; Lohengrin.* MASSENET: *Manon.* GOUNOD: *Faust.*
(M) (***) EMI mono CDH7 63495-2 [id.].

Most of the items here are taken from an early LP recital by de los Angeles that has rarely been matched in its glowing beauty and range of expression. The *Willow song* and *Ave Maria* from *Otello* have never been sung with more aching intensity than here, and the same goes for the Mascagni and Catalani arias. The final cabaletta from *Cenerentola* sparkles deliciously with de los Angeles, as so often, conveying the purest of smiles in the voice. The CD reissue is augmented by the valuable Mozart, Massenet, Gounod and Wagner items, all recorded in the days of 78s.

Spanish song recital: FALLA: excerpts from: *La vida breve; 7 Canciones populares españolas.* GRANADOS: *Goyescas: La maja y el ruiseñor.* TURINA: *Canto a Sevilla; Saeta en forma de Salve; Poema en forma de canciones: No. 3 Cantares.*
(M) (**(*)) EMI mono CDH7 64028-2 [id.].

This Spanish collection brings together many of the most ravishing of Victoria de los Angeles's very earliest recordings, made between 1948 and 1951. Though the CD transfer adds an unwanted brightness to the voice in some of the fortissimos, and the opening items from *La vida breve* betray their origin on 78-r.p.m. discs with a surface swish, the golden freshness of this most naturally beautiful of voices remains magical. Though recorded in London, the performances – thanks to the inspiration of the singer – are very idiomatic, not least the rare Turina suite, with the then recently founded Philharmonia Orchestra, conducted by Stanford Robinson, Anatole Fistoulari and Walter Susskind. Gerald Moore accompanies in the Falla folksongs, with Victoria de los Angeles at her most sparkling. The transfer adds an edge to high violin lines, as it does to the voice.

'On wings of song': MENDELSSOHN: *Auf Flügeln des Gesanges.* GRIEG: *Ich liebe dich.* BRAHMS: *Wiegenlied.* DVOŘÁK: *Als die alte Mutter (Songs my mother taught me).* MARTINI: *Plaisir d'amour.* HAHN: *L'enamourée.* DELIBES: *Les filles de Cadiz.* MONTSALVATGE: *5 Cançiones negras.* SADERO: *Irish lullaby.* YRADIER: *Era la vo.* OVALLE: *La paloma.* LUNA: *Azulao.* CHAPI: *De españa vengo.* RODRIGO: *Carceleras; Madrigales amatorios: Econ qué la lavaré?; Vos me metasteis; De donde vênis, amores?; De los alamos vengo, madre.*
(M) *** EMI CDM7 69502-2 [id.].

Opening with a glorious performance of Mendelssohn's *On wings of song*, followed by a delightfully lyrical *Ich liebe dich*, both of which immediately take wing, Victoria de los Angeles goes on to cover a wide range of repertoire, not all of which suits her quite so well: *Les filles de Cadiz*, for instance, needs a frothier approach than she manages. But later in the recital there are some delicious moments, especially in the Spanish repertoire in which she is so naturally idiomatic. The good things here easily outweigh the lesser and everything is sung with ravishing tone and fine musicianship, the voice vividly projected by the CD remastering.

'Ave Maria'

'Ave Maria': Sacred arias (sung by Leontyne Price, Sutherland, Pavarotti, Horne, Te Kanawa): SCHUBERT: *Ave Maria*. MOZART: *Exsultate jubilate*. GOUNOD: *O divine redeemer*. Arias from: HANDEL: *Samson; Messiah*. VERDI: *Requiem*. BERLIOZ: *Requiem*. BRAHMS: *German requiem*. ROSSINI: *Stabat Mater*. BACH: *Christmas oratorio*.
(M) *** Decca 425 016-2; *425 016-4*.

Decca are very good at creating anthologies of this kind and this 70-minute collection, superbly sung and splendidly recorded, makes a most enjoyable recital, with plenty of contrast between items. The programme is framed by Leontyne Price in rich voice in Schubert and admirably flexible in Mozartian coloratura; while Joan Sutherland's *Let the bright seraphim* also shows her in outstanding form. Pavarotti's golden tones bring distinction to the *Ingemisco* and *Sanctus* from the *Requiems* of Verdi and Berlioz respectively; and he is equally impressive in the livelier *Cujus animam* from Rossini's *Stabat Mater*. Kiri Te Kanawa contributes a memorable *I know that my Redeemer liveth*, taken from Solti's complete *Messiah*, and is in ravishing voice in Brahms's *Ihr habt nur Traurigkeit*.

Bach Choir, Sir David Willcocks

'Family carols' (with Philip Jones Brass Ens.): *O come, all ye faithful; Gabriel's message; Angelus and Virginem; Ding dong merrily on high; A virgin most pure; God rest ye merry gentlemen; In dulci jubilo; Unto us a son is born; Once in Royal David's city; Hush, my dear, lie still and slumber*. WILLCOCKS: *Fanfare*. RUTTER: *Shepherd's pipe carol; Star carol*. KIRKPATRICK: *Away in a manger*. GRUBER: *Stille Nacht*. arr. VAUGHAN WILLIAMS: *Sussex carol*. MENDELSSOHN: *Hark! the herald angels sing*.
(M) *** Decca Dig. 417 898-2; *417 898-4* [id.].

An admirably chosen and beautifully recorded collection of traditional carols. Fresh simplicity is the keynote here; the brass fanfares bring a touch of splendour but the music is not overscored. *Silent night* has seldom sounded more serene, and Rutter's infectiously rhythmic *Shepherd's pipe carol* makes a refreshing contrast. The digital sound is in no way clinical; indeed the resonance is perfectly judged.

Baker, Dame Janet (mezzo-soprano)

'An Anthology of English song': VAUGHAN WILLIAMS: *The call; Youth and love*. IRELAND: *A thanksgiving; Her song*. HEAD: *A piper*. ARMSTRONG GIBBS: *This is a sacred city (by a bierside); Love is a sickness*. DUNHILL: *The cloths of heaven; To the Queen of Heaven*. WARLOCK: *Balulalow; Youth*. HOWELLS: *King David; Come sing and dance*. GURNEY: *Sleep; I will go with my father a-ploughing*. FINZI: *Come away, come away Death; It was a lover and his lass*.
(M) *** Saga SCD 9012 [id.].

Like the companion collection of Lieder, this Saga recital served as the (then) Miss Janet Baker's gramophone début, and the recording's quality is considerably improved in the CD transfer. Although the recital is only 44 minutes long, it makes a charming collection, superbly sung. The singer's artistry reveals moments of pure enchantment in these unpretentious settings of English lyrics. Janet Baker chose them herself and, though the majority have not immediate popular appeal, they grow more and more attractive on repetition – the melismatic 'Alleluias' in Howell's *Come sing and dance*, the golden simplicity of Gurney's *I will go with my father a-ploughing*, the warm, flowing line of Warlock's *Balulalow*. Martin Isepp is an outstanding accompanist, always sympathetic. The balance is close; yet, although the acoustic is confined, the voice glows with presence, even if there are hints at times of too high a modulation on the analogue master tape, with the sound not absolutely stable. However, the artistry of the singing triumphs over any inadequacies in the sound-balance.

Lieder (with Martin Isepp, piano): SCHUMANN: *Frauenliebe und Leben* (song-cycle), *Op. 42* ❀. SCHUBERT: *Heimliches Lieben; Minnelied; Die Abgeblühte Linde. Der Musensohn*. BRAHMS: *Die Mainacht; Das Mädchen spricht. Nachtigall; Von ewiger Liebe*.
(M) *** Saga SCD 9001 [id.].

Janet Baker's inspirational account of *Frauenliebe und Leben*, part of this early Lieder recital for Saga, has never been surpassed. The Schubert songs are not quite on this level (*Der Musensohn* a little jerky), but the Brahms are beyond praise. This is singing of a quality that you find only once or twice in a generation and – whatever the price – this CD is a collector's piece. The stereo on the original LP was curiously balanced, with voice and piano unnaturally separated, but the CD transfer transforms the sound, with oddities ironed out. Set in a dryish acoustic, the quality is now full-bodied, with a vivid sense of presence to make the transcendental performances even more involving.

French song recital (with the Melos Ensemble): RAVEL: *3 Poèmes de Stéphane Mallarmé; Chansons madécasses*. CHAUSSON: *Chanson perpétuelle, Op. 37*. DELAGE: *4 Poèmes hindous*.

❀ (M) *** Decca 425 948-2 [id.].

This is a very beautiful record. Chausson's extended cantilena about a deserted lover has a direct communication which Janet Baker contrasts with the subtler beauties of the Ravel songs. She shows great depth of feeling for the poetry here and an equally evocative sensitivity to the songs about India, written in 1912 by Ravel's pupil, Maurice Delage, which are by no means inferior to the mélodies by his more famous contemporaries. With superbly atmospheric playing from the Melos group and an outstanding 1966 (originally Oiseau-Lyre) recording, this is a ravishing collection which must be placed among Dame Janet's most outstanding records.

Berganza, Teresa (mezzo-soprano)

Operatic arias (with ROHCG O or LSO, Gibson) from: GLUCK: *Orfeo ed Euridice; Alceste; Elena e Paride.* PERGOLESI: *La serva padrona.* CHERUBINI: *Medea.* PAISIELLO: *Nina pazza per amore.* ROSSINI: *Il Barbiere di Siviglia; L'Italiana in Algeri; Semiramide; La Cenerentola; Stabat Mater.*
(M) *** Decca 421 327-2 [id.].

This wide selection from Berganza's repertory comes mainly from recordings of the 1960s, when the voice was at its most beautiful, although the *Cenerentola* excerpt is from 1959. The musical intensity combines formidably with an amazing technique (shown throughout the Rossini excerpts), and only occasionally in the classical arias does one sense a lack of warmth. First-rate recording, vividly transferred.

Spanish and Italian songs (with Felix Lavilla, piano): CHERUBINI: *Ahi! che forse ai miei di.* CESTI: *Intorno all'idol mio.* PERGOLESI: *Confusa, smarrita.* A. SCARLATTI: *Qual mia colpa . . . Se delitto è l'adorati; Chi vuol innamorarsi; La Rosaura (Un cor da voi ferito); Elitropio d'amor.* GURIDI: *Canzones castellanas: Cómo quieres que adivine; Mañanita de San Juan.* LAVILLA: *4 canciones vascas.* TURINA: *Saeta en forma de Salve a la Virgen de la Esperanza, Op. 60.* GRANADOS: *El tra la la y el Punteado; El majo timido; La maja dolorosa.* TURINA: *Está tu imagen, que admiro (Farruca).*
(M) *** Decca 425 947-2 [id.].

This 1962 recital was made when Teresa Berganza's voice was at its freshest and most appealing. If anyone in the world could approach Victoria de los Angeles in Spanish song at that time it was Berganza, and her singing here is very nearly as spontaneous-sounding and imaginative. The second of the two Guridi songs included is especially beautiful with a movingly tender melody. The arias by Cherubini, Scarlatti and others would have gained from having more than just a piano accompaniment, but the classical quality of the singing is most beguiling. The recording was made in Decca's West Hampstead studio and is vivid and well balanced.

Bergonzi, Carlo (tenor)

Operatic arias from: VERDI: *Aida; Luisa Miller; La forza del destino; Il Trovatore; Un ballo in maschera; Don Carlo.* MEYERBEER: *L'Africaine.* GIORDANO: *Andrea Chénier.* CILEA: *Adriana Lecouvreur.* PUCCINI: *Tosca; Manon Lescaut; La Bohème.*
(M) *** Decca 421 318-2 [id.].

This recital of his early stereo recordings shows Bergonzi on peak form. He does not attempt the rare pianissimo at the end of *Celeste Aida*; but here among Italian tenors is a thinking musical artist who never resorts to vulgarity. The recording (of whatever vintage) has transferred well and retains the bloom on the voice. This is essentially a programme of favourites, but everything sounds fresh.

Bergonzi, Carlo; Giuseppe di Stefano; Bruno Previdi (tenors)

'Nessun dorma (Famous tenor arias)' from VERDI: *Aida; Luisa Miller; Un ballo in maschera; La forza del destino.* MEYERBEER: *L'Africaine.* MASSENET: *Werther.* BIZET: *Carmen.* GOUNOD: *Faust.* PUCCINI: *Tosca; La Fanciulla del West; Turandot.* GIORDANO: *Andrea Chénier; Fedora.* MASCAGNI: *Cavalleria Rusticana.*
(B) **(*) Decca 433 623-2; *433 623-4.*

Bergonzi sings stylishly, ardently and intelligently in arias from Verdi and Meyerbeer, though he does not attempt the rare pianissimo at the end of his vibrant *Celeste Aida.* Giuseppe di Stefano shows his feeling for the French repertoire and ends with exciting accounts of the two famous tenor arias from *Tosca.* Then Bruno Previdi takes over, a less charismatic artist but with an appealing voice and a finely spun line in excerpts like *Amor ti vieta* from *Fedora.* His *Nessun dorma* is potent too, though less individual than with Pavarotti. He is very well recorded, while the Bergonzi and Di Stefano items are much earlier (the late 1950s) and the orchestral sound is less ample. Good value (64 minutes).

Bernac, Pierre (baritone), Francis Poulenc (piano)

Mélodies: POULENC: *Banalités; Calligrammes (Guillaume Apollinaire); Chansons villageoises; Main dominée par le coeur; 4 Poèmes de Guillaume Apollinaire; Tu vois le feu du soir.* DEBUSSY: *Beau soir; L'échelonnement des haies; Le promenoir de deux amants.* RAVEL: *Histoires naturelles; Mélodies hébraïques.* SATIE: *Le Chapelier; Daphénéo; La statue de bronze.*
(M) (***) Sony mono MPK 46731 [id.].

This famous partnership recorded widely for HMV in the late 1940s, but these performances were made for Columbia Records in New York in 1950 and appeared on two LPs in America in the 1970s. Bernac's voice is fresher than ever and his powers of characterization remarkable. In addition to the two-dozen Poulenc songs, there are another fourteen by Ravel and a handful by Debussy and Satie. They sound very well indeed and should not be missed. Thirty-eight songs by a great interpreter in very acceptable recorded sound at mid-price is a real bargain.

Bjoerling, Jussi (tenor)

Operatic recital: Arias from: PONCHIELLI: *La Gioconda.* PUCCINI: *La Fanciulla del West; Manon Lescaut.* GIORDANO: *Fedora.* CILEA: *L'Arlesiana.* VERDI: *Un Ballo in maschera; Requiem.* MASCAGNI: *Cavalleria Rusticana* (with Tebaldi). LEHÁR: *Das Land des Lächelns.*
(M) *** Decca 421 316-2; *421 316-4.*

John Culshaw's autobiography revealed what an unhappy man Jussi Bjoerling was at the very end of his career, when all these recordings were made by Decca engineers for RCA. You would hardly guess that there were problems from the flow of headily beautiful, finely focused tenor tone. These may not be the most characterful renderings of each aria, but they are all among the most compellingly musical. The recordings are excellent for their period (1959–60). The Lehár was the last solo recording he made before he died in 1960. The transfers to CD are admirably lively and present.

Live recital (with Frederick Schauwecker, piano): VERDI: *Requiem: Ingemisco.* SCHUBERT: *Die Allmacht; An die Leier; An Sylvia; Was ist Silvia?; Die Forelle; Frühlingsglaube.* BEETHOVEN: *Adelaïde.* BRAHMS: *Ständchen.* RACHMANINOV: *Lilacs; In the silence of the night.* GRIEG: *Ein Traum.* TOSTI: *Ideale.* R. STRAUSS: *Zueignung.* Songs by SJOGREN; PETERSON-BERGER. Arias from: TCHAIKOVSKY: *Eugene Onegin.* PUCCINI: *Turandot; Tosca.* VERDI: *Rigoletto.*
(M) (***) BMG/RCA mono GD 60520 [id.].

Recorded at Carnegie Hall in March 1958, just over two years before Bjoerling died, this recital gives a warmer, more strongly characterized view of the great Swedish tenor than most of his studio recordings, immaculate and stylish as they consistently were. On record he has generally been remembered for his fine interpretations of central operatic roles, and he gave this recital in New York largely as a counterthrust to his much-publicized rupture with the Metropolitan Opera (over pay). His immaculate legato is a glory of his Lieder-singing here, as it always was of his operatic singing. It is thrilling to hear even Schubert songs treated to big, heroic tone, as in *Die Allmacht* or even *An die Leier*, though rhythmically Bjoerling is often erratic and he is not helped by the scrappy playing of his accompanist. The encores bring the biggest excitement, with the audience welcoming each of the Italian items with applause as they recognize them. The mono recording of the voice is splendidly forward and vivid.

Burrows, Stuart (tenor)

'Sacred songs' (with Ambrosian Singers, Wyn Morris): SULLIVAN: *The lost chord.* GOUNOD: *O divine Redeemer.* PARRY: *Jesu, lover of my soul.* Spirituals (arr. McCarthy): *Steal away; Jericho.* DVOŘÁK: *Goin' home.* MALOTTE: *The Lord's prayer.* WEATHERLY: *The holy city.* TCHAIKOVSKY: *Crown of roses.* LIDDLE: *Psalm 84: How lovely are thy dwellings.* SCHUBERT: *Ave Maria.* MONK: *Abide with me.*
(B) ** Decca 433 673-2; *433 673-4.*

Stuart Burrows's simplicity of style and tonal beauty are very telling in religious pops like *The lost chord*, *Abide with me* and *The holy city*. He also sings the Tchaikovsky carol appealingly and (with the help of the Ambrosians) is telling in the spirituals. Full, atmospheric recording helps this concert to make a good impact, but its appeal is limited to admirers of sentimental religious ballads.

Burrows, Stuart (tenor), John Constable (piano)

'The world of favourite ballads': TOURS: *Mother o' mine.* RAY: *The sunshine of your smile.* FOSTER: *I dream of Jeannie.* HAYDN-WOOD: *Roses of Picardy.* MARSHALL: *I hear you calling me.* BALFE: *Come into the garden, Maud.* ADAMS: *The star of Bethlehem; Thora.* SANDERSON: *As I sit here.* JOHNSON: *When you and I were young, Maggie.* DANKS: *Silver threads among the gold.* LINTON: *I give thanks for you.* WEATHERBY: *Danny Boy.* HANDEL: *Silent worship.* AITKEN: *Maire my girl.*

E. PURCELL: *Passing by.* DE KOVEN: *Oh, promise me.* GREEN: *Gortnamona.* COATES: *I hear you singing.* MOLLOY: *The Kerry dance.* DEL RIEGO: *O dry those tears.*
(B) *** Decca 430 090-2; *430 090-4.*

With his headily beautiful voice at its freshest – the recordings were made in 1978 – and much simple charm, Burrows makes an excellent interpreter of popular ballads like these. The engineers, recording in a London chapel, placed the microphones rather close, but the effect on CD is to give a most vivid presence. John Constable accompanies strongly.

Caballé, Montserrat (soprano), Shirley Verrett (mezzo soprano)

'Great operatic duets' (with Amb. Op. Ch., New Philh. O,, Guadagno) from: ROSSINI: *Semiramide.* DONIZETTI: *Anna Bolena.* BELLINI: *Norma.* OFFENBACH: *Contes d'Hoffmann.* VERDI: *Aida.* PUCCINI: *Madama Butterfly.* PONCHIELLI: *La Gioconda.*
(M) ** BMG/RCA GD 60818.

One might have thought that the vibrancy of Shirley Verrett's personality would have sparked off some real excitement here; in fact, however, it is the lyrical moments of the recital – obviously rehearsed with great care – that provide the highlight of this otherwise slightly disappointing collection. Both the Rossini and Donizetti scenes are slightly dull, but *Mira, o Norma* is gorgeously done, and the singers make equally ravishing sounds in the *Flower duet* from *Madama Butterfly*, by far the most memorable item in the second half of the recital. Vivid sound.

Callas, Maria (soprano)

Arias from: ROSSINI: *Il barbiere di Siviglia.* VERDI: *Macbeth; Don Carlos.* PUCCINI: *Tosca.* GLUCK: *Alceste.* BIZET: *Carmen* (with Nicolai Gedda). SAINT-SAENS: *Samson et Dalila.* MASSENET: *Manon.* CHARPENTIER: *Louise.*
(M) *** EMI CD-EMX 2123; *TC-EMX 2123.*

This compilation on the EMI Eminence label brings together at budget price some of Callas's most cherishable performances, mostly taken from recital material. An excellent sampler, well recorded and satisfactorily transferred on to a mid-priced CD.

'The incomparable Callas' (Arias from): BELLINI: *Norma.* DONIZETTI: *Lucia.* VERDI: *Ernani; Aida.* PONCHIELLI: *La Gioconda.* PUCCINI: *Tosca.* GLUCK: *Orphée et Eurydice.* GLUCK: *Roméo et Juliette.* THOMAS: *Mignon.* MASSENET: *Le Cid.* BIZET: *Carmen.* SAINT-SAENS: *Samson et Dalila.*
(M) *** EMI CDM7 63182-2 [id.].

One might quibble whether the title *'The incomparable Callas'* is apt when applied to these particular items, mostly taken from complete operas and recitals recorded in the 1960s. Her later sets of *Lucia* and *Norma* are both well represented here, but even finer is the *Suicidio!* from her second version of Ponchielli's *La Gioconda*, among her finest achievements. The *Carmen* items taken from the complete set are more questionable in their fierceness but are totally individual – as indeed, flawed or not, is the last-recorded item here, Aida's *Ritorna vincitor*, made in 1972. The transfers capture the voice well.

Arias from ROSSINI: *Semiramide; Il Barbiere di Siviglia.* CHERUBINI: *Medea.* BELLINI: *Norma.* DONIZETTI: *Lucia di Lammermoor.* VERDI: *La Traviata.* MOZART: *Il Seraglio.*
(BB) (*(*)) LaserLight 15 096 [id.].

These LaserLight CDs appear to derive from recordings taken from radio broadcasts that were made live from the operatic stage. Although *Bel raggio lusinghier* from *Semiramide* (1956) is impressive, the highlight here is Callas's 1958 performance of Rossini's *Une voce poco fa* at the Paris Opéra: her creamy coloratura will be a revelation for those who know only her later recordings; she adds the most engaging decoration towards the end. There is also a 1955 *Casta diva* and a powerful *Dei tuoi figli la madre* from *Medea*, conducted by Bernstein two years earlier. Unfortunately the excerpts from *Lucia di Lammermoor* and *La Traviata* are spoilt by poorly focused sound; but there is a fascinating coda in a wild but exciting performance, in Italian, of Constanze's Act II aria from Mozart's *Il Seraglio.*

Volume 1: Arias from: VERDI: *Macbeth; Ernani; Don Carlo; Un ballo in maschera.* DONIZETTI: *Poliuto; Anna Bolena.* CHERUBINI: *Medea.*
(BB) (*(*)) LaserLight 15 223 [id.].

Vieni t'affretta from *Macbeth* (1959) opens with a rare moment of spoken dialogue; although the following *Ah! non credea mirarti . . . Ah! non giunge* (from a 1957 La Scala performance of *La Sonnambula*) is impressive, especially the introduction, and a similar comment might be made about the 1962 *Surta lè la notte . . . Ernani, Ernani*, the highlight here is the fine 1963 *Tu che le vanità* from *Don Carlo*, impressively accompanied by Prêtre and the French National Radio Orchestra, though they are recorded very shrilly. A rare *Di quai soavi lagrime* from Donizetti's *Poliuto* (1960) is also worth having, though the excerpts from *Un ballo*, *Anna Bolena* and *Medea* are more variable.

Cambridge Singers, John Rutter

'Portrait': BYRD: *Sing joyfully; Non vos relinquam.* FAURÉ: *Cantique de Jean Racine; Requiem: Sanctus.* RUTTER: *O be joyful in the Lord; All things bright and beautiful; Shepherd's pipe carol; Open thou mine eyes; Requiem: Out of the deep.* PURCELL: *Hear my prayer, O Lord.* STANFORD: *Beati quorum via; The Bluebird.* TRAD.: *This joyful Eastertide; In dulci jubilo.* HANDEL: *Messiah: For unto us a child is born.* FARMER: *A pretty bonny lass.* MORLEY: *Now is the month of maying.* DELIUS: *To be sung of a summer night on the water.* VICTORIA: *O magnum mysterium.* TERRY: *Myn lyking.*
(M) *** Coll. Dig./Analogue CSCD 500; *CSCC 500* [id.].

This splendid mid-priced sampler makes a wonderfully rewarding concert. John Rutter has arranged the items here with great skill so that serene music always makes a contrast with the many exuberant expressions of joy, his own engaging hymn-settings among them. Thus the bright-eyed hey-nonny songs of John Farmer and Thomas Morley are aptly followed by the lovely wordless *To be sung of a summer night on the water* of Delius, and Stanford's beautiful evocation of *The Bluebird* (one of Rutter's own special favourites). The sound, vivid and atmospheric, suits the colour and mood of the music quite admirably. Not to be missed!

Carreras, José (tenor)

Arias from: PUCCINI: *Manon Lescaut; Turandot.* LEONCAVALLO: *Zaza; I Pagliacci; La Bohème; I Zingara.* GIORDANO: *Andrea Chénier.* PONCHIELLI: *La Gioconda; Il Fioliuol Prodigo.* MASCAGNI: *L'amico Fritz.* GOMES: *Fosca.* CILEA: *L'Arlesiana.* MERCADANTE: *Il Giuramento.* BELLINI: *Adelson e Salvini.*
(M) **(*) Ph. 426 643-2; *426 643-4.*

Including some attractive rarities, this is an impressive recital. Carreras is never less than a conscientious artist, and though one or two items stretch the lovely voice to its limits, there is none of the coarseness that most tenors of the Italian school would indulge in. Excellent sound and vivid transfers.

Caruso, Enrico (tenor)

'Opera arias and songs': Arias from: VERDI: *Rigoletto; Aida.* MASSENET: *Manon.* DONIZETTI: *L'Elisir d'amore.* BOITO: *Mefistofele.* PUCCINI: *Tosca.* MASCAGNI: *Iris; Cavalleria Rusticana.* GIORDANO: *Fedora.* PONCHIELLI: *La Gioconda.* LEONCAVALLO: *I Pagliacci.* CILEA: *Adriana Lecouvreur.* BIZET: *Les pêcheurs de perles.* MEYERBEER: *Les Huguenots.* Songs.
(M) (***) EMI mono CDH7 61046-2 [id.].

The EMI collection on the Références label brings together Caruso's earliest recordings, made in 1902 and 1904 in Milan with misty piano accompaniment. The very first were done impromptu in Caruso's hotel, and the roughness of presentation reflects that; but the voice is glorious in its youth, amazingly well caught for that period. It was the sound of these very recordings which, more than anything else, first convinced a wide public that the gramophone was more than a toy.

'Prima voce': Arias from: DONIZETTI: *L'Elisir d'amore; Don Sebastiano; Il duca d'Alba.* GOLDMARK: *La regina di Saba.* GOMEZ: *Lo schiavo.* HALÉVY: *La juive.* LEONCAVALLO: *Pagliacci.* MASSENET: *Manon.* MEYERBEER: *L'Africana.* PUCCINI: *Tosca; Manon Lescaut.* VERDI: *Aida; Un ballo in maschera; La forza del destino; Rigoletto; Il Trovatore.*
(M) (***) Nimbus mono NI 7803 [id.].

The Nimbus method of transfer to CD, reproducing ancient 78s on a big acoustic horn gramophone of the 1930s, tends to work best with acoustic recordings, when the accompaniments then emerge as more consistent with the voice. There is an inevitable loss of part of the recording range at both ends of the spectrum, but the ear can often be convinced. This Caruso collection, very well chosen to show the development of his voice, ranges from early (1904) recordings of Massenet, Puccini and Donizetti with piano accompaniment to the recording that the great tenor made in 1920, not long before he died, of his very last role, as Eleazar in Halévy's *La juive*, wonderfully characterized.

'Caruso in Song': Popular songs & ballads; Neapolitan songs. Arias by HANDEL and ROSSINI.
(M) (***) Nimbus mono NI 7809 [id.].

Caruso knew all about 'crossover' records generations before the term was invented. As the supreme Italian tenor of his time, perhaps of all time, he had the popular touch. A whole collection of drawing-room ballads – *For you alone* in English, *Because* in French – as well as Neapolitan songs like *Santa Lucia* and *O sole mio*, are sung here with transparent, heartfelt sincerity, and the voice even on these pre-electric recordings seems to ring out with extra amplification, not least in the riotous account of the American wartime song, *Over there* – one verse English, one verse French. But why did he wait till June 1918 to do it, when the war was nearly over? The recordings of the two arias, Handel's

Ombra mai fu and Rossini's *Domine Deus*, date from 1920, only months before the great tenor's death, and there the weighty, baritonal quality comes over impressively.

Chaliapin, Feodor (bass)

Russian opera arias: MUSSORGSKY: *Boris Godunov: Coronation scene; Clock scene; Farewell and Death of Boris.* Excerpts from: GLINKA: *Life for the Tsar; Russlan and Ludmilla.* DARGOMINSKY: *Russalka.* RUBINSTEIN: *The Demon.* BORODIN: *Prince Igor.* RIMSKY-KORSAKOV: *Sadko.* RACHMANINOV: *Aleko.*
❀ (M) (***) EMI mono CDH7 61009-2 [id.].

Not only the glory of the voice, amazingly rich and consistent as recorded here between 1908 (aged 35) and 1931, but also the electrifying personality is vividly caught in this superb Références CD. The range of expression is astonishing. If posterity tends to think of this megastar among basses in the role of Mussorgsky's *Boris* (represented here in versions previously unissued), he is just as memorable in such an astonishing item as *Farlaf's Rondo* from *Russlan and Ludmilla*, with its tongue-twisting chatter made thrilling at such speed and with such power. The presence of the singer is unwaveringly vivid in model transfers, whether the original recording was acoustic or electric.

'Christmas stars'

'Christmas stars': (i) Sutherland; (ii) Tebaldi; (iii) Pavarotti; (iv) Te Kanawa; (v) L. Price: (i) HANDEL: *Joy to the world.* TRAD. arr. Gamley: *Twelve days of Christmas; What child is this?; Good King Wenceslas.* (ii) TRAD.: *Adeste fidelis.* SCHUBERT: *Ave Maria; Mille cherubini in coro.* GOUNOD: *O Divine Redeemer.* (iii) ADAM: *O holy night.* YON: *Gesu bambino.* (iv) GRÜBER: *Silent night.* TRAD.: *Angels from the realms of glory.* (v) *Sweet little Jesus boy.* BACH/GOUNOD: *Ave Maria.* MENDELSSOHN: *Hark! The herald angels sing.*
(M) ** Decca 433 010-2; *433 010-4* [id.].

Not quite the sum of its parts, this collection still has several memorable highlights, including Joan Sutherland's brisk and sparkling *Twelve days of Christmas* and Pavarotti's two contributions, especially the appealing *Jesu bambino.* But while there is undoubted charisma in all these items and they are vividly recorded, it is Tebaldi's *Mille cherubini in coro* of Schubert which steals the show. She sings it quite delightfully; elsewhere her touch is distinctly heavy-handed. Leontyne Price, too, sounds rather ample, though *Sweet little Jesus boy* is affecting.

Clare College, Cambridge, Choir and Orchestra, John Rutter

'Carols from Clare': RUTTER: *Shepherd's pipe carol; Nativity carol.* TRAD., arr. Rutter: *Infant holy, infant lowly; Angel tidings; Quelle est cette odeur agréable; Once in Royal David's city; Il est né le divin enfant; I saw three ships; In dulci jubilo; Quem pastores Laudavere; Rocking; The twelve days of Christmas; Here we come a-wassailing; The coming of our King; O come, O come, Immanuel; The infant king; Noël nouvelet; O little town of Bethlehem; Gabriel's message; Sans day carol; Flemish carol; Past three o'clock.* CANTELOUBE: *Shepherd's noël.* GRÜBER: *Silent night.*
(M) *** EMI CDM7 69950-2; *EG 769950-4.*

This generous collection combines the contents of two LPs, recorded in 1967 and 1970. The sustained mood is pastoral, to evoke the Christmas Eve atmosphere, the shepherds in the fields and the Baby in the manger. Rutter's own *Shepherd's pipe carol* is delightful and here, as throughout, the discreet yet colourful use of the orchestral palette frames each set of words most tastefully. Rutter's own arrangements are very effective. The charming French carol *Il est né le divin enfant*, has a rustic dance flavour, and the presentation of *I saw three ships*, *In dulci jubilo*, *Rocking*, *Past three o'clock* and Grüber's *Silent night* is equally colourful. The recorded sound, while lacking a little in sharpness of focus, remains warmly atmospheric. An ideal collection for Christmas Eve: it plays for nearly 75 minutes.

'The Holly and the ivy' (Carols): RUTTER: *Donkey carol; Mary's lullaby.* TRAD., arr. RUTTER: *King Jesus hath a garden; Wexford carol;* (Flemish) *Cradle song; Child in a manger; In dulci jubilo; I saw three ships; The holly and the ivy.* TRAD., arr. WOODWARD: *Up! Good Christian folk.* TRAD., arr. WILLCOCKS: *Gabriel's message; Ding! dong! merrily on high; Quelle est cette odeur agréable.* TRAD., arr. PETTMAN: *I saw a maiden.* DARKE: *In the bleak mid-winter.* PRAETORIUS: *The noble stem of Jesse; Omnis mundus jocundetur.* TCHAIKOVSKY: *The crown of roses.* POSTON: *Jesus Christ the apple tree.* TRAD., arr. VAUGHAN WILLIAMS: *Wassail song.*
❀ (M) *** Decca 425 500-2; *425 500-4.*

This outstanding collection, recorded by Argo in the Lady Chapel at Ely Cathedral in 1979, is a model of its kind. The freshness of the sound, its warm ambience combined with natural detail, has been enhanced even further by digital remastering and the effect is far more transparent and real than Rutter's companion EMI carol record (although that offers 15 minutes' more music). There is surprisingly little duplication and Rutter's admirers, among whom we can be counted, will surely want both discs for the Christmas season. If only one is needed, then this Decca reissue is first choice. The opening arrangement of *King Jesus hath a garden*, using a traditional Dutch melody, immediately sets the mood with its pretty flute decorations. Moreover Rutter's own gentle syncopated *Donkey carol*, which comes fourth, is indispensable to any Christmas celebration, melodically as memorable as any of the great traditional examples of the genre. The whole programme is a delight – not always especially ecclesiastical in feeling, but permeated throughout by the spirit of Christmas joy. Some of the loveliest of seasonal melodies are included and the lyrical style of the music-making is very persuasive, especially when the sound is so refined.

Collegeum Aureum or Collegium Terpsichore

'Dances from Terpsichore' (with Siegfried Behrend; Siegfried Fink).
(B) *** Pickwick IMPX 9026.

An unexpectedly successful and rewarding collection of early dance music, some of it sounding quite primitive, but with the later items, collected by Praetorius, more sophisticated; yet all full of vitality and presented here with the most piquant instrumental effects. The performances by the Collegium Terpsichore are especially spontaneous, but the whole programme of 36 items encourages dipping into.

Divas

'Prima voce': Divas 1906–35 (Tetrazzini; Melba; Patti; Hempel; Galli-Curci; Ponselle; Lehmann; Turner; Koshetz; Norena; Nemeth; Muzio): Arias from: VERDI: *Un ballo in maschera; Rigoletto; Aida; Il Trovatore.* THOMAS: *Mignon.* MOZART: *Die Zauberflöte.* ROSSINI: *Il Barbiere di Siviglia.* MASSENET: *Manon.* PUCCINI: *Madama Butterfly.* BEETHOVEN: *Fidelio.* RIMSKY-KORSAKOV: *Sadko.* BORODIN: *Prince Igor.* GOUNOD: *Roméo et Juliette.* BOITO: *Mefistofele.* Songs: YRADIER: *La Calesera.* DENAUDY: *O del mio amato ben.*
(M) (***) Nimbus mono NI 7802 [id.].

The six supreme prima donnas on this compilation are all very well represented. The soprano voice benefits more than most from the Nimbus process, so that with extra bloom Tetrazzini's vocal 'gear-change' down to the chest register is no longer obtrusive. She is represented by three recordings of 1911, including Gilda's *Caro nome* from *Rigoletto*; and Galli-Curci has three items too, including Rosina's *Una voce poco fa* from *Il Barbiere di Siviglia.* The tragically short-lived Claudia Muzio and the Russian, Nina Koshetz, have two each, while the others are each represented by a single, well-chosen item. They include Melba in *Mimi's farewell*, the 60-year-old Patti irresistibly vivacious in a Spanish folksong, *La calesera*, and Frieda Hempel in what is probably the most dazzling of all recordings of the Queen of the Night's second aria from *Zauberflöte.*

'Prima Voce': Divas Volume 2, 1909–40 (Hempel, Galli-Curci, Farrar, Kurz, Garrison, Gluck, Ivogün, Onegin, Schoene, Norena, Ponselle, Leider, Vallin, Teyte, Koshetz, Flagstad, Favero): Arias from: BELLINI: *I Puritani.* MOZART: *Le nozze di Figaro; Die Entführung aus dem Serail.* PUCCINI: *Tosca.* VERDI: *Rigoletto; La forza del destino.* OFFENBACH: *Les contes d'Hoffmann; La Périchole.* GODARD: *Jocelyn.* BIZET: *Carmen.* J. STRAUSS, Jnr: *Die Fledermaus.* THOMAS: *Hamlet.* WAGNER: *Tristan und Isolde; Die Walküre.* MASSENET: *Werther.* PONCE: *Estrellita.* MASCAGNI: *Lodoletta.*
(M) (***) Nimbus mono NI 7818 [id.].

As in the first *Divas* volume, the choice of items will delight any lover of fine singing, a most discriminating choice. Maria Ivogün, the teacher of Schwarzkopf, contributes a wonderfully pure and incisive *Martern aller Arten* (*Entführung*) dating from 1923, and Lotte Schoene is unusually and characterfully represented by Adele's *Mein Herr Marquis* from *Fledermaus.* Frida Leider's *Liebestod* is nobly sung but is surprisingly fast by latterday standards. Maggie Teyte sings delectably in an aria from *La Périchole*; and though some of the pre-electric items in Nimbus's resonant transfers suggest an echo-chamber, the voices are warm and full.

Domingo, Placido (tenor)

Volume 1: Arias from: LEONCAVALLO: *I Pagliacci.* MASCAGNI: *Cavalleria Rusticana.* PUCCINI: *Il Tabarro.* VERDI: *Il Trovatore; La Traviata.* WAGNER: *Lohengrin.*
(BB) (**) LaserLight 15 230.

Although the voice projects vibrantly, the effect here is of being in a seat in the gallery. The highlights are some red-blooded excerpts from a performance of *Il Trovatore*, recorded in New Orleans in 1958 with Caballé and Sordello, and a quite impressive (1967) *Traviata* with Maralin Niska, recorded at the New York City

Opera, also the source of the performances of *Pagliacci* (1967), *Cavalleria Rusticana* and *Il Tabarro* (1968). The excerpts from a Hamburg *Lohengrin*, made in the same year, bring very indifferent sound.

Operatic recital (1970–80 recordings): Arias from: VERDI: *Aida; Giovanna d'Arco; Un ballo in maschera; Don Carlos.* GOUNOD: *Faust.* BOITO: *Mefistofele.* PUCCINI: *Manon Lescaut; Tosca.*
(M) *** EMI CDM7 63103-2; *EG 763103-4.*

Compiled from Domingo's contributions to EMI opera sets in the 1970s, this mid-price CD includes some 71 minutes of music. The remastering brings the advantage of negligible background noise, but otherwise there is no great gain in presence; however, the sound is admirably clear and well balanced. If Domingo has recorded such items as the *Manon Lescaut* excerpt more perceptively, and if his singing of *Faust* is less stylish here than it usually is in French music, the range of achievement is formidable and the beauties great. The Puccini arias sound especially real, combining a fresh clarity with a pleasing atmosphere.

Arias from: VERDI: *Rigoletto; Aida; Il Trovatore; La Traviata; Ernani; Macbeth.* DONIZETTI: *L'Elisir d'amore; Lucia di Lammermoor.* BIZET: *Carmen; Les Pêcheurs de perles.* MEYERBEER: *L'Africaine.* PUCCINI: *La Fanciulla del West.* LEHÁR: *Land des Lächelns.* Songs: LEONCAVALLO: *Mattinata.* LARA: *Granada.* CURTIS: *Nonti scorda.* GREVER: *Mucho.* CARDILLO: *Catari, catari.*
(B) *** DG Compact Classics *419 091-4* [id.].

A self-recommending Compact Classcs tape, offering nearly an hour and a half of Domingo in excellent operatic form. The programme includes obvious favourites but some less-expected items too, and the songs are welcome in showing the great tenor in lighter mood. A bargain, very useful for a long journey if you like to turn your car into La Scala Motorway.

Early Music Consort of London, David Munrow

'Music of the Crusades': Anonymous thirteenth-century French music, and music by: MARCABRU; CUIOT DE DIJON; WALTER VON DER VOGEL-WEIDE; FAIDIT; CONON DE BETHUNE; RICHARD COEUR-DE-LION; THIBAUT DE CHAMPAGNE.
(M) *** Decca 430 264-2; *430 264-4.*

Of all the Early Music groups, the Early Music Consort under the late David Munrow can be relied on best to entertain and titillate the ear without ever descending into vulgarity. Not all the music in this collection can be associated directly with the Crusades themselves but, in his scholarly and informative note, James Tyler does not make particular claims that it can. The characteristic combination of familiarity with their repertoire and imaginative flair which characterizes the work of this group informs the whole programme. Most of the accompaniments are purely speculative (only the melodic line survives in some cases) so that listeners should be prepared to approach these lively performances for what they are, resourceful and stimulating reconstructions rather than exact reproductions of what was heard in the thirteenth century. The performances, like the realizations, are brilliantly effective and the presentation deserves the highest praise for its blend of scholarship and inventiveness. The 1970 (Argo) recording sounds as fresh here as the day it was made.

Ewing, Maria (mezzo-soprano)

'From this moment on' (with RPO, Neil Henderson; Richard Rodney Bennett (piano): PORTER: *Medley.* YOUMANS: *More than you know.* KERN: *All the things you are; Yesterdays.* BURKE: *But beautiful.* HUPFIELD: *As time goes by.* WEILL: *It never was you.* ARLEN: *Come rain or come shine; When the sun comes out; One for my baby.* GERSHWIN: *The man that got away; Medley.* RODGERS: *Spring is here.*
(M) **(*) Pickwick Dig. MCD 18; *MCC 18* [MCAD 10154; *MCAC 10154*].

The RPO here attempt a crossover collection, not an easy area for success, but, with sophisticated orchestral backing, Maria Ewing's smoky mezzo is heard at its most seductive in Kern's *All the things you are* and *Yesterdays* (the latter with a sinuous violin solo from David Towse). In five songs, *More than you know*, *But beautiful*, *It never was you*, *When the sun comes out* and the gently expressive Rogers and Hart number, *Spring is here*, Richard Rodney Bennett provides intimately understanding piano accompaniments to give a sultry, night-club ambience. Ewing's dark timbre suits Arlen's *When the sun comes out* rather well; before that, in the livelier *Come rain or come shine*, the accompaniment needs the extra uninhibited bite an American group could provide. But clearly the London players are enjoying themselves, and both singer and orchestra are at their most vibrant and silkily sentient in the closing Gershwin medley. This is a string of five famous standards, to which the piano also contributes, and if *Our love is here to stay* is a shade drawn out, the following *S'Wonderful*, with a superb sally from the horns, comes off infectiously, and *Someone to watch over me* ends the recital in beguilingly gentle evocation, with its interweaving violin obbligati.

Ferrier, Kathleen (contralto)

Lieder, arias and songs: MAHLER: *Kindertotenlieder* (with VPO, Walter). GLUCK: *Orfeo ed Euridice:* excerpts including *Che faro.* PURCELL: *Ode for Queen Mary: Sound the trumpet. Indian Queen: Let us not wander* (with I. Baillie). HANDEL: *Ottone: Spring is coming; Come to me.* GREEN: *O praise the Lord; I will lay me down in peace.* MENDELSSOHN: *I would that my love* (with I. Baillie, G. Moore).
(M) (***) EMI mono CDH7 61003-2 [id.].

It was especially tragic that Kathleen Ferrier made so few recordings in which the technical quality matched her magical artistry. This disc includes many of her EMI mono records, which generally sound much better than the Decca repertoire listed below. The Gluck *Orfeo* excerpts (deriving from a broadcast) have undoubtedly been enhanced and the 1949 *Kindertotenlieder* also comes over very well. Particularly worth having are the duets with Isobel Baillie, as these artists obviously worked especially well together. Generally, the new transfers are vivid and show a considerable enhancement of their previous LP incarnations.

BBC Recitals (with (i) Frederick Stone; (ii) Ernest Lush): (i) STANFORD: *The fairy lough; A soft day.* PARRY: *Love is a bable.* VAUGHAN WILLIAMS: *Silent noon.* BRIDGE: *Go not, happy day.* WARLOCK: *Sleep; Pretty ring-time.* arr. BRITTEN: *O waly, waly; Come you not from Newcastle.* arr. HUGHES: *Kitty my love.* (ii) FERGUSON: *Discovery.* WORDSWORTH: *Red skies; The wind; Clouds.* RUBBRA: *Psalms 6, 23 & 150.*
(M) (***) Decca mono 430 061-2.

These recordings come from two BBC broadcasts, made on 5 June 1952 and 12 January 1953, in the last two years of Kathleen Ferrier's life. Her vocal line is immediately at its most ravishing in the opening Stanford song; throughout, the warm personality and wonderful sense of timing illuminate repertoire in which she was completely at home. No one has presented arranged folksongs so endearingly – just sample the ravishing pianissimo at the end of *O waly waly.* Most valuable are the rare William Wordsworth songs, of which *Clouds* is totally memorable, and the very characteristic Rubbra Psalm settings, *O Lord rebuke me not*, *The Lord is my Shepherd* and *Praise ye the Lord.* The recordings are of excellent quality and have a natural presence, so that the occasional click from the acetate disc original is, alas, the more noticeable.

'The world of Kathleen Ferrier': TRAD.: *Blow the wind southerly; The Keel Row; Ma bonny lad; Kitty my love.* arr. BRITTEN: *Come you not from Newcastle.* HANDEL: *Rodelinda: Art thou troubled? Serse: Ombra mai fu.* GLUCK: *Orfeo: What is life?* MENDELSSOHN: *Elijah: Woe unto them; O rest in the Lord.* BACH: *St Matthew Passion: Have mercy, Lord, on me.* SCHUBERT: *An die Musik; Gretchen am Spinnrade; Die junge Nonne; Der Musensohn.* BRAHMS: *Sapphische Ode; Botschaft.* MAHLER: *Rückert Lieder: Um Mitternacht.*
❀ (B) (***) Decca mono 430 096-2; *430 096-4.*

This selection, revised and expanded from the original LP issue, admirably displays Kathleen Ferrier's range, from the delightfully fresh folksongs to Mahler's *Um Mitternacht* in her celebrated recording with Bruno Walter and the VPO. The noble account of *O rest in the Lord* is one of the essential items now added, together with an expansion of the Schubert items (*Die junge Nonne* and *An die Musik* are especially moving). Her spoken introduction, together with the Jensen *Altar* (taken from a BBC broadcast) are now omitted, perhaps for copyright reasons. The CD transfers are remarkably trouble-free and the opening unaccompanied *Blow the wind southerly* has uncanny presence. The recital plays for 65 minutes and fortunately there are few if any technical reservations to be made here about the sound quality.

Ferrier, Kathleen (contralto), Bruno Walter (piano)

Edinburgh Festival recital, 1949: SCHUBERT: *Die junge Nonne. Rosamunde: Romance. Du liebst mich nicht: Der Tod und das Mädchen; Suleika; Du bist die Ruh'.* BRAHMS: *Immer leiser wird mein Schlummer; Der Tod das ist die kuhle Nacht; Botschaft; Von ewiger Liebe.* SCHUMANN: *Frauenliebe und Leben, Op. 42.*
(M) (***) Decca mono 414 611-2.

Though the mono recording – taken from a BBC tape of 1949 – leaves much to be desired, with the piano sound often hazy, this historic issue gives a wonderful idea of the intensity of a Ferrier recital. Her account here of *Frauenliebe* is freer and even more compelling than the performance she recorded earlier. Walter's accompaniments may not be flawless, but they are comparably inspirational. The recital is introduced by a brief talk on Walter and the Edinburgh Festival, given by Ferrier. The CD transfer does not seek to 'enhance' the sound, but most of the background has been cleaned up. There are moments when the vocal focus slips – and this is not exactly hi-fi, even in mono terms – but the ear adjusts readily.

French operatic favourites

'French operatic favourites' (sung by Obraztsova, Gedda, Freni, Schwarzkopf and Jeannine Collard, Massard, Callas, Vanzo and Sarabia; Paris Opéra Ch., Prêtre): Arias and choruses from: BIZET: *Carmen; Les pêcheurs de perles.* GOUNOD: *Faust.* OFFENBACH: *Contes d'Hoffmann.* MEYERBEER: *L'Africaine.* SAINT-SAENS: *Samson et Dalila.* MASSENET: *Manon.* THOMAS: *Mignon.*
(B) ** CfP CD-CFP 4562; *TC-CFP 4562.*

Elena Obraztsova is certainly a vibrant Carmen and the *Habanera* and *Seguidilla* have plenty of character; her Delilah, however, lacks sensuality. Gedda offers sensitive accounts of *O paradiso* from *L'Africaine* (not lacking fervour) and *Salut! Demeure chaste et pure* from *Faust.* Mirella Freni adds a sparkling *Jewel song* and there are two favourite choruses from the same opera; Freni also contributes a charming *Adieu notre petite table* from Masssenet's *Manon*; both her arias were recorded in 1968 when the voice was strikingly fresh. However, the chosen *Pearl-fishers' duet* (Alain Vanzo and Guillermo Sarabia) is taken from the 1863 original score and culminates not in a rich reprise of the big melody but in an insubstantial waltz theme. The highlights here are Callas's characterful 1961 recording of the *Polonaise* from *Mignon* and Schwarzkopf's ravishing account of Offenbach's languorous *Barcarolle* in duet with Jeannine Collard, which comes from an unsuccessful 1965 complete set of *Tales of Hoffmann.*

Galli-Curci, Amelita (soprano)

'Prima voce': Arias from: AUBER: *Manon Lescaut.* BELLINI: *I Puritani; La Sonnambula.* DONIZETTI: *Don Pasquale; Linda di Chamounix; Lucia di Lammermoor.* GOUNOD: *Roméo et Juliette.* MEYERBEER: *Dinorah.* ROSSINI: *Il Barbiere di Siviglia.* THOMAS: *Mignon.* VERDI: *Rigoletto; La Traviata.*
(M) (***) Nimbus mono NI 7806 [id.].

'Like a nightingale half-asleep,' said Philip Hope-Wallace in a memorable description of Galli-Curci's voice, but this vivid Nimbus transfer makes it much more like a nightingale very wide-awake. More than in most of these transfers made via an acoustic horn gramophone, the resonance of the horn itself can be detected, and the results are full and forward. Galli-Curci's perfection in these pre-electric recordings, made between 1917 and 1924, is a thing of wonder, almost too accurate for comfort, but tenderness is there too, as in the Act II duet from *La Traviata* (with Giuseppe de Luca) and the *Addio del passato*, complete with introductory recitative, but with only a single stanza. Yet brilliant coloratura is what lies at the root of Galli-Curci's magic, and that comes in abundance.

Ghiaurov, Nicolai (bass)

Operatic arias from: GOUNOD: *Faust.* MEYERBEER: *Les Huguenots.* BIZET: *La jolie fille de Perth.* VERDI: *Don Carlo; Macbeth.* PUCCINI: *La Bohème.* BOITO: *Mefistofele.* TCHAIKOVSKY: *Eugene Onegin.* BORODIN: *Prince Igor.* MUSSORGSKY: *Boris Godunov.*
(M) *** Decca 421 872-2.

The first five items here were studio (recital) recordings made in the early 1960s, with the LSO under Edward Downes, and if the singing has to yield to Ghiaurov's fellow Bulgarian, Boris Christoff, in detailed artistry, there is no doubt about its panache, nor indeed the vocal richness. As Mephistofeles from Gounod's *Faust*, Ghiaurov lacks something in biting humour but not in gusto (and he is equally good in the same role as set by Boito). The other items, apart from the extremely lively Galitzky's aria from *Prince Igor*, again with Downes, come from his various complete sets, ending appropriately with Boris's Monologue and the moving *Death of Boris* (with Karajan). Given Decca's consistently vivid projection of a magnificent voice, the whole programme is worth investigating.

Gigli, Beniamino (tenor)

Opera arias from: GOUNOD: *Faust.* BIZET: *Carmen; Les Pêcheurs de perles.* MASSENET: *Manon.* HANDEL: *Serse.* DONIZETTI: *Lucia di Lammermoor; L'Elisir d'amore.* VERDI: *Rigoletto; Aida.* LEONCAVALLO: *I Pagliacci.* MASCAGNI: *Cavalleria Rusticana.* PUCCINI: *La Bohème; Tosca.* GIORDANO: *Andrea Chénier.* PIETRI: *Maristella.*
❀ (M) (***) EMI mono CDH7 61051-2 [id.].

No Italian tenor has sung with more glowing beauty than Beniamino Gigli. His status in the inter-war period as a singing superstar at a time when the media were less keenly organized is vividly reflected in this Références collection of 18 items, the cream of his recordings made between 1927 and 1937. It is specially welcome to have two historic ensemble recordings, made in New York in 1927 and originally coupled on a short-playing 78-r.p.m. disc: the *Quartet* from *Rigoletto* and the *Sextet* from *Lucia di Lammermoor.* In an astonishing line-up Gigli is joined by Galli-Curci, Pinza, De Luca and Louise Homer. Excellent transfers.

'Prima voce': Vol. 1 (1918–24): Arias from: BOITO: *Mefistofele.* CATALANI: *Loreley.* DONIZETTI: *La Favorita.* FLOTOW: *Martha.*

GIORDANO: *Andrea Chénier*. GOUNOD: *Faust*. LALO: *Le roi d'Ys*. LEONCAVALLO: *Pagliacci*. MASCAGNI: *Iris*. MEYERBEER: *L'Africana*. PONCHIELLI: *La Gioconda*. PUCCINI: *Tosca*. Songs.
(M) (***) Nimbus mono NI 7807 [id.].

Gigli's career went on so long, right through the electrical 78-r.p.m. era, that his pre-electric recordings have tended to get forgotten. This collection of 22 items recorded between 1918 and 1924 shows the voice at its most honeyed, even lighter and more lyrical than it became later, with the singer indulging in fewer of the mannerisms that came to decorate his ever-mellifluous singing. In aria after aria he spins a flawless legato line. Few tenor voices have ever matched Gigli's in rounded, golden beauty, and the Nimbus transfers capture its bloom in a way that makes one forget pre-electric limitations. In the one item sung in French, by Lalo, he sounds less at home, a little too heavy; but the ease of manner in even the most taxing arias elsewhere is remarkable, and such a number as the *Serenade* from Mascagni's *Iris* is irresistible in its sparkle, as are the Neapolitan songs, notably the galloping *Povero Pulcinella* by Buzzi-Peccia. One oddity is a tenor arrangement of Saint-Saëns's *The Swan*.

'Prima Voce': Volume 2 (1925–40). Arias from: DONIZETTI: *L'elisir d'amore; Lucia di Lammermoor*. PUCCINI: *Manon Lescaut; La Bohème; Tosca*. VERDI: *La forza del destino; La Traviata; Rigoletto*. THOMAS: *Mignon*. BIZET: *I pescatori di perle*. PONCIELLI: *La Gioconda*. MASSENET: *Manon*. GOUNOD: *Faust*. RIMSKY-KORSAKOV: *Sadko*. GLUCK: *Paride ed Elena*. CILEA: *L'Arlesiana*. CACCINI: Song: *Amarilli*.
(M) (***) Nimbus mono NI 7817 [id.].

Issued to celebrate the Gigli centenary in 1990, the Nimbus selection concentrates on recordings he made in the very early years of electrical recording up to 1931, when his voice was at its very peak, the most golden instrument, ideally suited to recording. The items are very well chosen and are by no means the obvious choices, though it is good to have such favourites as the *Pearlfishers duet* with de Luca and the 1931 version of Rodolfo's *Che gelida manina*. The Nimbus transfers are at their best, with relatively little reverberation.

Arias and excerpts from: GIORDANO: *Andrea Chénier*. DONIZETTI: *La Favorita; L'elisir d'amore; Lucia di Lammermoor*. GOUNOD: *Faust; Roméo et Juliette*. LALO: *Le roi d'Ys*. PUCCINI: *Tosca*. PONCHIELLI: *La Gioconda*. BIZET: *Les pêcheurs de perles*. VERDI: *Attila; I Lombardi*. GOMES: *Lo schiavo; Il Guarany*.
(M) (***) BMG/RCA mono GD 87811 [7811-2-RG].

This RCA compilation with its bright, forward CD transfers of the original 78s underlines the astonishing consistency of Gigli's golden tenor over the whole of his long recording career, whether in heroic outbursts or in gentle *bel canto*. The selection ranges wide, from pre-electrics like Chénier's big aria, always a favourite with him, to ten items from the early electric period – 1925–30 – and with two little songs by Gomes from 1951 as a postscript. Specially notable from these American recordings are the duets and trios with his great contemporaries at the Met. in New York, Ezio Pinza, Titta Ruffo and Elisabeth Rethberg. The voice is consistently close and immediate, with an astonishing sense of presence, yet with none of the histrionic harshness one can expect from other tenors.

Gomez, Jill (soprano)

'Spanish songs' (with John Constable, piano): GRANADOS: *Tonadillas al estilo antiguo, Nos. 1–6*. TURINA: *Poema en forma de canciones, Op. 19*. FALLA: *Trois Mélodies. Siete canciones populares españolas*.
(M) *** Saga SCD 9007 [id.].

Jill Gomez's memorably delectable recital of Spanish songs (including Falla's *Seven Spanish popular songs*) is one of the highlights of the Saga catalogue. In its original, LP format, this issue was spoilt by noisy surfaces, but now one can hear the recording in its pristine glory, wonderfully fresh and naturally balanced. The performances are in every way outstanding and the repertoire a delight.

Great Singers

'Prima voce': Great singers 1909–38 (Tetrazzini; Caruso; Schumann-Heink; McCormack; Galli-Curci; Stracciari; Ponselle; Lauri-Volpi; Turner; Tibbett; Supervia; Gigli; Anderson; Schipa; Muzio; Tauber): Arias from: BELLINI: *La Sonnambula; I Puritani; Norma*. LEONCAVALLO: *Pagliacci*. MOZART: *Don Giovanni; Die Zauberflöte*. ROSSINI: *Il Barbiere di Siviglia*. PUCCINI: *Turandot*. VERDI: *Un ballo in maschera*. BIZET: *Carmen*. PUCCINI: *La Bohème*. SAINT-SAËNS: *Samson et Dalila*. MASCAGNI: *L'amico Fritz*. Song: REFICE: *Ombra di Nube*.
(M) (***) Nimbus mono NI 7801 [id.].

This was the first of Nimbus's series of archive recordings, taking a radical new view of the problem of transferring ancient 78-r.p.m. vocal recordings to CD. The best possible copies of shellac originals have been played on an acoustic machine with an enormous horn, one of the hand-made Rolls-Royces among non-electric gramophones of the 1930s, with thorn needles reducing still further the need to filter the sound electronically. The results have been recorded in a small hall, and the sound reproduced removes any feeling of boxy closeness. Those who have resisted the bottled or tinny sound of many historic recordings will find the Nimbus transfers more friendly and sympathetic, even if technically there is an inevitable loss of recorded information at both ends of the spectrum because of the absolute limitations of the possible frequency range on this kind of reproducer.

This compilation makes a good starting point, even if the method still does not provide the ideal answer. The Tetrazzini item with which the selection opens, *Ah non giunge* from Bellini's *La Sonnambula*, is one of the supreme demonstrations of coloratura on record, and the programme goes on to a magnificent Caruso of 1910 and an unforgettable performance of the coloratura drinking-song from Donizetti's *Lucrezia Borgia* by the most formidable of contraltos, Ernestine Schumann-Heink. Then follows John McCormack's famous account of *Il mio tesoro* from Mozart's *Don Giovanni*, with the central passage-work amazingly done in a single breath. Other vintage items include Galli-Curci's dazzling account of *Son vergin vezzosa* from Bellini's *I Puritani*, Eva Turner in her incomparable 1928 account of Turandot's aria, Gigli amiably golden-toned in *Che gelida manina* from *La Bohème*, and a delectable performance of the *Cherry duet* from Mascagni's *L'amico Fritz* by Tito Schipa and Mafalda Favero, riches indeed!

(A) Hundred Years of the Gramophone

100 years of the Gramophone (1888–1988): LEONCAVALLO: *Pagliacci: Vesti la Giubba* (Caruso). MARSHALL: *I hear you calling me* (John McCormack). KREISLER: *Liebslied* (Kreisler). CHOPIN: *Étude in A* (Cortot). BACH: *Cello suite No. 1: Prelude* (Casals). MUSSORGSKY: *Song of the flea* (Chaliapin). TARREGA: *Recuerdos de la Alhambra* (Segovia). ROSSINI: *Scala di seta overture* (Toscanini). LEONCAVALLO: *Mattinata* (Gigli). BEETHOVEN: *Sonata No. 14 (Moonlight): Adagio* (Schnabel). MOZART: *Così fan tutte: Soave sia il vento* (Schwarzkopf, etc.). DINICU: *Hora staccato* (Heifetz). PUCCINI: *Tosca: Vissi d'arte* (Callas). MOZART: *Horn concerto No. 4, K.495: Rondo* (D. Brain). SCHUBERT: *Ave Maria* (Menuhin). RACHMANINOV: *Prelude in C sharp min.* (Rubinstein). BIZET: *Carmen: Habañera* (De los Angeles). WAGNER: *Lohengrin: Prelude, Act III* (Boult). VERDI: *Aida: Celeste Aida* (Domingo). GERSHWIN: *Porgy and Bess: Summertime* (Te Kanawa). ORFF: *Carmina Burana: O Fortuna* (LSO Ch., LSO, Previn). SAINT-SAENS: *Carnival of animals: The Swan* (Du Pré).
(M) *** EMI CDH7 63018-2.

This celebratory sampler inevitably is an arbitrary selection, and every collector will have his or her own ideas about what should have been included. Even more striking is the roster of artists who are not here – Dame Janet Baker, for instance. Nevertheless there is plenty to fascinate the ear and give some idea of what a remarkable recorded legacy is held in the vaults of just one major company. Certain conductors (Beecham, for instance, with de los Angeles) are represented only in accompanying roles.

Italian Operatic favourites

'Italian operatic favourites' (sung by: De los Angeles, Del Monte, Gedda, Moffo, Campora, Grist, ROHCG Chorus, Merrill, Cavalli, Sereni, Corelli). Arias from: VERDI: *La Traviata; Rigoletto; Il Trovatore* (including *Anvil chorus*); *Aida*. ROSSINI: *Il Barbiere di Siviglia*. PUCCINI: *La Bohème; Tosca; Madama Butterfly*. PONCHIELLI: *La Gioconda*. MOZART: *Le nozze di Figaro*. DONIZETTI: *Lucia di Lammermoor*.
(B) *(*) CfP CD-CFP 4560; *TC-CFP 4560*.

A disappointing recital. Much of the male singing is undistinguished and often relatively coarse. That comment certainly does not apply to Victoria de los Angeles' excerpts from her 1960 recordings of *La Traviata* and *Madama Butterfly*, and *Un bel dì vedremo* is the highlight of the disc. Anna Moffo, recorded in 1961, provides the arias from Rossini's *Il Barbiere di Siviglia*, Mozart's *Voi che sapete* and the Mad scene from *Lucia di Lammermoor*, and there is some lovely singing here also. But while her tone is always creamy and beautiful, there is something too casual about the actual performances.

Jurinac, Sena (soprano)

R. STRAUSS: *Four Last songs (Vier letzte Lieder)*. Opera arias from: MOZART: *Così fan tutte; Idomeneo*. SMETANA: *The Bartered bride; The Kiss*. TCHAIKOVSKY: *Joan of Arc; Queen of Spades*.
(M) (***) EMI mono CDH7 63199-2.

This EMI Références issue, very well transferred, celebrates a magical, under-recorded singer. It brings together all of Jurinac's recordings for EMI outside the complete operas, and adds a live radio recording from Sweden – with Fritz Busch conducting the Stockholm Philharmonic Orchestra – of Strauss's *Four Last songs*, most beautifully done, if with rather generalized expression. Busch was also the conductor for the Glyndebourne recordings of excerpts from *Così fan tutte* and *Idomeneo*.

King's College, Cambridge, Choir, Philip Ledger

'Festival of lessons and carols' (1979) includes: TRAD.: *Once in Royal David's city; Sussex carol; Joseph and Mary; A maiden most gentle; Chester carol; Angels, from the realms of glory.* HANDEL: *Resonet in laudibus.* ORD: *Adam lay ybounden.* GRÜBER: *Stille Nacht.* MATHIAS: *A babe is born.* WADE: *O come all ye faithful.* MENDELSSOHN: *Hark! the herald angels sing.*
(M) *** EMI CDM7 63180-2 [id.]; *EG 763180-4.*

This most recent version on record of the annual King's College ceremony has the benefit of modern recording, even more atmospheric than before. Under Philip Ledger the famous choir keeps its beauty of tone and incisive attack. The opening processional, *Once in Royal David's city*, is even more effective heard against the background quiet of CD, and this remains a unique blend of liturgy and music.

'Procession with carols on Advent Sunday' includes: PALESTRINA (arr. from): *I look from afar; Judah and Jerusalem, fear not.* PRAETORIUS: *Come, thou Redeemer of the earth.* TRAD.: *O come, o come, Emmanuel!; Up, awake and away!; 'Twas in the year; Cherry tree carol; King Jesus hath a garden; On Jordan's bank the Baptist's cry; Gabriel's message; I wonder as I wander; My dancing day; Lo! he comes with clouds descending.* BYRT: *All and some.* P. NICOLAI, arr. BACH: *Wake, o wake! with tidings thrilling.* BACH: *Nun komm' der Heiden Heiland.*
(M) *** EMI CDM7 63181-2 [id.]; *EG 763181-4.*

This makes an attractive variant to the specifically Christmas-based service, though the carols themselves are not quite so memorable. Beautiful singing and richly atmospheric recording; the wide dynamic range is demonstrated equally effectively by the atmospheric opening and processional and the sumptuous closing hymn.

King's College, Cambridge, Choir, Sir David Willcocks

'The world of King's': HANDEL: *Coronation anthem: Zadok the Priest* (with ECO). ALLEGRI: *Miserere.* PALESTRINA: *Hodie Beata Virgo.* TALLIS: *Sancte Deus.* VIVALDI: *Gloria in D, RV 589: Gloria; Et in terra pax* (with ASMF). BYRD: *Ave verum corpus.* CROFT: *Burial service.* GIBBONS: *This is the record of John* (with Jacobean Consort of Viols). BACH: *O Jesu so meek.* HANDEL: *Chandos anthem No. 9: O Praise the Lord with one consent* (with ASMF).
(B) *** Decca 430 092-2; *430 092-4.*

A fine demonstration of the creative excellence of Sir David Willcocks's regime at King's, recorded for Argo between 1958 and 1966. The programme is well made, opening and closing brightly and colourfully with extrovert Handel, and including the famous performance of Allegri's *Miserere* with the ethereal treble solo of the young Roy Goodman, now better known – nearly thirty years later – for his music-making with the Hanover Band. The soaring lines of Tallis and the serenity of Byrd are to be heard alongside the most famous of Gibbons's verse-anthems (with accompanying viols) and William Croft's nobly austere *Funeral service* (given complete). The excellence of the sound throughout, bright and fresh, with the King's acoustics always an atmospheric asset, is a tribute to the original Argo engineering.

'Carols from King's': TRAD., arr. WILLCOCKS: *On Christmas night; Tomorrow shall be my dancing day; Cherry tree carol; The Lord at first; A Child is born in Bethlehem; While shepherds watched.* TRAD., arr. VAUGHAN WILLIAMS: *And all in the morning.* CORNELIUS: *Three Kings.* EBERLING: *All my heart this night rejoices.* GRÜBER: *Silent night* (arr. Willcocks). Trad. Italian, arr. WOOD: *Hail, blessed Mary.* TRAD., arr. SULLIVAN: *It came upon the midnight clear.* Trad. French, arr. WILLCOCKS: *Ding dong! merrily.* Trad. Basque, arr. PETTMAN: *I saw a maiden.* DARKE: *In the bleak midwinter.* Trad. German: *Mary walked through a wood of thorn.* BAINTON: *A Babe is born I wys.* PRAETORIUS: *Psallite unigenito.*
(B) *** CfP CD-CFP 4586; *TC-CFP 4586* [CDB 67356].

This recital was planned and recorded as a whole in 1969, and very successful it is. By then the EMI engineers had found the full measure of the King's acoustic, and the focus is clean while there is no lack of atmosphere. The programme has an attractive lyrical flavour, with plenty of delightful, unfamiliar carols to add spice to favourites like *Tomorrow shall be my dancing day* and *In the bleak midwinter*, which sound memorably fresh. The arrangements are for the most part straightforward, with added imaginative touches to charm the ear, like the decorative organ 'descant' which embroiders *Ding dong! merrily on high*. The King's intimacy gives much pleasure here, yet the disc ends with a fine, robust version of *While shepherd's watched.* Most rewarding and a real bargain.

'Christmas music from King's' (with Andrew Davis, organ, D. Whittaker, flute, Christopher van Kampen, cello, & Robert Spencer, lute): SWEELINCK: *Hodie Christus natus est.* PALESTRINA: *Hodie Christus natus est.* VICTORIA: *O magnum mysterium; Senex puerum portabat.* BYRD: *Senex puerum portabat; Hodie beata virgo.* GIBBONS: *Hosanna to the Son of David.* WEELKES: *Hosanna to the Son of David; Gloria in excelsis Deo.* ECCARD: *When to the temple Mary went.* MACONCHY: *Nowell! Nowell!* arr. BRITTEN: *The holly and the ivy.* PHILIP (The Chancellor): *Angelus ad virginem.* arr. POSTON: *Angelus ad virginem; My dancing day.* POSTON: *Jesus Christ the apple tree.* BERKELEY: *I sing of a maiden.* TAYLOR: *Watts's cradle song.* CAMPION: *Sing a song of joy.* PEERSON: *Most glorious Lord of life.* Imogen HOLST: *That Lord that lay in Assë stall.* WARLOCK: *Where riches is everlastingly.*
(M) **(*) EMI CDM7 64130-2 [id.]; *EG 764130-4.*

A happily chosen survey of music (63 minutes) inspired by the Nativity from the fifteenth century to the present day. As might be expected, the King's choir confidently encompasses the wide variety of styles from the spiritual serenity of the music of Victoria to the attractive arrangements of traditional carols by modern composers, in which an instrumental accompaniment is added. These items are quite delightful and they are beautifully recorded (in 1965). The motets, from a year earlier, were among the first recording sessions made by the EMI engineers in King's College Chapel, and at the time they had not solved all the problems associated with the long reverberation period, so the focus is less than sharp. Even so, this group demonstrates the unique virtuosity of the Cambridge choir, exploiting its subtlety of tone and flexibility of phrase.

King's College, Cambridge, Choir, Willcocks or Philip Ledger

'Christmas carols from King's College': GAUNTLETT: *Once in Royal David's city.* TRAD., arr. VAUGHAN WILLIAMS: *O little town of Bethlehem.* TRAD., arr. STAINER: *The first nowell.* TRAD., arr. LEDGER: *I saw three ships.* TRAD. German, arr. HOLST: *Personent hodie.* TERRY: *Myn Lyking.* HOWELLS: *A spotless rose.* KIRKPATRICK: *Away in a manger.* HADLEY: *I sing of a maiden.* TRAD. French, arr. WILLCOCKS: *O come, o come Emmanuel.* TRAD. arr. WILLCOCKS: *While shepherds watched; On Christmas night.* arr. WOODWARD: *Up! Good Christian folk and listen.* DARKE: *In the bleak midwinter.* GRÜBER: *Silent night.* TRAD. arr. WALFORD DAVIES: *The holly and the ivy.* TRAD., arr. SULLIVAN: *It came upon the midnight clear.* CORNELIUS: *Three kings.* SCHEIDT: *A Child is born in Bethlehem.* TRAD. German, arr. PEARSALL: *In dulci jubilo.* WADE: *O come, all ye faithful.* MENDELSSOHN: *Hark! the herald angels sing.*
(M) *** EMI CDM7 63179-2 [id.]; *EG 763179-4.*

With 71 minutes of music and 22 carols included, this collection, covering the regimes of both Sir David Willcocks and Philip Ledger, could hardly be bettered as a representative sampler of the King's tradition. Opening with the famous processional of *Once in Royal David's city*, to which Willcocks contributes a descant (as he also does in *While shepherds watched*), the programme is wide-ranging in its historical sources, from the fourteenth century to the present day, while the arrangements feature many famous musicians. The recordings were made between 1969 and 1976, and the CD transfers are first class. The two closing carols, featuring the Philip Jones Brass Ensemble, are made particularly resplendent.

King's College, Cambridge, Choir, Willcocks

The Psalms of David, Volume 1: *Psalms Nos. 15, 23–4, 42–43, 46, 61, 84, 104, 121–2, 137, 147–50.*
(M) *** EMI CDM7 63100-2; *EG 763100-4.*

Psalms of David, Volume 2: *Psalms Nos. 12, 22, 65–7, 78, 81, 114–15, 126, 133–4.*
(M) *** EMI CDM7 63101-2; *EG 763101-4.*

Psalms of David, Volume 3: *Psalms Nos. 37, 45, 49, 53, 93–4, 107, 130–1.*
(M) *** EMI CDM7 63102-2; *EG 763102-4.*

In pioneer days the early Christians took over the Psalter along with the Old Testament teachings from the Hebrew Temple, and the Psalms have always been an integral part of Anglican liturgy. Although they are called 'The Psalms of David' it has long been recognized that the original Hebrew collection (some 150 strong) was gathered together over a period of several hundred years, and the writings are from many different anonymous hands. The Anglican settings used on these recordings have offered their composers a fairly wide range of expressive potential, yet the music itself, perhaps because of the stylized metre and the ritual nature of its use, seldom approaches the depth and resonance which are found in the music of the great composers of the Roman Catholic faith, Palestrina, Victoria and so on. The King's College Choir, conducted by Sir David Willcocks from the organ, give an eloquent account of a cross-section of the Psalter on these discs. They are beautifully recorded and well transferred to CD.

Lehmann, Lotte (soprano)

Opera arias from: BEETHOVEN: *Fidelio.* WEBER: *Der Freischütz; Oberon.* NICOLAI: *Die lustigen Weiber von Windsor.* WAGNER: *Lohengrin; Tannhäuser; Tristan und Isolde.* R. STRAUSS: *Der Rosenkavalier; Ariadne auf Naxos; Arabella.* KORNGOLD: *Die tote Stadt; Das Wunder der Heliane.* J. STRAUSS Jnr: *Die Fledermaus.* LEHÁR: *Eva.*
(M) (***) EMI mono CDH7 61042-2 [id.].

Lehmann's celebrated account of the Marschallin's monologue from the classic set of *Rosenkavalier* excerpts recorded in Vienna in 1933 is an essential item here. Otherwise this collection of fourteen of her recordings, made in the days of 78s, concentrates on the Parlophone issues done in Berlin in the 1920s and early '30s. The earliest has the young George Szell accompanying her in Korngold (the only pre-electric here), but there are many other treasures. The Richard Strauss items are particularly valuable, with Arabella's *Mein Elemer* recorded within months of the opera's première in 1933. Though Isolde was not a role she would ever have considered singing on stage, the *Liebestod* here has wonderful poise and beauty, while it is good to hear her speaking voice in the 1928 recording of Lehár's *Eva.*

Song recital: CIMARA: *Canto di primavera.* SADERO: *Fà la nana.* GOUNOD: *Vierge d'Athènes.* PALADILHE: *Psyché.* DUPARC: *La vie antérieure.* HAHN: *Infidélité; L'enamourée; D'une prison.* GRECHANINOV: *My native land (Heimat).* WORTH: *Midsummer.* SJÖBERG: *Visions (Tonerna).* TRAD.: *Drink to me only; Schlafe, mein süsses Kind.* BALOCH: *Do not chide me.* WOLF: *Nun lass uns Frieden schliessen; Und willst du deinen Liebsten sterben sehen?; Der Knabe und das Immlein.* R. STRAUSS: *Wozu noch, Mädchen; Du meines Herzens Krönelein.* BRAHMS: *Das Mädchen spricht; Mein Mädel hat einen Rosenmund.* SCHUMANN: *Waldesgespräch; Du bist wie eine Blume; Frühlingsnacht.* SCHUBERT: *Im Abendrot; Der Jüngling an der Quelle; An die Nachtigall; Nacht und Träume; An Die Musik.*
(M) (***) BMG/RCA mono GD 87809 [7809-2-RG].

Bringing together Lehmann's 78-r.p.m. recordings, made for RCA between 1935 and 1947, this is a fascinating, often unexpected collection, with Italian, French and English songs as well as German Lieder. The transfers bring the singer vividly face to face with the listener, but this is not as full a portrait as the Références collection of her singing opera arias, recorded in the 1920s and early '30s (see above).

London Symphony Chorus and Orchestra, Richard Hickox

Opera choruses: BIZET: *Carmen: Toreador chorus.* VERDI: *Il Trovatore: Anvil chorus. Nabucco: Gli arredi festivi; Va pensiero. Macbeth: Che faceste?. Aida: Grand march.* GOUNOD: *Faust: Soldiers' chorus.* BORODIN: *Prince Igor: Polovtsian dances.*
(B) *** Pickwick Dig. PCD 908; *CIMPC 908.*

Most collections of opera choruses are taken from sets, but this is a freshly minted digital collection of favourites, sung with fine fervour and discipline. The opening *Toreador chorus* from *Carmen* is zestfully infectious and the *Soldiers' chorus* from *Faust* is equally buoyant. The noble line of Verdi's *Va pensiero* is shaped beautifully by Hickox, with the balance between voices and orchestra particularly good. In *Gli arredi festivi* from *Nabucco* and the famous Triumphal scene from *Aida* the orchestral brass sound resonantly sonorous, even if the fanfare trumpets could have been more widely separated in the latter piece. The concert ends with Borodin's *Polovtsian dances* most excitingly done. The recording, made at the EMI Abbey Road studio, has the atmosphere of an idealized opera house, and the result is in the demonstration bracket, with a projection and presence fully worthy of this polished but uninhibited singing.

Luca, Giuseppe de (baritone)

'Prima voce': Arias from: VERDI: *Don Carlos, Ernani, Il Trovatore, La Traviata, Rigoletto.* ROSSINI: *Il Barbiere di Siviglia.* DONIZETTI: *L'elisir d'amore.* BELLINI: *I Puritani.* DIAZ: *Benvenuto Cellini.* PUCCINI: *La Bohème.* PONCHIELLI: *La Gioconda.* WOLF-FERRARI: *I gioielli della madonna.* Songs: DE LEVA: *Pastorale.* ROMILLI: *Marietta.*
(M) (***) Nimbus mono NI 7815 [id.].

There has never been a more involving account on record of the Act IV Marcello–Rodolfo duet than the one here with de Luca and Gigli, a model of characterization and vocal art. The baritone's mastery emerges vividly in item after item, whether in the power and wit of his pre-electric version of *Largo al factotum* (1917) or the five superb items (including the *Bohème* duet and the *Rigoletto* numbers, flawlessly controlled) which were recorded in the vintage year of 1927. Warm Nimbus transfers.

McCormack, John (tenor)

'Prima voce': Arias and excerpts from: DONIZETTI: *Lucia di Lammermoor; L'elisir d'amore; La figlia del reggimento.* VERDI: *La Traviata; Rigoletto.* PUCCINI: *La Bohème.* BIZET. *Carmen; I pescatore di perle.* DELIBES: *Lakmé.* GOUNOD: *Faust.* PONCHIELLI: *La gioconda.* BOITO: *Mefistofele.* MASSENET: *Manon.* MOZART: *Don Giovanni.* WAGNER: *Die Meistersinger.* HERBERT: *Natomah.* HANDEL: *Semele; Atalanta.*
(M) (***) Nimbus mono NI 7820 [id.].

With the operas represented ranging from Handel's *Atalanta* and *Semele* to *Natomah*, by Victor Herbert, the heady beauty of McCormack's voice, his ease of production and perfect control are amply illustrated in these 21 items. His now legendary 1916 account of *Il mio tesoro* from *Don Giovanni*, with its astonishing breath control, is an essential item; but there are many others less celebrated which help to explain his special niche, even in a generation that included Caruso and Schipa. Characteristic Nimbus transfers.

'The art of John McCormack' (with Gerald Moore; O, cond. Walter Goehr; Fritz Kreisler): MARTINI: *Plaisir d'amour.* HANDEL: *Semele: Where'er you walk. Il pastor fido: Caro amor. Atalanta: Come, my beloved.* MOZART: *Oh what bitter grief is mine; Ridente la calma.* SCHUBERT: *Who is Sylvia?.* BRAHMS: *Die Mainacht; Feldeinsamkeit.* R. STRAUSS: *Allerseelen; Morgen; Du meines Herzen Krönelein.* WOLF: *Auch kleine Dinge; Herr was trägt der Boden hier; Schlafendes Jesuskind; Wo find ich Trost; Anakreons Grab.* RACHMANINOV: *Before my window; How fair this spot; To the children.* FRANCK: *La procession.* FAURÉ: *L'Automne.* DONAUDY: *O del mio amato ben; Luoghi sereni.* ELGAR: *Is she not passing fair?.* QUILTER: *Now sleeps the crimson petal.*
(M) (***) EMI mono CDH7 63306-2.

Even though it opens – winningly – with Martini's *Plaisir d'amour*, this McCormack anthology centres on his classical 78-r.p.m. discs, from finely spun Handelian lyricism through German Lieder and songs by Rachmaninov (with Fritz Kreisler ready at hand to provide violin obbligatos) to French mélodie and songs of Elgar and Quilter. His French pronunciation was hardly colloquial, nor was he ever entirely at home in German, yet his contributions to the Wolf Society recordings celebrated a unique feeling for this composer, readily shown here. Overall, the recordings span a long time-period and include a batch of pre-electrics from 1924. But transfers are exemplary. Desmond Shaw Taylor's notes are indispensable too.

Popular songs and Irish ballads. TRAD.: *The garden where the praties grow; Terence's farewell to Kathleen; Believe me if all those endearing young charms; The star of the County Down; Oft in the stilly night; The meeting of the waters; The Bard of Armagh; Down by the Salley Gardens; She moved thro' the fair; The green bushes.* BALFE: *The harp that once through Tara's halls.* ROECKEL: *The green isle of Erin.* SCHNEIDER: *O Mary dear.* LAMBERT: *She is far from the land.* HAYNES: *Off to Philadelphia.* MOLLOY: *The Kerry dance; Bantry Bay.* MARSHALL: *I hear you calling me.* E. PURCELL: *Passing by.* WOODFORD-FINDEN: *Kashmiri song.* CLUTSAM: *I know of two bright eyes.* FOSTER: *Jeannie with the light brown hair; Sweetly she sleeps, my Alice fair.*
(M) (***) EMI mono CDH7 69788-2.

McCormack's voice recorded with wonderful naturalness, partly because he mastered early the art of using the microphone. These 78-r.p.m. transfers, all but one from the 1930s and '40s, sound as fresh and real as the day they were made. In Irish repertoire like *The star of the County Down* McCormack is irresistible, but in lighter concert songs he could also spin the utmost magic. *Down by the Salley Gardens* and Stephen Foster's *Jeannie with the light brown hair* are superb examples, while in a ballad like *I hear you calling me* (an early pre-electric recording from 1908) the golden bloom of the vocal timbre combining with an artless line brings a ravishing frisson on the closing pianissimo. Many of the accompaniments are by Gerald Moore, who proves a splendid partner. Occasionally there is a hint of unsteadiness in the sustained *piano* tone, but otherwise no apology need be made for the recorded sound which is first class, while the lack of 78-r.p.m. background noise is remarkable.

Martinelli, Giovanni (tenor)

'Prima voce': Arias from: GIORDANO: *Andrea Chénier; Fedora.* LEONCAVALLO: *Pagliacci.* MASCAGNI: *Cavalleria Rusticana; Iris.* TCHAIKOVSKY: *Eugene Onegin.* VERDI: *Aida; Ernani; La forza del destino; La Traviata.*
(M) (***) Nimbus mono NI 7804 [id.].

This collection of 17 fine examples of

Martinelli's very distinctive and characterful singing covers his vintage period from 1915 to 1928, with one 1927 recording from Verdi's *La forza del destino* so clear that you can hear a dog barking outside the studio. The other two items from *Forza* are just as memorable, with Martinelli joined by Giuseppe de Luca in the Act IV duet, and by Rosa Ponselle and the bass, Ezio Pinza, for the final duet, with the voices astonishingly vivid and immediate.

Melchior, Lauritz (tenor)

'Prima voce': Arias from: WAGNER: *Siegfried; Tannhäuser; Tristan und Isolde; Die Walküre; Die Meistersinger; Götterdämmerung.* LEONCAVALLO: *Pagliacci.* MEYERBEER: *L'Africana.* VERDI: *Otello.*
(M) (***) Nimbus mono NI 7816 [id.].

The Nimbus disc of Melchior, issued to celebrate his centenary in 1990, demonstrates above all the total consistency of the voice between the pre-electric recordings of *Siegfried* and *Tannhäuser*, made for Polydor in 1924, and the *Meistersinger* and *Götterdämmerung* extracts, recorded in 1939. Of those, the Siegfried–Brünnhilde duet from the *Prologue* of *Götterdämmerung* is particularly valuable. It is fascinating too to hear the four recordings that Melchior made with Barbirolli and the LSO in 1930–31: arias by Verdi, Leoncavallo and Meyerbeer translated into German. As a character, Otello is made to sound far more prickly. Characteristic Nimbus transfers.

Muzio, Claudia (soprano)

Arias from: BELLINI: *La Sonnambula; Norma.* VERDI: *Il Trovatore; La Forza del destino.* BOITO: *Mefistofele.* MASCAGNI: *Cavalleria Rusticana.* PUCCINI: *La Bohème; Tosca.* CILEA: *L'Arlesiana; Adriana Lecouvreur.* GIORDANO: *Andrea Chénier. Songs.*
(M) (***) EMI mono CDH7 69790-2.

This is a superb celebration of one of the greatest Italian sopranos of the century, one who died tragically young and whose recording career failed to encompass the very period when she was, by all accounts, at her greatest. All 20 items on this Références CD come from her last years, 1934 and 1935 (she died of a heart complaint in 1936). *Casta diva* here would have expanded more generously a few years earlier; but, once that is said, every single item brings magical communication, highly individual in expression and timbre, with the voice shaded and varied in tone and dynamic so that one is mesmerized by phrase after phrase. There are few accounts of Mimi's arias from *La Bohème* to match these – with the close of the *Farewell* wonderfully veiled in tone; while the Cilea, Giordano and Boito items have a depth of expression never surpassed. The beauty of legato line in the Bellini items and the tonal variety in the Verdi arias, conveying tragic intensity, remain models for all time. Keith Hardwick's superb transfers bring the voice to us wonderfully refreshed and clarified, almost as though Muzio were still in our presence.

'Prima voce': Arias from: MASCAGNI: *Cavalleria Rusticana.* VERDI: *La forza del destino; Otello; Il Trovatore; La Traviata.* PUCCINI: *Tosca; La Bohème.* GIORDANO: *Andrea Chénier.* BOITO: *Mefistofele.* CILEA: *Adriana Lecouvreur; L'Arlesiana.* BELLINI: *La Sonnambula.* Songs by BUZZI-PECCIA; PERGOLESI; REGER; DELIBES; REFICE.
(M) (***) Nimbus mono NI 7814 [id.].

This Nimbus collection of recordings by the sadly short-lived Claudia Muzio duplicates much that is contained on the EMI Références CD of her. The main addition here is the Act III duet from *Otello* with Francesco Merli, but some cherishable items are omitted. The Nimbus acoustic transfer process sets the voice more distantly as well as more reverberantly than the EMI, with its distinctive tang less sharply conveyed.

Opera Choruses

'Famous Opera choruses' (various artists) from: VERDI: *Nabucco; Il Trovatore; Aida; Macbeth.* LEONCAVALLO: *Pagliacci.* PUCCINI: *Madama Butterfly.* GOUNOD: *Faust.* WAGNER: *Tannhäuser.* TCHAIKOVSKY: *Eugene Onegin.* MUSSORGSKY: *Boris Godunov.*
(B) ** Decca 433 601-2; *433 601-4.*

A generally rewarding bargain collection, given characteristically vivid Decca sound. Many favourites are here, with the *Aida* triumphal scene taken from Karajan's spectacular, early, Vienna set. The Waltz scene from *Eugene Onegin* comes from another early set, made in Belgrade, and includes the Introduction to Act II. The scene from *Boris Godunov* is a studio recording, with the Covent Garden Opera Chorus ably conducted by Edward Downes and with Joseph Rouleau as Boris. The inclusion of items (the Wagner and Leoncavallo excerpts) contributed by the perfectly adequate Kingsway Chorus under Camerata is the only curious choice.

L'Opéra français

'L'Opéra français' (sung by Corelli; Crespin; Ghiaurov; Horne; Krause; Pavarotti; Resnik; Di Stefano; Sutherland): excerpts from: BIZET:

Carmen; Les pêcheurs de perles. DELIBES: *Lakmé.* GOUNOD: *Faust; Sapho.* SAINT-SAENS: *Samson et Dalila.* MASSENET: *Werther.*
(M) ** Decca 421 876-2; *421 876-4.*

This is another generous (73 minutes) collection that looks enticing but which fails to add up to the sum of its parts. It opens with Marilyn Horne's vibrant account of the *Habanera* from Bizet's *Carmen*, taken from her highlights disc (see under the composer); but not everything else here is quite so riveting. The highlights are two of Régine Crespin's contributions, the enchanting *Air des lettres* from *Werther* and the no less engaging *O ma lyre immortelle* from *Sapho*, and her performance of the key aria from *Samson et Dalila* is pretty impressive too. Sutherland contributes a sparkling *Bell song* from *Lakmé*, and she is joined by Jane Berbié in the charming *Flower duet* from the same opera. But the other famous French duet, from Bizet's *Pearl fishers*, is represented, curiously, by a forthright mono recording by Libero de Luca and Jean Borthayre. There are some enjoyable excerpts from *Faust*, and everything sounds vivid, but this is a recital to pick and choose from rather than to listen to right through.

Operatic Duets: 'Duets from famous operas'

Duets sung by: (i) Nicolai Gedda, (ii) Ernest Blanc, (iii) Jussi Bjoerling and Victoria de los Angeles, (iv) Carlo Bergonzi, (v) Maria Callas, (vi) Mirella Freni, (vii) Eberhard Waechter and Graziella Sciutti, (viii) Tito Gobbi, (ix) Gabriella Tucci, (x) Franco Corelli, (xi) Evelyn Lear and D. Ouzounov, (xii) Antonietta Stella; (i; ii) BIZET: *Les Pêcheurs de perles: Au fond du temple saint.* (iii) PUCCINI: *Madama Butterfly: Bimba dagli occhi.* (iv; v) *Tosca: O dolci mani.* (i; vi) *La Bohème: O soave fanciulla.* (vii) MOZART: *Don Giovanni: Là ci darem la mano.* (v; viii) ROSSINI: *Il barbiere di Siviglia: Dunque io son'.* (ix; x) VERDI: *Il Trovatore: Miserere d'un'alma già vicina.* (xi) MUSSORGSKY: *Boris Godunov: O Tsarevich I beg you.* (x; xii) GIORDANO: *Andrea Chénier: Vicini a te.*
(B) **(*) CfP CD-CFP 9013; *TC-CFP 4498.*

There are not many operas that hold their reputation in the public memory by means of a male duet, but *The pearl fishers* is one, and a sturdy performance of *Au fond du temple saint* makes a suitable centre-point for this collection of purple duos. The CD, however, opens with the genial lyricism of *Là ci darem la mano*, from the 1961 Giulini set of *Don Giovanni* with Eberhard Waechter and Graziella Sciutti singing most winningly. The star quality of the artists is noticeable through most of these extracts. Highlights include this beautifully relaxed *Là ci darem*, the short Rossini item, and the *La Bohème* duet (which seldom fails). There is also a blaze of melodrama from *Andrea Chénier*. As a programme, the effect of a series of such full-blooded, passionate vocal embraces is perhaps a little wearing. But otherwise, with generally lively recording, few will be disappointed. The CD has been remastered admirably to make the most of the different recording sources – the vocal timbres are particularly smooth and natural, without loss of projection.

Operatic Duets: 'Great love duets'

'Great love duets' (sung by Sutherland, Freni, Pavarotti, Tebaldi, Corelli, M. Price, Cossutta): PUCCINI: *Madama Butterfly; La Bohème; Tosca; Manon Lescaut.* VERDI: *Otello; La Traviata.*
(M) *** Decca 421 308-2.

This collection in Decca's mid-price Opera Gala series is very well chosen, starting and ending with duets from two of Karajan's outstanding Puccini recordings for Decca, *Madama Butterfly* and *La Bohème*, both with Freni and Pavarotti. The *Bohème* item includes not only the duet *O soave fanciulla* but the two favourite arias which precede it, *Che gelida manina* and *Sì, mi chiamano Mimì.* Sutherland is represented by *La Traviata*, Tebaldi by *Manon Lescaut* and Margaret Price by *Otello*, all very well transferred.

Operatic Duets: 'Great operatic duets'

'Great operatic duets' (sung by Sutherland, Pavarotti, Freni, Ludwig, Horne, Bergonzi, Fischer-Dieskau, Del Monaco, Bastianini): from DELIBES: *Lakmé.* PUCCINI: *Madama Butterfly.* BELLINI: *Norma.* VERDI: *La forza del destino; Don Carlo.* OFFENBACH: *Contes d'Hoffmann.*
(M) *** Decca 421 314-2.

Again at mid-price, Decca provides a further excellent collection of duets, ranging rather more widely, from some of the company's finest recordings of the 1960s and '70s. The choice is imaginative and the transfers excellent, to bring out the fine quality of the original analogue sound.

'Great operatic duets' (sung by: (i) Sutherland/Pavarotti; (ii) M. Price/Pavarotti; (iii) Te Kanawa/Aragall; (iv) Te Kanawa/Carreras; (v) Caballé/Baltsa/Pavarotti/Milnes; (vi)

Sutherland/Caballé) from VERDI: (i) *La Traviata; Otello;* (ii) *Un ballo in maschera.* PUCCINI: (iii) *Tosca;* (iv) *Manon Lescaut.* PONCHIELLI: (v) *La Gioconda.* BELLINI: (vi) *Norma.*
(M) *** Decca 430 724-2; *430 724-4* [id.].

A splendid collection, with every item full of vibrant star-quality and offered in typically vivid Decca sound. Pavarotti and Sutherland are well matched in *La Traviata*, and later he makes an equally charismatic partnership with Margaret Price in *Teco io sto* from Verdi's *Un ballo in maschera*, while Sutherland duets equally impressively with Caballé in the *Norma* excerpt. Kiri te Kanawa, in glorious voice, and Carreras pair thrillingly in *Manon Lescaut*, and the 67-minute recital ends with a foretaste of Pavarotti's Love duet from *Otello*, but with Sutherland sounding not quite at her best, in a 1988 version recorded in New York with Bonynge.

Operetta: 'Golden operetta'

'Golden operetta': J. STRAUSS, Jnr: *Die Fledermaus: Mein Herr Marquis* (Gueden); *Csardas* (Janowitz). *Eine Nacht in Venedig: Lagunen waltz* (Krenn). *Wiener Blut: Wiener Blut* (Gueden). *Der Zigeunerbaron: O habet Acht* (Lorengar). *Casanova: Nuns' chorus* (Sutherland, Amb. S.). ZELLER: *Der Obersteiger: Sei nicht bös* (Gueden). LEHÁR: *Das Land des Lächelns: Dein ist mein ganzes Herz* (Bjoerling). *Die lustige Witwe: Vilja-Lied* (Sutherland); *Lippen schweigen* (Holm, Krenn). *Schön ist die Welt* (Krenn). *Der Graf von Luxemburg: Lieber Freund . . . Bist du's, Lachendes Gluck* (Holm, Krenn). *Giuditta: Du bist meine Sonne* (Kmentt). LECOCQ: *Le Coeur et la main: Bonsoir Perez le capitaine* (Sutherland). OFFENBACH: *La Périchole: Letter song. La Grande Duchesse de Gérolstein: J'aime les militaires* (Crespin).
(M) *** Decca 421 319-2.

A valuable and generous anthology, not just for the obvious highlights: Joan Sutherland's *Vilja* and the delightful contributions from Hilde Gueden – notably a delicious *Sei nicht bös* – recorded in 1961 when the voice was at its freshest; but also Régine Crespin at her finest in Offenbach (the duchess reviewing her troops) and the charming *Letter song* from *La Périchole*. In their winningly nostalgic account of the *Merry Widow waltz* Renate Holm and Werner Krenn hum the melody, having sung the words, giving the impression of dancing together. The recording throughout is atmospheric, with plenty of bloom and with the voices given a natural presence.

Pavarotti, Luciano (tenor)

'Mattinata': Songs by BELLINI; GIORDANI; ROSSINI; GLUCK; TOSTI; DONIZETTI; LEONCAVALLO; BEETHOVEN and others.
(M) **(*) Decca 417 796-2; *417 796-4*.

Pavarotti is at home here in the lightweight items. Giordani's *Caro mio ben* is very nicely done and the romantic songs have a well-judged ardour. Gluck's *Che farò*, the one operatic aria included, is rather less impressive. The tone is not always golden, but most of the bloom remains. Vivid transfers.

Donizetti and Verdi arias (with Vienna Op. O, Downes) from: DONIZETTI: *Dom Sébastien, roi de Portugal; Il Duca d'Alba; La Favorita; Lucia di Lammermoor.* VERDI: *Un ballo in maschera; I due Foscari; Luisa Miller; Macbeth.*
(M) *** Decca 421 304-2.

Though not as distinguished as either the full-price Sutherland or the Marilyn Horne (Rossini) recital in Decca's mid-price series, Pavarotti's 'Opera Gala' issue of Verdi and Donizetti presents the tenor in impressive performances of mainly rare arias, recorded in 1968, early in his career, with the voice fresh and golden. Good, full recording.

'King of the high Cs': Arias from: DONIZETTI: *La fille du régiment; La Favorita.* VERDI: *Il Trovatore.* R. STRAUSS: *Der Rosenkavalier.* ROSSINI: *Guglielmo Tell.* BELLINI: *I Puritani.* PUCCINI: *La Bohème.*
(M) *** Decca 421 326-2; *421 326-4*.

The punning title may not be to everyone's taste, but this is another attractively varied Pavarotti collection, now offered at mid-price, a superb display of his vocal command as well as his projection of personality. Though the selections come from various sources, the recording quality is remarkably consistent, the voice vibrant and clear; the accompanying detail and the contributions of the chorus are also well managed. The Donizetti and Puccini items are particularly attractive.

'Pavarotti in concert' (with Teatro Comunale, Bologna, O, Bonynge): BONONCINI: *Griselda: Per la gloria d'adorarvi.* HANDEL: *Atalanta: Care selve.* A. SCARLATTI: *Già il sol dal Gange.* BELLINI: Songs: *Ma rendi pur contento; Dolente immagine di fille mia; Malinconia, ninfa gentile; Bella nice, che d'amore; Vanne, o rosa fortunata.* TOSTI: Songs: *La serenata; Luna d'estate; Malia; Non t'amo più!* RESPIGHI: *Nevicata; Poggia; Nebbie.* ROSSINI: *La danza.*
(M) **(*) Decca 425 037-2; *425 037-4* [id.].

In the classical items Pavarotti is more subdued than usual: he finds an attractive lyrical delicacy for the opening Bononcini aria, though there is a hint of strain in Handel's *Care selve*. He is in his element in Tosti and, with evocative accompaniments from Bonynge, he makes the three Respighi songs the highlight of a recital which is nicely rounded off with a spirited but never coarse version of Rossini's *La danza*. The 1974 Decca sound is both atmospheric and vivid in its CD format. Incidentally, this collection is about the length of his usual live recitals of this kind – so the collector could count this good value, compared to the price of a seat for such an event!

'Tutto Pavarotti': Arias from: VERDI: *Aida; Luisa Miller; La Traviata; Il Trovatore; Rigoletto; Un ballo in maschera.* DONIZETTI: *L'Elisir d'amore; Don Pasquale.* PONCHIELLI: *La Gioconda.* FLOTOW: *Martha.* BIZET: *Carmen.* MASSENET: *Werther.* MEYERBEER: *L'Africana.* BOITO: *Mefistofele.* LEONCAVALLO: *Pagliacci.* MASCAGNI: *Cavalleria Rusticana.* GIORDANO: *Fedora.* PUCCINI: *La Fanciulla del West; Tosca; Manon Lescaut; La Bohème; Turandot.* ROSSINI: *Stabat Mater.* BIZET: *Agnus Dei.* ADAM: *O holy night.* DI PAPUA: *O sole mio.* TOSTI: *A vucchella.* CARDILLO: *Core 'ngrato.* TAGLIAFERRI: *Passione.* CHERUBINI: *Mamma.* DALLA: *Caruso.*
(M) *** Decca 425 681-2; *425 681-4* (2) [id.].

Opening with Dalla's *Caruso*, a popular song in the Neapolitan tradition, certainly effective, and no more vulgar than many earlier examples of the genre, this selection goes on through favourites like *O sole mio* and *Core 'ngrato* and one or two religious items, notably Adam's *Cantique de Noël*, to the hard core of operatic repertoire. Beginning with *Celeste Aida*, recorded in 1972, the selection of some 22 arias from complete sets covers Pavarotti's distinguished recording career with Decca from 1969 (*Cielo e mar* and the *Il Trovatore* excerpts) to 1985, although the opening song was, of course, recorded digitally in 1988. The rest is a mixture of brilliantly transferred analogue originals and a smaller number of digital masters, all or nearly all showing the great tenor in sparkling form. The records and tapes are at mid-price, but there are no translations or musical notes.

'Gala concert at the Royal Albert Hall' (with RPO, Kurt Adler): Arias from: PUCCINI: *Tosca; Turandot.* VERDI: *Macbeth; I Lombardi; Luisa Miller. Un giorno di regno: Overture.* DONIZETTI: *Lucia di Lammermoor.* CILEA: *L'Arlesiana.* DE CURTIS: Song: *Torna a Surriento.* BERLIOZ: *Les Troyens: Royal hunt and storm.*
(M) **(*) Decca 430 716-2; *430 716-4*.

This disc celebrates a much-hyped appearance by Pavarotti at the Royal Albert Hall in 1982, in the days when one tenor alone was enough! It would be unfair to expect much subtlety before such an eager audience, but the live recording conveys the fever well. There are bold accounts of the two most famous arias from *Tosca*, and the celebrated *Nessun dorma* from *Turandot*, and even simple recitatives as intimate as Macduff's in *Macbeth* are proclaimed grandly. The bright digital recording shows up some unevenness in the voice, but no one will miss the genuine excitement, with the electricity of the occasion conveyed equally effectively on disc or tape.

'Live, on stage': excerpts from: VERDI: *Rigoletto; La Traviata.* PUCCINI: *La Bohème.*
(BB) LaserLight 15 104 [id.].

Although the opening of the *Rigoletto* excerpts (with Scotto as Gilda) promises well, with Pavarotti's voice ringing out boldly, the sound soon begins to deteriorate, the *La Traviata* scenes are insecure and distorted, and the focus becomes very fuzzy indeed in *La Bohème*. Not recommended.

Volume 1 (Live recordings: 1964/67): excerpts from: DONIZETTI: *Lucia di Lammermoor* (with Scotto). VERDI: *Rigoletto* (with Rinaldi, Lazzarini, Cappuccilli). *Requiem* (with L. Price, Cossotto, Ghiaurov). MOZART: *Idomeneo* (with Richard Lewis).
(BB) (**) LaserLight 15 225 [id.].

It is good to hear Pavarotti's voice sounding so youthful, gloriously free and strong in these recordings from *Lucia di Lammermoor* and *Rigoletto*, recorded in 1967. His partnership with Renata Scotto in the former is impressive and in the duet, *Sulla tomba che rinserra*, she sings very affectingly. The Quartet from *Rigoletto* is also excitingly done, and the 1964 excerpts from *Idomeneo* show how well Pavarotti is suited to an opera he was to record for Decca twenty-five years later. The only write-off here is the excerpt from Verdi's *Requiem*, which is poorly focused. Otherwise the sound is good, if not refined.

Pavarotti, Luciano (tenor) and **Mirella Freni** (soprano)

Arias and duets from: PUCCINI: *Tosca; La Bohème.* ROSSINI: *Guglielmo Tell.* BOITO: *Mefistofele.*
(M) *** Decca 421 878-2; *421 878-4*.

Both artists come from the same small town in Italy, Modena, where they were born in 1935; less surprisingly, they studied under the same singing teacher. Their artistic partnership on record has always been a happy one, and perhaps reached its zenith in their 1972 *Bohème* with Karajan (unexpectedly, recorded in the Jesus-Christus Kirche, Berlin). Their great introductory love-duet as Mimi and Rodolfo, perhaps the most ravishing in all opera (from *Che gelida manina*, through *Sì, mi chiamano Mimì* to the soaring *O soave fanciulla*) is an obvious highlight here, but the much less familiar *Lontano, lontano* from *Mefistofele* shows no less memorably that the voices were made for each other. It was a very good idea to include a substantial selection from their 1978–9 *Tosca* (recorded in the Kingsway Hall), not a first choice as a complete set, but with some marvellous singing in Act III, of which some 17 minutes is offered (including *E lucevan le stelle* and the dramatic finale of the opera). The recital opens very spontaneously with 13 minutes from Act I (*Mario! Mario!*), the engagingly temperamental interplay between the lovers, in the Church of Sant'Andrea della Valle. The only slight disappointment is Freni's *Vissi d'arte*; otherwise this is 70 minutes of vintage material, given Decca's top drawer sound.

Ponselle, Rosa (soprano)

'Prima voce': Arias from: BELLINI: *Norma*. PONCHIELLI: *La Gioconda*. SPONTINI: *La vestale*. VERDI: *Aida; Ernani; La forza del destino; Otello*. Songs by: ARENSKY; RIMSKY-KORSAKOV; DE CURTIS; DI CAPUA; JACOBS-BOND.
(M) (***) Nimbus mono NI 7805.

One of the most exciting American sopranos ever, Rosa Ponselle tantalizingly cut short her career when she was still at her peak. Only the Arensky and Rimsky songs represent her after her official retirement, and the rest make a superb collection, including her classic accounts of *Casta diva* from Bellini's *Norma* and the duet, *Mira o Norma*, with Marion Telva. The six Verdi items include her earlier version of *Ernani involami*, not quite so commanding as her classic 1928 recording, but fascinating for its rarity. Equally cherishable is her duet from *La forza del destino* with Ezio Pinza.

Arias from: VERDI: *Ernani; Otello; La forza del destino; Aida*. MEYERBEER: *L'Africana*. SPONTINI: *La Vestale*. PONCHIELLI: *La Gioconda*. BELLINI: *Norma*. BACH-GOUNOD: *Ave Maria*. RIMSKY-KORSAKOV: *The nightingale and the rose* & Songs.
(M) (***) BMG/RCA mono GD 87810 [7810-2-RG].

The clarity and immediacy of the RCA transfers make a complete contrast with the warmly atmospheric Nimbus transfers of the same singer. Though the voice is exposed more, with less bloom on it, the character and technical command are, if anything, even more impressively presented. To sample the greatness of Ponselle, try her dazzling 1928 account of *Ernani involami* or her poised *Casta diva*. Notable too is the final trio from *La forza del destino* with Martinelli and Pinza, even more immediate than on Nimbus's Martinelli disc.

Price, Leontyne (soprano)

'Christmas with Leontyne Price' (with V. Singverein, VPO, Karajan); GRUBER: *Silent night*. MENDELSSOHN: *Hark! the herald angels*. HOPKINS: *We three kings*. TRAD.: *Angels we have heard on high; O Tannenbaum; God rest ye merry, gentlemen; Sweet li'l Jesus*. WILLIS: *It came upon the midnight clear*. BACH: *Vom Himmel hoch*. BACH/GOUNOD: *Ave Maria*. SCHUBERT: *Ave Maria*. ADAM: *O holy night*. MOZART: *Alleluja, K.165*.
(M) **(*) Decca 421 103-2 [411 614-2].

There is much beautiful singing here, but the style is essentially operatic. The rich, ample voice, when scaled down (as for instance in *We three kings*), can be very beautiful, but at full thrust it does not always catch the simplicity of melodic line which is characteristic of many of these carols. Yet the vibrant quality of the presentation is undoubtedly thrilling, and it can charm too, as in *God rest ye merry, gentlemen*, with its neat harpsichord accompaniment. The sound is admirably full, clear and vivid in its CD format.

Ricciarelli, Katia (soprano), José Carreras (tenor)

'Duetti d'amore' from PUCCINI: *Madama Butterfly*. VERDI: *I Lombardi*. DONIZETTI: *Poliuto; Roberto Devereux*.
(M) *** Ph. 426 644-2; *426 644-4*.

The two Donizetti duets are among the finest he ever wrote, especially the one from *Poliuto*, in which the hero persuades his wife to join him in martyrdom. This has a depth unexpected in Donizetti. Both these items receive beautiful performances here; the Puccini love-duet is made to sound fresh and unhackneyed, and the *Lombardi* excerpt is given with equal tenderness. Stylish conducting and refined recording.

Rogers, Nigel (tenor), Anthony Bailes (lute)

'Airs de cour' (songs from the reign of Louis XIII): MAUDUIT: *Eau vive, source d'amour*. DE COURVILLE: *Si je languis d'un martire incogneu*. ANON.: *C'est un amant, ouvrez la*

porte. BATAILLE: *Un jour que ma rebelle; Ma bergère non légère; Qui veut chasser une migraine.* GUÉDRON: *Si jamais mon âme blessée; Césses mortels de soupir; Quel espoir de guarir.* LE FÉGUEUX: *Petit sein où l'amour a bâti son séjour.* MOULINIÉ: *Paisible et ténébreuse nuit; Quelque merveilleuse chose; Je suis ravi de mon Uranie; Enfin la beauté que j'adore.* BOESSET: *Plaignez la rigueur de mon sort; N'espérez plus, mes yeux; Ennuits, désespoirs et douleurs.* GRAND RUE: *Lors que tes beaux yeux, mignonne.*
(M) *** EMI CDM7 63070-2.

A beautifully sung and most naturally recorded recital of *airs de cour* (Court songs) which will give much pleasure to the non-specialist listener who might not normally venture into this repertoire. The songs are simple in style, the settings, usually of popular anonymous verse, follow the text naturally without word repetition but often with a pleasing, elegant freshness. The songs are mostly about *l'amour* and the hedonistic pleasures of eating and drinking. There is sentiment, melancholy (though usually not so overt as in Elizabethan lute songs), gaiety and (cultivated) high spirits. The melodic writing has pleasing spontaneity, often helped by the light rhythmic feeling: *Ma bergère, non légère en amours* may have ingenuous lyrics but it goes with an engaging swing, while *Qui veut chasser une migraine* good-naturedly chooses to cure the headache with a well-laden table (sausages and ham), good wine and good company. The love-songs are nicely expressive, and the recital attractively intersperses the gay settings with the more dolorous expressions of feeling like the lovely *Quel espoir de guarir* or the two closing songs by Étienne Moulinié. The CD has great presence and realism; the balance between voice and the sympathetic lute accompaniments of Anthony Bailes is ideal. It is a great pity that translations are not provided; even so, the French words are easy to follow.

'A Musicall Banquet (1610)' (with Jordi Savall, viola da gamba): DOWLAND: *Sir Robert Sidney His galliard; Far from triumphing court; Lady, if you so spite me; In darkness let me dwell.* HOLBORNE: *My heavie spirite, oppress'd.* MARTIN: *Change thy mind since she doth change.* HALES: *O eyes, leave off your weeping.* BACHELER: *To plead my faith.* TESSIER: *In a grove most rich of shade.* ANON.: *Go, my flock, go get you hence; O dear life, when shall it be?; Passava Amor su arco desarmado; Sta notte mi sognava; Vuestros ojos tienen d'Amor; O bella più.* GUÉDRON: *Si le parler et le silence; Ce penser qui sans fin tirrannise ma vie.* MEGLI: *Se di farmi morire.* CACCINI: *Dovrò dunque morire?; Amarilli mia bella.*
(B) **(*) EMI CDM7 63429-2.

To quote from Anthony Bailes' notes: 'Robert Dowland's *Musicall Banquet* is unique among English publications for lute and voice: the only one to contain English, French, Spanish and Italian airs, it is truly a banquet!' Bailes introduces the recital with a galliard, and one might have expected this programme to be more varied in mood than the companion collection of Court songs, but the dolorous mood of Dowland and his contemporaries creates a rather melancholy atmosphere, and so this is a recital to be dipped into rather than taken at a single sweep. The singing is highly sympathetic and the accompaniments are expert, while the recording has fine naturalness and presence. However, again no translations are provided.

Royal Opera House, Covent Garden

Royal Opera House Covent Garden (An early history on record). Singers included are: Melba, Caruso, Tetrazzini, McCormack, Destin, Gadski, Schorr, Turner, Zanelli, Lehmann, Schumann, Olczewska, Chaliapin, Gigli, Supervia, Tibbett, Tauber, Flagstad, Melchior. Arias from: GOUNOD: *Faust.* VERDI: *Rigoletto, Otello.* DONIZETTI: *Lucia di Lammermoor.* VERDI: *La Traviata.* PUCCINI: *Madama Butterfly; Tosca.* WAGNER: *Götterdämmerung; Die Meistersinger; Tristan und Isolde.* R. STRAUSS: *Der Rosenkavalier.* MUSSORGSKY: *Boris Godunov.* GIORDANO: *Andrea Chénier.* BIZET: *Carmen.* MOZART: *Don Giovanni.*
(M) (***) Nimbus mono NI 7819 [id.].

Nimbus's survey of great singers at Covent Garden ranges from Caruso's 1904 recording of *Questa o quella* from *Rigoletto* to the recording of the second half of the *Tristan* love duet, which Kirsten Flagstad and Lauritz Melchior made in San Francisco in November 1939, a magnificent recording, never issued in Britain and little known, which repeated the partnership initiated during the 1937 Coronation season at Covent Garden. The Vienna recording of the *Rosenkavalier* Trio with Lehmann, Schumann and Olczewska similarly reproduces a classic partnership at Covent Garden, while Chaliapin's 1928 recording of the *Prayer* and *Death of Boris* was actually recorded live at Covent Garden, with the transfer giving an amazingly vivid sense of presence. Those who like Nimbus's acoustic method of transfer will enjoy the whole disc, though the reverberation round some of the early offerings – like the very first, Melba's *Jewel song* from *Faust* – is cavernous. Particularly interesting is the 1909 recording of part of Brünnhilde's Immolation scene, with Johanna Gadski commandingly strong.

'Sacred arias'

'Sacred arias' (sung by (i) Dame Kiri Te Kanawa; (ii) Lucia Popp; (iii) Elsie Morison; (iv) Richard Lewis; (v) Dame Joan Sutherland; (vi) John Shirley-Quirk; (vii) Dame Janet Baker; (viii) Dietrich Fischer-Dieskau; (ix) Montserrat Caballé and Fiorenza Cossotto; (x) Nicolai Gedda; (xi) Victoria de los Angeles; (xii) Robert Gambill): (i) MOZART: *Mass in C min., K.427: Laudamus te.* (ii) *Exsultate jubilate: Alleluja, K.165.* (iii) HANDEL: *Messiah: I know that my Redeemer liveth.* (iv) *Comfort ye . . . Ev'ry valley. Judas Maccabaeus: Sound an alarm.* (v) BACH: *Cantata No. 147: Bereite dir.* (vi) HAYDN: *The Creation: Now heaven.* (vii) *Elijah: O rest in the Lord*; (viii) *Draw near, all ye people . . . Lord God of Abraham.* (ix) VERDI: *Requiem: Agnus Dei*; (x) *Ingemisco.* (xi) FAURÉ: *Requiem: Pié Jesu.* (xii) ROSSINI: *Stabat Mater: Cujus animam gementem.*
(B) **(*) CfP CD-CFP 4532; *TC-CFP 4532.*

Although the contributions from Fischer-Dieskau and Gedda are impressive enough and Richard Lewis's *Sound an alarm* is vigorously stirring, it is the ladies who shine most brightly here. Joan Sutherland's account of Bach's *Bereite dir*, made in 1958 (an unexpectedly welcome contribution to an EMI record), is particularly lovely. Kiri Te Kanawa and Lucia Popp are also on top form, while Dame Janet's *O rest in the Lord* (from *Elijah*) is wonderfully poised and serene. The male contributions are more uneven, and Robert Gambill's histrionics in the closing Rossini *Cujus animam* has the feeling more of the opera house than of the concert hall.

St John's College, Cambridge, Choir, George Guest

'Christmas weekend': GRÜBER: *Silent night.* RUTTER: *Shepherd's pipe carol.* MENDELSSOHN: *Hark the herald angels.* TRAD.: *O little town of Bethlehem; Born on earth; The twelve days of Christmas; Up! good Christian folk; Good King Wenceslas; While shepherds watched; God rest you merry, gentlemen; The holly and the ivy; Away in a manger; The first nowell; I saw three ships; Suo Gan.*
(B) *** Decca 421 022-2; *421 022-4.*

This is first rate in every way, a wholly successful concert of mostly traditional carols, in sensitive arrangements without frills. The singing is straightforwardly eloquent, its fervour a little restrained in the Anglican tradition, yet with considerable underlying depth of feeling. The full character of every carol is well brought out; the expressive simplicity of *I saw three ships* and Rutter's *Shepherd's pipe carol* is most engaging. The recording is excellent, and on Decca's inexpensive Weekend label this is a bargain.

'Hear my prayer (Choral favourites)': MENDELSSOHN: *Hear my prayer.* TRAD.: *A tender shoot.* BACH: *Jesu, joy of man's desiring.* MOZART: *Ave verum corpus.* STAINER: *I saw the Lord.* BRAHMS: *German requiem: Ye now are sorrowful.* LIDÓN.: *Sonata de l tono.* CALDARA: *Crucifixus.* PURCELL: *Jehova, quam multi sunt hostes mei.* S. WESLEY: *Thou wilt keep him in perfect peace.* FAURÉ: *Cantique de Jean Racine.*
(B) **(*) Decca 433 608-2; *433 608-4.*

The refined style of the St John's Choir is here at its most impressive in the famous Bach chorale, the Goldschmidt carol and Mozart's *Ave verum.* In Mendelssohn's *Hear my prayer* the treble soloist sings with striking purity if without the memorability of Master Ernest Lough's famous Temple Church version (from the early electric 78-r.p.m. era). The substitute of a treble for a soprano voice in the Brahms excerpt is not wholly convincing, especially as the soloist sounds a little nervous. But the choir is on excellent form through this 1949 recital to which the last four items have been added (dating from 1964, 1976 and 1978). The singing remains consistently fresh and restrained, though the serenely beautiful Caldara *Crucifixus* would have gained from a degree more intensity.

Schipa, Tito (tenor)

Opera arias from: GLUCK: *Orfeo ed Eurydice.* A. SCARLATTI: *La Donna ancora e fedele; Pirro e Demetrio* (& Song: *Sento nel core*). BELLINI: *La Sonnambula.* DONIZETTI: *Don Pasquale; L'Elisir d'amore; Lucia di Lammermoor.* VERDI: *Rigoletto; Falstaff.* PONCHIELLI: *La Gioconda.* PUCCINI: *La Bohème; Tosca.* MASCAGNI: *Cavalleria Rusticana; L'amico Fritz.* MASSENET: *Werther; Manon.*
(M) (**(*)) EMI mono CDH7 63200-2 [id.].

This EMI collection is particularly valuable for containing Schipa's first recordings, made in 1913. Whether in *Lucia*, *Rigoletto* or *Cavalleria*, the voice and the interpretations are even fresher than they were later. The disc is also indispensable for containing one of the most delectable of all Schipa records, his delicious account of the *Cherry duet* from *L'amico Fritz* with Mafalda Favero. But his RCA account of the aria for which he was most famous, *Una furtiva lagrima* from *L'Elisir d'amore*, is preferable to this (see below), and the transfers are not as immaculate as one expects of this EMI series.

Arias from: MASSENET: *Werther; Manon.* CILEA: *L'Arlesiana.* ROSSINI: *Il Barbiere di Siviglia.* DONIZETTI: *L'Elisir d'amore; Lucia di Lammermoor.* LEONCAVALLO: *Pagliacci.* VERDI: *Rigoletto; La Traviata.* MOZART: *Don Giovanni.* HANDEL: *Xerxes.* BELLINI: *La Sonnambula.* Songs by TOSTI and others.
(M) (***) BMG/RCA mono GD 87969 [7969-2-RG].

RCA provides vivid, very immediate transfers of a sparkling collection of Neapolitan songs as well as arias. Few tenors have matched Schipa for the point and personality of his singing within his carefully chosen limits. It is like being face to face with the singer.

'Prima voce': Arias from: MASCAGNI: *Cavalleria Rusticana. L'amico Fritz.* VERDI: *Rigoletto; Luisa Miller.* DONIZETTI: *Lucia di Lammermoor; Don Pasquale; L'elisir d'amore.* LEONCAVALLO: *Pagliacci.* MASSENET: *Manon; Werther.* ROSSINI: *Il barbiere di Siviglia.* THOMAS: *Mignon.* FLOTOW: *Martha.* CILEA: *L'Arlesiana.*
(M) (***) Nimbus mono NI 7813 [id.].

The first nine items on this well-chosen selection of Schipa's recordings date from the pre-electric era. The voice is totally consistent, heady and light and perfectly controlled, between the *Siciliana* from Mascagni's *Cavalleria*, recorded with piano in 1913, to the incomparable account of more Mascagni, the *Cherry duet* from *L'amico Fritz*, made with Mafalda Favero in 1937. It says much for his art that Schipa's career continued at full strength for decades after that. The Nimbus transfers put the voice at a slight distance, with the electrical recordings made to sound the more natural.

Schock, Rudolf (tenor)

'Portrait': Arias from: MOZART: *Die Entführung aus dem Serail; Die Zauberflöte.* FLOTOW: *Martha.* CORNELIUS: *Der Barbier von Bagdad.* WAGNER: *Lohengrin; Die Meistersinger von Nürnberg.* GOLDMARK: *Die Königin von Saba.* KIENZL: *Der Evangelimann; Der Kuhreigen.* KORNGOLD: *Die tote Stadt.* THOMAS: *Mignon.* OFFENBACH: *Tales of Hoffmann.* BIZET: *Carmen; The Pearlfishers.* MASSENET: *Manon.* SMETANA: *The Bartered Bride.* TCHAIKOVSKY: *Eugene Onegin.* MEYERBEER: *L'Africaine.* DONIZETTI: *L'Elisir d'amore.* VERDI: *Aida; Don Carlos; Otello; Rigoletto; La traviata; Il trovatore.* LEONCAVALLO: *Der Bajazzo.* MASCAGNI: *L'amico Fritz.* PUCCINI: *La Bohème; The Girl of the golden West; Manon Lescaut; Turandot.* GIORDANO: *Andrea Chénier.* J. STRAUSS, Jr: *Cagliostro in Wien; Eine Nacht in Venedig; Der Zigeunerbaron.* MILLÖCKER: *Der Bettelstudent.* FALL: *Die Rose von Stambul.* LEHÁR: *Friederike; Giuditta; Das Land des Lächelns; Paganini; Der Zarewitsch.* KÁLMÁN: *Die Csárdásfürstin; Gräfin Mariza.* KATTNIGG: *Balkanliebe.* KÜNNEKE: *Die grosse Sunderin.*
(M) (**(*)) mono EMI CZS7 67183-2 (3) [id.].

With no translations included in the German documentation about this underappreciated, ringing-toned tenor, the present three-disc anthology is obviously primarily intended for the German domestic market, but there is much for all voice-lovers to enjoy. The first disc (containing mainly German repertory) and the third (containing operetta) are the most immediately recommendable. The opera items include a section from Rudolf Kempe's classic recording of Wagner's *Meistersinger*, containing Schock's fine account of the Prize Song. There are also rare items from Goldmark's *The Queen of Sheba* and Korngold's *Die tote Stadt*, as well as operas by Kienzl. The French and Slavonic items in translation are less valuable – but when it comes to the second disc, containing the Italian repertory, mostly sung in German, the results are fascinating. One rarity has Schock and the young Fischer-Dieskau in 1954 singing the Act IV duet from Puccini's *La Bohème* in German; and the baritone, Josef Metternich, makes a superb partner in the big duet from Verdi's *Don Carlos*, again in German, as does the soprano, Elisabeth Grümmer, singing Desdemona opposite Schock's Otello. The items recorded in England are done in Italian however, including two duets with Joan Hammond, the Cherry duet from Mascagni's *L'amico Fritz* and the final duet from Giordano's *Andrea Chénier*. But some may find themselves puzzled when the title of the Puccini opera from which Schock sings (in Italian) the aria, *Ch'ella mi creda*, emerges here as *Das Mädchen aus dem Goldenen Westen*.

Schumann-Heink, Ernestine (contralto)

'Prima voce': Arias from: DONIZETTI: *Lucrezia Borgia.* MEYERBEER: *Le Prophète.* WAGNER: *Das Rheingold; Rienzi; Götterdämmerung.* HANDEL: *Rinaldo.* Songs by: ARDITTI; BECKER; SCHUBERT; WAGNER; REIMANN; MOLLOY; BRAHMS; BOEHM & TRAD.
(M) (***) Nimbus mono NI 7811 [id.].

Ernestine Schumann-Heink was a formidable personality in the musical life of her time, notably in New York, as well as a great singer. 'I am looking for my successor,' she is reported as saying well before she retired, adding, 'She must be *the* contralto.' Schumann-Heink combines to an astonishing degree a full contralto weight and richness with the most delicate flexibility, as in the *Brindisi* from Donizetti's *Lucrezia Borgia*. This wide-ranging collection, resonantly transferred by the Nimbus acoustic method, presents a vivid portrait of a very great singer.

(Heinrich) Schütz Choir, Roger Norrington

'A Baroque Christmas' (with London String Players, Philip Jones Brass Ensemble; Camden Wind Ensemble; Charles Spinks): SCHÜTZ: *Hodie Christus natus est; Ach Herr, du Schöpfer aller Ding.* PURCELL: *Behold I bring you glad tidings.* ANON.: *Soberana Maria.* HAMMERTSCHMIDT: *Alleluja! Freuet euch, ihr Christen alle.* BOUZIGNAC: *Noé! Pastores, cantate Dominum.* G. GABRIELI: *O magnum mysterium.* MONTEVERDI: *Christe Redemptor.* PRAETORIUS: *Singt, ihr lieben Christen all.* HASSLER: *Angeles as pastores ait.*
❀ (M) *** Decca 430 065-2; *430 065-4* [id.].

A superlative collection which celebrates the joyful Renaissance approach to Christmas. The glorious opening number is matched in memorability by the engaging lullaby, *Soberana Maria*, and *Noé! Pastores* has a delightful interplay between Gabriel (Hazel Holt) and the Shepherds. Giovanni Gabrieli's *O magnum mysterium* is justly famous and sounds superbly sonorous here, while the Michael Praetorius carol has a tune most will readily recognize. The performances are splendid and the 1968 analogue recording remains in the demonstration bracket. There are few more unusual or more rewarding Christmas celebrations than this.

Schwarzkopf, Dame Elisabeth
(soprano)

'Romantic opera arias': from WAGNER: *Tannhäuser; Lohengrin* (with Christa Ludwig). SMETANA: *Bartered bride.* TCHAIKOVSKY: *Eugene Onegin.* WEBER: *Der Freischütz.*
(M) *** EMI CDM7 69501-2 [id.]; *EG 769501-4.*

This CD draws on a pair of LPs but centres on one of them, a classic recital containing Wagner and Weber, with Agathe's two arias from *Der Freischütz* given with a purity of tone and control of line never surpassed, magic performances. So too with the Wagner heroines. The second record found Schwarzkopf less keenly imaginative in more unusual repertoire. This was recorded eight years after the first (in 1967) and the voice had to be controlled more carefully. *The Bartered bride* aria is attractive (though sung in German) but the *Letter scene* from *Eugene Onegin* is less convincing: here the projected vocal personality seems too mature for the young Tatiana. The remastered sound is certainly vivid.

'Carnegie Hall recital': MOZART: *Così fan tutte: Come scoglio. Abendempfindung; Als Luise; Dans un bois solitaire; Un moto di gioia.* SCHUBERT: *An Sylvia; Der Einsame; Der Vollmond strahlt; Die Vögel; Gretchen am Spinnrade; Seligkeit.* GLUCK: *Einem Bach der fliesst.* R. STRAUSS: *Puhe, meine Seele; Schlechtes Wetter; Hat gesacht; Wiegenlied.* WOLF: *Herr, was trägt der Bodem hier; Bedeckt mich mit Blumen; In dem Schatten meiner Locken; Zum neuen Jahr; Philine; Kennst du das Land?; Wir haben beide lange Zeit geschwiegen; Was soll der Zorn, mein Schatz; Wiegenlied im Sommer; Elfenlied; Nachtzauber; Die Zigeunerin.* SCHUMANN: *Der Nussbaum.* BRAHMS: *Ich hab' in Penna; Vergebliches Ständchen.* HANDEL: *Atalanta: Care selve. Swiss folk song: 'S Schätzli.*
(M) (***) EMI (mono) CHS7 61043-2 (2) [Ang. CDHB 61043].

The live recording of Schwarzkopf's 1956 Carnegie Hall recital – long-buried treasure, finally unearthed – brings a marvellous supplement to her immaculate series of studio recordings of Lieder and opera. Inevitably, even with such a perfectionist there are tiny blemishes, not to mention intrusive applause from the enthusiastic New York audience; but the atmosphere and intensity of a great occasion are vividly conveyed, and with it an extra dimension in Schwarzkopf's powers of artistic communication. The programme is astonishingly generous, with substantial encores after each group. So, after the opening Mozart group, Schwarzkopf adds nothing less than *Come scoglio* from *Così* and, with piano accompanying her instead of an orchestra, her agility is even more phenomenal than in her masterly performances from her two complete opera sets. The range of expression is astonishing, through the items by Schubert, Gluck, Strauss and others, with inimitable touches of humour in the haunting Swiss folksong, *'S Schätzli*, and Brahms's *Vergebliches Ständchen.* The climax comes in the big group of 12 Lieder by Hugo Wolf, including above all the setting of Goethe, *Kennst du das Land?*, which here more than ever emerges as the greatest of all Lieder for a woman's voice. With George Reeves a most sympathetic accompanist, this is one of the most vivid examples of a live Lieder recital ever put on disc. The mono sound, while inevitably limited, is faithful and clear as presented on CD.

75th Birthday Edition: WOLF: 24 Lieder and Lieder by: SCHUBERT; SCHUMANN; R. STRAUSS. Arias from: MOZART: *Le nozze di Figaro; Così fan tutte; Don Giovanni.* HUMPERDINCK: *Hänsel und Gretel.* NICOLAI: *Die lustige Witwe.* J. STRAUSS, Jnr: *Die Fledermaus.* PUCCINI: *Turandot.* R. STRAUSS: *Ariadne auf Naxos; Der Rosenkavalier; Capriccio.* VERDI: *Requiem.* Various encores by BACH; BEETHOVEN; MARTINI; TCHAIKOVSKY; DEBUSSY; ARNE etc.
(M) *** EMI stereo/mono CMS7 63790-2 (5).

The five discs of the Birthday Edition, available in a box, provide a comprehensive survey of Schwarzkopf's astonishing achievement on record, not least in the early years of her career in the days before stereo was universally adopted. The individual discs – the Wolf Lieder collection as well as the four recitals listed below – are available separately. With excellent transfers, all can be warmly recommended.

Recital: BACH: *Cantatas Nos. 51, 68 and 208.* HANDEL: *Sweet bird.* MOZART: *Exsultate jubilate, K.165.* BEETHOVEN: *Ah! perfido, Op. 65. Fidelio: Abscheulicher!*
(M) (***) EMI mono CDH7 63201-2 [id.].

This collection, one of the five discs issued to celebrate Schwarzkopf's 75th birthday, brings together some ravishing examples of her very early recordings, with the voice exceptionally fresh and flexible. Most fascinating of all are the two Beethoven items, originally recorded as fill-ups for Karajan's Philharmonia recordings of the symphonies. The role of Leonore in *Fidelio* was not one that Schwarzkopf would ever have taken on stage, but the vehemence of her *Abscheulicher!* has never been surpassed on record, a searingly intense reading.

'Encores' (with Gerald Moore or Geoffrey Parsons): BACH: *Bist du bei mir.* GLUCK: *Einem Bach der fliesst.* BEETHOVEN: *Wonne der Wehmut.* LOEWE: *Kleiner Haushalt.* WAGNER: *Träume.* BRAHMS: *Ständchen; 3 Deutsche Volkslieder.* MAHLER: *Um schlimme Kinder artig zu machen; Ich atmet' einen linden Duft; Des Antonius von Padua Fischpredigt.* TCHAIKOVSKY: *Pimpernella.* arr. WOLF-FERRARI: *7 Italian songs.* MARTINI: *Plaisir d'amour.* HAHN: *Si mes vers avaient des ailes.* DEBUSSY: *Mandoline.* arr. QUILTER: *Drink to me only with thine eyes.* ARNE: *When daisies pied; Where the bee sucks.* arr. GUND: *3 Swiss folk songs.* arr. WEATHERLY: *Danny Boy.* J. STRAUSS, Jnr: *Frühlingsstimmen* (with VPO, Joseph Krips).
(M) *** EMI stereo/mono CDM7 63654-2; *EG 763654-4.*

Schwarzkopf herself has on occasion nominated this charming account of *Danny Boy* as her own favourite recording of her singing, but it is only one of a whole sequence of lightweight songs which vividly capture the charm and intensity that made her recitals so memorable, particularly in the extra items at the end. As a rule she would announce and explain each beforehand, adding to the magic. The range here is wide, from Bach's heavenly *Bist du bei mir* to the innocent lilt of the Swiss folksong, *Gsätzli*, and Strauss's *Voices of spring.*

Lieder (with Gerald Moore or Geoffrey Parsons): SCHUBERT: *Die Vögel; Liebhaber in allen Gestalten; Heidenröslein; Die Forelle; Der Einsame; Der Jüngling an der Quelle; An mein Klavier; Erlkönig; Was bedeutet die Bewegung & Ach, um deine feuchten Schwingen (Suleika I & II); Hänflings Liebeswerbung; Meeres Stille; Gretchen am Spinnrade.* SCHUMANN: *Der Nussbaum; Aufträge; 2 Venetian Lieder; Die Kartenlegerin; Wie mit innigstem Behagen (Suleika).* R. STRAUSS: *Hat gesagt, bleibt's nicht dabei; SchlechtesWetter; Wiegenliedchen; Meinem Kinde; Wiegenlied; 3 Ophelia Lieder; Die Nacht.*
(M) (***) EMI stereo/mono CDM7 63656-2; *EG 763656-4.*

With the Schubert selection including a high proportion of favourites, this compilation provides a fine survey of Schwarzkopf's unique achievement as a Lieder-singer outside the specialist area of Hugo Wolf. The earliest recordings, made in 1948, are of two Schubert songs, *Die Vögel* and a Goethe setting, *Liebhaber in allen Gestalten*, and the latest, Schumann's *Der Nussbaum*, from 25 years on in her career, all beautifully transferred.

Opera arias: MOZART: *Le nozze di Figaro; Così fan tuti; Don Giovanni.* HUMPERDINCK: *Hänsel und Gretel.* LEHÁR: *Die lustige Witwe*; J. STRAUSS, Jnr: *Die Fledermaus.* PUCCINI: *Turandot.* R. STRAUSS: *Ariadne auf Naxos; Der Rosenkavalier; Capriccio.* VERDI: *Messa da requiem.*
(M) (***) EMI stereo/mono CDM7 63657-2; *EG 763657-4.*

This fine collection of arias is taken from various sets Schwarzkopf contributed to in the 1950s. They range from Mozart operas, conducted by Karajan and Furtwängler, to the glories of her supreme recordings of Strauss operas, Ariadne's lament, the Marschallin's final solo in Act I of *Rosenkavalier* and the Countess's final aria in *Capriccio.* Also featured is the *Recordare* from de Sabata's early recording of the Verdi *Requiem.*

'Unpublished recordings' (with (i) Philh. O, Thurston Dart; (ii) Kathleen Ferrier, VPO,

Karajan; (iii) Philh. O, Galliera; (iv) Walter Gieseking, Philh. O, Karajan): J. S. BACH: (i) *Cantata No. 199: Mein Herze schwimmt im Blut: Auf diese Schmerzens Reu; Doch Gott muss mir genädig sein; Mein Herze schwimmt im Blut.* (ii) *Mass in B min.: Christe eleison; Et in unum Dominum; Laudamus te.* (iii) MOZART: *Nehmt meinen Dank, K.383.* (iv) GIESEKING: *Kinderlieder.* R. STRAUSS: *4 Last songs.*
(M) (**(*)) EMI CDM7 63655-2; *EG 763655-4.*

Long-buried treasure here includes Bach duets with Kathleen Ferrier conducted by Karajan, a collection of charming children's songs by Gieseking, recorded almost impromptu, and, best of all, a live performance of Strauss's *Four Last songs* given under Karajan at the Festival Hall in 1956, a vintage year for Schwarzkopf. Sound quality varies, but the voice is gloriously caught.

'To my friends' (with Parsons, piano): WOLF: *Mörike Lieder: Storchenbotschaft; Fussreise; Elfenlied; Bei einer Trauung; Jägerlied; Selbstgeständnis; Heimweh; Nixe Binsefuss; Mausfallen Sprüchlein; Nimmersatte Liebe; Lebe Wohl; Das verlassene Mägdlein; Auf eines altes Bild.* LOEWE: *Die wandelnde Glocke.* GRIEG: *Ein Schwan.* BRAHMS: *Mädchenlied; Am jüngsten Tag; Therese; Blinde Kuh.*
(M) *** Decca 430 000-2 [id.].

This glowing collection of Lieder was Schwarzkopf's last record and also the last recording supervised by her husband, Walter Legge. With excellent Decca sound, the charm and presence of Schwarzkopf, which in a recital conveyed extraordinary intensity right to the very end of her career, comes over vividly. Most cherishable of all are the lighter, quicker songs like *Mausfallen Sprüchlein* ('My St Trinians reading', as she herself says) and *Blinde Kuh* ('Blind man's bluff'). Superbly balanced, bringing the artists right into one's room.

Sopranos

'Great sopranos of our time' ((i) Scotto; (ii) Schwarzkopf; (iii) Sutherland; (iv) Nilsson; (v) De los Angeles; (vi) Freni; (vii) Callas; (viii) Cotrubas; (ix) Caballé): (i) PUCCINI: *Madama Butterfly: Un bel dì.* (vi) *La Bohème: Sì, mi chiamano Mimì.* (ii) MOZART: *Così fan tutte: Come scoglio.* (iii) *Don Giovanni: Troppo mi spiace . . . Non mi dir.* (iv) WEBER: *Oberon: Ozean du Ungeheuer.* (v) ROSSINI: *Il Barbiere di Siviglia: Una voce poco fa.* (vii) DONIZETTI: *Lucia di Lammermoor: Sparsa è di rose . . . Il dolce suono . . . Spargi d'amaro.* (viii) BIZET: *Les Pêcheurs de perles: Comme autrefois.* (ix) VERDI: *Aida: Qui Radames . . . O patria mia.*
(M) *** EMI CD-EMX 9519; *TC-EMX 2099.*

An impressive collection, drawn from a wide variety of sources. It is good to have Schwarzkopf's commanding account of *Come scoglio* and Nilsson's early recording of the Weber, not to mention the formidable contributions of Callas and the early Sutherland reading of *Non mi dir*, taken from Giulini's complete set of *Giovanni*. The CD transfers are bright and vivid, and this makes a fascinating mid-priced anthology.

Soprano arias: 'Famous soprano arias' (sung by: (i) Régine Crespin; (ii) Tebaldi; (iii) Maria Chiara; (iv) Sutherland; (v) G. Jones; (vi) Felicia Weathers; (vii) Suliotis) from: PUCCINI: (i) *Madama Butterfly;* (ii) *Gianni Schicchi;* (iii) *La Bohème;* (ii) *Tosca.* CATALANI: (iii) *La Wally.* VERDI: (iv) *Rigoletto;* (iii) *I vespri siciliani;* (v) *Aida;* (i) *Otello.* GOUNOD: (iv) *Faust.* PONCHIELLI: (viii) *La Gioconda.*
❀ (B) *** Decca 433 624-2; *433 624-4.*

The compiler of this 67-minute programme is to be congratulated for remarkable vocal discernment and awareness of the potential in the Decca back-catalogue. It would be difficult to conceive a more winning recital of miscellaneous popular arias derived from this source, opening with the most famous soprano aria of all, *Un bel dì*, excitingly and tenderly sung by Régine Crespin. It is gratifying to see the art of Maria Chiara acknowledged: she is enchanting in the *Boléro* from Verdi's *I vespri siciliani* and makes a ravishing Mimì. Felicia Weathers is both captivating and individual in her long scena from *Otello*, while Tebaldi's *O mio babbino caro* has great vocal charm. She ends the recital with a characteristically melting account of *Vissi d'arte*, made in 1960. Sutherland's two contributions were also recorded in that same year: her lyrical coloratura in *Caro nome* is quite delicious. Dame Gwyneth Jones is in glorious voice in the two major arias from *Aida* (1968), while Eleana Suliotis, sometimes an uneven singer, is at her strongest and most commanding in her searingly powerful *Suicido* from *La Gioconda*, vocally as well as dramatically thrilling.

Souzay, Gérard (baritone)

Mélodies (with Jacqueline Bonneau): FAURÉ: *Tristesse; Au bord de l'eau; Après un rêve; Clair de lune; Arpège; En sourdine; L'Horizon chimérique; Spleen; C'est l'extase; Prison; Mandoline.* CHAUSSON: *Nanny; Le charme; Sérénade italienne; Le Colibri; Cantique à l'épouse; Les papillons; Le temps de lilas.* Airs: BOESSET: *Me veux-tu voir mourir?.* ANON.: *Tambourin.* BATAILLE: *Cachez, beaux yeux; Ma bergère non*

légère. CANTELOUBE: *Brezairola; Malurous qu'o uno fenno.*
❀ (M) (***) Decca mono 425 975-2.

The great French baritone made these recordings for Decca when he was at the very peak of his form and they have been much sought after by many collectors (and much treasured by those fortunate enough to have bought them at the time). The Fauré were recorded in 1950 and the glorious Chausson songs in 1953. Lotte Lehmann is quoted as saying that she would travel miles to hear him, and one is tempted to say that this 70-minute recital offers the best singing of the year. Souzay was endowed with the intelligence of Bernac as well as his powers of characterization, the vocal purity of Panzera and a wonderful feeling for line. The Decca transfer does complete justice to the original sound, and it is good to have these performances without the surface distractions of LP. Full texts and translations are provided. A marvellous record worth as many rosettes as stars!

Stefano, Giuseppe Di (tenor)

Neapolitan songs (with New SO, Pattacini or Olivieri): DE CURTIS: *Torna a Surriento; Tu ca'nun chiagne; Sona chitarra! A canzone 'e Napule; Ti voglio tanto bene.* BONGIOVANNI: *Lacreme napulitane.* TAGLIAFERRI: *Napule canta; Pusilleco.* CALIFANO: *'O surdato 'nnammurato.* CARDILLO: *Catari, catari.* COSTA: *Era di maggio matenata; Scetate.* NICOLAVALENTE: *Addio, mia bella Napoli.* CESANNI: *Firenze sogna.* DI LAZZARO: *Chitarra romana.* NEN: *Parlami d'amore Mariu.* BARBENS: *Munasterio 'e Santa-Chiara.*
(M) *** Decca 417 794-2.

Di Stefano was still in magnificent voice in the mid-1960s when he recorded these popular Neapolitan songs – including many comparative rarities as well as obvious choices like *Torna a Surriento*, *Catari, catari*, and *Addio, mia bella Napoli*. Despite the inevitable touches of vulgarity, the singing is both rich-toned and charming. The recording is admirably clear and vivid.

Sutherland, Dame Joan (soprano)

The retirement of Joan Sutherland from the operatic stage has prompted Decca to make a bouquet of imaginatively assembled reissues, admirably surveying her thirty-year recording career.

'Greatest hits': Excerpts from: HANDEL: *Samson.* LEHÁR: *Merry widow.* J. STRAUSS Jnr: *Casanova.* DONIZETTI: *Fille du régiment.* DELIBES: *Lakmé.* BELLINI: *Norma.* GOUNOD: *Faust.* DONIZETTI: *Lucia di Lammermoor: Mad scene.* Song: ARDITI: *Il bacio.*
(M) *** Decca 417 780-2; *417 780-4* [id.].

A collection like this, well chosen to entertain, is self-recommending at mid-price. The recordings all come from the period when the voice was at its freshest: *Let the bright seraphim*, the *Bell song* from *Lakmé*, and the vivacious *Jewel song* from *Faust* in 1961; while the luscious version of *Vilja* (with chorus) was made in 1963. The lively excerpt from *La fille du régiment* comes from the complete set, as does the Mad scene from *Lucia di Lammermoor* – the 1961 first recording, under Pritchard. The sound is consistently vivid.

'Opera gala': Excerpts from: BELLINI: *Norma.* DONIZETTI: *Lucia di Lammermoor: Mad scene; Linda di Chamounix.* VERDI: *Ernani; I vespri siciliani.*
❀ (M) *** Decca 421 305-2.

Sutherland's 'Opera Gala' disc is one of the most cherishable of all operatic recital records, bringing together the glorious, exuberant items from her very first recital disc, made within weeks of her first Covent Garden success in 1959 and – as a valuable supplement – the poised account of *Casta diva* she recorded the following year as part of the '*Art of the Prima Donna*'. It was this 1959 recital which at once put Sutherland firmly on the map among the great recording artists of all time. Even she has never surpassed the freshness of these versions of the two big arias from *Lucia di Lammermoor*, sparkling in immaculate coloratura, while the lightness and point of the jaunty *Linda di Chamounix* aria and the *Boléro* from *I vespri siciliani* are just as winning. The sound is exceptionally vivid and immediate, though the accompaniments under Nello Santi are sometimes rough in ensemble.

'Romantic French arias' (with SRO, Bonynge) from: OFFENBACH: *Robinson Crusoé; La Grande-Duchesse de Gérolstein.* MEYERBEER: *Dinorah; Robert le Diable.* CHARPENTIER: *Louise.* AUBER: *Manon Lescaut; Fra Diavolo.* BIZET: *Les pêcheurs de perles; Vasco de Gama.* MASSENET: *Cendrillon.* MASSÉ: *Les noces de Jeannette.* GOUNOD: *Mireille; Le Tribut de Zamora; Faust.* LECOCQ: *Le coeur et la main.*
(M) *** Decca 421 879-2; *421 879-4* [id.].

This 73-minute recital encompasses much of the cream of a two-LP album, recorded in September 1969; for those new to the selection it will come as a delightful surprise to discover that Offenbach's *Robinson Crusoé* includes an irresistible waltz-song for the heroine as she steps ashore on Crusoe's island and is met by cannibals (*Take me to the man I adore*). Sutherland opens with that and sings here and in all the other brilliant numbers with great flair and abandon, relishing her virtuosity. The romantic side is represented by such enchanting items as Massenet's sad little Cinderella aria, Dinorah's sweet lullaby for her pet goat, a nightingale aria from Victor Massé's *Les noces de Jeannette* and a ravishing account of *Depuis le jour* from *Louise* to make most modern rivals sound pale and thin. Bizet's rare *Chanson bohème* from *Vasco da Gama* is most engaging, and the aria from his *Pearlfishers* is the only relative disappointment. The sound-balance in the Victoria Hall, Geneva, is quite well managed, but the CD transfer makes the voice sound brighter than usual.

'Operetta gala' (with New Philh. O, Bonynge): Arias from: OFFENBACH: *La Grande-Duchesse; La Périchole.* ZELLER: *Der Vogelhändler.* MILLOCKER: *Die Dubarry.* FALL: Medley. LEHÁR: *Eva; Paganini; Die lustige Witwe (The merry widow); Paganini.* O. STRAUS: *Ein Walzertraum; The Chocolate soldier.* HEUBERGER: *Der Opernball.* J. STRAUSS, Jnr: *Casanova.* KREISLER: *The King steps out.* POSFORD: *Balalaika.*
(M) *** Decca 421 880-2; *421 880-4* [id.].

Opening with the vivacious military song from *La Grande-Duchesse de Gérolstein* (which derives from her French compilation), Sutherland goes on to charm us with the *Letter song* from *La Périchole* and then offers a substantial selection from her 1966 (two-disc) lilting, whoopsing operetta compilation, originally entitled rather cosily *'Love, live forever'*. This covers very much the same ground as Schwarzkopf's (full-priced) operetta collection. Sutherland may not always match Schwartzkopf in the haunting Viennese quality which inhabits such an enchanting number as *Im chambre séparée* (although her sensuous charm is disarming); but she is splendid in a fizzing number like *The Dubarry*, with the Ambrosians providing enthusiastic support, and the Leo Fall potpourri has comparable élan. What is immediately obvious is Sutherland's own delight in singing this music, and the accompaniments have matching infectious qualities, with Bonynge obviously entirely at home, providing the necessary light touch and idiomatic feeling for rubato. The sumptuous recording catches the glory of Sutherland's voice to perfection against a sparklingly rich orchestral and vocal backing. The chorus are splendid throughout.

'The age of Bel canto' (with Marilyn Horne, Richard Conrad, LSO or LPO, Bonynge): Arias & excerpts from: PICCINI: *La buonna figliuola.* HANDEL: *Samson.* BONONCINI: *Astarto; Griselda.* SHIELD: *Rosina.* MOZART: *Die Zauberflöte.* BOIELDIEU: *Angela.* ROSSINI: *Semiramide.* WEBER: *Der Freischütz.* DONIZETTI: *Don Pasquale.* VERDI: *Attila.* BELLINI: *La straniera.* GRAUN: *Montezuma.*
(M) *** Decca 421 881-2; *421 881-4* [id.].

The original (1963) two-LP recital *'The age of Bel canto'*, from which virtually the whole of this mid-price reissue is taken, included arias for mezzo-soprano and tenor, as well as ensembles. It was understandable that Sutherland's contributions to the whole, not just solos but ensembles too, should one day be hived off like this; and a very impressive disc it makes. It is good to be reminded what a fine Mozartian Sutherland is, in the Queen of the Night's *O zittre nicht*, and the delightful point of Shield's *Light as thistledown* is irresistible. As for her duet, *Serbami ognor* from *Semiramide*, it brings a performance of equal mastery. Added to the items from the original set, to make up a total timing of nearly 72 minutes, comes a generous addition – two charming arias from the Sutherland/Bonynge 1966 records of *Griselda* and *Montezuma*. Here the balance is brighter, the voice more forward: in the main recital there is a more natural, concert-hall effect, very realistically transferred to CD.

'Command performance' (with LSO or New Philh. O, Bonynge): Arias from: WEBER: *Oberon.* MASSENET: *Le Cid.* MEYERBEER: *Dinorah; Les Huguenots.* LEONCAVALLO: *Pagliacci.* VERDI: *I Masnadieri; Luisa Miller.* ROSSINI: *La cambiale di matrimonio.* BELLINI: *Beatrice di Tenda.*
(M) *** Decca 421 882-2; *421 882-4* [id.].

The idea behind this 1963 'Command performance' recital was that Queen Victoria would have asked for just such a concert, had she been able to invite Joan Sutherland to Windsor. The LP issue was a presentation set of two records, provided with a lavishly illustrated booklet and notes by Andrew Porter. The reissue includes the contents of the first of the two LPs (thus omitting the frothier items) and, to make the concert more generous, her scena *O beau pays de la Touraine* from *Les Huguenots* (the opera with which she made her stage farewell in Sydney) is added as an appendix, ravishingly sung, taken from her (1969) complete set. There are now new, more succinct notes from Alan Blyth. As to Sutherland's singing, there was still too much of the 'mooning' style which had overtaken her in the early 1960s, words disappearing in the quest for ever more cooingly beautiful tone; but the coloratura is ecstatically beautiful, enlivening what would otherwise be too consistently languid an experience. The rare Verdi and Bellini arias are especially welcome. The recording is of Decca's best vintage, especially rich in the *Les Huguenots* excerpt.

'Tribute to Jenny Lind' (with various orchestras, Pritchard or Bonynge): Arias from BELLINI: *Beatrice di Tenda; I Puritani; La sonnambula.* DONIZETTI: *Rosamonda d'Inghilterra; La fille du régiment.* MOZART: *Le nozze di Figaro.* MEYERBEER: *L'étoile du nord.* ROSSINI: *Semiramide.* VERDI: *I Masnadieri.* Songs: ARDITI: *Il bacio.* BENEDICT: *The gypsy and the bird.* BISHOP: *Lo! here the gentle lark.*
(M) *** Decca 421 883-2; *421 883-4* [id.].

This recorded tribute from one great singer to another encompasses virtually the whole of Joan Sutherland's career onwards from her delectably fresh (1961) recording of Rosamonda's aria (Donizetti), complete with flute obbligato, and three frothier items from the original second LP of *'Command performance'* (1962) with Benedict's *The gypsy and the bird*, a piece of Victorian nonsense of course, but providing with its trills and roulades a glorious opportunity for display – one of her most inspired pieces of singing on record. The 1968 *Fille du régiment* is justly celebrated, while the Meyerbeer excerpts come from her (1969) two-LP set of French repertoire, the bulk of which is available on the CD listed above. It is good to have the Mozart arias, to experience her ravishing phrasing in this repertoire. The three Bellini scenas demonstrate her varying vocal production between 1966 and 1980, when the *La Sonnambula* excerpt, astonishingly agile, yet displayed a slight beat in the voice in the lyrical line. The careers of the two sopranos linked in the title were comparably successful, and their remarkable coloratura, impressive breath control and felicitous ornamentation had a good deal in common, but Sutherland almost certainly had the greater emotional range. Excellent sound throughout: all in all, a fascinating 74-minute collection.

'The art of the prima donna': Arias from: ARNE: *Artaxerxes.* HANDEL: *Samson.* BELLINI: *Norma; I Puritani; La Sonnambula.* ROSSINI: *Semiramide.* GOUNOD: *Faust; Roméo et Juliette.* VERDI: *Otello; Rigoletto; La Traviata.* MOZART: *Die Entführung aus dem Serail.* THOMAS: *Hamlet.* DELIBES: *Lakmé.* MEYERBEER: *Les Huguenots.*
❀ (M) *** Decca 425 493-2 (2) [id.].

This ambitious early two-disc recital (from 1960) remains one of Joan Sutherland's outstanding gramophone achievements, and it is a matter of speculation whether even Melba or Tetrazzini in their heyday managed to provide 16 consecutive recordings quite as dazzling as these performances. Indeed, it is the Golden Age that one naturally turns to rather than to current singers when making any comparisons. By electing to sing each one of the fabulously difficult arias in tribute to a particular soprano of the past – from Mrs Billington in the eighteenth century, through Grisi, Malibran, Pasta and Jenny Lind in the nineteenth century, to Lilli Lehmann, Melba, Tetrazzini and Galli-Curci in this – Sutherland is herself asking to be judged by the standards of the Golden Age. On the basis of recorded reminders, she comes out with flying colours, showing a greater consistency and certainly a wider range of sympathy than even the greatest Golden Agers possessed. The sparkle and delicacy of the *Puritani Polonaise*, the freshness and lightness of the Mad scene from Thomas's *Hamlet*, the commanding power of the *Entführung* aria and the breathtaking brilliance of the Queen's aria from *Les Huguenots* are all among the high spots here, while the arias which Sutherland later recorded in her complete opera sets regularly bring performances just as fine as – and often finer than – the later versions. The freshness of the voice is caught superbly in the recording, which on CD is amazingly full, firm and realistic, far more believable than many new digital recordings. Reissued at mid-price, it is surely an essential purchase for all who care for beautiful singing.

'Prima donna assoluta': Arias from OFFENBACH: *Contes d'Hoffmann.* DONIZETTI: *Fille du régiment; Lucia di Lammermoor.* GOUNOD: *Faust.* BELLINI: *I Puritani.* VERDI: *La Traviata.*
(B) *** Decca 425 605-2.

Issued on Decca's cheapest label, this captivating recital concentrates on excerpts from Sutherland's complete sets. However, the closing *Lucia di Lammermoor* Mad scene derives from her famous 1959 Decca début record, conducted by Nello Santi, representing one of the most magical and thrilling displays of coloratura ever recorded: the luminous freshness of the voice is unforgettable. The other recordings come from between 1960 and 1972, and this disc is in every way a bargain. The documentation, however, is entirely biographical.

Russian music (with LSO, Richard Bonynge, (i) Osian Ellis; or (ii) Josef Sivo, SRO, Horst Stein): GLIÈRE: *Coloratura concerto*; (i) *Harp concerto.* STRAVINSKY: *Pastorale.* CUI: *Ici-bas.* GRETCHANINOV: *Lullaby.* (ii) GLAZUNOV: *Violin concerto.*
(M) **(*) Decca 430 006-2 [id.].

The two highly engaging concertos are discussed in the composer index. Dreamy beauty perhaps goes a little far in Sutherland's account of Stravinsky's early *Pastorale* (there is too much vocal sliding), while the Cui and Gretchaninov songs are accompanied by

Richard Bonynge at the piano. The addition of Sivo's account of the Glazunov *Violin concerto* for the CD reissue is no great advantage. There is some less than ideal intonation, and the performance, though well recorded, is not distinctive.

Tebaldi, Renata (soprano)

'The Early Recordings': VERDI: *Aida: Act I, Ritorna vincitor!; Act III* (complete; with Stignani, Caselli, Protti, del Monaco, Ac. di Santa Cecilia Ch. & O, Erede); *Il Trovatore: Tacea la notte placida.* Arias from: GOUNOD: *Faust.* PUCCINI: *Madama Butterfly; Manon Lescaut; Tosca; La Bohème.*
(M) (***) Decca mono 425 989-2 [id.].

This fascinating collection includes the very first records Tebaldi made for Decca in November 1949, in effect the start of a new era in operatic recording. More recital recordings were made in 1951. (I. M. remembers the great impact her initial mono LP made on him at the time, with the ravishing bloom of her lyrical line bringing a frisson of excitement and sentient pleasure which he has never forgotten). This led to her early version of *Aida* of 1952, here represented by Act III, opposite two of her regular partners, neither showing anything like her finesse: the coarse Mario del Monaco and the colourless Aldo Protti, firmer here than he was to become. Though her later recordings are more refined in expressive detail, the freshness of these performances is a delight and, with the reservations noted concerning the mixed blessings of the *Aida* cast, our Rosette for her two-disc set, below, could be extended to cover many of the earlier items included here. Good transfers.

'La Tebaldi': (arias recorded between 1955 & 1968): PUCCINI: *Madama Butterfly; La Bohème; Tosca; Gianni Schicchi; Suor Angelica; Turandot; La rondine.* BOITO: *Mefistofele.* VERDI: *Aida; Otello; Il Trovatore; La forza del destino; Don Carlo; Un ballo in maschera; Giovanna d'Arco.* ROSSINI: *Guglielmo Tell.* CILEA: *Adriana Lecouvreur; L'arlesiana.* GIORDANO: *Andrea Chénier.* CATALANI: *La Wally.* PONCHIELLI: *La Gioconda.* MASCAGNI: *Cavalleria rusticana.* REFICE: *Cecilia.*
❀ (B) *** Decca 430 481-2 (2) [id.].

This two-disc collection superbly celebrates one of the sopranos with a special place in the history of recording, the prima donna who in the early days of LP most clearly reflected a great period of operatic expansion. Unlike her great rival, Callas, thrilling, dynamic, unpredictable, often edgy and uneven on record, Tebaldi was above all reliable, with her creamy-toned voice, exceptionally even from top to bottom, and with its natural warmth ideally suited to recording. The 24 items here, entirely devoted to the Italian opera, cover the full range of her repertory, from her justly famous assumption of the role of Butterfly to her personification of Leonora in *La forza del destino*, while she was an unforgettably moving Mimì in *La Bohème.* Many of the items are taken from the complete sets she recorded for Decca, generally more freely expressive than those originally issued on recital discs. The actual interpretations are totally consistent, though over the years the detail grew ever more refined. Excellent transfers. An indispensable set for all those who respond to this lovely voice, bringing a magical feeling of vulnerability to her personifications, when she creates a gentle, glowing pianissimo.

Tenors

'Great tenors of our time' (with (i) Carlo Bergonzi; (ii) Franco Corelli; (iii) Placido Domingo; (iv) Nicolai Gedda; (v) James McCracken; (vi) Luciano Pavarotti; (vii) Jon Vickers): (iii) VERDI: *Aida: Se quel guerrier . . . Celeste Aida.* (v) *Otello: Niun mi tema.* (i) *La Forza del destino: O tu che in seno.* (iv) BIZET: *Les Pêcheurs de perles: Je crois entendre.* (vii) *Carmen: Flower song.* (i) PUCCINI: *Tosca: E lucevan le stelle.* (ii) *Turandot: Nessun dorma.* (iii) *Manon Lescaut: Donna non vidi mai.* (ii) GIORDANO: *Andrea Chénier: Come un bel di.* (vi) MASCAGNI: *L'amico Fritz: Ed anche . . . oh amore.* (iv) GOUNOD: *Faust: Salut! Demeure.* (vii) SAINT-SAENS: *Samson et Dalila: Arrêtez, o mes frères.*
(M) **(*) EMI CD-EMX 2114; *TC-EMX 2114.*

EMI compiled this anthology ingeniously from many sources; for example, Luciano Pavarotti, an exclusive Decca artist from early in his international career, had earlier still taken part in EMI's complete set of *L'amico Fritz*, so providing the excerpt which completes this constellation of great tenors. Not that each is necessarily represented in the most appropriate items, and the compilation does have one wishing (for example) that Vickers rather than McCracken was singing *Otello*, though that excerpt is valuable for preserving a sample of Barbirolli's complete set of that opera. And although Vickers does not make an ideal Don José, it is useful to have his *Flower song*, since the set from which it comes is one of the less recommendable versions. The transfers are clear and fresh, the voices given immediacy, the orchestral backing suitably atmospheric. Considering the variety of the sources (dating from 1959 – Placido Domingo's fine *Salut! Demeure* – to 1974 – the same artist's stirring *Celeste Aida*, which opens the programme), the recording is remarkably consistent.

Tetrazzini, Luisa (soprano)

'Prima voce': Arias from: BELLINI: *La Sonnambula.* DONIZETTI: *Lucia di Lammermoor.* ROSSINI: *Il Barbiere di Siviglia.* THOMAS: *Mignon.* VERACINI: *Rosalinda.* VERDI: *Un ballo in maschera; Rigoletto; La Traviata; Il Trovatore; I vespri siciliani.* Songs.
(M) (***) Nimbus mono NI 7808 [id.].

Tetrazzini was astonishing among coloratura sopranos not just for her phenomenal agility but for the golden warmth that went with tonal purity. The Nimbus transfers add a bloom to the sound, with the singer slightly distanced. Though some EMI transfers make her voice more vividly immediate, one quickly adjusts. Such display arias as *Ah non giunge* from *La Sonnambula* or the *Boléro* from *I vespri siciliani* are incomparably dazzling, but it is worth noting too what tenderness is conveyed through Tetrazzini's simple phrasing and pure tone in such a tragic aria as Violetta's *Addio del passato*, with both verses included. Lieder devotees may gasp in horror, but one of the delightful oddities here is Tetrazzini's bright-eyed performance, with ragged orchestral accompaniment, of what is described as *La serenata inutile* by Brahms – in fact *Vergebliches Ständchen*, sung with a triumphant if highly inauthentic top A at the end, implying no closure of the lady's window!

Tibbett, Lawrence (baritone)

Arias from: LEONCAVALLO: *Pagliacci.* ROSSINI: *Il Barbiere di Siviglia.* VERDI: *Un ballo in maschera; Simon Boccanegra; Falstaff.* PUCCINI: *Tosca.* BIZET: *Carmen.* GOUNOD: *Faust.* WAGNER: *Die Walküre.* GRUENBERG: *Emperor Jones.* HANSON: *Merry Mount.* GERSHWIN: *Porgy and Bess.*
(M) (***) BMG/RCA mono GD 87808 [7808-2-RG].

The glorious, characterful timbre of Tibbett's baritone is superbly caught in RCA's clear, immediate transfers, with the vibrato never obtrusive as it can be on some records. It is sad that so commanding a singer was heard relatively little outside America; but this is a superb memorial, not just for the classic arias but for such an item as the excerpt from Louis Gruenberg's *Emperor Jones*, a role he created.

'Tibbett in opera': excerpts from: LEONCAVALLO: *Pagliacci.* BIZET: *Carmen.* PUCCINI: *Tosca.* VERDI: *Un ballo in maschera; Simon Boccanegra; Rigoletto; Otello.* ROSSINI: *Il barbiere di Siviglia.* GOUNOD: *Faust.* WAGNER: *Tannhäuser, Die Walküre.*
(M) (***) Nimbus mono NI 7825 [id.].

The scale and resonance of Lawrence Tibbett's voice come over vividly in this fine selection of his recordings made between 1926 and 1939. The Nimbus process allows the rapid vibrato in his voice to emerge naturally, giving the sound a thrilling richness in all these varied items. Particularly interesting is the longest, the whole of *Wotan's farewell*, with Stokowski conducting the Philadelphia Orchestra in 1934. It is an over-the-top performance that carries total conviction, even if the sheer volume produces some clangorous resonances in the Nimbus transfer. Also memorable is the celebrated *Boccanegra* Council chamber sequence, recorded in 1939 with Martinelli and Rose Bampton in the ensemble.

Turner, Dame Eva (soprano)

Opera arias and songs: Arias from VERDI: *Il Trovatore; Aida.* PONCHIELLI: *La Gioconda.* PUCCINI: *Tosca; Madama Butterfly; Turandot.* MASCAGNI: *Cavalleria Rusticana.* WAGNER: *Lohengrin; Tannhäuser.* Songs: GRIEG: *I love thee.* TOSTI: *Goodbye.* RONALD: *O lovely night.* DEL RIEGO: *Homing.* D'HARDELOT: *Because; Sometime in my dreams.*
(M) (***) EMI mono CDH7 69791-2.

The art of Eva Turner is superbly celebrated in this generous selection of recordings made between 1928 and 1933. They include not only her celebrated 1928 recording of Turandot's *In questa reggia* but also magnificent samples of her portrayals of Aida, Leonora in *Trovatore* and La Gioconda, as well as half a dozen songs and ballads. Most fascinating of all are her two Wagner recordings, of *Elsa's dream* from *Lohengrin* and *Elisabeth's greeting* from *Tannhäuser*, sung in English. These were never issued, and Dame Eva's copy of the latter, the only one surviving, was broken into three pieces. It was lovingly reassembled so that it could be played, if with persistent clicks. The CEDAR process was then used to eliminate the clicks, automatically filling in each microscopic gap with surrounding material in a way impossible if the process is to be done laboriously by hand. The finished result is among the most thrilling of all the recordings ever made by Dame Eva, rich and intense. It is a delight also to have Dame Eva's spoken introduction, recorded in June 1988 when she was in her ninety-eighth year. Keith Hardwick's transfers, quite apart from the help from CEDAR, are models of their kind, with the voice astonishingly vivid.

Welitsch, Ljuba (soprano)

Arias from: TCHAIKOVSKY: *Eugene Onegin.* VERDI: *Aida.* PUCCINI: *Tosca; La Bohème.* WEBER: *Der Freischütz.* R. STRAUSS: *Salome: Closing scene.*
(M) (***) EMI mono CDH7 61007-2.

It is sad that Ljuba Welitsch's career was far shorter than it should have been. The voice itself, strikingly individual in its timbre, conveys fire and intensity and, as these classic recordings consistently show, the vibrant personality matches that. This immaculately transferred collection gathers together the handful of studio recordings she made for EMI after the Second World War (notably *Tatiana's letter song* from 1948, done in German). As a splendid bonus comes the radio recording, made in Vienna in 1944, of the closing scene from Strauss's *Salome*, where the extra vibrancy of live performance is caught vividly, despite the fuzziness of sound, here reasonably clarified in the digital transfer.

York Minster Choir, Francis Jackson (organ)

'On Christmas night': TRAD.: *The first nowell; While shepherd's watched; Coventry carol; Good King Wenceslas; The holly and the ivy; O come, all ye faithful; In dulci jubilo; God rest you merry, gentlemen; On Christmas night (Sussex carol).* WAINWRIGHT: *Christians awake!* GAUNTLETT: *Once in Royal David's city.* HOPKINS: *We three kings.* GRÜBER: *Silent night.* WOODWARD: *Ding dong! merrily on high.* MENDELSSOHN: *Hark! the herald angels sing.*
(M) **(*) Chan. CHAN 6520; *MBTD 6520* [id.].

Those who prefer straightforward presentations of popular carols will find these performances pleasingly fresh. Because Francis Jackson is an imaginative player (and not because of the balance or any intrusive accompaniments) one is often more aware of the organ than usual; but the singing itself has an affecting, simple beauty and the words are clear. The York Minster acoustics are beautifully controlled by the Chandos engineers so that there is no overhang or blurring, yet the music-making is pleasingly coloured by the ambience. The effect is perhaps less individual than the King's or Clare records but is refreshing in its absence of the imposed personalities of arrangers.